Raymond Kévorkian is an historian who teaches at the Institut Français de Géopolitique, University of Paris-VIII-Saint-Denis. He is Director of the Bibliothèque Nubar – the Armenian Library in Paris – and the author of numerous works on the history of modern and contemporary Armenia and Armenians.

"This is a major, magnificent achievement of scholarship. It is hard to imagine this book being surpassed for decades in terms of the breadth and depth of its research and the scale of its undertaking."

**Donald Bloxham, Professor of Modern History,
University of Edinburgh**

"Raymond Kévorkian has made a major contribution to the developing historiography of the Armenian Genocide of 1915–1916. Using previously little-employed sources found in distant archives, he weaves a detailed and compelling account of the ideological background, the planning and execution of the first major mass killing by a modernizing, nationalizing state. An event of this magnitude, one would believe, could be neither denied nor forgotten, and yet through the systematic efforts of governments of the Republic of Turkey this "crime of crimes" has been obscured and rendered controversial. Reading this rich, convincing account makes this holocaust before the Holocaust undeniable."

**Ronald Grigor Suny, Charles Tilly Collegiate Professor of Social
and Political History, University of Michigan, and author
of *Looking Toward Ararat: Armenia in Modern History***

"This is the most comprehensive book to date on the Armenian Genocide of 1915. In this detailed account, Raymond Kévorkian describes the process which drove 1.5 million Armenians in the Ottoman Empire to their deaths."

Le Monde

"This mighty volume constitutes the most complete summary to date."

Histoforum, Paris

THE ARMENIAN GENOCIDE

A Complete History

Raymond Kévorkian

I.B. TAURIS

LONDON · NEW YORK

Published in 2011 by I.B.Tauris & Co Ltd
6 Salem Road, London W2 4BU
175 Fifth Avenue, New York NY 10010
www.ibtauris.com

Distributed in the United States and Canada
exclusively by Palgrave Macmillan
175 Fifth Avenue, New York NY 10010

French edition published in September 2006 by Odile Jacob as *Le Génocide des Arméniens*

ISBN: 978 1 84885 561 8

A full CIP record for this book is available from the British Library
A full CIP record is available from the Library of Congress

Library of Congress Catalog Card Number: available

Printed and bound in Great Britain by TJ International Ltd, Padstow, Cornwall

MIX
Paper from
responsible sources
FSC® C013056

Contents

Part V The Second Phase of the Genocide
Fall 1915–December 1916

Part VI The Last Days of the Ottoman Empire:
The Executioners and Their Judges
Face-to-Face

Introduction

The destruction of historical groups by states is always the culmination of complex processes that unfold in particular political and social environments – most notably, in multiethnic contexts. The translation of genocidal intentions into action is systematically preceded by periods of maturation rooted in diverse experiences, collective failures, frustrations, and virulent antagonisms. It is justified by an ideological construction that envisages the elimination of "internal enemies" from the social body. Each instance of genocidal violence, however, obeys an internal logic that lends it its singularity. The physical destruction of the Armenian population of the Ottoman Empire has, in its turn, a singular feature: it was conceived as a necessary condition for the construction of a Turkish nation-state – the supreme objective of the Young Turks. The two phenomena, in other words, are indissolubly linked: we cannot understand the one if we ignore the other.

The present book is informed by this assumption and its structure depends on it. "Destruction as self-construction" might have been the slogan adopted by the Committee of Union and Progress (CUP) and that is the guiding thread of this study. In adopting it, I have decided to situate myself at a level of observation that privileges the Young Turk and Armenian elites; I have chosen methodically to examine the internal evolution of these limited circles; I have attempted to assess the reactions of the two groups in crisis situations; and finally, I have studied the nature of the interrelations between the two groups, their points of convergence and divergence, and even their ideological similarities. Thus, it is domestic Ottoman politics, examined from the level of the Empire's elites, which serves as the frame of reference for this book and sets its problematic. This point of view distinguishes the present book from previous studies, which are generally organized around the "Eastern Question" and European interventionism in the Ottoman Empire. I have not felt the need here to evoke the historiographical traditions on the subject, so as perhaps to better distance myself from them. The historiography is, in any case, a complex matter calling for a study of its own, one that would divert us from our main subject.

That said, I have primarily interrogated the institutional, political, social, and even psychological mechanisms that culminated in the destruction of the Ottoman Armenians. In particular, I have sought to mark off the successive phases of the radicalization of Young Turk circles. I have paid special attention to decision-making processes, which are a complex phenomenon if ever there was one.

The debates over ideas within the Young Turk elite and the formation and subsequent radicalization of the Young Turks' ideology are here set against the parallel development of the nationalism fostered by the Armenian revolutionary movements. These elites, both when they were in opposition to Sultan Abdülhamid's regime and, later, when they were at the head of the state, endlessly discussed the destiny of their common society. I have tried to account for this. Particular attention has been paid to the troubling resemblance between the Armenian and Young Turk elites, both of whom saw themselves as the bearers of a "sacred" mission – saving the "nation." The present study accordingly moves back and forth between examinations of the practices of each.

As a lens for the examination of the Young Turk regime's political practices, the April 1909 Cilician massacres have been privileged over every other pre-war event. My choice was dictated by the fact that this violence was a major issue in the dialogue between Turks and Armenians, one that provoked a crisis of confidence. The abundant documentation available on this intermediate period, which affords us insight into phenomena that are harder to discern in later periods, was another reason for my choice.

The geographical problematic is the second frame of reference for the present work. The regional approach, which requires that one descends to the micro-historical level, has never been seriously integrated into a global study. The immensity of the geographical area to be considered, together with its local specificities, makes the task a formidable one that has no doubt intimidated more than one historian. The historical vacuum that prevails in this domain is perhaps also not unrelated to the enormous mass of material that has to be patiently sorted out and worked through in order to establish the facts in the different regions. The bloody nature of the events to be examined may, in turn, have dissuaded some. It is not without apprehension that I have set out on this long adventure myself. But a plunge into the Ottoman provinces is also necessary, in that it alone allows us to draw macro-historical lessons from the strategy pursued by the central authorities and to single out the modifications of it that came about one at a time. A regional approach also authorizes conclusions about the fates of the Armenian conscripts which varied with their native region; it helps us identify the categories of Armenians likely to survive (that is, to be drawn into the "Turkish world" in formation); it throws a harsh but revealing light on the relationship between executioners and victims and on the reactions that the party-state's genocidal policies elicited from both society and especially certain officials; and it brings out the roles played by the administrative, army, political, and paramilitary groups linked to the CUP in the context of the extermination plan. What thus comes into view is a repetitive mechanism that consisted in entrusting the "legal" side of the process to the agencies of the state (identification of people to arrest, formation of convoys, seizure of property) and the "shadowy" side to the Special Organization, to whose activities we have paid very close attention. In this vast inventory of the realities that emerged in the Armenian provinces of eastern Anatolia and the Armenian communities of western Anatolia, each regional study contributes something to our understanding of the global process.

To round out this approach, I have made an inventory of the civilians, military officials, and local notables implicated, in one capacity or another, in this mass violence, in order to better discern the sociological profile of the men who took part in the Young Turk experiment. In response to the legitimate curiosity of the victims' descendants, I have also tried to determine as precisely as possible the dates on which the convoys of deportees set out, region by region and locality by locality. I have endeavored to retrace their trajectories, establish the location of the killing fields to which they were sent, and identify both the officers commanding their "escorts" and the heads of the Special Organization's squadrons of irregulars permanently assigned to "managing" the gorges that were most commonly used as slaughterhouses.

I have also taken an interest both in the activities of the commissions created by the Ottoman administration to deal with what was termed "abandoned property" and in the broader economic effects of the spoliation of the Armenians' property, which was carried out within the framework of the Millî Iktisat ("national economy"). The importance of these expropriations can hardly be exaggerated: they constituted one of the major objectives of the Young Turk policy of ethnically homogenizing Asia Minor.[1]

Among the individuals and institutions representing the CUP at the local level, the Young Turk clubs and "responsible secretaries" delegated by the Ittihad's (Committee of Union and Progress abrege Turkish form) Central Committee have held my attention because their activity exposes the hidden underside of the genocidal program.

Among the most innovative aspects of this present work are the lessons it draws from an examination of the legal actions brought by the state against both civilians and military personnel in the course of the war. This examination allows us to pinpoint the reasons why miscreants were indicted and the nature of the penalties imposed for economic "infractions" – misappropriation of real estate or moveable assets. It shows, as well, that no one was ever indicted for mass murder.

In studying the procedures the CUP used to liquidate the Armenian population, it seemed worthwhile to take a long look at the fate of the deportees who, in the "second phase of the genocide,"[2] were interned in Syrian and Mesopotamian concentration camps controlled by the Aleppo Sub-Directorate. Here, I zero in on the final decision of the Young Turk leadership, made in the first half of March 1916, which sealed the doom of several hundred thousand deportees. This decision illustrates the flight to the front by the Young Turk leaders with decision-making power.

In accordance with the methodologies of this book, I have also systematically examined the activities of the clandestine humanitarian networks, both Armenian and foreign, which strove to save orphans and intellectuals in particular.

I could hardly have brought this study to a close without considering the legal dimension and political effects of the destruction of the Ottoman Armenians. Therefore, the last part of the book discusses attempts by both the Ottoman authorities and international institutions to bring the authors of the genocide to justice, as well as the judgment passed on them. Such a discussion is essential. It allows us to measure the will of the state and society to face up to their responsibility in the eradication of the Armenians. It offers an occasion to analyze not only the way all the trials organized in Constantinople from February 1919 to spring 1921 were conducted but also the procedures applied in carrying out preliminary court investigations and validating the evidence accumulated by the commissions of inquiry, as well as the methods used to interrogate defendants or witnesses. It affords us a glimpse of the mental universe of the defendants, by way of their explanations, self-justifications, and perceptions of the criminal acts for which they stood accused. Finally, it allows us to bring out the basic element of the founding discourse that inspires the Turkish authorities even today. We are thus led to reflect on the ideological and cultural foundations of a society that rejects its past and is unable to come to terms with its history.

This examination of the legal proceedings also allows us to assess outside interference in the postwar trials, notably in the trial of the Young Turks who had withdrawn to Anatolia or were still in the Ottoman capital. We further discuss their Anatolian and, soon, Kemalist sanctuary in connection with the sabotage of the judicial procedure, the theft of incriminating evidence, the rejection of the very idea that the suspects should be judged, and the organization of their flight to Anatolia by CUP militants active in the eastern provinces.

Several points must be made about the materials to which we had access in carrying out the present study. Many may find the slow progress of research on the Armenian genocide puzzling. It is perhaps unnecessary to point out that since Turkish sources are scarce – in particular, the archives of the Young Turk Central Committee and its paramilitary extension, the Special Organization, are unavailable; one has to go to great lengths to make up even partially for such a handicap. Fortunately, well-documented works, such as those by M. Şükrü Hanioğlu,[3] make it possible to understand the ideology that animated the Young Turk regime, its internal practices and gradual radicalization. For his part, Krieger (the pen-name of Father Krikor Gergerian); carried out the pioneering task of systematically collecting the available sources on the genocide of the Ottoman Armenians, even though he published only one work (in Armenian).[4] Vahakn Dadrian has taught the discipline to take its first steps, with his many scholarly articles and an essential book on the genocide.[5] The work of Erik J. Zürcher is no less important.[6] By carefully sifting through Turkish historiography, notably on Mustafa Kemal, he has succeeded in casting new light on many facts that historians considered incontestable and in clarifying historical questions that had long remained obscure. The principal merit of his work is that it brought out the ideological and personal links between the Young Turks and Mustafa Kemal. There can be no doubt about their importance, even if Kemal worked hard to establish legitimacy in his own right in order to construct the Turkish nation-state whose foundations were laid by his predecessors.

Taking Turkish-Armenian relations as our guiding thread, I try to go one step further here. My work is largely based on material that for all intents and purposes had not been exploited previously – the archives of the Information Bureau created by the Armenian Patriarchate immediately after the Mudros Armistice. The main mission of this bureau was to gather information on the deportation and massacre of the Armenians for the indictments of the Young Turk leaders. We must first say a word about the importance of these materials and their origins.

Let us begin by recalling that the Armenian Patriarchate in Constantinople was dissolved in 28 July 1916 by decision of the Ottoman Council of Ministers[7] and that the Patriarch, Zaven, was exiled to Baghdad on 22 August. The Patriarchate was restored only after the Mudros Armistice brought an end to hostilities. The British High Commissariat then set up an Armenian-Greek committee[8] charged with rehabilitating the survivors of the genocide. When, on 19 February/4 March 1919, Patriarch Zaven returned to Istanbul,[9] one of his priorities was to create an Information Bureau (*deghegadu tivan*). He appointed Arshag Alboyajian (1879–1962), a young historian, to head it. Alboyajian was assisted by Zora Zorayan and, later, by Asadur Navarian (1875–1955) and the jurist Garabed Nurian, who became a member of the Armenian Political Council in 1920.[10] The Information Bureau set about gathering old and new documents on demographic issues, the anti-Armenian persecutions, massacres, deportations, and stolen property. It also compiled facts about the principal authors of the massacres and eyewitness accounts, corroborating evidence and statistics on people who had been abducted and held against their will.[11] According to a report of Nurian's, the Bureau also prepared files on the Turkish authorities' treatment of the Armenians after the Armistice, submitting three hundred reports on attacks on Armenian survivors to the British High Commission. Furthermore, it accumulated documented files on the authors of the deportations "whom the Turks were trying to exonerate" and published two books on "the massacres in Caesarea and Dyarbekir."[12] Thus, it can be seen that, as soon as circumstances allowed, Armenian institutions began to collect materials with the expectation that the Young Turk leaders would be brought to justice before an international "High Court."

On 21 November 1918, a commission of inquiry into the government's conduct, the "Mazhar Commission," was created within the Department of State Security by imperial *irade* (official decree).[13] The following month saw the creation of courts martial charged with trying the Young Turk criminals. Pretrial investigations of a large number of suspects were now opened. The Mazhar Commission, as soon as it came into existence, set about collecting eyewitness accounts and other evidence. It focused its inquiries on state officials complicit in crimes against the Armenian population. It had rather broad prerogatives, inasmuch as it could serve writs, search and seize documents, and also order the arrest and imprisonment of suspects by the Criminal Investigations Department or other state agencies. At the outset, Hasan Mazhar sent an official circular to the provincial prefects and sub-prefects, demanding the originals or certified copies of all orders received by the local authorities in connection with the deportation and massacre of the Armenians. The commission also proceeded to question witnesses under oath. In a little less than three months, it compiled 130 files, regularly transmitting them to the court-martial. These files contained numerous official or semi-official documents, only some of which were published in the legal supplement to the

Official Gazette (*Takvim-ı Vakayi*). Many others appeared in the Istanbul press of the day, in Ottoman Turkish, Armenian or French.

In their capacity as plaintiffs, the Armenians represented by the Constantinople Patriarchate had access to the prosecution's files on the accused. They also had the right to make copies or take photographs of the original documents or of certified copies of them. Although the court was an "extraordinary court-martial," it was originally "mixed" – that is, both civilian and military judges sat on it. Such, at least, was the case until 24 March 1919.[14] Although the Patriarchate and its lawyers enjoyed access to the files compiled by the prosecution for only a brief period – 5 February to 23 March – the Information Bureau was able to assemble a rather substantial mass of official documents; they were supplemented by material from other sources and the eyewitness reports that came flooding into the Patriarchate's offices.

In November 1922, faced with the Kemalist forces' imminent entry into the capital, Patriarch Zaven sent the 22 trunks containing these documents to the Armenian primate in Europe, His Grace Krikoris Balakian, who was then in Manchester. When Balakian was elected bishop of Marseille in 1927, he took the documents with him. On the express request of the retired Patriarch, who wished to consult this material in writing his memoirs, it was sent, early in 1938, to the Patriarch of Jerusalem, Torkom Kushagian. By then, Zaven Der Yeghiayan was living in retirement in Baghdad.[15]

Acknowledgements

Thanks to Vahé Tachjian and Michel Paboudjian, who shared their expert knowledge of archives with me, provided me with innumerable documents, and kindly shared my interrogation of this history; Boris Adjémian, for patiently reading through the manuscript and making valuable suggestions; Stephan Astourian, Hamit Bozarslan, George Hintlian, Hrayr Karagueuzian, Hans-Lukas Kieser, Marc Nichanian, Ara Sarafian, Eric Van Lauwe and Vartkes Yeghiayan, for their generosity, advice and help of various sorts; Alice Aslanian and Serge Samuelian for their kindness and discrete, effective aid; and, last but not least, Gérard Chalian, for suggesting to Odile Jacob's publishing firm that it publish the present work and kindly agreeing to write the preface to the French edition.

PART I

Young Turks and Armenians Intertwined in the Opposition (1895–1908)

Chapter 1

Abdülhamid and the Ottoman Opposition

A great deal of ink has been spilled on the virulence and diversity of the opposition to the regime of Sultan Abdülhamid II. His accession to the throne was tainted by illegitimacy and probably a regicide, but illegitimacy and murder were, after all, common in Ottoman court circles. A good many historians have also stressed the fierce hostility of conservatives, the clergy, and, more generally, Muslim Ottomans to the "Tanzimat," a policy of reform and centralization designed to reorganize the state in central form and make all Ottoman subjects equal before the law. It can hardly be doubted that the centralization of power bred discontent among the *begs*, or tribal chieftains, accustomed to broad autonomy for centuries. It is still more certain that the foreseeable, if not indeed already accomplished, end of the traditional Ottoman system, based on a social hierarchy that put Muslim Ottomans at the top of the scale and "infidels" at the bottom, alarmed, the dominant group and its clerics.

While Abdülhamid II had not initiated the modernization process, he had nevertheless inherited its consequences, particularly the "Midhat Constitution," the restoration of which would later figure as one of the Young Turks' political demands. The fact that the sultan suspended this constitution in rather short order, dissolving parliament and relieving its author of his functions, did not prevent him from pursuing his predecessors' policies of reforming the administration, reorganizing the army, creating a modern educational system, and, more generally, adopting Western models. Yet this was evidently not enough to satisfy the Young Ottoman "modernists."

The Russo-Ottoman War of 1877–8, with which the sultan was confronted almost as soon as he acceded to the throne, reminded the dominant group that the Ottoman Empire had begun an irreversible decline and was losing its possessions one after another. The modernization of the Ottoman state and Ottoman society was, of course, a response to this decline. The new setback that the empire suffered in the Russo-Ottoman War indicated, however, that all the efforts it had made had not yielded the expected results, that the empire would continue to decline and was incapable of putting up effective resistance to the ambitions of the great powers. Such, at any rate, was the conclusion to which many figures associated with the government came, along with conservative and religious social strata.

How was the empire to be saved? Beyond a doubt, all the various Ottoman oppositions crystallized around this question, even if they answered it in diametrically opposed ways. As is often the case when a multicultural, multiethnic empire begins to fall apart, each of its component groups focused on its own future. This was most true, first and foremost, for the group that had held power for centuries.

The very nature of the system was such that the opposition to the sultan was, initially, internal and institutional. Thus, the most active opposition emerged from the ranks of state officials, civilian or military, belonging to the dominant group. Historians have noted that the very idea of opposition to the sovereign and caliph was altogether foreign to the Muslim masses. Under Abdülhamid, one could be exiled to the empire's remote provinces, such as Yemen or the eastern provinces of Asia Minor, on mere suspicion. Indeed, the sultan's pathological suspiciousness, to which his contemporaries often pointed, helped the oppositional groups recruit new members throughout the 30 years of his reign. Members of the Ottoman elite, all educated in accordance with the same modernist model, sometimes found themselves in the opposition quite simply because they had fallen into disgrace, even though they had no fundamental disagreements with the regime. Their political discourse came down to a demand for restoration of the constitution.

This did not hold for the clergy, beginning with those clerics who had roots in the religious orders. They could not accept, as we have said, egalitarian ideology and the attendant risk of losing the superior status that Islam conferred on them. Since the clergy enjoyed, to some extent, ascendancy over the Muslim masses, they played an important part in shaping the public opinion that rejected Western innovations and looked askance at the increasingly influential role played by non-Muslims.

In contrast, the Young Ottomans, who in 1889 founded the *Ittihad-ı Osmani*[1] at the *Tıbbyeyi Askeriye* (Military Medical School) – Mehmed Reşid,[2] the future vali of Dyarbekir, İbrahim Temo (1865–1939), Abdüllah Cevdet (1869–1932) and İshak Sükûti (1868–1903) – embodied the beginnings of a true political opposition. For they had assimilated a key source of the cohesion and, therefore, power of the Western societies of their day – namely nationalism. They had very little power in this period and were a school of thought rather than an organized movement, but their guiding idea was already making its way in the Ottoman world.

With regard to the burning question of the empire's future, however, the elements that were not associated with the dominant group were already wondering what was to become of them. Their status as *gâvurs* ("infidels") had improved somewhat since implementation of the *Tanzimat*, yet they continued to be perceived by the Turkish population as ungrateful, deceitful, and disloyal groups with a penchant for profiting from all the others.[3] While some of the members of these *millets* served in government, they had only subaltern functions and had no political responsibilities; in the everyday world, the courts and the administration in general maintained inegalitarian practices and taxed non-Muslims more heavily than others. The Muslim masses continued to regard the *millets* as foreign elements, almost as domestic foes.

For the non-Turkish groups living in the European part of the empire, the 1878 Treaty of Berlin had plainly put a dent in the dogma of the empire's territorial integrity; it remained only to work out the final details of their divorce with Istanbul. This was not the case with the Arab, Armenian, or Kurdish elements of the empire, whose destiny was much more closely bound up with that of the Ottoman state, thanks to their implantation in the Asiatic part of the empire. The organic religious bond that tied the Arab world, practically severed from its Egyptian component, to the Ottoman capital and its Sultan-Caliph was by no means superficial, but it appeared too loose to hold forever. Egypt's impressive economic development did not go unnoticed and was the envy of many people from the clan-based or tribal world of Syria and Mesopotamia, or even Arabia and Yemen. This was the more so in that it brought out the contrast between modernization at a forced pace and an Ottoman society stagnating under an administration that many deemed inefficient and corrupt.

The Armenian-Kurdish Ottoman world was, in its turn, awakening from a slumber of several centuries. The Armenians saw the progress that had been made in the eastern part of their historical territory ruled by Russia, even if this progress went hand-in-hand with assimilationist, repressive policies. Officially, the Tanzimat had freed them of their dependency on Kurdish *begs*, but the result was to revive an ancient rivalry that had over the centuries yielded to a sort of arrangement, or "symbiosis," from which both parties benefited. The Kurdish chieftains, who had been replaced by officials appointed by the central government, found it hard to accept the loss of their long-standing privileges for the sake of modernizing the state and centralizing it in line with a European model about which they knew nothing. Yet, neither Kurds nor Armenians had as yet begun to envisage their future outside the Ottoman framework.

The "Armenian Committees," which doubtless represented the most virulent wing of the opposition, were considered, both by the Hamidian government and many Young Turk opponents of the regime, to be terrorist organizations threatening the country's domestic security and territorial integrity, helping to create through their propaganda a deplorable image of the empire in the West. For their part, the committees deemed themselves part of the enlightened element of Ottoman society, a kind of avant-garde imbued with socialist values that was endeavoring to free the masses from the reigning obscurantism and build a federal state.

It can readily be seen, then, that an immense gulf separated the ruling group, which was desperately seeking to preserve the empire and defend its privileges, from the Armenian activists who reasoned in terms of intellectual categories altogether foreign to the world in which they operated. Sultan Abdülhamid's response to these movements was to massacre nearly 200,000 Armenians in the years 1894–6. These crimes, of which we still have no comprehensive study, had an organized character; it is beyond doubt that the Sublime Porte was directly implicated in them. Although they cannot be called genocidal, they seem to have been intended to reduce the Armenian population at large and weaken it at the socio-economic level. They also unleashed a debate within the Committees and the Armenian population about the revolutionary acts of self-defense supposed to have brought on this bloody repression. This debate lastingly poisoned relations within the Ottoman Armenian community: it of course raises questions about the psychological effects of mass murder, but also about the practices of the Hamidian regime, the role of violence in Turkish society, and that society's way of dealing with political questions.

That said, the mobilization of Western public opinion that resulted from these events transformed the massacres into a sort of moral touchstone or yardstick that was later used in judging Ottoman oppositional currents. The massacres were thus a central topic of debate when the Young Turks and Armenian activists in exile began to discuss the future of the Ottoman Empire.

Young Turks and Armenian Militants in Europe, 1895–1901

Until 1895, Paris remained a place of exile for the Young Turks, including the most famous of them, Ahmed Rıza, who founded the Ottoman Committee of Union and Progress (OCUP) in this period. Rıza had gathered only a small group of Young Turks around him, but it was a very select one: it included Dr. Nâzım, a native of Salonika, who joined him in 1894 in Paris, where he also hoped to complete his medical studies,[4] and Ahmed Ağaoğlu (Agayev), a native of Shushi (the capital of Karabagh) who took courses in history and philosophy at the Sorbonne and the National Institute of Eastern Languages and Civilizations.[5]

Among the Armenians in Paris in the same period, Stepanos Sapah-Giulian was undoubtedly the most interesting figure.[6] A leader of the Hnchak Social-Democratic Party (SDHP), Sapah-Giulian was the moving spirit behind the Hnchak club in Paris. Here he rubbed shoulders with the Young Turk exiles, whom he claimed to know better than anyone else because he had had dealings with them for so many years.

In early 1895, in Parisian political and intellectual circles, conversation turned on the appropriate reaction to the anti-Armenian massacres perpetrated in Sasun in summer 1894 and the publication, in a British parliamentary *Blue Book*, of the damning conclusions of the European consuls who had served on a commission of inquiry into these events. The Sultan, many said, had to be confronted with a demand for "reforms" in the eastern provinces of Asia Minor that would put an end to the "insecurity" reigning there.

For the first time, the Parisian Young Turks were forced to consider the vexing question of the "reforms" that the European powers were seeking to impose on the Ottoman Empire. With this question, it was their conception of the Ottoman state, and the place and status of non-Muslim elements in it, that was put to the test. The publication of an article on the reform plan of "11 May 1895," in the Parisian daily *Le Figaro*,[7] led to a meeting between the Parisian SDHP activists and the Young Turks, headed by Rıza and Nâzım, who had just been elected treasurer of the CUP. Sapah-Giulian's account of their meeting shows that the two Turkish leaders were staunchly opposed to this reform plan[8] – that is to say, hostile both to European interference in what they considered an internal Ottoman affair, as well as the creation of a special status for certain provinces of the empire. They continued to argue for a policy of centralization, contrary to the Hnchaks, who simply denounced the tribal system and the violence prevailing in the eastern provinces and condemned the Sasun massacres.

What is more, the official leader of the Young Turk movement, Ahmed Rıza, rejected the revolutionary methods espoused by part of the anti-Hamidian opposition. He advocated, rather, a conservative policy[9] that was ultimately not very different from the sultan's. However, Rıza needed support from the Armenians, among others, in order to make his political project credible in Parisian circles. He therefore asked to meet with Nubar Pasha,[10] an Armenian from Smyrna who had served as Prime Minister of Egypt and was the father of the Egyptian reforms, notably the creation of mixed courts. Rıza doubtless hoped to profit from the Egyptian pasha's many connections to French politicians, and from his generosity as well.

In fall 1895, the "Armenian Students of Paris" organized a lecture in a hall in the city's Grand Orient lodge. The invited speaker was Avetis Nazarbekian of London, one of the SDHP's founders. The lecture and the response to it offer us an opportunity to evaluate the positions taken by the Parisian Young Turks on the most recent persecutions of the Ottoman Armenian population. Nazarbekian denounced Hamid's policies, especially the generalized massacres of October and November and Europe's indifference to them. "If the Armenians must die," Nazarbekian concluded, "they will die, not as slaves, but as free men." Yet, it was the part of his talk in which he questioned the Sublime Porte's ability to govern its possessions that disturbed his Young Turk listeners, more than the crimes themselves. Sapah-Giulian later noted that the many Armenian students in the Young Turks' ranks were surprised by their Muslim comrades' negative reaction.[11]

The massacres contributed heavily to turning Western public opinion against the Ottoman Empire. This pained the Young Turk exiles in Paris. The violence also helped bring about a radicalization of the Armenian Committees, whose leadership bodies had established themselves in London, Geneva, and Paris. The Young Turk movement nevertheless profited from the diplomatic crisis that followed the Armenian massacres.[12] The French supplement to *Meşveret* (*Mechveret supplément français*), which Rıza had begun publishing in Paris in 1895, reveals the uncomfortable situation in which the Parisian exiles found themselves, torn as they were between patriotic feelings informed by official Ottoman discourse and their shame at the European reaction to the events. A May 1896 article by the movement's master thinker includes a long demonstration in which Rıza endeavors to show that the anti-Armenian massacres organized by Abdülhamid "flew in the face of the traditions of Islamicism and the precepts of the Koran ... We wish to see the sultan surrounded by counselors who are steeped in both Muslim precepts and the ideas of order and progress."[13] Rıza thus put forward the thesis that responsibility for the massacres lay with the sultan's entourage, which had supposedly failed on this occasion to respect national traditions. He thereby exonerated the sultan himself of all blame, illustrating in the process his conception of the government and his attachment to the function of the Sultan-Caliph.

A few weeks later, Rıza expatiated on his approach to the notion of responsibility, thereby revealing his perception of the empire's Christian subjects. He confessed that he "defended the Muslims more often than the Christians." "This may seem exaggerated," he went on, "but the fact is that, in our country, there is no comparison between the fate of the Ottoman Christians and that of the Muslims. The Christians are by far happier, or, if one prefers, less wretched... If Christians are the preferred targets of looting, the reason is that they enjoy greater wealth and material comfort than the Muslims and that, either out of fear or suspicion of the victor, they generally keep their doors shut."[14] What the Young Turk leader says here is obviously rooted in a centuries-old Ottoman tradition, marked by the concept of the Christian "guest" who "takes advantage" of his happy lot and displays his lack of gratitude toward his masters by refusing to share what he possesses with them. Thus, the violence exercised by the dominant group is legitimized.

Jules Roches delivered a lecture in December 1895 at the Hôtel des Sociétés Savantes in which he denounced the horrors perpetrated by the Hamidian regime. The reactions that his lecture elicited are as revealing as Rıza's essay. One of the Young Turks present, who had taken a seat beside Rıza, was unable to contain himself and shouted out: "All this information is false; it has been made up by the Hnchaks." He then blamed the Armenians for the events that were sullying Turkey's reputation.[15] This shows how deeply young "liberal" activists, albeit united in their combat against Abdülhamid's regime, were opposed on a great number of issues, prisoners of their respective cultural backgrounds and traditions.

For their part, the Armenian activists who sought to appeal to Western public opinion complained that the Parisian press depicted them as terrorists and willfully ignored the reality of the massacres.[16] According to Sapah-Giulian, this general trend was reversed by a conversation he had with Anatole Leroy-Beaulieu, his professor at the École des Sciences Politiques. Leroy-Beaulieu, known as an expert on the East, agreed to intervene in the debate.[17] His contribution also took the form of a lecture, "Armenia and the Armenian Question," delivered at the Hôtel des Sociétés Savantes. This event, which saw a distinguished French personality participating in the discussion, provided Young Turk and Armenian activists with a new opportunity to air their opposing views. It showed, as well, that Istanbul kept close tabs on its opposition in exile. Münir Bey, the sultan's ambassador, who had been given the task of monitoring the opposition's activities in Paris, recruited young Ottoman students, Sapah-Giulian reports, and had them introduced into the lecture hall, where Ahmed Rıza and his partisans were also present. One of Rıza's supporters, no doubt reflecting his comrades' mood as well, interrupted the lecturer to ask him whether a scholar like himself could seriously speak in such terms about a "religious group."[18] In thus seeking to downplay Armenian identity, the Young Turks were in fact voicing the apprehensions they felt at the campaign mounted by the Hnchaks, who, adding insult to injury, had invited a "foreigner" to join a debate on an "internal matter" and so incited the European chancelleries to intervene in Turkey.

Other examples, however, illustrate the solidarity prevailing between the oppositional groups in Paris and the fact that their relations, while sometimes stormy, were quite close. A meeting that took place between the Young Turk leaders and the Hnchak revolutionaries shortly after the events just discussed was one of the most revealing in this respect. Rıza and Nâzım proposed to the SDHP representatives that they collaborate and "make a joint contribution to the movement of national renewal." He suggested that, to this end, they "put old quarrels behind them."[19] In view of Rıza's frank aversion to his Armenian interlocutors' revolutionary methods, it is not easy to say what impelled the Ottoman Committee of Union and Progress to seek a rapprochement with the Hnchaks. Possibly Rıza and Nâzım were hoping to profit from the popularity that the Hnchaks enjoyed at the time or even from their relations with certain Parisian intellectual circles. They may also have been seeking to curb the Hnchaks' anti-Hamidian campaign, which they deemed anti-Ottoman.

The seizure of the Banque Ottomane by militants of the Armenian Revolutionary Federation (ARF) on 26 August 1896 is another event that serves as a yardstick with which to measure the Young Turk and Armenian positions. The operation, the kind that the press delighted in covering, found a much broader international echo than the massacres of autumn and winter 1895–6, doubtless because it struck directly at European financial interests.[20] This was, however, not a peaceful demonstration like the one that had taken place in October 1895; most of the French press reacted very harshly, painting the Armenians as terrorists. The Paris Hnchaks suddenly felt that they had lost the fruits of the public awareness campaign that they had been waging for the past year. The SDHP therefore requested a meeting with the leaders of the ARF, who agreed to make the trip from Geneva – their European headquarters and the city in which they published their official organ, *Droschak*. Sapah-Giulian asked them why they had mounted this operation. He seems to have received an embarrassed response; it came down to the idea that the ARF wanted to make an attention-grabbing appeal to Europe in order to bring an end to the Armenian massacres. In private, the Hnchak leaders did not hesitate to speak of "political immaturity."[21] It seems reasonable to suppose that the competition between the two organizations for leadership of the Armenians had helped motivate the ARF's spectacular strategy.

Leaving a meeting with the historian Ernest Lavisse and the academician Albert Vandale, Sapah-Giulian, who had asked the two Frenchmen to intercede on the Armenians' behalf, ran straight into Rıza and Nâzım, "arm-in-arm" in front of the main entrance to the French Senate building. Rıza exclaimed, "Mr. Sapah-Giulian, this time they are massacring people by the tens of thousands … What remains of the Armenian Question, the 11 May plan and European intervention?" Nâzım added, "The [death toll] of the massacres of the past few days is over one hundred thousand; it seems that they are not going to leave a single Armenian [alive]."[22] The Hnchak leader did not fail to note the ironic tone adopted by his interlocutors, who did not for a moment consider condemning these crimes, but had already begun calculating their demographic and political impact.

The Hnchak Committee finally decided to turn to a "heavyweight" in an effort to reverse the anti-Armenian trend. It sent a memorandum to Jean Jaurès defending the Armenians' struggle against Abdülhamid's regime and asking Jaurès to take a public stand in order to stem the flood of anti-Armenian propaganda in the French press. Sapah-Giulian points out that the socialist leader had previously rejected this suggestion because of his apprehensions about "Armenian nationalism." After a conversation with Sapah-Giulian, however, he decided to throw himself into the fray. At the same time, he confessed that he had misgivings about the fact that he would be defending the same position as certain conservative pro-Armenian circles in France.[23]

Jaurès's first intervention came on 3 November 1896, at the podium of the French Parliament, which was full to the point of bursting. The session was opened by Denis Cochin, but Jaurès did not take the floor until the conservatives had finished speaking. His entry into the lists came as a surprise, for no one had been expecting him to address a foreign policy issue. He made a strong impression on those present and on public opinion generally, in particular by indicting the French government for its policy on Turkey of the past four years.[24] Jaurès's one-and-a-half hour speech marked the real beginning of the pro-Armenian movement in France. The Parisian newspapers, which, as everyone knew, pocketed generous subsidies from agents of the Ottoman sultan, now struck a new tone.

There was a perceptible détente in relations between Young Turks and Armenian activists in late 1895. Changes within the Young Turk movement undoubtedly helped create the conditions for real cooperation among the various opponents of the Hamidian regime. Murad Bey Mizanci's arrival in Europe earlier in the year had already established a connection between OCUP circles in Istanbul and Europe, long isolated from each other. Unlike Rıza and Nâzım, Murad Bey, who had worked for a long time in the Hamidian administration, favored European intervention as well as rapprochement with the Armenian revolutionary committees and the formation of a united front. In December 1895, he began publishing the review *Mizan* (Balance) in Cairo, which had considerable impact in circles sympathetic to the Young Turks.[25] In this review, Murad Bey challenged Rıza's anti-revolutionary positions. He dealt Rıza the deathblow upon his return to Paris in July 1896, in the course of a meeting at which a new central committee was elected after Rıza had lost the support of the majority. Murad assumed leadership of this committee, with Nâzım as his second-in-command.[26] On his initiative, the Young Turks apparently established warmer relations with the ARF in particular.[27] In April 1897, the Turkish intelligence service intercepted a message from the ARF's Paris branch to the committee in Erzerum; it indicated that the Armenian organizations and the CUP had now come together around a common goal, dethroning the sultan.[28] No trace of such an agreement is to be found in Armenian sources, but it is the more plausible in that all branches of the CUP had been directly linked to Paris after the Constantinople branch was dissolved under pressure from the Hamidian political police.[29] For a long time to come, the ARF was the Young Turks' main Armenian interlocutor, even if we should not attach undue importance to this initial rapprochement.

That the ARF and CUP united around common goals is more likely; the social complexion of the Turkish organization had changed with the 1896–7 arrival in Paris of officers and army doctors.[30] However, thanks to the defection of *Mizanci* Murad, who in July 1897 agreed to return to Istanbul after negotiations with representatives of the sultan, Rıza had again assumed the dominant role in the CUP,[31] putting a damper on the plans for a rapprochement between Young Turks and Armenians. The salient feature of this period, however, was the growing influence of the CUP's Cairo branch, which helped change the Union's orientation.[32] As Hanioğlu points out, after first promoting a union of all Ottoman groups behind Rıza's idea of Ottomanizing society and secularizing the state, and then defending Murad Bey's conservative political line, which was favorable to outside intervention, the CUP adopted a new program that called for reconciling Islam with modernity on the basis of a constitutional system.[33]

The Armenian Committees probably took note of these transformations. At all events, a Turkish-Armenian oppositional delegation, headed by Rıza, participated in the 1899 Hague Peace Conference, where it distributed a joint memorandum. The Turkish leader was accompanied by an Armenian, Minas Tchéraz, a well-known yet independent figure to be sure, and Pierre Anmeghian, one of Tchéraz's most faithful followers. In other words, he was not accompanied by representatives of the Armenian revolutionary parties. Yet, the idea of sending a joint delegation to the conference was a success, for it attracted favorable attention from the European delegates.[34] The fact that the Armenian delegates were not altogether representative of their people should not obscure the novelty of this public initiative, from which the Young Turks, who were seeking to enlist European public opinion in their cause and profile themselves as liberals, derived the greater benefit. Abdülhamid seems to have understood this quite well, for he included Diran Kelekian,[35] a journalist well known for his perceptive analyses of Ottoman society, in the official Ottoman delegation.[36]

The positions that the Armenian Revolutionary Federation put forward, after the OCUP issued its call for a union of all oppositional forces in spring 1898,[37] provide a good index of the positive but skeptical attitude reigning in Armenian circles. The Armenian leadership thought that it had detected a change in the OCUP, which, it felt, "had resolved to abandon its passive position once and for all and enter an active phase." "To date," *Droschak* went on,

> we have tended to take a skeptical view of Young Turkey's capacities, course of action and principles, as well as the seriousness of its desire for reform. Long experience has convinced us of the need for this. In the last twenty years, we have never once seen this party attempt to protest the crowned murderer's unexampled injustices and outrageous crimes in *active* form. We have never laid eyes on Turkish revolutionaries; we have seen only Turkish "liberals" or "pacifists," who are present in large numbers among us [the Armenians] as well. We have had our fill of vain memoranda; we have had our fill of begging and imploring Europe, of sighs and lamentations ... The ideas that Young Turkey preaches have unfortunately not found fertile ground in the Turkish people or created a public movement among the Turks. The Young Turks' program was utopian. They made an enormous mistake in proclaiming "that the revolution would come from above" ... Today, however, we are happy to be able to point out that groups which ... have split off from this movement are professing more radical ideas [and] have invited us to show our solidarity with them ... If, today, there exists a degree of national antagonism between Ottoman Turks and Ottoman Armenians, the blame for it lies primarily with the government. We are convinced that, in future, once acceptable political conditions have been brought about in Turkey, our two nations will continue to live in peace and harmony and will, united in a common effort, make their way toward the highest form of civilization .... It matters little that certain decrepit representatives of Young Turkey, who are utterly ignorant of our activities, spread insinuations against us, holding up the Armenian Committees before all Europe as "destroyers of Turkish villages" and casting the word "separatist" in the Armenian revolutionaries' teeth ... Gentlemen, you have doubtless firmly resolved to have done with your old delusions, with moderation, slow progress, evolution and other such vague notions, in which your senile brothers are steeped. There are, among us Armenians as well, empty-headed philosophers who call themselves "evolutionists" and shun revolution. Evolution, however, is an undefined concept that everyone, the unbridled Tyrant included, can exploit to his own ends in elaborating programs, whether political or of some other kind ... You, too, should galvanize your own people, whose bitter sufferings you know very well. That unfortunate people is also being tortured ... Enslaved, it has, like the slaves of other faiths, crawled before tyrants and exploiters belonging to its own race ... Your clergymen, invoking the Koran, are unfortunately reinforcing and sacralizing hatred of all that is new. Rescue the people from this deadly immobility.[38]

This long response from the ARF, cast in the form of a lecture delivered in an occasionally peremptory tone, sums up the party's perception of the Young Turk movement. This perception, based on "long experience," confirmed, in the Armenian party's view, that "Young Turkey" had not adopted the "radical" methods of which the ARF considered itself the champion. It must be said that, in this period, violent clashes between the army and groups of Armenian *fedayis* in the eastern provinces were occurring almost daily; every issue of *Droschak* between 1890 and 1900 describes such clashes and gives the biographies of the fighters who fell in battle. The "martyrs" that the ARF's resistance to Abdülhamid's regime cost it no doubt explain the party's feeling that it was the sole opposition movement to combat the sultan's "tyranny" at the practical level.

The ARF's reaction to the 1899 Hague Peace Conference is also rather revealing of its irritation with the European powers. The tone of the "Declaration Addressed to the Public Opinion of the Civilized World" on the occasion of the conference is sarcastic, almost cynical, and in any case disillusioned in the passages that evoke the Europeans' foreign policy or their indifference to the 1894–6 massacres.[39] The "Declaration," however, says not a word about Rıza's decision to attend the conference as part of a delegation made up of Turks and Armenians.

Also worth pausing over, because they illustrate both the political game as it was played in the Ottoman family and the ARF's openness to dialogue, are the maneuvers that Sultan Abdülhamid undertook to silence the Armenian opposition in exile, as he had partially succeeded in doing with the Young Turks. He proceeded by engaging in political negotiations with the party even while pursuing repressive domestic policies. To open discussions between the Sublime Porte and the ARF, which did not become public knowledge until after they were broken off on 11 March 1899, Abdülhamid delegated his undersecretary of state for foreign affairs, Artin Pasha Dadian, a scion of one of the grand Armenian families that had served the Ottoman state for generations. On 28 October 1896, Dadian's son, Diran Bey Dadian, arrived in Geneva and met with the ARF's Western Bureau, which was grouped around the monthly *Droschak*. The message he bore was clear: the ARF had to abandon its violent activities. In exchange, the sultan pledged to carry out fundamental reforms in the country over the coming nine months.[40] According to *Droschak's* editors, the "Khanasor" operation – a commando raid on 25 August 1897 (6 September, new style), that had taken retaliatory measures against a Kurdish tribe that had participated in anti-Armenian massacres in the Van region the year before – and the abortive attempt to blow up Yıldız Palace on 6/18 August had forced Abdülhamid to take the ARF's demands seriously.

An accomplished politician, the sultan resorted to his usual methods, seeking to pull the wool over the eyes of the Armenian revolutionaries as he was also attempting to do with the Young Turks. On the sovereign's orders, Drtad Bey Dadian, a nephew of Artin Pasha's, spent almost eight months in Geneva, leaving only in March 1899. The length of his stay indicates the seriousness and determination of this initiative. While it proved unsuccessful, it nevertheless enabled the Sublime Porte to take the measure of the Armenians' demands: at Artin Pasha's request, the ARF drew up a list of the reforms that it was seeking.[41]

Manifestly, since *Mizancı* Murad's "surrender," the Young Turk movement in exile had once again adopted the positivist leader's moderate line, even if it did not command unanimous assent. In other words, the movement was paralyzed and found it difficult to recruit new members from the circles opposed to the sultan. It was repeatedly criticized for failing to commit itself to action.

In 1899 and 1900, the discussion between Young Turks and Armenians was carried on in their respective newspapers, which indicates that the parties were, despite everything, interested in each other. The old debate about whether or not it was necessary to build a common front of all those opposed to the Hamidian regime flared up frequently in these papers. Thus, an anonymous letter, published by *Droschak*, revealed that toward the middle of 1899, Tunalı Hilmi[42] had circulated in Cairo a declaration calling for a congress of "Muslims and non-Muslims" aimed at creating an "Ottoman Committee," and that Damad Mahmud Pasha and his two sons, members of the imperial family, had fled Istanbul to join the Young Turk opposition in exile. The anonymous author of the letter notes, finally, as if in response to his Armenian interlocutors' criticisms, that *Osmanlı* did not share *Meshveret's* anti-revolutionary positions and that "a good many Young Turks advocate revolutionary methods."[43] This is one index of the fact that the ARF embodied the idea of revolution for certain Young Turk circles, especially officers who had graduated from the Military Academy.

Damad Mahmud Pasha's "Open Letter to the Armenians," sent out from his Parisian exile in summer 1900, was the first credible sign that the Young Turk opposition wanted to pool the energies of all those opposed to the sultan, even if the letter blamed Abdülhamid alone for all the empire's ills. Mahmud expressed his regrets over the "appalling massacres" organized by the sultan, while also criticizing the Armenians for maintaining too great a distance from the Turks. He ended his letter with a call for unity, restoration of the constitution, and "federation with the Turks."[44] The last formula was unprecedented: coming from someone of Damad's stature, it was no mere rhetorical flourish, but a promising invitation to construct "the new Turkey."

The response of *Droschak's* editors shows that they took Prince Damad's offer seriously:

There was a time when we were constantly inviting the Turks, perplexed as we were by their indifference to Turkey's dire plight, to unite with us in struggle ... Now the roles have been reversed: Turkish calls for "union" are raining down on us, while we are unfortunately obliged, despite our deep-felt sympathy for the principle, to maintain an uncertain position ... "Let us unite": that is a superb idea. But with whom, and how? The Armenian revolutionaries have been on the scene for a long time and are already waging the struggle in whose name we are invited to unite. But where are the Turkish fighters? To date, we have encountered only individuals, groups, people busy making propaganda on paper; we have yet to see active fighters and agitators. Cut off from the real Turkish populace and depending for support on a negligible fraction of the Turkish intelligentsia, the Young Turks are still politicians who look to "the revolution from above"; they are weak, disorganized and, consequently, still inactive; they are men who prefer talk to action ... Would that they had, at the very least, waged a verbal propaganda campaign tending in the right direction and geared to the present cultural needs of the Turkish people. But read through the Young Turks' publications: you will not find a single challenge to the internal forces smothering Turkish society ... "Our history is superior to the Europeans', and we have more patience," someone writes. Someone else scurrilously repeats that "there exists no evil in Turkey that does not exist in still greater measure in so-called enlightened Europe." The only evil, we are told, is Sultan Hamid's person; the crisis that Turkey has been enduring for a quarter of a century is wholly due to his caprices. If Hamid disappears, Turkey will become a model country: this is what all the Young Turks repeat in chorus.[45]

The ARF was not the only organization to respond to Prince Damad's overtures. The SDHP also made itself heard in the person of Sapah-Giulian. He pointed out that the state was organized in such a way that there were no real bonds between its various constitutive elements, that no institution had sought to unite them in a bond of solidarity with the throne, and that, if the country were not reorganized on new foundations, it was condemned to disappear.[46] Finally, Sapah-Giulian reminded his readers that

the very moderate desires and the short-term goals put forward by the Armenian nation and the Armenians' fighting forces have never stood in opposition to the real, permanent interests of Turkey considered as a state. What the Armenians are demanding today is not in any way intended to weaken or paralyze Turkey, to dismember and, ultimately, destroy it, to pulverize the Turkish people and, on its ruins, re-establish the Home of the Armenians. The Armenian people's modest desires for reform and all the political, economic and social institutions to which it aspires contain, not the seeds of Turkey's destruction, but, abundantly, the seeds of its renewal.[47]

These reactions to Damad Mahmud Pasha's invitation sum up the Armenian Committees' political vision and reflect their determination to help rebuild a common state. The Ottoman dignitary's proposal to forge an "Armenian-Turkish federation"[48] doubtless reflected an option for founding the state anew shared by certain liberal circles that had emerged from the Ottoman elite. However, the Armenian Committees, still shaken by the violence inflicted on their compatriots in the eastern provinces, remained skeptical about the possibility of yoking their fate to that of this opposition, whose weakness and unrealistic objectives they had pointed out.

The end of the first stage of the rapprochement between Young Turks and Armenian revolutionaries throws up a crucial question: why did the largely legitimist Young Turk opposition seek to cooperate with the revolutionaries? On the face of it, everything separated a prince of the house of Osman from an Armenian intellectual who pleaded for socialism and even espoused revolutionary violence. Part of the answer no doubt lies in the common education and shared cultural references of the members of these two elites, who both spoke French and were steeped in European sociopolitical concepts. Another reason is to be sought in the existence of a vast network of Armenian militants, capable of operating in many different regions of the empire and characterized by their iron discipline, spirit of self-sacrifice and unwavering dedication: the Young Turk movement lacked any such base. We should also not overlook the fact that the Young Turk elite, especially the elite with roots in the Ottoman court or the upper echelons of the state administration, had necessarily come into contact with the high-ranking Armenian officials who had chosen to serve the state and did so with an effectiveness that no one dreamed of contesting. In addition, the same Young Turk elite was aware of the importance of the Armenian and Greek businessmen who were the moving spirits behind the industrialization of the country. Finally, we must not underestimate the pro-Armenian network that the Armenian Committees had succeeded in building up in Europe. Its by no means negligible ability to mobilize Western public opinion constituted the essential antidote to the propaganda campaigns of Abdülhamid and his agents, waged with the help of large "subsidies."[49]

The first phase of the Armenian-Turkish negotiations also revealed, however, the antagonistic positions of the two main Young Turk groups on basic issues such as foreign intervention or local autonomy. The organizing committee, indeed, had not so much as asked Rıza for his opinion before compiling the lists of invitees. It would seem that the members of the old OCUP were hostile to the Armenian Committees and, especially, the ARF.[50] But Damad Mahmud's whole strategy turned on the idea of a rapprochement between Young Turks and Armenians.[51] He therefore sought to neutralize Rıza while arranging to invite the three Armenian parties – the ARF; the Verakazmial Hnchaks, who accepted the offer; and the Hnchaks, who turned it down.[52] Each committee was represented by three delegates and agreed to work in coordination with the others. In January, they held preparatory meetings with the two princes and İsmail Kemal Bey to make certain that the negotiations would take Article 61 of the Treaty of Berlin and the Memorandum of 11 May 1895 as points of departure. Avetis Aharonian headed the Dashnak delegation.[53] The Armenian side was further represented by three Paris-based veterans of the anti-Hamidian opposition – Minas Tchéraz,[54] Garabed Basmajian[55] and Archag Tchobanian.[56] The Young Turk delegation included, among others,[57] Hüseyin Tosun,[58] İsmail Hakkı,[59] Hoca Kadri, Çerkez Kemal, Dr. Lütfi, Mustafa Hamdi, Ali Fehmi,[60] Dr. Nâzım, and Yusuf Akçura.

The congress was opened by Prince Sabaheddin (whose father had just died) on 4 February 1902. There were six sessions conducted, at the Armenians' request, in French as well as Turkish. Only a few Greek, Albanian, and Kurdish delegates took part. As for the Macedonians, they had not even been invited. Thus, the congress rapidly evolved into a tête-à-tête between the Young Turk groups and the Armenian delegation. One of the pivotal questions posed from the outset bore on the principle of foreign intervention. Sabaheddin and some of those participating in the congress were in favor of it. Those who voted against it, according to Bahaeddin Şakir's archives, were Abdülhalim Memduh, Abdurrahman Bedirhan (representing the newspaper *Kurdistan*), Ahmed Ferid, Ahmed Rıza, Ali Fahri (on the editorial board of *Osmanlı*), Albert Fua, Mustafa Hamdi, Dr. Nâzım, and Yusuf Akçura.[61] A majority of the 25 delegates voted down a motion, put forward at the third session of the congress by the 18 representatives of the minorities, to discuss the question of foreign intervention again.

A joint declaration was nevertheless hammered out, to "remind the European powers that it was their duty, and also in the general interests of humanity, to see to it that the clauses of the treaties and international agreements between them and the Sublime Porte be carried out in such a way as to benefit all parts of the Ottoman Empire."[62] The declaration had the merit of summing up both the question of outside intervention and the no less controversial question of how to implement the promised reforms – subjects that obviously concerned the Armenians and Macedonians above all others. Yet, it had undoubtedly been too heavily diluted from the standpoint of the Armenian delegation, which solemnly declared that the Armenians were "ready to collaborate with the Ottoman liberals in every joint activity aimed at changing the present regime"; that "beyond such joint actions, the Armenian committees [would] pursue their particular activities, it being well understood that these activities are directed against the existing regime, not the unity and organic existence of Turkey"; and that "their particular activity has no other goal than to bring about the immediate enactment of Article 61 of the Treaty of Berlin as well as the Memorandum of 11 May 1895 and the appendix to it."[63] This came down to agreeing to cooperate to preserve Turkey's territorial integrity while maintaining complete autonomy when it came to bringing about reforms in the eastern provinces.

Ahmed Rıza and his partisans were, obviously, opposed to this declaration,[64] so Sabaheddin had to propose a variant. It called for "realizing the Armenians' legitimate desires in connection with the organization and local administration of the provinces that they inhabit and of all other provinces; establishing a central government based on liberal ideas, the best way of guaranteeing the maintenance of national rights as well as the regular functioning of the provincial governments, from which the Armenians would benefit on the same footing and in the same measure as all the other peoples of the empire."[65] In this way, the prince tried to satisfy the Armenians' desire to have a hand in governing the provinces in which they lived while simultaneously envisaging an extension of the principle of "administrative" decentralization to the other provinces of the empire. But, in fact, he succeeded only in displeasing both sides: the Armenians left the congress before the last session, held on 10 February 1902. Nevertheless, the new organization's central committee was elected – by secret ballot.[66] The vote confirmed that Sabaheddin and a majority favorable to British intervention had taken control of the movement, which now included, among the accusations it leveled against the Hamidian regime, the sultan's policy of "suppressing the Armenians."

However, the majority also provoked the formation of a minority "coalition" within the movement.[67] This coalition brought together Ahmed Rıza and the activist young guard, which included many officers. It accused the majority of collaborating with the Armenians and Macedonians and consequently working against the interests of the empire. It accused it particularly of basing its strategy toward Europe on a defense of the Armenians, so as to legitimize the movement, as it were, in the eyes of the European chancelleries.[68] Thus, we see here the emergence of a group of Young Turks whose convictions were in every respect at variance with the activity of the Armenian committees – even if, like the ARF after the 1902 congress, this minority took positions shaped to some extent by the desire to remain open or even conciliatory.

In the wake of the congress, negotiations were opened between the majority and the ARF on the one side, and the Macedonian Committee on the other – represented by Aknuni (Khachadur Malumian) and Boris Sarafov, respectively.[69]

To arrive at a comprehensive view of the positions of the other Armenian Committees and understand their perceptions of the Young Turk movement, let us examine the way the SDHP reacted after the 1902 congress. A long article by the editorial board of the SDHP's official organ, published in London, begins by recalling that the SDHP had been the only party not to participate in the February 1902 congress and that it had made the decision not to attend "based on a thorough-going analysis of the situation." At the general congress that the SDHP held in the same period, the article declares, the party came to the conclusion that it was not possible to work with the Young Turks, for "dissatisfaction [with the current regime] is not sufficient grounds for collaboration," which could only be based on common leadership and common political goals. However, the editorial board contends there is "a towering barrier between the two groups," even if this is not obvious, for the Young Turks' "sole objective is to put the 'pitiful' Midhat Constitution into effect, without in any way altering the absolute tyrant's irresponsible status."[70]

The author then turns to the heart of the matter. He explains his party's position:

The Young Turks like to say that they want to propel the country by peaceful means down an evolutionary path toward a purely internal revolution of all state functions and all laws. But they do not for a moment consider giving up an inch of the state… The preservation of the state's territorial integrity is as much an article of faith for them as it is for the sultan and all the Old Turks. In that respect, they are as stubbornly patriotic as the sultan and the Old Turks, if not, indeed, more so. Their revolutionary aspirations and spirit are, consequently, strictly internal. They want to reform Turkey, revive it, and rejuvenate it, without, as we have said, calling state boundaries into question. It follows that, when the moment comes to defend the state against foreign encroachment or the kind of domestic discontent and revolt that threatens to violate its territorial integrity (elevated to the level of a sacred dogma) and undermine its organic unity – in a word, to divide or dismember that organic unity – then, we say, the Young Turks will readily forget, at once, all the divergences that distinguish them from their compatriots, the Old Turks and the sultan, and will join with them to defend, like a single man, their common *vatan* [fatherland] against foreign and domestic foes. The Young Turks say, "let us revolutionize the country, but first let us preserve its territorial integrity." We have nothing to object to this; how could we? One cannot ask them to unite with the enemies of the state in order to help dismember their fatherland.

There, however, at the root, at the foundation, lie the beginnings of the gaping abyss, the unbridgeable gulf that makes it impossible to envisage any sort of cooperative solidarity between the Young Turks and any revolutionary Armenian movement or political party. Given the Armenians' diametrically opposed aspirations, which are fundamentally national and fundamentally separatist, the two parties' basic, profound conflict of interest (economic, political and social) shows, as soon as they confront one another in any concrete domain, that they are nothing more nor less than enemies, deceptive outward appearances notwithstanding.

Certain revolutionaries, the author goes on to say, "are making a very big mistake." They wish "to overturn the regime currently dominating the Turkish state in order to replace it with a new regime of a high cultural level, like the regimes of the civilized nations of Europe." However,

the Armenian revolutionary does not have a mission of this kind. The Armenian revolutionary has no mission other than to shake off the servile yoke under which the Armenian people has been ... groaning for centuries ... It follows from all that has already been said that there can be no cooperative solidarity and no federation of any sort between us Armenian revolutionaries and the Young Turks ... The Young Turks themselves have understood very well where our aspirations lead; they have very clearly sensed the irreconcilable antagonism between us. The organizers of their Congress, their big wheels, those wily future candidates for posts as wily Turkish diplomats, capitalized on the naïve flirtation with Ottoman liberals in which the Armenian revolutionaries have engaged and are still engaging and invited the Armenian revolutionaries [to participate in their congress]. They invoked a general union of the peoples of the Ottoman Empire and general reforms in order to stifle or annihilate the Armenian cause, to evict it without a trace from the political arena.

Finally, the author affirms that,

> to date, in speaking of the Young Turks, we have assumed that they were an organized group. But that is not the reality of the matter. There is in fact no Young Turk organization and no organized Young Turk party. There are isolated individuals and small groups scattered here and there, without firm internal unity or an organizational structure based on rules and regulations. They are held together less by political or social ties than by a kind of familiarity typical of the East. There is no Young Turk party with branches reaching into the various strata of the Turkish population. The two entities known as Young Turkey and the Turkish people comprise two distinct worlds utterly foreign to each other.[71]

Compared to the moderate position laid out by Sapah-Giulian in February 1901, this declaration is surprisingly radical. How are we to explain this change in tone, this definite rejection of the Young Turk experiment? The line of argument developed in the text gives us an idea of the party's opinion of the Young Turks: they are accused of nationalism and of pursuing shadowy objectives designed to bury or instrumentalize the Armenian cause. By itself, however, this does not suffice to explain the disconcerting bluntness of the article, this "declaration of war." The internal debates and the reunification of the Hnchaks and the Verakazmial Hnchaks that took place at this time,[72] or even the information that reached the party's central committee at this time, may have induced the Hnchak leaders to radicalize their discourse and attack not only the Young Turks but also the ARF's policy of collaborating with them. As if to take their distance from ARF positions, the Hnchaks rejected, above all, the principle of Turkey's territorial integrity, which constituted the obligatory basis for dialogue between the Young Turk opposition and the Armenian activists.

The Young Turk Coalition: An Ideology in Gestation

The bitter debate that took place at the February 1902 congress of the Ottoman opposition, between the majority that had coalesced around Prince Sabaheddin and the minority led by Ahmed Rıza, finalized the break between the proponents of decentralization and dialogue with the other nationalities and the partisans of a centralized state hostile to non-Turks. This debate was all the more important in that it helped weld together the little group of activists who would produce the Young Turk ideology that dominated the movement between 1908 and 1918.

The August 1902 creation, in Paris, of a distinct central committee of the *Terakki Cemiyeti* (Committee of Progress), which comprised Rıza, Nâzım, Ahmed Ferid, Abdülhalim

Memduh, Mahir Sa'id, and Hikmet Süleyman, confirmed this divorce and illustrated the exclusively Turkish make-up of the minority.[73] The new central committee's official organ, *Şûra-yı Ümmet*, declared in its very first issue: "If Europe came to rescue us by accepting our invitation she would at first try to separate the Armenians and Macedonians from us."[74] This is a valuable index of the ideological evolution of the Committee of Progress. There was, to be sure, an antagonism of sorts between Rıza and the activists: Rıza remained opposed to revolution and violent action and "dreamed of creating a liberal 'public opinion' and thereby changing the regime," while the activists held that the time had not yet come to educate the population and bring a public opinion into being, since "a revolution to dethrone the sultan can be achieved only by high-ranking statesmen and the military." The two groups had, however, a point of convergence – Turkism. It was championed particularly by Yusuf Akçura, an eminent member of the new coalition.[75]

Nationalism and Turkism, the ideological expressions of centralization and the exclusion of non-Turks, constituted a kind of response to not only Sabaheddin but also the Dashnaks, who were struggling to win administrative autonomy for the eastern provinces. In fall 1908, the coalition's organ denounced the prince's political line, since,

> union with the non-Turkish opponents of the sultan was chimerical: "If a Christian ... is an Armenian, he dreams about the establishment of an independent Armenia ... Now the Bulgarians and the Armenians are engaged in armed rebellion. Turks are witnesses to all this, and naturally are saddened and feel that the Christians have hurt them."[76]

Unremarkable and widespread among the members of the coalition, these views show the similarity between their discourse and the Sublime Porte's when it came to the question of the nationalities – that is, the territorial integrity of the empire.

"Turkish" nationalism thus would appear to have coalesced in reaction to the emergence of national sentiment among the other groups in the empire. Doubtless because they were still marked by the Ottoman heritage, the Young Turk activists initially seem to have perceived only the movements formed by groups with roots in the Ottoman Christian world, which they clearly distinguished from Europe – itself perceived, first and foremost, as Christian. Both *Şûra-yı Ümmet* and the October 1903 issue of *Mechveret* introduced a nuance when they affirmed that to be anti-Islamic came down to being anti-Turkish. They also bitterly criticized Europe for discerning fanaticism in Islam alone: "if the Turks eradicated the Bulgarian race or massacre the Armenians, they are driven to do so by Muslim fanaticism."[77] In essence, they accused Europe of Turkophobia and attributed this attitude to the anti-Turkish propaganda of the Armenian Committees.

These committees had indeed been striving for more than a decade to capture the attention of the European intelligentsia. Especially in France and Great Britain, especially in the wake of the 1894–6 massacres, they had succeeded in creating a pro-Armenian network that directed its blows, first and foremost, against the Hamidian regime.[78]

Incidents that occurred during a summer 1904 Anglo-Armenian congress in London nicely illustrate the struggle between the Armenian Committees and the Young Turks of the coalition. Rıza, who had, after some hesitation, been invited to the London congress in his capacity as "leader of the party of Young Turkey," asked for the floor. The organizers suggested that he speak at the congress's closing banquet. During his address, delivered to an audience of Armenian activists, British intellectuals, and members of parliament, he faithfully repeated his faction's line. He was attacked by delegates from France and Italy, who criticized him for defending the sultan's policy and using the language of the Sublime Porte, and asked that he end his address.[79]

These circumstances reveal how difficult it was for the coalition to understand, even if it was somewhat familiar with the major intellectual debates agitating the West at the time, the objective reasons why much of Europe had rejected the sultan's policy toward the nationalities of the empire. In other words, they were hard put to see why what appeared to be "natural" to them as members of the "dominant group" was unacceptable to Western society. Doubtless, these Young Turks perceived anti-Hamidian discourse as anti-Turkish – and by extension, anti-Muslim – leading them to reject the West in turn. It is also probable that experiences of this kind eventually left them with a perception of Armenians as associated with Europeans and, concomitantly, with European colonial plans.

In any event, the coalition, which its opponents accused of continuing to be "nationalist, royalist, and Muslim," considered the problem a matter of pulling the wool over the eyes of a liberal Europe.[80]

The Cairo newspaper *Türk*, the organ of the Egyptian branch of the Young Turk movement, edited by Ali Kemal,[81] developed a still more radical nationalist ideology. "One day in the future," it wrote,

> history, the eternal mirror of the truth of events, will precisely show that one nation that has been unjustly confronted with the entire world's enmity is the Turks ... Is it not injust to ignore the distinct native talents of a nation which has developed from a small tribe into a magnificent state?[82]

In other articles in this newspaper, the Turks are presented as "the British of the East." We glimpse here the foundations of the Young Turks' ideological edifice, which associated consciousness of the past and of history with pain, but also with the frustration bred by the end of a golden age, which the new Turks dreamed of restoring in the guise of a modern state.

Türk repeatedly denounced Western economic penetration of the empire, which it said went hand-in-hand with a "crusade of European powers against the Turks."[83] This theme hit home because it reflected a frustration that many felt. Unable to offer a solution to these problems, the editors of *Türk* contented themselves with denouncing them. Many authors have pointed out the importance of Yusuf Akçura's famous manifesto, published in *Türk*, *Üç Tarz-ı Siyaset* (Three Political Systems). Here, the ideologue sketches the beginnings of an answer to the questions that one segment of the Turkish elite was asking itself. He lays out three alternatives – Pan-Ottomanism, Pan-Islamism, and Pan-Turkism – and identifies the third option as the right one.[84] Akçura's approach, which called for taking over certain features of the Western world for purely utilitarian purposes while rejecting the West's humanist values and, simultaneously, the political principles of Islam, illustrates the complexity of the equation to be solved and the intellectual flexibility required to close this yawning gap. Akçura attempted to do so by recommending that the Turks "take their inspiration from the West in order to become stronger and make progress."[85] This was, in some sense, an obligatory passage that would allow the pupil to acquire the means with which to hold his own with his teacher.

Turkism, however, also required a theoretical grounding on which to found its own procedures and build up its own intellectual constructs. To that end, it had no choice but to "take its inspiration" from the vast corpus of social science being developed in Europe in this period. It did so in the sense that one goes shopping to meet one's basic needs for food and clothing. Notions such as the state, the nation, race, and society, and their positivistic and, especially, evolutionist translation, became the new Turks' daily bread. A good many authors have dwelt on the new Turks' fascination for Social Darwinism and its biological and "scientific" conception of human societies.[86] These ideas were then popularized in the Turkish context. They were a source of inspiration for certain militants, who asked for nothing more than to translate them into practice in the Ottoman world.[87]

In the Young Turks' vision, the Turkish "dominant nation" had to assume the supremacy that Osman's descendants had exercised over the empire for more than five centuries. The Turkish nation was to be invested with the special status that had been reserved for the "Old Turks" and, above all, with the legitimacy that they had enjoyed – their "natural" right to govern. But the Young Turks had to ground this legitimacy whose transfer they were advocating in a Turkish identity whose contours were still blurred. The editors of *Türk* systematically highlighted the virtues of Turkish cultural heritage and presented the Turkish language, "with its present-day eloquence and perfection as the language of a civilized nation," as the most important and most highly developed eastern language.[88] This affirmation, which makes no mention of the Persian and Arabic contributions to Ottoman Turkish, contains the seeds of the thesis, put in final form by the Young Turks' Kemalist successors, claiming that Turkish is the "solar tongue" and the mother of all other languages.[89]

Clinging firmly to the notion of their legitimate authority, the Young Turks assumed only part of their heritage when it came to the non-Turkish nations of the empire – the part that gave them the right to "rule" and to take the state's destiny into their own hands. They did not accept the obligations that formed the pendant to it. Modernization of the state and society was a task incumbent on the "noble Turkish people."[90]

Behind the construction of a Turkish identity lay the need to transform the Ottoman Empire into a modern state with the help of a preferably Turkish entrepreneurial class. Thus, alongside the stock image of the terrorist Armenian revolutionary manipulated by the Western powers, there also appeared in Young Turk discourse that of the Armenian profiteer and usurer. Evoking this image, an editor of *Türk* wrote that, "the fortunes that they have made, the arts that they have mastered all arise from the fact that they have lived at our expense," and suggested that his readers draw their own conclusions and boycott these merchants and craftsmen who "would [otherwise] increase as a natural consequence."[91] We can already discern in such affirmations the theory of the Millî İktisat (National Economy), which would seek to replace Armenian or Greek businessmen with "Turks" and Muslims or, at the very least, to ruin the Armenians and Greeks. Also adumbrated is the rejection of the idea that personal merit had something to do with the Armenians' or Greeks' successes, which are here attributed exclusively to abuses whose victims are said to be Turks.

However, as we have already said, the principal determinant of the ideological orientations and mental universe of the Young Turk coalition was an obsession with the dismemberment of the empire, which the coalition sought to forestall by affirming a form of Turkish nationalism sustained by an elite that was cast as "the potential liberator of a fatherland that, inevitably, would be confronted with a catastrophe."[92] The Young Turks' frequent contact with Armenian activists and the sight of their determination and courage only reinforced Turkish apprehensions about the empire's future. In the face of these tightly structured organizations of devoted militants, revolutionary intellectuals, and *fedayis* fighting the Hamidian regime on a daily basis, the Young Turks probably questioned their own capacity to organize a movement and shape the destiny of the country. They may even have developed a sort of complex and erected the Armenian organizations into models whose methods they sought to adopt. Although such ideas could obviously not be expressed in public, they nevertheless made headway with the Young Turks and surely contributed to the evolution of their positions.

The positions taken by the Young Turks toward the Armenian initiatives that we have already described constituted an ideological corpus in their own right. Some of the concepts involved were already well developed while others were still emerging. These positions, too, were shaped by the Young Turks' relations with the Armenian activists.

In other words, the image of the Armenians as submissive, deceitful, and disloyal, handed down to the Young Turks by the Ottoman tradition, was being recomposed in this period.

Emerging out of it was a perception of the Armenians as an alien, albeit familiar, ethnic and religious group that threatened the ruling group – that is, the Young Turks – who saw themselves as the Turks' enlightened avant-garde.

Prince Sabaheddin's League for Personal Initiative and Decentralization: A Partner for the Armenian Committees, 1902–7

Historians have observed that the ascendancy of Prince Sabaheddin's majority over the movement was not immediately translated into a program of action and that the alliances concluded with the other elements of the Ottoman opposition produced no concrete effects.[93] Not only were no operations conducted against the Hamidian regime for three years (that is, until 1905), but the prince actually said very little about the situation in Turkey either.

Sabaheddin had, however, founded a League for Personal Initiative and Decentralization. Since the January 1902 congress, he had been assisted in this undertaking by Abdüllah Cevdet, the founder of the first small group of Young Turks. The name of the organization indicates what it considered the best way to pull the empire out of crisis. The prince, an avid student of the social sciences, was convinced that one of the conditions for the country's survival was the creation of a decentralized administrative system "guaranteeing the moral and material interests of the different races living on the soil of the empire."[94]

Prince Sabaheddin seemed to believe that the subordinate status imposed on non-Turkish groups in the empire was standing in the way of modernization process. Without abandoning the principle that the Turks should govern, he envisaged a kind of division of labor that would allow the empire to benefit from the "know-how" of each group. Thus, he observed that

> the Christians have developed private enterprise most fully; its absence is paralyzing the Muslims. Unlike the Muslims and, in particular, the Turks, the Christians do not expect to be rewarded with a civil service job, but attend to their own individual interests.[95]

In this way, Sabaheddin posed the question of how to transform the relation between the ruler and the ruled; only such a transformation, in his view, could liberate creative energies and bring non-Turks to commit themselves to the project of a common state. It goes without saying that this conception, although it ruled out division of the political sphere among the different groups, ultimately implied dismantling the Ottoman model and replacing it with a state not of subjects but of citizens.

From his position as a prince of the house of Osman, Sabaheddin analyzed the situation rather perceptively:

> If the minorities had discovered that the opposition wielded real power, they would have changed their minds. But they see a notoriously baneful force in the regime and, in the opposition, a vacuum in everything touching on the future. Hence it is not surprising that they should look to separatist solutions. We should also bear in mind that we have, for centuries, considered the Christians' privileges not as rights, but as gifts granted to them. We and the minorities have lived separately. We have thought separately. Nothing has ever succeeded in bringing our social perspectives closer together. Since we are the ones who have marched on their lands and conquered them, it is now incumbent on us to soften their hearts. Our duty and our interests alike require that we do so.[96]

This declaration may no doubt be regarded as the first introspective reflection of an Ottoman statesman about the dominant nation's traditional attitude toward the subject peoples, the fruit of an effort to understand their position.

As we noted in discussing the first congress of the Ottoman opposition, Prince Sabaheddin devoted special attention to the Armenians from the beginning. He continued to do so in the years ahead, proposing the creation of a "common fatherland" in which Armenians would have the same rights as Turks.[97]

Sabaheddin laid down conditions, however. In an "Open Letter to the Armenians," published in September 1905, he condemned terrorism while inviting the Armenians to participate in a common project: "Our Armenian compatriots, instead of pursuing a propaganda of the deed, would be acting in a way much more favorable to their interests if they pursued a propaganda of ideas in Turkish circles."[98] The Armenian Committees had in fact been striving, since their inception, to heighten awareness among the Turkish and Kurdish masses, but had not had much success with these conservative or tribal societies. Moreover, the prince observed:

> There exists, whatever the Armenians may say, a perfect harmony of interests between them and the Turks. These two groups make up a society of peaceful laborers who dream of order and peace and are exposed to the same danger: the periodical attacks of tribes of Kurdish nomads.[99]

Although he does not use the word, the prince probably had the complementarity of the two groups in mind.

Sabaheddin's political program was moderate in comparison with that of the Turkist members of the coalition. Hence, it was capable of appealing to the non-Turkish groups. The official organ that he began to publish in April 1906, *Terakki* (Progress), promoted individual freedoms, social prosperity, good relations among the empire's different groups, and the rights of the Ottomans in the face of the developed nations' aggression. Sabaheddin even proposed a platform for the defense of the rights of the empire's non-Turkish elements. His program called for political reform based on the principle of devolution and the idea that a decentralized system of administration should be established in the provinces, the election of local governments that would take part in the decision-making process, the consolidation of relations between the central government and the local authorities, proportional representation for different groups in local government, equal rights for all Ottoman subjects regardless of their ethnic background, and so on.[100]

Hanioğlu has surveyed the reactions that Sabaheddin's program elicited from the Turkist members of the Young Turk minority. They allow us to assess the Turkist positions on the questions raised by the program.

Rıza described it as "elastic, vague and obscure." Şakir, who had only recently arrived in Paris, noted that the prince's program would inevitably bring on division of the empire, would benefit non-Turks above all others, and could only be realized at the Turks' expense. In their secret correspondence, the Young Turk leaders, who considered themselves to be the legitimate defenders of their fatherland, repeated in chorus that Sabaheddin's plan could not but lead to disaster for the empire and that Sabaheddin was a traitor and a lackey of the separatist committees.[101] Şakir and Nâzım accused him of being "a British agent" and added that he "approved of the program of the Armenians, who want to leave us." The Unionists also flung an accusation at the prince that they believed robbed him of all credibility and legitimacy – namely, that he had Georgian blood in his veins. Finally, they urged that "this man be stopped, because he defend[ed] decentralization."[102]

The attacks of the Committee of Union and Progress were also directed against Sabaheddin's supporters: "Decentralization [was] a policy the Europeans and Armenians wished to see enacted in order to annihilate Ottomanness." Şakir went so far as to accuse the prince of accepting the principle that Christians were superior to Muslims, then launched an attack on the Armenian Committees. Alluding to the massacres of Armenians under Abdülhamid, he wrote:

> The real authors of the disaster of our Armenian compatriots are some stupid people among the leaders who were running and administering the Armenian community, the many vagabonds carrying out provocations under the title of committee members ... In his memoranda, Sabaheddin bey portrays Armenian committee members as innocent children and places all the responsibility on the government.

Şakir also contended that these militants were being manipulated by the Russian Armenians who controlled the movement. He added that they defended a rash political line that jeopardized the empire's territorial integrity, inasmuch as they were seeking to bring on a foreign intervention. They could therefore be considered, he concluded, a people in rebellion against "our nation."[103]

These reactions of the Young Turk coalition were apparently a response to Prince Sabaheddin's efforts to create an "organizational network from the west to the east of Asia Minor with agents" – to develop such an organization, the League depended on support from the ARF's local networks. Once again, the Young Turk movement was confronted with the problem of finding intermediaries in the population in order to promote its ideas. In the capital, Prince Sabaheddin's League tried to elude the surveillance of the sultan's political police by creating a student organization, the Cemiyet-i Inkilâbiye (Revolutionary Committee).[104]

Can the revolts that broke out between 1905 and 1907 in eastern and western Anatolia be imputed to the League and other revolutionary movements such as the Dashnaktsutiun? Despite the absence of conclusive documents, there is every reason to believe that Sabaheddin and the ARF leadership concluded a secret agreement to work together by the first half of 1905, at the latest. In May 1905, a member of the Western Bureau of the Dashnaktsutiun, Aknuni, accorded an interview to Abdüllah Cevdet, a close associate of Sabaheddin's, the tenor of which leaves little doubt about how close relations between the two parties were.[105] When a representative of the League, Captain Hüseyin Tosun,[106] was dispatched to eastern Anatolia to organize revolutionary activities there, the ARF took him under its wing. As soon as he arrived, Tosun was arrested by a military patrol, which suspected him of being an Armenian revolutionary. He emerged unscathed only because the commander of the patrol turned out to be an old classmate. All available sources indicate that it was Tosun who created the local committee and was at the origin of the revolt that erupted on 5 March 1906, where the rebels demanded exemption from local taxes as well as the tax on domestic animals. We should add, however, that the main lay and religious dignitaries in Erzerum put themselves at the head of this rebellion.[107] This indicates that the movement's founders took pains to lend the protest a social coloring, relegating whatever role the Dashnaktsutiun's militants may have played to the shadows. The reason, doubtless, was their fear of hostile reactions on the part of the populace if their collaboration with "infidels" became a matter of public knowledge.

The presence of just one delegate from Prince Sabaheddin's League cannot, however, explain the protest movement that erupted in Sinop, in the vilayet of Kastamonu, on 9 December 1905 and resurfaced in October 1906 and December 1907. There was, to be sure, nothing revolutionary about it.[108] At most, we can assume that these local phenomena inspired or encouraged the resolve of the two Young Turk movements to foment rebellions. The revolt that was smoldering in Dyarbekir in August 1905 is equally unconvincing, although it had the support of the city's *mufti*: it was a protest against acts of pillage and other crimes committed in the villages of the vilayet by the chieftain of the Kurdish Milli tribe,

İbrahim, whom Abdülhamid had elevated to the rank of pasha in 1902.[109] These were all ordinary phenomena in regions marked by tribal organization.

As to the events that occurred in Van after the 23 March 1908 murder of an informer by the name of David, they were merely one more chapter in the ongoing wrestling match between the ARF's revolutionaries and the government. In his memoirs, Goms (the pen name of Dr. Vahan Papazian) gives a detailed account of the skirmishing that took place at the time, as well as of the ARF's attempt to spring the famed Vartkes Seringiulian from prison. Seringiulian would later become one of the CUP's main Armenian interlocutors.[110]

Hanioğlu mentions a "bogus" Turkish organization, the Liberal Turkish Action Committee or Turkish Revolutionary Federation, which the ARF created out of whole cloth in an attempt to make its message more credible in the eyes of the Turkish and Kurdish populations of eastern Anatolia. Papazian, the chief of the party in Van in this period, reports that in summer 1904 a certain Haci Idris, a Turkish landowner, contacted him with the intention of collaborating with the ARF. Idris was soon joined by the *emlak müdüri* (the head of the land registration office) in Van, Şeref; the assistant chief of the telegraph office, Halil; and a tax official, Hakkı, all of whom were opponents of the regime.[111] He also notes that he had some of Sabaheddin's and Rıza's publications brought from Europe for his Turkish friends, adding that they were a distinct success and that, finally, in fall 1906, at Şeref's request, "we decided to publish a bimonthly periodical in Turkish, which we wrote, edited and printed ourselves, while they were responsible for distributing it."[112] *Sabah ul-Hayr* (Good Day), which called for joint Armenian-Turkish action, was well received, according to Papazian. Şakir, however, was convinced that "such a committee could never be Turkish or Ottoman."[113] Hanioğlu goes so far as to describe it as a "bogus organization of the Dashnaktsutiun" because he is unaware of the part, however modest, played in these anti-Hamidian propaganda campaigns by a handful of Turkish notables from Van.

The Parisian League seems to have been directly involved in the creation of the Ottoman Constitutional League (*Şûra-yı Osmani Cemiyeti*) in Cairo late in 1906 by Arab, Turk, Circassian, and Armenian intellectuals on the initiative of Ahmed Saib Bey and Abdüllah Cevdet, as is clearly indicated both by the identity of its founders and its program. It was doubtless not by accident that that the coalition's official organ, *Şûra-yı Ümmet*, which regularly described *Pro Armenia* as a newspaper "hostile to the Turks and an enemy of Ottoman institutions," described the League formed in Cairo in much the same terms. Moreover, the Ottoman Constitutional League had close ties with the ARF's Egyptian Committee. *Şûra-yı Osmani*, the organ of the Cairo League, illustrated how close they were when it declared that "a purely 'Turkish revolution might cause the end of the existence of the state"[114] – in other words, that a rapprochement with the Armenians could do a great deal more to maintain the unity of the country than unilateral action.

In his "Memorandum of the Turkish Liberals with respect to the Eastern Question," written in late 1906, Sabaheddin returns to the theme of the importance of coming to terms with the Armenians. "The Turks," he declared, were "an unquestionable and indispensable element of equilibrium" in the Ottoman Empire. The Armenians, for their part, were "persecuted for political reasons, which are not at all connected with religion ... An attempt was made at suppressing them because they were the future allies of the Turkish Liberals."[115]

The Committee of Union and Progress and the Armenians, 1905–6

The Young Turk Coalition, which from 1902 to 1905 only just managed to survive in the shadow of Prince Sabaheddin's League, was in the space of a few months transformed into so powerful an organization that it appeared by early 1907 as a credible committee of activists capable of attracting new members – or even taking power. According to Hanioğlu, this turn came about thanks to two little-known men who remained in the shadows and worked exclusively within the Central Committee of the Committee of Union and Progress until 1918.[116]

The first of these two men, Dr. Bahaeddin Şakir,[117] is without a doubt the one who succeeded in forging the synthesis on which all energies were focused. Şakir had had a career. Hardly had he graduated the Imperial Medical School then he became the personal physician of Prince Yusuf İzzeddin, second in the line of succession to the throne. He took advantage of his position to establish relations with Ahmed Celâleddin Pasha, the former head of the Ottoman Intelligence Service who had fallen into disgrace and, naturally, joined the opposition in Cairo. Şakir, who was in contact with the members of the coalition in exile in Paris, convinced the prince to finance their activities. Unmasked by the political police, he was arrested and banished to Erzincan. He managed to flee to Trabizond and, from there, board ship for Marseille. He arrived in Paris in September 1905.[118]

The young man of 26 presented himself in Paris as Yusuf İzzeddin's emissary, but also as an intermediary between the coalition and Ahmed Celâleddin. Two former Young Turks describe him as a "very vindictive character" and "a very narrow-minded individual."[119] Narrow-minded or not, Şakir understood the situation perfectly well. He himself confesses that he had already imagined uniting Rıza's coalition, Prince Sabaheddin's League, and the circles grouped around Celâleddin in Cairo. In Cairo, precisely, his privileged interlocutor was Diran Kelekian, responsible for the political section of the *Journal du Caire*.[120] Close to the former head of the Ottoman Intelligence Service and also to Prince İzzedin, Kelekian had agreed, at the prince's request, to help Şakir put his plans into practice. The doctor needed help publishing a revolutionary journal that appeared every ten days, and the idea was to convince the former chief of intelligence to help finance it. The members of the coalition, however, did not want to collaborate with Diran Kelekian, and wanted even less to be financed by Abdülhamid's former top spy. The Armenian journalist nevertheless suggested that Şakir remain in Paris and try to come to an agreement with the coalition.[121]

Şakir rapidly found acceptance in Paris with help from Nâzım, who encouraged Rıza to undertake the complete reorganization suggested by Şakir and join the new committee that had been created late in 1905 without his knowledge. In the newly founded organization were Sâmi Paşazâde Sezaî Bey, Prince Muhammad Ali Halim Pasha as its treasurer, Nâzım, and Şakir, who was put in charge of internal organization and relations with the sections.[122] Rıza now lost his position as head of the organization (the post of president had been abolished) and Şakir and Nâzım took de facto control of the committee. They would continue to control it until the party was dissolved in October 1918.

The next order of business was for Şakir to convince Prince Sabaheddin and his associates, Nihad Reşad and Ahmed Fazlı, to join his enterprise. He failed. With Ahmed Celâleddin Pasha, who had himself founded an oppositional party in Cairo together with "Bedri Bey" (the pseudonym of Diran Kelekian), he envisaged not a mere alliance, but a merger. It would, he hoped, put the financial resources of the Egyptian network at his disposal.[123]

In this matter as well as in many others, Kelekian, who had been active in Rıza's CUP in 1895–6 in Paris, became the Young Turk physician's confidant and counselor. He pointed out to Şakir, for example, that in its present form *Şûra-yı Ümmet* could not play the role of an "opposition journal [, which] should carry out the function of a banner." As for the new organization, he recommended that his friend find a prestigious successor for Ahmed Rıza and give the group a new name. Finally, he evoked the negotiations with Celâleddin Pasha and the possibility of bringing him into the Central Committee, although not necessarily as its leader.[124]

The former head of intelligence agreed to join the organization on four conditions. Firstly, that it abandon the form "Young Turkey"; secondly, that the ARF and the SDHP be included in the union, a move that, he said, could have very positive effects; thirdly that Rıza's role be restricted to that of a rank-and-file member – in other words, that he not be given any post allowing him to take part in the decision-making process; and finally, that *Şûra-yı Ümmet* continue to appear as the new party's organ. Finally, Cêlaleddin demanded that Kelekian draft a declaration calling on all the sultan's opponents to unite under the wing of the new organization. The coalition rejected these conditions. Cêlaleddin Pasha nevertheless agreed to provide a monthly subsidy to the newly formed Central Committee.[125]

To put the finishing touches on his project, Şakir drew up a draft agreement with the non-Muslim committees, in particular the Armenian organizations. He wrote a memorandum about this move, in which he asked Kelekian for advice. In his 9 April 1906 response, Kelekian noted that Şakir's text deviated from Rıza's program, which, if it was "more favorable toward the non-Muslims subjects, [was] not adequate for the purposes of achieving a union." If he wanted union, he would have to suggest a more far-reaching decentralization plan. Kelekian reminded Şakir, as if to lay his apprehensions on this score to rest, that there was nothing political about provincial government, which, "within the limits of *autonomie locale*, should be extended, with more substantial rights in appointing officials and in discussing and approving provincial budgets." He also suggested the possibility of using local languages in the provincial administration, alongside the country's official language, Turkish. More generally, he contended that the "nations" could receive equal treatment "without causing disorder in the government's administrative affairs," asking why some enjoyed this privilege – such as the Greeks on the Aegean islands or in Ionia and the Arabs in Beirut – whereas others, such as the Albanians and Armenians, did not. The follow-up to this exchange was equally frank. Kelekian wrote:

> I am aware that your friends would not agree with this opinion. Events would demonstrate to them, however, that the country can only be saved by such a liberalism, and that nobody can be deceived by a liberalism based on the principle of Turkification. The non-Muslim subjects are ready to become Ottomans, because they hope that by preserving their nationality and making their nationality a component of Ottomanness they would become Ottomans. Becoming Christian Turks by gradually forgetting their racial [origins], however, would not be found beneficial by them. Despite this fact, even if this program was accepted, most of the discontent caused by *Mechveret* would disappear.[126]

In response, Şakir asked Kelekian to draft a memorandum on the subject so that he could discuss it with the members of the coalition. This time, Kelekian dealt head on with the key questions, identifying what he considered and did not consider acceptable in the program of the Committee of Union and Progress. He noted that the

> Turkish nation, which has pursued a "dominant nation/religious community" policy since the establishment of the sultanate, wishes to save the freedom that it wishes for the country on this condition... The offer by the Turks to the non-Muslim nations is simply inviting them to a union based on "égalité individuelle." I wonder if the non-Muslim nations would accept such a union? The experience of the last ten years

indicates that they would not … . The elements which find individual equality inappropriate and demand "*égalité raciale et sociale*" would naturally act as they wish.

With regard to the risk of European intervention, Kelekian added that it could be obviated only by "basing domestic politics on maximal liberalism and unequivocal justice." He concluded his memorandum by emphasizing that "it is necessary to regard the fatherland as common for all, to abandon the claims of superiority and hegemony, and to limit oneself to being a 'partner' instead of a 'superior.'"[127]

The opinions formulated in this document by Diran Kelekian, the former editor-in-chief of the Istanbul daily newspaper *Sabah*, well known for his pertinent analyses of Ottoman society, sum up all the questions confronting the "non-Muslim nations." Hence they also shed light on the solutions proposed in the Young Turk organization's emerging program.

It hardly need be said that Kelekian's suggestions did not find grace in the eyes of the Young Turk leaders. Şakir, nevertheless, decided to engage a dialogue with the Armenian Committees after familiarizing himself with these revolutionary parties' founding principles, with Kelekian's help.[128] One of the members of the SDHP's Central Committee, Stepanos Sapah-Giulian, has given a detailed account of his meetings with the Young Turks,[129] in which another eminent member of his party, Murad, also took part.[130]

Late in July 1906, Şakir visited the SDHP's Parisian headquarters. He introduced himself as the former personal physician of the prince and heir to the throne Yusuf İzzedin, mentioning his clandestine activities in Constantinople and the Hnchak militants who had been hanged at Trabizond, as well as those he had known in Kirason and Samsun, on the shores of the Black Sea. After this preamble, he revealed that he was a member of the Committee of Union and Progress. The two Hnchak leaders pointed out that Rıza and Nâzım were very hostile to the SDHP. Şakir answered that Rıza and Nâzım were not representative of the party as a whole and that there were more open-minded people in it. After several informal meetings, he suggested that his interlocutors organize official meetings between the two parties. The first of these meetings was attended by Şakir, Rıza, and Nâzım, on the one hand, and Murad (Hampartsum Boyajian) and Sapah-Giulian on the other. Rıza began with the remark that, in view of the country's current plight, it was crucially important that they come to an agreement and that he was determined to do all in his power to bring one about. He added that he had received, from activists in the Caucasus,[131] Egypt, and Bulgaria, and from Turks in responsible positions as well, letters demanding that an accord be reached on the basis of mutual concessions. Şakir, for his part, said a few words on the party's situation in Salonika, Smyrna, and Macedonia.

Sapah-Giulian observes, in his description of this initial encounter, that the evolution of European policy toward the Ottoman Empire had certainly helped convince the Young Turks to modify their positions. They sensed, he says, that the empire would collapse and disintegrate if nothing was done. They were alarmed by the Arabs' anti-Turkish position, as well as by the agreements that the Armenians "had reached with Arab intellectuals." Without fully understanding the direction in which the Balkan states were moving, they had also perceived that the situation in Macedonia was explosive. Finally, Sapah-Giulian notes that they continued to believe that all was not lost and that they could still save their empire. The Armenians were, in their view, in a better position than the Arabs to help them do so, and it was no longer possible to postpone coming to an agreement with the forces of the internal opposition if the external dangers threatening the empire were to be warded off. Rıza also asked Murad – who had just spent ten years in prison – to forget the past and "act like a patriot." Finally, he said, "if I were Armenian, I would have taken the position that you have taken, but I don't think that you would have taken a position different from mine."[132]

It was decided that both parties would study all these questions one by one before any further meetings were held. The following points were to be examined in the following order: 1) the Armenian question and the goal of a single state; 2) autonomous Armenia and Turkey; 3) a democratic constitution and the Midhat Constitution; 4) the Armenian question and foreign intervention; 5) socialism and nationalism; 6) nationality and Ottomanism; 7) organization, propaganda, and revolutionary actions; 8) organs of liaison and relations between the parties; and 9) the question as to what parts of any agreement reached should be made public.[133]

With regard to the first point, the Young Turks proposed to resolve the Armenian question within the framework of a single Ottoman state. On the second, Nâzım sought to show that foreign intrigues would render reforms ineffective – until the state was reformed and modernized, he suggested, broad local reforms were all that could reasonably be hoped for. The Hnchak leaders contested this approach, which came down to postponing reform until the arrival of better days at some unspecified point in the future. Şakir then asked "what the Armenians were going to do with the Turks and Kurds living in Armenia." He was told they would stay where they were, enjoying all the political, economic, and social rights that Armenians did.[134] Nâzım raised the question again, in these terms: "Since the majority is Muslim, what purpose would autonomy serve?" Sapah-Giulian retorted: "The overwhelming majority is on our side, although the question is more meaningfully posed in historical, cultural and national, rather than in quantitative terms. Hence the number of non-Armenians can in no case play a decisive role." At this point, Rıza announced that in order to reach an agreement, the Young Turks were prepared to accept the principle of an autonomous Armenia, but that they wished to familiarize themselves with the details, such as the proposed region's borders (that is, the villages and towns it was to include), as well as the form of autonomy proposed, the conditions under which it was to be realized, and the nature of the proposed region's connection with, and relations to, the Ottoman state.[135]

This last discussion, although it created the impression that the Young Turk leaders were ready to make concessions, seems in fact to betray their underlying objective of making a precise assessment of the SDHP's position on these fundamental questions.

At the next meeting, Murad and Sapah-Giulian presented Kiepert's "Map of Historical Armenia,"[136] on which Russian and Persian areas were marked off. They showed their interlocutors the borders laid down in the agreement of 11 May 1895. The Young Turks reacted rather coldly – indeed, they even said that they were stupefied by these pretensions. The two Hnchak leaders replied that autonomy did not mean independence. Nâzım retorted that "if separation does not come about today, then it will come about in five to ten years."[137]

The basis for examination of the remaining points was, broadly, the plan of 11 May 1895 – administrative autonomy, participation in the general budget, a governor general whose appointment was to be confirmed by the Council of Ministers, a parliamentary regime, and so on. Disagreement persisted on Cilicia. Here, the Young Turks were willing to accept nothing more than local reform. For Armenia itself, they were prepared to accept "autonomy on non-secessionist bases." Sapah-Giulian concludes: "This was hard for them to swallow, but history and the general political situation forced them to come to this conclusion ... We understood that the knife had reached the bone." The solutions considered at these negotiations, which were, after all, binding on only two opposition groups, clearly showed just how far the Armenian demand for local autonomy went. This was no doubt what Şakir, Nâzım, and Rıza were after. It explains their willingness to "negotiate" with the most uncompromising of the Armenian Committees.

Calling for the adoption of a democratic constitution stripped of all references to divine right and theocratic institutions, the Hnchaks reminded their interlocutors that they advocated secularization of the state even as they envisaged the future in an Ottoman frame-work. The unanimous response of the Young Turk leaders showed that this demand was out of the question: adopting a constitution of that type, they replied, was tantamount to handing "state power over to the non-Turkish elements." The Midhat Constitution, "with which the Turkish population [was] already familiar," was more appropriate in their view.[138] Socialism was rapidly dropped from the discussions. The question of Ottomanism, on the other hand – the affirmation that there was only one nation in Turkey into which all the others should melt – remained a major, non-negotiable Turkish demand.

We cannot rule out the possibility that both sides sincerely wished to reach an agreement. The SDHP's proposals to create common propaganda organs and committees responsible for organizing revolutionary actions were not, however, seriously entertained. Confronted with the telling silence of his interlocutors, Sapah-Giulian told them that the ideological distance between their two formations was decidedly too great to be bridged.[139] We are accordingly inclined to believe that the sole purpose of the Hnchaks' proposals was to test the Young Turks' willingness to collaborate, while the Young Turks, for their part, were merely sound-ing out their interlocutors' positions. Indeed, in an essay published immediately after these negotiations, Sapah-Giulian felt obliged to rebut accusations of "nationalism" and isolation-ism.[140] Referring to the situation in the eastern provinces and the threats hanging over the Armenian population, he pointed out that,

> between Armenians, on the one hand, and Turks, Çerkez and Kurds on the other, there is an essential difference, even if all of them are in much the same economic and political situation. Unlike the Armenians, the other groups are not threatened with complete annihilation. The Turkish government does not have, vis-à-vis these other groups, a domestic policy the purpose of which is to liquidate them. "To resolve the Armenian question, it is necessary to eliminate the Armenians – to leave only groups of Muslims in the heart of the Taurus Mountain region." This sword of Damocles is not dangling over the heads of any group living in Turkey, with the exception of the Armenians.[141]

As for solidarity with the Muslim groups living in the eastern provinces, Sapah-Giulian observes that years of effort have failed to produce results. Such solidarity is fine in theory, he writes, but unattainable in practice: the internal workings of the Muslim societies in these provinces and the local context make it difficult to recruit individuals caught up in the clan or tribal system.[142] He points out that if Turkey is to preserve its territorial integrity, the dif-ferent elements it comprises have to want to live together. "But do they?" he asks. Macedonia wishes to secede; "this is clear as day." "As for Crete," he writes,

> it is now only a matter of time, of days... Arabia has a certain inclination to break away... Who is left? The Kurds, the Çerkez, the Avshars, the Laz? Are these groups capable of working toward the creation of a new state out of a crumbling Ottoman empire, when some of them are still not sedentary and others are still half barbarian?

Sapah-Giulian's essay delivers an uncompromising verdict on the Young Turk movement:

> As for the dominant Osmanlı element... there are currently two small groups among Turkish youth: one is gathered around *Terrakki*, the other around *Meşveret*. The first accepts, together with the Midhat Constitution, a system of administrative decen-tralization for the other peoples, but this movement... has attracted only a handful of

individuals and has no organization or local branches. The members of this movement have set all their hope on intervention from the outside by the European powers and their "great men." The *Meşveret* group, as is well known, is made up of out-and-out nationalists who are so intolerant that they do not even want to hear the Armenian question or [reform] plan of 11 May mentioned. They do not have a functioning organization, either … They want merely to restore the Midhat Constitution … which, in its [current] form, cannot satisfy any of the groups in the empire or bring about an improvement in the situation.

Sapah-Giulian further contends that the history of the past few decades has shown that all attempts to achieve reform in Turkey have failed: "Everything goes to show that it is impossible to reform Turkey in general, absolutely impossible." He concludes:

May Turkey continue to live; but we, too, must live. Yet, given that neither the old nor the new dominant element in this country will grant us even minimal conditions of existence and both are opposed to implementation of the project of 11 May, we are not the one who can reverse the historical current and, with our very limited forces, accomplish what the European powers themselves have not succeeded in accomplishing for centuries.[143]

After these negotiations came to an end in October 1906, Murad proposed to convene a congress of Armenian revolutionaries. This initiative, however, came to naught.[144]

In December 1906, Sapah-Giulian again considered the possibility of joint action with the Young Turks. He remained skeptical, however, in the face of those he called "radical nationalists," who had not evolved in the least, and went so far as to ask whether "it was wise" for the Armenians "to put [their] hopes of survival in general reforms."[145] He was equally skeptical about the Midhat Constitution, which he analyzed in considerable detail, only to reaffirm that "it would bring nothing of a constitutional nature, even if it was an application of [constitutional] principles." The Young Turks' attempt to bring the Armenians to commit themselves to the struggle to restore it, he added, was intended only to bury the Armenian question: the constitution "merely confirms, legalizes and popularizes the government's unreservedly theocratic, despotic and tyrannical principles." The Hnchak leader emphasized, in this connection, that the articles of this constitution, notably articles 3, 4, 7, 11, 27, and 87, which spelled out the sultan's political-religious prerogatives, were purely theocratic in nature, and that article 5, which absolved the sovereign of all responsibility for his actions, also gave him the power to appoint and dismiss ministers. The only important novelties introduced by this constitution, Sapah-Giulian contended, were its recognition of individual liberties, which had earlier been denied, and the fact that it acknowledged that state power was held and exercised by men, "not an entity desired and created by divine pronouncement."[146]

The event that left the deepest mark on the years 1905–6 was the ARF's assassination attempt against Sultan Abdülhamid. It took place on 22 July 1905, at 12:30 p.m., in the square before the Hamidiye Mosque, and left 78 people dead or wounded.[147] It might even be said that this operation constituted a turning point in the evolution of the anti-Hamidian opposition, for it showed that a well-organized group, even one whose members came from the ranks of a "subject people," could make an attempt on the life of a sultan. The archives of Operation Vishab (Dragon), an operation entrusted to the "cell for demonstrative operations" (tsutsagan marmin), illustrate the logistical problems that this ARF commando had to resolve. In summer 1904, for example, the members of the commando, meeting in Piraeus, discovered that it was not possible for people with Armenian names to enter Istanbul safely, since those who did so were immediately tailed by the secret police. The commando also observed that the sultan very rarely left Yıldız Palace. He went only twice a year to Dolma Bahçe during the Bayram festivities, in order to receive the homage of various state bodies, and was then escorted by thousands of armed men.[148] From the commando's report on the operation, we learn that the terrorists finally succeeded in making their way into Istanbul by presenting themselves as married couples, less suspect in the East than bachelors.[149] The report also contains a detailed description of the methods it used to bring explosives into the city.[150] It further points out that all the houses around the square in front of the Hamidiye Mosque had been demolished, so that it was impossible to come within more than a half a mile of it. Several options were therefore examined: shooting from rooftops a half a mile away, packing a car full of explosives (melinite), or launching grenades from a pavilion reserved for foreign visitors.[151]

Most instructive of all, however, are the Young Turks' reactions to this assassination attempt. Many members of the opposition, despite their hatred for the sultan, were shocked at the idea that Armenians had dared to get mixed up in what the Young Turks considered to be a purely "family affair."[152] Kâzım Karabekir declares in this connection that the Turks "would have regarded the assassination of a Turkish padishah by Armenians or other non-Turks as a blameworthy act."[153] In other words, as the Young Turks saw matters, the fact that "foreigners" had presumed to settle Turkish "family problems" was intolerable.[154] Or, if one likes, it was intolerable that others had very nearly succeeded in doing what the Young Turks themselves were unwilling or unable to do.

The Transformation of the Committee of Progress and Union and Its Fusion with the Ottoman Freedom Organization: the Decisive Turning-point

While Şakir's attempts to unify the Ottoman opposition did not produce the desired results, the reorganization of the CPU was successful. It succeeded, notably, in bringing the movement to adopt revolutionary practices, previously limited to the non-Turkish opposition, and to "secretly assemble under the same banner" men who had the same ideas. Drawing the lessons of its past failures, the CPU drew up new party statutes, including internal regulations of decisive importance. As Hanioğlu notes, the CPU was at this time more interested in order than in ideology.[155]

The new statutes provided for the nomination of a director and four autonomous sections of the Central Committee, each of which could work independently of the others and had the right to stamp the results of negotiations with the seal of the Central Committee. The first section, headed by Rıza, was responsible for publishing *Mechveret Supplément Français* and for relations with foreign groups. The task of the second, led by Sâmi Paşazâde Sezaî Bey, was to publish *Şûra-yı Ümmet*. The third, led by Nâzım, was responsible for party finances. The fourth, jointly directed by Şakir and Nâzım, was charged with working and corresponding with all the branches of the party – that is, with attending to internal business. The Central Committee also included two young officers who had broken with Istanbul, Lieutenant Seyyid Ken'an and Lieutenant Mehmed Fazlı, as well as two princes in disgrace, Mehmed Said Halim and Mehmed Ali Halim. In 1907, let us add, when the Central Committee decided that *Şûra-yı Ümmet* would henceforth be published in Paris, not Cairo, Şakir became its de facto editor-in-chief. Thus, he assumed effective, albeit unofficial, control of the party apparatus, seconded, as always, by Nâzım.[156]

At the time, the CPU did not have a single branch worthy of the name, except perhaps for the one in Cairo, which was, however, confined to the house and person of Ahmed Saib.

A specialist points out that the CPU took its inspiration from the organizational structure of the ARF, a revolutionary federation of branches linked in a network, as it was putting its own loose network of Young Turk groups in place.[157]

While there was progress in this domain, it should be emphasized that it was registered in the Balkans, among the Muslim population, in particular the officers in the many Ottoman units that controlled or tried to control this explosive region, regularly plundered by armed bands.

The 18 September 1906 creation of the Osmanlı Hürriyet Perverân Cemiyeti (Ottoman Freedom Organization/OFO) in Salonika was, precisely, the result of a fusion between these young officers serving in the Balkans and the "veterans" of the CUP.[158] The small group of the OFO's founders comprised Mehmed Talât,[159] Midhat Şükrü (Bleda),[160] Mustafa Rahmi (Evranos),[161] Lieutenant İsmail Canbolat,[162] Major *Bursalı* Mehmed Tahir,[163] Lieutenant Ömer Naci,[164] İsmail Hakkı,[165] Major Naki Bey (Yücekök), Captain Edib Servet (Tör), Captain Kâzım Nâmi (Duru), and Lieutenant Hakkı Baha (Pars). The composition of the first "Supreme Council," made up of Mehmed Talât, Mustafa Rahmi, and İsmail Canbolat, attested that leadership responsibilities were shared out among civilians, notables, and officers, while also evincing the radicalization of the movement, the statutes of which excluded non-Muslims and *dönmes* from the committee. Some of these men had been members of the first CUP cells and had kept up relations with Paris: thus, Midhat Şükrü was still in contact with Nâzım, and Mehmed Talât with Ahmed Rıza.[166] But it was the arrival in Paris of Lieutenant Ömer Naci (in May 1907), and Captain Hüsrev Sâmi (Kızıldog'an)[167] (in August 1907), and their adhesion to the movement, which speeded up the rapprochement between "Parisians" and "Salonikans." After Talât presented Nâzım with the proposal to merge the two organizations, Nâzım, himself a native of Salonika, left for the Balkans.[168] After discussions lasting several weeks, he sent, on 27 September 1907, a unification plan back to the CPU's Central Committee. Paris unanimously approved it on 16 October of the same year. From this point on, the CPU was represented by a domestic Central Committee based in Salonika and an external Central Committee based in Paris.[169] Thus, from 1908 to 1918, the members of the CUP's Central Committee came mainly from the two entities that fused at this time: Şakir, Nâzım, Rıza, and Naci had roots in the Parisian CPU, while Talât and Şükrü came from the OFO in Salonika.

It seems plain that Şakir and Nâzım played equally important roles in this unification process and that Şakir led the reorganization of the new party with firm resolve. Complaining that the domestic Central Committee took too many chances, he suggested that it adopt the underground methods of the non-Muslim committees, especially the program and statutes of the ARF, which were used in elaborating the internal operating principles of the unified CPU.[170]

Among the innovations inspired by the Dashnaktsutiun's methods was the creation of local sections made up of volunteers prepared to make the supreme sacrifice – the *fedayis*. The local executive committees alone knew the identity of these men, whose mission was to carry out "special operations." The ceremony at which new members of the committee were inducted also seems to have been modeled on that of the Armenian revolutionaries: new members swore an oath of loyalty to the party while holding a Koran in one hand and a dagger or revolver in the other. Also taken over from the Armenians was the custom of keeping Central Committee members' names and the location of party headquarters a secret.[171]

Among the profound changes the CPU underwent in this period, the most decisive would appear to be the growing influence of young officers on the Committee. Responsible for this freely made choice were, it seems, two physicians on the Central Committee who were convinced of the need to attract "young officers ready to sacrifice themselves" rather than pashas and *beys*. It was in this way that there began to flourish in the official organ of the party the militaristic discourse that made officers the "guides" of the nation and the "light of the eyes of our society," for the army was "the only institution capable of carrying out a revolution."[172] This choice also allowed the CPU to organize bands of irregulars, modeled after those Bulgarian, Macedonian, and Greek ones infesting the Balkans in this period, that were capable of carrying out armed raids and political murders. Involved here was both a response to what the Young Turks considered to be the challenge thrown down by the non-Muslims, and also a way of financing the party similar to the one used by the Armenian Committees.[173] The logical next step for these bands, under the command of young officers who were members of the party, was to recruit criminals and deserters who had become highwaymen. Major Enver (the future minister of war) and Major Eyüb Sabri (Akgöl) were the first to recruit such criminals, in Macedonia early in 1908.[174] Doubtless, these initial experiments can be considered the origin of the Special Organization, which was to constitute the military wing of the Central Committee of the CUP during the First World War. Then, however, it was no longer a question of armed raids, but of the systematic liquidation of a civilian population.[175]

Among the many officers who joined the OFO in fall 1906 were Ahmed Cemal[176] and Halil (Kut),[177] the uncle of Major Enver, who himself joined the organization on 9 October 1906 and founded a branch of the party at Manastır.[178] Unification with the OFO, a process in which Nâzım played a major role, enabled the CPU to put down deep roots in the Ottoman Balkans, but was obviously only the opening stage of the two CPU leaders' plan. In December 1907, Nâzım again went secretly to Smyrna, this time in order to create a Young Turk branch there. He turned for support to the ARF's local networks, which were solidly implanted in the port city.[179] A few months earlier, in May 1907, Şakir, for his part, had traveled to Istanbul on a false passport in order to reorganize the branch of the CPU there.[180] Profiting from the relations of his confidant in Cairo, Diran Kelekian, he met with Armenians from the capital who agreed to help create a local committee. Kelekian and Şakir also envisaged assassinating the sultan with the help of subsidies that Kelekian had obtained from Ahmed Celâleddin Pasha – the former director of Ottoman Intelligence was still living in Cairo – and Yusuf İzzedin.[181] These efforts did not, however, yield the expected results. It was, in the end, the OFO's networks that united the different groups in the capital under Silistreli Hacı İbrahim Paşazâde Hamdi's lead: they had a membership of 70 at the time, including a fair number of officers, such as Kâzım (Karabekir).[182] Moreover, on his return trip to Paris in June 1907, Şakir met in Bucharest with the famous İbrahim Temo, a historic figure of the CUP, and succeeded in convincing him to organize branches in Romania and among the Albanians. The historical CUP leader even obtained the support of leading Albanian Muslims for the CPU.[183]

Also indicative of the CPU's ambitions was, finally, Ömer Naci's November 1907 journey to eastern Anatolia for the purpose of founding local sections of the party.[184] These conservative tribal regions did not, however, offer the advantages that the Balkans did. Only the Armenian Committees could survive there.

The ARF's Fourth Congress: Vienna, 22 February to 4 May 1907

When the Fourth General Congress of the ARF opened in Vienna on 22 February 1907 in a building belonging to the Austrian Socialist Party,[185] the Young Turk opposition was, as we have just seen, going through a period of profound changes. The same held for the Dashnaktsutiun itself, which capitalized on the opportunity offered by the congress to draw up the balance sheet of its past actions in the field and also assess the evolution of the Young Turk movement. Those present at the congress – 24 delegates from the local committees and the party's Eastern and Western Bureaus[186] – were intellectuals and also militants active at the practical level. They held more than one hundred sessions, during which many issues were examined in depth, notably the question of collaboration with the Ottoman opposition.

Although the ARF was democratic in its internal functioning, it was handicapped by the fact that, first, socialists, anarchists, and nationalists – all with very different working methods – coexisted within it. Second, it was led by "a voluntaristic, traditional oligarchy."[187] This leadership comprised the party's two supreme bodies – the Western Bureau, which had jurisdiction over the committees in Europe and those in the Ottoman Empire lying west of a line that ran north-south from Kirasun through Harput to Dyarbekir, and the Eastern Bureau, which had jurisdiction over the regions to the east of that line and also over the committees in Russia (it appears from this division that the ARF conceived of Armenian political reality as a unity). These two bodies were elected by a congress that convened, in principle, every four years. This congress alone was empowered to define and adopt the party program and budget. The ARF consequently functioned in somewhat rigid fashion, even if its regional committees enjoyed broad autonomy of action. Thus, when the Young Turks in exile sought contact with the Dashnaktsutiun, they applied to its historical headquarters in Geneva, where the editorial board of *Droschak* had had its offices since the party's foundation. The Young Turks were probably unaware that Geneva also happened to be the seat of the party's Western Bureau.

The Fourth General Congress published a declaration of principles as soon as it had finished its work:

> To put an end to baseless misunderstandings widespread among the Turks, the Congress deems it necessary to declare that the Dashnaktsutiun has never had and does not now have secessionist aspirations in Turkey, but that its objective has, rather, always been complete equality among the nations constituting the country and, in accordance with the principle of broad local autonomy, the establishment of administrative autonomy in the six Armenian *vilayets*. This is not contrary to the rights of the other nations.[188]

This profession of faith, in which the ARF firmly rejected the recurrent accusations of secessionism that the "Turks" leveled at Armenians in general and the party in particular, ratified the conclusions reached at the congress. It reaffirmed a principle that had not once been challenged during the discussions held there. The logged minutes of the congress show that the party's primary concern was the disastrous economic and social plight of the Armenian provinces and the insecurity that permanently reigned there. The first delegate to address this subject, Vana Ishkhan, representing Lernabar (Rshtunik/ Moks), painted a bleak picture. He stressed, to begin with, that the situation had grown worse since the massacres of 1895–6. The Kurds, encouraged by the government, had acquired greater influence since then, and the mountain districts found themselves in the worst situation, since they lived almost exclusively from animal husbandry. Famine also was now chronic in the region because the population no longer had the right to seek work in other regions of Turkey, given the restrictions that had been imposed on circulation. Finally, Ishkhan brought up the land question, which he declared to be of vital importance. The shortage of arable land, he said, as well as pressure from tribes of mountain Kurds who harassed and plundered both the Armenians and sedentary Kurds aggravated the problem. He noted that, on the plain of Vasburagan, 70 per cent of the land belonged to village communities and 20 per cent to individual landowners or stock-breeders, whereas in the districts of Kiavash, Khizan, and Spargerd, where large numbers of Kurds lived, the Armenian peasants paid tribute to Kurdish chieftains. In Shadakh, Hayots Tsor, and Timar, the peasants lived in dire poverty and rejected the demands of the Kurdish tribal chiefs.[189]

Thus, the land question was at least partially bound up with the state of relations between Kurds and Armenians. The sedentary Kurds, with whom the Armenians worked on a day-to-day basis, did not represent a problem, according to Ishkhan, whereas the tribal populations harassed their sedentary neighbors, especially in areas where the latter had not organized their self-defense.[190] Antranig's contribution to the discussion, which bore on the situation in the region he represented, Mush-Sasun, confirmed that relations with the Kurds were quite simply power relations: the Armenians' erstwhile friends turned against them just as soon as an order from the national government authorized them to act with impunity.[191]

The seventh chapter of the Western Bureau's report, presented by Aknuni,[192] broached the subject of greatest interest to us here: the relationship between the party and the other organizations struggling against the Hamidian regime. The preceding congress had assigned Aknuni responsibility for this question.[193] A number of speakers focused on relations with the Young Turk movement. Aram-Ashod (Sarkis Minasian),[194] a delegate from the committee for the Balkans, recalled the antagonism between the CPU, which he described as "exclusively nationalistic and constitutionalist," and Prince Sabaheddin's liberal tendency, which "accepted a system based on a degree of decentralization." The CPU, he went on, was firmly opposed to the liberals' political program, because "it believe[d] it contained the seeds of a future partition of Turkey." Aram-Ashod noted that, in late 1902, an editorial committee including Turks, Armenians, Albanians, and Macedonians had been formed to publish *La Fédération Ottomane*, but that the Turks had suspended their collaboration after one or two issues had appeared. He nevertheless believed that it was necessary to cooperate with and even to take the initiative of reunifying the opposition. "The nationalities," he said, "by preserving their identity on their native soil – something that is vital for us – will also ensure the territorial integrity of the Ottoman Empire."[195] Aram (Manukian), the delegate from Van, approached the same question from a different angle, contrasting the Young Turks in exile with "the activists who live among the Turkish masses":

I place no great faith in the Young Turks who have found refuge in Europe; they are, for the most part, palace revolutionaries who in one sense or another have dynastic interests. If we begin with them, we are going to encounter a great many problems. In any case, it is more appropriate to begin with the activists who live in the country and among the Turkish masses as they actually are. I must say that these movements have no ties to the Young Turks abroad. Indeed, we are the ones who distribute the newspapers and literature of the Young Turks in exile inside the country. I propose that we create, with the Turks in Turkey, mixed committees in which our forces are united. These communities should deal, in particular, with questions common to all nationalities, such as propaganda, political terrorism, protests based on our united forces, boycotts, and so on.[196]

This approach, reflecting tendencies observed among activists doing practical work, was contested by Rupen Zartarian, a delegate from the committee for the Balkans. Zartarian said that he was skeptical about the "Turkish masses'" inclination to make a revolution in the near future. He also reaffirmed that the party had never had separatist goals, but on the contrary wished to keep within an Ottoman framework.[197] However, Avetis Aharonian, a delegate representing the Kars committee, pointed out that this was not how the Young Turks perceived the ARF:

> The Young Turks discern a separatist tendency in our movement because we are working toward the creation of a special administrative regime for the six vilayets inhabited by the Armenians... This is by itself enough to convince the Young Turks that we are not far from having separatist tendencies, while their objective is to maintain Turkey's territorial integrity. At the [1902] Paris Congress, in which I participated,[198] Rıza turned to us and said "you are Ottomans." Sabaheddin, who wanted to collaborate with the Armenian revolutionaries *à tout prix* [at all costs], remarked that "what you are demanding for the six vilayets, we should demand for all the others as well."[199]

At the ninety-ninth session of the congress, held on 23 April, the subject came up again during a discussion of two motions on "solidarity among the oppositional groups in Turkey." The first to take the floor was a figure of historical importance in the ARF, Rostom (Stepan Zorian).[200] He recalled that the party had proved more than once that it did not harbor "separatist tendencies," as the decisions of the 1904 congress "distinctly" showed. He added that he was in favor of a policy of solidarity with the opposition, but noted that the party had made great efforts to this end without having tangible results to show for it. He was even more dubious when it came to the creation of "mixed committees with the Turks and Kurds, because the Kurds are led by their affluent class and *begs*."[201] As for Zartarian, he was firmly opposed to the creation of local mixed committees, "for the Turkish masses are not sufficiently educated and, what is more, such collaboration could lead to new massacres." The socialist sensibility of certain party members makes itself clearly felt in their inclination to endorse a common struggle against the sultan, yet their awareness of the gap between these ideals and practical social realities is also evident.

Aram (Manukian), in defending his motion for unity of action with the whole Ottoman opposition, made an interesting remark about the protest movement that had emerged in Asia Minor over the past two years. "It is a fact," he said, "that the movements with a political coloration that have appeared in Turkey have been led by us. It is possible that a good many of our comrades are unaware of this." This very general remark should be taken with a grain of salt. A penchant for secrecy and the obvious desire of the author of the motion to convince his comrades of his point of view may have predisposed him to attribute all the acts of political "rebellion" observed in Turkey to the ARF, even if it was obvious that some of them lacked all "political coloration" and owed nothing to the party. Drawing the conclusion that followed from his premises, Aram argued that the ARF should meet the opposition's expectations and join it in its efforts.[202]

Murad Sepastatsi,[203] a delegate from Lernabar, declared that he found some of his comrades rather too optimistic. He did not share their feelings, he said (with, of course, Aram's remarks in mind), for he had doubts about "the revolutionary nature of the movements that [were] emerging among the Turks."[204] Arshag Vramian, invited to take part in the congress as a delegate-at-large, took a similar position. He urged prudence, suggesting that the party limit itself to making financial contributions to the opposition movements that sprang up in the provinces of the empire, without coming forward openly.[205] Aharonian returned to the accusations of separatism, refocusing the debate on the ARF's relations with the Young Turks in exile: "Yes, we are simply regarded as separatists. The Turks propose that we support

Sabaheddin's project. If we refuse, we will be considered separatists."[206] Vramian[207] reacted in these terms:

> No one is considering secession from Turkey. That would be stupid, not because we are not capable of achieving it, but because our socio-economic interests mandate that we remain part of the country. The Turks do not understand the nature of the federation we are demanding; they take it as evidence of separatism. It is crucial that we bring the Turks round and make them understand that this is the only way of [preserving] Turkey's territorial integrity. The alternative is the partition of Turkey.

Minasian added:

> Not even the Young Turks can grasp our conception of solidarity; how can the untutored Turkish populace be expected to? The Turks are still guided by religious thinking; if Turkey should go to war with a Christian state, any Christian state, they would immediately turn on the Armenians.[208]

After this discussion was closed, Manukian's motion in favor of concerted action with the opposition was carried. The ARF thereby effectively agreed to make concessions as to the type of reforms to be introduced in the eastern provinces so as to lay the accusations of separatism preoccupying the party to rest.[209] An article published in its official organ, *Droschak*, shortly after the congress was adjourned, tends to show that the party leaders had taken due note of the ongoing mutation of the Young Turk movement under the influence of Şakir in particular. They did not hesitate to declare:

> We have not forgotten the positions taken by the leaders of the "Turkish liberal parties" when the Armenian movement was in its infancy. While we applauded all their declarations of hostility to the sultan's regime, they constantly embittered and disappointed us. A Murad Bey, a well educated, pragmatic man considered to be the sole leader of "Young Turkey," declared one fine day, in the name of his party in Europe, in a brochure written in French, that the Armenian revolutionaries were vulgar bandits or criminals whose actions invariably targeted the Muslim peoples and whose objective was to massacre them. As for Murad Bey's faithful successors – Rıza Bey, Ottomanus [Pierre Anmeghian] and so on – they presented the Armenian revolutionaries to Europe as Russian government mercenaries...Now, however, things have changed...It would appear that a new generation is coming up that has renounced passivity...a generation quite different from its predecessors, who, only yesterday, under the flashy, seductive name "Young Turkey," were wasting their days bombing their surroundings with paper, in the form of naïve exhortations and appeals addressed to Europe. [The younger generation] takes its inspiration from new slogans; it appeals to the noble "principle" of self-reliance. Let us hope that our premonitions are not mistaken; let us hope that fate will at last smile on our unfortunate peoples and the whole of our bloodstained country, which has long stood in need of cooperative cultural action. Let us wipe the last remnants of prejudice from our hearts; let us stretch our hands out to our neighbors with love as they wake from their slumbers.[210]

This official declaration was, very probably, a direct consequence of the negotiations engaged a few months earlier with the CPU's new leaders. It was a profession of good will.

Chapter 2

The December 1907 Second Congress of the Anti-Hamidian Opposition: Final "Preparations for a Revolution"

We have already discussed, among Bahaeddin Şakir's other preparatory work, the fruitless overtures that he made to the leaders of the Hnchak Party in summer 1906. His exchanges with the ARF seem to have been more productive. According to Hanioğlu, the initial negotiations between the two parties were conducted amid the greatest possible secrecy; no public declaration was ever made about them.[1] We know only that Ahmed Rıza was sent to Geneva by the CPU to engage in discussions with the ARF's Western Bureau and that the ARF, for its part, sent Aknuni to Paris to continue the negotiations there.[2]

During his stay in Paris, the Dashnak leader had a conversation with his classmate from Tiflis's Nersesian Academy, the Hnchak Stepanos Sapah-Giulian, at the latter's request. The Dashnak representative informed Sapah-Giulian that he had come to carry out a decision reached at the Vienna Congress, which had voted to organize a second congress of the opposition in collaboration with the Young Turks, with the objective of coming to a general agreement with them. Sapah-Giulian and Aknuni wished to come to terms themselves before pursuing their dialogue with the CPU.[3] Before entering into the discussion proper, Sapah-Giulian asked his interlocutor if it was true, as Şakir had told the Hnchaks, that the ARF had already established relations with the CPU and had begun to negotiate an agreement "about the option of a centralized state, with preconditions such as abandoning the Armenian question." According to Sapah-Giulian, Aknuni confirmed that this was indeed his party's orientation.[4] Examination of the preparations for the congress makes this plausible.

Şakir's private correspondence suggests that he was, for his part, persuaded that the Armenian Committees had no choice but to rally to the CPU, since the Armenian people was threatened with destruction by the Czarist regime as well as by Abdülhamid, while the policy of the great powers was, at the time, non-interventionist.[5] We can form a more precise idea of the CPU's objectives and Şakir's strategy by examining their correspondence. It shows that the CPU leaders' maneuvers were informed by a certain cynicism: they invited the non-Turks to take part in joint actions revolving around Ottomanism, even while reaffirming, internally, that they had rejected this concept of the nation and adopted a clear policy of excluding non-Turks.[6]

The 1905–6 "events" in the Caucasus – that is, the eruption of violence between Armenians and "Muslims," especially the Turkish-speaking population of Baku – probably had a greater impact on Young Turk circles than has previously been supposed. While this violence resulted, on the analysis of the Armenian Committees, from a policy of provocation orchestrated by agents of the Czar's regime,[7] Turkish-speaking circles perceived it as a Turkish-Armenian conflict for control of the South Caucasus. Bahaeddin wrote, in response to a March 1906 letter in which the Tatars of the Caucasus complained about Armenian "encroachments," that "the authors of the detestable massacres are not you, but those Armenian revolutionaries who are enjoying themselves by offending humanity."[8] In public, the CPU's official organs took a vaguely neutral stance toward the Armenian-Tatar conflict. In private, however, Şakir suggested "putting an end to Armenian wealth and influence in the Caucasus." He also suggested to his "Muslim Brothers" that they propagate "the patriotic idea of unification with Turkey" while simultaneously declaring to the Russians that they were "loyal to the Russian government" and not engaged in a religious war, but "in a stuggle against Armenians only because [they] have wearied of Armenian acts of aggression, outrages, and atrocities, and only in order to defend [their property and honor."[9] These Turkist positions obviously did not prevent the CPU from negotiating with the Armenian Committees and even, as we have seen, from cooperating with independent Armenian personalities.

To date, the ARF has been credited with initiating the organization of the second congress of the Ottoman opposition, approved of in principle by the Party's Fourth General Congress. Documents presented by Hanioğlu seem to suggest, however, that it was in fact the CPU which took this initiative.[10] In any event, both organizations expressed a desire to collaborate. Thus, Şakir observed that Aknuni was "extraordinarily favorably disposed" and showed great flexibility during the preliminary discussions, so much so that the Young Turk leaders became rather suspicious of his motives. At the Dashnak leader's request, Prince Sabaheddin's League for Personal Initiative and Decentralization was associated with the mixed commission that was to prepare the congress. This commission comprised Ahmed Rıza and Sâmi Paşazâde Sezaî Bey, members of the CPU's Central Committee, Dr. Nihad Reşad and Ahmed Fazlı of the League, and Aknuni, the ARF's official representative. Şakir was not a member of the commission, but archival material shows that he was the real initiator of the congress.[11]

Interestingly, the twelve-point document drawn up by the mixed commission begins by laying down the principle of the territorial integrity of the Ottoman Empire and the inviolability of the order of succession to the throne, and concludes with a mention of the "legal and revolutionary" means to be mobilized to bring down the Hamidian regime and restore the constitution. It also rejects all foreign intervention and "terrorism," even while allowing for the possibility of violent action in certain circumstances requiring further definition. The last stipulation states that "the Armenians especially should not participate in the revolt in Erzerum unless we [the CPU] approve it."[12]

The three "puissances invitantes," – the CPU, the ARF, and Prince Sabaheddin's League – invited the committees of the SDHP and the Verakazmial to take part in the congress. Both refused. The Hellenic League in Paris also received an invitation. Given the League's relative lack of influence, the debates were in fact an exchange between the CPU and the ARF. A problem cropped up when it came to choosing a name for the national representative body of the "régime représentatif" with which the country was supposed to be endowed. The Young Turks categorically rejected the formula "assemblée constituante" proposed by the Dashnaktsutiun. After an exchange between the ARF's Western Bureau on the one hand, and the Salonika Committee on the other, an agreement was finally reached on the term "national parliament."[13]

Besides these questions of principle, which are indicative of the two parties' objectives, bitter debates raged around the decision to use "legal and revolutionary" means to bring down the government. It is easy to imagine the uneasiness that the ARF's revolutionary practices caused the CPU's leaders, and we may suppose that, in negotiating with the Armenian Party, they intended to bring these practices under control. Among the means proposed by the Armenian revolutionaries were civil disobedience, draft resistance, the organization of armed bands, a general insurrection, a general strike with the participation of government officials and the police, and, finally, terrorist acts with individual or institutional targets. This vast program, coming from militants who had already proved that they were capable of carrying out extremely difficult operations, panicked the CPU leadership, since it maintained, despite all, a legalistic approach and was preoccupied with the fate of the Ottoman Empire. Thus, it made sense that the Young Turks should demand that the activities of the armed bands be closely supervised, that there be no call to resist the draft (for reasons of national security and so as not to weaken the army), and that the ARF abandon collective terrorist action, limiting itself to actions targeting specific individuals.[14]

When all was said and done, the ARF had made major concessions, agreeing not to call for implementation of the reforms in the eastern provinces or great power intervention in the empire's internal affairs, while rallying to the idea of a centralized state.[15] In exchange, the Armenian party doubtless hoped that the future state would, at least to some extent, have a representative character and respect democratic rules. The ARF may even have expected to acquire a degree of influence over state affairs. Despite this conversion, the Young Turks, who were used to battling their Armenian compatriots' plans for administrative autonomy, apparently displayed some reluctance to collaborate with them. The Armenian Committee, in turn, had to find acceptable foundations on which to ground its legitimacy in its own community. Precisely because Sabaheddin's League was among the organizers of the congress, the inclusion of other non-Turkish components of the anti-Hamidian resistance among the prospective participants helped to legitimize the ARF's choices, since it was now acting in the framework of a vast Ottoman opposition rather than allying itself with the Young Turks alone, a move for which it was harder to gain acceptance.[16] Negotiations with opposition movements such as the Interior Macedonian Revolutionary Organization (IMRO) proved much more difficult and ended in failure despite the efforts of the ARF, which had long-standing ties to this movement. A few Jewish and Arab delegates took part in the work of the congress, but exercised no real influence over it.[17]

Once all the preliminaries had been completed and the work of the various commissions cleared away, the congress could finally take place. It lasted for three days, from 27 to 29 December 1907.[18] The preliminary work performed by the commissions notwithstanding, several proposals caused problems. Rıza's last-minute appeal to the Armenian delegates to acknowledge the rights of the Ottoman Sultan in his capacity as Caliph, for example, led to a heated exchange. These socialist militants, who considered religion proof of obscurantism, can only have perceived this demand as one more manifestation of the "positivist" leader's conservatism. Fazlı and Şakir managed to resolve the problem by wringing an admission of "the issues of the caliphate and the sultanate which have been considered sacred by [their] Turkish compatriots" from the Armenians. The other source of tension, needless to say, had to do with the adoption of revolutionary methods. In this connection, Hanioğlu nicely brings out the difference between the conceptions of the members of the CPU and the Dashnak militants – that is, between the approach of the former, for whom such methods were simply a form of activism by which to attain their objectives, and the socialist vision of the latter, who were revolutionaries in the true sense of the word.[19] The bitter discussion of this issue was carried to its conclusion during the closing banquet, a rhetorical exercise during which all the participants expounded their conceptions of society and the state, without calling the final declaration into question. This declaration called, on the one hand, for the abdication of the sultan, a radical transformation of the existing administration, and the establishment of a consultative system and a constitutional government; and on the other, as a means of arriving at these objectives, it envisaged armed resistance, a general strike, non-payment of taxes, and propaganda activities in the armed forces. Finally, the congress decided to create a "standing mixed committee" responsible for organizing propaganda work and sending out calls to all social classes and the constitutive groups of the empire.[20]

This *accord historique* found a by no means negligible echo in the Western press of all political tendencies, including the socialist press, which, as might be imagined, had no love for the CPU. At the same time, the Young Turk Central Committee instructed its local branches to monitor the Armenian Committees and, in particular, report whether they respected the Paris accord. It also called on them to launch a systematic boycott of Prince Sabaheddin, who continued to be accused of disseminating "seditious ideas."[21]

The active role played by the Young Turk Central Committee in Paris, especially when it came to relations with the other Ottoman groups, should not blind us to the Salonika Central Committee's growing influence in the party. On the eve of the July 1908 "revolution," a good many of the six thousand members of the OFO were army officers by background,[22] recruited from the forces concentrated in the Balkans that were supposed to keep these regions under control. The creation of numerous Balkan branches of the party, notably in Manastır,[23] Serres, Skopye, and Resen, was a direct result of this internal transformation. The Salonika Central Committee, which included Mehmed Talât, adjutant Major Hafız Hakkı, Captain İsmail Canbolat, Manyasizâde Refik, and Major Enver,[24] was, with its majority of officers, itself militarized like the party as a whole. Yet, the CPU was still far from being able to carry out spectacular operations capable of hastening the fall of the regime. Mehmed Talât's vain attempts to convince his friends in the ARF to launch bombs "to Salonika and Istanbul"[25] revealed a certain powerlessness, even as they attested to the CPU's utilitarian approach to its Armenian allies.

Most historians agree that the implementation of reforms in Macedonia (the Mürtzeg Plan), occurring against the background of the diplomatic crisis between Russia and Great Britain, facilitated the recruitment of rebel officers and made it possible to mobilize Muslim public opinion in the Balkans, which had been unsettled by the prospects opened by the European plans for the region. It is also commonly assumed that these reforms undermined the position of the Sublime Porte, whose main priority remained the maintenance of military control over the region.

The reinforcement of the British commitment to the reforms in Macedonia that came in March 1908 was perceived by the CPU's Central Committee as an imminent threat of "partition and extinction of the Ottoman State and expulsion of Turks from Europe."[26] The CPU's reaction showed what the Young Turks understood "reform" to mean: it was, for them, tantamount to "partition." They even feared that the European plan for Macedonia could well lead to the loss of Albania, push their capital out of Europe, and "make us a second or even a third class Asiatic power."[27]

The 9–12 July 1908 meeting at Reval between the Russian Czar Nicolas II and the British sovereign Edward VIII seems to have been the event that finally convinced the CPU to throw itself into the battle against the regime. It is also likely that the sultan, whose political acumen is universally acknowledged, concluded at the same moment that he was no longer in a position to resist the pressure of the great powers – in other words, he had no choice but to yield to the pressures of the CPU in the hope that he could take matters back in hand once the crisis had passed. When he decided to restore the Midhat Constitution and allowed the Young Turks to make their entry onto the stage of history, he was probably well aware that they were much more legalistically minded than many supposed and were by no means averse to maintaining the monarchy. The main objective was to call a halt to the reform process in Macedonia, sure to lead, ultimately, to the partition of the empire.

On of the best experts on the Balkans at the time, the journalist Aram Andonian, points out that "the Young Turks very adeptly took advantage of the enthusiasm [engendered by the revolution] to send the European officials who had just taken up residence in Macedonia politely back home."[28] The Young Turk revolution, which was supposed to make good the democratic deficit and ensure the security of all the empire's subjects, had another effect as well: it brought all armed activity conducted by Albanians, Macedonians, or Armenians to an end, for they all supported the new regime. However, as Andonian points out, "in putting a successful stop to the scheduled reforms in Macedonia, the Young Turk regime paved the way for events that eventually led to the Balkan War." In other words, in refusing to heed those who advised it to enact reforms in order to allay separatist tendencies, it simply postponed the day of reckoning. Austria-Hungary compensated for this Young Turk success by annexing Bosnia-Herzegovina, while Russia seized the occasion to intervene in the Balkans, well aware that the new regime would not implement reforms there and would thus spark new revolts with its political intransigence.[29]

However that might be, the CPU immediately understood that it was by setting out from the Balkans, where it had found a fertile breeding ground, that it was most likely to succeed in bringing down the regime and taking power. Its commitment to the region, especially Macedonia, made a rapprochement with the local committees indispensable, beginning with the Macedonian IMRO. The revolution would come from Europe, not Anatolia. The alliance with the ARF accordingly lost some of its relevance or even utility.[30] It is not our task here to review the circumstances that brought about the neutralization of the Macedonian committee, but it may be noted that the process was greatly facilitated by the assassination of its leaders Boris Sarafov and Ivan Garvanov, militants who were close to the Armenian revolutionaries. The Greeks, for their part, remained passive, refusing to take part in these operations.

The CPU nevertheless needed the support of local organizations struggling for autonomy, which of course comprised non-Muslim elements, and even had to recruit members or volunteers directly from their ranks. At the same time, it could not reject the principle of the exclusively "Turkish" nature of the party. As often in the past, the Albanians provided the contingents that would carry the day; they were backed up by Muslim recruits from the Balkans. A few promises from the CPU to satisfy the Albanians' demands, revolving around the preservation of their identity, allowed the Turks not only to weld together substantial local forces, but also to extinguish a revolutionary project that had been smoldering for months. The work of Ahmed Niyazi, himself of Albanian origin, facilitated recruitment in Resen, Manastır, and Ohrid. There can also be little doubt that Albanian notables played a crucial role in rallying local forces to the Young Turks' cause. They doubtless hoped to receive special treatment in return, particularly regarding the cultural rights that they had been calling for, a demand that the CPU already regarded as a separatist tendency.[31] The CPU leaders' discourse had not been quite as successful when it came to rallying Jewish circles in Salonika, who had already been giving the local Young Turks logistical support for several years, although the CPU had made no concessions to speak of. The relations they forged with the Jews were nevertheless sufficient to provide conservatives all the occasion they needed to describe the revolution as "a cabal of Salonikan Jews, Freemasons, and Zionists."[32]

The latent revolt simmering in the armed forces, the first signs of civil disobedience, and the fact that it proved impossible to carry out the Sublime Porte's orders to bring the situation back under control left the sultan no other choice than to sign the decree restoring the constitution. It was promulgated on 24 July 1908.[33]

In Paris, the opposition in exile packed its bags and set out for its native land. In late July 1908, the Ottoman Consul General and Ahmed Rıza visited the Paris headquarters of the SDHP in order to invite the party's leaders to return to Constantinople. They promised the Hnchaks that they could operate there as they saw fit, even, if they wished, as an opposition party. This invitation, extended to the CPU's most uncompromising opponents, can be interpreted in various ways. It is likely that, in opting for this course of action, the Young Turks were seeking to neutralize external sources of opposition – they doubtless preferred to have them close to hand in the capital, where it was obviously easier to keep an eye on them than if they remained abroad. When Murad and Sapah-Giulian paid their visit to the Young Turks, they learned from Rıza that a CPU Congress would soon be held in Salonika. True to form, the positivist leader asked that they cease to attack Abdülhamid, who was now their sovereign and caliph.[34]

The next day, the two Hnchak leaders met with Prince Sabaheddin, who told them:

> If the Ittihad controls the government for more than eight months and runs the affairs of state, rest assured that the future of all the nations making up the empire, especially the Armenians, will be compromised and then finished … Certain persons have held confidential conversations with me: we spoke openly with each other, as Turks. What I say appeared clearly in their declarations and admissions. That is why you must immediately consider your own situation and decide what you have to do.[35]

This prophetic warning, coming from a leader who had been relegated to the margins, bears witness, at the very least, to the mood prevailing among the Young Turk leaders from the moment they took power, and to the duplicity of their discourse.

On 15 August 1908, Sapah-Giulian and Murad left Paris for Constantinople.[36] The Dashnak leaders, too, turned their backs on Geneva and set out for the Ottoman capital. Bahaeddin Şakir reached it first.

PART II

Young Turks and Armenians Facing the Test of Power (1908–12)

Chapter 1

Istanbul in the First Days of the Revolution: "Our Common Religion is Freedom"

In an editorial published late in July 1908, doubtless a few days after the restoration of the constitution, the Hnchak leadership observed, clearly alluding to the CUP: "In order to develop, Turkish nationalism needs more liberal political conditions than those the Hamidian regime offered it." In the same text, the Hnchaks reminded their readers of the SDHP's positions: "We are opposed to 'Young Turkey' if it proposes to establish the rule of one nation or race over the others...Complete equality of all nations has to be an inalienable right. We reject the absolute centralism defended by the Party for Union and Progress." The Hnchaks also continued to advocate the establishment of local autonomy, of "autonomy for Armenia," and a truly democratic constitution. Thus, they returned to Constantinople without excessive enthusiasm.[1] Yet, they boasted that they had sparked the Young Turks' activism. "As far as revolution is concerned," wrote the official organ of the Hnchak party, "the Armenian people has been the educator of the Turkish people."[2]

Despite the fact that the SDHP maintained these positions, which illustrated the constancy of its leaders' political choices, the Young Turks did not give up hope of changing their Armenian compatriots' minds. Thus, the Hnchak leaders Stepanos Sapah-Giulian and Hampartsum Boyajian received a visit from Dr. Bahaeddin Şakir a mere ten days after their arrival in Istanbul. Şakir had arrived in the capital a little earlier and had already assumed leadership of the local Ittihadist clubs. He informed the Hnchaks that his colleagues on the Central Committee of Salonika had just arrived and wanted to meet them. Sapah-Giulian and Murad accepted the invitation, their reservations about the Young Turks notwithstanding. They were received at the headquarters of the Committee of Union and Progress by Şakir, Mehmed Talât, Şazâde Başi, and Enver. Talât informed them that the Central Committee of Salonika had sent him to the capital to meet with all the leaders of the various parties and study all the existing currents, and that he was therefore hoping that the Hnchak leaders would explain the basic principles of their movement to him. This way of broaching matters was no doubt designed to sound out the Hnchaks' attitude toward the CUP in its new role as a party of government and also to discover the nature of the relations between the SDHP and the ARF. Talât did in fact ask his interlocutors what they thought of the Dashnaks; the Hnchak leaders responded that he should address himself to them directly. He also wondered how the Dashnaks "could include the term 'revolutionary' in their name." "Has anyone ever seen the government of a country," he asked, "authorize the existence of a party calling itself 'revolutionary'?"[3]

To Talât's suggestion that the SDHP position itself on the terrain of Ottomanism, Sapah-Giulian and Murad replied that "Ottoman and Turkish were synonyms" for each other.

"There are no Ottoman Armenians," they said, "and there cannot be; there are Ottoman subjects, there are Armenians who are Ottoman citizens."[4] Despite this response, the Young Turk leader proposed that they try to come to an understanding and establish the basis for an agreement – he even promised them that the Hnchaks would have total freedom of action as a political party.[5] A few days later, Hagop Babikian, an Armenian jurist who was a member of the Young Turk movement, was sent to SDHP headquarters in order to bring his compatriots around. He affirmed that the Ittihadists wished to reach an agreement with the Hnchaks, were prepared to guarantee them the number of parliamentary seats they had demanded, and would make all other necessary concessions because they wanted to make sure that the country would enjoy a period of political calm.[6]

The basis of the deal that the Young Turks doubtless proposed to all the Committees consisted of a few verbal concessions, combined with a promise of support in the upcoming elections for the Ottoman National Assembly. Armenian circles surmised that the CUP was attempting to exploit the old antagonism between the ARF and the SDHP fanning the flames of their rivalry by promising more parliamentary deputies to both sides, all the better to bind each of them to itself. Thus, the official organ of the Dashnaktsutiun defended itself against the Hnchaks' acerbic criticisms of the ARF for its cooperation with the Young Turks.[7]

As we have already seen, the agreement reached at the December 1907 second congress of the opposition had no real impact on the course of events. The Dashnaks seemed to be aware of this. However, they consoled themselves with the observation that

> after hesitating for a long time, the Young Turks, once they felt that they had become strong enough to do so, adopted terrorism as the most appropriate means of struggling against the network of spies and terrorizing the regime's protectors as well as the Sultan's entourage.[8]

Droschak hastened to quote a statement that Dr. Nâzım had made in Smyrna: "We owe the Armenians rather than the Ottoman army a debt of gratitude, for it is the Armenians who accompanied us on the path to liberty."[9] These words are puzzling. Can we reasonably attribute such flattery to feelings of gratitude on the part of one of the oldest Young Turk militants still active? Probably not. Yet, Nâzım's remarks sufficed to give the Armenian committee the impression that it had played a role during the "revolution" in one way or another, and had accordingly acquired a new legitimacy. If it is borne in mind that the ARF's revolutionary activities in Sultan Abdülhamid's day were severely criticized in Armenian circles in the capital, it becomes easy to understand how important it was for the party to gain a degree of recognition. From this standpoint, the revolution represented a triumph for the ARF within the Armenian community. Overnight, it opened the doors of all the Armenian national institutions before the Dashnaks. This should not, however, blind us to the bitter debates that occasionally raged within the party leadership. Although some ARF leaders, such as Mikayel Varandian or Aknuni, both members of the Western Bureau, saw 1908 as a "golden age,"[10] others such as Ruben Ter Minasian and Antranig were more skeptical: they pointed out that the sole objective of the officers' *coup de force* was to preserve the territorial integrity of the empire, and expressed concern about "a revolutionary party's chances of survival in a period of peace."[11] The broad majority of the party leadership, however, crystallized around Ottomanism and the principle of the integrity of the empire. In other words, it decided to pursue its collaboration with the CUP on the Ottoman political scene, placing its bets on the establishment of a liberal regime.

The position taken by Aknuni, the leader of the ARF delegation to the December 1907 Paris Congress, doubtless played a determining role in the party's decision to collaborate with the Young Turks. Arriving in the Ottoman capital before all the others in August 1908,[12] he wrote to his colleagues at the Western Bureau in Geneva:

> You cannot imagine how happy I am to be able to write you from this city without the slightest censorship or control. After thirty-two years of silence, the city is chanting "Freedom"; the crowds are drunk with joy. No matter: thirty years of silence are well worth thirty days of inebriation ... When the reaction re-establishes its rule, we shall rejoin the "club of the mute."[13]

This enthusiasm becomes easy to understand when we recall that it was the enthusiasm of a militant who had spent long years in exile and whose party had been persecuted in both Russia and the Ottoman Empire. The restoration of the constitution opened up heady prospects: the ARF could now hope to lead a fully public existence, become a legalized political party, and play its role in the political, social, and cultural life of the Armenian nation, while also participating in the Ottoman political game.

Another event that occurred in the same period and had symbolic value was the September 1908 return of the exiled Prince Sabaheddin to the Ottoman capital. To mark the occasion, a ship with "occupants of the Palace and nobles" aboard went out to welcome Sultan Mecid's grandson. The SDHP created another powerful symbol when it decided to hire to go out to meet the prince a ship bearing Stepanos Sapah-Giulian and Murad, among others. The two revolutionaries were invited aboard the ship of the "occupants of the Palace," where they were received by Deli Fuad Pasha, who had just returned from exile. Before this constellation of dignitaries, including Ahmed Rıza and Bahaeddin Şakir, the pasha waxed eloquent on the role played by the Hnchaks: "[they have] done much to help rouse the country from its torpor and bring down the Hamidian regime."[14] These militants, villains only yesterday, were suddenly being celebrated as heroes. They were not alone: an Armenian delegation representing the Patriarchate had set sail from the Golden Horn on the Princess Maria on 2 September, around 11 in the evening, making for the Dardanelles in hopes of welcoming Prince Sabaheddin before the others. The delegation included the lawyer Krikor Zohrab, who had himself returned from exile a few days earlier.[15] These signs of Eastern courtesy, however, only thinly veiled the CUP's hostility. The very day the prince arrived, the Istanbul press launched a vilification campaign against him: it was rumored that he had arrived in the capital in the company of 300 French nuns with the intention of "modernizing" Turkish women and 300 *paters* who would lead Turkish youth to atheism. The authors of this campaign, which we have every reason to believe were of Young Turk origin, had not misjudged their audience. Their strategy for denigrating the prince, whose long stay in France was supposed to have warped his moral fiber, relied on the public's conservative reflexes, particularly its rejection of "Western ways."[16]

The CUP's first "secret" congress to be held on Ottoman soil opened on 18 September 1908. It showed that the Young Turk Central Committee was now controlled by the leaders from Salonika, as well as Dr. Nâzım and Dr. Şakir. Ahmed Rıza had been quite simply pushed aside. It was also clear that Mehmed Talât and the two physicians had come forward as the true masters of the committee and were more powerful than the Council of Ministers.[17]

The eternal question about these much-discussed "secret" conferences is just what was decided at them. Sapah-Giulian, about whose revolutionary activity we hardly need say anything more, was a privileged witness to these events; he affirms that he sent one of his agents, Bedir Bey Bedirhan,[18] to Salonika to gather information on the decisions made by the Young Turk congress. According to this informant, the CUP decided to check the development of other political parties, to continue to struggle against Sabaheddin and his liberal ideas, to bear with the Armenian parties until the committee was stronger, to keep the Hnchaks under surveillance, to propagate the principle of Ottomanism, to promote Muslim control of the economy and foster the development of industry and trade among the Turks, and to maintain a Turkish majority in the Ottoman National Assembly at all times.[19] Of course, this information must be taken for what it is – a series of "revelations" that were put in writing in 1915 – but it should not therefore be dismissed out of hand. The secret correspondence of the Young Turk leaders unearthed by Hanioğlu[20] clearly shows that they systematically used a double language or adapted what they said to the context, without deviating an inch from the pursuit of their political objectives. These documents indicate that the CUP decided to maintain its military character at this congress, and also to have loyal members of the committee as well as *fedayis* appointed to all important posts. This meant all rectors and university professors, as far as the posts under the authority of the Ministry of Education were concerned; all *valis*, *mutesarifs*, and *kaymakams* for those falling under the authority of the Ministry of the Interior; and, at the Ministry of Justice, all judges.[21] This is another way of saying that the CUP's objective was to bring the whole machinery of the state administration under its control and leave nothing to its political "allies."

We should note one last element that was characteristic of the Young Turks' debut on the Ottoman political scene – the CUP's attachment to the Ottoman throne. Those who had participated in the December 1907 second congress of the Ottoman opposition in Paris were not surprised by this, for they had already observed that, when all was said and done, the Young Turks had a rather conservative conception not of society, but of the state. It does not matter much that it was Ahmed Rıza who came forward as the sultan's main defender at the congress: he simply said what his young comrades thought but could not openly express without risking their credibility as determined activists. Thus, one understands why, "after 1908, Ahmed Rıza had become the beloved child of Abdülhamid, who carried courtesy to the point of personally serving him a glass of water."[22] The positivist leader, who came from a milieu with ties to the Ottoman court, was, after all, in his element when he was received at Yıldız palace. In contrast, young men who had barely reached their thirties, such as Talât, Nâzım, and Şakir, must have been intimidated by the idea of taking the reins of power directly, to say nothing of the aversion to appearing in public common to all these militants, who were used to secrecy and had become veritable *komitacis*. The weight of Ottoman tradition, the prestige of the Sublime Porte, the handicap represented by their age – an important factor in Eastern societies – and their lack of experience[23] unquestionably increased this hesitation to assume power forthrightly, which would be unprecedented in the Eastern world. Herein, no doubt, lies the explanation for the fact that no fewer than 11 cabinets were formed between July 1908 and June 1913.[24]

When the restoration of the constitution was officially announced, the reactions that most surprised observers were the scenes of wild rejoicing by the broad masses of the people as well as the demonstrations of fraternization that could be observed not only in the capital, but also in the provinces. How are we to interpret the display of mutual respect or the homage paid to the victims of the 1895–6 massacres in a capital in which a little more than ten years earlier thousands of Armenians had been publicly disemboweled? Can these reactions be explained as an effect of what sociologists call "the trauma of the executioner," a sort of public display of bad conscience? This was the case with some people, at any rate. Or was the phenomenon the result of instructions that the CUP had issued to its networks in order, say, to show the world the image of a country all of whose component groups had come back together after thirty years of Hamidian "tyranny"?

To make a public display of its bad conscience over its treatment of non-Muslims was unthinkable for the dominant group. Moreover, Ottoman society, which was sharply hierarchical, was known not for its tendency to react spontaneously to events, but rather for its inclination to follow instructions from its clerics or government officials. It is thus hard to imagine that Muslim clergyman suddenly drew closer to their Armenian compatriots on their own initiative. This no doubt explains the stupefaction of the Armenians in the capital when they learned that a mullah had summoned the faithful to go to pray on Armenian graves at the cemetery of Balıklı in homage to the victims of the 1895 and 1896 massacres. Another circumstance would seem to indicate that this was no spontaneous outpouring: in the eastern provinces of Van and Mush, it was the local civilian and military authorities who organized receptions, complete with bands and "fraternal" banquets, for the Armenian *fedayis* who had come down from the mountains. No popular movements of the sort were to be observed.[25] The explanation may well reside in the complete lack of Young Turk networks in these regions in this period. Thus, it is probable that the authorities were instructed by the national government to invite the Armenian militants to abandon the maquis.

The CUP seems to have taken special pains to convince the Armenians of its benevolent attitude. According to a French diplomat, one of the first proclamations that the CUP made during the July 1908 revolution had to do precisely with the Armenians: "You are no longer confronted by a troop of Armenians endeavoring to re-establish an Armenian kingdom, as the government led you to believe. From now on, the Armenians will be struggling alongside us to deliver our fatherland from tyranny."[26]

A report on a conversation that Dr. Nâzım, "one of the main leaders of the movement," had "with the representative of a great power" is our richest source of information on the CUP's role in the first days of the revolution:

> We found a terrain admirably prepared by the suffering that the Turkish people endured for more than thirty years. Yet it took the qualities of this admirable people [the Armenians], qualities of patience and firmness of character, integrity and honesty, to convince a people – one whose most savage instincts [its masters] had striven to arouse, one that had been set upon the Christians and taught to slaughter and plunder them – to mend its ways, comprehend the horror of the acts that it had been led to commit and prove itself worthy of the freedom that we allowed it to glimpse... Wherever, in times past, massacres had occurred, we organized ceremonies of expiation; and when I saw tears streaming down the cheeks of officers and soldiers rarely given to such manifestations of tender feeling, I only needed to put the question to them to confirm that they had taken part in these massacres and were cognizant of the crime whose active, irresponsible agents they had been.[27]

Such rhetoric leaves little doubt about the "pedagogical" intent of the scenes of fraternization staged in this period.

Whatever the origin of the phenomenon, the immense majority of the Armenians in the capital became convinced supporters of the new regime. The lawyer Krikor Zohrab, an emblematic figure of the Istanbul intelligentsia, had returned from exile on 2 August. Three days later, he announced that he wished to found an Ottoman Constitutional club. On 13 August, this club organized a public meeting in the Taksim gardens attended by 50,000 people of all origins. Zohrab addressed the crowd in Turkish, arousing its enthusiasm with the declaration: "Our common religion is freedom."[28]

Another example from the Armenian world is indicative of the way it responded to the revolution. On 30 August, the Sahagian Middle School in Samatia organized a lecture on the revision of the constitution. Zohrab, who had a reputation as an orator, spoke this time in Armenian; he underscored the necessity of recasting this Constitution, which no longer met contemporary needs. Two Dashnak leaders, Rupen Zartarian and Aknuni, were present at the meeting and engaged in a dialogue with Zohrab on the burning questions of the day.[29]

In the capital, the ARF was led by the *frères ennemis* Aknuni and Simon Zavarian; they were gradually joined by exiles from Europe and the Caucasus, all of whom were apparently optimistic about the future and in favor of collaborating closely with the CUP.[30] The central Committees of the eastern provinces were, moreover, put under the authority of a *badaskhanadu marmin* ("responsible Committee") in Istanbul that was headed by Aknuni.[31] The revolutionary network in the capital was dissolved immediately following the July 1908 crisis. The party had to think about finding civilian occupations for its fighters, since they had been ordered to give up their arms under pressure from the CUP.[32] "The ARF wishes," Aknuni declared, summing up his party's hopes, "to open a window between Turkey and the civilized world of Europe; Turkey is going to follow the example of the French Revolution."[33] Concretely, these tendencies led to an August 1908 meeting between Major Cemal (the future pasha) and Aknuni, at which the two parties envisaged carrying out common projects.[34]

The sultan's general amnesty for common-law prisoners also benefited Dashnak activists such as Aram Manukian, an ARF leader in Van, or the *fedayi* Farhad, who was released from prison on 1 August 1908 along with 19 other Armenians.[35] This goodwill gesture was very well received by the Armenians, but nothing indicates that the CUP was behind it. It was, more likely, a general measure taken by the government to mark the beginning of a new era, one that happened to redound to the benefit of Armenian revolutionaries as well.

In contrast, the 10 September 1908 arrest of one of the participants in the 1905 assassination attempt on Abdülhamid, Kris Fenerjian (alias Silvi Ricchi), on the orders of the prefect of police in the capital, Azmi Bey, stirred up a veritable storm in Istanbul. The day after Fenerjian was apprehended, the Council of Ministers ordered his release, the Patriarchate and Zohrab having interceded on his behalf.[36] As in the preceding case, there is every reason to believe that the move was initiated by the government or, more precisely, that what was involved was a knee-jerk reaction on the part of the Hamidian administration.

According to Vahan Papazian, the ARF maintained friendly relations with the Ittihad during the latter's first few months in power. The CUP preached patience. The country, it said, was in an anarchic state: the state apparatus had ceased to function properly and the conservative social strata were still influential. It was therefore necessary to strengthen the constitutional regime. To do so, it told the ARF it was counting on the Armenian party's support. This discourse was intended to bridle the impatience of the Dashnak leaders, who had to deal with the frustration of militants in the provinces irritated by the slowness or even total absence of the promised changes.[37] The Armenian activists were at a loss to understand certain events, among them the fall 1908 arrival in the Ottoman capital of people from the Caucasus, such as Mardan Bey Topçibaşev or Ahmed Agayev. Agayev had been accused by Papazian (who took part in the operations conducted by his party during the conflict between Armenians and Tatars in the Caucasus) of being one of the organizers of the 1905 massacres of Armenians in Baku.[38] The arrival of these men in Istanbul was the more perplexing in that they openly advocated Pan-Turkist ideas. Although a part of the Ittihad rejected such ideas, the mere presence of Agayev or Topçibaşev in the CUP alarmed even the most imperturbable observers.[39] Papazian later summed up the reasons for their uneasiness: "We clearly felt," he wrote in his memoirs, "that the dominant element would sooner or later curtail the rights of the minority nations."[40] However, the ARF had its priorities at the time, such as its desire to become an established Armenian institution and also to be represented in the Ottoman parliament, in which it hoped to play a political role. To ensure that its deputies would be elected, it had to come to an understanding with the CUP. In particular, it had to conclude agreements to cooperate with it in the provinces.

The Hnchaks took a fundamentally different approach to the political situation. Their Central Committee nevertheless drew its conclusions from the changes that had occurred in the country and abandoned all notions of subversion. It decided to develop a network

of cultural centers with libraries, reading rooms, and theater groups, which together constituted, in some way, the educational aspect of the SDHP's activity.[41] Yet it by no means
quit the political arena. On 24 November 1907, the party reached an accord with the
Verakazmial Hnchaks, represented by Bishop Mushegh (Seropian), Mihran Damadian, and
Vahan Tekeyan, to unite their forces or, at the very least, work together in the Ottoman
political sphere. The two parties renewed their relations as soon as they returned to the
capital. The SDHP suggested that its former dissidents found a Ramgavar ("liberal democratic") party capable of recruiting among the Armenian bourgeoisie and conservative social
strata, which could thus be brought into the political domain. In the following months, the
Armenian Democratic Liberal Party (ADLP) was indeed brought into being with the help of
the SDHP, which provided the elements required to develop the ideological bases of the new
party. With this, the Armenian political landscape took its final form. Shortly thereafter,
the ADLP enthusiastically embraced Ottomanism. This was a bitter pill to swallow for the
Hnchak leaders, who denounced Ottomanism as a form of Turkism.[42]

Rather soon, to be sure, opposition to the Young Turks broadened to take in certain
"Muslim" circles as well. Their combined hostility to the CUP was variously motivated, but
focused above all on the way the Young Turks distributed lucrative posts in exchange for
bribes and also on the fact that the highest offices were systematically handed out to the
Ittihadist leaders' close friends and relatives regardless of how little competence or experience they had.[43] Thus, there existed fertile ground for the emergence of an organized
opposition among the Turks. The SDHP in particular worked toward creating this with
Maniasazâde Retik Bey, a well-known lawyer respected by both Turkish liberals and Muslim
circles. After a meeting organized by the SDHP in Kadiköy that was attended by 6,000
people – the majority of them Turks – the party drew still closer to this lawyer, who had
defended Hnchak militants in court at no charge under Abdülhamid. In a series of meetings, Retik and the SDHP elaborated a platform capable of bringing together those dissatisfied with the prevailing situation in a dynamic party of opposition to the Ittihadists.
These circles made no secret of their hostility to Young Turk nationalism and especially to
Ahmed Rıza, who took a public position against the "modernity" of women, which he said
was contrary to Koranic law.[44]

The SDHP campaigned consistently for Retif Bey, a candidate in Istanbul during the first
November–December 1908 legislative elections.[45] Things did not take a serious turn, however, until Retif and the SDHP were joined by forces from the Çerkez and Albanian democratic opposition. They met quietly near Sirkeci, in the home of one of the CUP's historical
founders, Dr. İbrahim Temo, who had broken with his former Young Turk friends.[46]

To be sure, a key figure was absent from this nascent movement – Prince Sabaheddin.
The smear campaign launched against him as soon as he returned to Istanbul had of course
had its effects. However, as Sapah-Giulian points out, the prince did not follow through on
his ideas. Their exchanges did not produce the results Sapah-Giulian had been hoping they
would, for Sabaheddin, he writes, "had considerably watered down his principles." It must be
added that his palace had "accidentally" caught fire shortly after he resettled in Istanbul and
that he had been obliged to leave for Europe again for a certain period.[47] Moreover, by 1908,
"the committee considered even Muslim non-Turks as potential enemies or traitors."[48] That
is, at any rate, what the private correspondence of its leading members suggests.

Very quickly, the Young Turk Central Committee had taken to playing the role that
had earlier fallen to Yıldız Palace, issuing decisions by the hundreds just as the sultan had
issued his imperial decrees.[49] Apart from its methods of filling government posts mentioned
a moment ago, it had taken on the role of a kind of "Committee of Public Safety," interfering
in the nomination of all high-ranking officials, *valis*, diplomats, and so on. The committee
sent directives to the ministers, without paying undue attention to the grand vizier, with

whom it corresponded directly.[50] It governed without saying so by means of a "phantom cabinet" and sought to block the development of a pluralistic political system. By creating specialized satellite organizations for the *ulemas*, women, and guilds, it endeavored to control the networks that had influence over Ottoman society. In many respects, it evinced a desire for hegemony that even the most powerful sultans had not dared admit.[51]

One can readily imagine how hard it was for the parties of the opposition to maintain a place in the public sphere under these conditions. They were not mistaken when they said that the CUP conducted itself not like a political party, but like a cabal. Although the Ittihad officially created a parliamentary faction in 1909, it was merely a transmission belt for the Young Turk Central Committee, which continued to meddle in everything. Indeed, one faction in the committee, representing *fedayi* officers, was opposed to the transformation of the CUP into a classical political party; it rejected constitutional rights and tried to impose a more radical political line.[52]

It is also important to note that the CUP already saw itself as a "Holy Committee" which had the self-imposed duty of creating a governing civil-military elite.[53] With its *fedayis* and officers clubs, it was effectively a paramilitary organization, and set about restructuring not only the army – by placing members of these clubs in the military – but the civilian administration as well.[54] Nothing better illustrates this orientation than the fact that both soldiers and the sultan were obliged to take an oath of allegiance not to the constitutional regime but to the committee. Furthermore, schoolchildren were required to learn the CUP's military anthem, with its opening words: "Oh, glorious, grand, honorable organization / Your name and renown are the pride of a nation."[55] Such lyrics had probably been composed by one of the Ittihad's leaders. The oath that new CUP members had to take included, moreover, a clause revealing its conception *sui generis* of political struggle: "I swear," it ran, "to kill ... anyone who fights against the [committee] with my own two hands."[56]

A few statistics provide the best proof of the Young Turk Central Committee's program having indeed been translated into reality. Between July 1908 and March 1910, all the *valis* of the empire's twenty-nine vilayets were replaced. Ninety-three per cent of the directors of regional telegraph offices, 93 per cent of provincial directors of education, 100 per cent of the empire's ambassadors, and 94 per cent of its *chargés d'affaires* were dismissed and replaced by men loyal to the regime.[57]

It is thus easy to understand why one of the committee's pivotal figures, Bahaeddin Şakir, could proudly announce late in 1909 that the CUP had 360 clubs in the country and a membership of over 850,000, and that it had won the battle for "public opinion."[58]

The Revolution in the Eastern Provinces in the First Electoral Period

We have said that the July 1908 revolution was basically "Balkan," with the result that it was only feebly implanted in the provinces of Asia Minor. This state of affairs was a major handicap for a Committee that aspired to extend its influence throughout the empire. Hence, one of the first tasks the CUP undertook was to send delegates to Asia Minor to explain its political project there and set up local Young Turk clubs. It was not hard to create such clubs in these sometimes remote regions, which continued to function in accordance with clan-based and, even more frequently, tribal traditions. As frequently happens in environments of this kind, a number of traditional leaders lost no time rallying to the new regime. According to Hanioğlu, the resulting network was made up of local notables as well as high-ranking military and civilian officials. They so often took advantage of their new positions to enrich themselves or meddle in local affairs that the CUP was very soon forced to purge its ranks and put young officers known to its central leadership at the head of local party branches.[59] Of greater relevance to our purposes, these CUP projects also provided the Ittihad with an occasion to test the solidity of its alliance with the ARF.

How much real political strength did the ARF have in the eastern provinces in this period? According to historians of this party, it was implanted, above all, in areas that had a large Armenian majority, such as the Van region, the area south of Lake Van, the Sasun district, the plain of Mush, the Dersim district, and the Erzincan region. It often had, however, a merely symbolic presence limited to a few dozen militants whose relationship with the Armenian peasantry was ambiguous, to say the least. The villagers were proud of their heroes, these resistance fighters who defied insuperable odds. At the same time, they were aware that they themselves, as the targets of state retaliation, had to pay a heavy price for every operation the *fedayis* undertook. Opinion was accordingly divided among the populace. Some believed that self-defense was a necessity, even if it brought on reprisals; others considered the presence of the fighters to be a burden and held them responsible for every imaginable ill.

The clandestine Dashnak leaders, long the only ones to put up resistance to Abdülhamid's regime, now emerged from underground. In Van, Vahan Papazian[60] and his men were in their mountain refuge when they received confirmation of the news that the Constitutionalists had carried the day. Aram Manukian, one of the ARF's local leaders, had just been released from prison – he invited Papazian to join him in Van to celebrate the restoration of the constitution. Harassed by Ottoman troops only yesterday, the *fedayis* had a hard time persuading themselves of the reality of the new situation: they did not return to Van until 31 August. Papazian and Manukian were invited to the *konak* (local authorities building or palace), where the *vali* received them with honors. "We were foes; from now on, we are friends. Yesterday, tyranny reigned; today, the Constitution does. I am convinced that we shall defend it together," declared their enemy of yesterday before the stunned Armenian leaders.[61]

In Mush/Muş, the ARF's local military chief, Ruben Ter Minasian, was just as surprised by the news – it was some time before he decided that it was not a trap set by the Hamidian regime. A message sent by two militants, Dadrak and Carmen, read:

> God's grace is upon us. Today, the prefect visited the prelate; he told him that, thanks to a revolution, "Sultan Abdülhamid has promulgated the Constitution. All prisoners are going to be set free. Write to Ruben and tell him to remain calm; a decree amnestying him, too, is on its way."[62]

When he reached the center of Mush, Ruben was stupefied by the official reception, complete with a marching band, that the governor, Salih Pasha, gave him in front of the *konak*. No fewer than nine regiments marched past the Armenian *fedayis*, who watched them with mixed feelings: "There are the *fedayis*, our brothers. We used to point our bayonets at them, because there were blindfolds on our eyes. The old regime was to blame. Long live the Constitution! Long live the revolutionaries!"[63]

Ceremonies of the same sort were staged elsewhere as well. In Smyrna, the local ARF representatives, Hrach Tiriakian and Harutiun Kalfayan, listened as Dr. Nâzım, who had been living in the city since December 1907,[64] spoke of the "indissoluble bonds" between Armenians and Turks.[65] In Dyarbekir, in a Kurdish environment, Vartkes Seringiulian, the former head of the party in Van who had only recently been set free after spending several years in prison, enthusiastically participated in the official receptions alongside the local Young Turks. The Dashnak militants of Dyarbekir, however, remained on their guard, "refusing to reveal, notwithstanding the opinion of the future parliamentary deputy, their organizational structure or the source of their arms."[66] It must be added that these militants had witnessed the re-appearance on the local scene of two former executioners of Armenians, Arif and Feyzi Bey, who had recently rallied to the CUP's cause.[67]

This handful of examples leaves us with the general impression that the militants active in the field were skeptical and suspicious of the new regime, in contrast to the leaders who had returned from exile and settled in the capital.

A symptomatic episode says a great deal about the relations between the ARF and the CUP. Early in August 1908, Ömer Naci Bey, a member of the Ittihad's Central Committee responsible for inspecting the local CUP branches, arrived in Van together with Mirza Said, an Iranian Constitutionalist, and two leading Dashnak militants from Persia, Marzbed[68] and Sepastatsi Murad.[69] In the city, it became clear that Naci decided everything on the advice of Cevdet Bey, the son of the former *vali* of Van, Tahir Pasha. Papazian and other local party leaders were invited to a banquet given by the vali in Naci's honor. The conversation turned to local problems, in particular that of replacing government officials who had enforced Abdülhamid's repressive policies. The Young Turk propagandist declared, in a jocular tone:

> We Turks are lagging far behind European civilization, whereas you have made considerable progress. If it is true that it is indispensable to move forward together and live together as brothers, you will have to pause for a while and wait for us to catch up. If you don't, we shall have to latch on to your skirts to prevent you from advancing.[70]

Despite such scruples and second thoughts, the two movements cooperated. They needed each other: the CUP needed the ARF's help in putting down local roots, while the ARF needed the CUP in order to be able to play a political role in vilayet affairs. A few days after Ömer Naci's trip to Van, Cevdet Bey was named interim *vali* of Van and, of course, charged with founding a Young Turk club in the city.

It is probable that Naci's mission was not only to see to it that Young Turk clubs were set up in the area, but also to assess the ARF's real influence in the eastern provinces and rally local forces to the CUP. Thus, on 8 August 1908, Sarkis and Ghevont Meloyan, two local activists, as well as Murad and Marzbed, went to Erzerum to attend a regional ARF congress. They were accompanied by Naci Bey. There they met Colonel Vehib Bey (the future General Vehib Pasha), a CUP delegate who had been one of the small group of Young Turk officers at the head of the 1908 rebellion in Macedonia. Together, they tried to convince the local notables to collaborate with the new regime. At the congress, the Ittihadists and Dashnaks decided to rapidly organize in Bitlis a meeting of local Ittihad and ARF leaders as well as Kurdish *begs*.[71] The meeting was held in November 1908. Ishkhan,[72] Meloyan, Carmen,[73] Marzbed, Sarkis, and Pilos represented the ARF; Mehmed Sadik, a friend of the Armenians, was the Kurdish representative; the CUP sent Ömer Naci and Vehib Bey.[74] According to a 6 January 1909 letter from Simon Zavarian to ARF members in the Daron district, the purpose of the Bitlis meeting was to organize joint actions in the eastern provinces.[75] The reality of the matter, however, was a great deal more complex.

The meeting's aftermath offers a very different picture of the nature of the relations between the Young Turk military leadership and the leading Armenian *fedayis*. After the Bitlis meeting, Vehib Bey spent another ten days in Mush, then traveled through the surrounding area with Ruben, Ishkhan, and Aram – the chiefs of the ARF in the regions of Sasun-Mush, Lernabar, and Van, respectively. Relations between the Turks and the Armenians were characterized by a mixture of mutual admiration and mistrust. On the long horseback journey that took them from Mush to Van by way of the southern shore of Lake Van, Vehib Bey and his aide, Mustafa Kâmil,[76] had the time to make Ruben's and then Ishkhan's acquaintance. Ruben's detailed account of their conversations shows that one of his party's objectives was to convince the two Ittihadist officers that the ARF was influential in the region and that the local Armenian population was well disposed toward it. When the little group rode through Armenian villages, of which there were a great many on its route, it was indeed greeted by enthusiastic crowds. The Armenians had erected triumphal arches made of greenery and vegetables and crowned them with banners in Armenian that showed where they stood: "Long live the ARF and the Ottoman Revolution!" But it was Vehib Bey who was offered salt and bread, in the traditional gesture of welcome. In fact, Ishkhan had carefully prepared the reception of the visitors, giving precise instructions everywhere. According to Ruben, Vehib was favorably impressed by the Armenian population's hospitality and political maturity and surprised that the inhabitants of the Kurdish villages seemed indifferent to events and apathetic. The Armenian *fedayis* reminded him that the Constitutional regime could only be detrimental to the interests of the Kurdish *begs*, whom the old regime had privileged and allowed to act as they saw fit. In Vostan/Aghtamar, the halfway station, Ishkhan welcomed the little group, reminding Vehib that a few years earlier Vehib had shelled the island of Aghtamar, where Ishkhan and his *fedayis* had taken refuge.[77] The reception that the Armenian *fedayis* gave the official delegate of the Young Turk Central Committee had one overriding objective – to show him that Ishkhan's *fedayis* were the real masters of the region. Ruben's account of these events confirms, moreover, that the ARF leadership bodies in Istanbul had instructed their local activists to take Vehib Bey in hand on his trip through the eastern provinces.[78] The aim was to justify the agreement to collaborate concluded by the CUP and the Armenian party.

The picture of Vehib Bey that Ruben paints in his memoirs shows how well informed the militants were about their guests' history, and also reveals the interest that each side took in the other. "He called himself a Turk," Ruben remarks. He was educated, intelligent, experienced, and a good speaker, he added. He had served as a *vali*, had fought in the Balkans and Yemen; he affirmed that he was in favor of the equality of all the empire's subjects, but was opposed to political or administrative autonomy for the "nations," to socialist ideas, to foreign intervention in any form, and to a policy of decentralization.[79] What Ruben does not explicitly say, although we can read it between the lines of his account, is that he was made uneasy by an individual such as Vehib, who had a personality quite similar, in certain respects, to that of the *fedayis*. Evoking his state of mind at the time, the Armenian fighter confessed that the disarming of the *fedayi* commandos imposed by the ARF leadership in Constantinople had seemed to him to be a mistake and even an act of treason, for it left the party at the mercy of every shift in the political winds.

The *fedayi* leaders found the first months after the restoration of the Constitution difficult: after years of combat and a rough-and-ready life in the mountains of the area, they felt that they had suddenly become useless. Ruben was among the first to draw the consequences and left for Europe to study engineering. The *fedayis* had lost their motivation. Their romanticism had turned into bitterness. They had seen themselves as the incarnation of the nation, as its "saviors"; now they were forced to accept the strategy of collaboration dictated by the intellectuals of the capital.

It was in this state of mind that Ruben, Ishkhan, Vehib Bey, and Mahmud Kâmil were greeted at the gates of Van by Aram and the *vali* and then conducted to the city in horse-drawn coaches as if they were high-ranking dignitaries. In front of the *konak*, soldiers standing at attention and a huge throng listened to the speech begun by Vehib Bey under the ironic gaze of the Armenian leaders, with a formula that had been heard a thousand times before: "This is an exceptional day."[80]

To round out this brief evocation of the atmosphere reigning in the eastern provinces, we should also say a word about the working meeting held in Van during the same period in November 1908. It was attended by several members of the ARF's Eastern Bureau[81] and the three military chiefs of the southern zones – Ruben Ter Minasian, Ishkhan (Nikol Mikayelian), and Aram Manukian (these southern zones had heretofore been under the jurisdiction of the Eastern Bureau, but came under the de facto authority of the party's Istanbul leadership after the July 1908 revolution). The strategy of cooperating with the Young Turks adopted at the 1907 Fourth General Congress was confirmed at this meeting, which also ratified the more recent decisions to disarm the *fedayis* and engage in legal activities as well as to work toward improving the educational level of the population.

An interesting, revealing phenomenon appeared among the party's most emblematic personalities in this period: they returned to the homeland, setting an example for others by giving up their political functions in order to work amid the Armenian population. As one of them, Simon Zavarian, reports: "After twenty years of struggle, the militants were in sore need of the peace that now prevailed and the possibility of working under legal conditions; they threw themselves wholeheartedly into peaceful activities."[82] Thus, Zavarian himself volunteered to take a post as a school inspector in order to reorganize the Armenian school system in the Mush-Sasun area.[83] He introduced modern teaching methods, hired qualified teachers, and set up village commissions to manage local schools. Educated as an agricultural engineer, he devoted part of his energies to developing agriculture as well. His copious correspondence allows us to form an idea of the social and economic situation on the plain of Mush and the mountainous Sasun district, as well as the complex relations between the Armenians and the sedentary and nomadic Kurdish populations.[84] The other remarkable example is provided by Arshag Vramian, an ARF intellectual who moved to Van in 1909 and became its representative in the Ottoman parliament a few years later.[85]

Despite the official speeches and the friendly declarations by representatives of the CUP, Papazian notes that the Armenians' relations with the local authorities became less friendly after Naci's visit. He also remarks that the Kurds in the region hated the Ittihadists and that early in the fall the leaders of the Haydaran tribes – Kör Hüseyn Pasha, Emin Pasha, Mehmed Sadık, and Murtula Bey (all of them close to the Armenians) – paid him an impromptu visit in Van to discuss the credibility of the new regime.[86] Exchanges of this sort sum up the explosive political situation reigning in the "tribal provinces." The Kurdish *begs*, conservatives who had, generally speaking, been shown all the honors under Abdülhamid, were suspicious of these Young Turk militants, who spoke French with the Armenian revolutionaries and had dared to attack the Ottoman sovereign and caliph.

With the beginning of the electoral campaign for the Ottoman parliament in September 1908, immediate interests took precedence over all others. Papazian, an official ARF candidate, later described with a wealth of detail how the joint CUP-ARF meetings were organized in Van and the surrounding region. The campaign gave rise to almost comic situations: candidates harangued meeting halls that were full to bursting, preaching "solidarity" and defending the constitution before Armenian notables who passionately hated the Dashnak revolutionaries and Muslim notables notorious for having been the previous regime's staunchest supporters.[87] The two candidates endorsed by the CUP and the ARF – Tevfik Bey, a big landowner, and Papazian – were elected to represent the vilayet in parliament.[88]

To understand why the CUP was able to dominate these elections, we need to examine the electoral law that made the *sancak* (that is, the prefecture, subdivided into *kazas*, or subprefectures, and *nahies*, or counties) the basic electoral district and gave the right to vote to all males 25 and over. The electoral rolls identifying these male voters were established by the imams, priests, *muhtars* (village headmen), and other notables. On the basis of these lists, the *mutesarif* (prefect) decided how many parliamentary deputies a *sancak* would have, "in accordance with the following rules: one deputy for an adult male population between 25,000 and 75,000, two deputies for an adult male population between 75,000 and 125,000, and so on."

Candidates had to be at least 35 years old to be eligible. A parliamentary deputy's term ran for four years. Civil servants and officers, if elected to parliament, had to give up their posts.[89]

What gave the system a special twist, however, was the fact that each group of 500 voters designated an elector of the first degree who chose, in turn, an elector of the second degree in accordance with quantitative criteria: one elector for 500 to 750 voters, two for 750 to 1,250, and so on. The second-degree electors then met in the administrative seat of the *sancak* in order to elect the members of parliament (a quorum of 80 per cent was required). As a French diplomat who described the system points out, "applying these rules led to major difficulties that aggravated still further the absolute non-existence of anything resembling an accurate census." The result was widespread dissatisfaction and distortions in the distribution of seats.[90]

The two Armenian deputies elected in the capital, Krikor Zohrab and Bedros Halajian,[91] were not ARF members. Halajian belonged to the CUP. Interestingly, the Ottoman Constitutional Club nominated both men on 18 September in an election by secret ballot held at the Club.[92]

In the provinces, the ARF's candidates were not successful everywhere, despite official support from the CUP. While the Dashnaks carried the day in Erzerum, where Vartkes (Hovhannes Seringiulian)[93] and Armen Garo (Karekin Pastermajian)[94] were elected, and in Mush, with the victory of Kegham Der Garabedian,[95] the party was defeated in other areas. Thus, Spartal (Stepan Spartalian)[96] and the "Young Turk" lawyer Hagop Babikian[97] were elected in Smyrna, the Hnchak Murad (Hampartsum Boyajian)[98] won in Sis/Kozan, and Cilicia and Dr. Nazaret Daghavarian[99] carried the day in Sıvas.

Thanks to "judicious" utilization of the electoral system, the CUP won by a landslide, obtaining 160 seats, including those of Babikian and Halajian, both CUP members. Still more revealing are the figures that show that, of a total of 288 seats up for election, no fewer than one 140 went to Turks, 60 to Arabs, 27 to Albanians, 36 to Greeks, 14 to Armenians, 10 to Slavs and 4 to Jews. To put it differently, 220 Muslims and 46 Christians were elected to parliament. Thirty per cent of the deputies were clergymen, 30 per cent were big landowners, 20 per cent were civil servants, and 10 per cent belonged to one of the liberal professions.[100] The Ittihad's triumph was confirmed on 17 December 1908, when parliament opened its doors to the new deputies after 30 years of silence. It was inaugurated by a "speech from the throne," delivered by an Abdülhamid surprised by the ovation he received from the deputies. The Young Turks were not the slowest to take up his invitation to dine in Yıldız Palace on 31 December, following the example of the newly elected president of parliament, Ahmed Rıza.[101]

The European diplomats stationed in the provinces attentively followed these elections and sometimes made rather perceptive analyses of them. The French vice-consul in Erzerum began by noting that

> throughout the vilayet, the Muslim elections were monitored and controlled by the Young Turks. They skillfully foiled the intrigues of the partisans of the old regime ... As for the Armenian elections, they were run throughout the *sancak* by emissaries of the Dashnak Committee. The Committee used all the means at its disposal to reach its goal: it succeeded in having two of its members elected thanks to persuasion, pressure and, sometimes, the threats that its agents proffered during the first-degree elections. To obtain the required majority of votes in the second-degree elections, however, it needed the support of the Young Turks, and it is clearly thanks to this support that the vilayet now has two Armenians among its representatives.

Here we have confirmation of the methods used by the Young Turks and their Dashnak allies.

The social and political profile of the deputies elected in Erzerum also reveals the careful balance concocted and imposed by the central CUP authorities. Thus, we find among them a lawyer and "advocate of the liberal regime," Seyfulla Effendi; a *hoja*, Haci Sevket, a native of Lazistan, educated in *medreses* in Erzerum and later Constantinople, but considered to be a moderate; a magistrate, Haci Hafız Effendi, a native of Keghi/Kıgi, a judicial inspector in the vilayet of Baghdad "reputed to be a liar"; and our two Armenian revolutionaries, who, according to the French vice-consul, had "very advanced socialistic ideas; in parliament, they will be, not representatives of this province, but spokesmen and tools of the revolutionary Committees."[102]

The CUP was sometimes less generous vis-à-vis the minority candidates, or else unable to influence the political process in certain localities. Thus, in the vilayet of Angora, all 12 of the deputies elected in fall 1908 were Turks; the 125,000 Christians living in Angora did not obtain a single representative:

> The Young Turk Committee, which controlled these elections, had initially designated four candidates, of whom one was a Christian. But as it was unable to alter the Muslims' mentality, they did not fail to put a distinctly confessional stamp on these elections. Thus ... they refused to vote for Christians, whereas Christians did not hesitate to cast their ballots for Muslims.[103]

The circumstances surrounding the election of 11 or 12 deputies from the vilayet of Salonika offer further proof that the region had become a CUP stronghold. Elected here were Rahmi Bey (Evrenos), "descended of a family of conquerors"; Midhat Şükrü, the former assistant director of the public school system in Salonika and a "mason in the local masonic lodge"; Dr. Nâzım, "a physician and a major in the army [who had] enjoy[ed] great prestige since the proclamation of the Constitution"; and Mehmed Cavid Bey, a teacher at the Feyiziye school, of which he was also the principal. All were leaders of the CUP.[104]

The by-elections, held in the vilayet of Aleppo one year later in order to replace deputies who had resigned, are indicative of the CUP's strategy in "ethnic" provinces such as Syria. Of the two new deputies promoted by the CUP, one was a Turk and the other an Armenian: Bab Effendi Emirizâde, who worked in the vilayet's accounting office and was "fanatic and xenophobic," and Artin Effendi Boshg[h]azarian,[105] a lawyer from Ayntab who had settled in Aleppo after the 1895 massacres and been named to the Criminal Court of Appeals in 1908.[106] Yet the region was populated by Arabs. This choice of candidates can therefore appear surprising, unless one bears in mind that the CUP thus had these candidates in its grip, since they had no real electoral base, and simultaneously deprived the Arab nationalist movement of any opportunity to express itself through deputies elected from its ranks.

The Armenian National Institutions and the Integration of the Revolutionaries

For the non-Turkish elements of the empire, the Imperial Ottoman model, based on *millets*, or ethno-religious nations, had at least the advantage of allowing them a degree of autonomy. In the Armenians' case, the Constantinople Patriarchate was central to their collective existence. Under Abdülhamid, however, this institution, the workings of which were democratized from 1863 on, was dealt blow after blow. In September 1891, the Armenian constitution was suspended by the sultan. The Armenian chamber,[107] which had its seat in Galata, was forced to break off its activities, which paralyzed the internal administration of the *millet*. The chamber was convened only four times in over 17 years, after the sovereign had personally authorized it to meet on 7 December 1894 to elect Patriarch Mattheos

Izmirlian; on 6 November and 20 November 1896 to elect Patriarch Malakia Ormanian; and on July 1906 to settle major administrative problems.[108]

Thus, it was essentially under the Patriarchate of Malakia Ormanian that the nation had to come to grips with the situation that had been forced upon it. The leadership with which the patriarch had to work in this period was a truncated political council consisting of a few high government officials delegated by the Sublime Porte, such as Artin/Harutiun Dadian, Dr. Stepan Aslanian, and Gabriel Noradunghian.[109] Despite that undeniable handicap, this team did a great deal on behalf of an Armenian population that had been battered by the 1895–6 Hamidian massacres: it created schools for the 60,000 children orphaned in those years and organized a system of financial aid for families whose property had been looted or put to the torch.[110]

Given the nature of the relations that the patriarch and his "counselors" had to maintain with the Ottoman sultan, one can readily imagine that the Armenian revolutionaries held them in low esteem, and even understand why they organized an assassination attempt against Patriarch Ormanian on 6 January 1903. Struck by two bullets from the revolver of a young student as he was leaving the Sunday church service, the prelate survived.[111] The Political Council was, after ten years in office, finally renewed with the sultan's blessing: on 25 July 1891, the 61 deputies who were still alive – they had been elected 15 years earlier in 1891 – chose a new council, led by Gabriel Noradunghian and Diran Ashnan.[112]

It was thus to be expected that, after the July 1908 revolution, there would be changes not only at the head of the country, but in the Armenian *millet* as well. Patriarch Ormanian, who represented for militants of all stripes the Armenian face of Hamidian repression, was unjustly accused of collaborating with the tyrant and confiscating power to personal ends. A violent press campaign portrayed him as a declared partisan of the sultan's. On 16 July, at a meeting of the mixed council held while Dashnak militants demonstrated outside its chambers, Noradunghian, with his usual political acumen, demanded and received the patriarch's resignation.[113] This first blow, which the Armenian revolutionaries had of course helped prepare, heralded the Dashnak leaders' integration into Armenian national institutions. In the following weeks, the parishes proceeded to renew the Armenian chamber, electing a fair number of Dashnak and Hnchak activists who had abandoned their underground activity or returned from exile. As goes without saying, the laurels with which the Istanbul press and the Ittihadists had deliberately crowned the Armenian Committees helped boost their popularity and smoothed the way for their election.

Thus, even as it cultivated relations with the CUP, the ARF also sought to assert itself within its own group. But Istanbul Armenian society was a complex entity with peculiar sensibilities, and it was not easily convinced. It had its own networks; the ARF had had great difficulty recruiting members in Istanbul in the past. Aknuni and his friends had to compose with these realities and work patiently to gain a legitimacy that was not spontaneously accorded to them. After the Hamidian interlude, the Constantinople Armenians were rediscovering their democratic reflexes.

The Armenian national chamber reopened its doors on 3 October 1908. It had 80 deputies. At the head of the new political council was a liberal, Stepan Karayan,[114] along with two members of the Dashnak and Hnchak leaderships, Harutiun Shahrikian[115] and Murad (Hampartsum Boyajian), and, finally, Krikor Zohrab. For the first time, the political parties were taking a direct hand in running the nation's affairs, side by side with the still numerous conservatives. It was a period in which alarming reports of persistent insecurity continued to pour into the Patriarchate. During the session of 17 October, Zohrab, speaking on behalf of the political council, presented the chamber with a report on the general situation in Armenia and the means that would have to be mobilized to improve it. It thus became clear that, despite the proclamation of the constitution, nothing had really changed: the governors continued to implement Hamidian policies and famine had driven several thousand refugees to the capital, where they lived on alms from the Patriarchate. Zohrab proposed a number of ways of bringing the situation back to normal. They included creating a mixed Turkish and Armenian commission of inquiry invested with executive powers; dismissing *valis* and offic-ers of the *hamidye* (regiments) who had committed atrocities; trying looters and murderers in a Constantinople court; restoring confiscated land to its rightful owners; according exiles who wished to return to their villages rights and exemptions similar to those granted to the *muhacir* (Muslim migrants); taking measures to prevent the *beys* and *ağas* from continuing to extort money from Armenian peasants; helping populations on the brink of famine get through the winter by giving them wheat and seed; and, finally, issuing orders to the military authorities to carry out the decisions taken in the field by the mixed commission.[116]

The chamber accordingly designated a delegation to negotiate these matters with the Sublime Porte. Led by Zohrab, Hrant Asadur,[117] and Dr. Vahram Torkomian,[118] the delega-tion was assured that all available means would be mobilized to restore the Armenians' rights.[119] We thus see that the chamber's concerns about the Armenian population in the provinces were quite similar to the revolutionaries'. It was, however, the eminent members of the Constantinople Armenian community who were sent to present the nation's grievances to the Ottoman government.

Simon Zavarian, one of the ARF's historic leaders, sent a long report to the patriarch in November 1908, shortly after assuming his post in Mush. In it, he portrayed the general condition of the region as catastrophic. "I am not among those," he wrote, "who think that all the different problems that have killed a whole generation can be resolved by means of individual reforms."[120] Zavarian consequently advocated radical changes at the highest levels of the state, especially among the caste of high-ranking government officials who blocked all the reformist impulses of progressive circles. After evoking the chaos reigning in the Armenian provinces, he observed that,

> in Constantinople, it is possible to survive if one works. But what are the prospects for an inhabitant of Daron or Sghert [Siirt], where the barbaric system has filled the fields with nomads and their herds and brought all work and all production to a halt?

Indeed, after centuries of resistance, the Armenian peasants were giving ground to the Kurdish nomads. The Kurds, who had received favored treatment from Abdülhamid, had arrogated considerable rights to themselves and were not inclined to relinquish them, even after the changes that had come about in the country. Zavarian, for his part, asked the Patriarchate to make a priority of supporting the peasants who were trying to resettle in their villages in Armenia, while cutting back the aid it allocated to the many refugees who were present in Constantinople in 1908. The parliamentary deputies as well as the politicians knew only too well that the fate of these regions turned on developing the economy and re-establishing secure conditions.

The Armenian Deputies in the First Ottoman Parliament of the Young Turk Period

The restoration of the constitution, a Young Turk battle horse for as long as the CUP was in the opposition, should have made it possible in theory to democratize the country's political life and allow the opposition to be heard. The heart of democratic life, in which the appro-priate space for debate was supposed to be created, could only be the parliament, in which the people were represented. Like certain other groups, the Armenians, as we have said, hoped that they would have the means to promote the liberalization of the Ottoman system there. They very quickly discovered, however, that this tribune was reserved for others; the CUP[121] had seen to it that it would dispose of a majority large enough to enable it to reduce the number of non-Turkish deputies to a minimum while according the opposition merely symbolic status (the sole opposition party was the Osmanlı Ahrar Fırkası, the Ottoman Freedom Party).[122]

The four Dashnak deputies, it must be added, did not have a mastery of the official language of parliamentary debate, Ottoman Turkish; as a rule, they had to express themselves through the Armenian deputy representing the capital, Zohrab. They also had to deal with the demands of the Armenian chamber, which regarded them as the parliamentary representatives and spokespersons of the *millet*. These handicaps seem not to have prevented them from making an active contribution to the Armenian parliamentary delegation. One of them, Dr. Vahan Papazian, notes in his memoirs that the Armenian deputies concerned themselves exclusively with matters of general interest during the first parliamentary session, never once bringing up questions specific to the Armenian world.[123] He points out, for example, that Zohrab played a pivotal role on the committee charged with drafting a bill on the reform of the court system; that Garo, an engineer by training, worked on the "Chester" plan for a railroad connecting Istanbul to the Iranian border; that he himself worked on reforming and "secularizing" the school system; and that Daghavarian, a physician and agronomist, wrote most of the provisions of the basic law for the promotion of agricultural development, and another aimed at reforming the health system and improving hygienic conditions.[124] All this indicates the spirit ("what is good for the country is good for us") in which the deputies representing the Armenian *millet* worked, without ulterior motives, toward reforming the empire. The parliamentary activity of Krikor Zohrab, whose decisive role in the creation of the Ottoman Constitutional Club we have already pointed out,[125] is exemplary in this regard. Although certain conservative circles had no love for Zohrab, whom they criticized for "knowing only the literary aspect of Armenian life,"[126] he became the spokesman and guiding spirit of the group of Armenian deputies. Before attending the inaugural session of parliament, he had first to pay a visit to CUP headquarters on Nuri Osmaniye Street, no doubt in order to make it clear that he owed his election to the Ittihad; he left the headquarters sitting beside a Young Turk judge, Mustafa Asım, in a coach.[127] Also significant was the fact that he took his seat in parliament next to Hüseyin Cahit, the editor-in-chief of the Young Turk newspaper *Tanin*.[128] Both facts are indicative of the influence that the Ittihadist movement exercised over the Ottoman parliament. The Armenian lawyer's first parliamentary speech, on 24 December, illustrates the "misunderstanding" between the Young Turk and Armenian deputies that would grow worse as time went by. Zohrab denounced the obviously improper election of a certain Serdatazâde Mustafa, who had a reputation as a bandit and murderer in his electoral district of Şabinkarahisar. However, Zohrab was rebuked by his colleagues, who did not seem to have been shocked by Serdatazâde Mustafa's personal history.[129]

Istanbul circles were troubled by the fact that not a single deputy had spoken up in support of Zohrab's position, although it was common knowledge that Serdatazâde Mustafa had been deeply implicated in the November 1895 massacres in his native region. This first incident provided an occasion for muted expression of a criticism that would recur regularly in the debates: the Muslim deputies from the eastern provinces who had been elected on CUP lists were often former partisans of the Hamidian regime who had been more or less complicit in the 1894–6 massacres. The apparently baseless rumors to the effect that Zohrab had received death threats illustrate, in any case, the first signs of tension.[130]

While Armenian institutions and the Armenian deputies did not openly express their bitterness over the government's tolerant attitude toward those who had only recently been the Armenians' executioners, they deplored the fact that the "Red Sultan" – whom they, and especially the revolutionaries among them, had hated with a passion ever since his decision to decimate the Armenian people – was still being treated with kid gloves by their progressive Young Turk friends. The sultan, for his part, had probably been relieved to learn that the Armenian deputies, some of whom had organized an attempt on his life not long before, had coldly turned down the invitation to dine in Yıldız Palace with which he had honored all the newly elected deputies.[131]

There were, however, other contradictory signs that came as surprises, such as Zohrab's November 1908 appointment to a professorship of penal law at the Istanbul Law School and the success he enjoyed there. More than 700 students abandoned their classrooms to throng into the hall in which he delivered his inaugural lecture.[132] This was evidence of something like a thirst for knowledge, the polar opposite of the conservative reactions observable in the Ottoman parliament, something resembling a desire to sample knowledge coming from elsewhere.

An interview that Zohrab granted the correspondent of a Bulgarian newspaper late in December 1908 offers an even more precise illustration of the archaic side of Ottoman political life. Zohrab told his interviewer that he deplored the lack of organized political groups into which "the nationalities could melt" instead of working in the form of antagonistic national blocs. The Armenian deputies, he said, wanted "above all, to work toward the general welfare of the Empire. The particular interests of the Armenian nation come afterwards."[133] Thus, he took the floor in parliament on 21 January 1909 to demand that a commission of inquiry be formed to investigate the conditions under which the Hejaz railroad was being built, for it seemed that management of the project had been marred by serious financial corruption.[134] In other contexts, he suggested that the government establish a draft budget and submit it to a parliamentary vote, that it elaborate a genuine tax policy, and so on. If he was virtually the only Armenian deputy to intervene in the debates, he more than made up for his colleagues' silence.

The Stakes of Power: The CUP and the Opposition

The explanations given at the 13 February 1909 session of parliament, at which a vote of norconfidence toppled Kâmil Pasha's cabinet (formed on 5 August 1908), led Zohrab to intervene in the debate. His remarks disconcerted his Young Turk colleagues. It was well known that with its continual meddling in government affairs, the CUP's Central Committee had often exasperated the grand vizier, leading to abiding tension between the two sources of power. When Kâmil Pasha had sought to ram through the appointment of new ministers of defense and the navy against the committee's advice, the Ittihad had ordered its deputies to vote in favor of a motion of censure, because it would under no circumstances relinquish its control of the army.[135] The pasha had tried to free himself of a form of supervision too restrictive for his tastes and had immediately had to pay the price for his presumption; he fell victim to the Ittihadists' first "coup d'état."

Hüseyin Hilmi Pasha succeeded Kâmil on 14 February 1909. Although this officer was reputed to stand closer to the CUP, he was not treated any more gently by it. Hardly had he been appointed grand vizier than he learned, at a meeting at the Sublime Porte with the future Ottoman ambassador to Spain, Ali Haydar Bey (son of the famous Midhat Pasha), who had come to receive his letters of accreditation, that the diplomat had been ordered to wait for the arrival of Major Enver Bey, who would give him the instructions he needed about the line to take with the Spanish government. Faced with Ali Haydar's firm refusal to take his instructions from anyone other than the minister of foreign affairs, the new grand vizier had to confront, for the first time, the rage of the Young Turk Central Committee.[136] This episode, which is banal after all, offers only a glimpse of the chaotic functioning of the state in these first months, in which an administration still redolent of the old regime shared power with a committee that still lacked experience in handling state affairs.

Another structure put in place by the Ittihad reveals the general nature of the regime that was now being put in place: the systematic utilization of secret paramilitary forces entrusted by the committee with special missions ranging from making threats to murdering opponents or journalists. This underground structure had made great strides since it was founded in 1907. Its cadres were almost without exception graduates of Istanbul's Military Academy. After the officers who, like Eyüb Sabri (Akgöl) and Ahmed Cemal, had rallied to the committee in summer 1908, other officers now joined this paramilitary organization: Hüseyin Rauf (Orbay),[137] Monastırlı Nuri (Conker),[138] Kuşçubaşızade Eşref (Sencer),[139] Yenibahçeli Şükrü (Oğuz),[140] Kara Vasıf[141] and Kâzım (Özalp)[142] or, again, Abdülkadır († 1926), Ali (Çetinkaya), Atif (Kamçıl), Sarı Efe Edip, Sapbanclı Hakkı, Halil (Kut) (Enver's uncle), Filibeli Hilmi, Ismitli Mümtaz, Hüsrev Sâmi (Kızıldoğan), Süleyman Askeri, Yenibahçeli Nail (Şükrü's brother), Yakup Cemil († 1916), and Cevat Abbas (Gürer) (1887–1943).[143] We shall see the decisive role these men played in the eradication of the Armenian population during the First World War.

The Ittihadist Central Committee did not hesitate to use such extreme methods as murder to rid itself of its opponents. The oppositional journalist Hasan Fehmi was assassinated on 6 April 1909 and Ahmed Samin, a member of the opposition, was murdered shortly thereafter. These practices illustrate the conception of political struggle that held sway in the CUP. For the committee, the opposition was an assortment of "reactionaries, thieves, swindlers, drunks, gamblers, good-for-nothings and murderers."[144] One of the "saviors of the Empire," Enver, formulated the matter more precisely: "All the heads dreaming of sharing power must be crushed … we have to be harsher than Nero as far as ensuring domestic peace is concerned."[145]

Some of the Unionists confirm in their memoirs what people suspected of the CUP when certain events occurred. The Ittihad's former secretary general, Midhat Şükru, reports how one of his colleagues on the Central Committee, Kara Kemal, personally led a retaliatory action against the headquarters of the organization Fedakaran-ı Millet (Those Devoted to the Nation) at the head of a band that demolished its offices.[146]

According to one of the best connoisseurs of the political life of the day, "virtually all the opposition parties in the Unionist period advocated a liberal economy, were Westernizers, [championed] the unity of the [Empire's ethnic] groups and favored decentralization."[147] These parties initially came together in the Ahrar and, thereafter, under the banner of Hürriyet ve Ittilâf Fırkası (Liberal Alliance), which was the product of a fusion between İbrahim Temo's Democratic Party, Gümülcineli İsmail Bey's Party of the People (Ahali), the Mutedil Hürriyet-perveran Fırkası (Moderate Liberals' Party)[148] and the Independent Party.[149]

After the events of 31 March, which we shall be discussing later, General Şerif Pasha, a former "fellow traveler" of the Central Committee in Salonika, founded the Islahat-ı Osmaniye (Radical Party) together with other CUP dissidents such as Refik Nevzat, Albert Fua, and Mevlanzâde Rıfat. Exiled in Paris, they ferociously opposed the CUP, especially in their French language review, *Mécheroutiette*, which ceaselessly denounced the Ittihadists' political crimes and corruption. These "radicals" demanded, notably, that the army cease to meddle in politics, that the committee stop operating like a secret organization and designate deputies, and that the CUP abandon its project of Turk-ifying the country.[150] Indeed, these demands, cast in the form of accusations, were common to the entire opposition, including the Muslim circles that had come together in the Ittihad-ı Muhammedi (Mohammedan Association), founded on 5 April 1909. In its organ, *Volkan*, Ittihad-ı Muhammedi criticized the Young Turks' atheism and their rejection of Islamic values.[151]

In revolutionary Armenian circles, in particular among the Hnchaks, these movements sparked some hope that the Ottoman Empire would adopt a domestic policy more favorable to non-Turkish groups. The SDHP, which had been opposed to the Ittihad from the outset, clearly sought to combat the CUP so as not to leave it the leisure to apply its Turkish program.[152] Its rapprochement with Ahrar and then with the Ittilâf had no other purpose than to combat the nationalist Young Turk regime. Sapah-Giulian notes in this connection that the day the Ittilâf and the SDHP signed an agreement to cooperate, "the apprehensions were palpable in the Ittihadist milieu" and that by way of this cooperation, his party influenced the Ittilâf's politics, moving them in a more progressive direction, while playing a major role in organizing it and forming its branches in the provinces.[153] "While it is true that the Ittihad," says Sapah-Giulian,

> could, by massacring Armenians in the provinces and ordering pillage and kidnappings there, fairly claim to have advanced one of its projects, it suffered significant setbacks elsewhere, among them the uprising of traditional Turkish circles in Konya, the Constantinople rebellion and the events in Albania and Rumelia.[154]

Its practice of governing from behind the scenes notwithstanding, after eight months in power the CUP had undeniably succeeded in displeasing everybody. Despite appearances, it did not yet wield much power: while its policy of forging a broad alliance of forces initially enabled it to rally once loyal partisans of the sultan to its side, notably by offering them seats in parliament, the CUP was disillusioned by the alacrity with which these circles turned their coats. It also discovered that the society on which it wished to impose its vision of the future was even more unsympathetic to its projects than it had thought. The CUP learned this bitter lesson with the first violent blow struck against it, on 13 April 1909.

Chapter 2

Young Turks and Armenians Facing the Test of "The 31 March Incident" and the Massacres in Cilicia

The two events that took place in April 1909 – the "reaction" to the establishment of the Young Turk regime in Constantinople and, concomitantly, the massacre of the Armenians in Cilicia, better known as the "Adana events" – allow us, in many respects, to evaluate the transformations that had taken place in the Ottoman Empire since the restoration of the constitution. Since they antedated the laws on the press and freedom of association that were passed in summer and fall 1909, and since they occurred in plain view of external observers and a free oppositional press, they offer an ideal standpoint from which to observe Ottoman realities. They bring us to the question of the significance of the "reaction" of April 1909, of the Young Turks' responsibility in the organization of the Adana massacres and, consequently, of their national and international credibility. But it is the way in which the CUP handled these two matters that here has the most to tell us about its practices and its vision of the Armenian element of the empire. The Armenian institutions' management of the crisis is equally instructive, for it provides us insight into the Armenians' feelings about the Young Turk regime and their horizon of expectations. The question that obsessed the Armenians more than any other, as the declarations of their leaders in the Chamber of Deputies clearly indicate, was whether the massacres represented the last gasp of the old regime or were rather the inaugural act of a new policy of extermination.

"The 31 March Incident"

Most historians consider the reaction against the Young Turks, better known by the euphemism The "31 March Incident" (13 April by the Gregorian calendar), to have been an operation directed by circles loyal to the old regime that were described as reactionary by the press of the day: it leagued soldiers from the garrisons of Constantinople and officers who had risen through the ranks with the religious opposition, the *ulema* and sheikhs of the orders of Dervishes who took their inspiration from the Ittihad-ı Muhammedi and the Ahrar party. Some detect in this reaction a maneuver designed by the British Foreign Office to destabilize the CUP after the fall of the cabinet headed by its "protégé," Kâmil Pasha. Whichever hypothesis one adopts, the radicalization of the liberal and religious opposition in this period was undeniable, as was the growing antagonism between officers who had risen through the ranks (*alaylı*) and graduates of the military academy (*mektemli*) – the *alaylı* complained that the *mektemli* completely dominated the army.[1] The question remains how these diverse forces united in order to take to the streets, occupy the parliament building, and instigate a hunt for Ittihadists throughout the capital.

The reactionary aspect of the uprising was quite real (even if examination of the press of the day shows that it was probably retrospectively amplified by the CUP), inasmuch as the insurgents demanded a return to the sharia. First and foremost, however, what was involved was a hostile reaction to the Young Turks. Thus one of the principle architects of the movement, Vahdetti, issued a call to "Christian and Jewish Ottomans" in which he assured them that they need not fear for their property or their lives "thanks to our sharia" and recommended that they "not withdraw from the union with Islam ... or follow the enemies of civilization and traitors to the sharia." The Ittihad-ı Muhammedi also pointed out that the sharia protected the rights of Muslims and non-Muslims alike. These declarations prove that the leaders of the movement were well aware of the non-Muslims' demands. Their political platform even called for "justice for the Christians as well," predicting that "they will fraternize with us."[2]

The example that historians most often adduce to illustrate the reactionary nature of the movement is that incarnated by the public activist and journalist Mizanci Murad Bey, editor of the newspaper *Mizan*, who, "more deeply estranged from his former companions than ever, threw oil on the fire by stirring up religious passions and denouncing equality [between Muslims and] non-Muslims."[3] If the insurgents' official declarations are to be believed, this former Young Turk leader, who was exiled as early as October 1908 and did not reappear on the scene until April 1909,[4] was the only "reactionary" hostile to non-Muslims. He was, nonetheless, counselor to the ephemeral liberal grand vizier who emerged from these events, Ahmed Tevfik Pasha. To pin the same label of "reactionary" on both Muslim and liberal strata comes down to endorsing the arguments used by the Young Turks to discredit the opposition and liquidate it the more effectively. The liberals, who tended to favor a policy of decentralization and integration of non-Muslims, seem to have been unjustifiably lumped together with the reactionaries.

Let us recall that the Young Turk Committee was, to say the least, in a difficult position on the eve of these events. It was entangled in somber affairs involving the murder of journalists and political opponents and was under pressure from the opposition. Did it capitalize on the situation to take control of the country militarily and eliminate oppositionists of all stripes? Several circumstances suggest that this was indeed the case. After the insurgents had taken over the parliament building, killed a few deputies, and sacked the editorial offices of the main Young Turk newspapers, the situation was taken back in hand by Tevfik Pasha, at which point the rebels of the First Army Corps, based in Constantinople, returned to their barracks. The Ottoman parliament then convened, deciding at its April 17 session to send a delegation to Çatalca to meet with Mahmud Şevket Pasha and his troops in Rumelia. The delegation was to inform him that the rebels had returned to their barracks and asked for pardon, so that it was no longer necessary to march on the capital; this could only lead to a pointless bloodbath. Şevket, after initially accepting the proposals of the deputies who had been sent to confer with him – Yusuf Kemal, Krikor Zohrab, and Vartkes Seringiulian – decided to occupy Constantinople after all.[5] This general, a product of the old school who was surrounded by a general staff of Young Turk officers, probably consulted with the Ittihadist Central Committee before carrying out the repression that followed his arrival at the capital. Once the ephemeral Tevfik cabinet had fallen – named on 18 April, it resigned on 26 April – the declaration of a state of emergency and the creation of a court-martial made it possible to hang rebels, and especially members of the opposition, in droves. Among them were a number of journalists and liberal politicians who were first carefully tagged as anti-Constitutional "reactionaries," a useful charge that justified reprisals. In the name of the constitution, the CUP rid itself with little effort of the whole opposition; it contented itself with exiling the best-known personalities, such as Prince Sabaheddin, in order to prevent its basic objective from becoming too obvious.

How did Armenian circles react to these events? The daily press of 14 and 15 April 1909 evinces perplexity mixed with apprehension in the face of this rebellion. Some feared that it was a coup mounted by their *bête noire*, Abdülhamid, because he wanted to abrogate the constitution again. The general impression given by all the declarations in the press is that the Armenians' overriding concern was that the announced reforms should be carried through and lead to the creation of a state based on the rule of law and the restoration of civil peace. In an article entitled "The Current Crisis,"[6] the editor-in-chief of the Istanbul daily *Piuzantion*, Piuzant Kechian, reported that on the evening of 16 April the ARF organized in a room in the Hotel Splendide a meeting of 30 leaders of various Ottoman political currents – the CUP, the Ahrar, the ARF, the SDHP – with a view to bringing about a rapprochement based on "defense of the Constitution." The same newspapers also wrote that Armenian volunteers from Tekirdağ had joined the troops of Rumelia "to defend the Constitution"; on 27 April, the Armenian community of Constantinople organized a massive funeral for the volunteers who had fallen in the fighting in the capital.[7] From Dashnak sources we learn, more precisely, that the ARF, with the approval of the Ittihad, organized militias to support the Action Army, including 550 men from Adabazar who helped quell the insurgents from the Selimiye barracks.[8] Moreover, one of the ARF's military leaders, Ruben Ter Minasian, had been sent to Tekirdağ to recruit Armenian volunteers there; Şevket, however, had been unwilling to provide them with arms.[9] In Smyrna, finally, the *vali* and the local Ittihad club had asked the Dashnaks and Hnchaks to "form groups of volunteers in the next twelve hours": the following afternoon, 230 young Armenians from the city and the surrounding villages, as well as Turks, Greeks, and Jews, had been armed and sent to the Smyrna-Kartal train station.[10]

All this clearly indicates that Armenian circles approved of the constitution and the ARF's alliance with the CUP. But the clearest proof of their attachment to these positions was provided by the way the parliamentary deputy Bedros Halajian – who would later be named minister of public works – reacted when the insurgents invaded the Ottoman chamber, on the morning of 13 April 1909, to demand that the sharia be restored and that the president of the parliament, Ahmed Rıza, resign.[11] Although several deputies had just been killed in the city and most of those in the chamber lay down on the floor to protect themselves, Halajian stood up and, in a scene reminiscent of the French Etats Généraux, declared to the insurgents, who were quite impressed by his aplomb: "We have been elected by all the peoples of the Empire. A representative of the people does not have the right to let anyone tell him what to do [while threatening him] with bayonets...Look out the window! The rabble that is peppering our breasts with lead is over there...Go ahead, kill me, I'm on my feet."[12] Another circumstance illustrates, were there any need for further illustration, the close bonds between the Armenian deputies and their Young Turk colleagues as well as the confidence reigning between them: in the five days of anarchy that followed the outbreak of the insurrection of 13 April, at a time when the Unionist militants were being actively pursued, the leader of the Dashnak party, Aknuni, hid Mehmed Talât in his home,[13] while Zohrab took in another CUP leader, Halil Bey (Menteşe),[14] and the ARF militant Azarig provided refuge to Dr. Nâzım.[15]

In the days leading up to these events, the Young Turk press, particularly the daily *Tanin*, had not passed up the occasion to attack certain Armenian deputies in its columns. One of these attacks was aimed at Zohrab, who then figured as the leader of the Armenian parliamentary group, and the editor-in-chief of *Ikdam*, Ali Kemal (elected to succeed Rıza as president of parliament shortly afterwards). *Tanin* criticized the two men for taking advantage of their posts as professors at the law school to "manipulate their students and make use of them to defend their own political opinions."[16] What motivated these attacks on Zohrab, which had been orchestrated by his neighbor on the benches of parliament, Hüseyin Cahit?

Had the growing importance that Ottoman public opinion accorded the lawyer alarmed the CUP? Did it find him somewhat too enterprising? The nature of the attack does not tell us much; to all appearances, the students of the law school played no role in the events of 31 March. Had Zohrab's and Kemal's courses, which put the accent on the role of law in the creation of a democratic society, irritated the Young Turks?

In sum, it may be observed that the events of 31 March simply confirmed, at least as far as the leaders of the ARF were concerned, the solidity of the alliance with the CUP and the hostility of all Armenian circles to the possibility of a restoration of the old regime.

Young Turks and Armenians Facing the Test of the April 1909 Massacres in Cilicia

Understanding the origins of the explosion of violence that culminated in the massacre of 25,000 Armenians from Cilicia in April 1909 was an absolute priority for the Armenians. This massacre, all too reminiscent of the ways of the old regime, threatened to undermine their commitment to the Constitutional process, as well as the ARF's alliance with the CUP. To put it differently, it was the sincerity of the Young Turks' desire to collaborate with the Armenians – their real determination to improve the lot of the populations of the eastern provinces – that was thrown into question under the circumstances. The Armenian political institutions sought to make this issue a test of the Young Turks' intentions; they wanted to know to what extent the CUP was responsible for the Adana events. This indicates just how decisive an impact the crisis had on the way relations between the Armenians and the Young Turk government evolved.

A French diplomatic dispatch sent from Maraş, Cilicia on 4 January 1909 announced the threat of massacres and reported exactions against both the local Young Turk club and the Christians "who had been the most enthusiastic about the establishment of the new regime." No action was taken against those responsible for these excesses.[17] There were also reports on the anarchic situation prevailing in the vilayets of Dyarbekir and, a few weeks later, Mamuret ul-Aziz: there had been a settling of scores between Kurdish tribes, it was said, and hostile reactions to the Young Turks, accompanied by a rise in Muslim fundamentalism.[18]

In a 1 September 1908 dispatch, the consular agent responsible for the vice-consulate in Van, evoking the consequences of the July 1908 revolution in that city, remarked that "a Committee of Union and Progress" had been formed there. It had, he said, "twenty-one members: seven military personnel, seven Armenians and seven Turks." The Committee, he added, corresponded "with Salonika, from which it received its instructions."[19]

In Cilicia, the formation of local Young Turk Committees had made it possible, above all, to settle scores with the two main representatives of the state, whose policy of appeasing Christians was not particularly popular in this region, still steeped in tribal custom. Thus, the Young Turk Committee of Adana, made up of the principal Turkish notables of the region, had first arranged for the *ferik* (military commander) to be replaced and had then trained its sights on the *vali* of the vilayet, Bahri Pasha, demanding that he resign. Accused of "sympathizing with the Christians," Bahri had had to leave the city secretly, but was

arrested by villagers on the border of the vilayet at the request of his personal enemy, Bağdâdizâde,[20] and then released on orders from the Committee in Adana ... He [was] said to have resisted, for five hours running, pressure from the Committee in Adana that was demanding his resignation; he claimed that thirty thousand Armenians would rise up in his defense. The Committee is supposed to have retorted: "See if they will: you won't even find thirty."[21]

These few remarks are indicative of the mood reigning in Adana shortly after the revolution: they reveal the local Turkish notables' real assessment of the ability of Cilicia's Armenian population to stage a revolt, of which they were to make so much over the following months.

Later, on 15 October, Bahri Pasha's successor, Cevad Bey, arrived in Adana:

In anticipation of all eventualities, [Cevad] has asked Damascus to send him reinforcements... The pessimists were even speaking of a massacre of Armenians by that date [the end of Ramadan], but this eventuality seems rather unlikely, unless the Armenians maintain their outrageous attitude, which is as imprudent as can be... This attitude of the Armenians is just what is required to alienate the Young Turks. Young and Old Turks now seem to be putting their differences behind them on the basis of patriotism and Islamicism. Already, in the mosques, the mullahs are summoning the faithful to defend "their rights" with vigor... It is Bağdâdizâde who is urging the Turks on, the same Bağdâdizâde who, they say, arrested Bahri Pasha during his flight.[22]

All the elements of the problem come together in the passage just quoted – the first rumors of massacre and the first allusion to the "provocations" of certain Armenian militants. In other words, the official dialectic of "provocations, revolt, and massacre" is here put in place and echoed without second thought by the French vice-consul, whose inconsistency and cowardice during the April 1909 events would come in for comment from officers and missionaries among his compatriots.

The ambiance in Cilicia was indeed oppressive during the Ramadan celebrations of October 1908. The Muslims found the changes brought about by the Constitutional revolution hard to swallow, especially the fact that the Christians, beginning with the Armenians, had taken a rather high profile – that is, that they had vigorously defended the constitution. An unverifiable rumor was even making the rounds in Adana's Turkish neighborhoods: the Christians were getting ready to attack the barracks and bring it under their control before launching an assault on the Turkish population.[23]

This said, we need to examine the justification for the charges of provocation and revolt that certain Turks and also some foreign observers regularly repeated in Cilicia and elsewhere in the Armenian provinces, in order to understand the origins and content of those charges. In this connection, the dispatches that the French consular agents in the provinces sent to the French minister of foreign affairs and the ambassador in Constantinople are a by no means negligible source when it comes to gauging the tensions that persisted here and there, despite the proclamation of the constitution.

From Van, Captain Dickson, who presided over the French vice-consulate, reported to the minister on his conversations with the Armenian leaders. "To try to improve the very tense situation," he wrote,

I met with the Tashnak [*sic*] leaders, Aram [Manukian] and the Doctor [Vahan Papazian], and I gave them some advice. I advised them to conduct themselves with prudence and moderation, to drop, for the moment, their exaggerated ideas, to treat the compromised figures of the old regime gently, rather than with an eye to taking revenge, and not to call for excessive punishment. Fortunately, they lent an ear to my counsel.[24]

This first, revealing report reminds us that, under the old regime, Abdülhamid's policy of arming the Kurdish *hamidiye* regiments and setting them loose on the populations of the eastern provinces gave local Kurdish tribes a sense of impunity and omnipotence; they profited from the situation to seize a great deal of land and other real estate from the Armenians. With the restoration of the constitution, local Armenian leaders, as well as their colleagues in parliament in Constantinople, emboldened by their new-found legitimacy and the Ittihad's apparent support, demanded that these abuses be punished or, at the very least, redressed – that is, the property be restored to its rightful owners. This implied that thousands of suits had to be settled, threatening positions acquired by tribal chieftains who still had considerable power in their native regions and who were also in some cases members of the provincial Young Turk clubs or even members of the Ottoman parliament. Yet, as the French chargé d'affaires in Constantinople, Boppe, remarked:

> The Kurds were ill-prepared for the reforms that the constitution brought to the empire... The Kurds find it hard to forget the privileges that they enjoyed during Abdülhamid's reign. They miss the distinctions and gratifications that were sent to them from Yildiz as recompense for the crimes and depredations that they perpetrated against the Armenian population.[25]

Confronting local dignitaries by challenging the positions they had acquired was part of the tradition for the Armenian revolutionaries, who, as we know, did not hesitate to "punish" the Kurdish chieftains who had committed the most abominable crimes. It was also quite reasonable from the standpoint of these militants, who spoke in terms of social progress and were steeped in progressive ideas, to demand that they be given a role in running the affairs of their region. Obviously, former "terrorists," who had been received with honors on their return from exile or emergence from the underground and were once again in good odor, could only arouse distrust among high-ranking officials who had spent the previous 30 years persecuting and mistreating the Armenian population with the Sublime Porte's blessing. It must indeed have been difficult for such people, set in their ways, to grasp in a short span of time the transformations that Ottoman society was now supposed to undergo. It is equally probable that the integration of these former clients of Abdülhamid's into the new democratic institutions shocked the Armenians, who vehemently denounced the inclusion of these locally powerful men in the new arrangements. What was perceived as a "provocation" at the time was no doubt this demand for justice, unquestionably somewhat idealistic, especially in a society that still held that there could be no question of equality for all the empire's subjects. To come forward with demands was itself a "provocation."

The very fact that Hnchak or Dashnak militants returned to Cilicia and often joined local Young Turk clubs irritated certain consuls accustomed to reasoning along lines laid down by the state, whatever the nature of the state in question was. The French vice-consul in Mersin and Adana remarked, for example, that the Armenians' "ringleader is a certain [Garabed] Geukderelian, long imprisoned because of the part he played in the affairs of Armenia."[26] This is a curious way of judging a militant who had been persecuted for years, a renowned lawyer who, just after the revolution, was assigned the mission of founding a Young Turk club in Hacın together with Captain Abdüllah in order to promote a climate favorable to good relations between the various elements of the town's population. Let us note, however, that this same Captain Abdüllah, after being received by the local notables and drinking a cup or two, had betrayed how he really saw matters to the Armenian bishop: "*Si, sous la Constitution, les Arméniens continuent de cultiver des idées séparatistes, nous les tuerons tous jusqu'au dernier.*"[27] As a former Hnchak activist, Geukderelian in fact remained suspect in some people's eyes. Above all, he annoyed – or aroused the jealousy of – the local notables, who were rather hard put to accept his newfound influence, which threatened their own prerogatives.

Beyond such general accusations, an exceptional bundle of charges was leveled against the Turkish authorities' main *bête noire*, the bishop of Adana, Mushegh Seropian, who was universally accused of having done more than anyone else to provoke the Turks and thus bring on the massacres in Cilicia.[28] Seropian's case is even more revealing of the differences in "mentality" or the "misunderstandings" that emerged in the period. An educated man, the bishop represented a new generation of Armenian prelates. He did a great deal to develop the educational structures of the Armenian community and improve its general level of education, and missed no chance to promote the growth of democracy in the region. This "intelligent, energetic man of around thirty-five" was nevertheless supposed to be, according to the French Rear-Admiral Pivet – echoing, no doubt, what he had heard from the high-ranking Turkish officials in Adana whom he held in great esteem and from missionaries who were not a little embittered – "frenetically ambitions and, seemingly, a religious sectarian, although he has, in reality, no religion at all."[29]

An event reported in the liberal newspaper *Serbesti* and the daily *Piuzantion* provides some sense of Seropian's character. To protest against the press law, which restricted freedom of the press and imposed censorship, Turkish and Armenian liberals in Adana had organized, against the prefect's advice, a 14 February 1909 rally in the municipal park that drew nearly 10,000 people. A mixed committee had been founded for the occasion. It included Ihsan Fikri, the president of Adana's Young Turk Club and editor-in-chief of the CUP's official organ in the region, *Ittihal*; Tevfik, an imam; and, from Sis, Haci Süleyman. Representing the Armenians on the committee were two notables, the lawyer Garabed Chalian and Krikor Kljian, and also Bishop Mushegh. At the rally, the prelate said:

> The many crimes that have blackened Turkey's and the Ottoman fatherland's name have been its ruin. They were the consequence of the enslavement of the population. Slavery in whatever form is unbearable, but the slavery of the spoken and written word is the worst of all forms of servility. If, down to the present day, so many crimes and injustices have been committed, if the empire has, until today, slid steadily toward its ruin, the main reason is that we were deprived of the right to speak out, of the right to protest, of our capacity to defend the legitimate rights of our sacred fatherland. The tongues of those who demanded justice were cut off; the pens of those who inveighed against injustice were smashed.[30]

It was the same prelate and author of "provocations" who, on 10 January 1909, sent *vali* Cevad a famous report that listed the various provocations and exactions aimed at Armenians in the previous weeks, so that measures might be taken to bring them to an end. Mushegh's report denounced above all the machinations of the *mutesarif* of Cebelbereket, Asaf Bey, who had been inciting the Muslim population with declarations to the effect that it was unacceptable that Armenians should enjoy the same rights as Muslims did, and that Armenians were arming themselves in order to attack Muslims. This official intervention by the prelate seemed inadmissible to the *vali*, who sent several reports to the interior minister (notably on 16 January) demanding that the bishop be replaced because he was "inciting the Armenians against the government and laws and gradually poisoning the minds of his fellow citizens."[31] The commander of the French fleet in the eastern Mediterranean, Rear-Admiral Pivet, corroborated these accusations in his fashion. The Armenians, he said,

> although they were perfectly well aware that the Turks of Adana were, as a rule, attached to the old regime – or, rather, precisely because they were aware of this – have not tired, since the promulgation of the new constitution on 11 July 1908, of provoking and threatening them. At the instigation of their bishop, a man named Mushegh, they have created insurrectional Committees and circulated proclamations identifying the ministers and principal leaders of a future Armenian kingdom. What is more, they

have armed themselves with up-to-date weapons and enjoy showing them off to the Turks.[32]

In the report that *vali* Cevad sent to Constantinople on 16 January 1909, it is also said that Mushegh had donned the costume of a Cilician king and had himself photographed in it, that he had organized theatrical performances in which "mythical" kings of Armenia appeared on stage, and that he had encouraged the Christian population not to pay military and local taxes.

The charges leveled at Mushegh were serious, all the more so since the main blame for the massacres would also be laid at his door. Why was the Armenian prelate in particular the butt of these accusations? Were the accusations justified or did they stem from a mistaken interpretation of his acts? These are the questions to which we now turn.

Let us begin by noting that the bishop was a man with a strong personality. He was upright and perhaps stubborn, and, as his speech at the rally of 1 February 1909 clearly shows, he had a marked aversion to the old regime and those who had served it. He was plainly one in the group of young men who had inscribed the values of the Constitutional revolution on their banners and considered themselves the agents of a social mission. He had even been a member of the SDHP. As such, he had very probably clashed with the reactionary circles of Adana that, according to all witnesses, were still influential. *Vali* Cevad, for his part, was of another generation and, as the indictment of the court marital shows, a pure product of Abdülhamid's Yıldız. Thus, it would seem that everything set these men in opposition. Moreover, when the young prelate drew up his famous report of 10 January 1909, which noted all the excesses that had occurred in the vilayet, he offended the sensibilities of the old government official on two scores. First, the bishop put his finger on practices that were, for Cevad, perfectly legitimate as long as they affected only Armenians. Second, Cevad found it intolerable that a Christian cleric could meddle in affairs that he regarded as his own preserve. When the 16 January report in which the *vali* demanded that Mushegh Seropian be transferred to another post is read against the background of these tensions, it becomes easier to understand why Cevad, with considerable bad faith, leveled such exorbitant charges at the bishop's door – to say nothing of the pressure that certain Turkish circles in Adana must have been putting on the *vali*.

Thus the fable that Mushegh had donned the costume of an Armenian king is a far-fetched interpretation of the ceremonial dress that an Armenian prelate wears when celebrating religious festivals. As for the photograph of Mushegh that the *vali* denounced, taken under the portico of a church the bishop was leaving after celebrating mass, it was simply a picture taken to immortalize a religious holiday. The theatrical performance that was apparently a serious cause for alarm in the eyes of the Ottoman authorities and the local Muslim population was a dramatization of the holiday known as Vartanants, which memorializes those who fell at Avarayr, a battle that was fought against the Persian Zoroastrians in 451 and is celebrated every year by the Armenian Church. As for Mushegh's supposed exhortations against paying military and local taxes, they come down to the fact that he had demanded that the excesses committed when these taxes had been collected in the *sancak* of Cebelbereket be redressed.

In the end, it is Rear-Admiral Pivet's veritable denunciation of the bishop that seems to weigh the most heavily against both him and his flock. We have not taken the time to study the personality of this senior French officer, but one gains a clear sense of the man upon reading the reports he dispatched to his ministry. Let us point out only that central authorities' declarations, which, to be sure, were made late in the day, quashed these accusations that had been nothing more than the fruit of rumor. A high-ranking soldier who had made a career in a colonial France marked by massive prejudices, a conventionality and an arrogance that we can today measure, Rear-Admiral Pivet had taken the comments of his Turkish colleagues for good coin. The outrageousness of these comments about the "shadow cabinet" of "a future Armenian kingdom" can only bring a smile to the face of anyone with the slightest knowledge of the domestic situation of the Ottoman Empire. One of the most perceptive observers of the day, Major Doughty-Wylie, the British consul in Adana, universally praised for his intelligence and devotion, wrote in a report:

> I do not at all believe in the existence of an Armenian revolutionary movement bent on creating an independent kingdom with the help of foreign intervention. If the Armenians had been pursuing a goal of that sort, they would have withdrawn into the mountainous regions, where they would have been better able to defend themselves. They would never have left thousands upon thousands of scattered, unarmed peasants... in the countryside to bring in the harvest. What is more, it is ridiculous to suppose that even the Armenians who had arms – at best, revolvers and hunting rifles – could have believed that they were capable of confronting the Ottoman Army. As for foreign intervention, the least familiarity with the political situation would have convinced them of the absurdity of such a notion.[33]

It is, however, the well-meaning circular that the grand vizier sent to all the *valis* on 11 August 1909 that best describes (a few choice euphemisms notwithstanding) the problem of "a lack of understanding" that "engendered" the massacre of the Armenians:

> Under the old regime, in which the abuses of despotism were common practice, certain classes of the Armenian community were undoubtedly working toward political ends. Whatever the forms their activity took, however, it had but one aim: to put an end to the intolerable misdeeds and harassment of a despotic government. On the other hand, it has been observed that, in the recent past, the Armenians have done a great deal to help this nation obtain the Constitution, thereby demonstrating their sincere attachment to the Ottoman fatherland. Convinced, above all, after the restoration of the Constitution, that their nation could find neither salvation nor happiness outside the context of allegiance to the Ottoman Constitution, they concentrated their efforts on working on a common accord for the nation's welfare. Hence there is no grounds for the false opinion that leads those ignorant of the truth to suspect the Armenian community of nursing blameworthy political aspirations.
>
> As for the origin of the deplorable Adana events, the conclusions reached by the special commissions investigating them and the circumstances under which these regrettable events came about have shown that the elation and feelings of joy displayed by the Armenians were misinterpreted by naive individuals. These events were the last, deplorable vestiges of the days of an absolutism that wished to stamp out all feelings of patriotic fraternity. The populace that, until then, had been unaware of the name and program of the Committees "Tashnak-Zutiun" and "Hinchak" fell victim to an illusion when it saw the members of these Committees spontaneously emerging in broad daylight: it indulged in unfounded assumptions and mistaken interpretations.[34]

In addition to the charge of "provocations," whose limits and unlikelihood we have already pointed out, it is worth pausing over the accusations revolving around a nascent "Armenian kingdom" – the grand vizier's circular makes a veiled allusion to it – and the rumors about a planned insurrection that was supposed to give rise to an independent Armenian state going beyond the borders of Cilicia. This point is all the more important in that it is the core of the dialectic elaborated by the Cilician authorities and central government to substantiate the thesis that the Turks had been defending themselves against Armenians who had organized an attack on them.

One of the first rumors to this effect was reported by the French vice-consul in Sıvas, H. Rouland. "It is being whispered," he wrote to Pichon on 29 January, "that the Armenians intend, as soon as they are armed, to rise up against the Ottoman government, proclaim their independence and restore the ancient kingdom of Armenia. They are supposedly only waiting for a favorable opportunity."[35]

Suspicion of the Armenians was not, however, only the stuff of rumor. High-ranking officials in Cilicia apparently took seriously the idea that the Armenians represented a potential threat and elaborated policies designed to fend it off. The 16/29 March 1325/1909 telegram (no. 23)[36] that the *vali* of Adana sent to the interior minister is one of the most revealing in this connection:

> Response to Your Excellency's encrypted telegram of 13/26 March. Recently, at a meeting of the provincial general council, the Armenian representative of the kaza of Kozan proposed – citing the fact that Hacın is surrounded by rugged terrain and that arable land is in short supply there, a circumstance that deprives the poor population of the possibility of tilling the soil – that five hundred of these poor households be settled in either Kozan, another part of the *çiftlik* of Çukorova or some other place to be chosen by the local authorities ... All the Christian members [of the council] endorsed this proposal. However, given that there are nomadic tribes to be settled in the province and also that, if we accept this proposal in one area, populations from other areas that are also complaining about the lack of arable land will in their turn publicly demand that they be allotted uncultivated land, many different problems will arise, countless requests will be made and cases of villages moving from one place to another will multiply ... We [therefore] suggested that the poor people of Hacın improve their living conditions as best they can by engaging in trade and the crafts.

This apparently anodyne note betrays the prefect's desire to limit as sharply as possible the number of Armenians on the Cilician plain or confine them to their "mountain refuges" so as to favor the sedentarization of the nomad tribes that the government planned to settle on the plain. It illustrates the central government's "demographic" preoccupations and the reigning suspicion of the Armenians.

These arguments are more explicitly developed in the justifications elaborated by the court-martial charged with handling the Cilician question. The report it sent to Constantinople constitutes a sort of distillation of the various rumors that had been making the rounds in the months preceding the Adana events. The Armenians, the report affirmed, had been seeking to provoke incidents in the coastal regions through which the Baghdad Railway passed, regions in which "foreigners had relatively greater interests than elsewhere":

> They chose to focus the planned provocations and disorders on Adana ... Our investigation allows us to affirm that, thereafter, a large number of Armenians from regions near and far arrived and settled there, in order to reinforce the area's Armenian population ... However, the fact that they made such audacious use of the freedom and equality that they had just obtained was not at all appreciated by the Muslims, whose suspicions and hostility increased when the Hnchak, Droshak and Dashnak Committees, hated by the public in the past, opened clubs everywhere, [and] when Armenians began settling in large numbers in the same place ... Hardly had the constitution been restored ... than they began fomenting coups to obtain their independence,

diffusing imaginary Armenian coats of arms and illustrations representing imaginary kings and [national] heroes; they stirred up the Armenians' emotions.[37]

This discourse, although it was written after the fact to justify the violence unleashed upon the Cilician Armenians, reflects the mood dominating Muslim public opinion. It cannot be exclusively ascribed to provocations orchestrated by conservative circles. The Muslims were steeped in the Hamidian propaganda that had for decades cast the Armenians in the role of traitors and rebels, and their reactions continued to be informed by the old criteria of judgment. Thus, they could not understand how political parties that had only recently been described as terrorist could be suddenly legalized and allowed to create local clubs. We can sum up the problem by saying that the Ottoman society of the day was hard put to create even the semblance of a democratic society, and that this proved no easier in Cilicia than in the other Ottoman provinces. What is more, the leading members of the court-martial were asked to resign after the release of this report, to which the grand vizier's public circular, cited above, responded virtually point by point. This plainly shows that certain Ottoman circles were perfectly aware of the state of public opinion in the country and sometimes felt the need to make adjustments in order to calm people down or protect those in the line of fire.

That said, economic development had indeed attracted some Armenian migrants from the provinces of eastern Anatolia to Cilicia, while others struck out for Constantinople, Egypt, or even the Caucasus, fleeing chronic poverty and permanent insecurity. Is it, however, possible to speak of a concerted plan to increase the population of Cilicia? It is unlikely that there ever was such a plan. For one thing, these migratory movements were primarily seasonal – people came to Cilicia to work on the big farms on the Cilician plain from spring to fall – and were thus provisionally and economically motivated. Also, one finds no trace of a concerted plan in this region far from the Armenian provinces, and it is hard to see how such a plan could have been put into practice. Finally, from the moment the constitution was restored, the Armenians had shown, without the least ambiguity, that they wished to participate in the edification of a modern state in which they could assume their rightful place. On the other hand, thousands of Muslim families from Rumelia and the Balkans settled in Cilicia in 1908 and 1909.[38]

Provocations on the Eve of the April 1909 Massacres in Cilicia

The governmental commission of inquiry into the Adana massacres was made up of two judges, one Turkish – Fayk Bey, a member of the Council of State – and the other Armenian – Artin/Harutiun Mosdichian, a court inspector in the province of Salonika. Its report was published on 10 July 1909 – that is, three days after publication of the court-martial's. It provided an obviously more objective assessment of the situation in Cilicia on the eve of the massacres.[39]

After conducting investigations in Adana, Dörtyol, Osmaniye, Bağçe, Hamidye, Tarsus, Hasanbeyli, and Harnı, the two judges observed that since fall 1908 there had been strong antagonism between the Young Turk and liberal parties in Adana, led respectively by Ishan Fikri Bey – who was hostile to the *vali*, Cevad Bey – and Ali Gergerli, backed up by the Hnchak lawyer Garabed Geukderelian, both of whom supported the *vali*. The judges also noted the rather minor role played by the conservative current of Islamicist inspiration, made up of people who longed to restore the old regime, although this current did help spread rumors of massacre that poisoned the atmosphere. This conservative group was led by a powerful local notable, Abdülkadır Bağdadizâde,[40] the founder of Adana's Ziraat club and its weekly organ, *Rehber-i Ittidal*. This circle made no secret of its opposition to the constitution and to the equality before the law officially granted to Christians.

According to Armenian sources partially confirmed by the Constantinople press, it was in the context of this internal struggle that a number of events presaging what was to come occurred in Cilicia. The threats of massacre in October 1908 during the Bayram, mentioned above, triggered a chain of events – some of them apparently the result of deliberate provocations, others exploited by one or another party – that contributed to increasing the tension in Adana. Early in February 1909, Kör Ahmed, the son of the *mufti* of Hacın, wired the *vali* to tell him that the Armenians of Hacın were preparing a revolt.[41] The related rumor that these Armenians were going to march on Adana made the local Muslims jittery. Early in March, another provocation took place in the Grand Mosque, Ulu Cami: the door of the mosque was smeared with excrement at night, angering the population and leading to accusations that Christians had desecrated the mosque. The following night, a handful of guards surprised the two culprits as they were about to repeat their act, but since they were clergymen the authorities decided not to prosecute them. Almost immediately thereafter, a rumor began making the rounds in Adana's Turkish neighborhoods: the Armenians were supposedly getting ready to attack the city's arsenal the following night, using a secret underground passage. Many Turks thus concluded that they had to make preparations to defend themselves. In the early hours of the morning, the Armenians of Adana who read the local Young Turk organ, *Ittidal*, were stupefied to learn what had transpired that night. The Armenian bishop protested against these rumors, demanding in vain that an investigation be conducted to find out who was responsible for spreading them. It should be added that, in winter 1908–9, several Armenians had been murdered on the province's roads, creating an unhealthy atmosphere of insecurity. When the culprits behind the murder of three mule-drivers in the vicinity of Sis were apprehended, they contended that they had been acting "on the orders of a secret organization for massacring Christians," who deserved punishment because, by way of support for the constitution, they intended to abolish the sharia.[42] By the beginning of spring, serious incidents had been occurring almost daily in the immediate vicinity of Adana: several Armenian women and girls were abducted, and men were attacked and beaten.

All sources confirm, however, that the "April 1909 events" were touched off by the murder of two Turks by a young Armenian carpenter, Hovhannes, on the outskirts of Adana on 9 April, Easter Monday. On 4 April, as Hovhannes was on his way home, he encountered a group of bandits led by one Isfendiar, who surrounded him and demanded that he fulfill their pleasures. When he refused, he was bastinadoed and then abandoned. The following morning, the young man went first to the prefecture and then to the courthouse to swear out a complaint against the criminals, but he was unceremoniously shown the door. He decided to buy a pistol with which to defend himself. On the evening of Easter Monday, the group of bandits ambushed Hovhannes on the way home and stabbed him several times. The young man defended himself, killing the leader of the band and wounding two of the others. Hardly had the news become known than Isfendiar's body was recovered and exhibited in Adana's Turkish neighborhoods before being buried in a particularly oppressive atmosphere. After the burial, a large crowd set out in search of the homicide, who had fled. They looted his house and brutalized his family. *Vali* Cevad, who was informed of the situation, did not intervene. Four days later, one of the two wounded bandits also died. The burial led this time to a veritable riot. The mob made its way to the suburb of Tosbaghı Kalesi, where Hovhannes was living, and demanded that he be handed over to them. They threatened, if he was not, to put the whole quarter to fire and the sword.[43]

That very evening, the Young Turks of Adana held a meeting under the leadership of Ihasan Fikri, who made a fiery speech hostile to the *gâvurs*. On the night of 12 April, a handful of people, led by one Karakösehoğlu Mahmud, fired their guns in the air and then went to the police station to declare that two Turks had been killed by "the" Armenians.

It quickly appeared that this was false information. The American missionary Chambers, the minister Hampartsum Ashjian, and Dr. Hampartsumian went to see the *vali* in order to draw the tense situation in the city to his attention. On 13 April, market day, peasants from the surrounding villages poured into Adana as they did every Tuesday, but did not go back home when evening fell. A rumor had been making the rounds that day: four Muslims, two men and two women, had supposedly been murdered by the Armenians. An investigation showed that this information was wrong. The rumor naturally alarmed the Christian communities, whose representatives went to see the vali the same day in order to make the gravity of the situation clear to him. He answered only that he had "issued all the necessary orders."

On this Tuesday, observers noticed that certain Turks had put on white turbans so as to pass for *softas*. They killed an Armenian and then sounded the alarm, saying everywhere that another Muslim had been killed. The city's expert in forensic medicine, who was alerted and asked to confirm the causes of the victim's death, saw that it was one of his Armenian patients, who, moreover, had a tattoo in the form of a cross. Around nine o'clock that evening, a mob led by *hojas* went to the prefecture and demanded that the *vali* give them permission to go punish the Armenians, but Cevad sent them away. A first meeting was then organized in front of the offices of İhsan Fikri's newspaper, *Ittidal*, located in the *medrese* of Demircilar and the adjacent streets. That night, a rally was held in front of the prefecture. It was presided over by Cevad Bey. Also present were the *ferik* (major general, military governor) and judge, Mustafa Remzi Pasha, Adana's *mufti*, two of the most eminent men of the region, Abdülkadır Bağdadizâde and Gergerlizâde Ali, and the police chief Kadri Bey, among others. A spirited discussion began. Over the objections of a judge and the director of the post office, who were also on hand, the people at this assembly decided that the time had come to teach the Armenians a lesson. The *mufti* assured them that the massacre of Christians was in conformity with Islamic law and issued a fatwa confirming what he had said.[44]

However, in spite of the provocations and the rising tension, no Turk in Adana actually engaged in violence on 13 April. In the course of the day, *vali* Cevad sent four wires to the minister of the interior, informing him in very general terms of the chaos reigning in the city, in particular of the fact that he had had "to mobilize reserves throughout the vilayet to maintain order." The only answer he received was a 1/14 April telegram from the undersecretary of state in the Interior Ministry, Haci Adıl Bey (Arda),[45] instructing him "to take great care that foreign subjects, their religious establishments and their consulates suffered no damage."[46] Although these recommendations did not have the expected effect – most of the buildings belonging to foreigners, whether religious or not, were later burned down and two American missionaries were killed – they indicate the way in which this affair was handled at the Interior Ministry by a leading member of the CUP.

The First Phase of the Massacres of Cilicia: 14–16 April 1909

The outpouring of violence that engulfed all of Cilicia on 14 April cannot be characterized as spontaneous for the above reasons. Moreover, these events were not unlike the massacres that had been organized in 1895–6 in the Armenian provinces and elsewhere, both in the way they unfolded and by virtue of the methods employed: in both cases, false rumors were spread; the rural population of the surrounding area took part in the violence; the Muslim clergy spurred the mob on; and notables, the gendarmerie, and, of course, high-ranking officials – beginning with the *vali* and the sub-prefects – assumed the role of organizers and ringleaders.

The report of the father superior of the Catholic missions, Rigal, confirms this impression:

On Easter Wednesday, 14 April, around eleven o'clock in the morning, rifles and revolvers were fired throughout the city. People were firing from roofs, windows and minarets: the bullets fell thick as hail on roofs, streets and houses. It was a cross-fire that began all at once, as if a flash of electricity had armed all the inhabitants of Adana at the same time. For several days, people had been saying that there would probably be massacres: the Turks were threatening and the Christians were afraid. The alarm had already been given once or twice. In the morning, at market, people had noticed men with the faces of bandits wielding huge, iron-tipped clubs, of the sort with which so many Armenians had been beaten to death during the 1895 massacres. Leaving the mosque, Muslims who usually did not wear turbans were seen wearing mullahs' head-gear, so that they would not be mistaken for Christians. Finally, there was something like the smell of blood in the air and the shops in the market were closed.

At the sound of the fusillade, people's first impulse was to save their lives. They came pouring through all the doorways, while the surrounding rooftops sent waves of people flooding into the mission. The same thing happened at the American mission, in the churches and wherever else people thought they would be safer.[47]

Plainly, the order to attack the Armenian neighborhoods had just been given, although it was still not known who had given it. To get out of harm's way, the Armenian craftsmen and merchants wanted to close their stands and go home. The leading Christian notables, however, Ottoman subjects and foreigners alike, immediately convened a meeting at the Armenian bishopric and then sent a delegation to see the *vali* and ask him to organize protection for their neighborhoods and institutions. David Urfalian, the president of Adana's Armenian National Council and a magistrate at the audit office, represented his community. The *vali* told the delegation that he had the situation under control, that it was nothing very serious and that "it was very important to keep calm"; he ordered the delegation to go to the market around 3 p.m. to calm people down and invite them to resume their usual activities. At the market, Urfalian insisted that the pharmacy and shops in particular reopen for business. He was shot to death shortly thereafter, becoming the first victim of the events and, as such, a symbol. Meanwhile, the market was overrun by a quickly growing crowd and the Christians decided to lower the iron shutters before their shops. At this point, the handful of policemen and mounted troops at the market suddenly disappeared. The crowd, comprising men and women alike, began systematically plundering the shops.

In the interim, the dragomans from the British, French, German, and Russian consulates had in their turn formed a delegation and gone to see the *vali*. They told him how wrought up the populace was, adding that a *hoja* had been preaching from atop the minaret of the mosque of Tosbaği that it was time to liquidate the *gâvurs*. They accordingly asked him to authorize them to use firearms if necessary. After this meeting, the *vali* went to the *konak*. There, in his presence, Artin Shadakian, an Armenian member of the municipal council who had come to ask that the police and gendarmes be ordered to intervene, was shot to death by an official. Massacres had already begun in the city's outlying neighborhoods, where Armenian minorities lived among the Muslim population.

In fact, the first day of the violence, 14 April, was mainly devoted to destroying Armenian shops at the market – signs had been carefully nailed up on those belonging to Muslims – and to massacring the Armenians who lived dispersed throughout the quarters on the outskirts of the city or in inns such as Acem Han, Düz Han, Haydaroğlu Han, Deli Mehmed Han, Yeni Han, Pamuk Bazar Küpeli, and Vezir Han, which were visited one by one by the mob.

Around 300 people were killed in these Hans, mostly seasonal workers or mule-drivers from Hain, Kayseri, Dyarbekir, and other places, who had been on their way through the city.

According to the rare witnesses, the mob consisted, at this time, of between 20,000 and 30,000 people made up of some five to ten groups of assailants: Turks, Kurds, *Fellahs*, Çerkez, Avshars, nomads, and Muslims from Crete. They were led by local notables such as Abdülkadır Bağdadizâde and Boşnak Salih. These groups finally attacked the Armenian quarter of Şabanieh. After a moment of panic, the Armenians organized their defense: they set up barricades and, after arming themselves, fought off the assaults of their Muslim fellow citizens. The commander of the gendarmerie, Kadri Bey, who witnessed these disorders, resigned and was immediately replaced by Zor Ali, the former police chief of Adana who had been dismissed for earlier abuses and had returned from Istanbul on 10 March, at just the right moment.[48]

After retreating before the resistance put up by the Armenian quarter, this mob, led by men of second rank – Katib Effendi, Muzteba Effendi, and Dabbağzâde Ali – demanded that the authorities distribute weapons to them. The ammunitions dump was put at the assailants' disposal. They then made their way to the Sultane-Valide mosque near the Karalar neighborhood. Here the *hojas* preached the jihad and made all those present promise not to leave a single Armenian alive.[49]

Under the lead of Zor Ali, the mob now attacked the Şabanieh neighborhood. It was supported by soldiers under the command of Resim Selim Bey. The mob, however, was unable to make its way into the heart of the Armenian neighborhood, which was defended, according to internal Armenian sources, by 73 young Armenian men – those who had managed to arm themselves properly – posted at various points of access to the neighborhood. They had the backing of the entire population.[50] In the face of this vigorous resistance, the attackers decided to set fires all around the Armenian quarter and then launched a new assault. On 15 April, at around two o'clock in the morning, the exchange of gunfire became much more intense: the Armenian defenders were saluting the arrival of Major Doughty-Wylie, the British consul in Mersin and Adana. He had arrived in Adana shortly before in a special train that had been chartered in Mersin and immediately gone to see the *vali* to ask him to take the measures required to bring the disorder to an end. He then left on horseback, protected by a mounted escort, to make a tour of the Armenian quarter, where his arrival was taken as a hopeful sign.

In the morning, the *vali* told Doughty-Wylie that he no longer controlled the situation and was incapable of halting the violence, going so far as to propose that the consul himself step in and offering to put officers and soldiers at his disposal. The consul's voyage to Adana, however, only briefly interrupted the assault in places. In the course of the day, he abandoned the idea of intervening personally – he had been wounded by a stray Armenian bullet – and took the train back to Mersin. Meanwhile, a number of Armenians sought refuge in the churches of the Holy Virgin and St. Stepanos as well as in foreign institutions, especially the buildings of the French Jesuits and the nuns of St. Joseph, where some 8,000 people had been given refuge. The American mission, directed by Reverand Chambers, also granted haven to the refugees.[51] The middle school for girls that abutted the American mission was attacked that evening, though the girls who lived there managed to flee through a hole they had made in the party wall. However, Reverend Hovagim Kayayan and two missionaries, Roger and Maurer, were shot to death while trying to put out the fire that was destroying the school.

On the night of 15–16 April, most of the men had withdrawn to the courtyard of the cathedral and the immediate perimeter of the new Armenian middle school, which had been partly destroyed by a fire that the young men had managed to extinguish. A battle without mercy now began in the neighborhood. The defenders were hard put to recognize one another in the dark and used a password. In the first hours of the morning, the whistle of a train coming from Mersin nourished hopes that outsiders would step in and put an end to the violence. It was, however, only the British consul returning to Adana. The besieged Armenians thought that they had seen young "Greeks" coming to save them, but it quite soon appeared that these were Muslim attackers in disguise, and they opened fire on the young men who came out to greet them.

On the morning of 16 April, a good part of the Armenian quarter had come under the control of the attackers, but one last block was still resisting, although it was running low on ammunition. One of the rare Turkish notables who lived in the quarter, a certain Osman Bey Tekelizâde, decided to visit the *vali* and ask that he intervene. He found him at a meeting with the mob's main ringleaders, who accepted the principle of a cease-fire on condition that the Armenian notables sign a declaration in which they acknowledged that they were to blame for the outbreak of violence. After returning to the Armenian quarter, Osman Bey convinced the Armenians to send a delegation to negotiate an end to the hostilities with the *vali*. Agreement was rapidly reached, with one crucial additional proviso: the Armenians had to surrender their arms.

The approximately 200 regular soldiers and reserve troops, who had remained passive to this point now swung into action to bring the fighting to an end, accompanied by Turkish and Armenian notables. Around 10 p.m., in less than half an hour, calm was restored as the troops took up positions in front of the Jesuit middle school and the Armenian churches where the immense majority of the city's Armenians had taken refuge. The mob launched one last assault toward midnight, apparently without much conviction. By the morning of 17 April, Adana was once again calm. The witnesses who now emerged from their hideouts discovered an apocalyptic scene: houses had been burned down and the streets were strewn with countless corpses. More than 10,000 people were famished and without shelter.

The Armenian population of Adana had suffered relatively limited loss of life in these three days of deadly, uncontrolled violence. The Armenian villagers of the environs, however, as well as those living on the farms of the plain, had for the most part been killed in their fields, victims of a veritable manhunt. On 18 April, the authorities demanded that the Armenians hand in their weapons as agreed. With the encouragement of the British consul, who guaranteed their security in the name of his government, as well as that of the Armenian Patriarchate in Constantinople, the Armenians ultimately gave up their arms.[52]

The 17–24 April Interlude in Adana and the First Official Reactions in Istanbul

On 18 April, the first French battleships put down anchor in the harbor of Mersin. They were followed by British, Russian, German, American, and Italian ships. Aware of the irritation that their presence was causing not only to the local Muslim population but also to the authorities, the foreigners prudently limited their intervention to landing groups of observers, paying courtesy visits to high-ranking local officials and providing the victims with ad hoc relief funneled through the religious institutions. According to certain witnesses, the local authorities took the Westerners' relative reserve as encouragement to carry out a second massacre in Adana.

In the city, people were busy clearing the streets of corpses, which were thrown into the Sihun River – sailors reported seeing hundreds of corpses floating in the Bay of Mersina. Furthermore, the *vali* had just declared a state of emergency. Gradually, the Armenians returned to their homes, if they had not been burned down, while improvised hospitals were set up for the ill and wounded in the compounds of the missionaries or diplomatic missions, as well as in the Armenian schools that had been left standing, such as the St. Stepanos middle school for girls.

Despite the material and human losses that the first massacres had caused throughout Cilicia, local Turkish circles, far from being preoccupied by the consequences of their acts, rather seemed frustrated by the fact that it had proved impossible to kill many Armenians from Adana. This spirit made itself felt particularly in the incendiary articles published in the famous 20 April issue (no. 33) of the daily *Ittidal*, the Young Turk organ in the city.[53] Distributed free of charge both to the local Muslim population and throughout the empire, this "special" issue was a sort of compendium of all the criticisms that had been directed at the Armenian population, as well as an extraordinary barometer of the psychology of the local Turkish elite and its working methods. It is therefore worth our while to reproduce extracts from it here and comment on them.

It is easy to imagine the stupefying effect that the tone of the articles by İhsan Fikri and İsmail Safâ had on Armenians. Fikri was the director of the newspaper and president of Adana's Young Turk club; Safâ was the paper's editor-in-chief. As yet unaware of the part that Fikri had played in organizing the first massacres, the Armenians no doubt imagined that this "democrat" and partisan of the constitution would expose the role of certain "conservative or reactionary" circles in the region and demand that the guilty be tried and punished. They were instead surprised to find an indictment of the Armenians – the cynicism, incoherence, and implausibility of which revolted more than one observer. Indeed, the objective of this issue can be summed up as trying to "prove" that the Armenians alone were responsible for what had happened and to refute in advance accusations against the civilian and military authorities in the area, as well as the leading Turkish notables, by reversing the roles of victim and victimizer.

In an article entitled "A Terrible Insurrection," Safâ wrote:

> How sad that the upsurge of anger and the [desire] for independence that had stirred and then put down roots in the depths of the Armenians' hearts should have led to the ruin of the region...! Let us have a look at this insurrection that has condemned the inhabitants of Adana to dire poverty. Like the Turks, the Armenians were, during the thirty-three years of a tyrannical rule, crushed under tyranny's hellish burden; they raised their voices in protest. When the Ottomans entered a magnificent period of happiness and peace, the Armenians ceased to protest [literally: they shut their mouths] and cry out for revenge and, as equals with us, applauded our sacred revolution. But that was soon over, and they began preparing their own project. Sometimes, they created tensions by putting on dissatisfied expressions and making it understood that they could not possibly live alongside Muslims...Our demand for unity and mutual understanding was not enough to stem their dangerous inclinations and this led to a difference in the Turks' and the Armenians' ways of looking at things...The Armenians worked virtually without pause to acquire what they lacked, and devoted a great deal of effort to arming themselves. At market or in the public squares, the Armenians even outdid each other in purchasing Martinis, Mausers and other weapons of battle. After they had stockpiled such weapons, they lost their traditional restraint...They brazenly made threats of this sort: "one of these days, we shall massacre the Turks; we are no longer afraid; the old wounds are still bleeding." Thus they provoked the Turks as a way of casting off their own responsibility. The Turks, however, accepting and obeying the advice of their great men, who preached appeasement, sought to avoid incidents of all kinds. The Armenians, observing the unbearable silence and patience displayed by the Muslims, planned to commit various crimes in defiance of the law...The fact that the state was not sufficiently powerful

engendered fear and alarm among the Turks; among the Armenians, it was a source of strength and courage.[54]

One rarely finds articles in the press in which a Young Turk politician expresses himself as clearly as this. In the present case, to be sure, we can see a minor provincial leader straining, above all, to justify the acts committed by his group. In the process, he exposes the main springs of his logic and echoes the Adana Muslims' interpretation of what the Armenians said and wrote in the new context of freedom created by the July 1908 Constitutional revolution. He calls our attention to a key point that is occasionally emphasized by well-informed observers – namely, that every attempt to demand equality and justice was interpreted as "insurrection." In June 1909, the reporter dispatched to Adana by the French daily *Le Temps*, Edouard Barfoglio, wrote, after declaring that it would be a mistake to see "Yıldız's hand" behind the Adana events:

> The Turks, who have always been the dominant group, have the feeling that they are the losers in the newly established order. As a result of the Constitution, they have, in some way, ceded the predominance that was once theirs, and they feel that, in these conditions, the future can only visit destruction on them; in this context, they have risen up to defend their privileges by means of bloodshed and pillage. The Turks sensed this in the changes in the Armenians' behavior at the level of their daily relations.[55]

Seen from this standpoint, the underlying reasons for the killing in Adana and the comments in *Ittidal* become almost comprehensible. We understand better why the local population, generally speaking, heeded the watchwords of its local ringleaders, convinced that ultimately its predominance was in jeopardy. On the other hand, the retrospective accusation that the Armenians were preparing for war and wished to restore "an Armenian kingdom of Cilicia" could hardly have been taken seriously in Turkish political circles, which were perfectly familiar with the positions of the Armenian parties and well aware of the absurdity of such aspirations in a region where the Armenians were in a minority and had begun to benefit, or so they thought, from the advantages of freedom.

The rest of Safâ's article is cast in a more classic vein. It reviews the story of the killing of a bandit by a young Armenian attacked by a gang, identifying it as the point of departure for the "events," and making sure to note that "the Armenians firmly avowed that they would never turn in the murderer." We are also told that "until Wednesday, the police and the Muslims went about their business amid fear and trembling, on their guard lest they fire the first shot."[56] By Safâ's logic, insurgents barricaded themselves in fortified buildings in their neighborhood in order to launch a general assault. The fact that the Armenian shops were closed, the consequence of a justifiable fear rooted in Ottoman tradition (in the Ottoman Empire, massacres always began in the market, since the attackers were tempted by the goods that they could loot there), is cast in his article as an act of aggression presaging an insurrection. In other words, to continue to follow Safâ's logic, the Armenian shopkeepers, in anticipation of an Armenian offensive, closed their shops, leaving them at the mercy of the looters. Safâ's article also affirms that Turks and Armenians were engaged in unequal combat. As he tells it, "the Armenians, entrenched in their houses, fired without let-up through gun-holes and from the roofs, whereas we poor Turks were in the streets, armed only with sticks." Decoded, this means that civilian insurgents who had been surrounded in their neighborhoods and were armed to the teeth opened fire on unarmed Turks who happened to be walking through the streets of the Armenian quarter. Concluding this plea for peace, the Young Turk "journalist" affirms that, "besides all this, the fires set almost everywhere by the

Armenians have destroyed the whole city and left it in ruins."[57] This interpretation does not deviate from the official position of the local authorities. Father Rigal, who went to see the *vali* several times, remarks with considerable lucidity that "he never heard any other refrain from [the Muslims'] mouths" than:

> It is the Armenians who massacre the Muslims, the Armenians who fire on our soldiers, the Armenians who loot and burn and, finally, the Armenians who have ruined this country and are the source of all our woes. This means, in French: the Armenians are murderers because they do not go quietly to slaughter, but have the gall to defend themselves. It means, again: the Armenians loot their homes and stores and set fire to their buildings, for, after all, one has only to open one's eyes to see that hardly anything besides the Christian stores, homes, churches and schools have been destroyed by the flames; that the Muslim mosques have been spared and rise up proudly amid the ruins of the Christian quarter.[58]

Fikri's article appeared in the same issue of *Ittidal*, entitled "Signs of Anarchy." Written in a more political vein, it elaborated on the thesis of a plot against the unity of the Constitutional state and the gradual colonization of Cilicia by Armenian settlers. Above all, it threatened the survivors. In short, the accusations proffered in the Adana Young Turks' official organ by İsmail Safâ and İhsan Fikri and the interpretation of the events they put forward there raised a chorus of protests from Armenian circles in both Adana and Istanbul. For the Armenians, these methods of disinformation were only too reminiscent of the techniques of the old regime. This was all the harder to bear in that until then they had had the feeling that the period of tyranny was now behind them.

Two days before these articles appeared, on 18 April, the undersecretary of state in the Interior Ministry, Adıl Bey, who was serving as interim minister during the vacuum of power due to the "reaction," presented a report on the Adana affair to the grand vizier, Tevfik Pasha, who had been appointed the same day. The content of the report was interpreted in different ways. The Constantinople press declared the following day that Adıl had affirmed that the Armenians were the aggressors. "They are armed," he wrote,

> and are massacring defenseless Turks; they have surrounded the prefecture. Armenians from distant villages are attacking Turkish settlements – they are armed, whereas the Turks have only sticks… Armed Armenians have gone so far as to besiege the subprefecture of the sancak of Jebelbereket, whose terrified *mutesarif* has made repeated requests for assistance.[59]

This declaration, apparently inspired by telegrams sent by the *vali* and the local *mutesarifs*, does not seem to have convinced everyone, because *vali* Cevad was dismissed from his post on 18 April – although he continued to exercise his function for another two weeks. In these conditions, the 19 April session of the Ottoman parliament was supposed to clarify the situation, despite the anarchy that had reigned in the capital for the previous few days. The Armenian members of parliament, supported by the Turkish deputies Ali Münîf and Ali Hikmet, submitted a motion demanding that an immediate end be put to the massacres. At the same session, the deputy Vartkes Seringiulian exclaimed to his colleagues, "if we do not punish the people responsible for such acts, which breed hatred among the different Ottoman groups, regrettable events of this sort are likely to occur elsewhere as well."[60] Under threat from the troops from Macedonia who had pitched camp nearby in Çatalca, Tevfik Pasha's government was living on borrowed time. The day before, a parliamentary delegation had gone to see Mahmud Şevket Pasha in Çatalca. It was probably during their 18 April discussions, in which Zohrab and Vartkes took part,[61] that the decision was reached to send 850 from the second and third army regiments to Cilicia. According to the *Times* of 25 April, Mahmud Şevket decided to personally dispatch this battalion, stationed in Dede Ağac on the shores of the sea of Marmara, to Mersin, with instructions to restore order there.[62] These troops, part of the "Action Army," were commanded by Young Turk officers.

This battalion, after resolving problems connected with finding a transport ship, arrived in Adana around noon on 25 April. It was an official representative of Constitutional legality and, as such, its arrival was a source of great relief to the Armenian population. While it is true that a fragile calm reigned in Adana from 17 to 24 April, many areas in Cilicia were still in the hands of the *başibuzuk* and certain towns were still under siege – the siege of Hacın came to an end only on 28 April. In many different localities, tens of thousands of survivors were living out in the open in sanitary conditions that were little short of catastrophic. In Adana, the *vali* who, although he had already resigned, was still in office (his successor did not arrive until the end of the month) reacted pro forma to the provocations of *Ittidal*'s editors, shutting the paper down for three days. However, as soon as the Young Turk daily was able to reappear, it resumed its campaign of denigration, encouraging Adana's Muslim population to carry through its "mission." The French foreign minister, Pichon, in a note addressed to his Ottoman counterpart, complained that

> the director of the newspaper *Ittidal*, who took an active personal part in the massacre and, since then, has been publishing dangerously libelous articles against the Armenians, has not been deranged in any way and is pursuing his campaign. On the other hand, two Armenian newspapers in Constantinople, *Piuzantion* and *Manzume* [*Efkiar*], have just been suspended. The director of *Piuzantion*, Mr. Piuzant Kechian, was recently arrested and is being held in the Ministry of War.[63]

In the afternoon of 25 April, as the "soldiers of freedom" were pitching their tents on the leveled field known as Kışla Meydan, located on the banks of the Seyhan, they were fired on. No one was wounded, but it set the already nervous troops on edge. Somewhat further off, on the square near the clock tower, a crowd of considerable size was attending a rally. An Armenian who had heard the gunfire immediately went to the bishopric to inform the notables of what was afoot. They remained skeptical, convinced that the butchery could not begin again now that soldiers had arrived to ensure order. It was, however, already being rumored that the Armenians had fired on the soldiers. (Several weeks later, the report of the parliamentary commission of inquiry would show that this was a physical impossibility, given the location of the military camp and the fact that, for good reason, there had not been a single Armenian in this spot since the first massacres.) Another, even more far-fetched rumor had it that 15,000 Armenians, under the command of the lawyer Garabed Geukderelian, were marching on the city from the river – a rumor that was shown to be false by the crowd itself, which found nothing where the attack was supposedly taking place. Conditions were, nevertheless, ripe for a second massacre. A handful of provocateurs had only to go to the soldiers' encampment and declare that the Armenians were attacking the Turkish quarters to convince these soldiers to interrupt their meal and "go to the rescue of" their fellow Muslims.

The Second Adana Massacres (25–27 April) and the "Action Army"

On Sunday, 25 April, at six o'clock in the evening, although nothing had occurred to provoke new atrocities, the fusillade began again, as violent as it had been on the first day, with the difference that, this time, the Christians did not defend themselves and that, this time, the regular army was at the sides of the *bashi-buzuk*. Since the city was in a state of siege, people could not, on pain of being shot, leave it after sunset. All the streets were under guard; those who were in their homes could, therefore, escape only by fleeing from rooftop to adjacent rooftop, although the rooftops, too, were under surveillance. At the same time as the shots rang out, fires broke out again.[64]

This is how Father Rigal describes the onset of the second Adana massacres. The Armenians, who were now disarmed, were no longer in a position to defend themselves and sought refuge in the public buildings, schools, Armenian churches and, above all, the mission. The same French clergyman reports:

One of the first buildings to go up in flames was the Armenian school building, where a large number of refugees had found shelter. Fleeing the flames, these unfortunates ran toward our compound. When groups of them made their way into the street, the soldiers fired at them point-blank. I shouted at them to give the refugees free passage.

The next day, Father Rigal interceded with the *vali*. His commentary on their conversation plainly shows that there was a certain consistency to the behavior of this high-ranking official:

The next day, when the *vali* sang me his usual refrain – "it is the Armenians who are firing on our soldiers, looting houses and stores and setting fires" – I took the liberty of saying, not without a touch of humor: "Your Excellency, it is not the Armenians who are shooting at me in my own house, but the same soldiers who are shedding the Armenians' blood."

Threatened by the fire, the St. Paul middle school was likely to go up in flames at any moment. The monk again went to see the *vali*. "On the way," he writes, "I met municipal firemen who were laboriously dragging a pump in our direction." Later, both Father Rigal and the commission of inquiry reported that this pump was used, not to put out fires, but to feed the flames devouring the buildings in the neighborhood with paraffin. This time, the middle school – where 6,000 refuges had found shelter – the Marists' establishment, and the school of the Sisters of Saint Joseph were set on fire. Thanks to the British consul's intervention, their occupants were transferred to the gardens of the prefecture.

"Sunday night," Father Rigal goes on,

the next day and the following night as well, the fire continued to rage. It devoured a church and two immense Armenian schools, the boys' and the girls' school, the little chapel, the Catholic Syriacs' residence, the Protestant church, all our buildings, the free dormitory, middle and elementary schools, the Armenian Catholic church, the bishop's residence, the big Terzian middle school and the girls' school – in sum, seventy-five percent of the big Armenian quarter. I had almost forgotten the Orthodox Syriacs' buildings, which had only just been constructed: the dormitory, church and school...Tuesday, 27 April might be called the last day in this horrible series, the likes of which has, perhaps, not been seen in modern history.

Rigal concludes:

No one who has not lived through these days can imagine what they were like. The crackling of gunfire mixed with the crackling of the fire, incessantly, for days and nights on end, and the hell of a city in flames; the thunder of the crumbling walls, heaving clouds of fire heavenward; the piercing cries of the unfortunates felled by the bullets and, still louder, the savage cries of the men busy slitting people's throats; the wrenching appeals of a throng of people in a circle of flames, as their tormentors prepare to burn them alive; this frenzied, despairing population that stretches its arms out toward you and begs to be saved; the emotion that chokes you the more powerfully the closer the fire comes and the more helpless you feel, delivered up to a pack of arsonists and throat-cutters; the sinister gangs running past, laden down with booty; the arsonists who slip under doors, clamber over walls, break down everything that stands in their way and, sneering, contemplate the malignant flames; and these hordes of butchers who trample corpses underfoot, stab them full of holes, smash in skulls with their gun butts and then, the supreme insult, spit on their victims; the gaping wounds and quivering limbs; the head of a woman perforated by seven blows of a butcher's knife; a skull split in two; six men strung together like beads by a grave mullah doing an experiment to see how many bodies one bullet can pierce; the unfortunates daubed with oil and transformed into living torches; a mother whose belly has been cut open and made over into a cradle for her new-born baby; all these atrocities, all these horrors, all these ruins, and the disgust and emotions that they call forth; the pen is powerless to translate all that into words.

The report of the commission of inquiry called into being by the Ottoman parliament provides a rather similar description of the facts:

There are no words strong enough to describe the horror and ferocity of the second massacre, which went on for two days. It was in the course of this carnage that the sick and wounded who had arrived from the surrounding villages and found refuge in the school building were burned alive. Cevad Bey has deemed it superfluous to speak, in his report, of the terrible death that these wretched people met in the flames; he says not a word about the pregnant women whose bellies were cut open, the little children whose throats were slit and a hundred other unspeakable atrocities. He does, however, take pains to note that a large quantity of bombs and dynamite exploded as the Armenian quarter was consumed by the flames. The best refutation of this slander is the fact that the Armenians never made use of bombs or dynamite in their attempt to defend themselves. Since they used ordinary weapons in their self-defense, it is plain that, had they had arms of this sort at their disposal, they would have used them as well, with very easily recognizable effects. Since we do not have the least indication that they used such explosives, it is only natural to suppose that this is sheer slander, designed to pin the blame for what happened on the Armenians.[65]

The same report concludes:

All these details clearly show one thing: in Adana, the government officials and country squires took pains to create in advance conditions likely, as they saw it, to minimize their responsibility for massacres that they had premeditated and then decided to commit and to throw that responsibility – at least officially – on the Armenians. To attain that goal and somehow legitimize the Muslims' savage fury, all sorts of lies were put into circulation and someone hit upon the odious trick of firing on the soldiers' encampment.

This time, the direct participation of the president of Adana's Young Turk club, İhsan Fikri, was attested to by the official investigations. Like the others, Fikri had worn the white turban that was the mark of the aggressors. The final act was played out in the yard of the prefecture, before the *vali's* residence, where several thousand refugees from the Jesuit mission and Armenian church of St. Stepanos had been gathered together (those in the church owed their lives to the courage of Brother Antoine, a French Jesuit who had plunged into the fire to save them). After several hours of doubt – some contend that the *vali* was waiting for an order from Constantinople or somewhere else that would settle the fate of this population – the throng was sent away. Since there were no buildings left in the city capable of sheltering them – the Armenian quarter had been largely demolished and what was left of it was in flames – they were led out of Adana toward the railway station by the British consul, who invited them to take up temporary quarters in the Tripani factory and on the premises of a German establishment nearby. It was there that these survivors learned that Sultan Abdülhamid had just given up his throne and been succeeded by Mehmed Reşad. It was also from there that they watched for several days as their neighborhood burned to the ground.

The *Official Gazette* published, in its 18 May 1909 issue, a telegram that was devastating to the Ottoman authorities. Addressed to Denys Cochin (a French catholic leader), it read:

> All the information we have, which converges with that published by the European press, confirms the complicity of the troops in the appalling massacres that took place in Adana and the rest of the province. The second, 25 April massacre was carried out by the very troops sent from Dede Aghach to put an end to the disorders. There occurred scenes at which indescribable atrocities were committed. All Cilicia is in ruins, prey to famine and poverty.

Human and Material Losses

As will be readily imagined, the attempt to assess the human losses due to the "troubles" in Cilicia led, in this context, to an interminable battle of figures, with variations that were as much as 20 times higher in some cases than others, depending on the sources. The first statistics published by the local authorities – that is, under the supervision of Cevad Bey – in the daily *La Turquie*, indicated that a total of 1,000 people had been killed, 250 of them Muslims. In a cable to the minister of the interior, Cevad's successor, Mustafa Zihni Babanzâde, put the number of Muslim casualties at 1,980 dead and 553 wounded, and estimated the number of Armenian dead and wounded at 1,455 and 383, respectively.[66] At the 2 May session of parliament, the figures presented by the Armenian deputies on the basis of the information they had received indicated that 20,000 to 30,000 had died.[67]

The regime's new strongman, General Mahmud Şevket Pasha, also accepted the official statistics. In an interview with the newspaper *La Tribune* on 13 May, he declared:

> Things have been exaggerated. The official statistics on the number of victims show that not more than three thousand Armenians and Muslims were killed. Thus it is clear that remarks to the effect that thirty thousand people were killed are way off the mark.[68]

Obvious underestimations, these statistics, which deflate the number of Armenian and inflate the number of Muslim casualties, were plainly designed to substantiate the thesis that Muslims were victims of an Armenian attack. Mushrooming accounts in the independent Istanbul press and European newspapers, however, provided a very different picture of the situation that the authorities had to take into account in order to maintain a semblance of credibility. Thus, they felt obliged to take their distance from the conclusions of high-ranking Cilician officials and give a higher estimate of both the total number of casualties and the proportion of Armenian victims. By now, it had become grotesque to contend that there had been more Muslim casualities than Armenian ones.

The author of the report of the parliamentary commission of inquiry, Hagop Babikian, said the following on this subject:

> I have observed an enormous disparity between the official figures and common assessments of the number of victims. The Armenians and foreign newspaper correspondents concur on a figure that varies between twenty-five thousand and thirty thousand. As for the government, after initially hewing to the official figure of one thousand five hundred non-Muslims and one thousand nine hundred Muslims, it now admits, on the basis of new investigations, to a total of six thousand casualties. The government's statistics are based on information from the local registry office and lists provided by the *muhtars* and priests of certain localities. It goes without saying that local registries of births and deaths do not constitute reliable documents and it is only too clear that the authorities of Adana have made use of all sorts of methods to hide the real number of Christian victims.[69]

The government's commission of inquiry, which comprised two senior magistrates – Fayk Bey and Mosdichian Effendi – who were assisted by the *mutesarif* of Mersin, Esad Rauf Bey, affirms in its 10 July 1909 report to the interior minister:

> The total number of people killed during the regrettable events in the vilayet of Adana is, according to the registries of births and deaths, 5,623, including gendarmes and soldiers: 1,487 Muslims and 4,196 non-Muslims. However, as it is probable that many people who were only temporarily in the area and were therefore not listed in the registries were also killed, and as it is not possible at present to establish how many such individuals there were, we believe that the total number of those killed – Muslims and non-Muslims – is around fifteen thousand.[70]

Their official character notwithstanding, these figures were not publicly recognized by the government. Early in August, however, the government made yet another estimate of the number of those killed in Cilicia, raising it this time to 6,429 for the vilayet of Adana and 484 for the vilayet of Aleppo.[71] In the wake of publication of the two magistrates' report, the new *vali*, Mustafa Zihni Pasha Babanzâde, was forced to prolong local inquiries, which ultimately arrived at a figure, for the vilayet of Adana alone, of 20,200 (19,400 Christians, including 418 Orthodox Syriacs, 163 Catholic Syriacs, 99 Greeks, 210 Catholic Armenians, 655 Protestant Armenians and 620 Muslims). This is closer to the truth.[72]

According to the English journalist Ferriman, the most precise account of the casualties was produced by the commission of inquiry set up by the Armenian Patriarchate of Constantinople. It arrived at results quite similar to the *vali*'s. Of course, it did not dare to evaluate Muslim losses. It found that the total number of Christians killed in the vilayet of Adana was 21,361, including 18,839 Armenians, 1,250 Greeks, 850 Orthodox Syriacs, and 422 Catholic Syriacs.[73] It emphasized that it had been unable to make a proper estimate of the number of casualties among seasonal workers, but noted that 2,500 people were missing from the Hacın area alone, which accounted for a by no means negligible proportion of the seasonal workers of the Cilician plain, so that a total figure of 25,000 victims seemed to be closer to the truth. Let us add that in the following months, a few thousand more victims of the massacres succumbed to their wounds or to epidemics. Thus, 2,000 children died of dysentery in summer 1909.[74]

Material Losses and Social Consequences

Like the human losses, the material losses too gave rise to a frenzied give and take between the authorities and the victims. To accept the government's initial estimates would have been to admit that the Muslim populations sustained, in addition to their many human casualties, considerable material losses. But the reality on the ground left little room for doubt about the facts of the matter. Hilmi Pasha's government charged Cevad Bey's successor, Zihni Pasha, specifically with estimating the damages caused by the "disorders." For the city of Adana, he arrived at a figure of 96,000 Turkish pounds, rounded up to 100,000 in the semi-official government organ, *Tasviri Efkiar*.

As in the case of the number of victims, here too the government's official commission of inquiry proved more reliable than the local investigators. It concluded that, in the vilayet of Adana alone, a total of 4,823 houses, farms, agricultural complexes, schools, churches, factories, caravansarais, mills, shops, or stands had been wholly destroyed, including 386 that belonged to Muslims.[75] Measured against information collected for each of the localities involved, this figure probably still falls short of the truth, but has the merit of providing some sense of the magnitude of the economic catastrophe precipitated by the massacres and the series of fires and acts of plunder that accompanied them. The same sources evaluate the material losses at 5,600,000 Turkish pounds.

An international commission was created to aid the survivors. Considerable sums were allocated for the purpose but, given the extent of the damage, the money sufficed at best to ensure the bare subsistence of tens of thousands – approximately 90,000[76] – homeless people. The big problem was that because these people's work tools had been destroyed, they were not yet in a position to assure their own needs.

Another problem – that of the thousands of orphans created by the massacres – led to interminable debates among Armenians. To grasp the importance of this issue, we have to review the precedents, the 1895–6 massacres, which left around 60,000 children orphans, as well as the scandal caused by the admission of a certain number of these orphans to institutions founded by American, German, Swiss, French, and other missionaries. The Armenian nation, which had sustained considerable human losses (in addition to the massacres, many women and children had been abducted and forcibly converted to Islam), was dealt a blow that jeopardized its very survival. As a result, it withdrew into itself, in order, as it were, to reconstitute itself. Under these conditions, every child educated in a foreign culture by a non-Armenian institution appeared as one more member of the group destined to swell the ranks of other peoples and undermine the historical Armenian collectivity a bit further. Far from constituting a rejection of all things foreign, this reaction was rather the fruit of a new national impulse, a collective will to survive as a group. When the Cilician massacres happened, these painful memories were still very active, and were all the more easily revived in that they recalled all too well the tragedies that the Armenians had experienced under the Hamidian regime.

Another element to be taken into account is the Armenians' feeling of humiliation over the fact that they were not themselves in a position to educate "their" orphans. Again, although the Armenians were culturally fairly similar to Europeans, they found the colonialist mindset of most of the foreigners who intervened on their behalf – whether they were missionaries, merchants, or diplomats – very hard to bear, despite the undeniably positive aspects of their presence. This held especially for the best educated Armenians, who found it intolerable to be treated as natives and did not understand why their religious convictions earned them the label of sectarians. The religious aspect of this problem should not be underestimated. The Armenian Church, its numbers already reduced by the Catholic and

Protestant missionaries who had been carrying off members of its flock, considered a child educated in this environment to be a lost soul. A number of laypeople were thinking the same thing.

Thus, the Armenian Patriarchate of Constantinople and its Chamber of Representatives made the future of the orphans of Adana a national priority.[77] It set up a commission and then took the initiative of creating an International Relief Committee comprising not just Armenians, but also Greeks, ·Turks, and foreigners such as the director of the Banque Ottomane. The commission, chaired by Said Pasha, the president of the Ottoman Senate, met for the first time on 22 May 1909 in Constantinople.

It was the national commission that was responsible for the first relief efforts, sending a Committee to Cilicia on a preliminary fact-finding mission, followed by a medical team. It also organized the distribution of food and financial aid to the families who had been the hardest hit, at a total cost of 1,943,162 aspres.[78]

On 20 August 1909, the Armenian Chamber decided to create a Central Commission responsible for the orphans of Cilicia. The commission founded six orphanages: the first in Adana, in August 1909, with accommodation for 233 children; the second in Maraş, in September 1909, with places for 178; a third, the same month, in Hacın, for 350; the fourth in Ayntab, in October 1909, with room for 185; the fifth, also in October, in Hasanbeyli, for 207; and, again in October, a sixth in Dört Yöl, designed to accommodate 273 children. Thus, by mid-autumn 1909, the Armenian National Commission was running six institutions with accommodations for 1,426 orphans.

Five more institutions were created to care for orphans. American missionaries opened one in Hacın (350 wards), English missionaries opened another in Ayntab (100 wards), and German missionaries established one in Marash (727 wards). Two state-run orphanages took charge of another 216 children in Marash and Dörtyöl. Thus we obtain a total of 3,164 orphans who had lost both their parents. To this figure, we must add 3,977 children who had lost their fathers in the vilayet of Adana, and 762 in the vilayet of Aleppo, making a grand total of 7,903 orphans who were either placed in institutions or raised by their mothers alone.[79]

Chapter 3

The Ottoman Government's and the Armenian Authorities' Political Responses to the Massacres in Cilicia

We have already discussed the circumstances that led to the Cilician catastrophe, showing how the Ottoman government first tried to downplay the casualty figures, only to put forward statistics that in the end were close to those announced by Armenian and international circles. It is easy to see that the reason the government did not wish to reveal how heavy the human losses had been was its obvious desire to maintain the official thesis: that uncontrolled rioting had created a limited number of casualties in both camps. Its official statements, echoed by a good part of the Ottoman press, had, moreover, convinced a public used to seeing the Armenians cast in the role of troublemakers that the Armenians bore the main blame for these "disorders" as well. Very few Ottoman politicians, consequently, demanded that the whole truth about the Cilician affair be brought to light, apart from the ten or so Armenian parliamentary deputies and a handful of Greek and Turkish deputies who, as we shall see, displayed a fair degree of courage in an openly hostile environment.

In the preceding pages, by following the events in Cilicia step by step, we were able to show with considerable precision how the local civilian and military authorities were implicated in the massacres. We must now try to decrypt the real role of the government – or the political groups connected to it, such as the Committee of Union and Progress – in order to establish whether this violence was instigated locally or inspired by orders handed down by the national authorities. This comes down to asking the key question of the national government's responsibility for these events and, by extension, the question as to who ordered these crimes.

The Ottoman parliament provided the Armenian deputies, veritable representatives of their *millet* vis-à-vis the authorities, with a tribune from which to express their people's indignation over this new wave of violence and to demand explanations for the accusations identifying them as responsible for their own massacre. The charges that had been leveled at the Armenians in the period preceding the massacres – that they had been guilty of provocations and had been making secret preparations to resuscitate an "Armenian kingdom of Cilicia" – may have originated in a skewed interpretation of the attitude of the Cilician Armenians after the restoration of the constitution. With equal plausibility, the aggressiveness and violence toward the Armenians manifested at the time may be traced back to the Hamidian legacy. Finally, it may be supposed that the changing tribal world represented by the Cilicia of the day was shot through with antagonistic currents led by men eager to establish a local power base. While all these explanations are well grounded, none can solely account for the sudden explosion that occurred in Cilicia on 14 April 1909. At the turn of the twentieth century, no event of such proportions could have taken place without an order that came, or was supposed to have come, from the highest state authorities or, at the very least, one of the centers of state power.

The most paradoxical aspect of the matter is the fact that, even as it minimized the import of the events and pinned the blame for them on the Armenians, the Turkish political establishment and initially even the Armenian political establishment attributed the Cilician massacres, like the counter-revolution of 31 March, to a conspiracy hatched by Abdülhamid and those nostalgic for his reign. This thesis was, however, contradicted by the sultan's actual situation: the Young Turks had gradually isolated him in his palace of Yıldız by dismissing a good many of his collaborators and transferring his Albanian guard elsewhere, thus reducing his capacity to maintain his networks intact and exert an influence over the domestic political situation. Even that pragmatic Jesuit, Father Rigal, declared that

> the author of these massacres is the same individual who, thirteen years ago, sent one hundred thousand victims to their deaths and, in our time, sensing that the throne was collapsing, sought, as he fell, to wipe this excessively dynamic people, whose very name he found hateful, off the face of the earth.[1]

This explanation had the advantage of exonerating the new political establishment that had emerged from the July 1908 revolution while maintaining the credibility of its desire for reforms.

The First Reactions of the National Authorities

Given the brief tenure of Tevfik Pasha's cabinet, which was formed on 18 April and resigned on 26 April, it is clear that it did not have the time to take the government in hand, let alone follow events in Cilicia. As has already been pointed out, it was to all intents and purposes the undersecretary of state in the Interior Ministry, Adıl Bey, who handled the Cilician issue and reported on the events to the grand vizier and Ottoman parliament. The decision to send troops to Cilicia was, however, made by Şevket Pasha. Hence, we cannot pass judgment on Tevfik Pasha's cabinet and cannot assign it the least responsibility for what happened in Cilicia.

Furthermore, parliament did not concern itself with the affair in any real sense until its session on 2 May 1909. Ahmed Rıza, who was again presiding over the Ottoman chamber that day, had no choice but to read the report that had been sent to him on 26 April by the *vali* of Adana, who had been recalled but was still serving as *vali*. In terms hardly more measured than those used in his initial reports, Cevad Bey wrote: "We have learned from unimpeachable sources that a few Armenian *fedayis* bear the responsibility for the most recent events."[2] The Armenian deputies, who had the support of a few of their Turkish and Greek colleagues, reacted immediately: they firmly declared, to begin with, that the *vali*'s report was a tissue of lies, and then attacked undersecretary of state Haci Adıl Bey (Arda), reminding him of the notorious cable he had sent to Cevad Bey in which he had limited himself to recommending that the *vali* see to it that "foreign subjects were protected" and that he "restore calm," formulas that under the old regime had meant "massacre the Armenians, but leave foreigners alone."[3] The newly appointed minister of the interior, Rauf Bey, who was also a member of the Young Turk Central Committee, allowed Adıl to speak on behalf of the ministry. Adıl confined himself to the cautious statement that the grand vizier, Hilmi Pasha, and General Mahmud Şevket had conferred and decided to send a special commission to Cilicia to conduct an investigation.

The leader of the Armenian deputies in parliament, Zohrab, thereupon made the following declaration:

> There are two ways of ascertaining the truth – either by means of words or by means of testimony and circumstantial evidence. The counselor [Adıl] has read us telegrams from the prefect of Adana and the governor of Cebelbereket, as if these were trustworthy documents. He was asked approximately how many people were massacred; this all-powerful counselor,[4] who is in contact with this region ten times a day, was not able to provide us with that information.

In an article published in *Le Temps*, the Parisian daily's correspondent made the following comment on the parliamentary debates:

> At yesterday's session [of parliament], there was a spirited discussion of the Adana massacres. Several deputies, notably the Armenians, attacked the government and demanded that the ex-*vali* be brought to justice. The undersecretary of state at the Interior Ministry defended the government: he read out cables from the authorities ascribing the disorders to Armenian revolutionaries and everywhere presenting the Armenians as the aggressors.[5]

Thus, it is clear that, early in May, Hilmi Pasha's government was still defending the thesis put forward by ranking officials of the administration. However, a shift in its position, doubtless inspired by the information published in the international press and oral notes from the powers, could be perceived at the 13 May session of parliament, when the government announced to the deputies that it had decided to send a four-member commission of inquiry to Cilicia under the authority of the interior minister. Two Armenians and two Muslims were to be named to the commission, of whom two were to be civil servants and the other two members of parliament. Although the discussion that followed revealed that part of the Ottoman chamber openly opposed the creation of this commission, for which it saw no need, the deputies elected to it a militant Armenian Young Turk, Hagop Babikian, and another deputy from the CUP, Şefik Bey. At the same session, the president of parliament, Ahmed Rıza, insisted on the fact that "the Adana affair has given rise to a polemic with the European powers and the foreign minister is holding daily meetings with foreign ambassadors."[6] Rıza thus gave expression to the preoccupation of the authorities, who were concerned with preserving a good image in the West and consequently forced to maintain a degree of transparency. It was probably for this reason, rather than out of respect for the Armenian victims, that the government set up a commission of inquiry.

Grand Vizier Hilmi finally commented on the Cilician crisis in the 24 May 1909 address before parliament, in which he outlined his governmental program. Without once touching on controversial points, he listed the measures that had been taken, such as the declaration of a state of emergency in the province and the creation of courts martial in Marash and Ayntab as well as Adana. Hilmi also announced that the fact that ten brigades of soldiers had been sent to the area had made it possible to restore order and that "the property stolen during the events is gradually being recovered and given back to its owners" (witnesses indicate that this was merely a pious wish). The grand vizier recalled, finally, that in order to evaluate the number of victims and assess the responsibility of the local authorities, a commission of inquiry had been formed, made up of two deputies and two ranking magistrates. Their conclusions, he said, would serve as the basis for a prompt indictment of those found guilty.[7]

From this point on, neither the Ottoman parliament nor the Ottoman government made the slightest official declaration, pending the commission's conclusions. Appointing two Young Turk deputies with solid reputations to the commission, the former magistrate Hagop Babikian and the lawyer Yusuf Kemal, as well as two credible ranking magistrates, H. Mosdichian and Fayk Bey, Hilmi's cabinet was doubtless counting on the fact that these "responsible" men would provide conclusions exonerating the state and the pro-Constitutional Turkish political establishment, thus allowing them to emerge from this affair cleared of all guilt in the eyes of international public opinion. It is not known whether Hilmi issued instructions to the members of the commission to this end, but their work in the field and the conclusions reached in the two reports that were released (that of the two magistrates, officially handed in on 10 July, and the other, drawn up by Babikian and kept secret until 1911) allow us to judge how far the government was then prepared to go toward challenging the Turkish political establishment.

The members of the commission arrived in Cilicia in early June and for more than a month conducted a rather scrupulous investigation. The two magistrates, Fayk and Mosdichian, worked in tandem and produced a common report. This was not so for the two deputies, even though they were members of the same party. Babikian, who it is universally agreed was a fervent partisan of Ottomanism and its rejection of dividing walls between communities, clearly seems to have been in disagreement with his Turkish colleague. The French vice-consul in Mersin and Adana, Barré de Lancy, reports in a dispatch to the chargé d'affaires in Constantinople that Babikian "is said to have had rather sharp altercations with his Muslim colleague Yusuf Kemal, who is still in Adana."[8] Returning from Mersin on 4 July with the other members of the commission – the notable exception being Kemal[9] – Babikian confirmed in interviews he gave to two Young Turk journals during his stop in Smyrna that he and his colleague had had a few misunderstandings. In reply to a question from a journalist at the Izmir daily *Ittihad*[10] about the results of his investigation and the reasons for the massacre, he said:

> In view of the information I gathered during my inquiry, [it can be said] that, since the proclamation of the Constitution, the partisans of tyranny had given signs that they were discontent and planned massacres of Christians: this is obvious and has been proved by official court documents.

To another question from the same journalist on the local and national authorities' participation in the massacres, the deputy from Tekirdağ answered:

> The national government did not take part in them, but was the reason for them. The local authorities, for their part, were implicated in them. In particular, the *vali*, Cevad Bey, the military commander Mustafa Remzi Pasha, the *mutesarif* of Cebelbereket, Asaf Bey, Abdülkadır Bağdadizâde, Salih Effendi Boşnak and the owner of the newspaper *Ittidal*, Ihsan Fikri, are fully complicit in the massacres.

In the same interview, Babikian also alluded to the court-martial's lack of objectivity.

The remarks that Babikian made to the reporter from *Tasviri Efkiar*[11] were still more candid, offering a glimpse of the report to come. Babikian dodged a question about the rumors of his disagreements with his colleague Kemal, who was supposed to have precipitated his premature return, pointing out that he had accomplished his mission and that his colleague would be returning soon. About the situation in Cilicia, however, he was more forthcoming. After making a few rhetorical reservations, he declared, emphasizing from the outset that his comments should be interpreted as those of a loyal Ottoman concerned about the happiness and development of the fatherland, that "the details published in the articles in the European press about the Adana events [were] by no means exaggerated and even [fell] short of the truth when [he] compared them with what [he him]self saw." He thus pointed to an abiding characteristic of Turkish society, which found it hard to acknowledge its own acts and often perceived observations made by foreigners as attacks. By far the most pertinent part of Babikian's analysis, however, bore on the origin of the Adana events:

> The Adana affair has two major causes: the reaction and the tyranny ... The former mufti of Bağçe began going here and there and saying that freedom and the Constitution were inventions of the Christians, who are opposed to the sharia; in this fashion, he began to stir up the population and turn them against the Christians and the Constitution.

As to the possibility that Sultan Abdülhamid was involved, Babikian emphasized that, although that opinion was often heard, nothing proved it. There followed three questions that together constituted the grounds for the accusations that the Cilician authorities had laid before Ottoman public opinion:

> 1) *It is said that the Armenians caused the disorders: is that right?*
> The official documents that I have brought with me prove that this hypothesis is altogether mistaken.
>
> 2) *They say that the Armenians wanted to proclaim their independence in Cilicia: is that true?*
> Our investigation has shown that that charge is completely baseless.
>
> 3) *Is the primate of Adana, Bishop Mushegh, implicated in this business?*
> The results of our inquiry prove that the primate is not implicated. Quite the contrary: as early as January [1909], Bishop Mushegh had sent memoranda to the prefecture, the content of which has been established by our inquiry. At the time, the bishop declared orally to the *vali* that there was a risk that disorders would break out and suggested that he take the necessary measures; the prelate's remarks were, however, deemed to be exaggerations and it was judged pointless to mobilize the means required.

These initial observations form a sort of practical illustration of the problems engendered at the heart of Ottoman society by Young Turk modernity. They leave one with the feeling that the local members of the opposition attacked the Armenian population because they regarded it as a symbol of a modernity that they found alarming.

Babikian's response to the next question, about the number of victims and the proportions of "Muslims and non-Muslims," is the more interesting in that it refers for the first time to the statistics that were established by the new *vali*, Zihni, but carefully concealed by the central government. They put the number of those killed at a little over 20,000, including 620 Muslims. The last question bears on another controversial point that was amply exploited to portray the victims as villains: the fact that the British consul in Adana was wounded in the arm. The authorities presented this as an example of the Armenians' criminal attitude. Here is what Babikian had to say about the matter:

> I personally interrogated the consul about this. His response ran as follows: "The disorders had just begun. Terror held sway everywhere. I went out into the street; I saw someone whose look, behavior, acts and gestures gave the impression that he had gone completely mad. He was running towards me. He was fleeing. I wanted to approach

him to ask what was going on. The fugitive interpreted my move as the sign of my evil intentions, pointed his revolver at me, emptied it and then ran off." [12]

Shortly afterwards, *Tasviri Efkiar* interviewed Fayk Bey. He contended that these events could not be imputed to reactionary circles. They were rather due to "the ignorance of the local Muslim and Christian populations." [13]

Even before the investigators' reports were made public, all this had already provided unmistakable indications as to the tone they would strike. These interviews also give us a sense of the role played by the Young Turk press in Constantinople, which had until then by and large published articles reflecting the theses of *Vali* Cevad and the undersecretary of state at the Interior Ministry, Adıl Bey. It is true that the conclusions of the commission of inquiry's two reports, Fayk's and Mosdichian's included, challenged the line of defense that Turkish circles in Cilicia and Constantinople had maintained until July: neither report ever suggests that the Armenians were responsible for the events in Cilicia. Quite the contrary: both treat the Armenians as victims. However, for the Turkish circles in question, there was a yawning gulf between, on the one hand, the very general remarks that, sparing the political establishment, attributed the upsurge of violence to an ignorant populace and incompetent local officials in high places, and on the other, the kind of statements that Babikian made. Babikian, it seems, violated an unspoken rule against openly affirming that the local Muslim populations had received orders to massacre the Armenians, that the soldiers of the army sent from Macedonia to Cilicia had themselves staged the second massacre of Adana, that Cilicia's Young Turk leaders had taken a direct hand in organizing the atrocities, and so on. Had there not been such a rule, it would be hard to explain why only the Fayk-Mosdichian report, submitted on 10 July, was published after only a 20-day delay, while the manuscript of Babikian's report remained in a drawer at the Armenian Patriarchate for more than three years. Moreover, several convergent indices suggest that pressure was exerted in parliamentary circles, and probably at the level of the government and CUP leadership as well, to prevent Babikian's report from being made public.

To begin with, Yusuf Kemal tried to discredit Babikian and have him excluded from the commission of inquiry. He sent a wire to the Ottoman parliament on 3 July to inform the deputies that Babikian had left Cilicia prematurely before completing his mission (as we have seen, this was not Babikian's view of the matter). Kemal even suggested that the Jewish deputy from Salonika, Emmanuel Carasso, be sent to Adana as quickly as possible to replace him. [14] Parliament apparently did indeed consider replacing Babikian. Thus, the French vice-consul in Mersin and Adana pointed out, in a 9 July dispatch to the chargé d'affaires in Constantinople, [15] that

Mersin is awaiting the arrival of a member of parliament, Carasso. His Muslim colleague is still in Adana. He has declared that he is opposed to paying indemnities of any sort, on the grounds that a revolution has taken place and that the government cannot be held responsible. The *vali* says the same thing about the [French] nuns who are rebuilding.

Beginning in late June, Kemal would for his part contend that the disorders organized by the Armenians and a few Cilician Muslims were designed to benefit the Ahrar party and harm the Young Turk Committee – a statement that speaks volumes about the state of mind prevailing among Ittihadist militants. [16] Babikian's interviews, however, had a certain impact. All things considered, it is probable that the Young Turk committee of Salonika preferred not to alienate one of its militants, even if he was Armenian, by not coming out too openly in favor of the thesis that the Armenians were the culprits.

The Evolution of the Hilmi Cabinet's Position on the Adana events

The shift began in early July. To be sure, the Young Turk daily *Tasviri Efkiar* published, in its 1 July and 19 July issues, an article by the parliamentary deputy from Konya, Ebuzzia Tevfik Bey, which confirmed his party's position that "the Armenians alone were to blame." Indeed, Tevfik did not hesitate to congratulate the court-martial for the work it had accomplished in the field.[17] (We shall see that this first court-martial, basing itself on Cevad's reports, found that the Armenians were responsible for their own massacre.) Hakkı Bey, an eminent member of the Young Turk leadership, made a similar declaration in the 28 May issue of *Le Temps* in Paris. Doubtlessly feeling the pressure of Western public opinion during his stay in Europe, he had not hesitated to state, in order to exonerate his party: "People exaggerate. Your press is not always very favorably disposed. In fact, it is known today that the disorders in Adana were fomented in Constantinople. We have intercepted dispatches proving that the Armenian Committee was seeking to bring about a European intervention."[18] This declaration, in the most classic Hamidian style, naturally provoked a reaction from the ARF leadership, whose party was officially allied with the CUP: the Armenian party demanded that the Central Committee of Salonika disavow the statement made by this Ittihadist leader.

It would appear, however, that these declarations represented the Young Turk militants' last stand. After an anti-Armenian campaign that had lasted two months, the members of the commission of inquiry returned to Constantinople to present their reports. Yusuf Kemal, who left Mersin on 14 July, was among them.[19] Kemal took part in the 20 July session of parliament, announcing that he was going to present it with his conclusions in a few days.[20] At the 26 July session, at which Babikian was present, the Fayk-Mosdichian report had its first effects. It attributed the main responsibility for the massacres to, notably, the *vali* of Adana, Cevad, the military commander Mustafa Remzi Pasha, Abdülkadır Bağadizâde, and İhsan Fikri. Yet all four of these men had been exonerated by a court-martial created in May that was composed mainly of Young Turk officers.[21] The two magistrates' revelations were doubtless related to the fact that certain Young Turks, who had so far been rather conciliatory, now took more uncompromising positions. Speaking from the podium, İsmail Hakkı, the deputy from Gümülcina, criticized the government for meddling in the affairs of the Adana court-martial: the presiding judge and an eminent member of the court had resigned after the government had ordered those responsible for the massacres arrested. Half of the deputies, following Hakkı's lead, voted in favor of a motion against the Hilmi cabinet, which had simply acted on the recommendations put forward in the Fayk-Mosdichian report. It thus became clear that half the members of parliament rejected the idea that those responsible for the slaughter in Adana should be judged. Babikian rose and said, "Twenty-one thousand people have been killed in Adana and you are rising to the defense of two individuals." There followed a rather heated exchange, which showed that certain Turkish deputies contested even the number of victims and, more generally, the idea that "the" Armenians were not to blame for the carnage. To put an end to this tense moment, which revealed major differences of opinion, the assembly agreed to postpone the debate on the Adana events until after the parliamentary commission of inquiry had filed its reports. Thus, on 26 July 1909, the beginning of the debate on the events in Cilicia came to a close.[22]

However, damning documents were published in the Istanbul press the very next day. Among them were two encrypted telegrams from *Vali* Cevad to the *mutesarifs* and *kaymakams* of his province, and also to the Interior Ministry. The second stated, for example: "the Armenians have attacked; the government palace [that is, the prefecture] has been encircled; the Armenians are armed and are massacring unarmed Turks. Help us."[23] Such affirmations leave little doubt about the fact that the massacres were premeditated; they expose the manipulations in which the authorities engaged in order to justify crimes in which they seem to have had a hand. At this point, the last week of July, tensions were at their height. Everything goes to show that there could be no question of a debate in this country, in which virtually the entire political establishment, and an overwhelming share of public opinion, held that the massacre of non-Muslims was not a crime. The French ambassador, Bompard, reported specifically to the French foreign minister, Pichon, that the government had had to "follow the advice of the Committee of Union and Progress, which wanted to appease public opinion and spare the Chamber a dangerous debate over the report submitted by the commission of inquiry."[24]

The debate did not, in fact, take place, notably because Babikian died on 1 August, the day before his report was to have been presented.[25] His brother announced on the morning of 1 August that Babikian had sat down at his desk to put the finishing touches to his text and had then begun to complain about pains in his stomach and chest. He quickly fell into a deep coma and then died. In view of the circumstances, the 53-year-old deputy's sudden death was grist for rumors. Nothing, however, indicates that he died of non-natural causes. The most that can be said is that this death prevented his report from being made public at a time when (thanks to the interviews he had given) only its broad outlines were known.[26]

At the 5 August session of parliament, the president of the assembly informed the deputies that Yusuf Kemal had submitted the report on his inquiry and that the deputy Vartkes had requested that Babikian's report also be read. The parliament decided, however, to hear the conclusions of the two deputies on the following Saturday, 7 August. The next day, when the question was again put on the agenda, the president suggested to the assembly that these reports be submitted to a special parliamentary commission for examination before being read to the assembly.[27] This was the last time the Adana events were ever mentioned in the Ottoman parliament, for the two reports were never made public. We still do not know what was contained in Kemal's, although we do know, thanks to its author's public statements, that it was far from drawing conclusions similar to Babikian's.

As the French ambassador points out, it seems that, in the interim, behind-the-scenes negotiations took place with a view to preventing this extremely embarrassing affair from being fully aired in public. The CUP and its government apparently feared a popular reaction – at least that is what they said in private – and, above all, too broad an exposure of the patent complicity of the local Young Turk militants in the massacres.

These negotiations, which were secret by their very nature, seem to have gone on between the Young Turk leaders and their Armenian allies in the ARF, who were then drawing up the cooperation agreement that we have already discussed.[28] The Armenian deputies probably consented to non-publication of the reports and agreed that the parliamentary debate should not take place. Accepting the arguments of their Young Turk colleagues to the effect that a debate would not resolve anything and, indeed, was more likely to poison the atmosphere, they implicitly admitted that a majority of the members of parliament did not want to hear so unflattering a truth. In exchange, the Armenians were probably promised that a public declaration would be made that would clear them of all the accusations leveled at them since the events occurred, that a genuine climate of security would be created in Cilicia, that those who had lived through the massacres would receive help in recovering part of their looted property, and, above all, that justice would be meted out to the real culprits.

There are several indications that a turnabout in official government policy took place in the first days of August 1909:

1) A new prefect was appointed in Adana, Colonel Ahmed Cemal Bey, the future minister of the navy. Cemal was a very influential member of the Central Committee of the CUP and had a reputation for being energetic and liberal minded.[29]

2) A budget worthy of the name was set up to aid the tens of thousands of Armenians who had been left homeless.[30]

3) The courts martial created in Cilicia at last arrested those who bore the main responsibility for the massacres, even if they hanged only people who had played subaltern roles.

4) On 11 August, the grand vizier, Hilmi Pasha, published an official circular that cleared the Armenians of all the charges against them.[31] One sentence sums up the general tenor of this text: "There can be no doubt that in the days of the old regime, when despotic abuses were common practice, certain classes of the Armenian community were working toward political goals. Whatever form this work took, however, its sole aim was to achieve emancipation from the unbearable harassment and misdeeds of a despotic government." These words amounted to a confession. They implied that the Armenians had been massacred because, in 1909, people continued to regard Armenians generally as *fedayis* – that is, "terrorists" and revolutionaries.

5) On 12 August, the minister of justice, Nail Bey, publicly declared: "The Armenians are in no way responsible for these events."[32] This sentence closed the rehabilitation campaign.

The Work of the First Courts Martial Established in Cilicia

Nothing testifies more clearly to the existence of a political will than the establishment by a state of a system of justice capable of punishing those guilty of crimes and thus restoring civil peace and the rule of law. However, after the Cilician events, the work of the first local courts martial gave rise to "abuses" that more than one observer found shocking, to say nothing of the victims. "It is unfortunately only too certain," said a diplomat, "that the country's new rulers spend more time leveling charges at the Armenians than trying to find the real culprits. Armenians are being arrested by the hundreds, while those who instigated the massacres go unpunished and are even in charge of the work of the courts."[33] These courts martial had another unusual feature: they were composed of the main organizers of the massacres and all of them proceeded on the basis of reports provided by local commissions of inquiry whose members had themselves been involved in the massacres.[34] Thus, they had the power to decide who was "guilty." The reports by Babikian and Fayk-Mosdichian pointed out these anomalies, as well as the frequent recourse to perjury and the practice of extorting forced confessions from the victims. It was in the wake of diplomatic protests and a sharp reaction from the Armenian circles of Constantinople that Grand Vizier Hüseyin Hilmi finally announced to parliament, on 24 May 1909, the creation of a court-martial to be made up of five judges, all recruited from the Young Turks' ranks, with Yussuf Kenan named the presiding judge. It should be noted, however, that this court lacked the means it needed to conduct pretrial investigations, and so simply relied on the results of investigations carried out by its predecessors. It also set up three branch courts in Tarsus, Erzin, and Marash.

This court-martial's general line of conduct had probably been dictated to it by the national authorities. It consisted initially of dealing blows to both victims and executioners without distinction, so as to give the impression of even-handed justice or, more precisely, to preserve the fiction of Armenian responsibility. The best proof is the report – which no one had commissioned – that it published a few days before Fayk's and Mosdichian's. A sentence from this report (which we have already evoked to illustrate the nature of the indictment) aimed at the Cilician Armenians sums up the military judges' attitude: "Muslims did not much appreciate the fact that [the Armenians] made such bold use of the freedom and equality that they had only just acquired."[35] In other words, unidentified propagandists "explained" to an already exasperated population that the Armenians' behavior was the first sign of a plan to win independence and massacre Muslims. In this connection, the oral note that the French minister Pichon delivered to the Ottoman foreign minister offers valuable insight into the methods used by the Adana court:

> Six Armenians were just hanged in Adana by order of the court-martial, together with nine Muslims, for provoking massacres. Thus the court-martial has largely adopted the version of events put forward by the Adana authorities, who wanted to pin the blame for the catastrophe on the Armenians. We protest against this injustice, as a result of which six representatives of the cruelly mistreated Armenian population were punished along with representatives of the Muslim authors of the massacres. We know, moreover, that the Muslims who were punished were merely tools of no real import- ance and that those who are truly guilty have gone unpunished. The *vali* of Adana has not even been brought before the court-martial. The director of Adana's Turkish newspaper *Ittidal*, who personally participated in the massacre and, since then, has published dangerously slanderous articles against the Armenians, has not been dis- turbed in any way and is pursuing his campaign.[36]

Pichon's observations received concrete confirmation when the court-martial acquitted all the local authors of the massacres.

The execution of these six Armenians, like the submission of the Fayk-Mosdichian report, forced the government to adopt a new strategy, as we have seen. Hilmi's cabinet issued orders for the arrest of the individuals incriminated in the report – the *vali*, Cevad Bey, the mili- tary commander Mustafa Remzi, the president of Adana's Young Turk club İhsan Fikri, the influential notable Abdülkadır Bağdadizâde, the *mutesarif* of Cebelbereket, Adıl Asaf Bey, the police chief Kadri Bey, and their accomplices. Two weeks passed, however, before the former *vali*, Cevad, was arrested on 27 July, because the new *vali*, Zihni Pasha, and the judges on the court-martial refused to execute the orders they had received. The grand vizier con- sequently had no choice but simultaneously to replace, on 29 July, *Vali* Zihni[37] with Ahmed Cemal, and the presiding judge of the court-martial, Yusuf Kenan, with İsmail Fazlı Pasha, until then the military commander of Smyrna. The same day, Cevad, Zihni, and Kenan were taken into custody.

In August, the newly formed court-martial finally proceeded to try the authors of the mas- sacres. Obviously, nothing more was said about the Armenians' guilt, yet the old reflexes apparently continued to hold sway. The Armenian Patriarchate of Constantinople pointed out bitterly to the grand vizier that, despite everything, many Armenians were still languish- ing in Cilician prisons under appalling conditions, subject to the whims and brutality of their guards. The Patriarchate also protested the light sentences handed down by the court. Let the reader judge. Cevad was condemned to six years of ineligibility for any and all govern- ment posts; he was, however, granted a monthly salary. Mustafa Remzi was sentenced to three months in prison, but the sentence was not executed. Asaf Bey was declared ineligible for any civil service job for a period of four years. İhsan Fikri was banned from Adana. Fikri's colleague at *Ittidal*, İsmail Safâ, had to spend one month in prison. Osman Bey, the com- mander of the garrison in Adana, received a prison sentence of three months. Abdülkadır Bağdadizâde was exiled to Hejaz for two years, but he was granted amnesty on the first anni- versary of the constitution.[38] The French vice-consul in Mersin and Adana explained, in his reports to foreign minister Pichon, the workings of the court-martial: it was virtually impos- sible for an Armenian to testify, and some of the judges on the court were swayed by gifts from the accused. İhsan Fikri's Young Turk colleagues even summoned him to Constantinople after he had spent a brief period in Cairo, to make an official report there on what had happened.

No one, however, publicly disavowed him for his acts. Simultaneously, in Cilicia, the new *vali*, Cemal Bey, had more than one hundred people hanged in short order for participating in the massacre – yet, as the diplomats indicated, those punished had merely been second fiddles.

The limited nature of this justice is illustrated by a conversation that the patriarch held with the presiding judge of the court-martial, İsmail Fazıl Pasha, on 4 September, at a moment when Fazıl had just condemned 40 Turks and 3 Armenians to death. In response to a question from the Armenian prelate, the Turkish general said, "Of course, it has been established beyond a doubt that the Armenians were innocent; there were, however, Armenians who committed acts that the Turks themselves would not dare commit."[39]

In sum, by replacing the presiding judge of the court, the government had corrected the most blatant excesses while ensuring that its appointee would impose symbolic sentences rather revelatory of its preoccupations.

The Hilmi cabinet's ostensible good intentions notwithstanding, a witness comments:

The military courts continued to consider the Armenians rebels, without, be it added, giving them the opportunity to prove the contrary; to appeal to the most notoriously compromised officials in conducting investigations; to let themselves be guided by people who had provoked and organized massacres; and, finally, to base their judgments on false accusations.

Another American witness remarks:

Many people were held in prison on the basis of false accusations. Apparently anyone could be arrested and imprisoned as the result of a remark made by a Muslim. I know of no case in which the evidence of an Armenian called to the bar was accepted. In its haste to indict Armenians, the court went so far as to serve writs on people who had died several months before the disorders.[40]

The Hilmi Cabinet and the judges on the court-martial were incontestably more concerned with Western reactions than with the complaints lodged by their Armenian allies.

The Treatment of the Cilician Crisis in Armenian Circles

The Cilician massacres initially puzzled the Armenian authorities. Some Armenians, such as Krikor Zohrab, thought that they were yet another "Hamidian provocation," while others, more skeptical, questioned the role played by the Turkish authorities. The skeptics pointed out that the arrival in Cilicia of "liberation" troops commanded by Young Turk officers had not brought the carnage to a halt and, indeed, that these forces had helped perpetrate the second wave of violence, that many of those who were known to have been responsible for these acts had not been jailed, that many survivors of the massacres were arrested or even executed for no reason, that the Armenian delegates who had been sent to Cilicia had not been allowed to enter Adana, that sums of money which the Patriarchate had wired to the city's archbishopric had never arrived, and, finally, that the Turkish government and press generally put the blame for the "events" on the Armenians, whom they accused of having staged a rebellion.[41] The Armenian parliamentary deputies noted that this violence was accompanied by other forms of harassment: notables were arrested, schools were destroyed, churches and homes were burned down, houses that had been spared during the massacres were searched and plundered, women and children were abducted, taxes were levied immediately after the events, survivors were denied food and, in certain villages, Armenians were forced to assimilate. All this was reminiscent of the methods used in Abdülhamid's day.[42]

The Armenian deputies also observed that even the presence of several British, American, French, Russian, and Italian battleships near Mersin, two hours from Adana, had not prevented the army from perpetrating a second wave of massacres – they had even made it possible to provide food relief to the survivors who roamed the streets in a daze.[43] For the Armenian representatives, the priority clearly consisted in coming to the aid of the survivors with all possible speed. The Armenian Chamber of Deputies immediately sent medical teams and a relief column to Cilicia. Their mission was to distribute food and clothing to the area's inhabitants and care for the many orphans, whose numbers were put at 7,000 in June 1909, two months after the slaughter.[44] The chamber intended, above all else, to demand an explanation from the government, even while conducting its own investigation in the area.[45] In the memorandum it submitted to the Sublime Porte, it demanded that 1) imprisoned Armenians be released; 2) people who had been Islamicized by force be sent home; 3) young girls "married" to Muslims be returned to their families; 4) homeless survivors receive compensation and be given back property stolen from them; 5) the new *vali*, Mustafa Zihni, be recalled; 6) the guilty be arrested; 7) food relief be organized for the survivors; and so on.[46]

Early in June, Patriarch Yeghishe Turian, who had succeeded Izmirlian (elected as Catholicos of Armenia), was very courteously received by the sultan, grand vizier, and interior minister. The Armenian delegation stated a number of grievances: the courts set up in Cilicia in order to pronounce judgment on the rioters and other killers were made up of the main organizers of the massacres and had condemned and hanged six Armenians; several archbishops, including the archbishop of Marash, who had resisted the attacks, were currently being prosecuted by the courts; and the government and Turkish press continued to depict the massacres as an Armenian revolt.[47] The patriarch accordingly proposed that a mixed parliamentary commission of inquiry be given executive powers and dispatched to Cilicia, and also demanded that military courts based in Constantinople be charged with bringing the guilty to justice.

In the course of the 21 August 1909 debates in the Armenian Chamber, it was revealed that although Babikian's report had not been read before the Ottoman parliament, the handful of extracts from it published in the press had put the government in an embarrassing position. The government had told the Armenian representatives in private that it was hard for it to punish those responsible for the massacres because this might stir up the Muslims, who would not tolerate the least decision "favorable" to the Armenians.[48] In fact, all indications are that the Armenian Political Council and the Armenian parliamentary deputies were directly handling the issue in collaboration with the government and the CUP, although the chamber was probably not systematically informed of the course of their discussions.

Of course, the Armenian press was less prudent, taking advantage of the relative freedom it still obtained in this period. An editorialist at *Piuzantion*, Suren Bartevian, was one of the first Armenian journalists to give forthright expression to the indignation felt by most of his community. Referring to the second Adana massacres, which had targeted an unarmed population, he exclaimed:

> After this bloody trick, how can anyone accuse the supine corpses of people who, this time, could not make the least attempt at self-defense, fire a single shot or even throw a stone? How are we to describe these deceitful accusations? How are we to understand them? Tell us … if you no longer want us to live in this country or exist on the face of the earth … How long must our blood and tears flow because of a fanciful, half-cocked story about an "Armenian kingdom" that you do not believe yourselves, because you cannot imagine that the Armenians are stupid enough to believe it in their turn.[49]

These words reflect not only the indignation but also the despair that came over many Armenians who were discovering in the wake of these events how little the situation had changed. Others, such as the editorialist of the daily *Azadamard*, who evoked the activities of the parliamentary commission of inquiry, were instead cynically pessimistic. "It would be naive," wrote this editorialist, "to expect that justice will be done. The whole process underway at the moment is not designed to let justice triumph, but to throw a veil over this catastrophe, which has devastated the Armenian population of Cilicia."[50]

Besides these general declarations, however, accusations aimed directly at the government were beginning to make themselves heard. Zohrab, obviously beside himself, exploded at the podium of the Ottoman parliament: "The government remains faithful to the long-standing tradition of denying the facts, as in the case of the Adana events; for a long time, it refused to acknowledge the number of victims, although official information later confirmed it."[51] The reaction of many Young Turk deputies, who were in principle open to democratic practices, reflected the Ottoman reality of the day: Zohrab was quite simply interrupted, pulled from the podium, and roughed up. Another revealing fact could be observed at the following parliamentary session, held on 3 July. Zohrab and Vartkes Seringiulian tried to defend a bill to establish trade unions in the Ottoman Empire. A majority of the deputies were hostile to it, although it had been introduced by the Young Turk fraction.[52] The contrast between the arguments put forward by the two Armenian deputies and the reactions – conservative, to say the least, of some of their Turkish colleagues – illustrates the cultural abyss between the Armenians and their counterparts, not excluding deputies reputed to be modernists.

Despite the modest progress that had been made in the Cilician affair – we have seen how the Ottoman parliament and government handled it – Armenian circles continued to demand, as the autumn began, that the victims receive compensation for the damages they had suffered and that their property be restored to them. Given the political and social context, which these circles knew better than anyone else, their stubborn insistence that justice be done in a country that until recently had a restrictive interpretation of the word may seem surprising. The Armenians, however, had plainly decided to pursue the matter to the end without making concessions. After showing a certain flexibility in negotiating directly with the government or the Young Turk leaders throughout the summer, they now refused to settle for mere promises, for the affair seemed to them to represent too great a threat for the future and too blatantly to contradict the principles that the Young Turks officially espoused.

On 25 September, at a public session of the Armenian chamber, N. Jivanian, who was also a member of the Ottoman parliament and an Ittihadist, defended the Young Turk government. He took up the thesis that after the "Adana affair" the authorities had only just managed to avoid excesses and massacres in the eastern provinces. Interrupted in the midst of his plea by loud protests from all sides, he yielded the floor to the Dashnak leader H. Shahrigian, who spoke on behalf of the Armenian Political Council. After analyzing the situation, Shahrigian revealed that the members of the Council, acting in concert with their Armenian colleagues from the Ottoman parliament, had preferred to avoid discussion of the parliamentary commission's report (written by Babikian) at a session of the Ottoman chamber. The reason was that a majority of the Ottoman deputies were manifestly opposed to any public declaration openly impugning the Turkish authorities. The members of the council and the Armenian delegates had concluded that sidestepping a discussion would make it easier for the government to work toward what they considered desirable ends.[53] As soon as Shahrigian had finished speaking, the leader of the Hnchaks, Hmayag Aramiants, took the floor. He argued that there was continuity between the Hamidian and Young Turk regimes, although the policies of the latter, while they did not diverge from Abdülhamid's, were much more skillfully "packaged" and carried out behind a legal facade. This had been the case at the Adana trials, Aramiants said. It seems that the government could not legally overturn the verdicts they had rendered.

A few dissenting voices notwithstanding, a large majority of the Armenian deputies had tried to maintain relations with the Sublime Porte in seeking a resolution to the crisis.

However, to make it clearer that it was not inclined to give way before the authorities' arguments or threats, the Armenian Political Council suggested to Patriarch Yeghishe Turian that he resign. Turian did so on 4 September, as a sign of protest against the government's inertia.[54] Yet, parallel to these discussions, liberals and Dashnaks continued to maintain relations with the Ittihad's leadership, which they knew was influential. The lack of concrete results and – according to those opposed to the Armenian Political Council – the inadequacy of its policies, brought on the downfall of the liberal and Dashnak leadership of the chamber. It proceeded to elect a new council with a conservative majority, the unreconstructed Minas Cheraz.[55] Thus, the chamber's "soft underbelly" seems to have taken the government's threats seriously after all.

In the course of the debates that followed this change in the chamber's leadership, Aramiants, backed up by Zohrab, pointed out to the assembly that electing people from the old school was not the way to obtain the best results. Moreover, he said, such people were altogether ignorant of what daily life in the provinces was really like; it was no longer possible, he added, to exclude the political parties from the conduct of affairs. Zohrab, who was more conciliatory, recalled that, upon returning from exile the year before, he had tried to unite the intelligentsia and the parties in a single bloc, so as to bring them to participate in national political life in the framework intended for that purpose. After all, he said, electing party activists to the council did not imply turning it into an appendage of the parties, but was rather a means of channeling the parties' energies in a consensual direction.[56]

In fact, the crisis into which the Cilician affair plunged the Armenian institutions was an expression of profound unrest within the Armenian political establishment. *Piuzantion* reported Zohrab's revealing remarks before the chamber:

> There is no denying that the present government is well disposed towards us, for we know very well that, five months ago, there was a real danger that the Adana massacres would spread to all of Armenia, as telegrams and letters that have fallen into the hands of the national leadership show.[57]

Information relayed by the European consular network in Anatolia confirmed that this danger had indeed existed:

> For some time now, a sort of pessimism has been spreading among us: it has it that the Ottoman Committee [the CUP], if it did not organize the Adana massacres, was at the very least not opposed to them and took great satisfaction in them. It is crucial that this question be clarified, for it is undeniable that the Ottoman Committee controls the current leadership of the country and that its orientations and decisions are of vital significance for the Armenian people. If, in future, the Ottoman Committee wants to destroy the Armenians materially and morally, it is desirable that we be informed of this right now, so that we can take thought for our future, that is, get up and leave this country. For our part, we have been examining this question for six months. We have been informed of the telegrams and reports that the Patriarch has received and we ourselves constantly receive correspondence from very different groups in the regions with an Armenian population. We have not, however, drawn the conclusion that the Ottoman Committee wanted to massacre the Armenians.[58]

Kechian's editorial does not pronounce on the key question preoccupying everyone at the time – namely, whether or not the CUP was implicated in the massacres. It does, however, give expression to oppressive doubts and a vague sentiment that the Armenians' very presence in the empire was already a matter of controversy.

In December of the same year, on behalf of the council's new leadership, H. Khosrovian presented a report on the government's response to its requests and its demands for reparations. Khosrovian announced that five Armenians who had been condemned to death had been amnestied and that 42 people who had participated in the massacres had been hanged, that some of the prisoners had been released, but that basically the organizers of the carnage had not been bothered and that nothing had been done to help kidnapped children return to their families.[59] Despite everything, the Catholicos of Cilicia, Sahag II Khabayan, who had resigned in protest at the same time as the patriarch, had changed his mind and asked his counterpart in Istanbul, Yeghishe Turian, to do the same. Thus, the crucial question informing the chamber's debates in the 1908–9 period was posed: how far could it go in demanding that reparations be made and the security of the Armenians' life and property be ensured without provoking new massacres?

This was precisely the subject of a new, hour-long address by Zohrab, who asked that he be allowed to speak at a closed, off-the-record session.[60] This is understandable, because the execution of 42 killers in Cilicia was a very emotional issue for Turkish public opinion. To be sure, those who bore the main responsibility for the massacres had not been punished; the execution of the second fiddles, however, had sufficed to bring about the fall of the prime minister, Hilmi Pasha, who was replaced by Hakkı, the author of the famous declaration blaming the Armenians for the massacres.[61] Certain deputies believed that the Cilician affair constituted a precedent and that if the chamber did not wage its struggle to obtain reparations to the bitter end, there could be no counting on an improvement in the lot of the Armenian population in the provinces, whether what was involved was the restoration of confiscated lands or control of the Kurdish tribes. In the end, the chamber charged the Armenian deputies in the Ottoman parliament – especially Zohrab, Hampartsum Boyajian, and Vartkes Seringiulian – with approaching their Turkish colleagues again. Significantly, the Armenian Political Council simultaneously asked the patriarch to resume his functions.[62] The Armenians had obviously decided not to persist in their demand for amends for fear of provoking further violence.

The Role of the Committee of Union and Progress in the Cilician Massacres

On 11 March 1909, the Constantinople *Independent* reported the confidences of an Armenian parliamentary delegation leaving a meeting with the president of parliament, Ahmed Rıza. Rıza had told them, without beating around the bush: "Watch out; if you don't stop making trouble, all of you are going to be massacred." Very obviously, a declaration of this sort, which Rıza might have made because he had momentarily lost his temper, can in no way be taken as proof of the party's desire to settle a political issue with a massacre. Rıza's remark does, however, give us an idea of the state of mind of the second-most-important man in the state and make us wonder about the role that the CUP actually played in the Cilician affair. To be sure, apart from accusations like those leveled by Zeki Bey, an inspector at the Office of the Ottoman Debt and the editor-in-chief of the review *Şerah* – Zeki openly impugned the Young Turk Central Committee[63] – we have no proof that the Ittihad's leadership was directly responsible for the Adana massacres. Also at the time, people sought to identify the underlying causes of the carnage. An attentive observer who had been in Adana during the April 1909 massacres, Father Rigal, also tried to understand them:

> It has often been asked what could have caused an explosion of such ferocious fanaticism among the Muslim population. I was obliged to maintain fairly frequent contact with various authorities during those unforgettable days. I can say that I never heard

them utter any refrain other than "the Armenians are massacring the Muslims; the Armenians are firing on our soldiers; the Armenians are looting and burning..." This means, in a word, "the Armenians are the aggressors" – the exact opposite of the truth – or, again, "the Armenians are rebels and we are simply putting down a revolt," to cite, verbatim, something the *vali* once said to me.[64]

Like many other contemporary observers of the events, this missionary only raised the crucial question, throwing the authorities' description of the events into relief, without himself answering it. Indeed, this affair remains inexplicable if we do not look beyond the local context, at the level of the leadership of the Young Turk movement.

Given the lack of compelling evidence, in order to measure the extent of the CUP's involvement, we must closely observe the way the leadership or local organs of the party behaved during and after the massacres, the positions it officially took, the reaction of the Young Turk faction in parliament when the Cilician affair was put on the parliamentary agenda, and the way its press judged the events. Such circumstantial evidence will allow us, at a minimum, to detect signs of complicity or at least solidarity with the authors of these crimes.

As far as the local organs of the party are concerned, the Fayk-Mosdichian report, like Babikian's parliamentary document, shows without the least ambiguity that, in addition to the *vali* and the military commander of the vilayet, the presidents and members of the Union and Progress clubs of Tarsus and Adana took a direct hand in organizing massacres in those two towns. Yet, not only did the CUP deny this fact, it refused to condemn an individual as dubious as İhsan Fikri[65] – although it was known that he had stirred up local public opinion by publishing articles that accused the Armenians, notably of separatism and of preparing a massacre of the Turkish population.

Also troubling are the orders that the undersecretary of state in the Interior Ministry, Adıl Bey, issued the *vali* of Adana, demanding that he "protect the foreigners," which, in the Hamidian idiom, meant, "massacre the Armenians, but leave the citizens of foreign countries alone, for, if you do not, Europe is going to ask us to give an account of ourselves." Far from being sanctioned for what he said, Adıl was allowed to remain in his post and was later promoted to the rank of counselor to the grand vizier.[66] No less troubling was the behavior of the "Action Army" led by Young Turk officers, which proceeded to perpetrate the second Adana massacres on 25 April, the day it arrived in the area. What, finally, should we say of the reactions of the Young Turk faction in parliament, which roughed up an Armenian deputy who demanded that the truth be revealed and protested vigorously against the arrest of *vali* Cevad and the military commander, Remzi Pasha (although both had been explicitly found responsible for the Adana massacres)?

We can continue this list of the CUP's interventions by inquiring into the conduct of the Young Turk officers on the first court-martial established in Adana: sparing Cevad, Remzi, İhsan Fikri and consorts, they inflicted the death sentence on ordinary Muslim participants in the massacres and Armenians who had taken part in the resistance in their neighborhoods. Did the Central Committee of Salonika, which kept an eye on everything, fold its hands and watch as the sentences were meted out? It is more likely that it chose the members of the court-martial from the ranks of its militants and gave them instructions before sending them to Cilicia. İhsan Fikri's case is one of the most edifying: condemned to exile by the first court-martial after the general hue and cry provoked by his initial acquittal, he was summoned to Constantinople to meet with Grand Vizier Hilmi Pasha, whom he sought to intimidate by more or less openly threatening to make revelations. He was consequently exiled to Beirut, where he died soon after under mysterious circumstances.

It should also be pointed out that the Young Turks' press organs had a direct hand in the campaign, lasting from April to July, which consisted in depicting the Armenians as wholly to blame for their own massacre. When this position became untenable, they fell silent.

Nothing, in any case, seems to have been left up to chance. Yusuf Kemal himself, one of the two members of the parliamentary commission of inquiry, seems to have seen and said things that did not please the committee, his divergences with his colleague Babikian notwithstanding. Not only was his text not made public, but he was generously rewarded with the post of supervisor of Turkish students in Paris – he was already a middle-aged lawyer at the time – in order to remove him far from Istanbul. The committee's most significant act, however, was the promotion of the principal officers who had participated in the Cilician massacres and the demotion or dismissal of those who had succeeded in maintaining order in their military districts. Haci Muhammed, a major in the Albanian gendarmerie in Sis who had protected the local Armenian population, was relieved of his command; Lieutenant-Colonel Hursid Bey, who saved Hacın, was transferred to Rumelia. In contrast, the former *icra memur* of Marash, Hüseyin Effendi, whom the court-martial had earlier sentenced to a few months in prison for having helped organize the attack on the Armenians of his city, was appointed examining magistrate in Dyarbekir.[67]

All these factors, which we have discussed in the preceding chapters, suggest at the very least that the committee "provided accompaniment" for the massacres and handled the situation that resulted from them in accordance with Hamidian rules of conduct. Morever, there are reasons for presuming that it organized them.

Because Constantinople's "reaction" to the events was contemporaneous with the events themselves, contemporaries initially thought that those responsible for carrying out the massacres were the same people as those who had organized them. They also thought, in light of appearances and the Hamidian precedents, that these events could probably be chalked up to reactionary circles or circles regarded as such. The people who planned the massacres no doubt reasoned along similar lines. In any event, those who derived the greatest benefit from the Constantinople affair were the Young Turks, who, capitalizing on the occasion, simultaneously rid themselves of Abdülhamid (who was dethroned by parliament on 27 April 1909)[68] and the entire liberal opposition.

The thesis that the Cilician affair resulted from a spontaneous upsurge of violence is untenable. Only an order from the government that guaranteed the perpetrators impunity could have convinced the populace to plunder and kill its neighbors. Moreover, one is hard put to see how a governor, backed up by the region's military commander, could have taken the initiative to provoke a human and economic catastrophe of these proportions on their own (it was later proved that the two of them coordinated the massacres at the local level). In our view, there can be no doubt that these experienced men – General Remzi Pasha had helped organize the 1895–6 Hamidian massacres in Marash – were given the order to launch these massacres by their superiors. They were able to create the impression that they had been overwhelmed by an uncontrollable situation. They also succeeded in "managing" the flow of information the way it had been managed under Abdülhamid, on the basic principle that the victims should be portrayed as the aggressors and the aggressors as the victims.

Who gave the order? Who told high-ranking civilian and military officials, as well as the local notables, to organize these "spontaneous riots"? Was it the authorities, the state, the government, the CUP? Everything suggests that it was only the sole institution that controlled the army, the government, and the main state organs – namely, the Ittihadist Central Committee – that could have issued these orders and made sure that they were respected. In view of the usual practices of this party, the orders must have been communicated, in the first instance, by means of the famous itinerant delegates sent out by Salonika, whom no *vali* would have dared contradict.

What was the point of committing these massacres? Without giving a definite response to this question, we can hazard a few plausible explanations. The economic dynamism of the regions and its exceptional geographical situation, in which – Turkish circles frequently underscored this point – the Armenian population, although it was a minority, had acquired considerable influence in agriculture and commerce, could have incited the Young Turk party, obsessed with the Turkification of the country, to strike a blow at the development of a region that had been partially spared by the Hamidian massacres of 1895–6.

The Armenians Facing Young Turk Realities in the Wake of the Cilician Massacres

The Adana massacres necessarily led the ARF to do more than just question its strategy of alliance with the CUP and the plans of the Young Turks, whose assimilationist ambitions were, it seems, no longer a secret from anyone. In this connection, *Droschak*'s editorialist observed:

> "Union," as conceived by Rıza, simply means assimilation. [The Young Turks] wish to do what great nations with a high level of civilization have not succeeded in doing with ethnic minorities down to the present day. They think it has suddenly become possible – the curiosity and political absurdity of the matter lies here – for the Ottoman Empire to assimilate, at last, the other ethnic groups, although these groups have a centuries-old cultural heritage and are, collectively, at an incomparably higher intellectual level; they think the Empire will at last dissolve them in the predominant Turkism. *En attendant*, the fraction that dominates Young Turkey is attempting to build up, by any and all means, legal or illegal, a totally centralized system under the hegemony of the Turkish element, a system in which the Ittihadist party will be able to say, like Louis XIV, "l'État, c'est moi."[69]

It seems that, by late April 1909, the ARF had taken the measure of its partner. However, it must have said to itself that it had no choice but to maintain a dialogue with it. The only other alternative was to take up arms again and go back underground.

The same editorialist, drawing up a balance sheet of the Young Turk committee's work, affirmed that

> eight or nine months of the committee's rule illustrate its profound, revolting indifference to the other nations' most vital demands. The Armenian element was the main victim of the old regime; yet we have not observed, in the dictatorial committee's policy, the least plan or any serious, just attempt to help it survive, to bind up its bleeding wounds. The land of the Armenians remains a breeding ground for the crimes of the old regime; it is teeming with all the well-known hyenas of days past, the organizers of plunder and massacres, decked out in official uniforms.[70]

Thus, the ARF's criticisms of the Ittihadists had become more precise: the CUP was designated for the first time as the "dictatorial committee." Published in the ARF's official journal, this indictment, the first made by the ARF in the July 1908 revolution, also included the charge that well-known criminals had become deputies thanks to the support of the Young Turk "majority," which had decreed that "all those favorable to decentralization" were "traitors to the fatherland."[71]

The fall of the Hilmi cabinet, brought on by the execution of the Cilician criminals, obviously constituted a warning for the Armenian deputies, who now understood that the limits of the possible had been reached in their relationship with their Turkish colleagues. The Armenian leadership, even while it held a firm position on the Cilician question, continued to maintain that Armenia was an integral part of the Ottoman Empire and that the unity of the empire was important to it. This is why all Armenian leaders endorsed the bill that proposed to make military service obligatory for non-Muslims, too, and worked actively for its adoption (in August 1909). They supported this reform because they believed that it would help accelerate their integration and make them full-fledged Ottomans. It was their wish, however, that the conscription of young Armenians coincide with abolition of the military exemption tax, which had replaced the poll tax for non-Muslims, a levy that brought out the difference in status between Turks and Christians too starkly. Fearful that religious pressures would be brought to bear in the barracks, they also demanded that "mixed" battalions – the formula that the government finally chose – be assigned chaplains enjoying the same status as imams.[72]

Conscription, however, turned out to be a veritable nightmare for the young Armenian recruits. Simon Zavarian, who spent the years 1909–10 on the plain of Mush, told his comrades in Istanbul about the bastinados, the acts of violence of all descriptions, the catastrophic sanitary conditions (there were no barracks in Mush), and the cases of desertion that resulted. He observed that, in the past three months, there had been 30 deaths in a group of fewer than 800 draftees. He added, however, that "the most terrible situation was that of the Albanian [soldiers], half of whom had already disappeared." The Dashnak chief also reported Dr. Zavriev's account of the recruits in Erzerum, where the previous year over 2,000 soldiers had died. "That is a rate," he pointed out, "ten times higher than in foreign countries."[73]

During a brief stay in Sıvas, Sapah-Giulian encountered 500 Armenian conscripts from throughout the area who had been assigned to a barracks in the city in which there were only 60 to 70 Turks. Fearing a rebellion, the commander of the garrison had decided to disarm the Armenian soldiers. The tensions between Armenian draftees and their Turkish junior officers made themselves felt when the officers demanded that the draftees call themselves Osmanlıs, not Armenians. They made the Armenians do all the obligatory chores and meted severe punishments out to them on the slightest pretext.[74]

Other political issues were only allusively mentioned at sessions of the chamber or, when a party's interests required it, were cautiously revealed in newspapers with the help of leaks. There were, however, exceptional cases, as when on 25 November 1911, in a departure from the rules, Zohrab held an almost two-hour-long speech before the deputies on the subject of Turkish-Armenian relations.[75] Zohrab made a rather pessimistic, but pragmatic, assessment of the three years of the Constitutional regime. "It would be somewhat naive," he said, "to believe that, in this country, simply proclaiming the constitution could change the general attitude of the Ottoman population [in whose eyes] Christians can never be the equals of Muslims, the only ones who have rights." Evoking the security of the populations of the provinces, Zohrab recalled that the Armenian deputies in the Ottoman parliament had always collaborated to carry out unspectacular joint activities; he felt that the time had now explain things. The Armenians, he maintained, had to take the Turks' immaturity into account and to act with circumspection, since, as everyone knew, the constitution was an empty shell, like the proclamation of the equality of all citizens before the law. In this regard, it was significant that the Christian one-third of the empire's population was represented by only one-seventh of the parliamentary deputies, and that vice-presidencies or the chairmanships of committees were altogether beyond the reach of non-Turks. If parliament itself did not respect the rule of equality, it was not hard to imagine the mood of the Turkish population as a whole. Taking Adana as an example, Zohrab also observed that the parliament and government had been unwilling to condemn these infamies and, at best, had eventually brought only ordinary participants in the massacres to justice, while continuing to provide cover for the main organizers of these atrocities. He himself, he said, had made a public declaration before parliament, and everyone knew that he had been interrupted by his furious Turkish colleagues. The same day, the government had been loudly applauded when it blamed the Armenians for the violence. In these circumstances, Zohrab declared, he had been able to gauge the depth of the Turkish political establishment's blindness and, with the other Armenian deputies, had contented himself with bringing the government to admit, after several months of intense discussion, that "the Armenians bore no part of the blame" for their own massacre, as parliament itself had ultimately acknowledged. As for the Armenians who had been condemned to death in Hacın, he recalled it had been necessary to provoke the resignation of Patriarch Turian to keep them from being executed. Turian had returned to the patriarch's throne only after Cavid and Talât had provided formal assurances that the Young Turks would do what was necessary to restore calm in Cilicia and Armenia. All this had been obtained, Zohrab maintained, thanks to a prudent political line without public speechifying of the sort that could touch off violent reactions from the Turkish population. To improve the lot of the Armenians of the high plateau, he added, "we have succeeded in bringing about the appointment of honest *valis* in certain regions – Celal Bey in Erzerum, Bekir Sâmi in Van, İsmail Hakkı Bey in Bitlis, and Cemal Bey in Adana." It was all the more significant for him that, when the *valis* prevented the Kurds from looting or extorting money and tried to defend the Armenians' rights, the same Kurds threatened to emigrate or revolt. Moreover, Zohrab went on, there was a powerful pro-Kurdish "lobby" in Constantinople, with Young Turks in its ranks, that approved of the policy of harassment practiced by the nomads. Together with his colleagues, he had, he said, asked the government to propose a law that would make it possible to appoint inspectors with executive powers to avoid interminable judicial proceedings and, at the very least, put an end to land theft. At their insistence, the authorities had agreed to draw up a bill and had submitted it to parliament. However, it had been vehemently rejected by a large majority of the deputies. After this setback, Zohrab reported, the Armenians and certain Ittihadist deputies had considered proposing other formulas that might lead to a legal resolution of the problems. These efforts, however, had not yet borne fruit.

More broadly, Zohrab was of the view that the enfeeblement of the Young Turk party, overwhelmed by ultra-nationalist circles, was an alarming development and that a general massacre of the Armenians could erupt at any moment. To justify the government's conduct, he added that it feared it would provoke a Kurdish revolt in the east if it improved the Armenians' lot at the Kurds' expense, at the very moment when the situation in Thrace was explosive and war was imminent.

This balance sheet shows that the Armenian authorities had continued to cultivate relations with the Young Turks. Some of Zohrab's remarks indicated that their discussions had brought the Armenians to the conclusion that it would be preferable to make no further public mention of the Cilician question, to stop trying to bring about a discussion of it in parliament, and to resolve it discreetly with the Young Turks. In other words, Armenian circles had come round to the view of the heads of the CUP that the insistent Armenian demands for reparations and punishment for the criminals risked touching off new massacres.

We still have a trace of one of these meetings. It had been sought by a CUP delegate, who had been sent to Constantinople in August 1909 to suggest to the ARF that it send representatives to Salonika for a "friendly meeting." Harutiun Shahrigian and Armen Garo had several meetings with Midhat Şükrü and Dr. Nâzım there.[76] As in every major crisis, the CUP had made contact with the ARF in order, as it were, to assess its mood and renew its alliance with the Armenian party. Despite the negative balance sheet cited above, which the Dashnaktsutiun had published in its official organ shortly after the Cilician massacres, it had not broken off its dialogue with the CUP; indeed, ARF militants even saved Talât, Halil and Nâzım from the fury of the insurgents and answered the Ittihadists' call for volunteers to "save the constitution." It remained convinced that the CUP was the only partner capable of reforming the empire. After three long meetings, the representatives of the two committees finally drew up an agreement with the fundamental aims of carrying out a joint struggle against conservative circles "for the defense of the fatherland and its territorial integrity" and of reforming the administration "on the principle of decentralization." The Dashnak delegates had insisted that the last formula be included; the Young Turks had probably made the concession to convince their allies of their good will. It is, however, doubtful that the CUP had really taken a new tack on this question.

Chapter 4

The CUP's First Deviations: The 1909, 1910, and 1911 Congresses

Although the Armenian authorities dealt rather pragmatically with the events in Cilicia, the violence in Adana nevertheless had a lasting negative impact on relations between Young Turks and Armenians. It dashed the hopes of the Dashnaks and certain other circles in Istanbul that the new regime would reform the empire. Yet, as we have already suggested, there was no real alternative: once the CUP had again secured its hold on power and crushed the opposition in the wake of the events of 31 March, the Ittihadists were obligatory negotiating partners.

The second CUP congress was convened on Ottoman soil, in Salonika, from 13 to 25 October 1909. It afforded the committee an opportunity to make a first assessment of its work at the head of the country, but also to discuss questions basic to the party's future. We do not have much information on this congress, but it is an established fact that it was marked by bitter debates between those for and against keeping the Central Committee a secret organization and maintaining the armed forces' supremacy over politics. Among the newcomers to the CUP was Mehmed Ziya Gökalp,[1] a delegate from Dyarbekir; his vision of the future of the Turks' empire and his conception of Ottoman society attracted attention in Salonika.[2] The congress offered him an ideal platform from which to expose the ideological synthesis that would gradually gain sway over the movement in the following years. Another personality distinguished himself at this congress thanks to the positions he took – Mustafa Kemal, a delegate from Tripolitania. Against the advice of many, but in line with a recent imperial decree, he defended the principle that the armed forces and political power should be kept separate and that the former should be subordinated to the political authorities. He thereby effectively condemned the existing situation – that is to say, the presence of a large number of officers in the Merkez-i Umumî (the CUP's Central Committee), such as Enver Bey, who was a member of both the Ottoman general staff and the Central Committee.[3]

This congress also assessed the effects of the events of 31 March, and probably made decisions bearing on the events in Cilicia, in which the Hilmi government had become bogged down, as we have seen. Everything suggests that it was at this congress that the CUP first seriously considered replacing Hilmi Pasha, who had been criticized for making too many concessions and, among other things, publishing the famous circular of 11 August 1909[4] in which all ambiguity as to the Armenians' role – the "misunderstanding" of which they had been the victims – had been swept aside and emphasis placed on their loyalty.

The French ambassador, Bompard, who was, as it were, an eyewitness to the 28 December 1909 resignation of the Hilmi cabinet and the appointment of Hakkı Bey, notes that grand viziers were not CUP members, but

accorded total freedom of action to the cabinet members representing the CUP ... They [the CUP] had eventually come to ignore the authority of the grand vizier ... If he was not an obstacle, he remained a censor... Hence they decided to rid themselves of him.

This very diplomatic formulation reminds us that it had become risky to exercise the functions of a grand vizier under the Young Turks. Pleasing or satisfying the CUP was no easy task: "the whole problem consisted in finding a successor who was to the Committee's taste while ensuring that the grand vizier was not replaced by one of the 'old hands.'"

One of the few members of the committee already able to take on the role of grand vizier, Talât, either felt that he was not up to the task or had already taken the measure of the risks the position entailed, given that an omnipotent Committee monitored, from behind the scenes, the slightest move a government made. Hakkı Bey, a former law professor, had an advantage, as many Young Turks had been students of his.[5]

While we have some idea of the nature of the relations between the CUP and the cabinet of ministers, we are much less well informed about the internal practices of the Central Committee, which was secret by its very nature. Only the revelations of erstwhile Committee members who later joined the opposition allow us to form some notion of the Committee's methods and secret objectives. One member, General Şerif Pasha, who quit the CUP on 25 March 1909 and went into exile in Paris, is among the principle commentators on the party's Turkist projects and its desire to mobilize all available means to assimilate or Turkify the empire's non-Turkish elements.[6] In the CUP's first ten months in power, down to the "incidents of 31 March," its obsession, Şerif affirms, was with the Albanians. Examination of the Committee's Albanian policy in this period, particularly the propaganda campaign waged in the Young Turk press in Constantinople, reveals that the bloody repression that the Ottoman army carried out in Albania was legitimized by charges of separatism. An attentive contemporary observer remarked that "the slightest matter that happens to involve one or another Albanian is immediately ascribed to the whole race, which the Committee adamantly insists on casting in the role of an enemy of the new regime."[7] Notwithstanding the Albanians' decisive role in crushing the reaction of 31 March, to say nothing of their crucial contribution to the July 1908 revolution, in early June 1909 the CUP used its newspapers to launch a campaign of denigration against the Albanians. They were accused of having built up a reactionary movement opposed to the constitution. This, in turn, seems to have been sufficient grounds to launch a vast military operation in Albania, in which the country was put to fire and the sword. The Albanians, the most faithful of the faithful, and a majority of them Muslims, had until then been considered one of the pillars of the Ottoman Empire – Abdülhamid's personal guard, for example, was made up of Albanians. But, from the Young Turks' point of view, they had one major defect. Although they should have been the easiest group to "Turkify," they resisted Turkification, proving to be profoundly attached to their language and national traditions. Measured by the CUP's yardstick, the very modest demands that flowed from this attachment were regarded as manifestations of separatism.

The confessions of Dr. Nâzım, one of the main ideologues on the Ittihad's Central Committee, shed light on this matter:

The pretensions of the various nationalities are a capital source of annoyance for us. We hold linguistic, historical and ethnic aspirations in abhorrence. This and that group will have to disappear. There should be only one nation on our soil, the Ottoman nation, and only one language, Turkish. It will not be easy for the Greeks and Bulgarians to accept this, although it is a vital necessity for us. To bring them to swallow the pill, we shall start with the Albanians. Once we have gotten the better of these mountaineers, who think they are invincible, the rest will take care of itself. After we have turned our cannons on the Albanians, shedding Muslim blood, let the *gâvurs* beware. The first Christian to move a muscle will see his family, house and village smashed to smithereens. Europe will not dare raise its voice in protest or accuse us of torturing the Christians because our first bullets will have been expended on Muslim Albanians.[8]

The whole future strategy and ambition of the CUP is summed up here. This declaration also distills the main elements of the party's developing ideology. Social Darwinism plainly informs these remarks. Violence is legitimized in the name of the higher interests of Turkism, even if that violence is at this point envisaged only as a means of intimidation designed to foster assimilation.

The period was also marked by the entry of two members of the Ittihad into the government: Mehmed Cavid became minister of the economy in June 1909, while Mehmed Talât was appointed interior minister in August of the same year. This justifies the supposition that the CUP had decided to take a more direct role in running public affairs so that it could translate its plans into action and secure its influence over the cabinet. However, the Committee's first experience of government was catastrophic. The two new Ittihadist ministers engaged in financial misdealing that was exposed in public, permanently besmirching the party's reputation. The trial of the murderers of Zeki Bey, an inspector in the Ottoman Debt Administration and the editor-in-chief of the review *Şerah*, led to public revelations about the methods of the Committee and its ministers. The fact that two CUP *fedayis*, Mustafa Nâzım and Çerkez Ahmed, were taken to court meant that part of the Young Turk system had been put on public display.[9] The pretrial investigation had in fact revealed that the murdered man, Zeki Bey, a specialist in economic matters, had in the course of his duties been led to make a painstaking examination of the financial operations conducted by various ministries. Thus, he had come to work, at the request of certain members of the Ittihad's Central Committee, on the "Maimon Affair," the big loans taken out abroad by the minister of finance, Cavid Bey, and also on the circumstances surrounding the concession for the exploitation of bromine. In the course of this inquiry, however, Zeki Bey also discovered "proof of political crimes committed by the Committee" that would enable him, he said, to establish the guilt of Talât Bey, Cavid Bey, and "their friends." After reading Zeki's initial report, the Ittihad Central Committee is supposed to have decided to force both Talât and Cavid to resign (respectively, on 10 February and around 10 May 1911). The scandal, which was still limited to the inner circle of the Young Turk leadership, apparently bred severe internal tensions, as well as some bitterness toward Zeki. It was probably at this time that Talât and Cavid or, more probably, their clan within the Central Committee decided to have Zeki murdered.[10]

The two murderers have been irrefutably identified as *fedayis* of the Ittihad's branch in Serez, which was headed by Derviş Bey – by way of reward, he was "elected" to parliament after the murder. The investigation also revealed that the April 1909 murder of the liberal journalist Hasan Fehmi,[11] as well as many other politically motivated homicides, such as that of Ahmed Samin, had been the work of the same group of *fedayis*, which took its orders from an inspector of the Central Committee in Salonika, Dr. Tevfik Rüştü (1873–1926),[12] and the deputy from Serez, Midhat Şükrü (Bleda), the party's future secretary general and a close collaborator of the two ministers. These revelations, made at the 7 November 1911 session of the trial, momentarily shook the Committee.[13] The court, however, doubtless concluded that it was preferable to leave matters at that and refused "to subpoena the witnesses" capable of explaining the internal workings of the CUP. All that one learns, in passing, from evidence gathered at the court's request by the Ottoman ambassador in Paris, is that Zeki was on the point of publishing "important revelations about the Committee's intrigues, the revolutionary movement of 31 March and the Adana incidents," and that he knew that he "had been condemned to death by the Committee" as a result.[14] Despite the gravity of the charges against them, Talât and Cavid did not turn against the witnesses and lawyer who denounced them for ordering Zeki Bey's murder.

At any event, the murder allowed the finance minister, Cavid Bey, to avoid trial for the embezzlement that he had committed when the agreements on the foreign loans to the Ottoman Empire were signed.[15] It remains to be asked whether these "indelicacies" were the fruit of a personal initiative of the minister's or an order from the Central Committee. It is probable that the Committee or, more exactly, one of its factions, fell back on expedients of this sort to finance its own secret activities. Were this not the case, it is by no means certain that it would have dispatched two of its best *fedayis* to assassinate a high-ranking official with a reputation for integrity. In any case, even if very few of the facts were made public, this scandal led to a crisis at the ministerial level, radicalized the opposition, and sowed serious dissension in the CUP's ranks:

> Many officers who had risen up against the Hamidian regime, but not against the inalterable principles that had informed Turkish politics for centuries, sided with the dissidents, with the result that these dissidents attained a majority not only in the Chamber of Deputies, but even in the Party of Union and Progress.[16]

Between April and September 1911, this affair contributed to a split in the CUP. Zeki's investigation had been ordered by the faction of the party led by Colonel Mehmed Sadık,[17] either because this faction had doubts about Talât's and Cavid's integrity or because it was looking for a way to expel party members whose projects ran counter to its own. But Sadık and his partisans did not succeed in destabilizing Talât's faction, which kept control of the Central Committee despite the charges with which it was faced. The pressure of public opinion did, however, lead to Cavid's indictment for financial misdealing in October 1911.[18] The factional struggles were obviously older, but this affair had intensified existing antagonisms.

The CUP congress that had convened in November 1910 in Salonika had already heralded the tensions to come, especially the seditious tendencies of certain military party cadres. A speech that Talât held at a preliminary "secret meeting" of the CUP, before 27 of its members,[19] provides valuable insights into the problems then confronting the Committee and the questions that would be broached by the November congress. "According to the constitution," Talât said,

> there is to be perfect equality between Muslims and non-believers. You know and feel yourselves that that is absolutely impossible: both the sharia and our history stand in the way of such equality. Hundreds of thousands of believers rebel at the thought; however – this is the interesting point – it also runs counter to the feelings of the unbelievers. They do not want to become Osmanlis; all the means set in motion to develop a sentiment of Osmanliism have proved unsuccessful and will remain so for a long time to come ... There can be no question of equality until the day when the Ottomanization of all groups is an accomplished fact. That is a long, arduous task.

Speaking of the administration of the state, Talât emphatically declared that, "there are still many things that we ought to do in the country outside a governmental framework."[20] In other words, general Turkification was a necessary condition for the adoption of the principle of equality for all Ottoman subjects. While waiting for it to come about, the Committee had to operate in secret.

The congress opened on 1 November 1910. Forty representatives were in attendance: 30 delegates from the vilayets and the seven members of the Central Committee of Salonika, as well as Halil Bey (Menteşe),[21] in his capacity as the party's parliamentary leader, Ahmed Nesimi (Sayman),[22] the deputy from Constantinople, and Şeyh Safet, the deputy from Urfa.[23] One of the first to take the floor was the secretary general of the congress, İhsan Bey. His speech presaged the CUP's radicalization. "The Committee of Adrianople," he said,

> demands that we take steps to diminish the weight of the Bulgarian population, either by settling a large number of Muslim muhacirs in the vilayet of Adrianople or by liquidating all the Christians hostile to Young Turkey ... The Central Committee, while it is aware that these measures could prove useful, is unable to approve of them, because of their rather impractical nature.[24]

We thus can thus see how the local Committee envisaged regulating the demographic "unbalances" persisting in the vilayet of Edirne, their constant preoccupation being to ensure by whatever means necessary that the region remain a part of the empire.

The occasional resistance that the Committee encountered in the state administration also seemed to have interfered with its plans more than once. In order to realize its plans, the Committee intended to utilize all the mechanisms of power and to mobilize all the means available to the state. The congress consequently decided that "upper-level administrative posts should be reserved for Committee members and the authorities should consult the Central Committee before appointing anyone to them."[25] For the CUP, taking control of key positions and placing men from its ranks in the state apparatus was much more than a means of action; it was a crucial stake and an inevitable step on the way to harnessing the empire to its ends. It was a sort of practical realization of its elitist ideology.

Another aspect of this ideology, Turkish nationalism, was evoked at the congress when the conflict between the Central Committee and the Committee of Damascus was discussed. The CUP found itself torn between its desire, which had been confirmed at the 1909 congress, "to allow only Turks to serve on the Central Committee" and its hegemonic ambitions in the Arab vilayets. The Committee of Damascus, a majority of whose members were Arabs, "had expressed a desire to send Arab delegates to the Central Committee of Salonika" but had met with a firm refusal from the Ittihad's congress.[26] In the inner circles, Turkism obviously took priority over the immediate interests of the empire and the development of the movement.

"Defense of the fatherland" and the affirmation that Anatolia – especially its eastern provinces – was "Turkish" were at the center of the discussions. The Committee decided to ask the relevant ministers to increase the budget for settling *muhacirs* in the regions in question: "A new commission will be set up in Erzerum to help Muslim émigrés from the Caucasus and Turkestan who have already manifested a desire to come to Turkey to settle there."[27] The provinces with heavy Armenian populations already had the Committee's entire attention. The aim here was to reinforce, by means of this voluntarist policy, the "Turkish" presence in these areas and to implant culturally correct populations in the heart of the territory inhabited by Armenians – populations on which the movement could count in the future.

The "non-Muslim nationalities," for their part, were to see to it that they behaved – that is, that they consented to renounce their identity and language and melt into the Turkish element. To that end, it was necessary to convince them of the Committee's good will, even while enfeebling them.[28] One of the rare delegates to affirm that this position was hard to maintain was the delegate from Istanbul, Ahmed Nesimi (Sayman). "The number of Christian deputies in parliament," he observed, "is far from proportional to the number of Christians in the Empire ... If we exclude them everywhere, we will be very hard put to bring them over to our side."[29]

The Central Committee elected by the congress comprised[30] Haci Adıl (Arda), the new secretary general,[31] Dr. Nâzım, Eyüb Sabri (Akgöl),[32] Ömer Naci,[33] Mehmed Ziya (Gökalp), Abdüllah Sabri[34], and Midhat Şükrü Bey.[35]

This congress's decisions were, of course, not all translated into acts in the following months, which saw above all a recrudescence of repressive policies directed at the Albanians. The CUP's response to the local problems in Albania was violence. No fewer than 50,000 troops were sent to Albania in 1910 to "disarm" the population, leading to a veritable slaughter that was naturally followed by revolts in 1911 and 1912. The expenditures made necessary by these military operations caused, moreover, a serious economic crisis in the country. At the parliamentary session on 22 November 1910, one of the secretaries of the finance committee, Zohrab, announced that, to his regret, the military operations conducted that year had resulted in the loss of 5,000 men and had cost the budget 69 million franks.[36]

The French ambassador in Istanbul observed in a 3 September 1911 letter to his minister that

> increasingly, the Committee is turning toward Asia. The reason is that its activity in Macedonia is well and truly finished: Albanians, Epiriots, Bulgarians and Greek-speaking populations are openly opposed to the CUP ... The Committee has no illusions about the collapse of its prestige in the European provinces but it now seems inclined resolutely to counterbalance the always dubious sentiments of the Macedonians with the weight of its Asiatic loyalties.[37]

This observation illustrates the effects of the Young Turk government's repressive policies in the Balkans: a concrete translation, as it were, of the plans envisaged earlier by Dr. Nâzım.[38]

The disastrous consequences of the party's previous choices notwithstanding, the next CUP congress, inaugurated in late September 1911 in Salonika, did not consider modifying previous policy, reaffirming the party's position vis-à-vis non-Turks in general and Albanians in particular.[39] It was still a question of "teaching the rebels a lesson." Although tensions materialized in the course of the congress, they were due above all to the repercussions of the indictment of Mehmed Cavid, also known as the "Maimon affair," which occurred as the congress was underway, as well as the growing influence of the opposition led by former Ittihadists such as Colonel Sadık.

The stability of the Committee's positions doubtless explains why its make-up hardly changed. The seven members of the previous leadership body – Haci Adıl Bey (secretary general), Mehmed Ziya (Gökalp), Eyub Sabri, Dr. Nâzım, Abdüllah Sabri, Ahmed Midhat Şükrü, and Ömer Naci – were joined by Mehmed Talât, Ahmed Nesimi, Halil Bey (Menteşe), Ali Fethi (Okyar),[40] and Dr. Hüseyinzâde Ali (Turan).[41] It should be noted that the arrival in the CUP's upper echelons of Hüseyinzâde Ali, one of the two surviving members (along with Mehmed Reşid) of the original CUP, seems to have reinforced the hard-line Turkists' camp led by Ziya (Gökalp).

Chapter 5

Armenian Revolutionaries and Young Turks: The Anatolian Provinces and Istanbul, 1910–12

Despite the threats of massacre hanging over the Anatolian provinces after the violence in Cilicia, observers concur that the socio-economic situation there improved somewhat after the July 1908 revolution. One of the three founders of the ARF noted in a letter that "this devastated country is on the way to recovery. In the space of a year, the population's living standard has risen by at least twenty-five percent."[1] He also emphasized, rather optimistically, that the tribalism that had paralyzed the region for centuries was in decline, for, "among the Kurds as well, the level of consciousness has begun to rise. In many places, the Kurdish peasants are protesting side-by-side with the Armenians against the practices of the *ağas*."[2] He observed, finally, that even the openly Islamist discourse of tribal chiefs such as Musabeg and the sheikhs, who called for "unity around the sharia," "met with resistance from the Kurds in certain regions."[3]

The basic question preoccupying not only the local authorities but also the sedentary populations and the local Dashnak and Ittihadist Committees was the Kurdish tribal chieftains' attitude toward the new government and its policies. Thus, the Committee of Union and Progress found itself confronted with a complex equation: it wished to develop in the area, but could do so only if it successfully wooed local tribal forces, even while cultivating "privileged" relations with the Armenian Committees. These local constraints no doubt explain why the CUP was unable to apply a uniform policy of collaboration with the ARF. Hence, it is not surprising that the Dashnak Committees of the eastern provinces did not have close relations with the local Young Turk clubs, "whose members were all *ağas*."[4] It is no more surprising that whenever a high-ranking official tried to resolve problems such as restoring property seized by the Kurdish *begs*, as did Tahir Pasha, the *vali* of the vilayet of Bitlis,[5] which included Mush, the local CUP club put pressure on Salonika to have him recalled. It is probable that the resolution of land disputes, constantly postponed by the authorities, was thwarted by the political influence or barely veiled threats of the tribal chieftains. The control commissions that Istanbul dispatched to study the land question accordingly returned to the capital without having accomplished serious work.[6]

As far as security went, the situation was not the same everywhere. Generally speaking, the areas on the plains were less exposed to danger than the mountain districts. Thus, the Sasun district, especially the *kaza* of Khut, was almost constantly threatened by attacks from Kurdish tribes, who committed a number of murders there in summer 1911 and stole hundreds of sheep.[7] These were anything but isolated cases. Before the July 1908 revolution, one of the activities of the Armenian *fedayis* had consisted precisely in struggling against nomadic tribes who attacked villagers. Once the *fedayi* commandos were disarmed, however, this task devolved, in theory, on the gendarmerie or even the army, both of which were sometimes hard put to control the nomads and usually arrived too late. After discussing these problems, Zavarian concluded that the only way to put an end to these exactions would be to disarm the Kurdish tribes, such as the Şeko tribe, "since it is impossible to arm the Armenians."[8]

Indeed, the question of self-defense and the disparity between the situations of the armed Kurds and the defenseless sedentary population recurred again and again. A year never went by in which the Armenians, and particularly the ARF, did not raise the problem with the government or the Committee of Union and Progress. They did so, for example, in November 1812, when the Western Bureau demanded that the Council of Ministers agree to the stationing of guards in the villages, although they hardly had illusions about the kind of answer they would receive: "I doubt that they will accept," Zavarian wrote.[9] The ARF knew only too well that its activities under the Hamidian regime had left a lasting mark on the minds of the Young Turks, who did not want to hear about the legalization of village militias, over which the Dashnaks would inevitably gain control. The Dashnaks, for their part, had no other choice than to continue to work legally for the progress of the empire, from which a good part of the Armenian population was already profiting, especially in urban areas.

The social progress and the development of intellectual life and the educational system toward which many reconverted ex-revolutionaries were working did not go unnoticed by the Central Committee of Salonika. According to the parliamentary deputy from Van, Vartkes Seringiulian, the Committee found this alarming, and after its October 1911 congress adopted a more radical policy.[10] Seringiulian detected proof of this change in the fact that, after the congress, the Young Turk clubs in the provinces were more overtly hostile to Armenian circles.[11] He mentions a confidential circular sent to these local clubs by the Ittihad's Central Committee late in 1911, which asked them to work discreetly toward limiting Armenian activity in the educational, cultural, and economic fields.[12] Papazian also observed an unmistakable rapprochement with Kurdish circles that had until then maintained a sullen opposition to the CUP: the party drew closer even to notorious bandits, who now began persecuting the sedentary populations even more intensely than before, without intervention by the authorities. Moreover, alarming information from the provinces impelled the Armenian deputies to demand that the grand vizier, Ferid Pasha, send a commission of inquiry there. The proposition was, however, rejected by a majority of parliament.[13]

Still other signs pointed to the shift in CUP strategy for the provinces. Two important ARF cadres, Carmen[14] in Mush and Marzbed[15] in Bitlis, were subjected to outright administrative harassment, which prevented them from engaging in political activity of any kind in their respective regions. Further to the east, to the south of Lake Van, the young school inspector of Moks was murdered under atrocious circumstances: the party's press condemned the act, complaining above all about the fact that there was no real investigation of the crime.[16] Seringiulian was even imprisoned for two days in his capacity as director of the Istanbul daily *Azadamard*, which the authorities attacked for its critical tone. The CUP did not react in any way, ignoring the interventions of its official allies.[17]

The situation in the western Anatolian provinces, which had a more varied ethnic make-up and a large Turkish-speaking majority, seems to have been quite different. The interpenetration of the various historical groups there endowed these regions with a cultural cohesion that was clearly superior to that of the tribal zones in the east. Thanks to the account of the Hnchak leader Stepanos Sapah-Giulian,[18] who traveled through the regions of Samsun, Merzifun/Marzevan, Amasi, and Sıvas from May to August 1911, we understand better how the local Committees of the SDHP and the Ittihad clubs worked, and how the Turkish, Greek, and Armenian populations perceived both the changes that had taken place in the country since 1908 and also the activity of the "gentlemen" who came from the capital to preach the good word.

Hardly had he got off the boat on 10 May 1911 when Sapah-Giulian was invited to visit Samsun's Ittihadist club. He and the parliamentary deputy Murad (Hampartsum Boyajian) were welcomed to Samsun by the local Unionist leadership, made up of Muslim clergymen, a few military men, and above all the CUP inspector for the regions of Samsun, Sıvas, and Canik, Mustafa Necib. Necib "decided everything" there, and he was particularly concerned with replacing government officials with Ittihadists.[19] That very evening, the city's Hnchak club organized a meeting in a room in the elementary school where not long before the Young Turk propagandist Ömer Naci – a member of the Central Committee – had given a talk that had had some influence on Armenian circles, especially among Armenian merchants. Among the audience, Sapah-Giulian noticed many Turks, often civil servants and Ittihadists, sitting in the first rows, as well as Armenian-speaking Greeks. On the lecturer's own account of his talk, he unsparingly denounced the nationalism that was developing in the empire and conducing to its ruin. The Ittihadists listened in silence, taking notes.[20]

On Sunday, 11 May, in the same room, Sapah-Giulian gave a second lecture on "economic questions." There were again Young Turks in the audience, accompanied by interpreters. Faithful to his habits, the Hnchak leader condemned the Young Turks' policies in his lecture: they were calculated, he said, to bring about the economic ruin of non-Turks and put the economy in the hands of the dominant nation.[21] Obviously, these virulent attacks did not leave the Young Turk circles indifferent; they were worried about the impact that Sapah-Giulian's words would have on the local population. The occasion for an exchange on these questions arose naturally because it was the custom in these societies to pay a visit to one's "guests." An Ittihadist delegation, with Mustafa Necib at its head, went to Samsun's Hnchak club and began a conversation on the subject of Armenian-Turkish relations, "which are no longer as warm as they were in the first months of the Constitutional revolution." The reason, Sapah-Giulian writes, was that the Adana massacres had dampened the ardor of the most enthusiastic, as had the government's and the CUP's policy, especially its "narrowly nationalistic" position. There was no lack of arguments in defense of the Committee's centralizing policies, which according to Mustafa Necib were the sole means of maintaining the country's unity. Necib even contended that "the least step toward decentralization [would] spell the destruction of this country."[22] Even while criticizing the Hnchaks for their decentralization plan, the Ittihadist inspector conceded that the Hnchak clubs were carrying out work of considerable importance for the education of the people, whatever their nationality, and stimulating them to take initiatives to develop the country.[23]

On Tuesday, 16 May, Sapah-Giulian arrived in Merzifun, where he was welcomed by a representative of the *kaymakam* and a crowd of 3,000 people, including Turks, before receiving, that evening, a courtesy visit from the local Ittihadists, both Turkish and Armenian. On the morning of Wednesday, 17 May, he took part in a meeting of the city's Hnchaks; the local branch of the party had 450 male and 30 female members.[24] All the problems of daily existence were discussed there. Thus, we learn that, in setting local tax rates, Armenian houses were systematically over-evaluated and Turkish houses under-evaluated. In passing, Sapah-Giulian mentions that after the constitution was restored, mayoral elections were organized in Merzifun. An Armenian won the election against another candidate, but his victory was contested in a complaint lodged with the *mutesarif* of Amasia, on the pretext that people who were ineligible to vote had participated in the balloting. A commission of inquiry confirmed the Armenian's election, yet the *vali* of Sıvas invalidated it. According to information obtained locally, the *vali* had acted on instructions from the Central Committee of Salonika, which is supposed to have said that "posts of this kind should not be given to Armenians for the time being, since the Muslim population might find that somewhat irritating."[25]

Let us note, finally, that a boycott of Armenian companies and stores had been launched in Merzifun in 1911 and that Armenian tailors and shoemakers had been obliged to take on Turkish apprentices.[26] This indicates that the groundwork for the Young Turk project to "nationalize" the economy was already being laid in this period.

The theme of the meeting held in Samsun on 17 May 1911 in a room in the Sahagian school was "the national question and the social-democracy," one of the Hnchaks' favorite subjects. No fewer than 1,500 people were in attendance, including the local Turkish and Armenian Ittihadists. To buttress his attack on the CUP's Turkism, Sapah-Giulian pointed out in his talk that the empire was made up of several nations, not just one.[27] The Hnchaks' relations with the leader of Merzifun's Young Turks, Osman Effendi, were no more than courteous. Effendi, who supervised everything that went on in the city, followed the instructions he received from the Ittihadist Central Committee to the effect that all decisions "involving vital state interests" should be the sole province of members of the club.[28] The Hnchaks' meeting with the *kaymakam*, a Greek by the name of Constantine, was distinctly warmer: the *kaymakam* did not hesitate to evoke the problems he had been having ever since he had refused to join the CUP.[29] At a second meeting, which was attended by the police chief, Mahir Effendi, an Armenian from Van who had been kidnapped as a young child and raised in a Turkish family in Merzifun, people's tongues were untied: the *kaymakam* revealed to Sapah-Giulian that the Ittihadists were secretly striving to whet the Muslim population's hostility to non-Turks, adding that the clubs were arming their members. He warned him that he should be very careful and not be lulled by the Young Turk militants' demonstrations of courtesy and respect.[30]

The Hnchak revolutionary's next stop was the village of Sim Haciköy, where he was welcomed on 25 May 1911 by a large crowd of Greeks, Turks, and Armenians. Shortly thereafter, Mustafa Necib, who seemed to be keeping tabs on Sapah-Giulian, paid him an impromptu visit at the village's Hnchak club, accompanied by the mayor and municipal physician.[31] At the banquet that the Greeks and Armenians of the village gave in honor of their Armenian guest, the Young Turks and Hnchaks found themselves in a veritable face-off. The local Young Turk club had been working to create Committee schools in which "everyone was educated the same way, since all were Ottomans," whereas the Armenian and Greek social-democrats ran their own school. In this confrontation over the school system, two different conceptions of Ottoman society clashed. Apparently, only the mufti, who was also a rich landowner, was in a position to oppose the Young Turks without fear of reprisals.[32] When Sapah-Giulian met with him, the Muslim clergyman unsparingly criticized the Unionists, whom he considered to be usurpers "concerned about their personal interests before all else" and always intent on divesting people of their money on various pretexts: for example, to buy battleships, open a school, or support the army.[33] The mufti also pointed out that the public schools were being neglected because they had been replaced by Committee schools "where children are taught to say that they are Turks." Finally, he reported that Mustafa Necib and his supporters had come to see him to suggest that he not lease his land to Armenian farmers but instead to Muslim peasants.[34] All this incidental information, gleaned in passing, makes it possible to paint, touch by touch, a picture of everyday Ittihadism and the way the CUP's nationalist ideology was translated into practice in the provinces.

In late May, Sapah-Giulian arrived in Amasia, where he was welcomed by the city's parliamentary deputy, İsmail Pasha, members of the local Young Turk club and a group of Hnchak militants (the party had 350 members in the city) headed by Minas Ipekjian and Dr. Haigazun Tabibian.[35] This stay in a city that was reputed to be prosperous made it possible to get a sense of the climate prevailing in the provinces after the revolution. The traditional meeting that was held at the Hnchak clubhouse and attended again by many Young Turks had as its subject "the SDHP and the parliamentary system." It attracted big crowds and provided an occasion for sharp debates. But Sapah-Giulian's 31 May visit to the Ittihadist club was still more instructive. There he encountered people playing backgammon and smoking water pipes, all of them Turkish notables from the city.[36] Tabibian explained to his guest from Constantinople that most of the Armenians had joined the CUP at the time of the July 1908 revolution, the better to forget the horrors of the past. That, however, had lasted a scant two or three months. Their ardor had cooled when delegates dispatched from Salonika arrived, for the Armenian militants had not been invited to the meetings and were excluded from the leadership. A circular is even supposed to have been sent from the Ittihadist Central Committee demanding that local leadership bodies be limited to Muslims. The upshot was that the Armenians had left the CUP and since then were "less generous" toward it.

Yet another of Tabibian's revelations is worth pausing over. He affirmed that, in 1909, a friend and the president of Amasia's Young Turk club, Halim Effendi, had reported that during the Adana massacres the Central Committee of Salonika had sent the club a wire that it had also sent to other *eşrafs*, demanding that they attack the Armenians. It was, in any case, an established fact that the Muslim population had poured into the marketplace and that Halim and Tabibian had immediately gone to see the *mutesarif*, Çerkez Bekir Sâmi Bey[37] (who claimed he was of Armenian origin), to ask that he intervene. Sâmi had gone to the market and made a declaration: "If you want to attack the Armenians, you will have to pass over my dead body; if you dare to attack the Armenians, I will appeal to my Çerkez compatriots in Tokat and they will massacre all of you." After two tension-fraught days, calm was restored. Halim was relieved of his functions as president of the local CUP. It should also be noted that the parliamentary deputy İsmail and his entire family opposed the planned attack. Many suspected Mustafa Necib, who had already brought all the CUP clubs in the region under his control, of having instigated these "disorders."[38] Among other facts reported by Sapah-Giulian, one notes that the policy of "nationalizing" the economy was at work here as well, reinforced by systematic interventions of the Ittihadist club in local industrial and commercial affairs. Thus, people posted at the entry to the city advised arriving merchants not to sell their goods to Armenians while others at the market suggested to customers that they not buy from Armenians. There were also reports that orchards and vegetable gardens had been subject to repeated attacks.[39] While it is not possible to verify all this information, it nevertheless attests to a certain hostility to the Armenian population and great uneasiness, apparently warranted, among the Armenians.

Sapah-Giulian's stay in Tokat, the next stop on his journey, showed that here, as in the towns he had already visited, the SDHP held the dominant position among the Armenians and wielded indisputable political influence even if the party was opposed to the conservatism of local society. At the lecture organized in the public meeting room, not a single woman was present, for "custom still dominated life [in Tokat]."[40]

Sıvas constituted a crucial stage of Sapah-Giulian's journey. His arrival had obviously been announced beforehand: all the government officials and notables welcomed him at the city gates and escorted him to the Hnchak club, which had no fewer than six hundred members in 1911.[41] The atmosphere in Sıvas was very tense: a considerable degree of insecurity reigned in the city, so the Armenians made plans to organize surveillance of the neighborhoods and the market, especially at night.[42] In the region, in which the Armenian presence was much more conspicuous, trade, the crafts and transportation were largely in Armenian hands. At the market, the Armenians complained about endless shake-downs by Turkish officers and notables. They were often told that "the Constitution will not suffice to free you from our clutches; you are our merchandize; we will treat you as our needs dictate."[43] Such remarks illustrate the particular status each group had.

Upon his arrival in Sıvas on 28 June 1911, Sapah-Giulian learned that Mustafa Necib had come to town shortly before him and had tried to sow dissent among the two Armenian political parties. In this city on the borders of the Armenian homeland, the ARF, which was omnipresent in the eastern provinces, and the SDHP, implanted mainly in the western regions, coexisted without problems. The two Committees had even decided, the Hnchak leader writes, to organize a joint self-defense plan. While they had divergent positions – the Dashnaks remained attached to the idea of cooperating with the Ittihadists, while the Hnchaks maintained a frankly hostile position that they proclaimed in public – recurrent provocations and a number of suspicious signs had ultimately alarmed the local Dashnak Committee, which had moved closer to the SDHP, the dominant party in Sıvas.[44]

In the months preceding Sapah-Giulian's visit, the Armenians had noticed that numerous meetings were being held in the homes of the town's leading Turkish citizens. It had, however, finally become clear that the participants belonged to Sıvas's anti-Ittihadist circles; it followed that the meetings were not aimed directly at the Armenians. Another event had left its mark: poisoned sweets had been scattered through the streets of the city's Armenian neighborhoods and children had unsuspectingly picked them up and eaten them. Two had died and several others had to be treated for poisoning. People suspected the Ittihad of this vile act.[45] The tensions in Sıvas had not, then, been engendered by the Turkish-Armenian face-off alone, but were also due to a latent conflict between certain circles of notables and the Young Turk authorities. It would also appear that rumors had been put in circulation in order to turn Muslim public opinion against the Armenians. Sapah-Giulian reports that, at a meeting he held at the Hnchak club with Turkish *hojas*, the *hojas* asked, with obvious concern, if it was true that the Armenian patriarch had demanded the right to attend meetings of the Council of Ministers along with the *şeyh ul-İslam*. Many people were convinced that Mustafa Necib had been spreading rumors of this sort, although it was common knowledge that the SDHP was precisely the only party to advocate the abolition of all traces of religion from the Council of Ministers.[46] Sapah-Giulian, who had firsthand experience of the debate on the separation of church and state from his student days at the École des sciences politiques in Paris and, later, his exile in the French capital, knew what was meant by a secular state. But he was also aware that, in Sıvas, he found himself in a world for which such a debate was something altogether alien.

In the aggregate, all the details passed in review here provide a much clearer picture of the policies implemented by the CUP. It was the Ittihad's activities in the provinces that allowed the Armenian parties to evaluate the concrete contents of the program elaborated by the CUP's Central Committee. Here the Unionists found it harder than in the capital to veil their ethnic-nationalistic intentions.

However, the spring 1912 decision to call early elections for parliament forced the parties to find compromises and gloss over their differences. In Van, the authorities announced a census of the vilayet's male population. "In view of the care the inhabitants of the city take to hide, to avoid either military service or taxes, the numbers given below," the French vice-consul wrote in a report, "are most certainly underestimates." The incumbent members of parliament – Tevfik Bey, Vahan Papazian, and Şeyh Tahir – were hoping to be re-elected with the support of the Ittihad and the ARF, who had concluded an electoral pact. Their opponents – the Hnchaks, the Ramgavars, and the Liberal Entente – had likewise joined forces in support of their candidates.[47]

In Erzerum, Vartkes Seringiulian and Armen Garo were candidates for re-election and again had the support of both the ARF and the CUP.[48] Both men were re-elected, as were Murad in Sis-Kozan, Nazareth Daghavarian in Sıvas, and Kegham in Mush. Vahan Bardizbanian, a Dashnak physician elected in Smyrna on the CUP list, was among the newcomers to parliament.[49] In Siirt, a dark horse by the name of Nâzım Bey won a seat.[50] Nâzım was distinguished by the fact that he had a Muslim father and an Armenian mother, a situation that was extremely rare at the time. He was something of a symbol for the Ittihad, which dreamed of making all Ottoman subjects into Turkish citizens. In Van, Vahan Papazian was replaced by Arshag Vramian,[51] who had much greater prestige in his own party and also the advantage that he was Turkish-speaking and well known in Constantinople Unionist circles.

Armenians and Young Turks in Istanbul: A Marriage of Reason (1911–12)

When the Tripolitanian War broke out with the Italian landing on 4 October 1911, tension in the capital was at its height. This act of colonialist aggression led, as was often the case in Turkey, to increased hostility toward the empire's Christian population. Vahan Papazian notes how badly the non-Turk deputies were treated in parliament. "You would think," he writes, "that we were the ones who were fighting them in Tripolitania."[52]

The war came at the wrong time, for it upset the CUP's plans, whose initial effects in the Anatolian provinces we have just discussed. The creation of the Türk Yurdu Cemiyet (Association of the Turkish Homeland), founded on 3 July 1911 by Mehmed Emin (Yurdakul), Ahmed Ağaoğlu and Yusuf Akçura,[53] testifies to the nationalists' growing influence over the Young Turk movement, gained at the expense of the militants attached to Islam and existing institutions. Thus, the Committee was riven by antagonistic currents, and it seems reasonable to suppose that the radical orientation of the nationalists impelled many others to join the opposition. The conspicuous departure of Colonel Sadık and the young officers in his movement, who immediately joined the opposition, dealt the Ittihad a severe blow.

The opposition had been almost entirely renewed after its liquidation in April 1909. It was reorganized with the foundation, on 21 September 1911, of a new liberal party, Hürriyet ve Ittilâf Fırkasi (Party of Freedom and Understanding). Led by Damad Ferid Pasha (president), Colonel Sadık Bey (vice-president), Dr. Rıza Nur, Şükrü al-Aseki, and Rıza Tevfik, the new party brought together virtually all existing oppositional currents, conservative and liberal alike, and had the support of many different Greek and Armenian circles.[54] Sapah-Giulian notes that the day the Ittilâf and the SDHP signed an agreement to cooperate, "the Ittihadists' apprehension was palpable." He adds that his party was able to influence the Ittilâf's politics thanks to this collaboration, making it more progressive, and that the SDHP played a role in organizing and educating its branches in the provinces.[55] The CUP had united everyone against it; the upshot was a triumph for the opposition in the Constantinople by-elections of November 1911.

The ARF's sixth congress – the first congress of the party to be convened in Constantinople – was held in the same period, from 17 August to 17 September 1911. The party was now confronted with an issue it could no longer put off: whether or not it should maintain its alliance with the Committee of Union and Progress. In the ARF, too, the opposition to collaborating with a committee whose nationalistic ideology had become common knowledge was growing. Papazian writes in his memoirs that the party had already decided to break off relations with the CUP.[56] But this is highly unlikely. On more neutral accounts, many young people in the capital made it known that they were unhappy with the sixth congress's decision to pursue its dialogue with the CUP; the distinction between that and Papazian's statement is worth emphasizing.[57] Rostom, one of the ARF's founders, observed after arriving in Constantinople in order to take part in the congress that the ARF's bureau in Pera was no longer responding to invitations from the branches in the neighborhoods and had lost touch with its own militants. It was probably in order to deal with the *fronde*, which jeopardized the party's credibility, that a meeting was called at the ARF's club in Pera. At this meeting, Aknuni, H. Shahrigian, Arshag Vramian, Ruben Ter Minasian, and others finally agreed to renew the party's pact with the CUP if the Ittihadists agreed to their conditions of 1) a struggle against domestic insecurity; 2) tax reduction; 3) abandonment of the policy of Turkification and Islamicization; 4) creation of genuine equality before the law, a constitutional regime and civil liberties.[58] It might well be asked, however, whether this was not a mere tactic designed to reduce the internal opposition to the prevailing line. Indeed, the Dashnak leadership in Constantinople cultivated an ambiguous attitude toward the Young Turks. Its relations with the CUP had certainly cooled after the massacres in Cilicia, but the break between the two parties had never been consummated.

Isolated in the face of a reinvigorated opposition, the CUP regained the initiative by setting out to negotiate a new agreement with the ARF. The resulting discussions, however, remained secret: they are not mentioned in any official ARF publication. We have to turn to an oppositional newspaper to form some idea of them.[59] Sapah-Giulian revealed that there were in fact two agreements. One, signed on 11 November, was for internal use and bore on the coming legislative elections. The contents of the other, secret agreement, signed in January 1912, have never been made public. The Hnchak leader, however, describes them in detail in a series of articles on the relations between the Dashnaks and Ittihadists that was published 18 months after the agreement was concluded. Here we make the rather surprising discovery that most of the stipulations of this agreement concern Persia – more precisely, the activity of the Dashnak military chief Ephrem Khan. Thanks to this document, we see for the first time that the ARF's transnational dimension and its activities outside the Ottoman Empire constituted, in certain circumstances, a bargaining chip in its negotiations with the CUP. In other words, to win concessions from its Young Turk allies in the Ottoman context, the Dashnaktsutiun occasionally had to throw its influence in other areas into the scales. Persia, the case to hand, had become much more than a field of action for Dashnak *fedayis* on mission. Ephrem Khan and his commandos were the veritable initiators of the Iranian constitutional revolution; they comprised a force that put itself at the head of the country's progressive groups and familiarized them with revolutionary ideas.[60]

The January 1912 secret agreement stipulated, notably, that the ARF would curb Ephrem Khan's activities in Persia, which had encouraged Russian ambitions. The party agreed not to conduct armed operations in the country and not to involve Ottoman subjects in its other activities there. According to Sapah-Giulian, the Western Bureau immediately sent the corresponding instructions to its Committee in Persia and also decided to review its pro-Russian positions, calling a halt to the activity of Ephrem, who was reputed to be following directives from Moscow.[61] Thus, the Western Bureau is supposed to have firmly opposed Ephrem's attack on the city of Hamadan. Sapah-Giulian goes so far as to speculate that the ARF might have been involved in the 6 May 1912 assassination of the leader of the Persian revolution, which took place under mysterious conditions at the entrance to the city.[62]

The Committee of Union and Progress, however, apparently did not confine itself to concluding pacts with the Dashnaks. It is highly probable that it also encouraged the ARF to engage in a dialogue with the Hnchaks aimed at bringing them into an alliance with it. The ARF's way of approaching the SDHP is quite interesting. The maneuvering began at a time when the Hnchak leader, Sapah-Giulian, whose hostility to this plan was well known, was touring the provinces.[63] Officially, the two Armenian parties were negotiating an electoral agreement. However, the driving force behind this rapprochement was the Marxist journalist Parvus, a Russian Jew living in Germany. Parvus, a socialist who had entered into relations with a few Hnchak leaders in Constantinople, was the founder of Millî İktisat (A Journal *National Economy*) and also an arms dealer and an informer working for the German intelligence service.[64] He was known at the time for having, at the CUP's request, taken several Georgian socialist refugees under his protection in Istanbul and then dispatched them to Adjaria to foment an anti-Russian rebellion there. In arguing for his plan to bring the two Armenian parties to collaborate, he pointed to the need for a union of socialist forces, in accordance with the decisions of the Amsterdam Congress. A number of militants seem to have found this splendid demonstration convincing. To resolve the predictable problems connected with setting the number of Armenian parliamentary deputies, Parvus promised to serve as an intermediary with the CUP. The initial arrangement seems to have been that the Armenians would be given twenty seats, of which two or three would go to "neutral" candidates. Finally, written agreement was reached to the effect that the ARF would receive nine seats and the SDHP eight; the remaining seats would go to whichever party succeeded in taking them.[65]

When Sapah-Giulian returned to Istanbul, the pact had almost been finalized. On his account, the Ittihad was in a ticklish situation, but had adroitly secured the ARF's support and was now trying to rally the Hnchaks to its side by way of a pact between the ARF and SDHP. Thus Parvus, he writes, "was in the process of doing the CUP a great service."[66] Matters had advanced so far that the Hnchak leader had a great deal of difficulty in turning the situation around. At the September 1911 meeting at which the agreement was to have been finalized, K. Gozigian, who was representing the Hnchaks at the negotiations, as Sapah-Giulian had suggested, told the two Dashnak representatives, Papazian and A[knuni], that he was prepared to sign if he were shown a document from the CUP's Central Committee that "bore its official seal" and declared that it agreed to the establishment of "Armenian autonomy." The Dashnaks pointed out that they had obtained an oral promise and that they would vouch for the CUP. This provided Gozigian the opportunity to turn the offer down.[67] The next day, Parvus, in his capacity as former intermediary, rushed to the Hnchak club and upbraided his socialist comrades for having made light of his mediation by rejecting the agreement. He also argued that the presence of two socialist parties in the Ottoman parliament would have had an excellent effect in Europe, adding that, in rejecting the agreement "for narrowly nationalistic reasons," the SDHP was working against socialism.[68] Sapah-Giulian's reply was in the same vein: it was regrettable that a convinced socialist such as Parvus, he riposted, could support a nationalistic party "that has the Adana massacres on its conscience [as well as] murders, kidnappings and confiscations of property carried out to further the objectives of Turkish nationalism."[69]

From these examples, we learn a number of lessons about the political practice of the Committee of Union and Progress. The CUP, which already had the main mechanisms of the state apparatus in its hands and could utilize them as it saw fit, while throwing a few crumbs of power to those who agreed to serve it or collaborate with it, was now seeking to gain the time it needed to put its plans into effect. To that end, it did not hesitate to have its opponents who represented a real threat murdered or exiled, while guaranteeing the criminals impunity. We can thus legitimately ask if the permanent insecurity reigning in the eastern provinces – plunder, kidnapping, localized massacres – was not the result of a plan.[70] In 1912, in any case, the situation there had deteriorated so badly that a sharp debate broke out in Armenian circles as to whether an alliance should be concluded with the Ittihad or the Ittifâl. The SDHP was convinced that it was necessary to harass the CUP in order to deny it the leisure to translate its program into reality ("To distract its attention from Armenia," as Sapah-Giulian put it).[71] In provincial Turkish circles, too, the Ittihad had earned the enmity of groups exasperated by the constant meddling in their internal affairs of local Young Turks, who were often less than respectable sorts. There were even cases in which Armenians intervened in these Turkish circles as peacemakers, in order to re-establish calm: for instance, when the Unionist club in Erba refused to confirm the appointment of a religious leader who was not a member of the club; or again, after an attack on the Ittihadist club of Balıkeser.[72] Furthermore, certain government officials did not share Young Turkey's political vision, as was shown when, in spring 1912, the *kaymakam* of Niksar, İhsan Bey, and the commander of the corresponding military district, Sabih Bey, entrusted the SDHP leadership with "valuable" documents emanating from the Unionist Central Committee on the one hand and the government on the other.[73] According to Sapah-Giulian, these texts all had to do with the way the Armenians were to be treated and the means to be employed in order to "rid the country of the Armenians and gain control of all their real estate and other assets." Sabih Bey "doubtless thought," Sapah-Giulian adds, "that we had no information on that head."[74] An article in the Hnchaks' official organ stated even more clearly what the SDHP believed the Turkists' intentions to be:

> When the least occasion offers ... Turkish nationalism, which, today, has the government of the country in its grip, will, without hesitation, ruthlessly massacre the Armenians, as a historical *necessity*. And, this time, it will massacre them more mercilessly than in 1895–6, more violently than during the Catastrophe of Adana. The psychology that makes for massacres is an abiding one; it has deep roots ... It is also plain that the old and new representatives of Turkish nationalism have no desire whatsoever to accept the idea of the existence, development and vitality of the Armenian people.[75]

This viewpoint, however, remained that of a minority of Armenians, even if "no great benefits could be expected from the constitutional regime," in the words of Gabriel Noradounghian, who would soon become the first and last non-Muslim Ottoman foreign minister, who expressed that opinion at a dinner he gave early in 1912 for the four Dashnak deputies and Krikor Zohrab.[76]

In these conditions, it is easy to imagine the atmosphere reigning in the Ottoman Empire during the spring 1912 election campaign. This election, known as the *sopalı seçim* ("the big-stick election"), shocked more than one observer because of the violent methods and intimidation to which the CUP resorted to ensure the victory of its candidates.[77] The number one enemy was the Ittilâf, which counted many renegades from Unionist ranks among its members, notably non-Turks who had been excluded from any and all positions of responsibility in the CUP. In the weeks preceding the second legislative elections, the two parties traded blows with a vengeance. Unsurprisingly, the newly elected parliament had an Ittihadist majority and, in certain Armenian circles, electoral interests eventually gained the upper hand over questions of substance. Said Pasha formed the new cabinet; Mehmed Cavid was put back in charge of the Ministry of Finance.

It seems that, in this regime, power could only change hands by force. In May–June 1912, Colonel Sadık Bey, the Ittilâf's vice-president, stepped up his pressure on the cabinet to the point that this pressure could be described as a *coup d'état*; he had the support of young officers known as *Halâskâr Zâbitan* (Savior Officers), a majority of whom came from the army in Macedonia.[78] On 21 July, the grand vizier stepped down in favor of a liberal cabinet formed by Ǧazi Ahmed Muhtar Pasha, which included Noradounghian as foreign minister. In some sense, Prince Sabaheddin's outlook had come to power for the first time (if one ignores the brief existence of the Tevfik cabinet in April 1909). The object was to restore confidence, in particular among non-Turkish groups, by applying the prince's much ballyhooed decentralization program. Shortly after these events, it was learned that Mehmed Talât and Mustafa Rahmi had returned to Salonika; they were soon followed by Cavid and Dr. Nâzım.[79]

To make certain that he could count on the army, Ǧazi Muhtar appointed a graduate of Saint-Cyr, General Nâzım Pasha, as minister of war; Nâzım was a Çerkez from Istanbul whom Marshal Göltz considered to be the best officer in the Ottoman Army.[80] The ARF was not slow to draw the lessons of these changes. In an 18 July 1912 declaration, the Western Bureau announced that it had effectively broken with the Young Turks.[81] In the same period, several books were published, the obvious purpose of which was to get at the truth about the massacres in Cilicia.[82]

Significantly, the ARF waited until mid-September 1912 to create a special committee including Rupen Ter Minasian and Sepastatsi Murad. Its first working meeting took place in Constantinople. The "question of self-defense" was on the agenda, and this was the first time since the July 1908 revolution that the party discussed the issue. Those at the meeting agreed that a self-defense project would require "years and years" (of work), and that the party did not have "enough responsible cadres in the provinces or the necessary funds" to realize it.[83] Was the ARF's suddenly renewed interest in "self-defense" a consequence of the deterioration of the situation in the eastern provinces? Perhaps. One can, however, also speculate that the momentary elimination of the ARF from the Istanbul political scene gave it a margin to maneuver that it had not previously enjoyed.

The Armenians in the Balkan Crisis

The Ottoman Empire, which found itself confronting the threat of war from the moment that Ğazi Ahmed Muhtar's cabinet took the reins of government, was not, according to contemporary observers, in a position to fight. Its finances were at a low ebb and its army was poorly organized and demoralized after several years of lack of discipline. For the first time, however, non-Muslims would be taking part in a war; they were mobilized just as their compatriots were. The patriotic appeals thus concerned all Ottoman subjects, and the Armenians were not the last to rise to the "defense of the fatherland."

The Balkan alliance seems to have surprised even the European diplomats, who were concerned, to be sure, about the fate of the Ottoman Balkans, but from the standpoint of the reforms that they hoped to compel the Sublime Porte to carry out. The specialists on the conflict concur that Greek Prime Minister Venizelos hid his hand with consummate skill and played a decisive role in forging the unlikely Balkan alliance.

In September 1912 a festive atmosphere, laced with patriotic sentiments, reigned in Constantinople. The most enthusiastic counted on celebrating their victory in Sofia before the year was out, Bulgaria having been promoted to the rank of the empire's main foe. The liberal cabinets, made up of experienced men who were aware of the weakness of the army and its lack of modern arms and equipment, were opposed to the war, as was the majority of the Ottoman parliament. Only the Young Turks, who had lost most of their seats in the new assembly, actively campaigned in favor of going to war.[84] In an article published in the 21 September 1912 *Tanin*, a semi-official Ittihad organ, Enis Avni Bey wrote, under the pseudonym Aka Gündüz: "Every spot on which I tread shall spurt forth blood...If I leave one stone upon another, may the home I leave behind me be razed."[85] This longing for a good fight reflected the Young Turks' ambition to profit from the opportunity offered by the war to win back territory lost over the past few decades. The violence that had attended the interventions of the Ottoman army in Macedonia and Albania in the recent past perhaps explains the declaration that the foreign minister, Noradounghian, made in the foreign press to the effect that the Ottoman army would observe the rules of civilized countries in waging the war and that there would be no massacres in the areas it occupied. On the afternoon of 21 September, the Ittilâf organized a rally on the square in front of the Sultan Ahmed Mosque; 100,000 people took part. One of the first to speak was an old acquaintance of ours, Diran Kelekian, the editor-in-chief of *Sabah*, who declared that he was in favor of going to war and made a patriotic speech that ended with the elegantly defensive formula: "Either the Ottomans will leave 30 million graves behind them or they will show Europe what stuff they are made of by crushing the Balkan states."[86]

On the evening of the same day, in the same square, the Ittihad held its own meeting under Talât's lead. Those in attendance were younger. The list of speakers included Talât himself, Hasan Fehmi, Cemaleddin Arif, Hagop Boyajian, and the ARF's representative,

Dr. Garabed Pashayan.[87] "The ARF," Pashayan said, "is generally opposed to war, which produces misery and privation for the people. However, it can only affirm its approval of a combat the purpose of which is to defend the fatherland against external aggression." While Pashayan's speech, which hewed closely to the Dashnaktsutiun's line, was not character-ized by patriotic excess, it nonetheless reaffirmed the ARF's solidarity with its former allies in these difficult circumstances (the party had broken with the CUP on 18 July). The last speaker, Ömer Naci, who was considered one of the best CUP propagandists, appealed to the "spirit of a race" that had known only victory; Naci exhorted his listeners to "go spit in the faces of the handful of petty nations that insult the seven hundred years of existence of the Turkish race."[88] In this atmosphere of patriotic one-upmanship, many Armenians volun-teered for the army, as did many Çerkez and Kurds. It should be noted, however, that there was no draft in Syria, Mesopotamia, or the eastern provinces of Anatolia. Despite all this, the statements that foreign minister Noradounghian made to the reporter from *Le Temps* revealed that he was personally opposed to the war.[89]

Both the Ittilâf and the Ittihad solicited Armenian support for their positions. The Ittihadist opposition, however, knew much better how to mobilize large crowds. Moreover, it could, although it was no longer in power, rely on the networks that it had built up in all classes of society. Turning the first public demonstrations to account, it mobilized university students in particular in order to pressure and destabilize Ahmed Muhtar's liberal govern-ment. It knew better than any of its rivals what issues could bring people together, such as rejection of Article 23 of the Treaty of Berlin, which provided for reforms in Rumelia, or of the idea of equality for all the empire's subjects – a theme symptomatic of the state of Ottoman society in the period. By far the most impressive demonstration of the day was the students', started by one hundred or so Young Turk militants on 24 September 1912. It quickly turned into a semi-insurrection and put the government, whose hostility to the war was unpopular, in a delicate situation: the demonstrators accused it of "crawling before the Balkan states."[90]

Thus, the government was caught between the hammer of a public opinion burning to go to war and the anvil of the great powers, who were urging it to ratify the celebrated 23 August 1880 "law of the vilayets," which would reform the local administration and trans-late Article 23 of the Treaty of Berlin into practice in the regions that the Balkan states sought to acquire. Hence, it was forced to publish a declaration that cautiously affirmed that the reforms were still under examination and that there could be no question of ratifying an unconstitutional law. At the same time, however, Noradounghian promised the Western ambassadors that Article 23 would soon be applied; this sparked new demonstrations. In order to avoid war, the Council had no other choice than to make the concessions that the Balkan states were demanding, and, in particular, to enact Article 23.[91]

It will readily be imagined how easy it was for the Ittihad's networks to turn "Turkish" public opinion against reforms that were considered to be acts of treachery that profited the empire's non-Muslim groups, who were perceived as enemies enjoying the support of the Christian powers. Torn between hopes sparked by the liberal government's promises to enact reforms and alarm engendered by the public's hostility to the slightest concession, Armenian circles assumed their responsibilities and summoned their compatriots to do their duty. They were, however, unsettled by *Tanin*'s affirmation that, if Article 23 were to be applied in the vilayets of European Turkey, "Article 61 would follow on its heels" – that is, the Article of the Treaty of Berlin that concerned the Armenian provinces.[92] The cause-and-effect relation-ship was quite clearly spelled out, as was the parallel between events in the Balkans and the Armenian provinces in eastern Anatolia. *Tanin*'s remarks offered a glimpse of the Ittihad's vision of the empire's future and the depth of its determination to preserve its territorial integrity. It left the Armenians with little hope that even the smallest reform would be enacted in the east. A few weeks later, after the Ottoman army's defeat at the hands of the

Balkan Coalition, the CUP again assayed a rapprochement with the ARF, passing in silence over the positions it had taken in public on the eve of the war. The moving spirit behind this renewed invitation to collaborate was Mehmed Talât, who extended it to Zohrab as well. The situation was critical, and Talât accordingly made a number of promises that clearly contra-dicted the CUP's long-standing positions: he held out the prospect of enacting the 1880 law on the vilayets, resolving agrarian questions (land theft) and repressing looters.[93]

The ARF's Western Bureau had observed the Balkan Coalition's initial successes with a certain alarm, aware that the Armenians could not expect the slightest help from Europe or Russia if the Turks should turn against them. Caution was in order, in Simon Zavarian's estimation: "This is crucial, for, if the Turks are defeated, they will naturally seek to avenge themselves on the Armenians, who constitute the weakest group and cannot defend themselves."[94] There were grounds for these apprehensions. During the Balkan War and in the following months, the situation in the eastern provinces had deteriorated, due in part to the arrival of Bosnian *muhacirs* fleeing the fighting; large numbers of them had been sent pouring into the Armenian vilayets. These refugees, their feelings against Christians in gen-eral at a fever pitch, worried Vahan Papazian. "We feared," he wrote, "that, like locusts, they would devour everything the Armenians possessed and carry out a new massacre of them. Such was the government's diabolical plan."[95]

In the field, the Armenian soldiers did their duty, particularly in defending Janina. Observers unanimously declared that they had fought bravely and noted the competence of the Armenian officers, who were especially effective as artillerymen. Like the rest of the Ottoman army, they suffered many casualties.[96] In a defeated, humiliated country, however, that did not count for much.

The Ittihad's leaders in particular perceived these events as a national and personal tragedy, proof of the total failure of the grandiose plans. Many of them had spontaneously enlisted in the army, beginning with Talât,[97] while others such as Cemal did their duty as officers. Dr. Nâzım was even subjected to the humiliation of being arrested in the historical headquarters of the Committee of Union and Progress when the Greeks captured Salonika in October 1912; arrested with him was the Albanian deputy from Derviş Bey, the leader of one of the Committee's most active groups of *fedayis*. Nâzım and Serez, who were taken under heavy guard to Greece, had at least been spared the spectacle of the plunder of the Muslim and Jewish populations, as well as the murders and rapes committed by the Greek soldiers under the gaze of shocked witnesses.[98]

All of General Nâzım's courage and intelligence was required to halt the advance of the Bulgarian army in Çatalca, a few dozen kilometers to the west of Constantinople, and to free the other Young Turk leaders who had been apprehended during the battle[99] as they were attempting to flee to the capital. This minister of war, despised by the CUP leaders, now rescued the very men who would assassinate him a few months later. During these events, a new Young Turk paramilitary organization was to take its first steps in subversion, sabotage, and political murder. It would soon take the name Teşkilât-ı Mahsusa (Special Organization) and would play an important role in preparing the new conquest of Edirne in July 1913.[100]

In a declaration published on 25 December 1912, the Ittihad's *bête noire*, the Hnchak Central Committee, summed up the dilemma with which the Armenian authorities were confronted after this war, which put an end to the Turkish presence in Europe: "In this criti-cal hour, this appalling, fertile hour, fraught with consequences, the Armenian Question has also loomed up: it is one of the thorniest questions there is, one of the most difficult to resolve, caught as it is in the iron ring of the most unfavorable circumstances." The editors of the Hnchaks' official organ went on to point out that Young Turkey had been unable to carry out the slightest reform, observing that its constitution "was a military 'constitution,' one which proved, for that very reason, from the standpoint of the interests of the people of the state, wretchedly sterile." Alluding to the remedies the Young Turk leaders had prescribed for the country, they concluded that the Young Turks had "turned out to be, not doctors, but veterinarians; and not even that, but, rather, butchers killing animals in a slaughterhouse."[101]

PART III

Young Turks and Armenians Face to Face (December 1912–March 1915)

Chapter 1

Transformations in the Committee of Union and Progress after the First Balkan War, 1913

The humiliating defeat dealt to the Ottoman Empire by the states that emerged from its former European possessions led to what the Committee of Union and Progress had feared the most – the demise of European Turkey and the re-centering of the empire in Asia. The war had, moreover, set off vast population movements. According to official sources, 500,000 to 600,000 refugees had been expelled from Rumelia and Macedonia, and the state was looking for ways and means of settling them in Asia Minor. In an interview with a French diplomat, the Turkish ambassador to Austria-Hungary and former grand vizier, Hilmi Pasha, suggested "a project to revitalize Asia Minor" by resettling these refugees there, at a cost of 250 to 300 million franks. He suggested, as a likely place for the resettlement, "the district of Adana, [which] is so fertile that it is like a little Egypt," and expressed hope that French capital would back the project.[1] This geographical choice was probably not fortuitous, but rather part of the general Young Turk policy of relocating refugees from the Balkans in zones that were considered strategically important, even when that ran counter to the interests of their native inhabitants. Such was the case in vilayets with an Armenian population.

Kâmil Pasha's cabinet, after waging a war that it had not wanted, had to confront the Young Turk opposition, which renounced the terms of the armistice concluded after the rout of the Ottoman forces. The liberal government was also under pressure from the powers, which demanded that it accept the Balkan states' conditions. The coup d'état that brought down Kâmil's cabinet on 23 January 1913 thus put an end to a political crisis engendered by the Ottoman defeat. Once again, power changed hands by force of arms. But the importance of this particular event should not be downplayed: it marked the Ittihadist Central Committee's true assumption of control over the executive and went hand-in-hand with an unmistakable accentuation of the Committee's militaristic orientation,[2] which saw the armed forces claiming the role of guardians of the constitution (meşrutiyet) and freedom (hurriyet). The best proof lies in the methods that the Young Turks used to seize power. The ease with which Enver Bey and his accomplices were able to cross protective barriers, make their way into the Sublime Porte, and shoot the minister of war, Nâzım Pasha – they did not encounter the slightest resistance – is at the very least suspect. There is every reason to think that a part of the palace guard was in league with the military members of the CUP. The reinforcement of the position of the militarists also doubtless explains the appointment of General Mahmud Şevket, the strong man of the moment, to the office of grand vizier on the evening of 23 January 1913, as well as the early March nominations of Colonel Ahmed Cemal to the newly created post of "guardian [or military governor] of Istanbul" and Lieutenant-Colonel

Halil (Kut) Bey, a young uncle of Enver Bey's, to the post of commander of the garrison stationed in the capital.[3] However, the new grand vizier was soon recommending that officers be prevented from interfering in politics. It is quite possible that, in thus opposing the politicization of the army, he was responding to the concerns of a faction of the Ittihadist Central Committee that was trying to free itself of the intensifying domination of the "young officers" and diminish their influence. Pursuing his advantage and profiting from the demoralization of the officer corps engendered by the defeat in the Balkans, Şevket also proposed to carry out a thoroughgoing reform of the army if it proved impossible to depoliticize it.[4] It is likely that part of the Unionist Central Committee reacted favorably to this initiative and also to Şevket's appeal for German assistance, which it regarded as the natural sequel to the first experiments carried out by General Göltz.[5] The grand vizier and his supporters surely imagined that calling on someone from outside the Ottoman sphere would make it easier to limit or even halt the growing politicization of the officers. But in doing so, Şevket was launching a frontal assault on a faction of the party whose support he needed at a time when he had to defuse the explosive political situation bequeathed to him by Kâmil's cabinet. His overriding task was to bring about a final resolution of the Balkan conflict – that is, to sign a peace treaty confirming the surrender of Edirne – which is precisely what the young officers led by Enver were unwilling to accept.[6]

This question doubtless dominated debate at the Ittihad's 31 January 1913 Central Committee meeting. However, the effect of this meeting, to judge from what we know of it, was above all to confirm Talât's growing ascendancy over the Committee and force the party to appeal to religious sentiment to galvanize Muslim public opinion. It is even said that at the same meeting Ahmed Agayev (Ağaoğlu) argued that Islam was in peril and called for a holy alliance of all the groups in the empire as well as a declaration of jihad.[7] The creation by the Committee, on the very same day, of the Müdafa-i Milliye Cemiyeti (Committee for Public Welfare), along with the formation not long thereafter (in June 1913) of Türk Gücü (Turkish Strength), a paramilitary organization whose anthem was composed by Ziya Gökalp, were evidence of profound uneasiness and a radicalization of the movement. Talât's ever tighter grip on the party leadership doubtless resulted from these tensions. Talât profited from his increasing dominion over the party to impose on 16 March 1913 Major Ali Fethi (Okyar)[8] as both a member of the Ittihadist Central Committee and its secretary general, in the hope of counterbalancing the growing weight of the leader of the party's other major faction, Enver.[9]

The grand vizier, Mahmud Şevket, who had initially served as a guarantor for the Young Turk government, was from this point on nothing more than a pawn with no real political influence, pushed back and forth between the two main factions of the CUP. In his isolation, he shared his preoccupations with his confidant of the day, Ahmed Cemal, the real master of Istanbul, somewhat naively disclosing to him his planned reform of the Ottoman army, which consisted in putting one corps of the army in the hands of a German general and appointing German officers to the general staff. According to Cemal, the grand vizier believed that this would allow him to control the political activities of the officers associated with the CUP.[10]

Şevket, however, manifestly lacked the means to bend the officer corps to his will; notwithstanding the Kaiser's 6 June decision to appoint a general to head the German military mission, he was in no position to pursue his objectives. On the morning of 11 June, while riding through the streets of Istanbul on his way to the Sublime Porte, he was shot down by four gunmen.[11]

A few days earlier, on Friday, 6 June 1913, the principal Unionist leaders had held a meeting at Fener Yalu, near Haydarpaşa, with an agenda that read: "The political situation of the country is dangerous." On 10 June, around 10 p.m., the officers of the army of Çatalca, supporters of Enver, had made a show of their hostility and ordered Şevket's cabinet to resign. Should it fail to, the officers threatened, "the army will march on Constantinople." On the testimony of a well-informed diplomat, "the grand vizier wanted to quit the scene, but the leader of the party, Talât Bey, had urged Şevket to remain in office to the end, in accordance with his oath." The French intelligence service did, however, note that "the secret Committee is in constant contact with the army of Chatalja."[12] In other words, the Ittihad's Central Committee had incited the "young officers" under Enver's control to call on the cabinet to resign, while Talât, for his part, demanded that the grand vizier remain in his post. The tensions between the two factions of the CUP had obviously been set aside, and agreement had been reached within the Committee to get rid of General Şevket. The Central Committee must have decided that it would be more productive to have the grand vizier assassinated than to let him resign, an assumption that appears all the more likely when we recall that this murder, attributed to the opposition, made it possible for the Committee of Union and Progress to declare a state of emergency in the country and liquidate all its adversaries once and for all. The Ittihad had already vainly sought, early in March 1913, to credit the idea that Prince Sabaheddin's secretary, Safvet Lutfi Bey, had hatched an oppositional "plot."[13] But the affair had not produced the desired results, making it impossible to suppress the opposition. With the assassination of General Şevket, as with the "events of 31 March in 1909," the CUP had acquired the means it needed to deal a fatal blow to its political foes. On the day of the murder, a French diplomat noted, Talât and the leading members of the CUP "were, together with Enver Bey, constantly at the side of the military governor of Istanbul [Cemal Bey]."[14] Şevket quite clearly fell victim to a conspiracy that was squarely within the tradition of the Ittihadists, who took advantage of it to set up a military dictatorship. Events followed in rapid succession thereafter: the CUP, "which [held] power from the death of Mahmud Şevket Pasha on," saw to it that Prince Said Halim was given the post of grand vizier, and then proceeded to arrest several hundred people.[15] Three days later, Mehmed Talât was named minister of the interior and Halil (Menteşe) became president of the Council of State.[16] The courts also did their work much faster than usual: on 24 June, it was announced that 12 defendants had been condemned to death by court-martial and executed the same day by hanging in Sultan Bayazid square.[17] The "authors" of the murder and the leaders of the opposition were condemned and executed in a single, sweeping operation. The legal opposition was outlawed: Prince Sabaheddin and Şerif Pasha, accused of instigating the murder, were condemned to death in absentia – that is, invited to remain in exile in Paris.

The military defeats and recurrent domestic crises had probably convinced the Unionists of the need to reform the institutions and administration of the empire – or, in a word, to assume full control of the state and its institutions. The Committee of Union and Progress, which had until then been reluctant to transform itself into a political party or even to take the affairs of state directly in hand, now seemed finally to have accepted this option, or even actively sought it out.

The CUP's official assumption of power went hand-in-hand with a mutation in the party itself: the "young officers" led by Enver Bey[18] were no longer content simply to do the Central Committee's dirty work, but now demanded their share of the pie. The Committee's leaders, beginning with Mehmed Talât, had henceforth to reckon with Enver's faction. If only temporarily, Ahmed Cemal, who held the key post of military governor of Istanbul, also became, after the murder of the grand vizier, master of the capital and of the Committee's destiny and, as a result, another central CUP figure.[19] According to Turfan, even the composition of Said Halim's cabinet had to be submitted to the "young officers" for approval.[20]

The CUP general congress of 18 September–11 October 1913 was thus exceptionally important. Not much has ever been revealed about the decisions it took. It is known, however, that ideologues such as Ahmed Agayev, the editor-in-chief of *Tercuman Hakikat*, as well as Hüseyin Cahid and İsmail Hakkı Babanzâde, the editors of *Tanin*, enjoyed increasing ideological influence at this congress.[21] According to a French diplomat, the Young Turks "seemed to have been won over to the idea of administrative decentralization." He saw evidence of this in the project to give provincial governing councils the right to approve the local budget.[22] Fethi Bey, named the congress's secretary general, is even supposed to have recommended "that the government negotiate with the Armenians in order to conclude an agreement like the one reached with the Arabs."[23]

But the congress also came to the conclusion that the parliamentary system was hobbling its efforts, and accordingly proposed to limit sessions of parliament to four months. It further suggested giving the Council of Ministers the right to promulgate temporary laws between sessions "whenever there [was] an urgent necessity" for them[24] – we shall see how this decision was exploited in 1915 to deport and plunder the Armenian population. The most important decision of this congress, however, had to do with the internal transformation of the CUP, which now abandoned its status as a "secret" organization and officially became a political party.[25] A set of "by-laws of Union and Progress" was drafted and adopted. It provided for the creation of three governing bodies: 1) a 50-member General Council, headed by a president, which was empowered to settle questions involving the general administration of the party; 2) a nine-member Central Bureau, representing the parliamentary faction, which was designated by the president of the General Council and was supposed to provide a liaison between the CUP and parliament; and 3) a Central Committee, elected by the congress and headed by a secretary general, which was composed of nine members who were neither senators nor deputies to parliament and who were charged with overseeing all the organizations associated with the party in Constantinople or the provinces.[26]

The by-laws also provided for a reorganization of the activities of the clubs in the provinces, dissolving them at the level of the *kaza* and maintaining only the sections in the biggest *sancaks* and the capitals of the vilayets.[27] To ensure that its plans would be enacted, the congress established a "program committee" made up of İsmail Hakkı (Babanzâde); (Eyub) Sabri Bey; Mehmed Ziya (Gökalp); Emrullah Effendi, a former minister of education; Hüseyin Kadri Bey; (Kara) Kemal Bey, a parliamentary deputy from Constantinople; Ahmed Nesimi, a member of the Central Committee; Ahmed Agayev; Ali Bey, the CUP's representative in Mamuret ul-Aziz; and (Küçük) Talât Bey, CUP inspector in Smyrna.[28]

The "by-laws of Union and Progress" stipulated that the local committee in each *sancak* was to be headed by a "responsible secretary"[29] appointed by the Central Committee. The responsible secretaries, who were to be assisted by a committee comprising from four to six members, supervised the organizations in their district, convened committee meetings, drew up their agendas, organized the meetings, and named corresponding members. The by-laws further stipulated that local committees "were to follow the Central Committee's instructions."[30]

The congress elected the following people to the bureau of the general council: Ahmed Rıza, Cavid Bey, Hüseyin Cahid, İsmail Hakkı, (Bedros) Halajian, and Ahmed Agayev (who received the fewest votes of all those elected), as well as the secretary general of the Central Committee and a former parliamentary deputy from Serez, Midhat Şükrü. It also elected Dr. Bahaeddin Şakir; (Eyub) Sabri Bey; Dr. Rüsûhi Bey; Dr. Nâzım; Mehmed Ziya (Gökalp), formerly a parliamentary deputy from Dyarbekir; Emrullah Effendi, a former minister of education; Mehmed Talât Bey; (Kara) Kemal Bey, the Committee's inspector in Constantinople; and Riza Bey, its inspector in Bursa.[31]

The Ittihadist Central Committee, in creating a General Council by which it was elected in its turn, doubtless hoped to sideline the "young officers." Abandoning its status as a secret organization, it doubtless hoped to acquire a semblance of respectability. But the CUP's fifth congress, which concluded that the decision-making center should be transferred from the clandestine Central Committee to a General Council – "the parliament of the Party for

Union and Progress" – only reinforced the centralism of the system and its impact in the provinces, inasmuch as the responsible secretaries were appointed by the Committee itself and placed under its direct control.

These changes notwithstanding, Mehmed Talât and his faction remained dependent on the Unionist officers, notably when the Bulgarians attacked the Serbs and Greeks during the night of 29–30 June 1913. To make good on this unhoped-for opportunity to win back lost territory, the CUP needed the young officers' support. Despite the economic crisis, an attack on Edirne was launched at Talât's urging. On 17 July, Enver declared that the government would not yield to the pressure of the powers – they had called for a halt to the offensive – adding that he himself had ordered the troops to advance. The same day, Ziya Gökalp published an appeal, entitled "The New Attila," which urged the army to forge ahead. These statements were no doubt intended to encourage the cabinet, not all of whose members approved of this operation, to give unqualified support to this CUP initiative. In the end, it was Talât who obtained authorization for the Imperial Army's march on Edirne from the Council of Ministers. Ahmed İzzet,[32] the chief of staff and minister of war, remained hesitant about and even opposed to a resumption of hostilities, but had to bow to pressure from Enver, who threatened to relieve him of his post. The capture of the ancient Ottoman capital strengthened the position of the clan of young officers, which found its symbolic representative in Enver, even if the city fell almost without a fight.[33] But this unexpected success refurbished, above all, the prestige of the Committee of Union and Progress. It also made the anti-European and, more generally, anti-Christian current that dominated Ottoman public opinion still more vehement than it had been. The "victory" did not undo the collective humiliation experienced after the debacle of the first Balkan War. Rather, it whetted a spirit of revenge that found a target in the Christian groups in the empire, which were identified with the Balkan states and Christian Europe. The massacres perpetrated by the soldiers in Tekirdağ/Rodosto from 1 July to 3 July 1913 can perhaps be attributed to these reactions. As often occurred when persecutions of this kind were committed, the Istanbul press misrepresented "the Rodosto events," casting them as a revolt that the army had had to "put down." The correspondent of the newspaper *Gohag*, who had himself witnessed these events, denounced the Turkish press's misleading interpretation of them.[34] He reported that, on 1 July, a boat had arrived carrying men who had volunteered to help establish control over the city, which had been abandoned by the Bulgarian forces. The Greek metropolitan, the Armenian primate, and representatives of the local governing bodies went out to greet the new arrivals. *Gohag*'s correspondent reported that the soldiers had surrounded the city's neighborhoods, an Armenian was gunned down, the city's inhabitants panicked, and the stores in the bazaar were hastily abandoned by the Armenian shopkeepers. According to this journalist, the Armenians had been directly targeted and the soldiers, commanded by Şerif Bey, had been informed which houses belonged to them. The soldiers proceeded to pillage the Armenians' homes and stage massacres in the city and especially its environs, where the Armenians worked as farmers. Many Armenians saved themselves by taking refuge in the consulates or the homes of foreign residents. The clusters of refugees were presented by the military commander as proof of a revolt in the making. At any rate, such was the rumor that the officers started in the city, while simultaneously ordering that the Armenians immediately turn in their arms. To avoid all possible provocation, the Armenians remained in their widely scattered places of refuge for a whole week while stores were looted, fields were burned, and a mill was partially destroyed. Thanks to an intervention by foreign battleships, the Armenian population of Tekirdağ managed to emerge from this explosion of violence without greater losses. It was estimated at the time that around one hundred people had been killed, not counting the "missing."

The steps taken by Armenian organizations to bring about reforms in the provinces were doubtless the origin of this violence, which should probably be regarded as a clear message sent to the Armenians by the CUP as a Thracian the daily extension of in the east. Localized massacres also occurred at this time: one in Hacın in March 1913 and another in Bitlis the following month.[35]

The Situation in the Eastern Provinces during the Balkan Wars

The projected reforms in the Armenian provinces are in many respects comparable to similar reform plans that the powers vainly tried to have implemented in Macedonia. While it is undeniable that, in the Macedonian question as well as the Armenian case, the European interference was partly motivated by political and economic interests, the fact remains that in both regions real problems of security and a disastrous economic and social situation provided a basis for the pressure that the powers put on the Sublime Porte. Abdülhamid had in some sense responded as the Ottomans often did when confronted with such domestic questions. In the West (with the possible exception of Germany), his energetic methods were depicted as "bloody." From the Ottoman imperial point of view, however, the massacres merely constituted a legitimate response to demands that, coming from subjects of the sultan, were quite simply inconceivable, the more so in that they emanated from subaltern groups. The Young Turks had of course inherited these imperial traditions. Moreover, like Abdülhamid, they were fully conscious of the way such traditions were perceived by Westerners, who were objects of both contempt and admiration thanks to their scientific savoir-faire and efficient methods of colonial and military administration. During their years of exile in Europe, the Young Turks had come to appreciate the extent to which nationalism had focused energies and cemented identities there. When they contemplated importing this European model into the Ottoman Empire, however, they were confronted by, on the one hand, groups endowed by their history with a solid structure and, on the other, a "Turkish" people still unaware that it had become, at least in the view of certain ideologues, a racial category.

The Armenian elites, who had also been educated in conformity with the Western models then fashionable in the Ottoman capital, were rapidly confronted with the question of their future place in a disintegrating empire. Certain Armenian circles found personal ways of meeting their expectations: they entered state service. Others took up the revolutionary struggle with the objective of secularizing the institutions of the empire and introducing "progressive" social models in Turkey. Despite the retrospective Turkish historiography that portrays the Armenian revolutionaries as separatist nationalists, we have seen that, in the four years following the July 1908 revolution, Armenian community institutions defended loyalist positions and clearly indicated their desire to take part in the modernization of society and the state. However, the April 1909 massacres in Cilicia, the increasingly authoritarian tendencies of the Committee of Union and Progress, and the elimination of the liberal opposition ultimately convinced even the most optimistic political leaders, such as Aknuni, that the Young Turks had never seriously considered improving the condition of the Armenian population of the eastern provinces, but on the contrary were intent on making these Armenians' lives so difficult that they would opt for exile. The countless reports arriving from the provinces pointed to a marked deterioration of the situation. Its beginnings may be dated to 1912, the year of the First Balkan War. A circular that Patriarch Hovhannes Arsharuni addressed to the ambassadors of the powers sheds light on the position of the official Armenian organizations:

> The Patriarchate of the Armenians of Turkey begs to submit to Your Excellency a translation of the *takrir* that it presented to His Highness the grand vizier on Saturday

evening. It would be loath to see its initiative interpreted as a sign tending to confer new urgency upon the question of reforms in the eastern provinces. For more than two years now, the Patriarchate has declined to engage in an exchange with the Ottoman government on this subject. It regrets that it cannot expect it to make any sincere effort to reorganize these devastated regions. In the memorandum that the Patriarch presented to His Highness the grand vizier on 12 May last, it contented itself with pointing out to him, one last time, the threat of massacre hanging over the Armenians. It demanded that effective measures be taken to eliminate this danger, which is growing daily. Your Excellency is not unaware that the Armenians' situation deteriorated suddenly in the aftermath of the Balkan War. The unfortunate outcome of this war added a thirst for revenge to a centuries-old hatred. From one end of Anatolia to the other, a threat of massacre gathered over their heads. They became hostages in the Muslims' hands. If these massacres did not occur, it was due solely to the fact that the Armenians, albeit victims of the most reprehensible crimes, refrained even from demanding justice, for fear that their attitude might be interpreted as a provocation. To date, they have simply managed to avoid wholesale slaughter. The number of murders has not diminished but increased and, for some time now, these murders have been committed, significantly, with the manifest intention of sowing terror among the Armenians. Exposed to these outrages and the danger of mass slaughter, the Armenians cannot rely on protection from the state and do not even have the right to defend themselves. If they procure arms, they immediately find themselves accused of preparing a rebellion. The watchfulness of the government toward the Armenians never slackens. The government's action, which is such as to suggest that the Armenians are always ready to take up arms, only whips up the hatred of the fanatical masses ... From Aleppo to the shores of Lake Van, the Armenian people lives in fear of the future. Long convoys of families are once again making for the borders. The Armenians find themselves forced to abjure the ties that centuries of history and unremitting labor have forged between them and this land. This situation, which has become unbearable, and the negative result of the initiatives of the Patriarchate, [which], while it confidently awaits the forthcoming solution to the question of reforms in Armenia, begs Your Excellency to take the urgent measures that Your Excellency considers appropriate in order to avoid the danger of imminent massacres in Anatolia.[36]

Even as it appealed to the diplomats, the Patriarchate continued to keep records of the exactions committed in the provinces and to inform the Sublime Porte that it was doing so.[37] It called attention to "the harassment to which government officials subjected the Armenians alone," the "isolated murders, confiscations of property, kidnappings and acts of pillage," and the exodus of the population that these acts brought on. It did not, however, restrict itself to drawing up an inventory of such acts. It also interpreted them:

This situation suggests that the Armenians no longer have the right to live in the Ottoman Empire. This state of affairs can only lead to the annihilation of the Armenian element in the above-mentioned regions; the government's multiple assurances about the adoption of measures to preserve the honor, life and property of our countrymen have had no effect, and as there is nothing to add to the supplications, complaints and protests to which I have already drawn attention, it only remains for me to appeal, with an eye to the future destiny [of] the Armenian people – excluded from society – to the conscience and sense of responsibility of the Ottoman state and people, as well as the pity of the civilized world.

Thus, it was made clear that the Armenian organizations, which officially expressed their views by way of the Patriarchate, were leaving the door open to direct negotiations with the Sublime Porte even while appealing to the powers to intervene.

The complaints formulated in general terms by the Armenians reflected concrete realities. Among the excesses mentioned in the untold number of memoranda drawn up by the services of the Armenian patriarchate, we find the pillage of the villages of Kâmiköl and Bizer on 20 April 1329 (1913) by brigands from the *kaza* of Ğarzan (Bitlis); the transfer of the *kaymakam* of Çarsancak, Şükrü Bey, because he had attempted to restore Armenian "properties illegally seized by the *ağas*"; the "untold depredations that the famous bandit Said Bey" perpetrated in the village of Dad Bey, whose inhabitants had fled to Bitlis; the "crimes of the beys" in the village of Asrat (on the plain of Mush), which had been abandoned by its inhabitants; an attack carried out by Haso İbrahim, "well known for his crimes and subject to an arrest warrant," on the village of Elyoh, in the *kaza* of Beşiri (in the vilayet of Dyarbekir), which had resulted in two deaths; the murders and depredations in the *kaza* of Gavaş (to the south of Lake Van) committed by the "Grave" tribe, which had also made off with 2,000 sheep and killed two Armenian shepherds in the *kaza* of Şatak; the murder of an Armenian tax collector; the kidnapping of a 14-year-old girl in the *nahie* of Edincik (in the *kaza* of Erkek); the kidnapping and murder of five people from the village of Gorgor (Bitlis) on 13 May 1913; the murder of four Armenians in the *kaza* of Hizan, in the village of Banican, and four others in Haron; the theft of 1,000 sheep in the same region; numerous murders and acts of pillage in the *sancaks* of Mush and Siirt; the cutting off of communications, including the closure of all roads, between the Armenian villages in the regions of Dyarbekir, Bitlis, and Van; and so on.[38]

The same documents indicate that these acts of violence often interfered with farm work and that bands of brigands "acted everywhere with impunity," multiplying kidnappings and ransom demands to the point that the Armenians of Erzincan and the surrounding area, "desperate and no longer able to bear the exactions that they are made to endure," were emigrating to America. In the *kazas* of Silvan and Beşiri, the Kurds "are feverishly arming themselves and continue to kill, plunder or threaten the Armenians."[39]

Officially, the Sublime Porte was not indifferent to these grievances and passed them on to the relevant departments so that the necessary measures could be taken.[40] However, in his response to them, the grand vizier, Mahmud Şevket, basing what he said on a report drawn up by the interior minister, Haci Adıl Bey, did not hesitate to call the credibility of the Armenian complaints into question, so that we are left wondering, above all, about the good faith of the local and national authorities. The declarations that the minister made to the newspaper *La Turquie*, to the effect that there was no need for reforms in Armenia because there was no insecurity, everything was calm, and the gendarmerie was doing its job,[41] cast doubt upon the government's real intentions. The Istanbul press, for its part, pointed out the cynicism of the statement by this high-ranking Ittihadist, recalling his role during the Cilician massacres, in particular the famous telegram in which he urged the local authorities to see to it that foreign interests were spared![42]

The arguments developed in the grand vizier's response to the Patriarchate's grievances indicate the way the Sublime Porte handled this issue:[43]

Your Highness's complaints about the government's negligence in pursuing the bandits and criminals do not reflect the reality of the situation. Not only were military forces dispatched to Şirvan and Ğarzan in order to capture and punish bandits disturbing public order in the vilayet of Bitlis, such as Yaşar Çeto, Hahme, Mehmed Emin and Cemil, but the *vali* even went to Iluş in order to take steps to ensure the maintenance of public order. The governor general of Van, for his part, traveled to

Şatak in order personally to direct the pursuit of the destructive, plundering tribes. A force of four hundred men with two canons was put, for this purpose, at the disposal of Cevdet Bey, the governor of Hakkiari, and Sefvet Bey, the commanding officer of the regiment of sharpshooters. After these tribes have been put down, it will be the turn of the Girav tribe. Once the Giravli are punished, Mir Hehe will be left without support... In short, the local authorities are doing everything in their power to put a speedy end to the dangers threatening public order in the above-mentioned regions.

With respect to the question of illegal confiscations of property, the grand vizier pointed out that the issue had been "turned over to a special commission charged with resolving the agrarian problem in the eastern vilayets of Anatolia; the commission is now about to leave for that region." As for the alleged atrocities and murders perpetrated in the *kaza* of Hizan by Said Ali, the grand vizier remarked that Ali

was a respectable person; the Armenians have fallen into the habit of attributing every crime committed in the whole vilayet to him, and the Armenian element is nursing, as a result, an intense hatred for this individual. Nevertheless, the legal and civil authorities have not brought a single charge against Said Ali Effendi – who leads a sedentary existence – that would call for prosecution. And despite the Armenians' belief that the bandit Hahme, who operates in the Van and Bitlis regions, takes his orders from Said Ali, Ali's son Salaheddin, in an encounter with the aforementioned bandit's gang in the province of Van this week, killed one of Hahme's followers and wounded another. These two facts indicate that the Armenians' assumptions are ill-founded. Nonetheless, all Said Ali Effendi's actions are under surveillance and the authorities will not fail to deal severely with him should that become necessary.

Turning to the case of the famous Haso, Şevket wrote: "Not only has he had no hand in the aforementioned events; he is not even a bandit. He is the chief of a tribe that had nothing to do with the troubles of 1311 (1895), has never in any way harmed an Armenian and is well liked by all Armenians."

All the grievances formulated by the patriarch are given the same sort of response here: "the crimes committed must be attributed to ordinary personal motives"; the local authorities see to it that criminals are punished, dispatching troops, when called for, to punish the tribes; there is no significant emigration from the Erzerum and Erzincan regions – in a word, the Armenians are impugning people for their presumed intentions, not their acts.[44] The grand vizier's response implicitly claims to be purely factual and without political connotations to the Armenian protests. The Armenian organizations, however, far from regarding the "explanations" provided by the cabinet as satisfactory, expressed their surprise that the government had called the veracity of the information arriving from the provinces into question: "The answers given above," the Armenians remarked,

suggest that the communications received from our bishoprics and curacies are sheer invention and slander, and that the Imperial government, without making the least discrimination between Ottoman subjects, whatever their race or religion, is pursuing and arresting all bandits and criminals without exception, while sparing no means efficaciously to ensure the peace and welfare of the population. In view of this state of affairs, our patriarchate is invited to attach no importance to, and put no confidence in, these malevolent reports and inventions, and also to replace the bishops of Siirt and Bitlis.[45]

Besides registering these complaints about fundamentals, the Armenian authorities also sought to refocus the debate on local problems, particularly on the social sources of the insecurity reigning in the Armenian provinces:

We consider it essential to remind Your Excellency, without equivocation, of certain historical truths bearing the closest possible relation to the situation prevailing today. From time immemorial and in every province of the Empire, the *eşrefs* and large landholders have formed a class apart, a state within the state. This privileged class has gradually acquired such power that it has proved capable of foiling the projects and actions of the central state's best-intentioned members. Local civil servants – from those of the highest to those of the lowest rank – have unfortunately never been able to escape its influence. Those who have tried have, as a result of ruse or slander, been promptly dismissed or replaced, or else, obeying feelings of honesty or patriotism, have resigned their posts. All the investigations carried out by local authorities of crimes or offences committed in the provinces have had to be conducted under the influence of this privileged class, that is, in conformity with its illegitimate interests. Anyone who dared complain about the tyrannical actions of this class to either members of the local administration or the national authorities suffered more, perhaps, because he had lodged a complaint than from the act about which he had originally complained.

The Armenians concluded:

Given this state of affairs, it is only natural that the central government cannot form an accurate idea of the situation in the provinces ... Over the last thirty years, the absolutist government developed a system of oppression and exactions brought to bear, in particular, on the Armenians living in eastern Anatolia; it went so far as officially to instruct the provincial authorities that it was licit to make attempts on the life, honor and property of Armenians, or at least intimated that to them. Persuaded, however, that these actions carried out in violation of religion, conscience and the law had to be hidden from the eyes of the outside world as far as possible, the above-mentioned government had recourse to the basest, most monstrous means to deceive European public opinion. Thus the legitimate complaints addressed by Armenians to the local or national authorities were, on orders of the national authorities and under the influence of the large landowners, simply filed away; indeed, those who had shown the courage to lodge such complaints were accused of rebelling against the state. This policy of harassing the Armenians culminated in the organization of appalling massacres. And, so as to ensure the impunity of the perpetrators and instigators of these tragedies, the criminals were not prosecuted as they should have been, whereas the Armenians [who had] survived the massacres were. The aim was to bring these unfortunates to beg for a general amnesty from which their tormentors would also have benefited. This barbarous persecution, to which the Armenians were exposed for more than a quarter of a century, eventually acquired – especially in the vilayets of eastern Anatolia – the character of natural custom and, one might say, of a law superior to the civil and religious laws. The tragedy of Adana, which took place after the proclamation of the constitution, was one logical consequence of the transformation of this policy into natural law.[46]

The Armenian Council further noted that this law had "convinced the oppressors that everything was permitted when it came to our countrymen," adding that "the national authorities would not find it easy to make these tyrants change their minds today," the more so as the investigations in progress had been confided to low-ranking local officials who were under the influence of Kurdish *begs*. This

> made it impossible to maintain peace and public order. Most of these officials are sincerely convinced that patriotism and the law make it their duty to conceal crimes committed by Muslims against non-Muslims ... They use all sorts of tricks in an attempt to deny or cover up undeniable realities. However, they themselves are so well aware of the absurdity of a system under which the Armenians are presented as complaining of nonexistent facts that they are at pains to make it seem as if our countrymen were motivated by ill-will or invidious hatred.

The authors of this report underscored that the Armenians who had fallen victim to such exactions had to

> defend themselves unaided against the base slanders invented in order to force them to withdraw their complaints ... Matters have come to such a pass that these unfortunates, who know from experience that they will face all sorts of negative consequences as a result of these slanders ... do not even dare to present themselves to the authorities in order to identify their persecutors ... One has only to make an impartial examination, in the light of the circumstances described above, of the reports submitted by local government officials to the central authorities ... in order to appreciate the absurdity of these accusations.[47]

The ARF's official organ, *Droschak*, was still more direct. Pronouncing its mea culpa for its own past attitude, it made no attempt to play down the Ittihad's responsibility for the situation that had been forced on the Armenian population of the eastern provinces: "Constitutional Turkey has ... with greater deceitfulness and methodicalness ... been sucking the blood of the Armenian people like a vampire for the past four years ... and we, naive as we were and blinded by illusion, insensibly drew closer, a step at a time, to this fatal abyss." The Dashnak editorialist also took the full measure of the trap in which the Armenians found themselves: "Today we are confronted with a cruel, frightening dilemma. At stake is the very existence of the Armenian people: it will either secure real assurances of its survival as a nation or must prepare to disappear under the ruins of Turkey, like a sacrificial victim. There is no half-way solution, no half-way exit."

The conclusion is even more striking: "The hellish plot that is being forged against the Armenian people in the dark is no longer a secret. The Turkish government – the Young Turks – no longer feel the need to hide the crime they are meditating."[48]

In the internal reports drawn up by the Armenian Political Council, the facts are exposed in a still cruder light:

> According to information received in the past few days from absolutely trustworthy individuals ... the persecution of the Armenians in the six vilayets is proceeding in systematic fashion. It is not hidden, but takes place in broad daylight. Everything and anything now serves as a pretext for imputing subversive ideas to the Armenians and pursuing them before the law. If they kill a Kurdish brigand who has become the terror of their region, if they are found bearing arms, if they come together to commemorate a holiday, if they don a hat instead of a fez, they are immediately arrested and thrown into prison. What they have done is always described as a crime jeopardizing "state security," so that they may be kept in prison until the end of a judicial investigation that of course never ends. The Kurds, for their part, are armed to the teeth; they travel about

in compact groups...By sowing terror, they help keep the Armenians submissive. By plundering, they help the government wage the economic war it has declared against the Armenians. Thus they serve everywhere as stand-ins for the Turkish authorities.

The same report notes that the murders of Armenians all have one characteristic in common: those felled by the murderers' bullets are always people of distinction. The victims are drawn from the ranks of schoolteachers, priests, village *muhtars*, farmers – in short, all those who, by virtue of their education, profession, or social situation, perform functions useful to the community. "Systematic extermination is at work here. It is strikingly reminiscent of the procedures the Ottoman government recently used against the Balkan peoples," notes the author of this report. The land question, he writes, was also growing ever more acute. New illegal seizures of land were taking place in the vilayet of Van, in Nordüz, Aghbak, and Moks, in the vilayet of Bitlis, in Sasun, where "the Armenian villages...were wrested from their Armenian owners and turned over to Kurds." The situation was similar in the vilayet of Dyarbekir, in Beşiri and Ğarzan, as well as in the vilayet of Erzerum, in Bayburt and Bulanik. In fact, the Political Council seemed to be convinced that the authorities had no intention of giving the Armenians back their lands:

> In spite of the government's promises to carry out such restitution by administrative means, this procedure has never been applied. The Armenians have had to turn to the courts. The fate meted out to them by the courts is well known. It makes no difference whether they produce a title deed; the judge always finds an excuse to dismiss their complaints. Sometimes terrorism plays a role here: an Armenian plaintiff is killed on his way back from court...We also hear that the Ottoman government is getting ready to settle a good many of the emigrants from Rumelia in Armenian areas; entire caravans are already on their way to the vilayet of Sıvas.[49]

Finally, the Political Council observed that, taking its cue from the government, the Turkish press had launched an anti-Armenian campaign; that the tone of the Turkish newspapers was growing more vehement day by day, with articles making open threats of massacre[50] or a general boycott.[51] According to the Armenian leaders, the Turkish authorities were pursuing a twofold objective: they wanted to terrorize the Armenians on the one hand and, on the other, to be able to convince the powers that Ottoman public opinion made it impossible for them to accede to the Europeans' demands, however limited and modest they might be.[52]

In the latter half of 1913, the harassment of the Armenian population of the eastern vilayets seemed to be part of a general strategy elaborated by the national leadership – probably by the Ittihad's Central Committee.

Chapter 2

The Armenian Organizations' Handling
of the Reform Question

The two preceding chapters describe the situation prevailing in the Ittihad and the Armenian organizations after the crushing defeat in the Balkans. It is clear that the radicalization of the Ittihad alarmed the Armenians. The Armenian organizations, which had long hoped that the Young Turk regime would put the desired reforms into effect, finally decided to internationalize the question. From then on, the Armenians found themselves in an agonizing, merciless face-off with their Turkish "compatriots." As the editorialist of the Hnchak newspaper, *Gohag*, pointed out, the Balkan Wars had created a "new situation" and endowed the Armenian question with "new topicality."[1] For its part, the ARF organ *Droschak* drew up a balance sheet of the past few years. It reminded its readers that "since the establishment of the new regime, despite painful realities such as the Adana massacres ... the Armenians have provided eloquent, concrete proof of the sincerity of their feelings and their profound attachment to the Ottoman constitution."[2] Yet this, it added, had had no effect.

Krikor Zohrab writes in his diary that it was in a July 1912 interview in Istanbul with Alexander Guchkov, the president of the Duma, that he succeeded in tempering the Russian leaders' sharp hostility towards the Armenians.[3] The Russians, probably influenced by Ottoman diplomacy, suspected the Armenians of harboring separatist tendencies, to say nothing of the veritable war that the Czars had declared on the Armenian revolutionary committees, especially the ARF. The ARF's hatred of the Czarist regime, which had not abated since the party's foundation,[4] was a major obstacle for the official Armenian organizations. If Russian diplomacy was to play an active role in bringing about the Armenian reforms, the burden embodied by the ARF would have to be cast off, which is to say that the party would have to consent to establish normal relations with the Czarist state.

We have not found documents that allow us to draw clear-cut conclusions on this question, but the initial October 1912 negotiations between Catholicos Kevork V and the viceroy for the Caucasus, Vorontsov-Dashkov, would seem to indicate that the ARF found common ground with the Russians around this time. It is possible, if not indeed probable, that high-ranking Armenian officials in St. Petersburg stepped in here. It is known, in any event, that two eminent St. Petersburg personalities, Professor Nicolas Adontz (1871–1942) and the lawyer Sirakan Tigranian, were present in Istanbul on 21 and 22 December 1912[5] and were received in the Armenian chamber on the very day that it created the Security Commission it charged with handling the reform question.

On 21 December, a "historic" meeting of the Armenian chamber was held behind closed doors in its seat in Galata. The Political Council – comprising Stepan Karayan,[6] a judge on the court of appeals, the Hnchaks Murad Boyajian and Nerses Zakarian,[7] the Dashnaks Garabed Pashayan[8] and Vahan Papazian, and the "centrists" Diran Erganian,[9] Levon

Demirjibashian,[10] Oskan Mardikian,[11] and Sarkis Svin[12] – presented its plan for enacting reforms in the Armenian provinces.[13] It fell to Zohrab, whose role in the plan to put the Armenian question back on the agenda has already been discussed, to review the reasons for the Political Council's initiative. The proposed plan was unanimously approved by all the tendencies represented in the Armenian chamber, which agreed that there was no longer any alternative to radical measures in order "to put an end, once and for all, to the risks of a generalized massacre attested by all the credible reports received in the recent past."[14]

To deal with this question, the chamber moved to create an Advisory Committee that was to collaborate closely with the Political Council. It was to have five members – Harutiun Shahrigian of the ARF; Vahan Tekeyan of the Ramgavar party; David Der Movsesian, representing the political Center; B. Kalfayan of the SDHP; and finally, Zohrab. To coordinate the whole, the Mixed Council – a joint body comprising both the Political and Religious Councils – created a Security Commission with the former Patriarch Yeghishe Turian as its president. The commission included Krikor Balakian, Stepan Karayan, Oskan Mardikian, Levon Demirjibashian, Murad Boyajian, and Dr. Vahan Papazian, who was named its executive director.[15]

Since the 1895 efforts to bring about reform, made under pressure from the powers and with the cooperation of Patriarch Matteos Izmirlian, the Armenian national authorities had never again sought outside support of any kind to achieve their objectives. They saw only too clearly that the Western powers were simply exploiting moral arguments to wrest more and more advantages from the Ottoman state. This time, with the benefit of experience, the Constantinople Patriarchate went about matters in very methodical fashion, coordinating its activities with the Catholicosate in Etchmiadzin. Elected in November 1912, the Armenian political leadership and its Special Commission worked with the greatest possible circumspection. Thus, as Karayan admitted at the 21 April 1913 session, certain activities of the Special Commission were not reported to the Armenian chamber for security reasons.[16]

While the Commission pursued its task, Boghos Nubar[17] was appointed president of the Armenian Delegation by Catholicos Kevork V. Late in 1912, Nubar settled in Paris in order to conduct – in close coordination with Constantinople and Tiflis, where a commission had also been formed – the preparatory work that it was hoped would lead to the implementation of reforms in Armenia.[18] Thus a division of labor emerged: Nubar was responsible for diplomacy and discussions with the European governments, while the Political Council, seconded by the Constantinople and Tiflis commissions, was to negotiate the reform question with the authorities of the Ottoman and Russian Empires.

At the same time, the Council did everything it could to curb the massive emigration of the exhausted Armenian peasantry. It promised the peasants that a system of justice worthy of the name would soon be established, exhorting them to remain in their villages; it dispatched commissions to tour rural areas and assess their needs; it called on Armenian communities abroad to lend their compatriots in Armenia a hand; it tried to facilitate economic investment so as to encourage the population to stay put; it arranged for a patriarchal bull urging the Armenian population to stay in its homeland to be read out in the churches; it drafted plans for an agricultural bank; it initiated in February 1913 a census of the Armenians; and so on.[19]

While the Political Council's first overtures to Kâmil's cabinet had met with an encouraging response, things changed when Mahmud Şevket took the helm of state late in January 1913: the negotiations between the government and the Patriarchate ceased immediately.[20] Şevket did not meet with the leadership of the Political Council until May 1913. Karayan, who had been re-elected, took the opportunity to tender the grand vizier a very revealing memorandum.[21] It stated that the Armenians did not appreciate the fact that the press and public opinion it had helped form had blamed the defeat in the Balkans on them. They were even less enthusiastic, the memorandum went on, about intimations that it would be necessary to destroy the Armenian element in the empire to forestall a European intervention.

Indeed, at the 21 April 1913 session of the Armenian chamber, Karayan, who had become a member of the Council of State under Kâmil, had exclaimed: "All legal channels have been exhausted. Our initial impression of the government's attitude was a positive one. Today, however, Armenia's situation has become unbearable and dangerous. At this very moment, we face an imminent threat in an area extending from Cilicia to Van."[22] The situation in the provinces now seemed so tense that H. Khorasanjian, the leader of the center and a man with a reputation for moderation, declared at the 7 May session of the assembly that, "if we must perish, let us be cut down with honor: let us assume our responsibilities and die behind our breastworks."[23]

In the Caucasus, in Tiflis, the head of the Armenian church had also created a standing committee modeled on the one in Constantinople. It comprised nine members, including Alexander Khatisian, the mayor of Tiflis, the Dashnak leaders Nigol Aghbalian and Arshak Jamalian, and Hovhannes Tumanian, a poet and public activist.[24] Somewhat as they had done during the preparations for the 1878 Congress of Berlin, the Armenian authorities now entreated Czar Nicolas to see to it that the question of reforms in Armenia was put on the agenda of the London Conference, scheduled for April 1913.[25]

For his part, Boghos Nubar had, upon taking up residence in Paris, called on the Turkish ambassador in order to explain what he planned to do: work toward bringing the Russians, British, Germans, and French to a consensus on the reform issue.[26] After thus serving notice of his intentions, he circulated a memorandum summarizing the question. The argument he developed in it sought to show that, far from contravening the interests of the powers, the reforms would help promote peace and stability in the region.[27] This memorandum, which contained concrete propositions, had been drawn up by the Special Commission under the aegis of the Political Council and then submitted to André Mandelstam, a diplomat and jurist attached to the Russian embassy in Constantinople.[28] Officially, then, what was involved was a "Russian plan" that all parties treated as if it had been Mandelstam's.

The principle clauses of this plan may be summarized as follows:

1) unification of the six vilayets, with the exclusion of certain peripheral areas;
2) nomination of a Christian governor, Ottoman or European;
3) nomination of an administrative council and a mixed – that is, Muslim and Christian – Provincial Assembly;
4) creation of a mixed gendarmerie commanded by European officers;
5) dissolution of the *hamidiye* corps;
6) legalization of the use of the Armenian, Kurdish, and Turkish languages in the local administration;
7) the right for each community to establish its own schools, whose administration was to be financed by special taxes of the kind previously levied for the sole benefit of Turkish schools;
8) creation of a special committee charged with examining the land confiscations carried out in recent decades;
9) expulsion from the provinces of the Muslim refugees or immigrants who had been settled on Armenian-owned land;
10) application of identical measures in Cilicia; and
11) an obligation on the part of the European powers to see to it that the plan was enacted.

From the outset, Britain and France were associated with the discussions about the concrete implementation of the plan. Of course, without the agreement and support of these two powers, every reform would be condemned to remain a dead letter, even if the Russians briefly toyed with the idea of unilateral intervention.[29] The Germans, initially excluded from the negotiations, were finally brought into them in January 1913, after the German ambassador in Constantinople had got wind of what was afoot.[30]

The preliminary discussions of the reforms threw the diverging viewpoints and conflicting interests of the powers into sharp relief. Thus France, the Ottoman Empire's main creditor, was simultaneously negotiating to obtain a concession to build a railroad in Armenia, in direct competition with the Germans. Britain, while it had prudently begun scaling down its investments in Turkey in 1880, was treating the caliphate with kid gloves in order to avoid the least risk of Islamicist contagion in its own colonies in Egypt and the Indian subcontinent, to say nothing of the first concessions it was trying to obtain in the oilfields near Mosul, in these early days of the saga of "black gold." Britain and French diplomats were still seeking to maintain the territorial status quo in Turkey, which both Britain and France deemed crucial to their immediate and long-term interests. Thus they regarded the Russian initiative somewhat apprehensively, participating in it the better to control it. As for Germany, which was heavily involved in the construction of the Berlin-Baghdad Railway as well as the reorganization of the Ottoman army, it was hostile to the very idea of reforms, which could jeopardize its attempt to consolidate its economic control over part of Anatolia. Indeed, Germany, whose ties to the Young Turks had been growing steadily stronger, was attempting at their behest to torpedo the "Russian plan."

Thus, it is evident that the success of the plan was anything but a foregone conclusion, so that Boghos Nubar's efforts to allay Western apprehensions were by no means superfluous. In the memorandum that the Armenian leaders submitted to the European chancelleries, they were at pains to point up the "social aspect" of the reforms in order to dispel the fears of Russian annexation agitating France and Britain. Their efforts did not prevent these two powers from curbing Russian ambitions at the April 1913 London Conference, even while refusing to rally to the position defended by the Germans, who believed that what was involved here was meddling in the internal affairs of the Ottoman Empire, a serious infringement of its sovereignty and a green light for a partition of Anatolia that would leave the door open to subsequent Russian annexation. To counter this thesis, Russian diplomats contended that if the reforms were not rapidly put in place, there would be a sure risk of disorder, which would inevitably bring on armed Russian intervention.

In the end, the reforms were approved of, in principle, by all the powers, including Germany, on the condition that their execution be left to the Sublime Porte and that they be enacted under its supervision or, if need be, that of the powers. Evidently, this new proposal, endorsed by Britain and France, was categorically rejected by Russia, who saw in it nothing more than an underhanded way of refusing to seek concrete solutions to the problem of re-establishing security in Armenia.[31] Unwilling to pursue the matter any further within the framework of the London Conference, the powers decided, taking up a Russian suggestion, to charge their respective ambassadors in Constantinople with pursuing the discussions. Meanwhile, backing up his words with deeds, Czar Nicolas massed troops on the Turkish border and ordered his agents to organize Kurdish provocations in Armenia in order to step up the pressure.[32]

While this bargaining was underway, Nubar attempted, especially in the months following the London Conference, to soften the positions of the different powers. He sought support for his efforts from pro-Armenian national committees such as the British-Armenian Committee, of which Lord Bryce was a leading member, and the Armenian Committee of Berlin. He also brought his many personal relations into play. Both in his correspondence and at all the meetings he attended, Nubar insisted above all that it was essential that the reforms be overseen by the great powers if they could not be carried out under Russian supervision, an option that London and Berlin categorically rejected.[33] It should be added that Nubar was not genuinely displeased by this collective decision, since he himself opposed the idea of Russian hegemony over the Armenian provinces. For the leading Armenian circles in Turkey, Russian control was the solution of last resort when it came to imposing a normalization of the situation on Istanbul. From his Paris base, Nubar did not hesitate to travel repeatedly to London to meet Sir Edward Grey, the British foreign secretary.[34] Although he had the support of members of parliament who also belonged to the British-Armenian Committee, he was hard put to convince the British that his initiative was well founded. He was the more shocked by Britain's passive attitude, as the grand vizier himself, Mahmud Şevket, regarded the demands for reform as reasonable and let it be known, shortly before he was assassinated, that he was prepared to accept them.[35]

At all events, the discussions conducted by the ambassadors of the powers began in June 1913 in Constantinople. The basis for them was provided by the text of the 1895 memorandum, supplemented by the one that the Armenian Patriarch had just submitted to them.[36] Meanwhile, Nubar was sounding out Italian political circles in discussions with Galli, an Italian parliamentary deputy who had just made a declaration before the Roman parliament. Nubar reassured him that the Armenians were by no means pursuing autonomy, which was impracticable in the present situation, but rather sought the establishment of an administration capable of protecting their lives and property.[37] Nubar also appealed to his friends among the British to convince financial circles that it was crucial to promote the reforms in order to obtain better guarantees for their loans to Turkey.[38] He received solid support from the Armenian Committee of Berlin, presided over by G. V. Greenfield. His efforts to explain the situation to the Wilhelmstraße consisted of defense of the Armenian thesis: the surest way of ensuring Russian non-intervention was to enact the reforms.[39] In Constantinople, the press seized on the reform question in July; vehement opposition to the plan was expressed in certain quarters, and some went so far as to burn down the house near Hagia Sophia in which Talât was then living.[40] Plunged in to a disastrous financial crisis, the empire was hoping to obtain material aid from Europe, which Nubar advised the Europeans to provide in exchange for a Turkish political decision in favor of the reforms. This appeal was not taken seriously; the European chancelleries paid virtually no attention to it. St. Petersburg, whose Armenian Committee was headed by the historian Nicolas Adontz, was the only capital genuinely interested in the question of reforms in Armenia. Moreover, doubtless with a view to exacerbating the antagonism between the powers, the Sublime Porte began circulating a rumor to the effect that it intended to appoint British officers to head the gendarmerie in Armenia, and another alleging Armenian hostility to European supervision.[41] Thus, one sees that the Armenians' leaders devoted themselves body and soul to the extremely complex game in progress throughout 1913, and were busy seeking support wherever it was to be had.

Ultimately, the Sublime Porte chose to publish a counter-plan encompassing all the provinces of Asiatic Turkey, the Armenian vilayets included. The idea was to establish a network of inspectors-general who were supposed to resolve all the region's economic and social problems, ostensibly with a view of "decentralization."[42] At the same time, the German ambassador, Hans von Wangenheim, continued to block the Constantinople negotiations, notably by attacking the Russian diplomats, whom he accused of harboring ulterior motives. Nubar therefore decided to travel to Berlin early in August 1913 to meet with the German foreign minister and persuade him to modify his policy of obstructing the reforms.[43] This visit to the *Wilhelmstraße* proved decisive, for it unfroze the situation in Constantinople, bringing the European ambassadors there to undertake serious negotiations.[44] A few days later, Dr. Lepsius sent a telegram to Nubar, indicating that "the situation [was] favorable" to successful completion of the negotiations, and proposing that Nubar come to Constantinople as soon as possible in order to oversee operations there.[45] Nubar's response to the German Protestant minister was that he could not decently step in to replace the Political Council, which had been charged with handling the matter.[46]

Lepsius, specifically, seems to have played a major role in moving the negotiations forward, serving as an intermediary between the Patriarchate and the German embassy,[47] and working hand-in-hand with Krikor Zohrab.[48] Late in September 1913, it was reported that the German and Russian diplomats had reached a compromise:

> The country shall be divided into two sectors, one encompassing Trebizond, Erzerum, and Sıvas/Sepastia, and the other, all the rest. The Sublime Porte requests that the great powers appoint two inspectors, one for each sector. These inspectors shall be entitled to appoint and dismiss their subordinates. Participation in local administrative functions and representation in the assemblies and councils shall be half Christian, half Muslim.[49]

This news, confirmed by the correspondence of the St. Petersburg Armenian Committee, revealed the ambiguous but decisive part that Russian diplomats took in bringing about an agreement. Nubar informed the Russian foreign minister, Serge Sazonov, of his satisfaction at their 17 October meeting.[50] Certain details of the plan, however, had yet to be settled, especially those concerning the nature of the executive powers to be vested in the two inspectors-general. Zohrab set about working out these details with Dr. Schönberg after the German ambassador, Wangenheim, received instructions from the Wilhelmstraße to come to terms with the Russian diplomats.[51] France and Britain, which had been observing the Russian-German tug-of-war with interest, also rallied to the compromise. The French minister Pichon even pledged active French support.[52]

Late in October, after the "deal had been sewn up," the dossier was transmitted to the Western chancelleries, which had now to convince the Sublime Porte to enact the accord. To hasten the process, Nubar organized in Paris an international conference on Armenian reforms. On 30 November and 1 December 1913, the leading representatives of the Armenian Committees in Europe, as well as pro-Armenian associations, diplomats and politicians from Germany, Russia, Britain, and Italy came together in the French capital to coordinate their efforts.[53]

On 25 December, the Russians and Germans officially transmitted the plan for reforms in Armenia to the Ottoman government. After a few weeks of foot-dragging, the Sublime Porte ultimately approved of the agreement on 8 February 1914. It had not succeeded in obtaining suppression of the clause on Western supervision, however, which it considered decisive.[54]

The Negotiations over the Reforms with the Ottoman Cabinet and the Ittihad

In the preceding section, we examined to an extent the public and diplomatic aspects of the negotiations over the reforms. For the sake of clarity, we have chosen to devote a separate section to the parallel negotiations, informal but crucial, which took place between a few Turkish and Armenian protagonists.

As has already been pointed out, when the Armenian side decided to relaunch the idea of reforms in the eastern provinces, Kâmil Pasha's liberal cabinet constituted an ideal interlocutor, and the negotiations advanced quite briskly. Not by accident, Kâmil Pasha summoned a number of Armenian personalities to a 21 December 1912 meeting, on the initiative of his foreign minister, Gabriel Noradounghian, in order to discuss the reform plan. Not only the Political Council, but the ARF too was excluded from these discussions. The parties to them were the former Patriarch Malakia Ormanian, the editor-in-chief of *Sabah*, Diran Kelekian, the parliamentary deputy from Sıvas, Dr. Nazaret Daghavarian, and two senators, Azarian and Eramian.[55] This bypassing of the legal authorities caused quite a stir in Armenian circles, so much so that Zohrab and Vahan Papazian, a former parliamentary deputy from Van and executive director of the Security Commission, went to see Kelekian and Ormanian to demand an explanation. Kelekian and Ormanian affirmed that they had stressed, in their conversations with the grand vizier, that they were in no way authorized to speak on behalf of the nation and that he would have to "speak with the Armenian national representatives."[56]

The Ittihad, back at the helm of state after the 23 January 1913 coup d'état, profited from its close ties with the Dashnak leaders, as soon as it had gotten wind of the reform plan, to renew its contacts with the Armenian authorities, with whom it had broken off relations some time earlier.[57] As was often the case under such circumstances, Bedros Halajian, a parliamentary deputy and member of the Ittihad, had been drafted to serve as an intermediary. The first meeting was organized in his home, probably in late January 1913, bringing together, on the one hand, Mehmed Talât, Halil, the deputy from Menteşe, and the CUP's secretary general, Midhat Şükrü, and on the other, Aknuni, Vartkes, and Armen Garo. All indications are that the Ittihad was convinced, at the time, that it would once again succeed in destroying the unanimity about the reform plan that reigned in the Armenians' ranks. It was counting on the powers of persuasion of Talât, who reminded his Armenian comrades of the friendship that had long united them. Sensing, however, that the Dashnaks, who had silently suffered so many indignities since 1908, would not be persuaded all that easily, Talât informed them that he himself wished to introduce reforms, modeled after the 1880 plan for Rumelia. He also pointed out that they were all "children of the same fatherland, bound by mutual ties." In order to underscore the ideological proximity between the Ittihad and the ARF, and the corresponding distance between them and "conservative" circles, he launched an attack against Boghos Nubar, describing him as a "Russian tool." In a final overture to the Armenians present, after intimating that the reform project was Nubar's and that the ARF bore no responsibility for it, Talât suggested inviting the Egyptian statesman to Istanbul so that he might present his demands directly to the Young Turks.[58] Another meeting between the Dashnak leadership and the Young Turk leaders İsmail Hakkı, Hüseyin Cahid, and Mehmed Talât took place on 1/14 February at Zohrab's house. This time, the discussion turned on a point of crucial importance – the powers' intervention in the administration of reforms. The Ittihadists, of course, suggested settling the matter without external mediation.[59] The Dashnaks retorted that the Armenians had defended that position since 1908 but that the successive Young Turk governments had consistently rejected their proposals, even though they had been quite modest.

The Dashnaks were the more skeptical because they had seen the CUP resort to radical measures almost as soon as the reform plan was floated. Among them were the organization, late in 1912, of a parliamentary faction of Kurdish and Turkish deputies from the eastern provinces, and that of a Union for the Defense of the Rights of the Eastern Provinces.[60] But the most concrete manifestation of the CUP's attitude was a new policy of economic boycott of the Armenians and their products, backed up by a panoply of measures such as the refusal of bank loans and administrative harassment of those engaged in export. Religious circles "secretly preached" that all business and trade with Armenians should be broken off. Beginning early in 1913, commercial groups exclusive comprising Turkish merchants sprang up, and it was recommended that people patronize them and them alone, rather than "buying impure goods" from Christians.[61] Also noteworthy is the dismissal of all Armenian civil servants in the *kazas* of Agn, Arapkir, Divrik, and so on, to say nothing of more spectacular acts, such as setting fire to the bazaar of Dyarbekir, where the merchants and craftsmen were almost all Armenians, or the burning down of Edirne's Armenian quarter.[62] While all this was going on, the Council of Ministers was adopting the "Islahat kanoni," a sort of reform *avant l'heure*, the sole purpose of which seems to have been to sow confusion and provide an argument for suspending the Armenian initiative. Mehmed Cavid was even dispatched to the eastern provinces in the capacity of inspector in order to supervise the application of this "law."[63]

In inviting Boghos Nubar to resolve the problem of the reform plan "in the family,"[64] Şevket's cabinet was seeking to bring him to leave Paris and thus abandon the work he was pursuing in the Western chancelleries. In other words, the Ittihad's as well as the cabinet's strategy in this period was to train their fire on the key point of the powers' mediating role, which the powers had to be stopped from playing if the reform plan was to be foiled.

In Armenian circles, it was noted that the ARF maintained contact with the Young Turks, apparently without ceding to the pressures that the CUP was putting on it. It may also be presumed that the ARF had no ulterior motives in collaborating with the Political Council and the Security Commission, in which it was not merely represented, but also very active, with the Dashnak Vahan Papazian serving as the Commission's executive director. It was, moreover, in this capacity that Papazian traveled to Paris in February 1913 in order to meet with Boghos Nubar and hammer out certain crucial points of the memorandum that the Armenian organizations were then drawing up.[65] According to the memoirs of this former parliamentary representative from Van, their conversations, conducted in French (Nubar spoke Armenian poorly), went very well: they put the finishing touches on a joint project that they planned to submit to the powers. It bore, notably, on the nomination of European inspectors or counselors and the provision of guarantees by the European states.

In Istanbul, the Russian embassy was another crucially important interlocutor for the Armenian organizations. Two of the men working for these organizations played special parts. Ivan Zavriev,[66] a Dashnak leader who was very well placed in ruling circles in St. Petersburg (he was in Istanbul in 1913), played a decisive role in negotiations with the Russians, while Zohrab was the "semi-official voice" of the Armenians.[67] Zohrab, in his diary, remarks that Zavriev "was the first Dashnak I ever knew who admitted the truth that, under a Turkish government, the sole fate awaiting the Armenian world was annihilation"; he contrasts him with Aknuni, who was "the last to part with his Turkophile dreams."[68] Zohrab and Zavriev held many private interviews with the Russian ambassador B. Charikov and his adviser André Mandelstam, who was charged with handling the reform issue. Work sessions were also organized with the participation of various experts, such as that of 12 April 1913, at which Zohrab, the Russian ambassador, and a representative of the Patriarchate, as well as L. Demirjibashian, Zavriev, and Zavarian,[69] discussed demographic problems, which the diplomat considered to be of great importance, and also the census of the Armenian population that the Patriarchate had begun conducting in all the vilayets of Asia Minor in February.[70]

In spring 1913, after the London Conference, at which the Armenian project took a big step forward, the Ittihad naturally revived the practice of meeting regularly with the Dashnaks. Halajian served as an intermediary and a barometer of the CUP's reactions.[71] In particular, a dinner was organized on the Island of Prinkipo in June 1913, bringing together Ahmed Cemal, then military governor of the capital (accompanied by Vahan Tatevian,[72] one of his close associates) and the entire Dashnak leadership – Armen Garo, Aknuni, Vartkes, Hrach Tirakian and Vahakn, and Vahan Papazian. Cemal was evidently blunter than Talât; he made no bones about the fact that the CUP considered the Armenian initiative to be a serious error. It came down, he thought, to working for the Russians. His party would consequently use all available means to counter the project: "at stake," he said, "is the territorial integrity of Turkey, which has been imprudently endangered as a result of your actions." He agreed, to be sure, that the Young Turks had not succeeded in carrying out the required reforms. The explanation, he said, lay in the country's dire economic and social plight. "The Armenians should have understood this," he added, "rather than backing us up against the wall." Finally, he suggested that "the Armenians not broaden the existing gulf between Turks and Armenians ... The consequences may be irreversible."[73] Papazian would later confess that all the Armenians present had very well understood Cemal's barely veiled threats, but that they "were persuaded that Turkey was at the end of its rope."[74]

In an interview granted to the Istanbul daily *Azadamard* during a visit to Paris early in July 1913, Mehmed Cavid, who had gone to France to negotiate a loan, spoke in very different terms. He declared that the Ottoman government had decided to satisfy the Armenians' demands "because the political character of the Armenian question [had] changed since the last [Balkan] war, becoming one of the essential questions before the empire."[75] In the same interview, he also affirmed that he had met with Boghos Nubar and that they had reached full agreement on nearly every point, "with the exception of the question of guarantees."[76] This positive declaration seems, however, to have been inspired by the problem then confronting the Ottoman minister of finance: convincing the French government to float a loan on behalf of a Turkey that had been bled white and desperately needed cash with which to resume the war against Bulgaria. This priority no doubt explains Cavid's tone and the fact that he took the trouble to pay a visit to Nubar, whose weight in French political circles was by no means negligible.

The impression that Cavid wanted at all costs to convince his auditors of his government's good intentions, fueling hopes of positive developments in the reform question, is confirmed by a number of factors. It finds its explanation, above all, in the context – that is, the imminent offensive against Edirne, which had probably already been decided upon, and also the "Ambassadors' Conference" held in Yeniköy from 3 to 24 July for the purpose of putting the last touches on the plan for reforms in Armenia, in accordance with a decision made at the London Conference.

We find confirmation of the temporary change in the strategy of the Young Turks, who were obviously trying to gain time in which to realize their short-term projects, in another interview, accorded this time by the interior minister, Mehmed Talât, to the newspaper *L'Union* early in July 1913.[77] Summoned to provide answers to delicate questions about, for example, the reasons that the confiscated property of Armenian exiles had still not been restored, the impunity of criminals, and forced conversions to Islam, Talât clearly stated that he had assigned 500 more policemen to the eastern provinces; that the army was going to help repress banditry; that the agrarian question was due to be examined in the near future; that the government had shown that it had changed its attitude and that a commission of inquiry was going to be created to study these questions in the eastern provinces themselves; and that arrangements had been made to assign experienced civil servants to the region. In other words, the minister conceded that there were problems – he was no longer denying that fact – but added that he had now bent himself to the task of resolving them.

After the informal Prinkipo meeting attended by Ahmed Cemal, the Unionist Central Committee also resumed its negotiations with the ARF's Western Bureau in early summer 1913 – indirectly at first, by way of Zohrab and Halajian, and then in direct encounters with Aknuni, Vartkes, and Armen Garo, who met with Halil (Menteşe), Midhat Şükrü, and Talât.[78] At these meetings, the CUP's leaders demanded that the Armenians not try to profit from the empire's delicate situation, and refrain from appealing to outside forces, especially Turkey's mortal enemy, Russia. In exchange, they announced that they were prepared to come to an agreement with the ARF and the Patriarchate about putting the reforms into practice. But, they said, so as not to inflame public opinion the Armenians had to reject all forms of outside interference in the country's internal affairs. Talât concluded with the remark that, in any case, "they would find the means they needed to scotch the plan if the Armenians did not yield to their demands."[79] In private, then, even with their former Dashnak allies, the Unionists' discourse was distinctly less benevolent, yet was also marked by a certain consistency: now that the Ambassadors' Conference was imminent, they wanted to persuade the Armenians to abandon the idea of mediation by the powers. The Armenian leaders, conversely, were unanimously in favor of maintaining the principle of a negotiation guaranteed by the European states, since they were convinced that that was the sole way to ensure authentic reforms.

Parallel to these semi-official negotiations, the interior minister was making public appearances of a kind that were meant to impress. Thus, on 22 June 1913, he paid a visit, in his official capacity, to the Patriarch. He was received in the Patriarchate's official reception room, where he solemnly announced a reform of the judicial system and the gendarmerie in the provinces. The Patriarch responded that he would like to believe that there would be an end to the violence and pillage that had not ceased in the eastern provinces, touching off a massive exodus of the Armenian population. He added that if the problems had been resolved by the government as they arose, outside intervention of any sort would have been perfectly superfluous.[80]

The Dashnak leadership seemed to confirm, in its official organ, that it was not disposed to make new concessions to the Ittihad. In the September 1913 issue, it reminded its readers that

> the Party for Union and Progress, its untold solemn promises notwithstanding, has not met the most elementary demands of the Armenian people and the Dashnaktsutiun – for example, demands for guarantees of personal safety, a solution to the land problem, a redistribution of taxes to finance education or proportional Armenian representation in the civil service at the local and national levels.[81]

The real negotiations, however, began only after the Ambassadors' Conference came to an end – indeed, only after Germany and Russia reached agreement on the essential points on 25 October 1913.[82] The first version of the plan, endorsed by the ambassadors in July, stipulated that only people with fixed abodes had the right to vote and that the *hamidiye* regiments would be dissolved.[83] The Russian-German text did not, however, provide for the restitution of confiscated land, nor did it prohibit the settlement of *muhacir* from the Balkans in the eastern provinces. As for the *hamidiyes*, they were renamed "lightly armed troops."[84]

About the last phase of the negotiations, in which Zohrab was the main Armenian participant, we now have a valuable source of information in his recently published diary, which sheds new light on many different aspects of the acrimonious discussions between Armenians and Young Turks. Not by accident, the Ittihad appointed Halil (Menteşe), the president of the Council of State, to explain to Zohrab the party's opposition to certain aspects of the plan that it categorically rejected.[85] The two men knew each other very well.[86] The Young Turk leader went to see Zohrab at his home on 20 December 1913 and set out the Ittihad's position, summed up in a *formule* (Zohrab uses the French word in his diary): "The Turks would rather die than accept interference of any kind from the powers in the Armenian question, although they know that the country would die along with them. They regard this as ... a question of life and death for all of Turkey and their party."[87] After a year of negotiations, temporization, and advances and retreats, depending on the circumstances, the two sides had reached the end of the road. The Ittihad's new initiative had to be accordingly interpreted, Zohrab acknowledged, as "the final, supreme argument before the rupture between Turks and Armenians was transformed into a war."[88] Zohrab and Halil therefore envisaged ways of reducing "the reigning tension between Armenians and Turks" and cooperating on putting the reforms into practice.[89]

"I would have preferred," Zohrab wrote,

> that someone else had been in my shoes then; someone conscious of his responsibilities and familiar with all the discouraging details of our situation; someone who saw, as if it were right there in front of him, the imminent, inevitable clash that was going to take place between the Armenian and Turkish element, with, as its consequence, the definitive failure of the Armenian question.[90]

Coming from a man with as much experience as Zohrab, this disabused reflection testifies to the tension that marked the last phase of the negotiations. He doubtless sensed the unspoken hostility in the Committee of Union and Progress and the lack of political discernment characteristic of some Armenian leaders, who had initially refused to negotiate with the Ittihad.[91]

The "impasse" was produced by a demand "that constitutes the very basis of our question" and that "they have always opposed."[92] The issue was, in Zohrab's words, of a "guarantee" from the power. In Halil's formulation, it was one of "supervision." In an effort to persuade his interlocutor to accept the terms that the Armenians preferred, Zohrab set forth a number of different arguments. He was well aware, he said, that the Sublime Porte could curry favor with Russia and Germany by granting them certain advantages. It might be possible to bury the Armenian question in that way. But, he wondered, would that truly represent a success for the Turks? He suggested that they should rather try to regain the Armenians' confidence, and, to that end, carry out reforms without delay, since "it was not possible to leave the Armenians as dissatisfied as they were."[93] As for the role of the powers, Zohrab contended that it was not a question of "foreign supervision," but of a "guarantee," since the inspectors would be officially "designated by the Sublime Porte," while the ambassadors of the powers would merely signify their agreement orally. Halil, however, told him that these stipulations had been firmly rejected by his party.[94] "I believe," Zohrab nevertheless wrote, "that I succeeded in convincing him of a point that is the cornerstone of our cause, a point [the Ittihadists] have always opposed ... I prepared him to convince his party to consent ... to the principle of a *recommandation* [in French in Zohrab's text] from the powers ... and go back to the formula of a European *inspecteur général* [in French] to whom powers would be delegated."[95]

Zohrab writes that Halil then promised him to do everything in his power to convince his party, but adds:

> It was obvious that he would have to overcome a number of difficulties, many more than we thought. A military faction among the Turks, led by Cemal Bey, was the most firmly opposed, and the Committee was favorably inclined toward this faction. Halil Bey feared, precisely, that those in Cemal's faction, although fully aware of the consequences of their actions, would remain adamant.[96]

Zohrab was thus cognizant of the pressure that this military faction, associated with Enver, was bringing to bear on the Ittihad and the government to take total control of the army and adopt an even more radical political line.[97] Indeed, the Turkish press was, in this period, passionately inveighing against the Armenians in alarming terms,[98] while Vartkes, who met with Ahmed Cemal about the same time, around 20 December, heard the Young Turk officer speaking even more bluntly than usual, proffering threats of massacre in the event that the Armenians failed to abandon the clause about a guarantee from the powers.[99]

Zohrab was, however, also alarmed by the Armenian political parties' inclination to raise the stakes and their blindness to the results their decisions might have. The Armenians, he thought, had to be able to admit the possibility of not "obtaining everything" and treating the reforms as "a stage," as Ambassador Wangehneim had put it.[100] When, the very next day, on 21 December, Zohrab gave an account of his meeting with the president of the Council of State to the Patriarch, Karayan, Papazian, Boyajian, and Armen Garo, putting the accent on the impasse around the issue of "supervision" by the powers, he observed with dismay the intransigence of his colleagues and sighed, "may God grant that we emerge from all this with as little damage as possible."[101] He reminded them that Article 61 of the Treaty of Berlin, the basis for the reform plan, provided for an "international guarantee," not "international supervision."[102] He urged them to make concessions: this would enable them to "improve [their] relations [with the Turks], which had become extremely bitter and were taking on increasingly threatening forms." By way of response, he was told that the Turks' aim was to negotiate this difficult moment while eluding European "supervision," so as "to leave the Armenians in a face-off" with them alone.[103]

Halil's failure to obtain significant results no doubt prompted the minister of the interior to intervene in person. On 24 December 1913, Zohrab went to see Halil at his residence: there he found Talât, who confirmed that he wanted the inspectors-general to be named by the Sublime Porte. This came down to doing away with European mediation and limiting European supervision or guarantees.[104] Zohrab responded that it was essential that the reforms succeed; it was not enough merely to announce reforms, as had been the case with the army, where there had been no tangible results. "You will grant," he said to Talât, "that the Armenians' desire for security is legitimate. Agree, at a minimum, to make a ten-year commitment on the agrarian question and on language, military service, the school tax and the *hamidiye*."[105]

The next day, Zohrab, Vartkes, and the minister of finance, Mehmed Cavid, who was reputed to be a moderate, had a dinner meeting that represented the last chance to reach a compromise. Cavid said that he approved of the reforms, but suggested that the Armenians make the concessions the Ittihad had asked for.[106]

In his diary entry for 28 December/10 January 1913–14, Zohrab noted bitterly that he had had to bear with the anti-Czarist positions of the Dashnaks for five years and that the party had now broken off discussions with the Ittihad against his advice.[107] His misgivings were by no means unfounded, for a new factor had arisen to complicate the negotiations: the acrimonious discussions between the Russians and Germans on the subject of the German military mission in Turkey headed by Otto Liman von Sanders.[108] The Armenians doubtless considered that if the Germans showed willingness to compromise on this matter, the Russians might also be inclined to make concessions on fundamental points of the reform package.

There can be no doubt that the failure of the December 1913 Armenian-Turkish negotiations left profound traces at a time when the Ittihad had decided to take complete control over the army and the state. For Zohrab, the Armenians had made a serious political error and nothing could now be done to remedy it. This is what he said to Vahan Papazian and Armen Garo when they came to see him on 17 January 1914 and announced that they were prepared to accept the compromise that they had rejected three weeks earlier. The damage had already been done, and Zohrab flew into a rage when they suggested that he go to see Halil. He criticized them for refusing to bargain, and particularly for having dismissed the proposal to bring Boghos Nubar to Turkey in order to carry on direct negotiations with the government.[109]

Zohrab informed Papazian and Garo that the Young Turks had agreed to apply the fifty-fifty principle to local political institutions, and also in appointing civil servants and policemen in the vilayets of Bitlis and Van. A proportional system was to be applied in the other regions. At the meeting of the Security Commission held the same day, the Armenian side proposed that the problem of the Kurdish *hamidiye* regiments be resolved by, at a minimum, incorporating these regiments into the army. The Patriarch insisted that the fifty-fifty principle be applied in Erzerum as well.[110] But the Armenians had to act quickly, because the Russian ambassador was to call at the Sublime Port at three o'clock. Zohrab hurriedly drafted the Patriarchate's response to the proposals of the Sublime Porte as transmitted by the ambassador. This was, to say the least, an odd situation, although perhaps not such an unusual one in the last years of the Ottoman Empire: the representative of a foreign state was acting as an intermediary between a party of government and a party representing an Ottoman national group.

The final details of the reform plan were examined on 4 February 1914 in the presence of André Mandelstam and Zohrab, at a dinner given at the residence of the Russian ambassador.

In a telegram, St. Petersburg had instructed its diplomats to insist on three points: first, that the fifty-fifty principle be applied to the vilayet of Erzerum as well; second, that *muhacir* be prohibited from entering Armenia; and third, that Christians be guaranteed the right to sit on the general councils in the zones in which they were a minority – in Harput, Dyarbekir, and Sıvas.[111] The Sublime Porte rejected the first demand, gave an oral promise with regard to the second, and accepted the third.[112] On 8 February, the agreement was officially signed.

Since spring 1913, the Armenian leadership had also been conducting negotiations over Armenian representation in the Ottoman Chamber of Deputies, with an eye to the upcoming elections.[113] The Justice Ministry, however, let it be known that the electoral system was not a proportional one: parliamentary deputies were chosen to represent, not an ethnic group, but the whole Ottoman nation, and the ministry consequently saw no reason to allot the Armenians a number of seats proportional to their relative weight in the population. Moreover, the Turkish and Armenian authorities disagreed about the number of Armenians living in the empire. After numerous discussions – from which the Patriarchate was officially excluded, even though its political leadership was the Porte's official interlocutor – a meeting attended by the Armenian parties, national leadership, and a few Armenian dignitaries was held on 18 December 1913. There it was decided to demand at least 18 to 20 seats in parliament, with the deputies to be elected by the nation and distributed among the different vilayets in accordance with the demographic weight of the Armenian population in each. The Ittihad had initially accepted these propositions, but then changed its mind, doubtless when the negotiations over the reform plan were broken off. In February 1914, Stepan Karayan and the new Patriarch elected in August 1913,[114] Zaven Der Yeghiayan, held a meeting with Interior Minister Talât and the secretary general of the Ittihad, Midhat Şükrü, at which they finally agreed to set the number of Armenian deputies at 16. It was, however, also stipulated that the candidates recommended by the patriarchate would first have to be presented to the bureau of the Ittihad, so that they could be "officialized." For "good measure," the minister even promised, "as a show of his trust in the Armenians," that he would have one of these candidates elected vice-president of the Ottoman chamber; carry out the reforms, which were needed in Armenia, as quickly as possible; and revitalize the economy in these regions by building a railroad there.[115] According to Vahan Papazian's memoirs, Talât declared at this meeting that there was no good reason "that they could not also come to an agreement on the question of Armenian representation in the Ottoman parliament." The aim of all these declarations by Cavid, Talât, and even (in *Tanin*) Hüseyin Cahit was, however, to appease Europe, with which the Ottoman government had for months been negotiating to obtain new credits – the more so as Paris and London had given them to understand that one of the conditions for obtaining the desired loan was rapid implementation of the Armenian reforms. Papazian also informs us that rumors had even been making the rounds to the effect that Bedros Halajian might be named inspector general. "This," writes Papaian, "is how they succeeded in duping the Europeans and throwing sand in their eyes."[116]

By the end of this wrestling match, which had gone on for more than a year, the official Armenian organizations had, to be sure, had their way on the main points. In the meantime, however, the government had passed from the hands of the liberals into those of a radical Young Turk cabinet, which ultimately ceded only under heavy pressure from the powers. All indications are that the Ittihad remained deeply hostile to reforms, which it considered to be the first step in a separatist process. It seemed that nothing could reconcile Young Turks and Armenians, who were now in a tense face-off, like a couple that has already filed for divorce.

Chapter 3

The Establishment of the Ittihadist Dictatorship and the Plan to "Homogenize" Anatolia

From January 1913, when the CUP took the country firmly back in hand, to the congress of the Ittihad in October of the same year, the "young officers" led by Enver plainly attained a position of dominance in both the party and the conduct of state affairs. But this ascension was still far from having reached its apex, held back as it was by many different oppositional tendencies. The project to reform the army put forward by Mahmud Şevket accordingly aimed above all to keep the officers out of politics, just as the restructuring of the Ittihad had sought to reduce the risk that the army would bring the Central Committee under its control. Far from laying down their arms, Enver and his partisans kept up their pressure on the party and the government. Late in 1913, as the question of the Armenian reforms was entering a critical phase, the Ittihadist Central Committee found itself caught on the horns of a dilemma: it could either yield to the officers' bid for influence, at the risk of allowing a certain anarchy in the army, or reorganize the army by depoliticizing it.

The fact that the Ittihad and Said Halim's cabinet were indeed under pressure was confirmed when, toward the middle of December, Major Enver went to see the grand vizier Halim to insist that he be given the post of minister of war. The Egyptian prince pointed out that Enver was still too young for a position of that sort, but proposed to make him the chief of staff in order to show that he was aware of the young man's growing influence. Talât, for his part, hesitated to lend Enver his support,[1] probably because he was already wary of Enver's ambition and fearful of being sidelined in his own party.

These questions of personal ambition aside, what was at stake was the remodeling of the army already set in motion by Şevket. Halil (Menteşe), by now president of the Council of State, notes in his memoirs that "after the disastrous defeat in the Balkans, the question of the modernization of the army was on the agenda. The list of commanding officers to be sent into retirement had already been compiled."[2] But not everyone in the army shared the view that these officers should be shunted aside, beginning with the incumbent minister of war and chief of staff, Ahmed İzzet Pasha, who was reluctant to enact the decision. According to Halil, İzzet invoked the fact that all these high-ranking officers were "my friends."[3] More probably, he was of the view that if he eliminated the old guard of ranking officers to a man, he ran the risk, quite simply, of decapitating the army and aggravating the disorder that already reigned in it. Opposed, like Şevket, to the politicization of the officer corps, he doubtless constituted, after the assassination of the grand vizier, the last obstacle to the Young Turk leaders' assumption of total control over the army. Educated in Germany, İzzet was a close acquaintance of General Liman von Sanders, the head of the German military mission charged with reorganizing the Ottoman army. It was İzzet who went to receive von Sanders at the Sirkeci train station when the Prussian general arrived in Istanbul on 14 December 1913.[4] It may reasonably be supposed that, like many civilian and military leaders in the Hamidian period, he harbored serious apprehensions about the Young Turks and their ability to conduct affairs of state. Moreover, the Ittihadist Central Committee apparently wished to push İzzet aside. Indeed, Halil reports that, "One day, the late Talât said: 'Halil Bey, we will go to İzzet Pasha this evening. You know the problem. I will make this gentleman one last offer. If he shows the least hesitation, I shall suggest that he resign.'"[5] Obviously, the Ittihad was after more than just a reorganization of the Ottoman army; it was seeking to impose its own commanding officers on it so that it would no longer have anything to fear from that quarter. The army had become a major political stake, and control over it was now a prerequisite for holding power. The Committee, its mistrust of Colonel Enver notwithstanding, had no choice but to make use of him and the circles of officers supporting him in order to push General İzzet Pasha out the door.

İsmail Enver seemed confident of success. On 30 December 1913, he wrote to his fiancée and member of the imperial family, Naciye Sultan, that his appointment to the position of minister of war was certain and that he had been promoted to the rank of brigadier general. However, the daily *Tanin* did not report his appointment as war minister until 3 January 1914 and it was not until the day after that an official communiqué announced that Colonel Enver had become a brigadier general and been named minister of war.[6]

A diplomatic dispatch announcing İzzet's resignation noted with alarm: "the man whom the Committee has named as his successor is a threat: with Enver Bey in the position of minister of war, we may confidently look forward to adventures of the worst kind."[7] The dispatch also confirms the major role played by the Committee in this affair and the fame that Enver had already acquired despite his youth. Furthermore, there is every reason to believe that the Committee had also decided to make the radical purge of the army that was carried out a few days later: 280 ranking officers and 1,100 officers in all, "in whom [Enver] saw political adversaries," were "abruptly dismissed" on 7 January 1914.[8]

"We soon learned," Liman von Sanders writes, "that a number of officers had been confined in the cellar of the War Ministry – those who Enver feared might react."[9] We are inclined to suppose that, among these officers "who were no longer fit to serve or had become too old,"[10] some had played decisive roles in the "Halâskâr Zâbitan" (freedom officers), the group that brought down Said Pasha's cabinet in July 1912, and that the Ittihad at last saw its chance to liquidate them.

The head of the German military mission adds, bitterly, that he had "received no official notification of these measures," despite the clauses in the military mission's contract stipulating that it "was to be consulted on the choice of personnel for ranking positions"; he was never allowed, he writes, to interfere in this area.[11] There was good reason for this: the newly appointed officers were drawn, without exception, from the CUP's ranks. Moreover, von Sanders "later frequently had occasion to confirm that it was a waste of time to complain about an officer who belonged to the Committee," adding that he "was never able to determine how many members it had or who they were, apart from the main leaders whom everyone knew."[12] This time the Ittihadist Committee had taken a decisive step in its patient effort to subordinate the organizations of the state to the party. Never, perhaps, since the Ottoman Empire was founded, had civilians been so thoroughly under the thumb of the military, even if in January 1914 the army did not yet have the full apparatus of power in its grip.[13] With Enver's arrival at the head of the armed forces, Unionist ideology had finally been imposed on the Turkish army, which it would dominate for several decades to come.

For Enver and his partisans, according to Turfan, "reforming the military was equivalent to reforming the state."[14] The dissolution of the Council of Military Affairs, promptly decreed by Enver on 7 January 1914,[15] also directly served the CUP's purpose, which was to eliminate all alternate sources of power and all risk of interference with its policies. From this point on, to cite the no doubt exaggerated formulation of a historian,

> the destiny of the Ottoman state was under the control of the Committee of Union and Progress, the Committee of Union and Progress was under the control of the Central Committee, the Central Committee was under the control of the Triumvirate [in Turkish, *ücler*; that is, Enver, Talât and Cemal], and the Triumvirate under the strong will of the Minister of War, Enver pasha.[16]

It would seem that the CUP's strategy was to create the impression that it was a trustworthy partner and thus a first-rate, dependable ally for the German militarists. In his war memoirs, the head of the German military mission, who was also inspector general of the Ottoman army, stresses that the Ottomans systematically sought to hide the deplorable condition of the Turkish troops from him by systematically preparing his inspection tours in advance. To pull the wool over his eyes, Enver's staff would transfer one company's equipment to another so as to paper over deficiencies. The Turks also "hid sick soldiers, constitutionally feeble soldiers, and even the insufficiently educated," so that the German general would not see anything shocking or unpleasant. "In many units," van Sanders goes on, "the men were infested with vermin that bit them unmercifully. Not a single barracks had baths... The kitchens were as primitive as one could imagine," and even the equipment sent by the Germans sometimes remained "in its pristine packing," unused from when it arrived five years ago. Moreover, many buildings belonging to the army's service corps "offered, inside, a prospect of the greatest possible desolation, with piles of garbage in every corner."[17] Slovenliness and disorderliness constituted an obvious handicap for this army, an army that its Young Turk leaders hoped to make over into an instrument for conquering back what the empire had lost. "What was needed more than money," Von Sanders writes in this connection, "was a sense of order, cleanliness, and the importance of work. In those days, the Turks did not like to hear a German officer tell them to go to work; they preferred to find all sorts of excuses and pretexts for continuing to lead the contemplative life."[18]

The last important measure taken in December 1913, shortly after the arrival of the German military mission, was the subordination of the Ottoman gendarmerie, "an elite force of more than 80,000 men," to the Interior Ministry. Officially, the aim was to avert conflicts between the foreign officers serving in the gendarmerie, among them a commander of the gendarmerie, the head of the German military mission, and the French General Baumann.[19] It is more probable, however, that this administrative measure was intended to provide the interior minister with the military means he needed to deal with domestic matters, such as the Armenian civilians of the eastern provinces.

The effects of the reform agreement were not slow to make themselves felt. It is likely that the provincial authorities were ordered to harass the Armenian population. The "patriotic" fundraising campaign launched by the Trebizond Ittihadist club for the official purpose of "purchasing battleships" is a good illustration of this policy: the task of collecting the money was assigned to local delinquents,[20] who seized the opportunity to "extort large sums from Armenians and Greeks and occasionally to loot stores."[21] The Young Turk cabinet's official endorsement of "the plan to enact reforms in Armenia" did not preclude sharp tensions, probably provoked by the Ittihad's networks. A French diplomat remarked that

> the government again succumbed to the temptation to authorize the least respectable of those under its jurisdiction to meddle in public affairs, with the underlying design of then using the supposed resistance of Muslims to supervision [of the reforms] as a pretext for declaring itself powerless to ensure their enactment.[22]

In February 1914, wrote the French chargé d'affaires in Constantinople, "anti-Christian" agitation was on the rise and "isolated attempts to launch boycotts" could be observed. According to the same source,

> the chauvinistic excitement that the Committee's propagandists are trying to provoke among the masses, not without success, threatens to lead to an explosion of religious fanaticism and, in any case, to engender an anti-Christian mood. From this point of view, the propaganda that the agents of [the party of] Union and Progress are churning out in the provinces brings with it a danger that it is impossible to ignore.[23]

There can be little doubt about the Ittihadist cabinet's intention to sabotage the programmed reforms by inciting riots and other forms of violence, as Talât had indeed announced several months earlier in a discussion with his Armenian "friends."[24]

True to its usual methods, the CUP simultaneously announced the appointment of 80 civilian inspectors to posts in the provinces. Their mission was to supervise the maintenance of public order, the organization of the gendarmerie and the police, military recruitment and transportation, electoral activity, censuses, and the sedentarization of nomadic tribes.[25] In the provinces, however, there was widespread discontent, reflected in the many different complaints about a Young Turk administration that was constantly laying the country under contribution. Mass emigration was a problem plaguing not only the Armenian provinces, but the Arab regions as well, sparing no religious confession.[26] The minister of the interior hoped to settle immigrants from the Balkan countries in Syria, but this region, he was told by a well-informed interlocutor, was losing every week a thousand inhabitants fleeing dire poverty. "Those are Christians," Talât Bey is supposed to have replied, in a tone indicating that he was glad to be rid of them. But he was unaware that Muslims were also moving abroad. Emigration was proceeding so rapidly that, according to the same source, "the region would soon no longer need either farmers or craftsmen." The laws prohibiting people in certain social categories from leaving the country were powerless to halt the trend. Talât's interlocutor suggested that "it would be preferable to keep the people from considering emigration by improving the administration, reducing taxes and promoting agriculture."[27]

The more or less chronic discontent of the Kurds was itself exploited by the Ottoman government, which presented it as if it were "directed against the reforms," whereas it was above all a question, as General Şerif Pasha insisted, of anti-governmental agitation. The leader of the revolt, Mollah Selim, had to set the record straight in a letter addressed to the archbishop of Bitlis, Suren, before the government ceased to exploit the problem.[28] Taner Akçam's recent work,[29] based in particular on the memoirs of Kuşçubaşizâde Eşref (Sencer),[30] the head of the Special Organization in the Aegean region, reveals that a "plan to homogenize" Anatolia, cleanse it of its non-Muslim "tumors," and eliminate "concentrations of non-Turks" was discussed from February to August 1914 at several secret meetings of the Ittihad's Central Committee in the presence of the minister of war, although a number of other ministers were not informed of it. This "plan" was, as early as spring 1914, aimed first and foremost at the Greeks of Anatolia and the Aegean coast; it centered on Smyrna. It involved the implementation of 1) "general measures" carried out by the government (by *Vali* M. Rahmi); 2) "special measures" enacted by the army (the task of cleansing the region was put in the hands of Cafer Tayyar Bey); and 3) "measures" taken by the CUP (under the supervision of its delegate in Smyrna, Mahmud Celal [Bayar]). Halil (Menteşe) remarks in his memoirs that it was not supposed to look as if the government and administration were implicated in these exactions, which would take the form of massacres, deportations, forced exile, and the spoliation of hundreds of thousands of Greeks.[31]

It seems that the plan also provided for the transfer, at a later date, of the Armenian population to Syria and Mesopotamia.

From the Aborted Armenian Reforms to the Arrest of the Hnchak Leaders

As we have seen, the reform issue mobilized the official Armenian organizations for many months. They were, however, exhausted by the veritable battle that had pitted them against the Ittihad. There was even a degree of bitterness in the Armenians' ranks: some Armenians, such as Zohrab,[32] grasped the gravity of the situation and took anxious note of the Ittihad's radicalization.

Nevertheless, on 7 February, the day before the official decree announcing the reforms was signed, the Political Council made a public declaration before the Chamber of Deputies. In it, Karayan, the president of the chamber, confirmed that signature of the decree was imminent[33] and gave a public account of all the actions that the council and the Security Commission had taken in close collaboration with the Armenian National Delegation and the Tiflis and St. Petersburg committees.[34] All these efforts, in Karayan's view, had culminated in a globally positive result, even if it had been necessary to accept the division of the Armenian provinces into two "governorships," as well as the inclusion in these governorships of regions that were plainly located outside the boundaries of the Armenian high plateau. The patriarch, Zaven Der Yeghiayan, voiced the same cautious optimism at the 9 May 1914 spring opening session of the Armenian chamber.[35]

The task of finding candidates capable of exercising the functions of inspector general in the two "governorships" provided for by the reform agreement was entrusted to Boghos Nubar, who had many connections in Europe.[36] The two men who were chosen arrived in Constantinople in April. Zohrab received them. The Dutchman Louis Constant Westenenk, formerly chief administrator of the Dutch East Indies, was assigned to Erzerum (the northern sector), and Major Nicolai Hoff, a Norwegian officer, was assigned to Van (the southern sector, to which the vilayets of Bitlis, Dyarbekir, and Harput had also been attached).[37] The Sublime Porte signed the decree confirming the appointment of the two inspectors rather quickly, but only Hoff was able to assume his functions in Van early in August 1914, after assembling a supporting staff.

In 1914, Van seemed to be recovering from the disasters it had recently undergone. The *vali*, Tahsin Pasha, had restored law and order to the vilayet and showed signs of being well disposed toward the Armenians. Hoff, for his part, set about gathering information on the current situation and collecting the data he needed to implement the reforms.[38] On 16/29 August 1914, however, the Ministry of the Interior summoned the inspector general to quit his post and return to Constantinople without delay. His departure coincided with the arrival of the German consul in Erzerum, an occasion marked by a grand military review in which "twelve thousand goose-stepping soldiers paraded by." A few days later, Tahsin Pasha discovered that he had been semi-officially "seconded" at the head of the vilayet by Enver's brother-in-law Cevdet Bey, who was provisionally given the twofold title of military governor of Van and commander-in-chief of the Turkish troops massed along the Persian frontier.[39] It is hard to understand these developments as anything other than measures taken in anticipation of the gathering conflict, indicative of the Ittihad's intentions and its desire to throw the Ottoman Empire into the battle.

In the course of a meeting that Hoff had with interior minister Mehmed Talât after returning to Istanbul, the Armenian deputy Vartkes Seringiulian, who had also been invited to attend, saluted the Norwegian's return with a witty bon mot: "You have reformed Armenia, *inshallah*, and now you are back." In his diary, Zohrab wrote that "Hoff returned with, at the

very least, the conviction that Armenia needed reforms and that the Turks had no desire
to enact reforms there."[40] But the Armenian leaders sensed the threat hanging over their
nation. The fact that the sultan made no mention of "the appointment of two European
inspectors for the eastern vilayets"[41] in his 14 May 1914 speech to the Turkish parliament
inaugurating its new legislative period was itself a sign fraught with significance.

Nonetheless, until July, the staff of the Constantinople Patriarchate was very active around
the question of the reforms, as is attested by the many letters it exchanged with dioceses in the
provinces (in Trebizond or Gürün, for example) about the enactment of the reform plan and
the measures to be taken to smooth the way for it. These documents make systematic reference to a 17 February 1914 circular sent out by the Patriarchate.[42] It seems everyone's energies were mobilized for the purpose of establishing the beginnings of order in the Armenian
provinces. If all these tasks were to be successfully performed, it was of crucial importance to
establish a close relationship with the central Ottoman administration. Since the rupture of
December 1913, however, the Armenian leaders in the capital, and even the Patriarchate, had
been quite simply ignored and only rarely had an opportunity to confer with their Young Turk
colleagues. The situation was the more difficult in that the Ottoman parliament had recessed
on 2 August, the day before the proclamation of a general mobilization,[43] leaving it to the
cabinet to adopt "temporary" laws. The Cercle d'Orient, where it was possible to meet politicians, high-ranking officials, and foreign diplomats and gauge the situation in the country, was
in this period very faithfully frequented by its two Armenian members, Zohrab and Halajian.
Among the Dashnaks, Armen Garo and Vartkes Seringiulian maintained personal contacts
with certain ministers and members of the Young Turk Central Committee.[44]

What turned out to be the final session of the Armenian chamber was held on 4 July of the
same year. Gabriel Noradounghian, who chaired it, opened the debate in the hemicycle in
Galata in the presence of the leading lights of Armenian politics, Zohrab and Seringiulian.[45]
At a time when, in the wake of the ultimatum the Austrians had issued Serbia in late June,
warning signs of war had already appeared on the horizon, the Political Council duly noted
the first measures taken in the provinces in the framework of the reform plan. It was only
in mid-July that a sharp change in the nature of the threats hanging over the Armenians
became perceptible in Armenian circles. The press campaigns that, albeit malignant, were
business as usual, now yielded to a much more alarming sort of discourse: they portrayed the
Armenians in general as rebels conspiring with political exiles and foreign powers. The new
campaign, which seems to have been orchestrated in high places, began with the 16 July
1914 arrest of some 20 leading members of the Social Democratic Hnchak Party, promptly
followed by the imprisonment of about 100 activists of lower rank and searches of the party's
editorial offices and clubs as well as the homes of those arrested.

The story of the Hnchaks, which occupied the political stage for a full eleven months, had
multiple ramifications, culminating in the 15 June 1915 execution of 20 Hnchaks by hanging. Although it has rarely been studied by historians, this story constitutes one of the main
components of the official discourse designed to justify the measures the state took with
respect to the Armenian population in 1915. The basis for an examination of this episode is
provided, on the one hand, by explanations that the Hnchaks themselves furnished,[46] and,
on the other, by the grave accusations that the Turkish minister of the interior leveled at the
time of the events.[47] This question cannot, then, be ignored, the more so as it allows us to
follow the emergence and evolution of the official discourse stigmatizing the Armenians.

We have already seen that the SDHP was the Young Turks' *bête noire* during the period
in which the anti-Hamidian opposition was in exile, and no less during the "constitutional"
years, thanks to its positions, alliances with the liberal opposition, and political struggle
against the Ittihad. After the party's historical leaders, Murad (Hampartsum Boyajian) and
Stepanos Sapah-Giulian had returned from exile, this revolutionary committee found itself

confronting the need to make a political choice between becoming a legal organization or maintaining its underground structures. At their Sixth General Congress, which opened in Istanbul on 12 July 1909, the Hnchaks had unambiguously opted for legality and proceeded to draft new statutes in conformity with Ottoman law. The official declaration published at the end of this Congress did, however, point up the limits of the Constitution and the conservatism and benightedness of Ottoman society, as well as the religious hatreds that continued to dominate it, breeding clashes between its component groups together with the absence of "class consciousness."[48] In other words, the party remained critical while nursing hopes that the situation would evolve.

The party's discourse changed little over the next few years. At its Second General Assembly, convened in Istanbul on 26 September 1912, it condemned the "nationalistic, Pan-Turk" policies implemented by the Ittihad and reaffirmed its alliance with the Ittilâf.[49] The pact it signed with the Ittilâf nevertheless defended "the integrity of the Ottoman state and the rights guaranteed by the Constitution" and "rejected all separatist aspirations" (Article 2), "defended the civil rights of all nations comprising the Ottoman state" while "rejecting the domination of any one of its components over the others" (Article 3), and called for resolution of the agrarian question as well as settlement of the *muhacir* where land was available.[50]

The SDHP seems to have made a turn, however, at its Seventh General Congress, which opened on 5 September 1913 in Constanza, Rumania.[51] In the conclusions to which this Congress came, we read that the party had adopted a legalist course at its previous Congress and decided against pursuing "separatist policies." However, having observed over the preceding four years that "the promises made by the Ottoman Constitution [had] remained without concrete effect and [had] no real significance," and also that the Ittihad, the sole political force in power, had "no basic principles beyond that of safeguarding the Turkish bureaucracy... and [had] plainly set out not only to assimilate the constituent nations, but to annihilate them, to massacre them," the SDHP decided that it had become necessary to struggle against the Young Turks by illegal means, "until more favorable political and economic conditions [were] created." In obedience to its revolutionary logic, the party, which had denounced the Young Turks' nationalism when it was still in exile in Paris, decided to employ "violent revolutionary tactics" in an active struggle against the Ittihad. This was, in its view, the only way to foil the Unionists' criminal plans.[52]

According to the author of the official history of the Hnchak party, "all sections of the Hnchak party in Turkey, without exception, approved the [decisions of the] Seventh Congress, particularly the [use] of terror," while all possible precautions were taken to keep the latter decision secret. Party members chosen to carry out terrorist operations were "whisked off to the countryside."[53] However, this official account is contested by Hmayag Aramiants, who affirms that a majority of the local committees in Turkey – 44 of 61 – did not take part in the Congress and, accordingly, did not endorse its decisions.[54] A reading of these two versions reveals the existence of serious dissensions in the SDHP; it is probable that the organizers of the Congress had tried to exclude the militants likely to oppose the most extreme positions. The exclusion of Aramiants himself, who was clearly in the legalists' camp, as was the majority of the Istanbul party leadership, would appear to confirm this hypothesis. The Hnchak committee in the capital, which, in the person of one of its leaders, Nerses Zakarian, a member of the Patriarchate's Political Council, was actively working to settle the question of the reforms side by side with all other Armenian political forces, opposed the decisions reached at Constanza. They led to the dissolution of the official party in Turkey, henceforth placed under the tutelage of an underground committee.

What these Hnchak party officials did not, in any case, know was that interior minister Talât had succeeded in infiltrating the party with an officer from the intelligence service.

This officer, Arthur Esayan, alias Arshavir Sahagian,[55] had arranged to have himself named a delegate to the Constanza Congress by the party's Cairo committee. By way of the Ottoman consul in Dede Ağac, he provided Talât with a comprehensive account of the decisions adopted by the Congress and a list of the participants. Since most Armenian organizations were under surveillance by the minister's agents, one may suppose that the SDHP, uncompromisingly opposed to the Ittihad and made up of fearless activists, was watched more closely than all the others. There is even every reason to believe that after decapitating the liberal Ottoman opposition, the Young Turks had decided to rid themselves of the Hnchaks, who unremittingly condemned their political practices. The open letter to the European governments that the SDHP published in Paris in 1913 after the Constanza Congress[56] can only have strenghthened the Young Turks' resolve, given the considerable effects it produced in Europe. In this text, the party criticized Europe for the vacillations of its diplomacy since the adoption of Article 61 of the Treaty of Berlin, pointing out the devastating impact on the Ottoman Armenian population of the failure to honor the promises the treaty contained. A number of European newspapers even published editorials on the question of the "reforms in Armenia,"[57] reminding their readers of the powers' "moral" obligation to put an end to the exactions to which successive governments had subjected the Armenians, or had at least covered up. The Hnchaks' appeal, written by individuals with strong social values, denounced the archaic nature and conservatism of the Young Turk regime, the similarity of its practices to Abdülhamid's, and its instrumentalization of the Muslim masses. Although cast in quite sophisticated terms, the appeal could hardly have provided the basis for an indictment in a democratic society – not for an indictment for criminal conspiracy, at any rate. What is more, the source of this appeal was the "external" Central Committee, from which, according to the party statutes, the Turkish Committee was independent, and nothing justified the affirmation that the Turkish Committee condoned the appeal.

At this point in our discussion, the question obviously arises: if the documents that Arshavir Sahagian assembled were as compromising as the Ottoman government would later affirm, why did it wait until 16 July 1914 to arrest the Hnchak leaders of Istanbul?[58] Was the reason for the delay the imminence of the war, which the Young Turk leadership had already decided to enter? Was it the preparation of an assassination attempt on the minister of the interior himself, to which no allusion was made until after the interrogations had begun? It is certain, in any case, that this was a particularly opportune moment, since the attention of all Europe was fixed on the Austrian-Serbian crisis. From the detailed account of the interrogations to which the Hnchak leaders were subjected and from the nature of the offences for which they were subsequently indicted – Bedri Bey, the police chief in the capital, personally informed them of the charges against them – there emerges a general accusation of conspiring to endanger state security; criminal involvement with General Şerif Pasha, at the head of the opposition in exile in Paris; and attempted murder of a person whose identity was not revealed.[59]

The battery of charges was probably not particularly solid, inasmuch as a number of those accused were released after a few days or weeks of questioning – although their liberation can also be interpreted as a tactical decision of Talât's on the eve of a general mobilization to which all Armenians of draftable age were subject.[60] In any event, this first warning shot fired by the government alarmed the SDHP's Istanbul organization, which had been unceasingly taking its distance from the decisions of the Constanza Congress.

Perhaps with a view to clarifying its positions in the wake of these accusations, the SDHP of Turkey convened its Third General Assembly in Istanbul on 24 July 1914. It was attended by 31 delegates from its local committees[61] and elected a new committee comprising Murad (Hampartsum Boyajian), Nerses Zakarian,[62] Vahan Zeytuntsian[63] and Harutiun Jangulian.[64] Most probably, this initiative was taken after Dr. Benné,[65] delegated by the SDHP's Central

Committee to take control of the Turkish Committee, ordered that the party dissolve itself and go underground, in accordance with the decisions reached at Constanza.[66] The Istanbul branch of the party considered it imperative to thwart this process and dispel the serious suspicions hanging over the party. In any case, the Hnchaks' Ottoman networks had been virtually neutralized by July 1914; they were occupied with the defense of their imprisoned comrades, against whom very real charges had been brought.

The Armenian authorities were not indifferent to these events. The Political Council and the patriarch personally had stepped in to try to obtain the release of the Hnchak prisoners, or at least improve their conditions. Certain well-known magistrates were even approached and asked to intercede on their behalf. Often, in Eastern societies, those against whom extremely serious accusations have been brought, justifiably or not, can be "pardoned" as long as they or their friends have the means and connections required. It is probable that some of the Hnchaks were able to obtain their freedom in this way.

The second event exploited by the Ittihadist cabinet in order to make the Ottoman Armenians out as traitors to their country was the ARF's Seventh Congress, which opened in Erzerum in late July 1914. The Dashnaks, who still considered themselves privileged interlocutors of the Ittihad, were alarmed by the repression of the Hnchaks and the way the Istanbul press had been exploiting it. They had already understood that, by way of the SDHP, all Armenians were being portrayed as traitors and rebels. They therefore arranged for their party's congress, which had been scheduled long in advance, to disappear from public view. The delegates were dispersed after only two weeks of discussions. By the time they were, they had learned that war had broken out in Europe, that the reforms had been "suspended," and that, on 3 August, a general mobilization had been proclaimed. The congress, while reaffirming that Armenians should meet their civic obligations in the countries of which they were citizens in case of war, decided to dissolve the ARF's Constantinople-based Western Bureau.[67] It added that, if it should be confirmed that the government was obstructing the reforms, "the party should oppose the methods employed by the government to thwart realization of the plan and defend the rights of the Armenian people."[68] A special commission made up of nine members, including, notably, A. Vramian, Rostom, and Aknuni, was chosen to elaborate the party's politics in the light of the most recent developments. It was this commission that received Dr. Bahaeddin Şakir[69] and two famous CUP *fedayis*, Ömer Naci and Filibeli Ahmed Hilmi, who arrived in Erzerum on 8 August.[70] They had not come as emissaries of the CUP, but had been charged with preparing the future activities of the Teskilât-ı Mahsusa (Special Organization).[71] Şakir suggested to his Armenian interlocutors that they take part in the campaign of subversion then being planned for the Caucasus, offering to create an autonomous Armenia in exchange for Armenian help in destabilizing the area behind the Russian army's lines.[72] The ARF now found itself torn between its two poles, Russian and Ottoman. It had been asked to take an impossible position, to betray one of the two states with an Armenian population. The Dashnak leaders once again issued a public call to Armenians to remain loyal subjects of the empire, but this was not enough to satisfy their Young Turk colleagues. Şakir reported to the CUP's Central Committee on the Armenian delegates' rejection of his proposal.[73] In his coded response, dated 17 August 1914 and entitled "Orientations," Midhat Şükrü, the Central Committee's secretary general, wrote: "Beyond a doubt, the Armenians are not inclined to collaborate with us. [See to it] that our orientation is kept secret from them."[74] The Ittihad, the "orientation" of which seems already to have been set, had probably not expected the ARF to respond any differently and had no other aim than to lay the groundwork for the government's future propaganda campaign on the theme of the Armenians' treachery.

As soon as the ARF's leaders had returned from the Congress of Erzerum, they organized a series of meetings attended by Zohrab and the party's Istanbul officials. The same question was examined from every possible angle: what position should the Armenians take in the anticipated conflict, in which Armenian soldiers called up in both Turkey and Russia would have to fight in both the Ottoman and Russian forces? The discussions always led to the same conclusion: the Armenians in the empire should do their duty, accept conscription into the armed forces, and pay the special taxes to help finance the war effort.[75] On the evening of 13 August, aboard a steamboat bound for the island of Kınalı, Zohrab said to his fellow deputy Vahan Papazian, who was scheduled to leave the next morning for his electoral district, Van: "You can be sure that they're going to do something to us."[76] The Armenian elite had already understood that it had been taken hostage and was no longer in a position to influence the course of events. Vartkes and Armen Garo, whom Zohrab invited to his summer home on Prinkipo on 16 August, observed that "the Turks want to profit from this war. The objectives of some of them are modest, those of others are grandiose."[77] This apparently insignificant phrase pointed to a question of crucial importance for the Armenians: what aims were the Ittihadists really pursuing in preparing to enter the war?

The Dashnaks, for their part, wondered what the coming conflict held in store for them. They were being solicited from different quarters: both the Russians and the French made overtures to them. A party official, Parsegh Shahbaz, returned from Paris in early August 1914. He informed his comrades that Victor Bérard, a pro-Armenian militant, had met with French Prime Minister Gaston Doumergue at the latter's request, and Doumergue had asked him "whether the ARF would be willing to help the Entente." Bérard had then made contact with *Droschak*'s editorial board in Geneva and its director, Mikayel Varantian, had dispatched Shahbaz to the Ottoman capital.[78] Malkhas (Ardashes Hovsepian), who was present at the 22 August meeting called to discuss this question in the editorial offices of *Azadamard*, writes that the members of the committee were unanimously in favor of declaring that the Armenians had to remain "loyal citizens wherever they were found, especially in Turkey," adding that the leadership was opposed to the creation of groups of volunteers in the Caucasus.[79] Given the ambient hostility and the accusations that they were pro-Entente, the Dashnaks knew that, multiplying their efforts, they had constantly to "prove" their loyalty.

An article attributed to Simon Vratsian, the editor-in-chief of *Droschak*, gives us a rather good sense of the dilemma confronting the ARF as well as the Ittihadist leaders' mood at this time:

Turkey, too, has thrown itself into the fray. It has of course sensed – or, perhaps, its German mentors have brought it to understand – that the critical hour of truth has sounded for the Ottoman Empire as well. "If the French-English-Russian Entente defeats Turkey, it will be partitioned between those three victorious states. If the German-Austrian alliance wins the war, Turkey will be able to gain back some of the territory that it lost in the Balkans, and perhaps in Egypt and the Caucasus as well." Thus a straightforward calculation has convinced the Ittihadist government to lose no time jumping on the bandwagon of the German-Austrian alliance, justifying the decision with the arguments of the faction led by Enver Pasha, who is under the Germans' spell. Turkish troops are accordingly advancing toward the Caucasus, on the one hand, and Egypt on the other. The Russian army has entered Turkey, won a few battles, found itself confronted with the rigors of the climate, slowed its advance and even come to a halt here and there, but it is stubbornly pursuing its march on Erzerum, the citadel of Armenia, where Turkey has concentrated significant forces and created a powerful defensive system under the lead of German officers.

When will the Russians take Erzerum? How far will Russia advance into Armenia? What are St. Petersburg's plans for this region? These questions are so many crucial riddles for the Armenians today. In the liberal Russian press, voices favorable to Armenian autonomy have been raised, but there is no doubt that other circles are very differently disposed. The Czar's Manifesto was read aloud by the viceroy before an audience of Armenian dignitaries in Tiflis, but we should not overestimate the value of this kind of declaration, full of promises. Manifestos of this sort have been widely diffused among the other peoples of Russia. They are written to be forgotten. We should not delightedly and enthusiastically applaud such declarations or promises: there are painful historical precedents, such as the 1826 Russo-Persian War, during which the Armenian people, following its spiritual leader, rose as a single man and made a powerful contribution to the Russian conquest of the two khanates. This justified Armenian hopes of obtaining at least limited autonomy. Yet such hopes proved vain ... Two years later, the Russian army took Erzerum, but then quickly abandoned it and withdrew, leaving the Armenian population, which had shown unreserved sympathy for the Christian army, at the mercy of the vengeful local population.

Evoking the Russo-Turkish War of 1878, which had also led to "acts of violence, the exile of entire populations to the Caucasus, famine and endless misery," the writer calls for restraint:

> Thus we have no reason to meet the invaders of yesterday with childish manifestations of joy and thanksgiving ... The principal objective of the Armenian volunteers' legion, which was enthusiastically recruited from all quarters and has been put under the command of first-rate leaders, should be to protect the Armenian population in the event of Turkish massacres, especially in regions where the Armenians are weak, unarmed and in a minority ... It would be criminal naivety to rely on the Russian army to avoid massacres. The Russians have set out to conquer the Armenians' lands and their hearts will not grieve if Armenian blood once again flows abundantly here and there.[80]

The Dashnaks' mixed feelings about Russia find a perfect illustration here, as does their reading of the Ittihadists' intentions. The ARF was no longer, however, simply a tool that each of the powers could try to bend to its own use. Beginning notably in 1912, while certain party officials responsible for military matters envisaged the organization of a system of self-defense in the Armenian provinces, its leadership consistently rejected the idea, continuing to pursue the legalist political line that culminated in the adoption of the "reforms in Armenia."

The Secret Pact between Turkey and Germany and the General Mobilization

The negotiations between the German ambassador Hans Wangenheim and the Ittihadist cabinet, in particular the minister of war, İsmail Enver,[81] took place over a ten-day period beginning on 24 July[82] – which is to say, even before war broke out in Europe. According to the memoirs of the head of the German military mission, Liman von Sanders, both Sanders himself and ambassador Wangenheim had until then been opposed to an alliance with Turkey because they put no faith in the military capacities of an army that was as poorly equipped and undisciplined as Turkey's was.[83] Furthermore, as early as April 1914 Said Halim's government had made it known that the cabinet was leaning toward the Entente. In mid-May, Talât even sailed to the Black Sea on the imperial yacht in order to meet with the Czar and Sazonov.[84] Though his proposals were rejected, the presence of a Turkish delegation did not go unnoticed among the Germans of Istanbul. How, then, are we to explain the signing of the secret treaty that was a decisive step on the way to Turkey's entry into the war? While it is true that the tradition of putting the reorganization of the Ottoman army in the hands of German officers had by this time been firmly established for decades, that certain Ittihadist leaders genuinely admired the German Empire and its militaristic traditions, and that also Germany had more or less backed Turkey on the question of the Armenian reforms, these factors do not suffice to explain the German-Turkish treaty, which many observers both domestic and foreign regarded as irresponsible given the general state of the country. However, Germany's pledge to provide Turkey with "massive" economic aid opens up perspectives that we shall now go on to examine.

According to the testimony given at the November–December 1918 hearings before the Fifth Commission of the Ottoman parliament by former ministers in the war cabinets, the negotiations, which took place in Wangenheim's summer home in Tarabia and in the Yeniköy residence of Grand Vizier Said Halim, had been conducted at the urging of Enver Pasha, who is supposed to have taken the initiative leading to these discussions single-handedly.[85] What we know about the practices of Ittihadist circles, however, makes this explanation rather implausible. Although Enver did succeed in obtaining a sharp increase in military funding and financial advantages for army officers from Minister of Finance Mehmed Cavid,[86] it is unthinkable that he had acted without the approval of the Ittihad's Central Committee and the grand vizier. Moreover, Cavid himself notes that on 2 August 1914, when Said Halim invited him to his residence, he found Talât, Enver, and Halil (Menteşe) there, along with the dragoman of the German embassy, Weber. By Cavid's account, they were in the thick of a negotiation.[87] Thus, it is probable that, in this short period in which many different initiatives were being taken, the whole Ittihadist network had been activated. How else are we to explain the simultaneous signing at Said Halim's residence (on the evening of 2 August) of the secret German-Turkish accord and the decree proclaiming a general mobilization, as well as the imperial *irade* recessing the Ottoman parliament on the following day?[88] There were, furthermore, many different meetings between Young Turk leaders in this period. This tends to indicate that the debates were intense, but that decisions were taken collectively. Thus, on the evening of 3 August, Talât and Cavid went to see Enver at Ferid Pasha's *konak*, where Enver was then living (here they learned that Weber had come round that morning to pick up the treaty signed by Halim the previous evening). On 4 August, the same people met again at Halim's residence.[89]

According to the minister of public works, Çürüksulu Mahmud Pasha, "the signing of the treaty was never brought up before the Council of Ministers"[90] in order to keep the treaty secret and forestall resistance from ministers opposed to the war. For, in addition to Said Halim, Cavid, Çürüksulu Mahmud, Süleyman el-Bustani, and Oskan Bey (Mardikian)[91] made no secret of their desire to see Turkey remain neutral. A note in which the three Entente powers pledged to respect the territorial integrity of the Ottoman Empire if it maintained "absolute neutrality" was made public on 16 August 1914. It had been negotiated with the ambassadors of the Entente by Minister of Finance Cavid.[92] The negotiation and publication of the note had probably been intended as a means of evaluating the advantages that Turkey could reap from the powers in this context, but the aim may also have been to put the Germans under pressure. Significantly, in August the CUP also conducted negotiations with Bulgaria with a view to bringing it into the war on the German side. It also sought to secure the neutrality of Romania and Greece. On 1 September, Talât returned from a trip to Romania and Halil came back from Bulgaria.[93]

It is only too clear that Turkey was counting on German protection in order to conduct its own war and thereby acquire the status and capacities of the great power that it no longer was. But what precisely did the Ittihadists expect to gain from this adventure? Vahan Papazian, the parliamentary deputy from Van who was still in the Ottoman capital in early August, cites persistent rumors then circulating about Turkey's possible entry into the war and the recovery of lost territories – those in Bosnia-Herzegovina, those lost during the Balkan Wars, and even a conquest of the Caucasus.[94] Beyond such territorial ambitions, which are common during wartime, some authors also believe that Turkey's entry into the war was further motivated by domestic objectives, particularly a plan to annihilate the Ottoman Armenians. Vahakn Dadrian cites many accounts by different German and Austrian officers that provide solid support for this thesis.[95] In his memoirs, Marshal Pomiankowski, who was for a long time attached to the Ottoman general staff, reports "opinions expressed spontaneously by many intelligent Turks" to the effect that the subject peoples should have been forcibly converted to Islam or else "exterminated." "In this sense," he concludes, "there is no doubt that the Young Turk government had decided, well before the War began, to take advantage of the first occasion that came along to correct this error, at least partially." "It is also very probable," he adds, "that this consideration, that is, their project, decisively influenced the Ottoman government's decision to ally itself with the Central Powers."[96] We shall see later, when we examine the sources of the Ittihad's ideology and in particular the conditions surrounding the implementation of its project for a "national economy" or, again, the military operations it carried out in spring 1918, that the Unionist regime always gave absolute priority to its "domestic security" goals, privileging them above all other military and economic considerations.

The general mobilization order issued on 3 August 1914, the day after the secret German-Turkish agreement was signed, does not seem to have resulted from a hasty decision. According to Mehmed Cavid's deposition before the Ottoman parliament's fifth commission, the decision to issue the order was not made at a meeting of the Council of Ministers. Rather, Enver took the initiative that led to it, "arranging for each of the ministers to sign, separately, a draft of the imperial *irade*." The order was not published in the *Official Gazette* until after it had been publicly proclaimed.[97] This rapidity can doubtless be explained by the minister of war's desire to take advantage of the emotion generated by the announcement of war in Europe in order to generate an upsurge of national feeling. Zohrab, an attentive observer of the Ottoman world, remarked – with a good dose of fatalism and no little clairvoyance – that the mobilization took place under extremely chaotic conditions, "more like a coming together of forces getting ready to massacre and loot than a regular fighting organization."[98] The chaos probably resulted from the successive cultural grafts attempted onto the Ottoman army.

Men between the ages of 20 and 45 were the first to be affected by the mobilization order. This held for the eastern provinces as well. According to reports received from dioceses in the provinces, the mobilization seems to have proceeded calmly, but the conscription of the 20-to-45 year-olds led to an almost complete standstill of agricultural and commercial activity.[99] These reports also indicate that the Armenian draftees, who were not used to handling weapons or to life in the army, had a hard time adjusting to their new conditions.[100] The main problem in the eastern provinces was the lack of basic structures and organization. Papazian, who was in Mush in mid-November, saw groups of young conscripts arriving daily. They were lodged in mosques, khans, or dilapidated depots, often left to their own devices, in the cold and without food. Deserters were legion among all the population groups in the empire.[101]

Papazian notes further that requisitions had attained major proportions by early December 1914, for Mush had by then become a major recruitment and training center to which reluctant conscripts from Dyarbekir, Harput, Gence, and Hazo were brought in droves. The storehouses were filled with grain and other products that had been seized in the Armenian villages on the plain of Mush or from shops in the market that had been stripped clean of their merchandise.[102] In a country such as the Ottoman Empire, where officials had a reputation for dishonesty, the requisitions ordered by the government offered a golden opportunity for abuses. In Erzerum, a few days after the general mobilization had been decreed, the military authorities began to requisition carts, cattle, horses, and foodstuffs from the area's inhabitants, and rice, wheat, and sugar from Armenian and Turkish merchants, without offering them any compensation whatsoever.[103] The Armenian primate noted that the approaching winter season threatened to be particularly difficult for those peasants on the plains of Pasın, Khnus, and Tercan, for the requisitions had left them without reserves.[104]

Preparations for War: The Creation of the Special Organization

We have seen that the Committee of Union and Progress, since coming to power in 1908, often made use of its *fedayis* to do its dirty work, fight the opposition, liquidate critical journalists, give direction to its clubs in the provinces, and take control of key posts in the army. Yet everything indicates that this paramilitary structure retained an "amateur" organization down to the time of the Balkan Wars. The various sources at our disposal all confirm that it was the trauma brought on by the Balkan Wars that contributed decisively to a new radicalization of the Ittihad and prompted the party to create "special forces" that would be operational in case of war – that is, capable of both destabilizing an army's rear by organizing a network of spies behind enemy lines and struggling against "separatist movements" within the country itself.[105]

The first, still embryonic Special Organization was especially active in the second Balkan War, particularly during the July 1913 campaign to take back Edirne.[106] This first group was unsurprisingly made up of young officers, CUP *fedayis*, and partisans of Enver. It recruited for the occasion from the ranks of the Müdafa-i Milliye Cemiyeti (Committee of National Defense), which was led by well-known Ittihadist officers such as Halil (Kut), Enver's uncle, Filibeli Ahmed Hilmi, Yenibahçeli Nail, and Yakup Cemil.[107] We also know that, in the course of the year, Halil Bey terrorized the Greek villages of Thrace at the head of 5,000 çetes, indicating that the organization was already a force to be reckoned with. According to another source, hardly had Enver been named to head the War Ministry than he ordered, on 24 January 1914, Kuşçubaşızâde Eşref (Sencer), one of his *fedayis*, to found a branch of the Special Organization in Smyrna; Greeks and Armenians, the minister of war affirmed, had transformed the churches of the city into arsenals that had to be "cleaned out" (*temizleme*).[108] French consular sources, in turn, indicate that CUP *fedayis* were criss-crossing the provinces of Asia Minor as early as spring 1913. Yakup Cemil, "who had already come" to the city of Adana in Cilicia "in 1909, shortly before the massacres," returned on 11 April 1913, accompanied by three "officers in civilian clothing," for a meeting with the Ittihadist Şakir Effendi and the *vali*.[109] This suggests that the leaders of the Special Organization had set out to reinforce their local networks. We do not, however, know what they were trying to accomplish. Although this secret organization created on Enver's initiative[110] had not yet taken its final form, this handful of examples attests that it was no longer interested only in conducting sabotage and destabilization operations abroad, but was also already dealing with questions of "the domestic security of the Ottoman Empire."[111]

To judge from the documentary evidence presented at the Ittihadists' trial (sixth session, 17 May 1919), it would appear that from late July 1914 this first Special Organization, controlled by Enver and the army, had a second, subsidiary structure.[112] It was around this time, according to the indictment of the chiefs of the CUP, that the Ittihad's main leaders held a secret meeting at party headquarters in Nuri Osmaniye Street. The decisions taken at this meeting constituted a decisive step toward creating a new Teşkilât-ı Mahsusa and defining its tasks.[113] According to Arif Cemil, an official in the new organization, the secret meeting was held "the evening of the day on which the mobilization order was published" – that is, 3 August.[114] Cemil further notes that a ferocious battle was then raging in the CUP for control of the paramilitary groups linked to the party: Ahmed Cemal controlled the Türk Ocağı ("Turkish Hearth" society), while Enver sought to increase his personal power by means of the Special Organization, to which he hoped to transfer some of the CUP's prerogatives.[115] Thus we should not exclude the possibility that the second Teşkilât-ı Mahsusa was born of Talât's – and above all, Nâzım's and Şakir's – desire to curb Enver's megalomaniacal ambitions. Cemil also points out that from the moment the Special Organization came into being, its "main objective was [the creation] of an Islamic Union and the union of all the Turks living outside Turkey's borders."[116]

The Ittihadist leaders' trial also sheds light on the internal structures of the second Special Organization. It reveals that it answered to the Ittihad's Central Committee and was controlled by a political bureau headed by Bahaeddin Şakir. The trial also shows that the political bureau was made up of five members – that is to say, half – of the Central Committee, who were charged with the political leadership of the Special Organization: Dr. Nâzım, Dr. Şakir, Dr. Rüsûhi,[117] Yusuf Rıza Bey,[118] and Atıf Bey (Kamçıl).[119] They were assisted by Aziz Bey, head of the Interior Ministry's Office of State Security, and Colonel Cevad, who replaced Enver's uncle Halil Pasha (after the latter's departure for Van and Iranian Azerbaijan) as Istanbul's military governor and a member of the Teşkilât-ı Mahsusa's political bureau.[120] Finally, it should be noted that the Special Organization had its head office in the headquarters of the CUP in Nüri Osmaniye Street.[121] Here, Aziz Bey, Atıf Bey, Nâzım, and Halil (Kut) went about their duties, along with Colonel Cevad and Halimoğlu Yusuf Ziya Bey, who is mentioned only once in the course of the Unionists' trial, as a member of the Ittihad's Central Committee and also as the head of the Special Organization in Trebizond.[122] Moreover, all the telegrams and documents addressed to the networks in the provinces that were presented as evidence at the Unionists' trial bore the signatures of these officials based in the organization's headquarters. They show that the individuals who worked on Nuri Osmaniye Street planned and coordinated the operations carried out in the field, whereas the president of the political bureau of the Special Organization, Şakir, together with Rüsûhi and Yusuf Rıza Bey, led these operations directly.

After reading out the indictment of the Ittihadist leaders, the presiding judge at the court-martial summed up the results of the pretrial investigation:

> It has been established that the secret network was created by the leaders of Union and Progress under the name Teşkilât-ı Mahsusa, on the pretence that it was to participate in the War, as appears in the indictment. It was headed by Dr. Nâzım, Dr. Bahaeddin, Atıf Bey and Rıza Bey, members of the Central Committee, as well as Aziz Bey, the head of the Department of Criminal Investigations. Bahaeddin went to Erzerum to direct the forces in the eastern vilayets from there. Rıza Bey led the forces in the Trebizond area. Aziz, Atıf and Nâzım Bey worked in Constantinople, where their decisions had to be approved and executed by the local military commander, Cevad. This is proven by a secret decision, document no. 150; it is addressed to Bahaeddin Şakir, contains the words "the Committee should punish Galatalı Halil" ... and bears the signatures of Aziz, Atıf and Nâzım as well as Cevad's stamp of approval.[123]

Thus, the structure of the Special Organization and its organic connection with the Ittihad's Central Committee appear quite clearly. We shall go into these matters in greater detail later.

Can we, in light of the foregoing, speak of two Special Organizations that had different missions, or were even in competition? The trial of the Unionists and "responsible secretaries," the party's all-powerful representatives in the vilayets, does not allow us to give more than a partial response to this question, for a number of the accused fled Turkey before the trial began, while those present were manifestly unwilling to divulge the secret motives for their actions.

Two eminent CUP members admitted, albeit rather reluctantly, the existence of two organizations functioning independently of each other – Major Yusuf Rıza Bey, head of the Special Organization in the Trebizond region (on 17 May 1919, at the sixth session of the Unionists' trial),[124] and Colonel Cevad, the military governor of Istanbul and a member of the Special Organization's political bureau (at the fourth session of the same trial, on 8 May). Cevad added that the first of the Special Organizations fell under the jurisdiction of the War Ministry while the second answered to the CUP.[125] The Ittihad's secretary general, Midhat Şükrü, confessed, for his part (at the seventh session of the trial, held on the afternoon of 17 May), that certain members of the Central Committee had taken a direct hand in the creation of the Teşkilât-ı Mahsusa. The others did not react:[126] they either refused to testify about this subject, on the pretext that Enver's War Ministry was the body responsible for such matters, or else flatly denied that there had been two Special Organizations.

Arif Cemil's memoirs, albeit written with considerable caution and teeming with flagrant mistakes, contain information that sheds more light on the question of the Special Organization. According to this Ittihadist officer, Talât very quickly gained the upper hand over Enver in the match that saw them struggling for control of the second Teşkilât-ı Mahsusa. Initially, however, when the Ittihad's Central Committee decided, as the general mobilization was getting underway, that CUP members were to take part in the war effort in the framework of the Special Organization, two competing groups left Istanbul for Erzerum and Trebizond more or less simultaneously. The first, created on Talât's initiative, was led by Şakir – according to Cemil, it was Talât who asked Şakir to go to Erzerum to set up the Special Organization (after reminding him that he had been present at the siege of Edirne and thus had the required experience) – in association with Ömer Naci, the CUP's inspector general; Filibeli Ahmed Himli, a military official of the party; Emir Halmet and Çerkez Reşid, both leaders of çete bands, with their underlings; and finally, the officer Rüşdi Bey.[127] The second group, made up of Ittihadist fedayis, was sent east on the initiative of Enver and the minister of war.[128] Following Cemil's account, the Central Committee designated Ömer Naci and Rüsûhi Bey to direct operations on the Persian border. Süleyman Şefik Pasha, Hüseyin Rauf (Orbay), and Übeydullah were dispatched to Afghanistan; İbrahim and Yusuf Rıza were assigned to the Caucasus; and Celal Bey was given responsibility for Macedonia.[129] Finally, the Committee sent the responsible secretaries based in party headquarters on missions to the eastern provinces. All were instructed to travel incognito and reveal their identities to the local governors only when absolutely necessary.[130]

These details are not insignificant. They show that two structures coexisted in early August 1914. One was founded on a decision of the Ittihad's Central Committee with Talât's and Enver's approval and put under Bahaeddin Şakir's responsibility. The other, which had already been in existence for some time, was subordinated to the War Ministry, and Enver in particular, and led by a colonel on the general staff, Süleyman Askeri,[131] who was succeeded by Kuşçubaşızâde Eşref (Sencer). Can we, then, speak of distinct, competing organizations? The two organizations were indeed in competition, to the extent that the objectives of the second Special Organization were not fundamentally different from those of the first. They were distinct as well, except in the eastern provinces where they would merge in spring 1915. In fact, the first Special Organization pursued two very different goals at the same time: it conducted military counter-espionage and, secondarily, "harassed domestic foes," in Macedonia, Thrace, and on the Aegean coast. The second Special Organization also carried out operations behind enemy lines beyond the empire's borders; it sought in particular to foment rebellion among the Muslim and Turkish-speaking populations of the Caucasus, but then rapidly confined itself to liquidating or deporting "internal enemies." It only partially accommodated the demands of the military; above all, it carried out "internal" missions, but sometimes, in Turkish environments, "external" missions as well. Kuşçubaşızâde Eşref, the head of the Special Organization in the war ministry, confesses in his memoirs that

> the Special Organization was a black box that became the fundamental structure for ensuring the security of the Ottoman state at home and abroad ... To this end, it had its own officers, uniforms, treasury and secret code; it was a state within the state. In taking on missions that went beyond normal limits, it acquired a moral personality. Pursuing its three main objectives – concretely, the unification of Turkey, Islamic union and Pan-Turkism – the Organization put the domestic and foreign policy of the state into practice.[132]

By the Ittihadists' ideological logic, these "domestic" and "foreign" operations were two sides of the same coin. They were complementary contributions to the ultimate goal of the reign of Turkism, which was to impose, everywhere, the Ittihad's national ideal. In other words, the CUP saw no contradiction in its actions. Taking advantage of wartime conditions, it would use its secret weapon to accomplish its supreme mission in the name of the nation.

The antagonism between the Ittihad and the War Ministry was superficial, even though it sometimes makes it hard to understand the structure and workings of this apparatus. The Ittihad and its emanation, the political bureau of the Teşkilât-ı Mahsusa, maintained exclusive political and operational control of the organization's activities, with the help of the Interior Ministry and the local government agencies under its aegis. The military authorities, for their part, were responsible for recruitment, equipment, officer training, and, of course, financing the squadrons of killers with secret funds at the disposal of the War Ministry.[133] Collaboration in the field sometimes proved difficult but, as the examples adduced in the fourth part of this study show, political objectives always took precedence over military or ethical considerations. The overlap between the two sources of power, political and military, and the extraordinary skill with which the Ittihad camouflaged the Special Organization's operations as counter-espionage activities, no doubt explain why certain scholars have failed to perceive the existence of the second Special Organization.[134]

There was, however, a basic distinction between the first Teşkilât-ı Mahsusa and the second, one that reveals the narrower goals of the CUP's Central Committee from August 1914 on. This difference stemmed from the introduction of a crucially important innovation: convicts released from Turkish prisons were extensively recruited by the second version of the Special Organization for the purpose of making up its squadrons. Examining the way this innovation worked out in practice and the nature of the missions entrusted to the new organization is quite simply tantamount to assessing the Ittihad's genocidal intentions. It also allows us to identify the precise period in which the Young Turk regime made the decision to translate its plans into action.

A wire sent by the Bursa committee to the Ittihad's Central Committee in response to orders transmitted on 15 September 1914 is the first source to mention the recruitment of criminals. This document indicates that all the local committees had been apprised of the request to enroll convicts in the Special Organization, but that it proved hard "to find sufficient numbers of people who frequently engage[d] in murder and theft." The local Ittihadists nevertheless believed that they could furnish from the vilayet of Bursa between 500 and 1,000 recruits with the desired profile.[135] One sees, then, that the CUP's usual networks were still being utilized in the first weeks of the recruitment campaign, probably because the political bureau of the Special Organization had not yet come into existence or been organized.

There is, moreover, virtually no documentation of the Special Organization's activities prior to early autumn 1914. Thereafter, with the official declaration of war, the sources suddenly begin to proliferate. A coded 13 November 1914 dispatch from Halil (Kut) – who was not appointed commander of the Fifth Persian Expeditionary Corps until December – to Midhat Sükrü, the party's secretary general, ordered that the responsible secretaries in the provinces speed up the creation of squadrons of the Teşkilât-ı Mahsusa. This document was counter-signed by Dr. Nâzım, Atif Bey, and Aziz Bey, the head of the Office of State Security,[136] thus justifying the suspicion that, by the beginning of November at the latest, the political bureau of the Special Organization was already operational, while more and more convicts were being released from detention. Other telegrams, bearing mid-November dates, were read out at a session of the trial of the Unionists (during the interrogation of Colonel Cevad); sent by Bahaeddin Şakir, then based in Erzerum, or addressed to Midhat Şükrü, they bore on the CUP clubs in Bursa, Ismit, Bandırma, and Balıkeser,[137] and indicate both that the president of the Special Organization's political bureau was corresponding with the Ittihad's secretary general about matters connected with forming squadrons, and also that the Istanbul members of the political bureau were working directly with the responsible secretaries dispatched by the CUP to all the regions of the empire. A 20 November 1914 encrypted telegram from Musa Bey, the CUP inspector in Balıkeser, informs the political bureau that the *mutesarif* received, on 16 November 1914, an encrypted telegram from the interior minister containing an order to form bands in a week's time by enlisting convicts released from prison and sending them to the localities where they were to serve.[138] In other words, the minister of the interior and local government officials were also helping to create squadrons of *çetes* in the same period.

November thus marks a turning point in the implementation of the decisions of the Ittihad's Central Committee: it was in November that the process of releasing criminals from prison was accelerated. One hundred twenty-four were liberated from the prison of Binian (in the vilayet of Sıvas) in November alone, thanks to the *vali* Muammer, who interceded directly with the presiding judge of the local court.[139] Research conducted by Krieger indicates that no fewer than 10,000 imprisoned common-law criminals, most of them murderers, were set free and enrolled in squadrons of the Special Organization beginning in fall 1914.[140] It is worth pointing out that the health services, the army, the gendarmerie, and a judge participated in the release of each of these convicts, as can be seen in the case of Angora's central prison, whose 249 freed criminals appeared before a commission comprising Mahmud Celaleddin Bey, the head of Angora's Health Department; Captain Fehmi Bey; Colonel Mehmed Vasıf Bey, the commander of the Angora gendarmerie; and Ali Haydar Bey, a judge on the Imperial Court of Appeals.[141] Special committees were set up in all regions of the country to supervise the procedures by which felons were selected, released from detention, and incorporated into the squadrons. The CUP's secretary general, Midhat Şükrü, responding to the court's questions at the sixth session of the Unionists' trial, stated that once the *çetes* had been set free and integrated into the squadrons of the Special Organization, they were considered *namuslu* ("respectable people"), "for they massacre[d] Armenian women and children to serve the fatherland."[142]

The Special Organization thus benefited from the active collaboration of state agencies, especially the Ministry of Justice, without whose approval it would have been impossible to release felons from prison. Yet a minister, İbrahim Pirizâde, nevertheless affirmed, in responding to a question before the fifth commission of parliament in November 1918: "I knew nothing about this organization. The Council of Ministers did not know anything about it, either. We were completely unaware of its purpose and activities. I know absolutely nothing about it and, what is more, I am under no obligation to."[143] A deputy hereupon pointed out that "it was Ömer Naci Bey who initiated the implementation of measures connected with the Special Organization [and] it is rather odd that İbrahim Bey, who was a member of the Council of Ministers when all these events took place, found out about them only after the fact." Cornered, İbrahim Bey finally conceded the point: "I remained in the cabinet in order to counteract, to the extent that one could, acts of this kind of which I was informed. Rest assured that when I say that we did not know about the Special Organization, I mean that no decision was made by the Council of Ministers." When the Arab deputy Fuad Bey asked İbrahim Bey if he had authorized the release of common-law criminals, İbrahim admitted, in his fashion, that he had: "Yes. I no longer remember the vilayet involved. But when I learned of the intention to liberate convicts in this vilayet in order to send them to the front, I vehemently protested ... We then drafted a law on this matter that was ratified by your honorable assembly."[144]

Revelations made by Colonel Cevad, Istanbul's military governor (*muhafız*) and a member of the Special Organization's political bureau, show that certain provincial *valis* were unwilling to carry out the orders that they had received from the national leadership – that is, to perpetrate deportations and massacres. As we shall see, such men were promptly dismissed and sometimes replaced by responsible secretaries delegated by the Ittihad. The Young Turk government's response took the form of a special law intended to overcome the scruples of certain officials. Passed in December 1914, it legalized the enlistment of convicted criminals in the militia.[145] In other words, everyone knew the kind of task that the *çetes* were supposed to perform. A 7 December 1914 wire from an officer on the general staff, Colonel Behiç Erkin, to the Special Organization's political bureau is revealing in this regard. Informing the political bureau of passage of the law on the enrollment of criminals, the dispatch points out that provincial governors will henceforth be able "to act on a legal basis."[146]

Finally, as far as the role of the minister of war in the Special Organization's operations is concerned, the Ittihadists' trial reveals that Colonel Cevad acted as coordinator between his own ministry and the organization's political bureau, of which he was a member. Besides overseeing the operations of the Special Organization, which had its offices in the War Ministry (this supervisory task had initially been assigned to Süleyman Askeri, and, later, Kuşçubaşzâde Eşref), the second bureau, better known as the Intelligence Department (Istihbarat Şubesi), which was subordinated to the Ottoman army's high command and headed by Colonel Seyfi of the general staff, played a prominent part in carrying out propaganda work, ensuring logistical support for the Teşkilât-ı Mahsusa, and planning deportations. The same agency, as a captain working for it reported, controlled the secret funds earmarked for the Special Organization.[147]

In his testimony before the fifth parliamentary commission, Said Halim declared, with regard to the creation of the Special Organization: "It was brought into being by the military authorities ... The government had nothing to do with it. This matter was not discussed by the Council of Ministers." When the judge presiding at the court-martial asked Halim whether he had been informed of "the creation of such an organization," he admitted that he had, but only "after everything was over." And when he was asked about the fact that "no one was ever criticized in connection with this business," he responded, continuing to speak in abstract terms, that he had himself leveled such criticisms. He then pronounced a terrible conclusion: "but what use were they after all the evil that had already been done!" Answering one last question about how the Special Organization was financed, Halim confirmed that "the minister of war had large sums at his disposal."[148]

The elements just reviewed warrant the conclusion that the Special Organization founded in 1914 was meant to pursue, in complete independence, objectives related to the state's "domestic" security and "external" interests, to use the classical formula. In other words, it was to deal with both "domestic enemies" and Turkish populations outside Turkey. It was a kind of specialized branch or military extension of the Ittihad's Central Committee. This explains why the Special Organization depended on the Ittihad's local networks for support, especially the delegates or responsible secretaries whom the party had named in each region:[149] they have power over all civilian and military authorities to execute orders received from the Special Organization's political bureau.

To free the felons who were then enrolled in the squadrons, the political bureau relied on the services of the Interior and Justice Ministries; to select, train, and equip the killers, it called on the Ministry of War. Each of these institutions had representatives on the special commissions formed in every *kaza*, *sancak*, and vilayet. These representatives were, as a general rule, *valis*, military authorities, senior judges, police chiefs, and the heads of health departments, as well as local CUP delegates.

The interrogation of an important member of the political bureau, Atıf Bey (Kamçıl), provides valuable insights into the power relations or hierarchy within this complex network. When the presiding judge asked him why the Ittihad's Central Committee and the interior minister maintained direct contact with the squadrons, to which they transmitted orders by way of local government officials or CUP delegates even though the Teşkilât-ı Mahsusa was officially under the jurisdiction of the War Ministry, Atıf dodged the question with the remark that "it was not a question of orders, but of advice about certain matters." When it was then pointed out to him that the interventions of the party's authorized delegates with local authorities plainly took the form of orders, not expressions of opinion, and that furthermore the instructions of the Interior Ministry were sometimes countermanded by the party's Central Committee, Atıf gave no further response. Moreover, telegrams read in the course of the same session attest that certain delegates had expressly asked whether they should obey the Interior Ministry's directives or the Central Committee's.[150] In other words, the Special Organization's political bureau was sometimes conflated with the Ittihad's Central Committee. One might perhaps go so far as to say that there was at most a simple division of labor among the members of the party's highest body.

Nothing was said about the nature of the Teşkilât-ı Mahsusa's "domestic operations" until the fifth and seventh sessions of the Unionists' trial. It was at these sessions that a member of the Young Turk Central Committee, Yusuf Rıza Bey, whom the party had dispatched to Trebizond, brought himself to admit that there had existed two organizations bearing the same name, one active on the front and the other in the interior provinces. The second of the two was involved, he said, in deporting the Armenians, "for there were not enough gendarmes (*zinayr*) to accomplish this task."[151]

The trial of the Special Organization's leaders also shows that care was taken to destroy orders having to do with the *çetes*. In evidence he gave at the second session, Colonel Cevad, the member of the political bureau responsible for logistics, revealed that he had received a 21 January 1915 circular requesting that he "organize irregular forces in the First, Second, Third, Fourth and Fifth Armies." A copy of this circular, which bore the stamp of the general staff of the army in the War Ministry, had been sent to the commanders-in-chief of each army. "Once the information was received, we had to send it on to the addresses indicated... After the order had been distributed and carried out, we were supposed to destroy it." The same document, No. 1117, also includes the following instructions: "Send the squadrons of *çetes* whose training has been completed to the areas that have already been specified."[152]

In a written deposition submitted on 5 December 1918 to the ex-*vali* of Angora, Hasan Mazhar, the president of the Commission to Investigate Criminal Acts set up on 23 November 1918, General Vehib Pasha, who had assumed command of the Third Army on 20 February 1916, drew up a detailed list of the inquiries that he had conducted after his arrival in Erzincan. He affirmed that Bahaeddin Şakir, in his capacity as president of the Teşkilât-ı Mahsusa, had freed a number of convicts and integrated them into squadrons of *çetes* or, as the general put it, "butchers of men."[153]

In the prosecutor's 13 January 1920 concluding statement before the court-martial, in which he demanded that Şakir be condemned to death, he declared, referring to General Vehib's deposition, that

> the extermination of the Armenians and confiscation of their property and land flowed from decisions made by the Central Committee of Union and Progress. Bahaeddin Şakir organized battalions of butchers in the area under the jurisdiction of the Third Army [comprising the vilayets of Erzerum, Bitlis, Van, Dyarbekir, Harput, Trebizond, Sıvas and the *mutesarifat* of Canik] and coordinated all the crimes committed in this region. The state was complicit in these crimes. No government official, no judge, no gendarme ever stepped in to protect the populations subjected to these atrocities.[154]

The general added, in the "resumé of the convictions" contained in the complete, still unpublished version of his deposition

> it is obvious that all the disorders and troubles in the [jurisdiction] of the Third Army were brought on by the deceptive actions of Bahaeddin Şakir Bey. Traveling in a special automobile, he went from one local center to the next to communicate orally the decisions made by the Party for Union and Progress and the directives dispatched to the various sections of the party and the heads of government [the valis] in these localities ... The atrocities that were committed, on a premeditated plan and with absolutely predetermined intent, were first organized and ordered by delegates of the Party for Union and Progress and its highest bodies and then carried out by the leaders of the governorships, who had become pliant tools serving the designs and desires of this organization, which knew no law and had no scruples.[155]

Chapter 4

Destruction as Self-Construction: Ideology in Command

In the preceding chapters, we isolated certain salient traits of the ideology that prevailed among Young Turks, observing in particular that the need for a centralized state was for them a fundamental, unquestionable principle – in other words, that they were viscerally opposed to any and all decentralization schemes, such as the one put forward by Prince Sabaheddin and the Ottoman liberals. Whereas, for the liberals, decentralization was the price to pay for maintaining the integrity of the Ottoman Empire, Ittihadists of all stripes never considered making the slightest concession to the non-Turkish groups in the country. On the contrary, the policies they pursued in Albania, Macedonia, and Yemen bear witness to a radicalization that each collective failure only intensified. For, beyond the integrity of the empire, which had been maintained by dogma, a solid project to found a Turkish nation could be seen emerging. It was to replace the imperial model, characterized by a cosmopolitan society and a division of labor that had given rise to a nascent industrialization process favoring the country's Christians. Originally purely theoretical, especially during the period of opposition and exile, the Young Turk project naturally ran up against the harsh realities of the Ottoman Empire, which made the Ittihadist elite's objectives impracticable. The Ittihad accordingly had to conclude "tactical" alliances with groups that were hostile to its ambitions on principled grounds, and sometimes had to cast the veil of an acceptable, plausible discourse over those ambitions: the ideology of Ottomanism, developed by the Young Turks' modernist precursors, had, in some way, to be popularized and adapted to the needs of the Young Turk cause. It must be admitted that Ottomanism initially succeeded in capturing the attention, or even favor, of the empire's non-Turkish elements, thanks in part to their memories of the tyrannical Hamidian regime. In traditionalist circles, the egalitarian discourse that accompanied Ottomanism inevitably gave rise, in a society incapable of entertaining egalitarian perspectives, to aggressive protests. Yet paradoxically, as we have seen, the Ittihadists themselves profoundly despised this concept, which they regarded as an empty abstraction. Mobilizing nationalistic, Islamic, and egalitarian themes by turns, the CUP was often caught defending blatantly contradictory positions, unmasked by oppositional groups and, on two occasions, driven from power. It was not easy for the Committee gradually to eradicate all opposition and take control of the state apparatus and army. Although it is not possible categorically to affirm that the 1908–18 period was exploited to attain, step by step, the CUP's supreme goal of founding a "Turkish" nation within as yet unspecified borders, the course of events as well as the decisions made by the Young Turk elite in this period give the impression, at the very least, that that is what happened.

This is not the place to detail the origins of Turkism or, more generally, Young Turk ideology, subjects on which scholars have advanced clashing views.[1] We shall confine ourselves to considering the points directly or indirectly pertinent to our study – the conceptions of the state and army, and of society and the state, developed by the CUP.

In an Ottoman Empire that rested on the foundations of ongoing military conquest and built on past successes to obtain new ones, an empire in which only professional soldiers could hope to attain prestigious social positions, the military superiority of the West gradually made itself felt, engendering endless territorial losses and a long internal crisis whose culmination can be schematically dated to 1923, when the empire ceased to exist. Such was the curious destiny of a state that, although its grandeur was owed to the sultans' ability to mobilize all its internal forces, in the end implacably rejected a substantial segment of those forces. It is easy to imagine how bitter the clash of mid-nineteenth century civilizations must have been for the Ottoman elite when the West, which the empire had deeply penetrated and from which it had drawn much of its substance for centuries, now appeared not as an object of prey but as a predator solidly sustained by a form of national unity unknown in the East. What, this elite must have wondered, is the secret of the West's power and energy? Why have we been overwhelmed and subjugated by these nations that we dominated only yesterday?

All these questions, frustrations, and traumas formed the Ottoman heritage, which the Young Turks sought less to assume than to cast off. Paradoxically, this colonial empire, with its colonial character mitigated by an Islamic social base, found itself confronting another kind of imperialism – a modern one.

Although the central elements of this heritage can be traced to Abdülhamid's reign, some of its features can also be attributed to the Young Turks themselves, especially their elitist conception of society and their social conservatism. For the Unionists, it was never a question of making a popular revolution or educating the illiterate masses and affording them the opportunity to participate directly in the decision-making process. Nor was there any question of creating a mass organization. Their goal was an elitist, centralized party. In their view, society mattered only to the extent that it served the interests of the state.[2] Social Darwinism was the natural law that governed biological processes and also legitimized social inequality – or, if one prefers, the Young Turks' contempt for society. As an elite, they judged themselves to be the nation's "social physicians," the only ones capable of enlightening the "masses"[3] – on the condition, of course, that the masses consented to obey them unquestioningly.

Many – this holds for the ARF – blamed circumstances for the authoritarianism of the CUP, which was long perceived as a constitutional movement. Yet, "examination of the Young Turk secret correspondence and publications, as well as the private papers of the leading members of their organizations, clearly reveals that they viewed themselves above all else as the saviors of an empire." For this reason, the Young Turks did not regard themselves as bound by the Constitutional pact. At most, they made use of it to acquire a presentable image. As M. Sükrü Hanioğlu points out, "the Young Turks' inclination toward authoritarian theories was by no means a coincidence."[4] All the currents of thought that held their attention – biological materialism, positivism, social Darwinism, elitism – interested them to the extent that they could legitimize their conception of the state and society, at antipodes from the idea of the equality of all citizens that they defended in public. Their social Darwinism was founded on the idea of "human inequality," while sociological theories interested them only insofar as they made it possible to understand mass psychology and justify the activity of the elite – that is to say, their own activity. From this point of view, their readings of European authors, especially sociologists, might be called utilitarian. They were engaged in a sort of quest for magic formulas that could legitimize their own practice.

Hamit Bozarslan has discerned a crucial element in the mental universe of this Young Turk elite – its adoption of the positivist conception of the laws of historical development.

This allowed them "to engage in a given activity, but also to continue to deny their role as historical actors."[5] In other words, their positivism allowed them to act without considering themselves responsible for their acts, since they were the agents of a supreme mission.

For the closed circle of some 30 people who controlled the Ittihad, the idea of human rights was an abstraction, as was the motto of the republic. "Liberty, equality, fraternity" was an archaic "metaphysical fantasy" that had no other aim than "to win over various Ottoman ethnic groups to the cause of Ottomanism."[6] What mattered more than anything else, society included, was the creation of a strong authoritarian state[7] to be at the Committee's beck and call and be capable of realizing the Committee's ends. Nothing was to be allowed to interfere with this historical mission, especially not the opposition, as we saw in discussing the January 1913 attack on the Sublime Porte and the murder of the minister of war. Had it not been for certain contingencies of domestic and foreign politics, the dictatorship that was put firmly in place in January 1914 would have come into being much earlier.

Thus, it will be readily understood that the July 1908 revolution represented anything but emancipation for Ottoman society, even if it opened up spaces of freedom that had not existed under the regime of Abdülhamid. It is, moreover, quite symptomatic that this "revolution" succeeded only because of the young officers. As Hanioğlu has magisterially shown, when Bahaeddin Şakir and Nâzım restructured the CPU/CUP between 1905 and 1907, both of them understood very well that, without the army, their projects might well never get off the ground and they themselves might remain in exile forever. After attempting to induce a few high-ranking officials of the Hamidian administration to defect, they were forced to open the doors of the Central Committee to members of the armed forces.

The amalgam constituted by these Young Turks in exile, shaped by the theoretical debates between Ahmed Rıza and Prince Sabaheddin as well as their frequent contacts with their fellow Armenian exiles, was thus necessarily neither fish nor fowl. This was the more so as the "order and progress" the Young Turks called for would have required for their realization a social environment that did not exist in the Ottoman Empire. Thus was born the sociological oddity consisting of the "substitution of officers for an industrial class," with the role of "sole actor" devolving upon the army.[8] Turkey bears its stamp even today. The theories of the father of the reorganization of the Ottoman army, Colmar von der Goltz, which assigned the military a special role in pre-industrial societies, enjoyed great popularity among the young officers who had graduated from Istanbul's Military Academy. They also flattered the prejudices of the Committee of Union and Progress, which thought of itself as a semi-military structure[9] above the law. Hanioğlu observes in this connection that, "in the Ottoman Empire, where the military had traditionally played a more significant role in policy-making than the militaries of many European states did, the reemergence of the military as a dominant power was a relatively easy transition." Even "civilian" members of the Ittihadist Central Committee were steeped in militarist traditions. Had not two of the eminent founders of the "reformed" CUP, Şakir and Nâzım, graduated the Military Medical School, and were they not both army officers? In 1914–16, in any case, one finds them at the head of the Special Organization, which was carrying out "domestic missions," and was quite simply a paramilitary structure concocted by the "saviors of the nation."[10] To save the nation, however, a military elite did not suffice. What was required were men of exceptional capacities, the "supermen" about whom Şakir wrote, with disappointment and anger, that "the only Turk possessed of a will strong enough to become the *Übermensch* [was] Sultan Abdülhamid" himself.[11] Apparently, not even Enver Pasha found grace in Şakir's eyes.

Rejection of the Ottoman model and its linguistic and cultural plurality, which the Ittihadists sought to replace with "Ottomanism," was another key feature of the Young Turks' project. However, what they offered – in essence, the possibility without alternatives of adhesion to Turkism – ran up against solidly anchored identities, whether Arab,

Greek, or Armenian, and had the disadvantage of proposing fragile cultural bases to these groups. Moreover, rather than actually seeking to include non-Turks in their melting pot, the Ittihadists rejected all forms of particularism. Nâzım did not beat about the bush: "Nationalist protests and aspirations exasperate us. Only one nation and one language should exist on our soil."[12] "Ottomanism," of course, was merely a decorative flourish, as was the discourse about equality.

It might even be ventured that the slow erosion of the Ottoman world, which yielded its place to nation-states, together with the Ittihadists' frequent contact with Albanian, Macedonian, and Armenian revolutionaries endowed with solid national identities, helped catalyze the Young Turk project to found a Turkish nation. As Bozarslan forcefully points out, the Ittihadists who suggested this project discovered that there was, properly speaking, no Turkish "nation"[13] living on its ancestral lands, but a dominant Muslim Ottoman group that had never wondered about its identity and had long ceased to trace its origins back to its Central Asian ancestors. Thus, the construction of the Turkish nation could proceed only by way of opposition to other groups, which for their part had identities based on a culture and a homeland. The rejection of the rules defining a life in common – the cement that had ensured the cohesion of the empire – could not but lead to a clash. The transformation of a multicultural empire into a nation-state was an impossible task and inevitably a source of antagonism. There is every reason to believe that that antagonism was induced, or perhaps revealed, by the Ittihad's nationalist ideology.

Because the Ittihad conceived the modernity to which it claimed to aspire in terms of the creation of a Turkish nation, it pursued policies based on the rejection of groups that did not fit into its ideological scheme. It was no longer a question of dominating others, as in the Ottoman Empire, but of assimilating them. If this was the point of departure, how was it possible to conceive of a political arena, a zone of dialogue? Both of their led only a paper existence. As many have emphasized, on the rare occasions when power changed hands in the Young Turk period, the change came about through the use of force, as the result of a coup d'état. Significantly, the term adopted to designate "politics" (*siyasa*) denoted the art of governing or controlling a horse.[14]

Under these circumstances, there could be no question of granting equal status to non-Turks, let alone non-Muslims. Discussing the Young Turks, Tekin Alp, an ideologue of Turkism, points to one of the problems confronting them:

> Ottomanism was a truly bad bargain for them; here, they could only lose. They could not put themselves at the same level as their fellow citizens from other groups... The risk was that they would turn out to be the junior and not particularly brilliant partner in the association that they had proposed amid the hope and enthusiasm of the first embrace.[15]

While it is by no means certain that the Ittihad ever really proposed the kind of association that this prophet of the Turkish nation says it did, it is obvious that the idea of making all Ottoman citizens equal opened up perspectives that could not but alarm the less radical Young Turks. A member of the Ittihadist inner circle, Hüseyin Cahit (Yalçın), whose newspaper, *Tanin*, was a good barometer of the mood in the capital, offered the following interpretation of egalitarianism:

> Does the statement that non-Muslims will have the same rights as Muslims mean that this country will become Greek, Armenian or Bulgarian? No! This country will remain the Turks' country. We will come together under the label "Ottoman," but the form of the state will never be altered to the detriment of the special interests of the

Turkish nation. No measure jeopardizing the vital interests of Muslims will ever be taken ... Whatever people may say, the Turks are the dominant nation in this country, and will continue to be![16]

Everyone knew the basic rules of the game. There was never any question of creating a political space for the other groups making up the empire.

On the other hand, the Young Turk project involved the adoption of elements of European civilization and, as we have already indicated, social models described by European sociologists, as well as European technical know-how. Enver Pasha's pregnant, poetic formula, uttered in conversation with a German, summed up the conception of the majority of Young Turks: "Your civilization is a poison, but it is a poison that quickens men's spirits ... Because we have admitted the superiority of your civilization, we also tolerate its vices."[17] The Ittihadists were aware that their society lacked inspiration, as if its flame had been extinguished, and that it was in sore need of stimulation. They also knew that its most dynamic groups, the ones that precisely had been the most successful at assimilating Western achievements, happened to be the empire's Greeks and Armenians, while the nascent Turkish nation was the most resistant to such influence. How were features of European civilization to be combined with those of Muslim Ottoman civilization? How could Muslim Ottoman society become modern while remaining true to itself?[18] Such were the questions confronting Young Turk intellectuals.

Among the models proposed by the West, the notion of "race" plainly caught the Young Turks' eye, since it made it possible to construct a Turkish model transcending national boundaries. Exploiting this model, however, was problematic because the classificatory system adopted by European "scientists" put the Turks at the bottom of the scale, beneath even the "yellow race." Moreover, as Hanioğlu points out, the concept "Turkish race" was rarely evoked from 1907 on, since it was too patently at odds with the Young Turks' "Ottomanist" propaganda.[19] The Committee's ideologues could not put European racial theories to use in the empire, for they would generate effects contrary to those sought, threatening even to identify its non-Turkish elements as superior to its Turkish elements.

Indeed, in their search to forge a distinctly Turkish nation, the Ittihadists repeatedly butted up against an apparently insoluble problem: the multiethnic Ottoman heritage. It did not take them long to realize, after coming to power, that it was quite simply impossible to Turkify the Greeks and Armenians. Indeed, at least for some Young Turks, "Turkishness" probably replaced the idea of fraternity among the various components of Ottoman society[20] even before the 1908 revolution. To valorize the Turkish model, the alternatives had to be denigrated and rejected. The Young Turk poet Mehmed Emin captured this idea in four suggestive lines written in 1910: "The most beautiful face is ugly in our eyes / We love the Turkish face / The best essence is bad in our eyes / We want the Turkish essence."[21] Turkishness was thus plainly associated with a fascinating Western model – nationalism.

This nationalism was manifested, Bozarslan notes, in the fact that "merely demanding minority rights was immediately identified as separatism and, in a staggering amalgam, with defense of the old system."[22] However, since the Young Turks wished to imbue the whole nation with Turkish patriotism, which turned on use of the Turkish language, they were also aware that they had to lead a struggle against Ottoman cosmopolitanism while modernizing Turkish, a language, Ömer Seyfeddin wrote, that "was disastrous, miserable, baneful, illogical."[23] A further objective of this quest for modernity and identity was to enhance the status of the Turks and valorize their glorious past. To this end, it was necessary to obliterate the Ottoman historiographical tradition, in which the East is portrayed as the barbaric homeland of the bloodthirsty Mongols. In other words, it was necessary to break with the inherited, established Byzantine imperial model and turn to these famous Mongol cousins as well as the Tatars of Russia for inspiration. An affirmation by the writer Ahmed Midhat illustrates this aspiration. Midhat declared that it was Turkishness, rather than Islam, which endowed "four hundred tents of the Oğuz tribe, come from the Asian steppes," with the energy required to build one of the world's greatest empires.[24] In the space of a few years, the intense work carried out by the Young Turk networks incontestably contributed to the emergence, in Ottoman society, of a more flattering image of the Turks.

The next stage in the formation of Turkish nationalism, constructed as a reaction, doubtless owes a great deal to Yusuf Akçura (1876–1935), a pure product of the French school of political science. Akçura preached the unity of all Turks, wherever they might be found, and staunchly opposed the idea of an "Ottoman nation," which he deemed impracticable.[25] Ahmed Agayev/Ağaoğlu (1869–1939), who, like Akçura, was a Tatar, grew up in the Armenian environment of Shushi, the Karabagh district's "little Paris." He too received his higher education in Paris and preached Turkish nationalism, but called for its liberation from the grip of Islam, or at least demanded that Islam be transformed into a "national religion" – that is, subordinated to the Turkish nation.[26] For Ağaoğlu, Islam's universal dimension was intolerable because it was at odds with the project of establishing a distinctly Turkish culture.[27] As we have seen, however, Ağaoğlu did not hesitate to warn that Islam was in danger, launching an appeal for a jihad in January 1913 after the disaster in the Balkans.[28] There were obviously contradictions in the discourse of all these prophets of Turkish nationalism, torn between their patriotic feelings and their Islamic heritage, as there were within the Young Turk movement. Among the Tatars of Russia, who, as we have noticed, very early established ties with the Young Turk movement – Hüseyinzäde Ali (Turan) and Yusuf Akçura are prominent examples – Ahmed Ağaoğlu stood out, for he quite rapidly secured himself a place on the Ittihad's Central Committee. He was the only one of its members not only to have experienced but also to have taken a direct hand in a clash with Armenians in the Caucasus in 1905. Ağaoğlu can probably safely be called the very type of the Turkish nationalist formed through contact with Russian imperialism, and Russian and Armenian revolutionaries in Baku as well as Paris. He grew up in Shushi, one of the leading nineteenth-century Armenian cultural centers and a city that boasted a remarkable intellectual elite. It was probably here that he discovered the force that resides in the cultural cohesion of a nation and, by way of contrast, the road that his Tatar compatriots would have to travel before they could constitute themselves as a nation. The goal, as he saw it, was to take advantage of the territorial acquisitions of the Ottomans in order to unify all the Turks. The fact that he was descended of a family of *donmës*[29] – Turkish-speaking Jews of the Caucasus who had converted to Islam – may well have strengthened his determination to work toward this goal. The part he played in the July 1911 creation of the Türk Yurdu Cemiyeti ("Turkish Homeland Society"), alongside Mehmed Emin (Yurdakul) and Akçura,[30] also shows that he was not merely a theoretician and did not hesitate, notably in the massacres of the Baku Armenians, to get his hands dirty.

As Erik J. Züricher has observed, the most nationalistic of the Young Turks hailed from areas that had mixed populations or were situated on the borders of the empire, and it was their direct confrontation with the multiethnic character of these areas which showed them the basic problems of Ottoman society and familarized them with the "question" of the "nationalities."[31]

Tekin Alp, who was born in Serez, provided the "best exposé"[32] of the Pan-Turk program. He embodies a particularly striking example of the position of certain "minority" individuals who identified with the national ideal. Although he was a non-Turk and thus excluded from the leadership of the Ittihad, he came forward as a prophet of the grand Turkish national project.

Ziya Gökalp, Pan-Turk Ideologue, and Bahaeddin Şakir, Pan-Turk Activist

All the Young Turks espoused the principle of a strong, centralized state in which the army would have a special role, but the myriad contradictions thrown up by Pan-Turk ideology remained objects of controversy and a source of uneasiness until Mehmed Ziya Gökalp forged his celebrated synthesis, which turned on the supremacy of society over the individual. The matter was made more complicated, however, by the fact that, for Gökalp, "society" meant "nation" and "nation" meant "Pan-Turkism" – in other words, a combination of nationalism and exclusion. To explain the Turkish world's calamitous plight, Gökalp contended that the Turks possessed a highly developed culture but that this culture had been extinguished by the Islamic-Arab and Byzantine civilizations of the Middle Ages. As a means of rediscovering and regenerating it, he pleaded for a combination of modern European culture and this original Turkish culture, although he did not thereby exclude Islam from his project.

Gökalp's synthesis was intended for a Young Turk movement that included a great many military men and was consequently hostile to theoretical discourse;[33] yet it commanded virtually universal assent, for it entrusted the nationalist elite with the mission of pursuing an ideal common to all Turks. The fact that this modest parliamentary representative from Dyarbekir, who took part in the CUP's fall 1909 congress in Salonika, was elected a member of the Central Committee at the next congress, in November 1910,[34] shows just how well what he had to say answered to the expectations of the Unionist elite, justifying the CUP's single-party regime. Gökalp's "synthesis," Bozarslan writes,

> definitely eliminates Islam as a basis for legitimizing the social order but gives a large place to religion, because, with its help, the Committee [could] hope to rally most of the Islamicist opposition to its side, and also because it treats Turkishness and civilization as literally inseparable from Islam. The exclusion of religion from the political field comes at the price of assigning it a primordial role in the formulation of Turkish identity or even the definition of the political field.[35]

Far from being purely theoretical, Gökalp's model defined practical stakes, such as control over the economy, and set itself ambitious aims, such as conquest of the Russian provinces in which Turkic languages were spoken. In Gökalp's view, the only way the Turks could restore the ancestral virtues of the Turkish nation was to assimilate Western culture, as long as they took care not to lose their souls in the process.[36]

It is true, Bozarslan writes, that, "before the establishment of the constitutional regime, there were already many Turks [in Turkey]. But since the idea that 'we are the Turkish nation' was absent, there was no Turkish nation."[37] Thereafter, the Ittihad strove to constitute this nation while struggling against the "national consciousness" of the other groups in the empire. The goal was to establish *meşrutiyet*, a "unique Ottoman national personality"[38] – that is, a pact of adhesion to Pan-Turkism. As Gökalp saw it, there was no longer any place for the official representations of the *millets*, the non-Muslim communities, whose very existence was merely a historical anachronism inherited from the Ottoman Empire. The *millet* was "a secret state organization specific to the minorities," and, we would add, a highly suspect one.[39] Yet, it was no easy matter to do away with the Armenian and Greek Patriarchates any more then it was to forge a homogenous nation within the boundaries of the Ottoman Empire, since the indispensable precondition was assimilation of the non-Turks, including the Arabs and Kurds. The "Turkification of Islam"[40] was indeed part of Gökalp's program, and the CUP also made an attempt to realize this goal. The results, however, were disastrous. In these foreign environments with their own codes of behavior, the party managed at best to recruit marginal elements or delinquents alienated from their own cultural milieu.[41]

There was another strand in Gökalp's ideological project that was of crucial importance, for it legitimized the activity of the Young Turk elite. This was the substitution of the concept of the nation for that of society or, in other words, the rejection of the individual as a political agent in favor of the collectivity, the nation, with which the CUP, as we have seen, unreservedly identified. To be sure, Gökalp distinguished the "hero" or superman from this subjugated mass. The hero, unlike the mass, had total freedom of action, including the freedom

> to short-circuit society and legal institutions and place himself above society, and especially the law. For the legitimacy of the hero's acts does not reside in their legality, and even less in their conformity to a tradition; it resides in the historical import of his project. The realization of this project may call for the use of means that are altogether exceptional and non-traditional and thus naturally capable of undermining any social consensus; they may also be illegal, if that is what is called for.[42]

This ideological validation of practices that were already firmly established in the Ittihad is reminiscent of the self-justification of certain Armenian revolutionaries who also cast themselves as "heroes" struggling for the sake of their nation. The legitimization of the hero's activity, of his conviction that he has to act outside the law for the good of his people and in order to safeguard his nation's future, formed the core of what Talât had to say to Western diplomats and, later, his accusers. A comment that Dr. Reşid, the *vali* of Dyarbekir, made shortly before his suicide in 1919 falls into this category: "The Armenians will either sweep the Turks aside or will be swept aside by the Turks...I do not much care what the other nations write about me."[43]

The last element popularized by Gökalp, the grandiose plan to unify the Turks that had been adopted by the Ittihad as its supreme ideal in the years immediately preceding the First World War, was, of course, not completely new; Hanioğlu has brought out the part a review such as *Türk* played in popularizing this theme at the dawn of the twentieth century. However, with Gökalp (who, be it recalled, was a member of the Ittihad's Central Committee, where for a time he rubbed shoulders with another Pan-Turk thinker, Ahmed Agayev), this theoretical notion, which had until then been a sort of Pan-Turk rallying cry, acquired a practical dimension. It was no longer the watchword of an oppositional group, but of a Committee that had put it at the heart of its political program and had the apparatus of power in its hands. Gökalp even maintained that a state "called Turkiyya and a Turkish nation" would not be viable unless it embraced all the Turks, and unless these Turks spoke a common language, Islamic and Turkish, that had yet to be created; the whole would be based on a Turkish national economy and division of labor.[44] Agayev foresaw several stages on the road to the supreme ideal of the unification of the Turks: "*Türkiyacılık* (unification of the Turks of Turkey), *Oğuzculuk* (unification of the Turcs of Oğuz), and, finally, *Turancılık* (unification of all Turks)."[45] This was a vast program – one that the first Ottoman military operations in the Caucasus sought to realize, as we shall see. Gökalp's Pan-Turk project doubtless explains why he countenanced, at the very least, the extirpation of the Armenians, which was retroactively justified by their "treason."[46] Close to Şakir and Nâzım, Gökalp probably took part in the war "effort" like his uncle, the parliamentary deputy for Dyarbekir, Feyzi Pirincizâde,[47] who was the main accomplice in *Vali* Reşid's liquidation of the 120,000 Armenians in the vilayet.

Gökalp's nationalism obviously informed his radical view that it was impossible for the Turks to coexist with the other groups making up the empire. These non-Turkish groups constituted, in his estimation, a major obstacle in the development of Turkism and the crea-tion of a fatherland in which everything would be Turkish:

> A country whose ideals, language and religion are common to all. / Its parliamentary deputies are its own. / A land in which the Boşo[48] have no right to speak. / In which all the capital circulating in the market is Turkish, / Like the science and technology that guide its industry. / Its businesses help each other. / The arsenals, factories, ships and trains belong to the Turks! / Behold, sons of Turks ... There is your country.[49]

Behind this Turkism plainly lay another crucial feature of the program of the Unionists and their foremost ideologue, Gökalp: exclusion of non-Turks from the fatherland that was being constructed for the Turks. Implicit in Turkism, in other words, was the destruction or elimination of everything that stood in the way of building the Turkish fatherland.

The First World War provided the Unionist Central Committee with the opportunity to realize its unification plan. According to Arif Cemil, an officer in the Special Organization, "it had decided to carry out its plan to unite the Turks of Russia with those of Turkey on the first occasion that offered. [The members of the Central Committee] had become so firmly attached to this idea that they had gone so far as to draw up plans to make it a reality."[50] With the failure of the campaign of winter 1914–15, however, "the planned operations of the Special Organization ... in the Caucasus had become irrelevant, and the expansionist ambi-tions of the first weeks had given way to a preoccupation with defending the fatherland."[51] Once the Committee was confronted with the harsh realities of the war, the second face of its project, exclusion, seems to have replaced the drive for unification. Unable to link up with the Turks of Russia, the Ittihadist state committed itself to a project that was much more clearly within its grasp because it was domestic.

Before the president of the political bureau of the Teşkilât-ı Mahsusa returned to Istanbul from his mission to recruit *çetes* in all the eastern provinces, he decided – in terms that, albeit very general, are suggestive – "to convert the Special Organization's headquarters into an active, efficient [center]." He further decreed that

> preparation of the plans should be left up to the local authorities. It is incumbent on them, in particular, to identify the means that the Organization requires. It is essential that the *çetes*, the individuals and the corps that are to be dispatched to the eastern zone be subordinated to the eastern center[52] of the Special Organization.[53]

Cemil plainly notes the Ittihad's turn toward domestic objectives. "As for Dr. Bahaeddin Şakir Bey," he writes, he had decided, in Istanbul, that he would no longer concern himself with the operations aimed at the Teşkilât-ı Mahsusa's foreign enemies, but, rather, turn his attention to the country's internal foes. Bahaeddin Bey was now convinced," the Ittihadist officer insists, "that we had to worry as much about the enemy within as the external foe."[54] One could hardly state any more forthrightly that the time had come to "worry about" the Ottoman Armenians. Cemil is less forthcoming about what happened next. He remarks cautiously yet clearly that, "when Dr. Bahaeddin Şakir Bey returned to the Caucasian front several months later, the situation had been clarified. But we shall not go into this."[55] Cemil does, however, remark that "a grand national awakening can make it possible to eliminate the foreign microbes lodged within the Islamo-Turkish group."[56]

According to Bozarslan, the success attained by Gökalp's "synthesis" owes a great deal to the skill with which he combined "elements espoused by three different currents of thought" – Turkist, Islamicist, and Westernizing – while ably overcoming their contradic-tions. One particular element was, for Gökalp, crucial to the successful realization of his program – suppression of "Ottoman cosmopolitanism." Conceived as a "surgical operation," the Ittihad's eradication of "cosmopolitanism" allowed its number-one ideologue to "impose his formula 'Turkification, Islamification, Westernization' as if it were a magic spell."[57]

At the May 1919 trial of members of the Ittihad's Central Committee, the judge presiding over the court-martial repeatedly questioned Gökalp, asking in particular about his activities at the head of the review *Yeni Mecmu'a*, founded by his colleague Bahaeddin Şakir. He was asked if he had indeed "written essays in which he said that Turanism should become Turkey's program." Gökalp confirmed that in some of his essays he had developed his ideas on Turanism, which he "considered beneficial for Ottomanism." Asked if "this had not angered the non-Muslim groups," he declared: "These groups were constantly in pursuit of autonomy. Turanism was to have left the other nationalities their freedom while strengthening the Turkish element...I do not deny the existence or rights of the other nationalities." Before his judges, the ideologue denied that he had advocated the "exclusion" of the Armenians, which he had nevertheless defended as an imperative duty for all who aspired to the ideal of the "unification of the Turks." Questioned about the Central Committee's internal organization, Gökalp provided details of little interest: "The members of the Central Committee earned thirty pounds monthly before the War. During the war, they earned fifty to seventy pounds." Exasperated, the presiding judge ordered someone to read out a number of dispatches received by the Central Committee bearing on both the deportations and the Committee's connections with the Special Organization. Gökalp finally blurted out, "When it was called for, the Committee provided support." Asked to confirm "that the deportations had been decided on in the Central Committee" and, thereafter, whether the Central Committee had indeed ordered "massacres and acts of pillage," he answered that they had "learned about them afterwards and lodged a complaint with the minister of the interior. There were inquiries, but all that continued."[58]

While Gökalp did a great deal to elaborate and legitimize the projects of the Ittihad's Central Committee, especially its program to eradicate the Armenian population, there can be no ignoring the determinant role played by another Central Committee member, Dr. Bahaeddin Şakir, in putting the program into practice. Until Hanioğlu brought out Şakir's central role in the evolution of the Ittihadist movement between 1905 and 1908, very little was known about this "guardian of the Young Turk temple," distinguished by the fact that he never exercised ministerial functions or held high-ranking administrative posts. Indeed, Turkish historiography has almost entirely ignored him. A short biographical notice, recently supplemented by the "research" of an academic, presents him as a "Turkish scientist" who was born in 1880 (he was in fact born around 1870, in Bulgaria), completing his studies in the Military Medical School in 1896, where he graduated with the rank of captain, and was then named assistant professor of forensic medicine in that institution in 1900. He went on, we are told, to serve as Prince Yusuf İzzeddin's personal physician. The biographical notice further informs us that,

> since he espoused republican ideas, he was assigned to the Third Army, stationed in Erzincan. From there, he managed to flee to Paris. Returning secretly to Istanbul in [1907], he made contact with the leaders of the Committee of Union and Progress [which no longer had a branch in the capital]. After the proclamation of the 1908 Constitution, he returned to his fatherland and again took up his functions in the Military Medical School. One year later, he was appointed to its medical faculty as a professor of forensic medicine. He was the secretary general of this faculty from 1910 to 1921 [in fact, he fled to Berlin on 30 October 1918]. In this period, he published the newspaper *Şûra-yı Ümmet* and founded the periodical *Yeni Mecmu'a* (New Review) [an ultra-nationalist Pan-Turk review, which Şakir founded with Ziya Gökalp].

Finally, the biographical notice informs us that Şakir was "condemned by the forces of the Coalition" – that is, the Anglo-French alliance – which we must translate to read "condemned to death by the court-martial established in Constantinople against the advice of the British." "Fleeing Istanbul," the notice goes on, "he found refuge in Berlin. There he was shot and killed by an Armenian. He has left a book entitled *Lessons in Forensic Medicine*." Near the end of this notice, we are informed that, "during the First World War, he was charged with organizing the migration of the Armenians within Turkey."[59]

The report on Şakir prepared by the Information Bureau of the Armenian Patriarchate in 1919 strikes a different note. The Information Bureau mentions Şakir's functions as Prince İzzedin's personal physician and his activities in the Ittihad's Central Committee before the war, first in Paris and then in Salonika. It points out that a "Special Council [*incuman*] made up of Talât, Bahaeddin Şakir, Nâzım, Atıf, Rıza, Aziz and Cevdet" oversaw all the provincial *incumans* that had the squadrons of *çetes* of the Special Organization at their command, adding that Şakir was the Central Committee member responsible for carrying out the liquidation of the Armenians.[60] The same report indicates that he traveled to Erzerum as early as August 1914, accompanied by Çerkez Hüseyin Husni, in order to set up these *incumans* in the Armenian provinces and supervise the training of the squadrons of the Special Organization. The responsible secretaries or special delegates whom the CUP dispatched to each region acted as his intermediaries.[61]

A coded telegram that Şakir sent on 4 July 1915 from Erzerum to the *vali* of Mamuret ul-Aziz, Sabit Bey, requesting that Sabit forward it to Boşnak Nâzım Bey (of Resne), the Committee's delegate in the vilayet,[62] precisely indicates what kind of work the president of the Teşkilat-ı Mahsusa's political bureau carried out: "No. 5, for Nâzım Bey. Have you begun to liquidate the Armenians who have been deported from there? Are you eradicating the harmful individuals whom you say you have deported or exiled, or are you simply relocating them? Give me explicit information, my brother." This document, which survived the purge of the Special Organization's files, shows that its leader could not orchestrate all its operations by traveling from one place to another in his famous "special automobile,"[63] but had sometimes to use encrypted telegrams to communicate.

The Patriarchate's report further spells out that Şakir not only bore the main responsibility for the murder of 500,000 Armenians in the six vilayets, but also directly supervised the liquidation of hundreds of thousands of other deportees who had been sent to the camps of Syria and Mesopotamia. It also indicates that "he saw to it that a significant part of the Armenians' confiscated property made its way into the coffers of the Ittihad's Central Committee," and finally adds that he conducted propaganda tours through Persia and Afghanistan during the war in hopes of laying the groundwork for a vast Pan-Turanic movement against the British.[64]

Details in the biographies of Şakir published after he was assassinated in Berlin give us a better sense of the man. Thus we learn that he was employed in Parisian hospitals during his 1905–8 exile in the French capital; worked as an assistant in the field of forensic medicine before being named to a teaching post in 1909; served as the chief physician in the Red Crescent's hospital in Edirne when, in fall 1912, the city was besieged by the Bulgarians, who eventually took him prisoner; and became the director of Istanbul's morgue the following year and, in 1913, president of the Justice Ministry's medical commission.[65] In 1914, he was promoted to the rank of colonel.[66] Thus, this army doctor had had difficult moments: one can readily imagine how humiliating his capture by the Bulgarians must have been for him. Thanks to his field of specialization, he was thoroughly acquainted with the anatomy of the cadavers that it was his task to examine daily; one of his students says that he practiced autopsies with great skill. The gusto with which he supervised the summary slaughter of hundreds of thousands of Armenian civilians, carried out for the most part with knives, axes, or bayonets, testifies to his lack of inhibitions when it came to perpetrating mass violence, as well as his utter lack of scruples. This specialist in forensic medicine was doubtless the best incarnation of the faction of the Ittihad that was driven by racist, xenophobic, nationalistic, and criminal impulses.

The Millî Iktisat (National Economy), or the Spoliation of "Abandoned" Armenian Property

It has rarely been understood, or even considered, that the economic dimension of the destruction of the Ottoman Armenians conceived by the CUP was one of the major material and ideological objectives pursued by the Ittihad's Central Committee and, accordingly, one of the factors that triggered the genocidal act. The Armenians themselves clearly sensed that the spoliation of which they were the victims was not pillage of the usual sort carried out, for example, under Abdülhamid. The 1913 economic boycott of the Armenians had already made the most perceptive among them aware that they were facing a coordinated movement designed to ruin them financially. It is, however, by no means clear that they fully foresaw the consequences of the unilateral abolition of the Capitulations on 1 October 1914.[67] Traditionally depicted by Turkish historiography as a sign of the country's determination to free itself of the shackles imposed by the colonial powers, the abolition of these bilateral agreements stripped foreign investment and foreign property in the Ottoman Empire of all legal safeguards and, above all, cleared a path for their "nationalization." With the abolition of the Capitulations, the Ittihadist Central Committee set the first phase of its plan to "nationalize" the economy in motion. The aim of the second would be to seize the property of the Greeks and Armenians.

Coming to power after several decades of an economic liberalism based on modernized legislation encouraging trade and foreign investment, the CUP rapidly opted for "economic independence."[68] The Young Turks, in line with their nationalist ideology and Turkist discourse, decided to construct a national economy. Zürcher points out, however, that the "naïveté of Young Turk economic policies,"[69] was inspired in part by flamboyant figures such as Alexandre Helphand, who advocated building up a native merchant and industrial bourgeoisie. Yet it was Gökalp, a man deeply influenced by the German tradition of social solidarity, who convinced the Ittihad to "nationalize" the economic sphere, since, as he wrote, "every modern society in which organic [that is, non-ethnic] solidarity prevails runs the risk of disintegration."[70] He had well understood that without a bourgeoisie it would be impossible to realize his Turkish national project. Yet, from the Ittihad's standpoint, the Ottoman bourgeoisie patently lacked the requisite qualities – it was basically Greek and Armenian. Therefore, this state of affairs had to be remedied by "nationalization" of Greek and Armenian enterprises – that is, by putting them in the hands of Turkish entrepreneurs.

In fact, the program Gökalp defended was much more ambitious and thoroughgoing. He had given much thought to the way the Turks could gain access to civilization – or, if one prefers, acquire the "status of a modern nation" – and had grasped the "indissoluble bond between the emergence of capitalism, access to civilization and nation-formation."[71] He was aware that the Turks were "state-centered" by "nature," so much so that even their "revolutions" had been the work of the "state," which was predestined to play an important role in the economy, the formation of corporatist organizations, and the establishment of social order. These were all activities that "flow[ed] naturally from Turkish law."[72] The state interventionism advocated by Gökalp was explicitly directed against classical political economy, which it thought hindered the development of a national economy. Gökalp's program sought to lay the foundations of the emergent nation, which would have to be firmly controlled by its elites.

Another CUP ideologue, Tekin Alp, was well aware that credit for Turkey's nascent industrialization did not go to a Turkish bourgeoisie, a circumstance he deemed most unfortunate. Alp also regretted the fact that Turks preferred military or civil service careers[73] – a symptom, he thought, of their conception of the state as the source of all initiative. Yusuf Akçura stated the preoccupations of Young Turk circles more prudently: "We, too, consider the Turkish-Ottoman commercial and industrial class capable of competing with non-Turkish Ottomans to be essential to establishing equilibrium among the different groups making up the Empire."[74]

Undeniably, Western and non-Turkish firms basically dominated Ottoman economic activity on the eve of the First World War. The problem, however, ran still deeper. Even craftsmanship was to a large extent in Greek and Armenian hands. To appreciate the prevailing imbalance, one need only leaf through the huge directories listing Ottoman enterprises, such as the *Annuaire oriental de 1915*. They show that the Westernization of society eagerly pursued by the CUP had begun first and foremost among the Greeks and Armenians, the natural partners or competitors of Western entrepreneurs. Even the Banque Impériale Ottomane, which continued to function as a bank of issue during the war, was distinguished by the fact that most of its capital was held by two enemy countries, France and Great Britain. The empire was so dependent on foreign capital that the Council of Ministers, which had decided to nationalize the BIO on 11 July 1915, finally changed its mind in view of the stout opposition of the Germans, as well as the risk that the national currency would collapse if it acted on its decision.[75]

When the war broke out, the Ittihad doubtless concluded that the time had come to put an end to its dependency on the West and, at the same time, organize the transfer of the country's business enterprises to a Turkish middle class. The local Ittihadist clubs also attempted to open modern schools and get "Christian" master craftsmen to take on "Turkish" apprentices, to the sole end of preparing society to manage without non-Turks. The results of these initiatives, however, were evidently unsatisfactory. Raising the general educational level was an indispensable condition for developing Turkish society. Yet the education provided by prestigious schools such as Robert College or the Galatasaray lycée, to cite only those two examples, generally benefited non-Turks, since Turkish parents were reluctant to enroll their children in foreign schools. In the form of the economic question, then, the Young Turks who had taken it upon themselves to save the nation were confronted with a fundamental cultural choice.

Some progress had been made toward the creation of Turkish joint-stock companies. There were only two such companies in 1908. The number rose to 13 in 1909, and to 39 from 1915 to 1917, only to fall back to 29 in 1918.[76] But these figures hardly evince a new trend, even if Hüseyin Cahid declared, in an article that appeared in *Tanin* on 7 May 1917, that the war had had, along with its deleterious effects, "very positive effects on [the Ottoman Empire], especially in the economic sphere."[77] As it is well known that the Ottoman population endured severe shortages of all kinds during the conflict, no great acumen is required to understand that this well-turned phrase alludes to a "source" of revenue to which the Young Turks had easy access in the period: Armenian assets.

In everyday life, the plans to create a "national economy" took very concrete forms. Needless to say, prevailing political conditions as well as the Balkan Wars prepared the ground for boycotts of Greek and Armenian products and businesses. In the Armenian case, the reports of foreign consuls in Turkey abound in examples of such boycotts, especially in the period when negotiations over the reforms were underway. Thus, the Istanbul longshoremen's guild refused to unload a ship belonging to an Armenian merchant when it docked in the city's harbor because, as the diplomat who reported this incident put it, "this economic civil war is the talk of the town; according to information furnished by our vice-consul in Sıvas, it would appear to be the result of orders received from a Central Committee."[78] The French ambassador to Turkey, Bompard, held a meeting with Talât in which he called the minister's attention to "the boycott of the Christians and the violence and intimidation" of which they were the targets. Reporting on the interview immediately afterwards, he noted that Talât had told him that the government "was looking for ways to prevent the spread of the boycott." Talât had added, however, that he was

> confronted with a movement that had profound causes, beginning with the Muslims' resentment of the Greeks living of the coast, whom they suspect[ed] of wishing to throw off Ottoman rule ever since the Greek victories; moreover, the Turkish population ha[d] a legitimate desire to take advantage of the reigning situation to loosen the economic grip that Greek and Armenian merchants had acquired over it.[79]

Given the nature of the system, there is good reason to suspect that orders were issued to ensure the success of this boycott, which served as the occasion for a general call to "buy Turkish." A law passed in June 1914[80] was one of the first concrete manifestations of state interventionism, and was expressly intended to recruit a national bourgeoisie of entrepreneurs from the ranks of provincial Muslim merchants, economic guilds, and even civil servants. The June 1914 law sought to promote local industry by encouraging people to buy Ottoman products even when they cost as much as 10 per cent more than the competing foreign goods. Zürcher underscores that the principal victims of this economic policy were urban consumers as well as Greek and Armenian businessmen, who were forced to bring Turks into their firms at the management level before they were swept up in the terror campaign waged by the Special Organization during the war years. When some of them were deported, their businesses were then turned over to entrepreneurs who frequently proved incapable of running them.[81]

The program to develop the "national economy" launched in autumn 1915 was put under the responsibility of a member of the Ittihadist Central Committee, Kara Kemal, who was both minister of provisions and the initiator of the national companies formed under the aegis of the Heyet-i Mahsusa-i Ticariye (Special Trade Committee).[82] Kemal was in some sense charged with giving concrete form to the work of the emvalı metrukes, the commissions responsible for "abandoned property," whose activities we shall examine later. Between 1916 and 1918, 80 companies were founded with active CUP "support,"[83] started up with confiscated Armenian assets.

Thanks to the general mobilization and the abolition of the Capitulations, the Young Turks gained total control over rail transportation. The least one can say is that the Young Turk Cabinet used these circumstances to their advantage. It profited from its monopoly to take complete control of trade, seizing the opportunity to collect a "tithe" that considerably exceeded the traditional 10 per cent. According to Zürcher, only those provincial merchants in good odor with the CUP were now able to dispatch their goods to the capital or the army. By way of the National Defense Committee and the Guild Association, the CUP dominated virtually all trade and distribution in the cities. The consequence was not "the development of Turkish capitalism," but large-scale corruption. "The 'rich of 1916' – in other words, the war profiteers – became infamous. The price was, of course, paid by the wage-earners in the towns, who had to pay hugely inflated prices (prices rose by more than 400 per cent during the war)."[84] The testimony of various ministers in the war cabinets at the November 1919 hearings before the fifth commission of the Ottoman parliament reveals extensive economic corruption, made possible notably by a monopoly on flour that earned a fortune not for the state, but for the CUP.[85] Liman von Sanders, closely acquainted with İsmail Hakkı Pasha, a member of the party's Central Committee and the senior administrative officer of the general staff in the War Ministry, reports that Hakkı

> and the subordinates and agents he had everywhere in the empire requisitioned everything that came their way. Since he was also (as far as is known) the Committee's treasurer and, as such, responsible for paying for the purchases that Enver made, he had a hand in many different financial deals.[86]

The spoliation of Armenian and Greek businesses carried out from the very outset of the war in the guise of military requisitions was probably the first stage of a comprehensive CUP plan. It paved the way for the official confiscations of Armenian property undertaken a few months later, when the deportations began. Acting on the same authority as the Special Organization, the CUP supervised, working through various ministries, the creation of "commissions for abandoned property" in all the provinces. According to the Information Bureau of the Armenian Patriarchate in Constantinople, which conducted an inquiry into the matter late in 1918, Abdürahman Bey and his assistant Mumtaz Bey were the special delegates charged by the Ittihad's Central Committee with setting up *emvalı metrukes* in every province, and "enforcing" what was known as the law of "abandoned property."[87] From another document, we learn that the attendant procedures were worked out in detail by the *kiami siasi*, the head of the national police force's Department of Political Affairs, Mustafa Reşad. Reşad in particular was responsible for drawing up the lists of entrepreneurs to be arrested and setting up the *emvalı metruke* commissions.[88]

The document that most convincingly illustrates the connection between the CUP's policy of creating a "national economy" on the one hand and the confiscation of "abandoned" Armenian property on the other is a circular dated February 1916 and signed by the minister of the interior himself:

> The purpose of the directive about the creation of Muslim enterprises and the aid and facilities to be granted them to that end was to familiarize Muslims with commercial activity and increase the number of Islamic commercial companies. It has, however, come to my attention that this order has been misinterpreted; that, in certain regions, an attempt has been made to consign all abandoned property to these companies alone; that all trading firms and stores have been handed over to these companies, while the rest of the population has not been allowed to take part in the auctions; and that many of these companies were dissolved immediately after selling, at a price several times higher [than the purchase price], the assets thus acquired. Aid and facilities should be granted to Muslims to encourage them to create commercial firms; care should also be taken to protect individual businesses and special measures should be put in place to ensure that the aid extended to companies does not lead to commercial privilege or profiteering. Abandoned goods must be put up at auction and sold off individually. In particular, the rest of the population must be given the opportunity to participate in the auctions at the same time as people engaged in commerce. The Minister, Talât.[89]

The minister's bitterness no doubt reflects complaints that had reached Istanbul from individuals who had not been given a chance to take part in the "auctions" of Armenian property.

Shortly after the temporary deportation order was published, a directive dated 15 June 1915 authorized the creation of local commissions charged with "safeguarding" "abandoned property."[90] This simple administrative measure provided the basis for the confiscations carried out down to fall 1915. Thus, it can be said that the law that at the administrative level

formalized the pillage of Armenian property was passed ex post facto. It is worth pointing out that this "Temporary law on the property, liabilities and debts owed deported persons," dated 13/26 September 1331/1915 (17 Zilkade 1333),[91] was drafted by the Directorate
for the Settlement of Tribes and Refugees, an agency subordinated to the Interior Ministry
and responsible for planning the deportations. It was supplemented by a "Regulation on the
execution of the temporary law of 13 September 1331/1915 about the commissions charged
with the liquidation of property left behind by the deportees, and on their competencies,"
dated 26 October/8 November 1331/1915 (30 Zilhidiye 1333).[92] This regulation was the basis
for the creation of the commissions responsible for *emvalı metruke* (abandoned property); it is
comparable to the decrees that authorize application of a law in the French legal system.

The first article of the law alludes directly to individuals "deported in accordance with
the temporary law of 14/27 May 1331/1915,"[93] but does not refer to the directive of 10 June
1915, the provisions of which had certainly proved inadequate. The first phase of the deportations had in reality been nearly completed by the time the law on "abandoned property"
and the corresponding decree of application were promulgated, on 26 September 1915 and
8 November 1915, respectively. It may therefore be assumed that this battery of laws sought
to "legalize" the spoliation of property already in progress and provide for arbitration of the
litigation that might arise in connection with it.

None of these texts mentions the Armenian population. Article 1 of the law, however,
stipulates that "assets and liabilities abandoned by persons physical or moral shall be liquidated by the courts on the basis of *mazbata* (report) that the commissions created for this
purpose shall draw up separately in each case."[94] The "denationalization" of this property
thus concerns physical and moral persons alike – that is to say, it extends to "inalienable"
national property, the property of religious institutions or *wakıfs*. This is explicit proof that
the law was designed to despoil the Armenians individually, as well as to "requisition" their
historical patrimony, including hundreds of centuries-old churches and monasteries. Article
2 stipulates, to be sure, that the "officials of the Land Registration Office shall assume the
role of the adverse parties in the event that complaints are brought or other legal proceedings initiated in connection with the aforementioned assets."[95] In other words, provision was
made for the eventuality that "deported" persons might sue in court!

Another clause bore on fraud – specifically, the possibility that proprietors, "in the fortnight preceding their deportation," might have "alienated their real estate in bogus sales or
at fraudulently low prices." This means that a property-owner did not have the right to sell
his property before being deported. Implicitly, the text acknowledges that, in the conditions
in which the sellers found themselves, they could dispose of their property only at very low
prices, an act prejudicial to the interests of the state, which wished to be the beneficiary of
sales of such property.

Article 3 of the law, which applies to the "cash and property left behind by the deportees, as well as their deposits and the debts owed them," stipulates that the president of the
commission responsible for "abandoned property" is to collect these assets. This was tantamount to freezing all bank accounts (cash was harder to control). The law further states
that "all abandoned property not subject to litigation shall be sold off at public auction and
the proceeds of the sale deposited in the coffers of the Treasury in the name of the rightful
owners."[96] Article 9 provides that *wakıf* properties "can, in conformity with the regulation on
emigrants, be sold and distributed to immigrants [*muhacir*] free of charge."[97] In other words,
the displacement of the deportees, albeit "temporary," was to make room for the *muhacir*.
One can only conclude that, as those who wrote the law saw matters, such departures were
"definitive."[98]

The decree of application promulgated on 8 November 1915 also merits close examination.
It provides that the commissions created in each *kaza* to administer the deportees' assets are

to comprise officials from the tax office, land registration office, registry office, and *Evkaf* (*wakıf* administration). The first article stipulates that the fact that an individual has been deported "shall be confirmed by a written declaration emanating from the highest government official in the locality."[99] Article 2 provides for the "urgent" creation of registers of all property belonging to persons physical or moral, "in the form of buildings or any other form," and enjoins the establishment of "lists of the villages that have been completely evacuated in consequence of the deportation of their inhabitants,"[100] after which the documents are to be transmitted to the "commissions for the liquidation" of "property in default of heirs." Article 5 spells out that these commissions are to comprise a president "appointed by the Ministry of the Interior and two members appointed by the Ministries of Justice and Finance."[101] Article 7 stipulates that a record of "the documents [*mazbata*] relating to the liquidation shall be registered by the civil courts with jurisdiction over the deportee's legal place of residence."[102] Subsequent articles establish the procedures by which a deportee's creditors, in the event that he has unpaid debts, may submit claims on "the moveable assets or real estate abandoned by the deportee" to the presidents of the local commissions (Article 12).[103]

Article 13 is of crucial importance, for it authorizes the commissions both "to take delivery of the deportees' cash and merchandise entrusted to the government's safekeeping, as well as all other property belonging to the aforementioned deportees," and also "to demand, from private individuals, banks and other financial institutions, an inventory of the moneys and property abandoned by the deportees."[104] Article 16 further enjoins that "an inventory of the objects, images and holy books found in the churches shall be made and the aforementioned objects safeguarded. The right to dispose of schools, monasteries and all the material in these establishments shall be transferred to the Ministry of Public Education."[105]

Article 18 recommends that the property be sold at auction "at a price approximating its real value as closely as possible." Finally, Article 22 stipulates that the "activities of the commissions" shall be supervised by "the central administration."[106] There is no need to examine the provisions of the law in greater detail in order to grasp what they signified in a country whose administration, as contemporary observers unanimously agreed, was "infected" by the virus of a lust for lucre.

Accounts by a number of diplomats show that the formal aspect of these laws masked a very different reality. In Bursa, home to many prosperous Armenian silk mill owners, the Austrian consular official L. Trano reported on the deportation of the Armenians and the liquidation of their estates by the *emvalı metrukes* on 16 August 1915.[107] Three days later, he noted that the Armenians had been deported in two-tiered cattle cars and that the commission had confiscated their mills and other assets.[108] In late August, the Austrian diplomats observed that the Armenians' property had been cornered by members of the local Unionist club and other Turkish notables in Bursa.[109] Late in September, the same source informed Vienna that the authorities were turning the Armenians' homes over to *muhacir*.[110]

The text of the law on "abandoned property" and the corresponding decree of application betray the Ittihadists' economic objectives. The destruction of the Armenians obviously went hand-in-hand with the wholesale "nationalization" of the economic fabric of their community – that is, its transfer to Turkish entrepreneurs. Colossal sums also poured into state and CUP coffers, where they helped finance the eradication of the Armenians.

A historian of the BIO notes, without comment, a sharp increase in the price of food and basic commodities from August 1915 on. By February 1918, the cost of food was more than 20 times what it had been before the war.[111] This calls for two remarks. Its access to European manufactured products cut off, the domestic Ottoman market was thrown back on the production of its own craftsmen, which collapsed in August 1915 after the deportation of the Armenians. As for the increase in the price of foodstuffs, it originated in the monopoly on the trade in cereals held by CUP-connected firms. The same historian of the Banque

Impériale Ottomane observes that, beginning in September 1915, the Ottoman state, which had until then financed the war by borrowing heavily from Germany, no longer needed loans from the BIO and was even able to pay off its debts.[112] This economic historian seems to be unaware of the source of these funds, which also helped finance the rest of the Turkish war effort.

We shall leave detailed examination of the operating methods of the *emvalı metruke* commissions in the regions for the fourth part of the present work, where we also name their individual members whenever possible. We note it noted here that a rather distinct social profile emerges from such an examination: local notables, tendentially members of the Ittihad, and high-ranking civilian officials played a pivotal role in these commissions, and were the first to amass personal fortunes.

Chapter 5

Turkey's Entry into the War

Germany's Status

The secret treaty that the Ottoman Empire concluded with Germany is commonly regarded as the starting point of the process that led to the empire's entry into the First World War. This decision was far from commanding universal assent among the Ottoman elite. Some even considered the enterprise suicidal. The parliamentary deputy Krikor Zohrab, during a 3 November visit to Cavid, having just resigned from his post as minister of finance, remarked that the empire's entry into the war could have terrible consequences for Turkey and that the Ottomans might even lose their capital city. He was told that "Talât and his acolytes are supposed to have said that the present war would be 'winner take all.'"[1] This comment sums up the state of mind of the majority of the Ittihad's Central Committee members rather well: they considered the war an opportunity to restore the empire's lost grandeur, this time under the banner of Turkish nationalism.

In the course of the same conversation, Cavid revealed to the Armenian lawyer that Talât was the most ardent partisan of going to war. He was convinced "that this war [would] allow Turkey to become a Pan-Islamic world empire."[2] Indications are, however, that the minister of war, Enver, was on Talât's side. He, too, was spoiling for a fight. It is also known that at the war council convoked on 13 September 1914, in which Admiral Souchon, who had arrived with the battleships Goeben and Breslau a month earlier, took part, Enver promised his German colleague to put 800,000 men at the disposal of the new coalition.[3] A scrupulous examination of the sources has convinced Frank Weber that, in October 1914, the Turks wanted to go to war "at all costs."[4] While Germany's pledge to provide financial support for the Turkish war effort probably had something to do with Turkey's decision, it must be remembered that the Young Turks were above all motivated by their "national" objectives and their Turkist ideology. An alliance with Germany was merely an occasion to realize them.

Another point has received less attention than it deserves: the secret German-Turkish treaty of 2 August 1914 was directed at Russia alone. Not until 11 January 1915 was it extended to include Great Britain, France, and a possible Balkan coalition.[5] In other words, the Turkish objective had been, first and foremost, to go to war with Russia in hopes of putting its Pan-Turk plan into practice by establishing a physical link with the Muslim-Turkish populations of the Czarist empire. We can have no doubt about this when we observe that the cream of the CUP, including eminent members of the Central Committee, was dispatched to Trebizond, Erzerum, and Van as early as August 1914, or when we consider the Turks' military preparations in the field, as we shall below. The Ittihadist ministers' and party leaders' obstinate denial that the war with Russia had its origins in the 29 November 1914 attack on Odessa and other Russian localities by the Goeben and the Breslau can only be explained by their desire to hide their real ambitions. The reaction of the minister of public education, Ahmed Şükrü, a member of the Central Committee, before the fifth commission of the Ottoman parliament in November 1918 shows just how carefully the Young Turks had striven to mask their main war objective: Şükrü denied that the Young Turk cabinet bore any responsibility for Turkey's entry into the war, affirming in the face of all the evidence that "the Black Sea fleet was attacked by the Russians" ("but everyone knows that it was the other way around," the president of the commission shot back).[6] It was important to the Young Turks that their operation appear to be no more than a simple war maneuver.

The question of the precise part played by the Committee in Turkey's entry into the war has also been raised. According to Turfan, this was "Enver Pasha's war," for it was Enver who chose the empire's camp and issued the 25 October 1914 order to attack Russia.[7] It is regarded as an established fact that the minister of war took a decisive hand in initiating both this attack and the July-August negotiations with the Germans. However, given the way the Ittihad worked, it is all but impossible that Enver acted all alone. Moreover, at the fourth session of the Ittihadists' trial, the party's secretary general, Midhat Şükrü, reluctantly confirmed that the government ministers went to see the Central Committee to discuss Turkey's entry into the war.[8] In other words, a collective decision was taken on which the Committee then put its stamp of approval. This seems more in line with its customary practices and disinclination to play too conspicuous a leadership role.

A great deal of ink has been spilled over another question – that of Germany's role and status in the war in the east. We have already taken note of Ambassador Wangenheim's skepticism about Turkey's military capacities, as well as the reservations of the head of the German military mission, Otto Liman von Sanders, whom Enver had to work hard to overcome. Does it follow that what was involved was an *accord inégal* which left Turkey beholden to Germany – that is, made it a partner of second rank that had to comply with German demands? This is plausible. However, the thorough studies of German-Turkish relations conducted by Weber and Trumpener show not only that the Turks never intended to cede the least authority to foreigners,[9] but also that they frequently managed to wring enormous sums from the Germans that were not always justified by the war effort, that they hounded the German businessmen working in the eastern provinces, and that they never let German diplomats or military men meddle in their "internal" affairs. In other words, while Vahakn Dadrian's conclusions are not unfounded – Dadrian attributes great influence to the Germans, making them accomplices in the Young Turks' crimes, at least to the extent that they "closed their eyes" to what was happening or declined to intervene[10] – they should not obscure the fact that it was the Young Turk Central Committee that put the genocidal plan into practice. Weber, for his part, points out that Wangenheim was not as ill-disposed toward the Ottoman Armenians as is often said, even if people in his immediate entourage, such as the very influential Hans Humann, naval attaché at the Constantinople embassy, or certain German Turkophiles, such as Ernst Jaeckh or even Kaiser Wilhelm himself, nursed a veritable hatred for the Armenians.

These hardly negligible influences were counterbalanced by the German missionary networks dominated by Dr. Johannes Lepsius and the leader of the German *Zentrum* Party, Matthias Erzberger. The missionaries enjoyed the support of German public opinion, which was unfavorably disposed toward the alliance with the Turks.[11] The history of German-Turkish relations during the First World War is a long series of successful blackmail attempts adroitly mounted by the Young Turk Central Committee, which had its prey in its grip and, blowing hot and cold as circumstances dictated, set to harassing it as soon as the occasion offered. In view of the intransigent, irredentist nature of early twentieth-century Turkish nationalism, skilled at negotiation even in the most extreme situations (the manifest weakness of its position notwithstanding), we are inclined to believe that the CUP was always able to deflect or downplay the accusations or criticisms leveled at it by German diplomats, employing threats or boycotts when necessary. The fact is that each of the two phases of the genocide coincided with an extremely tense military situation that left Germany little room for maneuver. The first was the battle for the Dardanelles, which began in earnest in late April 1915 and continued until the fall. The second was the surprising capture of Erzerum by the Russian forces in mid-February 1916, which touched off the campaign to eradicate the Armenians who had been "resettled" in the Syrian and Mesopotamian deserts and called an abrupt halt to the efforts of the parliamentary delegation, carefully prepared by the centrist leader Erzberger, which met with Enver and Talât on 10 February 1916 to demand that the Turks immediately abandon their policy of "persecuting" the Armenians.[12] Plainly, strategic considerations took priority. The first military operations in the Caucasus, planned by the head of the Ottoman general staff, Fritz Bronsart von Schellendorff,[13] provided for an attack on Russian Transcaucasia, an objective that could not but gratify Enver and his colleagues on the Committee. Beyond the military advantage that Germany expected to obtain by tying down Russian divisions in the Transcaucasus, the Turkists' "grand design" was at last going to be put to the test – what is more, with support from a great power. The Turkey of the Young Turks, by allying itself with Germany, had in some sense attained great power status itself, and profited from the material advantages that this status brought with it. We are accordingly inclined to believe that the CUP entered the war on the side of the alliance that was in the better position to advance the Committee's Pan-Turkist projects.

The Armenians in the Capital: August 1914 to April 1915

In the Ottoman capital, the general mobilization and the arrests of the Hnchak leaders provoked considerable unrest in Armenian circles. It was reinforced by the news that a fire had ravaged the Dyarbekir bazaar on the night of 19 August 1914.[14] Other stories reported by the press in the capital increased the Armenians' alarm: for example, the announcement that Westenenk had been summoned to the Ministry of the Interior and notified of his dismissal by the minister, Talât;[15] the 23 September publication of an imperial *irade* granting amnesty to the Kurds who had been found guilty of murder (of Armenians) in the villages of Azım (Bitlis) and the *nahie* of Gargar (Van);[16] and the closure, on 1 October, of the foreign mail service in Istanbul, a measure that did a little bit more to isolate the Armenians, who used this more efficient, uncensored service more often than other groups.[17]

All this notwithstanding, the Armenians' sentiments were more a matter of the apprehension that people justifiably feel when their country is on the brink of war than the consequence of a precisely identifiable threat. Even the 9 October publication of Czar Nicholas's appeal to the Armenians (signed on 28 August) in the CUP's official organ, *Tanin*, failed to give rise to an anti-Armenian propaganda campaign. The Young Turk newspaper went so far as to express the hope that this appeal would have no influence on Ottoman Armenians – indeed, the paper noted that the Armenian press in the capital had reacted skeptically to it.[18] In this preparatory phase of the war, during which the mobilization was still underway, requisitions were proceeding apace and the ranking Young Turks led by Bahaeddin Şakir were fanning out through the eastern provinces, the CUP had obviously decided not to heighten tensions in the capital to no purpose.

News of continuing violence in the provinces or neighboring countries nevertheless continued to trickle in, creating a very different picture of the government's intentions. A 16 October attempt on the lives of members of British-Armenian Committee, Noel Buxton (a British liberal politician and deputy) and his brother Harold (a clergyman) in Bucharest, where they had gone to attend the funeral of King Carol, was a telling sign of things to come. Responsible for this act was an Albanian journalist by the name of Hasan Tahsin, a reporter for the Ittihadist paper *Tasfiri Efkiar*. Tahsin had only recently come to Bucharest from Istanbul and Salonika, which suggests that the assassination attempt had taken place on orders from the Ittihad. Moreover, the Constantinople press did not pass up the opportunity to point out that the two brothers had just published a book, *Travel and Politics in Armenia* (London, 1914), which *İktam* described as "hostile to the government's reform plan in the eastern provinces." The book unfavorably compared the condition of the Armenians of Turkey with that of the Russian Armenians.[19] The patriarchal vicar, Yervant Perdahjian, remarks in his memoirs:

> Although young Armenians obediently enrolled in the army when the call to serve came, while Armenian merchants were literally plundered within the framework of the law on military requisitions, and despite the line of conduct adopted by the Patriarchate, [Armenian] parliamentary deputies and political parties and their exemplary loyalty, we were informed by reliable sources, whose reports were later confirmed, that the government was in the process of recruiting *çetes* among convicted murderers (who were in principle exempt from military service) and dispatching them with special orders to the provinces inhabited by Armenians.[20]

Thus, the first, still vague reports about the government's machinations had begun to filter through, even if no one as yet suspected the existence of the Special Organization. The vicar further observed that the *çetes* were being sent to all the "provinces that had been promised reforms, especially the villages." Here, murders, kidnappings of young women and girls, and looting were proliferating. Finally, Perdahjian noted that, even before war was declared, "the Patriarchate was daily receiving reports of new atrocities and murders from the provinces."[21]

These circumstances finally led the Political Council to convene a session to discuss the course of action to follow. A number of outside personalities were invited to it, among them Krikor Zohrab, Aristakes Kasparian, Hampartsum Boyajian, Mihrtad Haygazn, Tavit Der Movsesian, Nerses Ohanian, Rupen Zartarian, Hagop Avedisian, Kevork Simkeshian, Aram Andonian, Sarkis Minasian, Mikayel Natanian, and Bishop Hmayag Timaksian.[22] Thus, all the Armenian currents in the capital were well represented. On 30 October 1914, Patriarch Zaven, on his way to the palace to extend his best wishes to the sultan on Bayram, in accordance with custom, learned that a naval clash between Russians and Turks had taken place the previous night.[23]

In his diary, Zohrab reports that he was promptly informed that the whole cabinet had met that very day at Said Halim's residence in Yeniköy. Two days later, after war had officially been declared, Zohrab encountered Mehmed Cavid, who had just resigned. Cavid told him that "foreign adventurers are running our country; the press is in the hands of Tatars and *dönmes*; we have an Aka Gündüz at *Tanin*, an Agayev at *Tercumanı Hakikat*, a Zeki at National Defense and a *dönme* of Yunus Nadi's ilk at *Tasfiri Efkiar*."[24] Although this was a surprising remark coming from a man who was himself descended from a *dönme* family, what Cavid confided to Zohrab is symptomatic of the rumors that must have been circulating in the capital at the time. They might be compared with the rumors about the Germans that began making the rounds a little later: they were blamed for the defeats on the battlefield and even for the annihilation of the Armenians.

At the Patriarchate, all had clearly perceived the danger. Another meeting of the Political Council, again with outside participation, took place on 2 November in the church at Galata where the council usually met. Those invited included Zohrab, Bedros Halajian, Dr. Seghposian, Manug Azarian, Piuzant Kechian, Hampartsum Boyajian, Tavit Der Movsesian, Hayg Khojasarian, Vartkes Seringiulian, Diran Kelekian, Hagop Hagopoff, Mgrdich Manukian, Harutiun Shahrigian, Mihran Muradian, and Bishop Timaksian.[25] Let us note that, even though they rarely frequented Armenian nationalist circles, Halajian, who had himself been a Young Turk and a minister until the day before the meeting, Diran Kelekian, the respected editor of the newspaper *Sabah* and a close friend of Bahaeddin Şakir, and the senator M. Azarian, had also accepted invitations to attend. They thus served notice that they were keenly aware of the gravity of the situation. The assembly concluded, after a long discussion, that it was vital to demonstrate to the government how loyal the Armenians were. A decision was made to publish a circular to be sent to all the provinces, urging everyone to renew his fidelity to the Ottoman fatherland and do his duty. The assembly also resolved to maintain good relations with the government and CUP and to found a field hospital at the expense of the Armenian nation.[26] The task of reviving relations with the CUP was naturally confided to Halajian. In a téte-à-tête, the patriarch asked him to assure the Ittihad's leaders that the Armenians would fulfill their civic duties. On 8 November 1914, Halajian went to see the patriarch in order to confirm that he had delivered the message and that the Young Turks had promised that they would continue to display unreserved good will toward the Armenians.[27]

The patriarch's circular of 10 November is worth pausing over, for it reveals how the Armenians perceived the situation:

> Our country has unfortunately not remained unaffected by the generalized war that broke out among the European powers three months ago. Issuing the call for a general mobilization, the imperial government has put the army under arms. All the telegrams and letters that have reached us in the past three months from throughout the provinces show that our people has obeyed the mobilization order by answering the call ... to serve in the armed forces, complying with the war requisitions and other governmental directives and gladly responding to the appeal for funds to meet the army's and the state's diverse needs. The course of events hitherto shows that the Armenian nation, as an indivisible part of the Ottoman fatherland, is, as the occasion demands, prepared to make every sacrifice to demonstrate its loyalty and patriotism.[28]

The patriarch accordingly exhorted his "people" to "fulfill its duties to the Ottoman fatherland," as it had been doing "for centuries"; to "respond wholeheartedly to the appeals made by the government in the name of the fatherland ... to give to the point of sacrificing its life, even if it was not accustomed to military life"; to "organize charitable societies ... attend to the needs of the families of mobilized soldiers without other means of support ... and the needs of sick and wounded soldiers in particular, even sheltering them and caring for them in its own homes." "There is of course no need," the patriarch went on, "to say that acts of compassion must be performed without regard for an individual's religious or national affiliation, for all are children of one and the same fatherland."

The patriarch also exhorted the

> faithful to maintain friendly relations with their neighbors and compatriots; to help them by giving selflessly and displaying a spirit of sacrifice; to respect their feelings, display more far-sightedness and circumspection than ever; not to leave the door open to misunderstandings; and, more generally, to exercise caution in word and deed, for it is well known that, in circumstances of this sort, people become more nervous and irritable.[29]

It goes without saying that this appeal to Ottoman patriotism, accompanied by a clear recommendation to be more careful and avoid provocations, was very well received by Istanbul's Young Turk press, which covered it with praise – especially in the daily, *Young Turks*.[30] In his memoirs, the patriarch stresses that with these initiatives the patriarchal authorities sought to convince the government of the Armenians' goodwill. A school offering accelerated training courses for future nurses, founded by Dr. Vahram Torkomian and Rupen Sevag (Chilingirian), was even opened on 29 November 1914 in Pera. In the provinces, the

Armenians undertook to produce warm clothing for the soldiers, including socks and even the underwear "that they lacked."[31] All these efforts were well received, the patriarch notes, "yet all indications were that the Turks' appreciation was just pretence. The mobilization went forward under increasingly severe conditions."[32]

The declaration of jihad, a holy war against the "infidels," officially proclaimed on 13 November 1914 by the Şeyh ul-Islam, Hayri Effendi – an Ittihadist who had nothing of the clergyman about him – attested to a discursive radicalization whose import was lost on no one. To be sure, General Liman von Sanders noted in his description of the "demonstrations" staged in response to this declaration the next day, Saturday, 14 November, that "the Turkish police organized, as usual, marches in the streets; the usual demonstrators and a few other individuals who happened to be available received a few piasters by way of recompense."[33] The press reported that these demonstrators made their way to Sultan Fatih's mausoleum, went on to the sultan's palace and even headed for the German embassy, which was exempted from religious anathema for the occasion; indeed, Dr. Nâzım[34] spoke fervently of his high esteem for Turkey's German allies. Zohrab, an old hand at Ottoman politics, wrote in his diary that on Saturday, 14 November,

> A grand comedy was staged. The Turks solemnly proclaimed a jihad against four belligerent states, Russia, France, Great Britain and Serbia. The first to laugh at this farce are the Turks themselves ... In my opinion, the people of the city took no part in this demonstration [which saw] attacks on commercial firms belonging to a number of enemy powers and peaked in the demolition of the Tokatlians' hotels.

Zohrab also observes that the police played "its traditional role, and, this time, smoothed the way for the work of the vandals. Poor Tokatlian," he adds, "who had for five years been selflessly serving all the members of the Ittihad, great and small ... all of whom had been his honored guests," was punished despite his pains.[35]

The head of the German military mission, a witness to these events, remarked that "these demonstrations were not really taken seriously by foreigners or in Germany, thanks to a tendentious account of them"[36] that should probably be attributed to someone on the Istanbul embassy staff.

We should not, however, underestimate the impact of the Şeyh ul-Islam's call, which had Pan-Islamic objectives and probably far-reaching effects in the Muslim world. After a long introduction of strictly religious inspiration, this document states in a more concrete, frankly anti-imperialist tone, that,

> over the course of the previous century, the band of oppressors known as the Triple Entente not only robbed the Muslim peoples of India, Central Asia and most of the regions of Africa of their political independence, their states and even their freedom, but has for more than half a century now, thanks to the support that each of the three powers making it up has given the others, been robbing us of the most valuable parts of the Ottoman Empire.

The text also recalls the traumas of a

> more recent past – only yesterday, one might say; during the Balkan War, which [the Entente] provoked by encouraging and protecting our neighbors, it was the moral and material cause of the annihilation of hundreds of thousands of innocent Muslims, the rape of thousands of Muslim virgins and the fanatical desecration of things sacred to Islam.[37]

Genuine pain makes itself felt here, despite certain rhetorical excesses: to begin with, pain occasioned by the loss of the greater part of European Turkey, but also by the semi-colonial situation which the Turks perceived as theirs.

That said, it is interesting to note the reaction of Constantinople's Armenian elites to these demonstrations. Aknuni, the Dashnak leader, confessed during a 16 November visit to Zohrab that he accepted the consequences of his misplaced trust in the Ittihadists, "those indefensible adventurers," and of his rejection of the liberal circles that had sought to save Turkey.[38] Two days later, he informed Zohrab, this time in the presence of the parliamentary deputy Vartkes Seringiulian, that he was hoping to leave the country and intended to "appeal" to Talât for a travel permit. This disarming naivety earned him only sarcastic comments from his two friends, who recalled the high hopes with which he had come back to Istanbul. "What can you expect of this country," Zohrab remarks,

> when its leaders are named Talât, Dr. Nâzım, Bahaeddin Şakir, Midhat Şükrü and Halil, while its ambitious officers, Enver, Cemal, Fethi and Hakık Hösken, were, only yesterday, greenhorns... And the second fiddles [are] freeloaders like Ahmed Agayev, now known as Ağaoğlu, Aka Gündüz or Yunus Nadi, that drunken newspaper editor[39]

Yet, Zohrab observes, precious few Turks had protested against the declaration of war. In a personal note of rare candor, the spirit of which was probably shared by part of the Armenian elite, he explains this as a consequence of the fact that

> the Turks, who have been raised and nourished on war and have lived on war, are expecting, in the midst of their current decline, to be rehabilitated by it. They do not see that sloth has brought them to the brink of extinction and that they can only be saved by hard work. But work is not for them; they would rather die than work. That is why they go to war so easily, considering war to be only a matter of courage and a little luck. It's an incorrigible gambler's psychology.[40]

The whole of the cultural gap and the difference in mentality between Turks and Armenians is encapsulated in this vehement outburst, written under the immediate influence of the events of the day.

The general feeling of the Armenian elite at the time was that what it was witnessing represented the "beginning of the last stage of Turkey's downfall." Zohrab even expected that he would once again have to give sanctuary to some of these leaders in his home, as he had done for Halil in April 1909, "when they were fugitives."[41] His words bear witness to the close relations that certain Armenian leaders had with the Young Turks and the tolerance they showed towards them.

An anecdote related by Zohrab sums up the situation in which the Ottoman Armenian population found itself at the beginning of the war. A middle-class Armenian came to see Vartkes Seringiulian to tell him about his apprehensions and ask for advice. Vartkes told him that nothing could be easier; he had a very good solution that would cost no more than five *kurus*: "Keep a white *tülbend* (turban) in your pocket. As soon as the Turks start the massacre, pull it out and wrap it around your fez to make a turban. Then declare you're a Muslim. No one will harm a hair of your head." The man replied, "I'll do no such thing, Vartkes. When the Armenians of Sasun were massacred, did they abjure their faith?"[42]

"There's another solution," Vartkes answered: "buy a weapon and defend yourself, if need be." After a moment's thought, the man replied, "I'll do no such thing, Vartkes, because then they'll massacre my kith and kin into the bargain."

Vartkes asked, "What are you going to do, then?" "God is merciful," the man replied. Vartkes brought their conversation to an end with the following words: "Everyone says that. The world is awash in blood and God is merciful. What if God is merciless?" To convert to Islam or pretend to, to defend themselves, or commend themselves to God's mercy, such were the Armenians' options. Another story doing the rounds in the capital illustrates the reigning mood: a twelve-year-old Turkish schoolgirl in a German school in Istanbul told one of her Armenian classmates, "After we win the war, we're going to massacre all the Greeks first." Bewildered, the young Armenian asked her, "and what are you going to do with us?" The bell announcing the lunch break interrupted the conversation.[43]

In the months following Turkey's entry into the war, Zohrab frequently encountered people in Young Turk circles who were opposed to the war, notably the former finance minister, Mehmed Cavid. Cavid was an invaluable source of information for him now that an implacable system of censorship had been put in place.[44] Thus, Cavid reported on a 4 December 1914 meeting convened in his home; those attending were from an "important Turkish milieu." The discussion revolved around the Germans' policy and the Ittihadists' criticisms of the ARF, which they accused of organizing groups of Armenian volunteers in the Caucasus; rumors of pillage and massacre in the Erzerum region were also brought up.[45] On 17 December, Zohrab met with Nami Bey, Said Halim's son-in-law, as well as Cavid, who revealed that, immediately after the outbreak of hostilities in Europe, the Turkish cabinet had pledged to take part in the war on the German side. The Christian ministers and even certain Muslims who were opposed to the Turkish-German alliance had not been invited to these cabinet meetings. According to Cavid, Said Halim, Talât, Enver, and Halil put the final touches on the agreement with the Germans. As for Turkey's entry into the war, it was decided upon in the course of a meeting of "part" of the Council of Ministers that Halil and certain members of the Ittihad's Central Committee also attended. For the former minister of finance, Talât was "indispensable to the proper functioning of the Committee." Without him, its members would tear each other to shreds. Talât kept an eye on everything. Albeit mild-mannered, he was the most powerful of all.[46]

The Armenian lawyer had had dealings with the Ittihadists for seven years and had come to know them well. He observes that they had introduced practices typical of the çetes in the way they governed, that "in every domain, 'strong-arm tactics' were the only method they ever used,"[47] and that this explained their "psychological affinity for the Germans, who employed similar methods of government. There is a 'solidarity'[48] between the Ittihadists and the Germans, a kind of 'complicity'[49] that is always stronger than all other bonds." Zohrab also noted that the heads of state of the Entente powers were incapable of understanding this and drawing the proper conclusions from it.[50]

In a period in which he lacked inside information, Zohrab recalled, upon receiving a letter from Vahan Papazian, who was then in Mush and wrote to inform him of the situation there, that it had taken three years of effort to convince the ARF to participate in the reform plan.[51] This detail has its importance. It suggests that the ARF had long rejected the plan, since it had promised to do so in the pact it concluded with the CUP and knew just how hostile the Young Turks were to the reform scheme.

Among the measures the Ittihad took in the opening months of the war, one must be singled out for special attention. Although the annual session of the Ottoman parliament, presided over by Halil (Menteşe), had been inaugurated on 14 December 1914, it was closed on 1 March of the following year, after the assembly passed on 11 February 1915 an amendment proposed by the Ittihad's secretary general, Midhat Şükrü, to cut the session short by a month and a half.[52] In his memoirs, Talât does not deny that the suspension of the parliament's activities was directly related to the measures directed against the Armenians.[53] It should also be noted that the military operations carried out between

December and February, which did not produce the expected results, led to the massacre of civilian populations in Ardahan, Artvin, Alashgert, Diyadin, Bayazid, Karakilise, and the eastern suburbs of Van. The murder of the vicar of Erzincan, Sahag Odabashian, also attracted attention in Constantinople. Odabashian was killed together with his coach-man on the Sıvas-Erzincan highway, in a place called Kanlıdere in the *kaza* of Suşehir, on the morning of 1 January 1915. He had been on his way to Erzincan to assume the post to which he had just been named. It was soon established that he had fallen victim to a band of *çetes* who had set out from Sıvas on 23 December.[54] The Patriarchate, however, refrained from drawing any conclusions from this murder, the more so as the authorities had obviously decided not to take any action that might alarm the Armenians in the capital itself. At most, the Agence D'informations Ottomane proffered veiled threats from mid-December 1914 on. As for the 19 Armenian merchants tried on charges of shel-tering groups of *fedayis*, they were acquitted by Constantinople's Criminal Court after a brilliant defense by Zohrab.[55]

The 18 March 1915 appointment of Halajian as the Ottoman delegate to the International Court of Justice in The Hague was more troubling.[56] The attempt to sideline this loyal Ittihadist, who had often served as a middleman between the CUP and the Armenians in times of crisis, may be interpreted as part of the arrangements then being made by the Young Turks to deal with the Armenians. The move eliminated, at any event, one of the Armenians' regular channels of dialogue with the government. The suspension of the Dashnak daily *Azadamard*, on the other hand, did not appear to be a departure from custom, since the paper resumed publication on 4 April.[57]

If one had to give a precise date for the opening of the campaign against the "enemy within," it would undoubtedly be 21 April 1915, when *Tanin* published an article entitled "The Accomplices." The article reported appalling details of the crimes that it claimed had been committed against the Muslim population by the Russian army on the Caucasian front. "The most astonishing thing," the author of the article wrote,

is that ... the Armenians of the Caucasus, years of persecution by the Russians notwith-standing, are also playing a part in this masquerade. It is truly stupefying that these Caucasian Armenians should be collaborating with the bloody hands that, in Siberia, strangle and silence their brothers who are struggling for freedom and civilization. How quickly have they forgotten those whose eyes were put out on the gallows with twisted, pointed iron bars.[58]

Tanin established a link between the operations in the Caucasus and the murder of a certain Mahmud Ağa and 14 other people in the village of Perkri (vilayet of Bitlis, *kaza* of Gargar); it accused the Russians' "accomplices" – that is, the Armenians – of the crime.

The battle for the Dardanelles that began in this period naturally also had an impact on the capital. When the question of transferring the government and the sultan to Konya was under discussion, the patriarch informs us that the Armenian Political Council and Armenian chamber decided to follow them if need be. The minister of justice was informed of their decision and submitted the matter to the Council of Ministers. The council is sup-posed to have accepted the Armenian proposal and asked for a list of people whom it might be appropriate to send to Konya.[59]

As early as 2/15 May 1915, Catholicos Sahag informed the Patriarchate of deportations that had been carried out in Zeitun, thus confirming rumors that had already reached Istanbul. However, as the patriarch later wrote, all communication with the provinces had been outlawed and his requests to be allowed to communicate with them in Turkish had all been rejected.[60]

Chapter 6

The Teşkilât-ı Mahsusa on the Caucasian Front and the First Military Operations

In Chapter 3 of this section, we reviewed the circumstances surrounding the creation of the Special Organization and saw that its activities were initially focused on the Caucasian front. We shall now observe what the Teşkilât-ı Mahsusa did in the field from August 1914 to early March 1915, with a view to identifying its leaders and examining the nature of the actions it carried out during the first military operations of winter 1914–15.

Arif Cemil's memoirs, which we have already exploited to determine the Special Organization's objectives, will prove extremely valuable here as well. They attest to the hastily improvised fashion in which army officers, "Enver's *fedayis*," were sent east without a precise destination. This momentary indecision was probably a consequence of the struggle between the Central Committee and the minister of war for control over the Special Organization. The precipitate departure of "Enver's *fedayis*" finds its explanation in the fact that two days previously the Central Committee's rival organization, led by Bahaeddin Şakir, had also set out for the east. Cemil, moreover, states that his group had to wait for 17 days in Erzerum before headquarters in Istanbul issued it the order to move on to Trebizond. In other words, it was in the latter half of August 1914 that the conflict between Enver and the Central Committee was laid to rest and the tasks of the Special Organization's officers were clearly defined. The arrival in Trebizond two weeks later of Kara Kemal, a Central Committee member and the head of the party in the capital, was no doubt also related to the Central Committee's desire to restore order in the Special Organization. Enver had apparently got a head start on his rivals by sending two of his officers, Yenibahçeli Nail and Yusuf Rıza Bey, both of them reputable Ittihad *fedayis*, to Trebizond early in the day.[1] Since Talât, however, had for his part urged Bahaeddin Şakir to go to Erzerum, there sprang up, de facto, zones of influence: Enver's partisans controlled the Trebizond region while Talât's controlled the region around Erzerum. The two groups nevertheless adopted the same recruitment procedures, swelling their ranks with brigands and criminals who had been released from prison on special authorization. This indicates that they were working on the basis of the same directives. Cemil also informs us that when Kara Kemal arrived in Trebizond, Colonel Süleyman Askeri of the general staff had just been appointed head of operations. He adds that the CUP's leader in the capital was accompanied by two Germans, Louis Mosel and Captain Oswald von Schmidt. The Germans had been charged with training and supervising 16 Georgians who had recently returned to the area from Istanbul and were supposed to conduct operations behind the Russian lines.[2]

According to Cemil, the groups in Trebizond and Erzerum were not collaborating effectively at this point, while the national leadership was taking its time settling the conflict between them. The situation was so tense that Süleyman Askeri had to step in and demand that a meeting be held to discuss coordinating their efforts. The meeting took place in Bayburt, halfway between Trebizond and Erzerum. It was attended by Şakir and his assistant, Filibeli Ahmed Hilmi, on the one hand, and on the other, Kara Kemal and Yusuf Rıza. They decided to summon representatives of their networks in Russia to Trebizond and Erzerum in order to plan with them, among other operations, the sabotage of ammunition depots as well as the rebellions the Turks hoped to trigger.[3]

The Special Organization's first operations were thus plainly designed to pave the way for an offensive in the Russian Caucasus that had probably already been decided upon in principle. War, however, had not yet been declared; hence there were still Russian consuls in Trebizond and Erzerum and the leaders of the Special Organization had to proceed with caution. Their first contacts with the Turkish speakers of the valley of Corok were apparently encouraging: these people indicated their willingness to revolt. Using Rize as his base of operations, Yenibahçeli Nail concentrated on enlisting the leaders of local bands.[4] Şakir's activities extended as far as Persian Azerbaijan, where he recruited an important local dignitary, Hoca Ali Khan, who was "very influential" in Khoy and Salmast.[5] This is an indication not only of the Special Organization's military objectives in the region, but also of the Turkist dimension of its operations. According to information Şakir sent back to Istanbul, the Georgians were ready to revolt as soon as military operations commenced. His direct collaborator, Şakir Niyazi, a Russian speaker, regularly moved back and forth between the border zones, where he met with the Special Organization's informers. Şakir also obtained information from the men he had infiltrated into the mass of Greek and Armenian refugees already making their way to the Caucasus.[6]

Another incident is worth pausing over – the attempt to murder the last Dashnak delegates to leave the Erzerum Congress for the Caucasus. Cemil gives us a precise account of it. Ahmed Hilmi, in a 3/16 September 1914 letter to his superior, confirmed that he had received the latter's encrypted telegram about "the persons leaving Erzerum" and informed him that "orders have been issued where necessary to ensure that we can apprehend them ... Like the objectives to be pursued outside the country, there are also people to eliminate in the country. That is our viewpoint, too."[7] While no definitive decision had yet been made about the fate to be meted out to the Armenian population, these two eminent CUP members displayed at the very least a hostile attitude toward the activists who had been the Committee's most dependable supporters from 1908 on. Cemil further states that Şakir personally demanded that the *vali* of Erzerum expel the last ARF delegates, who had been lingering in the city, and adds that the Central Committee had instructed Ömer Naci to engage discussions with them, doubtless because Naci and the Dashnak leaders were old acquaintances. However, the Caucasian delegates, who knew their Young Turk friends very well, took roundabout routes on their way out of the city, thus managing to escape Hilmi's *çetes*.[8]

Şakir, in the report he sent Talât in mid-September, described the inspection tours that he had made in the region of Narman, "whose killers are efficient," and also in Hasankale. The main subject of his report, however, was the theft of more than 1,000 sheep and 400 cows and water buffalos from the Armenian peasants living on the other side of the border. This operation seems to have delighted Şakir, who deemed these exploits a success even if they brought on a number of bloody skirmishes with the Cossacks at the frontier.[9]

According to Cemil commandos were already operating behind enemy lines by September 1914. The leaders of the Special Organization had now taken up their stations in the region: Şakir, Filibeli Ahmed Hilmi and Şakir Niyazi were at the command center in Erzerum, Halil Bey had been assigned to Kötek and Narman, and Dr. Fuad Bey and Necati were in Bayazid. Necati had arrived there the first week of September and recruited his squadrons of *çetes* from the local Kurdish population, who had been promised in exchange that they would be granted amnesty for the crimes of which they were accused.[10] Another Ittihadist *fedayi*, Abdül Gaffar, who had recently been dispatched to the region from Istanbul, met with Rostom in Erzerum in late August and suggested that searches be carried out in the villages with all possible speed in order to disarm the population. He asked for money for this purpose for himself and Ömer Naci,[11] who had been working in the Van region as an inspector for the Ittihad since late August, and he let it be known that he had recruited the men needed to do the job from among the very cooperative Kurdish tribes. He added that the Armenians of Van were "gentler than those from Erzerum."[12] Talât consequently recommended in a 6/19 September 1914 telegram that Naci accelerate the organization of the Teşkilât-ı Mahsusa in Persia and fan the flames of the revolt that had broken out near Urmia.[13] In the following weeks, a number of Kurdish tribes in Persian Azerbaijan, notably those led by Seyid Taha, rose up in revolt. They had begun to represent a problem for the Russian troops already present in the region and for the local Christian populations as well.[14]

In Trebizond, the *vali*, Cemal Azmi, played a significant role in recruiting *çetes* from the ranks of brigands living in the mountain districts of the vilayet by obtaining amnesties for them.[15] The only factor complicating operations here was the antagonism between Yenibahçeli Nail and Major Yusuf Rıza Bey, rivals for the position of commander of the Special Organization's squadrons in the region.[16] Their conflict was finally settled in favor of Rıza, who was a member of the Ittihad's Central Committee. Nail nevertheless managed to assemble 700 *çetes* by early November, all of them convicts released from prison, and prepared to lead them into the frontier zones via the coast.[17]

According to Cemil, Şakir was then focusing his efforts on the Olti and Artvin regions, but he also inspected the Special Organization's forces in Bayazid. Here, noticing that there were Armenian conscripts serving among the troops guarding the borders, he suggested that they be transferred to the garrisons "in the interior."[18] Our eyewitness and participant in the events, Cemil, affirms that the Teşkilât-ı Mahsusa was operational by late October, and adds that it was then that the minister of the interior, Talât, proposed to Şakir that he either accept an appointment as *vali* of Erzerum or continue to serve as the chief of the Special Organization.[19] In either case, the Ittihadist specialist in forensic medicine would remain in the important regional center, north of which, at Tortum, the Third Army had established its headquarters with jurisdiction over the six eastern vilayets. In a 17 November 1914 cable, the minister of the interior, in response to a message of Şakir's, asked him to proceed to Trebizond, where he said Yakub Cemil would give him extremely important oral instructions.[20]

We do not know the content of the message that Talât transmitted to his fellow Central Committee member. It is likely, however, that it briefed Şakir on his appointment to the presidency of the Teşkilât-ı Mahsusa's political bureau. Cemil says that Şakir was its president in February 1915, adding that its vice-president was Filibeli Ahmed Hilmi.[21] But it is possible that the decision to give Şakir the post was made earlier.

In the field, the first operations conducted by the Special Organization's squadrons were led by Major Yusuf Rıza, who advanced as far as Maradidi, a village dominating Batum. He and his men were soon joined by the 700 *çetes* under the command of Nail, who distributed arms to the Georgians in the village so that they could defend this highland area.[22] We know from another source that in early December 2,000 *çetes* who had set out from Istanbul arrived in Bortchka, not far from Maradidi, under Yakub Cemil's command. The plan was for these forces to link up with the squadrons that Şakir had concentrated in Artvin, Ardanush (captured on 3 December by Yusuf Rıza), and Olti.[23] By 5 December 1914, Şakir had settled into Artvin, which had been occupied on 24 November; he considered leading an attack on Ardahan from there.[24] With support from Cemil's forces and the Eighth Infantry regiment commanded by Colonel Stanger,[25] Şakir's troops launched a successful attack on Ardahan, which was defended by Cossacks. They took the city on 29 December,[26] but pulled back to Yusufeli almost immediately thereafter.[27]

Somewhat further to the southwest the Third Army, commanded by General Hawiz İsmail Hakkı,[28] repulsed a brief attack launched by the Russian forces on Köprüköy, between Kars and Sarıkamiş, in November.[29] It was, however, the offensive that the minister of war personally launched at the head of the Third Army in late December – an operation that Liman von Sanders described as "extremely difficult, if not altogether impossible"[30] – that determined the outcome of the military campaign. The nearly total destruction of this 90,000-man army, routed in Sarıkamiş on 4 January,[31] left a profound mark on people's minds. At Sarıkamiş, Enver lost some of his prestige and influence within the CUP,[32] but it was above all the Ittihad's ambitions in the region that had now to be scaled down. The vice-generalissimo's precipitate return to Istanbul in mid-January no doubt marks a turning point in the Ittihadists' psychological development. According to von Sanders, "the extent of this bloody defeat" was long kept a secret. "Very little information about the event," he wrote later, "ever reached Germany."[33]

As we have seen, all the operations just evoked were military in nature. To be sure, in the areas in which the Special Organization had been active, the çetes had perpetrated localized massacres, abductions, and acts of pillage against the Armenian population. A review of the reports on these exactions in military and diplomatic German and Turkish sources[34] does not, however, justify the assertion that what was involved were premeditated acts or a pre-established plan.

The crimes committed in the villages of the plain of Erzerum,[35] reported in early December 1914 by the German vice-consul in the city, Dr. Paul Schwarz – murders of priests and peasants and attempts to extort money by threats – must be classified, even if they occurred repeatedly, as excesses brought on by the presence of large numbers of troops in the region. In contrast, those committed by squadrons of the Special Organization under Şakir's command in late November and early December in the villages of Pertus and Yoruk, near Ardanush and Olti, were more like large-scale massacres. in these two villages, 1,276 Armenians were mowns down and 250 young women and girls were abducted.[36] The çetes, accompanied this time by Adjars, committed other atrocities in Artvin and Ardanush. Johannes Lepsius puts the number of Armenian victims in these frontier zones at 7,000 in the November-December 1914 period.[37] The majority of the massacres took place before Enver launched his offensive. In our view, they reflect the logic of the twofold objective that we outlined in Chapter 3 of this section. For the time being, priority was given to the offensive in the Caucasus. The "enemy within," however, was by no means ignored.

The exactions perpetrated in the *kaza* of Başkale, southeast of Van, in December 1914–January 1915 were similar to those that occurred further north. In the first week of December, massacres took place in the villages of Paz, Arak, Pis, Alanian, Alas, Soran, Rasulan, and Avak, which had a combined population of some 3,500 to 4,300 Armenians.[38] Their victims were primarily men.

The targets of the killing, looting, and kidnapping committed in the *kaza* of Saray-Mahmudiye, located just north of the *kaza* of Başkale on the Persian frontier, were the most remote Armenian villages in this region – Hasaran (15 December), Satmants (20 December), Akhorig and Hasan Tamran (30 December), and Avzarig (14 January 1915).[39] Perpetrated for the most part by Kurdish çetes, these crimes were very probably the fruit of the work that Ömer Naci had been carrying out in the area since August 1914 with a view of forming squadrons of çetes for the Special Organization, but they were also related to the offensive that had been launched against Iranian Azerbaijan. They affected isolated Armenian localities strung out the length of the frontier with Persia, not the big population centers of the interior.

Desertions of Armenian soldiers from the Third Army during the battle of Sarıkamiş, attested by Turkish and German sources,[40] as well as the fact that two battalions of Armenian volunteers entered the battle alongside the Russian forces, are commonly supposed to provide the explanation for these massacres, which are described as retaliatory measures. The desertions are supposed to have profoundly affected the Ottoman general staff and to have heightened their mistrust of the Armenian soldiers. Zürcher, however, in his discussion of the problem of deserters from the Ottoman army during the First World War, points out that desertion was a widespread phenomenon in all Ottoman armies beginning with the Third Army,[41] and that there were diverse reasons for it, notably the soldiers' deplorable living conditions and lack of food and equipment. While he provides no figures for the winter offensive of 1914–15, which, it is true, relatively few Ottoman soldiers survived (estimates have it that some 12,000 escaped death), he notes that, in the wake of the winter 1916 capture of Trebizond and Erzerum by the Russians, the same Third Army, in which there were no longer any Armenian troops, lost 50,000 to desertion – more than half of its strength.[42] Moreover, substantial numbers of soldiers in the Third Army were captured and interned in Siberia; these men were very probably counted as casualties or deserters. The Armenian soldiers held in Siberia with other Ottoman soldiers in similar conditions were, let us add, freed only in June 1916, after the Catholicos of Armenia had repeatedly interceded on their behalf with the Russian military authorities. They spent a total of 18 months as prisoners of war.[43] Finally, Enver himself survived the inferno of Şarıkamiş only because an Armenian officer from Sivas, a veteran of the Balkan Wars, carried him from the debacle on his back, something the vice-generalissimo noted in the letter of high praise that he wrote about this episode to the Armenian primate of Konya, Karekin *vartabed* (Doctor in theology).[44] Cemil, for his part, reports that there were many desertions even from the ranks of the Special Organization. One commander of a squadron of *çetes*, *Topal* Osman, who would make a name for himself in spring 1915 thanks to his operations against the Armenians of Trebizond, was brought before the court-martial of Rize established by Yusuf Rıze and charged with abandoning the front along with his *çetes*. He was condemned to 50 strokes of a stick.[45] The Laz deserters from the Special Organization were also punished: their moustaches were shaved off, the supreme insult in Laz society.[46] When the Special Organization decided to evacuate Artvin under Russian pressure on 23 March 1915, its interim president informed Şakir that *çetes* were deserting en masse.[47] Thus, it seems that the accusations of desertion, a widespread phenomenon at the time, should be treated with caution.

Donald Bloxham observes, in connection with the battalions of Armenian volunteers engaged in military operations against the Ottoman forces, that most of the massacres of November–December 1914 and January 1915 took place in the zones where these volunteers were fighting on the front – for example, in Karakilise and Bayazid, where by way of retaliation after the Russian retreat, 18 villages suffered exactions at the hands of the *çetes* of the Special Organization.[48] This, however, is not enough to explain why there were some 16,000 victims in the frontier regions between November and January. The many massacre victims in the far northern regions near Ardahan, for example, were killed in areas in which the offensive launched by the Turkish forces had met with resistance from Cossacks alone. It seems more probable that these atrocities were an expression of the hostility toward the Armenians that was deeply rooted in the Special Organization, even if it is beyond doubt that no plan yet existed systematically to destroy the Armenians.

The demonization of the Armenian population can be clearly seen in the retrospective discourse of Arif Cemil. He points out that the *çetes* of the Special Organization, retreating before the advancing Russian troops at Çaldıran, discovered "a large number of documents" in the possession of an Armenian pharmacist in Arcış, which "indicated that the Armenians were planning to conduct their movement in collaboration with the Russians and revealed how they would go about implementing their extermination policy."[49] Cemil makes a great deal of these "documents" and does not hesitate to publish them, for they seem to him to provide material proof of the Armenians' treachery. "The Armenians of the interior," he writes,

> tried, with the help of organized commandos, to put the rear of our army in danger and close off its avenues of retreat. A certain number of important orders regarding the Armenian çetes fell into our hands. These orders, which had to do with their future movements, contained absolutely everything, in great detail.[50]

Although this passage was written more than 15 years after the event and was doubtless influenced by the discourse on the Armenians' treason that Istanbul concocted ex post facto, it reflects a mood that must have been common among the Turks. There can be no doubt about the fact that Cemil and his companions-in-arms were convinced of the Armenians' treachery: that is what led Cemil to publish these "important orders" in their entirety.[51] A close reading, however, reveals that they are in fact the contents of a booklet, its meaning somewhat distorted by the military translator, that originated in Sultan Hamid's day and was intended for Armenian *fedayis* – *Rules of Battle*, by the celebrated Antranig.[52] This, then, is how Cemil's precis of the Young Turk perception of the Armenian conspiracy came into being. One would be hard put to say whether that perception was mere propaganda or genuine conviction symptomatic of a skewed perception of reality.

After the debacle at Sarıkamış, the Special Organization clearly acknowledged that it had been dealt a hard blow. The squadrons of çetes were assembled in Melo on the orders of Filibeli Ahmed Hilmi Bey, while Kara Kemal headed back to Constantinople and Şakir Niyazi Bey, Bahaeddin Şakir's assistant, went to Maraş "to rest."[53] On 11 February 1915, Dr. Şakir himself withdrew to Yusufeli, in the vicinity of Artvin, and began trying to put his squadrons back in order.[54] But, Cemil reports, a typhus epidemic had attained such proportions that Şakir was assigned to create, from his base in Erzerum, a healthcare system out of whole cloth and to coordinate the efforts of the physicians in the city.[55]

At the time, the Teşkilat-ı Mahsusa was, despite the desertions, one of the rare forces still capable of offering resistance to the Russians, who were cautiously waiting for winter to end before pursuing their advance. Cemil, moreover, voices a symptomatic apprehension: "There was no doubt that the Russians, if they succeeded in taking back the lands that we had conquered, were not going to leave a single Turk or Muslim alive."[56] It is not possible categorically to affirm that this apprehension was a direct consequence of the exactions that the çetes had perpetrated in these regions, but that certainly seems probable.

Without specifying a date, Cemil indicates that, ultimately, "the president of the Teşkilât-ı Mahsusa, Dr. Bahaeddin Şakir, left Erzerum for Istanbul in order to save the situation; he named Hilmi Bey temporary president of the organization."[57] Another military officer states that the president of the Special Organization left Erzerum for Istanbul on 13 March 1915.[58]

Hilmi stayed in touch with his superior and repeatedly appealed to him for help, particularly when he was confronted with the army's desire to incorporate the existing çete units, a project that in his opinion could only hinder the realization of their objectives. Clearly, the fact that the Special Organization operated autonomously was not to the military's liking. The question was presumably discussed at the highest levels, inasmuch as Avni Pasha and Kara Vasıf, two ranking members of the Ittihad, were now entrusted with the task of disciplining the Special Organization "as if it were a regular army."[59]

Cemil's conclusions should be cited here, for they sum up the Ittihad's evolution after Şakir's return to Istanbul. According to Cemil, the

> numerous documents that were discovered [plainly showed] that the domestic enemies who had organized inside the country were preparing to attack our army from the rear. After Dr. Bahaeddin Şakir had brought all this to the attention of the Ittihad's Central Committee in Istanbul, the Committee worked together with him on defining the measures to be taken; thanks to them, the Turkish army avoided a great danger. The result of their collaboration was the deportation law.[60]

While we cannot be certain that Şakir triggered the Central Committee's decision to translate words into deeds simply by showing it these "numerous documents," it is quite certain that his report did a great deal to bring this decision about. His colleagues on the Committee were doubtless more inclined than ever to heed his arguments.

It is just as clear that the "many agents [who] were sent to Persia or Batum to create Organizations there," as the former minister of public works, Çürüksulu Mahmud Pasha, put it in his deposition before the fifth commission of the Ottoman parliament,[61] had been given the mission of developing the Ittihadists' expansionist plans in a Turkish-speaking environment, whereas Şakir's activities in the area under the jurisdiction of the Third Army fell into the category of Ottoman domestic policy in an Armenian-speaking environment. The failure of the operations outside Turkey obviously accelerated implementation of the plan for the demographic homogenization of the eastern provinces.

Chapter 7

The First Acts of Violence

Military Operations and Massacres in Iranian Azerbaijan: September 1914–May 1915

We have already seen that the Ittihad delegated Dr. Rüsûhi and Ömer Naci, a former member of its Central Committee and a well-known *fedayi*, to form squadrons of *çetes* of the Special Organization in the region of Van and in Iranian Azerbaijan;[1] that Naci was officially charged with initiating a dialogue with the Dashnak leaders in the area;[2] and finally, that, on 19 September 1914, the minister of the interior instructed Naci to speed up the recruitment of Kurdish tribal leaders in Iranian Azerbaijan[3] for the purpose of harassing the Russian troops stationed in the area. A 26 September 1914 dispatch from the French vice-consul in Van, Barth de Sandfort, reported that a printed proclamation calling on the Muslim population to demonstrate "Islamic solidarity in order to drive the enemy from our land" was circulating in Persia.[4] The French diplomat stated that "the three Turkish bands" of 150 men each that had "so far been sent" to Persia were "very well armed and equipped with bombs" and that the "proclamation" given "to the members of these bands for distribution in Persia [had been] signed by a Persian revolutionary and was intended to foment rebellion in Azerbaijan."[5] His dispatch further stated that "three thousand four hundred Kurdish cavalrymen are supposed to be concentrated here under the command of the former inspector of the vilayet, Abdülkader Bey," who had been promoted to the rank of brigadier general. Thus, we see that the leaders of the Teşkilât-ı Mahsusa were extremely active in the Van region, where they depended on support from local notables, who they solicited in the name of religious solidarity, and that Van had been assigned a central role in these maneuvers.

Hostilities began in earnest in November–December 1914, when Russian troops stationed in Khoy launched an attack on Ottoman territory that directly threatened Van, even though their own rear was threatened by local Kurdish tribes who had been won over by the Special Organization. The Turkish counterattack was aimed at Qotur, a fortress near the border. The attack was carried out by regular forces, backed up by units of the Special Organization and Kurdish auxiliaries. In mid-December came the news that some 2,000 Armenian refugees from the Başkale area had arrived in Salmast, as had 200 prisoners of war, mostly Armenians or Catholic Syriacs who had been captured by the Russians.[6] It is, however, the military campaign waged south of Lake Urmia by the Turkish forces late in December – obviously coordinated with Enver's campaign in the north – which interests us here: it forced the Russians to evacuate Urmia on 2 January, Salmast on 2 January and Tabriz on 5 January.[7] The first Turkish contingents were soon reinforced by Cevdet, Enver's brother-in-law, who had at last been officially appointed both military governor of Van and commander of the Turkish troops on the Persian frontier on 20 December.[8] A proclamation issued in Tabriz on 25 January 1915[9] by İbrahim Fuzi, "commander of the Ottoman troops and the Muslim mujahid sent from Mosul," reveals how these "soldiers of Islam" recruited by the Ittihad planned to deal with the Armenians:

> The Armenians, subjects of a foreign power, who are at present resisting and fighting the Armies of Islam, unhesitatingly attack Muslims' property, life, reputation and honor: from the religious and legal standpoint, their property is a legitimate target for the soldiers of Islam. Their business assets are fair prey: the value incarnated in them must be spent on the wounded or to acquire goods needed by the army. According to a report we have received, certain inhabitants of the city, certain merchants, are safeguarding property belonging to the Armenians – foreign subjects – in their businesses or homes. We hereby inform all these inhabitants of the city that anyone who has goods from the commercial stock of the foreign Armenians in his keeping ... risks severe punishment and the confiscation of his own property.

Another proclamation, undated but issued around the same time and signed by Haci Mirza Abul Hasan, reads: "In the name of God, exalted be He. The aforementioned individuals must be killed and their property must fall prey to the Muslims. God knows best."[10] These frankly Pan-Islamic appeals were typical of the interventions of the Turkish army and the Special Organization in Iranian Azerbaijan. They leave no doubt as to the Ittihad's intentions in this peripheral region in January 1915. They also show that the Ittihad's objectives were not purely military. Finally, it should be said that the man who signed the first of these two texts was one of the propagandists recruited by the Ittihad to promote its Pan-Islamic campaign.

The Turkish advance naturally sowed panic among Azerbaijan's Christians, who had only recently experienced Turkish occupation under Sultan Abdülhamid. On 25 December, there began a massive exodus of these Christians over the Julfa Bridge toward the Arax river valley in the Caucasus. According to concurring sources gathered by Magdalena Golnazarian-Nichanian, a total of 53,437 Armenian and 9,658 Syriac refugees had made their way to the Caucasus by 30 January 1915.[11] Not until late April 1915 and the beginning of the Russian offensive did these refugees begin to go back home. A few hundred Armenians died en route; the others owed their lives to their flight. As for the economic effects of the Turkish incursion, they were disastrous: all the villages were plundered and then burned to the ground. The situation was the more difficult in that in the same short period several thousand refugees from the rural areas of Van thronged into Salmast-Dilman, fleeing the bloodbath that accompanied Cevdet's withdrawal from Azerbaijan in early April.[12]

The Pan-Islamic slogans and the license to attack Christians that was issued to the faithful did not, however, suffice to provoke an uprising among the local populations, who were unaccustomed to the kind of ritual massacre frequent in the Ottoman Empire. The dirty work was done by the Turkish forces, the çetes, and their local allies. With the 8 January 1915 arrival of the Turkish occupation troops in Tabriz, observers, diplomats, and missionaries discovered, masquerading as a regular army, "a band of Kurds of all ages and conditions, some on horses, the others on mules and the rest on donkeys. Almost all of these animals were also loaded down with crates, bundles of clothing, boxes of all sorts and carpets."[13] This is an indication that these irregular troops had seized whatever they happened upon in the Christian villages on their way. During the three-week occupation of Tabriz, however, order prevailed; there was no violence and only a little harassment of the Armenians. This was probably owing to the presence of many foreign observers in the city. The same cannot be said of Urmia, a point of convergence for peasants from the villages on the plain who had not been able to flee to the Caucasus in time. More than 17,000 Christians, including 2,000 Armenians, found refuge in Urmiah's Presbyterian mission compound; another 3,000, mainly Syriacs, thronged into the Lazarists' mission early in January 1915. The Presbyterians, as citizens of a neutral country, escaped the troops' rage. The Lazarists were not as fortunate; their residence was attacked on 11 February on the "pretense" that "they were hiding arms and ammunition in it."[14] Only a very few massacres occurred – the victims were for the most part elderly people who had refused to leave their homes – but the intention to commit them was evidently not lacking.

In Salmast, a small town located close to Dilman on a plain just north of the plain of Urmia, the Armenians were not molested until 14 February, since, in this community without a foreign mission, they were sheltered by their Muslim neighbors. It was here that, in the latter half of February, the biggest massacres were perpetrated. A stratagem devised by the commander, Rostom Beg, made it possible to arrest some 800 Armenians and pack them off to the neighboring villages of Haftevan and Khosrova. After being tortured and mutilated, they were killed and thrown into wells and cisterns.[15] According to a German source, 21,000 Christians fell victim to the Turkish operations in Azerbaijan between December 1914 and February 1915, especially in the plains of Salmast and Urmia – to say nothing of the women and children who were abducted and sequestered by Kurdish tribes.[16]

The last major Ottoman offensive was waged in April 1915 by Halil Bey (Kut), Enver's uncle, who had ceded his post as both military governor of Istanbul and as a member of the executive bureau of the Teşkilât-ı Mahsusa to Colonel Cevad in order to take command of the Fifth Ottoman Expeditionary Corps, called into existence for the purpose of attacking Iranian Azerbaijan.[17] The outcome of the Turkish offensive was decided at Dilman, where hostilities commenced on 18 April/1 May, at a moment when resistance in the Armenian city of Van had already begun. Halil and his 12,000 men, backed up by 4,000 Kurdish irregulars, confronted General Nazarbekov's Sixth Russian Division, reinforced by Antranig's First Armenian Volunteer Battalion.[18] The Turkish forces were defeated and retreated toward the vilayet of Van, where the situation was on the point of boiling over.

Was the violence that marked the first Azerbaijan campaign of the same order as that being perpetrated more or less simultaneously further north, on the Russian-Turkish frontier? Here as well, it was due to *çetes* of the Special Organization, commanded by Ömer Naci, but comprised Kurdish *hamidiyes*, Çerkez, and tribal forces from Azerbaijan. It should also be pointed out that it was legitimized by a Pan-Islamic ideology, as foreign witnesses noted.

The Situation in Van from the Mobilization Order to the April 1915 Siege

In fall 1914, Tahsin Bey, who had a reputation as a moderate, was still governor of Van. Throughout the northern part of this vilayet, in which the Armenians were in the majority and the ARF had considerable political clout, the authorities continued to treat the Dashnak leaders with consideration. The Dashnaks' relations with the local Young Turk club, headed by Colonel Jafar Tayar and Kücük Kâzım, were courteous.[19] Aram Manukian, Ishkhan (Nigol Mikayelian), and the parliamentary deputy Arshag Vramian, who had been elected in spring 1914, had taken care to smooth over the problems that had cropped up since the proclamation of the general mobilization order and the first requisitions. The Armenian leaders were even invited to the ceremonies organized when the troops left for the Caucasus in October.[20] A few incidents did, however, mar the calm reigning in Van – Hoff's recall to Istanbul on 29 August, which put a semi-official end to the Armenian reforms; the September 1914 murder in Bayazid of a local Dashnak leader, Aloyan; and the arrest of three Hnchak leaders in the city of Van. In a private conversation with Vahan Papazian, Vali Tahsin justified this arrest on the grounds that the three Hnchaks had held secret meetings in Romania and were plotting against the regime.[21] He was, however, careful to point out at the same time how much the authorities appreciated the ARF's loyalist political line.

One event provides a barometer of the situation in Van – the general mobilization. It took place very early there, beginning on Sunday, 9 August, under rather special circumstances. Troops took up their positions in the broad square in front of Ararots Cathedral shortly before the end of the church service, and all the men leaving the church as well as all the merchants who had a stall on the square were detained and led straight to the city's barracks. No distinctions of age were observed, so that it took several days to separate the men of draftable age from the rest. Some of the conscripts soon deserted and were actively pursued by the authorities. Meanwhile, the army began to requisition carts and draft animals in the villages.[22]

As happened elsewhere as well, the mobilization of the peasants interrupted work in the fields at the very moment that the harvest was getting underway. A substantial rise in the price of bread was the almost immediate result. To overcome these problems, the prelacy negotiated an agreement with the local authorities by which leaves were granted to farmers so that they could bring in the harvest and to schoolteachers so that they could maintain their classes, at least provisionally. The Armenian deputies and primate instructed the population to obey the mobilization order without a murmur.[23] An order from the commander-in-chief of the Third Army, Ahmed İzzet Pasha, the former minister of war, was handed down in late August: in addition to the tithe, 2.5 per cent of the harvest was to be sent directly to him in Erzerum. To carry out the order, virtually all the means of transportation still available were mobilized.[24] As in almost all the eastern vilayets, the departure of the men for military service led to serious security problems in the now undefended villages. The prelate accordingly requested that the *vali* station guards in the villages. The other problem that became especially pressing in November had to do with the requisitions for the army. This operation, which was carried out by the local authorities, did not, needless to say, take place under ideal conditions. The war offered an excellent occasion to loot Armenian property and acquire substantial revenues at small cost, and it was not necessarily the army that profited from these confiscations. On 2 December 1914, the merchants of Van sent a telegram to the Patriarchate, requesting that it petition the minister of justice in their name. The petition was deposed at the ministry on 14 December. In it, the merchants complained that the local authorities had requisitioned goods worth 20,000 Turkish pounds without offering the slightest compensation in exchange (in violation of the established rules), with the result that they were unable to pay the war taxes that had also been imposed on them.[25]

The situation grew much more tense after the late September arrival of Enver's brother-in-law, Cevdet. Cevdet was much more radical than the *vali* Tahsin Bey. Of Albanian origin, he was the son of the former *vali* of Van, Tahir Pasha, and had thus spent part of his youth in the city. He also happened to be a close friend of Arshag Vramian's, having been a classmate of his at Istanbul's Mülkiye. Thus, he was thoroughly acquainted with the situation in Van and aware that it would be necessary to maintain friendly relations with the local ARF leaders, who had long been involved in resolving day-to-day problems in the area.

Turkey's entry into the war gave rise, among other significant incidents, to the 21 November 1914 expulsion of all the French missionaries from the city. The American missionaries, however, stayed on.[26] In the same period, the first military operations led to the arrival in the city of refugees who were fleeing the fighting or had fallen victim to the violence that *çetes* of the Special Organization had inflicted on the Armenian villages in the eastern *kazas* of Başkale and Mahmudiye.[27] Those who offered shelter to the survivors listened with consternation to their detailed descriptions of the atrocities committed by the irregulars of the Special Organization, who, they reported, killed with a "refined cruelty without precedent." The preparations that Ömer Naci was making with a view to forming squadrons of *çetes* did not, of course, go unnoticed by the Dashnak leaders. Their priority, however, was to avoid all provocation and maintain their dialogue with the *vali* and the national authorities.

Several more or less serious incidents occurred in the vilayet of Van between December 1914 and March 1915. Each time, the Armenian leaders had to step in to pour oil on troubled waters. In Pelu/Pılı, a village straddling the border between the *kazas* of Ğarzan and Gevaş, the telegraph cable was severed early in December. The villagers were accused of the act by the *kaymakam*, who arrived accompanied by gendarmes and ordered that the whole village be burned to the ground, although most of the inhabitants managed to flee.[28] Another incident took place in mid-February in Gargar, on the border between the vilayets of Van and Bitlis. Here the young men riposted when the gendarmes attacked. The village was ultimately looted by Kurdish *çetes*, while the inhabitants fled to the *kazas* of Moks or Gevaş.[29] Ardzge, in the *kaza* of Adilcevaz northwest of Lake Van, a village whose Armenian *kaymakam*, Bedros Mozian, had been dismissed in August 1914, was the scene of a third episode.[30] Members of the Kurdish Çato tribe, who had already in December wrought havoc in Melazkırt, Erciş, Perkri, and Arcak, attacked the village of Kocer on 25 February 1915, looting, raping the women, and abducting the girls and cattle. A self-defense group of some 50 young men was immediately formed to defend the other villages in the area. On 26 February, when the same Kurds attacked two neighboring villages in the *kaza* of Adilcevaz, they were met with gunfire and left a number of dead behind. A final incident took place on 24 March in the *kaza* of Timar, northeast of Lake Van, where soldiers and gendarmes encircled the self-defense group that had come from Adilcevaz. Aram raced to the scene to restore calm and forestall a confrontation.[31]

These events kept tensions running high. Evidently, they were interpreted in diametrically opposed ways by the local authorities and the Armenians' representatives. In March, Vramian sent a memorandum to the minister of the interior about the massacres that had occurred in the *kazas* of Başkale and Mahmudiye and, more generally, the insecurity reigning in the region. This document is of special interest because it expresses the Armenian leaders' viewpoint on the events of the winter of 1914–15 and considers the validity of the charges leveled by the military and civilian authorities. Vramian began with the observation that 150 *hamidiyes* of the Kurdish Mazrik tribe, led by Sarıf Bey, took part in the attack on the Armenian villages of Başkale. Turkish military sources, he went on, pointed to the Armenian resistance to the successful Turkish attempt to recapture the little town to justify this intervention, while simultaneously criticizing the Armenians for ostensibly following the retreating Russian troops. Vramian pointed up this contradiction, asking whether it was conceivable that the Armenians had abandoned their families and fled with the Russians. He added that

> the local authorities in Başkale report[ed] only that they ordered the arrests of eleven men whose names are cited in their report. These men were ordered to go to Van and murdered on the way. This was why I made a number of personal appeals to Mehmed Şefik Bey, the interim *vali*, requesting that he authorize a local inquiry with a view to compiling a list of the killed and missing and providing their poverty-stricken families with aid.

Vramian remarked that his appeals had fallen on deaf ears, as had his proposal to transfer to Van a few "of these unfortunates, who could have given us information about the situation." He noted that he had gradually received confirmation of the fact that hundreds of women and children remained "in the ruins and ashes of the villages," clad in rags and dying of hunger.[32]

Turning to the massacres in the villages of the *kaza* of Saray – Akhorig, Hasan Tamran, Kharabsorek, and Dashoghlu – which occurred late in December, the Armenian deputy recalled the pretext on which the gendarmes of Saray, led by Abdül Gadir and Yaver Rasim, turned up in Akhorig. On orders from the *kaymakam*, the male inhabitants of Akhorig were instructed by the gendarmes to go to the little town of Saray to rebuild the barracks there that had been destroyed. The day before, they had been told not to leave Akhorig until they received further orders. "This [was] proof," Vramian wrote, "of premeditation." These men never arrived at Saray, he continued: they were killed in two groups by the Kurds at Avzarig. The very same day, 100 Armenians were slaughtered at Hasan Tamran. The *kaymakam* then ordered that the 300 survivors of the massacre be expelled to Persia. Unable to cross the mountains, which were buried in snow, they turned back and sought refuge in Ingize and Tarkhan. The gendarmes, however, denied them access to those two villages. Some 70 or 80 of them ultimately managed to make their way to Salmast. Vramian provided all these details in order to apprise the minister of the interior of the violence being visited on the Armenians. To the same end, he described the fate of a priest named Vartan, whose nose and ears had been cut off and whose eyes had been gouged out before he was shot to death, while his wife was forced to marry a porter.[33]

The Armenian deputy next described the massacres and looting that took place in Hazaren on 15 December: "Five thousand six hundred ten animals (sheep, oxen, cows, calves, water buffalos and horses), grain and all the farm implements were taken from this village," whose church was then demolished. The same thing happened at Setibeg, where, Vramian observed, "an inquiry has established that there were gendarmes among the Kurds." "Similar scenes," he wrote, "are being repeated everywhere; well organized massacres and looting, razed villages." After listing all the acts of violence committed in November and December, again on 9 January 1915 in Kangar and still later in Nordüz, Erciş, Ardzge, and on the northern shores of Lake Van, Vramian asked why the "local authorities" encouraged such acts. He noted that his demands for an explanation had met with the following responses: 1) the Armenians of Başkale were spying for the enemy; 2) some Armenians were supposed to have looted the Turkish army's depots when the Russians invaded the country; 3) some men had joined the Russian army; 4) others had mounted an armed resistance after the Russian retreat; 5) if hundreds of women had left, they had done so of their own accord, out of a desire to go to Salmast to join their husbands; and 6) the Kurds were fired up against the Armenians.[34] After assuring Talât that all these accusations were baseless, Vramian wrote:

> An anti-Christian policy will not help save the country ... The government must cease to consider the Armenian elements in the empire as enemies ... If the government is at present incapable of guaranteeing the Armenian people the exercise of its sacred rights – its life, honor, religion and property – then it ought to authorize them to defend those rights by itself; if it is to be presumed that low-level government officials have misinterpreted the central government's orders and understood nothing of its policies, then these officials must be punished and forcibly set back on the right path.

After emphasizing that it was in the interests of the country to put a stop to this violence, the parliamentary representative suggested 1) sending a commission of inquiry to the area and gathering up "the abandoned women and children with no source of support in all the ruined villages; the women who have been converted by force ..."; 2) restoring to the peasants of the razed villages their herds and their property; 3) collecting "the rifles that were issued to the sedentary Kurds on the government's initiative"; 4) arming militiamen only after they had been enrolled in the army; and 5) returning to the Armenians "the weapons that were taken from them by force."[35]

The foregoing summary of Arshag Vramian's long memorandum sheds light on the terror campaign waged by the local authorities; it also affords us a glimpse of the strange dialogue that he established with the national government. The Armenian leaders apparently had no other choice than to believe that what they were witnessing were deviations by the local authorities. Another important phenomenon may be observed here – the institution of a discourse collectively incriminating the Armenians of the border provinces and simultaneously justifying the violence perpetrated against them by portraying it as retaliation. We should, however, note that this was still a local discourse that had not yet appeared in the press of the capital. Thus, one has the impression that the Ittihadist government was provoking the Armenians of the provinces in hopes of bringing them to abandon their publicly professed loyalty and rebel. It is indeed symptomatic that Vramian himself drew up a catalogue of the various charges leveled by the local authorities – which in the aggregate tended to show that the Armenians were traitors to their country – in order then to redefine the problem as that of the security of the civilian population. In a document addressed to the minister of the interior, Tahsin Bey wrote: "Rather than deporting the Armenians in the middle of a war, I suggest, for my part, that they be maintained in their present situation until further notice and not be spurred to revolt by the illegitimate use of force. The condition of our army is well known."[36] Coming from a man who was eminently familiar with the local situation, this statement leaves little doubt about the government's desire to "spur a revolt by the illegitimate use of force." The behavior of the authorities in Van reflected this logic, which could only have been inspired by instructions from the national government. The replacement of Tahsin Bey by a radical partisan of the regime, Cevdet Bey, the minister of war's brother-in-law, was probably calculated to make it easier to implement such a policy of provocation. There is even every reason to believe that it was at the instigation of Ömer Naci, CUP inspector in Van and the head of the Special Organization in the region, that Tahsin was transferred to Erzerum in February 1915.

Referring to the "revolt" at Van that broke out on 19 April 1915, Tahsin Bey wrote:

> There would have been no revolt at Van if we had not ourselves created, with our own hands, by using force, this impossible situation from which we are incapable of extricating ourselves, and also the difficult position in which we have put our army on the eastern front. After enduring this painful experience and its deadly consequences, we are, I fear, making the mistake of putting our army in an untenable situation, like someone who has poked out her own eye while trying to apply mascara to her eyelids.[37]

In other words, the strategy adopted by the CUP was an error that only plunged the Turkish troops into greater disarray – the more so, Tahsin Bey insisted, in that the Armenians "ensured, with their grain and means of transport, our army's food supply." "This is a point," he insisted, "that ought to be duly considered, for, today, we are just barely able to maintain the food supply at the price of a thousand difficulties," to say nothing of the fact that "Armenians comprise 90 per cent of the artisans that are absolutely essential to the population and army. One or two grocers and butchers aside, there are no craftsmen among the Turks. This, too, has its importance."[38] Vramian, in a 26 March 1915 telegram addressed to his friend Cevdet, who was still at the Persian border, reminded him that he and his comrades had done everything in their power to avoid violence; criticized him for failing to take the measures needed to prevent the excesses that the militia and gendarmes had perpetrated against "property and persons" on the pretext of looking for deserters; noted that he had therefore had no choice but to refer the matter to Talât; and complained that the authorities had not reacted to the killing of 15 people in the village of Aghchaveran by Edhem Bey and his militiamen. Finally, Vramian demanded that a number of villages that had been burned down – Erer, Dılmachen, Adnagants, Payrag, and so on – receive compensation so that they could rebuild and, in closing, asked Cevdet to pay his respects to Naci Bey.[39]

Cevdet, in the answering letter that he wrote on 26 March in the monastery of St. Barthoghemeos, where he was stationed at the time, informed Vramian that the two of them would soon be able to discuss these matters in person, since he was leaving for Van the following day at the head of a large force. "Rest assured," he added, "of the government's fair, honest stance and inform the populace of it."[40]

On 30 March 1915, Cevdet was received by a delegation of government officials and local dignitaries who had gone out to meet him, Aram Manukian and Vramian among them. Vramian observed that he was wearing the khaki uniform "of a *çete*" and had 600 "elite" Çerkez equipped with three canons at his command. As soon as Cevdet and Vramian reached the *konak*, they disappeared into the *vali*'s office. The Armenian deputy left this meeting with the feeling that he had clarified matters and laid Cevdet's "apprehensions" to rest. On Easter Sunday, 4 April, Cevdet, in turn, paid a friendly visit to Vramian; they spent two hours together. The same day, however, 800 *çetes* who had returned from Persia arrived in the city.[41]

As soon as the *vali* returned from Azerbaijan, where Cevdet and Ömer Naci had perpetrated massacres on the plains of Salmast and Urmia, he demanded that 3,000 more Armenians be mobilized. He seemed adamant about this subject. The Armenian lay and religious leaders were reluctant to accede to this new demand. Everyone knew that Armenian conscripts were no longer sent into battle, but were in the best of cases assigned to military labor battalions, mistreated, and sometimes killed. "Accepted one day, [the propositions] were rejected the next." These negotiations dragged on until mid-April 1915, without yielding tangible results.[42]

In the meantime, Cevdet made certain that he could count on the cooperation of the commander of the gendarmerie, Ahmed, and Captain Uskudarli Arab Yaşar. He also armed the Çerkez tribes of the Van region, notably the tribe of Topal Rasul,[43] and appealed to several tried and true killers of the Ittihad for support: Çerkez Ahmed, Çolak Hafez, Selanikli Şevki, Çerkez İsmail, Çerkez Raşid, and Bandermali Haci İbrahim, who had once served as Talât's chauffeur.[44]

On 11 April, a revealing incident occurred in Shadakh, a *kaza* south of Lake Van: Hovsep Choloyan, a schoolteacher and Dashnak leader living in the administrative seat of the *kaza*, was unexpectedly arrested, together with five young men. The next day, the shops in the little town remained closed. People were surprised by the news. Until then, the Dashnaks had never been molested and had often played the part of conciliators. Everyone knew that the men could not have been arrested if Cevdet had not been informed beforehand. Vramian went to see him and they made a joint decision to send a peacemaking party to Shadakh. The Joint Armenian Council, which dealt with situations of this sort, also thought it best to cool tempers and "play for time."[45] Ishkhan was assigned the mediator's role. On the afternoon of 16 April, he set out for the village, accompanied by three experienced party activists,[46] Vafik Bey, and three gendarmes; they were escorted for a few miles by an honor guard provided by the *vali*. The eight men stopped for the night in the village of Hirj (in Hayots Tsor). Ishkhan and his men stayed in the house of a Kurdish friend of theirs, Kârimoğlu Raşid. That night, a group of Çerkez surrounded the house and killed the four Armenians.[47] There is every reason to believe that none other than Cevdet, the superior of these Çerkez, had ordered these killings. He had probably come to the conclusion that he could accomplish nothing in a city with an Armenian majority unless he first got rid of the three Dashnak leaders. His behavior the following day tends to confirm this suspicion. Early in the morning, he summoned two of the leading Armenian citizens of Van to the *konak* along with Aram and Vramian. He placed two separate telephone calls, although the men lived in the same neighborhood. Vramian promptly took up the invitation, but left Aram a message recommending that he ignore an invitation from the *vali* should he receive one.[48] Vramian was never seen again, except when someone caught a glimpse of him that evening guarded by 50 gendarmes at the port of Argants, where the parliamentary deputy was put aboard a vessel bound for an unknown destination.[49] He was murdered shortly thereafter in Arapu Tsor, not far from Bitlis.[50]

Aram did not go to the *konak*. Like the rest of the city, he very soon learned that Ishkhan had been murdered. The news shocked and dismayed the population.[51] The American missionaries in Van, Dr. Clarence Ussher and Miss Grace Knapp, who were eyewitnesses to these events, provide us details that leave little doubt as to the *vali*'s intentions. On 18 April, Ussher himself went to see Cevdet in order "to see if there was any way of quieting the apprehensions of the people" awakened by "rumors of massacre." While the American physician was in the *vali*'s office, a colonel from the "Vali's Regiment" came in; Cevdet himself had baptized it Kasab Taburi, the "butchers' battalion." The colonel was given the order to "go to Shadakh and wipe out its people."[52]

On 17 April, the *vali* stationed 150 Çerkez[53] in the Hamut Ağa barracks, which was located in Van's Armenian quarter and had remained empty until then. The Armenians interpreted this move as yet another threat. The next day, the primate Eznig *vartabed*, and two Armenian notables, Kevork Jidechian and Avedik Terzibashian, went to see Cevdet, who spoke in a threatening tone for the first time.[54] That same day, 18 April, generalized massacres broke out in the Armenian villages of the vilayet, beginning with Hirj, the village in which Ishkhan had been assassinated on the previous day. The following day, a Monday, they took a systematic turn throughout the area south of Van known as Hayots Tsor, "the valley of the Armenians." Systematic violence also broke out on that Monday to the north of Lake Van, in the *kazas* of Erçis/Arjesh and Adilcevaz/Ardzge;[55] to the east, in the region of Perkri; and to the south, in the *kazas* of Karcikan, Gevaş/Vostan, Şatak/Shadakh, and Moks.[56]

Rafaël de Nogales, a Venezuelan officer attached to the Third Army, arrived in Adilcevaz on the evening of 20 April. He beheld a Dantesque scene: fires were raging all around Lake Van. The next morning, he was informed that "the Armenians had attacked the town." Leaping onto his horse, Nogales rode through the city, where he discovered a very different spectacle: the shops had been sacked and Turks and Kurds were hunting down Armenians in the Armenian quarter. "The assassins penetrated into the houses," he wrote, and "knif[ed] the defenseless victims." When Nogales ordered the mayor, who was leading the "mob of villains," to stop immediately, the mayor told him that he had received an "unequivocal order emanating from the governor-general of the province 'to exterminate all Armenian males of twelve years of age and over.'" "At the end of an hour and a half of butchery there remained of the Armenians of Adil-Javus [Adilcevaz] only seven survivors." Returning to the *konak*, Nogales was nonplussed by the "effrontery" of the *kaymakam*, who "thanked me effusively for having saved the town from tremendous Armenian attack."[57]

On Saturday, 17 April in Van, the commander of the gendarmerie had already asked Ussher to authorize him to station, for "ten days," around 50 soldiers and a cannon in the "[American] mission compound, which was on a hill dominating the Armenian quarter of Garden City [Aykesdan]." Officially, the aim was to "protect [the Americans]," for "trouble between the Kurds and the Armenians" had broken out and the Kurds, the man told Ussher, "might injure you."[58]

Ussher and the Italian vice-consul, Sbordoni, now went to see Cevdet. They told him that the news about Ishkhan's murder and the massacres in the villages that had reached the city had "excited" the Armenians, who would never agree to the stationing of soldiers and a cannon on a height overlooking their neighborhood.[59] The next day, Sbordoni explained to the *vali* that "the course he was taking was calculated to arouse opposition and not allay it." According to Ussher, Cevdet had apparently changed his mind on 19 April and even urged the Armenians to open their shops, but had also ordered that Aykesdan, one of the city's Armenian quarters, be surrounded as soon as evening fell. It was precisely on 19 April that the city learned that thousands of "defenseless men" had been massacred throughout the province.[60]

On 20 April 1915, Aykesdan was attacked at dawn. Aram Manukian, however, had already made preparations to ward off an attack and was able to prevent the Turkish troops from entering the quarter. In the next few days, nearly 15,000 peasants found refuge in Aykesdan. On 21 April, the outbreak of an "Armenian revolt" in Van was front-page news in the Istanbul papers. Several months later, an official publication of the Interior Ministry presented matters this way:

> In March, again, an Armenian rebellion broke out in the *kaza* of Timar, administratively attached to Van. The movement then spread to the *kazas* of Gvash and Shatak. In the city of Van itself, the insurrectional movement was still more violent: large areas of the city were burned down and hundreds of people, both civilians and military personnel, were murdered... After a short-lived resistance, the Russians and Armenians occupied the city of Van. The Muslim population remaining in the city was ruthlessly slaughtered.[61]

This is virtually the only official version of the "revolt" of Van that we have. The "revolt" is described in the same pamphlet as one of the reasons for which "the commander of the Imperial army, observing that the Armenians had made common cause with the enemy forces, felt compelled, so as to protect its rear, to order the transfer of the Armenian groups settled in areas regarded as military zones to the south."[62]

The Situation in Mush: September 1914–May 1915

Like the region of Van, the *sancak* of Mush was an area with a majority Armenian population in which, in 1915, the ARF was by no means a negligible political factor. As such, Mush constitutes another exceptional point from which to observe and assess the evolution of the political situation in the eastern regions of the empire from the beginning of the war to May 1915. As was the case elsewhere, conscription took place amid the greatest imaginable confusion, but in the absence of significant conflicts. Around the middle of October 1914, however, the local authorities began circulating rumors that the Dashnaks were organizing bands of *çetes* in the region and that these irregulars were preparing to join the Armenian volunteers from the Caucasus in attacks on Muslim villages.[63] To be sure, these rumors were officially denied at the insistence of the primate of Bitlis,[64] but they engendered an abiding malaise.

When the parliamentary deputy Vahan Papazian arrived in Bitlis "on the day war was declared" (2 November 1914), he learned that Şeyh Said Ali Hizan's revolt had just been put down, and saw that one of the main moving spirits behind the revolt, Şeyh Selim, was still dangling from a gibbet in the middle of the city's central square. He also observed that the center of town was filled with squadrons of Kurdish *hamidiyes* who had been summoned to Bitlis by the authorities.[65] Their presence aroused the suspicions of the Armenian leaders. Here, too, the military requisitions paved the way for what can only be called the pillage of businesses and stores, while the treatment of draftees who were put to work repairing roads occasioned vociferous protest.[66]

Papazian was charged with presenting the grievances of the Armenian population to the local authorities. As soon as he arrived, he was received by the *vali* of Bitlis, Mustafa Abdülhalik, Talât's brother-in-law, "an educated, well-bred man." Papazian describes in particular the plight of the families who, because one of their members had tried to dodge the draft, had seen their property confiscated, their houses burned down, and their parents taken hostage.[67]

Toward mid-December 1914, Papazian reached Mush. He was welcomed by the Dashnak club, which met in the dispensary founded by Dr. Zavriev in 1912. The head of this club was none other than Ruben Ter Minasian.[68] In the small town of Mush, Armenians and Kurds lived side by side. Among the Kurds, one clan, the Kotans, dominated the local CUP club. The head of this clan, Hoca Haci Iliyas Sâmi, a deputy from Mush, had an Armenian mother (she had been abducted and had converted) and spoke fluent Armenian. He was the lead-ing personality in the city; the Young Turk *mutesarif*, Servet Bey, "a well-bred young man" "educated by Filibeli [Ahmed] Hilmi,"[69] was obliged to take his opinions into consideration. Another figure of note, the military commander Vasıf Bey, also had a certain importance in Mush; he was distinguished by the fact that he was not affiliated with the Young Turk party.[70]

The plain of Mush and its hinterland, the Sasun district, had a revolutionary history that was still present in everyone's mind. The 1894 resistance and the exploits that the Armenian *fedayis* performed in Sultan Abdülhamid's day helped give the Armenians of Mush a well-deserved reputation for bravery. Even if the ARF activists had mutated into teachers and responsible politicians after 1908, they still arouned a certain suspicion among high-ranking Turkish officials in Mush. We have a nice illustration of the phenomenon in the account that the bishop of Mush, Nerses Kharakhanian, gave Patriarch Zaven of his conversation with the German consul in Mosul, Hosten, who had been traveling through the region in 1914. The consul told him that the government did not trust the Armenians at all, adding that the Kurdish bandits in the Sasun district – in Hoyt/Khoyt and elsewhere – had been summoned to Mush and displayed frank hostility to the bishop's people. "There are clear signs," the bishop wrote, "that the government is seeking a pretext to bring a catastrophe down on the heads of the Armenians of the region."[71]

As in Van, these apprehensions by no means prevented the authorities from maintaining normal day-to-day relations with the Armenian leaders. On 25 November, a meeting took place between Papazian and the two leaders of the local Ittihadist club, Dido Reşid, the responsible secretary delegated by the CUP, and Paramaz, a relative of Ilyas Sâmi's. All three men reaffirmed the need to work together to organize the army's rear and collect and trans-port food and supplies. There was, however, also a discussion of the Armenian volunteers from the Caucasus, whose cooperation with the Russians enraged the CUP.[72] In his capacity as parliamentary deputy, but also as a leading ARF member, Papazian in fact played the role of an intermediary; he dealt as best as he could with controversial matters such as the draft and the requisitions, which by early December were proceeding apace.[73] Mush had become, by the beginning of the war, a training and recruitment center into which conscripts from Dyarbekir, Harput, Gence, and Hazo poured. However, the city lacked the basic services and structures required to accommodate these soldiers, who were therefore lodged in mosques, schools, and khans. News of the rout of the Caucasian army in January spawned a semi-anarchic situation in the town as well as the mass desertion of the *hamidiye* battalions, which had to be laboriously patched back together. According to Papazian, Haci Musa, a brother of the deputy Haci Iliyas Sâmi, had instigated these desertions.[74]

Turkish distrust of the Armenians in Mush did not, however, lead the ARF to alter its strategy of collaborating with the authorities. The Armenian deputy even accepted the *mute-sarif*'s proposal that he serve as president of the eight-member commission, which included two officers, that was responsible for organizing supplies for the front. In his memoirs, Papazian remarks that this put him in a position to establish rules governing the way draftees were used for transportation, the main means of transport at the time being men's backs. The rules set maximum load levels and provided for mandatory rest periods.[75] However, as the winter

wore on, the region's particularly harsh climate made such transportation increasingly ardu-
ous, while the Armenian soldiers in the labor battalions were increasingly exposed to risk:
they were often murdered in the villages through which they passed. Papazian observes that
discontent was growing rapidly but that the Armenian representatives continued to recommend that the government's demands be met as fully as possible. To be sure, the Armenians
did not appreciate the fact that the *mutesarif* of Mush had organized a splendid reception for
the chiefs of the Kurdish Jibran tribe, even though these *çetes* had just pillaged the villages of
the plain.[76] The Armenian deputy complained about this to the *mutesarif*, pointing out that
the authorities only encouraged the brigands to maintain the prevailing anarchy by adopting
such an attitude, and emphasizing the risks of destabilization of the Ottoman rear that such
anarchy entailed.[77]

After this stormy meeting, a conclave of all the Armenian leaders was held at the archbishopric. Here it was decided "not to cede to the provocations, but to put up with them ... and
not to voice [Armenian] discontent in too demonstrative a fashion."[78] The 1915 New Year's
festivities provided an occasion to re-establish friendly relations: the *mutesarif*, military leaders, judges, and notables of Mush all came to wish a happy New Year to their somewhat
skeptical Armenian counterparts.[79] The authorities' cynicism came to the fore even more
clearly in January, when the *mutesarif* suggested to Goriun, a well-known ARF official from
the Daron district, that he agree to head an Armenian-Kurdish militia that the *mutesarif*
wished to create in order to meet "the security needs of the plain of Mush." Goriun's response
was quite as absurd as the suggestion itself: he proposed creating an all-Armenian militia that
would be equipped by the army. The *mutesarif* prudently promised that he "would submit the
proposal to the *vali* of Bitlis."[80]

The Armenian leaders had of course evaluated the situation and considered organizing
their own defense. By February 1915, fairly serious discussions were being devoted to this
question. They are rather precisely described by Papazian, who informs us that the first to
raise the issue were former *fedayis* who lived in the villages on the plain and complained that
they were under close surveillance. The deputy and others who were of his mind pointed out
that there were not enough men capable of fighting and that they lacked arms: they had at
best 700 to 800 hunting rifles and 150 to 200 rifles that were "more or less suitable, but for
which they had little ammunition." In other words, they had just enough arms and ammunition to put up a brief self-defense. However, various epistolary exchanges with the committees of Erzerum and Van, as well as the bureau in Istanbul, convinced them that they would
do well to take steps allowing them to defend themselves if necessary.[81] It is obvious that the
Armenian leaders were not much inclined to credit the authorities' good intentions.

The tour through the villages of the region that Ruben and Goriun made in February
was undertaken with a view to applying their party's directives. Their departure, however,
did not go unnoticed. According to information that reached the Dashnak club of Mush,
seven or eight Kurdish gendarmes had been rushed off to Goms, Goriun's native village.
Papazian, who was summoned to the *konak* the following morning along with Archbishop
Kharakhanian, was told by the *mutesarif* that the previous evening Goriun and Ruben had
burned alive a corporal named Mustafa Fakhi, together with a few gendarmes. Servet Bey
threatened to burn down the village where this had happened if the two Armenian leaders
did not turn themselves in. He announced that he planned to hold the Armenian deputy
hostage until they did.[82]

These threats must, however, be put in perspective. Thus, Papazian notes that the *mutesarif* invited him to dinner at his house, where he was "put under the surveillance of the
chief of police," and also that he agreed to allow the deputy to go to the village where
the incident had occurred to conduct an investigation together with the military commander of Mush, Vasıf Bey. It would seem to follow that in this odd face-off the two camps

were both still trying to avoid a final break. Papazian and Vasıf Bey set out without delay, accompanied by the *kaymakam* of Bulanık, Esad Bey, the *mudir* of Hazo, Süleyman, and an escort of seven or eight policemen. Upon reaching Goms, they discovered hundreds of Kurds from the surrounding area in the process of methodically pillaging the houses in the village and carrying off the herds. These *hamidiye* units had taken around 50 male and female villagers hostage and let the others escape. The refugees were questioned in front of Papazian, who tried to put them at their ease and asked them to speak freely. The villagers then said that the gendarmes had arrived the evening before "to collect taxes." In accordance with tradition, Goriun had seen to it that they were lodged and fed. Shortly thereafter, one of the Kurdish gendarmes, an old acquaintance of Goriun's, came to see him at this house and warned him of the "evil intentions" of Corporal Fakhi, who was planning to murder both him and Ruben, "on the orders of the Ittihadist club in Mush." Goriun thereupon set the stable in which the gendarmes were spending the night on fire, after blocking the exits from it; the gendarmes who managed to get out of the stable alive were shot down. According to Papazian, the inquiry culminated in the conclusion that a "trap" had been set, and the hostages were freed a day later.[83] After Papazian and Vasıf had returned to Mush, the *mutesarif* listened to the results of their inquiry "without batting an eyelid." Papazian even says that he was surprised by Servet Bey's objective attitude, confessing that he did not understand until later that the *mutesarif*'s behavior was dictated by the fact that he was hoping to bring the two main military leaders of the region, Goriun and Ruben, to return to Mush so that he could take them prisoner.[84] A few days later, the police searched the ARF club. However, before the club was closed down and the doors sealed, the party militants managed to spirit away both the weapons that had been hidden there and the party archives.[85]

Among other signs of rising tension was the fact that in February the soldiers who had been drafted into the *amele taburis* (worker battalion) and assigned the task of transporting supplies from the plain of Mush to the front began to disappear, one by one at first, and then in whole groups. When their families and friends sought information about them, the *mutesarif* invariably answered either that the roads were blocked by snow or that the men had had "to cover greater distances than they had in the past in order to keep up with the advance of the Ottoman army" (apparently no one was aware that the army had retreated). Moreover, notables from the villages on the plain were being arrested on various pretexts – for example, that they had refused to turn over crops required by the army – and detained in the prison in Mush. The *mutesarif* remained courteous, however, declaring in response to Papazian's complaints that he lacked the forces he needed to restore order in a country that had settled into anarchy; that it was necessary to be patient and to help him accomplish his task; and that Ruben's flight had angered the Muslim population.[86] At the same time, he continued to draft more and more men to serve as porters. Papazian turned down none of his requests. To meet the *mutesarif*'s demands, he now had to turn either to peasants who were often 50 or even 60 years old or adolescents of 15 or 16. One of these new conscripts, a 60-year-old man, later testified that his battalion of 250 porters, all of them Armenian, had left Mush in January 1915 in the company of 20 gendarmes on horseback. Despite abundant snowfall, he got as far as Hasankale, after enduring a thousand difficulties. By that time, the group counted only 100 men, whose powers of resistance surprised the gendarmes. The others had perished en route, succumbing to exposure or exhaustion.[87]

As in Van, the situation did not truly deteriorate until March. In the region of Mush, it was the recruitment of the famous Kurdish chief Haci Musa Beg, who had gained notoriety in the 1890s for the atrocities he committed on the plain and in Sasun, which marked the beginning of the campaign of harassment directed against the *sancak*'s Armenian villages. Haci Musa was specifically responsible for an attack on Mushaghshen, in which he killed several villagers and burned down houses,[88] and for the murder of members of the family of the mayor of Avzud, Reis Malkhas, who were burned alive in their barn.[89] In response to these depredations, the veteran *fedayis* demanded that their leaders allow them to take to the mountains. Some 30 of them withdrew to the Monastery of the Apostles overlooking the city, without waiting for instructions from the party. When the *mutesarif* was informed of this, he immediately dispatched Lieutenant Çerkez Ahmed and a few dozen horsemen to capture or kill these men who were defying his authority. On the very steep road that led toward the monastery, the first shot fired threw the horses into a panic. The lieutenant tumbled into the abyss at the side of the road.[90]

Notwithstanding the tension caused by this incident, Papazian continued to meet regularly with Servet Bey, with whom he sometimes spoke French. The courteous relations that still prevailed did not prevent the Armenian doctor from demanding that the *mutesarif* establish law and order on the plain and put a stop to the looting of the villages if he wanted to prevent men from taking to the mountains.[91]

A fact reported by Papazian allows us to pinpoint the moment when Servet Bey was ordered by his superiors to move to a more repressive phase in the treatment of the Armenian population of his *sancak*. Late in March, Servet was summoned to Bitlis by the *vali* Mustafa Abdülhalik.[92] Although we do not know the precise nature of their conversations, the period in which they occurred coincided more or less exactly with the week in which, as we shall see, the Ittihad's Central Committee arrived at a decision to "deport" the Armenians. In early April, Papazian learned almost by accident that the Russian army had advanced as far as Bulanık, in the far northeastern corner of the vilayet of Bitlis, 60 miles from Mush,[93] and that the campaign to recruit squadrons of Kurdish *hamidiyes* had now been extended to the *sancak* of Hakkari and was being supervised by German officers charged with training these recruits.[94]

The patriarch, Zaven Der Yeghiayan, cites a "report drawn up by a high-ranking official" on the results of a meeting that began on 25 April 1915 and ran for two or three days. At the meeting, which took place on the road between Bitlis and Siirt, were Dr. Nâzım, a member of the Special Organization, the *vali* Mustafa Abdülhalik, and the commander of the battalion of the gendarmerie in Siirt. It would seem that the first reports to the effect that the Armenians had risen up in rebellion in the isolated mountain region of Hizan were diffused in the wake of this meeting. As a result, several hundred mounted gendarmes, as well as irregulars recruited from the Kurdish tribes living in the area, were sent to Hizan. An inquiry later revealed that these "rebels" were in fact some 20 Kurdish bandits who had been wreaking havoc throughout the region. The minister of the interior nevertheless spread the news of an Armenian revolt in the Hizan district.[95] The Istanbul press echoed this official version of events, which was transformed in turn, in the pamphlet put out by the Interior Ministry a few months later, into an assault on gendarmes carried out by "armed men in Mush and Hizan."[96] Clearly, the local authorities had not succeeded in prodding the Armenians of the vilayet to "revolt." Even Dr. Nâzım's personal intervention had failed to produce a credible pretext for future "acts of retaliation."

A conversation between Papazian and the *mutesarif* that took place late in the evening of 10 April marked a crucial stage in the evolution of the relations between the government and the Armenians. According to the physician's account of it, Servet Bey, who was carrying a pistol in the back pocket of his pants, had been intending to arrest him personally. However, in this tense face-off, Papazian conspicuously advertised the fact that he, too, was armed, and let the Turkish official know that his friends were waiting for him outside.[97] The moment of the break was drawing inexorably closer, but Servet probably did not yet feel that he was in a position to liquidate the last Armenian representative of the region – and a parliamentary deputy at that.

Thus, when Papazian contracted typhus in mid-April, the *mutesarif* contented himself with having him watched, while noting that Dashnak activists were carefully monitoring the condition of their bedridden leader. Servet even took the trouble to visit him twice while he was ill in order to inquire personally about the state of his health. At their second meeting, which took place in May, the *mutesarif* confided to him that, during a brief stay in Bitlis, he had encountered Arshag Vramian, who had just returned there from Istanbul – even though Vramian had in fact been executed one month earlier.[98] This lie, which was intended to reassure Papazian, shows how isolated the region was. In his memoirs, the Dashnak leader remarks that he had heard vague reports of generalized massacres in the neighboring vilayet of Van, yet was aware that he would be arrested as soon as his physical condition was deemed satisfactory. In mid-June, as he was recovering, he received a laconic message from the head of the Mush telegraph office advising him to change his place of residence. That very evening, he was invited to a meeting of local ARF leaders at Hayg Mirijanian's house, at which the measures to be taken to protect the 100,000 Armenians of the plain of Mush were discussed. All agreed that it was necessary to organize the Armenians' self-defense, but that it was very late in the day and that the Sasun district, which could be more easily defended than the plain, could not support and provide shelter for so many people.[99] At the time, there were very few regular troops in Mush and the *mutesarif* probably preferred to wait for more to arrive before proceeding to arrest Papazian and his companions. Among the Dashnaks opinions diverged as to the proper course to steer – whether the Armenians should try to take control of the city before the troops arrived or withdraw to the mountains of Sasun with the men who were capable of fighting. The shortage of arms and ammunition convinced them to choose the second alternative. On 20 June, some 15 policemen occupied the house where, officially, Papazian was recuperating from his illness.[100] This marked the beginning of the operations against the Armenians of the plain of Mush and the mountains of Sasun. Papazian and his companions now took to the maquis,[101] leaving the plain and city to fend for themselves.

In Bitlis on 20 April, the day the Armenians of Van entered into resistance, the "cream of the youth of Bitlis" – Armenag Hokhigian, Kegham Basmajian, and Hovhannes Muradian – were arrested on orders from the *vali* Mustafa Abdülhalik. They were paraded through the city in chains and subjected to the "insults of the Turkish population" before being led outside the city, where gallows had been set up. Their bodies were left hanging for two weeks and were partially devoured by dogs.[102]

Judging the crimes committed in the vilayet of Bitlis, General Vehib Pasha would later write that "Mustafa Abdülhalik Bey, the former *vali* of Bitlis, a man without fault and endowed with civic virtues, was not able to put a stop to these events, of which I shall never be able to approve."[103]

A number of lessons can be drawn from our review of the events that occurred in the vilayets of Van and Bitlis down to spring 1915. To begin with, it appears that the Armenian leaders and local authorities maintained almost daily contact until the government decided to have done with the Armenians. It can be seen as well that the Armenians patently sought to defuse the situation and tried to avoid provocations; that the information that the local authorities communicated to Istanbul in an attempt to portray the Armenians as traitors conspiring with the Russian foe was hastily seized on by the Ottoman government, which never sought to verify it; that the much ballyhooed Armenian "revolts" were merely – in the rare cases in which Armenians were involved – acts of self-defense carried out in extremis, as in the case of the city of Van; that local acts of violence did not, down to the month of April, have the systematic character they later assumed, except perhaps in Iranian Azerbaijan; that the massacres perpetrated in this period were concentrated in border areas and were thus bound up with military offensives and also, albeit to a lesser extent, with defensive operations; and that most of these crimes were committed by çetes associated with the Special Organization and recruited above all among the Laz, Çerkez, and Kurds, some of whom were acting as "gendarmes," or at any rate wore the uniform of the gendarmerie.

The maintenance of a kind of *cordon sanitaire* that blocked all communication between regions, together with a strategy centered on concealing the CUP's true objectives, were the two indispensable conditions for the success of the plan to liquidate the Armenians without provoking resistance.

The Mobilization of Armenian Soldiers: Between the Front and the Labor Battalions

In earlier chapters, we saw that the mobilization of men between the ages of 20 and 45 rapidly came to constitute a bone of contention in the eastern provinces between the local authorities and the Armenian leaders. We noted as well that conscription spawned violence in the rural zones and that, from March 1915 on, the theme of the Armenians' desertion and treachery became one of the arguments regularly put forward by the authorities to justify retaliatory measures. The official pamphlet of the Ministry of the Interior, published in winter 1916, sums up the authorities' position as follows:

> Most of the young Armenian men who were inducted into the army to fulfill their military obligations not only deserted but, after securing weapons distributed by Russia, joined the enemy forces in attacks on their own motherland. These young Armenians massacred the Muslim populations of the border regions into which the enemy had succeeded in advancing.[104]

These grave accusations, leveled by the authors of a propaganda brochure in time of war, reflect an official position that to the present day remains central to the discourse with which the Turkish authorities legitimize the violence perpetrated against the Armenians. An examination of the structure of this discourse is therefore worthwhile.

Obviously, conscription did not proceed in linear fashion everywhere. Draftees from the capital or western Anatolia (under the jurisdiction of the Fourth Army) were mobilized under relatively good conditions, whereas conscription in the eastern provinces (under the jurisdiction of the Third Army) suffered from insufficient preparation and a lack of proper structures needed to lodge and train recruits. The socio-economic level of the population from which the first group of recruits was drawn was distinctly higher: many young men in the western part of the empire paid the *bedel* (tax of exemption) and thus legally avoided the draft, or else found themselves serving as officers thanks to their educational level. Because of the lower standard of living of the group from the east, the young Armenians there were less frequently able to avoid conscription; vilayets such as Van and Bitlis, which had dense Armenian populations, provided soldiers in large numbers. Thus, the province of Bitlis alone furnished 36,000 men during the first wave of mobilization. Of the men between the ages of 20 and 45 who were called up, 24,000 were Armenians. All of these 24,000 Armenians were sent to Erzerum and from there to the Russian front. During the battle of Sarıkamiş, at least, not all of them served in labor battalions. Many were in combat units, and more often than not on the front lines.[105] We have, moreover, already seen that several hundred Ottoman Armenian soldiers captured by the Russians remained in captivity in Siberia for 18 months along with their Muslim companions-in-arms.[106]

The draftees from the vilayet of Van, for their part, formed no fewer than 20 battalions, in which the Armenians "represented up to two-thirds of the total." Stationed in Berkri (Fourth Battalion), Adılcevaz (Fifteenth and Sixteenth Battalions), Hoşab (Seventeenth and Eighteenth Battalions), and Başkale, they were about to be sent into battle against the Russian forces near Köprüköy when an order came down to disarm Armenian soldiers and assign them to *amele taburis*, charged with maintaining the roads, digging trenches, and transporting supplies.[107]

Thus, the Armenian conscripts were not systematically assigned to labor battalions, even if some of them were disarmed very early in the day. We can even affirm that, in the regions in western Anatolia under the jurisdiction of the Fifth Army, a fair number of conscripts were assigned to combat units. While it is true, as Zürcher emphasizes, that the 70 to 120 *amele taburi* units that traditionally made up this auxiliary service of the army responsible for transport and road construction essentially comprised Christians – one document even states that 75 per cent were Armenians[108] – this did not become the general rule in the First World War until after the first Caucasian campaign. That said, there can be no doubt that Christian soldiers – Armenian, Greek, and Syriac alike – were from the outset suspected of disloyalty.

Thus, when Enver decreed on 25 February 1915[109] that Armenian soldiers were to be disarmed, only a few thousand of them were likely to have been affected by the order, mostly recruits who were serving in the Third Army. Ultimately, a limited contingent was involved, for it seems quite clear that Armenians from Istanbul, Adabazar, Ismit, and elsewhere fought in the ranks of the Ottoman army during the Battle of the Dardanelles, which began in earnest in mid-April 1915, and on the Palestinian front until 1918,[110] well after the decree was issued. Thus, the order to disarm the Armenians has, in our view, greater symbolic than practical value. It was designed, in a certain sense, to substantiate the charge that the Armenians were traitors, which could hardly have been leveled at *amele taburis* since they necessarily served behind the lines. It also offered, perhaps, a welcome opportunity to hold the "traitors" accountable for a military disaster for which all observers agreed Enver personally was to blame.

On the account of an Armenian soldier from Mush who served in the regular army, Hayg Aghababian, five, ten or even 20 Armenian soldiers in his Erzerum-based unit were taken from their cantonment nightly and never seen again. The primate of Erzerum, Smpad Saadetian, appealed to Vali Tahsin Bey to rectify the situation. The *vali* acknowledged that such things had indeed happened, but added that instructions had been issued to put a stop to them – "Yet it went on until all the Armenian soldiers had disappeared."[111] We have in fact scant information about the fate of the soldiers who served in combat units. This one account does not allow us to draw general conclusions, yet it does at least seem to indicate that the combatants disarmed after 25 February on the Caucasian front were not enrolled in labor battalions but were rather quickly liquidated in small groups. A similar occurrence took place in early December. At Köprüköy, after a clash between Russians and Turks and the retreat of the Ottoman troops to the village of Eğan, 50 Armenian soldiers were executed for abandoning their posts. This was, to be sure, more a disciplinary measure than evidence of a general strategy. Yet the fact is that the Armenian soldiers alone were punished for the disbandment of an entire brigade.[112]

Another phenomenon has also rarely been studied – the successive mobilization waves and the gradual change in the nature of the missions assigned to each wave.[113] After men between 20 and 45 had been called up – they had all been inducted by early November at the latest – the authorities gradually recruited men from other age groups, especially from January 1915 on. The second phase of the mobilization took in men over 45; they were to be employed as "soldiers attached to the gendarmerie." There existed, however, two types of battalions, stationary and mobile. Most Armenians were assigned to the latter, which were subject to much harsher conditions since the conscripts in these battalions had to serve far from their homes, whereas the farmers remained in units close to where they lived.[114]

Several different accounts indicate that the newly mobilized units of the *amele taburis*, which as we said in the previous chapter were used to transport supplies and equipment (for instance, from Mush to Hasankale), comprised on average 250 men each. These were, as a rule, peasants well advanced in years or 16-year-old adolescents. The weight of the loads they carried was not as strictly regulated as Papazian liked to think. Every week, convoys of this kind left Mush for Khnus. Apparently, it was from these units and those assigned to do roadwork that the greatest number of desertions occurred,[115] although probably not at a rate much higher than the Ottoman average.

Can we, in light of the above, interpret Enver's order on 25 February as one of the first manifestations of the Ittihadist government's intention to liquidate the Armenians? This is Vahakn Dadrian's view of the matter,[116] which we have also endorsed elsewhere.[117] Zürcher notes, for his part, that although the document cited by Dadrian suggesting such a view – better known as the "Ten Commandments" – is "of extremely doubtful provenance," it is nonetheless "undeniable" that the state of affairs to which Enver's order gave rise proved an effective tool for implementing the policy of persecution that the government adopted vis-à-vis the Armenians.[118]

As for the accusations that the Young Turk cabinet leveled against the Armenian volunteers who fought side by side with Russian troops against the Turkish forces during the winter 1914–15 campaign, it must be said that the contribution of the four Armenian volunteer battalions – a total of 2,000 to 2,500 men – to the Russian successes on this front has been largely overrated. Let us add that there were virtually no Armenian soldiers in the Russian army of the Caucasus, since the 120,000 Armenians who fought for the Czar served on the Galician front against Austria-Hungary. As for the 75,000 "Asiatic" (Ottoman) Armenians denounced by Austro-Hungarian sources in February 1915 for going over to fight for the Russians, this was obviously deliberate disinformation.[119] Even if one counts women and children, 75,000 Armenians cannot have left Turkey for Russia in this period, since the Russian forces had not yet advanced far enough into Ottoman territory to make that possible. A-To, who had official Russian sources at his disposal, observes that after the Russian retreat from the Pasın region in early December, the Armenian population of the region left with the Russian forces for Kars and Sarikamış, followed on 29 December by the Armenians of Alaşkırt, Tutak, Karakilise, Dyadin, and Bayazid. The Russian statistics on the Ottoman Armenians who had found refuge in the Caucasus by late January 1915 identify their places of origin as follows – *kaza* of Pasın, 12,914 refugees (1,551 households); Narman, 655 refugees (84 households); Bayazid, 1,735 refugees (224 households); Dyadin, 1,111 refugees (130 households); Karakilisa, 6,034 refugees (781 households); Alaşkert, 7,732 refugees (956 households); and Başkale, 2,897 refugees (385 households). This makes a total of 33,078 refugees (4,111 households).[120] Among these Armenians, people in a condition or of an age to be drafted were rare, since the majority were women, children, and old men. The draftable men who had succeeded in avoiding conscription by paying the *bedel* were few and far between.

More generally, the measures taken by the Turkish authorities were aimed directly at the vital forces of the Armenian population, which found itself isolated and particularly vulnerable: the men left behind a population that was entirely at the mercy of hostile tribes and authorities who were rarely well disposed toward Armenians. This no doubt explains why there were precious few "revolts" or, to put it differently, why the Armenian capacity to organize self-defense efforts was sharply limited, if not practically non-existent. The precautions that the local authorities took to restrict the activity of the handful of official Armenian representatives, such as the parliamentary deputies or political leaders who had constantly to be putting out fires – that is, defusing provocations – proved effective, all in all. The one possible exception was Van, distinguished by the fact that it abutted the border regions.

Chapter 8

Putting the Plan into Practice, and the "Temporary Deportation Law"

T he historian who has to deal with a subject as sensitive as mass crime longs to unearth the irrefutable document(s) that will allow him to pinpoint the precise moment when the decision was made, as well as those elements of the executioners' discourse mobilized to justify implementing it. He is also aware, however, that the criminals in question have carefully cloaked their crime in the guise of a legal act mandated by the higher interests of the state. In other words, the historian hardly has illusions about his chances of discovering "the" document he wants. Yet, in the Armenian case, a document of this sort has been circulating for some 20 years now. It was sold in January 1919 by the head of the intelligence service of the Criminal Investigations Department of the Ottoman interior ministry, Ahmed Esad, to Arthur Calthorpe, a British officer working for the British High Commissariat in Constantinople.[1] Dubbed the "Ten Commandments" by the British, it is a digest of the ten measures to be taken in order to eradicate the Ottoman Armenian population. This document was in fact published in the Istanbul press[2] as early as March 1919. Even then, an opposition journal asked whether it was a forgery.[3] Sold for £10,000 sterling, the "Ten Commandments" also allowed Ahmed Esad to avoid legal prosecution for his part in the mass crimes organized by the Ittihadist government.[4] If the document is a forgery, as is highly probable, the fact remains that it was forged by a Young Turk whose functions gave him access to secret documents and who knew exactly what the British were looking for. In other words, the forger probably fabricated an "authentic fake" that summed up the measures for liquidating the Armenian population actually decided upon by the highest echelons of the CUP.

There can be little doubt that the Ittihadist Central Committee perfected its genocidal scheme in a series of meetings. As we have seen, the CUP envisaged, beginning in January 1914, a "plan to homogenize" Anatolia, and considered ways of "cleansing" it of its "non-Muslim" "tumors." According to the "plan," however, the operation was to have begun with the Greeks of western Anatolia; subsequently, the Armenian population was to have been transferred to Syria and Mesopotamia. This "secret" plan was in fact made public in a late January 1914 article published in the Russian newspaper *Kolos Moskoy* that did not go unnoticed in Turkey. Indeed, the article came in for so much attention that the Turkish daily *İktam* felt obliged to issue a disclaimer in its 17/30 January 1914 issue. The Young Turk journal denied that there existed a plan "that aimed to remove the Armenians from the provinces inhabited by them and deport them towards Mesopotamia [in order to] people Armenia with Muslims who, obviously, could unite with the Muslims of the Caucasus and put up serious resistance to encroachment by the Slavs." *İktam* added, rather naively, "the Ottoman government has no need to do anything of the sort, for, in the regions inhabited by the Armenians, Muslims constitute a majority." The most interesting point in the article is the conclusion: "Indeed, is it possible to expedite several hundred thousand Armenians toward Mesopotamia? Even if the Armenians agreed to go, [such a plan] would be impossible to put into practice. What point is there in publishing things as incoherent as this?"[5]

Thus, there was a radicalization of the CUP after the Ottoman Empire entered the war. The Armenians were now no longer to be sent elsewhere, but rather to be liquidated. Taner Akçam has detected that the Ittihad's Central Committee held a number of meetings around the middle of March 1915 in order to "evaluate" the development of the Armenian "menace."[6] According to Cemil, it was at these meetings, which took place after the painful Turkish defeat in the battle of Sarıkamiş, that the Ittihadist leaders familiarized themselves with the contents of a report drafted by Bahaeddin Şakir, who had returned to Istanbul after spending six months in Erzerum and on the Caucasian front. Şakir's report focused on the "domestic enemies" who were "preparing to attack [the Ottoman] army from the rear." Cemil also points out that the chief of the Special Organization worked together with the Central Committee after returning to the capital – he had left Erzerum on 13 March – to define "the measures that had to be taken, thanks to which the Turkish army avoided a great danger; the result of this collaboration was the deportation law."[7] At these famous meetings, which must have taken place from 20/22 March 1915 on, Şakir probably demanded that "measures" be taken to eliminate the "Armenian menace." In other words, the CUP decided not to confine itself to the simple "displacement" to the Syrian and Mesopotamian deserts provided for by the plan drawn up early in 1914, but to undertake a campaign of extermination that was to unfold in several stages.

Jay Winter attempts to explain the CUP's radicalization by pointing to the situation of "total war" that obtained during the First World War. If this situation was not enough by itself, he writes, to produce "genocide, it created the military, political, and cultural space in which it could occur."[8] He thus draws a connection between the Battle of the Dardanelles,[9] which was shaping up by late March, and the decision made by the Young Turk Central Committee. He further notes that the first utilization of deadly poison gas by the Germans, which occurred in April 1915 during the battle of Ypres, in Belgium, may have helped dissipate the last reservations in the Young Turk ranks.[10] There can indeed be no doubt that "total war" engenders a predisposition to commit atrocities, including genocide, and spawns a "cultural preparation of hatred" in society that may be likened to an "infectious disease," while considerably reducing tolerance and legitimizing violence.[11]

These rather innovative approaches to the question are by no means to be dismissed, but in our view do not suffice to explain the radicalization of the Ittihad that came about late in March 1915. They neglect the ideological dimension of the genocidal act and more particularly its Turkist aspect, which we have already discussed. In the case at hand, it was the Young Turk conception of control over the Turkish national space that was directly at issue, together with the Ittihadists' desire to Turkify the eastern regions by eliminating "foreign bodies." To be sure, this ethno-demographic concern of the Young Turks already informed the decisions on basic principles reached in early 1914. Yet it took a more radical turn during the meetings of late March 1915, probably under the impact of "total war." Indeed, the indictment read out by the chief public prosecutor Haydar Bey at the first June 1919 session of the trial of the members of the war cabinets points out that "the slaughter and destruction of an entire community and the confiscation of its property can come about only as a result of bloodthirsty measures taken by a secret association ... All this came about as a result of the coded dispatches that have been seized."[12]

The fact that the "temporary deportation law" was not adopted until late May[13] indicates either that it took time to implement the measures adopted by the Central Committee or that the CUP felt the need to create a legal cover for its plans. It is also significant that official publication of this governmental law-by-decree came one month after its adoption and that it was released even then in bowdlerized form.[14] Five of the eight paragraphs of the law – those bearing on the confiscation of Armenian property and the settlement of *muhacirs* in Armenian homes – seem to have been censored.[15] Not until passage of the Law of 26 September 1915[16] did the Ottoman government give presentable legal form to the confiscation of Armenian property, at a time when the deportation process was virtually complete. Although the Armenians were never mentioned by name, the wording of the censored paragraphs of the "temporary law" was no doubt too explicit; it must have seemed to go too far toward revealing the Ittihad's true objectives. Publishing rules for the immediate installation of *muhacirs* in Armenian homes came down to admitting that the "displacement toward the interior" of the Armenian population had nothing "temporary" about it, but that it was meant to be permanent.

The mass of documents that came to light during the 1919 Constantinople trials, confirmed by local observations of events, show that the deportation orders were issued well before publication of the temporary law-by-decree.[17] Hence the two laws about the deportation and the confiscation of Armenian property must be deemed tools designed not to establish rules to regulate a situation but to legitimize actions that were often already in progress, if not indeed already complete. The compulsion to legitimize or justify these acts plainly makes itself felt in the pamphlet distributed by the Ministry of the Interior in 1916: "The Armenians who remained in various parts of the Empire," we read there,

> carried their audacity to the point of engaging in revolts and fomenting disorder. The commander of the Imperial army, observing that the Armenians were making common cause with the enemy forces, felt compelled, so as to protect his rear, to order the transfer of the Armenian groups settled in areas regarded as military zones to the south.[18]

As for the way the temporary deportation law was applied, the order to appear before a court-martial that was rendered public in June 1919 stresses the crucial role that the CUP "played during the implementation of the law on the deportations." Conducted in "a uniform manner," these operations "were supervised by the delegates and responsible secretaries of Union and Progress" under the direction of Bahaeddin Şakir, "who had been appointed head of operations in these regions, the eastern vilayets, by the Special Organization, made up of the leaders of Union and Progress. Thus all the atrocities of which these regions were the theater were conceived and prepared by Union and Progress."[19] One could hardly state any more clearly that the CUP not only decided on the genocidal measures but that its members were also directly implicated in their implementation at the local level. As for the argument about the security of the Ottoman army's rear that the Ittihadist government invoked to justify the deportations, it does not hold up under attentive examination of the real situation of the Armenian population. The long telegram that the *vali* of Erzerum, Tahsin, addressed to the minister of the interior on 13 May 1915 illustrates the reticence of certain high-ranking government officials, who were aware of the disadvantages that this measure would bring in its wake and knew that it served no useful military purpose. Tahsin suggested that the government abandon the idea of deporting the Armenians, who did not represent a danger, since "they work mainly in trade and industry, and many of them understand the consequences that a movement initiated by themselves could have."[20] Tahsin also observed that "Erzerum is a fortified city and a powerful garrison. Hence the Armenians cannot create problems. As for the [other] districts [of the vilayet], they are inhabited by Armenians in small numbers living in miserable conditions."[21]

We are provided with another important piece of information by Tahsin Bey, who reminded Talât that the former commander of the Third Army, Hafız İsmail Hakkı, had himself voiced his "fears" of what might happen if the Armenians were deported from the vilayet of Erzerum. This shows that the idea of deporting the Armenians from the region was already being discussed in February 1915, at the moment of Tahsin's transfer from Van to Erzerum.[22] The *vali* says so explicitly in his telegram: "At the time, I had assured Your Excellency that if we decided to deport the Armenians to the interior, we risked creating precisely the kind of danger for the army that we wished to spare it ... These considerations are more valid than ever today."[23] Can we affirm that the government and military authorities were already weighing the possibility of extirpating the Armenian population on the pretext of carrying out a "deportation to ensure security"? The claim can certainly be advanced. It is, however, eminently possible that the Ittihad had not yet considered implementing such a measure elsewhere than in the eastern vilayets.

After receiving the order to deport the Armenians of his vilayet, Tahsin Bey informed the minister of the interior that the commander-in-chief of the Third Army kept insistently raising the issue "of the deportations" and that he, Tahsin, "had explained to him that the question was not as simple as he supposed ... and pointed out the dangers with which it was fraught ... One can't deport sixty thousand people from the borders of the Caucasus to Baghdad or Mosul with mere words."[24] Tahsin thus joined the ranks of the *valis*, *mutesarifs*, and *kaymakams* who displayed a degree of reluctance to apply the deportation orders because they were perfectly conscious of what these implied for the people involved. Tahsin also wondered "who would protect [the Armenians] and take charge of their goods and lands"? He even suggested that, "if the military authorities are capable of successfully carrying out the operation, then the responsibility should be given to them."[25] Here we are afforded a glimpse of another problem that the Ittihad had to face when the deportations commenced – the conflict of competencies between the military and civilian authorities. It was resolved by the responsible secretaries who the Central Committee had sent to the provinces, for they had authority in everything touching on "Armenian affairs."

The creation of the Teşkilat-ı Mahsusa and the treatment of Armenian recruits, important matters in whose light we can study the evolution of the decisions made by the Ittihadist Central Committee, have proved much more complicated than they appeared at first sight. The elements we have assembled here do not allow us to affirm that the decision to effect the plan to liquidate the Armenian population was reached before late March 1915. On the other hand, it may be said that, notwithstanding all the efforts on the part of the Armenian authorities to avoid all provocations and demonstrate their loyalty to the Ottoman government, the *Teşkilat-ı Mahsusa* began conducting operations to cleanse the border zones of Armenians very early with no real military justification. As for the fate meted out to the Armenian draftees in the winter of 1914–15, it varied from region to region. One cannot, in any case, speak of a generalized extermination policy in this connection. Even the 25 February 1915 decree ordering that Armenian soldiers be disarmed, which as we have seen had more symbolic value than anything else, seemingly cannot be taken as a sign that the final decision had already been reached, for it is not a sufficiently clear indication of this. It reflects at most the Ottoman general staff's deep distrust of its Armenian soldiers.

There are, in fact, much more telling signs. One is the dismissal or transfer, beginning in late March 1915, of many high-ranking officials in the provinces that were affected by the CUP's genocidal plans and their replacement by "hard-core" Young Turks. The most significant and most symbolic example is provided by the vilayet of Dyarbekir, where, on 25 March 1915, one of the CUP's historic founders, Dr. Mehmed Reşid, was named to replace Hamid Bey (Kapancı), a man who was in his successor's opinion much too kindly disposed.[26] Other *valis* suffered the same fate in the following weeks, such as Hasan Mazhar in Angora, who was replaced by the man who stripped him of his post, Atıf Bey, the CUP delegate in the vilayet of Angora; Atıf had observed that Mazhar refused to apply the deportation order.[27]

Also dismissed were a number of *mutesarifs*, such as Cemal Bey, the *mutesarif* of Yozgat, whom the responsible secretary of the vilayet of Angora, Necati Bey, evicted from his post by means of a simple directive sent to Istanbul. Sometimes a firm order sufficed to overcome nascent resistance: in Kastamonu, the local responsible secretary successfully brought the *vali*, Reşid Bey, to expel the handful of Armenians living in his vilayet.[28] There were, however, much more extreme cases. One was the murder by the *vali* of Dyarbekir, Mehmed Reşid, of the *kaymakam* of Behşiri and native of Bagdad, Naci Bey, and the *kaymakam* of Lice, Nesimi Bey. Both had refused to massacre (rather than merely deport) the Kurdish-speaking Armenian populations of their *kazas*.[29]

The 18 March 1915 appointment of Halajian as the Ottoman delegate to the International Court of Justice in The Hague[30] can serve as another chronological guidepost and confirmation of the party leaders' change of tack. In removing him from the political scene, the CUP rid itself of the sole Armenian member of the CUP's General Council, to which Halajian had been elected in November 1913.[31] At the same stroke, it effectively banished the only influential intermediary capable of maintaining relations between the Patriarchate and the Young Turk Committee.

Another revealing sign of the CUP's radical decision may be discerned in an apparently anodyne measure – the April 1915 "removal" of the Armenian inspectors working in the Post and Telegraph Office,[32] which employed a great many Armenians. This decision may be interpreted as a measure aiming to render communications between the capital and the provinces "safe" at a time when the government was getting ready to transmit confidential instructions.

To round off our discussion of the decision-making process, we should also mention information published by two journalists of the day. Both refer to one or more secret meetings of the Young Turk Central Committee or, at any rate, of its members present in Istanbul in February or March 1915. Let us begin by making it clear that neither of these two authors identifies the precise source from which he draws his information. In 1920, Sebuh Aguni, a former editor of the Istanbul newspaper *Zhamanag*, published at the request of the Armenian Patriarchate his *Documented History of the Massacre of One Million Armenians*, the first work of its kind. The author, one of the members of the Armenian elite deported on 24 April 1915, reveals that his work is based "on a large number of documents available to the Patriarchate."[33] In other words, Aguni was able to utilize materials assembled by the Information Bureau of the Armenian Patriarchate in Constantinople,[34] whose staff had until March 1919 had access to the files of the accused at the Istanbul trials. The other journalist, Mevlanzâde Rifat, was a liberal who had briefly flirted with the Ittihad before becoming one of its principle detractors.[35] Rifat affirms that he had access to the famous documents seized during a search conducted by Constantinople's police chief at the house of Ahmed Ramız Bey, Bahaeddin Şakir's son-in-law, in Pera. These documents came from the CUP's Nuri Osmaniye headquarters and included a file containing the minutes of the secret meetings of the party's Central Committee.[36] Rifat's account contains elements that seem plausible, but also approximations[37] that make it less than credible. It nonetheless constitutes one source among others. Published in 1929 in Syria under the French mandate, in a period in which the Armenian question had been shrouded in silence and Kemalism was triumphant, the journalistic essay does not have the ring of a settling of scores, but it is muddled and therefore unusable. Aguni's exposé is distinctly more rigorous, but the author contents himself with the statement that he is publishing the minutes of one of the Ittihad's secret meetings "based on solid information specially obtained for the purpose"; the only date he gives is the first three months of 1915.[38] It is therefore with reservations that we here provide a translation of the minutes of this meeting, supposed to have been held at the Nuri Osmaniye headquarters under the joint chairmanship of Mehmed Talât and Ziya Gökalp. Present were Midhat

Şükrü, Bahaeddin Şakir, and Mehmed Nâzım. Şakir and Nâzım were in favor of systematic eradication of the Armenians, whereas "Hüseyin Cahid, Kara Kemal and Halil [Menteşe] proposed restricting [operations] to the three border provinces of Erzerum, Van and Bitlis, whose Armenian populations, they maintained, should be deported westward."

Talât: I would like to point out to my brother Cahid that we entered the war in the absolute certainty that we would emerge from it as victors. In their own interests, the Germans are today appealing to us for help, but what assurances do we have that, after winning the war, they will not abandon us and stretch out their hand to the Armenians and Greeks? For we must not blind ourselves to the fact that they comprise the vital forces in this country, by virtue of their intelligence and, in equal measure, their ingeniousness and business acumen – indeed, in everything. We, on the other hand, are civil servants or officers.

Ziya Gökalp: We must bear in mind that Greece is always suspect and that it is sooner or later going to go to war against us. By giving the Armenians a good knock on the head, we will, by the same stroke, silence all our adversaries, and the policy we adopted toward the Armenians will become a nightmare for Greece, which obviously will not care to see the more than 2 million Greeks in Turkey suffer the same fate as the Armenians.

Kara Kemal: I grant that both Talât's point of view and yours may be right, but we also have to consider the opposite. If, God forbid, we should lose the war, we will simply have helped bring on our own destruction with our own two hands. I know the Armenians much better than you do: if we treat them with a little consideration, by fulfilling one of every five demands that they are likely to make, it is still possible to win them over to our side. Yes, to be safe, let's organize their deportation, but let's not massacre a group from which we'll be able to profit some day, after converting it to Islam. Don't forget that, according to one of the provisos of the statutes of our party, we can't force our responsible delegates in the provinces to carry out a decision made here if they refuse to. Let's first find out what they think; we'll make the important decisions thereafter.

Dr. Bahaeddin Şakir: I can already assure my brother Kemal that our delegates in the provinces will approve of our decision, as long as we maintain an internal system of decentralization.

Dr. Nâzım: I'm surprised to hear that some of our comrades are still standing up for the Armenians, when it is precisely the Armenians who are making life unbearable for our army in the border region and preventing us from advancing onto Russian territory. In Russia, besides the regular forces, thousands of volunteers are joining the fight against us, while thousands of Armenian deserters have simply upped and disappeared. We have to attack the Armenian question at the root, by wiping this nation out without a trace. I believe that I may speak for Beha Bey as well: the two of us can finish this job. You have only to make the decision.

Halil: Don't forget that this war is a game of poker in which you also have to consider the possibility that you may lose. Bulgaria has still not clarified its position. Tomorrow, it may turn against us and the Triple Entente will be able, thanks to the communication routes that Bulgaria possesses and the means it can put at the Entente's disposal, not only to put us under pressure, but also, using the road to Constantinople, to open the road to Berlin and win the war. What is to be gained by wiping out the Armenians? The radical elimination of the Armenian question? But isn't it true that, if the Entente carries the day, Anatolia will fall into Russian hands? I think that, by eliminating the Armenians, we'll only make the post-war situation of our country harder to bear, and that even harsher conditions may be forced on us as a result.

Ziya Gökalp: Germany has given us every assurance that Bulgaria will be fighting along-side us; I'm not worried on that score. But what if the Armenians are manipulated by the Russians into causing internal disorders and making our task more difficult?

Talât: In my capacity as minister of the interior, it is my personal responsibility to use what I consider to be the appropriate means of dealing with the Armenians. It's true that, so far, they seem to be loyal, but the Dashnaktsutiun can change its tactics tomorrow. When that party was on the point of adjourning its congress in Erzerum, we asked it whether, if we went to war with Russia, it was going to march with us against her. The answer we received did not give us much reason for hope. The Dashnaktsutiun responded categorically that it wasn't in a position to foment a rebellion against Russia in the Caucasus. As for its role in Turkey, it was to consist in advising the Armenians to enlist in the army and help our government in every way it could. However, the same Dashnaktsutiun was secretly sending volunteers to the Caucasian front under the command of its principal leaders.[39]

Attested by Turkish sources, the evolution of the position of certain members of the Central Committee – such as Ziya Gökalp, Midhat Şükrü, and Kara Kemal – who opposed "the form taken by the Armenian deportations," but also that of Halil (Menteşe) and Said Halim,[40] seems to be reflected in the exchanges supposed to have taken place at this meeting. If what is involved is a fabrication, its author was, at the very least, well acquainted with his protagonists.

The Intensification of the Anti-Armenian Measures and the Reactions of the Patriarchate in March–April 1915

A careful examination of the violence perpetrated outside the war zones in March–April 1915 is another important way of gauging the evolution of the Ottoman authorities' policy towards the Armenians. Most significant in this regard is the special treatment meted out to Zeitun, a city that had never retreated from its fighting tradition. The first intervention of the army in Zeitun took place on 13 March; the official motive was to bring deserters from the town to heel. These deserters did not just defend themselves but also killed several soldiers. On 12 March, the army occupied another celebrated Cilician town, Dörtyol, which put up very stiff resistance during the 1909 "events." A number of adult men were arrested and enrolled in Aleppo's *amele taburi*. They were never seen again. Thus, it seems that around mid-March the authorities had opted as part of their gradualist strategy to neutralize before all others the two Armenian localities with a reputation for rebelliousness. An examination of the facts reveals an intensification of the repression accompanied by rather skillfully dosed threats. The catholicos of Cilicia, Sahag Khabayan, consequently had no other choice than to pressure the leaders of Zeitun into complying with the authorities' demands. In other words, Zeitun was asked not to resist so as not to jeopardize Cilicia's Armenian population as a whole. A new stage began on 31 March, when Turkish forces entered Zeitun and arrested a number of local notables and teachers.[41]

Another telling sign of the intentions of the Ittihadist authorities appeared when one of the principal CUP leaders, Ömer Naci, left the Van region for Cilicia. Here he organized several public meetings, notably in Adana and Aleppo, at which he exhorted the Muslim population to mobilize against "the enemy within." The next stage opened on 29 March, in Aleppo, where Ahmed Cemal condemned the "revolt" of the Zeitun Armenians and announced that he had demanded that the military authorities take measures to "punish" them. Several brigades were dispatched to the Armenian city, where Turkish forces had already been stationed in January–February 1915. The people of Zeitun, respecting its prom- ise to Catholicos Sahag (who was later criticized for asking them to disarm) surrendered without a fight. Beginning on 8 April, 22,456 women and children from the town and its environs[42] were deported to central Anatolia, in the environs of Konya/Sultanieh[43] or, in the case of those who left later, to Aleppo and Der Zor, in the middle of the Syrian desert. Were these first deportation measures a consequence of the decisions that the CUP had reached late in March? We think that they were. The destination chosen for the men, Der Zor, is itself an indication that leaves little doubt about the fate in store for the mountaineers of Zeitun. Although the CUP continued to veil its intentions by presenting these operations as ad hoc interventions, it is clear that it was first and foremost seeking to crush the localities that were likely to resist when the party's goals became manifest.

For the Young Turk authorities, the first half of the month of April 1915 was in some sense an interlude, during which they took the preliminary measures required by their plan to liquidate the Armenians. They took care, however, not to give them too conspicuous a form. Among the events falling into this framework were doubtless the 3 April arms searches conducted in Armenian homes in Maraş and Haçin, followed by the arrest of many local dignitaries; the 8 April arrival of *muhacirs* from Bosnia in villages around Zeitun; and, the same day, the fire that raged in the famous monastery perched on the heights overlooking the city.[44]

As April wore on, the number of violent acts occurring in the vilayet of Sıvas steadily rose, including arbitrary arrests of political leaders and methodical looting of villages by bands of *çetes*.[45] The impression that this spiral of violence was an integral part of a policy of provocation orchestrated in the capital becomes a certainty when one considers the events occurring at the same time in the vilayets of Erzerum, Van, and Bitlis.

At any rate, such was the feeling that prevailed in the Armenian Patriarchate, which was receiving increasingly alarming reports from its dioceses in the provinces. It demanded explanations from the authorities or looked to the Germans to provide them. Among the rare foreign interlocutors of the Armenian leadership was the dragoman at the German embassy, Dr. Mordtmann, who was in charge of Armenian affairs; he often met with Patriarch Zaven in order to gauge the Armenians' mood. During one of their conversations, Mordtmann asked the patriarch why the Armenians sympathized with the Triple Entente.[46] On another occasion, he suggested that the patriarch publish a bull urging the Armenian volunteers in the Caucasus to refuse to fight in the Russian ranks.[47] The most revelatory action undertaken by Mordtmann came, however, on 24 April, when he paid a visit to Zaven in the Armenian chamber in Galata in order to propose that the patriarch send a Turkish-Armenian-German propaganda committee into the provinces to work toward a rapprochement between Turks and Armenians.[48] This might seem to indicate that Mordtmann was still unaware of the intentions of the minister of the interior, Talât Pasha, who was making preparations to arrest the Armenian elite of the capital that evening. A German diplomatic document, however, reveals that a conversation took place at the German embassy in Constantinople on 24 April between Mordtmann and General Passelt, military commander of the garrison in Erzerum. The general affirmed that the Armenians could remain in their homes "if the Turks did not put pressure on them," since their attitude was "irreproachable."[49] That is, the drago- man already knew of the government's deportation plan and was doubtless trying to decide whether this measure was justified when he put his proposal to the patriarch and Zohrab. Should his intervention be interpreted as a final attempt to save the Armenians? This seems doubtful. It is more likely that he wanted to test the good will of the Armenian leadership or else find out how much they knew.

The "incidents" occurring in Cilicia and elsewhere led the patriarch to summon Bedros Halajian on 1 April 1915 and ask him to intercede with the Young Turk party leadership so as "to spare the civilian population."[50] We can deduce from this that the patriarch already knew, albeit perhaps not exactly, what was being plotted in the offices on Nuri Osmaniye Street. On 9 April 1915, Halajian came to see the patriarch again in order to report Talât's response: the interior minister had said that he would confer with Enver about the proper policy to follow vis-à-vis the Armenians. On 13 April, Halajian called at the Patriarchate one more time. He had new information: he had seen Talât again. The minister, who had, he said, discussed the matter with Enver in the interim, had told him with a good dose of cynicism: "massacres cannot take place in the provinces, because the government does not condone them."[51] However, as the patriarch later wrote, the information that the Patriarchate was receiving through different channels (if somewhat belatedly) despite the strict censorship told a very different story. Yet the Armenian population continued to provide the army with clothing and supplies of various kinds while also offering it medical assistance and helping to care for the wounded. At the same time, violent requisitions akin to looting were on the rise.[52] The interview with the minister of the interior that the patriarch had requested took place a few days later, on 21 April 1915. Talât assured Zaven that the CUP did not have a policy toward the Armenians as such, that Armenian soldiers had been disarmed as the result of a hasty decision, and that he had no information about the murders committed in the Erzerum region.[53] These reassurances did not convince the prelate, who on 23 April 1915 convoked a meeting of the Mixed Council, to which the parliamentary deputies and senators Zareh Dilber, Krikor Zohrab, Vartkes Seringiulian, Harutiun Boshgezenian, and Hovsep Madatian were also summoned. The patriarch reviewed all the violence that had occurred recently in Kayseri, Mush, Bitlis, Van, Dortyöl, and Zeitun pointing out that it was evidence of patent ill will and that it bespoke the government's mistrust of all Armenians. All those present reaffirmed that it was necessary to continue to offer the government, as the patriarch already had, guarantees of unswerving allegiance to the Ottoman fatherland. Zohrab invited those present to do all they could to mitigate the government's hostility to the Armenians. He suggested that they draw up a memorandum, to be signed by all the deputies and senators, which would summarize the most recent events with supporting documentation. At the end of the day, Zohrab and Dilber were assigned to write this text.[54] Submitted at a meeting held on 26 April 1915 in Galata, the document they produced begins by citing the arrests that had just taken place in Istanbul. "The Armenian nation," it declares, "does not understand why the government is so suspicious of it," adding that "it is a mistake to attribute political significance to the desertions of Armenian soldiers" and that the Armenians "fear that all the violence inflicted on them is paving the way for a general massacre."[55] It should be pointed out here that the press campaign against the Armenians had not yet really begun, even if the Ittihadist government's accounts of the problems occurring in the provinces are marked by undisguised partiality.

The 24 April 1915 Arrests of the Armenian Elite

The round-up of Constantinople's Armenian elite that took place during the night of 24/25 April affected several hundred people – not only Dashnak, Hnchak and Ramgavar political activists, but also the most prominent Armenian journalists, as well as writers, lawyers, doctors, secondary school principals, clergymen, and merchants.[56] A handful of individuals, including Sebuh Aguni and Yervant Odian, slipped through this vast dragnet – but they would be arrested later. Two eminent Armenian leaders, the parliamentary deputies Zohrab and Seringiulian, were left at liberty. Early in the morning of Sunday, 25 April, the two deputies, who had been informed of the arrests made that night, in particular those of the

Dashnak leaders Aknuni, Rupen Zartarian, and Garabed Khan Pashayan, went together to Talât's house to ask their close acquaintance for an explanation. Talât temporized. Zohrab wrote with some bitterness in his diary that "the ARF, after working side by side with the Ittihad and in its interests, has now been dealt a heavy blow by it."[57] He claimed to know why he himself was still in freedom, but did not state the reason. We are inclined to think that, with his colleague Vartkes, he was being held in reserve because the government feared that the course of events might take an unfavorable turn for the empire: on 25 April, French and British forces had begun disembarking in the Dardanelles at Gallipoli, and preparations to transfer the government to Eskişehir, in the interior of the country, had been accelerated. After maneuvering and concealing its real aims for several weeks in order to forestall the possibility of an Armenian reaction, the Ittihad had at last decided to act. The first step was to neutralize the Armenian elite.

Quite obviously, this operation, which mobilized several hundred state agents, had been carefully prepared. According to reports that the Patriarchate's Information Bureau gathered after the Mudros Armistice, the minister of the interior had, at an unspecified date that we can put around February–March, created a special committee responsible for overseeing all those aspects of the Young Turks' plan that touched on administrative and police-related matters in the capital as well as the provinces. This committee was under the CUP's direct control.[58] It included eminent members of the CUP leadership – İsmail Canbolat,[59] general director of the Office of State Security and later governor of the capital; Aziz Bey, the head of State Security at the Interior Ministry; Ali Münîf, an undersecretary in the same ministry; Bedri Bey, the police chief in the capital; Bedri's assistant, Mustafa Reşad,[60] from early 1915 to June 1917 director of the national police force's Department of Political Affairs; and another close collaborator of Bedri's, Murad Bey,[61] assistant police chief in Constantinople. It was these officials who were responsible for compiling lists of the members of the Armenian elite to be arrested on 24 April. The Armenians had in fact been spied on for weeks. According to the memoirs of the journalist Yervant Odian, arrested a few weeks later, rumors to the effect that the police were putting together a "list of Armenians to be exiled" had already been making the rounds in Istanbul's Armenian community.[62] Odian also reports that when he learned of the arrests of the Dashnaks, including the editorial board of Azadamard, he assumed that these were "isolated cases." He gradually lost his illusions in the course of the following day, Sunday, 25 April, when he learned that among those arrested the previous night were well-known personalities such as Teotig, Barsegh Shahbaz, Daniel Varuzhan, Sarkis Minasian, the parliamentary deputy Nazaret Daghavarian, Dr. Torkomian, Piuzant Kechian, Diran Kelekian, Aram Andonian, Sebuh Aguni, Aknuni, Khazhag, Mikayel Shamdanjian, Dr. Jelal, Dr. Boghosian, director of the psychiatric ward at Surp Prgich Hospital, Hayg Khojasarian, Father Krikoris Balakian, Father Gomidas, and others.[63]

On 26 April 1915, the Mixed Council examined the memorandum prepared by Zohrab. It appealed to the government to treat the Armenians less severely, "out of respect for the memory of the thousands of Armenian soldiers who [had] died defending the Ottoman fatherland." The Council then chose four delegates to call on the grand vizier, Said Halim – the patriarch, Zohrab, Dr. Krikor Tavitian, president of the Political Council, and Archbishop Yeghishe Turian, president of the Religious Council.[64] Responding to protests from the Armenian leaders, Halim declared that arms and ammunition had been discovered in various localities, notably Van, and that the government, taking alarm, had decided to neutralize the political activists. Zohrab retorted that it was unjust to treat Armenians in this way when the community had since the general mobilization demonstrated that it was deeply conscious of its duties; that the Armenians had fulfilled their obligations as citizens and as soldiers; that they had often chosen not to protest despite the abuses they had suffered; that it was unwise to make the civilian population suffer the consequences of minor faults; and that these people should not be unnecessarily humiliated.[65]

Directly following this exchange with the grand vizier, the delegation met with Minister of the Interior Talât, who received the Armenians in the company of the president of the Senate, Rifat Bey. Talât struck a firm tone. "All those Armenians," he said, "who, by their speeches, writings or acts, have worked or may one day work toward the creation of an Armenia, have to be considered enemies of the state and, in the present circumstances, must be isolated." When the delegates replied that among those deported on 24 April were people who had never had anything to do with the national question, the minister answered that he did not know if "errors had been made," as in the case of the hapless cook of Senator Abraham Pasha, but that the matter would be looked into and the innocent released. He took pains to add that he continued to have confidence in the Armenians and that "only members of political parties had been affected by the measures taken." "Clearly," he said, "we have no indications of the existence of a real movement directed against the state, but, in the interests of state security, the decision was taken to isolate the party activists and dissolve the parties." The Armenian delegates pointed out that "it was pointless to examine the case of each individual deportee in the absence of evidence that the political parties had conspired against the state" and that, consequently, they favored the "return of all of them." At this point, the patriarch writes, Talât called the police chief in the Armenians' presence and was told that no further arrests were to be made.[66]

It has been established that the arrests were not as well prepared as they might have been, and that among those detained were people who happened to have the same names as the real targets of the repression, as well as others who had no connections with Armenian activist circles and were arrested and deported for no reason. Moreover, the list of those arrested included a number of very well-known personalities who could be described as being above all suspicion – for example, Diran Kelekian, the editor-in-chief of the Turkish-language newspaper *Sabah*, which, as we have seen, had, in collaborating with Bahaeddin Şakir, provided great service to the CPU/CUP when the party was in the opposition.[67] As for the declarations that the minister of the interior made to the Armenian delegates, they illustrate the classic strategy of the CUP, which sought to carry out its plan without "tipping its hand," so as to reassure its victims or leave them guessing.

Once the Constantinople Armenians had been arrested and banned, they were transferred to two places of internment. One, Ayaş, was in the vilayet of Angora, 12 miles west of the city; the other was in Cankırı, 60 miles northeast of Angora in the vilayet of Kastamonu. These operations unfolded in several stages – arrest, at home or at the workplace, by agents of the State Security Office and the Political Department of the police; an identity check at State Security headquarters; internment for 24 hours or more in Istanbul's central prison; transfer under police escort to the Haydar Paşa railroad station in the Asian part of the capital; and rail transport to Angora at the deportee's expense.

In Angora, the banned Armenians were divided into two groups: the "political prisoners" or those considered to be such (some 150 people) were interned in Ayaş; the "intellectuals" (also about 150 in number) were kept under surveillance in Çankırı, but allowed to circulate freely in the city on the condition that they report daily to the local police station. People as important as Aknuni, Rupen Zartarian, Harutiun Shahrigian, Hayg Tiriakian, Levon Pashayan, Khazhag, Murad (Boyajian), Harutiun Jangulian, and Nerses Zakarian – Dashnak and Hnchak leaders – as well as the parliamentary deputy Nazaret Daghavarian, were interned in Ayaş. The internees were quartered in an immense barracks divided into "dormitories" by means of a few separating walls. According to what one of the few survivors from the Ayaş group, Piuzant Bozajian, seems to affirm, a delegate of the Ittihad was sent to Ayaş to confer with the Dashnak leaders Aknuni and Pashayan. Their conversations remained secret, but Bozajian reports rumors that the Young Turk delegate once again proposed to the Armenian leaders that they collaborate with the Turks against the Russians. Aknuni is supposed to have replied that they had to be set free before all else. This information is, however, contradicted by another internee, Dr. Boghosian. In his view, what was involved was a simple interrogation, the purpose of which was probably to verify that the internee was indeed the Dashnak leader Aknuni.[68]

To provide a clearer picture of the circumstances surrounding the arrest of the Armenian elite of the capital, we shall take the case of Dr. Boghosian, a psychiatrist arrested in his home on 25 April around two o'clock in the morning. Three "policemen" "hauled him in," escorting him to the offices of the "police chief" on the pretext that he was ill and needed emergency care (such stratagems, designed to veil the real objectives of the police, were often employed in the course of these arrests). In the face of Boghosian's reluctance to leave the house with them so late at night, the arresting policeman finally served notice of their intention to use force. Boghosian's arrest involved an Ottoman subtlety. Since he held the rank of an officer in the health services, he was taken to the prison of the Ministry of War at Sultan Bayazid Square and detained in a building reserved for officers, where he was joined by Dr. Bardizbanian, the chief managing editor of *Azadamard* (the men would see each other again at Ayaş). Later, Boghosian was brought before İsmail Canbolat, the general director of the Office of State Security and a man who struck Boghosian as a "born criminal." When the psychiatrist protested about his arrest, which was perfectly illegal because no charges had been brought to justify it, Canbolat flew into a rage:

> If I killed you right here, like a dog, who would come looking for you? If I exterminated the entire Armenian race, as I aspire to do, who would call me to account? I used to think your people were intelligent. You're all stupid, one stupider than the next. Do you imagine that Europe is going to call me to account? Not at all: Europe's not as harebrained as you are. Get out of here.

Boghosian, apparently not unduly troubled by these words, retorted: "You can kill me and the whole Armenian people as well. But rest assured that, in a certain way, you will be killing Turkey if you do." [69]

This conversation, apparently authenticated, certainly provides an accurate summary of the mood of the Young Turk leaders in late April 1915. Long obliged to bridle their emotions in order to allay the Armenians' suspicions, it seems they now felt that the time had come to vent frustrations that had been accumulating for years on their victims.

In the fourth part of this study, we shall see the fate that was reserved for the provincial Armenian elite as well as all those deported to Ayaş and Cankırı. Let us here content ourselves with noting that on 1 May 1915, "secret" information arrived at the Patriarchate from the provinces: there had been a massive wave of arrests there. Zohrab, who was not deported until 2 June, wondered, "What date has been reserved for the massacre of the Armenians?"[70] Ibranosian and Brothers, one of the biggest firms in Turkey, suddenly discovered around 9 May that the directors of all its branches in the provinces were under arrest.[71] This was an indication that the Ittihad had now also begun to put its "economic" plans into practice.

The Trial of the Hnchaks, or the Armenians' "Guilt"

On Patriarch Zaven's account, all the precautions taken by the government to avoid alarming the Armenians of the capital were thrown to the wind with the announcement of the "rebellion" in Van.[72] If we were asked to name the event that convinced the Ittihad to put its genocidal program into practice precisely on 24 April, we would have to answer that the "rebellion" it had programmed at Van constituted the ideal alibi for it. In other words, the CUP chose what it deemed the propitious moment to resolve the problem that the Armenian presence in Turkey represented in its eyes. To that end, it had accumulated material enabling it to accompany its acts with an intense propaganda campaign. This propaganda comprises, even today, the heart of the "Turkish version of the story," which others call revisionist history.

The first sign that the authorities intended to demonstrate that "the Armenians" were guilty of wrongdoing and play up the outcry over the desertions and the Van rebellion came on 28 April 1915, when the presiding judge of the court-martial in Istanbul announced that the Hnchak leaders, most of whom had been behind bars since late July 1914, had been indicted for "disturbing public order and for subversion."[73] In a certain sense, this was the trial of all the Armenians. It lent the actions of the authorities judicial legitimacy while also providing them with the opportunity to give formal expression to their criticisms of the Armenian nation.

Shortly before noon on 11 May, the 28 accused – two of whom, Stepanos Sapah-Giulian and Dr. Varazdat, were "fugitives from justice" and therefore tried in absentia – were brought before the court-martial conducted by General Nafiz Bey. Two Armenian-speaking interpreters had also taken their places in the room, Sureya Bey and Mustafa Reşad Bey himself, the head of the national police force's Department of Political Affairs.[74] The presence of a "personal judge" (*teharri memüri*) surprised the accused: this was Arthur Esayan, alias Arshavir Sahagian,[75] the man who had revealed the secret decisions of the Hnchaks' December 1913 Constanza Congress to the minister of the interior. In his opening statement, the presiding judge regretted that the accused had had to wait in prison for ten months to be judged. He also made a point of reminding them that, "since the Ottoman government had conferred on all Ottomans the right to choose their political party freely, I declare that we do not consider the mere fact of belonging to the Hnchak party to be [grounds] for indictment." Combining courtesy with an insistence on the letter of the law, he also promised the accused that they would have the right to explain their actions and defend themselves and that they would be given a fair trial. The Hnchak activists responded with the observation that the charges brought against them were largely based on the content of their statutes and program in the form they took prior to the July 1908 restoration of the Constitution.[76] During the second session of their trial, however, held on 15 May, some extremely compromising documents were read into the court record: they revealed that certain members of the SDHP had planned to organize self-defense efforts among the Armenians and that they had also sought to overthrow the Ittihadist government.[77]

The indictment, which was read out during the fifth session of the trial, included the following counts: 1) a separatist conspiracy; 2) a plan to create an "autonomous or independent Armenia"; 3) a conspiracy to stage insurrections; and 4) terrorist plots elaborated in complicity with "traitors" (an allusion to Colonel Sadık and General Şerif Pasha). However, at the sixth session of the trial, held on 26 May, important information about the opposition of the Hnchak Central Committee of Turkey to the decisions of the Constanza Congress was entered into the court record. At its Third General Assembly, held in Istanbul from 24 July to 8 August 1914 with the participation of 31 delegates from local committees, the SDHP of Turkey declared that the Constanza Congress had been illegal. It had not attained a quorum, since only 17 of the SDHP's 64 branches in the Ottoman Empire had been represented at it.[78] One might, of course, suppose that the positions adopted at this Third General Assembly, which were made public in August 1914 and once again served notice of the desire of the Hnchaks of Turkey to operate within the bounds of the law, were motivated by the mid-July arrests of the party's activists. But that would be to ignore the fact that the Constanza Congress clearly excluded most of the Turkish branches of the party and tried to ram through positions to which, as it was well aware, the Ottoman activists would be opposed. The court acknowledged these facts while also observing that some Turkish branches of the party had endorsed the Constanza positions.

The last session of the Hnchaks' trial is particularly noteworthy, for it provides a perfectly clear illustration of the nature of the antagonism between "Turks" and "Armenians." In his opening statement, the vice-president of the court-martial, Çerkez Hurşid, said that he was moved by the "boundless patriotism" of the accused, yet could not understand what had impelled men "who were full of life and energy" to set off down "a dead end." "You have," he added, "suffered for the sake of the struggle against injustice; we, for our part, have always thought that particularistic tendencies have to pay their tribute to the onerous obligations that govern the world. That is where our ways part."[79] This striking formulation nicely sums up the two logics that clashed here: that of the state or those who control it is always the logic that "has to be respected."

The homage that the court thus paid to the accused did not leave them unmoved. In his response, Paramaz, who came forward as the leader of the Hnchaks in the dock, confessed that he had been touched by Hurşid Bey's words. He also pointed out how hard he and his comrades had struggled "for the happiness of this poor country," how much blood they had shed and how many sacrifices they had made "to make the brotherhood between Turks and Armenians a reality" and "foster mutual trust between them." However, he went on,

> you have, by your indifference, condemned our enormous effort to sterility and deliberately pursued [the goal] of exterminating us, forgetting that the liquidation of the Armenians is tantamount to the destruction of Turkey. It is you who have encouraged crimes and pillage and sought to silence every expression of our protest. For centuries, you lived off our lifeblood, but were never willing to give the fountain from which it sprang the right to stand firm and produce. You oppressed us when, as weak-willed *rayas* [members of a subjugated group], we endured all this servility with the patience of the wretched. You terrorized us the day we decided to demand from our masters the means of living half an existence. You flew into a rage when we sought to cultivate the seeds of Western civilization in the East, with a view to securing our future and yours. You began massacring us when, one day, we decided to assume a position that would allow us our self-respect. You excluded us from the protection of the law when we sought to benefit from the rights granted by Midhat's truncated constitution. Among the groups making up Turkey, we were the most dedicated and productive, and we were the ones you forced to suffer the most. Even today, brandishing the charge that we seek to create an independent Armenia, you want to crush us.[80]

It would be hard to produce a better description of the nature of the relationship between Armenians and Turks in the final years of the Ottoman Empire, a combination of close attachment and mutual exasperation. But the eloquent exchange between the judge and the Hnchak leader also resembled a last exchange before the divorce imposed by the Young Turk Central Committee. Twenty of the accused were condemned to death for "high treason and separatism." Around half past three on the morning of 15 June 1915, they were hanged in the courtyard of the War Ministry amid the greatest possible secrecy. The death sentence was, moreover, not officially announced until 17 June.[81]

While the Hnchaks' trial was in progress, an intense press campaign was set in motion – spearheaded, of course, by the Young Turk daily *Tanin*. Magisterially conducted by Hüseyin Cahid, it sought to expose the danger represented by the Armenians as a group. On 9 May, *Tanin* began publishing a series of articles entitled "The Grand Conspiracy." The "conspiracy" revolved around a plan woven by the leader of the opposition in exile, General

Şerif Pasha, and his partisans to overthrow the Ittihadist government and assassinate the Young Turk ministers. The article contended that this "conspiracy" had been hatched on the initiative of prominent anti-Turkish Europeans who wanted to "drive a wedge between Turkey and Germany." Above all, it indicated that Armenians were heavily involved in the plot: the Hnchaks Stepanos Sapah-Giulian, Paramaz and Varazdat were supposedly key players, alongside the famous Colonel Sadık, the organizer of the July 1912 coup d'état and the Ittihadists' *bête noire*.[82] Aram Andonian notes that the publication of these articles accusing the Hnchaks – "the Armenians" – of complicity in a plot against "state security" engendered smoldering hostility toward the Armenian population of the capital, poisoning the atmosphere. The articles charged Sapah-Giulian in particular with having dispatched terrorists to Istanbul, at Şerif Pasha's request, in order to assassinate the Ittihadist leaders and seize power. In "return for services rendered, he was to be given the portfolio of economy and finance in the new government."[83] It is not hard to guess the objective of these articles, teeming with improbable details: the Young Turks were trying to discredit both the opposition and the Armenian "conspirators" by exposing a vast "plot" directed against their party. The simultaneous publication in the same daily of several articles by one Mehmed Midhat (in fact a pseudonym used by the "traitor" Arshavir Sahagian) that insisted on the Hnchak leaders' complicity with Şerif Pasha[84] probably had no other aim than to underscore the key role played by the Armenian activists in this affair.

For his part, Sapah-Giulian, who was one of the main targets of these accusations and was condemned to death in absentia by the Istanbul court-martial in May 1915, affirms that after the 1913 attempt on Şerif Pasha's life in Paris, which was very probably engineered by the Ittihad, Prince Sabaheddin made a rapprochement with the Ittihadists, and was allowed to live since he was regarded as a possible alternative to the reigning sultan. Most importantly, Sapah-Giulian also reveals that in spring 1915, at a time when the Ottoman Empire was plunged in crisis, Talât summoned Sabaheddin and Şerif Pasha to Vienna, where it was agreed that Sabaheddin and his supporters would take power if the Entente succeeded in taking control of the capital. Sapah-Giulian even spells out that it "was their Arab friend Nazir Azuri" who informed them of these behind-the-scenes maneuvers.[85]

We have no other sources of information on these negotiations. In view of what we know about the Young Turks' usual operating methods, however, Sapah-Giulian's account is plausible. Let us add that the assassination attempt against Talât and Enver was conceived in late 1913 or early 1914, after the attempt on Şerif's life, but that the war broke out before it could be put into practice. In other words, the Ittihad launched a press campaign around an affair that was more than a year old. The objective was, without a doubt, to bolster the propaganda effort that aimed to make the Armenians out to be "domestic foes" while providing a context for the Hnchaks' trial, the legal component of the Ittihad's campaign. The Young Turks found it harder to stage a courtroom spectacle that would help it rid itself of its Dashnak "allies." The Dashnaks had consistently sought to defuse the provocations orchestrated by the Ittihad's representatives in the provinces; thus the Ittihad had to fall back on less "legalistic" methods in order to eliminate the ARF leaders, such as ruses or thinly veiled murders amid the confusion of the war.

Of the long list of charges officially leveled against the Armenians by the Ottoman Ministry of the Interior, let us, by way of example, mention the ostensible facts cited to justify what was undoubtedly the most appalling of the large-scale massacres perpetrated in summer 1915 against the Armenians of the *kaza* of Boğazlian and the surrounding area, including the vilayet of Angora. "Sizeable Armenian bands attacked Muslims. Before they were relocated, the Armenians attempted to destroy the houses and cities that they were leaving behind by setting huge fires."[86] The author of these lines obviously did not strain his imagination. At the trial of those responsible for this slaughter, during which more than

65,000 people were killed in the space of a few days (this trial began in February 1919 and was thus less constrained than were those that took place in the days of the "national movement" in Anatolia) an important witness gave testimony on Friday, 21 February 1919 that shed considerable light on the "Armenian revolt." When one of the judges asked Colonel Şahabeddin, the commander of the Fifteenth Division, assigned to this area, how many soldiers he had sent to put down the insurrection after learning of it, Şahabeddin admitted that he had sent 200. When the presiding judge went on to ask about the nature of this rebellion and the number of rebels involved, Şahabeddin needed a recess before he could bring himself to concede that "there were five or six Armenian insurgents, who had taken refuge in the mountains."[87] The rest of the interrogation showed, moreover, that the "revolt" of five or six individuals occurred only after the "displacement" of the Armenian population.[88]

Another grave accusation bore on the Armenians of the Kayseri region, where, according to the official propaganda account:

> The Imperial authorities discovered bombs, arms, gunpowder, and codes for encrypting secret correspondence destined for the revolutionary bands, along with other documents. It has been proved that the Armenian primate was at the head of the movement; moreover, the accused have confessed that the confiscated bombs were intended to obtain independence for Armenia.[89]

However, the information assembled during the pretrial investigation of the "vicar" in question, Bishop Khosrov of Caeserea, was not quite as categorical. In early summer 1914, Khosrov had gone to Holy Etchmiadzin to be consecrated bishop by the Armenian catholicos. It was on these grounds – travel to an enemy country, as the indictment put it – that nearly one year later, in spring 1915, "the Armenian bishop of Kayseri, Khosrov Effendi," came under suspicion of "complicity with the revolutionary movements." The court martial feared that its "jurisdictional prerogatives" were too narrow to allow it to try the case – that Khosrov could not be arraigned because of his status as a clergyman.[90] However, while waiting for the opening of the procedure against the bishop, the military commander of Kayseri voiced apprehensions that the prelate would use the time at his disposal "to sow disorder and make propaganda." He therefore suggested that Khosrov be exiled.[91] The bishop's rather summary trial ended one week after his arrest. It revealed that the "the Armenian bishop of Kayseri, Khosrov Effendi, had been apprised of [the] revolutionaries' preparations,"[92] which is to say that he had not found himself "at the head of the Armenian revolutionaries," as government propaganda put the matter several months after his trial. On these grounds, the court found "that there were extenuating circumstances" in the bishop's case and "condemned him to 13 years of detention in a fortress."[93] Oddly, when the commander of the Fifth Army informed the minister of war of the verdict rendered in the case of the Armenian bishop Khosrov Effendi, he depicted the bishop as "one of those who inspired the preparations for a revolution and the revolutionary movement that had set out to create a future Armenian state," contradicting the terms of the judgment delivered against the clergyman.[94] This supplementary judgment was surely designed to satisfy the minister of war, since he had transformed the sentence into a death sentence shortly after the trial, before the Council of Ministers, on 20 July 1915, finally commuted the bishop's punishment to life in prison.[95] In any case, Khosrov was one of the large numbers of clergymen murdered in the following months.[96]

The Kayseri revolutionaries mentioned in the official brochure of the Ministry of the Interior were themselves Hnchak activists. According to an account by Manuel Mgrian, a pharmacist in Everek, some 300 of these Armenians were being held in Kayseri's civilian prison in April–May 1915, where the feet of most of them were beaten to a pulp with truncheons. Sometime in May, Mgrian had also been sent to Kayseri's military prison to treat a prisoner with serious injuries. There he discovered the parliamentary deputy and Hnchak leader Murad (Hampartsum Boyajian), who had been recently transferred to Kayseri from Ayaş, where the "political" prisoners deported from Istanbul were being held. Murad refused to submit to a new round of questioning from the *mutesarif*, pointing out that he had already told Talât everything he had to say. For this outrage, he was tortured with a red-hot iron. The pharmacist provides us with a detailed description of the effects.[97] Boyajian did receive some treatment before being hanged at night some time later.[98]

One may well wonder about the capacity of the Armenians of Kayseri, a tiny Turkish-speaking minority surrounded by Muslims, to transform itself into a subversive force and go on to struggle "for the independence of Armenia."

The formulations employed to describe the resistance put up by some of the Armenian inhabitants of Şabinkarahisar also have a certain flair:

> Early in June of this year, the Armenians attacked the city of Sharki Karahisar, suddenly and for no ascertainable reason, burning down the Muslim neighborhoods. The 800 rebels who barricaded themselves in the city's citadel refused to listen to the fatherly advice and conciliatory proposals of the Imperial authorities. They were responsible for the deaths of 150 people, including the commander of the gendarmerie.[99]

We will come back to the fate of these people who are said to have attacked their own city by entrenching themselves in its citadel.

To conclude, the Young Turks' campaign to present the Armenians as collectively guilty often exploited old facts – sometimes dating back to before the 1908 revolution – that were revamped when necessary to suit present purposes. It also used all available means to exploit the least little detail capable of proving Armenian "treachery." Thus, the Ittihad succeeded not only in painting a plausible picture of the "enemy within" but also in whipping up the population against the "traitors," thus preparing them to stand by and watch the mass violence to come without qualms, or even to participate in it.

On 22 April and 6 May – that is, twice in the space of some two weeks – a decree was promulgated ordering that arms be requisitioned from the civilian population. The decree also stipulated that everyone possessing arms had to turn them in to the military commanders within five days, with the exception of those individuals holding special permits issued by the military authorities.[100] This constituted the true beginning of the campaign of persecution of the Ottoman Armenians. With the requisition order, which officially applied to the entire population, a pretext had been found for legalizing violence, as it were. Police raids now mushroomed in the capital as well as in the provinces. Once again, the Ittihad had shown great imagination in hiding its objectives behind what might appear to be almost normal wartime measures.

In the Vortex of the War: The First Phase of the Genocide

PART IV

In the Vortex of the War: The First Phase of the Genocide

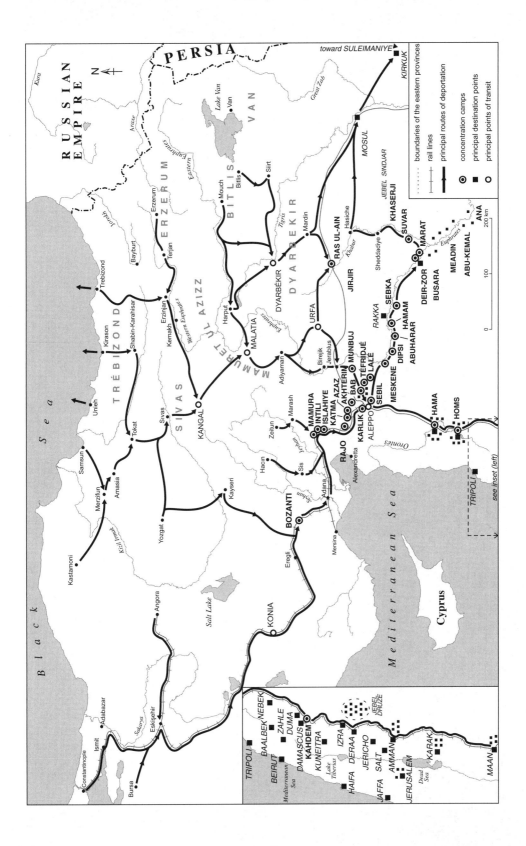

Chapter 1

The Armenian Population of the Empire on the Eve of the War: The Demographic Issue

The immediate pre-war distribution of the Armenian population in the Ottoman Empire presented a variegated picture. Although most Armenians still lived on the Armenian high plateau – then known as the eastern vilayets – communities of greater or lesser density had long since been implanted in western Asia Minor, European Turkey, and Constantinople. The capital of the empire had naturally attracted people from the provinces for centuries, but the wars between the Ottomans and the Safavids and, later, between the Ottomans and the Russians, also contributed to altering the demographic situation on the Armenians' lands. At the turn of the seventeenth century, the deportations carried out by Shah Abbas and the Jelali revolts resulted in major demographic shifts and the emergence of virtually depopulated areas, particularly in the crescent stretching from Erzincan to the plain of Ararat. The events gradually brought on a division of the Armenian habitat between its two historical poles, north and south. It was accentuated by the division of the high plateau into Persian and Ottoman spheres. The general tendency was an almost constant westward drift of the population. Furthermore, communities materialized in the seventeenth century to the east and southeast of the Sea of Marmara in historical Bythinia, which had itself sustained unprecedented demographic losses the century before.

Thus, there sprang up sharply contrasting situations within the Armenian world: peasants living on their ancestral lands contrasted with city-dwellers present in large numbers in the capital. The ways of life and cultural foundations of these groups were radically different. Indeed, one might even speak of mutually foreign worlds had the rural exodus not unceasingly replenished the Armenian population of the capital with people from the countryside who maintained familial ties with the regions from which they came. Until the 1878 Congress of Berlin, which not only hastened the end of the Ottoman presence in Europe but also put the Armenian high plateau on the political map, the existence of these Christian populations on the eastern confines of the Ottoman Empire had apparently not been a matter of concern to the Ottoman rulers. However, when the Europeans, especially the Russians, began to be "preoccupied" by the fate of the eastern provinces, the sultans reacted in short order. As was shown at length in the second part of this study, the question of the territorial integrity of the empire gradually became an obsession for the Ottoman elites, with every fresh territorial loss only intensifying the dominant group's trauma and humiliation. The process of radicalization was a long time in coming, but it was no less powerful for that.

The obsession with the empire's territorial integrity, which was obviously bound up with the question of its demographic composition, haunted the Young Turk movement as much as it had Sultan Abdülhamid's regime. Their modernization plans for the empire were not radically different. In any case, demographic considerations helped shape the sultan's policy vis-à-vis the Armenians, even if the massacres committed between 1894 and 1896 have often been presented as punishments meted out to "insurgents." The proof, we would suggest, is provided by the complementary Hamidian policy of very plainly encouraging emigration. The destruction of work tools, looting of stores and businesses, growing tax burden, and constant insecurity due to the bands of *hamidiyes* organized by the sultan drove hundreds of thousands of people into exile, depopulating both town and country.

From the day the Armenian question was posed, the Armenians' demographic weight in the population became a political problem and was treated as such. Thus, it is not surprising that the Ottoman authorities systematically falsified their own censuses. Their goal was to show that there was no Armenian question because the Armenians were only a tiny minority in an ocean of Turks. To attain this goal, they set up barriers that made it difficult to make a precise assessment of population trends in the empire. One of the most frequently used methods consisted in constantly redrawing the administrative boundaries of the Armenian vilayets. The result was that successive censuses bore on different regional entities. This makes it harder to study the demographic evolution of a region, the impact of massacres, and the consequences of emigration.

The Administrative Divisions

At the administrative level, under the cover of the *tanzimat* (reforms), the *eyalet* of Erzerum – the former governorship of Ermenistan – was in 1864–6 subdivided into seven *mutesarifliks* (department governed by a mutesarif) (Erzerum, Çaldıran, Kars, Bayazid, Muş, Erzincan, and Van). They included almost all of the Armenian plateau. Notably excluded from the *eyalet* were the regions of Harput, Arğana, Palu, Agn, and Arapkir, as well as the Sasun and Şirvan districts and Hizan, which were all incorporated into the *eyalet* of Dyarbekir. A European diplomat offers an instructive comment on these administrative boundaries:

> In Asia, the major [administrative] divisions corresponded to the territorial divisions as they had been at the time of the conquest and, like the European provinces, bore the names of the communities that originally inhabited these territories: for instance, the *eyalet* of Ermenistan (Armenia) or the *eyalet* of Kurdistan. These names survived down to the reign of Sultan Mahmud II. From that period on, however, the policy pursued by the Divan, which wanted to efface the names of the aforementioned major subdivisions because they provided too stark a reminder of the vanquished nationalities' historical importance, [consisted in] ... chopping up the *eyalets*.[1]

The 1864–6 administrative divisions, however, left too high a proportion of Armenians in a single region. Istanbul accordingly decided to divide up the vilayet of Erzerum in 1878 – that is, immediately after the Congress of Berlin, which ratified the loss to Russia of the regions of Batum, Kars, and Ardahan – by removing entire districts from it and adding others. Four new vilayets were now created: Erzerum, Van, Hakkari, and Muş. The following year, the Ottoman authorities created the autonomous *sancaks* of Dersim and Harput. In 1880, they attached Dersim to Harput and Hakkari to Van. The effect was to dilute two Armenian regions in two zones populated by Kurds. Later, in 1886, the Ottomans decided to divide up the Armenian Plateau once again, this time into smaller administrative units. The Euphrates Basin now found itself cut up and assigned to the new vilayets of Erzerum, Harput (Mamuret ul-Aziz), Dyarbekir, and Sıvas, to which the Dersim district, the Hakkari district, Bitlis, and Van were attached.

The last important division took place in 1895, on the eve of the great massacres. The eight existing vilayets were now condensed into six new administrative units – Van, Bitlis,

Dyarbekir, Harput, Sıvas, and Erzerum. The Dersim and Hakkari districts disappeared, "to the benefit of" Harput and Van.

With these manipulations in mind, we must now come to grips with the problem of the censuses and the other statistics on the Armenian population of the Ottoman Empire. The specialists who have treated this question all agree on certain points: the best known – Vital Cuinet,[2] Gustave Rolin-Jaequemyns,[3] and Abdolonyme Ubicini[4] – unhesitatingly speak of "the Turks' indifference to the demographical sciences," the dubious methods utilized by Ottoman government officials, the extreme difficulty with which they managed to obtain vague figures, and finally, the subjective nature of the standards of measurement used. In one instance, the number of households was counted; in another, Armenians were accurately distinguished from Greeks or Syriacs, and Catholics, Protestants, and Orthodox were separately counted, while the census-takers studiously avoided distinguishing Turks from Turcomans, Kurds, Kızılbaş, Zazas, Yezidis, and other sects. Thus, Muslims were set against the various Christian denominations as a monolithic block. Demography was here harnessed to purely political ends; the Ottomans produced statistics for the consumption of international public opinion alone.

The Pre-1895 Censuses

The first attempt to conduct a census in Turkey was made in 1844 by Rıza Pasha, the minister of war. It showed that there were some 2 million Armenians in Asiatic Turkey.[5] In 1867, the Turkish government commissioned publication of a volume on Turkey for the Universal Exposition in Paris. It, too, indicated that there were 2 million Armenians in Asia Minor and another 400,000 in European Turkey.[6] On the eve of the Congress of Berlin, the Patriarchate drew up a preliminary balance based on the empire's official *Salname* for the year 1294 of the Hegira (1878). It put the number of Armenians living in the Ottoman Empire in this period at 3 million:[7] 400,000 in European Turkey (primarily in Constantinople, Thrace, Bulgaria, and Rumania); 600,000 in western Asia Minor (the vilayets of Angora, Aydın/Smyrna, Konya, Adana, Aleppo, the *mutesariflik* of Ismit, etc.); 670,000 in the vilayets of Sıvas, Trebizond, Kayseri, and (southern) Dyarbekir; 1,330,000 on the Armenian plateau – that is, in the vilayets of Erzerum (excluding the regions annexed by Russia) and Van – as well as the northern part of the vilayet of Dyarbekir, comprising the districts of Harput, Eğin, Arapkir, and Arğana on the one hand and, on the other, the northern part of the *sancak* of Siirt, comprising the Sasun, Şirvan, and Hizan districts.

Population	Erzerum and Van	Dyarbekir (North)	Total
Armenians	1,150,000	180,000	1,330,000
Turks	400,000	130,000	530,000
Kurds	80,000	40,000	120,000
Greeks	5,000	–	5,000
Chald.-Syriacs	14,000	8,000	22,000
Zazas	35,000	2,300	37,300
Yezidis	13,000	2,000	15,000
Gypsies	3,000	–	3,000
Total	1,700,000	362,300	2,062,300

Oddly, the "official" census results published by Kemal Karpat provide radically different estimates for the years 1881/82–93,[8] a period during which the administrative organization of the Armenian provinces was considerably modified: almost all the former *mutesarifliks* of Chaldir, Kars and Bayazid now came under Russian rule, while the boundaries of the *eyalets* of Erzerum and Dyarbekir were redrawn. According to these documents, the Armenian population was distributed as follows: there were 179,645 Armenians in European Turkey (156,032 of them in Constantinople, 270,183 in western Asia Minor – the vilayets of Angora, Aydın, Konya, Adana, and Aleppo, the *mutesariflik* of Ismit, and elsewhere); 227,202 in the vilayets of Sıvas, Trebizond, and Dyarbekir (not including the northern part of the Dyarbekir vilayet) and the *sancak* of Kayseri; and 371,113 in Erzerum, Bitlis, Van, Harput, and the northern part of the vilayet of Dyarbekir. The Armenian population of the five vilayets was divided up as follows:

	Erzerum	Bitlis	Dyarbekir	Harput	Van	Total
Arm.	107,868	106,306	22,464	75,093	59,382	371,113
Muslims	445,548	167,054	101,065	300,188	54,582	1,068,437
Greeks	3,356			812	543	4,711
Total	556,772	273,360	124,341	375,824	113,964	1,444,261

Alongside these figures, we may range two other sets of statistics obtained in the same period. First, those of the Armenian Patriarchate, which date from 1878/79:[9]

	Erzerum	Bitlis	Dyarbekir	Harput	Van	Total
Arm.	280,000	250,000	150,000	270,000	400,000	1,350,000

Second, Cuinet's statistics, culled around 1890 from the *Salname* and other documents furnished by the Ottoman administration:[10]

Population	Erzerum	Bitlis	Dyarbekir	Harput	Van	Total
Armenians	135,087	131,390	83,226	69,718	80,000	499,421
Muslims	500,782	257,863	388,644	504,366	241,000	1,892,655
Gr. and Syr.	3,725	210	53,420	650	99,785	157,790
Total	639,594	389,463	525,290	574,734	420,785	2,549,866

An examination of the figures presented above reveals wide disparities. Thus, from 1844 to 1867, official Turkish sources affirm that there were 2,400,000 Armenians living in the empire, with 2,000,000 of them in Asiatic Turkey. In the census carried out between 1881 and 1893, however, the number of Armenians suddenly falls by one-half, to 1,048,143 (156,032 of them in Constantinople). Unless we assume that these figures resulted from political manipulation, it is hard to explain so great a difference from one census to the next, even if we take into account the 1878 loss of Kars and Ardahan and the exodus of several tens of thousands of Ottoman Armenians to Russia.

The *Salname* of 1294/1878 that the Armenian Patriarchate presented to the Congress of Berlin was a no less official Ottoman document. Produced for economic purposes before these "adjustments" had been made, it would seem to reflect the demographic evolution of the region much better: it puts the number of Armenians in Turkey at 3 million. This figure indicates a 25 per cent population increase over 30 years, as opposed to the decrease of 50 per cent reported in the other official Ottoman statistics. Similarly, for the Armenian plateau as we have defined it above, the Ottoman census of 1881–93 gives figures of 1,068,437 Muslims and 371,113 Armenians out of a total population of 1,500,000, whereas the statistics published in the 1294/1878 *Salname* presented by the Patriarchate in Berlin are quite different: they show 1,330,000 Armenians, 650,000 Kurds and Turks, 27,000 Greeks and Christian Syriacs, and 55,300 Zazas, Yezidis, and Gypsies. If we put Turks, Kurds, Zazas, Yezidis, and Gypsies in the same category – although the Gypsies were often Christians – as the Ottoman administration probably did, then we arrive at a figure of 705,300 out of a total 2,062,300 inhabitants. But we still fall far short of the total, even when we compare the Ottoman census to that conducted by the Patriarchate in 1882. The Patriarchate's census, which takes into account the fact that the Armenians of Kars and Ardahan had come under Russian rule in 1878, indicates that 1,350,000 Armenians were still living in the eastern provinces in this period. Attentive examination of Salaheddin Bey's statistics throws some light on this question. They state that a total of 13,223,000 Muslims lived in all of Asiatic Turkey out of a total population of 16,383,000.[11] Of this total, 10,907,000 people lived in western and central Anatolia and Cyprus – 1,000,000 were Greek, 80,000 Jewish, 700,000 Armenian, and 9,127,000 Muslim. In Syria and Iraq, 2,650,000 Arabs, Turks, Druze, and Kurds lived side by side with 100,000 Christians, while 900,000 Arabs inhabited the Hejaz and Yemen. If we add up these figures, it appears that, of the 13,223,000 Muslims said to be living in Ottoman Asia, 12,677,000 lived outside the boundaries of the "Anatolian East," which, according to Salaheddin Bey, had a total population of 1,906,000. Subtracting, we find that this province, comprising the vilayets of Van, Erzerum, Kurdistan, and Harput, was inhabited by 1,300,000 Armenians, 60,000 other Christians, and 546,000 Kurds, Turks, Turkomans, Çerkez, and so on. The Ottoman statistics in the 1294/1878 *Salname* submitted by the Armenian patriarch to the Congress of Berlin differ only slightly from these figures. They show a total of 1,330,000 Armenians, 650,000 Kurds, Turks, and so on, as well as 82,000 people belonging to diverse other groups (taking only northern Kurdistan in the vilayet of Dyarbekir into account). The census carried out by the Patriarchate in 1882 arrived at a similar result: it indicated that 1,350,000 Armenians were living in this region.

Once again, the official *Salnames* vouch for the credibility of the Armenians' censuses. The 1298/1882 *Salname* published the state budget figures for 1296/1880 as established by the Council of Ministers. This document indicated that the tax known as the *bedeli askeri*, paid by all non-Muslim males between the ages of 15 and 60, showed an annual yield of 462,870 Turkish pounds for all of Turkey. However, the Council of Ministers estimated, according to the same document, that this tax should have yielded twice as much.[12] Implicitly, the state thus acknowledged that it collected this tax from only half of its non-Muslim population – the half reported in its census.

While it is an established fact that the official statistics were falsified, it is important to determine the extent of the falsification. In the case to hand, only an examination of all the regions concerned would allow us to establish the actual dimensions of the fraud. Such an examination could, for example, provide irrefutable evidence of a substantial Armenian population, which the 1891–93 Ottoman census ignores or minimizes. Among the obvious falsifications, we can cite the Ottoman figures for Scutari, which indicate that no Armenians lived in the area,[13] even though it is known that entire neighborhoods were inhabited by these Christians and that there were many churches and schools there.[14] In Mersin, in the heart of Cilicia, the Ottomans counted 438 Armenians and 19,737 "Muslims."[15] In the *kaza* of Zyr, near Angora, the Turkish census put the number of Armenians at 2,214,[16] although the village of Stanoz alone, inhabited exclusively by Armenians, had a population of 3,000.[17]

The Post-1896 Censuses

In the present chapter on demography, we have chosen to distinguish the pre-1895 and post-1895 periods for an obvious reason: such a distinction makes it easier to assess the direct consequences of the 1894–96 massacres, which particularly affected the population of the Armenian high plateau.

Shortly before these massacres began, in 1894, an Ottoman census arrived at figures similar to those given for 1881/2–83 (with differences well under one hundred individuals). By and large, the statistics utilized for 1894 were the same as those cited from 1881 to 1894[18] in both official publications and the documents transmitted to foreign governments or specialists such as Cuinet. The demographic evolution of the Armenian high plateau is only perceptible in an official document said to have been produced in 1897, but is in fact based on results obtained in 1895, on the eve of the biggest massacres.[19] Interestingly, this document reveals radical changes that had supposedly come about in a single year: in the vilayet of Erzerum, the number of Muslims jumped from 445,648 to 509,948; in Van, the figure of 60,448 Armenians established by both the 1894 census and earlier censuses fell to 59,433, while the number of non-Christians soared from 59,412 to 80,773. Nothing about the events that the populations of the area lived through in 1895 allows us to explain this 36 per cent increase in the number of Muslims over a 12-month period. Thus, it is quite obvious that no serious census had been carried out for decades. Rather, the old figures were regularly recycled; the number of Muslims was methodically inflated and the number of Christians just as methodically reduced. We must, however, distinguish the way the Ottoman authorities handled statistics for European Turkey and western Anatolia from the methods it employed in the case of the Armenian high plateau: there were, it seems, fewer distortions in its figures for the former regions, whereas the census figures for the Armenian plateau were subject to careful manipulation.

The Ottoman census of 1906/07 is hardly more explicit. It indicates that the vilayets of Erzerum, Bitlis, Van, and Mamuret ul-Aziz had an Armenian population of 354,577 (352,035 in 1895) and a Muslim population of 1,194,778 (1,139,041 in 1895).[20] According to these figures, then, practically no demographic change had occurred in 11 or 12 years: this was tantamount to affirming that the massacres of 1895 had never taken place except in the Armenians' imagination, and in the Western newspapers that claimed to have described a slaughter organized by Sultan Abdülhamid. In fact, the Census Bureau of the Ministry of the Interior resolved the problem by reissuing the figures for previous years, which had already been reduced, on our estimate, by 200 per cent. Given the importance of the demographic weight of a given group in the resolution of a territorial conflict – consider the example of Bulgaria, Romania, and Greece in 1878 – it was simply not possible to obtain figures accurately reflecting the real situation from the states concerned. It was, no doubt, because the Armenian Patriarchate was aware of this fact that it carried out censuses of its own.

In the preceding pages, we have already discussed the patriarchal censuses for 1878/82, which, it should be added here, generally assessed only the overall Armenian population, without giving precise information as to how it broke down by *kaza*. Moreover, it is clear that the Armenians adopted a low profile under Abdülhamid. There could be no question of their conducting a census of any kind in the period. Thus, it was only with the Young Turks' assumption of power in 1908 that it became possible to engage in an undertaking of this sort. In 1912, the Patriarchate produced a preliminary assessment, hardly more precise than that of 1878/82, of the number of Armenians living in the vilayets of Van, Bitlis, Mamuret ul-Aziz, Dyarbekir, and Erzerum, arriving at a figure of 804,500.[21] Probably because it was dissatisfied by the imprecision of this document, the Patriarchate methodically carried out a second census, necessitated by the plan to reform the eastern provinces. According to Vahan Papazian, who was, as we have seen, executive director of the Security Commission directly responsible for the question of the Armenian reforms,[22] the Commission took the initiative[23] of organizing the 1913 census.[24] Of course, the government and the Patriarchate were in this period fighting a fierce battle around population statistics, since the future of the reform plan was inseparable from the number of Armenians living in the eastern provinces.[25] The main argument advanced by the Young Turk cabinet to justify its rejection of the principle of reforms in "Armenia" was that the Armenians represented a tiny "minority" there and that there was therefore little reason to make changes in the local administration, and even less to give the Armenians responsibilities in the management of local affairs. Papazian says that, while he was waiting for the results of the census then in progress, one of the best sources of information at his disposal was a census carried out under the sultan's authorization with a view of collecting "one per cent more" from each Armenian family in order to pay off the colossal debt of the Jerusalem Patriarchate. The records of this census, with lists of the sums collected, were preserved in the archives of the Patriarchate in Istanbul.[26]

On 20 February 1913, the offices of the Patriarchate sent a circular and the required forms to all the dioceses in the empire: the dioceses were charged with distributing these documents to the parish councils, collecting and synthesizing the results, and forwarding them to Constantinople. The census was supposed to be completed by May. In summer 1914, forms countersigned by the primates and the members of the diocesan councils were still arriving in Constantinople.[27] Most of the work, however, had already been done by then.[28]

Based for the most part on community structures, and especially the thousands of parish councils in the empire, the census was carried out more carefully in some regions than in others. Despite imperfections and lacunae, however, the document that resulted is of crucial importance, since no other one like it was produced in the period that interests us. It is the only source to reveal the real weight of the Armenian population, particularly that of the Armenian plateau. Furthermore, this census was taken precisely in a period when it was assumed that the reforms in the eastern vilayets would be supervised by two European inspectors. The Patriarchate accordingly had no interest in doctoring its figures, which it knew would be promptly verified by the two officials in question.

In light of the figures we have just given, it appears very plainly that the Armenian population of the high plateau, far from growing between 1874 and 1914, sharply diminished. Indeed, without adjustment for probable population growth under normal conditions, the Armenian statistics show a drop of more than a million individuals in the 37 years between these two dates. This drop cannot be explained by the massacres of 1894–96 alone. The 300,000 "émigrés" registered in this period also have to be taken into account,[29] together with the many villages forcibly converted to Islam.[30] It must further be noted that the representatives of the dioceses who conducted the censuses did not always have access to all the areas inhabited by Armenians, especially when Kurdish tribes controlled them. Consequently, not all Armenians were counted. This was particularly the case for the vilayet of Dyarbekir, from which the Turk authorities deported, to their surprise, 120,000 Armenians in spring 1915,[31] although there were only 106,867 in the vilayet according to the Patriarchate's 1914/1914 statistics and only 73,226 according to the 1914 Ottoman census.[32] The figures on tax revenues in 1914–16, published by the empire's Ministry of Finance, are no less significant. They indicate that, overall, the five eastern vilayets contributed diverse fees and taxes totaling more than 110 million piasters to the Ottoman budget: 64,683,935 piasters in 1915 and nothing in 1916.[33] Even if the war obstructed the collection of these taxes in the combat zones, it is hard to understand why the regions to the south, although spared by the fighting, contributed nothing to the war effort – unless we agree that the massacres and deportations of the Armenian populations of these vilayets, which was significantly underestimated in the statistics, brought on the financial ruin of these regions and their Muslim inhabitants.

The Armenian Presence in The Ottoman Empire on the Eve of the War, According to the Patriarchate's Census

Although the Patriarchate's census is organized by diocese, the statistical tables provided below reflect the administrative organization of the empire as it stood at the beginning of the First World War.[34] In other words, we have regrouped the localities identified in the Patriarchate's census according to *kaza*, with, it must be admitted, some doubt in the case of villages located near the boundary between two *kazas*. Some of the figures given here are not to be found in the documents housed in the Bibliothèque Nubar in Paris; they have been taken from those collected by the Constantinople Patriarchate's Information Bureau and are now housed in the archives of St. James Monastery in Jerusalem or other diocesan sources (such sources are indicated in the footnotes to the table). In the following chapters, our evaluations of the relevance of information on the number of deportees found in other sources are based on the statistics given below.

Administrative Unit	Localities	Armenians	Churches/ Monasteries	Schools
1. Constantinople	43	161,000	47	64 (25,000)
– Gelibolu/Dardanelles	6	2,670	6	
Total	49	163,670	53	64 (25,000)
2. Thrace				
– Edirne and W. Thrace	5	7,948	7	6 (565)*
– Tekirdağ and E. Thrace	4	22,368	7	9 (1,873)*
Total	9	30,316	14	15 (2,438)*
3. *Sancak* of Ismit				
– Ismit	12	25,399	14	18 (3,000)
– Adabazar	6	15,169	8	16 (2,000)
– Kandira/Kandere	9	3,652	8	7 (480)
– Geyve	7	8,628	10	6 (1,000)
– Karamürsel–Yalova	8	8,827	11	6 (1,000)
Total	42	61,675	51 and 1	53 (7,480)
4. Vilayet of Bursa/ Hüdavendigar				
A. *Sancak* of Bursa				16 (2,078)*
– Bursa	4	10,000	6	
– Bazarköy	6	22,209	11	–
– Gemlik	3	12,100	2	–
– Muhalic	6	3,218	1	–
– Kirmasti	1	1,016	1	–
Edrenos/Atarnos	3	4,225	1	–

Continued

Administrative Unit	Localities	Armenians	Churches/ Monasteries		Schools
B. *Sancak* of Ertuğrul/ Bilecik					10 (1,263)*
– Bilecik	5	13,110	5		–
– Yenişehir	3	4,750	3		–
– Inegöl	2	5,350	2		–
– Şögüt	5	6,872	5		–
C. *Sancak* of Kütahya					5 (1,174)*
– Kütahya	5	3,578	6		–
– Uşak	1	1,100	1		–
– Eskişehir	3	4,510	3		–
D. *Sancak* of Afion– karahisar	3	7,448	3		7 (850)*
E. *Sancak* of Karasi/ Balıkeser	8	20,006	4		8 (1,334)*
Total	58	118,992	54		50 (6,699)*
5. Vilayet of Aydın/ Smyrna					
A. *Sancak* of Smyrna	8	13,679	17		–
B. *Sancak* of Manisa	5	5,875	6		
C. *Sancak* of Aydın	2	1,043	2	1	
D. *Sancak* of Denizly	1	548	1		–
Total	16	21,145	26	1	27 (2,935)
6. Vilayet of Konya					
A. *Sancak* of Konya	6	11,650	6		
B. *Sancak* of Niğde	5	5,727	4	1	
C. *Sancak* of Isparta/ Burdur	2	2,600	2		
D. *Sancak* of Tekke/Elmaly	2	761	2		
Total	15	20,738	14	1	26 (4,585)
7. Vilayet of Kastamonu					
A. *Sancak* of Kastamonu	5	3,978	4	7	
B. *Sancak* of Çankırı	1	1,000	1	1	
C. *Sancak* of Inebolu	6	3,217	7	6	
D. *Sancak* of Sinop	6	5,266	5	4	
Total	18	13,461	17		18 (2,500)
8. Vilayet of Trebizond/ Trabzon					
A. *Sancak* of Trabzon					116 (6,000)
– Trebizond, Akçeabat, Surmene	37	20,158	25	1	
– Görele	2	562	3		
– Tirebolu	1	868	1		
– Giresun	2	2,335	3		
– Ordu	30	13,565	25		

Continued

Administrative Unit	Localities	Armenians	Churches/Monasteries		Schools
B. *Sancak* of Samsun/Canik					
– Samsun	1	5,315	1		3 (610)
– Bafra	1	2,035	1		3 (374)
– Çarşamba	21	13,316	21		33 (1,160)
– Terme	5	3,427	6		8 (310)
– Uniye	11	7,700	14		21 (?)
– Fatsa	3	1,330	3		3 (?)
C. *Sancak* of Gumuşhane	3	2,749	3		3 (?)
D. *Sancak* of Rize/Lazistan	1	35	1		
Total	118	73,395	106	31	90 (9,254)
9. Vilayet of Angora					
A. *Sancak* of Angora					
– Angora	2	11,319	72		15 (2,000)
– Kalecik	1	830	1	1	2 (120)
– Stanoz/Zyr	1	3,142	3		2 (500)
– Nallihan	1	1,030	1		2 (220)
– Mihaliççik	1	272	1		1 (59)
– Sivrihissar	1	4,265	1		2 (990)
B. *Sancak* of Kırşehir	2	4,400	2		4 (990)
C. *Sancak* of Yozgat					
– Yozgat	4	13,969	5		6 (3,300)
– Sungurlu	1	1,936	1		2 (170)
– Çorum	6	3,520	4		6 (380)
– Boğazliyan	32	35,825	36	1	22 (c. 5,000)
– Akdağmaden	5	3,361	3		6 (450)
D. *Sancak* of Kayseri	31	52,000	40	7	56 (7,119)
Total	88	135,869	105	11	126 (21,298)
10. Vilayet of Sıvas					
A. *Sancak* of Sıvas					
– Sıvas	37	31,185	13	4	19 (1,980)
– Yenihan	2	2,175	3		3 (186)
– Şeyhkeşla/Tonus	26	21,063	20		22 (1,988)
– Aziziye	1	1,106	1	2	8 (412)
– Bunian	5	4,781	6		
– Gürün	7	13,874	10		12 (1,120)
– Darende	2	3,983	2	1	2 (220)
– Kangal	9	7,339	7	1	8 (1,152)
– Divrig	18	10,605	18	2	10 (857)
– Koçgiri/Zara	9	7,651	10		
– Koçhisar	30	13,055	30	2	7 (590)
B. *Sancak* of Şabinkarahisar					28 (2,483)
– Şabinkarahisar	9	9,104	8	1	9 (1,085)
– Suşehir	35	13,430	24	1	23 (1,815)
– Alucra/Mehsudiye	3	627	3		2 (75)
– Köyulhisar	2	190	2		
– Hamidye/Alucra	2	520	2		2 (65)

Continued

Administrative Unit	Localities	Armenians	Churches/ Monasteries		Schools
C. *Sancak* of Tokat					
– Tokat	18	17,480	17	2	11 (1,400)
– Niksar	3	3,560	3		2 (715)
– Erbaa	9	6,948	6		2 (460)
– Zile	4	4,283	2		3 (600)
D. *Sancak* of Amasia					
– Amasia	1	13,788	5	2	12 (1,325)
– Merzifun/Marzevan	3	10,666	1		8 (1,221)
– Ladik	2	350	1		1 (40)
– Havza	1	333	1		1 (35)
– Vizirköprü	1	1,612	1		2 (150)
– Gümüşhaciköy	1	4,064	2		6 (550)
– Mecidözü	1	700	1		1 (75)
Total	241	204,472	198	21	204 (20,599)
11. Vilayet of Adana					
A. *Sancak* of Adana	6	27,990	4		25 (2,755)*
B. *Sancak* of Mersin	3	6,987	4		
C. *Sancak* of İçil	2	466	2		
D. *Sancak* of Sis/Kozan					
– Sis	11	5,600	2	1	7 (641)*
– Feke/Vahka	8	4,948	7	1	9 (661)*
– Hacın	5	27,850	8	1	4 (577)*
– Karsbazar	6	5,645	4		
E. *Sancak* of Cebelbereket	29	39,928	13	2	18 (1,200)*
Total	70	119,414	44	5	63 (5,834)*
12. Vilayet of Alep					
A. *Sancak* of Maraş					
– Maraş	23	32,844	20	2	23 (1,629)*
– Bazarcik	1	1,500	1		
– Göksun	18	9,505	12	1	
– Zeitun	18	22,456	14	3	10 (690)*
– Albistan	4	5,838	4		4 (265)*
B. *Sancak* of Ayntab					
– Ayntab	3	36,448	8		25 (5,000)
– Kilis	1	7,966	1		1 (380)
C. *Sancak* of Urfa					
– Urfa	10	38,680		6	20 (?)
– Birecik	2	1,600	2		
– Rumkale/Hromgla	4	1,460	3	2	
D. *Sancak* of Antioch/ Antakya					
– Antioch	8	8,532	7	2	10 (487)*
– Şuğur/Kesab	9	8,736	9		8 (?)
– Iskenderum/Alexandretta and Beylan	16	14,000	6		12 (?)
Total	117	189,565	93	16	113 (8,451)

Continued

Administrative Unit	Localities	Armenians	Churches/ Monasteries		Schools
13. Vilayet of Harput/ Mamuret ul–Aziz					
A. *Sancak* of Harput					
– Harput	57	39,788	67	9	92 (8660)
– Keban Maden	3	789	3		2 (122)
– Arapkir	5	10,880	9		14 (862)
– Pötürge	1	679	1		1 (120)
– Agn/Eğin	25	16,741	25	3	20 (1300)
B. *Sancak* of Dersim					
– Hozat	16	2,299	18	11	5 (180)
– Kyzilkilise/Nazimiye	1	89	5		
– Medzgerd/Mazgirt	9	1,835	14	22	2 (155)
– Çarsancak	43	7,940	51	15	23 (1114)
– Çemişkezek	22	4,494	19	2	17 (729)
– Ovacık	1	50			–
C. *Sancak* of Malatia					
– Malatia	5	17,017	7	2	8 (1370)
– Kahta	57	10,245	11		
– Hasanmansur/ Adiyaman	21	5,202	5		4 (370)
– Behisni	8	4,550	3	1	4 (320)
– Akçadağ/Arga	5	1,691	4		4 (330)
Total	279	124,289	242	65	204 (15632)
14. Vilayet of Dyarbekir					
A. *Sancak* of Dyarbekir					
– Dyarbekir	25	16,352	10	1	11 (1300)
– Severek	8	9,275	8		3 (250)
– Derik	3	1,782	2	1	1 (50)
– Viranşehir	1	1,339	1		2 (100)
– Beşiri/Chernig	40	5,038	15		14 (700)
– Silvan	70	13,824	28	2	35 (1600)
– Lice	33	5,980	24	1	5 (305)
B. *Sancak* of Arğana Maden					
– Arğana Maden	11	10,559	10	2	7 (700)
– Palu	37	15,753	38	2	26 (2,050)
– Çermik/Chermug	3	12,418	5	1	5 (900)
C. *Sancak* of Mardin					
– Mardin	2	7,692	3		4 (800)
– Nusaybin/Nisibin	1	90	1		5 (500)
– Cezire/Cizre	12	4,281	1		
– Midyat	1	1,452	1		2 (210)
– Savur	1	1,032	1		2 (195)
Total	249	106,867	148	10	122 (9,660)

Continued

Administrative Unit	Localities	Armenians	Churches/ Monasteries		Schools
15. Vilayet of Erzerum					
A. *Sancak* of Erzerum					
– Erzerum	53	37,480	43	3	52 (6355)
– Hinis/Khnus	25	21,382	21	4	17 (871)
– Kiği/Kghi	51	19,859	45	5	63 (2925)
– Tercan/Mamahatun	41	11,690	36	2	27 (1187)
– Bayburt/Papert	30	17,060	5	3	9 (844)
– Ispir/Sper	17	2,602	17	1	13 (459)
– Tortum	13	2,829	14	1	3 (?)
– Keskin	13	8,136	14		5 (?)
– Narman	2	748	2		2 (160)
– Pasinler/Pasen	57	16,740	16	1	20 (940)
B.– *Sancak* of Erzincan					
– Erzincan	38	25,795	53	24	37 (3863)
– Pülumur/Polormor	4	862	4	3	3 (103)
– Kemah/Gamakh	15	6,396	37	6	13 (802)
– Kuruçay	6	2,989	6		5 (?)
– Refahiye/Gerjanis	3	1,570	3	2	3 (?)
C. *Sancak* of Bayazid					25 (2839)
– Bayazid	5	4,884	14	8	6 (684)
– Diyadin	8	1,649	6	11	2 (200)
– Karakilise	12	8,180	9	1	4 (?)
– Eleşgird/Alashgerd/	12	9,914	13	1	11 (960)
Toprakkale					
– Tutak	20	1,624	7		2 (?)
Total	**425**	**202,391**	**406**	**76**	**322 (21,348)**
16. Vilayet of Bitlis					
A. *Sancak* of Bitlis					
– Bitlis	57	23,899	57	8	15 (979)
– Ahlat/Khlat	22	13,432	23	4	15 (898)
– Hizan	76	8,207	48	10	14 (500)
– Modgan/Mutki	27	5,469	26	4	1 (14)
B. *Sancak* of Muş/Mush					
– Muş/Mush	103	75,623	113	74	87 (3,057)
– Sasun	156	24,233	127	6	15 (1,300)
– Malazgird/Manazgerd	39	11,931	25	45	15 (527)
– Bulanik/Pulanegh	30	25,053	29	3	14 (575)
– Varto	9	4,649	7	3	4 (210)
C. *Sancak* of Genc/Ardushen	23	4,344	18	2	5 (300)
D. *Sancak* of Siirt/Seghert					
– Siirt/Seghert	9	4,437	3	1	2 (330)
– Harzan/Kharzan	76	8,343	22	1	14 (392)
– Pervari	15	2,538	7		2 (72)
– Eruh/Bohtan	20	3,393	4		2 (120)
– Şirvan	19	2,853	11		2 (60)
Total	**681**	**218,404**	**510**	**161**	**207 (9,309)**

Continued

Administrative Unit	Localities	Armenians	Churches/ Monasteries		Schools
17. Vilayet of Van					
A. *Sancak* of Van					
– Van	116	53,589	200	19	
– Perkri	41	5,152	40	8	
– Erciş/Arjesh	54	10,381	24	4	
– Adilcevaz/Ardzge	25	6,460	19	3	
– Mahmudiye	4	826	3		
– Kiavaş/Vostan	25	6,851	30	15	
– Karcikan/Garjgan	36	7,281	26	7	
(+ Lower Gargar)					
– Moks	45	4,459	36	14	
– Şatak (+ Norduz)	65	8, 433	49	5	
B *Sancak* of Hakkari					
– Çulamerk/Chulamerg	5	534	2		
– Hoşab	12	1,746	7		2
– Elbağ/Aghpag	20	3,505	19	3	2
– Kiavar/Gevar		2	1,680		
Total	450	110,897	457	80	192
TOTAL	2,925	1,914,620	2,538	451	1,996 (173,022)

Chapter 2

The Ottoman Armenians' Socio-Economic Situation on the Eve of the War

According to the figures presented in the previous chapter, of the 2,925 towns and villages of the empire in which Armenians lived, no fewer than 2,084 were located on the Armenian high plateau, properly speaking – that is, in the vilayets of Erzerum, Van, Bitlis, Mamuret ul-Aziz, and Dyarbekir. In these basically rural regions, 762,848 Armenians, 90 per cent of them peasants, lived side by side with the Turkish population and their turbulent Kurdish neighbors. In the adjacent regions, in the vilayets of Sıvas, Trebizond, and Angora, 413,736 Armenians lived alongside Turks, Greeks, and Kurds. Peasants represented a somewhat smaller proportion of the population of these provinces: according to figures provided by the Patriarchate's 1913–14 census, approximately 80 per cent of the Armenians there lived in the countryside. To the south in Cilicia, in the vilayet of Adana and the northern part of the vilayet of Aleppo, this figure fell to 60 per cent. Of the half a million other Armenians scattered throughout the other regions of the empire, 180,667 lived in the towns and villages of Bithynia, from Ismit through Kütahya to Bursa, 60 per cent of whom earned their living by tilling the soil. Another 215,131 lived mainly in urban environments in Constantinople, Smyrna, and Thrace. Thus, it clearly appears that Armenian society was predominantly rural on the eve of the First World War, not only on the high plateau, but also in the regions beyond it.

To date, there has been no serious study of the socio-economic situation of the vilayets of the Armenian high plateau in the early twentieth century. Aside from the fact that the Armenians lived in a basically rural society that was largely autarchic, even if they also boasted a few urban centers that exported manufactured products, we know virtually nothing about the macroeconomic equilibria prevailing at the time. Nor do we know how much each of these regions contributed to the budget of the Ottoman state. The modernization of the state had, however, made it necessary to gather statistics on a regular basis. The first such statistics to be released were for fiscal years 1326 and 1327 of the Hegira (14 May 1909 to 13 May 1910 and 14 March 1910 to 13 March 1911); they appeared in the *Annual Statistical Bulletin* (later quarterly), published by the Ministry of Finance. These official statistics allow us to draw a few conclusions about the economy. First of all, expenditures and receipts were more closely balanced in the five Armenian vilayets than elsewhere. For calendar year 1326 of the Hegira (1910–11), the vilayet of Erzerum (which, according to the official statistics for the year, had 781,071 inhabitants) contributed 48,324,826 piasters to the state budget and spent 49,040,755 piasters. The vilayet of Bitlis (410,079 inhabitants) paid out 20,756,439 piasters and received 19,316,833 in exchange; the vilayet of Dyarbekir (424,760 inhabitants) contributed 27,840,936 piasters and got back 24,184,027; the province of Mamuret ul-Aziz

(455,579 inhabitants) paid in 21,842,050 piasters and received 22,050,358; and finally, the vilayet of Van (285,947 inhabitants) paid out 12,998,311 piasters and had expenditures of 18,623,690. One can see at a glance that the average per capita contribution was much the same from vilayet to vilayet. By contrast, expenditures for these eastern vilayets were proportionally twice as high as in the other provinces of the empire, with the exception of Albania, the Edirne region, and certain Arab provinces. In theory, this should have facilitated development of the basic structures and economy of these regions. A closer look at expenditures in the east shows why it did not: of a total of 133,215,663 piasters allocated to the region, no fewer than 58,136,107 went to cover the expenditures of the Ministry of War in these five vilayets, while 17,010,324 piasters went to the gendarmerie and another 10,655,062 were allocated to local agencies of the Ministry of the Interior. Thus a total of 85,801,493 piasters – two-thirds of the total expenditures in the five vilayets – went exclusively to financing repressive apparatuses: to the army as well as the gendarmerie and other agencies of the Interior Ministry. This speaks volumes about the policies of the state in the eastern vilayets of the Ottoman Empire. Plainly, these non-productive "investments," proportionally three times higher than in the rest of the empire, left no leeway for collective or social programs. The absence of such state investments probably reflects the state's intention to block the economic development of these regions, among the most neglected in the empire, in which half of all tax revenues emanated from the agricultural sector.[1]

Families and Communities: Organization and the Economy

In Armenian society, the family is more than just a solidarity network based on blood ties. It is a community in itself, with a strict hierarchy that still bears the marks of Indo-European heritage.[2] It is patriarchal and assigns a very important place to the head of the household, the *danuder*, who determines the way the family's land or other property is used. All the male descendants of a family are grouped around the *danuder*, together with the wives of his younger brothers and his sons. The whole thus formed functions in accordance with well-established rules and a precise hierarchy. In the absence of this strict form of social organization, survival would have been all but impossible in the harsh climate of many Armenian provinces, as nomads of different origins have observed throughout history. This no doubt explains why certain regions remained Armenian down to the beginning of the twentieth century, despite the Ottoman authorities' attempts to colonize them from the sixteenth century on. The partial integration of the Kurdish nomads there was made possible only by the "symbiosis" imposed by the national government. Is eastern Turkey not very sparsely populated even today? Indications are that the sedentarization of the Kurds' descendants was not successful everywhere it was attempted. It doubtless took all the know-how of an ancient agricultural civilization such as the Armenians' to produce everything that was needed to survive in these climes.

In the region of Kayseri, a couple had on average "only" slightly over four children. In Erzerum, couples had five; in Pasın, Bayburt, Kemah, Hizan, Genc, Muş, Sasun, and the vilayet of Van, couples had eight. Households were correspondingly large. As many as 70 members of the same family lived together in some mountain districts – that is, several couples and their children, as in Sasun or Moks. In the plains and valleys, an average household generally contained 30 to 40 people. In urban centers, where tradition was weaker, the brothers or the youngest sons in a family often founded households of their own. Finally, in cities such as Smyrna or Constantinople, many families consisted only of a couple and their children; the eldest son would continue to live with his parents, or the other way around.

Statistics gathered during the 1913–14 census indicate that the average number of inhabitants in a village community also varied sharply from one region to the next. In high mountain districts, many villages contained only 250 to 500 people. Yet households containing from 50 to 150 individuals were not rare there. On the plain of Muş or Harput, in contrast, villages were much larger, containing on average 700 to 800 inhabitants. In such villages, mixed populations of Christians and Muslims were more frequent than in the mountains.

In villages with fewer than one thousand inhabitants, the Ottoman administration was nonexistent. The social hierarchy was organized around the "mayor," clergy, and a "council of wise men." After 1908, schoolteachers began to occupy an ever more important place in the social life of rural communities, as both educators and activists in the political parties. The "mayor," the *danuder*, was, as the title indicates, the head of a household – the richest or the most respected. It fell on him and his peers to run community affairs, whether it was a question of the equitable distribution of water for irrigation of the fields, relations with Ottoman officialdom in the *kaza* to which the village belonged, disputes between individual peasants, distribution of the collective tax burden among the households of the village, or renovation of the village church and construction of a school. This council of wise men maintained close relations with the village priest, who was, when he was not attending to his religious duties, himself a farmer and paterfamilias like the others. Deeply attached to its Christian faith, the rural world lived a life punctuated by religious holidays, which also marked off the seasons and thus the rhythms of farm life. When nomadic Kurdish brigands attacked a village, the church served as a refuge, for it was always the most solid building in the village.

The nature of the rural economy varied, of course, from region to region. In high mountain districts such as Sasun, Moks, or Şatak, the villagers raised sheep, pigs, horses, and water buffalo. These activities, very important economically, were practiced along with agriculture. The long, snowy winters condemned most of the villages in these regions to autarchy for several months of the year, and also favored the exercise of crafts such as rug-making, pottery, carpentry, and so on. Agricultural instruments were basically made of wood, but had certain metallic parts. Plows were drawn by animals, generally oxen or water buffalo, as on the plateaus or plains. On the plains, agriculture was naturally more highly developed than elsewhere, typically consisting in the cultivation of cereal plants, grapevines, fruit trees, and vegetables. The purpose of all this activity was, as a rule, the production of an autonomous food supply rather than a marketable surplus. It was rounded off by beekeeping, which furnished sugar as well as wax for candles. As for the salt needed to preserve food, it was found in surface mines or on the shores of Lake Van. The iron and copper used by blacksmiths, tinsmiths, silverers, and so on were extracted from lodes exploited with the help of primitive techniques already in use in ancient times. Over the centuries, in short, the rigorous climate and rugged relief helped forge a nearly self-sufficient society that was inward-looking, attached to tradition, and above all concerned with living under secure conditions.

It was precisely the quest for security, which was often severely threatened, that brought Armenian peasants to abandon their land, whether it was a question, as in the sixteenth century, of deportations and deliberately induced famines, or the policy of depopulation systematically pursued by Abdülhamid and the Young Turks in his wake. Rural areas were particularly vulnerable to the *talan*, the annual raid that was most often carried out by Kurdish nomads, who did not always content themselves with the payment of tribute. Thus, every year, as if subject to a ritual, the peasants would be confronted by their nomadic neighbors, who had for centuries been accustomed to living off the sedentary inhabitants of their region.

The Armenian population, although it was robust, lived in a land with an austere climate. Nature – especially epidemics – had eliminated the weakest. Until 1844, the plague regularly raged on the Armenian high plateau, sometimes mowing down as many as half of the inhabitants of urban centers, and a somewhat smaller proportion of the population in the countryside.[3]

The Urban Centers and the Beginnings
of Industrialization

In the Armenian provinces, villages were often entirely Armenian or had mixed Armenian-Kurdish and, less frequently, Armenian-Turkish populations. A very different situation prevailed in the urban centers, which were military garrisons and the seats of the Ottoman administration. Here, Christians were not always in the majority but in almost every case lived side by side with their Muslim neighbors. The Armenians, clustered together outside the city walls in neighborhoods of their own, went downtown only to exercise their professions in their craftsmen's shops or their stands at the bazaar. At the turn of the century, they still held a virtual monopoly on local and interregional commerce, and had unchallenged control of the craft guilds. Here they perpetuated traditions and craft techniques handed down over the centuries. In the little towns, however, a significant portion of the population engaged in agricultural work: they cultivated, notably, vegetable gardens, orchards, and vineyards, with the result that these towns had something of a rural air.

As far as craftsmanship went, every region had its specialties. Thus, Eğin/Agn was famous for its goldsmiths, who plied their trade in Constantinople as well; Van was known for its skilful tailors, tinsmiths, goldsmiths, and saddle-makers; Sıvas was celebrated for the dexterity of its blacksmiths, gunsmiths, and weavers; Kayseri's architects, masons, carpenters, stone-cutters, and tapestry-makers had an excellent reputation, as did the shoemakers of Harput; Amasia, Malatia, and Hacın were known for their textiles, Muş and Bitlis for their woolens, Gümüşhane and Erzerum for their silversmiths, Erzincan and Kemah for their wholesalers, and so on. These craftsmen, the *esnafs*, who had for centuries been organized in guilds governed by statutes, also played a significant political and social role in the Ottoman Empire.

Early in the twentieth century, Armenians were also still very active in the crafts in Constantinople. In Büyükçarşi, Vezirhan, Çuhacihan, Kürkçühan, and Çarsambabazar, there were no fewer than 1,850 Armenian workshops in which some 15,000 master artisans, journeymen, and apprentices plied their trades. In the city as a whole, there were 5,000 shops and 35,979 professional craftsmen. Competing Western products, however, made the industrialization of Turkey an imperative. As early as the 1870s, certain forms of craft production, notably in the textile branch, had begun to die out because they were unable to compete with European production. The first Ottoman "industrial" enterprises appeared in this context. The Armenians quite naturally joined the new movement, unhesitatingly introducing Western technical innovations into the empire. The Armenian bourgeoisie of Constantinople and Smyrna was at the front ranks here, but notables from Bithynia, Cilicia, and to a lesser extent the Armenian high plateau were also very dynamic. Inhabitants of the high plateau, lacking means of transportation and practicable roads, lived, as we have pointed out, in a state of permanent insecurity, and it did not easily lend itself to large-scale industrialization.

Steam engines, power looms, iron furnaces, and so on were slowly making their way into the empire. Tobacco factories, flourmills, textile factories (cotton mills, silk mills, and wool mills), as well as shipyards, were largely in Armenian hands.

Armenians also took an active part in trade and finance. The monopoly of local trade and international commerce characteristic of Armenians in the east was no less striking in Istanbul, Smyrna, and other cities in the west of the empire. These individual successes, which some tend to celebrate as proof of the benevolent attitude of the Ottoman government towards the Armenians, in no way reflect the policy of the sultans vis-à-vis the Armenian population.

As a result of local conditions as well as the subordinate status that the Armenians had had for centuries, even affluent Armenians rarely made a show of their wealth by building outwardly resplendent homes. The interiors of their homes, on the other hand, were often marked by great refinement, with harmonious inner courts, murals, and libraries fitted out with elaborately worked wainscoting. The sumptuous homes of the Armenian quarter of Kayseri, which were only recently torn down, bore witness to the affluence and tastes of this provincial bourgeoisie, as do the many still extant, albeit dilapidated and sometimes completely neglected, mansions in Sıvas, Erzerum, and Kars.

Chapter 2.1

The Eradication of the Armenian Population in the Provinces of the Ottoman Empire: Reasons for a Regional Approach

On the threshold of the fourth part of the present work, about the first stage of the genocide, we ought perhaps to explain why we have placed so voluminous a file in the middle of the book – a file that is, moreover, largely empirical. We could, of course, have omitted it and continued instead to examine the mechanisms put in place by the Young Turk regime to liquidate the provincial Armenian population. Had we done so, however, it would have been much harder, if not impossible, to take stock of the differences in the way the various regions were treated and to grasp the complexity of the machinery of destruction. Omitting this section would also have precluded an assessment of the precise role of local governments and the army, and would have obscured the activity of the Special Organization, especially in the eastern provinces. In the absence of regional studies, we might also have been tempted to make do with approximations: the socio-economic dimension of the genocidal enterprise, particularly the activity of the commissions responsible for "abandoned property," might well have escaped our notice, along with the possibility of accurately weighing up the demographic issues involved in evicting the Armenians from their homes and settling "Turkish" *muhacirs* in their place. Moreover, a regional approach makes it much easier to appreciate the victims' experience in each of the regions involved. Finally, it allows us to pinpoint the historical moment at which a world came to an end: the violent disappearance of an Armenian presence in the area that went back 3,000 years.

Obviously, the regional treatment proposed here presupposes knowledge of the mechanism of destruction. Starting out by considering the "operating instructions," however, has its disadvantages. While there is a pedagogical justification for beginning that way, from a methodological standpoint it is open to the objection that only micro-historical examination makes macro-historical observation possible. We have consequently chosen to draw the central lessons of the Young Turk experiment only after immersing ourselves in events in the provinces. Moreover, our discussion in the third part of this study of the nature of the Special Organization, its hierarchy, and its activities in the opening months of the war, together with our examination of the functioning of the *emvali metruke* commissions – that is, the apparatus of destruction and confiscation – has laid bare the foundations of the genocidal process. The CUP's driving role and the activity of the government ministries, local officials, and coordinators known as "responsible secretaries" or provincial delegates of the CUP have also been approached from a structural angle. Thus, the fourth part of our study draws a sort of line of demarcation between the entity that conceived the program of eradication and

ultimately set it in motion and the concrete realization of the plan by the structures thus
called into existence. Finally, approaching the matter from this angle focuses our attention
on the same set of problems that the Ittihad's Central Committee itself confronted when it
decided to carry out its plan to eliminate the Armenians at what it deemed the most opportune moment. We have, in some sense, once again pulled out the ethnographic maps that it
used to plan the liquidation of the Armenians and homogenize Anatolia.

To grasp all the different facets of this complex question, we had no choice but to examine
the traces left not only by the actors – the victims and their executioners – but also by "outside" witnesses whose own interests in the acts committed varied. American missionaries
or diplomats, as well as German or Austro-Hungarian officers or consuls, have viewpoints
shaped by their personal experiences and the status of the state or organization that they
serve. Similarly, the way the victims and executioners view events is largely conditioned
by their individual status and religious confession. In other words, the actors invested with
state legitimacy will tend to legitimize their actions by evoking the higher interests of the
state, just as the actor-victims will tend to condemn their "natural" predators, the more so as
they only rarely possess the means needed to grasp the real nature of the operations directed
against them.

The historian is of course often confronted with accounts that describe the same events as
seen through radically opposed interpretive grids, with Western observers as "umpires" – this
was often the case in the Ottoman Empire of the day – marked by their religious convictions
and specific military or political interests. There was virtually no town in the empire, however unprepossessing, that did not have its American or German eyewitnesses, although only
some of these eyewitnesses had experience (sometimes long-time experience) of the country
and, as a result, the ability to understand local phenomena "from the inside." Despite the
inherent weaknesses of some of these accounts, they remain indispensable when it comes
to establishing the credibility of survivors' testimony. But they have another by no means
negligible merit: they provide us with crucially important clues about the actions of the local
civilian and military authorities to whom the diplomats and missionaries often turned in
their capacity as spokespersons for the Armenian population.

As for information provided by the victims, which researchers long dismissed, it must
first be pointed out that only accounts made while the events related were still "fresh" – that
is, accounts dating from the immediate postwar period – are utilized here. These accounts
were collected by the Armenian Patriarchate of Constantinople and the Armenian National
Unions formed to care for the deportees in the same period, or else stem from evidence given
by survivors at the first 1919–20 Istanbul trials of Young Turks implicated in war crimes and
the massacre of Armenians. Such material sometimes allows us to draw valuable lessons
about the psychology of the executioners from the courtroom confrontations between the
victims and their executioners. Some of these documents have been published in their original language; many others remain in manuscript form.

Official and semi-official Young Turk sources are problematic. It is known that certain sets
of documents concerning the treatment of the Armenians that emanated from the Ministry
of the Interior or the CUP's Constantinople headquarters were destroyed or shipped to an
unknown destination. This point will be discussed in detail in Part Six. Yet, however many
precautions the Unionist leaders took, they were unable, for technical reasons, to destroy
all the documents produced by the government. In other words, only a small fraction of
this material is currently accessible; yet even this fraction provides insight into the way the
genocidal machinery worked.

The indictment and the supporting evidence presented to the court-martial on 27 April
1919 indicate that in the course of the criminal investigation it became obvious that a good
many of the "documents concerning this Organization as well all the documents of the Central

Committee were stolen."[1] It appears, then, that the archives of the Special Organization and the Ittihadist Central Committee, whose interrelations we have already discussed, were spirited away from the Nuri Osmaniye headquarters by a party official immediately following the resignation of Talât's cabinet on 7 October 1918. According to the Partriarchate's Bureau of Information, it was Midhat Sükrü who purged the files at party headquarters.[2]

The same indictment cites a note (No. 31) from the minister of the interior "which proves that files containing important information and the correspondence of the Organization were removed by Aziz Bey, the Director of the Department of Criminal Investigations [of the Department of State Security], before Talât resigned."[3] In question here are probably the thousands of instructions, circulars, and encrypted telegrams that the interior and war ministries sent to the valis of the provinces and the army commanders, as well as statistics concerning the deported and massacred Armenians. This material was apparently kept, according to the same judicial source, in the offices of the Political Department of the Interior Ministry, where it was deposited in the files of the Special Organization known as the "Special Secret Archives." It, too, was removed in early October 1918, two days before Talât resigned, loaded into light wooden crates and sent to an unknown destination. At any rate, such was the answer that the minister of the interior gave upon repeated questioning by the court-martial.[4]

Despite the precautions taken by the Young Turk leadership, as we have said, it proved technically impossible to eliminate all traces of the genocidal operations.[5] The first category of documents, encrypted originals, is extremely rare, for such documents were briefly kept in the files of the Post and Telegraph Office before being transferred to the files of the Interior Ministry or the Department of Security in Constantinople under the name *Mahrim dosieler* (secret files). In contrast, the second category of materials, the encrypted telegrams sent by the administration of the Post and Telegraph Office and then transcribed locally, is more common. Decoded by the addressees, who knew the code – as a rule, the vali of the province to which these telegrams were sent or his private secretary – they comprise the message received in coded form as well as the decoded version, written between the lines of the coded message if there was room enough or, if not, on the bottom or back of the page bearing the coded message. Once the originals of the encrypted telegrams were decoded, they were signed or initialed by the vali and his assistant and provided with one or more marginal annotations by the same vali and/or the assistant director of the Bureau of Deportees, who was responsible for carrying out the orders received. Sometimes the police chief or commander of the gendarmerie played this role.

The third category of document is still more common: it comprises copies of encrypted telegrams, accompanied either by another copy of the encoded text and the decoded text, or the decoded text alone. What are involved here are certified copies of the originals of the encrypted telegrams, authenticated by the secretary general of the vilayet before being transmitted to the Ministry of the Interior, the president of the Commission of Inquiry (the Mazhar Commission) or the judge presiding over the court-martial.

The investigative files prepared by the Mazhar Commission and court-martial include material falling into the two last-named categories. These documents came from virtually all the provinces, where it had obviously proved impossible to "clean house" thoroughly. It was the documents included in these investigative files, available to the plaintiffs, which the Armenian Patriarchate of Constantinople legally obtained in the form of certified copies in its capacity as representative of the community.

Only a few vilayets responded to the demand for materials formulated by the Ottoman legal institutions, notably the vilayets of Konya and Angora.[6] However, insofar as the documents involved were circulars sent to all the provinces, the materials transmitted from these vilayets to Istanbul are a source of first-hand information.

Chapter 3

Deportations and Massacres in the Vilayet of Erzerum

The vilayet of Erzerum was the major theater of the fighting between the Russians and Turks and, as such, constituted a central strategic stake of the First World War. The fortress of Erzerum and the surrounding plain constituted the rear base of the Third Army, which had its headquarters in Tortum, north of the regional capital. With the failure of the Turkish offensive in winter 1914–15, the Third Army was decimated and the Ottoman general staff had to make a strenuous effort to form new unities. In February, Enver suggested that Liman von Sanders, the head of the German military mission, take command of this front, but the German general rejected the offer since the troops with which he was supposed to rebuild the army were in a catastrophic state: "approximately one-third of the troops in the region's training camps were ill, while another third had deserted on their way to the recruitment centers."[1] The command of the Third Army had consequently been entrusted to Kâmil, a former classmate of the minister of war.[2] From the moment he took office in May, the new vali of Erzerum, Tahsin Bey,[3] had also been confronted with a typhus epidemic that was wreaking havoc on the soldiers and the civilian population (he had been briefly aided in his new post, as we have seen, by the president of the Teşkilât-ı Mahsusa, Bahaeddin Şakir, before Şakir's departure for Istanbul on 13 March 1915).[4] Thereupon, Filibeli Ahmed Hilmi Bey, a famous CUP *fedayi*, took the reins of the Special Organization as its interim president.

So far, we have seen that the violence inflicted on the Armenian population, which basically occurred during the military operations in the winter of 1914–15, affected border zones and can be explained in terms of strategic imperatives and the Ittihad's desire to eliminate potential enemies.[5] The rest of the vilayet of Erzerum had, generally speaking, been spared massacres. On the other hand, we noted the excesses that accompanied the military requisitions, as well as acts of violence, confirmed by German diplomats, in certain *kazas* of the Erzerum vilayet.[6] The incidents were serious enough that the German ambassador Wangenheim felt compelled "to address them in conversations with the Sublime Porte ... The Grand Vizier thinks that these incidents could not have taken place without provocation from the Armenians." The German consul Paul Schwarz, however, noted in a 5 December 1914 report to his ambassador that the Armenians were in a state of high alarm as a result of certain incidents "that they considered to be warning signs of new massacres." He mentioned in particular the murder of the parish priest in Odzni on 1 December by "three Turkish irregulars" who had spent the night in his house, as well as the exactions committed by other *çetes* of the Special Organization (for example, in the village of Tevfik, where a dozen irregulars had illegally locked up the men of the village because they were unable to produce the 100 Turkish pounds demanded of them).[7] Violence had also been perpetrated by regular Turkish troops, who compensated for the shortage of barracks by taking up quarters in Armenian villages, evicting the inhabitants and consuming their food reserves.[8]

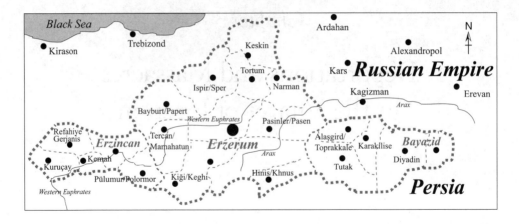

The celebrations and patriotic manifestations that had been organized in the capital after the capture of Ardahan[9] were now things of the past, as were the congratulations that Enver Pasha had extended to the Armenian primate of Konya on the conduct of the Armenian soldiers on the Caucasian front.[10] On his retreat to Erzerum, moreover, the minister of war had taken 200 Armenians from the Olti area hostage. They were imprisoned in Erzerum and later executed.[11] Enver also had 30 Armenian civilians from Ardahan, whom he had likewise taken hostage after the defeat at Sarıkamiş, hanged beneath the ramparts of Erzerum at the Istanbul Gate.[12] To be sure, the allegedly hostile activity of these foreign civilians was cited to justify the treatment meted out to them, but it did not frighten the Armenian population of Erzerum any less for that. The Armenians interpreted it as a clear sign of the Young Turk government's mood.

The intensification of the hostility toward the Armenians peaked, without a doubt, on 10 February 1915, when, in broad daylight, two soldiers murdered the assistant director of the Erzerum branch of the Banque Ottomane, Setrak Pastermajian, in the middle of the street. The directors of the bank in Constantinople learned that the local authorities had announced that Pastermajian had died of typhus,[13] which was then raging in the region. In private, however, as well as in diplomatic circles, it was rumored that he had been killed because his brother, a former parliamentary deputy from the vilayet, was working for the Russians. The military commander of the garrison, General Posseldt, who took an interest in the matter, observed that the murderers, whom everyone knew, had not been arrested.[14] This was an indication that the soldiers had been acting under orders. According to Constantin Trianfidili, a Greek notable from Erzerum, many more Turks than Christians had refused to enlist in the army ever since the 3 August announcement of the general mobilization, yet only the Christians were harassed. The same witness claimed that Pastermajian had been murdered in order to see how the Armenians would react, and they had not budged.[15] For his part, Alphonse Arakelian observes that "the deportations did not come out of a clear blue sky; the government first had recourse to provocations." Bands of çetes raped and looted in the rural districts, while murders of soldiers took place more frequently.[16] But "still no-one budged." The Armenians of Erzerum knew, says the same witness, that a large number of military units had pitched camp in the area; "what is more, almost all the young Armenian men were already in the army."[17] Thus, here, as in the vilayet of Van, provocations began mushrooming from February 1915 on, although the phenomenon did not take on the dimensions it did there.

As has already been said, a good many Armenian inhabitants of the *kazas* of Pasın (pop. 12,914), Narman (pop. 655), Bayazid (pop. 1,735), Dyadin (pop. 1,111), Karakilisa (pop. 6,034), and Alaşkert (pop. 7,732) – a total of 30,181 villagers in all (3,726 households) – followed the retreating Russian forces in late December and early January.[18] In the *kaza* of Pasın, however, only the Lower Pasın district was evacuated. In areas further to the west, not far from Erzerum, 4,000 people remained behind, notably in Ekabad, Hertev, Hasankale, and Badijavan.[19] In late March, the peasants of these villages in the Pasın district were deported on the pretext that "they lived too close to the border and there was good reason to be suspicious of the Armenians."[20]

These provocations notwithstanding, the Armenians of Erzerum were not unduly molested until April. When violence did occur, the primate, Smpat Saadetian, would go with a few other notables to lodge a complaint with Vali Tahsin, who "played dumb or pretended to be deaf, depending on the circumstances."[21] The first sign of alarm came in late February 1915, when 70 Armenian notables from Erzerum were arrested. Sixty of those detained were released after the prelate interceded on their behalf, but ten members of the editorial board of the Dashnak newspaper *Harach*, Aram Adruni and his comrades, were kept in prison and then transferred to an unknown destination.[22] The target of these actions was plainly the local Dashnak committee. For the time being, however, the local authorities seemed to content themselves with measures of intimidation.

As elsewhere, the Armenian elite of the region was arrested on 24 and 25 April 1915. Some 200 individuals were apprehended, including the Dashnak leaders Kegham Balasanian, Stepan Stepanian (known as Maral), Pilos, and Mihran Terlemezian.[23] The next day, Adruni, Stepanian, Balasanian, Hrant Koseyan and Boghos Papaklian, among others – 30 notables in all – were ordered to be transferred to Erzincan and were slain on their way there.[24] The others were held in the central prison of Erzincan and interrogated under torture about arms caches as well as alleged plans to revolt.[25] Four to five hundred prisoners were squeezed into squalid cells. Officially, the aim was to forestall a general insurrection. The real aim, however, was to obtain compromising "revelations" by means of torture. These confessions were meant to justify in advance the events that were about to unfold.

A telegram that Bahaeddin Şakir sent on 21 April 1915 from Erzerum to the CUP delegate responsible for the vilayet of Mamuret ul-Aziz, Resneli Boşnak Nâzım Bey, shows that the head of the Teşkilât-ı Mahsusa had returned to the region in the latter half of April.[26] He quickly set up a special deportation committee; Cemal Bey, secretary general of the vilayet (a sort of "vice vali") and an influential member of Erzerum's Ittihadist club, was named as its president. He was assisted by the *kaymakam* of Hasankale, Tahir Bey; Hulusi Bey, the police chief; Mustafa Efendi Ali Guzelzâde, an Ittihadist; and Jafer Mustafa Effendi, the commander of the squadrons of the Teşkilât-ı Mahsusa in Erzerum. All deportation orders were executed under the supervision of this committee, which handled the lists of deportees.[27] The *çetes* were under the supervision of Filibeli Ahmed Hilmi Bey, Şakir's assistant. Information communicated to ambassador Wangenheim by the German vice-consul Scheubner-Richter, who was reporting explanations given by Vali Tahsin, indicates that the deportation orders were issued by the military authorities – more exactly, by the commander of the Third Army, Mahmud Kâmil – whereas the civilian authorities, especially the vali, were reluctant to implement these measures.[28]

Thanks to information provided by an Armenian survivor from Erzerum, Boghos Vartanian,[29] we can give a more coherent explanation of the process that culminated in the application of the decision to eradicate the Armenians. According to Vartanian, the Sublime Porte sent a telegram to Erzerum about the treatment to be meted out to the Armenians. In response, a secret meeting was held at Vali Hasan Tahsin's residence from 18 April to 21 April 1915. In attendance were the local Ittihadist leaders and notables from the city, some 120 people in all. Those present fell into three groups. A group of 40 people argued for limiting the pending measures to removing the Armenians from the border zones. The 20 people in the second group recommended that the Armenians be left alone. A third block,

headed by the vali, the parliamentary deputy Seyfullah, and the principal Young Turk leaders of the city, demanded "that all the Armenians be eradicated, that all of them be taken
from their homes and then massacred, until not a one is left alive." The date of this conclave
gives us reason to think that Şakir and Filibeli Hilmi took a discrete part in the discussions,
submitting the "patriotic" arguments of the Young Turk Central Committee to the consideration of their friends from Erzerum. It is, consequently, probable that local officialdom and
the local elite were brought into the decision-making process in all the vilayets. The content
of the message that Şakir sent from Erzerum to the CUP delegate in Harput, Resneli Nâzım,
on the last day of the Erzerum conclave, 21 April 1915,[30] reinforces this suspicion.

Furthermore, a cable that Vali Tahsin sent to the minister of the interior on 13 May 1915[31]
seems to confirm that the army played the central role in the initial operations aimed at
cleansing the region of its Armenians. More exactly, it confirms that the CUP had chosen to
address its deportation orders to the military hierarchy as a way of legitimizing its discourse
about ensuring the security of the army's rear. Concealed behind this official facade, however,
as the instructions dispatched by the interior minister show, was an administrative apparatus
on the one hand and the Young Turk network on the other. Yet we must not neglect the real
hostility of certain high-ranking government officials to these measures, either because they
were loath to carry out such tasks or, as in the case of Hasan Tahsin, because they were aware
of all the negative consequences that this deportation could have for the local economy,
the provisioning of the army and, more generally, the maintenance of social peace in the
vilayet. Tahsin was also made uncomfortable by allegations of an Armenian insurrection,
which seemed too implausible to him; he suggested that the civilian population be allowed
to remain at home.[32] But the official response of the minister of the interior, dated 23 May,
recommended that the civilian officials of the eastern vilayets apply the orders issued by the
military authorities[33] – in other words, by the commander of the Third Army, which had
jurisdiction over the six eastern vilayets.

The collection of documents for the years 1915–20 published by the General Directorate
of the State Archives unfortunately does not include the deportation order transmitted to
the valis, probably because it did not have an official character. According to Sebuh Aguni,
who had a great many documents at his disposal in his time, this order arrived in Erzerum
on 5 May 1915,[34] even before the cabinet had officially decided, on 13 May,[35] to deport the
Armenian population and, on the 27 May, made the "law" on the matter public.[36] Thus,
there was a marked lag between the CUP's political decisions, the corresponding discussions
in the provinces, and their formal translation. The only information we have on the content
of the message sent to the local governments is provided indirectly by the resolution of the
Council of Ministers, which still bears the marks of the Ittihad's militant discourse and is
much less formal than the "temporary deportation law" published two weeks later. The resolution is, in fact, of the order of a propaganda declaration: it evokes, pell-mell, "Armenians
engaged in dangerous operations, collaborating with the enemy, slaughtering an innocent
[Muslim] population and plotting rebellions."[37]

It is probable that the Ittihadist leaders came to the conclusion, after publishing a resolution designed for internal consumption, that it was not likely to appear credible outside
Ottoman circles. In any event, the deportation orders in the three eastern provinces of Van,
Bitlis, and Erzerum were issued before any decision had been reached by the cabinet. The
Central Committee used its own channels to circulate them, but rapidly realized that, despite
the presence of its delegates in the provinces, it could not set its extermination program in
motion without offering local governments a legal justification for their acts. In other words,
the CUP was at the outset certainly planning to conduct operations in line with its usual
internal procedures – in secret and without the slightest legal grounding – but then changed
its mind.

It is doubtless no accident that on the very day on which Talât confirmed the deportations from the vilayet of Erzerum – 23 May – the minister of the post and telegraph office ordered that all its Armenian employees in the provinces of Erzerum, Angora, Adana, Sıvas, Dyarbekir, and Van be dismissed.[38] The desire to ensure the confidentiality of communications and the nature of the orders to come undoubtedly mandated such precautions.

The first operations targeting Armenian civilians were so violent that, notwithstanding the many measures taken in advance to keep them out of the public eye, the German vice-consul, Scheubner-Richter, felt compelled to alert his embassy. For his part, Dr. Mordtmann, who was responsible for the "Armenian file" at the embassy, demanded an explanation from the interior minister. Talât responded that very serious charges had been leveled against the Armenians of Erzerum, who were involved in a conspiracy.[39] He saw proof of this in the discovery of "bombs," a term to which the minister of the interior frequently resorted by way of explanation. Yet the German diplomat's reports and the official correspondence published by the General Directorate of the State Archives, which are rife with accusations of this kind, make no mention of such discoveries in Erzerum. No doubt Talât had been extemporizing. He informed the Germans in the same breath that the decision to deport the Armenians was irrevocable.

Deportations from Erzerum and the Surrounding Countryside

Once the decision had been made, the procedure that the authorities in Erzerum followed for deporting Armenian civilians seems to have unfolded in accordance with a pre-established plan. Indeed, a region-by-region chronology of the deportations rather clearly shows that the strategy was to evacuate the eastern *kazas* of the vilayet first, followed by the rural areas around the provincial capital, in order to isolate the Armenian population of Erzerum and eliminate any possibility that it might receive outside support. Examination of the facts also reveals that the organizers of the deportation sought to empty the towns and villages lying along the planned deportation routes, and also to vary those routes so as to isolate the convoys of deportees as much as possible from each other, thus reducing the risk of resistance. Furthermore, particularly in the case of Erzerum, the deportation committee chose to include people in certain social categories in the first convoy, such as big merchants and traders. We cannot explain this choice on the basis of the sources at our disposal, but the rapid expulsion of these prominent men, who were a burden on Tahsin and must have had support among the local Turkish population, would seem to have been a prudent next step after the arrest of the political and intellectual elite in late April. Yet gradually isolating Erzerum also had its disadvantages. News of the massacres of the villagers from the plain or the outlying *kazas* reached the Armenian authorities in short order. The primate, Smpat Saadetian, reacted, as usual in the Ottoman Empire, by going to see the vali and asking him whether the Armenians of Erzerum were to be subjected to the same fate. Saadetian asked Tahsin why there had been so many murders of Armenian draftees assigned to the *amele taburis* since 14 May, and why the Armenian villagers of the plain of Erzerum, who had set out for Mamahatun in three big caravans on 16 May, had been systematically massacred in the vicinity of Erzerum.[40] As happened elsewhere – we have already seen how valis and *mutesarifs* in Van and Bitlis/Mush maintained ostensibly friendly relations with the Armenians' civilian and religious leaders down to the last moment – Tahsin did his best to seem reassuring, explaining to the prelate that these had been regrettable incidents that would not be repeated, since he had taken all the measures required to prevent "Kurdish brigands" from again attacking the convoys of Armenian deportees.

The German vice-consul, Scheubner-Richter likewise informed the vali that he disapproved of the massacres that had been perpetrated against the deportees. In response, Tahsin

Bey expressed his regrets and declared that such things would not happen again. At the same time, he took refuge in the statement that it was Mahmud Kâmil who held "real power" in the region.[41] But all of this high government official's skill proved insufficient to mask the Ittihadists' true objectives. The one thing that neither the prelate nor the diplomat knew was that, behind the official figure of Tahsin, there existed a well-organized apparatus, that of the Teşkilât-ı Mahsusa, supervised by one of the three leading members of the Young Turk Central Committee, Bahaeddin Şakir.

The First Convoy from Erzerum

Obviously, the 14 June departure of this first group did not escape the German vice-consul's attention, the more so as it included the most influential Armenian families in Erzerum.[42] Such information as the vice-consul possessed, however, was quite superficial: all he really knew was that the men in the convoy had been killed on the road. Only the accounts of the survivors from this group give us an inside view of the way the executioners went about their work. Shushanig M. Dikranian and Adelina Mazmanian were both in this convoy, and endured the ordeals inflicted on it along with all the others. The two women provide converging information about the convoy's date of departure, 16 June 1915, and the number of families it included, 25, making a total of about 150 people.[43] They disagree, however, about the number of gendarmes escorting the convoy – one says 30, the other 50 – although both give the name of the gendarmes' commanding officer, Captain Nusret.[44] Mazmanian even identifies almost all the families in the convoy: Mazmanian, Kazanjian, Ohanian, Janisian, Arushanian, Seferian, Dikranian, Nalbandian, Oskerchian, Mesrikian, Stepanian, Sarafian, Danielian, Movsesian, Musheghian, Samuelian (the two last-named families came from Kghi), Karagiulian, Der Melkisetegian, Keoseyan, Mozian, and Chiregian. These families took 30 loads of goods with them on muleback. Beginning the very first time they pitched camp, a ritual seems to have been observed: each gendarme chose a family and sat down for dinner at the table that that family set up under a tent. Thus, this first convoy was rather special, since it was traveling under conditions characterized by a certain standard of comfort. Moreover, it did not take the northwestern route that led toward Erzincan, where the killing fields under the control of the Special Organization's "butchers' battalions" were to be found, but rather the route leading southwest toward Kığı and Palu.

On the third day, the relationship between the gendarmes and the notables in this first convoy began to change. Captain Nusret suggested to those "under his protection" that they entrust him with the sum of 600 Turkish pounds so that he could satisfy the demands of the Kurdish brigands dogging the convoy.[45] After 11 days on the road, the deportees arrived in the *kaza* of Kığı, near the village of Şoğ, where they were threatened by Kurdish *çetes*. According to Mazmanian, the headman of the neighboring village, Husni Bey, promised to protect them from the Kurds following them for one night in exchange for 260 Turkish pounds. It was in Şoğ that the caravan was looted and three men – Musheghian, Hagop Samuelian and Nazaret Keogishian (a native of Arapkir) – were killed.[46] Dikranian notes that during this first act of the deportees' drama the *çetes* reminded them that revolutionaries had massacred the population in Van, "tearing fetuses from their mothers' bellies and dishonoring the young women." They used these false rumors, spread by the Turkish press, to justify the crimes they themselves were committing.

The worst, however, was yet to come. The next day, at an hour's march from Şoğ, while the convoy was making its way through a thick forest, the Armenian deportees were surrounded by a thousand Kurds under the command of two *çete* leaders from the Special Organization, Ziya Beg of Başköy[47] and Adıl Bey (whose real name was Adil Güzelzâde Şerif).[48] The two men proposed to escort them safely as far as Harput in exchange for a certain sum. They also promised to bring 50 gendarmes from Kığı in order to protect the caravan from the local Kurdish and Turkish populace. Shortly thereafter someone blew a whistle. Nusret, the captain of the gendarmerie who was leading the convoy, stepped aside and the massacre began.[49] According to Mazmanian, the çetes killed one of the editors of *Harach*, Ardashes Kagakian, as well as Kalust Garabedian; Hovhannes, Armenag, Diran and Rupen Hanesian and three of the Hanesian children; Mkhitar, Aram, Mushegh, and Satenig Mesrigian and two of the Mesrigian children; Levon and Vahan Mazmanian (their sisters, our eyewitness and her younger sister Vartanush, were abducted by Kurds); Hagop Karagulian and his wife Armig (their two children, Nvart and Krikorig, disappeared); Yervant Keoseyan and his children Aram and Dikran; the Antranig brothers; Mardiros and Karnig Dikranian, their married sister Aghavni Mnatsaganian and her two children; Arshag, Sarkis and Krikor Seferian; Garabed, Levon and Siragan Arzanian; Pakrad Daniélian; Toros Ohanian (his daughter Mayranush was abducted by Ziya Beg); Siragan Geogushian; Bedros from Harput; Hagop Nalbandian and his son; Harutiun and Hagop Alzugian; Hovhannes Der Melkisedegian, his son Hampartsum and his grandson; Dikran Oskrchian and his sons Yervant and Harutiun; Harutiun Sarafian; Harutiun Stepanian; Kevork Ghazigian; and Garabed and Hagop Zeregian, as well as other old men, women and children whose "names" our witness had "forgotten."[50]

According to Shushanig Dikranian, the çetes were soon replaced by Kurdish women armed with knives, who swooped down on the rest of the convoy, shouting "Para, para!" (money, money) and rifling through the corpses.[51] Our two witnesses confirm that two men survived because they were dressed in women's clothing – Vahan Dikranian, who was wounded, and a servant named Parsegh, a native of Vartag. Shushanig alone adds that the men defended themselves and killed 17 Kurds before they were overpowered and killed.[52] A few women and their children took refuge behind Captain Nusret and thus escaped the carnage, but not the executioners' insults and their descriptions of the way they had "hacked [the women's] husbands and children to pieces." Several young women who had been stripped naked refused to follow Nusret nude. The gendarmes eventually brought them clothing stained with the blood of other, murdered members of the convoy. A few Kurds continued to attack a child. An old man told them to leave the child alone: "It's a pity," he said, "let me have him. Why kill him? He'll grow up and will be able to do all sorts of things." In the end, the child left with the remains of the convoy. Of the survivors, ten more women were carried off by Kurds. Among them were Nvart Karagulian, Mayranush Ohanian ("she is now with the çete Sayin, in a village in the Dyarbekir area"), and Vartanush Mazmanian.

After traversing Palu, the 30 or so survivors trekked through the village of Bazu, where the ground was littered with corpses and there was hardly a sign of life. A 25-year-old man, who had hidden in a mulberry tree, was apparently the only survivor.[53] When the group reached the plain of Harput – this is an interesting detail – and then the little town of Hiuseinig, the Armenian population had not yet been deported. When the people of Hiuseinig saw the condition of their compatriots from Erzerum, says Shushanig Dikranian, they began to realize what lay in store for them. In the principal city in the vilayet, Harput, the deportation of the population was just beginning when this group of survivors arrived. The prelate, Bsag *vartabed*, and other dignitaries had just been put on the road. The deportees now understood that their hopes of receiving help from their compatriots were in vain. These 30 women and children were soon Islamicized and parceled out among various Turkish households, where some of them (Gayane Nalbandian and Nazenig Zeregian) found new husbands.[54] After the deportees had remained there for 40 days, the deported women were apprehended by the police in the homes in which they had been placed. Vahan Dikranian, the only surviving man, was incarcerated with the 900 Armenians being detained in the prison of Harput. Every night, Shushanig Dikranian reports, small groups of these men were taken from the prison, led outside the city limits and killed. One night the prison caught fire. The authorities declared that *fedayis* were responsible for the blaze. This was true in a sense: the fire had spread to the prison from the pyre on which the corpses of 20 Armenian "*fedayis*" were being immolated.[55]

Shushanig Dikranian made several attempts to save her brother-in-law, Vahan Dikranian, by appealing to the military authorities. It turned out that the commander of the garrison in Mamuret ul-Aziz, Süleyman Faik, knew her family, the Der Azarians. Faik promised that he would see to it that Vahan Dikranian was not killed, even while reminding Shushanig, to show her how generous his act was, that the local authorities had in their possession "an order from Istanbul to the effect that [the Turks] should not leave a single Armenian alive on the face of the earth." Shushanig Dikranian asked him why, in that case, were she and the other women not dead? The brigadier general's answer was, as it were, a practical expression of the Ittihadists' Turkism: "Because our own women are utterly ignorant, we have to take Armenian women to improve our family lives." Shushanig herself was confronted with a practical application of this Young Turk officer's views. A Turkish family sought her 12-year-old daughter in marriage for their young son. The girl rebelled at the idea, saying that the people who wanted her to marry into their family had murdered her father. In fact, the approximately 200 women and girls from diverse localities who had found refuge in Harput by then were invited to convert to Islam.[56] A ceremony was organized by the authorities. It afforded Turkish families an opportunity to select a daughter-in-law for themselves.

These operations offer an occasion to evaluate the nature of the relations that were subsequently established between the families of the newlyweds. Shushanig's "in-laws," for example, demanded that she procure the means they needed to send her future son-in-law to pursue his studies Constantinople. Apparently some people were not unaware that these rich families had accounts in the Erzerum branch of the Banque Ottomane. What they did not know, however, was that the directors of this bank in Constantinople had set a limit of 25 Turkish pounds per person on withdrawals by Armenian deportees.[57] Shushanig Dikranian's request, made under her former name, to make a withdrawal from the bank was honored two weeks later, when she received 50 Turkish pounds from the bank, enough to rid herself of her "in-laws." These forms of pressure induced the Armenians to turn to the American consulate, where they were apparently well received. As the circumcision ceremony of her son Bedros drew closer, Shushanig decided to flee to Aleppo.[58] Adelina Mazmanian, for her part, chose to return to Erzincan, and then Erzerum by way of Dersim when she learned that Erzerum had fallen to the Russians.[59]

The Second Convoy from Erzerum

After the departure of the first convoy, the primate of Erzerum, Smpat Saadetian, who had received specific information about the massacres in the *sancak* of Erzincan, went to see the vali and the German vice-consul. The vali told him that the Armenians of Erzerum would be spared and that incidents of the kind he had been told about would not happen again. The German promised to protect the Armenian bishop. The primate let himself be persuaded and urged his flock to obey. The second convoy set out in the direction of Bayburt on 18 June 1915. It was made up of 1,300 middle-class families, who were joined en route by 370 families from the little town of Garmirk (in the *kaza* of Kiskim), making a total of some 10,000 people. They were escorted by hundreds of gendarmes commanded by Captain Muştağ and Captain Nuri, under the supervision of two leaders of the Special Organization, the *kaymakam* of Kemah and Kozukcioğlu Munir.[60] Two survivors from this convoy, Garabed Deirmenjian and Armenag Sirunian, later stated, referring to their arrival in Pirnagaban, a village halfway between Erzerum and Bayburt: "We encountered an automobile in which the famous Dr. Bahaeddin Şakir and Oturakci Şevket were sitting ... We learned a few days later that they were on their way back from Ispir, where they had organized the eradication of all the Armenians living in that district."[61] The caravan made its way through Bayburt, which had already been emptied of its Armenian population, and reached the bridge that spans the Euphrates at the entrance to the Kemah gorge without mishap. Here *çete* bands led by Oturakci Şevket and Hurukcizâde Vehib sorted the deportees into groups. Several hundred men were separated from the rest of the convoy. Guarded by *çetes*, the caravan continued on its way southwest as far as the area around Hasanova. There, the irregulars of the Special Organization extorted money from the deportees, who were traveling on foot or in carts and pitched their tents every night. They then proceeded to carry out the first massacre. Thereafter, the convoy continued on its way, passing close by Eğin/Agn and Arapkir, and finally arriving near Malatia. There, the deportees camped in a place known as Bey Bunar, where their guards from Erzerum turned them over to the local authorities, first and foremost the *mutesarif* of Malatia, Reşid Bey.[62]

When the caravan reached the mountain district of Kahta, south of Malatia and east of Adiyaman, the deportees were suddenly confronted with an appalling sight: the gorge just outside Fırıncılar was filled with the corpses of people from earlier convoys. They were, in fact, entering one of the main killing fields regularly used by the Teşkilât-ı Mahsusa. It had been put under the supervision of the parliamentary deputy from Dersim, Haci Baloşzâde Mehmed Nuri, and his brother Ali Pasha, who had two Kurdish leaders from the Reşvan tribe under their command, Zeynel Bey and Haci Bedri Ağa, as well as Bitlisli Emin, a retired gendarmerie officer.[63] Once the caravan reached the gorge, Zeynel Bey directed operations from a height, following a well-established ritual. He first had the men separated from the convoy and put to death. The operation went on for a full hour and a half. According to Alphonse Arakelian, who was in this convoy, 3,600 people lost their lives, but some one hundred men survived.[64] One of Arakelian's companions, Sarkis Manukian, later declared, for his part, that 2,115 men were slain that day in the Kahta gorge.[65]

The next day, the deportees, who the surviving men had rejoined, came face to face with a newly arrived inspector (*mufettiş*), "officially" representing the *mutesarif* of Malatia and the *kaymakam* of Adiyaman. The *mufettiş* ordered that the deportees be subjected to a body search, and had "tents, rugs and anything else that seemed as if it might have value" confiscated, including watches, jewels, money, and checks. The survivors then set out on their way again. They now encountered the *kaymakam* of Adiyaman, Nuri Bey, who had probably come in order to assess the effects of the treatment to which the deportees were being subjected, but also to claim the share of the Armenians' property due to the Special Organization. The deportees' route led them back to the banks of the Euphrates at Samsad, where the gendarmes threw "the sick and crippled" into the river and made off with young women and children. Four months after the second convoy left Erzerum, "what was left of some sixty families" arrived in Suruc (in the *sancak* of Urfa). From there they were set marching in the direction of Rakka and the Syrian Desert.[66]

Thanks to Boghos Vartanian's eyewitness account, we know what happened to the men who were separated from the convoy at Kemah. There were between 900 and 1,000 people in this group. Their escorts carefully searched them and stripped them of their belongings on the Kemah road. Three hundred Armenians were packed into a stable on the spot and left without food and water; they had to bribe their guards to open the door to let in a little air or give them water from the Euphrates, which they paid for by the glassful. The guards exacted 2,000 Turkish pounds in the form of checks from another group of 160 men who had been shut up in the church in exchange for a promise to set them free. In the small hours of the morning, when the commander arrived, a list of the deportees present was drawn up, specifying their age and place of origin. The same officer informed them that they were to be assigned to labor battalions but that for security reasons they would do better to turn their money and valuables over to him. Only half-convinced by these reassuring words, the deportees gave him a mere 14 Turkish pounds, along with rings and 14 watches. The *çetes* then entered the stable and brought the men out in groups of from 15 to 30, after tying them together. The wealthiest individuals were tied together in pairs, back to back, so that they could walk only with difficulty. This was on 18 July. The prison, too, was emptied of its last occupants, some 20 Dashnaks – Vagharshag Zorigian, Bedros Baghdigian, Shah-Armen, Vahan Dandigian and others – who had requested that they be tied together and killed together.

These groups of bound men were then taken under guard toward the Euphrates and the bridge over the Kemah gorge. The operation was directed by the strong man of the district, Çetebaşi Jafer Mustafa, who had chosen the heights where the groups of men were killed before being thrown down into the turbulent waters of the Euphrates.[67]

Vartan Der Azarian was one of the first to die. He asked that those who survived tell his family where he had been slain. The *çetes* circulated among the groups who were waiting for their turn to be killed, collecting the money that the deportees would no longer need. Some of these irregulars were perhaps sorry that they had to do a job of this sort: "We are only carrying out government orders," they said. Some even declared that they were collecting this money "in order to give it to [the men's] families, who had been detained elsewhere."

By nightfall, there were only ten "roped groups" left. The *çete* leader Jafer ordered his men to abandon the usual methods, which involved killing the people in these groups one by one, and execute them all at once instead. When the group of men in which our witness found himself reached the edge of the cliff overhanging the Euphrates, they saw hundreds of lifeless bodies down below; the *çetes* were inspecting them and finishing the wounded off with their bayonettes.[68] Of this last group, attacked at dusk, less carefully than had been the case in the preceding hours, four wounded men survived because the bodies under which they found themselves lying had protected them. These men were Boghos Vartanian, our witness, Bedros Baghdasarian, and two peasants from the plain, Yervant Kloyan and Harutiun Mnatsaganian. After walking east along the left bank of the Euphrates, the survivors finally decided to head toward Dersim, where the local Kurds were reported – accurately – to be protecting Armenian deportees. Bedros eventually collapsed in the sand, temporarily unable to go on.[69]

After a four-day trek, the men arrived in Dersim on 22 July, where the Kurds fed them and sent them on to their mountain pastures. Krikor, an Armenian orphan between 10 and 12 years old whom they met on their way, served Boghos Vartanian as a guide and gave him all the bread he had as provisions for the rest of his voyage. As Boghos penetrated ever deeper into the Dersim district, he met 16 Armenians from Kampor/Koghk (in the *kaza* of Ispir/Sper) and then, on 28 July, two families from Erzincan. The women fed him and tended his wounds.[70] The case of these Armenians who found refuge in Dersim was no rarity. Vartanian met others, such as Father Arsen Arshaguni from the village of Ergans (in the *kaza* of Erzincan), who was now living in the camp of Ali Said Ağa. Our witness remained in the same camp for ten months, until spring 1916, when the Russians took Erzincan. When he returned to Erzerum, Vartanian found its Armenian neighborhoods in ruins; the houses had been burned down.[71]

The Third Convoy from Erzerum

The third caravan left Erzerum on 29 June 1915. Made up of from 7,000 to 8,000 individuals, including 500 families from the Khodorchur district, it was conducted toward Bayburt and Erzincan. In Içkale, a ten-hour march from the city, 300 men were separated from the others and slain. Further on, in Kemah, all the remaining males were separated from the rest of the convoy and led into the gorges of the Euphrates, where they were supposed to be killed. However, hundreds of the men in this group defended themselves against the *çetes'* attacks before finally surrendering. The famous Zeynel Bey later liquidated the survivors in a gorge south of Malatia. Only a few dozen women and children in this convoy ever reached Mosul.[72]

The Fourth Convoy from Erzerum

The fourth caravan left Erzerum for Bayburt on 18 July. It was made up of 7,000 to 8,000 people, basically workers in military plants, the families of soldiers, army doctors and pharmacists, together with bishop Smpat Saadetian, the primate of the diocese, and Father Nerses, the prelate in Hasankale.[73] Saadetian was one of the first victims in this group; the *çetes* made him dig his own grave in the Erzincan cemetery before "tearing him to pieces and tossing him into it" under the gaze of a Greek army veterinarian, M. Nikolai.[74] The Special Organization's well-oiled apparatus then took charge of the convoy: the men were dispatched in Kemah and the women and children in Harput. Roughly 300 survivors, including two men disguised as women, managed to reach Cezire and then Mosul.[75]

Deportations from the Plain of Erzerum: the *Kazas* of Pasın, Tortum, Ispir and Erzerum

As we have seen, the rural areas of the vilayet of Ererum were emptied of their Armenian population well before the cities. Most of the population of the *sancak* of Bayazid found refuge in the Caucasus, whereas the last villages of the Pasın district began to be "displaced toward the interior" late in March.[76] However, the towns and villages in Pasın lying near the Russian border that were evacuated in December 1914 or January 1915 were not spared atrocities. Half of the livestock (800 sheep, 1,400 cows, and 230 water buffalo) belonging to the villagers of Khosroveran, where 40 families earned a living mainly from animal husbandry, were seized during the military requisitions in fall 1914 without the compensation provided for by the law. Eleven men were massacred during the Turkish army's retreat, the Mgrdichian family was Islamicized, seven people were killed while fleeing toward the Russian border, and five children were abandoned en route.[77] In the neighboring village of Ishkhu, where 1,100 Armenians lived before the war, 70 per cent of the community's livestock (2,600 cows and 2,700 sheep) was confiscated to meet the army's needs at the very outset of the mobilization. The village also contributed 45 conscripts and 20 to 30 porters to the war effort; the porters carried supplies to the front on their backs. Moreover, 30 adults were massacred on the spot during the January 1915 debacle, another 45 people died on the way to the Caucasus, and eight children were abandoned along the way.[78]

We have only an indirect account about the *kaza* of Ispir, which comprised 17 small villages with a total Armenian population of 2,602. Thanks to this account, we know that these villagers were exterminated where they were found toward mid-June 1915 under the direct supervision of Bahaeddin Şakir and the *çete* leader Oturakci Şevket.[79] Of the fate of the 13 villages in the *kaza* of Tortum (pop. 2,829), where the Third Army had its headquarters, and the two neighboring localities in the *kaza* of Narman (pop. 458),[80] we know nothing at all. At most, we can hazard a guess that the presence of Armenian peasants in the immediate vicinity of the army's headquarters was not tolerated for long. The complete absence of eyewitness reports even suggests that there were no survivors from these districts – that their fate was similar to Ispir's.

We know more about the fate of the 53 villages of the plain of Erzerum, with a total Armenian population of 37,480.[81] While the population of the localities in the immediate

vicinity of Erzerum was deported at the same time as that of the city itself, those remaining, roughly 30,000 people, were deported in the direction of Mamahatun in three convoys, beginning on 16 May 1915.[82] There seems, however, to be no geographical logic to
the route taken by one of the three caravans, given the location of the deportees' villages.
Inhabitants of localities west of Erzerum were put in the same convoy as inhabitants of
others north of it. Thus, it is likely that the authorities' strategy consisted – as in the case
of the plain of Erzerum, to be discussed later – in making their system invulnerable to
attack by treating the villages independently of each other, concentrating their forces on
just a few villages or little towns at a time and evacuating villages located far apart from
one another, probably to avoid all risk that the villagers would pool their forces and fight
back.

The first convoy included the inhabitants of the villages of Chiftlig, Gez, Kararz/Ghararz,
and Odzni; it seems to have reached Erzincan without losses. The second was made up of
villagers from Ilija, Tsitogh, Mudurga, Hintsk, Tvnig, and a few other places; they were massacred as soon as they reached Mamahatun. The third and final convoy evacuated the peasants of Umudam, Badishen, Tarkuni, Ughdatsor, Norshen, Yergnis and a few other villages.
A good many of its members were cut down in Piriz, a locality close to the banks of the
Euphrates a short distance north of Tercan. A few survivors nevertheless managed to return
to the plain, and eventually found refuge in the cathedral in Erzerum.[83]

Unlike the convoys that left the city in June, these caravans passed directly through
Mamahatun and proceeded to Erzincan without taking the route that led through Bayburt.
That difference aside, the treatment meted out to them was much the same as that to which
the other Armenians of the vilayet were subjected. Their numbers were first reduced as
they passed through the Kemah gorge. The survivors were then conducted toward Eğin and
Malatia and massacred in the Kahta gorge. Finally, the remnants of the convoys arrived in
the deserts near Rakka, Mosul, or Der Zor. Because Dersim was so close, a few hundred people managed to escape death by taking refuge with the Kurdish Zaza/Kızılbaş population of
that district.[84] A few eyewitness accounts by survivors from these villages, collected after the
arrival of Russian troops in the region in spring 1916, provide information about the experiences of the Dersim refugees. Thus, we learn that of the 2,050 people who lived in the village
of Mudurga before the war, 36 saved their lives by fleeing to Dersim. As for the inhabitants of
Shekhnots, which had a population of 700 before the deportation, there were no indications
one year later that any had survived. It seems that only a few women from Tuanch, which
had 695 Armenian inhabitants, 50 of whom had been drafted, managed to survive in the
deserts of Syria and Mesopotamia. Of the surviving inhabitants of Hinsk, we know of only
three Islamicized families who reverted to their original faith after the Russians arrived, and
33 refugees who fled to Dersim. Seventy-five survivors from Otsni/Odzni arrived in Syria, and
two more found refuge in Dersim.[85]

The *Kaza* of Bayburt

To this northern *kaza* with its roughly 30 Armenian localities and a total Christian population of 17,060,[86] the Young Turk government had sent one of its most faithful militants,
Mehmed Nusret Bey, a native of Janina, to serve as the *kaymakam* of Bayburt. The Special
Organization, for its part, put its squadrons in the area under the command of Lieutenant
Piri Necati Bey.[87] This district, through which ran the roads leading south from the shores
of the Black Sea as well as the main road between Erzincan and Erzerum, was cleansed of
its Armenian population earlier than most others. As early as 2 May 1915, the Armenian
villages in the northern part of the *kaza* were set upon by bands of *çetes*. The next day, the
military authorities issued an order to "remove" the Armenian population from all areas

within 75 kilometers of the border. The first to be arrested and murdered were the notables of the village communities.

What gives a particular twist to the events of May–June 1915 is the fact that operations in this period were directly supervised by Bahaeddin Şakir, who traveled from Erzerum to Bayburt in order personally to establish the procedures to be used during the deportations and massacres, first in the villages and then in the cities and towns. He had Nusret Bey appointed president of the deportation committee, which was made up of Piri Mehmed Necati Bey; Ince Arab Mehmed, a government official; Arnavud Polis, the police chief; Kefelioğlu Süleyman Paşazâde Hasib; Velizâde Tosun; Şahbandarzâde Ziya; Musuh Bey Zâde Necib; Karalı Kâmil; Kondolatizâde Haci Bey; and Ince Arab Yogun Necib.[88]

The trial of those who organized and carried out the massacres in Bayburt, which was held in July 1920 before Court-Martial No. 1 in Istanbul, provides us with information that we lack in the case of the other regions of the vilayet of Erzerum. The testimony of Adıl Bey, a captain in the gendarmerie stationed in Erzerum, shows that the massacres in the *kaza* of Bayburt were organized by Bahaeddin Şakir, the "president of the Teşkilât-ı Mahsusa" and a member of the party's Central Committee; Filibeli Ahmed Hilmi Bey, the party's delegate in Erzerum; Saadi Bey, a nephew of the senator Ahmed Rıza bey and a lieutenant in the reserve; and Necati Bey. The verdict handed down by the court-martial states, finally, that the massacres perpetrated in this region were the first to be discussed and decided upon by "the headquarters [of the Central Committee] of the Union and Progress party" and that they were organized under Bahaeddin Şakir's authority.[89]

In the course of this trial, it was established that Lieutenant Mehmed Necati voluntarily transferred most of the mobile battalions of the gendarmerie to the front so that he himself could escort the convoys of deportees. In other words, the Special Organization considered the gendarmes to be an obstacle to the realization of its plans. At their trial, of course, Necati and Nusret adamantly proclaimed their innocence of the crimes they were charged with. They were, however, contradicted by Salih Effendi, the commander of the brigade of the gendarmerie in Bayburt, who testified before the commission of inquiry that a few of his men had been charged with carrying out arrests of army deserters or draft dodgers. The gendarmes in the region had, however, not escorted the caravans of deported Armenians, who were taken in hand by Necati Bey. They never arrived in Erzincan.[90]

Other witnesses, such as Hasanoğlu Ömer, who was responsible for provisions and supplies in Bayburt, declared before the commission that Kefalioğlu Kiaşif, a lieutenant in a labor battalion, Iliasoğlu Sabit, and others, deported the Armenians from Bayburt in several convoys: "At two hours' distance from Bayburt, they took the children aged between one and five from the convoys and brought them back to the town." Ali Esadoğlu Effendi, a native of Baştucar (in the *kaza* of Surmene), added that Nusret was a close friend of Tahsin Bey's and that he sent 150 orphans to Binbaşihan, where he invited the inhabitants of the village to choose those they wished to "adopt." All reports concur about the fact that Deyirmendere, located on the first spurs of the Pontic Mountains to the north of the town, was the place where most of these deportees were put to death.[91]

It would thus appear that the CUP had from the outset planned to recover children of five and under in order to integrate them into the great Turkish family. The age limit mentioned here suggests that the condition for this "integration" was that the children be too young to remember their origins. Interestingly, Armenian women and children were sought-after commodities. When Armenians were rejected, what was rejected was their identity. It should be noted that Nusret Bey, the 44-year-old *kaymakam* of Bayburt who "committed crimes during the deportation of the Armenians from his *kaza*," helped himself to the 24-year-old Philomen Nurian of Trebizond and her younger sister "Nayime."[92] Accounts by survivors attest that Nusret sent the deportees to Binbaşihan and Hindihan, where he had all their money confiscated; that he was present while the massacres took place; and that, with the gendarmes' help, he secured the prettiest girls and young women for himself and carried them off. Nusret nevertheless maintained that the convoys of deportees from Bayburt were sent to Erzincan. The court pointed out in response that they never arrived there.[93]

The procedure employed here, at this experimental stage, was rather similar to the one that would be adopted in other areas in the weeks to come. The first concrete action taken was the arrest, on 18 May 1915, of the leading personalities of Bayburt – the primate, Anania Hazarabedian, as well as Antranig Boyajian, Hagop and Smpat Aghababian, Arshag and Manug Simonian, Ohannes and Serop Balian, Zakeos Ayvazian, Khachig Boghosian, Hagop and Aram Hamazaspian, Vagharshag Dadurian, Vagharshag Lusigian, Antranig Sarafian, Krikor Keynageuzian, Hamazasp Shalamian, and 60 other people. Those arrested were sent to the village of Tighunk, guarded by a squadron of çetes under Nusret's personal command. There they were shut up in a stable belonging to the mufti, Kuruca Koruğ, where a squadron of Turkish and Kurdish çetes stripped them of their belongings. On 21 May, the kaymakam had them hanged to the beating of drums on the banks of the Jorok.[94]

On 24 May came the first attacks on the villages Aruk/Ariudzga (pop. 370), Chahmants (pop. 502), Malasa (pop. 380), Khayek (pop. 361), and Lipan. On 25 May, Tumel (pop. 204), Lesonk (pop. 981), and another ten or so villages were attacked; a total of 1,775 people were evacuated and led to the gorge of Hus/Khus. Here they were massacred, under Nusret's and Necati's direct supervision, by bands of çetes commanded by Huluki Hafiz Bey, Kasab Durak, Derviş Ağa, Kasab Ego, Attar Feyzi, and Laze Ilias. On 27 and 28 May 1915, the inhabitants of 24 more villages were evacuated and led in the direction of Hus/Khus, but were massacred further off, near the village of Yanbasdi.[95]

According to the report of a survivor by the name of Mgrdich Muradian, the Turkish population of Bayburt was opposed to the deportation of the Armenians; the kaymakam is supposed to have had three Turks executed to bring people to reason.[96] The first caravan nevertheless left Bayburt on 4 June 1915, followed by a second caravan on 8 June and a third on 14 June. In all, some 3,000 people were deported. As early as 11 June, İsmail Ağa, İbrahim Bey, and Pırı Mehmed Necati Bey set about destroying the monasteries of Surp Kristapor in Bayburt and Surp Krikor in Lesonk, after plundering them. The aim was doubtless to gain possession of the monasteries' treasures, but also to set in motion without delay the effort to wipe out all traces of the Armenians' millennial presence in the region, especially the superb architectural monuments of the early Middle Ages.

According to Mgrdich Muradian, who was in one of the convoys that left Bayburt in the first half of June, his convoy followed the road leading from Erzincan over the Kemah Bridge to Arapkir, as far as Gümüşmaden. There, Kurdish çetes began systematically slaughtering the deportees. A few women and children managed to make their way to a village lying between Arapkir and Harput, Khule kiugh (Huleköy). From there, Kurdish ağas took them to Dersim. In this way, 80 people escaped with their lives. They eventually found refuge in Erzincan after the Russian forces captured the city.[97]

Keghvart Lusigian, who was probably in the same caravan as Muradian, reports that her group was taken to a place two hours distant from Bayburt; there the men were separated from the others and killed. In Plur, the convoy was attacked by Kurdish çetes, who slit the throats of the last men in the group, Hagop Aghababian, Zakar Sheiranian, and Keghvart's brother Garabed Lusigian. The çetes then robbed the deportees and abducted a number of young women. In Kemah, they put women, adolescent girls, and children in separate groups, which were then given as gifts to Turks who had come from Erzincan for the purpose. Four hundred women and girls were selected, but some of them succeeded in throwing themselves into the Euphrates. According to Lusigian, some 300 women from Erzerum were "married" to officers in Erzincan and another 200 were "married" to government officials. She herself "belonged" to a *kadi* by the name of Şakir.[98]

It seems that the stretch of the Euphrates near the Kemah gorge also served to drown 2,833 children from the *kaza* of Bayburt[99] who were too old to be "adopted."

The *Kaza* of Hinis/Khnus

The 25 Armenian villages in the *kaza* of Hinis/Khnus, which lay in an isolated area in the southern part of the *sancak* of Erzerum, had 21,382 inhabitants.[100] These villagers did not suffer the fate of the other localities in the region, but were massacred on their native ground. As elsewhere, operations began with the arrest of the local elites. In Khnus, the administrative seat of the *kaza*, Nusreddin Effendi, Haci Isa, Fehim Effendi, Şükrü Mahmud Ağaoğlu, and Egid Yusuf Ağaoğlu formed a deportation committee that was headed by Şeyh Said. This committee recruited *çetes* from the local Turkish population and made public declarations about the threat to Islam embodied by the Armenians, said to be preparing "to join with their brothers of Russia in order to massacre Muslims."[101] The first massacres were perpetrated in the *kaza* in April, when Hoca Hamdi Bey, the commander of a squadron of *çetes*, led his men, billeted in the Armenian village of Gopal in the eastern part of the *kaza*, in an attack on two neighboring localities, Karaçoban (pop. 2,571) and Gövenduk/Geovendug (pop. 1,556). The *çetes* massacred a number of peasants, abducted young women, and plundered the villages.[102] Tahir Bey, the *kaymakam* of Khnus, was by no means the least zealous when it came to liquidating Armenian villagers. It was Tahir who took command of the 600 to 700 *çetes* recruited by the deportation committee. In these remote rural mountain districts, the Turkist ideology of the Istanbul elites was a less powerful spring of action than Ottoman Islam, so that the latter rather than the former was exploited to mobilize local energies. Tahir was a classic example of the middle-level government officials with a rudimentary education who nursed a deep hatred of these Armenian villagers pretentious enough to try to give their children a proper education and make social life a little less rude. Faithfully following the strategy designed by the Special Organization, the *kaymakam* began by attacking his prey where it was weakest. The first victims of the "deportations" initiated on 1 June 1915[103] were the villagers of Karaçoban, or what was left of it: they were taken to the furrows that the waters of the melting snow had carved in the Çağ gorge and had their throats cut. The neighboring village of Geovendug was subjected to the same fate the very same day. The *çetes* next attacked the villages of Burnaz/Purnaq (pop. 449) and Karaköprü (pop. 1,161); their inhabitants were stabbed and clubbed to death in an isolated area.[104]

The task of massacring the remaining villagers had been entrarsted to a Kurdish chieftain, Feyzullah, who inaugurated his campaign in the village of Khert (pop. 408) at the head of a squadron of *çetes*, then attacked Khozlu (pop. 1,770), a village controlled by a Kurd named Moro. Feyzullah and his *çetes* first killed the men and then proceeded to slaughter the women and children, taking "the prettiest women for themselves" as they went along. The inhabitants of the village of Yeniköy (pop. 451), in turn, had their throats cut in the Kurdish village of Burhana, where their neighbors had invited them to take refuge. Some of the villagers of Çevirme (pop. 1,361) were subjected to the same fate at Kızmusa, while the rest were put to the sword by Feyzullah's bands. The most agonizing death was reserved for the inhabitants of Elbis (pop. 608): Şükrü Bey, their "protector," burned them alive in a barn.[105]

In the first days of May, Aghchamelik (pop. 318) and Pazkig (pop. 876) were attacked by Feyzullah's squadrons, as were Shabadin (pop. 391), Maruf (pop. 338) and Duman (pop. 398). The inhabitants of all these villages were put to death.

The Armenians of Yahya (pop. 305) were liquidated by the garrison established in this village. Khırımkaya (pop. 425), Salvori (pop. 245), Dorukhan and Gopal (pop. 1,375) were wiped off the map by soldiers under the command of Haci Hamdi. Thanks to accounts by three different eyewitnesses, we know that 75 men from Gopal, a village with a great deal of livestock, were arrested and shot during the Russian offensive of late April 1915 – Israel Sarksian, Dikran Avdalian, Tiko Kévorkian and Egho Barigian, among others – and that the remaining villagers were massacred by the soldiers quartered in the village. A few people managed to flee to the Russian lines, while a child, Harutiun Serovpian, was adopted by Kurds and converted to Islam.[106]

It seems that only the villagers of Sarlu (pop. 540) and Mezhengerd (pop. 75), both near Khnus, were deported, to an unknown destination.[107] The last village to be attacked, Haramig (pop. 898), valiantly withstood the çetes' assaults under the command of Hagop Kharpertsi, a hekim who practiced traditional medicine. The people of Haramig held out for two weeks until their ammunition ran out; they inflicted heavy losses on the Kurds.

A few old men and children who had survived these slaughters and been left to wander through the villages were gathered together in Hinis and deported a few weeks later.[108]

The Kaza of Tercan/Mamahatun

Lying astride the southern Erzerum-Erzincan road, the 41 Armenian villages of the kaza of Tercan/Mamahatun had a total Armenian population of 11,690 on the eve of the war.[109] The deportations began in these villages on 30 and 31 May. They were directed by the parliamentary deputy from Kemah, Halet Bey, the son of the former vali of Erzerum, Sağar Zâde, who had organized squadrons of çetes made up of Muslims from the Kemah and Erzincan areas as soon as the general mobilization was decreed.[110] These bands, under the command of the chief of the Balaban tribe, Gülo Ağa, were placed under the joint supervision of the mutesarif of Erzincan, Memduh Bey, and the kaymakam of Tercan, Aslan Hafız.[111]

According to survivors' reports, the men were massacred either where they were found or some 15 miles to the south in Goter/Gotır Köprü, where the squadron commanded by Gülo Ağa was waiting for them. Here they were stripped of their belongings, their throats were cut, and they were thrown into the Euphrates.[112] Survivors from the villages of Pulk (pop. 778),[113] Pakarij (pop. 1,060),[114] Sargha/Sarikaya (pop. 695),[115] and Piriz (pop. 855)[116] later affirmed that some of those who survived these massacres were driven as far as Erzincan and then on to the Kemah pass, where they were killed.

The Kaza of Kığı/Kghi

In the 50 Armenian villages of the kaza of Kığı, with a total Armenian population of 19,859,[117] the mobilization and requisitions took place under conditions of relative calm, thanks especially to the goodwill of the kaymakam. In May, however, he was replaced by the commander of a squadron of çetes of the Special Organization, Laze Midhat Mehmed Bey,[118] who created a deportation committee. The committee was made up of Çinazzâde Mustafa, the president of the local Ittihad club; Mehmedzâde Hilmi, a native of Kars; Husni İsmail Çavuszâde Şakir, an assistant of the kaymakam's; Haci Ahmedzâde Müdad, the mufti; and Davudzâde Hafız. The leaders of the squadrons of çetes involved in the massacre of the deportees from Kığı were Zeynelzâde Hasan;[119] Erzrumli Ömer; Şeyhzâde Necibet and his sons Hafız, Tevfik, Rıza, Beyti, and Mahmud; Dede and Ali Hamdi Abidoğlu, from Osnag; İsmail Hüseyin; Ahmedoğlu Mehmed, from Hoghas; Osman Bey, the müdir (administrator) of the nahie of Çılheder; Fazıl Bey, from Oror; Cemal Bey, from Tarman; Karaman Effendi; and Ulaşzâde Mustafa and İzzet Ağa, from Karmrug. Ziya Beg, a native of Başköy, and Adil

Güzelzâde Şerif, who participated in the massacre of the deportees from Erzerum, were also involved here.[120]

On 8 June 1915, the new *kaymakam*, Laze Midhat Mehmed Bey, announced the order to deport Armenians from the war zone to Harput to the primate, Kegham Tivekelian, and the other 25 notables whom he had convoked. The Armenians' safety, he said, would be assured. The muezzin helped spread the order, adding that the Armenian population was to be deported three days later. An order was also issued to stock food supplies in the church. In the same period, Kığı, the administrative seat of the *kaza*, was required to billet a battalion from Dyarbekir at Armenian expense.[121]

Tension had been running high in the villages of the *kaza* for a few days before the deportation order was made public: the authorities had sent *çetes* there to collect the inhabitants' arms, threatening to have the men shot if they did not surrender their weapons. The Armenians, however, turned in only their hunting rifles, hiding their other weapons in the fields. The young people who were left in the village made plans to defend themselves, but the prelate of Kığı requested that they do nothing of the sort. The *kaymakam* sent a lawyer by the name of Toros Sadghigian to the area to investigate the situation, but Sadghigian was murdered near the village of Sergevil by Zeynelzâde Hasan.[122]

According to Vahan Postoyan, a native of the village of Khups, Hıde Ibiz, a Kurdish chieftain from Dersim, attacked Akrag (pop. 350) with his followers on 3 June 1915, plundering the village and killing several men. On 5 June, similar atrocities were committed – again on the pretext of a search for arms – in the mixed villages of Hubeg (pop. 200), Kariköy/ Khasgerd (pop. 122) and Kholkhol/Kulkum (pop. 53). Sergevil (pop. 658) and its medieval monastery, Surp Prgich, were attacked on 6 June; three-quarters of the village's inhabitants were slain. On 7 June, Herdig/Herdif (pop. 700) met the same fate.[123]

However, when the bands of *çetes* attacked the village of Khups/Çanakci (pop. 1,216) at six o'clock on 7 June 1915, they were met with gunfire from the peasants, organized into six self-defense groups led by Suren Postoyan, Srabion Postoyan, Mesrob Matosian, Hovhannes Khoteian, Manug Elesigian, Baghdasar Der Garabedian, Yerazayig Kholkholtsi, and Zakar Postoyan. After two days of uninterrupted fighting, which cost 40 Kurdish *çetes* and one Armenian (Giragos Baghdigian) their lives, the villagers decided to break through the enemy lines. They succeeded, but were all killed somewhat further off in a mill, in which they fought to the last bullet.[124]

In the first days of June 1915, arrests took place in the other villages of the *kaza*. Among those arrested in Dzirmak were Melkon Aloyan, Garabed Tchavushian, Hovhannes Kalayjian, and Krikor Maghoyian and, in Tarman, Sarkis Endroyian, Sarkis Sarkisian, Arsen Varzhabedian, Mampre Bardizbanian, and others. These men were transferred to the town of Kığı in chains and killed with axes.[125] Finally, the irregulars proceeded to encircle the town and the remaining villages in the *kaza*. According to Vahan Postoyan, the initial operations conducted in the villages of the district of Kığı by the *çetes* of the Special Organization resulted in the deaths of 1,500 people.[126]

On 10 June 1915, the authorities arrested the heads of the town's affluent households.[127] They were put in the first caravan of 1,200 people that, accompanied by Bishop Tivekelian, set out from Kığı toward the southwest on 11 June. On 13 May, this group arrived near Tepe, in Deli Mizi, on the road to Palu. The bishop and a number of notables, including Smpat Musheghian, Antranig Yesayan, Aghaser, the director of the town's Armenian schools, Hovhannes Boghosian, Hovagim and Hagop Hovhannisian, Diran, Armen Srabian, Stepan Kurkjian, Vahram Kotan, Yesayi Yesayian, Vahan and Sarkis Dumanian, Avedis and Kegham Kachperuni, Harutiun Oynoyian, Kevork Tcheogurian, and Senekerim Kharpertsi were separated from the rest of the convoy, ostensibly in order to meet with the president of the deportation committee, the *kaymakam* of Kığı, who had just arrived in the area. Hagop

Hovhannissian was the first to be tortured and then shot in the head by İsmail Çavuszâde Şakir, who subjected the other prisoners to similar treatment, including the primate and young men from the villages of Tchan/Çanet and Chanakji/Çanakci.[128]

The deportees in the first convoy were, of course, unaware of the notables' fate. They continued on their way the next day. As they approached Palu Bridge, the men were separated from the caravan, led to the banks of the Euphrates and massacred, after which the caravan was plundered. All the subsequent caravans also passed through this area, where more than half of the deportees from Kığı were killed in the next few days.[129]

According to an eyewitness account by Mrs. Aghaser, many women drowned themselves by jumping into the river from Palu Bridge in order to avoid "being dishonored"; thus, of the 1,200 people who set out in the first caravan, there remained only 200 to 250. These survivors sought in vain to remain in Palu; they were sent on to Harput, where they arrived, naked and starving, after 25 days on the road. Although all the other surviving deportees were sent on in the direction of Dyarbekir and Aleppo, Mrs. Aghaser succeeded in staying behind in Harput along with four other women, after finding employment as a supervisor in the Turkish orphanage of Harput, which the Ittihad had founded in order to "educate" Armenian children in the spirit of Turkism. The 700 orphans living in the orphanage were left in the care of Armenian women. It was not long, however, before the *kaymakam* came to the conclusion that they "were raising up enemies" and ordered the institution closed. According to Mrs. Aghaser, he had the children sent on to Malatia, where they were thrown into the Euphrates.[130]

The second convoy from Kığı, which set out on 11 May, comprised 2,000 villagers, 700 of them men. The deportees came from 12 different localities in the western part of the district. On 15 June, they arrived in a place called Dabalu in the vicinity of Palu, escorted by Mehmedzâde Hilmi, an eminent member of the deportation committee of Kığı.[131] This group was harassed and plundered even more ferociously than the preceding caravan had been; the deportees, nearly naked, were in a wretched state. In the vicinity of Dabalu, near Palu Bridge, the squadrons of *çetes* liquidated the men, then allowed the local population to close in on the camp.[132]

The third convoy, which left on 12 June, comprised inhabitants of other villages and the town itself. Three hours from Palu, in Lıhan, the *çetes* escorting the deportees extorted 3,000 to 4,000 Turkish pounds from them. The next morning, the convoy came under heavy gunfire and the *çetes* then attacked it with knives and abducted young women. For the first time in this region, those escorting a convoy cut open women's bellies, for they had discovered that some women swallowed their gold coins during body searches. On 16 June, the deportees who survived the carnage (approximately one-quarter of the total) were brought together in Palu with the vestiges of the first two caravans. On 18 June, all of them then set out on the road leading south.[133]

On 13 June, a fourth convoy (the last to leave Kığı), made up of civil servants and merchants, was put on the road under the command of the *çete* leader Karaman Ulaşzâde Mustafa, a native of Karmrug. This caravan, however, was sent straight to Harput. By the evening of 13 June, then, there were no more than ten craftsmen and other indispensable individuals left in town, such as the municipal physician, Dr. Melikian, and an official in the municipal health department, Barkev Nenejian.[134]

The last convoy, comprising villagers from 35 localities, including Temran, Oror, and Arek, was put on the road on 16 June 1915. It was attacked and plundered for the first time in a place called Sarpiçay, in the *kaza* of Akpunar; responsible for the attack was the *müdir* of the *nahie* of Çılheder, Osman Bey, who ordered his Kurdish *çetes* to massacre the deportees.[135] During the shooting that followed, H. Sarkisian lost his father and uncle. He later evoked the indescribable panic that came over the deportees, who fled in all directions. That night, the *çetes* searched the corpses and finished off the wounded. Those in charge of the convoy recovered the women and children who had been given refuge in a nearby Kurdish village by threatening their rescuers and set them marching back down the road to Palu. Like previous caravans, this one was brought to a halt on the outskirts of the town, near the village of Dabalu, which was strewn with corpses. The church had been burned down and the houses had been pillaged. The deportees were slaughtered with axes on Palu Bridge and thrown into the Euphrates. Our witness, on his desperate flight toward Dersim, which seems to have been the only place where the fugitives could find a safe haven, saw workers busy destroying churches and cemeteries. A Kurd who briefly accompanied him on his way told him, "It is the government which has given orders to demolish them, so that no trace indicating that this was once an Armenian village will remain."[136]

On 20 June 1915, the survivors from the last convoys, 2,500 people, including 350 men disguised as women, were sent south by way of the notorious Palu Bridge. After three days on the road, they arrived at a spot three miles from Arğana Maden, where, after a careful identity check, the last men were knifed to death, while young women were sold to the local populace.[137] The last deportees arrived in Dyarbekir after a 50-day trek. They were confined to a field outside the city walls, where they were visited by the vali, Dr. Mehmed Reşid, and local dignitaries, who picked out a few young women for themselves. When the survivors, who had been stripped of their clothing en route, reached Maden, they were clothed and fed by Syriac Christians and lodged in partially burned houses whose cellars were stacked high with charred corpses. After another 20 days on the road, the caravan reached Ras ul-Ayn, where the last man in the group was murdered by Çerkez.[138]

Of all the deportees who had set out in the various convoys from Kiği, some 3,000 arrived in Ras ul-Ayn. A month later, no more than 700 were left; famine and typhus had carried off the rest. Four hundred survivors were sent by rail to Hama and Homs and another 300 were sent to Der Zor. There, in late 1916, some 15 to 20 were still alive.[139]

According to Vahan Postoyan, 1,500 people were killed in the villages before the deportation began, while 461 women and children were recovered from the Muslim population after Russian forces arrived in the region.[140] The deportees were slaughtered in Chan/Çan (3,000), Tepe (2,500), at Palu Bridge (10,000), and in Kasrmaden, near Harput (13,000).[141]

Deportations from the *Kaza* of Kiskim-Khodorchur

The *kaza* of Kiskim, in which the 13 villages of Khodorchur were located, had an Armenian population of 8,136. Most of these Armenians were Catholics.[142] Kiskim, a mountain district well suited for sheep breeding, was one of the most isolated areas in the vilayet of Erzerum. The villagers of Khodorchur were rich and peaceably inclined. When the general mobilization was announced, they chose to pay the *bedel* for both themselves and the emigrants from the area working abroad, rather than serve in the Ottoman Army. From late August 1914 on, they also lodged and fed several battalions of the Ottoman army – protesting mildly, and to no avail, when the army requisitioned all their horses and mules. In December 1914, the little town of Garmirk was also visited by some 30 *çetes*, who plundered and beat the villagers and imposed a tax of 300 Turkish pounds on them. But these were, after all, classic practices. The house searches conducted in February 1915 by gendarmes looking for arms had been more alarming, especially because they were accompanied by acts of torture and the arrest of village notables, as in Mokhragud (Harutiun Dzarigian) and Khodorchur (Joseph Mamulian).[143]

Because the majority of Armenians in Khodorchur were Catholics, they had until then benefited from the protection of French and Austro-Hungarian diplomats. Hence, they were probably hoping when they received the deportation order that the ambassador of Austria-Hungary would see to it that they were not harmed. Interestingly, negotiations conducted by the German vice-consul in Erzerum at the Austrian ambassador's request, though dragging on from June to September 1915, succeeded in saving only about a dozen Armenian Sisters of the Immaculate Conception and a few Mkhitarist monks;[144] the Catholics of Khodorchur as a whole were not spared. Quite the contrary: in May 1915, the local authorities proceeded to arrest 27 priests who had been educated in Rome or at the seminary of Saint-Sulpice in Paris – among them the primate, Harutiun Turshian, as well as some 30 schoolteachers.[145] Late in May, the *kaymakam*, Necati Bey, summoned the notables of Khodorchur and informed them of the deportation order, adding that they would not be allowed to sell their assets before setting out. A few local notables nevertheless encouraged Armenians to entrust their property to them pending their return. Besides Necati, among the main organizers of the deportation and spoliation of the Armenians were local dignataries such as Ali Beg, Sahuzoğlu Dursun, Kürdoğlu Mahmud, and Ömerzâde Mehmed.[146]

The Armenians of Khodorchur were deported in five convoys. The first two set out early in June. The first was made up of 300 families comprising 3,740 individuals from the villages of Khodorchur. There were 200 families comprising some 1,500 individuals in the second, almost all of them from Kudrashen and Kiskim; they were massacred between Kasaba and Erzincan.[147]

The third convoy, made up of villagers from Garmirk (pop. 600) and Hidgants, set out on 8 June 1915. It was soon incorporated into the second caravan from Erzerum, and shared its fate. Twenty survivors, after passing through Bayburt, Erzincan, Kemah, Eğin, Malatia, Arapkir, Samsad, Suruc, Raffa, Birecik and Urfa, were registered in Aleppo on 22 December 1918.[148]

The fourth convoy, which included villagers from Mokhrgud (pop. 350), Kotkan, Atik, Grman, Sunik, Gakhmukhud, Keghud, Jijaroz/Jijabagh, Gisag, Michin Tagh and Khantatsor, followed a route much like that taken by the third convoy as far as Samsad. It was then decimated on the banks of the Euphrates between Ğantata et Ğavanluğ by regular troops and *çetes* under the command of Samsadlı Haci Şeyh Içko.[149]

The fifth and final convoy included only a few deportees, the last inhabitants of the villages all but emptied by the fourth convoy, above all old people and the infirm. They were massacred in Poşin, on orders from the *mutesarif* of Severek, by Severekli Ahmed Çavuş and his *çetes*. Eight of those in this convoy survived. A total of around 100 people from all the Armenian localities in the *kaza* survived.[150]

Deportations from the Sancak of Erzincan

The *sancak* of Erzincan, which, with its 66 Armenian villages and a total Armenian population of 37,612, was rather sparsely settled, played an important role as a zone of transit for convoys of deportees from the vilayet, while the district's Kemah gorge served as a killing field. The main organizers of the massacres here were the *mutesarif* of the *sancak*, Memduh Bey, and the parliamentary deputy from Kemah, Halet Bey. They were backed up by Muhtar Bey, the commander of the gendarmerie of Erzincan, Mecid Bey, the *mutesarif*'s secretary, and the commanders of the *çetes* of the Special Organization, Ziya Beg, Adil Güzelzâde Şerif, Nazıf Bey, Nazıf's nephew Mazhar Bey, Eçzaci Mehmed, Kürd Arslan Bey, a cousin of Halet Bey's, and Kemal Vanlı Bey.[151] In a written deposition submitted to the Mazhar Commission, General Vehib Pasha, who succeeded Mahmud Kâmil at the head of the Third Army, stated that the officers of the gendarmerie received the order to deport the Armenians from "Memduh Bey, the former *mutesarif* of Erzincan," and that "those who committed the murders had received their instructions from Dr. Bahaeddin Şakir Bey."[152]

Both the general mobilization and requisitions were carried out with special rigor in this *sancak*. A witness reports that, when the requisitions were made in her village, which had

300 Armenian and 50 Turkish households, "it was plain that not much at all was taken from the Turks."[153] As elsewhere, the April 1915 order to collect arms was executed with extreme violence and accompanied by torture, bastinados, and arrests. None of the villages on the plain of Erzincan were spared these operations.[154]

On Sunday, 16 May, the last service was celebrated in the cathedral of Erzincan. In his sermon, Father Mesrob informed the population that the government had decided to deport it and that the most affluent 16 families had to go to Konya. On Tuesday, 18 May, the Der Serian, Papazian, Boyitian, and Susigian families, among others, were deported. On 21 May, they were followed by 60 other families whose names figured on a list drawn up by the local authorities. A few days later, the Armenian bishopric of Erzincan received telegrams, sent from Eğin, announcing that these families had arrived there safe and sound.[155] In Erzincan, the authorities had confiscated three of the city's four churches, leaving Surp Prgich Cathedral to the Armenians.[156] According to Kurken Keserian, Erzincan's Armenian quarter was now transformed into a veritable chaos; its schools and churches were systematically pillaged.[157] A week before the deportation of the Ezincan Armenians, Halet Bey had the city's notables arrested; among them were Krikor Chayan and Apkar Tashjian. These notables were massacred in Kemah and Sansar Dere soon after their arrest.[158]

On the evening of 23 May, the *kaimakam* of the *kaza*, Memduh, arrived on the plain of Erzincan at the head of a group of gendarmes, *çetes*, and Turkish peasants from the surrounding villages, a force of some 12,000 armed men. They surrounded the villages and monasteries. A few young men managed to flee to the mountains, but the men from the households on the plain were methodically killed on Sunday, 23 May, and Tuesday, 25 May, while the women and children were sent to Erzincan's Armenian cemetery.[159] According to eyewitnesses, surprise attacks were launched on the villages after the forces that had been mobilized for this operation had carefully isolated them from each other. The men were then executed in small groups – they were either shot or had their throats cut in trenches that had been dug in advance.[160]

Once this operation had been terminated, the authorities began, on Tuesday, 25 May, to concentrate the Armenian population of Erzincan in the Armenian cemetery of Kuyubaşi, a quarter of an hour from the city. By the evening of 27 May, the whole population of the city and nearby villages had been interned there, where they were guarded by *çetes*. The Armenians of the Surmen neighborhood, who had a reputation for unruliness, were the only exception: they were to be dealt a special fate. The deportees were sorted into groups by neighborhood.[161] Men between 40 and 50 were separated from the others and massacred by the gendarmes and *çetes*.[162] On 28 May, under the supervision of the parliamentary deputy Halet Bey, the remaining deportees were set marching at one-hour intervals in little groups down the road that led to Kemah; the aim was to prevent visual contact between the different groups.[163] The caravan in which one survivor found himself got as far as the khan belonging to Halet's brother Haci Bey; there the squadrons of *çetes* were reinforced by Kurds from seven villages in the Ceferli district. Deportees from the villages of Karni, Tortan, and Komar were integrated into the convoy. Further on, this convoy, escorted by Captain Mustafa Bey, was attacked by a squadron of *çetes* under the command of Demal Vanlı Bey, Kürd Aslan Bey, and Mazhar Bey, a cousin of Halet's; they extorted large sums from the deportees and carried off six of the prettiest young women.[164] The gorge that lay three hours distant from the city and extended as far as Kemah, eight hours away, became the graveyard of the deportees from Erzincan and its plain, who were thrown into it. Only a few women who had been abducted and taken to Turkish villages in the area temporarily cheated death.[165]

One by one, the groups of deportees piled into the Kemah gorge, actually a series of gorges that extend over an area that it takes four hours to traverse on foot. It was as if the Armenians were caught in a trap from which there was no escape: on the one side was the turbulent Euphrates and, on the other, the cliffs of the Mt. Sebuh mountain chain. As the deportees entered the gorge, they were stripped of their belongings by çetes under the command of Jafer Mustafa Effendi, who had squadrons of the Teşkilât-ı Mahsusa under his orders. Deeper in the gorges, veritable slaughterhouses had been set up, in which some 25,000 people were exterminated in one day. Hundreds of young women and children joined hands and leaped into the void together. A few young women even dragged çetes who were trying to rape them down into the waters of the Euphrates with them. At regular intervals, the butchers clambered down to the narrow banks of the river in order to finish off wounded people who had not been swept away by the current.[166] Almost all the convoys of deportees from Ispir, Hınis, Erzerum, Tercan, and Pasin passed through these gorges, one of the main killing fields regularly used by the çetes of the Special Organization.

The fate of very young children seems to have differed from that of all the others. A conscript employed, along with his colleague Garabed Vartabedian, as the secretary of a captain in the army noticed that Turks were picking up "abandoned" children in the streets of Erzincan and taking them home. The next day, the same witness obtained permission to leave his barracks and go to his home in the city's Armenian quarter. On the way, he passed by the Armenians' municipal park, where 200 to 300 children between the ages of two and four had been gathered; they had been given neither food nor water, and some were already dead.[167] A pharmacist from Erzerum who was serving in the Erzincan garrison, Dikran Tertsagian, told our witness that six-month-old or seven-month-old babies were less fortunate: they were being collected in sacks in the villages of the plain and thrown into the Euphrates.[168] In the week following the massacres, policemen and gendarmes hunted down people hiding in the orchards and fields of the plain of Erzincan. In one house, two young men fought off 100 gendarmes, killing seven of them before being burned alive.[169]

On Monday 14 June, there were still 800 Armenians in Erzincan who were employed in the army workshop located in the outskirts of the city; another 150 Armenians were working as street sweepers, while three more were serving as nurses or nurses' aids in the military hospital. They did not know what had become of their families. Other men from the region who had been arrested before the deportation were still rotting in jail; the authorities had led them to believe that the deportees had been transferred to Mosul in perfect safety.[170] It was on this day, 14 June, that Mamud Kâmil ordered that all Armenian conscripts working in the hospitals, military workshops, and street-sweeping brigades be confined in the Erzincan barracks, to be guarded by çetes. A few of these conscripts remained there; the others were gradually, day by day, tied together in small groups and led off. They were conducted eastwards to the Cerbeleg Bridge, where they were shot and thrown into trenches that had been dug in advance.[171]

The conscripts from the region who were working in the amele taburis were massacred in two different places. Approximately 5,000 of them were slaughtered in a plain lying a short distance to the east of Erzincan; their bodies were thrown into mass graves.[172] A second group of about the same size was slain in the Sansar gorge, located eight hours east of Erzerum on the boundary of the kaza of Tercan, at the mouth of the mountain pass. It seems that 15,000 old people from the vilayet were also put to death there.[173]

According to a conscript who survived the massacre, when the Russians arrived in the area in spring 1916, there were only a few dozen women left; they had been taken into the households of the gendarmes and the dignitaries with the heaviest responsibility for the massacres, now having finally been given permission to "marry" Armenian women.[174] Also left alive were some 300 indispensable craftsmen, such as Avedis Kuyumjian and the seven members of his family, and Nshan Buludian and the six members of his (the former was a goldsmith, the latter a tailor). These men directed state workshops. There were also some 50 doctors on the staff of the hospital in Erzincan, among them Sarkis Sertlian, an eye doctor from Constantinople, and Dr. Mikayel Aslanian of Harput. The authorities sent Aslanian on to Harput and Sıvas just before Erzincan fell to the Russians.[175]

Deportations from the *Kazas* of Kemah, Refahiye/Gerjanis, Kuruçay and Koziçan

In early June, the 15 Armenian towns and villages in the *kaza* of Kemah, with a total population of 6,396,[176] were also attacked by squadrons of approximately 200 çetes, under the command of Armedanli İsmail, Erzinganli Kasab Memduh, Ziya Hasan Çavusoğlu and Boyağlı Sefer, who had also taken part in the massacres in Tercan, Kığı, and Erzincan. The victims were massacred where they were found. A few young Armenian men nevertheless managed to cross the çetes' lines and flee to Dersim, as did 200 women from the little town of Kemah.[177]

In the *kaza* of Refahiye/Gerjanis, the eradication of the Armenians began on 3 June 1915. Three Armenian villages in the district – Gerjanis, Horopel, and Melik Sherif, with a total population of 1,570[178] – were surrounded by çetes, who killed their inhabitants on the spot.[179]

The inhabitants of the six villages of the *kaza* of Kuruçay, which had an Armenian population of 2,989 – Greater Armdan, Lesser Armdan, Apshda, Hasanova, Tughud, and Dantsi – as well as those in the six towns and villages of the district de Koziçan, which had an Armenian population of 4,700,[180] were not massacred in their villages, but deported. Most of the men were exterminated near Lecki Bridge while the women and children had their throats slit in the vicinity of Acem Dağ under the supervision of the parliamentary deputy from Kemah, Halet Bey, together with Şevki Abbas Oğlu, Hüseyin Ağa of Gerjanis, Elias Oğlu Mehmed Ağa, and Hüseyin Bey Zâde Hasan. Şevki Abbas Oğlu personally murdered the brothers Parsegh and Markar Avoyan and sent their heads to the *mutesarif*, Memduh, as a form of homage.[181]

The 862 Armenians living in the *kaza* of Pülumur/Polormor – in the villages of Perkri, Gersnud and Dantseg – were massacred there in late May.[182]

The Army's Role in the Eradication of the Armenians and the Fate of the Draftees from the Vilayet of Erzerum

We have already seen that the Armenian draftees from the eastern provinces, whom we clearly distinguished from those native to other vilayets, were assigned to both combat and transport units in the first months of the war. We must now say something about the treatment reserved for them after the deportations and massacres began in the Erzerum region. Let us start by pointing out that their fate was in the hands of the commander-in-chief of the Third Army, Mahmud Kâmil, as was that of the civilian population, inasmuch as the government had officially left it up to the army to decide how "urgent" the "displacement" of the "suspect" populations from the war zones to "the interior" was. Yet it was largely on the Armenian population that the Ottoman troops stationed in the vilayet of Erzerum depended for their maintenance; the Armenians billeted them in their own villages – the lack of barracks was no secret from anyone – fed them, provided them with draft animals, transported supplies for them on its backs, gave them medical care, and furnished them with products turned out by its craftsmen. In "displacing" the Armenian population "to the interior" – that is, in cutting off this source of logistical support – Mahmud Kâmil risked making the position of the Third Army untenable in very short order, as the vali of Erzerum, Tahsin, pointed out. In other words, from a strictly military point of view, the elimination of the Armenian civilians could be regarded as sheer folly. From a political and ideological point of view, on the other hand, it was perfectly consistent with the objectives of the Young Turk Central Committee, which sought to exclude non-Turks from the eastern provinces. Can we, moreover, imagine even for a moment that the handling of the Armenian question was really entrusted to Mahmud Kâmil or the army? This was impossible in a system in which the party's Central Committee reviewed all decisions. We must rather assume that the "security of the army's rear base" was merely an alibi designed to legitimize the extermination policy by providing it with a legal facade – the more so as the political decisions made in Istanbul clashed with the immediate interests of the military.

That said, we must ask who controlled the fate of the tens of thousands of Armenian conscripts who had been plucked from their natural environment and separated from their families. The examples at our disposal indicate that the army maintained its right to revise decisions bearing on these soldiers at least until May 1915, although we saw that, from winter 1914–15 on, the treatment meted out to them bordered on a policy of elimination by exhaustion or, for the less docile, incitation to desertion. During the deportations, the authorities sometimes even considered not deporting soldiers' families, although this held only for recruits from the provinces of western Anatolia, who fought in the Dardenelles or on the Syrian-Palestinian front. None of the contemporaneous accounts we have suggest that similar measures were ever considered in the eastern vilayets. It was as if the fate of the populations living in the Armenians' homeland had been clearly dissociated from that of the groups scattered throughout the west.

We have already seen that, from late February on, draftees in combat units who were natives of the vilayets of Erzerum and Bitlis were executed in small groups. However, the fate of these groups of combatants, who represented a minority of the Armenian draftees, has to be distinguished from that of the soldiers serving in the *amele taburis* or labor battalions. It would seem that the doom of the latter was sealed when that of the civilian populations was. Thus, the decision to liquidate them in the area under the jurisdiction of the Third Army was made around 15 May.[183] The most frequently used method consisted in turning them over in groups of 200 to 300 to *çetes*, who saw to their execution in the killing fields that we have already mentioned. This held, for example, for the 200 conscripts from Hınıs massacred in Çan, near Kiği,[184] as well as the 4,000 worker-soldiers from Harput who had been put to work on the road between Hoşmat and Palu; a deportee fleeing for his life saw their corpses, still in an early stage of decomposition, as he was making his way toward Dersim.[185] There were also intermediate cases, such as that of the drafted artisans employed directly by the army or in military workshops; the treatment of these people was less systematic. Thus, 60-year-old Eghia Torosian of Mamahatun, drafted despite his age, worked first in the hospital in Erzincan and was then, in May 1915, assigned to the 800-man-strong 35th Labor Battalion. These workers were employed in a military firm located 20 minutes from the center of the town of Mamahatun.[186] Despite the critical demand for experienced craftsmen, even this battalion was gradually shorn of a majority of its members, who were taken beyond the city limits at night in groups of 15 to 20 and quietly executed by *çetes* of the Special Organization. Nonetheless, 235 artisans survived.[187]

We also know about the case of Rupen Toroyan, a draftee from Erzerum. Along with his Muslim comrades, Toroyan was responsible for transporting supplies from Erzerum to the front. He witnessed the looting of the Armenian villages of Pasın, the sacking of the church in Olti, recently occupied by the Ottoman army, and the mistreatment of the 200 Armenians taken hostage in Olti.[188] In Odzni, where his regiment was based, he saw how Armenian villagers were expelled so that their homes could be taken over and their food stocks plundered.[189] In the nearby village of Ilija, he witnessed the expulsion of the inhabitants by gendarmes as well as the suffering these homeless peasants endured outside the village for six days before all of them were executed a short distance away. One of his Turkish companions, Corporal Ibrahim, confirmed what Toroyan had seen when he complained that he had had nothing of the windfall associated with the massacre of these Armenians, who were carrying a great deal of gold, "especially the women."[190]

After his return to Erzerum, Toroyan witnessed the departure of the convoys of deportees. Until then, he had not been molested in any way. His corporal nevertheless offered to save him if Toroyan brought him "a pretty girl." Arrested, like all the other Armenian draftees, he was sent off in a convoy comprising around 1,000 people, guarded by 60 gendarmes. The following morning, near Aşkale, *çetes* and soldiers encircled the caravan, stripped the deportees of their belongings and transferred the 200 to 300 conscripts in the convoy to the prison in Aşkale. Four or five of them starved to death every day. A few days afterwards, the conscripts from Erzerum – a detail in Toroyan's account indicating that there were other soldiers in the prison – were sent to work on the roads. They joined other Armenian workers under the surveillance of soldiers: one soldier for every ten recruits. Toroyan notes that he worked under these conditions for a period of five months, during which many of the Armenians, including his brother, were so badly mistreated that they died. The authorities then separated out craftsmen like Toroyan and sent the others "to the slaughterhouse of Kemah Deresi."

The remaining 200 men, who continued to work under appalling conditions, offered to convert to Islam. The question, says Toroyan, was referred up the hierarchical ladder until it reached the vali. Two days later, the men received a favorable response and a mullah arrived to initiate them into their new faith. Three months later came an order to assemble all the Armenian converts of Aşkale and send them to Erzerum. With seven of his companions, Toroyan worked in the state ironworks in Erzerum for some time. Ultimately, however, all of them were taken to a gorge near Aşkale, where hundreds of conscripts were shot on 15 February 1916. Toroyan, along with one of his comrades from Bitlis, escaped with his life because he had hidden under the corpses of his companions. He succeeded in finding refuge with a Turk from Aşkale who told him: "From now on, you're going to protect *me*: the Russians are coming."[191] There is every reason to believe that the sudden advance of the Russian army sealed the doom of the Armenian recruits still employed by the local authorities: they were liquidated despite their conversion to Islam.

There are a number of rather interesting stories of survival among the conscripts. The story of Krikor Keshishian from Pakarij is an example. When the general mobilization was announced, Keshishian was in prison. Although he was released in November, his status as a former convict meant that he could not legally serve in the army. He was mobilized nonetheless and sent to Mamahatun, where he joined the recruits assigned to transport military supplies to the front on their backs. Of a pragmatic turn of mind, Keshishian thought that it was ridiculous to impose an ordeal of that kind on soldiers, and bought three mules that could be used to transport supplies. The military authorities did not appreciate this display of initiative: they confiscated Keshishian's mules and he deserted. His parents then asked him to turn himself in, knowing that if he did not their house would be demolished. On 24 January 1915, the Keshishian family home was burned down with all the occupants inside, except for the men, who fled. According to Keshishian, 366 people from the villages of Tercan who had paid the *bedel* to avoid military service were arrested as deserters and sent to Erzerum on 15 February.[192]

Thus, it would seem that the commanders of the Third Army collaborated with the Special Organization, which was apparently responsible for executing the orders to eliminate the Armenian conscripts in the *amele taburis*. In certain instances, however, the military was able to retain a minimal number of craftsmen to ensure that its logistical needs would be met.

We do not have much material on the transmission of deportation-related orders in the area under the Third Army's jurisdiction. However, it seems that, at least until mid-summer, the commander-in-chief of the Third Army, Mahmud Kâmil, sent many cables ordering that

Armenians be exterminated, as was later admitted by General Süleyman Faik Pasha, commander of the garrison in Mamuret ul-Aziz.[193] Yet, beginning on 8 August 1915, the military authorities received orders no longer to concern themselves with the deportations but simply to cooperate with local government officials. It is likely that this decision was reached after an 18/31 July 1915 meeting in Erzincan attended by the valis of Erzerum, Trebizond, Harput, and Sıvas, as well as many *mutesarifs* and *kaymakams*, such as the *kaymakam* of Bayburt.[194] This meeting was without a doubt chaired by Bahaeddin Şakir. We do not, of course, know the substance of the discussion that took place in the fief of Şakir's main collaborator, in the *sancak* where most of the massacres of the vilayet's Armenians were carried out. However, given the date of the meeting, there is every reason to assume that it was called in order to draw up a preliminary balance sheet of the eradication of the Armenian population in the eastern provinces and, probably, assign the civilian authorities the task of completing the project conceived by the Ittihadist Central Committee. More particularly, the aim was to mop up the last Armenians who had somehow managed to elude the machine that Istanbul had put in place.

The circular telegram that the commander of the Third Army, Mahmud Kâmil, sent from his headquarters in Tortum on 10 July 1915 to the valis of Sıvas, Trebizond, Van, Mamuret ul-Aziz, Dyarbekir, and Bitlis[195] is the only official document on the question that we have. Submitted to the court-martial at the session of 27 April 1919, it is of inestimable value, for it provides proof of the Ittihadists' determination to pursue their project of destruction until they had eliminated the last Armenians left alive, even those who had converted to Islam or benn "integrated" into Turkish or Kurdish families:

> We have learned that, in certain villages the population of which has been sent to the interior, certain [elements] of the Muslim population have given Armenians shelter in their homes. Since this is a violation of government orders, heads of households who shelter or protect Armenians are to be executed in front of their houses and it is imperative that their houses be burned down. This order shall be transmitted in appropriate fashion and communicated to whom it may concern. See to it that no as yet undeported Armenian remains behind and inform us of the action you have taken. Converted Armenians must also be sent away. If those who attempt to protect Armenians or maintain friendly relations with them are members of the military, their ties with the army must be immediately severed, after their superiors have been duly informed, and they must be prosecuted. If they are civilians, they must be dismissed from their posts and tried before a court-martial.
>
> The Commander of the Third Army, Mahmud Kâmil, 10 July 1915.

This telegram bears a revealing annotation, dated 12 July and probably made by the vali or a high-ranking official of the vilayet of Sıvas: it requested that the order be transmitted "secretly, and in writing only in exceptional cases."[196]

The content of this circular leaves little room for doubt about the intentions of the commander of the Third Army, who probably did no more than carry out orders received from Istanbul to apprehend the last Armenians who had eluded the deportations by conversion to Islam, flight, or some other expedient. The severity of the punishment risked by Muslim families who were tempted to protect Armenians is a measure of the Ittihadist regime's determination to eliminate the entire Armenian population without exception. Revelatory in this regard is the case of two Armenians who were close to the German vice-consul of Erzerum – Sarkis Solighian, the owner of the building in which the consulate was housed, and Elfasian, the former dragoman. The vice-consul, Scheubner-Richter, was harassed for weeks by Hulusi Bey, the Erzerum police chief, who demanded that these two protégés of the consul's be deported without delay. They were finally arrested on 1 July 1915. Scheubner-Richter's appeals to Vali Tahsin notwithstanding, he proved unable to save the two Armenians, who, as everyone knew, were his only independent source of information about events in the region. As Hilmar Kaiser points out, the authorities' behavior was meant to demonstrate to local public opinion that even the German vice-consulate was incapable of protecting anyone.[197]

It is clear that the steps taken by the civilian and military authorities around mid-July 1915 were designed to carry the deportations to their term, eliminating the last Armenians in the vilayet. Witness two circular telegrams sent on 20 July by the interior minister to the local authorities, including those in Erzerum. They requested a precise assessment of the demographic situation in these regions before and after the deportations, as well as information on the number of Armenians who had converted to Islam and local government officials' attitude toward them. The aim, no doubt, was to evaluate the results of the work already accomplished, the better to decide on new measures.[198]

Conversion to Islam or the Struggle for Survival

In the preceding pages, we have noted instances (the most common) of conversion to Islam that took place while the deportations were underway; they involved, above all, women and children "adopted" by Turkish or Kurdish families. We have not, however, discussed the families that agreed to convert in order to escape the deportations or keep their property. While some of these families were sent to their deaths a few weeks after their compatriots, others, especially in the countryside or among the craftsmen of the urban centers, did indeed survive. As the reader will readily imagine, these converts who were allowed to remain in their homes did not often talk about their experience. One of the rare exceptions was Hovhannes Khanzarlian, a native of Erzerum, who confessed that he had been "compelled to abandon Christianity and adopt Islam."[199] Anticipating his critics, Khanzarlian says that they do not know what it means to spend days on end in a prison filled with nauseating odors, to be tortured daily, or to see one's companions strangled or sent off to die: "Ordinary mortals like me abandon their religion easily when they see that every other way out has been blocked and that conversion offers a glimmer of hope." Khanzarlian also notes, however, that he felt indescribable shame when he went to the mosque for the first time and began to pray; he had the feeling that "his ancestors shuddered." Our witness does not, however, refer only to his lineage. He also recalls what his teachers taught him and affirms that his national feelings also made it impossible for him to remain a Muslim. He points out, quite reasonably, that "in this infernal Turkey, nationality and religion are indissolubly linked." He also evokes the violence inflicted on his relatives, adding that he could not bear the fact that he bore the name "of those who had murdered his father and raped his sister"; that he felt as if he had "betrayed" their memory. The last argument advanced by Khanzarlian is, as it were, theoretical. It shows rather clearly how the Armenians of the provinces perceived their Muslim environment and the consequences of a possible conversion: "I was going to deprive myself of the benefit of exchanges with powerful minds."[200] In other words, he thought that if he accepted the law of the Prophet, he would be denied all access to modernity and the world of ideas – that to which the Ottoman Armenian world precisely aspired in this period.

The Banque Ottomane, the Local Authorities and the Spoliation of Armenian Property

The confiscation of Armenian property in the vilayet of Erzerum seems to have been a process that unfolded in several stages, depending on the type of assets in question.

Initially, it was doubtless the secret provisions of the Temporary Deportation Law[201] that provided an official as opposed to a legal framework for the operations of the local authorities; for the "Law on Abandoned Property" and its decree of application were not promulgated until fall 1915 – that is, well after the Armenian population had been deported.[202] It is probable that the extortion and various abuses from which civilian and military officials personally profited, and also the prevailing uncertainty as to who now owned what, compelled the Ittihadist authorities to adopt basic laws to protect the interests of the state and party, at least as far as real estate went. General Vehib Pasha, in the deposition he submitted to the Mazhar Commission, forthrightly stated how the cash and other valuables in the possession of the deportees from Erzerum and Trebizond were parceled out in the Kemah gorge:

> After [the deportees] were stripped of their money and jewels on the edge of the gorge there [and then] massacred and thrown into the waters of the Euphrates … the sums that had been taken from them were divided up on the basis of one-third for the Party of Union and Progress, one-third for the government, and one-third for the heads of the bands that carried out the massacres.[203]

In other words, those responsible for the deportations were invited, in some sense, to pay themselves for their labors out of what they took from the exiled Armenians.

Two men played key roles in organizing the seizure of Armenian assets in the vilayet of Erzerum: Hakkı Bey, the director of the customs office and future president of the local commission of the Emvalı Metruke, and Hüseyin Tosun Bey, the Ittihad's delegate in Erzerum and also "Milli agens müdiri" (head of the Milli Agency).[204] These two Ittihadist officials took a particular interest in the regional capital's well-to-do families – that is, in their real estate, stocks of merchandise, and bank accounts.

The information about the assets of these affluent families that Kaiser has brought to light – in particular, material from German consular archives[205] – shows that early in June, after it had been established that these families would be deported, the local authorities were obviously not prepared to handle issues related to their property. When the question of the confiscation of their holdings was raised, the director of the local branch of the Banque Impériale Ottomane (BIO), Pierre Balladur, went to Vali Tahsin with the suggestion that a mixed commission be created and charged with safeguarding the deportees' assets, although the bank would not insure them against loss.[206] Balladur fairly quickly obtained approval for the plan from his board of directors in Istanbul. Approval from Tahsin Bey's superiors was somewhat longer in coming: on 9 June, Tahsin received rather precise instructions from the Interior Ministry to the effect that all property belonging to the Armenians was to be auctioned off.[207] The stocks of Erzerum's major wholesale merchants had, however, already been transferred to the Armenian cathedral on the BIO's authority.[208] It seems that it was the BIO board, made up of three administrators in Istanbul – two of them Armenian[209] – which turned to the minister of finance (Talât had become interim finance minister after Cavid's resignation) with the request that he settle the dispute over the Armenian assets held by the bank. The board demanded that "a ruling be made to protect the bank's interests."[210] André Autheman, in his history of the BIO, notes that the question was more pressing in Erzerum than elsewhere because the bank had been entrusted with a "considerable amount" of property in that city – merchandise worth over 400,000 Turkish pounds – while "the Armenians' assets, after their departure, had been taken in hand by the local authorities, but under conditions that had not been defined."[211]

In other words, Talât no doubt conceived the idea of passing a Law on Abandoned Property after being thus approached by the BIO While the "considerable amount" of property entrusted to the bank was ultimately confiscated after the creation of the local commission of the Emvalı Metruke in October 1915,[212] over the stiff resistance by Pierre Balladur, it proved much harder for the authorities to lay their hands on the bank accounts of the Armenians deported from Erzerum and elsewhere. The only way to do so was to nationalize the BIO, which was distinguished by the fact that most of its capital was held by two enemy countries, France and Great Britain, while it continued to perform the crucial function of a bank of issue. On 11 July 1915, the Council of Ministers did indeed decide to take over administration of the bank – not, as Autheman rather naively seems to think, "in order to secure advantages from it,"[213] but rather in order to be able to deal with the Armenians' accounts as it saw fit. Let us add that the BIO decided in February 1916 to freeze the accounts of these "clients currently traveling," some of whom before then had succeeded in obtaining advances from its branches in Syria and Mesopotamia.[214]

According to a report written after the war by a well-informed survivor from Erzerum, the Armenians of the vilayet of Erzerum controlled 80 per cent of local commerce, as well as trade with the other provinces of the empire and foreign trade; they owned some 60 commercial firms with an annual turnover of more than 30,000 Turkish pounds, 500 firms with a turnover between 10,000 and 15,000 Turkish pounds, and 2,500 firms with a turnover between 800 and 1,000 Turkish pounds. The author of the report also underscores the generally elevated educational level of the Armenian population, the knowhow of its artisans, and the substantial amount of property belonging to national institutions, particularly monastic communities such as Garmir Vank and Lusavorichi Vank, as well as the cathedral of Erzerum.[215]

According to Alphonse Arakelian, the property "abandoned" by the Armenians of the vilayet had a total value of 17,503,000 Turkish pounds. The value of that held by merchants was 7,300,000 Turkish pounds; civil servants, 1,000,000 Turkish pounds; the three big religious institutions and 37 monasteries, 850,000 Turkish pounds; the diocese of the Armenian Apostolic Church of Erzerum, 310,000 Turkish pounds; the diocese of the Armenian Catholic Church, 50,000 Turkish pounds; and the Armenian Protestant Church, 10,000 Turkish pounds. To these sums we must add 372 village churches, with their properties, representing a value of 581,000 Turkish pounds; the holdings of 19,000 peasant families, with a value of 5,730,000 Turkish pounds; and the assets of 8,390 artisan families, with a value of 1,672,000 Turkish pounds.[216]

The Human Balance

In February 1916, when the Russian army took control of the better part of the vilayet of Erzerum, there remained only a few dozen Armenian craftsmen and doctors, together with 200 or 300 survivors, most of whom had found refuge in the mountains of Dersim. As we have said, 33,000 people from the vilayet, almost all of them from the *sancak* of Bayazid, had fled to the Caucasus, and somewhat over 5,000 women and children had survived in the places to which they were deported: Mosul (1,600), Urfa (300) and Aleppo (1,000), with another 2,200 scattered through Syria and Mesopotamia. Virtually the whole of the surviving male population consisted of 120 men.[217]

Chapter 4

Resistance and Massacres in the Vilayet of Van

With its 450 towns and villages and a pre-war Armenian population of 110,897, the vilayet of Van, characterized by its many mountains and rugged topography, was thinly populated. It had, however, an Armenian majority. The *kaza* of Van, with its 116 Armenian villages and 53,589 inhabitants, accounted by itself for almost half the total Armenian population.[1] In an environment of this sort, the Armenian committees had considerable influence on the decisions of the local authorities. As we have seen, down to early April 1915, outside the border zones, the *kazas* of Mahmudiye/Saray and Başkale,[2] the Armenian population suffered only from the excesses spawned by the war requisitions. Such excesses were, in the final analysis, common in conflicts of this sort.

An examination of the events that led the Armenian population of Van to entrench itself in the old city of Aykesdan on the morning of 20 April 1915[3] indicates that in all probability Enver's brother-in-law, Cevdet, returned to the region from Persia late in March with a mission: to have done with the Armenians of Van once and for all, and to begin by liquidating its three Armenian leaders, who had until then, in their role as intermediaries, helped smooth over the minor conflicts that cropped up here and there in the vilayet. The vali obviously knew, when he decreed on 18 April that the population had to turn in its arms, that he was facing the Armenians with a difficult choice. They knew that they were doomed if they obeyed; yet, if they failed to, they would provide the vali with the pretext he needed to attack the city's Christian quarters and the rural areas. In other words, the Armenian leaders' strategy of temporization had become obsolete. The murder of Ishkhan on the night of 16 April and the arrest of Arshag Vramian – Van still did not know that he had been murdered – probably convinced the last Armenian leader left alive, Aram Manukian, to reject the authorities' injunctions and prepare the city for an attack that was now certain to come.

In examining the course of events in Van, we cannot ignore the incidents that occurred from 11 April onwards in the administrative seat of the *kaza* of Shadakh/Şadakh in Tagh,[4] a little town with an exclusively Armenian population of 2,000 that was located in the mountainous area that towers up to the south of Lake Van. Here, Hovsep Choloyan and five other young men were arrested on 11 April 1915 on orders from the *kaymakam*, Hamdi Bey. The people of Tagh interpreted these arrests as a provocation. Choloyan was the director of the district's Armenian school system and also the head of the local Dashnak committee.[5] This was the first time that the authorities had arrested an Armenian leader from the ARF's ranks. There was no apparent reason for their action, which met with sharp protests from the inhabitants of Tagh. According to A-To, whose book on the events in Van, written shortly after they occurred, is the best-documented study of the subject, it was Cevdet who ordered Hamdi Bey to have Choloyan and the five other activists arrested. In A-To's view,

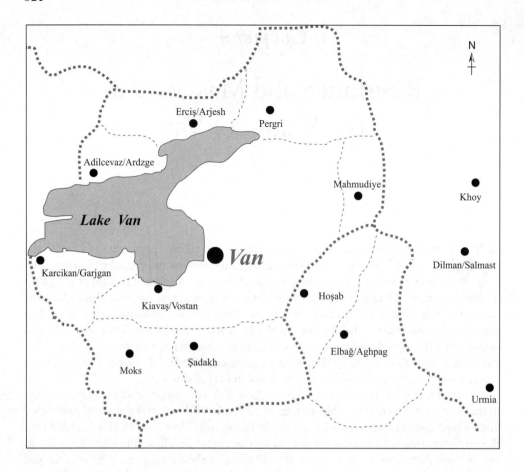

it is inconceivable that the *kaymakam* could have taken such a step on his own.[6] The director of the American hospital in Van, Dr. Clarence Ussher, affirms for his part that Cevdet
"thought this a good opportunity" to suggest that Ishkhan go to Shadakh and conduct an
inquiry so that he could have him murdered en route.[7] In other words, Cevdet had staged
this provocation, which targeted a regional Dashnak leader, in order to step up the pressure
without precipitating an immediate break with the ARF in Van. Moreover, there are indications that in late March Kaymakam Hamdi had already ordered the local Kurdish tribes who
had recently returned from the Caucasian front to "hold themselves at the ready."[8]

On 12 April, the authorities in Tagh demanded that the Armenian population turn in
its arms. It was common knowledge that the Kurdish tribes roamed this region armed; hence
obeying the order would, according to A-To, have been tantamount to "committing suicide."[9]
The messages exchanged between Hamdi and Cevdet, discovered in the sub-prefecture after
the Turkish evacuation of the area, seem to indicate that the *kaymakam* and the vali were
aware that calling on the Armenians to disarm amounted to instigating a confrontation.[10] A
native of Tagh, Dikran Baghdasarian, an officer who had been educated in Istanbul's Military
Academy and had recently returned from the Caucasian front after being wounded in Köprüköy,
was one of the first to meet with Hamid Bey, with whom he had maintained friendly relations
until then. Baghdasarian, who would become a few days later the soul of the defense of the
Armenian eagle's nest and its environs, suggested in vain that Hamdi free Hovsep Cholayan.
On 14 April 1915, the *kaymakam* demanded that the Armenians of Tagh open their shops and
go about their business as usual. The leaders of the self-defense committee agreed to do so on

two conditions: that Choloyan be set free and that the gendarmes and militiamen stationed in positions threatening the town be pulled back.[11] Until 16 April, the status quo was more or less respected: the *kaymakam* was apparently waiting for orders from Van. The day before, the villages located in the eastern part of the *kaza* – Vakhrov, Arikom, Akrus, Kerments, Sheghchants, Arosgi, Gvers, Baghg, Babonts, Paghchgants, Shino, Shamo and Eritsu, with a total population of about one thousand – had been attacked by Kurdish tribes; the inhabitants had been forced to take refuge in the villages of Kerments and Babonts.[12] The skirmishes in the administrative seat of the *kaza*, Tagh, did not begin until 17 April, when militiamen tried to surround the upper section of the Armenian town.[13]

It goes without saying that the two parties interpreted these early incidents in radically opposed ways. Cevdet was in the process of methodically laying the groundwork for his plan to liquidate the Armenians, who, for their part, scrutinized the authorities' gestures and acts in an attempt to make out their intentions and react accordingly. The incident at Tagh, which gave Cevdet the opportunity to eliminate two of the three Armenian leaders, certainly helped crystallize the Armenians' energies, while convincing Cevdet to make moves that would bring on a rupture. In any case, if we examine the violence that erupted in the surrounding districts beginning on 18 April, we can understand much better why, in the days leading up to 20 April, the Van Armenians prepared to withstand a siege of their neighborhoods.

Massacres in the *Nahies* of Arjag and Timar

The violence that preceded the siege of Van was not limited to the *kaza* of Shadakh. The *nahie* of Arjag (Erçek), located on the shores of Lake Arjag two hours to the northeast of Van, learned on 16 April from the Kurd Nuro Pisoğlanı, a notable who maintained close relations with Armenian circles, that the *kaymakam* of Perkri, Ziya Bey, had called a meeting of the *muhtars* of the area in order to warn them that, should massacres occur, Kurds must not give refuge to Armenians or protect them, on pain of being shot. The *kaymakam* of Mahmudiye, Kâmil Bey, had been assigned the task of massacring the inhabitants of the *nahie*; he was accompanied on his mission by 150 gendarmes, backed up by Kurdish contingents under the chieftains Şaraf Beg of Khanasor, Nacib Ağa of Mugur, and Arif Beg of Şav. The first village to be attacked, on 18 April, was Mandran (pop. 390), which had made a name for itself in the past by resisting Kurdish attacks. Fifteen people were killed and the village was mercilessly plundered, but the women and children managed to flee without being seriously threatened. On 19 April, Arjag was attacked by *çetes* under the command of the *kaymakam* of Perkri, Ziya Bey: one hundred people lost their lives, houses were burned down and many women were raped.[14] However, when, on the afternoon of the same day, these irregulars attacked the village of Kharagonis (pop. 1,525). Some 200 people were concentrated there, with the refugees from Mandran, Hazara, and Boğazkiasan, and they were met with heavy gunfire. On 20 April, all the forces under the *kaymakams* of Perkri and Saray were regrouped before Kharagonis, but did not launch their second assault until 21 April, when they attacked a village in which only old men, women, and children remained – a good part of the population had fled to Mt. Kızılja in the area north of the lake – slaughtering around 50 of them and burning the village to the ground.[15]

On 19 April, the villages of the northeastern part of the *nahie* of Timar, which were located on the eastern shore of Lake Van, were attacked in their turn: the villagers of Ardavez (pop. 118), Goj (pop. 137), Atikeozal (pop. 226), Giusnents (pop. 825), Seydibeg (pop. 56), as well as those from two villages bordering on the *kazas* of Perkri, Keaparig (pop. 379), and Kharashig, also sought refuge on the flanks of Mt. Kızılja. On 22 April, 300 Kurdish *çetes* attempted to attack them from the north, but were beaten back by heavy gunfire. On 23 April, the throng of refugees on Mt. Kızılja was further swollen with peasants from Napat (pop. 165), Yalguzarach (pop. 49), Kızılja (pop. 423), Boghants (pop. 451), and Paytag (pop. 195), who were fleeing the *çetes.*

The lack of hygiene and food, however, made the situation of those who had found refuge on Mt. Kızılja literally untenable, leading the village headmen to organize a withdrawal toward the little town of Averag (pop. 1,061), located on the plain, on the morning of 24 April. The result was that some 8,000 people in all found themselves crowded together in Averag, where they were notably joined by the inhabitants of Shahpagh. That afternoon, Averag was surrounded by squadrons of irregulars and a few gendarmes. They met with powerful resistance.[16] During the night, 7,000 people, escorted by a few young men under arms, made a successful attempt to break through their encirclement and reach Van.[17] On 25 and 26 April, the forces that had surrounded Averag went on to attack Tarman and Gokhbants, where the inhabitants of Lim (pop. 143), Zarants (pop. 240), Sevan (pop. 439), Ermants (pop. 24), Bakhezeg (pop. 98), Farugh (pop. 210), and Osgerag (pop. 270) had taken refuge, bringing the total number of people in Tarman and Gokhbants, defended by 70 men, to 3,000. Adopting the same tactics as the refugees who had been concentrated in Averag, this group succeeded in reaching the slopes of Mt. Varak, further south; villagers who had come from localities southeast of Lake Van were also concentrated here.[18]

The villages in the northern part of the *nahie* of Timar, Aliur (pop. 1,955), Marmet (pop. 811), Ererin (pop. 938), Khzhishg (pop. 775), Giusnents (pop. 825), Boghants (pop. 451), Khavents (pop. 633), and Janik (pop. 714), were not spared by the militiamen and squadrons of *hamidiyes* under Captain Amar and Arif Beg, reinforced by members of the Şavetli tribe (from Perkri). Inhabitants of mentioned villages were attacked on 21 April. They met with resistance, however, at Asdvadzadzin/Diramayr (pop. 462), Khzhishg, Aliuret, and Marmet, where the inhabitants of the surrounding villages had come together. Seventy people were killed in Asdvadzadzin and 73 more in Janik.[19] It was in this district, the furthest from the administrative seat of the *kaza*, that thousands of people who had come from the villages of Pirgarib, Sosrat, Shahkialdi, Janik, Asdvadzadzin/Diramayr, Norashen, Kochan, Norovants, and Koms found themselves massed on the lakeshore opposite the island of Lim toward the end of the day of 21 April. On 22 April, militiamen and *hamidiyes*, followed by a crowd attracted by the prospect of plunder and acquiring young women, marched on the encampment that had been hastily set up on the shores of Lake Van.[20] A few dozen armed men fended off the attackers while the villagers were transferred to the island by boat. It took a full three days to transfer all of these 12,000 people to the island of Lim, where the situation soon became critical for lack of food. On 25 April, after having cleaned out the Armenian villages of Upper Timar, the *kaymakam* of Perkri, Ziya Bey, with his militiamen and *çetes*, laid siege to Aliur, the biggest town in the district. Concentrated here were villagers from Paylag/Paytag (pop. 195), Adnagants (pop. 247), and Derlashen (pop. 657), protected by 160 armed men.[21] Unable to break their resistance, the *kaymakam* offered to spare the village if the armed men agreed to leave. As in other localities, the notables accepted the proposal; the militias and Kurds thereupon proceeded to lock the 160 men in the church and began looting the village. The population fled. On 28 April, the men in the church were tied together and taken in small groups to a place called Ekbağ, where they were massacred in the usual fashion with knives, bayonets, and axes.[22] On 27 April, the men who had conducted this attack, led by Ali Beg of the Şavetli tribe, launched an assault on the village of Marmet, whose mayor, Raïs Hovhannes, chose to negotiate. He asked the 60 armed men present to leave. One hundred men were thereupon arrested, locked into the church, and then led to Zhagatsi Tsor, half an hour from Marmet, where they were liquidated at the same time as 25 men from Zhirashen.[23]

Massacres in the *Kaza* of Erçiş

Located on the northeastern shore of Lake Van, the *kaza* of Erciş/Arjesh boasted 54 Armenian towns and villages on the eve of the war, with a total population of 10,381.[24] In the administrative seat of the *kaza*, Agants (2,078 Armenians), the *kaymakam*, a Young Turk from Istanbul, Ali Rıza Bey, ordered on 19 April that all the Armenian men in the small town gather before the sub-prefecture. Four hundred men were locked up on that day in the town jail. In the evening, the men were bound together in groups of ten and conducted by gendarmes and militiamen toward the lakeport, near the village of Khargen (pop. 285), where they were shot.[25] The same day, 700 to 800 men from the neighboring villages who had been confined in the barracks near the town's southwestern exit met the same fate. Among the men detained in the town jail and executed in the evening were the auxiliary primate, Father Yeghishe, and the other leading citizens of the town: Nicolas and Sarkis Shaljian, Harutiun, Nshan, Khosrov, and Serop. An eyewitness remarks that in the evening the *kaymakam* delivered a solemn speech to the militiamen assembled on Agants's central square, urging them to pursue their operation to help save the fatherland.[26] In the course of the day, these *çetes* of the Special Organization had systematically attacked all the Armenian villages in the *kaza* and massacred the rest of the population.[27]

According to A-To, of the 10,381 Armenians in the *kaza*, 2,378 had been massacred by 19 April, 518 (for the most part young women and children) had been abducted, 953 had been carried off by disease or starvation, and 693 were missing. This represented 4,542 people, nearly 45 per cent of the total Armenian population.[28] The survivors managed to flee northeast behind the Russian lines, which were then situated on a line running through Dyadin. Thus, a method that would be used elsewhere in the following weeks had already been applied here: it consisted in first liquidating the men and then wiping out the towns and villages.

Massacres in the *Kaza* of Perkri

According to a survivor from the Perkri area, Mushegh Mgrdichian of the village of Yegmal, most of the men of the 41 towns and villages of the *kaza* of Pergri/Perkri, which had a total population of 5,152,[29] had been working in the region's *amele taburis* since the August 1914 general mobilization. In early April, gendarmes nevertheless scoured the villages of this *kaza*, located at the northeastern extremity of Lake Van, in order to "mobilize" all the males over 15, "so as to beef up the battalions of worker-soldiers." The same informant states that approximately 1,000 men were working in the *amele taburis* at the time; they were repairing the roads in the Abagha Valley, where the snow was beginning to melt. On 19 April, these men were massacred in groups of 25 in the narrowest part of the Pante Mahu gorge, which extended to a point "two versts" southwest of Perkri, near the medieval Golod Bridge. Their executioners were gendarmes and militiamen commanded by Milis Iso Telun. A Kurdish commander of a squadron of *hamidiyes*, Tahar Beg, had been poisoned at a meal with the *kaymakam* and the commander of the gendarmerie, Amar Bey, for trying to protect some of these men.[30] On the same day, 80 men were murdered in the village of Khachan (pop. 600), including Usta Mgo, his five brothers, two sons, and several of his nephews.[31] On the morning of the 19 April, the village of Kordzot (pop. 790), located on the boundary of the *nahie* of Timar, received a visit from the *kaymakam*, Ziya Bey, and the commander of the gendarmerie, Amar Bey, accompanied by 200 men and the auxiliary primate, Der Manvel. The villagers scraped up 50 Turkish pounds and ten rifles, in the belief that that would be enough to satisfy the authorities. Eighty-six men were nevertheless arrested and locked up in the Meloyan family home. On the morning of 20 April, the gendarmes set them marching toward Yeghunatsor, where they were all massacred.[32]

The neighboring village of Bzdig Kiugh (pop. 447) was occupied on the morning of 20 April by 300 militiamen and *hamidiyes* under the orders of Süleyman from Irishad (Arjesh); 120 men were arrested in the village and shot in the vicinity, while the village itself was looted and 60 people were slaughtered. Those who attempted to flee down the road to Perkri were shot as they ran or executed on the Golod Bridge in the Pante Mahu gorge. The next villages to be attacked were Engizag (pop. 311), Surp Tatos (pop. 211), Antsav (pop. 108), and Panz; 60 men from these villages had their throats slit, while the villages were looted and burned down.[33] Some of the inhabitants of these villages found refuge in Kordzot; among them were 50 armed men. When, on 25 April, Kurdish *çetes* went to Kordzot to seize its wheat reserves, they were met with heavy gunfire. Doubtless busy wiping out the other villages in the area, Amar Bey and several hundred militiamen waited until 7 May to attack the village. They were met, this time, with spirited resistance that lasted three days. When the Armenian volunteers arrived in the village on 15 May, they were confronted with a morbid spectacle: its central square was strewn with corpses.[34]

Massacres in the *Kaza* of Adilcevaz

In 1915, there were 25 Armenian villages in the last *kaza* on the north shore of Lake Van – the one furthest west, Adilcevaz/Ardzge, which had a total population of 6,460.[35] As we have already seen, Rafaël de Nogales, a captain who had been assigned to the Third Army, arrived in Adilcevaz on the evening of 20 April, where he witnessed the massacre of the 500 Armenians who lived in the administrative seat of the *kaza*. The next morning, he watched as their quarter was looted and then burned down on direct orders from the *kaymakan*, who "thanked me effusively for having saved the town from the tremendous Armenian attack."[36]

The villages of the *kaza* of Adilcevaz had already come under attack on 19 April. In Norshechur, 40 men managed to flee to a mixed Kurdish-Armenian village, Kızıl Yusuf, located in the neighboring *kaza* of Manazgerd/Melazkırt (in the vilayet of Bitlis), where the massacres had yet to begin. The *kaymakam* of Adilcevaz, however, sent gendarmes after them; they killed the 40 fugitives in the village.[37] It thus appears that the orders received from Erzerum and Istanbul concerned only the Armenians of the vilayet of Van, and not at all those of the neighboring districts.

Massacres in the *Kaza* of Kiavaş/Vostan
and in Hayots Tsor

In the *kaza* of Kiavaş/Vostan, which boasted 25 Armenian villages with a population of 6,851,[38] generalized massacres began on 18 April in Hirj (pop. 205), where Ishkhan had been assassinated the previous day. Forty-six men were slain here. The same day, the other villages in the eastern part of the *kaza*, Atanan (pop. 372) and Spidag Vank (pop. 124), were attacked and set ablaze. A day later, Edhem, a captain in the gendarmerie, arrived in Van at the head of 300 militiamen equipped with two cannons and shelled Beltents (pop. 386). On 18 April, the Kurdish chieftain Lazkin Şakiroğlu attacked two localities in Hayots Tsor, on the Norduz road. In Angshdants (pop. 411), the notables, including the mayor, Murad, who tried to reason with the Kurdish leader, were shot. Twenty men, however, defended the village well enough to prevent the attackers from taking control of it.[39]

The same day, Lazkin and his men plundered the neighboring village of Eremeri (pop. 432), which was defenseless, and then massacred 80 people. A young man barricaded in a house, Sahag Kaprielian, was the only one to hold his own with the *çetes*; he killed seven Kurds. After nightfall, he led the survivors to Gurubaş.[40]

The next day, 19 April, Angshdants was encircled again. Its defenders fled that night, leaving the way open before Lazkin and his *çetes*. Seventy people were killed in the village, while the others fled northeast toward the mountainous region of Varak and the Kurdish village of Temkos. Lazkin's third target, Gghzi (pop. 312), was counting on the protection of a local Kurdish *beg*, Mahmad Şarif. Şarif intervened, but to no avail: on the afternoon of 19 April, 60 people were massacred in Gghzi, including Hovsep Aloyan, Harutiun Garabedian, Vartan Manukian, and Father Mgrdich. Retrenched in a house, eight young men resisted until nightfall, when they fled to Pertag and Varak.[41]

On 20 April, Lazkin attacked Gem (pop. 547) and Ankgh (pop. 678), which lay south of Van in Hayots Tsor. He was backed up by two other *çete* leaders, Jıhankir and Sadul. He had two cannons at his disposal. The inhabitants of Musgavents/Mashdag (pop. 394) and Gzltash/Kızıltaş (pop. 314) had also thronged into Gem, where they were defended by 60 armed men who were unable to fend off the *çetes'* attack. The survivors poured onto the road to Ankgh, where 150 people were massacred.[42] The same day, Ankgh was attacked in its turn; 270 villagers were slain there, while 300 fled toward the Khoshap River, where 100 more perished. Thus, a total of 700 people were massacred on 20 April.[43] What was left of the population of the villages in the vicinity gathered in Ishkhani Kom (pop. 409), located between the Semiramis Canal and the Khoshap. On the afternoon of 20 April, Lazkin, Jıhankir, Sadul, and their *çetes*, who had been joined by the contingent under Captain Edhem to form a force of around 1,000 men equipped with four cannons, attacked the village, defended by 80 men. Eight hundred men of all ages retreated to Varak, to the east, while the women and children set out for Ardamed, where 300 were massacred. Three thousand people, however, succeeded in reaching either Van or Varak.[44]

A total of some 2,000 survivors from Beltents, Gghzi, Spidag Vank, Atanan, and Kızıltaş took refuge on Mt. Gghzi, where they remained for around three weeks. On 10 May, the *kaymakam* of Kiavaş arrived with 200 militiamen and attacked the Armenian villagers. Some fled toward Van and Varak; the bulk of the group succeeded in reaching the plain of Pzantashd in the northwestern part of the *kaza* of Şatak/Shadakh, where people from Karcikan/Garjgan and the villages in the western part of the *kaza* of Kavaş had gathered.[45]

Massacres and Resistance in the *Nahie* of Varak

Varak, a mountainous district lying one hour east of Van, containing the monastery of St. Gregory and the villages of Tarman (pop. 482), Gokhbants (pop. 218), Tsorovants (100 Armenians and 240 Kurds), and Shushants (pop. 559), offered a haven to thousands of villagers from both the immediate vicinity and Hayots Tsor in the first days of the massacres in the area. This mountainous zone was the more important in that it communicated with the *nahie* of Arjag and the Persian border, while dominating the Khoshap/Hoşab-Başkale road, which the inhabitants of Van regarded as a possible escape route.[46] This no doubt explains why some 30 gendarmes took up positions in the monastery of Varak at a rather early stage in the fighting. On the evening of 20 April, these gendarmes murdered the monastery's two monks, Father Aristakes and Father Vrtanes, along with their four servants, and then, oddly enough, abandoned their position and returned to the city. It was precisely at this moment that 3,000 fugitives from Hayots Tsor, Nor Kiugh (pop. 413), Lim (pop. 143), Zarants (pop. 240), Sevan (pop. 439), Ermants (pop. 24), Bakhezeg/Baghezig (pop. 98), Farugh (pop. 210), and Osgerag/Osgipag (pop. 270) arrived in these heights, defended by 60 men. The 6,000 refugees on Mt. Varak even succeeded in establishing a nighttime link with the city.[47]

Spared by the early fighting, the mountainous area was attacked on 8 May on orders from Vali Cevdet by a substantial force, the "Erzerum Battalion," which comprised 300 cavalrymen and 1,000 militiamen and *çetes*, equipped with three batteries of cannons. The Armenian defenders facing them were deployed in three positions: 50 men under Hagop Blgoyan were stationed in Gokhbants; 250, under Toros's orders, were posted in the monastery at Varak; another 250, commanded by Shirin Hagopian of Arjag, had taken up positions in Shushants. The first attack was launched against Shushants, which was taken and burned down after putting up a feeble defense. The attackers then turned to Gokhbants and its monastery of St. Gregory, which also gave way; the ancient monastery of Varak and its collections of medieval manuscripts were given over to the flames. In the space of three days, the 6,000 people who had been concentrated here managed to reach Van, traveling by night.[48] One Armenian source has it that Cevdet made no attempt to hinder the refugees' flight into the city, "so that he could starve the population and overcome the obstinacy of the defenders faster and more easily."[49]

The Siege of Van

While most Armenians in Van were concentrated in the quarter known as Aykesdan (the "Gardens"), located in the eastern part of the city just below the fortress, some of them lived in the fortified old city, where the shops and main government offices were located. Between the two neighborhoods lay a virtually uninhabited area. Thus, the resistance movements that the Turkish forces battled for three weeks – one in the old city and the other in Aykesdan – could not, practically speaking, communicate.[50] The first clashes occurred on 20 April in Aykesdan, at dawn; the Armenians barricaded themselves in the old city three hours later, when Van was shelled from the western part of the Urartuan citadel in which one of the city's barracks and the ammunitions depot were found.[51]

Dr. Clarence Ussher, who had been the private physician of Tahir Pasha, the former vali of Van, had known his son Cevdet well when Cevdet was still a young man, as well as his wife, the sister of Minister of War Enver. In his description of this modern, refined Young Turk, the American physician remarks that he "had proved himself past-master of the art of concealment and dissimulation" by convincing the Armenians of his good intentions in order to assassinate Ishkhan the more easily, and by maintaining "pleasant social relations" with the missionaries before shelling this den of "infidels" and frankly voicing his real feelings about them.[52] In the missionary's view, everything went to show that Cevdet "had planned for 19 April a massacre of all the Armenians in the vilayet." At the missionaries' insistence, however, he agreed to discuss with them his proposal to station gendarmes in the American mission "for [their] protection," and even postponed executing his plans for the city for 24 hours, a "delay [that] had been responsible for the effective defense."[53] Of all the participants in these events, Ussher is the only one to have suggested this hypothesis. However, the chronology of the massacres in all the *kazas* of the vilayet of Van, with the exception of the Shadakh/Şatak massacre, seems to corroborate it.

Van's defenders, albeit heavily outnumbered and poorly armed, had an advantage – they found themselves in a densely urban environment – and a disadvantage: their positions communicated directly with all the government buildings in the city, such as the Administration of the Public Debt, the courthouse, the police station, and the regional government building, which constituted so many positions from which the Turkish forces could attack them. This explains why the leaders of the resistance decided on the very first day of the fighting to send out commandos with the mission of burning these buildings down.[54]

Shortly after the fighting began, during the night of 21–22 April, an eyewitness and central participant in the Van events, Rafaël de Nogales, the Venezuelan officer who had been put at the disposal of the vali of Van, arrived on a boat in the city's lakeport. After witnessing the massacre of Adilcevaz's Armenians the day before, he saw, while he was still crossing the lake, the bright light emanating from the "burning villages," especially the village of Ardamed, where affluent families from Van spent the summer (the village church was blazing "like a torch").[55] The next morning, while Nogales was inspecting positions in both parts of Van, he witnessed the arrival of several hundred Kurds who were supposed "to help in killing all the Armenians" and take part in the "bacchanal of barbarity" – a manhunt for the handful of Armenians who had not been able to make their way to one of the quarters that were resisting. A brave attempt notwithstanding, de Nogales was unable to rescue two young men from the hands Kurdish *çetes*, who ignored his orders to desist and killed both of them.[56] In the outskirts of Aykesdan, in front the American mission, he averted his gaze so as not to have to witness the spectacle of dogs fighting over corpses. Further on, he observed "the Musulman populace during [its] zealous search for treasure" in the Armenian homes outside the combat zone. He also noted the care the authorities took to have the corpses of the Armenian victims burned, in order to wipe away "the other traces of their crimes."[57]

When, a little later, de Nogales went to dine with Vali Cevdet, he discovered "a panther in human form" in his luxurious villa, dressed "à la dernière mode parisienne." Cevdet was flanked by one Captain Reşid and his battalion of Laz "Janissaries." Reşid's task was to carry out all the vali's "secret orders." The Venezuelan officer was struck by the contrast between the violence raging a few dozen yards away and the refined surroundings of the residence of the vali, who was an educated man. Among the guests was "a gentleman called Achmed Bey," who fascinated Nogales. Wearing a well-cut English tweed suit and fluent in several languages, "with his aristocratic manners and his rather blasé expression," this was "none other than the notorious bandit" Çerkez Ahmed, the leader of a group of "Circassian" *çetes*.[58] A native of Serez in Macedonia, this *fedayi* of the Ittihadist Central Committee and major in the army had made headlines a few years earlier by assassinating high-ranking government officials and journalists who had denounced the political practices of the Young Turks, and also by taking part in the 23 January 1913 coup d'état that cost the minister of war his life.[59] After fading back into anonymity for a time, the major was named one of the officers of the Special Organization and dispatched to Van with his squadron of butchers in order to lend Cevdet a hand.[60]

Nogales was well aware that the "only political offense … of hundreds of innocent women and children consisted in being Christians." This by no means prevented him from accepting the mission Cevdet assigned him: he was to take "the direction of the siege" and coordinate two companies of artillery that he set up in the citadel.[61]

A considerable force had been put at his disposal. It consisted of battalions of Circassian and Turkish volunteers, battalions of gendarmes, including a mounted battalion, regular troops, and 1,200 to 1,300 Kurdish *çetes*, almost all of them "attracted by the hope of sacking the town." Thus, he had the rough equivalent of a division at his command – 10,000 to 12,000 men.[62]

One of the major problems that the other camp, the Armenians, had to contend with was the Turkish artillery, which pounded their two fallback positions without let-up. The network of deep trenches that they had dug went only part of the way toward solving the problem: every night, brigades of masons repaired the holes that Turkish shells had ripped in the defense lines. The other major problem that the defenders of Aykesdan had to overcome was the fact that the Hamudağa barracks butted up against the eastern part of the Armenian quarter; from there the Turkish forces chipped away at the Armenian positions. However, a few audacious Armenian soldiers succeeded in making their way to the basement of the barracks, which had been built in 1904 in order to control Aykesdan; they crawled through the network of *kanas*, the tunnels traditionally used for the distribution of water in the city. On

22 April, at 4 p.m., mines that were placed with great precision under the foundations of the barracks exploded, setting off a fire that reduced the building to ashes and forced the Turkish troops to abandon the adjacent position of Şahbender.[63] This swift success both relieved and galvanized the Armenians. Nogales, for his part, noted that "the resistance of the Armenians was terrific ... Each house was a fortress that had to be conquered separately." He even had the feeling that the Armenians were always able to guess his intentions, because the positions that he considered attacking were consistently defended by men in large numbers.[64]

On the Venezuelan officer's own admission, Cevdet was unnerved by the "heroic resistance of Van" – the expression is Nogales's – which withstood the fierce assaults conducted by regular forces or *çetes* as well as the *déluge de feu* that rained down on the city. After five days of fighting and a by no means negligible loss of human life, the Turkish and Kurdish volunteers were visibly demoralized, as their commander observed: the Kurds "evaporated by the dozens, and toward the last by the hundreds, as the siege was prolonged."[65] Among the other measures taken by Cevdet, Nogales notes that he ordered the American mission shelled, although the vali himself claimed that the shelling resulted from an error; subsequent events showed that he was determined to liquidate the "American *giaours* [infidels]."[66] Cevdet also ordered the bombardment of St. Peter and Paul Cathedral, a building in the old city that had "a monument of unquestionable historical" value.[67]

Of course, relations between the authorities and the Armenians were broken off in the first days of the fighting. The Italian consular agent G. Sbordoni was the only European diplomat still working in Van. He had maintained friendly relations with Cevdet to this point, and decided on 24 April to attempt to intercede with him.[68] Sbordoni reminded the vali that his sole motive was a desire to restore peace and that he had already had occasion, during their conversations of the previous few weeks, to call his excellency the vali's attention to the fact that "regrettable incidents could arise in consequence of the militias' attitude and lack of tact," since the militiamen "were incapable of acting in strict accordance with [Cevdet's] orders." After assuring the vali that he had perfect confidence in him in view of his extensive experience and that he was certain that he would find a "solution," Sbordini added that he was convinced that his proposals "would be well received in Armenian circles." He emphasized, however, that there was no chance of bringing the Armenians to accept a proposal to lay down their arms "and unconditionally surrender in the prevailing situation." "If the Armenians have had recourse to arms," the Italian told the vali, "it is because they are convinced that the government, using military service as a pretext, wishes to eliminate every last one of them [and have therefore decided] to defend the lives of their families." "Five cannonballs," he went on to complain, "have struck our consulate." They had, however, caused only material damage, and the consul was happy to learn that the vali had now ordered that the cannons be pointed in a different direction. Finally, speaking on behalf of the American and German missions, he told the vali that they wished to inform him that they had not given shelter "to armed individuals," but only to women, children, and the ill, and asked that he be so good as to take "the measures required to ensure their protection."[69]

In Aykesdan, the Defense Committee had now been organized, but had to deal with the throng of 7,000 refugees who arrived on 25 April from the villages of the *nahies* of Arjak and Timar and the surrounding areas. The overriding concern was to feed all these people. The committee also had to use its ammunition sparingly or else replenish it; it therefore improvised a cartridge factory, a gunpowder factory (directed by a chemist), and an arms factory. A smithy was even converted into a cannon foundry. Although this project was of merely symbolic value, it seems to have sustained the morale of the populace, which was invited to donate its copper pots and pans; they were melted down to make an "Armenian cannon" that was used to shell the Hacibekir barracks on 4 May, albeit to no great effect.[70] Like the firing of this cannon after days of memorable effort, another feat of arms left its mark on people's minds, beginning with Nogales's: on 28 April, the Armenians dug a tunnel and blew up the Reşidieh barracks, where the notorious *kaymakam* of Perkri was stationed with his *çetes*, whose exactions in the Perkri district we have already examined.[71] In response to these acts of force, Cevdet ordered Çerkez Ahmed and his *çetes* to go to the villages in the environs of Van and liquidate the women and children still to be found there. According to Nogales, this squadron committed acts of such violence that even Cevdet felt obliged to give Major Ahmed a dressing down, "sincerely or not," for the horrors he had perpetrated.[72]

In early May, when the news from the front had begun to alarm the Turks, and both Kurdish *çetes* and Turkish volunteers were abandoning the city, Cevdet attempted one last maneuver: he told de Nogales that he had just signed an "amnesty" with the Armenians.[73] The Armenians' situation, too, was critical: by now, 15,000 refugees had poured into the city from the rural zones of the *sancak* of Van.[74] It was for this reason that they agreed to negotiate the terms of an "amnesty," although they were persuaded that this was another ruse of the vali's. Cevdet, for his part, ordered a cease-fire in all combat zones on 3 May.[75] The written proposal that he submitted to the Armenians is worth examining in detail, for it is symptomatic of Cevdet's turn of mind and the methods of disinformation he used. Maintaining his accusatory tone, the vali complained about the Armenians' "insurrection," which he said had produced a bloodbath. The district of "Arjag and part of the district of Timar have received the punishment they deserved," he went on, thus creating the impression that the massacres in this region had been retaliatory measures, although they took place on 19 April, before the Armenian population of Van had retrenched itself in its quarters. However, he struck a magnanimous pose, announcing that he was granting "a respite to the refugees on the island of Lim and in Timar"; he promised that if they surrendered, "no harm would be done to their women and children" – although he was perfectly aware that the 12,000 refugees who had flocked onto the island of Lim were doomed to perish for lack of an adequate food supply.[76] He then returned to the "insurrection" in Van, launching out on a discourse designed to justify his actions by presenting them as legitimate measures. He first affirmed, in defiance of all logic, that he had given orders not to return the "insurgents' fire"; however, when it became apparent that "these imbeciles continued to fire away to the sound of drums and trumpets," he had "given the order to shoot back." In other words, the assault launched against Aykesdan at dawn on 20 April had been a riposte. Continuing in the same tone, the vali accused the Armenians of having "fired on the guards" and of killing "a few policemen and passers-by," which left him with no choice but to use cannons. To lend credibility to his thesis that the Armenians were the aggressors, he added: "I know that there are many people from the villages in the city. I am convinced that they want to attack the fortress" – although the Armenian quarter was besieged, and had been saved thanks only to its defensive posture.

Cevdet employed a threatening tone in the rest of his missive: "Be warned that the artillery is on the way ... As soon as the cannons arrive, they will be turned on the city and will fire away until it is nothing but a pile of rubble."[77] The vali then listed his military exploits, as if trying to convince himself of his own strength: he announced that he had captured the villages of Tarman and Gokhbants, whose inhabitants, as we have seen, had fled to the slopes of Mt. Varak, and then described the exploits of those of his troops who had taken control of a zone stretching from the Hamudağa barracks to Cross Street. Here, too, he said, "we have proved to be stronger, and have burned everything down." In question, however, was an area of the city that was essentially unsettled.

Compounding threats with lies, the vali then told the Armenians, who had no external source of information, that Halil Bey's troops, "sweeping aside the Russian troops they had encountered on their path, had entered Khoy" the day before. In fact, Halil's Expeditionary Corps was in retreat after a heavy defeat in Dilman.[78] In his conclusion, Cevdet betrayed the true purpose of his letter: "Please understand that you must abandon all hope of being saved." The coda was a set of proposals prefaced with a preamble formulated in classically Ottoman style:

> To the present day, we have loved and protected this people as if it were the light of our eye; its sole response has been ingratitude and treachery. It must be punished. Think of your innocent families. What sin have they committed? If you have no pity on yourselves, take pity on them, at least.

In other words, if the defenders of Van did not surrender, "innocent families," who had already fallen victim to massacres throughout the vilayet, would suffer official retaliatory action brought on by the "insurrection." Cevdet accordingly proposed to the Armenians that they "1) give up all weapons and 2) surrender, placing [their] confidence in the generosity of the government to which [they had] to swear fidelity."[79]

The vicar Eznik, to whom Cevdet's letter was formally addressed, answered in his response on 4 May that the Armenians had never ceased to recognize the sultan's sovereignty[80] – that is, that they had simply reacted to the threat facing them. Rafaël de Nogales adds that the Armenians were willing to leave the city and go to Persia, but demanded that the vali accompany them in person to guarantee their safety. Nogales accordingly proposed, in vain, to accompany them in the vali's stead. "We all knew," the Venezuelan captain observes, "that Cevdet was hoping that the Armenians would leave the city "so that he might have them slain on the way."[81]

Even as he was negotiating, Cevdet ordered the execution of seven Armenians who had served in the mounted gendarmerie without the least criticism from anyone.[82] He also ordered that Armenian prisoners be executed, beginning with the Hnchaks whom he had had arrested well before the onset of the events. Their throats were cut in the city's outskirts.[83]

Sbordoni provides us with information that precisely contradicts the affirmations of the vali, who, the Italian consul wrote, "sought to create the impression that the government had extended its benevolent protection to the peaceful populations." "Unfortunately," he added,

> we are receiving, from outside sources, reports of acts of unheard of cruelty perpetrated in villages that were absolutely unarmed. The Armenians lost all confidence when they heard these reports; they are increasingly convinced that the government is pursuing a program of generalized massacre and are increasingly inclined to defend themselves.

Finally, Sbordoni gave the lie to the vali's denial that the inopportune shelling of the Americans had been deliberate, after he had personally inspected "the damage that the shells had done to the American church."[84]

Nogales, too, observed the practices of the local administration when he visited Van's military hospital on 1 May. There, two nurses – a German named Martha, and Grisell MacLaren, an American – told him that the hospital's senior physician, İzzet Bey, had "gotten rid" of his Armenian personnel and let his Christian patients die of gangrene, refusing to provide them with the least treatment.[85] But Nogales witnessed another spectacle that shocked him still more profoundly: Cevdet had the women and children who had been rounded up by his çetes during their raids on the villages brought to the city, where he had them executed in full view of the besieged Armenians.[86]

In his last letter to Cevdet, dated 4 May, the Armenian prelate gave him to understand that he had not been fooled by the vali's talk of a possible "amnesty." He reminded him of what really mattered: "If you truly wish to save my unfortunate country, put an end to the massacres of women and children – of an innocent population in its entirety."[87] The Armenians' problem was that the committees in the old city, where the prelate lived, and in Aykesdan, where Aram Manukian was, were unable to communicate, so that neither knew anything about the other's mood and intentions. For information, they accordingly depended on the affirmations of the vali, for whom, as we know, they had no great esteem, and, perhaps, the Italian consul, whose services Cevdet called on in negotiating with Aykesdan. When the vali warned the prelate that he was expecting a "definite answer" the following day, 6 May, reminding him that, "as he very well knew, the government could not contract agreements with its subjects," the military situation was alarming from the Turkish point of view.[88] Halil and his Expeditionary Corps had retreated toward Başkale after their defeat at Dilman and established their headquarters further to the south, in Tokaraga, in the upper Zab valley.[89] Moreover, the battalion of Armenian volunteers commanded by Vartan, backed up by several brigades of Cossacks, had been authorized by Major-General Nikolayev, the commander of the corps of the Russian army operating in the Igdir area, to open an offensive on Perkri, where violent fighting had occurred in early May.[90] As we have seen, Cevdet, who had probably given up hope of overcoming the resistance in Van, had on 8 May ordered the "Erzerum battalion" to attack the Armenian positions on Mt. Varak. It is true that the arrival in Van of several thousand refugees from this mountain district had further complicated the sanitary situation and made it harder to feed the population. Nonetheless, Cevdet no longer had the forces he needed to crush the Armenian resistance. All indications are that, by 7 May or the day after, the vali had understood that he could not bring the city to its knees. Nogales, at any rate, had come to that conclusion by now, and asked Cevdet to relieve him of his command. He was not, however, given permission to leave until 14 May.[91]

It was also on 14 May that the Muslim population and Ottoman forces began to evacuate Van. The last troops left the city on 16 May after burning down their barracks. According to Nogales, Halil had ordered Cevdet to abandon Van and link up with Halil's Expeditionary Corps by way of Khoşab.[92] The Armenian sources report the besieged Armenians' joy upon learning that the Turks had left, but also, with consternation, how the inhabitants of Van pillaged and sacked the city's deserted Turkish neighborhoods.[93] The vali had clearly anticipated the 18 May arrival from the north of the Russian vanguard, with the volunteer battalion under Vartan's command at its head. The next day, Major-General Nikolayev's division arrived. To avoid a political vacuum, the Russian commander appointed Aram Manukian provisional governor of Van and authorized him to create a local administration. It functioned to the end of July.[94]

Resistance in the Kaza of Şatak/Shadakh and the Fate of the Armenians of Moks

The *kaza* of Şatak/Shadakh, with its rugged relief traversed by deep gorges, was located in the foothills of the Taurus. In 1915, it boasted 65 Armenian localities with a total population of 8,433.[95] The administrative seat of the *kaza*, Tagh, which straddled the eastern branch of the Tigris, had just over one thousand inhabitants, almost all of them Armenian; a few government officials also resided there, including the *kaymakam*, Hamdi Bey.[96] It was in Tagh, as we have seen, that the first tensions between the authorities and the local population sprang up, beginning on 11 April, with the arrest of Hovsep Choloyan and the *kaymakam*'s attempt, the next day, to confiscate the weapons held by the population.[97] Although an armed peace prevailed here until 17 April, information that arrived in Tagh on 16 April about the attack carried out by Kurdish *çetes* on the Armenian villages in the eastern part of the *kaza* the day before only intensified the inhabitants' suspicions of the authorities. At this point, Dikran Baghdasarian, an officer who had been trained in Istanbul's Military Academy, decided to begin preparing Tagh to defend itself in case of attack. According to A-To, he had 70 Armenian fighters at his disposal, against the 150 gendarmes and militiamen present in the village.[98] On 16 April, the whole population was assembled in the quarter located on the left bank of the eastern Tigris, by far the biggest quarter in Tagh, which stood facing on the right bank the quarter known as "The Mills." Here, the local government and the forces at its disposal were to be found.[99] In other words, both sides were camped at their positions, and any attempt to enter one quarter from the other could only be perceived as an act of aggression. The balance was upset on 17 April, when the young men who controlled access to the upper quarter – that is, the three bridges linking the two parts of the town (only the central bridge was made of stone) – refused to let militiamen cross one of the bridges. The ensuing exchange of gunfire announced the beginning of hostilities. In the upper quarter of the town, where the inhabitants now dug in, communication took place through holes in the party walls of adjoining houses.[100]

The self-defense committee headed by Dikran Baghdasarian established a general defense plan that took account not only of the inhabitants of Tagh, but also those of the *kaza*'s villages. To cut off access to the area from the south, the committee decided to seize control of the Khlkdun/Hlkdun Bridge, which spanned the Upper Tigris. Only by crossing this bridge, located two hours south of Tagh, could the Kurdish Halili, Havşdun, Eztini, and Alani tribes, which were based in the south, reach the Tagh area. Thus, the safety of all the villages located on the right bank of the eastern Tigris was assured.[101]

A second defensive position was established at Pols, northwest of Tagh. It controlled the road from Moks and another road farther to the north, as well as two dams – one near Hashgants, an hour to the north, the other near Sozvants, half an hour to the west. These were the only access routes to the hinterland, in particular the plain of Pzantashd to the northwest, the key to communications in the area.[102]

On 20 April, the Armenians in Tagh burned the wooden bridge leading to "The Mills" in order to forestall an attack from the rear. On 22 April, their northern position at Hashgants was captured by Kurdish *çetes*, but Pols continued to resist, while the bridge located at the exit from Hashgants succeeded in holding off the Kurdish tribes until 1 May. The *kaymakam* let it be known that Hovsep Choloyan and his five comrades had been executed the same day in the jail in Tagh.[103]

By early May, the pressure brought to bear by the Turkish forces had become so intense that the self-defense committee decided to regroup its forces – joined by villagers from the valley of Gaghbi (to the southwest) – in an area near Dzidants, one hour west of Tagh. The objective was to reduce the length of the front.[104] On 19 April, the *kaymakam* of Norduz, Halet Bey, had arrived in the *kaza* with reinforcements of 60 men. Concentrating the Armenians from the surrounding villages in Tagh and other defensive positions had led to the desertion of the Kurdish contingents; the pressure on the Armenians did not, however, diminish as a result.[105] On 29 April, the fighting grew more bitter when the notorious Kurdish chieftain Lazkin Şakiroğlu, who had just finished attending to business in the villages in the *kaza* of Gevaş, arrived in Shadakh by way of Norduz and took Arikom and then Krments, forcing their inhabitants to flee to Tagh.[106] Cevdet, however, seems to have been late in delivering the ammuntion and two cannons that he had promised to *kaymakams* Hamdi and Halet. It was not until 5 May that he informed them that this materiel would soon arrive, while recommending to the two officials that they maintain Lazkin and his *çetes* in the area.[107]

At this point in the confrontation, control of the northern front, the key to access to the plain of Pzantashd, where a good number of refugees from the *kaza* of Gevaş were concentrated, constituted a major stake of the battle. This position was the more critical in that it dominated the access route from Vostan and Van. Beginning on 17 April, fierce combats took place here. They continued until 20 April, even as thousands of fugitives from the villages in the southern part of the *kaza* of Gvaş, such as Nor Kiugh, Mokhrapert, Kantsag, Varents, and Entsag sought haven in the district. They were joined at the end of the month by refugees from Hayots Tsor and Timar, raising the number of displaced persons in the area to approximately 6,000. Levon Shaghoyan led the resistance here, which was mounted by fighters from the *kaza* of Gvaş. It cut off direct access to Tagh for the reinforcements that had been sent from Van, forcing them to take roundabout routes.[108] The fighting focused on two key points in the valley: Shahrur Castle, which was subjected to the fiercest attack by Hüseyin Ağa on 29 April, and Paratodig, which was threatened the same day by 500 men equipped with a cannon, who had been sent from Van to reinforce the government troops. Unable to break the resistance at these two points, the reinforcements had to make their way through the rugged eastern Tigris river valley, and thus did not reach Tagh until 18 May.[109]

The other fronts did not hold up as well. In Pols, northwest of Tagh, and at the Hashgants Bridge on the road from Moks, Kurdish forces pushed the Armenian fighters back to Dzidzants, where there was extremely fierce fighting on 9 and 10 May. It was, however, the 11 May fall of Sozvants, to the west of Tagh, which destabilized the Armenian resistance and led to the complete encirclement of Tagh. Only the forces positioned to the north, in Sindgin and on the plain of Pzantashd, were able to break out of this encirclement.[110] On 18 May, these forces tried to recapture Sozvants. Meanwhile, the cannons dispatched from Van finally arrived in Tagh, where they immediately went into action.[111] Their belated arrival no doubt prevented the *kaymakam* from better exploiting his advantage. On the morning of 21 May, Armenian rearguard forces recaptured Sozvants and thus broke the siege of the town. On 23 May, Hamdi Bey and the *müdir* of the Alani, Şevket, resigned themselves to abandoning Tagh because Tro's (*dashnak* military chief) battalion of Armenian volunteers from the Caucasus had already reached Sindgin.[112]

By the end of the day, when Shadakh came under Russian control, all the villages of the eastern and western parts of the *kaza* had been razed. Their inhabitants were now crowded into Tagh. As for the villagers from the southern part of the *kaza*, they had either regrouped in Gaghbi, Gajet, and Armshad or fled to Moks and Sindgin.[113] The fate of the 45 villages of the *kaza* of Moks and its 4,459 Armenians[114] offers a telling indication of the influence of local officials or tribal chieftains: these Armenians were never molested, thanks to the protection of a Kurdish chieftain, Murtula Beg, who refused to execute orders he had received from Van.[115]

Balance Sheet of the Events of April–May 1915

According to the general balance sheet drawn up by the Russian army after it took control of the vilayet of Van, the advancing Russian forces discovered 55,000 corpses in May 1915, which they burned as they went.[116] This represents a little more than 50 per cent of the vilayet's Armenian population. In addition to the human losses, the vilayet's Armenian villages had been systematically plundered and then burned down, leaving the refugee population, concentrated in Van, Shadakh and Moks, in a precarious state. Indeed, the region had, for all practical purposes, been depopulated, inasmuch as its Muslim inhabitants had fled in the wake of the retreating Turkish army.[117]

The Turkish Retreat and the Russian Advance

Over the month of May, the military situation in the region evolved rapidly. After the defeat suffered by the Ottoman Fifth Expeditionary Corps, the troops led by Lieutenant-Colonel Halil (Kut) were forced to retreat to Tokaraga, south of Başkale,[118] fighting General Nazarbekov's

Sixth Russian Division and the auxiliary forces of the first battalion of Armenian volunteers as they withdrew.[119] Expressly dispatched from Istanbul, Halil's Expeditionary Corps was much better equipped than the other Turkish forces,[120] yet it did not obtain the expected results. Quite the opposite: it sustained the second major Turkish defeat on the eastern front, denying the Young Turks their primary objective of encompassing the local forces of Iranian Azerbaijan within their Pan-Turk strategy, to which they had given a Pan-Islamic patina.

When Rafaël de Nogales arrived in Tokaraga on 15 May, Halil, a fanatical and jealous individual,[121] had just given orders that his headquarters be transferred further south to Sova (today Sinova), which was apparently easier to defend.[122] At this point, the Sixth Russian Division was in Başkale. Nogales, who was retreating with the vanguard of the Expeditionary Corps, notes that they set out in the direction of the Norduz Mountains on 26 May, bivouacking on the way in Kişham, a village inhabited by semi-nomads of the Jewish faith who spoke a mixture of Kurdish and Armenian. It reached Şağmanis on 29 May.[123] On that day, the Russian vanguard was still in contact with the Ottoman Expeditionary Corps in the gorges of Norduz, but Halil seems to have abandoned the idea of putting up a defense, opting instead for a rapid withdrawal westward toward Siirt.[124] So as to retreat faster, the Expeditionary Corps lightened its load by jettisoning its war booty along the way. Sebuh, who was in the Russian vanguard that had set off in pursuit of the Turkish forces, had the impression that he was at an "open-air market": strewn along the edge of the road were costly Persian rugs, household goods, clothes, and so on.[125]

After weighing the possibility of returning to Vostan, Halil decided, probably in view of the Russian drive toward the northern shore of Lake Van, to follow the eastern Tigris river valley south of Şatak.[126] En route, the vali of Van and his troops, passing by way of Khoşab, linked up with the Expeditionary Corps.[127] According to Sebuh, the Turkish troops systematically slaughtered the inhabitants of all the Armenian villages they found on their path.[128]

After making a number of detours toward the southwest, the purpose of which was to take them ever further from the Russian forces, the Turkish troops crossed the Tigris on 7 June, arriving in Khisgir/Hisgir on 9 June, the same time as Colonel Isak and the "famed tribune" Ömer Naci,[129] an eminent member of the Special Organization who was probably returning to Turkey from Persia in order to take part in operations planned for the vilayet of Bitlis. As the Expeditionary Corps approached Siirt, in the *kaza* of Şirvan, it slew some 20 Armenian-speaking Nestorians in Gundeş/Gunde Deghan.[130] This violence was a harbinger of the crimes that would be committed throughout the vilayet of Bitlis in the following weeks.

The Russian Withdrawal and the Evacuation of Van and Its Environs

Altogether unexpectedly, on 24 July 1915, as the Russian forces advancing along the northern and southern shores of Lake Van met up at its western extremity, Tatvan, the offensive came to an abrupt halt and the Russians pulled back, beginning on 27 July, to Akhlat and Sorp.[131] According to A-To, there was a heavy concentration of Turkish forces on the northern front near Olti and Sarıkamiş. The Russian general staff, when it ordered the evacuation of the region on 30 July, gave fear of encirclement as the official explanation for its decision.[132]

Although military imperatives might conceivably explain the Russians' prudence, it remains puzzling that St. Petersburg ordered the evacuation of the whole Armenian population of the vilayet of Van, including its capital. Moreover, the Russian authorities' decision, which was at the very least unexpected, also seemed strange to certain experts at the time. Thus, the American military attaché, E. F. Riggs, noted in a report that it was the battalions of Armenian volunteers who went to great lengths to aid Van and, above all, that unnecessary retreats were twice organized,

> probably on purpose. For 24 hours the Turks were left to enter the city and wreak their
> will on the inhabitants. Those remaining in the city were subjected to indescribable
> misery while those attempting to escape were attacked on their way into Russia by
> Kurds. In this manner about 260,000 people, mostly women and children, were turned
> on the public charge in the Caucasus, who if left protected in their own country could
> have aided the Russian armies in Armenia by furnishing them with supplies from their
> farms.[133]

The Russian forces abandoned Van on 3 August, forcing the local Armenian government to evacuate the population of both the city and the surrounding rural zones. Several tens of thousands of people set off toward the north. They were attacked by Kurdish *çetes* and Turks in a gorge in the region of Perkri, where more than 1,600 people were massacred.[134] Cevdet Bey even recaptured Van, accompanied by 400 to 600 Çerkez and Kurdish *çetes*, who slaughtered a few hundred old men and sick people unable to leave the city.[135] However, a new defeat inflicted on the Turks on the Olti-Sarıkamiş-Alaşkert front changed the general situation a few days later, and the Russians again took control of the Van region, which was now deserted.

The refugees from Vasburagan and the survivors from Manazgerd and Mush who now arrived in the Caucasus swelled the ranks of those who had already found haven there – former inhabitants of the eastern zones of the vilayet of Erzerum and Armenians fleeing the advance of the Turkish troops in Iranian Azerbaijan. The result was a terrible humanitarian crisis.[136] In a two-week period from late August and early September, 2,613 deaths were recorded in the city of Echmiadzin alone, due essentially to epidemics. The situation of those who had fled to Yerevan and Igdir was no better.[137]

Chapter 5

Deportations and Massacres in
the Vilayet of Bitlis

The massacres of the Armenian populations of the vilayet of Bitlis are generally presented as a direct effect of the "events" in the neighboring region of Van, as an act of revenge for the military defeats suffered by the Turkish forces in Persian Azerbaijan and during the subsequent retreat of Halil's Expeditionary Corps. However, the fragmentary information available to us indicates that, from 25 to 27 April 1915, a long meeting took place halfway between Siirt and Bitlis between Dr. Nâzım and the vali of Bitlis, Mustafa Abdülhalik.[1] This provides grounds for supposing that the order to extirpate the Armenian population of the region, as well as the methods to be used in doing so, were discussed much earlier.

In Bitlis, late in April, Vali Abdülhalik had three local Armenian leaders arrested and hanged.[2] This was no longer the harassment or violence that typically accompanied the military requisitions or general mobilization, but a move designed to condition the population psychologically. The Dashnaks were the direct target, although curiously they were still being treated respectfully in Mush. The authorities probably posed the problem in terms of power relations. After deciding to eradicate the Armenians, they had to find the necessary means to carry out the operation. There was a tremendous difference between what was required in Bitlis and on the plain of Mush. In Bitlis, there was practically no danger that the Armenians would react if they were attacked, because there the ARF did not have a network worthy of the name. The plain of Mush, in contrast, was almost entirely Armenian and a Dashnak stronghold. Abdülhalik could do practically whatever he wanted with the forces at his command in Bitlis; he knew that he would have to mobilize a much stronger force to liquidate the Armenians of the plain of Mush and the mountains of Sasun. Close examination of the situation prevailing in the vilayet of Bitlis until early June 1915[3] leaves little doubt that there was a shortage of troops in Mush. In other words, the retreat of the Fifth Expeditionary Corps under Halil (Kut) and the 8,000 men in Cevdet's "butchers' battalions" (*kasab taburis*) – as we have seen, the two forces linked up in the eastern Tigris river valley – may be regarded as the result of a decision taken in consultation with Istanbul; it made it possible seriously to envisage translating plans into action in the vilayet of Bitlis. The sole foreign witness to this retreat of Cevdet's and Halil's joint forces, Captain de Nogales, describes the mood of the two Young Turk leaders and the massacres that their troops perpetrated on their retreat through the *kaza* of Hizan/Khizan. On 12 June, when the bulk of the troops struck out for Siirt, to the northwest,[4] several officers in the battalion from Başkale took a different direction, along with the Venezuelan. "With an air of great satisfaction," they told Nogales that the Bitlis authorities were preparing to commit massacres, and were only waiting for the final order from Halil to begin.

Rather than an act of vengeance, then, what was involved was the implementation of a pre-established plan. It was made possible by the arrival of Halil's and Cevdet's forces, whose

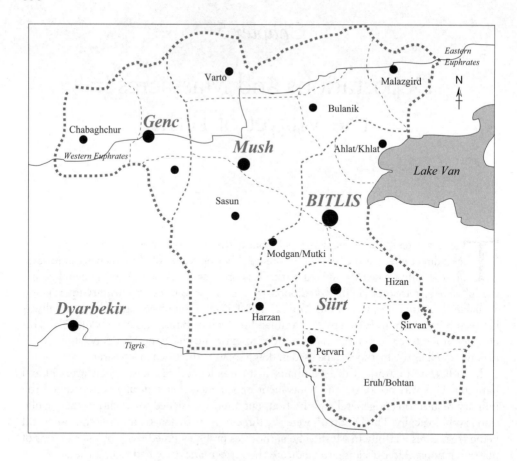

connections with the Special Organization were no secret. As Nogales was approaching Siirt, the massacres began. He discovered "thousands of half-nude and still bleeding corpses" of all ages, and in such numbers that he and his companion had to "jump our horses over the mountains of cadavers which obstructed our passage."[5] In the city, the Venezuelan also witnessed the sacking of "the houses of the Christians" by the police and the "populace." In the *konak*, he stumbled upon a meeting to which the *kaymakams* of the region had been summoned; it was chaired by the commander of the gendarmerie of Siirt, Erzrumli Nâzım Hamdi, who had directed the massacres in person. One can guess what the meeting was about. Nogales confesses that it was only now that he understood the true significance of the revelations that the officers escorting him had made the day before.[6]

The presence of a foreigner, even one in the right camp, had obviously not escaped the attention of the Young Turk military leaders, who probably arranged for him to take another route so that he would not witness massacres like the one at Siirt. According to Nogales, Halil, too, tried to have him killed, as Cevdet had in Van, to "prevent my revealing later on, in Constantinople or abroad, what had taken place."[7] Halil was planning, the Venezuelan claims, to have him assassinated at two or three days' distance from Siirt so that the murder could be attributed "to bandits or Armenian rebels."[8] Aware that he was "the only Christian ... to witness things that should never have been witnessed by any Christian," Nogales lost no time leaving the city. As he did, he passed groups of children and old men, both Armenian and Syriac, who were being taken out of town under guard.[9] But merely leaving Siirt did not suffice to extract this embarrassing witness from the clutches of Halil Bey.

Reporting a conversation that he had further west with the mayor of the village of Sinan, located several miles south of Beşiri, Nogales tells us that his interlocutor insisted on learning his "personal opinion about the massacres." Noticing that Nogales was not much inclined to say what he thought, the mayor, who was persuaded that Nogales did not understand a word of Turkish, ordered his secretary to call the minister of war immediately in order to inform him of the imminent arrival of this foreigner and his "full knowledge of everything" (*hepsi biler*).[10] In the end, Nogales emerged from this adventure unscathed; but it showed the lengths to which the leaders of the Special Organization were prepared to go in order to be able to act without witnesses or eliminate the witnesses who might talk.

We have another indication that the "blood-red general staff"[11] had arrived in the area in order methodically to liquidate the Armenians in the vilayet of Bitlis: Vali Mustafa Abdülhalik, who happened to be Talât's brother-in-law (his wife's brother), had for weeks been recruiting *çetes* among the Kurds and other groups. The recruits were put under the command of Behcet Bey, commander-in-chief of the Teşkilât-ı Mahsusa in Bitlis.[12] Abdülhalik had also ordered, in the first half of June, the systematic arrest of Armenian notables throughout the vilayet, as well as systematic massacres in the *kazas* in the northern part of the *sancak* of Bitlis.[13]

Nogales learned, moreover, from "résidents étrangers," that Abdülhalik had told them that Halil had issued the extermination order in person, and that his "vengeance" was in fact the realization of a "carefully laid-out plan."[14] Between mid-June and late July, 681 Armenian localities, with a total population of 218,404, and 510 churches, 161 monasteries, and 207 schools,[15] were to be wiped off the face of the earth with extreme violence.

Massacres in the Sancak of Siirt

As we have just seen, the event signaling the start of the massacres in the vilayet of Bitlis took place in Siirt. The *sancak* of Siirt, a mountainous region sandwiched between the Armenian and Kurdish settlement areas, had a mixed population: the Armenian presence was more pronounced in the *kazas* in the northern part of the *sancak* and very widely dispersed in the *kazas* in the south, which was also home to 15,000 Orthodox and Catholic Syriacs. On the eve of the war, there were 146 towns and villages in the *sancak*, inhabited by 21,564 Armenians, who maintained 45 churches and three monasteries.[16]

Side by side with the "blood-red general staff," the local Ittihadist club, led by İhsan and Servet Bey, took an active hand in organizing the massacres in the area. The club's efforts were seconded by government officials – Serfiçeli Hilmi Bey, the *mutesarif* of Siirt; Erzurumlu Nâzım Hamdi Bey, the commander of the gendarmerie; Rifat Bey, an officer in the gendarmerie; Emin Basri, a captain in the gendarmerie; Arslan Bey;[17] and Bitlisli Ali Effendi, the police chief; as well as several leaders of squadrons of *çetes* in the Special Organization (Ali Ziya, Haci Mustafazâde Ahmed, Abdüllah Sadık), making a total of some 40 local officials.[18] It was with the active cooperation of these men that Cevdet and his "butchers" set about executing the orders given them by Halil, who plainly outranked the valis Cevdet and Abdülhalik.

On their way to Bitlis, Halil and Cevdet carried out mass liquidations in the Siirt area. The 35 villages of the easternmost *kaza* of the vilayet – Pervari, Bohtan/Eruh and Şarnag, with a total population of around 6,000 Armenians – were literally annihilated when the forces commanded by Halil and Cevdet passed through them; the inhabitants were slaughtered on the spot. In Siirt, the local authorities had anticipated the arrival of Cevdet and his butchers. Four days previously, on 9 June, the Armenian primate of the diocese, Yeghishe, the Catholic Syriac bishop, Addai Şer, the orthodox Syriac Abuna, Ibrahim, and ten of the leading men of Siirt were arrested and shot the next day, half an-hour from the town. On

11 June, 670 men from Siirt, out of a total Armenian population of 4,032, were summoned to the barracks, ostensibly to transport military supplies to Bitlis. They were, however, arrested and shot the next day, at a half-hour's distance from the town in the Vedi Ezzreb gorge. When Cevdet arrived on 13 June he finished the job: over the next few days, he rounded up the remaining older men, whose throats were cut on the town's central square.

The women and children were assembled a few weeks later at the exit from the town and offered to the Kurdish population. Of those the Kurds did not fancy, some were massacred on the spot with axes and knives; around 400 people were deported toward Mardin and Mosul. No one in the group that was set marching in the direction of Mardin survived; its last surviving members had their throats cut a short distance from town. Fifty deportees in the other caravan reached Mosul alive.[19]

Nobody knows what became of the several hundred villagers from the eight villages in the vicinity of Siirt, or of the 2,853 Armenians from the villages and towns of the *kaza* of Şirvan/Shirvan.[20] It is known, however, that the 5,000 Syriacs in the *sancak* of Siirt, both Catholic and Orthodox, received the same treatment as the Armenians.[21] As for the 8,343 villagers from the 76 towns and villages of the *kaza* of Harzan,[22] they fled to the mountains of the neighboring district of Sasun, where they suffered the same fate as the local population. However, as was revealed at the Istanbul trials in 1919, it should be noted that Serfiçeli Hilmi Bey, the *mutesarif* of Siirt, was transferred to Mosul because he had displayed little enthusiasm for eliminating the Armenians or Syriacs in his prefecture. He was later to draw up a full report on the massacres in Dyarbekir and Mardin and submit it to the German vice-consul in Mosul, Walter Holstein, for transmission to the German ambassador, Hans von Wangenheim.[23]

Massacres in the Sancak of Bitlis

After "cleansing" Siirt of its Armenians and Syriacs – all things considered, rather rapidly – Cevdet and his "butchers' battalions" promptly set out for Bitlis, with Halil's Expeditionary Corps hard on their heels, for the Russian troops were also marching on the city. In the regional capital, Vali Abdülhalik had already taken the initiative by waging a campaign of destruction against the villages to the north. The members of the big American mission in Bitlis, which included a hospital and an Armenian girls' school, witnessed events in the region, as did a nurse in the military hospital who had recently arrived from Van, Grace H. Knapp. Knapp was the only one to leave a written account of what she saw.[24]

On 16 May, Knapp's boat arrived in Tatvan, located at the western extremity of Lake Van, at the same time as thousands of wounded or exhausted villagers from the 56 villages of the *kaza* of Bitlis, which had a total population of 16,651, and the 22 villages of the northern *kaza* of Akhlat, inhabited by 13,432 Armenians.[25] These Armenians, among whom there were virtually no men, had been attacked by Kurds and had fled to Bitlis to seek the protection of the government. "They had no idea," Knapp wrote, "that the affair had been ordered by the government." The American missionary was in fact witnessing the results of the first massacres in the northern areas of the *sancak* of Bitlis. She also noted that every evening the Kurdish squadrons returned from their expeditions to the villages after finishing "their work of murder and destruction."[26] In the space of a few days, some 12,000 refugees, many of them wounded, had thronged into Bitlis. Seven hundred of them were taken into the American mission,[27] while the others found a place in Armenian institutions in the last days of May 1915. The bishopric and the mission fed and cared for these refugees as best they could.

When the missionaries asked the vali for explanations of what they were hearing from all the rural zones of the *sancak* about atrocities perpetrated against the Armenians, Abdülhalik affirmed that Kurdish brigands were sowing disorder there and that he was doing all he could to "put an end" to it. Early in June, however, the throng of refugees in Bitlis was gradually moved out of the city on the road leading south, guarded by gendarmes. A woman who escaped from one of these convoys and fled to the American mission revealed that the convoys were being attacked and decimated en route by Kurds. At a meeting with Abdülhalik, Grace Knapp's father, George Knapp, the head of the American mission and a Protestant minister, and the Armenian Protestant minister in Bitlis, Khachig Vartanian, requested that he authorize the caravans to take the road to Mush so that they could avoid the Kurdish attacks – but to no avail.[28]

On 22 June, at a time when Bitlis was under serious threat from the Russian troops and the vali and local government were already making plans to leave, panic gripped the city with the arrival of the Kurdish chieftains of Modgan/Mutki. It was later learned that, shortly before coming to Bitlis, the Kurds had destroyed the 27 Armenian villages in their *kaza*, massacring the 5,469 villagers where they found them.[29] The same day, the destruction of the Armenians of Bitlis began. The first step was the arrest of Reverend Vartanian, followed a day later by an operation targeting the American mission: it was surrounded by soldiers and gendarmes, who took the handful of Armenian pharmacists, nurses, and teachers employed there into custody.[30] It would appear that the presence of these foreign missionaries was extremely troublesome from the authorities' point of view. When they proceeded to arrest all the males in Bitlis the same day, Reverend Knapp immediately went to see Abdülhalik to demand an explanation. Courteous as always, the vali justified the arrests by citing information to the effect that letters from Van had been received by "some Armenians" in the city: "the object of arresting all the men was to discover who the recipients [of these letters] were."[31] These feeble excuses, inspired by the official discourse, could hardly hide the true objective of the systematic round-up, accompanied by unprecedented acts of violence, of all males over ten from the streets, schools, bazaar, and houses of Bitlis[32] – namely, to eliminate all possibility of resistance from the outset. From 22 June on, the men were led out of the city under escort in small groups of between 10 and 15 individuals, depending on the length of rope available to tie them up. They were then shot to death or killed with axes, shovels, or sharp stakes. It took a full two weeks to liquidate the Armenian male population of Bitlis.[33] In the testimony that Colonel Nusuhi Bey, a witness for the prosecution who had served in the Bitlis region, gave to the court-martial in 1919 about the activities of the commander-in-chief of the Third Army, Mahmud Kâmil, he noted in passing that the Armenians of Bitlis were killed "in a valley at a half-hour's distance from the city," where "they poured oil on them and burned them."[34]

On 25 June, Cevdet arrived in Bitlis with his 8,000 "human butchers." The effect was not only to keep the Russian forces, then one hour away in Han Alam,[35] from marching on the city, but also to cut off the city's communications with the outside world. The authorities could now go serenely about their business. Cevdet, the better to mark his arrival, immediately had Hokhigian and a few other Dashnak leaders in the city tortured. They were subsequently hanged on a nearby promontory, Taghi Klukh.[36] He then turned his attention to the imprisoned Armenian notables, from whom he extorted 5,000 Turkish pounds[37] before demanding the "hand" of the daughters of two of them, Araxi and Armenuhi.[38]

Doubtless in order to bring matters to a conclusion as speedily as possible, 700 men were conducted to a spot six miles from the city, slain, and then thrown into pits that they had been made to dig themselves.[39] Not even very young children, it seems, were spared: all the boys from ages one to ten were taken from their families, led out of the city, thrown into a huge pit, doused with kerosene, and burned alive, "in the presence of the vali of Bitlis."[40] A different fate was reserved for women, and the children from the city and surrounding villages who did not fall into this category – some 8,000 people in all. The police began rounding them up on 29/30 June. They were initially left for two days in a few spacious houses in the city or in the courtyard of the cathedral, and then, early in July, conducted by gendarmes and policemen to the southern exit from Bitlis, at the entrance to the Arabi Gorge near the bridge of the same name, where they remained for two weeks. The gorge served as a market where anyone who wished to could help himself to the woman, girl or child of his or her choice. At the end of this vast auction, at which 2,000 people found takers, the 6,000 unfortunates who had not were attacked at dawn by Cevdet's çetes; several hundred perished. The survivors were led in a caravan down the road to Siirt, guarded by gendarmes. The caravan was again harassed by çetes at Dzag Kar. What was left of it trekked past Siirt to Midyat, where approximately 1,000 deportees were murdered, leaving some 30 survivors with the option of continuing on their way.[41]

By mid-July, only a dozen Armenian men were left in Bitlis – artisans whom the army considered indispensable[42] – together with the women and girls held by the former parliamentary deputy Sadullah, the *mal müdir*, the chief of the post office, Hakkı, the proprietor of the hamam, and others.[43] The authorities also had to hunt down a few children still roaming the streets of the city; they were thrown into the river, or into pits whose sides were so steep that they could not climb back out of them.[44] Finally, Cevdet and Abdülhalik insisted on evicting the handful of women who had found refuge in the American mission, together with the girls at the school. Grace Knapp's detailed report about the harassment to which the mission was subjected bears witness to the two Young Turk leaders' resolve to fulfil their mission: to wipe out the Armenian presence in Bitlis without leaving a trace behind.[45] Thus, we are told that gendarmes regularly called on the mission to arrest the women who had found refuge with the Americans. Some managed to stay where they were by bribing the gendarmes, but only for a few days, after which they met the common fate.[46] The arrest in the American mission of an orphan girl aged two or three, the daughter of an Armenian schoolteacher from Tatvan, illustrates the zeal displayed by the local police. It is true that the girl kept repeating, to whomever cared to listen, the name of the Kurd who had murdered her father.[47] The well-educated, polyglot girls at the American school aroused the desires of Young Turk officers, who even seem to have put pressure on the vali – this, at least, is what the Americans affirm – to turn the girls over to them.[48] It seems more likely, however, that these girls were destined to disappear like the others, even if the biological conception of Turkism then prevailing did not rule out such alliances. In the end, the girls of the American school escaped with their lives thanks to the chief physician at the Turkish Military Hospital, Mustafa Bey, an Arab who had been educated in France and Germany. Aware that "the presence of these girls in the school was a constant thorn in the flesh to the government," he nevertheless stubbornly opposed their deportation on the grounds that the hospital was absolutely incapable of operating properly without them: a stand that earned him the enmity of the Turkish officers who were impatiently awaiting their prize.[49] Thanks to Mustafa Bey's resistance, the matter took on a certain importance, so that Mustafa Abdülhalik was left with no choice but to refer the question to Cevdet, who came only occasionally to Bitlis because he had other business to attend to on the plain of Mush. We may thus note in passing that Cevdet, both a military leader and a former vali, outranked Abdülhalik. In any event, Cevdet decided in favor of the army physician.[50]

Around 15 July, when the liquidation of the Armenians of the *sancak* was virtually complete, the Russian forces stepped up their pressure and the local government made serious plans to evacuate the city. To this end, a battalion of 1,000 Armenian conscripts was sent southward with the vali's library and archives. All these men were massacred at some distance from Bitlis, and the governor's archives were destroyed.[51] The authorities would later accuse George Knapp of having hoisted the American flag over the roof of the hospital in which wounded soldiers and Muslims suffering from typhus were being treated in order to "guide the enemy." Yet the Turks were the first to express surprise when they learned on 24 July that the Russian troops had pulled back.[52] After this brief moment of panic, two staff members of the local branch of the Banque Impériale Ottomane returned to Bitlis and reported on the ghastly scenes that they had witnessed on the road leading south. The banks of the Bitlis Çay were covered with piles of rotting corpses; in many places, mountains of dead bodies blocked the road and the sides of the road were littered with the remains of the deportees from Bitlis and the surrounding region.[53]

We have little information about the fate of the villages in the vicinity of Bitlis, with the exception of the important town of Khultig, lying two hours southeast of the city, with an Armenian population of 2,598.[54] In May, gendarmes went to Khultig to collect arms; in exchange, they promised the villagers protection. With the first acts of violence in Bitlis, on 25 June, some of these villagers fled, only to be massacred in the countryside. It was not until 2 July that Khultig was occupied by 100 soldiers and Kurdish militiamen. The inhabitants were then packed into barns and burned alive by Humaşli Farso and his men.[55] Thirty young men managed to escape and subsequently joined the volunteer battalions. Some 100 women and children from the village were later found among the Kurdish tribes of the region, and another five women and ten orphan girls were found in Bitlis when the Russians took the city in 1916.[56]

Thus Rafaël de Nogales's estimate that 15,000 Armenians were massacred in the *sancak* of Bitlis alone seems quite plausible.[57]

The Butchers of Bitlis

In the first days of July, while the last convoys of women and children were being massacred at Dzag Kar (which means "perforated stone" in Armenian), those who bore the main responsibility for these crimes – Lieutenant Colonel Halil, the uncle of the minister of war; Cevdet Bey, the minister's brother; Mustafa Abdülhalik, brother-in-law of the minister of the interior; and Turfan, the police chief – were at a banquet with the main butchers in an inn located near the scene of the slaughter. To entertain the guests and put the finishing touches on their work, the Armenian prelate and a few of the leading men of the city who had been spared until then were shot there by gendarmes that night.[58]

The massacres organized in the vilayet of Bitlis cannot, however, be explained simply as a consequence of the activity of these high-ranking personalities, close to the highest state authorities. An entire political, administrative, military, and local governmental hierarchy was mobilized to perpetrate this violence. The executioners in the front ranks were to be found, of course, within the leadership of the local CUP club: Muftizâde Sadullah and Gidozâde Resul, Ittihadist parliamentary deputies, and Muftizâde Nasrullah, also an Ittihadist deputy and the president of the club. Among the civilian officials who played important parts, beside Mustafa Abdülhalik, were Hamdi Effendi, the president of the municipality, and Şemeddin Fatullah, the director of the *Evkaf*; both were members of the commission responsible for abandoned property (*emvalı metruke*), and were especially heavily involved in plundering Armenian assets. Among those in the military or related organizations, Behcet Bey, the commander-in-chief of the squadrons of the Special Organization in Bitlis, held the fairest claim to the title of chief organizer, closely followed by the Bitlis police chief Turfan Bey, who organized the arrests in the city and dispatched his men to execute the Armenians; he received help from Ahmed Refik, a police captain. Edhem Bey, the commander of the gendarmerie, and his assistant, Faik Bey, organized the convoys of deportees and provided them with their escorts; they took a direct hand in the mass slaughter.

In the Bitlis region, with its essentially Armenian and Kurdish population, tribal chieftains and local clans played a direct role in the massacres. Among them were Ilikzâde

Abdurahmanoğlu Şemseddin Şamo, Yaralızâde Mehmed Salih, İbrahimzâde Haci Abdül Gani, Yusufpaşazâde Musa Effendi, Haci Melikzâde Şeyh Abdül Bek Effendi, Tüfrevizâde Şeyh Abdül Bak Effendi, Haznodarzâde Tevfik Effendi, Kadri Şeyh Haci İbrahim, Terzi Naderzâde Haci Şemseddin, Fuadağazâde Haci Şemseddin, Karsondlizâde Haci Kasim, Karsondlizâde Haci Fato, and Molla Said.[59]

A captain at the staff headquarters of the Ottoman army in the Caucasus who visited Bitlis in fall 1915, after its Armenian population had been wiped out, reports that there were still 300 young Armenian women in the city. Placed under guard in Bitlis's Armenian cathedral, they served the pleasure of the officers and soldiers passing through town on their way to the front. By the time the captain visited Bitlis, most of these women had contracted venereal diseases. The local military commander felt obliged to eradicate this scourge, which was negatively affecting the soldiers. He had the young women poisoned or otherwise put to death, with the approval of Mahmud Kâmil, the commander-in-chief of the Third Army.[60]

Events in Spargerd in the *Kaza* of Hizan

In the *kaza* of Hizan, which straddled the vilayets of Bitlis and Van, there were no fewer than 76 Armenian villages, with a combined population of 8,207 in 1915. The available sources all discuss the district of Spargerd, in which there were 26 villages with an approximate total Armenian population of 2,600. The district lay in the southernmost part of the *kaza*.[61] There is every reason to believe that the fate of the Armenians of the other *nahie*s was similar to that of the inhabitants of Spargerd.

According to our main witness, conscription was a painful process in this district, because many men of draftable age were working far from home or even abroad, as was common in the rural areas of Armenia. The conscripts were sent to Van and from there to the Caucasian front. None came back alive. Despite the tensions that arose during the military requisitions, the leader of the local ARF committee, Lato, succeeded in maintaining relations with the *müdir* of Spargerd and in obtaining guarantees that the militias formed in the region would not mistreat the Armenian population.[62] As happened elsewhere, the authorities in this *nahie* organized a second conscription campaign late in March; its purpose was to enlist men over 45 years of age, who were supposed to serve in the military labor battalions.[63] When the Van events occurred, it seems that the local Kurds began to make preparations for war, perhaps in response to orders from their superiors. At the same time, Lato mobilized 120 armed men to ensure the safety of the population. Around 20 May, the region found itself under threat from "Kurds and Turks fleeing Van." However, the Armenian *fedayis* checked the offensive by maintaining control over a pass in the southern part of the *nahie*, the sole means of access to it. An agreement between the *müdir* and Lato finally resolved the matter. Our witness reports that in the same period a battalion of volunteers from the Caucasus had advanced as far as the neighboring *kaza* of Moks, but that the people of Spargerd were unaware of this until Tro's contingent arrived in Spargerd.[64]

The Russian forces effectively controlled the region for almost two months, between late May and late July. In July, however, the Russian general staff ordered the evacuation of all the inhabitants of Spargerd and Khizan. It is likely that the return of Halil's and Cevdet's unified forces alarmed the Russian commanders, who preferred to evacuate these villages to save them from certain death. After waiting for three weeks in Vostan, on the shores of Lake Van, the Armenians of Khizan set out on their exodus, bound for the Caucasus.[65] Like the refugees from Van, they fell victim to massacres in the Perkri pass. Over the following weeks, many others were mowed down by epidemics in Echmiadzin, where they had found refuge.[66]

Massacres in the Sancak of Mush

The eradication of the 141,489 Armenians of the *sancak* of Mush and the destruction of the 234 towns and villages in which they lived[67] constituted an objective that was incomparably harder to attain for the Turkish authorities than cleansing Bitlis and Siirt of their Armenian populations. The two conscription campaigns of August 1914 and March 1914 had drained the area of its vital forces, as we have already pointed out,[68] and considerably diminished the Armenians' ability to defend themselves. For the authorities, the priority was obviously to extirpate the population of Sasun and take control of its mountain fastnesses. In May, they launched their first attack on the area with support from Kurdish tribes – the Beleks, Bekrans, Şegos, and so on – which they armed. This attack was repulsed.[69] These operations were carried out at the same time as those that targeted the civilian populations of the *kazas* south of Sasun, Silvan and Beşiri,[70] and in the northern part of the *sancak* of Mush, in Bulanik. The timing of the two actions suggests that the next stage in the plan was the liquidation of the "big piece in the middle" comprising the 103 villages of the plain of Mush, with its 75,623 Armenians.[71] The failure of the offensive against Sasun conducted by the Kurdish *çetes* probably convinced the Young Turks to appeal exceptionally to "regular" troops in order to get the better of this dense cluster of Armenians. Here, no doubt, lies the explanation for the June lull in the action in Mush: the harassment and plunder of the villages in the district "suddenly ceased everywhere, and perfect order prevailed in Mush." The calm held for three weeks,[72] during which Halil's and Cevdet's forces were busy liquidating the Armenians of the *sancaks* of Siirt and Bitlis. They became available for other operations only in early July, at which point Cevdet and Lieutenant-Colonel Kâsim Bey, accompanied by a division, left Halil to finish his task in Bitlis and gained the plain of Mush.[73] It was not until 8 July 1915 that Halil and his Expeditionary Corps, equipped with mountain cannons, linked up with them.[74] But the authorities also needed to mobilize local forces to maximize their chances of success. They were greatly aided in this by the June arrival in Mush of a key personage, Hoca Ilyas Sâmi, a Kurdish religious dignitary and a member of the Ottoman National Assembly. Sâmi, who galvanized the Muslim populations of the region, does not appear to have returned from Constantinople by accident. One historian says that the *mutesarif*, Servet, called him to the rescue;[75] in fact, he had just been named CUP inspector in Mush.[76] As in the other vilayets, an operational committee was created, and Sâmi was named to head it; the other members included Servet; Halil (Kut); Falamaz Bey, Hoca Ilyas's first cousin; Derviş Bey; Haci Musa Beg, Hoca Ilyas's uncle; Dido Reşid, the CUP delegate in Mush; and Salih Bey – all of whom were tribal chiefs belonging to the Young Turk club in Mush.[77] The committee could also rely on the support of civilian officials such as Bedirhan Effendi, the head of the land-registry office; İbrahim Effendi, the director of the hospital; Esad Pasha, the *kaymakam* of Bulanik; Mahmud Effendi, the police chief; Kâzım Effendi and Rıza Effendi, police officers; and military personnel such as Behcet Bey, the commander of the gendarmerie, and Dr. Asaf, an army pharmacist.[78]

The Special Organization had squadrons of Kurdish *hamidiyes* at its disposal, as well as the members of local tribes rallied by Haci Musa Beg, the commander-in-chief of the irregular forces. Haci Musa Beg was seconded by the commanders of the *çetes*: Rustamoğlu Hayrullah; the sons of Haci Yasin, Kazaz Mahmud, Kotunlı Dursun, Şükrü, Mustafa and Arif from Haci Ali; Abdül Kerim; the sons of Topal Goto; Kotunlı Ahmed; Şeikh Niazi and his brother, Cemil Effendi, from Beyrakdar; Nurheddin from Slo; Arif from Asad; Haci İbrahim; Bakdur Hüseyin; and Deli Reşidoğlu Mahmud.[79] Some of these officers of the Special Organization, such as Dido Reşid, along with his 500 men, had already participated in the military operations at Van. Others were just arriving on the scene. All, however, received arms, ammunition and a salary from the prefecture, and were employed as "regular forces" on mission.[80]

Hoca Ilyas Sâmi continued to play an altogether central role in Mush. The fact that he was a high religious dignitary endowed him with considerable prestige, which he used to preach the jihad in the city's grand mosque.[81] Yet, like all the local notables, he was doubtless only executing orders received from Lieutenant-Colonel Halil (Kut), one of the leaders of the Teşkilât-ı Mahsusa. The first measure taken after the 8 July arrival of Halil's Expeditionary Corps in Mush was designed to bring all the access routes to the city under control and cut off communications between the localities of the plain, which were attacked the next day by squadrons of çetes under the command of Haci Musa Beg.[82] In the days preceding the attacks, the same çetes confiscated arms in all the villages after systematically torturing the villagers into revealing where they had hidden their rifles. In other words, steps were taken to make it possible to swing into action as soon as the upper echelons of the Special Organization gave the order. The task before these çetes was easier in that there were hardly any young men left in the localities they were to attack.[83] The various survivors' accounts at our disposal indicate that much the same method was applied throughout the plain. The çetes would encircle a village, round up the men, tie them together in groups of 10 to 15, lead them from the village, and kill them in a nearby orchard or field. Then they would shut the women and children up in one or more barns, picking out children and the "prettiest" young women for themselves before dousing the building(s) with kerosene and burning those inside alive. Finally, they would plunder the village and then burn it to the ground.[84]

An eyewitness account given to a French press correspondent who was in Istanbul during the trial of the Young Turk leaders describes the case of 2,000 women who were surrounded by these Kurdish çetes and "sullied and looted." The women were suspected "of having swallowed their jewels to keep them out of the bandits' hands." Disemboweling them proved to be too time-consuming a job. They were therefore doused with kerosene and burned alive. The next day, their ashes were run through a sieve.[85]

No fewer than six days, from 9 to 14 July, were required to extirpate the Armenians from the plain of Mush and the northwestern *kaza* of Varto (nine villages with a total Armenian population of 649). Roughly 20,000 people managed to flee to the Sasun highland, near Havadorig, where they crowded into an area with a circumference of three to three-and-a-half miles, a veritable trap in which they found themselves surrounded, along with the rest of the Sasun mountain district.[86]

A few people from villages in the northeastern part of the plain, such as Vartenis, succeeded in fleeing to the Russian lines near Akhlat.[87] Colonel Nusuhi Bey, in the testimony on the violence on the plain of Mush that he gave to the 1919 court-martial, states that he suggested to Mahmud Kâmil that the women and children be "left in peace." However, on his return to Mush, he found that preparations for the violence were in progress and met the leader of the çetes "charged with killing the Armenians," Musa Beg, together with his band.[88] This would seem to indicate that the orders to eradicate the Armenians were issued by an authority independent of the army, most probably the leadership of the Special Organization, whose highest-ranking representative in the region was Halil (Kut).

The chronology of events shows, moreover, that Halil personally supervised operations. Whereas the villages on the plain were razed on 9 July, he gave his men the order on 10 July to take control of the Armenian houses on the heights dominating the city, the strategically located quarter known as the "Citadel," with a view to setting up his mountain cannons there.[89] On 11 July, the local authorities had the *munedik* (town crier) announce that all males over 15 had to register for their departure, with their families, for Urfa, in compliance with government orders. The next day, 200 people who had shown up to register were arrested and sent the following night to a village on the plain, Alizrnan, where they were slaughtered.[90] The day before, the *mutesarif*, Servet Bey, had had 300 worker-soldiers from Mush, who had already been enrolled in *amele taburis*, executed on the road to Chabaghchur (in the *sancak* of Genc). He also turned a battalion of 700 worker-soldiers over to the police chief, Kâzım; the men were locked up for two days without food or water, tied up, and then sent to Garmir, where they were shot.[91] These initial operations were designed to complete the arrangements to eliminate all those who might offer resistance to the program of destruction. After the vicar and a few leading men of the city begged the *mutesarif* to spare the women and children, he finally agreed to grant them a respite of three days, until 14 July.[92] It seems reasonable to suppose, however, that the 12 July arrest of the bishop of Mush, Reverend Vartan, and 100 other people, all of them subsequently taken under guard to Khaskiugh and shot, was part of the general plan put in place by the authorities, who had never intended to deport the Armenian population of the region, but rather meant to liquidate it on the spot.[93]

Only after bringing these initial operations to their term and beginning to cleanse the Armenian villages on the plain of their population did the Young Turk leaders in Mush give the order, on 12 July, to shell the Armenian neighborhoods of the city, and then to send units of the army and squadrons of *çetes* into action against them. The 3,000 inhabitants of the neighborhoods located in the lower part of the city, Chikrashen and Prudi, were the first to be rounded up and escorted to Arinchvank, a short distance northwest of the city. Here they were separated into two groups: the men were shot in the village orchard, while the women and children were shut up in barns that were then set on fire.[94] *Çetes* and soldiers went through these neighborhoods house by house; they broke down doors and, without further ado, massacred all those who had barricaded themselves in their homes, using axes or bayonets.[95]

Part of the population of the city and the inhabitants of the villages near Mush succeeded in fleeing to Veri Tagh, Tsori Tagh, and St. Marineh, where resistance was organized around a core of some 60 armed men, led by Hagop Godoyan. The cannons in the upper city pounded these neighborhoods as the regular troops and *çetes* steadily advanced, taking first St. Marineh and then Veri Tagh. The civilian population fled in panic to the last Armenian enclave, Tsori Tagh, the "Quarter of the Little Valley." Many of the refugees were caught as they tried to escape, and were either killed on the spot or locked into houses "doused with kerosene" and burned alive.[96] Thus, a group of 1,100 women and children was detained in the courtyard of the police station and then sent to Karist, where these Armenians were shut up in barns and burned alive on the orders of Behcet Bey, the commander of the gendarmerie, who saw to it that the gold and jewels found in the ashes were collected.[97]

After several days of desperate resistance, the fighters defending the Tsor neighborhood abandoned their positions on 17 July, leaving the *çetes* and regular soldiers a clear field. The soldiers were followed by a mob intent on looting. Many of the Armenians perished in an attempt to flee into the mountains on the night of 17/18 July; those who survived were taken under guard to Komer, Kashkiugh, Norshen, Arinchvank, or Alizrnan, where 5,000 people were packed into barns and burned alive.[98] The heads of certain households opted to poison themselves and all the members of their family; others managed to escape to the mountains of Sasun. The stragglers and the wounded left behind in the city were stacked up on a "huge pyre" and set ablaze. This cycle of violence was brought to a close when the Armenian neighborhoods were systematically burned down.[99] Some 10,000 women and children from the villages on the plain of Mush – Sorader, Pazu, Hasanova, Salehan, Gvars, Meghd, Baghlu, Uruj, Ziaret, Khebian, Dom, Hergerd, Norag, Aladin, Goms, Khachkhaldukh, Sulukh, Khoronk, Kartsor, Kizil, Aghatch, Komer, Sheikhlan, Avazaghpiur, Plel, and Kurdmeydan – were "deported" westwards by way of the eastern Euphrates valley (the Murat Su) under Kurdish escort. Some of the women died or were abducted on the way. Others were massacred by Kurds who had come from Jabahçur in the gorges of the Murat Su, the entry to which lies west of Genc. These were the only Armenians of the *sancak* who were not put to death in their native region.[100]

Even the children and teaching staff of the Deutscher Hilfbund's orphanage in Mush, where the Swedish missionary Alma Johannsen (1880–1974) worked, were targeted for destruction. A squadron of regular soldiers went to see the Swedish missionary under the lead of a commanding officer who presented her with "a written government order" to "turn over" the orphan girls and Armenian women present in the institution (many women had found sanctuary there during the massacres) to him so that they could be "sent to Mesopotamia."[101] Apparently under no illusion as to the fate in store for these women and girls, Johannsen attempted to resist the orders of the commanding officer. The next day, she discovered that, apart from the handful of her protégés who had "found a protector," the others, several hundred in all, had been "assembled in a house and burned alive," or else buried alive in big mass graves outside the city.[102] Combing the city in search of possible survivors, she heard a gendarme boasting that he had burned the "little girls" of her orphanage alive.[103] The authorities had shown a certain respect for the formalities in dealing with this conscientious missionary, the only "foreign" witness to events in the region, who, moreover, worked for a German institution; they presented her with an official written order. They did not, however, succeed in preventing her from reporting on the bloody practices of the government and army, which here showed themselves to be pliable tools in the hands of the Ittihad's Central Committee. Johannsen notes, moreover, that Servet Bey tried to evacuate the German woman and another Swedish woman who ran the Deutscher Hilfsbund's orphanage with her to Harput, but that only the German obeyed his order to leave. The few conversations Johannsen had with the *mutesarif* also contain the only first-hand descriptions we have of the mood of this militant Young Turk. Johannsen made an attempt to save her orphan girls by wringing permission from Sevret to take them to Harput. He consented, but added, "Since they are Armenians, their heads may be, and indeed will be, lopped off on the way."[104] Thus, all pretences had been dropped; no further attempt was made to hide the CUP's true objectives. The Swedish missionary observes that, after the slaughter was over, "all the officers were boasting about how many victims they had personally massacred, thus helping rid Turkey of the Armenian race."[105]

Here, as elsewhere, the economic dimension of the program to eradicate the Armenians has to be taken into account. Certain local notables, such as the parliamentary deputy Hoca Ilyas Sâmi, even managed to reconcile their "patriotic" duty with their personal interests. On friendly terms with the leading Armenians of Mush, Sâmi had, from the very beginning of the massacres in the city, suggested to several of these notables that they come to stay in his home, where they would be safe. Nazaret Keshishian, Dikran Mezrigian, Aram and Bedros Baduhasian, and Mgrdich Amrighian and their families accepted the offer. In this fashion Sâmi succeeded in getting his hands on their property; he then turned his guests over to the government, which had them murdered on the edge of town.[106]

This handful of advantages in kind, like the goods that the mob of looters took from the Armenians' homes and boutiques, amounted to very little in comparison with the lion's share of the booty that the four men who organized and carried out the carnage took for themselves. A witness observes that after the butchers had finished their work, Abdülhalik, Hoca Ilyas, Cevdet, and Halil left the city, "followed by a long string of camels loaded down with eighteen big bundles. These bundles, covered with gaily colored sheets, were full of gold, silver, precious objects and antiques." The caravan was bound for Constantinople.[107] It is also easy to imagine the precious objects that were seized when the big monasteries were plundered; their treasures, which had in some cases been accumulating for 15 centuries, were of inestimable value, to say nothing of their unique collections of medieval manuscripts, of which today only fragments survive thanks to the determination of a handful of people. It is likely that the bulk of these stolen goods were earmarked for the Central Committee of the Ittihad and its individual members.

That said, how are we to explain the weakness of the resistance in Mush? To begin with, unlike the plain, Mush had a majority Muslim population, and the number of regular troops stationed there was much higher than in Van: counting the squadrons of *çetes* as well, there were more than 20,000 troops in the city. Vahan Papazian, who remained in Mush until mid-June, writes in his memoirs that opinions diverged within the Dashnak leadership of Daron about the steps to take to safeguard the population. Should the Armenians anticipate the arrival of the Turkish regular forces by trying to seize control of the city, or should they withdraw to the mountains of Sasun with the men capable of fighting?[108] It seems that the Armenian leaders had not definitely opted for one or the other alternative, but thought that the authorities were planning to attack Sasun before turning to the plain of Mush. They consequently assumed that it was preferable to withdraw into the mountains with the fighters and all available arms, since it was the mountain district that was in any event going to serve as a refuge for the villagers of the plain. The influence that the Russian advance had on the choices made by both the Armenians and the authorities must also be considered. Late in June, the Russian army occupied Manazgerd/Melazkırt, attaining on 18 July the westernmost point that it would reach during the first phase of the war, the *nahie* of Liz (in the *kaza* of Bulanik). From there, it was a 16-hour march to Mush.[109] Even if the Dashnak leaders in the region did not have exact intelligence, especially after their withdrawal to Sasun, they had set their hopes on a prompt rescue by their cousins from the north, with whom they had only recently had execrable relations.

Rafaël de Nogales, who continued to see Cevdet and Halil for the next few years despite his negative experiences at Van and Siirt, put the number of Armenians massacred in Mush and on the plain at 50,000. He did not count those who succeeded in fleeing to Sasun only to be eradicated a few weeks later.[110]

Massacres and Evacuation in the *Kaza* of Manazgerd

In the *kaza* of Manazgerd, in the northeastern part of the *sancak* of Mush, comprising 39 Armenian villages with a total Christian population of 11,930,[111] conscription spawned acts of extreme violence, as it did in other areas as well. According to an Armenian witness, men between the ages of 18 and 35 were inducted into combat units, while those between the ages of 35 and 50 were assigned to transport units; most of the latter were killed by Kurdish *çetes* upon their return from the front.[112] Arms were collected in Manazgerd as early as mid-April, which led to only limited violence. It was also in this period that the Turkish army beat a hasty retreat under pressure from the Russian forces, which had advanced as far as Tutak, in the northeastern part of Melazkırt. The army systematically plundered Armenian villages as it withdrew, while incorporating an average of 30 to 40 men in each village.[113]

Guided by the *kaymakam* Halet Beg and two *hamidiye* officers, Sarti Beg and Süleyman Beg, the army methodically looted the following villages: Noradin (pop. 1,671; 70 people were killed), Kharaba-Khasmig (pop. 234; 20 killed), Erzaghi-Khasmig (pop. 663), Sultanlu (pop. 116), Molla-Mustafa (pop. 217; 20 killed), Kotanlı (pop. 400; 20 killed), Terig/Gereg (pop. 922), Khanoghli (pop. 234), Rsdamgedig (pop. 1,800; 30 killed), Tundras (pop. 171), Agner-Sheytanava (pop. 421), Pert/Manazgerd (pop. 945), Ekmal (pop. 160), Aynakhoja/Eknakhoja (pop. 360), Oghzkhan/Okhkin (pop. 90), Mollapagh (pop. 110; 10 killed), Karakaya (pop. 725), Marmus (pop. 300; 20 killed), Dolazbash (pop. 300), Pakran (pop. 155) and Panzden (pop. 237; 30 killed).[114] Those killed in these villages were the young men still living in them – as a rule, adolescents. They were "recruited" by the commander of the *hamidiye çetes*, Haci Hamdi Beg, officially in order to carry out military transport. Conducted under guard to a place near Kotanlı, in the valley of the Murad Su, they were, on the testimony of a few survivors, shot and thrown into the river.[115]

One hundred families from the administrative seat of the *kaza*, Pert/Melazkırt, together with 250 from the villages mentioned above, were grouped together in Agner by two Kurdish chieftains, İbrahim Beg's sons Abdüllah and Hüseyin, who protected them from harm. They fled to Alexandropol in the Caucasus when the Russian forces took control of the region in May; so did the Armenians from the villages of Hasse (pop. 72), Gushdian (pop. 52), Hasan Pasha (pop. 47), Ganigor (pop. 54), Dugnug (pop. 438), Endris (pop. 105), Kharali (pop. 58), Yaramish (pop. 73), Sardavud (pop. 49), Premasian (pop. 27), Hajipot (pop. 79), Khanek (pop. 51), Keranlegh/Kirali (pop. 82), Mkhchin (pop. 145), Khoshajin (pop. 43), Poyi-Chabghun (pop. 57), and Dorokhan (pop. 268).[116]

Massacres and Evacuation in the *Kaza* of Bulanik

The *kaza* of Bulanik, which bordered on the *kaza* of Melazkırt, had, with it 30 towns and villages and 25,053 Armenians, a very dense Armenian population on the eve of the war.[117] The mobilization of men between the ages of 20 and 45 took place without noteworthy incident here. As elsewhere, so here, the younger conscripts were assigned to combat units and the others were put in labor battalions that were used to effect military transports. These labor battalions, which traveled back and forth between Bulanik and Hinis, had a high mortality rate in winter 1914–15.[118] Furthermore, the requisitions in Bulanik, supervised by the *kaymakam*, Esat Bey,[119] were so extensive that the area had suffered a severe grain shortage.[120]

Thanks to the rapid advance of the Russian forces into the region in May 1915, the population of the villages in Upper Bulanik escaped massacre: the inhabitants of the principle town in the *kaza*, Gop (5,000 Armenians) fled to Melazkırt between 14 and 16 May when the Russians arrived there, as did those of the localities of Yonjeli (pop. 1,560), Kharaba Shehir (pop. 572), Miribar (pop. 472), Sheykh Yakub (pop. 1,200), Plur (pop. 182), Odnchur (pop. 1,295), Teghud (pop. 1,168), Latar (pop. 700), Yegmal (20 households), Kekerlu (pop. 1,306), Plur (pop. 182), Khachlu (pop. 39), Shirvan Sheykh (pop. 1,300), and Maltlu (195 households).[121] The only exceptions were Karaghel and Hamza Sheykh. Hamza Sheykh, inhabited by 1,299 Armenians, was attacked by Kurds of the Jibran tribe and local Çerkez, who massacred its inhabitants on the spot, leaving only 14 people alive.[122] The villagers of Karaghel (pop. 1,312) fled along the banks of the eastern Euphrates (Murad Su), protected by 30 armed men led by Kevork Khlghatian, but were not immediately able to cross the river, which was in spate. Taking refuge on an island in the river, they fought off the assaults of Kurdish tribes for two weeks, and then succeeded in crossing to the other bank of the Euphrates, clinging to water skins that they had made with sheepskin.[123]

The men of Gop opted to escort their women and children to the Russian lines when they learned that the Russian army was in Melazkırt; meanwhile, under the command of Gniaz Mkhitarian, Bedros Markarian, and Mushegh Seropian, the little town fought off Musa Kâzım's assaults. Some 100 Armenians lost their lives during the fighting, but the others later managed to flee.[124] The villagers of the 11 localities in lower Bulanik, which lay much further to the southwest – Liz (pop. 1,499), Kerolan, Abri (pop. 203), Khoshkaldi (pop. 1,018), Adghon (pop. 754), Prkashen (pop. 517), Goghag (pop. 472), Akrag (pop. 267), Mulakend (pop. 200), and Pionk (pop. 457) – were less fortunate.[125] Khoshkaldi came under attack by Kurds commanded by Musa Kâsim Beg, the leader of the Jibran tribe, Haydar, and a well-known bandit, Jendi. The Kurds first massacred the males over five, and then turned to the women.[126] As for the members of the 60 households in Kerolan, they were massacred by Kurds under the command of local Kurdish sheikhs, with the exception of a few young women and girls who were carried off to Liz by their torturers.

Some of the villagers of Abri, Adghon, Prkashen, Goghag, Akrag and Mulakend were massacred in their villages around 10 May by Şeykh Hazret and Musa Kâsim. The survivors, after trying in vain to cross the Turkish lines, fled to Liz, the principle town in the *nahie*, where the commander of the local garrison protected them until 18 May, the day Russian troops arrived in Upper Bulanik. At that point, 1,200 men were put in chains and shot one verst (1,066km) from Liz; their bodies were dumped into two immense mass graves by regular troops.[127]

It is, without a doubt, possible to see these massacres as connected with the operations carried out in the same period in the neighboring *kaza* of Akhlat (in the *sancak* of Bitlis), with a view to eliminating the Armenian population before the Russians arrived.

Guerilla Warfare and Massacres in the *Kaza* of Sasun

Contrary to expectations, the high mountain district of Sasun, which dominated the plain of Mush to the north and the valleys in the northern part of the vilayet of Dyarbekir to the south, was not the first area in the vilayet of Mush to come under attack. Indeed, in summer 1915, Sasun even served as a haven for the tens of thousands of Armenians fleeing deportation and massacre in the vicinity. It seems as if the authorities' strategy consisted in trapping the survivors in this "mountain sanctuary." Later they sealed it off. As we have seen, on 2 June 1915,[128] Kurdish irregulars launched an offensive against the district of Psank/Busank in the southern part of Sasun in order to confiscate the arms held by the villagers. The failure of this offensive made the authorities more cautious. They had no doubt also learned the lessons of Cevdet's defeat in Van; this time, they would take as many precautions as they could to ensure the success of their plans. Alma Johannsen, while visiting the Ottoman general staff in Mush, where she hoped to find surviving women teachers from her orphanage, observed that all these high-ranking officers "were very proud that they had been able to eradicate the Armenians so quickly ... and were sorry that such extensive preparatory measures had been taken."[129]

To wipe out the Sasun district's 80,233 Armenians, who had repeatedly shown, notably in 1894,[130] that they were not inclined to let themselves be killed without a fight, the authorities took a series of measures. They managed to mobilize some 3,000 Armenian conscripts, who were officially to be enrolled in the military transport service but were in fact taken under guard to Lice and then split up into three groups that were executed between Harput and Palu in May 1915.[131] Early in May, they also organized the massacre of the Armenians of the *kazas* of Silvan and Beşiri, to the south of Sasun, probably to make it easier to close off the southern access routes to Sasun – to which several thousand of the Silvan/Beşiri Armenians nevertheless managed to flee.[132] That is, the authorities sought to bring all avenues of communication with Sasun under control without, however, preventing survivors from the plain from fleeing there. They hoped to starve the Armenians in the mountain district into submission, as they had tried to do in Van; for while Sasun had meat in abundance – it was a cattle-and sheep-breeding district – it was utterly dependent on the neighboring regions for its grain supply and salt.[133] If we add to these refugees the 8,000 and more Armenians of the *kaza* of Harzan (in the *sancak* of Siirt), who fled the first massacres in their area perpetrated in mid-June by Halil and Cevdet and found haven in Sasun,[134] we can readily imagine how critical the sanitary situation of these people must have been. It became far worse a month later, in mid-July, when, in their turn, some 20,000 villagers from the plain of Mush poured in through the pass of Havadorig.[135]

As soon as he arrived in Mush, Lieutenant-Colonel Halil (Kut) sent part of the forces under his command – several squadrons of cavalry – to bolster the siege of Sasun, which Kurdish irregulars had been maintaining unaided until then. In any case, it was only after the regular troops had finished cleansing the plain of Mush of its Armenians that they arrived in large numbers to crush the resistance in Sasun. The operation put in place to eradicate the tens of thousands of Armenians who had taken refuge there resembled a veritable military campaign. The Şeg, Beder, Bozek, and Calal tribes took up positions to the east of the mountain district; the Kurds of Kulp, led by Hüseyin Beg and Hasan Beg, dug in to the west, along with the Kurds of Genc and Lice; Khati Bey of Mayafarkin and the Khiank, Badkan, and Bagran tribes took up their positions to the south; finally, the regular army, equipped with mountain cannons, set out to take Sasun from the north. Additional troops were dispatched from Dyarbekir and Mamuret ul-Aziz to reinforce those already on hand.[136] Ruben Ter Minasian, one of the two leaders of the Armenian resistance, estimates that the Kurdish-Turkish force encircling Sasun comprised around 30,000 troops.[137] In the besieged district were approximately 20,000 natives of the *kaza* and some 30,000 refugees who, as we have seen, had come from the plain of Mush and areas to the south. According to Vahan Papazian, the other main Armenian leader, the self-defense effort was mounted by about 1,000 men who had very few modern weapons and a great many hunting rifles.[138]

The first general assault was launched on 18 July 1915. It was renewed the next day by way of Shenek. The attackers forced the Armenians to fall back to their second line of defense on Mt. Antok, where they held firm for several days running. By 28 July, Sasun was running low on ammunition and famine had begun to claim lives, especially among the refugees. On 2 August, the defenders decided to attempt a sortie with the whole population of the enclave. A few thousand Armenians succeeded in crossing the Kurdish-Turkish lines and making their way to the Russian positions in the northern extremity of the *sancak* of Mush, but the vast majority were massacred, notably in the valley of Gorshik, after the hand-to-hand fighting of the final battles of 5 August, in which the women, armed with daggers, also took part.[139]

A few days earlier, in late July, some of the refugees had gone back down to the plain in desperation. They had convinced themselves that the sultan's *firman* (order), in which he granted the Armenians "his pardon" and promised to spare the lives of those who returned to their homes, was no hollow promise. A few days later, the pyres on which the corpses of some of these gullible villagers were burning in Norshen, Khaskiugh, and Mgrakom sent up billows of foul-smelling smoke that polluted the whole plain.[140] Other Armenians, a few thousand in number, were deported, while a few hundred were "taken into" Kurdish families or seized as war booty by officers. At the time, the Russian lines, which ran through Melazkırt, were only 25 miles from Mush. It was this distance that the fugitives crossed at night in order to reach the front, when they were not intercepted. In mid-July, Vahan Papazian, Ruben Ter Minasian, and a few *fedayis* succeeded in doing so, going by way of the mountain district of Nemrud.[141] Sasun had by this time been emptied of its inhabitants, and its villages lay in ruins.

Massacres in the Sancak of Genc

The *sancak* of Genc, traversed by the eastern Euphrates, lay at the northwestern-most tip of the vilayet of Bitlis. It had lost the great bulk of its Armenian population to massacre or Islamicization in 1895. In 1915, there were only 23 modest Armenian localities left in the *sancak*, with a total Armenian population of 4,344.[142] The Armenians' feeble numbers facilitated the task of the main local Young Turk leaders – the parliamentary deputy Çerkez Ahmed Emin Bey, Hasan Bey, and Ahmed Bey – who organized the massacres in the *kazas* of Chabaghjur and Pasur under the supervision of Abdülhalik, and with direct support from the army. There is no trace of survivors from this region. We have only meager descriptions of the circumstances surrounding the massacres, which we owe to local Turks whom the inhabitants of Mush later encountered in Aleppo. The deportees were for the most part massacred at Palu Bridge.[143]

Balance Sheet of the Massacres in the Vilayet of Bitlis

In contrast to what transpired in the vilayet of Erzerum, very few Armenians were deported from the region of Bitlis. The density of the Armenian population, especially in the *sancak* of Mush, was one reason for the extreme violence with which the Armenians there were liquidated, but the main explanation doubtless resides in the character of the principal Young Turk leaders who carried out these operations, bound as they were by family ties to the minister of war and the minister of the interior, and also in the tribal practices that prevailed in the region. The inordinate military might brought to bear also indicates that the Ittihadist leadership feared that its extermination plan might well fail in this region, under threat from the Russian forces.

Statistics established by Armenian institutions after the war show that almost all the Armenians in the *sancak* of Bitlis were killed in the *sancak* itself. Six thousand people, 130 of whom survived, were deported to Mosul; 2,500 young women and children were "integrated" into Muslim families; and approximately 6,000 people from the *kaza* of Hizan/Khizan succeeded in fleeing to the Russian lines (half of them survived the harassment to which they were subjected on their retreat to the Caucasus). Of the Armenians from the *sancak* of Mush, around 25,000 survived, most of them because they came from the *kazas* in the northeastern part of the *sancak* and were saved by the Russian advance, another 5,000 because they succeeded in gaining the Russian lines after breaking out of the siege of Mush, and a few hundred more because they were deported to the Syrian desert and managed to survive the conditions there. In the *sancak* of Siirt, a mere 150 deportees (here, too, the overwhelming majority of the population was massacred where it was found) seem to have survived, along with perhaps a few dozen inhabitants of the *kaza* of Harzan who were able to escape the slaughter in Sasun. The few known survivors from Genc were all young women and children who had been abducted.[144]

In his December 1918 deposition, General Vehib Pasha pointed out, in describing the violence perpetrated in a village in the vilayet of Bitlis, that it represented "an example of atrocity of a kind never before seen in the history of Islam." Citing the role played by Mustafa Abdülhalik Bey, "a man without fault and endowed with civic virtues," Vehib said: "he was not able to put a stop to these events, which I shall never be able to approve." The general even reported that this man, whom he called

> resolute, caring, brave, charitable and human, devoted, patriotic and religious, began, with tears in his eyes, to chant the prayers of the Koran when he learned the facts mentioned above, no doubt in the belief that the divine wrath provoked by these atrocities was going to plunge the nation into catastrophes and ordeals that he sought to ward off with his prayers.

Vehib nevertheless concluded by wondering: "Was Mustafa Abdülhalik Bey not capable of calling a halt to these atrocities in his province, or of preventing them?"[145]

Whatever the truth of the matter, the Council of Ministers appointed Mustafa Abdülhalik vali of Aleppo on 17 October 1915.[146] Thus, he was given responsibility for the hundreds of thousands of Armenian deportees from western Anatolia who had arrived in Syria.

Chapter 6

Deportations and Massacres in the Vilayet of Dyarbekir

In 1914, the vilayet of Dyarbekir had a mixed population consisting of Kurds, Orthodox and Catholic Syriacs, and Armenians. The Armenians were basically concentrated in the northern and northeastern parts of the vilayet, the southernmost zones of the territory they inhabited; they lived in 249 towns and villages, with a total population of 106,867, according to the censuses of the Constantinople Patriarchate.[1] The Armenians of the northeastern *kazas* – Lice, Beşiri, and Silvan – were Kurdish-speaking. Their tribal mode of life suggests that they had adapted to their predominantly Kurdish environment. These regions, with a dense Armenian population that largely escaped the control of the central authorities, had been a source of profound irritation for the CUP from a very early date. In May 1913, French diplomatic sources observed an upsurge in the number of exactions perpetrated by the Kurdish tribes against the Armenian population; the violence of these acts can only have come about as the result of orders from the higher echelons.[2] In the capital of the vilayet, Dyarbekir, the situation was less tense. Since the assumption of power by the Young Turks, ARF party leaders had maintained friendly relations with the city's Ittihadist club and the local authorities. The Armenians comprised nearly one-third of the total population of 45,000. But they had an economic weight beyond their numbers, and held a virtual monopoly over Dyarbekir's craft production and commercial exchanges. Although the all-Muslim Association of the Renaissance (Intibah Şirketi) had been created on the CUP's initiative in Dyarbekir early in 1910 for the purpose of taking the local economy in hand, it had not produced the expected results.[3] In other words, one of the Ittihad's major objectives, the creation of a Turkish Millî İktisat (national economy), was, for lack of businessmen, not easily realized in the provinces. However, the general mobilization announced in Dyarbekir on 3 August 1914, together with the subsequent military requisitions, afforded local Young Turk circles an opportunity to undermine the social position of Armenian entrepreneurs. The mobilization emptied the city of part of its economically active Armenian population and left a number of craftsmen working for the army and state without compensation. Conscription had brought forceful interventions by the gendarmerie in the vilayet's villages and towns.[4] Two thousand young men from Dyarbekir were assigned to labor battalions on the front, in Hasankale and Karacasun,[5] while the others worked in the region itself. It was, however, the methods used during the requisitions that best illustrated the Ittihad's desire to ruin the local economy. Alongside the military commission responsible for "military contributions" (*teklif-i harbiyye*), a civilian committee (Ahz ve Sevki Asker) was created, officially for the purpose of collecting foodstuffs and other products to meet "the needs of military."[6] All the members of Ahz ve Sevki Asker had been handpicked by the Young Turk representatives in Dyarbekir, the responsible secretary of the Ittihad, Attar Hakkı, and the party's delegate, Circisağazâde Kör Yusuf. They in turn created branches of this committee

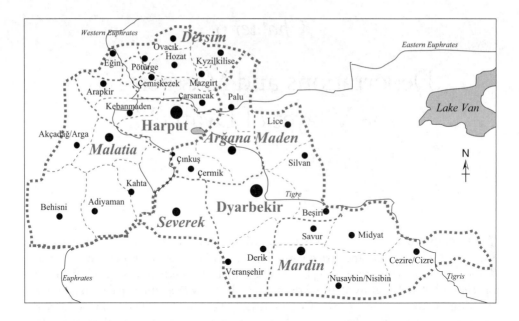

in all the *kazas* of the vilayet. The local branches were, in effect, delegations responsible for collecting the *teklif-i harbiyye*.[7] In other words, in carrying out these operations, the Ittihad replaced the military authorities.

In a letter to the patriarch of Constantinople, the Armenian vicar, Mgrdich Chlghadian, denounced the arbitrariness with which the commissions were emptying the shops and ware-houses of Dyarbekir's Christians and, especially, the violence with which the authorities had confiscated, in the 110 villages of the *kazas* of Beşiri and Silvan, reserves of wheat, flour, barley and oil, as well as horses, mules, sheep, and cows. They also denounced the resurgence of attacks by plundering Kurds and the devastation of the tobacco fields, the region's main resource, that were located in the area between Beşiri and Bitlis.[8] Furthermore, in certain localities, villagers had been taxed for the "tithe" (actually one-eighth rather than one-tenth of the harvest) three times in the space of a few months – here, too, in the name of patriotism and the war effort.[9] How should these methods be interpreted in a country in which arbitrary behavior was a deeply rooted cultural practice? Should we ascribe them to the exceptional circumstances brought about by the war, or should we consider them, rather, as one of the first manifestations of the CUP's plan to eradicate the Armenians? If we consider the proce-dures used against the Greek population of the Aegean sea coast in the first three months of 1914 – a combination of deportation and banishment to Greece accompanied by con-fiscations of these Greeks' property – we can have no doubt as to the Ittihad's intention to implement, to begin with, the economic component of its anti-Armenian plan. The Kurdish tribalism prevalent in the region of Dyarbekir only aggravated the phenomenon, while reduc-ing the share of the booty that the CUP had planned to take for itself. Even before war was declared, the first phase of the plunder of Armenian goods took place behind a respectable facade that was more or less based on legal rules, as interpreted by officials who did not have an unduly strict respect for the letter of the law.

The act that was most symptomatic of the Ittihad's real designs was the burning down of the Dyarbekir bazaar on the night of 18/19 August 1914. The fire reduced 80 shops and stands, 30 baker's ovens, three hans, and 14 carpenter's workshops to ashes. According to witnesses, the operation was organized by the police chief Gevranlızâde Memduh Bey, under the supervision of the president of the Association of the Renaissance (Intibah Şirketi) and the parliamentary deputy from Dyarbekir, Pirincizâde Feyzi[10] (Feyzi was, incidentally, an uncle of a member of the Ittihad's Central Committee, Ziya Gökalp),[11] along with two local Young Turk leaders, Attar Hakkı and Circisağazâde Kör Yusuf. Apparently no effort was made to fight the fire; the police and gendarmerie even prevented shop owners from trying to douse the flames or save their merchandise.[12] The new vali, Hamid Bey, appointed on 1 October 1914, was able to dismiss Memduh, whose involvement in this act of arson was a matter of common knowledge. Hamid Bey proved unable, however, to punish the three people who were the main culprits.

Memduh, although indicted, was set free at the request of parliamentary deputy Fayzi,[13] who was the most influential personality in the vilayet. The British vice-consul in Dyarbekir, Thomas Mgrdichian, was well acquainted with Fayzi. In his memoirs, he reports the conversation he had with him in the deputy's home on 27 August 1914 in the presence of his maternal uncle, a mufti by the name of İbrahim. Feyzi affirmed his confidence in Germany's military might and the outcome of the war. He also declared that "Turkey's higher interests require that it side with Germany," which had promised to help it recover the territories that the empire had lost – Egypt, Tripoli, Tunisia, Algeria, Rumelia, the islands of the Aegean archipelago, Crete, Cyprus, and the Caucasus, to say nothing of the Indies – and become a powerful state of 300 million Muslims.[14] Had Feyzi not been Ziya Gökalp's uncle, we might doubt the accuracy of the statement attributed to this deputy of Çerkez and Kurdish descent, who soon turned to a subject he found equally fascinating – "the Armenians." The British vice-consul learned straight from the source how bitter Feyzi was over the Armenians' refusal to foment an anti-Russian uprising in the Caucasus; this indicates that the Dashnak leaders' response to the recent proposals of Ömer Naci and Dr. Şakir had circulated rather quickly in Young Turk circles. The question of the recently approved reforms also inspired a very lively reaction from the Ittihadist deputy: "If the Armenians continue down this path, it will cost them very dearly. England, France and Russia are no longer in a position to rescue them or help them, whereas we can work our will on them; our German and Austrian allies will not say a word."[15] Noticing the diplomat's surprise at such candor, Feyzi informed him that he had traveled to Germany in the spring with a delegation of the Ottoman National Assembly, and that everything he had learned in the course of this voyage had brought him to these conclusions.[16]

At a second meeting, which took place at the British consulate a few days later – the parliamentary deputy Kâmil Bey was also on hand – Thomas Mgrdichian remarked that, at the present rate, the commission of the *teklif-i harbiyye* would soon have finished ruining the Armenians; that they would do well in their capacity as deputies representing all the inhabitants of the vilayet to have a word with the two heads of that commission, Attar Hakkı and Circisağazâde Kör Yusuf; and that, in thus bankrupting the Armenians, the authorities were ruining trade and agriculture, the sources of the region's wealth. This came down, Mgrdichian said, to "eliminating the source of the money needed to fight the war and, thus, to destroying Turkey." Feyzi's reaction revealed the logic that dominated Young Turk circles on the eve of the declaration of war:

> The Armenians should give the matter a little more thought, for there are not many of them. If they are liquidated, they will cease to exist. There are, on the other hand, many of us, and if half of us disappear, the other half will still be there – the more so as we are going to win back what we have lost in two hundred years, and then some.

The vice-consul said he was surprised at the aggressiveness of Feyzi's words, and then riposted quite undiplomatically: "Germany will swallow you up and make you one of its lackeys."[17]

The nature of this dialogue between a Young Turk, who shared the hope in the resurrection of the Ottoman Empire that his party had put at the center of its program, and a British diplomat who was a native of the country but had shaken off the status of Ottoman subject thanks to his functions, doubtless reflects the general state of mind reigning in the eastern provinces just before Turkey's entry into the war. One could express the threats hanging over the Armenian population no better.

The nature of the CUP's plans was confirmed by the testimony that the former civilian inspector of the vilayets of Bitlis and Mosul gave before the Istanbul court-martial on 18 February 1920. He reported that he had made the return voyage from Constantinople in August 1914 in the company of an eminent member of the Ittihad, Feyzi Bey, and an Armenian deputy from Dyarbekir – this was Stepan Chrajian, who was to be murdered in June 1915. On the way to the capital, Feyzi remarked to the Armenian deputy that the Armenians "had treated us badly ... and appealed for foreign intervention." "This will cost you dearly, my friend," he concluded; "your future is in jeopardy." When the group reached Urfa on 7 August and learned that the two inspectors, Hoff and Westenek, had just been dismissed, Feyzi exclaimed: "Now you'll see what it means to demand reforms."[18]

On 10 September, Thomas Mgrdichian went to see the head of the commission of the *teklif-i harbiyye* and the CUP delegate in Dyarbekir, Circisağazâde Kör Yusuf, in order to point out that the accounts turned in by his commission indicated that Muslim and Christian taxpayers were being taxed unequally: the Christians, who represented one-third of the population, were being asked to pay for five-sixths of the war effort. "The Armenians are richer," Kör Yusuf pointed out in response; "the whole market of the city and the vilayet, as well as trade, the crafts and agriculture are in their hands; they have a lot of money and so they ought to hand it over." The vice-consul's reply – that the big Kurdish landowners, the pashas and *beys*, were much richer and had huge cash reserves at their disposal, does not seem to have changed his interlocutor's mind any more than did Mgrdichian's conclusion: "In plundering the Armenians, [the Turks] are killing the goose that lays the golden eggs."[19]

Witnesses concur that Vali Hamid attempted the impossible in his six months in office (October 1914 to March 1915) – to limit the excesses committed by members of Dyarbekir's Young Turk circles – but that he was powerless in the face of men such as the parliamentary deputy Feyzi, who enjoyed the support of the Young Turk Central Committee. The official nomination of Dr. Çerkez Reşid, one of the historical CUP's founding fathers and a graduate of Istanbul's Military Medical School, to the post of vali of Dyarbekir on 25 March 1915,[20] was doubtless not unrelated to the decisions about the fate of the Armenians that had just been made by the Ittihadist Central Committee. In his capacity as *mutesarif* of Karesi (in the vilayet of Balıkesir), Reşid had actively contributed to the policy of liquidating the "Rum" (Greeks) of the Aegean sea coast in the first three months of 1914. He had applied a battery of rather efficient political and economic measures designed by the CUP to eliminate concentrations of the Greek population.[21] At the practical level, he had taken part in the activities of the Teşkilât-ı Mahsusa, which was still cutting its teeth, and had learned to appreciate the effectiveness of its methods of intimidation. His July 1914 nomination as counselor to the inspector general in Van, Nikolai Hoff, was a sign of the confidence that Young Turk circles in the capital had in this high-ranking official. While his stay in Van was too brief to allow them to evaluate his work there – he was recalled on 13 August by the ministry to which he answered[22] – we may nevertheless suppose that Talât assigned him the mission of sabotaging the Armenian reforms, which the CUP continued to regard as unacceptable interference by the powers in Turkey's internal affairs. In other words, when Reşid arrived in Dyarbekir on 28 March 1915, he had very likely received precise instructions as to the operations to be conducted there. The fact that he was accompanied by Colonel Çerkez Rüşdi Bey, who had been put in command of the vilayet's gendarmerie; Çerkez Şakir, an aide-de-camp; Bedreddin Bey, the secretary general (*mektubci*) of the vilayet (later the *mutesarif* of Mardin); and some 50 Çerkez *çetes*[23] sent to the area from Mosul, gives us some idea of the nature of his mission. That he had links with the Teşkilât-ı Mahsusa is hardly open to doubt. The 20 December 1915 report of Mazhar Bey, the president of the commission of inquiry established in Mamuret ul-Aziz and Dyarbekir, clearly accuses Vali Reşid of having organized, altogether illegally, squadrons of irregulars that were guilty of pillage and massacre.[24] A document presented at the Unionists' trial on 27 April 1919 also attests "that the massacres and atrocities perpetrated in Dyarbekir were carried out at Talât's instigation."[25] An Armenian source even affirms that Reşid set up a telegraph station in his governor's residence so as to be able to communicate directly with the Ministry of the Interior.[26]

Among the first steps the vali took was the creation of a "militia," as is confirmed by many witnesses, and Reşid himself;[27] this "militia" would seem to have been nothing other than a number of squadrons of *çetes* of the Special Organization. Early in April, the vali charged two well-known Dyarbekir criminals, Cemilpaşazâde Mustafa and Colonel Yasinzâde Şevki, with the task of forming 11 battalions of *çetes* recruited from the ranks of the delinquents and felons in the region; these battalions comprised, on average, 500 men, except for the eleventh, nicknamed the "butchers' battalion."[28] Officers carefully chosen for their aptitude for violence were put in command of these units. According to testimony by the civilian inspector, Colonel Rüşdi Bey, the vali's right-hand man and commander of the gendarmerie, had supervised the process, while the local leaders of the Ittihad, with the deputy Feyzi at their head, had actively contributed to the formation of these battalions of the Teşkilât-ı Mahsusa.[29] The leaders of these *çetes* were Feridzâde Emin Bey, Şeihzade Kadir, Mosuli Yehia Muştak Bey, Fatihpaşaoğlu Haci Bekir, Allahutonoğlu Salih, Mardinkapulı Tahir Bey, Abdülkadirzâde Kemal Bey, Osman Kanon Zabiti, Cemilpaşazâde Ömer Bey, Muftizâde Şerif Bey, Mosuli Muhamed, Dellalzâde Emin Bey, Zazazâde Muhamed, Kasab Niko, Kasab Şeko, and Çerkez Yaver Şakir, the vali's aide-de-camp.[30] Somewhat later, Pirincizâde Feyzi recruited two officers of the Special Organization from the district of Cesire – Ömer and Mustafa, famous bandits from the Ferikhanoğlu tribe who had been terrorizing the district for 20 years and repeatedly been condemned to death in absentia.[31] Reşid also had the police chief Gevranlızâde Memduh, whose role in the fire in Dyarbekir's bazaar we have already seen,[32] recalled from Adana. Armenian observers point out that these battalions were basically made up of Kurds and Çerkez émigrés from the vilayet.

The second measure taken by Reşid was the creation of a "supreme council" (*meclisi alı*) chaired by the vali himself. The council's vice-president was the deputy Pirincizâde Feyzi; the other members were the commander of the *çetes*, Cemilpaşazâde Mustafa, and the local leaders of the Ittihad and the delegates of the national government: Feyzi's nephew, Pirincizâde Sedki; Muftizâde Şerif; Harputli Hüseyin, Yasineffendizâde Şefki; Velibabazâde Veli Necet; Zulfizâde Adıl Bey; Kâtibzâde Şevket; Zulfizâde Zulfi Bey, a Unionist parliamentary deputy; Circisağazâde Abdül Kerim; Diregcizâde Tahir; Haciğanizâde Servet; Mosuli Mehmed; Mehmed Emin; Cırcisağazâde Kör Yusuf; and Attar Hakkı.[33] The creation of a council of this sort, which, as we have seen, existed in Erzerum as well, was apparently part of a general system, doubtless designed by the Ittihadist Central Committee to maintain control over the political situation in the regions while coordinating the anti-Armenian persecutions and providing justification for them. Since we do not have conclusive documentation, it is hard to grasp the exact nature of the Supreme Council's activity, but it seems reasonable to suppose that it was a kind of political leadership body, enlarged to include government officials and army officers, which represented both the CUP and government, and was charged with carrying out the national authorities' decisions.

The nature of the mission conducted by Pirincizâde Feyzi in Cezire from 29 April to 12 May shows that this council played a major role in diffusing the joint propaganda of the CUP and the government. Witnesses say that the parliamentary deputy visited all the villages he encountered on his way, exhorting the Kurdish tribes to perform their "religious duty." Feyzi incited these populations against the "infidels" with the help of religious references and with the support of the *hojas*, rather than Turkic discourse. One slogan was repeated everywhere: "God, make their children orphans, make widows of their wives through and give their property to Muslims." In addition to this prayer, legitimization of plunder, murder, and abduction took the following form: "It is licit for Muslims to take the infidels' property, life and women" ("giavurların malı, canı ve namuse helal dir islamlara"). The last element exploited by Young Turk propaganda – the fact that Turkey's allies, Germany and Austria, endorsed the policy of eradicating the Armenians[34] – shows the credibility of this alliance in the eyes of Turkish public opinion.

A civilian inspector who arrived in Cezire on 8 May 1915 reports that the *kaymakam*, Halil Sâmi, was especially alarmed by Feyzi's machinations. By that time, the deputy had already been in the city for some two weeks. Dispatched on a special mission "by the vali of Dyarbekir," Sâmi summoned the chieftains of the Kurdish tribes of the region to a preparatory meeting held in Cezire on 10 May. At this meeting, according to the inspector's testimony, he resorted to the kind of discourse described by Mgrdichian. The *kaymakam*, however, is supposed to have refused to support the plan or dismiss the district's Armenian and Syriac Catholic civilian officials from their posts. He was dismissed from his post on 1 May 1915.[35]

The Preparation of the Massacres in Dyarbekir

In the first half of April, the authorities began hunting down deserters in the towns and villages of the vilayet of Dyarbekir. On the 16 April, the manhunt took on altogether different proportions. The Armenian quarter of the city of Dyarbekir was surrounded by gendarmes, policemen, Çerkez çetes, and "militiamen." The object was to arrest the deserters who had taken refuge on the adjoining terraces – the flat roofs – in the Armenian quarter, but also to search for arms held in private homes, in accordance with the vali's early April order that the population surrender its weapons. Armenian witnesses observe that those arrested were young men, some of them not yet of draftable age, and that the house searches gave rise to extremely violent incidents, notably a series of rapes. According to the same sources, 300 men, a few notables included, were arrested during this operation and interned in the city's central prison. Three days later, on 19 April, members of the diocesan council, the parish councils, and humanitarian organizations were arrested and jailed in turn, either for "desertion" or for aiding and abetting deserters.[36]

On 20 April, in reaction to this first wave of arrests, a meeting was held in the Armenian prelacy. Chaired by the vicar of the diocese, it brought together the main leaders of the political parties and other Armenian notables, as well as the representatives of Dyarbekir's Catholic and Protestant communities. The purpose of the meeting was to settle on the measures to take under the prevailing circumstances, and especially to decide whether the Armenians should "put faith in the authorities' promises and allow themselves to be disarmed." The discussion dragged on for 24 hours. The vicar, the French vice-consul, Harutiun Kasabian, the dragoman of the vilayet, Dikran Ilvanian, and the Dashnak, Henchak, and Ramgavar parties, together with a few other leading personalities, argued for organizing a self-defense effort – that is, "selling their skins as dearly as possible." The Armenians should put no faith, they maintained, in the government's or the CUP's promises. Other notables, however, headed by Khachadur Dikranian, a member of the city council (*meclisı idare*), pointed out that the means of defense at their disposal were quite limited, and that in the best of circumstances they could hold out for a month at most. The second group carried the day; the Armenians decided to do nothing.[37]

On the morning of 21 April, the leaders of the political parties were arrested. Among them were the Dashnaks Mihran Basmajian, Giragos Ohannesian, and Dikran Chakejian; the Hnchak parliamentary deputy Stepan Chrajian and his sons Garabed, the *müdir* of the Tur Abdin district, and Khosrov, a judge on the Dyarbekir court; the Ramgavars Hagop Oghasapian and Dikran Ilvanian; the dragoman of the vilayet, Stepan Matosian; and Misak Shirigjian, the authorized representative of the Singer Manufacturing Company.[38] American and Turkish witnesses confirm that these men were tortured and put on display in the city streets.[39] The heights of cruelty attained by the vali's torturers, who were directed by the police chief, Resul Hayri, are indicative of the atmosphere then reigning in Dyarbekir. This torture must be interpreted as a preparatory measure, carried out on orders from Dr. Reşid, the purpose of which was to liquidate the Armenian political elite before moving on to the main phase of the extermination plan.

Massive arrests of the local Armenian elite began, accordingly, only 20 days later, on 11 May 1915. The targets were state officials, lawyers, intellectuals, merchants, bankers, architects, engineers, and landowners, famous and less famous. The last to be arrested were the vicar Mgrdich Chlghadian, the Catholic archbishop Andreas Chelebian, the Protestant minister Hagop Andonian, and other clergymen.[40] The official purpose of the torture inflicted on them was to bring them to reveal where they had hidden their weapons and to confess to their plans to "revolt." It seems the real reason that they were burned with red-hot irons, had their fingernails pulled out, their skulls crushed in vices, and horseshoes nailed to the bottoms of their feet, or that, after being "proven guilty," they were paraded through the streets of Dyarbekir, was rather the authorities' desire to terrorize the 10,000 Armenians still in the city. This cruelty was perhaps also the violent expression of a collective frustration that had various long-standing causes. For the vali, the torture was apparently also meant to provide grounds for an indictment that would retroactively legitimate the recourse to brute force. Thus, Dr. Floyd Smith observes that, under torture, an employee of the American mission "confessed" that the American Board of Commissioners for Foreign Missions was preparing an insurrection in Dyarbekir and that he himself was their "agent."[41] The absurdity and crudeness of this procedure should not be allowed to mask its ideological underpinnings – the rejection of everything foreign – or the Young Turks' desire to eliminate potential witnesses, here too, on the eve of the mass slaughter.[42]

A 17 May 1915 telegram from Dr. Reşid to the vali of Adana, İsmail Hakkı,[43] spells out the criminal intentions of the Young Turk physician. After informing his colleague about the situation in Van – Cevdet had just abandoned the city – Reşid insisted on the need to exterminate the Armenians, stressing that he had himself already begun to carry this policy into practice. But this was just a beginning. On 27 May 1915, a careful inventory was taken of the 980 people who were still being held in Dyarbekir's central prison (some of those interned had already died under torture).[44] A list was drawn up of 636 men for whom Pirincizâde Feyzi had made special plans. On 30 May, these people were taken out of the city at dawn, led toward the banks of the Tigris, and loaded onto 23 *keleks* (rafts that floated on inflated water-skins). Officially, these men were being banished to Mosul.[45] Reşid asked his aide-de-camp, Çerkez Yaver Şakir, to accompany them with his Çerkez *çetes*. Someone was missing when roll was taken – the vicar, Chlghadian. Although present when the *keleks* set sail, he had been taken back to prison. The torture inflicted on him at his point could only have been the product of some indefinable pathology: his torturers pulled out his teeth, pierced his temples with red-hot irons, gouged out his eyes, and then exhibited him in the city's Muslim neighborhoods in an atmosphere of collective revelry, to the beating of tambourines. His ordeal came to an end in the courtyard of Dyarbekir's principal mosque, in the presence of government officials and religious authorities: he was sprinkled with oil, a drop at a time, and then burned alive. Dr. Smith found him as he lay in agony in the stable of the Turkish hospital, but was unable to save him. The next day, the vali had an attestation drawn up and signed by several doctors; it stated that the prelate had died of typhus.[46]

The caravan of *keleks* arrived at a point upstream of Beşiri on 9 June, after being subjected to an attack by Kurdish "brigands," the only objectives of which seem to have been to allow Çerkez Şakir to obtain 6,000 Turkish pounds in "protection" money from the deportees, and to convince them to abandon the *keleks* in order to make their way to the riverbank by foot. The 636 men were taken ashore and pointed in the direction of the village of Shkavtan/Çalikan, which belonged to the Ömer brothers (nicknamed Amero and, sometimes, Eumeri) and Mustafa Ferikhanoğlu, the chieftain of a clan of the Ramma tribe who had been recruited by deputy Feyzi to deal with Dyarbekir's Armenian elite. After being stripped naked, carefully searched, and tied together in small groups, the deportees were taken under guard to the Rezvani gorge, where they had their throats cut or were shot by members of the Ferikhanoğlu clan and the *çetes* of the vali's aide-de-camp Çerkez Şakir, who personally oversaw the three-hour operation. The deputy Stepan Chrajian, Diran Kazarian, Atalian, Garabed Khandanian, and others were among the last victims; their executioners apparently wanted them to see the spectacle before they were finished off in turn.[47] The German vice-consul in Mosul later confirmed that these massacres had occurred.[48]

The epilogue to the execution of Dyarbekir's Armenian elite illustrates Reşid's cynicism. Around two weeks after the killings, on 24 June, the vali and Pirincizâde Feyzi invited the man who had been mainly responsible for carrying out the massacre, Ferikhanoğlu Amero (Ömer), to Dyarbekir to reward him for his services. A group of some ten Çerkez was supposed to go out to greet him somewhere outside the city limits. On Reşid's orders, they murdered him instead, near the Anbar Çay fountain.[49] It seems that the vali was incensed by the fact that the Kurdish clan had kept all the Armenians' property for itself.

Application of the Extermination Procedures and Resistance at the Local Government Level

A few days after these events, a general meeting organized in the Ulu Cami mosque under the chairmanship of deputy Feyzi was attended by all of Dyarbekir's leading citizens. The aim was apparently to associate the local elite with the decision to liquidate the vilayet's Armenians. At the meeting, the mufti, İbrahim, was asked to state whether the massacre of women and children was in conformity with the precepts of the Koran. The clergyman recommended sparing both children under 12, in order to Islamicize them, and the most beautiful young women, who could be integrated into harems. Overriding his opinion, the assembly decided to spare only the comely young women.[50]

Although the conditions required to liquidate Dyarbekir's Armenian population had been met, Reşid knew that certain *kaymakams* and *mutesarifs* in his province would be reluctant to put his program into practice. Hilmi Bey, the *mutesarif* of Mardin, was one of the first to refuse to carry out his orders. On 25 May, he was relieved of his post[51] – having been in office since 30 November 1914 – and replaced by Şefik Bey, who was himself dismissed one month later for the same reasons.[52] This time, Reşid took no chances. He had his right-hand man, İbrahim Bedreddin Bey, appointed interim *mutesarif* of the city of Mardin[53] and Captain Gevranlızâde Memduh named police chief of the *sancak* of Mardin.[54] If the *mutesarif* of Mardin ultimately got off lightly, despite his audacity, this was not the case with certain *kaymakams.* The *kaymakam* of Derik, Reşid Bey (who held office from 12 October 1914 to 2 May 1915), was not only dismissed for having demanded a written order from the national government, but was murdered on the road to Dyarbekir by Reşid's Çerkez.[55] Hüseyin Nesimî Bey and the Baghdad native Naci Bey, the *kaymakams* of Lice and Beşiri, respectively, were also murdered on the vali's orders.[56] Naci's successor was appointed on 20 June 1915 and remained in office until 1 July 1917; this indicates, at the very least, that the minister of the interior approved of his vali's methods and was willing to replace officials who had too many scruples. Reşid's denials, when he found himself confronting the magistrates of the commission of inquiry set up after the armistice, did not suffice to exonerate him of these crimes: Hüseyin Nesimî's son Abdin explained to the commission how his father had been summoned to Dyarbekir and assassinated on the way by an officer of the Special Organization, headed up in Dyarbekir by the vali himself.[57]

It is probable that Reşid's drastic methods had alarmed the province's *kaymakams* and *mutesarifs*, a considerable number of whom had demanded to see an order from the central government before carrying out the vali's instructions. In other words, Reşid's orders were so manifestly fraught with consequences that these officials sought to protect themselves against the possibility of being charged with crimes later on. This would seem to be the sole possible explanation for the exceptionally high proportion of *kaymakams* who were dismissed or executed in this province: in addition to the three sub-prefects who were executed, Mehmed Hamdi Bey was replaced at the head of the *kaza* of Çermik by Ferik Bey on 1 July 1915; Mehmed Ali Bey, the *kaymakam* of Savur, remained in office only from 2 May to 1 October 1915; İbrahim Hakkı Bey, who held office in Silvan, was dismissed on 31 August 1915.[58]

Massacres and Deportations in the Sancak of Dyarbekir

In the first two weeks of June, Armenian men in the *sancak* of Dyarbekir were systematically rounded up and taken daily in groups between 100 and 150 to the Mardin gate or the road to Gözle (today's Gözalan), where their throats were slit. A group of 1,000 men assigned to do maintenance work or administer military requisitions was also liquidated in similar conditions.[59]

Once the systematic elimination of the men had been completed, Dr. Reşid worked out a method of liquidating the remaining population that proved much more sophisticated and efficient than those utilized by some of his counterparts in other provinces. Armenian witnesses noted that, every morning in the latter half of June, the colonel of the "militia," Yasinzâde Şevki, accompanied by two other men, surrounded around 100 Christian homes in Dyarbekir and subjected them to methodical "house searches." Guards prevented the occupants from leaving their homes until nightfall; at a predetermined hour, the vehicles used for military requisitions arrived at the designated houses and the 100 families living in them were loaded up and led from Dyarbekir in remarkably orderly fashion.[60] This system had the advantage of forestalling disturbances in the city and leaving members of the other Christian confessions with the hope that they themselves would be spared. It was a method that made it practically impossible for anyone to escape from the trap, while allowing the authorities to call on a minimum of personnel to deal with the deportees.

The first group, deported by way of the road to Mardin, comprised the women and children of the leading families of Dyarbekir, the Kazazians, the Trpanjians, the Yegenians, and the Handanians; they were promised that they would be reunited with the male heads of their households. Members of the richest families were separated from the rest of the convoy and detained in a village, Alipunar, south of the city. They were not allowed to leave until they had revealed where they had hidden their valuables. They were then taken to a place nearby, where their throats were cut. The other members of this caravan, 510 women and children, were killed and thrown into the underground cisterns at Dara – vestiges of the Byzantine period located on the road to Cezire.[61]

The next convoys were sent in one of two directions – southwest, toward Karabahçe, Severek, and Urfa, or due south, toward Mardin, Dara, Ras ul-Ayn, Nisibin, and Der Zor. It seems that Kozandere, a place located one hour's distance south of Dyarbekir near the village of Çarakılı, was the principal slaughterhouse on the second of these two trajectories. Kurds from the region and squadrons of çetes of the Special Organization were permanently stationed near this killing field, which went into operation with the second convoy of deportees from Dyarbekir.[62] The massacre of these Armenians was bound up with a propaganda campaign orchestrated by Reşid, but no doubt ordered by Istanbul. Kozandere served as the stage for a macabre spectacle: the corpses of Armenians tortured and killed there were dressed in Muslim costume, capped with turbans, and photographed.[63] The pictures were then reproduced and widely distributed, first in Dyarbekir, later in Istanbul, and even Germany. They were supposed to show victims of atrocities committed by the Armenian "insurgents,"[64] "in order to incite the population against the Armeniens."[65] Rafaël de Nogales, who spent a few days in the barracks in Dyarbekir in late June, notes that Reşid, whom he compares to a "hyena," "killed without ever risking his own life," and that a commander in the gendarmerie, Mehmed Asim Bey, offered him two photographs of a scene that he had "composed almost entirely of fowling-pieces easily disguised" with no other aim than to "impress the public" and convince it that the Russians had, well before the war began, furnished to "Armenians, Chaldeans, and Nestorians of the provinces of Van and Bitlis, Dyarbekir, and Urfa, considerable quantities of arms and ammunition."[66] This documented example, which is probably not an isolated case, gives us an idea of the propaganda methods that accompanied the Young Turks' crimes.

Another killing field was located to the east, in the Bigutlan gorge, between the villages of Şeytan Deresi and Kaynağ. This spot, controlled by members of the Kurdish Tırkan tribe, is supposed to have seen the massacre of 80,000 deportees.[67] We do not, however, know whether the victims were Armenians from other vilayets or Christians from kazas north of Dyarbekir. The second hypothesis seems more likely.

The majority of deportees were massacred well before they reached the places to which they were officially being deported. Some of the many available documents on the deserts of Syria and Mesopotamia, where hundreds of thousands of deportees, above all from western Asia Minor, were sent, show that eight women from Dyarbekir were registered in Rakka in fall 1915,[68] that a 12-year-old child from the province was registered in Aleppo,[69] and that a few women and young girls reached Der Zor in late August 1915.[70] According to a local source, 12,000 deportees from the vilayet of Dyarbekir reached Der Zor by May 1916.[71] Those who reached Ras ul-Ayn were dispatched by the Çerkez of this small town, who plaited a rope 25 yards long with the hair of young women whom they had killed. They sent it as a present to their commander from the Caucasus, the parliamentary deputy Pirincizâde Feyzi.[72]

A few hundred Syriacs, both Orthodox and Catholic, were also deported from Dyarbekir, together with all the clergymen of these two communities. According to Father Jacques Rhétoré, more than 300 Armenian families in the city converted to Islam, together with a few Catholic Syriac households. The mufti İbrahim seems to have earned a veritable fortune by delivering attestations of conversion in exchange for substantial sums. These newly Islamicized Christians were nevertheless deported a few weeks later along with their compatriots, whose fate they shared.[73] Some craftsmen who agreed to convert were, however, allowed to stay on in Dyarbekir and a few villages in the vicinity.[74]

Around 400 children between the ages of one and three were rounded up and initially placed in various institutions, notably the former Protestant school. It seems, however, that such measures, which were supposed to make it possible to educate these children in conformity with the Ittihad's canons, remained in effect for only a short time. In the fall, these children were deported in two convoys. Those in the first were thrown off the old bridge spanning the Tigris near the exit from Dyarbekir. Those in the second were sent to Karabaş, one hour from the city, where they were sliced down the middle and fed to dogs in the vicinity.[75]

When Nogales arrived in Dyarbekir around 25 June, the bazaar was deserted and the silk-weaving and rug-weaving shops were closed. The economic life of the provincial capital had been paralyzed for lack of workers.[76] The plundering of Armenian property had already commenced. It was organized by a special committee created under the vali's lead. On it were Nebizâde Haci Said; Mosuli Mehmed; Harputli Hüseyin, the former police chief; Cırcisafiazâde Kör Yusuf, the CUP delegate in Dyarbekir; Ferid Bey, the defterdar of the vilayet; Muftizâde Şerif; Haci Hüseyin; Numan Bey, the chief prosecutor at the appeals court; and Necimi, the principal of a model school. The commander of the troops of the Teşkilât-ı Mahsusa, Yasinzâde Şevki, and the commander of the gendarmerie, Colonel Çerkez Ruşdi, personally took a hand in the pillaging of Armenian homes, often accompanied by Pirincizâde Sedki. Gold, silver, and precious objects fell into their hands. Moveable assets were stored in the church of Saint Giragos and the adjoining residences, then put up at auction "at derisory prices." Real estate went to "Turks" before all others, while the local Young Turks shared out the most richly appointed homes among themselves: the Kazazians' was taken over by Çerkez Ruşdi, the Minasians' by Bedreddin, and the Trpanjians' by Veli Necet Bey.[77] While it can hardly be doubted that there were many cases of personal gain, it appears that Reşid organized the transfer of 20 vehicles loaded with the precious objects to Istanbul, had them sold at auction, and turned the proceeds over to the Ittihadist network.[78] Indeed, indications are that the accusations of personal enrichment leveled at him in 1916 were baseless. According to information presented by Hans-Lukas Kieser, he would even seem to have been one of the rare Young Turks to have fought widespread corruption and shown himself to be a faithful servant of the Turkish state under construction.[79]

A report that Reşid sent the interior minister on 15 September 1915 speaks of the "deportation of 120,000 Armenians" from his vilayet.[80] This exceeds Dyarbekir's Armenian population. Since Reşid conducted affairs with rigor, it seems improbable that he would have made so loose an approximation, unless the vali had in mind not only Armenians but also all the other Christians affected by these "measures." In this province, the authorities apparently made no distinction between Catholic and Orthodox Syriacs on the one hand and Armenians on the other,[81] even if indications are that only some of the Syriacs were deported and massacred.

Reşid's genocidal activity was a matter of public record. A congratulatory telegram was sent to him on 19 October 1915 by a Young Turk magistrate from Mardin on the occasion of Kurban Bayramı. In a way, this telegram marks the end of the liquidation campaign. Halil Edip, somewhat too optimistically, but in a style revelatory of the spirit animating the Young Turk elites and motivating their acts, credits Reşid with the liberation of the "six vilayets," an accomplishment "opening the way to Turkestan and the Caucasus."[82]

Even as it perpetrated these atrocities, the Turkish administration displayed a certain respect for legal and administrative formalities, in accordance with the usual Young Turk practices. In July 1915, Ambassador Wangenheim seemed to take seriously information he received about an investigation conducted by the court-martial in Dyarbekir "of several leaders of the Dashnak party accused of high treason," and also about the "suicide" of the city's Armenian bishop.[83] In contrast, after the German press had published the official denials, the vice-consul in Mosul, Walter Holstein, expressed his surprise "over the naiveté of the Porte, which (festivity of the sacrifice) believes that it can efface the reality of the crimes committed with crude lies."[84]

Massacres and Deportations in the Kazas of the Sancak of Dyarbekir

When Captain de Nogales left Dyarbekir for Urfa on 27 June, he saw charred and still-deserted Armenian houses in the villages through which he passed.[85] In June, the whole Armenian and Syriac population of the *kazas* of the *sancak* of Dyarbekir was subjected to treatment similar to that inflicted on the Christian population in the regional capital. This holds, to begin with, for the 24 localities of the *kaza* inhabited by a few thousand Armenians, and also for the Syriac villages.

The *Kaza* of Viranşehir

The Armenian presence in the *kaza* of Viranşehir was limited to the administrative seat of the same name; 1,339 Armenians,[86] and at least as many Syriacs belonging to different denominations, lived here. Living in isolation in an essentially Kurdish environment, the Christians of Tella (the Syriac name for the little town) were first and foremost craftsmen and merchants who were rarely natives of the town. The first events of note occurred on 1 and 2 May: the Armenian and Syriac Catholic churches were subjected to police searches. We do not know what motivated these operations, but it would seem that they were carried out against the will of the *kaymakam*, İbrahim Halil, who had been in office since 29 February 1913. On 2 May 1915, he was replaced by Cemal Bey, very certainly on the instigation of Dr. Reşid. From then on, as elsewhere, one event followed hard on the heels of the last. On 13 May, the Armenian and Catholic Syriac notables were arrested and accused of belonging to a revolutionary committee. On 18 May, a second group of men was apprehended and imprisoned. On 28 May, the first group of notables was executed. On 7 June, "Circassians" – a term that probably designated Reşid's Çerkez – proceeded to arrest all males between 12 and 70, a total of 470 people. On 11 June, at dawn, these 470 men were taken under guard to the nearby village of Hafdemari and put to death. The same day, part of the remaining Armenian population was rounded up, taken to the caves in the outlying area and massacred there. On 14 June, the same fate befell a second convoy made up of women. On 16 June, the third and last convoy set out for Ras ul-Ayn, which a few survivors actually reached.[87] These operations were carried through to their term by the presiding judge of the court-martial in Dyarbekir, Tevfik Bey, who had been delegated by Reşid; he continued his work at Derik thereafter. The property of the Catholic and Orthodox Syriacs in the *kaza* was systematically looted, but the Syriacs were not affected by the June 1915 massacres. On the testimony of Father Armalto, at least some of them were expelled and sent to Mardin, where "men, women and children" arrived on 25 August.[88] Thus, the treatment reserved for the Syriacs differed somewhat from that inflicted on the Armenians: two months after the Armenians, they were deported as families and assembled in administrative centers such as Mardin. Though stripped of their belongings, they were not methodically liquidated but abandoned to their fate without means of support. Let us note in passing that this "soft" method would be utilized by the Kemalists from 1923 on in order to cleanse the region of Dyarbekir of its last Christians and induce them to leave for Syria, then under French mandate.

The *Kaza* of Severek

Severek, the medieval Sevaverag ("Black Ruins"), was the principal town in the *kaza*. The town had an Armenian population of 5,450 on the eve of the First World War; this represented more than half of the total population. Seven other localities in this basically rural district known for its red wine were home to 3,825 Armenians: Karabahçe, Çatak, Mezre, Simag, Harbi, Gori, and Oşin.[89]

We have very little documentation on the events that occurred in the *kaza* of Severek. We do know, however, that the *kaymakam*, İhsan Bey, in office from 1 May 1914 to 3 November 1916, played a crucial role in the destruction of the Armenian population, with the help of the troops of the Special Organization commanded by Yuzbaşi Şevket, a captain who was seconded by a number of leaders of squadrons of *çetes*: Ahmet Çavuş, Bıçakci Mehmed Çavuş, Bıçakci Kör Ömer Ağa, and Haci Tellal Hakimoğlu, nicknamed Haci Onbaşi. Several tribal chieftains, such as Ramazan Ağa, Kadir Ağa, and Kalpoğlu, as well as notables from the city, such as the mufti of Severek, Acemoğlu Haci Vesil, Terzi Osman, Osmanoğlu Abo, Kasanoğlu Zılo, and İbrahim Haliloğlu Mahmut, were directly implicated in the massacres and pillaging of Armenian property.[90]

According to the meager sources available to us,[91] the house searches and elimination of the men took place in May 1915, followed by the deportation of the women and children. A few survivors reached Urfa or Aleppo. The only credible eyewitness account, by Faiz el-Güseyin, an Arab Bedouin who had been a parliamentary deputy and a *kaymakam*,[92] describes Severek and the vicinity shortly after the elimination of its Armenian population (probably in July).[93] El-Güseyin observes that initially a multitude of corpses littered the road between Urfa and Severek, above all those of women and children. The Armenian bodies that he saw the next day on the road to Dyarbekir were probably not those of natives of Severek, but of people deported from regions to the north.

The *Kaza* of Derik

The *kaza* of Derik, which lay some 58 miles south of Dyarbekir, had in 1914 an Armenian population of 1,782, 1,250 of whom lived in the administrative seat of the *kaza*. The others lived half an hour's distance from the town in Bayraklı, known as Bairuk in Armenian.[94] As we have seen,[95] the *kaymakam* Reşid Bey (in office from 12 October 1914 to 2 May 1915) was dismissed from his post because he had refused to proceed with the deportation of the Armenians under his administration without a written order from the national authorities. He was later executed by Dr. Reşid's Çerkez on the road to Dyarbekir. His assassination was ascribed to the Armenians of Derik, providing the vali with an opportunity to send Tevfik Bey, the present of the court-martial in Dyarbekir, to the town.[96] Tevfik, who had just finished dealing with the Armenians of Viranşehir,[97] applied the usual procedures. From 20 to 30 June, he first eliminated the men in small groups, then turned to the women and children, who were deported and massacred a short distance from the town. The public hanging of clergymen of various denominations on 27 June crowned, as it were, the judge's activity.[98]

It is not without interest that the new *kaymakam*, Hamdi Bey, was appointed to his post on 30 June 1915 – that is, the day operations were terminated in Derik.

The *Kazas* of Silvan and Beşiri/Chernig

The 110 Kurdish-speaking Armenian villages of the rural *kazas* of Beşiri and Silvan, with respective Armenian populations of 5,038 and 13,824, lay on the eastern border of the vilayet of Dyarbekir, just south of Sasun.[99] The location of these villages may explain why they were attacked very early. As we noted when discussing the operations carried out in the *sancak* of Mush, the authorities appealed in May to the Kurdish Belek, Bekran, Şegro, and other tribes to attack not only Sasun but also the civilian populations of the *kazas* of Silvan and Beşiri.[100] While many fell victim to the massacres that the Kurds staged in these villages, several thousand Armenians from the area managed to flee to Sasun, where in August they met the same fate as its own population.[101]

Among Dr. Reşid's many victims was the *kaymakam* of Beşiri, Naci Bey, a native of Baghdad; as we have said, he was assassinated on the vali's orders[102] and was not replaced by Rasım Bey until 20 June 1915, after the district had been cleansed of its Armenian population (Rasım remained in office until 1 July 1917). The *kaymakam* of Silvan, Hakkı Bey, appointed on 4 October 1914, was not transferred elsewhere until 31 August 1915. He participated in the crimes committed here.

The *Kaza* of Lice

In 1914, nearly half of the 5,980 Armenians in the *kaza* of Lice lived in the administrative seat of the *kaza*, which bore the same name, along with 1,980 Orthodox Syriacs. The other half lived scattered in 32 small mountain villages or in deep gorges.[103]

The orders concerning the Armenians were apparently contested in this area as well by Hüseyin Nesimî Bey, the *kaymakam* of Lice, who was executed on instructions from the vali of Dyarbekir.[104] Subsequent events seem to have followed the usual pattern. According to a secret report by the head of the Administration of the Public Debt in Lice and a Catholic Syriac, Nâman Adamo, house searches were first conducted with a view to finding arms. They were followed by the arrests of the notables, who were assassinated in caverns located further south in Daştapise. Next came the elimination of all males over ten and, finally, the deportation of the women and children. The men still present in the Taurus mountain villages seem to have been massacred where they were found. We do not know what became of the women and children.[105]

Massacres and Deportations in the Sancak *of* Arğana

The *sancak* of Arğana Maden had an Armenian population of 38,430, living in some 50 towns and villages. Lying on the southern slopes of the Taurus mountains and traversed by the eastern branch of the Euphrates (Murad Su) in the north and containing the source of the Tigris in the east, the region was well-suited to agriculture and animal husbandry. Copper mines were also in operation there. The prefecture was located in Arğana Maden, a little town lying on the right bank of the upper Tigris that had an Armenian population of 3,300.

Argana/Arğin

The first wartime *mutesarif*, an Armenian named Dikran Bey, held office very briefly, from 20 August to 28 October 1914. On 30 December 1914, he was replaced by Nazmi Bey, who supervised the liquidation of the Armenian population in the region until he left it on 24 August 1915. The 10,559 Armenians of the administrative seat and ten other localities of the *kaza*[106] were eliminated in July 1915, at the same time as the inhabitants of Chnkush, in the place known as Yudan Dere; this was a chasm lying on the border between this *kaza* and the *kaza* of Çermik, where an underground river fed the sources of the Tigris.[107] However, no survivor seems to have left an account of these crimes, apart from one witness to the events that took place in Göljük, a little town lying on the shore of the mountain lake that is the source of the Tigris.[108] Göljük/Dzovk ("sea" in Armenian), famous since antiquity for the horses bred near the lake, lies halfway between Harput and Dyarbekir; it formed the sole practicable passage between the two regions and marked the administrative border between them. After the general mobilization order, things remained calm in the little town of Göljük, situated on the southern lakeshore. Only in April did the authorities collect all the Armenians' arms and proceed to arrest the notables. On the evening of Friday 4 June, Göljük was surrounded by some 50 horsemen and 70 "soldiers of the militia," come from Harput and commanded by the *müdir*, Begzâde Ali. They proceeded to arrest all males over 16, whom they imprisoned in a stable and systematically tortured. The official objective was to bring them to reveal where their arms caches were located.[109] Toros Toroyan, one of the principal notables in Göljük, committed suicide when his captors threatened to transfer him to Arğana Maden.[110] Krikor Mardikian, M. Buludian, Shahbaz Vartabedian,[111] and all the men who had been taken into custody were put on the road to an unknown destination, guarded by "militiamen" and a police officer.[112] The parish priest, Father Boghos Zhamgochian, was taken to Harput and subsequently slain at Deveboynu, near the village of Kharasagh.[113]

On Wednesday 7 July, the officials responsible for carrying out the deportations from Göljük arrived there, accompanied by Turkish and Kurdish *çetes*. They proceeded to count the deportees house by house, confiscated all their property and food reserves, and then announced that they were to be deported to Aleppo. The leaders of this operation were Halil Ağa and his two sons, Mahmed and Abdüllah, who were accompanied by their men. On Friday, 9 July, the first convoy, made up of 70 families, began moving eastward, hugging the lakeshore; the second, comprising the remaining 30 households, set out the following morning.[114] An order is then supposed to have come down from the capital of the vilayet authorizing the local population to "adopt" male children under 12 and females irrespective of their age on the condition that the Christians agreed to convert on the spot and had no relatives abroad, "especially in America." The "adoption" ritual then took place, legalized by an official who proceeded to register the new believers.[115] Remaining behind in the town, the six "chosen ones" saw two young girls and an 11 year-old boy, Aram Mardikian, who had left the previous evening with the first convoy, suddenly emerge from the lake. The children related how their companions had been massacred with axes a few hours from Göljük, in Gapan.[116]

The island on which the monastery of Saint Nshan was located, close to the southern lakeshore, eventually became a refuge for dozens of Armenians native to villages of the plain of Harput or areas further south.[117] Until Tuesday, 2 November 1915, they were not seriously molested. On that day, however, a brigade of army troops arrived. An emissary promised them that the sultan had proclaimed an armistice with all the "Syrian Armenians" (*Suriyani Ermeni*). Only a few young men managed to escape the ensuing attack and survive in the mountains.[118] The very detailed account we are following here contains an interesting piece of information: the Armenians of the southern lakeshore, which, as we shall see in the next chapter, served as a gigantic slaughterhouse for the Armenians from the plain of Harput, were "dealt with" by the authorities of the vilayet of Mamuret ul-Aziz, although they were officially under the jurisdiction of Dr. Reşid. The only exceptions were a few notables who had been sent in the direction of Arğana Maden or Dyarbekir.

Çermik

The *kaza* of Çermik, located just southwest of the district of Argana, was sparsely inhabited. Armenians lived in only three localities in Çermik in 1914: in the administrative seat, Chermug ("Hot Springs"), with an Armenian population of around two thousand and, above all, in Chnkush (today Çüngüş), where more than ten thousand Armenians were settled on an impressive rocky plateau that dominated the Euphrates valley.[119] In this remote region, the authorities' strategy seemed to consist in liquidating the Armenians where they were found: there was no trace of deportees from this *kaza* in the concentration camps of Syria and Mesopotamia.

Chnkush is the best-documented case, thanks to five survivors whose accounts were recorded by Karnig Kévorkian.[120] Conscription emptied the town of men between 18 and 45, including those who had paid the *bedel* to avoid the draft. The requisitions were the financial ruin of the tanners and fur traders (two of the town's specialties) and left the muleteers without their animals, but no exceptional event came along to disturb the calm reigning in Chnkush until June 1915. The anti-Armenian exactions began there as soon as the *müdir*, Karalambos, a Greek from Maden who had been in office since September 1909, was dismissed from his post by Reşid for refusing to organize police searches of the Armenians' homes. Twelve cavalrymen were waiting for him one morning in front of his home, and he was forced to follow them. He was replaced by the more flexible Ferik Bey on 1 July (Ferik remained in office until 25 June 1917). Systematic searches of the Armenians' homes began soon thereafter. The Armenian prelate Yeghia Kazanjian, the Protestant minister Bedros Khachadurian, and Father Pascal Nakashian, a Catholic priest, were all arrested. The Protestant was the first to die, under torture in the "prison" of Chnkush; the Apostolic clergyman was massacred along with his flock, and the Catholic priest was deported to Dyarbekir, where he was put to death somewhat later.[121] The Armenian notables were also arrested. Among them were Abraham Kaloyan, Hagop Gulian, and Hovsep Der Garabedian, who were sent to the administrative seat of the *sancak*, Arğana Maden.[122] Forty others were dispatched to Dyarbekir to stand trial before the court-martial. They were accused of being "revolutionaries."[123]

In July, the remaining men were methodically arrested. Then came the women and children's turn. All were deported in several convoys to the chasm of Yudan Dere (which the Armenians called "Dudan"), two hours northeast of the town. They were joined on the way by deportees from neighboring areas, notably Arğana Maden. The rare survivors report that the convoys were escorted by Circassian gendarmes, which should doubtless be taken to mean Çerkez *çetes* of the Teşkilât-ı Mahsusa wearing gendarmes' uniforms. These *çetes* were probably sent from Dyarbekir. It was these gendarmes who were also stationed on the promontory that towers over the chasm of Yudan Dere. The males were dealt with first, in accordance with a classic procedure: tied together in small groups of fewer than ten, they were handed over to butchers who bayoneted them or killed them with axes and then threw the bodies into the chasm. The method used on the women was quite similar, except that they were first systematically stripped and searched and then had their throats cut, after which their corpses were also thrown into the chasm. Some of them preferred to leap into the abyss themselves, dragging their children with them; thus they cheated their murderers of part of their booty.[124]

According to Karnig Kévorkian, 13 people survived – a few men who had taken refuge in the mountains and a handful of young women who had been abducted in Yudan Dere.[125]

Palu

Boasting 37 Armenian villages and towns with a total population of 15,753 in 1914,[126] the *kaza* of Palu, located at the northern extremity of the vilayet of Dyarbekir and traversed by the eastern branch of the Euphrates (Arsanias), was not a strategic stake of any special importance. The administrative seat, Palu, boasted 10,000 inhabitants, 5,250 of whom were Armenian. As elsewhere, the general mobilization drained the region of its vital forces: some of the recruits were sent to the Caucasian front and others to the front in Palestine, with the exception of the handful of men who were able to pay the *bedel*.[127] Until spring 1915, the only problem we know of was the violence of the military requisitions and, toward the end of February, the enrollment of new Armenian draftees in the *amele taburis*.[128] In the same period, the only two Armenian gendarmes in Palu were dismissed, for no apparent reason. This was, however, unspectacular in a country that was little accustomed to seeing non-Muslims bear arms. The first alarm came in April 1915, when the town's leading personality, the pharmacist Karekin Kiurejian, was arrested and sent to Dyarbekir. He was soon followed by two Hnchak activists, the brothers Hampartsum and Mgrdich Kozigian.[129] The order to search people's homes for arms was issued by the *kaymakam*, Kadri Bey, very shortly thereafter.[130] Two Kurdish chieftains, Haşim and Teffür Beg, were charged with accomplishing this task in the 36 Armenian villages in the *kaza*.[131] The biggest Armenian village, Havav, which had 1,648 inhabitants, was the first to be searched. It was surrounded by 150 armed men led by the mayor of Palu; 70 notables were arrested – among them Thomas Jelalian, Vahan Der Asdurian, Manug Navoyian, and Sisag Mkhitar Baghdzengian – and jailed in Palu. They were subsequently taken to Palu Bridge in a convoy of 200 men and slain in the nearby gorge of Kornak Dere, after which *çetes* commanded by Teyfeş Beg threw their bodies into the river.[132] The other Armenian villages of the *kaza* were cut off from each other and then, in the first half of June, were attacked by *çetes* under the command of İbrahim, Tuşdi, and Teyfeş Beg. All the men were stripped and shot on the banks of the Euphrates; their corpses were thrown into the river. In the village of Til, about which we have a detailed account, only one miller was spared, so that he could continue to provide the town with flour.[133]

On 1 June, 800 men of the *amele taburi* stationed in Khoshmat, north of Palu, all of them from Eğin or Arapkir, as well as 400 worker-soldiers based in Nirkhi, where they had been working for seven months, were tied together and killed with knives by the "butchers of men."[134]

Palu's prison rapidly filled with schoolteachers and merchants who had been arrested in the administrative seat of the *kaza*. The pivotal point the genocidal system set up in the *kaza*, however, was the famous medieval bridge with eight arches that spanned the eastern Euphrates near the exit from the town. Squadrons of *çetes* operated there in three killing fields under the immediate command of the *kaymakam* Kadri Bey, who sometimes took a hand in beheading his victims. He encouraged his men with a formula: "The body for the nation and the head for the state."[135] All the men of Palu were slain here.[136] In the first half of June 1915, Palu Bridge was also a point of passage or massacre for some 10,000 deportees from the vilyet of Erzerum, especially the *kaza* of Kiği.[137] The leaders of the butchers who performed their work on the bridge were Zeynalzâde Mustafa and his sons Hasan and Husni, Mahmud Çavus from Norpert, Şeyhzâde Hafız, Süleyman Bey, Saïd Bey, Kâzım Ali Mustafa Ağa, and Musrumli Karaman.[138] They worked under the authority of Kadri Bey, who was also a leader of Palu's Young Turk club.[139]

The women and children from the rural zones were first transferred to Palu and confined in the courtyard of the Church of St. Gregory the Illuminator for two weeks. The male population came to pick out young women, who were raped and then returned after a day or two. The turn of families from Palu came next: their houses were systematically plundered, with the exception of a few that had been earmarked for Turkish notables. Very young children were then separated from their mothers, packed into barrels, and thrown into the Euphrates. A few young men and a few families succeeded in fleeing to the mountains, where they survived by living in caves before reaching Dersim at the beginning of winter 1915.[140] In early July, several hundred women, old men, and children from the area were finally sent away in a convoy that passed by way of Maden, Severek, Urfa, and Bilecik.[141] Bishop Yeznig Kalpakjian and Father Mushegh Gadarigian were not arrested until late June. They were killed near Palu, in the vicinity of Sınam, by a certain Reşid.[142]

Massacres and Deportations in the Sancak of Mardin

Mardin, lying in the heart of Syriac territory, had a population of 12,609 Orthodox Syriacs and 7,692 Armenians, the vast majority of them Catholic. All were Arabic-speaking.[143]

Conscription proved quite difficult in this region that was far from the front. The search for the recalcitrant took violent forms that, all in all, took classic forms. The first genuinely alarming sign for the Christian population did not appear until late February 1915, when all non-Muslim civilian officials were dismissed from their posts. On the other hand, doubtless in order to reassure the Christians and create the impression that everything was in order, the sultan bestowed a high Ottoman decoration on Ignace Maloyan, the Armenian Catholic bishop. It was awarded to him at a 20 April ceremony.[144] On 22 April 1915, the first rumors began to circulate about the organization of secret meetings among the Muslims both in Dyarbekir and the villages. The police search of the Armenian bishopric that was conducted on 30 April only confirmed Maloyan's fears of anti-Christian violence. His testament, written on 1 May, shows that this Catholic was not fooled by the honor that the authorities had shown him; he was expecting the worst from them.[145]

However, as we have already seen, Dr. Reşid had to rid himself of the *mutesarif* of Mardin, Hilmi Bey (fired on 25 May), and also his successor, Şefik Bey (dismissed one month later), and then appoint one of his henchmen, İbrahim Bedreddin Bey, as interim *mutesarif* before he could put his extermination plan into practice in the *sancak* of Mardin. With the promotion of two men from Dyarbekir – the appointment of the police captain Gevranlızâde Memduh as Mardin's police chief, responsible for expediting the convoys, and that of Çerkez Şakir, Reşid's aide-de-camp, as commander of the town's gendarmerie – the vali put the finishing touches on his apparatus in Mardin.[146]

These three individuals – Bedreddin, Memduh, and Şakir – formed the core of the local "committee of execution," which also included Halil Edip Bey, a magistrate in Mardin and member of the local Young Turk Club. This committee was assigned the task of creating squadrons of *çetes*.[147] It was, however, the parliamentary deputy Feyzi who finally won over the Muslim notables of Mardin, at a meeting he convened in the town on 15 May at Abdo Hac Karmo Kasımoğlu's residence.[148]

The 500 men whom Halil Edip Bey recruited to the militia "Al Hamsin" were in fact *çetes* of the Teşkilât-ı Mahsusa, whose principal officers were Abdurrahman Kasab; Muhamed Hubaş; Çelebi Şahpiri Abdülrezah; Abdüllah Heder; Şeyh Kasur el Insari; Şeyh Tahir el Insari, director of Mardin's prison; and Şeyh Nuri el Insari.[149] The "committee of execution" could also count on the support of several important men in the area: Abdülkadir Bey, the commander of the gendarmerie, and his aides Faik Bey et Harun Bey; Hıdır Çelebi, the mayor of Mardin; Necip Çelebi Bey, a tax collector; Abdülkerim Bey, who was responsible for dispatching the convoys (under the supervision of Memduh Bey); Hüseyin, the mufti of Mardin; and tribal notables and chieftains such as Abdelrahman el Kavas, Abdelrazzak Şatana, Davud Şatana, Musa Şatana, Fares Çelebi, Mehmet Ali, Mehmed Raci, Abdallah Effendi, Hac Asad el Hac Karmo, the chieftain of the Daşiye tribe, Ahmed Ağa, İbn Nuri Bitlisi, and Osman Bey.[150]

Throughout the month of May, the authorities' main activity consisted in conducting police searches of the Christians' homes in a search for arms (which, apparently, were nowhere to be found in this law-abiding Catholic Syriac environment), arresting notables from all groups of the population and torturing them so that they would reveal their supposed arms caches. An extremely unusual circumstance involving weapons that the "militiamen" were trying to hide near the Syriac Catholic church on the night of 26/27 May sheds light on the methods used by the authorities to legitimize the imminent anti-Christian violence. In this case, the falsification was exposed, for *çetes* were surprised in the act of digging the trench that was supposed to contain the weapons. But this failure was soon made up for by the discovery of an arms stockpile on land owned by a Kurd named Mohammed Farah, thanks to a confession extorted from an Armenian, Habib Yune. The police lost no time photographing these arms and sending the prints to the Ministry of the Interior, along with the information that the arms in question had been discovered in the possession of the Armenians of Mardin.[151] All methods were allowed when it came to proving, more particularly, that the Armenian Catholic prelate, Ignace Maloyan, was involved in an ostensible plot against state security: among them was a fraudulent document attesting that "twenty-five rifles and five bombs" had been transported to "Mardin's Armenian Catholic bishopric."[152]

These two pieces of "incriminating" evidence seem to have been judged sufficient to seal the doom of the Armenians and their prelate. On the evening of Thursday 3 June, gendarmes and "militiamen" took control of all access routes to the city, while town criers announced that no one could leave Mardin on pain of death. The first round-up of Armenian notables occurred that very night. It was coordinated by Memduh Bey, who had just arrived. Bishop Maloyan and six of his priests were also taken under guard to the prefecture and imprisoned there.[153]

The next day, 4 June, and on 5 June as well, this first series of arrests was followed by new round-ups involving 62 people, clergymen and laymen alike. Not all were Armenian, although the majority were.[154]

The business of the "Armenians' arms" aside, the authorities conjured up two other incidents that repay close attention because they provide an excellent summary of the psychological amalgam that the Young Turk regime fabricated out of thin air. The Young Turks combined religious prejudice with ignorance, the better to manipulate a population that was, to say the least, unsophisticated. The local members of the Fraternity of St. Francis, whose membership lists, in Arabic, were discovered in the Capuchins' church during a police search, were transformed into militants of a "French Association" – that is, into accomplices of France. An association of the "precious blood" – the reference was obviously to Christ's sacrifice – was said to have no other goal than to "drink Muslim blood."[155] Ignorance of "the other" seemed to be so basic a feature of the society of the day that we cannot rule out the possibility that, apart from a few "enlightened" Young Turks, the local dignitaries were sincerely convinced of the accuracy of the accusations leveled against "the Christians."

The Orthodox Syriacs, 85 of whose leading men had also been arrested, persuaded the authorities, after considerable effort, of their loyalty to the state and their profound aversion to both Catholicism and France. Thus, they managed to avoid the fate meted out to the other Christians of Mardin. According to "Catholic" witnesses, some of these Orthodox Syriacs went so far as to sign a joint declaration together with Muslim notables proclaiming the Armenians' "guilt."[156] While these accusations are improbable, they reveal, above all, that the authorities had a good deal of talent for exploiting the long-standing divisions among the various Christian denominations, while confirming that they resorted to pressure tactics to leave their victims, in the end, no other choice than to distance themselves from the other groups.

The Young Turk authorities' determination to prove by all possible means that they were simply reacting in a legitimate way to the subversive machinations of "domestic enemies" was exposed in caricatural fashion during Bishop Maloyan's "trial." The bishop was confronted with the famous document "proving" that he had had 25 rifles and five bombs transported to his "room." The signatory, a certain Sarkis, could not appear in court because he had very conveniently been murdered by persons unknown.[157] On the basis of this document, police chief Memduh leveled a deadly charge at the prelate: he was the head of a "Fedawi" – that is, a revolutionary association.[158] Was Memduh Bey persuaded of the truth of this charge or was he merely being cynical? In other words, had he been entrusted with his mission because he was myopic but devoted, or because he was considered shrewd enough to make far-fetched accusations with a modicum of credibility? Answering this question would provide us in this case with a better sense of the criteria used to recruit local collaborators with the Young Turk regime in an area that was reputedly marked by tribalism.

The roughly 400 people who had been imprisoned – some of those arrested, for example the Orthodox Syriacs, had been released for various reasons – were finally led from the city under a guard of 100 çetes and gendarmes very early in the morning of 10 June 1915.[159] The departure of Mardin's elite was staged as a spectacle: tied together or in chains, the men were paraded through the town's Muslim and then Christian neighborhoods. It is hard to understand why. The sight of these important men in chains was perhaps meant to show the population that the government had the means it needed to neutralize its "domestic foes," stringing them out in a heavily guarded column, with Bishop Maloyan bringing up the rear. The methods used to execute these men – in Ahraşke, on the road to Dyarbekir, in the case of the first to perish; in Adırşek, near Şeyhan, in the case of the others – did not differ from those used elsewhere. The departure of the convoy provided police chief Memduh, who was in command of the escort, with an opportunity to press large sums from the deportees, especially Naum Jinaji, a member of one of the most powerful families in Mardin, and also to exhibit his rhetorical talents. As if pronouncing a verdict, he said to the deportees: "Yesterday, the empire accorded you a thousand privileges; today, it accords you three bullets."[160]

Mardin's leading citizens were killed in three groups: 100 were massacred in caves in Şeyhan; 100 more had their throats slit and were thrown into the "Roman wells" at Zırzavan, an hour from Şeyhan; the last 200 were liquidated the following morning on 11 June, in a gorge further north. Maloyan was the last to be dispatched, near Karaköprü, by police chief Memduh. It took a year for information about the fate dealt out to the men in this convoy to trickle through. The authorities even took the trouble to have a forensic pathologist sign a certificate declaring that Maloyan had died of a heart attack en route.[161]

After wiping out the elite, the authorities set about liquidating all the other males. On 11 June, 266 men, 180 of them Armenian, were taken into custody. After being tortured, they too set out on the road to Dyarbekir, on 14 June, escorted by Abdülkadir Bey, a commander in the gendarmerie. When they reached the caves of Şeyhan, they were stripped and methodically relieved of their valuables. On 15 June, at dawn, 84 of them were slain by Kurds from the surrounding area. The others were escorted to Dyarbekir: the non-Armenians were "amnestied," while the Armenians were brought back to the prison in Mardin. The account of this episode, described in detail by Syriac survivors, has it that gendarmes from Dyarbekir arrived in a great rush in Şeyhan with orders that made it possible, for the time being, to save the last members of the convoy.[162] Yves Ternon contends, citing a 12 July telegram from the minister of the interior,[163] that the execution of the Christian Syriacs had probably not been ordered by the national government but was rather an initiative of the local authorities, who had a degree of latitude in these matters. The sharp reactions called forth in certain diplomatic circles in Constantinople by the abundant information proving that Catholics had been put to death probably impelled the Young Turk government to suspend the operations carried out against non-Armenians, at least in towns in which there were foreign witnesses.[164]

In any case, the sudden suspension of operations on 15 June indicates that the orders from the national authorities were obeyed. The fact that the eradication program was not resumed until 2 July also tends to show that Istanbul's intervention upset the plans of Mardin's "committee of execution," which was perhaps supposed to have awaited instructions before going into action. On 2 July, things returned to normal: 600 men, among them some of the Armenian survivors of the second convoy, were this time taken under guard to the city walls, where they were summarily executed.[165]

What happened next was, as it were, classic: from 13 July on, Memduh Bey convened the women and extorted large amounts of money from them in exchange for "saving their lives."

The sums he received varied between 350 and 750 Turkish pounds in gold; the money was personally pocketed by Memduh, Bedreddin, and Çerkez Şakir, Mardin's three strongmen.[166] On 15 July, the wives of the notables, including women who belonged to Mardin's two richest Armenian families, the Jinajis and Kaspos, were invited to get ready to join their husbands in Dyarbekir; they were authorized to take money and valuables with them. As had happened in Dyarbekir, government vehicles were sent to pick up women, children, old men, and a few other men who had so far eluded the round-ups at their homes. The resulting convoy, 250 people strong, set out on 17 July, escorted by gendarmes under the command of Çerkez Şakir. But it was halted at the city limits by police chief Memduh. The police chief arranged for the deportees' money and jewels to be handed over to him, since they might excite the greed of "Kurdish or Arab looters." The convoy then continued on its way southwest.[167] It arrived at İmam Abdül, near Tell Armen, in the evening. Here, the presiding judge of the court-martial in Dyarbekir, Tevfik Bey – whose role in the massacres of Viranşehir and Derik we have already seen[168] – was waiting for it. Tevfik began by liquidating the few men in the caravan, including Boghos Kaspo and Dikran Jinaji, and then ordered the massacre of the others. Tevfik's çetes and gendarmes proceeded family by family: after being stripped of their last belongings, the deportees were taken off in vehicles, undressed, were sometimes raped, and then killed with knives or shot. Mrs. Jinaji was subjected to more refined treatment: first her hands were chopped off and then she was beheaded. While the slaughter was in progress, several young women and children were carried off by the Kurdish çetes, who later sold a part of their booty. By midnight, the convoy had been entirely decimated.[169]

The fourth convoy of men, comprising roughly 300 people, including the last survivors of 15 June and prisoners from Tell Armen, left Mardin on 27 July. These men were killed and their bodies were thrown into the underground cisterns at Dara, with their beautiful masonry arches. The last males still alive in Mardin, the conscripts, were massacred later in small groups on the road to Nisibin: 50 were slain behind the citadel on 12 August and another 12 were killed at the foot of the nearby monastery of Mar Mikayel on 24 August. Seventeen Armenian masons, who were busy building the minaret of the Mosque of el-Şahiya, were granted a reprieve: they were not done away with until October 1915.[170]

The rest of Mardin's Armenian population was deported very gradually, from late July to late October 1915. Some of the deportees in the second convoy of families made it to Ras ul-Ayn and then Aleppo. The third caravan, some 600 people strong, set out on 10 August; the fourth, comprising 300 deportees, on 23 August; the fifth, made up of 125 women and children, left on 15 September. Most of the deportees were slaughtered on the road, particularly in Salah and Harrin. A few reached Mosul or Aleppo, while others managed to take the least deadly route, the one leading to Homs, Hama, and Damascus.[171]

Amid this explosion of violence there were a few acts of humanity. Thus, the Chechens of Ras ul-Ayn saved 400 to 500 Armenians, whom they ushered to the mountain area of Sinjar, inhabited by Yezidis. To be sure, these Chechens, who took an active part in the operations organized by Dr. Reşid and would play a crucial role in the fall 1916 eradication of tens of thousands of deportees in the Ras ul-Ayn and Der Zor concentration camps, received a "bonus" of 10 to 20 Turkish pounds per person.[172] However, in other cases, money promised and given did not suffice to save people's lives. In Mardin, in any case, the other Christian denominations escaped the Armenians' fate, with individual exceptions.

Let it be observed finally that the çetes and Kurdish tribes posted in Mardin participated actively in the liquidation of the convoys of deportees that came from the north. Father Hyacinthe Simon drew up an instructive chronology: from 1 July to 5 July, two caravans of women containing from 2,000 to 3,000 people arrived in Mardin after a 35-day trek. They were left for several hours in the courtyard of the Armenian Catholic church before being sent to their deaths on the road leading south.[173] On 20 June, 12,000 women and children were massacred between Dyarbekir and Mardin. On 7, 8, and 9 July, convoys of women from Dyarbekir and Harput were slaughtered a short distance beyond Mardin, under the direct supervision of Memduh Bey.[174] On 10 September, 8,000 women and children from Harput and Erzerum were slain between Dyarbekir and Mardin. Two thousand others from the same convoy were exterminated on 14 September on the outskirts of Nisibin.[175]

The plunder of the Armenians' property in Mardin gave rise to grotesquely comic scenes and left the city looking like a construction site. Many people were hard at work digging up the grounds around or inside the Armenians' houses in a quest for hidden treasure. The myth of the Armenians' gold, which is still alive and well today, excited people's lust for gain. Once the period in which it was possible to make easy money had come to an end with the first phase of the massacres, the most enterprising turned to trafficking women. On 15 August 1915, for the first time in Mardin, a public sale of young Armenian women was organized. Buyers had to pay from one to three Turkish pounds per head, depending on the beauty and age of the female on offer.[176]

The only Armenian village in the *kaza* of Mardin, Tell Armen, was inhabited by both Muslims and more than 1,200 Catholics, most of them Armenian. It was not until 11 June that a handful of notables and the two Armenian parish priests, Father Anton and Father Minas, were arrested. They were put to death the same day at Şeyhan, along with the notables of Mardin. The arrests of men between 10 and 70 began on Friday, 18 June and continued over the next few days, on orders from Hıdıroğlu Derviş, the *müdir* of Tell Armen. After being confined in one of the two Armenian churches, these men were taken under guard to the Güliye (Ksor) road, where they were killed by Kurds from the area. Some of the women and children were slain in the other Armenian church or in the fields.[177] On 9 July 1915, the German ambassador informed Chancellor Bethmann Hollweg about the Tell Armen massacres.[178] He was unaware, however, that the town had been thoroughly looted and then burned down on the orders of an eminent member of Mardin's "committee of execution," Halil Edip Bey, who took the trouble to supervise these operations in person.[179]

In the whole *kaza* of Mardin, as we have seen, only the non-Armenian Christians of the administrative seat of the *kaza* were, to a certain extent, spared. Elsewhere, in the countryside, the inhabitants of the Syriac villages were condemned to a fate similar to the Armenians'. The procedures used were also similar. Yves Ternon has made an inventory of the massacres carried out, for example, in Güliye (Ksor) on 3 July, of more than 1,000 Orthodox Syriacs and Catholics; in Mansuriyeh, on 16 June and somewhat later as well, of more than 600 Orthodox and Catholic Syriacs; and in Kalat Mara, Maserte, Bafua, and finally Benebil, which put up resistance to the *çetes'* attack.[180]

Midyat and the Syriac "Revolt" in Tur Abdin

Midyat, the administrative seat of the *kaza* of the same name, was a town with a population of approximately 7,000. Most of the inhabitants were Orthodox Syriacs; there were also 1,452 Armenian Catholics and a few Protestants.[181] The *kaymakam*, Şukri Bey, who was appointed to his post on 28 February 1915 and remained in office until 10 July 1917, was well disposed toward them until early June. On 21 June, he ordered searches of the Christian homes and had around 100 men arrested, including Dr. Naaman Karagulian (a Protestant).[182] These men were slain outside the city, in the place known as the "Wells of Sayta." When news of their death reached the town, Midyat mounted a resistance that was sustained until late in the fall; the battalions of Kurdish irregulars, some of whom had come from a considerable distance away, were unable to take the town.[183] The inhabitants of other localities in the *kaza*, such as the 2,000 Orthodox Syriacs and Catholic Syriacs of Kırbüran, 600 of whom managed to flee, as well as the Catholic Syriacs of Kırzhaus, Batı,

Killet, and Hisn Kayfa, were massacred or fled to the mountainous district of Tur Abdin in June 1915.[184]

If we are to grasp the reasons for the vigorous resistance mounted by the Orthodox Syriacs of Tur Abdin from July 1915 on, we have to put the events that took place in both Aynwarda, an Orthodox Syriac village located in the eastern part of Midyat, and also Azakh, in the context of the massacres perpetrated by the authorities in the *sancak* of Mardin. Officially presented as the "revolt of Midyat," this resistance shows that the Kurdish irregulars and the regular army had failed to achieve their objectives – that is, the eradication of these rural populations, who had rapidly become quite certain that they were slated for elimination in their turn. In October, contingents of the Third, Fourth, and Sixth Armies were sent to Midyat to have done with these "rebels." Even the Turkish-German Expeditionary Corps, under the joint command of Ömer Naci, a member of the Ittihadist Central Committee and an officer in the Teşkilât-ı Mahsusa, and Max von Scheubner-Richter, the German vice-consul in Erzerum, was diverted from its original objective, Tabriz, in order to lend support to the attack on the Orthodox Syriac enclave, whose members were supposed to have "cruelly massacred the Muslim population of the region."[185]

This accusation, which was also trotted out in the north to legitimize state violence, has of course not been corroborated by any other source. Moreover, Naci, from whom the charge emanated, does not name the villages from which these Muslim victims were supposed to have come. In a subsequent report to the German Chancellor, Scheubner-Richter, obviously unaware that Naci had transmitted accusations as crude as this to Istanbul, observed that the "ostensible 'rebels' who had been presented to him as 'Armenians' had retrenched because they feared a massacre."[186] Naci, whom the German officer described as one of the moderates in the Ittihadist Central Committee, had nevertheless given Scheubner-Richter reason to believe that the defenders of Azakh were "Armenian rebels" in order to encourage him to take part in their liquidation with his German contingent.[187] However, Scheubner-Richter had understood that this maneuver, which he attributed to Halil (Kut), was simply designed to induce him to play "a compromising role in the Armenian business."[188] This episode from the history of German-Turkish military collaboration illustrates the methods of disinformation employed by the Young Turk leaders in their effort to implicate the Germans in the anti-Armenian violence. It shows how hard it was for German officers to grasp the complexity of the situation: in the case to hand, Scheubner had understood that he was being manipulated, yet remained unaware that the "rebels" were not Armenians, but Orthodox Syriacs. He also confirmed that the Young Turk propaganda about the "domestic enemy" was aimed exclusively at "the Armenian rebels"; the adjective "Armenian" legitimized, in some sense, the military operation planned against the Syriacs of Tur Abdin. The charge that Muslims had been massacred, leveled by a "moderate" of Ömer Naci's stamp, was also calculated without a doubt to furnish retroactive justification for the crimes already committed throughout the vilayet of Dyarbekir. That the German-Turkish Expeditionary Corps was diverted from its original objective is, moreover, indicative of the priorities of the Turkish general staff, which lavished greater attention on "its" Christians, who were hardly in an offensive posture, than on its military objectives. Held up by these operations, Naci and Scheubner's Expeditionary Corps was forced, with the approach of winter, to abandon the idea of launching an offensive on Tabriz.

Savur

As in the *kaza* of Midyat, Armenians lived only in the administrative seat of the *kaza* of Savur, where there were hardly more than a thousand of them shortly before the war.[189] The *kaymakam*, Yaver Bey, who had been in office since 15 January 1914, was dismissed on 2 May

1915, probably at the request of Dr. Reşid and for the same reasons as his colleagues from the other districts of Dyarbekir. He was replaced the same day by Mehmed Ali Bey, who held his post rather briefly, until 1 October 1915. This was, however, time enough for him to arrange to have all the men in the little town arrested and killed, Armenians and Orthodox Syriacs alike. The murders took place in June 1915, outside Savur. The long march of the convoy of women and children began thereafter. It culminated in Karabhond, outside Nisibin – more specifically in a huge well into which the bodies of the last of the deportees were thrown.[190]

Cezire/Cizre

In Cezire, the easternmost *kaza* of the vilayet of Dyarbekir, there was a higher concentration of Armenians than in the rest of the *sancak*. Besides the 2,716 Armenians living in Cezire and 11 villages nearby, 1,565 Armenian nomads, Kurdified Christians, roamed through the *kaza*.[191] The *kaymakam* of Cezire, Halil Sâmi, who had been in office since 31 March 1913, was dismissed from his post on 2 May 1915 and immediately replaced by Kemal Bey, who remained in his functions until 3 November 1915. That Tur Abdin was able to mount a resistance is doubtless not unrelated to the fact that this district was attacked late in the day. The massacre of the inhabitants of the rural areas began on 8 August and went on for the next several days. Few survived it.[192] The administrative seat of the *kaza*, also called Cezire, was left in peace until 28/29 June. The Orthodox and Catholic Syriac bishops were murdered on the first of those dates. On the next, all the Armenian men and a number of Orthodox and Catholic Syriacs were arrested, tortured, and killed.[193] In this tribal region, life revolved around weapons, and the authorities had always to take the power of the local tribes into account. Here more than elsewhere, what contemporary witnesses describe as "primitive populations" engaged in limitless violence barely tempered by religious considerations, at the instigation of the authorities and with "the participation of the regular army." On the out-skirts of town, the throats of the Christian men were slit with knives as if in a ritual sacrifice, and their bodies were thrown into the Tigris. In their turn, the women and children were deported on *keleks* toward Mosul on 1 September. The luckiest were abducted by Kurds; the others were drowned.[194] On 22 September, 200 worker-soldiers from Erzerum were liquidated, at three hours' distance from Cezire, before the eyes of Halil (Kut). It is easy to imagine the role he played in these late massacres.[195]

Nusaybin/Nisibin

In the southern *kaza* of Nisibin in Mesopotamia, there were only 90 Armenians, all of whom lived in the administrative seat of the same name.[196] Among the other inhabitants were Orthodox and Catholic Syriacs, Kurds, and some 600 Jews. The *kaymakam*, Nâzım, who held office from 2 March to 17 September 1915, organized a round-up of the Christian notables, including the Orthodox Syriac bishop, on 16 August. They were slain the same day at some distance from the little town. The women and children were killed over the next few days. Their bodies were thrown into 65 wells that also served as the final resting place of thousands of deportees who arrived from the north.[197]

Dara, in the northern part of Nisibin, was the scene of repeated slaughters; this suggests that the ruins of the ancient city had been chosen as a killing field. In addition to the car-nage evoked in the preceding pages, let us mention, for example, the 11 July 1915 massacre of 7,000 deportees from Erzerum in Dara, whose bodies were thrown into the town's immense Byzantine cisterns.[198] According to information gathered by the British intelligence service, Ali İhsan Pasha, who was serving in Mesopotamia with the Sixth Army at this time, was primarily responsible for the massacres perpetrated in the district of Nisibin.[199]

Questions about the Massacres in the Vilayet of Dyarbekir

In the predominantly Kurdish region of Dyarbekir, the repeated replacement of *kaymakams* and *mutesarifs* in May and June 1915 shows that the national authorities and their representative in Dyarbekir, Dr. Reşid, were hard put to secure local government officials' support for their policy of eradicating the Armenian or Christian population. The Kurdish-Çerkez family of Ziya Gökalp, notably Pirincizâde Feyzi, had to make a major personal effort[200] to bring the Kurdish tribal chieftains to collaborate on their project. In the end, however, the action taken by Dr. Reşid in his vilayet was among the most effective. General Vehib, in the deposition he read to the court-martial in Istanbul in April 1919, observed:

> The crimes committed in the province of Dyarbekir, by virtue of their magnitude and tragic character, number and nature, went beyond all the crimes I have just mentioned. As we have seen, even the Syriacs and Greeks fell victim to these crimes and families such as the Shazzazbanis, who had been known for centuries for their loyalty to the state and the services they rendered it, were killed, along with their children, and their property was illegally seized.[201]

As Hans-Lukas Kieser points out, however, Reşid was no exception among the Young Turk elite of the day. Contrary to what many contemporary Turkish academics affirm, he was highly representative of it.[202] The extreme forms of violence to which he resorted in order to eliminate the non-Turks of his vilayet were in his view justified by the higher interests of his party and the "Turkish nation."

The atrocities perpetrated in the vilayet of Dyarbekir also raise the question of the nature of the crimes committed against the Catholic and Orthodox Syriacs in a region in which they abounded, and which contained their principal historical monuments. The available sources on these events show that, on average, 60 per cent of these groups were eliminated during the persecutions organized by the local authorities. However, more than the dimensions of the crime, we need to assess the genocidal intention behind it – to determine, in other words, whether the Young Turk Central Committee made a decision to wipe out these population groups, as it had in the Armenians' case. We have already noted that Yves Ternon is inclined to think that the decision came from the local authorities, who he says enjoyed autonomy, at least to a certain extent. The substance of the telegram that Mehmed Talât sent Reşid on 12 July 1915[203] does indeed create the impression that the local authorities exceeded their prerogatives. It should, however, also be pointed out that Talât's order to halt the massacre of the Syriac population was probably inspired by the many reactions in diplomatic circles – especially on the part of the diplomats of Austria-Hungary and the Vatican – to crimes committed against Catholics and Monophysites.[204] For the national authorities, it was much harder to gain acceptance for the discourse about the "enemy within" in the case of these Christians, who, unlike the Armenians, had no political representation to speak of in Istanbul, little economic and demographic weight, and a narrow territorial base.

The fact that the killing came to a halt in Mardin almost one month before the arrival of the "official" telegram of the minister of the interior, even as it continued to rage in peripheral and rural areas, is reason enough to wonder whether Talât, in sparing Mardin's non-Armenian Christians – let us recall that their elites had perished together with the Armenians' – was not attempting to hide his party's objectives vis-à-vis the Syriacs and disguise the consequences of his own orders as local excesses. The Ittihadists' Turkist ideology, their determination to exclude and eliminate non-Turkish groups, inclines us to the view that the Young Turk Central Committee decided to eradicate the Syriac population along with the Armenians as a complementary measure. Reşid's character rules out the possibility that he simply took an ill-considered step; he was one of the founding fathers of the Young Turk movement, a disciplined, honest official of high rank who ceaselessly battled the negligence and venality of the Ottoman administration and was prompt to dismiss those who failed to obey him. It can even be said that he was one of the rare high-ranking officials to carry out all of the national authorities' orders to the fullest extent because he believed in their usefulness. It must also be borne in mind that Reşid doubled as the leader of the Special Organization in the vilayet of Dyarbekir and thus answered to two hierarchies, of which at least one, the Special Organization, had proved its effectiveness and imposed its decisions with unmistakable determination. Local pressures, inspired in particular by a lust for gain, might, at the limit, explain the violence, which was chronic in the region, but they can by no means explain the programmatic methods brought to bear on the Syriac population.

The fact that the Syriac-speaking population was divided up into many different Christian communities and that each denomination had its prejudices about all the others should not be allowed to mask the fact that the Syriacs, collectively speaking, were the victims of genocide. Much more clearly than the Armenian case, the eradication of the Syriacs, which was not tainted by accusations of irredentism, bears witness to the ideological nature of the genocide organized by the Young Turk Central Committee.

Chapter 7

Deportations and Massacres in
the Vilayet of Harput/Mamuret ul-Aziz

The available sources on the circumstances surrounding the eradication of the Armenian population of the vilayet of Harput are exceptionally abundant and diverse. In addition to many survivors' accounts,[1] we have the official Ottoman documents unearthed by the Constantinople court-martial during the November 1919–January 1920 "Harput" trial[2] and those published in the collection issued by the General Directorate of the State Archives of Turkey.[3] We also have the detailed reports drawn up by the United States consul, Leslie Davis,[4] and American missionaries who witnessed the events.[5] In Harput more than anywhere else, the fact that many citizens of a neutral country were present in the region represented an additional problem for the authorities, who had to simultaneously oversee their extermination program and bring the Americans' efforts to save as many Armenians as possible to naught. In other words, in studying the events of 1915 in the vilayet of Mamuret ul-Aziz, we need to take into account the problem of Turkish-American antagonism, which had a direct influence on the Armenians' fate. That antagonism is the more important in that the answers given by the local authorities to the questions raised daily by the American representatives allow us to grasp certain elements of the genocidal machinery that elude us elsewhere. Even if the American interventions privileged the survival of only one segment of the Armenian population, the members of the Protestant community, they compelled the vali to take certain precautions and also to elaborate a discourse justifying the violent measures he carried out and the mass crimes that the consul and missionaries witnessed firsthand. To be sure, the vali sometimes succeeded in convincing his Western interlocutors of the existence of an Armenian "revolutionary plot," but he lost all credibility when he leveled such accusations at, for example, the teachers at the principal American institution in Harput, Euphrates College, since the missionaries were personally acquainted with them and knew that they were absolutely incapable of getting mixed up in a "plot." It is in these rare moments, vividly depicted in the Americans' accounts of their experiences, that we can assess the coherence of the arguments that the authorities mobilized to justify their crimes.

The other regional particularity is the role of the pivot or hub of the deportations that fell to the vilayet of Mamuret ul-Aziz: in 1915, nearly all the convoys of deportees from the regions of Trebizond, Erzerum, Sıvas, and the eastern part of the region of Ankara passed through the "slaughterhouse province"[6] and lost some of their members there. The concentration in the *sancak* of Malatia of a large number of killing fields to which certain squadrons of the Teşkilât-ı Mahsusa were permanently attached tells us something about the procedures the authorities adopted to eliminate the deportees, the *çetes*' operational methods, and the routes taken by the convoys. Mezreh also served as the Third Army's main rear base; this was where soldiers wounded on the Caucasian front were sent, and it was also a place of refuge for the Muslim civilian population fleeing the Russian advance. The third salient characteristic of this vilayet has to do with its northern district, the *sancak* of Dersim, over which the authorities had practically no real control at the time; it was the only possible sanctuary for the Armenian deportees who came from the region of Harput or passed through it. This state of affairs obliged the authorities to devise a mechanism allowing them to control, at the very least, access to Dersim – since they could not establish military supremacy over the district itself – in order to make it as hard as possible for the deportees to escape from their system.

Relatively remote from the war zones, the vilayet of Mamuret ul-Aziz undermines the claims about security needs put forward elsewhere. Observed from the vantage point it offers, they manifestly do not suffice to mask the Young Turks' determination to "homogenize" the population. Located at the point of confluence of the two branches of the Euphrates, the region included on the eve of the First World War 270 towns and villages with a total Armenian population of 124,289. It boasted 242 churches, 65 monasteries, and 204 schools attended by 15,632 children.[7] Behind these statistics lay a variegated society: it comprised a majority of peasants, who were responsible for the great bulk of the vilayet's agricultural production; a broad stratum of craftsmen and merchants, who enjoyed almost total control of the local market; and finally, a class of serious intellectuals, most of whom had been educated at Harput's American Euphrates College or the Armenian Central College. The vilayet's Protestant Armenian community was exceptionally big; its importance was due not just to its size but, first and foremost, to its members' level of education. The cultural gap between the Armenian and Muslim – especially Kurdish – populations seems to have been widening in the years before the war, as were the socio-economic disparities between the two groups. The permanent ties between the region and its 26,917 emigrants, most of whom had settled in the United States,[8] help explain the accelerated modernization of Armenian society, or at least its urban segment.

The heart of the vilayet, its economic and political center, was made up of four adjoining towns: Harput, Hiuseinig, Kesrig, and Mezreh. They had a combined population of 17,198 Armenians, as against 13,206 Turks.[9] Mezreh/Mamuret ul-Aziz, located on the plain, was home to a number of institutions: the vilayet's governmental bodies; the Eleventh Army Corps, which was transferred to Mezreh between 26 July and 8 August 1914 and commanded by a brigadier general; the American hospital, Annie Tracy Riggs Memorial Hospital, headed by Dr. Henry Atkinson; the American Consulate; and the German mission, under the direction of Johannes Ehmann, a former officer who had become a Protestant minister.

The general mobilization of 3 August 1914 gave rise to scenes of chaos. A description by the president of the American mission, Henry R. Riggs, gives us a detailed view of the reigning confusion. Riggs begins by describing the posters pasted up in the city and the proclamations of the town criers announcing the mobilization of men between 20 and 45 – in other regions, the corresponding age limits were 18 and 45 – who had five days to enroll. The populace, Riggs says, responded "promptly and loyally" to the call, but the draft boards worked slowly and displayed a certain "laxity."[10] After waiting for several days to be mustered, a good many Kurds from Dersim simply went back home and never returned. The busiest army officers were apparently the doctors, who handed out exemptions right and left to those who proved sufficiently generous. Riggs attributes the disorder that characterized the mobilization to the officers' inexperience. He observes in particular that counter-orders followed orders, concerning first those under 40 and then those under 31, who were the first to be mobilized. Management of the lists of people exempted from military service for health reasons, because they had paid the *bedel*, or because they were too young or too old, was, at the very least, disastrous. The underlying reason was the "chaos" reigning in the office, where, one day, "the list of names prepared the day before had been lost." Thus, some of the men exempted from service were identified as deserters and arrested.[11] The officers' lack of comprehension of, or scorn for, the peasants, especially the Kurds who did not know Turkish, the appallingly inadequate accommodations for the new recruits, the fact that the soldiers' food supply depended on the generosity of the local populace, and a shortage of arms and equipment, explained why "only 15 percent of the men" actually arrived on the front.[12] Riggs also notes that there existed "a bond of sympathy" between the Armenian and Muslim conscripts, who shared the same fear of the fighting to come; the proclamation of a holy war did not undermine it.[13]

The abuses spawned by the military requisitions angered the local population and led the Armenian primate, Bsag Der Khorenian, to lodge an official protest with the local authorities.[14] The requisitions provided the occasion for massive misappropriations of foodstuffs, farm animals, clothing, wood, and various other products.[15] The corruption was orchestrated by the commission responsible for "military contributions" (*teklif-i harbiyye*), created in fall 1914 under the auspices of the local Ittihadist club.[16] This club was supervised by Boşnak Resneli Nâzım Bey, the CUP inspector in Mamuret ul-Aziz. He was seconded by Ferid Bey, the responsible CUP secretary and head of the vilayet's school system; Şedihizâde Fehmi, a member of the local Ittihadist council; Haci Baloşzâde Mehmed Nuri Bey, a parliamentary deputy from Dersim and the head of the regional Teşkilât-ı Mahsusa; Baloş Mustafa Effendi, a Unionist deputy; Mufti Hoca Bey Zâde; and Haci Feyzi, a member of the general council of the vilayet.[17]

The new vali, Sabit Cemal Sağiroğlu, who had been appointed to his post early in September 1914, had an interesting background.[18] Whereas the corresponding posts in Van, Bitlis, and Dyarbekir were held by Enver's and Talât's close friends or relatives – men who were considered to be educated and could speak French – Governor Sabit was perceived by the American consul as an "exceedingly ignorant and uncultured man … gross in his manners," but "of considerable natural shrewdness."[19] The American diplomat even informs us that the new vali had spent all his life in a Kurdish environment and that the "only public position" that he held before he was given the job in Mezreh was that of *mutesarif* of Dersim.[20] Davis was unaware, however, that Sağiroğlu came from a feudal family native to the Kemah area.[21] His familiarity with the Kurds of Dersim and his social position doubtless explain why the government made a man of his stamp vali of a region in which Turkish *ağas* and Kurdish *begs* had considerable political weight.

On 11 September 1914, the American consul, Leslie Davis, and the head of the American mission in Harput, Henry Riggs, had a chance to meet the new vali. They were introduced to him on the very day that the press agency Milli announced that the Capitulations had been abolished – the decision was to take effect on 1 October; news that put Sabit in a very good mood. Riggs was not mistaken when he said that the suppression of these privileges left the American charitable institutions at the mercy of the Turkish authorities.[22] In fact, the abolition of the Capitulations initiated a gradual takeover of the Americans' property, which was confiscated bit by bit by the authorities on more or less hollow pretexts; the manifest intention was to push these "foreigners" aside and reduce their influence in the region. In the following weeks, the consul and missionaries, threatened with the total loss of their buildings and land, could only make appeals to the "gracious generosity of the Governor" through certain Ottoman friends.[23]

The attempt to gain control of the Americans' assets was aimed, first and foremost, at Harput's Euphrates College, a symbol of American influence in the region. A request was made, "very politely," for use of one of the college's buildings, "Audience Hall," which the army wanted to convert into a barracks. In the weeks thereafter, the girls' school and the seminar were confiscated. To justify the confiscations, the vali mentioned the risk of typhus epidemics, which he said compelled him to take preventive measures and close the American schools. The government's effort culminated only on 26 March, when the authorities took possession of Euphrates College – by no means indispensable to the army, according to Riggs – and issued the order to shut down the schools once and for all. The American consul stepped in at this point, making an appeal to the Istanbul embassy, but his intervention did not stop the colonel and police chief, who came in person to take charge of the premises that the Americans refused to surrender "voluntarily."[24]

The other prestigious American institution, the Annie Tracy Riggs Memorial Hospital, which was located in Mezreh, partly escaped the fate of the institution in Harput, because the American Red Cross announced in December 1914 that it would assume responsibility for 100 beds reserved for wounded soldiers sent back from the Caucasian front.[25] Thus, the hospital served, until the winter of 1915–16, as a sanctuary for its Armenian personnel. Access to it, however, was closely monitored by a squad of soldiers permanently stationed on the premises. Also, Armenians able to prove that they were American citizens, and a few other members of the Protestant community who had been recommended to the consul by the missionaries, were allowed to stay in the American consulate, or, at any rate, the vast yard surrounding it. The gradual confiscation of the buildings that housed the American institutions can be explained by the Young Turks' desire to eliminate foreign influences from the country and, secondarily, by the army's needs for barracks and office space. However, the takeover of the American schools, decreed on 26 March 1915, was no doubt also designed to eliminate any and all zones beyond the authorities' control – that is, to leave the Armenians no way out. It is, moreover, telling that the first step the vali took was to arrest most of the Armenian faculty of these schools.[26]

The rising death rate, in late winter 1915, among conscripts charged with transporting supplies to Erzerum, Bitlis, and Mush seemed to the Armenians to be cause for alarm,[27] as did the public execution of three peasants from the village of Korpe who were executed by firing squad in front of the military hospital for "aiding and abetting deserters."[28] Riggs, one of a generation of American missionaries who had been born in Turkey and spoke Turkish and Armenian, notes that over the preceding years, "certain conditions had presaged the coming storm," although this was not at all the case in 1915, when "the relationship of the Armenian to his Moslem neighbor was more friendly and sympathetic than ever before."[29] Riggs also remarks that the mood changed in April, when rumors began to circulate about "seditious activity," followed by reports of the atrocities to which the Muslim population in the border zones had been subjected by the Russians and Armenians. He adds that he, too, had heard "fantastic tales" of this kind from the vali himself. These stories, of course, spawned some resentment among the Turks; they were, however, never spread by official publications.[30]

Armenians seem to have sensed the threat much earlier, for, on 5 February 1915, a meeting of the main Armenian political leaders was called at Jean Shirvanian's house in Mezreh in order to assess the situation and discuss the possibility of organizing a self-defense effort if it should deteriorate further. They came to the unanimous conclusion that the Armenians lacked the preparation needed to do so.[31] They were probably unaware that Vali Sabit was already busy organizing squadrons of çetes for the Special Organization, as is indicated by a 15 February 1915 telegram addressed to the mutesarif of Malatia;[32] it gave him three days to send the çetes to Mezreh. Of course, the Armenians could not have known that the vali would announce, in a 16 March conversation with a German diplomat passing through Mamuret ul-Aziz, that "[t]he Armenians in Turkey must be, and were going to be, exterminated." "They had grown in wealth and numbers," he said, "until they had become a menace to the ruling Turkish race; extermination was the only remedy."[33]

In any event, the vali, Sabit Sağiroğlu, maintained relations with the leading Armenian men in the vilayet until early April. Matters took a less friendly turn when he summoned these political and religious leaders to his offices in order to inform them that he had to begin collecting the weapons held in people's homes. Although he treated his interlocutors with respect, he had soon unleashed a campaign against Armenian political activists. "Shortly after Easter" (4 April) 1915, Armenian clubs were searched and their leaders were arrested. In Mezreh, the first to be arrested were the Dashanks Garabed Demirjian, Dikran Asdigian, Dr. Nshan Nahigian, Aram Srabian, and Garabed Geogushian, the Hnchaks Harutiun Semerjian and Garabed Tashjian, and the liberals Khosrov Tembekijian and Smpad Arslanian.[34] A rumor had been circulating to the effect that "bombs and guns had been found in the possession of certain persons who were thought to be members of Armenian revolutionary societies conspiring against the Turkish Government." "Looking at the matter in the light of subsequent events and comparing it with what happened in all others parts of Turkey at the same time," the consul adds, "I think it is probable that in many cases the bombs, which were found in the backyards of the persons accused, were actually buried there by the police so as to manufacture evidence against the Armenians."[35] The political activists arrested were held in Mezreh's central prison, where they were tortured, the official purpose being to get them to reveal where they had hidden their weapons. The house-to-house searches already underway in both the towns and villages were now transformed into occasions for destruction and plunder. The authorities looked not only for arms, but seized on the least little letter or printed document in their quest for compromising documents, which were turned over to a committee charged with examining them.[36] In a 5 May letter, the head of the German mission in Mezreh, Johannes Ehmann, informed the German ambassador in Constantinople that house searches had been conducted in Harput-Huysenig-Mezreh and that people "who seemed suspicious" had been arrested, despite the fact that the populace "obeyed the government" and had accepted conscription without complaint. Ehmann also noted that Vali Sabit, with whom he had met, "[was] himself convinced of the peaceful disposition of the Christian population of the region."[37]

Nazaret Piranian, a teacher at Euphrates College, reports in this connection a conversation that he had in mid-April with Feymi Bey, a local liberal, in the shop of a Mezreh pharmacist, Karekin Gurjian. Feymi Bey informed Piranian and Gurjian that he had recently attended a meeting in the city between the authorities and Turkish notables about disarming the Armenians. Aware of the alarm caused by the prospect, Ehmann, who had been invited to the meeting, offered to intercede, taking advantage of his status as a man of the cloth.[38] The Dane Hansina Marcher, who worked alongside the German pastor, gives a different interpretation of his role in this matter. As she tells it, the vali asked Ehmann to intercede with the Armenians (this is probable), and the minister then summoned the leading Armenians in the city to ask them to bow to the authorities' demands.[39] The Armenian sources, for their part, indicate that the former German officer played a much more active role; he is said to have gone to preach in the Apostolic and Protestant churches of Harput, Mezreh, Hiuseinig, Pazmashen, Korpe, Khulagiugh, and so on. In the village of Pazmashen, where he went in the company of Pulutlı Halil, the leader of a squadron of çetes in the Teşkilât-ı Mahsusa, and a few local government officials, he assembled the population in the church and "very skillfully" delivered a "sermon" in which he asked the Armenians to hand in their weapons, swearing on the Bible that he would personally guarantee their safety.[40] In Hiuseinig, he also promised that he would obtain the release of the men who had been arrested.[41] Piranian even affirms that the minister used Biblical quotations and his status as a Christian clergyman to wage a propaganda campaign for the benefit of the authorities, and that he was in fact an officer of the military propaganda department (like Scheubner Richter in Erzerum, as we have seen).[42]

The searches conducted in April thus seem to have had several different functions. They sought to completely disarm the population and gradually neutralize the Armenian elite, followed by all male Armenians, while at the same time lending substance to the charge that an "Armenian revolt" was in the making. An examination of the way events unfolded shows that the local authorities methodically enacted a plan that had probably been hammered out in Istanbul; it was distinguished by the fact each step paved the way for the next. Thus, the hunt for arms justified the arrests, tortures, and house searches. These made the thesis of an Armenian "plot" credible; the existence of the "plot" justified extending the measures taken to all males over the age of ten, followed by the deportation of the whole population. It was an almost perfect mechanism.

Observers of the situation, who concede that they had not yet understood what was in fact taking place, began to ask themselves questions after the arrests of 1 May 1915. Members of the Protestant Armenian elite, notably teachers at Harput's Euphrates College, were among those taken into custody; the arrests thus directly affected the American institutions and "men whose attitude on all political matters was well known to be scrupulously correct."[43] Undeniably, the sudden arrest of these intellectuals "admired by Moslems as well as Christians," against whom there existed no "suspicion of any clandestine activity against the government,[44] was an important feature of the genocidal system. While it deprived the Armenians of enlightened leaders, it showed above all that official talk of a "plot" was manifestly just a ploy: the vali, indeed, was no longer even pretending to legitimize his actions. Of Khachadur Nahigian,[45] Nigoghos Tenekejian,[46] Garabed Soghigian,[47] Mgrdich Vorperian,[48] Hovhannes Bujikanian,[49] and Donabed Lulejian,[50] only Lulejian managed to escape with his life.

The arrests and repression affected not just the Protestant elite of Harput, but all the Armenian leaders, such as the head of Mezreh's Central College (Getronagan Varzharan), Yerukhan (the pseudonym of the writer Yervant Srmakeshkhanlian); Hagop Janjigian, an important businessman whose premises were subjected to a police search; Dr. Artin Bey Helvajian, who was dismissed from his post; Dr. Mikayel Hagopian of Mezreh, who had directed a field hospital during the first Caucasian campaign; the well-known writer Tlgadintsi (whose real name was Hovhannes Harutiunian); Father Vartan Arslanian of Harput; Hagop Fermanian; Garabed Ekmekjian; Garabed Hovsepian; Armenag Terzian; Erzuman Erzumanian; Khachadur Nahigian; Serop Vartabedian; the lawyer Aleksan Nalbandian, who had made a name for himself with his defense of the insurgent Kurds of Dersim; Mardiros Muradian, who was tortured to death the night after he was arrested, and so on.[51]

Riggs, who happened to speak with a member of the "committee" responsible for examining the "papers" found in the possession of the arrested suspects, learned "that in all the papers examined there was absolutely nothing objectionable, but that the other members of the committee were showing a determination, by misinterpretation and by segregating isolated words, to make out an artificial case against the men on trial."[52] As an example of such misinterpretation, he cites the condemnation of the teacher Nigoghos Tenekejian, the leader of the Armenian Protestant community. According to information "revealed" to him by the parliamentary deputy for Harput, Haci (Baloşzâde) Mehmed (Nuri), Tenekejian was convicted on the basis of documents proving that he was the president of the "Cooperative Committee." But, as Riggs notes, Tenekejian's position at the head of this "ecclesiastical body composed of missionaries and representatives of the Protestant church organization, whose duties were purely ecclesiastical," had long been known to one and all, as had the nature of his activities in the organization. This did not prevent the judge from declaring that Tenekejian had confessed to "his complicity in seditious organizations."[53] The files assembled by the authorities to justify the arrests of well-known people above all suspicion were doubtless intended to influence local public opinion and convince the public that the government's anti-Armenian measures were legitimate. The arrests of 40 to 50 Armenian notables of the first rank, apprehended from May to early June,[54] helped bolster the story of a plot woven by seditious organizations that represented a threat to state security, such as the

Protestant "Cooperative Committee." According to Riggs, the campaign mounted by the authorities was successful: the Muslim population's friendly attitude toward the Armenians gave way to profound suspicion.[55]

As for the other question preoccupying the authorities, the confiscation of the Armenians' weapons, Ehmann's intervention, the torture inflicted on the Armenian prisoners and the house searches conducted in Mezreh, Hiuseinig, Harput and the surrounding villages from April on seem not to have produced the desired results. It is true that the Armenian notables had undertaken to consult their "Turkish fellow citizens" at a "mixed assembly" held in the first half of May to discuss the problem of arms, and had agreed to turn over their weapons if and when the Turks guaranteed their security.[56] The vali, however, claimed that they had not handed over all their weapons, but had kept their modern arms and "bombs." Sabit's threats and the Turkish notables' promises convinced the Armenian notables who had not yet been deprived of their liberty to visit the prisoners, accompanied by parish priests and the inevitable Reverend Ehmann, in order to beg them to reveal where they had hidden their arms. If they did not, the prisoners were told they would "be responsible for the destruction of the whole community."[57] The vali also promised "immunity" to everyone who voluntarily gave up his arms.[58] In the end, a miscellaneous "arsenal" was assembled and put on display at the police station in Mezreh; it allowed the parliamentary deputy Haci Baloszâde Mehmed Nuri to spread the idea that "a dangerous plot had been unearthed and was being vigorously prosecuted by the government."[59] Vali Sabit lost no time in photographing these war trophies, sending the pictures to Constantinople along with a report on the conspiracy that he had brought to light.[60] Consul Davis noted, for his part, that there was no telling "how many of the bombs may have been planted by the police themselves and how many weapons were obtained by innocent people for the purpose of having something to surrender to the police."[61]

The preliminary stage that we have just examined ran from late April to late May. It was followed by a second stage, the beginning of which may be dated to 6 June 1915. The second stage was characterized by a sharp increase in the number of arrests throughout the cities of Mezreh and Harput and a systematic search of all houses "without exception" – including the few buildings still in the hands of the American missionaries.[62] Riggs notes that he learned only much later that local officials had conducted the arrests on the basis of preestablished lists.[63] Kesrig and Hiuseinig were surrounded on 7 June and a good many of the men were arrested. The turn of the villages on the plain came on 8 June. On 10 June, Mezreh was surrounded by troops. All of its Armenian shops were closed and its leading citizens were arrested.[64] By 20 June, several hundred men were being held in the prisons of Mezreh; 200 were transferred to Harput on that date.[65]

These prisoners were put in several different prisons. The political prisoners, who in theory had to be brought before a court-martial, were held in solitary confinement in Mezreh's central prison. But most of the prisoners were locked up in the Kirmizi Konak ("Red Konak") near the western exit from Mezreh. Piranian, who was detained in this military barracks from 14 to 28 June 1915, says it was a hell through which both the worker-soldiers of the labor battalions as well as the men of Mezreh, Harput, and Hiuseinig passed. The day he was jailed, 3,000 men of the *amele taburis* were in custody there.[66] They were left for 30 hours without food or water, and crowded together under unspeakable hygienic conditions. On 15 June, they were joined by 500 newcomers, most of them craftsmen from Harput employed by the government and army. Every night, some 50 men were taken to the prison's torture chamber and brought back in the early hours of the morning, just before the passage of Mezreh's garbage collectors, whose task it was to collect the bodies of prisoners who had died overnight.[67]

News of the internment of these 3,500 men soon spread, resulting in thousands of wives and mothers descending on the *konak* with provisions in the hope that they would be allowed to give their relatives food and drink. On their third day of detention, the prison-ers were actually authorized to receive water and a little food.[68] On the morning of 18 June, Piranian noticed the arrival of Çerkez Kâzım, one of the commanding officers of the Special Organization's "militia," accompanied by cavalrymen and 200 infantrymen, who were in turn followed by a cart piled high with ropes. The authorities had apparently decided to empty the konak, which was full to the point of bursting, of the more than 2,000 prisoners who were still alive. These men were told that they were leaving for Urfa to help construct the railroad being built there. They were set marching southward in the afternoon, tied together in groups of four, under the command of Çerkez Kâzım.[69] Our witness, who managed to stay behind in the konak, did not learn what happened to these men. At first, Riggs had heard only rumors; then he obtained information about how they were massacred. He was told in the course of a conversation with the vali that "those prisoners had encountered some Kurds, and there had been some 'unpleasantness'."[70] In other words, the vali did not deny that these men had been put to death, but attributed the crime committed by the soldiers and Çerkez Kâzım's çetes to Kurds.

The next morning, on 19 June, the konak was again filled up with men from the surround-ing villages of the plain who had been arrested during the night. The next day they were joined by men arrested in Mezreh and Harput. By 22 June, some 1,000 Armenians, both urban notables and peasants, were being held in the Red Konak.[71] In the two weeks he spent there, Piranian observed the various ruses that the commander of the garrison, Mehmed Ali Bey, used to squeeze money from the prisoners. He announced that those who could pay the bedel of 42 gold Turkish pounds would immediately be set free, while the others would be sent to Urfa the next morning. Although all contact with the outside world had been forbidden until then, the men were now authorized to receive visits from their wives, obviously so that they could try to obtain the required sum. The 100 prisoners who succeeded in finding the money were put in a separate room. The other roughly 900 men were set marching south under heavy guard on 23 June.[72] According to the verdict handed down in the trial of the criminals of Mamuret ul-Aziz, these men were shot at the foot of Mt. Heroğli on 24 June.[73] Riggs, an outside observer of these events, remarks that the police went systematically to all Armenian homes, beginning on 24–25 June, and arrested all the men, who were then "herded into prison, and it would appear that when the prison [was] full it [would] be cleared out in the same fashion again."[74] News that the first groups of men had been murdered on the outskirts of Harput reached Mezreh in short order. Thereafter, it seems, the authorities decided to stage the massacres in more isolated sites, notably in Güğen Boğazi, a gorge near Maden.[75]

By 25 June, the konak was full again. The prison administration had announced that this time the military authorities wished to recruit craftsmen. Nursing the secret hope that they would escape the fate reserved for their fellow prisoners, 80 candidates, including our witness, were registered. The next day, however, the army declared that it needed only 40 men, and proceeded to dispatch them to their new posts. This episode would hardly be worth mentioning if it were not symptomatic of the cruel game that the military had decided to play with its prey. After the lucky 40 had happily left the prison, the officers in the konak revealed that it was the 40 artisans left behind who had in fact been chosen; the "happy few" were sent to the slaughterhouse.[76]

On 27 June, another 500 prisoners, who had been arrested over the preceding few days, left for "Urfa" at dawn.[77] This is the last convoy of men about whom we have information, but there is every reason to suppose that the same procedure was used to dispatch the others as well, and that the heart of the vilayet of Mamuret ul-Aziz had been virtually emptied of its male population by late June. It is probable that the authorities waited until this stage of their extermination plan had been brought to an end before initiating the next one.

On 26 June, the *munedik* (town crier), Mamo Çavuş, announced in every Armenian neighborhood of Mezreh that all Christians were to be deported to the south and that the first convoy would leave in five days. Çavuş began his announcement this way:

> Listen! My message is for the *gâvurs*, all the *gâvurs* ... By order of our sublime state and the king of kings, it has been decided to send all the *gâvurs* in Harput to Urfa. From babies in the cradle to the last of the old men, all must go ... The first group, to be formed of people from the Devriş, Nayil Beg and Market neighborhoods, is to set out on the first of July at dawn.[78]

Thus, it appears that not only the Armenians but also the Syriacs were deported from Harput. Riggs, however, informs us that the same day, 26 June, the decision to deport the Syriacs was confirmed and then rescinded,[79] probably after an exchange with the minister of the interior. In fact, as soon as the *beyanname* (deportation order) was made public, all the foreign residents of Mezreh-Harput joined together and demanded to be received by the vali. Riggs again best captures the mood prevailing in the city. Although the men were being liquidated, the city was basically unaware of the fate that had been reserved for them – it only knew about the tragic destiny of the first convoy, the blame for which had been put on the Kurds. Until the *munedik* announced the deportation order, the city knew even less what was in store for it. Davis and Ehmann sent telegrams to their respective ambassadors to ask that they intercede, but the authorities censored them; the American consul's telegram did not reach its intended destination. Moreover, the missionaries' telephone line was cut. Thus, it appears that, when the extermination program entered the crucial phase, the local authorities took all the measures necessary to isolate foreign residents and prevent them from communicating with the outside world.[80] "There was no possibility," Riggs writes, "of changing the order in any way, as it had been sent in just that form from Constantinople."[81]

The "memorable visit" that all the foreign residents paid Vali Sabit on the afternoon of 29 June began in a very chilly atmosphere. The only diplomat present, Davis, took pains to point out that his visit did not have an official character and that he had come solely to request that the vali show "mercy for the unfortunate Armenians." According to Riggs, the attitude that Sabit took and the words he uttered plainly gave them to understand that their "interference was not welcome."[82] On the evening of 27 June, Davis had already met with Sabit Bey to request that the American missionaries be allowed to accompany the convoys. He received a "categoric refusal."[83] During the "memorable visit," of which Riggs and Davis give converging accounts, the foreign residents began by broaching the problem from another angle. They suggested that the Armenians be granted extra time in which to prepare for this "difficult journey." Their aim was to gain time in the hope that possible "delay might give time for appeal in Constantinople and reversal of the edict." Very diplomatically, Sabit Bey said that he was aware of the difficulties, but added that he could not disobey his orders; at most, he would allow the women and children who had no male accompaniment to leave with the last convoys. There was, he said, no cause for concern because "they would be taken good care of."[84] Riggs notes the vali's statement to the effect that the Armenians were to blame for what was happening to them because of their acts of "disloyalty," especially in Van, and also that he had discovered "weapons and bombs" in their possession in Harput. The head of the American mission then asked if that was sufficient reason to condemn so many innocent women and children to death. "Indignantly," the vali answered "that they were not condemned to death, but to be sent into exile." Sabit Bey also assured his visitors that he had seen to it that the deportees would be provided with means of transportation and protected by a sizeable escort.[85]

The failure of these local efforts should not blind us to the fact that diplomats in Istanbul also interceded with the Young Turk government. For example, Riggs points out that Ambassador Morgenthau arrived at an agreement with the Sublime Porte exempting naturalized Americans from deportation. Similarly, the joint efforts of the Vatican's nuncio, His Eminence Angelo Maria Dolci, and Johann von Pallavicini, the Austro-Hungarian ambassador, were rewarded with an "imperial pardon" for the Armenian Catholics. Protestants, too, were officially granted exemptions.[86] Likewise exempted were Harput's Syriacs, particularly the Catholics among them. Thus, people in at least four categories were exempted, as were, finally, children "without families," whom the minister of the interior, Talât, personally authorized to remain in the city in a 26 June telegram to Sabit Bey.[87] However, as Riggs notes, the order exempting Catholics and Protestants was not made public until after the groups concerned had been deported; the local authorities paid no attention to the rights accorded to naturalized Americans.[88] As we shall see, for the children "without families" initially admitted to a Turkish orphanage, they were put to death in the fall. At this stage of our study, we can only conclude, given all that we have already established about the Young Turks' methods, that the sole purpose of the exemptions granted in Constantinople was to throw sand in the eyes of the diplomats in the capital and conceal the CUP's true objectives. There is even every reason to believe that the local authorities were ordered to ignore these exemptions and deport all the Armenians. It would appear, moreover, that the handful of people who did benefit from these measures because they were able to hide when the deportations began were finally rounded up and deported in fall 1915. It should also be pointed out that, as early as 27 June, even before the departure of the convoys of women and children, the minister of the interior ordered Sabit Bey to take the steps required to settle Muslim *muhacirs* in the "evacuated" Armenian villages[89] – that is, to "make a clean sweep of things."

The documents available on the events that occurred in Harput in 1915 provide insight into another interesting moment, hard to study in other areas, in the process of eradicating the population – the few days that preceded the departure of the convoys. As we hardly need point out, this phase was characterized by an initial transfer of Armenian assets to Muslims and Syriacs. It gives us a glimpse of the state of mind of the future deportees and the measures taken by the authorities to prevent Armenians from eluding the party-state and its representatives; it illustrates the American consuls' and missionaries' willingness to play the role of bankers; and finally, it shows us the varying responses of the Turkish population to the Armenians' distress. Thus, Riggs observes that it was the women who prepared their own and their families' departure in their imprisoned or "deported" husbands' stead. Although few of them had experience in commercial or economic affairs, they had to liquidate their husbands' moveable assets or business stock at, on average, a tenth of their real value.[90] Many Turks naturally saw this as an opportunity to enrich themselves on the cheap. Some did not merely attend the auctions held in the streets, but went to see these helpless women to extort what they could from them on various pretexts – and sometimes by straightforward threats. Others, however, particularly those Turks from the "better" social classes, were apparently horrified by the treatment being meted out to their Armenian neighbors and refused to profit from the situation by acquiring *haram* ("unlawful") goods. Some even neglected their own affairs for several days in order to help a neighbor's widow sell her property, without asking for the least compensation in exchange. Such people were, however, exceptions.[91]

While the fate of the men was sealed in advance, it seems that Istanbul left some leeway where young women and girls were concerned. In the short period before the departure of the convoys, the authorities encouraged conversions and "marriages" that would make these Armenian women the second, third, or fourth wife of a Turk. The immense majority, to be sure, refused this solution, preferring deportation. But others understood that it was the only way to save their lives. Alongside such cases, based on coercion, there were more unusual situations, such a young woman who survived by contracting a fictive marriage with a Turkish neighbor, a policeman, probably in exchange for money; or the official union of a young Armenian woman with a Muslim neighbor's minor son.[92] Although such agreements were sometimes respected, there were also more tragic cases: for example, that of the young women who, having brought their inheritance to their new husband's family as a "dowry," were ejected from the household that had taken them in and deported.

Unlike many other features of the deportation, the local authorities' attitude toward impromptu sales of Armenian assets evolved rather rapidly. On the first day, they were content to levy the legal tax of 5 per cent on all commercial transactions. However, the day preceding the departure of the first convoy, the town crier announced that "anyone who sells or buys anything, if caught, will be sent to the court-martial."[93] It is likely that the vali and his administration, or even the national government, had initially established rules that were somewhat too vague without anticipating their economic effects, and had understood only afterwards that it would not be easy for them to lay hands on the Armenians' moveable assets if they let matters stand as they were. The way the Armenian "taxpayers'" debts and accounts receivable were dealt with also spawned a certain number of abuses. A multitude of claims, from both real and imaginary creditors, came raining down on the Armenians. These were debts of the sort ordinarily incurred by business firms, representing only an insignificant fraction of their sales volume or value. Yet they served here as a pretext for numerous financial misdealings particularly wholesale confiscations of commercial property. The Banque Impériale Ottomane played a crucial role in these matters by "promptly" taking possession of businesses and stores and selling them after the departure of their proprietors. As Riggs points out, the BIO, after paying off the debts on these businesses – a tiny fraction of the value of the properties that it sold off – deposited the balance "in the coffers of the government."[94]

The large sums of cash, sometimes amounting to several thousand pounds in gold and held by people who were able to liquidate their assets, also presented a problem because the banks were not authorized to accept deposits. They were, however, allowed to accept "transfers" that certain Armenians made to themselves through a bank or post office for withdrawal in the locality to which they were ostensibly being deported.[95] Some survivors later managed to master the subtleties of the banking regulations set up by the authorities, and a handful of them – those who escaped the massacres or arrived in the place to which they were supposed to be deported – indeed profited from them. However, the bulk of these "transfers" benefited the state. The problem of traveling with cash was, moreover, one faced by almost all Armenian deportees, who knew their country and were aware that it was, to say the least, imprudent to circulate with large amounts of money in one's possession. These considerations and an objective analysis of the situation convinced a good number of future deportees to entrust sizeable sums to the American consul and American missionaries in Harput-Mezreh. According to Davis, at that "memorable visit" on 29 June, the vali did not object to the Armenians "leav[ing] their money," jewels, precious objects and documents to the Americans. Some even gave the consul or the missionaries the addresses of relatives in the United States, with the request that these deposits be sent there should nothing be heard from them for longer than six months. "All feel that they are going to certain death," Davis wrote in a report, "and they certainly have good reason to feel that way."[96]

Order of a kind was re-established after the rapid creation of a commission responsible for abandoned property, which set about trying to recover the funds that the Armenians had deposited in the post office or kept in their bank accounts, as well as the stocks of merchandise from their businesses.[97] The commission was officially charged with "safeguarding" the Armenians' property during their absence. According to Piranian, who had remained in Mezreh after the departure of the convoys, the authorities had the doors of Armenian homes sealed to prevent looting. A kind of race then began between the authorities and the Turkish population to see who could plunder faster – doors, windows, and everything else were carried off. Only those houses in the immediate vicinity of the prefecture remained in the authorities' hands.[98] The commission was not unaware that large amounts of money had been deposited with the American consul and missionaries and accordingly demanded, on behalf of the government, that these assets be turned over to it. In September 1915, the vali himself made the same demand in a letter addressed to the consul, who ignored it.[99] The missionaries had received much bigger deposits than Davis (Riggs writes that he was "simply deluged with money"), having resorted to tricks that facilitated access to the mission buildings in Mezreh and Harput by Armenian depositors or fugitives. Although the mission in the provincial capital had been left totally isolated and unprotected throughout June, it was surrounded by soldiers who had kept a close eye on the main entrance from the moment the deportation order was announced.[100] The vali's absolute, if tardy, interdiction notwithstanding, Henry and Ernest Riggs, as well as Henry Atkinson, continued to accept the Armenians' deposits. According to a rumor circulating in Mezreh, the missionaries had "fabulous sums" on their hands, and yet the orders of magnitude cited by the rumormongers "never surpassed" the sum that Riggs had actually forwarded to his treasurer in Constantinople by way of a local bank. The treasurer, in turn, took responsibility for transferring the money to America. The police never succeeded in ascertaining how much money was involved.[101] When the vali sent a request to Riggs, through the police chief, to turn the funds over to him, the head of the American mission declared that he had already transferred the money to the United States. All the police officer had in hand by way of "official" documentation was a claim filed by a young woman whose family had entrusted money to the Americans and who was now being held in a harem in Mezreh. Riggs notes that he was constantly assailed by demands of this kind from Turks holding Armenian women. He says that he invariably met them with the same response.[102]

To appreciate the state of mind of the Armenians who were about to be deported, we must take an important factor into consideration: they were absolutely ignorant of the crimes being committed in the other provinces. The first caravans from the vilayets to the north arrived in Mezreh immediately following the departure of the two first convoys. This was probably no accident. Piranian, who had made the acquaintance of two fugitives from Jabaghchur while a prisoner in the Red Konak in the latter half of June, remarks that it was only when he heard their story that he took the full measure of the Young Turk plan – in particular the fate reserved for those deportees on the road to "exile."[103] An event that occurred the day before the departure of the first convoy gives us a glimpse of the Armenians' mood. That day, since the authorities had requisitioned both the Armenian Apostolic and Armenian Protestant churches, the last prayer vigil was to be held in the German mission building. The theme of the vigil, conducted by Reverend Hovhan Sinanian from Mezreh, was: "Let us pray that evil vanish from the Armenian horizon."[104] During the service, Sinanian had turned to Ehmann and sarcastically asked him if he was inclined to serve as their guide in the desert. "The time has come," he said, "to prove the sincerity of your apostle's soul."[105] Ehman did not take up the challenge.

In his own fashion, Consul Davis also anticipated the announced departure of the Armenian population. He observes that, according to official statistics, 90 per cent "of the trade and of the business carried on through the banks is that of Armenians," whose businesses were now doomed to destruction "beyond the possibility of its being restored." Pessimistically, he prophesied a return to the Dark Ages.[106]

The *Kaza* of Harput

We have so far considered the events that took place in and around Mezreh and Harput, the administrative and economic heart of the vilayet of Mamuret ul-Aziz. It must, however, be recalled that the fate of these towns went hand-in-hand with that of 50 villages on the plain of Harput, which had a total population of 20,590 peasants.[107]

The first convoy, made up of people from three Mezreh neighborhoods – Devriş, Nayil Beg, and the markets – contained a total of some 2,500 deportees. They were escorted by infantrymen and mounted gendarmes under the command of Captain Adam Pasha. The convoy set out on the road to Dyarbekir on 1 July. Although the immense majority of people in this caravan were women and children, there were also a few older family heads. Notably among the deportees were the Mazmanian, Istambulian, Doertyolian, Khanigian, Darakjian, and Kalpakjian families. The convoy was followed by a cart full of rope, which served its purpose shortly after the deportees left Mezreh, when the males were separated from the others and put under separate guard.[108] The following day, the deportees passed by Lake Göljük, arriving that evening in Arğana Maden, in the vilayet of Dyarbekir. They reached the city of Dyarbekir in a week. There they were left in a cemetery outside the city walls; the guard was changed and the carts rented in Mezreh resumed their journey. In the week it took this convoy to travel from Dyarbekir to Mardin, the deportees were repeatedly plundered by *çetes*. Young women and children were abducted or sold to local populations. The youngest members of the caravan as well as old people were left on the side of the road. The survivors reached Ras ul-Ayn a fortnight later, and a handful of those arrived in Der Zor in another two weeks.[109]

On 2 July 1915, the second convoy set out from Mezreh, this time heading toward Malatia. The roughly 3,000 deportees in this convoy came from the Karaçöl, Icadiye, and Ambar neighborhoods. They were from the most affluent families: the Fabrikatorians, Harputlians, Kazanjians, Zarifians, Sarafians, Dingilians, Gurjians, Arpiarians, Totvians, Karaboghosians, and Demirjians. Reverend Hovhan Sinapian was also in this convoy.[110] The affluence of these Armenians doubtless explains why the caravan had a great many vehicles at its disposal and included many male family heads. It was not until it reached Malatia that the men were separated from the others. We know nothing about how they died. The rest of the caravan continued on its way towards Urfa. Some of those in it reached Der Zor several weeks later.[111]

On 4 July, the Armenian population of Hiuseinig was deported in turn, in a single convoy that set out on the road to Malatia.[112] The deportation of the Armenians of Harput was put off until late July. According to Riggs, Asim Bey, the *kaymakam* of Harput, maneuvered so as to delay departure of the population of the former provincial capital in hopes of relieving it of all its cash and precious objects before sending it on its way. It is more likely, however, that the authorities chose to deal with Mezreh and Huiseinig first, perhaps because of a shortage of personnel, and concentrate on Harput thereafter. The arrests of all males over 13 did not begin until the first days of July, apart from those of members of the elite, who had been apprehended very early. On Saturday, 6 July, Maria Jacobsen and Tracy Atkinson learned that 200 of those arrested, along with the men who had been in Mezreh, had been massacred the night before in a gorge near Hanköy by the squadron of *çetes* that accompanied them – in all, 800 people.[113] The same day, the town crier summoned the inhabitants of Harput to open their shops. All the men present were then arrested by soldiers of the regular forces and sent away the following night. In the evening, the Danish missionary finally learned that all males over the age of nine had been herded together in a mosque and dispatched from the city on Saturday 4 July. Their guards, "Kurds and gendarmes," came back from Içme on Sunday in clothes smeared with their victims' blood.[114]

After the first convoys had set out from Mezreh, it would appear that the authorities soon decided to attend to the people who had been officially exempted from deportation. Beginning on 8 July, the elderly, who had been allowed to "remain behind," received summons in their turn and were put on the road.[115] Jacobsen mentions the case of an old man of 80, Hagop Benneyan, who was killed in front of his house by the soldiers who had come for him. The handful of women and girls who had been authorized to remain were, for their part, invited to convert to Islam immediately.[116] Boys between the ages of four and eight were apparently not abandoned. They were rounded up, circumcised, and then admitted to two "Turkish" orphanages that had opened around 10 July.[117] The authorities even asked Consul Davis to contribute to their upkeep.[118]

It was not until 10 July that the deportation order was announced in Harput and the population was invited to convert to Islam.[119] A first convoy comprising 150 families from the "Lower Quarter" (Vari Tagh) was put on the road the same day, escorted by "Kurds and gendarmes."[120] The former *kaymakam* of Harput, Dr. Artin Bey Helvajian, a general practitioner who had been relieved of his post in May and replaced by Asim Bey, was also deported on 14 July, along with 40 other leading personalities. They were transported in horse-drawn coaches, all officially granted "safe conduct" and provided with guarantees of absolute security. Officially, Dr. Helvajian was deported to Aleppo, supposedly suffering from a lack of physicians. Traveling with him was his family and, notably, the Catholic primate of the diocese of Harput, Archbishop Stepan Israyelian, as well as Father Sarkis Khachadurian, Father Ghevont Minasian, and four nuns from the Congregation of the Immaculate Conception. The following day, 15 July, the convoy was brought to a halt near Kâzım Han, eight hours to the south of Harput, and massacred by the gendarmes who escorted it, according to testimonies given by one of the three women who survived the massacre and the gendarmes in the escort who had returned to Mezreh.[121]

The second convoy from Harput, made up of some 3,000 people, was expedited down the road to Malatia toward Urfa on 18 July, escorted by 100 gendarmes and three officers.[122] At dawn, the army surrounded the city's upper quarter and proceeded to expel its inhabitants one house at a time. Only five Armenian craftsmen and their families were allowed to remain in their homes, as were the Syriacs and Greeks. Jacobsen notes that, by 21 July, officers and government officials had already moved into the Armenian houses located in the neighborhood of Euphrates College.[123] According to a survivor from the second caravan, Mushegh Vorperian, it had reached Malatia in a week, having lost only 25 victims after the escorting officers had extorted money from it. At three hours' march from Malatia, in the place known as Çiftlik, all the males over 12 were separated from the rest of the caravan and locked up in a nearby barracks, where they were put to death. The 14 year-old sister of our eyewitness was "taken to wife" by one of the officers in the caravan's escort; the other women and children were turned over to the men, who were authorized to help themselves.[124]

In a 24 July report, Consul Davis indicates that 12,000–15,000 Armenians had already been deported from Mezreh and Harput by that date. Between 1,000 and 1,500 remained in the city "with permission or through bribery or in hiding."[125] He adds that thousands of other people from the neighboring villages had already been put on the road.[126]

Hardly had the deportations been completed then Davis expressed his surprise over the "total lack of resistance" on the part of the Armenian deportees, which in his opinion was due "very largely also to the clever way in which the scheme has been carried out." The overview of events that he drew up while they were occurring is doubtless one of the most edifying documents we have on the eradication of the empire's Armenian population. Davis was in the thick of what was happening and had a perfect grasp of a key aspect of the extermination plan: each stage of it paved the way for the next with almost clockwork precision. This led him to conclude that "everything was apparently planned months ago." He had also understood the authorities' first move. The arrest of "a few who were said to have been involved in a revolutionary plot"[127] had established the principle of the "Armenians' culpability" from the outset, legitimating the authorities' suspicions. In fact, the authorities were so little convinced of the justifications which they themselves advanced that they attempted to wring incriminating testimony from foreigners. For example, Davis reports that on 23 July, at a meeting with the vali, whom he had gone to see in order to ask him to leave the Armenians not yet deported in peace, he was asked to make a written request, which he was told the vali would be inclined to treat favorably if the diplomat spelled out that the authorities had deported only "all those who were guilty of anything."[128] The vali even suggested that he could send the police chief to see Davis "to explain the matter more fully." The vali's intentions then became much more explicit: he went so far as to have the police chief ask Davis to stress the fact that the Armenians "who were guilty of having been engaged in a revolutionary plot had been punished, together with their families," unlike those who had been allowed to remain behind.[129] This episode, written down almost as soon as it happened, suggests that the minister of the interior had asked high-ranking officials in the provinces to build up the story of an Armenian "conspiracy," utilizing, if at all possible, "testimony" from foreign residents. This perhaps explains why Mezreh's police chief responded to the consul's stalling tactics by stepping up the pressure and threatening to take severe measures against naturalized Americans and others.[130]

One last striking event occurred after the departure of the big convoys of deportees: Mezreh's central prison went up in flames. In this institution, located close to the seat of Governor Sabit, the leading Armenian citizens of Mezreh, Harput, and Hiuseinig – those deemed the most "dangerous" – were interned from April to July. Here they were systematically tortured in an attempt to elicit the "confessions" needed to bring them before a court-martial. By early August, however, the authorities doubtless considered these legal artifices superfluous. The time had come to liquidate these men, the same way the less important men imprisoned in the Red Konak had been liquidated. However, when soldiers came to announce to these prisoners, in the middle of the night of 3/4 August 1915, that they were to leave immediately for Urfa, Dr. Nshan Nahigian refused to obey. He demanded that all the prisoners be allowed to leave by day, "when they could be seen by one and all," or, if they were to be killed, that they be hanged in public. The prisoners had gleaned at least some information about the fate of the Armenian population by this time and were aware that transfer to Urfa meant death. Rather than let their executioners do with them as they pleased, the political elite of Harput-Mezreh chose to set the prison on fire and die in the flames.[131]

The few Armenians still present in the region were hiding in various places, such as on the plain or in abandoned homes, or else lived in the hospital or the American consulate. In the case of the hospital, these were doctors or nurses looking after soldiers sent back from the front and, in the case of the consulate, relatives of murdered American citizens,[132] or diplomats such as the British vice-consul of Dyarbekir, Thomas Mgrdichian, and his family.[133]

The 500 boys between four and eight, who had been rounded up in the countryside or the city's deserted neighborhoods in July after the deportations[134] and placed in what the authorities called "orphanages," had in fact been crammed into abandoned houses in Mezreh and left without food and water. In three days, 200 of them perished. The missionaries, Atkinson notes, were not allowed to visit these "institutions." The odor of the children's rotting corpses led to protests from the Turkish population, which demanded that the authorities bring this experiment to an end. The surviving children were ultimately deported to the southwest on 22 October. Those who did not die on the road were thrown into the Euphrates at Izoli, a short distance from Malatia.[135]

The Villages of the *Kaza* of Kharpert

We do not have information on what happened in every village on the plain of Kharpert in 1915. However, the existing documentation suggests that the same procedure was followed in all of them. Men between 30 and 80 years old were mobilized and sent to the front in fall 1914. Some of those between 35 and 40 had avoided the draft by paying the *bedel*, while the rest were used to transport military supplies. In early April, adolescents between 15 and 17 were also mobilized and assigned to transport units or labor battalions. Early in May, systematic searches were carried out in the villages; the leading men were arrested and tortured by the army or squadrons of *çetes*. In June, the remaining men were rounded up and interned in the Red Konak in Mezreh or murdered in isolated areas close to their villages. This was what happened at Içme and Habusi. On 26 June, several women from these localities arrived in Mezreh and reported that their husbands and brothers had been massacred in the mountains at an hour's distance from the two villages.[136]

As we have said, Johannes Ehmann, the head of the German mission in Mezreh, repeatedly helped confiscate arms in the villages of the plain of Kharpert, such as Pazmashen, Korpe, Khulakiugh, and so on. The German pastor, accompanied by the *çete* leader Pulutlı Halil and a few government officials, had there sworn on the Bible that the villagers would be spared if they surrendered their weapons. They complied, only to be arrested and killed.[137] The sole act of resistance we know of took place at Morenig, where a dozen adolescents barricaded themselves in the church and fought back until they were all killed – but not before inflicting a few casualties on the "gendarmes" who had come to arrest the village men.[138]

We owe the fullest account we have to a naturalized American citizen, Krikor Yeghoyan, from the village of Khuylu, which had 240 Armenian households in 1915 (1,201 people) and 10 Turkish households. Located two hours south of Mezreh, the village was well known for its tanners and its apostolic school, whose operating costs were paid out of income from a fund established by emigrants who had settled in the United States.[139]

During the general mobilization, 23 men in Khuylu paid the *bedel* and 36 others were mobilized. Of these, some were sent to the front while others were sent to the city. In April 1915, 34 adolescents and older men were also conscripted and assigned to carry out military transports to Mush, along with 260 other villagers from the plain, including one Turk. They were gradually eliminated as they returned to Mush by way of Bitlis and Dyarbekir. The 65 men who were not killed en route were subsequently shot on the road to Harput, with the exception of a 65-year-old-old man and two 15-year-old boys. These three survivors were apprehended and deported several weeks later, together with all the other men of Khuylu.[140]

Early in May, 85 soldiers and a dozen gendarmes under the command of Zunguldağli Haydar surrounded the village of Khuylu. The gendarmes conducted house searches, looking for arms. The village notables were tortured, with the worst treatment being reserved for the village priest. Next came the remaining men, who were taken to the Red Konak. Our eyewitness was able to hide for a time in the German orphanage, until Ehmann found out he was there and ordered him to quit the premises. However, the brief interlude that followed the mid-April proclamation of the imperial "pardon" for Catholics and Protestants provided him with an opportunity to leave the city and, with help from Kurds, make his way to Dersim.

On 16 July, the women and children of Khuylu were supposedly deported to Urfa. In fact, the *çetes* escorting them slaughtered them with axes in a gorge near the village of Kürdemlik shortly after they were deported.[141]

Piranian, who fled to a village northwest of Lake Göljük, passed through the deserted village of Yegheki on 16 July and later through a devastated Ertmneg, which had been emptied of its population. There he encountered an old woman who lay dying. At her side were three children between the ages of four and eight, naked and with swollen bellies.[142]

The Fate of the Worker-Soldiers of the Amele Taburis of the Vilayet of Mamuret ul-Aziz

According to an Armenian source, some 15,000 Armenian conscripts from the vilayet of Mamuret ul-Aziz were either sent to the Caucasian front in fall 1914 or assigned to logistical tasks in their native region.[143] In early April, 7,000 of them were gradually disarmed and brought back to the vilayet under guard to be put in *amele taburis*.[144]

The fate of these men depended on the military authorities; it was independent of the civil population. One man who played a major role in determining it was Brigadier General Süleyman Faik Pasha, the commander of the Eleventh Army Corps, which had been based in Mezreh since 8 August 1914. Appointed to his post in May 1915, this Bosnian, a Harbiye graduate, had also served as interim vali in Sabit Bey's absence, both while Sabit was on a mission to Dersim early in August 1915 and that November when Sabit took part in a meeting of the valis of the eastern provinces in Erzerum.

From the documents gathered during the pretrial investigation of those responsible for the massacres in Mamuret ul-Aziz, it appears that all military matters were under the direct supervision of Süleyman Faik and that he "could not deny that he had ordered the execution of seven thousand Armenian conscripts."[145] In May 1915, shortly after Faik assumed his functions in Mezreh, he ordered his subordinates to draw up a list of all Armenian soldiers, irrespective of their rank, who were serving in the various regiments and military formations in the vilayet. He also mobilized all the Armenians who had not yet been mustered because they were not of draftable age – that is, males between 16 and 18 and between 55 and 60 – and assigned them to *amele taburis*.[146] According to survivors from these labor battalions, the main units of worker-soldiers were based in Habusi, Hoghe, and Alishami, on the road to Palu.[147] Piranian, a former teacher at Euphrates College, together with three Turkish officers, was charged with drawing up the plans for the construction work to be carried out at Hoghe.[148] He joined his labor battalion, comprising about 2,000 men, on 26 May, accompanied by three young men from Mezreh. There were no barracks in this district, despite an office responsible for keeping track of the lists of conscripts having been established in Hoghe under the command of a Turkish officer, Huseynıklı Hüseyin. The worker-soldiers of the three battalions therefore lodged wherever they could. Piranian notes that they were totally isolated at the time and had no idea about what was happening in the city; they did not even know that the Armenian notables had been arrested there. He adds that one of the *amele taburi* officers, Garabed Kasoyan, was Armenian.[149]

On 11 June at dawn – we continue to follow Piranian's account – the battalion in Hoghe was surrounded by a group of cavalrymen commanded by Çerkez Kâzım. It was, however, only on Monday, 14 June that the worker-soldiers were taken under guard to a field, where they were joined by the battalions from Habusi and Alishami.[150] Çerkez Kâzım, who had a list of these worker-soldiers, escorted them, guarded by 200 infantrymen and 40 cavalrymen, to the Red Konak, into which all 3,000 of them were crammed.[151]

Information gathered during the pretrial investigation of the criminals of Mamuret ul-Aziz indicates that Süleyman Faik Pasha personally passed these 3,000 men in review in front of the Red Konak, his official residence. He told them that, as a "friend of the Armenians," he was going to send them "to a good place."[152] While waiting to be sent to this "good place," the men were left without food or drink for 30 hours. Every day, around a hundred corpses were piled into garbage trucks, taken to the outskirts of the city, and burned. Piranian observes that some 50 men were tortured nightly, often with big tongs that were used to pull off toes, fingers, and strips of flesh. Red-hot irons were used to smash skulls or run through abdomens, and saws were used to open skulls or amputate limbs. Axes were put to many different uses.[153]

As we have already seen,[154] these 3,000 men were put on the road to Dyarbekir on 18 June, and then slain. The indictment for the Mamuret ul-Aziz trial spells out that all the battalions of worker-soldiers sent to Urfa "to help build the railroad" were in fact dispatched in separate groups and put to death in the defile of Deve Boynu or a place known as Güğen Boğazi, a few minutes' distance from Maden. They were killed either by their guards or by the *çetes* stationed there for the purpose.[155]

An encrypted telegram that was sent by Süleyman Faik to the commander of the Third Army at Tortum and later unearthed by the court-martial provides a rather remarkable summary of the practices of the Ottoman military elite. It is worth citing *in extenso*:

> I have the honor to provide you with the following information, taken from a report by the agent responsible for the convoy of the battalion of workers put at the vilayet's disposal. This battalion, which was en route to Dyarbekir, reached Maden without incident. After it left Maden, near the place known as Güğen Boğazi, Armenian bands suddenly loomed up and opened fire from both sides, interfering with the orderly advance of the convoy. The workers of the battalion all deserted in order to join the bands. Since they refused to obey the order to "halt," arms were used against them and the bands. It proved impossible to stop a large number of the members of the battalion and the bands, despite the efforts of the contingent responsible for guarding the convoy as well as the reinforcements dispatched by the local authorities, for the fugitives were aided by the rugged terrain. However, detachments continued to pursue them. In the mêlée, one soldier disappeared, three weapons were destroyed and the sheath of a sword was broken. The agent escorting the convoy saw no point in remaining in the area and returned home.[156]

Taking this (rare) document as his starting point, the presiding judge at the court-martial, Nemrud Kürd Mustafa Pasha, cross-examined Süleyman Faik. He asked him in particular how, if the brigands were armed, the escort managed to kill all these men while sustaining no losses itself.[157] This odd way of informing one's commander-in-chief that a battalion had been exterminated could not, of course, fool a general in the Ottoman army.

The pretrial investigation file also reveals the role played by Haşim Beyzâde Mehmed, the leader of a squadron of *çetes* based at an hour's distance from Malatia, in the 11 June 1915 murder of 1,200 Armenian worker-soldiers in Izoli. Initially locked up in the mosque of the village of Pirot, the Armenians were led from it in small groups and brought down to the Euphrates, where they were killed and thrown into the river. These killings apparently took place on orders from Sabit Bey and the *mutesarif* of Malatia, Nabi Bey.[158] This accusation must, however, be taken with a grain of salt. It is quite possible that the person who made it, a soldier, wished to impute these crimes to the civilian authorities without knowing how much real power they had over the military units. The possibility that Sabit assumed the role of intermediary can by no means be ruled out, but the *mutesarif* of Malatia certainly did not. He was dismissed early in May 1915 and replaced by Reşid Bey on 20 June, when the veritable bloodbath began in the region of Malatia.[159]

The Convoys of Deportees in the Areas North of Harput

So far, we have rarely had occasion to consider descriptions in non-Armenian sources of the passage of convoys of deportees that had been on the road for weeks. Thanks to eyewitness accounts left by the American missionaries and consul in Harput, we have such descriptions for the vilayet of Mamuret ul-Aziz.

The composition of the caravans coming from the north, which had set out in mid-May, had obviously changed by the time they arrived in the plain of Mezreh. These caravans had, as a general rule, been formed anew out of what was left of various groups decimated en route. The first convoy from the north to arrive in Harput, on 2 July, was made up of 8,000 deportees from Erzerum and Erzincan. They had been on the road for about six weeks, having set out in different convoys and regrouped on the way. There were no males among them except for very young boys.[160] The groups that followed at ever-closer intervals, such as the convoy of 3,000 people that arrived on 9 July, also came from Ordu, Kirason, Trebizond, Kığı,

Erzincan, and Erzerum. The deportees remained in the Harput area for an average of two days, in a place on the outskirts of Mezreh known as the "Four Fountains."[161] The missionaries came to see them here, offering what comfort they could. But these stops also provided certain Turks from Mezreh with an opportunity to acquire women for their harems.[162] Leslie Davis, who paid several visits to the camp at Four Fountains, gives a graphic description of the deportees' condition: in rags, unable to wash or change their clothes, and malnourished, "to watch them one could hardly believe," he says, "that these people were human beings."[163] Hundreds of people on their last legs died in this improvised camp. The corpses were buried in a mass grave when they were not simply abandoned. The able-bodied were set marching again. Davis notes that the method was fool-proof, making it possible "to dispose of all of them in a comparatively short time."[164] A few people nonetheless escaped the common lot thanks to the missionaries who admitted them to the American hospital or to the German orphanage in Mezreh. Some of the women even succeeded in taking up residence in one of the city's abandoned houses by "marrying" an officer, such as Siranush Hoghgroghian, who was 13 years old and already pregnant.[165]

As these convoys from the north left Mezreh, they were directed toward one of two killing fields. One, as we have seen, lay eight hours southwest of Malatia, in the gorges outside Fırıncılar, near Kahta. Here squadrons of *çetes*, led by two Kurdish chieftains of the Reşvan tribe, Zeynel Bey and Haci Bedri Ağa, attended to business under the supervision of Haci Baloşzâde Mehmed Nuri Bey, a parliamentary deputy from Dersim, and his brother Ali Pasha.[166] The other killing field was made up of the many rocky little valleys that sloped down to Lake Göljük (present-day Hazar Gölü), which lay some 30 miles southeast of Harput, a short distance from the road to Dyarbekir.

The Slaughterhouse at Göljük

After Nazaret Piranian found sanctuary in Havtasar, a Kurdish village located on the heights overlooking the northwest shore of Lake Göljük, he learned from the Kurd who had given him refuge, Ğanli Cemo, that on that very morning – shortly after Ramadan, which in 1915 came to an end on 12 August – four Turkish officers had arrived in the valley and asked to meet the *ağas* of the Kurdish villages in the area. Accompanied by 200 *çetes*, they had conducted a caravan of about 3,000 deportees from Trebizond, Erzerum, and Erzincan to the lakeshore, and were now inviting the villagers to help them "finish" their work. The Kurdish villagers responded to the invitation in family groups, attacking the convoy with axes and knives. After the slaughter was over, Piranian notes, a very few children were brought back to the village. Suffering from deep physical and psychological wounds, all of them died in less than a week. A few days later, when Piranian left his refuge and went down to the shores of Lake Göljük, he discovered a huge mass grave: the bodies of these 3,000 deportees filled one of the little valleys that descended toward the lake to half its height.[167] This firsthand testimony does not, however, do justice to the extent of the crimes committed near the lake. Here, the narrative of Consul Davis provides us with information not available elsewhere. On 24 September 1915, Davis decided to inspect the area around the mountain lake on horseback after a Turk informed him that it was strewn with corpses.[168] Setting out at four o'clock in the morning so as not to be seen, the consul and his Turkish guide rode for four hours toward Kurdemlik, discovering hundreds of half-buried bodies as they went. Arms or legs stuck out of the ground, sometimes devoured by animals; some bodies had been burnt "in order to find any gold which the people may have swallowed."[169] Upon reaching the lake, the consul decided to hug the cliffs on its northwestern shore, which was broken up by "deep valleys." It seems that the method most often used by the *çetes* consisted in throwing the deportees from the towering cliffs down into the steep valleys, veritable traps from which there was no exit apart from the lake itself. On this first leg of his tour, Davis observed two valleys filled with about 1,000 bodies, in the first case, and 1,500 in the other. He saw a good many more that were not as full, but could not approach them for a long time because of the unbearable odor.[170]

The information that the consul gleaned from local Kurds confirmed that the çete "gendarmes" had delegated the task of liquidating the deportees to the Kurdish villagers living in the area. In exchange for a lump sum that varied with the size of the convoy, the "gendarmes" turned the convoy over to the Kurds, who in turn made their money from their victims. Davis also notes that the bodies he saw were naked, indicating that the victims were probably stripped before being killed. He even suggests that this method was applied in all the eastern provinces. He also remarks that practically none of the victims had been shot to death.[171]

Returning to Mezreh by way of Keghvank, southwest of Göljük, Davis discovered the bodies of several thousand half-buried victims in another mass grave; they were already skeletons. His assumption was that these were the remains of the men of Harput and the surrounding area who had been sent to their deaths before the big convoys of women and children set out.[172]

During his second trip to the area, undertaken with Dr. Atkinson on 24 October, the American consul decided to explore the eastern lakeshore. In the vicinity of the village of Göljük he saw the rotting bodies of hundreds of people who had been massacred more recently. Riding across the highlands, he discovered a little valley filled with the bodies of hundreds of killed women and children, their corpses bearing the mark of fresh bayonet wounds. Leaving the southern lakeshore behind, Davis and Atkinson reached a valley located at the lake's northwestern tip, in which they discovered "more dead bodies than [Davis] had seen in any other place on either trip." The two men estimated that 2,000 bodies littered these several acres of land. The papers found on them indicated that the victims were from Erzerum and other regions. Davis concludes the account of his second trip with the estimate that the remains of 10,000 massacred Armenians lay in the mass graves around Lake Göljük: "Few localities could be better suited to the fiendish purposes of the Turks in their plan to exterminate the Armenian population than this peaceful lake in the interior of Asiatic Turkey ... far removed from the sight of civilized man."[173]

It is worth pausing over one more eyewitness account, that of a *protégés francs* from Smyrna, S. Padova, who had been expelled from Bitlis by Vali Rahmi Bey along with A. Amado and D. Arditti. On 17 September 1915, these three men witnessed the massacre of a caravan of 3,000 Armenians on the shores of Lake Göljük. They had left Harput for Bitlis on 15 September, arriving at the lake's southern shore after a journey on which they stumbled upon corpses "almost every step of the way." They encountered the caravan on the lakeshore. Stationed on the mountains dominating the lake, bands of Kurds opened fire on the deportees and then encircled the convoy. "It was simply an attack by ferocious animals," Padova writes, "on a defenseless flock." The deportees were dispatched with axes while the "gendarmes" escorting the convoy stood by and watched. In half an hour, these 3,000 people had been "drowned in a pool of blood." The Kurdish women then ran down the mountainsides and proceeded to strip the bodies.[174]

Final Measures to Eradicate the Armenians

In an 18 September 1915 cable addressed to the interior minister, Sabit Bey drew up the first balance sheet of the operations conducted in his region. He estimated the number of deported Armenians at 51,000; 4,000, he thought, were still hiding in the villages.[175] From mid-August to mid-November, the authorities focused their efforts on the Armenians who had in one way or another escaped the deportations. To find these fugitives and flush them out of their hiding places, however, Vali Sabit needed to restore a climate of relative confidence. Thus, less than a month after the departure of the last convoys of deportees, on 18 August, the town crier announced that the Protestants – virtually all of whom had already been deported – were now free to remain in their homes.[176] Davis notes that on two occasions, notably on 26 September, the authorities had announcements made to the effect that there would be no further deportations.[177] And indeed, no noteworthy initiatives were taken for two weeks, although the police did stage a raid on the American hospital in order to verify that no "non-authorized Armenians" were to be found there.[178] A number of villages on the plain, such as Habusi, were now inhabited by Çerkez, Turks, and Kurds from the eastern provinces, but other villages, such as Hoghe, near Harput, were still occupied by Armenians.[179]

On 4, 5, and 6 November, however, the deportees from Trebizond, Erzerum, and Ordu who had found refuge in Harput's Upper Quarter – Armenians and Syriacs from the city and people who had returned to the villages of the plain – were rounded up in a raid and assembled in the police station.[180] On 4 November, the American hospital was also surrounded by troops and the United States consulate was put under surveillance. With the exception of a few doctors, the Armenians working there were women taking care of Turkish soldiers, such as the schoolteacher Anna, a widowed mother of three who had also adopted the six children of her deceased sisters. At half past one in the morning, the police burst into the hospital and demanded that all the men and boys present be turned over to them. A mother gave her eldest daughter to a gendarme so that he would help her and her other children remain in the city.[181] On 8 November, the 435 people who had been rounded up over the past few days were finally deported.[182] Davis, for his part, estimates that 1,000 to 2,000 Armenians were led off and killed in "isolated valleys" by "gendarmes" early in November.[183]

These events occurred on the orders of General Süleyman Faik, the commander of the Eleventh Army Corps and acting vali[184] in the absence of Sabit, who had left for Erzerum on 19 October.[185] Together with the vali of Erzerum, Tahsin, the vali of Sıvas, Muammer, and the vali of Trebizond, Cemal Azmi, Sabit was taking part in a meeting organized by Kâmil Pasha. According to an Armenian survivor, Mihran Zakarian, the discussions at this meeting turned, notably, on the measures to be taken to ensure that confiscated assets become state property.[186] The inadequacy of our sources about this meeting does not allow us to substantiate Zakarian's claim, but given the fact that it was held after the first phase of the eradication of the Armenians had come to an end, it is likely that its purpose was to ascertain the results of the operations and perhaps decide what needed to be done to finish the job. Thus, the October meeting would have been a kind of follow-up to the one organized in Erzincan in late July.[187] At any rate, such is the impression created by two telegrams brought to light by the Istanbul commission of inquiry in 1919. The first, dated 3 November, apparently refers to the conscripts, considered "deserters," who had managed to elude the fate reserved for worker-soldiers:

> We understand that, where you are, scattered here and there, Armenian males are living with Armenian females without guardians who have arrived from various places. This situation is likely to lead to disorder: in one or two days, individuals of this kind must be rounded up and sent off, under escort, by way of the road to Dyarbekir.[188]

This first telegram can, however, also be interpreted as an order to deport Harput/Mezreh's remaining Armenians. That, in any event, is how General Faik interpreted it, who answered Sabit the same day with:

> A search group has been created and assigned the task of flushing out Armenians in hiding, whether they are from the city or elsewhere; one convoy was recently

dispatched. In future, in accordance with Your Excellency's orders, we shall accelerate operations and bring this situation to an end.[189]

Other documents that bear on the *sancak* of Malatia are much more explicit. These clearly indicate that, "in conformity with the most recent orders received, not a single local [Armenian] has been left behind. Similarly, not a single person who has come from elsewhere has been allowed to remain."[190]

In light of the above, we are inclined to think that the participants in the Erzerum meeting decided, among other things, to liquidate the last Armenians in the eastern provinces. After the early November deportations of the 1,000 Armenians who had been left in Mezreh and Harput, there remained only 150 girls in the custody of American missionaries,[191] 300 to 500 children in Mezreh's German orphanage,[192] and a few orphans, who roamed the streets and occasionally came to the mission in search of a bit of bread – the sole survivors of the group that had been taken from Mezreh's Turkish orphanage on 22 October and thrown into the river at Izoli.[193]

With the departure of a number of American missionaries on 15 November, the authorities stepped up their harassment, demanding that the Americans hand over the girls in their institution.[194] As for the wards of the German orphanage, its Danish director, Genny Jansen, informs us that, in January 1916, the authorities officially requested that Reverend Ehmann hand the children over to them, so that they could "be sent to the places where their parents are." After obtaining "solemn assurances that these children would be delivered to their destination safe and sound," the orphanage's German staff entrusted the 300 boys to the "special agents" come to take them away.[195] Two days later, two of the orphans arrived at the German orphanage "covered with sweat from running so long" and informed their former protectors that "their comrades [were] being burned alive" at two hours' distance from Mezreh. Jansen confesses that she did not believe a word of this "very incredible story" at first, but that, when she went the next day with the German nuns to the place that the orphans had described, she saw a "still smoldering black heap" and the "poor children's charred skeletons."[196] Inexorably, the authorities were eliminating the last traces of an Armenian presence in the region.

The *Kazas* of Keban Maden and Pötürge

We have only scant information about the fate of the 789 Armenians who lived in Keban Maden, the administrative seat of the *kaza* of the same name, or in the villages of Argovan and Ashvan;[197] there is no record of survivors. An official report, probably dating from September 1915, tersely indicates that 308 Armenians were deported from the *kaza* of Keban Maden.[198] It would seem to follow that more than 400 people were allowed to remain in the *kaza* or, more likely, were put to death in their native villages under the supervision of the *kaymakam*, Tevfik Bey, who occupied his post from 2 May to 1 July 1915.

In the *kaza* of Tepürke/Pötürge, a mountain district, all 679 Armenians were concentrated in the village of Vartenig.[199] According to official statistics, 622 were deported in summer 1915.[200] These villagers were put on the road in a single convoy at the request of the *kaymakam*, Rüşdi Bey, who was probably appointed to his post in order to carry out this mission, having held it only from 8 July to 31 October 1915. Given the proximity of these districts to the much more heavily populated *kazas* of Arapkir and Eğin, it seems reasonable to suppose that their Armenian inhabitants received a similar treatment to that reserved for those in more populous districts.

The *Kaza* of Arapkir

In this agricultural *kaza* on the banks of the Euphrates, the Armenians were concentrated in the administrative seat, Arapkir, which had a population of 9,000 Armenians and 7,000

Turks. There were also four Armenian villages in the *kaza*: Ambrga (pop. 250), near Arapkir; Shepig (pop. 468); Vank (pop. 129); and Antshnti (pop. 510).[201] As everywhere else in these eastern provinces, trade and the crafts, especially silk-weaving, were in Armenian hands, the countryside was populated mainly by sedentary Kurdish peasants, and the government and administration were a Turkish monopoly. Around 4,000 Armenians from Arapkir had emigrated to America and Egypt after the 1895 massacres, but maintained close ties to their native land.[202]

During the general mobilization, 2,300 of the 3,000 men of draftable age in Arapkir left the *kaza* to serve in the Ottoman army.[203] Complaints lodged by the Armenians indicate that all the war requisitions were made to their detriment, whereas the handful of affluent Turks in the *kaza* were not affected.[204] Over the winter, gendarmes and policemen regularly visited Armenian homes looking for deserters, and profited from the occasion by helping themselves to whatever they found. According to Khachig Kardashian, Armenian business-men who had avoided the draft by paying the *bedel* were arrested on 26 April 1915. The next day, the town crier announced that people had five days to turn over the weapons stashed in their homes. Kardashian also informs us that in the same period, rumors began to circulate to the effect that Armenians and Kurds had massacred Turks.[205] Kalust Kaloyan notes, for his part, that the authorities did not have the manpower they needed to carry out house searches, so groups of *çetes* were formed, recruited from the most affluent Turkish families, to deal with "the Armenian business." They were reinforced by gendarmes, policemen, old soldiers, and the notables from nearby villages.[206] These *çetes* began to scour the different neighborhoods and conduct searches of people's homes, which were literally sacked in the process. Every night, some of them also tortured the men, who had been imprisoned in accordance with the usual procedures. The search for arms provided a pretext for blackmail-ing the inhabitants, who sometimes preferred to pay a bribe so that their homes would not be demolished.[207] Yet it was not until 19 June that 30 of the men who had been detained were taken from the prison in chains and escorted beyond the city limits. Officially, they were to be transferred to Mamuret ul-Aziz, in compliance with a request from the vali.[208] Only later did the inhabitants of Arapkir learn that this convoy was led to the banks of the Euphrates, piled onto a raft, and drowned in the middle of the river.[209]

Two days later, on 21 June, a second group of 300 men, also in chains, was supposedly dispatched to Malatia, but in fact disappeared in the waters of the Euphrates. The last two convoys, each containing 250 men, set out on 23 and 24 June and met the same fate as the previous two.[210] In other words, by this time there was hardly a man between 18 and 45 in Arapkir. The last men to be arrested, the Catholic priest Reverend Krashian, the auxiliary primate Father Goriun, and the municipal physician Dr. Hagop Aprahamian, a native of Kütahya and the only civilian doctor in the city, were deported in the second convoy.[211] The population was unaware of the fate these men suffered, but it witnessed the arrival, around 25 June, of a column of deportees from Erzincan, whose condition left little room for doubt about what was to come.[212]

On Sunday, 27 June, a town crier announced that the Armenians of Arapkir were to be transferred to Urfa, and that they had one week to sell their property and make prepara-tions for the journey. The sales took place on the square in front of the sub-prefecture, under surveillance by government officials, while the militia patrolled the town's neighborhoods to prevent looting.[213] A handful of older men made one last effort to save the Armenians of Arapkir from being deported: they wrote a telegram in which they offered to turn over all their assets and deeds to the government, entreating it to allow them to remain in their homes in exchange. But the *kaymakam* refused to send the telegram.[214]

The sole convoy from Arapkir, comprising more than 7,000 people, 250 of them adult males, set out on 5 July 1915 under the surveillance of approximately 150 *çetes* and gendarmes.[215] The authorities brought it to a halt some five hours from the city and informed the deportees that they could return to their homes if they agreed to convert to Islam. The police were already drawing up a list of families and their decisions when a counter-order arrived: the leaders of Arapkir's Ittihadist club found this solution unacceptable. A CUP inspector even arrived from Mezreh – probably Resneli Nâzim – to resolve the problem. It seems that the mufti had hard words for the Ittihadists and their project, but it made no difference: the deportation order was confirmed.[216] The very day the deportees set out, their houses and stores were put under seal. Members of the most affluent families, notably S. Chaghatsbanian, were carefully searched and then tortured by the police and certain members of the local Ittihad club in order to bring them to confess where they had hidden their cash reserves and valuables.[217]

After the deportees had been on the road for four days, the captain of the gendarmerie who was in command of their escort demanded 8,000 Turkish pounds in gold from them, threatening to abandon the men to the Kurds if they did not produce the money without delay. Jewelry as well as gold and silver coins were collected and handed over. On the sixth day, when the convoy reached the Euphrates, halfway to Malatia, the deportees discovered the bodies of Armenians from previous caravans on the riverbanks.[218] On the seventh day, the 250 men in the caravan, as well as the boys over 11, were separated from the rest of the caravan and led down to the Euphrates by the entire escort. The rest of the caravan continued on its way, guarded by Kurds, until it reached Kırk Göz ("Forty Arches") Bridge,[219] which spanned the Tohma Çay, a northern tributary of the Euphrates. This was one of the centers of destruction under the control of the *sevkiyat memuri* (director of the deportation). Here the *çetes*, sometimes wearing the uniform of the gendarmerie, transported groups of deportees to the other bank of the river. Most of the caravans that set out from the Black Sea coast or the vilayets of Angora and Sıvas passed through this point. Hundreds of half-buried bodies could be seen on the banks of the Tohma Çay. On the heights, in front of the guard post, several thousand deportees were resting, almost all of them women and children. This was a convoy of city-dwellers from Sıvas that had been on the road for 30 days.[220] The escort arrived somewhat late and took up its posts around the encampment as it did every evening, "so that the Kurds would not throw themselves" on the deportees. At dawn, it was announced that the "men" were to rejoin the group. This in fact refered to a group of about 30 boys aged 12 to 16 who had been led away the day before with adults, supposedly for transfer to Harput by boat. A gendarme revealed a little later that they had been shot and thrown into the river.[221]

On the eighth day, when the convoy from Arapkir was fewer than four hours away from Malatia, the guards directed the deportees southward on a route circumventing the city. A simulated Kurdish attack was staged that night, enabling the officers of the escort to demand additional "recompense" from the deportees for the protection they were providing. On the tenth and eleventh days the caravan was once again set marching east, toward the Euphrates. It had already lost a quarter of its members by the time it reached the village of Fırıncilar, around three hours southeast of Malatia, where convoys of Armenians from Tokat, Amasia, Agn, Samsun, Trebizond, and Sıvas had recently arrived, making an immense throng.[222]

The site was strewn with rotting corpses that gave off a terrible stench. An elderly Turkish man explained to our witness that the worst would come the next day, when he and the rest of his caravan set out on the "death route" that lay on the other side of the peaks of the Malatia Dağlari.[223] Doubtless attracted by the presence of so many caravans, a large number of merchants had set up shop in the village of Fırıncilar, where anything and everything could be found, but at exorbitant prices. Kaloyan also noted that a battalion of the "gendarmerie" was on hand here, along with a *müdir* who regularly received orders by telephone.[224] This was a Special Organization command center, which coordinated the departures of those convoys on the "death route." Our witness observes, moreover, that the "gendarmes" ordered the deportees rather courteously to leave their belongings on the spot, entrusting them to the commission responsible for "military contributions" (*teklif-i habriyye*). He puts the number of deportees camping at the foot of the mountains at between 80,000 and 100,000.[225]

On the twelfth day, 16 July, the authorities ordered the families to turn their daughters under 15 and boys under 10 over to them. The children were to be admitted to an orphanage in Malatia created especially for them. Between 3,000 and 5,000 children were loaded onto carts and taken away. In Kaloyan's opinion, some of them had been rounded up earlier in raids.[226]

One by one, the convoys headed for the gorge located outside Fırıncilar, one of the Teşkilât-ı Mahsusa's main killing fields. The site was under the supervision of Haci Baloşzâde Mehmed Nuri Bey, the parliamentary deputy from Dersim, and his brother Ali Pasha. They had two Kurdish chieftains of the Reşvan tribe, Zeynel Bey and Haci Bedri Ağa, under their command, with the Kurds' squadrons of *çetes*.[227]

Kardashian, one of the 17 worker-soldiers in the Arapkir barracks who had been allowed to remain there after the deportation of the Armenians thanks to the well-disposed commanding officer, Hüseyin, saw successive convoys of deportees from the provinces of Erzerum and Trabizond trekking through Arapkir. He also informs us that this old officer refused to shake down these convoys the way "the other Turks" did.[228] As they passed through Arapkir, the convoys left victims behind, and a certain number of children who were abandoned to their fate as well. Kardashian points out that the local authorities had therefore decided to create an "orphanage" that was rather more like a "slaughterhouse for children." Every day during the few weeks of its existence, some 50 corpses were removed from it. After it was closed, the surviving children were ostensibly sent to the orphanage in Malatia, but in fact were taken to Kırk Göz Bridge and thrown into the Tohma.[229] But what surprised cadet Kardashian the most was the convoy from Erzerum, which arrived in carts, was equipped with tents, and had an escort of well-armed gendarmes. These deportees, he thought to himself, had obviously been well protected en route; they constituted an odd exception in the midst of the flood of desolation that poured through Arapkir.[230]

Kardashian further observes that each time a convoy passed through Arapkir, the authorities took the trouble to register all those who had permission to settle there in order to make good for the absence of craftsmen, which was making itself felt after the deportation of the town's Armenian inhabitants. The residence permits issued to them, however, were valid for only a few weeks – such craftsmen were regularly sent off to "Urfa."[231] Our witness also reports rumors, making the rounds in Arapkir toward the end of the summer, to the effect that "the government deported the Armenians, but the Kurds massacred them on the way." The rumor is supposed to have irritated the Kurds and made them more hostile toward the Armenians seeking refuge with them.[232]

The campaign to eliminate the Armenians from the *kaza* of Arapkir was, without a doubt, organized by the *kaymakam*, Hilmi Bey, who was appointed on 2 March 1915 (and transferred elsewhere on 19 December of the same year). He was seconded by a number of government officials, notably Kadri Bey, the commander of the gendarmerie; Khorşid Bey, the police chief; Mehmed Effendi, *nufus memuri* (administrator of the registry office); Reşid Bey, the head of the telegraph office; and Bekir Effendi, the director of the post office.[233] But we have also seen that the Ittihadist leaders in the provincial town, who had been recruited from the ranks of the local notables – Riza Effendi, a lawyer; Nagib Hamdi Effendi, a landowner; Şakir Bey, the former head of the telegraph office; and Molla Ahmedzâde Tevfik Effendi, a clergyman – exercised considerable if not decisive influence.[234] These men were, at the very least, associated with the decision-making process, no doubt in order to enlist the Turkish population's support for the policies of the Young Turk government. Among the chief perpetrators of the crimes against the Armenians, the best known are Derebeyoğlu

Ali Effendi, Çuşi Ağasi Mustafa, Şeirli Mehmed Bey, Paşekizâde Lutfi Bey, Kuçubeyzâde Mehmed Bey, Kuçubeyzâde Tevfik Bey, Kuçubeyzâde Haci Bey, Paracuklı Haci Mehmed Effendi, Hiranlı Bekir, Şotiguli Mustafa Effendi, and several "policemen" – Selamlizâde Şerif Ağa, Denizli Fazlı, Bekir, a native of Malatia, Osman, Mehmed, Şaban, Ethem, and Mehmed, from Şeyhler.[235] According to the above-mentioned undated fall 1915 report to the minister of the interior, 8,545 Armenians were deported from Arapkir.[236]

The *Kaza* of Eğin/Agn

Traversed from one end to the other by the Euphrates, the *kaza* of Eğin/Agn boasted 25 Armenian towns and villages in 1914, with a total Armenian population of 16,741. The administrative seat of the *kaza*, known as Agn in Armenian and rebaptized Eğin, had a mixed population of 7,720 Armenians and approximately 6,000 Turks.[237] With an economy based on wine-growing and tanning, this mountain district, in which the villages were for the most part located in the highlands dominating the Euphrates, suffered from a shortage of arable land and had for centuries been sending emigrants elsewhere. Thus, many of the Armenians from Agn could be found among the prominent bankers and jewelers of the Ottoman capital, but also among high-ranking government officials; the last famous example was Gabriel Noradounghian, foreign minister from 1912 to 1913 in the last liberal Ottoman government.

The first arrests in the *kaza* were made on 22 April 1915, for no apparent reason. The same day, the town crier announced that arms had to be surrendered to the authorities. This order was followed by systematic house searches and new arrests.[238] According to our main witness, 248 people were arrested in the course of 24 hours in Agn alone. Similar events occurred in the *kaza*'s villages around the same time.[239] After this first phase of violence, the authorities unmistakably inaugurated the second stage of their plan on 1 June, when they arrested the auxiliary prelate, Father Bedros Karian, and another 30 of the town's leading citizens, including the *kaza*'s tax collector, Srabion Papazian, a member of the district council; Margos Narlian, the head of the Armenian orphanage; Mardiros Semerjian; and also B. and H. Diradurian, Gh. Vartabedian, B. Khanarian, K. Ardzruni, Avedis Palushian, Avedis Gananian, and Dr. Sahag Cholakian. Those arrested were promptly sent off to Keban Maden with 90 other men, loaded onto a raft, and drowned in the Euphrates.[240] Agn, however, knew nothing about what had become of them.

The town crier's 7 June announcement, that the draft was being extended to include males between 16 and 18 and between 46 and 60, suggests that the authorities had devised a new stratagem to eliminate the men in the *kaza*. Thus, 400 men were "mobilized" only to be taken under guard to three places on the banks of the Euphrates, tied together in groups of five, and thrown into the river. Since there had already been a conscription campaign the year before, this left virtually no adult males in Agn aside from a few old men.[241]

The deportation order was issued late in June. The authorities announced, however, that they were willing to allow those families who agreed to convert to Islam to remain in their homes. About 5 per cent of the population succeeded in avoiding deportation in this way.[242]

Three convoys were deported. The first included the population of the villages, the second was made up of people from the outskirts of Agn and one of the town's neighborhoods, and the third and last, dispatched on 5 July under the command of Halil Çavuş and with an escort of 30 "gendarmes,"[243] comprised the rest of Agn's Armenian population – that is, around 7,700 people.[244] All the houses and shops in the bazaar were put under seal as soon as the convoys had set out.

Our principal witness, a 17-year-old youth by the name of Levon Boghosian, left Agn with the last convoy, the fate of which he would share until the deportees reached Fırıncilar, where the 400 survivors from his group arrived after 27 days – that is, around 1 August

1915.[245] Boghosian's account allows us to observe the way the caravan was decimated day after day and the way the deportees were methodically stripped of their possessions. Thus, he notes that from the very first time the convoy pitched camp, the prettiest young women were abducted, while the families were charged 2,070 Turkish pounds gold by their guards for "protection from the Kurds." One week later, the convoy numbered fewer than one thousand;[246] dehydration, malnutrition, and exhaustion had carried off the youngest and oldest deportees. Suicides were also quite frequent. If the main reason for this was simply despair, many of those who took their own lives were young women, who chose to throw themselves into the Euphrates rather than submit to rape. Mothers also frequently refused to submit to the will of their torturers, killing themselves and their children instead.

Boghosian also observes that a caravan leaving Agn could by the direct route reach the Kırk Göz Bridge across the Tohma Çay in four to five days, whereas his caravan reached it only after a 24-day trek. Thus, it is probable that the escort had been ordered at regular intervals to prolong the deportees' trajectory in order to produce more casualites. Boghosian's description of the transit camp at Kırk Göz also suggests that the area was so crowded with deportees that the authorities were forced to "reroute" the convoys. "A human flood was to be found there," he writes, "consisting of people from all the cities of Turkey: tens of thousands of people, four hundred to five hundred of whom died every day.[247]

Boghosian's description of the camp of Fırıncilar is just as harrowing. He notes in particular that 12-year-old Turkish and Kurdish boys came to the camp to help themselves to girls.[248] It would appear that the extreme violence unleashed by the Young Turk government had swept taboos aside and unleashed behavior that was normally repressed, to the point that these children felt that they could have their way with these girls as the fancy struck them because the girls belonged to a group officially declared to be outside the law.

The government officials implicated in the crimes committed in Agn were, first and foremost, the *kaymakam* Asım Bey (who held his post from 23 July 1913 to 15 October 1915) and the commander of the gendarmerie Abdülkadir Bey, who supervised the departure of all the convoys and the local massacres of the men. Asım and Abdülkadir were backed up by Arnavud Mustafa and Mustafa Bey, two lieutenants in the gendarmerie, and the police chief Hurşid Bey, who organized arrests, torture, and house searches. The local Ittihad club, made up of Nurzâdeoğlu Bekir Çavuş, Musa Receboğlu Musa, Abçuğalı Mustafa, and Dr. Şerif, a member of the vilayet's regional council, distinguished itself by orchestrating the anti-Armenian propaganda campaign, seeing to it that the program of destruction decided upon by the CUP was carried out and setting up the commission responsible for abandoned property, with Tevfik Bey as its president, with Tavtili Yaşar's and Tevfik's father, Ahmed Bey, at his side.[249]

Among those who played especially prominent roles in slaughtering the people of Agn and the surrounding villages were Haci Mehmed Keleşağazâde, Haci Hasanzâde, İbrahim Ağa, Cemal Hasanzâde Osman Ağa, Akraklı Sadik Çavuş, Parakoç Ömer Ağa, Hezinin Kel Ahmed Ağa, Dardağanzâde Halid Ağa, Kürd Ali Ağa, Kel Hacizâde Mehmed Ağa, Kör Haci Ağa, Osman Ağa, Hakkı Ağa, Babaoğlu Ali Ağa, Arslanoğlu Mehmed Ağa, Kürd Osmanoğlu Receb Ağa, Çisenoğlu Mevlud Ağa, Boğoyi Hasanoğlu Mehmed Ağa, Ibooğlu Yaşar Ağa, İsmail Ağaoğlu Memo, and Selo and his three sons.[250] There were only a few Kurdish notables among these criminals. According to the Constantinople Armenian Patriarchate's sources, some 400 Armenian children were being held in Turkish homes in Agn in late 1918. There were an additional 900 Armenian survivors, half of them from the villages of the *kaza*.[251]

Deportations and Massacres in the Sancak of Malatia

The preceding pages have provided some information about the pivotal place that the *sancak* of Malatia occupied in the annihilation of the convoys of Armenian deportees from the four corners of Asia Minor. One can therefore readily imagine that the city of Malatia was itself a major coordination center in the system created by the Young Turk government. Only one foreigner resided in the city, a German pastor by the name of Hans Bauernfeind, the head of an institution for the blind run by the Deutscher Hilfsbund für christliches Liebeswerk im Orient. Bauernfeind would witness the events and record them in his diary.[252] A patriot and partisan of the German-Turkish alliance, he initially took a skeptical view of the evidence, describing the mayor of Malatia as "mad" when the Turkish official explained to him what was really going on beneath the soothing discourse of the authorities. He came to confess, however, that he had "been most horribly duped from first to last." His remarkably precise account allows us to chart the preliminary phase of the genocide, from the second mobilization to the requisitions, and from the arrests of the men to their liquidation, with a wealth of detail only rarely available for other regions.

What did Malatia represent on the eve of the war? It was, to begin with, the biggest city in the vilayet of Mamuret ul-Aziz, with a total population of 35,000 to 40,000 and an Armenian population of 15,000.[253] Although Armenians were a minority, the region, famous for its textiles, dyes, rugs, and gold jewelry, depended mainly on them for its economic development, which was reinforced by the remittances sent back to Malatia by Armenian emigrants to the Unites States. These ceased when the war broke out.[254] Near Malatia, 1,400 Armenians still lived Melitene – or at least what remained of the ancient city – and also in the villages of Kogh Lur (pop. 150), Orduz (pop. 400), and Chermekh (pop. 67). The city of Malatia had been largely spared the massacres of 1895. The Armenians in the rural zones, however, had been all but wiped out.[255]

During the general mobilization, a significant number of Armenians from Malatia were exempted from military service because they paid the *bedel*. A commission responsible for "military contributions" (*teklif-i habriyye*) was immediately created and proceeded to make requisitions that one Armenian source describes as "pillage" of almost exclusively Armenian property.[256] These operations, combined with the rise in the price of food, were partially responsible for the rapid impoverishment of the Armenian population. The harsh conditions imposed on the soldiers and, above all, the typhus epidemic that ravaged the Third Army in February 1915, spawned desertions as well, initially among the Kurdish recruits and then among the Armenians and Turks. An Armenian source claims that there were proportionally more deserters among the Turks but that the Armenians were the first targets of the disciplinary measures: thus, the family homes of two Armenian deserters were burned down and the soldiers went back to their barracks.[257] Shortly thereafter, the Postal Ministry outlawed correspondence in Armenian. Armenian conscripts in the region were disarmed around 19 April.[258] In May, the authorities nevertheless decided to draft men in age groups that had been spared hitherto, notably 18- and 19-year-olds and those between the ages of 46 and 50,[259] and assigned them to *amele taburis* to do roadwork between Malatia and Harput, three hours to the north.[260] The Ottoman Information Bureau also announced that the "Armenian insurgents [had] sabotaged the mountain passes and so hindered the soldiers' advance." The Muslim population clearly seems to have taken these claims for good coin, so that tensions in the city were raised a notch or two.[261]

On 4 May, Bauernfeind wrote, "It would appear that the government has lost all trust in the Armenians."[262] Hovhannes Khanghlarian, an eyewitness to events in Malatia, notes that police searches of Armenian homes were now undertaken with a view to confiscating letters, newspapers, and all printed documents using the Armenian alphabet; owners of such material were suspect, and were arrested and imprisoned.[263] Bauernfeind reports the arrest of a young Protestant woman, Veronika Bonapartian, who was accused of having "Armenian songs that were composed by her pastor and written out in his hand" in her possession.[264] The collective incrimination of the Armenians, observed elsewhere as well, constituted a first phase that was followed, on 20 May, by the town crier's announcement that weapons held in people's homes had to be turned over to the authorities "for the state's self-defense effort."[265] This decree unleashed a second wave of house searches that in turn provided the basis for the arrests of many more men. On 22 May, all Armenian government officials were imprisoned, together with important figures including the Armenian auxiliary primate, members of the district council, leaders of the political parties, and local men of means.[266]

This second phase of the persecutions seems to have gained momentum with the arrival in Malatia of the CUP inspector, Boşnak Resneli Nâzım Bey, who lodged with Haşim Bey, a parliamentary deputy and a rich landowner who lived near the German mission.[267] According to a judge on Malatia's court-martial, Captain Fazıl, the inspector organized a meeting of all the Young Turk leaders in the city at Haşim Bey's house:[268] Talât Bey, a member of the regional council; Haci Çakirdegin Effendi (who would later bury several hundred children alive); Mehmed Bey and Faik Bey, Haşim's sons; Eşaf Bey, another parliamentary deputy from Malatia; and Mehmed Effendi, a businessman.[269] Resneli Nâzım was apparently also interested in the attitude of Malatia's German resident, whom he took the trouble to meet. Bauernfeind's description of him as "the most pleasant, well-educated and manly Turkish official we have ever seen" indicates that the Bosnian succeeded in charming the German minister.[270] The sudden recall of the *mutesarif*, Nabi Bey, on 3 June, and his provisional replacement by Vasifi Bey, the *kaymakam* of Akçadag/Arga,[271] was doubtless related to Nâzım's visit. Perhaps the CUP inspector found that Nabi did not display sufficient initiative. It is also possible, however, that the *mutesarif* fell victim to the machinations of local Young Turk circles. In any case, the new prefect, Reşid Bey,[272] who arrived on 20 June from Istanbul, had the advantage of being Kurdish, a factor of no little importance in a predominantly Kurdish region. It should also be noted that the authorities released common-law criminals from prison around 6 June in order to incorporate them into squadrons of *çetes*. The German pastor writes of these irregulars that he was "initially surprised that all these people were immediately given arms, although they were robbers and murderers."[273] There can be little doubt that the creation of this squadron of the Special Organization resulted directly from initiatives taken by Resneli Nâzım. It is hard to imagine that a *mutesarif*, and an interim *mutesarif* at that, could open the doors of a prison except on orders from his superiors. However, in the party-state system of the day, a CUP inspector not only had the powers required to enroll convicts in the Teşkilât-ı Mahsusa; it was his duty to do so. The fact that this squadron (which, as we shall see, played an important role in the improvised slaughterhouses) had been put under the command of Mehmed Bey,[274] a son of the parliamentary deputy Haşim Bey and a local Young Turk leader, confirms that these irregulars answered to no other authority than that of the Special Organization. As Resneli Nâzım was preparing to return to Harput on 9 June, a ceremony was held in a schoolyard before all of Malatia's leading citizens. It illustrates the influence of the Young Turk network on – or even the fear it inspired in – the provincial notables. By way of a parting recommendation, Bauernfeind writes, Nâzım held up before his audience a "copy of a cheap cops-and-robbers magazine containing illustrations of a large number of rifles, bombs and similar objects that are said to have been discovered in the homes of Armenians from Kuharea [presumably Kütahiya], Dyarbekir and so on." The interim *mutesarif* put the crowning touches on Nâzım's demonstration when he told the German minister that the day before, "they had found nearly five thousand bombs in Mezreh."[275] The outrageous nature of the accusations was on a par with the violence that the authorities were perpetrating.

For Malatia's Armenians, the demand that they turn in their arms posed a major problem. Since the outbreak of the war, they had scrupulously performed their duties as Ottoman subjects in hopes of laying the authorities' lurking suspicions to rest. When it came to surrendering their weapons, however, the question of the government's intentions toward them arose: if they gave up their arms, they would be giving up all possibility of defending themselves. This brought back memories of the 1895 massacres, which, of course, were one of the Armenian population's obsessions. This concern was most palpably felt by the jailed Armenian leaders. In prison, where they were daily subjected to extremely violent forms of torture, these men, after taking counsel, decided to make the authorities a proposal: if they were set free, they would proceed to collect and deliver up the Armenians' arms. Four men were released on 27 or 28 May. Among them was the leader of Malatia's Dashnaks, Khosrov Keshishian, a Protestant pharmacist. The others remained behind bars. The Armenians apparently handed over all their weapons to the authorities[276] ("weapon" here means everything from hunting rifles to rifles of a more or less modern kind). Those who did not have any arms "secretly bought rifles, simply so that they would have one to turn in if they should be forced to do so by being put in jail or beaten with clubs."[277] The government was plainly seeking to neutralize the Armenian population, which, for its part, had doubts about the authorities' true intentions. The accusations of an Armenian conspiracy that were more or less officially put into circulation had fit the Young Turk strategy too well to be taken seriously. On the other hand, it goes without saying that the Armenian leaders, here as elsewhere, grappled with the question of self-defense. Yet the strategy of methodically undermining the Armenians' capacities seems to have made this option quite simply unfeasible.

According to Bauernfeind's diary, the arrests began to affect all strata of society from 27 May onward.[278] Khanghlarian mentions in particular the arrests of adolescents, old men, and the craftsmen and merchants of the bazaar. The result was that 1,300 men had already been taken into custody by late May.[279] An official at the government accounting office (*muhasebeci*) and a close friend of Bauernfeind's, who lived opposite the prison in which the Armenians were detained, asked the German minister to take him in for a few days because he could no longer bear the racket caused by the bastinadoes, which had already claimed their first victim – an "elderly" Catholic priest[280] named Stephan Baghdasarian.[281] The torturers demanded that the prisoners tell them where the "dynamite, bombs, arms stockpiles and cannons" had been hidden.[282] Six weeks later, Bauernfeind doubted "that all these stories about bombs and pogroms had a basis in the truth." "The Armenians here," he went on, "haven't done anything that need alarm the government."[283] According to Khanghlarian, the authorities ultimately secured 114 "outlawed" rifles and pistols; they laid them out next to "weapons from the barracks," photographed the whole, and sent the pictures to Istanbul. To be sure, "they did not find the bombs"[284] that seemed to obsess them. By the time the campaign to confiscate weapons was over, 60 Armenians had died under torture – including Manug Khantsian, Khosrov Keshishian, and Napoleon Bonapartian [sic], who threw himself from an upper story of the prison to avoid torture.[285]

An examination of the sources suggests that once the arms had been collected, the authorities moved on to the third stage of their plan: the systematic liquidation of the men – that is, both the conscripts in the new age groups, 18–19 and 46–50 – who had been mobilized in May and set to repairing the road to Harput in *amele taburis* (they were not immediately affected)[286] and the men arrested late in May or early in June who were locked up in Malatia's central prison. It was now no longer a question of torture, but of summary execution. On 16 June, Bauernfeind wrote in his diary: "We now take it to be an established fact that prisoners are dying and being buried in secret. On the other hand, we do not believe that the government is helping them die … We have now discovered where they bury the men." The first victims were ineptly buried in the southwest corner of the German mission grounds, in a mass grave dug overnight.[287] The repetition of these inhuman nighttime scenes and the nuisance caused by the stench of the rotting corpses finally pricked the conscience of the German pastor, who requested a "secret meeting" with *mutesarif* Reşid Bey. Bauernfeind's account of this "two-hour meeting on the Armenian question" betrays his first doubts about the authorities' intentions toward the Armenians. Following his indications, the *mutesarif* sent a *saptieh* to inspect the mass graves adjoining the mission. The explanation of the affair that he was given ("someone buried a horse there") was hardly credible. Reşid Bey therefore adopted a new strategy: he told the pastor that it did not lie "in his power to change things" that had taken place "before he assumed his post and that he [was] not claiming that nothing illegal had happened." The murders had been committed, Reşid said, "at the instigation of a few rich people." Moreover, his predecessor had "done a little something to help [the prisoners] die." After making these confessions, Reşid solemnly declared that, "for as long as he remain[ed] in his post, illegal acts of this sort [would] never again occur."[288]

After this well-educated *mutesarif* recently dispatched from Istanbul, Malatia's *belediye reisi* (mayor), Mustafa Ağa Azizoğlu, was the pastor's second-most-important interlocutor. Azizoğlu made no secret of his opposition to the measures aimed at the Armenians and frequently passed on information about the authorities' crimes. Thus, the day after Baurenfeind visited Reşid Bey, he was told by the mayor that "the bodies in the six graves had been decently buried; there were more than one hundred corpses." He also learned "with certainty" that 1,200 Armenian worker-soldiers who had been doing roadwork in Çiftlik, located on the Euphrates between Malatia and Çoğlu, had been massacred on 11 June 1915 near the village of Pirot. The crime had been committed by a squadron of *çetes* based in Taşpinar that had been recently created on orders from Haşim Beyzâde Mehmed, son of parliamentary deputy Haşim Bey.[289] The same squadron liquidated, in Haşim's presence, a second contingent of worker-soldiers from Malatia on the night of 13 June: 214 of them were killed with axes and knives at the quarry of Taş Tepe, after which their corpses were thrown into pits; 74 more were killed an hour and a half from Taş Tepe in Kızıl Göl, where their bodies were dumped in a pool used for breeding fish.[290]

Rumors of these first massacres spread through the city. According to Khanghlarian, the authorities had to go to considerable lengths to lay them to rest in order to keep people in doubt. On 26 June, they finally announced the order to deport the Armenian population of Malatia within three days. The next day, however, they announced that the families of young men who volunteered for labor battalions would not be deported. Four hundred young men under the age of 18 enlisted. They were divided into three groups. The first group from Indere, one hour's distance from Malatia, was responsible for keeping the barracks in Malatia supplied with water. The second was put to work building the city's CUP club. The third made uniforms in the workshop of a certain Osman.[291] There is every reason to believe that these men were recruited in order to remove as many adolescents as possible from town. An event that occurred on 1 July shows, moreover, that the authorities wanted to make certain that the Armenians' self-defense capabilities had been crushed before initiating the deportations. That day, mounted troops surrounded the Armenian neighborhoods and simulated an attack, obviously in order to see whether this would bring on an armed reaction. It did not.[292]

The liquidation of the men still imprisoned in Malatia seems to have followed on the heels of that of the worker-soldiers. In his diary entry for 2 July, Bauernfeind wrote: "The most horrible, appalling thing has happened: a massacre." Once again, he solicited an interview with the *mutesarif*, where he says he was able to "speak more frankly" since they were alone. Reşid Bey nevertheless began by dishing him up a lie about the fate meted out to the mission's steward, an Armenian. In the end, however, he revealed to him, in a confidential tone: "Don't tell anybody: they killed Garabed, and not only Garabed, but 300 other people last night and 180 the night before. All of them had been taken to Indära [Indere] and there...I didn't have the courage to ask whether they had been strangled or shot to death."[293] The *mutesarif*'s confidences were meant to create the impression that he was not implicated in the murder of "all the prisoners, that is to say, almost all the men" who were still in prison.[294] Bauernfeind, however, knew that, "in accordance with the reigning linguistic conventions," to be "'sent somewhere else' meant 'killed,'" and that "things did not happen any differently here than in Mezreh, Sıvas, Erzerum, Erzincan, Cesaerea and so on. This would appear to be an order received from above and, of course, carefully prepared. That is why we have not had visits from Turks for a long time now ... We have been abominably deceived and betrayed, with diabolical ill-will and cunning."[295] The German minister was even more explicit in an entry dated 5 July: "What pains us the most is that our 'allies and brothers' have betrayed us in the most unspeakably vile, loathsome way. This treachery ... has utterly destroyed our faith in the government."[296]

According to information gathered by the mayor Mustafa Ağa Azizoğlu, "in the preceding two weeks, more than 2,000 Armenians were killed; most were massacred and buried in Indere ... Taş Tepe and near Kündebeg."[297]

In the other provinces, the end of the massacre of the males heralded, in principle, the beginning of the deportations. Why, then, did the deportations in Malatia not begin until mid-August? A delay of a few days could perhaps have been explained by the fact that this prefecture had been assigned the role of slaughterhouse: it had to cope with the massive arrival, in the first half of July, of convoys of deportees from the west and the north. But this is probably not sufficient explanation for a delay of almost six weeks. Bauernfeind was now persuaded that the *mutesarif* was "unremittingly endeavoring to keep the women in the area."[298] He was, however, unaware that this "humane act" was motivated by the desire to wring huge sums from the Armenians for the *mutesarif*'s personal benefit, as we learn from an investigative report submitted to a court-martial on 25 November 1915, "exposing the illicit gains of the former *mutesarif* of Malatia, Reşid Bey."[299]

In July and early August, Bauernfeind observed the continuous passage of convoys from the north and west. On 12 July, he saw the first caravan from Sıvas arrive, 2,000 people strong, as well as a convoy of 3,000 to 4,000 deportees from Mezreh and the villages nearby.[300] On 17 July, he watched as a caravan of 2,000 peasants from the region of Sıvas trekked past. A Turkish gardener told him that the caravan had been sent half an hour's march north, where "a big grave [had been] dug." "They are," said the gardener, "all going to 'be lost' there."[301] On 21 July, "one or two thousand more," also from the region of Sıvas, pitched camp along the road.[302] On 22 July, 10,000 deportees from Sıvas passed close by Malatia, but were redirected toward the plain of Fırıncilar.[303] On 29 July, 10,000 to 15,000 people who had come from the north camped close to the mission.[304] On 30 July, Bauernfeind saw a convoy "comprising about 1,000 to 1,500" deportees coming from the northwest. In a single day, 1 August, he saw two caravans from the region of Sıvas, comprising 1,000 and 2,000 people, respectively.[305] Finally, on 3 and 4 August, the German pastor saw a caravan containing 1,000 deportees, and another "that took almost two hours to pass by."[306]

Obviously, all these columns, which arrived by the road from Sıvas, represented only a fraction of the convoys arriving in the region of Malatia. While all the caravans passed by way of Kırk Gök Bridge, a good many avoided the city of Malatia and headed directly for the plain of Fırıncilar. Moreover, the isolation in which the German mission found itself and the minister's obviously imperfect knowledge of the environment in which he was living prevented him from acquiring a comprehensive view of the situation. After the initial shock caused by his discovery that the men had been massacred, it took him some time to realize the significance of the deportations. In a diary entry dated 22 July, he reports a conversation he had had the day before with the mayor Mustafa Ağa, observing that "his lack of all power of judgment again came to the fore; he claims that Malatia is a deathtrap; that people are brought here from all over in order to be killed; that nobody ever reaches Urfa, and so on."[307] Evidently, Bauernfeind was hard put to admit the harsh reality of the situation, although he had already noted that the operations conducted by the authorities took "the form of a high-blown legal murder presented in public as a patriotic necessity and legitimized, with precious little justification, by references to the German example in Belgium."[308] Shortly thereafter, he wondered "whether all the confiscations of arms had been carried out with this in mind."[309]

The minister's observations are corroborated and completed by those of an Armenian witness. About the simultaneous arrival on 12 July of the first convoy from Sıvas and a convoy from Mezreh, Hovhannes Khanghlarian observes that the *mutesarif*, the Turkish notables of Malatia, and a squadron of *çetes* at full strength went out to "welcome" the deportees in the second group. After conscientiously stripping them of their belongings, they led them to the square in front of the barracks, where the last of the men were separated from the rest of the convoy and locked up in the garrison's prison, while the boys under ten were held in the city. The next morning, our witness, who at the time was in one of the three battalions of adolescents formed in late June, observed that the prison had been evacuated overnight.[310] The group from Sıvas, which had arrived two hours after the one from Mezreh, now consisted almost exclusively of women and old men, accompanied by a few young men. It was stationed for several days in the khan of the market, where most of the women were raped.[311] Khanghlarian does not describe all the following convoys in detail, but notes that they systematically took the road leading to the plain of Fırıncilar without entering Malatia, after being plundered near Kırk Göz Bridge.[312] It is likely that the large numbers of deportees, presumably together with considerations of hygiene, led the authorities to give up the idea of having the deportees transit through the city of Malatia around mid-July. On the other hand, they decided to assemble females under 15 and males under ten there. On 16 July, they rounded up the first group of these young deportees in Fırıncilar,[313] an estimated 3,000 to 5,000 children. These round-ups continued through the latter half of July and into early August. According to Khanghlarian, the children were put in the five Armenian Apostolic churches in the city at this time, as well as the Protestant church, the Armenian schools, and a few big residences, under the gaze of Malatia's Armenian population, which was still in the city. More than 4,000 children – the most fortunate ones – found themselves temporarily lodged with Armenian families. Turks and Kurds were officially authorized to pick out children for themselves. Those they took with them were promptly replaced by new arrivals from the subsequent convoys.

All in all, some 40,000 children passed through Malatia's "orphanages."[314] Bauernfeind, in whose diary flashes of insight alternate with professions of faith in the authorities, writes that these children were "voluntarily entrusted to the government by their mothers. This is, then, an act of social charity."[315] The reality of the matter was rather less heartwarming than his formula suggests. Witnesses say that the improvised establishments in which the authorities hoped to educate "true Turks" never possessed the necessary means to provide their wards' upkeep. Hygiene there was catastrophic, malnutrition chronic, and a terrible epidemic carried off a considerable number of the children. The infected children and the bodies of those who had died were thrown indiscriminately into mass graves in Göz Tepe; these children were immediately replaced by a batch of new arrivals.[316] A young man whose mother worked in one of these homes states that there was one "mother" for every 50 children, adding that he himself was for several weeks responsible for transporting children to Turkish and Kurdish villages, where they were handed out to the villagers.[317] The glut that resulted from these repeated distributions of children (again according to Levon Boghosian) compelled the authorities to take more radical measures in order to make space in their orphanages. At night, carts with a gendarme in each would be loaded with children and driven to the banks of the Tohma Çay, where "the infidels' progeny" were drowned in the river.[318] To the extent that one can hazard a judgment on the basis of this information, it would appear that the ideal of Turkification as envisaged at the highest level of the Ittihadist party-state came up against the harsh realities of the situation on the ground, particularly in the irresponsibility of local government officials, who preferred to pocket the limited funds earmarked for Turkification rather than spend it to lodge and board potential "Turks."

The authorities did not, however, concern themselves with children alone. For nine straight days in early August, young men from several *amele taburis* as well as their older comrades had their throats cut in Malatia's prison; the bodies were carted down to the Tohma and thrown into the river. The executions took place at an average rate of 300 victims nightly. The problem of evacuating their blood left the authorities with no choice but to dig canals capable of conducting the blood from the slaughterhouse to a point outside the city. Boghosian gives us a Dantean description of these nights: when he arrived in the courtyard of the prefecture, he saw hundreds of naked young men awash in their blood. The bodies gave off an unbearable odor; the atmosphere was so thoroughly impregnated with the stench that visitors were soon covered with it.[319]

For their part, Malatia's Armenians did not sit on their hands. Around 16 July 1915, they formed a delegation that personally submitted a petition to the *mutesarif*, and he was "said to have shown great kindness and been touched" by their initiative.[320] In fact, there is every reason to suppose that this petition was accompanied by a cash "gift" intended to persuade Reşid Bey to spare the petitioners. Several other means seemed to have been mobilized in an effort to escape deportation: a certain number of women found refuge in the homes of their Turkish acquaintances[321] by promising to give the master of the house all their property in exchange. As soon as the deportations began, however, virtually all the Turkish family heads turned their female "protégés" over to the authorities.[322] Other Armenians sought to convert to Islam, but the authorities, Bauernfeind writes, "were not interested in proselytizing the Armenians, but in putting them out of the way."[323] The Greeks and "Syrians," in contrast, were spared. As for the Germans, they were "in the worst of cases," Bauernfeind declares, "in danger only insofar as they were embarrassing witnesses."[324]

The minister points to certain rather telling signs of the prevailing mood in the city: for example, the curious "feeling that the Germans had become Muslims or were about to was very common among the populace."[325] This was probably the result of rumors spread by the authorities to convince the population of the legitimacy and power of the Young Turk government, which was supposed to have in some sense succeeded in gaining the upper hand over its powerful ally. This notion also had the merit of flattering conservative Muslim public opinion, which did not easily accept an alliance with a Christian state at a time when a good part of the population was taking part in the physical elimination of its many Christian subjects. The authorities could, however, avail themselves of another stimulant, represented by the idea that the "property of the slain Armenians legitimately belongs to the Turks." These words, uttered around 7 July by a mullah and parliamentary deputy from Malatia, Eşaf Bey,[326] speak volumes about the methods used to bring the populace to consent to a crime that was taking on collective dimensions.[327] As for the economic aspects of that crime, one of the most commonly employed methods in the days preceding the 15 August departure of the first convoy consisted in demanding the repayment of fictive debts from those about to leave, at a time when the authorities were willing to validate such claims. Others, more courteous, approached their Armenian neighbors and suggested that they give them their property rather than let the authorities confiscate it, since they were going to be killed in any case.[328] Bauernfeind notes that the determination of a few local notables "such as Haşim Bey and his sons, [who] sought to make a fortune by acquiring the property of the slain Armenians – war booty, as it were – played an important role in this business."[329]

The first convoy to leave Malatia was formed in three days. On the morning of 15 August, the army surrounded three neighborhoods on the outskirts of Malatia, among them the Niyali neighborhood, and put their population on the road to Sürgü, which lay some 40 miles southwest of Malatia near Behesni/Besni. On 16 August, the inhabitants of the Çavuşoğlu and Haraza neighborhoods were deported; those of the Market neighborhood followed the next day.[330] This first group of deportees was plundered and partially massacred at two hours' distance from Malatia in the Begler Deresi valley. Somewhat further south, the Kurds of Akçadağ took charge of the caravan, abducting the girls and women and dispatching the others with knives.[331]

The second convoy to leave Malatia was also formed in three days, beginning on 23 August. These deportees, however, were not led in the direction of Sürgü, but rather toward Fırıncilar. From there, a few survivors went to Kahta and then on to Samsat/Samosat.[332]

The last sizeable group of deportees, made up of the 400 volunteer workers who had been recruited in late June, was interned in the prison in Malatia on the evening of 17 August. The few Syriacs present were released thanks to an imperial decree that granted them "pardon." On 27 August, these workers learned that there were no Armenians left in the city – that is, their families, who had until then been exempt from deportation, had also been "sent away." On 29 and 30 August, these workers' throats were cut in the prison slaughterhouse.[333]

On 30 August, Muslim homes were searched by the authorities, who were looking for Armenians over the age of ten. Muslims who did not turn them over were threatened with severe punishment. The families holding young children registered them; those who had older girls in their possession formalized their unions (*nikah*) with them. The handful of artisans who had been allowed to remain in the city were invited to convert to Islam around 30 September.[334] These measures constituted the final stage of the program to liquidate the Armenians. One month later, on 31 October, Reşid Bey's replacement, Hüseyin Serri Bey, drew up a balance sheet of the deportation measures and an account of the families still in the city:

> In Malatia, 3,341 males and 3,594 females were registered in 1,582 houses. Of these people, the occupants of 1,550 households, 3,246 males and 3,492 females, were deported. The occupants of the 32 remaining households, 95 males and 102 females, were allowed to remain behind because they were artisans. Also present in the city are individuals [who should] have been deported and fugitives who have come here, a total of 30 males and 60 females; they have been arrested and are subject to deportation. [There] are also male and female children without guardians, approximately 600 males and 400 females, who have come from elsewhere and are now in orphanages or living with the populace. Finally, as a result of delays in the deportation and in accordance with orders received, 130 Catholic males and 185 Catholic females, 50 Protestant males and 80 Protestant females as well as 30 Levantine males and 27 Levantine females have been left in place by the commander of the gendarmerie.[335]

On the other hand, an order dated 12 November offers a glimpse of a more restrictive policy: "There is no objection to the presence of female artisans, if they are chosen, preferably, from among the Catholics and Protestants, and on the express condition that their number does not exceed ten or fifteen."[336]

The *Kaza* of Hüsni Mansur/Adiyaman

The *kaza* of Hüsni Manusr/Adiyaman boasted 21 Armenians localities in 1914, with a total population of 5,202. The administrative seat of the *kaza*, Adiyaman, had a population of 3,390. The *kaza*, which served as a transit zone for Armenian deportees, was also distinguished by the fact that the rural zones in the north were inhabited by Armenians who had been Islamicized at an undetermined date.[337]

The first striking event in the *kaza* occurred on 14 May 1915, when 400 Armenians in the *kazas* of Behesni and Adiyaman were massacred by *çetes*[338] commanded by Haci Mehmed Ali Bey.[339] The sub-prefect, Nuri Bey, was named to his post on 27 June 1915 and remained in office only until 17 December. With the leader of the *çetes*, Haci Mehmed Ali Bey, he was one of the four main criminals in the region; the others were Mehmed Effendi, the commander of the gendarmerie; Vasfi Bey, the police chief; Mehmed Alioğlu Haci Mustafa Effendi; and Nureddinoğlu Sıddık, a *çetebaşi* (*çete* chief) who supervised the massacre of thousands of deportees in transit in this district.[340] Sıddık could reckon on support from the Zırafkan and Zeynel tribes of Kolık, in particular. After the men were arrested and eliminated, the population was deported on 28 July 1915 toward Samsat and then Urfa. Two hundred people, adolescents and a few old men, were massacred in the Karakayık gorge.[341]

In a 3 November telegram, the *kaymakam* informed the *mutesarif* of Malatia that "there are no more local Armenians to deport: there are only four to five households belonging to Armenian craftsmen who have come here with their families and whose conversion took place after the required religious obligations were fulfilled."[342] Nuri Bey also notes that there were a few boys and girls who had been "placed with well-intentioned people." "As far as the young virgins who wish to marry are concerned," he added, "the process is nearing completion." He pointed out, however, that he would not take the older women who had offered to convert into consideration, since he preferred to marry off "younger females."[343]

Thus, most of the Armenians allowed to remain in Adiyaman were from other regions, particularly "women from elsewhere who had married after converting to Islam." Another telegram, however, is less forthcoming about "how to deal with people taken into custody."[344]

The *Kaza* of Kahta

In 1914, 2,250 Armenians out of a total population of 4,300 lived in the administrative seat, Kahta, of the *kaza* of the same name. There were 56 localities in this *kaza* in the *nahies* of Şiro, Gerger, Merdesi, and Zeravikan, where more than 10,000 Armenians lived alongside Catholic Syriacs, Kurds, and a handful of Turks.[345] The divergence between the Patriarchate's population figures and the official census is astonishing here: there were more children enrolled in the Armenian schools alone than there were, according to the official count, Armenians in the *kaza*. Yet the summary of the deportations submitted to the *mutesarif* of Malatia in September 1915 contains figures matching those in the official census: this summary speaks of 791 Armenians, of whom 715 had been expelled, as well as 74 boys under ten and girls under 15 "without father or mother" who were in the custody of "pious people."[346] More than 9,000 people seem to have simply evaporated without plausible explanation.

The *kaymakam*, Hakkı Bey, who was appointed to his post on 9 April 1915 and served until 12 June 1916, bore the main responsibility for the crimes committed in the region. These involved not only the liquidation of the local Armenians, however many of them there may have been, but also supervision of the killing fields in the gorge immediately adjoining the plain of Fırıncilar in the northernmost part of the *kaza*. In a 9 December 1915 report to the Sublime Porte, Hasan Mazhar mentions specifically the "crimes committed by the *kaymakam* of Kahta." The reference, however, is not to his role in eradicating the deportees. Rather, he is accused of having seized control of a convoy of Armenians from Erzerum that had been entrusted to the *kaymakam* of Hüsni Mansur, and thus of "exceeding his prerogatives." Mazhar notes that the two men clashed because they could not agree on how to "divide up" these deportees' property. Things became more complicated when Haci Bedri

Ağa,[347] who belonged to the Reşvan tribe involved in "sending off" the deportees, "stuck his nose" into the affair, so that Hakkı Bey was compelled to give him "part of the booty in order to calm him down." Mazhar's report charges the *kaymakam* of Kahta with "responsibility for substantial material losses" and also with seizing, "by legal or personal means, large sums of money and considerable amounts of property. According to information and proof of the most reliable kind, he transferred only 10,000 piasters to the treasury." Mazhar observed that, "in the *kaza*, the plunder of Armenian property, by both officials and the population, assumed incredible proportions."[348]

Thus, as we have just seen, the inquiry carried out by Istanbul centered on a sordid affair of illicit personal gain at the expense of the state treasury, to say nothing of the deportees. The fact that Haci Bedri Ağa and his men murdered these people in the Kahta gorge near Fırıncilar does not seem to have upset the central authorities much. It is clear that their main concern was recovering the property taken from deportees, wherever they might be. Jafar Abdallah, an officer in the gendarmerie accused of having organized the massacre of 1,500 Armenians in Karlık, was also unduly troubled by the military courts.[349]

This remote *kaza*, which saw hundreds of thousands of deportees plundered or slain in the Karlık gorge, is almost a caricature of Young Turk government and Ottoman society in the eastern vilayets. Two sub-prefects quarreled over the property of the deportees from Erzerum, who were killed soon after; an inquiry was undertaken, but only because this property was diverted from the state coffers; a Kurdish chieftain, who had been entrusted with the task of "expediting" the deportees – that is, with the dirty work of killing them – insisted that he be given his share of the "pie." Financial abuse and personal enrichment seem to have been the only crimes for which anyone could be brought before a court-martial, as if the authorities had legalized massacres in advance. A 12 December 1915 telegram would seem to indicate that while these matters were under investigation the minister of the interior was issuing new instructions to "deport" the handful of Armenians who had so far been left in their homes: "In accordance with the last orders received, not a single local [Armenian] has been kept here. Similarly, not a single person come from elsewhere has been allowed to remain."[350]

The *Kaza* of Besni/Behesni

In the *kaza* bordering on Kahta, Behesni, 3,750 Armenians, one-third of the total population, lived in its administrative seat in 1914, while another roughly 800 Armenians inhabited seven other localities: Kesun, Surfaz, Şamboyad, Tut, Pelvere, Raban Ovase, and Hoçgaşi.[351] The *kaymakam*, Edhem Kadri Bey, who was named to his post on 11 April 1915 and remained in it until 6 March 1916, ordered the arrest of Father Clement Singirian and 20 notables from Behesni in early May. They were sent to Kündebeg and massacred by *çetes* on 13 May.[352] Like his colleague from the *kaza* of Kahta, Edhem Kadri Bey faced court prosecution after the inquiry conducted by Mazhar in fall 1915.[353] Kadri, the president of the local commission responsible for abandoned property (*mahalli emvalı metruke*), was blamed "for significant losses of property abandoned by deported Armenians and abuses in connection with this property"; sealing only about ten houses, with as many stores "abandoned by the Armenians of his *kaza*, out of a total of 400 houses and 128 stores"; and leaving the remaining real estate "without surveillance." Mazhar also charged him with recruiting collaborators who were "widely known to be disreputable," with the result that the bulk of the "abandoned property" had disappeared; failing "to keep records that would have made it possible to make an inventory of the abandoned property"; and selling the property stored in the church "that was serving as a warehouse," thus facilitating "illicit gain on the part of certain individuals." The accusation also bore on government officials' participation in the auctions. These officials had "sold goods worth 13,232 piasters on credit" and had never tried to recover the debt from the buyers. Finally, the accusation noted that the *kaymakam* had "failed to take the interests of the Treasury into account"; it charged him with rigging auctions, "requisitioning the furniture and possessions of one of the richest Armenian houses in Behesni, without compensation" for his personal use and, more generally, "making illicit profits thanks to his involvement in Armenian affairs."[354]

Mashar's fall 1915 report thus exposes the ferocious struggle between the Treasury on the one hand and local notables and government officials on the other over the legalized plunder of the Armenians' "abandoned property." The real situation was a far cry from the formal statements of the authorities, who pledged to protect this property yet themselves behaved like predators. In a 5 November 1915 report, the *mutesarif* of Malatia laconically announced: "There are no Armenians left in Behesni."[355]

The Slaughterhouses of the *Kaza* of Akçadağ

There was, at best, only a symbolic Armenian presence in the *kaza* of Akçadag, which had a total Armenian population of 1,691. The Armenians lived in Arga (137 Armenians), the predominantly Kurdish village of Ansar, the administrative seat of the *kaza* (167 Armenians), Muşovga (380 Armenians), Hekimhan (770 Armenians), and Hasançelebi (237 Armenians).[356] However, as we have seen, the *kaza* straddled one of the main routes used to deport the Armenian population. The choice of a *kaymakam* for Akçadağ was therefore important. Vasfi Bey, who had been appointed on 27 March 1914, was dismissed on 23 July 1915 and immediately replaced by Asım Bey (who remained in office until 12 June 1916). Coming at a time when dozens of convoys were converging on Akçadağ from the north and west, this was a surprising change. One possible explanation is that Vasfi Bey had not carried out orders with sufficient rigor. It is, however, much more likely that the *kaymakam* was a victim of the financial issue – the question of how the deportees' expropriated assets were to be divided up. Ali Amruş, the commander of the gendarmerie in Akçadağ/Arga, also served as a financial inspector in Hekimhan, a place where many massacres were perpetrated. Complicit in the murder of several thousand deportees along with Haci Karib Ağa, the head of the squadron of *çetes* responsible for the site, he was brought before a court martial in Malatia and condemned for "abuses" (that is, misdealings), but was ultimately acquitted by the military authorities.[357] Haci Halil Kör, who openly boasted that he had executed 49 male Armenians in Hekimhan, was never prosecuted, probably because he had distributed part of the booty he took from the deportees to his superiors.[358] Tayar Bey, the secretary of the gendarmerie in Malatia who was charged with leading the *çetes* "disguised as gendarmes" stationed at Kırk Göz on the Tohma Çay, kept the 5,000 Turkish pounds he had taken from deportees whom he had ordered killed. Yet he was not indicted either.[359] According to the report of Captain Fazıl, who sat on the bench of the court-martial in Malatia, the sole grounds for indictment were personal gain, never murder or rape.

As we have seen, Kirk Göz Bridge, which the Armenians deported from Nigde, Tokat, Samsun, Amasia, Gürün, Arapkir, Sıvas, and Eğin crossed on their way to one of the killing fields near Malatia, was under the control of a *sevkiyat memuri* (director of the deportation).[360] With the aid of *çetes*, who may or may not have been wearing gendarmes' uniforms, the *sevkiyat memuri* transported groups of deportees to the other bank of the river after removing the males between 12 and 65 from the convoys. These males were massacred on the riverbank and thrown into the river, whereas the women and younger children were set walking again, bound for the plain of Fırıncilar, a six-hours march away.

The Main Authors of the Slaughters in Malatia

The report drawn up by Captain Fazıl, a former judge of the court-martial in Malatia, is without contest the richest document we have on the crimes committed in this *sancak*. Fazıl lists the names of 567 war criminals complicit by various degrees in the atrocities and crimes perpetrated in the vilayet of Harput. In addition to providing information that Fazıl acquired during the trials that some of these men faced for financial abuse, his 82-page report, completed on 30 November 1918, also describes the crimes that he himself had witnessed and the abuses about which their perpetrators had boasted in his presence.

Fazıl's report on the events that occurred in 1915 in the vilayet of Mamuret ul-Aziz and especially the *sancak* of Malatia begins with a general assessment that is not without interest:

> The 1915 abuses perpetrated against the Christians of the eastern provinces constitute one of the blackest pages in history... These abominations, acts contrary to justice and civilization, wounded Islam in its very heart. These thousands of Christians never showed the least resistance to the government's orders... They were deported from all over, one convoy after the next. All their personal belongings and property were plundered and more than 1 million people were exterminated to satisfy the bloodlust of a few brigands... Large numbers of children were smashed against walls and boulders. Barely pubescent girls drowned themselves after being raped; hundreds of thousands of men and women were massacred with swords or axes and cast into ditches or wells. Other corpses were strewn over mountains and plains and abandoned, food for birds of prey.[361]

The captain's report refers to a number of cases submitted to the court-martial in Malatia at the request of the ministers of justice, war, and the interior. Yet the court, he observes, never judged the people implicated in the massacres; it considered only the property-related abuses of which the Armenians were the victims, the seizures of real estate and movable assets. According to Fazıl, the cases submitted to the court-martial particularly involved people suspected of having cheated the CUP or government. Even when the proceedings attested the perpetration of massacres, they were never judged. In Fazıl's view, there existed a tacit agreement between the government, the CUP, and the leaders of the Special Organization, by which the courts martial would not deal with crimes but only "abuses." Moreover, when all was said and done, very few real condemnations were pronounced; the punishments inflicted were often limited to confiscation of the assets that had been illegally acquired by the accused.

The examples that Fazıl adduces give us an idea of the ordinary crimes that were often committed for no reason other than a lust for gain. Fevzizâde Muftizâde Effendi, a man accused of stealing the rugs and other belongings of an Armenian doctor to whom he had supposedly given shelter in order to save him, but whom he had in fact murdered, was condemned for theft but not for murder.[362] Hoca Mehmed Effendi Dellalzâde, who murdered an Armenian woman to come into the possession of her three houses, had all his property confiscated by the state but was not condemned for homicide.[363] Haci Ahmed, the son of Haci Kolağasi, confessed before the court-martial that he had shot several Armenians to death with a revolver in order to seize their property; the court ordered the property confiscated and sentenced him to 12 years in prison for theft (his sentence was later reduced by the military authorities).[364] Ziya Hararci, chief court clerk in Malatia's court of justice and an inspector of the convoys of deportees, had escorted a caravan of 1,500 Armenians to Indere, an hour's march from the city, and ordered the *çetes* there to kill them, dig a pit, and burn the bodies in it. Yet the court-martial saw no reason to indict him.[365]

This general mechanism of conditional impunity, established at the highest levels of the Ittihadist party-state, throws up the question of the personal legal accountability of government officials, if not that of the members of paramilitary groups such as the Teşkilât-ı Mahsusa, who were by law immune from punishment of any kind. It is hard to imagine that Constantinople was capable of appointing to the highest level of the local governmental hierarchy – that is, to the post of *mutesarif* – anyone it suspected of opposing its policy of eliminating the Armenians. In Malatia, Reşid Bey, Reverend Bauernfeind's spontaneous liking for him notwithstanding, was deeply implicated in the anti-Armenian persecutions, although not necessarily as their main instigator. The Ittihad inspector Resneli Nâzım's long stay in Malatia reveals that the key individual there, who was also probably the head of the Teşkilât-ı Mahsusa in the region, was none other than the city's parliamentary deputy and president of its Ittihadist club, Haşim Bey. A rich landowner and a very influential individual, Haşim was, according to the mayor Mustafa Ağa, one of the "principal authors" of the persecutions, the initiator of the arrest and massacre of Malatia's Armenians. According to Bauernfeind, he and his sons derived "great personal profit" from the seizure of the murdered Armenians' property.[366] The role played by his son Mehmed, who had been entrusted with commanding the squadron of *çetes* operating in Malatia and the vicinity, made Haşim and his sons the family with the heaviest responsibility for the murder of the Armenians, as well as the family that profited the most from the seizure of their assets. However, the house searches, the confiscation of Armenian weapons, the torture, and the deportations – in a word, all the "administrative" preliminaries – were carried out by civilian and military officials. The Young Turk state's responsibility for these mass crimes, as well as its duplicity, are nicely brought out by this statement of the German minister's:

> The outward appearances are beyond criticism: legal condemnation of those who have fomented sedition and banishment of the rest of the population to Urfa. [However,] en route or even right where they are, as many men as possible are secretly murdered. As a rule, the women are allowed to live, that is, to perish. The same holds for the children – or they are transformed into Turks.[367]

The military and civilian officials implicated in these crimes were Reşid Bey, *mutesarif* (no. 42); Serry Bey, *mutesarif* and Reşid's successor (no. 77); Hamdi Bey, a commander in the gendarmerie (no. 69); Abdülkadir, a commander in the gendarmerie and Hamdi's successor (no. 38); Tayar Bey, a secretary in the gendarmerie; Nâzım, a lieutenant in the gendarmerie (no. 69); Tevfik, an inspecteur in the gendarmerie (no. 60); Vasfi Bey, the *kaymakam* of Akçadağ; Salih Bey, vice *mutesarif*; Tahir, the ex-*mutesarif* of Kerbala (no. 72); Hrink Köylü Abdüllah, a police chief (no. 52); Ali Çavus, the head of the gendarmerie of Erğana (no. 106); Eginli Sadik Bey, an assistant police chief (no. 65); Ayvasin Hasan Effendi, Halil Effendi, and Haci Ibrahim, police captains; Şiroli Mahmud, a prison director (no. 53); Muhezin Yusuf (no. 54); Süleyman Effendi, an assistant prison director (no. 59); Ahmed Effendi, a director of the Agricultural Service; Arapkirli Cemal, an official in the land registration office (no. 74); the parliamentary deputy Eşref Hoca; the mufti who wrote the fatwa about the extermination of the Armenians in Malatia; Erzrumli Masud Effendi, a judge (no. 41); Gusikoğlu Ahmed, an interpreter; and Hoca Ali Effendi, a teacher (no. 17).[368] Of the multitude of underlings who carried out orders, a good many came from the tribes. Among them were Saricanli Kasab Hüseyin, the murderer of the Catholic bishop; Yazicezâde Tahir (no. 35); Demirci Ali Ahmed Ağa; Hasim Effendi, a policeman; Ağcadağli Velioğlu Hüseyin Ağa; Hakkı Effendi, a policeman; Velioğlu Kör Ali Ağa; Bekir Ağa, son of Kurbağli Köse; Süleyman, son of Kurbağli Köse; Ali Amruş, the commander of the gendarmerie of Akçedağ (no. 62); Dedeşarkhinli Yusuf Ağa; Becet, a policeman (no. 57); Delibaşli Süleyman Ağa; Boyrazin

Hasan Ağa; Mağmurlioğlu Yusuf Ağa; Muftizâde Fazıleddin Feyzi Effendi; Haci Hasan, son of Tommo; Hasan Onbaşi (no. 71); Çoloğlu Mahmud Ağa; Boranlı Kurd Hamo Ağa; Lutfi Bey, a retired *kaymakam*; Hüseyin Ağa, son of Çeşo; Küçügün Vahab Ağa; Tortunlı Haci Hafiz Ağa; Tellalzâde Hoca Mehmed Effendi; Kesecioğlu Kasab Süleyman; Bedri Ağa Kahtalı; Haci Abdüllahzâde Hasan Bey (no. 81); Selukizâde Ahmed Ağa; Reşuvaloğlu Haci Effendi; Haci Pasha; Haci Rol Ağasineoğlu; Haci Ahmed; Kandaroğlu Haci Abdüllah; Müdir Süleymanzâde Kadir; Alibeyzâde Haci Reşid; Mehmed Effendi; Erdegununioğlu Abdüllah; Mafuzeffendioğlu Yusuf; and Erzrumli Faik.[369]

The Sancak *of Dersim, a Haven for Armenian Deportees*

The *sancak* of Dersim represents a very special case in the millennial history of Asia Minor. This mountainous, forest-covered enclave has almost always been relegated to the margins of history; its population has remained isolated, displaying specific local characteristics inherited from time immemorial. Carved up into several different Armenian principalities in antiquity, the region was never completely Armenized, although an impressive number of churches (107) and monasteries in ruins (50) show that it was extensively Christianized. Cut off from the world and refractory to all outside influence, Dersim was never subjugated by the Ottoman state, which collected no taxes in the district and was unable to impose its authority on it. Although the district was reputed to be dangerous for anyone not native to it, a few Armenian merchants and hardy churchmen ventured into it under the protection of local *begs*.

Thanks to a handful of firsthand reports by such people, we can give an approximate description of the social and political situation prevailing in Dersim on the eve of the First World War. In this period, 16,657 Armenians lived there alongside two groups that together formed the majority – to the south and southeast, the Seyd Hasan tribe, supposed to have come from Persian Khorasan, and in the rest of the *sancak*, in the most inaccessible regions, the "Dersimli." Albeit partially Turkified, both groups, especially the Dersimli, had elaborated a very particular religious syncretism under various influences; it was the religion of the overwhelming majority of both the Dersimli and the Seyd Hasan. Several strata coexisted in it – pagan, Zoroastrian, Christian, and Muslim. Because of their secret religious practices, the Kızılbaş followers of this faith were deemed *gâvurs* ("infidels") like the Christians. Indeed, the mere trappings or outward manifestations of the faith of the Kızılbaş were enough to give pause to an orthodox Muslim. Parallel to the worship of Saint Serge, whose feast day was preceded every year by seven days of fasting, or that of the Twelve Apostles, the Holy Cross, and the Hake sun (the feast of the "red eggs") – that is, Easter, which the Kızılbaş celebrated in common with the Armenians – the followers of this syncretic religion turned toward the east when they prayed and went on pilgrimages to monasteries, which they protected against all incursions as if they were part of their own heritage. This did not prevent them from celebrating Ali, Hüseyin, and Moses, but they completely ignored Ramadan. At the same time, they had a ritual of their own, which according to the best-informed observers consisted of songs and dances performed secretly at night in accordance with an elaborate code. The members of a religious caste, all from the same tribe, saw to it that this code was properly observed. Among the 40 tribes in Dersim, two – the Mirakian and Der Ovantsik tribes – were Armenian. The Mirakians, whose territory lay near Dujik, Çukur, Ekez, and Torud, could mobilize 3,000 fighters. Earning their living almost exclusively from sheep-raising, as well as rugmaking and kilim-making, these mountaineers were partially liquidated in 1915, although a minority of them survived in Dersim.[370]

Thus, it is hardly surprising that, during the 1915 events, the region became a refuge for 10,000 to 15,000 Armenians from the plain of Harput and the western districts of the *sancak* of Erzincan,[371] and also for many inhabitants of the neighboring *kazas*, especially the Armenians of Pardi/Ovacık (pop. 50) and Nâzımiye/Kyzilkilise (pop. 89).[372] Did the welcome given to these refugees have political significance? Probably not. Both Reverend Riggs's and Nazaret Piranian's accounts state that these population transfers came at a high price: the first fugitives paid as much as 100 Turkish pounds for passage to the area, although Kurdish *begs* later reduced their price to as little as 10 pounds. On the other hand, there were cases in which people without means were welcomed in Dersim. But life there was harsh for one and all, and many Armenians survived only by entering the service of the local *ağas*. That said, the Kurdish chieftains of Dersim never allowed the authorities to enter their fiefdoms. It is likely that the objective of Vali Sabit's ten-day mission to Dersim, which began on 31 July 1915, was to persuade the local Kurdish chieftains to turn over their Armenians.[373]

In 1914, in the administrative seat of the *kaza*, Hozat, an ugly village of scarcely a thousand inhabitants, there lived 350 Armenians. There were also 15 mixed – that is, Armenian and Kızılbaş – villages in Dersim, with a total Armenian population of 1,949.[374] According to an official report, 1,088 Armenians were deported from the *kaza* of Hozat.[375] If the official count of the Armenian population is to be believed, which put their numbers only a little higher, it follows that all the Armenians of the *kaza* were either killed or deported. Given the geography of the district, this seems unlikely. It is more reasonable to suppose that about half the Armenians fell victim to the persecutions, while the other half was able to flee to the mountains of Dersim.

Of the 1,835 Armenians of the *kaza* of Medzgerd/Mazgirt, 1,200 lived in Hozat, which had been an important Armenian fortress town in the Middle Ages. The others lived in eight Armenian-Kızılbaş villages: Lazvan, Dilan-Oghche, Tamudagh, Dana-Buran, Shordan, Khozenkiugh/Kushdun, Pakh, and Chukur. The ruins of some 15 medieval monasteries were to be found in the vicinity of these villages.[376] Here as well, the official statistics would suggest that the deportation carried off virtually all the Armenians – that is, 1,423.[377] Above all, the figure seems to attest to the zealousness of the people responsible for the deportations in the area; they were doubtless more eager to show Istanbul how well they were performing their task than to establish a precise count.

The *Kaza* of Çarsancak

In 1914, there were 1,763 Armenians in Peri, the administrative seat of the *kaza* of Çarsancak, and around 6,200 living in 42 villages in the *kaza*.[378] The *kaymakam*, Ali Rıza, held office from 2 March to 15 July 1915. He was therefore present when the first massacres took place, in Pertag/Pertak, near the landing of the ferry that linked Harput to Dersim over the Euphrates.[379] In this *kaza*, the official count of the deportees, 6,537,[380] seems quite as unlikely as the census figures cited a moment ago if one bears in mind the number of conscripts in the *amele taburis* and the number of people who were able to retreat into Dersim's mountainous areas.

The *Kaza* of Çemişkezek

Chmshgadzak/Çemişkezek, the administrative seat of the *kaza* of the same name, had an Armenian population of 1,348, representing about one-third of the *kaza*'s total population; another 3,146 Armenians lived in its 21 villages. It was set apart by the fact that it had a population of 4,935 Islamicized Armenians by the late eighteenth century. Most of them inhabited the *nahie* of Saint-Toros, in the northwestern part of the district, near the little town of Barasor on the left bank of the Euphrates. There were also Orthodox Armenians – called "Greeks" in the Ottoman statistics – in the villages of Mamsa, Khntrgig, and Setrga, where they lived alongside their Apostolic compatriots. The other villages were Dzaghari, Ardga, Sisna, Strkeh, Garmri, Miadun, Pazapon, Morshka, Kharasar, Mezra, Baghcha/Bardizag, Ekrek/Yeritsakrag, Murna, Brekhi, and Tsntsor.[381]

The first rumors to the effect that Armenian soldiers serving in the battalions stationed in the regions of Erzerum and Erzincan were being disarmed reached Chmshgadzak during the Easter holidays, around 4 April. Shortly thereafter, stories began to make the rounds about Armenian soldiers who were going over to the enemy and betraying "military secrets".[382] It was at this point that the *kaymakam*, Selim Ahmed, opened the first phase of the anti-Armenian persecutions. On 1 May 1915, searches were conducted in the Armenians' schools, officials' homes, and shops in the bazaar. Eighteen leading citizens were arrested. The authorities were looking in particular for the official seals of the Hnchak and Dashnak parties and the Armenians' supposed arms caches. The next day, as many as 100 people were taken into custody.[383] The torture to which they were subjected seems to have been more violent than anything observed elsewhere – several men were nailed to a wall – and went on until 20 June, when the *kaymakam* announced that the prisoners were leaving for Mezreh to be tried.[384]

On 1 July 1915, the town crier announced the deportation order and outlawed sales of real estate or moveable assets, which were henceforth "government property." On Friday, 2 July, around 1,000 people were put on the road to Arapkir after a few children and young women had been abducted by Turkish families. The convoy took four days to reach Arapkir, remained there for another three, and then set out for Harput. Ordinarily a journey of a day and a half, the caravan walked for three weeks before arriving in Harput, taking wildly improbable detours. In Mezreh, it was stationed at an hour's distance from town. It then set out on the road to Dyarbekir, going by way of Hanlı Han, where the males between ten and 15 and between 40 and 70 were removed from the convoy and shut up in a khan. The rest of the caravan continued on its way until it reached Argana Maden, where it was confronted with a horrifying vision of hundreds of bodies rotting on the banks of the Tigris.[385]

After a six-weeks trek, the convoy reached Severek, where all the deportees were plundered and some had their throats cut. The next waystation was Urfa. There, what was left of the caravan was divided into two groups: one set out for Suruc, to the southwest, while the other headed due south, toward Rakka. Our witness notes that by now there were no longer any old men in the convoy. After passing through the camps of Mumbuc and Bab 150 women reached the transit camp in Aleppo.[386]

We have an account of events in the rural zones of the *kaza* by three eyewitnesses from the village of Garmrig, located a mile or two west of Chmshgadzak.[387] Here, the searches for weapons took place on 19 June. On Sunday, 4 July, 200 men from the surrounding villages joined the men of Garmrig, who had been taken into custody the day before. They were then "sent to work," escorted by gendarmes and *çetes*.[388] The same day, all boys under 10 years of age were taken from their families. On 5 July, the women were summoned to the church in order to register their belongings there before preparing to leave for Urfa. A convoy of female deportees from the villages of the Chmshgadzak district was put on the road around 10 July. The same evening, when they reached the banks of the Euphrates, the guards showed them the bloodstained clothing of their men.[389]

Witnesses say that their convoy and another comprising more villagers from the *kaza* of Chmshgadzak were combined in Arapkir. Several weeks later, 12 of the 100 women who had left Garmrig on 5 July reached Aleppo after passing through Urfa, Mumbuc, and Bab.[390]

A number of villagers from the *kaza*, especially those from localities in the north, managed to flee to the Kurdish areas, where they survived as best they could until spring 1916. They moved on to Erzincan when the Russian army took control of the region.[391]

Destroying the Traces

The file on the pretrial investigation of the criminals responsible for the massacres and deportations includes correspondence between the vali of Mamuret ul-Aziz and the *mutesarif* of Malatia, and also between Sabit Bey and the minister of the interior. The sole subject of this correspondence is how to wipe away the traces of the crimes, particularly how to bury the bodies littering the roads. The first telegram on this subject was sent by Sabit to Mutesarif Reşid of Malatia on 21 August 1915 – that is, shortly after the main convoys of deportees from the north and west had entered the *sancak* of Malatia. To begin with, we learn from it that "there are many corpses strewn along the roads" in this *sancak*, "with all the problems that that entails." Sabit also makes it understood that these corpses have not been buried with "care" and that "officials guilty of negligence" ought to be punished without delay.[392] It would seem, however, that his instructions had no effect. On 10 September, he repeated his admonitions to Reşid: "It has come to our attention that there are corpses rotting on the boundary between [the *kazas* of] Hüsni Mansur and Besni ... It is not appropriate, either from the government's standpoint or for health reasons, that putrefying [corpses] be left out in the open."[393] In all fairness to the *mutesarif* of Malatia, it should be acknowledged that the repeated passage of convoys necessitated regular clean-ups of the roads, a chore that was curiously assigned to the gendarmes. "From the government's standpoint," these putrefying bodies betrayed rather too plainly what the real objective of the deportations was.

Three months later, doubtless in reaction to information that had reached Istanbul through diplomatic channels, the minister of the interior reprimanded the vali of Mamuret ul-Aziz, complaining that "there are still bodies out in the open ... or remains."[394] It seems that transmitting these instructions to the *kaymakams* and the commanding officers of the gendarmerie, who were threatened with court-martial,[395] finally convinced them "to re-open the trenches and dig them deep enough that dogs could not get into them."[396] The mode of transport generally used to deport the Armenian population – walking – certainly reduced the logistical problems involved in providing them with an escort, but it also generated a number of secondary effects: epidemics broke out in the deportees' wake, ravaging the civilian population.

The Authors of the Massacres in the Vilayet of Harput

Although we can quite clearly discern the role that Vali Sabit Cemal Sağiroğlu,[397] General Süleyman Faik Pasha,[398] the commander of the Eleventh Army Corps, and the police chief Süleyman Bey Zâde Reşid Bey played in the arrests, torture, and house searches, as well as the organization of the deportations and "orphanages" and the "protection of the convoys," it is harder to asses their part in the atrocities to which the imprisoned men and the deportees were subjected. Obviously, the national authorities wanted to separate the administrative procedures, where a semblance of legality was maintained, from the massacres entrusted to the Teşkilât-ı Mahsusa, which were generally committed in remote areas in the absence of witnesses.

In the vilayet of Mamuret ul-Aziz, several prominent members of the Young Turk club took an active hand in those clandestine massacres. As the driving force behind these crimes, one stands out from all the others – the deputy from Dersim, Haci Baloşzâde Mehmed Nuri Bey,[399] who was assisted by his brother Ali Pasha. It was Mehmed Nuri Bey who organized and supervised the squadrons of *çetes* led by the two Kurdish chieftains of the Reşvan tribe, Zeynel Bey and Haci Bedri Ağa; their field of operations was the plain of Fırıncılar and the gorge immediately adjoining it.[400] At a lower level, the deputy from Malatia, Haşim Bey, and his son Haşim Beyzâde Mehmed, head of the squadron of *çetes* based an hour's distance from Malatia, in Taşpinar, played similar roles in this *sancak*.[401] It is harder to assess the criminal activities of the other Young Turk protagonists of Mezreh and Malatia, whose names we have listed.[402] The case of the CUP inspector in the vilayet of Mamuret ul-Aziz, Boşnak Resneli Nâzım Bey, is even more problematic. Although a fair number of foreigners resided in the vilayet's capital, none of the reports we have mention Boşnak Resneli even once. All we know, thanks to the diary of the German minister Hans Bauernfeind and the account of a judge who officiated on the court-martial in Malatia, is that he spent more than two weeks in this city; he organized a meeting of all the Young Turk leaders at Haşim Bey's house, where he also lodged, and facilitated the training of the squadron of *çetes* who notably massacred the worker-soldiers of the region's *amele tarburis*.[403] There is every reason to believe that he engaged in similar activities in Mezreh, where, however, he seems to have come in for criticism (like Haci Baloşzâde Mehmed Nuri) from General Süleyman Faik Pasha and various other officers, who charged both men with profiting from their positions to extort large sums "in the name of the Committee of Union and Progress," and thus "personally enriching themselves at the expense of the Armenian deportees and the Syrians." These officers even demanded that Resneli Nâzım be recalled and that Hasim Bey be punished, suggesting to the vali that he refer the matter to "the honorable Committee."[404]

We likewise have only scant documentation on inspector Nâzım's relations with the twin hierarchies on which he depended, the Ittihad's Central Committee and the political leadership of the Teşkilât-ı Mahsusa. The only known telegram, dated 21 Haziran/4 July 1915, was addressed to Nâzım Bey by the head of the Teşkilât-ı Mahsusa, Bahaeddin Şakir; it was twice authenticated by the court-martial of Istanbul in 1919. It has apparently never been examined by historians, who, in citing it, copy one from the next the erroneous date of 21 April, thus robbing the telegram of all significance. The real date shows it to have been sent the day after the second convoy of deportees left Mezreh. The message is explicit and provides direct insight into the way Bahaeddin Şakir supervised, from Erzerum, the criminal operations underway in the area under the jurisdiction of the Third Army: "No. 5, for Nâzım Bey. Have you undertaken the liquidation of the Armenians who have been deported from the region? Are you eradicating the harmful individuals whom you say you have deported or exiled, or are you limiting yourselves to displacing them? Give me clear information, my brother."[405] The connection between the Special Organization and the representatives of the Ittihadist Central Committee appears clearly here, as does the nature of their relations.

Officers present in the area often witnessed the way the state's policy toward the Armenian population was translated into practice. Not all of them necessarily approved of these measures. Many took, at the very least, a rather lucid view of them. Araks Mgrdichian, the 21-year-old Euphrates College-educated daughter of the former British vice-consul in Dyarbekir, Thomas Mgrdichian, reports conversations she had or overheard while treating Turkish officers in the American hospital in Mezreh in summer 1915. Responding to colleagues who asked if the Armenians were truly guilty of the charges the government was leveling at them, Captain Ahmed Rıza said wryly, "Even the Armenians have started wondering whether they are truly guilty of having fabricated bombs and dynamite. The poor imbeciles!"[406] On another occasion, Mehmed Ali, an officer who had abducted and "married" the daughter of Professor Vorperian, a Euphrates College teacher, exclaimed: "Do you imagine that we weren't capable of punishing only those who were guilty – if any actually were? Why do you suppose that the civil court did not resolve the problem, but passed it on to the court-martial, which, in this war, had become savage? The plan was four years old."[407] Such statements, which were perhaps not particularly rare among Ottoman officers, show to what extent the propaganda meant to stigmatize "the" Armenians came to influence broad sectors of the population, until it came to affect the Armenians themselves.

Among the civilian officials working alongside the vali and implicated to one or another degree in the anti-Armenian persecutions were Cemal Bey, the secretary general of the vilayet; the head of the post office, Mektubci Şevkı Bey, who was also an influential member of the Young Turk club; Hasan Effendi, the warden of the Mezreh prison; Asim Bey, the *kaymakam* of Harput until August 1915; Hikmet Bey, the head of the department of commercial litigations (*umum hukukiye*); and Edhem Kadri Bey, the *kaymakam* of Behesni. Among military officials and officers in the gendarmerie, some played crucial roles in the arrest and torture of the men, especially in the Red Konak: Süleyman Faik Pasha, the commander of the Army's Eleventh Corps; Major Ferid, a division commander; Arapkirli Mehmed, a secretary in the gendarmerie; Arapkirli Ali Effendi; and Colonel Mehmed Vehib, who replaced Süleyman Faik late in November 1915. Of course, the commission responsible for abandoned property, headed by Mehmed Ali, assisted by Süleyman Sudi Effendi, Kuheddin Bey and his son, and Şerif Bey and his two sons, supervised the confiscation of Armenian property, in part to the personal benefit of its members. Among those who carried out the massacres were the commanders of the squadrons of *çetes* of the Special Organization: Mulazim Ethem Şevket; Haci Kahya from Izoli; Akçadağlı Sinanoğlu; Pulutlı Halil; Haci Şeih Ağa; Mehmed Bey; and Zeynel Ağa and Haci Bedri Ağa, chieftains of the Revan tribe. They were aided and abetted by a number of band leaders: Arab Mustafa Effendi; Arapkirli Genco Ağa; Haci Feyzi; Arapkirli Çobanzâde Halil Pasha; Asim Bey; Arapkirli Kenan; and Arapkirli Nalbandbaşi Mehmed Ali.[408]

The indictment that Fazıl drew up against Sabit Bey indicates that the vali took 15,000 Turkish pounds gold from Hovhannes Harputlian after killing him and deporting his family.[409] Another document accuses Sabit of depositing large sums at the Erzerum post office, including orders of payment signed by people who were deported and killed on the road to Malatia. The vali was also charged with ordering the head of the post to deposit 8,000 Turkish pounds gold in his account in October 1915.[410] The judgment that General Vehib Pasha passed on the crimes committed in the vilayet of Mamuret ul-Aziz confirms that local officials acted with total impunity, having been protected by the supreme authorities of the party-state:

> The atrocities perpetrated in Mezreh, Harput and the surrounding area and, in particular, in Malatia, eminently deserve to be singled out and recorded. The fact that this murderous apparatus, which was brought to bear even on women and children, sometimes operated under the very eyes of the leaders of the executive and responsible state officials, with their full knowledge, like the fact that, despite pressing reasons to the contrary, no legal prosecution was ever undertaken by either the gendarmerie or legal authorities, means, at the very least, that the leaders of the government and government officials closed their eyes to what was going on. The criminals, thus encouraged, committed their crimes without restraint, because those crimes were tolerated.[411]

Thus, one is not surprised to learn that at the trial (which ran from 20 November 1919 to 14 January 1920) of the men implicated in the deportations from the vilayet of Mamuret ul-Aziz,[412] only two of the authors of these crimes – the parliamentary deputy Mehmed Nuri and the head of the department of education, Ferid – were actually sitting in the dock.[413] It is no more surprising to observe that Bahaeddin Şakir, condemned to death "in accordance with Articles 171 and 181 of the Ottoman penal code," and Resneli Nâzım, condemned to 15 years in prison, were both absent. As for Haci Baloşzâdeh Mehmed Nuri Bey, he was acquitted.[414]

Inasmuch as all the mechanisms of the party-state were involved in these acts, the verdict was predictable. Moreover, when Enver Pasha passed through Mezreh in May 1916, accompanied by the German military attaché Hans Humann, the minister of war gave the American consul to understand that he knew about the reports on the atrocities perpetrated against the Armenians in the region that the consul had transmitted to Istanbul. He was also not unaware of the fact that the people whose honored guest he was that day had massacred the owners of the house in which he was being received (it was later acquired by Sabit Bey).[415] One more detail is symptomatic of the Young Turks' determination to liquidate the Armenians down to the last man, woman, and child: when Leslie Davis left Mezreh on 16 May 1917, he was not allowed to take with him the "American" citizens who had been living in his home since early summer 1915.[416]

Chapter 8

Deportations and Massacres in the Vilayet of Sıvas

The vast Sıvas vilayet, one of the most densely populated in Asia Minor, had approximately 1 million inhabitants in 1914, including 204,472 Armenians and about 100,000 Greeks and Syriacs. The Armenians in the urban centers were the most conspicuous, but non-negligible numbers of Armenians inhabited the countryside as well; they lived in some 240 villages and hamlets, boasting 198 churches, 21 monasteries, and 204 schools with a total enrolment of 20,599.[1] Unlike the vilayets we have examined so far, the Armenians in the Sıvas vilayet lived side-by-side with a Turkish-speaking (rather than Kurdish-speaking) Sunni Muslim population, including 10,000 *muhacirs* who had settled in the region in the wake of the Balkan War.[2]

The 30 March 1913 nomination of a new vali, Ahmed Muammer Bey – he held his post until 1 February 1916[3] – seems to have exacerbated the degradation of the non-Muslims' situation. In accordance with the wishes of Young Turk circles, as soon as he took office the vali initiated a policy of boycotting Christian entrepreneurs and merchants after the Ottoman defeat at the hands of the Balkan coalition. Muammer, a native of Sıvas and the son of a magistrate, played a decisive role in creating a network of Ittihadist clubs in his native vilayet from 1908 on.[4] Thirty-two years old when he assumed his post, the vali was the very prototype of the new sort of man the CUP needed to implement its policy of creating a "national economy" in the provinces: he was simultaneously the vali and the representative of the Unionist Central Committee in this vilayet in the middle of Asia Minor, through which he traveled extensively in order to broaden the circle of Ittihadist party activists and spread party propaganda.[5] According to Armenian sources, the real problems began only after the adoption of the reforms in the eastern provinces. Like the Greek populations living on the coasts of the Aegean, the Armenians of the Sıvas vilayet were the victims of the increasingly harsh policies of the Young Turks. In particular, Ahmed Muammer carried out a plan of economic harassment, the objective of which was to put an end to the Armenians' "prosperity" and bring Turkish cooperatives into existence.[6] He even seems to have called on the *hojas* of the vilayet to give their sermons a corresponding slant.[7] This determined vali also created schools in which Armenian teachers trained apprentices.[8] He thus sought to eliminate what seemed to him to be an Armenian monopoly over craft production. But Muammer also attacked religious institutions; such as when he confiscated the land belong to the monastery of St. Nshan, located near the city, in order to build a barracks for the Tenth Army Corps on it.[9] But the veiled economic boycott imposed by the authorities apparently did not completely ruin the Armenians. In April and May 1914, several suspect fires broke out, one after the next, in the bazaars of Merzifun/Marzevan, Amasia, Sıvas, and Tokat. In Tokat, according to an Armenian middle school teacher, 85 stores, 45 homes, and three khans were reduced to ashes by a fire that raged in Baghdad Cadesi, the street where many of the city's

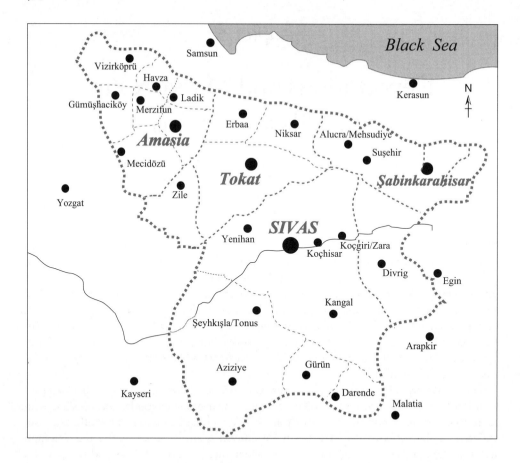

businesses were located, on 1 May 1914.[10] Three big flourmills were also ravaged by fires in Merzifun, Amasia, and Sıvas.[11] We have no proof that the local authorities had a hand in these criminal fires, but Armenian circles were not unduly persuaded to believe that the fires had been set on Ahmed Muammer's initiative. When the general mobilization order, the *seferbelik*, was announced in Sıvas on 3 August, every male of draftable age went to enroll at the recruitment center that had been set up in the Ulu Cami mosque, formerly the Church of St. Eranos. Over the next few weeks, the Church of the Holy Cross and some of the schools that belonged to the 20,000 Armenians of Sıvas – such as the Aramian middle school or the Sanasarian *lycée* – were gradually confiscated by the military authorities, who wished to use them as barracks.[12] By paying the *bedel*, some of the Armenian conscripts avoided mobilization or were assigned to the Red Cross. As elsewhere, the *Teklif-i Harbiyye* provided an opportunity for obvious abuses, to Armenian merchants' cost: all means of transportation in both the cities and the villages were requisitioned.[13] Furthermore, the national Armenian hospital assumed the costs of maintaining 150 hospital beds, which were put at the army's disposal.[14]

Among the striking measures observed in Sıvas after the Ottoman Empire entered the war was to dispatch to the Caucasian front the Tenth Army Corps, made up of recruits from the vilayet, including some 15 Armenian doctors and numerous Armenian soldiers.[15] In addition, 2,500 worker-soldiers were assigned to two labor battalions. The first improved the road leading from the konak to the stone bridge at Kızılırmak; the second built a pipeline two kilometers long to provide the city with drinking water.[16] Sıvas also served as a rear base for the Army of the Caucasus; in particular, the soldiers who fell victim to the dysentery and typhus epidemics decimating the army because of catastrophic sanitary conditions were sent here.[17] Once the French Jesuit fathers had left,[18] Reverend Ernest Partridge's American mission was the only foreign institution remaining in Sıvas. The national Armenian hospital and the establishment of the American Red Cross, directed by Dr. Clark, played a major part in fighting the epidemics. Nevertheless, 25,000 epidemic victims were recorded.[19]

Two events that occurred in the Sıvas vilayet attest to the tension-fraught atmosphere reigning in the regional capital. Since no one held the office of primate in the region, the Armenian Patriarchate had named two auxiliary primates to head the dioceses of Sıvas and Erzincan – Bishop Knel Kalemkiarian and Father Sahag Odabashian. In this troubled period, the patriarchate deemed it indispensable to maintain an official presence in these areas, in which the authorities recognized its right to represent the community. On 20 December, the two prelates arrived in Sıvas together. Odabashian, a native of the city, stayed with his family for a few days while waiting to find a vehicle that could take him to his new post. It seems, however, that the Interior Ministry had raised doubts as to the prelate's real mission. An encrypted telegram that it sent Muammer on 21 December 1914 informed the vali that, "there are serious reasons for thinking that [Odabashian] plans to precipitate disorders among the Armenians" and requested that he "put him under surveillance as soon as he arrives."[20] The task of watching the 38-year-old vicar was entrusted to Halil Bey, the commander of the *çete* squadrons; Emirpaşaoğlu Hamid, the leader of the Çerkez of Uzunyayla; and the *çetes* Bacanakoğlu Edhem, Kütükoğlu Hüseyin, and Zaralı Mahir. They assassinated Odabashian on the road between Suşehir and Refahiye, near the village of Ağvanis, on the morning of 1 January 1915.[21] The investigation that followed this murder, which had also taken the life of Odabashian's driver, Arakel Arslanian, offers a striking example of the formalism and duplicity of the administration.[22] The initial evidence indicated that "the weapons used were of two different kinds, resembling a Mauser and a Martini"; however, "since weapons of this kind are not just lying around, except in the Armenians' homes, it is possible that the authors of these murders are Armenians who committed the crime with a particular purpose in mind."[23] The investigation proceeded to focus on the surrounding Armenian and Greek villages, asking how people who had been absent from their village on the day of the murder had "spent their time."[24] The *kaymakam* of Suşehir, the investigating magistrate, and the commander of the gendarmerie went to the scene of the crime and interrogated witnesses. Thus, it was established that the murder was "committed by two individuals riding gray horses, while the other mounts were of various colors," that this band was armed with "Mauser Gras and Martini" rifles, and that the individuals in question had spoken Armenian, Greek, and Turkish. Zehni, the judge, observed, "the fact that they had not touched the victim's seven piasters gold, watch, baggage, or other personal belongings seems to indicate that the motive for the crime was not theft, but that the murderers had some other objective."[25] Suspicion focused on a Greek, Kristaki Effendi, from the village of Alacahan in the *kaza* of Refahiye, who had been "recognized by his voice"; however, the *kaymakam* of Suşehir thought that "the guilty parties were Armenians or Greeks from the region of Erzincan."[26] The Armenians of Sıvas understood very well that this "investigation" was a masquerade staged by the authorities to cover up their own role in the murder of the prelate, an event that, under other circumstances, would have caused a commotion. Yet no one dared protest, whether in Constantinople or Sıvas.[27] The accusations were, to be sure, so implausible that Muammer felt a need to engage in diversionary tactics. Patriarch Zaven notes in his memoirs that immediately after the murder of Sahag Odabashian, the local authorities accused the Armenians of taking revenge by poisoning the bread delivered to the Turkish soldiers, an accusation that spread through the population, leading to open hostility toward the Armenians.[28] On the night of 5/6 January, several soldiers from one of the Kavakyazı barracks had shown signs of indigestion. This "poisoning" was blamed on the bread, in which there were blue streaks, and taken as proof that a suspect substance had been mixed in with the dough. Ahmed Muammer, who went to the barracks without delay, observed that the Armenian soldiers there did not have the same symptoms, and concluded that the Armenians had doubtless committed a crime against the Turkish recruits. The Armenian soldiers were immediately confined to the basement of the barracks, while their Turkish colleagues were put on a state of alert; armed men surrounded Armenian neighborhoods and the authorities told the Turkish populace to get ready to react if the Armenians staged an "insurrection." In the course of the night, the accused bakers were arrested and tortured in order to make them confess as to which party, the Dashnaks or the Hnchaks, had ordered them to poison the soldiers' bread.[29] In the space of a few hours, Sıvas was transformed into a city under siege; massacres would probably have ensued if Constantinople had not stepped in to prohibit them. The investigation conducted the next day by Haci Hüsni, an army physician, Dr. Harutiun Shirinian, and Turkish and Armenian pharmacists revealed that the bread in question had been made from a mixture of wheat and rye flour, which caused the blue streaks in it, but that it was perfectly safe to eat. They further noted that the symptoms that had cropped up the night before had disappeared and that no one had been poisoned.[30] The local press, which was soon echoed by the press in Istanbul, nevertheless reported the official version of events, according to which Armenian bakers had poisoned the soldiers. This version was never retracted, despite Bishop Knel Kalemkiarian's repeated appeals to the vali.[31] A witness also reported that a mutilated body found near the suburb of Hoğtar had been exhibited in front of the town hall for 24 hours "in order to incite the Turks against the Armenians."[32]

The Armenians' situation was not improved by the event that occurred shortly thereafter – an 18 January 1915 reception held in Sıvas for Vice-Generalissimo Enver, who was on his way back from the front after the Ottoman defeat at Sarıkamiş. The famous Murad Khrimian (Sepastatsi Murad), a former Dashnak *fedayi* who had been rehabilitated after the proclamation of the Constitution,[33] went out to greet Enver and had a conversation with him. The minister emphasized that two members of the Dashnak leadership in Sıvas, Vahan Vartanian and Ohannes Poladian, had shown great courage during the fighting, but also stressed that the troops had been poorly trained.[34] When Enver received a visit by the Armenian religious and political leaders, he reminded them that he had been saved a few days earlier by Lieutenant Hovhannes Aginian, who had died of his wounds shortly thereafter, adding that the Armenian recruits had fought bravely.[35] These remarks, however, remained confined to the context of this courtesy visit. As was the case in other provinces, the Dashnaks remained the local authorities' privileged interlocutors in the first few months of the war. Murad Khrimian often met with Muammer to clear up "misunderstandings" with him – that is, to defuse provocations. Thus, in fall 1914, he was able to negotiate the staggered mobilization of different age cohorts with the authorities, the vali's hostility to the idea notwithstanding.[36] Yet mistrust continued to be perceptible on both sides. Like the valis of Dyarbekir and Trebizond, Ahmed Muammer too was the local leader of the *Teşkilât-ı Mahsusa*. It was on his orders that, in November 1914, the president of the vilayet court released 124 criminals from the prison of Bünyan to incorporate them into a unit then being formed.[37] An Armenian source observed that the squadron of *çetes* created in late fall 1914 had initially conducted operations "amid the greatest possible secrecy, and, later, in the open."[38] But Sıvas was also a city through which irregular troops sent from the western parts of the empire passed in transit. For example, on 10 December 1914, a unit of 1,200 *çetes* en route for Erzerum arrived in Sıvas and was given a hero's welcome by the Turkish populace. In contrast, the Armenian villagers' memory of these men's passage through the area was a much less happy one, for they wreaked havoc on the villages of the plain.[39] Bekir Sâmi Bey's group, comprising 800 irregulars, 20 of them officers, spent the month of January in Govdun, the village near Hafız in which Murad Khrimian lived. The *çetes* were, however, careful not to mistreat the population, with which they were billeted, and even showed the celebrated former *fedayi* respectful deference.[40] The handful of abuses noted in this period may, moreover, be put down to these men's criminal past. The vilayet of Sıvas did not really begin to feel the effects of the war until after the failure of the Sarıkamiş offensive. Thus, from 2 February on, the Armenian villages on the plain of Sıvas were surrounded by what was left of the Third Army, which took up quarters there and lived off the residents. Typhus raged among these soldiers and soon spread to the villagers as well. The villages of Kızılbaş also had to help feed and lodge these men. Turkish localities, however, were spared.[41] Govdun seems to have been required to make a particularly heavy contribution to the war effort, perhaps because Murad lived there. Although one-and-a-half battalions of the regular army had already been billeted in the village, a new squadron of *çetes* arrived from Istanbul to take up quarters there on 30 January. Now, however, the tone changed: the Çerkez officer in command of the unit immediately attacked Murad for having struggled "against Islam for twenty years," and threatened the villagers. The *fedayi* answered that the sole purpose of his fight had been to establish the "constitution," adding that "the village was not in revolt" and appealing for corroboration to the officer responsible for the regular troops stationed in the village. The next day, when Murad visited the commander of the brigade posted in the sector in order to request that he send these *çetes* away, he was told that this squadron answered directly to the vali, not to the military authorities.[42] Murad therefore left for Sıvas in order to meet with Muammer. He described the unbearable situation of the rural populations of the vilayet, who were expected to feed and quarter thousands of soldiers. By way of his answer, the vali remarked: "It seems that the Armenian population is unhappy over our successes." In other words, the Ottoman "successes" – the defeat at Sarıkamiş had not yet been publicly announced – supposedly irritated the Armenians, who were suspected of harboring sympathies for the Russians. Murad understood the message very clearly and immediately convoked a meeting of the Armenian representatives of all confessions in order to evaluate the authorities' intentions, which were deemed alarming. The Armenian leaders decided to remain vigilant in order to defuse provocations,[43] the more so in that they had already observed that the authorities had not reacted when, during the January 1915 debacle, Armenian soldiers responsible for transport had been massacred near the Erzincan-Sıvas road.[44] The Armenians' alarm was heightened when they learned on 8 February that the village of Piurk, located in the *kaza* of Suşehir, had been destroyed under suspect circumstances by a recently formed group of *çetes* that included Zaralı Mahir, one of the men who had murdered Sahag Odabashian.[45] This massacre, during which several men had been killed, was all the more symbolic in that Piurk had had a reputation as an Armenian *fedayi* center in Abdülhamid's day.[46] The Armenians were also worried because of alarmist remarks that German officers stationed in Sıvas were supposed to have made, according to Dr. Hayranian, an army doctor educated in Germany who was a friend of Dr. Paul Rohrbach's.[47] A German doctor, whom Hayranian had asked to intercede with the authorities after the attack on Piurk, had answered: "What can I do? What can I say? Think rather about how to die with honor."[48]

In the first half of February, the arrival of between 1,500 and 1,700 Russian prisoners-of-war on the plain of Sıvas offered the local authorities another opportunity to paint the Armenians as suspect. Certain villages had been asked to lodge and feed these Russians. Eight men who had arrived in terrible condition, suffering from typhus, died the first night, despite the care the villagers gave them. The soldiers escorting them were nevertheless opposed to the idea of burying them. Having ignored this prohibition to bury them, the Armenian villagers were immediately accused of rebelling and treated accordingly.[49] The authorities pretended not to know that the Christian funeral rite required that the dead be buried regardless of identity. It is, however, also possible to chalk these events up to the bitterness engendered by the defeat at Sarıkamiş.

In March, the Young Turk members of parliament from Çangırı, Harput, and Erzerum were invited to come to Sıvas by the CUP's responsible secretary, Erzrumlı Gani, in order to speak before the Young Turk club and in the mosques.[50] According to a number of concurring sources, Fazıl Berki, the representative from Çangırı, declared: "Our true enemies are close to us, among us – they are the Armenians...who are sapping the foundations of our state. That is why we must first wipe out these domestic foes."[51] These remarks, based on a speech that Bahaeddin Şakir had made in the same period,[52] circulated so openly in Sıvas that Bishop Kalemkiarian felt the need to go to see the vali and ask what they meant.[53] The role of Erzrumlı Gani Bey appears here for the first time. This Young Turk leader, a native of Erzerum who had received his officer's training at Istanbul's Military Academy (Harbiye), arrived in Sıvas in fall 1914.[54] There, he organized a lecture that Dr. Şakir had delivered before the Ittihadist club, probably on his way back to Istanbul in early March 1915.[55] Gani worked with the vali, Muammer, and his henchmen – the parliamentary representative from Çangırı, Dr. Fazıl Berki; the representative from Sıvas, Rasim Bey; and Colonel Ali Effendi, the deputy commander of the Tenth Army Corps – on the plan to extirpate the Armenians.[56]

Muammer, however, entrusted the organization of new squadrons of çetes in the vilayet to the parliamentary representative Rasim Bey in March 1915.[57] Approximately 4,000 çetes were recruited and given gendarmes' uniforms. This group was drawn, notably, from the Kurdish population of Darende, Karapapak who had come from the Caucasus, and freed felons. Two thousand of these "gendarmes" were to go to Sıvas, while the others were to be dispatched to the neighboring villages.[58] In the same period, there was a sharp rise in desertions among the Armenian recruits, who had suffered increasing harassment and persecution. The medreses of Şifahdiye and Gök were converted into detention centers for Armenian soldiers.[59] Thus, by March, the first signs of the events to come could be discerned. The most symbolic act was the arrest, around 15 March, of 17 political leaders and teachers in Merzifun and Amasia – among them Kakig Ozanian, Mamigon Varzhabedian, and Khachig Atamian – who were immediately transferred to Sıvas and interned in the medrese of Şifahdiye.[60] The Armenian sources say nothing about the motives that the authorities invoked to justify these arrests, but note that they preceded the arrests of the political and intellectual elites of Sıvas by two weeks. In the provincial capital, the alleged flight of a Russian officer served as a pretext for the arrests of a hotelier, Manug Beylerian; Cholak Hampartzumian; and, on 28 March, of the pharmacist and Dashnak leader Vahan Vartanian, along with his colleagues Hovhannes Poladian and Harutiun Vartigian; the Hnchaks' Krikor Karamanugian, Murad Gurigian, and Dikran Apelian; and the dragoman of the vilayet, Mardiros Kaprielian, all of whom were summoned before Muammer and then immediately placed under arrest. On 7 May, after spending 40 days in the central prison, these men were put in chains and sent to Yeni Han on the Sıvas-Tokat-Samsun road. Muammer, the CUP's responsible secretary Gani Bey, and Colonel Pertev, the commander of the Tenth Army Corps, joined them in a place called Maşadlar Yeri, where they interrogated the Armenian leaders about their plans for an insurrection and the quantity of arms in their possession, and then put them to death.[61] Bishop Kalemkiarian's protests to the vali proved to be in vain, as did the request from Dr. Haranian to liberate the detainees; indeed, Haranian's bold intervention cost him his life.[62] It was Murad Khrimian, however, who was Muammer's greatest cause of concern. On Monday, 29 March – that is, the day after the Sıvas leaders were arrested – the vali sent Keleş Bey, the commander of the gendarmerie, to Sıvas, accompanied by a squadron. Keleş Bey told Murad to go with him to Sıvas because Muammer "wished" to see him. After giving orders to set a resplendent table for his guests, the *fedayi* disappeared without a trace.[63] The forces of the gendarmerie sent to look for him arrested the male population of the village of Khandzar, which was suspected of having given Murad shelter, and proceeded to kill the men in the Seyfe Gorge, a spot two hours to the east of the village.[64] This massacre, which occurred in early April, marked the end of the first phase of operations, the main target of which had been the political elites of Sıvas and conscripts from the city.

Deportations and Massacres in the Sancak of Sıvas

In 1914, the Armenian population of the *sancak* of Sıvas alone was 116,817. The Armenians lived in 46 towns and villages.[65] The *kaza* of Sıvas had 37 towns and villages, with a total Armenian population of 31,185, almost 20,000 of whom lived in the regional capital.[66] Demographic considerations perhaps explain why the first operations, the official purpose of which was to track down deserters and collect weapons, targeted only the Halys/Kızılımak valley, focusing on the villages in the northern part of it. Moreover, early in April 1915 the authorities took all the measures required to completely cut off relations and correspondence between Sıvas and the neighboring villages: "no one knew what was going on, even in a village just an hour away."[67]

We have information about one of the battalions of *çetes* created on Muammer's initiative, the one commanded by Kütükoğlu Hüseyin and Haralı Mahir, the murderers of Father Sahag Odabashian.[68] This battalion conducted its operations in the localities of the Kızılırmak valley from 2 April onward.[69] It had been given the mission of arresting the adolescents, village priests, schoolteachers, and notables who had not been conscripted. According to Armenian sources, these operations were accompanied by looting, rapes, and murders, and were followed by the transfer of the men who had been arrested to Zara/Koçhisar or Sıvas. Some of these men were killed in the Seyfe gorge or at the level of the Boğaz bridge. The others were interned in the city, in the *medreses* of Şifahdiye and Gök.[70] We also know that a battalion of gendarmes commanded by Ali Şerif Bey carried out operations in this valley. The killing of the men of the villages of Khorasan and Aghdk, located on the outskirts of Koçhisar, were its work; the villagers were put to death in the Bunağ Gorge.[71] It is probable that the 4,000 *çetes* stationed throughout the *sancak* were given similar missions in other districts during these operations, which took place in April and May. A squadron even took up a position near Sıvas, on the banks of the Kızılırmak in a place called Paşa Çayiri, which was converted into a slaughterhouse for prisoners who had been interned in the regional capital.[72]

The Armenians of the city of Sıvas were not really targeted until May 1915. One of the first measures taken concerned the Armenian employees of the Post and Telegraph Office. The minister responsible for it issued an order by telegraph calling for their immediate dismissal,[73] which was followed by that of all other Armenian civil servants, such as municipal physicians and pharmacists, gendarmes, and so on.[74] The monastery of St. Nshan came under full army control. Finally, the authorities ordered that the population turn in its weapons on pain of court-martial. At the vali's request, Bishop Kalemkiarian asked his flock in a Sunday sermon to obey the government's orders. Armenians and Turks handed over their weapons (for the sake of appearances, the decree applied to the entire population). Of course, Muammer invoked the Armenians' lack of cooperation to justify launching a vast confiscation campaign that led in turn to the arrests of the city's notables (one of the first to be imprisoned was the famous arms-maker of Sıvas, Mgrdich Norhadian).[75] The government's propaganda now took on a more vehement tone. The authorities began by putting the weapons turned in by the Armenians on display, adding to these the battle arms in the barracks and photographing the pile. The vali also sent a report to the Sublime Porte in which he accused the Armenians of treason.[76]

There also exist reports of a meeting held in Sıvas sometime in May that was attended by Turkish notables and Çerkez and Kurdish chiefs (from the *kaza* of Koçkiri), to whom the vali issued directives about the treatment to be meted out to the Armenian population. After the Armenians had been demonized for several weeks, the situation seemed ripe for the transition to the practical phase of the extermination. A Turkish liberal, Ellezzâde Halil Bey, told one of his Armenian friends, "You cannot imagine what they are preparing to do to you."[77] Among the Armenians, a rumor was making the rounds about how "black lists" containing the names of the first men to be arrested were being drawn up for every quarter of the city. It would appear that a general list was produced by combining material from three sources: the heads of the various neighborhoods; artisans' associations, which the CUP club had asked to produce names; and the police. Hnchak Party and Dashnak Party clubs were searched and their archives impounded.[78] Down to the end of May, however, the arrests carried out across the vilayet had involved only 400 to 500 men.[79] Finally, there are indications that Muammer made a tour of the *kaza*s of his vilayet, notably Merzifun[80] and Tokat,[81] in late May and early June.

Here, too, the first victims of this operational phase were those people most deeply involved in local political and social life, as well as those with connections to foreign institutions, such as the physicians at the American hospital or the teachers at Merzifun's Anatolia College. Thus, the authorities sought to isolate these establishments. They gradually requisitioned their buildings and then forced the missionaries to leave the region.[82] On 15 June, 12 people were publicly hanged. These men were political activists, four deserters from Divrig/Divriği, and people who had been accused, apparently unjustly, of a murder that had occurred several years earlier.[83] This spectacle took place shortly before the beginning of the systematic operations conducted by the police and the gendarmerie that began on Wednesday, 16 June 1915. On that day, 3,000 to 3,500 men were arrested in their places of work or their homes and interned in the central prison or the cellars of the *medreses* of Şifahdiye and Gök.[84] Among them were teachers from the Aramian and Sanasarian *lycées*, including Mihran Isbirian, Mihran Chukasezian, Hagop Mnjugian, and Hayg Srabian; Mikayel Frengulian, a teacher from the American middle school; Avedis Semerjian, Krikor Gdigian, and Senig Baliozian from the Jesuit middle school; the members of the Diocesan Council, including its leading members Voskan Aslan and Benyamin Topalian; and staff members of charitable organizations, political activists, doctors, pharmacists, and all those who counted in Sıvas, such as the police officers Ara Baliozian and Mgrdich Bujakjian, the surveyor Serope Odabashian, the lawyer Mgrdich Poladian, the Telegraph Office employee Aram Aginian, the municipal architect Hovhannes Frengulian, the photographer H. Enkababian, and the former dragoman of the French consulate, Manug Ansurian.[85] Ernest Partridge notes that no proof whatsoever of the guilt of these men was put forward, that they were never indicted, and that no one knew why the authorities had arrested them. The vali repeatedly assured the American minister that they would be "freed and sent on their way with their families."[86] The Armenian bishop was given a more original explanation: Muammer told him that he had had the men interned to protect them from the possibility of a massacre, since "prison was the safest place" for them. He also advised the prelate not to get involved in these matters, especially because he was not yet acquainted with the Armenians of Sıvas. Only he, the vali, knew "just how dangerous this element was."[87]

The first round-up was followed by a second wave of arrests, launched on 23 June, that led to the apprehension of around 1,000 men. Thus, a total of some 5,000 people were crammed into the city's central prison and the cellars of the *medreses*.[88] Similar operations were conducted in the second half of June in Tokat, Amasia, Merzifun, Zile, Niksar, Hereke, and so on, with the apprehended men rapidly killed in the environs of these localities.[89] In Sıvas, Muammer seems to have opted for another method: as we shall see, it was only after carrying out the deportations that he concerned himself, early in August, with the fate of these prisoners. Despite its proven utility, Sivas' Armenian national hospital, which had put 150 beds at the army's disposal and played an important role in fighting the typhus epidemic, was confiscated by the authorities. Most of its staff were arrested[90] and put to death shortly thereafter.

The pretrial investigation of Gani Bey, the CUP's responsible secretary in Sivas, mentions a trip that he made to Istanbul in the second half of June 1915 in order to take part in a coordinating meeting with his colleagues from other vilayets.[91] We do not have further details about the directives that were issued to the Ittihadist delegates there, but it seems reasonable to suppose that they bore on the deportations that began in very many different locales in early July.

The first to be deported were the inhabitants of the villages located in the upper part of the Halys/Kızılırmak valley in the *kazas* of Koçhisar and Koçkiri. These deportees were put on the road in the latter half of June, before the official publication of the expulsion decree. As elsewhere, first the adolescent and adult men were arrested and killed, after which women and children were set marching southward. By 29 June, the deportation of the villagers from the Kızılırmak valley had already been completed.[92]

The official deportation order was not promulgated until late June – 30 June, to be exact.[93] On 1 July, Ahmed Muammer convoked the Armenian orthodox primate, Bishop Kalemkiarian, as well as his Catholic counterpart, Bishop Levon Kechejian, to inform them that the first convoy would have to leave the city on Monday, 5 July, bound for Mesopotamia. On Kalemkiarian's account, the vali justified this measure by recalling that the Armenians had been living "for six hundred years under the glorious protection of the Ottoman state" and had profited from its sultans' tolerance, which had enabled them to preserve their language and religion and to prosper to the point that "trade and the crafts were entirely in [their] hands." Finally, Muammer pointed out that if he had not been vigilant and anticipated developments, an "insurrection would also have broken out and you would have – God forbid – stabbed the Ottoman army in the back."[94] This condensed historical overview no doubt reflected the sentiment prevailing among the Young Turks at the time, as well as the leitmotif of official propaganda.

Armenian sources depict the desperate attempts of some Armenian women to intervene with the vali and Sivas's Turkish dignitaries, who advised them to convert while waiting for "the storm to blow over." It would appear that a few dozen craftsmen at most were authorized to remain in the city after agreeing to become Muslims. In any event, this possibility of escaping deportation was briefly but vigorously[95] debated by the detainees, who brought the debate to a swift close since they seemed to have understood that this semi-official opening was a lure. On Sunday, 4 July, a final church service was held in the cathedral. When it was over, the bishop took the keys of the building to the vali, who refused to accept them.[96] According to G. Kapigian, who observed these events with a certain perspicacity, Muammer had deftly profited from the general despair in order to spread rumors to the effect that the anti-Armenian measures were just temporary, even justifying the deportees' hopes of a swift return. Indications are that the vali had worried until the last moment that the Armenians might rise up in revolt despite the fact that the community's most vigorous elements had been jailed. As in Harput/Mezreh, the Armenians tried to put their most valuable belongings in the safekeeping of the American missionaries, especially Dr. Clark and Mary Graffam, but the police limited their ability to do so by blocking the entrance to the American mission. Funds deposited with the *Banque Ottomane* were also frozen and then confiscated on Muammer's orders. The vali recommended that the Armenians register their property and deposit it in the cathedral, which had been transformed into a warehouse to that end. Many Armenians, however, chose to bury their savings. It must be added that the authorities had prohibited the sale of moveable property in advance and this ordinance was, by and large, respected.[97] In other words, the Armenians' assets were turned over in their entirety to the commission charged with "administering" them. It must finally be noted that, shortly before the departure of the first convoy, three regiments commanded by Neşed Pasha set out for Şabinkarahisar in order to put down the Armenian resistance that had been organized there.

The Deportation of 5,850 Families from Sıvas

Between Monday, 5 July and Sunday, 18 July, Sıvas's 5,850 Armenian families were deported in a total of 14 convoys, at a rate of one convoy daily, with an average of 400 households in each caravan.[98] The operation was carried out neighborhood by neighborhood – even street by street – in an order that suggests the most affluent families were deported first and the most modest quarters dealt with last. However, some 70 artisan households were allowed to remain behind, along with nine students from the Sanasarian lycée, the vali's son's violin teacher K. Koyunian, four physicians (Harutiun Shirinian, Karekin Suni, N. Bayenderian, and Gozmas Mesiayan), the 80 orphans in the Swiss orphanage, three officers (Dikran Kuyumjian, Vartan Parunagian, and Vartan Telalian), the pharmacists Hovhannes Mesiayan and Ardashes Aivazian, and above all the approximately 4,000 recruits from the region assigned to labor battalions.[99] The inhabitants of a village near the city, Tavra – millers who provided the city and the army with its flour – were also temporarily allowed to stay behind, as were the peasants from Prkenik, Ulash, and Ttmaj, who produced the bulk of the vilayet's wheat.[100]

On the morning of 5 July, Muammer oversaw the departure of the first convoy from the balcony of his residence. A dense crowd watched the spectacle, apparently with satisfaction, exclaiming, "The thermalistes [hydrotherapists] are leaving." A bridge known as Twisted Bridge served as a checkpoint: the government officials stationed there recorded the names of men, women, boys, and girls on separate lists.[101]

The first measure taken by the vali was to post a squadron of the Special Organization in the Yırıhi Han Gorge on the other bank of the Kızılırmak river. This group, dubbed Emniyet Komisioni, was commanded by Emirpaşoğlu Hamid, the chief of the Çerkez of Uzunyayla; Halil Bey, the commanding officer of the squadrons of çetes and Muammer's yaver (assistant); Bacanakoğlu Edhem; Kütükoğlu Hüseyin, who spoke Armenian and was the most knowledgeable about Sıvas' Armenians; and Tütünci Haci Halil. These çetes' mission was to single out the men still present in the convoys, especially if they were young, and to suggest that the deportees leave their money and valuables behind. They first looted the groups of deportees even before they were put on the road.[102] All the convoys from the sancak of Sıvas followed, grosso modo, the same trajectory and were subjected to the same fate. The deportations were carried out along a route that ran through Sıvas, Tecirhan, Mağara, Kangal, Alacahan, Kötihan, Hasançelebi, Hekimhan, Hasanbadrig, Aruzi Yazi, the Kirk Göz Bridge, Fırıncilar, Zeydağ, and Gergerdağ (the mountains of Kanlı Dere where the Kurdish chieftains of the Reşvan tribe, Zeynel Bey and Haci Bedri Ağa, officiated), then headed toward Adiyaman and Samsat, crossed the Euphrates near Gözen, and took the road running through Suruc, Urfa, Viranşehir, and Ras ul-Ayn, or the road to Mosul, or, again, the road that led to Aleppo via Bab and Mumbuc. The few known survivors were those who reached Hama, Homs, or, in the case of the most unfortunate, Rakka or Der Zor.[103] We shall here content ourselves with describing in detail the fate of the eleventh caravan, which left Sıvas on 15 July, which comprised 400 families from Karod Sokak, Dzadzug Aghpiur, Holy Savior, Ğanli Bağçe, Hasanlı, Taykesens, and Han Paşi. Among them was the family of Garabed Kapigian, a privileged witness to the events that transpired in Sıvas. Kapigian, a former Hnchak party activist who had lived for a long time in Istanbul, was one of the rare adult men over 40 still "free." The escort of gendarmes was commanded by Ali Çavuş, a Turk well known by a certain number of the deportees.[104] After being looted for the first time in the outskirts of Sıvas, the eleventh convoy continued its journey via Maragha and Kangal, whose Armenians had already been deported. Kapigian notes, however, that a banker from Sıvas, Ghazar Tanderjian, who had left with the first convoy, managed to remain in Kangal by converting with his whole family to Islam. In the field near the village that served as a campground, the deportees from Sıvas discovered two caravans who had arrived the day before from Samsun, Merzifun, Amasia, and Tokat. The scant information that they gleaned from the deportees of these convoys confirms that the same scenario had unfolded in those towns as well. It should be noted, however, that all males over the age of eight in these convoys were separated from the others and killed in Şarkışla by Turkish and Çerkez villagers on the orders of Halil Bey. Before the convoy left, Kapigian saw a brigade of Armenian worker-soldiers arrive. They had been charged with demolishing the church in Kangal.[105]

On 24 July, the eleventh convoy from Sıvas arrived in the Yırıhi Han Gorge, located outside the village of Alacahan. Like the groups that had preceded it, the caravan had to pass through this filter, where the *çetes* commanded by Emirpaşaoğlu Hamid Bey were waiting for it. Hamid immediately ordered the men to step out of the convoy and line up in front of the khan because he wished to address them. His remarks, reported by Kapigian, are worth briefly pausing over. Very courteously, the *çete* leader apologized for his failure to safeguard the roads against "the permanent attacks of the Kurdish savages." It was because of these attacks, he went on, that the government, "always solicitous of your welfare," had dispatched the *Emniyet Komisioni* to the Yırıhi Han Gorge and charged it with taking in hand and registering in the deportees' names all the gold, money, jewels, and other valuables they had with them ("everything you have in your possession"). Hamid Bey promised that these items would be restored to their owners as soon as the convoy reached Malatia. In a less friendly tone, he warned everyone that systematic body searches would be conducted and that anyone discovered to have held back the least little coin would be shot on the spot. Even before the group was dispersed, Kapigian reports, a mounted "gendarme" galloped onto the scene and announced that the convoy from Samsun, which had set out that very morning, had been attacked by Kurds, who had looted the deportees and massacred a number of people. Kapigian says that this carefully staged show, which was supposed to illustrate the dangers to which the deportees were exposed around Yırıhi Han, hardly convinced the deportees. Rather, it plunged them into a dilemma:[106] how, in such an environment, should they hide their possessions, the means of guaranteeing their survival? Obviously, this question confronted all the deportees – or at any rate, all who possessed means. In this curious game that consisted in relieving the deportees of all their possessions in order gradually to deprive them of the means of survival, the victims and their executioners were in a one-way face-off. Kapigian lists the stratagems to which the Armenians resorted: some swallowed gold coins, others hid jewels on their children, and still others hastily buried their purses. The government's solicitude evaporated at this point. The *çetes* proceeded to carry out systematic body searches on the deportees. Already experienced, they no doubt knew better than the victims the various ways of hiding money and jewels. Threats, blackmail, and violence were enough to change the minds of those deportees who had been trying to hold back at least some of their possessions in order to be able to proceed on their way.

Thus, the *Emniyet Komisioni* served as a framework for the official pillage of the deportees before they were turned over to the looters. In other words, the system that Muammer had put in place in Yırıhi Han was designed to secure the lion's share of the booty for the Ittihadist party-state before the deportees were turned over to the *çetes* or peasants mobilized along the routes that the convoys went down. However, the CUP's official bodies had to overcome the recurrent problem of the indelicacy or cupidity of the "civil servants" in charge of these official stations set up for the seizure of Armenian property. This explains the extraordinary formality that characterized the operations by which the deportees were stripped of their property and the fact that someone close to the vali was generally on hand with the obvious mission of supervising the operations. Kapigian notes the great care taken by the commission to register the deportees' property, counting and recounting their cash and describing their jewels in great detail.

This formality, however, gave way to more muscular methods when the family heads were summoned, one by one – a few of them were men, but most were women – to appear before the members of the commission presided over by Hamid Bey in order to relinquish their possessions. Systematically, they were told that what they had turned over was far from being everything they owned, a remonstrance that was usually accompanied by a bastinado with which the commission obtained an additional effort from the deportees. The commission worked all the more effectively because its members knew their victims rather well; they were aware of the position they occupied in society and consequently had a rather precise notion of the means at their disposal. After this ritual, which lasted for several hours, the çetes conducted searches of the other members of the convoy, down to the most private parts of their bodies. In the final stage of the operation, the notables who had escaped the round-ups in the city were removed from the convoy and summarily killed.[107] Kapigian's brief description of the fates reserved for the preceding and following convoys shows that the same procedure was followed every time.

When the convoy reached Kötü Han on the boundary between the vilayets of Sıvas and Mamuret ul-Aziz, its escort was relieved. Kurdish gendarmes now took the place of the Turkish gendarmes. According to Kapigian, *bakshish* in the usual amount was not enough to satisfy this new escort and convince it to step in when local villagers tried to profit from the passage of a convoy by acquiring a few valuables or abducting a girl. The intervention of a mullah made it possible, however, to curb these appetites, so that the profits were made by the sale of fresh produce – at obviously exorbitant prices.[108]

It was, however, only after they reached Hasançelebi, in the northern part of the *sancak* of Malatia, that the convoys began to be systematically decimated. In theory, it was a 30-hour journey from Sıvas to Hasançelebi, but the eleventh convoy from Sıvas needed no fewer than 15 days to make the trip, indicating that the individual stages of the journey were not long and were probably even bearable for old people. Moreover, during this first stage of the trek, human losses were limited to the dignitaries killed at Yırıhi Han. It was as if it had been decided to bring the deportees out of their native *sancak* before moving on to the exterminatory phase in the proper sense of the word; it was as if the local authorities wished to pin the blame for the programmed crimes on the civil servants of the neighboring region or the Kurdish population, which systematically took the role of the "black sheep."

Hasançelebi was a site that had been chosen for the systematic extermination of all the males in the convoys from Samsun and the *kazas* of the Sıvas vilayet. The advantage of the valley that ran from the village outward was that it lay squeezed between high mountains: deportees from the convoys that had arrived from Samsun, Tokat, Amasia, Sıvas and their rural zones in the preceding days were concentrated in the immense camp located in it. Amid indescribable chaos, the groups camped in two distinct areas. Kurdish çetes crammed in young boys, adolescents, adults, and old men from this multitude; they were escorted from the camp in small groups and briefly interned in a stable pressed into service as a prison. According to Kapigian, those in charge of the camp granted the new arrivals a day's respite – that is, enough time to unload their carts and pitch tents. Around 300 men in the eleventh convoy from Sıvas were led off in this fashion.[109] Here, too, the procedure followed was almost mechanical. Every night, the people arrested in the morning were removed from the stable, tied together in pairs, and escorted to a spot behind a promontory in a gorge. There the executioners killed their prisoners with knives or axes and threw them from the promontory. The next morning new arrests were made, and so on. On Kapigian's estimate, more than 4,000 males in the 14 convoys from Sıvas were killed in Hasançelebi. Boys under ten, however, were spared.[110]

Reverend Bauernfeind, who left his mission in Malatia on 11 August, went to Kırk Göz at dawn the same day,[111] and better understood

> why our coach-drivers wanted to reach Hasanbadrig before the heat of noon at all costs. The stench of the corpses – which is all too familiar to us – from about a hundred, or perhaps more, individual and mass graves to the left and right, were so poorly dug that, here and there, parts of the bodies stuck up out of them. Further on, the graves disappear, but not the dead: men, women, and children lie stretched out beside the road, in the dust, either in rags or stark naked, in terrible condition, more or less decomposed. In the space of a four hours' journey to Hasanbadrig (roughly twenty kilometers), we counted one hundred bodies. It goes without saying that in this region full of valleys, many of the corpses escaped our gaze.

Further north, shortly before Hekimhan, Bauernfeind again saw corpses, "as a rule, in pairs – again, males – in a state that inevitably led one to suspect that they had met a violent death. Because the terrain was so rugged, we were not able to see many others, but we could smell them." However, subsequent observations made by the German minister, who went the other way, down the route the convoys had taken, confirm that no significant violence had been inflicted on the deportees beyond Hasançelebi.[112]

Hekimhan, the next stage, seems above all to have served to eliminate the handful of men who escaped being killed at Hasançelebi.[113] For its part, the transit camp, located further to the south, near the Kırk Göz Bridge over the Tohma Çay, where the secretary of the Malatia gendarmerie Tayar Bey presided over operations with a squad of *çetes* "disguised as gendarmes,"[114] served to regulate the flow of convoys that converged on it from the regions of the Black Sea coast, Erzerum, and the northern part of Harput. This no doubt explains why the authorities appointed a *Sevkiyat Memuri* ("director of the deportation") there.[115] From that point on, the convoys from Samsun and the different *kaza*s of Sıvas took the route followed by everyone, else and shared their fate.

The deportees from Sıvas, like their compatriots from other regions, were also concentrated in the immense camp at Fırıncılar, one of the main killing fields chosen by the *Teşkilât-ı Mahsusa*. It was supervised by Haci Baloşzâde Mehmed Nuri Bey, a parliamentary representative from Dersim, and his brother Ali Paşa.[116] As was the case with other groups, the authorities removed the boys under ten and the girls under 15 from the convoys in order to send them on to Malatia, where they were ultimately killed.[117] Kapigian, who had survived up to this point by disguising himself as a woman, confirms the miserable plight of the refugees, who had been weakened by the journey, deprived of means of transport, and stripped of virtually all their belongings as a result of the successive acts of pillage to which they had been subjected.[118] It was in Fırıncılar that the deportees from Sıvas had been deprived of their means of transport, which were officially confiscated by the requisitions commission to meet the needs of the army.[119]

Here Kapigian observed the arrival of caravans of deportees from the Black Sea coast – particularly Kirason, Ordu, and Çarşamba – as well as the villages of Şabinkarahisar. They were in a more than wretched state because the women and children – there was not a single man in these groups – had made the entire journey on foot. Fırıncılar also served as a graveyard for the oldest deportees, who were unable to go on, and the small children abandoned by their mothers because they could no longer carry them.[120]

Kapigian's convoy left Fırıncılar on 18 August, just before the third caravan from Erzerum arrived there. All the groups took a mountain trail known as Nal Töken ("which makes the horseshoes fall off"), then entered the appropriately named Kanlı Dere ("blood valley") Gorge, where Zeynel Bey and Haci Bedri Ağa, two Kurdish chieftains of the Reşvan tribe, were waiting for them with their squadrons of çetes.[121] One by one, the deportees were stripped of their clothing and divested of their last possessions. The handful of men still among them was killed, and the most attractive girls and young women were carried off.[122] The sites of Fırıncılar-Kanlı Dere went out of operation in September once the flood of convoys had tapered off. According to Mrs. Aristakesian, who worked as a cook for the commander in charge of the Fırıncılar "camp," the last deportees who left, basically the sick and elderly, were put to death in a nearby valley.[123]

Thus, the deportees who arrived at the next way-station, Samsat, were physically diminished and psychologically weakened, if not traumatized. From Samsat, they took the road to Urfa through Karakayık Gorge. On the way, these groups were attacked at precise points and gradually decimated, with the killing taking place notably on the banks of the Euphrates south of Samsat, near the village of Oşin. A few remnants of these convoys nevertheless managed to reach Suruc, Urfa, and then Ras ul-Ayn or Der Zor.[124] In the fifth part of the present study, we shall see the fate reserved for these survivors in the second phase of the genocide.

The *Kaza* of Koçhisar

This *kaza*, which borders on Sıvas, was located in the upper Halys/Kızılırmak valley. In 1914, it boasted 30 Armenian localities with 13,055 inhabitants and 28 schools with a total enrollment of 2,483. The principal town in the *kaza*, Koçhisar, had barely 3,000 inhabitants, 2,037 of whom were Armenian.[125]

The main organizers of the deportations and massacres here were Vefa Bey, the interim *kaymakam*; Kukuşoğlu Şükru, the mayor and a member of the Ittihad; Salaheddin, a sergeant in the gendarmerie in Koçhisar; Mustaf, an employee in the Tobacco Régie; Adalı Hasan, who organized the deportations in the *kaza* itself; the Turkish notables Hamdi Effendi, Rıza Effendi, and Sehid Osman Nuri; and the chief of the çetes, Mehmed Çavuş.[126]

As we have already noted,[127] the first arrests here came at the very beginning of April, in both the city and the villages. They were carried out under the leadership of the çete leaders Kütükoğlu Hüseyin and Zarah Mahir. Some of those arrested were put to death in Seyfe Gorge or near the Boğaz Bridge; others were interned in the city in the *medreses* of Şifahdiye and Gök. But the systematic arrest of the males did not begin until June, particularly in the villages, when 2,000 men, including all the village priests in the *kaza*, were confined in Koçihisar's prison and slain before the deportations, in line with the usual procedure. Every night, these men were taken from the city in groups of 100 and killed in Seyfe Gorge or near the Boğaz Bridge.[128]

The first convoy, made up of villagers, left around 20 June. It was followed by a caravan made up of inhabitants of Koçhisar, 500 of them males. After suffering a first attack by Çerkez from Kuştepe, this convoy reached the village of Ulash, the population of which had, for the time being, been allowed to remain so that it could bring in the wheat harvest. Here the convoy was combined with another comprising 1,000 women and 200 men from the rest of the *kaza*. Two days later, the group arrived in Hasançelebi, where 200 adolescents were removed from the convoy and killed. The next day, at Hekimhan, the old men were removed from the convoy and massacred. After crossing the Kırk Göz Bridge on the fifth day, the deportees reached Fırıncılar in 36 hours. They remained there for seven days, during which a number of girls and boys were abducted.[129] This convoy was in fact one of the first to test the system put in place by the authorities crossing the mountains of Nal Töken. According to a survivor, Zeynel Bey – not Haci Bedri Ağa – ordered that the 200 men still alive be killed, the deportees be pillaged, and the women be stripped in Kanlı Dere Gorge, where thousands of corpses were already strewn over the ground.[130] After passing through Adiyaman, the convoy reached the Göksu, near Akçadağ. A number of women were thrown into the river there by Kurds; others were abducted. As they went on toward Suruc, the survivors were combined with what was left of other convoys, thus forming a caravan of 1,500 people. About half of them remained in Suruc, while others continued their trek toward Birecik, Bab, and finally Hama, their "place of residence," which a few dozen women from Koçhisar managed to reach in fall 1915.[131]

The *Kaza* of Koçgiri/Zara

In this rather mountainous *kaza* in the upper valley of the Halys there were, in 1914, a mere dozen Armenian localities with a total population of 7,651. The principal town in the *kaza*, Zara, had 6,000 inhabitants, 3,000 of them Armenian. Traversed by the road leading from Sıvas to Erzerum, Zara was mainly a farming town, but it also served as a way-station, with an immense khan that belonged to the Chil Hovhannesians.[132]

As we have seen, the Armenians in this region were attacked very early on by *çetes*, notably by the squadron commanded by Zaralı Mahir, a native of the region who, from 2 April 1915, played a crucial role in putting the men of the *kaza* to death in Seyfe Gorge or near the Boğaz Bridge.[133] We do not know the exact date on which the convoys left Zara, though it was probably between 20 and 29 June. We do know, however, that they took a different route than the deportees from Sıvas, because they headed toward Divrig/Divriği and then Harput, Maden, Severek, Urfa, Viranşehir, and Rakka.[134]

Apart from Mahir, those mainly responsible for the persecutions were the *kaymakam*, Hüseyin Hüsni (who served in this post from 13 October 1912 to 5 August 1916), Kör Hakkı, Kebabci Ahmed, and Bakkalci Ahmed.[135] Because the army needed their services, a few craftsmen, notably a blacksmith, were allowed to remain in the *kaza* on the condition that they convert to Islam.[136]

The *Kaza* of Yeni Han

The two Armenian localities in the *kaza*, the administrative seat Yeni Han (pop. 1,461) and Kavak (pop. 630), were located near the road leading from Sıvas to Tokat and Samsun.[137] Responsible for organizing the deportation of the *kaza*'s Armenians toward the end of June 1915, after the men had been put to death in Maşadlar Yeri, near Yeni Han, was its *kaymakam*, Reşid Bey, who held his post from 2 December 1914 to 12 November 1915.

The *Kaza* of Şarkişla/Tenus

This agricultural *kaza*, close to Sıvas and traversed by the Halys, boasted 26 Armenian localities in 1914, with a total population of 21,063. The most important of these was Gemerek, which was then home to no fewer than 5,212 Armenians. The *kaza* had some 20 churches and 21 schools with a total enrolment of 1,988.[138]

The *kaymakam*, Cemil Bey, who served from 8 May 1914 to 4 September 1915, first organized the arrest of 400 villagers in the environs of Şarkışla, who were killed there night after night in groups of twenty. The deportation took place early in July. In Kangal, one of the first convoys was combined with a caravan from Sıvas, forming a group of 5,000 Armenians.

This convoy then followed the usual route, passing through Alacahan, where the men were removed and liquidated, and Kötü Han, where Emirpaşaoğlu Hamid Bey's *çetes* were waiting for them. There, 2,000 men from Sıvas and the environs of Şarkışla were seized, tied up, and brought before Hamid, who knew most of them from Sıvas and thus how much each of them possessed. He managed to extract seven bags of gold from them before dispatching convoys toward Hasançelebi, Hekimhan, Hasanbadrig, Kırk Göz, and Fırıncılar. Almost all were eliminated during these stages of their trek; none reached Samsat.[139]

Gemerek, which together with the surrounding villages formed a dense group of Armenians, was given separate treatment. Its *müdir*, Çerkez Yusuf Effendi, called on his Çerkez compatriots from Yayla (in the *kaza* of Aziziye) for help in slaying the men of Gemerek, Çisanlu, and Karapunar. A few notables from Gemerek were even publicly hanged, after which the women and children were put on the road to Kangal, joining the flood of deportees from Sıvas and regions to the north.[140] Besides the *müdir* of the *nahie* of Gemerek, the main organizers of the massacre of the males – adolescents over age 13 met the same fate as adults – were Kör Velioğlu Ummet, Kayserli Cemal Effendi, Talaslı Mükremin, Şarkışlayi Mehmed Effendi, Colonel Talaslı Behcet Bey, and the *müdir* Ahmed Effendi.[141]

Approximately 3,000 Armenians from the villages of Shepni, Dendel, Burhan, and Tekmen took refuge in a huge cave in the highlands around Ak Dağ, where they fought off some 2,000 regular soldiers backed up by irregulars for several days. Some 15 men survived the massacre that followed the fighting. The women and children were deported.[142]

The *Kazas* of Bünyan and Aziziye

On the eve of the First World War, there were only 5,887 Armenians in Bunyan and Aziziye; 1,106 lived in the latter *kaza*, almost all of them in the principal town.[143] The arrest of the Armenian notables here was orchestrated by the head of the local Ittihad club, Havasoğlu Haci Hüseyin, with the support of the *kaymakam*, Hamid Nuri Bey (who held his post from 17 October 1914 to 22 October 1915). The pillage of Armenian property was directed by Hayreddin Bey, the head of the *emvali metruke*. It mainly benefited, however, a few Turkish *eşrefs* from the district: Sofoyoğlu Mehmed, Feyzi Effendi, Haznedarzâde Kadir, Imamzâde Hakkı, Haci Ahmed Arif, Yusufbeyzâde Adil, Yusufbeyzâde Sadık, Çarçi Hasanin Ali, and Hacimusaoğlu Haci Ömer.[144] The deportation route led through Gürün and Akçadağ to Fırıncılar.

Armenians from five localities in the neighboring *kaza* of Bünyan – Bunyan, the seat of the *kaza*, with its 500 Armenians, as well as Gigi (pop. 350), Sarıoğlan (pop. 336), Seveghen (pop. 829), and Ekrek/Akarag (pop. 2,700) – were also deported toward Gürün on orders from the *kaymakam*, Nabi Bey, who held his post from 4 June 1915 to 31 August 1916.[145]

The *Kaza* of Kangal

In 1914, the *kaza* of Kangal had an Armenian population of 7,339; 1,000 of these Armenians lived in the administrative seat of the *kaza*, Kangal, from which they were deported in late June. The others lived in the district's villages: Magahar (pop. 951), Yarhisar (pop. 703), Bozarmut (pop. 224), Komsur (pop. 343), and Mancılık (pop. 1,919).[146] In the last-named village, the liquidation of the men took place in May and early June. One of the notables, Stepan Hekimian, was even nailed to a cross and paraded through the village. The execution of some 100 men in Daşli Dere was personally supervised by the leader of the squadron of *çetes* in Sıvas, Kütükoğlu Hüseyin. Among those killed were Murad, Asdur, and Hovhannes Karamanugian, Misak Dzerunian, and Vartan Stepanian. The rest of the population, including the men, was deported on 14 June. Only the 2,000 inhabitants of Ulash were temporarily spared, so that they could bring in the wheat harvest needed by the army. In September 1915, they were deported in turn toward the Syrian desert by way of Malatia, Adiyaman, and Suruc, on orders from the *kaymakam*, Mohamed Ali Bey, who held his post until 11 March 1917.[147]

The *Kaza* of Divrig

The administrative seat of this *kaza*, Divrig/Divriği, had a population of 12,000, almost one-third of whom were Armenian. Together with its 18 Armenian-inhabited villages, the district boasted a total Armenian population of 10,605.[148] Among the countless vestiges of the medieval period sprinkled through the region was the monastery of St. Gregory the Illuminator, a jewel of medieval Armenian architecture build in the eleventh century that was perched on a rocky outcrop three hours north of Divrig near the village of Khurnavil (pop. 320). The neighboring village of Kesmeh (pop. 580), and the native village of the Noradounghians also boasted medieval churches, as did Zimara/Zmmar (pop. 1,250). Binga/Pingian (pop. 1,300), on the right bank of the Euphrates, was a medieval citadel that was nearly inaccessible because it was pressed up against a rock face close to the Euphrates. Its only access route ran over a suspended bridge that had been built in the eleventh century. In the southwestern part of the *kaza* was a string of Armenian villages on the two banks of the Lik Su: Arshushan (pop. 310), Kuresin (pop. 240), Odur (pop. 215), Parzam (pop. 510), and the village around the monastery of St. James that the Turks called Venk (from the Armenian word *vank*, monastery) (pop. 290). Finally, there were five Armenian villages on the right bank of the Çaldi çay, in the easternmost part of the district: Armdan (pop. 1,605), Palanga (pop. 480), Sinjan (395 Armenians), Mrvana, and Shigim.[149] When the general mobilization order was issued, the recruits from the district of Divrig were assigned to an *amele taburi* based in Zara.[150]

In the administrative seat of the *kaza*, Divrig, the primate Krikor Zartarian was summoned before the *kaymakam* Abdülmecid Bey (who held his post from 1 March 1914 to 29 November 1915) in late March. Abdülmecid demanded that the weapons held by the Armenians in the town and the villages be handed over to him in one week's time, along with the deserters. The Armenians' response was apparently judged unsatisfactory, because the auxiliary primate, Father Serovpe Prigian, and several political leaders, such as Khachadur and Armenag Menendian; Garabed Hayranian; Mgrdich and Hagopos Kljian; Krikor, Dikran, and Mgrdich Kakanian; Melkon and Suren Guzelian; Mihran Doktorian; Kevork, Haig, Toros, and Tatul Hayranian; Nshan Tahmazian; Sarkis Lusigian; Hovhannes Shahabian; Khachadur Deombelekian; and Karekin and Aram Torigian, among others – a total of 45 people – were arrested, tortured for two weeks (some, including the auxiliary primate, died as a result), and then dispatched to Sıvas.[151]

The victims of the second wave of arrests were Divrig's craftsmen and merchants, as well as its adolescents under draft age – a total of some 200 people. After being tortured for several days running, these men were taken from the village, tied up, and led an hour's distance to the Deren Dere Gorge, where they were killed with axes. According to our witnesses, the men were all eliminated in this fashion, with the exception of 200 who managed to flee to the mountain villages inhabited by Alevites; some of them survived by pillaging Turkish localities in the region.[152]

The deportations from the *kaza*'s villages, however, did not begin until 28 May 1915. The peasants were first of all concentrated in Divrig, where the men and adolescents between the ages of 14 and 18 were separated from the others and confined in a church before being killed. The rest of the rural population was deported toward Malatia by way of Agn/Eğin and Arapkir.[153] The townspeople of Divrig were put on the road a little later. On 28 June, the city was practically emptied of its men. On the morning of 29 June, the town criers announced the deportation order, which gave people three days to make preparations to leave. On 1 July, the Armenian quarters of Divrig were surrounded by regular troops who proceeded to expel the inhabitants. They were regrouped near the southwestern exit from the town and were dispatched from there toward Arapkir after the abduction of young women and girls for the harems of local dignitaries. The convoy was pillaged shortly after it set, at Sarı Çiçek, by Kurdish villagers from the surrounding area.[154]

According to Hmayag Zartarian, the anti-Armenian operations in the region were conducted by a squad of *çetes* commanded by Kör Adıl, a native of Trebizond. He was backed up by Çadıroğlu Abdüllah, Topcuoğlu Hüseyin, Ğasab Süleyman Çavuş, Hafız Effendi, Leblebici Polis Mohamed, Köroğlu Polis Ülusi, İzet Bey, Sıvaslı Küregsiz Hafız, and others.[155]

We also know about the fate of the 1,300 Armenians of Binga/Pingian, located on the right bank of the Euphrates, thanks to the testimony of a survivor named L. Goshgarian. According to Goshgarian, 100 recruits from the village were put to work on the Erzincan-Erzerum road in a place called Sansa Dere, sharing the fate of the 4,000 to 5,000 worker-soldiers assigned to the *amele taburis* stationed in the region. However, a few dozen young men and adults did manage to flee to the mountains and go to Dersim. The rest of the population was deported toward Arapkir on 23 June 1915.[156]

The *Kaza* of Darende

In 1914, the *kaza* of Darende had a population of only 3,983 Armenians. Somewhat more than 2,000 of them lived in the seat of the *kaza*, also called Darende, while another 1,100 lived in the neighboring village of Ashodi.[157] The *kaymakam*, Receb Bey, who had been appointed on 8 February 1913, was dismissed on 21 May 1915 and replaced by Süleyman Bey on 14 June. This might be taken as an indication that Receb refused to carry out Muammer's orders. We do not know anything at all about the circumstances under which the Armenian population of the *kaza* of Derende was eliminated. The fact that it lies on the road between Gürün and Malatia, however, suggests that it was dealt a fate similar to that meted out to the Armenians of its northern neighbor.

The *Kaza* of Gürün

With its five exclusively Armenian villages and a handful of dispersed communities, the *kaza* of Gürün had a total Armenian population of 13,874 in 1914. The seat of the *kaza*, Gürün, isolated in a narrow, steep-sided valley, had 12,168 inhabitants, 8,406 of whom were Armenian. The town was strung out along the two banks of the Melos/Tohmak, made up of a succession of neighborhoods scattered through little valleys. The Armenians had 12 schools in Gürün. The town preserved its prestigious past, seen in the ruins of a medieval citadel that had been restored early in the eleventh century and the "desert" (monastery) of the Holy Mother of God in Saghlu. It was known not only for its commerce and craftsmanship, but also for the manufacturing of rugs, cotton fabric, and wool products. There were three Armenian villages in the immediate vicinity of Gürün – Kavak (pop. 220), Karasar (pop. 410), and Kristianyören (pop. 80) – and two more villages to the north on the road to Mancılık: Karayören (pop. 560) and Çahırınköy (pop. 140).[158]

In contrast with what happened in many other regions, the *kaymakam*, Şahib Bey, who held his post from 30 August 1912 to 7 November 1915, does not seem to have played a determining role in the persecutions. According to Armenian sources, it was the military commander of Sıvas, Pertev Bey, who went to Gürün personally to transmit the order to begin the operations against the Armenian population. Avundükzâde Mehmed Bey, a Turkish notable from the town, and his three sons, Özer, Hüseyin, and Eşref, organized a meeting at which, with the help of the local Ittihadist club, a local branch of the *Teşkilât-ı Mahsusa* was formed under the name of *Milli Cendarma*. Captain İbrahimoğlu Mehmed Bey was appointed the commander of this militia. The group charged with carrying out the massacres and deportations brought together other notables who were members of the Young Turk club: İbrahimbeyoğlu Dilaver, Küçükalizâde Bahri, Eminbeyoğlu Mehmed, Mamoağazâde Emin, Köseahmedzâde Abdüllah, Sadık Çavuş, who was also the commander of a squadron of *çetes*, Yehyaoğlu Mehmed, Karamevlutoğlu Talât Effendi, and Nacar Ahmed Abdüllah Karpuzzâde.[159] This committee charged Kâmil Effendi, the commander of the gendarmerie and a well-known Young Turk, with drawing up the lists of Armenian notables to be arrested. The first arrests took place in May. The first to be detained were the Armenian primate Khoren Timaksian and Reverend Bedros Mughalian,[160] followed by the town's notables, who were imprisoned in the Minasian khan, located in the Sagh neighborhood, and also in the Turkish baths at Karatepe. Delibekiroğlu Mehmed Onbaşi in particular was charged with supervising the torture sessions, which here too were designed to make the victims confess the location of possible arms caches and the nature of the "plot" they were supposed to have hatched.

The killing of the notables of Gürün began on 10 June 1915. Seventy-four men were massacred in the Ulash/Ulaş valley near the village of Kardaşlar by 12 *çetes* in gendarme's uniforms under the command of Cendarma Ali Çavuş. On 27 June 40 more notables met the same fate near Çalikoğlu.[161] On 22 June 1915, some 20 men were put to death on the road to Albistan by Tütünci Hüseyin Çavuş and his irregular troops.[162] İbrahimoğlu Mehmed, the leader of a squadron of *çetes*, as well as Gürünlü Üzeyer Effendi, Ömer Ağa from Setrak (a village in Albistan), and Hakkı Effendi, a native of Ayntab, also played outstanding roles in slaughtering the males of the region of Gürün and then Akşekir.[163]

It would appear that the committee subsequently decided to have boys between ten and 14 arrested and killed. Kasap Osman, one of the Special Organization's killers, indeed took on the job of dispatching a group of 120 boys to the valley of Saçciğaz, a Turkish village located two hours from Gürün, where they were slain with knives and axes.[164]

Küçükalizâde Bahri, one of the most influential members of the local Ittihad and the *Milli Cendarma*, personally murdered three of the principal Armenian leaders of the main town in the *kaza* – Hajji Hagop Buldukian, Hagop Shahbazian, and Haji Artin Gergerian – in Tel, near Aryanpunar. It was also Bahri who supervised the looting of the two convoys of deportees from the *kaza* in Kavak, a Turkish village located on the road to Albistan. Early in July, after the males were liquidated, the deportations were carried out under Bahri's supervision with the help of local policemen (Abdüllah, Hamdi, and Sabri). Katırci Nuri Effendi, the inspector of the convoys, and Deli Bekir Mustafa, aided by Hacioğlu Yusuf, conducted the two convoys.[165] The first passed through Albistan, Kanlı Dere, Kani Dağ, Ayranbunar, Sağin Boğaz, Aziziye, Göbeg Yoren, and Fırıncilar, and then through Ayntab, Marash, Urfa, and Karabıyık to Der Zor. The second convoy started off on the same route, but was then set marching in the direction of Hama, Homs, and the Hauran. Many of the deportees from Gürün were massacred in the vicinity of Marash.[166]

Deportations and Massacres in the Sancak of Tokat

The statistics compiled by the Patriarchate indicate that the *sancak* of Tokat had an Armenian population of 32,281 in 1914, which lived in 27 towns and villages that boasted 28 churches, two monasteries, and 14 schools with a total enrolment of 3,175.[167] Thus, the Armenian presence in this western district of the vilayet of Sıvas was relatively modest, although, from an economic point of view, it was not negligible. Tokat, where the prefecture was located, was spread over a valley two kilometers long; its various neighborhoods lay on the sides of the valley, forming a sort of amphitheater. On the eve of the war, there were 11,980 Armenians and about 15,000 Turks in the city. But there were another 6,500

Armenians in the rest of the *kaza* of Tokat. They lived in 17 rural communities: west of the city, in the valley of the Tozanlu Su and on the plain of Ğanova, in Endiz (Armenian pop. 280), Gesare (pop. 100), Söngür (pop. 160), Varaz (pop. 90), Çerçi (pop. 220), Biskürcuk (pop. 550), Bazarköy (pop. 130), Kurçi (pop. 80); south of the city, in the Artova valley, on the road to Yeni Han, Bolus (pop. 300), Yartmeş (pop. 400), Kervanseray (pop. 350), Çiflik (pop. 326), Tahtebağ (pop. 262), Gedağaz (pop. 308); and, east of the city, near the road between Tokat and Niksar, in Krikores (pop. 600), on the left bank of the Iris, and on the right bank, Bizeri (pop. 280).[168]

The most striking event in the months preceding the outbreak of the war was the fire on 1 May 1914 that ravaged the street where many of Tokat's businesses were located, Baghdad Cadesi. As we have seen, this was not an isolated act.[169] There is even every reason to believe that these events reflected the general strategy adopted by the Ittihad in February 1914 with a view to diminishing the economic importance of the Greeks and Armenians. When the general mobilization was announced, many Armenians paid the *bedel* in order to avoid conscription; hence there were only 280 worker-soldiers from Tokat and Krikores in the *amele taburi* that was formed to build a barracks in the city. In line with directives issued by the Patriarchate, the military requisitions, despite the abuses to which they gave rise, did not occasion protests.[170] The situation deteriorated in late April 1915, when the CUP sent its parliamentary representatives into the provinces of Asia Minor to preach elimination of the "domestic foe." Several Armenian witnesses attended a meeting organized in the Paşa Cami at which a CUP representative attacked "those who, in our midst, seem to be friends," but whom "the Turkish people must make it a priority to purge."[171] This declaration led the young Armenian primate, Father Shavarsh Sahagian, to multiply gestures of goodwill toward the local authorities. The decree summoning the population to turn in all the weapons in its possession, pasted up in every public building, compelled the primate to organize a discussion with all the community leaders. According to Hovhannes Yotghanjian, who took part in this meeting, all were aware of the impending threat, but there was disagreement as to what to do about it. Shavarsh Sahagian and the local Hnchak leader M. Arabian were opposed to giving up the weapons and suggested taking measure to organize the self-defense of the Armenian neighborhoods. A majority of those present, however, pointed out that there were no Armenian fighters available in the city apart from a few deserters who had taken refuge there. The weapons were finally deposited in the Church of St. Stepanos and delivered up to the authorities.

The subsequent events resembled those we have seen elsewhere. Irregulars carried out search and seizure operations in the rural areas while gendarmes or soldiers ransacked the Armenian households in Tokat for arms and all documents printed in Armenian. Early in May, the Hnchak leaders Beyekh Simon and Garabed Gövjian and the Dashnaks Khachig Seraydarian (an army pharmacist) and Garabed Arenderian were arrested, tortured, and executed in prison.[172] During a visit that Muammer paid to Tokat in this period, the vali demanded that the Armenian primate turn over "imported arms" and dismissed all the Armenian civil servants in the police force and gendarmerie. Apparently, the authorities considered the situation sufficiently ripe by this time: on 18 May 1915, they proceeded to arrest all of Tokat's Armenian notables and teachers. The method they employed in carrying out this round-up was also rather classic. The *mutesarif*, Cevded Bey (who held his post from 2 May 1915 to 4 February 1916),[173] very courteously summoned all these notables – Kevork Pasbanian, Hagop Boyajian, Hovhannes *Kazanjian*, Avedis Khdrian, Nazar Shishmanian, and others – to the *konak*, but at the end of the meeting had them arrested and interned in police stations. In the course of the day, the adolescents were also arrested in the streets and confined in the food warehouse near the central square, where they were systematically tortured.[174] The remarks that Ahmed Muammer made to the Armenian primate early in June during a working visit to Tokat clearly show that the authorities did not judge the number of weapons they had so far confiscated to be satisfactory. The vali demanded that the prelate, "on whom everything depends," do what he had to convince his flock to give up their arms. On Sunday, 13 June, Sahagian, in the last sermon he delivered, stated his conclusions, as it were, before a distraught multitude: he told them that he had discreetly met with Muammer three times, that the vali had tried to convince him to turn over "arms and deserters," and that the community leaders had decided to submit to the government's orders "in order to ward off the danger" threatening them, but that he could still not utter "the least little word of consolation, because we are lost."[175] The prelate seems to have made an accurate assessment of the situation. The next morning, when 300 deserters gathered before the cathedral, ready to turn themselves in, he refused to go with them to the military authorities "so as not to be their executioner." On Wednesday, 16 June, a new stage opened with the systematic arrest of the men, beginning with Father Sahagian. That afternoon, Sahagian was summoned to the *konak*, where the police chief Mehmed Effendi informed him that he had to go to Sıvas immediately to meet with the vali. He was killed that very evening on the way there, in Kızın Eniş.[176]

Arrests continued to be made on 17 June. Died together in groups of ten, 1,400 men were conducted out of the city in four convoys to Ardova, Ğazova, and Bizeri, where they were shot. According to Lusia Zhamgochian, 17 clergymen, including the auxiliary bishop Nerses Mgrdichian (1861–1915) and Father Andon Seraydarian, were murdered on 18 June in Tokat's citadel, after having been subjected to refined tortures. Subsequently, the young men between 14 and 20 were put to death. By the end of June, only the 280 worker-soldiers employed in constructing the Şube barracks, three army doctors – Seraydarian, Eminian, and Misak Panosian – and a few artisans working for the army or the authorities, were still "free."[177]

The rest of the population was not deported all at once but according to age cohorts. The Azar khan served as a detention center for older women, who were arrested by the police and put on the road two days later; they were followed by the young women and then the last remaining Armenians, who were marched down the Sıvas road by way of Çiftlik-Yeni Han toward Şarkışla-Marash or, more frequently, Kangal-Malatia.[178]

Besides the *mutesarif*, Cevded Bey, those primarily responsible for the violence in Tokat were Hoca Fehmi, a parliamentary deputy and member of the Ittihad; Osman Bey, the commander of the gendarmerie; Mehmed Effendi, the police chief; Muteveli Nuri Bey, a notable and member of the commission responsible for "abandoned property"; Latifoğlu Ibrahim, a CUP member; the policemen Uzun Mahmud, Nuri, Ziya, and İbrahim; the gendarmes Reşidoğlu Fehmi (a sergeant), Salih, Muftioğlu Asem, and Hayreddin; the *müdir* of Ğazova, Gurci Ahmed, who oversaw the massacres in his district; the *çetes* of the Special Organization Salih Ağa, a butcher, Çerkez Mirza Bey, Çerkez Osman Bey, Çerkez Mahmud Bey, Çerkez Elmaylizâde Haci Effendi, Salih Mehmed Bey, Alipaşazâde Enus Bey, Debelege Effendi, Elmaylizâde İzzet, Elmaylizâde Tevfik, Elmaylizâde Osman, Karaderviş Şükrü, Ekmeci Güzeller, Haci Bey Apulçavusoğlu Mustafa, Geproğlu Osman Nazıf, Abdüllah, Kör Binbaşi Ferid, Cinçoğlu Ahmed, Latifzâde Osman, Latifzâde Filmi, Kaimakamzâde Tacir Bey, Celani Haci, Istambolu Hikmet Bey, Muftizâde, and Cigeroğlu Osman Bey, the son of Osman Bey.[179]

The *Kaza* of Niksar

Of the 3,560 Armenians in the *kaza* of Niksar, 2,830 lived in the principal town, also called Niksar. Known in antiquity as Neocaesarea, Niksar lay 53 kilometers northwest of Tokat in the fertile plain of the Kelkit Çay. Almost all the Armenians here were Turkish-speaking, and, with few exceptions, earned a living as craftsmen, businessmen, or farmers. The 8 June 1896 massacres ruined the community, whose property was systematically pillaged; there-after, the Armenians failed to recover the prosperity that they had enjoyed in the past. There were also two Armenian villages in the *kaza*: Kapuağzi (with an Armenian-speaking population of 650) and Karameşe (pop. 80).[180] Here the men were slain and the rest of the population deported in late June;[181] the operations were carried out under the direction of the *kaymakam*, Rahmi Bey, who held his post from 4 May 1914 to 8 August 1915.

The *Kaza* of Erbaa

In this *kaza* in the northern part of the vilayet, long a part of the vilayet of Trebizond, there were nine Armenian localities in 1914 with a total population of 6,948. Half of the *kaza*'s Armenians lived in its principal town, Herek, located on the left bank of the Iris river 55 kilometers from Tokat. In addition to their traditional crafts, the Armenians of Herek, who were Turkish-speaking, cultivated hemp and opium. The *kaza*'s eight Armenian villages were all inhabited by Armenian-speakers from Hamşin who had settled in the region early in the eighteenth century: Ağabağ (pop. 279), Çozlar (pop. 292), Ayvaza (pop. 313), Sarıkaya (pop. 263), Saharçal (pop. 180), Hayatgeriz (pop. 120), Gerasan (pop. 220), and Cibrayl (pop. 320).[182] The procedure applied by the authorities was the same as was followed elsewhere; here, too, the women and children were put on a trajectory leading through Sıvas-Kangal-Hasançelebi-Fırıncilar and beyond.[183] Apparently, the *kaymakam*, Abdel Settar Bey, who had assumed his post on 19 April 1914, disobeyed orders, for he was dismissed on 1 June 1915 and replaced on 9 August 1915 by Rahmi Bey, who was trans-ferred from Niksar.

The *Kaza* of Zile

In 1914, 4,283 Turkish-speaking Armenians lived in the *kaza* of Zile, located 30 kilometers west of Tokat. All of them lived in the seat of the *kaza*; their principal occupation was rug-making.[184] The men, among them the Hnchak pharmacist Dikran Seraydarian, were arrested in June and conducted, with their local priest at the head of the procession, to the marsh of Ğaz Göl, where they were killed.[185]

Deportations and Massacres in the Sancak of Amasia

The *sancak* of Amasia, with its roughly 200,000 inhabitants, including 31,717 Armenians and 39,676 Greeks, was on the eve of the First World War an extraordinary museum of the cus-toms of the native populations of Asia Minor. In the *kaza* of Amasia, all 13,788 Armenians lived in the administrative seat of the *kaza*, also called Amasia, which was strung out in a narrow valley traversed by the Iris. The biggest Armenian neighborhood, known as Savayid, covered both slopes of a little dale. Located here were the Cathedral of Our Lady, the bisho-pric, the Church of Saint James, the Armenian hospital, the big Bartevian middle school, a Protestant church, a Jesuit middle school, and an Armenian Catholic church. There was also a big Armenian population in the Deve neighborhood. Altogether, there were 12 schools attended by more than 1,600 children. At the time, Amasia owed its prosperity in large measure to weaving, which the Armenians had partially mechanized.[186]

We have already noted that the first arrests occurred early in Amasia, around 15 March. The targets were political leaders and teachers: Krikor Jerian, Minas Ipekjian, Harutiun

Baghchegiulian, Nshan Adzigian, the pharmacist Toros Kaymakian, Tateos Mserian, the elementary schoolteacher Krikor Vartabedian, and others. These men were systematically tortured in order to induce them to turn over the archives of their parties and reveal where the weapons they supposedly had were located. Shortly thereafter, they were transferred to Sıvas and interned in the *medrese* of Şifahdiye.[187] The other notables of Amasia were arrested on 18 May, tortured for a few days, and then killed with axes on 23 May in an isolated spot three hours from the city at Saz Dağ.[188] Only after the vali had expressly paid a visit to the city on 14 June did the arrests, torture, and systematic killing of the men – especially the craftsmen – begin. On 29 June, 360 of them were taken from the city by night and tied together in groups of four, with four other convoys of this sort having to be organized before all were liquidated.[189] The city, however, was unaware of the fate reserved for these men. Rumor had it that they were safe and sound. There was even talk of an imperial pardon in the air, but in the end the *mutesarif* Celal Bey announced the deportation order to the auxiliary primate, Mampre Fakhirian. Fakhirian ordered that the bells of the cathedral be rung; the population streamed to the cathedral, where it learned that it would have to leave the city in short order.[190]

The deportations began on 3 July and proceeded at the rate of one convoy per day for five days. The last caravan, our witnesses, comprised approximately 1,000 people, among them 200 adolescents and old men who had not been killed with the rest of the men.[191] After passing through Kangal, all the males over the age of eight in the convoys from Amasia were slain in Şarkışla around 15 July by Turkish and Çerkez villagers under the orders of Halil Bey, the commander of the squadrons of *çetes* in the vilayet of Sıvas. The killings took place in the presence of the *kaymakam*.[192] Thereafter, these convoys took the route that the deportees usually followed, but did not arrive in Hasançelebi until 28 August, or in Fırıncılar until 7 September, which shows how slowly the authorities led them on.[193] Zeynel and Bedri were waiting for them further on, in the Kanlı Dere gorge, where, our witnesses confirm, not a single male over eight was left alive.[194] The remainder of the trajectory of these convoys from Amasia was classic: they passed by way of Suruc and Arabpunar, after which the handful of survivors moved on to Bab, Aleppo, or Meskene-Der Zor.[195]

As one can readily imagine, the considerable economic stake represented by the seizure of Armenian property commanded the authorities' undivided attention. Celal Bey the *mutesarif*; Serri Bey, a member of the deportation commission (he became the *mutesarif* of Çangırı in 1919); Osman Nuri, also known as Körguzi Raşi Nuri, the commander of the gendarmerie; the *muftis* Müneverzâde Haci Tevfik Hafız and Ğüzluglu Hafız Hoca; Rüşdi Hafız; Salim or Saleh Bey, the president of the local Ittihad club; Nalband İzzetoğlu Kâmil; Tıntın Hasan and Haci Tevfik, two Unionists; Nalband İzzetzâde Haci Kismil, a Unionist and the mayor of Amasi; Nafız Bey, a parliamentary representative from Amasia; Fatar Rezmi, an engineer; Hamdi Bey, the head of the *belediye*; Topcioğlu Mustafa, the secretary general in the town hall; Kürdoğlu Serhoş Hasan, a former parliamentary deputy from Amasia; and Ali Effendi, the director of the orphanage, all bore a large share of the responsibility for the arrests, house searches, torture, and the pillaging of the Armenians' property.[196]

The Special Organization's representative in Amasia, Timarhaneci Halil, who was also an eminent member of the local Ittihad club and responsible for the squadron of *çetes* based in the city, as well as Topcioğlu Şükrü, an officer in this squadron, played a central role in the massacre of the men and boys of Amasia, along with their main collaborators: Topcizâde Halil, Osman, Konfikten Rıza, Tlatıs Hasan, Kontraci Hasan and his brother, Ğabaş Ali; Cin Sarac; Tatar Arabaci Mehmed; Topcioğlu Ziya; Göv Ömeroğlu Hasan; Bakal Kör Ahmed; Kel Osmanoğlu Besim; Arpacızâde Haci Osman and his four sons; Tutunci Mustafa; Bazadoğlu Mehmed and his brothers; Deli Beyler; Çaycızâde Nuri Bey; Abdoğlu Hulusi; and Ladikli Ekizler.[197]

The *Kaza* of Merzifun

In 1914, the seat of the *kaza* of Merzifun, Marzevan/Merzifun, had an Armenian population of 10,381, with eleven schools boasting a total enrolment of 1,221. There were also small numbers of Armenians in the only two Armenian villages in the district – Yenice (pop. 140) and Lidj/Korköy (pop. 145), located near the monastery of the Holy Mother of God, which served as the seat of the bishop of the joint diocese of Amasia and Marzevan.[198]

Thanks to fuller documentation than we have for other areas, we may note a concrete case of despoliation of Armenian property for the benefit of a few local notables. It occurred even before the outbreak of the war. When, in autumn 1914, military requisitions began, four men set out to appropriate 8,000 to 10,000 sacks of flour produced by seven large flour mills owned by Armenians from Merzifun. Salihbeyzâde Hüseyin, the president of the municipality; the CUP's local responsible secretary; the commander of the gendarmerie, Mahir Bey; and a Young Turk merchant named Kiremicizâde Hadi officially confiscated these stocks of flour to meet the "needs" of the army before quickly reselling them "at high prices" and dividing up the profits among themselves.[199] There is every reason to believe that this documented episode hides abuses on a much larger scale that were committed by local Young Turks who took advantage of their status as activists in the party in power.

The first arrests in Merzifun came in April: the targets were some 50 notables who were either tortured to death or dispatched to Sıvas to answer for acts endangering state security. In May, the local authorities proceeded to recruit 100 *çetes* from among the villages. Meanwhile, the decree ordering that people turn in any weapons they kept at home was published, providing the *çetes with* an opportunity to conduct house searches and make arrests in the Armenian community.[200] Muammer, after visiting Amasia on 14 June, also paid a visit to Merzifun, apparently to accelerate the elimination of the men there. Indeed, the 1,200 men arrested on 12 June, shortly before his arrival in the city, were eliminated on Monday, 15 June.[201] The first group, comprising 300 young men, was conducted to Elek Deresi, near the village of Tenik on the road to Çorum, under the direct supervision of Fayk Bey, the *kaymakam*,[202] and Mahir Bey, the commander of the gendarmerie. The men were stripped and killed with axes. Over the next few days, the other men met the same fate.[203]

The deportation order was made public shortly thereafter, on 21 June. The convoys were rapidly put on the road and followed the same route as those from Amasia. Around 20 men and fewer than 100 women and children reached Aleppo.[204] According to an anonymous witness who remained in the city,

> the furniture and the other properties abandoned [by the women], without being officially inventoried in any way, was loaded on carts and piled up in the city's Armenian church, while the Armenians' stores were looted by Turkish officials and the populations. The stores that were thus emptied were put under seal as 'abandoned property.'[205]

Aside from the few Armenians who were allowed to remain in Merzifun because they had agreed to convert to Islam, a non-negligible number of schoolchildren, teachers, and members of the Anatolia College medical staff, directed by Dr. George E. White, were also left in the city. These people benefited from the protection of the American embassy and the consular agent in Samsun, William Peter, who was responsible for watching over the interests of these institutions and had repeatedly traveled to Merzifun to negotiate with the *kaymakam*.[206] The authorities had soon set their sights on Anatolia College, administered by the American Board of Commissioners for Foreign Missions. They wished to take control of it and at the same time get rid of the Armenians they found there. For the Americans, however, there could be no question of accepting the least encroachment by the authorities. Dr. White and Dr. Marden, responsible for the college and the hospital, reminded the *kaymakam* of Merzifun in a letter that, "the Embassy telegraphs that necessary and precise orders have been given, by the Ministry of the Interior and by the Pasha the Minister of War to the local authorities, assuring in definite form the protection of our institution, the College, together with all the persons connected with it without exception."[207] Refusing to make an exception for Anatolia College, the Turkish administration demanded that all the Armenians on its staff and all the Armenian students be deported with their compatriots in the rest of the city. The question was therefore referred to the vali of Sıvas, to whom Marden and White sent a telegram in which they declared:

> on the ground that it is necessary for all Armenians to go to an appointed place, the kaimakam had informed us regarding certain of our workers, ministers and professors, who have been many years in our congregation and are graduates of advanced schools … that the local government has no authority to give them exemption.[208]

Marden and White also tried the same day to send a wire to the American ambassador Morgenthau. The *kaymakam*, however, refused to transmit their cable, which pointed out that "the employees of our Hospital would be included in the general despatch of Armenians to an appointed place," and, furthermore, that "if these persons are sent away without regard to the needs of the institution, all our buildings for philanthropic purposes and our place of worship for religious exercises will be closed and useless."[209]

On 31 July, William Peter arrived in Merzifun in hopes of changing the minds of the local authorities – specifically, the *kaymakam* Fayk Bey – so that the Armenians working at the college would be spared deportation. The record of his interviews with the *kaymakam*, related carefully and in detail by the American consular agent in his dispatches to Morgenthau, illustrate the obstinacy with which the authorities endeavored to have the teachers, medical personnel, and young girls of the college handed over to them.[210]

In the long report that Peter addressed to Morgenthau after his first visit to Merzifun,[211] he noted that Professors Manisajian and Hagopian, both of Anatolia College, were among the first to be arrested and that they had been "set free, after interventions on their behalf, but only temporarily," after he had "greased the palm of the commander of the gendarmerie, Mahir Bey, arranging for him to be given the sum of 275 Turkish pounds by their lawyer." It seems that the American believed that, as a result, "the Armenian question had been settled as far as they were concerned, but this was a royal error, for this was only the prelude to further maneuvers." The *kaymakam* accused the Americans of agreeing to safeguard "a mass of objects belonging to the Armenians" and giving refuge to "a mass of refugees." According to the reports of the American doctors, the *kaymakam*, the commander of the gendarmerie Mahir, and the mayor Hüseyin Effendi, "consoled the Armenians," assuring them that "they could remain where they were, while relieving them of as much money as possible and, when no more was to be had, sending them off." Emin Bey, the military commander, also gave him certain indications about the methods used by these unscrupulous civil servants to pillage the Armenians: "this trio had pried at least 500 Turkish pounds per capita from thirty-five individuals, which amount to the neat sum of no less than 17,500 Turkish pounds." Emin, apparently shocked by these methods, had declared that he was ready to testify and suggested that the American diplomat inform his superiors. The consul's report reveals that the *kaymakam* had indeed held "a few hundred Armenians in a monastery" for some time [undoubtedly the monastery of the Holy Mother of God near Korköy] where they were "again shaken down for as much as possible before being sent off."[212]

In a conversation that took place on 2 August, Peter asked the *kaymakam* not to interfere in "American interests"; Fayk answered that he had to deport "all the Armenians in the college and hospital – nurses and so on – and that nothing could be done about that." Peter's remark, the purpose of which was to show that under these circumstances Dr. Marden would have no choice but to shut down the hospital, with the result that Merzifun would remain "without medical help," obviously did not suffice to save the medical staff. "He was, more-over, at a loss to understand what call foreigners had to be in [and] I could see that we had to do with a very fanatic individual here."[213] Indeed, the authorities in Merzifun seemed to be applying methods that had been tried and tested elsewhere, methods calculated to precipi-tate the immediate departure of the missionaries, to make it possible to take over their build-ings, and to liquidate the Armenians connected with their institutions. On 10 August, the police chief and his men turned up at Anatolia College and demanded that the Armenians in the college and hospital be turned over to them. According to White, 72 people, including a number of professors, turned themselves over in order to prevent the police from investing the institution. They were immediately put on the road to Zile, escorted by gendarmes. The men were removed from the group in Yeni Han, tied up, and killed.[214]

According to information gathered by Peter, the *kaymakam* "demanded another 2,000 to 3,000 Turkish pounds in exchange for letting the girls in the school go." The diplomat, however, was persuaded that "it was pointless to give him any more money, since, ultimately, they were going to send everyone away."[215] His prediction was on the mark: on the morn-ing of 12 August, policemen and gendarmes entered the college by force and took the 73 student boarders into custody, along with a number of teachers. Apparently, Peter observes, "the *kaymakam*, the commander of the gendarmerie, and the *beledier-reis* could not agree as to how the money was to be divided up … and, while they were arguing over it, the girls were put on the road."[216] According to White, the *kaymakam* came to see him in order to suggest that the girls "change their names" – that is, convert to Islam – since most of them no longer had fathers and were "subjects of the Turkish government and were the objects of particular attention from the Turkish officials." Apparently the officers, gendarmes, and officials working in Merzifun had shown an inclination to "take in" these schoolgirls from the American school, who had a reputation for being well bred. But, none of them agreed to convert, and they "were sent off in the direction of Amasia." Miss Gage, Miss Willard, and Dr. White managed to accompany their wards as far as Amasia, where the *mutesarif* Celal Bey had tried to arrest them. However, the Americans were able to accompany them further, as far as Sıvas.[217]

After Anatolia College had been liquidated, only the American hospital remained (briefly) in operation, thanks to a medical staff of 52 Armenians, on whose behalf White and Peter interceded with the authorities, pointing out that deporting them would mean closing the hospital. Nevertheless, during the night of 18/19 August, the first attempt was made to arrest the Armenians. "However," Peter notes, "since I was present, they did not dare risk it."[218] The second attempt proved successful. In a letter that Peter sent the vali on 26 August, he told him that he "deeply regretted that you did not make an exception for the American college and hospital … which have brought only blessings and benefits to the region. How many of your soldiers were welcomed [to them] last winter and given all the care they needed."[219]

According to Peter and White, some 1,000 Armenians, nearly all girls and young women, agreed to "register" as Muslims and enter harems, thus escaping deportation.[220]

The *Kazas* of Vezirköprü and Gümüşhacıköy

Constructed on the ruins of the ancient Neapolis, the seat of the *kaza* of Vezirköprü (also called Vezirköprü) had only 6,300 inhabitants in 1914, 1,612 of them Armenians. The Armenians had two schools (with an enrollment of 150) and the Church of Saint George.

The *kaymakam*, Bekir Bey, who held his post from 16 May 1914 to 21 January 1916, organized the elimination of the men and, thereafter, the deportation of the rest of the Armenian population toward Sıvas and Malatia by way of Havza, Amasia, and Tokat.[221] In 1914, the 4,064 Armenians of the *kaza* of Gümüşhacıköy all lived in the principal town of the *kaza*, near Merzifun, which boasted two churches and six schools. This district was well known for its silver and copper mines. The *kaymakam*, İbrahim Niyazi Bey, who held his post from October 1914 to 2 July 1916, oversaw the massacres and the deportation along the same route taken by the Armenians of Merzifun.[222]

The *Kazas* of Ladik, Havza, and Mecitözü

In the *kazas* of Ladik and Havza, which lay on the Amasia-Samsun road, there were no more than 250 Armenians: 300 of them lived in Ladik and 50 more at an hour's distance in Yaremcaköy. Another 333 Armenians lived in the seat of the *kaza* of Havza, which was known for its spa, constructed near the ancient Roman baths. Seven hundred Armenians lived in the last of the *kazas* in the *sancak* of Amasia, Mecitözü, all of them in Hacıköy.[223] We have no information about the fate of these small communities; they were probably swept up in the flood of convoys from Samsun.

Resistance and Massacres in the Sancak *of* Şabinkarahisar

In 1914, the *sancak* of Şabinkarahisar, located in the easternmost part of the vilayet of Sivas, had 23,169 Armenian inhabitants. They lived in 44 towns and villages, placed under the jurisdiction of a diocesan council based in Şabinkarahisar that administered 38 parishes, two monasteries, and 36 schools with a total enrollment of 3,040. In this mountainous, wooded region, there was only one plain of any importance, the plain of Akşari/Sadağa, which lay south of Şabinkarahisar. The town of Enderes/Suşehir lay in the western part of this plain. Almost all of the *sancak*'s Armenian population was concentrated there.[224]

On the eve of the First World War, Şabinkarahisar, where the prefecture was located, had an Armenian population of 4,918; the Armenians formed a majority here. They were concentrated at the foot of the medieval citadel, perched on a rocky outcrop in the upper quarter around the Cathedral of Our Lady. Piled up one beside the next, their houses, with contiguous flat roofs, were all interconnected: the roofs of one row of houses served as a street for the next-highest row. To the northwest, a new Armenian neighborhood, known as Kopeli, had sprung up in the latter half of the nineteenth century.

In 1914, there were also five big Armenian villages in the immediate periphery of Şabinkarahisar, with a total population of 9,104. Four kilometers northwest of the city lay Tamzara (with an Armenian population of 1,518). Buseyid (pop. 510) and Anerği (pop. 646) lay five kilometers southwest. Ziber (pop. 752) and Şirdak (pop. 667) were located to the south.[225]

According to our main witness, who took part in the resistance in Şabinkarahisar, 300 Armenian conscripts left for Erzincan and Bayburt in November 1914, after the general mobilization (a good many older men were able to pay the draft exemption tax of 43 Turkish pounds).[226] In a report to the patriarch in Constantinople, the primate of Şabinkarahisar, Father Vaghinag Torigian, noted that "every day brings fresh proof of rancor toward the Armenians" in the form of requisitions resembling pillage, especially in the villages in the vicinity of the city, which the authorities required to transport the requisitioned goods using means of their own, despite most of their carts, horses, and oxen having already been taken by the army.[227] This, however, could hardly be called shocking in a country in which the state had a reputation as a predator. The news of the 1 January 1915 murder of the designated primate of Erzincan, Sahag Odabashian, between Suşehir and Refahiye[228] – that is, very close to the city – was obviously much more alarming for the Armenian leaders of Şabinkarahisar. It was, moreover, Father Torigian, who went to the scene of the crime to make arrangements for the victim's burial.[229] On his return, the prelate informed the political leaders about his apprehensions. The massacre of Armenians soldiers that took place on the road between Erzincan and Sıvas in January 1915, after the debacle at Sarıkamiş, followed by the 8 February destruction by a band of çetes, under alarming circumstances, of the village of Piurk, located in the neighboring kaza of Suşehir,[230] convinced the Armenians of Şabinkarahisar that preparations were being made to massacre them. However, as A. Haygaz observes, no one anticipated the scope of the Young Turks' extermination plan. Rather, the Armenian leaders were expecting "traditional" massacres of the Hamidian kind, which generally lasted from one to three days, and against which well-organized resistance could prove effective if it held out until orders came from the capital to put an end to the violence.[231]

The assassination in May of the priest of the nearby village of Anerği, Father Seponia Garinian,[232] the arrest and murder of Nazaret Hiusisian, an emblematic figure in the city, and the arrest of well-known personalities such as Asadur Tiutiunjian, Ardashes and Mirijan Burnazian, Krikor Dakesian, Garabed Garmirian, Rafayel Odabashian, and Garabed Skhdorjian, compelled the Armenian leaders to take refuge in the quarter around the citadel. Khosrov Medzadurian, Hmayag Margosian, Pitsa, Ghugas Deovletian, Hmayag Karageozian, Vahan Hiusisian, and Shabuh Ozanian went underground.[233] The authorities thereupon launched the next phase of operations, which consisted in confiscating weapons and hunting down deserters. This led to extremely violent search-and-seizure operations. Torigian went to see the mutesarif, Mektubci Ahmed Bey, in an attempt to bring them to a halt. He proposed to the mutesarif that he personally see to the confiscation of weapons,[234] obviously a matter of crucial importance for both parties. The Armenians finally decided to turn in their handguns, hunting rifles, and a few Martinis, bringing them to the prefecture in a cart escorted by two gendarmes. Haygaz wonders if the authorities really believed that this charade meant that the Armenians were laying down their arms. The fact that the authorities proceeded to recruit a militia of "volunteers" (gönülüler) made up of social outcasts, whose pitiful condition was a subject of comment by witnesses,[235] suggests that the mutesarif deemed it necessary to reinforce his troops before taking new initiatives. The feeble potential of these recruits, however, led him to increase the military capacity of the militia by freeing common-law criminals.[236] These initiatives left little doubt as to his intentions, which took concrete form when, on the evening of Sunday, 6 June 1915, the mutesarif summoned his traditional interlocutor, the prelate, to the konak "for consultations."[237] He "consulted" Torigian by interning him upon his arrival and having him tortured in the cellar of the konak. After undergoing this ordeal, the prelate was dragged by two policemen – a Zaza and a Çerkez – into Ahmed Bey's office.[238] With the mutesarif in his office was a delegate of the Young Turk Central Committee, Nuri Bey, "an educated native of Istanbul," who had arrived in Şabinkarahisar only recently. Ahmed Bey mockingly asked the prelate how he was, without provoking the slightest reaction from him. Then, more aggressively, he demanded that Torigian provide him with a list of the insurgents and the number of weapons in the Armenians' possession. The exchange that followed showed that each man was perfectly well aware of his own position.

> *Torigian:* Pasha, I know what you are going to do; give the order to have me killed right now.
>
> *Ahmed Bey:* We are interrogating you.
>
> *Torigian:* I am not in a condition to answer.

Ahmed Bey: To refuse to respond to representatives of the law is a crime of treason that merits appropriate punishment.

Torigian: Gentlemen, what do you expect from a miserable clergyman who has been broken, crushed, and dishonored? You speak in the name of the law. But what law authorized you to turn a prelate over to policemen and order that he be beaten to death? By what right do you accuse a whole nation of crimes that it has not committed? Over the centuries, the Armenians have more than once experienced the justice of this country and are convinced that justice has never existed in the Ottoman Empire and never will…We Armenians are guilty of having failed to understand, over the centuries, that this is a system that has been at work from the outset. After the constitution was restored, not only ordinary people, but even our Hnchak and Dashnak revolutionaries were duped; they believed that an end would be put to unjust practices…But the Adana events go to show that, in this country, in which neither conscience nor God exists, there can be no justice.[239]

Several blows from the Ittihadist delegate, accompanied by the exclamation "Shut up, dog," led to a new reply from the prelate: "You see, effendi, you have proved that I am right. An educated, cultivated young man, ci-devant an official representative of the Istanbul Ittihad, raises his hand against a people's spiritual shepherd."[240] It would be an understatement to say that these exchanges express all the accumulated rancor of the Armenians toward the regime and the predator's mentality of the young delegate of the Ittihad and the high-ranking official, both fully aware of how much power they had.

The Armenian clergyman, who was 45 years old, understood perfectly well the fate that awaited him and refused to play the role of the guilty party any longer. On Monday, 7 June, he left the city, guarded by some 15 gendarmes, and was murdered the same day near Enderes, the seat of the *kaza* of Suşehir, by Kucurzâde Kâmil Beg.[241] It was not until the morning of 16 June that the population of Şabinkarahisar learned what had happened to its primate.[242]

In this densely populated urban center with an Armenian majority, the systematic arrest of the men, the prelude to deportation, required that the authorities display a certain tactical skill. The meager results of the searches conducted in the upper quarter around the citadel compelled the *mutesarif* to limit himself to launching an operation against the centers of craft and commerce located below the city. On 14 June, soldiers and *çetes* surrounded these buildings and hurriedly arrested 300 men, who were then imprisoned in the basement of the *konak*. A squadron of *çetes*, commanded by someone named Kel Hasan, also made its way into the city's lower quarters and carried out arrests throughout the night. Hasan was, however, unable to penetrate the quarter around the citadel.[243] On the morning of 15 June, an Armenian commando tried to free the prisoners confined in the *konak*; the prisoners, however, were executed when the commando reached the area.[244] On 16 June, the inhabitants of Şabinkarahisar saw, in the distance, the village of Anerği in flames, while the news of the murder of the primate made the rounds. According to Haygaz, the inhabitants of the city now spontaneously barricaded themselves in their neighborhoods; people from nearby villages, attacked by irregulars, took refuge in the city; and the Armenians of the city's lower quarter, known as the "Orchards," began to withdraw to the heights.[245] There were, moreover, skirmishes between the squadron of *çetes* commanded by Kel Hassan and Armenian butchers in the city's Middle Quarter. On Thursday, 17 June, more villagers from the vicinity arrived in Şabinkarahisar. A military council was then created, made up of Ghugas Deovletian, Hmayag Karageozian, Vahan Hiusisian, Hmayag Margosian, Krikor Baronvartian, Aleksan Dakesian, and Khosrov's lawyer, Divrig.[246] The fire that had broken out that same day in the lower quarters, where the houses were mainly built of wood, spread, accelerating the concentration of the Armenian population in the upper quarter and, later, in the citadel, where according to Armenian sources between 5,000 and 6,000 people, three-quarters of them women and children, found refuge.[247] An abrupt shift in the wind drove the flames toward the Turkish quarters, destroying all the government buildings located in the city's lower quarters.[248] The Armenians were, however, unaware of the extent of the panic that had swept over the local authorities. It should further be noted that during the massacre of the prisoners in the *konak*, when someone named Karnig Beylerian seized a gendarme's rifle and killed the commander of the gendarmerie and his assistant, the *mutesarif* and the mayor fled.[249]

The main problem confronting the military council, which was made up of local notables, was the lack of fighters, especially young men. According to Haygaz, there were fewer than 500 people capable of "bearing arms," and they had only 200 weapons in their possession, including 100 Mauser rifles.[250] The other problem was the lack of water: the Armenians were forced to go down to the springs every night in order to procure enough to meet their minimum needs.[251]

After five days of relative calm, Vali Muammer of Sıvas arrived in Şabinkarahisar on 20 or 21 June, with army units equipped with cannons in order to conduct the siege of the citadel. He immediately sent a message to the insurgents, demanding that they lay down their arms and surrender, promising that their lives would be spared in exchange.[252] The military council rejected the offer, and the Ottoman artillery began to pound the Armenians' positions. It seems, however, that this shelling did not produce the anticipated results. Rather, the scraps of metal from the hundreds of shells that came raining down on the citadel appear to have served as raw material with which to make crude bullets.[253] The army units that had come from Suşehir launched the first assault on 25 June.[254] They pressed the attack for several days, affording the Armenians an opportunity to recover arms and ammunition from the attackers killed beneath the citadel. On 27 June, Muammer sent a new message to the military council, this time threatening to inflict exemplary sanctions on the men who had precipitated these "disorders" and were responsible for the fire and the destruction of the city.[255] Thus, he blamed the fire on the Armenians, even though it had broken out in the Armenian quarters and wreaked havoc there before spreading to the lower part of the city.

As far as the strategy adopted by the two parties is concerned, it would seem that Muammer favored a massive assault aimed at quickly crushing the Armenian resistance, whereas the local notables wanted to conduct a classic siege that would inevitably lead to water and food shortages. At all events, the authorities waited for several army battalions that had been dispatched from Erzincan to arrive, along with several squadrons of *çetes*[256] and three regiments from Sıvas commanded by Neşed Pasha,[257] before launching the assault to break the Armenian resistance. This offensive was opened on Sunday, 4 July, with 6,000 men thrown into the battle.[258] Around 300 Armenian combatants and, probably, more than 300 attackers fell in the course of these violent clashes. The citadel was now defended by only 200 men, many of them adolescents.[259] On the night of 8 July, the last Armenian fighters, running out of food and ammunition, attempted a sortie. On the morning of the 11th, the twenty-seventh day of the siege, a white flag was hoisted above the citadel.[260] After hesitating, soldiers and *çetes* surround the citadel: the handful of males over fifteen were shot on the spot, while some 300 boys between the ages of three and 15 were separated from the others.[261] According to our witness, who was in this group, there followed heated discussions involving a *hoca*, the military men, and the local notables about what to do with these children, who were ultimately reintegrated into the group of women assembled in the cathedral and the adjacent buildings. Some of the women chose to take poison. The rest were exiled to the deserts by way of Agn and Fırıncilar.[262]

Among those who bore the main responsibility for what happened in the *sancak* of Şabinkarahisar, in addition to the *mutesarif* Mektubci Ahmed Bey, the CUP delegate Nuri Bey, the lawyer Edhem Bey, Pel Hasan, Gugug Mustafa, Tatar Haliloğlu Tahsin,

Hacihaliloğlu Mahmud, Ciğuloğlu Şerif, Aydınoğlu Şerif, Saleh Kasab Asim, Karamil Azımzâde İsmail, Faik Çavuş, Tamzaralı Müdir Ali Osman, Ömer Feyzi (a deputy in the Ottoman parliament), and Tokatlı Komiser Sâmi played crucial roles in arrest and killing the men of the city, and also in the looting and deportations that took place in the rest of the region.[263]

The *Kaza* of Suşehir

The 35 Armenian villages in the *kaza* of Suşehir, almost all of which lay in the plain of Sadağa to the east of the seat of the *kaza*, Andreas/Enderes, had in 1914 a total Armenian population of 13,430. Located some 30 kilometers southwest of Şabinkarahisar, Enderes had an Armenian population of 2,784 in 1914. Together with the inhabitants of the 18 biggest Armenian villages in the *kaza* – Sis (pop. 785), Piurk (pop. 1,716), Mshagnots/Muşagemiz (pop. 844), Gtanots/Krtanos (pop. 325), Alamlik (pop. 219), Ezbider (pop. 352), Ğaraş (pop. 104), Sevindig (pop. 375), Aziller (pop. 2,489), Abana (pop. 444), Yeniköy (pop. 214), Tmluc (pop. 173), Aghvanis (pop. 700), Komeshdun (pop. 107), Beyçiftlik (pop. 76), Aghravis (pop. 923), Avand (pop. 126), and Hamam (pop. 197) – the Armenians of Enderes were massacred or deported by way of Agn and Fırıncilar in the latter half of June 1915, under the supervision of the *kaymakam*, Ahmed Hilmi, who held his post from 10 November 1913 to 23 November 1915.[264]

The *Kaza* of Mehsudiye

The Armenian population of this *kaza*, put at 627, was essentially concentrated in the seat of the *kaza*, Mehsudiye (pop. 140), and in Karamahmud (pop. 350). These Armenians too were massacred or deported late in June 1915 by the *kaymakam*, Nafi Bey, who held his post from 9 April 1914 to 19 July 1916.[265]

The *Kazas* of Köyulhisar/Kızılhisar and Hamidye

In these two districts in the western part of the *sancak* of Şabinkarahisar there were only a few dozen Armenian households left by 1914: 20 in Köyulhisar, the seat of the *kaza* (pop. 100), 15 in Mushal (pop. 90), and 70 in Masudiya, the seat of the *kaza* of Hamidye.[266]

The *kaymakam* of Kızılhisar, Sermed Yaşar, who held his post from 1 June 1915 to 9 July 1916, and the *kamaykam* of Hamidiye, Celal Bey, who held his post from 7 April 1914 to 11 April 1916, organized the massacre of the men and the deportation of the rest of the population by way of Agn and Fırıncilar in these two *kazas*.[267]

Sivas in the Aftermath of the Deportations

As we have seen, the system used to eliminate the Armenians of the vilayet of Sivas had a distinctive feature: some 5,000 men were held in the central prison and the cellar of the Şifahdiye and Gök *medreses* in Sivas for almost a month after the departure of the convoys of deportees.[268] We do not know what brought Ahmed Muammer to leave them alive for so long, and we have no information about the conditions in which they lived in prison. We do know, however, how these men were methodically liquidated in two stages, at two different sites relatively close to Sivas. Those interned in the *medrese* of Gök were the first to be massacred. From 2 to 7 August, groups of 100 to 200 men were taken from this *medrese* every night and led up to Karlık, on the heights of the monastery of St. Hagop in the Çelebiler valley, approximately four hours northwest of Sivas. There they were killed with axes.[269] The second group, the prisoners held in the *medrese* of Şifahdiye, was liquidated between 8 August and 12 August. These men were led in groups of 200 to 300 to a school for apprentices located near a farm three hours away from Sıvas. There they were put to death under the supervision of the Ittihad's responsible secretary, Gani Bey,[270] Şekeroğlu İsmail, Halis Bey, Sobaci Şükrü (the *müdir* of Sğcakışla), Ğarza Dürger Hasan – Şükrü and Hasan destroyed the villages of Dendil, Burhan, Karagöl, and Chepni – as well as the commander of the garrison, Ali Bey; Haci Ömer; Ömer's sons Veysel and Hanif; Nurioğlu Süleyman; Tekkeşin İbrahim; Evilya Effendi; Tayib Effendi; the grocer Nuri; Arpacı Şükrü; Ziya Effendi, the director of the Sultaniye middle school; and the Unionists Bakal Aziz and Bakal Behcet.[271]

Around the middle of August, according to the Islamicized craftsmen who were allowed to remain in Sıvas, Muammer organized a big banquet after liquidating all the Armenian men, expressing his satisfaction over his accomplishment.[272] It is possible that the slaughter of these men was postponed until the vali's return from Erzincan, where he participated, around 31 July, at the meeting of the valis of Erzerum, Trebizond, Harput, and Sıvas chaired by Bahaeddin Şakir.[273] It is reasonable to suppose that the meeting was held to assess the first phase of operations and decide on complementary measures, such as the fate of the worker-soldiers.

Reverend Bauernfeind, who traveled through Ulash and Sıvas on 16 August 1915, wrote in his diary, "There are no more corpses, but adult Armenians working to bring in the harvest." Of course, Bauernfeind could not know that these peasants from Ulash would be dispatched southwards a few days later, after the harvest had been brought in.[274] He observed at the entrance to the city that "the road [had] been repaired by Armenians" (who would be killed the following year) and that "male and female Armenian employees, including adult males, are still employed at the [American] hospital," but would "have to leave in the next few days."[275] The German minister thus saw the last traces of the Armenian presence in Sıvas, which Vali Muammer, who had made judicious use of these Armenians' labor power, was now preparing to eliminate by overcoming the resistance of the American missionaries.[276]

Arriving in Gemerek, on the road to Kayseri, on 18 August 1915, Bauernfeind discovered a city "whose Armenians [had] now departed"; it "gave him the impression of being deserted and destroyed." He had nevertheless been able to converse "in French and in Turkish with the commander and an army doctor," an Armenian "who belonged to a battalion of Armenian laborers." Bauernfeind had encountered an *amele taburi* in Gemerek that comprised 900 men from Kayseri.[277]

On 28 September 1915, Muammer sent a coded wire to the interior minister, informing him that so far 136,084 Armenians from Sıvas and the areas administratively attached to it had been deported toward Mesopotamia (the vali wrote "Cizre").[278] If we make allowance for those who were massacred locally, the conscripts incorporated into labor battalions, and the Islamicized young women and children, this figure seems altogether plausible.

In the written deposition he submitted to the Mazhar Commission in December 1918, General Vehib Pasha, who had succeeded Mahmud Kâmil as the head of the Third Army in February 1916, observed: "In the province of Sıvas, all the Armenians, with the exception of those who had converted to Islam, were deported ... The officials employed in this province had a direct, pernicious relation with the crimes committed and knowingly helped perpetrate them. That is my conviction."[279] He also noted that, "as 'abandoned property,' the sums collected and precious objects and jewels transformed into cash were amassed and preserved, and, consequently, were not looted." This, he said, confirmed that Muammer, someone with "an exalted sense of honesty, honor, and loyalty," had followed the instructions he had received from the capital.[280] Other sources, to be sure, incline us to make a less flattering assessment of Muammer's activities. While it seems to be an established fact that the vali, defending the interests of the party-state, succeeded in preventing in the area under his jurisdiction the kind of pillage that went on elsewhere, as we have seen, indications are that he nevertheless imitated a number of his colleagues, personally appropriating the property of some of those under his administration. He also managed to cover up, with undeniable skill, the massacres perpetrated on his orders, thus creating the impression that he had carried out an administrative deportation in legal form. From this point of view, Muammer Bey proved to be one of the most effective valis, the one who executed the orders he received from the capital with the greatest fidelity, the debacle of Şabinkarahisar aside.

Shortly after the Mudros Armistice was signed, at a time when Turkey was still endeavoring to settle its accounts with its Young Turk elite, a Turkish officer posted in Sıvas during the war wrote an open letter to the ex-vali of Sıvas. "In the name of humanity," he declared, "I have the right to ask you for an account of the number of people you massacred."[281] To make what he said more credible, this witness reminded the vali of the acts of theft he had committed and "made others commit," and went on to ask him, "where are the twenty-eight rugs that belonged to the money-changer Dikran Effendi? Or the eighteen jewels of various kinds that belong to Baghchegiulian Effendi? Or the jewels worth four thousand pounds that belonged to Miss Virgin, Mgrdich Effendi Mardikian's sister-in-law?" Finally, this officer, whom Muammer had had brought before a court-martial in Sıvas, recalled that he had been in the vali's office when Muammer had summoned the "jeweler Lifter and asked him to assess the value of the jewels contained in eleven walnut chests," threatening to kill Lifter "if he dared reveal anything about the matter."[282]

In a report submitted to the Istanbul court-martial, Captain Fazıl was hardly more tender with the vali of Sıvas: he portrayed him as the main culprit in the destruction of the Armenians, a man who had ordered the "gendarmes" to kill and had amassed a fortune of 60,000 Turkish pounds at the deportees' cost.[283]

These revelations, doubtless inspired less by moral considerations than by a spirit of revenge, do not only tarnish the bright image of an exemplary vali, but also illustrate the day-to-day practice of most of the Young Turk leaders. General Vehib's favorable declaration about Ahmed Muammer remains a mystery, especially in view of the vehemence with which the general denounced the vali's role in the destruction of the Armenians of the region, and in light of the serious conflict between the two men after the July 1916 massacre of several thousand Armenian worker-soldiers in a gorge lying between Sarkışla and Gemerek.

The July 1916 Liquidation of the Amele Taburis of Sıvas

We have noted that the great majority of Armenian worker-soldiers who served in the *amele taburis* of the five other eastern vilayets, including those males under 18 and over 45 who were recruited late in the day, were put to death in the wake of the deportations. It must be emphasized that, in contrast, Armenians in the labor battalions who were liquidated in the vilayet of Sıvas perished a full year after the deportations had come to an end.

Aside from the *amele taburi*, comprising 900 men from Kayseri who were put to work in Gemerek,[284] a labor battalion of some 500 men was present in Hanlı, halfway between Sıvas and Gemerek.[285] Additionally, a considerable number of craftsmen-soldiers were employed by the army, especially in Sıvas. These units were under the orders of Colonel Behcet Bey and the commanding officers Hikmet Bey, Nuri Bey, and Ali Şefik Bey.[286]

For as long as the Third Army was under the command of Mahmud Kâmil, it seems that the elimination of the worker-soldiers posed no problems for the military authorities. When, however, General Vehib Pasha became the commander-in-chief of the Third Army, it is clear that the Special Organization, the CUP delegates, and the valis were no longer able to decide the fate of these men without first consulting the supreme commanding officer under whose orders these recruits were serving. We have virtually no official documents about the circumstances surrounding the destruction of the *amele taburis* in fall 1915; virtually all our information comes from survivors' reports. Thus, the military inquiry into the massacre of the worker-soldiers from the vilayet of Sıvas that was conducted in fall 1916 on Vehib's orders, and reopened by the Mazhar Commission in November 1918, is of even greater interest than it otherwise would be.

In the deposition he submitted to the Mazhar Commission, Vehib stated, "Military imperatives made it necessary to send Armenians serving in the labor battalions to the Fourth Army. It was decided to bring them together in Sıvas in order to send them from there to Aleppo. Orders to this effect were issued to the vali."[287] It can clearly be inferred from this formulation that the military authorities deemed it necessary to remove these men from the front line, which ran through Enderes/Suşehir at the time. Muammer, who often appeared at the headquarters of the Third Army to resolve problems having to do with provisioning the troops, was precisely at Zara when this decision was made. According to Armenian sources, he had even telephoned orders from Zara to concentrate the Armenian worker-soldiers in Sıvas in the *medreses* of Şifahdiye and Gök in order to send them from there to Bozanti and Syria.[288] While grave charges weighed against the commander of the gendarmerie of Şarkışla, Mescizâde Nuri, who carried out the massacre of the Armenian worker-soldiers of Sıvas, the vali of Sıvas was also under heavy suspicion. Thus, Nuri declared that Muammer had telephoned him and told him to send the *amele taburis* "to Kayseri in one hour."[289] Translated into plain language, this was an order to liquidate them (it was a several days' march from Kayseri to Sıvas). In response to inquires by the Mazhar Commission into the death of these soldiers, Vehib declared that he had demanded an explanation from Nuri and that the commander had "said that the order had been communicated to him orally by Muammer Bey in the course of a telephone conversation"; however, Vehib added, Muammer had denied "ever having issued such an order."[290] In view of the special position of the vali, who was also the head of the Special Organization in the region under his jurisdiction, it is more probable that Muammer did indeed issue orders to massacre these thousands of men after himself receiving such orders from his superiors. The decision of the Third Army's commander to assemble the worker-soldiers under his jurisdiction in the vilayet of Sıvas with a view to putting them at Cemal Pasha's disposal was certainly perceived by the Young Turk network as an opportunity to eliminate them. Doubtless, Istanbul assumed that it would not occur to the commander of the Third Army to inquire into the fate of these men who were supposed to have been transferred to Syria. However, three months after the departure of these labor battalions, Vehib, who had "received no news indicating whether or not they had arrived at Aleppo," began to wonder what had become of them.[291] He asked Ahmed Cemal, the commander-in-chief of the Fourth Army, for "an explanation." Cemal replied that these "soldiers had not arrived in the area under his jurisdiction." Vehib therefore turned to Muammer, who "informed [him] that all the Armenian soldiers had been massacred between Şarkışla and Gemerek by Nuri Effendi, a captain in the gendarmerie who was under orders to dispatch them [to Aleppo]." The inquiry conducted by Vehib "established that he had intentionally massacred the soldiers in question."[292] Nuri Bey was summoned to the headquarters of the Third Army in Suşehir and brought before the Military Council, which condemned him to death. "I took the responsibility," Vehib wrote, "before my conscience, of issuing an order to carry out the sentence, so that this would serve as a clear example for others."[293]

But Vehib did not content himself with punishing someone who had merely carried out orders. He demanded that the man who had given the order, Ahmed Muammer, be brought before a military court. According to Bishop Knel Kalemkiarian, who met with Talât in this connection, the fact that the interior minister and İsmail Hakkı visited Sıvas on 29 November 1916 was directly related to this affair.[294] On the pretext of carrying out a "general inspection tour," the two Young Turk leaders "in fact came in order to smooth over the dispute between Vehib Pasha and Muammer." Vehib supposedly demanded that the capital "immediately relieve [Muammer] of his duties" and is said to have remained "inflexible to the end," so that the interior minister was finally forced to transfer the vali to Konya.[295]

After the Mudros Armistice, when the governmental commission of inquiry began to investigate Muammer's activities during the war, its president, Hasan Mazhar, turned to Vehib for additional information on the vali's role in the murder of the worker-soldiers. He notably asked him whether there was "anything having to do with Muammer Bey in the minutes of the interrogation of Nuri Effendi" and, furthermore, whether the vali had "interceded in his favor" with Vehib when the death sentence was handed down. The general responded: "Nuri Bey simply declared that he had received the liquidation order from Muammer Bey." However, Vehib went on, Nuri had not been able to show him a written order, so that "Nuri's affirmations remained mere words, without the least proof to back them up and lacking all legislative or official character; thus they were considered to be worthless."[296] The prudent general was, however, careful to say nothing about the steps he had taken in Istanbul with a view of obtaining Muammer's resignation after the Armenian soldiers' "lamentable end." He did, however, testify that when he asked the vali to send Captain Nuri to his headquarters, Muammer had wanted to "know why he was being sent for." A few days later, when Muammer went to the headquarters in Suşehir to resolve "problems having to do with provisioning the army," the vali "stated orally that the investigation that he had conducted had revealed that Nuri Effendi was the author of the crime in question ... and that he had informed the interior minister of this."[297] These confidences in the form of justifications were apparently not enough to convince the general. They reflect a concrete situation of a kind we rarely have the opportunity to observe, one in which a Young Turk leader, suddenly confronted with his responsibility for issuing orders to commit a crime, unhesitatingly sacrificed one of his subordinates to protect himself and his party.

According to reports collected by N. Kapigian, 500 craftsmen-soldiers from the city of Sıvas, among the 3,000 men interned in the city's *medreses* early in July 1916, were quite promptly released. The others were sent to the gorge located on the southern slopes of the Dardaşlar mountain chain and massacred at Taşlı Dere, on the road to Şarkışla, near Gemerek, on Captain Nuri's orders.[298] It seems that German officers witnessed these summary executions.[299] Bishop Kalemkiarian reports that, accompanied by the German vice-consul, Karl Wert, he went to see the vali, who had returned from the headquarters of the Third Army the day before, to ask why the Armenians had been imprisoned. The vali declared that "the commander of the Fourth Army had asked that the soldiers be sent to him so that they could be put to work on building the railroad in the Bozanti area," but that they had in fact "been massacred with unimaginable savagery, with axes, swords, clubs, and bullets, or were thrown over cliffs by criminals."[300]

According to a file assembled by the British authorities, the CUP's responsible secretary in Sıvas, Gani Bey, participated personally in the liquidation of another *amele taburi* in Yon Yukuş, three hours from Sıvas.[301] In the same period, the 500 worker-soldiers working near Hanlı were put to death at Kayadipi, seven hours from Sıvas,[302] while the 900 men in the battalion based in Gemerek met the same fate near the Ortaköy spring.[303]

Three army doctors, Baghdasar Vartanian, Maksud, and Hayranian, were the last victims of these mass murders; they were first relieved of their duties and then murdered in Sıvas's central prison. High-ranking German friends of Hayranian's, who had close relations with German officers based in the city, had interceded directly with Enver Pasha on his behalf.

But even this powerful protection does not seem to have sufficed to restrain Muammer.[304] There is every reason to believe that the vali did not want to see a physician on such good terms with the empire's German allies survive, the more so as Hayranian had been a witness to the vali's criminal activities.

Thus, a total of around 5,000 Armenian recruits, who may be considered the remnants of the Third Army's *amele taburis*, were liquidated in the course of July 1916.

Those Responsible for the Massacres in the Vilayet of Sıvas

In a document addressed to Sıvas's police chief, Rifat Bey, in December 1918, Hasan Mazhar, the head of the government commission of inquiry, asked 39 questions that, as it were, outline the basic structure of the program to liquidate the Armenian population of the region.[305] We do not know if Rifat Bey responded to this questionnaire. But some of the questions are virtually answers in and of themselves. They not only echo a number of the events we have just reviewed, but also provide more precise information about them, and show, in the process, how familiar Hasan Mazhar was with the mechanism put in place by the CUP. We list below all these questions. Some have been followed by the beginnings of an answer or more precise information, when we were in a position to supply it.

1) Who was the president of the Union and Progress Club in Sıvas? Şekerlıoğlu İsmail.[306] 2) Who were the members of the Committee of Union and Progress in Sıvas? Kol Agasi Ali Effendi, Sopaci Şükrü, police lieutenant Hafız, police lieutenant Mahmud, Muammer's *yaver*, his hit-man, Çerkez Mahmud, who executed Manuel Dedeyan and his students at the Sanasarian *lycée*, Ali Şerif Bey, who supervised arrests and tortures, as well as search-and-seizure missions in the villages, Sadullah Bey, Behcet Bey, the commander of the *amele taburis*, and Pertev Bey, the commander of the Tenth Army Corps stationed in Sıvas.[307] 3) Did the vali, Muammer Bey, go to the Club every day? Very probably. 4) How many days did Dr. Bahaeddin Şakir, a member of the Central Committee, spend in Sıvas, and in whose house did he stay? This corroborates that the head of the *Teşkilât-ı Mahsusa* paid a visit to Sıvas. 5) What did he say when he was there? 6) How many days did Talât Bey, the minister of the interior, spend in Sıvas, and in whose house did he stay? We do not know if this is an allusion to Talât's visit of November 1916, connected to the decision about Muammer's fate, or an earlier stay. 7) Who formed the bands of *çetes* known as the *Teşkilât-ı Mahsusa*? Muammer, with Rasim Bey, the parliamentary deputy from Sıvas who organized the squads of *çetes* in the vilayet.[308] 8) What is the name of the parliamentary deputy from Kangal who made a speech before the Union and Progress Club and in the mosques (in Sıvas)? He said there: "O Muslims, your enemies are not the foreigners, not the Russians or the British. Your enemies are in your midst." This was most likely the deputy from Çanğırı, Dr. Fazıl Berki Bey, who made more or less the same remarks in Uli Cami.[309] 9) How did Muammer Bey react when Talât gave speeches in the mosque and before the Club? In them, he said: "O Muslims, we have completely exterminated the Armenians; we give you all their property, their shops, stores, and houses. From now on, trade is in your hands and will be exclusively yours." 10) Who released the convicts (from prison) so that they could be enrolled in the Special Organization? 11) How many prisoners were recruited by the Special Organization, and how many were recruited by the gendarmerie? 12) What tasks were the battalions of worker-soldiers assigned? 13) How many churches were demolished in Sıvas? 14) Why did Muammer Bey demolish all the houses in the village of Tavra and transform this village of 300 households into farmland? 15) What is the secret of the destruction of the big Armenian churches and the 300 to 500 houses of the Hülluklik neighborhood (in Sıvas)? 16) Of you and Muammer Bey, who issued the order to replace the crosses on the church

belfries with crescents and called on the people to pray from these belfries? 17) The gravestones in the (Armenian) cemetery were torn down and their epitaphs were effaced by certain people. Then these monuments and stones from the destroyed churches were brought to the area in front of the prefecture building, where the Turan Hotel, the Committee of Union and Progress Club, the prefecture's printing-house, and the drafts-men's office was constructed. Was this operation carried out on orders from Muammer Bey? 18) Were worker-soldiers employed (for this purpose)? When were they summoned to Sıvas to build these buildings, before their deportation and massacre? 19) Was it not on Muammer Bey's orders that 52 Armenian soldiers who had fought in Çanakkale and been wounded in battle were forced to join a labor battalion? 20) Who presided over the groundbreaking ceremonies for the Turan Hotel and the Union and Progress Club? 21) Who presided over the inauguration of these buildings when they were completed? 22) Who attended the groundbreaking and inauguration (ceremonies) of these build-ings? 23) When did you learn, in Sıvas, the news of the massacres and liquidation of the workers of the battalions that was carried out by Nuri Effendi in the Tenus district? 24) When did Muammer Bey learn of these major crimes? Did he order that investigations be conducted, and were they really carried out? 25) Were the *mutesarifs* of Azizyie, Kerdun, and Tenus questioned? 26) If an investigation really was carried out, what was the rea-son for it? 26) When were weapons collected? How many days after the deportation did this procedure begin? 27) We have been apprised that, during the deportation of the Armenians from Sıvas, Muammer Bey declared to the populace: "Any Muslim who hides an Armenian in his house will be hanged in front of it." This proclamation was published in the provincial newspaper by the Şeyh press. Do you have this newspaper? 28) In your capacity as director of the police, did you issue travel permits (*vezika*) to nine people who were with the Bishop, Mr. Karnig Tughlajian, and Aram Musheghian, who wished to use these permits to Constantinople? 29) What happened in the monastery of Saint Nshan? 30) What was the role of the Special Organisation? What was the position of Dr. Bahaeddin Şakir, the president of this organization? 31) What was the date on which the head of the postal service between Kayseri and Sıvas laid down his functions? 32) How many Armenian officials were serving in the administration of the vilayet? How many Armenian judges were there on the bench? What were their names? 33) Who was the dragoman of the vilayet? 34) Which judges were relieved of their official duties and deported with Oskan Aslan Effendi, the director of the forests and mines? 35) Why were these judges and Oskan Aslan Effendi imprisoned before being deported? Who ordered that they be deported? 36) Is it true that Vartanian, Vartoyan, and Manug Beylerian, the dragoman of the vilayet, were deported and murdered with four or five other Armenians? 37) Twenty or twenty-five days after they were deported, were other men arrested and imprisoned? 38) Hulusi Bey, with 150 of his men, went to Kangal to find the caravan of Armenian women deported from Sıvas; he mistreated them and took from them a con-siderable quantity of gold and precious objects which were loaded into three vehicles, one with springs and two without. What portion of this plunder was allotted to the vali? Do you know if a register was established in which the quantities of gold and valuable objects were noted? 39) The Union and Progress delegate in Sıvas was Gani Bey. Who asked you to include him on the police commission?[310]

This "questionnaire" reconstructs the mechanism that was set in motion at the regional level while spelling out the role played by the administration, on the one hand, and the secret centers, on the other, in the plan to liquidate the Armenians and seize their prop-erty. It is usefully completed by a list of those who bore the main responsibility for the massacres and deportations in the vilayet.[311] In addition to the leader of the local Ittihad Club, Muammer, and the CUP representative, Gani, the following people were involved:

Bacanakzâde Hamdi, the president of the municipality; Mustafa Hoca of Turkal, a member of the Deportation Committee that compiled a list of the city's Armenian elite to be liquidated; Colonel Ali Effendi, a member of the Deportation Committee; Rıza Effendi, Colonel Ali's brother, the leader of a squadron of *çetes*; the mullahs Derindeli Hoca, Gamalı Hoca, İzzet Hoca and Öçenoğlu Mustafa, who urged that the Armenians be eliminated in the sermons that they preached in the mosques; Halil Bey, the commander of the gendarmerie; Ali Şevfik, a major in the gendarmerie, one of those who organized the massacres in the *kaza* of Suşehir; Rifat Bey, the police chief, who had the Armenian notables arrested and organized the seizure of their property; the *defterdar* (administrator of the land register) Tevfik, a member of the commission responsible for abandoned property; Akıpaşazâde Murteza, Tevfik's secretary; Nür Bey, the director of the newspaper *Sıvas*, "who published many articles about the atrocities that Armenian *çetes* inflicted on Turks"; Emin Bey, an auditor; Hayri Effendi, an official on the committee to sell "abandoned property" who was responsible for settling *muhacirs* in houses that had belonged to Armenians; Mahmud Çete, a police lieutenant at the head of the convoys of deportees who engaged in pillage and perpetrated massacres near Hasançelebi; Celal, an assistant of Muammer's who perpetrated massacres at Çelebiler and Tavra; Keleş Bey, an officer in the gendarmerie who ordered and supervised massacres; Halis Bey, an officer in the squadron of *çetes*, the director of the commission of the *Teşkilât-ı Mahsusa* in the vilayet; Emirpaşaoğlu Hamid, the chief of the Çerkez of Uzunyayla; Bacanakoğlu Edhem, a *çete*; Kutugünoğlu Hüseyin, a *çete*; Zaralı Mahir, a *çete* (the last five people were all implicated in the murder of the vicar Sahag Odabashian); Cizmeci Haci, a carrier or car; Çerkes Kadir, a *çete* accused of having received and transferred, along with the five last-named people, 48 sacks full of jewels and a sack containing 30,000 (Turkish) pounds in gold from Hasançelebi and Hekimhan to Sıvas, where they were turned over to Muammer; Sobaci Çil Şükrü, an auxiliary gendarme who was charged with establishing the whereabouts of the people to be arrested; the *müdirs* of Ulaş/Ulash and Agcakışla, who were implicated in the massacres in their districts; Garga Durğere Hasan, a *çete* who perpetrated massacres in the Armenian villages around Ulaş; Haciömeroğlu Veysel, a *çete*; Hanif; Nuribeyoğlu Süleyman and Nuribeyoğlu Kâzım, who slit the throats of people interned in the prison of Sıvas near the farm of the Balahor, on the road leading from Eni Han to Sıvas, together with Kurdish emigrés; Tekeşen İbrahim, an accomplice of the people just named, along with Tayib Effendi, an official at the town hall; Nuri, the grocer; Arpaci Şükrü; Bakal Aziz; Bakal Behcet; and Berber Şükrü (one of those who murdered a Sanasarian *lycée* teacher named Menjukian).

We should also mention the activities of Sâdullah, an officer in the gendarmerie and the head of the prison guards in the fortress of Sıvas (the prison of the court-martial), where he murdered Armenian prisoners in July 1916, as well as Colonel Pertev Bey, the military commander of the Tenth Army Corps; Tevfik Bey, the director of farms (*çiftlik müdüri*); Aherpaşazâde Halid, his secretary, who took part in the massacres of worker-soldiers in the gorge of Çelebiler; Aherpaşazâde Murteza, one of those who stole Armenian property in Sıvas; Avndukzâde Nusin and Handenezâde Hasan, who looted stores; Kâzım, an assistant to the vali and a *çete* who was implicated in the massacres in Kangal; and Ahmed Bey, the head of the Turkish orphanage in Sıvas, who was implicated in the murder of Armenian children.[312]

The French-language Istanbul daily announced in its fifth issue, published on Friday, 13 December 1918, that Muammer Bey had been arrested in the Ottoman capital. With his colleague from Dyarbekir, Dr. Reşid, he was one of the first of the accused to be placed under arrest.

Chapter 9

Deportations and Massacres in the Vilayet of Trebizond

Wedged between the Black Sea and the Pontic mountain chains, the vilayet of Trebizond, which had a surface area of 32,400 square kilometers and 1,500,000 inhabitants, was one of the most densely settled regions in the Ottoman Empire on the eve of the First World War. It was at the time divided into four *sancaks*: Trebizond, Canik, Lazistan, and Gümüşhane. Its population was essentially made up of Greeks, Turks, Lazes, Ajars, and Abkhaz, but it also had a flourishing Armenian minority 73,395 strong. They lived in 118 towns and villages and had 106 churches, three monasteries, and 190 schools with a total enrolment of 9,254, and a few Catholic and Protestant schools as well.[1]

In Trebizond alone, where the vali resided, there were 5,539 Armenians, including 750 Catholics and 150 Protestants.[2] The city was an important port of transit in which there were a large number of khans, consulates of all the great powers of the day, the offices of the fleet owners, and the homes of the richest Greek and Armenian merchants, located near the port around Central Square, popularly known as Gâvur Meydan.

In the first years of the constitutional regime, the Armenian political parties took an increasingly important part in the affairs of the Armenian community. During the legislative elections, the ARF also established close ties with the local Young Turks, who had a very narrow social base outside the circles of notables. Among the Armenians, the ARF too faced the opposition of conservative circles and even of the primates who came and went in rapid succession until the 8 July 1913 election of a young prelate, Kevork Turian.[3] The Balkan War afforded the Trebizond Armenians an opportunity to show their attachment to the Ottoman fatherland by serving in the army. Trebizond's Dashnak club even offered lodging to Ottoman officers.[4] When the newly elected patriarch, Zaven Der Yeghiayan, passed through the port in December 1913, the prelate was given a very respectful welcome by the local authorities and the CUP delegate, Ömer Naci.[5]

However, with the agreement on the reforms in the Armenian provinces, a policy of harassing the Armenian population of Trebizond was initiated. It took various forms. Thus, the "patriotic" fundraising drive that Trebizond's Ittihadist club launched in February 1914, officially organized for the purpose of "purchasing warships," was entrusted to local delinquents[6] who "extracted large sums of money from the Armenians and Greeks, sometimes going so far as to loot their stores."[7] It also seems that, as had happened elsewhere, instructions were issued in the capital to boycott Greek and Armenian merchants in Trebizond.[8]

When war broke out with Russia, Trebizond obviously constituted a strategic port of the first importance for the Ottomans; the Young Turk government planned to launch large-scale operations from the city. We have, moreover, seen that even before hostilities commenced, the CUP sent some of its most eminent members here: Major Yusuf Rıza Bey, a member of the Ittihad's Central Committee, who was put at the head of the *Teşkilât-ı Mahsusa*,[9] and

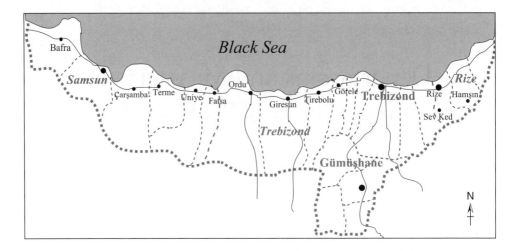

Yenibahçeli Nail, a renowned CUP *fedayi*, who served as the party's delegate in the vilayet.[10] The two men were briefly involved in a conflict about which of them was to command the squadrons of the Special Organization in the region; Major Rıza emerged victorious.[11] Nail managed to assemble 700 *çetes* by early November, all of them convicts released from prison.[12] The real political boss of the vilayet nevertheless appears to have been the vali, Cemal Azmi, who also played a significant role in recruiting *çetes* by appealing to the bands of brigands who infesting the vilayet's mountainous regions and obtaining an amnesty for them. Appointed to his post on 7 July 1914, shortly before the general mobilization (he held his post until 2 February 1917), Azmi was to be one of the main architects of the liquidation of his vilayet's Armenian population.[13]

As if to announce events to come, one of the buildings of the Armenian middle school, which abutted the Russian consulate, was burned down a few days before the general mobilization order was issued. The local Young Turks came under heavy suspicion.[14] But it was the shelling of the city by Russian warships in early November 1914 that revealed the first signs of hostility toward the Armenians. The home of a notable, Sarkis Injearabian, was searched and its proprietor arrested, accused of having flashed signals to the Russian ships.[15] The inquiry that followed proved that the charges were baseless, but it had poisoned the atmosphere nonetheless. Must this incident be interpreted as a sign of the authorities' deliberate wish to heighten suspicion of the Armenian population, or should it simply be attributed to the climate of tension spawned by the war? Let us leave the question in suspense.

The Young Turk plan went into its operational phase in Trebizond on 2 May 1915. On that date, the gendarmerie proceeded to conduct a systematic search of Armenians' homes in both the towns and villages, looking for possible deserters, arms, and "Russian spies." The operation turned out to be fruitless, but Cemal Azmi refused to make a public statement on the subject, as the primate, Turian, had requested. The operation nevertheless helped sow a climate of terror within the Armenian population.[16] Apparently in order to allay its fears, the vali took the initiative of creating a propaganda committee made up of notables and clergymen, including Turian, and asked it to go to Armenian towns and villages to assure the inhabitants of "the government's good will."[17]

On 5 June, the CUP delegate Nail organized a meeting in the city park. There he made a speech of a Turkist and Islamicist bent in which he alluded to Tamerlane, "the Russian infidel, and his friends; the time has come to show them the strength of our swords." In line with the constitutional tradition, a Dashnak Armenian schoolteacher, Toros Effendi, was invited to speak on the glorious past of Osman's descendants and "the Armenian people's loyalty to the courageous Turkish people."[18] This ambiguous initiative was supposed to inspire local Armenian leaders with new confidence. But the fact that on 17 May 1915, Trebizond's Armenian notables approached the vali in order to suggest that they cede all their real estate and moveable assets "if the authorities limited themselves to imprisoning them under the surveillance of gendarmes" shows that Armenian circles were aware of the danger threatening them.[19] A few days later, around 15 June, their apprehensions were confirmed when Azmi issued an order to conduct Father Turian[20] to the court-martial in Erzerum "in order to give testimony," and then had him murdered on the road between Erğana and Gümüşhane by the gendarmes guarding him.[21] Several witnesses, both Turkish and Armenian, affirm that the course of events was accelerated after Bahaeddin Şakir paid a visit to Trebizond around 22/23 June. According to Dr. Avni, Şakir "kept in permanent touch with the vali and Nail Bey while he was there; then he left."[22] Philomene Nurian affirms, for her part, that "the vali, after holding a long conversation with Şakir, who had arrived from Erzerum, issued orders to expel the Armenians."[23] Siranush Manugian even states that Şakir arrived in Trebizond "with a sealed envelope....The deportation committee then went to work in line with the instructions contained in the envelope."[24] Apparently, the working visit of the leader of Trebizond's *Teşkilât-ı Mahsusa* did not go unnoticed, and its effects rapidly made themselves felt. On 24 June 42 notables, including the Dashnak leaders, the city's leading businessmen, and teachers, were summoned to the *konak* and informed that they were to be "immediately transferred to Samsun for an investigation already in progress." Put aboard a boat the next morning, these men were killed on the Black Sea opposite Platana, 15 kilometers west of Trebizond,[25] by *çetes* under the command of Tekkeli Neşad.[26] These facts were corroborated by Louis Vidal, a French citizen who worked for the Singer Company in Trebizond, at the 7 April 1919 sixth session of the trial of the criminals of Trebizond.[27] According to Vidal, the men were put aboard a barge that set sail for the open sea and then drowned. However, "one of these Armenians managed to swim ashore...He reported that all of those who had been with him had been drowned." The man took refuge with a sailor named Bedros before "the police then transferred him to the hospital," where "he was poisoned by Ali Saib," the director of the Health Department, as member of the medical staff, Der Tavitian, informed him.[28] Nâzım Bey, the former president of the committee responsible for "abandoned property," and Dr. Avni Bey, a health service inspector, gave an account this episode that was quite similar, that culminated in the drowning on the open sea of the Armenian elite, and also of the tragic end of the restaurant owner Vartan, who died the day after he was admitted to Trebizond's military hospital.[29] It is all but certain that the police transferred him to the hospital for no other purpose than to prevent him from testifying about what he had seen. While maintaining a humanitarian facade, Cemal Azmi was thus able to have him personally poisoned by one of his henchmen, the director of the Health Department.

On the testimony of a witness at the Trebizond trial, a meeting was organized under the chairmanship of the vali immediately after Şakir's departure, and was attended by Trebizond's leading Young Turks. Azmi held another meeting with the *mutesarifs* and *kaymakams* of the vilayet. At these meetings, the vali declared that he favored deporting the Armenians and staging a massacre outside the city. The "Agent" Mustafa as well as Mehmed Ali were "partisans of an immediate massacre, while others suggested that the Armenians not be massacred in the vilayet."[30] This observation indicates something interesting about the methods chosen by the local Ittihadist leaders, divided between those who espoused radical methods and the partisans of a more prudent approach. Azmi himself suggested draping the deportation of the Armenians in a semblance of legality and avoiding massacres too close to the city, where so many foreigners could witness them. Thus, he complied with the recommendations of the Ittihad's Central Committee. It is also noteworthy that the committee that decided the Armenian population's fate was made up almost exclusively of civil and military officials belonging to Trebizond's Ittihadist club. Besides the vali, the club included the CUP delegate, *Yenibahçeli* Nail Bey;[31] Imamzâde Mustafa, who managed the *Teşkilât-ı Mahsusa's* armory in Lazistan and later those in Trebizond;[32] Mehmed Ali, chief customs officer and president of the local Red Crescent; Pirizade Şevki, an officer; Talât Bey, the commander of the gendarmerie; and Dr. Yunüz Vasfi Bey, the head of the Health Department.[33]

The legal basis for the persecution of the Armenians orchestrated by the local Ittihadists was here provided by the official decree, promulgated on 26 June 1915, ordering that the Armenians be exiled within five days.[34] Trebizond's Armenian notables, as well as the German, Austro-Hungarian, and American consuls who were informed of the conditions under which this decree had been executed in the neighboring region of Erzerum, appealed to the goodwill of the ministers Talât and Enver and interceded with the vali in hopes of obtaining more favorable arrangements for people in certain categories, such as women, children, old people, Catholics, and Protestants. As we have seen elsewhere, the local authorities and the CUP delegate Nail gave them reason to hope that the elderly, Catholics, and Protestants would be spared.[35] Here, however, we see a notable difference from other vilayets: there were no systematic arrests of the men before the deportations began. Apart from the political activists apprehended on 24 June, only 300 young men were arrested the day the deportation order was issued, put aboard a cargo ship that proceeded to cast anchor opposite Platana. The *çetes* charged with murdering these men and throwing them into the sea were then transported to the spot on motorboats.[36]

Among the other arrangements made at Trebizond that are significantly different from those made elsewhere was the fact that the Armenian population was not authorized to sell its moveable assets or purchase any means of transportation before being deported.[37] In contrast, it was authorized – "whenever the parents so desire" – to leave children – girls up to the age of 15 and boys up to the age of ten – in homes baptized "orphanages by the Turks."[38] The Greek metropolitan, Bishop Chrysantos, who seems to have been well aware of the nature of the orders that Şakir had issued, had interceded with the vali on the eve of the departure of the first convoy of deportees to convince him to spare the children and create an orphanage for them, claiming his prelacy and the Greek community were willing to take charge of the institution. A committee chaired by Cemal Azmi himself, with Chrysantos as its vice-president, was formed in order to organize the functioning of the orphanage. But the local Ittihad Club and its leader, the CUP delegate Nail Bey, opposed this initiative and succeeded in having the orphanage closed. Its children were distributed among the Turkish "homes."[39] For their part, Dr. Crawford, the director of Trebizond's American school, and his wife admitted several dozen Armenian children into their institution, and also accepted deposits in the form of money and jewels from the future deportees, in violation of the rules laid down by the authorities. The authorities thereupon successfully demanded that the children and the Armenian goods left on deposit be turned over to them.[40] In other words, the humanitarian initiatives encouraged by the vali were rapidly transformed into an opportunity to buttress the program of "Turkification" of children espoused by the Ittihadist Central Committee in Istanbul. Informed of the massacres that had recently been committed in the neighboring region of Erzerum, the Trebizond Armenians had no illusions about the fate that awaited them and gladly turned over their children when the Greek metropolitan and the American missionary offered them that alternative. The ostensible magnanimity of Cemal Azmi, which was highly praised by Bishop Chrysantos, was in the end only an artifice designed to get control of the children, whom Nail parceled out among the "homes" known as *baş baba* or *orta baba*.[41] They were sometimes also placed in Turkish households as adoptive children or sexual objects, or else admitted to the Red Crescent's hospital, where they were given "medical care" or invited to make a last voyage to the Black Sea.

The Functioning of the Young Turk Machinery in Trebizond

The trial of the criminals of Trebizond, which was held before Istanbul's Court-Martial no. 1 from 27 March to 22 May 1919, led to revelations that shed light on the role of Trebizond's Young Turk leaders and the "deportation committee" that they set up. The testimony of the principal authors of these mass crimes, corroborated by the evidence given by high-ranking officials and officers as well as Armenian survivors and other Ottoman subjects, constitute the fullest body of information we have for a single region. It makes it possible to comprehend the internal functioning of the local structures created to extirpate the Armenian population.

It must, however, be noted that, of the 19 sessions of the Trebizond trial, only the final verdict, handed down on 22 May 1919, was published in the 6 August 1919 (no. 3616) *Takvim-ı Vakayi* [Official Gazette].[42] The trial record and incriminating evidence presented during the various sessions of the trial were published, in whole or in part, by semi-official or independent Turkish newspapers.[43]

The Poisonings at the Red Crescent's Trebizond Hospital and the Drownings at Sea

When the deportation of the Armenians from Trebizond began, the hospital of the Red Crescent apparently served as a reception center for Armenians who were old and incapacitated or pregnant, as well as for Armenian children. These "hospitalizations" were probably intended to prove to foreign diplomats – who, as we have seen, launched appeals to the vali and their respective embassies – that the authorities were making allowances for the problems of the weakest. These humanitarian considerations did not, however, deter the Young Turks from pursuing their initial goal of the systematic destruction of the Armenians. The person bearing the main responsibility for the murders committed in this hospital was incontestably Mehmed Ali, who was simultaneously the chief customs officer, president of the local Red Crescent, director of the hospital, and one of the leaders of the Ittihad in Trebizond.[44] The second protagonist was Dr. Ali Saib, an inspector in the health service and a member of the deportation committee. Also involved was Dr. Yunüz Vasfi Bey, the director of the Health Department.[45]

At the fourth session of the Trebizond trial, held on 3 April 1919, Abdülkadir, a soldier and native of Trebizond who managed the supplies department of the Red Crescent hospital, told the presiding judge "Many Armenians were brought to the hospital and then transferred elsewhere ... I know that examinations were carried out and prescriptions delivered by Dr. Avni and Dr. Ali Saib. There were fatal cases."[46] But when the presiding judge remarked that "certain Armenians were poisoned at the hospital," Abdülkadir answered, "I did not see anything; I do not know anything." He agreed, however, that the staff obeyed the hospital's director, Mehmed Ali, "who received his own orders from the vali."[47]

Sofia Makhokhian, a member of the richest Armenian family in Trebizond, testified at the third session of the trial that she had stayed in the hospital before being "adopted" by Mehmed Ali. There she witnessed how people "who were often old" were ejected from the hospital and sent "to Deyirmen Dere, where they were all massacred, without exception," noting, however, that others "were poisoned." When the presiding judge asked her what allowed her to "affirm that they had been poisoned," she answered:

> Because all of them exhibited the same symptoms before dying. The bodies of all of
> them turned black. Dr. Ali Saib gave the orders that they be poisoned; the nurses

refused to carry out his orders, and it was someone named Şatizâde Kenan who took on the task of making them drink the potion proposed to them.

When Dr. Saib protested his innocence, Makhokhian added that, "[t]here were four year-old and five-year-old children in the hospital who had been poisoned." Saib then asked her how many patients there had been in the hospital. The young woman answered that "there were twenty women in my ward, but the terrace was full of patients whom Saib had given orders to deport." Saib confirmed what she said, but pointed out that it was the vali who had ordered him "to examine the people who had been hospitalized in order to separate those who were not ill from the others. I considered some of them to be in a condition to be transported and informed the vali of this." This face-off continued in the same tone; it brought to light that "the bodies of those who had been poisoned," such as those of Araksi and Hranush Yesayan, "were thrown into the sea" (Araksi Yesayan was pregnant at the time), and that 15 boys had also been "put aboard a barge and drowned in the sea by Inceli Mehmend."[48]

At this stage of the trial, another person under indictment, Niyazi Effendi, an innkeeper, made his apparition. His main task had been to transport Armenian property by sea,[49] but he had also been responsible for taking groups of Armenians out to sea. During his examination at the fourth session of the trial on 3 April 1919, Niyazi, like the rest of the accused, denied the charges leveled against him and even affirmed that if asked, the Department of the Navy could establish that he "had not been at Trebizond when these events occurred." But this defense strategy did not hold up for long: the official report of the Department of the Navy confirmed that Niyazi had indeed been present in Trebizond when the acts in question were committed.[50] The evidence given by Satenig, a native of Gümüşhane, at the 1 April 1919 session of the trial, confirmed that she had been put aboard a barge with other young women "under Niyazi's orders," and that she had been saved only because the person at the wheel of the boat in which she found herself was Ali Bey from Surmene, a friend of her father's.[51] The examination of Dr. Avni, a health service inspector, provided further, crucially important details. Avni, an army doctor who had been responsible for quarantining the infected, revealed that he had not witnessed "deportations by sea" because "the Armenians were not put aboard the barges in the port." In other words, care was taken to board them in a more secluded spot so that there would be no witnesses. When the presiding judge asked Avni if Niyazi Bey had conducted the deportations by sea, he answered: "I think that these deportations were carried out by the men of the Special Organization." Without denying the role played by the innkeeper Niyazi, the doctor thus put blame for the drowning of these groups at sea on the organization that had been charged with liquidating them. When the judge asked Avni about his failure to react to these "painful events," the doctor observed: "That was impossible. The Committee for Union and Progress was running the city and I was not on good terms with its [members]. I interceded with Nail Bey and asked him to save certain women. He refused."[52] Dr. Ali Saib interrupted the proceedings at this point and asked if it was true that Dr. Avni, who lived in an Armenian household, had found "certain documents" there. When the presiding judge insisted that he answer, the doctor confirmed that he had found certain documents signed by Nail Bey and "a few other people," which ordered: "allot such-and-such a person so many girls."[53]

Imamzâde Mustafa, who managed the *Teşkilât-ı Mahsusa's* armory, was examined on 1 April 1919, at the third session of the trial.[54] His evidence, too, contained a number of revelations. After denying that he had participated in any way in the "business of the deportations," the Agent Mustaf, who as everyone knew was an intimate of the vali's, admitted that he had seen barges with 50 to 60 Armenians on board leaving for Samsun. However, when the presiding judge told him that "those who were drowned were not the victims of an accident, but were deliberately killed," Mustafa said that he "did not know."[55] Father Laurent, who had been in Trebizond during the deportations, was examined on 8 April 1919. He stated that he had seen how "many women and children were put aboard barges that then headed for the open sea." He testified that he had learned these boats "returned to port empty."[56]

Mehmed Ali, the president of the local Red Crescent and director of its hospital in Trebizond, was also one of the key figures in the Ittihad. At the fourth session of the trial, when the innkeeper Niyazi was at the bar, it was revealed that he had said to the Armenian women who had found refuge in the hospital, "We do not want to transform the city into a graveyard; you are going to leave," thus giving them "to understand that they would not be killed in the city, but outside it."[57] All indications are that he quite simply saw to the liquidation of the Armenians who had been admitted to his hospital by poisoning or drowning them. This is suggested in particular by a question from the presiding judge, who asked him at the same session of the trial: "Why did you have the hospital evacuated? Was it not in connection with giving the Armenians refuge?" To which Mehmed Ali answered, "We evacuated only the lower ward"[58] – that is, the ward where pregnant women were concentrated. When, at the tenth session of the trial, General Mustafa Nâzım asked Ali about the massacre of the deportees and the harshness of the orders that had been issued, the director of the hospital declared that if he had not "obeyed, he would immediately have been murdered."[59] Coming from one of the main criminals of Trebizond, this reaction gives some idea of the pressure that threatened even eminent members of the Ittihad.

The Singular Case of Dr. Ali Saib, a "Persecuted" Official

Dr. Saib was then questioned by the presiding judge,[60] who asked him, in his capacity as "a member of the deportation committee," what had become of the children after the deportation. The inspector answered, "At first...I distributed them in [Muslim] villages. Later, certain Muslims took girls into their homes. I adopted a girl, Satenig Giulian. There were no more homeless Armenians in the city. The girls were married and the children were placed in shelters." Asked about the fate of "the four-year-old to five-year-old children," about whom the magistrate observed that there was "no information at all," Saib said: "I do not know; I was only a health service inspector." The presiding judge reminded him that the children had, after all, been entrusted to the Red Crescent hospital. "Where are they now?" he asked. He received no answer. Obviously exasperated, the military judge exclaimed: "This is extraordinary. You inspected insignificant things; you examined questions involving two or three piasters, yet you took no interest in innocent children who were exterminated." How, he went on, was "an institution that was dedicated to public service converted into a house of death? Why didn't you intervene?"[61]

At the 19 April 1919 thirteenth session of the trial, Virginie Odabashian, responsible for caring for 30 to 40 boys between the ages of two and four who had been taken in by the American school, testified that Dr. Saib came to look for them in person and then had them "sent away by sea."[62] The investigative reports drawn up by the inspector Ziya Fuad Bey and Adnan Bey, Director General of the Health Department, which had been read before the court at the third session, further incriminated Saib, who reacted by asking why the name of his successor, Dr. Sadreddin Bey, had not been mentioned. Is it, he asked, "because he is, even today, the secretary of the *Teceddüt* Party[63] in Trebizond?"[64] In other words, the doctor expressed his surprise that he was being asked to account for acts committed on CUP orders, whereas one of his colleagues had been left alone because he still belonged to the Ittihadist movement. Saib also asked that the former military commander of Trebizond, Avni Pasha, who had become one of the sultan's aides-de-camp, and Dr. Yunüz Vasfi Bey, the director of the Health Department, be heard in his defense; they "could testify that all the atrocities inflicted on the Armenians resulted from decisions made by the Central Committee of the Party of Union and Progress and were executed by the government."[65] Saib complained, moreover, "My whole life, I have never been able to live in peace anywhere for six months with this government." He even affirmed that he had been persecuted by the committee since 1908, in particular because he had been the publisher of the newspaper *Hukuki Ümümieh*.[66] His line of defense throws the CUP's role in these crimes into relief. It also reveals the state of mind of the executioners and the sentiment prevailing among them that they had acted legitimately because their acts had been decided by the party.

This "persecution," however, does not seem to have prevented the doctor from profiting from his position in order to improve his lot in life. The presiding judge, General Mustafa Nâzım Pasha, was well aware of this when he asked Saib if he had taken in "the late Dr. Leo Arslanian's wife." Saib denied that he had. The evidence given by others of his peers, however, throws a harsh light on the methods that many of these cadres employed in order to get their hands on a woman or enrich themselves without effort. Only rarely do we have reliable documentation of the sort that enables us to observe the methods that these predators used to divest one of their victims of his property or, perhaps, lay their hands on a member of his family. However, from the well-furnished court file in the trial of the criminals of Trebizond, we learn in detail how doggedly Ali Saib and Imamzâde Mustafa, a member of the *Teşkilât-ı Mahsusa*, pursued both Dr. Arslanian, despite being a municipal physician well-known for having organized a number of Red Crescent hospitals,[67] and – even more – his wife, who obviously constituted a highly coveted prize.

At the sixth session of the trial of Trebizond, Louis Vidal, a French citizen who worked for the Singer Company, revealed that his brother-in-law Arslanian, who was married and the father of two children – a boy of ten and a girl of seven – was quite affluent, and that his wife, too, possessed a heritage of 1,200 pounds gold. Nicknamed "*la belle dame*," Mrs. Arslanian was, in Vidal's words, "a victim of her beauty."[68]

Vidal also reported that Arslanian had been appointed to a post as military physician in Erzerum, despite having already contracted typhus. Despite his poor health, Dr. Avni, an inspector in the army's health service, "had given him two weeks" to pack his bags. This ostensible transfer had led straight to the void: the doctor had been "deported and killed on the road," most probably on instructions from his superiors in Trebizond. Since this news was not official, Vidal had been surprised to learn that Mrs. Arslanian had been arrested, since the wife of an officer on active duty was, at least in theory, exempt from deportation. But he was still more stunned when he went to the police station, "where he was told that Dr. Arslanian was in Sıvas and that his wife and children would be joining him there." The lie seemed still cruder because Arslanian's wife would have taken the road running along the Black Sea coast, not the road to Sıvas. Vidal concluded that "now his wife's turn had come." Hence he decided "to save his two children when he learned that they were alive." To that end, he sent a request to the vali, who answered: "The mother who cares for them has been massacred; what point is there in leaving the two children alive?"[69] But the case of "*la belle dame*" involves a good deal more. The examinations of the main actors in this drama, which took place at the fifth trial session on 5 April 1919, afford us a glimpse of the role played by each one in this woman's ordeal. The Agent Mustafa almost invariably met the presiding judge's questions with an "I do not know." In particular, he denied that Mrs. Arslanian had asked him to help her "by going to get a sum of money that she kept in her home and giving it to her." The most he would admit was that he knew that "she had been exiled" and that he "never saw her again." The presiding judge pointed out to him that "Some people say that Mrs. Arslanian, her son, and you yourself set out on a boat for the open sea ... You and Ali Saib Bey exiled this woman with a secret purpose in mind." Mustafa denied this. But subsequent examinations of the witness revealed that "Mrs. Arslanian was in the Agent Mustafa's household." Saib, questioned in turn, said that he did not know whether that was true, but added: "I have, however heard that a man was willing to pay 300 or 400 piasters to marry her and thus get control of her heritage." He admitted that he had then consulted Nuri Bey, the police lieutenant, who had told him that the man in question was a relative of Mustafa's by the name of Ruşdi, but that the vali had got wind of the affair and given orders to "expel Mrs. Arslanian from Mustafa's house." Saib nevertheless believed that Mrs. Arslanian had "seven hundred or eight hundred Turkish pounds" at her disposal. Given the accused man's disinclination to talk, the presiding judge finally exclaimed: "Some people say that you tried to marry the beautiful lady, and that she turned you down. Mustafa had his eye on her heritage. Then the two of you decided to exile Mrs. Arslanian."[70]

The next day, the man thus incriminated, Abdüllah Ruşdi, a 65-year-old native of Daghestan, was examined by the court. The examination revealed that Mrs. Arslanian had been deported twice. The first time, she had "returned to the city with her son, hold-ing a letter from Nail Bey" – that is, the Ittihad's delegate had personally stepped in to save her, probably at Mustafa's or Saib's request. It may also be presumed that Mustafa placed this woman in a relative's house in order to save her from the other predators interested by her fortune or good looks. Ruşdi revealed that gendarmes came looking for her while she was gone and asked him to go with them to see the vali, "who wanted to talk to him." He further revealed that, "on the vali's orders, sailors took her out to sea and threw her overboard."[71] Spilling secret after secret, Ruşdi also said that he knew "that she had inher-ited," because in her household there was "a nine-year-old boy whose mother had been a domestic in the house of the health service inspector." In veiled terms, the witness thus informed the court that Saib was familiar with Mrs. Arslanian's financial situation and was not enamored of her charms alone.[72] A few days later, one final witness, Major Edhem Bey, "who was the president of the deportation committee and organized departures toward the interior of the country," confessed "that he had heard Mrs. Arslanian shouting on the boat that was heading for the open sea; she was crying for help."[73] From all these elements, it transpires that the vali and his collaborators were in sharp competition for control over the property of a widow such as Mrs. Arslanian. She had certainly been brought back from deportation, with the accord of the CUP delegate Nail, so that what she possessed might be extorted from her, but the personal ambitions of Mustafa and Saib were curbed by Cemal Azmi, who had "*la belle dame*" executed, perhaps after getting her to give him her property.

The Roles of the Government and the Teşkilât-ı Mahsusa in Liquidating the Armenians

According to the evidence given to the Istanbul court-martial on 3 April 1919 by Colonel Vasfi, the commander of the Seventeenth Battalion who was stationed in Trebizond in June 1915, "the Trebizond *Teşkilât-ı Mahsusa* was under the command of Bahaeddin Şakir," who "got in the way of [the armed forces'] military operations. Initially, all the valis were under his authority, along with the squadrons of the *Teşkilât-ı Mahsusa* that found themselves in his jurisdiction. We opposed this process, but did not fully succeed [in putting an end to it]."[74] Dr. Avni, the health service inspector, added that these "gangs ... set out with the Armenian deportees. People everywhere were talking about the massacre of the Armenian deportees on the highway, and of the fact that they had been attacked and looted."[75] The American consul Oscar Heizer also had an opinion on the question: " The real authority here seems to be in the hands of a committee of which Nail Bey is the head and he apparently receives his orders from Constantinople and not from the vali."[76]

The Special Organization and the CUP's delegate in Trebizond obviously played a crucial role in the anti-Armenian persecutions, taking their orders from the capital. Arif Bey, the *kaymakam* of Kirason, maintained, however, that it was Cemal Azmi who gave him "the order to deport the Armenians toward Mosul by way of the Black Sea" – that is, to drown them.[77] Kenan Bey, a court inspector in the region, stated that he was well acquainted with Cemal Azmi, who had earlier been the *mutesarif* of Lazistan, and that the vali "was responsible for the deportations and massacres of Armenians." He also remarked that the reports that local magistrates sent to the Justice Ministry had produced no "results" and that the vali "did exactly as he pleased; he could bring anyone he cared to before the court-martial." He added that "the *kaymakam* of Bafra, who had tried to intercede on the deportees' behalf, was killed."[78]

Yusuf Rıza Bey, a member of the Ittihadist Central Committee and for a time the head of the *Teşkilât-ı Mahsusa* in Trebizond, faced judgment in the trial of the Unionists. In testimony he gave at the first session of the trial of Trebizond, he declared that the decision to deport the Armenians had not been adopted by the Party's Central Committee, but rather that "it was the government that made it." He was, moreover, not in Trebizond when the deportations took place – "Nail represented the Committee in the area."[79] If we follow his reasoning, the Ittihad had nothing to do with this business and he was not even its representative in Trebizond, Nail was; the implication is that Nail was responsible for the mass violence. After Nail, Talât Bey, an inspector in the gendarmerie, denied all involvement in the events,[80] even though it was he who had been entrusted with the mission of seeing to the security of the convoys of deportees. Talât had difficulty responding when he was asked whether "the separation of the men and women and the confiscation of the deportees' property had not been carried out in line with the government's orders." "That is beyond my remit," he answered; "I do not know."[81]

Already impugned as a pliable tool in the vali's hands, the Agent Mustafa contended that he had "never had anything to do with the deportations." On the contrary, he said, he "had tried to save all [his] friends, but unsuccessfully ... I worked for the Armenians." He said that his friends "Ibranosian and the Kamburian brothers" could testify in his behalf; they had "named him to safeguard their property,"[82] pending, no doubt, their improbable return from exile. Examined again at the fourth session of the trial, Yusuf Rıza, albeit a member of the Unionist Central Committee, merely "thought" that he had been appointed CUP responsible secretary in Trebizond by Haci Adil Bey, "on the orders of the congress and orally." He claimed to have been "involved in the opening of schools and the 'intellectual advancement of the population,'" and said that he had collected "sizeable sums of money" to create "a foundation for the schools." The presiding judge, obviously not convinced by these arguments, thereupon asked him if there was a record of his activities and, if so, who had made it. Rıza stated that it was Tali, the treasurer, and later, "Nail Bey and others," who had recorded these operations.[83] He was not to say anything more about this.

The president of the military recruitment office, Necmeddin Bey, stated, at the fifth session of the trial, that "[t]he army commanders received an order not to interfere with the deportations." When the presiding judge asked if he had "authorized searches for Armenian soldiers who had deserted," Necmeddin Bey confirmed that he had, while adding that "[t]he gendarmes came back empty-handed." The judge asked why, and whether he had been alarmed by the fact, doubtless in order to make him confess that the gendarmes had killed the deserters they found. But Necmeddin Bey contented himself by answering: "I learned that they had been exiled." This brought a stinging response from Mustafa Nâzim: "The Armenians were massacred and looted. Did you never hear anything about that?" Without losing his composure, the officer answered: "I knew that the Armenians had been deported by land or by sea. I did not see that with my own eyes, but many rumors about the subject were making the rounds." The military judge was the more surprised by this ignorance because there had existed a court-martial in Trebizond, presided over by the vali in person, to which Necmeddin Bey had been, on his own witness, a member. He did, however, seem to recall that one of the leading members of the "evacuation committee" (that is, the deportation committee) was the police chief Nuri Bey, and that he had "given accounts" to his superior, the military commander of Trebizond, Avni Pasha, who had "told him what he had written" on this subject.[84] Thus, information about the mass crimes committed in the region had trickled through only in veiled terms.

In his concluding statement, the prosecutor, Feridun Bey, recapitulated the proceedings. He noted:

> The Young Turk government made the decision to deport the Armenians. The men were deported first, followed by the women and children. Most of the men were massacred in the spot known as Deyirmen Dere. Some women and children were taken out to sea on barges and drowned; other children were turned over to the Red Crescent hospital and poisoned there. The jewels and other property belonging to the Armenian deportees were pillaged. Some of those guilty of these crimes are fugitives. Cemal Azmi and Nail Bey are considered to be the main culprits: they organized the squadrons of *çetes* and recruited accomplices in order to put their criminal plans into effect.[85]

The pleas of the defense lawyers, made at the eighteenth session of the trial, consisted, in sum, of blanket denials of the charges, accompanied by expressions of regret over "the atrocities committed."[86] The verdict, handed down on Thursday, 22 May 1919, pointed out that the two main culprits in the dock had issued "secret orders to liquidate the Armenians" and proceeded to form squadrons of *çetes*.[87] At the sixth session of the trial of the Ittihadist leaders on 17 May 1919, Yusuf Rıza, who was judged in his capacity as a former member of the Young Turk Central Committee and also as someone who had organized and headed the squadrons of the *Teşkilât-ı Mahsusa* in Trebizond, did not deny that the organization that he directed had "operated independently" of the organization of the same name engaged in carrying out sabotage behind the enemy lines.[88] Ultimately, it appears that the local administration and the Young Turk network (be it the local Ittihad club or the *Teşkilât-ı Mahsusa*), their frequent conflicts of interest notwithstanding, divided up the work between them, as it were. The task of coordinating operations fell to the vali Cemal Azmi; the task of executing them devolved upon the CUP delegate, *Yenibahçeli* Nail Bey – who, during the trial, was in Baku with Nuri, Enver's younger brother.

Among the state officials, Mehmed Ali, the chief customs officer and president of the Red Crescent, who was condemned to ten years of hard labor, had a political role and participated directly in the decision-making process; Dr. Ali Saib, health service inspector and member of the deportation committee, was both a decision-maker and an executor, who probably had children poisoned on the orders of the deportation committee; Dr. Yunüz Vasfi, the director of the Health Department, only carried out orders; Dr. Sadreddin, Saib's successor, probably had no part in this business because he was appointed to his post late in the day.[89] Among the military men and police officers, Avni Bey, the military commander of the region – he was the Sultan's aide-de-camp when the trial was held – does not seem to have had a hand in the mass violence, but was careful not to denounce it. Sentenced to one year in prison, Nuri Bey, the police chief, who was responsible for arresting the notables of Trebizond, probably helped compile lists of those to be liquidated and assisted the commission responsible for "abandoned property" in confiscating Armenian assets. He declared at the seventh session of the trial that he had "never had anything to do with the deportation." The *defterdar* Lutfi Bey, however, contradicted him, contending that "he played a major role ... He was on good terms with the vali and [was] one of his intimate associates."[90] Major Talât Bey, the commander of the gendarmerie, was acquitted; yet he had a crucial role in organizing the deportation of men to Gümüşhane and massacring them with the help of Major İbrahim Bey, the chief of the supply dump. Rublis Esad Bey, the commander of an *amele taburi*, was directly responsible for the liquidation of the Armenian worker-soldiers under his orders.

Among the local civilians implicated in the massacres perpetrated by the *Teşkilât-ı Mahsusa*, the best known were Pirizâde Şevki, Mustafa (who was deported to Malta), Kirşlaye Arif, Abdüllah Bey, Mehmed Ali Bey, Hakkı Haci Ali Hafızâde, Kahiya Reys, Zekeria, Arslan Fayikci, İnce Mehmed Tahir, İzzet Çavuş, Tekkeli Neşad, Keresteci Hafız Cemal, Şekerci Mustafa, Kel Mustafa, who was charged with drowning children, Keçecizâde Ahmed, Esad Bey, Abdülkerim, İsmail Effendi, and Mirza Effendi.[91]

Dealing with "Abandoned Property"

The takeover of Armenian property, the economic dimension of the plan to eliminate the Armenians, had its armed branch, the commission responsible for "abandoned property," one of whose presidents in Trebizond was Lutfi Bey, who was also the vilayet's *defterdar*. As the president of this commission, Lutfi too was questioned before the court-martial, at the eighth session of the trial of Trebizond. He revealed, at the outset, that the deportation committee "collected the abandoned property." In other words, his own commission was a sort of specialized branch of the local Young Turk leadership that managed the commission at the political level. Lutfi also pointed out that the "abandoned property" collected by the commission was stored in "special warehouses; the goods were piled up in the Armenian church." He added that no "detailed inventory" of these goods had been made since their orders did not call for that. He also noted that it was "the police that was [sic] responsible for the warehouses" and for "guarding" them until another commission responsible for liquidating (*tasfiye*) them proceeded to auction them off. Lutfi denied ever having received the least sum "of money confiscated from the deportees." The police chief Nuri Bey, who was also a member of the commission, understood that his role was being called into question at the trial. Indignant, he "energetically rejected these accusations," taking care to underscore as he did so that "the population of Trebizond is honorable, virtuous, and honest. It never seized Armenian goods." He pointed out, however, that, "during the deportation of the Armenians, the goods that were transferred to the warehouses were stockpiled in very disorderly fashion; it was therefore impossible to register these goods in their owners' names," despite the fact that "guards" were stationed "before the doors" of Armenian homes. Lutfi concluded by observing that "the orders we had were favorable to the Armenians, but it proved impossible to carry them out."[92] The presiding judge then asked him whether the police were held responsible "when a household was looted if the family to which it belonged had to leave, abandoning it." Nuri's answer, which accentuated the fact that Trebizond had "thousands of households, twenty thousand homes," implied that despite what he had declared at the outset, he had been unable to prevent these homes from being looted with the forces at his command. Lutfi intervened at this point to say that "[c]ertain Armenians took fright and fled to the mountains ... Certain policemen in civilian clothing took advantage of the circumstances" – in other words, helped themselves to whatever they wished. He also confirmed that the population did not "participate in the looting of Armenian property," but that it was "in particular, members of the deportation committee, government officials, policemen, and a few privileged people who looted." As proof of what he said, Lutfi read one of the telegrams that he had sent to the finance minister, "denouncing, day after day, the financial abuses and the other illegal activities of the vali and his accomplices."[93] The examination, at the fifteenth session of the trial, of Nâzım Bey, the former president of the commission responsible for "abandoned property" in Trebizond, proved disappointing. That of his successor, Hilmi Bey, was richer in information. Hilmi stated that he had not been able to "offer resistance" because the vali controlled the court-martial, so that he would have "risked" his life if he had. He also admitted to "confiscating, in the American school," Armenian property, but could not recall having established "an inventory." He nevertheless assessed the value of "these jewels" at "between four thousand and five thousand pounds gold." General Mustafa Nâzım then pointed out to him that jewels "worth one thousand, seven hundred pounds gold were transferred to Constantinople." "What," he asked, "became of the rest?" His words were followed by a heavy silence.[94] Here we see a classic case of the division of the spoils between the local actors and the CUP, which demanded its share of the loot, generally assessed at one-third its real value.

The other testimony given at the various sessions of the trial of Trebizond yielded further information about the methods used to "sell" the confiscated goods. According to the innkeeper Niyazi, whose particular task had been to organize the transport of Armenian merchandise by ship and drown the deportees out at sea, it was the policeman Ali Effendi who "supervised" the auctions "on orders from the military commander": "The abandoned goods were sold without a list. They put them in the storehouse; the merchants suggested a price and bought them."[95] It would seem, then, that besides being supervised by the deportation committee, the commission responsible for "abandoned property" was assisted by the police, and that it had also received orders from the army when it sold this property off. It is hard to explain why the military commander, Avni, played this role, unless we assume that the military too was interested in the results of these sales.

Significant quantities of goods stemming from the pillage of Armenian merchants' warehouses were, according to information obtained in the course of the trial, exported to Samsun or Istanbul under Niyazi's supervision, especially after the capture of Trebizond by the Russians had become inevitable. Yet, Niyazi said that he did not know whether "the vali had transferred forty-two barges loaded with goods before the city was occupied."[96] Lutfi, however, confirmed that Niyazi "had secretly organized the transportation of goods … he traveled back and forth between the cities on the Black Sea coast … He was particularly close to the vali … He played a role in everything."[97] The examination of Nuri also revealed that the innkeeper had amassed a personal fortune worth several thousand pounds gold by acquiring "on the vali's orders" some of the Tahmazian store's stock of "textiles worth five thousand to six thousand pounds gold" for only "two hundred pounds gold."[98] Nuri himself, we read, had "personally appropriated [goods] worth three thousand pounds, as well as eighty jewels."[99] At the ninth session it was also revealed that the Agent Mustafa, who was the commander of the port,[100] had "taken the vali a box belonging to Vartivar Muradian," and had received "five hundred pounds gold and jewels" from Cemal Azmi in exchange.[101] Nuri said that the box in question had first been opened at the police station on orders from the vali; he did not remember very well if he had informed the commission responsible for abandoned property about this.[102] The vali clearly seems to have benefited personally from this gift from one of his subordinates. Arusiag Kilijian, an 18-year-old orphan "taken in" by Azmi who had traveled with Azmi's family from Trebizond to Istanbul, reported that the vali's house was full of "stolen goods, rugs, and so on," part of which he took with him to the capital.[103]

Finally, Avni, the health service inspector, was accused of having demanded 500 pounds gold from the Makhokhian family in exchange for saving it, as well as of being among those who looted the Makhokhian's stockhouses. He denied having participated in this pillage in any way, although the president of the commission responsible for abandoned property affirmed that the stocks of the Makhokhians' firms had never been turned over to him for safekeeping. The ensuing discussion further revealed that the Makhokhian's daughter had excited people's lusts. She had been provisionally put in the Red Crescent hospital and then Islamicized before being "adopted" by the director of the hospital, Mehmed Ali.[104] At the eleventh and twelfth sessions of the trial, witness after witness took the stand in order to state that they, or certain other indicted individuals, had not been in Trebizond when the deportations took place.[105]

The *Kazas* of Trebizond, Surmene, and Akçabat

According to the report of the American consul, Oscar Heizer, the first convoy of deportees was put on the road on 1 July 1915. On that day, troops surrounded certain Armenian neighborhoods of Trebizond and proceeded to expel 2,000 inhabitants of the city, who then were taken in small groups to a place known as Deyirmen Dere, located ten minutes outside the city, and from there led off in the direction of Gümüşhane. A total of 6,000 people left the city between 1 July and 3 July; approximately 4,000 more left the surrounding villages.[106] Initially, the authorities had declared that Catholics and Protestants, as well as incapacitated old people, children, and pregnant women, would be "maintained." In the end, however, no exceptions were made, and these "exempted" individuals were dispatched with the last convoy that set out on 5 July.[107]

Besides the 5,539 Armenians of the city of Trebizond, these measures were applied to the 17,779 Armenians of the rural areas of the vilayet. Involved were, first, 20 villages located east of Trebizond, not far from the city in an area between Deyirmen Dere and the Yanbol River, centered on the little port of Drona (pop. 184) in the foothills of the Pontic Mountains: Zifanus (pop. 951), Komra (pop. 147), Shana (pop. 600), Kalafka (pop. 400), Surmene (pop. 1,210), Sifter and Abion (Church of St. Gregory). These villages claimed a total Armenian population of more than 6,500, of whom 323 lived in three other villages of the *kaza* of Surmene.[108]

The deportation measures were also applied to 16 localities located south and west of Trebizond, with an Armenian population of around 7,000, 3,517 of which lived in the *kaza* of Akçabat.[109] In contrast to what happened in Trebizond, however, the men here were apparently killed in their villages by bands of *çetes* belonging to the Special Organization, as in Tots.[110]

According to Louis Vidal, a Frenchman allowed to remain in Trebizond and who testified before the Istanbul court-martial on 7 April 1919, approximately 15,000 Armenians were deported from Trebizond and the vicinity: "Not a single man survived, [but] a number of orphans [were] in the villages, in Muslim households, because the sailors sometimes brought them to shore and took them into their homes."[111] Tahsin Bey, the vali of Erzerum, who testified at the third session of the trial of Trebizond, said he believed that the Armenians deported from Trebizond had been attacked on the road to Gümüşhane.[112]

According to survivors' reports, the 15,000 deportees from the region of Trebizond were dispatched in three convoys comprising 4,000 to 6,000 people. These convoys were formed at the exit from Trebizond in Deyirmen Dere, where all the convoys were assembled.[113]

On the testimony of the 42-year-old Nvart Makhokhian of Trebizond, 500 men were taken from her convoy of 5,000 near Gümüşhane – this was apparently the first convoy – and killed a half-hour's march away while the caravan was looted by çetes. After Fırıncılar, in the Kanlı Dere Gorge, where the Kurdish chieftains of the Reşvan tribe Zeynel Bey and Haci Bedri Ağa were in charge of affairs,[114] the 1,500 men still in the convoy were separated from the others by Zeynel Bey and his squadron of Kurdish çetes and massacred in plain sight of their families. After four months on the road, after losing hundreds of people on the way and being repeatedly pillaged, Nvart Makhokhian and her companions reached Aleppo.[115]

Philomene Nurian left Trebizond with the third convoy of 6,000 people, all of them Armenian Catholics, guarded by gendarmes under the command of İsmail Effendi from Platana. According to her, the men preceded the women, girls, and children at some eight-to-ten hours' distance. At Gümüşhane, İsmail turned the males over to a band of çetes commanded by Mirza Effendi, who massacred them in the vicinity.[116]

The third caravan from Trebizond reached the entrance to Kemah Gorge on 22 July, where it was systematically pillaged and then sent on to Harput. American missionaries and the American consul note that it was in the place called "Four Fountains," at the exit from Mezreh; they say that the deportees were in a pitiful state.[117] Philomene Nurian also observes that after a three-day trek the boys were separated from the others and killed before their mothers' eyes. The next morning, the Catholics were separated from the Apostolic Armenians. Nurian said she knew "nothing of what became of them." She does not say where these events occurred, but there is good reason to believe that it was in the vicinity of Lake Göljük, where, according to reports, deportees from Trebizond arrived and were massacred at this time.[118] Nurian reports that the Catholic deportees, whose escort was under the command of Lieutenant Harputlu Hasan Effendi, were ordered to strip, "so that a more systematic search could be made for the money that we had managed to hide until then [Hasan] then turned us over to a Kurd by the name of İsmail Bey, who had been waiting for us with his band of çetes ... It was then that we understood that our last hour had come: they attacked, and the massacre began."[119]

Nurian's mother and younger brother were killed with iron bars in front of her. She herself was repeatedly stabbed, but was saved along with her younger sister by İsmail Bey. On the way, the gendarme Şefik Bey, "who knew [her]," took her back from the Kurds and turned her over to his mother, with whom she went to Arğana Maden, where she remained for a year, abandoning her religion ("I was called Nacieh") and repeatedly changed masters "so as to maintain [her] moral integrity." In early March 1916, she fell into the hands of Mehmed Nusret Bey from Janina, who had become the *mutesarif* of Arğana Maden,[120] "an inhuman creature representative of his masters." Nusret Bey had also taken her sister, now called Nayime, "on the pretext that he had to send her to Aleppo ... I never saw [her] again." Later, Philomene Nurian managed to find refuge in Kütahya, where she survived by giving piano lessons; she arrived in Constantinople in October 1918, "without anyone's help."[121]

So far, we have only rarely had occasion to observe the behavior of the gendarmes who guarded the convoys or that of the squadrons of çetes except through survivors' reports. The investigative file assembled for the court-martial of the Twenty-Ninth Division, based in Erzincan, in July-August-September 1915, affords us a glimpse of the conditions in which a convoy from Trebizond was looted and some of its members killed. It might seem surprising that such an investigation was conducted immediately after the deportations, unless we bear in mind that a certain legal order still subsisted in the Ottoman Empire. In fact, provincial courts martial were extremely active during the First World War and significant numbers of people were brought before them. However, as is indicated by the few documents we are aware of, it was not mass crimes that were judged by these military courts but "abuses" – that is to say, the seizure of Armenian goods to the detriment of either local Ittihadist leaders or the CUP itself. All indications are that instructions came down from the highest echelons to mete out severe punishment to economic criminals. At all events, the affair of the escorts from Trebizond enables us to observe, cases of personal enrichment aside, how the deportees in a convoy from Trebizond were treated and, incidentally, to also grasp the role assigned the squadrons of çetes based in Gümüşhane, whose mission was to liquidate the men in the gorges near Maderınkil, near Teke.[122]

The object of the investigation conducted by the Erzincan court-martial was the group of gendarmes who escorted the first convoy to leave Trebizond, mentioned above. This convoy left the city guarded by an escort under the orders of Captain Agah Bey, the commander of the second company of the first battalion of the regiment of the mounted gendarmerie of Trebizond.[123] Officially, the presiding judge of the court-martial of the Twenty-Ninth Division, Lieutenant-Colonel Fehmi, opened proceedings against the men who had "pillaged the caravan." Some of those indicted were arrested in Erzincan, but Fehmi Bey demanded that the vali of Trebizond send him two other suspects "immediately and without fail," and inform him as to whether çetes had been employed in his region.[124] Cemal Azmi answered: "We have confirmed that, to the present day, no çetes have been employed in the capital or any of the districts of the vilayet and that there has been no looting."[125] A few days later, he informed his correspondent that the gendarmes he had requested had left Trebizond on 19 July.[126] These brief exchanges create the impression that Azmi was somewhat discomfited, probably because of the rigor with which the judge presiding over the court-martial of Erzincan was carrying out his investigation. Here we can also glimpse the possibility of a manipulation by the CUP and its network, which had officially given the army the right to "displace civilian populations" – the better to cover up the extermination undertaken by the Special Organization. It is in any case noteworthy that Captain Agah, whose role in the liquidation of the men near Gümüşhane was pointed out by those under indictment, was never deranged by the army's courts. The highest-ranking soldier among the accused was Osmanoğlu Mehmed Faik, a 24-year-old unmarried junior lieutenant in the second company of the first battalion of the regiment of mounted gendarmes in Trebizond. His examination revealed that approximately 2,000 pounds gold were extorted from the deportees; that, half an hour from Gümüşhane, they were "plundered" by the gendarmes; and that, the next day the men were separated from the women. "In Gümüşhane," Faik said,

> there were two bands charged with killing the Armenian men. One was from Trebizond; the other was made up of a Kurdish band under the orders of Mikho [Mirza] Bey. They looted the Armenians who passed by. The chief of the band from Trebizond had a conversation with the commander of the company. The commander then told me to leave and collect the money during the next stage. We were supposed to keep one-third of it; the second third was to go to the bands, and some would go to the community ... It was also stated that the government did not want any of their money; it only wanted to throw them into the Euphrates.[127]

The examination of the junior officer Faik thus reveals that there was clearly collaboration between the gendarmerie and the leaders of the çetes. Another witness, Osman, a gendarme, pointed out that a çete named Rizeli İsmail, a member "of Murad Bey's band," who "had been added to our group by the authorities," also took part in slaying the men in the convoy.[128] Faik noted that the commander of his company had, after "a conversation with the *mutesarif* of Gümüşhane and Mirza Bey," ordered "the men be put on one side and the women on the other," although the oldest men were left with the women. "The band from Trebizond [that of Murad Bey, with Rizeli İsmail]" then proceeded, in the Maderenkil valley, "to kill the men and take their money." In a sentence uttered in passing, Faik revealed that the number of men killed in this secluded spot by these two çete bands "exceeded three thousand."[129] Thus, we see the outlines of the system for liquidating the men established by the "authorities" of Gümüşhane. There is every reason to believe that the Trebizond deportation committee opted for the solution of eliminating the men outside the city to avoid the accusations that foreign witnesses would inevitably have leveled had the vali had followed the example of Mezreh/Harput.

Significantly, the indications about what happened to the men that were given in passing by those facing court-martial came in the course of interrogations focused on the pillaging of the deportees. A certain antagonism between the *çetes* and the gendarmes can also be observed: the gendarmes were, so to speak, frustrated by the fact that only the *çetes* benefited from the property extorted from the deportees. Ayub Sabri, a gendarme, pointed out that he and his comrades protested to their superiors, asking why "these *çetes* are taking this money that we should be getting for [ourselves]." Faik answered, according to Sabri, "that this money was not destined for them, but would go to the government, the fleet, and the national relief organization," although he gave "one pound to every gendarme."[130] The balance of Sabri's examination shows that this gendarme was not satisfied with his one pound gold because, when he was arrested, there was discovered on his person "fifty-three Ottoman pounds, a check for one hundred pounds, eleven and a half Russian pounds, three and a half pounds sterling, a gold watch, earrings, and other gold ornaments."[131] As for the technique used to extort property from the deportees in the convoy from Trebizond, Osman, a gendarme, pointed out that Rizeli İsmail and Faik Effendi "searched the Armenians and took their money and valuables ... telling them that he was acting on government orders; that each of them should keep no more than sixty piasters and give them the rest of their money and valuables, and that the government would make arrangements to feed them in their place of destination."[132] As will have been remarked, this discourse was often used in other regions as well in order to justify the seizure of the deportees' property and make them increasingly dependent on their executioners. Osman confirms, moreover, that "most of the money was taken by the *çetes*; the rest remained in Faik Effendi's hands."[133] Hafız Seyfeddin, a gendarme, also indicated that Rizeli İsmail and Faik threatened those deportees who were slow to obey orders, telling them that "those who did not hand [their money] over would be shot."[134]

Osman reveals another interesting detail: of the 50 gendarmes who left Trebizond in the escort, 23 accompanied the caravan as far as Erzincan; "the others remained with the Armenian men who had been segregated in Gümüşhane."[135] In other words, the "other" gendarmes very certainly took part in the liquidation of the men, along with the two bands of *çetes* stationed in Gümüşhane.

Finally, the examination of Junior Lieutenant Mehmed Faik provides a graphic illustration of a rarely appreciated aspect of the abduction of young women by their executioners. Thus Faik reported that on the way he met "a young woman from the Arabian family; I found her attractive; I wanted to marry her, by the grace of God. The girl's mother and father consented." Faik also said that "her father was killed at Gümüşhane and, as she was too little, she cried and did not want to leave her sister." Preoccupied by his professional duties, the Junior Lieutenant entrusted "the two girls to a gendarme in the guard, asking him to take them to the house of the photographer Kadus Bey [in Erzincan] and leave them there," while he escorted the convoy to Kemah. He also "considered giving" his future wife's sister "to a doctor" or "a lieutenant."[136]

After accomplishing his mission in Kemah, Faik lost no time rejoining the Arabians' daughter, who was being held in Kadus Effendi's house. He was there when the gendarmes came to arrest him. Before the court-martial, Faik justified his actions as follows: "As for the girls, I can assure you that they can be found in every house, all along the route. For my part, I have read no government order [on this subject] and I did what the whole population did: I kept this little girl whom I had known even before [these events]."[137]

The *Kaza* of Ordu

The Armenians of the *kaza* of Ordu, most of whom had roots in *Hamşin* and whose ancestors had settled relatively late in this area, numbered around 13,565. Three thousand of the *kaza*'s Armenians resided in the principal town, also known as Ordu; the others lived scattered about 29 villages. The development of the seat of the *kaza* dates from the second half of the nineteenth century, when Armenians who had come from Tamzara and Kirason settled in the quarter known as Boztepe. It was these Armenians who introduced the cultivation of hazelnuts to the region, founded the city's weekly market, and developed limestone, silver, and manganese mining and export. As for the 29 villages in the hinterland (located at least one hour and at most ten hours from Ordu), they were organized in six rural clusters to the south, southwest, and west of Ordu, notably in the valleys of the Melet Irmak and its tributaries: Ak Punar (pop. 109), Kulcoren (pop. 476), Kara Tipi (pop. 263), Kara Kiraz (pop. 93), Kesacık (pop. 219), Kızılen (pop. 680), Kadencık (pop. 240), Kran (pop. 105), Kolaca (pop. 96), Kater Köy (pop. 156), Tepe Köy (pop. 753), Taşoluk (pop. 762), Hocoğlı and Yazık (pop. 303), Güğören (pop. 271), Musakılıc (pop. 584), Şeyiler (pop. 116), Uzunmusa (pop. 66), Uzunmahmud (pop. 388), Çavuşlar (pop. 727), Çatalı (pop. 114), Bultan (pop. 55), Bazarsu (pop. 354), Sayaca (pop. 581), Seraycık (pop. 236), Darıkca (pop. 182), Oprama (pop. 224), Kiraz Dere (pop. 327), and Hacoğlu (28 households).[138]

According to a report by E.B. Andreasian, Ordu was gradually isolated from the rest of the country in the first months of the war. The first arrests there took place around mid-June 1915. Five hundred regular soldiers took control of the Armenian neighborhoods and proceeded to arrest a number of men, who were then interned in the barracks jail. This operation lasted some six days; only after it was over was the decree ordering the deportation of the Armenian population toward Mosul made public. The first to leave were the men, who were tied together in groups of four and led off in convoys of 80 to 100 people each. According to our witness, it was learned only much later that these men had had their throats slit in the woody valleys in the vicinity.[139]

Certain prisoners succeeded, however, in gaining their release by means of bribes and thus were able to leave Ordu with their families in the convoys that were put on the road a few days later. The first caravan contained the families of the men who had been arrested and massacred. All these groups set out on the road that led by way of Mesudiye to Suşehir, which lay 30 kilometers to the west of Şabinkarahisar. Near Suşehir, in the *nahie* of Elbedir, many of these deportees were massacred and large numbers of girls and women were abducted.[140] A small group managed to continue its journey. Reverend Hans Bauernfeind encountered this group near Kangal, south of Sıvas, on 14 August 1915, together with the deportees from Trebizond.[141]

The old, the sick, and the infirm, who had been briefly admitted to the hospital of Ordu or other institutions, were shortly thereafter officially sent by boat to Samsun. In fact, they were drowned out at sea in conditions similar to those we observed in Trebizond.[142] A group of women and, especially, children of both sexes between the ages of three and 12, went into hiding in the homes of Greek, Georgian, or Turkish friends; these people remained in Ordu after the convoys left. But the authorities' threats apparently convinced their friends to get rid of them. In some cases, the authorities distributed these children to families in Kirason and in others took them out to sea and killed them. At the fourteenth session of the trial of the criminals of Trebizond on 26 April 1919, Hüseyin Effendi, a merchant from Ordu, certified that Faik Bey, Ordu's *kaymakam*, dispatched two barges loaded with Armenian women and children toward Samsun, which "came back empty two hours later."[143] These boats could not have made the journey to Samsun and back in so short a lapse of time; their passengers were, in other words, "lost at sea." A few dozen adolescents nevertheless managed to flee to the nearby Pontic Mountains, where they survived for three years.[144]

The following government officials bear the brunt of the responsibility for the anti-Armenian persecutions: Ali Faik Bey, who was the *kaymakam* of Ordu from 29 January 1913 to 5 July 1915; Postuzâde Yusuf, the mayor; Rahmi Effendi, a court clerk; Rüstem Effendi, an investigating magistrate; Mustafa Bey, head of the supplies department; Osman Effendi, the director of the Tobacco Régie; Salim Effendi Başizâde; and Çapanoğlu Küçük Hüseyin and Gurci Murad Effendi, tax collectors. Among the notables enrolled in the Special Organization, the following played distinctive roles: Mustafaağazâde Ruşdi Bey; Mustafaağazâde Mehmed Bey; Hacikodazâde Haci Bekir Effendi; Hacikodazâde Küçük Mehmed; Akağzâde Abdüllah; Körahmedzâde Mustafa; Atta Bey; Haci Teza Bey; Kâtibzâde Tevfik; Rafikzâde Tevfikoğlu; Avundukzâde Hüseyin Bey; Mumcizâde Ali; Mollah Veli Zâde; İzzet Bey, the head of the *Emvalı metruke*; Celazâde Haci Kadir Bey; Sabaheddinağazâde Alaeddin; Mahmudbeyzâde Bekir; and Neçatzâde Mustafa. Among the leaders of the *çetes*, those most deeply involved in the massacres were Fotuzâde Haci Haron; Fotuzâde Haci Ali Osman; Boyraszâde İzzet Ağa; Alaybeyzâde Mehmed Ağa; Alaybeyzâde Sadik Ağa; and Bozulizâde Haydar Ağa.[145]

It should finally be noted that after the Russians captured Trebizond, the innkeeper Niyazi was dispatched by Cemal Azmi to Ordu with the mission of deporting the Greeks and selling off their property "at ridiculously low prices."[146]

The *Kazas* of Kirason, Tireboli, and Gorele

As in many other Black Sea ports, the Armenian colony of Kirason developed after 1850 with the arrival of Armenians from Tamzara and Şabinkarahisar. The Armenians numbered 2,075 on the eve of the First World War, plus 40 families in a peripheral village, Bulancak, where they worked in trade, hazelnut and cherry production, and anchovy fishing. The Armenian communities of the *kazas* of Tireboli and Gorele were even more insignificant: there were 312 Armenians in Elu, the seat of the *kaza* of Gorele, and 250 in the village of Elev. Eight hundred sixty-five Armenians lived in Tireboli, where they were very active in commerce.[147]

At the fourteenth session of the trial of the criminals of Trebizond on 26 April 1919, Arif Bey, the *kaymakam* of Kirason, confirmed that he had received an order from the vali, Cemal Azmi, to deport the Armenians of his region toward Mosul "by way of the Black Sea."[148] The shortcut suggested by his hierarchical superior should not, however, lead us to believe that the *kaymakam* simply carried out the vali's orders. Surrounded by convinced Young Turks such as Sarı Mahmudzâde Hasan, the president of the local Ittihad club, or Eşref Sarı Mahmud and Tarğınzâde Hakkı, influential members of the club, as well as by government officials who were every bit as zealous – among them Sıdkı Bey, the chief customs officer; Husni Bey, the *müdir* of İkisu; Salih Çavuş, the *müdir* of Kulakkaya; Hayri Bey, the imperial prosecutor; Hoca İbrahimzâde Ziya, the general secretary of the sub-prefecture; and Mehmed Bey, the imperial vice-prosecutor – Arif Bey engineered the liquidation of the Armenians of his *kaza*.[149]

The procedure used to eliminate the Armenian population here was classic. In the second half of June 1915, the police searched Armenian houses in Kirason, officially looking for arms and deserters. Males between 16 and 50 were arrested and confined in the courtyard of the town hall. One hundred fifty to 160 notables were murdered the next night outside the city; the other men were set free. Only after these operations had been completed was the deportation order made public.[150]

The caravan in which our main witness found herself – the fourth and last – was guarded by gendarmes under the orders of Hasan Sabri. It comprised 1,200 people, 500 of them males. The males were separated from the others near İki Su, halfway to Şabinkarahisar, and massacred by 82 "gendarmes" near Eyriboli. The convoy then took the road to Tamzara and was pillaged in a Kurdish village in the environs of Şabinkarahisar, where girls and women were also abducted. In Kavaklık, near Ezbider, the convoy was attacked by *çetes* from Kirason who were led by Sari Mahmudzâde Eşref and his brother Hasan, Kâtib Ahmed, the commander of the gendarmerie Kemal Bey, Major Faik, and an officer named Osman. They burned the last eight men in the convoy alive. After a 28-day trek, when our witness reached

Kuruçay, between Şabinkarahisar and Divrig, there were only 500 deportees left in the caravan; they were natives of Kirason and the *kazas* of Tireboli and Gorele. According to Mariam Kokmazian, they were attacked again, on the *kaymakam*'s orders, by Kurdish villagers; the 40 survivors in the caravan then set out for Demir Mağara, located somewhat south of Divrig, a place that had been given the name "Slaughterhouse of the Armenians" by the local population because several thousand Armenians had had their throats cut there. On the 36 day these survivors reached Agn/Eğin. Our witness was placed in the city's Turkish orphanage, where 500 Armenian children were living in appalling conditions. When, somewhat later, these children were poisoned and thrown into the Euphrates, Mariam succeeded in escaping. At first she survived by working for a tailor in the city and later made her way to Sıvas dressed as a Turk before moving on to Konya and, finally, Istanbul.[151]

In addition to the Young Turks mentioned above, several officers in the army and gendarmerie played important roles in eliminating the Armenians of Kirason and the surrounding *kazas*: Faik Bey, the commander of the gendarmerie; Kemal Bey, a lieutenant in the gendarmerie; Arap Mustaf Bey, a major in the gendarmerie; and Nihad Bey, the head of the recruitment office. Among the notables in the city, Haci Ali Ağazâde Kiağifi played a leading role in looting Armenian property in his capacity as president of the *Emvalı metruke*. The leaders of squadrons of *çetes* who were the most deeply involved in the massacres or drownings at sea were Topal Osman and Ishak Çavuş. They were assisted by Kızılcioğlu Buni Hasan Hüseyin; Harputlu Paşa Reis; Eğinli Hüseyin; Eşref Çelebi; Kolci Yusufzâde Yusuf; Bulanoğlu Şaban; and Pehlivan İsmail.[152]

Massacres and Deportations in the Sancak of Gümüşhane

An enclave in the Pontus mountains, the *sancak* of Gümüşhane, which had enjoyed a long period of prosperity thanks to its silver mines, had been largely emptied of its Armenian population after the Russo-Turkish War of 1828. In 1914, 1,817 Armenians were still living in the town of Gümüşhane. There were another 450 in Şeyran, the seat of the *kaza* of the same name, and 482 in Kelkit, the southernmost district in the *sancak*.[153]

As we have seen, the *mutesarif* of Gümüşhane, Abdülkadir Bey, who held his post from June 1915 to 16 January 1917, played a decisive role in the liquidation of the men deported from Trebizond[154] and, naturally, the Armenians of his own district. He was seconded by Nazmi Bey and Refik Pasha, who were backed up in turn by two squadrons of *çetes* stationed there under the command of Mirza Bey and Murad Bey.[155]

The Sancak of Rize, a Haven for a Few Armenian Fugitives

According to the Ottoman census of 1914, there were only 35 Armenians in the whole *sancak* of Rize.[156] This statistic, however, masks a much more complex reality: the mountainous region of Hamşin was home to an Armenian-speaking population that was converted by force to Islam between 1680 and 1710, and was distinguished by conspicuous cultural traits. Despite the activity of the *mutesarif*, Süleyman Sâmi Bey (who held his post from 16 July 1914 to 16 July 1915), this population unhesitatingly took in a number of Armenians from the regions of Kiskim, Bayburt, and Erzerum, which made these mountains a locus of resistance to the government forces that set off in pursuit of the Armenian fugitives.[157]

Massacres and Deportations in the Sancak of Canik/Samsun

According to the statistics of the Patriarchate and the 1914 Ottoman census, there were 35,907 Armenians in the *sancak* of Canik. They lived both in the towns – Samsun, Bafra,

Çarşamba, Uniye, and Fatsa – and in the countryside in ten villages around Uniye, four in the vicinity of Terme, and 20 in the Çarşamba district; refugees from *Hamşin* had founded almost all of these early in the eighteenth century. The *sancak* boasted, in 1914, 49 churches and 74 schools.

The development of the port of Samsun in the latter half of the nineteenth century owed a great deal to the opening of a road that could be traveled by wagon between Samsun and the interior of the country. In 1914, the Armenian population here numbered 5,315. It was settled in the Armenian quarter located in the northwestern part of the city, near the shore. Solidly anchored in its hinterland, the city exported notably tobacco, cotton, pearls, and lumber.[158]

The few known sources on the deportation of the Armenians of Samsun are, above all, German,[159] hence the importance of the abundant correspondence, in French, due to the American consulate in Samsun, William Peter.[160] It is all the more important in that most of the American consular documents were destroyed at the request of the State Department when the United States entered the war in 1917. As the American consul in Aleppo, J. B. Jackson, said:

> There was no alternative, however, for I had had the terrible example of the failure of the French Consul-General at Beirut, Syria, to do likewise, as a result of which his archives had been seized by the Turks and more than sixty estimable men of Syria were exposed and hanged, and some 5,000 more were deported and all had their property confiscated by the Turkish Government. With this before me I did not intend that any act of omission of mine should be the cause of a like catastrophe.[161]

Peter, a Swiss citizen, took up his duties as a consular agent in Samsun in spring 1915.[162] As the representative of a neutral country, he also found himself charged with representing the interests of the English, French, Russians, Italians, and so on. Already very busy defending the commercial interests and property of those countries in the Samsun area, Peters was in late June 1915 suddenly confronted with, in his own words, an "Armenian question." The consul was at first puzzled by the "measures of displacement to the interior" of the Armenian population. Certain signs, however, indicated that an operation by the Turkish authorities was imminent. An 11 May 1915 letter from the American consul in Trebizond, Oscar Heiner, informed Peter that "upon instructions from the Embassy I enclose herewith copy of a Note Verbal from the Sublime Porte dated 18 April requesting that American Consular Officers refrain from making trips into regions in which the Imperial Ottoman armies are operating."[163] The tone of this "circular verbal note" from the Sublime Porte, dated 18 April 1915, was revealing:

> Pursuant to a communication from the vice-commander of the Imperial Army, the minister of foreign affairs respectfully requests that the embassy of the United States of America be so good as to send all necessary instructions to the American consuls so that they refrain from making journeys to the zone[s] in which the Ottoman Imperial Armies are engaged in carrying out operations with a particular purpose.[164]

What were these "operations [carried out] with a particular purpose"? The answer came on 26 June 1915, when Peter wired the American ambassador Henry Morgenthau: "Authorities demand internment Armenians, women, children. Because measure too serious, request intervention with government to preserve freedom innocent people."[165] Two days earlier, Peter had already sent this cable: "Authorities demand internment Armenians [under] American protection, stop. Moreover, authorit[ie]s demand delivery keys monastery, Latin church, advise. Peter."[166] In other words, Peter had been asked to abandon the idea of protecting American citizens of Armenian origin and to turn over property belonging to enemy countries.

The American consul in Samsun, although he was the representative of a neutral country, was put under ever-tighter surveillance, while his communications with the embassy in Istanbul were impeded. In August 1915, there were even frictions between Peter and the *mutesarif* of Samsun, who, Peter claimed

> Must have received instruction from Sıvas no longer to accept my sealed letters ... I would have communicated this to you by telegraph, but my dispatch would certainly not have arrived. My two trips to Merzifun have given the Turks the idea that I went there for the Armenians alone, in order to persuade myself of the reality of the matter on the spot. Indeed, the *kaymakam* of Merzifun said this to one of my Turkish friends.[167]

It is no less interesting to observe how a consul who initially did not have a global vision of the events in progress gradually modified the vocabulary he used to describe the liquidation of the Armenians. Convinced, at first, of the truthfulness of the declarations of the local authorities by the spectacle they staged – Armenian deportees leaving the city on ox-drawn carts – he wrote in his report of 27 June 1915:

> On orders from Constantinople, the *mutesarif* decreed on Thursday evening, the 24th of this month, that the population, regardless of social position, religious sect [sic], or foreign protection, had, within five days, to leave the city and prepare for exile. This spontaneous order, composed in extremely severe fashion, not only stunned all the Armenians and plunged them into a state of anguish, but also deeply touched the humanitarian feelings of all the other Christians and a good part of the Muslims who still possess upright judgment – which is unfortunately not the case with all of them.

The consul found especially cruel the "expulsion, on pack wagons, [of] women, children, and old people, accompanied by a prohibition to sell in order to acquire the financial means needed to survive during the journey, the length and destination of which are unknown."[168] By 10 July, already using more categorical language, he announced:

> They have formed groups of Armenian males and have had all of them massacred by peasants. They are certainly going to take the kind of measures against women and children that will have these creatures dying of hunger or despair, a horrible massacre reminiscent of the period in which they rid Constantinople of its dogs and left them all on an island to die![169]

The information contained in his report of 26 August is more precise. The deportees of

> Samsun, Amasia, Merzifun have all arrived in Amasia. Then, the men separated, tied up, some clubbed to death between Amasia, Turchal, Tokat. Everyone that arrived in Tokat was sent from Tokat to Chiflik or Gishgisha and butchered. The women and children transported by oxcart as far as Scharkysschla [Şarkışla, near Sıvas] and then send on foot to Malatia by detours, then thrown in the Kırk Göz or the Euphrates.[170]

In the same document, abandoning the generally reserved tone he used when writing to the ambassador, Peter gave vent to his indignation in these terms: "If Turkey is, in general, not up to scratch in matters of organization and talent, this time, when it was a question of massacres, theft, and so on, it showed nicely coordinated, nicely accelerated savoir-faire in swiftly expediting hundreds of thousands of creatures to the next world."[171]

Thus, in the space of two months, Peter seems to have taken the measure of the event. His correspondence provides valuable information about the methods the authorities used to disguise their crimes. Initially, it was a question of temporarily expelling the Armenian population and sending it on oxcarts "to the interior," as far as Amasia, so as to buttress the conviction of foreign observers that nothing more was involved here than preventive security measures that were undoubtedly painful, but not inhumane. Armenian Catholics and Protestants, whose fate interested certain Western consulates in particular, were not spared in this first phase, but the authorities sustained doubts as to whether they would be down to the last minute. Only those "who wish to convert to Islam can remain here; this government decision has no other purpose than to efface the name Armenian."[172] It was necessary to wait no more than two weeks to learn that

> even converts, according to what the *mutesarif* says, cannot remain here, but have to go to Trebizond, Kerasund, Merzifun, Bafra, etc., etc. The Turks are working hard to convert people. A great many of the people who have left would very much like to [follow] the example of the one hundred fifty families that have converted, but it seems that it is already too late and that they are not being allowed to return here even if they embrace Islam.[173]

As for "American subjects [*sic*] [of] former Armenian origin, [they] will probably be expelled," Peter wrote in a 4 July 1915 telegram to Morgenthau.[174]

The longer second phase now began. The aim of it was to finish the job – that is, to deport those who had been spared so far or had managed to elude the roundups. This phase is particularly revelatory of the authorities' determination to finish what they had started by relentlessly tracking down the handful of individuals who had benefited from some sort of protection. The letters exchanged with Constantinople in the archives of the Samsun consulate about one threatened "protégé" or another are past counting. To illustrate the fierce determination and cynicism of the Turkish authorities, it is enough to present the case of a single man, the dragoman of the Russian consul in Trebizond, G. Tokatlian. Initially, on the insistence of the American embassy (which had been charged with defending Russian interests as well), Tokatlian had been placed under house arrest in Kayseri. His two sons, Hrachia and Michel,

> were living with Mr. T[okatlian]'s sister … When the Armenian deportation began, the *mutesarif* had promised to let these two children remain here, but, later, he suddenly wanted to dispatch them to Urfa, and it was only with great difficulty that Peter secured permission for them to stay in Samsun. While Peter was away in Merzifun, the *mutesarif* had them deported after all; today, we do not know where his sister and two children are.[175]

It was now December 1915 and Tokatlian was still alive. A few months later, in October 1916, Peter informed the American ambassador that he had until then been sending Tokatlian "his usual salary via the Banque impériale ottomane in Sıvas, that is, to the end of June. But the money for July was returned to me, and the bank wrote to me to say that Tokatlian had left Cesarea two months earlier and had sent no news."[176] Tokatlian had indeed "left" Cesarea, accompanied by his guards, in July. Abram Elkus even confirmed this in a letter to Peter:

> In reply to your enquiry relative to Messrs Simeonidès and Tokatlian, formerly dragomans of the Russian consulate at Samsun, I have to inform you that the Embassy has

received a report stating that about July 9th last they were sent in chains from Cesarea to Bunian. From there they started under guard towards Azizie. Nothing more has been heard from them except that it is commonly reported that they were killed at a place near Burian [Bunyan]. There are strong reasons to suppose that this was the case, although the local Government states that they were to have been deported to Der Zor.[177]

Like Leslie Davis in Mezreh, the American consul in Samsun answered requests for information sent to the embassies by relatives of Armenians living in Samsun. The files in the archives in Washington, D.C. are replete with letters of this kind, the responses to which are, as a rule, identical: "Please inform M. Gregoire Kherian, the head of the International Transportation Company in your city, that Murad Kherian's family has been sent to the interior together with a goodly number of other Armenian families."[178] Or again, in response to a request for information from the American Diplomatic Agency in Cairo:

I would respectfully like to inform you that Mrs. Filomenish G. Hekimian, with her daughter, as well as Mrs. Antoinette M. Hekimian, whose maiden name was Misir, are in Aleppo, where they are living with Mr. Nurian. Two of Mrs. Antoinette Hekimian's children died on the way there. Nothing is known about the fate of the men, Onig, Mygerditch [that is, Mgrdich], and [H]agop, and it is supposed that they took the path that so many others have had to tread.[179]

In a few rare cases, the consul managed to save someone by pulling the wool over the authorities' eyes. Thus, he succeeded in dispatching Koharig Kamberian, the sister of a Romanian subject, to Romania; otherwise "she, too, would have been deported, or would have lost her life in the interior … It was to save a human life that we had to resort to these means; it would be convenient if this person had a passport in hand."[180]

One of the major questions that the American consulates had to handle is connected with the economic consequences of the war, in particular the debts due the Armenians. Economic life in Samsun, still vibrant despite the war, seems to have come to a sudden halt at the end of June 1915. We possess letters on this subject that are not without a certain piquancy. The headquarters of the Bank of Salonika, located in Constantinople, drew the consequences of the deportation of the Armenians, informing its correspondents as early as 6 July that "Mr. J. Zekian, formerly a teller at our branch in Samsun, has quit our establishment of his own accord; thus his signature is no longer valid."[181] Of course, not all the Armenians had the good grace to leave their post "of their own accord" – most of them even went off without leaving a forwarding address. This spawned curious epistolary exchanges, involving notably an American company in Richmond that harassed Consul Peter because some 50 families of the Armenian upper crust in Samsun had rented pianos from it but had stopped paying their monthly bill as of July 1915. The managers in Richmond, no doubt poorly informed about the course of the war in this part of the world, accordingly demanded that their property be returned to them as soon as possible. It is easy to guess the tenor of Peter's response, which confirmed that these people had been deported and were probably dead, and also that "the private homes of the Armenians, as well as their stores and warehouses, have been sealed by the government, but a start has already been made on settling emigrants in a good number of these homes, which are being stripped by these people."[182] These remarks illustrate another stake of the genocide – the acquisition of Armenian property by the central or local authorities and private persons.

The documents of the American consulate in Samsun address another ticklish subject, the question of the life insurance policies that Armenians had taken out with companies in various countries: Britain (The Star and The Equitable[183] in London), the United States (the New York Life Insurance Company),[184] Hungary, and so on. In most cases, Peter's demands that these companies pay indemnities received the same response: "We would request that would consider that the above-mentioned insurance policy has lapsed because the premium has gone unpaid." Peter unfailingly pointed out that the sole survivor of one family or another was currently living in the greatest imaginable poverty in some corner of the Syrian desert and that in paying out an indemnity the companies "would in any case be doing a good deed."[185] This question was even the subject of a 29 December 1915 circular that the Ottoman minister of commerce sent to all the insurance companies doing business in Turkey, bearing on the accounts of the Armenians "who had been transported elsewhere." The aim was to flesh out the arrangements already in effect in order to put the crowning touch on the seizure of Armenian property: "As per instructions from the minister of the interior, you are under obligation to submit us a list showing all deposits, credits, and indemnities of Armenians with your company involving the provinces of Rodosto, Adana, Jebelbereket, Kozan, and Samsun."[186]

The memoirs of a survivor, Payladzou Captanian,[187] show how the convoys of deportees who left Samsun were treated on their journey through Tokat, Sıvas, and Malatia/Fırıncilar. Many different accounts indicate that the convoys of deportees from Samsun traveled through Kangal,[188] south of Sıvas, Alacahan,[189] Hasançelebi,[190] Kırk Göz,[191] and Fırıncilar.[192] They show that the men of Sasun were, after passing through Tokat, liquidated in Çiftlik, near Tonuz; that the old men and adolescents were killed in Hasançelebi; and that a few dozen survivors managed to reach their provisional destination, Aleppo.[193]

Vehib Pasha declared, after the armistice, that the *mutesarif* of Canik, Süleyman Necmi Bey, "thanks to his intelligence, sense of justice, and good will, succeeded in escorting all the caravans of Armenians to the borders of his jurisdiction safe and sound."[194] He did, however, observe that "the civilian population was put in the hands of irresponsible vagabonds, who had no consideration for either the honor or dignity of the state."[195]

What the American consul did not know is that the *mutesarif* Süleyman Necmi Bey and the president of the local Ittidhad club, Sıdkı, coordinated operations for the whole *sancak* of Canik. In Samsun, the police chief, Sabri Bey, oversaw the departure of the convoys with the Armenian primate Hamazasp Vartabed, who left with the first convoy at their head, followed by Father Mgrdich Meghmuni, the Catholic exarch. Many of the men were slain south of Tokat, near the village of Çiftlik, the point of arrival of the caravans from Samsun, Bafra, Çarşamba, Merzifun, Amasia, and the countryside.[196]

In October 1915, there remained, in Samsun, only eleven Islamicized families, two Armenian families whose members were Persian subjects, the families of two doctors working on the front, Dr. Kasabian and Dr. Ajemian, and about 100 children from three to six years of age who were first taken in by Greek families then taken from them by the authorities and handed over to Turkish families.[197]

The *Kaza* of Bafra

In this westernmost *kaza* on the Black Sea coast, only one locality was inhabited by Armenians in 1914: it was Bafra, a city lying at the mouth of the Kızıl İrmak,[198] which had an Armenian community 2,000 strong. These Armenians were deported at the same time as those of Samsun. According to testimony given at the trial of the criminals of Trebizond by Kenan Bey, a court inspector in the region, Bafra's *kaymakam* was murdered after he tried to intercede on behalf of the Armenians deported from his *kaza*.[199] A handful of adolescents nevertheless managed to flee into the Pontic Mountains, where they formed with other young men from the region a group of resistance fighters.[200]

The *Kaza* of Çarsamba

Çarsamba, the former seat of the government of the *sancak* of Canik, was founded by Armenian peasants from *Hamşin*, who colonized the regions from 1710 on. Located four hours from the Black Sea on the banks of the Yeşil İrmak, Çarsamba had in 1914 an Armenian population of 1,800, which was settled in the western part of the town. But this district also boasted 20 Armenian villages, also founded by people from *Hamşin*, with a total population of 13,316 and 21 churches and 33 schools: Gurşunlu (pop. 2,800), Khapak, Ortaoymak, Erinçak, Kıyıkli, Martel, Tekvari, Takhtalık, Odiybel, Konaklık, Kapalak, Ağlac, Kabacniz, Eyridere, Olunpar, Kökceköy, Ağcagöne, Çeşmesu, Daşcığıç; and Kıstani Kıriş.[201]

The entire population of Çarsamba was deported, with the exception of a few hundred people who took refugee in the mountains under the lead of Father Kalenjian, Khachig Tulumjian, Abraham Khachadurian, and Hagopos Kehiayan.[202]

The *Kazas* of Terme and Uniye

Of the 3,427 Armenians in this *kaza* in 1914, only some 100 people lived in the principal town in the *kaza*, Terne. Most of the Armenian population was concentrated in four villages lying nearby: Kocaman (1,965 Armenians), located on a height half an hour from the sea, Alemdaz (pop. 560), Suluca (200), and Hoyla.[203] We know nothing about what became of these villagers.

In 1914, there were 7,700 Armenians in the *kaza* of Uniye. A scant 700 lived in the seat of the *kaza*, the port of Uniye. The Armenian population was to be found, above all, in ten villages of the hinterland that were inhabited by stonecutters, weavers, and peasants who cultivated tobacco and hazelnuts: Ozanı, Yamurcan, Eyrubeyli, Tekedamı, Düztarlan, Khachdur, Yusuflar/Köklük, Seylen, Gözderen, and Manasdere.[204] Thanks to an account by two adolescents aged 15 and 16 at the time, Serop Karakehiayan and Kalust Kosian,[205] we have a few indications about the conditions under which the Armenians of this district were deported. In the absence of the men, who had been mobilized, it seems that the authorities had no trouble whatsoever removing these villagers from their homes.

Even before the deportation order was published, 25 notables from both the seat of the *kaza* and the villages were summoned to appear before the *kaymakam*, who had them imprisoned and then shot in Alaçami. A survivor from this group, Zakar Tumanian, provides an account of what happened.[206] The Armenians were deported in four caravans, with the exception of the inhabitants of the village of Köklük, who were murdered there, and some old people who were allowed to remain in their homes. Approximately 150 people withdrew to the mountains under the leadership of Avedis Chakrian, Garabed Tahmazian, Kevork Koseyan, and Dikran Zeytunjian; they succeeded in saving a few deportees.[207] For several years, this group survived in the Pontic hinterland, carrying out occasional operations in Turkish villages to seize food, and sometimes confronting the forces of the state. One of these skirmishes, which took place near Köz Tepe in late September 1915, is quite revealing. A squadron of *çetes* commanded by someone named Gürci Torunoğlu Süleyman took the Armenian fugitives by surprise. Its mission had been precisely to hunt down fugitive Armenians. In the course of the fighting, Süleyman was shot down by Dikran Zeytunjian.[208] On other occasions, these groups freed girls or children being held in the villages and executed men whom they held responsible for the violence inflicted on their people.[209] It would be an understatement to say that these young men were filled with a powerful spirit of revenge. The most serious incident occurred on 23 and 24 February 1916, on the heights of Köz Tepe, in the hinterland of Uniye: around 150 men confronted several brigades of the regular army that had been sent from Sıvas. The unexpected arrival of two hundred Armenian resistance fighters from the neighboring regions of Fatsa, Çarsamba, and Bafra enabled the group from Uniye to resist. Several years later, under the Kemalist regime, these Armenians would be forced to leave the region for Abkhazia.[210]

The *Kaza* of Fatsa

The 3,330 Armenians of the *kaza* of Fatsa lived in the principal town of the *kaza*, Fatsa, and the villages of Çubukluk and Kaya Ardi.[211] It seems that part of the population agreed to convert to Islam in order to avoid being deported, but that these people were finally deported to the south somewhat later, with the exception of a miller.[212] As in the *kazas* of Bafra, Çarsamba, and Uniye, so here, too, between 100 and 200 people took to the maquis under the command of Yaghjian, Minasian, and Hamalian. The handful of survivors discovered after the war came from this group.[213]

Chapter 10

Deportations and Massacres in the Vilayet of Angora

The sprawling, densely populated vilayet of Angora had, in 1914, an Armenian population of 105,169. They lived in 88 towns and villages, and had 105 churches, 11 monasteries, and 126 schools with a total enrollment of 21,298. Although there had long been an Armenian population in the *sancak* of Angora, it was now concentrated in a few urban centers – in Angora, of course, but also in Kalecik, Stanoz, Nallihan, Muhalic, and Sivrihisar. The *sancaks* of Yozgat and Kayseri, in contrast, had a non-negligible rural Armenian population that went back to the Middle Ages.

In the *sancak* of Angora, there were, in 1914, 20,858 Armenians, more than half of whom lived in the city of Angora, where the vali had his residence. Here they engaged in trading manufactured good, cottage industry, rug-making, and so on. Angora's Armenian population comprises a case apart due to the size of its Catholic community, which represented 70 per cent of the 11,246 Armenians living in the city in 1914, having been converted by French missionaries early in the eighteenth century. The Red Monastery, dedicated to the Holy Mother of God, had served as the Armenian Apostolic bishopric since the fourteenth century. This prosperous community maintained schools with an enrolment of two thousand on the eve of the First World War.[1]

In many respects, an examination of the destruction of this population is of particular interest because of its location at the heart of Anatolia and its Catholic majority. These two features might have enabled the Armenians of the vilayet to escape "displacement to the interior," the more so as these Turkish-speaking Armenians, who wrote Turkish with the Armenian alphabet, were by common consent not highly politicized and enjoyed the protection of both Austria-Hungary and the papal nuncio. Hence this community was not deeply marked by the tensions that we have observed in the eastern vilayets. Only the settlement of 10,000 Muslim *muhacirs* late in the day – that is, after the Balkan Wars – created tensions having to do with land distribution.[2]

Here, perhaps more than elsewhere, the discourse that sought to paint the Armenians as a seditious group remained most unconvincing. The vali, Hasan Mazhar Bey, who had been appointed to his post on 18 June 1914, was, moreover, so little persuaded of it that he resisted the Interior Minister's deportation orders. Istanbul's response was no less firm. Early in July 1915, the Young Turk Central Committee sent one of its most eminent members, Atıf Bey [Kamçil], whose role within the political leadership of the *Teşkilât-ı Mahsusa* we have already seen, to Angora as a delegate.[3] This choice speaks volumes about intentions in the capital. Like Bahaeddin Şakir in Erzerum or Yusuf Rıza in Trebizond, the leaders of the Special Organization did not hesitate to travel to a locality in person in order to translate their program into action. But what is even more interesting in the case of Angora is that, as a result of direct intervention by a member of the Young Turk Central Committee, the

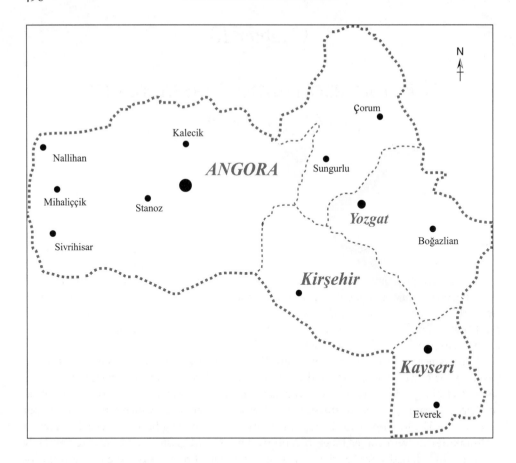

interior minister immediately relieved Vali Mazhar of his duties on 8 July 1915, naming the CUP's delegate to the region, Atıf Bey, interim vali.[4] Atıf, who held his post from 14 July to 3 October 1915, accomplished nothing more nor less than the mission entrusted to him by the Ittihad – that is, the extirpation of the Armenian population from the vilayet of Angora. According to Mehmed Necib Bey, an official of the Tobacco Régie then posted to Angora, "the atrocities committed by this vali are unforgettable ... Atıf Bey, Angora's interim vali, demonstrated incomparable mastery."[5]

Even Armenian observers were surprised to see this 27-year-old arrive in Angora in early July, accompanied by "another child, twenty-five years old, animated by the same hatred for Christians and greed for what they owned." This was someone named Bahaeddin Bey, whom the CUP had delegated to take the reins of the vilayet's police force.[6] It seems that Şemseddin, a member of the local Ittihad club and the vilayet's general council, and Necati Bey, the CUP's responsible secretary in Angora,[7] had not succeeded in modifying Mazhar's position. It was said that this compelled the party to send people in positions of authority to the region.

The two representatives of the committee had not, however, remained completely inactive. They oversaw the liberation of 249 felons from Angora's central prison on 3 March 1915 by a commission made up of Mahmud Cellaleddin Bey, the director of Angora's health services; Captain Fehmi Bey; Colonel Mehmed Vasıf Bey, the commander of the gendarmerie in Angora; and Ali Haydar Bey, a judge on the appeals court. These criminals, recruited as çetes of the Special Organization, were sent to Çorum; we will see later the mission entrusted to them there. According to a report signed by the members of the commission, the prisoners agreed to join the "army." They were given "a medical examination, and a list of their names, the nature of their crimes, and the sentences they had been given was compiled."[8] This commission was still functioning in spring 1915; on 15 May of that year, it freed another 65 murderers for the same purpose.[9] The interim *mutesarif* of Yozgat, Kemal Bey, later confirmed that the responsible secretary of the Party of Union and Progress in Angora, Necati Bey, had intervened directly in this matter. Questioned by Hasan Mazhar on 16 December 1918, he did not deny that Necati had gone to Yozgat "before the deportation of the Armenians, orally communicated secret orders and instructions about the deportation of the Armenians, and held a meeting in Yozgat with the members of the Party of Union and Progress, the heads of Union and Progress and of the *Teşkilât-ı Mahsusa*."[10]

It seems that the Young Turk leaders and the local and central authorities opted for a strategy calculated to first liquidate the Armenian populations of the *sancaks* of Kayseri and Yozgat in order to deal with the Armenians of the *sancak* of Angora afterwards. Probably informed as early of May 1915 of the exactions committed in the border regions, the Armenians of Angora briefly succeeded in convincing themselves that they would be spared thanks to the protection of Mazhar and certain foreign diplomats. But when, a few days after assuming office in mid-July 1915, Atıf Bey had the non-Catholic Armenian notables of Angora arrested, the Catholics no doubt suddenly understood that they were vulnerable. According to a foreign witness, 500 men were arrested in the space of a few days by the police and gendarmerie, notably the director of the *Banque impériale ottomane*, Shnorhokian, under the supervision of the new police chief, Bahaeddin Bey, and the CUP's responsible secretary, Necati Bey, assisted by the mufti of Kirşehir, Nuffid Hoca, Şamseddin, and Çingene Hakkı.[11] In the next few days, the list of those interned grew longer, eventually coming to include around 200 men.[12] We also know that on 14 August, CUP volunteers left the city in a car, carrying shovels and picks and that toward midnight on the same day, several hundred Armenians were led from the city by an escort of police and gendarmes, tied together in pairs. At dawn, their guards turned them over to *çetes* who had been waiting for them in a secluded spot.[13] These recruits of the Special Organization were, according to another source, butchers and tanners from Angora, "given special pay" for executing these Armenians with the help of villagers in the vicinity. In five or six days, they massacred around 1,200 Armenians.[14] Armenian witnesses affirmed that, after these atrocities had been committed, Osman Bey, the commander of the gendarmerie, immediately tendered his resignation, while the recruits of the Special Organization came back to the city bearing their trophies, notably their victims' shoes and pants. Rumors about the deportation of Catholics were also beginning to make the rounds.[15] Bishop Gregoire Bahabanian and a few Catholic notables went to see Atıf Bey, suggesting that he intervene in Istanbul. The vali was reassuring: he promised that the authorities had no complaints about them and for that reason there was no point in taking steps in Constantinople.[16]

Yet, on Friday, 27 August, gendarmes and policemen invested the Armenian neighborhoods and summer residences where many families were staying at the time. The same day, approximately 1,500 Catholic males, including the bishop and 17 priests, were arrested and grouped in the city.[17] After being invited to convert, in vain, these men were stripped of their belongings and on 29 August set on the road, tied together in pairs. They had walked for 18 hours and were in the village of Karagedik when "an officer arrived at full speed and communicated the government's counter-order to [them]: he told [them] that the order for a general massacre had been rescinded in [their] favor and that [their lives] were no longer in danger."[18] It seems that these men's fate had been sealed, but that the intervention of Angelo Maria Dolci, the papal nuncio, had made it possible to save them[19] – that is, to deport them to the deserts of Syria rather than liquidate them. The German embassy was rapidly apprised of the deportation of these Catholics,[20] as was the ambassador of Austria-Hungary, Pallavicini, who informed his minister that he had asked Talât "to spare the Armenian Catholics and Protestants, and that Talât had promised to write to the prefects and sub-prefects of the province... about this matter."[21] Thus, it is probable that the convoy of 1,500 Catholics from Angora was momentarily spared on an order issued by Talât in order to give satisfaction to Pallavicini and Dolci, so that it was able to continue on its journey via Kırşehir, Kayseri, and Biğa as far as the gates of Cilicia, in Bozanti.[22] According to survivors from this caravan, the men took nearly one month to reach Tarsus and then Katma, a village near Aleppo. Most were then sent on by Hakkı Bey, "the inspector of the deportees to Syria," to Ras ul-Ayn or Der Zor. Four of the priests and some 30 of the laymen among them survived in Meskene, managing to reach Aleppo after Hakkı had been replaced.[23]

In early September, the Armenian women, children, and old people of Angora, Catholics and Protestants alike, were expelled from their homes, which were sealed by the police. These thousands of people were then concentrated in the railroad station near the exit from the city, where they remained for no less than 25 days, the time required to extort their property from them and convince the most attractive women to convert and marry Muslims. Those who accepted this offer were authorized to return to the city; the others were ultimately sent to Eskişehir and Konya, where they were put on the deportation route leading to Syria. A few hundred families were, however, allowed to remain in Angora "as the families of military men," although the men in question had been "massacred or deported."[24] It is probable that these exceptions were made to deceive foreign diplomats and ward off possible protests from them. Essentially, the procedures employed in the *sancak* of Angora can be interpreted as local adaptations that did not fundamentally alter the determination of the authorities to extirpate the Armenian population of Angora. Locally less radical, the measures taken merely put off the elimination of the Armenians in time and space.

The method used to get hold of Armenian property scarcely differed from that observed elsewhere. Moveable assets and real estate were systematically seized. Moreover, the most richly appointed Armenian homes were allotted to civilian and military authorities. The fire that raged in the Armenian neighborhoods almost eight months after the deportations was no accident. It took no less than four days to realize the plan, the objective of which was, without a doubt, to hide the extent of the looting that had gone on for the personal benefit of certain individuals.[25] Some witnesses noted that the record books of the Registry of Abandoned Property were indeed opportunely consumed by the flames. During the examination of the former justice minister, İbrahim Bey, on 10 November 1918, the members of the Fifth Commission of the Ottoman Parliament, who had been charged with investigating certain crimes committed during the war, went so far as to ask the minister why those responsible for this blaze, the aim of which was to "lay hands on their assets," had not been arrested.[26]

Among the Young Turks implicated in the deportations and massacres, in addition to Şemseddin Bey and Necati Bey, whose role we have already mentioned, the principal instigators were Kara Mehmed; Mufid Hoca, the mufti of Kırşehir; Tabib Effendi, a deputy in the Ottoman Parliament; Çingane Hakkı Bey; Şefket Bey, a municipal pharmacist; and Ahmed Neşed, the director of forestry.[27] Among the government officials, apart from Atıf Bey, who was at once interim vali, a member of the political bureau of the Special Organization, and a special CUP delegate, the main organizers of the deportations and massacres were Topcu Ziya, the head of the committee responsible for settling Muslim immigrants; Rasim Bey, the president of the municipality; Bahaeddin Bey, delegated by the CUP to assume leadership of the vilayet's police force after the "resignation" of his predecessor; Mustafa Turhan Bey and Rahim İbrahim Bey, police lieutenants; İbrahim Bey, the director of prisons; Kara Böbrek Hasan Effendi, the assistant director of the *Banque Ottomane*; and Çerkez Kahmi, a captain in the gendarmerie. The members of the *emval-ı metruke* who oversaw the pillage of the Armenians' assets were Karabekir Hasan Bey; Fincancizâde Mehmed Şemseddin Bey; and Nasreddin Bey, a parliamentary deputy from Sıvas who resigned his post as *kaymakam* of Çorum in order to assume the presidency of the committee responsible for "abandoned property" in Angora. The main organizers of the local squadrons of *çetes* and the massacres were Kütükcuoğlu Ziya Bey, a pharmacist from Sivrihisar; İsmail Bey; Tufenkci Ali Bey; and Eczacizâde Şevket.[28]

The Kazas of Angora

The *Kaza* of Stanoz/Zyr

Lying 30 kilometers west of Angora, Stanoz was, on the eve of the First World War, an exclusively Armenian village with a population of 3,142 Armenian-speakers. Established late, at the end of the fourteenth century, this prosperous village had three churches, one of them Protestant, and two schools with an enrollment of 500. Stanoz had since the seventeenth century been mainly known for its *sofe*, a kind of cloth made from the fur of Angora goats, and also for rug-making, embroidery, dying, and leather-working.[29]

As early as August 1914, much of Stanoz's economically active population was mobilized and incorporated into the Third Army.[30] Thanks to its proximity to the Sincanköy railroad station, the village was rather well informed of the course of the war and even had news of the 120 to 150 members of the Istanbul Armenian elite who had been imprisoned some 15 kilometers to the west in Ayaş. Father Khoren Avakian, the stationmaster, had been on hand when they arrived and had even been able to inform Dr. N. Daghavarian's family of their arrival.[31] It was the Armenians of Stanoz who provided the prisoners in Ayaş with food and other necessities until they set out for an unknown destination. In May, house searches were carried out in Stanoz. Father Khoren was one of the first to be arrested. Late in the month, 15 notables from Stanoz, including Giragos Kabzemalian, Arsen Turkmenian, and Harutiun Avakian, were arrested and interned in the Zencirli G̃uyu barracks.[32]

Not until around 15 August, however, were the males over 15 – around 700 people – summoned to present themselves in the *konak's* courtyard, where they were arrested and transferred to Angora under guard. A few days later, after the Protestant Armenians had been released, these men were led off to the Çayaş Bahcesi valley and massacred there. The Protestant males were invited to convert to Islam. When they refused, they were taken to Seyirce, in the vicinity of their village, and their throats were cut.[33]

Many of the women and children of Stanoz owed their lives to the *müdir*, İbrahim Şah. Şah succeeded in keeping the families of the conscripts in the village and in finding homes for the rest of the population in the Turkish villages of the *nahie*.[34] Unlike the Armenian population of many other *kazas* in the *sancak*, that of Stanoz was, ultimately, partially spared.

The *Kazas* of Nallıhan and Mihalıççık

In 1914, there were only two small Armenian colonies in the *kazas* of Nallıhan and Mihalıççık, which lay northwest of the *sancak* of Angora. The colony in Nallıhan had an Armenian population of 1,030; the Armenian population of Mihalıççık was 272.[35]

According to a survivor from Nallıhan, rumors were making the rounds among the Turks as early as April, while certain local notables had gone so far as to claim this or that house for themselves in advance.[36] But it was not until 2/15 August that a colonel who had been appointed *sevkiyat memuri* [director of the deportations] arrived in Nallıhan. Shortly thereafter, the church bells began pealing and all the Armenians were assembled in the church, where the colonel informed them that the families of soldiers would be allowed to remain in the town and that, with the exception of males fourteen and older, all could freely choose to stay or go. According to our witness, the Turkish notables immediately laid common plans to establish check points at the different entrances to the city in order to keep outsiders from coming to take part in the auctions of Armenian property, so that they could obtain it at low prices themselves. In the space of three days, all the Armenians' assets had passed into Turkish hands, at the instigation of Beyzâde Ahmed Bey. It should also be pointed out that the Turkish notables had initially proposed to "buy" the Armenians' real estate before it was put up for auction.[37]

On 6 August, all males fourteen and over were arrested and put on the road the evening of the same day, with around three hundred women and children; they were guarded by a squadron under the orders of Abdül Selim Tevfik. Ten hours from town, in Yardib, Kör Haci Seyid Köpecli and the Turkish villagers in the environs began methodically looting the goods that the Armenians had taken with them. The convoy was then allowed to continue on its way.[38] According to M. Manugian, who was in this convoy, it took them no less than thirteen days to reach Angora, where they were interned in a granary. The Turkish officers and notables of the city lost no time coming to the granary in order to suggest to the most attractive girls and women to convert to Islam and leave with them.[39] Two hundred sixty men were separated from the group, led off to the *konak*, and then locked up in the central prison, where seven "individuals" methodically searched them and took all they had: money, watches, and so on. On 23 August, the men were removed from the prison, tied together in pairs, and set marching in the direction of Kirşehir. Five of them perished the first day, including two Catholics from Angora, clubbed to death by their escort, which was made up of a police lieutenant, three more policemen, and twenty gendarmes.[40] When they reached Kirşehir, the surviving men were confined in the military warehouse, before continuing their journey through Kayseri, Incesu, Eydeli, Bozanti, and, finally, Tarsus, where they remained for one month, before being dispatched to Hama or Meskene, in the Syrian deserts.[41] There are no reports on what became of the women and children left behind in Angora. It seems reasonable to suppose that some were "integrated" into Muslim families, while others were put on the road to Syria in a bigger convoy. We do know, however, that the people allowed to remain in Nallıhan – basically the families of recruits – were rapidly parceled out to the Turkish villages in the vicinity.[42] The main beneficiary of the pillage of Armenian property seem to have been a certain Said, who "took the Manugians' farm for himself, as well as the flocks of sheep and goats and the herds of cows" belonging to the Nallıhan Armenians.[43]

The *Kaza* of Sivrihisar

Located in the middle of a vast plateau in the southwestern part of the *sancak*, Sivrihisar nestles in a loop of the Sakaria. The Armenian community of Sivrihisar, like the rest of the Armenian population in these western regions of the vilayet of Angora, did not begin to solidify until the early seventeenth century, when Armenians from Kantsag/Genje and from Karabagh settled here. In 1914, this colony boasted a population of 4,265. The Armenians of Sivrihisar were reputed to be prosperous; some earned a living farming land on the outskirts of the town.[44]

According to the memoirs of Father Hovhannes Kizirian, the situation remained relatively calm until late July. There were frequent and, apparently, cordial meetings between the Armenian notables of the city and the *kaymakam* Ali Rıza Bey, the military commander Besim Bey, and the commander of the gendarmerie Cemal Bey.[45] On 12 August, the deportation order was published. On Saturday, 14 August, Kizirian was received with all the honors at the *konak*, where the vali, Ali Rıza, informed him that the Armenian population had a week to make preparations to leave. The clergyman tried in vain to obtain an exemption for the families of conscripts. He himself left with the last convoy on 19 August. In the meantime, he witnessed the looting of Armenian homes.[46] All the caravans were directed toward the railroad station in Eskişehir, where thousands of deportees from the west were camped out under precarious conditions. At this point, there arrived an order to the effect that the families of conscripts should be dispersed in the surrounding villages.[47] Thereafter, the fate of the Armenians of Sivrihisar was indistinguishable from that of those deported either by rail – in two-tiered stockcars originally meant for sheep – or on foot to Bozanti, the gateway to Cilicia. According to survivors' reports, the deportees from Sivrihisar were dispatched toward Rakka and Der Zor. The overwhelming majority of them died on the way when they were not killed before setting out, victims of the final massacres perpetrated in fall 1916.[48]

Beside the *kaymakam* and the commanders of the gendarmerie and army, several government officials played concrete roles in the deportations to various degrees: Yakup Çavuş and Besim Çavuş, officers in the gendarmerie; Şakir Effendi, a civil servant employed in the Régie; Dr. Hasan Tahsin, a municipal physician; and Potizâde Ahmed Effendi, an *Evkaf* official.[49] Among the Young Turk notables who took part in the deportation of the Armenians, the most active were Nişanzâde Mehmed Effendi, the secretary of the local Ittihad club, and the following members of the club: Nişanzâde Ali Effendi, Haci Çakir Kâtibi, Mehmed Ali Effendi, Ali Kânli Effendi, Zâde Haci Bekir, Amasialızâde Sabit Ali Effendi, Çarpikzâde Ali Effendi, Zafer Hamid Harieli Edhem Ağa, Arif Effendi, and Nevzat Effendi.[50] The seizures of Armenian property were supervised by the *emval-ı metruke*, headed by Ahmed Husni Effendi, with the assistance of Nureddin Effendi, a land registry official; Mehmed Ali Effendi, a mufti; Amasializâde Talât Effendi, a secretary in the Tobacco Régie; Fuadzâde Mustafa Effendi; Sarı Paşazâde Abdüllah Effendi; Canzâde Ali Effendi, a tax collector; and Canzâde Tahir Effendi.[51]

Balahisar, a village southwest of Sivrihisar, had, in 1914, 300 Armenian households. On orders from the *kaymakam*, Kâmil Bey, the men of the village were arrested and massacred near Köprüköy in August 1915 with the complicity of Faik Bey, a civil servant employed in the Registry Office, and Mehmed Bey, an official in the Land Registry Office.[52]

The *Kaza* of Kalecik

In the *kaza* of Kalecik, lying to the north of Angora, there were only 830 Armenians on the eve of the war. All of them lived in Kalecik, on the banks of a tributary of the Kızıl Irmak. Nothing is known about what became of them.[53]

Massacres and Deportations in the Sancak of Yozgat

At an altitude of around 1,500 meters and furrowed by valleys, the *sancak* of Yozgat was famous for the fertility of its land. Its Armenian population, much more rural than elsewhere in the vilayet, lived in nearly 50 villages concentrated in the *kazas* in the southern part of the *sancak*, around Yozgat, Boğazlian, and the environs. This cluster of villages was simply the northern continuation of the Armenian-inhabited areas in Cappadocia. Armenians were also scattered, however, in the principal towns of certain other *kazas*, including Çorum, Süngürlü, and Akdağmaden. The total Armenian population of the *sancak*, according to local Armenian sources, was 58,611 in 1914, whereas the Ottoman census of the same year put the figure at only 36,652.[54]

The principal town of the *sancak*, also called Yozgat, was founded in the first decades of the eighteenth century by Armenian artisans. In 1914, the 9,520 Armenians residing in the town represented 40 per cent of its population. Near Yozgat, there were three Armenian villages: Incirli (pop. 1,000), Daneşman (pop. 250), and Köhne (pop. 2,000). There were also a few small Armenian communities scattered throughout the *kaza*.[55]

It should be noted at the outset that the extirpation of the Armenian population of this *sancak* gave rise to the first trial conducted by the Istanbul court-martial, the proceedings of which ran from 5 February to 8 April 1919. The government commission of inquiry headed by Hasan Mazhar was able to complete its pretrial investigation in short order, gathering initial proof and testimony from civilian and military officials as well as surviving victims and transmitting them to the court-martial. As often happened in the case of secondary trials, the court record of the 18 sessions of the Yozgat trial was not published in the *Takvim-ı Vakayi*; only the verdict handed down by the court-martial on 8 April 1919 appeared there.[56] Istanbul newspapers, however, published, either wholly or in part, the exhibits and documents presented before the court.[57] Thus, we have a quite exceptional corpus of material for the events that occurred in this region. As in Angora as well, the *mutesarif* Cemal Bey, appointed on 27 May 1915, refused to liquidate the men and was dismissed on 5 August by the interim vali Atıf Bey. On the very same day, he was replaced by the *kaymakam* of Boğazlian, Kemal Bey,[58] who had already begun zealously to apply the orders in his *kaza*. In the case of Yozgat, we possess documents that offer insight into the circumstances under which the local Ittihadists managed to obtain the dismissal of the *mutesarif*. According to evidence given by Azniv Ibranosian, the wife of the director of the Ibranosian Brothers' firm in Yozgat, at the fifteenth session of the trial of those who perpetrated the massacres in Yozgat on 28 March 1919, Vehbi Bey, the Chief of the Treasury, organized a secret meeting at his house at which the local Young Turks agreed to oversee the operation.[59] Involved were Ali Münîf, Necati Bey's Yozgat correspondent; Yeşil İmamoğlu Kadi; Hüseyin İmamoğlu Kadi; Ömer Lufti, a teacher in the Turkish *lycée*; Akıf Pasha; Kitabci Asim; Çerkez Sarı Ahmed; Rıza; Şeyh Ahmed; Divanlızâde Ahmed; Mehmed Effendi, the director of Yozgat's Turkish orphanages; Ceridzâde Husni; Uzun Ahmed, the secretary general of the municipality; and Uzun Rahcet.[60] It appears, however, that the *mutesarif* Cemal Bey and the secretary general of the prefecture, Mustafa Bey, refused to carry out this decision. According to the director of the Turkish orphanage, Şevki Bey, it was an open secret that Cemal had been dismissed because he had balked at implementing the orders of "the government and the Committee."[61] There is, moreover, every reason to believe that the local Young Turks referred the question to their superior in Angora, for on Thursday, 5 August, Necati Bey had arrived and organized a secret meeting with them, as was confirmed by the interim *mutesarif* Kemal Bey, who added that Necati then communicated oral instructions to "the leaders of Union and Progress and the *Teşkilât-ı Mahsusa*."[62] Vehbi is supposed to have said of Cemal Bey, according to what the secretary general of the prefecture "confidentially reported" to Ibranosian: "This *mutesarif* isn't Turkish. He must be driven from Yozgat."[63] Another official mentioned a conversation between Necati and Cemal was held the same day, in which the Ittihadist allegedly declared: "Although the government's orders seem to call for exiling the Armenians, the true objective of the Central Committee of the Party of Union and Progress and the interior minister is to extirpate the Armenians and thus render a service to our country."[64]

Most likely, it was these informal instructions that the *mutesarif* refused to follow, forcing Atıv and Necat to dismiss him from his post that very evening so that Yozgat's Ittihadists would have their hands free.

The statement made by the military commander of Yozgat, General Salim Mehmed, likewise provides much information about the way the Ittihadists interfered in local affairs while also showing just how plainly the "temporary deportation law" was a legal cover for crime.[65] The general began by noting that Articles 1 and 2 of the "deportation law" transmitted to him by Şahabeddin, the commander of the Fifteenth Division, based in Kayseri, authorized commanders "to employ military force immediately" against all those acting "counter to the interests of, or endangering the security of, the country," It also authorized them to deport groups of the population "if they were suspected of spying or treason." Mehmed observed that telegram no. 193, dated 18 July 1915, had stipulated, "Government officials do not have the right to interfere in matters involving public order and discipline. Entire responsibility for these questions should be entrusted to the military administration." Nevertheless, "people who proudly affirmed that they were members of the Party of Union and Progress interfered in these matters and, without the least hesitation, made illicit gains and disturbed law and order in the *sancak*." The general also stated that these people sought to "compromise the Armenians" and have them "accused of subversive activities." To that end, they "sent fictitious, official or semi-official reports to the government, stating reasons that sufficed to have the provisions of the aforementioned law applied to the Armenians." Mehmed further observed that the inquiries conducted by the police and gendarmerie "in response to questions that had been repeatedly raised" showed that

> the Armenians of Yozgat did not have ties to the Dashnak or Hnchak committees. Yet, by way of Necati Bey, the same people addressed denunciations to the commanders of the army corps and the division, exposing [the existence] of an imaginary Armenian committee that the authorities treated as real. They ordered that a search for arms be carried out, but the only arms found were those that had been 'planted' by the people conducting the searches. Ultimately, they obtained an order to deport the Armenians.[66]

While the "temporary deportation law" could be rather easily applied in the eastern provinces, it was much harder to evoke it to justify the deportation of civilian populations living in the heart of Asia Minor. The intervention of local CUP representatives was therefore all the more imperative there, especially when it became necessary to manufacture a file capable of legitimizing the deportation order. These difficulties help explain why genocidal measures were carried out late in a vilayet such as Angora.

The position taken by the *mutesarif*, Cemal, gives one indication as to the limits that certain state officials were disinclined to transgress. Thus, Cemal, from the moment he took office in May 1915, imposed restrictions on the circulation between villages and enforced the prohibition on taking herds out to graze. It was likewise under his authority that from late May on the Armenian villages in the *sancak* were methodically invested by *çetes* of the Special Organization. To the questions that Bishop Nerses Tanielian, the Armenian prelate of the diocese of Yozgat, asked about the presence of these irregulars in the countryside, the *mutesarif* responded that they were there "to protect [the Armenians] from their Turkish neighbors."[67] But when the local Young Turks, led by the commander of the gendarmerie Mehmed Tevfik Bey, set out to deal with the 12,000 Armenian conscripts from the *sancak* of Yozgat who were assigned at the time to the *amele taburis* attached to the Fifth Army,[68] Cemal blocked the attempt. On 1 July 1915, according to General Salim Mehmed, the Ittihadists submitted to him "a report in which they recommended that the Armenian soldiers of the Ninth Labor Battalion be transferred to the Second and Fourth Brigades of the same battalion in Kırşehir. Otherwise, they could instigate disorders that might disturb the peace in the *sancak*."[69] The same witness affirmed that, notwithstanding the *mutesarif*'s orders that Major Tevfik "act within the limits of the instructions he had received," Tevfik "ignored him, turning to Muammer Bey, the vali of Sıvas, to whom he complained about the *mutesarif*, requesting instructions."[70] These indications thus seem to suggest that Muammer, in his capacity as the head of the *Teşkilât-ı Mahsusa* in the region, had played a direct role in the destruction of the Armenian worker-soldiers from Yozgat. Sâmi Mehmed points out, moreover, that Tevfik "overstepped the limits" by executing 13 Armenians "during the incidents of the farm of Sarı Hamza" and then massacring 72 others "on Muammer Bey's orders."[71] In other words, the hierarchy established by the CUP overrode the administrative chain of command and the local authorities whenever it was deemed necessary. Obviously, the fact that Hasan Mazhar was replaced in Angora also made it possible to get rid of Cemal Bey in Yozgat.

The choice of Kemal Bey as interim *mutesarif* due to Atıf Bey leaves little doubt as to the CUP's determination to impose its own men when a government official refused to carry out the party's extermination orders, while also confirming that it had the power to intervene in local affairs. Kemal Bey, who was the *kaymakam* of Boğazlian, had been in charge of the *kaza* with the largest number of Armenians, who were, moreover, peasants. From mid-May to late July, the *sancak*'s 48 villages, with around 40,000 Armenian inhabitants, were first emptied of their male population, then followed by women and children, under Kemal Bey's direct supervision.[72] General Mehmed notes that Tevfik Bey, commander of the gendarmerie in Yozgat, had himself made a tour of these Armenian villages and ordered a number of people killed "with no reason whatsoever, on the pretext that they were Committee members."[73] In contrast to other regions, however, virtually no one was deported from these villages: Kemal organized a vast slaughterhouse in the vicinity of the village of Keller, where tens of thousands of Armenians of all ages and both sexes were slain with knives, sabers, and axes. Thus it can be seen that Atıf and Necati here appealed to a state official whom they deemed "exemplary," although he had not even resorted to the usual administrative formalism to veil his crimes. After liquidating the Armenians in the countryside, Kemal and his men completed their task by extirpating the Armenians of Yozgat.

Massacres and Deportations in the *Kaza* of Boğazlian

In 1914, the *kaza* of Boğazlian boasted 32 localities inhabited by 35,825 Armenians, all of them Armenian speaking. The recently founded village in which the prefect resided, also named Boğazlian, lay in the middle of an immense plain. Two thousand Armenians with roots in Sıvas and Hungary lived in the "upper quarter" of Boğazlian. Two adjacent Armenian villages lay to the south: Beyloren (pop. 750) and Gurden (pop. 1,000). To the northeast was the village of Rumdigin: the 2,000 Armenians who lived here represented two-thirds of the population. Kiurkci (pop. 200) was still further north.

Thirty kilometers east of Boğazlian, in Iydeli, there lived around 1,500 Armenians, most of them wine makers. Karahalı, a stone's throw away, had a population of 2,000, Uzunlu, 3,000, and Gövenci, 550. The biggest Armenian villages in the rest of the *kaza* were Çakmak (pop. 1,000), Çokradan (pop. 1,000), Fakralı (pop. 800), Melez (pop. 350), Brunkışla (pop. 2,000), Keller (pop. 1,500), Eylence (pop. 600), Kümküyü (pop. 900), Kediler (pop. 500), Şatlı (pop. 500), Saçli (pop. 600), Magaroğlu (pop. 450), Karabüyük (pop. 800), Pöhrenk (pop. 800), Çat (pop. 3,500), Terzilli (pop. 2,000), Bebek (pop. 1,300), Karayağub (pop. 900), Sarı Hamza (pop. 1,250), Daşlıgetçit (pop. 250), Menteşe (pop. 1,100), Urnec (pop. 1,200), and Çatak (pop. 1,025).[74]

According to a witness from Pöhrenk, Enver visited Yozgat in the first half of April 1915, when the witness himself happened to be in the city. Shortly thereafter, soldiers and gendarmes invested the Armenian villages "to collect weapons." These operations, the witness reports, were accompanied by extreme violence, notably the rape of young women, and also looting. Their other objective is supposed to have been to mobilize males under 20 and over 45 and, according to this account, to make it impossible to travel from one village to another.[75] The same witness also affirms that Turkish friends told him: "Finally, they are going to massacre you, but they are going to confide the task to the *başibozük*, so that the government will later have a way to justify itself." The revelations made at the fifteenth session of the trial of

Yozgat on 28 March 1919 do indeed indicate that one of the first operations carried out in the *kaza* of Boğazlian took place on 19 April 1915. On that day, the *kaymakam* Kemal, the commander of the gendarmerie in Yozgat, Tevfik, and the *müdir* of Şayir Şeyhli, accompanied by 200 gendarmes, searched homes in the village of Çat. Officially, they were looking for weapons and bandits. When they came away empty-handed, they proceeded to arrest part of the male population and committed "every imaginable outrage."[76]

A report by Major Tevfik, read out at the fifteenth session of the trial on 28 March 1919, referred to a rebellion by "bandits" from Çat and suggested deporting the Armenians of this village and replacing them with Muslims. But Cemal Bey, the former *mutesarif* of Yozgat, had pointed out to Tevfik that "[t]he people whom you are today calling bandits were Armenian deserters and deportees."[77] Questioned about this "rebellion" at the eighth session of the trial of Yozgat on 21 February 1919, Colonel Şahabeddin, commander of the Fifteenth Division, based in Kayseri, admitted that Major Tevfik had asked him "to dispatch soldiers to put down a rebellion," and that he had sent 200 men to Boğazlian. When a defense lawyer, Levon Remzi, asked him "how many Armenians took part in the revolt," the Colonel asked permission to leave the court "for a breath of fresh air," answering only after coming back into the room that "the number of Armenian insurgents was five or six; these people had taken refuge in the mountains."[78] This episode, revolving around a handful of fugitive deserters, shows that Major Tevfik had "concocted" a story of rebellion to justify in advance the exactions carried out first in Çat, and then in the other Armenian villages.

The operation aimed at eliminating males from the rural areas did not in fact begin until 28 June 1915, when Tevfik and a battalion of "gendarmes" returned to Çat and the neighboring village of Terzilli. A town crier, Hasan Çokradan, demanded that all Armenian males between ages 15 and 65 agree to join the army. One thousand one hundred fifty people complied. They were immediately tied together in pairs and then divided into two groups. The first, conducted by Sergeant Kemal, was sent toward Kemal Goğazi, where *çetes* massacred the men. The second was personally escorted by Tevfik Bey to the village of Eşikli, where they had their throats cut, after which their bodies were dumped into a mass grave.[79]

Two weeks later, the authorities came back and promised the women that they would be spared if they handed over between ten and 50 Turkish pounds. The *kaymakam* Kemal, who had recently returned to Boğazlian with an escort of 15 gendarmes, now arrived in Çat. There he singled out 995 women and children to be put to death in the Akdere gorge.[80]

According to evidence that the Indian Colonel Mehmed – a British subject and prisoner-of-war – gave during the fifteenth session of the Yozgat trial on 28 March 1915, the town crier had demanded that the Armenians of Boğazlian enter their names in a register, after which they were taken prisoner and then led from the village in small groups. A few days later, the Indian colonel learned that "all the prisoners were led up into the mountains and massacred." Naturally curious, Colonel Mehmed had followed a group of men "who were massacred in a valley nearby." He also said that Turkish travelers from the surrounding villages who arrived in Boğazlian had reported that the corpses of Armenians could be found throughout the area and that it had been unbearable to travel through it because of the stench filling the atmosphere."[81] Asked by the presiding judge to provide further details, Mehmed affirmed that on the day in question, 50 to 60 people had been massacred; that the following day, women and children had been murdered in the same spot; and that the murderers, who had been wearing military uniforms, had been under the command of İhsan Çavuş. This testimony was contradicted by Kemal, who affirmed that the Indian prisoner-of-war "could not have left the city" and thus not have followed a convoy. The colonel retorted, "I was perfectly free and could come and go as I pleased in Boğazlian." To prove that what he had said about these crimes was true, he declared that he could take anyone to the place where they had been committed: "The Armenians' bones are visible there even today."[82]

A Turkish notable from Yozgat also pointed out that Major Tevfik had ordered the village of Kümküyü burned down in the middle of the night while the inhabitants were asleep. Six hundred people died.[83] It was without a doubt that after this testimony was given, on 4 February 1919, the court-martial sent the *mutesarif* of Yozgat a letter, asking for detailed information about Tevfik's accomplices. The major, they wrote, "had scattered inflammable material around the Armenian village of Kümküyü ... burned it down ... hacked the surviving children to pieces in their cradles and ordered others to do the same."[84]

Another source says that the inhabitants of 23 villages in the *kaza* of Boğazlıan were massacred from 5 July on.[85] From still another source, we learn that the worker-soldiers recruited to transport the wheat harvest to Angora were murdered on their way back,[86] and also that a squadron of *çetes* invested the villages of Sarıhamza, Daşlıgetçit, and Pöhrenk to "recruit soldiers" – that is, to arrest all the males and liquidate them in a secluded valley.[87] According to Movses Papazian, a native of the village of Pöhrenk, around 1,000 *çetes*, accompanied by gendarmes, took part in these operations to purge the villages of their Armenian population.[88] Major Tevfik, interrogated during the pretrial interrogation conducted by the Istanbul court-martial, implied that he had been the "president of the Organization's Bureau" – which is to say, the local head of the *Teşkilât-ı Mahsusa* – and had had the commanding officers of several squadrons of *çetes* under his orders: Sükrü, Ceridzâde Hasan, and İbrahim.[89] But it is probable that Tevfik deliberately hid the identities of his accomplices, who are known from other sources as the leader of the Unionists in the *kaza* Aya Bey, as well as Major Şükrü Bey and the assistant to the imperial prosecutor Refik Bey, both of whom helped Kemal Bey organize the massacre of the Armenian population of the *kaza*. They were assisted by the following *çete* chiefs: İzzetbeyoğlu İbrahim; Zekioğlu Ormanci Hasan; Kadioğlu Haydar Bey; Mehmedoğlu Ibrahim Bey; Mehmedoğlu Said; Hasan Bey; Tevfik Bey; Ali Bey; Fahri Bey; Kâtibi Ahmed Damadi; Hoca Abedinzâde Tevfik; Mazhar Bey, a judge; Şevket Bey, a former commander of the gendarmerie; Nizami Ali Bey; Kara Sabri Bey; Abdüllah Effendi; Selimli Yusuf; Bakırcizâde Mahmud; Tevfikzâde Abdüllah; Ahmedzâde Abdüllah; Arapoğlu Abdurrahman; Çapanlardan Derviş Bey; Şevket Bey; Avadalluoğlu Mehmed; Şükrü Çavuş; Yemenici Ahmed Usta; Çerkez Kelçeçe; Kürt Hüseyin; and Zeyn Ağa Ahmed, who were considered to bear the main responsibility for the massacre of around 30,000 people in the *kaza* of Boğazlıan.[90]

According to an Armenian witness, every day, in methodical fashion, the *çetes* dealt with five villages. The proceeded to arrest both the men who were exempt from military service and also the notables, who were all tied up and put to death outside the villages, after which their bodies were stripped and thrown into mass graves. The *çetes* then rounded up the males over 12, who were led off to a "slaughter-house for adolescents" located in Hacılar, halfway between Akrak Maden and Boğazlıan.[91] Thereafter, the rest of the population – women and girls of all ages, old men, and boys 12 and under – was assembled in a field near the village. Here the children were separated from their mothers; the women who tried to interfere with these abductions were killed on the spot. Kızılbaş and Çerkez villagers from the vicinity were thereupon invited to come loot the abandoned villages. With the help of pack animals, they took all the available goods from the villages and then helped massacre the survivors and burn the bodies.[92] A number of children of both sexes up to the age of 11 were taken off to the city and placed in "orphanages."[93] Dr. M. Kechyan dates the end of operations in the rural areas of the *sancak* to 7 August, estimating the number of victims at 40,000.[94]

The military authorities seem to have taken a special interest in the fate of the men apprehended in the villages. Telegrams exchanged within the Fifth Army show that its chief commanding officer personally inquired into the destination of the smallest group of these men and also into the number of men slain, so that he could provide his minister with an account. In other words, the army was at least implicated in the liquidation of the men, conscripts or not. The military commander of Boşazlian, for example, informed his superior in a 27 July 1915 telegram that the *kaymakam* had publicly announced the massacre of 1,500 Armenians, whose names were recorded in a register that the military authorities twice asked Kemal Bey to hand over to them, unsuccessfully.[95] Another document mentions the arrest of 14 "suspects" in Boğazlian and its environs; the men, we read, were "dispatched to their place of exile tonight."[96] The interim commander-in-chief of the Fifth Army, Halil Recayi, plainly found this response unsatisfactory; he insisted that a subordinate of his inform him as soon as possible in what direction "the individuals in question had been sent off."[97] His 5 August wire to the interim commander of the Fifteenth Division in Kayseri, Colonel Şehabeddin, reveals that the military commander of Boğazlian, Mustafa Bey, had informed him that these Armenians had been murdered by a gendarme, Hüseyin Avni, "because they were dangerous."[98] Examined at the seventh session of the trial of Yozgat on 18 February 1919, Halil Recayi Bey acknowledged that the [government] commission of inquiry had questioned him "about the telegrams connected with the massacre of the Armenians in Boğazlian," especially a message that he had received from Colonel Şehabeddin in which Şehabeddin informed him that 130 Armenians from Yozgat who had been dispatched to Boğazlian had been massacred by gendarmes near Cevizli Han.[99] An 8 February 1919 exchange between the court-martial and the new *mutesarif* of Yozgat further indicates that certified copies of 16 telegrams between Şehabeddin Bey and the *kaymakam* of Boğazlian had been forwarded to the court. But they seem not to have been made public.[100] They were at most mentioned at the sixteenth session of the trial on 29 March 1919 in the state prosecutor's indictment. The magistrate described these telegrams as "proofs still more terrible than the testimony that has been heard." Despite this damning evidence, Colonel Şehabeddin denied, at the eighth trial session on 21 February 1919, of "having received an official deportation order for the Armenians of Yozgat or having had contacts with the authorities" of that city. At the seventh session on 18 February 1919, the interim commander of the Fifth Army, Halil Recayi Bey, declared that he had informed his superiors of the crimes committed in the Boğazlian area, probably in an attempt to protect himself from being accused of anything. As he told it, his superiors had instructed him "not to interfere in matters connected with the deportation," because that was "the task of the civilian authorities."

In light of this handful of documents, we can put forward the hypothesis that the army, in coordination with the local structures of the Special Organization, had been involved in particular in eliminating the men of the vilayet, while leaving the chore of liquidating the women and children in the *Teşkilât-ii Mahsusa*'s hands.

As for the role of the civilian administration, the complicity of the *kaymakam* Kemal Bey in the massacres of Boğazlian has been attested to by many witnesses. At the fifteenth session of his trial on 28 March 1919, Kemal attempted to deny that "such an event" had taken place, but was confronted with testimony from his "colleagues" that established that "a majority of the Armenian deportees from Boğazlian were liquidated." When the presiding judge asked him if he had "received instructions from a department" of the government in this connection, Kemal responded that he had not received any such instructions; to the contrary, the central government had told him to transfer the money once the deportees had been settled in the localities earmarked for them. "We deported the Armenians for military reasons," he declared.

The parliamentary deputy from Yozgat, Şakir Bey, questioned at the fourth session of the 11 February 1919 trial of Yozgat, stated that he had "sent a protest to Atıf Bey, the vali of Angora," but that Atıf had not taken it "into account," like the protest that he had sent to

Talât, who "had not given it any account," and had asked him: "Are you the protector of the weak?" As far as the *çetes* were concerned, he did not deny that "criminals had been released from prison," but said he had been "persuaded that they were sent to the front."

The only known case of resistance by victims occurred in Kümküyü, in the Akdağmaden area, where a few young men managed to escape when their village was burned down and took to the maquis. As we have seen, this incident was "blown up" by Tevfik Bey to justify the intervention of the army reinforced by *çetes*.[101] A witness who also took an active part in these events, Movses Papazian, states that their group soon included some 30 people. He adds that on 25 November 1915, they were attacked by 150 gendarmes in the Akdağ area, and were then attacked again on 10 December 1915 in the Maden area by four battalions of regular troops under the orders of the military commander of Yozgat. Each time they succeeded in escaping.[102] Certain members of the group even tried to free, by violent means, relatives of theirs being held in villages of the region.[103] Over the next few months, worker-soldiers who had deserted their labor battalions in the Kayseri area swelled their ranks until they constituted a sizeable fighting force.[104] On 15 June 1916, the military commander of Kayseri arrived in the Maden region at the head of a considerable force with the intention of liquidating the Armenian resistance group. This time, a number of young men were unable to escape their pursuers.[105] A dozen of those who did then decided to head for Samsun. On 1 July 1916, they left the region by way of Zile, wearing gendarme's uniforms. Five days later, they crossed the Amasia Bridge without hindrance; procuring food and basic necessities in the Turkish-speaking Greek villages they encountered along the way. Finally, after a 13-day trek, they joined the resistance groups in Samsun, Ordu, and Sinop.[106]

Massacres in the *Kaza* of Yozgat

The 5 August 1915 appointment of Kemal Bey as *mutesarif* of Yozgat coincided, as we have said, with the end of operations in the rural areas of the *kaza* of Boğazlian. With that, the fate of more than 9,000 Armenians of Yozgat and the surrounding localities seem to have been sealed. On 8 August, Bishop Tanielian and 471 notables from the city were arrested and "deported."[107] According to Azniv Ibranosian, the gendarmes told the Armenians to report to Vehbi Bey, the Director of the Treasury, and then arrested them in Yozgat's marketplace.[108] For his part, an Armenian who served in the army on Captain Husni Bey's staff in Yozgat observes that he crossed paths with Uzun Ahmed, the secretary general of the municipality, at the head of a group of *çetes* who shouted "our mothers brought us into the world for this day" as they arrested Armenians in their homes.[109] In addition to the interim *mutesarif* Kemal and the commander of the gendarmerie Tevfik, a third individual, Feyaz Ali Bey, an official in the *Evkaf* (Land Registry Office), seems to have played a major role in the liquidation of the city's Armenians. According to a 4 February 1919 letter sent by the presiding judge at the Istanbul court-martial to the *mutesarif* of Yozgat, during the deportations Feyaz Bey was the head of a committee "that met and worked in the Armenian church." This committee alone was empowered to issue a *vesikat* or a "suitable for deportation."[110] We have other information that allows us to give an exact description of the procedure that culminated in the arrest and execution of the men. According to Major Tevfik, "the Armenians to be deported were first registered." At the fourteenth session of the Yozgat trial on 26 March, Kemal even stated that it was a lieutenant in the gendarmerie, Hulusi Bey, who "drew up the registers with the lists of deportees."[111] Tevfik added that he then informed "the high authorities of the number of Armenians who had been deported toward Der Zor" and that he also gave "instructions to the *müdirs* of the *nahies*, who, in turn, transmitted "orders and instructions to the officers in their respective branches of the gendarmerie," with the help of "registers prepared in advance."[112] Thus, we see the machinery maintained by the civilian and military authorities, rounded out by the parallel structures of the Special Organization, which for its part was concerned with the illegal dimension of the process.

At the same trial session, the prosecutor presented a document written by the interim *mutesarif* of Yozgat contained in an envelope bearing three red stripes. The following was written between the stripes: "When you arrive in the village of Battal, this letter should be remitted to the Effendis Bakırcizâde Mahmud, Abdüllah, and Mehmed. The envelope should be opened after the date, hour, and seal have been recorded." The sealed envelope contained two letters: one, addressed to Şükrü, the commander of the gendarmerie, ordered him to obey the three people just named; the other said that "women and girls should be divested of their possessions, which should be transferred to the city of Yozgat." The prosecutor pointed out the contradiction in this order: "The possessions of these women and girls were already available in the city from which they had been deported. Consequently, when he says that their possessions should be transported to Yozgat, he simply means that these women and girls should be killed, and that their possessions should be collected and sent on to the city."[113] To the best of our knowledge, this is the only document of this sort currently available. Composed in a style characteristic of the Young Turks, it strikes an administrative tone to express criminal intent. Kemal Bey was not in error when he declared, in the face of all the evidence, that the seal in question was not his and that the handwritten note on the envelope was not in his writing. He went even further, affirming that he had not "issued these instructions," since his "orders had been to protect the Armenians."[114] It is, moreover, noteworthy that one of the three men whom he said should be obeyed, Bakırcizâde Mahmud, was the head of a squadron of *çetes*,[115] whom he had probably orally entrusted with the task of liquidating the Armenians in the village involved. It is precisely in this case that we can observe firsthand the collusion between the administration and the paramilitary groups of the *Teşkilât-ı Mahsusa*. The main governmental actors here were Tatar Mehmed Said Bey, the police chief; his assistant Numan Bey; Nuhlis Bey and Hulusi, lieutenants in the gendarmerie; Haci Abedinzâde Tevfi, a secretary at the courthouse in Yozgat; Mazhar, a *şeri* [bailiff]; and Dağistanlı İsmail, the head of the deportations office.[116] Shortly after the departure of the first convoy of men, a second group made up of 300 men was sent to Dere Mumlu, a four-hour march from the city, where all those in it were massacred with the exception of a handful of survivors, such as our witness.[117] According to the same source, 600 prisoners from Yozgat were still confined in the town jail, along with 42 people from Istanbul,[118] who were probably among the elite of the capital who had been deported on 24 April 1915. Another witness indicates that Kemal Bey was present at the departure of one of these convoys, which was expedited to a secluded valley near the village of Keller. The men were there tied together and escorted by gendarmes with bayonets fixed to the barrels of their rifles.[119] In February 1919, the judge presiding at the Istanbul court-martial discovered that a register containing the name of more than 1,500 Armenians killed in the vicinity of Boğazlian was to be found in Yozgat, in the possession of the military commander. However, despite insistent, repeated demands, the judge was unable to obtain it.[120]

Concerning the role of the gendarmerie, in particular that of its commander, Tevfik, the non-Turkish witnesses indicate that Tevfik had with his men escorted most of the convoys to Taş Punar and Keller, where the deportees were massacred with knives and axes.[121] One of the survivors of these death caravans, Simon, states that in Yozgat people did not use the word *tehcir* (deportation) to describe the Armenians' fate, but, rather, *kasim* (massacre).[122] Azniv Ibranossian sums up the role of the *mutesarif*'s two collaborators this way: "Tevfik took charge of killing them and Feyaz, of looting them."[123] The detailed interrogation to which Major Tevfik was subjected at the thirteenth session of the trial did not reveal anything new. He contented himself with the statement that he had received the order to deport the Armenians and that he had carried it out and that a committee had been created to "collect the deportees' money in order to shield it against possible acts of pillage and, later, restore it to its owners." He declared that he had "in no way been responsible for the deportation carried out when Kemal was *mutesarif* of Yozgat" and that he had "carried out deportations when Cemal Bey was *mutesarif*." Tevfik added that he had only done his "duty." When he was criticized for leaving these deportees without any of the basic necessities, he retorted that he had not received "any instructions to distribute food to the deportees," but supposed that "the population came to their aid in Anatolia."[124] His contradictory remarks were obviously intended to exonerate him of the blame for the massacres committed under Kemal's authority, despite the evidence that had accumulated against him, the leader of the *Teşkilat-ı Mahsusa* in the *sancak* of Yozgat.

Thanks to the trial of the criminals of Yozgat, we also have a broad range of information about the activities of the committee responsible for "abandoned property," headed by the leader of the city's Young Turk club, Feyaz Bey, who was assisted by several local notables: Kara Salih, Çarşi Ağasi Şevket, Kambur Kalfa Nuri, Savfet, Nazıf and Nizanin Ali Kara Fabri.[125] We know that the committee supervised by Feyaz established its headquarters in the Armenian church,[126] where goods confiscated from the massacred deportees were stocked.[127] Examined at the thirteenth session of the Yozgat trial, Feyaz denied that he had been a member of the CUP or played a "role in the deportations." When the presiding judge asked him how he happened to possess "the episcopal ring of Yozgat's Armenian primate," he declared that he had bought "a ring from the liquidation committee," not "taken it from the primate's finger."[128] The inquiries carried out after the armistice also show that Feyaz had appropriated, on the farm of Ellin in the village of Eşekciler, near Keller, "the money and valuables of certain convoys of Armenian deportees who had perished or been slain" with the complicity of the tinsmith Mahmud, Major Tevfik, and his assistants Haydar and Hüseyin, as well as the gendarmes Adıl, Abdüllah, Nuri, Hakkı, Mustafa, Hasan, İmamzâde Şakir, Başı Kel Ahmed, and Kara Ali.[129]

On the testimony of Dr. Mgrdich Kecheyan, it was only on 20 August – that is, after the men had been liquidated – that the Armenians of Yozgat were informed of the order to deport them, except for families of conscripts. Once the news had been made known, the women sold their moveable assets at low prices and the committee immediately had their houses sealed.[130] The first convoy from Yozgat, comprising approximately 2,000 women and children, left the city on 22 August by the road leading south.[131] Waiting for it on the highway at Armağan, an hour's distance from Yozgat, was a colleague of Feyaz's, Vehbi Bey (we have already noted Vehbi's part in the dismissal of the *mutesarif* Cemal Bey, as well as his influence in the local Ittihadist club).[132] The head of the committee responsible for "abandoned property," Vehbi was charge with relieving the deportees of their cash and valuables. As we have seen elsewhere, he and his assistant Etam, who were well informed about the worth of each family, suggested that the Armenians entrust their possessions to them in order to avoid being looted on the road. Observing the exiles' reluctance, they ordered a dozen brigades to subject them to a methodical search.[133] It took the malefactors no less than five days to divest the deportees of most of what they possessed. Thereafter, the convoy was sent on to Incirli. On 27 August, these women and children were surrounded somewhat further south in Karahacılı by Turkish and Çerkez villagers of both sexes, who proceeded to stage a slaughter survived by only a few girls and children abducted in order to be sold.[134]

The second convoy from Yozgat left on 27 August; it comprised around 1,700 women and children. In Armağan, it was subjected to the same treatment as the first caravan and then sent in the direction of Keller, a village lying a few kilometers off the main road not far from Boğazlian. Emptied of its Armenian population more than a month earlier, the village was serving as a camping ground for several squadrons of Çerkez recruited by the Special Organization and commanded by someone named İliyas. Around 1,000 deportees were methodically massacred there. Spared were a few young women and children to be later sold to the Turks of Boğazlian at around eight and ten *mecid* (Turkish silver money) each. The only remarkable incident to occur during this carnage involved a young man by the name of Dikran who had slipped into the convoy disguised as a woman. He had decided to defend himself, leading a number of the women to fight back as well, by throwing stones or biting their executioners.[135]

A peasant in Eşekciler, Stepan, who was deported to Keller, reports that Kemal had a trumpet that he used to issue the order to begin a massacre.[136] In other words, the *mutesarif* personally made the journey to supervise the liquidation of the deportees. Eugenie Varvarian of Yozgat also testified before the court-martial that Kemal, whom the local populace had nicknamed *Kasab Kaymakam* [the butcher *kaymakam*], had organized massacres with Major Tevfik.[137] There ensued a rather sharp exchange between the young survivor and the state official, who met these accusations with a blanket denial. He protested that he had "never left Yozgat during the deportations and that the girl was a liar who didn't know what she was talking about." The young woman responded: "Kemal is lying when he says that he didn't massacre Armenians. Did all the Armenians commit suicide? Where are most of them now?" She conceded, however, that he did not kill these Armenians "personally," but added that she had heard him shout: "Kill them, kill them; if you don't, I'll kill you."[138] After this butchery, Kemal proceeded to deal with Armenian families who had converted. According to depositions made by Yakub Hoca from the village of Paşa and other witnesses such as the barber Misak from the village of Incirli, and transmitted in an 8 February 1919 report by the presiding judge of the local court-martial, Faik Bey, to the *mutesarif* of Yozgat, Kemal had 70 Protestant families from Incirli massacred before turning his attention to the 250 Armenian families from the village of Karabüyük whom Yakub Hoca had converted to Islam. Kemal met the protests of the Muslim clergyman, who declared that this was not in accordance with the precepts of Islam, with the remark that "you convert the Armenians in accordance with Islamic law and I liquidate them in accordance with my policy."[139] The inspector Nedim Bey, in conclusion to the inquiry he conducted in the locality in December 1918, declared: "Before my conscience, beyond a doubt ... the Armenians had been eliminated in groups and that the person who committed the crime was the *kaymakam*, Kemal Bey. Specifically, it was Kemal Bey who issued the secret orders and informed the commanders of the gendarmerie, who were constantly called on to carry out the crimes."[140]

According to official figures cited before the court-martial during the Yozgat trial, around 33,000 Armenians from the *sancak* of Yozgat were deported, and a majority of them were massacred in Boğazkemin, lying in a valley near Keller, where the *çetes* also engaged in raping little girls and killing babies.[141] Captain Şükrü, who served in Yozgat's gendarmerie, says in his "confessions" that the massacres were carried out on the orders of the interior minister and that the traces of these massacres "were wiped out in late October, when huge mass graves were dug in which the bodies were thrown and then burned, but that the winter rains exposed rotting corpses and bones." Şükrü affirms that, with the exception of the first convoy from Çorum deported in early July 1915, very few of the deportees escaped death:

> It is a secret for no one that 62,000 Armenians were massacred in our *sancak*. This surprised even us, because the government itself did not know how many Armenians there had been in the province of Angora. A few thousand of them came from other provinces; the necessary steps were taken to ensure that they would pass our way, because we wanted to slaughter them. We received the orders to exile the Armenians, or, to employ the precise formulation, to conduct the Armenians from the towns and villages and then to massacre them, from the headquarters of the committee of the Ittihad or the minister of the interior.[142]

Şükrü also observes that after the news of the massacres of Angora had made its way to Constantinople: The German embassy protested and the government sent a commission of inquiry to Angora, but we knew perfectly well that the real motivation for this commission was simply to show that the government had not in any way taken part in the massacres." Thereafter, he adds, "instructions were issued by Constantinople to take the measures required to prevent Europeans and, especially, American missionaries, from being given information about the massacres perpetrated in the interior of Anatolia."[143]

The commission of inquiry that was dispatched to Yozgat late in 1915 concluded that "illicit gains" had been made there "at the cost of the committee responsible for abandoned property" and judged Kemal and his accomplices for these acts. However, it never accused them of homicide.[144] Kemal, after admitting in his initial deposition that he had only been tried for "illicit gain," retracted his statement and incessantly affirmed that he had already been tried for homicide and thus did not understand why he was being tried again for a matter that had already been judged before the courts. Asked about this by the Istanbul court-martial, the investigating magistrate in the Yozgat trial, Nedim Bey, responded that "[n]o murder investigation was conducted or could have been, because the higher orders that [he] had received bore only on an investigation of illicit gain." Nedim further stated that Kemal had appeared before the court as an "accused party in liberty"; it is inconceivable that he would not have been in detention if he had been indicted for homicide.[145] As we have pointed out elsewhere, the 1916 proceedings against Kemal confirm that the court-martial had instructions to judge state officials for "illicit gain" while ignoring the mass crimes that they had committed.

While the pillage of Armenian property in Yozgat took place under basically the same conditions as had obtained elsewhere,[146] it is noteworthy that in this *sancak* the *mutesarif* was personally implicated in the plunder. Questioned at the fifteenth session of the trial of those who had organized the Yozgat massacres on 28 March 1919, Vehbi Bey, the president of the committee responsible for "abandoned property," maintained that Kemal Bey "remitted the lists of Armenian deportees, and it was only after receiving them that [he] collected the superfluous moneys [sic] in the possession of the Armenian deportees and recorded them in a special registry."[147] He also admitted at the next session that he had sought out Armenians who had refused to put their "trust" in him – that is, to entrust their assets to him – but he only mumbled a few unintelligible words when asked if these acts were lawful.

Among those who made "illicit gains," Major Tevfik was charged with having collected five Turkish pounds from thousands of recruits or deserters of all confessions in exchange for keeping them from being sent to the front.[148] A well-informed witness also evoked the gifts that Tevfik gave his brothers, the goods that he sent to Constantinople and Eskişehir, the rugs and kilims that he sent to Çorum, and the real estate that he sold off, such as the Apkarian farm in Yozgat that he sold for 5,000 Turkish pounds. Mufteri Rifât observes that, with Necati's consent, Tevfik laid hands on many other Armenians' goods and property, which he registered in his brother Hosrov Bey's name.[149] At the seventh trial session on 18 February 1919, it was also revealed that this simple major in a gendarmerie had acquired a farm worth from 30,000 to 40,000 Turkish pounds.[150] Another member of the committee responsible for "abandoned property," Nazif Bey, was accused of "accumulating enormous wealth" and sending 36,000 pounds to Constantinople.[151]

In the face of these multiple accusations of illicit gain and mass murder, Kemal adopted a line of defense that was particularly symptomatic of the climate of the period. At the sixteenth trial session on 29 March 1919, he justified his acts as follows: "The Armenians were domestic foes of the Turkish people and the Muslim religion; the members of the Armenian political parties were separatists." Repeating Young Turk discourse for the occasion, he no longer denied the acts of which he was accused, but gave his listeners to understand that he had simply implemented government policy. The defense strategy adopted by Major Tevfik's lawyer, Hami Bey, was in the same vein. He began by legitimating the seizure of Armenian assets on the grounds that the government's concern had been to prevent the deportees from being pillaged on the road. Above all, he accused the Armenians of being responsible for the massacres by virtue of their provocative revolutionary activities. He also contended that "[t]he Armenians massacred one million Muslims, whereas the Turks massacred only two hundred thousand [Armenians]." The Istanbul press with Ittihadist sympathies published more or less the same sort of discourse in its newspapers.

At a banquet organized to celebrate the end of the operations, it was revealed that Kemal Bey, Major Tevfik, and Feyaz Bey had made a toast to "the Armenians' health."[152]

Several sources indicate that a second operation was carried out in February 1916 by Kemal's successor, Agah Bey, also a Unionist, against 1,300 to 1,500 women and children working as slaves in Turkish households in the region. These survivors, arrested on the new *mutesarif*'s initiative, were massacred locally.[153]

The *Kazas* of Süngürlü, Çorum, and Akdağmaden

The main Armenian community in Süngürlü, 1,000 strong, was to be found in the principal town in the *kaza*, located at its southernmost tip. There were a few other small, dispersed groups in the *kaza*, bringing the total Armenian population to 1,936.[154] All were liquidated in the *kaza* itself in the course of July 1915.[155]

The 3,520 Armenians in the *kaza* of Çorum lived in five localities: 1,020 in Çorum, 1,500 in Ekrek, and the rest in Bozok, Hüseyinabad, and Alaca (pop. 400).[156] With the exception of the first convoy from Çorum, which set out early in July for the Syrian deserts by way of Boğazlian and Bozanti,[157] the groups of deportees were liquidated by *çetes* from Angora under the supervision of the *kaymakam* Nureddin Bey, who held his post from 22 November 1913 to 27 March 1916.[158] The 3,361 Armenians from the *kaza* of Akdağmaden lived mainly in Akdağ, the seat of the *kaza* (pop. 1,300), Delihamza (pop. 250), and Karaçayer (pop. 300).[159] Major Ahmed, the military commander in Akdağmaden, informed the *mutesarif*, Cemal, in a cable dated 11/12 July 1915, that "public order" had in no way been perturbed in his *kaza*, that there had never been an attack by an "Armenian band," and that it was only after the looting of the village of Terzilli by gendarmes that the villagers fled into the mountainous areas of his district.[160] Despite these denials, Major Tevfik arrived with a band of *çetes*, burned down the Armenians' houses in Akdağmaden, and slaughtered the population.[161]

Massacres and Deportations in the Sancak *of Kayseri*

Since ancient times Armenians had peopled the outlying *sancak* of Kayseri in the southwestern part of the vilayet of Angora, which covered part of the area of the ancient province of Cappadocia. In this respect, Kayseri differed from the other districts in the province. The presence of an Armenian population here is attested since the third and fourth centuries of our epoch. It increased over time: after the Arabs conquered part of Asia Minor, Armenian colonists were settled here by the Byzantines in order to strengthen the military marches of the Taurus. On the eve of the First World War, there were still 31 towns and villages inhabited by more than 52,000 Armenians in this *sancak*. These possessed 40 churches, seven monasteries, and 56 schools with an overall enrolment of 7,119.[162]

In the city of Kayseri, located in the central *kaza*, the 18,907 Armenians were concentrated in 28 of the city's 114 neighborhoods in 1914, representing approximately 35 per cent of the total population. Cesarea's economic importance hardly needs to be demonstrated. By this time, the city's international trade had declined sharply, but this regression was partially compensated by Anatolian commerce. Gold-working, leather-tanning, and rug-making were especially thriving crafts. Five kilometers southwest of Cesarea, the village of Talas, albeit on the decline in the early twentieth century, still had an Armenian population of 1,894, representing 42 per cent of its total population. In the upper quarter, where the most affluent social strata resided, were magnificent homes, located on streets that bore the names of the most prestigious families: the Gulbenkians, Turabians, Selians, and so on. The village of Derevank (310 Armenians), just northeast of Talas, dominated the entry to a valley in which there lay a string of Armenian villages: Tavlusun (pop. 115), Germir (pop. 365), Balages (pop. 923) – on the outskirts of which lay the immense monastery of St. Daniel, established in the mid-eleventh century and demolished a few days after all the inhabitants of Balages were deported – Mancesen (pop. 386), Nirze and the adjoining village of Darsiak (pop. 835), with the monastery of St. Gregory, founded in 1206, a quarter of an hour away. The villages of Muncusun (pop. 1,669) and Evkere/Gasi (pop. 2,154) closed off the northern extremity of the valley that began above Talas, with the famous monastery of St. Garabed, the region's most important spiritual and educational center and also the seat of the diocese's archbishop since the twelfth century. The last of these villages, Erkelet (pop. 300), lay in the northern part of the *kaza*.[163] Thus, there was a non-negligible rural Armenian population, particularly in the *kaza* of Kayseri.

As in many other regions of the Anatolian east, a simmering hostility toward the Armenian population sprang up when the reform plan was signed in February 1914. It found expression notably in the economic boycott launched by local Young Turk circles. More than the ban on buying products in Armenian shops, marked with red crosses painted on the storefronts, it was the barely veiled threats that reminded the Armenians just how much their fate depended on the *milletı hakime* [ruling nation]. Curiously, in the same period, the Ittihad agreed to promote the election of the teacher Garabed Tumanyan to the Ottoman parliament as the deputy for Kayseri, and he was elected in 20 March 1914.[164] In the weeks following the general mobilization, the Armenian population noticed more obvious signs of discrimination. The requisitions made in the name of the war effort resembled, according to Armenian witness, outright pillage, and the treatment of conscripts, who were mishandled and left without food, was tantamount to a call to desert. In contrast to the regions in the northern part of the vilayet, there were in the *sancak* of Kayseri well-organized networks of Hnchak and Dashnak activists who construed the attitude of the local authorities as a provocation calculated to exasperate the Armenians. A mixed committee made up of the Hnchaks M. Minasian, G. Chidemian, H. Kazazian, and E. Sutjian and the Dashnaks K. Vishabian, G. Khayerlian, and K. Bosdanian was formed in order to apply the instructions these activists had received from the leaderships of their respective parties – to avoid "a revolt and meet the government's demands."[165]

It would appear that, during the mobilization, the Armenians of draftable age left for the army without protest and that no particular incident troubled order in the region. However, it is noteworthy that Armenian civil servants were dismissed in April.[166] By all accounts, an incident that occurred in Everek in February touched off an extremely violent repressive campaign. A young man who had recently returned from the United States, Kevork Defjian, blew himself up while manipulating a handmade explosive device. Immediately, the *kaymakam* of the *kaza* of Develu was dismissed and replaced by Salih Zeki Bey, who was charged with carrying out an inquiry that was given extraordinary public notice.[167] It is probable that Zeki had instructions to exploit the incident to put the party activists under pressure. In the first half of March, he had a number of Armenian homes in Everek searched and arrested a certain number of politicians and notables, who were interned in the *konak*'s jail. According to several witnesses, gendarmes beat prisoners to death every evening in the courtyard of the *konak* under the eyes of local Young Turks and the *kaymakam* Zeki, who, glass of cognac in hand, seemed to find the spectacle entertaining. Hovhannes Barsamian and Hovagim Chilingirian died under torture; Hagop Bozakian was quartered; Asadur Minasian's chest was covered with live coals on which the executioners made coffee; Hagop Madaghjiyan had horseshoes nailed to his feet and tried to commit suicide to put an end to his ordeal.[168] The official objective was to make these men confess where they had hidden their weapons. On 30 March 1915, Zeki Bey ordered the arrests of a few notables in the surrounding villages, especially Çomaklu/Chomakhlu and Incesu. He ordered a second round of arrests on 14 May, imprisoning all those taken into custody in Everek, where they were tortured to make them reveal where they had concealed their arms.[169] Several incidents illustrate the local authorities' determination to whip the Muslim population up against the Armenians. For example, a sort of infernal "machine" was exhibited in the courtyard of the *konak*, and the multitudes were invited to come inspect it. It was in fact a machine for making sugar imported from Europe. Zeki, however, told one and all that the machine was used to send wireless telegrams and "make thousands of rifles daily." The machine's owner, who had been arrested, was urged to confess this.[170] A second example testifies to the spirit reigning at the time and the way the public's naivety was exploited: the village of Tashkhan was attacked and the authorities announced that a "cannon" had been seized there – what was involved was in fact a salt cauldron. The upshot was the condemnation of 42 men by Kayseri's court-martial.[171]

These events were obviously not without consequence in Kayseri, where the *mutesarif*, Ahmed Midhat, deftly exploited the effect that they produced in order to attack the city's Armenian elite. The first to be arrested was a leading public activist, Garabed Jamjian, the president of the diocesan assembly and the local branch of the Armenian General Benevolent Union. This respected businessman was arrested on Thursday, 29 April in his home in Kayseri and paraded through the Muslim neighborhoods of the city in chains as a dangerous separatist, under a hail of insults from the crowd.[172] It was probably no accident that the authorities' choice had alighted on Jamjian, who was deeply involved in civic affairs, but not at all in the local Armenian political clubs. There is good reason to think that by neutralizing someone capable of presenting the authorities with a credible point of view, Midhat wanted to deal the community a severe blow at the outset and show that even someone regarded as respectable was implicated in the Armenian "separatist" movement. The announcement that the Hnchak leaders had been indicted in Istanbul on 28 April 1915 – the day before Jamjian was arrested – for "disturbing public order and rebellion"[173] marked the beginning of an operation aimed at neutralizing the Armenian elites in the provinces. The arrests of Kayseri's Dashnak leader, Kevork Vishabian, and his Hnchak counterpart, Minas Minasian,[174] clearly reflected the authorities' concern to act with a semblance of legality so as not to drive the Armenian population into despair and precipitate the revolt of which "the" Armenians had been accused in advance. Without a doubt, it was this maneuver that convinced other Armenian leaders that the only targets of these operations were a handful of ranking politicians and that, consequently, they had an interest in remaining circumspect and complying with the authorities in order to safeguard the security of the population. According to an unconfirmed source, the order to turn in weapons was immediately made public. Between 20 and 25 May, a general meeting of Armenian leaders was held in Kayseri and a majority of those present came out in favor of obeying the order by handing over all weapons. A witness, Vahan Elmayan, reports that all the weapons were delivered up "regardless of the fact that we could then no longer count on help from anyone."[175] According to the American missionary Clara C. Richmond, who had been working in Talas and Kayseri for several years, the Armenians had indeed acquired large numbers of weapons after the 1909 massacres in Cilicia in order to defend themselves should the need have arisen.[176] It is probable that the authorities were aware of this and sought to bring this arsenal under control before revealing their true objectives.

In the process of bringing the Armenians under suspicion, a campaign that had been fabricated out of thin air against the primate, Bishop Khosrov Behrigian, the details of which we have already noted,[177] doubtless also played an important role. Accused in mid-June of collusion with the enemy, and also "of complicity ... with the revolutionary movements,"[178] the bishop of Cesarea constituted another choice target for the authorities. For lack of concrete evidence, the court-martial in Kayseri finally "granted Behrigian the benefit of mitigating circumstances,"[179] but official discourse continued to present him as "one of those who had inspired the preparations for revolution and the revolutionary movement, the object of which was to create in the future an Armenian state."[180] The accusation of separatism, leveled against the Armenian population in the middle of a war, was the core of Young Turk discourse. Clearly, the actions of the authorities in Kayseri were designed to credit this charge. The "discovery" of "cannons" and other supposedly lethal machines was also intended to buttress the official propaganda campaign, which a few months later painted Behrigian as the leader of a "movement" that aspired to "obtain the independence of Armenia."[181] The 15 June hanging of 11 members of the Armenian elite in the Kömür Bazar[182] – that is, on the day when the bishop was condemned and the 20 Hnchak leaders were executed in Istanbul – was probably another move designed to leave a strong mark on people's minds and credit the thesis of an Armenian conspiracy. The political and sociological profile of the 11 men condemned to death in Kayseri, among whom were only two local political leaders of the ARF and SDHP, Kevork Vishabian and Minas Minasian, indicates that the authorities were most likely seeking to implicate all the Armenian circles in their accusation of separatism as a generalization of the phenomenon. Thus, we find four important businessmen among the executed Armenians – Hagop Khayirlian, Avedis Zambakjian, Karnig Kuyumjian and Garabed Jamjian; a banker, Hagop Merdinian; a footwear manufacturer, Garabed Shidemian; a rug merchant, Hagop Sudjian; a goldsmith, Garabed Muradian; a jeweler, Hovhannes Nevshehirlian; and a musician, Mirijan Yoghuralashian.[183]

From June 1915 on, when it condemned Bishop Behrigian, the court-martial in Kayseri was uninterruptedly in session. Under, first, the presiding judge Colonel Şehabeddin, succeeded by Lieutenant-Colonel Tevfik Bey, with Ziya Bey as chief prosecutor, Captain Kuçuk Kâzım, the vice-president of the recruitment office and the director of deportations, as judge, and Gübgübzâde Sureya, nicknamed Topal Lutfi, as commander of the gendarmerie, the court-martial condemned in rapid succession the entire Armenian political and economic elite of Kayseri, under the direct supervision of the Ittihad's special delegate, Cemil Bey.[184]

In the end, the court-martial in Kayseri condemned 54 people to death. Nine more men, mainly from Everek, fell victim to the second round of executions – Krikor Munjihanian, a judge; Krikor Ghachrekian; Harutiun Dayan; Asadur Minasian, a photographer; Harutiun Keleyan, a merchant; Garabed Akhcharian; Manug Euchakjian; Hagop Chibukjian; and the Hnchak deputy Murad (Hampartsum Boyajian) – all of whom were executed before the citadel at three o'clock on the morning of 24 July 1915.[185] Fifteen notables from Kayseri perished in the third round of executions, which took place on 13 August: Toros Nazlian, a physician; Krikor Kuyumjian, a rug merchant; Garabed Nevruzian, a merchant; Mardiros Zurnajian, a carpenter; Vahan Amaduni, a teacher; Avedis Elmajian, a rug merchant; Harutiun Yoghuralashian; Kevork Turkejian, a rug merchant; Parsegh Mutafian; Ghazar Mayisian; Hagop Kazezian; Hovhannes Zeytuntsian; Hovhannes Tavitian; Father Ghevont Gemjian; and Sarkis Tulumjian. The fourth round of executions took place on 2 September. Six men were hanged: Vahan Kumjian, a teacher; Hagop Urzanjian; Hovhannes Boyajian, a teacher; Hagop Balukjian; Garabed Uzunoghlanian; and Hagop Yesayan, a teacher. On 17 September, Dr. Suren Nshanian was hanged; on 26 September, the lawyers Garabed Tashjian and Mardiros Kundakjian, as well as Sarkis Atmajian, a manufacturer of matchsticks, were hanged. On 28 November, it was the turn of the teacher Hagop Berberian and Sahag Kayserlian of Rumdigin to be executed. In the last round of executions, which took place on 16 December 1915, six Armenians from Everek perished: Mihran Kuzian, a merchant; Levon Varzhabedian, an architect; Setrak Chechejenian, a butcher; Sarkis Karagozian, a farmer; Misak Bahanjian, a goldsmith; and Karnig Shemshian, also a goldsmith.[186]

By late September, the court-martial in Kayseri had already condemned 1,095 more people, of whom 857 were executed in the same period.[187] On 21 June 1915, 24 condemned men left by night for Dyarbekir by way of Gemerek; on 11 July, 83 prisoners left by night for Aleppo by way of Nigde and Sıvas; on 12 July, 14 prisoners left by night for Aleppo by way of Azizye; on 13 July, 46 men left by night for Çorum by way of Erkilet; on 17 July, six men left by night for Dyarbekir by way of Gemerek; on 19 July, 36 adults left by night for Dyarbekir by way of Gemerek; on 21 July, 134 condemned men left by night for Aleppo by way of Albistan; on 22 July 54 prisoners left by night for Aleppo by way of Azizye; on 22 July, another group of 28 men left by night for Aleppo by way of Sıvas; on 23 July, 21 people left by night for Aleppo by way of Azizye; on 26 July, 22 people left by night for Aleppo by way of Azizye; on 27 July, 73 prisoners left for Dyarbekir by way of Sıvas; on 28 July, eight people left by night for Aleppo by way of Azizye; on 4 August, 22 men left by night for Aleppo by way of Sıvas; on 15 August, five men left by night for Dyarbekir by way of Gemerek; on 25 August, 11 men left by night for Aleppo by way of Cevizlihan; on 26 August, eight men left by night for Aleppo by way of Cevizlihan; on 28 August, 130 men left by night for Aleppo by way of Cevizlihan; on 4 September, 30 men left for Aleppo by way of Dyarbekir; on 7 September, four men left for Aleppo by way of Dyarbekir; on 7 September, four men left for Aleppo by way of Dyarbekir; on 8 September, four men left by night for Dyarbekir by way of Azizye; on 15 September, four men left by night for Aleppo by way of Dyarbekir; on 24 September, 21 men left by night for Aleppo by way of Nigde; and on 5 October, 620 men left by night for Aziziye by way of Hamidiye. The last-mentioned 620 men were youths between the ages of 14 and 18, most of them Catholic or Protestant, who had been working in an *amele taburi*. They were led to Kayadipi, a valley lying between Gemerek and Şarkışla, and put to death there. This was the same spot on which certain groups of condemned men from Kayseri were executed.[188] The German minister Hans Bauernfeind, traveling through Gemerek on 18 August, encountered 900 worker-soldiers from Kayseri who were working in an *amele taburi* – "most of them merchants" – and 4,000 to 5,000 more "just before Cesarea ... who came from Nigde."[189] We do not know what happened to these men, but it is probable that they too were executed on the road to Sıvas under the supervision of Muammer, whose intermittent interventions in the neighboring vilayet we have already noted.

According to the American missionary Theda Phelps, males over 14 began to be systematically arrested in the first half of July. This gave rise to nightly departures of small caravans, which were dispatched without ado.[190]

Manuel Mgrian, a pharmacist from Everek, observes that 300 Armenians under indictment were held in Kayseri's civilian prison in May 1915, where they were subjected to the most terrible forms of torture. Summoned to the military prison to care for a seriously wounded man, he discovered the Hnchak leader Murad (Hampartsum Boyajian) there – Murad had recently been transferred from Ayaş – as well as a number of Hnchak militants whom the authorities were holding in a separate section of the prison.[191] Gübgübzâde Sureya Bey, a captain in the gendarmerie and the head of the *çetes* of Kayseri and the Special Organization, oversaw the torture sessions with the aid of Küçük Kâzım Bey and his 165 *çetes*; Ali Garib Bey, a parliamentary deputy from Kayseri; Kâtibzâde Nuh; and Camız Imamzâde Reşid.[192] Once the elite had been condemned and eliminated, the police chief Mehmed Zeki Bey and the *mutesarif* of Kayseri Ahmed Midhat took over the court-martial's role. Zeki compiled the lists of people to be executed; Midhat approved them; and for his part, the military commander Colonel

Şehabeddin gave the orders required to have the condemned men deported and murdered. To this end, he communicated with the gendarmerie and the Special Organization, both directed by Gübgübzâde Sureya Bey.

After being held in prison and tortured for several months, the Armenian primate Khosrov Behrigian was put on the road for Urfa on 26 August, accompanied by Bedros Gumshian, Parsegh Tabibian, Dr. Stepan Tabibian, and Parsegh Tokatlian. All five men were murdered together between Urfa and Aleppo a few days later. The auxiliary primate, Father Aristakes Timarian, Panos Kuyumjian, and Hagop Balekjian were murdered around 2 September in the vicinity of Sıvas. Most of the Armenian males of the region were liquidated, however, at a killing field at Kanlı Dere located in the gorge that forms an extension of the plain of Fırıncilar, south of Malatia.

That said, the dimensions of the system that the CUP set up in Kayseri would seem to suggest that the region had been chosen very early on by the leaders in the Nuri Osmaniye as a suitable place in which to fabricate a damning case incriminating "the" Armenians. Thus, one notes the presence in Kayseri of a special party delegate, Yakub Cemil Bey, a former CUP *fedayi* and an important military chief of the Special Organization;[193] Imamzâde Ömer Mumtaz Bey, a Unionist parliamentary deputy; and Draçzâde Nusrullah Bey, the CUP's responsible secretary. These three ranking Ittihadists had the support of local notables: Gübgübzâde Rifât Bey, the president of the Ittihadist club; İbrahim Safa Bey; Çalıkoğlu Rifât Bey, the president of the municipality and one of the organizers of the Special Organization in Kayseri; Katibzâde Nuh; Gözüböyükzâde Sadet; Imamzâde Reşid Bey; Talaslızâde Şaban; Akça Kayalı Rifât; Karabeyzâde Mustafa; Camız Imamzâde Reşid Bey; Dr. Feyzullal, a municipal physician; Draçzâde Sâmi; Nakıbzâde Ahmed; Taşcizâde Ömer; Taşcizâde Mehmed; and Hacılarlı Mustafa.[194]

The involvement of all the ranking civilian and military officials with posts in Kayseri in the organization of the deportations and massacres seems to indicate that the CUP's decision to privilege the area had been a wise one. These officials included Ali Sabri Bey, the *mektubci* [head of the bureau of correspondence]; Colonel Şahabeddin, the commander of the Fifteenth Division; Colonel Şahab; Lieutenant-Colonel Tevfik, the presiding judge at the court-martial; Captain Kuçuk Kazım, the Director of Deportations and the commander of a squadron of 165 *çetes*; Major Lutfi Gübgübzâde Sureya, the commander of the gendarmerie; Major Nureddin, who murdered many Armenian notables; Mehmed Zeki Bey, the police chief; and Zeki's assistants Giritli Sâmi Bey, Çerkez Ahmed Aşım Bey, Besim Bey, Yegenoğlu Mustafa, and Elçizâde Muheddin.[195]

Once the elimination of the men had been secured, the governmental machine went into motion. The general deportation order was made public in both Kayseri and Talas on 8 August 1915.[196] The deportations began five days later in the city's outlying neighborhoods and came to an end with Taldon and the central districts. Armenian assets were confiscated and the Monastery of St. Garabed was converted into an orphanage for "Islamicizing Armenian children," while certain churches (such as St. Gregory's) were transformed into mosques or military depots. While Catholics and Protestants were spared, their property was still confiscated and they were banished to the city's outskirts.[197] Approximately 20,000 people were deported from Kayseri and Talas.[198] The caravans set out on the road that ran through Incesu, Develi, Nidge, Bor and Ulukışla, under the personal supervision of the CUP delegate Yakub Cemil Bey.[199] According to the American missionary Clara Richmond, some of the women converted to Islam on the way and were allowed to return to Kayseri and Talas; children enrolled in the American school were removed from it by the authorities and put in a Turkish orphanage, except for the oldest, who were transferred to a school in Adana; and that still other schoolchildren escaped to the mountains, where they gradually formed a band of 200 children who would later be hunted down and liquidated.[200] In late August and early

September, the American missionaries managed to save a few women and children by admitting them to their hospital in Kayseri. In February 1916, however, the authorities confiscated the American buildings and summoned the last remaining Armenians to convert.[201]

The survivors who got as far as the Syrian frontier were for the most sent on in the direction of Hama, Damascus, Maan, Dera'a, and Kerek. Among the men, only a few physicians were able to remain in Kayseri by converting, such as Dr. Abraham Göcheyan and Sarkis Kaltakjian.[202]

The task of seizing Armenian property was entrusted to a committee responsible for "abandoned property" headed by Nagibzâde Ahmed and Kadili Daniş Bey. Thirteen of their collaborators – Murad Bey, an official in the Land Registry Office; Abdülaziz Bey; Taşcizâde Mehmed; Attarzâde Kâmil; Bohcelizâde Ahmed; Imamzâde Reşid; Imamoğlu Ali; Elekcioğlu Hüsezin; Hacılarlı Mustafa; Ibrahim Safa; Şeyh İbrahimoğlu Fuad; Kâtibzâde Nuh; and Kürkcüzâde Ömer Hulusi – founded a corporation, the *Birlik Cemiyeti*, which acquired the Armenian assets put on sale for virtually nothing. They first acquired a khan and then "purchased" the manufacturing establishments of the Yazejian, Mendigian, Balian, and Jamjian brothers.[203]

Massacres and Deportations in Talas and in the Villages of the *Kaza*

In the neighboring village of Talas, whose population was reputed to be affluent and little interested in politics, it seems that there were great tensions between Sabri Bey, the head of Kayseri's Bureau of Correspondence and a well-known Young Turk, and the *müdir*, Faik. Sabri had been charged with ordering the murder of this official, who demurred at carrying out the orders bearing on the Armenians of his district. Sabri would later be accused of being an accomplice of Yakub Cemil's and of having personally organized the massacres in the villages near Kayseri. The murders of well-known entrepreneurs in Talas or Kayseri, such as Vahan Janjian, Gabriel Kurkjian, Markar Yazejian, Vahan Kehayan, or Kevork Janjian, were chalked up to his account.[204] It is, moreover, patent that the prosperity of the Armenians of Talas had aroused the appetites of certain village notables. Armenian sources note in particular the rapacity of Talaslı Haci Ahmed Effendi; Zâde Osman; Salih Mehmed; Seyeddin Evladları Ali; Mehmed; Tafiloğlu Tevfik; Alizâdeoğlu Kâzım; the president of the municipality of Talas, Ali; Mahmud, a sergeant in the gendarmerie; Hekim Balıhın Hasan; and Eli Küçük Mehmed, who were both the executioners of the Armenians of Talas and also the main beneficiaries of their elimination.[205]

According to the missionary Clara Richmond, employed in the American school in Talas, the notables, beginning with Boghos Agha, were arrested on Sunday, 13 June.[206] The American school's Armenian teachers were arrested shortly afterwards and imprisoned in Kayseri. They were then sent to Gemerek, where they were shot.[207]

In the month of July, the authorities turned their attention to the men of the village of Derevank, located 20 minutes from Talas, and also to the men in other localities in the valley. However, as was also the case in Kayseri, it was not until 8 August that the deportation order was published. On 11 August – that is, on the eve of the departure of the first deportees – Catholics and Protestants were exempted.[208] An Armenian source states that, on the intervention of Dr. Ringate, the departure of the first convoy of deportees was postponed until 18 August and that the deportation was organized neighborhood by neighborhood in three convoys: the most affluent families were deported on 18 August, the poorest families (approximately 1,000 men, women, and children, guarded by gendarmes) were deported on 28 August, and the last Armenians remaining in Talas were deported on 29 August. Our witness was spared, as were some ten other young people, because he volunteered for combat duty. He notes that a handful of Protestant women eluded the deportation by taking employ-ment as servants or nurses.[209] Finally, it should be pointed out that until February 1916, the administration of Talas's American middle school for girls succeeded in protecting 150 of its students. But when the authorities invited them to convert and marry Turks, they all refused to submit and took poison together "to escape from their ferocious guides."[210]

The *Kaza* of Everek/Develi

Five hours southeast of Kayseri, on the southern slope of Mt. Argus, there was still in the early twentieth century a little cluster of 17 localities inhabited by 19,841 Armenians. The principal town of the *kaza* of Everek/Develi, Everek-Fenese, was in fact an agglomeration of two villages that had merged over the years. There were 8,305 Armenians there in 1914, including the nearby hamlet of Ilibe. In the modern period, the neighboring village of Develu, the seat of the *kaymakam*, was also incorporated into the Armenian agglomeration around Everek. At the time, the agglomeration had four quarters: 1) Everek Ermeni (1,000 Armenian households); 2) Everek Islam or Develu (120 Turkish households); 3) Fenese (700 Armenian households); and 4) Aykostan (120 Greek households).[211]

On the eve of the war, the town was thriving, thanks to its production of wine and liqueurs and also to its silkworm production, which provided the raw material for the local silk manufactories. An American orphanage, opened in 1910 for Armenian children whose parents had been massacred the year before in Cilicia, was closed in summer 1914 on orders from the authorities. Çomaklu, which lay 90 minutes from Everek in the foothills of Mt. Argus, was home to 1,679 Armenians in 1914, farmers or artisans from Cilicia. A short dis-tance south of Çomaklu, the village of Incesu had a Turkish-speaking Armenian population of 1,202. Only 273 Armenians lived in Gömedi, located to the southeast. Another 1,115 Turkish-speaking Armenians from Cilicia lived in Cücün.[212]

We have already seen that the accidental explosion of a homemade bomb in Everek touched off a wave of persecution of the Armenians. The main organizer of this was Salih Zeki, the new *kaymakam*. Zeki was assisted by local officials and a few Young Turk nota-bles, such as Ziyali Tosun;[213] Osman Bey, the mayor of Everek; and a few notables who benefited materially from the liquidation of the Armenians: Hafız Effendi; Kantarcı Ali; Kantarcı Mustafa; Pırıncı Mehmed Usta; Hoca Abdüllah; Puruncu Ali Usta Oghlu; Mehmed Tahrirat; and Kantarcı Osman Effendi.[214] The main organizers of the massacres and deporta-tions were, however, members of Everek's Ittihadist club, who created a "secret committee" for the purpose:[215] Hakim Bey, the president of the club; Süleyman Vehbi, the director of the Régie; Mufti Haci Effendi; Ankaralı Ömer; Hafız Effendi; Haci Cafar Abdüllah; Mustafa Effendi; and Stambolu Ahmed.[216]

In March 1915, Salih Zeki began by arresting certain local notables, especially politi-cal activists. He accused the notables of Incesu of "fomenting disorders" and proceeded to arrest the village headman and the village priest, who were tortured in order to make them "reveal" the names of the "troublemakers." Around mid-May, Zeki went to the village in person, accompanied by a brigade of gendarmes. The priest and his family were murdered, followed by the occupants of the other houses. Their bodies were then loaded onto carts and used to stage a spectacle in the vicinity: rifles and boxes of cartridges that had been ripped open were arranged around the bodies as proof that the gendarmes had eliminated a band of Armenian rebels. Upon returning to Everek, Salih Zeki informed his hierarchy that he had had to put down a revolt of Armenians in Incesu, setting up a commission of inquiry and drawing up a report.[217] He then proceeded to systematically arrest the men and confiscate weapons. Imprisoned in the *konak* and tortured, some of the men died, while others were dispatched to Kayseri and "judged" before the court-martial. While some were condemned to death and hanged with their compatriots in Kayseri, others were "deported to Dyarbekir" – that is, slaughtered by their guards shortly after having been put on the road. Two groups of condemned men were thus murdered on the very day they set out: Yeghia Yusufian, Garabed Gelderian, Avedis Verdiyan, Krikor Melegian, Yeghia Chebukjian, Garabed Shaldibian, Toros Keshishian, Hovhannes Kazajian, and Avedis Mgrdichian; and Hagop Cherkezian, Hagop Kalayjian, Krikor Kalayjian, Garabed Gebredanian, Ohannes Oknayan, Mariam Dzerunian, and Aghavni Dzerunian.[218]

In the course of July, Zeki ordered the deportation of the *kaza*'s rural population, arranging for the convoys to take mountainous routes so as to force them to abandon the goods that they had taken with them on setting out. In Everek, the deportation order was not published until early August. Twenty Protestant families were authorized to remain behind; the rest of the population was put on the road on 18 August. According to the survivors, the convoy reached Tarsus in 16 days. In several places, the local authorities had the deportees sign obviously "fictitious" documents attesting that they had received aid, when in fact some of them died of disease or malnutrition and most of the others had been massacred in Der Zor.[219] Of the 13,000 people deported from the *kaza*, approximately 600 seem to have survived in Aleppo and another 400 in Damascus.[220]

A survivor observes, "We Armenians knew well that the Turks had not decided to liquidate us because they feared an Armenian insurrection, as they claimed." In support of what he says, he reports remarks that Zeki is supposed to have made when notables from Everek came to plead with him to abandon his plans. Nothing proves that this account is true, but the substance of it doubtless sums up the spirit then reigning among many ranking Young Turks:

> You, the Armenians, are a people who love progress; you are an industrious, hard-working people. I wish that we, the Turks, were like you. I appreciate your good qualities, but what use are they, since they don't correspond to our interests. Was it conceivable that the Turk, who is master in this land, should serve you? As everywhere else, so here, too, I see that the Armenians have beautiful houses, while the Turks have huts; that the Armenians are well dressed, while the Turks are in rags; that the Armenians eat well, while the Turks [content themselves] with a crust of bread. So, since we now have the opportunity, we have decided to eliminate all of you, for the three following reasons: 1) your civilization and culture; 2) your wealth; 3) your pro-Entente penchants. Yes, we have taken an oath to eliminate you, but we do not want to kill you fast. There is still time for that. First, we are going to torture you and make you suffer; one day, when the Russian army goes on the offensive, it will be easy to wipe all of you out.[221]

The determination with which Zeki carried out the enterprise of extirpating the entire Armenian population of his *kaza* is illustrated by the political tug-of-war in which the *kaymakam* was engaged with the commander of the Fifteenth Division of Kayseri, Colonel Şehabeddin. Şehabeddin, notwithstanding his role in the Kayseri court-martial, which we have already mentioned, was opposed to deporting the families of soldiers and converts. Zeki accordingly turned to Istanbul to obtain an order authorizing him to expel these Armenians to Meskene, in the Syrian Desert, where most of those deported had died.[222]

In 1914, the town of Tomarza, in the easternmost part of the *kaza* of Everek, still constituted an altogether singular case because of its social structure and autonomous mode of functioning. Its 4,388 Armenian inhabitants lived in four neighborhoods that had been ruled since the twelfth or thirteenth century by four hereditary "princely" families: the Dedeyans, Kalayjians, Maghakians, and Tamuzians. There were also seven Armenian villages in the environs of Tomarza: Söyüdlu (pop. 481); Çayrioluk (pop. 100); Tashkhan (pop. 750); Yenice (pop. 473); Yağdıburun (pop. 227); Karacıyoren (pop. 275); Musahacılı (pop. 173); and Sazak (pop. 400).[223]

Among those who bear the main responsibility for the violence visited upon Tomarza and the environs, the *müdir*, Ali Effendi; the secretary general in the town hall, Büyük Emin Haci Ömer; the corporal Kayserli Ali; the gendarmes Mehmed, Hasan, İsmail İsmet, Halil Çavuş, Haci Bekir, Ahmed Çavuş, and Süleyman Çavuş; among others – a total of 32 people[224] – organized the searches for arms in the Armenians' homes and arrested 200 of the city's notables. These people were tortured and threatened with death. Twenty were then set free after paying bribes, and the rest were sent to the *kaymakam* of Everek. In the end, 70 Martini rifles were handed over to the authorities. It seems, however, that Zeki was not satisfied with this result. The *müdir*, Ali, was dismissed and replaced by a certain Osman Effendi, who undertook new house searches. In the course of this second operation, 196 men were arrested and deported to Hacın by night. Only after liquidating nearly 400 men was the deportation order for the rest of the population issued. On 27 August 1915, the inhabitants of Tomarza were put on the road to Aleppo by way of Hacın, after being divested of their possessions in Çibaraz, not far from the city, under the supervision of the 32 officials and notables mentioned above.[225] Those in villages in the vicinity such as Tashkan[226] apparently met a similar fate.

By the time the convoy arrived in Aleppo, only 300 of the deportees were still alive. They were sent to Der Zor, Raffa, or Meskene, where most of them died.[227]

According to a number of survivors, the worker-soldiers who were employed in an *amele taburi* charged with putting up telephone lines in the region were put to death near Tomarza.[228]

Of all the people implicated in the atrocities inflicted on the Armenian population of the *sancak* of Kayseri, only Colonel Şakir Bey was indicted by the Istanbul court-martial in 1920. He was ultimately acquitted.[229]

Massacres and Deportations in the Sancak of Kırşehir

Wedged between the districts of Angora and Kayseri, the *sancak* of Kırşehir had only two localities with substantial Armenian populations – the prefecture, Kırşehir, with a population of 7,150, and to the north, Keskin, the principal town in the *kaza* of Denek Maden, with a population of 2,650.[230]

In June and July, Armenian homes were searched, but the authorities found no trace of arms or "revolutionaries." They proceeded to arrest from 15 to 17 young men nonetheless. Guarded by Ahmed Çavuş, the men were sent to face court-martial in Angora because every Saturday they had collected alms for the poor that were suspected of having been used for revolutionary purposes.[231] When they arrived in Gülhisar, these young men were stripped of their belongings and slaughtered. The victims of the next stage of the operation were 14 notables from the city who were deported to Arpaçuhu, where they were slain by the head of the recruitment office, Muncur Sadir Bey. There followed a new wave of arrests: sixty-five adults were taken into custody and then massacred by the *çetes* Şakir Receb and Hasan Çavuş. The last group to be apprehended (135 males) was taken under guard 20 minutes outside the city to a place called Gülhisar, near Muncur, and were liquidated by *çetes* with the assistance of Turkish locals from a nearby village.[232]

In Kırşehir, the *mutesarif* then had the girls and women transferred to the town barracks, while the children were conducted an hour's march from the city and left in the middle of a field to starve to death. The authorities first sealed the Armenians' houses, after which officials and notables plundered homes and stores and divided up the booty among themselves, leaving objects without value to the committee responsible for liquidating "abandoned property." According to survivors, the girls and women confined in the barracks were told that they would have to convert if they wanted to escape with their lives. The pressure was the greater in that thousands of villagers from the vicinity had come to town to "acquire women." But after the women and girls had pooled all their jewels and handed them over to the local Union and Progress club, they were granted a reprieve.[233] Seventeen adolescent boys between the ages of 15 and 19 who were still in the town were rounded up on the orders of the leaders of the Unionist club, which suggested that they also convert. After firmly refusing, they were conducted to Çallıgedik, where they were put to death by Şakir Receb and his *çetes*. By the time these operations had been terminated, the only Armenians left in Kirşehir were five or six families of artisans who had converted and a few other women.[234]

After organizing the August 1915 massacres, the members of the local Ittihadist club – Remzi Bey, the head of the post office: Bahirzâde Ziya; Musiroğlu Süleyman; Kara Muhammer Bey; and Osman Saib Bey, the president of the committee responsible for "abandoned property" – appointed themselves to the *emval-ı metruke* with the blessing of the *mutesarif*, Hilmi Bey, and seized the Armenians' assets.[235]

Of the government officials implicated in these mass crimes, the most active were Burhaneddin Rumli, the commander of the battalion of Kirşehir (he was arrested by the inter-Allied police on 4 March 1919); Asadullah Bey, the commander of the gendarmerie; Ali Nazmi Bey, the assistant imperial prosecutor and president of the local Ittihad club (who was deported to Malta in 1919); Hami Bey, the police chief; Kadir Bey, the head of the office that recruited and organized *çete* bands; Hilmi Bey, the *mutesarif* (also deported to Malta in 1919); Ali Rıza, the assistant police chief; and Rıza's aides Nuri, Husni Bahirzâde Ziya, and İsmail Hakkı, also the director of the Tobacco Régie. Among the notables recruited to lead bands of *çetes*, Kâzım, the school director (he was later transferred to Smyrna, where he had been appointed principal of the Sultaniye lycée), İzzet Bey, Sarkıçirzâde Vehbi, Şakir Receb Bey, Hasan Çavuş, Seifalioğlu Kara Ahmed, Molla Ahmed, Nurizâde Mehmed Ağa, and Aset Ağa Kara Fakinin Muharrem were the murderers of the Armenian population of Kirşehir.[236]

When Yervant Der Mardirosian, a native of Talas, and his military convoy approached Kirşehir on the evening of 26 August 1915. They encountered a brigade of 900 worker-soldiers whom a squadron of *çetes*, accompanied by Turkish adolescents, was getting ready to liquidate. In town, Der Mardirosian observed that "all males twelve and older" were massacred, while the women and children were deported.[237]

In Keskin, events unfolded in much the same way. The *kaymakam*, Talât Bey, distributed weapons to the Turkish villagers in the vicinity so that they would be prepared to carry out a massacre. A member of the town council, Borzakian, who had grasped the gravity of the situation, had a conversation with Talât Bey and gave him a sizeable sum to head off the "danger." One week later, Talât Bey nonetheless proceeded to make mass arrests: four hundred eighty men were imprisoned in a *han*, while the local populace was invited to pillage the Armenian quarter. The first convoy, comprising 130 men, was then put on the road, escorted by a captain in the gendarmerie, Urfan Bey, who had them slaughtered not far from the city. The second, third, and fourth groups were sent off under the same conditions, on the basis of lists drawn up by the council under the supervision of the *kaymakam*.[238] In addition to Talât Bey, this council comprised Irfan Bey, the police chief; Hafiz Bey, the head of the recruitment office; Baltalızâde Nuri Bey, the mayor; Sadık Effendi, a mufti; and Şevket, the assistant police chief. The massacres themselves were perpetrated by *çetes* under the orders of four men: Hacializâde Mehmed, Hacializâde Kâmil, Alişan Bey, and Ali Rıza Bey.[239] Upon his arrival in Keskin on 27 August, Der Mardirosian accordingly discovered a town that had been emptied of its Armenian population with the exception of a few women and children. Lodged with someone named Osman Effendi, who took him for a Turk, he learned from his host how he had taken part in the massacre of the men and abducted the prettiest women.[240]

The Fate of the Armenian Elite Incarcerated in Ayaş

Ayaş, which, as we have said, is located near the Sincanköy railroad station, 15 kilometers from the Armenian village of Stanoz and some 50 kilometers west of Angora, was chosen as the place of imprisonment for the Armenian political elite of Istanbul – some 120 to 150 people. The prisoners arrived in Ayaş in several waves, after a stay – short or long, depending on the prisoner – in Istanbul's central prison. Vrtanes Mardikian, a survivor, arrived in Angora by train with 40 companions on the evening of 5 May and was transferred to Ayaş by car two days later.[241] All the prisoners were confined to an immense barracks at a point opposite the *konak* of the subprefecture, in cramped conditions: for lack of space, the men slept two to a bed in beds ranged one over the next. After repeated requests, they were allowed to leave the barracks for an hour or two a day, under the surveillance of gendarmes, to walk in the field surrounding their prison.[242] Although they were cut off from the world and lacked all means of subsistence, Khoren Avakian, the station chief in Sincanköy, managed to transmit information to the capital about the fate of these men. Somewhat later, the Armenians of Stanoz, who had not yet been deported or massacred, supplied the political prisoners in Ayaş with basic necessities.[243] Very soon, however, the men obtained permission to send two of their number to the market every morning to buy groceries.

A few details provided by Vrtanes Mardikian show that the prisoners had not lost their sense of humor. Reveille, sounded every morning by the police chief Ali Rıza himself, gave rise to comic scenes. The many different pseudonyms used by the political activists interned in Ayaş made it hard to identify them, the more so as the police chief had some trouble pronouncing their names (Marzbed, for example, became "Marizabad"). The explanations offered every morning by people who had been arrested in someone else's stead, because their names sounded more or less like those of the Armenians who were supposed to have been arrested, were also an occasion for general hilarity. Every morning, Nshan Odian, who had been mistaken for Yervant Odian, reminded Ali Rıza, who persisted in calling him Yervant, that he wasn't the man in question, and was, moreover, a member of the Social-Democratic Hnchak Party.[244] Politicians of every stripe, writers, and journalists lived more or less harmoniously side-by-side, all taking part in the chores and also the gymnastics led by the jurist Shavarsh Krisian. Dr. Avedis Nakashian notes that the members of this elite, who often belonged to antagonistic political currents, had by this time understood that their fate was in no sense due to the positions they had held earlier, but solely to the fact that they comprised the elite of the Armenian nation. "Representatives" chosen by the internees were even invited to write to the interior minister to request that he initiate legal proceedings to judge their acts and have them released. The atmosphere changed when the news that the 20 Hnchak activists had been hanged reached them.[245] Murad (Hampartsum Boyajian), the Hnchak leader, had been transferred to Kayseri on 11 May, as had his comrade Marzbed one week later, in order to be "judged" before the court-martial there.[246] It was, however, the 2 June departure of the six main political leaders – Rupen Zartarian, Nazareth Daghavarian, Karekin Khajag, Aknuni (K. Malumian),[247] Harutiun Jangulian, and Sarkis Minasian – that marked the beginning of the liquidation of the Istanbul Armenian elite. Officially, these six men were sent to Dyarbekir to face court-martial there.[248] In fact, after passing through Aleppo, where they remained for a short time, the men were murdered, on orders from Captain Şevket, halfway between Urfa and Severek in a place called Karacur, by Haci Tellal Hakimoğlu, known as Haci Onbaşi,[249] a *çete* chief in the forces of the Special Organization based in Severek.[250]

We know, moreover, that Parsegh Shabaz, a Dashnak leader, was brought before the court-martial of Mezreh/Harput on 19 June and that the Armenians who had been arrested by mistake or who had benefited from the intercession of people in high places – such as Mardikian or Nakashian, a non-partisan parliamentary deputy from Istanbul – were released in July.[251] Mardikian confirms that the psychiatrist Boghosian, who was later sent to Aleppo as a municipal physician, was transferred to Çangırı, adding that, when he left Ayaş there were still 53 or 54 prisoners there, the poet Siamanto among them.[252] Shortly thereafter, at an unspecified date, the authorities informed these men (none of them would survive) that they were going to be released and transferred to Angora, where they could board trains. At some distance from the ancient city of Ankyra, in the Elmadağrı valley, Harutiun Shahrigian, Hrach (Hayg Tirakian), Dr. Garabed Pashayan, Nerses Zakarian, and some 30 of their companions were tortured and then executed by a squadron of *çetes* of the Special Organization.[253]

Chapter 11

Deportations and Massacres in the Vilayet of Kastamonu

I n this immense vilayet, with a surface area of 60,000 square kilometers stretching along the Black Sea coast, there remained on the eve of the First World War some Armenian colonies with a total population of 13,461. The prosperous Armenians of the vilayet maintained 17 churches and 18 schools, with a total enrollment of over 2,500 boys and girls. Most of the vilayet's Armenian communities had been founded by Armenians from Nakhichevan and Yerevan early in the seventeenth century.[1]

The *sancak* of Kastamonu boasted 18 Armenian communities. They were to be found in the principal town of the *kaza* (pop. 653/140 households), Kadinsaray (pop. 154/35 households), Mururig (pop. 35/6 households), Kurucik (pop. 800/130 households), Daday (pop. 208/40 households), Gerizköy (pop. 102/20 households), Karabüyük (pop. 238/45 households), Devrekianu (pop. 183/38 households), Taşköprü (pop. 1,250/250 households), and the surrounding villages, Çuruş (pop. 33/6 households), Belençay (pop. 95/18 households), Gücüksu (pop. 79/16 households), Iregül (pop. 91/17 households), Malahköy (pop. 77/14 households), Ğaracı (pop. 97/18 households), and Yumacik (pop. 99/18 households).[2]

The *sancak* of İnebolu on the Black Sea coast had four Armenian parishes: İnebol (pop. 198); Daşköprü, located some 30 kilometers northeast of Kastamonu (pop. 1,497), Eskiatfa (pop. 434); and, in the southwestern part of the *sancak*, Tosya (pop. 130).[3] Barely 1,000 Armenians lived in the southernmost *sancak*, Çanğırı. Almost all of them in the prefecture; the others lived in the *kazas* of Koçhisar and Tuhtenli (pop. 129).[4]

In other words, the vilayet had only isolated communities of little demographic weight, located in a Turkish-speaking region far from the war theater. This no doubt explains why the CUP chose to intern a good part of the Constantinople Armenian elite in a town in this region, Çanğırı, some 100 kilometers south of Kastamonu, late in April 1915.[5] The Ittihad had, moreover, sent one of its leading members, Cemal Oğuz, to Çanğırı as the party's responsible secretary, notably in order to oversee the treatment these men received.[6] It also established its inspector Hasan Fehmi, one of the party's chief propagandists, in Kastamonu.[7] It was Fehmi who instructed the vali, Reşid Bey, to proceed with the liquidation of the Armenians living in his vilayet and who ultimately had him recalled when he refused to obey the order.[8] The appointment of Atıf Bey, who had served as interim vali of Angora until 3 October 1915, to the post of vali of Kastamonu in place of Reşid Bey confirms, were there any need, the real objectives of the Young Turk leadership in the region. What is more, Atıf received this promotion as a reward for "applying the program to extirpate the Armenians" in Angora, according to an official of the Tobacco Régie.[9] The vilayet's secretary general (*defterdar*), Fuad Bey, briefly served as interim vali with the support of the Unionist representatives Hasan Fehmi and Cemal Oğuz.[10] On occasion, Dr. Fazıl Berki, the CUP's special delegate, also came to Kastamonu to supervise

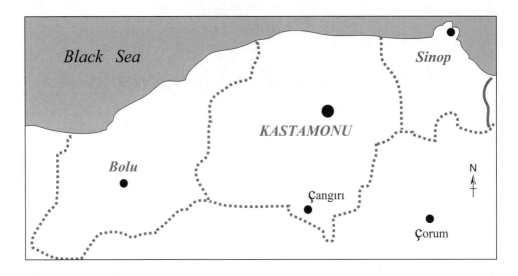

the departure of the political prisoners. The vilayet's Armenian population, however, had been spared until Atıf's arrival. Atıf initially called on the help of the local Ittihad club in carrying out the liquidation of the Armenians of Kastamonu. At the head of it were Sultan Effendi; Vasfi Effendi; Mehmed Ekşioğlu, the president of the municipality; Hasan Fahri Bey; Mustafa Effendi, the police chief of the vilayet; Nureddin, the police chief in Kastamonu; and Dolmacizâde Cemal, a member of the regional council.[11] The Armenians of Çangırı had managed to escape the first wave of deportations by raising a sum of 460 Turkish pounds and turning it over to Cemal Oğuz and his coworkers.[12] Early in October, however, a week after Atıf assumed office, 2,000 men were deported, 300 of them from Kastamonu. These deportees from the Kastamonu and Çangırı areas took the following route: Çorum, Yozgat, Incirli, Talas, Tomarza, Hacın, Osmaniye, Hasanbeyli, Islahiye, and then Meskene, Der Zor, and Abuharar. Twenty-one political internees from Çangırı, including Vahram Asturian, Azarig, Yervant Chavushian, and Khachadur Khachadurian, were incorporated into this convoy.[13] Clara Richmond confirms that they passed through Talas in October 1915.[14]

The Fate of the Elite Interned in Çangırı

It is of course the fate meted out to the roughly 150 members of the Armenian elite confined in Çangırı that gives a special twist to the events that occurred in this vilayet. We have already noted that these "intellectuals" here lived under conditions of house arrest, unlike the political prisoners in Ayaş who were confined in a barracks.[15] Each internee had to provide his own means of subsistence and rent lodgings from a local landlord. Several witnesses say that the prisoners formed groups based on personal affinities, with each man playing a particular role in these reconstructed households. After a brief stay in Çangırı, eight people were authorized to return to Istanbul on 11 May: Dr. Vahram Torkomian, the journalist Piuzant Kechyan, the musicologist Gomidas Vartabed, the pharmacist Hagop Nargilejian, the journalist Yervant Tolayian, the minister Keropian, Dr. Misak Jevahirjian, and the dentist Zareh Bardizbanian.[16] Shortly afterward, a second group comprising some 20 people was also authorized to return to the capital.[17] Interpretations as to why these men were released vary widely, depending on the source. In the cases of Gomidas or Torkomian, for example, it is said that diplomatic circles in Istanbul or court circles interceded on their behalf. It is also possible that after CUP bodies or the interior minister examined the matter it was concluded that this or that individual had been rather hastily added to the list of those to be banned. According to Armenian sources, a member of the Unionist Central Committee, İsmail Canbolat, was charged with reviewing the files of those interned in Çanğırı,[18] so it is possible that Canbolat allowed the Armenians whom he considered the most innocuous to return to Istanbul. It is also noteworthy that one of those detained, Stepan Tatarian, was transferred to Kayseri early in July in order to face court-martial there, and that in the same period four men – Dr. Boghosian, Melkon Giulesarian, Onnig Maghazajian, and Jirayr (Onnig Gholnagdarian) – were allowed to return from Ayaş, probably because they had nothing to do with the political prisoners.[19]

Once these adjustments had been made, it was decided to proceed with the liquidation of the remaining detainees. According to an Armenian survivor, the first group of those exiled to Çanğırı, comprising 56 people, was put on the road on 11 or 18 July 1915 and slain to a man shortly thereafter.[20] The second convoy of "intellectuals" set out on 19 August. In this group were, among others, Baruyr Arzumanian; Dr. Stepan Miskjian; the pharmacist Krikor Miskjian; Krikor Yesayan; N. Der Kaprielian (Shahnur); the teacher and writer Mihran Tabakian; the pharmacist Hagop Terzian; Harutiun Kalfayan; the journalist Aram Andonian; Mihran, Levon, and Kevork Kayekjian; the pharmacist Asadur Arsenian; the Russian consulate's translator, Momjian; and Parunag Sarukhan.[21] We know a great deal more about the fate of the second group because, while none in the first group survived, there were two survivors in the second. Thus, we know that these men were interned in the prison in Angora from 20 to 24 August and that on the evening of the 24th, with the exception of Andonian, who had accidentally broken his leg and been transferred to the hospital in Angora, all were put on the road and killed a few days later in the vicinity of Yozgat.[22]

It seems that a special fate was reserved for five men, among them the physician and writer Rupen Sevag (Chilingirian) and the poet Daniel Varuzhan. These two were put on the road after the second convoy set out and murdered by twelve çetes six hours from Çanğırı, near the khan of Tüney, on 26 August.[23] There were only 37 internees left at Çanğırı by the time Atıf Bey was named vali of Kastamonu early in October.[24] Among them was Diran Kelekian, who was also subjected to special treatment. Officially, Kelekian had been authorized to leave Çanğırı, but was banned from Istanbul. A close friend of Atıf's, Kelekian took advantage of the appointment of his friend to ask for permission to settle in Smyrna.[25] According to an official in the Tobacco Regie, Mehmed Necib, it was Atıf who decided to send this Mulkiye professor away and have him killed.[26] Aram Andonian, however, maintains that Kelekian's murder should not be blamed on Atıf. He reports that the commander of the gendarmerie, Nureddin, and five other men came to search his room in Çanğırı, arrested him, and put him on the road the night of 20 October, officially so that he might stand trial at Çorum. According to testimony from the navy captain Mustafa Ethem and a coworker of his on the staff of "Hospital Number 2," the pharmacist Haroutiun Beshirian, Diran Kelekian was murdered at eight o'clock that night on the road between Yozgat and Kayseri, near the Çokgöz Bridge over the Kızılirmak.[27] It is probable that the order to kill him came from Istanbul.

The Main Culprits for the Deportations in Çanğırı

Among those most deeply implicated in the violence visited on the Armenians of the *sancak* of Çanğırı, apart from Cemal Oğuz, the CUP's responsible secretary, we must underscore the roles played by the mufti Atta Effendi, president of the local Ittihad club;

Süruri, the president of the municipality; Kürd Köylü Hasan Effendi, a member of the city council; Palancızâde Haci Şakir; Dolmacızâde Cemal; Cincircizâde İsmail; Abdüllah Effendi; Haciefezâde İsmail; Ali Effendi; Nureddin Bey, the commander of the gendarmerie; and Manasebeci Rifât. Among the notables who took advantage of their positions on the committee responsible for "abandoned property" in order to enrich themselves were Sarı Yasefoğlu Yasef, İzzet Effendi, Yuzbaşizâde Hamdi, Halvacioğlu Cevad, Haci Effendi Zâde, Haci İsmail Effendi, Tellal Ahmed, and Semerci Çivici Mehmed Usta. Şükrü Bey, the *mutesarif*; Abdülrahim, an imam; Hafiz Ahmed, a muezzin; and Salih Effendi, Mehmed Fahri, and Salih Sabri, all of them government officials, also took part in "divvying up" the Armenians' property. Among the police and military officials, *Binbaşi* Lutfi, the commander of the gendarmerie; İzzet, the head of the Recruitment Office; Remzi, the police chief; and Remzi's assistants Vehib and Fehmi, oversaw the deportation and certain massacres together with their subordinates Husni Çavuş, Salih Çavuş, Süleyman Çavuş, and Lutfi Şükrü. The local operations of the Special Organization were supervised by Osman Talât, a jurist; Ömeroğlu Zeki; Sirri Bey, the former *mutesarif*; Arabaci İsmail, a *çete*; and Ali, who murdered Rupen Sevag (Chilingirian).[28]

After the armistice, only Cemal Oğuz had to answer for his acts. His trial before the court-martial in Istanbul began in December 1919. He was notably charged with having "committed major abuses connected with the provision of supplies."[29] At the 3 February 1920 session of his trial he denied "ever having participated in the Armenian affair." But a witness recalled the considerable influence that he exerted over state officials and described how he, in unison with the interim vali and the commander of the gendarmerie, had taken several hundred pounds gold from the Armenian populace in exchange for a promise not to deport them. Yet he had, this witness went on, deported the Armenians from Çangırı. They were massacred near the *han* of Tüney.[30] Oğuz was condemned and sentenced to five years of hard labor, but was allowed to remain in the hospital of Gümüşsu.[31]

Massacres and Deportations in the Sancak of Bolu

In 1914, Bolu's Armenian colony had barely 1,220 members. It profited from the city's geographical location on the main road through Asia Minor to engage in very profitable trade. Duzce, northwest of Bolu, had an Armenian population of 392; Deverek, 50 kilometers further east, had an Armenian population of 670; Zonguldak, on the coast, had a community with 512 members; finally, Bartin had a community of 420.[32]

The elimination of the men was carried out behind a facade of legal proceedings. A "commission of inquiry" headed by someone name Mehmed Ali Bey was created in Bolu. Its leading member was the police chief, İzzet Bey, who was responsible for house searches and arrests. The court-martial, under the presiding judge Sopaci Mehmed, was responsible for condemning those indicted. Its activities were overseen by Dr. Ahmed Midhat, chief of police in Constantinople, who had been sent by the CUP to Bolu to supervise the 24 September deportation and massacre of the *sancak*'s Armenian population, with the help of Suraya Effendi, a member of the district's general council; Habib Bey, a parliamentary deputy from Bolu; and İbrahim Bey (who had been implicated in the 1909 Adana massacres) and Tahir Bey, the leaders of a squadron of *çetes* that counted among its ranks, notably, Hafız Ali, Sarı Mehmed, Postaci Nuri, and Cendarma Kancarci Emin.[33]

An Armenian survivor, held in the prison of Bolu until the end of his trial on 23 January 1916, reports that some of those indicted were accused of being members of the Armenian Benevolent Society and condemned to hard labor for that reason, and that others were condemned to death and executed for reasons just as trivial. He notes, for example, the 28 September/11 October 1915 execution of Siragan Papazian, a native of Adabazar, and

Aliksan Harutiunian; on 21 December 1915/3 January 1916, of Stepan Ahtzaian, Divrig, Nshan Markarian, Mgrdich Bartevian, Sarkis Lazian, Karekin Papelian, and Stephani (a Greek); on 28 December 1915/10 January 1916, of Father Goriun of Adabazar, Sarkis Kozayian, Ohannes Kozayian, Nazaret Tashjian, Mihran Tashjian, Garabed Haotzian, Mihran Kiremijian, and others; on 21 March/3 April 1916, of Bedros Genjian, Boghos, Ohannes Muradian, Khachig Mardirosian, and Hampartsum Cheian; and, on 3/16 October 1916, of Siragan Stambultsian, Armash, Hagop Bijoyan, Kangal, Iskander Tumanian, and Garabed Zenian, Chengiler.[34]

According to another account, the police chief İzzet Bey played a crucial role in concocting the indictments by planting "prohibited objects: weapons, bombs, and so forth, and English, French and Russian flags" in Armenian homes. He is also supposed to have summoned the Armenian notables to the prefecture, where they were arrested and then handed over to the *çetes*.[35] It is probably that İzzet's superiors in Istanbul had demanded that an indictment be fabricated in order to justify the deportation order that Ahmed Midhat took it upon himself to carry out. The same source has it that Mondays were "holidays for the Turks, since Monday was hanging day." The gallows were erected on the square where the city government was based, toward which "a crowd overflowing with sinister joy" streamed. Many children were "adopted" by Turkish families, while young Armenian women were "imprisoned in the harems."[36]

Massacres and Deportations in the Sancak of Sinop

In Sinop, a wooded peninsula, there were three Armenian colonies in 1914, in Kuyluci, Aliseylik, and Göldağ, with a total population of 1,125. Gerze, on the Black Sea coast, had an Armenian population of 491. The densest Armenian population in the *sancak*, however, was to be found in the interior, in Boyabad and the surrounding villages: the total Armenian population here was 3,650.[37] Boyabad constituted Atıf's first target. As soon as he was appointed in early October 1915, he had 800 men arrested and interned in the mosque. Officially, some of them were sent to Angora in order to face court-martial. They disappeared on the way there.[38] The rest of the population was deported by way of Çangırı, where prisoners from Istanbul saw it pass by in mid-October. These people were probably massacred near Yozgat, as were many other deportees from these areas near the Black Sea.[39]

We have no reports about the fate of the Armenian men of Sinop and Bartin. We do know, however, that the rest of the population of these two localities was deported by way of Sıvas[40] and, consequently, must have endured the hell of Fırıncilar.

Chapter 12

Constantinople in the Period of the Deportations and Massacres

We have discussed the circumstances surrounding the arrests of the Armenian elite of the Ottoman capital, as well as the deterioration of the climate brought on by the May-June 1915 trial of the Hnchaks.[1] Official government statements and the press campaign orchestrated by the government for the purpose of collectively portraying the Armenians as "traitors" were obviously intended to convince the public of the need for present and future violence.

By early May 1915, of the Armenian elite of Constantinople, only two figures of importance – the parliamentary deputies Krikor Zohrab and Vartkes Seringiulian – were still present in the capital. Their interventions with the interior minister and the grand vizier had not produced the expected results. On the contrary, they seemed to have convinced the two Armenians of the Young Turk government's real intentions. Both Zohrab and Seringiulian were encouraged by their entourage to flee the country but, reacting in much the same fashion, both refused even to contemplate leaving. On 18 May, Zohrab told Martin Hagopian, a notable who offered to help him flee: "To whom do you want me to abandon this people, without leadership or a chief? I do not want to leave; it is my duty to remain on the front lines to the very last."[2] The public announcement of the temporary deportation law on 27 May, and the information then reaching the Armenian Patriarchate about the massacres in the provinces, left little doubt about the Young Turks' intentions. In the course of a stormy exchange on 1 June with Talât and the CUP's secretary general, Midhat Şükrü, Zohrab demanded an explanation for the crimes that had been perpetrated against Armenians in the eastern provinces. He pointed out to the interior minister that he would eventually have to account for his actions and when that day came he would not be able to "justify his crimes." Sure of himself, Talât responded that he did not see who could possibly ask him to given an account of himself. The Armenian lawyer answered: "I can, in parliament, in my capacity as an Armenian deputy."[3] The next day, Zohrab, the Senator Zareh Dilber, the parliamentary deputy Bedros Halajian, and the newly resigned minister Oskan Mardikian met at the "Petit Club." The purpose of this meeting of men close to the Young Turk government was to evaluate the situation.[4] There is every reason to think that these individuals, who knew the political mores of the leaders of the CUP better than anyone else, concluded that a program to extirpate the Armenian population was being put into effect. Nevertheless, that evening, Zohrab went to the "Cercle d'Orient," where he played cards with the interior minister. Two hours after he went back home, the police chief in Pera, Kel Osman, knocked at his door. Osman searched Zohrab's apartment, confiscated his personal papers, and then asked the Armenian lawyer to follow him. At the same moment, Vartkes was also arrested in his home.[5] After being briefly detained in the police station in Galatasaray, the two men were transferred by boat to the train station at Haydarpaşa under police escort.[6] Officially, they were sent to Dyarbekir in order to face a court-martial. They were murdered on 19 July on the road to Dyarbekir, shortly after setting out from Urfa, by the famous Çerkez Ahmed,[7] who had become the head of a group of "Circassian" çetes.[8]

Patriarch Zaven's Impossible Undertaking

On his own witness, the Armenian patriarch found himself singularly isolated on the Istanbul political scene after Zohrab and Vartkes were deported.[9] To the multiple takrir (requests) that the Patriarchate had addressed to the government from late April 1915 on, the minister of justice had ultimately given an oral response, delivered to the Chief Secretary of the Armenian Patriarchate, Kamer Shirinian. The statutes of the Patriarchate, the justice minister said, did not authorize it to make "such political" takrir.[10] Of the diplomats then residing in Istanbul, Dr. Mordtmann, the dragoman at the German embassy who was responsible for Armenian matters there, met with Patriarch Zaven more frequently than anyone else; it appears that he had been charged with feeling out the reactions of Armenian circles.[11] His 10 June 1915 visit to the Armenian prelacy was all the more important in that it took place shortly after Zohrab and Vartkes were deported – that is to say, at the moment when the authorities decided definitively to close off all channels of dialogue with the Armenian elite. It also coincided with Dr. Johannes Lepsius's arrival in Istanbul in early June,[12] which gave the patriarch reason to hope that the Germans had taken a less-hostile position to the Armenian population or had might even been prepared to intervene on its behalf. Doubtless in order to allay the patriarch's apprehensions, Mordtmann suggested to him that the deportation of the population of Erzerum that had begun on 1 May, "toward the south, far from the front," was a desirable measure, given the military situation on the front. The "information" he had about a commission of inquiry sent to Zeitun "to assess the value of the land owned by the population of the town and its environs," so that it might be more justly "indemnified," was probably also dictated by his desire to relieve the patriarch's fears. Zaven Yeghiayan, for his part, pointed out to the German diplomat that Ambassador Wangenheim had assured him that there would be no massacres, but that "what is happening now is much worse than the massacres." In fact, Armenian circles in the capital were apprised of the situation in the provinces until the last days of May, thanks to wires from the provincial prelates. But this source of information dried up when all communication by telegraph with the provinces was outlawed. From then on, assessments of the situation could only be based on reports from people arriving from the provinces.[13] It is probable that, with only these scraps of information at his disposal, the patriarch could not take the full measure of the eradication program, so that there remained at least a little doubt as to the intentions of the Young Turk government. Even the joint declaration that the powers of the Triple Entente had published on 24 May 1915, which held the Ottoman government responsible for the "crimes against humanity" committed against the Armenians,[14] could be construed as an almost classic wartime propaganda maneuver. The Young Turk government's reaction, which consisted in denying that there had been massacres and attacking Great Britain and Russia for inciting the Armenians to revolt, had itself been transformed into an anti-Armenian campaign. Furthermore, Patriarch Zaven later conceded that at the time of his conversation with Lepsius in mid-June, he was still very much in the dark about the events that had occurred in the provinces, having only taken measure of the crime when his nephew Dikran, a student at Harput's Euphrates College, arrived in the capital in August 1915.[15] It was from his nephew that the patriarch learned how the notables of the city – such as the primate Bsag Der Khorenian or Nicolas Tenekejian, a teacher – were arrested and killed, the state in which the deportees who arrived from the north found themselves, or, again, the fact that countless corpses lay strewn along the road running through Malatia that his nephew had taken on his way to the capital.[16]

After making several fruitless bids to obtain an interview with the interior minister, the patriarch was finally referred to the minister of justice and religious confessions, İbrahim Pirizâde, who received him on 8 July 1915. In other words, the authorities proved willing to receive Zaven only in his capacity as a religious leader. Moreover, the minister initially refused to say anything about the fate of the civilian population, although he ultimately admitted the fact of the deportations, which he claimed had taken place "in the best of conditions, because the government ha[d] given the necessary orders."[17] The response of the patriarch, who stressed that "all these measures show that the government does not have confidence in our nation and wants to wipe our people out,"[18] suggests that he had a clear perception of events. For İbrahim Pirizâde, "All this [was] the work of the military authorities, who took the measures that they considered necessary ... While the empire is making tremendous efforts to ensure its survival, and is shedding its blood, one has to be careful not to antagonize it." Zaven answered by pointing out that the Armenians, too, were shedding their "blood for the fatherland," while their women and children were being "expedited to the deserts." He also said that he understood that the military authorities had to employ "the means they deem[ed] necessary in the combat zone," but could not understand why they should do this "everywhere," thereby condemning "more than a million people" to death. Finally, he asked the minister "why the government was punishing women and children, who could not be accused of engaging in activity directed against the government?"[19] The minister's answer was calculated to justify the authorities' decision: he pointed out that they did not want to "deprive families of their men" and had accordingly opted for a "collective displacement." This answer shows how little credence could be put in the justifications advanced by the government. Pirizâde also reminded the patriarch that it was a question of the measures taken by the military authorities in view of the military imperatives with which they were faced.[20]

Two days later, on 10 July 1915, the Zaven was granted an audience with the grand vizier, Said Halim, to whom he revealed his underlying concerns at the very outset of their conversation. His people's plight, he said, obliged him to beg for "the government's mercy." He was now alone, he added, and left to wonder why the state had decided to inflict this fate on his people, "why it had been condemned to death."[21] Halim's answer was the more interesting in that it traced the measures taken against the Armenians back to the reforms in the eastern provinces. While the grand vizier did not deny that the Armenians' situation was a "painful" one, he maintained that they were to blame for it. They had demanded reforms and their "one segment of the population had taken up arms" against the empire. Zaven Yeghiayan of course rejected the charge that there had been a "general uprising," noting that "the reports sent to the government distort the facts or are deliberately misleading." He regretted above all that the authorities were punishing "a whole people" and suggested that they take their example from "Sultan Abdülhamid, contenting themselves with massacring only the men."[22] Halim denied that the government had set itself "the objective of liquidating the Armenian people," but admitted, "that since means of transport were nonexistent, the *muhaciret* [migration] could prove difficult." The rest of the two men's exchange, as described in the patriarch's memoirs, shows a prelate who was trying desperately to bring the authorities to abandon the idea of deporting the Armenian population living outside the border regions. Halim, however, told him that "the government [had] made an irrevocable decision." "Whatever happens," he said, "they will have to leave." At the end of the conversation, the grand vizier finally asked the patriarch why he had not gone to see Talât, thus giving him to understand that it was Talât who had the power to bring the persecutions to an end. "When I told him that he would not receive me," Zaven writes, "he answered: 'none of this should ever have happened.'"[23]

Yeghiayan also interceded with the president of the Ottoman Parliament, Halil [Menteşe],[24] a Young Turk leader who was reputed to be less radical than the others;[25] for, according to Wangenheim, the patriarch now seemed to "have given up hope of bringing about an improvement in the situation by intervening with the Turkish government."[26] According to the patriarch, Halil had received Zohrab, Vartkes, and Halajian after the declaration of war in order to encourage them to think about the fact that the Armenians were now "defenseless." Yeghiayan writes that upon returning from Germany, however, he found that the situation had deteriorated and endeavored to save the deputies Zohrab and Vartkes "by, at the very least, having them confined to Aleppo."[27] Like Said Halim, he suggested that the patriarch "discuss the matter" with Talât, and "immediately reached for his telephone" and obtained an appointment for him for the next day, while also promising, "to do all that [was] in [his] power." On 2 October 1915, the Zaven went to see the interior minister. At the beginning of their conversation, Talât declared that the Armenians "bore the blame for the situation" and that he knew that they had decided to "precipitate a revolution" and "support the Russians," stockpiling "arms and bombs everywhere" for that purpose. He also attacked them for their "responsibility for the fact that part of the country [had] fallen into the Russians' hands." In response, Yeghiayan pointed out that "these things [were] the doings of a few individuals," which provoked the retort: "Not of a few, not of a few thousand, and not of a few hundred thousand. Today, it is one political party; tomorrow, another will come into existence. Those who don't belong to a party will join one."[28] Without a doubt, Talât was here expressing, with a ring of sincerity, the central preoccupation of the CUP, which perceived all Armenians as a future threat for the country. The patriarch pointed out to him that even if his accusations were legitimate, nothing could justify the fate that had been inflicted on the women, or the fact that "children [were] being abducted and entrusted to others." Punishment, he said, should be "proportionate to the crime." Talât thereupon declared that "nothing of the sort was occurring," to which the patriarch rejoined that it was enough to note that many of these children were now to be found in the capital. The minister promised that he would commission an inquiry into the matter and punish the "guilty." Zaven also told him that "[t]he Armenians [had been] devastated at seeing that they had received this blow from one of the figures whom they held in highest esteem." Talât confirmed that he "loved the Armenians, because [he knew] just how useful they were to the country," but added that he "[loved] the fatherland even more than the Armenians."

At this point in the conversation, the Zaven drew to the minister's attention the situation of the Armenians of Rodosto/Tekirdağ, then being deported. Talât had accused these Armenians of having "inflicted all kinds of brutalities on the Muslims during the Bulgarian occupation," contesting the patriarch's claim that "some deported families [had], at the time, provided financial aid to the families of the muhacirs." He also requested that the authorities aide the deportees and that they not leave young women "scattered through the villages," defenseless and without resources.[29] The minister promised that the government would consider the request, on condition that the patriarch not interfere in these matters. As to the fate of the Armenian clergymen, Talât declared that many, such as the prelate of Kayseri (whose trial we have discussed),[30] were traitors and members of political parties.[31] Thus, he implicitly identified the reason for which the Armenian religious leaders had been "punished."

In summer and fall 1915, the Armenian patriarch, besides making these appeals to the key Young Turk political leaders, sought counsel from people reputed to be close to the CUP, such as the former minister of the Postal and Telegraph Service, Oskan Bey Mardikian. Mardikian suggested that he turn to the Şeyh ul-Islam, Musa Kâzım, a convinced Ittihadist. Kâzım, however, refused to intervene.[32] The patriarch also appealed to someone who was close to the Sultan and, to the heir apparent, Prince Yusuf İzzeddin, Senator Abraham Pasha

Yeramian. However, Yeramian shirked his responsibilities on the grounds that his interven-tion could produce no results.[33] Among the Armenian notables who had been spared, it seems that the only one to work regularly at the patriarch's side was Vahram Torkomian, who had been briefly detained in Çangırı. At Zaven's request, Torkomian, the private physician of Prince Abdülmecid, second in line to the throne, went to see the prince on 22 August 1915, in an attempt to persuade him to intercede with the Sultan on the Armenians' behalf. According to Yeghiayan, Abdülmecid did not meet with Sultan Reşid to raise the question of the Armenians' plight until 8 October, when the sultan supposedly told him that he would do "what was necessary" and that he had "already repeatedly spoken with Talât," but that the Talât had "turned a deaf ear" to his appeals.[34] In his memoirs, the patriarch notes bitterly that people such as Hrant Asadur, a member of the Council of State, blatantly ignored him, and that Bedros Halajian, a deputy from Constantinople, former minister, and a member of the Ittihad, avoided him and did not lift a finger to save anyone. Among the Armenian deputies still alive, only Onnig Ihsan, who had been elected in Smyrna, endeavored to save people, sometimes successfully. Kegham Der Garabedian, a Dashnak deputy who had been spared because he had tuberculosis; Bishop Yeghishe Turian, the former patriarch; Hayg Khojasarian, the president of the Armenian Chamber; Dr. Krikor Tavitian, the president of the Political Council; the patriarchal vicar, Yervant Perdahjian; and the chief secretary of the Patriarchate, Kamer Shirinian, who had a reputation as a Turkophile, also gave the patriarch valuable help and rendered him numerous services.[35]

Although he was unable to temper the Young Turks' positions, the patriarch neverthe-less took it upon himself to inform the outside world of the information he had about the Armenian population's plight. In his memoirs, he reports that he sent his unsigned reports to the bishop of the Armenians of Bulgaria, Ghevont Turian, by way of the Italian embassy.[36] His sources of information were quite varied: they included reports by an Islamicized woman from Bayburt, a young woman from Zile who had been abducted by a Turkish officer and was living in Istanbul, a Muslim traveler who had come from Harput, foreigners who had arrived from Erzincan, and so on.[37] The details that he provides show that the patriarch was, from early fall 1915 on, informed about the fate of the Armenians in the vilayets of Erzerum, Trebizond, Sıvas, Mamuret ul-Aziz, Bitlis, and Dyarbekir, as well as that of the soldiers of the *amele taburis* based in the regions of Erzerum, Dyarbekir, and Harput, or, again, about the situation in Aleppo, Ras ul-Ayn, and Der Zor. In a report of his dated 15 August 1915, he was already estimating the human losses at around 500,000.[38]

The patriarch had, moreover, helped organize a network to distribute aid to the depor-tees who had reached Syria. In this connection, he affirms that the American embassy's legal advisor, Arshag Shemavonian, played a crucial role in obtaining Gomidas's release, which others had also sought, and that he had, above all, persuaded the American Red Cross to send the deportees material aid. Initially, this aid was funneled to the Ottoman Red Crescent, in accordance with this international organization's standard procedure. But the Americans saw that their Ottoman counterparts were not passing on any aid at all.[39] A committee made up of American and German missionaries was therefore created in Aleppo with the support of the U.S. and German consulates. It served to channel the aid sent by the Constantinople patriarch and the American-Armenian community. It is also known that Ambassador Morgenthau intervened on the deportees' behalf, even if his actions failed to produce the desired results.[40]

The patriarch is much less indulgent when it comes to the papal nuncio Angelo Maria Dolci. He notes that Dolci was incapable of gaining access to the Sublime Porte and interven-ing to save deportees.[41] On the other hand, he has words of praise for the Austro-Hungarian ambassador, Johann von Pallavicini, whom he was able to approach thanks to a Mkhitarist monk in Vienna, Father Khoren. While the Austrian diplomat did not succeed in convincing the authorities to allow Armenians who had not yet been deported to remain in their native regions; stabilizing the situation of the deportees in concentration camps so that they would not be forced to move again; facilitating wire transfers of funds; making it possible to receive requests for aid; putting an end to compulsory conversion; or liberating women and children held in Muslim families, he was able to obtain advantages for people in certain categories, especially Armenian Catholics.[42]

On the other hand, it has been definitely established that the German Ambassador Hans von Wangenheim, the only person who, in the American Ambassador's words, "could have put a stop to these crimes," did not, until his death on 24 October 1915, make the least effort to help the Armenians, who were in his view, "nothing but treacherous vermin."[43] The death of this influential diplomat and his replacement by Count Paul Wolff-Metternich, a man whose views were said to be less rigidly aligned with those of the German chiefs of staff, emboldened the patriarch to appeal to the newly arrived ambassador. In a 23 November 1915 letter to Metternich, Yeghiayan once again requested that the Germans intercede with the Sublime Porte.[44] Four or five days later, Dr. Mordtmann paid him a visit in the Armenian Chamber of Galata to inform him that the ambassador wished to have a more detailed report on the Armenians' situation. Two days later, the patriarch transmitted a first document to the embassy, followed by another entitled "The Annihilation of the Armenian Element in Turkey."[45] Metternich's correspondence with Berlin indicates that the German ambassador rapidly delved into the Armenian file, met with the main Young Turk leaders, and "seriously discussed the massacre of the Armenians" with them.[46] Yeghiayan confirms that the German and Bulgarian Ambassadors interceded with the Ottoman government in December 1915 "so that the crimes against the Armenians would come to an end." According to him, the information that had begun to circulate in the Western press had put Germany in a difficult position. The German Social Democratic Party had also publicly addressed questions to the German government on the subject in the wake of an article published on 11 January in the *Volkszeitung*.[47]

By the end of 1915, the Armenian Patriarchate, more isolated than ever, was the last legitimate representative of the Armenians still in a position to speak out and take action, even if its margin to maneuver was extremely narrow.

Armenian Assets and Solidarity Networks

According to Zaven Yeghiayan's memoirs, again, the Patriarchate learned, early in 1916, that the moneys that Armenian institutions had deposited with Ottoman state banks were going to be confiscated. On 29 January, the Armenian Political Council decided to make an immediate transfer of the funds held by educational or humanitarian institutions such as the *Tbrotsaser*, *Azkanver*, Zavarian Fund, *Oknenk Sasuni*, and so on, to the Patriarchate's accounts. Thus, when a week later the government sent the state banks a circular inquiring into the balances of the associations and institutions just named, it was told that no funds belonging to these organizations were on deposit with the banks. Fearing confiscation of the treasury bonds and other assets that the Patriarchate, the parish councils, the Patriarchate's humanitarian organizations, and its clergymen had deposited with the banks, Zaven decided to gather up all these securities and deposit them temporarily with the American embassy. The *Miatsial* Educational Association had itself been the target of several police searches. The patriarch accordingly suggested that the members of the association who were still present dissolve the association and transfer their archives to the Patriarchate, along with those of the *Akzanver* Association. Shortly thereafter, Zaven deposited two paintings by Aivazovsky with the American embassy, together with archives connected with the reform plan in the Armenian provinces. Another part of the

Armenians' assets and archives was, the patriarch writes, temporarily deposited with the Swedish embassy.[48]

With the 24 April arrests and the subsequent deportation of Vartkes, the only Istanbul Dashnak leaders still in Istanbul were Sarkis Srents, Shavarsh Misakian, and Hagop Siruni, who had had time to go into hiding and form an underground committee. According to the Patriarchate, they had forged a solidarity network, centered on Hovhannes Cheugiurian, the purpose of which was to provide financial aid to the families of party militants who had been "deported," help people wanted by the police to flee the city, and retrieve Armenian orphans held in Turkish households. However, by putting the accounts of *Oknenk Sasuni* or the Zavarian Fund in the Patriarchate's name, Yeghiayan had involuntarily deprived this network of its principal source of revenue. When representatives of the committee asked him to turn over the money on deposit, the patriarch found himself in an embarrassing situation. "It is obvious," he writes, "that any attempt to transfer such a sum would put the Patriarchate in perilous situation; it was, in fact, practically impossible to effect such an operation secretly, and we were surrounded by government informers, not to mention the fact that some of them had positions in the Patriarchal administration." After several fruitless conversations and a menacing letter from the committee, it was agreed that the Patriarchate would directly forward financial aid to families in need on the basis of a pre-established list, demanding receipts in return.[49]

In his memoirs, the patriarch also discusses the arrest of Shavarsh Misakian, who had been making preparations to travel clandestinely to Bulgaria with the local archives of the Dashnak Party, which had been entrusted to the head of the *Kısm Siasi*, Reşad Bey, for translation. These documents do not seem to contain shocking revelations about the ARF's putative treachery. It has, however, been established that a copy of the threatening letter that had been sent to the Zaven was discovered, leading the authorities to publish a declaration in which they stated, among other things, that "[t]he patriarch was under the revolutionaries' thumb."[50]

We have only a few reports about the clandestine Armenian networks operating in Istanbul during the First World War, among them that by the leading Dashnak activist Marzbed[51] and the memoirs of Berjuhi, the wife of Sarkis Barseghian, a journalist and political militant.[52] The network to which Marzbed [Ghazaros Ghazarosian] belonged[53] was above all active on the railway that traversed Asia Minor from Istanbul to Cilicia. It drew much of its support from Armenian railway employees who worked on this line and counted people from many different walks of life in its ranks.

According to information provided by the author of a monograph on Marzbed, the patriarch was the soul of this network in the capital, while at the other end of the railway, in Mosul, the police chief Mehmed Effendi – a converted Armenian from Khnus – worked for it.[54] According to Berjuhi, the Istanbul network sought, in particular, to find hiding places for people who had eluded the 24 April roundups and were wanted by the police. The havens they found were, as a rule, private homes, preferably ones owned by non-Armenians. When fugitives were transferred to them, it was *de rigueur* to disguise them as "Turkish women" or bearded "old men." The fugitives never spent more than a week in the same hideout. It is noteworthy that young women ensured the network's communications and transported weapons earmarked for the banned activists.[55]

Indications are that the network profited from the benevolent attitude of certain neutral countries' legations, which generously provided it with passports thanks to which a number of young men were able to leave the country. The unwritten rule seems to have been to save the youngest first; the oldest men were left where they were.[56]

A more specifically feminine network, led by women who were the heads of families, also concerned itself with abducting children who had been brought from the provinces and entrusted to Turkish families.[57] It was, however, impossible to find and retrieve the thousands of boys and girls who had been transported to the capital. The Istanbul network therefore decided to compile lists of the homes in which they were living, including as much information as it could about these children. After the armistice, Berjuhi notes, this information helped mothers who had survived to find their children, while the Patriarchate was able to retrieve large numbers of orphans.[58]

The Deportation of the Armenians of Constantinople and Its Environs

Armenians have lived in Constantinople almost from the day on which the Ottomans captured the city. Under the reign of the Ottoman Sultans, successive Armenian deportations (in the sixteenth century) or emigration (in the seventeenth century) led to the formation of six Armenian neighborhoods in the city. The first exiles constituted the famous *altı cemât* (six communities) of Samatia, Balat, Kumkapı, Langa, Hasantipi, and Galata, each inhabited by people who had emigrated from a single region. At the turn of the seventeenth century, a new influx of Armenians fleeing the Turkish-Persian wars settled in the outer districts of the capital: Edirne Kapı, Top Kapı, Eyub, Beşiktaş, Ortaköy, Kuruçeşme, Üsküdar, and Kadiköy.

According to the Patriarchate, 161,000 Armenians were living in Istanbul in 1912, not counting the emigrants who has recently arrived from the provinces.[59] The 1914 Ottoman census put the number of Armenians of all confessions in the capital and its suburbs at 84,093,[60] a number well below all known estimates. The density of the Armenian population, combined with the affluence of certain circles and the confessional hierarchy established by the empire's Ottoman masters, constituted the very basis for the survival and development of an Armenian identity in the capital. Community life was centered mainly on the Armenians' 47 parishes.[61] Spread across the European and Asiatic shores of the Bosphorus, the Armenians boasted, on the eve of the First World War, 42 neighborhood elementary schools, ten secondary schools, and a dozen Catholic and Protestant middle schools and *lycées*, with a total enrollment of about 25,000.[62]

The Patriarchate, located since 1641 in Kumkapı, was the pivot of the community's political and religious life, with its chamber of elected deputies that met in Galata. The administration of the Patriarchate put out a weekly *Official Gazette*, in which it published a record of the sessions of the chamber, financial reports, the results of the work carried out by the commissions, and election results. Another important Armenian institution, the National Hospital of the Holy Savior in Yedikule, was one of the most modern medical centers in Constantinople; it extended over several acres and comprised ten buildings, a huge park, a chapel, a farm, a professional school, a school for nurses, an orphanage, an old people's home, and an asylum. The leading names in Ottoman medicine, educated almost exclusively in France, practiced all the medical specialties of the day there.

In inner Constantinople, the Armenians were mainly concentrated in the southern part of the city near the sea, in Gedik Paşa, Kumkapı, Yeni Mahale, Samatia, Narlıkapı, Altı Mermer, Topkapı, and Salma Gömrük, and, to the north, Balat. Outside the perimeter of the old city, they could be found in Eyub, Balıklı, Yedikule, Makriköy, San Stefano, and, further to the west, Silivri. On the other side of the Golden Horn they were concentrated in Hazköy, Kasim Paşa, Galata, Pera, Pangaltı, and, further to the north, Şişli, Dolab Dere, Feriköy, Beşiktaş, Ortaköy, Kuru Çeşme, Bebek, Rumeli Hisar, Boyaciköy, Stenia Yeniköy, Tarabia, Büyük Dere, and Sarıyar-Yeni Mahale. On the Asiatic side of the city, there were Armenians in Beykoz, Kandili, Kuzguncuk, and Üsküdar, in the quarters of Melamihe, Icadiye, and Yeni Mahale, Kadiköy. To the east of Scutari, in Alemdağ, the "Armenian Village" (Ermeniköy) was divided up between innkeepers and woodcutters. Finally, on the shores of the Sea of Marmara, there was a big colony in Kartal and on the Prince's Islands, in Proti (Kenalı) and Prinkipo (Büyükada). This arid inventory of the areas in which the Armenian population of Greater Constantinople lived gives a rather poor idea of a distinct community marked by an original way of life. Grouped around their churches, given direction by their deputies and clergymen and administered by their parish councils, the Armenians in the city exercised almost all the trades, from the *hamal* (porter) who had just arrived from Mush to the government minister descended from one of the capital's old aristocratic families. Many Armenians were craftsmen: primarily goldsmiths, silversmiths, bakers, weavers, tailors, compositors, boot-makers, shoemakers, masons, tile-makers, carpenters, cabinet-makers, potters, and ceramists. The Armenian elites were active in international commerce, trade, shipping, banking, and industry, as well as in the liberal professions, especially medicine, architecture, and law. The yearbooks of industry and trade provide a good indication of the key positions that the capital's Armenian community held in these fields. The intellectual and artistic professions, for their part, had undergone rapid growth from the middle of the nineteenth century on: an increase in the number of schools, newspapers, and publishing firms, together with the creation of professional theaters, offered new opportunities to young people who wished to pursue intellectual careers. Finally, since the 1850s, the number of Armenians employed at the upper levels of Ottoman government had increased significantly, notably in the technical, economic, and diplomatic ministries. It was, moreover, from the spheres of finance, the liberal professions, the higher levels of government, and the press that the Armenian deputies in the Ottoman parliament and Armenian Chamber were recruited.

The Ottoman capital, in constant relation with Europe, was of course subject to the influence of Western ways, especially as far as its affluent and intellectual strata were concerned. The members of these groups almost all spoke French and were steeped in French culture, wore European dress, and, more generally, lived "*à la franca*," to employ the expression immortalized by the humorist Hagop Baronian. They frequented the fashionable restaurants of the Bosphorus and spent their holidays on the islands (on Proti, in the Armenians' case, where the patriarch had his summer residence).

The center of the political and intellectual life of the empire's Armenians, and also the site of the biggest Armenian urban concentration anywhere, Constantinople exerted a constant pull on the provinces, the population of the High Plateau included. When circumstances allowed, as was notably the case after 1908, the political parties established their headquarters and press organs here. The first reflections about the Armenians' development and future were forged in this crucible.[63]

Finally, 2,300 Armenians lived in the *kaza* of Kartal, on the northeastern shore of the Sea of Marmara. They were primarily winemakers, particularly in Maltepe and Kartal.[64]

According to a well-informed Armenian source, the patriarch appealed to the German Ambassador, then to Bishop Dolci, and finally to the American Ambassador with the request that they intercede with the government when, around 15 May, the Ittihad was making preparations to deport the Armenians of the capital. It seems, however, that Hüseyin Cahid, Kara Kemal, and Enver expressed opposition to this decision. According to credible sources, cited by Aguni, Enver even raised the question at a meeting of the Council of Ministers, where he is said to have insisted on the disastrous effects that such an undertaking would have in the capital's Western circles.[65] The writer Yervant Odian, who had eluded the 24 April roundup and was living more or less underground, notes in his souvenirs that in Istanbul in May 1915 the authorities ordered the mobilization of new age cohorts and the men who had so far been exempted from the draft because they had paid the *bedel*. Thus, spontaneous roundups conducted in the streets beefed up the contingents of men sent to the Dardannelles, which was the scene of intense fighting in this period.[66]

According to Aguni, the Patriarchate "learned within an hour," through various channels, about all government decisions having to do with the capital's Armenians. He also
reports that the grand vizier, Said Halim, took pains to convoke the patriarch by way of
Senator Zareh Dilber in order to inform him that the Armenians of Constantinople would
not be deported.[67] It can be affirmed with virtual certainty that bitter debates about the
fate of the Armenians of Istanbul raged in both the government and the Unionist Central
Committee. Not humanitarian considerations, but most assuredly fear of the negative effects
of hunting down Armenians in the middle of Constantinople militated in favor of allowing
at least part of the capital's Armenian population to stay put. It is also noteworthy that, after
this collective decision was reached, Interior Minister Talât announced that "all Armenians
who, by virtue of what they say, write, or do, seem likely to work toward the creation of an
Armenia and are considered dangerous" should be deported. In other words, all the active
elements of the Armenian population were to be eliminated. The authorities added to the
list of those subject to deportation all the Armenians who came from the provinces to work
in the capital, especially the men. Lists were compiled quarter by quarter, and deportations
began in the month of June. They affected a second group of the Armenian elite, such as the
lawyer Diran Yerganian, Hagop Ardzruni, or Sarkis Svin.[68] Unlike the elites deported in late
April, however, these deportees were sent by rail to Syria, via Konya and Bozanti.

According to Armenian sources, it was a member of the Unionist Central Committee,
İsmail Canbolat, the general director of the Department of State Security and the governor of the capital, who was charged with deporting natives of the provinces from the
capital. He is also said to have ordered the murder of those interned in Çankırı.[69] Bedri
Bey, the Constantinople police chief and one of the architects of the deportations in the
provinces; Murad Bey, Bedri's assistant police chief;[70] Muftizâde Şükrü [Kaya] Bey, the head
of the Directorate for the Settlement of Tribes and Emigres (Iskân-ı Aşâyirîn ve Muhâcirîn
Müdîriyeti) and the CUP's delegate in the provinces of Adana and Aleppo in fall 1915; and
İbrahim Bey, the director of Istanbul's prisons, played pivotal roles in these operations.[71] At
a lower level, Tevfik Hadi, the police chief in Constantinople's Bayazid neighborhood who
worked primarily in the police administration, was very active in carrying out deportations
and in engineering the murders of members of the Armenian elite.[72]

Yervant Odian was arrested in his home in Şişli on 26 August. The historian Arshag
Alboyajian was arrested the same day. Odian soon found himself in prison with Dr. Kelejian,
a well-known physician, and the journalist Sebuh Aguni. A few days later these men left
by rail for Konya under police guard.[73] It seems that Mehmed Talât had not abandoned the
idea of deporting the Armenians of the capital. In September 1915, Halil had nevertheless
succeeded, with the help of the internal opposition to the Ittihad, in taking the Ministry of
Foreign Affairs in hand, having been controlled until then by Said Halim. Halil was one of
the main opponents of the policy of liquidating the Armenians. The result was that, between
September 1915 and May 1916, partisans of deporting the Armenians from the capital were
locked in a ferocious struggle with those who opposed the idea. In the cabinet, the battle
lines ran between Talât on the one hand and Enver and Halil on the other. In the Ittihad's
Central Committee, they ran between Talât and Nâzım.[74]

On 8 September 1915, at a time when many caravans had already set out, Ambassador
Pallavicini noted that "the expulsion of Armenians from Constantinople has been called to
a halt, thanks to the energetic actions of the American Ambassador, according to rumors circulating within the Committee of Union and Progress. Yet members of the said Committee
have declared: 'We have stopped for the moment, but we will still find a way of ridding
ourselves of all the Armenians.'"[75] A few weeks later, these threats were put into practice.
"According to a credible source," the German chargé d'affaires Neurath wrote, "the Turkish
government, all its assurances notwithstanding, has decided to deport the Armenians of

Constantinople as well."[76] On 7 December 1915, the German Ambassador Wolff-Metternich informed Berlin that, "According to information provided by the police chief, four thousand Armenians were recently expelled from Constantinople and sent to Anatolia; the eighty thousand still here will be gradually evacuated, to say nothing of the thirty thousand who were deported over the summer and another thirty thousand who have fled."[77] Ernst von Nahmer, a reporter for the *Kölnische Zeitung*, stated in a confidential report dated 5–6 September 1915 that the targets of the first deportations were natives of the provinces, followed by unmarried men and married men with their families. He added that "the most inoffensive people are being deported in altogether systematic fashion, such as the two employees in my boarding-house. They simply disappeared after being summoned to the police station ... The discretion with which [the arrests] are being carried out finds its explanation in the presence of the ambassadors."[78] An account by Yervant Der Mardirosian, a native of Talas and a cadet at Istanbul's Yakacık Military Academy who was enrolled in the armed forces on 10 September 1915 along with another 40 young Armenians from the provinces, indicates the complexity of the situation of Armenian males. Like his fellow students, Der Mardirosian agreed to convert, thereby saving his life. The other cadets nevertheless continued to show the Armenian converts a frank hostility that reflected the effects of the propaganda campaign waged in Turkish circles. Moreover, every day, down to their departure from the capital in January 1916, Der Mardirosian and his classmates witnessed the house searches that the police conducted in Armenian homes in Istanbul and the systematic arrests of young men and provincials.[79]

In addition to the inhabitants of the "Armenian village" of Alemdağ, located outside Üsküdar, the Armenians in the villages surrounding the capital seems to have been deported more systematically than others. The "trial of Büyükdere/San Stefano," which culminated in a verdict rendered on 24 May 1919, was based exclusively on charges of financial "abuse." Nevertheless, it revealed the way Selanikli Refik Bey, the *kaymakam* of Büyükdere, Hafız Mehmed, Abdül Kerim, a police lieutenant, and Rizeli Celal Effendi "shortened the period authorized by the government for deporting non-Muslims from the Büyükdere area and appropriated the assets of the deportees."[80] The accused strove to demonstrate that they had been at pains "to protect the life and property of the persons who were displaced," yet were in some cases condemned to pay fines and serve prison sentence of one to two years – in others, they were simply acquitted. There was never any question of the damages incurred by the Armenian deportees.[81]

In closing the present chapter on the Ottoman capital, we must point out that, despite the human and material losses inflicted on the Istanbul Armenians, the approximately 100,000 of them who were able to maintain their residence or find refuge there until war's end provided invaluable aid to the surviving deportees eking out an existence in Syria or Mesopotamia.

Chapter 13

Deportations in the Vilayet of Edirne and the *Mutesarifat* of Biğa/Dardanelles

I n the Ottoman epoch, the Armenian community in the vilayet of Edirne developed from the sixteenth century on, when the famous architect Sinan called on 250 of his compatriots to help build the mosque of Sultan Selim in Edirne. At the turn of the seventeenth century, Armenians from the Kemah and Erzincan areas, victims of the series of famine years that had followed the looting by the *celali* (revolts), also settled in Tekirdağ/Rodosto and Malgara on the shores of the Sea of Marmara and further west in Çorlu and Silivri.

On the eve of the war, 800 Armenian families (4,536 Armenians) were living in Edirne, the seat of government of the vilayet of the same name.[1] They were concentrated in two inner city neighborhoods, Kale Içi and At Bazar, and also in the suburb of Kara Ağac. The inhabitants of Kara Ağac were truck farmers, whereas the Armenians who lived in the inner city were craftsmen, tradesmen, or railroad employees when they were not employed in tobacco manufacture.[2] The biggest Armenian colony was to be found in the port of Rodosto, the principal town of the *kaza* of Tekirdağ; the approximately 17,000 Armenians who lived in the town represented half its total population. Rodosto's Armenian community, founded in 1606, had settled on the shore, in the Takavor neighborhood in the southwestern part of the city, and also to the northeast in the suburb known as Çiftlik, the name of which indicates its connection with agricultural activities. The Armenians here were tinsmiths, blacksmiths, goldsmiths, and millers, but also ship captains or even fleet owners and bankers.[3]

In 1914, some 3,000 Armenians lived in the town of Malgara, which lay northwest of Rodosto. Almost all were descended of natives of Pakarij (a district of Kemah). They, too, had settled in the region in 1606.[4]

To the south lay the *kaza* of Gallipoli, which formed a slightly elevated peninsula. Its population was overwhelmingly Greek, with a mere 1,190 Armenians living there in 1914.[5] They worked principally in commerce and the crafts.

On the road that led to Constantinople, in Çorlu, there lived in 1914 from 1,678 to 3,005 Turkish-speaking Armenians, whose ancestors had come from Yozgat. Finally, 1,000 Armenians lived in Silivri, in the easternmost part of the vilayet; they were reputed to be among the best *kayıkci* (boatsmen) on the Sea of Marmara.[6]

The Deportations in Edirne

During the Balkan Wars, the city of Edirne, which had passed from Turkish to Bulgarian hands and then won back by the Young Turks, had been the scene of violent acts that had affected all the groups in the city. The bitterness that had accumulated in the course

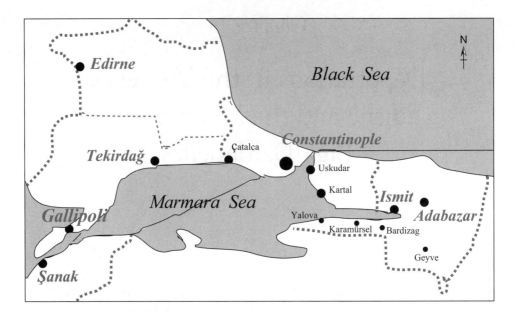

of these events, especially among the Muslims, resurfaced in fall 1915, when the fate of Edirne's Armenians was hanging in the balance. Here the deportation order was made public much later than elsewhere, on 14 October. There was at least one objective reason for this. Bulgaria's late entry into the First World War on the Ottoman side probably forced the Young Turk authorities to postpone anti-Armenian operations in European Turkey, so as not to impede the negotiations aimed at inducing Bulgaria to rally to the Ottomans. Moreover, a 24 October 1915 note from the Austrian Ambassador to the empire reveals that, "With the cession of Kara-Agatsch [Kara Ağaç] to Bulgaria, all the Armenian families in that locality were expelled to Anatolia."[7] The expulsion orders had been issued by the vali of Edirne, Haci Adıl Bey [Arda],[8] a jurist of Cretan origin, Unionist parliamentary deputy from Edirne, former general secretary of the CUP, close friend of Talât's, and, for a time, minister of the interior, who had, moreover, been implicated in the 1909 Cilician events.[9] The choice of so eminent a CUP leader as vali was probably also a sign of the importance that the Ittihad attached to this vilayet. In addition to Adıl Bey, the CUP had sent Abdül Ğani to serve in Edirne as its responsible secretary, with Hayrullah Bey as his assistant. The Ittihad could also count on Haci Ali Bey, the president of the Unionist club in Edirne, and two influential Young Turks from the city, İzzeddin Bey, the head of the Health Department, and Rifât Bey, the mayor. Among the military men involved in the anti-Armenian violence, Dr. Ertogrül Bey, an army doctor who worked in the Kalayçi hospital, also played a role in liquidating the soldiers in the labor battalions. Among the magistrates and civilian state officials, Tevfik Bey, the chief prosecutor at the court-martial and a member of Edirne's *emvalı metruke*; Şakir Effendi, the *mektubci* (head of the correspondence bureau); Emin Bey, the vilayet's *defterdar* and the president of the *emvalı metruke*; Tevfik Effendi, the assistant police chief; and the police lieutenants Niazi Effendi and Nuri Effendi all had a hand in organizing the deportations and pillaging the Armenians' "abandoned property."[10]

Departing from the methods employed in Anatolia, the local authorities here did not give the Armenians any time at all to prepare for the deportation. The order for immediate deportation was issued on the night of 27–28 October 1915, giving rise to acts of pillage that profited the local Ittihad club and Turkish schools. Three hundred Armenian shops in the Ali Paşa bazaar were demolished.[11]

A report written "of a common accord" by the Bulgarian general consul M. G. Seraphimoff and the Austro-Hungarian consul Dr. Arthur Nadamlenzki and sent to the Austro-Hungarian embassy in Constantinople on 6 November 1915, reveals how the CUP organized the liquidation of the Armenians of Edirne:[12]

The fact that what is happening is obviously only the implementation of a carefully meditated program, a program the aim of which is the "annihilation of the Christian elements in Turkey," is so serious that the undersigned believe it their duty to refer the matter to the interested powers ... The new system adopted by the ruling circles, which frightens not only the Jews and the other Christians living here, but also the overwhelming majority of the Muslim population, was exhibited in all its cruelty and cynicism on the occasion of the expulsion of the Armenians of Adrianople ... The procedures that the undersigned were able to observe here bear witness to a desire, not merely to expel, but, clearly, to eradicate an entire race. On the night of 27–28 October, the organs of the police knocked at the doors of the city's rich Armenian families and forced them to abandon, without delay, their homes, their belongings, and all their assets in order to be transported to an unknown destination. The scenes that took place on that and the following nights defy description. There took place things that only an altogether deprived mind and a barbaric, brutal soul could conceive.

Women still bed-ridden because they had given birth the day before were torn from their beds; small children who were seriously ill were carried off by force in carts; semi-paralysed old men were forced to leave their homes. Little girls in the city's boarding schools had no idea that their parents had been forced to leave and were thus separated forever from their fathers and mothers. The unfortunates did not even have the right to take money or objects dear to them when they left. With a few piasters in hand, men who had considerable fortunes – four thousand Turkish pounds were discovered in the chest of one Armenian alone – had to leave the house of their fathers in order to be led off into dire poverty ... The belongings of those expelled were sold off at ludicrously low prices in public auctions at which the Turkish buyers were once again privileged over the others. Thus fortunes were squandered which, by rights, ought to have been inventoried.

On the very night on which the Armenians were expelled, the Turkish authorities staged little feasts in homes bereft of their masters: people played the piano there, emptied the cellars, and ate whatever provisions they found. The same scenes were repeated in broad daylight the next day. We were told by a completely reliable source that many valuables and a great deal of money have disappeared. The only salvation the Turks offered the Armenians was to embrace Islam! So far, not a single family has bowed to this pressure.

The vali and the police chief have declared that widows and their children will be spared. The Young Turk Committee has found a way to make even this category of people miserable. It is trying to abduct the young girls and marry them off to Turks. Two of the Menziljian daughters were able to escape these new dangers only because they happened to be at the school of the Sisters of Agram and were protected by the consulate of I. and R. Austria-Hungary. The Bulgarian authorities are doing everything they can to obtain the return of all the Armenian families whose sons and husbands are fighting in the Bulgarian army for the common cause. The fact that the children enrolled in the Turkish schools and, in particular, those in the Committee's schools were taken out to watch the departure of hundreds of Armenians crazy with sorrow and despair as if it were a spectacle is, in the opinion of the undersigned, a matter of extreme gravity! It makes it possible to infer and gives us a glimpse of the secret designs animating the domestic policy Young Turk Committee, which is inculcating a spirit of hatred for the Christians in children's hearts and minds, a hatred that may one day also be directed against the friends of today. That this circumstance is no mere accident, but itself part of a pre-established program, is proven by the fact, known to one and all, that during the persecutions of the Greeks, Turkish schoolchildren were made to take part in the looting of the Greek villages on the city's outskirts... Here, in the vilayet of Adrianople, almost all the big, wealthy trading houses were, in the past few years, in Armenian hands. Almost all the rich Jewish and Greek bankers and merchants left the vilayet after the Balkan War. With the expulsion of the Armenians who worked together with the big Austro-Hungarian and German factories, the most important merchants have left Adrianople, without, of course, first settling accounts with their suppliers, creditors, or debtors.[13]

This remarkable report needs no comment. Let us point out only that these deportees took the Istanbul-Konya-Bozanti route, by foot or rail, and ended up in Syria or Mesopotamia. A last wave of deportations, which targeted the families of craftsmen and soldiers, was carried out during the night of 17–18 February 1916 on the initiative of the interim vali, Zekeria Zihni Bey, formerly the *mutesarif* of Tekirdağ.[14] It emptied the city of its last Armenians.

Deportations in the Sancak of Rodosto

In the most important Armenian colony of the region, that of Tekirdağ/Rodosto, with an Armenian population of roughly 17,000 in 1914, the deportations were preceded by a number of alarming events. We must first recall the massacres perpetrated from 1 to 3 July by soldiers in Rodosto, which the Istanbul press quickly painted as a revolt that the army had had to "put down."[15] We cannot ignore the fire in the Armenian quarter that broke out on 26 August 1914, in the midst of the general mobilization – it was, to say the least, of suspicious origin.[16] Nor can we ignore the direct threats hanging over the heads of the Armenian population in the same period, which had compelled the interior minister to come to the port in person, accompanied by the patriarchal vicar, Perhajian, to reduce tensions.[17] According to a survivor, most of the conscripts from Rodosto were assigned to the region's labor battalions from fall 1914 on; very few managed to avoid them.[18] Yet, the first arrests, which targeted the city's notables, were not made until Monday, 20 September. Officially, it was a question of "punishing" people who were said to have "facilitated the Bulgarians' entry into Terkirdağ" during the Balkan war. The day after they were arrested, these men and their families were put aboard trains bound for Anatolia.[19] On Wednesday, 22 September, a second wave of arrests took place, targeting once again entrepreneurs such as the Keremian Brothers, Krikor Shushanian, the Jamjian brothers, Hovagim Karanfilian, Hovhannes Papazian, or the lawyer Bedros. All were immediately put on the road.[20] Thereafter, the deportations took a more systematic form. They went on until 31 October and affected nearly 10,000 people, who followed the Istanbul-Konya-Bozanti-Aleppo route and ended up in the Syrian Desert. By 10 November, 3,000 more people had been expedited; only the families of a few dozen soldiers were spared.[21] On 20 February 1916, a final group of 120 was sent to Ismit by ship, where it was then sent on its way to Syria.[22]

The soul of these operations was the former *mutesarif* of Tekirdağ and the interim vali of Edirne, Zekeria Zihni Bey, an Ittihadist of Circassian origins and a graduate of the *Mulkiye*.[23]

He was assisted by İsmail Sidki Bey, an *evkaf* official and CUP delegate in Rodosto, and also by two local Unionists, Ahmed Hilmi Bey and İbrahimzâde Ahmed Tevfik. The *mutesarif* also benefited from the collaboration of Kâzım Bey, his assistant; Ömer Naci, Rodosto's mufti; Mehmed Effendi, a civil servant employed in the Registrar's Office; Nahir Bey, a captain in the fortress; Arif Bey, the head of the Department of Public Education; Ziya Bey, the head of the Agriculture Department; Remzi Bey, the head of the Department of the Public Debt; and Ferdi Bey, the head of the Tobacco Régie. Among those implicated in the pillage of Armenian property, we must note, above all, the activities of Sahir Bey, the president of the committee responsible for "abandoned property"; İbrahim Nâzım Bey Zâde, the auctioneer; and Süleyman Bey, Fuad Bey, Haci Mehmed, and Tutunci Eyub Osman, members of the committee. Among the military men, Natan Bey, the commander of the local brigade; Haci Hüseyin Bey Baban, the head of the military workshops; Derviş Bey, the commander of the gendarmerie in Rodosto; and Mehmed Bey, the Head of the Recruitment Office, carried out the deportations. The men were arrested and tortured by Tahir Bey, Rodosto's police chief, who was responsible for recruiting the squadrons of the Special Organization. He was assisted in turn by Süleyman Bey and Ali Rıza Bey, the assistant police chiefs; Sandalci Hasan Bey; Nusret Bey; Fehmi Bey, the son of the parliamentary deputy Haci Adıl Bey; Hilmi Bey, a lawyer; Haci Norheddin; Selanikli Haci Mehmed; and Selanikli Haci Hilmi.[24]

According to statistics published by the Armenian Patriarchate, approximately 3,500 Armenians from Rodosto survived the deportations.[25]

Deportations in the *Kazas* of Çorlu and Gallipoli

What we know of the fate of the Armenians of Çorlu is that they too were deported rather late, on 15 October 1915, initially by ship to Ismit, and then on foot or by rail to Bozanti and Syria via Konya.[26] Among those chiefly responsible for the exactions perpetrated in Çorlu were, of course, the Unionists and *çetes* who were active in Tekirdağ as well. Among the Ittihadists, the main instigators of these exactions were Sandalci Hasan Bey; Nusret Bey; Rahmi Bey, the son of the parliamentary deputy Ali Bey; Tahir Bey; Hilmi Bey, a lawyer; Furuncizâde Fuad; Ahkincizâde Haci Nusreddin; Selanikli Haci Mehmed; and Selanikli Kanlı Hilmi. Among the civilian and military officials, we should note the roles played by Ali Sakıb Bey, the *kaymakam* of Çorlu; Cemal Bey, the commander of the gendarmerie; Eşref Hasan Bey, Cemal's second in command; General Osman Nuri Bey, the head of the railroad; Mehmed Nesip Bey, a judge; Şefik Bey, the police chief; Enver Effendi, the president of the municipality; Dr. Mustafa, a municipal physician; and Rahim Effendi, a tax collector. The committee responsible for "abandoned property" was in the hands of Zöhdi Bey, a lawyer; Mehmed Nazmi Halim; Ağazâde; and Mehmed Şefik Yegenzâde.[27]

The fate of the Armenians of the peninsula of Gallipoli was sealed in early April 1915. When the battle for the Dardanelles began, they were temporarily transferred to Biğa and Lapsaki, and, later, deported.[28]

According to an Armenian source, several thousand of the more than 30,000 Armenians of the vilayet of Edirne escaped deportation thanks to the energetic intervention of the Bulgarian authorities.[29]

Deportations in the Mutesarifat *of* Biğa/Dardanelles

In 1914, the Armenian presence in the Dardanelles was limited to some 2,500 people, half of whom lived in Çanak Kale and the environs. This port, long simply a fortress defending the entry to the Sea of Marmara, had gradually grown in size and importance, attracting artisans and merchants who had come from Persia in the first half of the sixteenth century. The Armenians in the rest of the peninsula were to be found in 1914 in Ezin (pop. 670), Ayvacık, Bayramiş (pop. 200), Biğa (pop. 409), and Lapsaki.[30] As in the case of the Armenians of Gallipoli, the battle for the Dardanelles precipitated an evacuation of the district's entire civilian population. The Armenians were later deported to Syria.[31]

Chapter 14

Deportations in the *Mutesarifat* of Ismit

Like the Armenian colonies in Thrace, those in Bithynia came into existence between 1590 and 1608, with the arrival of large numbers of peasants from Agn, Arapkir, Sıvas, Kemah, and Erzerum. Settling in this very fertile but depopulated area, they formed a continuous string of villages that stretched from the Black Sea coast through Adabazar and Ismit to Bursa. Early in the twentieth century, Nicomedia/Ismit, the former capital of the eastern empire, was still the region's administrative and economic center, profiting from its exceptional geographical location as a port serving as the entryway to Anatolia. Its domination, however, was threatened by Adabazar, which, thanks to the railway, was establishing itself as the new transit center for Anatolian exports and imports.[1] On the eve of the war, the *mutesarifat* of Ismit boasted a total Armenian population of 61,675, settled in 42 localities.[2] The Armenians had 51 churches, a monastery, and 53 schools.[3]

The *Kaza* of Nicomedia/Ismit

Set deep back in the Gulf of Ismit, Nicomedia had 12,000 inhabitants in the early twentieth century. The town's 4,635 Armenians lived in the Kadibayir/Karabaş neighborhood, around the Cathedral of the Holy Mother of God in the western part of the city. Ismit's Armenian population, which was Armenian speaking, was made up of industrious craftsmen and merchants. With the Greeks, they dominated the bazaar, which lay at the foot of the ancient acropolis that looked down on Nicomedia. The chief economic activities were silk-making and the silk trade, as well as the production and sale of tobacco and salt. Eleven Armenian villages lying within a radius of 15 to 20 kilometers maintained close relations with the town.[4] To the south, the little town of Bardizag/Bağçecik, with its 9,024 inhabitants, was the last station on the steamboat line that ran between Ismit and the capital. Located six kilometers from the coast near Mt. Minas and surrounded by forests and fertile farmland, Bardizag was known above all for its production of silkworms, its vineyards, and its truck gardens. A large American mission, with a middle school and hospital, was active in the town on the eve of the First World War.[5] Half an hour from Bardizag, the village of Döngel had a population of 419. To the south and southeast lay the rural centers of Zakar (pop. 404), Manushag (pop. 591), Ovacık (pop. 3,303), and Jamavayr (pop. 264); Arslanberg (pop. 3,218) lay to the northeast.

In the northern part of the *kaza* of Ismit was the Monastery of Armash, founded in 1611. Its special importance was due to its position as the one and only Armenian seminary in western Anatolia. In 1910, the village adjacent to the seminary had a population of 1,505. Its villagers raised silkworms on lands belonging to the monastery. It was the seat of the *müdir* of the *nahie* of Armash, Fakreddin Effendi, who was to become one of the main organizers of the expulsion of the region's Armenian population. A few kilometers to the west of Armash lay the villages of Dagh (pop. 380) and, hard by Dagh, Khach (pop. 202). Hazkal/Pirahmed (pop. 811) lay an hour to the northeast.[6] Thus, on the eve of the war, the total Armenian population of the 12 localities of Ismit (including Catholics and Protestants) was 25,399, out of a total population of 70,000 inhabitants, including large numbers of Çerkez who had settled in the area in the late 1870s[7] and the *muhacirs* from Salonika and Rumelia who settled here after the 1912–13 Balkan Wars.[8]

The *Kaza* of Adabazar

In the period that interests us, Adabazar, located 45 kilometers east of Ismit in the immediate vicinity of the Sakaria River, was, together with Bardizag, undeniably the most important regional urban center for the Armenians, who represented 50 per cent of the town's total population. Many of Adabazar's 12,450 Armenians lived in the center of town, near the bazaar, in the parish of the Holy Archangel; the others were to be found in Nemçeler and Malacılar. The town's prosperity, which was owing to the construction of the Anatolian railway that reached Adabazar in 1898, greatly benefited its Armenian craftsmen and merchants, who had grown rich thanks to their silk workshops, provided with thread by the silk-raisers of the surrounding villages.[9] Southeast of Adabazar, on the southern shore of Lake Sabanca, the Armenians had, in 1710, founded a village of the same name, which, with its southern "New Quarter," had 360 inhabitants. East of the town, in the *nahie* of Handık, were two more Armenian villages, Hayots Kiugh (pop. 1,007) and Hoviv (pop. 288). A few more Armenians lived scattered in other localities. To the southwest, in the *nahie* of Akyazi, the little village of Kup was inhabited by 1,064 Orthodox Armenians, whose ancestors had come from Agn.[10]

Until spring 1915, this region, lying close to the capital, was relatively calm. With the August 1914 general mobilization, most of the young men were conscripted and assigned to the region's labor battalions. The military requisitions spawned abuses, but nothing hinted at the violence to come. The *mutesarif* of Ismit, Deli Mazhar Bey, who held his post from 10 June 1913 to 28 September 1916, was a typical civil servant who obeyed the orders he received from the capital without crises of conscience. Until spring 1915, a few notables and political activists had been arrested, but the Armenians seemed to be convinced that these men had fallen victim to narrowly focused repression. Everything changed with the arrival of two CUP delegates – İbrahim Bey, the former director of Istanbul's prisons, and Hoca Rifât Effendi[11] – who had plainly been sent to the area to oversee the deportation.

The order to deport the Armenians from the 42 localities of the *sancak* of Ismit, signed by the interior minister on 5/18 July 1915,[12] crowned two months of activity designed to undermine its Armenian communities. Here too this activity had consisted in a campaign to confiscate arms that served to legitimize the increasingly systematic arrests of men throughout the region. İbrahim Bey and Hoca Rifât, who were also officers of the *Teşkilât-ı Mahsusa*, could call on the services of several squadrons of *çetes*, commanded by Şevket Bey; Faik Bey, the commander of the gendarmerie in Ismit; *Çeteci* Mehmed; *Çeteci* Edhem; and *Çeteci* Pehlivan Hasan Çavuş, who were charged with carrying out the operations in the region.[13]

Major Mustafa Emir, Eşref Adıl Bey, and Beha Bey, commanders of military units; Hüseyin Çavus, the head of the militias; and Reşid Bey, Ismit's police chief, took charge of the "legal" dimension of operations, particularly the arrests. Ismit's Unionist leaders, who were also members of the *emvali metruke* – İsmail Ali Bey, a navy official; Şerif Bey, a lawyer, and Cavid, a pharmacist – conducted the party propaganda campaigns and organized the seizures of Armenian property.[14]

The first operations targeted the Armenians of Adabazar rather than those in Ismit. In early May, some 50 Adabazar notables were taken into custody and deported to Sultaniye (in the vilayet of Konya) and Koçhisar. Shortly thereafter, soldiers of two divisions of the Ottoman Army were billeted in the Armenian neighborhoods, apparently for the sole purposed of guaranteeing order in the town. İbrahim Bey, upon his arrival in Adabazar in late May, proceeded to arrest another group of notables, including the merchant Bedros Afeyan, the banker Bedros Muradian, and the president of the municipality, Stepan Demirjian. According to an Armenian source, İbrahim Bey, accompanied by the police chief Reşid Bey, went to see the Armenian notables, who had been confined in the Church of the Holy Archangel. He introduced himself to them as a "*çete* leader" who had long "operated in Macedonia" and had a great deal of experience in conducting house searches. He also claimed that he had worked side-by-side with Hnchak militants during the "reaction of 31 March" 1909 and had distributed arms. He therefore knew who had arms and demanded that the Armenians turn over "two hundred fifty Mausers" without delay.[15] That İbrahim held such a speech about taking back the weapons that the CUP had distributed to the Armenian "committees" is the more plausible in that it legitimized the arrests that followed in a way we have had occasion to observe elsewhere. According to our Armenian source, 600 to 700 men were arrested and interned in the Church of St. Garabed in the space of a few days. The auxiliary primate, Father Mikayel Yeramian, and a notable, Antranig Charkejian, were the first victims of the torture that İbrahim ordered his men to carry out in order to make the prisoners confess where they had stashed their weapons. Two weeks later, 10 notables were brought before the Istanbul court-martial.[16]

On 11 August 1915, the order to deport the Armenians of Adabazar and the surrounding villages was published. Soldiers surrounded the Armenian neighborhoods and guarded the exits from them, blocking all possibility of flight. The authorities did not allow the populace to take its moveable assets with it. In two weeks, more than 20,000 people, beginning with those who lived in the neighborhoods of Nemçer and Malacılar, were put on the road to Konya. Twenty-five families of craftsmen who worked for the army were spared and allowed to remain in their homes, as was the one family that agreed to convert, that of Haci Hovhannes Yeghiayan.[17]

As soon as the deportees had left, Necati Sezayi Bey, *kaymakam* of Adabazar from 19 January to 22 November 1915, and Reşid Bey, *müdir* of the *nahie* of Hanlık, set about methodically demolishing the Armenian houses and churches – which were in some cases converted into stables or granaries – and transferred ownership of the schools to the local authorities. This procedure was apparently motivated by the authorities' desire to make it impossible for the exiles to return.[18] Hamid Bey, the responsible secretary whom the CUP had dispatched to Adabazar, and the members of the town's Ittihadist club, Kalıbcı Hafız, Mehmed Ziyaeddin, Haci Numan, and Arapzâde Said, helped İbrahim carry out these operations and above all saw to the seizure of Armenian property.[19] In the *kaza* of Ismit, violence was focused in particular on two exclusively Armenian localities, Bardizag and Arslanbeg, which the authorities seemed to think should be evacuated before all others. The first problems cropped up in Arslanbeg in May, when a few dozen notables were arrested and jailed in Ismit, where men from Bardizag and Ovacık had also been locked up. Shortly afterward, all these men were transferred to the *kaza* of Geyve and interned in the Turkish village of Taraklı, where the local elites of Ismit, Yalova, Çengiler, and so on were already concentrated.[20] On 18 July 1915, under the orders of a commander in the gendarmerie, İbrahim Bey, 200 soldiers and gendarmes surrounded Arslanbeg. The deportations began the next morning while the village was looted by Çerkez *çetes* of the Special Organization, relayed by Turkish villagers from the vicinity who completed the task of demolishing Arslanbeg.[21] Like the other deportees from the region, more than 2,000 natives of Arslanbeg were deported by way of Eskişehir, Konya, and Bozanti, and then were scattered in Rakka, Meskene, Der Zor, Mosul, and Baghdad. Very few of them ever returned.[22]

Bardizag/Bağçecik met a fate similar to that dealt out to Arslanbeg. Approximately 1,000 young conscripts were sent to work on construction sites; some 20 doctors, elementary schoolteachers, merchants, and craftsmen were arrested and deported in May; and the con-fiscation of weapons led to arrests, house searches, and looting. The CUP's delegate, İbrahim Bey, went to Bardizag to oversee operations in early July.[23] The Armenian middle school was a special target of the *çetes* accompanying the Ittihadist leader, who repeated the threats he had proffered in Arslanbeg, following them up with torture of the kind we have observed elsewhere. The searches conducted in the churches did not yield the expected results: the "discovery" of a fragment of a theater prop led to a good deal of unpleasantness for Father Madatia Keondiurian, the auxiliary primate, who was accused of possessing a painting depict-ing "a king of Armenia."[24]

From 13 to 15 August, more than 8,000 natives of Bardizag were put on the road. Hard on their heels was the populace of Döngel and Ovacık, who had first had to turn their house keys over to the local authorities. A few families took the precaution of depositing their most valuable belongings with the American mission. Thanks to an Armenian source, we also know that Ali Şuhuri, the *müdir* of the *nahie* of Bağçecik, promised the deportees that they would be taken no further than Konya, probably in order to calm them down and get them to submit to him more readily.[25] Assembled in Ismit's train station, the exiles were told to pay for their train tickets to Konya. An order arrived to the effect that soldiers' families had per-mission to return to their homes. But when it became apparent that almost all the families qualified, the local Young Turk leaders decided not to follow these instructions. This order was probably a mere deceptive maneuver designed to sow confusion in the deportees' minds about the authorities' real plans for them.[26]

In Ismit, where the Armenians represented a smaller proportion of the total population, 38 notables were arrested in May on orders from the CUP delegate, İbrahim Bey. The depor-tations, however, did not take place until 6–9 August, when three convoys were dispatched to Konya. The authorities then began methodically burning down the houses in the Armenian quarter and also the bishopric, devastating the graveyard and generally seeing to it that all traces of the Armenians' presence in the town were wiped out.[27]

Arthur Ryan, an American missionary who was in Bardizag from 6 October to 20 November 1915, notes in a report[28] that only about 60 Armenians were left there, of whom 30 were handicapped and under the care of the American mission. Ryan also witnessed "Turkish Officials collecting the moveable property of the deported Armenians," stocked in the Armenian church and then sent by ship to Istanbul. Finally, he notes that 60 Muslim families had already been installed in the Armenian houses still standing, while the women and children were held in villages in the vicinity but were not given anything to eat because they refused to convert.[29] His description of Ismit, where he went several times during his stay in Bardizag, confirms that the shops in the bazaar had been thoroughly looted and that the Armenian neighborhood, which was burned down immediately after the deportations, was a pile of rubble. He found no trace of Armenians here, apart from 2,500 deportees from Thrace who briefly camped in the churchyard before continuing their trek to Konya.[30]

A witness mentions that 900 male deportees from Ismit and Angora passed through Kirşehir, where they were stationed behind the town's *konak*; 380 were massacred nearby, in Muncur, and had their bodies thrown into the lake by İzzet Hoca, Haci Halil, Derviş Effendi, and Nuri Effendi.[31] The victims may have been men taken from the caravans, but it is more likely that they were worker-soldiers, for we have no evidence that males were treated differ-ently than females on the Istanbul-Ismit-Konya-Bozanti route.

The *Kaza* of Kandere

In 1914 there were two clusters of Armenian villages, one on each side of the Sakaria, in the *kaza* of Kandere on the Black Sea coast. One, two hours south of Incirli, comprised four rural centers founded in the mid-nineteenth century by "Armenian Laz" – that is, natives of Hamşin: Açambaşi was inhabited by 42 Islamicized families; Kegham had 596 Christian Armenian inhabitants; Çukur had 40 households, and Aram/Kızılcı had a population of 347. The other group of villages, lying northeast of Kandere on the left bank of the Sakaria, comprised five hamlets that had been founded in the seventeenth century: Fındıklı (pop. 500), Ferizli (pop. 872), Tamlek (pop. 416), and Almalu (pop. 471). Thus, a total of more than 3,500 Armenians were living in the *kaza* of Kandere on the eve of the war. They were deported down the Konya-Bozanti route in August 1915 under the supervision of the *kaymakam* of Kandere, Kâmil Bey, who held his post from 9 January 1913 to 10 March 1917.[32]

The *Kaza* of Geyve

The *kaza* of Geyve, which straddled the Sakaria in the southeastern part of the *sancak* of Ismit, boasted in 1914 seven villages occupied either exclusively or partially by Armenians. Geyve and Eçme, on the banks of the river, were inhabited by 2,168 "Armenian-speaking Greeks," or Orthodox Armenians whose ancestors had come from Agn. Ortaköy and Saraclı Karyesi were located in the hills nearby. On the opposite bank of the Sakaria, facing Eçme, was the village of Kıncılar, inhabited by 2,265 Armenians, whose roots were also in Agn.

To the south, on both sides of the railroad, were the villages of Kurdbelen, on the left bank of the river, and Gökgöz, on the right bank, with a total population of 3,923. The last village, Akhisar, lay on the left bank of the Sakaria one hour south of Gökgöz. It had 272 inhabitants. As in the rest of the *sancak* of Ismit, these Armenians too were deported in August 1915. The *kaymakam* of Geyve, Said Bey (who held his post from 19 September 1913 to 21 August 1915) refused to carry out the deportation order and was replaced by Tahsin Bey (who served as *kaymakam* until 5 September 1916).[33]

The *Kazas* of Karamursal and Yalova

Lying close to Constantinople, the *kazas* of Karamursal and, further to the west, Yalova, were in constant communication with the capital thanks to the steamboat lines that served them, Yalova in particular. Karamursal had an Armenian population of 1,378. Yalakdere and Merdeköz, which lay two kilometers from the coast, had Armenian populations of 1,125 and 3,000, respectively. Yalova was made up of a cluster of villages on the Black Sea coast – Şakşak, Kuruçeşme, and Kılıc – with a total population of 1,640 Armenians. Five kilometers to the south, on the road to Bursa, were two more Armenian villages – Çukur, home to 420 Kurdish-speaking Armenians from an area south of Van, and Kartsi/Lalıdere, which had 1,264 inhabitants.[34] The deportation of these Armenians was carried out by the *kaymakam* of Karamursal, Necib Bey, who held his post from 27 May to 2 October 1915, with the assistance of Mehmed Cemal Bey, the commander of the gendarmerie; Ahmed, a mufti; Salaheddin Effendi, an imam; Nuri Bey and Tahir Bey, members of the local *emvalı metruke*; Mazlum Bey, a *mal müdiri*; Ahmed Effendi, Mazlum's assistant; and the *çete* officers Tokatlı Ahmed Çavuş, Bursalı Ahmed Onbaşi, Boşnak Hafız Onbaşi, and Tufenkci Mustafa.[35] In Yalova and its environs it was Ruşdi Bey, holding the post of *kaymakam* from 9 February 1913 to 31 December 1917, who organized the deportation of the Armenians and oversaw the seizure of their property.

From November 1919 to February 1920, several of those responsible for the deportations and the pillage of Armenian property in the *sancak* of Ismit were brought before the court-martial in Istanbul. The first of those indicted, Hamid Bey, the CUP's responsible secretary in Adabazar, went on trial on 6 November 1919 for having acquired the Armenians' assets at "indecent prices." The former *kaymakam* Necati Sezayi Bey was the witness for the prosecution.[36] On Tuesday, 17 February 1920, the court-martial, with Esat as its presiding judge, acquitted Hamid.[37]

The trial of the authors of violence and "abuses" in the *kazas* of Ismit and Karamursal that ran from 15/28 January to 29 February/16 March 1920 culminated in the condemnation of Hoca Rifât, the CUP's delegate in Ismit, who was then being held on the island of Malta and was convicted *in absentia*; İbrahim Bey (sentenced to 15 years in prison), arrested on 4 March 1919 in Istanbul; and a number of less important criminals: İmam Salaheddine; Ali; the navigator İsmail Bey; Ali Şuhuri Bey, *müdir* of the *nahie* of Bağçecik (two years in prison); Faik Çavuş (three years and 200 days in prison); Ahmed Çavuş and Hasan Effendi (four months in prison and 20 strokes of the rod for each). The witnesses who gave evidence at the trial revealed no more than that İmam Salaheddine had "committed no offense against the Armenians, but that he did not attend the mosque and drank without respecting the fast."[38] The only noteworthy information to come out at these "trials" had to do with Ali Şuhuri Bey, *müdir* of Bağçecik, who, according to several witnesses, bore the responsibility for the systematic pillage of Armenian property by people who had been charged with organizing the deportations.[39]

Chapter 15

Deportations and Massacres in the Vilayet of Bursa and the *Mutesarifat* of Kütahya

At the dawn of the twentieth century, the vilayet of Bursa had, according to statistics compiled by the Armenian Patriarchate, an Armenian population of 82,350. Located some 20 kilometers from the Sea of Marmara at the foot of Mt. Olympus, the city of Bursa had until 1915 an Armenian population of 11,500, settled mainly in the Setbaşi and Emir Sultan neighborhoods. The city's Armenians and Greeks represented more than one-third of its population, which also included a large number of *muhacirs* who had recently come from the Balkans. The Armenian colony of Bursa, founded prior to the fifteenth century, grew considerably in the early seventeenth century with the arrival of exiles fleeing the Turkish-Persian wars.

Bursa's prosperous Armenian community possessed, in the middle of the Setbaşi neighborhood, a group of buildings, including a cathedral, a large *lycée*, and elementary schools. The Armenians' main economic activities were silk-making, diamond-cutting, tapestry-making, and the production of gold jewelry. Their summer residences were located in the suburb of Çekirge, with its hot springs and spa. There were also two Armenian villages in the immediate environs, Mulul and Cerahköy.[1]

According to a French military source, there were 42 functioning silk-mills in Bursa before the war, but only 12 in 1919, for "lack of a labor-force" and because cocoon production had "fallen off by 50%."[2] This laconic observation reflects the profound changes that the First World War brought to the vilayet of Bursa, where the anti-Armenian persecutions began early. By 15 April 1915, searches were already being conducted in the houses of the local elite, and teachers and notables were being arrested on various pretexts. Interrogated by the chief of police in the vilayet, Mahmud Celaleddin, and the senior investigating magistrate, Mehmed Ali, some 200 of these notables were transferred to Orhaneli, south of Bursa near Atranos, by the end of May. Others were sent to Bandırma for court-martial.[3] According to an Armenian witness, local magistrates would declare: "You have done nothing wrong, but given the disadvantages that your presence in Bursa brings with it, you will be deported to Atranos, where you will remain for fifteen or twenty days." The arrival in Bursa in early July of a Unionist delegate from the First Division of the Department of State Security, Mehmedce Bey, marked the beginning of the veritable expulsion of the Armenians from the region. Mehmedce's arrival seems, moreover, to have been timed to coincide with the order, sent to the vali of Bursa on 5 July 1915, to deport the Armenian population from the Asian regions near Istanbul.[4] It may in any case be assumed that the Ittihadist delegate judged that the preparatory actions, such as the confiscation of weapons or the systematic arrest of the men, had not proceeded far enough to justify moving immediately to expel the Armenians. Early in

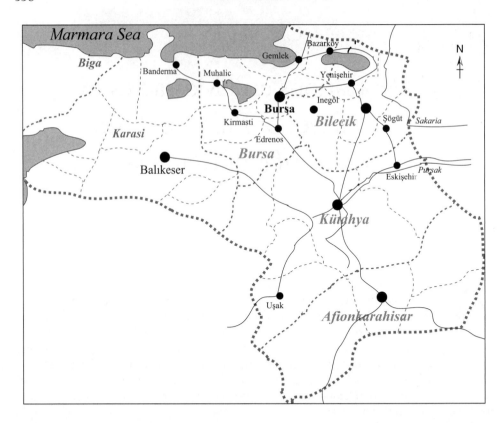

July, Mehmedce had summoned the Greek and Armenian prelates of Bursa, Doretheos and Barkev Tanielian, as well as certain notables such as Mikayel Neshterjian, and ordered them to hand over "the weapons of the revolutionary committees" to the authorities. It would appear that the Armenians complied, but not fully enough to satisfy the Ittihad's delegate, who proceeded to arrest hundreds of men. They were confined in a building known as the Kırmızı Fener, where they were methodically tortured.[5]

On 22 July, Mehmedce Bey, accompanied by çetes of the Special Organization, went to Orhaneli, where some 400 men were being held. Their liquidation began the next day. Every day, they were taken in groups of 40 to the Karanlık Dere gorge, where they were shot by çetes, who then burned their bodies. Among the victims were many merchants: Antranig Hanjian, Onnig Baltayan, Abraham Nalbandian, Hagop Kapujian, Toros Pekmezian, Karnig Pekmezian, Stepan and Levon Dingiuilian, Lutvig Lutfian, Minas Keuleyan, Hrant Arabian, Azniv Philibelian, Onnig Philibelian, Gabriel Michigian, the Lapatians, father and son, and Simenet Bedros Shamamian. Among those shot were also state officials and members of the liberal professions, teachers, and craftsmen: Minas Findeklian (an employee at the *Banque Ottomane*), Harutiun Yazejian, Harutiun and Armenag Luftian (pharmacists), Mihran Luftian (an elementary schoolteacher), Artine Uzunian (a lawyer), Stepan Hisian (a secretary), Mikayel Hanjian, Sarkis Michigian (a student), Piuzant Morukian (a student), Eduard Beyazian (an official in the Office of the Public Debt), Karnig and Garabed Pachajian (butchers), Aram Kamburian (a secretary), Sarim Kelejian (a blacksmith), Garabed Ebeoğlu (a secretary), and Krikor Andonian (an official in the Department of the Public Debt).[6]

Around the same time, the 100 men interned in the prison of the Bandırma court-martial, including 20 notables from Bursa who had been incarcerated since late April, were condemned to death or prison terms. The prelate of Bursa, Barkev Tanielian, and Sukias Diulgerian were condemned to five years in prison and then deported to Der Zor, where they died of typhus a few weeks later. As for those condemned to death, they were brought back to Bursa and finally hanged on 24 October 1915.[7] The hanged men were Dr. Stepan Meliksetian (a physician), Parunag Ajemian (a pharmacist), Simonig Seferian (a commission agent), Misak Mermerian (a goldsmith), Misag Der Kerovpian, Krikor Beoliukian, and four peasants; they were symbolically hanged on the Setbaşi Bridge, at the entrance to the old Armenian quarter.[8]

The deportation order, which was published on 14 August 1915, gave the Armenians three days to prepare their departure. The looting of Armenian homes began even before the evacuation. The first convoy left Bursa for Eskişehir on 17 August. One thousand eight hundred families left the city in the space of three days; 150 Protestant and Catholic households were exempted from the deportation on orders from Istanbul.[9] Like all the convoys of deportees, those from Bursa followed the railway as far as Konya and Bozanti and then crossed Cilicia to Aleppo; the most unfortunate were sent on to Der Zor.[10] According to an Armenian source, several hundred deportees managed to go into hiding in the regions of Konya and Kütahya. Most of the post-war survivors from Bursa were drawn from their ranks.[11]

The Austro-Hungarian consul, L. Trano, announced the imminent deportation of the Armenians of the vilayet and the creation of a committee responsible for "abandoned property" as early as 16 August.[12] In another message to the Austro-Hungarian Ambassador in Istanbul three days later, Trano stated that approximately 9,000 people had been deported by way of Bilecik and Konya, more than 7,000 of them in two-tiered stockcars, and around 1,800 by foot. The consul further noted that the committee responsible for "abandoned property" had immediately proceeded to "confiscate manufactories and other Armenians' property."[13] With regard to these "confiscations," a 31 August cable from Pallavicini to the minister Burian indicated, on the basis of information that Trano had provided on the 23rd, that "the Armenians' property was seized by the members of the Union and Progress Club and certain other Turkish notables" from Bursa.[14] Trano spelled out, above all, the methods used by the members of the committee responsible for "abandoned property" to get hold of Armenian assets even before their proprietors were deported. The Armenians were first summoned to the office of the vilayet's secretary general in the *konak*. A bag filled with money had been placed on the table in this office. A state official asked the person who had been summoned to sign a prepared document indicating that he was voluntarily ceding his property to a Turkish buyer, present in the office, who counted out the contents of a purse and handed the sum over to him. When the "involuntary seller" left the room, he was intercepted by another official who took the money from him and put it back on the table in the office, and so on.[15] Thanks to this exceptional document, we can gather some notion of the methods employed by Bursa's Young Turk circles. It seems reasonable to suppose that these practices, a combination of formalism and cynicism, were widely utilized to lay hands on the assets of the most important Armenian businessmen. It is probably no accident that the CUP dispatched Mumtaz Bey to Bursa and other places in order to set up "committees responsible for abandoned property" with the help of two other party cadres, Abdurahman Bey and Receb Bey, who also came from the capital,[16] as well as that of the parliamentary deputies Memduh Bey and Hamid Rıza Bey.[17]

Here better than elsewhere, one can observe the precision with which the capital organized operations, dispatching its delegates to supervise this or that aspect of the general plan to deport the population and seize its assets. In charge of the political dimension of the plan were Ali Osman, the vali; İbrahim Bey, an Ittihad inspector; Muhtar Bey, the president of the city council; and İsmail Hakkı, the commander of the gendarmerie. Mahmud

Celaleddin Bey, the police chief; Mehmedce, a CUP delegate; Mehmed Ali, a magistrate; and Tevfi, a police lieutenant, assumed responsibility for arresting the men, and for the interrogations and torture that went hand-in-hand with the arrests. Mumtaz Bey and his men, as we have said, took charge of the economic aspects of the program.[18] Dr. Ahmed Midhat, the former Constantinople police chief, whose role in the deportation from Bolu we have already discussed,[19] was also delegated by the CUP to Bursa to keep an eye on the progress of operations there.[20] This goes to show how many precautions the Young Turk committee took to make certain that nothing would hinder realization of its plan. But this multiplication of party cadres in the area also indicates how deeply the Ittihadist leaders were concerned about the obstacles that certain local circles could put in the way of the plan, especially for financial reasons. The CUP seems not to have trusted the members of the local Ittihad club – Haci Selim Semerci; Bakhal Necip; Haci Safti, the head of the Deutsche Bank; Defterdar Arif; Attar Haci Sabit Bey; Haci Abdüllah Bey; Sfahanlı Haci Emin; Urganci Abdüllah; Hafız Sabit; Celal Salih; Sfahanlı Hakkı – who were, in fact, the first to benefit from the spoliation of Armenian property.[21]

Government officials also seem to take advantage of the circumstances to enrich themselves. In addition to Ali Osman Bey, the vali, the following people both organized the deportations and were at the same time the main beneficiaries of the liquidation of Armenian property: Seyid Bey, the director of the vali's cabinet; Ahmed Muhtar Bey, the mayor; Niazi Bey, *evkaf memuri* (director of religious and charitable institutions, the *wakıf*); Reşad Bey, a *vergi memuri* (tax collector); Ahmed Haci Effendi, an investigating magistrate; Safet Effendi, the principal of a *lycée*; Haydar Bey, the *zirât memuri* (director of agriculture); Nureddin Effendi, the *belediye memuri* (secretary general at town hall); Edib Bey, the head of the Tobacco Régie; Ali Gulvi and Hasan Fehmi, magistrates; Hulusi Bey, the *marif müdüru* (director of education); İsmail Hakkı, the commander of the gendarmerie; Ziya Bey, the military commander; Arap Fuad, an officer in the gendarmerie; Mahmud Celaleddin, the police chief; Çerkez Tevfik, the assistant police chief; and Haci Tevfik and Hidayet Tevfik, police officers.[22]

At the trial of those responsible for the anti-Armenian persecutions held before the court-martial in Bursa, the two people who received the heaviest sentences, the CUP's delegate Mehmedce Bey, who was condemned to death, and İbrahim Bey, the Ittihad's inspector, who was sentenced to eight years in prison, were, significantly, judged in absentia. Similarly, the police lieutenant Haci Tevfik, the policemen Yahia and Sadık Süleyman Fevzi, and the gendarme Hasan indeed received sentences of ten years of hard labor, but were officially "fugitives from justice," whereas the people present at the trial who were the most heavily implicated in the deportations and violence were all acquitted.[23] Moreover, a report drawn up by the French Navy's intelligence service in April 1919 indicates that these men were all in Bursa, where they were living without being put out in any way by the new authorities. They even seem to have been involved in the murders of Armenians then returning from exile, which occurred daily.[24]

The *Kaza* of Bazarköy

Lying in the northern part of the *sancak* of Bursa, around Lake Iznik, the six Armenian villages in the *kaza* of Bazarköy constituted the biggest demographic concentration in the region. In 1910, a total of 22,209 Armenians lived here; their ancestors, who came from Agn, Arapkir, Palu, Harput, and Erzerum, settled in the area between 1592 and 1607.[25]

To the northeast of Lake Iznik, Keramet had 1,215 inhabitants. Two hours further west lay Medz Norkiugh – Cedik Kariye for the Ottoman administration – with its 2,937 Armenians, almost all of whom earned their living either from the cultivation of grapes and olives or as craftsmen. Three kilometers further west, Michakiugh/Ortaköy had a population of 3,000.

Çengiler, also in the immediate vicinity, was a large village of 5,000 inhabitants known for its silk workshops, which employed several hundred workers, and its 500 to 600 steam-driven wheels in the workshops of the village. Around 1914, the village exported more than 2,000 kilograms of raw silk annually to Marseille, Lyons, Milan, and London by way of a cooperative that local craftsmen had founded to secure supplies and promote sales. The 1,000 inhabitants of the village of Benli/Gürle, on the southwest shore of the lake, lived mainly from fishing. Finally, the village of Sölöz, two hours further south, boasted a population of 4,000.[26] The August 1914 general mobilization very quickly drained all these Armenian villages of their young men, but there is no record of any particular problems occurring in any of them until late May 1915. At that point, house searches and arrests began; the official objective was to induce the population to hand over its weapons to the authorities.[27]

The first target of these operations was Çengiler. On 4 August 1915, 2,000 soldiers and gendarmes surrounded the village[28] under the supervision of Haci Alaeddin, the CUP's temporary delegate and a member of Bazarköy's Ittihadist club, and Abdülhamid Bey, the military commander of Bursa, who had been charged with carrying out the deportation in Çengiler.[29] After a short exchange with the local notables, they put some one thousand two hundred families on the road with a sizeable escort. These deportees were not allowed to take their moveable assets with them. The men were separated from the rest of the convoy a half-hour from the village and slain on the banks of a stream in the place known as Barzudag.[30] About 100 men were maintained in the village in order to transport the Armenians' belongings to the church, where they were divided up among peasants, soldiers, and gendarmes. After that, the village was methodically plundered and put to the torch. The 100 men were led from the village under guard and slaughtered.[31]

The inhabitants of Ortaköy, Medz Norkiugh, Keramet, Sölöz, and Benli were deported shortly after the population of Çengiler.[32] In Medz Norkiugh, the deportation order was issued on 16 August; the villagers were given three days to make preparations for their journey, under the supervision of the *müdir*, Mehmed Fahri. On 19 August, these convoys, escorted by squadrons of *çetes*, set out for Eskişehir, and proceeded from there down the Konya-Bozanti-Aleppo route on foot.[33]

It is noteworthy that a few dozen young recruits from Çengiler, Ortaköy, and Sölöz took to the maquis when they learned that their families had been deported, and that the inhabitants of Benli put up a degree of resistance, burning their harvest before leaving their homes. According to Aguni, the Armenian recruits resisted for about one year in a mountain district, securing their food supply by raiding Turkish villages and, sometimes, inflicting losses on the forces that came looking for them. Many of them died fighting on a farm in Sölöz where they had been surrounded.[34]

Armenian sources give the names of those bearing the main responsibility for the atrocities inflicted on the *kaza* of Bazarköy: Kürd Sâmi Bey, an officer in the gendarmerie; Refik Bey, a former director of the Department of the Public Debt; Tahir Effendi, the secretary of a regiment; Softaoğlu Mehmed; Ali Bey; Hüseyin Bey; Giridli Adıl Bey; Recepoğlu Salih; Urufat; Tabuk İbrahim; Halil Effendi; Küçük Ahmed; and Onbaşi Musa Ali.[35]

The *Kaza* of Gemlik

In the district of Gemlik, lying just west of the *kaza* of Bazarköy on the coast not far from Bursa, there were three Armenian villages on the eve of the war with a total population of 12,100. In the basically Greek port of Gemlik, there were barely 100 Armenians. The big village of Beyli, in contrast, located three kilometers to the west, was entirely Armenian; its 7,000 inhabitants were blacksmiths, animal breeders, farmers, and craftsmen, whose ancestors had come from Agn and settled there around 1600. Two kilometers farther south, Karsak had an Armenian population of 5,000. These three groups were deported at the same time as the Armenians of the *kaza* of Bazarköy, in mid-August 1915.[36]

The *Kazas* of Muhalic, Kirmasti, and Edrenos/Atarnos

The three districts of Muhalic, Kirmasti, and Edrenos/Atarnos, located west and south of Bursa, boasted a total Armenian population of 8,459 on the eve of the war. The principal town of the *kaza* of Muhalic, a small Greek town with 8,000 inhabitants, had an Armenian population of 400. There were another five rural communities scattered throughout the area. The densely populated *kaza* of Kirmasti had only one modest Armenian colony with around 1,000 members, all of whom lived in the seat of the *kaza*. More than 4,000 Armenians, however, lived in three localities in the *kaza* of Edrenos, south of Bursa, most of them peasants who earned a living by raising silkworms.[37] In these three *kazas*, the deportations were carried out in August 1915 by the local authorities, acting under supervision from Bursa. In Kirmasti, the *kaymakam*, Kâmil Effendi; Osman Effendi, the mufti; Kambur Reis, a *muhtar*; Ayaşköylu Mehmed Bey; Ziya Effendi; Muezzin Mehmed; and Haci Muharım organized the expulsion of the Armenian population to Eskişehir and down the Konya-Bozanti route.[38]

The Deportations in the Sancak *of Ertuğrul*

The 13 Armenian villages in the *sancak* of Ertuğrul had also been founded at the turn of the seventeenth century. According to the 1914 Ottoman census, they had a total Armenian population of 25,380 in that year. The statistics of the Constantinople Patriarchate put their number somewhat higher, at 28,629. Most of these Armenians were Turkish-speaking, unlike those in the *sancaks* of Ismit and Bursa.[39]

Located on a hillside on the left bank of the Karasu river, Bilecik, the seat of the *mutesarif*, had somewhat more than 10,000 inhabitants in 1914; 4,080 of them were Armenians who lived in the Balipaşa neighborhood. They were chiefly occupied in raising silkworms and spinning silk in the seventeen silk-mills, almost all of them Armenian owned.

There was also a small number of Armenians in the northern part of the *kaza*: in Mekece, on the right bank of the Sakaria, in Lefke, ten kilometers further south, and in Gölbazar or Nor Kiugh, a village with an Armenian population of 500. Further to the southwest lay the village of Göldağ, with an Armenian population of 2,200, and the big village of Decir Hanlar, with an Armenian population of 2,500. Ten kilometers further to the east, the village of Turkmen was, despite its name, exclusively Armenian; it had a population of 2,630.[40]

In August 1915, these 13,110 people found themselves deported in the space of a few days. To carry off this operation, the CUP sent Ahmed Mercimekzâde as its responsible secretary to Bilecik; there he was able to count on the support of Ali Kemal Bey, the president of the local Ittihadist club, and other influential members of the club, such as Fuad Mercimezâde, Haci Ahmed, and Saraf Imam Abdüllah.[41] The administrative dimension of the plan to extirpate the Armenian population was seen to by the *mutesarif*, Cemal Bey, Teymuz Bey, the *kaymakam* of the *kaza* of Bilecik, and Binbaşi Rifât, the commander of the gendarmerie of the *sancak* of Ertuğrul, who served for a time as interim *kaymakam*.[42]

A Mkhitarist monk who witnessed the events notes that he was in Bilecik on 16 August 1915, the date on which the notables and the auxiliary primate, Father Simon, were summoned by the *mutesarif* Cemal Bey and told that they had to leave in three days. The monk observes that there were very few men in the town, since they had been mobilized; that, for a week, it had been impossible to travel outside the town; and that the Armenians of Bilecik had witnessed the passage of convoys of deportees from the west in a state that gave them some notion of what lay in store for them. Once the deportation order had been made public, the Armenians began to sell off their furniture to their neighbors, who had flocked to buy what they could at extremely low prices. Scenes of the pillage of Armenian homes began to multiply from 17 August on, when the villagers from the environs came to take their part of the loot.[43] On 18 August, according to the Mkhitarist monk, who was spared because he was a Catholic, the Armenian church was full for the last service. The next morning, all the Armenians of Bilecik left the town in a single convoy bound for Eskişehir. The schoolchildren were invited to help demolish the Armenian quarter. In particular, they were given the task of removing house windows and doors; the women followed them into the abandoned houses. This pillage, and the sacking of the Armenian quarter, went on for ten days. Only the cathedral, which had been converted into a depot, and the homes of a few notables, occupied by government officials, escaped destruction. The orchards surrounding the city and the Armenian cemetery were also sacked.[44] With the exception of a few Catholic families, Bilecik was emptied of its Armenian population.

The *Kazas* of Yenişehir, Inegöl, and Şögüt

Lying on both shores of the eastern half of Lake Iznik, the *kaza* of Yenişehir had, in 1914, three Armenian colonies with a total population of 4,750. Two hundred fifty Armenians lived in Nor Kiugh ["New Village"], just outside Nicea/Iznik; 2,500 were to be found in the village of Marmaracık. Finally, in Yenişehir, the seat of the *kaza*, with a mixed population, there were more than 2,000 Armenians, most of whom earned their living as farmers.[45]

A heavily wooded region lying about 40 kilometers east of Bursa, halfway between Bursa and Bilecik, the *kaza* of Inegöl had, in 1914, two Armenian villages, Yenice (pop. 2,000) and Ceran (pop. 2,500).[46]

In the westernmost *kaza* in the *sancak* of Ertuğrul, Şögüt, there were on the eve of the genocide four Armenian villages, located to either side of the Sakaria. To the south, Çalgara had 900 inhabitants. On the right bank of the river lay Muraca, with a population of 2,600; Asarcık, inhabited by 1,200 of the faithful; and Yenibazar (pop. 700). One thousand four hundred seventy-two Armenians, including a handful of Protestants, lived in the seat of the *kaza*, Şögüt.[47] The deportation of this population and the seizure of its property was supervised by Young Turk cadres from Bilecik, who delegated Emin Effendi, the CUP responsible secretary, and the parliamentary deputy from Inegöl, Mehmed Bey, to oversee operations. They were assisted by the members of the local club, Ahmed Alizâde ali Effendi, Sadıkzâde Haci Hüseyin Effendi, Sabri Effendi, and Tüfenkcibaşizâde Molla Yusuf. Among the government officials, Said Bey, the *kaymakam* of Inegöl; Nuri Effendi, a civil servant in the Department of Finance; Süleyman Effendi; Mustafa Effendi, director of the Office of the Public Debt; and Osman Nuri, the commander of the local gendarmerie, all played pivotal roles in the deportation carried out in August 1915.[48]

The Deportations in the *Sancak* of Karasi/Balikeser

According to the Patriarchate's 1913–14 census, there were approximately 20,000 Armenians in the *sancak* of Karasi, almost all of whom were concentrated in the *kazas* of Bandırma and Balıkeser. The colonies of this *sancak*, which had close ties to Istanbul and Bursa by virtue of their geographic location, had been founded in the first years of the seventeenth century.[49]

In the Balıkeser prefecture, known for its cotton production, there were in 1914 3,684 Armenians, who were settled in the Alifakiye neighborhood. The only Armenian-populated villages in the environs were Bali Maden (pop. 480) and Babaköy/Burhaniye (pop. 320).[50]

Set deep in the Cyzique Gulf, Bandırma served as the port of the *sancak* of Karasi; a steamboat line ran between the port and the capital. In 1914, 3,450 Armenians lived here, most of them earning a living either raising silkworms or in weaving, embroidery, or the silk-trade. In the northern part of the *kaza*, in Erdek, on the peninsula of the same name, a colony of 1,000 Armenians was established in a Greek environment. Opposite Erdek, on the coast, the port of Eydincik had an Armenian community with 1,470 members. Finally, south of Lake Manias, in the environs of the city of the same name, there was an Armenian population of 1,200; another 1,302 Armenians lived in the village of Ermeniköy, located on the shores of the Sea of Marmara. To these figures, we must add the few thousand Armenians who lived scattered throughout the rest of the *sancak* – for example, in Sultançayr Maden (pop. 450), Susurlu (pop. 100), Armudova (pop. 250), or Edremid (pop. 65).[51]

Here, too, the deportations were organized in August 1915,[52] under the direction of Ahmed Midhat Bey, the *mutesarif* of Balıkeser; Dyarbekirli Cemal Bey, the secretary general of the *sancak*; Necib Bey, the head of the Regie; and Rıza Bey, a retired battalion commander. The murder of several dozen men and the seizure of the Armenians' property were the work of the members of Balıkeser's Young Turk club – Arapzâde Sabaheddin Bey, the president, assisted by Atıf Bey, a parliamentary deputy from Biğa; Hasan Bedu Bey; Recayi Şükrü Bey; and Laz Haci Mustafa Effendi.[53]

In Bandırma, the main organizers of the extirpation of the Armenians from the region were Ömer Lutfi Bey, the CUP's responsible secretary; Servet Bey, the president of the municipality and president of the committee responsible for "abandoned property"; as well as the local Young Turk notables Mehmed Bey Mulkizâde, Mehmed Bey Velibeyzâde, Haci Sâmi Bey, Giritli Celal Bey, Selanikli Sabri Bey, Reşad Bey Taşcizâde, Mehmed Bey, Balıklı Tahir, İsmail Effendi Hakkızâde, Eberlerin Içak Hadi, Hacinâzımbeyzâde Teza Bey, Musazâde Tevfik Bey, and Dabağ Dervişoğlu Ahmed. Among the government officials, Nizameddin Bey, the *kaymakam* of Bandırma; Tahtaci İsmail Effenci, the president of the commercial court; Hüseyin Çavuş, the commander of the local gendarmerie; and Reşid Bey, the police chief, saw to the administrative aspect of operations, leaving it to the club and the Special Organization to carry out the massacres. The local *Teşkilât-ı Mahsusa* was headed by the following commanders of squadrons of *çetes*: Adal Haci Ahmed, Tellal İsmail Bey, Hanci Ali Çavuş, and Boykotci Mehmed.[54]

In the *nahie* of Eydincik, the deportations were organized by the *müdir*, Necip Effendi; Haci Yusuf, the mayor; Behcet Effendi, an official in the *Tapu* (Land Registry Office); Tatar Mustafa Çavuş, the commander of the gendarmerie; Veli Effendi, an official in the Telegraph Office; and Ali Effendi, a civil servant employed in the Office of the Public Debt. They were aided and abetted by the local Unionist notables, who committed several murders: Kara Mustafa Bey, Nuri Ömer Effendizâde, Ramzi Abdo Mollaoğlu, and Karabaşoğlu Rağıb.[55]

Deportations in the Mutesarifat of Kütahya

Kütahya's Armenian colony, founded at the turn of the fifteenth century, was one of the oldest in the region. It was famed, above all, for its production of faience. There were also two small rural centers in the vicinity of Kütahya, Alinca and Arslanik Yayla, and two Armenian colonies in the northwestern part of the *kaza*, in Tavşanlı (pop. 320) and Virancik (pop. 200). Thus Kütahya had a total Armenian population of 3,578.[56] Located in the southernmost tip of the *sancak* of Kütahya, the Armenian colony of the *kaza* of Uşak, with 1,100 members, was essentially concentrated in the seat of *kaza*, also named Uşak; economic activity here was organized around rug-making and the fabrication of woolens.[57]

The Armenian population of the *sancak* of Kütahya was not deported – a fact rare enough to be singled out for mention. The *mutesarif*, Faik Ali Bey, was one of the state officials who refused to carry out the orders he received from Istanbul; yet, contrary to expectations, he was not dismissed. According to Aguni – who after the war asked the *mutesarif* in person how he managed to maintain the region's Armenians in their homes – the local Turkish population firmly opposed the deportation of the Armenians, with the encouragement of two families of notables, the Kermiyanzâdes and Hocazâde Rasik. This had its effects on the central government. Yet, while Mehmed Talât threatened the *mutesarif* and these notables with retaliation, he seems to have exhibited a certain indulgence in this particular case, a sort of exception that proves the rule. Although, initially, fewer than 5,000 people were supposed to benefit from this exception, several thousand deportees from Bandırma, Bursa, and Tekirdağ also profited from the benevolent attitude of the *mutesarif* and the local population, thus escaping the fate that awaited them on the Konya-Bozanti-Aleppo route. It was ultimately the Grand Assembly of Ankara that would liquidate, a few years later, this oasis of life, after extorting a heavy contribution from it "for the defense of the fatherland."[58]

The histories of a few individuals detained in Çanğıri who were among the rare prisoners released, on condition that they reside elsewhere than in Istanbul – the architect Simon Melkonian, Sarkis Arents, the pharmacist Hajian, Kasbar Cheraz, Mikayel Shamdanjian, and Father Vartan Karageuzian – illustrate the uniqueness of the case of the *sancak* of Kütahya. After passing through Eskişehir and being expelled from Smyrna on 31 October, these men arrived, on 3 November, in Uşak, whose population had also not been deported, because, at the administrative level, the city was attached to Kütahya. Thanks to the station-master, M. Dedeyan, and the priest, Father Harutiunian, who vouched for them with the authorities, the local police granted them permission to settle in Uşak, where they remained for three years – the only deportees present in the town – and even founded a school for the Armenian children there.[59]

Deportations in the Sancaks of Eskişehir and Afionkarahisar

It is revealing that, despite what was just said, the Armenian population of the *sancak* of Eskişehir did not benefit from the privilege accorded the Armenians of the neighboring *sancak*, although Eskişehir was administratively attached to the *mutesarifat* of Kütahya. In the Armenian quarter of Eskişehir, founded early in the seventeenth century, there were barely 1,000 Armenians. They worked mainly in the bazaar, which they ran together with Greeks. There were another three Armenian villages in the rest of the *kaza*, Artaki Çiftlik, Karaharac, and Bey Yayla; the total Armenian population of the district was 4,510.[60] These Armenians were deported on 14 August 1915, under extremely harsh conditions; they were not authorized to take any belongings at all with them.[61] Rifât Bey, the *mutesarif* of Eskişehir, and Halid Ziya, the mayor, played important roles during the administrative phase of operations, but the veritable architect of the deportation was Dr. Besim Zühtü, the CUP's responsible secretary in Eskişehir.[62] Zühtü had the support of the members of the local Unionist club: Abdüllah Sabri Bey, who was also a member of the *emvalı metruke*; Derecioğlu Ali Velioğlu, the president of the local club; and Reşid Bey. Among the government officials, Edhem Effendi, the director of the Department of Public Education, and Zeki Bey, the head of the Committee for Emigration, played crucial roles in preparing the deportation. Reşid Bey, the police chief; İsmail Hakkı, the assistant police chief; Besim Bey, the commander of the gendarmerie; and Ömer Lutfi, an officer in the gendarmerie, were chiefly responsible for carrying out the deportations. The seizure of Armenian property was organized by Elvadcizâde Abdülrahman, Telcizâde Haci Hakkı, Mustafa Besim (a lawyer), Fakreddin Haci Nebi, Emin Bey, Hocazâde Arif, Kenanzâde Süleyman, Abdüllah Sabri Bey, Kianizâde Halil İbrahim, Megalici Halil, Bayrakdarzâde Ali Ulvi, Haci Çakerlar, Haci Hafız Ömer, Yaver Hoca, Hasan Effendi, Hafız Osman Nuri, Haci Edhem Bey Zâde Faik, Dedelikzâde Arif, Erdemzâde Muslin, and Hasköylı İbrahim.[63]

When Father Vartan Karageuzian passed through Eskişehir around 25 October, the city had been entirely emptied of its Armenians, with the exception of a few Catholic families.[64]

The *sancak* of Afionkarahisar was no more spared the deportations than was Eskişehir. The Armenian colony of Afion, the prefecture, boasted 6,500 members in 1914; it was reputed for its production of furniture and objects made of wood inlaid with silver. There were also two small communities in the *kaza* of Azizye, to the north of Afion, in Muzlice and Sandıklı (pop. 170). Thus, 7,448 Armenians lived in the *sancak* as a whole; all were Turkish-speaking.[65] The population of the villages of the *kaza* of Aziziye was deported on 13 August 1915, with the exception of twenty-seven artisans and their families, who had to convert. The Armenians of Afion were deported on 15 August.[66]

The violence and deportations were organized by Dr. Moktar Besim, the CUP's responsible secretary in Afion, At Osman Zâde, the president of the local club, and the town's other Unionists, most of whom were Bosnian *muhacirs*: Boşnak Muhacir Salih, Pambuk Mehmed Effendi, Boşnak Mehmed Ali, Boşnak Hilmi, and Boşnak Mehmed Effendi. The *mutesarif*, Hakim Bey; the mayor, Rizazâde Alaheddin Effendi; İbrahim, the director of the Agricultural Bank; Elmas Effendi, a magistrate; Dr. Mustafa, the municipal physician; and Hayreddin Effendi, the president of the *emvali metruke*, carried out the administrative operations, while Bahaeddin Bey, the commander of the gendarmerie; Osman Nuri, an officer; Hasan Fehmi, the police chief; and Mustafa Effendi, the assistant police chief, implemented the deportation order. The main beneficiaries of the spoliation of the Armenians' property were the following notables: Nyasi, Boşnak Eyba, Köroğlu Halil Ağa, Gübeleoğlu Ahmed, and Şeyh Derviş.[67]

Chapter 16

Deportations and Massacres in the Vilayet of Aydın

The fact that there was very little anti-Armenian violence in Smyrna during the war was attributed by those who took part in the events of the day to the energetic activity of the vali, Mustafa Rahmi [Evranos], one of the founders of the CUP in Salonika and an influential member of the party.[1] The correspondence of the Consul General of the United States in Smyrna, George Horton,[2] like that of his colleague Vladimir Radinsky, who managed the Austro-Hungarian consulate,[3] tends to show that the Armenians of the vilayet of Aydın owed their survival and the fact that they could remain in the city exclusively to the influence of Rahmi Bey, who is supposed to have resisted the orders he received from Istanbul. This was also the opinion of both circles close to the Patriarchate, in particular the journalist Sebuh Agnuni, who does, however, point out how much this "cost" Smyrna's affluent families.[4]

The story of Smyrna, however, can obviously not be reduced to the action of a single man, however powerful he may have been or whatever the personal profit he may have reaped from his acts. The fact that a member of the CUP as influential as Mustafa Rahmi should have been appointed vali of Smyrna in the aftermath of the Balkan Wars probably had to do with the Young Turks' plans to "homogenize" the regions of the Ottoman Aegean coastline. Put into practice in spring 1914 by a decision of the Young Turk Central Committee, this plan, the objective of which was to eradicate the Greek population of the coast, was entrusted to Rahmi's "administrative" leadership.[5] There is every reason to think that the vali himself helped draw up this plan. In other words, it was the Greek dimension of the plan for the ethnic "homogenization" of Anatolia, which was then at the center of Rahmi's preoccupations and also those of the commander-in-chief of the Fourth Army Corps, General Pertev Pasha [Dermirhan]. If these operations had slowed by the eve of the war, the reason was doubtless the crucial stake represented by Greece's neutrality or even entry into the war on the German side. Moreover, the forced exile of tens of thousands of Greeks to the Kingdom of Greece and the deportation of hundreds of thousands of others to the interior allowed the CUP to realize its basic political and economic objectives: the assets of this population group were seized. Having accomplished that goal, the Ittihadist party-state could have spared Smyrna and what remained of the vilayet's Greek population, which it indeed did. Rahmi promoted this policy by magisterially manipulating the local press.[6] An Austro-Hungarian diplomat noted that "Rahmi Bey has had a reputation for being an inveterate Grecophobe ever since the expulsions from the coast, [but] he knows how to make the editor-in-chief of *Réforme* publish laudatory articles certifying that the Orthodox Greeks of Smyrna and the environs are happy with their government."[7] The vali also displayed a benevolent attitude toward the Englishmen whom the war caught by surprise in Smyrna. He was in fact so successful at this that the Foreign Office thought he might be a "potential interlocutor" on bad

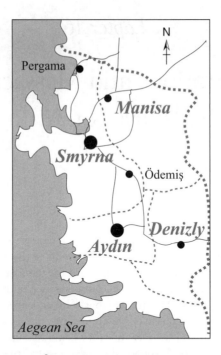

terms with the Ottoman capital.[8] In Smyrna, accordingly, during the first year of the war, a sort of armed peace reigned with the Greeks, who were on their guard and overall hostile to the Young Turk regime.

In such a context, the elimination of the city's Armenians would no doubt have spawned tensions in Greek circles, where it would have been perceived as a danger that could affect the Greeks as well. According to the 1914 Ottoman census, corroborated in this case by the Patriarchate's statistics, there were nearly 21,000 Armenians in the vilayet of Aydın, more than 11,000 of whom lived in Smyrna and its suburbs, Burnabad and Cordelio.[9] Playing the card of fidelity to the empire for all it was worth, the Armenian archbishop organized in November 1914 a church service for the victory of the Ottoman Army, which was attended by the vali and Pertev. The service was followed by a reception at which Rahmi took pains to point out that whenever the government launched a patriotic appeal, "the Armenians were always the first Christian group to answer it.[10] It goes without saying that declarations of this kind were intended to reassure the Armenians, but also to indicate how much less interested the Greeks were in the fate of the "fatherland." This state of grace ended in April 1915, when Rahmi summoned Archbishop Mattheos Injeyan and a few notables to destroy all the arms and ammunition in their possession.[11] On 2 and 3 May, police searches were carried out in the homes of Armenian political leaders; 100 people were arrested and 20 were brought before the court-martial in Smyrna.[12] According to information relayed by the American and Austro-Hungarian consuls, explosives and grenades had been found. It seems, however, that the explosives in question had been entrusted to the Smyrna ARF by the local CUP club during the 1909 "counter-revolution" for the purposes of the struggle against the "reactionaries." What is more, the devices had been buried for six years and could apparently no longer be detonated.[13] It is well known that relations between the local CUP and ARF committees were close and that in April 1909 the local Ittihad club had appealed to the ARF and Hnchaks to "form volunteer groups in the next twelve hours."[14]

Nevertheless, after a two-month pretrial investigation and two trial sessions held on 4 and 5 July 1915, the Smyrna court-martial condemned seven of the indicted men to death for having explosives in their possession.[15] Smyrna's Armenian notables tried to obtain "imperial clemency" for them, arguing that the men had been unjustly condemned. To that end, they appealed to the vali, Rahmi, and foreign diplomats, brandishing a "memorandum" in support of their position. This appeal for mercy seems to have been inspired by the fear that the threatened executions would "create the impression, among the most ignorant Turkish fanatics, that the Armenians were plotting against the government, something that could precipitate a massacre."[16] The vali informed the notables that he would do what he could, but added that the decision to execute the sentence was in the hands of the commander of the Fourth Army Corps, Pertev Pasha. On 4 August 1915, the sultan finally commuted the death sentence to 15 years of hard labor, and five of the condemned men were sent to Konya to serve out their sentences.[17]

This episode shows that the authorities employed the usual methods in Smyrna in order to portray "the" Armenians as conspirators and traitors, but without translating the implied threat into action by deporting them. It is probable that, as in Istanbul, they had staged this spectacle in order to justify actions they were taking elsewhere, while at the same time making a show of their magnanimity to foreign observers. Mustafa Rahmi seems to have played the role of protector exceedingly well and thus assured himself of the generosity of Smyrna's leading Armenian families.

However, the Armenians of the vilayet of Aydın were not yet delivered of the threat hanging over them, and were subjected to regular harassment until fall 1918. It should be recalled in this connection that all unmarried men from other regions living in Smyrna were gradually arrested and deported to the Syrian deserts[18] by the police chief, Yenişehirli Hilmi, and two of his henchmen, Bazarlı Haci Abdüllah and Spahanlı Haci Emin.[19] Also noteworthy is the fact that, on 1 November 1915, the city's main Armenian neighborhood, Haynots, where the Cathedral of St. Stephen and the adjacent archbishopric were located, was surrounded by the army, which proceeded to carry out a systematic search and to arrest some 2,000 people.[20] These operations had been sparked by an anonymous proclamation, written in Turkish and French and pasted up in a few places with Smyrna, which took issue with the government's pro-German policies. The author of this lampoon, a certain Stepan Nalbandian, was identified in rather short order. The ensuing investigation showed that he had acted on his own. That, however, did not prevent the vali from deporting several hundred people in different convoys sent in different directions on 28 November and then again on 16 and 24 December. Among them were a considerable number of British, Italian, and Russian subjects, many of whom died on the road. This suggests that Rahmi had profited from the occasion to eliminate these "foreigners" and lay hands on their property, distributing part of it to police officials and members of the Ittihadist club, such as Ali Fikri or Mahmud Bey.[21]

After every police action, the Archbishop Mattheos Injeyan and Armenian notables Diran Achnan, Misak Morukian, and Nazaret Hilmi Nersesian assiduously solicited the vali's intervention, heedless of the expense, in order to save members of their community. Rahmi took advantage of every such occasion to pocket large sums.[22] Armenian Apostolic circles, however, were not the only ones targeted. The Armenian Catholics, who had previously been spared because they were relatively well protected by the Austro-Hungarian consul, came under attack in September 1916. The police searched the Catholic cemetery on 16 and 17 September and claimed to have found bombs there. There is reason to think that this was a provocation engineered by the vali and the Unionists of the port city, for this "discovery" provided justification for the arrest of 300 Armenian Catholics from Smyrna, Cordelio, and Karataş, some of whom were deported to Afionkarahisar, where they were followed on 9 and 10 November by 300 to 400 people from the affluent classes.[23] The choice of the people to be deported seems to have depended on the assets they possessed, coveted by this or that local notable or government official.

These deportations did not just affect Armenians from Smyrna. In the rest of the *sancak*, the 1,000 Armenians of Pergamon and the 1,500 of Ödemiş, as well as the members of the little colonies of Menemen, Kuşadası, Bayındir, and Söke, were also targeted.[24] The Armenians of Söke, like those of Pergamon, were quietly deported in mid-August 1915, followed by those of Ödemiş in February 1916.[25] The deportations were carried out under the supervision of Farah Bey, the *kaymakam* of Kuşadası/Dikili, and Arif Hikmet Bey, the *kaymakam* of Pergamon.[26]

The Deportations in the *Sancak* of Manisa

Located northeast of Smyrna, the *sancak* of Manisa boasted an Armenian colony 2,875 strong. The Armenians here were concentrated in the lower quarter of the town, known as Malta, and in the upper quarter, which was entirely Armenian. In the rest of the *sancak*, there were also small colonies of 1,000 members each in Kasaba, Akhisar, and Kırkağac.[27]

In Magnesium, an Armenian witness states that the *mutesarif*, Tevfik Bey, succeeded in saving the Armenian population by only going through the motions of carrying out his orders. Four hundred people were expelled from their homes rather late, on 15 October 1916, and on the initiative of the commander of the gendarmerie, Fehmi Bey.[28] Furthermore, the weaver's workshop that belonged to M. Sariyan, who was deported from Smyrna on 24 December 1916, was turned over on 29 December to two influential members of Smyrna's Unionist club, Husnizâde Ali Fikri and the officer Ahmed Bey, on "an order come from Smyrna." But the Armenians in the other towns and villages of the *sancak* were spared,[29] except for those from Kırkağac, who were deported to Konya in November 1915.[30]

The Deportations in the *Sancaks* of Aydın and Denizly

Only a few Armenians lived in the southern part of the vilayet of Aydın. They were to be found in the seat of the *sancak*, also called Aydın (pop. 500), Nazilly (pop. 543) and, 25 kilometers to the east, in Denizly (pop. 548).[31] These Armenians had, however, already been partially eliminated along with the Greek population in spring 1914. As in the region of Manisa, a local official named Nuri Bey succeeded in preventing the *mutesarif*, Reşid Bey, a former director of the political division of the Istanbul police force, from carrying out the deportations.[32] In Denizly, a few dozen men were arrested during the house searches carried out in early May 1915, and one of them was even executed in public on 16 September 1916. The colony as a whole, however, was spared.[33] In other words, the balance of the Ittihadists' anti-Armenian policies in the region is a mixed one, serving chiefly to put Greek and Armenian businesses and the inherited wealth of the leading families in Turkish hands.

Chapter 17

Deportations and Massacres in the Vilayet of Konya

During the deportations of summer and fall 1915, all the deportees from Thrace and western Anatolia who were following the Adabazar-Konya-Bozanti route to exile in Syria were concentrated in the vilayet of Konya. Konya's train station, which lay on the last trunk of the railway, also served as a transit or regrouping center for the deportees. By the same token, it played a crucial role in the system put in place by the government to expel the Armenians from western Anatolia. An examination of the methods employed here by the local authorities and the CUP delegates sent to Konya offers an opportunity to examine the way the Special Organization and the ministries responsible for the armed forces and police intervened in these operations. This examination is the easier to make because there were around 24,000 local Armenians in the vilayet of Konya, according to the Patriarchate's statistics (nearly 14,000, according to the Ottoman census),[1] even if a large proportion of them were deported as well. The reports by these Konya Armenians, as well as the observations of American missionaries or deportees who spent time in Konya, shed light on the system set up by the Ottoman government.

In the city of Konya, where the vali had his seat, 4,440 Armenians lived in the upper quarter known as Allaheddin. There were also nearly 5,000 in Akşehir, in the northwestern tip of the *sancak*, somewhat more than 1,000 in Karaman, in the south, and another 1,000 in Eregli, in the southeast.[2] Since 6 August 1914, the vali, Azmi Bey, formerly prefect of police in Istanbul,[3] had been mistreating the Armenian population of the vilayet and had extorted large sums from it "for the war effort." In early May 1915, he organized house searches that went on for several nights, especially in the Armenian schools and the homes of notables. Officially, the purpose of these operations was to locate illegally held weapons. In reality, Azmi's instructions were probably to work up a compromising case against the Armenians in order to justify arresting the Armenian elite here as well.[4] On the basis of a list apparently compiled earlier by the local Ittihadist club, 110 merchants, financiers, and elementary schoolteachers were summoned to the police station, then taken to the train station and sent off toward Sultaniye, east of Konya. In the same period, 4,000 Armenian deportees from Zeitun arrived in Konya in a pitiable state, after having trekked through Tarsus and Bozanti with no means of subsistence whatsoever. In an exchange with the vali that took place on 6 May, the chief physician of the American Red Cross Hospital in Konya, Dr. William S. Dodd, asked Azmi for permission to go out to meet these deportees and provide them with food and basic necessities. The vali categorically refused.[5] For his part, the Armenian primate, Karekin Khachadurian, went to great lengths to win the deported men the right to return home. He made an appeal to this effect to Azmi, who had just returned from a trip to Istanbul. "The policies adopted with regard to the Armenians," the vali answered, "cannot now be modified. The Armenians of

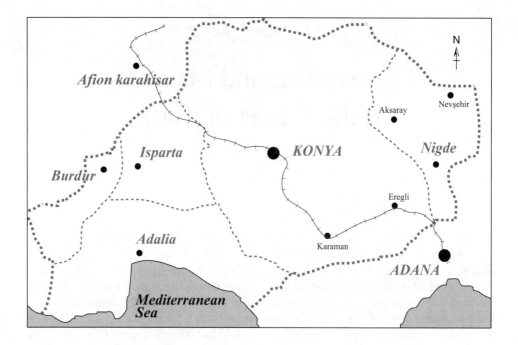

Konya should consider themselves lucky because they have been deported no further than to a neighboring province."[6]

On 18 June 1915, Azmi, who had been appointed vali of Lebanon, was replaced by Celal Bey, who had until then been posted to Aleppo (from 11 August 1914 to 4 June 1915). The result was a shift in the policies of the authorities in Konya. The new governor was a well-meaning man who refused to deport the Armenians of his province. It was while he was absent – he left for "medical care" in Istanbul – that the first convoys of deportees from Adabazar arrived in Konya, around 15 August, after being pillaged on the way. Dr. Dodd, who describes their physical condition, also notes that 2,000 of them had been put in a *medrese* in Konya and left there without any food at all. "All reports," he writes in this connection, "that the Government are providing food are absolutely false, those who have money can buy, those who have none beg or starve [...] How many can survive it?"[7]

The urgent dispatch to the capital of several Syrian divisions forced the authorities to call a temporarily halt to the movements of the convoys of deportees.[8] Taking advantage of the fact that Celal was in Istanbul, the local Young Turks hastened to put nearly 3,000 Armenians from Konya on the road on 21 August. Although Azmi had already assumed his new functions in Beirut, indications are that he continued to exert a great deal of influence in Konya.[9] Ferid Bey, known as *Hamal* Ferid, the CUP's responsible secretary in Konya, organized these deportations. He was assisted by the main Unionist notables in the city: Muftizâde Kâmil Bey, the mayor and president of the Ittihadist club; Haydarbeyzâde Şükrü Bey, the president of the "Committee for National Defense"; Köse Ahmedzâde Mustafa Bey; Akanszâde Abdüllah Effendi; Haci Karazâde Haci Mehmed Effendi; Dr. Rifki, who had been charged with supervising the deportations; Hamalzâde Ahmed Effendi; Momcizâde Ali Effendi; Şükrüzâde Mehmed Effendi; and Dr. Servet, who had been responsible for the massacre of the worker-soldiers in the *amele taburis*.[10] Among the state officials from whom he received support were Edib Effendi; Rifât Effendi, the secretary general in the town hall; Mehmed Effendi, the registrar; and İsmail Hakkı, the head of the Régie. Ali Vasfi, the head of the office of military recruitment; Saadeddin, the police chief; and Hasan Basri, the assistant police chief, carried out the deportation procedures.[11] The most active among the notables, especially in the seizure of Armenian assets, were Hacikarazâde Haci Bekir Effendi; Molla Velizâde Ömer Effendi; Kâtibzâde Tevfik Effendi; Ruşdibeyzâde Mustafa Effendi; Allaeddin Ağa; Mustafa Ağazâde Bedreddin Effendi; and Hacikaransinoğlu Deli Ahmed Effendi.[12]

In the few days that preceded the departure of the first convoy from Konya, the city was transformed into a marketplace. Improvised sales took place everywhere. Often, the city's Turkish inhabitants went to inspect the Armenians' houses and suggested that their owners give them their belongings, for which they would have no further use, "since [they] would be left alive, at best, only a few more days."[13] Archbishop Khachadurian, accompanied by the Reverend Hampartsum Ashjian, sought in vain to bring the commanding officer of the German contingent stationed in Konya to step in. Even the American missionaries could only stand by helplessly and watch as the Armenian presence in Konya was wiped out. The committee responsible for "abandoned property" laid hands on the deportees' houses and arranged the transfer of bank accounts and the precious objects they had deposited with the banks before going to watch the demolition of the Armenian cathedral ordered by a *çete* leader, Muammer.[14]

A second convoy, comprising the last 300 Armenian families from Konya, had been assembled at the railway station and was ready to set out when the vali, Cemal, returned from Istanbul around 23 August. Saved by his intervention, these families were given permission to return to their homes, which had already been stripped of a good deal of their furniture. For as long as Cemal held his post – that is, until early October – these people remained in Konya and, side-by-side with the American missionaries, rendered great service to the tens of thousands of Armenians from the western provinces who passed by way of Konya's train station. As soon as the vali was transferred elsewhere, they were deported in turn, on the initiative of the CUP's responsible secretary, Ferid Bey.[15] It is, however, noteworthy that lists of people to be exiled were regularly drawn up beforehand and Celal was unable to prevent them from being deported.[16] In this regard, Dr. Dodd writes, "The vali is a good man but almost powerless. The Ittihad Committee and the Salonika Clique ruel all. The chief of Police seems to be the real head."[17]

The *Kaza* of Karaman

In line with the schedule of anti-Armenian operations observed elsewhere, the houses of Karaman's Armenians were subject to police searches on Sunday, 23 May 1915, and a number of men were arrested. The operation was organized and overseen by the local Unionist club, which was under the control of the mayor, Çerkez Ahmedoğlu Rifât, Helvadızâde Haci Bekir, and Hadimlizâde Enver. An enormous bribe paid out to the Young Turks nevertheless made it possible to limit the number of men who were "sent away." The veritable deportation of the Armenian population was not set in motion until 11 August 1915. The convoy took the Eregli-Bozanti-Tarsus-Osmaniye-Katma-Aleppo route and eventually reached Meskene in the Syrian Desert. Armenian property in Karaman was pillaged immediately after the deportees' departure.[18]

The *Kazas* of Akşehir and Eregli

In the principal town of the *kaza* of Akşehir, also called Akşehir, which had a big Armenian population, the deportations began on 20 August and went on until October. The members of the first convoy, after traveling a short distance by rail to Eregli, where the *kaymakam*,

Faik Bey, the police chief, İzzet Bey, the commander of the gendarmerie, Midhat Bey, and Mustafa Edhem Bey stripped them of their belongings, continued their journey on foot as far as Osmaniye. They were left there until 23 October and were then sent off to Katma and the Syrian deserts. Of Akşehir's 5,000 to 6,000 Armenians, 700 were allowed to remain in the town. In 1919, there were, furthermore, 960 survivors, almost all of the women and children who had been abducted: three hundred were in Aleppo, 460 were in Damascus, and 200 more were scattered throughout Syria. One hundred young girls were also held by families in Akşehir.[19]

As elsewhere, the CUP's responsible secretary, Haydarbeyzâde Şükrü Bey, and his local henchmen, Kürd Topal Ahmedoğlu Ömer and Fehmi Effendi, the *müdir* of the *nahie* of Cihanbey, played decisive roles in expelling the Armenians of Akşehir. They had the active help of government officials, above all Ahmed Rifât Bey, the *kaymakam*; Kütahyalı Tahir, the director of the Agricultural Bank; Nâzım Bey, a magistrate; İzzet Bey, a Treasury official; Hasan Vasfi Effendi, the police chief; Ömer Effendi, the *kaymakam*'s secretary; Kâmil Effendi, the head of the Telegraph Office; Rifât Effendi, the secretary general of the municipality; Kâmil Effendi, the director of the Turkish orphanage; and Mehmed Effendi.[20]

When Reverend Hans Bauernfeind passed through the Eregli train station on the afternoon of 23 August 1915, he observed that "everything here is simply terrible. Armenians are camping without shelter by the thousands; the rich have lodgings in town ... They do not suspect the imminent danger [they are in]."[21] The 1,000 Armenians of the Eregli community had been dispatched toward Syria a few days earlier by the *kaymakam* Faik Bey; the police chief İzzet Effendi; Yusufzâde Nadim, the head of the Office of Deportations; and Major Hasan Bey, the military commander of Ulukışla.[22]

The Deportations in the Sancaks of Burdur, Niğde, Isparta, and Adalia

In 1914, the Armenian presence in this *sancak* in the southwestern part of the vilayet was concentrated in Burdur (pop. 1,420).[23] Toward mid-August, the *mutesarif*, Celaleddin Bey (who held his post from 23 April 1915 to 27 August 1916) summoned the vicar, Father Arsen, and informed him that he would have to leave the city with his flock in 24 hours. The Armenians' property was confiscated on the spot and sold off for next to nothing. The convoy was first sent to Konya, where it remained for two weeks on the premises of the *Sevkiyat* (the organization responsible for carrying out the deportations), while a political battle raged between Celal Bey, who was trying to have the Armenians sent back home, and the police chief, Saadeddin, a Unionist, who ultimately obtained permission from Istanbul to deport them. By foot or rail, these 1,000 deportees traveled through Rakka and Ras ul-Ayn and were then sent in the direction of Der Zor. By January 1919, only seven families were still alive.[24] Haci Ahmed, the president of the local Ittihad club; Major Murad Bey, the head of the recruitment office; and Mehmed Bey, the police chief, helped the *mutesarif* conduct these operations.[25]

In the prefecture of the *sancak* of Niğde, 1,500 Armenians made a living as stockbreeders. Located close by, Bor had an Armenian population of nearly 900; 1,500 Armenians lived in Aksaray, located in the northern part of the *sancak*; perhaps another 2,000 lived in Nevşehir. The total Armenian population of the *sancak* was thus over 6,000.[26]

Bauernfeind, who traveled through Niğde on 22 August, noted that the Armenians "had all been sent into exile" and observed the same thing in Bor. On the way, he came across a group of Armenian men. "Even the young, intelligent *çavuş* accompanying us," the Protestant minister wrote, "shares the view that they are all going to be killed."[27] Nazmi Bey, the *kaymakam* of Niğde, and Lieutenant-Colonel Abdül Fetah, the head of the deportation office in Aksaray, organized the massacres in Aksaray in late August.[28] The Armenians of Nevşehir were deported to Syria in mid-August 1915 by the *kaymakam* Said Bey, who held his post from 17 April 1914 to 17 November 1915.

The 200 Armenians of Adalia, the 500 of Elmaly, and the 1,180 of Isparta were spared, possibly thanks to the *mutesarifs* of Adalia, Kâmil Bey (who held his post from 3 September 1913 to 3 April 1916), and Isparta, Hakkı Kilic Bey (who held his post from 5 November 1914 to 28 December 1915).[29]

According to Dodd, the many Çerkez living in the province were the backbone of the squadrons of *çetes* who harassed, pillaged, and massacred the deportees in the convoys that crossed the region on their way to Bozanti.[30]

Chapter 18

The Deportees on the Istanbul-Ismit-Eskişehir-Konya-Bozanti Route and Along the Trajectory of the Bagdadbahn

The railway generally known by its German name, the *Bagdadbahn*, ran between Istanbul and Bozanti, where there was a gap in the line. The tracks began again north of Adana and ran to a point further south in the Amanus district, where the line was once again interrupted. In the First World War, the *Bagdadbahn* served as a crucial instrument in the German-Turkish military operations on the eastern front. It was also a pivotal element in the deportation plan elaborated by the Young Turk party-state. An examination of this railroad is all the more worthwhile in that it illustrates the contradiction between military imperatives and political goals, between the empire's strategic objective and its policy of eradicating the Armenian population.

From the earliest phase of its construction, the *Bagdadbahn* was an enterprise dominated by German capital held by the Deutsche Bank. The Deutsche Bank, however, was not merely a financial company. Its vocation was also to serve as a tool for the German policy of penetrating Turkey while breathing life into Germany's economic ambitions there. Because it was closely tied to the German government, the Deutsche Bank was subject to constraints imposed by the alliance between Germany and Turkey. Moreover, by way of the Bagdadbahn Company, which it owned, it was implicated in both the conflict and, quite against its will, the genocidal treatment of both the deportees from Thrace and western Anatolia and also its own employees.[1]

During the war, the board of directors of the *Bagdadbahn* had to overcome three major obstacles that constituted so many impediments to the proper functioning of the company: 1) the threat of deportation hanging over the heads of its Armenian employees; 2) the interruption of work on the tunnels through the Amanus due to the deportation of Armenian workers and managers; and 3) the authoritarian, unpaid for utilization of its means of transportation to expedite the Armenian population to the Syrian deserts.

German sources suggest that the decision to deport personnel – managers, office staff, and manual workers – employed by the *Bagdadbahn* was made by the minister of war in May 1915. Early in July, workers from Kilis who were employed on the railroad's Amanus construction site were forced to quit their jobs in order to follow their families, who had received a deportation order. In Osmaniye, the military authorities resorted to a different method: they confiscated the property of the railroad company's Armenian employees in order to force them to leave. To be sure, M. Winkler, the engineer responsible for construction of the railroad in the vilayet of Adana, contacted the vali and pointed out to him all the disadvantages that interrupting the construction work would entail. The vali, however, told him that there was nothing he could do because his orders came from the minister of the interior and the minister of war, Talât and Enver.[2] Subsequent events showed that the Armenian workers on the Amanus site were also targets of the deportation order: on 7 and 8 July 1915, all the company's employees from Zeitun, Hacın, Hasanbeyli, Intilli, and Bahçe were deported and the houses were turned over to Muslim *muhacirs*. Indeed, the vali suggested to Winkler that he hire these *muhacirs* to replace the deportees, a move that Hilmar Kaiser translates in these terms: "Clearly, the company's operations had become a target of CUP chauvinism."[3] The momentary interruption of work on the line brought on by the deportation of the Armenian workers, and the resignation of certain engineers, do not seem to have disturbed the government unduly. On the contrary, it threatened to seize the railway if the company proved unable to resume work on it. The threats were so serious that Franz Günther, the head of the Anatolian Railway Company, demanded that Winkler put the construction site back into operation at all costs. This tactic, which consisted in creating a problem in order then to exploit it, illustrates the methods that the Young Turk leaders used to nationalize the economy, whatever the consequences might be. In order to meet his obligations, Winkler had no other choice than to recruit qualified personnel from the ranks of the Armenian deportees who now began to arrive from the west – that is, to violate the government ban on hiring Armenians. Many of them were employed under false names or assigned a fictitious nationality. Doctors were recruited to keep the company's hospital in Intilli in operation, and engineers, accountants, secretaries, foremen, carpenters, and so on were invited to come work on the Amanus site. It was the more urgent that this work go forward in that the October 1915 defeat of Serbia opened a direct rail connection to Germany that could be used to move troops and *matériel*. The sole obstacle to these movements toward the Egyptian front was the incomplete section of the railroad represented by the planned Taurus and Amanus tunnels; for Germany, finishing these tunnels now became a strategic priority.[4] Despite their obsessive desire to carry through with their program to eradicate the Armenians, the Young Turk authorities temporarily closed their eyes to the illegal recruitment policies prevailing at the Amanus site. They refused, however, to spare the employees and managers working on the *Bagdadbahn* Company's lines. As in the case of Armenian civil servants, the authorities ordered that these Armenians, too, be deported. They were, however, once again confronted with the resistance of the board of the *Bagdadbahn*, which pointed out that it could not assure a proper flow of traffic without these competent staff workers. The better to impose "nationalization" of the railway's staff and to exclude non-Turks, the government decreed that the company's correspondence and bookkeeping had to be conducted in Turkish rather than French – in other words, it decreed that Armenian employees be dismissed and replaced by Muslims.[5] Among the measures adopted to this end, the local authorities first isolated employees from their families, then deported them separately. Thus, in Angora, the vali Atıf Bey had 19 Armenian employees of the *Bagdadbahn* arrested and deported on 3 September; according to a witness, they were in fact put to death near the train station. This operation naturally led to protests from a company representative. Atıf Bey answered: "It is impossible to bring them back. Impossible, do you hear me? They will never return."[6]

Alarmed by the scope of the operation, Günther requested a meeting with the interior minister in order to convince him that systematic deportation of the railway's Armenian employees could paralyze transportation. The argument seems to have convinced Talât, who in a 25 September letter ordered the local authorities to suspend deportation of personnel in certain categories while waiting for an ad hoc committee to rule on the issue. Winkler, however, suspected that Talât had issued a secret counter-order, for he observed that the local authorities and the CUP clubs continued to deport the families of his employees who could not abandon their loved ones.[7] The ad hoc committee confirmed the deportation order at its 17 October meeting, but granted delays that varied with the employees' specialties in order to allow the board of the *Bagdadbahn* to train "Turkish" replacement personnel.[8] Given the *Bagdadbahn*'s military importance, Lieutenant-Colonel Böttrich, the head of the railway transport department of the Ottoman general staff, was asked for his advice. Böttrich not only gave an opinion favorable to deportation but also signed the document that made it official. Günther pointed out to both the Deutsche Bank's board of directors and the German Embassy in Istanbul that the office had committed an act of extreme irresponsibility in signing such a document, which implicated the Germans in "the Armenian persecutions."[9]

In addition to the fate of the manual and white-collar workers on the Amanus construction sites, Günther, the director of the Anatolian Railway Company, was also concerned about the use of the company's means of transportation to deport Armenian populations from the west. In August 1915, he received many reports from his coworkers about the exactions perpetrated against the deportees on the railway. In a 17 August 1915 letter to Arthur von Gwinner, the president of the Deutsche Bank, Günther uses the term "bestial horribleness" to describe "the extermination of the Armenians in today's Turkey."[10] He also draws his superiors' attention to the responsibility of the company, involuntarily transformed into a tool of the Young Turks' extermination program. Arthur von Gwinner seems, however, not to have taken the full measure of the crime being perpetrated in Turkey and its consequences for his enterprise. On 30 October 1915, Günther therefore sent von Gwinner a photograph of Armenians packed into cars. He wrote about this photograph: "Enclosed I send you a picture illustrating the Anatolian Railway as a bearer of culture in Turkey. These are our so-called mutton cars, in which for example 800 human beings are transported in 10 cars." This letter proved effective; Günther obtained financial aid for the deportees from the Deutsche Bank, accompanied by the recommendation that the humanitarian actions he undertake not give the impression that the bank was hostile "to an allied government."[11]

A military commissar who answered to the Ministry of War was charged with informing the board of the Eastern Railway of the rules to be applied in replacing its Armenian personnel. For example, a 7 November 1915 letter instructed the authorities in the vilayet of Edirne to suspend the deportation of three traffic managers who had been sent away and were in Tekirdağ at the time.[12] The same officer demanded that he be provided, in accordance with the committee's decisions, with a list of agents "in both of the categories working on your railway, and also a list of those who have been dismissed from your service after the expiration of the delays accorded them."[13] It seems, then, that the authorities were following the *Bagdadbahn*'s Armenian employees particularly closely. An 8 November circular from the military commissar for rail transportation spells out the general regulations established by the ad hoc committee.[14] After confirming that the "government is engaged in changing the place of residence of Armenians living in certain parts of the empire," the commissar states that plans have also been made to deport Armenians working for the railroad companies, "whose numbers are considerable." However, he notes, "in view of the fact that this would disturb the service exploiting the railway, my ministry is of the opinion ... that a sound method and pre-established rules would be preferable." In accordance with the committee's decisions, "the Armenian agents employed on the railway" were assigned to two different categories: "one [is] to be replaced within twelve months and the other within two to four years." Consequently, the railway companies must be made "to recruit people (naturally, from the Muslim population or other trustworthy groups) before the prescribed deadlines, without exception." Aware of the problems that this program could be expected to cause, the committee envisaged, "notwithstanding the fact that the greatest possible effort must be deployed to find people to take the places of the individuals to be replaced ... allowing the latter to continue to work for the company for a certain period. But this derogation should in no case be applied across the board."[15]

The same day, the interior minister approved the committee's decisions (which thereupon ceased its activities) about "the [gradual] replacement of the Armenian employees working for all railway companies, including the Anatolian company, in such a way as not to perturb railway service."[16] In the wrestling match between the *Bagdadbahn's* German administrators and the Turkish authorities, the decisions adopted may be qualified as compromises. It is impossible, obviously, to say how strictly this "replacement" program was carried out in practice, but there is every reason to believe that it proved unable to replace many white-collar workers and that the program's main victims were to be found among the unskilled.

Notwithstanding a few concessions that had become indispensable, the Young Turk authorities' obstinate desire to deport both those working on the Amanus construction sites and also the employees of the *Bagdadbahn* appears on balance as one of the clearest expressions of their genocidal policy and their project of a "national economy." In the case at hand, these objectives had priority over all other considerations, including the war effort. This experience also showed them how long it would take to "replace" the Armenians whom they had decided to exclude.

If this affair caused some tension between the German government and its Turkish ally, it ultimately showed the Young Turks that German political and military circles were willing to close their eyes to the crimes perpetrated against the Armenian population, even when those crimes were detrimental to German interests. The most that can be said is that the *Bagdadbahn's* engineers and managers, who daily witnessed scenes of horror, showed a certain concern for the Armenian deportees.

The Istanbul-Ismit-Eskişehir-Konya-Bozanti Deportation Route

The fact that Armenian employees worked on the Istanbul-Bozanti-Aleppo railway line proved highly beneficial to the deportees. We read in many different accounts that stationmasters, engineers, or doctors working for the company provided their compatriots with assistance. The network based in Konya and later in Aleppo served above all to transmit detailed reports to Constantinople and extract a few deportees from the convoys.[17] It was, however, the actions of the vali, Celal Bey, who held his post in Konya from 18 June to early October 1915, which enabled tens of thousands of deportees to remain at least briefly in Konya.[18]

The number of deportees who took this route in August, September, and October might be put at around 400,000. Some of them followed the railroad tracks on foot and then took the train as far as Bozanti. Others traveled by rail. Still others walked the entire distance, following the railway as far as the Taurus mountain chain. Obviously, the money or valuables at their disposal determined the means of transportation these deportees used. While the *Bagdadbahn's* German administrators complained that the authorities required them to transport the deportees without compensation, leading to financial losses for the company,[19] the fact that the deportees were transported free was a windfall for the gendarmerie or the local authorities, who systematically made them pay for their "tickets," sometimes demanding four times the official tariffs.[20] Apart from a few "political" deportees, who were under close guard, those who were able to take the train traveled in two-tiered sheep cars, at 80 to a car.[21] Under normal conditions, a train could make the journey from Haydarpaşa to Bozanti in fewer than 24 hours. However, the war and troop movements considerably interfered with traffic on this line, which consisted in many places of a single track, so that convoys of deportees were often forced to remain in the middle of a field for hours on end without food or, even worse, water.[22]

The deportees were not, then, transported directly and without interruption, but in several stages. This led to the formation of improvised transit camps around the main train stations. The first, northernmost station where such a camp was formed was in Eskişehir. Late in August, Dr. W. Post, who was traveling to Konya, counted 12,000 to 15,000 deportees camping there under precarious conditions. He observed that the local police "protected" the deportees during the day but every night helped the local populace pillage the camp and abduct or rape young girls. According to this American physician, 30 to 40 people died daily in the Eskişehir camp.[23] He noted the presence of 5,000 or more deportees, most of them natives of Bursa, trapped in the Alayun train station under similar conditions. Further south, in Konya, there were already 5,000 to 10,000 deportees from Bursa, Ismit, and Bardizag by 2 September; dysentery and malaria were wreaking havoc among them.[24] Toward mid-September, the number of deportees there had risen to around 50,000. They lived in an immense "tent" camp.[25] The absence of even elementary sanitation, lack of food, and, above all, water, led to many deaths every day. The bodies were burned in the city's Armenian cemetery.[26] According to Dr. Post, the CUP's responsible secretary and his henchmen took advantage of the vali's absence in late September to dispatch most of these 50,000 deportees to Cilicia and Syria. Post notes that two German officers posted near the train station witnessed the methods employed and protested, but it was in vain. This human tidal wave was dispatched on foot in a few hours, by way of the Konya desert. A handful of families who still had money or valuables negotiated the right to travel by rail with the gendarmes or the police.[27]

Dr. Dodd, the director of Konya's American Hospital, reports that a "committee responsible for exiles" had arrived from Istanbul. Its coming had been announced by a telegram from Enver stating that the committee had been given the mission of settling the deportees in the vilayet. However, Dodd observes, it soon became apparent that these men had been sent from the capital in order to clear the route and "speed up the traffic" coming from Bozanti and Adana. "It is reported" he writes, "that now the destination is Arabia."[28] Given the CUP's known modus operandi, it seems reasonable to suppose that the minister of the interior and the minister of war decided to dispatch these party cadres to organize the expedition of the convoys to the south and recall the undisciplined vali of Konya to Istanbul.

The sources at our disposal do not allow us to state the number of deportees who traveled by foot. A survivor reports that the 11,000 people in his convoy, natives of Balıkeser, Bandırma, Erencik, Bursa, Gemlik, Benli, Marmarcık, Gürle, Yenice, Adabazar, Darasu, Yalova, Çengiler, Ortaköy, and so on, walked all the way to Konya, because the trains had been requisitioned by the army.[29] We know from other sources that the tens of thousands of men deported from Istanbul "arrived in Konya after this journey of 400 miles" on foot, where they lived for a while with funds sent by their families.[30] It was these convoys of people on foot that were the last to arrive in Konya, in the second half of October; an example is provided by a group of 16,000 deportees that was briefly held up in Afionkarahisar.[31]

By late October, the camp around the Konya train station was empty. A few thousand Armenians had managed to hide in the city, now under the control of a new vali. These were, above all, affluent families from Bursa who paid a certain sum to officials every month in exchange for the right to stay.[32] But also among them were Protestants who had come from the west and Catholics from Angora, who sometimes succeeded in settling there on the strength of the late order by the interior minister concerning these population groups. According to Dodd, to "relieve the congestion thus created in the city," the authorities scattered these deportees through the rural areas, where they were attacked by çetes, who abducted the young women among them. Some of them managed to find work that enabled them to survive; others had no access to their bank accounts, which had been frozen. It seems that local Turkish businessmen had been given strict orders not to hire deportees.[33] A number of Turkish families nevertheless employed girls or women as domestics.[34]

Further south, the Eregli train station, like the train station in Konya, was the site of a vast tent camp. Fifteen thousand deportees were living there by early September. The men from Konya who had long been held in Sultaniye were sent to this camp in the same period and incorporated into the "ninth convoy," which left for Bozanti.[35] Post, who traveled to Bozanti on 20 November, counted 250 "refugees" there, and nearly 2,000 in the Eregli train station nearby, mainly craftsmen who worked for the army.[36] Post also says that, according to the statistics gathered by Bagdadbahn officials, 500,000 deportees passed by way of Bozanti. If, to the 400,000 Armenians deported from the west, we add the convoys from the north that traveled through this town, Dodd's figure seems reasonable. The municipal physician, Dr. Manug, who had been recruited from among the deportees' ranks, saved many deportees in transit, according to witnesses, providing them with medical care and material aid.[37] The commander of the gendarmerie, Musa, had arrogated unto himself the right to pillage the convoys that passed by way of Bozanti,[38] the last train station the deportees saw before confronting the mountain passes of the Taurus region.

We have very few accounts by deportees of their passage down the Istanbul-Bozanti route. We do know, however, that the losses they sustained were rarely due to physical violence. They died, rather, of hunger and thirst.

Another American physician, Dr. Hoover, who was returning to Istanbul by rail, witnessed the spectacle of deportees in transit in every train station. He saw, notably, the abduction of a 15-year-old girl by a captain who tried to justify himself on the grounds that by abducting her he was saving her life. In his own words, it was only then that the doctor began "to realize the enormity of the crimes." "Why," he asked the captain, "are you taking such brutal measures to accomplish your?" The officer answered, "Why, don't you understand, we don't want to have to repeat this thing again after few years. It's hot down in the deserts of Arabia, and there is no water, and these people can't stand a hot climate, don't you see?"[39]

The majority of the available accounts of the Istanbul-Bozanti route are due to the members of the Constantinople elite who were deported much later than the hapless colleagues of theirs who were arrested on 24 April 1915. These people were deported by rail under police escort and imprisoned at every station of their journey. We are, for example, familiar with the case of the journalist Levon Mozian, who traveled through Konya in July, guarded by two policemen, benefiting from the help of the prelate Karekin Khachadurian and the director of the Armenian middle school, Mgrdich Barsamian, before being sent on to Eregli and Bozanti.[40] The same holds for Krikor Zohrab and Vartkes Seringiulian, who were in Konya on 9 June 1915. Writing from that city, Zohrab informed his wife that he had met in the Baghdad Hotel his fellow parliamentary deputy, Mustafa Fevzi, the representative from Saruhan, whom he had asked to intercede on his behalf.[41] In a letter to his friend the interior minister, he expressed his surprise over the plans to send him to Dyarbekir without first informing him of the charges against him. "According to the information making the rounds," he wrote, "[I am being sent to Dyarbekir for] plotting against the government and exhibiting an unfriendly attitude. I do not accept this accusation in any way."[42] The Istanbul humorist and writer Yervant Odian, who was deported early in September with the journalist Sebuh Aguni and the pharmacist Nerses Chakrian, also traveled by rail under police guard, at a time when the Istanbul-Bozanti route was clogged with traffic.[43] In prison in Konya, he met Vahan Balabanian, a Dashnak militant from Smyrna who had been condemned to death and then pardoned.[44] At the station, in a khan, the three companions encountered a throng of families from Adabazar and Bandırma, as well as Lieutenant Hrant Samuel, the former editor of the daily *Zhamanag*, in an officer's uniform, and the parliamentary deputies from Aleppo, Harutiun Boshgezenian, and Adana, Mattheos Nalbandian, who were on their way to Istanbul to participate in the opening of the new parliamentary session.[45] All the complexity of the system set up by the Young Turks is summed up in these unlikely encounters. Among all these exiles, two deputies and an officer – remnants of normalcy, as it were – were free to come and go as they pleased. Further south, in Eregli, Odian witnessed the misery reigning in the hundreds of tents in which the deportees were living, many state officials and lawyers from Bursa and Ismit among them. He also saw an Istanbul businessman who could still communicate with the Patriarchate thanks to Armenian railway officials.[46]

On 24 September, Odian arrived in Bozanti without impediments, thanks to the friendly attitude of the Armenian stationmaster and ticket collectors. He joined the mass of deportees there.[47]

Chapter 19

Deportations from Zeitun and Dörtyol: Repression or Genocidal Program?

We have already seen how the events that occurred in Zeitun and Dörtyol in March and April 1915 were perceived in Istanbul.[1] We shall now look in some detail at the way they unfolded, with a view to assessing the credibility of the accusations that the local and, later, national authorities leveled against the Armenian population of these regions.

Let us begin by noting that the region of Maraş/Marash, of which Zeitun was a part, had been elevated to the rank of a *mutesarifat* early in March 1915.[2] Until then, the *sancak* of Marash had been under the jurisdiction of the vali of Aleppo, Celal Bey, who himself seemed to believe that the capital had "recently" granted this district autonomy for the sole purpose of preventing him from interfering with operations there.[3] Celal thus implied that the "incidents" that took place in Zeitun had their origins in a general plan established in Istanbul. The dates on which they occurred likewise suggest that their objective was to incriminate "the" Armenians – that is, to prepare the "legal" groundwork for the genocidal measures to come. Indeed, the very special attention that the capital lavished on Zeitun's Armenians was anything but fortuitous. The inhabitants of this mountainous region had been heard from more than once in the nineteenth century; they had consistently displayed a strong spirit of independence and a capacity for self-defense that had caused one sultan after the next no small amount of trouble. A latter-day remnant of the Armenian Kingdom of Cilicia, Zeitun, the Armenian Ulnia, had in 1618 received confirmation of its autonomy from Sultan Murad IV in exchange for an annual tribute. This state of affairs had persisted down to 1862. In the course of that year, the inhabitants of Zeitun successfully withstood the assaults of several tens of thousands of Ottoman soldiers. During the 1895 massacres, they also successfully beat back the large armed force that Constantinople had sent to crush them. The CUP, obviously drawing the lessons of these military debacles, had made Zeitun one of its primary objectives in 1915.[4]

On the eve of the First World War, the *kaza* of Zeitun, which was almost entirely Armenian, had more than 22,000 inhabitants. They lived in the town of Zeitun and six rural communities. Located at the foot of the southern face of Mt. Berid, the town was built, level after level, on the slopes of two valleys. To the north, on the heights, lay the monastery of the Holy Mother of God. In 1914, the town of Zeitun had a population of 10,600. It was divided into four neighborhoods (located in the two upper and the two lower quarters) governed by a city council headed by the bishop of the region. It was known for horse-shoeing, stonecutting, and the production of agricultural tools, but its inhabitants also cultivated olive trees, fruit trees, and a few different types of grain. They also raised horses, cattle, sheep, and goats, and produced brandy, wine, raisins, honey, wool, and leather.

An hour southeast of Zeitun laid the villages of Avakenk, Kalustenk, Hacidere, Avakhal/ Mehal, and Alabash (3,200 Armenians). Finally, in the northernmost part of the *kaza* laid the village of Yarpuz (1,100 Armenians).[5]

In August 1914, the induction of the men old enough to bear arms took place without resistance, although these mountaineers, required to serve in the army for the first time, were hardly used to military discipline. According to the minister Dikran Andreasian, a preacher in Zeitun, a non-negligible number of men from Zeitun nevertheless dodged military service, a circumstance that did not fail to produce tensions.[6] The *mutesarif*, Ali Haydar Pasha, went to Zeitun in person, accompanied by an army brigade. He summoned the Armenian notables there, who were arrested and tortured in the barracks located in the city's heights. Officially, it was a question of bringing them to confess that they were preparing a rebellion, and also of forcing them to give up their arms. A total of 42 notables, notably the charismatic leader of the inhabitants of Zeitun, Nazaret Yeniduniayan, were taken to Marash in chains. Most of them were poisoned or killed in some other way in the following weeks.[7] In other words, the authorities utilized a method in Zeitun that would be brought to bear on other regions the following year. These events did not fail to produce a certain indignation in Zeitun, but the catholicos of Cilicia, Sahag I Khabayan, reacted immediately, making it clear to the faithful in Zeitun that the least sign of a revolt would have "disastrous consequences for all Armenians." In the fall, witnesses noted that the gendarmes stationed in the town were openly provoking incidents: they entered houses without warning, committed thefts, and treated women disrespectfully.[8] The absence of the men of fighting age, who had either been mobilized or had fled to avoid being recruited, naturally gave the gendarmes and troops the impression that they were free to do as they pleased. Yet, the possibility that they had received instructions from Maraş to provoke the populace cannot be excluded. The fact that weapons held by the people of Zeitun were confiscated in August 1914 indicates, at the very least, that the town had been under close surveillance from the beginning, unless we are to suppose that Istanbul was thus paving the way for the operations it would carry out later.

The choice of Zeitun as the region's recruitment center, into which recruits streamed from all sides,[9] was probably no accident and helped keep tensions running at a high pitch there. The number of rapes committed by gendarmes[10] perhaps also contributed, after a fashion, to the rise of a powerful feeling of exasperation among the Armenian populace. Initially, the *kaymakam*, Hüsni Bey (who held his post from 15 June 1914 to 14 March 1915) and the military authorities closed their eyes to the 100 to 200 deserters from Zeitun who roamed through the region and staged raids in order to get food. Early in 1915, however, skirmishes began to multiply between these fugitives and the forces of order. Yet, it was not until March that the situation became genuinely tense: on Monday, 8 March, a squadron of the army was attacked in the vicinity of Zeitun by a group of deserters. According to Aghasi, who participated in these events, the attackers were seeking to obtain arms. They killed twelve soldiers before withdrawing to an impregnable monastery situated on the heights overlooking Zeitun to the north.[11] The American consul in Aleppo, Jesse B. Jackson, states in a letter that these 25 deserters were worker-soldiers who had been working on a site in Bazarcık between Ayntab and Marash before deciding to take to the maquis.[12] The killing of the soldiers obviously sowed panic among Zeitun's populace, which unanimously condemned the act and dispatched a delegation to the deserters to ask them to cease all attacks on the army or gendarmerie. On the evening of 9 March, two squadrons arrived from Marash, followed on 13 March by the *mutesarif* himself.[13] By intervening as promptly as they did, Armenian circles had doubtless hoped to limit the retaliation that inevitably awaited the region's Armenian population. The immediate destitution of the *kaymakam*, Hüsni, on 14 March – he was replaced by Hilmi Bey on 7 April – might have left them with the impression that the authorities had understood that the many different provocations orchestrated by this high-ranking official since fall 1914 had contributed to the deterioration of the situation. The delegations from the town that, one after the other, went to see the rebels and ask them to turn themselves in might also have encouraged people to believe that the authorities wished to settle the matter without using force. But the leaders of Zeitun had, according to Aghasi, already understood that the authorities had a solid pretext for liquidating their town, and that after getting the better of the 25 deserters they were doubtless going "to exterminate [them] as well." Their only hope was to limit the retaliatory acts to the men and prevent "the town from being reduced to ashes"[14] by exhibiting unwavering loyalty.

Moreover, the gradual arrival of some 5,000 troops from Aleppo between 17 and 22 March 1915[15] was a sign of the authorities' intentions. It is more than obvious that so large a force was not needed to bring 25 deserters barricaded in a monastery under control. On the night of 23–24 March, the people of Zeitun further observed that all the state officials had "fled" to the barracks overlooking the city, an indication of events to come. The townsmen immediately made contact with the *mutesarif*, with whom they held an impromptu meeting at which it was decided to wire the Patriarch, Zaven, and the catholicos, Sahag Khabayan, in order to request that the catholicos send representatives to Zeitun capable of persuading the deserters to surrender. Aware of the gravity of the situation, the catholicos had, with the approval of the *mutesarif* of Marash, already dispatched a five-man delegation to Zeitun, which arrived the morning of 24 March. It was made up of the auxiliary primate, Sahag Der Bedrosian, the catholic vicar Khoren, the Protestant minister Aharon Shirajian, and the director of the German hospital and orphanage in Marash, Reverend H. Blank.[16] While the delegation was able to meet with Zeitun's notables, who persuaded it that the problem was confined to the men who had barricaded themselves in the monastery, they were not given permission to meet with the insurgents and were soon firmly requested to leave.[17] It is probable that the *mutesarif* and General Hurşid, the commanding officer of the troops dispatched to Zeitun, had already received the order to launch the assault, which began at dawn on 25 March.[18] Some 20 men, most of them from the Yeniduniayan family, had joined forces with the deserters, embittered by the earlier murder of a member of their clan, Nazaret Çavuş. The Turkish forces, after shelling the monastery with a mountain cannon and destroying part of its outer wall, charged up the slope with the intention of capturing it, but encountering stiff resistance they retreated, leaving behind a captain, Süleyman, and a few dozen other casualties.[19] The next day, when the troops launched a second assault, they discovered that the rebels had burned down the monastery and fled overnight.[20] Immediately thereafter, the army brigades surrounded Zeitun. The townspeople hoisted a white flag to make it clear that they had no intention to resist.[21] The catholicos contacted the commander of the Fourth Army, Ahmed Cemal, and implored him to order the Turkish forces to spare the population of Zeitun. Armenian sources report that Cemal agreed to meet the Armenian prelate's request and sent a cable to this effect to Zeitun's military authorities on 31 March.[22] There is, however, every reason to believe that the Young Turk general had made a purely formal declaration, unless we are to suppose that conflicting orders later arrived from the capital. For, on 8 April, the deportation of the Zeitun Armenians commenced. The 35 leading citizens of the town, including our witness and the director of the orphanage, were put on the road to Osmaniye with their families; from there, they were sent on to Konya. A second convoy, including three priests, arrived in Marash on Monday, 11 April, and a third, with the "suspects," arrived on Wednesday, the 13th.[23] The patriarch notes in his memoirs that "[i]t was a golden occasion to deport all the Armenians from Zeitun."[24] Thus, a total of around 18,000 people was put on the road in three days: nearly 6,000 were set marching in the direction of Konya and

Eregli, and thence to Sultaniye;[25] 5,000 more were set toward Aleppo, and all the others to Rakka, Der Zor, Mosul, and as far as the environs of Baghdad.[26] In the second half of April, the Armenian population of the two neighboring *kazas*, Göksun and Elbistan, was deported in its turn.[27]

In the *kaza* of Göksun, which lay in the Anti-Taurus and took in the whole northwestern part of the *mutesarifat* of Marash, 9,500 people living in 18 localities were affected by the deportations. The principal town of the *kaza* and the surrounding villages had a total Armenian population of nearly 3,000. Göksun (pop. 380), Hüyük (pop. 120), Kirec (pop. 650), Gölpunar (pop. 150), Taşoluk (pop. 600), and Seyirmendere (pop. 400), together with the outlying farms, were the first localities to be evacuated. Further to the south, the deportations targeted the town of Geben, with a Turkish-speaking Armenian population of 3,000, as well as the villagers of Deyirmenbaşı, Çukur, and Bunduk (pop. 245). The last big group of Armenian villages affected by the deportations was located near the town of Furnuz, in the southern part of the *kaza*. A total of 3,000 Armenians lived here, including the inhabitants of six outlying villages, among which were Çağlağan and Telemelik, and on some 15 farms located somewhat further off, where 300 people lived.[28] The *kaymakam* Garib Bey, who held his post from 7 February 1914 to 25 October 1915, played a central role in organizing these operations, carried out by the army. Dr. Fred Shepard of the American Hospital in Ayntab notes, for example, that in Geben the women were doing their wash in the laundry when the order for immediate deportation was issued, and they were forced to leave without being able to take anything at all with them. As for their men, they were deported separately.[29]

In the *kaza* of Elbistan, located in the northeastern part of the *mutesarifat* of Marash, the deportations targeted nearly six thousand Armenians, nearly four thousand of whom lived in the seat of the *kaza* and the neighboring village of Bavurköy. Operations here were overseen by the *kaymakam*, Hüseyin Derviş Bey.[30] Kate Ainslie, a missionary, notes that the authorities made the deportees from Elbistan take a particularly mountainous route, circumventing Zeitun, so that they needed almost a week to reach Marash.[31] From there they were sent toward Ayntab and Aleppo.[32]

Several witnesses have pointed out that the Armenian localities of the *kazas* of Zeitun, Göksun, and Elibstan were immediately occupied by Muslim *muhacirs* from Macedonia and Rumelia. Ainslie observed as she left Marash on 14 June that Zeitun was now inhabited by Macedonians, who chopped down the fruit trees for firewood.[33] Reverend John Merril, from Marash, noted that the *muhacirs* who took the place of the Armenians of Furnuz and Geben had been temporarily left in Ayntab while waiting for the Armenian houses to be emptied of their occupants. He states that, "From confidential sources in Marash, the secret report is made that is the intention to deport the Christian population of all the Marash villages, extending as far north as Hasan Beyli."[34]

Arnold Toynbee has quite rightly observed that the fact that *muhacirs* were thus early stationed in the vicinity of Zeitun as early as 8 April is "one special feature about the execution of the scheme in Cilicia which is evident that it was carried out deliberately and thought out far ahead." "Immediately the Armenians were evicted from their villages," Toynbee continued, "their houses were assigned to Moslem refugees [...] from Roumelian vilayets," while these refugees from the Balkan Wars had until then been "on the Government's hands" in camps in Thrace or along the Aegean coast. In other words, high-ranking authorities had organized the transfer of these *muhacirs* "from the western fringes of the empire to the other extremity of the Anatolian Railway" so that they would be ready "to occupy the homes of the Armenians in Cilicia immediately their rightful owners had started on their road to exile."[35] In endeavoring to provoke a reaction from the inhabitants of Zeitun, the authorities no doubt singled out the population assuring them the best chance of success. However limited the reaction to the provocation was, it afforded the Young Turk government the opportunity to light a fire that it carefully kept burning thereafter.

As for the fate of the deportees from Zeitun, a European witness saw some of them pass through the Adana train station bound for Konya in "pig-cars," and others who were headed for Aleppo by way of "Arabia." The last convoy of these deportees passed by in mid-May, made up of old people and children in a lamentable state.[36] According to a survivor, the inhabitants of Zeitun who were held up in Sultaniye lost around 700 of their number in two months' time before being put back on the road on 8 August, bound for the deserts of Syria and the Dera'a district by way of Adana and Aleppo.[37]

The decision to rename Zeitun Süleymanlı after the officer who was killed during the assault on the monastery marks, no doubt symbolically, shows the beginnings of the program of Turkifying the Anatolian region by way of the liquidation of its Armenian population and also by changing place names there.[38]

The Deportations from Dörtyol

When the Ottoman Empire entered the war, the *sancak* of Cebelbereket, like the whole of the region of the Gulf of Alexandretta, found itself under pressure from the British and French fleets. The Allied ships were positioned near shore and regularly shelled the railroad that ran southward, skirting the coast. The shelling deeply alarmed the local population, which feared an Anglo-French landing. The other element contributing to the tension reigning in the region was the presence of some 40,000 Armenians who lived in 29 towns and villages of this coastal *sancak*, who were suspected of harboring sympathies for the Triple Entente. From the outbreak of the war, the inhabitants of the *kazas* on the coast, Yümürtalık and, especially, Payas, had been placed under close surveillance by the army. Payas, which lay a few kilometers from the sea on the western slopes of the Amanus mountains, boasted an Armenian population of 11,000, settled in three localities all in the same area: Dörtyol (pop. 7,000), Ocaklı (pop. 2,545), and Özerli (pop. 1,560).[39] According to Armenian sources, from November 1914 on, the coast near Alexandretta, Payas, Dörtyol, and Ayas was under the surveillance of a British warship, the *Doris*. As a result, the Ottoman military authorities had set up a system of obligatory passes; it was illegal to travel without one. Early in November, the *kaymakam* summoned the auxiliary primate, Father Mesrob Esefian, two members of the diocesan council, and four *muhtars* in order to tell them that there was a risk that the British would attempt a landing. The *kaymakam* suggested, consequently, that the Armenians "temporarily seek refuge" in the Amanus region, like the other inhabitants of the coastal region. He warned them that if they did not do so "spontaneously," the authorities would not hesitate to use force.[40] This threat was not carried out, but the Armenians perceived it as a clear warning. In February 1915, after the port of Alexandretta and its railroad had been shelled, the authorities mobilized 600 Armenians from Dörtyol to repair the damage.[41]

As in Zeitun, an incident accelerated events. Late in February, someone named Saljian, a native of the region who made his home in Cyprus, was arrested by the troops guarding the coast just after a British warship put him ashore.[42] The authorities immediately proceeded to arrest Armenians living in coastal areas and organized a public execution of peasants from villages near Payas, accused of having created a spy ring. The dragoman of the German vice-consulate in Alexandretta escaped a similar fate thanks only to the intercession of the German Ambassador in Constantinople.[43] As in the Zeitun affair, the primate of Adana, Father Kevork Arslanian, was summoned by the vali, Colonel İsmail Hakkı, and asked to send a reliable representative to Dörtyol to convince the local population to submit to the authorities. The chief secretary of the Catholicosate was chosen to accomplish this mission. He learned, before setting out, that Colonel Hüseyin Avni Bey, commander of the vilayet's gendarmerie and presiding judge at the Adana court-martial, had himself gone to Dörtyol, where he had proceeded to arrest all the men between the ages of 18 and 65 "in order to conduct them to the interior" and confiscate weapons.[44] The chief secretary wrote in his report on his mission that he had taken the train as far as the station in Toprakkale, and continued his journey from there in a car, after laboriously making his way past the military checkpoints that had been thrown across the road here and there. In Ocaklı, he had encountered two cars in which Father Mesrob and a handful of notables from Dörtyol were sitting. They had been summoned to appear before the court-martial in Erzin on the initiative of the Bosnian Colonel Hüseyin Avni.[45] The chief secretary of the Catholicosate, after a brief conversation with the *kaymakam*, Colonel Avni, and the commander of the gendarmerie in Dörtyol, Çerkez Murad Bey, convinced the town's notables to turn in their arms, essentially hunting rifles and daggers.[46] In a letter to his ambassador, the German consul in Adana expressed doubts as to the reality of the ostensible revolution that the authorities accused Dörtyol's Armenians of planning, and wondered whether it was legitimate to arrest all the men in the town, when they "had demonstrated their submission to the authorities and not shown them the least resistance."[47] One thousand six hundred adult males were sent to the *kaza* of Osmaniye, in Hasanbeyli, to work on building a section of the road 23 kilometers long; only a handful of the men in Dörtyol were spared this fate. The accusation of an "insurrection" was plainly baseless; nothing indicated that the least preparation had been made for armed resistance. On the other hand, it was notably Talât Bey himself who issued the order to launch the operation against Dörtyol, in a 2 March 1915 letter to the vali of Adana.[48] This makes it highly probable that the whole business had been concocted in the capital. It must further be pointed out that chief among those brought before the court-martial in Adana were the leading notables of Dörtyol, who were judged and publicly hanged over the following weeks.[49] Osmanağazâde Hasan; Dellaloğlu İsmail, who organized the death squadrons of the Special Organization in the region beginning in January 1915; Şükrü Bey, the *mutesarif* of Cebelbereket; Hüseyin Avni Bey, the presiding judge at the Adana court-martial; Haci Ali Effendi, the mufti of Dörtyol; Divlimoğlu Haci; Köisenoğlu Ahmed; Köisenoğlu Mevlat Effendi; Muftizâde Mustafa Effendi; and Haci Hamdi Effendi led this operation before bringing these men back to Dörtyol in order to deport them with their families to Adana and then Meskene, Rakka, Ras ul-Ayn, and Hama. In all, 20,000 Armenians from the *kazas* of Payas, Yümürtalık, and Hasa were deported to the south late in April. Around three thousand five hundred of them – basically people who had been deported to the Damascus area – were still alive when the armistice was signed.[50]

That said, it must be pointed out that very few local massacres took place in the course of these operations. They nevertheless prefigured, by virtue of the methods used in them, especially the way that they were prepared, the extermination program carried out elsewhere in the following weeks.

Chapter 20

Deportations in the *Mutesarifat* of Marash

After the operations that early in the day had affected the Armenian populations of the *kazas* of Zeitun, Göksun, and Elbistan, the regions of Marash and Bazarcık in turn fell victim to the Young Turk extermination plan. A region forming a kind of pivot between the worlds of Cilicia, Cappadocia, and the Armenian plateau, in an enclave between the Antitaurus and the Taurus, the *mutesarifat* of Maraş/Marash was inhabited in 1914 by more than 70,000 Armenians living in 64 towns and villages. When the last two *kazas* began to be emptied of their Armenians, there were fewer than 35,000 of them left in 24 localities. Most of them were living in the city of Marash, whose 22,500 Armenians represented in 1914 around 50 per cent of its population. Almost all of them were concentrated in a neighborhood west of the citadel that extended to an area below the monastery of Saint James, on the outskirts of the city. Within this perimeter were no fewer than five churches, several Armenian schools, an American College, and a German hospital and orphanage.

The other Armenian localities of the region were Fındıkcak, located 22 kilometers from Marash, with an Armenian population of 2,500; Kişifli (pop. 560), Dereköy (pop. 1,000), Camustul (pop. 250), and Döngel (pop. 1,500). There was a second group of Armenian villages around Yenicekale (pop. 800) and Mucukdere (pop. 500), between which lay the Red Monastery of Kesun: Arablı (pop. 100), Kötekli (pop. 150), Yeğialar (pop. 150), Çurukköz (pop. 300), Demerek, Punarbaşı (pop. 100), and Dikilitaş (pop. 100). Still further to the southwest, on the boundary-line of the *kaza* around Enderun (70 Armenians) were three other villages: Acemli (pop. 84), Dırtadlı (pop. 280), and Deyirmendere (pop. 140). The last Armenian village, Chivilgi, lying in a northerly extension of the Enderun mountain chain, had an Armenian population of 1,760.[1]

Taking in the entire southern part of the *mutesarifat* of Marash, the *kaza* of Bazarcık was home to 1,500 Armenians, all of whom lived in the seat of the *kaza*, also called Bazarcık.[2]

In Marash, whose Muslim inhabitants had a reputation for being very conservative, the German consul in Aleppo, Walter Rössler, who visited the city on 31 March 1915, observed the tension that had been reigning there since the events that had occurred in the neighboring town of Zeitun. A state of siege had been declared in the city and a court-martial had been formed.[3] According to two American doctors, Marash's Muslim leaders took advantage of the situation to pressure the *mutesarif* into imposing harsh treatment on the Armenian population. A military committee had been sent to the town around 7 April and proceeded to conduct searches in Armenian institutions and the homes of certain notables, looking for evidence indicating that a rebellion was being organized. The committee gave the population three days, from 9 to 11 April, to turn its arms over to the authorities. On 8 April, Hagop Horlakhian (Kherlakian), a notable who even had access to the imperial palace, was summoned to appear before this committee, which demanded that he see to it that the

Armenian population comply with the government's orders.[4] There is every reason to believe that the military commission began to cooperate closely with local Young Turk leaders. Dr. C. F. Hamilton and Dr. C. F. Ranney report that on 13 April the Armenians of Marash learned that "a black list of 300 to 600 names" was circulating in the city. Some Armenian notables nevertheless downplayed the significance of a document of this sort, making a game of trying to guess who was on the list.

Arrests in Marash took diverse forms. One of the methods most often employed was to invite all the men of draftable age, including those who had paid the *bedel*, to register for the draft. In fact, the registration campaign, which took place on 15, 16, and 17 July 1915, allowed the authorities to isolate these men, the better to liquidate them.[5] Among the first to be arrested were 11 notables, including the auxiliary primate, Father Ghevont Nahabedian, the Protestant minister Aharon Shirajian, Garabed Nalchayan, Armenag and Nazareth Bilezigji, and Konstan and Hovnan Varzhabedian, all of whom were sent to Aleppo.[6] In the course of a 21 April conversation with the vali of Aleppo, Celal Bey, the Protestant minister John Merril learned, moreover, that there was a plan to deport the "refugees" from Zeitun, but that the government's policy was above all, "to prevent such public and unordered violence." The American missionary's long experience taught him how to translate this remark: "This is a plan for the breaking down of the Christian population without bloodshed and with the color of legality." He had already observed that "false" reports about the Armenians had been transmitted to Istanbul "to be the basis for the orders now being carried out." Finally, he noted that the first to be deported were the best educated men, especially those who were close to American missionary circles.[7]

In the neighboring localities, where the villagers were deported at the same time as the Armenians of Marash, the only unusual occurrence was the resistance put up at Fındıkcak.[8] It was quickly crushed by the army, which massacred part of the population on the spot and deported the women and children.[9]

Some 30 men organized the squadrons of *çetes*, with some 20 irregulars in each, which wreaked havoc in the region. These 30 men, who also supervised the massacres and served as the members of the committee responsible for "abandoned property," were Ali Haydar Pasha, the *mutesarif* of Marash; Kocabaşizâde Ömer Effendi, the president of the Unionist club of Marash; Şevketzâde Şadir Effendi, parliamentary deputy from Marash; Ğarizâde Haci Effendi, a former parliamentary deputy from Marash; Dayizâde Hoca Baş, *ulema*; Haci Bey, the mayor of Marash; Eczaci Lutfi, a pharmacist; Sarukâtibzâde Mehmed; Eşbazâde Haci Hüseyin; Bulgarizâde Abdül Hakim; Sarukzâde Halil Ali; Şismanzâde Haci Ahmed; Şismanzâde Nuri; Ap Acuz Haci Effendi; Mazmanzâde Mustafa; Evliyazâde Evliya; Hoddayizâde Tahsin Bey; Hodayizâde Ahmed; Nazifzâde Ahmed; Hocabaşzâde Ahmed; Karaküçükzâde Mehmed; Derviş Effendi, the former mayor; Saatbeyzâde Şükrü; Eviliyazâde Ahmed, an imam; Bayazidzâde Ğadir Pasha; Bayazidzâde İbrahim Bey; Çuşadarzâde Mustafa; and Çuşadarzâde Mehmed.[10]

The principal local leaders of the *Teşkilât-ı Mahsusa* were Vehbizâde Hasip Effendi; Dr. Mustafa; Karaküçükzâde Mustafa; Koçabaşzâde Cemil Bey; Hoddayizâde Okbeş; Mazmanzâde Mustafa; Mazmanzâde Hasan; Haci Niazi Bey, secretary of the Department of Finance; Şakir Effendi; Cevdet Bey, the director of correspondence; Atıf Effendi, from Kilis; Ömer Effendi, an officer in the gendarmerie; Ömer's two sons; and Fatmaluoğlu Mustafa. Those mainly responsible for perpetrating the exactions were Bayazidzâde Şukri Bey; Bayazidzâde Kasim Bey; Bayazidzâde Kerim Bey; Bayazidzâde Hasan Bey; Buharizâde Abdül Hakim Effendi; Kocabaşzâde Haci İbrahim; Ayntablıoğlu Ahmed, the assistant police chief; Çuşadarzâde Mehmed, a member of the local CUP; Safiyeninoğlu Alay Mustafa Effendi, a regimental secretary; Kusa Kurekzâde Ahmed, a *belediye mufettişi* (municipal inspector); Cemal Bey, a criminal court judge; and Hayrullah Effendi, a teacher in the Idadi middle school.[11]

Chapter 21

Deportations in the Vilayet of Adana

According to the censuses conducted by the Catholicosate of the Great House of Cilicia, more than 80,000 Armenians lived in the vilayet of Adana in 1913. They were settled in 70 towns and villages, with nearly 28,000 of them in the *sancak* of Adana alone.

The city of Adana itself, with an Armenian population of more than 26,000 on the eve of the First World War, held a significant place in the political and economic life of the vilayet. There were only a handful of Armenian villages in its environs: to the north, Kristianköy (pop. 190); to the east, Incirlik (pop. 250), located on the *Bagdadbahn*, and Misis (pop. 480); and to the southeast, Abdoğlu (pop. 340) and Şeyhmurad (pop. 300).[1]

Since the April 1909 Cilician massacres, which took an especially heavy toll in Adana, tensions in this coastal region, exposed to the maneuvers of the French and British navies, had never really subsided. Local Young Turk leaders under the lead of İsmail Safâ [Özler], whose heavy involvement in the 1909 violence we have already discussed,[2] had maintained their influence intact. Even before the Ottoman Empire's entry into the war, the tone of things to come had been set at a 10 September 1914 meeting by Safâ, the president of Adana's Unionist club and an active proponent of unilateral abrogation of the Capitulations (the abrogation of which was officially made public on 1 October) and "nationalization" of the economy.[3] In other words, Safâ advocated eliminating the entrepreneurial middle classes, the main partners of the European enterprises implanted in Cilicia. These social strata, made up above all of Greeks and Armenians, complained precisely about the economic crisis spawned by the war, which they blamed on the Germans. Probably for economic reasons, their critique did not go unnoticed. According to the German consul in Adana, a German officer deemed it an act of "high treason" that called for punishment.[4] While the diplomats were not of the same mind as the military men here, this affair nonetheless revealed how suspect Greeks and Armenians were in the eyes of the Ottoman Empire and its allies.

A report by an American resident of Adana allows us to grasp the reasons for the bitterness that Greek and Armenian businessmen felt at the time. She observed that the mobilization and requisitions had been a veritable catastrophe for them, pointing out in particular that "[t]he Armenian shops were robbed at pleasure without payment."[5] Yet, while the Dörtyol "affair," the frequent public executions of condemned Armenians, and the repercussions of the events in Zeitun had disconcerted certain Adana Armenians, it must nevertheless be pointed out that no particular measures were taken against them until late April. The first harbinger of the future persecutions was the arrest, at the end of April, of 400 members of the elite of Adana, especially teachers and entrepreneurs such as Samuel Avedisian, Yesayi Bezdigian, Garabed Chalian, Mihran Boyajian, and the Bedrosian brothers. William

Chambers, who had been working in Turkey for 37 years, points out that those arrested were first and foremost men who had survived the 1909 massacres and been kept under close surveillance by the authorities.[6] Contrary to what happened in other regions, however, these men were freed after one week in detention.[7] The vali, İsmail Hakkı Bey, an Albanian with a reputation as a moderate,[8] probably had something to do with this. Also involved, in all likelihood, was Cemal Pasha, the commander-in-chief of the Fourth Army, who had himself served as vali of Adana for a year after the 1909 massacres and had cultivated relations with a few leading Armenian families. It is also reasonable to suppose that the vali had Cemal's support, which was indispensable if he wished to keep his post and withstand the pressures exerted by the local Unionist club. To the extent that one can deduce his position from his acts, Hakkı was not systematically opposed to the orders he received from the capital. Thus, he organized the deportation of more than 4,000 "non-resident" Armenians in Bozanti in May 1915, but succeeded in bringing them back to the town a few weeks later.[9] He likewise proved willing, early in May, to deport 30 of the richest Adana families, most of who returned in three weeks' time, apparently as a result of the intervention of the American Ambassador in Constantinople.[10] Another revealing sign of the vali's benevolent attitude came late in April 1915, when the Istanbul court-martial sent him a dispatch demanding that Adana's primate, Archbishop Khachadur Arslanian, be immediately transferred to the capital. His response was to instruct the Public Health Inspector to issue a certificate attesting that the prelate was physically unable to undertake the voyage to Istanbul.[11]

The first convoy of deportees from Adana, comprised more than 4,000 Armenians, left the city on 20 May under police escort, but with the money the deportees had obtained from the sale of their moveable assets.[12] The German consul, Dr. Eugen Büge, informed Wangenheim in an 18 May cable that the deportation had begun throughout the province, that the prisons were full, and that death sentences were being executed daily.[13] The interior minister, for his part, sent an inquiry to the local authorities about how far their implementation of the deportation program had advanced. In particular, he wanted them to inform him of the names of the localities whose inhabitants had been deported, and also the number of deportees.[14] According to the chief secretary of Adana's Armenian archbishopric, the catholicos of Cilicia, Sahag Khabayan, had called a meeting of the diocesan council and officers of the *Banque Ottomane* and Tobacco Régie on 23 May/5 June. He told them that it seemed to him inevitable that the Armenians of the vilayet would be deported and that the businessmen would therefore do well discretely to transform their stocks into cash. He added that he himself had decided to take up residence in Aleppo in order to organize there as best he could a program of assistance for the deportees passing through the city.[15] The arrest of 18 notables from Adana, which took place almost immediately after this meeting, and the deportations set in motion in the rest of the vilayet nevertheless prompted the city's Armenians to send the chief secretary of the archbishopric, Kerovpe Papazian, to see the catholicos and ask him to intercede with the commander of the Fourth Army, Cemal Pasha.[16] With the help of the parliamentary deputy Artin/Harutiun Boshgezenian, Sahag I wrote a letter addressed to Ahmed Cemal. In early June, Papazian was able to meet with Cemal in Aley, Lebanon, and deliver the catholicos's message to him. On his account, Cemal immediately sent a wire to the vali of Adana and the military commander of the region in which he ordered them not to deport a single Armenian "without informing [him] of it."[17] According to information provided by the American consul, Edward Nathan, a temporary halt was called to the deportations from Adana alone around 28 May. Over the opposition of the influential members of Adana's Unionist club, Nathan even announced the return of the families of the notables that had been expelled three weeks earlier and hinted that advocates and opponents of the deportations had had a rather sharp confrontation on the issue.[18] Armenian survivors would later confirm that İsmail Hakkı Bey and the police chief, Cemal Bey, were hostile to the deportations and had clashed with members of the Ittihadist club led by Safâ.[19] The vali was apparently powerful enough to withstand the pressure put on him by the local Unionists. He had an additional advantage in that the CUP had no responsible secretary in Adana looking over his shoulder. It is probable that Cemal Pasha's intervention made his task easier.

Without a doubt, it was with the intention of putting an end to this situation that made Adana an exception – between April and July, the Armenian population of Dörtyol, Hacın, Zeitun, Hasanbeyli, and Sis had been deported – that Talât's second in command in the Interior Ministry, Ali Münîf, who was also a parliamentary deputy from Adana, was dispatched to the city. His presence there produced effects virtually overnight: late in July, some hundred "suspects," including N. Geokderelian and the lawyer Garabed Chalian, were arrested and deported to Aleppo. Public hangings also began again. A 14-year-old adolescent from Dörtyol was executed together with adults after being condemned by a court-martial headed by Colonel Hüseyin Avni.[20] Münîf, "a member of the Special Commission on Deportations" who was there to "superintend the matter," served notice of a general deportation from Adana, Tarsus, and Mersin. Two hundred fifty families received an order to leave Adana. The same number was ordered to leave Mersin and Tarsus, where accusations of spying and insurrection were again being bandied about.[21]

Around the same time, the Austro-Hungarian vice-consul in Adana, Richard Stöckel, informed his superior in Aleppo that Muslim *muhacirs* continued to arrive in order to settle in localities "abandoned" by the Armenians.[22] The "non-residents," who had initially been spared, were deported for good in mid-August; on 2 and 3 September 1915, they were followed by the bulk of the Armenian population of Adana, Catholics and Protestants included. Eight convoys, comprising some 5,000 families, were thus put on the road under the direction of Münîf and the police chief, Adıl Bey, between early September and late October. However, Around 1,000 craftsmen and their families, as well as the families of skilled personnel working for the army or the government, were exempted from the deportation, together with some 40 people who had agreed to convert.[23] According to the missionary William Chambers, the Armenians of Adana were authorized to sell their moveable assets before leaving, but their real estate was confiscated before they set out.[24] A foreign resident estimated that 20,000 Armenians were deported from Adana in the last days of August 1915, during which it seemed as if the city were the site of a massive clearance sale.[25] Another witness noted that the authorities seized the Adana Armenians' bank deposits and the valuables they had deposited in bank safes, and had also requisitioned, in addition to the population's real estate, the Armenian schools and churches in the city.[26]

However, unlike the deportees from other Ottoman provinces, it seems that a non-negligible proportion of the Adana Armenians was sent to the Damascus region and areas further south on Cemal Pasha's "personal application."[27] Once again, the former vali of Adana seems to have shown generosity toward those he had formerly governed. By allowing a number of them to avoid the passage through the concentration camps strung out along the Euphrates, he very plainly saved their lives. This special arrangement, the exclusive privilege of his "friends" from Adana, indicates that Cemal Pasha was very well aware of the fate in store for the deportees who were being led toward the camps in the Syrian Desert. After traveling to the camp at Osmaniye by train, the deportees from Adana discovered what was waiting for them as they continued their journey on foot toward the concentration camps of Intilli and Katma and, thereafter, the transit center at Karlık, located near the Aleppo railroad station. We shall see later the role that Karlık played during the second phase of the genocide.[28]

Among the Armenians who had the right to remain in Adana beyond the craftsmen and specialists who were indispensable to the army's needs, the parliamentary deputy from Kozan/Sis, Matteos Nalbandian, was able to save a few people by passing them off as members of his family.[29] The American mission of Adana also managed to save some of the little girls who attended the mission's school.[30]

In a report written early in 1916, the Austro-Hungarian vice-consul in Adana, R. Stöckel, drew up a list of 205 Armenian businesses in Adana and Mersin that went out of operation as a result of the deportations, many of them having worked together with German and Austro-Hungarian firms. Their shutdown caused these European companies considerable losses. Stöckel also observed that the Mersin branch of the Deutsche Orientbank suffered heavy losses because the government committees had confiscated the Armenian assets that had served as collateral for their loans in order to transfer them to *muhacirs* from Macedonia.[31]

The Adana Region, a Place of Transit for the Deportees

The procession of the hundreds of thousands of deportees from the provinces of western Anatolia who passed through the vilayet of Adana was headed by the Armenian elites of Istanbul. They found themselves in transit through the regional metropolis in June 1915 – that is, well before the local population itself was deported.

One of the most reliable witnesses, the chief secretary of Adana's archbishopric, Kerovpe Papazian, reports, for example, the circumstances under which Nazaret Daghavarian, Rupen Zartarian, Karekin Kazhag, Aknuni, Harutiun Jangiulian, Sarkis Minasian and five of their companions, all of whom had been expelled from Ayaş on 2 June, were held for a few days in the *konak*.[32] Papazian relates how, having gone to see the vali to settle certain administrative questions, he was hailed by Daghavarian, an old acquaintance of his, who asked that the catholicos, Sahag I, intercede with the vali to secure permission for him and his companions to go pray in the cathedral. İsmail Hakkı readily agreed to grant them an exceptional three hours' leave. The political deportees were immediately escorted to the archbishopric in "two closed cars."[33] In fact, it seems that Daghavarian's real objective had been above all to meet with the catholicos. The chief secretary, who was present at the conversation that these men held with the prelate after briefly praying, notes in his memoirs that the parliamentary deputy from Sıvas seemed to him to be the most serene and courageous person in the group, although he was well aware of the fate that awaited all of them. According to Papazian, the ranking Dashnak Rupen Zartarian and Sarkis Minasian were in contrast very agitated, and said nothing throughout the audience.[34] One can readily imagine that the dejection of these dyed-in-the-wool party activists showed was not unrelated to the bitterness they felt over the policy of their former allies, the Young Turks, whose ideological motivations they understood better than anyone else, and also to the feeling that they had been tricked.

The Adana stopover of the parliamentary deputies Krikor Zohrab and Vartkes Seringiulian, who arrived shortly thereafter, makes it possible to gather some idea of the psychological state of the two main Armenian leaders. Interned in a room of the local barracks, where their meals were served to them, they had access to the press and were visited by the secretary of the archbishopric. Zohrab seemed demoralized to Papazian, more worried about his family's fate than his own; Vartkes, fatalistic and courageous, seemed worthy of his reputation, and little concerned by the prospect of imminent death.[35]

Others among the deportees from Istanbul, however, had better luck because they were less closely guarded: they managed to slip away to one place or another with the help of Armenian railroad employees or local businessmen working for the army. For instance, the writer and publicist Yervant Odian and the journalists Levon Mozian, Aram Andonian, and Sebuh Aguni benefited from the assistance of a physician, Dr. Boghosian, who had been temporarily assigned to the transit camp in Tarsus. Thanks to Boghosian, these four intellectuals found refuge, late in September 1915, with the Shalvarjian brothers, who owned a large flourmill that provided the 25,000 troops stationed in the region with flour. For this reason, the Shalvarjians had permission to send and receive money by wire. They allowed the deportees to take advantage of this possibility, cashing on their behalf the sums sent to them by relatives in the capital or elsewhere. Thus, they participated in a vast assistance network that most certainly helped prolong or save the lives of many Armenians in transit in the region. These Armenians lived in a camp containing 6,000 tents belonging to deportees from Bardizag, Ismit, Adabazar, Bursa, Edirne, Rodosto, Bandırma, and so on, surviving by working as amateur barbers, grocers, or by selling liquor (*rakı*). This camp lay near the Gülek railroad station, one hour from Tarsus. Dr. Boghosian gave unreservedly of his time and energy, treating many patients, especially victims of epidemics, as best he could. According to Odian, people in the camp were dying at the rate of around 70 every day, with their bodies being buried in the surrounding fields.[36] H. E. Wallis, who witnessed the events, puts the number of those living in the camp, out in the open, at 10,000 to 15,000; no one else had the right to approach it, much less provide the Armenians with material assistance. The foreign witnesses seem to have been the most profoundly shocked by the sight of the deportees crammed into the sheep-cars parked in the train station, who, forbidden to leave the cars, begged passerby for a little water.[37] Odian, who spent several weeks among them before he was saved, notes that every day, day and night, around 1,000 people were led off toward Osmaniye by the agents of the *Sevkiyat* (Deportation), whose local chief was someone named Hutsi Bey. With the October rains, the camp became a scene of death in which the deportees had to wade through the mud.[38] Elizabeth Webb observes that the camp, like certain others, was also regularly attacked, and that villagers from neighboring localities carried off young women and girls.[39]

One of the few men allowed to remain in Tarsus was a typographer who put out the Ottoman Agency's daily bulletin: he was apparently the only person in town who knew the ins and outs of the modern printer's trade. There were also a few deportees who had been saved thanks to two Greek businessmen, Simeon Oğlu and Tripani, who passed them off as Greek employees of their firms.[40] Late in October, the camp at the Gülek train station was closed for good. The handful of deportees who had managed to find hideouts in the city was flushed out by systematic police manhunts.[41] Among those captured were the four intellectuals mentioned above. The last arrival, Aram Andonian, had managed to find lodgings with a Greek from Tarsus after a short stay at the train station and later joined Sebuh Aguni and Levon Mozian, who had somehow managed to rent a room.[42] They had already been reunited with Yervant Odian, who had found refuge in the industrial flour mill belonging to the Shalvarjian brothers, Aram and Ardashes. Located half an hour from the city, it turned out 50 to 60 tons of meal daily to meet the army's needs.[43]

Adana's American mission also gave a few deportees temporary shelter, and provided others with material assistance. Elizabeth Webb mentions, among the people with whom she had contact in this period, a young woman from Ismit named Osanna and her four children, who had come to Adana on foot (two of her children died on the way) and found work as a domestic with an Iranian family living in the city; or, to cite another example, a 13-year-old girl from Tekirdağ whom an Arab from Ras ul-Ayn had sold "for about $2.00" to a Turk from Adana who had tried to force her to "marry" him until the child managed to find refuge in the mission; or the adventures of two sisters, Mariam and Khatun, from a village near Sıvas, who had reached Adana in such a state that it had taken them several weeks for them to "regain physical and mental equilibrium"; or, finally, Mariam from Mush, kidnapped and "married" by a Kurd who had been unable to prevent her from fleeing with the child she had had by him, who had died during their flight.[44] American sources also describe the fate of the schoolboys at Talas's American school, who had been transferred to a Turkish school in Adana.[45] The school administration had made a "great effort" to convert them, and then decided to murder the oldest, who resisted Turkification, while sending the youngest to other institutions after giving them Turkish names. The orphanage for Armenian children, which Ahmed Cemal had created in 1909 while still the vali of Adana, had been converted into a "Turkish orphanage" in turn after its director was hanged for being in "possession of two pernicious Armenian books."[46]

The 19 March 1916 appointment of Cevdet Bey, the former vali of Van, to head the vilayet of Adana marked the end of these exceptions. It was the prelude to the creation of the apparatus required to enact the second phase of the genocide.

The Deportations in the Sancaks of Mersin and İçil

Mersin, which served the capital of Cilicia, Adana, as a port of transit, developed late in the day, but rapidly. In 1914, 2,300 Armenians lived there; another thousand Armenians lived in villages nearby. Syrien and Çerkez immigrants as well as Greeks from Cyprus also lived in the city. Halfway between Mersin and Adana, Tarsus, known as Darson in Armenian, had in 1914 an Armenian population of only a little over 3,000. This was a direct result of the 1909 massacres, which had also claimed many victims at Kozoluk (Armenian population 290), a village near Tarsus.[47] A total of 6,987 Armenians living in the sancak of Mersin were affected by the deportation measures decided on in Istanbul. While the vali of Adana showed a degree of moderation that benefited the local Armenian population, the same did not hold for Mersin, where the mutesarif, Tevfik Bey, the president of the Unionist club, Dr. Hayri, the police chief, Mehmed Bey, the commander of the gendarmerie, Çalip Bey (a brother of the Young Turk leader Küçük Cemal), and a few notables such as Ğalib Effendi, Hoca Ahmed, Kalaycı Abdüllah, and Hamdi Effendi worked untiringly to liquidate the port city's rich Armenian community, not without ulterior motives of a financial nature.[48]

In late April, six "suspects" fell victim to a first wave of arrests. They were sent off to Adana, where they were imprisoned in the former French lycée together with 30 men from the city.[49] The American consul Edward Nathan also notes the deportation of a few dozen families from Mersin and Tarsus around 18 May 1915.[50] In August and September 1915, 600 families were gradually deported from Mersin, with the result that only around 30 craftsmen and their families were still living there by the fall, including the only Armenian in the town to have converted, Khoren Sarafian.[51] A second wave of deportations, organized in February 1916 after the British had shelled Mersin, put a definite end to the Armenian presence in the city.[52]

Apart from a few dozen notables who were deported around 18 May, the Armenians of Tarsus were put on the road at the same time as those of Adana, with the further exception of a handful of craftsmen and employees working in state enterprises, as well as their families. The Shalvarjian brothers, who were millers, were also spared; all of them boasted of the great generosity that they showed both the intellectuals mentioned earlier and the deportees in the camp at the Gülek train station, through which all the convoys traveling by rail to Osmaniye had to pass.[53]

In September 1915, the American consul was still hoping to save the last Armenians threatened with deportation, the "pupils" of the Institute of St. Paul of Tarsus, whom the local authorities were seeking to lay hands on and deport using all the means at their disposal.[54] The *kaymakam*, İbrahim Edhem Bey, who had taken office in November 1911, had probably been deemed too soft, for he was replaced on 4 November 1915 by the former *kaymakam* of Adabazar, Necati Sezayi Bey, a man who had proved that he possessed the qualities required that the post called for. Seyazi was able to count on the collaboration of Ahmed Emin Bey; Kurkli Hoca Effendi; Sadık Pasha, a parliamentary deputy from Tarsus; Hamdi Bey, the police chief; Ahmed Şükrü and İbrahim Çavuş, policemen; and Hakkı Bey, a member of the city council. These men were also the chief beneficiaries of the despoliation of the Armenians.[55]

The Armenian presence in the neighboring *sancak* of Içil was limited to two colonies – Selefke (371 Armenians), the ancient city of Seleucia, and Mala (pop. 95). These Armenians were expelled in September under the supervision of Ata Bey, who had been appointed to replace Rauf Bey on 17 September 1915.

The Deportations in the Sancak of Sis/Kozan

Sis, located in the very heart of Cilicia, was in 1914 the seat of the *sancak* of Kozan. The ancient capital of the Armenian kingdom of Cilicia and the official residence of the catholicos, it formed a monumental architectural ensemble. Overlooking the town at the dawn of the twentieth century was the royal citadel, surrounded by a colossal wall with 44 towers. In 1914, Sis was still almost three-quarters Armenian, with an Armenian population of 5,600 out of a total population of nearly 8,000, and it still clearly preserved its medieval character. In the rest of the *kaza* of Sis were a dozen Armenian villages, of which the most important were Karacalın and Gedik. In the ancient capital of the Rupinian dynasty, Anavarza, which lay 30 kilometers further to the south, one could still see traces of the extraordinary fortress built on the rocky outcrop towering over the plain, which was covered with Greco-Roman ruins.[56]

The *kaza* of Feke, located in the northern part of the *sancak* of Kozan in the foothills of the Antitaurus mountain chain, had in 1914 around 5,000 Armenian inhabitants, 1,150of whom lived in the principal town of the *kaza*, Vahka/Feke. Three hours to the south, on the banks of the Saros River, the village of Yerebakan had a Turkish-speaking Armenian population of 735. Halfway between Feke and Yerebakan, Kaladere was home to 300 Turkish-speaking Armenians. Ten hours to the north, in the forests of the Antitaurus, three Armenian villages still existed in 1914: Karaköy, Dikmen, and Sazak (pop. 349). Finally, four hours southeast of Feke laid the village of Tapan (267 Turkish-speaking Armenians).[57]

Still further north in the valley of the Şatak Su laid Hacın, the seat of the *kaza* of the same name. It was located in a site in the form of an amphitheater on a rock spur that lay at the intersection of two valleys. A mountain fastness par excellence, particularly well suited to self-defense, Hacın lay on one of the three routes between Cilicia and Cappadocia. The 1914 Ottoman census put the total number of Armenians in the *kaza* at 13,550, but the diocesan statistics, which are corroborated by missionary sources, indicate that the town of Hacın alone had an Armenian population of 26,480.[58] Four hours north of Hacın, Rumlu (comprising three villages: Köroğlu, Seki and Kuşkaya), lost in the forests of the Antitaurus, had an Armenian population of 250. On the northern boundary of the *kaza*, Şar, the antique Comana, had an all-Armenian population until 1915 (pop. 1,120).

In other words, Sis and Hacın, which had put up successful resistance to the 1909 massacres, were the two Armenian towns in the region on which the authorities concentrated their attention after extirpating the Armenians of Zeitun and Marash. The first incident to occur in this eagle's nest came in January 1915: a leaflet written in Turkish with Armenian characters – the Armenians here were Turkish-speaking – was plastered to a wall in the courtyard of the Cathedral of St. George, calling on Hacın's Armenians to "remain vigilant" and "focus their efforts on self-defense." The primate, Bishop Bedros Sarajian, tried to hush up the affair, but the authorities soon got wind of it.[59] The primate was summoned to the *konak*, where the *kaymakam*, Kemal Bey (who held his post from 15 February 1914 to 13 April 1915), gave him two days to find out who the authors of the text were and turn them in. The investigations carried out by the local Hnchak chiefs, under Garabed Kizirian's lead, had soon revealed that the provocative document had been produced on the police chief's initiative and that a child by the name of Aram Boyajian had been entrusted with the task of pasting it up at the church. Handed over to the authorities, the adolescent is nevertheless supposed to have told the police chief – that is, the person who had ordered him to post the incriminated leaflet up at the church – that the "Hnchaks" had given it to him. It does not much matter how this "revelation" was obtained; it provided the local Young Turks a pretext to arrest 35 ranking Hnchaks. Twenty-four of them were released, but 11 were brought before the court-martial in Adana on a charge of "rebellion." Four of these 11 were condemned to death and hanged; the others received a sentence of "life in exile."[60]

According to different witnesses to these events, the Hacın authorities adopted a method *sui generis* that consisted in deporting the Armenian population in small groups, staggering their departures so as to reduce the risks of a "general rebellion." The fact that the task of supervising operations in the region was entrusted to Colonel Hüseyin Avni, the commander of the vilayet's gendarmerie and presiding judge of the Adana court-martial (whom we have already observed in action in Dörtyol, in the Cebelbereket region, from 7 to 12 March),[61] suggests that direct orders about this matter had come down from the capital. The Bosnian colonel had come to Hacın on 14 May, accompanied by a judge on the Aleppo court-martial, Alay Bey, and left several brigades of soldiers there at five o'clock. According to Edith Cold, an American missionary in Hacın, Avni and Alay immediately held a series of meetings with the police chiefs and local notables. They then summoned Sarajian and gave him from 18 to 20 May to deliver up deserters and the weapons held by the population. At a long meeting, these notables decided to yield to the authorities' demands so as not to provide a pretext for accusations of rebellion and, above all, to ward off the threat of an intervention by the 3,000 to 4,000 men than returning from Zeitun.[62] Urged by their elders to comply with the authorities' orders, the handful of deserters in town turned themselves in on 23 May, while those who had rifles gave them up (a total of 70 weapons were delivered up to the authorities). The same day, the cavalry and infantry squadrons that had come from Zeitun invested Hacın and requisitioned the Armenian school for boys, the orphanage-monastery, and an American institution, which they converted into barracks.[63] The missionaries' protests against the army's confiscation of one of their properties were in vain. Their interlocutor, Sâmi Bey, the commanding officer of the cavalry unit, was, to be sure, "very courteous," but not at all disposed to give these complaints a hearing.[64]

Once these preliminary operations were completed, the arrests of the local elites began on 27 May. Two hundred notables were interned in the Monastery of St. James and 50 more were jailed in the *konak*, where they were systematically tortured.[65] The following day, the American missionaries requested a meeting with the military men responsible for these opera-tions, Hüseyin Avni and Ğalib Bey, in order to "obtain" explanations of these arrests from them.[66] This intervention was fruitless, and did not prevent the authorities from issuing a general deportation order on 3 June. The first convoy comprised only 30 of the most impor-tant Apostolic and Protestant Armenian families, among whom were people employed by the American mission. On 10 June, a mere 150 families were put on the road. But the departures of convoys proceeded steadily throughout the summer, under the orders of the new *kaymakam*, Kemal Bey, who had been appointed to his post on 13 April 1915. By early October, only a few craftsmen and their families were left in Hacın, along with 250 widows and soldiers' wives.[67] All the deportees were dispatched on foot toward Osmaniye and Aleppo, by the Kiraz mountain road rather than the road to Sis, which was practicable by wagon. The obvious intention was to make it impossible for them to use means of transportation.[68] Edith Cold reports that the American missionaries refused to let the Armenians deposit valuables at the mission because they had no instructions on this subject.[69] She further observes that the mufti of Hacın had refused to give his approval to the deportations and even took the assets of one of his Armenian friends in hand to prevent them from being plundered.[70] The case of two men mentioned by Cold reveals a great deal about the effects that the deportation order had on people who were serving their country. The first, Bedros Terzian, a graduate of the Constantinople law school who had fought in the imperial cavalry in winter and spring 1915, returned to Hacın on leave in May and was deported with the first convoy on 3 June. The second, Bedros Boyajian, a government official in Hacın, had been on mission in a village when he learned that his wife had been ordered to leave and reached the city a few hours after the convoy she was in had set out.[71] In the other Armenian localities in the region, especially Şar and Rumlu, the deporta-tions took place shortly after the beginning of operations in Hacın.[72] The convoys all took the same route to their final destinations of Ras ul-Ayn, Rakka, Meskene, or Der Zor.[73] According to Sebuh Aguni, 5,000 of the more than 28,000 Armenians of the *kaza* of Hacın survived the deportations.[74] The 5,000 Armenians of the *kaza* of Feke were deported relatively late, and were even able to benefit from the assistance of Hacın's American mission.[75] According to Cold, the Muslims of Feke and Yerebakan exhibited their hostility to the deportations, with the Turks of Feke behaving in "honourable" fashion.[76]

After overseeing the task of disarming and deporting the Armenians of Hacın, Colonel Hüseyin Avni attacked the Armenians of Sis and the *kaza* of Kozan. On 2 May 1915, the *mutesarif*, Safvat Bey (who had assumed office on 2 December 1914), was dismissed, prob-ably because he was judged unreliable, and replaced the same day by Salih Bey. In Sis, the Bosnian colonel also secured the support of local state officials and notables, particularly that of Hüseyin Bey, the head of the municipality; Ali Bey, its secretary general; Halilağazâde Haci; Kâmil Effendi; Halil Effendi; Yegenzâde Mehmed; Yegenzâde Ahmed; Hayta Çavuş; Yarumzâde Ahmed; and *çetes*[77] recruited in the area on Avni's initiative.

The official order to deport the Armenians of Sis, confirmed by the interior minister in person, did not reach the prefecture until 17 June 1915. As in Hacın, the inhabitants of the city and the surrounding villages were gradually expelled in the direction of Osmaniye and Aleppo. From these towns they were dispersed over the different deportation routes.[78]

The somewhat more than 5,500 Armenians of the *kaza* of Karsbazar lived in six localities: Kars/Kadirli (1,800 Armenians), Hamidiye, Çokak (pop. 650), Akdam (pop. 420), and the com-munities of Boğazdelik and Kuyumjian. They were deported in the course of June 1915.[79]

The Deportations in the Sancak *of Cebelbereket*

We have already seen that 20,000 Armenians from the coastal *kazas* of Payas, Yümürtalık, and Hasa were dispatched southward in late April 1915, in the wake of the "events" that occurred in Dörtyol. There were some 20,000 more Armenians in the Amanus region, comprising the *kazas* of Yarpuz, Islahiye, Bahçe, and Osmaniye. They were, however, deported somewhat later. These Armenians were above all concentrated in the northern part of the *sancak*, in the northern part of the *kaza* of Yarpuz, around Hasanbeyli, and in the Bahçe district located in its northern extremity. There were a great many fewer of them in the eastern *kaza* of Islahiye and the western *kaza* of Osmaniye.[80] Many were working, as we have seen, on construction of the series of tunnels being dug through the mountainous Amanus region, yet even they were not spared. On 7 and 8 July 1915, all of those employed on the tunnel construction sites from Hasanbeyli, Intilli, and Bahçe were deported with their families and their houses were immediately turned over to Muslim *muhacirs*.[81] A report drawn up by three ranking Armenian employees of the Bagdadbahn provides a rather complete inventory of the exactions that the officers and *çetes* of the Special Organization perpetrated against the Armenian populations of the region.[82] The Armenians underscore in particular the role played by a captain in the gendarmerie who had been sent from Adana, a certain Rahmi Bey, but also that of local officials: Vehib Rumi Bey, the *kaymakam* of Bahçe; Nusret Bey, the *kaymakam* of Islahiye; Fetih Bey, the *kaymakam* of Osmaniye; Ali Mumtaz, the director of the Department of State Property in Bahçe; and Mustafa Effendi, a tax collector in Bahçe.[83]

Hasanbeyli seems to have been the first locality affected by the deportations. Our witnesses note that some 60 men were arrested and tortured there, after which eight of them were brought before the court-martial in Adana.[84] They further observe that Colonel Hüseyin Avni came to oversee the July operations in person, probably after accomplishing his mission in Hacın and Sis.[85] We have no documents proving that the presiding judge at the Adana court-martial was the head of the Special Organization for the entire vilayet of Adana. It should be pointed out, however, that this judge was present during the deportations and personally oversaw them in all the districts of the region. It was doubtless in the Amanus district that his obscure role appeared the most clearly, for it was there that he had the leaders of the squadrons of *çetes* under his command.

We have a list of these *çete* leaders, district by district. In Hasanbeyli: Haci Ömeroğlu Osman; the brothers Akca and Hasan Bey; Hanefioğlu Nuri; Kayipoğlu Halil; Mustafa Effendi; Cani Bekir; Abdurrahman Effendi; Abdıcioğlu Mustafa; Hasanoğlu Nuri; Alikehyaoğlu Kara Mehmed; Kol Hoca.

In Bahçe: Mehmed Effendi; Kadi Effendi, a judge; Haci Ali; Berber Ali; Mustafa Effendi, a tax collector; Ömer Effendi; Said Effendi, a member of the *Emvali Metruke*; Farsah Ali; Hüseyin Effendi, a "procureur" in the Tobacco Régie; Kel Hüseyin, a Régie official; Haci Rıza; Yaşar Bey, the commander of the gendarmerie in Bahçe; Tekenoğlu Mustafa Çavuş; Musa Onbaşi; Kara Itli Mehmed Ali; Çil Ahmedoğlu Kara Mehmed; Halil Onbaşi; Abuş Effendi; Haci Effendi; Ali Çavuş; Kara Osman; Ökleş Ahmedoğlu Hasan; Haci Ömer and Mehmed Ali; Çakoloğlu Haci Mehmed; Arnavud Haci Yusuf; Tahsildar Burdu; Tahsildar Haci; Kurt Ökleş; Nasir Effendi; Colak Ali; Alioğlu Şükrü; Çavuş Hüseyinoğlu Mehmed; Molla Hasanoğlu Abdüllah; Süleyman Effendi, an official in the census bureau; Küçük Haci Ahmed and his son; Ali Calali; Bikir; Ağil Ali; Fattuhzâde Ali.

In Islahiye: Mustafa Ağa; Hurşid Ağa; Süleyman Ağa; Balanoğlu Mehmed Ağa; Balanınoğlu; Çerçi Oğlu; Amirşınoğlu Mustafa; Eşbaşzâde Mehmed; Hasan; Alişoğlu Mehmed; Sarı Kadı; Ahmed Effendi; Murad Ağa; Şeyh Ağa; Kesacık Ibo; Hasan Ağa; Mehmed Effendi, a judge on the court in Islahiye; Şih Ca. In the rural zones: Haydar Kehya;

Akçe Kehya from Kişniz; İsmail Ağa from Kaltan; Salman Çavuş from Folan; Milla Haliloğlu from Arıklı Kaşlı; Ömer Effendi; Miktat Ağa.

In Osmaniye: Fetih Bey, the *kaymakam*; Haci Hüseyin; Fettuhoğlu Ahmed; Haci Kehyaoğlu Haci Kehya from Adana; Çalıkoğlu Haci Ahmed; Çalikoğlu Süleyman; Mubaşir Kadiroğlu Tahak; Mubaşir Kadiroğlu Ağa; Polis Ömer; Semerci Kör Ahmed Çavuş; Mehmed Effendi; Kürd Hüseyin; Hamisli Deli Mehmedoğlu Deli Mehmed; Mulazim Haci Ali Ağa from Adana; Mubaşir Kadir Ağa from Adana; Ahmed Çalikoğlu; Arabacı Haci Oksen Effendi; Arapoğlu Mehmed Ali; Topal Haci Ahmed; Topal Haci Küçük Onbaşi; Haliloğlu Torun, an officer in the gendarmerie; Kızıl Ağa, a member of the deportation committee in his city; Mehmed Effendi from Yozgat; It Berber Küçükoğlu; Dolamoğlu Haci Effendi; Kürd Haci Ali Ağa; Ibisinoğlu Musa; Çunakı Kara Hasan; Haci Ökleş; Divilim Hocaoğlu Hoca Effendi; Kara Yağitoğlu Mehmed; Ince Arap; Şaban Çavuş; Topal Haci Mahmudoğlu Dide; and Ahmed Effendi.[86]

After the Mudros armistice, none of the criminals who had been active in Cilicia or Syria was brought to trial. The investigation opened there on 21 September 1915 on orders from the interior minister supposedly did not bring to light a single abuse warranting court proceedings.[87] Asım Bey,[88] who was named to conduct the investigations of the fourth investigative committee and charged with inspecting the provinces of Adana, Aleppo, and Damascus, was a Laz from Şoppa said to be close to the CUP leadership. It is perhaps for this reason that his mission more closely resembled a local inspection of the demographic effects of the deportations than a judicial investigation of possible crimes. Thus, Asım explained to Talât that he had first gathered information about the number of Armenians deported and "whether there was anyone who had complaints on this score." He observed that the sum of the number of deportees from the vilayet of Adana recorded in the official registers (47,258) and that of the remaining Armenians (18,000) did not match the figures in the "registers of 1915." In other words, the censuses had obviously underestimated the number of Armenians in the vilayet, unless the disparity was to be attributed, he wrote, humorlessly, to "an extraordinarily high birthrate since 1915 and the postponement of the deportation of certain individuals." According to the local authorities, the latter hypothesis was the more plausible of the two. It was to be explained, Asım wrote, by the

> multiple, frequent orders issued by your Ministry, the Ministry of War, the General Directorate for Military Equipment, and the Imperial Command of the Fourth Army, to the effect that the families of soldiers and the relatives of Armenians overseeing the construction and operation of the Baghdad railway be maintained where they were, along with family members of the owners of factories working for the military authorities, people involved in providing the army with food and supplies, people commissioned by the railroad company to cut and transport timber, as well as the families of parliamentary deputies.[89]

This listing of the categories of people provisionally exempted from the deportation is corroborated by survivors' accounts, confirming that the population of the vilayet of Adana was treated with relative clemency in comparison to those of other regions. It also shows how preoccupied the capital was by the demographic transformations brought about at the local level once the deportation plan had been carried out.

The same report notes the existence of "the families of three hundred soldiers, one thousand five hundred Catholic and Protestant exiles, Armenian workers in the factories producing goods for the military authorities, as well as the indispensable craftsmen in the *kaza* of Tarsus"; of "six households, comprising the families of five soldiers and that of an artisan" in the *kaza* of Cihan; of "a few craftsmen and woodcutters and their families, as well as four hundred employees working on the Intilli construction site on special orders" in the *kaza* of Islahiye; of 725 "people in the usual categories" in Kozan/Sis; of 38 in Karsbazar; of 863 in Hacın, including the families of soldiers, craftsmen, and converts; and of 228 in Feke, to which it is necessary to add people in other classes, comprising a total of 868 Armenians, "plus one living" in Dörtyol.[90] If the estimation of the number of Armenians allowed to remain here and there in the vilayet is most certainly too low, it nevertheless indicates, once again, the authorities' desire to limit these exceptions to people indispensable to the army. Thus, for the city of Sis (in the *kaza* of Kozan) alone, the extremely precise Armenian sources produced by the Catholicosate mention 4,000 deportees as opposed to 2,530 left in place[91] – that is, almost four times more than the figures given for the entire *kaza* by the judicial inspector Asım. The fact that an administration attached to the Catholicosate was maintained in Sis does not by itself suffice to explain both the singular generosity from which the inhabitants of the former Armenian capital benefited or the considerable disparity between the Ottoman government's figures and the Catholicosate's. The most likely explanation would appear to be that certain officials in the almost exclusively Armenian city of Sis forwarded underestimations to the government in Adana – in other words, that it proved possible to bribe these officials into distorting the real figures. While general conclusions can hardly be drawn from this one documented case, it seems more than probable that the fact that part of the Armenian population of Cilicia was allowed to stay home, and that another part of it was deported to the least deadly zones, resulted from buying off local government officials on a broad scale.

Chapter 22

Deportations in the *Sancaks* of Ayntab and Antakya

Armenians had been living in this region wedged between the Taurus and Amanus mountain chains since the tenth century, their arrival here coinciding with the creation of military *themata* occupied by Armenian soldier-colonists. In 1914, 44,414 Armenians lived in the *sancak* of Ayntab, which was administratively subordinate to the vilayet of Aleppo. More than 36,000 of them lived in the *kaza* of Ayntab alone, while another 8,000 were to be found in the *sancak* of Kilis.[1]

Thirty-six thousand of Ayntab's 80,000 inhabitants were Armenians from diverse religious backgrounds of whom 4,000 were Protestants. The community maintained several churches and 25 schools with a total enrolment of 5,000. Another several hundred young men and women attended Central Turkey College, which had been founded in 1876 by American missionaries and included a medical school as well as a hospital. The Armenian population of Ayntab, which had been Turkish-speaking since the mid-eighteenth century, had partially recovered its mother tongue thanks to the intense development of education encouraged by the Constantinople Patriarchate down to 1915; this held for the youngest in particular. The Armenians of Ayntab, an especially active population, were employed above all in trade and the crafts and held a key position in the economic life of the city.

The second *kaza* in the *sancak*, Kilis, boasted 8,000 Armenians. Almost all of them were concentrated in the seat of the *sancak*, also called Kilis, which lay on the road to Aleppo. In the early twentieth century, Kilis was a thriving town, famed for its production of tinned copper tools, textiles, and rugs.[2]

A well-informed Armenian witness reports that on the eve of the war a *Türk Yurdu* club was created in Ayntab by the parliamentary deputy Ali Cenani. Its main task was to orchestrate harassment of the Armenian institutions, promote the confiscation of farms on various pretexts, and generally promote Turkism.[3] The same source says that at the beginning of the war the local Young Turk club launched, a furious campaign against French and British organizations, and then conducted an anti-Armenian propaganda tour in the villages at the beginning of the spring. The Ittihadists also recommended that Turkish debtors not settle their debts to Armenians and cease cultivating land belonging to them, for, "before long, there will not be a single Armenian in Ayntab." It appears that the city's mosques produced the same sort of discourse.[4]

Like the rest of the vilayet of Aleppo, the *sancak* of Ayntab was not one of the areas originally included in the deportation plan. Ayntab's Armenian inhabitants, like Aleppo's, were to have been left in their homes. While various factors, especially the presence of large numbers of foreign witness and a sharp debate within the institutions of the CUP itself, can explain such a decision in the case of cities such as Istanbul, Smyrna, or Aleppo, it is hard to find reasons for this choice in the case of the Ayntab and Kilis Armenians. These two groups were, to be sure, isolated in a Turkish-Arab environment, but they nevertheless represented a non-negligible concentration of Armenians. The administrative autonomy that the neighboring *sancak* of Marash was granted in early spring 1915 would seem to indicate that the CUP had from the outset planned to spare the Armenians of the vilayet of Aleppo, forcing the most hard-bitten Unionist circles to resort to various artifices in order to include the zones that had been exempted in their program. According to our principal Armenian witness, the leaders of Ayntab's Ittihadist club, backed by the parliamentary deputy Ali Cenani and the former *kaymakam* of Kilis, Fadıl Bey, repeatedly appealed to the capital to obtain the deportation of the Armenians of these regions. However, the *mutesarif*, Şükrü Bey, and above all the military commander, Hilmi Bey, are said to have put up stiff opposition to such schemes.[5] These Unionists, who seem to have been lacking in experience in organizing provocations, are supposed to have been urged by their colleagues in Marash to send telegrams to Istanbul announcing that Armenians were making preparations to "attack mosques, kill Turks, rape women, and plunder and burn down Turkish homes." The affair, however, reached the ears of the higher-ups, including the military commander Hilmi, who requested that the head of the Fourth Army, Cemal Pasha, sanction such provocations. Cemal sent Fahri Pasha to the area to look into the matter – that is, to establish whether the accusations leveled against the Armenians were true. Police searches of the Armenian neighborhoods failed to provide confirmation of them.[6] Armenian sources also indicate that a ranking member of the *Teşkilât-ı Mahsusa*, Çetebaşi Ali Bey, arrived in Ayntab in late April with a squadron of *çetes*, who committed the first murders outside the city. Partial police searches were conducted on 1 May 1915, and some ten men were arrested and brought before the court-martial in Aleppo. The head of the local branch of the *Banque Ottomane*, Dikran Kherlakian, had no choice but to flee the city after receiving threats from Ali Bey.[7] Around the same time, on 3 May 1915, the Ayntab Armenians saw a first convoy of 300 deportees comprising only women and children from Zeitun pass by the city. In the next weeks, it was followed by caravans made up of several hundred deportees each, from Zeitun, Marash, Elbistan, Gürün, Sıvas, and Furnuz.[8] The first systematic arrests and police searches came on 12 May: around 200 people were arrested in the space of three days,[9] although the vali of Aleppo, Celal Bey, succeed in obtaining the release of most of those apprehended.[10] Two Americans from Ayntab furnish a few details about the caravans of deportees who arrived from the north and passed through the city, though it had been hard to approach them or provide them with relief. Miss Fearson notes that the Armenians managed to create a relief committee for the deportees, while Elvesta Lelie points out that J. Merril and Dr. Hamilton made great efforts, along with the American hospital's nurses, to aid the exiles, many of whom, children included, were suffering from serious knife wounds.[11] The deportees were stationed 15 minutes from the city in a place known as Kavaklık, near a copious spring that they could approach only if they paid the gendarmes guarding them "a quarter of a *mecidiye* per glass." At night they were attacked and pillaged, according to an Armenian witness, while young women were raped or abducted to fill the city's harems with the active complicity of gendarmes and government officials.[12]

The sight of these convoys regularly punctuated life in the city of Ayntab until late July – that is, until the CUP's responsible secretary in Aleppo, Cemal Bey, arrived in the city. This Ittihadist cadre had apparently come with the mission of convincing the notables to request that Istanbul issue a deportation order. A meeting called on 29 July by the local Young Turks confirmed the reception of a deportation order emanating from Istanbul. At the meeting, a list of the first Armenians to be sent off was drawn up.[13] The German consul in Aleppo confirmed this information, informing his superiors the next day that the order to deport the Armenians from the coastal zones of the vilayet of Aleppo, Ayntab, and Kilis "had just been issued."[14] The American representative passed this news along to his ambassador a few days later, adding that the order also applied to Antakya, Alexandretta, and Kesab.[15]

Manifestly, the *mutesarif* and military commander resigned so as not to have to carry out[16] the deportation order that was posted up and announced by the town crier the morning of 30 July.[17] The first convoy, made up primarily of notables and the members of the deportee relief committee,[18] left the same day by the city's western exit. A member of the city council, Nazaret Manushagian, was attacked and murdered there by the men of the Special Organization. The second convoy was methodically pillaged by *çetes* less than a day's march from Ayntab.[19] Every day, from 100 to 300 families were put on the road; at the same time, the city's Armenian neighborhoods were transformed into huge bazaars. As elsewhere, assets were sold off at laughable prices. These who tried to deposit valuables with the American mission were intercepted in the street and relieved of their property. The authorities requisitioned all non-Turkish schools and all churches; they confiscated the stocks of the stores; they rented the most beautiful houses "at extremely low prices" and attributed the others to Turkish families. The Armenian cathedral was transformed into a warehouse for "abandoned" property and then converted into a stable after all the objects deposed there had been sold off.[20] To facilitate certain transactions, the main beneficiaries of these acts of despoliation saw to it that the director of the Ayntab branch of the Deutsche Bank, Levon Sahagian, was rapidly deported. Sahagian would later be killed at Der Zor.[21]

Apart from the first two groups, which were sent toward Damascus, all the Armenians deported from Ayntab were sent toward the Akçakoyun railroad station, where they were put in a transit camp surrounded by barbed wire while waiting to be loaded into stockcars and transported to Aleppo, and then sent on foot to the region of Zor.[22] The American consul, Jackson, notes that nine trains passed through Aleppo between 1 and 19 August. Several of them were carrying thousands of Armenians from Ayntab, who had been put on board the trains in Akçakoyun, where they were pillaged by villagers in what he described as "a gigantic plundering scheme as well as a final Blow to extinguish the race." Jackson observes that, unlike the other convoys, those that came from Ayntab included men, women, and children over ten.[23] In a communication dated 1 September, the vali of Aleppo, Bekir Sâmi, also informed the interior minister that there were several thousand deportees from Kilis in the Katma train station and thousands of families from Ayntab in the Akçakoyun station.[24]

Only after the Apostolic Armenians had been expelled did the authorities issue the order, on Sunday, 19 September, to deport the few hundred Catholics of Ayntab who had initially been spared.[25] By late September, three-quarters of the Armenian population had already been deported. It is noteworthy, however, that the Protestants were still exempt, a circumstance that did not fail to irritate Ayntab's Turkish notables.[26] Indications are that the central authorities intended to spare the Armenian Protestants temporarily in order to liquidate them more effectively when they deemed the situation more favorable. The very personality of the new interim *mutesarif*, Ahmed Bey, hand-picked by the interior minister, provides an initial indication in this regard: the new vali had been a high-ranking police official in Istanbul,[27] who, moreover, arrived in Ayntab with the parliamentary deputy Cenani, the CUP's representative in the region. Ahmed promptly organized a second wave of deportations to Der Zor, on the principle that "if one is guilty, all are guilty."[28] The first measure he took, around mid-October, was to mobilize the males between 16 and 20 who were still to be found in the vilayet and assign them to a labor battalion that was put to work on the *Bagdadbahn* construction site in Rajo.[29] He also saw to it that the homes of Protestants were subjected to police searches, which happened immediately after the 13 December 1915 arrival of Ğalib Bey, who had played a leading role in carrying out massacres in Urfa.[30] The first Protestant affected by this measure was Dr. Movses Bezjian, a respected pharmacist and former parliamentary deputy; his house was searched from top to bottom, and even the land around it was plowed up.[31] Ğalib and the *mutesarif* had, however, to confront the hostility of the new military leaders, Yusuf and Osman Bey, who were opposed to deporting the Protestants. Ğalib, who had arrived with 500 *çetes* and mountain cannons that on his orders had been positioned on the heights overlooking the city, threatened to shell the Armenian neighborhoods that were still inhabited. This argument carried the day.[32] The Protestants were ultimately deported via the Akçakoyun railroad station, in falling snow, beginning on 19 December 1915, the day after Dr. Shepard was buried.[33] According to Miss Fearson, the *mutesarif*'s son personally participated in plundering the convoys of Protestants, which departed under the missionaries' gaze, along with all the teachers and medical personnel in the mission. The American resident of Ayntab notes that the deportees paid "exorbitant sums" in order to be sent south of Damascus – that is, somewhere other than Der Zor.[34] It is obvious that by December Ayntab's Protestants had had ample time to learn what it meant to be "expedited" to Der Zor and did not hesitate to mobilize all the means at their disposal in order to be deported by way of the Homs-Hama-Damascus route instead.

As far as the seizure of Armenian assets is concerned, Armenian sources state that the authorities forbade the deportees to sell their real estate before being expelled.[35] The new director of the local branch of the Banque Ottomane, Leon Maher, seems, moreover, to have played a big role in confiscating Armenian property. After encouraging businessmen to deposit their most valuable assets, such as silver, gold, jewels, account books, and acknowledgements of debt in his bank, he created a company together with Turkish partners and purchased these assets at one-fiftieth of their real value, thus amassing a personal fortune.[36] The method used "officially" to gain control of real estate is illustrated by the case of the Kenderjian brothers, Minas and Hovsep, who had been living in Adana for years but who owned a vast farm in Ayntab. Summoned to the city, they were deported most probably after being invited to consign their property deeds to the state or a private individual. The *mutesarif*, Ahmed Bey, is supposed to have expressed his surprise over the fact "that two hundred Muslims can work, while a Christian reaps the fruits of their labors";[37] the remark was most assuredly inspired by the doctrine of the "national economy," according to which assets were to be transferred to Turkish entrepreneurs. It appears, in any case, that the notables of Ayntab wanted to make sure that they could use the Armenian deportees' property as they saw fit however the war went. Thus, the members of the Ittihadist club and the local notables took a direct hand in the liquidation of around 15,000 Armenians from Ayntab who were deported to Der Zor. They organized, for that purpose, an executive committee made up of Dabbağ Kimâzâde, Nuribeyoğlu Kadir, and Hacihalilzâde Zeki, who went to Zor to make certain that the Armenians had indeed been put to death[38] so that they would not have to worry about returning their property to them.

The deportation of the Armenians was not without consequences. To provide minimal services and meet the army's needs, the authorities decided to exempt three main classes of Armenians from the deportation.[39] The first, comprising 370 people, was made up of craftsmen employed in a factory that was responsible for furnishing the army with clothing, shoes, and ironware. In the second were 65 to 70 doctors, pharmacists, dentists, goldsmiths, tinsmiths, kettle-makers, and bakers, accompanied by their families, whom the city needed to meet its daily needs but who did not live among the Turks.[40] Only 30 to 35 households, christened "soldiers' families," were in the third category of those exempted from the deportation. Of course, in the case of Armenian draftees, the term "soldier" could only apply to workers in the *amele taburis* no older than 18, which held the number of possible exemptions to a minimum.

Thus, a total of around 2,000 people were allowed to remain in Ayntab either throughout the war or for a few months, depending on circumstances.[41] From January to July 1916, the *mutesarif* continued to deport small groups of Armenians to the south on various pretexts while sending bakers by force to Urfa and Birecik, since bakers were in very short supply in these cities after the massacres that took place there.[42] The case of the auxiliary primate Father Garabed Kizirian, an aged paraplegic who was expedited to Zor for celebrating a marriage, is symptomatic of the local authorities' attitude toward those exempted from the deportation. When the priest's daughter came to see the *mutesarif* in order to beg him to show her father mercy, he answered: "Such is the punishment that I inflict on anyone who thus tries to increase the numbers of a people whom I am doing my best to wipe out. Armenian sources indicate that the priest died while being deported and that his daughter made a Turkish officer a very happy man.[43] In fact, the authorities proved much more lax in Ayntab than in other regions in dealing with deportees from the north who passed through their city. Many women and children naturally tried to take refuge in the city or were "adopted" by Turkish families, yet were not systematically rounded up. As a rule, the authorities contented themselves with conducting occasional raids, sending those rounded up to the south. The city's Armenians nevertheless had to take a great many precautions and show extreme discretion in organizing relief for their needy compatriots.[44] Finally, it should be noted that *muhacirs* from Rumelia were not settled as systematically in Ayntab as in Zeitun and elsewhere. Nevertheless, no fewer than 500 such families were settled in the city's Armenian neighborhoods in late fall 1915.[45]

The only information we have about the fate of the worker-soldiers from Ayntab bears on two *amele taburis*, comprising, respectively, 800 young men and 900 men between the ages of 30 and 45. Both of these labor battalions were sent to an area beyond Urfa and wiped out in the latter half of June 1916.[46]

In the end, according to Armenian sources, around 12,000 Armenians from Ayntab survived the war and deportations. Survivors were especially numerous among those deported by the Homs-Hama-Damascus route.[47] The deportations organized in the *sancak* were supervised by a *Sevkiyat komisionu* (Deportation Committee) headed up by the *mutesarif* and comprised Bilal Hilmi, a judge; Haci Fazlızâde Nuri Bey, the leader of the squadrons of *çetes* (400 men); Mollaşeyhzâde Arif, the mufti of Ayntab; Şeyh Ubediyet; and Haciağazâde Ahmed. Besides Ahmed Bey, the second *mutesarif*, those chiefly responsible for the deportations and pillage were Mustafa Effendi, the president of the municipality; Besim Bey, the head of the Treasury; Bilal Hilmi Bey, a judge; Kâzım Effendi, an official in the Census Office; Eyub Sabri Bey and Haci Yusuf, secretaries in the Department of Finances; Kemal Bey, a commander of the gendarmerie; Bilazikzâde Arif; Bulbul Hoca Effendi, the former mufti; Mehmed Effendi, the Şeyh of the bazaar; Habibzâde Mustafa, an *ulema*; Batamzâde Mehmed, an *ulema*; Fahreddin Hoca, the first secretary of the court; Major Bekir Bey, the commander of the regiment of Kızılhisar; Kâsim Bey, a member of the general staff; Hakkı Bey, regimental secretary; Hamid Bey, a municipal physician; Kerim Bey, a judge; Kâsim Bey from Urfa, a magistrate; Emin Effendi, the director of the Agricultural Bank; Izrapzâde Vahid Effendi, a secretary of the *Evkaf* (religious charitable institutions); Mahmud Effendi, the municipal treasurer; Şahin Hafız Effendi, the director of the Turkish orphanage; Talıpzâde Arif, the head of the *mutesarif*'s cabinet; Fevzi Effendi; Körukci Hafizzâde Mustafa and Haci Sabitzâde Ahmed, police lieutenants; Muşluzâde Mehmed, a sergeant in the gendarmerie; Necip Effendi; Bazarbaşi Mehmed and Emin Effendi, officials in the Tax Department; Nalçaci Ali, an official in the Correspondence Office; Abdallah Agha, a court official; Haci Halil Effendi, a commander of the gendarmerie; Haci Halil Effendi Oğlu, prison warden; Ömar Şevki, a lawyer; Ahmed Effendi, an imam from the *nahie* of Kozanlı; Şeyh Mustafa Baba, an imam from the *nahie* of Alaybey; Şeyh Mustafa Babaoğlu, a *çete*; Hafız Ahmed Effendi, *muhtar* of Alaybey; Ali Cenani Bey, a parliamentary deputy from Ayntab; Rıza Bey, a brother of Ali Cenani's; Dayızâde Sadıkoğlu Hasan Sadık, a Unionist leader; and Taşcizâde Abdallah, the president of Ayntab's Committee of Union and Progress.[48]

As for the 6,000 Armenians of Kilis whose fate was closely bound up with that of their compatriots from Ayntab, it must be pointed out that on the eve of the deportations the second in command of the Fourth Army, Fahri Pasha, also went to Kilis. There he held talks with the Armenian notables, guaranteeing the safety of their lives and property and yet, on the evening of the same day, he held "a secret meeting," in the *Mevlahane*, with Unionist leaders and local notables, during which the deportation of the Armenians was approved in principle, with the blessing of the CUP's responsible secretary in the vilayet of Aleppo, Cemal Bey.[49] Two days later, the leading Armenian personality in the city, Kevork Keshishian, was arrested on his farm and jailed in Kilis after being publicly humiliated.[50]

It should be emphasized that the deportation of the Armenians of Kilis began on the same day as it did in Ayntab, 30 July 1915. The convoys were initially led toward the Katma railway station, where a primitive camp had been hastily set up. Thus, the convoys from Kilis found themselves submerged in the flood of the hundreds of thousands of deportees from the four corners of Asia Minor who passed through this camp, most of them on foot, a few by rail. Around 300 people, essentially craftsmen, were allowed to remain in Kilis for some time, "charged with meeting [local] needs." They were eventually deported in turn.[51] The church was stripped of all its Christian symbols and ritual objects. Real estate was seized after its owners were killed under the supervision of the local Unionists, so as to make all protest impossible.[52]

During the war Kilis earned a name for itself because of the beauty of the Armenian women abducted from the convoys of deportees and placed in the bordello reserved for Kilis's Unionists and soldiers passing through the city.[53] Armenian survivors from Kilis compiled a list of the 107 people who were chiefly responsible for the crimes committed in the course of the deportation and were the primary beneficiaries of the despoliation of Armenian property.[54]

The Deportations in the Sancak of Antakya

The *sancak* of Antakya/Antioch took in, roughly speaking, the whole of the southern part of the Amanus mountainous region and the Mediterranean coast from Alexandretta to the mouth of the Orontes River. On the eve of the First World War, the 31,000 Armenians of the region were concentrated above all in the two mountainous regions just mentioned, as well as in a few towns, beginning with Alexandretta and Beylan. In the prefecture, Antioch, there were just over 200 Armenians, but there were also six little towns as well as several small villages to the west, in the foothills of Mt. Moses (Musadağ), in which 8,500 Armenians lived – Yoğunoluk, Hacihabibi, the two neighboring hamlets of Trzhnik and Karaçay, Bitias, Nor Zeitun/Şalihan, Kıdırbek, Vakıf, Kebusia/Körderesi, and the little port of Çevlik, which served the villages of Mt. Moses as their outlet to the sea. It was in this mountainous region that, beginning in late July 1915, the Armenians resisted the attacks and shelling of the Turkish troops for 40 days, and were then saved thanks to a spontaneous intervention by French warships.[55]

On the other bank of the Orontes, in the mountainous regions around Mt. Cassius (Cebelakra) in the western part of the *kaza* of Şuğur, lay a second cluster of nine Armenian villages located around the little town of Kesab. In 1914, nearly 9,000 Armenians lived in these localities: Kesab (pop. 4,760), Karaduran (pop. 1,505), Ekizoluk (pop. 560), Kulkene (pop. 525), Kayacık (pop. 119), Eskîyören (pop. 245), Çakalcık (pop. 140), Çinarcık (pop. 350), and Duzağac (pop. 532). Mt. Cassius, a mountain refuge par excellence, offered another advantage: it extended into the Mediterranean and thus offered access to a well-protected little harbor that was inaccessible from the coast. The relative security offered by these mountains was counterbalanced by the fact that these villages were all but isolated from the rest of the world and lived in virtual autarchy. Communications with Antakya and Latakiye were maintained thanks only to narrow mule paths.[56]

Although there were more than 14,000 Armenians in the *kazas* of Iskenderum/Alexandretta and Beylan, there were only two important colonies, found in the principal towns of the two *kazas*, Alexandretta and Beylan, as well as a number of scattered rural communities. There were some 2,000 Armenians in the city of Alexandretta, but the *kaza* also boasted several Armenian villages: Nargellik (pop. 180), Kışla (pop. 60), and Fartınlı (pop. 200). In the interior, on the road between Alexandretta and Aleppo, Beylan had an Armenian population of 1,800 on the eve of the war. There were a few Armenian villages in the vicinity of the town: Atık (pop. 231), Kırıkhan (pop. 176), Kanlıdere (pop. 127), Güzeli (pop. 121), and Söukoluk (pop.174).[57]

As we have already pointed out,[58] the Armenians in these coastal areas of the vilayet of Aleppo were initially to have been exempted from deportation. Ultimately, however, in late July 1915, the authorities issued an order to deport them as well.[59]

On the morning of 9 May, regular troops and the gendarmerie invested the Armenian villages of Musadağ. Their mission was to conduct searches of homes, churches, schools, and all other places in which arms might have been stashed. The operation was apparently set in motion after Muslims from villages in the area informed on their Armenian neighbors. A few hunting rifles aside, however, the searches produced no tangible results, apart from the fact that they intensified the already existing suspicions of the Armenians.[60]

A witness of, and participant in, the events that occurred in Musadağ, Dikran Andreasian, a Protestant minister in Zeitun who came from Yoğunoluk, reports that when the order to deport the villagers from the region was issued on 30 July, many, such as Harutiun Nokhudian, a Protestant minister from Bitias, thought that it would be "folly" to resist it.[61] Thus 332 families from Kebiusia/Körderesi (pop. 240), Yoğunoluk (2), Hacihabibli (80), and Bitias (10) submitted to the order and were conducted somewhat later to Antakya, where they were subsequently deported to Der Zor on the route running parallel to the Euphrates.[62] What the minister from Zeitun does not say, however, is that after finally returning to his native village, Yoğunoluk, on 25 July, thanks to the intercession of American missionaries from Marash, he informed his compatriots of the way that Zeitun had been emptied of its population.[63] This information apparently had a crucial impact on the Armenian village leaders' decision to withdraw to positions on the mountain with the villagers who chose to go with them – the 868 families or around 4,200 people who took to the maquis beginning on 31 July.[64] According to Reverend Andreasian, the Armenians who had decided to put up resistance had some 120 modern rifles and also old hunting rifles, enough to arm, at best, half of the men (there were 1,054 men over 14 years of age among them).[65] All these people immediately began organizing the defense of the mountainous area, notably by digging trenches at strategic points and naming a "Defense Committee."[66] After the week's reprieve that they had been granted by the authorities had expired, 200 regular soldiers launched a first attack on them on 8 August. Although the assault was pursued for six hours, the attackers were unable to break the Armenians' defense. Two thousand troops were sent to the area from Antioch over the next few days, setting up a bivouac on the mountain about 600 meters below the Armenian lines. The defense committee immediately decided to launch a surprise attack during the night, which threw the soldiers into a panic and caused heavy loss of life. The attackers also captured some arms and ammunition.[67]

At this point, the authorities adopted new tactics. According to Andreasian, around 15,000 men from the surrounding villages were armed and positioned around the mountainous area defended by the Armenians, creating a hermetic siege. Then, on Tuesday, 10 August, after the Armenian positions had been pounded by artillery, a second assault was launched.[68] It was at this point, Andreasian reports, that the besieged Armenians considered the possibility of opening a path on which they could make their way toward the coast and escape by sea. Before they had been completely surrounded, they had sent a messenger to the outside world, bearing an appeal written in English by Andreasian, which declared that as a result of the "policy of annihilation which the Turks are applying to our nation," the inhabitants of Musadağ had withdrawn into the mountains, where they were under siege.[69] Two immense white flags, one bearing the words "Christians in distress: rescue" and another bearing a red cross, were fabricated and hoisted on the mountaintop to make them visible from the sea below. On the morning of 10 September, a French battleship, the *Guichen*, sighted this appeal for help from the besieged Armenians of Musadagh, who sent a delegate to the ship. In the next 24 hours three other cruisers, including the *Jeanne-d'Arc*, arrived in the area and set about bringing more than 4,000 villagers on board. It took no fewer than 36 hours to complete the operation, and another two days to make the journey to Port Said, Egypt.[70]

The military exploits of this Armenian resistance aside, it must be pointed out that the unlooked for rescue of the inhabitants of Musadağ obviously owed a great deal to the geographical position of these Armenian villages not far from the coast. Furthermore, we cannot ignore the fact that the decision to resist was made only after the leaders of the resistance had clearly understood that the authorities planned to send them to their deaths. In other words, the villagers of Musadağ were among the rare Armenians who had no doubt about the authorities' real intentions toward them, which is what brought them to fight at all costs. The late date on which the authorities chose to deal with this region, as well as the laxity they exhibited in the case of Reverend Andreasian, who had witnessed the events in Zeitun, also help explain why the standard precautions that they took in order to mask their real intentions did not suffice here to convince the Armenians to submit to deportation, as they did elsewhere. The 1 August arrests of the Armenian notables of Antakya, a town with which Musadagh had close relations, only reinforced the arguments of the partisans of armed resistance.[71]

According to Mardiros Kushakjian, when rumors that the Armenians of the region were to be deported began making the rounds – Reverend Andreasian had arrived the day before – a meeting of the Armenian leaders of the villages of Musadağ and Kesab was immediately convened in Antioch on 26 July. The leaders of the villages on the right bank of the Orontes suggested to their neighbors of the left bank, the villagers of Kesab, that they collaborate in organizing a common defense effort if the information in their possession proved true. The notables of Kesab, however, rejected this suggestion and decided to submit to whatever orders the authorities might issue. They wished to demonstrate the loyalty that Armenian political and religious leaders had demanded that they show under all circumstances since the outbreak of the war.[72] Thus, the entire population of Kesab was deported – however, toward Homs and Hama – in the first half of August 1915, as was that of Alexandretta, by its *kaymakam*, Fatih Bey (who held his post from 14 April 1913 to 15 November 1915), and of Beylan, by its *kaymakam*, Ahmed Refik Bey (who served from 28 February 1915 to 21 January 1916).

Chapter 23

Deportations in the *Mutesarifat* of Urfa

The ancient city of Edessa was long a political and cultural center of the first importance. A sort of bridge between Mesopotamia and Asia Minor, it was inhabited by
very diverse populations. The Armenians and Syriacs who lived here still shared early
in the twentieth century an attachment to the Near Eastern cultural heritage, which they
zealously propagated. The Armenians arrived in the region of Edessa very late – that is, early
in the eleventh century. On the eve of the First World War, the *mutesarifat* of Urfa, which
had been detached from the vilayet of Aleppo in 1908, boasted nearly 42,000 Armenians,
25,000 to 30,000 of whom lived in Urfa and its environs. The city itself lay in a vast, fertile
plain, except for the Armenian quarter, most of which rose, level after level, up the slopes of
Mt. Telfedur in the northern part of the city. Overlooking the lower part of the Armenian
quarter was the Cathedral of the Holy Mother of God, the archbishopric, and the Armenian
middle school.

Commercial activity in Urfa, the economic center of Upper Mesopotamia, was then
largely dominated by the Armenians, who were also active in certain craft guilds, such as
those of the stonecutters, architects, boot-makers, copper tinners, goldsmiths, rug weavers,
and blacksmiths. The fertility of the surrounding plain, irrigated by the Berik, made it possible to cultivate immense vineyards and orchards, as well as cereals and cotton. There were
many thriving industries centered on weaving, the production of cotton prints, and dying.
On the eve of the 1915 massacres, the Armenians of Urfa appeared more than ever as the
dynamic element in the region. Nothing suggested at the time that these law-abiding citizens
would be transformed into resistance fighters when they received the deportation order and,
simultaneously, the news of the murder of 1,500 young recruits from the city who had had
their throats cut in small groups.

There were only a few Armenians in the northern plain of Mesopotamia, in Garmuc, an
hour and a half northeast of Urfa (pop. 5,000), Mankush (60 households), Tlbaşar (100 families), and in the *nahie* of Bozova, in Hoghin and Hovig, whose Turkish-speaking inhabitants
were winegrowers or raised silkworms.[1]

Indelibly engraved on the memories of the Armenians of Urfa were the deliberate destruction of their cathedral by fire on 28 and 29 December 1895, which caused 3,000 deaths, and
the massacre of 5,000 more Armenians in the city.[2] They nevertheless participated in the
general mobilization in the months immediately following the Ottoman Empire's entry into
the war and unflinchingly provided the contributions to the war effort that the authorities
demanded of them. As elsewhere, Armenian businesses were subject to outright plunder; as
a rule, it had precious little to do with the army's needs, serving above all the interests of
a few officers and civil servants.[3] According to one survivor's report, while the Armenians
feared a massacre like the one that had occurred in 1895, it occurred to none of them in this

period that the government would this time implement a program of an entirely different scope and kind. Thus, in spring 1915, when the court-martial in Bitlis demanded that two young men, Mgrdich Najarian and Kevork Shadarevian, be remanded to it, the Armenian authorities were convinced that there had been a "misunderstanding." Aram Sahagian notes that the news that the Armenian elites of the capital had been arrested surprised the people of Edessa, who were shocked when a convoy of women, children, and old men from Zeitun arrived in their city in late April on their way to Zor via Ras ul-Ayn.[4] The Danish missionary Karen Jeppe, who had tried to provide the deportees relief, notes that the sight of them profoundly revolted the Armenians of Urfa, the younger generation in particular. All had tried to help the deportees from Zeitun, notwithstanding the fact that it was absolutely forbidden to approach them.[5] As the weeks went by, the Armenians of Urfa hid thousands of deportees from the north in their homes. The primate, Ardavast *Vartabed*, had tried in vain to obtain permission from the *mutesarif* to provide the deportees with assistance.[6] An Austrian engineer then vacationing with his family in the vineyards of the Urfa region reports that "bandits lay in wait for an Armenian convoy" between Urfa and Arabpunar, swooping down on it when it passed by. He also notes how those guarding the convoys of deportees took bribes in exchange for letting men enter a khan or camp in order to "appropriate" deported "women or girls."[7]

From May to October 1915, Urfa was effectively transformed into a transit center for convoys of deportees. In this period, the city experienced a number of alarms. On 27 May, the police began to carry out systematic house searches in the Armenian neighborhoods, officially because they were looking for weapons and evidence of a possible conspiracy.[8] These initial measures, similar in every respect to those we have seen elsewhere, seem to have been triggered by the appointment of a new *mutesarif*, Ali Haydar, a Young Turk[9] who had probably received orders to speed up the operations. Ephraim Jernazian, then serving as the minister of Urfa's Protestant Syriacs, received a request from the *mutesarif* and the police chief, Şakir Bey, who was also the son-in-law of the parliamentary deputy Mahmud Nedim, to translate Armenian, French, and English documents confiscated from the Armenians into Ottoman Turkish. Together with a Syriac who also knew English, İbrahim Fazıl, at the time the head of Urfa's school system, he was ordered to go to work for a newly created military committee.[10] According to Jernazian, the authorities were trying to find compromising evidence of Armenian involvement in a plot against state security, but the documents submitted to him were of no great interest.[11] In the wake of this first major offensive mounted by the authorities, several meetings with the principal Armenian leaders were held at the archbishopric under the chairmanship of the primate, Ardavast Kalenderian. A large sum was collected and put at the prelate's disposal, so that he could, if necessary, bribe government officials. This gives some sense of the means the city's notables had considered using in order to parry an eventual threat.[12] They engaged in sharp debates with Mgrdich Yotneghperian, then wanted by the authorities, who tried to persuade the assembly to organize a revolt if the arrests continued. However, a majority of the notables present as well as the political parties refused to take that option into consideration. Mgrdich, his brother Sarkis, and Arush Rastgelenian accordingly took it upon themselves to prepare for a rebellion.[13] According to Jernazian, a written order to carry out a second wave of arrests the following day arrived at the court one week after he took up his post as a translator – that is, around 3 June. Targeted were the Armenians' political leaders. Jernazian thereupon warned Antranig Ferid Bozajian, the local leader of the ARF and director of the Armenian schools, to leave town without delay. Bozajian, however, said that he was not in danger since the local Young Turks were his friends.[14] Around 4 June, in the morning, the police surrounded the Monastery of Saint Sarkis located near the entrance to the city, where Bozajian and Kaspar Rsdigian, a Dashnak teacher, had their homes. They proceeded to arrest these two men and seize archival documents. Police commander Şakir Bey notably gave Bozajian's notebook to Jernazian and asked him to translate it. On the minister's own admission, this document "contained everything the Turkish government wanted" – that is, a list of all local ARF members and the outline of a plan to defend the Armenian quarter that had been drawn up after the 1909 massacres in Cilicia.[15] This discovery left the translator "in a cold sweat." He went to see the Armenian primate Ardavast Kalenderian that very evening in order to suggest that he bribe Şakir Bey or burn down the room in which the notebook was kept. The first of these two options was chosen; two notables went to see Şakir and İbrahim Fazıl, who accepted the offer.[16]

Massive arrests began on 8 June. Sixteen notables and high-ranking officials were apprehended: Garabed Izmirlian, the president of the diocesan council; Soghomon Knajian; Khosrov Dadian, the city's treasurer; Arush Sarafian; Arush Kaghtalian; Kevork Donavakian; Kevork, Nerses, and Hovhannes Yotneghperian, Mgrdich's brothers; Aghajan Der Bedrosian; and Hagop and Nazar Kulahian; Sarkis Ejzaji; Yezekiel Boyajian; Garabed Kataroyan; and Kazanji Kambur. Mgrdich Yotneghperian, disguised as a Bedouin, succeeded in making his way into the prison where these men were being held and suggested carrying out an operation to free them, but all refused, fearing that such an action would bring on a general massacre.[17] In a 14 June letter, Francis Leslie, a missionary acting as the American consul, confirmed that "the reign of terror has begun in this city" and also that the police and gendarmerie had conducted violent house searches in the Armenian neighborhoods, looking for arms; that certain notables had been brought before the court-martial and others had been tortured with red-hot irons; and that, in all, 100 "of the best citizens of the city" were in jail by mid-June.[18]

The 16 notables arrested on 8 June were tortured and then deported to Rakka on the 13th; their families joined them there a few days later.[19] While some of them were brought back to Urfa around 26/27 June, the others were liquidated one hour from Rakka in a place known as Cır Tosun.[20] The news reach Urfa in short order and a second meeting was organized at the archbishopric, called this time by the ARF. The only item on the agenda was how to organize a self-defense effort. Mgrdich Yotneghperian again suggested that they wait no longer, for it seemed clear to him that the authorities were trying to weaken the Armenians gradually by arresting the men. The ARF members present, however, decided not to take any action until the deportation order was published and to prepare for all eventualities.[21] Yotneghperian's analysis of the situation had not been wrong: on 25 June, in the space of two hours, some 100 Armenians were arrested. Involved this time was businessmen, craftsmen, members of the professions, and so on.[22]

According to Kate Ainslie, who left Marash on 14 June, "the man" who deported and killed the Armenians in Dyarbekir was transferred to Urfa in mid-June "with the evident purpose of letting him continue his work there."[23] The missionary does not give the name of this "man." It might well have been the parliamentary deputy Pirincizâde Feyzi, who played a pivotal role in the crimes committed in the vilayet of Dyarbekir together with the vali of the province, Reşid. Ainslie's observation indicates, in any case, that the leading bodies of the CUP were growing impatient and had decided to send experienced men to Urfa. It is true that Mgrdich Yotneghperian and the few dozen men loyal to him came and went with impunity, in particular laying their hands on arms stockpiles; the authorities proved unable to apprehend them.[24] The tension at the time was running at so high a pitch that the primate Kalenderian suggested to Yotneghperian that he leave the city and not return until calm had been restored. The *fedayi* and his men withdrew to a place near Garmuc, an Armenian village in the vicinity of the city. There they were discovered and surrounded on 6 July, but managed to flee through the army's lines. The troops relieved their frustration on the inhabitants of Garmuc: by way of reprisal, the mayor, Kevork Nersesian, was massacred and the village was razed.[25]

The next stage, the confiscation of weapons, began on 10 July, when the *mutesarif* summoned the Armenian primate and gave him 48 hours to turn over the arms in the possession of his flock. According to Armenian sources, the community limited itself to handing over a few old hunting rifles, which were then piled up in the courtyard of the cathedral. An artillery officer, Mihran Herardian, suggested that the Armenians not repeat the mistake they had made in 1895: after turning in their weapons, the Armenians of Urfa had been massacred.[26] In this strange face-off, in which each party was aware of the other's intentions, the tactics adopted by the authorities nevertheless persuaded certain Armenian circles to submit. The debate between these circles and the partisans of a self-defense effort remained sharp, despite the many arrests that continued without let up. The primate went so far as to try to bribe the authorities into freeing those arrested. The *mutesarif* responded by summoning him on 26 July and immediately imprisoning him. Thus, Kalenderian joined the hundreds of Armenians who had been arrested in the course of the preceding weeks and subjected to tortures that drove some of them, such as the gunsmith Nazar Tufenkjian, to suicide. Using all the means at their disposal, the authorities tried to make these men confess where they had hidden their weapons. Yet, according to the Danish missionary Karen Jeppe, none had talked.[27] This failure notwithstanding, the local authorities put the next stage of their plan into practice. On 28 July, they sent all the prisoners to Dyarbekir. Among them were the primate; Soghomon Kenajian; Garabed Izmirlian, the very wealthy president of the diocesan council and a member of the regional council; Giragos Tertsagian; Kevork Cherchian, a craftsman; Kevork Yotneghperian, a blacksmith and Mgrdich's brother; and the businessmen Hagop Kulahian and Harutiun Der Khorenian.[28] These men were massacred on 30 July on the road to Dyarbekir in a place near Urfa known as Şeytan Deresi.[29]

The fact that two high-ranking officers of the *Teşkilât-ı Mahsusa*, Lieutenant-Colonel Halil Bey [Kut], Enver's uncle, and Çerkez Ahmed, had come to Urfa from Dyarbekir was probably not unrelated to these massacres.[30] According to an Armenian witness, Halil had promised the primate just before the latter's arrest to save the lives of most of these men in exchange for 6,000 Turkish pounds. He pocketed the money and proceeded to organize the liquidation of the prisoners in question.[31] Thus, it seems that, after carrying out the campaign to extirpate the Armenian population of the vilayet of Bitlis in the first half of July, Halil and his expeditionary corps of *çetes* headed to regions to the south in order to conduct similar operations. Moreover, Çerkez Ahmed, an accredited CUP killer whose role in Van we have already seen,[32] personally attended to liquidating the two Armenian parliamentary deputies, Zohrab and Vartkes, who arrived in Urfa from Aleppo on 1 August.[33] Received with all the honors by their colleague the deputy Mahmud Nedim, who invited them to dinner, the two Armenian leaders were approached by Mgrdich Yotneghperian, who proposed to help them flee. Zohrab answered: "Our flight would make the situation of the population even more difficult."[34] Like many of Urfa's notables, the two deputies were apparently more concerned about the safety of the population than their own future. On 2 August, Zohrab and Vartkes were put back on the road, escorted by Şakir Bey, the police chief, and killed by Çerkez Ahmed and his men in a deep gorge lying two hours from the city, Şeytan Deresi, at virtually the same spot where Urfa's Armenian elite was put to death.[35] There can be absolutely no doubt that the two close acquaintances of the Young Turk leadership were executed on orders from the capital.

The next operation conducted by Halil and Çerkez Ahmed is just as symptomatic of the special missions entrusted to the *Teşkilât-ı Mahsusa*. On 10 August, a battalion of the Special Organization, under Halil's orders, set out to execute the 1,500 Armenian and Syriac worker-soldiers in two *amele taburis* working in Karaköprü and Kudeme, in the vicinity of Urfa. After surrounding the camp in Karaköprü, the *çetes* tied these men up, lined them up in front of ditches that had been dug in advance, and shot them.[36] When they attacked the camp in

Kudeme the next day, however, a number of worker-soldiers defended themselves with their tools or their bare hands. Some even managed to seize their executioners' weapons and take up positions on a promontory, where they put up a three days' resistance before committing suicide. Two survivors from these *amele taburis*, the brothers Sarkis and Krikor Daraghjian of the Sanderchonts family, were able to return to Urfa and inform the population about the massacres that had been perpetrated in Karaköprü and Kudeme.[37] Obviously, the news of these crimes reinforced the dedication of those who advocated resistance. According to Jernazian, Cemal Pasha, who also had authority over the autonomous *mutesarifat* of Urfa, which lay within the limits of the vilayet of Aleppo, was not in favor of such violence. Shortly thereafter, he had Çerkez Ahmed brought before a court-martial and executed for his crimes. To overcome the obstacle embodied by Cemal, the "fanatical members of the Ittihad" – it seems reasonable to suppose that Halil took this initiative – appealed to the interior minister, who decided to detach the region of Urfa from Aleppo and attach it to the vilayet of Dyarbekir.[38] The same witness, who, let us recall, was employed by the local court-martial and heard and saw the orders that came down from the capital, notes that after this decision a meeting of all Urfa's Turkish notables and officials who had come from Istanbul was held at city hall. He also points out that one of the participants, who did not know him, told him that an "secret order from Constantinople" indicating that the government had decided "to get rid of all the Armenians [...] because the Fatherland is in great danger" had been read out during the meeting and that the mayor had forced those attending to add lists of their Armenian friends to the "official register" as proof of their loyalty.[39] It is possible that Urfa's Armenian notables had opposed all attempts at rebellion only after receiving assurances from their Turkish friends that they would be spared. They were doubtless hoping to spare the Armenian population the fate of their compatriots from other regions. But it is also not inconceivable that a number of Turks from Urfa sought to spare their Armenian friends because they shared the same financial interests or had received bribes. It was presumably in order to overcome this passive resistance, the intensity of which is hard to evaluate, that the CUP took matters in hand and sent people of confidence to the area in August.

Jernazian says in his memoirs that he had hoped at the time that the "Armenians of Urfa did finally realize that appeasement and peaceful compliance had brought only increased oppression and gradual elimination of leaders and Young men."[40] Indeed, as the facts piled up, they persuaded even the most cautious that "all hope of survival was lost... The choice was between ignominious exile and murder or an honorable death through active resistance."[41]

On 19 August, while Mgrdich Yotneghperian and his right-hand man, Harutiun Rastgelenian, were busy reorganizing the defense of the Armenian neighborhoods, hard hit by the arrests of large numbers of men, they were discovered and encircled in a house in Urfa. The assault launched on the two banned men by Çerkez Ahmed and the warden of Urfa's prison, Bakır Çavuş, marked the commencement of hostilities. The two Armenian resistance fighters managed to vanish into thin air after killing their guard and forcing Çerkez Ahmed and his *çetes* to flee.[42] The next day, according to Franz Eckart, several hundred Armenians were massacred by *çetes* who had invested Urfa.[43] Dr. J. Vance, leaving the American hospital to go to the city, saw many Armenian corpses in the streets and observed that a first series of deportations toward Mardin had been set in motion.[44] The American consul Jackson was given similar information by his vice-consul in Urfa, Francis Leslie, who had not yet observed resistance on the part of the Armenians.[45]

Contrary to expectations, at a time when the situation favored systematic deportation or the beginning of resistance in the Armenian neighborhoods, it seems that an order from Istanbul called a sharp halt to the developments in progress. According to Jernazian, this order was motivated by the "great need" of the army, which only Armenian craftsmen could meet.[46] We do not know, however, whether this "great need" was that of Cemal's Fourth

Army or of the Third Army commanded by Mustafa Kâmil. It was not until 29 September that the church bells in the Armenian quarter all began pealing: since the December 1895 massacres, their use had been outlawed, which explains why the Armenians chose this symbolic signal to announce the beginning of the insurrection in Urfa. The insurrection was to last for 25 days. In the preceding weeks, Mgrdich Yotneghperian had reorganized the defense of the Armenian neighborhoods and redeployed his men, arms, and ammunition thanks especially to the girls and women, who transported materiel under their chadors.[47] After months of preparations aimed at decapitating Urfa's Armenian community, the authorities were surprised to encounter resistance. Between conscription, the liquidation of the elites, the massacre of the worker-soldiers, and the first deportations having largely emptied the city of its vital forces, only a few hundred men capable of fighting remained in Urfa.[48] The surprise here came from the girls and women, who participated directly in the fighting, to say nothing of their role in the logistical organization of the self-defense effort. This "last battle of despair,"[49] as Karen Jeppe describes it, mobilized everyone's energy to a single end, resisting until the last fighter had fallen.

Ali Haydar, the *mutesarif*, gave an old Syriac a message to take to Mgrdich Yotneghperian. In it, he referred to the "regrettable events" that had recently occurred, blaming them on the "gendarmes" – that is, the *çetes* – who had not "gone about fulfilling their duties properly." He also promised that he would guarantee the Armenians' lives and property if they surrendered.[50] This discourse, of a species that might be called the Ittihad's trademark, obviously did not have the intended effect on Yotneghperian, whose considerable lucidity and solid tactical sense would be shown by events to come. Rather than throwing up barricades before the main entries to the Armenian neighborhoods, he decided to leave the entries to them unguarded. He asked the military leaders of these neighborhoods – Kevork Alahaydoyan for the Father Abraham neighborhood, Sarkis Yotneghperian for Pos Paghents, Harutiun Rastgelenian for Masmana, Vagharsh Mesrobian and Harutiun Simian for the neighborhood in which the American institutions were located in Tlfıdur, and Movses Siujian for the Samsat Gate – to station their fighters in the houses that looked down on these entries.[51] The next morning, thousands of the city's inhabitants, armed with sabers and rifles distributed by the authorities, attacked the three main Armenian neighborhoods. It seems that the *mutesarif* had activated the traditional springs of religious fanaticism, inviting the Muslim population to punish the unbelievers: at the head of the advancing columns, clerics invoked God's blessings. The defenders, after letting the attackers penetrate the Armenian neighborhoods to a considerable depth, threw homemade bombs down on the crowd. The result was a general panic during which around 450 people fell victim to the explosives or, in the case of most of the casualties, were trampled underfoot by the throng.[52] On 1 October, the authorities adopted new tactics. Drawing from the lessons of their first failure, they decided to focus their assault on a single point, the neighborhood around the Catholic church, and to carry it out at night. Yotneghperian apparently learned of this plan beforehand, because he set up a veritable trap around this church. After letting the attackers take control of the building and its vast courtyard, the defenders sent grenades and heavy gunfire raining down on them, causing new casualties.[53] The next offensive came on 3 October. That morning, a Kurdish chieftain from Suruc, Süleyman Beg, arrived with 600 men from his tribe. The first shells, launched from the citadel, fell on the Armenian quarters, paving the way for the assault that was launched on the Father Abraham neighborhood by these more battle-steeled Kurdish fighters as well as newly arrived units of the regular army. Probably convinced that the shelling had shattered the Armenian positions in these sections of the city, the attackers sought, above all, to invest the houses. Positioned on the rooftops, the Armenians again used grenades to disperse the intruders.[54] The German Captain Wolffskeel, a member of the Fourth Army's General Staff, reported in a 1 October letter to his wife that he had been sent to Urfa to "restore order" and that he had personally commanded the attack that day, coming up against a "defense very well prepared."[55] On 4 and 5 October, the Turkish forces contented themselves with trading a few gunshots with the Armenians, probably because they were awaiting the announced arrival of 6,000 men equipped with modern German cannons under the command of the inevitable general Fahri Pasha.[56] As Hilmar Kaiser emphasizes, Eberhard Count Wolffskeel von Reichenberg was the "only German officer know to have served in Ottoman uniform and directly participated in the killing of Armenians."[57]

In fact, General Fahri Pasha's forces arrived in Urfa only on 6 October and did not launch their first assault until the morning of the 8th, after the Armenian neighborhoods had been heavily shelled. According to Captain Wolffskeel, the efficaciousness of the batteries of cannon under his direction enabled the Turkish forces gradually to reduce the defensive perimeter. Fighting was now limited to a few pockets of resistance.[58] It is true that the Armenians did carry out a number of spectacular operations, such as the 6 October attack that a commando made up of six men in Kurdish dress launched on the batteries of cannon before they were brought into the city.[59] But their fate was already sealed. In no hurry, Fahri Pasha put his cannons in place and then sent a message to Yotneghperian, in which he expressed his admiration for the insurgents' exploits but added that they should now surrender. An exchange even took place on the front lines between the two men, who were protected by their respective positions. To the promises of Fahri, who went so far as to propose to promote Yotneghperian to the rank of captain, the Armenian responded by listing all the crimes that had been committed in the course of the preceding weeks, such as the massacre of the worker-soldiers, and by reaffirming that he could not put the least faith in the word of the high-ranking Ottoman officer. "You know," he concluded, "that we will fight to the last man."[60] After this first failure, Fahri tried to convince F. Eckart and J. Künzler to act as go-betweens. He also gave Francis Leslie a few hours – until noon on 8 October – to evacuate the American mission together with the 14 foreign nationals to be found there.[61] Leslie and his companions' situation was indeed ambiguous, to say the least. In the view of one side, they were the Armenians' hostages; in the view of the other, they were friends protecting the hundreds of women and children who had taken refuge behind the mission's walls. It is entirely possible that Leslie pretended to be a hostage of the Armenians in order to justify staying put, doubtless in the hope that his mission would be spared thanks to his status as the consular agent of a neutral country. It is also reasonable to suppose that General Fahri was not happy about the existence of this potential sanctuary for Armenians, even if only women and children were involved. According to an anonymous American missionary, Leslie never considered leaving his mission.[62] J.B. Rebours is more precise: he observes that the American mission, in which "a number of women and children" had taken shelter, was a direct target of shelling.[63] Rebours affirms, in other words, that the mission was one of the main targets singled out by General Fahri, whose probable objective was to force the foreign nationals to leave the premises. Captain Wolffskeel von Reichenberg, who met Leslie when the American decided to leave the mission on 15 October, observes that "the Turks" suspected him of complicity with the Armenians, yet believed that Leslie was "surely innocent."[64] On 30 October – that is, a week after the end of the fighting – it was officially announced that Leslie had committed suicide.[65] There are legitimate grounds for the suspicion that Fahri Pasha and the local authorities liquidated one of the main and best-informed witnesses to the events that had unfolded in Urfa since the beginning of the crisis.

On the insurgents' side, Mgrdich Yotneghperian was wounded during an 9 October offensive that was, however, successfully beaten back.[66] On 11 October, Franz Eckhart came in hopes of convincing the Armenian leader to lay down his arms. He was sharply rebuffed and even accused of collaboration.[67] At this point, Fahri set out to destroy the Armenian neighborhoods by methodically subjecting them to heavy shelling. On 13 October, after they had been pounded for 24 hours, the Turkish troops launched a violent assault, gaining control of a number of Armenian positions. A second general offensive launched on 19 October left most of the Armenian neighborhoods in the assailants' hands.[68] By the evening of 23 October, after 25 days of fighting, all the Armenian positions had been taken by the army.[69] Most of the defenders had either died in combat or committed suicide, beginning with Mgrdich Yotneghperian, who shot himself in the head after the last bastion fell.[70] A few survivors, such as Sarkis Yotneghperian, Mgrdich's brother, were hanged in front of the *konak*. Reverend Soghomon Akelian, whose rope broke twice, exclaimed: "All the acts of your state are like this rope – rotten."[71] Elvesta Leslie, the American vice-consul's collaborator, openly accused Captain Wolffskeel, who had commanded the artillery, of having participated in the massacres.[72] She also noted that a number of women and children had been locked up in the city's hans, where many of them died of hunger or typhoid fever; that soldiers, officers, gendarmes, and civilians had come to the hans to carry off girls, as in a slave market; and that, after being put on the road, the others died like flies, with only a few managing to hide in Arab villages.[73] Wolffskeel informed his wife, more soberly, that after the fall of the city, "the unpleasant part began again, though." "The evacuation of the inhabitants and the courts-martial" and that what he had seen, "having nothing to do with me," was "not very pleasant."[74] He also noted that all industrial and craft production had come to a complete standstill in the city of Urfa.[75] On the testimony of Father Hyacinthe Simon, a convoy of 2,000 women and children from Urfa passed through Mardin on 20 October, followed by another comprising 3,500 people on 28 October. Their official destination was the Mosul region.[76] It is, however, impossible to determine the number of people massacred in the neighborhoods that the army invested from 13 October on, and quite as impossible to establish the number of those who were really deported to the deserts of Syria and Mesopotamia.

While a commission responsible for liquidating Armenian assets was established rather late, in December 1915,[77] it seems that its task was facilitated by the fact that the Armenians had taken care to burn all their property in the final days of the siege,[78] leaving very little to the authorities in the way of booty. Jernazian observes, moreover, that the defenders threw gold coins on the pavement and dared the soldiers to come plunder them.[79] This speaks volumes about the fury that had taken possession of the Armenians and their awareness of their desperate plight. Franz Eckhart, a member of Urfa's Deutsche Orient-Mission and the director of a carpet factory, was a particular target for diverse criticisms from the Armenian survivors. He was notably accused of having agreed to let Armenian entrepreneurs and families deposit property in his home and then denouncing them to the authorities so that he could appropriate their assets. Others charged him with collaborating with Captain Wolffskeel during the siege, and also with having kept part of the sums in gold sent from America, Germany, and Switzerland to assist the deportees who had taken refuge in the city.[80]

Throughout the events described here, Urfa had continued to serve as a city of transit for tens of thousands of deportees. In mid-June, around 2,000 deportees from Zeitun had passed through Urfa, whom the city's inhabitants had undertaken to assist.[81] In the following weeks, Armenians in a state beggaring description flooded into the city. They were put in particular in a large khan located at the exit from the city on the road to Aleppo, which all the caravans had to take; the courtyard of this khan was slowly transformed into an open-air morgue.[82] A few of these deportees managed, after the fall of the Armenian neighborhoods, to hide in the city, but they were later dispatched southward after a surprise roundup organized in June 1916 by the local authorities.[83] The others left Urfa, often falling victim to the squadrons of çetes who had taken up permanent quarters near Şeytan Deresi. Finally, it was reported that several thousand Armenian worker-soldiers from the *Bagdadbahn* construction sites[84] passed through Şeytan Deresi in July 1916 and were liquidated a short distance away.

In addition to the civil and military officials already mentioned, the list of people involved in the anti-Armenian persecutions in the region[85] includes Şeyh Savfet; Kurkcizâde Mahmud Nedim, a parliamentary deputy; Ömer Edip; Arabistan Haci Ali; Fesadizâde Haci Halil; Haci Kâmil Delizâde Haci Mustafa; Jdedavizâde Mehmed; Jdedavizâde Ömer; Hüseyin Fehmi, a captain in the gendarmerie; Halil Ağa Hakim; Şakir Bey, the police chief; Rasdgelmezâde Hüseyin; Haci Esad Effendi; Beyazbeyzâde Haci Bey; Ali Effendi, from Severek; Basmacizâde Hasan Çavuş; Basmacizâde Halil Effendi; Parmazkşxzzâde Şeyh Muslim; Kalaboyunda Arabizâde Reşid; Karalökzâde Haci Mehmed; Kazaz Irvanzâde Haci; Kazaz Haci Muslimzâde Haci; Haci Kâmilzâde Küçük Haci Mustafa; Barutcuzâde Haci Imam; Barutcuzâde Muslim; Gustonunoğlu Ömer; Isa Effendi; Arabizâde Mehmed; Kemanci Alizâde Kadri, a police lieutenant; Hacijomazâde Haci Mehmed; Keklik Emin; Saatcizâde Mehmed; Binbaşizâde Halil; Haci Saidağazâde Mehmed; Parmaksuz Mehmed Ali; Dişi Kurukun Halil; Dişi Kurukun Şeyh Muslim; Haci Kaplamazzâde Yahya; Musurlu Haci Alizâde Hasim; Musurlu Haci Alizâde Halil; Kiriscizâde Haci Ahmed; Hocazâde Çenesiz Halil; Hocazâde Çenesiz Abdurrahman; Lutfi Bey, the commander of the gendarmerie; Gökoğlu Halil, a Kurdish chieftain; Birecikli Bakher; Imam Effendi, the chief prosecutor; Zazanunoğlu Mehmed; Dellal Küçük Ahmed; Jurnalluzâde Kamer Usta; Nacar Maheninoğlu Haci Reşid; Nacar Maheninoğlu Haci Mustafa; Tekayid Yuzbaşi Juman; Yağlıcı Haci, the president of the city government; Haci Hasan Zedenzâde Haci Muslim; Sofizâde Osman; Molla Osmanzâde Mehmed Çavuş; Arab Alizâde Mehmed; Haci Karaazzame Yusuf; Bozuntuzâde Sanduk Emini Kadri; Osro Kuçizâde Fuad Bey; Haci Mumbarekzâde Mustafa; Alay Bey Zâde Mahmud; Gendarm Haci Nadir (who was responsible for burning down the cathedral in 1895); Police Nuri; Haci Fazlazâde Fazla; Ateşbeyzâde Ali Tahir, a *çete* chief; Haci Isazâde Hato; Dimmozâde Baklor Agha; Ali Ballizâde Ibrahim Kurdo; Bedirağazâde Halil Ağa; Haydarzâde Arif; Güllüzâde Hoca Ibrahim; Güllüzâde Hoca Abdüllah; Şekerci Eyup Effendi; Şekerci Mehmed Emin; Bekir Hatibinoğlu Nazif; Nebi Bey Zâde Hüseyin Pasha, from Suruc; Kurkcizâde Nediminoğlu Celal; Çibukci Hasan; Hacializâde Celal, the *malmüdürü* who appropriated abandoned property in Suruc; Haci Çaderzâde Salih Bey, a Kurdish chieftain; Haci Kâmilzâde Haci Bey; Ğaribbeyzâde Gesto Osman; Ğaribbeyzâde Mustafa; Mehmed Kasey; Salih Bey, a Kurd; Güllüzâde Mustafa; Namuk Agha, a Kurd from Samsat; Zeynel Bey, from Kahta; and Siza Bekir Ağa, from Çiba.

The *Kazas* of Birecik and Rumkale

Halfway between Ayntab and Urfa, on the banks of the Euphrates, the seat of the *kaza* of Birecik boasted, in 1914, an Armenian community 1,500 hundred strong. Birecik, on the Euphrates, was an obligatory way-station to Mesopotamia. A few kilometers to the west, on the road to Ayntab, the roughly 100 Armenians still living in Nisibin were mere vestiges of the ancient Armenian presence here. The northern *kaza* of Rumkale was inhabited by 1,500 Armenians who lived primarily in Eneş, Cibin, and Rumkale (the Armenian Hromgla), which had served as the seat of the catholicos between 1151 and 1292.[86] According to information communicated to the American consul Jackson by an American missionary, the biggest group of Armenians – that from Birecik – was deported in mid-August after being invited to convert, and that it was subject to the same "methods" used in Dyarbekir.[87] The Armenians of Eneş, and probably of Cibin and Rumkale as well, were also deported in mid-August, after the last men had been liquidated[88] under the direction of the *kaymakam*, Midhat Bey, who held his post from 22 August 1913 to 24 February 1916.

PART V

The Second Phase of the Genocide
Fall 1915–December 1916

Chapter 1

The Aleppo Sub-Directorate for Deportees: An Agency in the Service of the Party-State's Liquidation Policy

Throughout the process that culminated in the liquidation of the Ottoman Armenians, the chances of escaping the common fate were extremely rare, if not nonexistent. As is well known, a few Armenians escaped with their lives thanks to diplomats representing Bulgaria, then an ally of the Ottoman Empire; again, certain notables deported on 24 April 1915 were saved thanks to one diplomatic or political intervention or another. But the common lot of the several hundred thousand deportees who ended up in Syria or Mesopotamia was to help fill the dozens of hastily established concentration camps managed by the Sub-Directorate for Deportees that was created in Aleppo in fall 1915. This was an organization of an official character, subordinate to the Directorate for the Settlement of Tribes and Emigrants (*Iskân-ı Aşâyirîn ve Muhâcirîn Müdîryeti*), which answered in turn to the Ministry of the Interior. The IAMM's mission was to organize the deportations, but also to turn Armenian assets over to *muhacirs* – in other words, to settle *muhacirs* in the Armenians' places. It was the IAMM that coordinated, for example, the deportations of Muslim emigrés from Rumelia or Çerkez from Palestine to areas in Asia Minor that had been emptied of their Greek or Armenian inhabitants.[1] Thus, the IAMM was the agency charged with enacting the Ittihadist Central Committee's policy of "demographic homogenization." Its official name indicated that its mission was to settle uprooted Muslims, but it was also – indeed, primarily – responsible for uprooting the Armenian population and coordinating its deportation, a term whose meaning we now know varied with the areas in which the deported Armenians lived. Thus, when we observe the chronology of the Muslim population movements carried out on in authoritarian fashion on the IAMM's orders, it appears that this process was virtually parallel to, and synchronized with, the ethnic cleansing of the Armenians from regions to which the *muhacirs* displaced by the IAMM were to be sent.[2] The Directorate's link with the CUP was marked by the very nature of its mission of Turkifying the country, and also by the choice of its director, Muftizâde Şükrü [Kaya] Bey, a Young Turk cadre close to Mehmed Talât[3] whom the CUP sent as a delegate to the vilayets of Adana and Aleppo in summer 1915,[4] like a number of his colleagues from Istanbul who were sent to the provinces when the situation called for urgent intervention and implementation of the policy decided on by the Ittihad's central organs.

The countless telegrams dispatched by the interior minister himself concerned the rules to follow in handling the Armenian deportees. These rules had most assuredly been elaborated by the services of the IAMM. An order transmitted on 23 May 1915, for example, states that the deportees could be settled in the vilayet of Mosul, with the exception of the northern part of the vilayet, which bordered on the province of Van; it adds that the localities "in which the Armenians are to be settled" have to lie "at least twenty-five kilometers from the Baghdad railway or its branches."[5] A 7 July directive extends the zones where the Armenians were supposed to be "taken in" to the "southern and western parts of the vilayet of Mosul," localities in the *sancak* of Kirkuk "at least eighty kilometers distant from the Iranian border, the southern and western parts of the *sancak* of Zor at least twenty-five kilometers from the boundaries of the vilayet of Dyarbekir, including the villages in the Euphrates and Kabur basins, all the villages and towns in the western part of the vilayet of Aleppo, as well as regions to the south and east, with the exception of the northern zone of the vilayet and the Syrian lands, and the *sancaks* of the Hauran and Kerek, except for territories fewer than 25 kilometers from the railway. Here, then, are the regions in which the Armenians should be scattered and settled in a proportion equal to ten percent of the Muslim population."[6]

An account by Johann H. Mordtmann, a diplomat employed in the German embassy in Constantinople who was responsible for keeping track of Armenian affairs, of his 30 May 1915 exchange with İsmail Canbolat, director general of State Security in the Interior Ministry, illustrates the Ittihadists' approach to homogenization of the country. Mordtmann notes that Canbolat Bey had a map on his desk showing how far the deportations already initiated had progressed. This proves that the deportation plan was coordinated at the highest state levels and also attests its systematic dimension, which was in no sense "justified by military considerations."[7]

Muftizâde Şükrü Bey, generally given the title of Director General of the Deportations (*Sevkiyat Reisi Umumisi*), was also named to the post of special CUP delegate[8] so that he could organize the dispersion of the deportees who reached Syria. This establishes the direct role that the CUP played in conducting these operations, as well as the tight ties between the Unionist Central Committee and certain administrations of which it gained control by appointing its cadres to them.

That said, the chronology of the deportations indicates that there was a lag between the operations carried out in May and June in the eastern provinces and those targeting the populations of western Anatolia and Cilicia, which were expelled in August and September 1915. The methods employed in each of these regions explain, moreover, why the proportion of deportees from the eastern provinces who reached the gates of Syria was distinctly lower – on the order of 10 to 20 per cent – than that of Armenians from western Anatolia, which was around 80 to 90 per cent. It is, consequently, obvious that between early June, when the first deportees from the east arrived in Syria (with the notable exception of the deportees from Zeitun), and September, the central authorities had found reason to establish a structure, which they had not necessarily envisaged at the outset, for managing the streams of deportees. The mission entrusted to Muftizâde Şükrü Bey probably had no other purpose, like the arrival of Bahaeddin Şakir in the vilayets of Adana and Aleppo in the course of summer 1915.[9] The authoritarian terms employed in a telegram that Dr. Şakir sent Cemal Pasha, a telegram which was referred to by Cemal's chief of staff, even authorize the hypothesis that the chief of the Special Organization had acted for a time as the true director of deportations, profoundly irritating the master of the region, Cemal.[10] As we have seen elsewhere, interference by the CUP and its representatives spawned a certain antagonism with local civilian and military authorities. In Aleppo, Şükrü Bey found himself confronted with the ethically motivated reticence of the vali, Celal Bey, who was rapidly transferred to Konya, as well as his successor, Bekir Sâmi, who had been transferred from Beirut to Aleppo and remained in his post only from 24 June to 25 September 1915. In other words, the mere presence of a director of deportations in Aleppo did not suffice, as it had in the provinces from which the deportees originated, to manage what appeared by summer 1915 to be an increasingly vast task. It was necessary to create an organization such as the Sub-Directorate for Deportees. Such was the task with which the party charged Şükrü Bey.

Witnesses of the day mention two *Sevkiyat müdürü* (director of deportations) in Aleppo – Ahmed Eyub Sabri, who had been sent by Istanbul in June 1915,[11] and Abdüllahad Nuri. However, while Sabri bore the same title as Nuri, it seems that he did not dispose of an infrastructure worthy of the name with which to carry out his task. Indications are that this infrastructure was only put in place after Nuri was appointed to head the Sub-Directorate of Deportees in fall 1915. Nuri, who was the brother of the State Secretary in the Justice Ministry, the Young Turk parliamentary deputy Yusuf Kemal,[12] told the *kaymakam* of Kilis, when he assumed his functions, that he was "in touch with Talât Bey" and had received "liquidation orders from Talât in person."[13] The deputy-at-large, Avedis Nakashian,[14] emphasized in the accusation that he brought against Nuri in July 1920 that this man, "whose task consisted in sending all the Armenians to the deserts of Meskene and Der Zor," had committed "a deliberate crime" in dispatching them to the area and was well aware of what awaited them there.[15] In a 31 November 1915 note, the Austrian Ambassador reported that "Noury Bey, the former secretary general of the Mahsoussé," had told him: "A general directorate of emigration has been created in Aleppo; its mission consists in dealing with the dispatch of all the Armenians to Mesopotamia ... This flows from an irrevocable decision of the Committee of Union and Progress. After finishing with the Armenians, we shall begin with the mass expulsion of the Greeks."[16] This definitely establishes the direct part that the Central Committee and the *Teşkilât-ı Mahsusa*, from which Nuri came, played in organizing the concentration camps. Moreover, when one examines how these camps functioned in Bab, Munbuc, Ras ul-Ayn, Der Zor, and so on, it appears that *çetes* from the Special Organization were directly involved in liquidating deportees, showing that the activities of the Special Organization and the Sub-Directorate for Deportees were intertwined. We can also observe intertwining functions in the case of Colonel Hüseyin Avni, the commander of the gendarmerie of the vilayet and presiding judge of the court-martial in Adana, who was also the central coordinator of the deportations in the northern regions of his vilayet and a *çete* commander.[17]

In other words, it was only after Muftizâde Şükrü arrived in Aleppo that a veritable sub-directorate of the *Sevkiyat* was put in place there. In this sub-directorate, Eyub Sabri took on the role of Nuri's assistant, as the German consul Rössler gives us to understand.[18] It seems reasonable to assume that Nuri also had something to do with the fact that the valis Celal Bey and, after him, Bekir Sâmi, were transferred elsewhere, even if it is obvious that Mehmed Talât himself chose to appoint his brother-in-law, the former vali of Bitlis, Mustafa Abdülhalik, to Aleppo. Abdülhalik assumed office on 17 October 1915.[19] That date roughly corresponds with the appointment of Nuri to head the *Sevkiyat*.[20]

Chapter 2

Displaced Populations and the Main Deportation Routes

In a late note dated 4 February 1917, the Austrian Ambassador in Constantinople relates the confidences of an inspector of the Ottoman Army, Namik Bey, who had completed a tour of the vilayet of Sıvas "during the recent expulsions and massacres of the Armenians." In his report, which was simply deposited in the archives of the Office of Inspection – that is to say, buried in silence – Namik Bey wrote:

> Seven hundred thousand Armenians in a most pitiable state passed through Ak-Kyschla [Kışla] on their way into exile in the *sancak* of Zor. Bands, with the *kaymakam* of Azizié at their head, literally stripped them of all they had as they passed by. There was not a single Turkish house in the vilayet of Sıvas that was not holding young girls who had been wrested from their parents as well as property belonging to the Armenians.[1]

This account bears, of course, on the deportees from regions in northern and northeastern Asia Minor whose convoys converged near Akkışla, around 80 kilometers southeast of Sıvas; it provides a rough indication of the size of the deportation flows, but can in no case be taken as a basis for determining the number of deportees who in fact reached Syria or Mesopotamia. The role of the slaughterhouse sites such as the one near Malatia in Fırıncilar, the functioning of which we have examined, the massacres perpetrated en route by squadrons of the Special Organization or simple villagers, as well as the conditions of transportation, which claimed many victims, make precise calculations impossible. The examination of the local context undertaken in the fourth part of this study does, however, allow us to estimate the proportion of deportees who arrived "in their areas of relegation."

Of the approximately 740,000 Armenians from the vilayets of Trebizond, Angora, Sıvas, Mamuret ul-Aziz, and Erzerum, around 40,000 of them succeeded in fleeing and crossing the Russian border. We also know about the fate reserved for the tens of thousands of men who were mobilized and for the most part gradually liquidated, as well as the systematic massacres to which males over 10 or 12 were subjected. Finally, we know that in many regions some or all of the deportees were liquidated in slaughterhouse sites near their point of departure: for example, the Armenians of Trebizond were drowned off the coast of the Black Sea, those of Yozgat had their throats slit in Boğazlian, and those of the Erzincan region were massacred in the Kemah Gorge. Given the distances that these people had to travel on foot and the harassment to which they were subject en route, we can evaluate the proportion of those who reached the deserts of Syria by way of Urfa or Birecik at 20 per cent (about 130,000 people, essentially women and children). In a 16 October 1915 report entitled "Armenian Exodus from Harpoot," the American consul Jesse B. Jackson describes with precision, day after day, the trajectory of a convoy of 3,000 deportees that was put on the road on 1 June

1915 in Harput and integrated on the fifteenth day of its ordeal into a much larger caravan of 18,000 people (including only 300 men) who had come from Sıvas, Agn, and Tokat. On their sixty-fifth day on the road, after being systematically harassed by the çetes of the Special Organization, the deportees arrived in Ras ul-Ayn, where the last survivors were put on the train for Aleppo. Arriving in the Syrian metropolis on the seventieth day, the caravan now included only 35 women and children from the Harput convoy and 150 women and children from the main group – that is, fewer than 1 per cent of the deportees.[2] This, however, is no doubt an extreme case that should not be generalized to all the convoys that took the same route. The proportion of survivors was sometimes slightly higher: of a convoy of 400 people that came from Arğana Maden, 32 arrived in Aleppo; three of a group of 250 people expelled from Çımışkadzag in the Dersim area reached Aleppo.[3]

The second deportation route concerned approximately 425,000 Armenians from the vilayets of Dyarbekir, Bitlis, and the southern part of the vilayet of Van, some of whom were sent to Ras ul-Ayn in Syria by way of Dyarbekir and Mardin, while others were massacred locally or were able to flee. It is easier to evaluate the number of deportees in this case. We know that fewer than 20,000 people were deported from the region of Van and that fewer than 50 per cent of them reached their destination, while some 55,000 villagers from the vicinity of the city of Van were killed in April 1915[4] and some of the others reached Russia or were massacred en route. We have seen that in the vilayet of Bitlis a few thousand Armenians, primarily natives of Sasun, escaped the deportations and massacres carried out by the army and local Kurdish tribes in the plain of Mush and the region of Siirt.[5] At the very most, 60,000 people from Bitlis were sent southward; fewer than half arrived in Mesopotamia. This route was, in fact, taken essentially by the Armenians of Dyarbekir, the number of deportees from which, as we have seen, turned out to be substantially higher than the Armenian Patriarchate's population statistics indicate: the Patriarchate put the number of Armenians in Dyarbekir at 106,000, whereas the official Ottoman government figures put the number of deportees from this vilayet at 120,000.[6] Thus, we arrive at a total of 150,000 deportees who reached the gates of Syria or Mesopotamia.

The third deportation route, which followed the trajectory of the Bagdadbahn, concerned around 330,000 Armenians from Thrace, Constantinople, the Dardanelles, the mutesarifat of Ismit, and the vilayets of Bursa, Konya, Aydın, Kastamonu, and the western part of the vilayet of Angora. (Armenians from the other part of that vilayet, including Yozgat, were massacred in the region or sent down the first route by way of Malatia.) We have seen that these deportees were dispatched by rail or on foot toward Syria by way of Konya as far as the last station of the railroad, Bozanti.

Finally, it should be recalled that around 200,000 Armenians from the vilayet of Adana and the northern districts of the vilayet of Aleppo – with the exception of those allowed to remain in their homes – were, beginning in June 1915, sent by rail or on foot toward Syria in succeeding waves that followed one of two main routes. The first, taken by both deportees from the west and Armenians from the vilayet of Adana, led toward Bahçe; the second was taken by deportees from various regions who converged on Ayntab and proceeded toward Kilis. The deportees who followed this third route, because they traveled by rail or lived in the immediate vicinity of Syria, sustained relatively few losses en route. The losses they did suffer were due mainly to epidemics and famine, which raged notably in the transit camps of Konya and Bozanti, as well as to massacres perpetrated in Dörtyol, Zeitun, and Urfa. Thus, it seems reasonable to suppose, making allowances for the women and children abducted on the way, that around 600,000 Armenians concerned by the third deportation route arrived in Syria.

In other words, around 880,000 Armenians found themselves – in early summer 1915 in some cases, in fall 1915 in the others – "resettled" in Syria. This represents more than

40 per cent of the Armenians living in the Ottoman Empire on the eve of the First World War. Of the remaining 1,100,000 Ottoman Armenians, around 300,000 were not deported or managed to flee. This means that in fall 1915, during the first phase of the genocide, nearly 800,000 Armenians, the great majority from the eastern provinces, had already been liquidated or, in the case of a few thousand women and children, were being held in families, in harems, or by tribes.

The Arrival of the First deportees and the Establishment of the First Camps North of Aleppo

Between the deportations undertaken in the Armenian provinces in April-May 1915 and the creation of the Sub-Directorate for Deportees and its network of concentration camps from September 1915 on, a non-negligible flow of exiles reached the northern part of Mesopotamia and Syria over the course of the summer. Of course, no basic structures had been set up in advance to receive them. It seems, indeed, that the Interior Ministry gave thought to the problem of providing for the survivors only when it discovered that they were utterly disorganizing the strategic route by which the southern front communicated with Asia Minor. The growing numbers of rotting corpses on the sides of the road and the ensuing typhus epidemic that spread rapidly among the local populations also alarmed the prefects and sub-prefects, who were assailed by complaints from all sides. Thus, it became absolutely necessary that the ministry "disinfect" the region and take the measures required to establish a degree of order amid the reigning anarchy. The man concerned by these developments above all others, Cemal Pasha, wrote in his memoirs: "I was furious when I learned that the exiled Armenians were to come to Bozanti on their way over the Taurus and Adana to Allepo; for any interference with the line of communications might have the gravest consequences for the Canal [of Suez] Expedition."[7]

In fact, the first arrivals were the corpses that came floating down the Tigris or the Euphrates, depending on the regions concerned. By 10 June 1915, the German consul in Mosul, Holstein, was already wiring his ambassador to the effect that

> 614 Armenians (men, women, and children) expelled from Dyarbekir and conducted toward Mosul were all killed during the voyage by raft [on the Tigris]. The *keleks* arrived empty yesterday. For several days now, corpses and human members have been floating down the river. Other convoys of Armenian 'settlers' are currently en route, and it is probable that the same fate awaits them, too.[8]

The situation was still worse on the Euphrates, as a report by the German consul in Aleppo, Rössler, attests:

> The aforementioned presence of corpses in the Euphrates, which has been observed in Rumkale, Birecik, and Jerablus, continued for twenty-five days, as I was informed on 17 July. The bodies were all tied together in the same way, in pairs, back to back. This systematic arrangement shows that it is a question, not of random killings, but of a general extermination plan elaborated by the authorities... The corpses have reappeared, after an interruption of several days, in ever greater numbers. This time, it is essentially a question of the bodies of women and children.[9]

Thus, while the Euphrates made it possible to get rid of the corpses encumbering the northern provinces at small cost, they created problems for the local authorities in Syria and Mesopotamia. Certain authenticated documents mentioned during the trial of the Young

Turks, which confirm the information given by the German consul, show that this method was not to the taste of Cemal Pasha, the commander-in-chief of the Fourth Army, who had authority over the whole region. In a 14 July 1915 telegram to the vali of Dyarbekir, Reşid, the minister of the navy, complained about the fact that corpses were floating down the Euphrates. Two days later, Reşid wired back: "The Euphrates has very little to do with our vilayet. The corpses coming down the river have probably come from the provinces of Erzerum and Harput. Those who drop dead here are either thrown into deep abandoned caves or, as often happens, cremated. There is rarely any reason to bury them."[10]

Late in July, convoys of deportees from the regions to the north began reaching their destinations. On 27 July, Rössler stated:

> Recently, Armenians from Harput, Erzerum, and Bitlis passed through Ras ul-Ayn (currently the last stop of the Bagdad[bahn]). Reports about the Armenians from Harput indicate that the men were separated from the women in a village a few hours south of the city. They were massacred and their bodies were laid out on both sides of the road down which the women later marched.[11]

On 30 July, Rössler, again, evaluated the number of deportees who had arrived in Aleppo at 10,000, putting the number of those who had reached Der Zor at 15,000.[12] In a 24 July report, M. Guys, the retired French consul, reported "the passage of thousands of people, all Armenian Gregorians, through the city of Aleppo itself." He further noted that

> after a stay of two or three days in places set aside for them, these unfortunates, most of them boys, girls, women, or old men (the young men were assigned other destinations, where they are ostensibly to fulfill their military obligations), are ordered to leave for Idlib, Mârra, Rakka, Der Zor, Ras ul-Ayn, or the Mesopotamian desert, places that, it is generally assumed, are destined to become their tombs.[13]

In late May 1915, the first improvised camp for Cilician deportees from Zeitun, Dörtyol, and Hasan Beyli materialized north of Aleppo, in Bab.[14] The bulk of the convoys, however, arrived in July and August:

> Thousands of widows, without a single adult male, arrived in Bab; they came from the regions of Armenia by the Munbuc road, in an appalling state, half naked. They were supposed to go to Aleppo. A number of the first arrivals told us that they were natives of Kirg, located in the vilayet of Van. These people, as well as the ten to twenty groups who arrived after them, were in convoys made up of from five hundred to three thousand individuals, including hapless children in an indescribably miserable state.[15]

On 31 August, according to a precise evaluation made by Jesse B. Jackson, the American consul in Aleppo, 32,751 deportees had arrived in Aleppo by rail alone; 23,675 of them were adults and 9,076 were children.[16]

The Network of Transit and Concentration Camps North of Aleppo

Before arriving in Aleppo, the convoys passed through transit camps. Which one they passed through depended on the route they took. Thus, the deportees from Western Anatolia or Thrace who arrived by the third route in late summer and fall 1915 stayed in the camps of Konya and Bozanti before being sent on to Osmaniye, located in the foothills of the Amanus mountains in the easternmost part of the Cilician plain.[17] A transit camp had been set up in a place known as Kanlıgeçit near the Mamura railroad station. In the months of August, September, and October 1915, it received, on average, several tens of thousands of deportees: "Many of them were starving, many sick, and the sanitary conditions can be imagined ... One moment the tents were all in place, the next moment all could be seen was a mass of fleeing people. Some were pierced by the bayonets and killed, families were separated and lost each other, babies and old people were abandoned."[18] This improvised camp was regularly emptied of its population between July and December 1915, on orders from the Sub-Directorate for Deportees, which in this way pushed the survivors toward Islahiye, on the eastern slopes of the Amanus mountains. The *Sevkiyat müdürü* went to Kanlıgeçit to supervise evacuations in person: "He instructed a large number of policemen and hundreds of militiamen to surround this miserable throng of practically moribund people and, under threat of whip and club, ordered them to set out for Islahiye."[19] According to Yervant Odian, who passed through the camp in October, of the 40,000 deportees sent to Islahiye on the other side of the Amanus mountain chain, only half arrived.[20] However, according to reports by Paula Schäfer and Beatrice Rohner, who spent several weeks working to provide the deportees of Mamura with food and medical care, the camp again held "thousands of tiny low tents, made of thin material" between mid-November and mid-December.[21] Around 40,000 deportees seem to have found their final resting place there in the course of fall 1915.

To reach Islahiye and then the Syrian plain, the deportees followed a route that obliged them to cross the Amanus Mountains. According to Swiss missionaries, it was strewn with rotting corpses. The survivors took the road that led over the mountain crests through Hasanbeyli, then descended to the plain where the Bagdadbahn began again. Islahiye was the first concentration camp in the vilayet of Aleppo. "It is," a German missionary said, "the saddest thing I have ever see. Right at the entrance a heap of dead bodies lay unburied ... in the immediate neighbourhood of the tents of those who were down with virulent dysentery. The filth in and around these tents was something indescribable. On one single day the burial committee buried as many as 580 people."[22] Father Krikoris Balakian, who spent several months in the region and visited the camp in fall 1915, reports that the Sub-Directorate for Deportees, taking the lack of militiamen and means of transportation as an excuse, deliberately let the convoys that arrived in quick succession throng the camps, making it impossible to provide the deportees with the basic necessities and creating conditions that encouraged the spread of epidemics:

> People arrived by the thousands in Islahiye; only a few hundred were marched off every day ... There were days on which deportees in the tens of thousands of tents died, not by the dozens, but by the hundreds, while no healthy people could be found to collect and bury the dead ... The victims were, first and foremost, Armenian children ... The area spread out before us looked like a battlefield. The plain just beyond Islahiye was covered with countless earthen mounds, large and small. These were the graves of Armenians, containing fifty or a hundred bodies each ... Some, unfortunately, were as high as hills.[23]

We may estimate that 60,000 deportees died of starvation or typhus in the ten months that the Islahiye camp was in operation, from August 1915 to spring 1916.[24]

The camps in Rajo, Katma, and Azaz, located some 20 kilometers south of Islahiye on the road to Aleppo, were in operation only briefly in fall 1915, although a great many people lost their lives there in that short span. In an 18 October 1915 telegram, the interim consul in Aleppo, Hoffmann, informed his ambassador that the Director of Political Affairs in the vilayet (of Aleppo) estimated that there were 40,000 deportees concentrated in the camps of Rajo and Katma, and that other convoys "from Western, Central, and Northern Anatolia were on the way. Three hundred thousand people have to continue their route southward."[25] The camp in Rajo lay approximately one kilometer from the railroad station. At this time of the year, it was a vast marshland covered with tents. A deportee from Bandırma reported: "Corpses piled up in the tents. People who did not have tents had taken up quarters under the railroad bridge in order to protect themselves a little from the cold. A torrent caused by the rains suddenly inundated the spot and swept them off: they all drowned. There were bodies on all sides. Very few escaped with their lives."[26]

The neighboring camp of Katma, which also lay close to the railroad, offered a similar spectacle. Vahram Dadian, who arrived here on 6 September, observed that for every ten deportees who left the camp for the south, "a thousand arrive."[27] The shortage of food and the utter lack of hygienic conditions reigning in this tent city naturally bred disease, causing considerable human losses. At the sight of this spectacle, our witness understood that, unless he succeeded in leaving the camp in very short order, he would suffer the common fate – that is, starve to death or be carried off by an epidemic.[28] On 9 September, the catholicos, Sahag Khabayan, visited the camp at Katma but confesses that all his attempts to intercede with the authorities to improve the deportees' lot were in vain.[29]

Witness accounts give the impression that the strategy of the chiefs of the *Sevkiyat* was to let the deportees waste away in the camps so as to create conditions favoring the spread of epidemics. Thus, convoys never left the area promptly after arriving: the people the *Sevkiyat* chose to send further south were rather those who had already been sufficiently weakened by a prolonged stay in the camp. Two months after the catholicos's visit, on 8 November, Rössler informed the German Chancellor, Berthmann Hollweg, that "the concentration camp in Katma is an indescribable sight."[30] In a few weeks, the number of deportees there had indeed soared, briefly reaching a maximum of 200,000 internees. These people were ultimately "transferred, in the space of a few days, to Azaz, an hour's march away."[31] The accumulation of corpses and the general conditions prevailing in Katma no doubt convinced the heads of the *Sevkiyat* to transfer the camp to Azaz in order to resume operations on a virgin site.

The concentration camp in Azaz remained in operation somewhat longer, until spring 1916, but with fewer deportees. When the camp was created, a survivor noted that he could not say "with precision" how many tents had been pitched there, but that estimates ran between 15,000 and 20,000, "a number that [he] did not find exaggerated, because ... with the naked eye, it was impossible to see from one end to the other of this gigantic tent camp," in which dysentery was omnipresent, poverty "absolute," and the dead "past counting." A survivor reported that

> at night, [the population of the camp] was subject to attacks from people bent on plun-
> der ... The ground beneath the sagging tents, made of whatever was to hand, was strewn
> with the dead and dying. Many people were wasting away amid excrement, wracked
> by hunger. Odor and death reigned everywhere. Some used the dead as pillows; others
> stretched their dead over them as covers, to protect themselves as best they could from
> the cold ... The gravediggers were unable even to remove all the bodies ... Every day, a
> convoy was led away by force.[32]

According to Aram Andonian, 60,000 deportees perished in these two camps, carried off by famine or disease, in fall 1915.[33] Eyub Sabri, one of the chiefs of the Sub-Directorate for Deportees, seems to have personally supervised the departure of convoys from these camps. A witness describes one of Sabri's interventions as follows:

> I had never seen, anywhere, the methods that Eyub Bey used on the handful of con-
> voys under his escort. Astride a horse, surrounded by his accomplices, he attacked

the tents, trampling the sick lying on the ground under his horse's hooves... This was not enough to satisfy Eyub Bey; more exactly, galvanized by this spectacle, he would occasionally take his revolver from its holster and empty it on the throng of deportees.[34]

These camps were closed in late fall 1915 and the survivors were deported, for reasons that did not escape the German consul, Rössler. "In November and early December [1915]," he writes,

> deportees were massed the length of the railroad between Adana and Aleppo, especially in Islahiye and Katma[-Azaz]. For military reasons, the authorities wanted to remove them from this zone, so as to clear the army's rear and protect it from epidemics. They had begun to evacuate them to Ras ul-Ayn by rail, but, since what awaited them there was death and also because the train could not transport both soldiers and Armenians, the Armenians were finally conducted from Islahiye and Katma to Akhterim by foot, and from there to Bab.[35]

In other words, it was complaints from the military that prevented the *Sevkiyat* from accomplishing its mission in the area.

The camp in Bab is a case apart. Even before the influx, beginning in late May 1915, of deportees into the area, a transit camp had been set up a half-hour's distance from the city; it took in deportees who, until July, had been promptly scattered throughout the surrounding Arab villages.[36] The camp was run by the *kaymakam*, Şafi Bey, who held his post from 15 October 1914 to 27 March 1916, and the *Sevkiyat memuri*, Muharrim Bey. In August, when the deportees' numbers begin to increase, they were no longer allowed to settle in the Arab-speaking villages in the vicinity, but were held in a concentration camp set up by Muharrim. Established in a field of clay, the camp was transformed into a veritable lake whenever it rained. "The tents were immersed in water and filled with snow," remarked a survivor who had arrived in the camp late in December 1915.[37] In July and August, the population of the camp had momentarily soared as a result of the arrival

> of thousands of widows, without a single adult male; they came from the regions of Armenia by the Munbuc road, in an appalling state, half naked... These widows, as well as the ten to twenty convoys that arrived in their wake, were in caravans comprising from five hundred to three thousand individuals, including hapless children in an indescribably miserable state who resembled human monsters.[38]

They pursued their route toward Aleppo and the Syrian deserts after spending a few days or weeks in the camp. According to Andonian, it was in October 1915 that Bab acquired the status of a transit camp for convoys arriving from the north. The first director of the camp was a certain Jafer; he had soon been replaced by Şevket Bey.[39]

With the beginning of winter and the arrival of deportees from the camps of Islahiye and Katma-Azaz, typhus broke out in Bab. Four hundred to 500 people died there daily. So many deportees arrived every day that it was not enough to send convoys to the south to reduce the camp's population.[40] The head of the Sub-Directorate for Deportees, Abdüllahad Nuri; the director of the camp, Şevket Bey; and the new vali of Aleppo, Mustafa Abdülhalik, criticized Bab's *kaymakam*, Şafi Bey, for the slowness with which the deportees were being sent on to the south. It was probably due to the fact that the *kaymakam* was extorting money from them. The more determined director of the neighboring camp of Akhterim, Muharrim Bey, needed only two and a half months to empty his camp.[41]

In the system created by the heads of the *Sevkiyat*, designed to push the deportees from one camp to the next in stages, Bab and Akhterim were, in late autumn 1915, the last stations on the way to Aleppo. After the evacuation of the camps of Mamura, Rajo, and Katma, all the deportees who arrived from the north were crowded together there in sanitary conditions that witnesses describe as something out of Dante; they led to massive loss of life. Everything suggests that, in forcing the deportees to live in such dense human groups, the chiefs of the *Sevkiyat* had no other intention than gradually to eliminate them, relying on the effects of such massive concentrations and the action of nature. The system, which was undeniably effective, nevertheless generated undesirable side effects similar to those observed in the camps to the north. Epidemics spread throughout the region, affecting the civilian populations and the army. We know, for example, that 20 to 30 Arab villagers were dying daily of typhoid fever in Bab in winter 1915–16, despite snows that were unusually tenacious for these southern zones. The chiefs of the *Sevkiyat* must therefore have received categorical orders to improve the disastrous health conditions that they had themselves artificially created. To meet the emergency, Nuri appointed Muharrim to head the camp in Bab and charged him with liquidating it. It took him several months to complete the task. According to Aram Andonian, in January 1916, Aleppo decided to "completely cleanse the whole province of Aleppo of its Armenians." Even the first deportees, who had found refuge in the villages of the region, were ferreted out "and sent to the slaughterhouses of Der Zor." It must, however, be added that Muharrim's activity in Bab did not by itself suffice to implement this decision. Nuri Bey therefore appointed the military commander Süleyman Bey to assist him, along with 200 muleteers, as well as the *kaymakam* of Munbuc, Nebih Bey. Nebih "accomplished a remarkable feat in carrying out, in a week's time, the order he had received to send all the deportees of his region, Aleppo, to Meskene," in his capacity as *memuri maksus* (special delegate). The *kaymakam* of Kilis was also entrusted with a special mission. Thus, it appears that, after granting the deportees the possibility of settling as best they could in the villages of the region north of Aleppo, the authorities decided to send them further south to Meskene, while preventing them from passing by way of Aleppo itself.[42]

At the very least, 50,000 to 60,000 deportees lost their lives in Bab between October 1915 and the beginning of spring 1916, according to an account by Father Dajad Arslanian, who took it upon himself to bury the dead between late November 1915 and early February 1916.[43] These figures are confirmed by both the camp's chief gravedigger, a certain Hagop (the gravediggers, recruited from the ranks of the deportees, were allowed to stay with their families until the camps were shut down), who counted 1,209 deaths in two days, 11 and 12 January 1916, and the German consul, Rössler, who stated in a 9 February report that 1,029 people died in two days in the same camp.[44]

The deathtraps of Lale and Tefrice, located nearby on a secondary road that connected Bab and Meskene without passing through Aleppo, were, in the words of one deportee, "a veritable graveyard." People who had, "generally speaking, a life expectancy of a few days at best" were dumped here, "so that the destiny of these thousands of people would be accomplished far from the centers." According to Hovhannes Khacherian, a native of Bardizag, a scant 20 per cent of the people who passed through these camps ever reached Meskene.[45] This type of intermediate camp was basically a stretch of wasteland that could be supervised by only a minimal staff of a few militiamen or gendarmes. It made it possible to concentrate the dying in one place, so that the authorities could avoid leaving too many corpses lying on the sides of the roads. The information at our disposal indicates that these two sites, whose activities were closely bound up with those of the camps in Akhterim and Bab, were in operation from December 1915 to March 1916.

The last of the camps located north of Aleppo, Munbuc, is a very special case, because its main function from the outset had been to serve as a place of internment for Armenian clergymen, from the simple village priest to the primate of a diocese. Lying a few dozen kilometers northeast of Aleppo on the road to Ras ul-Ayn, the camp was set up in fall 1915 on Cemal Pasha's express demand, for the purpose of isolating the clergymen from the general population. At the high point of its activity, it was inhabited by as many as 1,000 *kahanas* (married priests) and their families. It was ultimately evacuated in January and February 1916 by the *kaymakam* of Munbuc, Nebih Bey, who personally saw to transferring the interned clergyman to Meskene, on the axis of the Euphrates.[46] In 1917, only 70 to 80 Armenians were still alive there, thanks to an Armenian patron who paid local officials regular bribes.

Yervant Odian, who found himself in this human flood in late November 1915, reports that rumors then making the rounds among the deportees indicated that they should do everything they could not to go beyond Aleppo and to avoid Der Zor and the camps in Katma and Rajo at all costs.[47] This indicates not only that information circulated among the exiles, but also that some of them were still capable of escaping the fate that the *Sevkiyat* had reserved for them. Despite local officials' laxity, which was probably motivated by the bribes they received, it was difficult to violate certain orders. For example, selling Armenians train tickets to Aleppo was prohibited – an order that was scrupulously respected. It was impossible to travel to the city clandestinely, Odian writes, for very thorough searches were carried out in every railroad station. The deportees therefore had to go on foot, without ever entering the city; it was even more difficult for them to stay in hotels, whose owners had received strict orders not to accommodate them.[48]

Chapter 3

Aleppo, the Center of the Genocidal System and of Relief Operations for the Deportees

Getting to Aleppo and finding refuge there was a life-and-death issue for many deportees. They hoped to melt into the urban tissue of this big city and take advantage of the aid that the Armenian community and foreign diplomats or missionaries living there were able to extend them. As for the authorities, after the improvisations of the first few weeks, during which thousands of deportees poured into the city, they quickly understood that, if their extermination plan was to succeed, it was indispensable to mobilize all available means to prohibit the deportees from entering the Syrian metropolis.

Around 5 June 1915, the American consul in Aleppo Jesse Jackson observed that several streams of deportees from Marash, Zeitun, Hasanbeyli, Osmaniye, Bahçe, Adana, Dörtyol, and Hacın were converging on Aleppo on foot and that 2,600 refugees to the city had been allowed to remain there.[1] When Kerovpe Papazian, the chief secretary of the archbishopric of Adana and the catholicos's representative with Cemal Pasha, passed through Aleppo on his return from Aley in mid-June, he witnessed the arrival of the first deportees from the north, basically of "women and children between the ages of eight and ten." They camped in the courtyards of the churches and schools and, above all, a monastery that belonged to the Congregation of St. James in Jerusalem (the *Hokedun*). Catholicos Sahag went to great lengths to ease the deportees' lot, even writing to Kaiser Wilhelm on the advice of the German consul, Rössler. Fifty to 70 people in Aleppo were dying of typhus or typhoid fever every day, despite the efforts of the Armenian relief committee that had been formed under the leadership of Sarkis Jierjian in order to provide the deportees with basic necessities and medical care. These deportees were for the most part only in transit in Aleppo; the police saw to it that they were rapidly expelled from the city.[2] According to Rössler, these first groups of exiles were dispersed in the villages to the east,[3] probably on the initiative of the vali, Cemal, or his successor. As late as the beginning of July, the American missionary Kate Ainslie saw convoys arriving in Aleppo, notably groups of deportees from Hacın.[4]

The parliamentary deputy Krikor Zohrab's correspondence with his wife during his one month's stay in Aleppo (from 16 June to 16 July 1915), where he was accompanied by Vartkes Seringiulian, provided an omen of things to come in the region. Zohrab wrote, lucidly, "The curtain is coming down."[5] While Zohrab was in Aleppo, Celal was transferred to Konya, after having admirably resisted the orders he had received from the capital.

The pace of events quickened from this point on. More and more deportees were streaming into the city every day. According to the American and German consuls Jackson and Rössler, who were surely the two men who knew the most about the treatment to which the Ottoman government had subjected the Armenian deportees, the authorities in Aleppo had gradually lost control over the situation. Rössler further noted that the deportees were not all treated the same way, but that the treatment they were meted out depended on where they came from: the Cilicians received aid from the authorities, albeit irregularly, whereas the Armenians native to the eastern provinces were denied all assistance.[6] Under these conditions, the cholera epidemic that broke out in the camps to the north reached Aleppo in September, forcing the authorities to evacuate the deportees from the city at a rate of around 4,000 to 5,000 a week. They were loaded onto stockcars or freight cars and sent to Damascus or the Hauran.[7] In September 1915, Dr. Martin Niepage, a German teacher in Aleppo's Deutsche Realschule, observed:

> I was told that there were large numbers of starving people in different quarters of Aleppo, the miserable vestiges of what were called "the columns of the deportation"...To see if the opinion I had formed on the basis of this information was justified, I visited every part of the city in which Armenians – what was left of the columns of deportees – were to be found. In run-down caravansaries [khans], I found piles of putrefying dead bodies and, among them, people still alive on the point of breathing their last. In other places, I found piles of sick and starving people left to fend for themselves. Around our school were four such khans, with seven hundred to eight hundred starving deportees in them...Opposite our school, in one of these khans, were the remains of one of these columns of deportees, around four hundred emaciated creatures, among whom were some one hundred children between the ages of five and seven. Most were suffering from typhus or dysentery. If one enters the courtyard, one has the impression that one is entering a madhouse. If one takes them food, it appears that they have forgotten how to eat. Their stomachs, weakened by months of hunger, can no longer bear food. If one gives them bread, they put it aside, indifferently; they lie there, quietly, waiting for death...And what will become of the unfortunates, now just women and children, who are being hunted down throughout the city and its environs and driven into the desert by the thousands? They are pushed from place to place until the thousands are reduced to hundreds, and the hundreds to a little group, and this group is still driven elsewhere, until nothing at all is left of it. With that, the purpose of the journey has been attained.[8]

Not until early November 1915 did the authorities deny the deportees access to Aleppo, while also prohibiting them from taking trains to the south in the direction of Damas and the Hauran. From this point on, they were systematically dispatched by foot or rail, either "along the trajectory of the Bagdadbahn" toward Ras ul-Ayn or along the "trajectory of the Euphrates" toward Der Zor.[9] These radical measures were probably not unrelated to the simultaneous arrival two weeks earlier of the new vali, Mustafa Abdülhalik, and Abdüllahad Nuri, now at the head of a reinforced Sub-Directorate for Deportees. From now on, we no longer have to do, as in the provinces of the interior, with a mere representative of the Istanbul IAMM, even if he bore the title of *Sevkiyat müdürü*, but with a veritable administrative apparatus that proceeded to create the network of concentration camps along the Euphrates. Preventing the deportees from taking the roads leading south, which had a reputation for being less murderous because there were no concentration camps strung out along them, and replacing those roads with the trajectories of the Bagdadbahn and the Euphrates as destinations, were measures with the sole aim of more effectively destroying the deportees. Moreover, in an 8 November 1915 dispatch to his embassy, the German vice-consul in Alexandretta, Hoffmann, reported remarks made by Abdüllahad Nuri's newly appointed assistant Ahmed Eyub Sabri that left no doubt as to the policy the government had decided to pursue: "You still don't understand what we want; we want to eradicate the Armenian name," Nuri had said.'"[10]

Despite the hopes that Aleppo inspired in the deportees who wished to avoid being sent to the camps to the east or southeast, it was difficult to access. The city was swarming with policemen and undercover agents who were kept abreast of developments by a vast network of informants, including Armenians such as Arshavir Sahagian.[11] Once one had managed to enter the city, however, it was always possible to find a hideout. In actual practice, the presence of thousands of Armenians living underground was the more readily tolerated in that it provided a host of city officials, policemen, and even military personnel with an unhoped-for source of income. What might be called "the rules of the game" were gradually established, and it was very rare that someone who had been able to retain money or valuables was unable to come to an understanding with local officials. Such, at any rate, was the situation that prevailed until Abdülhalik and Nuri were named to their posts in October 1915. Their arrival did not, however, suffice to put a complete stop to the self-interested benevolence of local government officials. They had to wage no less than a ten-month struggle to call a real halt to the stream of deportees who had succeeded in hiding in Aleppo.

The Official and Underground Armenian Information and Relief Networks Operating in Aleppo and the Surrounding Region

Early on, at the initiative of the Catholicos Sahag II Khabayan, who had taken refuge in Aleppo in late June, a Refugee Relief Committee was formed by eminent members of the city's Armenian community,[12] which then numbered around 13,000 and had a reputation for being well organized. Community members who had resided for at least ten years in the Syrian metropolis had been exempted from deportation. The Refugee Committee's activities consisted of taking in orphans and finding lodgings for deportees who had gotten as far as Aleppo. Sahag II repeatedly met with Cemal Pasha, the master of the region, in this period; on each occasion, he tried to bring him to take measures that would alleviate the deportees' suffering. The Armenian Protestant and Catholic churches organized their own relief networks.[13]

Early in November, however, probably at the initiative of the new vali Abdülhalik, Sahag II and his entourage were forced to move to Jerusalem.[14] In the meantime, the arrival in Aleppo of many deportees from Istanbul, such as Dr. Boghosian, who was appointed interim municipal physician,[15] made possible the creation of an underground network that gradually solidified its structures and extended its operations throughout not only Aleppo but the whole of the surrounding region as well – indeed, it had connections that reached as far as the capital.[16] In addition to Boghosian, a psychiatrist, the group included experienced militants such as Marzbed[17] and Ghazar Charek. Above all, it could count on the help of local notables, such as the brothers Onnig and Armenag Mazlumian, the owners of the famous Baron Hotel and close friends of Cemal Pasha's, a host of Armenian railroad officials[18] whom the government could not do without, and widely respected individuals such as the Protestant ministers Aharon Shirajian, who had come from Marash, and Hovhannes Eskijian. A sort of division of labor sprang up among these men: some concentrated their efforts on orphans (the two ministers), the others on saving and hiding young men and intellectuals, gathering information, and setting up a network that distributed direct assistance to deportees as far away as Der Zor. The benevolent attitude of the consul Jesse Jackson and – with certain, easily understandable reservations – Walter Rössler facilitated the transfer of the considerable sums that the network needed to help the deportees.[19] The Swiss missionary Beatrice Rohner and her colleague Paula Schäfer played an exceptionally important role in organizing the relief operations and obtaining extensive financial aid. Both of them belonged to the German missionary organization known as the *Deutscher Hülfsbund für christliches*

Liebeswerk. This, as well as the backing of Dr. Fred Shepard of the American hospital in Ayntab, helped them secure resources that had been collected in the United States by the American Board of Commissioners for Foreign Missions.[20]

Although the interior minister found out, late in July 1915, that two Armenian emissaries sent from Aleppo to Der Zor were distributing money to the deportees there and had issued orders for their arrest,[21] many others were not discovered and accomplished their missions without arousing suspicion. Thus, Marzbed masqueraded as a Kurdish animal trader from Bitlis by the name of Haci Hüseyin. He traveled under this identity as far as the construction site of the *Bagdadbahn* in Intilli, where he was recruited as a financial controller by the German firm.[22] Educated in Germany and fluent in German, Marzbed/Haci Hüseyin very certainly benefited from the protection of the Company's German officers and took advantage of his privileged status in order to travel without constraint and render his compatriots untold services.

The writer Yervant Odian, for example, succeeded in making his way into Aleppo thanks to the help of Pilig Arpiarian, a railroad official, and was then taken in hand by Dr. Boghosian, who found him a hiding place in the city. There he was often in the company of Reverend Kruzian, the director of an orphanage under the patronage of a German woman and a friend of Cemal's, who tolerated this Armenian institution. There he also met the one man deported from Trebizond to have arrived safely in Aleppo, Gaydzag Arabian. When he encountered problems, he turned, as a matter of course, to Onnig Mazlumian, whose Baron Hotel, while frequently occupied by the general staff of the Fourth Army, was a haven for intellectuals who had been swept up in the stream of deportees.[23] One of the network's activities consisted in saving the lives of men of letters, out of an awareness that the "survival of the nation" could be assured only if they were given priority over others.

Aram Andonian, who, protected by the Mazlumian brothers, had remained in hiding for months, began to collect material bearing on the liquidation of his compatriots very early in the day. Extensive use of this material has been made in the fourth part of the present study. In the Baron Hotel, Andonian saw those chiefly responsible for the genocide strolling past or dining at the expense of the hoteliers. Some did not hesitate to declare what had brought them to Syria.

It was of course impossible that the energetic efforts of Mazlumian brothers, the Barons, would go unperceived by the Young Turk government. When they were discovered, the two brothers were exiled to Zahle, in the Bekaa Plain, in September 1916. Another personality in the city, Dr. Samuel Shmavonian, who provided free medical care to the children in an orphanage founded by Reverend Aharon Shirajian, was brought to trial and sentenced to 15 years in prison. After being regularly tortured, he was "set free," but in such a state that he soon succumbed to his wounds.[24] His liquidation led to the elimination of certain sources of aid.

The repressive actions undertaken by the vali Abdülhalik did not completely cut off the flow of refugees into Aleppo because of the sheer size of the city, which prevented the authorities from controlling everything. Some managed to enter the city in secret; the more affluent were able to bribe government officials. But the greatest number of deportees was saved above all thanks to the solidarity network forged in Aleppo with the active support of American diplomats and missionaries. This network worked so effectively that by late 1915 Aleppo had been thronged by 40,000 illegal deportees.[25] The authorities, informed of the support that foreign consular services were giving these pariahs, issued them strict instructions not to give any form of assistance to the Armenians. Notwithstanding this prohibition, some Western diplomats and missionaries, particularly the Americans, unhesitatingly made personal commitments to aiding the victims. The American missions were even able to collect 100,000 dollars for the benefit of "disaster victims" in the Near East.[26] The U.S. consul Jesse Jackson administered this fund.

The most important task, however, was to hide the thousands of widows and children who had taken refuge in the city. Many were placed with families, Christian families in general and Armenian families in particular; the girls and women were most often employed as domestics. But the food shortages affecting the city thwarted the development of this system, which was also hampered by harassment from the authorities, who sought to block humanitarian activities benefiting the Armenians by all means at their disposal.[27]

The American consul subsidized the German *Hülfbund* and provided a monthly stipend to the Relief Committee that had been founded by Aleppo's Armenian prelacy. Jackson notes that in the same period two Armenian notables from Aleppo interceded with Ahmed Cemal, the commander of the Fourth Army, on behalf of their compatriots who had found refuge in the city. They suggested that Cemal put these deportees to work for the army without pay. The American consul does not say who these notables were, but Armenian sources indicate that one of them was Dr. Altunian.[28] Cemal Pasha accepted the suggestion and, in the space of two months, six factories went into operation that employed more than 10,000 people, mostly women and girls.[29] They spun wool and made clothes to meet the army's needs. As for the rare Armenian men in the city, they worked as blacksmiths, tailors, or carpenters. Treated like slaves and working in abominable conditions, they received as their sole recompense just enough food for subsistence.[30]

The typhus epidemic brought on by the massive numbers of Armenian deportees in Aleppo naturally drew the attention of the commander of the Fourth Army and the German officers on his general staff, especially when it began to affect their troops and precipitated a veritable health disaster.[31] Urgent measures were needed to get the better of this scourge. Cemal consequently had no choice but to approve of plans to open a hospital, directed by Dr. Altunian, for the purpose of treating the Armenian deportees.[32]

The other major problem was the catastrophic situation of the thousands of orphans who had crowded into Aleppo and been abandoned to their fate. These children wandered through the streets famished and ill. Some were adopted by local families, but most had to go without assistance of any kind. One of them, Antranig Dzarugian, would later write that, in order to obtain food, they formed gangs that attacked stores in the city, sometimes at the cost of their lives.[33] In this domain, the most important initiative taken in Aleppo was beyond a doubt the 31 July 1915 creation of an orphanage by Reverend Aharon Shirajian. The fact that an institution of this sort could be founded in a period when the authorities were enacting their plan to liquidate the Armenians may seem paradoxical. However, the orphanage was opened at a time when deportees were flooding into Aleppo and before the appointment of Abdülhalik to the post of vali. Most importantly, the initiative was supported by the American and German consuls, as well as the German-Swiss mission. It was because they interceded with Cemal Pasha that the institution was created.[34] But its creation was above all due to Shirajian's courage and determination. A deportee from Marash who had himself found refuge in Aleppo, he lost no time in organizing humanitarian action, gathering up abandoned children, usually sick or dying, in a house located beside the German consulate in the Akaba neighborhood that had been put at his disposal free of charge by a Swiss businessman established in Aleppo, Emil Zollinger.[35] Every day, children suffering from cholera, typhus, trachoma, or dysentery, often reduced to skin and bone, arrived at the orphanage, where Shirajian took in all of them without exception, while Dr. Shmavonian treated them until his arrest. This improvised orphanage was in fact a modest building with a straw-covered floor that served as a dormitory. Although children frequently died there, the orphanage nevertheless rendered great services. In the following months, Shirajian enlarged his institution by renting two more houses, thanks especially to Dr. Asadur Altunian, an Armenian notable who was known to have friendly relations with Cemal. Altunian, the director of a reputable hospital in which several high-ranking Ottoman leaders had received treatment, had many relations on which he was able to call throughout the war in order to protect Shirajian's orphanage. Ranking Ottoman officials made a number of attempts to have the orphanage shut down, and Shirajian himself was repeatedly imprisoned and threatened with deportation. On one occasion, local government officials entered certain of the buildings and removed 80 orphans, who were then expedited to the desert.[36] Every time, however, Altunian and the German consul both interceded with Cemal and succeeded in saving the orphanage and its director.

Furthermore, throughout the war, Altunian's daughter Nora provided the minister with competent help in running the orphanage by organizing fundraising campaigns in the Armenian community.[37] When the number of children in the institution increased to the point that this aid did not suffice to support all of them, the young woman went so far as to appeal directly to Cemal, who thereupon ordered the army to furnish the orphanage with the food and supplies it needed. But the most important act in the history of the orphanage occurred no doubt when Cemal signed a decree ordering the local authorities to cease interfering in its activities.[38] It is, of course, unimaginable that a charitable institution of this kind could have survived on Ottoman territory without the active backing of Aleppo's Americans and Germans. Zollinger, who, though a Swiss citizen, had served as a German consul in Aleppo, played the role of a middleman between the Americans, Germans, and Swiss on the one hand, and Shirajian on the other, making possible the transfer of significant amounts of money to the orphanage.[39] At war's end, the number of orphans in the institution had reached 1,500.[40] One detail is symptomatic of the general situation: all Shirajian's efforts to introduce courses in Armenian into the orphanage were strictly forbidden by the authorities. Their involuntary tolerance obviously had its limits.

Yielding to insistent demands from the German *Hülfsbund*'s Swiss missionaries Paula Schäfer and Beatrice Rohner, Cemal authorized them, in late December 1915, to open another orphanage in Aleppo. It, too, was destined to take in abandoned Armenian children, albeit under the supervision of the local authorities. The need to improve health conditions in the city was the main argument that the two missionaries had used to bring the pasha round.[41] Around 400 children found shelter in this institution. It had the backing of the German consul, Rössler, and benefited from American financial support.[42] It will, however, readily be imagined that the German mission's promotion of humanitarian actions benefiting the Armenian deportees was perceived by the central Ottoman authorities as a dangerous precedent to be stopped at all costs. It was probably with a view to putting an end to this undertaking that the interior minister, Talât, sent two circular telegrams, dated 23 March and 3 April 1916, to the local authorities, "reminding" them that the Ottoman government alone was authorized to administer aid to the deportees and that, consequently, all authorizations granted foreigners were illegal. The circulars called for punishing all government officials who had broken this rule.[43]

The Aleppo Relief Committee also cared for a few hundred orphans in the school adjoining the Church of the Forty Martyrs. These orphans were under the supervision of K. Kruzian.[44]

The Transit Camps on the Outskirts of Aleppo

While the first deportees to arrive in Aleppo in summer and early fall 1915 were temporarily settled in its caravansaries, as we have seen from November on, the vali Mustafa Abdülhalik prohibited the convoys from entering the city and systematically redirected them down the Euphrates or Baghdad railway toward Mosul. It was probably on his orders that the Sub-Directorate for Deportees created the first transit camp an hour to the east of the city in Sibil, a vast plain leading on to the Syrian Desert. This camp was put under the supervision of Selanikli Eyub Bey, a çete leader and an assistant to the *Sevkiyat müdüri*. Cemil Hakim Bey, the *Sevkiyat memuri*, administered it.[45] Every day, a convoy arrived at the camp while another left it, bound for Meskene and Der Zor. Hence there were always several thousand deportees in Sibil.

An institution set aside for Armenians was nevertheless maintained in the city – the immense caravansary in the Achiol neighborhood. In the courtyard of this caravansary, christened Kaşıldıh, stood a number of huge tents that served as a prison. This camp was reserved for both adult Armenian males who, miraculously, were still to be found in the convoys arriving in Aleppo and people hiding in the city who the police or gendarmerie had apprehended on one of their countless nighttime roundups. After being held for around three weeks in these frightful surroundings, these men were also put on the road, under heavy guard.[46] So many people died in Kaşıldıh that, Rössler writes, "it was decided in mid-October to create a new cemetery outside the city. However, before the authorities could begin to bury the dead there, the corpses were dumped in it in one big pile and lay out in the open for several days."[47]

A second camp was set up near Aleppo, in Karlık, near a village in the city's northern outskirts. The camp lay skirted the railway. According to the American consul Jackson, an average of 500 tents were to be found in Karlık at any given time. Two thousand to 3,000 deportees lived in them under appalling conditions, with virtually no water. One hundred people died there every day.[48]

Yervant Odian, who spent time in Sibil in late November 1915, saw thousands of tents there, occupied by Armenians from Bardizag, Rodosto, Adabazar, and Edirne, with a "small number" of others from Harput, Dyarbekir, and Afionkarahisar.[49] According to Odian, Cemal had authorized 300 families to go to "Sham" – that is, toward Homs-Hama and Damascus – to work as craftsmen in military enterprises. Tailors, shoemakers, tinsmiths, and so on were in especially high demand. Of course, everyone tried to get his name on the list of people setting out for the south, since that was the equivalent of a passport for life. This administrative *vezikat* was so sought after that the *vezikats* made out to individuals who had subsequently died were, as a Turkish book attests, negotiated at very high prices. Odian, who had no skills as a craftsman, renamed himself Asadur and gave himself out as a native of Bahçecik/Bardizag.

While waiting to leave the camp in his turn, Odian witnessed terrible scenes. He mentions notably a ditch dug on the edge of a camp into which every morning those who had died the night before were thrown; the dead were first and foremost victims of the dysentery epidemic that raged in Sibil in early December 1915. He also observes that Turks, Arabs, and Jews from Aleppo who wanted children came to the camp to buy boys and girls from their parents. Storms, the cold, and rain particularly decimated those who did not have tents; the food shortage did in the rest. In this environment, ethical and moral standards went by the boards. Mothers often opposed the sale of their children and did not always allow themselves to be convinced by the prospective buyers, who argued out that they were going to die in any case and that their children at least would be saved. Some of the mothers who initially agreed to such sales went mad or became feeble-minded shortly after handing over their progeny. The children in greatest demand were those between seven and ten years of age, especially girls. Thousands of boys and girls were sold in this way by their parents.[50] A few lucky deportees from Harput were saved by Dr. Klejian, a municipal physician in Aleppo, himself a Harput native, who took them into his home.[51] To a certain extent, Aleppo's Relief Committee managed to alleviate the suffering of these Armenians in transit in the city by mobilizing various methods to funnel them the financial aid that the Armenian Patriarchate of Constantinople regularly sent the committee by different channels wherever the heads of the camps were willing to take bribes – which is to say, virtually everywhere.[52]

In the camp in Mârra, a short distance to the west of Aleppo, there were, on average, 600 families of deportees at any given time in winter 1915–16 – that is, around 3,000 to 4,000 people – under the authority of Tevfik Bey, the *kaymakam*. Settled there on an express order from Cemal Pasha, who also ordered that wheat be distributed to the deportees, these exiles constituted an exemplary case of population "displacement"; the camp in no way resembled the typical immense camps that were nothing but deathtraps. Despite Cemal's orders, the *kaymakam* organized a number of small convoys and dispatched them to the Syrian deserts, probably as the result of an intervention by the Sub-Directorate of Deportees. It seems likely that he did so, however, in order to frighten the other deportees and relieve them of substantial sums in exchange for a promise not to send them off, too. This particular situation lasted only until the following spring, when Consul Rössler informed his ambassador that "on 16 April, the Armenians 'settled' in Mârra and the surrounding villages were forced to depart in the direction of Der Zor."[53]

By preventing the deportees from passing by way of Aleppo, the authorities were probably also seeking to hide their actions from foreign witnesses as best they could. We have seen, in this connection, that thanks to the Armenian underground network the patriarch continued to be informed of the situation and could communicate the information he received to diplomatic circles. Zaven reports that he regularly received news about Konya from Mesrob Naroyan, thanks to Armenian railroad employees, and about Aleppo, albeit less frequently, thanks to Catholicos Sahag II. For example, Sahag was able to forward to the patriarch, with the help of Rössler's wife and the dragoman of the German embassy, Hayg Taykesenian, a precise description of the situation at the moment when the convoys stopped arriving in Aleppo.[54] Mehmed Talât complained, in a wire that he sent Mustafa Abdülhalik, his brother-in-law, on 1 December 1915, that "[t]he American consuls are obtaining information by secret means," a statement that makes his denials that he knew about the conditions under which the deportation took place still more dubious. "It is," he wrote,

> crucial to our policy of the moment to convince foreigners traveling in that area that the sole purpose of this deportation is to change people's places of residence. For this reason, it is important, for the time being, to exhibit tactful behavior in order to preserve the forms, and to apply the known methods only in localities where they are appropriate. To this end, I firmly recommend that you arrest people who reveal information or conduct investigations and bring them, on other pretexts, before a court-martial.

An interesting detail should be noted here: this document bears a marginal note by the Sub-Director General for Deportees, Abdüllahad Nuri, to whom the telegram was transmitted.[55]

Chapter 4

The Camps in Suruc, Arabpunar, and Ras ul-Ayn and the Zones of Relegation in the Vilayet of Mosul

As the deportations came to an end, the Armenian deportees were grouped in several centers along the eastern trunk of the Bagdadbahn. One of these centers was Suruc, a small town of 10,000 inhabitants located a few dozen kilometers south of Urfa, ten hours' distance from the railroad. The families of some 30 Armenian craftsmen from Urfa had been settled here in 1915. Apart from the men who had been mobilized, a dozen heads of families had been murdered well before the convoys of deportees arrived; the women and children had then been invited to convert.[1]

The Deportees of Suruc

A witness from Sıvas, G. Kapigian, related how he lived for three months in this primarily Kurdish town, the seat of a *kaza* that was administratively attached to the mutesarifat of Urfa. This convoy of *yesir* (prisoners of war) – the local population's word for the Armenian deportees – that arrived in Suruc on 5/18 September 1915 was stationed in a field located near the exit from the city, where four big tents had been set up. Pitching the tents was more or less all that the authorities had done to accommodate these *yesir*, many of whom were ill. The municipal physician could only remind them that "we are not allowed to give sick deportees medicine."[2] It was also impossible to send a telegram to a friend or family member in the capital to request that he or she send money. The survivors in this convoy, who had been pillaged on the way, had all but run out of resources and understood that they were going to suffer the fate of a group of the few hundred women and children who had arrived before them, whose corpses lay rotting behind the city's khan as food for dogs.[3] The khan, consisting of miniscule cells, was in fact a deathtrap into which the authorities packed those deportees who were devoured by lice and disease and had only a few hours to live.[4] These deportees were Armenians from Sıvas and Zara who had been brought to Suruc by way of Fırıncilar, where Kapigian had crossed their path a few weeks earlier. Wryly, he expressed his surprise over the magnificent "creation of the scientific spirit" that this "microbe incubator" invented by the Young Turks represented.[5] For Kapigian, there could be no doubt that an institution like the khan in Suruc, which the authorities had christened a "hospital," had been conceived of as microbe factories for the purpose of killing their "patients."[6] Once still-healthy deportees had been put in these houses of death, they rapidly lost their capacities and sank into a physical and moral decline that could end only one way. The Interior Ministry's incessant requests for information from local government officials about how many depor-tees had recently arrived, where they had come from, and how many were still alive were doubtless motivated by only one desire – to evaluate the effects of these genocidal practices and add to the ministry's statistics.

The deportees' camp had received two visits. One was from the municipal physician, a Jew, who had explained to the camp's inmates that the local authorities lacked the means required to feed them and that they would have to continue to fend for themselves until they reached Aleppo. A few days later, Kapigian encountered six Armenian women that the physician was keeping in his home. The other visit was from the commander of the gendarmerie, who contented himself with touring the camp and picking out one or two young women for his harem, which had already acquired respectable dimensions. The *kaymakam* himself was holding five such women. Furthermore, many Turkish and Kurdish families helped themselves to children, especially little girls under ten.[7] This phenomenon was so widespread that it gives us reason to wonder whether this infatuation with young Armenians, with its biological connotations, did not originate in a campaign conducted by the authorities.

The fact that the second caravan from Erzerum, comprising Armenians from throughout the Erzerum region, arrived in Suruc in late November was itself a curiosity. Originally made up of around 10,000 people who had been put on the road on 18 June 1915,[8] the convoy had, to be sure, been partially purged of its men, who were massacred after it passed through Fırıncılar, in Kanlıdere, by the *çete* chief Zeynel.[9] Yet, its members had reached Suruc after suffering only a minimum of losses, in good order and even apparently good health, at least in comparison with their kinsmen from the Sıvas region. This case, which proves that it was not, in fact, impossible to "displace" Armenians populations without destroying them, indicates what conditions were required to escape the common fate.

The first explanatory factor put forward by the members of the convoy was money: deported very early, at a time when certain measures affecting the Armenians' assets had not yet been adopted by the central authorities, this group had benefited from a certain indulgence on the part of the vali, Tahsin Bey, who had suggested to the deportees that they deposit their money in the bank and take checks with them. In so doing, he had saved them from being looted en route and made it possible for them to make use of their means as effectively as possible in order to bribe the various government official and tribal chiefs whom they encountered from one end of their journey to the other. Whereas the deportees who were carrying cash were quite likely to pay and be massacred nonetheless, the Erzerum Armenians maintained an ability to negotiate that stemmed from their financial independence.

The second decisive factor had to do with the means of transport that the deportees were able to obtain upon setting out and keep until they reached Suruc. Thanks to their horse-drawn wagons or ox-carts, they had been able to take with them what they needed for the journey: bedding, tents, food and supplies. Above all, they had been able to avoid travelling thousands of kilometers on foot, maintain minimal health standards, and avoid epidemics.[10] In other words, this group was never caught up, unlike the great majority of the other convoys, in the spiral leading to physical and moral degradation. Kapigian observes that the savoir-faire possessed by the men, who had experience in conducting the toughest kinds of negotiations, provides the rest of the explanation for their success. Aware of the danger awaiting them in the deserts of Syria or Mesopotamia, a delegation from the second convoy from Erzerum paid the *kaymakam* of Suruc a "courtesy visit." After conferring with one another, these men had come to the conclusion that they would have to negotiate the right to stay where they were with the local authorities. They were able to "convince the *kaymakam* of their loyalty to the fatherland and provide him with testimonials of their esteem for him" by tactfully offering him gifts out of range of prying eyes. The *kaymakam* of Suruc could obviously not issue an "official order" allowing these exemplary individuals to remain as long as they wished, but he could, for example, look the other way when these families rented houses in the town – the more so as the populace also benefited from this unlooked for source of income. The *kaymakam*'s "benevolence" also profited deportees from other regions who had managed to flee the camp in Arabpunar and take refuge in Suruc. Late in December, they were even able to make use of the services of the local agricultural bank in order to cash checks and found commercial enterprises.[11] On several occasions, particularly when the authorities set out to defeat the Armenians of the neighboring city of Urfa, tensions rose somewhat in Suruc, and the roughly 15,000 Armenian deportees in the city were threatened with expulsion to the desert.[12] They even camped for almost one month at a half-hour's distance from the city. Many of them, however, were able to go back to Suruc and its environs once the tensions had abated.[13] In winter 1915–16, the local authorities had to organize several convoys to the desert, probably in order to avoid sanctions that the capital threatened to impose; they did not, however, empty the region of all its deportees. Kapigian notes that a number of people from the poorest families fell victim to malnutrition and disease. Thereafter, the interior minister demanded an exact count of the Armenians in the region.[14] Certain deportees tried to make themselves indispensable by creating a trade school in which the young women of the city could acquire manual skills and learn to read and write. Although these proposals were hard to reconcile with local social practices and surprised a good many people, others, such as the mayor of Suruc, turned the occasion to account, encouraging the initiative.[15]

As a result of pressure from the deportees, Suruc was transformed accordingly over the months into a place of relegation that was more or less secure for a number of them. According to Kapigian, of the nearly 700 Armenians who had set out from the region of Sıvas, listed in his account by their family names, 120 survived until they were expelled from Suruc for good.[16] But even these vestiges of the convoys eventually attracted the central authorities' attention. A military inspector dispatched by the court-martial in Urfa came to conduct an investigation in Suruc. The *kaymakam* and commander of the gendarmerie were the first to be threatened, accused of having benefited from the Armenians' generosity. The deportation order was finally made public on 1 January 1916: it applied to the refugees and the handful of (Islamicized) local families, who were ordered to set out for Rakka in five days at the latest.[17] Not even Erzerum's businessmen were able to escape this ultimate roundup. On Sunday, 9 January, the convoy, comprising a total of 1,851 people, was put on the road to Rakka, guarded by gendarmes.[18]

The Transit Camp in Arabpunar

Some ten kilometers further south, near the Arabpunar train station, another transit camp had been set up near a small lake.[19] Around 25 September 1915, 15,000 deportees, most of whom came from the vilayet of Sıvas, camped here under conditions that were precarious, to say the least. Shortly thereafter, epidemics broke out, carrying off between 120 and 170 victims daily; Kapigian says that 4,000 people died here in six weeks. By mid-November, the camp was empty. Some of its population had been sent to Ras ul-Ayn and on to Der Zor or Mosul; others succeeded in hiding for a while in Suruc and villages in the vicinity.[20]

The Camp in Ras ul-Ayn

Located east of Urfa and south of Dyarbekir, in a particularly desolate region near the outer limits of Syria and Mesopotamia, Ras ul-Ayn had been, before the Baghdad Railway went in, a simple way station comprising 20 or so households of Chechens who had been settled here by the Ottoman sultans after the 1877–8 Russo-Turkish War. In 1914, it was still the modest seat of a *kaza*; the following year, it became one of the main concentration camps for Armenian deportees. A remote spot far from the eyes of the curious, the village was gradually transformed into a vast "resettlement" center in late summer and in fall 1915. First, however, countless convoys from the Armenian provinces passed through it; the routes they took converged near Urfa and Ras ul-Ayn. The first deportees to arrive here came in mid-July; they were natives of Harput, Erzerum, and Bitlis.[21] In approximately the same period, the American consul in Baghdad, Charles P. Brissel, noted in a report that the vali of Baghdad, when he had been the prefect of the *sancak* of Mardin, "began at and near Mardin, persecutions against the Armenians and sent them to Ras ul-Ayn. There is a report in Baghdad that the Armenians sent to Ras ul-Ayn were massacred some time after their arrival at that place or en route to it."[22] Subsequently, many other convoys coming from Urfa, where the first and second deportation routes intersected, also arrived in Ras ul-Ayn. We have, however, less information about the operations conducted in this region than about those in the camps in the western areas, for the diplomats who were stationed the closest to Ras ul-Ayn, the German consul Holstein and the American consul Brissel, lived in Mosul and Baghdad, more than 300 and 500 kilometers away, respectively, on the edge of the Mesopotamian desert, while Rössler and Jackson found it extremely difficult to follow developments from Aleppo. In his 13 August 1915 report, Rössler nevertheless revealed that he had been "able to obtain precise information about another group that had left Adiyaman [northeast of Urfa]. Of the six hundred ninety-six people who set out, three hundred twenty-one arrived in Aleppo: two hundred six men and fifty-seven women were killed."[23] These figures attest the harassment to which the deportees were subjected on this road, which connected Malatia, a place of junction for the caravans of deportees, to Urfa and Ras ul-Ayn by way of Adiyaman. In the same report, Rössler wrote: "A group from Sıvas which arrived here [in Aleppo] on 12 August had been en route for three months and was utterly exhausted. A few of them died almost as soon as they arrived."[24] The only outside account is provided by an Austrian officer who spoke Turkish, Lismayer, who had for 20 years been working on building the railroad in the area. For obvious reasons, his name is not mentioned by Rössler or the missionary from Urfa, Jacob Künzler, who transmitted the information that he was given by this engineer to Aleppo.[25] However, Balakian, who met him several weeks later, reveals his name when he mentions his account:[26]

> It was in the last days of October [1915]. Lismayer had been busy constructing a narrow-gauge railway between Sorğana and Ras-ul-Ayn when he saw a large column coming from the north and slowly descending toward Ras-ul-Ayn ... This mass of people moved slowly down the road, and only when it had drawn near did the Austrian realize that the army was made up, not of soldiers, but of an immense convoy of women guarded by gendarmes. On some estimates, there were as many as forty thousand women in the convoy ... There was not a single man among them.[27]

Another engineer working on the Bagdadbahn, M. Graif, informed Dr. Niepage, a professor in Aleppo, "that along the entire trajectory of the railroad leading to Tell Abida and Ras ul-Ayn were piles of naked corpses of raped women," while the German consul in Mosul, who had traveled on the road between Mosul and Aleppo, "had seen, in several places on the way, so many severed children's hands that the road could have been paved with them."[28] Another German consul and military officer, Scheubner-Richter, reports in a 5 November 1915 travel account: "From Erzerum to Mosul, traveling by way of Hinis, Mush, Bitlis, and Siirt, I saw that all the villages and houses once inhabited by Armenians had been sacked and were completely empty. I did not see a single Armenian man who was still alive."[29] In the opposite direction, the Sub-Directorate of Deportees in Aleppo carried out the orders it had received from the capital: beginning in November-December 1915, the trend was reversed, and the deportees interned in the camps in Islahiye, Katma, and Azaz were sent to Ras ul-Ayn so that the strategic route between Adana and Aleppo could be cleared and decontaminated.[30] "They had started evacuating them by rail to Ras ul-Ayn," a survivor writes.[31] The city had, moreover, a very bad reputation,

> based on the fact that all the unfortunate convoys from the interior provinces [that is, those which took the road from Urfa] that had been dispatched in that direction had, without exception, been massacred. The same fate awaited the deportees arriving by the Konya-Bozanti route who had had the bad luck to be conducted to Ras ul-Ayn. Arab gendarmes, government officials, and even a good part of the population sardoni-cally gave them to understand the fate awaiting them. Some of them related episodes from previous massacres … It had become impossible to obtain information about the first massacres in Ras ul-Ayn. The last fragments of the convoys from the interior who had gotten that far had basically all been massacred. There were no witnesses left.[32]

On the account of J. Kheroyan, who in late October 1915 was appointed head of the con-centration camp in Ras ul-Ayn under rather surprising circumstances, the camp contained, 10,000 tents when he assumed his post – that is, around 50,000 Armenian deportees – which were set up on a height ten minutes from the village.[33] As elsewhere, the deportees had pitched their tents practically one next to the other for reasons of security. The *kaymakam*, Yusuf Ziya Bey, who held his post until February 1916, proved to be above all a well-meaning man; his benevolence was encouraged by the *mutesarif* of Der Zor, Ali Suad Bey, who had authority over Ras ul-Ayn at the time. Ziya, who had control over all state officials, includ-ing those employed by the Sub-Directorate for Deportees, even allowed those deportees who could afford it to live in town. He also tolerated petty commerce at the local level and did his best to protect the camp against Arab marauders, who had been used to taking what they wanted from the deportees. For four months, from November 1915 to late February 1916, the Ras ul-Ayn camp operated under almost normal conditions for this sort of structure, in comparison to other institutions of the same kind. Convoys were, to be sure, regularly expe-dited to Der Zor, but without excessive brutality. However, an impromptu visit by Cevdet, the brother-in-law of Vice-Generalissimo Enver, seems to have had a very negative impact on the camp in Ras ul-Ayn. When he arrived in Ras ul-Ayn, Cevdet, who was on his way to Adana to assume his functions there, is supposed to have been shocked by the conditions the Armenian deportees enjoyed in the camp: the death rate, at the time, was only 100 a day[34] (around 13,000 to 14,000 people nevertheless lost their lives in the four months in which the camp functioned "normally").[35] The importance of Cevdet's intervention, said to be key to explaining why the deportees of the camp in Ras ul-Ayn were liquidated, should not be overestimated. The vali's reputation as a bloodthirsty murderer, acquired in the Van region, influenced Kheroyan's judgement. Obviously, Kheroyan could not know that at the same moment, as we shall see, Istanbul was setting the second phase of the genocide in motion, in both Asia Minor and Syria-Mesopotamia.

It may, however, be affirmed that former vali of Van had something to do with the fact that the *kaymakam* of Ras ul-Ayn was dismissed ten days after Cevdet passed through the area. He was replaced by a dyed-in-the-wool Young Turk, Kerim Refik Bey. This measure was a necessary precondition for carrying out the programmed events to come. Refik assumed office in mid-March and immediately set about accomplishing the task with which he had been entrusted – liquidating the deportees in the camp in Ras ul-Ayn. The preparations began on 17 March 1916 and continued until 21 March, when the operation intended sys-tematically to eliminate the 40,000 internees who were still present commenced.[36] The *kaymakam* received a great deal of support here from Adıl Bey, the Director of Deportees, an "educated" native of Istanbul; the local Chechens, whose leader was none other than the mayor of Ras ul-Ayn, Arslan Bey; and the vice-mayor, Arslan's brother Hüseyin Bey.[37] Officially, these irregulars were supposed to protect the deportees who were sent southward. In fact, they carried out decisions made by the Sub-Directorate of Deportees. A few months later, these irregulars would go on to play outstanding roles in the July 1916 massacres of those deported to Der Zor.

Initial reports of the liquidation of the deportees in the camp of Ras ul-Ayn reached Aleppo only in early April. The first dispatch from consul Rössler, dated 6 April 1916, refers only to a massacre perpetrated by "Cherkez."[38] In his 27 April report, the consul was more precise:

> On the report of a perfectly trustworthy German who spent several days in Ras ul-Ayn and the vicinity ... [e]very day, or nearly every day, three hundred to five hundred people are removed from the camp, taken to a place around ten kilometers from Ras ul-Ayn, and slaughtered. The bodies are thrown into the river known as Jirjib el Hamar ... The Chechens settled in the Ras ul-Ayn region are playing the executioners' roles.[39]

To form some idea of the dimensions of the carnage, one has to turn to the accounts left by the handful of survivors. Thus, the camp's director, Kheroyan, states: "There were only a few hundred people left by 23 April [6 May]: the sick, the blind, invalids, and a few children ... After each convoy was sent off, we counted hundreds of victims, for whom big mass graves were dug." Kheroyan concludes: "A few days after the departure of the last convoy, it was announced, on the *kaymakam*'s orders, that the operations of the concentration camp had been discontinued; he asked me to turn the registries over to him."[40] The luckiest survived for a few more days, getting as far as the region of Sheddadiye in the Kabur valley, where they were killed.[41]

The Deportees "Relegated" to Mosul

The vilayet of Mosul was part of the zone officially set aside as a place of "relegation" for the Armenian deportees. Because of its particular geographical situation on the edge of the Mesopotamian desert, it was supposed to serve as a place of exile for the deportees who followed the second deportation route – that is, Armenians from the vilayets of Bitlis and Dyarbekir and the southern part of the vilayet of Van, along with the vestiges of the two convoys that had set out from Erzerum. In other words, Mosul was the intended destination for deportees from zones in which massacres *in situ* had been especially frequent and the percentage of survivors who had reached their official destination was extremely low. Our main source of information about the region, the German consul in Mosul, Holstein, counted barely 600 women and children from Siirt and Mardin in the city on 21 July.[42] According to Patriarch Zaven, who spent the last months of the war in Mosul, the deportees who arrived here after taking the route that led through Ras ul-Ayn and Cezire were the least numerous,[43] probably because those who followed that route fell victim to the squadrons of çetes whom the vali of Dyarbekir, Dr. Reşid, had sent out to intercept them. The third and fourth convoys from Erzerum, which arrived in Mosul by a more southerly route, suffered far fewer losses, but there was not a single man among them, only women and children.[44] According to Armenian sources, there were 1,600 deportees from Erzerum in the city of Mosul in February 1916 and 2,200 more in the region.[45]

According to Holstein, 15,000 deportees had reached the region by the end of December 1915. A second wave of deportees, comprising Armenians from all the regions of Asia Minor, the western part of it in particular, arrived in Mosul and the vicinity in spring 1916; it had set out from Der Zor. Holstein reports that only 2,500 deportees, who, when Ali Suad was still mutesarif, had been sent from Der Zor down the desert road running from Zor through Suvar, Şeddadiye, Hassiçe, and Zamukha to Mosul, actually arrived in Mosul on 22 May 1916,[46] whereas all those who followed under Salih Zeki's administration were killed on the way. In the same period, the American consul, Jackson, reported that there were around 5,000 deportees in Basra.[47]

The information provided by Holstein in a 4 May 1916 report produced in response to a questionnaire from the Swiss charitable organization *Schweizerisches Hilfswerk 1915 für Armenien*, indicates that the death rate among the deportees was around 67 per cent. Holstein puts the number of deportees from the regions of Erzerum and Bitlis who had landed in Mosul, Kirkuk, or Süleymaniye at between 4,000 and 5,000. He also provides valuable insights into the way these groups were handled. They were "[composed] mainly of women and children [in] desperate plight." "If one is to intervene usefully," he added,

> the deportees would, at the very least, have to have the right to remain once and for all in a single place and not be tossed back and forth – as was and is still the case – from one place to another, on the whim of the Turkish "special commissions" charged with dealing with these questions, which settle them without the least scruple ... Aid of any sort would only prolong their ordeal and postpone their miserable end for a few days more.[48]

In other words, the authorities here applied methods of treatment similar to those employed in the concentration camps: the exiles never stayed for long in any one place and were regularly driven from one camp to the next. There is every reason to believe that this procedure was designed to prevent the deportees from acquiring means of survival after familiarizing themselves with their new environment.

The vali, Hayret Bey, the former *mutesarif* of Marash,[49] who held his post from May 1915 to August 1917, together with his successor Memduh Bey, were the main architects of the gradual destruction of these groups.[50] Captain Nevzâde Bey, the military commander in Mosul, and Colonel Abdülkadri Hilmi Bey personally took charge of executing the Armenian worker-soldiers who were building a highway between Mosul and Cezire.[51] Captain Nâzım Bey, the commander of Mosul's gendarmerie; Mehmed Kâmil, a Unionist journalist; and Nuri Bey, the *mutesarif* of Kirkuk, were also implicated in these killings.[52]

In March 1917, when the British took Baghdad, several thousand Armenians were eking out an existence between Mosul and Basra, scattered here and there in the countryside or the towns. Patriarch Zaven, who went to Mosul shortly before the British captured the city, saw Armenian women (from Erzerum in particular) and children begging in the streets. With the help of donations received from the catholicos, Sahag Khabayan, he was able to ease their lot and to feed and clothe them. Although the Chaldeans did not provide him with the least assistance, the patriarch notes that the Jacobite Syriacs went so far as to put their churches at the deportees' disposal. Zaven also points to the active role that the police chief, Mehmed Halid, a converted Armenian, played in the relief operations for the Armenians of Mosul.[53] He further observes that the Yezidi population showed the deportees kindness and that a Yezidi sheikh, İsmail Bey, regularly came to see him during his stay in Mosul; he adds that the Yezidis of Sinjar took in and protected many Armenians.[54] Finally, the patriarch notes that 50 to 60 men who had so far managed to survive in Mosul were rounded up in a raid and assigned to an *amele taburi* working on road construction. The deportees in the best situation were women from Erzerum and Siirt employed as servants by German and Austrian officers or local government officials.[55]

Shortly after Baghdad was captured in March 1917, Hali Pasha arrived with his general staff. He was soon followed by Cevdet, who had been named commander of the area in

June.[56] The two men, who had already collaborated closely in extirpating the Armenians of the vilayet of Bitlis, seem to have been reunited in order to carry out a new operation of the same kind. According to information revealed during the April 1919 trial of Nevzâde Bey, a former military commander, immediately upon arrived in the area, Halil had launched a fierce repression campaign aimed not only at Armenian deportees, but also at Jewish and Kurdish refugees living in Mosul. On the evidence given by several officers, he had inaugurated the campaign by having five Jews hanged; their bodies were then thrown into the Tigris. Colonel Abdülkadri Hilmi Bey is also supposed to have directed fierce attacks on Armenian deportees in the Zakho gorge, located further to the north.[57]

The most important of the criminals brought to trial was Nevzâde Bey, a former CUP *fedayi* who according to chief prosecutor Reşad Bey had committed several political murders. He was charged with having organized the massacre of the deportees in Mosul, "where he last found himself," as well as that of the Armenian soldiers in a labor battalion.[58] On Şerif Bey's testimony, the dragoman of Mosul's military governor, Nevzâde, who "was Halil's favorite," made a fortune by pillaging the deportees before "exiling them to a remote place" and also by imprisoning several merchants from the city who were "dreadfully" tortured every night. A second witness, an officer by the name of Bekir Bey, told the court that Nevzâde was notorious in Mosul for the atrocities to which he had subjected "thousands of Kurds who had emigrated from Bitlis and Erzerum. He cut off their food supply, condemning them to starve to death." Be it added that the accused did not protest when the presiding judge of the court asked if it was true that, acting in concert with Halil Pasha, he had confiscated all food supplies arriving in the city and sold them for personal gain, dividing the profits up with Halil."[59] In other words, Halil, who was obviously in command of these operations, did not limit himself to attacking Armenian deportees, but also initiated a policy of eliminating Kurds, inspired by the "Turkism" of which he was a partisan.

This repressive campaign peaked in September 1917, when Halil ordered his aide-de-camp, Lieutenant-Colonel Basri Bey, to proceed to massacre the Armenian deportees scattered throughout the Mosul region.[60] Cevdet was apparently also deeply involved in this new liquidation campaign, which began on 11 September 1917.[61] According to reports gathered by the Swiss historian S. Zurlinden as the events were unfolding, Halil had 15,000 Armenians killed in two nights by Kurds and irregulars; they were tied together in groups of ten and thrown into the Tigris.[62] These details remind us that Halil, although he had donned a military uniform, was still working for the *Teşkilât-ı Mahsusa*.

The Patriarch, Zaven Yeghiayan, who was held under house arrest in Baghdad from 9 October 1916 to early March 1917, notes that a few Armenian notables from Baghdad were deported to Ras ul-Ayn and Der Zor in summer 1915, but that they were able to go back home a few weeks later thanks to the intercession of Der Goltz. According to the patriarch, the arrival of Ali Suad Bey as vali of Baghdad – he was replaced in Der Zor by Salih Zeki – in early summer 1916 alleviated the suffering of the city's Armenians.[63]

Chapter 5

The Concentration Camps along "The Euphrates Line"

Officially, the "Euphrates line" constituted, as we have said, the principal region in which the Ottoman authorities chose to "settle" the Armenian populations that had been "displaced to the interior." In theory, the assets confiscated from the Armenians were to have been used to settle the new migrants in these desert regions of Syria and Mesopotamia, inhabited by a few thousand sedentary Arabs and Circassians and thinly sprinkled with tribes of Bedouin nomads.

Deportees were to be found on the Euphrates line from an early date. There were 15,000 of them there in early August 1915;[1] by late September, the number had risen to 23,300,[2] soaring to 310,000 by early February 1916.[3] These exiles were split up between Meskene and Der Zor. Throughout the period in question, this trajectory was synonymous with death for all the deportees. Strung out along this line was a succession of camps: Meskene, Dipsi, Abuharar, Hamam, Sebka/Rakka, and finally, the camps of Der Zor/Marât. The number of those interned in them did not, however, significantly increase until the winter of 1915–16: as we have observed, it was then, in January 1916, that the authorities decided to purge northern Syria of its deportees. The camps of Mamura, Islahiye, Rajo, Katma, Azaz, Bab, Akhterim, Munbuc, and Mârra, all located in the outskirts of, or at a relatively short distance from, Aleppo, were now shut down one after the next, and the survivors of these camps were sent down the Euphrates line or the trajectory of the *Bagdadbahn* toward Ras ul-Ayn.

The Camp in Meskene

The camp in Meskene was the first important way station on the line leading to Zor; it lay at the point where the road from Aleppo intersects the Euphrates. Thinly inhabited at first, the camp grew rapidly in winter 1916. When Hocazâde Hüseyin Bey, a Çerkez from Munbuc, was named Meskene's *Sevkiyat memuri* in January 1916 – he succeeded Muhtar Bey – barely 20,000 deportees were living in the camp. In the following weeks, its population jumped to 100,000.[4] The Sub-Directorate for Deportees thereupon decided to add several officers to its staff, including Naim Sefa, well known because he served as Aram Andonian's informant, and another Çerkez from Munbuc named Ömer. After directing the camp for one year, Hüseyin was relieved of his duties in December 1916, at a moment when the camp had been virtually emptied of its internees. He was replaced by another Hüseyin, known as the One-Eyed Man (*Kör*). Kör Hüseyin had already distinguished himself as a convoy leader in the camp in Karlık on the outskirts of Aleppo, "where, with his brutality, he had acquired a reputation for terror. He was a short, fat, powerfully built, one-eyed man, and extremely depraved."[5]

The camp in Meskene was one of the most deadly on the Euphrates line. Hüseyin Bey's official estimate of the number of Armenians who died there in 1916, carried off by typhus, cholera, or hunger, was 80,000, "although the real figure was much higher than the well-known çeles[6] kept by the chief gravedigger [*mezarcı başı*] suggest." Since the chief gravedigger was illiterate, Andonian wrote, he "contented himself with cutting a notch on one of his çeles for every body of which he took charge. Certain people learned from him that the number of bodies that had been simply buried did not include those that had been thrown into the Euphrates: approximately one hundred thousand people, at the very least." Andonian also indicates that there were only 2,100 people in the camp in Meskene in April 1916,[7] most of them craftsmen who would be liquidated by Kör Hüseyin early in 1917. The German consul, Rössler, confirms that "a Turkish army pharmacist who had been serving in Meskene for six months told [him] that 55,000 Armenians were buried in Meskene alone. A Turkish vice-commander had, moreover, cited the same figure."[8] These estimates of the number of people buried in the city or drowned in the Euphrates indicate that the daily death toll was as high as that registered in the other camps in the area north of Aleppo in which deportees were interned. The American consul Jackson reports similar statistics in a 10 September 1916 dispatch: "Information obtained on the spot permits me to state that nearly 60,000 Armenians are buried there, carried off by hunger, privations of all sorts, intestinal diseases and the typhus that results. As far as the eye can reach, mounds can be seen containing 200 to 300 corpses buried pell-mell, women children and old people belonging to different families."[9] Patriarch Zaven, who traveled through Meskene shortly thereafter on 22 September 1916, saw, above all, "bodies and bones" there.[10] Two reports by Armenians from Konya indicate that the *Sevkiyat's* "inspector general," Hakkı Bey, a çete chief from Istanbul, arrived in Meskene on 16 August 1916 and had 200 orphans rounded up and "expedited" to Der Zor. Hakkı reminded the deportees that he was now their "second god" – that is, that he had the right of life and death over them. Hardly had the order to set out been issued then he took the lead of a squadron of çetes and proceeded to massacre all the males in the convoy on the banks of the Euphrates.[11] Hakkı embodies the symbiosis between the leadership of the *Sevkiyat* and that of the Special Organization. Indeed, he does it so clearly that one might well ask if the former was not merely an extension of the latter adapted to the context of the camps and camouflaged as an organization of the Ministry of the Interior.

According to a report by Karekin Hovhannesian, a native of Sivrihisar who had been deported on 5 August 1915 and had arrived in Meskene in early December, some convoys had been sent southward on *şahturs* – "two boats tied one to the other" that the deportees had to rent from Arab boatmen at their own expense – whereas the others either traveled down the right bank of the Euphrates through Dipsi, Abuharar, Hamam, and Sebka, or, more rarely, the left bank of the Cezire. The latter trajectory haunted the deportees' nightmares, for it required that they trek along mountain ridges where there were no bodies of water at all and where they were at the mercy of local nomads with a well-earned bad reputation.[12]

Like many other way stations, Meskene was both a concentration camp and a transit camp. Initially, the internees had been settled in a camp near the highway, in the highlands. Hüseyin Bey subsequently had them transferred to the bank of the Euphrates, while the transit camp was left in the highlands, near the barracks and the craftsmen's tents. In theory, the internees were to be placed in this center, as in all the others, for just a few weeks or even only a day or two, the time required to purge the convoys of their weakest members. They were then supposed to be put on the road to the next station and so on, until they reached Zor. But it was usually in the camp directors' interest to keep the internees who were capable of paying a kind of "fee" for the right to stay put. The longer these people remained in a camp, the bigger the "fee" that the head of the camp collected. It was, moreover, by no means rare for the camp directors to complain that their colleagues were keeping the wealthiest deportees too long, those who still possessed means of payment requiring their signature. Before Salih Zeki Bey was appointed *mutesarif* of Zor in June 1916, a certain laxity was observable among the "officials" of the Sub-Directorate for Deportees for the reasons just mentioned. Nevertheless, two to three convoys containing a few hundred people each were sent toward Zor every week. They were basically made up of the least "interesting" deportees, since Hüseyin Bey saw to it that his most affluent wards remained in Meskene until nothing more was to be had from them.[13]

The Camp in Dipsi

Located five hours from Meskene, the camp in Dipsi lay on the right bank of a dry riverbed "which was transformed, after storms or heavy rains, into an immense stream that flowed into the Euphrates."[14] Transfers from Meskene to Dipsi were usually made by land under conditions succinctly described by Krikor Ankut, a young intellectual from Istanbul who spent more than a year in the area:

> In mid-March [1916], we were transferred from Meskene to Dipsi. There were around one thousand people on foot and some fifty carts...Every step of the way, we came upon corpses, the dying, or exhausted men and women who no longer had the strength to walk and were waiting to die on the road, hungry and thirsty. On the road leading from Meskene to Dispi, we had encountered wandering gravediggers, whose job was, notably, to bury the dead. They were so utterly without pity that they buried the dying with the dead so that they would not have to do their job twice over. We constantly came upon the bodies of people whose heads had been bashed in. There were large numbers of dogs; they fed on the corpses.[15]

In this period, the camp comprised, Ankut says, 2,000 tents, that is, around 10,000 to 12,000 people:

> The tents all belonged, without exception, to poor people; not a one was presentable. Each was inhabited by from two to ten sick people lying side-by-side and waiting for death. This bank was known as the *Hastahane* [hospital]. All the unfortunates who had been displaced from Meskene on foot or in wagons were brought to this place called the Hospital and abandoned. They remained there, naked, hungry, and thirsty, until death came and mowed them down. Every step of the way, we saw corpses; there were so many of them that the gravediggers were unable to bury all the dead. Absolute poverty reigned in this place, and had sunk to unprecedented levels. Day after day, with the arrival of people from Meskene, the number of tents in the Hospital increased. The poor people contented themselves with eating, unsalted, a plant called *ebemkömeci*, which grew plentifully on the banks of the Euphrates in springtime.[16]

It was understood that Dipsi was the place to which people from Meskene were brought to die; it was run the same way that Suruc was. This camp remained in operation for only six months, from November 1915 to April 1916, yet 30,000 people died there, according to Ankut. Toward the end of April, some 20 "gendarmes" came to evacuate the camp for good and all; they sent one last convoy to Abuharar, after burning the tents and those of their occupants who could no longer walk.[17]

The Camp in Abuharar

In theory, the convoys dispatched from Meskene made a stop in Abuharar, after a trek of approximately nine hours. The place known as Abuharar in fact amounted to no more than two dilapidated caravansaries perched on the banks of the Euphrates. The concentration camp had been set up on a stretch of land very close to the river. On average, 500 to 600 tents – or around 3,000 people – were to be found there, even though Abuharar was originally supposed to be a transit camp. The reason was that people who had means of some sort could here too purchase the right to remain longer by bribing the sergeant in charge of the camp, one Rahmeddin Çavuş, who sent deportees on only after relieving them of everything they owned.[18]

The Camp in Hamam

Setting out from Abuharar, one had to walk another nine hours to reach Hamam by a route one hour from the Euphrates on which there was not a single body of water. Hamam was an unimportant village lying on a height located five hours before Rakka. The camp there was used exclusively as a transit camp. It had been set up in a vast plain that stretched into the distance before the village; convoys stopped here for one or two days. The camp was run by a Çerkez named Isak Çavuş.[19] By spring 1916, the camp had been totally emptied of its inhabitants. A few families managed to survive by working on the construction of army camps established on the Euphrates line from May 1916 on in anticipation of a new British offensive on Baghdad.[20] Patriarch Zaven, who traveled through Hamam during the night of 23–24 September 1916, counted only 150 tents inhabited by deportees, for the most part women from Marash and Ayntab.[21]

The Town of Rakka and the Camp in Sebka

By 1915, Rakka was already a fairly big town lying on a plateau located near the left bank of the Euphrates, half an hour from the river. The first deportees to reach it, in fall 1915, were Armenians from the regions of Sıvas (Zara, Kangal, Yenihan, Koçhisar), Thrace, and Urfa, as well as female Armenian gypsies from Tokat whose men had been killed. A total of 7,000 to 8,000 deportees were, at the time, able to find lodging in the town after bribing the local authorities (the *kaymakam* and the commander of the gendarmerie) and the head of the *Sevkiyat*, who ruled over the camp in Sebka on the opposite bank of the river. These first Armenian arrivals provided the city with a non-negligible labor force, which was more important in the view of the population and the local authorities than the instructions received from Aleppo. In March 1916, while Krikor Ankut was living in Rakka, a military inspector came to investigate the most flagrant cases of corruption.[22] A new *kaymakam*, Deli Fahri ("The Madman"), had been appointed but, in exchange for a handful of gifts that were more than modest, he continued to protect the deportees, even when orders to deport them arrived from Der Zor. Since Rakka, located on the left bank of the Euphrates, was officially independent of Urfa, Fahri refused to carry out these orders, appealing for protection to the mutesarif, who did not wish to knuckle under to ukases from Zor.[23]

Officially, Rakka was one of the zones of relegation for the deportees. In theory, then, they should have benefited from the aid that the government had promised to give them to help them resettle. In fact, the modicum of aid that arrived came, as we have seen, from relief networks created by the Armenians of Aleppo with the support of Swiss and American diplomats and missionaries. Rakka nonetheless constituted, in many respects, a rather exceptional case, in that a few thousand deportees were indeed resettled there, even if the authorities had nothing to do with this. A deportee stated the matter very well: to gain admittance to Rakka was to escape being sent to Der Zor and one's death. Until June 1916, at least, this population once again enjoyed, in some way, normal conditions of existence, and had the feeling that it could continue to live in the town on a permanent basis.[24]

A very different situation prevailed on the opposite bank of the river, in Sebka. The convoys of the last survivors from Asia Minor, who had been marching for weeks, succeeded one another there under much more appalling conditions. Our witness, Krikor Ankut, reports that a number of new corpses were observed there every day and that famine drove some people to cannibalism. In comparison, Rakka seemed like a paradise. All had sought to gain entry to it by bribing the head of the camp or *Sevkiyat* officials. In March 1916, when Istanbul decided to have done with the last deportees on the Euphrates line, the camp in Sebka was definitively evacuated and its last denizens were sent to Zor. Rakka's Armenian population found itself facing a similar fate, but momentarily escaped it thanks to the *kaymakam*, Fahri (who would soon be dismissed), and the populace, which did not wish to do without the resources that the deportees had brought to their town. Some of the exiles, the neediest ones, were recruited as craftsmen or assigned to help construct army camps on the Euphrates line. The result was that there remained only about 8,000 to 9,000 Armenians in Sebka by autumn 1916.[25] On 25 September 1916, when the patriarch traveled through the area, he saw only six families in Sebka, all of them from Karsbazar.[26]

Garabed Kapigian, who lived in Rakka for several months, provides very valuable details about the Armenian deportees' daily life in the city.[27] Kapigian, who had arrived in Suruc on 18 January 1916, together with somewhat over 1,800 other deportees, had had the good fortune to end up on the right side of the Euphrates and to be in a convoy that included Armenians from Erzerum who still had means at their disposal. He saw how on the opposite bank convoys arrived from the north every day, while others were sent southward. He notes in passing that those who could pay one pound gold were transported southward on rafts.[28]

At first, Kapigian's group was invited to pitch camp three hours from Rakka. Erzerum's notables, however,[29] rapidly secured permission to go to Rakka, where they made preparations to approach the *kaymakam*, Fehmi Bey, who agreed to allow the deportees from Erzerum – and them alone – to settle in the town in exchange for 500 Turkish pound gold, to be paid in cash. In other words, 400 deportees from Sıvas, Tokat, Amasia, Samsun, Bafra, Niksar, and Suruc were not covered by the agreement and were therefore sent to camp in Sebka on the opposite bank of the river, whence they were deported to Der Zor.[30] It was with bitterness that our witness observed this incident,[31] which revealed certain character traits of the men from Erzerum. Their lack of solidarity and their extreme parochialism found, under the circumstances, unrestrained expression.

There were at the time 3,000 homes in Rakka, a large minority of which belonged to Çerkez *muhacirs* who had been settled in an isolated quarter 20 years previously. When the thousand and more Armenians from Erzerum entered the city, it had already been inhabited for months by around 15,000 deportees who had been "recruited" by the *kaymakam* Fehmi and the head of the local *Sevkiyat*, Abid Agha: every day, the two officials crossed the Euphrates and brought back with them families willing to pay five to ten pounds gold per head. This was "like a gold mine" for the two men, Kapigian observes.[32] These Armenians were from Thrace (Rodosto, Malgara, Edirne), Bythinia (Ismit, Adabazar, Bardizag, Bursa, Bilecik, Bergame, Eskişehir), Angora, Konya, Isparta, Burdur, Sivrihisar, Nevşehir, Yozgat, Kayseri, Everek, Tomarza, Marash, Ayntab, Birecik, Adana, Hacın, Antioch, Kesab, Dörtyol, and Kastamonu and the surrounding areas – that is, from regions in western Asia Minor whose inhabitants had suffered much less from massacres and pillage than their compatriots from the eastern provinces. According to Kapigian, the local Arab population, particularly Rakka's notables, had given the Armenian deportees a good reception and had rapidly grasped all the advantages that it could obtain from these unexpected arrivals. Kapigian also emphasizes that the city's businesses and crafts had benefited from the savoir-faire of the newcomers, who were obviously prepared to work for a minimal salary. Availing themselves of the services of the Post Office, Agricultural Bank, and Department of the Public Debt, the deportees who had relatives in the capital received transfers of money from the capital that redounded to the benefit of commerce in Rakka, as well as aid that was sent from Aleppo by various channels.[33] These overlapping interests did much to strengthen the bonds between Arabs and Armenians; the appointment of three new *kaymakams* in short order did nothing to change matters.

People's situations within the community of deportees differed widely. Women raising young children on their own were, of course, the most vulnerable: these undernourished families did not have the means to rent lodgings and in some cases lived in the street. It is in these circles, which could not maintain minimal health standards, that epidemics made most of their victims. These people were regularly rounded up in the streets, transported to the opposite bank of the river, and then sent to Zor.[34] A few pharmacists and doctors among the deportees, under the lead of Dr. Sarkis Selian from Arslanbeg, who had been appointed municipal physician, and Harutiun Bakalian from Amasia, nevertheless managed to combat disease and establish a basic health regimen. Our witness dwells in particular on the devotion of Dr. Selian, who remained in Rakka until spring 1919.[35] In this relatively peaceful desert area, the deportees were not completely cut off from the rest of the world. They were authorized to carry on correspondence, albeit only in Turkish, and some even received newspapers, such as the Istanbul daily *Zhamanag*[36] – one of the rare papers in Armenian authorized to appear during the war. In their day-to-day lives, deportees from the same localities usually stuck together and accepted all forms of work that could help them earn enough to eat. For example, a former teacher from the orphanage in Sıvas was employed as a porter, thus ensuring the subsistence of both his family and his deceased brother's.[37]

This Armenian society was in fact a disparate structure made up of specimens of the Armenian communities in the provinces of Asia Minor and Thrace, speaking different dialects and originating in all the different social classes. What they had in common was the fact that they had all been torn from the environment with which they were familiar and were living together in a world recomposed by the hazards of the deportations. Garabed Kapigian's subtle account leaves its reader with the impression that all were aware that they were the last representatives of the society they had come from and had ended up in the Syrian Desert, where they were barely separated from the road to death by the Euphrates. As time went on, these peasants and city-dwellers came to know each other and established congenial relations. In this nascent community, a few personalities clearly stood out – a young Hnchak from Istanbul, Karnig Shahbazian, who had by some miracle gotten as far as Rakka and taken up the jeweler's trade; a resistance fighter from Urfa, Mgrdich Kiulahian, who was adopted and given privileged treatment by the deportees.[38]

The marriage of the Istanbul party activist with a young woman from Erzerum no doubt marked a new stage in the life of this community. Kapigian and the members of his household, where the bridegroom lived, acted as his parents and as such negotiated the conditions of the marriage. At the same time, they brought the bride's parents to agree that the ceremony would respect practices customary in Sıvas. A village priest from Eskişehir, Father Ghazaros, who was living in Rakka under his secular name, gladly undertook to celebrate the match. The deportees were well aware of the symbolic dimension of this act. With the help of Biblical references, they compared their situation with that of the Jews deported from Babylon; the ruins of the ancient city were not all that far from Rakka.[39]

Another, more tragic human-interest story, which unfolded in spring 1916, is symptomatic of the atmosphere prevailing in Rakka. In 1916, the waters of the Euphrates rose unusually high; this, followed by a storm, led to the death on 18 April of a German officer who was serving on a boat carrying ammunition and war supplies of other kinds to Baghdad. An Armenian priest officiated at the religious ceremony, which culminated in a eulogy delivered in German by Professor Sarkis Manugian, a teacher at the Sanasarian *lycée* in Erzerum, before the stupefied German officers attending the funeral.[40] One can readily imagine what was going through the minds of both the Germans, who had been privileged witnesses of the exactions perpetrated against the deportees on the other bank of the Euphrates and, from a very different standpoint, those of the Armenians, who continued to wonder at the German military's apparent indifference to these crimes.

Kapigian, a careful observer, notes the spring 1916 arrival of four Turks in hunters' uniforms. In his view, they were probably military men or delegates of the Ittihad sent to evaluate the deportees' situation. He finds support for his thesis in the fact that, during their one-week's stay, these men methodically visited the bazaar, which was mainly occupied by Armenians, and also the cafes that the Armenians had opened.[41] It is obviously impossible to verify this hypothesis, but it is easy to imagine that the capital wanted a precise assessment of the effects its policy was having on the deportees, as is shown by the many requests for information transmitted to the local authorities by the interior minister.

Kapigian also confirms that the *kaymakam*, Fahri, was locked in a wrestling match with the new *mutesarif* of Zor, Salih Zeki, throughout summer 1916. He also mentions the resistance that Rakka's Arab notables put up to the order to deport the Armenians from the city.[42] He sheds a great deal of light as well on the antagonism that developed between the army and the administration of the *Sevkiyat* around the question of the Armenian deportees – in other words, between the ranking Turkish and German officers charged with defending the Iraqi front on one hand, and the men of the *Sevkiyat* on the other, who, it was understood, answered to the orders of the CUP and its paramilitary branch, the Special Organization. At stake was obviously the Armenian deportees' labor-power and savoir-faire, both of which were indispensable to the military if it was to construct the basic structures it needed, especially the fortified stations stretching from one end of the Euphrates to the other, which were to be used to stock ammunition and supplies. Rakka's Armenians promptly grasped what was involved and, in a period when the "grand massacres" of Der Zor had already begun (in July), undertook to bribe the military commanders – and, simultaneously, the *Sevkiyat memuri* – in order to make sure that they would be enrolled in the labor battalions.[43] Needless to say, the question was referred all the way up to the authorities in Istanbul. An "inspector general" of the *Sevkiyat*, Hakkı Bey, who had been dispatched by the central authorities, arrived on the Euphrates line in August 1916.[44] Hakkı must have had orders from the very top of the party-state, inasmuch as he succeeded in having his way with the military and personally coordinated the systematic liquidation of all the concentration camps, from Meskene to as far away as Zor. The operation was carried out in extremely violent fashion, as all witnesses have noted. The special case represented by Rakka obviously did not escape the attention of the "inspector," who had probably got wind of the firm resistance shown by the local notables. In November 1916, when the liquidation of the deportees who had been driven to Zor was virtually complete, he went to Rakka and tried to convince the new *kaymakam*, Ali Kemal, to hand the city's Armenians over to him. The *kaymakam* cited the decree making Rakka a zone of relegation for the deportees to justify his refusal to comply.[45]

A count of these refugees, carried out at the request of the *mutesarif* of Urfa, provides interesting insights into the makeup of this population. Out of a total population of 8,000 to 9,000, there were a mere 400 Armenians from the vilayets of Sıvas, Harput, and Dyarbekir, including 16 men aged between 16 and 60, as well as 45 boys under 15.[46]

The community in Rakka was fully abreast of the massacres perpetrated in Zor, which claimed, as we shall see, 200,000 victims. They were informed of them thanks to reports from Çerkez in Rakka, who went to take part in these orgies of violence, and also by the survivors who had found refuge in the city. Shortly thereafter, the mufti invited the group to convert "as a guarantee" of their collective future. A total of 30 families accepted the offer. Dr. Levon Ohnigian, a native of Sıvas and former student of Garabed Kapigian's, did not hesitate to tell his teacher how much he had suffered after thus bowing to his fears.[47] However that may be, the Armenian community in Rakka was allowed to remain in the city, only to be then sucked into the serious crisis that affected the region when the fighting with the British forces around Baghdad grew more intense. Like the local populace, the Armenians too were victimized by the military requisitions that literally emptied Rakka of its food reserves, precipitating a terrible famine. Large numbers of children were left to fend for themselves as a result. The most generous deportees adopted them. Turkish and German officers on their way to the Baghdad front also showed these children great generosity, but such occasional assistance was not enough to save their lives.[48] The missionary Elvesta Leslie, who traveled through Rakka in early spring 1917, observes that the deportees there were dying like flies.[49]

In January–February 1917, the *mutesarif* of Urfa came to Rakka to recruit craftsmen; his city, he said, was in desperate need of them. Seven hundred to 800 women and a few men who had been reduced to dire poverty volunteered to go. One hour from Urfa, this convoy was detained in a khan and invited to convert in order not to "offend" the religious sensibilities of the Turkish population. Yet, even after this collective operation had been carried out, the new arrivals were not well received. Had instructions been given to impose a boycott? With the exception of a few specialists needed by Urfa and people who were recruited by the city government and army, the Armenians were sent to Karaköprü to "build a road."[50] It seems that this operation was a trick, the sole purpose of which was to eliminate a segment of the Armenian deportees from Rakka.

The last event of note was the June 1917 mobilization of people of both sexes between the ages of 15 and 60. Operation Yıldırım, the purpose of which was to defend the Iraqi front, required massive supply transports via the Euphrates, which the military envisaged making by *şahtur*, the well known "raft" used since antiquity for river transport. Apparently, no one still knew how to make this kind of primitive vessel, and 2,500 deportees from Rakka were sent to Birecik and Jerablus to accomplish the task. Five hundred more were sent to Meskene for the same purpose. Among the remaining deportees, 600 were of draftable age.[51] The last of Rakka's deportees were harassed by the new *kaymakam*; some fled to Aleppo. By October 1918, there were only 200 families left in Rakka.[52]

Der Zor, the Last Stop on the "Euphrates Line" and the Culminating Point of the Second Phase of the Genocide

With the camps in Der Zor and its environs, we broach the final episode in the 1915–16 massacres, the culmination of the second phase of the genocide. This phase began after six months of relative stability that might well have left the impression that the anti-Armenian persecutions were over. Before the deportees in the Syrian Desert met their tragic end, Zor had constituted the last stop for the Armenian survivors who reached it after crossing the desert. Despite the killings that reduced the number of deportees in the groups moving from one end of the line of the Euphrates to the other, camp after camp, tens of thousands of deportees arrived in Zor. According to a German witness who related his trip there to the German consul, Rössler, in early November 1915 there were already around 15,000 Armenians in this corner of the Syrian Desert in which "from one hundred fifty to two hundred people die every day. This, incidentally, is what explains the fact that the city can absorb the deportees, who continue to arrive by the thousands."[53] As a result of the attrition due to the killings, but also of famine and epidemics, Zor by and large respected the orders to main-tain a "reasonable" proportion of Armenians in the area. When the norms were exceeded, the local authorities' solution to the problem was to send small convoys to Mosul to restore the balance. This situation lasted for as long as the influx of new arrivals was compensated, as it were, by the more or less temporary placement of deportees in the concentration camps in the Aleppo and Ras ul-Ayn regions. As a result, around 15,000 Armenians were able to settle in Zor and even organize themselves there, while a transit camp was maintained, as in Rakka, on the left bank of the Euphrates.

Aram Andonian states that before the war there existed in Zor an Armenian Catholic church that served around 150 households, as well as to other churches belonging to Jacobite and Nestorian Syriacs. He adds that, among the Syriacs, a local notable, Georges Sevkkar, showed the deportees special generosity and mobilized all the influence he had to protect them.[54] What is more, Zor was set apart by the fact that its police chief was named Nerses Kiurdian – a kind of anachronistic survival from times past. As in Rakka, the Armenians had soon galvanized the local crafts and trade, encouraged by the *mutesarif* Ali Suad Bey, whom most sources describe as a well-educated man with a benevolent attitude. Alongside versatile people who were able to adapt rapidly to the new circumstances and find some sort of occupation, there was also a considerable number of women and old people, accompanied by children, eking out an existence under dreadful conditions in huts made of branches, outside in city limits on the left bank of the Euphrates. When Salih Zeki was appointed to succeed Ali Suad in July 1916, he judged that their situation was still too enviable:

> The day he arrived, he toured the various neighborhoods, especially the one around the market, where he was especially irritated to see that the Armenians were flourish-ing. They had, in fact, created a veritable Armenia, and the market was largely in their hands. Most were craftsmen, who were, generally speaking, active, offering an odd contrast with the local population.[55]

Levon Shashian, a young Istanbul intellectual and comrade of Aram Andonian's, with whom Andonian had organized a communications network connecting the different con-centration camps – the celebrated "human newspapers" constituted by the young orphans who went back and forth between Meskene, Rakka, and Zor[56] – organized a system for the purchase and sale of the deportees' assets. Thanks to it, the Armenians were not forced to sell their property for next to nothing. Located near the town hall, Shashian's little agency was, above all, an office that handed out social assistance to the neediest. In exchange for a few gifts, Shashian succeeded in winning the favor of certain influential personalities in Zor, becoming an invulnerable figure who effectively served as the leader of the Armenian colony.[57] Thus, the Armenian deportees were in the process of settling permanently in this small town in the Syrian Desert. However, as the course of events was to show, the Young Turk government did not intend to allow them to put down roots there.

For lack of sources that might shed light on the CUP's objectives, we have no choice but to decrypt the strategy worked out and implemented by the Sub-Directorate of the *Sevkiyat* through examination of its operations on the ground. The October–November 1915 estab-lishment of the *Sevkiyat*'s operational structures in Aleppo, along with the creation of con-centration camps, constituted the first stage of this plan. The aim was apparently to eliminate the deportees by creating health conditions of the kind that bred disaster.

The second stage plainly came in January 1916, when the authorities decided to shut down the concentration camps north of Aleppo and to begin expelling those interned there down the line of the Euphrates.[58] The third stage, the objective of which was the physical elimination of the surviving deportees, was probably discussed and decided upon between late February and early March 1916. A formulation used in a 22 February 1916 wire from the interior minister,[59] which the prosecution cited as incriminating evidence at the trial of the Young Turk leaders, is one indication of this: "The text of the general communiqué about the cessation of the deportation of the Armenians has given rise, in some places, to an interpretation that has it that not a single Armenian more should be expelled from now on. For this reason, a number of harmful individuals among the people in question have not been sent away." Marked by administrative formalism, this document is ultimately nothing more than an order to resume expediting people to the south; it announces the second stage in the plan. The Ottoman archives contain records showing that a total of 4,620 deportees arrived in Zor on 20, 21, 24, and 25 February 1916.[60] These figures give some sense of the rate at which people were being expedited at the beginning of the operation designed to concentrate them in Zor. The first large-scale massacres perpetrated in Ras ul-Ayn from 21 March on, which claimed 40,000 victims, represent the enactment of a decision that was necessarily made earlier.[61] The multiple deportation orders that in February and March 1916 affected categories of Armenians who had previously been allowed to remain in their homes, such as the families of soldiers, or Protestants, Catholics, craftsmen, and so on – we indicated the regions involved in the Fourth Part of the present study – constitute another indication that a decision had been made at the highest level of the party-state. The scope of the operation, however, and the massive number of deportees to be displaced meant that much more time was needed to complete the operations than had originally been anticipated: they went on for eight months – that is, until December 1916.

According to information that a Turkish officer gave the German consul, Rössler, there were in mid-April only 15,000 deportees in the city of Zor[62] – that is, about as many as in fall 1915. This figure, however, probably fails to take into account those interned in the camp on the left bank of the river. The *mutesarif*, Ali Suad, sought to respect the rules that allowed for a maximum of 10 per cent of deportees in the various localities of the region. The German vice-consul in Mosul informed Aleppo the German consulate that of the two convoys that had left Zor on 15 April 1916 and taken two different routes, 2,500 people had arrived in Mosul on 22 May, but that since then not a single convoy had,[63] although 21 groups had set out in that direction in summer 1916. In other words, only the convoys put on the road when Suad was *mutesarif* reached their destination. The case of 2,000 people who left for Mosul in mid-June and were brought back to Zor at the request of Salih Zeki, although that they had, after a month's march, reached the region of Sinjar, halfway to Mosul, would even seem to indicate that the new mutesarif had been instructed not to let a single deportee escape.[64]

The liquidation in spring and summer 1916 of the concentration camps located on the way to Zor of course led to an exceptional increase in the number of convoys arriving there. The groundwork for this last stage was, moreover, plainly laid by an order that Talât Bey sent to the prefecture of Aleppo on 29 June, to the effect that the last Armenians should be expelled toward the line of the Euphrates.[65] It was probably with a view to managing this concentration of people at Zor, then evaluated at around 200,000 deportees,[66] that the interior minister called on Salih Zeki, whose activities at Everek we have already discussed, to replace the *mutesarif* Ali Suad in early July. The August arrival, on the line of the Euphrates, of the *Sevkiyat*'s "inspector general," Hakkı Bey, was also most probably an ancillary measure taken by the central authorities in order to ensure that their orders would be properly carried out.[67] Acting in the guise of a state official, this *çete* leader was, on reports by Artin Manasian of Adabazar, Aram Manugian of Aslanbeg, and Hovsep Sinanian of Kütahya, the main organizer of the deportations from Aleppo to Meskene and on to Zor. They accuse him of having committed crimes against the convoys of deportees, set tents on fire, conducted Armenian children under guard from Meskene to Zor to be burned alive, and, finally, of having organized the massacre of 1,500 children from the orphanage in Zor.[68]

Before going to Zor to assume his functions, Zeki spent several days early in July 1916 in Aleppo (where he stayed in the Hotel Baron)[69] in order to meet with the vali, Abdülhalik, and the head of the Sub-Directorate for Deportees, Nuri. Thereafter, he went to Meskene. According to Andonian, Zeki there met with the director of the camp, Hüseyin, and then all the directors of the concentration camps set up along the line of the Euphrates as far as Zor.[70]

According to Armenian sources, Zeki made a priority of liquidating the men still present in Zor as soon as he arrived there, but clashed on this point with the military authorities, who, like their counterparts in Rakka, were then recruiting able-bodied individuals to construct the basic structures needed to implement Operation Yıldırım. According to information gathered by Andonian, when Zor's military governor learned that a first convoy of 18,000 people was about to be sent to Marât – that is, toward the killing fields in the Kabur valley – Nureddin Bey sent a telegraph to his superior, General Halil Pasha, requesting permission to create a battalion of worker-soldiers without delay. One thousand two hundred family heads volunteered for the battalion. Assembled in Salihiye in the northernmost tip of Zor, they were supposed to leave for Hamam to join the recruits from Rakka. It seems, however, that Zeki refused to obey the military men's orders. Significantly, he had these recruits locked up in the hospital in Salihiye and then issued orders to send them to Marât with their families – in other words, to massacre them. A second attempt to recruit soldiers among the deportees in Zor, which involved 550 young men between the ages of 21 and 30, failed in much the same way. Assembled in the barracks in Kışla, also to be found in the Salihiye quarter, these men were left without food or water for seven days; the survivors were finally sent in chains to Suvar by the direct desert route. On the way, Chechen çetes recruited by Zeki in Ras ul-Ayn killed them in small groups, despite an attempt at resistance.[71] Cast in the guise of recruitment campaigns, these two operations probably had no other purpose than to liquidate all the adult deportees in Zor while eliminating all risk of resistance. It cannot, however, be ruled out that the military authorities had indeed wanted to make use of this labor-power, but came up against contrary orders from the Minister of the Interior.

After getting rid of these men, Zeki surely drew the lessons of these initial massacres, coming to the conclusion that he would need additional recruits to finish the job. In the course of a short trip to Ras ul-Ayn, he recruited 100 more Chechen çetes from the ranks of those who had taken part in the massacre of the inmates of the camp in Ras ul-Ayn a few months earlier.[72] With that, the genocidal apparatus had been set in motion. As soon as some 10,000 deportees had been concentrated on the other side of the Zor Bridge, Zeki organized their expulsion to Marât, another camp lying five hours to the south at some distance from the Euphrates. As a general rule, the gendarmes there put the deportees entrusted to them in the hands of Zeki's Chechens, who set about selecting the people who still possessed financial means: these people were methodically stripped of their property and killed on the spot, so as not to risk leaving these resources to the Bedouins who had been charged with accomplishing the final liquidation of these convoys deeper in the desert. Marât was a camp in which the deportees were sorted out and put in new groups. Big convoys were broken down into groups of 2,000 to 5,000 people and gradually expedited to Suvar, a place in the Kabur Valley at a two days' march by the desert route. In Suvar, the last surviving men were separated for good – that is, killed in the surrounding area – from the women and children. Thereafter, continuing to sort and divide, the authorities grouped people together on the basis of their place of origin.[73] Women and children, after spending around ten days on a scanty diet in these desert areas, were put on the road to Sheddadiye, where they were, as a rule, killed behind the hill that looked down on this Arab village. A total of 21 convoys were dispatched from Zor, six big ones and 15 smaller ones. The first convoy, comprising around 18,000 people, left the camp near the Zor Bridge around 15 July 1916, bound for Marât. Only one group of women escaped the common fate: led off to Haseke, north of Sheddadiye, they were turned over to the local tribes, probably as booty.[74] These operations were carried out by the Chechens; there were not, however, enough of them to liquidate tens of thousands of deportees. Zeki therefore called on the services of nomadic tribes living in the region lying between Marât and Sheddadiye, "especially the Beggaras, who lived between Zor-Marât and Suvar, the Ageydids, who wandered between Suvar and Sheddadiye, and the Jeburis, established in Sheddadiye and its environs; he dazzled them with the prospect of plunder."[75]

Zeki had not only to contend with the problem of managing the convoys that came from the north and, generally speaking, camped on the other side of the Zor Bridge, but also faced the urgent task of clearing the city of Der Zor of the thousands of deportees who had been living there for months. To be sure, he had already gotten rid of their leader, Levon Shashian, and most of the heads of families, but there remained a large number of women and children who had entered fully into the city's social and economic life. Andonian provides a summary of the way Zeki went about his work:

> [Zeki] had the town criers announce that the city was full of rubbish, which could cause epidemics; that the regions of Sheddadiye and Ras ul-Ayn been set aside as settlement areas for [the deportees]; that they would no longer face privations there; that those who had money could build homes there; and that the government would provide for the poorest. The town criers also announced that on such-and-such a day, the people living in such-and-such a neighborhood would have to set out, and should accordingly make the necessary preparations for their journey. He first expelled the natives of Zeitun from their homes, assembling them in the street in a pouring rain. On the other side of the [Zor] bridge, Chechens had been gathering like ants, but no one knew anything about that, for they had been subject to close surveillance and not one had the right to leave [his neighborhood]. Zeki had also brought a group of Chechens into the city and charged them with guarding his residence. One or two weeks later, Arabs informed the Armenians that the Chechens had been mobilized to liquidate them. In the space of around two weeks, all the Armenians in the city were gradually transferred to the area on the other side of the bridge. Only Armenian women who had married a Muslim or were working as maids in Muslim homes were allowed to remain behind. The local Arabs had a considerable number of Armenians in their homes and could have taken in still more. Thanks to extremely thorough searches, however, these Armenians were discovered. [Zeki] promulgated an order to the effect that no Arab had a right to more than one [Armenian] woman as a wife or domestic; those who had more would be brought before a court-martial. The others were registered. The domestics were simply given passes guaranteeing them safe conduct, while those who had married received documents identifying them as Muslims. Thereafter, whenever an Armenian women was spotted at market, she was immediately arrested and subjected to a serve interrogation.[76]

In this way, Zeki managed to expel a large proportion of the deportees who had settled in Zor. He did not, however, manage to empty the city of all its Armenians. Those who remained were harassed for several weeks.

In a 29 July 1916 dispatch, the German consul Rössler states that Zeki had taken rather swift action. "On 16 July," Rössler wrote, "we received a wire informing us that the Armenians had been ordered to leave the city. On the 17th, all the clergymen and notables were thrown into prison ... Those who were left behind are now to be liquidated tin their turn. It is quite possible that this measure is bound up with the arrival of a new, pitiless *mutesarif*."[77] Late in August, the interim consul, Hoffmann, reported that

> on the official version of events, they were conducted to Mosul (a route on which only a small minority has any chance of arriving at its destination); the general view, however, is that they were murdered in the little valley lying southwest of Der Zor, near the spot where the Kabur flows into the Euphrates. Gradually, all the Armenians are being evacuated in groups of a few hundred people each and massacred by Çerkez bands recruited especially for that purpose. A [German] officer received confirmation of this information from an Arab eyewitness who had only recently been present at a scene of this sort.[78]

These dispatches, however, represent no more than bits and pieces of what actually happened; only first-hand accounts by survivors can give a true picture of the events. We have published a volume of such accounts.[79]

It is worth pausing over the liquidation, under dreadful conditions, of the 2,000 orphans living in Zor and of a few hundred others whom Hakkı Bey had brought together on the Meskene-Zor line. A witness has described the conditions under which these children had been living in the "orphanage" in Zor:

> Their miserable plight was beyond description. They walked about, for the most part, barefoot and naked, the burden of fatigue on their shoulders, and lacking even the spirit to run away and beg for a crust of bread in the vicinity. The arms and legs, as well as the reddened shoulders of many of them were covered with untold wounds that had become horrible sores. Since the wounds had not been treated, these sores were devoured by worms that the poor little children pulled out with their fingers. Before throwing them to the ground, however, they hesitated, standing stock still in order to observe the fat bodies of these worms that wrapped themselves around the tips of their fingers. They gazed at them as if they had the feeling that it was a terrible waste, as if they would have liked to eat them: they were so hungry ... They endured, for a while, a great many hardships in this hell that had been christened an orphanage, and were then ... packed off in carts and put on the road.[80]

Long protected by the mayor of Zor, Haci Fadıl, these children survived on the strength of their wits – scavenging something to eat, for example, from garbage and animal excrements – before being sent to Suvar. There, some of them were blown up in their carts with dynamite in an utterly uninhabited spot in the desert, while others were put in natural cavities in the ground, sprinkled with kerosene, and burned alive. "Zeki Bey found a legal reason for sending them off," Andonian writes,

> He had the *müdir* of Zor, a Turk, write a report indicating that, given the increase in the orphans' numbers, there was a danger that they would spread contagious diseases. Only two children survived this massacre. One of them, thirteen or fourteen years of age, was a boy from Rodosto [Tekirdağ] by the name of Onnig who had not died of smoke inhalation because he had managed to withdraw to a remote corner of the cavity and then make his way to the surface. This boy was able to return to Zor on his own, but was so sick and had been so badly traumatized that he lived for only another three or four months. The other survivor was a girl from Şabinkarahisar named Anna, the sister of an army officer. She escaped death under the same conditions and was able to flee all the way to Urfa.[81]

Investigations conducted after the Mudros armistice revealed that it was the police chief, Mustafa Sidki, who supervised the slaughter of these children from the orphanage in Zor on 9 October 1916, followed on the 24th of the same month by that of some 2,000 more orphans whom Hakkı had rounded up in the camps to the north. Here they had been tied together in pairs and thrown into the Euphrates.[82]

According to information gathered by Aram Andonian, 192,750 people fell victim to the massacres in Zor in the five months that it took Salih Zeki to cleanse the region, from July to December 1916.[83] The indictment of the Young Turk leaders, read out at the first session of their trial on 27 April 1919, states that 195,750 people were murdered in Zor in 1916:[84] 82,000 people were liquidated between Marât and Sheddadiye and another 20,000 were liquidated at the fort of Rav near Ana under the supervision of Lieutenant Türki Mahmud.[85] A report drawn up by the Information Bureau of the Armenian Patriarchate in Constantinople indicates that, in addition to the *mutesarif* of Zor, Salih Zeki Bey, a Çerkez, the Young Turk deputy from Zor, Muhammad Nuri; Şükrü Bey, Zeki's assistant; Tiki Mahmud, the local chief of the *Sevkiyat*; Muhammad, a mufti; Hasim Hatar, a magistrate; Ali Saib, the *mutesarif*'s secretary; Muhammad El Kheder, the *müdir* of Hindin; Abdüllah Pasha; Ayntabli Mustafa Sidki, the police chief; Bedri and Mahmud Abad, police lieutenants; Salaheddin, the military commander; and Muhammad el Senia, an officer in the gendarmerie, were mainly responsible for organizing the liquidation of more than 195,000 Armenian deportees. They were aided and abetted by several notables from Zor: Yasin, the son of the mufti Muhammad; Hasan Muhammad; Halif Abdüllah; Helal el Kerzat; Halid Tetarye; Hamad; Mustafa Natar; and Yapusli Abdüllah. The *çete* chiefs who directed the massacres were Yeas Yekta (a Chechen from Heczet), Süleyman Sadullah (from Fevren), Muhammad Gaza (from Murad), Şeyh Süleyman (from Sıvad), Rebban Lefe, and the şeyh of Yegidar.[86]

Patriarch Zaven traveled through the city of Zor on 27 September on his way into exile. He was lodged in the town hall and received with a degree of respect by Salih Zeki. There, he even encountered a dozen priests from western Anatolia, apparently the last surviving Armenian men in Zor.[87] On the other hand, further south in Miadin, where Zaven arrived on 29 September, he observed that all the Armenians had been expelled, as had all those in Abukemal, where he had encountered (on Sunday, 1 October) only a boy from Aslanbeg, a blacksmith from Adabazar, and a few bakers who had been allowed to stay behind because they were indispensable. The next day he discovered, first in Kayim and then in Nehiye, six worker-soldiers from a battalion of 150 Armenians and 100 Greeks, most of them from Afionkarahisar and Kütahya, who were constructing a road to Ana. He learned that, two months earlier, the 1,600 Armenians there had been deported to Der Zor. Eight bakers, blacksmith, and masons and their families had, however, been allowed to remain behind, along with three female "servants" of the *kaymakam*'s from Urfa, and two wagon-drivers from Ayntab and Tarsus.[88] In other words, a number of the Armenians who had been sent toward Mosul had thronged into these localities before being wiped out in summer 1916.

In the following months, however, the authorities brought deportees of the Hama-Homs-Damascus line back into the region. Odian, who spent more than a year in Hama, was himself deported to Zor by way of Aleppo early in 1917. On his way there, he observed that 1,500 Armenians were still living in Meskene;[89] they were presumably deportees from Rakka who had been working for the army. Further south, in Hamam, he met Hayg Goshgarian, a bookseller and the editor of the humor magazine *Gigo*, as well as Sahag Mesrob, who had just arrived.[90] In Zor, these men were recruited as street repairmen, although they were rather more accustomed to wielding the pen.[91] The Armenian presence in Zor had by then been reduced to a young woman from Adabazar who had escaped the massacres in Marât and been taken to wife by a gypsy with whom she exhibited a monkey and bears, and 100 emaciated Armenians held in the *konak* in Zor and awaiting their departure for Ana.[92] Odian and his companions, who were relegated to Miadin somewhat later, where 100 survivors of the massacres in Marât were also living, somehow eked out an existence in this village in the midst of the desert.[93] In May 1917, the government had Odian brought to Busara, a few dozen kilometers south of Zor. He later wrote that one year earlier the little town had boasted as many as 8,000 to 10,000 Armenians; they had been massacred at Suvar and Sheddadiye by the Chechen çetes, although a few Armenians were still left there. The *müdir*, for example, was holding a young woman, a little girl, and a 14-year-old adolescent from a well-to-do Bursa family that had been massacred; all three had been sold by Chechens.[94] Odian, who did not know Arabic and was little used to this country way of life, was hard put to find a place in this society. Like many others, he had gotten wind of the benevolence with which the Yezidis of Sinjar treated Armenian refugees and dreamed of going there. Notwithstanding the risks involved, he set out on this long journey, which would lead him down the banks of the Euphrates to Baghdad disguised as an Arab beggar. Promptly robbed by two Bedouins, who took money and tobacco from him, he was thereafter stripped of all his clothes and forced to return naked to Busara, where this intellectual found himself literally dying of boredom.[95] His second attempt to escape his bitter fate led him, on 31 August 1917, to Zor, where his friends Sahag Mesrob and Hayg Goshgarian were still living. With their help, he found work in a military enterprise in which some 20 Armenians from Ayntab worked manufacturing uniforms. Around 400 women, primarily widows, were still to be found in the city.[96] Shortly thereafter, Odian was drafted as a translator for Zor's military commander, who was not able to communicate with the German officers serving there.[97] Now sporting a uniform, Odian took advantage of his good knowledge of French at meetings between Turkish and German soldiers.[98] Somewhat later, he even became the *ordonnance* (assistant) of the military commander Edwal, a former Swedish officer in the Iranian gendarmerie and the commander of the German garrison in Zor.[99] One can readily imagine the oddity of his situation, which had made an Armenian exile the indispensable interpreter at meetings between Turkish and German military men. Odian was, moreover, a witness to the sharp tensions between the German officers and the Turkish civilian authorities, especially over the Armenian wagon-drivers who had been given responsibility for military transports between Aleppo and Zor, contrary to the authorities' wishes.[100] The authorities also prohibited the Armenians working in the German barracks from leaving the city or even crossing the bridge across the Euphrates.[101] The *mutesarif* repeatedly demanded, Odian observes, that the Armenians working for the Germans be turned over to him, reminding the Turkish officers that Armenians were not allowed to serve in the army. The antagonism between civilian and military authorities over the status of the Armenians is palpable here. Moreover, the local commander pointed out to the high-ranking civilian officials that a number of Armenians were serving in all the Ottoman armies as doctors, pharmacists, and dentists and that no objections had been heard from the War Ministry.[102] According to Odian, the nephew of the former parliamentary deputy Armen Garo was the last of the deportees from Istanbul to be murdered in the prison in Zor, on orders from the police chief Ayntablı Mustafa Sidki; he was killed in January 1918, at the moment that news of the fall of Jerusalem reached the city. The famine that broke out here, Odian further reports, drove a number of women and children living among the Bedouins to rally in Zor. After providing relief to an emaciated woman from Istanbul, Odian took charge of three brothers from Smyrna, the Atamians, who had until then been living as refugees in the Suvar area. When the British forces reached Ana and the Germans began to evacuate their garrison in Zor, the lives of the Armenians working there were endangered, the more so as the Germans never considered taking them with them.[103] Basing his estimate on the "best available sources," Odian puts the number of Armenians living in Arab and Turkish homes in Zor at this time, such as that of the head of the post office or of the mayor, at around 2,000, to which we must add some 10,000 Arabized children. There was not a police officer or government official who was not keeping a woman from Harput, Bursa, Bardizag, Adabazar, Ismit, or Ayntab in his house.[104]

The World of the Concentration Camps

Our inventory of the 20 or so concentration camps set up by the Sub-Directorate of the *Sevkiyat* in the northern part of the vilayet of Aleppo, on both sides of the Amanus mountains along the trajectory of the Bagdadbahn in Ras ul-Ayn, and on the line of the Euphrates, has not allowed us to broach certain crucial points – who ran these camps, how they were organized, and what their social life was like. Without making any claim to exhaust the subject, which calls for a much more thoroughgoing study, we think it is useful to sketch a few essential points as have been suggested by the many survivors' accounts that we have published.[105] After examining, in the fourth part of the present book, the day-to-day experience of a few convoys of deportees bound for the south, we now need to observe from the inside the concentration camps, which functioned like a system of connecting vessels. This examination is all the more necessary as around 700,000 people passed through these camps.

Those in Charge of the Camps

In most survivors' accounts, the armed men who escorted the convoys are identified either as "gendarmes" or as Çerkez or Chechen *çetes*. However, on the basis of the information found in these accounts, it can be said that the generic term "gendarme" used by the deportees bears in the present case on people recruited locally, in Syria or Mesopotamia, as "gendarmes," leaders of convoys, or camp directors, by the Sub-Directorate for Deportees in Aleppo. The same accounts show that such recruitment proceeded in line with methods like the ones employed by the Special Organization: irregular militiamen and auxiliaries were recruited from among common-law criminals, notables, and local Arab, Çerkez, or Chechen tribes. In other words, the Sub-Directorate for Deportees operated the same way the Special Organization did in this respect, behind a legal facade: it supposedly answered to the Interior Ministry, yet in fact clearly seems to have been under the direct authority of the CUP's Central Committee or that of the *Teşkilât-ı Mahsusa*. In this connection, it is not really surprising to see that the collection of documents published by the *Başbakanlik Develt Arşivleri* contains virtually no telegrams from the General Director of Deportations, Şükrü Bey, to his subordinate Nuri. This suggests, at the very least, that the orders received in Aleppo came directly from another agency.

The personnel recruited in this fashion basically constituted two corps: one was responsible for the convoys, the other for the camps. The convoys were conducted by a leader and an escort of auxiliaries whom the deportees call "gendarmes." As for the camps, they were run by a director (*Sevkiyat-ı müdürü*), backed up by coworkers dispatched from Aleppo or a locally recruited staff. The director, moreover, chose a supervisor and guards from the ranks of the Armenian deportees, offering, in exchange for their services, to provide them with food and guarantees that they would not be killed. These Armenians were responsible, notably, for watching over the camps at night. The logic informing the selection of supervisors seems to have been to recruit them from the most modest social strata, so as to exacerbate the already existing antagonism between the affluent deportees – that is, those who could still buy themselves something to eat, and the others, who were literally starving to death. By all accounts, these Armenian auxiliaries were just as brutal as their "Ottoman" colleagues and particularly aggressive toward their compatriots. One hardly need say that special circumstances of this kind favored the emergence of the basest instincts and promoted boundless aggressiveness among the deportees. This aggressiveness came on top of the traditional social antagonisms and ran through all social groups, as if the victims blamed each other for the fate to which their executioners were subjecting them.

There were, finally, recruits of whom the deportees were less critical: these were the gravediggers, whose task it was to go from tent to tent every morning and collect the bodies – on average, 200 per day and per camp – of the people who had died the previous night, in order to bury them in the mass graves that were dug in the immediate vicinity of each camp. In exchange for their work, the gravediggers were given food and were temporarily exempted from further deportation. Obviously, the information provided by these recruits constitutes one of our most reliable sources when it comes to evaluating the number of victims in their respective camps. When priests were to be found in a camp, they took on the task of celebrating simplified funeral services.

The Organization of the Camps and Social Life

Except for the two transit centers in the immediate vicinity of Aleppo, the concentration camps were all located in desert areas and always outside towns and villages, access to which was strictly controlled. To enter a city was to have a chance to vanish into the crowd and, especially, to bribe someone living there into hiding one. In fact, the camps usually consisted of nothing more than a bare stretch of land without facilities of any kind. They were generally located a quarter or half hour's march from a small village or town and covered with a multitude of "tents" made of different pieces of cloth sewn together that were pressed one up against the next for reasons of security. We have already observed that the camps were often attacked at night by local tribes and that it was not at all common for the director of a camp to see effectively to the security of those under his "administration."

As for food and supplies, no provisions had been made to provide the deportees with them, rare exceptions aside. The exiles themselves had to obtain the bare necessities from the local population. In exchange for a generous payment to the director of the camp, newly minted merchants sold flour, bread, or even water at exorbitant prices to the deportees, who had no choice but to buy what they were offered at any price simply in order to survive. Thus, a sort of hierarchy of misery was established. Only the most "well-to-do" could eat as much as they liked; the others were reduced to begging, with small success.

As for lodging, the least needy could also buy themselves a decent tent – that is, a form of shelter capable of protecting them somewhat from storms or the heat of the sun in these harsh regions characterized by sharp climactic variations. We also know that some managed to hide in the Arab villages if they had paid their "hosts" a substantial rent.

Money was also the reason for big differences in the treatment meted out to the deportees. By paying the director of their camp a kind of fee ensuring the right to stay put, the most affluent could avoid being put immediately in one of the convoys that were regularly sent south toward death in order to make room for new arrivals, especially when the "natural mortality rate" was not high enough to lighten the camp population sufficiently. Every time a convoy was scheduled to set out, the director had an opportunity to make money. On this basis, a relation of shared interest was established between the director and some of those he "administered": the director had an obvious interest in keeping these families in his camp as long as he could, or at least as long as they could find the means to satisfy his appetites. That is why directors rather frequently failed to comply with the orders they received from Aleppo, keeping the deportees in a camp even though they had been told to evacuate it. The situation is comparable to the problems that the Sub-Directorate for Deportees encountered when it tried to dislodge the tens of thousands of Armenians who had managed to "take refuge" in the Arab villages north of Aleppo and whom the local peasants refused to hand over because they represented a non-negligible source of revenue. Andonian, too, escaped the common fate because he was, as he readily confesses, protected by an affluent family that had succeeded in negotiating its survival, taking refuge in Aleppo. Alongside these exceptions, however, among whom many of the survivors were to be found, how many poor people ended up in mass graves in Islahiye, Meskene, or Ras ul-Ayn, after enduring, in the case of the youngest and most resilient, months of hell spent looking daily for something, anything, to eat? How many cases of cannibalism were there? How many mothers ate their children or sold them to some nomad for a crust of bread? Famine, malnutrition, and unspeakable hygienic conditions seem to have been among the panoply of measures that the Sub-Directorate for Deportees took to eliminate these "new migrants," to whom the authorities had officially assigned the task of making the deserts of Syria and Mesopotamia bloom, although only a few thousand Bedouins actually managed to survive there. By itself, the image of orphaned or abandoned children digging through animal excrements in search a few grains of barley with which to ensure their survival sums up the situation of those interned in the desert.

Alongside the dramas of daily life, of death stalking its victims day and night and haunting people's minds, of the petty ignominies that were the price of survival, we must also point to certain aspects revelatory of a rather impressive desire to survive and a sense of organization and talent for adaptation that seems to have been second nature for a number of deportees. The information that Andonian provides about the system of communication set up by a few intellectuals – the "living newspapers," children of ages 10 or 12 who went back and forth between the camps to ensure an exchange of information – offers an excellent illustration of the kind of organization established by the deportees, despite the appalling conditions reigning in the camps, in an attempt to avoid the moral traps set for them. In the same register, we might also point to the admirable work accomplished in Der Zor by the young Istanbul intellectual Levon Shashian, who directed a kind of humanitarian organization that sought to ensure the deportees' survival.

Finally, how can one fail to be impressed, as was Cevdet when he traveled through the area in late February 1916, by the handful of Armenians in Ras ul-Ayn who, turning the *kaymakam*'s benevolence (or sense of his own interests to advantage), succeeded in the few months accorded them in settling down and even instilling life and activity into a poverty-stricken little village? Even if political contingencies had an impact on their fate, "Cemal Pasha's Armenians," whose story we shall examine later, were probably spared in part because they represented a non-negligible potential for development in these zones which the Turkish general dreamed of ruling. Deported in convoys comprising people from the same town or village, subject to incessant attacks from çetes or the tribes living in the regions through which they passed, the survivors of the Syrian or Mesopotamian deserts always maintained, despite circumstances at the limits of the human, a strong sense of solidarity with those of their compatriots who came from the same region. Geographical origins constituted, in these years of suffering, a sort of major reference point in the social organization of the Armenian deportees.

Chapter 6

The Deportees on the Hama-Homs-Damascus-Dera'a-Jerusalem-Amman-Maan Line

As we have seen, the system established in October 1915 by the Sub-Directorate for Deportees had soon ruled out sending convoys southward, after those consisting mainly of Cilicians had been expedited in that direction.[1] On this route, which was more directly under the jurisdiction of the commander-in-chief of the Fourth Army Cemal Pasha, there was never any question of creating concentration camps; the deportees were simply widely dispersed among localities in the countryside and care was taken that they not make up more than 10 per cent of the total population. This marginal deportation route, which also began in Aleppo, passed through Hama, Homs, Damascus, Jerusalem, and Amman, in that order; moreover, it fed into the Jebel Druze and the western Hauran. As early as 18 July 1915, in a circular, Mehmed Talât's right-hand man informed the prefects in the area that the southern part of the vilayet of Aleppo and the western regions of the Hauran and Kerek (or Karak, a locality slightly to the south of the Dead Sea) had been chosen as zones of relegation for the Armenian deportees.[2] These instructions seem to have been scrupulously respected: a 2 October 1915 telegram probably sent by the vali of Sham – that is, Damascus – to the interior minister reveals that 21,000 deportees had arrived in the vilayet: 8,858 had been sent to Kerek and 10,289 to the Hauran, while 494 women had been dispersed in the *kazas* of Kuneytra, Bâlbek, Tebek, and Doma.[3] A 20 September 1915 report by the American consul in Damascus, Greg Young, confirms these official facts and figures. The report states that since 12 August, from two to three convoys arrived weekly, containing between a few hundred to 2,000 deportees, all of whom were concentrated in the outskirts of Damascus in Kahdem. Kahdem, a vast, dry field, was for Damascus what the camps of Sibil and Karlık were for Aleppo.[4] According to Young, who went to this camp because he wanted to make a more precise assessment of the deportees' situation – the camp's director received him with "courtesy," but did not allow him to enter the camp – there were only a few makeshift tents there, together with a multitude in rags. Young's informants put the number of deportees who had so far arrived in Damascus at 22,000. Finally, in the same dispatch, the consul revealed that, according to "well informed sources," another 30,000 Armenians were then interned in a camp in Homs.[5] A 28 October 1915 report that refers to accounts by Arab deputies in the Ottoman parliament states that "the train brings large numbers of Armenians to the mountain areas and leaves them there without food or water ... We saw many women, old people and children dying of hunger the length of the railway."[6] The American consul in Aleppo, Jackson, wondered in a report that he sent to his ambassador on 29 September how he might help the deportees, in view of the fact that "they are rapidly pushed on to Hama, Homs, Damascus, etc. and on to Amman."[7] In attachments to this report, the American diplomat estimated the number of Armenians who had been sent to the Damascus region before late September 1915 at 40,300, and the number of children among them at 6,150.[8] The rate at which conveys were sent south seems, moreover, to have remained fairly high in the following weeks, inasmuch as Jackson, again, counted, "from the reliable sources," 132,000 deportees in February 1916, of whom more than 100,000 found themselves in the areas that extended from Damascus to Maan (probably included in this figure were the deportees in the camps of Jebel Druze, the western Hauran, Jerusalem, Kerek, and Amman), another 12,000 in Hama and its environs, and 20,000 more in Homs and the vicinity.[9] Unlike their compatriots on the lines of the Euphrates and Ras ul-Ayn-Mosul, these deportees were not subjected to systematic liquidation.

The Fourth Army's need for to recruit qualified personnel seems to have enabled a few thousand additional deportees to move south, despite the ban imposed in November. Yervant Odian, who spent time in the camp in Sibil in late November 1915, was able to introduce himself into a convoy of one thousand one hundred craftsmen, with their wives and children, who had been recruited by the army.[10] These deportees, from Edirne, Bardizag, Adana, Ayntab, and Kayseri, with their distinct dialects, were sent south in a freight train, 100 to a car – that is, in extremely crowded conditions: it was impossible to sit down, and there were many sick people in the group. All were well aware that they had cheated death.[11]

The Armenian Deportees in Damascus

In the more southerly city of Damascus, too, there was a heavy concentration of deportees who had managed to avoid the line of the Euphrates and the Mesopotamian desert. As in Homs and Hama, certain deportees who had a reputation as skilled craftsmen were recruited to serve further north on the orders of the Fourth Army command and were sent to Damascus to help meet the Ottoman army's needs for various kinds of equipment. All knew that it was a privilege to reach Damascus, a gauge of survival,[12] all the more so as the city had before the war boasted an Armenian community of some 400 members[13] who were likely to help the new arrivals.

The Armenian church and its dependencies were soon filled with a multitude of refugees. During a November 1916 visit to Damascus, Bishop Yeghishe Chilingirian put the number of deportees in the city at more than 20,000. One year later, in November 1917, he estimated their numbers at 30,000, and observed that the deportees had adapted well to local life. Thus, he noted that Armenian merchants rather largely dominated the market in Bab Tuma in the Christian quarter.[14] The immense majority of deportees, however, worked in enterprises run by the army or indispensable from its point of view, such as the *Bagdadbahn* Company. One well-known firm of this sort was a railroad equipment factory that employed 150 Armenians, who represented one-fifth of its labor force.[15] After a few months, during which these deportees in Damascus were left more or less in peace, they were confronted with a painful choice: either to convert to Islam or set out again for an unknown destination.[16]

Like Ahmed Cemal, the vali of Damascus, Tahsin Bey, who had previously been the vali of Erzerum, was more interested in exploiting these deportees' labor-power than in liquidating them. Chilingirian notes that the vali had opened an orphanage for homeless children and a shelter for widows in which the women did embroidery or made carpets[17] without having to face threats of expulsion.[18] According to Patriarch Zaven, the Constantinople Patriarchate sent money to *vartabed* Aristages Khachadurian of the Jerusalem congregation in order to provide relief to the neediest deportees, including, he says, several hundred intellectuals, writers, and elementary and secondary school teachers.[19] This suggests that Aleppo's underground network had succeeded in preventing these people from being sent down the line of the Euphrates and having them dispatched to Damascus instead. In addition to the widows and orphans cared for in the institutions created by the vali, a commission for social welfare set up by the community took the poorest families and women without support in hand.[20]

In November 1917, in the wake of a joint Arab-British offensive on the Palestinian front, the authorities transferred the patriarch-catholicos, Sahag Khabayan, and the former patriarch, Malakia Ormanian, from Jerusalem to Damascus.[21] Khabayan had become the head of the Armenian millet after the dissolution of the Constantinople Patriarchate (we shall discuss these changes below). In February 1918, however, after the Ottoman army had been dealt a series of defeats, Damascus was threatened in its turn, and the situation of its inhabitants suddenly worsened. The Arab rebellion had made it difficult to bring food and supplies into the city, and prices had soared.[22] On the morning of 2 March, the police and army rounded up all the Armenians in the city without advance notice, on the pretext that they had a mobilization order. The 1,700 women and orphans who had survived on state aid until then ceased to receive food.[23] The fact that the orphanage and widows' shelter were no longer receiving food can be blamed on the military situation, but the "mobilization" of the men in the face of the Arab-British advance seems rather to indicate that the civilian and military authorities had decided to liquidate them before the enemy arrived.

The Armenian Patriarchate of Jerusalem and the Deportees

In Jerusalem, the Armenian Patriarchate was on the eve of the war going through an acute crisis of the sort that was endemic to this venerable institution. The former Patriarch Malakia Ormanian had been delegated as an inspector in Jerusalem by the Armenian authorities in Constantinople. His mission was to restore order to the Monastery of Saint James and put its finances back on a sound footing. After a stop in Alexandria, where he was received by Boghos Nubar on 3/16 May 1914, Ormanian bent himself to his task.[24] In fall 1915, he had to take in 80 notables from Adana with their families: as a special favor, Cemal had authorized these Armenians to move into apartments in the Patriarchal monastery that were traditionally reserved for pilgrims.[25]

On 9 November 1915, the catholicos and his entourage, who had been expelled from Aleppo by the vali Mustafa Abdülhalik, was finally authorized, on special orders from Cemal Pasha, to take up residence in the Monastery of Saint James.[26] It appears that, until April 1917, the institution had been more or less spared. On 25 April, all the students in the Patriarchal seminary were "mobilized" and the seminary was shut down as a result;[27] as was just noted, the Armenian religious dignitaries were evacuated to Damascus in November of the same year. According to information provided by a teacher who had taken refuge in Jerusalem, hundreds of orphans were living in the city's streets without any form of aid in March 1918, and would continue to do so until war's end.[28] Presumably, the fact that the superiors of the Congregation of Saint James were absent had prevented the venerable institution from taking these children into its care.

The Armenian Orphans in Ayntura

Before the war, Beirut was, with Damascus, one of the rare cities in the region that boasted an Armenian colony; the small community here numbered 1,500. Not far from the city, in Ayntura, the authorities had opened a "Turkish" orphanage in what had formerly been a French monastery; it had been put in the hands of one of the Young Turk movement's muses, Halide Edip. This well-supported model institution was a kind of laboratory in which Edip endeavored to Turkify the children who had been entrusted to her care – that is, around one thousand "rebaptized" Armenian orphans, but also a few Kurdish children. The missionary Harriet Fischer, who paid a visit to the orphanage in January-February 1916, reports that the

Young Turk feminist finally told her, in the course of a conversation about the fate meted out to the Armenians: "It is our nation or the Armenians'." "They are children," Edip added; "they don't know what religion means."[29] It was to this institution that children from the orphanage directed by Beatrice Rohner in Aleppo were transferred after the Aleppo orphanage was shut down by the Ottoman government in February 1917.[30]

The Armenian Deportees in Hama and Homs

The situation was palpably different in an Arab city such as Hama, which had 60,000 to 70,000 inhabitants, many of whom were orthodox Syriac Christians.[31] A majority of the deportees who ended up here in autumn 1915 were from Cilicia. A good many of them were the victims of epidemics or malnutrition; others were under heavy pressure from the authorities, whose objective was to convert them to Islam by force.[32]

Odian, who arrived in Hama on 21 December 1915, observes that around 5,000 Armenians from Adana, Kayseri, Ayntab, and Antioch had preceded him there.[33] Before long, half of the shops in the bazaar were in the hands of Armenians from Adana and Ayntab who had not endured the suffering inflicted on the others and had even been able to sell some of their assets before leaving. Pharmacists, dentists, tinsmiths, and so on provided services to the city, which faced a shortage of qualified personnel. Deportees opened the first photographer's shop and the first restaurants in town in the same period. Odian notes that, when Enver or Cemal traveled through Hama, the local authorities appealed to Armenians to organize a reception. But, alongside these quick-witted deportees, how many others found themselves in a terrible predicament – the 30 young women from Samsun, for instance, who reached Hama only after going through an ordeal lasting several months?[34] Our witness also points to rather exceptional cases, such as that of a convoy of 30 men from Kayseri, dentists and artisans whose wives, still in their homes, had either converted or been deported to Rakka. Because the overriding priority was to survive, and because a specialty such as medicine was often the ticket to survival, Odian writes that one of the men even palmed himself off as a doctor and prescribed his admiring patients remedies that were anything but orthodox. This determined charlatan was so successful that he was named to the post of municipal physician in Hama. There Odian also crossed paths with families from Ismit and notables from Adana.[35]

The deportees were all but cut off from the rest of the world here. The rare information that reached them was provided by the Agence Ottomane's French-language dispatches, which a reading cabinet created by the Germans made available to the deportees who spoke French and also to Armenian officers, doctors, and, especially, pharmacists who arrived from Constantinople on their way to the Palestinian front.[36]

There were only a few hundred Armenian men in Hama. They were given only a few months' respite. Early in April 1916, roundups of Armenians were organized in Hama's streets by the city's military commander, Osman Bey: the official purpose of these actions was to mobilized men between the ages of 18 and 45. The decision was, however, postponed on Cemal's orders.[37] In July 1916, the deportees were abruptly confronted with another threat. It was proffered by the president of the Young Turk club, Şevket Bey, who proposed to Islamicize them. The *mutesarif*, Hayri Feruzan, a former colonel who was reputed to be well intentioned, a man "whose advice revealed the danger that threatened the deportees," pointed out to the Armenian notables that if they refused this offer they could no longer remain in Hama. While we have precise information about conversions organized in one place or another, Odian's account allows us to observe in detail how the deportees in Hama reacted to this offer, as well as the methods used to convince them to convert. By itself, the fact that the proposition came from the local Young Turk chief is revelatory.

The deportees were given two days to make up their minds. Initially, they made a collective decision to refuse the offer. According to Odian, the *mutesarif* strongly insisted, confessing to his interlocutors that he was ashamed to make such a request of them but adding that it was the only way to save them and that their conversion would in any case be temporary. In the meantime, the deportees in Hama learned that collective conversions had begun in Homs.[38] Patriarch Zaven's advice was certainly sought: he confides in his memoirs that he suggested to the endangered deportees to accept while waiting for the storm to blow over.[39] Odian does not tell us whether the patriarch's opinion decided the matter, but notes that a majority of the Armenians showed a willingness to accept the offer to "save its skin." A member of the Unionist Central Committee who was in Damascus, Ali Kemal, made a personal appearance in Hama in order to supervise the conversion, which must obviously be understood as a sign of adhesion to Turkism. Those who showed the greatest alarm were men who headed families; they apparently feared that their daughters would soon face forced marriages.

Under duress, Odian became Aziz Nuri and even received identity papers under that name. To some extent as an act of defiance, and doubtless even more as a sign of derision, Odian notes that all the men took Abdüllah as their patronymic. Three priests and two Protestant ministers who were suspected of having urged their compatriots to resist conversion were arrested just before the commencement of the Islamicization procedures, which took place in Hama's Young Turk club.[40] Of the 5,000 deportees in the city, only 30 Armenian women from Samsun categorically refused to give in. "They killed our husbands and children," they exclaimed, "and carried off our daughters; let them kill us now." The Arab population was apparently shocked by these methods and refused to grant access to the mosques to these converts, who were spared circumcision for the moment, the appropriate period for that ceremony being March or April.[41] The case of Levon Mozian, which Odian describes, is one of the most interesting. Mozian, who belonged to the underground network working on the Intilli construction site of the *Bagdadbahn*, managed to escape when the Armenian workers were liquidated and took refuge in Hama in August 1916.[42] After Odian was arrested in Mersin – considered to be a deserter, he was also accused of spying for the British – and interned in Tarsus with a German driver who was also arrested as an English spy, although no one could converse with him, his talents as an interpreter saved his life. In Adana, he met Levon Zakarian, alias Ali Haydar, an inspector in the Department of the Public Debt who traveled back and forth between Adana and Beirut or Damascus. Thanks to Zakarian, Mozian was able to go to Hama, where he became, under the name of Ali Nureddin, a mathematics teacher in the city's only middle school.[43] The travels of this committed journalist, who spoke French and knew how to live by his wits, doubtlessly offer some sense of the way deportees in this category managed to survive.

Another group of survivors was made up of the 2,000 to 3,000 children, principally girls between the ages of four and eight, who were in the hands of Arab families from Hama, and also street urchins who sought to survive by any and all means. Among them, an 11-year-old boy caught Odian's attention, having survived by selling his younger sister to couples who wanted children, then retrieving her and selling her again.[44]

A number of women without families survived by working as domestics in Greek Melchite and Syriac homes in the city. In early 1917, the new *mutesarif* had them all rounded up on the pretext that they had all converted to Islam and could no longer work in Christian families.[45] One last group straggled into Hama late in 1916. Involved here were a few people who had escaped the massacres of Der Zor by miracle;[46] their accounts of what they had experienced terrified the Armenians who had been relegated to Hama.

The situation of these deportees was then especially insecure. All of them were at the mercy of the local authorities and, above all, the orders from the central authorities, who continued to pay close attention to the fate of the "lucky ones" dispatched down the route leading south.

Despite local conditions that hardly favored humanitarian action, in 1917 the deportees personally took in hand around 150 orphans in Hama. The children were lodged in a makeshift shelter. Once again, Zollinger, the philanthropist from Aleppo, stepped in to save lives: the monthly stipends of from 60 to 100 Turkish pounds that he provided for the orphans' support were instrumental to their survival. For lack of funds, about the same number of children were condemned to wander through the city's streets.[47] When the armistice was declared, the number of Armenian deportees in the region of Hama was estimated at 10,000.[48]

In the neighboring city of Homs, estimates put the number of surviving Armenians in the same period at between 2,000 and 3,000. These Armenians, too, had been converted under duress. Most of them survived by working in military firms until the British troops and the Arab forces arrived in the area.[49]

The Deportees Relegated to Jordan and the Hauran

In addition to the zones of relegation in Syria that we have just discussed, deportees were sent to several other regions further south. Patriarch Zaven reports that 1,000 families had been scattered throughout the regions of Salt, Kerek, Amman, and the *sancak* of Saray.[50] According to Hasan Amca, a Circassian officer working in Cemal Pasha's service, between 20,000 and 30,000 of them were living in several localities in the Hauran and Jebel Druze in May 1916. Amca was the better informed about the fate of these deportees, in that Cemal had entrusted him with the task of organizing their transfer to Beirut and Jaffa in summer 1916.[51] It was with a view to carrying out these instructions that he traveled in late August to Dera'a, the principal town in the Hauran, in his capacity as a delegate of the Special Commission responsible for the deportees in the Hauran. There he was confronted with the hostility of the chief of the Damascus branch of the *Sevkiyat*, Neşad Bey, who was also the Ittihad's regional delegate. Neşad was all the more hostile to the idea of a transfer in that he had just completed the procedures involved in the conversion of the deportees. "An Armenian priest," Amca recalls, "had been deprived of food until he died for systematically refusing to convert to Islam."[52] In the first localities he visited, he discovered thousands of people who were mere skin and bones, "with sunken cheeks, arms and legs that looked like sticks, resembling nothing more than mummies, and close to death."[53] Later, in the very rugged Jebel, which looks down on the desert of the Hauran, he came across a series of villages where "thirty thousand to forty thousand deportees had died of typhus, relapsing fever, or the malaria raging in the region." In Hazraköy, an hour from Kefrence, he learned that 417 of the 500 people who had been relegated to this village had died: "Living corpses, leaning on crutches, made their way down the narrow lanes of the village with great effort."[54] Amca nevertheless managed to recover 400 widows and orphans from the mountainous region known as the Jebel and bring them back to Dera'a; from there, they left in three convoys for Damascus, Tripoli (Syria), Haifa, Jaffa, and Akkia. This modest operation, which Cemal Pasha had decided to conduct at a time when Istanbul was in the process of liquidating the deportees in the camps on the line of the Euphrates, led to a serious conflict between Amca and the Ittihad's delegate in Damascus, Neşad Bey. Neşad is said to have given Amca a written order to bring these operations to a halt but, running up against the officer's stubborn refusal to comply, the two of them went to Damascus and submitted their difference of opinion to Cemal for judgement. Amca's account of the meeting seems to confirm that the commander of the Fourth Army had firmly resolved to carry out his plan to resettle Armenian deportees from the Hauran in Lebanon and Palestine. Indeed, Cemal succeeded in having the Ittihad's delegate relieved of his functions and had the vali of Damascus, Tahsin Bey, appointed to the post of director of the deportees. According to Amca, he went to Dera'a with Tahsin on 25 September 1916, and the convoys were once again put on the road south.[55]

Although this plan did not go forward as expected – too many deportees had already died and there remained only 3,000 to 4,000 Armenians in the Hauran – it reveals that there was a marked opposition between Cemal and the CUP leadership. When we recall Cemal's repressive practices toward the Arab elites of Syria and Lebanon, it seems reasonable to ask what motivated him to launch a campaign that ran counter to the line adopted by his party. In his memoirs, he contents himself with the statement: "I thought it better to bring a large number of them into the Syrian vilayets of Beirut and Aleppo," while saying nothing about the objectives he was then pursuing.[56]

Chapter 7

The Peculiar Case of Ahmed Cemal: The Ittihad's Independent Spirit or an Agent of the Genocide?

Ahmed Cemal, who simultaneously held the posts of minister of the navy and commander-in-chief of the Fourth Army, was in theory the sole master of Syria, Lebanon, and Palestine. Yet, we have already noted that he very often had no other choice than to bow to the demands of the Ittihad's radical branch. His political prerogatives seem almost always to have overridden the military priorities of which he and the empire's German allies were in charge. One can, however, ask whether he favored the liquidation of the Armenians. Before we try to answer this question, we should recall that Cemal's policy toward the Arab populations, Muslim and Christian alike, was at the very least harsh, and that it was an open secret that liquidating the Arab elites was, as the Young Turks and especially Cemal himself saw it, another "national priority." In his memoirs, Ohannès Pacha Kouyoumdjian, the last Ottoman governor of Lebanon (1913–15) and a remarkable observer of the prevailing situation in the first year of the war, leaves little doubt about the intentions that Cemal and the Young Turk regime harbored toward the Arabs in general and the Lebanese in particular.[1] The information that he provides on the debate about the famine in Lebanon buttresses the thesis that a deliberate land blockade – a blockade of the railroad – had been put in place for the purpose of decimating the Lebanese population, which was suspected of being pro-French and fomenting rebellion. As in the Armenian case, so here too the Young Turks' virulent nationalism sought to punish these inassimilable "traitors." The alibi that the British fleet had imposed a naval blockade, to which certain historians still frequently resort to explain the famine in Lebanon, offered the CUP perfect camouflage. The mere fact that Cemal felt obliged to publish, in 1916, a pamphlet in French justifying his anti-Arab exactions[2] shows that the General was concerned about his reputation and also wished to take his distance from the acts of his colleagues on the Unionist Central Committee. Nothing, however, suggests that Cemal was opposed to the policy of ethnic homogenization put into practice by his party, the liquidation of the Armenian population included. Rather, his opposition to prevailing policy seems to have been rooted in a certain military rationale that consisted in profiting from the Armenian deportees' labor-power before liquidating them. Cemal's frequent intercession on behalf of Armenian "friends" in Adana or in Aleppo, many examples of which we have already adduced, does not necessarily mean that he was not an advocate of the Ittihad's Turkism. Old friendships, dating from the days when he was vali of Adana, may suffice to explain his generosity vis-à-vis some of the Cilicians, who perhaps were also generous toward him, while playing on the amour-propre of a man who was made uncomfortable by the great influence that Enver enjoyed. The part he played in setting the trap for the people of Zeitun shows that, in accord with his party, he participated in fabricating the scenario of a revolt and then personally conducted the military operation.

That said, it must be pointed out that, unlike those on the line of the Euphrates or that of the *Bagdadbahn*, the 130,000 to 150,000 Armenians on the southern deportation line, which was more directly under Cemal's jurisdiction, were not radically liquidated. Indeed, in summer 1916, Cemal even undertook to mount a veritable rescue operation for a few thousand deportees in the Hauran, as we have just seen. On the other hand, the policy of systematically carrying out forced conversions to Islam that was applied from May 1916 on to the Armenian deportees of the Aleppo-Damascus-Jerusalem-Maan line does not seem to have met with his disapproval. Earlier, this possibility, which the authorities went so far as to codify by publishing a sort of book of instructions about demands so formulated that it was always possible to reject a request to convert,[3] had benefited only a few Armenians from localities scattered throughout western Anatolia. The spring 1916 campaign was, however, of altogether different dimensions because it affected all of "Cemal's Armenians" – that is, around 150,000 people.

At all events, this operation did not escape the attention of diplomatic circles. According to Ambassador Metternich, it was in May 1916 that recurrent reports of forced conversions reached the German embassy. However, Metternich writes, "The central government in Constantinople has consistently denied the accuracy of these reports. Halil Bey and Talât Bey have both repeatedly assured me that they did not have the slightest intention of harming the Christian elements of the Armenian population."[4] On 26 June 1916, the consul in Jerusalem, Dr. Brode, informed his superiors that the deportees who had settled in Transjordan had been converted by force, notably 3,500 people living in Dera'a.[5] Similar reports were making the rounds in Damascus, where consul Loytved indicated, in a 20 June note, that "the Armenians are more or less all obliged to become Muslims."[6] The interim consul in Aleppo reported facts indicating that a systematic campaign had been set in motion:

> Over the course of the past few weeks, in Hama, Homs, Damascus, and so on, depor-
> tees facing the threat of being sent to still remoter regions had to convert *en masse*
> to Islam (the information comes from several concurrent sources). The procedure is
> purely bureaucratic: a request is filed, followed by a name change ... Apparently, those
> promoting this plan have examples dating from the time of the Ottoman conquest in
> mind.[7]

These telegrams, which all corroborate Odian's account, leave no doubt about the fact that what was involved here was a planned operation and that the decision had been made at the highest levels of the state – without a doubt by the Ittihad's Central Committee – in March or April 1916. It is even probable that it coincided with the plan to liquidate the Armenians held in the concentration camps on the line of the Euphrates and to close down all foreign humanitarian institutions providing relief for orphans and other deportees. In other words, the method adopted to make "Cemal's Armenians" disappear was much less radical. Can we attribute this generosity to Cemal Pasha? That is quite possible. We are even tempted to suppose that it was in the wake of this decision that Cemal assigned Hasan Amca the mission of saving a few thousand Armenians, with the ulterior motive of showing that he himself, who had no small amount of Arab blood on his hands, did not endorse the genocidal policies of his party, thus arming himself in advance against fresh accusations of war crimes.

It is known, moreover, that the catholicos, Sahag Kahabayan, was assigned a residence in Jerusalem thanks to the commander of the Fourth Army, who later engineered the official 30 July 1916 decree ordering the merger of the Armenian Patriarchates of Jerusalem and Constantinople under the authority of Sahag II, promoted to the rank of "patriarch-catholicos" of all the empire's Armenians, with his seat in Jerusalem. It seems reasonable to suppose that this measure suited the CUP, for it made the elimination of the Armenians of Asia Minor official while preserving a semblance of legality. This patriarch-catholicos was apparently to govern the vestiges of the Armenian population settled in the Arab provinces of the Ottoman Empire. In his memoirs, Patriarch Zaven does not deny that the deportees were spared, relatively speaking, in the regions under Cemal's control. According to Zaven, Cemal had applied only the decision made by the Council of Ministers – to remove the Armenians from the frontier zones – but not the decision to liquidate them, which had been "taken by the Ittihad and implemented by the interior minister."[8]

The constant interference of the delegates of the Unionist Committee or the interior minister in local affairs, as in Dera'a, doubtless also helped make Cemal's relations with the CUP more tense. A wire that Talât sent Cemal on 18 February 1916 suggests that the two men disagreed about the fate to be meted out to the deportees.[9] In this telegram, the interior minister requests the Commander of the Fourth Army stop moving the Armenian deportees from "their places of residence." Which deportees are involved is not specified, but it may be presumed that Talât had in mind craftsmen or specialists who had been recruited to meet the army's needs. At all events, this was a way of reminding Cemal that he was exceeding his prerogatives and slowing down his work by taking control of deportees who did not fall under his jurisdiction. We shall see, moreover, that Cemal also endeavored, from December 1915 to spring 1916, to prevent the immediate liquidation of the worker-deportees who had been put to work digging tunnels through the Amanus. While military contingencies may explain these decisions, they were presumably also inspired by personal ambition. The same cannot, however, be attributed to moral repulsion over the criminal acts of Cemal's colleagues in Istanbul.

The Negotiations between Ahmed Cemal and the Entente Powers

The exploration of many different Western archives carried out in the past few years enables us today to point to a possible explanation for Cemal's peculiar positions. A Foreign Office document,[10] as well as a strange exchange of letters between Dr. Ivan Zavriev,[11] a Dashnak leaders close to Imperial circles in St. Petersburg, and Boghos Nubar, the president of the Armenian National Delegation based in Paris,[12] supplemented by notes preserved in the Archives of the French and Russian Foreign Ministries,[13] reveals that, in December 1915, Ahmed Cemal conducted negotiations in great secrecy with an eye to bringing together the English, French, and Russians in a common plan to destabilize the Ottoman Empire from within. Among the topics broached in these negotiations, it must above all be noted that Cemal showed a willingness to carry out a military expedition against Constantinople, obviously for the purpose of overthrowing the Young Turk regime in exchange for guarantees of the territorial integrity of Asiatic Turkey – that is, "Syria, Palestine, Mesopotamia, Arabia, Armenia with Cilicia and Kurdistan" – and another promise that he would be proclaimed sultan in place of the house of Osman, with hereditary rights for his family. What is more, one of the clauses of the proposal bears on the deportees' fate: Cemal offered to "take measures, beginning immediately, to save the Armenian population and provide it with basic necessities until the end of the war."[14] The seven-point plan preserved in the archives of the French Foreign Ministry,[15] as well as the letters exchanged between the Russians, French, and English, clearly indicate that the initiative here came from the Russians, but was inspired by Armenian circles in Russia. But this attempt interfered with the French and English Sykes-Picot negotiations over the future of the Near East.

The soul of this operation was Dr. Ivan Zavriev, a Moscow aristocrat with a background unusual in Armenian circles.[16] Zavriev had already played a very active role in St. Petersburg during the negotiations that led, on 8 February 1914, to the promulgation of an Ottoman Imperial decree providing for reforms in the eastern provinces. In 1915–16, he redoubled his activities. Aware of the deportations and massacres to which the Ottoman Armenians had been subject since spring 1915, he set out, with his party's approval, to find means of saving what might still be saved. To this end, he traveled to London in August 1915, but obtained no concrete results.[17] It seems, however, that the situation improved somewhat in December 1915, at a moment when Zavriev was in Bucharest. The first piece of information on the question came from the Russian ambassador in the Rumanian capital, S. A. Poklevsky, who indicated in an 11 December 1915 cable to the Russian foreign minister, Sazanov, that

> Zavriev has received information about the rupture just consummated between Cemal Pasha and the Turkish government; this opens up the possibility that he can be turned against Constantinople if the Entente powers promise him that he will rule over the Near East. Zavriev wants to know to what extent this measure corresponds with the audacious [plans] of the imperial government. If it does correspond, the Armenians are in a position to broach discussions with Cemal.[18]

This approach soon produced effects. In the next few days, Sazanov instructed the Russian ambassador to France, Alexandre Isvolsky, to contact the French and English in order to find out whether they were inclined to follow Russia's lead on this issue.[19] While the proposal was not without interest, it apparently had the disadvantage of conflicting with the "arrangements" that the members of the Entente had made for the dismemberment of the Ottoman Empire. To promise Cemal the eastern regions of the empire came down to depriving France and England of their "advance." Thus, the initially hostile reaction of Aristide Briand, president of the French Council of Ministers and also foreign minister, came as no surprise.[20] The response of the French ambassador in Petrograd, Paléologue, to Aristide Briand shows that "Cemal Pasha's suggestions were brought to the attention of the Russian government by one of its secret agents in Armenia, a physician [Zavriev] who is currently residing in Bucharest."[21] Presented at first as a Russian plan, the affair was ultimately described as "an Armenian plan ... that by no means implies adoption of all the points put forward by the Armenians."[22] From these first approaches, it is clear that it was Zavriev who had succeeded in establishing direct contact with Cemal in Bucharest as soon as he got wind of the discord between him and his Ittihadist colleagues. Doubtless he had also understood that, circumstances allowing, Cemal envisaged carving out a personal fief for himself that would straddle the Arab world and Asia Minor. In taking this initiative, Zavriev was obviously hoping to save the hundreds of thousands of Armenians who were still concentrated in the Syrian and Mesopotamian deserts, where they were wasting away. His correspondence with Boghos Nubar and the echoes of their February 1916 conversations in Paris indicate that the Armenian National Delegation, headed by Nubar, and the leadership of the Dashnak party, which had put this matter in Zavriev's hands, were working hand in hand. In a letter sent from Stockholm on 8 February 1916, Zavriev informed Nubar that he was coming to Paris "in connection with a matter that interests our government, with the consent of [his] comrades."[23] After arriving in Paris a few days later, he quickly obtained an interview with Alexandre Isvolsky.[24] In a 24 February note to Nubar, he informed him of his interview with the Russian ambassador and the hopes that it had aroused in him.[25]

All this tends to show that, early in 1916, a rift had appeared between the Ittihad, led by Mehmed Talât and Ahmed Cemal, and that it had widened to the point that Cemal could envisage the unlikely eventuality of turning against Istanbul if he obtained guarantees.

His memoirs breathe not a word about this chill in their relations – no more than Talât's do. Hence we do not know the underlying motivations for his behavior, which are probably unrelated to the fate of the deportees, now mere bargaining chips, in Syria and Mesopotamia. It was perhaps because Cemal was considering raising this question again that he decided to have nothing to do with the Armenians' liquidation and even to launch the Dera'a rescue operation.

That said, we need to point out that Aristide Briand's and Lord Gray's reluctance to endorse this plan was never really overcome. Their Russian counterpart Sazonov failed to convince them to enter into negotiations with Cemal, although an agreement with him would have committed them to very little, while the possibility of destabilizing the Young Turk regime was hardly one to be neglected. To be sure, the Russian forces had taken control of Trebizond and Erzerum by this time; the Russians had the greatest interest in a conflict between Cemal and the central authorities that could open the gates of Constantinople to them. But the English and French could not afford, precisely, to let the Ottoman capital fall into Russian hands. This was probably the decisive element leading to the failure of Zavriev's plan, which definitely sealed the Armenian deportees' fate.[26]

Chapter 8

The Armenian Deportees on the *Bagdadbahn* Construction Sites in the Taurus and Amanus Mountains

We have seen how the Ottoman government took advantage of the *Bagdadbahn* and proceeded, in July 1915, to deport the Armenian employees working on the railroad construction sites in both the Taurus and Amanus mountain regions. We have also noted that the company's directors, threatened with confiscation, had no other choice than to violate the ban on hiring Armenian workers if they wanted to resume construction of the trunks of the railway running through the mountains.[1]

On the Taurus construction sites, where some ten tunnels were being dug, there were hundreds of Russian, Georgian, Rumanian, French, English, and Russian-Armenian prisoners of war, but also thousands of Ottoman subjects, Armenian, Turkish, and Greek.[2] Located in the immediate vicinity of the points through which the deportees from western Anatolia passed, the Taurus building sites embodied a hope of survival for the Armenians. According to Sebuh Aguni, who had himself been recruited on one of these sites as a timekeeper, 3,000 Armenians were working between Bozanti and Dorak.[3] Two brothers from Adana, Dr. Benyamin Boyajian, the chief physician in the German hospital in Belemedik, and Kevork Boyajian, a manager employed by the German Bagdadbahn Company, played an eminent role in recruiting Armenian employees, especially intellectuals, and in providing hundreds of deportees with places of refuge.[4]

Aside from the Boyajian brothers, who were close friends of the chief of the building site, the Swiss engineer Lütneger exhibited a consistently benevolent attitude. The director of the "Technical Bureau," Hayg Kalenderian, but also translators such as Toros Avedisian, a manager in charge of supplies, Krikor Chakerian from Edirne, the pharmacist Onnig Papazian, the engineer and topographer Sebuh Sayabalian, the furnace supervisor Yervant Papazian, and the vice-treasurer Onnig Postagian were agents of the Armenian network who gave unsparingly of their time and energy in order to save their compatriots.[5]

In the Amanus region, where several tunnels were being dug, around 20,000 Armenian deportees had been recruited to work on the building sites of Intilli, Ayran, Yenice, Bahçe, and Keller in autumn 1915.[6] From Ismit, Bardizag, Adabazar, Bilecik, Eskişehir, Konya, or Eregli – that is, regions in western Asia Minor – these carpenters, woodworkers, blacksmiths, skilled workers, surveyors, and draftsmen were recruited directly in the camps of Mamura or Islahiye by foremen from the German company, who authorized them to bring their families with them. Thus, two camps were rather quickly set up in the Amanus region. According to Aguni, the engineer Philippe Holsmann, whose firm was responsible for building two of the Amanus tunnels, took the initiative of recruiting Armenian deportees and later did all he could to save their lives.[7] The same witness reveals that the deportees handled the dynamite, "for there was no one else to carry out such dangerous operations."[8] An orphanage was even created in Intilli on the engineers' initiative to care for homeless children roaming through the area.[9] Dr. P. Hovnanian, a physician working for the *Bagdadbahn* in the hospital in Intilli, and Vartivar Kabayan and Garabed Geukjeian, who were responsible for supplies on the Amanus building sites, played central roles in recruiting deportees.[10]

While Franz Günther, the head of the Anatolian Railway Company, obtained in fall 1915 the backing of the German military hierarchy and the War Minster for the idea of putting the building sites of the Taurus and Amanus regions back into operation by hiring deportees, M. Winkler, the engineer responsible for construction in the vilayet of Adana, had to put up with harassment from local government officials on a day-to-day basis.[11] The arrangements to which the military men closed their eyes were apparently tolerated only provisionally by the civilian authorities. When the interior minister learned, in January 1916, that 15,000 to 20,000 deportees had been concentrated around the Amanus building site, he conducted an "inquiry" and demanded that those who were "illegally" present on the site be deported to the "destination planned" for them.[12] The presence of 20,000 deportees massed around Bozanti and the Taurus building sites – some of whom were employed on the sites – also came to the attention of Talât Bey, who ordered that they "be dispatched, convoy by convoy, to the areas to which they are to go." The minister also demanded "the competent individuals" to furnish him "information about the number of Armenian émigrés who are to be found in these places and about how and from where they have come to the area."[13] It is clear that this procedure was part of the operation that the government launched in the same period in order to evacuate the camps north of Aleppo and shift the deportees toward the line of the Euphrates or Ras ul-Ayn. However, because in this particular case the procedure affected workers on the sites of the *Bagdadbahn*, it sparked opposition from the German leadership of the company as well as the German general staff.[14] German sources reveal that Winkler and his engineers faced down gendarmes who came to the building sites to arrest deportees. Ultimately, however, they agreed to compile a list of their employees.[15]

The fact of the matter seems to be that Talât had by no means abandoned his plan to liquidate the last deportees in the Taurus and the Amanus regions, but had simply suspended it. The 19 March 1916 appointment of Cevdet Bey, the former vali of Van, to the head of the vilayet of Adana was no doubt connected with this plan, the more so as Cevdet arrived with a battalion of Kurdish *çetes* who had been following him since Van.[16] Cevdet, associated with Colonel Hüseyin Avni, the commander of the vilayet's gendarmerie, as well as the presiding judge at the Adana court-martial and the local chief of the Special Organization, and Colonel Şekerci Ağia Bey, the commander of the Amanus labor battalions,[17] undertook in the following months to organize the liquidation of the Armenian workers on the *Bagdadbahn* construction sites. On 28 April 1916, he sent Colonel Avni to these sites to make an official count of the workers to be found there.[18] These operations, which took weeks to complete, had no other purpose, according to the explanations that the officials gave the German engineers, than to provide these deportees legal identity papers that would presumably protect them.[19] Aguni writes that it was only after taking 1,600 British and Indian prisoners-of-war in Kut el-Amara that the authorities decided to deport the Armenian workers and replace them with these captives.[20]

German sources indicate that additional gendarmerie brigades commanded by Colonel Hüseyin Bey arrived in the area in early June 1916 and surrounded the camps where the workers were living. On 13 June, the first convoy of deportees was put on the road, interrupting work on the site from the 19th on. Winkler estimates the number of Armenians dispatched by 17 June at 2,900.[21] The cessation of activities on the building sites had predictable effects on the war effort; this and probably complaints passed on by ranking German officers led Enver to issue the vali of Adana a counter order. It had, however, only a very short-term effect. The first convoy passed through Islahiye, where a British officer learned from members of the escort that these deportees were being sent to their deaths and would be replaced by British and Indian prisoners.[22] Discussion probably took place within the Ittihadist leadership because, in obedience to a 29 June 1916 counter-order from Enver, the remaining 15,000 workers were immediately dispatched. The last to leave were skilled personnel from Kilis and Marash whose families had been deported in early July.[23]

Kalust Hazarabedian, who found himself in the third convoy, reports that they had hardly left Bahçe when they saw "naked bodies sprawled on the sides of the road, some of which had been treated with the most appalling savagery and were ringed by dogs and vultures." "I knew," Hazarabedian goes on,

the fate that had been reserved for the preceding convoys. The state of these bodies entirely confirmed the information that I had received. Our escort had already begun its bloody work. Those who could not follow the group, because they were ill or too old, were killed within the minute, either shot or, more frequently, bayoneted to death ... We had advanced as far as the frontiers of the territory of the Orçans, suffering a good many casualties. From that point on, the situation grew still worse. Sabers, rifles, shovels, picks, stakes or sticks in hand, the Orçans attacked the group and began killing and looting. The guards hailed their intervention with a certain pleasure. Not only did they not try to stop them; on the contrary, they encouraged them. Involved here were, for the most part, criminals who had been released from prison for the precise purpose of dealing with the Armenians ... After slowing down the progress of the convoy and lining up to one side of it, they passed its members in review, one by one, as they went by. They began to single out, in particular, the young men whose clothing and faces looked clean and who seemed more or less affluent. They separated them from the others and shot them straightaway.[24]

According to the same witness, the great majority of the deportees who had been working between Islahiye and Yarbaşi were massacred between Bahçe and Marash in "a little less than one month." The others were driven to Birecik, Veranşehir, Urfa, or even, in the case of the last of them, Mardin.[25] Minas Tilbeian, however, who found himself in one of the next convoys, reports that his group was liquidated much further off in the vicinity of Mardin,[26] perhaps because it was made up of more resilient single men. It goes without saying that the liquidation of these workers, carried out by local tribes and, above all, gendarmes and the *çetes* commanded by Colonel Avni, was part of the vast campaign coordinated by Talât in summer 1916, the purpose of which was to extirpate the last groups of survivors to have reached the south. Be it added that the worker-soldiers of the *amele taburis* operating in the region were also put to death in summer 1916.[27]

Paula Schäfer, a Swiss missionary in Adana, confirms that the workers of the *Bagdadbahn* were deported with their families in July 1916 under the direct supervision of the vali of Adana, Cevdet Bey.[28] Three ranking Armenian employees of the German company working in the Amanus region provide a detailed account of the circumstances in which the workers of the *Bagdadbahn*'s construction sites were liquidated.[29]

Teotig and Aguni, who were employed on the Taurus building sites, state that the workers on the Belemedik site, very close to Bozanti, were supposed to meet the same fate, but that Dr. Boyajian and the Swiss engineer in charge of the site succeeded in convincing Colonel Şekerci Ağia Bey, who had himself been entrusted with the task of liquidating the Taurus sites, to postpone application of this order. In the end, only the Armenians working on the second trunk of the line were deported, with the exception of a few white-collar workers.[30] Cevdet Bey even personally "dealt with" Yervant Papazian, one of the management employees on this site.[31] Several thousand men working on the first, third, and fourth sites escaped this operation.[32] According to Teotig, early in 1918, the two kilometer-long trunk of the line on which he had been working had been practically completed, at minimum cost.[33]

The obstinacy with which the capital conducted these operations, against the advice of some military authorities – notably the commander of the Fourth Army – and in the face of all operational logic, illustrates, perhaps even better than the large-scale massacres perpetrated in Zor and Ras ul-Ayn, the desire of the civilian authorities – that is, the Young Turk leadership – to implacably carry through to the bitter end their plan to extirpate the Armenian Ottoman population.

Chapter 9

The Second Phase of the Genocide: The Dissolution of the Armenian Patriarchate and the Decision to Liquidate the Last Deportees

By a decree published in the *Official Gazette* on 28 July 1916, the Ottoman government reformed the Armenian community's internal constitution.[1] After cleansing Asia Minor of its Armenian population and undertaking liquidating the deportees who had arrived in Syria and Mesopotamia, the Young Turk government plainly decided to draw the consequences of these demographic changes. The decree that it issued provided for eliminating the Constantinople Armenian Patriarchate, with its legal representative body, the Chamber of Deputies, and its Political Council, notably charged with the mission of serving as the Ottoman authorities' official interlocutor. In eliminating the Patriarchate, the government simply ratified an accomplished fact. In the new arrangement, the Armenian Patriarchates of Jerusalem and Constantinople were to be merged under the authority of Sahag II Khabayan, who had been promoted to the rank of "patriarch-catholicos" of the Armenians; he was to have his seat in Jerusalem. According to the former Patriarch Malakia Ormanian, who was in Jerusalem when the telegram announcing the appointment of Sahag II arrived on 11 August 1916, it was Cemal Pasha who had suggested naming him catholicos of Cilicia and locating his seat in the Holy City.[2]

In addition to the memoirs of Patriarch Zaven of Constantinople,[3] the account handed down to us by the patriarchal vicar, Yervant Perdahjian,[4] constitutes a source of the first importance when it comes to understanding the circumstances surrounding this event and the situation prevailing in Istanbul on the eve of the dissolution of the Patriarchate. Perdahjian observes in particular that a petition, drawn up by the secretary of the central direction of the police, was submitted under duress early in 1916 to high-ranking clergymen and influential laymen for signature. The basic purpose of the petition was to condemn "Armenian troublemakers"; it seems likely that it was intended to contradict information about the mass crimes committed in Turkey that had filtered into the European and American press. According to Perdahjian, the patriarch, the president of the Religious Council, Archbishop Yeghishe Turian, and the president of the Political Council, Krikor Tavitian, "legitimized the petition, in some sort, by signing a *takrir* accompanying it. The patriarch in person then transmitted the petition to the prime minister, who expressed his satisfaction." This text, Perdahjian notes, "condemned all the Armenians of Turkey and insulted the memory of all the innocent martyrs, without making the least proposal to improve the situation of those who had survived the catastrophe."[5] Rumors had apparently been circulating since summer 1915 to the effect that the Armenian National Constitution was going to be suppressed and even that the Patriarchate might be transferred to Syria, "at least for the duration of the war," but no one had believed that the authorities would go so far as to abolish the Patriarchate of the Armenians of Turkey. The first signs pointing to an abrogation of the Constitution appeared when the Patriarchate asked for permission to begin organizing elections to renew the Religious and Political Councils in May–June 1916.[6] Before "giving an official cast" to this request, the Patriarchate's chief secretary had sounded out the Director of Religious Cults, who had promised to come to "an arrangement." But, after the official request was filed, it appeared that "authorization from the government" would have to be secured before the National Chamber could convene. Moreover, a police lieutenant came to the Patriarchate on behalf of the general directorate of the police to tell him that since the terms of those elected to the chamber had expired, they would "not be able, from now on, to convene the assembly."[7] In other words, the patriarchal bodies, beginning with the Political Council, found themselves paralyzed. According to Perdahjian, the patriarch "nonetheless continued to conduct the affairs of the nation until the Patriarchal institution was abolished, until the moment he left," and virtually single-handed at that: "four members of the Political Council had been deported," one had died, and only its president, Dr. Tavitian, "came to the Patriarchate twice a week." "After the deportation of the intellectuals and politicians," the vicar observes, "no one dared associate with the patriarchal administration." According to the *Müdur-i mezahib* (the Director of Religious Cults), these restrictions had been triggered by the steps taken by the Armenian authorities.[8] It is much more likely, in fact, that the government simply took advantage of this occasion to carry its plan to abolish the Patriarchate into practice.

The coup de grace came on the afternoon of 28 July/10 August 1915. The Director of Religious Cults, Beha Bey, and the police chief, Ahmed Bey, arrived at the Patriarchate "without warning," while the neighboring streets were invested by policemen.[9] According to the vicar, who was present at the scene, the director of religious cults handed the patriarch an official document signed by the minister of justice and religious cults. "Former Patriarch Zaven Effendi" was written on the envelope containing it. The content of the document was "more or less" as follows: "in accordance with the provisions of the law published in the today's *Official Gazette*, the Catholicosates of Cilicia and Aghtamar, as well as the Patriarchates of Constantinople and Jerusalem, are merged under the authority of Catholicos Sahag; your functions have been abolished."[10] The two officials further demanded that all the doors "of the official offices of the Patriarchate" be sealed "with the seals of the Patriarchate and the police chief" until a new vicar was appointed. The members of the Patriarchate's staff were invited to remove their personal effects from their desks, and the premises were put under the surveillance of three policemen, who were regularly rotated.[11]

On 13 August, "former Patriarch Zaven" was informed that he had to leave for Baghdad "in the next three days" and that his residence had been placed under surveillance by the police.[12] The Patriarch's imminent exile, which was the logical consequence of the abolition of the Patriarchate, attracted the attention of Constantinople's diplomatic corps, especially the American embassy and the papal nuncio, who, says Perdahjian, "repeatedly" interceded "with the interior minister in order to prevent his departure and secure a promise that he would be allowed to live after withdrawing to one of the islands in Constantinople." The diplomats, however, were only able to obtain guarantees that "the Patriarchate would be left alive." For his part, the Patriarchate's chief secretary, Kamer Shirinian, sounded out the state secretary in the Justice Ministry, Halil Bey, who is supposed to have told him: "The patriarch need not worry: the Council of Ministers has not decided to have him assassinated. If we were to put Archbishop Zaven to death, we would be murdering the patriarch, and this affair would lead to reactions abroad. Tell him that he will arrive at his destination safe and sound."[13] Zaven Yeghiayan was finally put on the road on Monday, 4 September, bound for the Haydarpaşa train station under the guard of two officials. A crowd watched, weeping.[14] We know about the rest of the Patriarch's journey to Baghdad from his memoirs, thanks to which it has also been possible to assess the effects of the second phase of the genocide along the route that he took.[15] After his departure, all the sums that had proceeded from the inalienable funds at the Patriarchate's disposal were frozen thanks in particular to one of the directors of the *Banque Ottomane*, Berj Kerestejian. The remittances that had been going to Aleppo by way of Dr. Peet now ceased for good and all.[16]

The Decision to Liquidate the Last Deportees

We have examined the fate reserved for the Armenian deportees who reached Syria and Mesopotamia, especially those from western Anatolia. In particular, we saw that in early spring 1916 a systematic campaign to liquidate the deportees held in the concentration camps north of Aleppo was carried out. It culminated, beginning in June-July 1916, in the elimination of the exiles in Zor and the workers on the construction sites of the *Bagdadbahn*. The chronology of these events indicates that it had been decided, probably in the first half of March 1916, to enact the second phase of the genocide. However, as with its first phase, set in motion in the second half of March 1915, we have no materials that would allow us to state the exact date of the meetings that approved implementation of this ultimate stage of the genocide. To broach the problem, therefore, we must once again sift through the context for a few revealing signs.

It must be recalled that, shortly before this decision was made in February 1916, nearly 500,000 deportees were still alive, scattered between Aleppo and Damascus or the Euphrates and Zor. More than 100,000 were scattered between Damascus and Maan, 12,000 were in Hama and the surrounding region, 20,000 were in Homs and the villages in the vicinity, 7,000 were in Aleppo, 5,000 were in Basra, 8,000 were in Bab, 5,000 were in Munbuc, 20,000 were in Ras ul-Ayn, 10,000 were in Rakka, and 300,000 were in Der Zor and its environs.[17] These numbers correspond, of course, to a given state of affairs on a precise date; the deportee population was subject to constant fluctuations, as was the geographical location of the deportees.

In other words, more than 300,000 deportees out of a total of over 850,000 had died in autumn 1915 and winter 1915–16 on the routes of Syria and Mesopotamia or in the concentration camps. The elements that we have discussed above indicate that by late 1916 the number of those who had perished exceeded 600,000.[18] At the very least, around 250,000 people were still alive at the beginning of the second phase of the genocide: 20,000 to 30,000 young women and children who had been sold to local villagers or abducted by tribes; 40,000 people who had managed to hide in the villages in the northern part of the vilayet of Aleppo; 30,000 people living underground; around 5,000 in the Basra region, and a majority of "Cemal's Armenians," who had officially been Islamicized on the line Hama-Homs-Damascus-Beirut-Haifa-Jaffa-Jerusalem-Tripoli-Dera'a-Amman-Salt-Kerek-Maan.

The CUP's initial plan had no doubt not foreseen that so many Armenians would survive. This probably touched off a debate within the Young Turk leadership. It seems to us worthwhile to examine the events preceding this debate.

When the Ittihad's annual congress opened in the club in Nuri Osmaniye Street on 23 September 1915, it is probable that one of the main subjects on the agenda was the ongoing program to liquidate the empire's Armenian subjects. In contrast, when the Ottoman parliament inaugurated its autumn session on 28 September under the presidency of Halil [Menteşe], the matter was not mentioned at all, even if the absence of most of the Armenian deputies, who had been executed in remote spots in Asia Minor by CUP killers, did not go entirely unnoticed. On 4 November, Tahsin Bey, the vali of Erzerum, and Cevdet, the former vali of Van, were invited to Istanbul to receive a decoration; it is easy to guess why. The only dissident voice amid this constrained unanimity seems to have been that of the heir to the throne, Yusuf İzzedin, who dared to say in public that Enver Pasha bore most of the blame for the defeat at Sarıkamiş.[19] On 1 February 1916, the Istanbul press announced the "suicide" of the prince, who had once employed Dr. Bahaeddin Şakir as his private physician.

On the foreign front, after the 24 October death of Hans von Wangenheim, his successor, Count Paul Wolff-Metternich, proved to be more conscientious. He intervened repeatedly with the Sublime Porte after his 14 November arrival in Istanbul, especially on the issue of forced conversions. The repeated denunciations in the press of the Entente countries of the atrocities that the Young Turk state had carried out against its Armenian population – acts of violence with which Germany was associated – called forth a few reactions. Count E. R. Rowentlow published a long article in the 19 December 1915 *Deutsche Tageszeitung* in which, after listing the accusations of criminal activity published in the American, Swiss, and British press, he wrote:

> Turkey had not only had a right, but a duty to punish the bloodthirsty Armenians ... How long will it take us to understand that it is not our business to bewail the fate of Armenian usurers and revolutionaries who constitute a grave danger for our faithful Turkish ally and are the tools of our mortal enemies, England and Russia .... There you have the reason that we Germans have to consider the Armenian question as a matter of interest to not only to Turkey, but all its allies as well, and to defend Turkey against external attacks.[20]

This reaction, of a cast that brings to mind subsequent events in Germany, did not, however, suffice to hide the fact that people at the highest levels of the German state were beginning to be alarmed by the consequences of their "laxity" in the face of the crimes committed by their Turkish ally. Wolff-Metternich's reports had not a little to do with this new awareness.[21] The circular telegram that the interior minister, Talât, sent out to the Ottoman provinces must no doubt be attributed to the concern now manifested by the German diplomatic establishment. Talât here refers to "the rumors" circulating

> in certain places about the fact that the deportations of Armenians are being carried out under pressure from the German government. Everyone should be aware that the means approved by the Imperial government, and by that government alone, are being applied only for reasons and in consequence of obligations of a military nature, as well as for security reasons, and that no foreign government can meddle in the situation and our internal affairs. This should be communicated in the form of a circular, using the appropriate means, to all the responsible state officials.[22]

But the public debate in Germany, postponed because of the imperatives of the war, eventually broke out in January 1916. German missionary circles – specifically, Dr. Lepsius's *Deutsche Orient Mission* and Dr. Friedrich Schuchardt's no less powerful *Deutscher Hülfsbund für christliches Liebeswerk im Orient* – received information from their two networks of institutions in the Ottoman Empire that left little room for doubt about the nature of the events underway there. The voyage of these two missionary leaders to Istanbul and the conversations that they conducted with Armenian circles and American missionaries convinced them to make an appeal to public opinion in their country.[23] Following publication of an article on 11 January in the *Volkszeitung*, the socialist deputy Liebknecht put a question to the government about the Armenian question in the Reichstag the same day, causing it considerable embarrassment.[24] Talât published an interview in the 24 January *İkdam* in which he declared: "I shall here prove that the remarks about the Armenians to be found in the enemy press are baseless." He stuck, however, to the official discourse that accused "the" Armenians of collaboration with the enemy. The interior minister subsequently published a pamphlet entitled *Vérité sur les mouvements révolutionnaires arméniens* (The truth about the Armenian revolutionary movements).[25]

Confronted by the Christian charitable organizations working in the Ottoman Empire, German diplomacy reacted to the campaign of forced conversion undertaken by the Young Turks. The German foreign minister, who had not seen fit to react to the far more violent liquidation campaign that preceded it, went so far as to instruct the German embassy in Constantinople to make it known in high places that "all the Turkish denials notwithstanding, the deported Armenians are still being forced to convert to Islam."[26] These complaints, formulated rather late in the day, were perhaps not merely *pro forma*, since in February a German parliamentary delegation under the conduct of the parliamentary deputy Matthias Erzberger arrived in Constantinople. Erzberger was successively received by the government ministers Talât and Enver, which speaks volumes about the importance that the Young Turk leaders accorded their German ally. They had no choice but to listen to the criticisms of the centrist German deputy, who suggested notably that they put an end to the forced conversions and persecutions.[27] There can be no doubt that this external pressure, which surely reminded the two Young Turk chiefs of the pre-war situation, only exacerbated their easily offended nationalism.

It must also be pointed out that in the first days of February, the news of the unexpected fall of Erzerum, which was soon followed by that of Trebizond, came like a dagger blow. After the Turkish victory over the French and British forces in the Dardanelles, Bulgaria's entry into the war on the side of the Allies and, in consequence, the inauguration of a direct rail connection to Germany, the wildest hopes had seemed justified; now this painful defeat, news of which was not made public until war's end, darkened the Ottoman military horizon. Yet there was no longer a domestic foe to blame for the setback, only internal weaknesses. Our familiarity with the individuals involved leads us to think that that idea of having done with the Armenians who had reached Syria and Mesopotamia materialized with the surprising February 1916 fall of Erzerum, somewhat in the manner of the radicalization that an exceptional event can inspire in certain individuals. By this logic, what had been lost on one front had to be made up for by a "positive" operation in another, better-controlled theater of the war.

In view of the role that Cevdet, the former vali of Van, played in the Special Organization, as well as his family ties with Vice-Generalissimo Enver, one can venture the hypothesis that his 19 March appointment to head the vilayet of Adana constituted a *terminus ad quo* for the decision to liquidate the deportees in the south. The successive directives that Talât sent to the local authorities in these regions for the purpose of liquidating the concentration camps north of Aleppo in March 1916, and then clearing out the camp in Ras ul-Ayn at the end of the same month before proceeding to eliminate the deportees on the line of the Euphrates from June to December 1916, are so many chronological markers betraying the methodical application of a pre-elaborated plan. The harassment of foreign humanitarian organizations, which helped prolong the deportees' lives, and the seizure of the orphans who had been living in these organizations' orphanages may be construed as proof of a desire to show the diplomats and missionaries in Syria that all their efforts were in vain. The campaign launched in the interior provinces of Asia Minor in late February 1916 to deport the last of the Armenians, who had been allowed to remain in their homes for various reasons – because they were Protestants, Catholics, members of soldiers' families, craftsmen, physicians, pharmacists, and so on – after several months of calm mark, in our opinion, the beginning of the second phase of the genocide.

The Banque Ottomane's February 1916 decision to freeze the accounts of these "clients on voyage," some of whom had hitherto been able to make withdrawals in the bank's agencies in Syria and Mesopotamia,[28] was probably also the work of the interim Minster of the Economy, Mehmed Talât, part of his policy of extirpating the Armenian deportees.

In the realm of German-Turkish relations, Wolff-Metternich did not long withstand the pressure exerted by the Sublime Porte to obtain his recall.[29] According to the former vali of Konya, Celal Bey, who published a series of articles in *Vakıt*, Count Metternich was recalled to Berlin after Halil Bey had made a voyage to Germany during which he had vigorously protested against the ambassador's comportment. The ambassador had "offended" the Sublime Porte by his frequent interventions regarding the fate dealt out to the Armenians.[30]

Mehmed Talât's 22 January 1917 accession to the post of grand vizier appears, in this light, as a kind of reward for everything that he had so far accomplished. Having reached the summit of the state hierarchy, the chief of the Ittihad demonstrated, in private, his positive attitude, if not indeed his magnanimity. "As far as the Armenians are concerned, he will do everything he can to satisfy them: he will allow the Armenians who have been removed to return to those provinces where that is possible," the Austrian Ambassador reported in a 14 February 1917 note.[31] Nothing seemed to faze the Committee of Union and Progress, which, as the Austrian diplomat told it, did not hesitate, three days later,

> even while proclaiming justice for all Ottomans in its program, [to promote] those who helped expel and annihilate the Armenians in obedience to its orders. Thus the vali of Aleppo, Mustafa Abdülhalik Bey (Aleppo was the central point through which all the Armenians bound for exile in the sancak of Zor had to pass), would be named undersecretary in the Interior Ministry. Thereafter, Hamdi Bey, the assistant director general of the central office for emigrations in Constantinople, a close associate of Abdülhalik's and one of the most important agents of the Armenians' annihilation, has been promoted to the post of general director of this office.[32]

In his Damascene exile, the former patriarch, Ormanian, wrote in March 1918: "I have said and I repeat: 'The stone of which the imperial edifice is made is the Turk; the mortar is the Armenian. Without mortar, buildings have no support, and cannot be erected.'"[33]

The Last Days of the Ottoman Empire: The Executioners and Their Judges Face-to-Face

Chapter 1

Grand Vizier Talât Pasha's New Turkey; or, Reanimating Pan-Turkism

Mehmet Talât's 22 January 1917 accession to the office of grand vizier marks a turning point in the history of the Committee of Union and Progress. After long leaving the management of day-to-day affairs in the hands of grand viziers and ministers who were more or less submissive, the CUP publicly affirmed its power by putting its president at the head of government. The committee, in its forward march toward the construction of a new Turkey, had the opportunity to draw up a balance sheet of its work at its annual congress, which was held on 24 September 1917 in Istanbul under the chairmanship of Midhat Şükrü, its general secretary. The composition of the new bureau elected by the assembly did not reveal any striking changes. The general council elected its bureau, made up of Musa Kâzım, Said Halim (the former grand vizier), Hayri Effendi (the *şeyh ul-Islam*), Haci Adıl[1] (the vali of Edirne who organized the deportations in Thrace in fall 1915), İsmail Enver (minister of war), *Giritli* Ahmed Nesimi [Sayman],[2] Ahmed Cemal Pasha (minister of the navy), Mehmed Cavid (minister of the economy), Halil [Menteşe] (minister of foreign affairs), Ahmed Şükrü (minister of education), Mustafa Şeref, Hüseyin Cahid (vice-president of parliament), and Atıf Bey[3] (first the CUP's delegate in, and then the vali of Angora and Kastamonu, whose Armenian population he ordered deported or massacred).[4]

The Central Committee also remained stable. In addition to Mehmed Talât and Midhat Şükrü, the party's secretary general, the following men were elected or reelected: Dr. Nâzım, [Kara] Kemal (minister of supplies, who was charged with creating "Turkish" enterprises), [Yusuf] Rıza[5] (who was active in the Trebizond region), Ziya Gökalp (the committee's ideologue), Eyub Sabri [Akgöl][6] (a *fedayi* who served without interruption as a member of the Central Committee from 1908 to 1918), Dr. Rüsûhi[7] (who was active in Azerbaijan and the Van region), Dr. Bahaeddin Şakir (the president of the Special Organization), and Filibeli Ahmed Hilmi[8] (the vice-president of the Special Organization, who was in charge of operations in Erzerum).[9] The only noteworthy promotion within the party's supreme body was that of Hilmi, Şakir's right-hand man. It is also worth remarking that the Central Committee now comprised ten members and that the men who had reputedly opposed the liquidation of the Armenian population were all in place in both the bureau of the general council and the Central Committee. Even Mehmed Cavid, who had taken his distance at the outbreak of the war, joined the bureau again. Thus, the opposition of certain leaders of the party to the anti-Armenian measures must not be accorded too much importance, the more so as our knowledge of its existence is based largely on accounts produced later by certain of its protagonists.[10] It is also possible, however, that, by early fall 1917, the Armenian question was considered closed and that the most prudent no longer felt any need to remain on the edges of the government.

The Grand Vizier's Address; or, the Legitimization of State Violence

The address delivered by Talât can provide only faint indications of the nature of the debates within the party because it was to be made public the following day.[11] To begin with, the minister repeated, in the face of all the evidence, the official thesis about the conditions under which Turkey had entered the war: "The Russian naval attack in the Black Sea and the land-based attack on our borders forced us to embrace the party toward which our historical destiny was carrying us and take our place alongside the Central Powers."[12] As for the main count in the indictment brought against the Ottoman Empire, state violence, Talât felt the need to devote more than half of his address to the government's behavior toward its non-Turkish subjects. It is worth pausing over his remarks, which are both a balance sheet and a justification. "Our enemies everywhere," he began,

> are saying that we mistreat belligerent subjects and enemy combatants and that we have committed all sorts of atrocities against the empire's Armenians and Jews. Fortunately, however, people in many different places are beginning to understand the invidious, pernicious nature of these reports, which we and many neutral personalities have contested in the name of humanity and justice.

According to the grand vizier, the American Ambassador Abraham Elkus and American consuls Jackson and Bordon had exposed the libelous nature of the charges leveled against the country.[13] These affirmations, contradicted by the dispatches of the diplomats in question, were an integral part of the Young Turk method of justification, which systematically appealed to "foreign" witnesses. It mattered little whether those witnesses had said the opposite of what the Young Turks claimed. In the case to hand, Talât's statement was the easier to make because the diplomats he named had not been in Turkey since the Unites States' entry into the war and thus were not in a position to contradict him. The appeal to "humanity" and "justice" reveals another characteristic trait of the Young Turk leaders: the recourse to values to which they were altogether insensitive in order to convince their interlocutors of their ethical modernity. Indeed, the Young Turk regime never assumed its ideology of exclusion through violence; it consistently took refuge behind "the necessities of the war," as if it were ashamed of the ideological monster that it had engendered and that animated it.

"The Armenians," the grand vizier reminded his listeners in a long historical expose on the Armenian question, "have for centuries comprised a vital element under the Imperial flag; they benefited fully from the state's solicitude, as industrious, peaceful elements, for as long as they were not carried away by separatist suggestions that came from the outside."[14] Talât then made the inevitable argument:

> The Armenians, whom we did not think capable of taking audacity to the point of committing acts of treason against the fatherland during this World War, were integrated, like other groups, into the structures of the army, and arms, too, were distributed to them. The 'comitajis' who had kept quiet until we entered the war went from calm to revolution, from loyalty to sedition, as soon as the Russians crossed our borders and occupied a few of our towns and villages. In the third month of the war, the parliamentary deputy from Van, Vramian, presented the vali of this vilayet with a memorandum detailing the Armenian claims; it was identical to the one that had

earlier been submitted to the Sublime Porte. The presentation of this memorandum was followed by the desertion of the Armenian soldiers enrolled in the army, who fled to the mountains with their weapons, and by attacks on gendarmes and the Muslim population. The Imperial government thereupon explained to the patriarch and the deputies on the committee, in Constantinople, the gravity of the situation, advising them to take preventive measures. We waited one and a half months for the result. It was only after the revolt in Van, before the army's lines, and in Zeitun, behind them, that police searches were undertaken everywhere, because the commanders of the army had pointed out that they were necessary. Arms, bombs, and explosives were found in Dyarbekir, Urfa, Kayseri, Ismit, Adabazar, Bağçecik, Amasia, Sıvas, Merzifun, Trebizond, Samsun, Arapkir, Malatia, Dörtyol, Hacın, Bursa, Erzerum, Erzincan, and other localities. These devices were discovered, for the most part, in monasteries and churches.[15]

Pursuing his demonstration, Talât concluded:

> Once it became obvious that the flanks and rear of the army were in jeopardy, we proceeded to carry out deportations from the war zone for the good of the troops. We cannot claim that this deportation took place under normal conditions, for order could not be assured as we would have wished, since most of the gendarmes had been incorporated into the army. The central government, however, sent out several investigative commissions, which brought all those who had committed acts of violence before a court-martial. Those who were convicted of crimes were condemned and meted out the most severe kind of punishment, such as death or hard labor. Every government has the right to defend itself against those who stage armed revolts.[16]

These affirmations, whose accuracy we assessed in the fourth part of the present study, call for a few comments. Talât does not deny that some excesses occurred, due to the lack of the "gendarmes ... incorporated into the army." He clearly perceives that to issue a blanket denial of the mass crimes that he coordinated would put him in an untenable position. However, he limits this budding confession by emphasizing that the central authorities severely punished the guilty, going so far as to inflict capital punishment on some of them. In the process, he obscures the original objectives of the commissions that had been sent out to conduct inquiries, the sole function of which, as we have seen, was to identify the civilian and military officials who had taken advantage of circumstances to make personal gains at the expense of the party-state. The trials had probably also been intended to intimidate people tempted by these examples. At all events, the judges imposed only light sentences and never, to the best of our knowledge, condemned anyone to death.

Invoking the right to legitimate self-defense in the face of an armed revolt, Talât asked whether "the English, who committed cruel acts of all sorts against the Irish, without taking the least thought for the lives of their women and children, would not have deported them beyond the war zone if revolution had broken out there and had spread as far as the flanks and the rear of the army fighting the Germans."[17] By taking as his point of reference the acts of a great power with little concern for the lives of "women and children," Talât, too, claimed the right to exercise state violence and sought to legitimize the violence he had ordered. He even referred to the "concentration camps in the Transvaal" in which the British let women and children "starve to death" without scrupling over "humanitarian considerations."[18] This rhetoric, which lays the groundwork for a justification of the crimes committed under the CUP's lead and with the support of the administration, is surely a response not only to the persistent accusations expressed outside the country, but also to the

muted rumors that must have been circulating within it as well. Profiting from the opportunity to express himself for the first time before the CUP in his capacity as grand vizier,
Talât sought to sever all connection with the past and convince skeptics that the actions of
the party had been justified.

In his conclusion, he hammered home the idea that "in our country, the Union and
Progress Party represents the new ideas and constitutes a factor for progress ... Social experience clearly shows that the rule of 'law' in a country can be guaranteed only by the rule of
knowledge and morality. The essential mission of a state is to institute justice and freedom
based on law."[19] Talât thus described the CUP's "sacred" goal, which it was the vocation of
the party's elite to achieve.

The Military Campaign in the Caucasus or
the Rebirth of Pan-Turkism (1918)

The party's "sacred" goal obviously did not consist in its ambitions for social progress alone,
but also in uniting the Turkish-speaking peoples under its banner. We have seen how the
partisans of Pan-Turkism, beginning with Enver Pasha, were disabused of their illusions and
lost influence after the bloody defeat at Sarıkamiş. The order of the day was now Turkism
and the much more accessible objective of "homogenizing" Anatolia. The 1917 Bolshevik
Revolution and its military consequences, however, put a project that had hitherto been out
of reach for the Young Turk regime back on the agenda. The hasty evacuation of the front
by the Russian army was perceived in Istanbul as an unimagined opportunity to link up with
the "Turks of the Caucasus." Arif Cemil, an officer in the *Teşkilât-ı Mahsusa*, notes in this
regard: "The question of the Turks in Russia had resurfaced. Those who were well informed
about the situation of the Turks in Russia had presented reports to the Central Committee
of Union and Progress in which they explained how it was possible to profit from this historic opportunity."[20] After Turkey and the Bolsheviks concluded the truce of Erzincan on
18 December 1917,[21] the government of Transcaucasia, which filled a political vacuum, was
also approached in mid-January by the Commander of the Third Army, Vehib Pasha, who
suggested that they sign a peace treaty.[22] The aim of these advances was doubtless simply to
calm the fears of the Caucasian leaders while gaining time in which to reorganize the Third
Army, which was very weak when the Erzincan truce was signed.[23] The Young Turk leadership lost no time. The minister of war proceeded to carry out a full-scale reorganization of
the army of the Caucasus, which was initially restructured in three army corps – the first,
under the orders of Kâzım [Karabekir], had Erzerum and Kars as its objectives; the second,
led by Yakub Şevki Pasha, was directed toward Trebizond and Batum; the third, commanded
by Ali İhsan Pasha, set its sights on Northern Persia. Later, it was reorganized as four army
corps and put under the command of the War Minister's uncle, Halil [Kut]: 1) the remains
of the Third Army were entrusted to General Esad; 2) the *Islâm Ordusi* (Army of Islam)
was to be led by General Nuri [Killigil], Enver's half-brother; 3) the Ninth Army was to be
commanded by General Yakub Şevki Pasha; and 4) the Sixth Army was placed under the
orders of General Ali İhsan Pasha [Sabis]. In other words, the two Turkish divisions that
had been stationed on the Galician and Moldavian fronts were not, once they were freed
up by the Peace of Brest-Litovsk, sent to reinforce the Palestinian and Mesopotamian fronts;
indeed, the Sixth Army was transferred from the Mesopotamian front and used to beef up
the army of the Caucasus.[24] The further course of events might have been a scenario written in advance. In February, Vehib Pasha, who had not yet been replaced by Halil, sent the
commander of the Caucasian forces, General Lebedinsky, several notes of protest in which
he accused "Armenian bands" commanded by Sepastatsi Murad of massacring 15,000 Turks.
These accusations, which seem to have been on the order of a psychological feint, served as

a pretext for breaking the truce. On 13 February, an offensive was launched on Erzincan, leading to the panicked flight of several thousand Armenian genocide survivors who had returned to the region in spring 1916.[25]

All that the Turkish forces had to contend with was an Armenian corps of 20,000 men that had been hastily formed beginning in December 1917 under the direction of General Nazarbekov, after the commander-in-chief of the army of the Caucasus, General Lebedinsky, had given his approval to the idea.[26] This corps was supposed to defend a long cease-fire line that stretched from Erzincan to Van, while also maintaining order in the Caucasus. The nature of the Transcaucasian Federation, in which Armenians, Azeris, and Georgians coexisted, was such as to guarantee the absence of cohesion of this improbable improvised state that was, in addition to everything else, under pressure from two antagonistic Russian blocs, Bolshevik and Czarist. The Armenians' situation, of course, was the most precarious. Caucasian Armenia had to provide for some 200,000 Ottoman refugees and establish security in a country including a large Turkish-speaking minority that was far from deaf to the sirens of Pan-Turkism.

After Erzincan in February, Enver launched a general offensive that culminated in the capture of Trebizond and Erzerum on 12 March.[27] The Turkish forces took Kars on 25 April, opening a path to the Transcaucasus,[28] and Van on 4 April, prefiguring the Ottoman army's general offensive in Azerbaijan. Thus, when the Batum "Peace conference" opened on 11 May 1918, the Ottoman plenipotentiary, General Halil [Kut], was in a position of strength and could dictate his conditions to the Transcaucasian delegates with their diverging interests, the more so as in the midst of the negotiations on 15 May, the army of the Caucasus launched an offensive on Alexandropol.[29] That said, it must be recalled that while the apparent objective of these military operations was to win back Ottoman territories, they also took their place, as we shall see, in a Pan-Turk plan that aimed among other things to liquidate the last surviving Armenians, whether Ottoman refugees or Russian subjects in the Caucasus. General von Lossow, the German representative at the Batum conference, wrote in this period that the Turks had undertaken "la liquidation totale des Arméniens en Transcaucasie également."[30] Lossow stated the matter more precisely in the following weeks: "The aim of Turkish policy, as I have always maintained, is to take possession of the Armenian districts in order to extirpate the population living on them";[31] "Talât's government wants to destroy all the Armenians, not only in Turkey but also outside it";[32] "after completely encircling the vestiges of the Armenian nation in the Transcaucasus, the Turks intend ... to starve the Armenian nation to death – that much is obvious."[33] General Friedrich Freiherr Kress von Kressenstein, the former chief of military operations in the Ottoman War Ministry who was appointed to head the German Imperial delegation to the Caucasus in June 1918, was himself convinced that "the Turkish policy that consists in provoking a famine is evidence, were there any need for further proof, of the will to annihilation that the Turks harbor toward the Armenian element."[34] He saw proof of what he said in General Esad's refusal, "on the flimsiest of pretexts," of his proposal to provide the Armenians aid; it was at most a question, he thought, of a change in method.[35] In the preparatory stages, Kress von Kressenstein reports, the Turkish civilian and military authorities fell back on a tried and true rhetoric in their reports to Istanbul, of the species "military necessity" or "threat to our communication lines and our rear" that was meant to "justify the murder of hundreds of thousands of human beings."[36] There are similarities here in the techniques used to present the facts and the smear campaign that preceded the crimes of 1915. The leaders of the Caucasian campaign evoked problems of military security in their communications with their superiors in order to legitimize the exactions that they would go on to commit on instructions received from those superiors. The only noteworthy difference observable in 1918 is the methodical use of the army, which was both an instrument of conquest and a machine for extermination.

It is, however, impossible to understand the significance of the Caucasian operation unless one is aware that the CUP seized the occasion provided by the Russian withdrawal to attempt to achieve the Pan-Turanian plan that it had failed to early in 1915. Lieutenant-Colonel Ernest Paraquin, who had been Halil [Kut's] chief of staff first in Iraq and then in the Caucasus, had "benefited" from the confidences of this general, who had, moreover, founded the *Teşkilât-ı Mahsusa* and later felt the need to make them public. Familiar with the Young Turk military leaders, the German officer points out how deeply obsessed an individual such as Halil was by "Turan," whose "frontiers he traced in blue pencil" in an English atlas.[37] The military and demographic occupation of the space that he dreamed of appears as a new form of colonialism *à la turque*, now based, however, on a "racial" homogeneity that was itself legitimized by the myth of a return to the sources of the race. For Halil, Paraquin notes, "the conquest of Turkestan, the Turks' cradle, was the most important item on the agenda." In Halil's eyes, "the Tatars of the Caucasus, related to the Turks by their origins," were destined "to be included" in the "federation" he envisaged. As for the "national minorities in the countries in between," they would have to "submit." Halil further noted that "the Armenian question" was on the "verge of being solved, thanks to the war, through the total annihilation of the Armenian race. All the interested Turkish departments are working to this end, with implacable resolve."[38]

"These imperialist dreams, which Halil laid out for me one evening, his eyes sparkling with enthusiasm," writes Paraquin, "were not merely the product of a very fertile Oriental imagination; their realization was pursued systematically and objectively." The German officer's account emphasizes, moreover, that the Young Turk leaders were prepared to make every sacrifice to achieve their Pan-Turk project, including abandoning their Arab possessions.[39]

According to Paraquin, Enver sent his younger brother Nuri, who had been promoted to the rank of lieutenant general at the age of 27, to Baku in order to lay the groundwork in secret. He even gives us to understand that the "Tatar Republic" had been baptized "Azerbaijan" by the Young Turks: "the name is well chosen, no?" Halil Pasha is supposed to have exclaimed, "alluding to Persian Azerbaijan, the incorporation of which into the new republic was not merely planned, but had already been initiated by all means possible."[40] Well before the Turkish troops arrived in Baku, Nuri "was undisputed master of a new Tatar state that, when I visited it in summer and fall 1918, left me with the distinct impression that I was in a Turkish province." All the strategic points in the region, Paraquin goes on, "had been occupied by the Turkish troops, who had been given the name 'Army of Islam,' as the cause required. The war minister, a Tatar lawyer, sported the uniform of a Turkish Pasha; everywhere, Turkish officers and 'softas' preached submission to the Caliph in Istanbul; the Turkish crescent waved over all public buildings. Similar procedures were used among the Muslim peoples of the North Caucasus."[41]

The "Azerbaijan" that was included in the Transcaucasian Federation in spring 1918 was clearly already under Istanbul's undisputed control and working from within to help realize the Pan-Turk project. It is probable that Istanbul suggested that the country's leaders maintain a certain reserve until the Armenian sanctuary had been completely liquidated. The April–May 1918 capture of Alexandropol and Kars led to a massive exodus of the Armenian population, which withdrew toward Yerevan, and also to massacres perpetrated with the complicity of, notably, Colonel Abdülkadri Hilmi, a member of the Ottoman general staff sent to reinforce the Turkish forces.[42] The Turkish side appealed to the terms of the Brest-Litovsk peace treaty (ratified on 15 March 1918 by the Bolsheviks), which awarded it the districts of Kars, Ardahan, and Batum, as well as to the "military need" for access to the Kars-Julfa-Baku railway in order to justify its inexorable advance, behind which the plan to liquidate the Armenians was coming into focus. An examination of the military operations shows that the army of the Caucasus sought to drive the population that the army expelled from its homes into a circumscribed area around Yerevan. The Turkish forces, after arriving in the Ararat plain on the left bank of the Arax River on 16 May, demanded free passage to Julfa. If it was not granted them, they could not guarantee the "invulnerability of the population."[43] Halil Pasha, in his exchanges of notes with the Caucasian Federation, promised a "friendly advance" of his troops, yet had them take control of the route between Yerevan and Tiflis and march on Bash Abaran, clearing the way to Yerevan.[44] Even as Istanbul was "negotiating" a peace treaty in Batum with the Transcaucasian Federation, it tightened its grip on Georgia and Armenia, enjoying the notable advantage of being informed hourly of the nature of the debates taking place within the Transcaucasian delegation, thanks to the delegation's Azeri members, who met discreetly with Halil Pasha.[45] To legitimize these operations, which could no longer be legitimized as a strict application of the terms of the Brest-Litovsk Treaty, Enver Pasha put forward, in a 20 May exchange with German interlocutors, a twofold argument – the Bolshevik danger in the Caucasus and "the sufferings that innocent Muslims had endured at the hands of vicious Armenians."[46] There is every reason to think that the Turks' strategy consisted at the time in shattering the Transcaucasian Federation so that they could better manipulate the local populations. The ultimatum that Halil delivered on 26 May had probably intended to serve that end. Like his nephew, he referred to the suffering endured by "hundreds of thousands of Turks and Muslims in Baku and its environs" and to the "irreparable tragedy" underway there to justify his demand for free access to the Transcaucasian railway. No government, he said, could remain "indifferent in the face of such atrocities."[47] Georgia's 26 May declaration of independence and, the following day, that of the state of "Southern and Eastern Transcaucasia," which was to become the Republic of Azerbaijan, put an end to the experience of federation and to ties with Russia. Nuri Pasha himself undertook to form, in Ganja, the "Azeri" cabinet, which immediately demanded the "assistance" of the Turkish forces in liberating the country from the Bolsheviks.[48] In other words, the formation of the "independent" republics was the fruit of a Turkish initiative. The "liberation" of the Transcaucasus from Bolshevik dominion must be understood as a liquidation of the Armenians who had a central place in the region's economy, and who also provided the main source of support for the Bolshevik revolution in the Caucasus. It was indeed a strange situation, which illustrated the extreme fragmentation of Armenian society, made up of groups with divergent interests, in the face of a Pan-Turkish movement that was cohesive but hampered by the fact that its capacities were not equal to its ambitions.

The Armenian National Council cautiously proclaimed itself the "supreme" authority in the "Armenian provinces" on 28 May, with an eye to filling the political vacuum created by the Russian withdrawal and making the last square of territory around Yerevan appear at least minimally representative. This new authority set about organizing the defense of the city. On 24 May, the Armenian forces stopped the Turkish advance a few dozen kilometers west of Yerevan in Sardarabad, and to the north in Karakilisa, thirty kilometers east of Alexandropol.[49] This sudden turn in the course of the fighting doubtless saved the Armenians from being trapped in an entirely isolated enclave that would have constituted a vast concentration camp in which they would unfailingly have starved to death. The Armenian authority nevertheless had no choice but to sign, on 4 June, the Treaty of Batum, which reduced "Armenia" to a territory with a surface area of some 10,000 square kilometers. Vehib Pasha, whose remarks during the "negotiations" at Batum have been reported by Khatisian, forthrightly justified Turkey's enterprise: "Our blood, our religion, our language are here. That exerts an irresistible pull. Our brothers are in Baku, Daghestan, Turkestan, and Azerbaijan ['Azerbaijan' here undoubtedly designates northwestern Persia]."[50]

Turkish ambitions were not limited to Armenia. Georgia, which had dense Armenian populations in Akhalkalak, Akhaltskhik, and Tiflis, was another objective for the army of the Caucasus. Paraquin notes that it was the "unexpected" arrival of German troops on 10 June that made it possible "to stop a victorious Turkish march on Tiflis." The tense relations that had sprung up between the Turks and their German allies as a result of Turkey's ambitions in the Transcaucasus issued in an armed conflict here, after which "the victorious Turks swallowed their pride, while loudly gnashing their teeth."[51] Although the Turkish army did not succeed in establishing a full blockade of the Armenian enclave, it did a great deal to provoke a food shortage that led to famine and epidemics. At the very least, around 200,000 people, first and foremost Ottoman Armenian refugees, lost their lives in the enclave between spring and fall 1918. Marshall Hindenburg, head of the German army's general staff from 1916 to 1918, writes that "les événements atroces ... qui se sont aussi étendus vers la fin de la guerre à la partie arménienne de la Trancaucasie ... étaient considérés par les Turcs simplement comme une affaire interne."[52] In late May 1918, an Austrian diplomat announced that, according to information received in Berlin, "la Turquie souhaite annexer entièrement le Caucase et exterminer les Arméniens avec tous les moyens imaginables."[53]

Vice-Marshal Pomiankowski, the Austrian plenipotentiary and military attaché in Turkey, observed in August that it would be necessary to "protect the Armenians again the massacres and also again starvation."[54] Half a million Armenians, mostly women and children, had been living scattered throughout the northern Caucasus since the Turkish offensive in the spring; Yerevan was trying to persuade the Germans to permit these refugees to return to their homes before the onset of winter. Armenia also sought Berlin's help in bringing the Turks to evacuate certain districts in Yerevan and Alexandropol in which exactions were taking place daily, and struggled to obtain food supplies that failed to arrive.[55]

The Spring 1918 Turkish Military Operations in Iranian Azerbaijan

While the Russian forces and battalions of Armenian volunteers commanded by General Nazarbekov had stopped the first spring 1915 Ottoman offensive in Azerbaijan, the vacuum created by the Russian retreat in late December 1917 led to a new Turkish occupation. As in the Caucasus, the Young Turks once again activated their local networks and urged the Iranian Democrats to support their campaign. The 4 April 1918 capture of Van marked the beginning of the Turkish offensive in Azerbaijan and triggered the precipitate flight of the 25,000 Armenians who had returned to their homes in the wake of the Russian army in summer 1916.[56] In February and March 1918, the Ottoman Sixth Army, commanded by General Ali İhsan Pasha [Sabis], who was notorious for the exactions that he had committed (notably in the Mosul region),[57] advanced along the northern and southern shores of Lake Van. He accelerated his advance from 1 April on. After the Russian troops dispersed, the defense of the entire region was assured by a mere 2,000 men who resisted in only two places, Vostan and Arjesh, before yielding before the enemy's greater numbers.[58] On 23 December 1917, France and Great Britain had, to be sure, signed an agreement providing that the Transcaucasus would become part of the British sphere of influence, yet Britain limited itself to setting up the "Dunsterville Mission," comprising 150 senior and junior officers, far to the south in Hamadân, in order to ensure the maintenance of communications between Baghdad and the Caspian sea.[59] In other words, the 10,000 to 12,000 men in the Turkish Sixth Army encountered only one obstacle during their invasion of Azerbaijan: the Christian battalions made up of Armenians and Syriacs that had been formed on a British initiative. Late in March, small Turkish contingents were spotted in Azerbaijan, in Oshnu. Somewhat later, 1,000 men were reported present in Sulduz; their advance on Khoy apparently alarmed the local authorities. The Iranian Democrats seem to have had something to do with this operation, which, an observer reported, "today does not (no longer) threatens anything but Persian territory, which does not interest them much, and the Christian populations, a circumstance that they find agreeable."[60]

On 14/27 February 1918, the Armenians of Salmast intercepted a messenger who was bearing a letter from a local Kurdish chieftain, Sımko, referring to a future intervention that "no Christian would be able to resist."[61] As Magdalena Golnazarian points out, the Turks "had already acquired some experience in the art of utilizing the Kurds to massacre and plunder the Christians." The Christians therefore tried to neutralize Sımko by making him interesting offers.[62] The attempt seems to have failed, for Sımko, who had for a time worked for the Russians, attacked the 25,000 Armenians from Van who were trying to reach the Caucasus by way of Julfa. Held up in Qotur, on the border, the Armenians were surrounded by Sımko and his men: "On that day, Sımko killed until sunset, and the Qotur River turned red with the blood of those killed ... Sımko was not satisfied with all these crimes. He sent his horsemen into the Armenian villages around Khoy to kill more Armenians."[63] This eyewitness account, however, omits to note that there was an armed contingent among the 25,000 refugees, which put up resistance to Sımko's 700 to 800 men. According to one Armenian refugee, 400 prisoners, primarily civilians, were killed on this day, 11 April 1918, while the others went to swell the ranks of the Ottoman Armenians living in the Armenian villages on the Salmast plain.[64]

The bulk of the Turkish force did not officially enter Persia until May; their declared objective was to "free the Persians of the obstacle represented by the armed Christian forces."[65] Several tens of thousands of Syriacs – perhaps 35,000 – were living on the plains of Salmast and Urmia after their flight from the southern part of the vilayet of Van in 1915, and there were at least as many Armenians there, both natives and refugees,[66] who constituted a preferential target for the Ottoman Sixth Army. The occasion was the more propitious in that there had been violent clashes between Nestorians and Muslims in the wake of the 17 March 1918 murder of the Nestorian Mar Shimun by the notorious Sımko. These were followed by massacres of the civilian population and by looting, especially in the Muslim villages of Jara and Soma, where Sımko usually lived.[67] One can of course ask why the religious leader of the Jelos was slain, and speculate that this provocation, which spawned a spiral of violence, was organized by Azerbaijan's Young Turk networks. However that may be, the native Armenians and Ottoman refugees, who had at first tried to keep their distance from the conflict, were eventually swept up in the storm.

On 4 May, part of the Sixth Army directly threatened Salmast and its principal town, Dilmân, as well as the city of Urmia. It faced forces made up of Armenian volunteers (above all from Van) and Syriacs who had defended the city for more than one month. On 21 June their defense crumbled, leading to the exodus of tens of thousands of Armenians and Syriacs. Shortly thereafter, a battalion commanded by General Antranig reached a spot near Khoy, 30 kilometers north of Salmast, but its Christian inhabitants had already abandoned the region. The inhabitants of several villages were massacred and the Armenians of Salmast and Khoy as well as the refugees from Van withdrew to Urmia.[68] After a first clash with Ali İhsan Pasha's Sixth Army on 23 June, the Armenian forces headed back to Julfa, together with the refugees whom they encountered on the way. Antranig's vain intervention, carried out against the advice of Yerevan, constituted, according to Golnazarian, "an excellent pretext for mobilizing the Persians against the 'invader'" and massacring the local Armenian population.[69] According to M. Riâhi, Antranig's arrival had been announced during the festivities organized in Khoy on 21 June to celebrate the defeat of the Christians in Salmast. That very evening, Turkish soldiers organized an anti-Armenian manhunt in Khoy. The Armenians were removed from their homes, led out of the city, and massacred to a man.[70]

In Urmia, where 10,000 to 12,000 regular troops and around 3,000 irregulars who had been recruited from the area confronted some 4,000 Syriac and Armenian combatants, the situation was critical, the more so as the city was also subject to the pressure of the tens of thousands of refugees from the plains to the north. Beginning on 18 July 1918, after several days of fighting, approximately 60,000 to 70,000 refugees left Urmia for Hamadân, where they hoped that the British would protect them. On 31 July, when the Turkish army marched into the city, only 1,000 Christians were left, having taken refuge in the foreign missions there. Bishop Sontag and nearly 600 Syriacs who had crowded into the French mission were liquidated.[71] Apart from the case of Khoy, then, it would seem that regular Ottoman troops did not participate directly in the massacres, but rather sought to incite the tribes against the Christians.

The Occupation of Tabriz by the Turkish Forces and the Taking of Armenian Hostages

Tabriz, the seat of government of the province of Azerbaijan, had a big, long-standing, and well-integrated Armenian community in 1918, which had nevertheless not escaped Turkish dominion over the region. According to contemporary reports, the atmosphere in the city was tense after the publication of inflammatory articles on the events in Salmast and Urmia, especially in the daily *Kelid-e Sa'âdat*, which endeavored "to rekindle hostility toward the Christian population of Tabriz, the largest component of which was represented by the Armenians."[72]

Pan-Turkish propagandists were also at work here. A physician from Baku, Dr. Melik-Aslanov, held a meeting in the Aramian theater about "Islam's victory over the Christians" before an agitated audience. To counter provocations of this kind, the Armenian community immediately organized an evening benefit in the same theater, entitled *Shab-e Irân* (Iranian night), for poverty-stricken Persians. Patriotic speeches and the singing of the Anthem of the Constitutional Revolution may have helped overcome "the negative effects of Turkish propaganda."[73] At all events, it was not until 7 June 1918 that some 40 Turkish soldiers appeared in Tabriz. A few days later, foreign nationals were invited to leave the city, at a time when the Turkish presence there was becoming increasingly conspicuous.

Initially, the Turkish army conducted itself in disciplined fashion and saw to it that law and order were maintained. In June 1918, P. Franssen notes, when the Turkish troops made a triumphant entry into Tabriz,

> a letter signed by a so-called Revenge Committee, primarily made up of Muslims who had come from the Caucasus, was sent to the city's Armenian notables; it demanded that they remit ten thousand toumans [Iranian money] to the aforementioned Committee within twenty-four hours, adding that, if they did not, the Bishop and the notables would be held responsible for everything that happened...On the evening of the following day, Saturday, they began by attacking the Armenians.

Several Armenians were killed in this way.[74]

The territory of a neutral country such as Persia was, so to speak, open to one and all. Although Istanbul had found an excellent pretext for intervening militarily in the regions of Khoy, Salmast, and Urmia and expelling their Christian populations, it found it harder to justify an occupation of Tabriz, fearing to display its Pan-Turkish ambitions too openly. A declaration bearing the signature of Tufik Bey, the commander of the contingent stationed in Tabriz, was posted up in the city on 23 June 1918. It gives some indication of the argument advanced by the Young Turks: "The principal objective of the Ottoman Army is to drive the English from Persian soil, which is inhabited by our Muslim brothers and under the authority of a government that is also Muslim; and, at the same time, to come to the aid of the inhabitants of Tauris."[75] Thus, it was the discourse of Islamic solidarity in the face of the aggressor that predominated here, with no mention of Turkism. Of course, Iranian Democrats such as Beluri, who were faithful allies of the Turks, would not necessarily have appreciated a different sort formulation. The efforts of the Young Turk officers to recruit from the ranks of structures such as the *Ettehâd-e Eslâm* (Union of Islam), which were supposed to obey orders issued by the Turkish authorities, did not produce the expected results.[76]

Another declaration, published in Tabriz on 30 June 1918 by the Ottoman military commander Munir Bey, illustrates the radicalization of the same discourse of Islamic solidarity: "It goes without saying that all Muslims ought to take part, with devotion and sentiments worthy of them, in the holy war currently being waged against Islam's true enemies, and should massacre them in order to prevent them from realizing their perfidious intentions and cruel, tyrannical designs."[77] Golnazarian remarks that "the official representatives of the Entente countries had already left Tabriz" and that "the Armenians, lumped together with the 'enemies of Islam,' comprised the only big Christian group in the city"; as such, they were the primary targets here. The military authorities, then, were capable of expressing themselves with less restraint. These barely veiled allusions took open form in another declaration published on 7 July 1918, again by Munir Bey. It revealed the real objectives of the military incursion into Azerbaijan:

> The cursed, rabid Armenians are always doing whatever they can to violate the political and religious rights of our poor brothers in Azerbaijan; what is more, they are trying to seize their land. The victorious army of the Ottoman Empire, which is striving to defend our holy religion and liberate our fellow Muslims in Azerbaijan, and also to liquidate the Armenians, has already laid siege to the city of Urmia.... Thank God, all of them were massacred as the result of a little attack by our Turkish heroes.[78]

In accordance with approved practice in the Ottoman Empire, the military authorities also threatened to impose "severe sanctions" on those who dared provide assistance of any kind to the infidels.[79] This incitement to violence, however, was not enough to engender more than a certain animosity toward the Armenians. The arrival in early August of Ali İhasan Pasha had been preceded by a demand from Munir, who demanded that Bishop Franssen provide him with 84 Armenian hostages chosen from among the notables, in line with orders he had received from his superior. According to Golnazarian, İhsan had reasons to fear acts of revenge for massacres that had been perpetrated in the province on his orders. The Armenian community perceived this demand as the first act of a preprogrammed death. It was hard for it to shed the image of the domestic foe that Young Turk propaganda had assigned it. Archbishop Melik Tangian and Bishop Franssen vainly tried to convince the Turkish military command that the taking of hostages was pointless. They were left with no other alternative than to beg the prince apparent and the governor of Tabriz to intercede with the Turkish authorities and "vouch for their Armenian subjects' loyalty toward the occupiers." Mohtasham ol-Saltane and the prince apparent's treasurer, Ehzâm ol-Molk, ultimately managed to reduce the number of hostages required to ten.[80]

For nine days running, the Diocesan Council maintained permanent contact with the Iranian authorities, who demonstrated on this occasion that they were clearly ready to protect their Armenian subjects. It was, without a doubt, thanks to the concern exhibited by the central authorities, Golnazarian remarks, "that this community was spared the worst and the hostages were never in danger."[81]

When İhsan made his official entry into Tabriz on 11 August, a delegation representing the Armenian community was among those that went out to receive him. The speech that the general delivered to these delegates was extremely frank:

I thank you for having come out to greet me, but listen to what I am going to tell you: above all, prove the truth of your words by your deeds. You are not unaware of all the afflictions that the Armenians of Urmia, Salmast, and Khoy have brought down upon the Muslims... In retaliation, we killed the Armenians of Khoy, and I gave the order to massacre the Armenians of Maku. If you wish to be well treated, honor the promises that you have just made. If you do not, I cannot offer you any guarantees.[82]

As soon as he arrived, İhsan called for the transfer of the hostages, who had hitherto been in the hands of his Democratic allies, and demanded that the Armenians of Tabriz pay a tribute of 60,000 toumans. As in the case of the hostages, the authorities opposed this demand made by the forces of occupation, apparently because they feared that the measure would be extended to Persian businessmen as well. Moreover, the French consul in Tabriz notes in an 8 March 1919 report that İhsan said, in the course of a conversation with Archbishop Tangian, that took place a few days after his arrival: "I have had half a million of your co-religionists massacred. I can offer you a cup of tea, if you'd like."[83] While the general obviously wanted to exaggerate his deeds, he plainly expressed the spirit animating a number of Young Turk military cadres. Lieutenant Colonel Paraquin, in turn, reveals the CUP's desire to exclude the Germans from its operations in "Persian Azerbaijan, which it considered to be its own sphere of influence," so much so, indeed, that the German Ambassador, Bernstorff, worried that the nomination of a German consul in Tabriz would "cause new problems with the Turks."[84] Even more than in the Caucasus, Istanbul wanted to be able to operate in Azerbaijan without outside interference. Only after the Mudros armistice, signed on 30 October 1918, did the Turkish expeditionary corps begin to evacuate Tabriz.[85]

The human and material costs of the occupation of Azerbaijan were extensive. Without distorting the facts, one can affirm that the centuries-old Armenian presence in the regions of Urmia, Salmast, Qaradâgh, and Maku had been dealt a blow from which it would never recover.[86] In this region, the İhsan had threatened sardâr and other khans with death because they had granted the Armenians refuge. In Keshmish Tape, the sardâr reports, "Ottoman soldiers who had come from Bayazid and Ottoman émigrés living in Maku... attacked and committed an abominable act," the massacre of 500 people, followed by the plunder of their property and the nearby monastery of St. Thaddeus, which had been seized by the Turkish soldiers.[87]

According to a report by M. Riâhi, despite the intervention of certain "wise men of the city," the very day the Turkish soldiers arrived in Khoy and nearby villages, the Armenian population was massacred by "Sımko and his men, a few fanatics in the city, and those under the influence of Ottoman propaganda."[88] The local population, which had given a warm welcome to its Turkish "liberators," rapidly soured when it was forced to provide for the maintenance of this expeditionary corps. In his memoirs, Mollâ Ja'far, an inhabitant of Khoy, says that on Wednesday, 10 July 1918, "Ottoman soldiers discovered seven Armenians in the home of Mashadi Khalil Âqâ, Hâji Fath ollâh-e Mâku-yi's son, who lived in Maqbare Street. They found two of them hidden in the well and five in the basement. The owner of the house was in Maku. They arrested his son Hâji Âqâ, the police chief... they caught five other Armenians in the same street and killed all of them."[89] The report that the Archbishop of Tabriz, Melik Tangian, submitted to the catholicos on 19 June 1919 drew up a general balance sheet that corroborates information available in other sources: 500 people had been killed in the region of Maku, where women and children had been Islamicized; 1,000 people had been massacred in Khoy and the vicinity, and an unknown number had been Islamicized; 5,000 inhabitants of Salmast, Urmia, Sulduz, and Sovuj-Bulâq had died while trekking toward Hamadân and Bakuba; 30 villages in the Qaradâgh district had been looted and 60 people had been killed in Âghâghân. Nearly half of the 30,000 Armenians of Azerbaijan had died or gone into exile by mid-June 1919.[90]

Turkish Military Operations in the Provinces of Elizabetpol and Baku in Summer 1918

General Korganoff, the former vice–chief of staff on the Caucasian front, considered that the Turkish forces lost precious months because they wanted to "bring Armenia to submit" before turning to their "main task" of taking control of Persian Azerbaijan and the Baku region.[91] We may add that this resistance also made it impossible for the Turkish forces to utilize the railway that ran along the Arax River to advance rapidly on Baku, forcing them to go by way of northern Armenia and march down the Kura River valley toward Elizavbetpol (Ganja), where the "Azeri" government controlled by Enver's brother Nuri Pasha had its seat. It was the delay that this caused that doubtless allowed the Bolsheviks briefly to take control of Baku on 25 April 1918. Whereas the military face-off had so far opposed Turks and Bolsheviks, the Commissariat for Transcaucasia, led by Stepan Shahumian, resigned on 31 July, and the Bolshevik troops withdrew.[92] The result was that the confrontation took on the character of a clash between Armenians and Tatars. On 5 August, General Mürsel Pasha tried to break through the enemy lines and march on Baku, but was thrown back by forces that were almost exclusively Armenian. The arrival of British units, which had an interest in seizing the city and its offshore oil, as well as the 27 August treaty between the Bolshevik regime and Germany that notably guaranteed the Germans oil shipments, considerably complicated the situation. The Bolsheviks made it a condition that the Germans prevent any "third force" (Turkey) from occupying Baku. In other words, all parties wanted the city – or, more exactly, wanted to prevent "others" from capturing it. Neither the Bolsheviks nor the Germans, however, were capable of defending it. Baku's fate was, as it were, left in suspense, and its big Armenian community, which was far from being a coherent whole with its big oil magnates and working classes, understood that its physical and economic existence was in jeopardy. The affair took the form of a tug-of-war between the Germans and the Turks. The conflict was so acute that Grand Vizier Talât had to go to Berlin to negotiate recognition of the "specific interests" of his country with regard to the Muslims of Russia and "Ottoman" influence in the Transcaucasus.[93]

While Talât was finalizing an agreement providing for the creation of "separate states" in the "Northern Caucasus and Turkestan," recognizing Turkish interests in the Crimea, and calling for an evacuation of Persia and "Azerbaijan" (after operations against the British were concluded), Enver was ordering his uncle Halil Pasha to take the reins of an offensive against Baku. General Dunsterville's thin British force set out for Enzeli, Persia, on 14 September, but left almost as fast as it had come, abandoning the civilian population to its fate. Halil Pasha, his nephew Nuri Pasha, and General Mürsel did not rush to take the city. There is every reason to suppose that they deliberately let Baku "settle its scores" – in other words, they encouraged the ensuing carnage, which caused from 10,000 to 20,000 Armenian deaths. The troops did not enter Baku until 16 September, meeting no resistance.[94] According to the most reliable sources, the regular troops confined themselves to controlling the populace. A note from the Bolshevik regime denouncing the war crimes perpetrated by the Turkish forces in the districts of Kars, Ardahan, and Batum, the fate of which was supposed to be decided later by referendum, was a response to the Turks' violation of the subsidiary Brest-Litovsk agreement concluded with Germany. The note also pointed out that the invasion of Transcaucasus constituted a violation of the treaty itself. Istanbul maintained that the exactions committed in Baku had been the work of irregular bands.

These diplomatic and military gestures aside, a certain number of remarks are called for here. It must first be pointed out that many of the actors of these events, especially France and Germany, did not have the means to match their ambitions, and that the two veritable protagonists in this struggle, Turkey and Bolshevik Russia, had both convergent and divergent interests. Both regimes were interested, if for different reasons, in pillaging the European and Armenian oil firms. The Russians were probably not unhappy to see the Turkish forces and populace do the work in their stead. The Turks continued to pursue the logic of physical and economic elimination of the Armenians so as to open a path toward their Tatar brothers, now baptized "Azeris," in order to pave the way for annexation of Iranian Azerbaijan.

Lieutenant Colonel Paraquin, chief of staff of the Eastern Army Group's Commander-in-Chief Halil [Kut], informed his superiors in a report written between 15 and 17 September 1918 – that is, while the massacres were underway in Baku – that General Mürsel, the commander of the Fifth Division, had informed him of the Tatars' plans to carry out massacres. Paraquin observed that it was only after Armenians had been hunted down in the streets for three days that the commander of the "Army of Islam," with Nuri's approval, had imposed martial law. Paraquin concluded that "the carnage was planned weeks in advance and stood in no relation whatsoever with the tactical operations."[95]

The clearest symptom of the genocidal logic masked by the military campaigns was Bahaeddin Şakir's presence in Baku. Şakir had arrived on the heels of the Eastern Army Group in order to assume the post of "Director General of the Police" in Baku.[96] Is there any need to point out that the head of the *Teşkilât-ı Mahsusa* was there, together with two of his CUP comrades, in order to honor the promise that he had made to his Caucasian interlocutors in 1906, that he would "put an end to the importance and the influence of the Armenians in the Caucasus"?[97] It is more than probable that Şakir personally coordinated the butchery in Baku in the three days preceding the regular army's entry into the city. It would even seem that Şakir became very popular with Baku's Turkish-speaking population thanks to the "services" he rendered the cause.[98]

After Turkish troops were stationed in Baku and martial law was imposed, the government of Azerbaijan ordered the arrest of the city's Armenian elite: lawyers, engineers, bankers, and business leaders. Nuri, moreover, led contingents of the Army of Islam to Karabagh, where massacres were reported in the villages.[99] Information that reached the German representation in the Caucasus indicated that a system of extortion had been established: it targeted affluent Armenian circles, which had to pay protection money to avoid being arrested.[100] Delinquents certainly took advantage of the situation to make money, but it is more likely that the government controlled by Istanbul initiated a campaign aimed at ruining Armenian businessmen since it could not officially confiscate their assets.

The defeat of the Central Powers and the British forces' march on Syria called a sharp halt to the formation of a Pan-Turkish federation dominated by Istanbul. But, the invasion of the Transcaucasus and Persian Azerbaijan allowed Istanbul to come close to completing its program of homogenizing its territory and helped create another homogeneous Turkish-speaking entity.

This chapter of history came to an end with an event that was, to say the least, odd – Halil Pasha's incongruous October visit to Yerevan, where he was received by Aram Manukian, Armenia's interim head-of-state. Arshavir Shakhatuni, Yerevan's military commander, who was present at the reunion of the two men, gives a rather surprising version of the motives that induced the Young Turk war leader to travel through Yerevan after asking Aram to guarantee his safety.[101] In these last days of the war, the military situation of the Turks in the Caucasus was by no means catastrophic, inasmuch as their forces controlled the region and were not threatened by any outside force. At most, they were concerned about the imminent defeat of their country and apprehensive about having to give accounts for the crimes that they had committed or encouraged.

Chapter 2

The Refounding of the Young Turk Party Shortly Before and Shortly After the Armistice

The military successes scored in the Caucasus and Azerbaijan and the explosion of joy among the people at the announcement that Turkish troops had entered Baku momentarily obscured the fact that, in order to obtain these results in the north, Enver had had to thin out his forces on the Palestinian front, opening the way before General Allenby's British troops. The British, after occupying Jerusalem on 9 December 1917, treaded water for quite some time before capturing Damascus on 1 October 1918. The Bulgarian surrender, which was made official on 2 October, suddenly reminded the Young Turk regime that its ten-year long adventure at the head of the country was drawing to a close, at least in its Ittihadist guise. Yet this experience of exacerbated Turkish ethno-nationalism was not over. Almost all key posts in the country's civilian and military administration, both in Istanbul and the provinces, were held by Unionists, the majority of whom had been appointed during the war and had participated in the common adventure, for reasons that were acceptable in some cases and less so in others. On 7 October 1918, Talât and his cabinet resigned. The next day, the new Sultan, Mehmed VI Vahideddin, asked Tevfik Pasha, the former Turkish ambassador to Britain, to form a new cabinet. Apparently, the sultan preferred to close his eyes to the fact that, for the Ittihadists leaders, it was by no means a question of ceding power to a hostile cabinet, but only of taking shelter behind a team with less blood on its hands. General İzzet Pasha, a former war minister and close associate of Enver's, was charged on 9 October with negotiating the terms of the anticipated armistice. By including several Ittihadists in his cabinet – Fethi Bey [Okyar] as interior minister, Mehmed Cavid as minister of the economy, Hayri Bey as justice minister, and Hüseyin Rauf as minister of the navy – the new grand vizier secured the support of Young Turk circles. Losing no time, the Ittihadist Central Committee organized the party's last annual congress. Between 21 October and 3 November, the CUP carried out a complete overhaul of its structures in both the capital and the provinces. It then dissolved itself, reemerging under the name *Teceddüt Fırkası* (Party of Renovation). Its assets were transferred to the new party, led by Fethi Bey.[1]

Officially, all relations between the new party and the CUP were severed. Moreover, the congress restricted membership by former CUP members, who were accused of having "ruined the country" with their arbitrary personal acts and said to have acquired wealth or positions illicitly.[2] The nationalist movement was obviously aware that identification with the CUP now constituted a serious handicap.[3] Hence it had to keep its distance from the Ittihad, even while assuming the Young Turk ideological heritage. Erik Zürcher remarks that *Teceddüt Fırkası* was basically made up of influential CUP members distinguished by their opposition to the policies pursued by Enver: Yunus Nadi [Abahoğlu] (1880–1945), a parliamentary deputy from Aydın; Faïk [Kaltakkıran], a parliamentary deputy from Edirne; Galip Bahtiyar; Dr. Tevfik Rüştü [Aras]; and a former interior minister, İsmail Canbolat.[4] Let us note that, of these opponents of Enver's adventurism, the two last-named were close associates of Talât's and were heavily implicated in the liquidation of the Armenians. It is clear that the head of the CUP had prepared the "second phase of the war" in the provinces, utilizing both public institutions and underground organizations.[5] In this undertaking, they relied, notably, on the powerful Army of the East, stationed in the Caucasus, and, in particular, on two divisions that had been repatriated from Galicia and Moldavia and been appropriately equipped and trained; they were practically out of reach of the troops of the Entente.[6]

Returning to their practices of the past, the CUP leaders melted into apparently inoffensive organizations with humanitarian or cultural missions, such as the Hilâli Ahmer (Red Crescent). The president of this organization was Dr. Esad [Isık]; its treasurer was Dr. Tevfik Rüştü [Aras], while Dr. Abdülhak Adnan [Adıvar], the former inspector general of the Turkish army's Health Department, served as its counselor. This honorable institution apparently provided cover for clandestine payments and provided a means of communicating with the Unionists who had fled abroad.[7] Another organization, the Millî Talim ve Terbiye Cemiyeti (National Association for Instruction and Education), was controlled by Esad [Isık] and the CUP's former secretary general, Midhat Şükrü [Bleda]. It brought together magistrates and university professors who took the initiative, after the armistice was concluded, of creating the Millî Kongre (National Congress).[8] The Türk Ocağı, whose moving spirit was Mehmed Ziya Gökalp, also sprang back into existence and played a major role, with its 28 regional sections, in organizing the National Congress. Esad Pasha, Ahmed Ağaoğlu, Halide Edip, and Ziya Gökalp and his cousin Süleyman Nazıf (1870–1927), who held the post of vali in several regions and directed Young Turk newspapers, undertook to reorganize the Young Turk networks.[9]

However, the major decision made by the Unionist leaders before they fled the country was the creation of Karakol (The Guard). Its objectives rather clearly revealed the spirit it animating it at the time. It sought to 1) protect the Ittihadists against possible prosecution for their involvement in war crimes by bringing them from the capital to the provinces; 2) organize a resistance movement in Anatolia and the Caucasus by transferring leaders, money, weapons, and ammunition to the provinces; and 3) ensure the defense of the rights of the Turkish population in areas that Greeks, Armenians, Frenchmen, Italians, and the British were threatening to annex.[10]

It was Talât who took the initiative of founding Karakol, in the course of a meeting in Enver's villa in Kuruçeşme in the last week of October 1918. Also attending this meeting were Colonel Kara Vasıf,[11] an eminent CUP leader; the inevitable Kara Kemal, one of those in charge of the party's finances and a great organizer of the "National Economy"; Colonel Baha Said; General Halil [Kut]; and, "according to certain sources," Dr. Adnan [Adıvar].[12] Before going back underground, these men created an organization made up of independent cells, with two distinct branches. One was urban. It had its center in the Topkapı and was directed by Lieutenant Colonel Hüsammeddin [Ertürk]. The other, called Menzil Hattı (Line of Communication) had as its guiding spirit Yenibahçeli Şükrü [Oğuz], and ran the system that brought CUP cadres to Anatolia.[13]

Before leaving the country, Enver and Talât also ordered the Teşkilât-ı Mahsusa to stockpile arms and ammunition in secret depots in different places in Anatolia; it did so prior to its October 1918 dissolution, when it was renamed Umum Alemi Islam Ihtilâl (General Revolutionary Organization of the Islamic World). According to the memoirs of one of its leaders, Hüsameddin [Ertürk], Enver issued orders to maintain the organization intact and prepare "the second phase of the war" with his uncle Halil [Kut] and his brother Nuri [Kiligil], who had significant forces under their command in the eastern provinces and the Caucasus.

After the armistice, the Special Organization aided *Karakol*, informing it of where arms and ammunition were hidden, sending it money, and offering it the benefit of its savoir-faire when it came to clandestine activity or the ethnic cleansing of non-Turkish population groups.[14]

The secret arms depots created on Talât's and Enver's orders were established in Angora, Kayseri, Erzerum, Kastamonu, and Bandırma under the control of the Special Organization. They were intended to be of use to the resistance movements.[15]

According to Zürcher, the clandestine activities of the Unionists, club members, and officers of the Ottoman Army seem to have been coordinated on a general plan prepared in advance and put into practice by the chiefs of the party even before their flight from the country. In other words, the protagonists of the budding national resistance movement in Anatolia simply carried out a plan drawn up by the CUP.[16] Zürcher also observes that Unionist politicians and officers reacted in fairly uniform fashion – concentration in Anatolia, mobilization of public opinion around the creation of a nation-state, rejection of demobilization and disarmament, creation of a resistance network, and the conviction that the defeat was only temporary.[17]

Zürcher is convinced that all the measures taken by Enver and Talât were based on a plan, worked out as early as 1915, to defend Anatolia, "the true Turkish fatherland." This scheme is supposed to have been conceived, down to its least details, when the battle for the Dardanelles broke out in spring 1915, as it anticipated a possible collapse of the Turkish forces with an eye to continuing the war in Anatolia. In other words, Talât and Enver simply reactivated a long-standing plan on the eve of the armistice and confided its realization to *Karakol*. It would appear that generals such as Kâzım [Karabekir], Ali Fuad, Mustafa Kemal, and Yakub Şevki were aware that they were proceeding in accordance with a plan established in advance by the CUP leadership.[18] This comes down to saying that there existed a relation of consanguinity between the Young Turk regime and the beginnings of the nationalist movement, one thinly disguised by a few cosmetic touches. Or, if one likes, it means that the Young Turk cadres did not wait for the arrival of a providential leader to put Anatolia in a state in which it could rebel. This is a phenomenon that Turkish historiography tends to obscure so as not to undermine the image of the hero who saved the "fatherland," Mustafa Kemal.

The CUP plan was financed out of the war treasury that the party had accumulated in the course of the First World War, thanks to shady financial practices, the acquisition of monopolies on grain, tobacco, rail transportation, and, above all, the pillage of Armenian and Greek assets. The German journalist Harry Stuermer, who lived in Istanbul in 1915–16, exposed the mechanism established by the two succeeding chiefs of the Commission for Supplies, İsmail Hakkı and Kara Kemal, to secure funds for the Ittihadist Central Committee. Hakkı and Kemal founded the *Bakal* (Grocers') Union, a semi-official organization that artificially created a food shortage the better to speculate on rising prices to result of enormous profits.[19] A British Secret Service document notes that the main beneficiaries of these monopolies were CUP members.[20] These practices, worthy of criminals, constituted one of the chief counts in the indictment of the Young Turk leaders when the Fifth Commission of the Ottoman parliament summoned them to testify at hearings in November 1918.[21] As we have seen, the primary task of this union of the *Esnafs* (guilds), founded in 1915 to foster the formation of a middle class of Turkish businessmen,[22] was to confiscate Armenian and Greek assets in the name of a policy of *Millî İktisat* (National Economy).[23]

The British sources again indicate that some of the assets and capital obtained in the framework of these operations was converted into foreign currency or French and British treasury bonds in September 1918, with the help of Istanbul moneylenders such as Jacques Manache and Aslan Fresco. These moneylenders bought the bonds in Switzerland or the Netherlands at the behest of their clients, essentially Young Turks whom the documents designate by name: Mehmed Cavid, İsmail Hakkı, Enver Pasha, and so on.[24]

It is probable that these individuals made such purchases with their own financial security in mind. But, they no doubt also considered this to be a way of preparing to finance the preprogrammed resistance movement in Anatolia.

The Mudros Armistice or the Effects of the Defeat

The signing of the Mudros armistice on 30 October by Admiral Calthorpe and Hüseyin Rauf Bey marked the beginning of the second phase of the war and redeployment of the means at the Ittihad's disposal. Although the principal leaders of the CUP left Istanbul on a German submarine during the night of 1 November, the fact remains that all the key posts in the state apparatus were still controlled by Unionists, for it had not proved possible to carry through with the purge begun in early 1919.[25]

The list of fugitives is based on how heavily they were involved in the exactions committed against the civilian population during the war. It includes: Mehmed Talât; İsmail Enver; Ahmed Cemal; Dr. Bahaeddin Şakir; Dr. Nâzım; Aziz Bey; Bedri Bey; Cemal Azmi the vali of Trebizond; İsmail Hakkı; Salih Zeki Bey, the *mutesarif* of Der Zor; İsmail Muştak Bey, the secretary general of the Senate; Resneli Nâzım Bey, the CUP's responsible secretary in Mamuret ul-Aziz; and Haydar İbrahim, Azerbaijan's representative in Istanbul.

Zürcher, in his study of the origins of the Kemalist movement, notes that from the outset, the leaders of the CUP, the Special Organization, and *Karakol* sent military cadres to the provinces to help organize the resistance in various regions. He notably cites the case of a CUP inspector, Yenibahçeli Nail, who was sent to Batum, and that of his colleague, Filibeli Ahmed Hilmi in Erzerum.[26] Let us recall that these were two eminent members of the Special Organization who had already been active on the Committee of National Defense in Thrace in summer 1913 and, in 1915, on the Caucasian front, where Hilmi served as Şakir's assistant.[27] As for the fate of the Turkish forces, which, according to the Mudros armistice, were to be disarmed or stationed in Asia Minor, it should be noted that Yakub Şevki [Sübaşı], the commander of the Ninth Army, which had its headquarters in Kars, was supposed to evacuate the Caucasus and the provinces of Kars, Ardahan, and Batum, but refused to execute these clauses of the agreement. On 26 November 1918, he even ordered his troops to defend the three provinces. When, on 25 January 1919, he received the second injunction to evacuate them, he complied only after entrusting the administration of them to the leadership of the *Millî Şura* (National Council), which had just been formed by the Young Turk networks in Anatolia. He also distributed arms to the population and turned over the stocks of arms and ammunition in the citadel in Kars to the "new" authorities. Once he had withdrawn to Erzerum, he created and armed militias, in line with instructions he had received from the Ittihadist hierarchy.[28] The CUP's influence in Asia Minor thus appears to have been unshaken and was even reinforced by the continuous transfer of Unionist officers, most of the them wanted for war crimes, who were taken in hand by *Karakol* with the complicity of the Ottoman administration.[29]

The political translation of the Ittihadist enterprise in Anatolia found expression in the convening, at *Karakol's* initiative, of a *Millî Şura* (National Council) on 11 December 1918. The council brought together the representatives of 63 political, social, cultural, and professional associations, which obviously were of Unionist inspiration, such as *Türk Ocağı*, *Teceddüt Fırkası*, and *Millî Müdafaa Cemiyeti* (National Defense Committee). Also present were "regional" organizations, with the notable exception of the liberals.[30] Among the associations for "Defense in the East," the most important were *Kars İslâm Şûrası* (Kars Muslim Council), which had received money and weapons from General Yakub Şevki, and *Vilayâti Şarkiye Müdafaai Hukuku Milliye Cemiyeti* (Association for the Defense of the National Rights of the Eastern Provinces), initiated by Süleyman Nazıf, a cousin of Ziya Gökalp's.[31] There is perhaps no need to point out that the purpose of these two organizations was to oppose the creation of an Armenian state in the six eastern vilayets the Armenian population of which had paid for the CUP's policy of homogenization with its life and property. One of the uppermost concerns of the Young Turk networks was, moreover, to silence the newspapers that now began to publish articles about the *tehcir* (deportation policy)[32] carried out by the Young Turk state-party – that is, about the liquidation of the Armenian population.

The whole of the system erected by the CUP not only allowed the party to maintain a presence on the Ottoman political scene, but also to work, first and foremost, toward throttling the release of information on the genocide it had committed, and even, as we shall see, to thwart the timid attempts to punish those responsible for it as well as those who carried out their orders. The Turkish nation-state in the Anatolian sanctuary was constructed on the basis of a discourse legitimizing violence that many endorsed. Of course, the movement's principal leaders and their objective allies, Kurdish and Çerkez tribal chieftains and other local notables, would have had a great deal to lose if justice had been done.

In other words, the governments that succeeded each other in Istanbul beginning in October 1918 had an extremely narrow margin of maneuver. Sultan Mehmed VI Vahideddin, Abdülhamid's younger brother, who acceded to the throne on 4 July 1918, had spent most of his life within his four gilded walls, but seems to have been resolved to reassert the influence of the House of Osman. He nevertheless submitted without flinching to the desires of the Ittihadist leaders, who imposed General Ahmed İzzet Pasha – the minister of war in 1913 – as the head of government. İzzet put together a cabinet made up of Unionists of second rank: Ali Fethi, Rauf Bey [Orbay], and Mehmed Cavid. It may be presumed that this carefully tailored Young Turk cabinet had no other goal than to negotiate an armistice before ceding its place. After the British and French High Commissioners had taken up residence in Istanbul, it became obvious that a new cabinet had to be formed without Ittihadists. On 11 November 1918, a new council of ministers was formed by Ahmed Tevfik [Okday] (1845–1936), who had served briefly as grand vizier in 1909 and had political sympathies that made him presentable. The Ottoman parliament, as well as the upper levels of the civilian and military administration, still dominated by Young Turks, made this cabinet and its successors fragile. The CUP did not hesitate to threaten the sultan and the authorities even after its members were arrested. The only grand vizier in the true sense of the word to emerge in the course of the year 1919 was Damad Ferid Pasha, who held office from 4 March to 10 October 1919, after repeatedly facing votes of no confidence.[33] It was above all under his government that the Young Turks began to be called to account for their deeds, that arrests were made with greater and greater frequency, and that the Ittihadist organizations were challenged.[34] At the request of the French and British, the Ottoman police proceeded to arrest, on 10 March 1919, Said Halim; Hayri Bey, a former şeyh ul-Islam; Musa Kâzım, the şeyh ul-Islam; Rifât Bey, a former minister of finance; Halil Bey [Menteşe], a former foreign minister; Ahmed Şükrü Bey, a former minister of public education; Ahmed Nesimi Bey, a former foreign minister; İbrahim Bey, a former justice minister; İsmail Muştak Bey, the general secretary of the Senate; Habib Bey, a parliamentary deputy from Bolu; Ali Münif, a former state secretary in the Interior Ministry; Hilmi Bey, a parliamentary deputy from Angora; Ahmed Emin Bey, a parliamentary deputy from Istanbul and the editor-in-chief of *Vakıt*; Celal Nuri Bey, the editor-in-chief of *Atti*; Osman Bey, general secretary in the Interior Ministry; Fethi Bey [Okyar], a former foreign minister and president of *Teceddüd*; Salah Cimcöz, a former parliamentary deputy; Fuad Bey, the director of the telephone company; Sabancali İsmail Hakkı, the publisher of *İstiklal*; İzzet Bey, a member of the CUP; Hoca Hasan Fehmi, a parliamentary deputy from Sinope; and Mustafa Reşad Bey, the director of the political section of the Police Department.[35] In other words, the "big fish" were not arrested until after Ferid arrived at the helm of government. Previously, with the exception of Dr. Reşid, the vali of

Dyarbekir, and İsmail Canbolat, both of whom had been arrested on 29 January,[36] only those who had merely carried out orders to liquidate the Armenians had been taken into custody: Major İzzet Bey, the director of the hospital in Van, arrested on 4 February;[37] Emmanuel Carasso, a former Unionist parliamentary deputy from Salonica,[38] on 6 February; Ahmed Celaleddin Bey, the *mutesarif* of Tomarza, on 9 February;[39] Colonel Tevfik Bey, the commander in Ras ul-Ayn, on 19 February;[40] Nâzım Bey, the head of the orphanage in Aleppo, on 25 February;[41] İbrahim Bey, the leader of a squadron of *çetes* in Ismit, on 3 March;[42] and Sabur Sâmi Bey, the *mutesarif* of Adalia, on 11 March.[43]

In March and April, Ferid's government trained its sights on men of still higher rank. It ordered the arrests of members of the Ittihad's Central Committee and high-ranking party cadres: Ahmed Ağaoğlu, on 20 March;[44] Cevad Bey, the military commander of the capital; Yusuf Ziya Bey, a member of the Central Committee; Necati Bey, on 27 March;[45] İlyas Sâmi Bey, a parliamentary deputy from Mush, on 1 April;[46] Nusret Bey, the *mutesarif* of Urfa, on 2 April;[47] Midhat Sükrü Bey, the CUP's secretary general; and Kuçuk Talât Bey and Ziya Gökalp, members of the Ittihadist Central Committee, on 17 April.[48] Manifestly, in this brief period there existed a real desire among certain Istanbul liberal circles to purge the country of the Young Turks who had remained where they were and whose criminal past tarnished the image of the Ottoman Empire, but who were also held responsible for its predictable dismemberment and for considerable human losses. According to Ahmed Bedevi Kuran, the war caused the deaths of around 550,000 soldiers, produced nearly 900,000 invalids, and left over 100,000 missing and 2,176,000 wounded.[49] M. Larcher, for his part, estimates the number of combat deaths at 725,000 (doubtless including the missing in this figure), and the number of those who died of illness or were carried off by epidemics at 240,000, out of a total of 2,850,000 conscripts.[50]

These arrests did not, to be sure, prevent *Karakol* from organizing the escape of many of these suspects, whom it set about bringing to safety in Anatolia. It would even seem that this organization succeeded in introducing an informer into Ferid's residence,[51] and that its military activities in Anatolia were supported by the army's general command, with which it was in "objective collaboration."[52]

The dissolution of parliament, many of the members of which were deeply implicated in the war crimes, became inevitable when *Teceddüd* held a general assembly on 20 December/ 2 January and decided to call for a vote of no confidence against the Tevfik cabinet.[53] The next day, Mehmed VI signed the decree announcing the dissolution of the Ottoman parliament.[54] The November–December 1919 legislative elections stood as a revealing sign of popular support for the Young Turk movement, or at least of its capacity to influence the masses: they returned a parliament that was still more heavily dominated by the triumphant Unionists.[55]

Chapter 3

The Debates in the Ottoman Parliament in the Wake of the Mudros Armistice

Although the main Ittihadist criminals had fled in the night of 1–2 November,[1] the Arab parliamentary deputy from Divaniye, Fuad Bey, made a motion in the Ottoman parliament to bring the ministers who had held their posts during the war years before the High Court of Justice.[2] Did the parliament address the question of legal proceedings against the Young Turk leaders thanks to this deputy or a few party cadres who regarded this assembly as the most appropriate place in which to initiate legal action that could be kept under control? We shall attempt to answer this question by analyzing the course of the debates and the remarks made by different groups present in the Ottoman parliament.

While it is true that most of the individuals indicted had been ministers or high-ranking state officials – a circumstance that justified bringing them before the High Court – it must also be said that this option offered many advantages: because it could be realized very rapidly, it allowed parliament to seize the initiative, orient the debates in line with the wishes of a majority of deputies, and, by the same token, thwart the legal initiatives that might be taken by much less well disposed circles.

In fact, the Ottoman parliament had been in session since 10 October 1918, yet no steps had been taken in the three weeks preceding the departure of the Young Turk leaders. The president of the assembly, Halil Bey [Menteşe], an eminent member of the Young Turk Central Committee and a former foreign minister, saw to that. Apart from Fuad's motion, he had to deal with the five-point request endorsed by 14 deputies,[3] including two surviving Armenians and two Greeks. It bore on acts committed during the war by the Ottoman government, and evoked, notably, the liquidation of 1 million Armenian subjects of the empire, the expulsion of 250,000 Greeks and the wartime seizure of their assets, the massacre of 550,000 Greeks from the Pontus at war's end, and the 1915 murder of deputies such as Krikor Zohrab and Vartkes Seringiulian. This request, which bore directly on war crimes that the Young Turk regime had committed against civilians, holding the Ottoman state responsible for its acts, was voted down after stormy debates that lasted for several sessions, although Fuad's motion – eight of the ten counts in the indictment submitted to parliament declaring the Committee of Union and Progress and its Young Turk ministers guilty of seizing control of the state apparatus, deciding to enter the war, concluding a secret agreement with Germany, engaging in financial misdealing for their own benefit, imposing censorship, publishing false information about the course of the war, and so on – had passed. It was the easier to reject the request in that the two charges that more or less directly concerned the liquidation of the Armenians and the violence perpetrated against the Greeks and Syriacs – the fifth, on the "temporary deportation law," and the tenth, which referred to the creation and criminal activities of the Special Organization – were formulated rather vaguely, with no mention of the principal victims, and focused, especially as far as the first point was concerned, on a panoply of laws put in place by the Young Turk government itself in order to legalize its crimes, or at least pass them off as administrative measures rendered indispensable by the war. This is, as we shall see later, when we analyze the declarations that the ministers made before the Fifth Parliamentary Commission, a way of avoiding drawing too much public attention to the mass murders and mentioning the victimized group by name, and, at the same time, an attempt to situate the debates on a terrain that the executioners had prepared in advance to justify their acts.

Notwithstanding this motion's obvious advantages, the Young Turk majority in parliament resisted, or pretended to, before finally adopting it on 4 November as the basis for its work. In response to the *takrir* [motions] made by the rare deputies from minority groups in the parliament, which summoned the government to state its position on the crimes committed by its predecessors, the interior minister Fethi Bey [Okyar] said that the victims had not only been Armenians, Greeks, or Arabs, but Turks as well, and the government would do all it could to remedy the injustices and send the deportees back to their homes.[4] Thus, he laid the groundwork for the position that the accused and, more generally, successive Turkish governments would defend at all costs in the months and years ahead. It might be translated as follows: we all suffered in the war; we are going to correct the abuses, punish the guilty, and make certain that such things never happen again. Confronted with this approach, which already contained the seeds of a denial of the facts, the Armenian deputies sought to place the government before its responsibilities. After Fuad's motion was adopted, the deputy from Sis/Kozan, Mattheos Nalbandian, together with five of his colleagues, filed a written request that the government state how it regarded the crimes committed after the passage and enactment of the Temporary Deportation Law (27 May 1915) and the Law on Abandoned Property (26 September 1915). Thus, they invested the terrain marked out by Fuad's motion, a tactic that had the merit of placing their Turkish colleagues before their responsibilities, since it was with reference to these two laws that parliament should have voted that crimes had been committed. The question these deputies put to the government was the more justified in that the text of the 26 May 1915 decree had been transmitted to the president of parliament a few days after the decree was promulgated, but had been submitted to the deputies only after the deportations had been carried out.[5] When the deputies demanded that the government take the necessary steps to return the survivors who were scattered here and there to their homes, the interior minister answered that that would take some time. These deputies were no doubt unaware that the deportation law in question had been published in an official form that deliberately left out four of its articles, which had been transmitted in the form of a handwritten circular accessible only to the authorities who had been charged with carrying out the deportations. This was no accident: the four secret articles contained the instructions the authorities needed to attribute the homes of the Armenian deportees to Turkish refugees and other refugee groups without delay,[6] thus giving them to understand that these "displaced persons" were not expected to return. In any case, the 4 November session of parliament ended with a vote that abrogated the truncated decree of the former interior minister, which had subsequently been transformed into an Imperial law.

There is, naturally, something surreal about the fact that Armenian deputies, whose most important colleagues had been murdered in cold blood, should have been addressing a chamber of which some members had been directly involved in the liquidation of the Armenians and had for the most part reaped personal benefits at the deportees' expense. Moreover, they did so in order to raise a question that no one really wanted to hear, but that had to be posed in appropriately minimal form to meet the needs of the moment.

By the time the next session of parliament devoted to this question was held on 18 November 1918, the composition of the cabinet, as we have said, had changed: it no longer included the well-known Young Turk leaders. In theory, a vote of confidence in the new government should have been conducted. But, the Armenian deputies, particularly Artin Boshgezenian, a Young Turk deputy from Aleppo whose previous interventions had been marked by extreme caution, decided to raise the question of the collective murder of their compatriots, putting their fingers on the sore spot. In a very long speech, Boshgezenian first recalled that the country would soon be invited to attend the peace conference and that it would be better that it not turn up there empty-handed; that the Turkish people were in the situation of an accused party – this affirmation provoked sharp protests, to which the speaker respond that his colleagues should first listen to him, and thrash him thereafter, if they wished; that they were "today facing a major crime, one of the saddest, bloodiest pages of Ottoman history ... the Armenian massacre"; that the country as a whole was being held responsible for these acts; that many Turks and, notably, the inhabitants of a city such as Konya, as well as some prefects, had nonetheless opposed the government's orders and tried to protect Armenian deportees; that the government had enacted its programs with the help of its prefects, the local military authorities, the gendarmerie, groups of çetes (released convicts organized in bands) and, more generally, state officials; and that it would therefore be difficult to put the blame on the Young Turk leaders alone, the more so as the population had taken part in the violence alongside the çetes in a number of localities. The Armenian deputy then demanded that the country cease to encourage "the dishonorable people" who continued to organize provocations and issue blanket denials that the crimes had occurred, although they themselves had perpetrated them. He concluded that the essence of the matter resided in the fate that would be meted out to these people; that Turkey's destiny depended on whether they were punished; and that it was necessary to arrest the guilty, most of who were still circulating freely, with all impunity.[7]

For the first time, a deputy had, while taking a few rhetorical precautions, raised the question of the liquidation of the Ottoman Armenians. This was no minor matter in a society characterized by a conception of justice and penal practices at quite some distance from European standards. The very idea that the Ottoman state might be accused of wrongdoing was for many inconceivable. The reactions of certain Turkish and Kurdish deputies, who echoed official Young Turk discourse about the Armenians' treason to justify the "punishment" that had been meted out to them and considered these events secondary, were symptomatic of Ottoman society's inability to take the measure of the mass murder that had just been committed in its name. Much the same thing might be said about the concordant reaction of the Young Turk deputies such as Hoca Ilyas Sâmi, a Kurdish tribal chieftain from Mush who, as was revealed when he was later brought to trial, had played a major role in the murder of the Armenians of his region.[8]

The 9 December session of parliament was just as interesting. It began with a reading of a *takrir* submitted by Dikran Barsamian, a deputy from Sıvas and former member of the Ittihad, and Kegham Der Garabedian, a deputy from Mush who had just died after a long illness thanks to which he had been spared in 1915. Although their motion was dated 5 November, it constituted a response to Ilyas Sâmi's intervention from a man who had known him well. It expressed surprise over the statistics on the number of Armenians who, according to their Muslim colleagues, had fallen victim to the exactions – 100,000 – pointing out that about as many Armenians had been slain in the coastal area of the Pontus alone, from Samsun to Trebizond,[9] and recalling how the Armenians from the plain of Mush had been killed.

Theoretically, the 11 December session was to focus on the violence to which the Greeks had been subjected, particularly in Tekirdağ, Edirne, and Çatalca, but it soon turned to a consideration of the Armenian case. The famous poet and deputy from Mosul, Mehmed Emin [Yürdakül] finally asked for the floor. An able, respected speaker, Emin insistently repeated that the violent acts perpetrated by a criminal band, especially the liquidation of the Armenians, could not be attributed to the government, let alone the Turkish nation, which had indeed been the primary victim of the conflict (he meant battle casualties in particular), and that it was unthinkable that they should blamed today for the crimes that had been committed.[10] Emin thus voiced the parliament's major preoccupation, its desire to clear the state's name by attributing the crimes, which Emin acknowledged, unlike some of his colleagues, to the group that had dragged the country into the war. Compared to the usual discourse of Turkish circles, this represented a kind of concession that should not be taken lightly. At the same session, the deputy from Trebizond, Mehmed Emin (who should not be confused with the deputy from Mosul) declared that he had personally witnessed the murder of the Armenians of Samsun, whom the governor had had drowned off the Black Sea coast. Emin had also learned, he said, that the governor of Trebizond, Cemal Azmi, had done the same thing in his vilayet.[11] This account, which indicated that the local authorities had taken a direct hand in organizing the massacres, did not go unnoticed: for the first time, a deputy, one who also had a reputation as a brilliant jurist, had spoken out without restraint.

The next day, 12 December, parliament debated these questions again. The Greek deputy from Tekirdağ, Efkalidis, addressed the government, focusing his remarks on the events that had occurred since 1913, which had in common the fact that all had been denied or interpreted in tendentious fashion, to say the least: the expulsion, beginning in 1913, of 500,000 Greeks (and the plunder of their assets), which had been interpreted as the voluntary departure of men wishing to serve in the Greek army; the deportation of the Armenians, which had been presented as a punitive measure similar to those adopted by the English in Ireland; and the minimization of the violence endured by the Greek and Armenian populations, which turned on the idea that there had also been many victims among the Turks, although it was a question of, on the one hand, subjects of the empire murdered by the authorities, and, on the other, soldiers who had fallen in the war. The Greek deputy, resolved to make his Turkish colleagues uncomfortable, asked whether they were trying to convince themselves of the truth of what they said, or whether they thought that they could thus fool the whole world.

Efkalidis's intervention was a way of staking out a clear position at a time when a sharp debate raged in the capital between the editors of the Young Turk newspapers and liberal circles, both Armenian and Greek. The next speech, by the deputy from Sis/Kozan, Mattheos Nalbandian, also sought to respond to the articles that put forward the Young Turks' classic argument: they were traitors; we had to take administrative measure to removes these potential traitors from the war zones; abuses were committed when these measures were carried out but when they came to our attention we punished those responsible for them, and so on. Nalbandian provided, for the first time, a historical summary of what had transpired, beginning with the arrest and execution of the whole Armenian elite in both the capital and the provinces; the systematic deportation of all the populations, wherever they were found; and the liquidation of convoys in the Black Sea, the Tigris and Euphrates, and the Syrian deserts. Directly addressing his colleagues, Nalbandian declared: "Gentlemen, these things are not tales from *One Thousand and One Nights*; these are the facts, just as they occurred, and our distinguished assembly should express regret over them and weep." The deputy went on to say that his own family had been deported; that he himself had survived thanks only to the intercession of Halil Bey (who was presiding over the session of parliament at which Nalbandian spoke), then foreign minister; that in the course of his voyage to Constantinople, he had witnessed unimaginable scenes – men and women in their death agonies on the road, children abducted from their mothers – and that upon his arrival in the capital he had described his experiences to Halil. Turning to Mehmed Emin (Yürdakül), he asked him how he could say that only three to five people were responsible for these horrors and that the Turkish people was a victim, given that it was the nation that dominated the empire, whereas the Armenians were among the subjugated nations.[12]

Hoca Ilyas Sâmi took the floor after Nalbandian. This time, the deputy from Mush did not present the usual thesis about an Armenian conspiracy. On the defensive, he first developed the theme of the benevolence shown to the minorities by religious circles from which he himself came, taking as his (dubious) example the 1895–6 Armenian massacres. He also asked that the war situation be taken into account and that attention be paid to the reasons that had led to the anti-Armenian violence. In so doing, he took a conciliatory step, admitting the crimes that had been committed against the Armenians; accusations that the Armenians had massacred Turks, which had been strewn through his first speech, were absent from this one. "I am under an obligation," he declared, "to speak the truth. Yes, the eastern provinces were transformed into a graveyard." Nevertheless, he added, "this is not the moment to settle accounts." That should be done "only after the fatherland has dressed its wounds."

The new interior minister, Mustafa Arif Bey, who attended these debates, closed the session with remarks that once again reveal an overriding concern to dissociate, from a penal standpoint, the Turkish nation from the Young Turks:

Both your august assembly and the government have confirmed that certain of the events connected with this question indeed took place. No one is saying that they did not happen. I think, however, that if we go so far as to admit that, among the millions of Turks, one hundred thousand [were involved], it is inadmissible to hold the entire race responsible for the acts committed by those one hundred thousand people.[13]

The Work of the Fifth Commission of the Ottoman Parliament

Parallel to the debates just discussed, the Ottoman parliament decided to create a commission of inquiry, known as the Fifth Commission. On the basis of the ten points in the motion by Fuad that had been adopted by the assembly, the Fifth Commission conducted hearings of the ministers of the war cabinets still living in the capital. To the best of our knowledge, the record of these hearings was not immediately published in the Ottoman parliament's *Official Gazette*, but was rather turned over to the court-martial, which in a sense pursued the commission's work in the judicial field. However, as can be readily imagined, the British and French intelligence services (the S.I.S. and the S.R. Marine, respectively)[14] followed the commission's work, carried on from November to December 1918, with great interest. In addition to the official publications of the Ottoman parliament, which have been exploited by the Armenian-American historian Vahakn Dadrian, we also possess, thanks to these intelligence services, a complete record of the interrogations of 15 ministers. An analysis of them is rich in lessons about the defense strategy adopted by Young Turk circles, even if these materials reveal nothing new about the facts themselves. They also shed a great deal of light on the atmosphere prevailing within the Fifth Commission and the objectives that parliament sought to obtain in agreeing to refer to the "abuses" committed against the empire's Armenian subjects, even if these references were drowned in a sea of issues revolving around the way the Young Turks had conducted the war.

Before considering the work of the Fifth Commission, it should be emphasized that the ministers it could interrogate – that is, those still living in the Ottoman capital – were the ones who had been the least directly involved in the crimes committed against the Armenians (even if they were perfectly well aware of the facts). The ministers themselves pointed this out every time they had the chance.

At one of the first hearings, held on 24 and 25 November 1918, the commission interrogated Mehmed Cavid, the former minister of finance, who had resigned as soon as the
Ottoman Empire had entered the war early in November 1914. This provided him the occasion to describe the circumstances that had led to Ottoman entry into the war and to remark
that "the Russian aggression was simply a lie spun out of thin air." He added that decisions
were made privately, at Said Halim's house, not at sessions of the Council of Ministers.[15]
Cavid next affirmed, in response to a question from the deputy from Ertuğrul, Şemşeddine
Bey, about the conditions surrounding the general mobilization in the empire, that the mobilization decree had not been decided upon by the Council of Ministers, but that it was Enver
who seems to have initiated it by having each of the ministers sign, separately, the draft of an
Imperial *irade* (command); the decree was signed and published in the *Official Gazette* only
after it had been publicly proclaimed.[16] As for the temporary deportation laws, "contrary to
the rules of law and humanity, and a violation of the letter and spirit of our Constitution,
which turned the country into a field of tragedies," Cavid pointed out that he was no longer
a member of the government "when the Armenian affairs took place ... At no time and place
did I ever endorse them; every time the occasion offered, I brought this subject to my colleagues' attention."[17] Cavid went on to emphasize that after his 1917 return to the ministry, he had applied "the laws and regulations pertaining to the Armenian deportees' assets
as generously as possible." "I even convinced Talât Pasha," he went on, "to authorize the
Armenians and Arabs to return to their homes ... I was not a minister ... when these laws were
applied."[18] For good measure, Cavid concluded that he had written to Talât when he was
appointed grand vizier and that Talât had informed him that the new cabinet "would see to
it that individual rights were scrupulously respected and that every Ottoman would benefit
from the rights conferred upon him by Constitutional law." "For the moment, the Armenian
and Arab questions," Talât had added, would "be resolved to the extent that the state of war
allows, and, shortly before peace is concluded, in fundamental fashion."[19]

To the last question posed by the president of the commission, "about participation in the
crimes resulting from the disorder in the administration and the assistance given to bands
that violated the population's freedom, life, honor, and property – in question is the Special
Organization," Cavid gave a categorical answer: "this was not the government's doing."[20]
Even while seeming to take his distance from this colleagues on the Young Turk Central
Committee – Cavid, remember, had resigned from the government at the beginning of the
war – and without denying the criminal plans aimed against the Armenians, to which, he
gave his listeners to understand, he had been opposed, Cavid pointed out with a certain
cynicism that in 1917 he had even helped restore the rights of the Ottoman subjects who
had disappeared more than a year earlier or lived on in harsh surroundings several thousand
kilometers from their homes. However, in response to the key question about the Special
Organization, of whose criminal activities he could not have been unaware, Cavid contented
himself with saying that the government had nothing to do with these bands. The members
of the Fifth Commission seemed to find that answer satisfactory.

One day earlier, on 23 November, the acting president of parliament, Halil Bey [Menteşe],
had testified before the commission.[21] Halil first denied the existence of the Temporary
Deportation Law, but then admitted that it had been promulgated before he joined the cabinet. To the insistent questions of the members of the commission, he ultimately responded
that, when he had been the president of the parliament, he had "used all his influence to
improve the deportees' lot." He added: "When I returned from Bern, the deportations were
a *fait accompli* and there were only a few isolated cases left ... If you ask the Armenians about
this, I believe that all of them will tell you about my efforts to that end." Finally, when he
was asked about the Special Organization, Halil asked in return, "in what regions were these
bands organized?" for he had no memory of the creation of such an organization. When

he was told that felons were released from prison and employed with the approval of the minister of justice, he said that he had not joined the cabinet until October 1915 and that "in the period during which I was minister, nothing of that sort took place."[22] Halil, an important member of the Young Turk Central Committee, seems to have been one of those opposed to the plan to liquidate the Armenians. Yet he limited himself here to protesting his innocence and covering for his colleagues.

The first accused person to testify before the commission, Said Halim, who had been grand vizier until early 1917, could not, for his part, hide behind the excuse that he had assumed his functions late in the day in order to argue that he knew nothing. Halim was the only eminent member of the war cabinet still in Constantinople, and his testimony is of crucial importance. Asked about his responsibility in state affairs, he tried to present himself as a man who had had no power in his hands (the implication being that power had been in the hands of the other Young Turk leaders): "The grand vizier presides over the Council of Ministers, but the ministers pay attention to him only if it pleases them. They can perfectly well turn a deaf ear to him on the pretext that only parliament is empowered to call them to accounts...No one ever asked me my opinion."[23] When Halim was asked about "certain inhuman temporary laws bearing on the transportation of families living near the frontiers or in strategic places," he repeated the official thesis: "this law was passed in order to ensure the security of the army while in combat."[24] However, the ensuing debate forced the grand vizier to take the floor. A deputy, Râgib Neşaşibî, even declared:

No such temporary law was ever brought before parliament, although it was in session for four years running; yet so important a law should have been submitted to it ahead of all others. The government must punish those who interfere with the movements of the army, but why did it punish people who were powerless to cut off the army's rear base? What motivated its acts?

One of Neşaşibî's colleagues, Rıza Bey (a deputy from Bursa), reminded him that "the law in question was presented to parliament; it is the law on the deportations." Either unconvinced or feigning ignorance, Neşaşibî now drew a fine distinction: "There exists a law on the deportations, but the law that allows the commanders of the army to hang and kill was not submitted to parliament." Rıza felt obliged to point out: "That wasn't a law. The commanders could, taking the first law as the basis for their acts, apply whatever sentence they wished."[25] Stubbornly pursuing his line of reasoning, Neşaşibî replied: "The courts martial could condemn and exile certain individuals. But does the law say that one has the right to hunt down woman and children in their homes and have them executed?" It took this sharp exchange to bring Halim to say, finally, after taking certain precautions: "You no doubt wish to talk about the Armenian question."

Alarmed, the president corrected the formulation – "the question of the deportations." Nevertheless, the grand vizier's response was rather enlightening: "The vice-generalissimo [Enver] and the commanders declared that the presence of the Armenians constituted a danger for the army and suggested transporting them elsewhere. But no one said that they should be killed. The problem lay in the way the law was applied." This was a step forward. Neşaşibî pressed his advantage: "But hadn't you heard that the enactment of the law was accompanied by atrocities?" The grand vizier now assumed his role of straw man again, exhibiting clear signs of amnesia: "As with everything else, so here too, I only learned about these atrocities after everything was over...Only the minister of war can explain his motivations; you will have to get your information there, for I can say nothing that you are likely to find convincing. I no longer have any memory of all that." The president thereupon pointed out to him that the law had been adopted by the Council of Ministers and that "someone must have presented the reasons for adopting it." Was this question "discussed at a meeting of the Council of Ministers?" As the Grand Vizier's memory continued to fail him, he finally said:

> Yes, that is all that I know. When I assumed the post of grand vizier, I undertook to carry out reforms in the six vilayets... At the moment when discussions were being conducted with the ambassadors about the laws to be applied by the governors, the general war broke out. This thwarted important reforms that the Imperial government had intended to enact. It was natural that the government, which was firmly resolved to ensure the welfare and happiness of its Armenian subjects, should, after the war, have pursued the reforms that it had initiated before it. Consequently, the proper policy would have been to wait calmly for the war to end. Unfortunately, that is not what happened. Commissions of inquiry were formed after the massacres of the Armenians took place. These commissions returned to Constantinople after accomplishing their task; despite my insistence, the interior minister did not want to make the results of their investigations public. I understood that, for as long as Talât Pasha was in charge of the Interior Ministry, the investigations would serve no purpose.

After a great deal of hemming and hawing, and notwithstanding a few euphemisms, Said Halim at last confessed, while implying that the search for culprits should focus on Talât.[26]

Another deputy, Nuri Bey, now took over from his predecessor and asked the grand vizier if the events in Syria and Iraq had taken place by virtue of a decision of the Council of Ministers? Halim, correcting himself, said: "Those events were never discussed in any way by the Council of Ministers. No correspondence was ever exchanged with the Sublime Porte about the Armenian affair, or the Syrian and Iraqi affairs." Nuri now drove him into a corner: "Yet, when the Armenian and Arab questions loomed up on the horizon, you maintained that they constituted a reason for you to withdraw from the cabinet." Halim then said: "Yes, I was horrified by these two questions." Nuri insisted: "You have just said that the Arab and Armenian questions induced you to withdraw from the cabinet." Halim answered: "Yes, excesses were perpetrated without my knowledge. How could I approve of crimes like those committed against [the] poor [parliamentary deputy] Zohrab Effendi?" This exchange put the grand vizier in an embarrassing position, and he once again evoked, "with horror," what he called "those two questions," a euphemism for the liquidation of the Armenians and the crimes perpetrated against part of the Syrian population, notably among the Arab notables of Damascus and the Christians of Mt. Lebanon. He tried to cover for those of his colleagues who were the most deeply implicated and was unable to confess that he had, at the very least, done nothing to stop what had happened.[27]

Although the rest of the interrogation, which concerned attempts to hide military defeats or territorial losses, is not directly related to our subject, it is worth examining, because it is revelatory of Ottoman practices during the war. Referring to the capture of Baghdad, which was not made public, Ragib Neşaşibî asked Halim: "How could such events be kept secret from the grand vizier's office?" Without yielding an inch, Said answered, in the tone that he had assumed at the beginning of the hearing: "They could, absolutely. They were hidden from us as they were hidden from all of you." Another member of the commission, Hilmi Bey, thereupon remarked that they had all heard that "at such-and-such a moment, Basra had fallen, that the enemy had reached Kurna and then Amara. The government must certainly have been informed of this." He added that he had also noticed that new valis had been appointed in Erzerum and Baghdad, and that their names had been published in the press. "How," he said, "is it possible to appoint valis to places that have been captured by the enemy?... Yet people knew about that."[28]

To the tenth question put to him, which concerned the Special Organization, Halim initially answered by repeating an apparently standard formula: "The government is in no way to blame here. That question was not discussed by the Council of Ministers." The president of the commission then asked him: "But were you not informed of the creation of such an organization?" The grand vizier then altered his line of defense: "We were, but after everything was over ... As soon as I learned of the existence of an organization of this type, I took measures: it ceased to operate." The president pursued his line of questioning: "Nobody was criticized in connection with this business?" Halim answered: "Of course we made criticisms. But what good were they after the harm had been done ...? I told Enver Pasha that these were reprehensible acts. I told Enver, insistently, that an end had to be put to these goings-on."[29] In the course of this hearing, Halim had finally said many things, but in veiled terms that left his listeners to draw the lessons of his partial confessions. His remarks almost leave one with the feeling that he had been the only person in the cabinet who had been unaware of what was happening and that he had nonetheless condemned "the harm done."

The next accused person to testify, Ahmed Şükrü Bey, a former minister of public education (1913–18), was doubtless one of the least well-known cabinet members. He had nonetheless played an important role in the liquidation of the Armenians, because he had served on the Young Turk Central Committee along with Dr. Şakir and Dr. Nâzım.[30] More than anyone else in Istanbul, he was in a position to provide information about the deportations and the Special Organization's operating methods. At his 12 November hearing, however, he clung to an untenable line of defense.[31] Thus, he said without flinching, in response to the first question put to him, which had to do with the empire's entry into the war, that the Russians had attacked the Ottoman fleet in the Black Sea. The president of the commission felt obliged to remark that everyone knew that it was the other way around. Asked about the notorious deportation law, Şükrü responded that it had been necessary to draft a law to meet the expectations of the army and general staffs, which wanted to make sure that they had a safe avenue of retreat. He then referred to information that had been received about "the events in Van, Bitlis, Kara-Hissar-Şarki and the Black Sea coast" in order to justify the measures that had been taken. Rağib Neşaşibî thereupon asked: "But how could one apply them to women and children? Even if these questions had not been discussed by the Council of Ministers, the ministers could not have been unaware of them. Did the Council make a decision that might have seemed to betoken approval of the acts of the military commanders?" To illustrate what he meant, Neşaşibî invoked the case of the vali of Dyarbekir, "who had been removed from his post for his criminal activity in that province":

> Less than two weeks after he was dismissed, he was appointed vali of Sıvas on a decision of the Council of Ministers. Yet, inasmuch as Reşid Bey had been dismissed because of his conduct in Dyarbekir, the Council of Ministers could not have been unaware of the acts of which the vali was guilty! How could it appoint him to a new post?

Without disputing these charges, Şükrü even pointed out that "Reşid Bey was then sent to Angora, but I do not know if this was a result of the part he played in the atrocities." The next question, about the fact that Reşid had bought a house for 9,000 Turkish pounds when "the interior minister knew that this man found himself in a very delicate position," was a ginger allusion to the fortunes that high-ranking state officials had acquired during the deportation of the Armenians. It received, however, no response, no more than did the one about the Special Organization that closed the hearing: "That is a question for the minister of war and the army commanders," Şükrü answered, "for the Council of Ministers made no decisions in these matters. Hence I know nothing about the crimes attributed to them."[32]

The commission pursued its task with the 12–13 November interrogation[33] of a former minister of commerce and Agriculture, followed by that of a former foreign minister, Ahmed Nesimi Bey, who from the outset hid behind the fact that he had joined the cabinet on 5 November 1914, well after the (August 1914) general mobilization, in order to justify his ignorance of the abuses committed during the military requisitions. With regard to the deportation law, the former minister offered the classic justifications, including collaboration with the Russians and regular espionage on the military situation. For good measure, he added:

> Nearly everywhere, we discovered arms, bombs, flags of an independent Armenia, and preparations for revolt... People insisted on the need to take extraordinary measures; the commander-in-chief suggested that, in the military zones, the local population, wherever the army was in danger, be removed and settled elsewhere, individually or en masse. This, as well as all other extraordinary measures of the same kind, were to be applied only in cases of absolute necessity and in proportion to the necessity involved. On the insistent urging of the commander-in-chief, who invoked the welfare of the army and the security of its operations, we felt compelled to grant this authority to the commanders of the various army corps... We were assured that, if this measure was not taken, our army would effectively have been caught in a crossfire... Thus the law in question was a measure of military security... Some time after this law was promulgated, I went to Carlsbad on the recommendation of my doctors and remained there from July to late August. Hence I was not in Constantinople during most of the period in which the events objected to occurred. On my return, I learned that, when this measure was applied, certain fundamentally evil people had committed all kinds of abuses.

Thus, the army was supposed to have instigated the "measures." Like others, Ahmed Nesimi spontaneously came up with an alibi – that he had been abroad in the summer of 1915 – to clear himself – in other words, he admitted that a collective crime had been committed, but declared that he had had nothing to do with the whole business. Moreover, he added, "it is obvious that I was in no way responsible for the application of this measure."[34]

The notorious deputy Ilyas Sâmi, whose role in the liquidation of the Armenians of Mush we have already seen, now took over from his colleague, asking a question that was, to say the least, odd:

> How, in deciding to deport a population to save the army from danger, as if what were involved were the withdrawal of a cabinet, could the government not have taken into account the fact that his population, this element had been settled in the region for years? The result was that women, innocent children, a defenseless Muslim [sic] population, were liquidated by bands. Before proceeding with the deportation, all that should have been seriously considered. The deportees should first have been protected against attack from armed bands, and only then transferred. It was this negligence that led to the liquidation of half of the total population. Not a Muslim [?] remains.

This intervention, which cast the executioner in the victim's role and probably went beyond the bounds of decency, provoked no reaction. After this grotesque intermezzo, Neşaşibî resumed his interrogation, asking: "In your view, were the deportation measures applied to everyone, including women and children, or only to male combatants?" Nesimi came up with a rather disarming response:

> As for the women, it was said that it would be still worse to leave them alone in their villages, and this affirmation was in fact justified by the general state of the region.

What is more, it was said that the women would engage in espionage and that a few of them had already been arrested. However, the law left this point to the discretion of those who applied it, after taking military necessities into consideration. I say, turning to my Armenian colleagues, you are familiar with my ideas and my sentiments. If you are not familiar with them, you can inform yourselves of them. I struggled against the adoption of a measure of this kind... If abuses were committed and if the deportation also took place outside war zones and without regard for military necessity, the culprits deserve to be punished.

With this hearing, a further step had been taken. Although the deputies were not always very curious, they sometimes managed to discomfit the ministers. By revealing that he had struggled to prevent "a measure of this kind," Nesimi clearly implied that there had been a debate over this question within the government or the Young Turk party. The rest of his testimony also indicates, cautiously, that this "measure" was applied "outside war zones and without regard for military necessity." His interrogation came to an end with questions about the Special Organization: he said he was "unaware that such bands had been created."[35]

The hearing that took place on 10 November seems to mark a discursive shift, and it cannot be excluded that this shift stemmed from preparatory meetings in Young Turk circles. The hearing is the more important in that it was an interrogation of İbrahim Bey, a former justice minister.[36] Like the witness who preceded him, İbrahim affirmed at the outset that the Russians had attacked Turkey. In connection with the deportation law, he recalled that, in the wake of events in Erzerum, Şabinkarahisar, and Bitlis, as well as

proclamations by the Armenian Committees, the government had no choice but to promulgate a deportation law. There followed a decision by the Council of Ministers about the amount to be raised from the émigrés' assets to ensure the subsistence and comfort of the people deported... We were informed about certain atrocities and I was deeply disturbed, for, truly, this was inacceptable.

Thus, a new element had been mentioned: without saying that the Council of Ministers had discussed the deportation law, yet evoking, with a mélange of cynicism and humor, a decision intended to provide for the "comfort of the people deported," İbrahim ultimately gave the commission to understand that debates about the Armenians' fate had indeed taken place, without saying anything more precise than that. But he went still further, affirming that he had created a commission of inquiry comprising civilian officials, including court officials, whom he had chosen himself, "among them Assime Bey, the presiding judge at the criminal court, a very high-minded, honest individual, and Nihad Bey, the assistant general prosecutor... These commissions were attached to the Interior Ministry, and sent their reports to this department." Following up this response, Rağib Neşaşibî asked "how the army commanders had been able to let people be massacred," but was called sharply to order by the president of the commission, who was obviously apprehensive that the question would lead to disclosures he had hitherto been able to prevent: "The subject before us is not massacres. We are talking about the law." In his capacity as justice minister, İbrahim was then asked if the laws had been submitted to the Council of State and which laws had been promulgated without first being submitted to him. But, İbrahim, too, was suffering from amnesia. He was also asked if the Council of Ministers had made a decision "bearing on the deportations and other atrocities. For this question is crucial and all the ministers are responsible for them." The former minister thereupon stated that "the exceptional treatment that was sometimes meted out when the deportation law was applied occurred without the government's knowledge." Neşaşibî, however, undaunted by these responses, went on to mention the case of

Dr. Reşid, the vali of Dyarbekir, "who was brought here to face serious charges. Fifteen or twenty days later, however, he was appointed vali of Angora. The Council of Ministers no doubt made this appointment." Once again, İbrahim Bey "could not remember very well."

The author of the ten-point motion, Fuad Bey, now entered the debate. "Two of these temporary laws," he recalled, "are extremely important. One is that on abandoned property; the other is that authorizing the execution of death sentences without an *irade*." He was given the following answer: "There was indeed a law bearing on the deportees' assets, but the purpose of this law was to safeguard their property and protect it from being pillaged." This very honorable preoccupation seems not to have convinced İbrahim's interlocutors. Harun Hilmi Effendi pursued the interrogation of the accused: "İbrahim Bey says that the deportations took place in military zones, for the security of the army." İbrahim answered, "We were not the ones who ordered them; the military ordered them carried out for that reason." Hilmi pursued his advantage: "The commanders had indeed been given very broad prerogatives; in the war zones, they were authorized to punish those who were under their command as they saw fit. But many people were deported or executed in areas that were not in war zones." This remark, however, produced no effect; İbrahim simply replied: "We did not know that." Hilmi then broached the issue of the government's attitude with him, asking: "After being apprised of these events, did the Council of Ministers not conduct deliberations for the purpose of putting an end to them?" İbrahim answered: "What was not said! But nothing at all of an official character." It was then pointed out to him that documents had been published and distributed to parliament. İbrahim responded: "It was not the government, but the Interior Ministry which published them." This provided Neşaşibî with an opportunity to relaunch the debate: "Was the Interior Ministry not part of the government? People say that there were a great many more massacres and that there exist many documents on this subject. How was that?"

İbrahim's answer was dumbfounding:

> The Interior Ministry had published documents about the atrocities that the Armenians had inflicted on the Muslims in the eastern vilayets. This question does not concern my ministry; moreover, it was not discussed by the Council of Ministers. The documents were given both to us and to the deputies ... I believe that the deputies were better informed about these questions than the government.

An investigation of crimes committed against the Armenians had suddenly turned into proceedings focused on "atrocities inflicted on the Muslims" about which the justice minister was, however, less well informed than parliament. İbrahim thus found himself in a difficult situation. Hilmi pressed his attack: "People say that, when the non-Muslims were deported in Angora, their neighborhoods were set on fire so that their property could be seized. Is that right?" The former minister did not know.

Queried about the Special Organization, İbrahim answered: "I knew nothing about this organization. Nor did the Council of Ministers. We were utterly ignorant of the goal and activities of this organization. I know absolutely nothing about it and, what is more, it is not my duty to know anything about it." Irritated, no doubt, by the evasive answers given by the accused, Ilyas Sâmi concluded:

> İbrahim Bey has answered most of the questions put to him by saying that he was unaware of the facts or that they occurred after he left the ministry ... Moreover, the whole cabinet has to answer for an event such as the fall of Erzerum. It was Ömer Naci Bey who began to apply the measures pertaining to the Special Organization. It is rather curious that İbrahim Bey, a member of the Council of Ministers when these events occurred, learned about them only after the fact.

Without meaning to, the deputy from Mush had just broken the law imposing silence and had clearly mentioned the name of the head of the Special Organization in Erzerum (its headquarters), Ömer Naci. When, somewhat later, he was asked why, under these circumstances, he had not resigned, İbrahim finally blurted out: "I remained in the cabinet in order to prevent the acts of this kind of which I was informed, to the extent that that was in my power. Rest assured that when I say that we knew nothing about the Special Organization, I mean that no decision was made by the Council of Ministers."[37]

One of the last ministers to testify before the commission, a former Constantinople police chief and interior minister, İsmail Canbolat, interrogated on 27 November, should also have shed new light on the events that interest us. It was under Canbolat's authority that the Armenian elite of the capital was rounded up during the night of 24–25 April 1915. However, to the questions he was asked about the deportation law, Canbolat contented himself by replying, with rare cynicism, that "during the 4 August [1917] meeting of the Council of Ministers, [he] had decided to arrange for the men arrested to be brought back home, and that no one had objected. First steps had even been taken to carry this measure out: the Directorate for Emigrés had begun to make the necessary preparations. The order authorizing the return of the deportees from Samsun and its environs had already been issued."[38] Was it possible that an eminent member of the CUP did not know that the Armenians from Samsun and the surrounding region had been drowned in the Black Sea or liquidated on the roads?

Although, as we have just seen, the investigation conducted by the Ottoman parliament and its Fifth Commission at least had the merit of initiating a debate about the crimes committed against the Armenian population, the sultan and Grand Vizier Tevfik's cabinet had soon come to the conclusion that, given its makeup, the standing parliament, which had notorious criminals in its ranks, was incapable of rendering justice. But the fact that a peace conference would in all likelihood soon be held meant that it was necessary to bring the war criminals to trial before the Allies themselves did. It must be added, finally, that the cabinet was not in a position to secure passage of any law whatsoever by the existing parliament. The sultan accordingly decided to dissolve it. In so doing, he intended to take the task of judging the Young Turks from the legislature's hands and, by the same token, strip the deputies of their parliamentary immunity; this led to the immediate arrests of no fewer than 24 of them.[39] On 21 December, the foreign minister, Mustafa Reşad, appeared before parliament in order to respond to the motion of no confidence brought by Hüseyin Kadri. He pointed out, notably, that the actions of the preceding governments had been exposed "with the help of Diogenes' lantern" and that the amplitude of the atrocities inflicted on the Armenians was now coming to light, "atrocities which," the minister said, "have aroused the indignation of the whole human race; the country entrusted to our care has been transformed into a gigantic slaughter-house." "This was," Istanbul's French-language daily concluded, "an official confession."[40]

Chapter 4

The Mazhar Governmental Commission of Inquiry and the Creation of Courts Martial

In the rather unusual context of a party-state that had signed the Mudros armistice even while organizing the "second phase" of the war in Anatolia, the Tevfik government encountered strong opposition when it relieved parliament of the responsibility of judging the Young Turk criminals and planned bringing them before a special court. It is quite obvious that the new authorities in Istanbul were aware of the threat of dismemberment hanging over the empire and the need to purge the country of a clique that had led it to ruin and extirpated part of its population. The crimes committed during the war constituted a heavy onus on Turkey's future and there was every reason to believe that the High Court controlled by the Ittihadist deputies was going to culminate, as the hearings held by the Fifth Commission had shown, in a parody of justice that would not suffice to appease the Allied Powers and justify hopes of a certain generosity on their part. In other words, purging the Young Turk officials who were omnipresent in the government and army, and then conducting credible trials, were the two requisite conditions for putting the Western governments in the best possible disposition and presenting a less degraded image at the upcoming peace conference.

The option of bringing the criminals before national courts no doubt appeared as the least unattractive choice at a time when the victors were considering the possibility of creating an international "High Tribunal." If it settled for this option, however, the Tevfik government would have to deal with the opposition of the Young Turk network, which could count on the support of the hundreds of thousands of Ottoman subjects at all levels of society who had been involved in the violence, had profited from the plunder of Armenian or Greek assets, or were still holding women and children captive. Manipulated by the Young Turks, this solidarity network constituted a block of refusal that rejected its responsibility across the board. Despite this barrier, the Tevfik government chose to act quickly, without waiting for the Allies to set up their own legal machinery on the basis provided by the principles of The Hague.

The Commission of Inquiry's Pretrial Investigation of the Young Turk Criminals and the Court-Martial

It was no doubt with these considerations in mind that, on 23 November 1918, even before parliament was dissolved, the sultan created a governmental commission of inquiry. The Council of State had apparently discretely compelled the Sultan to promulgate a *firman* setting up such a commission of inquiry within the Department of State Security. Hasan Mazhar Bey, the former vali of Angora, was appointed president of the Commission.[1] As soon as it was created, the "Mazhar Commission" set about gathering personal accounts and other evidence, focusing its investigations above all on the state officials implicated in the crimes committed against the Armenian population. As shown in Vahakn Dadrian study of the Commission,[2] it took paragraphs 47, 75, and 87 of the Ottoman Penal Code as the basis for its work, and enjoyed rather broad prerogatives, since it could subpoena witnesses, search and seize documents, and even arrest and imprison suspects with the help of the judiciary police or other state agencies. At the outset, Mazhar sent an official circular to the governors and vice-governors of the provinces, demanding that they send him originals or certified copies of the orders concerning the deportation and massacre of the Armenians that had been received by local government officials. The commission also set about examining witnesses under oath. In a little less than three months, it had constituted 130 pretrial investigative files, which it gradually transmitted to the court-martial that had been formed in the meantime. These files contained numerous official or semi-official documents, only some of which were published in the legal supplement to the *Takvim Vakayi* (Official Gazette) and the Ottoman Turkish, Armenian, or French press of the day.[3] In the provinces, where many of the valis, *mutesarifs*, and *kaymakams* appointed during the war were still in office, some had kept the orders received from the capital out of negligence or in order to defend themselves against possible charges, despite the instructions they had received to destroy or return them after reading them. Thus, the commission was able to secure a number of telegraphic orders the nature and origin of which we have examined;[4] these cables had been sent out from provincial governmental centers, notably in Konya, Angora, Dyarbekir, and Sıvas.

It was these provincial materials that served as the basis for the indictments drawn up in the various trials later conducted before the Istanbul court-martial. The indictment and the copies of telegrams presented before the court-martial on 27 April 1919 indicate that, in the course of the investigation, it became clear that many important "documents bearing on this organization and all Central Committee documents were stolen."[5] The archives of *Teşkilât-ı Mahsusa* and the Ittihadist Central Committee, two organizations that, as we have seen, were closely intertwined, were removed by the Ittihad's secretary general, Midhat Şükrü, from the Nuri Osmaniye headquarters after Talât's government resigned.[6] A note (no. 31) from the interior minister attached to the indictment of the Unionists exposes the facts "proving that files containing important information and the Organization's correspondence were removed by Aziz Bey, the Director of the Department of Criminal Investigations [in the State Security Service] before Talât resigned."[7] In other words, files were purged in the two places where decisions had been made and therefore where directives, circulars, and telegrams sent out by the Ittihadist Central Committee and the specialized departments of the Interior Ministry were preserved. Also removed in early October 1918, two days before Talât's resignation, were the statistics on the deported and massacred Armenians that had been kept, according to the same judiciary source, on the premises of the Political Section of the Interior Ministry, where they had been kept with the files of the Special Organization (*Mahrim Dosieler*) known as the "Special Secret Archives"; these documents were packed into crates by night and transported to an unknown destination. Such, at any rate, was the response with which the Interior Ministry met the repeated demands of the court-martial.[8] It will have been understood that Talât and Enver had, among the other arrangements they made before fleeing the country, given the necessary instructions to wipe away the traces of their crimes. In an article that appeared in the daily *Sabah*, the president of *Hürryet Ittilaf* (which was liberal in tendency), Mustafa Sabri, declared that İzzet Pasha, in the brief period before the signature of the Mudros Armistice in which İzzet had headed the government, "made it possible to, and provided the means required to, destroy a large number of official documents connected with the events of the war."[9] While this statement by a member of the opposition might seem questionable, it nonetheless indicates that the opposition to the Ittihad suspected that the authorities and administration were conniving with the fugitives.

It is probable that some of the documents spirited away by the Ittihadists were destroyed, but there exist various indications that others were stored in a safe place by *Karakol* or confided to the fugitives' friends or family members. Concurring accounts suggest that a police search of the CUP's headquarters in Nuri Osmaniye Street was carried out immediately after the Young Turk leaders' departure. They attest the discovery of official documents and telegrams. However, those conducting the search do not seem to have found more sensitive material. On the other hand, the police search of the home of Bahaeddin Şakir's son-in-law, Ahmed Ramız Bey, in Sabon Hane Street in Şişli, which was carried out on Saturday, 14 December 1918 by the Constantinople police chief, seems to have been more fruitful: it turned up a large sack containing many and secret files which obviously had come from the Nuri Osmaniye headquarters, among them the minutes of the committee's secret meetings.[10]

Destroying or removing the central archives bound up with the liquidation of the Armenians was not the only measure taken by the Ittihad's leaders. While the operations were being carried out, strict instructions had been issued, notably to the party's responsible secretaries and delegates, to destroy the telegraphic orders they received once they had been understood. It should be pointed out here that the process of decoding encrypted telegrams led to the production of several different types of documents;[11] this made it difficult to destroy all the copies in the provinces, especially in the case of circulars that were, by their nature, widely distributed. Among the known documents, a distinction must be made between those that emanated from the leaders of the *Teşkilât-ı Mahsusa* and those, formalistic and bureaucratic in tone, which originated notably in the Interior Ministry. We have only a very few documents of the first category – we have described them in Part Four – and more of the others. However, since the system of extermination had two faces, one of which was governmental and public, while the other was secret and violent, the first and better documented face of it allows us to assess the activities of those responsible for the second. The precautions that were taken to mask liquidation orders, so that only the official orders would come down to later generations, reflects the general image of the CUP, a vast manipulative operation that it is not easy to grasp.

The presiding judge at the court-martial before which the Unionist leaders still to be found in Istanbul were tried was probably familiar with their practices as well as the hierarchy that supervised the crime. At the fifth trial session on 12 May 1919, the court-martial conducted a close examination of Colonel Ahmed Cevad,[12] the military commander of the capital and a member of the Special Organization's Political Bureau, for it knew that all the orders dispatched to the provinces had necessarily passed through his hands.[13] The presiding judge first had the court clerk read out several telegrams and then asked Cevad if the signature they bore was indeed his. "It is possible," the Colonel replied; "I do not remember, a good deal of time has gone by since." In the end, however, he agreed that he was indeed the person who had noted in the margin that it would be necessary to return "the originals of such important telegrams… in compliance with the rules." He referred, however, to military instructions when the presiding judge asked him if this had been one of *Teşkilât-i Mahsusa's* standard procedures. The colonel affirmed that he had received on 21 January 1915 an order from the General Staff of the Army, "sealed with the seal" requiring him "to return the document in question… a copy of the order issued by the minister was addressed to every army commander. Once the information had been received, it had to be sent back to the places indicated… After an order had been diffused and implemented, it had to be effaced." The presiding judge, however, pointed out to Cevad that the court had a copy of this circular about the organization of squadrons of *çetes* that had emanated from the War Ministry (no. 1117), and added that "it said absolutely nothing about the destruction of orders." He accordingly asked the colonel if he had destroyed orders on his "own initiative." Cevad was unable to reply.[14] Thus, it emerges from this interrogation that it had been necessary to send the "originals" back to Istanbul, whereas "orders" issued in non-coded form were supposed to be destroyed locally. Let us note that Cevad carefully avoided mentioning the Special Organization, systematically referring his questioner to the War Ministry, although the telegrams read out at this session of the trial had been signed, as the presiding judge remarked, by the leaders of *Teşkilât-i Mahsusa*.

In order to authenticate the official or semi-official documents sent out by ministers, state officials, and officers or leaders of the Special Organization, the court-martial established a standard procedure: after a document was read out, the accused or witnesses were asked to confirm that it did indeed bear their signature. If they denied it, the court appealed to the recipient(s) of the document in question and often succeeded in establishing their authenticity in this fashion. By comparing and confronting often contradictory statements by different people, it managed to draw conclusions it regarded as reliable. The investigating magistrates of the court-martial and the governmental Commission of Inquiry were thus able to examine 293 files.[15]

An incident that occurred in February 1919 in Ayntab, where the British military authorities had seized official documents in the possession of the city's (italicize), suggests that initiatives had been taken, if only on the local level, to destroy correspondence between the interior minister and the provinces dating from the war years. A 17 June 1919 note of protest to the Sublime Porte reveals that a British officer had gone to see the mutesarif of Ayntab in order to "ask him to turn over all the telegrams and letters exchanged between the vilayet and the Imperial Interior Ministry on the one hand and the *mutesarifat* on the other in the period running from 1330 to 1334 [1914–19]." Confronted with the Ottoman official's refusal to comply, the officer had the building surrounded and the exits from it sealed off and then seized the documents in question. This procedure had been decided on after the dispatch of "a circular telegram from the head of the telegraph office in Dyarbekir instructing the agencies under his jurisdiction to destroy the originals of obsolete documents."[16]

Demands for documents made by the Commission of Inquiry or court-martial were only rarely heeded by the provincial authorities. A few vilayets nevertheless responded positively, remitting locally held telegrams and other materials. According to a British intelligence document exhumed by Dadrian, the commission retrieved, from the vilayet of Angora alone, 42 encrypted telegrams.[17] The vilayet of Konya also "conducted a search for copies of telegrams" and sent them to the Interior Ministry.[18]

The documents gathered in certain vilayets were addressed to the Interior Ministry and the governmental Commission of Inquiry headed by Mazhar Bey, which had its offices in the "special bureau of the headquarters of the Department of State Security" otherwise known as the "directorate general of investigations."[19] This bureau transmitted them in turn to the court martial after certifying that they were authentic.[20] A 2 April 1919 letter that the interior minister, Cemal Bey, sent to the presiding judge of the court-martial[21] reminds him that

It has been communicated to all concerned that the originals of encrypted telegrams pertaining to the question of the deportation sent by the Ministry to the valis between May 1331 [1915] and late April 1333 [1917] – which should be available in the telegraph offices – must be collected and expedited by a state official empowered to do so. We send you herewith all the documents sent to us by the Postal and Telegraph Ministry: forty-two telegrams dispatched by the prefecture in Angora in a special file and, in connection with the same question, correspondence that was sent to us by the prefecture in Konya (containing copies of the encrypted documents).

It seems that the Postal, Telegraph, and Telephone Ministry was also asked to collect and turn over correspondence dating from the war years. Thus, the general directorate of the Dyarbekir post office transmitted to the ministry from which it depended on 17 April 1919 a 17 May 1915 telegram from Dr. Reşid to İsmail Hakkı, the vali of Adana.[22]

The Creation of the Ottoman Courts Martial

The formation of courts martial was obviously the logical extension of the work of the Mazhar Commission. Early in December, the office of the chief prosecutor of the Istanbul Court of Appeals took the first steps toward creating them. They took definite form at a meeting between the director of the Justice Ministry's Division of Criminal Affairs and the Interior Ministry's chief legal counselor. On 13 December 1918, Armenian circles close to the Patriarchate announced that "individuals accused of having taken part in the Armenian massacres whose guilt has been established by the Commission of Inquiry" would be brought before an extraordinary court-martial under the presidency of Mahmud Hayret Tiranli; it was to comprised five members – three military men and two civil magistrates.[23] On 16 December 1918, the sultan formally established a court-martial and declared on 25 December 1918 that, for regions that were not under martial law, the existing courts were charged with organizing the trials. It was only on 8 January 1919, however, that the extraordinary court-martial was officially called into being.[24] On a decree issued by the sultan, three courts martial were established in Constantinople, as well as ten jurisdictions in the provinces, with their prosecutors and investigating magistrates:

1) the vilayet of Angora and Kastamonu, the *sancak* of Bolu;
2) the vilayet of Trebizond and the *sancak* of Samsun (Nusret Bey, chief prosecutor; Kevork Effendi, investigating magistrate);
3) vilayet of Bursa and Edirne, *sancak* of Çatalca;
4) vilayet of Aydın (Smyrna), *sancaks* of Çanakkale and Karasi (Mustaf Remzi, chief prosecutor; Aram Ipekian, investigating magistrate);
5) vilayet of Konya, *sancaks* of Eskişehir, Karahisar, Kütahya, and Antalia;
6) vilayet of Sıvas, *sancaks* of Kayseri and Yozgat;
7) vilayets of Kharpert and Dyarbekir;
8) vilayets of Erzerum, Van, and Bitlis;
9) vilayet of Adana and *sancak* of Maraş (İsmail Bey, chief prosecutor; Apostolaki Effendi, investigating magistrate);
10) *mutesarifat* and *sancaks* of Urfa, Ayntab, and Zor (İzzet Bey, chief prosecutor; Krikor Effendi, investigating magistrate).

Each of these jurisdictions was to have its own operating budget.[25] It is noteworthy that several Armenian investigating magistrates were appointed to provincial courts martial. It should also be pointed out that the jurisdictions of the easternmost vilayets remained *pro forma* because they were not assigned prosecutors and officiating magistrates. It seems reasonable to suppose that the objective of these local courts was to make it possible to carry out local investigations in places where the governmental Commission of Inquiry had been unable to function, and that the Sublime Porte was, at the time, resolved to shed light on the crimes committed in certain regions in the course of the war. In February, the judge presiding at the court-martial asked the Interior Ministry to transmit the originals or certified copies of documents pertaining to the deportation of the Armenians to its services. The 3 March 1919 resignation of the Tevfik government, and its replacement by a cabinet headed by Damad Ferid Pasha, seem to have been due to its opposition to a project to create a special jurisdiction to judge the Ittihadists. As early as 5 March, the new Council of Ministers examined a report drawn up by Sâmi Bey proposing to abolish the provincial courts and bring all cases involving massacres and deportations before an exclusively military, rather than a mixed, court-martial based in Constantinople.[26]

On 8 March 1919, the sultan ratified the accreditation of this new court-martial, with extended competencies and exclusively military judges.[27] It is further noteworthy that the mixed court-martial, which had begun to try the organizers of the massacres in Yozgat only two months earlier, suddenly suspended its operations on 6 March, during the twelfth session of the trial. When the trial was resumed, the court was made up of exclusively military judges. The most basic change, however, was the absence of the plaintiff, who was represented from now on by the prosecutor.[28]

According to the daily *Sabah*, the court put the accused who were to be tried separately on charges of "massacre and illegal personal gain" in different categories:

1) those who had really instigated the crimes against the Armenians;
2) those who had worked in the shadow of the main culprits, such as the influential members of the Committee of Union and Progress;
3) members of secret organizations, such as the Special Organization, as well as high-ranking military men and felons released from prison;
4) parliamentary deputies who failed to protest and acquiesced in the crimes committed;
5) journalists who applauded and encouraged these crimes and inflamed public opinion with misleading, provocative articles;
6) those who took advantage of these crimes to enrich themselves; and
7) the legions of pashas and beys who supervised these crimes.[29]

The judicial procedures were unmistakably sped up when Damad Ferid took the reins of government, while Young Turk leaders who had until then been spared were arrested. The Istanbul military prison and the prison of the court-martial – known as the Bekirağa Section – where the suspects and the accused were held, turned out to be unreliable. The complicity of people in the administration allowed many of the accused to escape, especially from the court-martial's prison. The circumstances surrounding the 25 January 1919 flight of Dr. Reşid, the former vali of Dyarbekir, from the Bekirağa Section bear witness to a certain laxity, at the very least. While Reşid was being taken under guard "to the Hamam," three men grabbed him and pushed him into "a black car" that disappeared before his guards could react.[30] This was clearly the work of the *Karakol* network.

It is noteworthy that, subsequently, the court-martial acquitted Lieutenant Colonel Ali and Lieutenant Yusuf Ziya, respectively warden and assistant warden of the house of detention attached to the court-martial. The two men were tried for helping Halil [Kut] escape.[31]

As for the competencies of the three courts martial created in Istanbul, only Court Martial No. 1 tried people accused of committing crimes against the Armenian population. Court-Martial No. 2 was apparently specialized in cases involving the illegal seizure of assets. A 15 May 1919 imperial decree initially set up two commissions charged with investigating economic abuses and "internal questions."[32] According to the Istanbul press, 1,700 officers who had enriched themselves during the war "thanks to financial misdealing" were under criminal investigation in early August 1919.[33] The creation of Court-Martial No. 2 was not, however, officially recognized until 27 October, with the appointment of a chief prosecutor, İsmail Vasif Bey, and two investigating magistrates, Ali Rıza and Hüseyin Bey. It addressed the "affair of the secret military committee *Nigehban*" and that of the *Red Khanjar*.[34]

Court-Martial No. 3 judged senior officers. It conducted, notably, the pretrial investigation of General Vehib Pasha.[35] Vehib, who appeared before the court-martial's Commission of Inquiry on Wednesday, 3 December 1919,[36] was jailed after the court unanimously decided to try him.[37] There are no clear reports of the reason for this indictment in the press, but it is highly probable that it was related to the long report[38] that Vehib submitted to the Mazhar Commission in early December. In breaking the law of silence and making precise revelations of the crimes perpetrated by the CUP, the ranking Young Turk officer committed an act bordering on treason; the colleagues of his sitting on Court-Martial No. 3 apparently wished to make him pay for it.

As for the provincial courts martial, it must be pointed out that the judges presiding over some of them were appointed only in late November or even early December 1919: Lieutenant Colonel Mustafa Tevfik Bey in Bolu,[39] Colonel Abdül Vahid Bey in Tekirdağ, and Colonel Kemal Bey in Samsun.[40] Early in February 1920, Major General İbrahim Pasha was appointed presiding judge at the Angora court-martial.[41] One can, of course, ask what significance these appointments had when one recalls that the central government was unable to assert its authority over cities such as Bolu, Samsun, and Angora, which were controlled by the nationalist movement.

In any event, these nominations went hand-in-hand with the abolition of the chief prosecutors' and investigating magistrates' posts in the provinces,[42] apparently because they had completed their investigations of those responsible for the massacres of Armenians and Greeks.

The account given by Setrag Karageuzian, who was appointed investigating magistrate in Trebizond in March 1919, provides valuable insights into the atmosphere that reigned in certain provinces immediately following the armistice.[43] Karageuzian's colleague Nusret Bey, the chief prosecutor in Trebizond, who had been appointed two months earlier and charged with beginning the investigation, "did nothing and did not even remain in the city." The Armenian magistrate, whose "mission it was to conduct an investigation into the crimes of deportation and massacre of the Armenians," immediately began to collaborate with his colleague. However, he says,

> none of my efforts and none of the work I did produced results. After a tortuous three-and-a-half months of labor, I came to the following conclusions: 1) the Ottoman government did not intend to punish those responsible for the massacres or the other culprits or to see that justice was done. Its sole aim was to deceive Europe and America and public opinion in the civilized countries; 2) the program of Union and Progress is a crystallization of the mentality of the Turkish people; 3) the great majority of the state officials, gendarmes, officers in the gendarmerie, police chiefs and policemen who organized and carried out the deportation and massacres are still in the posts they held then. Consequently, they will never want the investigations to succeed. The state officials have created as many difficulties as possible in order to bring our mission to naught. The police and gendarmerie, instead of arresting the accused, producing witnesses, and carrying out the orders given them, forewarn the guilty, that is, their former accomplices, of all pending actions; 4) with the means currently available, nothing can be done to apply the principles of justice.

Here are a few proofs of what I have just said. 1) A poor Greek woman who had the courage to tell me everything she knew about the massacres was killed. 2) So far, none of the guilty has been arrested by the police or gendarmerie. Hardly had I summoned two criminals without informing them of the reason for the summons and proceeded to arrest them than a universal feeling of anger and irritation made itself felt among all classes of the people, from the governor to the poorest peasant. The policeman who was working for me and had served the summons on the two criminals whom I had had arrested was promptly replaced by another who was supposedly more competent. Now they are busy inventing a thousand different ways of getting the arrested men released. It goes without saying that I categorically refused all the propositions that were made to me in this regard, but they are working ceaselessly to attain their goal. 3) On 22 May, I ordered the major of the gendarmerie to produce the eight accused, one of whom, a man by the name of Haci Mehmed, had been a receiver of contributions. On 23 May, I had to issue the same order again; there was, however, no response. I thereupon wrote to the prosecutor on 25 May, again without results. I next wrote to the Colonel of the gendarmerie (26 May). Finally, on 28 May 1919, the following response reached me: "One of the eight accused is in Of, another has gone to Russia, a third is dead, and the other five are facing prosecution." The prosecution in question, however, has produced no results to date. I again appealed to the gendarmerie and to Of, but my requests were not even answered. Disappointed by the attitude of the gendarmerie, I wrote on two occasions to the police to ask them to arrest and produce the receiver of contributions Haci Mehmed. I was told that he was not in the village. I again wrote to the gendarmerie, but received no answer. Finally, on 14 June, I wrote directly to the superior of the wanted man at his place of work [defterdar], who, on 6 July, sent me a response dated 21 June in which he said: "Haci Mehmed is ill; he will be back in a few days." But, no one ever came, and the man who organized massacres is still in his post; he has not been inconvenienced in any way. I related all this to the governor, who told me: "we lack the forces required to carry out your orders." I replied: "But not even the criminals who come and go as they please in the city have been arrested, and the accused state officials regularly receive their salaries." The governor contented himself with saying: "I will say something about that." But there have been no changes. Later, I informed the chief prosecutor of everything that had happened, but without seeing any results or receiving a response from him. 4) I called a famous Unionist and organizer of massacres by the name of Kelim, the first secretary of the Public Works Administration. After interrogating him, I demanded a written order from the governor authorizing me to arrest him. The prosecutor sent the accused man back home, kept his file for two days, and sent it back to me later. Two days after that, I was obliged to issue the arrest order, but Kelim was not arrested. He stands accused of a crime; there exists a warrant for his arrest; he is apparently a fugitive, but, at the same time, he has employment. 5) On 26 May, I demanded a copy of a few orders concerning massacres issued by the previous government. I was simply told that "no such orders exist." 6) I issued an order to arrest a notorious organizer of massacres named Hakkı. One month later, I was told: "ten days ago, Hakkı left for Erzerum." Why did they wait until he had left to answer me? 7) I issued an order to arrest notorious organizers of massacres such as Reşad, Kahya, Ömer, Hakkı, Haireddin, Süleyman and Murad, and I wrote a number of letters on this subject, but was unable to obtain any results at all. 8) Before my arrival, the police chief conducted an investigation of the crimes committed by police lieutenant Rauf. I asked the governor and police chief to send me the file three times, but my request went unanswered. According to information provided by witnesses, the file was burned ... 9) Although I issued an order for his arrest, the famous Unionist and organizer of massacres Haci Ali Hofuz Zâde Ëumer comes and goes in a car in the city as he pleases, is not arrested, and is not inconvenienced in any way. Recently, he came to the city with Reşat, Kahya, Süleyman, and others, and went to the government building to speak with the governor. 10) The well-known organizer of massacres and brigand *Topal Osman* was officially appointed mayor of Kirason. Is there any need to produce further proof?

If the government does not arrest brigands and people who have committed massacres, if it does not punish criminals, if bloodthirsty monsters who should be arrested on orders from a competent authority at liberty and even hold conversations with people in official posts, why were we sent here? If the aim is not to fool Europe and America, why do the Turks want to stage this well-constructed farce? But an Armenian can never serve as a pliant tool in the hands of people who wish to commit a shameful injustice. A judge can never play a cowardly, ignoble role.[44]

This provincial experience of an Ottoman Armenian magistrate was certainly no isolated case. If the Istanbul authorities had objective reasons for prosecuting people before the law, in order, as it were, to purge the state and appear more presentable at the peace conference, it is obvious that the provinces were still under the CUP's control, and that its elites were by no mean inclined to be tried. Whatever the divergences between the different Turkish nationalist currents, they concurred on one point – a categorical refusal to assume their responsibilities; an implacable desire to see their common project of building a Turkish national state through to the end.

Chapter 5

The Armenian Survivors in their Places of "Relegation" in the Last Days of the War

The British forces under the command of General Allenby, in the course of their march northward in late 1917 and throughout 1918, occasionally encountered deportees who had ended up in various places in Palestine and the Sinai. These were in fact survivors from the convoys that had been driven down the Hama-Homs-Damascus-Hauran-Salt-Kerek-Maan-Sinai route three years earlier.

A first group of 40 survivors was liberated by the British forces in November 1917, in Jordan's Wadi Musa region, which marked the northern limits of the zones of relegation. They had subsisted in cave dwellings or the ruins of the city of Petra.[1] Bit by bit, other information about the survivors that had been gathered up by General Allenby's army reached Cairo,[2] and the first humanitarian operations were launched from the Egyptian capital with the support of the British military authorities.[3] For example, the capture of Jerusalem on 9 December 1917 led to the discovery of around 500 deportees who had found refuge in buildings attached to the Armenian Monastery of Saint James.[4] Three months later, their number had risen to 650.[5] About 100 orphans who had been found in the region of Salt, west of Amman, were lodged in the monastery shortly thereafter. In the course of the February 1918 military operations, 900 deportees were also found in Tafile on the southern tip of the Dead Sea, all in terrible health. They represented the remains of a convoy of nearly 10,000 people from Gürün, Marash, Hacın, Dörtyol, Kayseri, and Mardin that had gotten as far as Tafile.[6] In April 1918, the British provided relief to 1,500 Cilician deportees eking out an existence in Salt, and a few others further south, in Kerek, natives of Adana, Marash, Ayntab, Kesab, and Karsbazar.[7]

It must also be pointed out that, during the British offensive, Armenians in another category fell into the hands of the Allied forces: the hundreds of Armenian soldiers who had been serving in the Ottoman Fourth Army, who had been taken prisoner at the same time as their Ottoman comrades, and who had been interned just as they had.

The first big group of deportees – nearly 30,000 people – was discovered in Damascus, which fell to the Arab and British forces on 1 October 1918. Their situation was all the more appalling in that they had survived until then by working for the Ottoman army.[8] Finally, in fall 1918, French forces discovered 4,000 Armenians in Beirut when they entered the city on 8 October, and another 1,000 in Baalbek and Zahle. In the next few days, 2,000 were found in Homs, 5,000 in Maara, and 1,000 in Hama.[9] Aleppo and the surrounding area were the last to be liberated, on 26 October. Forty thousand Armenians were found there. All in all, on the eve of the armistice, 100,000 deportees remained on the Alep-Damascus-Sinai axis.

In Aleppo, the 26 September 1917 departure of the vali, Mustafa Abdülhalik, reduced the danger to which the deportees were exposed. A number of Armenian survivors of the massacres in Zor, and others who had hidden in the nearby countryside, gradually came looking for aid and refuge in the regional metropolis. The fact that Beatrice Rohner's German orphanage had been shut down, that the Mazlumian brothers had been exiled to Zahle, and that the moving spirit behind the humanitarian operations in Aleppo, the auxiliary bishop of the city, Father Harutiun Yesayan, had been arrested in February 1917 had put all but a complete end to the relief programs for the deportees and led to the dissolution of the committee charged with organizing the aid.[10] A few private initiatives benefiting the deportees nevertheless made it possible to compensate, to some extent, for the absence of organized structures. Yervant Odian, who had returned to Aleppo in mid-March 1918, notes that Aram Andonian was there, living in the Baron hotel, as were Dr. Boghosian, Dr. Hekimian, Mikayel Natanian, Andon Rshtuni, and Krikor Ankut. This indicates that the underground network had succeeded in saving these intellectuals. But Odian also notes that the authorities were rounding up Armenians of draftable age in the streets and sending them to Bozanti.[11] The situation was thus far from being normal. The notorious informant Arshavir Sahagian, who had denounced the Hnchaks to the authorities, was tracking down Armenian deportees there. Odian, known for his impru-dence, fell into Sahagian's hands and found himself condemned to exile in Dyarbekir.[12] While waiting to be exiled, thanks to the complicity of an Armenian doctor who worked for the Aleppo police force, he observed the practices of the local police and noted that individual cases, such as that of a young Greek from Alexandria who was described as "dangerous," were decided in the Interior Ministry.[13] Odian also describes the situation of the Armenian soldiers who had been serving on the Syrian front for more than three years without ever being granted a leave.[14]

The second big group of survivors was found in Mesopotamia, in the Mosul and Baghdad areas. The Turkish forces abandoned Mosul on 21 October; General Ali İhsan Pasha tried to take up positions there again upon his return from Azerbaijan, but was driven out by the British troops.[15] The former patriarch, Zaven, now exiled to Baghdad, set out to recover the women and children who had been scattered throughout the region. He rented five houses in which he lodged the deportees who had arrived from the deserts, including young women who had prostituted themselves in order to survive.[16] Late in December, 1,700 survivors were recovered. The number reached 40,000 by January 1919, 1,000 of them orphans.[17]

Recovering the thousands of women and children held by Arab tribes in the region – the Anezes, Albu Diabs, and Zobas – constituted another thorny problem. Initially, a joint dec-laration by local religious leaders and notables, especially in the regions of Dehok and Zakho, whom a colonel in the military Security Forces and the British civilian governor, Nolder, had turned to for help, made it possible to organize a campaign to recover these women and chil-dren, sometimes by force.[18] The British authorities, however, soon curbed such operations, especially when the Armenians involved were converts or "married" young women, in order not to alienate the local population.[19] In Baghdad, the patriarch estimated the number of deportees recovered there at 2,000.[20]

The biggest problem, however, was constituted by the 75,000 Armenians and Chaldean Syriacs from the plains of Urmia and Salmast who had fled to Hamadân and Bakuba on 18 July 1918 in order to escape the threats of massacre from the Ottoman troops under Ali İhsan Pasha. After evacuating Iranian Azerbaijan, these Christians made a long trek in search of protection. Pursued by the Turkish forces, a number of them were killed in the vicinity of Heydarâbâd or in the attacks by Kurdish tribes to which they were subjected en route. Others dies of exhaustion or fell victim to stratagems, as in the case of the 400 horsemen wearing British uniforms who killed the former governor of Van, Kosti Hampartsumian, near the Sahin Ghal'e mountain pass. Around 5,000 people lost their lives during this opera-tion, carried out jointly by Turkish forces and Kurdish irregulars.[21]

In September 1918, Colonel Chardigny, the head of the French Military Mission in the Caucasus, estimated the number of Christian refugees in Hamadân at 50,000.[22] He also noted that they were being gradually evacuated to Baghdad, except for the men capable of bearing arms: thus, 7,000 men, including three thousand Armenians, were "recruited" by the British military authorities. According to the Armenian Republic's plenipotentiary repre-sentative in Persia, Araratian, of the 18,000 Armenian refugees who left Azerbaijan, 12,000 arrived in Bakuba, most of them from Van; the roughly 4,000 Armenians from Salmast and Urmia remained in Ghazvin and Hamadân.[23]

By late 1918, some 15,000 Armenian refugees, a majority of them from Van, inhabited the tent camp set up by the British in Bakuba, northeast of Baghdad.[24] The Lord Mayor's Relief Fund provided considerable sums to ensure these deportees' subsistence. A breakdown of the Armenians living in Bakuba in December 1919 according to place of origin shows that 10,247 came from the Van region; 2,530 from Iranian Azerbaijan; 547 from Bitlis; 385 from Aleppo; and 290 from Cilicia, while the others were natives of the Caucasus, Erzerum, Sıvas, Kharpert, Bursa, Angora, and the capital.[25] The camp also had an orphanage, founded in October 1918 and run by the *Vorpakhnam* (Association for the Protection of Armenian Orphans), which was based in Egypt. One thousand two hundred children, mostly from the Van and Azerbaijan regions, lived here in tents. When Patriarch Zaven visited the camp in January 1919 on his way back to Constantinople,[26] he spoke with General Austin about the conditions under which the British might create an Armenian battalion. Eight hundred fifty Armenian soldiers refused to serve elsewhere than in their native regions.[27]

In Basra, where the patriarch was getting ready to board ship for Constantinople and resume his functions, he discovered another group of survivors from Van, who had been provided relief by the Belgian consul, Dervishian, as well as Arshag Safrastian, who was for his part on his way to Paris to rejoin the Armenian National Delegation.[28]

One hundred fifteen thousand is no doubt a realistic estimate of the number of Armenian survivors living in the area stretching from the Sinai through Syria to the Persian Gulf when the armistice was signed. But this figure leaves one category of survivors out of account – the women and children in these regions held in Bedouin tribes. We shall discuss them separately.

The Armenian Presence in Asia Minor Shortly after the Armistice

A French-language daily in Istanbul puts the Armenian survivors in the following categories: 1) those who had converted and were living in Muslim localities; 2) those who were scattered throughout the empire, living in isolation and looking for their families, whose fate they did not know; 3) those who had returned to their homes, which they generally found in ruins or inhabited by "new owners who did not intend to be pushed out"; 4) those who had regained possession of their goods (an exception); 5) those who did not have the means they needed to return to their native regions; 6) those who had returned but had been unable to regain their homes and had left again, bound for areas in which their safety was assured.[29]

In examining, region by region, the way the deportations were carried out, we observed that certain categories of Armenians, notably those working for the army or municipalities, had been allowed to remain in their homes on a more or less temporary basis – as a rule, after agreeing to convert to Islam. We have also noted many cases in both cities and the country-side in which young women and children were abducted, placed in orphanages, or "taken up" in families. Finally, we can neglect neither the populations that fled to the Caucasus early in the war – some briefly returned to their homes in the vilayets of Erzerum and Van before fleeing again in early 1918 during the Turkish offensive – nor the Armenians from Istanbul or Thrace, who found refuge first and foremost in Bulgaria; all in all, they found it the easiest to return home. In sum, we find ourselves, in November 1918, facing a complex problem in which people found themselves widely scattered and in sharply contrasting personal situations. Reconstructing the pre-war Armenian world was a task obviously made difficult not only by the demographic disaster that resulted from the genocide, but also by the new situation created during the conflict. The CUP's policy of settling *muhacirs* in formerly Armenian homes made the elimination of the Armenians irreversible. The seizure of their assets by local Young Turk networks was another *fait accompli* that it was difficult to reverse by peaceful means. This multifaceted issue has yet to be seriously studied but merits examination, for it is extremely revelatory of the atmosphere reigning in the provinces of Asia Minor that were still controlled by Young Turk networks.

An account by a young officer from Talas, Yervant Der Mardirosian, who had been enrolled in the Nineteenth Brigade on his return from the Dardanelles, shows that in spring 1916 there were little islands of deportees scattered throughout Anatolia. Bound for Osmaniye with his unit on 19 April, Der Mardirosian met a compatriot there, Garabed Hergimian, who told him that his mother and two brothers had passed that way before setting out for Zor. Upon arriving in Marash on 29 May, the young man witnessed the departure of a convoy of 2,000 deportees for the south.[30] In Malatia in early June, he encountered a few Islamicized Armenians from Trebizond and saw that the cathedral had been transformed into a stable. Further north, in Harput, he noted the presence of a handful of Catholic and Protestant families, as well as Islamicized Armenians, living in dire poverty. In Palu, on 15 June, he does not mention seeing a single compatriot, but learned that young women were being held in the harems of government officials and officers, as was also the case further east in Jabaghchur, where the front lay at the time.[31]

Yervant Odian, whose wanderings from Istanbul to Der Zor we have followed over a three-year period, notes that in spring 1918 5,000 to 6,000 survivors of the Syrian Desert were living in Sultaniye, south of Konya. The vali of Konya, Muammer (who had previously been the vali of Sıvas), had adopted a policy of uninterrupted harassment toward them. The only Armenian men present were a deportee from Bursa, Karnig Shishmanian, who had a boutique in Sultaniye, as well as a few pharmacists and agronomists. They helped the women and children who had taken refuge in the town as best they could, and these people tried to subsist by taking small jobs.[32] Around 6,000 natives of Zeitun, who had been deported to Sultaniye in April 1915, had died of hunger there; their bodies had been buried in mass graves.[33] Odian spent the last months of the war in the town and still worked as an interpreter when German officers, sometimes taken for "Englishmen," traveled through it. It was from German officers that the deportees in Sultaniye learned one day that Aleppo had just fallen to the British. From the Istanbul press, they learned that the İzzet government had decreed on 14 October that the Armenian deportees could go back home. However, Odian writes, these were "just words."[34]

With the end of hostilities, an unending stream of soldiers and civilians began pouring out of Syria into Asia Minor. For example, on 19 January in Cilicia, "all the trains were subjected to close searches; if Armenian women or orphans were found in the possession of Turkish officers or soldiers...they were immediately set free." Cautiously, the newly formed National Council in Adana forbade Armenians to set foot beyond a line running through Bozanti, "with the result that all the Armenians who ended up in Cilicia were maintained there. Thus there are currently 35,00 thousand to 40,000 [deportees] there."[35] This prohibition was imposed rapidly in reaction to the frequent murders of deportees who had returned home. Of course, the situation was not the same everywhere. The vilayets of Erzerum, Bitlis, and Van were calm, for not a single Armenian was still to be found in them. Elsewhere, it was obvious that the Young Turk networks had not been hard put to implement a policy of intimidation calculated to prevent the deportees from returning and, thus, from laying claim to their property. Reports arriving in the Patriarchate in Constantinople clearly implied that the exactions and murders committed in certain provinces were the result of a concerted plan.

In the vilayet of Sıvas, in February 1919, a group of *çetes* commanded by Nalband İzzedin Kâmil, "famous for the crimes he had committed during the deportations," murdered 12 Armenian deportees who had just returned to Zara. The judge presiding at the court there, who was also Kâmil's uncle, had not deemed it worthwhile to hold these criminals in detention. In Sıvas, when the Greek forces occupied Smyrna, the authorities had organized rallies during which former CPU propagandists had aroused "Muslim fanaticism" and preached holy war against Christians in the mosques. In July in İnebazar, the *çete* leader Kâmil attacked a group of Armenian deportees returning to their homes and killed several of them.[36] Immediately after the 4 September 1919 Congress of Sıvas, Armenian sources note, Mustafa Kemal, Fahri Pasha, and Rauf Bey set about creating a provisional government, entrusting the important posts to those bore the main responsibility for the massacres.[37] It is quite obvious that Kemal moved in step with the "resistance" initiated by the CUP,[38] even if the Kemalists proclaimed their independence of the Young Turk network.[39]

In Tokat, the situation was rather similar to the one in Sıvas. The local Unionist leaders, deeply implicated in the 1915 massacres; Gurci Ahmed, the vilayet's accountant; Faik, the president of the *emvali metruke*; and İmam Bekir, who held property belonging to the Monastery of Saint John Chrysostom, prevented survivors from returning and blocked restitution of their confiscated property.[40] Later, in Merzifun, 2,000 returning survivors fell victim to a massacre; "the Turks burned down all that was left intact of the old Armenian quarter."[41] Finally, it should be noted that the courts martial set up by the new "nationalist" authorities condemned nearly 2,000 Armenians to death in the vilayet of Sıvas alone, and that many young people were enrolled in labor battalions.[42]

In the vilayet of Trebizond, as is indicated in another report, the induction into labor battalions of Greeks between 20 and 25 years of age confirms that in January 1919 the criminals involved in the massacres of Greeks and Armenians were not prosecuted and were even appointed to important posts.[43] The repatriates, wrote a French diplomat,

> had a hard time of it recovering their property because [of] silent opposition from petty Turkish officials, who had the support of the heads of the local branch of the Committee of Union and Progress. Those who had taken an active part in the Armenian massacres, which had been frighteningly cruel in this city, and who had an interest in keeping what they had stolen and blocking the return [of] witnesses, endeavored, by means of terrorist acts, to spread alarm among those who had returned, some of whom fled a second time.[44]

In March, the Young Turk networks distributed arms to the peasants, while 300 soldiers took to the maquis on the urging of three Unionist officers, who were joined by Ekrem Bey and his band of *çetes*. A similar situation reigned further west in Ordu, Kirason, Bafra, Samsun, Uniye, and Çarsamba.[45] While murders were less systematic in Trebizond than in the interior, they were no less frequent, as was observed by an American who traveled through the city on 21 June 1919. The officer also noted that returning survivors' real estate and moveable assets had still not been returned to them.[46]

In Ismit, where *muhacirs* from Salonika and Rumelia had been settled during the war, replacing the Armenians, barely 30 deportees had returned by 30 September 1920;[47] none were to be found in the surrounding region, where acts of pillage and murder had multiplied in the course of the year 1919.[48] The court-martial in Bilecik, after first imprisoning the local Young Turk leaders, freed, on 15 October 1919, "Unionist leaders of the city by the names of Mercimakzâde Ahmed, Dedeoğlu Ali, Cadizâde Haci Ahmed, and their accomplices." These men immediately took "the head of the nationalist movement and sowed terror among the Armenians." Observers further noted that they organized public demonstrations "with flags and a band, to cries of 'long live the Ittihad!'"[49]

The situation in the neighboring region of Bursa was appreciably different. Initially, the new vali had ordered the arrests of the local Unionist chiefs, who stood accused, notably, of the massacre of Atranos:[50] Dr. Midhat Bey; the lawyer Osman Nuri; Muheddin and Hakkı Baha; Sadık Bey, who had formed a squadron of 300 çetes; and others. The French intelligence service noted, however, the formation of "clubs made up of reserve officers"[51] – in other words, the local Young Turks had not thrown in the towel. In April 1919, between 800 and 1,000 deportees had returned – that is, around 10 per cent of the pre-war population.[52] A few months later, bands of çetes began to harass these survivors, demanding protection money from them, while the local press published inflammatory articles about them and the youngest were drafted into the Kemalist forces. It is also noteworthy that the trial of those responsible for the massacres in Atranos culminated in an acquittal on 8 March 1920, leading to a repression campaign that forced the Armenians to leave Bursa for good. They were immediately replaced by muhacirs.[53]

The sole information we have about the eastern provinces comes from Harput, where the French consul's former dragoman, Kevork Aharonian, began working again as an "information agent" in March 1919.[54] In his first report, dated 1 May, he notes that he is having problems because the state officials, "all of them Unionists," have not been replaced ("we are almost living under the rule of the Talaats and Envers," he writes). Aharonian also emphasizes that the returning deportees had enormous problems in recovering "real estate and moveable assets [and] the girls and women who had been abducted, finding food and supplies and realizing of the Armenian orphans. In the courts," he adds, "lawsuits brought by Christians were never taken into consideration." Aharonian notes a few murders and also reports that five Armenian prisoners who had been arrested by Ali İhsan Pash in Dersim early in 1918 – Ihsan had had most of the refugees seized in Dersim shot – were found guilty of "espionage" and were still behind bars.[55] He reveals, finally, that the CUP had reorganized in Harput under new names, such as Hurryet Itilaf (Liberal Entente) and "Association of Kurdistan" – parties that defended Turkish and Kurdish interests.[56] In August, Aharonian informed his superiors of the arrest of the vilayet's police chief, Hulusi Bey,[57] formerly a police lieutenant in Erzerum, where he had a notable hand in the massacres in the Kemah Gorge.[58]

Statistics produced jointly by the Ecumenical and Armenian Patriarchates early in 1919 indicate that around 255,000 Greek and Armenian survivors had managed to return to their homes or were living in the following regions: Constantinople, 2,339 Greeks and 470 Armenians; Edirne, 52,907 Greeks and 2,355 Armenians; Erzerum, 6 Greeks and 3,193 Armenians; Adana, 133 Greeks and 45,075 Armenians; Angora, 140 Greeks and 1,735 Armenians; Aydın, 26,790 Greeks and 132 Armenians; Bitlis, no Greeks and 762 Armenians; Bursa, 20,034 Greeks and 13,855 Armenians; Dyarbekir, no Greeks and 195 Armenians; Sıvas, 731 Greeks and 2,897 Armenians; Trebizond, 10,890 Greeks and 2,103 Armenians; Kastamonu, no Greeks or Armenians; Konya 2,346 Greeks and 10,012 Armenians; Mamuret ul-Aziz, no Greeks and 1,992 Armenians; Van, no Greeks and 732 Armenians; Eskişehir, no Greeks and 216 Armenians; Erzincan, no Greeks and 7 Armenians; Urfa, no Greeks and 394 Armenians; Içil, no Greeks or Armenians; Ismit, 184 Greeks and 13,672 Armenians; Bolu, no Greeks or Armenians; Teke, no Greeks or Armenians; Canik, 2,286 Greeks and 801 Armenians; Çatalca, no Greeks or Armenians; Ayntab, no Greeks and 430 Armenians; Karahisar, no Greeks and 298 Armenians; Dardanelles, 741 Greeks and 222 Armenians; Karasi, 32,165 Greeks and 899 Armenians; Kayseri, 14 Greeks and 47 Armenians; Kütahya, no Greeks and 721 Armenians; Karasi, no Greeks and 241 Armenians; Menteşe, 804 Greeks and no Armenians; and Nigde, no Greeks or Armenians. This makes a total of 152,510 Greeks and 103,456 Armenians.[59] It goes without saying that the number of repatriates was constantly changing as a result of late returns, especially those of deportees who had still been in Syria, Mesopotamia, and Transjordan in early 1919 or, again, women and children who were only gradually released by the families that had been holding them. After the repatriation campaign that affected, above all, deportees in Syria and Mesopotamia as well as refugees in Bulgaria and, to a lesser extent, the Caucasus, the repatriation of Armenian populations on the eve of the Treaty of Sèvres presented the following picture:[60] Constantinople, 150,000; vilayet of Edirne, 6,000; *mutesarifat* of Ismit, 20,000; vilayet of Bursa, 11,000; *sancak* of Bilecik, 4,5000; *sancak* of Karasi, 5,000; *sancak* of Afionkarahisar, 7,000; vilayet of Aydın, 10,000; vilayets of Kastamonu and Bolu, 8,000; *sancak* of Kirşehir, 2,500; *sancak* of Yozgat, 3,000; *sancak* of Angora, 4,000; vilayet of Konya, 10,000; *sancak* of Sıvas, 12,000; *sancak* of Tokat, 1,800; *sancak* of Amasia, 3,000; *sancak* of Şabinkarahisar, 1,000; *sancak* of Trebizond, none; *sancak* of Lazistan, 10,000; *sancak* of Gümüşhane, none; *sancak* of Canik, 5,000; vilayet of Erzerum, 1,500; Van (the city alone), 500; vilayet of Bitlis, none; vilayet of Dyarbekir, 3,000; *sancak* of Harput, 30,000; *sancak* of Malatia, 2,000; *sancak* of Dersim, 3,000; vilayet of Adana, 150,000; *sancak* of Aleppo, 5,000; *sancak* of Ayntab, 52,000; *sancak* of Urfa, 9,000; *sancak* of Marash/Maraş, 10,000; Jerusalem, 2,000; Damascus, 400; Beirut, 1,000; and the Hauran, 400. This makes a total of 543,600 Armenians.

This breakdown calls for a few remarks. Two hundred thousand of these Armenians were concentrated in Cilicia, to which the British and, later, French forces had encouraged them to return. According to Vahe Tachjian, by repatriating the Armenian survivors to Cilicia, France avoided the risks of tensions in Syria, since letting the deportees remain there would not have been a popular measure, At the same time, the French were certain that they could rely on the support of the Armenian population in Cilicia, notably for the purpose of obtaining a mandate over the region.[61] As in the non-occupied regions of Asia Minor, the repatriation of so large a number of Armenians, whether or not they were natives of Cilicia, raised a hue and cry from the local Young Turk networks, which benefited from the discontent caused by the issue of the restoration of Armenian property acquired during the genocide and also of the young women and children who had been abducted.[62] During the two years and more during which the French occupied Cilicia, the local branches of *Karakol* systematically thwarted the efforts of the French administration, led by Colonel Brémond, to promote peaceful coexistence between the different groups that had long been present in Cilicia. The colonial administration, despite its good faith, was hard put to ensure the restitution of property as well as people. The psychological condition of the Armenian repatriates, enraged in particular by the fact that their wives, daughters, and sisters were still being held in harems, also engendered countless conflicts and led to the settling of scores. Cilicia became the scene of a confrontation between victims and victimizers that intensified the long-standing rancor responsible for the unbridgeable gulf between the two groups. The Armenians' feeling that they had been unjustly treated was expressed more freely here than elsewhere thanks to the French military presence. Conversely, the local Young Turk leaders sought to preserve what they had acquired, throwing off the French colonialist yoke with all possible speed and simultaneously expelling the Cilician Armenians, who, during the genocide, had received better treatment than others. The local Turkish elites began working more closely with the Young Turk movement, which had in part rallied to the Kemalist banner.[63] As Tachjian has brilliantly shown, the Kemalist movement inexorably pursued the CUP's policy of demographic homogenization. By force or through administrative measures, it methodically strove to make it impossible for the repatriates to remain in their native towns and villages, terrorizing these non-Turks in hopes of making them flee. The CUP's strategy of harassing representatives of the League of Nations' High Commission for Refugees as well as humanitarian organizations that, as we shall see, provided the refugees assistance, speaks volumes about its desire to purge Turkey of "foreign bodies." The "war of national liberation" prepared by the Young Turks and carried through by Mustafa Kemal was, a few skirmishes with the French forces and the war with Greece aside, a vast operation with the purpose of completing the genocide by expelling the Armenian survivors. The policy adopted toward the Greeks of Asia Minor merely confirmed the existence of this political objective, which the Ottoman Empire's defeat in the war had not been enough to thwart. According to a report produced by the Armenian Patriarchate, 37,957 Greek and Armenian repatriates were murdered in the vilayets of Konya, Sıvas, Kastamonu, and Trebizond – the vast majority of them in Trebizond.[64] Herbert Gibbons, a reporter in the area, telegraphed to the *Monitor* in Boston: "Angora Turks continue deliberately their pitiless politic of extermination of the Greeks."[65]

The Patriarchate's Political Management
of the Post-War Situation

As soon as the Mudros armistice was signed, the Constantinople Armenian Patriarchate, an institution that had been dissolved by the authorities in 1916, was reestablished at the demand of the Entente Powers. It was all the more urgent that it be called back into existence since several questions of vital importance for hundreds of thousands of survivors were being posed at the same time. In a declaration published in November 1918, the French and British High Commissioners demanded that the Ottoman government see to the repatriation of the deported Greeks and the Armenian survivors; that it give them back the property that it had confiscated from them, together with their bank deposits; and that it obtain the release of the women and children abducted during the deportations.[66] The Armenian authorities' priorities were to restore the rights of those survivors who were returning to their homes, ensure them adequate support, and establish means of legal action against those who had perpetrated violence or seized property.

An Armenian leadership body was created even before Patriarch Zaven, who was still in exile in Mosul, returned to Constantinople. In January, it sent the Entente powers a memorandum that illustrates its position.[67] While it had no doubts about "Grand Vizier Tevfik's good intentions," it wondered whether the victims could be rehabilitated when "eighty percent of state officials today are Unionists and were deeply implicated in the same crimes." A purge of the administration seemed the more necessary to the Armenian leaders in that the inquiries into war crimes were making no progress and the preliminary files being assembled by investigating magistrates were being transmitted only very slowly to the court-martial. In the rather peculiar situation that had come about as a result of the appointment of Entente High Commissioners, the Armenians had the feeling that the experience of the war had not modified the authorities' behavior. "It goes without saying," the Armenian leaders observed, "that if the Allied powers had not been eyewitnesses to these tragedies, it would have been affirmed, in line with age-old practice, that nothing of the sort had ever happened and that these were only false rumors, or else that what was involved was a minor event brought on by the Armenians." They went still further, declaring to the powers that "the government [was] not going to punish the culprits."[68] The skepticism thus voiced by the Armenian leadership barely veiled the gulf that the violence had put between the Ottoman Armenians and the Turkish authorities. The patriarch doubted not the government's good faith, but rather the state itself, which was still entirely controlled by the Young Turks. He observed, accordingly, that if a radical purge were not conducted, it was out of the question that the CUP leaders would be brought to trial. The other argument advanced by the Armenian leadership to justify its skepticism was no less important: what it called a "centuries-old habit" that consisted in considering mass crimes committed against entire peoples as legitimate "punishment." The editorialist of the *Spectateur d'Orient* understood this well when he wrote:

> This is the first time in Turkey's history that a former grand vizier and former ministers have been brought to trial and risk being punished for crimes committed against the population of this country... Today, former Turkish leaders are being prosecuted for having ordered the massacre of Christians. It is the only time in the empire's history that this has happened, and represents a profound change in this country's customs. Where is the reason for this to be found? The sole reason is the outcome of the world war.[69]

It other words, it was the prospect that the Ottoman Empire might be dislocated that had impelled the new authorities to bring the Ittihadist leadership to trial in spite of prevailing public opinion. Reading the Istanbul press had convinced the Armenian leadership that it had no chance of obtaining retribution from the Ottoman courts. It had from the outset advocated creation of an "International Court of Justice" and had begun working to that end. In a 6 January 1919 public declaration, Dr. Tavitian, the president of the Political Council, pointed out that, despite the departure of those who bore the main responsibility for the massacres, a majority of the Turkish population had not changed its views and remained threatening: "We can see, especially in the provinces, the same bad faith as far as restoration of the 'loot,' orphans, girls, and women is concerned; the same threats are hanging over the heads of the human wrecks who escaped the carnage with their lives."[70]

Admiral Calthorpe rapidly set up a Greek and Armenian committee[71] that was charged with attending to the problems of the refugees, but also with seconding his own efforts to identify, arrest, and indict the authors of crimes against humanity. Dr. Krikor Tavitian was the Armenian representative on this committee.[72] It was, however, necessary to wait for Patriarch Zaven to return, as he did on 19 February 1919, in order to create the *Deghegadu divan* (Information Bureau), which was headed by Arshag Alboyajian (1879–1962) and placed under the direct authority of the Armenian Political Council.[73] Zaven Yeghiayan was welcomed by a large crowd, in conditions "likely to offend the religious and national sensibilities of the inhabitants of Istanbul,"[74] as the authorities complained.

The Information Bureau had been given the mission of collecting old and recent documents on demographic questions, the Armenian persecutions, the massacres, the deportations, and the real estate and moveable assets that had been seized, as well as facts about those mainly responsible for the massacres, eyewitness accounts, proofs, and statistics victims of abductions and sequestered orphans.[75] It also regularly produced reports on the situation in the provinces and the exactions perpetrated by the "nationalist forces," sending 300 reports on this subject to the British High Commission. Above all, it complied 292 files on the authors of the deportations, "whom the Turks are trying to whitewash."[76] Thus, the Armenian authorities had decided to gather documents and other evidence in anticipation of the creation of an international court of justice charged with judging the crimes committed by the Ottoman state.

The patriarch remarks in his memoirs that the new authorities did nothing to help the survivors return to their homes, especially in the eastern vilayets, with the result that many of them had thronged into Istanbul, making the Armenian authorities' task still more difficult. He notes that the government did not attempt to improve their lot, behaving as governments "did in the past, in the days of the Ittihad, except for the fact that the massacres have ceased."[77] Zaven sums up the situation as follows: "With the Turkish defeat, we were in a position to make demands; the Turkish government, for its part, had the feeling that we were working against it by bringing charges against it before the European powers." He concludes that under these circumstances it was hard for him "to cultivate friendly relations with it," the more so as the majority of Armenian circles were, opposed to reestablishing relations with the Sublime Porte, preferring to wait and see what the Entente would decide.[78] The one attempt at a rapprochement took place in spring 1919. Senator Manug Azarian came to see the patriarch on behalf of Grand Vizier Damad Ferid in order to propose that they reestablish relations "as they were before the war." As a goodwill gesture, the grand vizier informed the patriarch that a commission charged with "settling the Armenian question," of which Azarian was a member, had been created and attached to the Sublime Porte. The patriarch answered that the grand vizier knew very well what had happened to the Armenian nation and that, under these conditions, he wondered why he was doing nothing to help the thousands of survivors living in Constantinople in appalling conditions; why he had not budged "an inch" to provide them with relief and food, clothing, and shelter. He pointed out that the government had not made the "least sacrifice" for them, nor expressed "the least regret for the acts that had been committed." "How can you expect us," he exclaimed, "to cultivate relations with a throne and a government that have mortally wounded us and that do not seem to have put the sword back in its scabbard or to regret what they did? If the grand vizier wishes to do something, let him show some solicitude for these people. If he does, I will be the first to show him my gratitude."[79]

The Armenian authorities' position on the wartime persecution of the Armenian population is clearly laid out in a 27 December 1918 report[80] that merits examination. The description of the CUP's structures and the way it operated that serves as the introduction to this report aims to show that "in every city, big or small," "the bureaucracy," the army, "all the government's civilian agents, the police, the gendarmerie, all the notables, clergymen, representatives of the press and even criminals" were admitted to the Ittihadist clubs, for one could not "be a civil servant without being a Unionist."

The Central Committee was described as the "highest state council," in charge of "all domestic and foreign affairs." The report further points out that the

> Committee was able to win the support of the entire Turkish nation, with the exception of an insignificant minority, and for good reason: 1) it was the only organization that offered posts to all its members; 2) it wanted to strengthen the economic position of the Turkish element at the expense of the others; it gave Turkish merchants every advantage, while oppressing non-Muslims; 3) it flattered the Turkish soul with its Pan-Islamic ideas and Pan-Turk propaganda; 4) it aroused the fanaticism of the Turkish peasants and the populace; 5) by abolishing the Capitulations, it granted the Turks unrestrained freedom of action.

Formulated in the terminology current at the time, this description is not irrelevant and shows that the Armenians wished to communicate their experience of Turkism to the representatives of the Entente. As for the "crimes perpetrated against the Armenians, Greeks, and other nations," the report contends that "the program was decided upon after long reflection and its application was pursued with consummate skill." The report puts criminals in several different categories: 1) the deciders and organizers; 2) the cadres who provided "the means with which to massacre, plunder, and rape"; and 3) those who merely executed orders. In the first category, it puts Central Committee members and the war cabinets, parliamentary deputies, responsible secretaries, "the majority" of valis and *mutesarifs*, and certain journalists. According to the report, the immense majority of civilian and military officials, as well as police chiefs and commanders of the gendarmerie, fall into the second category. In the third category it puts all Kurdish, Çerkez, Chechen, and Laz *çetes*, as well as the officers and enlisted men of the regular army.[81]

This hierarchization of the criminals is developed in a subsequent report containing a list of those chiefly to blame "for the massacres and deportations."[82] It must first be pointed out that the Patriarchate, delegated by "the nation," addressed this report directly "to the justice of the Allied Powers." The introductory part of the text insists on "the moral and political effect" that a "judgement and punishment" could have on the development of "mentalities in Turkey," influencing "its future conduct toward the 'minorities.'" We do not know whether this document was produced on a demand from the Entente's High Commissioners, but it at least attests to the continuity of the policy adopted by the Armenian authorities, who apparently never contemplated anything other than an international court. The Armenians do not, moreover, hide the fact that they face a choice, drawing up an exhaustive list of the accused, "great or small," or "selecting" the most deeply implicated organizers, along with their main accomplices. In the first case, the scope of the crimes and the "tens of thousands of murderers" involved would remain inaccessible to "human justice." Consequently, the report declares, the Patriarchate has voluntarily restricted itself to presenting a selection "of the documents in its possession" and compiling a list of the main culprits while neglecting their "agents."[83]

The Information Bureau further states that it has opted for a province-by-province classification of the CUP's responsible secretaries, as well as the governors, military commanders, commanders of the gendarmerie, police chiefs, high-ranking officials, clergymen, and other notables involved locally in the "liquidation committees" that organized the plunder of Armenian assets or the creation of the *Teşkilât-i Mahsusa* "gangs" that massacred the population.[84]

A subsequent report broaches the crucial problem represented by the need to collect "proofs" of the guilt of the "high-ranking personalities," now fugitives, "who planned, organized, and ordered the deportations, massacres, and despoliation of the Armenians." It points out that it is hard to find "definitive proof... black on white," of the orders that they issued, since there was nothing to prevent them from "destroying most such proofs" before the armistice was signed. The Information Bureau also suggests that the "tribunal designated by the League of Nations" interrogate the members of the four commissions of inquiry dispatched to the provinces after the deportations, in reaction to the "indignation" voiced in Europe and America when "news of the atrocities" committed against the Armenians reached them.[85] After "officially declaring that no massacres had occurred, the Turkish government" sent commissions to the provinces so that they might produce "reports confirming the official declarations."

We have mentioned certain reports drawn up by the presidents of these investigative teams in late 1915 or early 1916. The interrogations of these men before the Fifth Commission prove that the reports were never published, but remained "buried" in the Interior Ministry.[86] The Bureau of Information proposed that the members of these commissions be interrogated in the knowledge that some of them took the mission entrusted to them seriously and submitted devastating reports. This held for Mazhar Bey, who had been chosen to conduct an inquiry in Harput and Dyarbekir.[87] The conclusions he reached probably convinced Talât to keep them to himself. The functioning of the second commission of inquiry, responsible for conducting investigations in the regions of Angora and Konya, also attracted the attention of the Armenian Bureau. According to declarations that Radi Bey made before the court-martial, the court's presiding judge, Hulusi, Tahsin Bey's brother-in-law, had contented himself with interrogating a few gendarmes who had been punished for "irregularities," passing over in silence, the Patriarchate's report notes, the "carnage in Keller and Boğazlian, although, for these two sites, at any rate, we have flagrant proof of what went on."[88]

With regard to the third commission, which held inquiries in the vilayets of Erzerum, Van, and Bitlis, "where the most barbaric massacres were perpetrated," the bureau observed that the commission's president, Nihad Bey, the brother-in-law of İsmail Muştak, the secretary general of the Senate, officially discovered no irregularities "during the deportations." He had also been invited after the armistice to assume the post of prosecutor at the first court-martial, the presiding judge of which was Mahmud Hayret Pasha, but "he refused this post so as not to have to plead against his colleagues on the Committee of Union and Progress."[89] By reporting this information, the bureau sought to show that these inquiries were conducted, as a rule, by creatures of the CUP. The case of the president of the fourth and last commission, Asim Bey, charged with inspecting the provinces of Adana, Aleppo, and Damascus, is even more flagrant in this regard. Asim, a CUP member, former court inspector in Salonika, and former director of the Justice Ministry's Department of Criminal Affairs, submitted a report in which not a single offence was mentioned. It would even seem that it was Asim who called Istanbul's attention to the fact that, in the Der Zor region, the Armenian deportees represented from 50 to 60 per cent of the total population, a proportion that was "not desirable." According to the Information Bureau, it was after this report was filed that Talât cabled Zeki, the *mutesarif* of Der Zor, the order to liquidate the Armenians.[90] It may therefore be affirmed that the patriarchal authorities played a major role in collecting information about the Young Turk criminals and had as early as 1919 a precise notion of the facts and the respective responsibilities of the main CUP leaders.

The memorandum sent to the British intelligence services by Dr. Avedis Nakashian, a former nonpartisan parliamentary deputy from the capital, developed a more legalistic line of reasoning with respect to the anti-Armenian exactions.[91] According to Nakashian, if the liquidation order was formulated in a special law, the affair could be considered legal, but one could also hold that what was involved was a crime, whether it was carried out "on an order formulated as a law or not." In the first case, only the late sultan and certain cabinet members would be considered responsible, since the others had only obeyed orders and done their duty. In the second, there would exist a "collective responsibility," about which Nakashian flet the need to make a few remarks.

1) Every official, from the minister to the simple gendarme, knew perfectly well that this law was nothing more than a pretext to murder and plunder an entire nation. Everyone knew that the law opened the doors of the prisons for criminals so that they could be enrolled in the Special Organization; that these bands were stationed at precise points on the roads in order to attack convoys, kill, rape, and plunder; this was done openly; consequently, those who delivered the Armenians up to these criminals are just as responsible as those who committed the murders.

2) Every Turkish official was absolutely certain that the Armenians he dispatched were going to die in one way or another; no one can be expected to walk from Samsun to Mosul hungry and survive. There is no doubt about the intention to kill and, consequently, no doubt that all who put these people on the road are criminals like the others.

3) The Turks knew perfectly well that there was no military imperative to deport the Armenians, but that this initially served as a pretext to liquidate a nation; it is a question of a crime committed by a whole nation, and everyone participated in carrying it out.

4) No *force majeure* mandated such acts: certain valis and lower-ranking officials resigned and did not commit such crimes, such as the valis of Konya, Angora, and Kastamonu, Celal Bey, Mazhar Bey, and Reşid Pasha. Other did not resign, but also did not obey orders, such as Faik Ali in Kütahya. We have before us a case of intentional homicide by thousands of criminals.

5) Most officials who played an active role in the liquidation measures and the pillage have not showed any signs of repentance.

Dr. Nakashian concluded that Ottoman society did not have "the same conception of justice." "There are millions of people in this country," he wrote, "who consider what happened a punishment that had to be meted out, as one would have punished an animal."[92] This position, which put the accent on "collective responsibility," was also that of the Armenian authorities. In order to defend the interests of the victims with a single voice, the Patriarchate concluded an agreement with the Catholic and Protestant authorities that led to the creation of a joint council in which the leaders of all three communities held seats.[93] It also cooperated rather closely with the Ecumenical Patriarchate. The two prelates even sent a common declaration to the peace conference on 24 February 1919 in which they called for the creation of a court of justice to try the Young Turk criminals.[94] This, of course, did not fail to excite the hostility of Young Turk circles.

The Restoration of "Abandoned Property"

The second thorny issue that the Patriarchate had to handle dealt with the restoration of property illegally seized during the genocide. It brought in its wake the question of reparations for the material damages that the Armenian population had suffered. It challenged, in other words, the idea of constructing a "National Economy" and also the transfer of Armenian assets of which circles bound up with the Young Turk movement had been the primary beneficiaries. The first step to take was, obviously, to abrogate the Law on Abandoned Property, decreed on 26 September 1915, which had legalized the seizure of these assets.[95] In February 1919, a mixed commission, comprising representatives of the Armenian-Greek committee set up by the British, submitted to the Council of Ministers a draft bill suppressing the September 1915 law; it sought to provide a legal mechanism for the restoration of the property illegally held by the state or private individuals.[96] It is easy to imagine the host of problems thrown up by such a measure, particularly in regions in which *muhacirs* had been settled in Armenian homes, and it will readily be understood that the prospect that the Armenians' property might be restored to them did much to unite the local notables and tribal chiefs who held the bulk of the assets in question. The murders and intimidation of which the survivors who had returned to their homes were the targets – we have offered a few examples – were no doubt motivated, first and foremost, by economic considerations. Abrogating the Law on Abandoned Property was tantamount to attacking local elites, calling into question the ownership of goods that their owners believed that they had definitely acquired, and raising a hue and cry in these circles. It was thus an extremely hazardous operation for the Ottoman government to give satisfaction to the survivors. The government was therefore careful not to ratify the law that would have enabled the survivors to recover their property throughout the empire and regularly pushed back the date on which it would, even while making a show of its good faith,[97] thereby exasperating the Armenians and Greeks. It must further be emphasized that these acts of confiscation had involved not just personal assets, but also "national property," in theory inalienable and the legal proprietor of which was the Constantinople Armenian Patriarchate. There was a good deal of such property: around 2,500 churches; 400 monasteries, with the lands belonging to them; 2,000 schools; and land and rental properties.[98] In July 1919, the Political Council of the Patriarchate sent an official note to the government demanding material aid and the transfer of revenues that had accrued to the national property confiscated during the war, so that it could assume the enormous costs engendered by the return of the survivors concentrated in the capital. According to the patriarch, the council never received a reply from the Sublime Porte.[99]

In the absence of a law, the Patriarchate tried to recover its assets as best it could. When it learned that there were still warehouses in Istanbul and the provinces in which Armenian property was stocked, it did not hesitate to make use of "illegal" means to recover this property. But it never managed to win its case as far as personal property was concerned,[100] the more so as the Entente powers demonstrated a certain reticence on this point so as not to promote the development of the Kemalist-Unionist movement and to preserve social peace.

Thus, an Information Bureau report indicates that the warehouse of the Central Commission for Abandoned Property, located in Istanbul, in the Grand Bazar, Kurkci Han, second floor, still held after the armistice some 30 safes that had remained "without a proprietor," some of which had not been cracked open. Also stocked on the same floor of the *han* were antiquities, ancient manuscripts, and sacred vases, some of the booty plundered during the war.[101] Only after hemming and hawing for a year did the authorities ultimately adopt, on 8/21 January 1920, in response to a final complaint lodged by the Patriarchate,[102] the Law on the Restoration of Abandoned Armenian Property. It comprised 33 articles.[103] Those concerning moveable assets constitute a sort of legal, post-genocidal *vade-mecum*:

> Article 1. Any letter of indemnity or receipt issued by a deported Armenian, and any alienation of his moveable assets made by his own hand, is null and void if the letter of indemnity or receipt was issued, or rights to the property were acquired, during the deportation or in the month preceding it.
>
> Article 2. Every deported Armenian, and, in the case of his death, his heir, is entitled to lodge a claim to a moveable asset of which he was deprived, in one manner or another, by the administration or an ad hoc committee, against the person in whose possession he discovers said asset, except against the administration or the committee.
>
> Article 3. Every deported Armenian, and, in the case of his death, his heir, is entitled to demand compensation from the government for any loss that he may have suffered in consequence of the sale of his moveable assets by the ad hoc committees. A commission comprising the presiding judge of the civil court, the president of the local municipality, and a delegate from the Armenian Patriarchate shall assess the value of the objects of which the plaintiff may have been deprived.
>
> Article 4. Any violation of the stipulations of Articles 1, 2, and 3 shall be punishable by a fine of five hundred Turkish pounds and two years in prison.[104]

The minister of finance sent the text of this law to the provincial authorities,[105] but for obvious reasons it was never applied in regions over which the central government had long since ceded its authority to the Kemalist-Unionist movement. It was the non-application of this law that made it necessary to include a special clause about abandoned property in the Treaty of Sèvres.[106]

Armenian Prisoners

Even after the armistice was signed, there remained a considerable number of "political" prisoners in Ottoman prisons, notwithstanding the fourth article of the armistice that provided for their release. We have already seen that the courts martial operated unceasingly throughout the war and condemned a number of Armenians to death or to prison terms of varying lengths that were generally commuted into deportation. For obscure reasons, the administration continued to hold a few hundred men (above all deserters) and a few dozen women in detention. A February 1919 report lists 25 prisoners, five of them women, in the Ismit prison; 48 in Kayseri, condemned to sentence of from 5 to 15 years in prison; 32 in

Konya, 22 of them imprisoned for "ordinary" offenses; 15 in Bolu; 18 in Bursa; and 6 in the prison of the Istanbul court-martial, called the Bekirağa Section.[107]

These cases – limited in number, to be sure – are puzzling. If it had been a question of common-law prisoners, it might be supposed that the Ottoman administration was simply executing a sentence and that the deportation law did not apply to them. However, the handful of details provided in a file that an Armenian organization sent to the Turkish authorities indicates that many of these prisoners were accused of, or had been condemned for, desertion. These were exclusively prisoners held in western Anatolia, where Armenian men had not been systematically massacred. This might explain the fact that the prisoners in question were held until February 1919, as if nothing had changed in the empire of the sultans.

Abducted Women and Children and the Construction of a Turkish Nation

The fate reserved for the women and children abducted during the genocide of the Armenians constitutes a dimension of the Young Turk plan which is essential in understanding the fundamental nature of the crime. The Turkish program called for a demographic homogenization that would also take the form of assimiliationist policies, conceived as an alternative to physical elimination. Such assimilation was premised on conversion to Islam, equivalent for the Young Turks to an acceptance of Turkism, which implied that the victims abandon their Armenian identity in order to melt into the dominant group. It must, moreover, be pointed out that, behind the discourse demonizing the Armenian nation, there lay concealed a paradoxical esteem for the victimized group, or at least certain of its members taken individually. We have already seen how certain categories of women and children were treated, in particular that a number of officers and Unionist officials sought to "marry" educated young women in order to found "Turkish" families with them. In other words, Turkism did not impose any "racial" prohibitions and even encouraged modernizing society by assimilating selected victims. A number of Ittihadists were convinced that these women could create the ideal family environment in which they could fashion the modern Turkish household of which they dreamed. To put it differently, the CUP's objective was to eliminate Armenian identity and its territorial bases, while taking over its cultural achievements as well as its material property in order to construct Turkism. At work here, then, was an ideology not based on the rejection of a race, but on the desire to eliminate the foundations of an identity that implied the physical elimination of some and the assimilation of others. What the "Ottomanism" that was characteristic of the beginnings of the Young Turk revolution had not succeeded in bringing about for lack of a common cultural base would be accomplished by physical elimination or coercion. The will to assimilate part of the victimized group constitutes one of the particularities of the Armenian genocide. The consequence of this particularity was that some of the victims experienced or became a part of the private lives of their victimizers, on the basis of a temporarily or permanently imposed identity. This group made up a large proportion of those who survived to the end of the war. In other words, a good part of the human resources, with which the Armenian nation reconstructed itself as best it could, was previously supposed to have served the construction of the Turkish nation as a factor of modernity and an element of the Ittihadists' demographic politics.

That said, it should be pointed out that the plan to assimilate Armenian women and children did not always yield the expected results because of resistance on the part of some victims or the lack of enthusiasm of certain victimizers.

The deportees' fate varied with the category into which they fell. Among those who survived, we may distinguish, on the one hand, the women and children abducted during the first phase of the genocide and held in Turkish and Kurdish families, and, on the other, women and children taken captive in the second phase of the genocide by Arab families or Bedouin tribes. The former were above all victims of a Turkish logic of assimilation, while the latter were perceived as products endowed with a certain commercial value. Common to people in both categories was the fact that they had survived for objective reasons, ideological or material, even while they underwent radically different experiences, depending on the environment in which they found themselves.

The young women, who were invariably converts and were transformed into slaves, held in harems, or "married," often gave birth to children whose fathers were simultaneously the women's torturers and their saviors. Thus, at war's end, scattered throughout the Near East, children of converted Armenian mothers were to be found in Turkish, Kurdish, and Arab environments, while older, abducted children were to be found in families or tribes, or else in Turkish orphanages.

Gathering Up Women and Children
Held in Syria and Mesopotamia

The fate of the Armenian women and children held in tribes or families is an aspect of the genocide that was ignored prior to the work of Vahe Tachjian. It proved impossible to determine how many there were or where they were to be found, geographically speaking. However, thanks to the British intelligence service, there exist lists of women and children, identified by name, which also provide the names of the Bedouin chiefs who refused to give up their hostages. With the help of these documents, we can establish the typical profile of these victims. They were, for the most part, young women around 20 years old, held in the Wadi Musa, Maan, or elsewhere,[108] who served as objects of a lucrative trade that went beyond the bounds of Transjordan. Thus, these young women were often sold in the slave markets in Arabia. Traces of some of them can even be found in Tunisia or Algeria, where they were taken by pilgrims returning from Mecca.[109]

On the basis of this information, reconnaissance and recovery groups, supervised by Egyptian Armenians,[110] were formed in spring 1918 out of deserters from the Ottoman Army, most of them from Urfa.[111] The first group, led by Levon Yotneghperian, a soldier who had served in the Fourth Ottoman Army in Damascus,[112] benefited from the support of Emir Faysal and the British General Staff and was able to pursue its operations after the armistice.[113]

Further north, in the Syrian Desert around Zor, another reconnaissance and recovery group had been formed in April 1919 under the command of Rupen Herian. The operations of retrieval here met with an undisguised reluctance to cooperate on the part of the Bedouins. The *Mufettish el-Ermen* ("Inspector of the Armenians," as was nicknamed by the native population) had sometimes to make use of strong-arm tactics to convince tribal chiefs to give up the Armenians they were holding.[114] Between June and August 1919, Herian succeeded in sending no fewer than 533 women and children back to Aleppo.[115] He also carried out missions in the vicinity of Mosul, where he recovered hundreds of people, including 400 orphans admitted to the orphanage in Bakuba.[116]

In 1919, on the initiative of the French military authorities, Armenian investigators were sent to Upper Mesopotamia in order to continue looking for captive Armenians there. Levon Ajemian, the former Persian consul in Aleppo, was thus charged with recovering the hostages held in Ras ul-Ayn and Nisibin.[117]

On the eve of the Treaty of Sèvres in July 1920, the Constantinople Patriarchate estimated the number of orphans still living scattered throughout the Syrian and Mesopotamian deserts, among the Jibur and Shammar tribes, at 5,800.[118] The Patriarchate did not know how many young women were still to be found there. The children were taken in hand by, notably, Armenian institutions[119] and American Near East Relief, which opened a number of orphanages in Aleppo, Beirut, and Jerusalem.[120] The Armenian General Benevolent Union in particular made a commitment to create shelters for young women and their children that were assigned the task of rehabilitating these deeply traumatized people.[121]

The Recovery and Maintenance of Women and Children Found in Asia Minor and Constantinople

In letter written in January 1920 – that is, more than a year after the armistice was signed, the Armenian Patriarchate put the number of orphans cared for by its services at around 100,000; another 100,000 women and children, it estimated, were still being held captive.[122] A few months later, it estimated that 6,000 women and children were still being held against their will in the regions of Constantinople, Ismit, Bursa, and Eskişehir; 2,000 in Karahisar; 1,500 in the district of Bolu; 3,000 in Konya; 5,000 in Kastamonu; 2,000 in Trebizond; 3,500 in Sıvas; 3,500 in Kayseri; 3,000 in Erzerum; 25,000 in Dyarbekir-Mardin; 3,000 in Harput; and 5,000 in the vilayets of Bitlis and Van.[123] The Patriarchate had to organize, in short order, a relief effort for the refugees concentrated in Istanbul while also opening orphanages. To run so vast an undertaking, it founded a *Vorpakhnam* (Committee for Orphan Relief) and a *Darakrelots getronagan hantsnazhoghov* (Central Committee for Deportees), which together created, in mid-May 1919, a *Azkayin khnamadarutiun* (National Relief Mission), whose operations were financed out of the revenues generated by a newly instituted national tax. Patriarch Zaven observes in his memoirs that the means of the Constantinople and Smyrna Armenian communities, the only ones that were still organized, did not suffice to cover the considerable costs of the program to rehabilitate the survivors.[124] Fortunately, American Near East Relief took an active part in the relief operations not only in Syria, but also in Asia Minor, notably by opening orphanages in Harput and Sıvas that cared for several thousand children.[125] The *Azkayin Khnamadarutiun* itself founded some fifteen orphanages in Constantinople in 1919–20:

1) the central orphanage in Kuleli, on the Asian side of the city, which was opened in July 1920 and cared for 1,000 children, on average;
2) the orphanage in Beylerbey, also on the city's Asian side, a former training school for policemen and gendarmes requisitioned by the English that provided shelter to some 250 children;
3) the orphanage attached to the National Surp Prgich Hospital in Yedi-Kule, which took in 300 children, many of whom were ill;
4) the girls' orphanage in Beşiktaş (120 wards);
5) the girls' orphanage in Kumkapı (100 girls);
6) the girls' orphanage in Uskudar (100 girls);
7) the girls' orphanage in Hasköy (130 girls);
8) the girls' orphanage and trade school in Arnavud Köy (100 young women);
9) the girls' orphanage in Balat (100 girls);
10) the girls' orphanage in Kuruçeşme (50 girls);
11) the orphanage for boys and girls in Makriköy (attached to the Bezazian middle school, with 80 wards);
12) and 13) the orphanages of the Sisters of the Immaculate Conception in Pera and Samatia (500 girls);
14) the agricultural orphanage in Armash (60 boys).

The *Tbrotsaser* Association took responsibility for hundreds of other orphans who were placed with foster families. Two more orphanages were run by the Lord Mayor's fund, a British charitable organization (later transferred to Corfu) and a Swiss-Armenian organization.[126]

All of these institutions admitted children found in the orphanages created by the Young Turk regime or in Muslim families, in the capital or the provinces. A 30 December 1918 French intelligence report provides an initial list of more than 50 orphans who were being held in Istanbul or the vicinity, as a rule by officers or state officials, or even by pashas. These orphans generally had forenames indicating that they had been converted. Thus, Azaduhi/Ayşe, a girl of around ten years of age, was living in the home of Cemal Bey at 31 Bekmez Tarlasi Street in Kadiköy. Sometimes (see no. 24) these captives were young women "married" to an officer whose father had killed the parents of his Armenian daughter-in-law with his own hands.[127]

The situations of these children and young women held in Turkish homes were extremely varied. While some of them were sexual objects, others were very officially married; still others were simply domestics or were treated like the children of the family. Alarmed by the arrival of the British, certain families spontaneously handed over the children whom they had been holding. According to Patriarch Zaven, the English high commissioner played a pivotal role in the search for these orphans.[128] However, the Armenian authorities themselves had to organize to carry out the rescue missions, somewhat like the groups operating in Transjordan, Syria, and Mesopotamia.

The group charged with conducting these operations was led by a young man, Arakel Chakrian, a former chemistry professor at the University of Istanbul. In the months following the armistice, he recovered no fewer than 750 children from state orphanages and Turkish homes in the capital.[129] Registers that came into the possession of the Patriarchal authorities seem to attest the existence of an organized system since they list the original names, place of origin, and new identities of the Armenian children who had been entrusted to Turkish families.[130] In other words, there certainly existed an official adoption program and, alongside it, unregulated kidnappings.

The Patriarchate's initiatives were soon the subject of complaints from the Turkish authorities, who argued in particular that the children taken from households were "true Turks." The High Commission consequently decided to create a "neutral home" in which the children involved in doubtful cases would be temporarily lodged, pending the results of investigations into their origins. This home was co-administered by two women, one Armenian, the other Turkish. According to statistics compiled by the Armenian Patriarchate, around 3,000 children were thus recovered in the space of three years; it proved impossible to locate or identify 1,000 to 2,000 others.[131]

In early June 1919, a vehement polemic sprang up in the capital's newspapers around the question of these children. It merits close attention, for it was certainly initiated, as the tone of the discourse attests, by Young Turk circles. An initial, anonymous article, "The Patriarchate's Mistreated Children," which appeared on 3 June 1919 in the daily *Ileri*,[132] was the opening shot in a smear campaign aimed at the Armenian authorities; it indicated that Unionist activity was again on the increase in the capital. "We reported," *Ileri* wrote,

> that two hundred twenty Muslim orphans who had been living in Kayseri were brought to Constantinople and turned over to the Patriarchate. Yesterday, we obtained very unpleasant information on this subject: the Patriarchate's staff has made energetic efforts to make these children admit that they are of Armenian origin, subjecting its victims to very harsh treatment, with the result that many were bruised and battered. The staff told these children that all Muslims had been killed, and that they had no choice but to agree to accept Armenian nationality and would be killed if they refused. One of our editors, who saw some of the children in question, observed that there were

marks on their bodies and that their faces were covered with wounds. Only forty-two of the children insisted that they were Turks, while the others, yielding to these threats, were carried off. The medical report on them affirms that the children who had been beaten required medical treatment and had to be hospitalized. We would like to know what measures the government plans to take in the face of facts like these.[133]

The reports of death threats and other forms of abuse to which the Patriarchate is supposed to have resorted to bring these "Turkish" orphans to convert is reminiscent of the Turkism in which CUP cadres were steeped. The outrageous nature of the accusations offers a rather faithful reflection of the state of public opinion. The restitution of children converted during the genocide was perceived as a serious blow to the Turkish nation.

As proof of what it said, *Ileri* presented the case of a young woman of 22, "Jemile Hanum," who had been placed in the "Neutral Home" on the presumption that she was Armenian. According to the newspaper, "to convince her to agree that she was Armenian, propagandists promised to give her in marriage to a rich Greek," but Jemile "categorically refused this offer." The author of the article asked, in conclusion, "by what right Armenians strive to Christianize a young Muslim woman of twenty-two, certainly old enough to have complete freedom of conscience."[134] It seems safe to assume that the fate of this unfortunate woman moved the paper's readers and helped convince them that they were the victims of oppression brought to bear by "the" Armenians. In updated form, this discourse manifestly sought to prolong the campaign to stigmatize the Armenian population launched in 1915. It confirms the cynicism of certain circles, which cast the "Turkish nation" in the role of victim.

A 5 June article by Süleyman Nazıf, a cousin of Ziya Gökalp's and one of the CUP cadres charged with reorganizing the party,[135] rules out all doubt about the fact that this was a campaign orchestrated by *Karakol* or one of its satellite organizations.[136] In the article, the Young Turk leader describes the "tragic story" of a 12-year-old boy originally from Şabinkarahisar living in the orphanage in Ortaköy who says that his name is Salem. The child was supposedly first admitted to the orphanage in Konya and then brought to Constantinople. "When they arrived in Haydarpaşa," Nazıf writes,

they were received by a certain number of Armenians, men and women. The Muslim children, despite their innocent protests and tears, were led off with the Armenian children. For these children, the orphanage in Shishli became a place of temptations and, at the same time, tortures. Young six-year-old and seven-year-old children, tempted by cakes and grapes, said that they were Armenians. These children were petted and given a rug on which to sleep. Those who did not wish to renounce their religion were beaten and deprived of food; they were placed on a hard sofa and tortured. There is no doubt about these facts. These children, boys and girls, aged from six to sixteen, raised their teary, trembling voices and related their misadventures with expressions of pain and revolt. It would be impossible to overestimate the sentiments of faith and amour-propre that have developed in so striking a fashion in these tender, cultivated hearts. They have already brought their martyrdom to the attention of the pubic and demanded the release of those of their comrades whom it has not yet been possible to liberate from pitiless hands. Among those comrades, there existed not only the sentiment that they were brothers in religion, but also blood brothers. "I got away, but my brother and my sister are still in their hands," some of them said, sighing. The merciful Armenian mission that is supposedly seeing to feeding these children and watching over their welfare does not have the time to concern itself with their physical conditions of existence, absorbed as it is by discussions of faith and religion. Disease, such as leprosy, eye ailments, and so on, from which the Muslims are suffering, continue to consume their victims and prolong their ordeal. Some may imagine that we are exaggerating, but the affair has been referred to the police and an official investigation is underway. We would be happy to see the foreigners in our city take an interest in these matters, if only for humanitarian reasons. It would then be possible to give the world a fair, accurate idea of the Turks and their enemies. Can the Armenians, who broadcast laments about their suffering to the four corners of the globe in order to attain their goal, prove their innocence in the court before which these small, innocent children have arraigned them? If so, we will drop all our complaints and admit all the allegations.[137]

To round off his demonstration, Süleyman Nazıf mentioned one of his visits to the orphanage in Ayntura, in November 1918. Armenian children "with no one to support them ... were fed, comforted, and educated in this institution," he said, "which was spotlessly clean"; this had not failed to "strengthen" his "love ... and respect for his race."[138] The underlying sources of his discourse recall the accusations of ritual murder of children of which anti-Semites in the same period accused the Jews.

In the 6 June 1919 edition of *Jagadamard*, an Armenian editorialist wrote: "from the moment that *Alemdar*, too, joined *Tasvir*, *Ileri*, *Hadisat*, and so on, all that remains is to shout: continue, gentlemen, to lie, cheat, massacre and loot, for, in that way, you will certainly be able to save what is left of your fatherland." The 6 June 1919 issue of *Zhamanag* remarked that "those who invent or echo all these lies and slanders are the same people who, yesterday, accused the Armenians of massacring millions of Muslims."[139]

Thus, one sees that, far from turning over a new leaf, Young Turk circles continued to produce Turkist propaganda and clung firmly to the positions developed by the Unionist Central Committee in 1915. As on other issues, such as that of abandoned property or the indictment of the party cadres who were the authors of the genocide, they apparently had no intention of yielding to the claims of the victims or the victors.

Chapter 6

The Great Powers and the Question of "Crimes Against Humanity"

In a joint declaration published on 24 May 1915, the members of the Triple Entente denounced the first massacres carried out in the rural areas of the vilayet of Van ("this new crime against humanity and civilization committed by Turkey") and warned "the Sublime Porte that they [would] hold all members of the Turkish government as well as civil servants who participate in the massacres of Armenians personally responsible."[1] Although this warning was issued in wartime, it is indisputably historic because it introduces the concept of a "crime against humanity" into the juridical lexicon. It is also innovative in that it points to a government's collective responsibility for a mass crime. That said, it is not at all certain that France and Great Britain were aware, when they issued this declaration, that they were confronting a crime of modernity inspired by a nationalist ideology. It is even probable, given the early date of the warning, that they had in mind the kind of traditional massacres that had been committed under Abdülhamid.

At war's end, the victors had a much more precise idea of the events and, of course, wondered how they should treat acts of this sort and of such scope at the political and legal levels. Great Britain, which had negotiated the armistice of Mudros virtually single-handedly, wondered from early October 1918 on what clauses should be included in the peace conditions. Initially, it was above all intent on obtaining guarantees that there would be no "future massacres," particularly in the eastern provinces of Asia Minor and the Caucasus, where it did not have significant military forces.[2] While strategic objectives continued to be the top priorities for Britain and France, they also contemplated instituting a system to apprehend war criminals and bring them to justice.[3] The British high commissioner in Constantinople, Admiral Calthorpe, rapidly created an Armenian-Greek committee to help him assemble files in support of the indictments of the Young Turk criminals.[4] It was, however, in the framework of the peace conference that the procedure to be used in order to bring members of the CUP to justice had to be decided.

The Work of the Committees of the Preliminary Peace Conference

From the outset, beginning in January 1919, the Preliminary Peace Conference set up several specialized committees charged with examining complex questions and reporting their conclusions.[5] On 3 February 1919, a Committee on the Responsibility of the Authors of the War and on Sanctions was created. It engendered in turn several subcommittees: 1) the Subcommittee on Criminal Matters, which was supposed to determine the acts, with their proofs, that led to the war, as well as the acts committed during it; and 2) the Subcommittee on Responsibility for the War, the task of which was to study "violations of the laws and customs of war and the laws of humanity." Another study group, the Committee on Reparations and Compensation, set up on 25 January 1919, was charged, as its name indicates, with evaluating the material damages caused by the war.[6]

The Committee on the Responsibility of the Authors of the War and on Sanctions, which is of particular interest to us here, announced its intentions from its very first working session, held on 3 February. Its provisional president, André Tardieu, recalled that the committee was to "translate the principles of justice, equality, and peace into acts." How, he exclaimed,

> can we turn a deaf ear to the appeal that comes from the graves to punish the guilty and protect humanity from a repetition of the crime? The committee must study the facts, using the victims' accounts, in order to establish that the guilty acted with premeditation and violated treaties, both those governing human rights and those establishing the laws of war. The committee's objective is to find those responsible for the crimes committed, that is to say, those who organized them and those who carried them out; finally, it is to establish the rules in accordance with which sanctions will be defined and applied.[7]

Beyond "human rights" and the "laws of war," the jurists present were doubtless aware that they had to establish norms for "new" crimes. As at the two Conferences of The Hague (held in 1899 and 1907), the jurists understood that, as the famous "Martens Clause" puts it, they were confronted with "cases not covered by the customary dispositions of the law" because they went beyond the war crimes that had already been codified. On the committee, which was chaired by the American Secretary of State, Robert Lansing, were Nicolas Politis, the Greek foreign minister, who was also a jurist, and a general rapporteur, the Belgian Edouard Rolin-Jaequemyns; they were seconded by Sir Ernest Pollock and M. Amelio.[8] Placed under the authority of this group, the third subcommittee (known as the "Committee of Fifteen"), which was charged with examining violations of the laws and customs of war, held six sessions between 14 February and 8 March 1919. Very quickly, a unanimous decision was reached to demand that sanctions be applied for the crimes committed and the violation of the laws and customs of war defined at The Hague.[9]

At the 7 February 1919 session of the Subcommittee on Criminal Matters, Nicolas Politis took the floor to spell out that "criminal matters" should be understood in the more general sense of criminal acts. As an example, he cited "the massacres organized by the Turkish authorities in Armenia" that did not enter "into the categories covered by the provisions of the Penal Code." The Subcommittee therefore had to look for "all acts that should be condemned, even if they do not constitute crimes in the proper sense of the word; one of its tasks would be to define, for the conference, the limits on persecution and de facto criminality or guilt."[10]

The Committee on Responsibility defined, in Point 3 of its 5 March 1919 report, the "acts constituting violations of the laws and customs of war," referring to norms already established in Section IV E of The Hague Convention of 1907: systematic terrorism; murders and massacres (Article 46); torture (Article 46); the use of civilians as human shields (Article 46); [violations of the] honor of women (Article 46); confiscation of private property (Article 53); pillage; collective punishments, including taking and executing hostages (Article 50); contributions without written orders, receipts, or a basis in law (Article 51); requisitions leading to forced participation in military operations (Article 52); confiscation of property belonging to communities or educational and charitable institutions (Article 56); wanton destruction of public or private property; deportation and forced labor (Article 46); and executions of civilians on false allegations of war crimes.[11] To punish these infractions, the report advocated, in its resolutions, creation of a "High Court."[12]

The memorandum presented on 1 March 1919 by J.B. Scott on behalf of the "Committee of Fifteen" identified questions hitherto ignored or that had been only inadequately taken into account in international conventions: 1) massacre and mutilation of human beings; 2) cases in which the methods of destroying human life and property are deemed unjustifiable; 3) the need to utilize physical force in order to guarantee national security or the preservation of national rights; 4) the reprehensible character of acts of cruelty is a question of degree that cannot be accurately determined by a fixed line of demarcation; 5) the criterion of guilt in the accomplishment of an act that is inhuman or improper; 6) the assertion, by the author of an act, that that act was necessary for military reasons does not exonerate him of guilt; 7) an arbitrary act is a crime against civilization and does not admit of any excuse; 8) it is a question of determining to what extent such an act is criminal and the improper motives that inspired it.[13]

The work of these committees bears witness to a desire to refine existing legal categories or develop new concepts. However, the jurists were hard put to abstract from "acts constituting violations of the laws and customs of war" – that is, from the context – in order to perceive crimes committed against civilian populations as autonomous categories.

To a certain extent, the 14 March 1919 memorandum submitted by the Greek delegation perceived this problem in exposing its grievances and distinguishing "common-law crimes, such as murder, rape, arson, theft, or kidnapping" from "public-law crimes," such as "the maintenance of famines, deportation, ill treatment, and 'crimes against the laws and customs of war,' such as mass deportations and illegal abductions."[14]

The memorandum that the Armenian delegation submitted to the peace conference through the intermediary of the Greek delegation – the Armenians had not been invited to participate in this phase of the conference's work – stressed that the object of the crime that had been committed against them had been the liquidation of the entire civilian population. The Armenian delegation accordingly insisted that those responsible for these massacres be judged by the Allied governments in accordance with the category into which they fell: those who conceived of the plan, those who issued the orders or organized the killings, those who directed the massacres, and those who carried them out. For reasons of principle, the Armenian memorandum contested the judicial procedure put in place by the Ottoman government and "earnestly" besought "the Allied governments to take the task of rendering justice into their own hands as soon as possible, so as to forestall the new, terrible catastrophe threatening the Christian populations in the East"[15] as a result of the operations conducted by Mustafa Kemal. In its final, 29 March 1919 report, the Committee on Responsibility laid out its views on 1) the responsibility of the authors of the war; 2) violations of the laws and customs of war; 3) personal responsibility; 4) the constitution of an appropriate court and its procedures; and 5) questions related to the creation of a High Court.[16] On the third point, the report concluded: "all people from enemy countries, however important their positions, regardless of rank, chiefs of state included, who are responsible for infractions of the laws and customs of war or the laws of humanity, are liable to legal prosecution."[17] The principal innovation in the project, of course, was constituted by the fact that state officials, including chiefs of state, could also be punished.

The problem of choosing the competent jurisdiction for this type of crime occasioned the proposal to create a "High Court" empowered to judge "charges brought against individuals from enemy countries, civilian or military authorities." The project envisaged the formation of a court comprising American, English, French, Italian, and Japanese magistrates, as well as magistrates from smaller countries chosen from among "the members of their national military or civilian courts or tribunals, already existing or specially created."[18] The report suggested, furthermore, that "no national court should proceed to judge an individual, whoever he may be, designated to be judged by the High Court." Finally, it recommended that the peace treaty stipulate

that the enemy governments must, even after peace is declared, recognize the jurisdiction of the national courts and the High Court, and that all enemy individuals presumed guilty of crimes against the laws and customs of war and the laws of humanity shall be excluded from any amnesty accepted by the belligerents and that the governments to which these individuals belong shall engage to deliver them up to be judged.[19]

Rules were also proposed that would require "enemy governments" to communicate the "names of persons entrusted with a command or a charge"; "all orders, instructions, copies of orders, reports, and documents presumed to have been produced or executed in violation of the laws and customs of war or the laws of humanity"; and "information tending to indicate which individuals committed these acts or operations, or were responsible for them."[20]

The work of the committees and their conclusions, while they did not set out openly and exclusively to sanction the crimes committed against the Greek, Armenians, Syriac, or even Belgian civilian populations, were certainly influenced by the information at the disposal of the committee members. A few points even seem to have been inspired by the Armenian experience.

The "Council of Four" and the Trial of the Young Turk Criminals

Obviously, it was incumbent on the "Council of Four" – made up of Woodrow Wilson, David Lloyd George, Georges Clemenceau, and Vittorio Emanuele Orlando – who took de facto the decisions that the peace conference would impose on the defeated countries, to translate these legal principles into political practice. From 24 March to 28 June 1919, these men daily exchanged ideas on the future of the world.[21] While the national interests of the four powers comprised the basic subject of their discussions, legal and even moral questions were not altogether absent from them. In the 2 April session, the question of responsibility was raised and there was a discussion of the principle of creating a court of justice as proposed in the conclusions of the Committee on Responsibility. Lloyd George accepted the principle of such a court, stating that he had no objection "to the idea that the court should be created by the League of Nations." "If we want," he added, " the League of Nations to have the power we hope it will, it must show from the outset that it is capable of punishing crime."[22] When the question of "punishable" crimes was broached again, on 8 April, the British prime minister suggested distinguishing between two categories of punishable acts: "first, criminal acts properly so called; secondly, general orders in violation of human rights." Wilson took what he regarded as a more pragmatic stance: "I fear," he said, "that it will be hard to punish those who are truly guilty, for nothing is easier than to destroy the trace of orders given. I fear that we will not have sufficient evidence."[23] In spring 1919, the Allies were aware that they would not find it easy to indict criminals who had taken care to wipe out the traces of their crimes.

In mid-June, the "Council of Ten" had to deal with the unforeseen arrival of an Ottoman delegation. It was invited to express its views on 17 June 1919. This first contact is particularly interesting because it allows us to observe the positions adopted by the Istanbul government and the reactions it called forth from the "four." Wilson noted, during a meeting of the four, that "a sort of general protest of the kind we just heard is absolutely worthless. The Turkish delegates say: 'Do not judge on the basis of what happened in the past few years, but on that of the whole history of the Ottoman Empire.'" "I believe," Wilson observed, "that that would be still worse" – a remark that speaks volumes about the Allies' opinion of Turkey and its past. What most irritated Wilson, however, was the discourse developed by the delegation in order to exonerate itself of guilt for past events. The delegation had in fact insisted that "the tyrannical government of a single party is responsible for the errors and crimes committed;

we are innocent." As Wilson saw it, "all they did was complain. They were the ones who asked to come here to present their case and that is all they had to say. It doesn't amount to anything." Lloyd George suggested that they be given a response. Georges Clemenceau even proposed that they "do so in writing"; in his view, it was necessary that the Turkish delegates "leave with an answer to their document, which is a veritable confession."[24] About the Turkish delegation's memorandum, the Council of Four noted that it "glorified Turkey's past, recalling that Turkey had been able to create and administer a great empire and that it had respected the existence of every religious community." Lloyd George exclaimed about this subject: "This delegation and its memorandum are good jokes." He was followed by Wilson, who added: "I have never seen anything stupider." "It is," said Lloyd George, "the best possible proof of the Turks' utter political incapacity."[25]

The strategy of the liberal Ottoman government, which sought to put all the blame for the liquidation of the Armenians on the Young Turk Central Committee and to present the policy implemented vis-a-vis the minorities as an accident, had obviously not convinced the "four." Later, during one of their final discussions, which took place on 25 June 1919, Lloyd George showed that he harbored no further illusions about Turkey's intentions: "If we tell the Turks that 'from 1 July on, Armenia is no longer yours,' they will immediately send people there to start massacring again."[26]

A few months later in March 1920, a "Committee for the Protection of the Minorities in Turkey," created by the League of Nations, presented a series of recommendations that it suggested should be inserted among the clauses of the peace treaty with Turkey.[27] In an accompanying letter, the delegates emphasized "the experience of the armistice and, especially, the recent massacres of Armenians clearly show that there is a need for certain guarantees for the effective performance in the interior of paper pledges signed by the Government of Constantinople."[28] Certain of the articles proposed summed up the problems facing the genocide survivors and put forward proposals. Article 3 reads:

> In view of the fact that, from 1 November 1914 to the date of signature of the armistice, a terrorist regime was in existence in the Ottoman Empire, and given that no conversions to Islam could take place under normal circumstances, no conversion that took place between those two dates is acknowledged as valid ... The Ottoman government shall assist in every possible way the recovery of men, women, and children wholly or partially of non-Muslim origin who have embraced Islam since 1 November 1914 and have been reclaimed by their communities or families. It shall also, by virtue of the present treaty, acknowledge all rights to visit or search either private homes or institutions of any kind whatsoever for the purpose of looking for missing persons. These searches shall be conducted by a representative of the interested community and an official of the Ottoman government, in the presence of a delegate or representative of the League of Nations (see Article 12).[29]

Article 5 reads as follows:

> The Ottoman government acknowledges the inequitable nature of the 1915 law on abandoned property (*Emvali metruke*) and the related regulations and declares them null and void, in the past as well as the future. It solemnly pledges to facilitate, as fully as possible, the return to their homes of Ottoman subjects of non-Turkish races who have been violently driven from them since 1 August 1914, whether for fear of being massacred or by all other forms of constraint, and also to facilitate the resumption of their business or commerce. It acknowledges that the real estate or moveable assets of said Ottoman subjects of non-Turkish races or of the communities to which these

subjects belong must, to the extent that they can be discovered, regardless of who has possession of them, be restored with all possible speed, free of all charges or liens to which they may have been subject and without compensation of any sort for the present owners of said property, transactions between the present owner and the seller of the property excepted... The Ottoman government admits the creation of arbitration commissions designated by the League of Nations or its representative (as provided for by Article 12) whenever that shall be deemed necessary. Each such commission shall be composed of a representative of the Ottoman government, a representative of the community affected or one of whose members has been affected, and a president appointed by the representative of the League of Nations... These commissions of arbitration shall have power to mandate... the removal of all persons who, after inquiry, shall be acknowledged to have taken an active part in massacres or expulsions, or to have precipitated them, with specification of the measures to be taken as to his property, including the possibility of ordering the transfer of all goods and assets having belonged to any and all members of a community who have died or disappeared since 1 August 1914 without leaving heirs to said community rather than to the state.... No decision by the Ottoman judiciary or administrative authorities can contravene the decisions of the commission of arbitration.[30]

Article 6 further suggests recalling that it is absolutely necessary that the empire grant "all Ottoman nationals equal rights before the law."[31] These measures, which sought to impose the rehabilitation of the survivors, show that, 17 months after the armistice, the Ottoman government and Turkish society had, far from moving in the direction of reform, refused to resolve basic issues, and that the Allies found themselves facing a "front of refusal" organized by the Young Turk network, Kemalists included. Indeed, the British high commissioner, John de Robeck, notes in a 17 March 1920 dispatch to London that the law on abandoned property adopted by the Ottoman government in January has not produced "satisfactory results," and that he accordingly plans to recommend including these questions in the peace treaty currently being drawn up.[32]

As for the punishment of the Young Turk criminals, the February–March 1920 London Conference suggested that the Allies submit to the Ottoman government draft articles on sanctions for inclusion in a future peace treaty. The government would recognize, in the first article of such a treaty, the freedom to try people accused of acts contrary to the laws or customs of war before the military courts. In the second article, it would further pledge to "deliver up all individuals deemed responsible for the massacres that, in the course of the war, were committed on former Ottoman territory and to recognize the right of the Allied Powers to designate the Tribunal charged with judging these crimes."[33] In March 1920, the Allied powers were still advertising their intention to bring those responsible for crimes "contrary to the laws or customs of war and the laws of humanity" before an International High Court. In an 11 March 1920 letter, Jules Cambon, the French foreign minister, submitted "draft articles" completing the propositions made in London to the British prime minister, Lloyd George, "to be inserted in the conditions for peace and submitted to Turkey." Cambon pointed out to Lloyd George that Article 2b had been drawn up separately "in case the Supreme Allied Council intends to include, among the said conditions for peace, a clause mandating a search for those responsible for the massacres committed in Asiatic Turkey." It would seem to follow that all were agreed about Articles 1 and 2, but that the Frenchmen contemplated adopting a more active policy mandating the pursuit of fugitive criminals. Article 4 even looked ahead to something like an obligation to extradite criminals, or to "take all necessary measures to ensure, at the request of the Allied powers and in accord with them, that they are prosecuted and punished." Article 2b further stipulated that the "Allied powers reserve the right to designate the court to be charged with judging the ... accused. Should the League of Nations have created, at the appropriate time, a court with the competency to judge the aforementioned massacres, the Allied Powers reserve the right to bring the accused aforesaid before this court."[34]

Ultimately, the Allies sent the Ottoman government, on 11 May 1920, a draft treaty that, generally speaking, contained the points we have just reviewed. In its response, the Ottoman government expressed, in the chapter devoted to "responsibility," a viewpoint that rather clearly reveals its line of defense:

> Turkey acknowledges the principle that there exists an obligation to make amends for damages resulting from acts that violate human rights ... If, contrary to its will and, no less, its patent interests, the Turkish people were dragged into the international conflagration, this was due to an oligarchy that took its orders from abroad. And if inhuman acts for which there is no excuse were perpetrated, they are entirely imputable to the same political clan. They are in no way a manifestation of religious fanaticism, but exclusively the work of a revolutionary faction that wrought havoc in Turkey ... The Turkish people, however, even as it acknowledges this responsibility toward human rights, has the right to distance itself morally from acts that it vigorously condemns. To make reparations for unjustly caused damages and to prevent them from occurring again – such is the twofold obligation recognized by Turkey.[35]

This minimalist approach, which sought to put responsibility on the shoulders of the Unionist leaders, who were supposed to have been manipulated by Germany to boot, sparked a response from the Allies, who were apparently not disposed to clemency. On behalf of all of them, the president of the peace conference, Lloyd George, sent a stinging reply to the "observations" of the Ottoman delegation on 16 July:

> The Ottoman government seems to be of the opinion that its responsibility for the war is less than that of its allies and that it can, consequently, expect to be treated less severely. The Allies cannot accept this pretension ... It would seem that the Ottoman Delegation has not taken the full measure of the losses and suffering that Turkey's intervention has caused mankind ... The Allies see clearly that the time has come to put an end, for good and all, to Turkey's domination over other nations. The history of the relations between the Porte and the Great Powers in the long years before the war is nothing other than a series of repeated but vain attempts to put an end to the atrocities in Bulgaria, Macedonia, Armenia, and elsewhere, atrocities that have shocked and revolted the conscience of all mankind ... In the past twenty years, the Armenians have been massacred under unspeakably barbarous circumstances. During the war, the Ottoman government's exploits in the way of massacres, deportations, and ill treatment of prisoners of war transcended even their previous accomplishments in crimes of this kind. It is estimated that, since 1914, the Ottoman Government has massacred, on the flimsy pretext of a putative revolt, 800,000 Armenians, men, women, and children ... The Turkish Government did not only fail to perform its duty to protect its subjects of non-Turkish races against plunder, violence, and murder; there is a great deal of proof that it took it upon itself to organize and lead attacks of the most savage kind on a population that it ought to have protected.[36]

These exchanges show that, on the eve of the conclusion of the Treaty of Sèvres, the Turkish government and the Allies had irreconcilable positions.[37]

The memorandum that the grand vizier, Damad Ferid Pasha, presented to the peace conference did not reveal any fundamental changes in the Turkish positions. Ferid began his address by admitting that, "in the course of the war, virtually the entire civilized world was troubled by the stories of the crimes that the Turks are supposed to have committed. I do not wish – perish the thought – to make light of these crimes, which were such as to make the human conscience tremble forever. I am even less inclined to diminish the guilt of the authors of this great tragedy." The grand vizier was, however, quick to add that he wanted to "show the world, offering proof of what [he said], who was really responsible for these dreadful crimes." He "deplored the murder of a large number of his Christian compatriots," but also "the murder of Muslims properly so called."[38] To make such a confession in public, even with restrictions, called for a certain political courage that, be it added, immediately cost Ferid Pasha his post. It doubtless constitutes, down to our own day, the fullest confession to have come from any Turkish authority whatsoever. At the same time, this confession takes up the thesis of the limited guilt of the CUP leaders, who, according to Ferid, supposedly also perpetrated mass crimes against "Muslims properly so called."

The British and the Question of the Young Turk Criminals

In circumstances prevailing in the first postwar years, whether an international court would be created depended largely on the political will of the Allies, particularly Britain and France. As soon as their High Commission had been set up in Constantinople, the British demonstrated their resolve to bring the Young Turk criminals to justice. On 18 January 1919, Admiral Arthur Calthorpe informed the Sublime Porte that his government was "resolved that those responsible for the massacres of the Armenians be duly punished."[39] It would even appear that the British Crown was determined to pursue its logic to the end, with or without the international community, by punishing the criminals individually and collective punishing the Ottoman Empire by dismembering it.[40]

Translating this political will into deeds, to be sure, called for the creation of an authority capable of conducting the requisite legal action. As we have seen, the work of the committees and subcommittees that had operated within the framework of the Preliminary Peace Conference from February 1919 on culminated in a recommendation that a "High Court" be created and placed under the auspices of the League of Nations. To the extent that one can judge on the basis of the available sources, the British were not hostile to this idea, which would have made it possible for the first time in history to try political leaders for criminal acts perpetrated against a segment of their own population. The Armenian-Greek Committee working alongside the High Commission was supposed to second the British Crown's efforts. Admiral Calthorpe, however, had clearly requested that the Armenian and Greek authorities follow the recommendations of the Foreign Office and restrict themselves to identifying Turkish criminals and performing investigative tasks.[41] The recommended procedure suggested that the arrests should be carried out "in every case" by the Turkish authorities, on their own initiative, "on our formal demand made in writing" or on "our verbal suggestions made through" Mr. Ryan (a British intelligence officer). On Calthorpe's account, 30 CUP members were apprehended "for complicity in massacres either by direct or indirect action," while others were arrested at the demand of his services.[42] Calthorpe also reminded London that, in compliance with instructions from the Foreign Office, he had demanded in a 5 February telegram (no. 233) that the Turkish government turn over the "prisoners selected by us for detention in Malta," but that the government had not responded to his demand because it was then in the process of inaugurating their trials before the court-martial.[43]

All these apparently insignificant details show that the British authorities did not wish to see a Turkish court-martial take on the task of judging war criminals; they simply wanted Constantinople to collaborate with them in furnishing evidence and apprehending suspects. It is even probable that it was the fact that the first trial against those who had organized the massacres in Yozgat had already begun on 5 February 1919, which induced the Foreign Office to demand that the Turkish authorities turn over their prisoners so that they could be transferred to Malta. In early February, London envisaged nothing less than the creation of a "High Court," while Istanbul was manifestly determined to do all in its power to avoid one, so that it could conduct the trials as it saw fit. It could thus validate its thesis that responsibility was limited to the Young Turk party, thereby exonerating the Ottoman state.

Several factors suggest that that the Turkish government was then trying to make its judicial project seem credible in order the more effectively to thwart the Allies' plans. The fact that it asked countries such as Spain, the Netherlands, Denmark, Sweden, and Norway to send it two judges who could serve on the Istanbul court-martial is one good indication of this.[44] It is quite as revealing that the European countries politely refused the Turkish request, whose political implications they had probably understood. It is not, on the other hand, known why the British waited until May 1919 to bring the accused back to Turkey and set the first trial in motion. Moreover, Admiral Calthorpe notes in a message that he sent to Balfour on 26 March 1919 that two members of the investigating committee were implicated "in the massacres of Armenians."[45] In other words, certain judges were not in a position to preside over legal proceedings of this type or, again, the administration was still under the control of Young Turk networks. Indeed, in August 1919 the high commissioner concluded that the trial conducted by the "Turkish" court-martial was nothing more than "une farce et une insulte à notre prestige."[46] He went so far as to call the judges who presided over the trial "incompetents" and the "methods of guarding the offenders so inadequate."[47] He also noted, however, that his French colleague was of the opinion that "the trial and punishment of these offenders was a matter for Turkish Authorities under the supervision and control of the Allied Military Authorities."[48] Thus, it is probable that the British plans to have the Young Turk criminals tried before a High Court were brought to naught by France's lack of enthusiasm for the idea. The jurists in the Foreign Office were also reluctant to create British courts martial in the occupied zone, and authorized judging suspects in only two categories – those who interfered with the application of clauses of the armistice and those supposed to have shown insubordination toward British officers. The jurists of the Crown thought, on the other hand, that these courts martial could not judge people accused of "outrages to Armenians or other subject races both in Turkey and Transcaucasia" – stipulations that bore on crimes committed after the Armistice.[49]

The increasing frequency with which suspects were released from prison – 41 people under indictment were freed on 22 May 1919 – and escapes occurred with official complicity convinced the British high commissioner to react. He had proposed that his government deport the criminals held by the court-martial in a "safe" place."[50] On 28 May, the Young Turk cadres were put aboard a war ship and sent to Malta.[51] This operation led to the arrests of several dozen more Young Turk criminals, who were also deported to the British island. It seems reasonable to suppose that London proceeded in this fashion in order to show that it would no longer put up with what increasingly seemed to it to be a "farce" undermining its credibility. The British could hardly reconcile themselves to the fact that the Turkish authorities were, on the one hand, proceeding to arrest war criminals and, on the other, releasing them from prison – to say nothing of the "escapes" that had certainly been engineered by *Karakol* networks. By stepping in promptly, the British wished to make certain that the Ittihadists would face judgement when the moment came. The Turkish Justice Minister's explanations to the effect that "the English took the Unionist prisoners in hand only because we went about judging them too slowly"[52] were obviously not credible and could not have convinced too many.

What is more, a letter than Admiral Calthorpe wrote Lord Curzon on 21 September 1919 shows that the high commissioner was still studying the case of the "Turks of every degree implicated in the deportations and massacres of Christians during the war." He reminded his superiors that it was of "the great importance of obtaining some guidance as to the intentions of His Majesty's Government and their Allies,"[53] as if the trials of the Young Turk leaders had never taken place. Furthermore, the British were working with the Greek and Armenian committees to amass as many incriminating documents as they could in anticipation of trials of the Young Turk criminals before a high court or some other tribunal.[54] In the course of a debate that took place in the House of Commons on 4 March 1920, the question of the trials of the Turks who had been deported to Malta was raised once again. Certain MPs recalled that the "majority of those interned were implicated in massacres [...] The question of their trial was "under consideration."[55] In an 11 March 1920 cable to Lord Curzon, the high commissioner John de Robeck "recommended for continued detention [in Malta] could not be prosecuted for participation in atrocities but in some cases their return to Constantinople would be inexpedient."[56]

After 18 months, during which the British had left the Turkish authorities with a certain latitude to take initiatives, putting faith in their sense of responsibility, the Allies had come to the conclusion that they could not impose the least peace treaty on Turkey if they left the Young Turkish networks intact. To struggle against the omnipresence of the Young Turks and put an end to their criminal activities in the Anatolian provinces, the British had to cut them off from their bases in the capital by taking military control of it. According to Erik Zürcher, the British had long known that the minister of war was working together with the nationalists; in January 1920, they called for the resignation of Cemal Pasha and Cevad Pasha, the chief of staff. The telegrams exchanged between the War Ministry and the provincial military commanders illustrate the development of Istanbul's collaboration with Anatolia and, more particularly, with *Karakol*, whose liaison officer with the ministry was none other than Colonel Galatalı Şevket. Moreover, the head of *Karakol*, Kara Vasıf, had been communicating directly with Cemal Pasha when Cemal was War Minister.[57] Under these circumstances, the 16 March 1920 Franco-British occupation of the capital by 50,000 men[58] was virtually inevitable, as was the arrest, by the British security services, of Hüseyin Rauf and Kara Vasıf, two of the main leaders of the Ittihad's networks, together with 11 other party leaders including General Cemal Pasha, a former war minister, and Hasan Tahsin, a former vali of Erzerum.[59] Cemal and Tahsin were transferred to Malta, where they were soon followed by Celal Nuri Bey, General Ali Said, Ebuziyazâde Velid Bey, and, most importantly, Süleyman Nazıf Bey.[60]

Later, the 16 May 1922 *Daily Telegraph* published a declaration of Chamberlain's before the House of Commons in which he read two telegrams, dated 10 May 1922, from the British high commissioner in Constantinople. One had been written after a conversation with Dr. Ward, a member of the Near East Relief committee who had just arrived from Harput. In it, the high commissioner reported, "The Turks seem to be acting in accordance with a deliberate plan to get rid of the minorities ... The Turkish official who heads the department of education in Harput told Dr. Ward, in order to illustrate the Turks' incompetence, that they had not done a good job of carrying the massacres through to the end in 1915, but that, this time, they would do things to perfection."[61]

In a 9 April 1924 debate in the House of Commons about the ratification of the Treaty of Lausanne, Lloyd George no doubt felt the need to justify his country's Turkish policy as well as the fact, minimized by the success of the Kemalist movement, that it had finally been dismantled. "We negotiated," he said,

> a series of treaties with Russia, Italy, France, and the Arabs; in all these treaties, it was stipulated that the non-Turkish areas of Asia Minor and European Turkey would be detached from Turkey. I maintain that that was a good policy... Was it a sound decision? I ask the honorable members whether they can show me a single province governed by Turkey whose wealth, population, freedom, happiness, and all that makes a country great and prosperous have not declined under Turkish rule. There is not a single one! Can they name me a single province detached from Turkey in the last fifty or more years that is not richer, more populous, and has not increased in power and prosperity, and, above all, become more free? There is not a single one! That constitutes a serious accusation against an empire.[62]

This statement of Lloyd George's, refocusing the debate on Turkey's incapacity to respect the groups making it up and increase their prosperity barely veils the bitterness of the British politician, who did not succeed in enforcing the principle he evokes and in punishing those responsible for crimes "against human rights."

The 1948 Convention on the Prevention and Punishment of the Crime of Genocide and the Experience of 1919

A number of authors have observed that Raphael Lemkin knew about the crimes committed against the Armenians in the First World War and that he had paid particular attention to the trial of Soghomon Tehlirian.[63] Annette Becker notes, however, that he made no reference to these matters in his seminal work, *Axis Rule in Occupied Europe*, in which he cites "the destruction of Carthage in 146 B.C.; the destruction of Jerusalem by Titus in 72 A.D.; the religion wars of Islam and the Crusades; the massacres of the Albigenses," rounding off his list with the horrors committed by Tamurlane.[64] In an essay published two years later, Lemkin repeated his list of early cases of mass murder. This time, however, he adds: "et plus près de nous encore, celui des Arméniens."[65] He further observes that "There were also diplomatic representations by various states in favor of the Greeks and the Armenians, when the latter were massacred, specifying the obligations which they were committed assuming as for the treatment of their own nationals,"[66] without, however, adding that these crimes were also examined by the jurists of the committees created by the preliminary peace conference. However, in an unpublished talk that he gave in New Haven in 1949, when the convention on the prevention and punishment of genocide was adopted, he observed that "it was only after the extermination of 1,200,000 Armenians during the First World War that the victorious Allies promised to the survivors of this abominable massacre an adequate law and a court. But that did not happen." Referring to the assassination of Talât by Soghomon Tehlirian, who was judged "not responsible for his acts" and acquitted, Lemkin underscored the irony of the situation: "A man, to have acted in the name of the human conscience, a conscience which had not found yet its legal expression in the international law, was declared insane."[67] Thus, Lemkin pointed out the fact that the crime against the Armenians had gone unpunished because the Allies had not carried their logic through to the end, while the international community had not yet provided a legal definition of that crime.

This last affirmation is open to question. An examination of the discussions and reports of the committees of jurists who worked within the framework of the preliminary peace conference show that these delegates were plainly aware that they were faced with "cases not covered by the customary dispositions of the law" and consequently sought to define "crimes against humanity," henceforth distinguished from war crimes.

Moreover, Resolution 96 (I), which was adopted by the United Nations General Assembly on 11 December 1946, repeats the formula "offense against human rights." The 9 December 1948 Genocide Convention is still more directly inspired by the conclusions of the Committee on Responsibility, which were published on 29 March 1919: Article 3 of this convention provides a similar definition of the categories of criminals involved in a genocide; Article 4 takes up the idea of punishing the culprits regardless of their rank in the state hierarchy; finally, Article 6 provides for the creation of an international judicial body, the formation and prerogatives of which are described in virtually the same terms as those already found in the 29 March 1919 report proposing the creation of a "High Court."[68] While the recommendations bearing on crimes "against human rights" were not translated into realities in their day, they did serve as the basis for the rules adopted by the U.N. after the Second World War. There is even every reason to believe that failed attempt to create an international jurisdiction immediately after the First World War was still on everyone's mind when the Allies decided not to leave the crime that the Nazi had committed against the Jews unpunished.

In the interwar period, moreover, the Fifth Commission of the League of Nations continued to work on the subject. It was no doubt aware that insufficient progress had been made in 1919.[69]

Chapter 7

The First Trial of the Young Turk Criminals Before the Istanbul Court-Martial

In May 1919, while the trial of the members of the Ittihadist Central Committee was in progress, Dr. Cemal Şehabeddin Bey, a writer whenever he had a little time to spare, published in *Alemdar* one of the rare texts that expressed what no one dared to – or wanted to – say: "Those who have even slightly open minds can understand that at all levels of the country, the mortal disease of Unionism continues to rage."[1] *Sabah's* editorialist, for his part, sought to understand why a court-martial had been created: "We stand accused of a crime and are suffering from a disease worse than the plague ... Yes, we are infected with the plague. Humanity hesitates to come close to us ... That is why we have organized an extraordinary court-martial to punish the culprits among us, depending on the degree of their guilt, as justice demands."[2] Ali Münîf Bey, prisoner no. 2762 and a former undersecretary of state[3] who had efficaciously assisted Mehmed Talât during the genocide, naively attempted to exonerate himself in a 19 October 1919 letter to the British authorities written in Malta. Yet he did not deny that the party-sate had committed a collective crime: "During the massacres that took place in 1915," he wrote, "I was not in a position to decide on or to commit these acts, directly or indirectly. Consequently, I cannot be held responsible for them; I had neither decision-making power nor the means to carry out decisions."[4] This Young Turk leader, held by the British far from home, understood that it was not possible in this context to deny the crime in the usual manner. Unable to claim that he had not held his post when the events took place, he tried to convince the high commissioner that his position as second-in-command at the Interior Ministry meant that he had been incapable of acting.

These three reactions suggest that Turkish public opinion was to some extent aware of the consequences of the mass crime organized by the CUP, particularly of the fact that it would be necessary to give accounts to the victims and the Great Powers. This, however, should not be allowed to mask the existence of the denialist camp – that is, the CUP networks – which rejected all accusations across the board and immediately laid plans to transform the trials into a tribune for the defense of Turkism, while preventing revelations of this kind from coming out; the methods envisaged included threats and blackmail. Only if we take this unremitting pressure into account can we grasp the way Istanbul's court-martial no. 1 functioned from February 1919 on, as well as some of its decisions.

That said, it may be asked why the court-martial chose to begin with the trial of the organizers of the Yozgat massacres – that is, with crimes committed in one particular area – rather than taking on the case of the decision-makers at the very outset. This choice may be explained by the scope of the Boğazlian massacres known to one and all. But it was also, perhaps, the result of a strategy that aimed to pin the blame for the "excesses" that had occurred in the course of the deportations on local government officials.

The Yozgat Trial

We have already discussed the conditions surrounding the liquidation of the Armenian population of the *sancak* of Yozgat, stressing that they were distinctly different from those observed in Anatolia.[5] We shall now examine the Yozgat trial with an eye to what it reveals about the line of defense adopted by the accused, the government's legal delay tactics, and the way public opinion reacted to the trial.

From the very first trial session, held on 5 February 1919, the lawyer defending Kemal Bey, Yozgat's interim *mutesarif*, objected that the court-martial was illegitimate. He argued that the sultan's decree provided for the creation of ten courts martial to judge acts committed in the different provinces and that, consequently, the trial should take place where the crime had been committed or the accused had been arrested.[6] The defense lawyers also contested the legitimacy of the plaintiff's lawyers, especially Hayg (Hmayag) Khosrovian, who supposedly had no mandate to counsel his clients. In this particular case, the Armenian Patriarchate, which had assumed the plaintiff's role, represented the people who had been liquidated; the dates and places of whose deaths were as a rule unknown.[7] After overruling the defense's objections, the court-martial proceed to identify the accused: Kemal Bey, 35 years old, born in Beirut, who had recently acted as general inspector of the deportations from Konya; Mehmed Tevfik, 44 years old, born in Istanbul, the commander of the gendarmerie in Yozgat; and Feyaz Bey, the head of Yozgat's Land Registration Office. All three were accused of crimes committed during the deportation of the Armenians. The presiding judge then had the list of Armenian and Turkish witnesses read out, among them the parliamentary deputy from Yozgat, Şakir Bey, and Halil Recayi, the inspector general of the prison camps, after which he presented the exhibits, consisting notably of documents sent to the Mazhar Commission by Şakir on 8 December 1918; these had been certified authentic by the civil inspector in Official Document No. 233, dated 14 December 1918. Finally, the prosecutor, Sâmi Bey, read out the indictment in which he observed that "the ongoing development of the intellectual and financial situation of the non-Muslim elements and the religious privileges that they enjoyed did not prevent them from constantly complaining that they did not have equal rights." The prosecutor's review of the historical context was followed by rather revealing remarks about the movements created by the "Armenian traitors" who had disturbed "public order." According to the prosecutor,

> It became clear that they wished to free themselves from Ottoman domination; the Armenian Committees' publications in foreign languages contributed to creating problems both domestically and in our foreign relations; in the early stages of the general mobilization, the Armenians put up armed resistance to military service; a group of Armenians crossed the frontier to join the enemy forces; they destroyed bridges and put our military equipment and supplies in danger. The authorities accordingly took preventive measures. The decision to deport the Armenians bore only on the vilayets of Erzerum, Bitlis, and Van; however, on 24 May 1915, the military authorities authorized the deportation of the non-Muslim populations of Kayseri.

Under these conditions, it was "natural," the prosecutor went on, that "certain elements should take advantage of the situation...to plunder and commit other crimes."[8] The French intelligence services, which had closely followed this first trial, noted that the indictment read out by the chief prosecutor, which was reproduced in the newspapers the next day, "was more like an indictment of the victims, and paved the way, at the same time, for an acquittal or acknowledgement of attenuating circumstances."[9]

At the 8 February and 10 February trial sessions, the court took due note of the complaint of Garabed Kuyumjian: converted to Islam by force, he demanded retribution for the massacre of his family. Three young Armenian survivors, represented by the lawyer Levon Remzi, had also lodged complaints: during the deportations, the three brothers had been soldiers, but their families had been deported in violation of the official orders. The evidence given by Mustafa Remzi, a judge, at the 10 February trial session confirmed the role of supervisors of the extirpation of the local Armenian populations played by the responsible secretaries delegated to each province. Remzi also testified to the criminal nature of these party militants, revealing that the CUP's responsible secretary in Angora, Necati Bey, went to Yozgat three days before the deportations began, that he had been the mayor's guest while there, and that he returned in the company of the new vali of Angora, Necmeddin Bey, on his way back from Samsun, after the deportees had set out.[10]

The parliamentary deputy from Yozgat, Şakir Bey, testified at the fourth trial session on 11 February. He said that "the massacres were already a fait accompli" when he tried to intervene with Atıf Bey, the interim vali of Angora, who "did not take my protest into account." When the lawyer for the defense, Levon Remzi, asked him whether the Armenians had committed acts of banditry at this time, he answered that, to the best of his knowledge, it had happened "only near the border," as the refugees told it. It was, however, the evidence given by the 18-year-old Eugénie Varvarian, a native of Yozgat, that rendered Feyaz's and Kemal's position untenable: she testified that her convoy had been plundered at Çiftlik and massacred in Keller. The *kasab kaymakam* ("butcher kaymakam") protested that "the girl is a liar, she doesn't know what she's talking about." Varvarian responded by reminding him of certain precise facts, and then asked him: "Did all the Armenians commit suicide? Where are most of them now?" This face-to-face between victim and executioner was, however, broken off by the prosecutor, who suggested that the young woman be given a medical examination. Kemal's lawyer, Saadeddin Bey, said that "Eugénie is seventeen years old today; she was too young at the time of the deportations to remember what happened." The witness nevertheless continued to cite the names of many criminals "who are today free to come and go as they please in Yozgat," notably that of Feyaz, one of the Unionist leaders in Yozgat who gave orders to the *çetes*.[11]

At the fifth trial session on 15 February, the court heard the testimony of a peasant from Elekciler, Stepan, who had found refuge with a Greek in Ankara for nine months after being deported to Keller. He explained that Kemal had a trumpet with which he gave the signal to begin the massacres.[12] Several high-ranking military men testified at the following sessions, such as the interim commander-in-chief of the Fourth Army, Halil Recayi, based in Angora, and Colonel Şehabeddin, based in Kayseri; we have already discussed the telegrams that they exchanged as well as their confessions.[13] The examination of these witnesses showed how closely the military brass and local state officials were associated with the operations. Finally, the Yozgat trial indicates that the declarations promising that those Armenians who agreed to convert to Islam would not be killed were above all intended to facilitate the departure of the convoys; that the plan was to liquidate these converts thereafter; and that, in any case, one rule had to be respected: the proportion of converted Armenians allowed to remain in a locality was never to exceed 5 per cent of its total population.

The makeup of the first court-martial was altered after an imperial decree reforming it was signed on 8 March. Were these alterations due to incidents that occurred during the Yozgat trial? This is unlikely since the reform of the court statutes was ready by 5 March.[14] But we can, in any event, observe the effects that the decree had on this trial, which was suspended at the end of the twelfth trial session on 6 March 1919, after an intervention by the lawyer Levon Remzi that attracted considerable attention.[15]

According to Colonel Hüsameddin Ertürk, a Special Organization officer who helped organize Kemal Bey's funeral, the presiding judge at the court-martial, Mahmud Hayret, was opposed to sentencing Kemal to death and ultimately decided to resign after an acrimonious discussion with Colonel Receb Ferdi.[16] Thus, it is clear that the presiding judge endorsed the Unionsts' positions to the effect that there could be no question of punishing these high-ranking officials or officers who had merely carried out the party's orders. At the very least, it may be said that he was swayed by the pressure to which Unionist circles must have subjected him.

When the trial resumed on 24 March 1919, the composition of the court had been considerably altered. General Nâzım Pasha was the new presiding judge, and military men had replaced his civilian magistrates. Furthermore, the chief prosecutor had asked the lawyers of the Armenian plaintiffs to leave the courtroom, since the court was now purely military and he would take it upon himself, in his capacity as chief prosecutor, to defend their interests. The lawyers argued in vain that the court-martial was not exclusively military, even if the judges were, since it was to judge not only officers, but also civilian officials, ministers, and politicians from the rank of vali to grand vizier, in accordance with the civil law code.[17] The lawyers then withdrew.

The fourteenth trial session on 26 March 1919, during which Kemal Bey and Tevfik Bey were examined, made it possible to establish the facts of the case. It showed in particular that the "revolt" taken to justify the massacres had been an invention carefully prepared by Kemal Bey himself. The examination of other witnesses at the fifteenth, sixteenth, and seventeenth sessions led to confrontations with the accused and a painful exchange between victims and their victimizers. The conclusions of the civil inspector Nedim Bey, who had been charged with investigating the massacres perpetrated in the *sancak* of Yozgat, drove yet another nail into the coffin of the accused. "I solemnly declare, with absolutely certainty about what I affirm," Nedim wrote, "that the Armenians were liquidated in groups and that the *kaymakam*, Kemal Bey, was the author of these crimes. It was, specifically, Kemal Bey who gave the secret orders and informed the commanders of the gendarmerie, who were constantly called upon to carry out these crimes."[18]

The court-martial, under the presiding judge General Mustafa Nâzım Pasha, withdrew for deliberations on 8 April 1919. The verdict it pronounced caused a sensation: it condemned the *kaymakam*, Kemal Bey, to death, and sentenced the commander of the gendarmerie Tevfik Bey to 15 years at hard labor.[19] After reiterating the customary formulas, the verdict pointed out that,

> although the accused and their counsel have denied all wrongdoing and demanded to be acquitted, the court is respectful of Islamic law and especially those of its provisions that protect the life, honor, and property of all the nation's subjects, without discrimination, against all forms of violence and expropriation, with a view to guaranteeing justice for all.

The verdict further stated:

> A deportation order was communicated to Kemal Bey, the *kaymakam* of Boğazlian and interim *mutesarif* of Yozgat, as well as Major Tevfik Bey, commander of the gendarmerie in Yozgat. In the exercise of their functions, they exiled defenseless women, the weak, and young women whom they had been ordered to deport; they exiled individuals who had been exempted from deportation; they plundered money, jewels, and other valuables belonging to the deportees in the Armenian convoys, without respect for personal rights; and they capriciously expedited certain individuals and gave secret orders

and illegal instructions to certain cunning people. They never saw the need to take measures to preserve and protect the population they were sending into exile. They not only refused to take the least measure of that kind, but wholly deprived [the deportees] of all means of defending themselves. They separated the men from the others so as to be able to commit their misdeeds. After their crimes were exposed, when they were asked to provide an explanation for them, they denied the truth. Rather than apply the law, they ordered irresponsible gendarmes to commit atrocities, guaranteeing them full impunity ... They were responsible for massacres and looting, which Muslims consider to be the greatest of crimes. The witnesses' statements show, without the least doubt, that certain military officials exchanged numerous telegrams whose contents the accused have denied. An examination of the various questions put to them shows that the women and children in the convoys were deprived of their protectors and parents and that crimes of massacre and plunder were committed ... The defense has argued that subversive activity took place. Reference was made to the fact that certain members of the [Armenian] committees, in areas under enemy occupation, urged [the Armenian population] to go over to the enemy and participate in the agitation, with the result that the Armenians rose up in revolt and pursued the treacherous objectives set for them by their compatriots living on the other side of the Ottoman borders. The cases cited do not constitute sufficient justification for the crimes committed. Even if a certain proportion of the Armenian population joined them, the rest demonstrated its loyalty ... In his defense, Kemal Bey has accused the Armenians of Van, Erzerum, and Bitlis of acts of cruelty against Muslims. With respect to the Armenians of Yozgat, in whose case we have no proof of a subversive movement, there is no legal or moral foundation for the charges leveled by the accused. Beside the fact that he acted in a spirit of revenge and for personal gain, he did so not only with the intention of inciting the district's Muslims, but also of inducing the Muslim population in general to kill Armenians; they took the massacres to be something natural and necessary. The content of the documents proves that these three irresponsible individuals controlled the activities of the government officials who escorted the convoys and obeyed the orders they received [from their superiors]. Documents written in their own hand prove that the gendarmes accompanied the convoys for the purpose of liquidating them. This has been proved beyond the shadow of a doubt. The proofs and the documents mentioned earlier definitely establish the guilt of the accused. The arguments put forward by the defense are worthless. The prosecutor has demanded that the accused be condemned in conformity with Article 56 of the Penal Code, but this Article has been judged inapplicable to the case before us. The accused, Kemal Bey and Tevfik Bey, have been condemned on the basis of Article 45, by a unanimous vote of the judges: death for Kemal and fifteen years at hard labor for Tevfik, military code, Article 170 and 171.[20]

Along with this sentence, the presiding judge produced a commentary that strongly suggested that the accused were motivated by a desire to avenge the suffering of Muslims in the vilayets of Van, Bitlis, and Mush. Above all, it should be noted that the verdict confirms the thesis of local excess, thereby absolving the central authorities, and breathes not a word about the role played by the CUP and its responsible secretaries, although the evidence presented at the trial leaves no doubt about their involvement.

This first trial, which took place at a time when the nationalist movement was still reeling under the effect of the recent defeat, established the limits of what the Ottoman court system was prepared to accept. Indeed, the reactions observed when the most important of the accused, Kemal, was executed, mark the Young Turk networks' first public manifestation against the very idea of bringing the men who carried out the liquidation orders to justice.

The British intelligence services, like the press of the day, fully grasped the import of these reactions. Kemal was executed on 10 April on Bayazid Square, in the presence of the commander of the Constantinople gendarmerie accompanied by an honor guard. Also present were the police chief, Halil Bey; the military governor of the capital, General Osman Şakir, accompanied by many high-ranking officers; the prefect of the capital, Yusuf Ziya; the presiding judge of the tribunal; magistrates; Constantinople's mayor; a number of leaders of çete squadrons; religious leaders; and a throng made up of members of Teceddüt Fırkası. In all, more than 10,000 people witnessed the execution. The "martyr" was buried the next day in the cemetery in Kadiköy, where a ceremony was organized at which a bouquet bearing the inscription "for the innocent Muslim martyr" was laid on his tomb.[21] All these groups considered the execution of Kemal to be an injustice because he had obeyed the government's and the party's orders. Hüsameddin Ertürk, a colonel in the cavalry and an officer in Teşkilât-ı Mahsusa, made a remark to Samih Hafız Tansu that probably reflected what all the members of the Young Turk networks felt, doubtless together with a segment of public opinion: "This hero, a son of the Turkish nation, is a victim of the enemy occupation; he has been hanged, but his memory will live forever in nation's heart."[22] A moment later, however, Ertürk dropped this conventional discourse to reveal why he found Kemal's execution inadmissible. "The order came from high-ranking authorities," he pointed out, "the headquarters of the party of Union and Progress. No one could oppose such an order."[23] "How," he added, "could the kaymakam of a little town have opposed the order given in this encrypted telegram? How could he have disobeyed his instructions? The guilt of Boğazlian's kaymakam [resides in] this: he carried the order out."[24] The question of personal responsibility was thus posed for those who endorsed the liquidation plan and patriotically put themselves in its service. Kemal's last words before his execution carried the same message: "Dear citizens: I am a Turkish official. I carried out the orders I was given; I conscientiously did my duty. I swear that I am innocent. This is my last declaration for today and tomorrow. To please foreign peoples, [our government] is hanging me. If this is justice, may justice perish forever."[25] Here lay the core of the criticisms leveled by the Young Turk networks at the governments that succeeded one another at the Sublime Porte: namely, that they were collaborating with "foreigners." In seeking to put the blame on the CUP's leaders, the different governments hoped to save the empire from being radically dismembered. The national movement, for its part, had opted for uncompromising resistance and a blanket refusal to assume its responsibilities. Hüsameddin Ertürk remarks: "The Unionist activists were worried, for the threat of arrest hung over their heads like a sword of Damocles. Every Unionist responsible for deporting and massacring Armenians expected to be arrested at any moment, imprisoned, and hanged."[26]

According to the French intelligence services, certain "Turkish circles" attributed the death sentence to "pressure from the English, and others to the government's desire to provide proofs of its good faith by punishing the guilty." The Armenian daily Jagadamard, for its part, published an article under the title, "He Has Commended his Soul to God." The editorialist here recalls that the Armenians

> [have no] confidence in the justice of the Turkish government, for they are well aware that it means only to play one more clever trick to pull the wool over Europe's eyes ... We feel no joy ... However, the simple word hadisat, "he has commended his soul to God," reflects the Turkish mentality, which can never change or forgive the fact that a Turk, even a monster, should be hanged for the Armenians' sake.

The editorialist further remarks that Sabah "is calling, in this connection, for punishment for the Armenians who have massacred thousands of Muslims. Thus it is playing out the time-honored farce of accusing the victims."[27] The very least one can say is that the execution of

Kemal, the first and nearly the last execution, generated sharp tensions and most certainly contributed to reviving the Young Turk movement in Anatolia.

A few months after these events, Kürd Mustafa Pasha, the only member of the court-martial to have sat on it both before and after 8 March 1919, summed up the course of events and the difficulties encountered by the courts martial in a declaration to the daily *Peyam*:[28]

The [members] of the commission of inquiry were designated in advance by the Justice Ministry, the Interior Ministry, and the Ministry of War, and their choices were confirmed by the grand vizier. We, the members of the court, did not have the right to interfere with their prerogatives. These commissions sent us their investigative files for examination; we studied them in order to do what was necessary straightaway. The court did not neglect a single document. However, whenever we opened the trial of an [accused] state official, exchanges of correspondence and reports considerably slowed things down and interfered with the usual procedures. A number of those accused and summoned to appear before the court were remanded to us either late or not at all. Moreover, as a result of regrettable escapes from the War Ministry prison, we had to postpone making certain judgements and fell further and further behind in our work. I remember very well that we had ordered a certain number of officers to appear before the court: they stood accused of the deportations in Büyükdere. But these accused officers were never turned over to us. This is just a minor case. There were far more serious cases.[29]

Chapter 8

The Truncated Trial of the Main Young Turk Leaders

The main trial, that of those directly responsible for the genocide – the members of the Council of Ministers and the Ittihad's Central Committee, that is, the heads of the party-state – was opened on 27 April 1919 before the extraordinary court-martial of Istanbul. These legal proceedings should have brought together the 23 titular members of the Ittihad's Central Committee and its Political Bureau, most of whom had held posts as ministers or administrators. But, 12 of them – Mehmed Talât (a member of the Central Committee), İsmail Enver (a member of the Central Committee), Ahmed Cemal (a member of the Central Committee), Dr. Bahaeddin Şakir (a member of the Central Committee), Dr. Ahmed Nâzım (a member of the Central Committee), Aziz Bey (the head of the Department of State Security), Bedri Bey (the police prefect in the capital), Cemal Azmi (the vali of Trebizond), İsmail Hakkı (a state secretary in the Ministry of War in charge of food and supplies), Dr. Rüsûhi (a member of the Central Committee who had operated in Azerbaijan and the Van region), Eyub Sabri [Akgöl], (a *fedayi* and member of the Central Committee without interruption from 1908 to 1918), Filibeli Ahmed Hilmi (the vice-president of the Special Organization who was in charge of its operations in Erzerum and a member of the Central Committee) – had fled abroad or already withdrawn to Anatolia. Nevertheless, when the "trial of the Unionists" – a formula widely used in the press of the day – opened on 27 April, ranking personalities were to be found in the dock: Halil [Menteşe] (a former president of parliament, former foreign minister, and member of the Central Committee), Midhat Şükrü (the Central Committee's secretary general), Ziya Gökalp (the rector of the University of Istanbul and a member of the Central Committee), Kara Kemal (a former minister of supplies and a member of the Central Committee), Yusuf Rıza (a member of the Central Committee's Bureau and the head of the Special Organization in the Trebizond region), Said Halim (a former grand vizier and a member of the Central Committee), Ahmed Şükrü (a former minister of education and a member of the Central Committee), *Giritli* Ahmed Nesimi [Sayman] (a former Foreign Minister and a member of the Central Committee), Atıf Bey (CUP delegate and, later, vali of Angora and Kastamonu, and a member of the Central Committee), Ahmed Cevad Bey (the military commander of the capital), İbrahim Bey (a former justice minister, and, at the time, president of the Council of State), and Küçük Talât Bey (a member of the Central Committee).[1] To this group were added, somewhat later, on 3 June, Hayri Effendi (a former *şeyh ul-Islam* and a member of the Central Committee), Musa Kâzım (a former *şeyh ul-Islam* and a member of the Central Committee), Mustafa Şerif Bey (a former minister of commerce and agriculture and a member of the Central Committee), as well as İsmail Canbolat (general director of the Department of State Security and a CUP cadre), Abbas Halim Pasha (minister of public works, Said Halim's brother), Ali Münîf Bey (a former state secretary in the Interior Ministry), Hüseyin Haşim (minister of the post and telegraph office), and Rifât Bey (the president of the Senate).[2]

These two exhaustive lists show that the chief prosecutor of the extraordinary court-martial initially concentrated on indicting members of the CUP's leading bodies, including the leadership of *Teşkilât-ı Mahsusa*,[3] probably in line with the strategy of Damad Ferid's government, which consisted in blaming them for the deportations and massacres of the Armenian population in order to exonerate the state. The indictment, which was read out at the first trial session, began by pointing to the existence, within the CUP, of two "Special Organizations, one of which was publicly acknowledged and, thus, official, and another that was secret and based on oral instructions." It went on to accuse "the moral person of this Committee" of a "series of massacres, acts of plunder, and financial abuse" for which its "leaders" were responsible.[4] In other words, the moral person represented by the Ittihad was the object of the indictment.

The rest of the indictment, a sort of detailed presentation of several dozen documents and depositions, sought illustrate the operating method that the CUP used to "fulfill" its "secret goals," especially the creation of *Teşkilât-ı Mahsusa*, whose leading members are mentioned by name. About this corpus, systematically utilized in Parts Three and Four of the present study, the indictment states:

> The essential point that emerges from the recent investigation is that the crimes committed in various places and at various times during the deportation of the Armenians were not isolated, local occurrences; rather, a central, organized force, made up of the above-mentioned individuals, planned them in advance and issued secret orders or gave oral instructions to carry them out.[5]

The last part of the indictment responded to the question about the competency of the extraordinary court-martial that had been posed by the accused who had exercised ministerial functions. Their request to be tried before the "High Court" created by the parliament was rejected on the grounds that their acts were not "offenses of a political nature committed during the exercise of their functions," but "common-law offenses" for which they "did not have the benefit of any legal privileges."[6]

"In view of the participation in the massacres ... of the accused Bahaeddin Şakir, Nâzım, Atıf, Yusuf Rıza, Cevad, Aziz Bey, and Enver, Cemal, and Talât Pasha," the chief prosecutor concluded, "it has been decided to judge them on an indictment for criminal activity," in accordance with the first paragraph of Article 45 and Article 170 of the penal code. For their part, Midhat Şükrü, Dr. Rüsûhi, Küçük Talât, Ziya Gökalp, Kara Kemal, Said Halim, Ahmed Nesimi, Ahmed Şükrü, and İbrahim and Halil [Menteşe] were charged with complicity and judged in accordance with Article 45, Paragraph 2 of the Penal Code.[7] Thus, from the outset, a clear hierarchy of responsibilities was established between those who organized the crime while working in a secret organization, and their accomplices, who represented the CUP's official face. However, in contrast to the hearings conducted by the Fifth Commission of the Ottoman parliament, the domain examined by the judges in this case was largely restricted to the liquidation of the Armenians. The accused were nevertheless also charged with manipulating public opinion in order the better to carry out their secret plans; confiscating to their advantage all the internal mechanisms of the state; taking advantage of the situation in order to enrich themselves; and, finally, hiding the disastrous course of the military campaigns. In a word, the Ittihadists were accused of having dragged the empire into an adventure and of violating all the articles of the Ottoman Constitution.

The head of the French navy's intelligence service, Lieutenant Rollin, noted in an assessment of the situation drawn up after the first trial session: "The indictment charges the accused with common-law offenses or crimes alone, but mentions no political questions."[8] Rollin also pointed out that the lawyers for the defense had demanded, despite the reasons adduced in the indictment, that the case of their clients, most of whom had been ministers, be referred to the High Court of Justice.[9] The defense lawyers argued, notably, that involved here were acts of state and they should be treated as such. After deliberating for a few days, the court held a second session on 4 May, at which it rejected the defense's arguments and published a decree about its competency that is not without interest.[10] Dated 4 May 1335 [1919], this document recalls that it was the moral person represented by the CUP "that [had been] charged with various crimes and that the accused [were] charged with having been the cause of these crimes in their capacity as members of the Committee's central body." The decree accordingly rejected as inadmissible the defense's argument to the effect that it was a question of "abuses and errors committed by members of the Council of Ministers in the exercise of their functions." It went on: As for the special organizations [*Teşkilât-ı Mahsusa*], whether they were under the immediate control of the Committee's central body or attached to an official department, they were, while ostensibly pursuing war aims, in fact exclusively concerned with deportations and massacres." After rebutting the defense's four objections, the court deemed itself "competent to discover and punish the authors of the crimes that shocked all Ottomans and also foreigners."[11] While admitting that the massacres were an extension of the deportations, the court deemed that these crimes were not secondary, unintentional effects of an act of state but, on the contrary, acts planned and ordered by the country's supreme authorities within the framework of a comprehensive plan one of the objectives of which was the liquidation of civilian populations. The angle of approach taken by the court-martial, doubtless on instructions from Damad Ferid's government, was probably designed to root out the Ittihad's networks and purge the administration and army of their members and sympathizers.

More surprising is the fact that the court decided to separate the trial of the Central Committee members from that of the former ministers, who were also affiliated with the Ittihad's highest body. It justified this decision by declaring that it wished to conduct complementary investigations of the accomplices of the most important of the accused, so that they could be judged at the same time as their hierarchical superiors. A French intelligence officer wrote: "it seems – such is the general impression called forth by this measure – that they are trying to save the former ministers' skins." "This is," the same witness noted, "the vicious circle characteristic of the trial now underway; it has been traced clearly enough to allow everyone to pull his chestnuts from the fire."[12] Formally speaking, this decision came down to judging separately, for the same acts and by means of two distinct trials, the CUP considered as a moral person on the one hand, and the members of the government on the other.

The Unionists' Trial

From 4 May to 17 May 1919, there took place seven sessions of the trial of six members of the Ittihad's Central Committee – Midhat Şükrü, Ziya Gökalp, Ahmed Cevad, Küçük Talât, Yusuf Rıza, and Atıf Bey – all of whom were still in the capital.[13] The last part of the 4 May trial session was taken up by a very technical examination of Şükrü,[14] Gökalp,[15] Küçük Talât,[16] and Atıf Bey[17] centered on the question of the codes employed for the orders that the Central Committee or Special Organization sent to the provinces. The next trial session, held on 6 May, involved nothing of fundamental importance, except perhaps for the fact that Atıf Bey corroborated the nature of the activities carried out by Bahaeddin Şakir and Yusuf Rıza in Erzerum and Trebizond.[18] A journalist described this session of the trial as a "pantomime ... with words," observing, somewhat ironically, that Rıza, "who was a member of the Special Organization, does not know whether he belonged to it or not." Atıf contradicted the presiding judge when the latter reminded him that, at the War Ministry, it was said, "this organization had two sections, one based in the Ministry and the other in the Committee itself."[19]

The debate seems to have become livelier at the fourth, 8 May trial session.[20] Gökalp, the first to be examined, declared that he had known nothing about Atıf's activities in Angora; the strong-arm interventions of the party's responsible secretaries in Trebizond, Erzerum, Erzincan, or Sıvas; or, again, the fact that Şakir used a specific code. He also denied knowing anything at all about the committee's relations with the *Milli* enterprises or the "humanitarian corporations" that engaged in speculation.[21] His colleague Midhat Şükrü admitted, however, that Kara Kemal took his orders from Talât Pasha.[22]

In this curious confrontation with accused men who had lost their memories, the presiding judge nevertheless succeeded, at the fifth trial session on 12 May,[23] in bringing Cevad to admit that there had indeed existed a system within the Special Organization whereby the originals of orders were sent out and copies of them were destroyed; he did so by holding up before him documents that Cevad himself had signed.[24] Later the same day, Şükrü found himself hard put to explain why he had received wires from the leaders of *Teşkilât-ı Mahsusa* that attested to the relations that the headquarters of the Central Committee had maintained with this organization.[25] The transcript of the exchange between the presiding judge and Şükrü gives some idea of the attitude of the accused:

> *The judge:* Certain responsible secretaries took part in the massacres; when they did so, they sent secret instructions to both the valis of the provinces and the mutesarifs. They immediately had the valis who did not want to obey them dismissed. Are you aware of all this?
>
> *Şükrü:* Yes, we dismissed a few of our delegates who interfered in government business.
>
> *The judge:* That is not what I am asking you: for example, Mazhar Bey, the vali of Angora, was dismissed the very next day, because he had refused to carry out the secret orders that he had received, and Atıf Bey was appointed vali in his place. The same thing happened to Reşid Pasha, the vali of Kastamonu.
>
> *Şükrü:* Your Honor, how can a delegate dismiss a vali? The secretaries, moreover, did not have the right to appeal to the interior minister. If Bahaeddin Şakir Bey and Dr. Nâzım did appeal to him, that happened without our knowledge.
>
> *The judge:* Do you know where Aziz Bey, the former head of State Security, is now?
>
> *Şükrü:* No.

The presiding judge then had a lettercard that Aziz Bey had sent Şükrü from Vienna, as well as a telegram sent to him by the CUP's inspector in Balıkeser, Musa Bey, and subsequently sent to Dr. Nâzım, whose answer to it read: "Collect money, dress bandits in the uniforms of the soldiers of the regular army, send them to Constantinople. We will arm them here. Yakub Bey will tell you when to send them." The presiding judge then said: "These documents prove, very precisely, that you were part of *Teşkilât-ı Mahsusa*."[26] In the evening, the presiding judge even brought Atıf Bey to confess that "under cover of the law, [the Unionists] released thieves and other criminals from the prisons."[27]

A few minor revelations were also made at the sixth trial session on 17 May. Yusuf Rıza finally admitted that there had indeed existed two *Teşkilât-ı Mahsusas* functioning "independently of each other."[28] The seventh and last trial session was more productive: Şükrü acknowledged that three of the ten members of the Central Committee had participated materially in the creation of the Special Organization, which had the mission of liquidating the Armenians, and that the seven others had not "reacted."[29]

The Trial of the Young Turk Ministers

When the court-martial resumed its work on 3 June 1919, the situation had changed considerably. To begin with, the chief prosecutor, Nazmi, had been dismissed for mysterious reasons. Rumor had it that he had received relatives and representatives of the accused in his home and collaborated with them on a strategy for lightening the charges brought against them.[30] A second, much more decisive event also took place: on 28 May, most of the Young Turk ministers were apprehended by the British and sent to Mudros or Malta.[31] Of the accused sent back to be tried with the ministers, only three second fiddles remained in the dock, as the prosecutor's replacement, Feridun Bey, remarked at the 3 June trial session: Musa Kâzım, a former *şeyh ul-Islam*, Hüseyin Haşim, the minister of the post and telegraph office, and Rifât Bey, the president of the Senate.[32] The trial that now began could only seem like a judicial "farce" as a result of the absence of Said Halim, Hayri Effendi, Halil [Menteşe], Ahmed Nesimi, İsmail Canbolat, Abbas Halim, İbrahim Bey, Ali Münif, Ahmed Şükrü, Mustafa Şerif, and Kara Kemal, which came on top of the absence of Talât, Cemal, Enver, and Nâzım.[33] The British high commissioner, in putting these prisoners out of reach of the Ottoman courts, was reacting to a government decision to release 41 of the accused following demonstrations that had taken place in the streets of the capital from 20 May on – a decision rendered urgent by the fact that the demonstrators were threatening to take the prison of the court-martial, Bekirağa, by assault.[34]

Under these conditions, the public prosecutor's indictment, presented in a courtroom in which the accused were no longer present, was thrown into still sharper relief. The charges brought against the absent prisoners had been stiffened and were now formulated in much less ambiguous terms. After stressing that "the government was not at all concerned to prevent massacres and acts of pillage or to punish those guilty of them," the prosecutor Haydar Bey recalled, "the massacre and destruction of an entire community and the pillaging of its assets can only have been the consequence of bloodthirsty measures taken by a secret association." There followed an order requiring the accused to appear before the court-martial; it stated that "Talât Pasha, Cemal, Enver and Company, leading members of Union and Progress, are summoned to appear before the court-martial on charges of massacre, pillage, destruction by fire of buildings and of corpses, devastation of villages, indecent assault, and torture."[35] The same document affirms that,

> one manifestation of the Committee's activity is the role it played while the deportation law was being carried out. The deportations, especially in places where they were conducted with greater intensity, that is, the eastern vilayets, took the same form. They were directed by delegates and responsible secretaries of Union and Progress. In these districts of the eastern vilayets, the task of supervising them was entrusted to Bahaeddin Şakir Bey, appointed head of the Special Organization, which comprised the leaders of Union and Progress.[36]

Thus, it was in the framework of these trials, in line with the additional charges brought by the Public Ministry, that the main Young Turk leaders were tried in absentia. The examinations of the former *şeyh ul-Islam*, Musa Kâzım, Hüseyin Haşim, and Rifât Bey were, unsurprisingly, altogether unproductive.[37] In the absence of the main authors of the crime, the court asked Hüseyin Haşim at the next trial session on 5 June 1919 why the Central Committee had issued the deportation order and burned documents. It received no answer.[38] Musa

Kâzım was embarrassed when the presiding judge showed him a "sentence to deport and massacre Armenians" (*Ermenilerin Tehcir ve Taktili fetvasını*) that he had issued during his tenure as *şeyh ul-Islam*.[39] The record of the third,[40] fourth,[41] and fifth[42] sessions of the ministers' trial, held on 9, 12, and 24 June, does not provide any significant new information about the facts. The court's inspiration appears to have dried up in the face of the wall of silence that nothing seemed capable of piercing. The next, 25 June trial session was livelier, because at this session the chief prosecutor Reşid Bey appeared instead of his substitute, Feridun Bey, and delivered an indictment aimed not at the culprits but at the victims. Nevertheless, this indictment provides, in passing, corroboration of the fact that the CUP's plans for the Armenian population were worked out in the first half of February 1914 – that is, immediately the reform plan for the eastern provinces was adopted.[43] The prosecutor mentioned the antecedents of this plan, massacres "of hundreds of thousands of Muslim women, children, and old people" (omitting to say where they are supposed to have taken place), but conceded that "that was no reason to massacre other innocent people in their turn."[44]

Musa Kâzım had the last word. At the seventh and last trial session held on 26 June, he recalled that "the cabinet and the leaders of the party, when the party is in power, are nothing but a 'phonograph of the [party] caucus'; the ministry is completely deprived of its independence and responsibility. Parliamentary debates are just a formality; everything is decided before hand in the caucus."[45]

On 5 July 1919, after more than two months of proceedings marked by several modifications of the initial indictment, the court delivered a verdict that applied only to those accused in the trial of the ministers,[46] ignoring those in the trial of the Unionists, whose fate seems to have disappeared in the meanders of the Turkish court system.

The court-martial's verdict recalls the various indictments affirming "that the disbanded association known as Union and Progress committed numerous offenses and crimes and that the members of the General Council representing said association were the authors of these crimes." The document then launches into a long historical account of the successive setbacks suffered by the Ottoman Empire. It recalls that "the Ottomans, thirsting for freedom and justice, considered the pure waters of freedom as, and perceived the movement that sprang up on 9 July 1324 as manna from heaven." However, it went on, they also saw the "disastrous consequences of the Italian and Balkan wars" and observed that the Young Turks had "led the government astray and, while pretending to respect freedom, succeeded in putting together a committee" that seized power and reached its "goal by subsuming the Council of Ministers under the General Council, making the former a slave" to the decisions of the latter.

> As the finance minister, Cavid Bey, openly said in the declarations that he read into the record of the fifth section of the Chamber of Deputies, dated 24 and 26 October 1334, this group of activists within Union and Progress was so bold and infallible in making decisions concerning the destiny of the nation and the country that they [the CUP leaders] saw no reason to submit the decision to declare war to the Council of Ministers, although even sovereigns do not make such decisions on their own. Since everyone had understood that this method of governing could not produce positive results, the acts of the Committee that even the opposition had respected seemed objectionable to people of sound judgment...Competent, honest, and experienced state officials were dismissed and replaced by people affiliated with the committee. The result was justified general complaints about a government so arbitrary and tyrannical as to make people regret the despotic regime, to give offense, in particular, to the non-Muslim nationalities, and, especially, to lead the Armenians, who now realized that nothing justified their conviction that freedom was a guarantee for security and

justice, to look for the first favorable opportunity to realize the national aspirations that they had nursed earlier. The fact that the national question came between the diverse elements and even between Muslims sowed division and distrust among them. Thus a serious blow was dealt to Ottoman unity ... Given that these facts have been established by research and inquiries as well as the aforementioned indictments, and that it is impossible to refute the five points exposed and examined by our court-martial, or to affirm that they are null and void, we have come unanimously to the solemn conviction that the aforementioned personal crimes, attributed to the Committee of Union and Progress, were committed in a way that sullies that Committee's honor ... It has consequently been decided, after deliberation, that, considering the phases of this trial, the aforementioned assertions of the defense counsel are an inadequate defense.

The five charges were as follows: 1) The crimes represented by the massacres whose reality has been established before the court-martial, massacres that were perpetrated in Trebizond, Yozgat, and Boğazlian, were organized and carried out by the leaders of Union and Progress; 2) The decision to enter the war was taken by the Committee without "deliberation of the Council of Ministers"; 3) The party interfered in government business for the purpose of obtaining the resignation of a minister of war, Ahmed İzzet; 4) The party congress decided to entrust [Kara] Kemal Bey, "who had been charged by the headquarters of Union and Progress with supervising questions involving supplies," with the mission of creating "a council of commerce and, later, a few companies and associations that gained a monopoly over commercial transactions, enabling them to confiscate all the wealth of the population," and 5) The party had interfered in affairs of state.[47]

The court accordingly condemned Talât, Enver, Cemal, and Dr. Nâzım to death in absentia, and Cavid, Mustafa Şerif, and Musa Kâzım to 15 years at hard labor. It acquitted Hüseyin Haşim and Rifât Bey.[48]

The only sentence that could be executed was that of Musa Kâzım, who had perhaps spoken too freely at the last trial session. The court-martial's verdict calls for a few remarks. Although the core of the trial consisted in shedding light on the massacres perpetrated by the Ittihadist leaders, the principal charge was included in a sort of contextualization of their criminal activities; the identity of the victimized groups, Armenian, Syriac, and Greek, was quite simply ignored.

This judicial episode, which anticipates the experience of the Leipzig trials, shows that, after committing a mass crime such as genocide, a state cannot find within itself the strength required to bring its own nationals to justice.

The Trial of the Responsible Secretaries and the Vicissitudes of the Subsidiary Trials in the Provinces

The eagerly awaited trial of the CUP's responsible secretaries and delegated inspectors began on 21 June 1919,[1] before the trial of the ministers had come to an end. It was, however, interrupted at the end of the third session, on 28 June 1919.[2] As Vahakn Dadrian rightly observes, only 11 of the 29 accused were responsible secretaries, and many were absent.[3]

Among those in the dock on 21 June were Dr. Ahmed Midhat, the Constantinople police chief, who was delegated by the CUP to Bolu and then to Bursa to supervise the deportations there;[4] Dr. Besim Zühtü, the responsible secretary in Eskişehir;[5] Avni Bey, the responsible secretary in Manisa;[6] Abdül Gani Bey, the responsible secretary in Edirne;[7] Hasan Salâheddin Bey, the responsible secretary in Beyoğlu/Istanbul; Hüseyin Cevdet Bey, the inspector in Mürgün; and Mehmed Cemal Bey, the responsible secretary in Aleppo.[8]

These men, who had had a direct hand in implementing their party's policy in the provinces, could have provided essential details about the mechanisms of liquidation and the seizure of assets, and could probably also have furnished precise statistics on the operations they had carried out. In any event, many new elements emerged from the proceedings at this trial. We do not know why it was interrupted on 28 June, to be resumed in November and concluded with a verdict pronounced on 8 January 1920.[9] This verdict confirmed that the Ittihad's Central Committee had created an executive leadership charged with liquidating the Armenians and "managing" their assets, which communicated directly with the responsible secretaries and delegates in order to implement its decisions in the area under the jurisdiction of the Third Army. The verdict also reveals that these "responsible secretaries," who were directly dispatched by the party, also had authority over the valis and could take all measures required to execute the orders they received: "they were free to conduct their criminal activities as they saw fit; these activities [implied] the organization and utilization of bands of brigands [*çetes*] whose task it was to massacre."[10]

Among the 13 accused still present in January 1920,[11] Midhat and Fehmi were condemned to ten years of prison, Avni was given nine months, and Gani's trial was adjourned. All the others were acquitted.[12]

For reasons that escape us, Cemal Oğuz, the responsible secretary in Çangırı, was tried separately at a later date. It is true that Oğuz had organized the murder of the capital's Armenian elites, who had been held for a few weeks in the area under his control.[13] His trial before the court-martial did not truly begin until 26 January 1920. He had tried to pass himself off as insane and then as deaf, but witnesses affirmed that he had been guilty of major abuses in the supply scandal.[14] He was, moreover, tried for his involvement in that scandal.

At the 3 February 1920 session of his trial, he contended that he had never had anything to do with the "Armenian business"; the magistrates did not see the need to look any further into the matter. A witness recalled, however, the influence he had had over state officials and the way he had, in concert with the interim vali and commander of the gendarmerie, extracted between 600 and 800 Turkish pounds gold from the Armenian population in exchange for a promise not to deport it. Despite this transaction, the Armenians were put on the road and massacred at the Tüney station.[15] The court-martial finally condemned Oğuz, in a verdict rendered on 8 February 1920, to five years of hard labor,[16] ; he remained, however, in the hospital of Gümüş Su.[17]

The Trial of Those Who Organized the Massacres in Trebizond

In addition to the trial of the criminals of Yozgat, the court-martial initiated a number of different proceedings against other people responsible for liquidating Armenians in other regions. The accused in Trebizond were among the first targets of these proceedings. The presence in this port of British forces and many diplomats goes part of the way toward explaining the haste with which the Trebizond trial was organized. Begun in April, it was brought to and end on 22 May 1919 in circumstances that we have discussed at length.[18] It culminated in a death sentence in absentia for the former vali of Trebizond, Cemal Azmi Bey, and the CUP's delegate in the city, Nail Bey.[19] It should be added that Dr. Ali Saib, indicted in the Trebizond affair for poisoning, was tried much later, between 16 and 21 December 1919,[20] and that Major Tevfik was tried still later, in September 1920.[21]

The Trial of Those Who Organized the Massacres in Mamuret ul-Aziz

Bahaeddin Şakir was, his flight to Germany notwithstanding, the most important of those facing indictment in this trial.[22] Accused along with him were Boşnak Resneli Nâzım, the CUP's inspector in Mamuret ul-Aziz; his assistant Ferid Bey, a responsible secretary and the head of Public Education in the region, Haci Baloşzâde Mehmed Nuri, a parliamentary deputy from Dersim and the head of the region's *Teşkilât-ı Mahsusa*;[23] and the vali, Sabit Cemal Sağiroğlu, then detained in Malta.[24] There was never any question at this trial of the killing fields south of Malatia.

According to the Istanbul press, the pretrial investigation had been concluded by mid-June and the trial of these men was imminent;[25] yet it did not begin, before Court-Martial No. 1, until 22 October 1919, in the presence of two of the accused, Ferid and the parliamentary deputy Nuri, who had been indicted "for massacres and deportations."[26] The proceedings were conducted briskly, on 30 October, 21 November, and 10 January, but the facts of the case were not really broached.[27] The only element that deserves mention is the famous 4 July 1915 telegram that Şakir sent the CUP's inspector in Harput, Resneli Nâzım; it constitutes one of the rare documents from the archives of *Teşkilât-ı Mahsusa* the authenticity of which has been certified.[28] It was probably the presence of this exhibit in the investigative file compiled for the Mamuret ul-Aziz trial that explains why Şakir's case was included in these proceedings.

The verdict, handed down by the court-martial on 13 January 1920, imposed the death sentence on the man who had incontestably been the most zealous organizer of the liquidation of the Ottoman Armenians. General Vehib Pasha's written deposition also contributed heavily to attesting the Şakir's role as well as the fact that these crimes stemmed from decisions made by the CUP's Central Committee. "The state contributed to the commission of these crimes," the verdict added. "No state official, no judge, no gendarme ever stepped in to protect the populations that fell victim to these atrocities."[29] At the moment when the British high commissioner, John de Robeck, learned that Şakir had been condemned, he believed that Şakir was in Germany or Holland. "Bahaeddin Şakir," he wrote, "is one of the members of a small secret committee known as *Teşkilât-ı Mahsusa*, or Special Organization, which was created by the CUP Central Committee to organize the liquidation of the Armenian race."[30] Resneli Nâzım, for his part, was sentenced to 15 years in prison; two of his underlings, who were present, received light sentences.

The Trial of Those Who Organized the Massacres in Bayburt

After these secondary trials, in which the accused who were present received particularly light treatment, Damad Ferid's return to power on 18 April 1920 made it possible to set the judicial machine back in motion. Immediately, the grand vizier appointed General Nemrud Kürd Mustafa[31] as presiding judge of the extraordinary court-martial. Mustafa was the only member of the team that had condemned the *kaymakam* of Boğazlıan, Kemal Bey, to death one year earlier who was still in place. The first case to be judged by the new court involved two people whose role in the massacre of the Armenians of Bayburt was common knowledge – Mehmed Nusret Bey from Janina, the *kaymakam* of Bayburt and, subsequently, *mutesarif* of Arğana Maden, and Lieutenant Piri Mehmed Necati Bey, the leader of a squadron of *çetes*[32] who were accused of having "committed crimes during the deportation of the Armenians of the *kaza*: murders, massacres, pillage, abductions."[33] The verdict, made public on 20 July 1920, unsurprisingly condemned Nusret and Necati to death; both had been found guilty of perpetrating massacres in the *kaza* of Bayburt. The verdict emphasized that the massacres carried out in this area were the first to be debated and decided upon by "CUP Party headquarters," and that they had been organized under Şakir's authority. The verdict further noted that Nusret "had subsequently been promoted to the post of *mutesarif* of the *sancak* of Arğana Maden (in the vilayet of Dyarbekir); [there] he had abducted the 24-year-old Philomene Nurian of Trebizond and her younger sister 'Nayime.'" With regard to Mehmed Necati, "thirty-five, an officer who [had] resigned his commission and [was] accused of organizing the deportation and massacre of the Armenians in the *kaza* of Bayburt," the court observed that most of the mobile units of the gendarmerie were voluntarily transferred to the front "and that the task of escorting the convoys had been entrusted to Mehmed Necati Bey."[34]

It should be noted that, unlike the other verdicts, the decree containing the court-martial's verdict was not published in the *Official Gazette*, but in an Istanbul daily, *Tercüman-ı Hakikat*, some two weeks later. Still more revealing, the Censorship Office stepped in to stop distribution of this issue of the paper.[35] Presumably, Damad Ferid's government, then in the midst of preparing the Treaty of Sèvres, was worried about the predictable public reactions that a new death sentence would arouse and opted to execute the sentence as quietly as possible. After Nusret was hanged in Bayazid Square, certain newspapers affirmed that these officials had been hanged after being denounced by the Armenian Patriarch, Zaven.

The Trial of Those Who Organized the Massacres in Erzincan

Another trial of local officials, the Erzincan trial, was held at almost exactly the same time as the Bayburt trial; General Nemrud Mustafa was the presiding judge in this case, too. The sentence, which was published on 27 July 1920, confirmed that the *kaymakam* of Erzincan, Memduh Bey, had ordered the gendarmes and policemen to massacre the Armenians in the convoys of deportees.[36] It nevertheless imposed the death sentence on the only indicted man present, Hafız Abdüllah Avni, the general secretary of the Erzincan gendarmerie (and the brother of Abdül Gani Bey, the party's responsible secretary in Edirne), who was accused of having "personally committed a number of atrocities, including infanticide."[37]

Avni was executed on 22 July 1920, again in Bayazid Square, after declaring: "Long live the party of Union and Progress. In massacring the Armenians, I did my country a great service."[38] Avni was the third and last "martyr" of the trials held before Court-Martial No. 1 in Constantinople.

The Other Subsidiary Trials, Judicial "Farces"

On 10 April 1919, the "Mosul trial" began before Court-Martial No. 1. The most important of the men facing indictment were Halil Pasha [Kut] and Nevzâde Bey, who were accused of having organized the massacre of deportees in Mosul and the Armenian soldiers in a labor battalion, as well as the murder of Bedirkhanzâde Abdül Rezak Bey.[39] This trial was, however, suspended in early June, in the wake of tensions spawned by the deportation of the Young Turk criminals to Mudros and Malta. When it resumed, only a few subalterns were still facing judgement;[40] Halil Pasha had managed to escape from the prison of the court-martial and flee to Anatolia in August 1919.[41]

In November 1919, there began a series of trials of the authors of exactions committed in the Ismit and Bursa areas. From 6 November 1919 to 17 February 1920 the court-martial, now presided over by Esad pasha, first tried Hamid Bey, under indictment for having acquired, in his capacity as the CUP's responsible secretary in Adabazar, the assets of 3,000 deported Armenian families at derisory prices. Despite the incriminating evidence provided by the former *kaymakam*, Necati Bey, the accused was acquitted on 17 February 1920.[42] On 15 January 1920, Court-Martial No. 1 opened the trial of people implicated in the acts committed in Ismit and Bağçecik.[43] The sentences were somewhat harsher in this case. In its verdict, rendered on Sunday, 29 February 1920, the court condemned İbrahim Bey, the prison warden, to 15 years at hard labor; Faik Çavuş, his accomplice, to three years and 200 days in prison; Ali Sururi Bey, *müdir* of the *nahie* of Derbend, to one year at hard labor; Vecihi Bey, *müdir* of the *nahie* of Bağçecik, to two years of prison; and Ahmed Çavuş and Hasan Effendi to four months of prison and 20 strokes of the rod each. The accusations referred to in this verdict show that this team, which had been charged with organizing the deportations, had in fact systematically pillaged Armenian assets for its personal profit.[44] In other words, it had contravened state interests and been condemned for "financial abuses."

The Karamursal-Yalakdere trial was held simultaneously; the accused were also charged with having committed "abuses" in the course of the deportations. Since the most important of those under indictment, Hoca Rifât, the CUP's delegate in Ismit, had been deported to Malta, he was tried *in absentia*. İbrahim Bey, the warden of the Ismit prison; İmam Salaheddin, Ali; and the navigation agent İsmail Bey were notably accused of having speculated on sales of wheat; they were, however, cleared of accusations of exactions against the Armenian deportees.[45] On 3 March, the court-martial rendered its verdict. İbrahim, who had been condemned in the Ismit trial, was not given a heavier sentence. Two of his accomplices were acquitted, and İmam Salaheddin, implicated in the "grain affair," was referred to a competent court.[46]

The court also took up the cases of 40 people involved in the deportation and massacres of Armenians from Bursa. However, only the fugitives among those indicted were condemned. The Unionist delegate, Mehmedce Bey, a member of the First Section of the Department of State Security, was condemned to death in absentia; the police lieutenant Haci Tevfik, the policemen Yahia and Sadık Süleyman Fevzi, and the gendarme Hasan were given ten years at hard labor; and the CUP's responsible secretary İbrahim received eight years in prison.[47]

Among the criticisms leveled at the court-martial until it was taken back in hand by Nemrud Mustafa in April 1920, the 30 March acquittal of Colonel Şakir Bey, who had been accused of massacring Armenians in Kayseri, caused a sensation.[48] The indictment of Bedros

Halajian, a former minister and former member of the Ittihadist Central Committee, for having been deeply involved in the deportation of Armenians and "attempting to modify the form of government," illustrates the cynicism of the court presided over by Esad Pasha, an Ittihadist. It acquitted the former deputy on 5 February 1920, but only after attaining its objective of encouraging the belief that an Armenian could have helped organize the massacres.

Also noteworthy is the court-martial's treatment of the deportations in Büyükdere/San Stefano. The verdict in this case, delivered on 24 May 1919, considered only charges for financial "abuse." It nevertheless reveals how Selanikli Refik Bey, the *kaymakam* of Büyükdere, Hafız Mehmed, the police chief Abdül Kerim, and Rizeli Celal Effendi "shortened the period set by the government for the deportation of non-Muslims from the Büyükdere area and the appropriation of the assets of the deportees."[49] The court-martial did not see fit to judge the substantial issues here – that is, the deportations and murders – and did all it could to limit the grounds for the indictment; it also omitted to broach the question of the damages and property losses sustained by the Armenian deportees.

Among other legal oddities, the case of Sabancali Hakkı Bey, a senior officer who belonged to the exclusive circle of the CUP's military cadres, is worth mentioning.[50] Among the rare people who demonstrated hostility to his party's plan to deport the Armenians,[51] Hakkı was brought before Court-Martial No. 1 on 9 August 1919,[52] at a time when dozens of other party cadres deeply implicated in the massacres were left untouched. After five trial sessions, which brought no serious charge against the officer to light,[53] Hakkı was acquitted.[54] In view of the practices cultivated by postwar Turkish governments, we are inclined to explain this indictment as a show for public consumption, designed to prove that an important party leader was not implicated in the liquidation of the Armenians. Much later, in February 1921, before Court-Martial No. 1 was dissolved, the Istanbul press reported other trials based on events that had taken place in Koçhisar, Sıvas, Kiği, and Agn, all of which culminated in acquittals.[55] It was as if Turkey felt an obligation symbolically to settle its scores with this violent past – or, if one prefers, to carry out a massive whitewash of those under indictment. Finally, to round off our succinct account of the results of the Turkish legal proceedings, we need to glance at the work of the provincial courts martial. The documented example of Trebizond, where the local authorities systematically thwarted the chief prosecutor's pretrial investigations,[56] shows that the Ittihadist networks made all local action virtually impossible. Of the ten regional courts martial initially created to judge crimes committed in the province, we know of only two that actually functioned – the court in Çorum, which tried and acquitted the Unionist Ziya Şakir, an editor of *Ertogrul* in Bursa who was implicated in the deportation of the local Armenians;[57] and the court in Eskişehir, which indicted 40 people involved in the deportations in Mihalıcık and Sivrihisar. Four of the accused were present at the Eskişehir trial, but those who had acquired the biggest fortunes, such as Sayaklı Emin, Çaputlı Hüseyin, and Mihalıcıklı Safet, were not inconvenienced and even threatened survivors who had returned to the city.[58] Still more clearly than in the Istanbul, it was impossible in the provinces – with the exception of the immediate vicinity of the capital and the zones occupied by the Allies – to bring notables to trial. It was out of the question that the courts should require them to render accounts for their crimes or for the goods they had acquired at the Armenians' expense.

The Judicial Vicissitudes of the Presiding Judge of the Court-Martial and a Discomfiting Witness, General Vehib

We have already seen that, in December 1919, Vehib Pasha was detained while awaiting trial after the court reached a unanimous decision to indict him, while carefully avoiding giving

clear indications of its reasons for doing so. Adeptly, Court-Martial No. 3, which was responsible for trying senior officers, even created the impression that he had been implicated in
the Armenian massacres.[59] There is, however, little room for doubt that his Young Turk colleagues wished to "punish" him in this way for having broken the law of silence. A still more
flagrant case of the Kemalist-Unionist network's interference in legal matters came to light
in summer 1920, at the trial, before the court-martial then presided over by General Nemrud
Mustafa, of people implicated in the massacres and deportations in the Aleppo region. One
of the accused, who had been arrested in the capital in August 1920 at the request of the
parliamentary deputy and physician Avedis Nakashian, was none other than Abdüllahad
Nuri, the former director of the Sub-Directorate for Deportees in Aleppo, whose role in Syria
we have already discussed.[60] Nuri's brother, Yusuf Kemal, a parliamentary deputy and CUP
leader, was working alongside Mustafa Kemal in Angora at this time. Given the major role
that Nuri played in liquidating deportees in Syria, many expected that the presiding judge at
the court-martial, Nemrud Mustafa, would have him condemned to death. Indeed, a journalist reports that Nuri, overwhelmed by the charges against him, broke into tears before the
court. At this point, an Armenian priest from Kastamonu arrived in Istanbul with a message
from the "foreign minister" in Angora, Yusuf Kemal, in which Kemal threatened to execute
the 2,000 to 3,000 Armenians under his control if his brother was not released from prison
in very short order.[61]

The fall of Damad Ferid's government, brought on by its signature of the Treaty of Sèvres,
and its replacement by a government favorable to the *Milli* movement, made it possible to
change the make-up of the court-martial and, in the process, "save" the last of the men
facing prosecution. Hardly had the Tevfik government taken the helm of state than it concerned itself with the case, of General Mustafa in particular. Mustafa, who had sat on the
court-martial since its February 1919 creation and had a reputation for honesty, was indicted
by the court, now presided over by Esad Pasha, of which he himself was a member. No official
reason was given for the indictment. The accused profited from the tribune this offered him
in order to read a memorandum, after first pointing out that he, for his part, had "not steeped
his hands in blood." This barely veiled accusation addressed to his colleagues on the court
apparently produced the desired effect: they declared themselves incompetent to judge one
of their own members. Mustafa's memorandum was nevertheless published in two Istanbul
newspapers, causing a stir. We read there that

> the pashas who have perpetrated unheard-of, unthinkable crimes and dragged the
> country into its present situation in order to protect their personal interests continue
> to wreak havoc. They have established tyrannies of all kinds, organized deportations
> and massacres, burned suckling infants to death with oil, raped women and girls in
> front of their wounded parents, after tying them up, separated young women from their
> mothers and fathers, confiscated their real estate and moveable assets, and exiled them
> to Mosul in a pitiable plight, subjecting them to violent acts of all sorts in the process.
> They have put thousands of innocent people on sailboats and thrown them into the
> sea; they have forced others to convert; they have made famished old people to walk
> for months on end; they have used them as slaves; they have cast young women into
> houses of prostitution established under appalling conditions, unprecedented in the
> history of any nation on earth.

Mustafa concluded that, in such conditions, he considered it an honor to be tried by the
court-martial.[62] Even if the general never once uttered the word "Armenian" in his speech,
the Unionist press did not neglect the opportunity to point out that he was acting as a
"champion of the Armenians."[63]

Unmistakably alluding to the indictment of General Mustafa, the daily *Peyam Eyam* remarked:

> We have not been able to hold anybody responsible for these tragedies that make the whole universe shudder, and we have not been able to punish anyone; we have either helped the pashas and beys whom we have haphazardly arrested escape from prison or have set them free on purely formal conditions and guarantees. If, after fulfilling our duty to render justice in rather lukewarm fashion, or, to tell the truth, failing to fulfil it at all, we go on to condemn a Mustafa Pasha for what the French call 'a crime of opinion,' we will be the laughingstocks of the whole world.

"General Mustafa's first crime," the editorialist concluded,

> is not to have defended the interests of the sacred Committee; his second crime is to have acted, on the contrary, in diametrically opposed fashion." The same source indicated, moreover, that there was no longer anyone "in the prison of the court-martial, but [that] Vehib Pasha has been left there, because, during his detention, he dared express himself irreverently about the aforementioned sacred Committee. In our country, all crimes can be forgiven, but *that* audacity is unforgivable... Our judgements and decisions do not go past the ends of our noses; it is probable that, tomorrow, they won't get even that far. In the face of such misfortune, we would do well to give ourselves a shake, throw off our famous *ocak* mentality, and behave like men, if only where the question of justice is involved.[64]

Thus, one can see more easily why Ferid Pasha, as soon as he took up the reins of government again, appointed General Mustafa presiding judge of the extraordinary court-martial on 18 April 1920 – doubtless in the hope that he could thus restore the credibility of the Turkish judicial apparatus. One can also see that with Ferid's fall and the nomination of a government favorable to the *Milli* movement, Mustafa's days at the head of the court-martial were numbered.

In its 25 October 1920 issue, *Le Bosphore* declared that rumors were making the rounds about the imminent "dismissal" of this judge who had, "in the course of the proceedings, provided an example of independence of spirit and a desire to see justice done which, although they did not carry the day, are nonetheless deserving of the highest praise." Queried on this subject, the judge said that he had received no information about it, but declared that

> such a decision, if it is taken by the Council of Ministers, can have been taken for only two reasons: first, the fact that [he was] of Kurdish nationality; second, the fact that [he] considered it [his] duty to subject Avni Pasha, the minister of the navy and son-in-law of Şakir Pasha, the minister of war, to a long interrogation in the matter of the massacres and deportations in Trebizond, the province whose military forces were under Avni's command when these events took place.[65]

The suspense did not last for long. By a 27 October 1920 imperial decree, signed by the grand vizier, Tevfik, and the minister of war, Ziyaeddin, General Hurşid Pasha was named presiding judge of Court-Martial No. 1, with the following judges to assist him: General Abdülkerim; the commander of the Twelfth Army Corps on the Caucasian front during the war, and thereafter the representative of the Ottoman military mission in Georgia; Tevfik Bey; General Ömer Cemil Bey, who served in the Third and Fourth Armies; and others.[66]

On 30 October, Hurşid and his team assumed their functions at the court-martial. Mustafa, for this part, was arrested along with certain of his collaborators[67] at the request of the minister of war, Şakir Pasha.

On 6 November, the War Council examined Mustafa Pasha, who "reiterated" his protest against his "illegal arrest" and demanded to be released.[68] A few days later, the former presiding judge of the court-martial and his colleagues were transferred to the *Sareskerat* prison.[69] Bit by bit, the Istanbul press revealed a few of the general's character traits. Thus, it was revealed that, during the war, he had refused all command posts because he was opposed to the Ottoman Empire's entry into the war; that he had already been arrested on charges of having made "subversive" political declarations – a charge he denied publicly by way of the press; and that he had threatened to make "sensational revelations about the massacres and deportations." The reporter at *Le Bosphore* was hardly exaggerating when he wrote that "the former presiding judge of the court-martial has many documents pertaining to this tragedy in his possession, documents that throw a great deal of light on the responsibilities in this affair, and on just *who* is responsible." According to *Le Bosphore*, Mustafa had also earned the hostility of certain Unionist circles after he initiated proceedings against the authors of thefts committed in Yıldız from the imperial treasury.[70] The general was, manifestly, the Young Turks' *bête noire*. This time, the proceedings initiated against him were conducted by the War Council. It seems, however, that they were not to the taste of the council's president, Marshal Kâzım Pasha, who resigned from it, thereby postponing ratification of the sentence.[71] Mustafa was charged, as were two other members of the court, with having rendered two distinct verdicts in the Bayburt trial, one of which declared that the court had unanimously found Nusret guilty and condemned him to death, while the other condemned him, without unanimity, to 15 years at hard labor. On 9 January 1921, the presiding judge at Court-Martial No. 1, Nemrud Kürd Mustafa, was finally sentenced to three months in prison; the verdict of 20 July 1920 was overturned and Nusret was officially cleared, posthumously, of the charges against him.

The neutralization of the general and the appointment to the court-martial of ranking officers devoted to the Young Turk cause marked the effective end of the symbolic efforts of the capital's liberal circles to render justice to the non-Turkish victims. Among the concrete effects of the changes in the makeup of the court-martial was the fact that Mustafa Abdülhalik, whose role in the liquidation of the Armenians was known to one and all, was set free after paying 1,250 Turkish pounds in bail,[72] as was Mustafa Reşad Bey, the former head of the political department of the police force.[73]

A few central features emerge from the evolution of the different kinds of legal procedures initiated by the Ottoman authorities after the signature of the Mudros armistice to autumn 1920 Mudros armistice. Manifestly, the different governments that succeeded each other in Constantinople were, with a few minor variations, all concerned to fit the Ottoman Empire out with a more decent image on the eve of a peace conference that was going to seal their country's fate. In the eyes of Turkish political leaders, strong domestic opposition notwithstanding, it was preferable to institute national legal proceedings that were likely to play down the crime or even veil its most monstrous episodes than to be forced to collaborate with a foreign court and comply with its demands – for example, to furnish it with the official documents it might ask for and turn indicted Ottoman subjects over to it.

The harassment campaign orchestrated against General Nemrud Mustafa and General Vehib Pasha marked the limits beyond which it was not possible to go. It shows that there was never any question of revealing the full scope of the crimes that had been committed during the war. It stands as one index of a consensus in Turkish society, which refused to assume its responsibilities and remained firmly rooted in its ethnic-nationalistic logic.

Chapter 10

Mustafa Kemal: From the Young Turk Connection to the Construction of the Nation-State

There can obviously be no question of discussing the vast subject of the development of Kemalism and the formation of the Turkish nation-state here. Yet it is impossible to bring the present study to an end without briefly examining the connections between Kemalism and the Young Turk movement, which official historiography has studiously ignored. Without entering into the construction of the myth around Mustafa Kemal, the excesses and silences of which have been laid bare by the pioneering work of Erik Zürcher, it should be pointed out that, as soon as he had returned to Istanbul in November 1918, the future Turkish leader drew closer to the Young Turk leaders in whose hands Talât and Enver had put the movement before going into voluntary exile. He joined the *Osmanlı Hürriyetperver Avam Fırkası* (Liberal Party of the Ottoman people), the CUP's successor organization, alongside Ali Fethi, Hüseyin Rauf, and İsmail Canbolat, and immediately initiated a campaign to bring down Ahmed Tevfik's government.[1] He also established relations with Kara Kemal, in charge of the CUP's finances, and Sevkiyatçı Rıza, considered one of the founding members of *Karakol*, although it has not been proven that he collaborated directly with this underground agency of the Unionist movement.[2] In any event, the exactions that Turkish bands committed against Christian villages in the Samsun region were not unrelated to his appointment as inspector of the Ninth Army. The Entente supposedly demanded that Damad Ferid put an end to these attacks, whereupon Ferid came up with the idea of sending a senior officer capable of restoring order to Samsun – that is to say, one who could call a halt to the operations that had certainly been planned by the Unionist network.[3] Zürcher suggests that the arrest of several of Kemal's close associates, such as Ali Fethi (on 17 April) induced him to accept the post, probably with *Karakol's* approval. Karakol was then looking, according to Şeref [Çavuşoğlu], for an eminent personality capable of heading up the resistance in Anatolia. The first person approached to take on the task, the former grand vizier Ahmed İzzet, is said to have refused the offer, paving the way for the nomination of Mustafa Kemal, who had the support, notably, of Dr. Esad [Işık], one of the leaders of *Karakol*.[4] Kemal, who is known to have been a Unionist from the early days of the movement, but who had no part in the genocidal policies implemented by Talât and Enver, was a logical "second choice."[5] But what calculations led Ferid to appoint a Young Turk inspector in Anatolia and to give him full powers? It is hard to imagine that the grand vizier was unaware of the general's long-standing ties to the CUP. Was he deceived by his entourage or even influenced by Unionist networks? Did he underestimate Kemal's capacities or did he think, rather, that his authority would lead to a conflict with the existing networks? There seems to be no satisfactory explanation for the choice, unless we supposed that Ferid was not hostile to the emergence of a resistance movement in Anatolia, even if the Young Turks control-led it. He doubtless hoped to take advantage of this situation to wring concessions from the Allies during the peace conference.

At any rate, the Congress of Erzerum, which Kemal convened two months after his arrival in Samsun on 19 May, was held, symbolically, on 23 July 1919, the anniversary of the 1908 revolution.[6] It may therefore be safely said that, given the urgency of the situation, the gen-eral had from the onset rallied the support of a part of the Unionist movement that had withdrawn to Anatolia, even if the movement did not recognize him as its legitimate leader. According to Zürcher, the Young Turk networks were of the view that Kemal owed his posi-tion to them and that this unprecedented situation could not last long. Kemal, for his part, was aware of the fact that he had no legitimacy within the Unionist movement and that, in order to acquire the authority he needed, he would have gradually to eliminate all those who contested his power: *Karakol* in April 1920, Enver's supporters in 1921, and the surviving Unionist leaders in 1926.[7]

Hardly had the Congress of Erzerum ended then Kemal found himself confronting an initiative by the *Karakol* that had been no doubt calculated to remind him that that organi-zation alone was the legitimate successor to the Young Turk heritage and thus had consider-able military and financial means. In August 1919, it sent a circular to all military units in which it announced that it had its own civilian and military structures, with officers, central headquarters, and general staff. Kemal was unaware at the time that the organization had decided to use him as a figurehead in hopes of acquiring a more presentable image. It was probably with a certain irritation that the general learned from Kara Vasıf, the head of the *Karakol*, that he had become, unbeknown to himself, the commander-in-chief of a group that took its orders from Berlin – that is, from Talât in person.[8] Thus, in refusing to submit to the *Karakol*'s orders, Kemal entered into conflict with the Central Committee members in exile. He thus effectively joined the already existing current of Unionist cadres who wanted to free themselves from the control of the organization's old leadership, which was labor-ing under the burden of its recent crimes and whose credibility was open to question. We can sum up the situation by saying that the current that came together around Kemal had wanted to pursue the Ittihad's national Turkish plan without having to assume responsibility for the atrocities perpetrated by its elders. The strategy of drawing closer to the Bolsheviks that the *Karakol* put into practice in January 1920 no doubt also contributed to accentuating the rupture between the two nationalist movements. In this instance, the Kemalists were not necessarily hostile to this policy as such, which took concrete form in the retreat from Azerbaijan of forces led by Nuri Pasha and Halil [Kut], respectively Enver's brother and his uncle, leaving the way open for the Red Army.[9] These concessions, imposed by the circum-stances, were no doubt intended to strengthen Azerbaijan's position in Moscow and at the same time leave independent Armenia in an untenable position on the eve of the Treaty of Sèvres. Kemal's perceptible irritation thus had more to do with form than with substance. He doubtless found it intolerable that the exiles continued to exert an influence from abroad on the policies adopted by Turkey and had an organization that was supposed to be acting along the same lines as he was under their direct orders. In deciding to dissolve the *Karakol* in April 1920,[10] Kemal patently sought to assert his authority and unify the nationalist movement. In so doing, he took the risk of offending the CUP's military leaders, especially those who had worked in the Special Organization during the war, with whom Enver remained very popu-lar.[11] In other words, in the first year of its existence, the Kemalist movement was far from enjoying unanimous support and had to wage a stiff battle in order to assert itself vis-a-vis the partisans of the Berlin exiles who had been reconverted into left-wing militants.

A misadventure of Filibeli Ahmed Hilmi's, the vice-president of the Special Organization and Şakir's right-hand man in Erzerum in 1915, shows that Kemal was suspicious of the exiles' close associates. In November 1920, when Hilmi arrived in Trebizond, intending to go to the Caucasus in order to convince Enver not to get involved in Anatolian affairs, Kâzım Karabekir, the commander-in-chief of the eastern front, prevented him from carrying out his plan.[12] There is good reason to suppose that Hilmi did not let him go north on orders from Kemal.

The result of the January 1920 elections to the Ottoman parliament shows, however, that the exiles' supporters continued to control political life in both the provinces and the capital. Furthermore, a report emanating from the British intelligence services indicates that, of the 164 newly elected deputies, a majority "as such approved of the Policy of extermination of the Armenian population, but their names have not been included in this list," and that 24 had been directly implicated in the violence:[13] Adıl Bey and his son Rahmi, elected in Tekirdağ;[14] Süleyman Sirri, released from prison on 6 April 1919 and elected in Ismit;[15] Bayrakdar Haci Veli, elected in Eskişehir, who had murdered the former *mutesarif* of Siirt, Serfiçeli Hilmi Bey;[16] Yusuf Kemal, elected in Kastamonu, implicated, according to a report produced by Lieutenant Slade on 29 December 1919, "in the policy of deportation"; Ahmed Şükrü, a member of the Central Committee who had been deported to Malta, elected in Kastamonu; Suad Bey, elected in Kastamonu, who had had a hand in the deportations; Besim Bey, elected in Kastamonu, the former secretary of Atıf Bey, the vali of Angora during the massacres; Bafrali Emin Bey, elected in Samsun; Kiresunli Eşref Bey, elected in Trebizond, who was implicated in the atrocities perpetuated in Kirason; Hilmi Bey, elected in Angora, who had been arrested on 16 March 1919 and then freed by the Kemalist forces; Hamitli Ali Rıza Bey, elected in Kirşehir, a leader of *çetes* belonging to the Special Organization and the author of the massacres that took place in Gölbaşi; Haci Tevfik, elected in Çanğırı, who was also implicated in the deportations in his city; Ömer Lutfi Bey, elected in Amasia; Halil Bey, elected in Erzincan; Mustafa Kemal, elected in Erzerum; Celal [Bayar], elected in Saruhan, a former CUP delegate in Smyrna; Alizâde Reşid, elected in Saruhan, the former military commander of Eskişehir, involved in the massacres and deportations; Hamdullah Subhi Bey, elected in Adalia, in exile in Germany, where he assured Talât's liaisons with Istanbul; Fayk Bey, elected in Denizli; Yünüs Nadi, the editor of *Yeni Gun*, elected in Smyrna; Tahsin Bey, the former vali of Erzerum, elected in Smyrna; Haydar Bey, the former vali of Mosul and Bitlis, elected in Van; Hasim Bey, the former police chief of Smyrna, elected in Karasi; and Fuad Bey, the former *kaymakam* of Burhaniye, also elected in Karasi.[17]

The outcome of these elections constitutes an excellent index of the state of Turkish public opinion, which had rallied massively to the nationalist movement and refused to accept the dismantling of the empire planned by the Allies. The elections also sanctioned the Liberal Ottoman Entente and its conciliatory policy toward the victors. Far from disavowing the Kemalist-Ittihadist movement, public opinion threw its support behind the movement's policy of harassing the Greeks and Armenians who were trying to reestablish themselves in their homes and recover their assets. When one takes a close look at the nationalist movement, it becomes clear that removing non-Turks from its Anatolian sanctuary continued to be one of its main activities: session after session, the Greek-Armenian committee attached to the British High Commission compiled lists of the exactions committed by the Kemalists-Ittihadists in the provinces.[18] It is noteworthy that, early in March 1920, operations were even conducted in the immediate outskirts of Istanbul, in Üsküdar and Yalova, whose Christian inhabitants continued moving to the European side of the Bosphorus.[19] In the interior, the harassment of non-Turks took much more violent forms: massacres were reported in Cilicia in February–March 1920, and acts of pillage and murder were committed throughout the country.[20] In Boğazlian and Kayseri in mid-April, the Kemalist forces even proceed to conscript Armenians by force.[21] In Bursa, the *Milli* set up committees that summoned taxpayers and demanded 25 per cent of the estimated value of their assets. Those who resisted were turned over to toughs who took on the task of ensuring that the directives were carried out.[22]

In a report dated 10 March 1920, the British authorities attempted to evaluate the possible effects of the drastic conditions imposed by the peace treaty with Turkey. They were of the opinion that serious threats of massacres of Christians existed in the areas controlled by the Kemalists.[23]

In other words, in mid-March 1920, the inter-allied forces had no choice but to take military control of Istanbul[24] by landing troops and increasing the size of their fleet there.[25] Questions of security aside, the Allies were also acutely aware that they were going to have to make a show of force should Turkey refuse to sign the peace treaty.[26] This deployment of Allied military forces, effected on the morning of 16 March 1920, did not meet with any real resistance in Istanbul, where five Turkish soldiers were killed during the landing.[27] The deployment of French and English forces in the capital and the subsequent arrest of war criminals did not, however, destabilize the nationalist movement. Apparently confident of their capabilities, the nationalists were not convinced, according to the British intelligence services, that the Allies were prepared to occupy more than just the capital.[28] It is even probable that the nationalist movement turned the repercussions of this operation to advantage in order to reinforce its position in Anatolia, make its actions more credible, and distract attention from the heavy charges leveled at most of the leaders of the movement. The remarkably well-orchestrated communications about the Anatolian resistance to European imperialism made it possible to make many forget the accusations of mass murder. The progressive Islamic posture adopted by the *Milli* movement also made it possible to mobilize support for Turkey in the Muslim countries under the yoke of European imperialism. The position taken by the "Young Turk government now in Berlin," as described by a British diplomat stationed in the German capital, was unambiguous: "The terrible war which broke out after the armistice in Asia, it is the product of the English policy of the last eighteen months."[29] In other words, the Kemalist-Ittihadist movement gave the British seeking to dismantle the Ottoman Empire as good as it got, by attempting, in particular, to destabilize some of Britain's colonies.

There can be no question of examining these matters in detail here. It may, however, be observed that a French diplomat stationed in Berlin had no doubt that an alliance had been forged between the Kemalist-Ittihadists and the Soviets, who were considering attacking the Entente "in two direction: toward Asiatic Turkey and western Persia by way of Azerbaijan and Georgia, and toward eastern Persia and India by way of Turkestan." There had even been discussion of the idea of putting "the leadership of the movement... in the hands of the Turkish leaders who were already present in the area: Enver Pasha in Tashkent and his brother Nuri Pasha in Azerbaijan." Also mentioned was "a sort of Pan-Islamist conference" in Munich, in Bavaria, and another "in Partenskirchen, a small town near the border where Cemal Pasha [was] living"; the participants included Talât, Dr. Nâzım, Bahaeddin Şakir, Cemal Azmi, Bedri Bey, Aziz Bey, "three Russians, two of them officers, two former German officers, a Tunisian, an Indian, a Persian, an Egyptian, and a Bulgarian." During a meeting of the Ittihadist Central Committee in which non-members also participated, Talât is supposed to have declared: "Lenin and Trotsky have agreed, in a treaty concluded with Enver, to provide 150,000 men for the Asian campaign," including 40,000 Turkmen "whom the former commander of the Army of Mesopotamia, Halil Pasha, is currently organizing with the help of several German officers." According to information obtained by the French diplomat just mentioned, Talât "is said to have described this policy as revolutionary opportunism, affirming that the Young Turks had to try to sow confusion everywhere so as to cause the English and French as many complications as possible."[30] Also worth noting is a short trip that Talât made to Naples around 16 April 1920, and then to Florence between 22 and 24 April, where he was to meet with a representative of Enver's, Zami Bey, for the purpose of coordinating their activities.[31] These grand Islamic-progressive maneuvers were crowned by the famous Baku Congress, which, the British S.I.S. reported served, above all, to strengthen the collaboration between Unionists and Bolsheviks. The terms of this collaboration, according to the same source, were negotiated in Baku by Cemal Pasha, Bedri Bey, and Halil [Kut]; the main objective was an insurrection against the British in Afghanistan and an invasion of northwestern Persia under Halil's command. Another member of the Ittihadist Central Committee, Küçük Talât, was appointed head of the Baku "translation bureau" – that is, a propaganda agency.[32] These operations were less an anti-imperialist campaign than a prolongation of the party's Pan-Turkish ambitions. Another S.I.S. report, based on documents confiscated from "a Turkish agent who had recently returned from Baku by way of Grozny, Novorsik, and Trebizond," shows that the Anatolian movement was in constant relation with its Caucasian networks.[33] It also reveals, citing "first-hand information," that the Bolshevik-Turkish agreement provided for "simultaneous attack upon Georgia and Armenia by the Soviet and the Turks [...] in order, however, to 'liquidate' Armenia."[34]

That said, it is by no means certain that Mustafa Kemal was associated with or even informed of these projects, which show that at the time the members of the Young Turk Central Committee believed that although they had briefly gone into exile, they and they alone had legitimate authority over Turkey. There must, however, have been a degree of collaboration between the Ittihadist and Kemalist movements in Anatolia, where Kemal was in the ascendant. It is, on the other hand, not certain that Kemal controlled the Ottoman League, whose general secretariat, based in Geneva, sought to convince the peace conference of the validity of the Turkish point of view. A 6 January 1920 Ottoman League circular declares that "300 million people, from the depths of Asia and the Pacific to the remotest parts of Africa – a whole world – today have their eyes riveted on Constantinople and its Caliph; a whole world is following, with breathless emotion, the great drama that will unfold in Paris and the fate that the Conference will mete out to the valiant Turkish people."[35] The June 1920 assassination of Grand Vizier Damad Ferid shows that the Kemalist organization already had active branches in Istanbul that were independent of the Ittihad's structures.[36] In 1920, the competition between Ittihadists and Kemalists was obvious. Among the documents intercepted by the S.I.S. about "a Turkish Bolshevik delegate" who had gone from Baku to Istanbul, the intelligence officers found a letter dated 27 July 1920 in Baku addressed to "Herrn H-Jafer Sa'iyd," Hardenburgstraße 4, Berlin. This was known to be Talât's address. The letter had been sent by a certain "Dr. Mehmed"; the British thought that Mehmed was Bahaeddin Şakir. The letter alludes to the activities of a certain Ali – most probably Enver – and a plan to create new "information organizations," one of them in Bern, Switzerland.[37] This suggests that the Ittihad also maintained a structured network in Istanbul, but did not control the Ottoman League, which was based in Geneva and directed, rather, by the Liberals.

The military operations targeting Armenia in fall 1920 were, in contrast, clearly conducted by the Fourteenth Army Corps under the command of Kâzım Karabekir, which received its orders from the Kemalist government. While these operations took place in the strategy aimed to make the clauses of the Treaty of Sèvres inoperative, they had another much more ambitious, albeit veiled, objective. "Armenia should be eliminated politically and physically," ordered a wire sent by the Kemalist government to Kâzım Karabekir on 8 November 1920.[38] Another cabled order that was intercepted by Ottoman and British intelligence services is just as revealing when it comes to the Kemalist regime's intentions. Dated 25 September 1920 and signed by Kemal in person, it gave the army commanders instructions about the operations planned against Armenia[39] (which is described in it as an "obstacle to communications with the Muslim peoples" to which Turkey had "promised" aid) and defined the mission of the "Army of the Arax," charged with "opening and maintaining

communications with the Allied forces toward the east and northeast."⁴⁰ These orders were
supplemented by an encrypted 8 November telegram that recommended "achieving our goal
stage by stage ... while acting as if we wanted peace."⁴¹ The military operations that followed,
culminating in the Sovietization of Armenia, were simply the logical consequence of these
orders. By offering itself to the Bolsheviks, Caucasian Armenia escaped a third phase of the
genocide, this time planned in advance by the Kemalist government. In a way, the Kemalists'
commitment to genocidal action against the Caucasian Armenians marked the passage from
witness of the original Young Turk movement to the new Unionist wave unified by Mustafa
Kemal. While there were manifest fine differences between the practices of these two, sometimes intermingled, groups, both had basically the same ethnic-nationalist ideology. Kemal
continued to build up the Turkish nation-state of which his predecessors had dreamed, even
if it did not have the proportions originally envisaged.

By executing Mehmed Talât in Berlin on 15 March 1921, Bahaeddin Şakir and Cemal
Azmi in Berlin on 17 April 1922, and Ahmed Cemal in Tiflis on 25 July 1922 – Enver
was killed on 4 August 1922 by a Bolshevik brigade – the Armenians quite involuntarily
rendered a service to the Kemalists, ridding them of their main Ittihadist rivals. Another
element doubtless helped strengthen Kemal's position within the Young Turk movement:
the British liberated the criminals they had been holding on Malta. It was Kemal's government that had negotiated the release of these men, from which the Young Turks of
the first generation profited. In mid-June 1921, the British military had suggested the idea
of an exchange of prisoners to Britain's diplomats.⁴² The politicians agreed on the condition that the Young Turk be brought to trial before "Turkish or other" courts, the more so
as the S.I.S. was having "trouble amassing evidence" capable of ensuring that "exemplary
sentences" would be pronounced, in conformity with "the clauses about [the] sanctions"
provided for in the Treaty of Sèvres. H. Rumbold agreed, notwithstanding, that it would be
necessary to have the British prisoners released "before winter."⁴³ The intransigence of the
government in Ankara had paid off; in the end, London agreed to release, unconditionally,
the 112 prisoners on Malta. On the afternoon of 25 October, 70 men were put aboard the
Chrysanthemum and another 42 aboard the *Montenol*; both ships were bound for Istanbul.⁴⁴
This unconditional liberation enhanced Mustafa Kemal's growing prestige but at the same
time exposed him to the renewed ambitions of the Ittihadist leaders who had been freed
thanks to him. When Kara Kemal met with his namesake, the general, in Ismit between
16 and 20 January 1923 – Zürcher points out that Mustafa Kemal does not breathe a word
about this in his memoirs – he was invited to confer with his friends about the CUP's
future role.⁴⁵ A Congress of the "CUP" was organized in April 1923 in Constantinople in
the home of Mehmed Cavid, the biggest home. All the members of the Ittihad's Central
Committee and Political Bureau came, except, of course, for those who had been executed
by the Armenians. In attendance, in addition to the man who hosted the congress, Mehmed
Cavid, were Dr. Nâzım, Dr. Rüsûhî, Ahmed Şükrü, Kara Kemal, Hüseyin Cahid [Yalçin],
Filibeli Ahmed Hilmi, Yenibahçeli Nail, Çolak Selâheddin, Vehbi Bey, Ahmed Nesimi
[Sayman], Hüseyinzâde Ali [Turan], Rahmi [Evranos], Küçük Talât [Muşkara], and, prob-
ably, İsmail Canbolat.⁴⁶

After two days of deliberations, the congress decided not to take part in the upcoming
legislative elections and, rather, decided to establish a new program for the reformed CUP; it
offered to make Mustafa Kemal the leader of the party, in the hope that it would thus obtain
a chance to revive it. Kemal obviously refused, as was foreseeable. He did not pass up the
occasion to recall that the CUP had been dissolved in 1918, so that no one now had a right
to speak on its behalf; this was one way among others of telling these criminal "patriots"
that their time had passed. Zürcher observed that a new opposition, taking the form of an
Ittihadist network, nevertheless emerged shortly after the elections to the Grand Assembly,

in June 1923, although the candidates it put forward had all been approved of by Mustafa Kemal in person.[47]

The adventure of the CUP did not really come to an end until 1926, when most of its ranking leaders were executed. Officially, a plot on Kemal's life was discovered in June 1926. It led to the arrest of the Ittihadist leadership and gave rise to a first trial that took place from 26 June to 13 July 1926 before the court in Smyrna, with Kel Ali [Çetinkaya],[48] a former member of the Special Organization who had gone over to the Kemalists, as its presiding judge.[49] The man assigned the task of killing Kemal, Ziya Hurşid, ostensibly confessed that he had planned the assassination with Abdülkadır and Ahmed Şükrü, a member of the Central Committee who supposedly provided the conspirators with weapons and money. It clearly seems, however, that this "plot" involving members of the CUP's Central Committee was nothing but a show staged by the Kemalists, who wanted to rid themselves of the last Ittihadists "legally."[50] The first trial culminated in death sentences for 11 men, who were executed on 12 July, the night after the verdict was handed down: İsmail Canbolat, Ahmed Şükrü, Ziya Hurşid, Halis Turgut, Colonel Arif, Rüştü, Hafız Mehmed, Rasim, and Abdülkadır.[51]"

It was, however, the second part of the trial, which began in Ankara on 1 August 1926, which made it possible to do away with the *crème de la crème* of the CUP for good and all. In the dock this time were Hüseyin Rauf, Abdülhak Adnan, Mehmed Cavid, Dr. Nâzım, Hüseyinzâde Ali [Turan], Yenibahçeli Nail, Filibeli Ahmed Hilmi, Hüseyin Cahid, Küçük Talât, Hüseyin Avnı, Kara Vasıf, Midhat Sükrü [Bleda], and Ahmed Nesimi [Sayman]. Especially harsh treatment was meted out to these CUP leaders, who were judged on three counts: 1) "the CUP's irresponsible wartime" policies and "abuses of power"; 2) planning to replace Mustafa Kemal in 1921; and 3) planning Kemal's murder at the 1923 Unionist Congress.[52] Thus, Kemal did not hesitate to question the actions of the CUP leadership during the first First World War; in so doing, he obviously wished to settle accounts with these criminals and dissociate his regime from them, even while lending credibility to the thesis that a conspiracy had been hatched against him. By having Cavid, Nâzım, Nail, and Hilmi hanged on 26 August 1926 – the other accused men were given prison terms – he punished the main organizers of the Armenian genocide still alive, without making direct reference to it. Zürcher seems convinced that the "complot de Smyrne" was merely a pretext for liquidating the first generation of Young Turks.[53] This internal purge of the Ittihad's ranking hierarchy should not, however, be allowed to obscure the fact that the purge itself made it possible for the CUP to survive under the new name "People's Republican Party." The party's cadres were basically Young Turks, almost all of whom had been implicated in the destruction of the Ottoman Armenians: Colonel İsmet [İnönü], prime minister and, later, president of the republic; Ali [Çetinkaya], the presiding judge at the supreme court; Celâl [Bayar], finance minister and, later, president of the republic; Tevfik Rüştü [Aras], foreign minister; Cemil [Urbaydın], interior minister; Ali Fethi [Okyar], prime minister; Kâzım [Özalp], president of the National Assembly; Receb [Peker], the party's secretary general and, , later, a minister; and Şükrü [Kaya], foreign minister and, subsequently, minister of the interior.[54]

We could add the names of dozens of deputies and high-ranking state officials to the list, among them Hüseyin Cahit [Yalçin], a former member of the Central Committee; Sabit Sağıroğlu, the former vali of Mamuret ul-Aziz; and Mustafa Abdülhalik, the former vali of Bitlis and Aleppo, who later became finance minister and then president of parliament.

Conclusion

At the end of the grueling task that writing a book like this one represents, I have the feeling that I have made a new contribution to research on the subject, but I am also well aware that many of the historical points touched on here will call for further work from scholars for a long time to come. The corpus of documents that provides the basis for the present volume is, to be sure, extensive, and helped me shed light on hitherto unexplored aspects of this outbreak of mass violence, but it did not allow me to penetrate to the depths of the Young Turk system; many unknowns remain. I was able to observe the activities of the Young Turk Central Committee only through indirect sources – as a rule, European intelligence services – in the case of a revolutionary organization like the CUP, such activities are by nature secret. Similarly, such access as we have to the internal procedures of the Special Organization continues to depend exclusively on the memoirs of its former members or foreign observers. There are no known archival funds for these two organizations, the veritable instigators and organizers of the destruction of the Ottoman Armenians, and this constitutes a major lacuna. A few hints, however, as we have indicated now and again in the course of this study, suggest that materials emanating from the Young Turk movement have survived and are probably held in Ankara today. When the time comes, they will surely shed decisive light on the circumstances surrounding the liquidation of the Armenians.

On the other hand, I believe that I have provided a very close analysis of the construction of the CUP's ideology and the party's ethno-nationalistic radicalization. I also think that I have brought out the nature of the friendly or conflictual relations that the Armenian Committees, Hnchak or Dashnak, maintained with the Ittihadist movement. When one compares these experiences, one discovers a striking cultural and even, in certain respects, ideological affinity between the groups in question. By exhuming the most important of the texts that express the Armenian revolutionaries' profound convictions about their Young Turk colleagues, and vice versa, I think that I have seized their points of convergence and, above all, the latent antagonism haunting them. It is clear that their respective conceptions of the empire's future were not all that different and that in both groups there were men convinced of the possibility of going a part of the road together, before circumstances conspired to promote a radicalization of the Young Turk Central Committee.

That said, it is no longer possible today to defend the thesis that a programmed destruction of the Armenian population was set in motion by Abdülhamid and brought to completion by the Young Turks. The Hamidian practice of partial amputation of the Armenian social body for the purpose, as it were, of reducing it to politically acceptable proportions, cannot be put on the same level as the policy of ethnic homogenization conceived by the CUP. Moreover, it has been established that the process that culminated in the perpetration of the genocide was signposted by a series of decisions that reveal the progressive radicalization of the Young Turk party-state, motivated notably by the serious military setbacks that it suffered on the Caucasian front. This affirmation must, however, be tempered in view of the lessons furnished by an attentive examination of the ideological development of the men in control of the state. Their desire to homogenize Asia Minor, to Turkify this territory, obviously went back a long way and certainly constituted the starting point for the collective thought process that eventually culminated, after going through a number of stages, in the plan for the physical destruction of the Ottoman Armenians. The plan to deport Greeks from the Aegean seacoast and Armenians from the eastern provinces concocted by the Young Turk Central Committee in February 1914 apparently reflected – as Taner Akçam has clearly shown – its desire to modify the demographic makeup of Asia Minor, to make it a "Turkish" space but not necessarily to liquidate its non-Turkish elements. The Armenians, who were initially one of the party's secondary priorities after the Greeks, were, it seems, initially supposed to go settle the Syrian and Mesopotamian deserts, areas considered to lie outside the Turkish heartland. But the CUP's ambitions were not limited to these population shifts alone. Muslim non-Turks, ranked according to their perceived capacities for assimilation to the proposed "Turkish" model, were also deported in order to fill the vacuum left in various places by the deportation of the Greek and Armenian populations. This vast internal manipulation of historical groups, reflecting a nationalist ideology and a geo-strategic logic, took its place within a still more ambitious plan that sought to create a geographic and demographic continuum with the Muslim or Turkish-speaking populations of the Caucasus. The stinging defeat dealt out to the Ottoman army in Sarıkamış in late December 1914 not only convinced the Young Turk Central Committee of the impossibility of achieving its ambitions, but no doubt also induced it to compensate for these reverses by adopting a more radical policy toward the Armenian population. This stage in the radicalization process may be dated 22–25 March 1915. If the new, more radical policy did not enjoy the unanimous support of the Young Turk Central Committee, it also did not elicit strong opposition.

The region-by-region examination of the process of deportation and extirpation also tends to show that at the outset, the Young Turks' liquidation plan bore only on the populations of the six eastern vilayets considered to be the Armenians' historical lands. However, the two-month lag observable in the operations affecting the Armenian colonies in Anatolia, which were integrated into their predominantly Turkish environment, can also be interpreted as the consummation – late, to be sure – of the liquidation program. The difference in the treatments meted out to conscripts enrolled in the Third Army and men from the eastern provinces, almost all of whom were eliminated locally, whereas the recruits from the communities of Anatolia served on the front in the Dardanelles or in the Fourth Army without being subjected to serious mistreatment, plainly shows that the Young Turk plan had been intelligently elaborated. Depending on where the people affected came from, the plan provided for immediate liquidation of the men, recruits or not, or rational exploitation of their skills and labor-power. Differential treatment is also observable as far as the rest of the population – women, children, and old people – is concerned. Study of the methods and means employed to deport these people indicates that the convoys that set out from the eastern vilayets were systematically destroyed en route and that only a small minority of deportees arrived in their "places of relegation." It can be seen, in contrast, that the Armenians from the colonies in Anatolia or Thrace were sent to Syria with their families, often by rail, and that they got at least as far as Cilicia.

The ultimate stage of the destruction process, which we have called the "second phase of the genocide," was aimed precisely at these survivors, most of who came from Anatolia or Cilicia. The material context for these new acts of violence, the concentration camps in Syria or Upper Mesopotamia, was long *terra incognita* for scholars. Returning to a preliminary study of this subject, I have situated, on the basis of a few converging indices, the ultimate decision to destroy these remaining deportees in late February or early March 1916. This decision affected some 500,000 surviving deportees who had reached Syria and Mesopotamia six months and more earlier, and sometimes even adapted to their new environment so well as to be able to support themselves there. In this precise case, two clashing logics – military needs and the desire to liquidate all the survivors without exception – can clearly be discerned, against the background of the rivalry between the leaders of the Central Committee and the region's military commander, Ahmed Cemal. The arrival of delegates of the Young Turk party in Syria and the fact that the Council of Ministers appointed the main executioners of the eastern vilayets to head the regions in which deportees were to be found are so many concrete signs announcing the "second phase of the genocide," which ran from April to December 1916. In many respects, this phase illustrates the Young Turk Central Committee's genocidal will even better than the first, for the Central Committee could not, in this case, take shelter behind its discourse about security and its theory about a plot against the Turkish state. Concretely, it set out to liquidate a population of which the great majority was made up of women and children. The general slaughter organized, notably, in Syria even seems to flow from a virtually pathological animosity toward the survivors, at antipodes from anything resembling rational governance.

More generally, it appears that the procedure elaborated by the Central Committee was the fruit of extended reflection on the demographic composition of Anatolia and Asia Minor, with the ambition of remodeling the human geography of these regions. It is this geographer's logic, the basis for the conception of the liquidation plan, on which we have focused precisely in order to reconstitute the process of destruction itself, the object of the fourth part of the present study.

A study of mass crimes such as genocide can obviously not be restricted to an examination of the acts of the "criminal state," even if the circumstances that led to the unleashing of such violence inevitably fascinate the historian. The historiography of the genocide of the Armenians long left the victims' experience to one side. Vahakn Dadrian, to whom we owe a great deal, long affirmed that sources provided by the survivors themselves could not be taken into account in so controversial a case. He himself deliberately limited himself to Turkish sources on the one hand and German and Austro-Hungarian sources on the other, all the better to "prove" that the genocide really occurred. In so doing, he focused his gaze almost exclusively on the executioners and ignored the real fate of the victims. Their fate, in contrast, has its place in my overall project. The aim here is to let the victims speak, thereby recovering their lived experience, something that does not require proof of any kind whatsoever. After steeping myself for several years in accounts produced "as the events unfolded" – just what that means is defined in the present work – I came to the conclusion that it was not only possible, but essential to exploit the Armenian sources, comparing them with materials provided by diplomats and missionaries and also with each other. The two main archives that I have exploited here, held respectively by the Armenian Patriarchate in Jerusalem (the Monastery of Saint James) and the Nubar Library of the Armenian General Benevolent Union in Paris, comprise a unique corpus that allowed me to make a comprehensive study of the geography of the genocide, thanks to some 10,000 pages of handwritten documents. In other words, they enabled me to compile an account of the summary executions in the eastern regions, of each convoy of deportees, the routes they took, the killing fields through which they passed, and, more generally, the experience of the "long march"; it revealed the natural selection that took place en route and the characteristics of those categories of Armenians whom the Young Turk Central Committee considered leaving alive, the better to integrate them into its plan to Turkify Asia Minor. As the Young Turks saw matters, young children – preferably little girls – and older girls or women were destined to reinforce the "Turkish nation" after going through a ritual of integration into the dominant group that was borrowed from the Muslim religion. As a Young Turk officer put it, Armenian women with a certain level of education were predestined to accelerate the modernization of the Turkish family and Turkish society. The many different cases described in the present volume show that Young Turk nationalist ideology is rooted in a form of racism directed against the collective identity of a group rather than in individual biological rejection of the kind later practiced by the Nazi regime. Careful examination of all these secondary effects of the genocide best illustrates how closely the murder of the Armenians was bound up with the construction of the Turkish nation.

Another aspect of the Young Turk plan seems to me to have been brought out clearly here – the systematic seizure of the individual and collective property of the Ottoman Armenians, which went hand-in-hand with the attempt to form a Turkish middle class of businessmen. The regime's sociologist, Ziya Gökalp, provided the theory for this program, baptized *Millî İktisat* (National Economy). We have analyzed the way it worked. It obviously constituted the socio-economic complement to the mass crimes. It served as both a justification and an incentive. It has been shown here that it benefited the Young Turk elite and the party-state above all, but all other social strata as well, notably those who participated in the Young Turk movement without necessarily sharing the extremist ideology of its leaders. The lust for gain no doubt did much to radicalize men who under other circumstances would not have acted as they did because they would have been held back by moral principles of religious inspiration. The action of the party-state itself and the propaganda that it methodically orchestrated to stigmatize the Armenians as a group did the rest.

On the basis of an inventory of those chiefly to blame for this genocide, whether civilian and military officials or local notables, it can be affirmed that the individuals who were the most deeply implicated in the mass violence often came from the most marginal social groups and, it must be emphasized, were often members of minorities with roots in the Caucasus. This holds for the Çerkez and Chechens in particular, who it seems safe to say had accounts to settle with their painful history and were easily led to identify the Armenians with their Russian oppressors. The major role played by "the" Kurds, which is stressed by Turkish historiography and also by many Western scholars, turns out, upon examination, to be much less clear-cut than has been affirmed. Indeed, it comes down to the active participation of nomadic Kurdish tribes and only rarely involves sedentary villagers, who were encouraged by the Special Organization to take what they could from deportees already stripped of their most valuable assets. There can be no doubt that Turkish historiography ultimately contaminated independent scholars who were not necessarily in a position to assess the accuracy of this dogma that had its practical uses for those seeking to shake off the burden of a violent past at the expense of a group that is itself stigmatized in our day.

Examining the last issue discussed in the present study, the trials of the authors of the genocide or, more specifically, the attempts to bring them to justice undertaken by both the Ottoman authorities and international institutions, has allowed me to evaluate the determination of the Ottoman state and Turkish society to assume their responsibility for the liquidation of the Armenians. This chapter of the history treated here clearly illustrates the incapacity of the great majority to consider these acts punishable crimes; it confronts us with a self-justifying discourse that persists in our own day, a kind of denial of the "original sin," the act that gave birth to the Turkish nation, regenerated and re-centered in a purified space. That said, these parodies of justice made it possible to assemble a great deal of judicial material – evidence given to a formalistic court-martial that was interested above all in pinning the blame for the crimes committed on a small group of men, the better to free the Ottoman state from its obligations and provide the nascent Turkish nation with a certain "virginity."

Parallel to these legal proceedings, the repeated attempts to interfere in them by Unionist circles show that the new authorities never succeeded in throwing off the Young Turks' tutelage. The sabotage of the legal proceedings, the theft of incriminating evidence, and the organization of the flight and transfer to Anatolia of the accused that were undertaken from the Anatolian and, soon, Kemalist sanctuary attest the influence of the Young Turk network that at most sought, by promoting Mustafa Kemal, to flee the gaze of the international community.

Finally, I would like to insist on the preparations made mainly by the British and French governments to bring the Young Turk criminals before an international "High Court." The legal categories elaborated from February 1919 on by the Committee of Responsibilities and its various subcommittees operating within the framework of the preliminary peace conference did not, it is true, find practical application. They did, however, provide direct inspiration for the Convention on the Prevention and Punishment of the Crime of Genocide adopted by the U.N. in 1948.

The mass of material[1] emanating from the Information Bureau of the Patriarchate of Constantinople that has been exploited throughout this study shows that the reconstructed Armenian institutions were resolved to identify those responsible for the extirpation of the Armenian population. The Armenians continued to be those best informed about the issue, those most familiar with the Young Turk elites. In addition to numerous lists of those responsible in the various regions, the Information Bureau also drew up lists of the "major culprits," while explaining the philosophy on which the compilation of such lists was based.[2] The Turks have elevated some of these individuals to the rank of national heroes; others formed the exclusive circles that helped Mustafa Kemal forge contemporary Turkey.

The formula "destroying in order to build" perhaps best reflects, with only a touch of exaggeration, the logic that dominated the Young Turk regime in 1915 and that still permeates the ideological and cultural foundations of a society which rejects its past.

Notes

Introduction

1. The historian Fuat Dundar has just exhumed, from the Archives of the prime minister in Istanbul, ethnographic maps and censuses carried out just before or during the First World War. Previously, we knew of their existence only from accounts by those who had seen them (see especially the report of the German diplomat H. Mordtmann, *infra*, p. 626, n. 7). These maps and censuses were put to use in the effort to modify the demographic make-up of certain regions and eradicate certain populations in order to replace them with others: Fuat Dundar, "La dimension ingénierie de la Turcisation de l'Anatolie: Les cartes ethnographiques et les recensements," paper presented at a conference in Salzburg, 14–17 April 2005.

2. Raymond Kévorkian, *L'Extermination des déportés arméniens ottomans dans les camps de concentration de Syrie-Mésopotamie (1915–1916), la Deuxième phase du génocide*, RHAC II (1998).

3. M. Şükrü Hanioğlu, *The Young Turks in Opposition*, Oxford University Press 1995; M. Şükrü Hanioğlu, *Preparation for a Revolution: The Young Turks, 1902–1908*, Oxford University Press 2001.

4. Krieger, Եղղռատի Հայասպանութեան Վաւերագրական Պատմութիւնը [*Documentary History of the Massacre of the Armenians of Yozgat*], New York 1980.

5. Vahakn Dadrian, *Histoire du génocide arménien*, Paris 1996; Vahakn Dadrian, "The Naïm-Andonian Documents on the World War One Destruction of the Ottoman Armenians – The Anatomy of a Genocide," *International Journal of Middle Eastern Studies*, vol. 18:3, pp. 311–60 (1986); Vahakn Dadrian, "The Role of Turkish Physicians in the World War I Genocide of the Armenians," *Holocaust & Genocide Studies*, vol. 1:2, pp. 169–92 (1986); Vahakn Dadrian, "The Role of the Special Organization in the Armenian Genocide during the First World War," in *Minorities in Wartime*, P. Panayi (éd.), Oxford 1993; Vahakn Dadrian, "Documentation of the Armenian Genocide in German and Austrian Sources," in The *Widening Circle of Genocide*, I. Charny (ed.), New Brunswick, NJ, 1994; *The Armenian Genocide in Official Turkish Sources. Collected Essays*, special issue of *Journal of Political and Military Sociology*, 1995; Vahakn Dadrian, Հայկական Ցեղասպանութիւնը Խորհրդարանային եւ Պատմագիտական Քննարկումներով [The Armenian Genocide in Parlementary and Historiographical Sources], Watertown 1995.

6. Erik J. Zürcher, *The Unionist Factor: The Rôle of the Committee of Union and Progress in the Turkish National Movement, 1905–1926*, Leiden 1984; Erik J. Zürcher, *Turkey: A Modern History*, London and New York 1999.

7. Cf. *Takvim-ı Vakayi*, no 2611, 28 July 1916, pp. 1–5, text of the decree modifying the internal Constitution of the millet. The circumstances surrounding this dissolution are explained at length below, pp. 850–851.

8. Public Record Office, FO 371/4174, n° 118377, letter from High Commissioner Calthorpe to Lord Curzon, 1 August 1919. See *infra*, pp. 801, etc., on the activities of this committee.

9. Zaven Der Yéghiayan, Պատրիարքական Յուշերս [My *Patriarchal Memoirs*], Cairo 1947, p. 277.

10. *Ibidem*, pp. 301–2 at 304. Not until the session of 17/30 August 1919 did the Political Council decide to put the Bureau under its direct authority.

11. Reports prepared by the Bureau were often published in the French-language daily *The Renaissance*, which appeared from December 1918 to spring 1920 under the direction of Garabed Nurian and Dikran Chayan, a former member of the Council of State; they were assisted by Dr. Topjian.

The patriarch informs us that the Patriarchate financed publication of this newspaper (*ibidem*, pp. 302–3).

12. *Ibidem*, p. 304. *Faits et documents. épisodes des massacres arméniens de Dyarbékir*, Constantinople 1919; Thomas Mgrdichian, Սիզրանակերսի Նահանգին Ջարդերը [*The Massacres in the Province of Dyarbekir*], Cairo 1919; Sebuh Aguni, Միլիոն մը Հայերու Ջարդի Պատմունիւնը [*History of the Massacre of One Million Armenians*], Constantinople 1920. The author, the former editor of the daily *Zhamanag*, was the first to publish a global study of the massacres, basing his work "on a large number of documents at the Patriarchate's disposal."

13. On the formation of the commission of inquiry, see Taner Akçam, *Insan Haklari ve Ermeni Sorunu*, Ankara 1999, pp. 445–6.

14. On 5 March 1919, the Council of Ministers nevertheless examined a report by Sâmi Bey that suggested abolishing the provincial courts martial and bringing all the cases involving the massacres and deportations before an exclusively military (rather than a mixed) court-martial based in Constantinople (*La Renaissance*, no. 82, 7 March 1919).

15. Zaven Der Yéghiayan, *Memoirs*, *op. cit.*, p. 303. These archives are still there today. They were "rediscovered" by Krieger in the 1960s, microfilmed, and then classified in some fifty boxes.

Part I   *Young Turks and Armenians Intertwined in the Opposition (1895–1908)*

1   *Abdülhamid and the Ottoman Opposition*

1. Hanioğlu, *The Young Turks in Opposition*, *op. cit.*, p. 71.
2. Dr. Çerkez Mehmed Reşit Bey (1872–1919), vali of Dyarbekir in 1915. We shall later have occasion to observe his impressive resolve to liquidate the Armenians of his vilayet.
3. Stephan H. Astourian, "Sur la formation de l'identité turque moderne et le génocide arménien: du préjugé au nationalisme moderne," acte du colloque *L'Actualité du génocide des Arméniens*, Paris 1999, pp. 35–7.
4. Sêlanikli Nâzım (c. 1870–1926), a physician trained in the Military Medical School in Constantinople, an emblematic figure of the Committee of Union and Progress from 1905 to 1922 and, as we shall see, one of the main organizers of the eradication of the Armenians. On his presence in Paris, see Hanioğlu, *The Young Turks in Opposition*, *op. cit.*, p. 74.
5. Ahmed Agayev (1869–1939) became one of the ideologues of Turkish nationalism and an eminent member of the CUP's Central Committee; as such, he was arrested and deported to Malta by the British in 1919. A leader of the Social Democratic Hnchak Party, Stepanos Sapah-Giulian, often met with Agayev during his stay in Paris: see Stepanos Sapah-Giulian, Պատասխանատուները [*The Responsibles*], Providence 1916, p. 134.
6. S. Sapah-Giulian (1861, Shahuk [Nakhichevan]–1928, New York) was educated in Tiflis, where he joined the SDHP; banished by the Czarist police, he fled to Paris, where he attended the Institute of Political Science as a student of Anatole Leroy-Beaulieu's: Sapah-Giulian, *The Responsibles*, *op. cit.*, p. 151.
7. This plan, which was made public on 11 May, had been prepared by the ambassadors of the powers stationed in Constantinople on the basis of Article 61 of the 1878 Treaty of Berlin, which provided for limited autonomy for the eastern vilayets inhabited by Armenians.
8. Sapah-Giulian, *The Responsibles*, *op. cit.*, p. 140.
9. Hanioğlu, *The Young Turks in Opposition*, *op. cit.*, p. 78.
10. Sapah-Giulian, *The Responsibles*, *op. cit.*, p. 145. Nubar granted the SDHP an annual subsidy of 300 pounds sterling to help finance publication of its newspapers.
11. *Ibidem*, p. 148.
12. Hanioğlu, *The Young Turks in Opposition*, *op. cit.*, p. 76.
    The fall 1895 massacres were aimed, first and foremost, at the Armenian population of the six eastern vilayets. They were launched in October, at the very moment that the sultan was signing (on 17 October) the reform plan of "11 May" after several months of resistance

to it. The correlation reform-massacre did not go unnoticed by the diplomats stationed in the empire; it constituted a challenge for the Young Turks, who were seeking at the time to create a unified organization against Abdülhamid around the themes of union and order.

13. Ahmed Rıza, "Chrétien, musulman et humanité," *Mechveret*, I/11, 15 May 1896, p. 3.

14. Ahmed Rıza, "Atrocités contre les chrétiens," *Mechveret*, I/14, 1 July 1896, p. 4.

15. Sapah-Giulian, *The Responsibles, op. cit.*, pp. 150–1.

16. On 1 October 1895, the Hnchaks had organized a demonstration in front of the Sublime Porte before presenting it with a petition bearing on the Sasun massacres the dismal plight of the survivors. Four thousand people participated in this peaceful march, which the organizers had announced to the authorities beforehand. The police, little accustomed to this type of protest – Dadrian points out that it was the first of its kind in the empire – stepped in; it was soon followed by the Muslim population. A general massacre was organized in all the neighborhoods of the capital in which Armenians lived. Istanbul's 40 Armenian churches were filled with refugees for two weeks, until the Palace issued the order to bring the manhunt for Armenians to a halt: V. Dadrian, *Histoire du génocide arménien*, Paris 1996, pp. 216–18, provides a general view of these events based on reports by European diplomats stationed in the capital.

17. *Ibidem*, p. 151. The scholar did sound out the French minister of foreign affairs, Hanoteaux, before agreeing to speak. Notwithstanding the negative response he received from Hanoteaux, who suggested that his participation in the debte might perturb the negotiations then underway, Leroy-Beaulieu decided to throw himself into the battle.

18. *Ibidem*.

19. *Ibidem*, p. 163. In his memoirs, Sapah-Giulian affirms that he felt at the time that Rıza needed them and was no longer treating them with the scorn he usually reserved for them.

20. Dadrian [1996], pp. 245–65, summarizes the events and provides a good overview of the sources available on both the act and its consequences.

21. Sapah-Giulian, *The Responsibles, op. cit.*, p. 164.

22. *Ibidem*, pp. 166–7.

23. *Ibidem*, pp. 172–3.

24. *Ibidem*, p. 173.

25. Hanioğlu, *The Young Turks in Opposition, op. cit.*, pp. 79–81. Murad Bey Mizanci (1853–1912), was a Turkish speaker from the Caucasus, born in Tiflis. The editorial board reacted positively to Murad Bey's call for union with the Armenian revolutionary committees, launched in the first issue of the *Mizan* published in Cairo. It appreciated, in particular, his clear condemnation of the large-scale massacres organized by the sultan: "Բաց նամակ Մուրադ Բէին [Open letter to Murad Bey]," *Hnchak*, no. 4, 29 February 1896, pp. 25–7.

26. Hanioğlu, *The Young Turks in Opposition, op. cit.*, pp. 83–4. In the empire, branches of the CUP were created, notably, in the towns to which the Young Turks had been exiled, such as Angora, Kastamonu and Mamuret ul-Azîz; they were also created in garrison towns, such as Erzerum, where the Local Committee established relations with the Armenian organizations. In March 1897, Setrak Pastermajian was arrested because he had received a sum of money from Europe and distributed it to members of the Erzerum CUP: *ibidem*., p. 87.

27. Mikayèl Varantian, Հայ Յեղափոխական Դաշնակցութեան Պատմութիւն [*History of the Armenian Revolutionary Federation*], II, Cairo 1950, p. 2, points out that in Geneva, where he himself was living in 1896, Tunali Hilmi and his Young Turk friends often visited *Droschak's* editorial offices, adding that after the attack on the *Banque Ottomane*, Ahmed Rıza came to see them in order to suggest that they join his struggle against the sultan, on condition that they renounce both the reforms provided for by Article 61 of the Treaty of Berlin and also revolutionary methods.

28. Hanioğlu, *The Young Turks in Opposition, op. cit.*, p. 87.

29. A branch created in Salonika in 1897 provided the occasion for Talât Bey's first appearance on the historical stage; Talât was corresponding with Ahmed Rıza in 1902. From 1897 to 1906, the branch failed to function properly: *ibidem*, p. 88.

30. *Ibidem*, p. 89.

31. *Ibidem*, pp. 100, 110. It was not until 1898 that Rıza again assumed leadership of the committee, with the support, as in the past, of Dr. Nâzım.

32. *Ibidem*, p. 102. The local opposition movement, which was almost entirely under the control of the *ulema* led by Hoca Muheddin, was in favor of the revolution because it would make it possible to spread Islam and preach "the word of God"; this movement finally became part of the CUP's Egyptian branch on the condition that the CUP stop recruiting Christian members and defend a political line based on unifying the Muslim elements of the Ottoman Empire.

33. *Ibidem*, p. 103.

34. *Ibidem*, p. 128. Rıza succeeded in persuading the *ulema* of al-Azhar to represent all the branches of the CUP: had Rıza convinced the *ulemas* that he represented the whole movement, a move that testified to his new approach. Dr. Nâzim, his confidant, notes that Rıza was suspicious of non-Turks, whom he considered unreliable (*ibidem.*, p. 136).

35. Diran Kelekian (1862, Kayseri–1915, near Sıvas), initially a Hnchak activist, joined the Young Turk movement after 1896, during his stays in London and Paris; he was part of the group that returned with Mizanci Murad; it was at this point that he drew closer to Ahmed Celâleddin, the chief of the intelligence service (*Droschak*, supplement of 40 pp. of 15 April, 15 July, 15 November to15 December 1899, p. 35; *Droschak*, no. 9/89, 30 September 1898, "Lettre de Constantinople, 1/13 octobre 1898"; editor-in-chief of the famous daily *Sapah* (1897–1899 and 1909–1915). During his exile in Cairo, he headed the political section of *Journal du Caire* (1904–1909). Close to certain Ottoman court circles, he helped Bahaeddin Şakir organize the CUP in 1905–1906. He was deported in April 1915 (A. Alboyadjian, Պատմութիւն Հայ Կեսարիոյ [*History of Armenian Caesaria*], II, Cairo 1937, pp. 2071–4).

36. Hanioğlu, *The Young Turks in Opposition*, *op. cit.*, p. 128.

37. "Երիտասարդ Թուրքիա [Young Turkey]," in *Droschak*, Organe de la Fédération Révolutionnaire Arménienne, no. 4/84, 30 April 1898, pp. 42–3.

38. "Առաջին քայլ [First Step]," in *Droschak*, no. 6/86, 30 June 1898, pp. 59–60, points out that *Mechveret*, "which, only a few months ago, was quite unreservedly attacking the Armenians and Bulgarians," had itself called for solidarity among all those opposed to the Hamidian regime.

39. "Քաղաքական Դրամա թէ Ֆարս [Political Tragedy or Farce?]," in *Droschak*, no. 4/95, 30 April 1899, pp. 50–1. In the section containing general information, p. 56, the editors point out that the local Armenian communities organized many meetings just before the conference, notably in Bulgaria, in order to vote on a memorandum to be sent to the president of the conference; they note that, at these meetings, Minas Tchéraz was chosen to represent them at the conference and charged with presenting their demands; "Declaration addressed by the ARF and the Macedonian High Committee to the public opinion of the civilized world on the occasion of the Peace Conference," in *Droschak*, no. 5/96, May 1899, pp. 1–2, distributed to the delegations on 3/15 June 1899.

40. *Ibidem*, p. 59. Another emissary, Vaghinag Ajemian, renewed the sultan's offer on 4 February 1897 (p. 60); a third emissary, Drtad Dadian, a cousin of the first, met with the *Droschak* leadership in Geneva on 26 October 1897.

41. *Ibidem*, pp. 60–1.

42. Hamit Bozarslan, *Les Courants de pensée dans l'Empire ottoman, 1908–1918*, doctoral thesis, Ecole des hautes études en sciences sociales, 1992, vol. II, p. 34, note 313, points out that Tunalı Hilmi was then one of the rare Young Turk militants to advocate armed insurrection (Ş. Mardin, *Jön Türklerin Siyasi Fikirleri, 1895–1908*, Ankara 1964, p. 96). Thus, it is quite possible that Tunalı Hilmi was the anonymous author of the letter discussed below.

43. "Jeune Turquie," in *Droschak*, no. 1/102, January 1900, p. 5, the letter of "a jeune Turk" also indicates that the Young Turk Committee had, the year before, sent a delegation to meet with Ottoman diplomats stationed abroad in order to suggest that they join the committee.

44. *Droschak*, no. 7/108, September 1900, pp. 101–2.

45. "Միութիւն Թիւրքերի հետ [Unity with the Turks]," in *Droschak*, no. 8/109, October 1900, pp. 113–16.

46. S. Sapah-Giulian, "Երիտասարդ Թիւրքիա [Jeune Turquie]," *Hnchak*, no. 7, 15 December 1900, pp. 71–5; the rest of the study was published in instalments in the issues of January (pp. 2–7), February (10–13) and March (18–22) 1901.

47. S. Sapah-Giulian, "Երիտասարդ Թիւրքիա [Jeune Turquie]," *Hnchak*, no. 2, 10 February 1901, p. 11.

Նիւթեր Հ. Յ. Դաշնակցութեան Պատմութեան համար [*Documents concerning the History of the Armenian Revolutionary Federation*], II, Beirut 1985, pp. 379–80, a circular distributed by the ARF's Western Bureau, Geneva, 3/16 October 1900, announces the publication of *Pro Armenia* in French at the party's expense, and asks the local committees to send in information about the situation in the provinces.

48. Hanioğlu, *The Young Turks in Opposition, op. cit.*, p. 170.

49. *Ibidem*.

50. *Ibidem*, pp. 173–83.
   Prince Sabaheddin explained, in the call convening this congress:
   > Given that it is all the Ottomans whose civil rights will continue to be denied if the current situation persists, it is imperative that all the elements of the Ottoman world succeed, on behalf of the communities they represent, in forging a general union of their forces.

   The call is reprinted in Y. H. Bayur, *Türk Ënkilabı Tarihi*, IV, Ankara 1966, p. 294, cited in Bozarslan, *Les Courants de pensée, op. cit.* I, note 871, p. 223.

51. *Ibidem*, p. 182.

52. Sapah-Giulian, *The Responsibles, op. cit.*, p. 182. The SDHP kept its distance from the Young Turk movement until 1906.

53. Report by the Armenian delegation: "Օսմանցի Ազատականների Համաժողովը [The Congress of the Ottoman Liberals]," *Droschak*, no. 2/12, February 1902, pp. 23–6; Mikayel Varantian, Հայ Յեղափոխական Դաշնակցութեան Պատմութիւն [*History of the Armenian Revolutionary Federation*], II, Cairo 1950, p. 2.

54. Minas Tchéraz (1852, Constantinople-1929, Paris), member of the Armenian delegation that sought to participate in the Congress of Berlin in 1878; exiled in London in 1889, he published the newspaper *Arménie* in French; after settling in Paris in 1898, he published the same periodical there until 1906. He returned to Istanbul in 1908: *Haykakan Hanragitaran*, IX, Yerevan 1983, p. 11.

55. Garabed Basmajian (1864, Constantinople–1942, Paris), physician, pharmacist and philologist who published the newspaper *Panaser* in Paris from 1899 to 1907: *Haykakan Hanragitaran*, II, Yerevan, 1976, pp. 304–5.

56. Arshag Chobanian (1872, Constantinople–1954, Paris), writer and publisher exiled to Paris in 1895 (*Haykakan Hanragitaran*, IX, Yerevan, 1983, pp. 59–60). Since he was close to Hnchaks who left the party in September 1896 to found the Verakazmial Hnchak Party, it may be assumed that he represented this party at the congress.

57. Hanioğlu, *The Young Turks in Opposition, op. cit.*, p. 184.

58. Parliamentary deputy from Erzerum, director of the Milli Agency in 1915.

59. İsmail Hakkı (1889–1948): E. Zürcher, *The Unionist Factor*, Leyde 1984, p. 78.

60. Editor of *Muvazene* (Geneva), Pan-Turk propagandist who was in Afghanistan in 1908: Zürcher, *op. cit.*, p. 74.

61. Hanioğlu, *The Young Turks in Opposition, op. cit.*, pp. 189–92.

62. *Ibidem*, p. 193.

63. *Ibidem*, pp. 193–4, and the joint report of the ARF and Verakazmial Hnchak, "Օսմանցի Ազատականների Համաժողովը [The Congress of Ottoman Liberals]," *Droschak*, no. 2/122, February 1902, p. 25.

64. *Ibidem*, p. 155: at a meeting held in the wings of the Congress, Hüseyin Tosun, Ismaïl Hakkı, Hoca Kadri, Şeyh Şevki Celâleddin, Çerkez Kemal, Dr Lütfi, Mustafa Hamdi, Dr Nâzım, Yusuf Akçura, Ali Fehmi, Halil Ganim, Ahmed Rıza, Ali Fahri, Mahir Said, Babanzâde Hikmet, Celâleddin Rıza, Zeki, Yaşar Sadık Erebera, Derviş Hima, decided, in *Mechveret's* editorial offices, to publish a four-point program reaffirming the legitimacy of the Imperial Ottoman family, to remain faithful to it, and the need to exalt Islam, Muslim civilization and the Muslim tradition of protecting other religions.

65. *Ibidem*, p. 195; Mikayel Varantian, Հայ Յեղափոխական Դաշնակցութեան Պատմութիւն [*History of the Armenian Revolutionary Federation*], II, Le Caire 1950, p. 2, confirms that the agreement did not come about, although the Armenian representatives accepted the principle of the territorial integrity of the Ottoman Empire, noting that Rıza denied the existence of an Armenian Question and would not even discuss foreign intervention.

66. Hanioğlu, *The Young Turks in Opposition, op. cit.*, pp. 195–6: Sabaheddin, İsmail Kemal, Ali Haydar Midhat, İsmail Hakkı, Hüseyin Siyret, Musurus Ghikis and Georges Fardis were elected. A compromise was worked out later, and an Armenian member was chosen to replace Siyret Bey.

67. Şükrü Hanioğlu, *Preparation for a Revolution: The Young Turks, 1902–1908*, Oxford University Press, 2001, p. 13.

68. *Ibidem*, p. 14, 28. For example, Dr. Mehmed Nâzım, an eminent member of the minority, sharply criticized the replacement, under pressure from the great powers, of the valis of Aleppo and, thereafter, of Dyarbekir, "for persecuting the Christians and committing atrocities against them."

69. *Ibidem*, chap. 2, note 90; *Droschak*, no. 3/123, March 1902, pp. 37–8, announces, somewhat emotionally, the death, in San Remo, of Dr. İshak Sükutî, a Kurd born in Dyarbekir who founded the original nucleus of the CUP; *Droschak*, no. 5/136, May 1903, p. 75, comments with interest on articles published in the newspaper *Fédération Ottomane*, which was published in Geneva under the aegis of the majority.

70. Հ. Խ., "Երիտասարդ Թիւրքիա եւ Երիտասարդ Հայաստան Անտագօնիզմը [The Antagonism between Young Turkey and Young Armenia]," *Hnchak*, no. 2, 1 May 1902, pp. 11–14.

71. *Ibidem*, pp. 13–14.

72. *Hnchak*, no. 2, 1 May 1902, pp. 1–3, announces an accord that led to the reunification of the Hnchak party and Verakazmial Hnchaks in May 1902, after a rupture lasting six years.

73. Hanioğlu, *Preparation for a Revolution, op. cit.*, p. 33. Two non-Turks in the minority, Khalil Ghanim and Albert Fuad, were excluded from it.

74. N° 1, April 1902, pp. 1–2, cited in Hanioğlu, *Preparation for a Revolution, op. cit.*, p. 34.

75. *Ibidem*, p. 39. *Şûra-yı Ümmet* valorized nationalism and made increasingly frequent use of the term "Turk," which now came to replace "Ottoman" (p. 40).

76. *Ibidem*, p. 40.

77. *Ibidem*, p. 45.

78. The subject is vast. It has been discussed by, notaby, Akaby Nasibian, *Britain and the Armenian Question, 1915–1923*, London 1984, and Edmond Khayadjian, *Archag Tchobanian et le mouvement arménophile en France*, Marseille 1986.

79. Hanioğlu, *Preparation for a Revolution, op. cit.*, p. 46; Նիւթեր Հ. Յ. Դաշնակցութեան Պատմութեան համար [*Documents concerning the History of the Armenian Revolutionary Federation*], IV, Beirut 1985, p. 95, Dr. Jean Loris-Melikov, elected a member of the ARF's Western Bureau at the party's Third Congress, responsible for propaganda in Europe, ARF representative at the London Conference, also reports this incident and notes that the French, Italian, and British delegates were shocked by the tenor of the Young Turk leader's remarks.

80. *Ibidem*, p. 47. The author points out, p. 48, that until 1906, the Young Turks in the coalition struggled to enlist European public opinion in their cause; thereafter, they abandoned the effort.

81. Ali Kemal (1867–1922), a teacher and journalist, joined the opposition to the Unionist regime after the 1908 revolution. Accused of collaborating with the enemy after the Mudros armistice, he was lynched by the Kemalists: Bozarslan, *Les Courants de pensée, op. cit.* II, p. 133.

82. *Ibidem*, p. 65, according to the 5 November 1903 *Türk*.

83. *Ibidem*, p. 66.

84. *Ibidem*, p. 67. According to the author, the manifesto sought to propagate his nationalism among Turks living outside the Ottoman Empire; he himself was descended of a Turkish family from abroad. It is also noteworthy that he employs the term "ırk" in the in *Türk* to designate all ethnic Turks as a whole, irrespective of their religion.

85. Y. Akçura, *Üç Tarz-ı Siyaset*, Ankara 1976, p. 19.

86. Notamment H. Bozarslan, *Les Courants de pensée, op. cit.*

87. Hanioğlu, *Preparation for a Revolution, op. cit.*, pp. 67–8, notes that one of the editors of *Türk*, Ahmed Ferid, confessed that "the term 'Ottoman' is an expression which has recently been given a new connotation to camouflage Turkish domination," and that Social Darwinism was quite influential among the Tatarsde Russie.

88. *Ibidem*, p. 69.

89. H. Bozarslan, "Autour de la 'thèse turque de l'Histoire'," *L'Intranquille*, I (1992), pp. 121–50.

90. Cited in Hanioğlu, *Preparation for a Revolution, op. cit.*, p. 71.

91. *Ibidem*, pp. 69–70, cited in *Türk*, 3 October 1905.

92. Bozarslan, *Les Courants de pensée, op. cit.*, II, p. 24.
93. Hanioğlu, *Preparation for a Revolution, op. cit.*, p. 82.
94. *Ibidem.*
95. Bozarslan, *Les Courants de pensée, op. cit.*, II, pp. 60–1.
96. P. Fesch (Sabaheddin's secretary), *Constantinople aux derniers jours d'Abdulhamid*, Paris 1907, p. 50; Bozarslan, *Les Courants de pensée, op. cit.*, II, p. 61.
97. *Ibidem*, p. 62.
98. Hanioğlu, *Preparation for a Revolution, op. cit.*, p. 83.
99. *Ibidem*, pp. 84–5.
100. *Ibidem*, pp. 87–8.
101. *Ibidem*, pp. 88–9 and n. 50: late in 1905, Bahaeddin Şakir approached Prince Sabaheddin, but confessed that his only objective was to obtain financial support from the prince so that he could carry out the reorganization of the CUP.
102. Bozarslan, *Les Courants de pensée, op. cit.*, I, p. 219; cites the records of the Committee's correspondence, maintained, as a rule, by Şakir and Nâzım; lengthy extracts from them are reprinted in Bayur, *op. cit.*, p. 425; Ë. H. Danişmend, *Izahlı Osmanlı Tarihi Kronolojisi*, Istanbul, Türkiye Yayınları, vol. 4, 1969, p. 358: Prince Sabaheddin's mother was a Georgian (Nâzım and Şakir cites by A. B. Kuran, *Osmanlı İmperatorluğu'nda İnkilâp Hareketleri ve Millî Mücadele*, Istanbul 1956, p. 40.
103. Hanioğlu, *Preparation for a Revolution, op. cit.*, pp. 90–91, article of Bahaeddin Şakir, in *Şûra-yı Ümmet*, no. 114, 1 June 1907, pp. 4–6.
104. *Ibidem*, p. 91.
105. *Ibidem*, pp. 94–6. Despite their explicit criticisms of the Armenian Committees, the coalition and Bahaeddin Şakir sought a tactical alliance with them, in part to drive a wedge between them and Prince Sabaheddin.
106. *Ibidem*, p. 97; see also *infra*, p. 817, n. 58. A graduate of the Military Academy of Istanbul, Tosun would later become an important leader of the CUP's Turkist faction.
107. *Ibidem*, p. 97, 115–17; Hüseyin Tosun traveled to the Caucasus under the pseudonym Şeikh Ali. The ARF provided him with a Russian passport, and he entered Turkey thanks to the *fedayis*. Abdullah Cevdet has left an account of Tosun's role in the Erzerum revolt. He notes that Sabaheddin's emissary initially posed as a grocer; with the help of Armenian friends, he then found employment as a deliveryman for the Russian consulate in Erzerum, a post that made it easier to distribute illegal literature. According to official sources, those responsible for the revolt came from Alevi circles; this, however, is anything but certain (see p. 115); Vahan Papazian, Իմ Յուշերը [*Memoirs*], I, Boston 1950, pp. 280–1, confirms both that he was present in Erzerum and that the local ARF played an important role, helping him to escape, among other things.
108. Hanioğlu, *Preparation for a Revolution, op. cit.*, pp. 104–6. The movement brought together 2,000 "Muslim and non-Muslim" demonstrators from the city and surrounding villages; taking up a position in front of the subprefect's house, they exclaimed that his corrupt practices were responsible for their plight. The following day, the members of local guilds occupied the post office while waiting for a positive response to the telegram that they had sent the vali of Kastamonu. The leaders of the movement – notably, the head of the butchers' guild – were exiled to various provinces.
109. *Ibidem*, pp. 106–7. In November 1907, new complaints at last convinced the Cabinet to banish İbrahim Pasha to Aleppo. It should be noted that Ziya Gökalp and Pirinçizâde Ârif Bey, future leaders of the CUP, took an active part in this last demonstration.
110. Papazian, *Memoirs, op. cit.*, I, pp. 512–35.
111. *Ibidem*, pp. 282–5; Hanioğlu, *Preparation for a Revolution, op. cit.*, pp. 97–9.
112. Papazian, *Memoirs, op. cit.*, I, p. 285; containing mostly articles translated from the Armenian by David Papazian.
113. Hanioğlu, *Preparation for a Revolution, op. cit.*, pp. 99–100. Joint actions of the same sort took place in Pasinler, Khnus/Hınıs (April 1906) and Çemişgezek/Tchmechgadzak or Seghert/Siirt (see *ibidem*, pp. 120–1).
114. *Ibidem*, pp. 97–9.
115. *Ibidem*, p. 128.

116. Hanioğlu, *Preparation for a Revolution, op. cit.*, especially pp. 130–2. The author has the personal archives of Bahaeddin Şakir and Ahmed Rıza at his disposal.

117. Born in Istanbul in 1879, executed in Berlin in 1922. A member of the CUP's Central Committee practically without interruption from 1907 to 1918, he led the *Teşkilât-ı Mahsusa* during the First World War. His decisive role in the eradication of the Ottoman Armenians is discussed at length below.

118. Hanioğlu, *Preparation for a Revolution, op. cit.*, pp. 131–2.

119. *Ibidem*, p. 131, note 13: Albert Fuad and the general Şerif Pasha.

120. See *infra*, p. 816 n. 35. Even as he collaborated with the Young Turks, Kelekian maintained ties with his Hnchak friends. When, in the fall of 1904, he set out to publish an oppositional newspaper in Cairo, where he spent his second period in exile, he appealed to Yervant Odian for help (Նամակներ [*Correspondence*]), ed. Ofelia Karapetian, Yerevan 1999, letter from Bombay, 29 October 1904, to Mikayel Giurjian, p. 196.

121. Hanioğlu, *Preparation for a Revolution, op. cit.*, p. 131.

122. *Ibidem*, pp. 132–3.

123. *Ibidem*, p. 133. Ahmed Saib was to found the Ottoman Constitutional League a few months later.

124. *Ibidem*, Private Papers of B. Şakir, letter from Bedri [D. Kelekian] to B. Şakir, Cairo, 9, 16, 17, 19 December 1905.

125. *Ibidem*, p. 135.

126. *Ibidem*, Private Papers of B. Şakir, letter from Bedri [D. Kelekian] to B. Şakir, Cairo, 9 April 1906.

127. *Ibidem*, p. 136, Private Papers of B. Şakir, undated memorandum, April 1906.

128. *Ibidem*, p. 136, n. 46. In a 12 September letter to Kelekian, Bahaeddin mentions discussions with a committee, without naming the party in question.

129. Cf. Sapah-Giulian, *The Responsibles, op. cit.*, pp. 182–95. It should be recalled that the SDHP moved its headquarters and official organ, *Hnchak*, from London to Paris in June 1904 and that Sapah-Giulian took over the task of editing the newspaper: cf. *Hnchak*, nos 9–10–11, September–October–November 1904, p. 1.

130. Murad (pseudonym of Hampartsum Boyajian), 1867, Hajın–1915; one of the founders of the Hnchak party; the leader of the 1894 Sasun rebellion; condemned to life in prison; *Hnchak*, 5, May 1906, announced that he had been set free after twelve years in prison and had settled in Paris, where he was put in charge of revolutionary operations; from 1908 to 1915, deputy in the Ottoman parliament; hanged in Kayseri in June 1915: Raymond Kévorkian, *IBN, Index bio-bibliographicus notorum hominum, Sectio Armeniaca*, III, Osnabrück 1986, p. 135.

131. Hanioğlu, *Preparation for a Revolution, op. cit.*, p. 40: during the fall 1905 events in the Caucasus, *Şûra-yı Ümmet* and *Mechveret supplement français* took a pro-Tatar, anti-Armenian position.

132. Sapah-Giulian, *The Responsibles, op. cit.*, pp. 185–6.

133. *Ibidem*, p. 187; from this point on, the meetings took place in a room in a café in the Paris suburb Les Lilas.

134. *Ibidem*, p. 190.

135. *Ibidem*, p. 191.

136. A renowned German geographer, author of many detailed maps of the Middle East.

137. *Ibidem*, p. 192.

138. *Ibidem*, p. 193.

139. *Ibidem*, pp. 194–5.

140. S. Sapah-Giulian, "Մենք եւ մեր Քննադատները [*We and our critics*]," *Hnchak*, no. 9–10, September-October 1906, pp. 91–5.

141. *Ibidem*, pp. 92–3.

142. *Ibidem*, p. 94.

143. *Ibidem*, p. 95.

144. *Ibidem*, pp. 197–8. Murad's proposal was not officially transmitted to the ARF until 16 March 1907. The ARF waited until 15 June 1907 to respond to it; it considered the proposal "premature." It was also on Murad's initiative that the SDHP signed, on 27 November 1907, a reunification agreement with its dissidents, who had founded the Verakazmial Hnchak party;

S. Sapah-Giulian, "Հրատապ Խնդիրը [The urgent problem]," *Hnchak*, no. 11, novembre 1906, pp. 104–8.

145. S. Sapah-Giulian, "Հին Ցաւը [The old grievance]," *Hnchak*, no. 12, December 1906, pp. 114–18.

146. S. Sapah-Giulian, "Միտհատեան Սահմանադրութեան Առիւ [On the Midhat Constitution]," *Hnchak*, nos 3–4, March–April 1907, pp. 26–36.

147. Նիւթեր Հ. Յ. Դաշնակցութեան Պատմութեան համար [*Documents concerning the History of the Armenian Revolutionary Federation*], III, Beirut 1985, p. 198. This volume of archival documents is wholly devoted to the Fourth Congress of the ARF, held from 22 February to 4 May 1907 in Vienna, in a building belonging to the Austrian socialist party. The volume includes detailed reports delivered to congress by the leaders of the attempt to assassinate the sultan (see pp. 194–223).

148. *Ibidem*, pp. 194–5. The commando comprised Ellen (Kristapor Mikayelian), Safo (Martiros Margarian), Torkom, Hovnan Tavtian, Ashod Bagratuni (Ashot Yeghikian): see p. 220, n. 1.

149. A total of 18 to 20 people, counting those who provided only occasional help.

150. *Ibidem*, pp. 196–7. Their materiel was twice confiscated; those who carried out the trials in Bulgaria were arrested and the addresses of the members who had been slipped into Istanbul were found in their possession. During the dry runs, one of the three founders of the ARF, the head of the commando, Kristapor Mikayelian, was killed as the result of an error in the handling of the explosives.

151. *Ibidem*, p. 198.

152. Bozarslan, *Les Courants de pensée, op. cit.* II, p. 31.

153. K. Karabekir, *İttihat ve Terakki Cemiyeti, 1896–1909, Neden Kuruldu? Nasıl Kuruldu? Nasıl İdare Olundu?* (ed. F. and E. Özerergin), Istanbul 1982, pp. 73–4.

154. See the letter of Dr. B. Server (=Bahaeddin Şakir), 25 March 1906, in A. B. Kuran, *İnkilâp Tarihimiz ve İttihat ve Terakki*, Istanbul 1946, p. 197.

155. Hanioğlu, *Preparation for a Revolution, op. cit.*, p. 137–8.

156. *Ibidem*, pp. 138–139. The grandson of the founder of modern Egypt, Mehmed Said Halim Pasha, who had also been exiled by Abdülhamid in 1905, accepted a position as inspector of the Central Committee, joining his brother Mehmed Ali Halim. The prestige of the two princes living in Cairo rapidly restored the CUP's credibility, without disturbing the physicians settled in Paris. The creation of a real office also allowed Şakir to take control of the CUP's correspondence, which had until then passed through the hands of Ahmed Rıza. Certain well-informed (mainly German) sources even present Mehmed Said Halim as the leader of the CUP during the First World War (*ibidem.*, p. 140, n. 73).

157. *Ibidem*, p. 146. Although the CUP was not implanted in the east, Şakir tried to make potential members of the committee believe that it had powerful branches in Anatolia, "especially in Erzerum, Bitlis, Van and Trebizond" (letter from B. Şakir to Mesud Remzi, Paris, 27 November 1907 (*ibidem.*, p. 115, n. 365). It was not until June 1907 that the official organ *Şûra-yı Ümmet* was brought back to Paris (*ibidem.*, p. 183).

158. Erik J. Zürcher, *The Unionist Factor: the Role of the Committee of Union and Progress in the Turkish National Movement, 1905–1926*, Leiden 1984, p. 22.

159. Mehmed Talât (1874–1921), member of the first CUP in Edirne around 1895, founding member, founder of the SOL in Salonika in 1906, parliamentary deputy from Edirne, minister of the interior, grand vizier, one of the main organizers of the Armenian genocide (*ibidem.*, p. 37 and *infra*, p. 815, n. 29).

160. Midhat Şukrü [Bleda] (1874–1956): then director of Salonika's municipal hospital, thereafter parliamentary deputy from Serez (1908), Drama (1912) and Burdur (1916), member of the CUP's Central Committee, close associate of Talât, secretary general of the CUP. After the armistice, Şukrü was given the task of destroying the CUP's archives (Zürcher, *The Unionist, op. cit.*, p. 38).

161. Mustafa Rahmi [Evranos], parliamentary deputy from Salonika (1908 and 1912), governor of Smyrna from 1915 to 1918 (*ibidem.*, p. 38).

162. İsmail Canbolat (1880–1926), parliamentary deputy from Smyrna (1912), chief of police (1914), governor of Istanbul (1915) and then vali (1916), minister of the interior (1918), deported to Malta in 1919, hanged in 1926 (*ibidem*, p. 38).

163. Bursalı Mehmed Tahir (1861–1926), appointed director of the Military Academy of Salonika in May 1906 (*ibidem*, p. 38).

164. Ömer Naci (1880–1916), officer educated in Harbiye, CUP propagandist, twice elected a member of parliament, member of the Central Committee from 1910 to 1912, one of the leaders of the Special Organization in 1915–16 (*ibidem*, p. 35).

165. İsmail Hakkı (1889–948), member of the CUP, undersecretary of state in the War Ministry, one of the leaders of the Special Organization (*ibidem*, p. 78).

166. Hanioğlu, *Preparation for a Revolution, op. cit.*, pp. 210–14.

167. Hüsrev Sâmi [Kızıldoğan] (1884–1942), artillery office, friend of Ömer Naci's, renowned CUP *fedayi* (Zürcher, *The Unionist, op. cit.*, p. 35).

168. *Ibidem*, p. 41; Hanioğlu, *Preparation for a Revolution, op. cit.*, p. 214. Nâzım first arrived in Greece in mid-June 1907 disguised as a dervish, then went on to Macedonia disguised as a sailor.

169. *Ibidem*, pp. 214–15.

170. *Ibidem*, pp. 216–17. In 1906, Talât defended the necessity of organizing the committee in the form of a Masonic lodge; "otherwise, Europe will crush the Ottomans" (cited in Karabekir, *İttihat ve Terakki Cemiyeti, op. cit.*, p. 175).

171. *Ibidem*, p. 218. The main CUP *fedayis* were Abdülkadır († 1926), Ali [Çetinkaya], Atif [Kamçıl], Sarı Efe Edip, Kuşçubaşızâde Eşref [Sencer], Sapanclı Hakkı, Halil [Kut], Filibeli Hilmi, Ismitli Mümtaz, Hüsrev Sâmi [Kızıldoğan], Nuri [Conker], Kâzım [Özalp], Süleyman Askeri, Yenibahçeli Sükrü and Nail, Yakup Cemil († 1916), one of the best-known *fedayis* of the party (Zürcher, *The Unionist, op. cit.*, p. 50).

172. Hanioğlu, *Preparation for a Revolution, op. cit.*, p. 220.

173. The *Potorig* ("storm") commando created in 1903 by the ARF's Third Congress was given the mission of collecting the revolutionary tax, by threat if necessary. A few Armenians who refused to contribute were executed.

174. Hanioğlu, *Preparation for a Revolution, op. cit.*, p. 226. Eyüb Sabri [Akgöl] (1876–1950), one of the officers who rebelled in summer 1908, member of the CUP's Central Committee without interruption down to 1918 (Zürcher, *The Unionist, op. cit.*, p. 43).

175. In 1906, Mustafa Kemal founded, together with three other officers who had graduated from Harbiye, a Young Turk branch of the *Vatan ve Hürriyet* in Salonika: Hakkı Baha [Pars], Hüsrev Sâmi [Kızıldoğan] and İsmail Mahir (1869–1916), who joined the SOL soon after. Kemal nevertheless remained on the periphery of the party to the end of the First World War (*ibidem*, p. 35).

176. Ahmed Cemal (1872–1922), member of the CUP's Central Committee, vali of Uskudar (1909), Adana (1909) and Baghdad (1911), prefect of Istanbul (1913), minister of the navy, commander of the Fourth Army (Syria-Palestine). Cemal is said to have engineered the famine that carried off thirty percent of the Lebanese population in the courses of the First World War (*ibidem*, p. 43).

177. Halil [Kut] (1881–1957), Enver's uncle, organizer of the squadrons of *çetes* of the Special Organization, responsible for massacres in the regions of Van and Bitlis in 1915 (*ibidem*, p. 43).

178. *Ibidem*.

179. Hanioğlu, *Preparation for a Revolution, op. cit.*, p. 153.

180. *Ibidem*, pp. 150, 167.

181. *Ibidem*, p. 168.

182. *Ibidem*, p. 169. Kâzım Karabekir (1882–1946), Turkish army general who played an important part in the activities of the Young Turk officers in the Balkans, architect of the Turkish victory in the War of Independence, pushed to the sidelines by Mustafa Kemal after the proclamation of the Republic (Bozarslan, *Les Courants de pensée, op. cit.* II, p. 130).

183. Hanioğlu, *Preparation for a Revolution, op. cit.*, pp. 152–3.

184. *Ibidem*, p. 161.

185. Նիւթեր Հ. 3. Դաշնակցութեան Պատմութեան համար [*Documents concerning the History of the Armenian Revolutionary Federation*], III, Beirut 1985.

186. *Ibidem*, III, pp. 4–5. Aknuni was the representative of the Western Bureau, based in Geneva; Rostom that of the Eastern Bureau, based in Tiflis; Hovhannes/Ivan Zavriev represented the Committee of Yerevan, Arshag Vramian, the Committee of the United States. The Committee

of the Lernabar (= Rshtunik-Moks) was represented by Ishkhan, Sham (= Van) by Aram Manukian, Mush-Sasun by Antranig (Ozanian) and Murad (Sepastatsi).

187. *Ibidem*, IV, p. 90. In his report on the work accomplished by the party since the previous congress, Dr. Jean Loris-Melikov (physician and scientist at the *Institut Pasteur* in Paris, nephew of the prince and general Loris-Melikov), who had been a member of the Western Bureau responsible for "managing" the newspaper *Pro Armenia*, criticized this "oligarchy" quite sharply.

> Loris-Melikov also gave an account of his activities as a member of the delegation, created on the initiative of the catholicos, sent to petition the powers after the Sasun affair. He reviewed his discussions with the president of the Council of Ministers in Paris, facilitated by V. Berard, E. Lavisse and Destournel; with the archbishop of Canterbury and the British prime minister, facilitated by Lord Bryce; and with Roosevelt, facilitated by James Reynolds. He then turned to his participation, on the advice of Clemenceau, Jaurès and Pressense, in the Boston Peace Conference as "the elected representative of Armenia." (*ibidem*, IV, pp. 96, 125).

188. *Droschak*, no. 5, mai 1907, Report on the decisions of the ARF's Fourth General Congress, Geneva, 4 May, pp. 66–8, cited on p. 72.

189. *Documents concerning the History of the Armenian Revolutionary Federation*, op. cit., III, pp. 17–20, proceedings of the eighth session, held on 26 February 1907. Ishkhan, whose real name was Nigol Mikayelian (1883–1915), born in Shushi, head of the ARF in the Lernabar district (Rshtounik/Moks) south of Lake Van from 1902 to 1908, and in the city of Van from 1908 to 1915. Murdered in April 1915.

190. *Ibidem*, III, pp. 21–2.

191. *Ibidem*, III, pp. 30–1, Antranig spoke at the thirteenth session of the Congress, held on 1 March 1907.

192. Aknuni (1863–1915), member of the Western Bureau from 1901 to 1915.

193. *Ibidem*, III, pp. 33–6. Described at the fifteenth session, held on 2 March 1907. The incumbent Western Bureau comprised Avetis Aharonian, Rostom (Zorian), Aknuni, Mikayel Varantian (Hovhannesian), and Jean Loris-Melikov.

194. Sarkis Minasian († 1915), born in Constantinople, journalist and teacher.

195. *Ibidem*, III, pp. 234–6.

196. *Ibidem*, III, p. 239. Aram Manukian (1879–1919), born near Ghapan, in the Zangezur district, officer in Iran and Van, where he led the self-defense effort in April 1915, interior minister of the Republic of Armenia in 1918.

197. *Ibidem*, III, p. 240.

198. Aharonian was of course alluding to the First Congress of the Ottoman Opposition, in which he took part as a representative of the ARF (see *supra*, p. 19).

199. *Documents concerning the History of the Armenian Revolutionary Federation*, op. cit., III, pp. 245–6.

200. Rostom (1867–1919), born in Tseghna, agronomist, founded the ARF in 1890.

201. *Ibidem*, III, p. 247.

202. *Ibidem*, III, p. 247.

203. Murad (1874–1918), born in Godvun (Sıvas), officer in the Lernabar district (1904), one of the defenders of Baku in 1918.

204. *Ibidem*.

205. *Ibidem*.

206. *Ibidem*.

207. Arshag Vramian (1871–1915), born in Constantinople, member of the Western Bureau in 1899, representative of the ARF in the United States until 1907, thereafter official of the party in Van (1909), executive director of the Western Bureau in Istanbul, parliamentary deputy from Van (1913), murdered in April 1915 of the orders of the vali of Van, Cevdet Bey.

208. *Documents concerning the History of the Armenian Revolutionary Federation*, op. cit., III, pp. 247–8.

209. *Ibidem*, III, p. 248. The congress elected the following people to the Eastern Bureau: Hamo Ohanjanian, Simon Zavarian, Garo (Karekin Pastermajian), Yeghishe Topchian and Arshag Vramian; to the Western Bureau: Mikayel Varantian (Hovhannisian), Aknuni (Khachadur Malumian), Hovnan Tavtian and Aram-Ashod (Sarkis Minasian) (*ibidem.*, III, pp. 286–7).

At the Fourth Congress, the ARF decided, in view of the way the situation had evolved in the empire and of the evolution of the Young Turks, to take the initiative of convoking a General Congress of the Ottoman Opposition (Mikayel Varantian, Հայ Յեղափոխական Դաշնակցութեան Պատմութիւն [*History of the Armenian Revolutionary Federation*], II, Cairo 1950, p. 43).

210. *Droschak*, no. 6–7, June-July 1907, pp. 82–3.

2 The December 1907 Second Congress of the Anti-Hamidian Opposition: Final "Preparations for a Revolution"

1. Hanioğlu, *Preparation for a Revolution, op. cit.*, p. 191.
2. *Ibidem*.
3. Sapah-Giulian, *The Responsibles, op. cit.*, pp. 199–204.
4. *Ibidem*, p. 208.
5. Hanioğlu, *Preparation for a Revolution, op. cit.*, p. 193.
6. *Ibidem*, p. 181.
7. *Documents concerning the History of the Armenian Revolutionary Federation, op. cit.*, III, pp. 94–5: about the Armenian-Turkish clashes in the Caucasus and the provocations organized by the Russian government.
8. Hanioğlu, *Preparation for a Revolution, op. cit.*, pp. 158–9.
9. *Ibidem*, p. 160, letter of 23 November 1906, sent from Paris to the Turkish-speaking correspondents of the Caucasus.
10. *Ibidem*, pp. 191–2.
11. *Ibidem*, p. 194.
12. *Ibidem*, pp. 194–5.
13. *Ibidem*, pp. 195–6.
14. *Ibidem*, p. 196.
15. Sapah-Giulian referred to this formula during his exchange with his former classmate Aknuni, cites above. M. Varantian, *History of the Armenian Revolutionary Federation, op. cit.*, p. 9, confirms that the ARF had ceased to advocate the reform and agreed to suspend the publication of *Pro Armenia*.
16. Hanioğlu, *Preparation for a Revolution, op. cit.*, p. 197. Hanioğlu insists above all here on the CUP's fears of the ARF; he deals more cursorily with the Dashnaks' approach.
17. *Ibidem*, pp. 198–203.
18. *Ibidem*, p. 203, notes that the sessions of the Congress were chaired by Prince Sabaheddin, Aknuni and Ahmed Rıza by turns and that Pierre Anmeghian served as the secretary of the Congress; Varantian, *History of the Armenian Revolutionary Federation, op. cit.*, II, p. 5, confirms this. The ARF delegation also included Hrach (Haïg Tiriakian [1871–1915], an agronomist born in Trebizond), Vahram (Harutiun Kalfayan), Aram-Ashod (Sarkis Minasian [c. 1875–1915], a member of the ARF's Western Bureau in 1907), H. Sarafian and Rupen Zartarian (known as Aslan [1874–1915], a journalist born in Severek, the founder of *Azadamard* [1909], a member of the Western Bureau in 1911).

    S. Sapah-Giulian, "Թուրք Բռնապետութիւնը եւ Երիտասարդ Թուրքերը [The Turkish tyranny and the Young Turks]," *Hnchak*, no. 1, January 1908, pp. 2–10, affirms, on the basis of the invitation recieved by his party, that *Droschak*, the CUP and the League for Private Initiative and Decentralization convened the Congress.

19. Hanioğlu, *Preparation for a Revolution, op. cit.*, pp. 204–205.
20. *Ibidem*, p. 205; *Droschak*, no. 1, January 1908, "The Congress of the parties [of opposition], 27–29 December 1907," pp. 1–5, published the texts of the decisions of the Congress.
21. Hanioğlu, *Preparation for a Revolution, op. cit.*, pp. 206–8.
22. Bozarslan, *Les Courants de pensée, op. cit.* I, p. 197, of a total of 56,000 Ottoman officers.
23. Hanioğlu, *Preparation for a Revolution, op. cit.*, p. 229. This branch, founded by Major Enver and Captain Kâzım [Karabekir], had more members and was more active than the Central Committee of Salonika.

24. *Ibidem.*
25. M. Talât, *Talât Paşa'nın Anıları*, (ed.) par M. Kasım, Istanbul 1986, p. 58, cited in Bozarslan, *Les Courants de pensée, op. cit.* II, p. 32.
26. Hanioğlu, *Preparation for a Revolution, op. cit.*, p. 236.
27. *Ibidem.*
28. Aram Andonian, Պատմութիւն Պալքանեան Պատերազմին [*History of the Balkan War*], I, Istanbul 1912, p. 315.
29. *Ibidem*, pp. 315–16.
30. Hanioğlu, *Preparation for a Revolution, op. cit.*, p. 242.
31. *Ibidem*, pp. 254–8.
32. *Ibidem*, pp. 259–60.
33. *Ibidem*, pp. 269–78.
34. Sapah-Giulian, *The Responsibles, op. cit.*, pp. 218–19.
35. *Ibidem*, pp. 220–4. The prince concluded his remarks with the words: "The country is on the road to its destruction, its dismemberment." The same day, the Hnchak leaders sent their Kurdish colleague Bedr Bey Bedrkhan to Salonika to gather information on the Ittihad's congress bring it back to them in Constantinople.
36. *Ibidem*, pp. 230–1.

Part II   Young Turks and Armenians Facing the Test of Power (1908–12)

1   Istanbul in the First Days of the Revolution: "Our Common Religion is Freedom"

1. "Սահմանադրական Թիւրքիա եւ Հայկական Խնդիր [Constitutional Turkey and the Armenian Question]," *Hnchak*, no. 6–7, June–July 1908, éditorial, pp. 49–50.
2. *Ibidem*, p. 51.
3. Sapah-Giulian, *The Responsibles, op. cit.*, pp. 232–3.
4. *Ibidem*, p. 233.
5. *Ibidem*, p. 234.
6. *Ibidem*, p. 235.
7. *Droschak*, no. 7/195, July 1908, pp. 97–106: note p. 100.
8. *Ibidem*, p. 101.
9. *Droschak*, no. 8/196, August 1908, p. 121; Mikayel Varandian, Վերածնունդ Հայրենիքը եւ մեր Դերը [*The Renascent Fatherland and Our Role*], Geneva, 1910, p. 69, writes, the "victory of July 1908 is that of the Young Turks and also of the Dashnaktsakans, who together showed the Muslim world for the first time, in 1907, that solidarity is something real."
10. *Ibidem*, p. 101; Gaïdz F. Minassian, "Les relations entre le Comité Union et Progrès et la Fédération révolutionnaire arménienne à la veille de la Première Guerre mondiale d'après les sources arméniennes," *Revue d'histoire arménienne contemporaine* I (1995), pp. 45–99.
11. Roupèn Ter Minassian, *Mémoires d'un partisan arménien*, trad. W. Ter-Minassian, Marseille 1990, p. 26; Roupèn Ter Minassian, *Mémoires d'un cadre révolutionnaire arménien*, trad. Souren L. Chanth, Athènes 1994, p. 607.
12. Hratch Dasnabédian, *évolution de la structure de la FRA*, Beyrouth 1985, p. 59.
13. Varandian, *History of the ARF, op. cit.*, I, p. 427.
14. Sapah-Giulian, *The Responsibles, op. cit.*, p. 238. This exchange took place in French.
15. A. S. Sharurian, Գրիգոր Զոհրապի Կյանքի եւ Գործունեության Տարեգրություն [*Chronology of The life and work of Krikor Zohrab*], Echmiadzin 1996, pp. 160–1. Krikor Zohrab (1861–1915), lawyer, writer, deputy in both the Ottoman parliament and the Armenian Chamber who, as we shall soon see, played an important role in Ottoman public life, defended Armenian, Young Turk, Bulgarian, and Macedonian political prisoners, notably Apig Unjian, accused of "aiding and abetting a Revolutionary committee" in September–October 1896, as well as Garabed Basmajian,

charged with the same crimes in October (p. 80). In 1902, the Sublime Porte initiated a procedure to exclude him from the Constantinople bar (p. 117).

16. Sapah-Giulian, *The Responsibles*, op. cit., pp. 263, 279.
17. Hanioğlu, *Preparation for a Revolution*, op. cit., p. 279. According to the CUP statutes, the precise functions of each party official were to remain a secret.
18. Descended of the Kurdish Bedırhan family from Bohtan, a former principality governed by the Bedırhan dynasty.
19. Sapah-Giulian, *The Responsibles*, op. cit., pp. 245–6.
20. Hanioğlu, *Preparation for a Revolution*, op. cit.
21. *Ibidem*, p. 286.
22. Bozarslan, *Les Courants de pensée*, op. cit. I, p. 151, cites A. B. Kuran, *Osmanlı İmparatorluğu'nda İnkilâp Hareketleri ve Milli Mücadele*, Istanbul 1956, p. 411. "The Sultan's rights constituted one of the thorny issues confronting the Young Turk Congress of 1907. The Armenians replied to the Turkish delegates at the time that 'a revolution that wishes to protect the Padişa's rights is not a revolution.'"
23. Erik J. Zürcher, *Turkey: A Modern History*, London and New York 1998, p. 99.
24. Said pasha (from 22 July to 5 August 1908), Kâmil pasha (from 5 August 1908 to 13 February 1909), Hilmi pasha (from 14 February to 13 April 1909), Tevfik pasha (from 14 April to 5 May 1909), Hilmi pasha (from 5 May to 28 December 1909), Hakkı pasha (from 12 January 1910 to 30 September 1911), Said pasha (from 30 September 1911 to 17 July 1912), Ğazi Ahmed Muhtar Pasha (from 21 July to 29 October 1912), Kâmil pasha (from 29 October 1912 to 23 January 1913), Mahmud Şevket pasha (from 23 January to 11 June 1913), and after the imposition of the dictatorship of CUP, Said Halim pasha (from 11 June 1913 to 4 February 1917) and Mehmed Talât pasha (from 4 February 1917 to October 1918): Feroz Ahmad, *The Young Turks*, Oxford 1969.
25. Vahan Papazian, Յուշեր [Memoirs], I, Boston 1950, pp. 591–8, II, Beirut 1952, pp. 32–3; Ter Minassian, *Mémoires*, op. cit., trad. W. Ter-Minassian, p. 255; Ter-Minassian, *Mémoires*, op. cit., trad. S. L. Chanth, p. 590.
26. Centre des Archives diplomatiques de Nantes (CADN), Ambassade de Constantinople, E 130, report from the French vice-consul in Uskub, G. Rajevof, to M. Boppe, chargé d'affaire in Constantinople, 28 June 1909, no. 65, *Histoire du mouvement révolutionnaire du mois de juillet 1908*, p. 15.
27. *Ibidem*, pp. 16–17.
28. Sharurian, *Chronology of the Life and Work of Krikor Zohrab*, op. cit., pp. 155–6, according to both Zohrab's correspondence and the Istanbul press of 14 August.
29. *Ibidem*, pp. 159–60.
30. A. Asdvadzadurian, "Հ. Յ. Դաշնակցութեան եւ Իթթիհատի Յարաբերութիւնները [The Relations between the ARF and the CUP]," *Hairenik* December 1964, p. 176. The ARF's main offices in Istanbul were located at 51 Sakız Ağac Street in Pera (Papazian, *Memoirs*, op. cit., II, p. 48).
    Simon Zavarian (1866–1913), a native of Lori, one of the founders of the party, studied agronomy in Moscow and served as a member of, first, the Eastern Bureau (1892–1902), and then the Western Bureau (Geneva, 1902–08). From November 1909 to July 1911, he was the inspector of the Armenian schools in the Daron district and, thereafter, an editor of *Azadamard* in Istanbul, a post he held until his death.
31. Papazian, *Memoirs*, op. cit., II, p. 36.
32. Ter Minassian, *Mémoires*, op. cit., trad. S. L. Chanth, p. 606.
33. Papazian, *Memoirs*, op. cit., II, pp. 46–54.
34. Varandian, *Histoire de la Fédération*, op. cit., I, p. 429.
35. *Ibidem*, I, p. 448.
36. Sharurian, *Chronology of the Life and Work of Krikor Zohrab*, op. cit., p. 162.
37. Papazian, *Memoirs*, op. cit., II, p. 51.
38. *Ibidem*, II, p. 82.
39. *Ibidem*, II, p. 83.
40. *Ibidem*, II, p. 51.
41. Sapah-Giulian, *The Responsibles*, op. cit., pp. 246–7. According to Sapah-Giulian, their main offices and all the meetings they organized were closely watched, probably on CUP orders.

42. *Ibidem*, pp. 249–50.
43. *Ibidem*, p. 253.
44. *Ibidem*, pp. 254–5.
45. *Ibidem*, pp. 254–5. He even became justice minister, but held the post only briefly since he died suddenly two months later under circumstances that some consider suspect.
46. *Ibidem*, p. 261. These developments led to the creation of the Ottoman Democratic Party on 6 February 1909. Among its leaders were two of the founders of the CUP, İbrahim Temo and Abdullah Cevdet.
47. *Ibidem*, p. 263. We mention the smear campaign *supra*, p. 57. He refused the presidency of the only oppositional party of the day, the *Osmanlı Ahrar Fırkası* (Ottoman Freedom Party).
48. A. B. Kuran, *İnkilâp Hareketleri ve Millî Mücadele*, Istanbul 1956, p. 483, in Bozarslan, *Les Courants de pensée, op. cit.* I, p. 207.
49. Hanioğlu, *Preparation for a Revolution, op. cit.*, p. 286.
50. *Ibidem*, pp. 280–2. The Post and Telegraph Ministry even received an order to give priority to exchanges between party branches, as it already did to intragovernmental exchanges.
51. *Ibidem*, pp. 282–3.
52. *Ibidem*, pp. 284–5. The same leading officers took it upon themselves to execute members of the opposition, especially the journalists who criticized the "Holy Committee." For Enver, the deputies were "people of average intellectual abilities" (p. 311).
53. *Ibidem*, p. 311.
54. *Ibidem*, p. 286.
55. H. A. Yücel, *Geçtiğim Günlerden*, Istanbul 1990, p. 149, in Bozarslan, *Les Courants de pensée, op. cit.* I, p. 208.
56. *Ibidem*, I, p. 210.
57. Hanioğlu, *Preparation for a Revolution, op. cit.*, p. 287.
58. *Ibidem*, p. 288.
59. Hanioğlu, *Preparation for a Revolution, op. cit.*, p. 282.
60. Papazian, *Memoirs, op. cit.*, II, p. 27. Vahan Papazian (1876–1973), better known by his pseudonym, Goms, born in Tabriz to a family from Van, physician, party cadre in Van (1903–1905), deputy from Van in the Ottoman parliament from 1908 on, he managed to cross the Turkish lines and regain the Caucasus in summer 1915. He died in Beirut.
61. Papazian, *Memoirs, op. cit.*, I, p. 480.
62. Ter Minassian, *Mémoires, op. cit.*, trad. S. L. Chanth, p. 590.
63. *Ibidem*, p. 597. Among the notables of Mush, Hoca Iliaz, a Kurdish tribal chief, seemed the most hostile to the Armenians and only reluctantly took part in staging an enthusiastic welcome for the *fedayis*. According to Ruben, Iliaz's mother was Armenian and he spoke the Armenian dialect of Mush, but he was a "fanatic." In 1915, this parliamentary deputy was to be the main organizer of the extirpation of the Armenian population from the plain of Mush; he killed his half-brother Sulukhi Stepan with his own hands (p. 604).
64. *Supra*, pp. 38, 52, on Dr. Nâzım's activities in Smyrna in this period.
65. For further details on the local ARF, see Hovhannes Boyajian, "Հ. Յ. Դաշնակցութիւնը Զմիւռնիային մէջ [The ARF in Smyrna]," *Hairenik* October 1958, pp. 88–9.
66. Minassian, "Les relations entre le CUP," *art. cit.*, p. 53.
67. Hovhannes Yeretsian, "Հ. Յ. Դաշնակցութիւնը Տիգրանակերդին մէջ [The ARF in Dikranagerd]," *Hairenik*, April 1956, p. 49.
68. Marzbed, the pseudonym of Ghazaros Ghazarosian (1878–1918), born in Tomarza (*sancak* of Kaiseri), a teacher trained at the University of Leipzig; ARF cadre in Persia, Van and Bitlis; deported in 1915, he managed to escape and work under an assumed name on construction of the Baghdad Railway in Cilicia.
69. *Infra*, p. 915, n. 33, for a brief biography.
70. Papazian, *Memoirs, op. cit.*, II, p. 30.
71. *Ibidem*, p. 34.
72. *Infra*, p. 816, n. 35.
73. Pseudonym of Dajad Melkonian (c. 1870–1916), doctor of theology, defrocked in 1906, ARF delegate first in Iranian Azerbaijan and then in the Mush-Sasun area (1908–1911); executed in Urfa.

74. Minassian, "Les relations entre le CUP," *art. cit.*, p. 58.

75. Simon Zavarian, Սիմոն Զաւարեան. Մահուան Եօթանասունամեակին Առթիւ [*Simon Zavarian: On the Occasion of the Seventieth Anniversary of His Death*], edited by Hrach Dasnabedian, III, Beirut 1997, pp. 31–3, letter from Constantinople, 6 January 1909

76. Mahmud Kâmil, a classmate of Enver's at the Military Academy of Istanbul became, in 1915, commander-in-chief of the Third Army, based north of Erzerum, in Tortum, after the failure of the offensive on the Caucasus launched in December 1914.

77. Ruben Ter Minassian, Հայ Յեղափոխականի մը Յիշատակները [Memoirs of an Armenian Revolutionary], vol. V, Los Angeles 1951, p. 184–96.

78. *Ibidem*, V, p. 198.

79. *Ibidem*, V, pp. 199–200.

80. *Ibidem*, V, pp. 226–7. Rupen ignored the official ceremonies, preferring to visit Van's police chief, Mehmed Effendi, an old acquaintance. Mehmed Effendi reminded him that Turkish officials governed the region and were perfectly familiar with the mentality of the local populations, as well as the fact that people from Van were interested only in their own region. He confirmed that police officials had produced all the propaganda aimed at glorifying Aram and Ishkhan and that its sole purpose was to allay the Armenians' suspicions. Ruben concludes his account of this conversation by revealing that the police chief in question was an Armenian who had converted to Islam after the 1895 massacres and regularly informed the *fedayi* leaders of the government's plans (*ibidem*, pp. 250–9).

81. *Ibidem*, pp. 244–5. Present were, notably, Dr. Hovsep Ter Davtian, Arshag Vramian, Vahan Papazian, and Vartan Shahbaz.

82. *Ibidem*, pp. 118–19, letter from S. Zavarian to the Balkans Central Committee, Constantinople, 10 October 1912.

83. *Infra*, p. 826, n. 30.

84. *Simon Zavarian: on the occasion of the seventieth anniversary of his death, op. cit.*, pp. 315–429, see the series of letters that Simon Zavarian wrote from Mush between 25 November 1909 and 6 July 1911.

85. *Infra*, p. 817 n. 53; Papazian, *Memoirs, op. cit.*, II, p. 37, for his action in Van.

86. *Ibidem*, pp. 38–9.

87. *Ibidem*, pp. 42–3.

88. *Ibidem*, p. 40.

89. CADN, Ambassade de Constantinople, E 130, report from the French vice-consul in Uskub, G. Rajevof, to M. Boppe, chargé d'affaires in Constantinople, 28 June 1909, no. 65, "Histoire du mouvement révolutionnaire du mois de juillet 1908," pp. 70–2.

90. *Ibidem*, p. 72.

91. Bedros Halajian (1852–1920), deputy in the Ottoman parliament, minister of public works, member of the Young Turk party.

92. Sharurian, *Chronology of the life and work of Krikor Zohrab, op. cit.*, p. 163. It should be added that initially, the patriarch interfered in the political process by taking a hand in creating the rules for choosing the Armenian candidates (at an informal meeting to which, notably, Zohrab, Rupen Zartarian, and Murad [Hampartsum Boyajian] had been invited) (*ibidem*).

93. Vartkes (1871–1915), born in Erzerum, head of the party in Van (1901–1903), arrested and condemned to death (a sentence commuted to life in prison), deputy in the Ottoman parliament from 1908 to 1915, deported toward Urfa and then murdered.

94. Armen Garo (1872–1923), born in Erzerum, doctor in chemistry (educated in Geneva), responsible for the occupation of the Banque Ottomane (1896), member of the Western and Eastern bureaus (1898–1901 and 1907, respectively) and deputy in the Ottoman parliament from 1908 to February 1914.

95. Kegham (1865–1918), born in Khebian (Mush), leader of the ARF in his native region, deputy in the Ottoman parliament from 1908 to 1918 (ill with tuberculosis, he was not deported).

96. Descended of a family of rich merchants from Smyrna.

97. Hagop Babikian (1856–1909), born in Edirne, lawyer in Constantinople, member of the CUP, deputy in the Ottoman parliament (1908), a leader, together with Yusuf Kemal, of the parliamentary commission of inquiry into the massacres of Cilicia.

98. *Supra*, I, n. 130.

99. Nazareth Daghavarian († 1915), born in Sıvas, writer, agronomical engineer, and Paris-trained physician, founder and secretary general of the A.G.B.U. (1906), deputy from Sıvas in the Ottoman parliament (1908–1915), deported on 24 April 1915 and murdered.

100. Ahmad, *The Young Turks, op. cit.*

101. Minassian, "Les relations entre le CUP," *art. cit.*, p. 60. The Armenian deputies of course refused the invitation.

102. CADN, Ambassade de Constantinople, série E/126, letter from the French vice-consul in Erzerum to Constans, French ambassador in Constantinople, 21 November 1908. The mufti elected in Erzincan was described as "very fanatical."

103. CADN, Ambassade de Constantinople, série E/126, letter from the French vice-consul in Erzerum to Constans, French ambassador in Constantinople, 20 November 1908.

104. CADN, Ambassade de Constantinople, série E/126, letter from the French consul in Salonika to Constans, French ambassador in Constantinople, 23 September 1908.

 Mehmed Cavid (1875–1926), graduated from Mülkiye at the same time as Hüseyin Cahid, member of the OOL in 1906, deputy first from Salonika (1908 and 1912) and then from Çanakkale (1914), minister of finance in June 1909 and again in 1913–1915 and 1917–1918; took part in the plot against Kemal and was executed in 1926 (Zürcher, *The Unionist, op. cit.*, p. 49).

105. The consul describes Harutiun/Artin Boshghazarian as an "intelligent man, a good speaker and a patriot. It is said that he owes his success to the vali's support.": CADN, Ambassade de Constantinople, série E/126, letter from the French consul in Aleppo to Bompard, ambassador in Constantinople, 25 November 1909.

106. *Ibidem.*

107. The Armenian Chamber had 140 members: the parish councils of Constantinople designated 80 deputies, the clergymen of the capital designated 20 more and the provincial dioceses designated another forty. The chamber elected the Political Council, a kind of national government with executive powers. The 20 people on the Political Council oversaw the naming and the work of four committees while also maintaining regular relations with the Ottoman government. The Political Council was sometimes combined with the Religious Council, made up of 14 clergymen, to form a Mixed Council.

 The four committees were the School Committee, which administered 2,000 schools; the Administrative Committee, charged with managing and maintaining national property and revenue (collecting rents and taxes), buying and selling real estate, keeping a strict watch over the national legacy, monitoring receipts and expenditures, and administering the hospitals; the Judiciary Committee, comprising eight members – four clergymen and four lay jurists required to have a doctorate in law – was charged with settling family disputes and dealing with the litigation involving Armenians that the Sublime Porte referred to it; and the Committee on Monasteries, charged with supervising the management of the hundreds of Armenian monasteries in the empire.

 The internal organization of the Armenian community in the provinces – the 45 dioceses – was modeled after the organization in the capital. The metropolitan of each diocese presided over the diocesan council, a majority of whose members were lay dignitaries, and had executive power: Raymond Kévorkian and P. B. Paboudjian, *Les Arméniens dans l'Empire ottoman à la veille du génocide*, Paris 1992, pp. 7–9.

108. *Adenakrutiun Azkayin Zhoghovo* [*Minutes of the National Chamber*], 1887–1896, Constantinople 1896.

109. M. Ormanian, *Azkabadum*, III, Jérusalem 1927, coll. 5066–506.

110. Kévorkian-Paboudjian, *Les Arméniens dans l'Empire ottoman, op. cit.*, pp. 15–19.

111. Ormanian, *Azkabadum, op. cit.*, col. 5153.

112. *Adenakrutiun Azkayin Zhoghovo* [*Minutes of the National Chamber*], Constantinople, July 1906, pp. 1–4.

113. Ormanian, *Azkabadoum, op. cit.*, coll. 5380–5388. This prelate (1841–1918), a convert from the Catholic Church educated in Rome, reformed the seminary in Armash where he trained the future leaders of the Armenian Church along modernized lines; he served as Archbishop of Erzerum, founding Erzerum's Sanasarian School, an elite establishment with a curriculum based on German

models. Ormanian is the author of standard works on the history of the Armenian Church. After being forced to resign, he spent several years in exile at the Patriarchate of Jerusalem, then returned and settled in the capital, where he lived modestly in a one-room apartment in Pera.

114. Stepan Karayan (1855–1933), jurist, law professor, judge on the court of appeals, president of the Political Council almost without interruption from 1908 to 1914.

115. H. Shahrikian, known as Nitra (1860–1915), born in Şabin-Karahisar, Istanbul-educated jurist, member of the Eastern Bureau (1898–1905), murdered in 1915.

116. *Adenakrutiun Azkayin Zhoghovo, Verapatsoum 1908–1909 Nstachrtchani* [*Minutes of the inaugural session of the National Chamber 1908–1909*], Constantinople 1909, pp. 39, 49–54.

117. Hrant Asadur (1862–1928), born in Constantinople, Paris-educated jurist, member of the Ottoman Constitutional Council, editor of the newspaper *Masis*, literary critic.

118. V. Torkomian (1858–1942), born in Constantinople, Paris-trained physician, Prince Abdül Mecid's private physician, president of the Imperial Medical Academy founder of the Armenian Red Cross, deported in 1915, exiled to France (1923), author of many scholarly works.

119. *Ibidem*, p. 57.

120. Report, 20 November 1908: Bibliothèque Nubar, CCG 5/4, file 1, 16 pp., in Kévorkian-Paboudjian, *Les Arméniens dans l'Empire ottoman, op. cit.*, pp. 26–7.

121. The first veritable crisis facing the CUP broke out in early October 1908, when, in short order, Bulgaria declared its independence (5 October), the Austro-Hungarian Empire proclaimed that it had annexed Bosnia-Herzegovina, and Crete proclaimed itself a part of Greece (6 October).

122. Founded on 14 September 1908 by Nureddin Ferruh, Ahmed Fazıl, Celâleddin Arif: Bozarslan, *Les Courants de pensée, op. cit.* II, p. 123; Erik J. Zürcher, *Turkey, a Modern History*, London and New York, ed. 1998, p. 100.

123. Papazian, *Memoirs, op. cit.*, II, p. 101. We have observed that the Armenian delegation had opted for direct negotiations with the government or even the Young Turk Central Committee in order to circumvent the tensions that reigned in the parliament to which many conservatives, especially from the provinces, had been elected on the CUP's lists.

124. *Ibidem*, pp. 99–100.

125. His candidacy was initally blocked by the CUP (*Piuzantion*, no. 3700, 8 December 1908, p. 1). However, in the face of the Patriarchal Political Council's insistence, and after a 6 December meeting that the Council's president, Stepan Karayan, held with "an important figure" at the CUP's Istanbul headquarters, the Young Turks agreed not to veto his election (*Piuzantion*, no. 3701, 9 December 1908, p. 1). In its 9 December issue, the CUP's organ, *Şûra-yı Ümmet*, announced that there were two Armenian candidates on the committee's list of candidates for the capital.

126. Under the feather of the editor-in-chief, Puzant Kechian, de *Piuzantion*, no. 3706, 15 December 1908, p. 1.

127. A Laz born in Şoppa, a judge who served in Damascus, Salonika, and Skopie (Uskub) as president of the penal court; after 1908, member of the CUP, court inspector in Salonika and interim vali of Kosovo; traveled frequently to Lazistan as a CUP propagandist; director of the Department of Criminal Affairs in the Ministry of Justice; member of the commission for the nomination of magistrates; charged with investigating the "abuses" committed during the First World War at the expense of the Armenians; presiding judge of the criminal and the appeals court: APC/PAJ, PCI Bureau, Ɜ 25–26–27–28–29–30–31–32–33–34, Second Report on Turks Responsible for the Armenian Atrocities.

128. Hüseyin Cahit bey [Yalçın] (1874–1957), parliamentary deputy from the capital, vice-president (1914–1916), and, later, president of parliament, member of the Young Turk Central Committee, one of the main CUP propagandists, editor of *Tanin*. Interned in Malta in 1919.

129. *Piuzantion*, no. 3714, 24 December 1908.

130. *Zhamanag*, no. 54, 29 December 1908.

131. *Piuzantion*, no. 3721, 4 January 1909.

132. *Piuzantion*, no. 3686, 21 November 1908.

133. *Zhamanag*, no. 61, 6 January 1909.

134. *Piuzantion*, no. 3736, 22 January 1909.

135. Bozarslan, *Les Courants de pensée, op. cit.* II, p. 123; Hanioğlu, *Preparation for a Revolution, op. cit.*, p. 292.

136. Naim Turfan, *Rise of the Young Turks: Politics, the Military and Ottoman Collapse*, London and New York 2000, p. 232, n. 63.

137. Hüseyin Rauf (1881–1964), agent in Persia during the First World War, signatary of the 31 October 1918 Mudros Armistice, one of the founders of the Karakol and the resistance in Anatolia (1919): Zürcher, *The Unionist, op. cit.*, p. 45.

138. Monastırlı Nuri (1882–1937), born in Salonika, Unionist *fedayi*, parliamentary deputy, first director of the *Teşkilât-ı Mahsusa*, Enver's secret service secret after 1914: *ibidem*.

139. Kuşçubaşızade Eşref [Sencer] (1873–after 1963), important director of a section of the *Teşkilât-ı Mahsusa: ibidem*.

140. Yenibahçeli Şükrü [Oğuz], Unionist *fedayi* and CUP inspector, member of the *Teşkilât-ı Mahsusa*, and, later, of Karakol: *ibidem*.

141. Kara Vasıf (1872–1931), colonel, member of the CUP prior to 1908, member of the court-martial that judged the fiasco of the Balkan War, founder of *Karakol* in 1919: *ibidem*.

142. Kâzım [Özalp] (1880–1968), member of the CUP, officer, member of the *Teşkilât-ı Mahsusa*, president of the National Assembly (1924–1935), minister of war (1922–1924, 1935–1943): *ibidem*.

143. *Ibidem*, p. 50.

144. Published by Ali Birinci, in *Tarih ve Toplum*, no. 70, 1989, p. 60, cited in Bozarslan, *Les Courants de pensée, op. cit.*, I, p. 210, n. 818.

145. "Enver Paşa'nın Gizli Mektupları," (ed. by Ş. Hanioğlu), *Cumhuriyet*, 9 October 1989, in Bozarslan, *Les Courants de pensée, op. cit.*, I, p. 210, n. 815.

146. Midhat Şükrü Bleda, *İmparatorluğun Çöküşü*, Istanbul 1979, p. 26. This group, founded early in 1909, had the support of Hasan Fehmi and was dissolved after the events of "31 March" on charges of plotting, not against the government, but against the CUP: Bozarslan, *Les Courants de pensée, op. cit.*, II, p. 138.

147. T. Z. Tunaya, *Hürriyetin İlânı*, Istanbul 1959, p. 41, in Bozarslan, *Les Courants de pensée, op. cit.*, I, p. 233.

148. Founded in November 1909, the moving spirits behind this party were Lütfi Fikri, Şükrî Al-Aseki: *ibidem*, II, p. 123.

149. This party was led by Ferit pasha Sadık bey, Şükrü al-Aseki, Rıza Nur, Lütfi Fikri and Gümülcineli İsmail: *ibidem*, II, p. 123.

150. *Ibidem*, I, p. 234.

151. *Ibidem*, II, p. 123.

152. Sabah-Gulian, *The Responsibles, op. cit.*, p. 284.

153. *Ibidem*, pp. 285–6.

154. *Ibidem*, p. 287.

2 Young Turks and Armenians Facing the Test of "The 31 March Incident" and the Massacres in Cilicia

1. Turfan, *Rise of the Young Turks, op. cit.*, p. 238, n. 89.

2. M. Sabri Efendi, "Menkibelerimiz ve Ayıblarımız," in S. Albayrak, *31 Mart Vak'ası Gerici Bir Hareket mi?*, Istanbul 1989, p. 33, discourse of Rasim Efendi in Ottoman parliament, in Bozarslan, *Les Courants de pensée, op. cit.*, II, pp. 69–70.

3. François Georgeon, "Le dernier sursaut (1878–1908)," in Robert Mantran (dir.), *Histoire de l'Empire ottoman*, Paris 1989, p. 582.

4. Ahmad, *The Young Turks, op. cit*, pp. 43–4. The grand vizier, Kâmil Pasha, expelled him again, perhaps under pressure from the CUP.

5. See the Istanbul press of 19 April 1909, in particular *Piuzantion*, no. 3806, p. 3; Zürcher, *Turkey: A Modern History, op. cit.*, p. 102.

6. *Piuzantion*, no. 3805, 17 April 1909, p. 2.

7. *Piuzantion*, no. 3812, 27 April 1909, p. 3.

8. Papazian, *Memoirs*, II, *op. cit.*, p. 109.

9. *Simon Zavarian: On the Occasion of the Seventieth Anniversary of His Death, op. cit.*, III, pp. 60–1, letter of S. Zavarian, Constantinople, 14/27 April 1909.

10. *Ibidem*, p. 61.

11. Papazian, *Memoirs*, II, *op. cit.*, p. 105, notes that Ahmed Rıza in particular was targeted by the insurgents, who were led by the grand mufti of Istanbul. No more than 50 or 60 deputies were present when the parliament building was occupied, including Halajian, Armen Garo, and Papazian himself.

12. *Azadamard*, no. 66, 9 September 1909, p. 1, published Papazian's eyewitness account; Papazian repeats what he wrote here in his *Memoirs*, II, Cairo 1957, pp. 103–8; a vote in favor of the reintroduction of the ṣaria as the basic law of the land took place nevertheless.

13. Minassian, "Les relations entre le Comité Union et Progrès et la Fédération," *art. cit.*, pp. 62–3.

14. Diary of K. Zohrab, in *Garun* 5/1991, p. 67.

15. Minassian, "Les relations entre le Comité Union et Progrès et la Fédération," *art. cit.*, p. 62.

16. Reprinted in *Mshag*, no. 67, 15 April 1909.

17. CADN, Ambassade de Constantinople, série E/131, letter from the French vice-consul in Marash, Marcial Grapin, to Constans, French ambassador in Constantinople, 4 January 1909.

18. CADN, Ambassade de Constantinople, série E/131, letter from the French vice-consul in Dyarbekir to Bompard, French ambassador in Constantinople, 20 April 1909.

19. Archives du ministère des Affaires étrangères (AMAE), Correspondance politique, Turquie, n. s., vol. 83, politique intérieure, Arménie, Anatolie, Cilicie, f° 69 r°, letter from the French vice-consul in Van, captain B. Dickson, to the minister of foreign affairs, Pichon.

20. Ten months later, Baǧdâdizâde, too, would be among the organizers of the massacres.

21. AMAE, Correspondance politique, Turquie, n. s., vol. 83, f° 64 r°-v°, letter from the French vice-consul in Mersina and Adana to French ambassador in Constantinople and to the minister of foreign affairs, Pichon, 18 August 1908.

22. *Ibidem*, ff. 84–85, letter from the French vice-consul in Mersina and Adana to French ambassador in Constantinople and to the minister of Foreign affairs, 23 October 1908.

23. Duckett Z. Ferriman, *The Young Turks and the Truth about the Holocaust at Adana, in Asia Minor, During April, 1909*, London 1913, p. 14; Hagop Terzian, Կիլիկիոյ Աղէտը [*The Catastrophe of Cilicia*], Constantinople 1912, p. 12.

24. AMAE, Correspondance politique, Turquie, n. s., vol. 83, f° 86, dispatch of 3 November 1908.

25. AMAE, Correspondance politique, Turquie, n. s., vol. 83, f° 159, letter from French embassy, Therabia, 31 July 1910.

26. AMAE, Correspondance politique, Turquie, n. s., vol. 83, f° 84, letter to minister Pichon, 23 October 1908. Despite the witch hunt and the corresponding climate that prevailed in Cilicia after the massacres, and despite the political condemnations pronounced by the court-martial, G. Guvderelian, who was held in prison for approximately one year before being cleared and released, was described by the members of the commission of inquiry come from Constantinople as a man who enjoyed great prestige.

27. Duckett Z. Ferriman, *The Young Turks and the Truth about the Holocaust at Adana*, *op. cit.*, pp. 13–14.

28. *Azadamard*, no. 9, 2 July 1909, p. 3, published an interview of the editorial board with Grand Vizier Hilmi Pasha and General Mahmud Şevket about the condemnation of Bishop Mushegh, "considered to be responsible for the massacres" to "101 years in prison."

29. Service historique de la Marine (Vincennes), SS ED 100, 13 pp., Escadre de la Méditerranée occidentale et du Levant, dispatch no. 716, Alexandretta, 8 May 1909, Contre-Amiral Pivet, commander of the Escadre légère de la Méditerranée, to the minister of Navy.

30. *Piuzantion*, no. 3764, 27 February 1909, p. 1.

31. Report from the vali Cevad bey to minister of the Interior, end of April 1909, in H. Terzian, La catastrophe de Cilicie, *op. cit.*, p. 752.

32. Service historique de la Marine (Vincennes), SS ED 100, 13 pp., Escadre de la Méditerranée occidentale et du Levant, dispatch no. 716, Alexandretta, 8 May 1909, Contre-Amiral Pivet, commander of the Escadre légère de la Méditerranée, to the minister of Navy.

33. A. Adossidès, *Arméniens et Jeunes-Turcs, les massacres de Cilicie*, Paris 1910, pp. 117–18.

34. AMAE, Correspondance politique, Turquie, n. s., vol 283, ff. 164/22–23v°, reprinted in *Azadamard*, no. 42, 12 August 1909, p. 1.

35. AMAE, Corr. pol., Turquie, n. s., vol 283, f° 94.

36. *Azadamard*, no. 39, 8 August 1909, p. 1.

37. Terzian, *The Catastrophe of Cilicia*, op. cit., pp. 717–24, published the entire proceedings of the court-martial, dated 7 July 1909; the proceedings were also published by the Istanbul press beginning in mid-July (see *Azadamard*, no. 22, 17 July 1909, p. 3).

38. FO 195/2280, letter from British consul in Mersina and Adana, Doughty-Wylie, Konya, 15 June 1908.

39. Terzian, *The Catastrophe of Cilicia*, op. cit., pp. 689–99, published the entire proceedings of the court-martial, dated 10 July 1909; the proceedings were also published by the Istanbul press beginning in mid-July (see *Azadamard*, nos 33 et 34, 31 July and 2 August 1909).

40. As early as 1906, Bağdâdizâde was sending reports to Sultan Abdülhamid accusing the Armenians of Cilicia of harboring separatist intentions : Ferriman, *The Young Turks*, op. cit., p. 12.

41. *Ibidem*, p. 19.

42. Terzian, *The Catastrophe of Cilicia*, op. cit., pp. 10–19.

43. *Ibidem*, pp. 19–20.

44. This information is provided both by Ferriman, *The Young Turks*, op. cit., pp. 22–3 and by the parliamentary commission in its report, written by the judges Fayk Bey and H. Mosdichian (see n. 37).

45. Haci Adıl (1869–1935), former vali of Edirne, participed in the Union and Progress congress in Salonika in November 1910, becoming, at that time, both a member of the Central Committee and Dr. Nâzım's successor as the CUP's secretary general (AMAE, Turquie, n. s., vol. 7, ff. 154–8, report from the French consul in Salonika, Max Soublier, to Pichon and to the French ambassador in Constantinople, Bompard, Salonika, 17 November 1910). Adıl served as president of the reform commission in Albania and briefly, in January 1913, as interior minister (*Gohag*, 30 January 1913, no. 3 [128], pp. 25–6), and president of parliament in fall 1915. Under Mustafa Kemal, he became Director-General of the State Monopolies. He was one of the defendants in the "Smyrna plot" trial of 1926: Zürcher, *The Unionist*, op. cit., p. 160.

46. This famous telegram was cited by virtually the entire Istanbul press and in the report of the parliamentary commission; it was also at the heart of the debates in the Ottoman parliament at the session of 19 April 1909, during which Adıl Bey was asked to provide an explanation in place of his newly named minister of the interior, who was not familiar with the details of the affair (see the precise account *Piuzantion*, no. 3806, 19 April, p. 2 and the publication *in extenso* of the parliamentary debates in Terzian, *The Catastrophe of Cilicia*, op. cit., pp. 592–607).

47. Rigal (P.), "Adana. Les Massacres d'Adana," *Lettres d'Ore, relations d'Orient* [Confidential Review of the Jesuit Missions Edited in the Order in Lyons and Published in Brusells], November 1909, pp. 359–91. Another series of reports was published in the July 1909 issue, pp. 199–223.

48. This summary of events is based on many different sources: the reports of the parliamentary commission, the Armenian Council, the missionaries and consuls, and, of course, on the articles and reports published in the Istanbul press, as well as the crucially important eyewitness accounts reproduced in Terzian, *The Catastrophe of Cilicia*, op. cit., pp. 26–36, Ferriman, op. cit., pp. 23–5.

49. According to the pharmacist Hagop Terzian, it was the 300 Armenians living in the quarter near the Sultane Valide mosque in Hazır Bazar, almost all of them natives of Hacın, who witnessed these events (cf. Terzian, *The Catastrophe of Cilicia*, op. cit., p. 37). After resisting for two hours, they succeeded in the course of the night in making their way into the house of the dragoman of the Russian consulate, Yanko Artemi, after making an opening in a side wall. They remained there for three days, until the massacres were over.

50. Terzian, who was in the Armenian quarter at the time, gives a very precise description of the positions, street by street, of the defenders (pp. 38–9). The English consul, for his part, confirms that the Muslims launched an assault on the Armenian quarter: FO 195/2306, letter from Doughty-Wylie to the ambassador Lowther, 21 April 1909.

51. See the French missionaries' narratives published in Raymond Kévorkian, *Les Massacres de Cilicie d'avril 1909, Revue d'Histoire Arménienne Contemporaine*, III (1999), pp. 144–7.

52. To present a full account of the Cilician events, we would also have to discuss the events that occurred simultaneously in the other towns and villages of the region; that would, however, take us too far afield. We therefore refer interested readers to our study: Kévorkian, *Les Massacres de Cilicie d'April 1909*, op. cit., pp. 5–141, and especially pp. 65–82, for the other towns and villages.

53. A facsimile reproduction, with a translation of the incriminating articles, is included in Terzian, *The Catastrophe of Cilicia, op. cit.*, pp. 64–92.
54. *Ibidem*, pp. 64–8.
55. Reprinted in *Azadamard*, no. 4, 26 June 1909, p. 2.
56. Terzian, *The Catastrophe of Cilicia, op. cit.*, pp. 68–9.
57. *Ibidem*, p. 69.
58. *Infra*, p. 833, n. 47, relation of Father Rigal.
59. Published especially in *Piuzantion*, no. 3806, 19 April 1909, p. 2.
60. Report on the Session in *Piuzantion*, no. 3807, 20 April 1909, p. 1.
61. *Supra*, p. 72.
62. *Piuzantion*, no. 3816, 1 May 1909, p. 1.
63. AMAE, Correspondance politique, Turquie, n. s., vol. 83, ff. 121–122, Paris, 16 June 1909.
64. Kévorkian, *Les Massacres de Cilicie d'avril 1909, op. cit.*, p. 149, Some of the following passages are also taken from Rigal's *Mémoire*.
65. *Ibidem*, p. 173, complete report by Hagop Babikian. This information is confirmed in the "Report on the Massacres in Adana" by major Doughty-Wylie: FO 424/220.
66. These figures are given in Interior Minister Ferid Pasha's report, read during the 11 May 1909 session of the Ottoman parliament. The full record of this session may be found in Terzian, *The Catastrophe of Cilicia, op. cit.*, p. 607; see also *ibidem*, 300; Ferriman, *op. cit.*, p. 80.
67. Figures cited by Zohrab in his contribution to the parliamentary debate; he identified his source as a letter, received in Constantinople, from the dragoman of the French vice-consulate in Mersin and Adana: Terzian, *The Catastrophe of Cilicia, op. cit.*, pp. 604–5
68. Reprinted in *Piuzantion*, no. 3827, 14 May 1909, p. 2.
69. Kévorkian, *Les Massacres de Cilicie d'April 1909, op. cit.*, p. 167, text of the report.
70. *Ibidem*.
71. *Tasviri Efkiar*, 12 August 1909.
72. Figures given by the charge d'affaire Boppe, in a letter to the minister Pichon: AMAE, Correspondance politique, Turquie, n. s., vol. 83, f° 147.
73. For the complete compilation, see *ibidem*, p. 83.
74. *Ibidem*.
75. See n. 30; Ferriman, *op. cit.*, pp. 85–7.
76. Figures given by the governmental commission of inquiry (see note 173). Ferriman, pp. 91–3, 97, furnishes the details region by region.
77. On the question of the orphans, see Zabel Essayan (administrator of the Armenian Red Cross in Cilicia in this period), correspondence and notes, Levon Kecheyan (ed.), in Kévorkian, *Les massacres de Cilicie d'avril 1909, op. cit.*, pp. 217, Suiv.
78. Terzian, *The Catastrophe of Cilicia, op. cit.*, pp. 814–16.
79. *Ibidem*, pp. 819–24.

3   The Ottoman Government's and the Armenian Authorities' Political Responses to the Massacres in Cilicia

1. Kévorkian, *Les massacres de Cilicie d'avril 1909, op. cit.*, p. 152.
2. The allusion is to the second massacres of Adana, underway as Cevad wrote.
3. Kévorkian, *Les massacres de Cilicie d'avril 1909, op. cit.*, p. 57, n. 59, p. 152.
4. Zohrab is alluding to the fact that Adıl was then de facto in charge of the Interior Ministry.
5. 3 May 1909, p. 1, "The Turkish Crisis: The Armenians Protest in the Chamber."
6. A complete translation of the records of the debates of the Ottoman parliament was published by the Istanbul press the next day, notably in *Piuzantion*, nos 3836, 3837, 24 and 25 May, pp. 2–3; see also Terzian, *The Catastrophe of Cilicia, op. cit.*, pp. 611–15.
7. *Ibidem*.
8. AMAE, Correspondance politique, Turquie, n. s., vol. 83, f° 159/2, from Barré de Lancy to Boppe, 3 July 1909.
9. *Ibidem*.

10. *Azadamard*, no. 13, 7 July 1909, p. 3.

11. *Azadamard*, no. 15, 9 July 1909, p. 3.

12. *Ibidem*.

13. *Azadamard*, no. 18, 13 July 1909, p. 3.

14. Records of the debates of the Ottoman parliament, 105 session, in *Azadamard*, no. 11, 5 July 1909, p. 2.

15. AMAE, Correspondance politique, Turquie, n. s., vol. 83, f° 159/3. Gabriel-Georges Barré de Lancy (born 8 Sept. 1865), vice-consul in Mersin and Tarse.

16. FO 195/2306, letter from Doughty-Wylie to the British ambassador in Constantinople, 30 June 1909.

17. *Azadamard*, no. 10, 3 July 1909, p. 3.

18. Reprinted in *Azadamard*, no. 12, 6 July 1909, p. 1. According to the editorialist of this daily, the members of the government admitted in private that all these accusations were false, but refused to say so publicly.

19. AMAE, Correspondance politique, Turquie, n. s., vol. 83, f° 159/7, report from Barré de Lancy to Boppe, Mersin, 16 July 1909.

20. *Azadamard*, no. 25, 21 July 1909, p. 2.

21. Three of these individuals and many others murderers were, oddly, appointed to the local commissions of inquiry charged with investigating crimes for which they too were under suspicion.

22. Reports in the Istanbul press of 27 July, especially in *Azadamard*, no. 29, 27 July 1909, p. 2. According to Şerif pasha, İsmail Hakkı is a member of Young Turk Central Committee: *Mécheroutiette*, no. 38, January 1913, p. 16.

23. *Azadamard*, no. 29, 27 July 1909, p. 3.

24. AMAE, Correspondance politique, Turquie, vol. 83, f° 162, Thérapia, 11 August 1909.

25. *Azadamard*, no. 34, 2 August 1909, p. 3.

26. *Azadamard*, no. 34 and 36, 2 and 4 August 1909, p. 3. Babikian's 4 August funeral was the occasion for a grand ecumenical ceremony at which members of parliament, senators, members of the government, and the diplomatic corps were all present. During the ceremony, Yusuf Kemal and Krikor Zohrab delivered eulogies in which they paid tribute to Babikian's selflessness and political courage.

27. Records of the debates of the Ottoman parliament were published by Istanbul press and by Terzian, *The Catastrophe of Cilicia, op. cit.*, pp. 621–3.

28. A complete translation was published in *Azadamard*, no. 63, 5 September 1909, p. 1.

29. *Azadamard*, no. 38, 6 August 1909, pp. 1–2, announced Cemal appointment and published an interview with him; ambassador Bompard also announced this appointment in a letter to minister Pichon, 11 August 1909: AMAE, Correspondance politique, Turquie, n. s., vol. 283, f° 162.

30. The funds were put in the hands of commissions made up of local notables more or less deeply implied in the massacres; most of the money was embezzled. Let us also point out that there occurred only symbolic restitution of the booty seized during the massacres: FO 195/2306, letter from Doughty-Wylie to Lowther, Adana, 9 May 1909.

31. French version in AMAE, Correspondance politique, Turquie, n. s., vol. 283, ff. 164/22–23v°; Armenian version in *Azadamard*, no. 42, 12 August 1909, p. 1.

32. *Azadamard*, no. 42, 12 August 1909, p. 3.

33. FO 195/2306, letters from Doughty-Wylie to Lowther, 4 and 21 May 1909.

34. Adossidès, *op. cit.*, p. 106, cites the report of the American mission.

35. Terzian, *The Catastrophe of Cilicia, op. cit.*, pp. 689–99, for the full report, 10 July 1909, and in the Istanbul press in the end of July (see *Azadamard*, no. 33, 34, 31 July and 2 August 1909).

36. AMAE, Correspondance politique, Turquie, n. s., vol 283, ff. 121–3, 16 June 1909.

37. A big Kurdish landowner said to be particularly corrupt.

38. AMAE, Correspondance politique, Turquie, n. s., vol. 283, f° 16421, 24, 33, Mersine, 11 and 21 September 1909.

39. *Azadamard*, no. 63, 6 September 1909, p. 3.

40. Adossidès, *op. cit.*, pp. 119–20.

41. *Adenakrutiun, op. cit.*, records of the 8 May 1909 Session, pp. 322–7.

42. *Ibidem*, pp. 328–35.

43. M. Ormanian, *Azkabadum*, III, Jérusalem 1927, col. 5432; diplomatic sources indicate that some of the victims from others regions were repatriated. "Some sixty people, widows as well as girls and boys whose parents had been massacred during the events in Adana and the surrounding area were taken to Sıvas by the local authorities in a terrible state" and then conducted "as far as their native district of Terjan, in the vilayet of Erzerum. Fleeing the poverty and famine prevailing in region from which they came, these families had gone to the vilayet of Adana the previous fall to work during the harvest."

44. *Adenakrutiun, op. cit.*, records of the 12 June 1909 Session, pp. 404, 409.

45. Sarkis Svin, a delegate traveling with a prelate, was put under "military surveillance" as soon as he arrived in Cilicia, and prevented from traveling freely (*ibidem*, p. 407).

46. *Ibidem*, records of the 24 April 1909 Session, pp. 305–6.

47. *Ibidem*, records of the 12 June 1909 Session, pp. 389–409.

48. *Ibidem*, records of the 21 August 1909 Session, pp. 484, suiv.

49. *Piuzantion*, no. 3823, 10 May 1909, p. 1.

50. *Azadamard*, no. 2, 24 June 1909, p. 1.

51. *Azadamard*, no. 9, 2 July 1909, p. 2, records of the 104 Session.

52. *Azadamard*, no. 10, 3 July 1909, p. 2, records of the Session.

53. *Ibidem*, records of the 25 September 1909 Session, pp. 517–18, 522–4.

54. *Ibidem*, records of the 4 September 1909 Session, pp. 493–4.

55. *Ibidem*, records of the 30 October 1909 Session, pp. 46–7.

56. *Ibidem*, pp. 49–50.

57. N° 3924, 20 September, p. 1, editorial.

58. *Ibidem*, p. 1.

59. *Ibidem*, records of the 18 December 1909 Session, pp. 127–9.

60. *Ibidem*, p. 130.

61. Declaration published in the *Temps* and reprinted in *Azadamard*, no. 12, 6 July 1909, p. 1, see *supra*, p. 103.

62. *Ibidem*, pp. 143–53, 161.

63. Zeki Bey was preparing to publish "important revelations concerning the Committee's intrigues, the revolutionary movement of 31 March and the Adana incidents." As a result, "he would be, in his own words, condemned to death by the Committee": *Mécheroutiette, Constitutionnel ottoman*, no. 51, February 1914, p. 34.

64. Kévorkian, *Les Massacres de Cilicie d'avril 1909, op. cit.*, p. 152.

65. *Piuzantion*, no. 3946, 16 October 1909, p. 3, published the declaration of the Central Committee in Salonika.

66. *Azadamard*, no. 3, 25 June 1909, p. 3, article of Rinat de Vall, correspondant of the *Giornale d'Italia*.

67. *Azadamard*, no. 125, 18 November 1909, p. 1.

68. Hanioğlu, *Preparation for a Revolution, op. cit.*, p. 285; Papazian, *Memoirs, op. cit..*, II, p. 114, points out that Zohrab was one of the main authors of the act destituting the Sultan.

69. "Երկրորդ Յեղափոխութիւն [Second Revolution]," *Droschak*, no. 4/201, April 1909, pp. 41–45.

70. *Ibidem*, p. 43.

71. *Adenakrutiun, op. cit.*, p. 43. the allusion is probably to the tribal leaders and notables in the provinces who had been closely associated with the old regime. "The traitors tothe fatherland" in favor of decentralization are probably the liberal circles that the CUP liquidated after the "reaction" of 31 March.

72. *Ibidem*, records of the 21 August 1909 Session and records of the 12 February 1910 Session, pp. 190–5. The correspondence of the French consuls sheds light on the first experiments in this domain. It also indicates that "the Christians also find the abnormal moeurs of the Muslim soldiers repulsive." These and similar remarks about the Turkish soldiers are confirmed by the frequent references to cases of rape or attempted rape of the Armenian conscripts. The authorities avoided airing them in public. They also maintained silence about the conditions imposed on Christian soldiers, illustrated by "the example of the seventeen recruits from Diarbekir who were sent to Musch [*sic*] last year; fourteen of them succumbed to fatigue and privation, [a circumstance that is] hardly likely to reassure the others": cf. AMAE, Correspondance politique, Turquie, n. s.,

vol. 85, pp. 37, 52, 105, letter from the French vice-consuls in Erzerum and Dyarbekir, 10 March, 6 April and 7 August 1911.

73. *Simon Zavarian: On the Occasion of the Seventieth Anniversary of His Death*, III, *op. cit.*, pp. 385–6: Letter to the Western bureau, section of Constantinople, 25 October 1910.

74. Stepanos Sapah-Giulian, Փորք Հայրի Յիշատակներ. Մաս Ա. 10-Մայիս-1 Օգոստոս [*Memories of Armenia Minor, Part 1, 10 May–1 August 1911*], Chicago 1917, p. 323.

75. *Adenakrutiun, op. cit.*, records of the 25 November 1911 Session, pp. 430–44.

76. Papazian, *Memoirs, op. cit..*, II, p. 126.

4 The CUP's First Deviations: The 1909, 1910, and 1911 Congresses

1. Mehmed Ziya [Gökalp] (1876–1924), sociologist, main CUP ideologue, member of the Central Committee from 1910: Zürcher, *The Unionist, op. cit.*, p. 77.

2. Bozarslan, *Les Courants de pensée, op. cit.* II, p. 124.

3. Turfan, *Rise of the Young Turks, op. cit.*, pp. XV–XVI. The author points out that Kemal's position is contradictory, since he himself was an officer and a delegate from Tripolitania. More prosaically, we might ask if his reaction is not due, above all, to his long-standing conflict with Enver, who shut him out of the committee's supreme body. An imperial decree of 29 May 1909 called on the officers to stop meddling in politics; Mahmud Şevket seemed to be one of the most determined high-ranking officers in this regard: Ahmad, *The Young Turks, op. cit.*, p. 55.

4. *Supra*, p. 105.

5. ADN, Ambassade de Constantinople, série E/126, letter from the French ambassador in Constantinople, Bompard, to the minister of Foreign affairs, 5 January 1910.

6. *Mécheroutiette, Constitutionnel ottoman*, no. 38, January 1913, p. 16.

7. *Ibidem*, no. 39, February 1913, p. 21, article of Sam Lévy, in *Journal de Salonique*.

8. *Ibidem*, p. 27, collected by Sam Lévy.

9. Records of the trial, 27 June 1911, in *Mécheroutiette, Constitutionnel ottoman*, no. 25–32, November 1911 to July 1912. Zeki had also collaborated for quite some time on Murad Bey's *Mizanci*. It was for this reason that he was arrested, like many other members of the opposition, after the events of 13 April 1909, and accused of being a "reactionary." He was not, however, found guilty, thanks to his reputation for integrity and his past as an opponent to the Hamidian regime.

10. *Mécheroutiette, Constitutionnel ottoman*, no. 51, February 1914, p. 34. The day after Zeki Bey was murdered, "police searches" were carried out in the victim's bureau and home, and all his files were confiscated; the court, however, did not make use of them at his trial. Ahmad, *The Young Turks, op. cit.*, p. 74, explains Cavid's resignation as the result of disagreement between him and the minister of war, M. Şevket, over the military budget.

11. His murder gave rise to a chorus of protests and a stormy debate in parliament, during which the CUP was openly accused of ordering the murder. To disparage Hasan, the Young Turk press fell back on its old propaganda arsenal, describing him, like many others, as a Hamidian reactionary opposed to the Constitution.

12. Dr. Tevfik Rüstü [Aras] (1883–1972), Dr. Nâzım's brother-in-law and a comrade of Mustafa Kemal's; an important member of the committee's inner circle, a leader of the war of liberation in Anatolia, foreign minister under Mustafa Kemal.

13. *Mécheroutiette, Constitutionnel ottoman*, no. 51, February 1914, pp. 15–53.

14. *Ibidem*, p. 34.

15. CADN, Ambassade de Constantinople, série E/126, letter from the French ambassador in Constantinople, Bompard, to the minister of Foreign affairs, 10 May 1911.

16. *Ibidem*.

17. Mehmed Sadık (1860–1940), born in Istanbul, *Harbiye* graduate, leader of the CUP in Manastır, member of the Central Committee in July 1908, influential in Salonika in 1909–1910; after breaking with the CUP, he became a one of the leaders of the Liberals: Ahmad, *The Young Turks, op. cit.*, pp. 89–90 et p. 178.

18. AMAE, Correspondance politique, Turquie, n. s., vol. 8, f° 121, letter from French consul in Salonika, Josselin, to Selves, minister of Foreign affairs, Salonika, 5 October 1911.

19. CADN, Ambassade de Constantinople, série E/126, letter from the French vice-consul in Üsküb to Bompard, 20 September 1910, "translation of a speech attributed to Talât Bey, minister of the interior"; the same speech is cited by a British source: Ahmad, *The Young Turks, op. cit.*, p. 85, n. 1, notes that he has found no Turkish sources on this discourse; Vahakn Dadrian, *Histoire du génocide arménien*, Paris 1996, pp. 301–3, n. 2–7, adds Austrian consular sources that are independent of the other diplomatic documents.

20. CADN, Ambassade de Constantinople, série E/126, letter from the French vice-consul in Üsküb to Bompard, 20 September 1910.

21. Halil bey [Menteşe] (1874–1948), jurist, member of the Young Turk Central Committee (1910), deputy from Menteşe, president of the Young Turk parliamentary group, president of the Council of State (June 1913), president of parliament, foreign minister (October 1915–February 1917), deported to Malta in 1919: Ahmad, *The Young Turks, op. cit.*, p. 171; AMAE, Correspondance politique, Turquie, n. s., vol. 9, f° 220, telegram from the French chargé d'affaire in Constantinople, to Boppe, 17 June 1913.

22. Giritli Ahmed Nesimi (?–1958), born in Crete, educated at the Ecole des Sciences Politiques in Paris, member of the Young Turk Central Committee (1911), foreign minister (February 1917–October 1918), deported to Malta in 1919: Ahmad, *The Young Turks, op. cit.*, pp. 175–6.

23. AMAE, Correspondance politique, Turquie, n. s., vol. 7, f° 124, letter from the French consul in Salonika, Max Soublier, to Bompard, 1 November 1910. Dr. Nâzım was then secretary general of the Central Committee. The consul notes that the Committee of Union and Progress and the party for Union and Progress had functioned independently of one another until then: *ibidem*, ff. 132–4, letter from Max Choublier to Pichon, Salonika, 7 and 8 November 1910.

24. AMAE, Correspondance politique, Turquie, n. s., vol. 7, f° 149 v°, letter from Max Choublier to Pichon, Salonika, 16 November 1910, speech of Ihsan bey.

25. *Ibidem*, f° 150.

26. AMAE, Correspondance politique, Turquie, n. s., vol. 7, f° 151 v°, letter from Max Choublier to Pichon, Salonika, 17 November 1910.

27. AMAE, Correspondance politique, Turquie, n. s., vol. 7, ff. 152–3, letter from Max Choublier to Pichon and Bompard, Salonika, 17 November 1910.

28. *Ibidem*, f° 154. The consul states that this information is corroborated by information that his European colleagues in Salonika had obtained from others sources (f° 157).

29. *Ibidem*, f° 164 v°, speech.

30. *Ibidem*, f° 158.

31. *Infra*, p. 833, n. 45.

32. *Infra*, p. 822, n. 174.

33. *Infra*, p. 822, n. 164.

34. A newcomer about whom very little is known, apart from the fact that during the First World War he was one of the pivotal members of the commissions responsible for "abandoned property" (*Emvali Metruke*), and thus for "nationalizing" the economy–in other words, for confiscating the moveable assets and real estate of the Armenians and then the Greeks: APC/PAJ, PCI Bureau, Ի 201, list of murterers in Eskişehir, and Ֆ 177–178.

35. *Infra*, p. 821, n. 160.

36. Aram Andonian, Պատմութիւն Պալքանեան Պատերազմին [*History of the Balkan war*], II, Istanbul 1913, pp. 349, 355.

37. AMAE, Correspondance politique, Turquie, n. s., vol. 8, f° 107, letter from the French consul in Salonika, Max Soublier, to Selves, minister of Foreign affairs, and to Bompard, Salonika, 3 September 1911.

38. *Infra*, p. 814, n. 4.

39. AMAE, Correspondance politique, Turquie, n. s., vol. 8, f° 117, letter from the French consul in Salonika, Josselin, to Bompard, Salonika, 30 September 1911. The consul also points out that the congress decided to increase the number of members on the Central Committee from 7 to 12: *ibidem*, f° 117v°.

40. Ali Fethi [Okyar] (1880–1943), member of the CUP in 1907 (Salonika), of the Central Committee in 1911, deputy, ambassador and minister in 1917, helped found the CUP again in October 1918, one of the organizers of war of liberation: Zürcher, *The Unionist, op. cit.*, p. 28.

41. AMAE, Correspondance politique, Turquie, n. s., vol. 8, f° 121, letter from the French consul in Salonika, Josselin, to Selves, minister of Foreign affairs, Salonika, 10 October 1911.

    Hüseyinzâde Ali [Turan] (1864–1941), Turkish-speaker born in Russian Azerbaijan, close associate of Ziya Gökalp's, physician trained at the Military Medical School in Constantinople, one of the four founders of the CUP (1889), member of the Central Committee in 1911: Zürcher, *The Unionist, op. cit.*, p. 78. Hüseyinzâde Ali introduced Russian populism and the accompanying revolutionary ideology to Turkey: cf. Ş. Mardin, *Jön Türklerin Siyasi Fikirleri 1895–1908*, Ankara 1964, pp. 32–3.

5 Armenian Revolutionaries and Young Turks: The Anatolian Provinces and Istanbul, 1910–12

1. *Simon Zavarian: on the occasion of the seventieth anniversary of his death, op. cit.*, III, p. 345, letter from Zavarian to Hovnan Tavtian, Mush, 20 May 1910.
2. *Ibidem.*
3. *Ibidem.*
4. *Ibidem*, pp. 347–8, letter from Zavarian to the Bureau oriental of the ARF, Mush, 25 May 1910.
5. *Ibidem*, p. 361: letter from S. Zavarian to the Occidental Bureau of the ARF, Mush, 4 August.
6. *Ibidem.*
7. *Ibidem*, pp. 427–8, letter from Zavarian to the Bureau oriental of the ARF, Mush, 6 July 1911.
8. *Ibidem*, p. 428.
9. *Ibidem*, p. 438, letter from Zavarian to Avetis Aharonian, Constantinople, 19 November 1912.
10. Papazian, *Memoirs, op. cit.*, II, p. 151.
11. *Ibidem*, p. 154.
12. *Ibidem*, p. 161.
13. *Ibidem*, p. 154.
14. *Infra*, p. 827, n. 73.
15. *Infra*, p. 827, n. 68.
16. Papazian, *Memoirs, op. cit.*, II, p. 161.
17. *Ibidem*, p. 162.
18. Stepanos Sapah-Giulian, *Memories of Armenia Minor, Part 1, 10 May-1 August 1911, op. cit.*
19. *Ibidem*, p. 80.
20. *Ibidem*, p. 93.
21. *Ibidem*, p. 96.
22. *Ibidem*, pp. 97–8.
23. *Ibidem*, p. 99.
24. *Ibidem*, pp. 103, 114, 116. On the way, he passed through a village of Nogayi *muhacirs* from Roumelia whom the government had authorized to loot in order to meet their basic needs.
25. *Ibidem*, pp. 123, 140.
26. *Ibidem*, pp. 130–1.
27. *Ibidem*, p. 127.
28. *Ibidem*, pp. 137–8.
29. *Ibidem*, pp. 154–6.
30. *Ibidem*, pp. 157–8. Meeting of 23 May.
31. *Ibidem*, pp. 168–9. The Greeks of this village were almost all Armenian-speakers and often members of the Hnchak club.
32. *Ibidem*, pp. 171–3.
33. *Ibidem*, p. 176.
34. *Ibidem*, p. 178.
35. *Ibidem*, pp. 184–5, 188.
36. *Ibidem*, pp. 191–4.

37. Bekir Sâmi (1865–1933), a native of Daghestan, received his higher education in Paris. A Young Turk leader, successively *mutesarif* of Amasia (1909), vali of Van (1911), Trebizond, Bursa, Beirut (1914), and Aleppo (24 June to 25 September 1915), where he was replaced by Mustafa Abdülhalik (nicknamed "the butcher of Bitlis") after being criticized for not carrying out the orders of the interior minister to liquidate the Armenians. Immediately following the First World War, he joined the Kemalist movement and became foreign minister (1920–1921). Arrested in 1926 in connection with the Smyrna plot, he was eventually released.

38. *Ibidem*, pp. 195–197. Ohannes Pasha Kuyumjian, governor general of Mount Lebanon when Bekir Sâmi was vali of Beirut (1913–1915), notes that Bekir Sâmi, after zealously serving the CUP, refused to implement CUP policy–to do "the Committee's dirty work"–vis-à-vis the Lebanese and then the Syrian population: Ohannès pacha Kouyoumdjian, *Le Liban à la veille et au début de la Grande Guerre. Mémoires d'un gouverneur, 1913–1915*, Raymond Kévorkian, V. Tachjian, and M. Paboudjian (eds.), *RHAC* V, Paris 2003, p. 154.

39. *Ibidem*, pp. 199–203.

40. *Ibidem*, p. 214. Let us note in passing that most Hnchak leaders in Amasia were Protestants (*ibidem*, p. 205). As he crossed the plain of Ardova on the road to Sıvas, Sapah-Giulian saw five Armenian villages. In the first, Çiflik, the inhabitants had been burned alive in the village church in 1895 (*ibidem*, p. 245).

41. *Ibidem*, pp. 256–61.

42. *Ibidem*, p. 294.

43. *Ibidem*, pp. 296–7.

44. *Ibidem*, pp. 317–18.

45. *Ibidem*, p. 319.

46. *Ibidem*, p. 322.

47. AMAE, Turquie, Politique intérieure, n. s., vol. 9, ff. 42–5, letter from the French vice-consul in Van, to Poincaré, Van, 15 March 1912. This document puts the number of men in the city at 17,240 and the number of those in the 33 surrounding villages at 6,760. The joint Hnchak-Ramgavar candidate was Nigoghos Aghasian, the *kaymakam* of Ispir (Erzerum) (*ibidem*, f° 45v°).

48. AMAE, Turquie, Politique intérieure, n. s., vol. 9, f° 56, letter from the French vice-consul in Erzerum to the ministry, 2 March 1912.

49. *Ibidem*, report from the French general consul in Smyrnia, June 1911, f° 73.

50. AMAE, Turquie, Politique intérieure, n. s., vol. 9, f° 110, letter from the French vice-consul in Van to the ministry, 20 June 1912; CADN, Ambassade de Constantinople, série E/132, letter from the French vice-consul in Van to Bompard, 20 June 1912. A native of Constantinople, 35-years old, official in the Interior Ministry, former inspector of the public debt in Siirt, and *başmudir* in Erzerum, son-in-law of Haci Adıl Bey, he spoke French, which he had learned from the Jesuits in Beirut; one of the founders of the club at Siirt.

51. Papazian, *Memoirs, op. cit.*, II, p. 182.

52. *Ibidem*, II, p. 151.

53. Bozarslan, *Les Courants de pensée, op. cit.*, II, p. 124. AMAE, Turquie, Politique intérieure, n. s., vol. 9, f° 177, letter from the French consul in Salonika, Josselin, to Poincaré, Salonika, 26 September 1912 announced the creation of *Türk Ocaği*, the "Turkish National Association."

54. Bozarslan, *Les Courants de pensée, op. cit.*, II, p. 233, Lütfi Fikri and Gümülcineli İsmail were also members of the party; Zürcher, *Turkey: A Modern History, op. cit.*, p. 107.

55. Sapah-Giulian, *The Responsibles, op. cit.*, pp. 285–6.

56. Papazian, *Memoirs, op. cit.*, II, p. 158.

57. Ռոստոմ. Մահուան Վաթսունամեակին առթիւ [*Rostom: On the occasion of the sixtieth anniversary of his death*], ed Hrach Dasnabedian, Beirut 1999, pp. 295–9, report of Kurken Mkhitarian. Mkhitarian, a student in Constantinople in fall 1911, underscores the spirit of revolt characteristic of young Armenians, who were critical of parties such as the ARF.

58. *Ibidem*; Papazian, *Memoirs, op. cit.*, II, p. 159, notes: "At the time, we were naive enough to believe that there could be progressive circles among the Turks."

59. [S. Sapah-Giulian], "Իթթիհատ-Դաշնակցական Գաղտնի Համաձայնութեան Պարունակութիւնը եւ Անոր Հետեւանքները [The Content of the Secret Accord between the Ittihadists

and the Dashnaks and Its Consequences]," in *Gohag*, 23 January/6 February 1913, no. 2 (127), p. 18, The sequel appears in the following issues.

60. *Gohag*, 6/19 February 1913, no. 4 (127), p. 41, reviews the history of Ottoman penetration into Persia after the Russian defeat at the hands of the Japanese in 1904, and also the role played by Ephrem Khan and his commandos, whose activity basically benefited Russia, making it possible for the Czarist Empire to return to the forefront of the local stage and conclude an agreement with Great Britain delineating Russian and British zones of influence.

61. *Gohag*, 13/26 February 1913, no. 5 (130), p. 54. Ephrem was the head of the Persian gendarmerie and, as such, all-powerful in Teheran. He seems to have opposed his party's pro-Turkish policy; he was, in any case, excluded from its ranks in this period: *Gohag*, 20 March/2 April 1913, no. 10 (135), p. 114.

62. *Gohag*, 30 January/12 February 1913, no. 3 (128), p. 27. Under pressure from the British, who had clearly seen that the Armenians' activity furthered Russian interests, St. Petersburg finally ceased to support the *fedayis*, effectively handing the CUP what it had hoped to obtain from the ARF; the CUP accordingly failed to honor its pledge to give its Armenian ally twenty seats in parliament: *Gohag*, 3/16 April 1913, no. 12 (137), p. 138.

63. Sapah-Giulian, *The Responsibles*, op. cit., p. 269.

64. *Ibidem*, p. 270. Parvus, the pseudonym of Alexander Helphand, was in fact an agent of the German intelligence service who took advantage of his undeserved reputation as a socialist to make his way into non-Turkish circles of all kinds. He was working for the CUP at the time and was rewarded for it during the war, when he was granted a monopoly on importing certain goods. Vahan Papazian, who was introduced to him by a Bulgarian deputy, Vlakhov, limits himself to saying that Parvus often came to visit *Azadamard*'s editorial offices. He does, however, acknowledge that they had not understood who he was in 1914; he suddenly became a millionaire in his capacity as a commercial agent responsible for the purchase of coal and grain for the government. When Papazian encountered him in Berlin in 1923, he was living "with a much younger woman in a private villa surrounded by a park with a pond": Papazian, *Memoirs*, op. cit., II, pp. 173–4; Zürcher, *Turkey: A Modern History*, op. cit., pp. 129–30.

65. Sapah-Giulian, *The Responsibles*, op. cit., p. 270.

66. *Ibidem*, p. 272.

67. *Ibidem*, p. 275.

68. *Ibidem*, p. 276.

69. *Ibidem*, p. 280. Parvus cultivated his relations with the Armenian militants for some time after this, but eventually came to the conclusion that it was impossible to manipulate the SDHP.

70. *Ibidem*, pp. 280–3. The author raises the question and provides arguments in its favor.

71. *Ibidem*, pp. 284, 291–2.

72. *Ibidem*, pp. 299–301.

73. *Ibidem*, pp. 302–3.

74. *Ibidem*, pp. 302–3. In summer 1911, when Sapah-Giulian was on mission in Anatolia, the *mutesarif* of Kayseri, an Albanian, is supposed to have told him: "If these Ittihadists remain [in power], they are going to create a new catastrophe, one still more terrible for the Armenian people. Endeavor to save your people from this danger as fast as you can."

75. "Preuves et réalité," *Hnchak*, no. 3, March 1913, p. 6.

76. Papazian, *Memoirs*, op. cit., II, p. 173.

77. Zürcher, *Turkey: A Modern History*, op. cit., p. 107.

78. *Ibidem*, p. 108; Bozarslan, *Les Courants de pensée*, op. cit., II, p. 124. The secret committee of "freedom officers" included, notably, Kemal Bey, Hilmi Bey, Receb Bey, İbrahim Aşkı Bey, Kudret Bey. It demanded that the army withdraw from politics and sent threatening letters to the Unionist leaders.

79. AMAE, Turquie, Politique intérieure, n. s., vol. 9, f° 177, letter from the French consul in Salonika, Josselin, to Poincaré, Salonika, 26 September 1912.

80. Aram Andonian, *History of the Balkan war*, op. cit., III, Istanbul 1913, pp. 484–90. Exiled to Erzincan in 1908, he succeeded in fleeing in May with the help of Armenians from the city, in particular, one Suren Sarafian, thanks to whom he was able to take refuge in Batum, again in an Armenian milieu, and arrived in Istanbul shortly after the armistice. It was Nâzım who managed to calm the rebels after the events of 31 March 1909. H was strongly opposed to Mahmud Şevket and did not enjoy the favor of the Ittihadists.

81. Papazian, *Memoirs, op. cit.*, II, p. 158.
82. See in the chapters devoted to this question.
83. *Simon Zavarian: on the occasion of the seventieth anniversary of his death, op. cit.*, III, pp. 117–18, letter from Zavarian to Mikayel Varantian, Constantinople, 22 September 1912.
84. Aram Andonian, *History of the Balkan war, op. cit.*, III, p. 433. Aram Andonian (1873–1951) was a journalist and, from 1911 on, a deputy in the Armenian Chamber.
85. *Ibidem*, p. 434.
86. *Ibidem*, pp. 437–8.
87. Garabed Khan Pashayan (1864–1915), also known by the pseudonym Taparig, was a physician. He was an ARF military leader in the region of Erzincan and later in Cilicia under Abdülhamid. He was a member of the editorial board of *Azadamard* and the Central Committee in Constantinople at the time. He was elected as a deputy from Harput in the 1912 elections.
88. *Ibidem*, pp. 439–40.
89. *Ibidem*, p. 442.
90. *Ibidem*, pp. 458–9. The day after this demonstration, Talât, Nâzım, and other Young Turk leaders left for their fief of Salonika. It is possible that they were thus seeking to assure their safety in the event that the government reacted: AMAE, Turquie, Politique intérieure, n. s., vol. 9, f° 177, letter from the French consul in Salonika, Josselin, to Poincaré, Salonika, 26 September 1912.
91. *Ibidem*, p. 461.
92. *Ibidem*, pp. 498–9.
93. Papazian, *Memoirs, op. cit.*, II, p. 164.
94. *Simon Zavarian: on the occasion of the seventieth anniversary of his death, op. cit.*, pp. 118–19, letter from S. Zavarian to the ARF's Balkanian Committee, Constantinople, 10 October 1912.
95. Papazian, *Memoirs, op. cit.*, II, p. 181.
96. Andonian, *History of the Balkan War*, V, *op. cit.*, pp. 889–91.
97. Georges Rémond and Alain Penennrun, *Sur les lignes de feu: le carnet de champ de bataille du colonel Djémal bey, de Kırk-Kilissé à Tchataldja*, Paris 1914, pp. 188–90. Cemal encountered Mehmed Talât in Viza on 2 November 1912, in the middle of the night. Talât, completely downcast, "seated on a large rock" in "a volunteer's uniform," and brought him back to the capital. We are then told that, during the battle, Talât was with Mahmud Muhtar Pasha's general staff. On their way back to the capital, they discovered an army in complete disarray: "It was the end of everything, the ruin, the collapse of the fatherland."
98. Andonian, *History of the Balkan war*, IV, *op. cit.*, pp. 826–7. The *Times* of London and *Le Temps* of Paris gave detailed accounts of these exactions.
99. *Ibidem*, III, p. 490.
100. Zürcher, *The Unionist factor, op. cit.*, pp. 114–15
101. 25 December 1912 Declaration of the SDHP's Central Committee, published in *Hntchak*, no. 1, January 1913, pp. 1–2.

Part III Young Turks and Armenians Face to Face (December 1912–March 1915)

1 Transformations in the Committee of Union and Progress after the First Balkan War, 1913

1. CADN, Ambassade de Constantinople, série E/86, letter from the French ambassador in Vienna, Dumaine, distributed by the Direction des Affaires politiques of the minister of Foreign Affairs, 26 March 1913. The massive arrival of Muslim refugees from Thrace is abundantly attested by the French consulates in the provinces; their dispatches clearly bring out the tensions that resulted: AMAE, Correspondance politique, Turquie, n. s., vol. 85 and 86 especially.
2. Turfan, *Rise of the Young Turks, op. cit.*, p. 286; Hanioğlu, *Preparation for a Revolution, op. cit.*, p. 285, notes that from 1908 to 1918, power changed hands only through the use of force, as in June–July 1912, with the Liberals, or the 23 January 1913 "raid" on the Sublime Porte.

3. The reporter for the *Diary de Paris*, Paul Erio, gives a detailed account of the intervention. Some 100 Young Turks led by Enver and Talât are supposed to have succeeded in forcing their way past the barriers. An exchange of gunfire is supposed to have followed, leading to the death of five men, among them Mutafa Negib, a close associate of Enver's: *Le Diary*, daté du 27 January 1913. AMAE, Turquie, Politique intérieure, n. s., vol. 9, f° 204, letter from the French ambassador in Constantinople, Bompard, to Quai d'Orsay, 3 March 1913, announced Cemal nomination to the post of military governor of Constantinople.

4. *Ibidem*, p. 322.

5. *Ibidem*, pp. 310–11. The decision to reorganize the Ottoman Army was taken on 14 February 1913 (1 Şubat 1329) – that is, several months before the arrival of the German mission headed Liman von Sanders, a general in the cavalry. It was initially kept secret, prepared by the Ministry of War and the general staff, confirmed by the council of ministers, and, finally, ratified by the sultan and officially announced on 11 December 1913.

6. *Infra*, p. 839, n. 40.

7. AMAE, Turquie, Politique intérieure, n. s., vol. 9, f° 199, letter from the French consul in Salonika, Josselin, to Poincaré, Salonika, February 1913.

8. *Supra*, p. 200, n. 26.

9. Turfan, *Rise of the Young Turks*, *op. cit.*, p. 404, n. 2. It is revealing that Ali Fethi took care to resign from the army.

10. *Ibidem*, p. 319. The grand vizier did not, however, dare to make an official declaration on this subject and even recommended to the German ambassador that he say nothing in public about his plan. The Chief of Staff, Ahmed İzzet Pasha, was himself opposed to the appointment of a foreigner to the supreme command. He favored, at most, a nomination to the head of a corps of the army that would have served as an experimental model (*ibidem*, pp. 324–5).

11. *Ibidem*, p. 326. CADN, Ambassade de Constantinople, E 132, three communiques of 11 June 1913 from the Ottoman Wire Agency, announcing the assassination of the grand vizier and the probable nomination of Prince Said Halim to the post; AMAE, Turquie, Politique intérieure, n. s., vol. 9, f° 211, telegram from the French chargé d'affaires in Constantinople, Boppe, to Quai d'Orsay, 11 June 1913.

12. CADN, Ambassade de Constantinople, E 132, rapport des services de renseignements "donné à M. Nichan par Tahir bey, Tarla Bachi, Ladjar Djadessi, no. 4 bis."

13. AMAE, Turquie, Politique intérieure, n. s., vol. 9, ff. 202–4, letter from the French ambassador in Constantinople, Bompard, to Quai d'Orsay, 3 March 1913. Frank G Weber, *Eagles on the Crescent: Germany, Austria and the Diplomacy of the Turkish Alliance, 1914–1918*, Ithaca & London, 1970, pp. 27–8, cites diplomatic sources that note that it was Enver who benefited the most from this murder, for the grand vizier had been standing in the way of his ambitions; they add that the committee criticized him for his willingness to make concessions to non-Turks, but that Mahmud Şevket had made up his mind to accept the German and Russian propositions.

    In a 7 January 1914 dispatch to his minister, the Austro-Hungarian ambassador, Pallavicini, reputed to be very knowledgable about on Turkey, explicitly accused Enver of having had the grand vizier assassinated in order to arrive at his ends: *ibidem*, p. 31.

14. AMAE, Turquie, Politique intérieure, n. s., vol. 9, f° 213, telegram from the chargé d'affaires in Constantinople, Boppe, to Quai d'Orsay, 11 June 1913.

15. AMAE, Turquie, Politique intérieure, n. s., vol. 9, f° 215, telegram from the chargé d'affaires in Constantinople, Boppe, to Quai d'Orsay, 14 June 1913.

16. AMAE, Turquie, Politique intérieure, n. s., vol. 9, f° 220, telegram from the chargé d'affaires in Constantinople, Boppe, to Quai d'Orsay, 17 June 1913.

17. AMAE, Turquie, Politique intérieure, n. s., vol. 9, f° 224, telegram from the chargé d'affaires in Constantinople, Boppe, to Quai d'Orsay, 24 June 1913.

18. Turfan, *Rise of the Young Turks*, *op. cit.*, p. 346: Enver's partisans were, above all, the young officers of the general staff and the *fedayis* of committee; from this point on, Enver was a preeminent, indispensable member of the CUP.

19. *Ibidem*, p. 329.

20. *Ibidem*, p. 331. Weber, *Eagles on the Crescent*, *op. cit.*, p. 34, notes that "la haute autorité [de Said Halim] reposait sur ses mains bien manucurées."

21. AMAE, Turquie, Politique intérieure, n. s., vol. 9, ff. 230–44, report from Guy de Feriec to Stéphane Pichon, 3 November 1913.
22. *Ibidem*, f° 232.
23. *Ibidem*, f° 232v°.
24. *Ibidem*, f° 233. In *Tanin*, İsmail Hakkı Babanzâde, who participated in the Congress, condemned "exaggeration of the principle of equality."
25. *Ibidem*, f° 235v°.
26. *Ibidem*, f° 236v°. For the full text, see pp. 240–2. Said Halim was elected president of the General Council. The General Congress was made up of the members of the General Council, the inspectors of the party, the responsible secretaries in the *sancaks*, and the delegates of the provincial congresses. The General Congress elected the members of the General Council, its president, the general secretary, and the members of the Central Committee.
27. *Ibidem*, f° 239.
28. *Ibidem*, f° 239, annexe 1.
29. In 1915, these party cadres acquired, as we shall see, powers greater than those of the valis and military commanders in everything that bore on the eradication of the Armenians. They were judged at a special trial in 1919–20.
30. *Ibidem*, f° 240. "The party had correspondents in all the towns and villages of the interior; they served as intermediaries between the Committee and rank-and-file party members." All of these decisions as well as the party program were adopted on 3 November 1913, indication that the congress was continued beyond the official date of adjournment.
31. *Ibidem*, f° 244.
32. Ahmed İzzet pasha (Furgaç) (1864–1937), minister of war (1913), commander on the Caucasian front during the First World War, grand vizier in November 1918: Zürcher, *The Unionist, op. cit.*, p. 46.
33. Turfan, *Rise of the Young Turks, op. cit.*, pp. 332–7.
34. *Gohag*, 10/23 July 1913, no. 36 (161), p. 345, editorial on the Rodosto massacres, which occurred 1–3 July. Other massacres took place in 1912 in a town nearby, Malgara, and in Ada-Bazar, 55 miles east of the capital. Period: Տեղեկագիր Հ․ Ա․ Ֆ․ Հ․ Ա․ 1912–1914 Շրջանին Ազգային Կեդրոնական Վարչութեան [*Report on the Activity of the Central Leadership of the Nation for the Period 1912–1914*], Constantinople 1914 (November 1912–February 1914), pp. 69–71.
35. *Ibidem*, pp. 32–3.
36. Archives of the Patriarchate of Constantinople (hereinafter abbreviated: APC), Armenian Patriarchate of Jerusalem (hereinafter abbreviated: APJ), The Patriarchate's Constantinople Information Bureau (hereinafter abbreviated: PCI Bureau), Է 336–7, file no. 5, letter from Patriarch Arsharuni to the Russian, British and French ambassadors, 14 May 1913.
37. APC/APJ, PCI Bureau, Է 338–9, file no. 17, *Takrir* to the grand vizier Mahmud Şevket, 18/31 May 1913.
38. APC/APJ, PCI Bureau, Է 340–2, List of the murders, acts of banditry, kidnappings, illegal seizures of property and other crimes committed in the various vilayets of Anatolia since 29 April 1913.
39. *Ibidem*. The consular sources of the day abound in similar examples, notably in AMAE, Correspondance politique, Turquie, n. s. 85, 86, 87. Thus, we read in a 10 May 1913 letter from the French ambassador to the minister to whom he answered, that "in Hajin and Sis, speeches were made; mysterious figures who are said to be emissaries of the Committee of Union and Progress, hold conclaves with the Muslim notables and visit the villages where the Armenians tried to defend themselves in 1896 and 1909. Hence, throughout eastern Anatolia, the Christian population is living in terror. The accounts given by the Patriarchate and the reports of the consuls paint a similar picture of the general malaise prevailing in Armenia" (see. vol. 87, p. 21 sq). Better than the euphemism describing the situation in the Armenian provinces as a "malaise," the consular correspondence reports the incendiary speeches that influential figures from the Committee of Union and Progress made on many different occasions in the intention of enflaming the local populations against the Armenians, Greeks, and Syriacs (see vol. 87, pp. 31, 69). The calls for murder were published in the newspaper *Babaghan* is confirmed in the correspondence of the French vice-consul in Mersina and Adana (see vol. 86, p. 217).

40. APC/APJ, PCI Bureau, Է 343, file no. 901, an extract from the *teskere* of the grand vizier, addressed to the department of justice and religious dominations, in connection with the correspondence between the grand vizier's office and the Ministry of the Interior on the *takrir* of 18/31 May 1913 (1229) presented by the Armenian Patriarchate to His Highness the grand vizier.

41. Hmayag Aramiantz, "Ծրագիրներու Շարանը [The Series of Projects]," an editorial in *Gohag*, 30 January 1913, no. 3 (128), pp. 25–6. *Infra*, p. 833, n. 45, for biographical information on Haci Adıl, elected a member of Central Committee and general secretary to replace Dr. Nâzım in November 1910.

42. "Մահաբեր Պատրանք [Deadly Illusion]," *Droschak*, no. 4/231, April 1913, pp. 49–51.

43. APC/APJ, PCI Bureau, Է 344–50, the grand vizier's response to the Patriarchate's *takrir*, *teskere* of the Ministry of Justice and religious denominations, 22 June 1329 (1913), file no. 78.

44. *Ibidem*. At the 21 July 1913 session of the Armenian Chamber, information from the provinces indicated that, on a single day, 100 people left Kghi for the Americas, that 1,000 left from Erzincan in a single week, and that, between 1908 and 1912, some 20,000 people emigrated to the United States alone: Papazian, *Memoirs, op. cit.*, II, p. 215.

45. APC/APJ, PCI Bureau, Է 356–60, file no. 78, response of the Mixed Council to the *teskere* of the Ministry of Justice and the religious denominations (22 June 1329/1913), no. 78, Patriarcat, 3/16 August 1329/1913.

46. *Ibidem*.

47. *Ibidem*.

48. "Մահաբեր Պատրանք [Deadly Illusion]," *Droschak*, no. 4/231, April 1913, p. 49.

49. APC/APJ, PCI Bureau, Է 406–12, internal report of the Patriarchate, 21 November 1913.

50. *Tanin*, 1/14 November 1913.

51. *Tasfiri Efkiar*, 12/25 and 13/26 November 1913.

52. APC/APJ, PCI Bureau, Է 406–12, internal report of the Patriarchate, 21 November 1913.

2   The Armenian Organizations' Handling of the Reform Question

1. Hmayag Aramiantz, "Իթթիհատը եւ Ազգերը [The Ittihad and the Nations]," *Gohag*, 6/19 November 1913, no. 69 (174), pp. 601–2.

2. "Հայերու Կացութիւնը Թիւրքիոյ մէջ 1908–1912 [The Situation of the Armenians in Turkey, 1908–1912]," *Droschak*, no. 2–3/230, February-mars 1913, p. 31.

3. Krikor Zohrab, Երկերի Ժողովածոյ [*Complete Works*] ed. Albert Sharurian, vol. 4, Yerevan 2003, pp. 341–432 [AU: 342?], Diary, 1912–1915 (Museum of Litterature and Art, Fonds Zohrab, ms. 17, 1–70 and ms. 5, 7–12), p. 344 (9 December 1912) and p. 572, nn. 19–20.

4. One has only to leaf through the party's official organ, *Droschak*, to see that the Dashnaks stood squarely in the tradition of the other Russian revolutionary movements; they, too, were struggling against the Czarist regime and did not hesitate to use terror to achieve their ends. Also worth noting are the harshness of the policy that St. Petersburg adopted toward the Armenians of the Caucasus and the incessant efforts of the secret police to dismantle the revolutionary committees and imprison or exile their militants, for whom Ittihadist Turkey represented a safe haven.

5. Sharurian, *Chronology ... of Krikor Zohrab, op. cit.*, p. 388, from the Archives of the Armenian Catholicosate, Matenadaran, vol. 20, f° 238.

6. See p. 65, n. 62.

7. Nerses Zakarian (1883–1915), teacher, writer, journalist, member of the Hnchak Central Committee.

8. See p. 207, n. 3.

9. Diran Erganian (?–1915), lawyer born in Istanbul, professor in the Istanbul Law School, and member of parliament. He was deported in April 1915 and murdered in Damascus.

10. Levon Demirjibashian (1863–1926), architect, member of the Ottoman parliament in 1914.

11. Oskan Mardikian (1867–1947), born in Erzincan, jurist, writer, minister of the postal and telegraph office (1913–1915) who resigned in August 1915 and later found refuge in Cairo (1920).

12. Sarkis Svin or Sunkujian (1870–1915), Istanbul physician, high-ranking official in the Ministry of Health, journalist, deported and executed in 1915.

13. Papazian, *Memoirs, op. cit.*, II, pp. 182–3.

14. *Ibidem*, p. 183.

15. *Ibidem*, p. 184. Vahan Papazian's memoirs are thus a basic source of information on the hidden aspects of the reform question.

16. *Report on the activity of the central leadership of the nation for the period 1912–1914, op. cit.*, p. 49 ff.

17. Boghos Nubar Pasha (1851–1930), engineer, a son of the Egyptian prime minister, was the head of the Egyptian railways and one of the founders (in 1906) of the Armenian General Benevolent Union.

18. The best overview of the question is still R.H. Davison, "The Armenian Crisis, 1912–1914," *The American Historical Review*, LIII/3 (April 1948), pp. 481–5. For the details, the Archives of the Délégation arménienne (Bibliothèque Nubar, Paris), files 2 and 3, are essential (hereinafter cites as ADA/BNu).

19. *Report on the activity of the central leadership of the nation for the period 1912–1914, op. cit.*, pp. 73–90.

20. Papazian, *Memoirs, op. cit.*, II, p. 234.

21. Ատենագրութիւն Ազգային Ժողովոյ [*Minutes of the National Chamber*], Constantinople 1913, 17 May 1913, Session, speech of S. Karayan, p. 49 sq.

22. Papazian, *Memoirs, op. cit.*, II, p. 213.

23. *Ibidem*, p. 216.

24. Richard Hovannisian, *Armenia on the Road to Independence, 1918*, Berkeley-Los Angeles-London 1967, pp. 32–5.

25. *Ibidem*. It was Zohrab who negotiated St. Petersburg's diplomatic intervention with the Russian Ambassador to Turkey, N. Tcharikov, and it was under his leadership that the bargaining with the representatives of the powers took place: Zohrab, *Complete works, op. cit.*, IV, Diary, p. 343. The passage that the Patriarch Zaven Der Yeghiayan, *Memoirs, op. cit.*, devotes to this affair is worth reading, as is L. Etmekjian, "The Armenian National Assembly of Turkey and Reform," *Armenian Review* 29/1 (1976), pp. 38–52. Les volumes 86, 87 ff. of the AMAE, Turquie, Correspondance politique, n. s., also make it possible to follow the question of the reforms very closely.

26. ADA/BNu, file 2, letter of 2 August 1913 from Boghos Nubar to A. Williams, president of the British-Armenian Committee, which also reveals that the plan was elaborated by the Patriarchate.

27. Hovannisian, *op. cit.*, p. 32; Gabriel Lazian, Հայաստանը եւ Հայ Դատը [*Armenia and the Armenian Question*], Cairo 1957, p. 155.

28. Papazian, *Memoirs, op. cit.*, II, pp. 543–83.

29. Davison, *art. cit.*, p. 500 sq.

30. *Ibidem*.

31. *Ibidem*, pp. 491–6.

32. *Ibidem*, p. 491.

33. ADA/BNu, file 2, letter from B. Nubar to V. Karanfilian, 16 June 1913, in which Nubar clearly indicates that in April, in the wings of the London Conference, he conferred with Johannes Lepsius on the proper course to follow in order to convince Western diplomats that his analysis was accurate.

    The principal members of the British-Armenian Committee were Lord J. A. Bryce, N. Buxton, Sir E. Bayle, T. P. O'Connors, A. Williams, and A. G. Symonds; the president of the French Committee was Robert de Caix, the co-presidents of the German groups were Dr. G. V. Greenfield and Lepsius, and the president of the Swiss Committee was Léopold Favre: AMAE, Turquie, Correspondance politique, vol. 86, pp. 253–5.

34. ADA/BNu, file 2, letter from B. Nubar to A. Williams, 19 June 1913, in which Nubar again mentions the results of his second voyage to London in mid-May.

35. Davison, *art. cit.*, pp. 500–1.

36. ADA/BNu, file 2, Letter from B. Nubar to A. Williams, 26 June 1913.

37. *Ibidem*, letter from B. Nubar to Galli, 25 June 1913.

38. *Ibidem*, letter from B. Nubar to A. Williams, 6 July 1913.

39. *Ibidem*, letter from B. Nubar to G.V. Greenfield, 23 June 1913.

40. *Ibidem*, letter from Kevork Nubar to B. Nubar, San Stefano, 3 July 1913.

41. *Ibidem*, confidential letter from. Williams to B. Nubar, 29 July 1913; see also *Les réformes arméni-ennes et l'intégrité de la Turquie d'Asie*, Constantinople 22 March 1913, 4 pp.; *Les réformes arméni-ennes et les populations musulmanes: les émigrants (mohadjirs) dans les provinces arméniennes*, Constantinople, 5 May 1913; *Les réformes arméniennes et le contrôle européen*, Constantinople, 14 June 1913, 4 pp.

42. *Ibidem*, review of the newspapers between 2 June and 10 July 1913; *Note sur quelques objections faites au projet de réformes arméniennes*, Constantinople, 5 August 1913, 4 pp.

43. *Ibidem*, letters from Greenfield to B. Nubar, 31 July and 5 August 1913.

44. *Ibidem*, letters from B. Nubar to A. Symonds, member of the British-Armenian Committee, 12 August, and to Yakoub Artin Pasha, in London, 13 August 1913.

45. *Ibidem*, telegram, 14 August 1913.

46. *Ibidem*, letter from B. Nubar to J. Lepsius, 22 August 1913.

47. *Ibidem*, letter from B. Nubar to Baron Robert de Caix, general secretary of the Comité de l'Asie française, section du Levant, 27 August 1913.

48. *Ibidem*, letter from *vartabed* Krikoris Balakian, secretary of Special Committee of Constantinople Patriarchate, to Nubar, 24 August 1913, Berlin, brings out the behind-the-scenes role played by Zohrab, an eminent member of the Special Committee.

49. *Ibidem*, letter from James Greenfield to B. Nubar, 28 September 1913, in Berlin.

50. *Ibidem*, letters from B. Nubar to Lepsius, 13 and 18 October 1913, which reveals the tenor of Sazonov's remarks of theirng his interview in Paris.

51. *Ibidem*, letter from Lepsius to B. Nubar, October 1913.

52. *Ibidem*, letter from B. Nubar to Lepsius, 18 October 1913, in which he mentions his 17 October conversation with Minister Pichon.

    Weber, *Eagles on the Crescent*, op. cit., pp. 20–1, shows that German policy was modified in favor of the Armenians and that the ambassador's attitude toward them changed. At this time, says Weber, Berlin considered looking to the Armenians to support its plans for economic development around the *Bagdadbahn*. To prevent the Germans from drawing closer to the Armenians, the Ottoman government is supposed to have proposed that the British send inspectors to Armenia. We are even told that the minister of foreign affairs, Jagow, ordered that negotiations be conof thected with Kurdish leaders so that they would "stop playing their favorite sport, murdering Armenians and burning down their villages" (p. 24).

53. *Ibidem* for the correspondence with these personalities and the preparations for the Paris Conference.

54. Davison, *art. cit.*, pp. 501–3.

55. Papazian, *Memoirs*, *op. cit.*, II, p. 200.

56. *Ibidem*, pp. 201–2.

57. Papazian, *Memoirs*, *op. cit.*, II, p. 190. Let us recall that the ARF had officially broken off its relations with Ittihad on 5/18 May 1912, publishing a memorandum of them on the occasion: "Դաշնակցութեան Դիրքը Իթթիհատի Հանդէպ [The Position of the Dashnaktsutiun vis-à-vis the Ittihad]," *Droschak*, no. 9–10, Septembre-October 1913, p. 147.

58. Papazian, *Memoirs*, *op. cit.*, II, p. 190.

59. Charourian, *Chronology ... of Krikor Zohrab*, *op. cit.*, p. 393; *Azadamard*, no. 1127, 2/15 February 1913.

60. Papazian, *Memoirs*, *op. cit.*, II, p. 197.

61. *Ibidem*, p. 198.

62. *Ibidem*, pp. 198–9.

63. *Ibidem*, p. 199.

64. *Ibidem*, p. 215.

65. *Ibidem*, p. 223.

66. He founded a clinic in Mush, where he spent two years before he came to Istanbul in December 1912, probably in order to participate in the negotiations between the Russians and Armenians. He met with Zohrab at Zohrab's home on 9 December 1912 in order to bring this question up with him: Zohrab, *Complete works*, *op. cit.*, IV, p. 343.

67. Papazian, *Memoirs*, *op. cit.*, II, p. 229.
68. Zohrab, *Complete works*, *op. cit.*, IV, p. 343.
69. Papazian, *Memoirs*, *op. cit.*, II, p. 267, announces the September 1913 death of this founder of the ARF and his imposing funeral in Galata.
70. Sharurian, *Chronology ... of Krikor Zohrab*, *op. cit.*, pp. 396–7.
71. Papazian, *Memoirs*, *op. cit.*, II, p. 191.
72. *Ibidem*, p. 191. This Dashnak leader was hanged in Adana in June 1915 by the vali, Avni Bey. His "friend" Cemal, the region's strongman, did not intervene.
73. *Ibidem*, p. 191.
74. *Ibidem*, p. 192.
75. *Ibidem*, pp. 192–3; *Azadamard*, 15 July 1913, pp. 1–2, interview conducted by Parsegh Shahbaz.
76. *Ibidem*.
77. Reprinted in *Azadamard*, 25 June/7 July 1913, p. 1; Papazian, *Memoirs*, *op. cit.*, II, p. 193.
78. *Ibidem*, p. 235. The meetings took place at Zohrab's house and at Vartkes's by turns; both men lived in Pera.
79. *Ibidem*, pp. 235–6.
80. *Gohag*, 23 June 1913, no. 31 (156), pp. 307–8.
81. "The position of the Dashnaktsutiun vis-a-vis the Ittihad," *art. cit.*, p. 147.
82. Papazian, *Memoirs*, *op. cit.*, II, p. 253.
83. *Ibidem*.
84. *Ibidem*, p. 255.
85. Zohrab, *Complete works*, IV, *op. cit.*, pp. 344–5, Diary, 7/20 December 1913. AMAE, Turquie, Politique intérieure, n. s., vol. 9, ff. 249–50, letter from the French Ambassador, Bompard, to S. Pichon, 16 December 1913, announces the publication of an imperial *irade* ratifying certain modifications of Articles 81 and 103 of the law of the vilayets. The *irade*, reprinted in a communique issued by the *Agence Ottomane*, provided for 1) utilization of local languages in the administration; recruitment of gendarmes and policemen among the Muslim and non-Muslim population "in proportion to their numbers"; 2) proportional distribution of the budget for elementary education among the different communties; and 3) the attribution of subsidies to non-Muslim elementary schools.
86. *Ibidem*, p. 305, letter in French to German Ambassador, Hans Wangenheim, Aleppo, 14/24 June 1915: one night in April 1909 – during the events of 31 March – he brought Halil Bey home with him; "for twenty days, we extended him hospitality to protect him from persecution by the Helaskiars." The author informed the diplomat of this fact in order to show him how close he was to the Ittihadists.
87. *Ibidem*, pp. 344–5, 379.
88. *Ibidem*, p. 379.
89. *Ibidem*, p. 345.
90. *Ibidem*, p. 379. This section of the diary was written a few weeks after the interview, around February 1914, after signature of the official decree ordering reforms.
91. *Ibidem*, p. 349, Diary, 8/21 December.
92. *Ibidem*, p. 353, Diary, 8/21 to 11/24 December 1913, that is, the day after his conversation with Halil.
93. *Ibidem*, pp. 351–6.
94. *Ibidem*, p. 353.
95. *Ibidem*, p. 379, a section of the diary written after the interview, around February 1914.
96. *Ibidem*, p. 379.
97. Turfan, *Rise of the Young Turks*, *op. cit.*, p. 353.
98. Zohrab, *Complete works*, *op. cit.*, IV, Diary, p. 377.
99. *Ibidem*, p. 379, a section of the diary written around February 1914.
100. *Ibidem*, p. 385.
101. *Ibidem*, pp. 346–7, Diary, 8/21 December 1913.
102. *Ibidem*, p. 386.
103. *Ibidem*, p. 349, Diary, 8/21 December.
104. *Ibidem*, pp. 356–7, Diary, 11/24 December.

105. *Ibidem*, pp. 356–7, Diary, 12/25 December, in which he completed his notes of the previous evening.
106. *Ibidem*, pp. 358–9, Diary, 13/26 December.
107. *Ibidem*, p. 365, Diary.
108. *Ibidem*, p. 366, Diary, 2/15 January 1914. Weber, *Eagles on the Crescent…*, *op. cit.*, pp. 35–6, gives details about the circumstances surrounding the nomination of Otto Liman von Sanders as well as his surprising appointment, by an imperial decree of 4 December 1913, to the post of commander of the First Army, based in Constantinople. The appointment provoked a sharp reaction from Russia and generated diplomatic tensions.
109. Zohrab, *Complete works*, *op. cit.*, IV, Diary, pp. 367–8, Diary, 4/17 January 1914.
110. *Ibidem*.
111. *Ibidem*, p. 370, Diary, 22 January/4 February 1914.
112. *Ibidem*, p. 370, Diary, 24 January/5 February 1914.
113. *Adenakrutiun*, *op. cit.*, record of the 3 May 1913 Session, p. 3 ff.
114. *Adenakrutiun*, *op. cit.*, record of the 30 August 1913 Session, p. 200.
115. *Report on the activity of the central leadership of the nation for the period 1912–1914*, *op. cit.*, pp. 98–9, We learn from this report that the posts of the deputies representing the Armenians were to be distributed as follows: two for Constantinople, one for Arghana, two for Bitlis, one for Smyrna, two for Erzerum, one for Kayseri, one for Aleppo, one for Marash, one for Ismit, one for Sıvas, two for Van, and one for Sis/Kozan; Féroz Ahmad, *The Young Turks*, *op. cit.*, p. 144, alludes to these discussions about the number of Armenian deputies in the Ottoman parliament, which had a total of 259 members in 1914, but included only 14 Armenians, as opposed to 144 Turks, 84 Arabs, 13 Greeks, and 4 Jews.
116. Papazian, *Memoirs*, *op. cit.*, II, pp. 194–5.

3   The Establishment of the Ittihadist Dictatorship and the Plan to "Homogenize" Anatolia

1. Turfan, *Rise of the Young Turks*, *op. cit.*, p. 351. On 15 December, Enver was promoted to the rank of colonel.
2. *Ibidem*, p. 348.
3. *Ibidem*.
4. Liman von Sanders, *Cinq ans de Turquie*, Paris 1923, p. 12.
5. Turfan, *Rise of the Young Turks*, *op. cit.*, p. 348.
6. *Ibidem*, pp. 352–3. The act of nomination, however, was never published in the *Official Gazette*, whereas an *irade* of 5 January announced Colonel Cemal Bey's promotion to the rank of brigadier general. The fact that no *irade* ever mentioned Enver's promotion to the rank of pasha would seem to indicate that the decision was made without the sultan's agreement (p. 354). This is confirmed in Sanders, 16, where the Sultan's reaction is cites: "I've read that Enver has become minister of war. This is simply not possible; he is still much too young for that." On the 8th, Enver was appointed Chief of Staff (*ibidem*, p. 354).
7. AMAE, Turquie, Politique intérieure, n. s., vol. 9, f° 252, telegram from the French chargé d'affaires in Constantinople, Boppe, to S. Pichon, 3 January 1914.
8. Turfan, *Rise of the Young Turks*, *op. cit.*, p. 312: a 7 January 1914 *irade* lists the commanders of the different army corps, the inspectors of four armies, and the generals and ranking officers assigned to the reserves (280 people); they were blamed for the defeat in the Balkans. L. von Sanders, *op. cit.*, p. 16, puts the total at 1,100.
9. *Ibidem*, p. 17.
10. *Ibidem*.
11. *Ibidem*, pp. 16–17.
12. *Ibidem*, p. 16.
13. Turfan, *Rise of the Young Turks*, *op. cit.*, p. 315, attributes this mutation to Enver above all, thus downplaying the role of the committee in bringing about this shift.
14. *Ibidem*, p. 355.
15. *Ibidem*, pp. 358–9; L. von Sanders, *op. cit.*, pp. 17–18.

16. Turfan, *Rise of the Young Turks*, op. cit., p. 359; Weber, *Eagles on the Crescent*, op. cit., pp. 38–9, cites German diplomatic dispatches which indicate that Enver was approached by Mikaël de Giers, the Russian Ambassador, as soon as he was nominated in January 1914; de Giers offered him money and proposed to support him in the attempt to overthrow the dynasty of Osman and reign in its place. The Russians also offered to support him against Austria in the Macedonian affair and to promote the creatin of an Albania under Ottoman sovereignty (p. 47).

17. L. von Sanders, op. cit., pp. 18–19.

18. *Ibidem*, pp. 20–1. The author also points out that "the situation was appalling in most military hospitals. Insalubrity and bad odors of all imaginable kinds made it impossible to remain in the overfilled wards," to say nothing of the fact that "the education given to Turkish army doctors... was very different from [The German Equivalent]."

19. *Ibidem*, p. 23.

20. AMAE, Turquie, Politique intérieure, n. s., vol. 9, f° 257, report from the French consul in Trebizonde to the president of Conseil and minister of Foreign Affairs, Doumergue, 2 February 1914.

21. AMAE, Turquie, Politique intérieure, n. s., vol. 9, f° 261, letter from the chargé d'affaires in Constantinople, Boppe, to the president of Conseil and minister of Foreign Affairs, Doumergue, 14 February 1914.

22. AMAE, Turquie, Politique intérieure, n. s., vol. 9, f° 257, report from the French consul in Trebizonde to the president of Conseil and minister of Foreign Affairs, Doumergue, 2 February 1914.

23. AMAE, Turquie, Politique intérieure, n. s., vol. 9, ff. 261 et 262v°, letter from the chargé d'affaires in Constantinople, Boppe, to the president of Conseil and minister of Foreign Affairs, Doumergue, 14 February 1914.

24. *Supra*, p. 161.

25. AMAE, Turquie, Politique intérieure, n. s., vol. 9, f° 263, letter from the chargé d'affaires in Constantinople, Boppe, to the president of Conseil and minister of Foreign Affairs, Doumergue, 14 February 1914. Six were Arabs and a majority were non-Turks. Among the latter were several Armenians: Hrachia Effendi in Van, Hagop Effendi in Stamboul-Ismit, Krikor Sidky Bey in Bitlis, Karnig Fikri Effendi in Trebizonde (f° 265).

26. Kouyoumdjian, *Le Liban à la veille et au début de la Grande Guerre. Memoirs d'un gouverneur*, op. cit., pp. 26–8, "This revolution made itself felt immediately in Syria in the form of measures more or less openly directed against the national feeling of the Arab people. An effort was made to promote the use of the Turkish language in the schools, town halls and courts, in the ridiculous, vain intention of improvising, all at once and from one day to the next, an 'Ottoman patriotism.' School curricula were modified to this end; the signs on street corners and in stores had to be written in the dialect of the ruling people. Finally, the Committee for 'Union and Progress,' which had its tentacles in every part of the empire and was taking control of the state in the guise of a much more powerful, influential state than the official one, began to play an active role in Beirut as well, turning things topsy-turvy and making life more difficult. It offended everybody and contravened the interests on one and all, recruiting its partisans and agents from the least respectable strata of the population, from the déclassés."

27. CADN, Ambassade de Constantinople, série E/86, letter from the French consul in Damascus to Bompard, the French ambassador in Constantinople, 21 March 1914, conversation between Talât Bey and the owner and publisher of the newspaper *Moktabay*, Mohamed Effendi Kürd Ali, who reported the substance of their conversation to the French consul in Damascus.

28. AMAE, Turquie, Politique intérieure, n. s., vol. 9, f° 284, letter from the general Sherif Pasha, "chef de l'Entente Libérale ottomane," to the minister of Foreign affairs, Paris, 16 April 1914. The same document points out that "Monsignor Zaven declaree that the agitation is directed against the government, not the Armenians."

29. Akçam, *From Empire to Republic*, op. cit., pp. 144–9.

30. Cemal Kutay, *Birinci Dünya Harbinde Teşkilât-ı Mahsusa ve Heyber'de Türk Cengi*, Istanbul 1962, pp. 60–3.

31. Akçam, *From Empire to Republic*, op. cit., p. 150.

32. Diary, 27 February/12 March 1914, in Zohrab, *Complete works*, IV, op. cit., p. 373.

33. On a suggestion of Zohrab's, the Armenian Chamber considered, during its 4 February 1914 session, creating posts for legal consultants in all the dioceses; their task was to consist in monitoring

cases of illegal land confiscations, various trials, and the treatment of population statistics: Papazian, *Memoirs*, *op. cit.*, II, p. 264.

34. *Adenakrutiun*, *op. cit.*, record of 7 February 1914 Session, p. 438 sq.

35. *Ibidem*, record of 9 May 1914 Session, p. 1.

36. Papazian, *Memoirs*, *op. cit.*, II, pp. 271–2; Armen Garo (Karekin Pastermadjian), "Մեր վերջին տեսակցութիւնը Թալեաթ Փաշայի հետ [Our Last Conversation with Talât Pasha]," *Hayrenik* 2 (1922), p. 41, points out that he left for Europe with Dr. Zavriev in order to meet the inspectors there and inform them of the situation in the region. This is the reason, he says, that the CUP did everything it could to prevent his reelection.

37. Davison, *art. cit.*, pp. 504–5; essential to grasping the context in which the two inspectors found themselves during their stay in Constantinople are "Diary Concerning the Armenian Mission," from L. C. Westenenk, in the *Armenian Review* 39/1 (spring 1986), pp. 29–89, and W. van der Dussen, "The Question of Armenian Reforms in 1913–1914," *ibidem*, pp. 11–28. Armen Garo, "Our last conversation with Talât Pasha," *art. cit.*, pp. 41–2, indicates that he was supposed to become Major Hoff's advisor, but that Talât was opposed to this.

38. *Ibidem*.

39. APC/APJ, PCI Bureau, Յ 470–2, Faits et documents, no. 37, the Van affair.

    The French ambassador confirms that Hoff was recalled, without giving a precise date, and that Westenenk was put on "half-pay" and then furloughed: AMAE, Guerre 1914–1918, Turquie, vol. 846, f° 234, letter from the French ambassador in Constantinople, Bompard, to the president of Conseil and minister of Foreign Affairs, Doumergue, 30 September 1914. A-To [Hovhannes Ter Martirosian], Մեծ դեպքերը Վասպուրականում [*The Major Events in Vasbouragan, 1914–1915*], Yerevan 1917, p. 72, points out that Hoff arrived in Van on 4 August, but did not make his official entry into the city until 9 August and was recalled to Constantinople on 16/29 August.

40. Diary, 3/16 November 1914, in Zohrab, *Complete works*, IV, *op. cit.*, p. 411, reports this conversation, which someone else present at it, the Dashnak leader Aknuni, recounted to Zohrab. A definite end was put to the reforms only on 16 December 1914, by imperial decree: V. Dadrian, *Histoire du Génocide*, *op. cit.*, p. 349 and n. 1.

41. AMAE, Turquie, Politique intérieure, n. s., vol. 9, f° 290r°-v°, letter from the French ambassador in Constantinople, Bompard, to the president of Conseil and minister of Foreign Affairs, Doumergue, 17 May 1914.

42. APC/APJ, PCI Bureau Ս 979–82, letters from the bishop of Erzerum to the patriarche Zaven Der Yeghiayan, about the reforms in the Armenian provinces, no. 543, 16 July 1914 and another 2 May 1914, APJ Ս 970–2; APC/APJ, PCI Bureau, Ց 296, correspondence of 8 June 1914 between the A.G.B.U. on the one hand and Catholicos Kevork V and Patriarch Zaven on the other, about plans to be carried out in connection with the reforms in the provinces.

43. Papazian, *Memoirs*, *op. cit.*, II, p. 275.

44. *Ibidem*.

45. *Adenakrutiun*, *op. cit.*, record of 4 July 1914 Session, pp. 15–20.

46. Arsen Gidur (ed.), Պատմութիւն Ս. Դ. Հնչակեան Կուսակցութեան [*History of the Social Democratic Hnchak Party*], I, Beirut 1962, constitutes the official history SDHP. The editor was himself the secretary of the Third Congress of the Branches of Turkey, which was held In Istanbul in July 1914, and was informed of the decisions of his party. Other, more detailed information is provided by Hmayag Aramiants, Վերածնունդի Երկունքը [*La cruelle douleur de la Renaissance*], I, Constantinople, 1918, p. 64; ibidem, Դեպի Կախաղան [*Towards the Gallows*], II, Constantinople 1918, p. 48; ibidem, Անկախ Հայաստան [*Independent Armenia*], III, Constantinople 1919, p. 48. Excluded from the SDHP at the September-December 1913 Congress of Constanza, the author diverges from other's official account on a few important points.

47. *La vérité sur le mouvement révolutionnaire arménien et les mesures gouvernementales*, Constantinople 1916. This brochure was widely distributed in Europe to justify the government's measures against Ottoman-Armenian population.

48. Gidur (ed.), *History of the Social Democratic Hnchak Party*, *op. cit.*, I, pp. 323–35. A Central Committee for Turkey was created and held its first general assembly in 1910 (pp. 336–8).

The SDHP was officially registered by the Ministry of the Interior, receiving its authorization (no. 90) on 26 January 1910: Aramiants, *La cruelle douleur de la Renaissance*, *op. cit.*,
p. 39. On the Sixth Congress, see pp. 39–41.

49. Gidur (ed.), *History of the Social Democratic Hnchak Party*, *op. cit.*, I, pp. 343–8.

50. *Ibidem*, pp. 348–9. The agreement was signed on 7 February 1912.

51. *Ibidem*, pp. 364–6. Fifty-nine delegates, representing the same number of regional committees,
were present at the opening of the congress, but only 17 branches from Turkey (of a total of 61
branches) were represented there.

    The congress had been officially announced in the Istanbul press and the Ministry of
the Interior was informed that it would be convened: Aramiants, *La cruelle douleur de la
Renaissance*, *op. cit.*, p. 46. The Eighth Congress appointed the following people to the
SDHP's Central Committee: S. Sapah-Giulian, Varaztad, Paramaz [Mattheos Sarkisian],
Kakig Ozanian et Siunik: *ibidem*, p. 48.

52. Gidur (ed.), *History of the Social Democratic Hnchak Party*, *op. cit.*, I, p. 365.

53. *Ibidem*, I, p. 373.

54. Aramiants, *La cruelle douleur de la Renaissance*, *op. cit.*, pp. 48–9.

55. In 1911, Arshavir Sahagian appeared to be a Hnchak militant in Cairo and Alexandria. In this
capacity, he was chosen by the Committee of Egypt to represent it at the Congress of Constanza
in September 1913. Shortly after returning to Cairo, he met in Alexandria with Cemal Azmi Bey,
the head of State Security (who, as the vali of Trebizond, would organize the eradication of the
Armenian population of the Black Sea Coast in 1915). After Sahagian was unmasked, he managed
to make his way to Istanbul, thanks to the Ottoman charge d'affaires in Cairo (pp. 377–9). He was
executed by Hnchak militants in Adana on 25 December 1919, shortly after being liberated by the
French authorities: CADN, Mandat Syrie-Liban, 1er versement, Cilicie-administration, vol. 133.

56. Gidur (ed.), *History of the Social Democratic Hnchak Party*, *op. cit.*, I, pp. 371–3, full text of the open
letter.

57. This call, along with other evidence, provided the grounds for the indictment at the Hnchaks'
April-May 1915 trial.

58. Aramiants, *La cruelle douleur de la Renaissance*, *op. cit.*, pp. 56–9. Nerses Zakarian, Murad, H.
Aramiants, Mgrdich Pnaguni, Samuel Tumajian, Ardzruni (Hagop Avedisian), Dr. Jelalian, H.
Jangulian, Dr. Benne, etc., were the first to be arrested. Murad and Dr. Jelalian were released the
same evening. In the next few days, a total of 120 militants were imprisoned, including Paramaz
(Mattheos Sarkisian [1863–1915] a military official of the SDHP, a native of Karabagh, who was
executed on 15 June 1915).

59. *Ibidem*, p. 61. The 1913 attempt on the life of General Şerif Pasha, the leader of the opposition in
exile, was probably ordered by the *Ittihad*: Sapah-Gulian, *The Responsibles*, *op. cit.*, p. 267.

60. Hmayag Aramiants, *Towards the gallows*, II, *op. cit.*, pp. 6–7. Fewer than 20 of the accused remained
in prison.

61. Gidur (ed.), *History of the Social Democratic Hnchak Party*, *op. cit.*, I, p. 374.

62. *Infra*, p. 845, n. 7.

63. Vahan Zeytuntsian (1882–1959), born in Gürün, teacher, journalist, writer: IBN, IV, p. 280.

64. Harutiun Jangulian (1855–1915), born in Van, a historian educated in Paris, deputy in the
Ottoman parliament in 1908, executed on 15 June 1915.

65. Dr. Benne, pseudonym of Bedros Manukian (1881–1915), born in Huseynik (Harput), a physician
trained in Beirut and the United States, member of the Hnchak Central Committee, executed on
15 June 1915.

66. Gidur (ed.), *History of the Social Democratic Hnchak Party*, *op. cit.*, I, pp. 376, 380–1. See pp. 380–90
for an account of the trial.

67. Hratch Dasnabédian, *Histoire de la Fédération révolutionnaire arménienne dachnaktsoutioun, 1890–
1924*, Milan 1988, pp. 107–8.

68. Simon Vratsian, Հայաստանի Հանրապետութիւն [*The Republic of Armenia*], Paris 1928,
pp. 6–7.

69. Dasnabédian, *Histoire de la Fédération révolutionnaire arménienne ...*, *op. cit.*, p. 107–8.

70. Arthur Beylérian, *Les Grandes puissances, l'Empire ottoman et les Arméniens dans les archives
françaises (1914–1918)*, Paris 1983, p. XXIV.

71. The indictment, drawn up on 12 April 1919 and presented before the court-martial on 27 April 1919, proves that the late July 1914 meeting of the main leaders of the party in the offices of the Central Committee in Nuri Osmaniye Street constituted a crucial step toward the "founding" of the new Special Organization: *Takvim-ı Vakayi*, no. 3540, du 5 May 1919, p. 6. The three Ittihadists must have left for Erzerum immediately after the party made these decisions. We shall examine this question in detail later.

72. Beylérian, *Les Grandes puissances…*, op. cit., p. XXIV, gives a complete bibliography on these proposals.

73. According to a 15 August 1914 telegram of Dr. Şakir, that was read at the fifth session of the trial of the Unionists, 12 May 1919: *Takvim-ı Vakayi*, no. 3554, du 21 May 1919, p. 69; this document was presented at the beginning of the interrogation of Colonel Ahmed Cevad Bey, who had succeeded Halil [Kut] as the military commander of Istanbul and was a member of the Special Organization's Executive Committee.

74. Encrypted telegram read at the Sixth Session of the Trial of the Unionists, 14 May 1919, published in *Takvim-ı Vakayi*, no. 3557, 25 May 1919, p. 98. At the fourth session of the trial, Midhat Şükrü gave rather similar testimony about the CUP's relations with the Dashnaks: "We could see that they did not want to take part in the war; they wanted to remain neutral": transcription in SHAT, Service historique de la Marine (Château de Vincennes), Service de Renseignements de la Marine, Turquie, 1BB7 232, doc. no. 676, Constantinople, May 1919, lieutenant Goybet, adjoint du chef du S.R. Marine, p. 2.

75. Papazian, *Memoirs*, op. cit., II, p. 280. Papazian also indicates that Talât, in a conversation with his friend Armen Garo that took place after Garo's return from Erzerum, made it clear to him that he was not happy about the position the ARF took at the Congress of Erzerum: *ibidem*, p. 276.

76. *Ibidem*, pp. 280–1. Vartkes Seringiulian and Armen Garo were also present. Dr. Papazian took "the last Italian ship bound for Batum" in 14 August.

77. Diary, 3/16 August 1914, in Zohrab, *Complete works*, IV, op. cit., pp. 383–4. In the course of the evening, Zohrab noted that "all the Turks, like the Jews, are Germanophiles."

78. Gabriel Lazian, Հայաստան եւ Հայ Դատը [*Armenia and the Armenian Question*], Cairo 1957, p. 175.

79. *Ibidem*, p. 176. Malkhas succeeded in making his way to the Caucasus shortly afterwards; he gave a report to the Eastern Bureau in Tiflis, at Arshak Jamalian's house, in the presence of Dr. Zavriev, Ishkhan, and a score of local notables (*ibidem*, p. 177).

80. "Հայութիւնը Ռուս-Տաճկական Պատերազմի Հանդէպ [The Armenians in the Face of the Russo-Turkish war]," *Droschak*, no. 9–12, September–December 1914, pp. 129–30.

81. U. Trumpener, *Germany and Ottoman Empire, 1914–1918*, Princeton 1967, gives a detailed description of the circumstances surrounding the signature of the treaty. SHAT, Service historique de la Marine (Château de Vincennes), Service de Renseignements de la Marine, Turquie, 1BB7 236, doc. no. 1593 B-9, Constantinople, 16 January 1920, lieutenant Goybet, adjoint du chef du S.R. Marine, annexe 5, "Explications de Saïd Halim pacha" to the Fifth Commission of the Ottoman parliament, 24 November 1918.

82. Weber, *Eagles on the Crescent…*, op. cit., pp. 60–8.

83. L. von Sanders, op. cit., p. 31.

84. Weber, *Eagles on the Crescent…*, op. cit., pp. 54–5.

85. Osman Selim Kocahanoğlu (ed.), *Ittihat-Terakki'nin sorgulanması ve Yargılanması (1918–1919)*, Istanbul 1998. Weber, *Eagles on the Crescent*, op. cit., pp. 63–5, indicates that on 22 July Enver threatened Wangenheim, saying that Turkey would turn toward the Triple Entente if Germany rejected its offer of an alliance; that Kaiser Wilhelm gave the "green light" on 24 July, against the advice of his minister of foreign affairs; and that the naval attache, Humann, a friend of Enver's, played a decisive role thanks to his relations with the minister the navy, Tirpitz, a friend of his father's.

86. Turfan, *Rise of the Young Turks*, op. cit., p. 360.

87. SHAT, Service historique de la Marine (Château de Vincennes), Service de Renseignements de la Marine, Turquie, 1BB7 236, doc. no. 1593 B-9, Constantinople, 16 January 1920, annexe 4, "Explanations provided by Cavid Bey, the minister of finance," in testimony given to the Fifth Commission of the Ottoman parliament on 25 November 1919. That same morning, Liman von Sanders went to the German embassy in Tarabia, where Wangenheim and Enver asked him for

his opinion on the plan to make a secret treaty of alliance between Germany and Turkey: L. von Sanders, *op. cit.*, p. 31.

88. At the fourth session of the of the Ittihadists' trial, the party's secretary general, Midhat Şükrü, eventually confirmed that the ministers went to the Central Committee to discuss Turkey's entry into the war: SHAT, Service historique de la Marine, Service de Renseignements de la Marine, Turquie, 1BB7 232, doc. no. 676, Constantinople, May 1919, lieutenant Goybet, adjoint du chef du S.R. Marine, p. 3.

89. *Ibidem*, annexe 4, "Explications fournies par Cavid bey, ministre des Finances," pp. 2–3.

90. *Ibidem*, annexe 6, "Déclaration du ministre des Travaux publics," p. 1.

91. *Ibidem*, annexe 7, "Déclaration du ministre des Travaux publics," "Les dessous de la politique unioniste," p. 2.

92. *Ibidem*.

93. *Ibidem*.

94. Papazian, *Memoirs, op. cit.*, II, p. 276.

95. V. Dadrian, *Histoire du Génocide, op. cit.*, pp. 335–44, cites, notably, the ambassador of Austria-Hungary, who indicated that the Turks were using the alliance like a "trampoline" to "deal in the harshest possible manner" with the Armenians; the German consul in Aleppo remaked that the Turks wanted to " solve the Armenian question while benefitting from the war and [that] their government uses alliance with the central powers to this end."

96. J. Pomiankowski, *Der Zusammenbruch des Ottomanischen Reiches*, Vienne 1969, p. 162; Dadrian, *Histoire du Génocide, op. cit.*, p. 341.

97. SHAT, Service historique de la Marine, Service des renseignements de la Marine, Turquie, 1BB7 236, doc. no. 1595 B-9, Constantinople, 17 January 1920, lieutenant Goybet, adjoint du chef du S.R. Marine, annexe 11 and 1BB7 236, doc. no. 1651 B-9, Constantinople, 24 January 1920, annexe 14, p. 7, déposition du ministre des Finances. At the fourth session of the Ittihadists' trial, the CUP's secretary general, Midhat Şükrü, confirmed that "the [mobilization] order came abruptly": SHAT, Service historique de la Marine, Service des renseignements de la Marine, Turquie, 1BB7 232, doc. no. 676, Constantinople, May 1919, lieutenant Goybet, adjoint du chef du S.R. Marine, p. 3.

Yervant Odian, Անիծեալ Տարիներ, 1914–1919, Անձնական Յիշատակներ [*The Cursed Years, 1914–1919, Personal Recollections*] published in instalments in *Jamanag*, 6 February 1919, no. 3440. According to Odian, the posters announcing mobilization were put up the same day in the provinces, which would tend to indicate that they had been prepared and distributed earlier (first installment).

98. Diary, 3/16 August 1914, in Zohrab, *Complete works*, IV, *op. cit.*, pp. 383–4.

J. Pomiankowski, *Der Zusammenbruch des Ottomanischen Reiches, op. cit.*, p. 162. Pomiankowski was Austria-Hungary's military attache in Constantinople for ten years – at the beginning of the war, there existed around 120 Christian battalions, made up mainly of Armenians.

Odian, *The cursed years, 1914–1919, op. cit.*, no. 2. According to Odian, most of the young conscripts in the capital were persuaded that the war would not last long and had chosen to enlist rather than pay the 50 pound *bedel* required to avoid the draft.

99. Zaven Der Yeghiayan, *Memoirs, op. cit.*, p. 61, letter from the Bishop of Bayazid to the Patriarch Zaven, 19 August 1914.

100. *Ibidem*, p. 60, letter from the Bishop of Erzerum, Smpad Saadetian, to the Patriarch Zaven, 28 September 1914; APC/APJ, Ֆ 334 (in French), no. 35, Rapport sur Les événements de Keghi depuis la mobilization jusqu'à la déportation (récit d'une rescapée), affirms that mobilization took place under good conditions.

101. Papazian, *Memoirs, op. cit.*, II, pp. 312, 316.

102. *Ibidem*, p. 326.

103. Zaven Der Yeghiayan, *Memoirs, op. cit.*, p. 59, letter from the Bishop of Erzerum, Smpad Saadetian, to the Patriarch Zaven, 1/14 August 1914.

104. *Ibidem*. Bishop Smpad Saadetian affirms that the ARF's Congress had left a very bad impression on the local authorities and that Aknuni, who had expressed a desire to remain in Erzerum for some time, was told to leave the city in 24 hours. He found the authorities' mistrust alarming.

105. Philip H. Stoddard, *The Ottoman Government and the Arabs, 1911–1918: Preliminary Study of the Teşkilât-ı Mahsusa*, Ann Arbor, MI, 1963, pp. 6, 50.

106. Zürcher, *Turkey: A Modern History, op. cit.*, pp. 114–15.

107. Halil Paşa, *Ittihad ve Terraki'den Cumhuriyet'e: Bitmeyen Savaş [From the Ittihad to the Republic: The Endless Struggle]*, M. T. Sorgun (ed.), Istanbul 1972, p. 125; T. Z. Tunaya, *Türkiyede Siyasi Partiler [The Political Parties in Turkey]*, 3 vol., 2nd completed edition, Istanbul 1984, p. 123.

108. Cemal Kutay, *Birinci Dünya Harbinde Teşkilât-ı Mahsusa ve Heyber'de Türk Cengi, op. cit.*, pp. 60–3

109. AMAE, Turquie, Correspondance politique, n. s., vol. 86, p. 244, letter from the vice-consul in Adana to the Minister Pichon, 19 April 1913.

110. Zürcher, *Turkey: A Modern History, op. cit.*, pp. 114–15. The author also indicates that the Special Organization played an important role in liquidating separatist movements during the First World War, especially in the Arab provinces, and also in the terror campaign directed against Greek businessmen in western Asia Minor.

111. Cemal Kutay, *Birinci Dünya Harbinde Teşkilât-ı Mahsusa, op. cit.*, p. 36.

112. Sixth Session of the Trial of the Unionists, 14 May 1919: *Takvim-ı Vakayi* no. 3557, 25 May 1919, p. 98, statement of Midhat Şükrü.

113. The indictment, drawn up on 12 April 1919, was presented to the court-martial on 27 April 1919, along with a series of letters and various other documents substantiating the charges: *Takvim-ı Vakayi*, no. 3540, 5 May 1919, p. 6.

114. Mil [= Arif Cemil], *Umumi Harpte Teşkilât-ı Mahsusa [The Special Organization in the General War]*, published in instalments (90 issues) in *Vakıt*, from 2 November 1933 to 7 February 1934, and almost simultaneously reprinted in V. Ishkhanian's Armenian translation in *Haratch* from 19 November 1933 to 7 April 1934 (92 issues), then published separately as: Arif Cemil, *Dünya savası'nda Teskilat-ı Mahsusa [The Special Organization during the First World War)*, Istanbul 1997.

115. *Ibidem.*

116. *Ibidem.*

117. A physician trained in Istanbul's Military Medical School, a classmate of Bahaeddin Şakir's, executed in 1926 in connection with the plot against Mustafa Kemal.

118. Retired officer, CUP inspector in Bursa, an associate of Enver's, nicknamed "Sevkiyatçı Rıza" for his role in the deportation of the Armenians, one of the founding members of the *Karakol*, the successor to the Special Organization after the latter was officially disbanded.

119. CUP *fedayi* in 1908, deputy first from Çanakale, then from Angora, member of the CUP's Central Committee.

120. First Session of the Trial of the Unionists, that was held on 27 April 1919, beginning at 1:50 p.m.: *Takvim-ı Vakayi*, no. 3540, 5 May 1919, p. 5.

121. First Session of the Trial of the *kâtibi mesulları* ("responsible secretaries"), 21 June 1919 (21 Haziran 1335), in *Takvim-ı Vakayi*, no. 3586, 28 June 1919, p. 168.

122. First Session of the Trial of the Unionists that was held on 27 April 1919, beginning at 1:50 p.m.: *Takvim-ı Vakayi*, no. 3540, 5 May 1919, p. 5. Ziya Bey is not referred to again in the following sessions.

123. *Ibidem*, p. 5, col. 1, lines 1–28. *Teskere* 59, bearing the signatures of Halil, Nâzım, Atıf, and Aziz and addressed to Midhat Şükrü, proves that Halil [Kut] was a member of the Political Bureau of the *Teşkilât-ı Mahsusa* when he was a commander of the garrison in Constantinople, before he set out for the Iranian border on mission.

124. Sixth Session of the Trial of the Unionists, 14 May 1919: *Takvim-ı Vakayi*, no. 3557, 25 May 1919, statement of Rıza, pp. 104–7.

125. Third Session of the Trial of the Unionists, 8 May 1335/1919, statement of the colonel Cevad: *Takvim-ı Vakayi*, no. 3547, 15 May 1919, pp. 63–6. The same day, Yusuf Rıza was interrogated by the presiding judge (pp. 59–62), but refused to say anything else on the subject.

126. Seventh Session of the Trial of the Unionists, 17 June 1919, statement of Midhat Sükrü: *Takvim-ı Vakayi*, no. 3561, 29 May 1919, pp. 115–26. For the declaration of the CUP's Secretary General, see p. 119. Information revealed at the trial suggests that the Central Committee of the Political Bureau of the Special Organization had five members.

The term "Central Committee" has to be treated with caution, because it seems that it was used indiscriminately to refer to both the 40-man-strong General Council and the Central Committee or bureau of the CUP, which had only about ten members in fall 1914: Trumpener, *Germany and Ottoman Empire, 1914–1918, op. cit.*, p. 44, n. 5 cites a secret report that spells out the way the party functioned internally.

127. Arif Cemil, *The Special Organization, op. cit.*, *Vakıt/ Haratch* pp. 2, 3 (nos 2350–1, 21 and 22 November 1933). Şakir's group ("some twenty people in disguise") set foot in Angora two days before the group of *fedayis* (which took three days to reach the city). It was there, says Cemil, that it learned that the two German battleships, renamed the *Yavuz* and the *Midilli*, had reached the Bosphorus (on 16 August 1914). This allows us to say that Şakir's group left Constantinople around 11 August, the group of *fedayis* on 13 August.

128. *Ibidem, Vakıt/Haratch* 3. Most of these military cadres were already active in the CUP in 1908, in Salonika, and cited *infra*, pp. 821–822, n. 160–167: Ismitli Mümtaz, Hüsrev Sâmi [Kızıldoğan], Abdülkadır, Ali [Çetinkaya], Atıf [Kamçıl], Sarı Efe Edip, Sabancalı Hakkı, Nuri [Conker], Kâzım [Özalp], Yenibahçeli Sükrü, and Yakup Cemil. The responsible secretaries mentioned are: Kemal Ferid, Hasan Basri, Memduh Şevket, Ethem, and Ihsan Bey.

129. *Ibidem, Vakıt/Haratch* 3.

130. *Ibidem, Vakıt/Haratch* 3.

131. Son of General Vehib Pasha; Young Turk *fedayi* prior to 1908; member of the general staff of the Tenth Army in the Balkans in 1913, under Enver's command. The vali of Basra in 1914, he led the unsuccessful battles against the British troops in Basorah, committing suicide in April 1915: Zürcher, *The Unionist ..., op. cit.*, p. 48, n. 14 (a typographical error puts his death a year earlier, in April 1914). One describes him as the leader of the military branch of the Special Organization in fall 1914: Arif Cemil, *The Special Organization, op. cit.*, *Vakıt/ Haratch* no. 11, affirms that this close associate of Enver's lost both his legs in the course of the fighting with the British, and committed suicide thereafter.

132. Kutay, *The Special Organization, op. cit.*, p. 36; Vahakn Dadrian, "Documentation of the Armenian Genocide in Turkish Sources," in *Genocide: A Critical Bibliographic Review*, II, I. Charny (ed.), Londres 1991, p. 126. Arif Cemil, *The Special Organization, op. cit.*, *Vakıt/Haratch* no. 69–70, confirms that Enver initially resisted the Ittihadist Central Committee's absolute control over the Special Organization, but that the defeat at Sarıkamiş caused him to lose his influence in the committee, along with a good deal of his credibility, so that he was forced to cede.

133. Vahakn Dadrian, "The Role of the Special Organization in the Armenian Genocide during the First World War," in *Minorities in Wartime*, P. Panayi (ed.), Oxford 1993, pp. 50–82, provides a number of references on these questions, notably in Turkish sources.

134. Zürcher, *The Unionist ..., op. cit.*, p. 59. His more recent manual on contemporary Turkish history suggests, however, that his approach to the question of the Special Organization has evolved.

135. Sixth Session of the Trial of the Unionists, 14 May 1919: *Takvim-ı Vakayi* no. 3557, 25 May 1919, p. 98.

136. First Session of the Trial of the Unionists, 27 April 1919, à 13h 50: *Takvim-ı Vakayi*, no. 3540, 5 May 1919, p. 5, col. 2, lines 8–14; Fifth Session, 12 May 1919: *Takvim-ı Vakayi*, no. 3554, 21 May 1919, p. 69.

137. Fifth Session of the Trial of the Unionists, 12 May 1919: *Takvim-ı Vakayi*, no. 3554, 21 May 1919, pp. 67–9. The telegram from the bureau, which bears the signatures of Aziz, Atıf, Nâzım, and Halil, is dated 13 November 1914. The presiding judge ordered another telegram read out and then asked Colonel Cevad if he was the one who had written "destroy" in the margin of the encrypted telegram and if he had received orders to do so (p. 68).

138. Sixth Session of the Trial of the Unionists, 14 May 1919: *Takvim-ı Vakayi* no. 3557, 25 May 1919, p. 97.

139. APC/APJ, PCI Bureau, U 497.

140. Krieger, Եոզղատի Հայասպանութեան Վաւերագրական Պատմութիւնը [*Documentary history of the massacre of the Armenians of Yozgat*], New York 1980, p. 215.

141. *Ibidem*.

142. Sixth Session of the Trial of the Unionists, 14 May 1919, questioning of Midhat Şükrü (pp. 91–9): *Takvim-ı Vakayi* no. 3557, 25 May 1919, p. 92.

143. SHAT, Service historique de la Marine, S.R. Marine, Turquie, 1BB7 236, doc. no. 2054 B-9, Constantinople, 3 May 1920, L. Feuillet, statement of İbrahim bey, pp. 40–2; *Ittihat-Terakki'nin sorgulanması, op. cit.*, pp. 133–69.
144. *Ibidem*, p. 42.
145. Second Session of the Trial of the Unionists, 4 May 1919, *Takvim-ı Vakayi*, no. 3543, 12 May 1919, pp. 28–9; Dadrian, "The Role of the Special Organisation...," *art. cit.*, pp. 30–1.
146. *Ibidem*.
147. Dadrian, "The Role of the Special Organisation...," *art. cit.*, pp. 26–7, cites, notably revelations in the Istanbul press, reports by the British intelligence service, and Fuat Balkan's *Hatıralar* (Memoirs), II, Istanbul 1962, p. 297.
148. SHAT, Service historique de la Marine, S.R. Marine, Turquie, 1BB7 236, doc. no. 1805 B-9, Constantinople, 26 February 1920, L. Feuillet, annexe 20, statement of Said Halim, pp. 18, 29–30.
149. A telegram sent by the responsible secretary in Samsun, Ruşdü, to the Central Committee of the Committee of Union and Progress, and forwarded on 16 December 1914 by Midhat Şükrü to Dr. Nâzım, the head of the *Teşkilât-ı Mahsusa* (First Session of the Trial of the Unionists, 27 April 1919: *Takvim-ı Vakayi*, no. 3540, 5 May 1919, p. 6, col. 2, lines 4–13), reads: "The fifth squadron, on Tufan Ağa's orders, comprising fifty-five men, was today dispatched by automobile." Thus, the CUP and the *Teşkilât-i Mahsusa* were working closely together to form squadrons.
    A 20 November 1914 letter from the CUP inspector in Balıkeser, Musa sent to Midhat Şükrü and forwarded to Dr. Nâzım, also suggests that the Ministry of the Interior and CUP were directly involved in organizing squadrons (*Ibidem*).
150. Sixth Session of the Trial of the Unionists, 14 May 1919, questioning of Atıf Bey (pp. 99–104): *Takvim-ı Vakayi* no. 3557, 25 May 1919, p. 102.
151. Seventh Session of the Trial of the Unionists, 17 June 1919: *Takvim-ı Vakayi*, no. 3561, 29 May 1919, p. 124; Fifth Session of the Trial of the Unionists, 12 May 1919: *Takvim-ı Vakayi*, no. 3554, 21 May 1919, pp. 88–9.
152. Second Session of the Trial of the Unionists, 4 May 1919: *Takvim-ı Vakayi*, no. 3543, 12 May 1919, p. 28. The presiding judge then ordered that the document be read before the court.
153. First Session of the Trial of the Unionists, 27 April 1919, abstract of the report of Vehib pasha: *Takvim-ı Vakayi*, no. 3540, 5 May 1919, p. 7, col. 2.
154. *Takvim-ı Vakayi*, no. 3771, 9 February 1920, p. 48, col. 2.
155. APC/APJ, PCI Bureau, Ձ 171–Ձ 182, a deposition of 12 handwritten pages, in Ottoman Turkish, addressed to *Emiyeti Umumîye Dairesinde, Sevkiyat Komisyonı Riyasetine*, followed by French and Armenian translations of the text, probably of thee to the Information Bureau of the Armenian Patriarchate in Constantinople, whose members had access to the pretrial investigation files until mid-March 1919 because, as employees of the Patriarchate, they were acting on behalf of the victims and therefore of the plaintiffs.

4 *Destruction as Self-Construction: Ideology in Command*

1. Bozarslan, *Les Courants de pensée, op. cit.*, 2 vol.; Hanioğlu, *Preparation for a Revolution, op. cit.*
2. *Ibidem*, p. 310.
3. *Ibidem*, p. 308.
4. *Ibidem*, p. 313.
5. Bozarslan, *Les Courants de pensée, op. cit.*, I, p. 91.
6. Hanioğlu, *Preparation for a Revolution, op. cit.*, p. 295.
7. Bozarslan, *Les Courants de pensée, op. cit.*, I, p. 95.
8. *Ibidem*, I, p. 97.
9. Hanioğlu, *Preparation for a Revolution, op. cit.*, p. 294.
10. *Ibidem*, p. 295.
11. M. Ş. Hanioğlu, *Bir Siyasal Örgüt Olarak Osmanlı Ittihat ve Terakki Cemiyeti ve Jön-Türklük*, Istanbul, s.d., pp. 52–4; Bozarslan, *Les Courants de pensée, op. cit.*, I, p. 102.
12. Albert Fua, Dr. Refik Nevzad, *La trahison du gouvernement turc Comité Union et Progrès*, Paris 1914, p. 13.

13. Bozarslan, *Les Courants de pensée, op. cit.*, I, p. 113.

14. *Ibidem*, I, p. 122.

15. P. Risal [Tekin Alp, ps. of Moïse Cohen], "Les Turcs à la recherche d'une âme nationale," in, Jacob M. Landau, *Tekin Akp, Turkish Patriot 1883–1961*, Istanbul 1984, pp. 66–7; Bozarslan, *Les Courants de pensée, op. cit.*, II, p. 37.

16. S. Akşin, *Jön-Türkler ve İttihat ve Terakki*, Istanbul 1980, pp. 168–9.

17. Letter from Enver pasha, in O. Koloğlu, "Enver Paşa Efsanesinde Alman Katkısı, 1908–1913," *Tarih ve Toplum*, no. 78 (1989), p. 19.

18. Zürcher, *Turkey: A Modern History, op. cit.*, p. 133.

19. Hanioğlu, *Preparation for a Revolution, op. cit.*, p. 297.

20. B. Kuran, *İnkilâp Hareketleri ve Millî Mücadele*, Istanbul 1956, p. 483; Bozarslan, *Les Courants de pensée, op. cit.*, I, p. 207.

21. See *ibidem*, II, p. 52. Mehmed Emin [Yurdakul] (1869–1914), writer and Pan-Turkist poet.

22. *Ibidem*.

23. *Ibidem*.

24. *Ibidem*, II, p. 54.

25. Yusuf Akçura, *Yeni Türk Devletinin Kurucuları, 1928 Yazıları*, Ankara 1981, p. 143; Bozarslan, *Les Courants de pensée, op. cit.*, II, p. 57.

26. Ahmed Ağaoğlu, "Islâm'da Davay-ı Milliyet," in İ. Kara, *Türkiye'de İslâmcılık Düşüncesi ? Metinler/ Kişiler*, Istanbul 1986, p. 452; Bozarslan, *Les Courants de pensée, op. cit.*, II, p. 58.

27. Ahmed Agayef, "Türk Alemi," *Tarih ve Toplum*, no. 63 (1989), pp. 18–21, in Bozarslan, *Les Courants de pensée, op. cit.*, II, p. 59.

28. *Infra*, p. 847, n. 3.

29. This is what is indicated by the file that the British authorities file prepared on him when he was imprisoned in Malta in spring 1919: FO 371/6500, no. 2764.

30. *Supra*, p. 194, n. 25.

31. Zürcher, *Turkey: A Modern History, op. cit.*, p. 136.

32. Tekin Alp, *Türkler bu Muharebede Ne Kzanabilirler ? [What Can the Turks Hope to Gain in This Struggle?]*, Istanbul 1914.

33. Bozarslan, *Les Courants de pensée, op. cit.*, II, p. 81.

34. *Infra*, p. 837, n. 1.

35. Bozarslan, *Les Courants de pensée, op. cit.*, II, p. 81.

36. Bozarslan, *Les Courants de pensée, op. cit.*, II, p. 90, in Ziya Gökalp, *Makaleler*, IX, ed. Ş. Beysanoğlu, Istanbul 1980, p. 41.

37. *Ibidem*, p. 28, in Bozarslan, *Les Courants de pensée, op. cit.*, II, p. 95.

38. Ziya Gökalp, *Makaleler*, I, ed. Ş. Beysanoğlu, Istanbul 1976, p. 70, in Bozarslan, *Les Courants de pensée, op. cit.*, II, p. 92.

39. Ziya Gökalp, *Ziya Gökalp Külliyatı, II, Limni ve Malta Mektupları*, F. A. Tansel (ed.), Ankara 1965, pp. LVI, in Bozarslan, *Les Courants de pensée, op. cit.*, II, p. 92.

40. According to the formula of Bozarslan, *Les Courants de pensée, op. cit.*, II, p. 93.

41. Kouyoumdjian, *Le Liban à la veille et au début de la Grande Guerre. Memoirs d'un gouverneur, op. cit.*, explains this very well with regard to Lebanon and Syria.

42. Bozarslan, *Les Courants de pensée, op. cit.*, II, p. 100.

43. Midhat Şükrü Bleda, *İmparatorluğun Çöküşü*, Istanbul 1979, p. 58.

44. Ziya Gökalp, *Makaleler*, X, ed. F. R. Tuncer, Ankara 1981, p. 76, in Bozarslan, *Les Courants de pensée, op. cit.*, II, p. 103.

45. Ziya Gökalp, *Türkçülüğün Esasları*, Istanbul 1976, p. 20, in Bozarslan, *Les Courants de pensée, op. cit.*, II, p. 103.

46. E. B. Şapolyo, *Ziya Gökalp, İttihat ve Terakki ve Meşrutiyet Tarihi*, Istanbul 1974, in Bozarslan, *Les Courants de pensée, op. cit.*, II, p. 103.

47. Sebuh Aguni, Միլիոն մը Հայերու Զարդի Պատմութիւնը [*History of the Massacre of One Million Armenians*], Constantinople 1921, p. 62.

48. Greek Deputy hostile to the Unionists: Bozarslan, *Les Courants de pensée, op. cit.*, II, p. 104, n. 720.

49. Ziya Gökalp, *Yeni Hayat Doğru Yol*, ed. M. Cunbur, Ankara 1976, p. 11, in Bozarslan, *Les Courants de pensée, op. cit.*, II, p. 104.

50. Arif Cemil, *The Special Organization, op. cit., Vakıt/ Haratch* 89. According to Cemil, the Ittihad's Pan-Turk projects for Russia, which aimed to unify the "Turks" of the Caucasus, Volga Basin, Siberia, Turkestan, and Crimea, were thwarted by the "penetration of foreign elements that hindered the development of the Turks, who do not possess the attributes of a nation": *Ibidem, Vakıt/ Haratch* 88.

51. *Ibidem, Vakıt/Haratch* 88.

52. Based in Erzerum.

53. *Ibidem, Vakıt/Haratch* 88.

54. *Ibidem, Vakıt/Haratch* 83.

55. *Ibidem, Vakıt/Haratch* 88.

56. *Ibidem.*

57. Bozarslan, *Les Courants de pensée, op. cit.*, II, p. 120.

58. Transcription of the third Session of the Trial of Unionists: SHAT, Service historique de la Marine, S. R. de la Marine, Turquie, 1BB7 232, doc. no. 676, Constantinople, May 1919, lieutenant Goybet, adjoint du chef du S.R. Marine, pp. 3–5, questioning of Ziya Gökalp.

59. The Meydan Larousse, the Turkish version of the French Larousse, seems to be the only biographical dictionary to mention this figure, whose name it spells "Bahaittin Şakir."

    Arslan Terzioğlu (holder of the chair of the history of medicine and medical ethics at the Faculty of Medicine in Istanbul, and also a diplomat), "The Assassination of Dr Bahaeddin Şakir in Berlin and the Armenian Relocation in line with National and Foreign Sources of Information," internet, 2002. Concerning the doctor's date of birth, he points out that the date "1878" engraved on his tombstone is obviously wrong: Şakir finished his study of medicine in 1896. His family probably emigrated to Istanbul after the war of 1877–1878, when Bulgaria became autonomous. Terzioğu notes that he specialized in forensic medicine and psychiatry in Paris. He concludes his notice with the suggestion that the mortal remains of this "great patriot" be repatriated to Turkey

60. APC/APJ, PCI Bureau, Ջ 947–950, file of Bahaeddin Şakir, pp. 1–2.

61. *Ibidem*, p. 3.

62. APC/APJ, PCI Bureau, file XXIX, Ս 576, encrypted telegram no. 5, from the head of the *Teşkilât-ı Mahsusa*, Bahaeddin Şakir, from his headquarter in Erzerum, 21 Haziran 1331 (4 July 1915), to the vali of Mamuret ul-Aziz, Sabit Bey, for transmission to the delegate of the CUP in Mamuret ul-Aziz, Resneli Nâzım Bey, encrypted, with the decoded version, in *Takvim-ı Vakayi* no. 3540 (session of 12 April 1919), 5 May 1919, p. 6, col. 1–2, and no. 3771, 13 January 1920, p. 48, col. 1, with Bahaeddin Şakir's condemnation to death.

    Be it noted that this document is often dated 21 April 1915, although the telegram indicates "21 Haziran 1331."

63. *Supra*, p. 187, n. 155.

64. APC/APJ, PCI Bureau, Ջ 947–950, file of Bahaeddin Şakir, p. 3. *The Bosphore* of 20 April 1922, published shortly his assassination in Berlin on 17 April 1922, cites Vehib Pasha's report when it evokes his criminal activities throughout Asia Minor and associates Dr. Nâzım with him. The daily also refers to a document discovered by General Nâzım Pasha, minister of war in the Kâmil cabinet, shortly before he was assassinated on 23 January 1913 by the Ittihadists. This document, which bears Şakir's signature, reads: "For the moment, try to win over the Armenians. We know what we will do to them later."

65. *Joghovourti Tsayn*, 21 April 1922 and *Vakıt*, 20 April 1922. In 1909, the Military Medical School and the Medical School merged and the new institution was established in Haydarpaşa: Terzioğlu, *art. cit.*

66. Bibliothèque Nubar, ms. 17, 18, PJ 1–3, Aram Andonian, Ժամանակագրական Նոթեր [*Chronological Notes, 1914–1916*] [written in 1925], f° 53, points out that Şakir's father was burned alive at the age of 83 when, on 30 July 1915, the Şakirs' family home in Kasım Paşa was destroyed in a fire. The colonel was "on mission" in the eastern provinces at the time.

67. Weber, *Eagles on the Crescent…, op. cit.*, pp. 77, 165, points out that this also led to problems with the empire's German and Austro-Hungarian allies.

68. Zürcher, *Turkey: A Modern History*, op. cit., p. 127.

69. *Ibidem*, p. 129.

70. Bozarslan, *Les Courants de pensée*, op. cit., II, p. 87.

71. *Ibidem*, II, p. 91.

72. *Ibidem*, II, p. 102.

73. Tekin Alp, "Tesanütçülük," in Z. Toprak, *Türkiye'de "Millî İktisat" (1908–1918)*, Ankara 1987, pp. 08–9, cité par Bozarslan, *Les Courants de pensée*, op. cit., I, p. 215.

74. Y. Akçura, "Pour une bourgeoisie nationale," in F. Georgeon, *Yusuf Akçura, Aux origines du nationalisme turc (1876–1935)*, Paris 1980. p. 129.

75. André Autheman, *La Banque impériale ottomane*, Paris 1996, p. 239. The author notes that on 9 January 1915, the three members of the board who were French or English nationals had to give up their posts at Talât's request. The three highest-ranking officials, all Ottoman subjects – Cartali, the bank's director, Hanemoğlu, its inspector general, and Kerestejian, the head of the operational division – then formed a collegial board, with Kartali as its president. On 17 July 1915, Talât, then interim minister of finance, summoned Kartali to his office to inform him of the decision of Council of Ministers, which, in the end, remained a dead letter (*ibidem*, pp. 233–4).

76. Bozarslan, *Les Courants de pensée*, op. cit., I, p. 217.

77. In Bozarslan, *Les Courants de pensée*, op. cit., I, p. 217.

78. AMAE, Turquie, Politique intérieure, n. s., vol. 9, f° 252, telegram from the chargé d'affaires in Constantinople, Boppe, to S. Pichon, 3 January 1914.

79. AMAE, Turquie, Politique intérieure, n. s., vol. 9, ff. 277–8, letter from the French ambassador in Constantinople, Bompard, to the president of Conseil and minister of Foreign Affairs, Doumergue, 31 March 1914.

80. Zürcher, *Turkey: A Modern History*, op. cit., p. 130.

81. *Ibidem*.

82. *Ibidem*. Akçam, *From Empire to Republic*, op. cit., p. 141, notes that the first sign of a plan for a "national economy" was the 3 July 1913 creation of the İstiklal-i Milli Cemiyeti (Committee for National Independence), the task of which was to promote the founding of new companies. The biggest companies were created by Kara Kemal, the minister responsible for food and supplies during the War.

83. Zürcher, *Turkey: A Modern History*, op. cit., p. 130. Yervant Odian notes that, in late July 1915, the authorities began to arrest certain businessmen and merchants in the capital in order to take control of their companies (Odian, *The cursed years*, op.cit., no. 17). Odian also relates a discussion he had in May 1915 with Oskan Mardikian, a former minister who had long moved in Young Turk circles. Mardikian told him that he was convinced that the CUP leaders were going to attack merchants and entrepreneurs: "they are going to appropriate the Armenians' property."

84. *Ibidem*, p. 131.

85. Especially the "Explications fournies par Cavid bey, ministre des Finances," Cinquième commission du parlement ottoman, 25 November 1919: SHAT, Service historique de la Marine, Service des renseignements de la Marine, Turquie, 1BB7 236, doc. no. 1593 B-9, Constantinople, 16 January 1920, annexe 4. Let us note that Cavid was the head of the Ottoman National Credit Company, which he founded as a minister after resigning from the cabinet until he returned to government in January 1917: Autheman, *La Banque impériale ottomane*, op. cit., p. 240.

86. L. von Sanders, op. cit., pp. 52–3.

87. APC/APJ, PCI Bureau, Ւ 125–30, a list of war criminals complicit in the massacres and deportations.

88. APC/APJ, PCI Bureau, Յ 202, file no. 31/1–2, Turks Responsible for the Armenian Atrocities. Born in Ortaköy, Reşad learned Armenian. He was a *kaymakam* in the vilayet of Erzerum, an interim *mutesarif* in Bayazid, and in 1913 was charged with reorganizing the police force in three departments. One of these was the Department of Political Affairs, where he served as an assistant to the police chief of the capital, Bedri. He was appointed *mutesarif* of Aydın in June 1917. Under the Kemalist regime, he adopted the surname Mimaroğlu and continued to hold important posts before being elected parliamentary deputy from.

89. APC/APJ, PCI Bureau, Ƶ 144, certified copies of the encrypted telegram from the Sublime Porte, minister of the Interior, Talât, to the vilayet of Konya, 6 February 1916, certified on 27 March 1919 by the departement of the Ministry of the Interior, published in *Takvim-ı Vakayi* no. 3540, pp. 1–14.

90. *Askeri Tarih Belgeleri Dergisi*, no. 81 (December 1982), doc. 1832.

91. Original in Ottoman Turkish: *Takvim-ı Vakayi*, no. 2303, 14 September 1915, pp. 1–7; Armenian transcription: APC/APJ, PCI Bureau, Ɑ 177–9; French version of the Law of 13/26 September 1915, published on 2 April 1923, supplément B, de La Législation turque, Constantinople, édition Rizzo & Son, pp. 1–6 (Archives of the SHAT, série E, carton 320, Turquie, 260, ff. 49–51v°).

92. Original in Ottoman Turkish: *Takvim-ı Vakayi*, no. 2343, 28 October 1915, in 25 articles; APC/APJ, PCI Bureau, Ɑ 205; French version of the Law of 13/26 September 1915, published on 2 April 1923, supplément B, de La Législation turque, Constantinople, édition Rizzo & Son, pp. 7–15 (Archives of the SHAT, série E, carton 320, Turquie, 260, ff. 52–6). Dadrian, *Histoire ...*, *op. cit.*, p. 361, speaks of a complementary law of 26 September, based on an erroneous source that is not cites.

93. Original in Ottoman Turkish: *Takvim-ı Vakayi*, no. 2189, 19 May/1 June 1915/2 Moharrem 1333. We will examine the provisions of this law later.

94. French version of the Law of 13/26 September 1915, published on 2 April 1923, supplément B, de La Législation turque, Constantinople, édition Rizzo & Son, p. 3.

95. *Ibidem.*

96. *Ibidem*, pp. 3–4.

97. *Ibidem*, p. 6.

98. *Ibidem*, p. 6, the text bears the signature of Sultan Mehmed Reşad, and of "Ibrahim, ministre de la Justice, Talaat, ministre de l'Intérieur, Mehmed Saïd [Halim], grand vizir, Haïri, ministre de l'Evkaf."

99. *Ibidem*, p. 7.

100. *Ibidem*, pp. 7–8.

101. *Ibidem*, p. 9.

102. *Ibidem*, p. 10.

103. *Ibidem*, p. 11.

104. *Ibidem*, p. 12.

105. *Ibidem*, p. 13.

106. *Ibidem*, p. 14.

107. Österreichisches Staatsarchiv, HHStA PA Beilage, file 69 D, report no. 441 P, from the Austrian consular agent in Bursa, L. Trano, 16 August 1915, to the ambassador in Constantinople and the Baron Burian, minister of foreign affairs, ff. 333–4.

108. Österreichisches Staatsarchiv, HHStA PA Beilage, file 70 B, report no. 453 P, from the Austrian consular agent in Bursa, L. Trano, 19 August 1915, to the ambassador in Constantinople and the Baron Burian, minister of foreign affairs s.

109. Österreichisches Staatsarchiv, HHStA PA XII 209, no. 71 P-B, report from the Austrian ambassador in Constantinople, Pallavicini, to the minister, Burian, 31 August 1915, f° 352.

110. Österreichisches Staatsarchiv, HHStA PA XII 209, no. 7P P-A, report from the Austrian ambassador in Constantinople, Pallavicini, to the Minister Burian, 30 September 1915, f° 367.

111. Autheman, *La Banque impériale ottomane*, *op. cit.*, p. 242.

112. *Ibidem*, pp. 244–5.

5 Turkey's Entry into the War

1. Diary, 3 November 1914: Zohrab, *Complete works*, *op. cit.*, IV, pp. 400–1. Zohrab reports that Cavid resigned in order to be in a position to "do something in case of catastrophe."

2. *Ibidem*, the same day, around midnight, p. 403.

3. Weber, *Eagles on the Crescent...*, *op. cit.*, p. 73.

4. *Ibidem*, p. 82.

5. *Ibidem*, p. 64, n. 14; Trumpener, *Germany and Ottoman Empire, 1914–1918*, *op. cit.*, pp. 108–12.

6. SHAT, Service historique de la Marine, Service des renseignements de la Marine, Turquie, 1BB7 236, doc. no. 1662 B-9, Constantinople, 19 March 1920, lieutenant de vaisseau Feuillet, annexe 20.

7. Turfan, *Rise of the Young Turks*, op. cit., p. 363; Weber, *Eagles on the Crescent...*, op. cit., pp. 83–5, confirms, on the basis of many different sources, that it was Enver who gave the order to attack the fleet.

8. SHAT, Service historique de la Marine, Service des renseignements de la Marine, Turquie, 1BB7 232, doc. no. 676, Constantinople, May 1919, p. 3. Trumpener, *Germany and Ottoman Empire, 1914–1918*, op. cit., p. 56, n. 33, notes that the General Council – that is, the broader leadership body of the CUP, which, in theory, had some 40 members – was convened on the morning of 30 October and that, by a vote of 17 to 10, it opted to enter the war on the German side.

9. Weber, *Eagles on the Crescent...*, op. cit., p. 65; U. Trumpener, *Germany and Ottoman Empire, 1914–1918*, op. cit.

10. Vahakn Dadrian, *German Responsibility in the Armenian Genocide*, Watertown 1996.

11. Weber, *Eagles on the Crescent...*, op. cit., pp. 184–7.

12. Weber, *Eagles on the Crescent...*, op. cit., p. 65; Trumpener, *Germany and Ottoman Empire, 1914–1918*, op. cit., pp. 234–6.

13. Zürcher, *Turkey: A Modern History*, op. cit., p. 119.

14. Sebuh Aguni, op. cit., p. 60.

15. Andonian, *Chronological notes, 1914–1916*, ms. cit., f° 10.

16. *Ibidem*, f° 12.

17. *Ibidem*, f° 13.

18. *Ibidem*, ff. 13–14.

19. *Ibidem*, ff. 14–16.

20. Yervant Perdahdjian, *Evénements et faits observés à Constantinople par le vicariat [Patriarcal] (1914–1916)*, transl. by Raymond Kévorkian, *Revue d'Histoire Arménienne Contemporaine* I (1995), pp. 251–2.

21. *Ibidem*, p. 252.

22. Zaven Der Yeghiayan, *Memoirs*, op. cit., p. 72.

23. *Ibidem*, p. 73.

24. Diary, 30 October and November 1914: Zohrab, *Complete works*, op. cit., IV, pp. 392, 396–7.

25. Zaven Der Yeghiayan, *Memoirs*, op. cit., p. 74.

26. *Ibidem*.

27. *Ibidem*, pp. 74–5.

28. We have published a French translation of the circular in its entirety: Yervant Perdahdjian, *Evénements et faits observés à Constantinople*, op. cit., pp. 250–1.

29. *Ibidem*.

30. Zaven Der Yeghiayan, *Memoirs*, op. cit., pp. 76–7; Andonian, *Chronological notes, 1914–1916*, ms. cit., ff. 20–1, notes that, on 6 November 1914, *Piuzantion* had published an initial circular that called on the Armenians to demonstrate "loyalty and a sense of patriotic of thety"; it received, he says, a warm reception in the press.

31. Zaven Der Yeghiayan, *Memoirs*, op. cit., p. 77. Andonian, *Chronological notes, 1914–1916*, ms. cit., f° 22: Dr. Torkomian launched the project of founding a training school for nurses on 13 November.

32. *Ibidem*, p. 78.

33. Sanders, op. cit., p. 45. He adds, with a touch of humor: "That is why these demonstrations, in Constantinople – whatever they are about – almost always involve the same people."

34. Andonian, *Chronological notes, 1914–1916*, ms. cit., f° 22.

35. Diary, 16 November 1914: Zohrab, *Complete works*, op. cit., IV, pp. 408–9; Sanders, op. cit., p. 46, also notes that it was these "demonstrators who broke all the windows and mirrors in the Tokatlian Hotel" (Sanders mistakenly dates the event to 20 November).
    Odian, *The cursed years*, op. cit., no. 6, reports that the demonstration was organized by the CUP together with the members of those guilds, notably the butchers' guild and the porters' guild, whose leaderships the Ittihad controlled.

36. Sanders, op. cit., p. 46.

37. The text of the call for a jihad was read out at the first session of the trial of the cabinet, on 3 June 1919 (3 Haziran 1335) and published in *Takvim-ı Vakayi*, no. 3571, 11 June 1919, pp. 127–40. The text was not published until 23 November 1914; the Information Bureau of the Patriarchate assembled prepared a file on Hayri Effendi in which he is described as a member of the Central

Committee: APC/APJ, PCI Bureau, Ƹ 139, with a French translation of the full text of the declaration of jihad, signed by şeyh ul-Islam Hayri, Ziyaeddin and Musa Kâzım. Kâzım would later succeed Hayri as şeyh ul-Islam and launch a more explicit call to murder Armenians.

38. Diary, 16 November 1914: Zohrab, *Complete works, op. cit.*, IV, pp. 409–10.
39. Diary, 18 November 1914: *ibidem.*, IV, pp. 412–13.
40. *Ibidem.*
41. *Ibidem.*
42. *Ibidem*, p. 414.
43. Diary, 19 November 1914: *ibidem*, IV, p. 419. Since the declaration of jihad, notes Zohrab, it is preferable not to look like a European. In the streets of Pera, he remarks, hats have been replaced by *fezes*: *Ibidem*, p. 415.
44. Diary, 5 December 1914: *ibidem*, IV, p. 419.
45. Diary, 7 December 1914: *ibidem*, IV, p. 421.
46. Diary, 17 December 1914: *ibidem*, IV, pp. 421–2.
47. In French in the original.
48. In French in the original.
49. In French in the original.
50. Diary, 18 November 1914: *ibidem*, IV, p. 416.
51. Diary, 20 December 1914: *ibidem*, IV, pp. 424–5.
52. Dadrian, *Histoire ..., op. cit.*, p. 382, n. 6.
53. C. Kutay, *Talât Paşanin Gurbet Hatiraları* [*The Memoirs of Talât Pasha in Exile*], II, 1983, p. 907; Dadrian, *Histoire ..., op. cit.*, p. 382, n. 5.
54. APC/APJ, PCI Bureau, file 23, The indications of the horrors to come in Sıvas; see *infra*, pp. 431–3.
55. Sebuh Aguni, *op. cit.*, p. 25.
    On 5 January 1915, the Istanbul press revealed a somber affair: poisoned bread had been distributed to soldiers in a barracks in Sıvas. Armenian bakers were accused of the crime. An investigation would later show that the bakers, who had been tortured, were the victims of false rumors, and clear their names. This affair is indicative of the state of public opinion in this period.
56. Andonian, *Chronological notes, 1914–1916*, ms. cit., f° 33.
57. *Ibidem.*
58. *Ibidem*, ff. 34–5.
59. Zaven Der Yeghiayan, *Memoirs, op. cit.*, p. 77.
60. *Ibidem*, p. 79.

6 *The* Teşkilât-ı Mahsusa *on the Caucasian Front and the First Military Operations*

1. Arif Cemil, *The Special Organization, op. cit.*, Vakıt/ Haratch 4–5. Kara Kemal arrival may perhaps also be explained by the fact that the National Defense Committee, of which Kemal was an eminent member, provided the Special Organization with financial support: see the 12 May 1919 declaration made at the fifth session of the trial of the Unionist leaders by Atıf Bey, a CUP delegate and, later, vali of Angora, who was elected to the Ittihadist Central Committee in September 1917: *Takvim-ı Vakayi*, no. 3554, 21 May 1919, pp. 6–8.
2. *Ibidem*, Vakıt/Haratch no. 4–5.
3. *Ibidem*, Vakıt/Haratch no. 6–7. Kemal returned rather soon to Istanbul.
4. *Ibidem*, Vakıt/Haratch 8.
5. *Ibidem*, Vakıt/Haratch no. 9–10, cites Şakir 23 August/5 September 1914 telegram to Askeri, in which he informs him of the imminent arrival of the Azerbaijani dignitary.
6. *Ibidem*, Vakıt/Haratch no. 11.
7. *Ibidem*, Vakıt/Haratch no. 12.
8. *Ibidem*, Vakıt/Haratch no. 13.
9. *Ibidem*, Vakıt/Haratch no. 13, 14.

10. *Ibidem*, *Vakıt/Haratch* no. 15. These methods of recruitment are indirectly confirmed by the parliamentary deputy Vahan, who was in Bayazid in September. There he met a former *fedayi* leader, Tro, a Dashnak who was very well known and highly respected by the Kurds for his past. Tro informed him that a number of leaders of squadrons of *hamidiye* had been in Bayazid for a few days: Papazian, *Memoirs*, *op. cit.*, II, p. 285.

    A 17 September 1914 letter from the primate of Erzerum, Smpad Saadetian, to Patriarch Zaven, reveals that in Kghi/Kığı, an Ittihadist by the name of Midhat who had recently come back from Erzerum was organizing meetings and forming militias to which he was distributing the weapons that he had brought back with him: Zaven Der Yeghiayan, *Memoirs*, *op. cit.*, p. 67

11. *Ibidem*, *Vakıt/Haratch* no. 14. He also suggested dismissing Erzerum main commissaire, Yeghishe, who happened to be an Armenian; he complained that İsmail Canbolat, the head of State Security and second in command at the Ministry of the Interior, was not responding to his suggestions on this subject.

12. *Ibidem*, *Vakıt/Haratch* 17, 34, for his role as leader of the Special Organization in Van. On the way to Van, in Berkri, Papazian met one of the leaders Kurdish *Haydaranlı*, Mehmed Sadık, an old acquaintance; Sadık told him that his tribe, which maintained squadrons of *hamidiye*, had been asked to make sure that is was prepared for all eventualities. He himself, he said, had been summoned to Bayazid: Papazian, *Memoirs*, *op. cit.*, II, p. 285.

13. Arif Cemil, *The Special Organization*, *op. cit.*, *Vakıt/ Haratch* no. 17.

14. *Ibidem*, *Vakıt/Haratch* no. 23.

15. *Ibidem*, *Vakıt/Haratch* no. 27.

16. *Ibidem*, *Vakıt/Haratch* no. 32.

17. *Ibidem*, *Vakıt/Haratch* no. 37.

18. *Ibidem*, *Vakıt/Haratch* no. 33.

19. *Ibidem*, *Vakıt/Haratch* no. 22, 23.

20. Document read au cours in Fifth Session of the Trial of Unionists, 12 May 1919: *Takvim-ı Vakayi*, no. 3554, 21 May 1919, p. 70.

21. Arif Cemil, *The Special Organization*, *op. cit.*, *Vakıt/ Haratch* no. 82.

22. *Ibidem*, *Vakıt/Haratch* no. 37, 43. Cemil adds that these Georgians abandoned the positions as soon as the troops Russian advanced.

23. *Ibidem*, *Vakıt/ Haratch* no. 44; Dadrian, "The Role of the Special Organization," *art. cit.*, p. 13.

24. *Vakıt/ Haratch* 46, letter to his wife, in which he reveals that he soon hopes to see the Turks take control of the whole Caucasus; Dadrian, "The Role of the Special Organization," *art. cit.*, p. 13.

25. Vahakn Dadrian, "Documentation of the Armenian Genocide in German and Austrian Sources," in *The Widening Circle of Genocide*, I. Charny (ed.), New Brunswick, NJ 1994, pp. 110–11, cites a 23 August 1915 report by Stanger about the operations carried out during this campaign and the massacres perpetrated by the *çetes* of the Special Organization, to which he had been assigned to carry out sabotage operations in the Caucasus.

26. Arif Cemil, *The Special Organization*, *op. cit.*, *Vakıt/Haratch* no. 51–2.

27. *Ibidem*, *Vakıt/Haratch* no. 54. A Turkish officer captured by the Russians confirms that the Russian army operating in the region was made up of Cossacks and regular troops, including Turkish-speaking troops from the Caucasus: *ibidem*, *Vakıt/Haratch* no. 57.

28. Cemil indicates that Hakkı died of typhus after a little more than a month as commander of the Third Army; his death, he says, had a deep impact on Şakir, who was very close to the general.

29. Sanders, *op. cit.*, p. 47.

30. *Ibidem*, p. 48.

31. *Ibidem*, p. 50.

32. Among his harshest detractors was Lieutenant Colonel Şerif Bey of the general staff, who sharply criticized the way he had conducted the offensive: Turfan, *op. cit.*, p. 357.

33. Sanders, *op. cit.*, p. 51.

34. Dadrian, "The Role of the Special Organization," *art. cit.*, pp. 12–14; Hilmar Kaiser, "A Scene from the Inferno," The Armenians of Erzerum and the Genocide, 1915–1916," in H.-L. Kieser et D. J. Schaller (ed.), *Der Völkermord an den Armeniern und die Shoah*, Zürich 2002, p. 130–1.

35. Dadrian, "The Role of the Special Organization," *art. cit.*, p. 12; Kaiser, "A Scene from the Inferno"..., *art. cit.*, p. 130.

36. Johannès Lepsius, *Rapport secret sur les massacres d'Arménie*, Paris 1919, p. 90; Dadrian, "The Role of the Special Organization," *art. cit.*, pp. 13–14.

37. Lepsius, *Rapport secret, op. cit.*, p. 90; Dadrian, "The Role of the Special Organization," *art. cit.*, p. 14.

38. BNu/ Fonds A. Andonian, P.J.1/3, file 40, Deportations in Başkale, ff. 1–12; Henry Barby, *Au Pays de l'épouvante*, Paris [1917], p. 234; Kévorkian & Paboudjian, *Les Arméniens dans l'Empire ottoman, op. cit.*, p. 564 puts the number of Armenians in the *kaza* at 3,505; Kemal Karpat, *Ottoman Population, 1830 1914, Demography and Social Characteristics*, Wisconsin 1985, p. 182, puts it at 4,297.

39. Barby, *Au Pays de l'épouvante, op. cit.*, pp. 235–40; Kévorkian & Paboudjian, *Les Arméniens dans l'Empire ottoman, op. cit.*, p. 544, estimates that 800 Armenians were living in these towns and villages in 1914.

40. Bloxham, "The Beginning of the Armenian Catastrophe," *art. cit.*, p. 115, n. 45–6.

41. Erik J. Zürcher, "Between Death and Desertion. The Experience of the Ottoman Soldier in World War I," *Turcica* 28 (1996), pp. 235–57.
    For an overview of the operations conof thected by the regiments of Armenian volunteers, see Magdalena Golnazarian-Nichanian, *Les Arméniens d'Azerbaïdjan: histoire locale et enjeux régionaux, 1828–1918*, thèse de doctorat, Université Paris III 2002, pp. 145–52.

42. *Ibidem*, p. 244, n. 29.

43. "The liberation of the Armenian prisoners," an article published in the Tiflis Armenian daily *Horizon*, 30 June 1916.

44. Zaven Der Yeghiayan, *Memoirs, op. cit.*, p. 96; Krieger, *op. cit.*, p. 29. This soldier was Lieutenant Hovhannes Aginian, who died at the front shortly thereafter.

45. Arif Cemil, *The Special Organization, op. cit.*, *Vakıt/ Haratch* no. 58–9.

46. *Ibidem*, *Vakıt/Haratch* no. 77.

47. *Ibidem*, *Vakıt/Haratch* no. 82.

48. Bloxham, "The Beginning of the Armenian Catastrophe," *art. cit.*, p. 117.

49. Arif Cemil, *The Special Organization, op. cit.*, *Vakıt/ Haratch* no. 71.

50. Arif Cemil, *The Special Organization, op. cit.*, *Vakıt/ Haratch* no. 83.

51. *Ibidem*, *Vakıt/Haratch* no. 83–5.

52. Original title of the work: Մարտական Հրահանգներ [*The Military Orders*], Genève 1906. This manual for *fedayi* commandos recommends, for example, traveling at night, maintaining group discipline, and obeying one's commanding officer. It was utilized in the Hamidian period, when the ARF maintained mobile units in the regions of Van and Bitlis.

53. Arif Cemil, *The Special Organization, op. cit.*, *Vakıt/ Haratch* no. 83.

54. *Ibidem*, *Vakıt/Haratch* no. 73.

55. *Ibidem*, *Vakıt/Haratch* no. 77.

56. *Ibidem*, *Vakıt/Haratch* no. 82.

57. *Ibidem*, *Vakıt/Haratch*.

58. Dadrian, "The Role of the Special Organization," *art. cit.*, p. 18, cites Ali İhsan Sabis, *Harp Hatiralarım* [*War Memoirs*], II, Ankara 1951, p. 192.

59. Arif Cemil, *The Special Organization, op. cit.*, *Vakıt/ Haratch* no. 82.

60. *Ibidem*, *Vakıt/ Haratch* no. 88.

61. SHAT, Service des renseignements de la Marine, Turquie, 1BB7 236, doc. no. 1689 B-9, Constantinople, 2 February 1920, lieutenant de vaisseau Goybet, annexe 18, complétant les annexes 6, 7, "Déposition de Tchuruk Soulou Mahmoud pacha."

7 The First Acts of Violence

1. *Supra*, p. 175, n. 70. They arrived with Dr. Şakir.

2. *Supra*, pp. 218–9.

3. *Supra*, p. 219, n. 13.

4. AMAE, Perse, n.s., vol. 18, ff. 112, 113, for the proclamation.

5. *Ibidem*, f° 112.

6. AMAE, Perse, n.s., vol. 18, f° 201v°, letter from the French consul in Tabriz, Nicolas, to MAE, 14 December 1914. For more details, see Golnazarian-Nichanian, *Les Arméniens d'Azerbaïdjan, op. cit.*, p. 109. We owe much of this information to Mary Schauffer Platt of the Presbyterian mission in Urmia: her account covers the events of 9 January to 3 June 1915. It was published in V. Bryce, *The Treatment of Armenians in the Ottoman Empire, 1915–1916*, Londres 1916.

7. Golnazarian-Nichanian, *Les Arméniens d'Azerbaïdjan, op. cit.*, pp. 110–11. Sanders, *op. cit.*, p. 57, affirms that Turkish troops entered Tabriz on 15 January. The reference, however, may be to Cevdet's forces.

8. Andonian, *Chronological notes, 1914–1916, ms. cit.*, f° 24, says that he was already in the post, but had not been immediately confirmed in his functions.

9. AMAE, Perse, n.s., vol. 18, f° 142.

10. AMAE, Perse, n.s., vol. 18, f° 142v°. A-To, *The Major Events in Vasburagan, 1914–1917, op. cit.*, pp. 97–8, indicates that the deputy from Van, Vramian, received a cable from Ömer Naci on 17 December, sent from Bazergan, on the Turkish-Persian border; Naci was there with the "army of Mosul," probably made up of local çetes.

11. Golnazarian-Nichanian, *Les Arméniens d'Azerbaïdjan, op. cit.*, pp. 111–14.

12. *Ibidem*, pp. 127–30.

13. *Ibidem*, pp. 132–4.

14. *Ibidem*, pp. 136–9.

15. *Ibidem*, pp. 139–40, cites ACEHA, fonds 121, vol. 2, file 153, published *in extenso*, p. 305.

16. *Ibidem*, pp. 140–2.

17. *Supra*, p. 184.

18. Golnazarian-Nichanian, *Les Arméniens d'Azerbaïdjan, op. cit.*, pp. 151–3. That is, 8,000 regular Russian troops, including many Cossack cavalrymen, and 1,000 Armenian volunteers.

    Sebuh, Էջեր իմ Յուշերէն [*Pages from My Memoirs*], I, Boston 1925, pp. 188–243. Sebuh, a brigade commander in this campaign, describes in detail the battles in which the First Battalion took part as well as spectacle offered by the villages whose Armenian population had just been massacred during their march into Ottoman territory way of the district of Nordüz.

19. Papazian, *Memoirs, op. cit.*, II, pp. 291–2.

20. *Ibidem*, p. 293.

21. *Ibidem*, p. 295.

22. Zaven Der Yeghiayan, *Memoirs, op. cit.*, p. 52, letter from the Archbishop of Van to the Patriarchate, 27 September 1914. Initially, mobilization concerned all of the males up to the age of 45, but the local authorities took the initiative of reducing the upper limit to 42, and then to 36, so as not to paralyze the local economy. However, orders arrived from Istanbul to maintain the upper limit at 45.

    A-To, *The Major Events in Vasburagan, 1914–1917, op. cit.*, is the fullest Armenian source on the Van events. A-To affirms that the population resisted conscription and that Aram took it upon himself to assemble 300 young men in front of the *konak* so that they could be enrolled (*ibidem*, p. 71).

    Clarence D. Ussher, *An American Physician in Turkey*, London 2002 (2nd ed.), pp. 116–18, observes that gendarmes invested the villages in the southern part of the vilayet and took the Armenian conscripts without further ado to the recruitment center in Van; those responsible for logistics, however, were unprepared to feed or equip the recruits. A-To also notes that the proportion of Turks and Kurds who refused to perform their military service were therefore considered to be deserters was higher than among the Armenians. The Armenian conscripts of Van served on the Caucasian front (p. 117).

23. Zaven Der Yeghiayan, *Memoirs, op. cit.*, p. 52.

24. *Ibidem*, p. 53; Ussher, *An American Physician in Turkey, op. cit.*, p. 118, confirms that conscription and the requisitions touched off an "economic crisis" in the region and that all means of transport were confiscated by the authorities.

25. Zaven Der Yeghiayan, *Memoirs, op. cit.*, p. 54.

26. APC/APJ, PCI Bureau Ց 470–2, *Faits et documents*, no. 37, L'affaire de Van.

27. *Supra*, pp. 220, 225. A-To, *The Major Events in Vasburagan, 1914–1917, op. cit.*, p. 80, indicates that Naci went to Persia before war was declared at the head of several squadrons of *çetes* comprising, above all, Çerkez and Laz, as well as Kurdish tribes "known for their cruelty."

28. A-To, *The Major Events in Vasburagan, 1914–1917, op. cit.*, pp. 132–3 (Pelu), pp. 134–6 (*kaza* of Gargar, mid-February).

    This incident is presented as follows in an official brochure published in 1916: "Late in the year [1914] gendarmes were attacked by armed men in Mush and Hizan. Communications between Van and Bitlis were cut off and telegraph wires were severed" (*La Vérité sur le mouvement révolutionnaire arménien et les mesures gouvernementales*, Constantinople 1916, pp. 16–17).

29. *Ibidem*, pp. 134–6.

30. *Ibidem*, pp. 136–41.

31. *Ibidem*, pp. 141–5.

32. APC/APJ, PCI Bureau, Ջ 58, Memorandum from Vramian, representative for Van, to Talât Bey, minister of the interior, March 1915. The author states that very many women and girls were raped, forced to convert to Islam, and carried off to various areas.

    When the vali of Van, Tahsin Bey, was transferred to Erzerum and replaced by Cevdet, the newly designated vali was in Persia; he named an interim vali to conof thect affairs in his absence: Ussher, *An American Physician in Turkey, op. cit.*, p. 126.

33. APC/APJ, PCI Bureau, Ջ 58, Memorandum from Vramian, representative for Van, to Talât Bey, minister of the interior, March 1915. Vramian notes that only the miller in Akhorig, Bedros, and another artisan, Yegho, remained in the village: "they were needed."

34. *Ibidem*.

35. *Ibidem*.

36. Encrypted telegram from the vali of Erzerum, Tahsin Bey, to the Ministry of the Interior, 13 May 1915: APC/APJ, PCI Bureau, file XLIX, Ս 285, original in Ottoman Turkish, transcription in the Armenian alphabet and French translation.

37. *Ibidem*.

38. *Ibidem*.

39. A-To, *The Major Events in Vasburagan, 1914–1917, op. cit.*, pp. 146–8. Thus the CUP delegate and head of the Special Organization in the region returned from the Persian campaign with Cevdet.

40. *Ibidem*, pp. 148–50.

41. *Ibidem*, pp. 150–1.

42. APC/APJ, PCI Bureau Ց 470–2, *Faits et documents*, no. 37, L'affaire de Van; Ussher, *An American Physician in Turkey, op. cit.*, p. 126, puts the number of additional draftees at 4,000.

43. It was *Topal* Rasul who murdered Ishkhan several weeks later.

44. APC/APJ, PCI Bureau Ց 563, Report on Cevdet bey.

45. A-To, *The Major Events in Vasburagan, 1914–1917, op. cit.*, pp. 152, 372 for more details.

46. *Ibidem*, p. 155: Boghos Tutunjian, Vahan Khranian, and Mihran Der Markarian.

47. *Ibidem*, p. 155; Aguni, *op. cit.*, p. 34; Zaven Der Yeghiayan, *Memoirs, op. cit.*, p. 92; Lepsius published a 26 April 1915 telegram from the German vice-consul in Erzerum, Max Erwin Scheubner-Richter, announcing the murder of Ishkhan and the siege of the Armenian quarter; Ussher, *An American Physician in Turkey, op. cit.*, p. 127.

48. A-To, *The Major Events in Vasburagan, 1914–1917, op. cit.*, p. 156.

49. *Ibidem*, p. 158.

50. *Ibidem*. We do not know where Vramian was murdered. For more details on the murder of Vramian and Cevdet's involvement in the crime: APC/APJ, PCI Bureau Ց 561–2, accompanied by an article from the daily *La Renaissance*.

51. APC/APJ, PCI Bureau Ց 563, Report on Cevdet Bey.

52. Ussher, *An American Physician in Turkey, op. cit.*, p. 127; for a more general view, see: Grace H. Knapp, *The Tragedy of Bitlis*, London 2002 (2nd ed.), pp. 13–27.

53. A-To, *The Major Events in Vasburagan, 1914–1917, op. cit.*, p. 153.

54. *Ibidem*, p. 158.

55. Rafaël de Nogales, *Four Years Beneath the Crescent*, trad. Muna Lee, London 1926, pp. 59–60.

56. A-To, *The Major Events in Vasburagan, 1914–1917*, *op. cit.*, pp. 168–90.

57. Rafaël de Nogales, *Four Years Beneath the Crescent*, *op. cit.*, pp. 59–61. In the following weeks, Nogales took part in the siege of the Armenian quarter; in particular, the batteries of canons positioned in the citadel were under his responsibility.

58. Ussher, *An American Physician in Turkey*, *op. cit.*, p. 129.

59. *Ibidem*, p. 130.

60. *Ibidem*, p. 131.

61. *La vérité sur le mouvement révolutionnaire arménien et les mesures gouvernementales*, Constantinople 1916, pp. 17–18.

62. *Ibidem*, p. 15.

63. Zaven Der Yeghiayan, *Memoirs*, *op. cit.*, p. 68, cites a 21 November 1914 letter that he received from the primate of Mush, Nersès Kharakhanian.

64. *Ibidem*, p. 69.

65. Papazian, *Memoirs*, *op. cit.*, II, p. 303.

66. *Ibidem*, p. 304.

67. *Ibidem*, pp. 305–6. The vali's tenure in Bitlis ran from 19 March 1914 to 1 September 1915. He later served as minister of finance and then as president of the Grand Assembly of Turkey.

68. *Ibidem*, p. 320.

69. Assistant of Bahaeddin Şakir, vice-president of the Special Organization, based in Erzerum.

70. Papazian, *Memoirs*, *op. cit.*, II, pp. 322–3.

71. Zaven Der Yeghiayan, *Memoirs*, *op. cit.*, p. 71, cites a 21 November 1914 letter that he received from the primate of Mush, Nerses Kharakhanian.

72. Papazian, *Memoirs*, *op. cit.*, II, p. 325.

73. *Ibidem*, p. 326.

74. *Ibidem*, p. 327.

75. *Ibidem*, p. 327. Logistical support for the Third Army was apparently coordinated from Hnis, approximately halfway between Erzerum and Mush.

76. *Ibidem*, p. 328.

77. *Ibidem*, p. 329.

78. *Ibidem*, p. 332.

79. *Ibidem*, p. 333.

80. *Ibidem*, p. 335.

81. *Ibidem*, pp. 336–7.

82. *Ibidem*, pp. 338–9.

83. *Ibidem*, pp. 338–40.

84. *Ibidem*, p. 340; another report has it that one Mehmed Emin, the leader of a squadron of Kurdish çetes, followed Goriun to Goms and was killed there: BNu/Fonds A. Andonian, P.J.1/3, file 51, Mush-Daron, f° 4, according to information provided by Mushegh Turnian.

85. Papazian, *Memoirs*, *op. cit.*, II, p. 341.

86. *Ibidem*, p. 341.

87. BNu/ Fonds A. Andonian, P.J.1/3, file 51, Mush-Daron, f° 2, according to information provided by Mushegh Turnian.

88. Papazian, *Memoirs*, *op. cit.*, II, p. 341; another source states that most of the Kurdish leaders recruited had been wanted criminals for years and were "amnistied" for the occasion. These bands of çetes carried out "indirect massacres" that the *mutesarif* ofscribed as "acts of banditry." He never punished them, confining himself to sending gendarmes to the towns and villages in which the "çetes had not succeeded in doing what they had set out to": BNu/ Fonds A. Andonian, P.J.1/3, file 51, Mush-Daron, f° 3, according to information provided by Mushegh Turnian.

89. *Ibidem*, f° 3.

90. Papazian, *Memoirs*, *op. cit.*, II, p. 341. We estimate the height of the precipice halfway to the monastery at 150 yards.

91. *Ibidem*, p. 343.

92. *Ibidem*.

93. *Ibidem*, p. 345.

94. *Ibidem*, p. 347. While a guest of *Schwester* ("nun/nurse") Kristin, who directed Mush's German mission, Papazian met one of these officers, who mistook him for a Turk; a few days later, he made the acquaintance of the German consul in Mosul, Holstein, who " wanted information about the military situation behind the lines."

95. Zaven Der Yeghiayan, *Memoirs, op. cit.*, p. 72.

96. *La vérité sur le mouvement révolutionnaire arménien et les mesures gouvernementales, op. cit.*, pp. 16–17.

97. Papazian, *Memoirs, op. cit.*, II, p. 350.

98. *Ibidem*, pp. 351–4.

99. *Ibidem*, p. 355.

100. *Ibidem*, pp. 356–63.

101. *Ibidem*, p. 357.

102. APC/APJ, PCI Bureau, Ɜ 529–530, file no. 26, 27.

103. First Session of the Trial of the Unionists, 27 April 1919, Extract from the 5 December 1918 deposition of Vehib Pasha: *Takvim-ı Vakayi*, no. 3540, 5 May 1919, p. 7, col. 2 and the full deposition of handwritten pages: APC/APJ, PCI Bureau, Ž 171–Ž 182, 5 December 1918, in French.

104. *La vérité sur le mouvement révolutionnaire arménien et les mesures gouvernementales, op. cit.*, p. 15.

105. BNu/Fonds A. Andonian, P.J.1/3, file 51, Mush-Daron, f° 1, according to information provided by Mushegh Turnian. Sending soldiers recruited from "minorities" into the most dangerous combat zones is a practice that is still widespread in certain countries.

106. *Supra*, p. 221.

107. A-To, *The Major Events in Vasburagan, 1914–1917, op. cit.*, pp. 99–100.

108. Zürcher, "Ottoman Labour Battalions in World War I," in H.-L. Kieser and D. J. Schaller (ed.), *Der Völkermord an den Armeniern und die Shoah*, Zürich 2002, pp. 190–2.

109. *Ibidem*, p. 187.

110. *Ibidem*, p. 192.

111. BNu/Fonds A. Andonian, P.J.1/3, file 51, Mush-Daron, f° 1.

112. A-To, *The Major Events in Vasburagan, 1914–1917, op. cit.*, p. 101.

113. Taner Akçam, *İnsan Hakları ve Ermeni Sorunu. İttihat ve Terakki'den Kurtuluş Savaşına*, Ankara 1999, p. 243, in Zürcher, "Ottoman Labour Battalions in World War I," *art. cit.*, p. 187, n. 2.

114. A-To, *The Major Events in Vasburagan, 1914–1917, op. cit.*, p. 78.

115. BNu/Fonds A. Andonian, P.J.1/3, file 51, Mush-Daron, f° 2; Papazian, *Memoirs, op. cit.*, II, pp. 304, 307.

116. Vahakn Dadrian, "The Secret Young-Turk Ittihadist Conference and the Decision for the World War I Genocide of the Armenians," in *Holocaust and Genocide Studies*, 7, 2 (fall 1993).

117. "Recueil de témoignages sur l'extermination des amele tabouri ou bataillons de soldats-ouvriers de l'armée ottomane pendant la Première Guerre mondiale," in *RHAC* I (1995).

118. Zürcher, "Ottoman Labour Battalions in World War I," *art. cit.*, p. 187.

119. HHSA, PA XL 272, Constantinople, 23 February 1915, in Donald Bloxham, "Power Politics, Prejudice, Protest and Propaganda: a Reassessment of the German Role in the Armenian Genocide of WWI," in H.L. Kieser and D. J. Schaller (ed.), *Der Völkermord an den Armeniern und die Shoah*, Zürich 2002, p. 220, n. 47.

120. A-To, *The Major Events in Vasburagan, 1914–1917, op. cit.*, pp. 107–8, 113–14.

8   Putting the Plan into Practice and the "Temporary Deportation Law"

1. Arthur Beylerian, *Les grandes puissances, l'Empire ottoman et les Arméniens dans les archives françaises (1914–1918)*, Paris 1983, pp. XXIX–XXX, publish the French translation of the "Ten commandments," from FO 371/ 4172/31307; Vahakn Dadrian, "The Secret Young-Turk Ittihadist Conference and the Decision for the World War I Genocide of the Armenians," *Diary of Political and Military Sociology* 22/1 (summer 1994), pp. 173–201.

2. French translation of this document: SHAT, Service historique de la Marine, Service de Renseignements de la Marine, Turquie, 1BB7 231, doc. no. 508, Constantinople, 27 March 1919, Armenian translation in *Verchin Lur,* 25 March 1919.

3. *Ibidem,* the *Yeni Gazetta* from 26 March.

4. Dadrian, "The Secret Young-Turk Ittihadist Conference," *art. cit.,* p. 175.

5. See *supra,* p. 171; the article in *Iktam* is reprinted in Teotig, Յուշարձան Նահատակ Մտաւորականութեան [*Monument to the Martyred Intellectuals*], Constantinople 1919, pp. 114–15.

6. Taner Akçam, *Armenien und der Völkermord,* Hamburg 1996, p. 43; Akçam, *From Empire to Republic, op. cit.,* pp. 166–7.

7. Arif Cemil, *The Special Organization, op. cit., Vakıt/Haratch* 88.

8. Jay Winter, "Under Cover of War: the Armenian Genocide in the context of Total War," in Jay Winter (ed.), *America and the Armenian Genocide of 1915,* Cambridge 2003, p. 39.

9. Efraim Karsh & Inari Karsh, *Empires of the Sand, The Struggle for Mastery in the Middle East, 1789–1923,* Cambridge 2001, pp. 142–6, provides a good description of the context in which this battle occurred.

10. Winter, "Under Cover of War: the Armenian Genocide," *art. cit.,* p. 41; Bloxham, "The Beginning of the Armenian Catastrophe," *art. cit.,* p. 106, also mentions this escalation in the means used to wage war.

11. Winter, "Under Cover of War: the Armenian Genocide," *art. cit.,* p. 42.

12. First session of the trial of the Cabinet members, 3 June 1919 (3 Haziran 1335): *Takvim-ı Vakayi,* no. 3571, 11 June 1919, p. 141.

13. Dadrian, *Histoire du Génocide, op. cit.,* p. 362 shows that news of the law was disseminated by the Istanbul press even before the Council of Ministers adopted it.

14. *Takvim-ı Vakayi,* no. 3586, 21 June 1919.

15. Haigazn K. Kazarian, Ցեղասպան Թուրքը [*The Genocidal Turk*], Beirut 1968, who was an agent of the British intelligence service in Istanbul in 1919–20, affirms that he had access to this document in the archives of the Ottoman Ministry of the Navy, where his division of the intelligence service had its headquarters (*ibidem,* pp. 27–8). The reference is perhaps to the terms of the 10 June 1915 directive that created committees charged with "protecting" "abandoned property"; the text of the directive was published rather late in the day, in *Askeri Tarih Belgeleri Dergisi,* no. 81 (December 1982), doc. 1832.

16. See *supra,* p. 204.

17. See *infra,* Part 6 of the present work.

18. *La vérité sur le mouvement révolutionnaire arménien et les mesures gouvernementales, op. cit.,* p. 15.

19. First Session of the Trial of the Cabinet members, 3 June 1919 (3 Haziran 1335): *Takvim-ı Vakayi,* no. 3571, 11 June 1919, p. 141.

20. Encrypted telegram from the vali of Erzerum, Tahsin bey, to the Ministry of Interior, 13 May 1915: APC/APJ, PCI Bureau, file XLIX, U 285, original in Ottoman Turkish, transcription in the Armenian alphabet and French translation.

21. *Ibidem.*

22. *Supra,* p. 231. Hakkı died of typhus on 12 February and was replaced by a classmate of Enver's, Mahmud Kâmil (Sanders, *Cinq ans ..., op. cit.,* p. 61).

23. Encrypted telegram from the vali of Erzerum, Tahsin bey, to the Ministry of Interior, 13 May 1915: APC/APJ, PCI Bureau, file XLIX, U 285, *doc. cit.*

24. *Ibidem.*

25. *Ibidem.*

26. Hans-Lukas Kieser, "Dr Mehmed Reshid (1873–1919): A Political Doctor," in H.-L. Kieser and D. J. Schaller (ed.), *Der Völkermord an den Armeniern und die Shoah,* Zürich 2002, pp. 245–80, especially p. 261.

27. Verdict in the trial of the responsible secretaries and delegates of the CUP, handed down by the court-martial of Constantinople, 8 January 1920: *Takvim-ı Vakayi,* no. 3772, February 1920, p. 2, col. 2, p. 3, col. 1, pp. 53–66.

28. *Ibidem.*

29. The murder of the two *kaymakams* was mentioned at the first session of the trial of the Unionists, 27 April 1919: *Takvim-ı Vakayi*, no. 3540, 5 May 1919, p. 8, col. 1, lines 15–20; we also have, on this subject, the report of a committee of inquiry into the exactions committed by Dr. Reşid: APC/APJ, PCI Bureau, , Ձ 119 (original ottoman) and Ձ 465 (transcription).

30. *Supra*, p. 214, n. 52.

31. *Supra*, p. 144.

32. Krieger, *op. cit.*, p. 30.

33. Aguni, *op. cit.*, p. 25.

34. About Information Bureau, see *supra*, introduction.

35. Mevlanzâde Rifat, Ouմանեան Յեղափոխութեան մութ ծալքերը [*Les dessous obscurs de la révolution ottomane*], Armenian translation of the ottoman edition, Aleppo 1929 (*Türkiye Inkilabinin iş yüzür*), Beirut 1968.

36. *La Renaissance*, no. 7, 15 December 1918, p. 1, and *Ariamard*, 18 December 1918, p. 2, reports the police search and the nature of the confiscated documents.

37. Krieger, *op. cit.*, pp. 76–7, notes that Aguni gives an account of only one meeting, whereas Mevlanzâde Rifat, who provides lengthier extracts, apparently conflates the minutes of a number of different meetings.

38. Aguni, *op. cit.*, p. 26.

39. *Ibidem*, pp. 26–9.

40. Stepan Astourian, "The Armenian Genocide: An Interpretation," *The History Teacher*, 23/2 (February 1990), pp. 138–40, n. 64–5, 122–3. The author points to factors indicating that CUP officials such as Sabancalı Hakkı and Hüsrev Sâmi were also opposed to the "deportations" (p. 141, n. 72–3).

41. Letter from the catholicos Sahag to the patriarch Zaven, 21 April 1915: J. Lepsius (ed.), *Archives du génocide des Arméniens*, Paris 1986, doc. 34, pp. 79–84; Aguni, *op. cit.*, p. 47.

42. Kévorkian & Paboudjian, *Les Arméniens dans l'Empire ottoman, op. cit.*, p. 313. By 20 April, the deportation of the Armenians of Zeitun and the surrounding area had been completed.

43. As we shall see, they were later set marching toward Der Zor and were all killed.

44. *Infra*, pp. 585–6.

45. *Infra*, pp. 431–2.

46. Zaven Der Yeghiayan, *Memoirs, op. cit.*, p. 84.

47. *Ibidem*, p. 85.

48. *Ibidem*, p. 86, extract from his Diary. The patriarch states that Zohrab received the same proposition; it was agreed that the Armenian deputies would discuss the matter with the government in order to obtain its authorization.

49. J. Lepsius (ed.), *Deutschland und Armenien*, Berlin-Potsdam 1919, pp. 51–2, doc. 31, report of Mordtmann, Constantinople, 26 April 1915. Moreover, the general denied that the Armenians had opened fire on their Turkish comrades and that they had always served behind the lines.

50. Zaven Der Yeghiayan, *Memoirs, op. cit.*, p. 93. After being appointed Ottoman representative to The Hague on 18 March, he declined to leave Turkey.

51. *Ibidem*.

52. *Ibidem*, p. 93.

53. *Ibidem*, pp. 94–5.

54. *Ibidem*, pp. 95–6.

55. *Ibidem*, p. 86.

56. Téotig, *Monument to the martyred intellectuals, op. cit.*, pp. 20–70, gives biographical information on 143 of those arrested in Constantinople and executed, and of another 618 people apprehended and executed in the provinces, but does not discuss those who survived (pp. 71–111).

57. Zohrab, *Complete works, op. cit.*, IV, Diary, 25 April 1915, pp. 431–2.

58. APC/APJ, PCI Bureau, Յ 202, file no. 31/1–2, Turks Responsible for the Armenian Atrocities.

59. İsmail Canbolat (1880–1926): see *infra*, p. 821, n. 162; Born in Kosovo, of Circasian origin, graduate from *Harbiye*, deputy from Constantinople, Canbolat was a member of the Ittihadist Central Committee; he was responsible for deporting Armenians from the provinces living in Constantinople and for the murder of those imprisoned in Çankırı: APC/APJ, PCI Bureau, file no. 13/1, Յ 144 and Ֆ 279–80 (in English).

60. See *supra*, p. 203, n. 88.
61. Born in Smyrna, a jurist by profession, Murad Bey became, after 1908, police chief in Salonika, and then Bedri Bey's assistant in Constantinople; he was one of the organizers of the roundup of 24 April: APC/APJ, PCI Bureau, file 3/1, Ց 822.
62. Odian, *The cursed years, op. cit., Jamanag*, no. 7.
63. *Ibidem*, no. 8.
64. Zaven Der Yeghiayan, *Memoirs, op. cit.*, p. 98.
65. *Ibidem*, p. 99.
66. *Ibidem*, p. 100.
67. *Supra*, pp. 30–2.
68. The present synthesis is based on Piuzant Bozajian: Teotig, *Monument to the martyred intellectuals, op. cit.*, pp. 113–25. Dr. Boghosian, "Պատմութեան համար Ճշդում մը [A Correction for History]," in *Baykar*, 16 July 1927.
69. Dr. Boghosian, "Իսմայիլ Ճանպոլաթի Իտէալը [İsmail Canbolat's Ideal]," in *Arev*, no. 2267, 3 August 1926, p. 1.
70. Zohrab, *Complete works, op. cit.*, IV, Diary, 1 May 1915, p. 432.
71. *Ibidem*, IV, Diary, 9 May 1915, p. 432.
72. Zaven Der Yeghiayan, *Memoirs, op. cit.*, p. 97.
73. Andonian, *Chronological notes, 1914–1916*, ms. cit., f° 36.
74. A complete record of the proceedings is given by one of the two defendants ultimately amnestied by the court: Hmayag Aramiants, Դէպի Կախաղան [*Towards the Gallows*], II, Constantinople 1918, pp. 41–2.
75. Cf. *supra*, p. 174, n. 55.
76. Aramiants, *Towards the gallows, op. cit.*, pp. 43–4.
77. *Ibidem*, pp. 44–6.
78. *Ibidem*, p. 276; Hmayag Aramiants, Անկախ Հայաստան [*Independent Armenia*], III, Constantinople 1919, pp. 30–2.
79. *Ibidem*, pp. 37–8.
80. *Ibidem*, pp. 39–40.
81. "Պոլսոյ Կախաղանները [The Gallows of Constantinople]," *Hnchak*, no. 3, August 1915, p. 1; Andonian, *Chronological notes, 1914–1916*, ms. cit., Armenian translation of the announcement of the Constantinople military high command, on two sheets glued to f° 49.
82. Andonian, *Chronological notes, 1914–1916*, ms. cit., ff. 38–46, gives lengthy extracts from this series of articles; Aguni, *op. cit.*, p. 30, also mentions these articles.
83. *Ibidem*, pp. 39–40.
84. Hmayag Aramiants, Վերածնունդի Երկունքը [*The Cruel Pain of the Renaissance*], I, Constantinople, 1918, p. 51.
85. Sapah-Gulian, *The Responsibles, op. cit.*, pp. 267–8. We have not been able to obtain information on Azuri.
86. *La vérité sur le mouvement révolutionnaire arménien et les mesures gouvernementales, op. cit.*, p. 19.
87. Eighth session of the trial of Yozgat: *Jamanag*, 22 February 1919, p. 4, col. 1–4.
88. *Ibidem*.
89. *La vérité sur le mouvement révolutionnaire arménien et les mesures gouvernementales, op. cit.*, p. 17.
90. APC/APJ, PCI Bureau, Մ 451, encrypted telegram from the commandant by interim of the 15th division, the Colonel Şahabeddin, in Kayseri, to the commandant by interim of the 5th Army, in Angora, Halil Recayi Bey, 2 June 1915 [2 Haziran 1331], no. 945/1/2 (Ց 58, in French).
91. APC/APJ, PCI Bureau Մ 451, encrypted telegram from the commandant by interim of the 5th Army, in Angora, Halil Recayi Bey, to the Ministry of the War, 3 June 1915 [3 Haziran 1331].
92. APC/APJ, PCI Bureau Մ 452, encrypted telegram from the commandant by interim of the 15th division, the Colonel Şahabeddin, in Kayseri, to the commandant by interim of the 5th Army, in Angora, Halil Recayi Bey, 9 June 1915 [9 Haziran 1331].
93. *Ibidem*.
94. APC/APJ, PCI Bureau Մ 456, encrypted telegram from the commandant by interim of the 5th Army, in Angora, Halil Recayi Bey, to the Ministry of the War, 25 June 1915.
95. APC/APJ, PCI Bureau, Մ 757, no. 48, p. 43.

96. Teotig, *Monument to the martyred intellectuals*, *op. cit.*, pp. 110.
97. Յուշամատեան Նուիրուած Սոցեալ Դեմոկրատ Հնչակեան Կուսակցութեան Քառասնամեակին [*Book of Memory for the Fortieth Anniversary of the Founding of the Social Democratic Hnchak Party*], Paris 1930, pp. 234–5.
98. *Ibidem*, p. 238.
99. *La vérité sur le mouvement révolutionnaire arménien et les mesures gouvernementales*, *op. cit.*, pp. 18_19.
100. Andonian, *Chronological notes, 1914–1916*, ms. *cit.*, f° 37.

Part IV In the Vortex of the War: The First Phase of the Genocide

1 The Armenian Population of the Empire on the Eve of the War: The Demographic Issue

1. Ministère des Affaires étrangères, *Livre jaune, documents diplomatiques, 1875–1877*, Paris 1877, p. 135, annexe I au 7ᵉ protocole de la Conférence de Constantinople, séance du 11 janvier 1877. Let us note, in connection with the eyalet of *Ermenistan*, that the name "Armenia" has, in the re-editions of seventeenth-century and eighteenth-century Turkish authors published in the past few decades, quite simply become "Eastern Anatolia." This holds, notably, for the second edition of the work of the seventeenth-century author Kâtip Çelebi (*Hayati ve eserleri hakkinda incelemeler*, Ankara 1957, p. 127) in which the title of Chapter 41, "About the Land of Armenia," has been replaced by "Eastern Anatolia (cf. the first edition, Constantinople, 1732, p. 227). For more detail, see A. Papazyan, "Քյաթիբ Չելեպիի "Ճիհան–Նուման Որպես Աղբյուր Հայաստանի Պատմական Աշխարհագրության [The "Jihan–Numa" of Kâtip Çelebi of the Geographical History of Armenia]," *Badma–Panasiragan Hantes* 3 (1983), pp. 229–32. For more detail on the administrative subdivisions of the Ottoman Empire, see the excellent article by K. Patalyan, "Վանի Նահանգը 1840–ական–1914 թթ. [The Province of Van in the Years 1840–1914]," *Panper Erevani Hamalsarani* 3 (1986), pp. 13–20 which makes systematic use of the Ottoman *Salname*.
2. *La Turquie d'Asie*, 4 vol., Paris 1890–1895, in the introduction to vol. 1.
3. *Armenia, the Armenians and the Treaties*, London 1891, pp. 8–10.
4. *Lettres sur la Turquie*, Paris 1853.
5. *Ibidem*, pp. 20–7. Ubicini also puts Constantinople's Armenian population at 222,000 in 1844, of whom 17,000 he says were Catholics, making a total population of 866,000 inhabitants.
6. Salaheddin Bey, *La Turquie à l'exposition universelle de 1867*, Paris 1867, pp. 214–17.
7. *Projet de règlement organique pour l'Arménie turque*, Constantinople 1878, pp. 18–23; Rolin-Jaequemyns, *op. cit.*, pp. 8–10; the major Ahmed Cevad, later grand vizier of the empire, also says that it counted 3 million Armenians in 1873 (cf. *Malûmat-i el-Kâfiyé fi Memalik-i el-Osmaniye*, Istanbul 1298/1873, p. 85, cited by A. Beylérian, *op. cit.*, p. XXII.
8. Karpat, *op. cit.*, pp. 122–46.
9. This census was carried out from April 1878 to late 1879 by Archbishop Karekin Srvantsdiants at the request of Patriarch Nerses Varzhabedian. The Armenian census takers, however, were unable to travel to certain regions that the Kurds had rendered unsafe. On the basis of these statistics, Srvantsdiants published two volumes in Constantinople in 1879 (*Toros Aghpar*). The censuses of Pasın, Tercan, Kemah, Bayazid, Alaşkert, Ispir, Keskin, and Erzerum, as well as those of their dioceses, were left in manuscript form in the archives; they were only recently published by Emma Gostantyan, "Արևմտյան Հայաստանի Հայաբնակ Վայրերի Վերաբերյալ Գ. Սրվանձտյանցի Կազմած Վիճակագրություններից [K. Srvantsdiants's Population Statistics on the Regions Inhabited by Armenians]," *Panper Hayastani Arkhivneri* 45/2 (1976), pp. 62–93 (see also *Réponse au mémoire de la Sublime Porte*, Constantinople 1919, p. 43); *Ararat* 9 (1914), p. 808 sq. Minutes of the session of Armenian National Chamber, 12 December 1908 (*Adenakrutiun*, *op. cit.*, p. 152) also show us that Bishop Srvantsdiants and two assistants were charged with carrying out this census, which he himself conducted in the field with help from the diocesan administrations.

10. These numbers summarize information available in the four volumes of *La Turquie d'Asie*, *op. cit.* *Le Livre jaune français*, *op. cit.*, uses Cuinet's figures, but adds: "Generally speaking, the preceding figures must be treated with caution, since the statistical information we have on Asia Minor is, as is well known, most inadequate" (pp. 1–8 for the commentary).

11. Karpat, *op. cit.*, p. 25; Salaheddin bey, *op. cit.*, pp. 210–14.

12. Léart, *op. cit.*, pp. 10–11 and annexe 1, p. 64 (extrait du *Salname de 1298 [1882]*, pp. 413–14).

13. In the census of 1881/1882–93: Karpat, *op. cit.*, pp. 126, 152.

14. Kévorkian & Paboudjian, *Les Arméniens dans l'Empire ottoman*, *op. cit.*, p. 75.

15. Karpat, *op. cit.*, p. 124.

16. *Ibidem*, p. 126.

17. The photographic documents of the period that we have published in Kévorkian & Paboudjian, *Les Arméniens dans l'Empire ottoman*, *op. cit.*, in the chapter on the vilayet of Angora, reveal a great deal about the importance of the village and the number of households it contained.

18. To verify this, it is enough to compare the figures in the censuses published by Karpat, *op. cit.*, pp. 122–46 (statistiques 1881/2–1893) and p. 152 ff.

19. *Ibidem*, pp. 196–7 and footnote.

20. *Ibidem*, pp. 162–7; *Ararat* 1–2 (1914), pp. 49 ,132.

21. Léart, *op. cit.*, pp. 60–1; *Réponse au mémoire de la Sublime Porte*, *op. cit.*, pp. 44–5.

22. *Supra*, pp. 158–9.

23. Papazian, *Memoirs*, *op. cit.*, II, p. 232.

24. Census available in the archives of the Bibliothèque Nubar: APC, DOR 3/1–3/4.

25. Papazian, *Memoirs*, *op. cit.*, II, p. 231.

26. *Ibidem*, p. 233.

27. Letter accompanying the census: Bibliothèque Nubar, APC, DOR 3/1–3/4.

28. We published this work in 1992: Kévorkian & Paboudjian, *Les Arméniens dans l'Empire ottoman*, *op. cit.*, p. 75. To exploit this census, we had to overcome the handicap represented by the inadequacy or the total lack of figures for certain regions. Since the problem was confined to the vilayet of Van and certain areas in western Anatolia, we have chosen to fill in these lacunae, wherever possible, with figures provided by the dioceses and published in various sources, so as to arrive at globally significant results. The number of schools and schoolchildren and churches and monasteries has been established on the basis of the official statistics of 1913/1914 or earlier documents published by the Patriarchate.

29. A. Hamparian, "Արեւմտահայերի Թուազանակի Հարցի Շուրջ [On the Question of the Number of Western Armenians]," *Panper Erevani Hamalsarani* 2 (1969), pp. 98–113.

30. *Ibidem*.

31. *Takvim-ı Vakayi*, no. 3540, p. 7, col. 1, published the encrypted telegram of 15 September 1915 sent by the vali, Dr. Mehmed Reşid, to the Ministry of the Interior; it indicates that the 120,000 Armenians of the vilayet have been deported.

32. APC/BNu, DOR 3/2, f° 47 and Karpat, *op. cit.*, p. 176.

33. *Bulletin trimestriel de statistique*, 6e année, Constantinople, X–XII (1332/1916), pp. 30–1.

34. APC/BNu, DOR 3/1–3/3, for details concerning the figures listed in the tables below, see Kévorkian & Paboudjian, *Les Arméniens dans l'Empire ottoman*, *op. cit.* Statistics on the schools that are marked with an asterisk have been drawn from an official publication of the Patriarchate dating from 1901/1902. Where the number of churches and monasteries was lacking, we have made use of the census conducted by the Patriarchate in 1912/1913 at the request of the Ministry of Justice and Religions. We have preferred to use the work of Kemal Karpat rather than Justin McCarty, *Muslim and Minorities: The Population of Ottoman Anatolia and the End of Empire* (New York and London 1983) in comparing or completing some of the figures that we publish here.

2   The Ottoman Armenians' Socio-Economic Situation on the Eve of the War

1. *Bulletin trimestriel de statistiques*, 2e année, Constantinople 1913.

2. J. P. Mahé, "Structures sociales et vocabulaire de la parenté en arménien contemporain," *REArm* 18 (1984), pp. 339–40.

3. J. D. Tholozan, *Histoire de la peste bubonique au Caucase, en Arménie et en Anatolie*, Paris 1876.

2.1 The Eradication of the Armenian Population in the Provinces of the Ottoman Empire: Reasons for a Regional Approach

1. The indictment, drawn up on 12 April 1919, was presented to the court-martial on 27 April 1919, along with a long series of letters and other documents substantiating the charges: *Takvim-ı Vakayi*, no. 3540, 5 May 1919, p. 6.
2. APC/APJ, The Patriarchate's Constantinople Information Bureau (hereinafter abbreviated: PCI Bureau), Ց 152 and Գ 281 (in English), doc. no. 14/1, file on Midhat Şükrü Bey.
3. The indictment presented to the court-martial on 27 April 1919, along with other documents substantiating the charges: *Takvim-ı Vakayi*, no. 3540, 5 May 1919, p. 6.
4. *Ibidem.*
5. The long report by Captain Fazıl, a judge at the court-martial of Malatia during the war and a local notable, as well as that of General Vehib Pasha, comprise two of the main Turkish accounts. Fazıl's report was completed on 30 November 1918 and later sent by courier to the grand vizier, the interior and justice ministries, the president of the Senate, and "various interested parties." It clearly indicates how orders were transmitted from Constantinople APC/APJ, PCI Bureau, file XXIII, Ց 432–64, copy in Ottoman Turkish and English translation probably made by the Information Bureau.
6. APC/APJ, PCI Bureau, Ձ 183–5, documents transmitted to the court-martial by the authorities in Konya, certified on 27 March 1919 by the department of the Ministry of the Interior; response of 9 February 1919 from Zami Bey, the vali of Angora, to the encrypted telegram of 2 February 1919 from the president of the court-martial in Constantinople, confirming that certified copies of documents and telegrams were posted to him the same day.

3 Deportations and Massacres in the Vilayet of Erzerum

1. L. von Sanders, *op. cit.*, p. 61. The German vice-consul in Erzerum, Max Erwin von Scheubner-Richter, informed him of the state of the troops. BNu/Fonds A. Andonian, P.J.1/3, file 59, Erzerum, f° 58, report by Boghos Vartanian, from Erzerum, 5 august 1916, indicates that the Armenian soldiers represented a mere 10% of the conscripts serving in combat units, but constituted 100% of the battalions of worker–soldiers.
2. *Ibidem*, pp. 127–8; APC/APJ, PCI Bureau, Ց 165–6, file of the General Mahmud Kâmil, born in Aleppo, of Arab origin.
3. Tahsin Bey held his post until 14 July 1916.
4. *Supra*, pp. 222–3.
5. *Supra*, pp. 220 and 221.
6. Letter from Hans von Wangenheim to Chancellor Bethmann Hollweg, Pera, 30 December 1914: Joannes Lepsius (ed.), *Archives du génocide des Arméniens*, Paris 1986, doc. 14, pp. 68–9. A hospital with a capacity of 350 to 400 beds was nevertheless created by the Armenian authorities in Erzerum to provide care for the soldiers: BNu/ Fonds A. Andonian, P.J.1/3, file 59, Erzerum, f° 63v°, report by Boghos Vartanian, from Erzerum, 5 August 1916.
7. *Ibidem*, p. 69. Localities in the Russian zones occupied in the early stages of the conflict were also sacked: the church in Olti, for example, was systematically demolished as soon as it was occupied BNu/Fonds A. Andonian, P.J.1/3, file 59, Erzerum, ff. 39–45, report by Rupen Toroyan, from Erzerum, 5 February 1917, f° 39.
8. *Ibidem*, f° 39v°: this happened, for example, in Mansur, where the church was converted into a lumberyard, or in the village of Odzni, where Rupen Toroyan's regiment took up quarters after expelling the villagers: *ibidem*, f° 41.
9. Yervant Odian, *The Accursed Years*, *op. cit.*, Zhamanag no. 7.
10. *Ibidem*, no. 48. Karekin *vartabed* was not in Konya when Enver traveled through the city on his way back from the Caucasus: he excused himself for his absence in a polite note that the minister of war answered.

11. BNu, Fonds A. Andonian, P.J.1/3, file 59, Erzerum, ff. 39–45, report by Rupen Toroyan, from Erzerum, 5 February 1917, f° 39; BNu/Fonds Andonian, P.J.1/3, file 59, Erzerum, f° 61v°, report by Boghos Vartanian, from Erzerum, 5 August 1916, says that Enver arrived in Erzerum one evening in mid-January, defeated and silent, spending the night there before setting out for the capital.

12. Aguni, *History of the Massacre of one Million Armenians, op. cit.*, p. 139.

13. André Autheman, *La Banque impériale ottomane*, Paris 1996, p. 235; Aguni, *History of the Massacre of one Million Armenians, op. cit.*, p. 138.

14. Hilmar Kaiser, "'A Scene from the Inferno,' The Armenians of Erzerum and the Genocide, 1915–1916," in H. L. Kieser and D. J. Schaller (eds.), *Der Völkermord an den Armeniern und die Shoah*, Zürich 2002, p. 130–1.

15. BNu/Fonds A. Andonian, P.J.1/3, file 59, Erzerum, ff. 35–6, report by Constantin Trianfidili, and written down by Kr[ikor] Ghamarian, from Erzerum, 16 January 1917.

16. See the examples that we have given, *supra*, p. 246.

17. BNu/Fonds A. Andonian, P.J.1/3, file 59, Erzerum, f° 3v°, report by Alphonse Arakelian, "Armenian deported from Erzerum, an eyewitness to most of the events described in the narrative," Alep, 24 February 1919.

18. See *supra*, p. 242.

19. Zaven Der Yeghiayan, *Memoirs, op. cit.*, p. 83.

20. BNu/Fonds A. Andonian, P.J.1/3, file 59, Erzerum, f° 35, report by Constantin Trianfidili, and written down by Kr[ikor] Ghamarian, from Erzerum, 16 January 1917. It was later learned that these peasants were massacred in the vicinity of Malatia, where most of the slaughterhouses maintained by the Special Organization were located; Kaiser, "'A Scene from the Inferno'," *art. cit.*, p. 134, cites a 14 May dispatch from vice-consul Scheubner that states that these deportees were bound for Mamahatun.

21. *Ibidem*.

22. *Ibidem*, f° 36.

23. BNu/Fonds Andonian, P.J.1/3, file 59, Erzerum, f° 19, report by Kh. Oskanian, Sarıkamiş, 3 November 1916; APC/APJ, PCI Bureau, ᕱ 348–9, *Sur le chemin du calvaire: Erzerum*; Aguni, *History of the Massacre of one Million Armenians, op. cit.*, p. 139; Kaiser, "A Scene from the Inferno," *art. cit.*, p. 133, exploits above all the dispatches of the German vice-consul to the German ambassador in Istanbul.

24. *Ibidem*, p. 134, dispatch from Scheubner to embassy, 9 May 1915.

25. Aguni, *History of the Massacre of one Million Armenians, op. cit.*, p. 139; Kh. Oskanian, arrested in Trebizond, was himself imprisoned along with Vartazar Dakesian, Hampartsum Balasanian, Khachig Ghugasian, a former activist from Trebizond, and Archag Zelpichigian: BNu/Fonds A. Andonian, P.J.1/3, file 59, Erzerum, f° 19.

26. APC/APJ, PCI Bureau, Ʊ 576, encrypted telegram no. 5 of 21 April 1915 from Erzerum, from the head of the Special Organization, Bahaeddin Şakir, to the vali of Mamuret ul-Aziz, Sabit Bey, for transmission to the delegate of the CUP on 21 April 1915, encrypted, with the decoded version: *Takvim-ı Vakayi* no. 3540, p. 6, col. 1–2, and no. 3771, p. 48, col. 1.

27. APC/APJ, PCI Bureau, Ʒ 775, doc. no. 14 (in English), ᕱ 347 (in French) and Ե 89, Report about facts to prove the Culpability of Cemal Bey in the Deportation of Armenians of Erzerum and Dercan; Kaiser, "A Scene from the Inferno," *art. cit.*, pp. 141–2, brings out Hulusi's role in the killing fields of Mamahatun and Kemah.

28. *Ibidem*, p. 134.

29. BNu/Fonds Andonian, P.J.1/3, file 59, Erzerum, f° 62, report by Boghos Vartanian, from Erzerum, 5 August 1916.

30. *Takvim-ı Vakayi* no. 3540, p. 6, col. 1–2 (*cf.* n. 26).

31. Encrypted telegram from the vali of Erzerum, Tahsin bey, to minister of the Interior, 13 May 1915: APC/APJ, PCI Bureau, file XLIX, Ʊ 285, original in Ottoman Turkish, transcription in the Armenian alphabet and French translation.

32. See *supra*, pp. 231–2.

33. BOA, DH. şfr no. 53/93, telegram from Talât to the vilayets of Van, Erzerum, and Bitlis, 23 May 1915: *Osmanli Belgelerinde Ermeniler (1915–1920)*, T.C. Başbakanlik Devlet Arşivleri Genel Müdürlüğü, Osmanli Arşivi Daire Başkanliği, *Armenians in Ottoman Documents (1915–1920)*, no. 25, Ankara 1995, pp. 36–7.

34. Aguni, *History of the Massacre of one Million Armenians, op. cit.*, p. 134.

35. BOA, Meclis-i Vükelâ Mazbatası, 198/163, the Cabinet's deportation decision of 13 May 1915: *Armenians in Ottoman Documents (1915–1920), op. cit.*, pp. 33–5.

36. See *supra*, p. 204, n. 93.

37. BOA, Meclis-i Vükelâ Mazbatası, 198/163, the cabinet's deportation decision of 13 May 1915: *Armenians in Ottoman Documents (1915–1920), op. cit.*, pp. 33–5.

38. BOA, DH. şfr no. 53/89, 23 May 1915 circular from the Ministry of the Post and Telegraph Office: *Armenians in Ottoman Documents (1915–1920), op. cit.*

39. Kaiser, "'A Scene from the Inferno'," art. cit., p. 137, cites two letters from Mordtmann and Wangenheim to the vice-consul in Erzerum, 29 and 30 May 1915.

40. BNu/Fonds Andonian, P.J.1/3, file 59, Erzerum, ff. 64–7, report by Boghos Vartanian, from Erzerum, 5 August 1916.

41. Kaiser, "'A Scene from the Inferno'," *art. cit.*, p. 139, dépêche à l'ambassade, 22 June 1915. Süleyman Nuran Pasha, a *dönme* physician born in Salonika and a member of the Ittihad's General Council, was at the time officially director of the military health services of the Third Army; it is probable, however, that he was also in Erzerum to assist Dr. Bahaeddin Şakir. He was, moreover, considered responsible for executing Armenian army doctors and for poisoning civilian populations in tests involving microbes carried out in the regions of Erzerum, Sıvas, and Erzincan: APC/APJ, PCI Bureau, Ց 154–6, file of Süleyman Nuran Pasha.

42. *Ibidem*, p. 139 and n. 21. BNu/Fonds Andonian, P.J.1/3, file 59, Erzerum, ff. 56–70 and 78–91, report by Boghos Vartanian, from Erzerum, 5 August 1916, f° 65 v°: the leading families received the order to get ready to leave on 28 May.

43. BNu/Fonds Andonian, P.J.1/3, file 59, Erzerum, ff. 9–17, report by Shushanig M. Dikranian, *Les premiers exilés partis d'Erzerum*; BNu/Fonds Andonian, P.J.1/3, file 59, Erzerum, ff. 52–5, report by Adelina Mazmanian.

44. According to Scheubner-Richter, there were 15 gendarmes and 500 deportees in the convoy: Kaiser, "'A Scene from the Inferno'," art. cit., p. 139. A survivor from the fifth convoy, Armenag Madatian, who left Erzerum early in July, gives an erroneous date of departure, 14 June: APC/APJ, PCI Bureau, Ձ 107 APJ, doc. no. 56.

45. Report by Shushanig M. Dikranian, *doc. cit.*, f° 9v°.

46. Report by Shushanig M. Dikranian, *doc. cit.*, f° 10; report by Adelina Mazmanian, *doc. cit.*, f° 52: proposals of marriage and conversion naturally followed, but were rejected.

47. APC/APJ, PCI Bureau, Ֆ 348–9, *Sur le chemin du calvaire: Erzerum*, states that one of the leaders of çetes in the vilayet was Kürd Ziya Beg, a relative of a parliamentary deputy from Erzerum, Seyfullah.

48. APC/APJ, PCI Bureau, Ի 218–19, those responsible for the deportations and massacres in the region of Erzerum.

49. Report by Adelina Mazmanian, *doc. cit*, f° 53. The massacre of Şoğ is also described by a witness born in Kiği, who states that heads of family were murdered by çetes under the command of Yazilci Zâde Husni Bey: APC/APJ, PCI Bureau, Է 351–6, report in English on the massacres in the region of Erzerum.

50. *Ibidem*.

51. Report by Shushanig M. Dikranian, *doc. cit.*, ff. 10–11.

52. *Ibidem*.

53. *Ibidem*, f° 12v°.

54. Report by Adelina Mazmanian, *doc. cit*, f° 55.

55. Report by Shushanig M. Dikranian, *doc. cit.*, f° 13.

56. *Ibidem*, f° 12v°–13. Others Armenian sources make brief reference to the fate of this convoy and what happened to surviving members of it in Harput: APC/APJ, PCI Bureau, Է 358–60, report in English on the massacres in the region of Erzerum, Ց 723–6, *Faits et documents*, doc. no. 29, *Les déportations des Arméniens d'Erzerum*; APC/APJ, PCI Bureau, Ֆ 348–9, *Sur le chemin du calvaire: Erzerum*; BNu/Fonds A. Andonian, P.J.1/3, file 59, Erzerum, f° 3, report by Alphonse Arakelian, from Erzerum, Aleppo, 24 February 1919.

57. The author of the study of the Banque Ottomane notes that the total amount that could be paid out to clients "presently voyaging" was limited to 1,500 pounds, because, "no doubt, the decision to grant the advance was made late in the day" and because the accounts were frozen in February 1916: André Autheman, *La Banque impériale ottomane*, Paris 1996, p. 238.

58. Report by Shushanig M. Dikranian, *doc. cit.*, f° 13. When she wrote this report, some of these women were still being held in Harput.

59. Report by Adelina Mazmanian, *doc. cit,* f° 55.

60. Aguni, *History of the Massacre of one Million Armenians, op. cit.,* p. 141; BNu/ Fonds Andonian, P.J.1/3, file 59, Erzerum, ff. 3–4v°, report by Alphonse Arakelian, Aleppo, 24 February 1919; APC/ APJ, PCI Bureau, Է 358–60 and Յ 723–6, *Faits et documents,* doc. no. 29, *Les déportations des Arméniens d'Erzerum.*

61. *Ibidem.* On the outskirts of Erzincan, on the road to Kemah, where the convoy came to a stand for some time, the deportees also saw the valis of Erzerum and Trebizond, the *kaymakam* of Bayburt, and later, the vali of Sıvas as well as various mutesarifs and *kaymakams* pass by. These officials probably came to the area to coordinate their actions: BNu/Fonds Andonian, P.J.1/3, file 59, Erzerum, f°–68v°, report by Boghos Vartanian, Erzerum, 5 August 1916.

62. APC/APJ, PCI Bureau, Է 358–60 and Յ 723–6, *Faits et documents,* doc. no. 29, *Les déportations des Arméniens d'Erzerum.*

63. BNu/Fonds A. Andonian, P.J.1/3, file 59, Erzerum, f° 4v°, report by Alphonse Arakelian. The convoys of deportees from the regions of Erzerum, Sıvas, Bitlis, and Harput almost all passed by way of the Kahta gorge, where they were decimated by the same squadrons.

64. *Ibidem;* APC/APJ, PCI Bureau, Է 358–60 and Յ 723–26, *Faits et documents,* doc. no. 29, *Les déportations des Arméniens d'Erzerum.*

65. Kaiser, "A Scene from the Inferno," *art. cit.,* p. 157, n. 109, report from German consul in Aleppo, Walter Rössler to Bethmann Holweg, 30 November 1915.

66. BNu/Fonds Andonian, P.J.1/3, file 59, Erzerum, f° 4v°, report by Alphonse Arakelian; The encrypted telegram of 23 June 1915 [23 Haziran 1331] from the *kaymakam* of Bayburt to the vali of Erzerum seems to have to do with this second convoy. It contains information about the monitoring of the deportations by the local government: "I hereby inform your Excellency that the convoy from Erzerum that was here until recently set out today under the supervision of the imperial district attorney, accompanied by a sizeable escort": APC/APJ, PCI Bureau, Է 758, no. 49.

67. BNu/Fonds Andonian, P.J.1/3, file 59, Erzerum, ff. 84–5, report by Boghos Vartanian, Erzerum, 5 August 1916.

68. *Ibidem,* f° 85 r°–v°.

69. *Ibidem,* f° 86–7.

70. *Ibidem,* ff. 88v°–9.

71. *Ibidem,* f° 91.

72. Aguni, *History of the Massacre of one Million Armenians, op. cit.,* p. 142; APC/APJ, PCI Bureau, Ֆ 348–9, *Sur le chemin du calvaire: Erzerum;* BNu/Fonds A. Andonian, P.J.1/3, file 59, Erzerum, f° 4v°, report by Alphonse Arakelian.

73. Aguni, *History of the Massacre of one Million Armenians, op. cit.,* pp. 142–3; APC/APJ, PCI Bureau, Ֆ 348–9, *Sur le chemin du calvaire: Erzerum.*

74. APC/APJ, PCI Bureau, Ձ 107 APJ, doc. no. 56, *The Murder of the Bishop Simpad Saadetian, prelate of Erzerum,* report by an escapee, Armenag Madatian.

75. Kaiser, "A Scene from the Inferno," *art. cit.,* p. 159.

76. *Supra,* p. 242. APC/APJ, PCI Bureau, Ֆ 321, provides a list of those who bore the main responsibility for the deportations in late March 1915 in the district of Pasın: Kerim son of Mehmed Bey, Behdi Bey, Ahmed Bey, Reşad son of Abdullah.

77. BNu/Fonds Andonian, P.J.1/3, file 59, Erzerum, f° 71, report by Nigoghayos Bazarian, 55 years old, from the village of Khosroveran.

78. BNu/ Fonds Andonian, P.J.1/3, file 59, Erzerum, f° 72, report by Harutiun Minasian, 55 years old, from the village of Ichkhu.

79. *Supra,* p. 296; Kévorkian & Paboudjian, *Les Arméniens dans l'Empire ottoman, op. cit.,* p. 442.

80. *Ibidem,* pp. 442–3, 449.

81. *Ibidem,* pp. 429–33.

82. BNu/ Fonds Andonian, P.J.1/3, file 59, Erzerum, f° 64, report by Boghos Vartanian, Erzerum, 5 August 1916.

83. *Ibidem,* ff. 64–5.

84. Aguni, *History of the Massacre of one Million Armenians, op. cit.,* p. 141.

85. BNu/Fonds Andonian, P.J.1/3, file 59, Erzerum, ff. 47–51, villages of the plain of Erzerum.

86. Kévorkian & Paboudjian, *Les Arméniens dans l'Empire ottoman*, op. cit., pp. 439–42.

87. In the first months of the war, İsmail Bey Arpaci and his son İbrahim organized the squadrons of çetes in the region of Bayburt.

88. APC/APJ, PCI Bureau, Ֆ 322, 325, Ֆ 336–7 (report in French): *Responsables des déportations et des massacres dans la région de Bayburt*.

89. The verdict of the court-martial, dated 20 July 1920, condemning to death "Mehmed Nusret Bey, *kaymakam* of Bayburt and later *mutesarif* of Arğana Maden, and Lieutenant Necati Bey, the leader of a squadron of çetes, both of whom bear responsibility for the massacres of Bayburt," was published in *Tercüman-ı Hakikat* no. 14,136, 5 August 1920. Distribution of this issue of the periodical was, however, blocked by the censorship office. Haigazn Kazarian, who was working for the British authorities in Constantinople at the time, kept a copy of the issue and later published a facsimile reproduction and an Armenian translation in his book on the genocide: Kazarian, op. cit., pp. 292–300.

90. *Ibidem.*

91. *Ibidem.*

92. *Ibidem.*

93. *Ibidem.* The witnesses were Shushanig, Aghavni, Varsenik, Armenuhi, Khachadur Seferian, and an adolescent by the name of Hampartsum. Nusret was condemned to death and hanged at 5 a.m. in Bayazid square on 5 August 1920: *La Renaissance*, no. 522, 6 août 1920. The verdict of the court-martial also notes that Nusret was promoted to the post of *mutesarif* of Arğana Maden and, later, Urfa, where "he committed tragic crimes against fifteen thousand to twenty thousand Armenian deportees from various regions; he received a promotion after the commission of each crime, as is proven by irrefutable documents."

94. SHAT, Service Historique de la Marine, Service de Renseignements de la Marine, Turquie, 1BB7 231, doc. no. 258, Constantinople, 7 February 1919, p. 1, report about *Les Responsables des massacres de Bayburt*.

95. APC/APJ, PCI Bureau, Ֆ 322, 325, Ֆ 336–7.

96. BNu/Fonds Andonian, P.J.1/3, file 11, Bayburt, f° 1, report by Mgrdich Muradian.

97. BNu/Fonds Andonian, P.J.1/3, file 11, Bayburt, ff. 1v°–3, report by Mgrdich Muradian.

98. APC/APJ, PCI Bureau, Ֆ 343–4 (in French), dos. no. 101, *Le récit navrant d'une survivante à Bayburt*.

99. Krieger, op. cit., p. 10.

100. Kévorkian & Paboudjian, *Les Arméniens dans l'Empire ottoman*, op. cit., pp. 434–5.

101. BNu/ Fonds Andonian, P.J.1/3, file 59, Erzerum, report by Vahan Mirakents, "Ինչպես ջարդուեցան Խնուսցիք [How the Inhabitants of Khnus Were Massacred]," Constantinople 1919, p. 1.

102. *Ibidem*, p. 2.

103. Kaiser, "A Scene from the Inferno," art. cit., p. 138, cites German consular sources.

104. BNu/Fonds Andonian, P.J.1/3, file 59, Erzerum, report by Vahan Mirakents, p. 2.

105. *Ibidem*, p. 5.

106. BNu/Fonds Andonian, P.J.1/3, file 59, Erzerum, f° 74, report by Sharo Nazarian, and f° 75, report by Simon Mekhitarian, f° 75v°, Harutiun Serovpian, from Gopal. A few inhabitants of Ashkhalu, a primarily Turkish village, saved their lives by converting to Islam in Serıncek: BNu/Fonds A. Andonian, P.J.1/3, file 59, Erzerum, f° 76, report by Arshag Derderian, from Ashkhalu.

107. *Ibidem.*

108. *Ibidem*, p. 6.

109. Kévorkian & Paboudjian, *Les Arméniens dans l'Empire ottoman*, op. cit., pp. 437–8. Some of the men of these villages had immigrated to Romania and Bulgaria; a smaller number had settled in the United States: BNu/Fonds Andonian, P.J.1/3, file 15, Tercan, ff. 1–3, reports on the situation in the *kaza* after the Russians arrived.

110. APC/APJ, PCI Bureau, Կ 588 and Ֆ 327–8 (in French), *Les exploits du député de Kemah Halet bey*.

111. BNu/Fonds Andonian, P.J.1/3, file 15, Tercan, f° 2v°.

112. *Ibidem*; BNu/ Fonds A. Andonian, P.J.1/3, file 15, Tercan, f° 10v°, report by Father Hampartsum Harutiunian, village priest in Vartig (Tercan).

113. *Ibidem*, f° 11.

114. *Ibidem*, f° 12v°, report by Vartan Avedisian, from Pakarij.

115. *Ibidem*, f° 13, report by Hovhannes Rasian, from Sargha.

116. *Ibidem*, f° 13, report by Hovhannes Gozeghian, from Piriz.

117. Kévorkian & Paboudjian, *Les Arméniens dans l'Empire ottoman, op. cit.*, pp. 435–7.

118. APC/APJ, PCI Bureau, Ϙ 334, dossier no. 35, Events in Kığı from the mobilization order to the deportation; Zaven Der Yeghiayan, *Memoirs, op. cit.*, p. 180, cited the report by Ms. Aghasser, the wife of the director of the Armenian schools in the *kaza*.

119. *Infra*, p. 399, his activities in the Kahta gorge.

120. BNu/Fonds Andonian, P.J.1/3, file 61, Kığı, f° 16v°–17, report by Vahan Postoyan; APC/APJ, PCI Bureau, Ϙ 321, those responsible for the region of Kığı.

121. BNu/Fonds Andonian, P.J.1/3, file 61, f° 16v°, Kığı, report by Vahan Postoyan; APC/APJ, PCI Bureau, P 334, dossier no. 35, Events in Kığı from the mobilization order to the deportation; Zaven Der Yeghiayan, *Memoirs, op. cit.*, p. 180.

122. BNu/Fonds Andonian, P.J.1/3, file 61, ff. 2–4, Kığı, report by Vahan Postoyan.

123. *Ibidem*, f° 64 r°–v° and ff. 72v°–73v°, report by Sarkis Arsigian, who states that İsmail Ağa, a local Kurdish *beg*, suggested that the villagers come to his village so that he could protect them, but then handed them over to the *çetes*.

124. *Ibidem*, f° 65 r°–v°.

125. BNu/ Fonds Andonian, P.J.1/3, file 61, f° 16r°–v°; another report bears on the 12 June 1915 massacre of the village of Ljig, 12 June 1915: BNu/Fonds Andonian, P.J.1/3, file 61, Kığı, ff. 68v°–70v°.

126. BNu/Fonds Andonian, P.J.1/3, file 61, f° 66v°, Kığı, report by Vahan Postoyan

127. BNu/Fonds Andonian, P.J.1/3, file 61, ff. 2–4, Kığı, report by Vahan Postoyan.

128. *Ibidem*, f° 16 and 66v°; Zaven Der Yeghiayan, *Memoirs, op. cit.*, p. 181.

129. *Ibidem*; APC/APJ, PCI Bureau, Ϙ 334 (in French), no. 35, report on *Les événements de Keghi depuis la mobilisation jusqu'à la déportation*.

130. Zaven Der Yeghiayan, *Memoirs, op. cit.*, p. 181; APC/APJ, PCI Bureau, Ϙ 334 (in French), no. 35, the events in Kığı from the mobilization order to the deportation, puts the number of orphans at 400.

131. APC/APJ, PCI Bureau, Է 351–6, report in English on the massacres in the region of Erzerum.

132. *Ibidem*; BNu/ Fonds Andonian, P.J.1/3, file 61, ff. 2–4, Kığı, report by Vahan Postoyan.

133. *Ibidem*; APC/APJ, PCI Bureau, Է 351–6, report in English on the massacres in the region of Erzerum.

134. BNu/Fonds Andonian, P.J.1/3, file 61, ff. 2–4 and 16v°, Kığı, report by Vahan Postoyan; APC/PAJ, PCI Bureau, Է 351–6, report in English on the massacres in the region of Erzerum: three men, Mihran Vartanian, Sarkis Krikorian, and Abraham Simonian, succeeded in fleeing to the forest of Darman, where they lived in a cavern for four months.

135. BNu/Fonds Andonian, P.J.1/3, file 61, Kığı, ff. 46–9, history of Hovhannes Sarksian, from Temran; APC/APJ, PCI Bureau, Է 351–6, report in English about the massacres in the region of Erzerum.

136. BNu/Fonds Andonian, P.J.1/3, file 61, Kığı, ff. 46–9, history of Hovhannes Sarksian.

137. APC/APJ, PCI Bureau, Է 351–6, report in English on the massacres in the region of Erzerum.

138. *Ibidem*.

139. *Ibidem*.

140. BNu/Fonds Andonian, P.J.1/3, file 61, Kığı, ff. 67v°–68, list of the villages, with the number of survivors from each one.

141. *Ibidem*, f° 66v°.

142. Kévorkian & Paboudjian, *Les Arméniens dans l'Empire ottoman, op. cit.*, pp. 446–7.

143. BNu/Fonds Andonian, P.J.1/3, file 24, report drawn up by the Committee of deportees from the Dayk district, Constantinople, August 1919, f° 11r°–v°.

144. Kaiser, "A Scene from the Inferno," *art. cit.*, pp. 145–6.

145. BNu/Fonds Andonian, P.J.1/3, file 24, Khodorchur, report drawn up by the Committee of deportees from the Dayk district, Constantinople, August 1919, f° 12.

146. *Ibidem*, f° 12v°–13v°.

147. *Ibidem*, f° 15v°.

148. *Ibidem*.

149. *Ibidem*; see Raffaelle Gianighian, *Khodorciur*, Venedig 1992, pp. 51–69. The author, from the village of Gisag/Kisak, was in this convoy.

150. *Ibidem*, f° 16. Among the survivors, there were also 1,540 people from Khodorchur who had worked in the Caucasus before the war.

151. APC/APJ, PCI Bureau, Ի 221 and Թ 322, those responsible for the deportations and massacres in the region of Erzincan.

152. Extract from the 5 December 1918 deposition of Vehib Pasha: *Takvim-ı Vakayi*, no. 3540, 5 May 1919, p. 7, col. 2 and the full deposition of handwritten pages: PAJ/APC, PCI Bureau, Չ 171–82.

153. BNu/Fonds Andonian, P.J.1/3, file 16, Erzincan, f° 83, report by Kevork Mardirosian, from Meghutsig.

154. *Ibidem*, f° 83v°; BNu/ Fonds Andonian, P.J.1/3, file 16, Erzincan, ff. 19–20, report by Kurken Keserian, *Deportations and massacres in the region of Erzincan*.

155. BNu/Fonds Andonian, P.J.1/3, file 16, Erzincan, ff. 85–6. The main witness stated that he later learned that the authorities had purveyed this false information in order to reassure the local population. The 300 families who had agreed to convert should, in theory, have been exempt from deportation.

156. *Ibidem*, f° 88.

157. BNu/Fonds Andonian, P.J.1/3, file 16, Erzincan, f° 28, report by Kurken Keserian, those responsible for the deportations and massacres in the region of Erzincan.

158. APC/APJ, PCI Bureau, Ч 588 (in English) and Թ 327–8 (in French), *The Exploits of an Deputy, Halet bey*.

159. BNu/Fonds Andonian, P.J.1/3, file 16, Erzincan, ff. 83–4, report by Kevork Mardirosian, from Meghutsig, and 89v°–90.

160. *Ibidem*, f° 90v°.

161. *Ibidem*, ff. 31, 91–2.

162. APC/APJ, PCI Bureau, Ч 588.

163. BNu/Fonds Andonian, P.J.1/3, file 16, Erzincan, ff. 31, 92.

164. APC/APJ, PCI Bureau, Ч 588.

165. BNu/Fonds Andonian, P.J.1/3, file 16, Erzincan, ff. 32–4.

166. BNu/Fonds Andonian, P.J.1/3, file 16, Erzincan, ff. 93–4. The secretary of the health commission of the central hospital of the Sixth Army Corps (Sıvas) related what he was told by Major Rifat Bey, a physician who witnessed the crimes committed in Kemah: APC/ PAJ, PCI Bureau, Յ 732, *Faits et documents*, no. 36, *Les atrocités de Kemah*.

167. BNu/ Fonds Andonian, P.J.1/3, file 16, Erzincan, ff. 34–5, report by Kurken Keserian, *Deportations and massacres in the region of Erzincan*.

168. *Ibidem*, f° 37.

169. BNu/Fonds Andonian, P.J.1/3, file 16, Erzincan, ff. 38–9, report by Kurken Keserian, *Deportations and massacres in the region of Erzincan*.

170. BNu/Fonds Andonian, P.J.1/3, file 16, Erzincan, f° 95.

171. BNu/Fonds Andonian, P.J.1/3, file 16, Erzincan, ff. 38–9, report by Kurken Keserian, *Deportations and massacres in the region of Erzincan*.

172. *Ibidem*, ff. 39–40. There were 17 survivors.

173. BNu/Fonds Andonian, P.J.1/3, file 16, Erzincan, ff. 85–6, 91.

174. *Ibidem*, f° 68.

175. *Ibidem*, ff. 63, 69 and 94v°.

176. Kévorkian & Paboudjian, *Les Arméniens dans l'Empire ottoman, op. cit.*, pp. 455–6.

177. APC/APJ, PCI Bureau, Է 364–5, *The Deporation in the Sancak of Erzincan*; BNu/ Fonds A. Andonian, P.J.1/3, file 25, Kemah/Gamakh, report by Harutiun Altiokganian.

178. Kévorkian & Paboudjian, *Les Arméniens dans l'Empire ottoman, op. cit.*, pp. 455–6.

179. APC/APJ, PCI Bureau, Է 364–5, *The Deporation in the sancak of Erzincan*.

180. Kévorkian & Paboudjian, *Les Arméniens dans l'Empire ottoman, op. cit.*, p. 456.

181. APC/APJ, PCI Bureau, Է 364–5, *The Deporation in the sancak of Erzincan*.

182. Kévorkian & Paboudjian, *Les Arméniens dans l'Empire ottoman, op. cit.*, p. 455.

183. APC/APJ, PCI Bureau, Թ 348–9, *Sur le chemin du calvaire: Erzerum*.

184. *Ibidem.*
185. BNu/Fonds Andonian, P.J.1/3, file 61, Kığı, ff. 46–9, history of Hovhannes Sarksian, from Temran (in Armenian).
186. BNu/Fonds Andonian, P.J.1/3, file 15, Tercan, f° 8, report by Yeghia Torosian.
187. *Ibidem,* f° 9.
188. BNu/Fonds A. Andonian, P.J.1/3, file 59, Erzerum, f° 39, report by Rupen Toroyan, 5 February 1917.
189. *Ibidem,* f° 41.
190. *Ibidem,* f° 41v°.
191. *Ibidem,* f° 42r°–v°.
192. BNu/Fonds Andonian, P.J.1/3, file 15, Tercan, ff. 4–7, report by Krikor Keshishian who confesses that he survived by plundering Turkish deserters and seizing their weapons until April 1916, when the Russians arrived in the region.
193. *La Renaissance,* no. 144, 20 avril 1919.
194. BNu/Fonds A. Andonian, P.J.1/3, file 59, Erzerum, f° 20v°, report by Kh. Oskanian, Sarıkamış, 3 November 1916; ff. 67–8, report by Boghos Vartanian, Erzerum, 5 August 1916.
195. APC/APJ, PCI Bureau, Ձ 133 and 154, Direction of the National Security, Ministry of the Interior, letter to the president of the court-martial of Constantinople, 23 February 1919, certified to be a faithful copy: "Excellency: Enclosed please find, in accordance with your orders, a copy of an encrypted telegram, written by the former commander of the Third Army, Kâmil Pasha, bearing on the deportation of the Armenians. We found the telegram, which we think may prove useful, among the documents transmitted by the prefecture of Dyarbekir."APC/APJ, Ձ 155, copy of an encrypted telegram from Mahmud Kâmil, published in *Takvim-ı Vakayi,* no. 3540, Sublime Porte, Direction of the National Security, Ministry of the Interior, to be a faithful copy of the document sent him by the authorities in Sıvas on 23 February 1919 at the request of the Ministry of the Interior, and forwarded to the court-martial.
196. *Ibidem.* The telegram also bears the words: "This document is certified to be a faithful copy, 23 February 1919," as well as the stamp of the special bureau of the Chief of Security, charged with assembling official documents.
197. Kaiser, "A Scene from the Inferno," *art. cit.,* pp. 146–9, cites notably the correspondence between the vice-consul and the German ambassador in Istanbul.
198. *Ibidem,* p. 151, n. 84–5, cites the references of these two official documents.
199. BNu/Fonds A. Andonian, P.J.1/3, file 59, Erzerum, ff. 189–90, report by Hovhannes Khanzarlian, Erzerum, 2 May 1917, "Why I was unable to remain a Muslim?"
200. *Ibidem.*
201. *Supra,* pp. 243–4.
202. *Supra,* pp. 203–4.
203. Extract from the 5 December 1918 deposition of Vehib Pasha: *Takvim-ı Vakayi,* no. 3540, 5 May 1919, p. 7, col. 2 and the full deposition of handwritten pages: PAJ/APC, PCI Bureau, Ձ 171–82.
204. APC/APJ, PCI Bureau, Ҍ 218–19, those responsible for the deportations and massacres in the region of Erzerum.
205. Kaiser, "A Scene from the Inferno," *art. cit.,* pp. 152–5.
206. *Ibidem,* p. 152.
207. BOA, DH. şfr no. 53/303, telegram from minister of interior to Tahsin Bey, 9 June 1915: *Armenians in Ottoman Documents (1915–1920),* no. 25, Ankara 1995, p. 40.
208. Kaiser, "A Scene from the Inferno," *art. cit.,* p. 153.
209. Autheman, *La Banque impériale ottomane, op. cit.,* pp. 233–4.
210. *Ibidem,* p. 239.
211. *Ibidem.*
212. Kaiser, "A Scene from the Inferno," *art. cit.,* pp. 153–4.
213. Autheman, *La Banque impériale ottomane, op. cit.,* p. 239.
214. *Ibidem,* p. 238.
215. BNu/Fonds Andonian, P.J.1/3, file 59, Erzerum, report by Alphonse Arakelian, an Armenian deported from Erzerum, Alep, 24 February 1919, f° 2.
216. *Ibidem,* f° 6v°.
217. *Ibidem,* f° 6.

4   Resistance and Massacres in the Vilayet of Van

1. Kévorkian & Paboudjian, *Les Arméniens dans l'Empire ottoman*, op. cit., pp. 507–13. The vilayet also boasted 457 churches and 80 monasteries, some of which were very old.
2. The four Armenian towns and villages in the eastern *kaza* of Mahmudiye (pop. 826) were burned down late in December 1914 and their inhabitants were massacred or displaced: *supra*, p. 220.
3. *Supra*, pp. 233–4.
4. A-To, *The Major Events in Vasburagan, 1914–1917*, op. cit., pp. 168–90.
5. *Ibidem*, pp. 371–2. Hamdi Bey, an educated native of Istanbul who had spent several years in Europe, made a name for himself at the outbreak of the war by forming squadrons of çetes sent into battle in Iranian Azerbaijan. He was assisted in his struggle against the Armenians of Shadakh by the secretary general of the subprefecture, Şevket Bey, the judge Ahmed Tevfik and a mufti, Hasan.
6. *Ibidem*, p. 372.
7. Ussher, *An American Physician in Turkey*, op. cit., p. 127. Ussher met with Cevdet on 18 April, after news of the crime had reached people's ears.
8. A-To, *The Major Events in Vasburagan, 1914–1917*, op. cit., p. 380.
9. *Ibidem*, p. 381.
10. *Ibidem*, pp. 383–4.
11. *Ibidem*, pp. 382–3.
12. *Ibidem*, p. 389.
13. *Ibidem*, p. 382.
14. *Ibidem*, pp. 192–3.
15. *Ibidem*, p. 194.
16. *Ibidem*, p. 195.
17. *Ibidem*, p. 196.
18. *Ibidem*, p. 197.
19. *Ibidem*, pp. 210–11.
20. *Ibidem*, p. 212.
21. *Ibidem*, p. 213.
22. *Ibidem*, p. 214.
23. *Ibidem*, p. 215.
24. Kévorkian & Paboudjian, *Les Arméniens dans l'Empire ottoman*, op. cit., pp. 542–44.
25. A-To, *The Major Events in Vasburagan, 1914–1917*, op. cit., pp. 169–73. An account of these events was later provided by one of the few survivors from this group of men, Mgrdich Hovhannesian, a native of the village of Panon (pop. 180). Hovhannesian would later manage to reach the Russian lines near Dyadin, along with 23 other people from the village of Sosgun.
26. *Ibidem*, p. 175. 60 men from the village of Aragha were also detained in the prison in Agants.
27. *Ibidem*, pp. 176–7.
28. *Ibidem*, pp. 186–8.
29. Kévorkian & Paboudjian, *Les Arméniens dans l'Empire ottoman*, op. cit., p. 542.
30. A-To, *The Major Events in Vasburagan, 1914–1917*, op. cit., pp. 179 and 184. The administrative seat of the *kaza*, Perkri, had 110 Kurdish and 25 Armenian households. The handful of survivors managed to flee to Maku, on the Turkish-Persian border.
31. *Ibidem*, p. 181.
32. *Ibidem*, pp. 208–9.
33. *Ibidem*, pp. 209–10.
34. *Ibidem*, p. 216.
35. Kévorkian & Paboudjian, *Les Arméniens dans l'Empire ottoman*, op. cit., p. 544.
36. Cf. *supra*, p. 233; Rafaël de Nogales, *Four Years Beneath the Crescent*, op. cit., pp. 59–61.
37. A-To, *The Major Events in Vasburagan, 1914–1917*, op. cit., p. 189.
38. Kévorkian & Paboudjian, *Les Arméniens dans l'Empire ottoman*, op. cit., pp. 545–48.
39. *Ibidem*, pp. 197–9.
40. *Ibidem*, pp. 200–1.
41. *Ibidem*, p. 201.

42. *Ibidem*, pp. 202–3.
43. *Ibidem*, pp. 204–5.
44. *Ibidem*, pp. 205–6.
45. *Ibidem*, pp. 207–8.
46. *Ibidem*, pp. 216–17.
47. *Ibidem*, pp. 217–18.
48. *Ibidem*, p. 219, states that the Turkish offensive against Varak began on 8 May; Rafaël de Nogales, *Four Years Beneath the Crescent*, *op. cit.*, p. 92 dates the departure of the "battalion of Erzerum" for Mt. Varak to 3 May; Ussher, *An American Physician in Turkey*, *op. cit.*, pp. 143–4.
49. M. G., *La défense héroïque de Van (Arménie)*, Genève 1916, p. 10; A-To, *The Major Events in Vasburagan, 1914–1917*, *op. cit.*, pp. 300–1, also believes that the vali thus hoped to starve Aykestan into submission.
50. A-To, *The Major Events in Vasburagan, 1914–1917*, *op. cit.*, pp. 219–24.
51. *Ibidem*, pp. 274–5.
52. Ussher, *An American Physician in Turkey*, *op. cit.*, p. 141.
53. *Ibidem*.
54. A-To, *The Major Events in Vasburagan, 1914–1917*, *op. cit.*, pp. 281–2.
55. Rafaël de Nogales, *Four Years Beneath the Crescent*, *op. cit.*, p. 63.
56. *Ibidem*, pp. 64–5.
57. *Ibidem*, pp. 66–7.
58. *Ibidem*, pp. 72–4. Several weeks later, Çerkez Ahmed would murder the parliamentary deputies Zohrab, Vartkes, and Daghavarian (see *infra*, p. 534).
59. *Supra*, p. 21.
60. Dadrian, "Documentation of the Armenian Genocide in Turkish Sources," in *Genocide: A Critical Bibliographic Review*, *art. cit.*, pp. 118–20, provides an annotated bibliography of Çerkez Ahmed's criminal activities, first in Van and then in the province of Dyarbekir. APC/APJ 3 563, PCI Bureau, Report about Cevdet Bey, it was the vali who asked that the major be released from his usual obligations and sent on mission to Van.
61. Rafaël de Nogales, *Four Years Beneath the Crescent*, *op. cit.*, p. 74. The only two Armenians he met were a disarmed gendarme who served as the vali's butler and the merchant Terzibashian, who occasionally served as an interpreter (*ibidem*, p. 88).
62. *Ibidem*, pp. 75–6.
63. A-To, *The Major Events in Vasburagan, 1914–1917*, *op. cit.*, pp. 250–3. Ussher, *An American Physician in Turkey*, *op. cit.*, p. 137, gives a convergent account of these events.
64. Rafaël de Nogales, *Four Years Beneath the Crescent*, *op. cit.*, p. 80.
65. *Ibidem*, pp. 76, 81, desertions increased from 25 April on.
66. *Ibidem*, p. 78. On 17 April, as we have seen, Cevdet had asked the missionaries if he could station 50 gendarmes and a cannon in their building, which dominated Aykestan: see *supra*, p. 233.
67. *Ibidem*, p. 82.
68. Archives of the Italian Ministry of Foreign Affairs, letter from the Italian consul in Van, G. Sbordoni to Cevdet Bey, 11/24 April 1915.
69. *Ibidem*.
70. A-To, *The Major Events in Vasburagan, 1914–1917*, *op. cit.*, pp. 340–1.
71. Rafaël de Nogales, *Four Years Beneath the Crescent*, *op. cit.*, pp. 85–6.
72. *Ibidem*, p. 86.
73. *Ibidem*, p. 89.
74. Ussher, *An American Physician in Turkey*, *op. cit.*, p. 149.
75. Rafaël de Nogales, *Four Years Beneath the Crescent*, *op. cit.*, p. 90; A-To, *The Major Events in Vasburagan, 1914–1917*, *op. cit.*, pp. 320–1.
76. Cf. *supra*, p. 325.
77. These were Krupp cannons, which were modern and of larger calibre than those already in place.
78. Rafaël de Nogales, *Four Years Beneath the Crescent*, *op. cit.*, p. 93, notes that news of Halil's defeat in Dilman reached Van in early May. On the military campaign, see *supra*, p. 227.
79. A-To, *The Major Events in Vasburagan, 1914–1917*, *op. cit.*, pp. 325–6, provides the full text of Vali Cevdet's letter to the bishop and prelate Eznik *vartabed*, 20 April/3 May 1915.

80. Eznik's exact words were: "We are not insurgents. We have always obeyed the Ottoman state; we have always respected its laws; our desire is to continue to do so, as in the past": A-To, *The Major Events in Vasburagan, 1914–1917, op. cit.*, p. 324, states that no one put faith in Cevdet's offer, but that the old city hoped it could thus learn what was happening in Aykestan. It also hoped that Cevdet's emissaries would be Colonel Ahmed and Kalust Jidechian, an Armenian notable whom the authorities had not molested.

81. Rafaël de Nogales, *Four Years Beneath the Crescent, op. cit.*, p. 90.

82. A-To, *The Major Events in Vasburagan, 1914–1917, op. cit.*, p. 327, notes that one of them, a native of Hinis, managed to escape and flee to the Armenian lines.

83. *Ibidem.*

84. Archives of the Italian Ministry of Foreign Affairs, letter from the Italian consul in Van, G. Sbordoni, to Cevdet Bey, 20 April/3 May 1915.

85. Rafaël de Nogales, *Four Years Beneath the Crescent, op. cit.*, p. 91.

86. *Ibidem*, p. 93.

87. A-To, *The Major Events in Vasburagan, 1914–1917, op. cit.*, p. 328.

88. *Ibidem*, letter from Cevdet to Eznik, 5 May 1915. The vali notes in his letter that de Sbordoni has already transmitted his conditions to Aykestan. The negotiations were broken off on 6 May.

89. Rafaël de Nogales, *Four Years Beneath the Crescent, op. cit.*, p. 104.

90. A-To, *The Major Events in Vasburagan, 1914–1917, op. cit.*, pp. 319–20.

91. Rafaël de Nogales, *Four Years Beneath the Crescent, op. cit.*, p. 96. Thanks to the indiscretion of an officer, de Nogales learned that Cevdet had given orders to have him murdered en route.

92. *Ibidem*, p. 107; Ussher, *An American Physician in Turkey, op. cit.*, p. 153, also notes that the Russian and Armenian prisoners were executed the day preceding Cevdet's departure.

93. A-To, *The Major Events in Vasburagan, 1914–1917, op. cit.*, p. 360.

94. *Ibidem*, p. 436.

95. Kévorkian & Paboudjian, *Les Arméniens dans l'Empire ottoman..., op. cit.*, pp. 550–5.

96. A-To, *The Major Events in Vasburagan, 1914–1917, op. cit.*, p. 365.

97. See *supra*, pp. 232 and 319.

98. A-To, *The Major Events in Vasburagan, 1914–1917, op. cit.*, p. 375.

99. *Ibidem*, p. 390.

100. *Ibidem*, p. 391.

101. *Ibidem*, p. 378. Two more bridges, both of wood, were destroyed, so that it was impossible to cross the river in the south.

102. *Ibidem*, p. 379.

103. *Ibidem*, p. 392.

104. *Ibidem*, p. 393.

105. *Ibidem*, p. 396. Hamdi Bey, in a 19 April letter to the vali of Van, pointed out that the tribes were deserting their positions to go plunder the villages abandoned by the Armenians; he therefore requested that regular forces and a mountain cannon be put at his disposal.

106. *Ibidem*, pp. 398–9, notes that the Kurds fighting in Tagh once again abandoned their positions to go plunder these two villages.

107. *Ibidem*, p. 400.

108. *Ibidem*, pp. 402–7.

109. *Ibidem*, pp. 411–2.

110. *Ibidem*, p. 416.

111. *Ibidem*, p. 429.

112. *Ibidem*, pp. 432–3. This battalion made its entry into Tagh on 25 May.

113. *Ibidem*, p. 434. In Pshantashd, 7,000 refugees survived.

114. Kévorkian & Paboudjian, *Les Arméniens dans l'Empire ottoman, op. cit.*, pp. 549–50.

115. Ussher, *An American Physician in Turkey, op. cit.*, p. 143; A-To, *The Major Events in Vasburagan, 1914–1917, op. cit.*, p. 427.

116. APC/APJ, PCI Bureau, 3 549–51, *Les massacres d'Arméniens dans le vilayet de Van*; Ussher, *An American Physician in Turkey, op. cit.*, p. 143, writes: "We have absolute proof that fifty-five thousand people were killed" in Van vilayet.

117. Rafaël de Nogales, *Four Years Beneath the Crescent*, op. cit., p. 98. On his way down the road leading to Halil's headquarters, de Nogales crossed Hayots Tsor, where he saw the remains of the Armenian villages that had been burned down. In Başkale, he witnessed the execution of 300 to 400 women and children, and also of a few craftsmen who had been left alive until then to help meet the army's needs (*ibidem*, p. 100).

118. *Ibidem*, p. 104.

119. Sebuh, *Pages from my memoirs*, I, op. cit., pp. 218–19, Sebuh, who participated in these combats, states that the Russian forces let pass an occasion to destroy the Ottoman Expeditionary Corps when they failed to cut off its retreat. He attributes this mistake to Antranig.

120. Rafaël de Nogales, *Four Years Beneath the Crescent*, op. cit., p. 105.

121. *Ibidem*, p. 104.

122. *Ibidem*, p. 109.

123. Rafaël de Nogales, *Four Years Beneath the Crescent*, op. cit., pp. 110–12.

124. Sebuh, *Pages from my memoirs*, I, op. cit., pp. 230–3.

125. *Ibidem*, p. 236.

126. Rafaël de Nogales, *Four Years Beneath the Crescent*, op. cit., p. 114.

127. *Ibidem*, pp. 107–8.

128. Sébouh, *Fragments de mes souvenirs*, I, op. cit., p. 237.

129. Rafaël de Nogales, *Four Years Beneath the Crescent*, op. cit., pp. 119–21.

130. *Ibidem*, p. 121. Nogales does not distinguish these Nestoriens from Armenians.

131. A-To, *The Major Events in Vasburagan, 1914–1917*, op. cit., pp. 466–7.

132. *Ibidem*, pp. 468–9.

133. APC/APJ, PCI Bureau, Ց 908–13, report from the American military attaché of the embassy of Petrograd, Lieutenant E. F. Riggs, to the ambassador, Odessa, 26 April 1917, p. 4.

134. Ussher, *An American Physician in Turkey*, op. cit., pp. 167–8 puts the number of Armenians killed during the Russian retreat at 7,000; A-To, *The Major Events in Vasburagan, 1914–1917*, op. cit., p. 480.

135. *Ibidem*, pp. 480–1. Ussher points out that a terrible typhus epidemic wrought havoc among the Turkish refugees who had been given refuge in the American mission in Van in June. His wife, who had been caring for them, died of typhus herself on 14 July (Ussher, *An American Physician in Turkey*, op. cit., pp. 160–1).

136. *Ibidem*.

137. *Ibidem*, pp. 485–6.

5   Deportations and Massacres in the Vilayet of Bitlis

1. See *supra*, p. 238.

2. See *supra*, p. 238, n. 105.

3. See *supra*, pp. 238–9.

4. Rafaël de Nogales, *Four Years Beneath the Crescent*, op. cit., p. 122.

5. *Ibidem*, p. 123.

6. *Ibidem*, p. 124.

7. *Ibidem*, p. 124. The author affirms it was the officers with whom he had been fighting side-by-side in Van who warned him of Cevdet's intentions.

8. *Ibidem*, p. 126. Nogales therefore decided to head in another direction and set out for Dyarbekir. As he was passing through the *kaza* of Beşiri, he encountered a caravan of several hundred women and children in desperate condition; a government official "told [him] confidentially that a number of similar caravans had marched past toward Sinan during the week" (*ibidem*, pp. 130–1).

9. *Ibidem*, p. 125.

10. *Ibidem*, p. 132.

11. This name was used by a survivor to describe the Halil-Cevdet-Naci troika: "The story of the first victims in Bitlis, by an eyewitness," *La Renaissance*, no. 39, Saturday 18 January 1919.

12. APC/APJ, PCI Bureau, Ց 506–7, those responsible for the deportations and massacres in the region of Bitlis.

13. BNu/ Fonds Andonian, P.J.1/3, file 43, Bitlis, f° 3v°; cf *infra*, pp. 343–4.

14. Rafaël de Nogales, *Four Years Beneath the Crescent*, op. cit., p. 134, 136.

15. Kévorkian & Paboudjian, *Les Arméniens dans l'Empire ottoman...*, op. cit., p. 463.

16. *Ibidem*, p. 502; BNu/Fonds Andonian, P.J.1/3, file 43, Bitlis, f° 8 v°.

17. APC/APJ, PCI Bureau, 3 509–10, those responsible for the deportations and massacres in the region of Siirt.

18. BNu/Fonds Andonian, P.J.1/3, file 43, Bitlis, f° 7 v°.

19. *Ibidem*. Father Jacques Rhétoré (*Les chrétiens aux bêtes ! Souvenirs de la guerre sainte proclamée par les Turcs contre les chrétiens en 1915*, pp. 295–9, ms. conserved in Bibliothèque du Saulchoir, Paris), affirms that the *sancak's* 15,000 Catholic Syriacs and 20,000 Orthodox Syriacs were meted out the same fate as the Armenians. Y. Ternon, *Mardin 1915*, RHAC, V (2002), pp. 207–13 and annexe, pp. 368–70, cites Syriac sources, both Catholic and Orthodox, which say that the Syriacs of Siirt were deported in three caravans from 11 July on, in part along with convoys of Armenians that had come from the north. Some of the people in these three caravans were killed en route. It would seem, then, that there was no difference in the way the Armenians and the Syriac-speaking population were treated in this *sancak*; there was, at most, a month's difference between the dates of departure of the convoys of deportees.

20. Kévorkian & Paboudjian, *Les Arméniens dans l'Empire ottoman*, op. cit., pp. 502–6. Villages of the *kaza* of Siirt: Til, Dershimsh, Khushenan, Tihok/Dehok, Derghalib, Kochik, Bekend, Husenik. Village of Shirvan: Kefra, Gunde-Deghan, Giurinan, Geli, Birke, Derik, Khandak, Smkhor, Kikan, Baytarun, Gerian, Avin/Teravel, Nibin, Siserk, Jum, Pul, Derzin, Deraba, Mnar et Madar.

21. BNu/Fonds Andonian, P.J.1/3, file 43, Bitlis, f° 8.

22. Kévorkian & Paboudjian, *Les Arméniens dans l'Empire ottoman*, op. cit., pp. 504–5.

23. APC/APJ, PCI Bureau, 3 321–2. Hilmi was vali of Eskişehir when, in October 1919, Halil Pasha and Küçük Talât, having fled Istanbul, joined the Kemalists who had just captured the city. But Hilmi had told the court-martial of the crimes that Halil had committed. Halil ordered his men to look for him and had him murdered three days later on the road to the *konak*.

24. Grace H. Knapp, *The Tragedy of Bitlis*, London 2002 (2nd ed.) Knapp, who was sent by boat to Tatvan, the closest port to Bitlis, witnessed the killing of the monks of the island of Aghtamar and the orphans who had been given shelter there (*ibidem*, p. 29).

25. Kévorkian & Paboudjian, *Les Arméniens dans l'Empire ottoman*, op. cit., pp. 469, 472–4.

26. Grace H. Knapp, *The Tragedy of Bitlis*, op. cit., p. 31.

27. *Ibidem*, p. 33.

28. *Ibidem*, pp. 34–5. The situation was, moreover, complicated by the typhus epidemic affecting the city and, above all, the refugee–deportees, whose corpses were burned.

29. BNu/Fonds Andonian, P.J.1/3, file 43, Bitlis, f° 6; on the number of Armenians, see Kévorkian & Paboudjian, *Les Arméniens dans l'Empire ottoman*, op. cit., p. 477.

30. Grace H. Knapp, *The Tragedy of Bitlis*, op. cit., p. 31.

31. *Ibidem*, pp. 36–7. in the course of this exchange, Abdülhalik is said to have warned Knapp: "Songez à vous même, car le même sort vous attend" (*La Renaissance*, no. 39, 18 January 1919, "Récit d'un témoin oculaire sur les premières victimes de Bitlis").

32. *Ibidem*, pp. 36–7.

33. Rafaël de Nogales, *Four Years Beneath the Crescent*, op. cit., p. 133; APC/APJ, PCI Bureau, 3 524–7; *La Renaissance*, no. 39, 18 January 1919, *art. cit.*; BNu/Fonds Andonian, P.J.1/3, file 43, Bitlis, f° 11, report by Garabed Saroyan, from Bitlis.

34. Krieger, op. cit., footnote, p. 20.

35. BNu/Fonds Andonian, P.J.1/3, file 43, Bitlis, f° 11, report by Garabed Saroyan, from Bitlis. According to the witness, the Russians had retreated north by this time.

36. APC/APJ, PCI Bureau, 3 524–7; *La Renaissance*, no. 39, 18 January 1919, *art. cit.*, states that their bodies were left hanging for two weeks but does not give the name of the Dashnak leader; Rafaël de Nogales, *Four Years Beneath the Crescent*, op. cit., p. 133, confirms these facts, but spells the Dashnak leader's name wrong (Kakighian); Arnold Toynbee, *Le Traitement des Arméniens dans l'Empire ottoman (1915–1916)*, Livre Bleu du gouvernement britannique, Laval [1917], p. 206, interview with Ruben Ter Minasian by A. S. Safrastian, 6 November 1915, in Tiflis, we find the correct spelling, Hokhigian.

37. Rafaël de Nogales, *Four Years Beneath the Crescent*, *op. cit.*, p. 133: Cevdet shared the money with Halil.
38. *La Renaissance*, no. 39, 18 January 1919, *art. cit.*, states that the girls "whom Cevdet married" were already with him.
39. Grace H. Knapp, *The Tragedy of Bitlis*, *op. cit.*, p. 40.
40. BNu/Fonds Andonian, P.J.1/3, file 43, Bitlis, f° 10, report by Sophia Yeghiazarian, the wife of the Russian [ex-]*kavas*, Alep, 13 December 1918.
41. BNu/Fonds Andonian, P.J.1/3, file 43, Bitlis, f° 5; APC/APJ, PCI Bureau, Ց 524–7; *La Renaissance*, no. 39, 18 January 1919, *art. cit.*; Grace H. Knapp, *The Tragedy of Bitlis*, *op. cit.*, pp. 42–7.
42. Rafaël de Nogales, *Four Years Beneath the Crescent*, *op. cit.*, p. 133.
43. BNu/Fonds Andonian, P.J.1/3, file 43, Bitlis, f° 6–7, lists the names of 78 abducted young women and girls, and, in certain cases, the names of their proprietors as well.
44. *La Renaissance*, no. 39, 18 January 1919, *art. cit.*
45. Grace H. Knapp, *The Tragedy of Bitlis*, *op. cit.*, pp. 42–4.
46. *Ibidem*, p. 44.
47. *Ibidem*, pp. 44–5.
48. *Ibidem*, pp. 45–7.
49. *Ibidem*, p. 89.
50. *Ibidem*, pp. 90–1. In January 1916, when the Russians were about to take Bitlis, Cevdet did not omit to order Mustafa Bey to "be put to death " this women (*ibidem*, pp. 95–6).
51. *Ibidem*, p. 87. George Knapp was wounded in the course of these events and sent to Dyarbekir by the authorities for treatment. The official thesis is that he died of acute indigestion the day he arrived: "a German, eyewitness to the events." This German was in fact Alma "Johanson" (the spelling used in the document held in the American National Archives): RG59/867. 4016/226), Constantinople, 9 November 1915 (see V. Bryce [= A. Toynbee], *The Treatment of Armenians in the Ottoman Empire, 1915–1916*, Uncensored Edition, ed. by A. Sarafian, Princeton 2000, p. 124, and footnote; Toynbee, *Le Traitement des Arméniens dans l'Empire ottoman*, *op. cit.*, p. 212. It seems more likely that this embarrassing witness to the massacres in Mush was eliminated on orders from Dr. Reşid, the vali of Dyarbekir, with the approval of Halil and Cevdet.
52. *Ibidem*, pp. 49–50.
53. *Ibidem*, p. 86.
54. Kévorkian & Paboudjian, *Les Arméniens dans l'Empire ottoman*, *op. cit.*, p. 469.
55. BNu/Fonds Andonian, P.J.1/3, file 43, Bitlis, ff. 6, 13, report by Asbadour Prudian, from Ghultig, 40 years old.
56. *Ibidem*, f° 14.
57. Rafaël de Nogales, *Four Years Beneath the Crescent*, *op. cit.*, p. 133.
58. APC/APJ, PCI Bureau, Ց 524–7; *La Renaissance*, no. 39, 18 January 1919, *art. cit.*
59. APC/APJ, PCI Bureau, Ի 224, Ց 506–7, those responsible for the deportations and massacres in the region of Bitlis.
60. APC/APJ, PCI Bureau, Հ 107, *Faits et documents*, *Les trois cents vierges*.
61. Kévorkian & Paboudjian, *Les Arméniens dans l'Empire ottoman*, *op. cit.*, pp. 475–7. These villages were Jazhvan (pop. 300), Godents-Verin (pop. 350), Godznts-Nerkin (pop. 80), Pazents/Baghents (pop. 120) Luar (pop. 45), Sevkar (pop. 120), Tagh (pop. 20), Geghis/Kervis (pop. 11), Dantsis/Tanzik (pop. 35), Dosu/ Doru (pop. 120), Talars/Keparis (pop. 100), Harkin/Araken (pop. 32), Hoghant/Okand (pop. 90), Hiuriuk-Verin/Ure (pop. 325), Hiuriuk-Nerkin/Ure (pop. 85), Usp/Esb (pop. 80), Badranants/Bedran (pop. 100), Khoit (pop. 70), Suzants (pop. 75), Arnchig (pop. 90), Tashd/Kish (pop. 90), Mad (pop. 80), Madatsmin/Tsmen (pop. 73), Dvaghus (pop. 75), Gran/Keran (pop. 9), Nerpan (pop. 25).
62. BNu/Fonds Andonian, P.J.1/3, file 43, Bitlis, f° 15r°–v°, report by Toros Hovhannisian, writes Suren Meloyan.
63. *Ibidem*, f° 15v°.
64. *Ibidem*, f° 16.
65. *Ibidem*, f° 16v°.
66. *Ibidem*, ff. 16v°–17; report by Mikayel Ghugasian, ff. 18–21.
67. Kévorkian & Paboudjian, *Les Arméniens dans l'Empire ottoman*, *op. cit.*, pp. 477–501.

68. See *supra*, pp. 240–2.

69. Toynbee, *Le Traitement des Arméniens dans l'Empire ottoman (1915–1916)*, *op. cit.*, p. 207, interview with Ruben Ter Minasian.

70. *Ibidem.*

71. Kévorkian & Paboudjian, *Les Arméniens dans l'Empire ottoman*, *op. cit.*, pp. 477–85.

72. Toynbee, *Le Traitement des Arméniens dans l'Empire ottoman (1915–1916)*, *op. cit.*, p. 207, interview with Ruben Ter Minasian.

73. *Ibidem*, mentions only the Kâzim's arrival, with "10,000 men"; Rafaël de Nogales, *Four Years Beneath the Crescent*, *op. cit.*, p. 134, states that Cevdet and Kâzim arrived together in Mush in order to "chastise the rebels." Cevdet later told him what he had done there.

74. BNu/Fonds Andonian, P.J.1/3, file 51, *Les massacres du Daron*, f° 5, report by Mushegh Turnian, from Mush; Grace H. Knapp, *The Tragedy of Bitlis*, *op. cit.*, p. 91.

75. Aguni, *History of the Massacre of one Million Armenians*, *op. cit.*, p. 162.

76. *Meclisi Mebusan Zabıt Ceridesi* [*Record of the Sessions of the Ottoman Parliament*], vol. 1, 14th session, 18 November 1334 [1918], pp. 143–61, 109, cited in V. Dadrian, *op. cit.*, pp. 21–42, n. 17.

77. APC/APJ, PCI Bureau, Э 561–2, *The organizer of the massacres in Mush, the deputy Hoca Ilyas.*

78. APC/APJ, PCI Bureau, Э 508–9, those responsible for the deportations and massacres in the region of Muş; BNu/ Fonds Andonian, P.J.1/3, file 51, *The massacres in Daron*, f° 7.

79. *Ibidem.*

80. BNu/Fonds Andonian, P.J.1/3, file 51, *The massacres in Daron*, f° 4, report by Mushegh Turnian, from Mouch.

81. APC/APJ, PCI Bureau, Э 561–2, *The organizer of the massacres in Mush, the deputy Hoca Ilyas.*

82. Papazian, *Memoirs*, *op. cit.*, II, p. 365; BNu/Fonds Andonian, P.J.1/3, file 51, *The massacres in Daron*, ff. 20–1, report by Serop Harutiunian, from the village of Mkrakom, was the only survivor of a family of 36. The çetes gouged out Father Kerovp's eyes, cut off his nose and ear and pulled off his fingernails.

83. Manug Der Ananian, "Էջեր Հայաջինջ Սարսափներէն, 1914–1920 [*A Partial Description of the Horrors That Wiped out the Armenians, 1914–1920*]," *Haratch*, 10 April 1934, no. 3.

84. Papazian, *Memoirs*, *op. cit.*, II, p. 365; BNu/ Fonds Andonian, P.J.1/3, file 51, *The massacres in Daron*, ff. 20–1, report by Serop Harutiunian, from Mkrakom; ff. 17–19, report by Smpat Khandilian, from Ziarat (of more than 1,500 inhabitants, 12 men escaped with their lives; ff. 22–8, report by Father Krikor Der Krikorian, 25 January 1917, in Tseti Hank.

85. *La Renaissance*, 31 January 1919, no. 52, reportage by Maurice Prax in *Le Petit Parisien*.

86. Papazian, *Memoirs*, *op. cit.*, II, pp. 365–70; BNu/ Fonds Andonian, P.J.1/3, file 51, *The massacres in Daron*, f° 17v°, report by Smpat Khandilian, from Ziarat, relates the attack on the Monastery of St. Garabed, the murder of all the monks, the seminarians, the teachers, and his superior, Vartan *vartabed*, who was burned alive with his fellow *vartabed*, Yeghishe.

87. *Ibidem*, p. 381.

88. Krieger, *op. cit.*, footnote, p. 20.

89. BNu/Fonds Andonian, P.J.1/3, file 43, Bitlis, f° 6; BNu/Fonds Andonian, P.J.1/3, file 51, *The massacres in Daron*, f° 5, report by Mushegh Turnian, from Mush The witness's father was executed during this operation.

90. BNu/Fonds Andonian, P.J.1/3, file 43, Bitlis, f° 6v°; BNu/Fonds Andonian, P.J.1/3, file 51, *The massacres in Daron*, f° 6, report by Mushegh Turnian, relates the same facts but speaks of men between the ages of 15 and 70.

91. *Ibidem*, f° 6.

92. Aramaïs, *Les massacres et la lutte de Mousch-Sassoun*, 1915, trad. by Arev in Baku, Geneva 1916, pp. 16–17.

93. BNu/ Fonds Andonian, P.J.1/3, file 51, *The massacres in Daron*, f° 7. The vicar was given special treatment: he was burned alive in the bishopric, which was burned down.

94. *Ibidem*, f° 6v°; BNu/ Fonds Andonian, P.J.1/3, file 43, Bitlis, f° 6.

95. Aramaïs, *Les massacres et la lutte de Mousch-Sassoun*, *op. cit.*, pp. 20–2.

96. *Ibidem*, pp. 25–6.

97. BNu/Fonds Andonian, P.J.1/3, file 51, *The massacres in Daron*, f° 6, report by Mushegh Turnian.

98. BNu/ Fonds Andonian, P.J.1/3, file 43, Bitlis, f° 6; Papazian, *Memoirs*, *op. cit.*, II, p. 377; Aramais, *Les massacres et la lutte de Mousch-Sassoun*, *op. cit.*, pp. 27–9.

99. *Ibidem*, pp. 26–9; Alma Johannsen, *Ett folk i Landsflykt* [*A People in Exile*], Stockholm 1930, pp. 28–9, trans. Bedros Zartarian, in *Achkhar*, from 29 March to 28 June 1980.

100. Toynbee, *Le Traitement des Arméniens dans l'Empire ottoman*, *op. cit.*, pp. 216–18.

101. Johannsen, *Ett folk i Landsflykt*, *op. cit.*, pp. 28–9.

102. *Ibidem*, p. 32.

103. *Ibidem*, p. 34; Alma Johannsen left behind another more general account, which was published anonymously in Toynbee, *Le Traitement des Arméniens dans l'Empire ottoman*, *op. cit.*, pp. 211–13, "Report by a German, eyewitness to the events": Alma "Johanson" [orthographe of the document]: American National Archives: RG59/867. 4016/226), Constantinople, 9 November 1915 (see V. Bryce [= A. Toynbee], *op. cit.* [n. 51 *supra*], p. 124, footnote).

104. *Ibidem*, p. 212.

105. *Ibidem*, p. 213.

106. BNu/Fonds Andonian, P.J.1/3, file 51, The massacres in Daron, ff. 6–7, report by Mushegh Turnian, from Mush; APC/APJ, PCI Bureau, Ꝫ 561–2, *The organizer of the massacres in Mush, the deputy Hoca Ilyas*.

107. APC/APJ, PCI Bureau, Ꝫ 528, *La Renaissance*, "Bitlis-Mush, The camels laden with gold."

108. Papazian, *Memoirs*, *op. cit.*, II, p. 363.

109. BNu/Fonds Andonian, P.J.1/3, file 51, Les massacres du Daron, f° 43v°, reports of Garabed Saroyan and Mkhitar Ohanian, elementary school teachers in Gop, 20 August 1916, in Karavansaray; BNu/Fonds Andonian, P.J.1/3, file 51, The massacres in Daron, f° 9.

110. Nogales, *Four Years Beneath the Crescent*, *op. cit.*, p. 135.

111. Kévorkian & Paboudjian, *Les Arméniens dans l'Empire ottoman*, *op. cit.*, pp. 497–8.

112. BNu/Fonds Andonian, P.J.1/3, file 32, Manazgerd, ff. 1v°–2v°, report by Mher Ayvazian, from Noradin.

113. *Ibidem*, f° 2 r°–v°.

114. *Ibidem*, f° 2v°.

115. *Ibidem*, f° 1v°.

116. BNu/Fonds Andonian, P.J.1/3, file 32, Manazgerd, f° 1, report by Hagop Khochiants, from Manazgerd.

117. Kévorkian & Paboudjian, *Les Arméniens dans l'Empire ottoman*, *op. cit.*, pp. 498–500.

118. BNu/Fonds Andonian, P.J.1/3, file 51, The massacres in Daron, f° 42v°, reports of Garabed Saroyan and Mkhitar Ohanian, *doc. Cit.*

119. Aguni, *History of the Massacre of one Million Armenians*, *op. cit.*, p. 161.

120. BNu/Fonds Andonian, P.J.1/3, file 51, The massacres in Daron, f° 43.

121. *Ibidem*, f° 42.

122. *Ibidem*, f° 44.

123. *Ibidem*.

124. *Ibidem*, f° 44v°.

125. *Ibidem*, f° 42.

126. *Ibidem*, f° 43v°. Among the victims were Hovhannes Boyajian and Saghatel, a schoolteacher.

127. *Ibidem*, f° 44v°.

128. See *supra*, pp. 352–3; Aguni, *History of the Massacre of one Million Armenians*, *op. cit.*, p. 164. Four thousand inhabitants of the district of Psank succeeded at this time in withdrawing to the interior of the Sasun district, but half of them were then massacred by Kurdish çetes (Aramaïs, *Les massacres et la lutte de Mousch-Sassoun*, *op. cit.*, p. 35).

129. Johannsen, *Ett folk i Landsflykt*, *op. cit.*, p. 35.

130. Raymond Kévorkian, "The Armenian Population of Sassoun and the Demographic Consequences of the 1894 Massacres," *Armenian Review* vol. 47/1–2, Spring-Summer 2001, pp. 41–53. Let us note that of the 209 villages mentioned in the census of 1894, 53 no longer existed in 1914 (*ibidem*, pp. 42–3).

131. Aguni, *History of the Massacre of one Million Armenians*, *op. cit.*, p. 164; Aramaïs, *Les massacres et la lutte de Mousch-Sassoun*, *op. cit.*, p. 33.

132. Rafaël de Nogales, *Four Years Beneath the Crescent*, *op. cit.*, p. 134; Toynbee, *Le Traitement des Arméniens*, *op. cit.*, p. 207, interview with Ruben Ter Minasian by A. S. Safrastian, 6 November 1915, in Tiflis. These two *kazas* boasted 13,824 and 5,038 Armenians, respectively.

133. *Ibidem*, p. 209.

134. See *supra*, p. 337.

135. See *supra*, p. 346.

136. Aramaïs, *Les massacres et la lutte de Mousch-Sassoun, op. cit.*, p. 39.

137. Toynbee, *Le Traitement des Arméniens, op. cit.*, p. 210, interview with Ruben Ter Minasian.

138. Papazian, *Memoirs, op. cit.*, II, pp. 365–70.

139. Aramaïs, *Les massacres et la lutte de Mousch-Sassoun, op. cit.*, pp. 57–63; BNu/ Fonds Andonian, P.J.1/3, file 47, Sasun, ff. 1–9, reports of Father Mgrditch Muradian, Dikran Eretsian, Manuel Mardirosian, and Movses Stepanian, Aleppo, 24 February 1919; Toynbee, *Le Traitement des Arméniens, op. cit.*, p. 210.

140. Papazian, *Memoirs, op. cit.*, II, pp. 391–2.

141. *Ibidem*, pp. 397–9.

142. Kévorkian & Paboudjian, *Les Arméniens dans l'Empire ottoman, op. cit.*, p. 502.

143. BNu/Fonds Andonian, P.J.1/3, file 43, Bitlis, f° 8; Nazareth Piranian, Խարբերդի Եղեռնը [*Kharpert's Holocaust*], Boston 1937, pp. 168–9. The author was a prisoner in the "Red Konak" of Mezreh/Mamuret ul-Aziz when two men from Jabaghchur arrived in chains and under guard on 21 or 22 June. They told the author how the army had rounded up the local population, which was deported and massacred for the most part on Palu Bridge (on the massacres carried out on this bridge or in the area around it, see *infra*, p. 371).

144. BNu/ Fonds Andonian, P.J.1/3, file 43, Bitlis, f° 8.

145. Extract from the 5 December 1918 deposition of Vehib Pasha: *Takvim-ı Vakayi*, no. 3540, 5 May 1919, p. 7, col. 2 and the full deposition of handwritten pages: PAJ/APC, PCI Bureau, Հ 171–82.

146. Andonian, *Notes chronologiques, 1914–1916*, ms. cité, f° 56.

6   *Deportations and Massacres in the Vilayet of Dyarbekir*

1. Kévorkian & Paboudjian, *Les Arméniens dans l'Empire ottoman, op. cit.*, pp. 392–416, coted 148 churches, 10 monasteries, and 122 schools (9,660 students), not counting Islamicized Armenians and other Armenians not included in a parish. Attached to the indictment of the Young Turk leaders, in an appendix, is a 15 September 1915 telegram from Dr. Reşid informs the minister of the interior that the 120,000 Armenians of the vilayet have been deported: *Takvim-ı Vakayi*, no. 3540, daté du 5 mai 1919, p. 7, col. 1, this figure is higher than the Armenian census figures, a fact that shows, at the very least, how unreliable the official statistics published by certain authors such as Justin McCarty are (*Muslim and Minorities. The Population of Ottoman Anatolia and the End of Empire, op. cit.*, pp. 69–70). McCarty assigns these figures an extremely implausible margin of error (from 73,000 to 89,000).

2. AMAE, *Correspondance politique*, Turquie, n. s. vol. 87, pp. 31, 69.

3. Thomas Mgrdichian, Տիգրանակերտի Նահանգին Զարդերը [*The Massacres in the Province of Dyarbekir*], Cairo 1919, pp. 20–1. At the time, the author was British vice-consul in Dyarbekir.

4. Zaven Der Yeghiayan, *Memoirs, op. cit.*, p. 55.

5. BNu/Fonds Andonian, P.J.1/3, file 54, Dyarbekir, f° 7, report by N. Shaporlamajian and Z. Basmajian.

6. *Ibidem*, pp. 18–19.

7. *Ibidem*, p. 19.

8. Zaven Der Yeghiayan, *Memoirs, op. cit.*, pp. 54–5, letter from vicaire of Dyarbekir, Mgrdich Chlghadian, 27 September 1914.

9. *Ibidem*, p. 57.

10. Thomas Mgrdichian, *The Massacres in the Province of Dyarbekir, op. cit.*, pp. 21–2; *Faits et documents. épisodes des massacres arméniens de Dyarbékir*, Constantinople 1919, pp. 6–7; Aguni, *History of the Massacre of one Million Armenians, op. cit.*, pp. 60–1.

11. See *supra*, p. 196. Arif, Feyzi's father, was himself one of the main organizers of the massacres of 1895 in Dyarbekir; he was elected as a Young Turk deputy to parliament in 1908, leaving his seat to his son in the spring 1914 elections (*Faits et documents. épisodes des massacres arméniens de Dyarbékir, op. cit.*, p. 8).

12. *Ibidem*, p. 6.
13. APC/APJ, PCI Bureau, Ӡ 786–7, Massacres in Dyarbekir: Feyzi Bey Pirinji Zade, 18 February 1920 testimony by the former civilian inspector of the vilayets of Bitlis and Mosul.
14. Thomas Mgrdichian, *The Massacres in the Province of Dyarbekir*, op. cit., pp. 22–3.
15. *Ibidem*, p. 24.
16. *Ibidem*, p. 26.
17. *Ibidem*, pp. 26–7.
18. APC/APJ, PCI Bureau, Ӡ 786–7, Massacres in Dyarbekir: Feyzi Bey Pirinji Zade, 18 February 1920 testimony by the former civilian inspector of the vilayets of Bitlis and Mosul.
19. Thomas Mgrdichian, *The Massacres in the Province of Dyarbekir*, op. cit., p. 27.
20. Kieser, "Dr Mehmed Reshid (1873–1919)," art. cit., p. 261; See *supra*, p. 238.
21. *Ibidem*, p. 257, citing a wide variety of sources. On the persecutions the aim of which was to expel the Greeks from the region, see Taner Akçam, *İnsan Hakları ve Ermeni Sorunu. İttihat ve Terakki'den Kurtuluş savaşı'na*, op. cit., pp. 178–9.
22. Kieser, "Dr Mehmed Reshid (1873–1919)," art. cit., pp. 260–1.
23. Thomas Mgrdichian, *The Massacres in the Province of Dyarbekir*, op. cit., p. 36, states that they were wearing policemen's uniforms.
24. APC/APJ, PCI Bureau, Ӡ 113, 119, report by the commission of inquiry in Mamuret ul-Aziz, Ottoman original and transcription in Latin scripts, signed Mazhar, 20 December 1915, proposing that Reşid Bey, the vali of Dyarbekir, be brought before the court-martial.
25. First session of the trial of Unionists, 27 April 1919: *Takvim-ı Vakayi*, no. 3540, 5 May 1919, p. 6, col. 1, telegram from the *mutesarif* of Zor, Ali Suat, to the minister of interior.
26. *Faits et documents. épisodes des massacres arméniens de Dyarbékir*, op. cit., p. 13.
27. Mehmed Reşid, *Hayatı ve Hâtıraları*, ed. Necet Bilgi, Izmir 1997, p. 89, in *Mülâhazât: Ermeni Meselesi ve Dyarbekir Hatıraları*, cited in Kieser, "Dr Mehmed Reshid (1873–1919)," art. cit., p. 264; *Faits et documents. épisodes des massacres arméniens de Dyarbékir*, op. cit., p. 13.
28. Aguni, *History of the Massacre of one Million Armenians*, op. cit., pp. 61–2; Reşid, *Mülâhazât…*, op. cit., pp. 103, 107, gives only Cemilpaşazâde Mustafa's name; Thomas Mgrdichian, *The Massacres in the Province of Dyarbekir*, op. cit., pp. 37–8.
29. APC/APJ, PCI Bureau, Ӡ 786–7, Massacres in Dyarbekir: Feyzi Bey Pirinji Zade, 18 February 1920 testimony by the former civilian inspector of the vilayets of Bitlis and Mosul.
30. APC/APJ, PCI Bureau, Ӡ 537–41, 544, List of those responsible in the vilayet of Dyarbekir, file 29; Aguni, *History of the Massacre of one Million Armenians*, op. cit., p. 62.
31. APC/APJ, PCI Bureau, Ӡ 542–3, 546, Les terreurs de Dyarbekir, file 8.
32. Thomas Mgrdichian, *The Massacres in the Province of Dyarbekir*, op. cit., p. 37.
33. APC/APJ, PCI Bureau, Ӡ 537–41, 544, List of those responsible in the vilayet of Dyarbekir, file 29; *Faits et documents. épisodes des massacres arméniens de Dyarbékir*, op. cit., pp. 14–15; Thomas Mgrdichian, *The Massacres in the Province of Dyarbekir*, op. cit., pp. 40–2.
34. *Ibidem*, pp. 46–7; Aguni, *History of the Massacre of one Million Armenians*, op. cit., p. 62.
35. APC/APJ, PCI Bureau, Ӡ 786–7, Massacres in Dyarbekir, Feyzi Bey Pirinji Zade, 18 February 1920 testimony by the former civilian inspector of the vilayets of Bitlis and Mosul.
36. Thomas Mgrdichian, *The Massacres in the Province of Dyarbekir*, op. cit., p. 48; Aguni, *History of the Massacre of one Million Armenians*, op. cit., p. 62. Dr. Floyd Smith, who was in the employ of the American Board of Commissioners for Foreign Mission (ABCFM), witnessed these early operations; he affirms that the "false accusation of desertion" was used to justify the arrest of the notables: archives of ABCFM, letter to James Barton, 18 September 1915, cited in Kieser, "Dr Mehmed Reshid (1873–1919)," art. cit., pp. 264–5.
37. Thomas Mgrdichian, *The Massacres in the Province of Dyarbekir*, op. cit., pp. 49–53; Aguni, *History of the Massacre of one Million Armenians*, op. cit., p. 64.
38. Thomas Mgrdichian, *The Massacres in the Province of Dyarbekir*, op. cit., pp. 49–53; Aguni, *History of the Massacre of one Million Armenians*, op. cit., p. 64.
39. Archives of ABCFM, letter to James Barton, 18 September 1915, cited in Kieser, "Dr Mehmed Reshid (1873–1919)," art. cit., p. 265, n. 61; "Rapport de Rifaat effendi, 'defterdar hakani Mémouri'… sur les massacres… à Diarbékir et Mardine": SHAT, Service Historique de la Marine, Service de Renseignements de la Marine, Turquie, 1BB7 231, doc. no. 65, Constantinople, 2

January 1919, notes "every night, they were stripped, left naked, sprinkled with cold water and covered with blows."

40. Thomas Mgrdichian, *The Massacres in the Province of Dyarbekir, op. cit.*, pp. 53–5; Aguni, *History of the Massacre of one Million Armenians, op. cit.*, p. 63; *Faits et documents. épisodes des massacres arméniens de Dyarbékir, op. cit.*, pp. 21–3. The main Armenian leaders tortured in the central prison were: Mihran Basmajian, Giragos Ohannesian, Dikran Chakejian, the deputy of Dyarbekir Stepan Chrajian, Hagop Oghasapian, Dikran Ilvanian, and municipal councilor Stepan Matosian: the heads of others were crushed in vices, some were crucified, still others had their arms and legs amputed.

41. Archives of ABCFM, letter to James Barton, 18 September 1915, cited in Kieser, "Dr Mehmed Reshid (1873–1919)," *art. cit.*, p. 265, n. 62.

42. *Ibidem.*

43. APC/APJ, PCI Bureau, Հ 253, encrypted telegram, 17 May 1915, no. 38, from the *muteşar* of the Ministry of the Interior, to the president of the court-martial, signed by the vali of Dyarbekir Reşid and addressed to the vali of Adana İsmail Hakkı.

44. Aguni, *History of the Massacre of one Million Armenians, op. cit.*, p. 63.

45. Thomas Mgrdichian, *The Massacres in the Province of Dyarbekir, op. cit.*, p. 59; Aguni, *History of the Massacre of one Million Armenians, op. cit.*, p. 66; APC/APJ, PCI Bureau, Յ 542–3, 546, "Les terreurs de Dyarbekir (dépositions des témoins turcs et arméniens)," file 8.

46. *Ibidem.* Dr. Smith was expelled a few days later, on the vali's orders: *Faits et documents. épisodes des massacres arméniens de Dyarbékir, op. cit.*, p. 27. The author of this booklet affirms that the American physician also signed the attestation in order to escape the vali's clutches.

47. APC/APJ, PCI Bureau, Յ 542–3, 546, "Les terreurs de Dyarbekir (dépositions des témoins turcs et arméniens)," file 8; Thomas Mgrdichian, *The Massacres in the Province of Dyarbekir, op. cit.*, p. 58, states that Amero was received with honors by the vali, who presented him with gifts and asked him to give these men "a reception" in his region; APC/APJ, PCI Bureau, Յ 786–7, Massacres in Dyarbekir: Feyzi Bey Pirinji Zade, 18 February 1920 testimony by the former civilian inspector of the vilayets of Bitlis and Mosul, confirms Ferihanoğlu's role in these massacres; Aguni, *History of the Massacre of one Million Armenians, op. cit.*, p. 66.

48. Telegram from W. Holstein, to Istanbul embassy, 10 June 1915: J. Lepsius (ed.), *Archives du génocide des Arméniens*, Paris 1986, doc. 78, p. 93. Holstein says that 614 people were killed and that he saw the "empty" *keleks* arrive in Mosul.

49. Aguni, *History of the Massacre of one Million Armenians, op. cit.*, p. 67; Thomas Mgrdichian, *The Massacres in the Province of Dyarbekir, op. cit.*, p. 61.

50. *Ibidem*, pp. 61–3; Aguni, *History of the Massacre of one Million Armenians, op. cit.*, p. 68.

51. Ishaq Armalto, *Al-Gosara fi nakabat annasara* [*The Calamites of the Christians*], Beirut 1970 (reprint of the anonymous 1919 edition), p. 145; Ara Sarafian, "The Disasters of Mardin during the Persecutions of the Christians, Especially the Armenians, 1915," *Haigazian Armenological Review* XVIII (1998), cites a Catholic Syriac witness who stated that Dr. Reşid asked one of his colleagues from Mesopotamia to have Hilmi murdered on his way to Mosul.

52. Rhétoré, *Les chrétiens aux bêtes, ms. cit.*, pp. 200–1.

53. Bedreddin was confirmed in his functions on 12 September 1915 and held his post until 11 January 1916.

54. Thomas Mgrdichian, *The Massacres in the Province of Dyarbekir, op. cit.*, p. 65.

55. Armalto, *The Calamites of the Christians, op. cit.*, p. 149. Let us note that the man who replaced him, Hamid Bey, was not appointed until 30 June 1915 (he remained in his post until 2 May 1916) – that is, the day on which the liquidation of the Christians of Derik was terminated.

56. The murder of the two *kaymakams* was mentioned at the first session of the trial of the Unionists, 27 April 1919: *Takvim-ı Vakayi*, no. 3540, 5 May 1919, p. 8, col. 1, lines 15–20; we also have on this subject the report by a committee of inquiry led by Mazhar Bey on the exactions perpetrated by Dr. Reşid: APC/APJ, PCI Bureau, Հ 119 (Ottoman original) and Յ 465 (transcription).

57. Mehmed Reşid, *Hayatı ve Hâtıraları*, cited in Necet Bilgi (ed.), Izmir 1997, pp. 79–91, in *Mülâhazât: Ermeni Meselesi ve Dyarbekir Hatıraları*, cited in Kieser, "Dr Mehmed Reshid (1873–1919)," *art. cit.*, p. 265; n. 66.

58. Mehmed Reşid, *Hayatı ve Hâtıraları, op. cit.,* pp. 87–9.
59. *Faits et documents. épisodes des massacres arméniens de Dyarbékir, op. cit.,* p. 38.
60. Thomas Mgrdichian, *The Massacres in the Province of Dyarbekir, op. cit.,* pp. 68–70; Aguni, *History of the Massacre of one Million Armenians, op. cit.,* p. 69.
61. Hyacinthe Simon, *Mardine, la ville héroïque. Autel et tombeau de l'Arménie durant les massacres de 1915,* Jounieh, s. d., pp. 137–8.
62. Aguni, *History of the Massacre of one Million Armenians, op. cit.,* p. 69; Thomas Mgrdichian, *The Massacres in the Province of Dyarbekir, op. cit.,* pp. 74–5.
63. APC/APJ, PCI Bureau, B 542–3, 546, "Les terreurs de Dyarbekir (dépositions des témoins turcs et arméniens)," file 8; Aguni, *History of the Massacre of one Million Armenians, op. cit.,* p. 67; Thomas Mgrdichian, *The Massacres in the Province of Dyarbekir, op. cit.,* pp. 74–5.
64. Semi-official Young Turk publications and the Istanbul press seized on these photographs to launch a campaign depicting the Armenians as criminals, see *La vérité sur le mouvement révolutionnaire arménien et les mesures gouvernementales,* Constantinople 1916.
65. "Les terreurs de Diarbékir (dépositions des témoins turcs et arméniens)": SHAT, Service Historique de la Marine, Service de Renseignements de la Marine, Turquie, 1BB7 231, doc. no. 279, Constantinople 1919, f° 2.
66. Rafaël de Nogales, *Four Years Beneath the Crescent, op. cit.,* pp. 139–40.
67. Thomas Mgrdichian, *The Massacres in the Province of Dyarbekir, op. cit.,* p. 75; Aguni, *History of the Massacre of one Million Armenians, op. cit.,* p. 69.
68. BNu/Fonds Andonian, P.J.1/3, file 58, Rakka, ff. 1–15, report by Krikor Ankut; Raymond Kévorkian, *L'Extermination des déportés arméniens ottomans dans les camps de concentration de Syrie-Mésopotamie (1915–1916), la Deuxième phase du génocide,* RHAC II (1998), p. 165.
69. BNu/Fonds Andonian, P.J.1/3, file 52, Der Zor, ff. 108–10, report by Aram Andonian; R. H. Kévorkian, *L'Extermination des déportés arméniens ottomans dans les camps de concentration de Syrie-Mésopotamie (1915–1916), la Deuxième phase du génocide, op. cit.,* p. 215.
70. *Ibidem,* p. 220.
71. *Ibidem,* p. 224.
72. Aguni, *History of the Massacre of one Million Armenians, op. cit.,* p. 69.
73. Rhétoré, *Les chrétiens aux bêtes,* ms. cit., pp. 35–6; *Faits et documents. épisodes des massacres arméniens de Dyarbékir, op. cit.,* pp. 40–1.
74. Aguni, *History of the Massacre of one Million Armenians, op. cit.,* p. 70.
75. *Faits et documents. épisodes des massacres arméniens de Dyarbékir, op. cit.,* pp. 51–2.
76. Rafaël de Nogales, *Four Years Beneath the Crescent, op. cit.,* p. 145.
77. *Faits et documents. épisodes des massacres arméniens de Dyarbékir, op. cit.,* pp. 45–8.
78. "Rapport de Rifaat effendi, defterdar hakani mémouri à Mardin, démissionnaire, sur les massacres d'Arméniens, de Grecs et de Syriens à Diarbékir et Mardine": SHAT, Service Historique de la Marine, Service de Renseignements de la Marine, Turquie, 1BB7 231, doc. no. 279, Constantinople, 2 January 1919.
79. Kieser, "Dr Mehmed Reshid (1873–1919)," *art. cit.,* pp. 268–9.
80. Telegram from Dr. Reşid, 15/28 September 1915, to the minister of interior: *Takvim-ı Vakayi,* no. 3540, 5 May 1919, p. 7, col. 1.
81. J. Naayeim, *Les Assyro-Chaldéens et les Arméniens massacrés par les Turcs,* Paris 1920, p. 138.
82. Telegram from Halil Edip to Dr. Reşid, 17 October 1915, cited in Necet Bilgi (ed.), *Reşid, Hayatı ve Hâtıraları, op. cit.,* p. 29.
83. Telegram from Wangenheim to chancelier Bethmann Hollweg, Pera, 9 July 1915: Lepsius (ed.), *Archives du génocide des Arméniens, op. cit.,* doc. 108, pp. 102–3.
84. Telegram from Holstein to Constantinople embassy, Mosul, 14 August 1915: Lepsius (ed.), *Archives du génocide des Arméniens, op. cit.,* doc. 139, p. 134.
85. Rafaël de Nogales, *Four Years Beneath the Crescent, op. cit.,* pp. 147–8.
86. Kévorkian & Paboudjian, *Les Arméniens dans l'Empire ottoman, op. cit.,* p. 400; Karpat, *op. cit.,* p. 176, gives the official figure of 1,128 Armenians in 1914.
87. Armalto, *The Calamites of the Christians, op. cit.,* pp. 350–9; Rhétoré, *Les chrétiens aux bêtes,* ms. cit., pp. 39–42; Simon, *op. cit.,* pp. 82–3; Ternon, *Mardin 1915, op. cit.,* pp. 98–100.
88. Armalto, *The Calamites of the Christians, op. cit.,* p. 94.

89. Kévorkian & Paboudjian, *Les Arméniens dans l'Empire ottoman*, *op. cit.*, p. 400; Karpat, *op. cit.*, p. 176, gives the official figure of 2,853 Armenians in 1914.

90. APC/APJ, PCI Bureau, Ց 537–41, 544, List of those responsible in the vilayet of Dyarbekir, Severek. Haci Tellal Hakimoğlu, nicknamed Haci Onbaşi, murdered the six leading political prisoners held in Ayaş: Rupen Zartarian, Dr. Nazareth Daghavarian, Karekin Khazhag, Aknuni, Harutiun Jangiulian, and Sarkis Minasian. They were killed in a place known as Karacur, half-way between Urfa and Severek: BNu/Fonds Andonian, P.J.1/3, file 3, prisoners of Ayaş, ff. 48–52 (see *infra*, p. 524).

91. Ternon, *Mardin 1915*, *op. cit.*, pp. 101–2.

92. Faiez el-Ghocein, *Les Massacres en Arménie*, traduit de l'arabe par A. El-G, second ed., Beirut 1965, pp. 16–18; Fa'iz el-Ghusein, *Martyred Armenia*, Bombay 1916, pp. 22–7, reprinted by Richard Kloian, *The Armenian Genocide. News Accounts from the American Press (1915–1922)*, Berkeley 1985.

93. On the way from Severek and Dyarbekir, the witness encountered a caravan of women and children from this city, from which most of the Armenians were deported in July.

94. Kévorkian & Paboudjian, *Les Arméniens dans l'Empire ottoman*, *op. cit.*, p. 400.

95. See *supra*, p. 363, n. 55.

96. APC/APJ, PCI Bureau, Ց 537–41, 544, List of those responsible in the vilayet of Dyarbekir, file 29.

97. See *supra*, p. 366.

98. Armalto, *The Calamites of the Christians*, *op. cit.*, p. 345; Rhétoré, *Les chrétiens aux bêtes*, ms. *cit.*, p. 43; Ternon, *Mardin 1915*, *op. cit.*, pp. 100–1.

99. Kévorkian & Paboudjian, *Les Arméniens dans l'Empire ottoman*, *op. cit.*, pp. 400–2.

100. Toynbee, *Le Traitement des Arméniens dans l'Empire ottoman (1915–1916)*, *op. cit.*, p. 207, interview with Ruben Ter Minasian.

101. Rafaël de Nogales, *Four Years Beneath the Crescent*, *op. cit.*, p. 134; Toynbee, *Le Traitement des Arméniens dans l'Empire ottoman (1915–1916)*, *op. cit.*, p. 207.

102. See *supra*, p. 363, n. 56.

103. Kévorkian & Paboudjian, *Les Arméniens dans l'Empire ottoman*, *op. cit.*, p. 402.

104. See *supra*, p. 363, n. 56.

105. J. Naayeim, *Les Assyro-Chaldéens et les Arméniens massacrés par les Turcs*, *op. cit.*, pp. 169–76; Rhétoré, *Les chrétiens aux bêtes*, ms. *cit.*, p. 49; Ternon, *Mardin 1915*, *op. cit.*, pp. 102–3.

106. Kévorkian & Paboudjian, *Les Arméniens dans l'Empire ottoman*, *op. cit.*, pp. 403–6. The villages were Göljük, Topelan, Pirnushan, Payam, Eğil/Ankgh, Aypega/Hiredan, Tilbaghdad, Piran, and Gaplan.

107. Karnig Kévorkian, Չնքուշապատում [*History of Chnkush*], Jerusalem 1970, pp. 92–101.

108. Guregh Khrayian, Ճովք եւ Կէոլճիք [*Dzovk-Göljük*], Marseille 1927.

109. *Ibidem*, pp. 145–58.

110. *Ibidem*, pp. 159–62.

111. *Ibidem*, p. 165. He was accused notably by the Kurds in the area of possessing a cannon. What was involved was in fact a still used to make rakı; these uneducated men seem to have mistaken it for a weapon.

112. *Ibidem*, pp. 165–6.

113. *Ibidem*, pp. 167–70.

114. *Ibidem*, pp. 171–9.

115. *Ibidem*, pp. 180–4.

116. *Ibidem*, pp. 184–7.

117. *Ibidem*, pp. 204–27.

118. *Ibidem*, pp. 229–51.

119. Kévorkian & Paboudjian, *Les Arméniens dans l'Empire ottoman*, *op. cit.*, pp. 400–2, a total of 12,418 Armenians, counting the 280 inhabitants of the neighboring village of Chnkush, Adish.

120. Kévorkian, *History of Chnkush*, *op. cit.*, pp. 92–101.

121. *Ibidem*, pp. 94–5; Jean Naslian, *Les Mémoires de Mgr Jean Naslian*, I, Vienna 1951, pp. 302–4.

122. K. Minaguian "Չնքուշի Կոտորածը [*The Massacre in Chnkush*]," *Bahag*, 29 August 1919, p. 1.

123. Kévorkian, *History of Chnkush, op. cit.*, pp. 95–6.
124. Naslian, *Memoirs*, I, *op. cit.*, pp. 344–5, report by an escape; Kévorkian, *History of Chnkush, op. cit.*, pp. 94–9.
125. *Ibidem*, pp. 100–1.
126. Kévorkian & Paboudjian, *Les Arméniens dans l'Empire ottoman, op. cit.*, pp. 406–8.
127. Mesrob Grayian, Բալու [*Palu*], Antelias 1965, p. 495.
128. *Ibidem*, p. 502.
129. *Ibidem*, p. 505.
130. APC/APJ, PCI Bureau, Յ 537–41, 544, List of those responsible in the vilayet of Dyarbekir, Palu.
131. Misak Khralian, Բալահովիտ [*Palahovid*], Sofia 1938, pp. 71–2.
132. BNu/Fonds Andonian, P.J.1/3, file 12, Palu, f° 2v°, report by Kevork M. Garabedian; Grayian, *Palu, op. cit.*, pp. 508–9.
133. *Ibidem*, pp. 77–8; BNu/ Fonds Andonian, P.J.1/3, file 12, Palu, f° 2, report by Kevork M. Garabedian. The village of Nirkhi was encircled on 21 May by a captain in the gendarmerie and 12 men who tortured the village priest and leading men and then got drunk: BNu/ Fonds Andonian, P.J.1/3, file 12, Palu, ff. 4–7, report by Zakar P. Fndkhian, from Nirkhi.
134. *Ibidem*, f° 2 v°; Simon, *op. cit.*, p. 82; Grayian, *Palu, op. cit.*, p. 509.
135. BNu/Fonds Andonian, P.J.1/3, file 12, Palu, f° 7, report by Zakar P. Fndkhian. It would even seem that this all-powerful official had a pronounced taste for young boys; he came to the bridge to pick them out.
136. BNu/Fonds Andonian, P.J.1/3, file 12, Palu, f° 11.
137. BNu/Fonds Andonian, P.J.1/3, file 61, Kığı, ff. 66v°.
138. APC/APJ, PCI Bureau, Է 351–6, report in English on the massacres in the region of Erzerum; APC/APJ, PCI Bureau, Թ 334 (in French), no. 35, report on *Les événements de Keghi depuis la mobilisation jusqu'à la déportation.*
139. Grayian, *Palu, op. cit.*, pp. 514–15.
140. BNu/Fonds Andonian, P.J.1/3, file 12, Palu, f° 3, report by Kevork M. Garabedian.
141. Grayian, *Palu, op. cit.*, p. 519.
142. *Ibidem*, pp. 515–16.
143. Kévorkian & Paboudjian, *Les Arméniens dans l'Empire ottoman, op. cit.*, pp. 412–15.
144. *Congregatio de causis sanctorum. P.N. 1 704. Ciliciae Armenorum seu Mardinen. Beatificationis seu Canonizationis servi Dei Ignatii Choukrallah Maloyan, archiepiscopi mardinensis in opium fidei, uti fertur, interfecti (1915); Positio super vita, martyrio eiusque causa necnon super fama martyrii ex testibus et documentis historicis*, I, Roma 1998, pp. 98–100.
145. For a full review of the sources on these events as well as Archbishop Maloyan's testament in Arabic, see Yves Ternon, *Mardin 1915*, RHAC, V (2002), pp. 110–1.
146. See *supra*, p. 363, n. 51–4.
147. APC/APJ, PCI Bureau, Յ 539, List of those responsible in the vilayet of Dyarbekir, Mardin. Halil Edip would later order that Tell Armen and El Kusru be burned down.
148. *Ibidem.*
149. The officers and leading members of the Special Organization were: Haydar Şeyheffendioğlu, Mehmed Kabulo, Mehmet el Mully, Şevket Bey Mehmet Ağaoğlu, Mehmet Bey, brother of Şevket Bey Mehmet Ağaoğlu, Beşo Sarac, the sons of Şeyh Hattap, Sadık Ali Terzioğlu, Hac Celdo, Kadi Amşaki, Hamdi el-Şarabi, Halil Halafo, Faris Paşa Fameyoğlu, Ömer, uncle of Faris Paşa Fameyoğlu, Vasi Muhar Saïdağa, Ali Bayrakdar, Osman, Mustafa, Aziz Ayo, Dervis Hamo, Yusuf Çavuş, Hüseyin Belalo, Hüseyin Belalo Halil, Hüseyin Belalo Osman, the sons of Ali Memo, Mehmet Şerif, Faranioğlu, Kade Bakır family, Aziz Bero Hüseyinbeyoğlu, Halil, "Hallo," and Haci Abdelkadir: APC/APJ, PCI Bureau, Յ 539, List of those responsible in the vilayet of Dyarbekir, Mardin.
150. *Ibidem.*
151. Sarafian, "The Disasters of Mardin," *art. cit.*, cites a Catholic Syriac who witnessed this fraud; Ternon, *Mardin 1915, op. cit.*, p. 117.
152. *Ibidem.*
153. *Positio super vita, op. cit.*, I, p. 353, report by Ibrahim Kaspo.

154. See the many sources on these events listed in Ternon, *Mardin 1915*, *op. cit.*, pp. 118–19, n. 3 to 6.

155. *Positio super vita*, *op. cit.*, I, p. 133, translation of Ishaq Armalto's narrative, *The Calamites of the Christians*.

156. *Ibidem*, I, p. 389; Rhétoré, *ms. cit.*, p. 68; Sarafian, "The Disasters of Mardin," *art. cit.*, p. 263, declaration of Chaldean witness; Ternon, *Mardin 1915*, *op. cit.*, p. 120.

157. *Ibidem*.

158. *Ibidem*.

159. *Ibidem*, p. 123, n. 20. The author catalogues various sources, which speak of 404 (Simon) to 480 men (the testimony of the "Chaldean"), of whom 35 were Catholic Syriacs and 20 were Protestants; the others were Armenians. There were also 11 clergymen in the convoy.

160. *Ibidem*, pp. 124–5, n. 22 à 27 for the sources.

161. *Ibidem*, pp. 126–7.

162. *Ibidem*, pp. 134–5.

163. Ternon cites the text of the telegram as given in S. Aydın, *Mardin*, *op. cit.* For the original, see: BOA, DH. şfr no. 54/406, encrypted telegram from the Ministry of Interior to the vilayet of Dyarbekir, 12 July 1915: *Armenians in Ottoman Documents (1915–1920)*, *op. cit.*, p. 75.

164. Ternon, *Mardin 1915*, *op. cit.*, p. 136.

165. *Ibidem*, p. 139.

166. *Ibidem*, pp. 140–1.

167. *Ibidem*, pp. 142–3.

168. See *supra*, pp. 368–9.

169. Ternon, *Mardin 1915*, *op. cit.*, p. 143–4.

170. *Ibidem*, pp. 145–6; Simon, *op. cit.*, pp. 89–90.

171. *Ibidem*, pp. 146–7; Rethore and Simon are our main sources for these events.

172. Sarafian, "The Disasters of Mardin," *art. cit.*, p. 266, declaration of Chaldean witness.

173. Simon, *op. cit.*, p. 55.

174. *Ibidem*, pp. 56, 85.

175. *Ibidem*, p. 90.

176. Simon, *op. cit.*, p. 78.

177. Ternon, *Mardin 1915*, *op. cit.*, p. 158–61, cites numerous accounts, notably that of Father Simon, 49–50, which indicates that 1,500 Catholic Armenians were executed beginning on 1 July.

178. Telegram from Wangenheim to chancelier Bethmann Hollweg, Pera, 9 July 1915: Lepsius (ed.), *Archives du génocide des Arméniens*, *op. cit.*, doc. 108, pp. 102–3.

179. APC/APJ, PCI Bureau, Β 539, List of those responsible in the vilayet of Dyarbekir, Mardin.

180. Ternon, *Mardin 1915*, *op. cit.*, p. 161–6.

181. Kévorkian & Paboudjian, *Les Arméniens dans l'Empire ottoman*, *op. cit.*, p. 415.

182. Simon, *op. cit.*, p. 87.

183. Ternon, *Mardin 1915*, *op. cit.*, pp. 167–70.

184. *Ibidem*, pp. 170–3.

185. Telegram from colonel Ömer Naci, 12 October 1915, to the General Commandment, with the encrypted telegram from Haydar Bey, vali of Mosul, to General Staff, 12 October 1915: Ataşe Arşivi, KOL: BDH, KLS: 17, dos.: 81/FIH: 27, cited in Israfil Kurtcephe, "Birinci dünya savaşinda bir süryani ayaslanmasi," *Osmanlı Tarihi Arastirma ve Uygulama Merkezi Dergisi* 1993/4, pp. 291–6.

186. Report from Scheubner Richter to Chancellor Bethmann Hollweg, Munich, 4 December 1916: Lepsius (ed.), *Archives du génocide des Arméniens*, *op. cit.*, doc. 309, pp. 234–40, especially p. 236.

187. *Ibidem*, p. 236.

188. *Ibidem*, p. 236. The encrypted telegram from the minister of war, Enver, to the commandant of the Third Army, Mahmud Kâmil, 28 October 1915, does indeed mention Syriac rebels fighting side-by-side with Armenians: Ataşe Arşivi, KOL: BDH, KLS: 17, dos.: 81/Fhr. 32, cited in Israfil Kurtcephe, "Birinci dünya savaşinda," *art. cit.*, p. 293.

189. Kévorkian & Paboudjian, *Les Arméniens dans l'Empire ottoman*, *op. cit.*, p. 415.

190. Ternon, *Mardin 1915*, *op. cit.*, pp. 175–6, cites Armalto, *op. cit.*, p. 413.

191. Kévorkian & Paboudjian, *Les Arméniens dans l'Empire ottoman*, op. cit., p. 415. These villages were: Arnabad, Mezer, Giundekşeyh, Tıldar, Perek, Berebt, Cerahi, Hntuk, Ceder, Keoçer and, Zakho.

192. Simon, op. cit., p. 88.

193. Report from Hohenlohe to Chancellor Bethmann Hollweg, Istanbul, 11 September 1915: Lepsius (ed.), *Archives du génocide des Arméniens*, op. cit., doc. 167, pp. 146–7; Ternon, *Mardin 1915*, op. cit., pp. 179–80.

194. *Ibidem*, p. 180–2.

195. Simon, op. cit., p. 91.

196. Kévorkian & Paboudjian, *Les Arméniens dans l'Empire ottoman*, op. cit., p. 415.

197. Ternon, *Mardin 1915*, op. cit., pp. 182–4; Simon, op. cit., p. 12.

198. *Ibidem*, p. 86.

199. Public Record Office, FO 371/6503, no. 264, the file of prisoner no. 2,667, Ali Ihsan, interned in Malta, accused of committing massacres in the regions of Van, Nisibin, and Urmia, where he personally murdered an American patient in the hospital, John Nooshy.

200. APC/APJ, Ց 158, the file of Ziya [Gökalp], born in Dyarbekir, a member of the Ittihadist Central Committee.

201. Extract from the 5 December 1918 deposition of Vehib Pasha: *Takvim-ı Vakayi*, no. 3540, 5 May 1919, p. 7, col. 2 and the full deposition of handwritten pages: APC/APJ, PCI Bureau, Հ 171–82.

202. Kieser, "Dr Mehmed Reshid (1873–1919)," art. cit., p. 268.

203. BOA, DH. şfr no. 54/406, encrypted telegram from the Ministry of Interior to the vilayet of Dyarbekir, 12 July 1915: *Armenians in Ottoman Documents (1915–1920)*, op. cit., p. 75.

204. See in particular the many exchanges between the diplomats posted in Constantinople and Berlin, especially the 4 September 1915 letter from Hohenlohe to Chancellor Bethmann Hollweg, in which Hohenlohe informs the chancellor that he has received the German transla-tion of "various telegraphic orders" issued by Talât: "he thereby sought to prove that the central government was making a serious attempt to put an end to the excesses." Yet only a few days earlier, Hohenlohe adds, the minister declared in his presence: "the Armenian Question no longer exists.": Lepsius (ed.), *Deutschland und Armenien*, Berlin–Potsdam 1919, doc. 160, p. 147; also Weber, *Eagles on the Crescent: Germany, Austria and the Diplomacy of the Turkish Alliance, 1914–1918*, op. cit., pp. 150–2.

7   Deportations and Massacres in the Vilayet of Mamuret ul-Aziz

1. Nazareth Piranian, Խարբերդի Եղեռնը [*The Holocaust of Kharpert*], Boston 1937, 541 pp., writ-ten by a former Euphrates College teacher, is the most comprehensive and reliable source. The 70 ff. reports in BNu/Fonds A. Andonian, P.J.1/3, file 23, Harput, are also uniquely illuminating sources on the events that occurred in the towns and villages of the plain of Harput and the mas-sacres perpetrated around Lake Göljük. Levon Gjigian, Մօրենիկ եւ իր Սեւ Տարին [*Morenig and Its Black Year*], Antelias 1969 and Anna Mirakian, Վէրքեր եւ Յաւեր [*Wounds and Griefs*], Antelias 1960, are also essential.

2. *Takvim-ı Vakayi* no. 3540 (at the session of trial of 12 April 1919), 5 May 1919, pp. 4–6 especially, in annexe of the Young Turk trial act of accusation, *Takvim-ı Vakayi* no. 3771, 13 January 1920, pp. 48–9 especially, indictment of the trial of Harput, again Bahaeddin Şakir.

3. *Osmanli Belgelerinde Ermeniler (1915–1920)*, T. C. Başbakanlik Devlet Arşivleri Genel Müdürlüğü, Osmanli Arşivi Daire Başbakanliği, *Armenians in Ottoman Documents (1915–1920)*, op. cit.

4. Leslie A. Davis, *The Slaughterhouse Province, An American Diplomat's Report on the Armenian Genocide, 1915–1917)*, ed. By Susan K. Blair, New Rochelle, New York 1989; Ara Sarafian (ed.), *United States Official Documents on the Armenian Genocide, III, The Central Lands*, Watertown 1995.

5. Henry H. Riggs, *Days of Tragedy in Armenia, Personal Experiences in Harpoot, 1915–1917*, Ann Arbor 1997; Maria Jacobsen, *Diary of a Danish Missionary, Harpoot, 1907–1919*, Ara Sarafian (ed.), Princeton-London 2001.

6. The expression often recurs in the reports of Davis, *The Slaughterhouse Province*, op. cit.

7. Kévorkian & Paboudjian, *Les Arméniens dans l'Empire ottoman, op. cit.*, pp. 353–91. Karpat, *op. cit.*, p. 182, puts the number of Armenians at 87,864 in 1914.

8. *Ibidem*, p. 358.

9. *Ibidem*, p. 360.

10. Riggs, *Days of Tragedy in Armenia, op. cit.*, pp. 3–4.

11. *Ibidem*, pp. 4–6.

12. *Ibidem*, p. 7.

13. *Ibidem*, p. 15, mentions, notably, the case of a Turkish soldier from Egin whom an Armenian companion-in-arms saved "like a brother."

14. Vahé Hayg, Խարբերդը եւ անոր Ոսկեղէն Դաշտր [*Kharpert and Its Golden Plain*], New York 1959, p. 1415.

15. Piranian, *The Holocaust of Kharpert, op. cit.*, pp. 73–4.

16. *Ibidem*, p. 78.

17. APC/APJ, PCI Bureau, 3 430, 467, 474, those responsible for the deportations and massacres in the region of Harput.

18. Also known as Sağırzâde, Sabit was born in Kemah (in the *sancak* of Erzincan) in 1881. Under the Kemalist regime, he served as the vali of Erzerum and was the founder and director of the Ziraat Bankası. He served several terms as a parliamentary deputy from Erzincan and, later, Elazığ. He died in Istanbul in 1960: Adnan Işık, *Malatia, Adıyaman, Akçadaği, Arabkir, Besni, Darende, 1830–1919*, Istanbul 1998, p. 761, n.

19. Davis, *The Slaughterhouse Province, op. cit.*, pp. 107–8: report to State Department, 9 February 1918.

20. *Ibidem*.

21. Işik, *Malatia, op. cit.*, p. 761, note.

22. Riggs, *Days of Tragedy in Armenia, op. cit.*, pp. 32–3; Davis, *The Slaughterhouse Province, op. cit.*, p. 107; Jacobsen, *Diary of a Danish Missionary, op. cit.*, p. 36, gives the date of the interview, in which M. Pierce also participated.

23. Riggs, *Days of Tragedy in Armenia, op. cit.*, p. 33.

24. *Ibidem*, pp. 34–5. However, the authorities ultimately ceded one floor to the school for girls; Davis, *The Slaughterhouse Province, op. cit.*, p. 117.

25. *Ibidem*, p. 117. During the winter of 1915, typhus wrought havoc among the soldiers and, later, the population of Mezreh in particular. The situation was so serious that the authorities appointed the general practitioner Artin Helvajian, a native of Dyarbekir trained in the Military Medical School of Constantinople, to the post of chief physician of the vilayet's hospitals, requesting that he take the necessary measures to stop the spread of the epidemic: Piranian, *The Holocaust of Kharpert, op. cit.*, pp. 73–4, 77–8, 84.

26. Piranian, *The Holocaust of Kharpert, op. cit.*, pp. 36–43, 43–58.

27. *Ibidem*, p. 79.

28. *Ibidem*, pp. 82–3.

29. Riggs, *Days of Tragedy in Armenia, op. cit.*, p. 45.

30. *Ibidem*, p. 47.

31. Hayg, *Kharpert and its golden plain, op. cit.*, p. 1417, cites the account of one of the participants in the meeting, Harutiun Pekmezian.

32. APC/APJ, PCI Bureau, file XXIX, Ս 579/4, copy of encrypted telegram from vali, Sabit Bey, to *mutesarif* of Malatia, 15 February 1915 (2 Şubat): "How is the training of the squadron proceeding? Is it about to bear fruit? I would ask you to devote all your energy and to concentrate all your efforts [on training it] and also to send men to the capital of the vilayet in, at the latest, three days."

33. Report by Miss Hansina Marcher, a Danish missionary working for the German Red Cross in Harput, in which she repeats remarks made by the German vice-consul as he was dining with the missionaries shortly after holding a conversation with Sabit Bey on the evening of 16 March 1915: Bryce [= Toynbee], *The Treatment of Armenians in the Ottoman Empire*, Uncensored ed., *op. cit.*, doc. 64, pp. 286–7; the French translation, Toynbee, *Le Traitement des Arméniens dans l'Empire ottoman, op. cit.*, doc. 22, p. 261, is imprecise; Aguni, *History of the Massacre of one Million Armenians, op. cit.*, p. 152.

34. Piranian, *The Holocaust of Kharpert*, op. cit., pp. 99–100; Davis, *The Slaughterhouse Province*, op. cit., p. 118: report to State Department, 9 February 1918. The chronological detail is provided by Maritza Kejejian: Toynbee, *The Treatment of Armenians in the Ottoman Empire*, op. cit., doc. 68, p. 299.

35. Davis, *The Slaughterhouse Province*, op. cit., p. 118: report to State Department, 9 February 1918.

36. Piranian, *The Holocaust of Kharpert*, op. cit., p. 100: many even burned their bibles so as not to give the authorities a pretext for violence; Riggs, *Days of Tragedy in Armenia*, op. cit., p. 47.

37. Letter from the director of Mezreh's German orphanage, Johannes Ehmann, to Wangenheim, Mamuret ul-Aziz, 5 May 1915: Lepsius (ed.), *Archives du génocide des Arméniens*, op. cit., doc. 42, pp. 86–7.

38. Piranian, *The Holocaust of Kharpert*, op. cit., p. 231.

39. Toynbee, *The Treatment of Armenians*, op. cit., doc. 64, p. 287.

40. Piranian, *The Holocaust of Kharpert*, op. cit., pp. 187–8, states that the village was attacked as soon as the population surrendered its arms.

41. *Ibidem*, pp. 219–20.

42. *Ibidem*, pp. 229–33; BNu/Fonds A. Andonian, P.J.1/3, file 23, Harput, ff. 49–50. Hagopian, a member of the German mission in Harput, affirms that the Armenians were convinced that the measures taken by the authorities were directed only at political activists and that the Armenian population had nothing to fear. B. Hagopian likewise had the feeling that Ehmann was, at the time, unaware of the Turks' criminal intentions (*ibidem*, f° 49 v°).

43. Riggs, *Days of Tragedy in Armenia*, op. cit., p. 47; Jacobsen, *Diary of a Danish Missionary, Harpoot, 1907–1919*, op. cit., p. 61, affirms that the arrests were made by soldiers who escorted them directly to the governor's palace, adding that in the evening these men were taken back to their places of residence so that they would be present when the police searched them.

44. *Ibidem*.

45. Piranian, *The Holocaust of Kharpert*, op. cit., pp. 43–4: teacher in Euphrates College, born in 1856, executed on 20 June 1915 on the northern shore of Lake Göljük, near Kezinhan.

46. *Ibidem*, pp. 46–7: born in 1864, leader of the Protestant community since 1895, teacher at Euphrates College, executed on 20 June 1915 on the northern shore of Lake Göljük, near Kezinhan.

47. *Ibidem*, pp. 48–9: born in 1868, teacher at Euphrates College, died on 25 January 1916, after one year in prison.

48. *Ibidem*, pp. 52–3: born in 1868 in Malatia, teacher at Euphrates College, killed in the second convoy from Mezreh, in early July.

49. *Ibidem*, pp. 54–5: born in 1873 in Chnkush, teacher at Euphrates College, executed on 20 June 1915 on the northern shore of Lake Göljük near Kezinhan.

50. *Ibidem*, pp. 57–8: born in 1875 in Harput, educated at Yale and Cornell, arrested on 1 May, a refugee in the American consulate until February 1916, thereafter a refugee in Erzerum, where he was the director of an orphanage; died on 22 March 1917.

51. Piranian, *The Holocaust of Kharpert*, op. cit., pp. 101–2.

52. Riggs, *Days of Tragedy in Armenia*, op. cit., p. 47.

53. *Ibidem*, pp. 47–8.

54. *Ibidem*, p. 48.

55. *Ibidem*, p. 49.

56. Report by Miss Hansina Marcher: Toynbee, *The Treatment of Armenians*, op. cit., doc. 64, p. 287; Toynbee, *Le Traitement des Arméniens*, op. cit., doc. 22, p. 262.

57. *Ibidem*. Jacobsen, *Diary of a Danish Missionary, Harpoot, 1907–1919*, op. cit., p. 67, mentions a proclamation of the vali's that was read out in the churches on 6 June to encourage the population to turn in its arms.

58. Davis, *The Slaughterhouse Province*, op. cit., p. 53: letter from Davis to Morgenthau, Harput, 24 July 1915.

59. Riggs, *Days of Tragedy in Armenia*, op. cit., p. 49.

60. *Ibidem*, p. 77.

61. Davis, *The Slaughterhouse Province*, op. cit., p. 157: letter from Davis to Morgenthau, Harput, 24 July 1915.

62. Jacobsen, *Diary of a Danish Missionary, Harpoot, 1907–1919*, op. cit., p. 67.

63. Riggs, *Days of Tragedy in Armenia*, op. cit., p. 75.
64. Jacobsen, *Diary of a Danish Missionary, Harpoot, 1907–1919*, op. cit., pp. 68–70; Piranian, *The Holocaust of Kharpert*, op. cit., p. 104, points notably to the arrest Hovhannes Harputlian, intellectuals and businessmen, and all the other men who had paid the *bedel* to avoid conscription.
65. Riggs, *Days of Tragedy in Armenia*, op. cit., pp. 77–8.
66. Piranian, *The Holocaust of Kharpert*, op. cit., pp. 117–18 and 133–7.
67. *Ibidem*, pp. 137–8. The author's sister, Sara, a schoolteacher in Mezreh's German school, appealed to Reverend Ehmann to intercede on behalf of those imprisoned in the *konak*, so that they might at least be allowed to drink; Ehemann denied that the authorities could be so brutal as to deny the men water (*ibidem*, p. 139); Tracy Atkinson, "The German, the Turk and the Devil Made a Triple alliance": *Harpoot Diaries, 1908–1917*, Princeton 2000, p. 38.
68. *Ibidem*, pp. 141–6.
69. *Ibidem*, pp. 98–9, 151–7.
70. Riggs, *Days of Tragedy in Armenia*, op. cit., p. 78.
71. Piranian, *The Holocaust of Kharpert*, op. cit., pp. 156–8, 167–8, 170.
72. *Ibidem*, pp. 171–6. On the night of 22 June, 75 men who had paid the *bedel* were taken out of Mezreh's central prison and liquidated shortly thereafter (*ibidem*, p. 177).
73. *Takvim-ı Vakayi* no. 3771, 13 January 1920, p. 48–9 especially, indictment of the trial of Mamuret ul-Aziz; Davis, *The Slaughterhouse Province*, op. cit., p. 79: report to State Department, 9 February 1918, confirms the destruction of this convoy, in which most of the notables of Harput and Mezreh were to be found, along with the Armenian Apostolic primate, Bsag Der Khorenian, whom Davis does not name, like Atkinson, "The German, the Turk and the Devil Made a Triple alliance," op. cit., p. 38.
74. Riggs, *Days of Tragedy in Armenia*, op. cit., pp. 77–8.
75. APC/APJ, PCI Bureau, ♂ 99, ♋ 229, ♋ 243–5 (in French), dossier des Turcs inculpés dans le procès des massacres de Mamuret ul-Aziz, 13 September 1920, file 2.
76. Piranian, *The Holocaust of Kharpert*, op. cit., pp. 179–82.
77. *Ibidem*, pp. 185, 206–7; BNu/Fonds A. Andonian, P.J.1/3, file 23, Harput, f° 53, report by Araks Mgrdichian, points out as well that in the same period boys between 13 and 15 were rounded up, imprisoned, and deported.
78. Piranian, *The Holocaust of Kharpert*, op. cit., pp. 206–7.
79. Riggs, *Days of Tragedy in Armenia*, op. cit., p. 119. Although the Orthodox Syriacs were officially exempt from deportation, Piranian notes that they were nevertheless stripped of all their possessions and that some of them were killed: Piranian, *The Holocaust of Kharpert*, op. cit., p. 203; APC/APJ, PCI Bureau, ♂ 99, ♋ 229, ♋ 243–4–5 (in French), dossier des Turcs inculpés dans le procès des massacres de Mamuret ul-Aziz, 13 September 1920, file 2, states that the brigadier general Süleyman Faik Pasha demanded that Harput's Catholic Syriacs who were not deported provide him with a written declaration to the effect that he had treated them "with kindness."
80. Davis, in a 6 September 1915 dispatch to Morgenthau sent from Mamuret ul-Aziz, notes that the dispatches he sent after 29 June had obviously not arrived at their destination and that even the "sealed" letters that he had sent after that date had passed through the vali's hands and had not all arrived: Davis, *The Slaughterhouse Province*, op. cit., pp. 67–9. Riggs also notes that the American mission's telephone had been cut off early in June: Riggs, *Days of Tragedy in Armenia*, op. cit., p. 64.
81. *Ibidem*, p. 80.
82. *Ibidem*, p. 81; Davis, *The Slaughterhouse Province*, op. cit., pp. 126–7, confirms that, in addition to the American missionaries, Reverand Ehmann, the director of the German mission, and the Austrian Charles Picciotto, assistant director of the local branch of the Banque Ottomane, took part in this conversation.
83. Letter from Davis to Morgenthau, Mamuret ul-Aziz, 30 June 1915: *ibidem*, p. 33; Ara Sarafian (ed.), *United States Official Documents on the Armenian Genocide, III, The Central Lands*, Watertown 1995, p. 3.
84. Report to State Department, 9 February 1918: Davis, *The Slaughterhouse Province*, op. cit., p. 54.
85. Riggs, *Days of Tragedy in Armenia*, op. cit., p. 81.
86. *Ibidem*, p. 103; report from Davis to Morgenthau, Mamuret ul-Aziz, 7 September 1915: Davis, *The Slaughterhouse Province*, op. cit., p. 73.

87. BOA, DH., şfr. no. 54/163, encrypted telegram from the minister of interior, Talât, to the vali of Mamuret ul-Aziz, Sabit, Istanbul, 26 June 1915: *Osmanli Belgelerinde Ermeniler (1915–1920)*, T.C. Başbakanlik Devlet Arşivleri Genel Müdürlüğü, Osmanli Arşivi Daire Başkanliği, *Armenians in Ottoman Documents (1915–1920), op. cit.*, no. 47, p. 56. Jacobsen, *Diary of a Danish Missionary, Harpoot, 1907–1919, op. cit.*, p. 73, indicates for his part that at the "rencontre memorable" of 29 June, the vali promised Ehmann that old people and "women without husbands" would be exempt from deportation; Piranian, *The Holocaust of Kharpert, op. cit.*, who worked at the American hospital in the following weeks, often mentions these two categories; some of the people in them were still living in Mezreh and Harput.

88. Riggs, *Days of Tragedy in Armenia, op. cit.*, p. 103; report from Davis to Morgenthau, Mamuret ul-Aziz, 7 September 1915: Davis, *The Slaughterhouse Province, op. cit.*, p. 73. Davis, for his part, notes that the orders did not arrive in time.

89. BOA, DH., şfr. no. 54/189, encrypted telegram from the vice-minister of the interior, Ali Münîf, to the vali of Mamuret ul-Aziz, Sabit, Istanbul, 27 June 1915: *Osmanli Belgelerinde Ermeniler (1915–1920)*, T.C. Başbakanlik Devlet Arşivleri Genel Müdürlüğü, Osmanli Arşivi Daire Başkanliği, *Armenians in Ottoman Documents (1915–1920), op. cit.*, no. 51, pp. 58–9. The document does not state where these emigrants came from. It is likely that they were inhabitants of provinces further to the east who were fleeing the advancing Russian army.

90. Riggs, *Days of Tragedy in Armenia, op. cit.*, pp. 84–5.

91. *Ibidem*, pp. 85–6; report to State Department, 9 February 1918: Davis, *The Slaughterhouse Province, op. cit.*, pp. 54–5, uses the expression "the vultures swooping down on their prey."

92. Riggs, *Days of Tragedy in Armenia, op. cit.*, pp. 98–9.

93. *Ibidem*, p. 89.

94. *Ibidem*, p. 89.

95. Riggs employs the term "remittances," although the operations described here are rather more like transfers: *ibidem*, p. 89; in his report to State Department, 9 February 1918: Davis, *The Slaughterhouse Province, op. cit.*, p. 54, confirms what the missionary says, adding that some Armenians left carrying large sums of money and "were robbed, almost without exception, soon after they left."

96. Letter from Davis to Morgenthau, Mamuret ul-Aziz, 30 June 1915: Davis, *The Slaughterhouse Province, op. cit.*, pp. 36–7. The whole second part of Davis's 9 February 1918 report is about the difficulty of "managing" these sums of money and responding to the demands of deportees who had arrived in Syria or Mesopotamia.

97. Report to State Department, 9 February 1918: Davis, *The Slaughterhouse Province, op. cit.*, pp. 128–9, cites the case of an American murdered in Çarsancak, Garabed Urfalian, whose wife, accompanied by the consul, had noticed that the 150 Turkish pounds deposited in her husband's bank account were paid out to the commission responsible for abandoned property. No doubt in order to evaluate the way this commission worked, the consul went to see its president and also the vali, as the representative of the interests of an American citizen, and demanded that the sum be paid to the widow and her children, who had taken refuge in Harput. "Inquiries" were undertaken "to verify" that the deceased had not left debts; it was promised that, if he had not, his widow would receive five to ten Turkish pounds. However, notes the consul, after six months of efforts, the commission had still not paid the widow anything.

98. Piranian, *The Holocaust of Kharpert, op. cit.*, p. 238.

99. *Ibidem*, p. 57, states that he had as much as 200,000 dollars in deposits.

100. Riggs, *Days of Tragedy in Armenia, op. cit.*, pp. 66–7, 90

101. *Ibidem*, pp. 91–2. Riggs states the bank's Armenian teller, to whom he entrusted these sums, respected the clients' right to secrecy and "have any reason" to reveal the amount of the deposits in question.

102. *Ibidem*, pp. 92–3. Reverand Ehmann was also asked to accept deposits: *ibidem*, p. 94.

103. Piranian, *The Holocaust of Kharpert, op. cit.*, p. 203; see *supra*, p. 388, n. 71.

104. Piranian, *The Holocaust of Kharpert, op. cit.*, pp. 208–10. The minister was erudite; he knew Greek, Latin, Italian, French, English, Turkish, Farsi, and Arabic. He was highly respected in Mezreh.

105. *Ibidem*, p. 211.

106. Letter from Davis to Morgenthau, Mamuret ul-Aziz, 30 June 1915: Davis, *The Slaughterhouse Province*, *op. cit.*, p. 148.

107. Kévorkian & Paboudjian, *Les Arméniens dans l'Empire ottoman*, *op. cit.*, pp. 353–73.

108. Letter from Davis to Morgenthau, Mamuret ul-Aziz, 11 July 1915: Davis, *The Slaughterhouse Province*, *op. cit.*, pp. 41–3; Piranian, *The Holocaust of Kharpert*, *op. cit.*, pp. 212–14, report by Aghavni Boyajian.

109. Piranian, *The Holocaust of Kharpert*, *op. cit.*, pp. 215–19; BNu/Fonds A. Andonian, P.J.1/3, file 23, Harput, ff. 13–15, report by Kohar Halajian.

110. *Ibidem*, pp. 222–5.

111. *Ibidem*, pp. 226–7.

112. *Ibidem*, pp. 219–20; Atkinson, "The German, the Turk and the Devil Made a Triple alliance," *op. cit.*, p. 40.

113. Jacobsen, *Diary of a Danish Missionary, Harpoot, 1907–1919*, *op. cit.*, p. 73, was informed of the fate of these men by the pharmacist at the hospital, "baron Melcon" [Liulejian, one of the survivors of this convoy]; Atkinson, "The German, the Turk and the Devil Made a Triple alliance," *op. cit.*, p. 40; Riggs, *Days of Tragedy in Armenia*, *op. cit.*, p. 103.

114. Jacobsen, *Diary of a Danish Missionary, Harpoot, 1907–1919*, *op. cit.*, p. 75.

115. *Ibidem*, pp. 76–7.

116. Atkinson, "The German, the Turk and the Devil Made a Triple alliance," *op. cit.*, p. 46.

117. *Ibidem*. Letter from Davis to Morgenthau, Mamuret ul-Aziz, 11 July 1915: Davis, *The Slaughterhouse Province*, *op. cit.*, p. 46, Davis notes that the day before he had met with the vali and tried to persuade him to authorize opening an orphanage for all the children who were roaming through the region or had ended up in Harput.

118. Letter from Davis to Morgenthau, Mezreh, 11 July 1915, p. 7, included in the report from Morgenthau to Secretary of State, 10 August 1915: National Archives (Washington), RG 59, 867. 4016/122 (microfilm 353, bobine 43). They were deported in early September (*ibidem*, p. 73, Davis to Morgenthau, 6 September 1915). In a report by 9 February 1918, Davis noted that these boys were sent to the slaughterhouse at Lake Göljük: *ibidem*, p. 142.

119. Jacobsen, *Diary of a Danish Missionary, Harpoot, 1907–1919*, *op. cit.*, pp. 76–7; The missionaries observed with relief that not many people converted.

120. *Ibidem*, p. 78; Atkinson, "The German, the Turk and the Devil Made a Triple alliance," *op. cit.*, p. 46.

121. *Ibidem*, pp. 46–7; Piranian, *The Holocaust of Kharpert*, *op. cit.*, pp. 236–8; Davis to Morgenthau, Harput, 24 July 1915: Davis, *The Slaughterhouse Province*, *op. cit.*, pp. 55–6: a Frenchwoman, Marguerite Gamat, who had been unable to leave Harput since the outbreak of the war, was among the victims.

122. BNu/Fonds A. Andonian, P.J.1/3, file 23, Harput, f° 47, report by Mushegh Vorperian.

123. Jacobsen, *Diary of a Danish Missionary, Harpoot, 1907–1919*, *op. cit.*, pp. 78–9; Riggs, *Days of Tragedy in Armenia*, *op. cit.*, p. 103.

124. BNu/Fonds A. Andonian, P.J.1/3, file 23, Harput, f° 48, report by Mushegh Vorperian.

125. Davis to Morgenthau, Harput, 24 July 1915: Davis, *The Slaughterhouse Province*, *op. cit.*, p. 157.

126. Jacobsen, *Diary of a Danish Missionary, Harpoot, 1907–1919*, *op. cit.*, pp. 82–3. 869. Davis to Morgenthau, Harput, 24 July 1915: Davis, *The Slaughterhouse Province*, *op. cit.*, p. 157.

127. *Ibidem*, p. 157. Davis states that the vali asked Ehmann and Picciotto to do the same thing.

128. *Ibidem*, p. 161.

129. *Ibidem*, p. 73. Davis notes that the head of the police was "sitting in my office that night … until nearly two o'clock in the Morning … He wanted me to speak in the letter about the bombs and weapons"; if he did not, the thousand or so Armenians still present in the city would face "more severe measures than ever" beginning the following day.

130. *Ibidem*, p. 162.

131. Jacobsen, *Diary of a Danish Missionary, Harpoot, 1907–1919*, *op. cit.*, p. 84; Piranian, *The Holocaust of Kharpert*, *op. cit.*, pp. 296–300. The prisoners who died in this fire included: Father Vartan Arslanian, Hagop Fermanian, Hagop Najarian, Mardiros Muradian, Harutiun Der Kaprielian, Dikran Asdigian, Dr. Nshan Nahigian, Hayrabed Hovsepian, Melkon Frengian, Shahpaz Bedrosian, Toros Tanielian, Levon Totovents, Edvart Tachjian, Garabed Geogiushian, Garabed Demirjian, Dr. S. Jelalian, Asadur Darakjian, Jean Parakian, Jean

Shirvanian, Nigoghos Kalenderian, Hagop agha, Pilibbos Nalbandian, Hovhannes Tanielian, Garabed Boyajian, etc.

132. BNu/Fonds A. Andonian, P.J.1/3, file 23, Harput, f° 50v°, the account by Reverand Bedros Hagopian, a member of the German mission of Harput, has rather severe words for Davis, who closed his doors to several naturalized Americans. One, Simon Sargavakian, tore up his U.S. passport and threw it in the consul's face.

133. BNu/Fonds A. Andonian, P.J.1/3, file 23, Harput, ff. 51v°–6, Araks Mgrdichian, the consul's daughter, depicts Davis as someone who was unwilling to take risks and who therefore refused to take in his colleague's family at the crucial moment. The family was saved in the end by Dr. Atkinson at the American hospital.

134. Atkinson, "The German, the Turk and the Devil Made a Triple alliance," op. cit., p. 46.

135. Piranian, The Holocaust of Kharpert, op. cit., pp. 247–8; Jacobsen, Diary of a Danish Missionary, Harpoot, 1907–1919, op. cit., p. 99.

136. Atkinson, "The German, the Turk and the Devil Made a Triple alliance," op. cit., p. 38.

137. Piranian, The Holocaust of Kharpert, op. cit., pp. 187–8.

138. BNu/Fonds A. Andonian, P.J.1/3, file 23, Harput, f° 42, report by Mihran Zakarian; Levon Gjigian, Morenig and his Black Year, op. cit.

139. BNu/Fonds A. Andonian, P.J.1/3, file 23, Harput, ff. 65–6, report by Krikor Yeghoyan, a native of the village of Khuylu, returned there from the United States on 25 December 1913.

140. Ibidem, f° 69v°; Davis to Morgenthau, 30 December 1915: Davis, The Slaughterhouse Province, op. cit., pp. 178–83, confirms that this was the fate of these drivers.

141. Ibidem, ff. 67–8v°.

142. Piranian, The Holocaust of Kharpert, op. cit., pp. 256–9. Piranian notes that the inhabitants of Khuylu were being deported when he passed through the vicinity on 16 July (ibidem, p. 259). Consul Davis later visited several villages on the plain and observed that they were in ruins and that the churches had been systematically demolished, as if to "remove all traces" of an Armenian presence: report from Davis to the State Department, 9 February 1918: Davis, The Slaughterhouse Province, op. cit., p. 79.

143. BNu/Fonds A. Andonian, P.J.1/3, file 23, Harput, f° 39, report by Mihran Zakarian, a theology student at Euphrates College.

144. Ibidem, f° 49v°. Consul Davis notes that several of the battalions of worker-soldiers who arrived from Erzrrum in November and December were put to death: Davis to Morgenthau, 30 December 1915: Davis, The Slaughterhouse Province, op. cit., pp. 178–83.

145. APC/APJ, PCI Bureau, ♂ 99, Ց 229, Ց 243–5 (in French), dossiers des personnes inculpées dans le procès des massacres de Mamuret ul-Aziz, 13 September 1920, no. 2, file I and II.

146. Ibidem.

147. Piranian, The Holocaust of Kharpert, op. cit., pp. 111–18.

148. Manug Jizmejian, Խարբերդը եւ իր Զաւակները [Kharpert and Its Children], Fresno 1955, pp. 434–5.

149. Piranian, The Holocaust of Kharpert, op. cit., pp. 111–18.

150. Ibidem, pp. 120–2.

151. Ibidem, pp. 127–8.

152. APC/APJ, PCI Bureau, ♂ 99, Ց 229 and Ց 243–5 (in French), dossiers des personnes inculpées dans le procès des massacres de Mamuret ul-Aziz, 13 September 1920, no. 2, file II.

153. Piranian, The Holocaust of Kharpert, op. cit., pp. 132–3.

154. See supra, pp. 387–8.

155. APC/APJ, PCI Bureau, ♂ 99, Ց 229, Ց 243–5 (in French), dossiers des personnes inculpées dans le procès des massacres de Mamuret ul-Aziz, 13 September 1920, no. 2, file I.

156. APC/APJ, PCI Bureau, Կ 360, encrypted telegram no. 33 (original Կ 361) sent by Süleyman Faik Pasha, the military commander of Harput, to the commander-in-chief of the Third Army in Tortum on 16/29 August 1915; James L. Barton, "Turkish Atrocities." Statements of American Missionaries on the Destruction of Christian Communities in Ottoman Turkey, 1915–1917, Ann Arbor 1998, pp. 33, testimony of Mary Riggs, who speaks of the cadavers of people who had been shot to death just before she passed through the area in early November 1915.

157. APC/APJ, PCI Bureau, ♂ 99, ♀ 229, ♀ 243–5 (in French), dossiers des personnes inculpées dans le procès des massacres de Mamuret ul-Aziz, 13 September 1920, no. 2, file I. The president announced that he had further information indicating that not just one convoy, but, rather, all of them had been liquidated under conditions like those described by Süleyman Faik. He therefore decided to arrest Faik immediately.

158. APC/APJ, PCI Bureau, ♀ 465, doc. no. 3, a passage of Fazıl's report about Sabit Bey. Lazare, 22, a native of Arapkir, escaped execution and succeeded in reaching Malatia, where he testified about these events.

159. Aguni, *History of the Massacre of One Million Armenians*, op. cit., pp. 158–9.

160. Atkinson, "The German, the Turk and the Devil Made a Triple alliance," op. cit., pp. 40–2; this convoy was put back on the road on 9 July; Barton, "Turkish Atrocities," op. cit., p. 42, report by Dr. Tracy Atkinson.

161. Piranian, *The Holocaust of Kharpert*, op. cit., p. 243.

162. Atkinson, "The German, the Turk and the Devil Made a Triple alliance," op. cit., p. 40.

163. Davis to Morgenthau, Mamuret ul-Aziz, 11 July 1915: Davis, *The Slaughterhouse Province*, op. cit., p. 150.

164. *Ibidem*, p. 151. The convoys that arrived in August were initially stationed near the village of Hulakiugh/Hulaköy, one hour west of Harput, to be moved late in September to the walled cemetery of Mezreh's Armenian Church: Barton, "Turkish Atrocities," op. cit., p. 57, report by Ruth A. Parmelee.

165. *Ibidem*, p. 160.

166. See *supra*, p. 297.

167. Piranian, *The Holocaust of Kharpert*, op. cit., p. 256.

168. Atkinson give the exact date of this trip ("The German, the Turk and the Devil Made a Triple alliance," op. cit., p. 55); report from Davis to state Department, 9 February 1918: Davis, *The Slaughterhouse Province*, op. cit., p. 79.

169. *Ibidem*, p. 80. Davis indicates that he initially believed that this was a "sanitary measure," but soon learned the truth about the murderers' methods.

170. *Ibidem*, pp. 81–2.

171. *Ibidem*, pp. 82–3. Davis' observations seem to indicate that these people had been on the road for several weeks and were therefore not Armenians from the region of Harput.

172. *Ibidem*, p. 84.

173. *Ibidem*, pp. 86–7; the exact date of the two men's departure is given in Atkinson, "The German, the Turk and the Devil Made a Triple alliance," op. cit., p. 58.

174. *La Renaissance*, no. 43, 22 January 1919, article of S. Padova, "Le lac ensanglanté," reprinted from *La Liberté de Smyrne*; BNu/ Fonds A. Andonian, P.J.1/3, file 23, Harput, ff. 23–6, doc. 45, "Le lac ensanglanté."

175. BOA, DH. EUM, 2 şb. no. 68/70, telegram from the vali of Mamuret ul-Aziz, Sabit, to the minister of the interior, Talât, Mamuret ul-Aziz, 18 September 1915: *Osmanli Belgelerinde Ermeniler (1915–1920)*, T.C. Başbakanlik Devlet Arşivleri Genel Müdürlüğü, Osmanli Arşivi Daire Başkanliği, *Armenians in Ottoman Documents (1915–1920)*, op. cit., no. 114, p. 106. This estimate is plausible if one adds to it the worker-soldiers, who were dealt with separately, the men killed before the official deportations began, and the populations massacred where they were found and the Armenians who managed to flee to the Dersim district. Another document, emanating from APC/APJ, PCI Bureau, file 57, report to the minister of the interior, mentions 50,024 Armenian deportees in the *sancak* of Harput and 74,206 in the whole of the vilayet.

176. Jacobsen, *Diary of a Danish Missionary, Harpoot, 1907–1919*, op. cit., p. 89.

177. Davis to Morgenthau, Mamuret ul-Aziz, 30 December 1915: Davis, *The Slaughterhouse Province*, op. cit., pp. 178–83.

178. Jacobsen, *Diary of a Danish Missionary, Harpoot, 1907–1919*, op. cit., pp. 91–2, Diary of 25 September.

179. *Ibidem*, p. 100; report from Davis to state Department, 9 February 1918: Davis, *The Slaughterhouse Province*, op. cit., pp. 85–6.

180. Barton, "Turkish Atrocities," op. cit., p. 57, report by Ruth A. Parmelee and, p. 70, report by Isabelle Harley; Davis to Morgenthau, Mamuret ul-Aziz, 30 December 1915: Davis, *The Slaughterhouse*

Province, *op. cit.*, pp. 178–83. The inhabitants of Harput were finally freed on condition that "se faire turc."

181. Jacobsen, Diary of a Danish Missionary, Harpoot, 1907–1919, *op. cit.*, pp. 105–6.

182. *Ibidem*, p. 108, The 35 men in the convoy had become Muslims several weeks earlier.

183. Davis to Morgenthau, Mamuret ul-Aziz, 30 December 1915: Davis, *The Slaughterhouse Province*, *op. cit.*, pp. 180–3.

184. Jacobsen, *Diary of a Danish Missionary, Harpoot, 1907–1919*, *op. cit.*, p. 99.

185. APC/APJ, PCI Bureau, ♂ 99, Ӡ 229, Ӡ 243–5 (in French), dossiers des Turcs inculpés dans le procès des massacres de Mamuret ul-Aziz, 13 September 1920, no. 2, file II. The general was accused, notably, of entering the American hospital, arresting the Armenians on the staff and having them killed.

186. BNu/Fonds A. Andonian, P.J.1/3, file 23, Harput, f° 42 v°, report by Mihran Zakarian, theology student at Euphrates College.

187. See *supra*, p. 314.

188. APC/APJ, PCI Bureau, file XXIX, U 578, certified copy of decoted telegram, and U 577, copy of encrypted telegram from the vali of Mamuret ul-Aziz, Sabit Bey, to the vilayet of Mamuret ul-Aziz, 3 November 1915, in Erzincan. in view of the date of the telegram, it is possible that Sabit took advantage of the meeting to visit his family in Kemah, near Erzincan, after finishing his work. He did not return to Mezreh until 16 November, with 200 young Armenians whom he ordered imprisoned in the Red Konak: Jacobsen, *Diary of a Danish Missionary, Harpoot, 1907–1919, op. cit.*, p. 110.

189. APC/APJ, PCI Bureau, file XXIX, U 578, certified copy of decoded telegram, U 577/2, copy of encrypted telegram from the temporary vali of Mamuret ul-Aziz, Süleyman Faik, to Sabit bey, Erzincan, 3 November 1915.

190. APC/APJ, PCI Bureau, file XXIX, U 579/3, copy of the encrypted telegram from the kaimakam of Kahta to the *mutesarif* of Malatia, 12 December 1915.

191. Report from Davis to state Department, 9 February 1918: Davis, *The Slaughterhouse Province*, *op. cit.*, pp. 79–80.

192. *Ibidem*, p. 94.

193. Jacobsen, *Diary of a Danish Missionary, Harpoot, 1907–1919*, *op. cit.*, p. 99, 112; cf. *supra*, p. 395.

194. *Ibidem*, p. 110.

195. BNu/Fonds A. Andonian, P.J.1/3, file 23, Harput, doc. 19, f° 27, "An Autodafé."

196. *Ibidem*.

197. Kévorkian & Paboudjian, *Les Arméniens dans l'Empire ottoman*, *op. cit.*, pp. 373–5.

198. APC/APJ, PCI Bureau, file 57, report to the Ministry of the Interior.

199. Kévorkian & Paboudjian, *Les Arméniens dans l'Empire ottoman*, *op. cit.*, p. 377; Karpat, *op. cit.*, p. 182, gives the official figure of 679 Armenians.

200. APC/APJ, PCI Bureau, file 57, report to the Ministry of the Interior.

201. Kévorkian & Paboudjian, *Les Arméniens dans l'Empire ottoman*, *op. cit.*, pp. 375–6 – that is, 10,880 Armenians; Karpat, *op. cit.*, p. 182, gives the official figure of 10,091 in the *kaza*.

202. BNu/Fonds A. Andonian, P.J.1/3, file 10, Arapkir, f° 5, report by Kalust Kaloyan, Papert, 17 June 1917.

203. *Ibidem*, f° 5v°.

204. *Ibidem*.

205. BNu/Fonds A. Andonian, P.J.1/3, file 10, Arapkir, f° 17, report by Khachig Kardashian, born in Arapkir, educated at Euphrates College, a cadet at the Officer's Training School in Erzincan from September 1914 to February 1915, was recovering from typhus in Arapkir.

206. BNu/Fonds A. Andonian, P.J.1/3, file 10, Arapkir, report by Kalust Kaloyan, ff. 6v°–7.

207. BNu/Fonds A. Andonian, P.J.1/3, file 10, Arapkir, report by Khachig Kardashian, f° 17v°.

208. BNu/Fonds A. Andonian, P.J.1/3, file 10, Arapkir, report by Kalust Kaloyan, f° 7v°, and report by Khachig Kardashian, f° 19, gives the date of departure.

209. *Ibidem*, f° 8.

210. *Ibidem*, f° 8 and 19 and 20v°. These events were related by the gendarmes in the escort shortly after they occurred.

211. BNu/Fonds A. Andonian, P.J.1/3, file 10, Arapkir, report by Khachig Kardashian, f° 19v°–20. Jacobsen, *Diary of a Danish Missionary, Harpoot, 1907–1919, op. cit.*, p. 65, reports that on 3 June,

the missionaries received a message informant them of the arrest of the Armenian ministers in Peri and Arapkir.

212. BNu/Fonds A. Andonian, P.J.1/3, file 10, Arapkir, report by Khachig Kardashian, ff. 20v°–1.
213. *Ibidem*, f° 21
214. *Ibidem*, f° 21v°.
215. *Ibidem*, ff. 21v°–2; Atkinson, "The German, the Turk and the Devil Made a Triple alliance," *op. cit.*, p. 39, notes that the missionaries learned of the massacre of the men of Arapkir on 26 June.
216. BNu/Fonds A. Andonian, P.J.1/3, file 10, Arapkir, report by Khachig Kardashian, f° 22.
217. *Ibidem*, f° 22v°.
218. BNu/Fonds A. Andonian, P.J.1/3, file 10, Arapkir, f° 9, report by Kalust Kaloyan.
219. *Ibidem*, ff. 9r°–v° and 22v°.
220. *Ibidem*, f° 9v°.
221. *Ibidem*, f° 10.
222. *Ibidem*, f° 11r°–v°.
223. *Ibidem*, f° 12.
224. *Ibidem*, f° 12v°.
225. *Ibidem*. Their escort headed back to Arapkir.
226. *Ibidem*, f° 13. At this point, the witness' sister was turned over to a young captain who agreed to take Kaloust with him as well. The Malatia Armenian population had not yet been deported.
227. See *supra*, p. 297, for an account of the destruction of a convoy from Erzerum in this gorge. BNu/Fonds A. Andonian, P.J.1/3, file 10, Arapkir, ff. 1–4, reports by three survivors from the convoy from Arapkir who reached Urfa and then Aleppo after crossing the Kahta gorge.
228. BNu/Fonds A. Andonian, P.J.1/3, file 10, Arapkir, report by Khachig Kardashian, f° 23–r°–v°. The handful of artisans who were allowed to remain behind after converting to Islam, most of whom were masons, were ultimately deported in their turn.
229. *Ibidem*, f° 23v°.
230. *Ibidem*, ff. 23v°–24. In view of the route they took, this must have been the "second convoy" from Erzerum. It was later decimated in the Kahta gorge, although it had paid Haci Bedri Ağa 30,000 Turkish pounds gold in protection money (*ibidem*, f° 25): see *supra*, p. 294.
231. *Ibidem*, f° 25.
232. *Ibidem*, f° 26.
233. APC/APJ, PCI Bureau, Һ 215 and Յ 469–70, 473 (in Arm.), list of those responsible for the massacres and deportations in Arapkir.
234. *Ibidem*.
235. *Ibidem*.
236. APC/APJ, PCI Bureau, file 57, report to the Ministry of the Interior.
237. Kévorkian & Paboudjian, *Les Arméniens dans l'Empire ottoman*, *op. cit.*, pp. 377–81; Karpat, *op. cit.*, p. 182, gives the official figure of 9,888 Armenians and 676 "Greeks" for the whole of the *kaza*. The Armenian villages were Abusher/Apchaka (Armenian pop. 1,920), Gamaragab (pop. 1,260), Gurshla (pop. 256), Lijk (pop. 526), Perga/Pekir (pop. 1,170), Narvid/Navril (pop. 207), Vank (pop. 150), Tsorag (pop. 70), Shrzu (pop. 320 Arm. orthodoxes), Mushaghga/Mechenkana (164 Arm. orthodoxes), Aghn/Aghin (pop. 319), Vaghshen/Vakshen (pop. 276), Kushna/Sowuk (pop. 397), Dzablvar/Zabiliar (pop. 16), Grani/Kir Ali (pop. 92), Hasgni/Haskini (pop. 70), Ehnetsig/Ihnesik (pop. 231), Khoroch/ Khoruch (pop. 115), Dzak/Eyin (pop. 687), Mashgerd/Mashgir (pop. 496), and Saghmga/Samuku (pop. 279).
238. Aguni, *History of the Massacre of One Million Armenians*, *op. cit.*, p. 174.
239. BNu/Fonds A. Andonian, P.J.1/3, file 2, Agn, report by Levon Boghosian, f° 1.
240. Aguni, *History of the Massacre of One Million Armenians*, *op. cit.*, p. 175.
241. *Ibidem*.
242. *Ibidem*.
243. *Ibidem*.
244. *Ibidem*; Atkinson, "The German, the Turk and the Devil Made a Triple alliance," *op. cit.*, p. 38. Atkinson notes that the missionaries in Harput learned on 26 June that massacres had taken place in the region of Agn: she is probably referring to the murders of the men in the city as well as in the villages. BNu/Fonds Andonian, P.J.1/3, file 2, Agn, report by Levon Boghosian, ff. 2–5.

245. *Ibidem*, f° 6.

246. *Ibidem*, f° 5r°–v°.

247. *Ibidem*, f° 6.

248. *Ibidem*, f° 6v°. Levon Boghosian succeeding in fleeing to Malatia at this time. There he gathered, as we shall see, valuable information about the central prison and state "orphanage."

249. APC/APJ, PCI Bureau, Þ 215 and Ӡ 468–9 (in French), list of those responsible for the massacres and deportations in Eğin/Agn.

250. *Ibidem*. Most of these criminals were Turkish notables from Agn and the environs; there were also a few Kurdish chieftains among them.

251. Aguni, *History of the Massacre of one Million Armenians*, op. cit., p. 176.

252. Hans Bauernfeind, *Journal de Malatia 1915*, edited by Méliné Pehlivanian & Tessa Hofmann, in Raymond Kévorkian, *L'Extermination des déportés arméniens ottomans dans les camps de concentration de Syrie-Mésopotamie (1915–1916), la Deuxième phase du génocide*, RHAC II (1998), pp. 245–325.

253. Kévorkian & Paboudjian, *Les Arméniens dans l'Empire ottoman*, op. cit., pp. 387–91. That is, 17,017 in 1914.

254. BNu/Fonds A. Andonian, P.J.1/3, file 31, Malatia, report by Hovhannes Khanghlarian, f° 2v°.

255. Kévorkian & Paboudjian, *Les Arméniens dans l'Empire ottoman*, op. cit., pp. 387–91.

256. BNu/Fonds A. Andonian, doc. cit., file 31, report by H. Khanghlarian, f° 2, indicates that the auxiliary primate protested these requisitions, only to be reprimanded by Captain Cavid, who described the Armenians as "traitors."

257. *Ibidem*, f° 3.

258. *Ibidem*; Bauernfeind, *Journal de Malatia 1915*, op. cit., p. 270, notes this fact in his Diary of 19 April 1915.

259. *Ibidem*, pp. 259 and 272, speaks of the mission's domestic, the 17-year-old Krikor; his "mobilization" took the form of imprisonment in the barracks in Malatia; BNu/Fonds A. Andonian, doc. cit., file 31, report by H. Khanghlarian, f° 6v°, confirms that the second age group was drafted.

260. BNu/Fonds A. Andonian, doc. cit., file 31, report by H. Khanghlarian, f° 3v°.

261. *Ibidem*, ff. 3v°–4.

262. Bauernfeind, *Journal de Malatia 1915*, op. cit., p. 271.

263. BNu/Fonds A. Andonian, doc. cit., file 31, report by H. Khanghlarian, f° 4.

264. Bauernfeind, *Journal de Malatia 1915*, op. cit., p. 271, Diary of 16 May.

265. BNu/Fonds A. Andonian, doc. cit., file 31, report by H. Khanghlarian, f° 4.

266. *Ibidem*, f° 4.

267. Bauernfeind, *Journal de Malatia 1915*, op. cit., p. 272, Diary of 26 May. The minister does not name Nâzım; he describes him as a "Müfetisch [representative] delegated by Constantinople."

268. APC/APJ, PCI Bureau, files XIX, XX/3 and XXIII, Ӡ 432–66 (transcript from modern Turk and English translation), report, completed on 30 November 1918, of Captain Fazıl, a retired notable from Malatia and former member of the town's court, addressed to the grand vizier, the interior and justice ministries, and the president of the Senate. [The report was later sent by courier to the addresses just mentioned and to various other interested parties, such as the Patriarchate Armenian and the Catholic Patriarchate], no. 45 from the list of 567 criminals recensed by Captain Fazıl, which states that Nâzım took 20,000 Turkish pounds gold for his own personal use.

269. APC/APJ, PCI Bureau, file XXIII, Ӡ 470–1, responsible for the *sancak* of Malatia.

270. Bauernfeind, *Journal de Malatia 1915*, op. cit., p. 272, Diary du 26 mai.

271. *Ibidem*, pp. 261–2, does not know the name of the interim *mutesarif*, describing him as the *kaymakam* of "Arrha" [that is, Agha, the administrative seat of the *kaza* of Akçadağ].

272. Aguni, *History of the Massacre of one Million Armenians*, op. cit., pp. 158–9, confirms that the prefect was replaced.

273. Bauernfeind, *Journal de Malatia 1915*, op. cit., p. 279, Diary of 25 June.

274. BNu/Fonds A. Andonian, doc. cit., file 31, f° 6.

275. Bauernfeind, *Journal de Malatia 1915*, op. cit., p. 274, Diary of 9 June.

276. Bauernfeind, *Journal de Malatia 1915*, op. cit., pp. 257, 272, Diary of 26 May, indicates that Keshishian was arrested on 25 May and then freed; it is Khanghlarian who reports that the four

men decided on a common course of action in prison: BNu/Fonds A. Andonian, *doc. cit.*, file 31, f° 4v°.

277. Bauernfeind, *Journal de Malatia 1915*, *op. cit.*, p. 273, Diary of 28 May.

278. *Ibidem*, p. 273, Diary of 27 May.

279. BNu/Fonds A. Andonian, *doc. cit.*, file 31, f° 4v°.

280. Bauernfeind, *Journal de Malatia 1915*, *op. cit.*, p. 273, Diary of 28 May.

281. BNu/Fonds A. Andonian, *doc. cit.*, file 31, f° 5.

282. *Ibidem*, ff. 4v°–5.

283. Bauernfeind, *Journal de Malatia 1915*, *op. cit.*, p. 287, Diary of 10 July.

284. BNu/Fonds A. Andonian, *doc. cit.*, file 31, f° 5v°.

285. *Ibidem*, ff. 5v°–6.

286. *Ibidem*, f° 6, estimates the number of worker-soldiers from Malatia assigned to this labor battalion at 1,200, adding that most of them were "between 20 and 35."

287. *Ibidem*, p. 277, Diary of 16 June.

288. *Ibidem*, p. 278, Diary of 24 June. "When I stubbornly insisted," Bauernfeind writes, "that the men's poor wives be informed, at the very least, exactly where their husbands were, he gave me to understand that he could not, because this was a rotten business."

289. *Ibidem*, p. 278, Diary of 25 June; this massacre was brought up before the court-martial, in 1919; APC/APJ, PCI Bureau, Ց 465, doc no. 3, report by Captain Fazıl on Sabit bey; BNu/Fonds A. Andonian, *doc. cit.*, file 31, f° 6; Մալաթիոյ Իթթիհատական Ջոկիրի Սարքած Դիւային Անեռլի Ջարդը [The Appalling Massacre Organized by the Ittihadist Band in Malatia]," *Tashink*, 31 May 1919. Tied together in groups of ten, these men were led a short distance to the banks of the Euphrates; there the çetes cut their throats and threw them into the river.

290. *Ibidem*; BNu/Fonds A. Andonian, *doc. cit.*, file 31, f° 7r°–v°.

291. *Ibidem*, ff. 8–9. The author says that the volunteers had to pay a bribe of ten Turkish pounds in order to enlist in the labor battalions.

292. *Ibidem*, f° 10.

293. Bauernfeind, *Journal de Malatia 1915*, *op. cit.*, p. 280, Diary of 2 July.

294. *Ibidem*.

295. *Ibidem*.

296. *Ibidem*, p. 282, Diary of 5 July.

297. *Ibidem*, p. 283, Diary of 7 July.

298. *Ibidem*. He also reports that "Mehmed Beg made a gift of the horse that belonged to the murdered municipal physician to someone from Mezreh; the horse that had belong to the Catholic bishop who was killed at night was given to Mustafa Ağa: he was already riding it today."

299. APC/APJ, PCI Bureau, file XXIX, Ջ 138 and 139 (file XXIII), encrypted telegram from president of the enquiry commission, H. Mazhar, to the Sublime Porte, Ministry of the Interior, 9 December 1915, in Mamuret ul-Aziz.

300. Bauernfeind, *Journal de Malatia 1915*, *op. cit.*, p. 289, Diary of 12 July.

301. *Ibidem*, p. 292, Diary of 18 July. The minister states that the squadron of çetes (he uses the term "baschi bosuk") followed the convoy, "probably because the escort of gendarmes had not managed to massacre so large a group of people unaided."

302. *Ibidem*, p. 294, Diary of 21 July.

303. *Ibidem*, p. 295, Diary du 22 July. The minister says that the group was headed for "Frudschir." "Miss Graffen," an American missionary from Sıvas, whose real name was Mary L. Graffam, was traveling with this group.

304. *Ibidem*, p. 306, Diary of 29 July.

305. *Ibidem*, p. 307, Diary of 1 August.

306. *Ibidem*, p. 307, Diary of 5 August.

307. *Ibidem*, p. 300, Diary of 22 July. Bauernfeind also observes that Mustafa Ağa "is in any case hated because he is a gâvur [unbeliever] and is in constant danger" (*ibidem*, p. 283, Diary of 7 July).

308. *Ibidem*, p. 285, Diary of 2 July. The allusion is obviously to the atrocities inflicted on Belgium's civilian population by the German troops.

309. *Ibidem*, p. 287, Diary of 10 July.

310. BNu/Fonds A. Andonian, *doc. cit.*, file 31, f° 10. These men, divided into three groups, were killed in Taş Tepe in the Kızıl Göl basin and at the huge well in Kündebeg (*ibidem*).

311. BNu/Fonds A. Andonian, *doc. cit.*, file 31, f° 10v°. The soldiers in the escort demanded five kuruş per head for allowing the men to enter a khan.

312. *Ibidem*. The author confirms the reports of others survivors to the effect that the last surviving men and adolescents were killed there and thrown into the Tohma Çay (see *supra*, pp. 404–5). The property taken from the deportees was brought to the state warehouse near Malatia.

313. See *supra*, p. 405; Bauernfeind, *Journal de Malatia 1915, op. cit.*, p. 291. On 16 July, Bauernfeind witnessed the arrival of "nine carts full of children from the region of Sıvas. The children confirmed that they were separated from their parents on the way so that they could go to school here; they don't know what became of their parents."

314. BNu/Fonds A. Andonian, *doc. cit.*, file 31, f° 12.

315. Bauernfeind, *Journal de Malatia 1915, op. cit.*, p. 300, Diary of 22 July.

316. BNu/Fonds A. Andonian, *doc. cit.*, file 31, f° 12v°.

317. BNu/Fonds A. Andonian, P.J.1/3, file 2, Agn, report by Levon Boghosian, ff. 8v°–9. His young brother and his sister starved to death there. He himself converted to Islam to obtain this post as a driver.

318. *Ibidem*, f° 9r°–v°. Bauernfeind also remarks that some eight hundred orphans were roaming the city around 29 July: Bauernfeind, *Journal de Malatia 1915, op. cit.*, p. 306, Diary of 29 July.

319. BNu/Fonds A. Andonian, P.J.1/3, file 2, Agn, report by Levon Boghosian, f° 8r°–v°.

320. Bauernfeind, *Journal de Malatia 1915, op. cit.*, p. 290, Diary of 16 July.

321. *Ibidem*.

322. BNu/Fonds A. Andonian, *doc. cit.*, file 31, f° 13.

323. Bauernfeind, *Journal de Malatia 1915, op. cit.*, pp. 290 and 294, Diary of 8 and 20 July.

324. *Ibidem*, p. 294, Diary of 18 July.

325. *Ibidem*, p. 294, Diary of 18 July.

326. *Ibidem*, p. 283, Diary of 7 July, does not give his name, which may be found in list of those responsible for the massacres and deportations in Malatia: APC/APJ, PCI Bureau, file XXIII, Ց 470–1.

327. Bauernfeind, *Journal de Malatia 1915, op. cit.*, p. 281, Diary of 4 July, note: "According to Habeş [a Turk employed in the mission], only 80% of the Turks approve of the measures taken against the Armenians."

328. BNu/Fonds A. Andonian, *doc. cit.*, file 31, f° 13.

329. Bauernfeind, *Journal de Malatia 1915, op. cit.*, p. 286, Diary of 8 July.

330. BNu/Fonds A. Andonian, *doc. cit.*, file 31, f° 13v°, states that the families of the young men serving in the labor battalions formed late in June were spared, as were a few households that managed to bribe local officials, adding that the doors of the Armenians' homes were sealed and that guards were posted around them.

331. *Ibidem*, f° 14.

332. *Ibidem*, f° 14r°–v°.

333. *Ibidem*, ff. 15–16v°.

334. *Ibidem*, f° 16v°.

335. APC/APJ, PCI Bureau, file XXIX, Ս 578, certified copy of the decoded telegram, Ս 577, copy of encrypted telegram from the *mutesarif* of Malatia, Hüseyin Serri Bey, to the vilayet of Mamuret ul-Aziz, 31 October/13 November 1915 (trad. in French: *ibidem*, Ֆ 150).

336. APC/APJ, PCI Bureau, file XXIX, Ս 579/2, copy of encrypted telegram from the vali of Mamuret ul–Aziz, Sabit Bey, to the *mutesarif* of Malatia, 12/25 November 1915 (trad. In French: *ibidem*, Ֆ 152).

337. Kévorkian & Paboudjian, *Les Arméniens dans l'Empire ottoman, op. cit.*, p. 391; the Armenian villages are: Vartan, Kevik/Gevrig, Samosat/Samsat, Kantara, Khrafi, Shabi, Kilisan, Dardghan, Gozan, Marmara, Gölbunar, Hayg, Zurna, Beshrin, Tavdir, Uremn, Zarkov, Ishek, Terpetil and Bozuk; Karpat, *op. cit.*, p. 182, says that there were 3,384 Armenians in the *kaza*.

338. APC/APJ, PCI Bureau, Ց 432–66, *doc. cit.*, report by Captain Fazıl.

339. APC/APJ, PCI Bureau, file XXIII, Ց 470–1, list of those responsible for the massacres and deportations in the *sancak* of Malatia, list of murderers in Adiyaman.

340. *Ibidem*.

341. APC/APJ, file XXX, Ց 432–66, *doc. cit.*, report by Captain Fazıl; Garabed Kapigian, Եղեռնապատում Փոքուն Հայոց եւ Նորին Մեծի Մայրաքաղաքին Սեբաստիոյ [*History of the Holocaust of Armenia Minor and Its Grand Capital, Sıvas*], Boston 1924, pp. 258–60.

342. APC/APJ, PCI Bureau, file XXIX, Մ 577, certified copy of the decoded telegram, Մ 577/1, copy of the encrypted telegram from the *kaymakam* of Hüsni Mansur to the *mutesarif* of Malatia, Hüseyin Serri Bey, 3 November 1915 (supplement to the telegram of 31 October).

343. *Ibidem.*

344. APC/APJ, PCI Bureau, file XXIX, Մ 578, certified copy of the decoded telegram, Մ 579/1, copy of the encrypted telegram from the *mutesarif* of Malatia, Hüseyin Serri Bey, to the vilayet of Mamuret ul-Aziz, 5 November 1915 (supplement to the telegram of 31 October), confirms this information.

345. Kévorkian & Paboudjian, *Les Arméniens dans l'Empire ottoman*, *op. cit.*, pp. 390–1; *Nahie* of Şiro: Keferdiz (400 Arm.), Aghvan (400), Umrun (350), Damlu (30), Mamaş (40), Tepehan (100), Kraj (130), Kiavuz, Deretepe, Çamçik, Arguçay; *Nahie* of Gerger: Gargar (450) and 2,400 Armenians in Komik, Karun, Kardigi, Bayiki, Bizman, Tillo/Daro, Terkidin, Mişrakli, Pütürge, Temşias, Vank, Kheçdur, Koragli, Cermekan, Çapan, Pirakhi, Şafkan, Arkavuni, Azmay and Halur; *Nahie* of Merdesi: there were 2,425 Armenians (312 households) in Böyuk Bağ, Hasandigin, Hores, Helim, Karatülbe, Teltela/Til, Salmadin, Narnka, Perag/Piris, Ulbiş, Kulbuc, Kekerdiş, Hut, Kordiye; *Nahie* of Zeravikan: 100 households, soit 820 Armenians, in Bervedol/Bawdol, Geyikan, Kolik, Karaçor, Havank, Blika, Meşrag, Karatur, Gudiş, Perdeso/Berbender, Seyd Mahmud; Karpat, *op. cit.*, p. 182, puts the number of the Armenians in the *kaza* at 750.

346. APC/APJ, PCI Bureau, file XXIX, Մ 578, certified copy of the decoded telegram, Մ 578/1, copy of the encrypted telegram from the *kaymakam* by interim of Kahta to the *mutesarif* of Malatia, 15 September 1915.

347. See *supra*, pp. 297 and 405.

348. APC/APJ, PCI Bureau, file XXIX, Զ 138, 139 (file XXIII), encrypted telegram from the president of the enquiry commission, H. Mazhar, to the Sublime Porte, Ministry of the Interior, 9 December 1915, in Mamuret ul-Aziz.

349. APC/APJ, files XIX, XX/3 and XXIII, Ց 432–66, *doc. cit.*, report by Captain Fazıl, accused no. 475.

350. APC/APJ, PCI Bureau, file XXIX, Մ 578, certified copy of the decoded telegram, Մ 579/3, copy of encrypted telegram from the *kaymakam* of Kahta to the *mutesarif* of Malatia, 12 December 1915 (trad. In French: *ibidem*, Ձ 153).

351. Kévorkian & Paboudjian, *Les Arméniens dans l'Empire ottoman*, *op. cit.*, p. 391; Karpat, *op. cit.*, p. 182, gives the official figure of 1,970 Armenians in the *kaza*.

352. Avédis Tékéian, Պեհէսնիի Հայութեան Գողգոթան [*The Calvary of the Armenians from Behesni*], Beirut 1956.

353. APC/APJ, PCI Bureau, file XXIII, Զ 156, telegram no. 545, from the president of the enquiry commission, H. Mazhar, to the Sublime Porte, Ministry of the Interior, 30 December 1915, in Dyarbekir, report on the *kaymakam* of Behesni, Edhem Kadri Bey, and his illicit gains at the expense of the commission responsible for abandoned property.

354. *Ibidem.*

355. APC/APJ, PCI Bureau, file XXIX, Մ 578, certified copy of the decoded telegram, Մ 579/1, copy of encrypted telegram from the *mutesarif* of Malatia, Hüseyin Serri Bey, to the vilayet of Mamuret ul-Aziz, 5 November 1915 (trad. in French: *ibidem*, Ձ 152).

356. Kévorkian & Paboudjian, *Les Arméniens dans l'Empire ottoman*, *op. cit.*, p. 391; Karpat, *op. cit.*, p. 182, gives the official figure of 466 Armenians in the *kaza*.

357. APC/APJ, file XIX, XX/3 and XXIII, Ց 432–66, doc. cit., report by Captain Fazıl, accused no. 102.

358. *Ibidem*, accused no. 406.

359. *Ibidem*, accused no. 438.

360. See *supra*, p. 404.

361. APC/APJ, PCI Bureau, file XIX, XX/3 and XXIII, Ց 432–66, The long report by Captain Fazıl, a judge at the court-martial of Malatia during the war and a local notable, as well as that of General Vehib Pasha, comprise two of the main Turkish accounts. Fazıl's report was completed

on 30 November 1918 and later sent by courier to the grand vizier, the interior and justice ministries, the president of the Senate and "to various interested parties." It clearly indicates how orders were transmitted: from Constantinople.

362. *Ibidem*, accused no. 122.

363. *Ibidem*, accused no. 125.

364. *Ibidem*, accused no. 126.

365. *Ibidem*, accused no. 282.

366. Bauernfeind, *Journal de Malatia 1915*, *op. cit.*, p. 245, Diary of 8 July.

367. *Ibidem*, p. 291, Diary of 16 July.

368. APC/APJ, PCI Bureau, file XXIII, Э 470–1, list of those responsible in the *sancak* of Malatia. The numbers refer to parts of Captain Fazıl's report: APC/APJ, file XIX, XX/3 and XXIII, Э 432–66.

369. *Ibidem*. The numbers in parentheses correspondent to those in the lists of the guilty provided by Fazıl; the names without numbers are given in the Patriarchate's report.

370. Kévorkian & Paboudjian, *Les Arméniens dans l'Empire ottoman*, *op. cit.*, pp. 381–2.

371. Riggs, *Days of Tragedy in Armenia*, *op. cit.*, pp. 108–17; Piranian, *The Holocaust of Kharpert*, *op. cit.*, pp. 516, 522.

372. Kévorkian & Paboudjian, *Les Arméniens dans l'Empire ottoman*, *op. cit.*, pp. 382, 387.

373. Jacobsen, *Diary of a Danish Missionary, Harpoot, 1907–1919*, *op. cit.*, p. 83, gives the date of departure and states that "no one knew the real reasons" for this voyage.

374. Kévorkian & Paboudjian, *Les Arméniens dans l'Empire ottoman*, *op. cit.*, p. 382. The villages are: Enjeghag (240 Armenians), Ergan (30), Aghzunig/Arsunik (65), Havshakar (260), Peyig (35), Sigedig (66), Sorpian (130), Zembegh (81), Tashdag (135), Sin (55), Halvori (32), Halvorivank (78), Haghtug (297), Akrag (42), Dekke (42); Karpat, *op. cit.*, p. 182, gives the official figure of 1,151 Armenians in the *kaza*.

375. APC/APJ, PCI Bureau, file 57, report to the Ministry of Interior.

376. Kévorkian & Paboudjian, *Les Arméniens dans l'Empire ottoman*, *op. cit.*, p. 383; Karpat, *op. cit.*, p. 182, gives the official figure of 1,483 Armenians in the *kaza*.

377. APC/APJ, PCI Bureau, file 57, report to the Ministry of Interior.

378. Kévorkian & Paboudjian, *Les Arméniens dans l'Empire ottoman*, *op. cit.*, p. 383; Karpat, *op. cit.*, p. 182, gives the official figure of 7,105 Armenians in the *kaza*.

379. Atkinson, "The German, the Turk and the Devil Made a Triple alliance," *op. cit.*, p. 39.

380. APC/APJ, PCI Bureau, file 57, report to the Ministry of Interior.

381. Kévorkian & Paboudjian, *Les Arméniens dans l'Empire ottoman*, *op. cit.*, pp. 386–7; Karpat, *op. cit.*, p. 182, gives the official figure of 3,772 Armenians and 215 "Greeks" in the *kaza*.

382. BNu/Fonds A. Andonian, P.J.1/3, file 39, Chemshgadzak, f° 14, report by Shavarsh Sgheribarmalian.

383. BNu/Fonds A. Andonian, P.J.1/3, file 39, Chemshgadzak, f° 1, report by V. Papazian.

384. *Ibidem*, f° 2. D'après BNu/Fonds A. Andonian, P.J.1/3, file 39, Chemshgadzak, f° 17, report by Shavarsh Sgheribarmalian, these men were murdered on the banks of the Euphrates the day after their departure, around 20 June.

385. BNu/Fonds A. Andonian, P.J.1/3, file 39, Chemshgadzak, ff. 2–3.

386. *Ibidem*, ff. 4–5.

387. BNu/Fonds A. Andonian, P.J.1/3, file 39, Chemshgadzak, ff. 6–8, report by Azniv, Annig, and Marta Mardikian.

388. *Ibidem*, f° 6.

389. *Ibidem*, f° 7.

390. *Ibidem*, f° 7.

391. BNu/Fonds A. Andonian, P.J.1/3, file 39, Chemshgadzak, ff. 18–22, report by Shavarsh Sgheribarmalian.

392. APC/APJ, PCI Bureau, file XXIX, Ʋ 578, certified copy of the decoded telegram, Ʋ 578/3, copy of encrypted telegram from the vali of Mamuret ul-Aziz, Sabit Bey, to the *mutesarif* of Malatia, 21 August 1915, in Mezreh.

393. APC/APJ, PCI Bureau, file XXIX, Ʋ 579/3: copy of encrypted telegram from the vali of Mamuret ul-Aziz, Sabit Bey, to the *mutesarif* of Malatia, 10/23 September 1915, in Mezreh.

394. APC/APJ, PCI Bureau, Ʊ 578, certified copy of the decoded telegram, Ʊ 578/4, copy of encrypted telegram from the minister of the interior, Talât, to the vali of Mamuret ul-Aziz, Sabit Bey, 19 December 1915.

395. APC/APJ, PCI Bureau, file XXIX, Ʊ 578, certified copy of the decoded telegram, Ʊ 578/2: copy of the 20 December 1915 encrypted telegram from the *mutesarif* of Malatia to the commanders of the gendarmerie in the districts subordinate to Malatia, as well as to the *müdir*.

396. APC/APJ, PCI Bureau, Ʊ 578/5, copy of encrypted telegram from the vali of Mamuret ul-Aziz, Sabit Bey, to *mutesarif* of Malatia, 20 December 1915, in Mezreh.

397. P.R.O., FO 371/6500, Turkish War Criminals, the file of no. 2686, Sabit Bey, interned in Malta: Vartkes Yeghiayan, *British Foreign Office dossiers on Turkish War Criminals*, La Verne 1991, pp. 20–38.

398. *Ibidem*, no. 2807, pp. 358–70.

399. See *supra*, pp. 383, 405; *Ibidem*, no. 2816, Mehmet Nuri bey, interned in Malta, pp. 413–28.

400. SHAT, Service Historique de la Marine, Service de Renseignements de la Marine, Turquie, 1BB7 231, doc. no. 314, Constantinople, 14 February 1919, report by Dr. Zaven Vahram, physician in Mezreh's military hospital ("Harputh" in the text), which confirms Bedri role in the massacres in Malatia.

401. See *supra*, pp. 398, 409, 411, 414, 420.

402. See *supra*, p. 419.

403. See *supra*, pp. 409–10: Let us note that Bauernfeind, although he mistakenly believed that Resneli Nâzım was a government official, provides crucial details about his activity in Malatia; APC/APJ, file XIX, XX/3 and XXIII, З 432–66, copy of the report by the Captain Fazıl, retired and notable from Malatia: Nâzım bey, no. 45 robbed 20 000 Turkish Lira.

404. P.R.O., FO 371/6500, Turkish War Criminals, no. 2686, Sabit Bey, interned in Malta, annex C, letter from Faik to Sabit, in Dersim [thus probably datable to the first days of August]: Vartkes Yeghiayan, *British Foreign Office dossiers on Turkish War Criminals*, La Verne 1991, pp. 31–2.

405. APC/APJ, PCI Bureau, file XXIX, Ʊ 576, encrypted telegram no. 5, from Erzerum headquarter, from the head of the *Teşkilât-ı Mahsusa*, Bahaeddin Şakir, to the vali of Mamuret ul-Aziz, Sabit Bey, for transmission to the delegate of the CUP, Resneli Nâzım Bey, encrypted, with the decoded version, 21 Haziran 1331 (4 juillet 1915), in *Takvim-ı Vakayi* no. 3540 (at the session of the trial of 12 April 1919), 5 May 1919, p. 6, col. 1–2, and in annex of the verdict of the trial of Mamuret ul-Aziz, *Takvim-ı Vakayi* no. 3771, 13 January 1920, p. 48, col. 1. After the verdict of the trial of Mamuret ul-Aziz was published, the Istanbul press mistakenly dated this document to 21 April; the mistake has been perpetuated to the present day, making the content of the document seem improbable.

406. BNu/Fonds A. Andonian, P.J.1/3, file 23, Harput, f° 54, report by Araks Mgrdichian, 21, educated at Euphrates College, was the daughter of the British vice-consul in Dyarbekir, Thomas Mgrdichian.

407. *Ibidem*.

408. APC/APJ, PCI Bureau, З 430, 467, 474, list of responsible in the vilayet of Harput.

409. APC/APJ, PCI Bureau, З 465, doc no. 3, report by Captain Fazıl on Sabit Bey.

410. APC/APJ, PCI Bureau, ♂ 99, З 229, З 243–5 (in French), dossier des Turcs inculpés dans le procès des massacres de Mamuret ul-Aziz, 13 September 1920, no. 2, file 2.

411. Extract from the 5 December 1918 deposition of Vehib Pasha: *Takvim-ı Vakayi*, no. 3540, 5 May 1919, p. 7, col. 2 and the full deposition of handwritten pages: APC/APJ, PCI Bureau, Ζ 171–82.

412. *Le Spectateur d'Orient*, 13 June 1919: that "the preliminary investigation" – in other words, the pretrial investigation of the case – was terminated in June, and that, in this period, Resneli Nâzım, Bahaeddin Şakir, and Mehmed Nuri were "fugitives from justice," whereas Sabit Bey had been transferred to Malta by the British.

413. *La Renaissance*, no. 302, 21 November 1919, "Procès de Mamuret ul-Aziz," announces that, on 20 November, the ex-deputy from Dersim, Nuri Bey, and head of the public educational system, Ferid Bey, were to go on trial for perpetrating "massacres and deportations."

414. Verdict of the trial of Mamuret ul-Aziz, 13 January 1920: *Takvim-ı Vakayi*, no. 3771, 9 February 1920, pp. 48–9.

415. Davis, *The Slaughterhouse Province, op. cit.*, pp. 223–4.

416. *Ibidem*, pp. 229–31.

8 Deportations and Massacres in the Vilayet of Sıvas

1. Kévorkian & Paboudjian, *Les Arméniens dans l'Empire ottoman*, op. cit., pp. 261–3.
2. APC/APJ, PCI Bureau, Ҧ 370. Also found here were Kyzilbaş and a Kurdish minority.
3. P.R.O., FO 371/6500, Turkish War Criminals, the file of prisoner no. 2719, Muammer Bey, interned in Malta: edited by Vartkes Yeghiayan, *British Foreign Office dossiers on Turkish War Criminals*, La Verne 1991, p. 89.
4. APC/APJ, PCI Bureau, doc. n° 23, *Les signes prédisant les horreurs futures à Sıvas*; BNu/Fonds A. Andonian, P.J.1/3, file 49, Sebaste, ff. 1–103, [Report] by Garabed Kapigian (1919), reprinted in Եղե ունապատում փոքուն Հայոց եւ նորին մեծի մայրաքաղաքի Սեբաստիոյ [*History of the Holocaust of Armenia Minor and His Great Capital, Sebastia*], Boston 1924, pp. 17 et 24; Kapigian adds that Muammer had earlier served as an assistant prefect and a prefect in Kangal, Aziziye, and Kayseri, as governor of Adana, and, later, of Konya.
5. Kapigian, op. cit., pp. 18–19.
6. *Ibidem*, p. 21. Muammer created, notable, co-operatives in Aziziye.
7. APC/APJ, PCI Bureau, doc. n° 23, *doc. cit.*
8. Kapigian, op. cit., p. 21.
9. APC/APJ, PCI Bureau, doc. n° 23, *doc. cit.*; Kapigian, op. cit., p. 27.
10. *Puzantion*, n° 5340, 2 May 1914; Kapigian, op. cit., p. 23; Arakel Patrik (ed.), Պատմագիրք-Յուշամատեան Սեբաստիոյ [*History of Armenians of Sebaste and Its Provinces*], I, Beirut 1974, pp. 717–18.
11. Kapigian, op. cit., p. 24.
12. *Ibidem*, p. 30; APC/APJ, PCI Bureau, doc. n° 23, *doc. cit.*
13. Kapigian, op. cit., pp. 31–3. Kapigian says that the Armenian merchants' stocks were unsparingly plundered.
14. *Ibidem*, p. 42.
15. *Ibidem*, pp. 34–5. A few weeks later, news of the virtually complete destruction of this army corps arrived.
16. *Ibidem*, pp. 44–5.
17. *Ibidem*, pp. 43–4.
18. *Ibidem*, pp. 39–40. Their real estate was immediately confiscated and the Jesuit chapel was transformed into a mosque. The interim vice-consul of France, Manug Ansurian, was forced by the vali to hand over the keys of the vice-consulate to the authorities (*ibidem*, pp. 40–1).
19. *Ibidem*, pp. 42–4.
20. APC/APJ, PCI Bureau, Ҧ 716, , encrypted telegram n° 47, from the minister of the interior, Talât, to the vali of Sıvas, Muhammer, 8/21 December 1914 (8 Kanuni Evvel 1330). French translation: *ibidem*, Ω 32).
21. APC/APJ, PCI Bureau, doc. n° 23, *doc. cit.*, reveals that the Armenian priest of Suşehir informed those concerned of the circumstances surrounding the murder. The prelate of Sıvas, Bishop Kalemkiarian, promptly went to see the vali, who told him: "We have no official information; I will, however, place a call immediately, and communicate the answer to you."; Kapigian, op. cit., pp. 46–7; Zaven Der Yeghiayan, *Memoirs*, op. cit., p. 66; APC/APJ, PCI Bureau, Մ 720, encrypted telegram from the judge Hüseyin Zehni, to the *kaza* of Suşehir, 20 December 1914/ 2 January 1915 (20 Kanuni Evvel 1330). French translation: *ibidem*, Ω 36–7.
22. APC/APJ, PCI Bureau, Մ 718 (Ottoman original, n° 230), encrypted telegram from the *kaymakam* of Suşehir, Ahmed, to the *mutesarifat* of Karahisar, n° 230, 2 January 1915 (20 Kanuni Evvel 1330). French translation: *ibidem*, Ω 34).
23. *Ibidem*.
24. APC/APJ, PCI Bureau, Մ 719, encrypted telegram from the *mutesarif* of Karahisar, Hilmi, to the vilayet of Sıvas, 20 December 1914/2 January 1915 (20 Kanuni Evvel 1330). French translation: *ibidem*, Ω 35).
25. APC/APJ, PCI Bureau, Մ 720, encrypted telegram from the judge Hüseyin Zehni, to the *kaza* of Suşehir, 20 December/2 January 1915 (20 Kanuni Evvel 1330).
26. APC/APJ, PCI Bureau, Մ 728, encrypted telegram from the *kaymakam* of Suşehir, Ahmed, to the *mutesarif* of Karahisar, 25 December/7 January 1915 (20 Kanuni Evvel 1330); Մ 729, encrypted

telegram from the *kaymakam* of Suşehir, Ahmed, to the *mutesarif* of Karahisar, 26 December 1914/8 January 1915.

27. Kapigian, *op. cit.*, pp. 48–9.

28. Zaven Der Yéghiayan, *Memoirs*, *op. cit.*, p. 66.

29. Kapigian, *op. cit.*, pp. 49–50; Aguni, *op. cit.*, pp. 77–8.

30. Kapigian, *op. cit.*, pp. 50–1.

31. *Ibidem*, from the newspaper *Kızıl Irmak*; Aguni, *op. cit.*, p. 25.

32. *Ibidem*, p. 30; APC/APJ, PCI Bureau, doc. n° 23, *doc. cit.*

33. Born in Govdun, Murad Khrimian (1874–1918) had since 1907 been one of the leaders of the ARF in the eastern provinces. At the time, he was living in Govdun, an Armenian village near Hafik, some 40 kilometers east of Sıvas. It was probably here that Murad went out to meet Enver.

34. BNu/Fonds A. Andonian, P.J.1/3, file 49, Sebaste, Սեբաստիա եւ իր գիւղերը [*Sebaste and His Villages*], f° 10v°.

35. *Cf. supra*, p. 221, n. 44; Kapigian, *op. cit.*, pp. 52–3; BNu/Fonds A. Andonian, P.J.1/3, file 49, *doc. cit.*, f° 10v°.

36. *Ibidem*, ff. 5v°-6.

37. APC/APJ, PCI Bureau, U 497, document transmitted by the vilayet of Sıvas to the Administrative Enquiry Commission directed by Hasan Mazhar.

38. BNu/Fonds A. Andonian, P.J.1/3, file 49, Sebaste, *doc. cit.*, f° 9.

39. APC/APJ, PCI Bureau, doc. n° 23, *doc. cit.*

40. BNu/Fonds A. Andonian, P.J.1/3, file 49, Sebaste, *doc. cit.*, f° 11. Among the officers commanding these men were Muavinli Sıdkı Bey and Muheddin Bey, as well as Dr. Rüşdi Bey, who "spoke in French."

41. *Ibidem*, f° 11v°.

42. *Ibidem*, f° 12. This means that the squadron was under the orders of the Special Organization.

43. *Ibidem*, f° 12v°. This meeting must have taken place in early February.

44. APC/APJ, PCI Bureau, doc. n° 23, *doc. cit.*

45. BNu/Fonds A. Andonian, P.J.1/3, file 49, Sebaste, *doc. cit.*, ff. 12v°-13; Aguni, *op. cit.*, p. 79.

46. *Ibidem*, p. 80.

47. Rohrbach was a staunch advocate of German penetration of Asia Minor and headed an association that promoted it; Hayranian belonged to this association: *cf.* Vahakn Dadrian, *German Responsibility in the Armenian Genocide*, Watertown 1996, p. 114.

48. BNu/Fonds A. Andonian, P.J.1/3, file 49, Sebaste, f° 13.

49. *Ibidem*; Kapigian, *op. cit.*, p. 55, points out that 300 of these prisoners survived and were interned in the Sanasarian *lycée* or in the monastery of St. Nshan; the monastery had been confiscated by the military authorities and converted into a prison.

50. *Ibidem*, p. 53; Aguni, *op. cit.*, p. 79.

51. *Ibidem*; Kapigian, *op. cit.*, p. 53; P.R.O., FO 371/ 6501, Turkish War Criminals, the file of prisoner no. n° 2719, Muammer Bey, interned in Malta: Vartkes Yeghiayan, *British Foreign Office dossiers on Turkish War Criminals*, *op. cit.*, p. 92.

52. *Cf. supra*, p. 191.

53. Kapigian, *op. cit.*, p. 53.

54. APC/PCI Bureau, those responsible for the deportations and massacres: BNu, ms. 289, ff. 27–3, those responsible in Sıvas.

55. APC/APJ, PCI Bureau, 3 168, file of Gani Bey must not be confused with Abdül Gani, the responsible secretary in Edirne who was brought to trial in 1919; the verdict in the trial of the CUP responsible secretaries and delegates, handed down on 8 January 1920: *Takvim-ı Vakayi*, n° 3772, February 1920, pp. 1–5, mentions Abdül Gani Bey, whose trial was adjourned.

56. APC/APJ, PCI Bureau, doc. n° 23, *doc. cit.*

57. P.R.O., FO 371/6500, Turkish War Criminals, the file of prisoner no. 2726, Gani Bey, interned in Malta: Vartkes Yeghiayan, *British Foreign Office dossiers on Turkish War Criminals*, *op. cit.*, p. 105; BNu, ms. 289, ff. 27–33, those responsible in Sıvas.

58. APC/APJ, PCI Bureau, doc. n° 23, *doc. cit.*

59. Kapigian, *op. cit.*, p. 57.

60. BNu/Fonds A. Andonian, P.J.1/3, file 6, Amasia, f° 2, testimony of Heghine Begian; Aguni, *op. cit.*, p. 81; Kapigian, *op. cit.*, p. 58. These men were put to death in early April, in a place known as Çerçi Deresi, two hours from Sıvas on the road to Kayseri (*ibidem*).

61. APC/APJ, PCI Bureau, doc. n° 23, *doc. cit.*; Aguni, *op. cit.*, pp. 81–2; Kapigian, *op. cit.*, pp. 59–60. The city learned of these murders from Greek woodcutters who had been working near the place where the massacre took place. According to an account by Lusaper Boghosian, the wife of the municipal physician, it was Gani who ordered the 12 notables from Sıvas arrested and organized their execution: P.R.O., FO 371/6500, Turkish War Criminals, the file of prisoner no. 2726, Gani Bey, interned in Malta: Vartkes Yeghiayan, *British Foreign Office dossiers on Turkish War Criminals*, *op. cit.*, pp. 104–5.

62. APC/APJ, PCI Bureau, doc. n° 23, *doc. cit.*

63. BNu/Fonds A. Andonian, P.J.1/3, file 49, Sebaste, f° 13v°, "Sebaste and his villages"; Aguni, *op. cit.*, pp. 82–3; Kapigian, *op. cit.*, pp. 62–3.

64. Kapigian, *op. cit.*, p. 64.

65. Kévorkian & Paboudjian, *Les Arméniens dans l'Empire ottoman*, *op. cit.*, p. 233; Karpat, *op. cit.*, p. 178, gives the official figure of 82,915 Armenians in the *sancak*.

66. Kévorkian & Paboudjian, *Les Arméniens dans l'Empire ottoman*, *op. cit.*, p. 235; Kapigian, *op. cit.*, p. 64.

67. APC/APJ, PCI Bureau, doc. n° 23, *doc. cit.*

68. *Supra*, p. 431.

69. BNu/Fonds A. Andonian, P.J.1/3, file 49, Sebaste, f° 14, "Sebaste and his villages"; Kapigian, *op. cit.*, p. 67.

70. *Ibidem.*

71. *Ibidem*, p. 68.

72. *Ibidem.*

73. *Ibidem.*

74. *Ibidem*, p. 70.

75. *Ibidem*, pp. 70–1.

76. APC/APJ, PCI Bureau, doc. n° 23, *doc. cit.*

77. Kapigian, *op. cit.*, p. 76.

78. *Ibidem*, pp. 77–8.

79. BNu/Fonds A. Andonian, P.J.1/3, file 49, Sebaste, f° 14, "Sebaste and his villages." Several encrypted telegrams dated 2, 3, and 4 May 1915 stating the number of Armenians arrested in the Sıvas region are now held in Jerusalem: APC/APJ, PCI Bureau, Ս 457; there also exists a list, prepared in advance by a commission, approved by the vali [of Sıvas], and signed by Captain Fazıl, of 160 Armenians who were deported at night to the place where they were massacred: APC/APJ, PCI Bureau, Յ 440.

80. P.R.O., FO 371/6500, Turkish War Criminals, the file of prisoner no. 2719, Muammer Bey, interned in Malta: Vartkes Yeghiayan, *British Foreign Office dossiers on Turkish War Criminals*, *op. cit.*, pp. 93–5, testimony of Arusiag Iskian.

81. "Ինչպէս նահատակուեցաւ Թոքատի Առաջնորդը, Շահարշ Ծ. Վրդ. Սահակեանը [*How the Primate of Tokat, Father Shavarsh Sahagian, Was Martyred ?*]," *Zhoghovurt*, no. 41, 13 December 1918, p. 1.

82. Liliane Sewny, an American who was married to an Armenian doctor, wrote about this to James Barton, 10 March 1916: Toynbee, *The Treatment of Armenians in the Ottoman Empire, 1915–1916*, *op. cit.*, p. 336

83. Aguni, *History of the Massacre of one Million Armenians*, *op. cit.*, p. 86.

84. *Ibidem*, p. 87; Kapigian, *op. cit.*, p. 79; BNu/Fonds A. Andonian, P.J.1/3, file 49, Sebaste, f° 179, "Ամբաստանագիր-Տեղեկագիր Սեբաստիոյ Կուսակալութեան [Accusation Report about the Vilayet of Sıvas]"; "Sebaste and his villages." According to Reverend Ernest C. Partridge, the head of the American mission in Sıvas, between 1,500 and 2,000 men were imprisoned; the vali promise to Partridge "de bien traiter" these prisoners: letter from Ernest C. Partridge, 13 July 1915, in Toynbee, *The Treatment of Armenians in the Ottoman Empire, 1915–1916*, *op. cit.*, p. 326, did not, however, have the inventory of the archbishopric at his disposal.

85. *Ibidem*, p. 87; Kapigian, *op. cit.*, pp. 79–81.

86. Letter from Ernest C. Partridge, 13 July 1915, in Toynbee, *The Treatment of Armenians in the Ottoman Empire, 1915–1916, op. cit.*, p. 326

87. Kapigian, *op. cit.*, p. 82, notes that most of the policemen came from Rumelia.

88. *Ibidem*, p. 85.

89. *Ibidem*, p. 86.

90. *Ibidem*, p. 89.

91. P.R.O., FO 371/ 6500, Turkish War Criminals, the file of prisoner no. 2726, Gani bey, interned in Malta: Vartkes Yeghiayan, *British Foreign Office dossiers on Turkish War Criminals, op. cit.*, p. 103.

92. BNu/Fonds A. Andonian, P.J.1/3, file 49, Sebaste, f° 179, "Ամբաստանագիր-Տեղեկագիր Սեբաստիոյ Կուսակալութեան [Accusation Report about the Vilayet of Sıvas]," Aleppo, 27 February 1919; Kapigian, *op. cit.*, pp. 90–1.

93. BNu/Fonds A. Andonian, P.J.1/3, file 49, Sebaste, f° 179, *doc. cit.*

94. Kapigian, *op. cit.*, pp. 91–2. Also convoked by the vali and present at this scene were Khachadur Tanderjian, Garabed Shahinian, and Mirijan Odabashian, as well as the parliamentary deputies Hoca Emindedip and Rasim, the commander of the gendarmerie Halil Rifat, and the police chief, Rifat: Memory of Mgr Knel Kalemkiarian, edited by Arakel Patrik, II, *op. cit.*, pp. 11–12.

95. *Ibidem*, pp. 95–6.

96. *Ibidem*, p. 98.

97. *Ibidem*, pp. 100–1.

98. *Ibidem*, pp. 103–4: on 5 July, 400 households from Küçük Bengiler; on 6 July, 500 households from Böyük Bengiler; on 7 July, 550 households from the lower quarter of Böyük Bengiler, as well as the Protestant community and the male and female boarding students at the American middle school; on 8 July, 450 households from Böyük Bengiler as well as the Catholic community; on 9 July, 400 households from the Hoğtarı and Ard neighborhoods; on 11 July, 350 households from Köse Dere and Davşan Bayir; on 12 July, 400 families from Pekmez Sokak and Blejents; on 13 July, 400 households from Kayseri Kapı, Ace Mahale, and Çavuş Paşa; on 14 July, 350 households from the parish of St. Sarkis; on 15 July, 400 households from Karod Sokak, Dzadzug Aghpiur, Holy Savior, Ğanlı Bağçe, Hasanlı, Taykesens, and Hin Paşi; on 16 July, 500 households from the quarter around the cathedral, Hendek Kenar, Ğurşunlu, and Jivani Dzag; on 17 July, 250 households from Ermeni Mahale; on 18 July, 400 households from Sarı Şeyh, Baldır Pazar, and Sev Hogh.

99. *Ibidem*, pp. 104–5.

100. *Ibidem*, pp. 106–8. They would be killed after bringing in the harvest.

101. *Ibidem*, pp. 108–10.

102. BNu/Fonds A. Andonian, P.J.1/3, file 49, Sebaste, f° 179r°-v°, "Accusation report about the vilayet of Sıvas," *doc. cit.*

103. *Ibidem*, ff. 179v°-180v°; Kapigian, *op. cit.*, pp. 115–420.

104. *Ibidem*, pp. 115–27.

105. *Ibidem*, pp. 129–33.

106. *Ibidem*, pp. 139–41.

107. *Ibidem*, pp. 142–9. Kapigian observes that the president of the commission granted his convoy "an exceptional amnesty"; he did not have any of the men in it killed (*ibidem*, p. 149).

108. *Ibidem*, pp. 163–6.

109. *Ibidem*, pp. 173–8.

110. *Ibidem*, pp. 179–201, lists the names of hundreds of people from Sıvas who were put to death in Hasançelebi.

111. Bauernfeind, *Journal de Malatia 1915, op. cit.*, p. 308, Diary of 11 August 1915.

112. *Ibidem*, pp. 309–10.

113. Kapigian, *op. cit.*, pp. 208–13.

114. Cf. *supra*, p. 420.

115. Cf. *supra*, p. 404.

116. Cf. *supra*, pp. 399, 405, 423

117. Cf. *supra*, pp. 405, 413; Kapigian, *op. cit.*, p. 243, notes that it's the boys under 8.

118. Kapigian, *op. cit.*, pp. 232–5.

119. *Ibidem*, p. 237.

120. *Ibidem*, pp. 236, 238.

121. *Cf. supra.*

122. Kapigian, *op. cit.*, pp. 241–2.

123. *Ibidem*, pp. 263–4.

124. The survivors from these convoys took two distinct routes: one led from Birecik through Nissbin, Rumkale, Ayntab, Bab, Mumbuc, Aleppo, and Rakka to Der Zor, the other from Urfa to Ras ul-Ayn by way of Viranşehir.

125. Kévorkian & Paboudjian, *Les Arméniens dans l'Empire ottoman*, *op. cit.*, pp. 247–8; Karpat, *op. cit.*, p. 178, states that there were a total of 11,376 Armenians in the *kaza*. The Armenian villages were Govdun (pop. 1,901), Tavshanlu (114), Tuzhisar/Aghdk (2,077), Akpunar (853), Kotni (770), Torosi (202), Khorsana (1,335), Gavdara (600), Khandzar (790), Gavra (783), Yenije (226), Yarhisar/Chejghenig (1,250), Prapert (622), Voghnovid (130), Baghchejik (600), Horohon (458), Todorag (720), Shahin/Jenjin (278), Kemeris (673) Borazur (34), Stanoz (710), Ttmaj (780), and Sarıhasan (151).

126. APC/APJ, PCI Bureau, Ɜ 168, file 37, the criminals of Koçhisar.

127. *Cf. supra*, p. 437.

128. BNu/Fonds A. Andonian, P.J.1/3, file 49, Sebaste, f° 123.

129. *Ibidem*, f° 124.

130. *Ibidem*, ff. 124–5.

131. *Ibidem*, f° 125.

132. Kévorkian & Paboudjian, *Les Arméniens dans l'Empire ottoman*, *op. cit.*, p. 247; Karpat, *op. cit.*, p. 178, states that there were a total of 6,056 Armenians in the *kaza*. The Armenian villages were Alakilise (pop. 1,146), Karhad (718), Tekeli (168), Karaboğaz (462), Keçeyurd (1 100), çayköy (95), Emin çiftlik (60), and Miadun.

133. *Cf. supra*, p. 437.

134. Kapigian, *op. cit.*, p. 234.

135. APC/APJ, PCI Bureau, ⴺ 168, those responsible in Zara.

136. Account by Sahag Hovhannesian, the blacksmith's nephew, given to his grandson in August 1973.

137. Kévorkian & Paboudjian, *Les Arméniens dans l'Empire ottoman*, *op. cit.*, p. 240; Karpat, *op. cit.*, p. 178, states that there were a total of 1,379 Armenians.

138. Kévorkian & Paboudjian, *Les Arméniens dans l'Empire ottoman*, *op. cit.*, pp. 240–1: the principal villages were Şarkışla (pop. 257), Temejik (227), Yapaltun (1,386), Karapunar (690), çisanlu (1,516), Karagöl (2,040), Alakilise (275), Shepni (1 350), Dendel (1 989), Burhan (1016), Tekmen (819), Paşa (383), Topadj (656), Kurtlukaya (316), Kantaroz (463), Patrenos (845) and Ğazımağara (790); Karpat, *op. cit.*, p. 178, states that there were a total of 13,694 Armenians in the *kaza*.

139. BNu/Fonds A. Andonian, P.J.1/3, file 49, Sebaste, f° 127.

140. *Ibidem*, f° 129.

141. APC/APJ, PCI Bureau, file 33, pp. 1–25, report on the massacres and deportations in the vilayet of Sıvas, Aleppo, 27 February 1919, p. 1 (in arm.). Those known to have carried out the massacres were Hacibeyoğlu Arslan bey, Hacibeyoğlu Adil bey, Hacibeyoğlu Şevki bey, Cadıbeyoğlu Yahya bey, Cadıbeyoğlu Mahil bey, Cadıbeyoğlu Osman bey, Mahmudoğlu Fazla, Mahmudoğlu Mehmed bey, Mahmudoğlu Hafi, Mulazım Bahri, Deli Beşiroğlu Ömer, Deli Beşiroğlu Seyfi, Deli Beşiroğlu Fikri, Deli Beşiroğlu Mükhtar, Köse Ahmedoğlu Sarı Mehmed, Sarnınoğlu Emir, Sarnınoğlu Hasan, Kayserlı Cemaloğlu Kenan, Cabaroğlu Yusuf, Cabaroğlu Haci Nezir, Seyidağaoğlu Seyfi, Seyidağaoğlu Husni, Tütüncioğlu Şehir Ali, Beyleroğlu Ömer, Cücükci İsmail and his sons, Cücükci Şaban (brother of İsmail), Hoca Ahmedoğlu Fayk, Şabanınoğlu Bahri, Cafaroğlu Seydi Halil, Isamoğlan Haci Mustafa, Kör Velioğlu Beşir çavuş, Hoca Mehmed, Biraderi Haci Kürd, Kalfa Ahmedoğlu Behran, Cırıkhoğlu Mustafa, Azkaglaoğlu, Bekir and Keltesal, Kazıkcıoğlu Mehmed and his sons, Kazıkcıoğlu Halil, Abdioğlu Ali, Tütüncioğlu Arif and his brothers, Tütüncioğlu Kadir Osman, Bostancıoğlu Sansar, Bostancıoğlu Bahar, çopüroğlu Ömer, Mustafa, Kuyucı İbrahim and Hamid, Sıvaslı jandarma Ladiker, Şarkışlayi Hüseyin Çavuş, Eyercilı Adıl Çavuş, Kareozlı Mahmud and Kenan Pehlivan, Kör Muzayiroğlu Ömer Osman, Kör Muzayiroğlu Kara Fazlı, and Ekizcelı Veli and his sons, Terkianlıoğlu Veli Mehmed.

142. Patrik (ed.), *op. cit.*, II, pp. 434–6.

143. Kévorkian & Paboudjian, *Les Arméniens dans l'Empire ottoman, op. cit.*, p. 241; Karpat, *op. cit.*, p. 178, states that there were a total of 1,102 Armenians in Bünyan.

144. APC/APJ, PCI Bureau, Ի 4, list of responsibles in the vilayet of Sıvas.

145. Kévorkian & Paboudjian, *Les Arméniens dans l'Empire ottoman, op. cit.*, p. 241.

146. *Ibidem*, p. 244.

147. BNu/Fonds A. Andonian, P.J.1/3, file 33, Mancılık, ff. 1–6; for Ulaş, *cf. supra*, p. 460.

148. Kévorkian & Paboudjian, *Les Arméniens dans l'Empire ottoman, op. cit.*, pp. 245–7; Karpat, *op. cit.*, p. 178, states that there were a total of 8,354 Armenians in the same area.

149. Kévorkian & Paboudjian, *Les Arméniens dans l'Empire ottoman, op. cit.*, p. 247.

150. BNu/Fonds A. Andonian, P.J.1/3, file 55, Divrig, f° 23, report by Hmayag Zartarian, Constantinople, 10 September 1919.

151. *Ibidem*, ff. 24–5; BNu/Fonds A. Andonian, P.J.1/3, file 55, Divrig, ff. 2v°-3, report by Vartan Shahbaz, 11 January 1917. These men were put to death later, in August, along with all the prisoners from the city.

152. *Ibidem*, ff. 6–7; BNu/Fonds A. Andonian, P.J.1/3, file 55, Divrig, ff. 25–6, report by Hmayag Zartarian.

153. *Ibidem*, ff. 4v°-5, report by Vartan Shahbaz.

154. *Ibidem*, ff. 26–7, report by Hmayag Zartarian.

155. *Ibidem*, ff. 30–1.

156. BNu/Fonds A. Andonian, P.J.1/3, file 13, Pingian, ff. 2–8, report by L. Goshgarian, Erzincan, 16 January 1917.

157. Kévorkian & Paboudjian, *Les Arméniens dans l'Empire ottoman, op. cit.*, p. 244; Karpat, *op. cit.*, p. 178, puts the number of Armenians in the *kaza* at 2,862.

158. Kévorkian & Paboudjian, *Les Arméniens dans l'Empire ottoman, op. cit.*, p. 243; Karpat, *op. cit.*, p. 178, puts the number of Armenians in the *kaza* at 8,905.

159. APC/APJ, PCI Bureau, file 59, list of the responsible in Gürün.

160. Kapigian, *op. cit.*, p. 86.

161. APC/APJ, PCI Bureau, file 59, list of the responsible in Gürün.

162. Two survivors later gave accounts of this massacre: Anania Mavisakalian and Nahabed Nahabedian (*ibidem*).

163. *Ibidem*.

164. *Ibidem*.

165. *Ibidem*.

166. APC/APJ, PCI Bureau, file 33, *doc. cit.*, pp. 20–1.

167. Kévorkian & Paboudjian, *Les Arméniens dans l'Empire ottoman, op. cit.*, p. 251.

168. *Ibidem*, pp. 251–4; Karpat, *op. cit.*, p. 178, puts the number of Armenians in the *kaza* at 12,925.

169. *Cf. supra*, p. 431; *Puzantion*, n° 5340, 2 May 1914; Kapigian, *op. cit.*, p. 23; Arakel Patrik (ed.), *op. cit.*, I, pp. 717–18. The editor of this volume was a schoolteacher in Tokat at the time and witnessed the fire.

170. Arshag Alboyajian, Պատմութիւն Եւդոկիոյ Հայոց [*History of Armenians of Tokat*], Cairo 1952, pp. 1224–5.

171. *Ibidem*, p. 1228.

172. *Ibidem*, pp. 1230–3.

173. He replaced Cemal Bey, who had been named to his post on 24 October 1914.

174. Alboyadjian, *History of Armenians of Tokat, op. cit.*, pp. 1233–4.

175. *Ibidem*, pp. 1234–5; "Ինչպէս նահատակուեցաւ Թոգատի առաջնորդը, Սահակ Ծ. Վրդ. Սահակեանը [How the Primat of Tokat, Father Shavarsh Sahaguian, Was Martyrised]," *Zhoghovurt*, no. 41, 13 December 1918, p. 1.

176. *Ibidem*.

177. *Ibidem*, pp. 1240–2.

178. APC/APJ, PCI Bureau, file 33, *doc. cit.*, p. 19.

179. *Ibidem*.

180. Kévorkian & Paboudjian, *Les Arméniens dans l'Empire ottoman, op. cit.*, p. 254; Karpat, *op. cit.*, p. 178, puts the number of Armenians in the *kaza* at 3,183.

181. Alboyadjian, *op. cit.*, p. 1249.

182. Kévorkian & Paboudjian, *Les Arméniens dans l'Empire ottoman, op. cit.*, pp. 254–5; Karpat, *op. cit.*, p. 178, puts the number of Armenians in the *kaza* at 3,704.

183. Alboyadjian, *op. cit.*, p. 1249.

184. Kévorkian & Paboudjian, *Les Arméniens dans l'Empire ottoman, op. cit.*, p. 255; Karpat, *op. cit.*, p. 178, puts the number of Armenians in the *kaza* at 2,921.

185. Kapigian, *op. cit.*, p. 23.

186. Kévorkian & Paboudjian, *Les Arméniens dans l'Empire ottoman, op. cit.*, pp. 255–60; Karpat, *op. cit.*, p. 178, puts the number of Armenians in the *kaza* at 9,979.

187. *Cf. supra*, pp. 436–8; BNu/Fonds A. Andonian, P.J.1/3, file 6, Amasia, f° 1, report by Heghine Begian, Aleppo, 24 January 1919.

188. *Ibidem*, ff. 14–15, report by Dikran and Kerope Tellalian.

189. *Ibidem*, ff. 2v°-3, report by Heghine Begian; f° 14, report by Dikran and Kerope Tellalian.

190. *Ibidem*, ff. 3v°-4 et 15.

191. *Ibidem*, ff. 4v°-5 et 15.

192. *Ibidem*, ff. 7–9; *cf. supra*, p. 443.

193. BNu/Fonds A. Andonian, P.J.1/3, file 6, Amasia, ff. 10–12, report by Heghine Begian, and ff. 15–16, report by Dikran and Kerope Tellalian.

194. *Ibidem*. The witnesses saved their lives by paying 300 Turkish pounds gold each to the two Kurdish *çete* leaders.

195. *Ibidem*, ff. 18–19.

196. BNu, ms. 289, ff 27–33, list of the murderers in Sıvas.

197. *Ibidem*; BNu/ Fonds A. Andonian, P.J.1/3, file 6, Amasia, f° 15, report by Dikran and Kerope Tellalian, which states that these were the men who killed the men from Amasia at Saz Dağ.

198. Kévorkian & Paboudjian, *Les Arméniens dans l'Empire ottoman, op. cit.*, pp. 261–3; Karpat, *op. cit.*, p. 178, puts the number of Armenians in the *kaza* at 9,726.

199. SHAT, Service Historique de la Marine (Château de Vincennes), Service de Renseignements de la Marine, Turquie, 1BB7 231, doc. no. 326, Constantinople, 15 February 1919, written by Colonel Foulon, naval attaché, pp. 1–2.

200. *Ibidem*, p. 2; P.R.O., FO 371/ 6500, Turkish War Criminals, the file of prisoner no. 2719, Muammer bey, interned in Malta: Vartkès Yeghiayan, *British Foreign Office dossiers on Turkish War Criminals, op. cit.*, annexe A, pp. 93–5, report by Arusiag Iskian, from Merzifun.

201. SHAT, Service Historique de la Marine, Service de Renseignements de la Marine, Turquie, 1BB7 231, doc. no. 326, p. 3; Barton, *"Turkish Atrocities," op. cit.*, pp. 75–86, notably p. 78, statement by Dr George E. White, headmaster of the Anatolia College of Merzifun, doc. 818.

202. It's in function from 29 April 1913 to 2 August 1916.

203. SHAT, Service Historique de la Marine, Service de Renseignements de la Marine, Turquie, 1BB7 231, doc. no. 326, p. 3; P.R.O., FO 371/6500, Turkish War Criminals, the file of prisoner no. 2719, Muammer bey, interned in Malta: Vartkès Yeghiayan, *British Foreign Office dossiers on Turkish War Criminals, op. cit.*, annexe A, pp. 94–5.

204. SHAT, Service Historique de la Marine, Service de Renseignements de la Marine, Turquie, 1BB7 231, doc. no. 326, p. 4.

205. *Ibidem*, p. 4. Salih Bey, a lieutenant in the police, took an especially active part in these operations.

206. We have his correspondence with the American Ambassador in Constantinople, available under the shelf mark Record Group 84 at the National Archives (Washington D.C.), Record of Foreign Service Posts of the Department of State, Consular Posts, Samsun, Turkey, Miscellaneous Documents, c49, c8. 1, box 5, 6 and 7 for the years that interest us (US NArch., RG 84, Samsun, c49, c8. 1).

207. US NArch., RG 84, Samsun, c49, c8. 1, box 5.

208. US NArch., RG 84, Samsun, c49, c8. 1, box 5, English translation (at the time, dispatches could only be sent in Turkish) of the telegram from Drs Marden and White to the vali, 14 July 1915.

209. US NArch., RG 84, Samsun, c49, c8. 1, box 5, English translation of the telegram to Morgenthau, 4 July 1915, whose the "transmission [was] refused by the *kaimakam*."

210. In his *Diaries*, held in "The Papers of Henry Morgenthau, Sr." (reel number 5–6), in the Library of Congress, Manuscripts Division, Washington D.C., the American Ambassador

devotes considerable space to the affair of the American College. He reveals, notably, that he ordered Peter to go to Merzifun on 29 July and that he carried out personally negotiated the fate of these young women with the war minister, Enver Pasha. Some of them were saved as a result.

211. US NArch., RG 84, Samsun, c49, c8. 1, box 5, from W. Peter to H. Morgenthau, Samsun, 12 August 1915, " Concerne Hôpital-Collège Merzifoun."

212. *Ibidem*. Peter also notes that "These people were not to receive anything in the way of food and diseases broke out. Dr. Marden wanted to dispatch a nurse, but that was not allowed.": *ibidem*; Barton, *"Turkish Atrocities,"* op. cit., p. 79, report by the Dr. George E. White.

213. US NArch., RG 84, Samsun, c49, c8. 1, box 5, from W. Peter to H. Morgenthau, Samsun, 12 August 1915.

214. Barton, *"Turkish Atrocities,"* op. cit., pp. 80–1, report by the Dr. George E. White; US NArch., RG 84, Samsun, c49, c8. 1, box 5, report from W. Peter to H. Morgenthau, Samsun, 13 August 1915, notes that "the *kaymakam* must have indicated, in his report to the vali, that there were six hundred Armenians in the college, but this is not true, because there are only two hundred twenty in all" (*ibidem*, Peter to Morgenthau, 12 August 1915).

215. US NArch., RG 84, Samsun, c49, c8. 1, box 5, report from W. Peter to H. Morgenthau, Samsun, 13 August 1915.

216. US NArch., RG 84, Samsun, c49, c8. 1, box 5, report from W. Peter to H. Morgenthau, Samsun, 26 August 1915; Barton, *"Turkish Atrocities,"* op. cit., pp. 82–3, the report of Dr. White states that 72 people were deported

217. US NArch., RG 84, Samsun, c49, c8. 1, box 5, report from W. Peter to H. Morgenthau, Samsun, 26 August 1915; Barton, *"Turkish Atrocities,"* op. cit., p. 83, report by the Dr. White, notes: "I thought of the difference between an American high school girl, safe and comfortable and happy, and an Armenian girl of some education, character and family standing in the hands of officials of the Turkish government."

218. US NArch., RG 84, Samsun, c49, c8. 1, box 5, report from W. Peter to H. Morgenthau, Samsun, 26 August 1915. Peter lists the teachers who took part in the "collection" for the benefit of the "trio" of Merzifun: Mihran Daderian, Boghos Piranian, Misak Ispirian (still in the hospital) and the professors Mannisejian, Dahlian, Mixarlian, Hagopian, Arosian, Mirakian, Kostschyan, Nerso and Gurekian, "sent to the interior."

219. *Ibidem*.

220. *Ibidem*; Barton, *"Turkish Atrocities,"* op. cit., p. 81, report by the Dr. White.

221. Kévorkian & Paboudjian, *Les Arméniens dans l'Empire ottoman*, op. cit., p. 263; Karpat, op. cit., p. 178, puts the number of Armenians at 1,632.

222. Kévorkian & Paboudjian, *Les Arméniens dans l'Empire ottoman*, op. cit., p. 263; Karpat, op. cit., p. 178, puts the number of Armenians at 3,722.

223. Kévorkian & Paboudjian, *Les Arméniens dans l'Empire ottoman*, op. cit., p. 263.

224. *Ibidem*, p. 248.

225. *Ibidem*, pp. 248–9; Karpat, op. cit., p. 178, puts the number of Armenians at 8, 494; APC/APJ, PCI Bureau, Կ 564, no. 123, " Şabinkarahisar or Karahisar Şarki."

226. Aram Haygaz, Շապին Գարահիսար ու իր Հերոսամարտը [*Şabinkarahisar and His Heroic Fight*], New York 1957, pp. 138–41.

227. Zaven Der Yeghiayan, *Memoirs*, op. cit., p. 62.

228. Cf. *supra*, p. 215.

229. Haygaz, *Şabinkarahisar*, op. cit., p. 143.

230. Cf. *supra*, p. 433.

231. Haygaz, *Şabinkarahisar*, op. cit., p. 145.

232. *Ibidem*, pp. 146, 361.

233. *Ibidem*, pp. 146–7.

234. *Ibidem*, p. 148.

235. *Ibidem*.

236. *Ibidem*, p. 149.

237. *Ibidem*, p. 150.

238. APC/APJ, PCI Bureau, Ի 234, list of the murderers, vilayet of Sıvas, Şabinkarahisar.

239. S. Ozanian, Շապին Գարահիսարի առաջնորդին նահատակումը [*The Martyrdom of the Primat of* Şabinkarahisar]: BNu/Fonds A. Andonian, P.J.1/3, file 36, Şabinkarahisar, ff. 1–2.

240. *Ibidem*, p. 2.

241. Haygaz, *Şabinkarahisar, op. cit.*, p. 150. The author, who was in a labor battalion, states that the murderer personally boasted to him about what he had done.

242. Ozanian, *doc. cit.*: BNu/Fonds A. Andonian, P.J.1/3, file 36, Şabinkarahisar, f. 3.

243. Haygaz, *Şabinkarahisar, op. cit.*, pp. 151–3.

244. *Ibidem*, p. 167.

245. *Ibidem*, pp. 171–4.

246. *Ibidem*, p. 184.

247. *Ibidem*, pp. 176–8, 180, 191; Aguni, *op. cit.*, p. 216. The villagers of Ziber, a village lying below the citadel to the south, also managed to join the inhabitants of the city in the refuge (Haygaz, *Şabinkarahisar, op. cit.*, p. 191).

248. *Ibidem*, p. 178. The buildings that were spared by the fire were the mosque, the cathedral, two commercial buildings, and a few dozen homes built of stone (*ibidem*, p. 187).

249. *Ibidem*, p. 183.

250. *Ibidem*, p. 192.

251. *Ibidem*, pp. 208–9.

252. *Ibidem*, pp. 206–7.

253. *Ibidem*, pp. 216–17.

254. *Ibidem*, p. 222.

255. *Ibidem*, p. 226.

256. *Ibidem*, pp. 228, 232; Aguni, *op. cit.*, p. 216.

257. *Cf. supra*, p. 440.

258. Haygaz, *Şabinkarahisar, op. cit.*, pp. 232–4.

259. *Ibidem*, p. 243.

260. *Ibidem*, pp. 256–8. A few dozen men succeeded in fleeing to the mountains, "where the Greek villages were located." Some were killed in skirmishes with the gendarmes; others survived in the Pontic Mountains until the arrival of the Russians in spring 1916.

261. *Ibidem*, pp. 260–3.

262. *Ibidem*, pp. 264–2.

263. APC/APJ, PCI Bureau, file 33, *doc. cit.*, pp. 22–3.

264. Kévorkian & Paboudjian, *Les Arméniens dans l'Empire ottoman, op. cit.*, pp. 249–50.

265. *Ibidem*, p. 250.

266. *Ibidem.*

267. Kapigian, *op. cit.*, p. 234.

268. *Cf. supra*, p. 438.

269. Kapigian, *op. cit.*, p. 569.

270. It is symptomatic that the Ittihad's representative, Gani Bey, was one of the first to benefit from the elimination of the Armenians. In 1919, Lusaper Boghosian testified before a commission of inquiry that Gani and his wife often visited her house, which seems to have been to their taste since they moved in after Dr. Boghosian was executed and his wife was deported:: P.R.O., FO 371/ 6500, Turkish War Criminals, the file of prisoner no. 2726, Gani bey, interned in Malta: Vartkès Yeghiayan, *British Foreign Office dossiers on Turkish War Criminals, op. cit.*, pp. 104–5.

271. "Ինչպէս տեղահան ըրին Սեբաստիան [How They Deported Sebaste]," *Zhoghovurt*, no. 41, 13 December 1918, p. 2.

272. Kapigian, *op. cit.*, p. 570.

273. *Cf. supra*, p. 314.

274. Bauernfeind, *Journal de Malatia 1915, op. cit.*, p. 311, Diary of the 16 August.

275. *Ibidem.*

276. Report by Liliane Sewny, an American married to an Armenian doctor, to James Barton, 10 March 1916: Toynbee, *The Treatment of Armenians in the Ottoman Empire, 1915–1916, op. cit.*, p. 337. Sewny states that the Armenian orphans in the American orphanage were deported or forced to marry Turks; officers even took some of them in order to dispatch them to Istanbul.

277. Bauernfeind, *Journal de Malatia 1915, op. cit.*, p. 311, Diary of the 18 August.

278. BOA. DH. EUM, 2.Şb. 68/84, in *The Armenians in Ottoman Documents (1915–1920)*, *op. cit.*, doc. no. 122, p. 111. This was a response to a telegram that he had received on 24 June 1915 from Ali Münîf, *nâzır* at the Interior Ministry, requesting information about the number of localities and people in the vilayet to be deported [*sevk*]:: BOA. DH. Şfr. nr.54/136, in *The Armenians in Ottoman Documents (1915–1920)*, *op. cit.*, doc. no. 44, p. 54.

279. Extract from the 5 December 1918 deposition of Vehib Pasha: *Takvim-ı Vakayi*, no. 3540, 5 May 1919, p. 7, col. 2 and the full deposition of handwritten pages: APC/APJ, PCI Bureau, Հ 171–Հ 182, 5 December 1918, in French.

280. *Ibidem.*

281. Modenizâde Fuad, "Les vols de Muammer," in *Söuz*, 19 January 1919.

282. *Ibidem.* The president of the governmental commission of inquiry set up on November 1918, Mazhar Bey, requested some additional information about the events from Sıvas's police chief. Mazhan mentioned, notably, Hulusi Bey's squadron, made up of 500 *çetes*, which harassed a convoy of women all the way to Kangal and laid hands on enough jewels and other precious objects to fill three wagons. Part of this booty was delivered to the local prefecture. Mazhar asked for more exact information on the quantity of objects deposited with the authorities: APC/APJ, PCI Bureau, Մ 317.

283. APC/APJ, PCI Bureau, Մ 465, doc. no. 2, report by Captain Fazıl, a judge at the court-martial of Malatia during the War, about Ahmed Muammer.

284. *Cf.* note 1440.

285. Bauernfeind, *Journal de Malatia 1915*, *op. cit.*, p. 311, Diary of the 17 August.

286. "Ինչպէս տեղահան ըրին Սեբաստիան [How They Deported Sebaste]," *Zhoghovurt*, no. 41, 13 December 1918, p. 2.

287. Extract from the 5 December 1918 deposition of Vehib Pasha: *Takvim-ı Vakayi*, no. 3540, 5 May 1919, p. 7, col. 2 and the full deposition of handwritten pages: APC/APJ, PCI Bureau, Հ 171–Հ 182.

288. Kapigian, *op. cit.*, p. 570.

289. *Ibidem*, p. 571.

290. Letter from the president of the enquiry commission, H. Mazhar, to the general Vehib pasha, 22 December 1918, include in the investigative file of those responsible for the massacres in Erzincan: APC/APJ, PCI Bureau, Մ 372–4, 376–401, 555–70, file XXIII, no. 151.

291. Extract from the 5 December 1918 deposition of Vehib Pasha: *Takvim-ı Vakayi*, no. 3540, 5 May 1919, p. 7, col. 2 and the full deposition of handwritten pages: APC/APJ, PCI Bureau, Հ 171–Հ 182.

292. *Ibidem.*

293. The investigative file of those responsible for the massacres in Erzincan: APC/APJ, PCI Bureau, Մ 372–4, 376–401, 555–70, file XXIII, no. 151. According to Vehib Pasha's report, the documents bearing on this trial were held in the archives of the president of the recruitment office for the Ninth Army Corps, Alaheddin Bey, who was also president of the war council. These documents were later remitted to the judicial department of the Third Army, but since this unit was abolished, the minister of war took them in hand.

294. "Le martyrologe des Arméniens de Sébaste," from the primate of Sebaste, Knel Kalemkiarian, 1919, 51 pp., chapitre XV: "Recueil de témoignages sur l'extermination des amele taburi," ed. by Raymond Kévorkian, *Revue d'Histoire arménienne contemporaine*, I (1995), pp. 299–300. Another extract, about his interview with Talât, has been published by Patrik, *Sebaste*, II, *op. cit.*, pp. 16–18.

295. "Le martyrologe des Arméniens de Sébaste," *art. cit.*, pp. 299–300.

296. Letter from the general Vehib pasha to the president of the enquiry commision, H. Mazhar, 24 December 1918, include in the investigative file of those responsible for the massacres in Erzincan: APC/APJ, PCI Bureau, Մ 372–4, 376–401, 555–70, file XXIII, no. 151.

297. *Ibidem.*

298. Kapigian, *op. cit.*, p. 571.

299. BNu/Fonds A. Andonian, P.J.1/3, file 49, Sebaste, f° 14v°, *Sebaste and his villages*, doc. cit.

300. "Le martyrologe des Arméniens de Sébaste," *art. cit.*, pp. 299–300.

301. P.R.O., FO 371/6500, Turkish War Criminals, the file of prisoner no. 2726, Gani bey, interned in Malta: Vartkès Yeghiayan, *British Foreign Office dossiers on Turkish War Criminals*, *op. cit.*, pp. 100–6.

302. *Cf. supra*, p. 462; Kapigian, *op. cit.*, p. 571.
303. *Ibidem*, p. 772; *cf. supra*, p. 461.
304. Kapigian, *op. cit.*, p. 465; in a 10 March 1916 letter to James Barton, Liliane Sewny, an American married to an Armenian doctor, confirms that these three doctors were Muammer's last victims: Toynbee, *The Treatment of Armenians in the Ottoman Empire, 1915–1916, op. cit.*, p. 336; BNu/ Fonds A. Andonian, P.J.1/3, file 49, Sebaste, f° 136.
305. APC/APJ, PCI Bureau, Ս 317, "Questions addressed to the police prefect of the vilayet of Sıvas by the commission of inquiry, December 1918."
306. BNu/Fonds A. Andonian, P.J.1/3, file 49, Sebaste, f° 135v°.
307. *Ibidem*.
308. BNu, ms. 289, ff. 27–33, list of the murderers in Sıvas.
309. *Cf. supra*, p. 434.
310. APC/APJ, PCI Bureau, Ս 317, "Questions addressed to the police prefect of the vilayet of Sıvas by the commission of inquiry, December 1918."
311. BNu, ms. 289, ff. 27–33, list of the murderers in Sıvas.
312. *Ibidem*.

9 Deportations and Massacres in the Vilayet of Trebizond

1. Kévorkian & Paboudjian, *Les Arméniens dans l'Empire ottoman, op. cit.*, pp. 179–81; Karpat, *op. cit.*, pp. 180, 184, puts the number of Armenians in the vilayet at 68,813 in 1914.
2. Kévorkian & Paboudjian, *Les Arméniens dans l'Empire ottoman, op. cit.*, p. 187.
3. Hovagim Hovagimian, Պատմութիւն Հայկական Պոնտոսի [*History of Armenian Pontus*], Beirut 1967, pp. 205–6.
4. *Ibidem*, p. 208.
5. *Ibidem*.
6. AMAE, Turquie, Politique intérieure, n. s., vol. 9, f° 257, report from the French consul in Trebizond to the president of Conseil and minister of Foreign Affairs, Doumergue, 2 February 1914.
7. *Ibidem*, f° 261, letter from the chargé d'affaire in Constantinople, Boppe, to the president of Conseil and minister of Foreign Affairs, Doumergue, 14 February 1914.
8. *Cf. supra*, p. 202; Hovagimian, *op. cit.*, pp. 214–15.
9. *Cf. supra*, pp. 219.
10. *Cf. supra*, p. 214.
11. *Cf. supra*, p. 218.
12. *Cf. supra*, p. 218.
13. Mehmed Cemal Azmi (born in Dyarbekir and executed in Berlin in April 1922), was a graduate of the *Mülkiye* (1891), the head of the Salonika Law School before 1908 and a member of the CUP, parliamentary deputy from Preveze (1908–1909), vali of Bursa, parliamentary deputy from Çorum in 1914, vali of Konya (1914): Feroz Ahmad, *The Young Turks, op. cit.*, p. 167; police prefect in Istanbul in 1908: Zürcher, *The Unionist, op. cit.*, p. 107; when he was assassinated, it was learned that he had been vali of Bolu before taking up residence in Berlin early in 1918 (it is not stated in what capacity he went there); most of the Istanbul newspapers affirmed that he and Dr. Şakir had been the real leaders of the CUP and that Talât and Enver treated them with respect because "they were afraid of them": *Vakıt*, 20 April 1922.
14. Hovagimian, *op. cit.*, pp. 215–17.
15. *Ibidem*, p. 218.
16. *Ibidem*, p. 218. A few people were arrested and the ARF's reading room was thoroughly searched.
17. *Ibidem*, p. 219.
18. *Ibidem*, pp. 219–20.
19. APC/APJ, PCI Bureau, Թ 363–4, no. 3, "Comment les Arméniens de Trébizonde furent anéantis?"
20. Born in Rodosto in 1872, this prelate studied theology at the University of Rochester in the United States and participated in a number of archeological digs before being elected primate of Trebizond: Hovagimian, *op. cit.*, pp. 220–1.

21. *Ibidem*, p. 220; APC/APJ, PCI Bureau, Ч 618, no. 69, Bloody pages of Trébizonde.
22. Report by the Dr. Avni, a health inspector in Trebizond, at the fourth session of the trial of Trebizond, 3 April 1919: *La Renaissance*, no. 104, 4 April 1919.
23. Report by Philomene Nurian, Constantinople, 1 May 1919, at the fourth session of the trial of Trebizond, 3 April 1919: APC/APJ, PCI Bureau, doc. n° 34, Ց 769–70.
24. Report by Siranush Manugian, at the fourth session of the trial of Trebizond, 3 April 1919: *La Renaissance*, no. 104, 4 April 1919.
25. Hovagimian, *op. cit.*, pp. 220–1; APC/APJ, PCI Bureau, Ч 618, no. 69, Bloody pages of Trébizonde; APC/APJ, PCI Bureau, Ց 363–4, n° 3, "Comment les Arméniens de Trébizonde furent anéantis." Those killed were Setrag Yesayan, an official in the Office of the Public Debt and Dashnak leader, Puzant Jermagian, bookseller and Dashnak leader, Arshag Bedrosian, tailor and Dashnak leader, Shahen Azaplarian, accountant and Dashnak leader, Vren Kasbarian, merchant and Dashnak leader, Karnig Jizmejian, Suren Karageozian and his five brothers, Russian subjects, the four Meghavorian brothers, Russian subjects, Hrant Malkhasian, henchakist, Manug Baloyan, Aram Vorperian, Levon Diradurian, Hrant Sarafian, Hagop Kedeshian, and the three Sarian brothers.
26. APC/APJ, PCI Bureau, Ի 214, Ց 354–5 and 358, those responsible for the deportations and massacres at Trebizond in June-July 1915.
27. *Nor Giank*, no. 168, 8 April 1919; *La Renaissance*, no. 109, 8 April 1919.
28. *Ibidem*.
29. Report by Nâzım bey, at the fifteenth session of the trial of Trebizond, 30 April 1919: *Nor Giank*, no. 182, 1 May 1919; *La Renaissance*, no. 132, 6 May 1919; Report by the Dr. Avni, a health inspector in Trebizond, at the fourth session of the trial of Trebizond, 3 April 1919: *La Renaissance*, no. 104, 4 April 1919.
30. Report by Philomene Nurian, Constantinople, 1 May 1919: APC/APJ, PCI Bureau, doc. no. 34, Ց 769–70; *La Renaissance*, no. 49, 28 January 1919.
31. APC/APJ, PCI Bureau, Ի 214, Ց 354–5, 358, those responsible for the deportations and massacres at Trebizond in June-July 1915.
32. Examination of Imamzâde Mustafa at the fourth session of the trial of Trebizond, 3 April 1919: *La Renaissance*, no. 104, 4 April 1919.
33. APC/APJ, PCI Bureau, Ի 214, Ց 354–5, 358, those responsible for the deportations and massacres at Trebizond in June-July 1915.
34. Report by the Dr. Avni, a health inspector in Trebizond, at the fourth session of the trial of Trebizond, 3 April 1919: *La Renaissance*, no. 104, 4 April 1919; interview of G. Gorrini, Italian consul général in Trebizond, 25 August 1915: Toynbee, *Le Traitement des Arméniens, op. cit.*, doc. 27, pp. 285–7; letter from German consul in Trebizond, the Dr. Bergfeld, 9 July 1915, to the chancelier Bethmann Hollweg: Lepsius (ed.), *Archives du génocide des Arméniens, op. cit.*, doc. 109, pp. 104–7; letter of American consul in Trebizond, Oscar S. Heizer, 7 July 1915, in Ara Sarafian (ed.), *United States Official Records on the Armenian Genocide, 1915–1917*, Princeton 2004, pp. 126–7.
35. *Cf.* ref. of the n. 34.
36. Hovagimian, *op. cit.*, p. 227.
37. Letter from the American consul Heizer to Morgenthau, 28 July 1915: Sarafian (ed.), *United States Official Records, op. cit.*, pp. 178–9.
38. Letter from the American consul Heizer to Morgenthau, 7 July 1915: *ibidem*, pp. 126–7.
39. Hovagimian, *op. cit.*, pp. 227–8.
40. Letter from the American consul Heizer to Morgenthau, 7 July 1915: *ibidem*, pp. 126–7.
41. Report by Nuri bey, the head of the police in Trebizond, at the first session of the trial of Trebizond, Istanbul, 26 March 1919.
42. Verdict of the Trebizond trial, 22 May 1919: *Takvim-ı Vakayi*, no. 3616, 6 August 1919, pp. 50–2, condemning to death in absentia Cemal Azmi bey and Yenibahçeli Nail bey, Mehmed Ali, the director of customs, to ten years of hard labor, and the others accused to minor punishment.
43. The legal material connected with the Trebizond trial was compiled by the PCI Bureau: APC/APJ, PCI Bureau, file XXXII, Ց 540–70 and 811–33 (newspapers in Osmanlı, Armenian, and French on the Trebizond trial).

44. APC/APJ, PCI Bureau, Ϧ 214 and ℗ 354–5, 358, those responsible for the deportations and massacres at Trebizond.

45. *Ibidem*; *cf.* as well the informations collected at the trial who enlighten the responsibility of each one.

46. Report at the fourth session of the trial of Trebizond, 3 April 1919: *La Renaissance*, no. 104, 4 April 1919.

47. *Ibidem*.

48. Report by Sofia Makhokhian, at the third session of the trial of Trebizond, 1 April 1919: APC/APJ, PCI Bureau, doc. no. 34, ℨ 769–70. The witness stated that the accused had also "seized merchandise from his father's store."

49. We shall address this question somewhat later, especially in connection with the sixth session of the trial of Trebizond, 7 April 1919.

50. Report at the fourth session of the trial of Trebizond, 3 April 1919: *La Renaissance*, no. 104, 4 April 1919.

51. Report at the third session of the trial of Trebizond, 1 April 1919: APC/APJ, PCI Bureau, doc. no. 34, ℨ 769–70.

52. Report at the fourth session of the trial of Trebizond, 3 April 1919: *La Renaissance*, no. 104, 4 April 1919.

53. *Ibidem*.

54. Report at the third session of the trial of Trebizond, 1 April 1919.

55. *Ibidem*.

56. Report at the seventh session of the trial of Trebizond, 8 April 1919: *La Renaissance*, no. 110, 9 April 1919.

57. Report at the fourth session of the trial of Trebizond, 3 April 1919: *La Renaissance*, no. 104, 4 April 1919.

58. *Ibidem*. In the 4 January 1919 issue of *Verchin Lur*, an article signed by "Dr. A. Kh." mentions Vasfi Bey, a health inspector in Trebizond, who poisoned orphans in the Red Crescent Hospital. But this is the only accusation leveled at Vasfi Bey.

59. Examination at the tenth session of the trial of Trebizond, 12 April 1919: *La Renaissance*, no. 114, 13 April 1919; *Nor Giank*, no. 168, 13 April 1919.

60. Examination of the Dr. Ali Saib, at the third session of the trial of Trebizond, 1 April 1919: *Nor Giank*, 4 January and 25 February 1919, the testimony given by Adnan bey again Ali Saib, and *La Renaissance*, 14 February 1919.

61. *Ibidem*.

62. *Nor Giank*, no. 174, 20 April 1919; *La Renaissance*, no. 120, 22 April 1919.

63. After the departure of its leaders, the CUP organized its last congress on 1 November and decided to disband on 5 November in order to found the *Teceddüt Fırkası* (the Party of Renewal), officially registered on 11 November 1918: Zürcher, *The Unionist*, *op. cit.*, p. 73.

64. *Nor Giank*, 4 January and 25 February 1919, the testimony given by Adnan bey again Ali Saib, and *La Renaissance*, 14 February 1919.

65. *Ibidem*.

66. *Ibidem*.

67. Report by the Father Laurent at the seventh session of the trial of Trebizond, 8 April 1919: *La Renaissance*, no. 110, 9 April 1919.

68. Report by Louis Vidal at the sixth session of the trial of Trebizond, 7 April 1919: *Nor Giank*, no. 168, 8 April 1919, and *La Renaissance*, no. 109, 8 April 1919.

69. *Ibidem*.

70. Examination at the fifth session of the trial of Trebizond, 5 April 1919: *La Renaissance*, no. 108, 6 April 1919; *Nor Giank*, no. 162, 6 April 1919.

71. Report by Abdüllah Ruşdi at the sixth session of the trial of Trebizond, 7 April 1919: *Nor Giank*, no. 168, 8 April 1919, and *La Renaissance*, no. 109, 8 April 1919. The witness points out that his wife wanted to follow the men who were taking him away but that she was prevented from doing so.

72. *Ibidem*.

73. Report by the Major Edhem Bey at the fifteenth session of the trial of Trebizond, 30 April 1919: *La Renaissance*, no. 132, 6 May 1919; *Nor Giank*, no. 182, 1 May 1919.

74. Report by the Colonel Vasfi, 39 years old, to be retired of service, at the fourth session of the trial of Trebizond, 3 April 1919: *La Renaissance*, no. 104, 4 April 1919.
75. *Cf.* note 1509.
76. Letter from the Consul Heizer to Morgenthau, 10 July 1915: Sarafian (ed.), *United States Official Records, op. cit.*, p. 146.
77. Report by Arif Bey at the fourteenth session of the trial of Trebizond, 26 April 1919: *La Renaissance*, no. 125, 27 April 1919; *Nor Giank*, no. 179, 27 April 1919.
78. Report by Kenan Bey at the sixteenth session of the trial of Trebizond, 5 May 1919: *La Renaissance*, no. 134 and 141, 8 and 16 May 1919; *Nor Giank*, no. 186, 6 May 1919.
79. Report by Yusuf Rıza Bey at the first session of the trial of Trebizond, 26 March 1919.
80. Report by Talât bey at the first session of the trial of Trebizond, 26 March 1919.
81. Report at the fourth session of the trial of Trebizond, 3 April 1919: *La Renaissance*, no. 104, 4 April 1919.
82. Report at the fourth session of the trial of Trebizond, 3 April 1919: *ibidem*.
83. Report at the fourth session of the trial of Trebizond, 3 April 1919: *ibidem*. The reading of General Vehib Pasha's report on the atrocities perpetrated in Trebizond and Erzerum annoyed Yusuf Rıza, who declared that the CUP had played a "glorious role in [Ottoman] history" and that the crimes were committed without the knowledge of the Central Committee: second session of the trial of Trebizond, 28 March 1919, in *La Renaissance*, no. 102, 30 March 1919.
84. Report by Necmeddin Bey at the fifth session of the trial of Trebizond, 5 April 1919: *La Renaissance*, no. 108, 6 April 1919; *Nor Giank*, no. 162, 6 April 1919.
85. Prosecution address by the general prosecutor, Feridun Bey, at the seventeenth session of the trial of Trebizond, 16 May 1919: *La Renaissance*, no. 144 and 146, 20 and 22 May 1919. The prosecutor also mentioned their main accomplices, Agent Mustafa, Niyazi Bey, Mehmed Ali and the Dr. Ali Saib, noting that it had not been proven that Dr. Ali Saib carried out the poisonings of which he stood accused.
86. Speech for the defense at the eighteenth session of the trial of Trebizond, 18 May 1919.
87. Verdict of the trial of Trebizond, 22 May 1919: *Takvim-ı Vakayi*, no. 3616, 6 August 1919, pp. 50–2.
88. *Takvim-ı Vakayi*, no. 3557, 25 May 1919, pp. 91–113, notably pp. 104–7, the examination of Yusuf Rıza, and p. 113, on the independent functioning of the Organization.
89. APC/APJ, PCI Bureau, Һ 214 and Ҩ 354–5, 358, those responsible for the deportations and massacres at Trebizond.
90. Report by Lutfi Bey at the seventh session of the trial of Trebizond, 8 April 1919: *La Renaissance*, no. 110, 9 April 1919. Nuri Bey admitted, during his examination at the ninth session of the trial of Trebizond, 10 April 1919 (*Nor Giank*, no. 166, 11 April 1919; *La Renaissance*, no. 112, 11 April 1919), that the police had had a hand in "the business" of the deportation: "Armenians were arrested on the basis of lists transmitted to us. Two battalions of soldiers were waiting there; the police turned the Armenians over to these soldiers. This happened day after day. The police did not participate in anything else."
91. APC/APJ, PCI Bureau, Һ 214 and Ҩ 354–5, 358, those responsible for the deportations and massacres at Trebizond.
92. Report by Lutfi Bey at the eighth session of the trial of Trebizond, 9 April 1919: *La Renaissance*, no. 111, 10 April 1919; *Nor Giank*, no. 165, 10 April 1919.
93. *Ibidem*.
94. Report by Nâzım Bey, at the fifteenth session of the trial of Trebizond, 30 April 1919: *Nor Giank*, no. 182, 1 May 1919; *La Renaissance*, no. 132, 6 May 1919.
95. Examination of Niyazi, at the sixth session of the trial of Trebizond, 7 April 1919: *Nor Giank*, no. 168, 8 April 1919; *La Renaissance*, no. 109, 8 April 1919.
96. *Ibidem*.
97. Report by Lutfi Bey at the seventh session of the trial of Trebizond, 8 April 1919: *La Renaissance*, no. 110, 9 April 1919.
98. Examination of Nuri Bey, at the ninth session of the trial of Trebizond, 10 April 1919: *Nor Giank*, no. 166, 11 April 1919; *La Renaissance*, no. 112, 11 April 1919.
99. *Ibidem*.

100. *Ibidem.*

101. *Ibidem*, examination of Agent Mustafa.

102. Report by Nuri Bey at the seventh session of the trial of Trebizond, 8 April 1919: *La Renaissance*, no. 110, 9 April 1919.

103. Report by Arusiag Kilijian, at the third session of the trial of Trebizond, 1 April 1919: APC/APJ, PCI Bureau, doc. no. 34, ꝛ 769–70.

104. Report by the Dr. Avni Bey at the eighth session of the trial of Trebizond, 9 April 1919: *La Renaissance*, no. 111, 10 April 1919; *Nor Giank*, no. 165 and 166, 10 and 11 April 1919. Afterwards, Mehmed Ali took Makhokhian's daughter to Samsun, then Constantinople.

105. Eleventh session of the trial of Trebizond, 13 April 1919: *Nor Giank*, no. 169, 14 April 1919; *La Renaissance*, no. 115, 15 April 1919; twelfth session, 16 April 1919: *Nor Giank*, no. 171, 17 April 1919; *La Renaissance*, no. 117, 17 April 1919. It's the case of Nemlizâde Cemal Bey and of the Trebizond deputy, Naci Bey.

106. Letter from the Consul Heizer to Morgenthau, 28 July 1915: Sarafian (ed.), *United States Official Records, op. cit.*, pp. 178–9.

107. Letter from the Consul Heizer to Morgenthau, 12 July 1915: *ibidem*, p. 146.

108. Kévorkian & Paboudjian, *Les Arméniens dans l'Empire ottoman, op. cit.*, pp. 189–90.

109. Zavria (pop. 403), Mala et Orus (325), Satari (130), Anifa (221), Azret (95), Elmanos (124), Tots (149), summer home of the Armenians of Trebizond, Ile (101), Ichaksa (150), Ilanos (130), Ilana (40), Laghana (400), Kharaga (40), Khorghorud (20), Kavlala (114), Kukhla (67), Krobi (147), Jochara (363), Mahmad (60), Makhtele (300), Mader (160), Mimira (186), Mancheler (84), Nokhadzana (134), Bodamia (17), Samarakha (289), Verana (115), Pirvane (180), Kaloyna (40) and Olasa (42): *ibidem*, p. 190.

110. Letter from the Consul Heizer to Morgenthau, 28 July 1915: Sarafian (ed.), *United States Official Records, op. cit.*, pp. 178–9.

111. Report by Louis Vidal at the sixth session of the trial of Trebizond, 7 April 1919: *Nor Giank*, no. 168, 8 April 1919, and *La Renaissance*, no. 109, 8 April 1919.

112. Report at the third session of the trial of Trebizond, 1 April 1919.

113. PC/APJ, PCI Bureau, ꝛ 363–4, *How the Armenians of Trebizond were destroyed.*

114. Deportees from other regions noted that this convoy from Trebizond was present in Fırıncilar; *cf. supra*, p. 418. We have already mentioned Zeynel Bey's and Haci Bedri's activities in this gorge.

115. Report at the third session of the trial of Trebizond, 1 April 1919.

116. Report by Philomene Nurian, Constantinople, 1 May 1919, at the fourth session of the trial of Trebizond, 3 April 1919: APC/APJ, PCI Bureau, doc. n° 34, ꝛ 769–70; *La Renaissance*, no. 49, 28 January 1919.

117. *Cf. supra*, p. 399. It would appear that a few deportees from Trebizond managed to hide for some time in Harput's upper quarter; they were deported from there in November 1915: *cf. supra*, p. 401.

118. *Cf. supra*, p. 400.

119. *Cf.* n. 116.

120. *Cf. supra*, pp. 301–2; the verdict of the court-martial, dated 20 July 1920, condemning to death "Mehmed Nusret Bey, *kaymakam* of Bayburt and later *mutesarif* of Arğana Maden, and Lieutenant Necati Bey, the leader of a squadron of *çetes*, both of whom bear responsibility for the massacres of Bayburt," was published in *Tercüman-ı Hakikat* no. 14136, 5 Frürio 1920. Nusret was hanged on 5 August 1920, at 5 o'clock in the morning, on Bayazid Square: *La Renaissance*, no. 522, 6 August 1920.

121. *Cf.* n. 116.

122. We have already pointed out that Cemal Azmi used squadrons of *çetes* "to commit atrocities, and that many deportees were massacred on the road between Trebizond and Gümüşhane." Report by Nuri Bey at the first session of the trial of Trebizond, 26 March 1919: *La Renaissance*, no. 99, 27 March 1919.

123. Testimony given to the court-martial by the junior officer Mehmed Faik. son of Osman, of the second company of the first battalion of the Trebizond regiment of the mounted gendarmerie, a native of Trebizond, 24 years old, single, on 21 and 22 July 1915 (8/9 by the Julian calendar): APC/APJ, PCI Bureau, file XXXII, Ʊ 561–2.

124. APC/APJ, PCI Bureau, file XXXII, Ս 563/2, telegram no. 1700, from the president of the enquiry section of Erzincan court-martial to the vali of Trebizond, Cemal Azmi, 5/18 August 1915.

125. APC/APJ, PCI Bureau, file XXXII, Ս 563/1, from the vali of Trebizond, Cemal Azmi, to the president of the enquiry section of Erzincan court-martial, 5/18 August 1915.

126. APC/APJ, PCI Bureau, file XXXII, Ս 563/3, telegram no. 1453, from the vali of Trebizond, Cemal Azmi, to the president of the enquiry section of Erzincan court-martial, 9 August 1915.

127. APC/APJ, PCI Bureau, file XXXII, Ս 561–2, testimony given to the court-martial by the junior officer Faik, son of Osman, of the second company of the first battalion of the Trebizond regiment of the mounted gendarmerie, a native of Trebizond, 24 years old, single, on 21 and 22 July 1915.

128. APC/APJ, PCI Bureau, file XXXII, Ս 558–60, Testimony given to the court-martial by the accused Osman, son of Ruşen, from the İmaret neighborhood of Trebizond, a third-degree graduate of the School of Economy, civil servant, 22 years old, single.

129. *Cf* note 1602.

130. APC/APJ, PCI Bureau, file XXXII, Ս 560, testimony given to the court--martial by the accused Ayub Sabri, son of Mufid Hasan, of the second company of the first battalion of the Trebizond regiment of the mounted gendarmerie, 20 years old, married.

131. *Ibidem.*

132. APC/APJ, PCI Bureau, file XXXII, Ս 558–60, Testimony given to the court-martial by the accused Osman, son of Ruşen, from the İmaret neighborhood of Trebizond, a third-degree graduate of the School of Economy, civil servant, 22 years old, single.

133. *Ibidem.*

134. APC/APJ, PCI Bureau, file XXXII, Ս 558, copy of the testimony given to the court-martial by the accused Hafız Seyfeddine, son of İbrahim, of the second company of the first battalion of the Trebizond regiment of the mounted gendarmerie, 22 years old, married.

135. *Cf.* note 1607.

136. Testimony given to the court-martial by Mehmed Faik, *doc. cit.*: APC/APJ, PCI Bureau, file XXXII, Ս 561–2.

137. *Ibidem.*

138. Kévorkian & Paboudjian, *Les Arméniens dans l'Empire ottoman, op. cit.*, p. 196; Hovagimian, *op. cit.*, pp. 488–518.

139. *Ibidem*, pp. 519–20.

140. *Ibidem*, pp. 520–1. The witness pointed out that the lawyer, Kevork Biulbiulian, hastily left for Mosul "to find a house there." This says a good deal about the state of mind of certain Ordu Armenians, who were convinced of the authorities' good intentions.

141. Bauernfeind, *Journal de Malatia 1915, op. cit.*, p. 308, Diary of 15 August 1915.

142. Hovagimian, *op. cit.*, p. 522.

143. Minutes in *Nor Giank*, no. 179, 27 April 1919 and *La Renaissance*, no. 125, 27 April 1919.

144. *Ibidem*, pp. 523–5, reports of some survivors.

145. APC/APJ, PCI Bureau, Ֆ 359–60, lists, in Latin letters, the names those responsible for the deportations and massacres in the *kaza* of Ordu.

146. Report by Lutfi Bey at the eighth session of the trial of Trebizond, 9 April 1919: *La Renaissance*, no. 111, 10 April 1919; *Nor Giank*, no. 165, 10 April 1919.

147. Kévorkian & Paboudjian, *Les Arméniens dans l'Empire ottoman, op. cit.*, pp. 192–5; Hovagimian, *op. cit.*, pp. 462–77.

148. Minutes in *Nor Giank*, no. 179, 27 April 1919 and *La Renaissance*, no. 125, 27 April 1919.

149. APC/APJ, PCI Bureau, Ի 217 and Ֆ 358, lists of the names those responsible for the deportations and massacres in Kirason.

150. Hovagimian, *op. cit.*, pp. 477–81.

151. APC/APJ, PCI Bureau, Ֆ 365, "L'extermination des Arméniens de Kirason, récit d'une rescapée"; BNu/Fonds A. Andonian, P.J.1/3, file 27, Kirason (text nearly similar); The details of the report given by Mariam Kokmanian of Kirason and published in the 17 January 1919 issue of *Jagadamard* (no. 54), suggest that Kokmanian is the author cited in the two documents mentioned above.

152. APC/APJ, PCI Bureau, Ի 217 and Ֆ 358, lists of the names those responsible for the deportations and massacres in Kirason.

153. Kévorkian & Paboudjian, *Les Arméniens dans l'Empire ottoman, op. cit.*, pp. 202–4; Hovagimian, *op. cit.*, pp. 543–54.

154. *Ibidem*, pp. 737, 740. He replaced Mihran Zohrab (the brother of the parliamentary deputy Krikor Zohrab), who was relieved of his duties on 2 June 1915, the day his brother was arrested: Sharurian, *Chronology ... of Krikor Zohrab, op. cit.*, p. 467.

155. APC/APJ, PCI Bureau, Ի 216, lists of the names those responsible for the deportations and massacres in Gümüşhane.

156. Karpat, *op. cit.*, p. 184.

157. Kévorkian & Paboudjian, *Les Arméniens dans l'Empire ottoman, op. cit.*, pp. 204–5.

158. *Ibidem*, pp. 196–202.

159. Two reports sent directly to the Imperial Chancellor Berthmann Hollweg by the German vice-consul in Samsun, Kuckhoff , 27 June and 4 July 1915: *cf.* Politisches Archiv des Auswärtigen Amtes, Türkeï 183, band 36, J. nr. 269. The second in Lepsius, *Deutschland und Armenien, op. cit.*, pp. 104–6; Lepsius, *Archives du génocide des Arméniens, op. cit.*, pp.108–11. These reports corroborate the information provided by the American consul: "All the Armenian without exception had to leave ... According to the *mutesarif*, the deportees who left Samsun were led toward Urfa. It is quite clear that no Armenian will get that far" (*cf. ibidem*, pp. 109–10).

160. We have his correspondence with the American Ambassador in Constantinople, available under the shelf mark Record Group 84 at the National Archives (Washington D.C.), Record of Foreign Service Posts of the Department of State, Consular Posts, Samsun, Turkey, Miscellaneous Documents, c49, c8. 1, box 5, 6 and 7 for the years that interest us.

161. US NArch., RG 59, 867. 4016/373.

162. Peter had been living and working in Samsun as a businessman for some time.

163. US NArch., RG 84, Samsun, c49, c8. 1, box 5, letter from Trébizonde, 11 May 1915, [ref. no.] 811.1.

164. US NArch., RG 84, Samsun, c49, c8. 1, box 5, [Copy] of the " Circulaire, note verbale" no. G1. 64141 and no. S1.85 from the Sublime Porte, minister of Foreign Affairs, to the American ambassador in Constantinople, 18 April 1915.

165. US NArch., RG 84, Samsun, c49, c8. 1, box 5, telegram from W. Peter to H. Morgenthau, 26 June 1915.

166. US NArch., RG 84, Samsun, c49, c8. 1, box 5, telegram from W. Peter to H. Morgenthau, 24 June 1915.

167. US NArch., RG 84, Samsun, c49, c8. 1, box 5, letter from Peter to Morgenthau, Samsun, 31 August 1915.

168. US NArch., RG 84, Samsun, c49, c8. 1, box 5, report from Peter to Morgenthau, 27 June 1915, p. 3.

169. US NArch., RG 84, Samsun, c49, c8. 1, box 5, report from Peter to Morgenthau, 10 July 1915, p. 1.

170. US NArch., RG 84, Samsun, c49, c8. 1, box 5, report from Peter to Morgenthau, 26 August 1915, p. 5. It is corroborated by "the report by an American from Samsun who arrived in Dedeagaç on 27 October 1915" which indicated that, "all along the road from Samsun to Angora, one comes upon large numbers of Armenian corpses" (cf. A. Beylerian, *Les grandes puissances, l'Empire ottoman et les Arméniens dans les Archives françaises (1914–1918)*, Paris 1983, p. 139).

171. US NArch., RG 84, Samsun, c49, c8. 1, box 5, report from Peter to Morgenthau, 26 August 1915, p. 6.

172. US NArch., RG 84, Samsun, c49, c8. 1, box 5, letter from Peter to the "Honorable légation du royaume de Roumanie, [à] Constantinople," Samsun, 30 June 1915, "Concerne affaires arméniennes."

173. US NArch., RG 84, Samsun, c49, c8. 1, box 5, report from Peter to Morgenthau, Samsun, 10 July 1915, "concerne expulsion Arméniens."

174. US NArch., RG 84, Samsun, c49, c8. 1, box 5.

175. US NArch., RG 84, Samsun, c49, c8. 1, box 5, letter from Peter to Morgenthau, 4 December 1915.

176. US NArch., RG 84, Samsun, c49, c8. 1, box 7, letter from Peter to Abram Elkus, new American ambassador, 14 October 1916, "G. Tokatlian et Dr Siméonides du consulat de Russie [in Samsun]."

177. US NArch., RG 84, Samsun, c49, c8. 1, box 6, letter from Elkus to Peter, 2 December 1916.
178. US NArch., RG 84, Samsun, c49, c8. 1, box 5, letter from Peter to the American consul in Geneva, F. B. Keene, Samsun, 28 July 1915.
179. US NArch., RG 84, Samsun, c49, c8. 1, box 5, letter from Peter to Morgenthau, 17 December 1915.
180. US NArch., RG 84, Samsun, c49, c8. 1, box 5, letter from Peter to the Rumanian general consul in Constantinople, 13 November 1915.
181. US NArch., RG 84, Samsun, c49, c8. 1, box 7, circular from the *Banque de Salonique* to his correspondents in Samsun, Constantinople, 16 July 1915.
182. US NArch., RG 84, Samsun, c49, c8. 1, box 5, letters between Peter and the Richmond.
183. US NArch., RG 84, Samsun, c49, c8. 1, box 6, letter from Peter to Elkus, 14 October 1916, about the contract of "Ovakim Kevork Masatian, insured with Equitable Ass. C., no. [of contrat] 1626139, Frs. 6 000 [et] The Star Ass. C. London, no. [of contrat] 114645, Frs. ?"
184. US NArch., RG 84, Samsun, c49, c8. 1, box 7, letter from the N. Y. Life Insurance to Elkus, 21 December 1916; letter from Elkus to Peter, 5 January 1917; letter from Peter to Elkus, 25 January 1917.
185. *Ibidem*, letter from the N Y Life Insurance Company to Elkus, 21 December 1916.
186. Archives du ministère des Affaires étrangères (Paris), Guerre 1914–1918, Turquie, vol. 888, f° 16, in Beylerian, *op. cit.*, pp. 175–6.
187. Payladzou Captanian, *Mémoires d'une déportée arménienne*, Paris 1920. Captanian was one of the rare survivors from Samsun to have reached Aleppo.
188. *Cf. supra*, p. 441.
189. *Cf. supra*, p. 441.
190. *Cf. supra*, p. 440.
191. *Cf. supra*, pp. 404, 413.
192. *Cf. supra*, p. 404.
193. Captanian, *Mémoires d'une déportée, op. cit.*
194. APC/APJ, PCI Bureau, Ց 167–8, file of Safet Pasha, military commandant of Samsun.
195. *Ibidem*.
196. Hovagimian, *op. cit.*, pp. 677–9.
197. *Ibidem*, pp. 683–4.
198. Kévorkian & Paboudjian, *Les Arméniens dans l'Empire ottoman, op. cit.*, p. 201.
199. Examination of Kenan Bey, at the sixteenth session of the trial of Trebizond, 5 May 1919: *Nor Giank*, no. 186, 6 May 1919 and *La Renaissance*, no. 134 and 141, 8 and 16 May 1919.
200. Hovagimian, *op. cit.*, pp. 725–33.
201. Kévorkian & Paboudjian, *Les Arméniens dans l'Empire ottoman, op. cit.*, p. 201.
202. Hovagimian, *op. cit.*, pp. 713–14.
203. Kévorkian & Paboudjian, *Les Arméniens dans l'Empire ottoman, op. cit.*, p. 201.
204. *Ibidem*.
205. Hovagimian, *op. cit.*, pp. 726–41.
206. *Ibidem*, p. 726. Among the shooted men: Sarkisian, Siragian, Mgrdich Ekserian, Onnig Parseghian, Nazareth Mutafian, Vartan Simonian, Armenag Eoksuzian, Sarkis and Nighogos Mutafian.
207. *Ibidem*, p. 728.
208. *Ibidem*, p. 731.
209. *Ibidem*, pp. 732–3.
210. *Ibidem*, pp. 733–8.
211. Kévorkian & Paboudjian, *Les Arméniens dans l'Empire ottoman, op. cit.*, p. 202.
212. Hovaguimian, *op. cit.*, pp. 721, 723.
213. *Ibidem*, p. 729.

10 Deportations and Massacres in the Vilayet of Angora

1. Kévorkian & Paboudjian, *Les Arméniens dans l'Empire ottoman, op. cit.*, pp. 207–10; Karpat, *op. cit.*, pp. 172, 182, 186 give similar figures.
2. APC/APJ, PCI Bureau, Ղ 370, "Muslims who emigrated during the Balkan war and the general war."

3. *Cf. supra*, pp. 186 and 246. Born in Makriköy, a small town to the west of Istanbul, Atıf Bey, an officer and CUP *fedayi*, was later to serve as the parliamentary deputy from Angora or Biğa. In his capacity as a member of the Ittihad's Central Committee, he became one of the five leaders of the Special Organization in fall 1914. After serving as interim vali of Angora, he was appointed vali of Kastamonu. His role in the Special Organization was revealed at the second session of the trial of Unionists, 4 May 1919: *Takvim-ı Vakayi*, no. 3543, 12 May 1919, pp. 29–31, during the examination of Atıf Bey, about the code used by the *Teşkilat-ı Mahsusa*, and during the examination of Cevad Bey, at the fourth session of the trial of Unionists, 8 May 1919: *Takvim-ı Vakayi*, no. 3549, p. 63. Cevad named the leaders of the Special Organization: the head of the Department of State Security, Aziz Bey, Dr. Nâzim, Atıf Bey, and so on.

4. The examination of Midhat Şükrü, general secretary of CUP, at the fifth session of the trial of Unionist, 12 May 1919, clearly revealed that the CUP intervened directly in local affairs: *Takvim-ı Vakayi*, no. 3554, 21 May 1919, p. 85.

5. APC/APJ, PCI Bureau, Ֆ 370, file about Atıf Bey, who was vali of Kastamonu and also interim vali of Angora.

6. BNu/Fonds A. Andonian, P.J.1/3, file 7, Angora, "Angora, récit du massacre et de la déportation des Arméniens," Aleppo, 17 February 1919, by eight survivors, father G. Kasabian and al., f° 1. These witnesses confirmed that Hasan Mazhar resisted orders.

7. APC/APJ, PCI Bureau, Ֆ 396 and Գ 19, List of the responsibles in the vilayet of Angora, Ֆ 451 and 460, Դ 179–80, List of the responsibles in the vilayet of Angora.

8. Report by Ali Haydar, the Colonel Mehmed Vasıf, the Captain Fehmi and Mahmud Celaleddin, 12 March 1915: APC/APJ, PCI Bureau, Մ 733; Krieger, *op. cit.*, p. 215. We have the list of the people released from prison: APC/APJ, PCI Bureau, file no. XLIV, Մ 532, report from Ali Haydar to Istanbul, 5 February 1919.

9. APC/APJ, PCI Bureau, file no. XLIV, Մ 534, list of the people released from prison on 15 May 1915 in order to be incorporated into the Special Organization: Kara Haliloğlu Mehmed Ali, Bebekoğlu Halil, Veli Kehiaoğlu Mustafa, Hüseyinoğlu Mehmed Magdülmemak, Koç Oğlanoğlu Ahmed, etc.

10. The verdict in the trial of the CUP responsible secretaries and delegates, handed down on 8 January 1920: *Takvim-ı Vakayi*, n° 3772, February 1920, p. 2, col. 2, p. 3, col. 1; APC/APJ, PCI Bureau, file no. XLIV, Մ 482–94, examination of Kemal by Hasan Mazhar, 16 December 1918.

11. APC/APJ, PCI Bureau, Յ 458–61 and Ֆ 420–3 (continued on pp. 2–5), *Faits et documents*, no. 46, Angora, signed J. Valence.

12. BNu/Fonds A. Andonian, P.J.1/3, file 7, Angora, "Angora, récit du massacre et de la déportation des Arméniens," Aleppo, 17 February 1919, f° 1v°.

13. APC/APJ, PCI Bureau, Յ 458–61 and Ֆ 420–3, *doc. cit.* J. Valence specifies that the Russian subjects stay in prison.

14. BNu/Fonds A. Andonian, P.J.1/3, file 7, *doc. cit.*, f° 1v°.

15. APC/APJ, PCI Bureau, Յ 458–61 and Ֆ 420–3, *doc. cit.*

16. *Ibidem*; BNu/Fonds Andonian, P.J.1/3, file 7, *doc. cit.*, f° 1v°.

17. *Ibidem*, f° 2; APC/APJ, PCI Bureau, Յ 458–61 and Ֆ 420–3, *doc. cit.*, give 15/28 August, for the arrest of Catholic Armenians (approximately 2,000).

18. BNu/Fonds Andonian, P.J.1/3, file 7, *doc. cit.*, ff. 2–3.

19. APC/APJ, PCI Bureau, Յ 458–61 and Ֆ 420–3, *doc. cit.*

20. Letter from the German chargé d'affaires Hohenlohe, Pera, 4 September 1915: Lepsius (ed.), *Archives du génocide des Arméniens*, *op. cit.*, doc. 160, pp. 144–5.

21. Letter from Pallavicini to the minister Burian, 3 September 1915: Österreichisches Staatsarchiv, HHStA PA LX, Interna, file 272, no. 72 A-H, f° 346.

22. Report by Frances Gage, with the letter of Henry Morgenthau to the State Department, 22 December 1915: Toynbee, *The Treatment of Armenians in the Ottoman Empire*, *op. cit.*, doc. 96, p. 404; APC/APJ, PCI Bureau, Յ 458–61 and Ֆ 420–3, *doc. cit.*

23. BNu/Fonds Andonian, P.J.1/3, file 7, *doc. cit.*, ff. 3–4.

24. *Ibidem*, f° 6.

25. *Ibidem*, f° 7.

26. SHAT, Service Historique de la Marine, S.R. Marine, Turquie, 1BB7 236, doc. no. 2054 B-9, Constantinople, 3 May 1920, L. Feuillet, report by İbrahim Bey, pp. 12, 27–8; *İttihat-Terakki'nin sorgulanması*, *op. cit.*, pp. 133–69.

27. BNu/Fonds Andonian, P.J.1/3, file 7, *doc. cit.*, ff. 9–10; APC/APJ, PCI Bureau, Թ 396 and Գ 19, "List of responsibles in the vilayet of Angora," Թ 451, 460, Ւ 179–80, French version.

28. *Ibidem*.

29. Kévorkian & Paboudjian, *Les Arméniens dans l'Empire ottoman*, *op. cit.*, pp. 210–12.

30. Garabed Terzian, Պատմագիրք Ստանոզի Հայոց [*History of Armenians of Stanoz*], Beirut 1969, pp. 56–61.

31. *Ibidem*, pp. 63–4.

32. *Ibidem*, pp. 66–7.

33. *Ibidem*, pp. 67–9.

34. *Ibidem*, p. 71.

35. Kévorkian & Paboudjian, *Les Arméniens dans l'Empire ottoman*, *op. cit.*, p. 212.

36. BNu/Fonds A. Andonian, P.J.1/3, file 7, Angora, report by Manug Manugian, 28 December 1918, f° 11.

37. *Ibidem*, f° 12; APC/APJ, PCI Bureau, Թ 426, the responsibles for the deportations in Nallıhan.

38. *Ibidem*.

39. BNu/Fonds A. Andonian, P.J.1/3, file 7, Angora, report by Manug Manugian, 28 December 1918, ff. 13–14.

40. *Ibidem*, ff. 14–16.

41. *Ibidem*, ff. 16–17.

42. *Ibidem*, f° 18; APC/APJ, PCI Bureau, Թ 426, the responsibles for the deportations in Nallıhan.

43. *Ibidem*.

44. Kévorkian & Paboudjian, *Les Arméniens dans l'Empire ottoman*, *op. cit.*, p. 213.

45. Krikor Der Hovhannesian, Պատմագիրք Սիվրիհիսարի Հայոց [*History of Armenians of Sivrihisar*], Beirut 1965, p. 328.

46. *Ibidem*, pp. 330–1.

47. *Ibidem*, pp. 333–5.

48. APC/APJ, PCI Bureau, Ի 549, no. 80/3, and Ց 523.

49. APC/APJ, PCI Bureau, Թ 396 and Գ 19, " List of responsibles in the vilayet of Angora," Թ 457–9, 432, file 70, French version.

50. *Ibidem*.

51. *Ibidem*. In January-February 1920, the trial of the 40 people who carried out the massacres in Sivrihisar was held before the Eskişehir court-martial; four of the accused who had had subaltern roles were present. The others continued to threaten the Armenians who were still present: *La Renaissance*, no. 383, 27 February 1920.

52. APC/APJ, PCI Bureau, Թ 448, 451, "Déportation du village de Balahisar."

53. Kévorkian & Paboudjian, *Les Arméniens dans l'Empire ottoman*, *op. cit.*, p. 210.

54. *Ibidem*, pp. 213–14; Karpat, *op. cit.*, p. 172.

55. Kévorkian & Paboudjian, *Les Arméniens dans l'Empire ottoman*, op. cit., p. 214.

56. Verdict of the Yozgat trial, 8 April 1919: *Takvim-ı Vakayi*, no. 3617, 7 August 1919, pp. 1–3, who condemned the *kaymakam*, Kemal Bey, to death, and sentenced the commander of the gendarmerie Tevfik Bey to 15 years at hard labor.

57. Krieger, *op. cit.*, provides a virtually exhaustive account of these newspaper reports, session by session.

58. Ata Bey was not officially named to his post until 26 September 1915 – that is, after the massacres had ended; he remained in it until 15 March 1917.

59. *Zhamanag*, 29 March 1919, p. 1, col. 3–4 and p. 4, col. 1–3. These remarks were disputed by the interim mutesarif, Kemal Bey, who objected that Azniv Ibranosian could not have knowledge of such things; Ibranosian retorted that she had had "occasion to visit the wife of Vehbi Bey, the director of the Treasury (*muhasebeci*)," while Kemal and Tevfik, the commander of the gendarmerie, "conversed with Vehbi."

60. APC/APJ, PCI Bureau, Ց 560 and Թ 452–3, List of responsibles in the *sancak* of Yozgat.

61. Reprinted in *Jagadamard*, 4 January 1919.

62. Verdict in the trial of the CUP responsible secretaries and delegates, handed down on 8 January 1920 [Kanunusanî 1336]: *Takvim-ı Vakayi*, n° 3772, February 1920, p. 2, col. 2, p. 3, col. 1; APC/APJ, PCI Bureau, file XLIV, Ս 482–94, examination of Kemal by Hasan Mazhar, 16 December (Kanunuevvel) 1918.

63. *Cf.* n. 59.

64. Letter from Cebbarzâde Edib Bey, from Yozgat, *kaymakam* of Silivke, to the *mutesarif* of Yozgat, 10 February 1919, in which the author states that it was Cemal Bey who informed him of the substance of Necati's remarks. APC/APJ, PCI Bureau, Ս 534. This puts Necati's arrival in Yozgat around 3 August.

65. APC/APJ, PCI Bureau, Ս 574–7, declaration of the General Salim Mehmed, military commandant of Yozgat, before the judge of preliminary investigation of Yozgat, 9 December 1918.

66. *Ibidem*. His testimony is the more believable in that he himself refused "to participate in the program": seventh session of the trial of Yozgat, 18 February 1919: report by Halil İbrahim Recayi Bey, 45 years old, from Monastir, commander of the 5th Army.

67. BNu/Fonds A. Andonian, P.J.1/3, file 17, Yozgat, report by the Dr. Mgrdich Kechyan (*sancak* of Yozgat), f° 28.

68. *Ibidem*, f° 27.

69. APC/APJ, PCI Bureau, Ս 574–7, declaration of the General Salim Mehmed, military commandant of Yozgat, 9 December 1918.

70. *Ibidem*.

71. *Ibidem*.

72. BNu/Fonds A. Andonian, P.J.1/3, file 17, Yozgat, report by the Dr. Mgrdich Kechyan, f° 35.

73. APC/APJ, PCI Bureau, Ս 574–7, declaration of the General Salim Mehmed, military commandant of Yozgat, 9 December 1918.

74. Kévorkian & Paboudjian, *Les Arméniens dans l'Empire ottoman*, op. cit., pp. 215–16; Karpat, *op. cit.*, p. 172, puts the total number of Armenians in the *kaza* at 15,670.

75. BNu/Fonds A. Andonian, P.J.1/3, file 17, Yozgat, report by Movses Papazian, from Pöhrenk (*sancak* of Yozgat), f° 1.

76. Report published in *La Renaissance*, no. 122, 24 April 1919.

77. *Ibidem*.

78. Report published in *Zhamanag*, 22 February 1919, p. 4.

79. Report published in *La Renaissance*, no. 122, 24 April 1919; APC/APJ, PCI Bureau, Ս 350–1, report by Mufteri Rifât from Yozgat, 1 December 1918 to the Ministry of the Interior, confirmed that the two villages were attacked, adding that Turkish villagers from the vicinity came to the attacked villages because the cries and the odor associated with the massacre had become unbearable, and told Tevfik that what he was doing was contrary to the sharia. He answered that they were interfering with his work, took his revolver from its holster and fired on the delegation, wounding several people: BNu/Fonds A. Andonian, P.J.1/3, file 17, Yozgat, report by Movsès Papazian, from Pöhrenk (sancak de Yozgat), f° 1v°, says that the second groups was murdered in Kadılı.

80. *Ibidem*, f° 6.

81. Report published in *La Renaissance*, no. 122, 24 April 1919.

82. *Ibidem*.

83. APC/APJ, PCI Bureau, Ս 350–1, report by Mufteri Rifât from Yozgat, 1 December 1918 to the Ministry of Interior.

84. APC/APJ, PCI Bureau, file XXVI, Ձ 326, letter from the court-martial of Constantinople to the *mutesarif* of Yozgat, 4 February 1919.

85. SHAT, Service Historique de la Marine, Service de Renseignements de la Marine, Turquie, 1BB7 231, doc. no. 312, Constantinople, February 1919, "Boghazlian, sandjak de Yozgad (vilayet d'Angora)."

86. BNu/Fonds A. Andonian, P.J.1/3, file 17, Yozgat, report by Movses Papazian, from Pöhrenk (*sancak* of Yozgat), f° 2.

87. *Ibidem*, ff. 2r°-v° et 4v°.

88. *Ibidem*, f° 4v°.

89. APC/APJ, PCI Bureau, Ձ 324, testimony of Tevfik Bey.

90. APC/APJ, PCI Bureau, Ց 560, list of responsibles in the *kaza* of Boğazlian, Damas, 5 March 1919.

91. APC/APJ, PCI Bureau, Ֆ 446–7, file no. 71, "L'extermination des Arméniens de Bozuk et Çakmak," states that the massacres of the males by the *çetes* were directed by İbrahim Bey from Boğazlian and Ahmed Bey from Kozan; APC/APJ, PCI Bureau, Ֆ 324, examination of Tevfik Bey, which reveals that the adolescents were systematically rounded up and that most of them were "crammed into prisons and cellars" before being killed.

92. BNu/Fonds A. Andonian, P.J.1/3, file 17, Yozgat, ff. 1–21, report by Movses Papazian, f° 5; BNu/ Fonds A. Andonian, P.J.1/3, file no. 17, Yozgat, report by Dr. Mgrdich Kechyan, f° 29.

93. *Ibidem*, ff. 29–30. Kechyan indicates that the most "intelligent and promising" of the Islamicized children were later transferred to the orphanage baptized Şifa Yurdisi in Talis, but that those who remained in Yozgat were in such a state that none of the "survived" the privations to which they were subjected.

94. *Ibidem*, f° 35; APC/APJ, PCI Bureau, Ֆ 446–7, file no. 71, "L'extermination des Arméniens de Bozuk et Çakmak," states that Kulis Bey, an officer in the department of military security, supervised the operations together with Kemal Bey.

95. APC/APJ, PCI Bureau, Մ 511, chiffred telegram from Mustafa Bey, military commandant of Boğazlian, to the commandant by interim of the 5th Army, via Şahabeddin, in Kayseri, 14/27 Temmuz/July 1915, no. 18; request no. 377, 12/25 July, and no. 379, 13/26 July.

96. APC/APJ, PCI Bureau, Մ 511, telegram from Mustafa Bey, to the commandant by interim of the 5th Army, in Angora, Halil Recayi Bey, 22 Temmuz/4 August 1915, no. 16.

97. APC/APJ, PCI Bureau, Մ 511, chiffred telegram from Halil Recayi Bey to Mustafa Bey, Angora, 22 Temmuz/4 August 1915, no. 16.

98. APC/APJ, PCI Bureau, Մ 540, chiffred telegram from Halil Recayi Bey to the commandant by interim of the 15th division, the Colonel Şahabeddin, in Kayseri, Angora, 23 Temmuz/5 August 1915.

99. APC/APJ, PCI Bureau, Ձ 631.

100. APC/APJ, PCI Bureau, Մ 478, file XXXV, chiffred telegram from the *mutesarif* of Kayseri, Kemal Bey, to the president of court-martial, in Constantinople, 8 February 1919.

101. *Cf. supra*, p. 503.

102. BNu/Fonds A. Andonian, P.J.1/3, file 17, Yozgat, report by Movses Papazian, from Pöhrenk, ff. 5v°-7v°.

103. *Ibidem*, ff. 8v°-9.

104. *Ibidem*, f° 18v°.

105. *Ibidem*, f° 19.

106. *Ibidem*, ff. 19v°-20v°. Involved were the witness, his brother Aristakes, his cousins Hovsep and Hampartsum Stambolian, and also Parsegh Parseghian, Benjamin Karadedeyan, Zamita Baliozian, Taniel Torosian, and Rafayel Arzumanian.

107. Report by the director of Yozgat Turkish orphanage, Şevki Bey, in *Jagadamard*, 4 January 1919.

108. Report by Azniv Ibranossian, the wife of the director of Ibranossian Fathers in Yozgat, at the fifteenth session of the trial of Yozgat, 28 March 1919: *Zhamanag*, 29 March 1919, p. 1.

109. Report at the eighth session of trial of Yozgat, 21 February 1919, in *Zhamanag*, 22 February 1919, p. 4.

110. APC/APJ, PCI Bureau, Ձ 326, file XXVI, no. 74, letter from the president of the court-martial to the *mutesarif* of Yozgat, 4 February 1919.

111. *Zhamanag*, 27 March 1919.

112. *Ibidem*.

113. *Ibidem*. Government officials often used formulations of this sort, introducing incoherencies that only the correspondents would notice, in order to issue an extermination order. In this particular case, the prosecutor clearly understood that the order to send the women's and girls' "possessions" to Yozgat meant, given that they had already been stripped of their possessions before leaving for Yozgat, that they were to be killed.

114. *Ibidem*. The presiding judge reminded Kemal that in his first [December 1918] declaration he had said that he had burned many of the documents having to do with the deportations: "you have," he said, "signed a statement to this effect." Kemal answered that he had been extremely

tired and had expressed himself "hastily." The prosecutor, who was a member of the governmental commission of inquiry, observed that Kemal had taken three to four hours to write out his answers.

115. APC/APJ, PCI Bureau, Ꞡ 560, list of responsibles in the *kaza* of Boğazlian, Damas, 5 March 1919.

116. APC/APJ, PCI Bureau, Ꞡ 560 and Ꝑ 452–3, list of responsibles in the *sancak* of Yozgat.

117. BNu/Fonds A. Andonian, P.J.1/3, liasse 17, Yozgat, report by Dr. Mgrdich Kechyan, f° 38.

118. *Ibidem.*

119. APC/APJ, PCI Bureau, ♂ 478–9.

120. APC/APJ, PCI Bureau, Ꝑ 266, telegram from the president of the court-martial to the vali of Angora, 22 February 1919.

121. Reports of Christaki, an employee of the German company, and Simon, a 29-year-old deportee from Harput studying law in Constantinople, who were in Yozgat in 1915, at the seventh session of the trial of Yozgat, 18 February 1919; report by Azniv Ibranosian, at the fifteenth session of the trial of Yozgat, 28 March 1919: *Zhamanag*, 29 March 1919.

122. Report by Simon, a 29-year-old deportee from Harput, at the seventh session of the trial of Yozgat, 18 February 1919.

123. Report by Azniv Ibranosian, at the fifteenth session of the trial of Yozgat, 28 March 1919: *Zhamanag*, 29 March 1919.

124. *Zhamanag*, 25 March 1919; *La Renaissance*, no. 97, 25 March 1919; *Jagadamard*, 25 March 1919; *Nor Giank*, 25 March 1919; APC/APJ, PCI Bureau, Ꝑ 324, examination of Tevfik in the court-martial.

125. APC/APJ, PCI Bureau, Ꞡ 560 and Ꝑ 452–3, list of responsibles in the *sancak* of Yozgat.

126. APC/APJ, PCI Bureau, Ⴟ 326, file XXVI, no. 74, letter from the president of the court-martial to the *mutesarif* of Yozgat, 4 February 1919.

127. Reports of Christaki, an employee of the German company, at the seventh session of the trial of Yozgat, 18 February 1919.

128. *Cf.* n. 124.

129. *Cf.* n. 126.

130. BNu/Fonds A. Andonian, P.J.1/3, liasse 17, Yozgat, report by Dr. Mgrdich Kechyan, f° 45.

131. *Ibidem*, f° 47.

132. *Cf. supra*, p. 508.

133. BNu/Fonds A. Andonian, P.J.1/3, liasse 17, Yozgat, report by Dr. Mgrdich Kechyan, f° 46.

134. *Ibidem*, f° 47.

135. *Ibidem*, ff. 47–8.

136. Report by Stepan at the fifth session of the trial of Yozgat, 15 February 1919.

137. Report by Eugenie Varvarian, 18 years old, an native of Yozgat, whose caravan was pillaged in Çiftlik and massacred near Keller, at the first session of the trial of Yozgat, 11 February 1919.

138. *Ibidem.*

139. Report at the eighth session of the trial of Yozgat, 11 February 1919.

140. APC/APJ, PCI Bureau, Ʊ 350, letter from the civil inspector Nedim Bey, in charge to investigate criminals in the sancak of Yozgat, to Emin Bey, 28 December 1918.

141. SHAT, Service Historique de la Marine, Service de Renseignements de la Marine, Turquie, 1BB7 231, doc. no. 259, Constantinople, 7 February 1919, "Rapport sur les atrocités de Yozgat, dressé par un fonctionnaire turc," 30 December 1918.

142. Confession of Şükrü, commander of gendarmerie in Yozgat, in Balakian, *op. cit.*, pp. 221–30. It was the mission of the second commission, headed by Hulusi Bey, to investigate the atrocities perpetrated in the Angora and Konya regions. Hulusi Bey, a court inspector, the brother-in-law of Tahsin Bey, the vali of Erzerum, and a CUP member since 1908, seems to have covered up the mass crimes committed in the region and contented himself with punishing a few gendarmes for "abuses": APC/APJ, PCI Bureau, Ꞡ 25–34, "Second report on Turks responsibles for the armenian atrocities of the Bureau of Information: the question of Turkish witnesses (Part 1)."

143. *Ibidem.*

144. APC/APJ, PCI Bureau, Ⴟ 326, file XXVI, no. 74, letter from the president of the court-martial to the *mutesarif* of Yozgat, 4 February 1919.

145. *Ibidem.* Letter from the president of the court-martial to the *mutesarif* of Yozgat, 5 February 1919.

146. BNu/Fonds A. Andonian, P.J.1/3, file no. 17, Yozgat, report by Dr. Mgrdich Kechyan, ff. 48–9.

147. Examination published in *Zhamanag*, 29 March 1919.

148. APC/APJ, PCI Bureau, Ս 350–51, report by Mufteri Rifât, from Yozgat, 1 December 1918, to the minister of interior.

149. *Ibidem.*

150. Reports of Christaki, an employee of the German company, at the seventh session of the trial of Yozgat, 18 February 1919.

151. SHAT, Service Historique de la Marine, Service de Renseignements de la Marine, Turquie, 1BB7 231, doc. no. 259, Constantinople, 7 February 1919, "Rapport sur les atrocités de Yozgat, dressé par un fonctionnaire turc," 30 December 1918.

152. Report by Vehbi, at the fifteenth session fo trial of Yozgat, 28 March 1919: *Zhamanag*, 29 March 1919.

153. APC/APJ, PCI Bureau, Թ 433, file 45–6; SHAT, Service Historique de la Marine, Service de Renseignements de la Marine, Turquie, 1BB7 231, doc. no. 312, Constantinople, February 1919, "Boghazlian, sandjak de Yozgad (vilayet d'Angora)."

154. Kévorkian & Paboudjian, *Les Arméniens dans l'Empire ottoman, op. cit.*, p. 214.

155. SHAT, Service Historique de la Marine, Service de Renseignements de la Marine, Turquie, 1BB7 231, doc. no. 312, Constantinople, February 1919.

156. Kévorkian & Paboudjian, *Les Arméniens dans l'Empire ottoman, op. cit.*, p. 215.

157. Confession of Şükrü, commander of gendarmerie in Yozgat, in Balakian, *op. cit.*, pp. 221–30.

158. *Cf. supra*, pp. 501–2; SHAT, Service Historique de la Marine, Service de Renseignements de la Marine, Turquie, 1BB7 231, doc. no. 312, Constantinople, February 1919.

159. Kévorkian & Paboudjian, *Les Arméniens dans l'Empire ottoman, op. cit.*, p. 216.

160. APC/APJ, PCI Bureau, Չ 599, telegram from Major Ahmed, military commandant of Akdağmaden, to the *Mutesarif* Cemal bey, 11/12 July 1915 (11/12 Temmuz). This was probably the group we mentioned on p. 631, above.

161. APC/APJ, PCI Bureau, Ս 350–1, report by Mufteri Rifât, from Yozgat, 1 December 1918, to the minister of interior.

162. Kévorkian & Paboudjian, *Les Arméniens dans l'Empire ottoman, op. cit.*, pp. 217–20.

163. *Ibidem*, pp. 220–5.

164. Arshag Alboyajian, Պատմութիւն Հայ Կեսարիոյ [*History of Armenian Caesarea*], II, Cairo 1937, p. 1435.

165. *Ibidem*, pp. 1437–8.

166. BNu/Fonds A. Andonian, P.J.1/3, file 26, Kayseri, report by Yervant Der Mardirosian, a 23-year-old native of Talas who taught in Talas's American College, f° 42.

167. Aris Kalfayan, Չոմախլու [*Tchomakhlou/çomaklu*], New York 1930, p. 81; Alboyajian, *op. cit.*, II, p. 1445; BNu/Fonds A. Andonian, P.J.1/3, file no. 26, Kayseri, report by Kalust Merjikian, Bassorah, 1917: "Ce qui s'est passé à Césarée," f° 4v°.

168. Kalfayan, *op. cit.*, p. 84; BNu/Fonds A. Andonian, P.J.1/3, file 20, Tomarza, collective report, Aleppo, 25 December 1918: "Brief report on the district of Everek," ff. 20v°-21.

169. *Ibidem*, f° 22.

170. *Ibidem*, f° 22v°.

171. *Ibidem*, ff. 22v°-23. A machine for knitting socks was also presented as a deadly device, and the person who owned it was arrested in Kayseri: BNu/Fonds A. Andonian, P.J.1/3, file 26, Kayseri, report by Hovhannes Asadrian, Constantinople, 1919: "Les sauvageries commises à Kayseri," f° 34.

172. Alboyajian, *op. cit.*, II, pp. 1412, 1439–40.

173. *Cf. supra*, p. 255.

174. BNu/Fonds A. Andonian, P.J.1/3, file 26, Kayseri, report by Yervant Der Mardirosian, *doc. cit.*, f° 42v°.

175. Alboyajian, *op. cit.*, II, p. 1442.

176. Barton, "*Turkish Atrocities*," *op. cit.*, pp. 121, report by Clara C. Richmond, missionary in Talas and Kayseri, 11 May 1918.

177. *Cf. supra*, p. 258.
178. APC/APJ, PCI Bureau, Մ 541, chiffred telegram from the commandant by interim of the 15th division, the Colonel Şahabeddin, in Kayseri, to Halil Recayi Bey, in Angora, 2/15 June 1915 [2 Haziran 1331], no. 945/1/2.
179. APC/APJ, PCI Bureau, Մ 452, chiffred telegram from the commandant by interim of the 15th division, the Colonel Şahabeddin, in Kayseri, to Halil Recayi Bey, in Angora, 9/22 June 1915 [9 Haziran 1331].
180. APC/APJ, PCI Bureau, Մ 456, chiffred telegram from the commandant by interim of the 5th Army, Halil Recayi Bey, in Angora, to the Ministry of War, 25 June 1915.
181. *La vérité sur le mouvement révolutionnaire arménien et les mesures gouvernementales*, Constantinople 1916, p. 17.
182. BNu/Fonds A. Andonian, P.J.1/3, file 26, Kayseri, report by Melkon Asadur, Constantinople, 1919: "L'abattoir de Césarée avec des noms seulement," f° 9; Alboyadjian, *op. cit.*, II, p. 1447.
183. BNu/Fonds A. Andonian, P.J.1/3, file 26, Kayseri, article of Diruhi Safrasdian, f° 41, edited in *Jagadamard*, 5 February 1919.
184. APC/APJ, PCI Bureau, Գ 19 and Թ 396, List of responsibles in the vilayet of Angora, in French, Թ 457–9, 432; Krieger, *op. cit.* Aris Kalfayan, a schoolteacher in Çomaklu who was interned on 26 May 1915 in Kayseri's "depot," a military prison next to the *konak*, gives detailed information about the forms of torture utilized there and the courageous behavior of Murad Boyajian (SDHP), Garabed Jamjian (ADL), and Kevork Vishabian (ARF), who sustained the morale of their fellow prisoners. He also describes the devotion shown by doctors who were themselves prisoners, Garabed Demirjian, Toros Nazlian, and Levon Panosian, the pharmacist Sarkis Torosian, who gave the tortured men medical care, and the services provided by the lawyers Arsen and Mattheos Kalfayan, Aram Mendikian, Garabed Tachjian: Kalfayan, *op. cit.*, pp. 101–2.
185. Alboyajian, *op. cit.*, II, pp. 1416–17.
186. BNu/Fonds A. Andonian, P.J.1/3, file 26, Kayseri, article of Diruhi Safrasdian, f° 41, edited in *Jagadamard*, 5 February 1919.
187. *Ibidem*; Alboyadjian, *op. cit.*, II, pp. 1421–2.
188. Ibidem; BNu/Fonds A. Andonian, P.J.1/3, file 26, Kayseri, report by the Dr. Harutiun Sarkisian, from Kayseri, f° 54, confirms that certain groups of men were liquidated between Gemerek and Şarkışla.
189. Bauernfeind, *Journal de Malatia 1915*, *op. cit.*, Diary of the 18 and 20 August, p. 312.
190. Barton, "*Turkish Atrocities*," *op. cit.*, p. 133, report by Theda B. Phelps, missionary in Talas, Philadelphia, April 1918.
191. Յուշամատեան նուիրուած Սոցեալ Դեմոկրատ Հնչակեան Կուսակցութեան Քառասմնեակին [*Book of Memory for the Fortieth Anniversary of the Founding of the Social Democratic Hnchak Party*], Paris 1930, pp. 234–5; BNu/ Fonds A. Andonian, P.J.1/3, file 26, Kayseri, report by Kalust Merjikian, Bassorah, 1917: "Ce qui s'est passé à Césarée," gives information about the forms of torture used in the military prison.
192. Alboyadjian, *op. cit.*, II, pp. 1420, 1442–3.
193. BNu/Fonds A. Andonian, P.J.1/3, file 26, Kayseri, report by the Dr. Harutiun Sarkisian, from Kayseri, f° 55; *ibidem*, report by Melkon Asadur, Constantinople, 1919: "L'abattoir de Césarée avec des noms seulement," ff. 14–15. No source states that the person involved was Yakub Cemil, whose activity in Cilicia in 1909 we have already discussed (p. 227), in the Special Organization (p. 227), especially in Trebizond. However, given his role in the region, there can be little doubt that the man was Cemil.
194. APC/APJ, PCI Bureau, Գ 19 and Թ 396, List of responsibles in the vilayet of Angora, in French, Թ 457–9 and 432; In addition to the leaders of the Special Organization, Gübgübzâde Sureya bey, Kâtibzâde Nuh et Imamzâde Reşid, several local notables took part in the operations designed to liquidate the Armenian males: Hacilerlizâde Mustafa, Mehtirzâde Osman, Şahinoğlu Mustafa, Bıçakcioğlu Mehmed, Uşakizâde Osman, Durgârzâde Hilmi bey, Mollazâde Ahmed Emin, Ak Alininzâde Haci Ali, Diklilizâde Ömer bey, Feyzizâde Osman bey, İmamzâde Osman, Dedestenizâde Mehmed, Dedestenizâde Mustafa, Dedestenizâde Cemal bey, Dedestenizâde Mahmud, Imamzâde Mehmed, Yahiya bey Kadir, İmamoğlu Ali, Çerkezoğlu Mustafa, Oğulduğı Katib Mehmed, Karahimseli Mehmed, Yağmurzâde İsmail, çavuşzâde Hamid, Arapzâde Abdurraman.

195. *Ibidem.*
196. Barton, *"Turkish Atrocities,"* *op. cit.*, report by Theda B. Phelps, missionary in Talas, Philadelphia, April 1918, p. 134.
197. BNu/Fonds A. Andonian, P.J.1/3, file 26, Kayseri, report by Kalust Merjikian, Bassorat, 1917: "Ce qui s'est passé à Césarée," f° 6.
198. Barton, *"Turkish Atrocities,"* *op. cit.*, report by Clara C. Richmond, missionary in Talas and Kayseri, 11 May 1918, p. 124.
199. BNu/Fonds A. Andonian, P.J.1/3, file 26, Kayseri, report by the Dr. Harutiun Sarkisian, from Kayseri, f° 54.
200. Barton, *"Turkish Atrocities,"* *op. cit.*, report by Clara C. Richmond, missionary in Talas and Kayseri, 11 May 1918, p. 127.
201. *Ibidem,* report by Theda B. Phelps, missionary in Talas, Philadelphia, April 1918, pp. 136–7.
202. BNu/Fonds A. Andonian, P.J.1/3, file 26, Kayseri, report by Melkon Asadur, Constantinople, 1919: "L'abattoir de Césarée avec des noms seulement," ff 17–18.
203. *Ibidem,* f° 13; APC/APJ, PCI Bureau, Գ 19 and Թ 396, List of responsibles in the vilayet of Angora, in French, Թ 457–9, 432.
204. APC/APJ, PCI Bureau, Թ 427, report on Sabri Bey, chief of the correspondence Bureau in Kayseri.
205. APC/APJ, PCI Bureau, Յ 560, in Armenian, report, Damas, 5 March 1919: "The killers and accapareurs of Talas."
206. Barton, *"Turkish Atrocities,"* *op. cit.*, report by Clara C. Richmond, missionary in Talas and Kayseri, 11 May 1918, p. 121.
207. *Ibidem,* p. 122.
208. *Ibidem,* pp. 122–3.
209. BNu/Fonds A. Andonian, P.J.1/3, file 26, Kayseri, report by Yervant Der Mardirosian, a 23 year-old native of Talas who taught in Talas's American College, f° 43r°-v°.
210. BNu/Fonds A. Andonian, P.J.1/3, file 26, Kayseri, report by Kalust Merjikian, Bassorah, 1917: "Ce qui s'est passé à Césarée," f° 7.
211. Kévorkian & Paboudjian, *Les Arméniens dans l'Empire ottoman, op. cit.*, pp. 225–7; Alex Krikorian & Setrak Karageozian, Յիշատակարան Էվէրէկ-Ֆէնէսէի [*Memorial of Everek-Fenese*], Paris 1963.
212. *Ibidem,* pp. 227–9.
213. APC/APJ, PCI Bureau, Գ 19 and Թ 396, List of responsibles in the vilayet of Angora, in French, Թ 451, 460, 432, Ղ 179–80.
214. APC/APJ, PCI Bureau, Յ 560, in Armenian, report, Damascus, 5 March 1919.
215. APC/APJ, PCI Bureau, Թ 443, 452, file 111, Everek.
216. BNu/Fonds A. Andonian, P.J.1/3, file 20, Tomarza, collectif report, Aleppo, 25 December 1918, "Brief report on the district of Everek," f° 23.
217. *Ibidem.*
218. *Ibidem,* 23v°.
219. *Ibidem,* 24r°-v°. The document observed that, amid the panic sown by these departures, local Ittihadists abducted a few young women, who they raped and then killed.
220. *Ibidem,* f° 25.
221. *Ibidem,* f° 25r°-v°.
222. *Ibidem,* f° 31. In this group were ten female schoolteachers employed at Kayseri's American school. None survived; Kalfayan, *op. cit.*; English translation: Aris Kalfayan, *Chomaklu*, New York 1982, gives a detailed account of the way Salih Zeki liquidated the Armenian population of the little town and published several official documents; that they are authentic is plausible.
223. Kévorkian & Paboudjian, *Les Arméniens dans l'Empire ottoman, op. cit.*, pp. 228–30; Hovhannes Tomardzatsi Torosian, Պատմութիւն Հայ Տոմարծայի [*History of Armenian Tomarza*], 3 vol., Beirut 1959–1969.
224. BNu/Fonds A. Andonian, P.J.1/3, file 20, Tomarza, report by Garabed Zorajian, f° 1.
225. *Ibidem,* ff. 2–3.
226. *Cf. supra,* p. 522.
227. BNu/Fonds A. Andonian, P.J.1/3, file 20, Tomarza, report by Garabed Zorajian, f° 4.

228. *Ibidem*, f° 25, collective report, Aleppo, 25 December 1918, "Brief report on the district of Everek," f° 25.

229. *La Renaissance*, no. 410, 31 March 1920.

230. Kévorkian & Paboudjian, *Les Arméniens dans l'Empire ottoman*, *op. cit.*, p. 213.

231. APC/APJ, PCI Bureau, ℗ 443 and 452, file 116, the deportations in Kırşehir; SHAT, Service Historique de la Marine, Service de Renseignements de la Marine, Turquie, 1BB7 231, doc. no. 340, Constantinople, 19 February 1919, "Les massacres de Kirchehir et de ses dépendances, déposition d'un témoin."

232. *Ibidem*, f° 1.

233. *Ibidem*.

234. *Ibidem*, ff. 2–3.

235. APC/APJ, PCI Bureau, Ձ 560, in Armenian, report, Damascus, 5 March 1919, in French, ℗ 459–60–1, list of those responsible for the massacres and deportations in Kırşehir.

236. *Ibidem*.

237. BNu/Fonds A. Andonian, P.J.1/3, file 26, Kayseri, report by Yervant Der Mardirosian, a 23 year-old native of Talas who taught in Talas's American College, f° 45.

238. APC/APJ, PCI Bureau, ℗ 395, the killers of Keskin/Denek Maden.

239. APC/APJ, PCI Bureau, ℗ 449, Keskin/Denek Maden.

240. BNu/Fonds A. Andonian, P.J.1/3, file 26, Kayseri, report by Yervant Der Mardirosian, f° 45.

241. Téotig, *Memorial*, *op. cit.*, provides a list of those detained in Ayaş, with their biographies; BNu/Fonds A. Andonian, P.J.1/3, file 3, the prisoners of Ayaş, letter from V. Mardikian to A. Andonian, Bruxelles, 26 April 1947, f° 6. More than 70 men, among the best known, had already arrived.

242. Dr. Boghosian, "Պատմութեան համար. Հշուում մը [*An Accuracy for History*]," *Baykar*, 16 July 1927.

243. Terzian, *Stanoz*, *op. cit.*, pp. 61–7.

244. BNu/ Fonds A. Andonian, P.J.1/3, file 3, the prisoners of Ayaş, letter from V. Mardikian to Aram Andonian, Bruxelles, 26 April 1947, ff. 6–7.

245. Dr. Avedis Nakashian, Այաշի Բանտը [*The Prison of Ayaş*], Boston 1925, pp. 32–42.

246. *Cf.* n. 244, f° 8 and *supra*, p. 516.

247. At the time, Aknuni continued to defend his former positions; he was convinced that Talât was a "noble character," citing as proof the fact that Talât had come to see him two weeks earlier, when Aknuni was sick in bed: Dr. Avedis Nakashian, *op. cit.*, pp. 43–4,

248. *Ibidem*; BNu/ Fonds A. Andonian, P.J.1/3, file 3, the prisoners of Ayaş, f° 40. German circles were rather quickly learned of their departure, as is shown by a letter from the Dr. J. Lepsius to the German Ministry of Foreign Affairs, 15 June 1915: Lepsius, *Deutschland und Armenien*, *op. cit.*, p. 85.

249. BNu/ Fonds A. Andonian, P.J.1/3, file 3, the prisoners of Ayaş, f° 48.

250. *Cf. supra*, p. 367, n. 90.

251. BNu/ Fonds A. Andonian, P.J.1/3, file 3, the prisoners of Ayaş, letter from V. Mardikian to A. Andonian, Bruxelles, 26 April 1947, ff. 6–7; Nakashian, *op. cit.*, pp. 47–8, notes that P. Shabaz, an intellectual educated in Paris, was first interned in the prison in Ayntab, then taken to Adiyaman, and finally executed near Malatia under appalling conditions.

252. BNu/ Fonds A. Andonian, P.J.1/3, file 3, the prisoners of Ayaş, letter from V. Mardikian to A. Andonian, Bruxelles, 26 April 1947, f° 8

253. *Ibidem*, f° 9.

11 Deportations and Massacres in the Vilayet of Kastamonu

1. Kévorkian & Paboudjian, *Les Arméniens dans l'Empire ottoman*, *op. cit.*, pp. 175–8; Karpat, *op. cit.*, pp. 180, 184, gives the same figures; APC/APJ, PCI Bureau, Կ 544, statistics by vilayet.

2. APC/APJ, PCI Bureau, Կ 789–90, Armenians before the war in the vilayet of Kastamonu.

3. *Ibidem*.

4. *Ibidem*; Kévorkian & Paboudjian, *Les Arméniens dans l'Empire ottoman*, *op. cit.*, pp. 175–8.

5. *Cf. supra*, pp. 253–4.

6. Trial of Cemal Oğuz, responsible secretary of the CUP in çangırı: *La Renaissance*, no. 330, 24 December 1919, and no. 365, 6 February 1920.

7. We have seen that Fehmi was one of the speakers at the meeting organized by the CUP at Bayazid Square on 21 September 1912, on the eve of the first Balkan War: *cf. supra*, p. 135; He was found guilty at the trial of the responsible secretaries and condemned to ten years of hard labor, the 8 January 1920: *Takvim-ı Vakayi*, no. 3772, February 1920, p. 2, col. 2, p. 3, col. 1.

8. Examination of Atıf Bey, one of the leaders of the Special Organization, with regard to the circumstances surrounding the recall of Reşid Bey, who "refused to carry out his orders": sixth session of the trial of Ittihadist, 17 May 1919, *Takvim-ı Vakayi*, no. 3557, 25 May 1919, pp. 99–104. An Armenian account confirms that Reşid blocked the deportation of the vilayet's Armenians: BNu/ Fonds A. Andonian, P.J.1/3, file 38, çangırı, f° 34.

9. APC/APJ, PCI Bureau, ₽ 495, "Document sur l'ex-vali de Kastamonu, Atıf bey," signed Mehmed Necib.

10. APC/APJ, PCI Bureau, ♂♀ 95–8, "List of responsibles in the vilayet of Kastamonu."

11. *Ibidem*.

12. BNu/Fonds A. Andonian, P.J.1/3, file 38, Çangırı, f° 25.

13. *Ibidem*, ff. 37–9; f° 107v°, letter from the Father Vartan Karagueuzian to Aram Andonian, 25 February 1947.

14. Barton, "*Turkish Atrocities*," *op. cit.*, report by Clara C. Richmond, missionary in Talas and Kayseri, 11 May 1918, p. 126.

15. *Cf. supra*, pp. 253–4.

16. BNu/Fonds A. Andonian, P.J.1/3, file 38, Çangırı, ff. 1 and 21.

17. *Ibidem*, ff. 21–2: Dr. Krikor Jelal, Dr. Parsegh Dinanian, Vrtanes Papazian, Hayg Khojasarian, Nshan Kalfayan, Armenag Parseghian, Garabed Deovletian, Vaghinag Bardizbanian, Norig Der Stepanian, Hagop Beylerian, Vahan Altunian, Manug Basmajian, Hagop Korian, Hovhannes Terlemezian, Samuel Tomajan, Simon Melkonian, Apig Jambaz, Melkon Guleserian, Avedis Zarifian.

18. APC/APJ, PCI Bureau, Ꝫ 144, file about İsmail Canbolat and Ꝩ 279–80, file no. 13/1 (in English): of Circassian origin, born in Kosovo, a graduate of Harbiye and parliamentary deputy from Constantinople.

19. BNu/Fonds A. Andonian, P.J.1/3, file 38, Çangırı, ff. 29–30.

20. *Ibidem*, f° 26; f° 107, letter from Father Vartan Karagueuzian to Aram Andonian, Cairo, 25 February 1947, states that this group left on 11 July.

21. BNu/Fonds A. Andonian, P.J.1/3, file 38, Çangırı, f° 23.

22. *Ibidem*, f° 28.

23. BNu/Fonds A. Andonian, P.J.1/3, file 38, Çangırı, f° 107, letter from father Vartan Karagueuzian to Aram Andonian, Cairo, 25 February 1947. In a second, 1 April 1947 letter to Andonian, Father Vartan states that they saw Sevag's and Varuzhan's guards return to Çangırı the evening of the same day: *ibidem*, f° 113.

24. *Ibidem*, f° 107v°.

25. *Ibidem*, f° 110. *Cf. supra*, pp. 30–1, n. 1, on D. Kelekian's role in the Young Turk movement.

26. APC/APJ, PCI Bureau, ₽ 495, "Document sur l'ex-vali de Kastamonu, Atıf bey," signed Mehmed Necib.

27. BNu/Fonds A. Andonian, P.J.1/3, file 38, Çangırı, f° 62, list of the çangırı internee established by A. Andonian.

28. *Ibidem*, f° 34; APC/APJ, PCI Bureau, ♂♀ 95–6–7–8, "List of responsibles in the vilayet of Kastamonu, çangırı."

29. Trial of Cemal Oğuz, responsible secretary in çangırı: *La Renaissance*, no. 357, 27 January 1920.

30. Trial of Cemal Oğuz, responsible secretary in çangırı: *La Renaissance*, no. 363, 4 February 1920.

31. Verdict of the trial of Cemal Oğuz: *La Renaissance*, no. 369, 8 February 1920.

32. Kévorkian & Paboudjian, *Les Arméniens dans l'Empire ottoman*, *op. cit.*, pp. 177–8; APC/APJ, PCI Bureau, Ꝩ 789–90, Armenians before the war in the vilayet of Kastamonu. Only the Armenians of Zonguldak were spared, thanks to the *kaymakam*, İbrahim Bey, who had close relations with an Armenian from the port: Aguni, *op. cit.*, p. 289.

33. APC/APJ, PCI Bureau, ՃԴ 95–6–7–8, "List of responsibles in the vilayet of Kastamonu," Bolu, and Ի 212.

34. APC/APJ, PCI Bureau, Թ 489, "Les condamnations de Bolu, témoignage d'un rescapé. Sur Ahmed Midhat, ex-chef de la police d'Istanbul": APC/APJ, PCI Bureau, Գ 19 and Թ 396, "List of responsibles in the vilayet of Angora," Թ 457–9 and 432 (in French).

35. APC/APJ, PCI Bureau, Թ 491–2, on İzzet bey, chief of the police in Bolu.

36. Ibidem.

37. Kévorkian & Paboudjian, Les Arméniens dans l'Empire ottoman, op. cit., pp. 177–8; APC/APJ, PCI Bureau, Ч 789–90, Armenians before the war in the vilayet of Kastamonu.

38. BNu/Fonds A. Andonian, P.J.1/3, file 38, Çangırı, f° 36.

39. BNu/Fonds A. Andonian, P.J.1/3, file 38, Çangırı, f° 107v°, letter from Father Vartan Karagueuzian to Aram Andonian, Cairo, 25 February 1947.

40. Ibidem, f° 37.

12   *Constantinople in the Period of the Deportations and Massacres*

1. Cf. *supra*, pp. 254–9.

2. Sharurian, *Chronology ... of Krikor Zohrab*, op. cit., p. 465.

3. *Ibidem*, pp. 466–7.

4. *Ibidem*, p. 467.

5. *Ibidem*, p. 467–8.

6. Ibidem, p. 469.

7. Cf. *supra*, p. 327. According to Yervant Odian, *The cursed years, 1914–1919*, op. cit., no. 17, Talât or his aide in the Interior Ministry, Ali Münif, personally telephoned K. Zohrab's wife to tell her that "her husband had died of a heart attack in Urfa."

8. Sharurian, *Chronology ... of Krikor Zohrab*, op. cit., pp. 492–3. We shall come back to the passage of the two deputies through Aleppo; it allows us to grasp the reactions in the provinces to the CUP's policies.

9. Among those authorized to return to Istanbul, Dr. V. Torkomian and Hayg Khojasarian, of whom the latter went to the Patriarchate to receive the aid earmarked for schoolteachers living underground (Sarkis Srents, Hagop Kiufejian, known as Oshagan, and so on), were the only ones to assist the Patriarchate: Zaven Der Yeghiayan, *Memoirs*, op. cit., p. 101.

10. *Ibidem*, p. 103.

11. Cf. *supra*, p. 293.

12. Letter from Wangenheim to the Chancellor Hollweg, Pera, 17 June 1915: Lepsius (ed.), *Archives du génocide des Arméniens*, op. cit., doc. 81, p. 96, comments on this visit; Weber, *Eagles on the Crescent: Germany, Austria and the Diplomacy of the Turkish Alliance, 1914–1918*, op. cit., p. 151.

13. Zaven Der Yeghiayan, *Memoirs*, op. cit., pp. 103–4.

14. *Ibidem*, p. 105.

15. *Ibidem*, pp. 110–11.

16. *Ibidem*, p. 113.

17. *Ibidem*, pp. 116–17.

18. *Ibidem*, p. 118.

19. *Ibidem*, p. 119.

20. *Ibidem*, p. 120.

21. *Ibidem*, p. 121.

22. *Ibidem*, pp. 121–2. "Last year," Said Halim recalled, "I told Monsieur Giers, the Russian Ambassador: 'The Armenian people belongs to us, and it is incumbent on us to see to its welfare.'"

23. *Ibidem*, p. 123.

24. Andonian, *Chronological notes, 1914–1916*, ms. cit., f° 51.

25. Cf. *supra*, p. 249.

26. Letter from Wangenheim to the chancelier Hollweg, Pera, 17 June 1915: Lepsius (ed.), *Archives du génocide des Arméniens*, op. cit., doc. 81, p. 96.

27. Zaven Der Yeghiayan, *Memoirs, op. cit.*, p. 124.

28. *Ibidem*, pp. 124–5.

29. *Ibidem*, p. 126.

30. *Cf. supra*, pp. 257–8, 516–7, 791.

31. The patriarch mentions that Khosrov Behrigian, his seminary fellow student in Armash, was not in any case "henchakiste": Zaven Der Yeghiayan, *Memoirs, op. cit.*, p. 127.

32. *Ibidem*, p. 129.

33. *Ibidem*, p. 130.

34. *Ibidem*, p. 130. The patriarch also mentions the role of Professor A. Khachadurian, the director of the Getronagan school, who communicated with him whenever he traveled to Galata until he, too, was deported; he apparently had means of transmitting information to the ARF's Central Committee.

35. *Ibidem*, pp. 189–90.

36. *Ibidem*, pp. 131, 142. He mentions, in particular, his reports of 7 June and 15 August 1915, which reached France and Britain under Bishop Turian's signature.

37. *Ibidem*, p. 136.

38. *Ibidem*, p. 137–49.

39. In the sixth part of the present study, we shall see that the Red Crescent had been transformed into an agency in the CUP's service; at its head were ranking members of the party.

40. *Ibidem*, pp. 154–8; Aguni, *op. cit.*, p. 100, notes that the patriarch turned to Morgenthau to in the attempt to prevent the Armenians of the capital from being deported.

41. *Ibidem*, p. 159.

42. *Ibidem*, p. 160.

43. Dadrian, *Histoire du Génocide, op. cit.*, pp. 429–34, quotations pp. 432, 434.

44. Zaven Der Yeghiayan, *Memoirs, op. cit.*, pp. 161–2.

45. *Ibidem*, p. 164.

46. Letter from Metternich to the Chancellor Hollweg, Pera, 7 December 1915: Lepsius (ed.), *Archives du génocide des Arméniens, op. cit.*, doc. 209, pp. 185–6.

47. Zaven Der Yeghiayan, *Memoirs, op. cit.*, pp. 165–6.

48. *Ibidem*, p. 182.

49. *Ibidem*, p. 183. *circa* 1,000 Turkish £.

50. *Ibidem*, p. 184, points out that Reşad Bey was rather well disposed and saved a number of individuals such as Yervant Perdajian, Kevork Mesrob, Mesrob Naroyan and Apig Moubahiajian.

51. Ghazar Charek, Մարզպետ Հաճի Հիւսէին [*Marzbed (Hadji Hüseyin)*], 2 vol., Beirut 1945.

52. Berdjouhi, *Jours de cendres à Istanbul*, French trans. By Armen Barseghian, Marseille 2004.

53. Barseghian, a native of Tomarza and ARF cadre in Persia, Van, and Bitlis, was deported in 1915, but managed to escape and work on the *Bagdadbahn* construction site under a false name: *cf. supra*, p. 60, n. 68.

54. Charek, *op. cit.*, pp. II–III.

55. Berdjouhi, *Jours de cendres à Istanbul, op. cit.*, p. 55.

56. *Ibidem*, p. 56.

57. *Ibidem*, pp. 60–2, relates the case of a little girl of three or four from Tamzara who was taken to Istanbul by the executioner of her parents, who offered her as a gift to his wife.

58. *Ibidem*, pp. 70–1.

59. M. Ormanian, *The Church of Armenia*, London 1912, annexe II, pp. 239–40.

60. Karpat, *op. cit.*, pp. 170, 184–6. The city had around eight hundred thousand inhabitants at the time.

61. Safrastyan, "Կոստանդնուպոլսի Հայոց Պատրիարգարանի Կողմից Թուրքիայի Արդարադատութեան եւ Դաւանանգների Մինիստրության ներկայացուած հայկական Եկեղեցիների եւ վանքերի ցուցակները ու դագիրները, 1912–1913 [*Takrir* and Listings of the Armenian Churches and Monasteries Presented to the Ministry of Justice and Religious Denominations by the Armenian Patriarchate of Constantinople]," *Echmiadzin* 1 (1965), pp. 43–5.

62. Armenian Patriarchate of Constantinople, Վիճակացոյց Թաղային Վարժարանաց Կոստանդնուպոլսոյ [*Statistics on Constantinople's Parish Schools*], January 1907.

63. Kévorkian & Paboudjian, *Les Arméniens dans l'Empire ottoman, op. cit.*, pp. 87–91.

64. *Ibidem*, p. 93.
65. Aguni, *op. cit.*, p. 100. The author was an editor at the daily *Zhamanag*.
66. Yervant Odian, *The cursed years, 1914–1919, op. cit.*, no. 13.
67. Aguni, *op. cit.*, p. 101.
68. *Ibidem*, p.102.
69. APC/APJ, PCI Bureau, ℨ 144, file on İsmail Canbolat and Ꝥ 279–80, file no. 13/1 (in English): of Circassian origin, born in Kosovo, a graduate of *Harbiye* and parliamentary deputy from Constantinople.
70. APC/APJ, PCI Bureau, ♂ 60–2, list of the accused, "secret-confidential."
71. APC/APJ, PCI Bureau, Ƅ 125–30.
72. APC/APJ, PCI Bureau, ℨ 197, file no. 30/1, Dossiers of Turks Responsible for the Armenians Atrocities. Tevfik was probably an Armenian orphan from Amasia who had been abducted after the 1895 massacres and adopted by a Turkish family in the capital.
73. Yervant Odian, *The cursed years, 1914–1919, op. cit.*, no. 17, 19, 22, 23.
74. Aguni, *op. cit.*, p. 105.
75. Österreichisches Staatsarchiv, HHStA PA XL, file 273, no. 327.
76. Politisches Archiv des Auswärtigen Amtes [A.A.], Türkei 183/40, A33705.
77. A.A. Türkei 183/40, A36184, ed. by Lepsius, *Deutschland und Armenien, op. cit.*, p. 187, and *Archives du génocide des Arméniens, op. cit.*, p. 185.
78. A.A. Türkei, 183/38, A30432, pp. 3–4, coted in Dadrian, *Histoire du génocide arménien, op. cit.*, p. 371, n. 2.
79. BNu/Fonds A. Andonian, P.J.1/3, file 26, Kayseri, report by Yervant Der Mardirosian, from Talas, *doc. cit.*, f° 45v°.
80. Verdict of the trial of Büyükdere/San Stefano, 24 May 1919: *Takvim-ı Vakayi*, no. 3618, 8 August 1919, pp. 6–7.
81. Aguni, *op. cit.*, p. 105.

13 Deportations in the Vilayet of Edirne and the Mutesarifat of Biğa/Dardenelles

1. Karpat, *op. cit.*, p. 170.
2. Kévorkian & Paboudjian, *Les Arméniens dans l'Empire ottoman, op. cit.*, p. 119.
3. *Ibidem*, pp. 120–1; Karpat, *op. cit.*, p. 184, puts the number of Armenians in the vilayet at 10,289.
4. *Ibidem*, p. 170, puts the number of Armenians in Malgara at 2,658; Kévorkian & Paboudjian, *Les Arméniens dans l'Empire ottoman, op. cit.*, p. 121.
5. Karpat, *op. cit.*, p. 170.
6. *Ibidem*, pp. 170, 186; BNu/Fonds A. Andonian, P.J.1/3, file 18, Edirne, a document by several hands produced on 19 February 1919 in Aleppo bay survivors from Edirne, f° 2, indicates that there were 3,500 Armenians in Çorlu and 3,000 in Gallipoli.
7. Österreichisches Staatsarchiv, HHStA PA LX, Interna, dossier 272, no. 388.
8. APC/APJ, PCI Bureau, ℨ 137, biography of Haci Adıl bey.
9. *Cf. supra*, p. 83, n. 45 (biography), p. 123 (his November 1910 entry into the Central Committee) and p. 148 (his activity as a minister in Mahmud Şevket's cabinet).
10. APC/APJ, PCI Bureau, Ƅ 131, Ƿ 560, Ꝥ 160–1, list of responsibles in the vilayet of Edirne.
11. APC/APJ, PCI Bureau, Ƿ 568–9, Andrinople.
12. Report written of a common accord by the Bulgarian consul general [in Edirne], M. G. Seraphimoff, and the Austro-Hungarian consul, Dr. Arthur, a knight of Nadamlenzki, also responsible for German interests [sent to the embassy in Constantinople on 6 November 1915]: Österreiches Staatsarchiv, HHStA PA XII, dossier 209, Z.98/P.
13. *Ibidem*. This information is corroborated by a document by several hands produced on 19 February 1919 in Aleppo by survivors from Edirne: BNu/Fonds A. Andonian, P.J.1/3, file 18, Edirne, ff. 2–8v°.
14. Aguni, *op. cit.*, pp. 258–9.
15. *Cf. supra*, p. 145.

16. Zaven Der Yeghiayan, *Memoirs, op. cit.*, p.67.

17. Sarkis Papazian, Յուշամատեան Ռոտոսթոյի Հայերուն [*Memorial Book of Armenians of Rodosto, 1606–1922*], Beirut 1971, p. 62.

18. *Ibidem*, p. 63.

19. *Ibidem*, p. 65.

20. *Ibidem*, pp. 65–6.

21. *Ibidem*, p. 66.

22. *Ibidem*.

23. APC/APJ, PCI Bureau, Ի 131, Թ 560, Դ 160–1, list of responsibles in the vilayet of Edirne.

24. *Ibidem*.

25. Aguni, *op. cit.*, pp. 262–3.

26. Ibidem, p. 265; Österreichisches Staatsarchiv, HHStA PA LX, Interna, file 272, no. 388

27. APC/APJ, PCI Bureau, Ի 134, Թ 564–5, list of responsibles in the region of çorlu.

28. Aguni, *op. cit.*, p. 265.

29. BNu, Archives de la délégation nationale arménienne, "Statistique de la population arménienne en Turquie [en 1920]," IV. 46. 2, f° 1.

30. Karpat, *op. cit.*, p. 186; Kévorkian & Paboudjian, *Les Arméniens dans l'Empire ottoman, op. cit.*, p. 118; APC/APJ, PCI Bureau, Կ 131, Dardanelles.

31. Aguni, *op. cit.*, p. 265.

14   Deportations in the Mutesarifat of Ismit

1. Kévorkian & Paboudjian, *Les Arméniens dans l'Empire ottoman, op. cit.*, p. 124.

2. APC/APJ, PCI Bureau, Յ 914, Կ 627/3, statistics on Armenian population in the region of Ismit, 29 May 1913; Karpat, *op. cit.*, p. 186, puts their number at 58,000.

3. Kévorkian & Paboudjian, *Les Arméniens dans l'Empire ottoman, op. cit.*, p. 124.

4. *Ibidem*, pp. 124–8.

5. *Ibidem*, pp. 128–1; Krikor Mkhalian, Պարտիզակ ու Պարտիզակցին [*Bardizag and Its People*], Cairo 1938.

6. Kévorkian & Paboudjian, *Les Arméniens dans l'Empire ottoman, op. cit.*, pp. 131–6; K. Fenerjian, Պատմութիւն Արսլանպէկի [*History of Arslanbeg*], Paris 1971.

7. Kévorkian & Paboudjian, *Les Arméniens dans l'Empire ottoman, op. cit.*, p. 136.

8. APC/APJ, PCI Bureau, Յ 914, report on the situation in Ismit, 30 September 1920.

9. Kévorkian & Paboudjian, *Les Arméniens dans l'Empire ottoman, op. cit.*, pp. 136–8.

10. *Ibidem*, pp. 128–31.

11. APC/APJ, PCI Bureau, Ի 136, list of responsibles in the region of Ismit.

12. T. C. Başbakanlik Arşivi, 22Sh1333, 5 July 1915, IAMM, circulaire of Ali Münîf (*nazir namina*), [şf 54/ 315], doc. no. 63.

13. APC/APJ, PCI Bureau, Ի 136–7, list of responsibles in the region of Ismit.

14. *Ibidem*.

15. Aguni, *op. cit.*, pp. 266–7. Among them were, notably, Krikor Kherkha, Hovhannes Tombulian, Antranig Genjian, Hampartsum Dimijian, Zareh Kochian, Misak Parseghian.

16. *Ibidem*, pp. 268–70.

17. *Ibidem*, pp. 270–1.

18. *Ibidem*, p. 271; Ardashes Biberian & Vartan Yeghisheyan, Պատմագիրք Աստուածաստեղծ Ասստ լաարեալ Քաղաքին [*History Book of God-Created City of Adabazar*], Paris 1960, pp. 702–18.

19. Aguni, *op. cit.*, p. 271.

20. Fenerjian, *op. cit.*, pp. 148–9. These men were then sent to Eskişehir in little groups, where they melted into the flood of deportees arriving in the railroad station there.

21. *Ibidem*, pp. 273–4; APC/APJ, PCI Bureau, Թ 553–4, no. 59, The deportation of Armeniens in Arslanbeg; Fenerjian, *op. cit.*, pp. 150–1, states that seven hundred young men from the village were mobilized in fall 1914, many of whom worked in the wool mill in Ismit (*ibidem*, p. 147).

22. *Ibidem*, pp. 152–3.

23. Mkhalian, *op. cit.*, pp. 624–6.

24. *Ibidem*, pp. 627–32.
25. *Ibidem*, pp. 635–6.
26. *Ibidem*, pp. 636–7; SHAT, Service Historique de la Marine, Service de Renseignements de la Marine, Turquie, 1BB7 231, doc. n° 280, Constantinople, 1919, "Ali Chououri, gouverneur de Bardizag, 1914–1918" [this was Ali Şuhuri, the *müdir* of the *nahie* of Bardizag] gives information, probably based on an Armenian source, about the exactions and "abuses" committed by this government official.
27. Aguni, *op. cit.*, pp. 266–7.
28. Barton, *"Turkish Atrocities," op. cit.*, pp. 181–5, report by Arthur C. Ryan, missionary in Istanbul, 28 March 1918.
29. *Ibidem*, p. 182.
30. *Ibidem*, p. 183.
31. SHAT, Service Historique de la Marine, Service de Renseignements de la Marine, Turquie, 1BB7 231, doc. no. 340, Constantinople, 19 February 1919, "Les massacres de Kirchehir et de ses dépendances, déposition d'un témoin," ff. 1–2.
32. Kévorkian & Paboudjian, *Les Arméniens dans l'Empire ottoman, op. cit.*, p. 139.
33. *Ibidem*, pp. 139–40.
34. *Ibidem*, pp. 140–1.
35. PCI Bureau, List of responsibles for the massacres and deportations: BNu, ms. 289, f° 15, Karamursal.
36. *La Renaissance*, no. 290, 7 November 1919.
37. *La Renaissance*, no. 375, 18 February 1920.
38. *La Renaissance*, no. 347, 16 January 1920 (first session); *La Renaissance*, no. 369, 11 February 1920; *La Renaissance*, no. 386, 2 March 1920 (verdict of the trial of Ismit, 29 February); *La Renaissance*, no. 387, 3 March 1920.
39. *La Renaissance*, no. 382, 26 February 1920 (trials of Bahçecik and Arslanbeg).

15 Deportations and Massacres in the Vilayet of Bursa and the Mutesarifat of Kütahya

1. Kévorkian & Paboudjian, *Les Arméniens dans l'Empire ottoman, op. cit.*, pp. 143–6.
2. SHAT, Service Historique de la Marine, Service de Renseignements de la Marine, Turquie, 1BB7 231, doc. no. 574, Constantinople, 15 April 1919, "Information sur la situation à Brousse à la date du 10 avril," signed by the naval lieutenant Rollin.
3. APC/APJ, PCI Bureau, ℗ 518, file 24; BNu/Fonds A. Andonian, P.J.1/3, file 45, Bursa, report by Rupen Donabedian, 4 January 1919, "Deportations and massacres of Armenians in Bursa"; Aguni, *op. cit.*, p. 239.
4. T. C. Başbakanlik Arşivi, 22Sh1333, 5 Temmuz [Juillet] 1915, IAMM, circulaire of Ali Münîf (*nazir namina*), [şf 54/ 315], doc. no. 63.
5. Aguni, *op. cit.*, pp. 241–2.
6. *Ibidem*, p. 242; APC/APJ, PCI Bureau, ℗ 518, file 24; BNu/Fonds A. Andonian, P.J.1/3, file 45, Bursa, report by Rupen Donabedian, 4 January 1919.
7. *Zhamanag*, 13 November 1919, "Funeral ceremony in Bursa."
8. *Ibidem*; Aguni, *op. cit.*, p. 242.
9. The United States consul arrived in Bursa as the deportations were just beginning; it seems that this induced the "Turks" to somewhat "temper their actions and abandon the idea of deporting the Armenian Protestants and Catholics": APC/APJ, PCI Bureau, ℗ 518, file 24; BNu/Fonds A. Andonian, P.J.1/3, file 45, Bursa, report by Rupen Donabedian, 4 January 1919.
10. *Ibidem*.
11. Aguni, *op. cit.*, p. 244.
12. Österreichisches Staatsarchiv, HHStA PA XII 209, dispatch no. 441/P, from the consular agent in Bursa, L. Trano, 16 August 1915, to the Ambassador in Constantinople, Pallavicini, ff. 333–4, with the dispatch no. 69/P-D, from the ambassador Pallavicini to the baron Burian, 24 August 1915.

13. *Ibidem*, dispatch no. 53/P, from the consular agent in Bursa, L. Trano, 19 August 1915, to the Ambassador in Constantinople, Pallavicini, ff. 336–8, with the dispatch no. 70/P-B, from the ambassador Pallavicini to the baron Burian, 27 August 1915.

14. *Ibidem*, dispatch no. 464/P, from the consular agent in Bursa, L. Trano, 23 August 1915, to the Ambassador in Constantinople, Pallavicini, ff. 342–4, with the dispatch no. 71/P-B, from the Ambassador Pallavicini to the Baron Burian, 31 August 1915.

15. *Ibidem*.

16. APC/APJ, PCI Bureau, ℗ 518, file 24.

17. APC/APJ, PCI Bureau, ℏ 202, list of responsibles in Bursa.

18. APC/APJ, PCI Bureau, ℗ 518, file 24.

19. *Cf. supra*, p. 530.

20. Examination of Dr. Ahmed Midhat, at the second session of the trial of the *kâtibi mesullari*, 23 June 1919 (23 Haziran 1335): *Takvim-ı Vakayi*, no. 3589, 5 juillet 1919, pp. 172–3; Midhat was sentenced to ten years at hard labor: the verdict in the trial of the CUP responsible secretaries and delegates, handed down on 8 January 1920: *Takvim-ı Vakayi*, n° 3772, February 1920, p. 2, col. 2, p. 3, col. 1, pp. 53–66.

21. APC/APJ, PCI Bureau, ℏ 202, list of responsibles in Bursa.

22. *Ibidem*.

23. Review of the trial: *La Renaissance*, no. 402, 20 March 1920. Let us also note that the Unionist Ziya Şakir, an editor of *Ertogrul* in Bursa who was implicated in the deportations, was acquitted by the court of Çorum (*La Renaissance*, no. 340, 7 January 1920), and, furthermore, that Osman Bey, the former vali of Bursa, İbrahim Bey, the CUP's responsible secretary in Bursa, and the comrades who were interned in the prison of the court-martial, were transferred to Bursa in order to face the court-martial there (*La Renaissance*, no. 132, 6 May 1919).

24. SHAT, Service Historique de la Marine, Service de Renseignements de la Marine, Turquie, 1BB7 231, doc. no. 574, Constantinople, 15 April 1919, *doc. cit.*, "Information sur la situation à Brousse à la date du 10 avril."

25. Kévorkian & Paboudjian, *Les Arméniens dans l'Empire ottoman*, *op. cit.*, pp. 146–7; Karpat, *op. cit.*, p. 176, states that there were a total of 22,883 Armenians and 11,884 Turks.

26. Kévorkian & Paboudjian, *Les Arméniens dans l'Empire ottoman*, *op. cit.*, pp. 146–7.

27. Aguni, *op. cit.*, p. 245.

28. SHAT, Service Historique de la Marine, Service de Renseignements de la Marine, Turquie, 1BB7 231, doc. no. 367, Constantinople, 24 February 1919, "La déportation des Arméniens de Tchinguiler."

29. PCI Bureau, List of the responsibles for the massacres and deportations: BNu, ms. 289, f° 13, çenkiler; APC/APJ, PCI Bureau, ℏ 197 and ℗ 561–2 , list of responsibles in çenkiler.

30. SHAT, Service Historique de la Marine, Service de Renseignements de la Marine, Turquie, 1BB7 231, doc. no. 367, Constantinople, 24 February 1919; Aguni, *History of the Massacre of one Million Armenians*, *op. cit.*, p. 247, states that Sahag Trayents and Usta Tavit were among the men massacred.

31. SHAT, Service Historique de la Marine, Service de Renseignements de la Marine, Turquie, 1BB7 231, doc. no. 367, Constantinople, 24 February 1919.

32. Aguni, *op. cit.*, p. 248.

33. *Ibidem*, p. 249. A few soldier's families were allowed to settle in the villages of Eskişehir, after an order to that effect arrived from Istanbul (*ibidem*, p. 247).

34. *Ibidem*, p. 246.

35. PCI Bureau, List of the responsibles for the massacres and deportations: BNu, ms. 289, f° 13, çenkiler; APC/APJ, PCI Bureau, ℏ 197 and ℗ 561–2 , list of responsibles in çenkiler.

36. Kévorkian & Paboudjian, *Les Arméniens dans l'Empire ottoman*, *op. cit.*, p. 147; Karpat, *op. cit.*, p. 176, states that there were a total of 3,348 in the *kaza*.

37. Kévorkian & Paboudjian, *Les Arméniens dans l'Empire ottoman*, *op. cit.*, p. 147; Karpat, *op. cit.*, p. 176.

38. APC/APJ, PCI Bureau, ℏ 197 and ℗ 561–2 , list of responsibles in Kirmasti.

39. Kévorkian & Paboudjian, *Les Arméniens dans l'Empire ottoman*, *op. cit.*, p. 147; Karpat, *op. cit.*, p. 176.

40. *Ibidem.*
41. APC/APJ, PCI Bureau, Ի 198, 144 (English version) and Թ 562–3, list of responsibles in Bilecik.
42. *Ibidem.*
43. Father Y. P., "Պիլէճիկի Աղէտր, 1915 [The Catastrophe of Bilecik, 1915]," *Pazmaveb* 1921, p. 117.
44. *Ibidem*, pp. 118–19.
45. Kévorkian & Paboudjian, *Les Arméniens dans l'Empire ottoman*, *op. cit.*, p. 150; Karpat, *op. cit.*, p. 176.
46. *Ibidem*; Kévorkian & Paboudjian, *Les Arméniens dans l'Empire ottoman*, *op. cit.*, p. 150 .
47. *Ibidem*; Karpat, *op. cit.*, p. 176.
48. APC/APJ, PCI Bureau, Ի 198, List of responsibles in İnegöl.
49. Kévorkian & Paboudjian, *Les Arméniens dans l'Empire ottoman*, *op. cit.*, p. 157; Karpat, *op. cit.*, p. 186.
50. *Ibidem*; Kévorkian & Paboudjian, *Les Arméniens dans l'Empire ottoman*, *op. cit.*, pp. 158–9 .
51. *Ibidem*; APC/APJ, PCI Bureau, Ի 627/2 and Յ 989, Balıkeser, bilan.
52. Aguni, *op. cit.*, pp. 287–8; APC/APJ, PCI Bureau, Յ 920.
53. APC/APJ, PCI Bureau, Ի 138–9 and Թ 556–7, list of responsibles in Balıkeser.
54. APC/APJ, PCI Bureau, Ի 138 and Թ 558–9, list of responsibles in Bandırma.
55. APC/APJ, PCI Bureau, Ի 138 and Թ 558–9, list of responsibles in Eydincik.
56. Kévorkian & Paboudjian, *Les Arméniens dans l'Empire ottoman*, *op. cit.*, pp. 150–1; Karpat, *op. cit.*, p. 186, states that there were a total of 3,449 in the *kaza*.
57. Kévorkian & Paboudjian, *Les Arméniens dans l'Empire ottoman*, *op. cit.*, pp. 150–1.
58. Aguni, *op. cit.*, pp. 287–8; APC/APJ, PCI Bureau, Յ 920.
59. BNu/Fonds A. Andonian, P.J.1/3, file 38, çangırı, ff 107v°, 112–13, letter from Vartan Karageuzian to Aram Andonian, 25 February 1947.
60. Kévorkian & Paboudjian, *Les Arméniens dans l'Empire ottoman*, *op. cit.*, pp. 150–1; Karpat, *op. cit.*, p. 186.
61. Aguni, *op. cit.*, p. 286.
62. Examination of the Dr. Besim Zühtü, responsible secretary in Eskişehir, at the second session of the trial of the *kâtibi mesullari*, 23 June 1919 (23 Haziran 1335): *Takvim-ı Vakayi*, no. 3589, 5 July 1919, pp. 171–17?; Dr. Nesim Zühtü was released: the verdict in the trial of the CUP responsible secretaries and delegates, handed down on 8 January 1920: *Takvim-ı Vakayi*, n° 3772, February 1920, p. 2, col. 2, p. 3, col. 1 and pp. 53–66 (the full verdict).
63. APC/APJ, PCI Bureau, Ի 201 and Ղ 177–8, list of responsibles in Eskişehir.
64. BNu/Fonds A. Andonian, P.J.1/3, file 38, çangırı, f° 110, letter from Vartan Karageuzian to Aram Andonian, Cairo, 1 April 1947.
65. Kévorkian & Paboudjian, *Les Arméniens dans l'Empire ottoman*, *op. cit.*, p. 156; Karpat, *op. cit.*, p. 182.
66. Aguni, *op. cit.*, p. 286; SHAT, Service Historique de la Marine, Service de Renseignements de la Marine, Turquie, 1BB7 231, doc. no. 257, Constantinople, 6 February 1919, "Déportations d'Afionkarahissar."
67. APC/APJ, PCI Bureau, Ի 198 and Ի 147 (English version), list of responsibles in Afionkarahisar.

16   Deportations and Massacres in the Vilayet of Aydın

1. *Cf supra*, p. 37, n. 161.
2. Letter from George Horton to Henry Morgenthau, Smyrnia, 30 July 1915 (U.S. State Department Record Group 59, 867.4016/130: Ara Sarafian (ed.), *United States Official Documents on the Armenian Genocide*, II, *The Peripheries*, Watertown 1994, pp. 107–9.
3. Letter from Vladimir Radinsky to Stefan Burian, Smyrnia, 30 August 1915: Staatsarchiv, HHStA PA 1915.
4. Aguni, *op. cit.*, p. 279.

5. Taner Akçam, *From Empire to Republic: Turkish Nationalism & the Armenian Genocide*, Londres & New York 2004, pp. 144–6; the American consul George Horton, *The Blight of Asia*, London 2003, pp. 24–33, reports his impressions of these events.

6. Hervé Georgelin, *La fin de la Belle-époque à Smyrne*, doctoral thesis, II, Paris/EHESS 2002, pp. 378–9, cited the Austro-Hungarian consul Vladimir Radinsky.

7. Letter from Vladimir Radinsky to Stefan Burian, Smyrnia,10 January 1916: Staatsarchiv, HHStA PA 1916, coted in Georgelin, *op. cit.*, p. 379.

8. FO. 371.2772, report no. 19 547, from Adam Block to the Foreign Office, 28 January 1916, coted in Georgelin, *op. cit.*, p. 379, n. 4.

9. Kévorkian & Paboudjian, *Les Arméniens dans l'Empire ottoman*, *op. cit.*, p. 156; Karpat, *op. cit.*, pp. 182, 184.

10. Letter from Vladimir Radinsky to Pallavicini, Smyrnia, 1 December 1914: Staatsarchiv HHStA K 405, coted in Georgelin, *op. cit.*, p. 381, n. 12.

11. Georgelin, *op. cit.*, p. 393.

12. SHAT, Service Historique de la Marine, Service de Renseignements de la Marine, Turquie, 1BB7 245, doc. no. 109, Smyrne, 29 April 1919, "Report on the unjust and criminal acts perpetrated by the Unionist Turkish government against the Armenians of the province of Smyrna," by Garabed Balabanian, pp. 5–6; letter from Vladimir Radinsky to Stefan Burian, Smyrnia, 3 May 1915: Staatsarchiv, HHStA PA 1915.

13. "Mémoire" appended to G. Horton's letter to H. Morgenthau, Smyrnia, 5 August 1915: Ara Sarafian (ed.), *United States Official Documents on the Armenian Genocide*, II, *The Peripheries*, Watertown 1994, pp. 112–13; letter from V. Radinsky to S. Burian, Smyrnia, 21 May 1915: Staatsarchiv, HHStA PA 1915, coted in Georgelin, *op. cit.*, p. 393, n. 1.

14. *Cf. supra*, p. 52, 59, 73, n. 10.

15. SHAT, Service Historique de la Marine, Service de Renseignements de la Marine, Turquie, 1BB7 245, doc. no. 109, Smyrna, 29 April 1919, "Rapport sur les actes injustes," pp. 8–9.

16. *Cf.* n. 13 "Mémoire" and G. Horton's letter to H. Morgenthau, Smyrnia, 30 July 1915: Ara Sarafian (ed.), *United States Official Documents on the Armenian Genocide*, II, *The Peripheries*, Watertown 1994, p. 108.

17. SHAT, Service Historique de la Marine, Service de Renseignements de la Marine, Turquie, 1BB7 245, doc. no. 109, Smyrna, 29 April 1919, "Rapport sur les actes injustes," p. 9.

18. Aguni, *op. cit.*, p. 280.

19. APC/APJ, PCI Bureau, ℗ 539, no. 12, "Liste des responsables unionistes, vilayet d'Aïdın."

20. Aguni, *op. cit.*, p. 281; SHAT, Service Historique de la Marine, Service de Renseignements de la Marine, Turquie, 1BB7 245, doc. no. 109, Smyrna, 29 April 1919, "Rapport sur les actes injustes," p. 9.

21. *Ibidem*, pp. 10–11, cited Daniel, Garabed and Berdj Bali, British citizens, Ardashes Karunian and Ardashes Isakian, Russian citizens, Giovanni Shaoum, Italian citizen, all of whom died in Islahiye, Birecik or Der Zor.

22. *Ibidem*, p. 12.

23. *Ibidem*, pp. 12–14; Aguni, *op. cit.*, pp. 282–4.

24. Kévorkian & Paboudjian, *Les Arméniens dans l'Empire ottoman*, *op. cit.*, pp. 169–70.

25. Aguni, *op. cit.*, p. 282; SHAT, Service Historique de la Marine, Service de Renseignements de la Marine, Turquie, 1BB7 245, doc. no. 109, Smyrna, 29 April 1919, "Rapport sur les actes injustes," pp. 17–19.

26. APC/APJ, PCI Bureau, ℗ 539, no. 12, "Liste des responsables unionistes, vilayet d'Aïdın."

27. Kévorkian & Paboudjian, *Les Arméniens dans l'Empire ottoman*, *op. cit.*, pp. 170–1.

28. SHAT, Service Historique de la Marine, Service de Renseignements de la Marine, Turquie, 1BB7 245, doc. no. 109, Smyrna, 29 April 1919, "Rapport sur les actes injustes," pp. 19–20.

29. *Ibidem*, pp. 20–1.

30. Aguni, *op. cit.*, p. 282.

31. Kévorkian & Paboudjian, *Les Arméniens dans l'Empire ottoman*, *op. cit.*, pp. 171–2.

32. SHAT, Service Historique de la Marine, Service de Renseignements de la Marine, Turquie, 1BB7 245, doc. no. 109, Smyrna, 29 April 1919, "Rapport sur les actes injustes," p. 21.

33. *Ibidem*, pp. 21–2.

17 Deportations and Massacres in the Vilayet of Konya

1. APC/APJ, PCI Bureau, Ч 780, vilayet of Konya; Karpat, *op. cit.* , pp. 180, 182, says there were 13,855.

2. APC/APJ, PCI Bureau, Ч 780, vilayet of Konya, estimates the Armenian population of this sancak at 14,809, including the two colonies of Seydişehir (pop. 175) and Ilgun (pop. 142).

3. Azmi left his post on 18 June and immediately assumed the responsibilities of the vali of Lebanon, where he had 11 Arab nationalists executed on 21 August 19195 in Beirut's Square of the Canons.

4. APC/APJ, PCI Bureau, Ֆ 388–9, no. 85, "The deportations in Konya"; Gaydzag [=Mgrdich Barsamian], "Գոնիայի Հայութեան Ողբերգութիւնը. Ականատեսի մը Յուշատետրէն [The Tragedy of the Armenians of Konya (according to the notebook souvenirs of a witness)]," *Zhoghovurt*, 20 December 1918. The author was the director of Konya's Armenian College in this period.

5. Letter from the Dr. W. Dodd to H. Morgenthau, 6 May 1915, in Ara Sarafian (ed.), *United States Official Records on the Armenian Genocide, 1915–1917*, Princeton-London 2004, pp. 37–8.

6. Cf. n. 4, *art. cit.*, *Zhoghovurt*, 20 December 1918.

7. Letter from the Dr. W. Dodd to H. Morgenthau, 15 August 1915, in Ara Sarafian (ed.), *United States Official Records on the Armenian Genocide, 1915–1917*, *op. cit.*, pp. 192–5.

8. *Ibidem*, p. 194.

9. BNu/Fonds A. Andonian, P.J.1/3, file 14, Konya, collective report, Aleppo, 14 December 1918, f° 6. They were transferred to Abuharar; 200 survivors were to be found in Aleppo after the armistice (*ibidem*); APC/APJ, PCI Bureau, Ֆ 388–9, no. 85, "The deportations in Konya."

10. APC/APJ, PCI Bureau, Ի 4, List of responsibles in the vilayet of Konya.

11. *Ibidem*.

12. *Ibidem*.

13. Cf. n. 4, *art. cit.*, *Zhoghovurt*, 20 December 1918.

14. *Ibidem*; Letter from the Dr. Wilfred M. Post to Henry Morgenthau, 3 September 1915, in Ara Sarafian (ed.), *United States Official Records on the Armenian Genocide, 1915–1917*, *op. cit.*, pp. 246–50.

15. APC/APJ, PCI Bureau, Ֆ 388–9, no. 85, "The deportations in Konya" .

16. Cf. n. 4, *art. cit.*, *Zhoghovurt*, 20 December 1918.

17. Letter from the Dr. W. Dodd to H. Morgenthau, 8 September 1915, in Ara Sarafian (ed.), *United States Official Records on the Armenian Genocide, 1915–1917*, *op. cit.*, p. 254.

18. BNu/Fonds A. Andonian, P.J.1/3, file 14, Konya, report by T. Tajirian, from Karaman, [Aleppo in 1919], f° 10.

19. BNu/Fonds A. Andonian, P.J.1/3, file 14, Konya, collective report by inhabitants from Akşehir, Aleppo, 23 February 1919, f° 2v°.

20. APC/APJ, PCI Bureau, Ի 4, List of responsibles in the vilayet of Konya. Among the main beneficiaries of the pillage of Armenian property were: Mustafa Ağazâde Ruşdi Bey, Haci Kurazâde Haci Bekir Effendi, Haci Kurazâde Haci Rusçük Ahmed, Akağazâde Abdullah, Küse Ahmedzâde Mustafa, Atta and his brother Haci Rıza, Kâtibzâde Tevfik, Raif, İsmail Hakkı, director of the Regie, Avındikzâde Hüseyin bey, Momcizâde Ali, Molla Veli Zâde, İzzet Bey, director of property (*mal müdüri*), Celalbeyzâde Haci Kadri Bey, Sabaheddinağazâde Alaheddin, Mahmudbeyzâde Behir, Nacarzâde Mustafa.

21. Bauernfeind, *Journal de Malatia 1915*, *op. cit.*, Diary of the 23 August 1915, p. 312.

22. APC/APJ, PCI Bureau, Ի 4, List of responsibles in Eregli.

23. APC/APJ, PCI Bureau, Ч 780, vilayet of Konya, puts 132 Armenians in Hamidiye.

24. *La Renaissance*, no. 48, 27 January 1919: "La déportation des Arméniens de Burdur."

25. APC/APJ, PCI Bureau, Ի 4, List of responsibles in Burdur.

26. APC/APJ, PCI Bureau, Ч 780, vilayet of Konya.

27. Bauernfeind, *Journal de Malatia 1915*, *op. cit.*, Diary of the 23 August 1915, p. 312.

28. APC/APJ, PCI Bureau, Ի 4, List of responsibles in the vilayet of Konya.

29. APC/APJ, PCI Bureau, Ч 780, vilayet of Konya.

30. Letter from the Dr. W. Dodd to H. Morgenthau, 8 September 1915, in Ara Sarafian (ed.), *United States Official Records on the Armenian Genocide, 1915–1917*, *op. cit.*, p. 254.

18 The Deportees on the Istanbul-Ismit-Eskişehir-Konya-Bozanti Route and Along the Trajectory of the Bagdadbahn

1. Gerald D. Feldman, "The Deutsche Bank from World War to World Economic Crisis, 1914–1923," in *The Deutsche Bank, 1870–1995*, London 1995, pp. 138–9; Hilmar Kaiser, "The Bagdad Railway and the Armenian Genocide, 1915–1916," in R. G. Hovannisian (ed.), *Remembrance and Denial: the Case of the Armenian Genocide*, Detroit 1998, pp. 78–92.

2. *Ibidem*, p. 78 and n. 2.

3. *Ibidem*, p. 79.

4. *Ibidem*, pp. 85–6.

5. *Ibidem*, p. 79.

6. Letter from Franz Günther to the president of the Deutsche Bank, 4 September 1915: *ibidem*, pp. 79–80, and n. 6.

7. *Ibidem*, p. 81.

8. *Ibidem*, p. 82.

9. *Ibidem*, p. 82.

10. Feldman, "The Deutsche Bank," *art. cit.*, p. 142.

11. *Ibidem*, pp. 142–3.

12. APC/APJ, PCI Bureau, 2 575, telegram no. 1068, 25 October 1915, from the Assistant Military Commissar of Rail Transport (War Ministry), Lieutenant Şükrü, to the Board of Directors of the Eastern Railways.

13. *Ibidem*.

14. APC/APJ, PCI Bureau, 2 576, telegram, 8 November 1915, from the Military Commissar of Rail Transport (War Ministry) to the Board of Directors of the Eastern Railways.

15. *Ibidem*. The commission recommended, finally, "following the matter constantly," "that the points indicated be fully applied and carried out."

16. APC/APJ, PCI Bureau, 2 577, telegram, 8 November 1915, from the minister of interior to the minister of war.

17. Ghazar Charek, *Marzbed (Hadji Hüseyin)*, *op. cit.*, pp. 9–13.

18. *Ibidem*, pp. 9–10; Zaven Der Yeghiayan, *Memoirs*, *op. cit.*, p. 115.

19. Feldman, "The Deutsche Bank," *art. cit.*, pp. 138–42.

20. Yervant Odian, *The cursed years, 1914–1919*, *op. cit.*, no. 26, states that he also had to pay for the tickets of the policemen guarding him and provide them with their daily wages; Letter from the Dr. W. Dodd to H. Morgenthau, 8 September 1915, in Ara Sarafian (ed.), *United States Official Records on the Armenian Genocide, 1915–1917*, *op. cit.*, p. 254, mentions that it cost four times the ordinary fare to travel in a sheep-car.

21. Photograph sent, with a dedication, to the president of the Deutsche Bank by the director of the *Bagdadbahn*: Feldman, "The Deutsche Bank," *art. cit.*, p. 142.

22. Report by the Dr. W. Dodd, doctor in the American Hospital of Konya, 21 December 1917, Montclair (New Jersey): Barton, "Turkish Atrocities," *op. cit.*, pp. 145–6.

23. Letter from the Dr. W. Post to H. Morgenthau, 3 September 1915, in Ara Sarafian (ed.), *United States Official Records on the Armenian Genocide, 1915–1917*, *op. cit.*, p. 246.

24. *Ibidem*, p. 247.

25. Report by Dr. W. Post, doctor in the American Hospital of Konya, 11 April 1918, Lawrenceville (New Jersey): Barton, "Turkish Atrocities," *op. cit.*, p. 155. Dr. Post points out that the temporary deportation law was used to send French and British citizens from the capital "to the interior." (*ibidem*, p. 153); Report by the Dr. W. Dodd, 21 December 1917 (*ibidem*, pp. 145–6), puts the number of deportees at 45,000 in Konya.

26. *Ibidem*.

27. *Ibidem*; Report by the Dr. W. Post, 11 April 1918: Barton, "Turkish Atrocities," *op. cit.*, p. 156.

28. Letter from the Dr. W. Dodd to H. Morgenthau, 8 September 1915, in Ara Sarafian (ed.), *United States Official Records on the Armenian Genocide, 1915–1917*, *op. cit.*, p. 255.

29. Anonymous letter, Afionkarahisar, 23 September 1915: Toynbee, *The Treatment of Armenians in the Ottoman Empire, op. cit.*, doc. 106, p. 431.

30. Report by the Dr. W. Dodd, 21 December 1917: Barton, "*Turkish Atrocities,*" *op. cit.*, p. 147. Dr. Dodd treated many of these Armenians, those suffering from injured feet in particular.

31. Letter from the Dr. W. Post to H. Morgenthau, 27 October 1915: Toynbee, *The Treatment of Armenians in the Ottoman Empire, op. cit.*, doc. 111, p. 445.

32. Report by the Dr. W. Dodd, 21 December 1917: Barton, "*Turkish Atrocities,*" *op. cit.*, pp. 147–8.

33. *Ibidem.*

34. BNu/Fonds A. Andonian, P.J.1/3, file 14, Konya, f° 7, collectif report, Aleppo, 14 December 1918.

35. Letter from the Dr. W. Dodd to H. Morgenthau, 8 September 1915, in Ara Sarafian (ed.), *United States Official Records on the Armenian Genocide, 1915–1917, op. cit.*, p. 254.

36. Letter from the Dr. W. Post to William Peet, 25 November 1915: Toynbee, *The Treatment of Armenians in the Ottoman Empire, op. cit.*, doc. 112, pp. 447–8.

37. *Ibidem*, p. 449.

38. BNu/Fonds A. Andonian, P.J.1/3, file 14, Konya, f° 7v°, collective report, Aleppo, 14 December 1918.

39. Report from Hoover to J. Barton, n. d.: Toynbee, *The Treatment of Armenians in the Ottoman Empire, op. cit.*, doc. 104, pp. 426–7.

40. Levon Mozian, Աքսորականի մը Ոդիսականը [*The Odyssey of an Exiled*], Boston 1958. The author was a reporter for the Constantinople daily *Azadamard*.

41. Letter from Krikor Zohrab to Clara Zohrab, Konya, 9 June 1915: Zohrab, *Complete works, op. cit.*, IV, pp. 290–1.

42. Letter from Krikor Zohrab to the Minister of Interior, Talât bey, Konya, 27 May/9 June 1915: *ibidem*, pp. 292–6.

43. Yervant Odian, *The cursed years, 1914–1919, op. cit.*, no. 23 and 26.

44. *Ibidem*, no. 29.

45. *Ibidem*, no. 30–2.

46. *Ibidem*, no. 34.

47. *Ibidem*, no. 37.

19 Deportations from Zeitun and Dörtyol: Repression or Genocidal Program?

1. *Cf supra*, pp. 249–50.

2. Letter from Kate E. Ainslie to J. Barton, 6 July 1915: Toynbee, *The Treatment of Armenians in the Ottoman Empire, op. cit.*, doc. 121, p. 484.

3. Letter from the American consul in Aleppo, J. B. Jackson, to H. Morgenthau, 21 April 1915: Ara Sarafian (ed.), *United States Official Records on the Armenian Genocide, 1915–1917, op. cit.*, p. 13.

4. Kévorkian & Paboudjian, *Les Arméniens dans l'Empire ottoman, op. cit.*, p. 313.

5. *Ibidem*, pp. 314–18.

6. Summary of the story of the Rev. Dikran Andreasian, from Zeytoun, by father Stephen Trowbridge, Cairo, 6 July 1915: Toynbee, *The Treatment of Armenians in the Ottoman Empire, op. cit.*, doc. 121, p. 489.

7. Agassi, Զէյթուն եւ իր Շրջակաները [*Zeytun and His Surrounding area*], Beirut 1968, pp. 386–9; Aguni, *op. cit.*, p. 46. Haydar was latter appointed vali of Mosul, where he took part in the liquidation of the deportees who arrived in his region; *La Renaissance*, no. 153, 30 May 1919.

8. Aguni, *op. cit.*, p. 46.

9. Agassi, *Zeytun, op. cit.*, p. 389.

10. Aguni, *op. cit.*, p. 47.

11. Agassi, *Zeytun, op. cit.*, pp. 390–1; Summary of the story of the Reverend Dikran Andreasian, from Zeytoun, by Father Stephen Trowbridge, Cairo, 6 July 1915: Toynbee, *The Treatment of Armenians in the Ottoman Empire, op. cit.*, doc. 121, p. 489.

12. Letter from the American consul in Aleppo, J. B. Jackson, to H. Morgenthau, 21 April 1915: Ara Sarafian (ed.), *United States Official Records on the Armenian Genocide, 1915–1917, op. cit.*, p. 10.

13. Agassi, *Zeytun*, *op. cit.*, pp. 390–1.

14. *Ibidem.*

15. *Ibidem*, p. 392; A letter that Wolffskeel von Reichenberg wrote to his father Karl from Damascus on 30 March 1915 (Hilmar Kaiser (ed.), *Eberhard Count Wolffskeel Von Reichenberg, Zeitoun, Mousa Dagh, Ourfa: Letters on the Armenian Genocide*, Princeton 2001, p. 4), reveals that the German chief-of-staff of the Fourth Ottoman Army had sent four battalions, a few squadrons, and a battery of cannon to surround Zeitun and get the better of the deserters; Summary of the story of the Rev. Dikran Andreasian, from Zeytoun, by Father Stephen Trowbridge, Cairo, 6 July 1915: Toynbee, *The Treatment of Armenians in the Ottoman Empire*, *op. cit.*, doc. 121, p. 489.

16. Letter from the American consul in Aleppo, J. B. Jackson, to H. Morgenthau, 21 April 1915: Ara Sarafian (ed.), *United States Official Records on the Armenian Genocide, 1915–1917*, *op. cit.*, p. 10; Agassi, *Zeytun*, *op. cit.*, p. 392.

17. *Ibidem*, pp. 393–4. According to the author, who attended this meeting, H. Blank was persuaded, when he arrived, that what was involved was a rebellion. This suggests that the authorities exaggerated the importance of the event (*ibidem*); Summary of the story of the Rev. Dikran Andreasian, from Zeytoun, by father Stephen Trowbridge, Cairo, 6 July 1915: Toynbee, *The Treatment of Armenians in the Ottoman Empire*, *op. cit.*, doc. 121, p. 489.

18. *Ibidem*; Agassi, *Zeytun*, *op. cit.*, p. 394; Aguni, *op. cit.*, p. 47.

19. Report by the Dr. J. R. Merill on the la situation in Zeytou and Marach, Ayntab, 14 June 1915: Ara Sarafian (ed.), *United States Official Records on the Armenian Genocide, 1915–1917*, *op. cit.*, p. 67, speaks of one hundred dead and as many wounded in the Ottoman ranks.

20. Summary of the story of the Rev. Dikran Andreasian, from Zeytoun, by father Stephen Trowbridge, Cairo, 6 July 1915: Toynbee, *The Treatment of Armenians in the Ottoman Empire*, *op. cit.*, doc. 121, p. 489.

21. Aguni, *op. cit.*, p. 48.

22. Agassi, *Zeytun*, *op. cit.*, p. 396.

23. Letter from the American consul in Aleppo, J. B. Jackson, to H. Morgenthau, 21 April 1915: Ara Sarafian (ed.), *United States Official Records on the Armenian Genocide, 1915–1917*, *op. cit.*, p. 11.

24. Zaven Der Yéghiayan, *Memoirs*, *op. cit.*, p. 91; This was also Wolffskeel's sentiment: Kaiser (ed.), *Eberhard Count Wolffskeel … Letters*, *op. cit.*, p. 14, letter to his wife, 24 April 1915.

25. In August 1915, the survivors of the camp of Sultaniye were dispatched to the deserts of Syria in their turn.

26. Aguni, *op. cit.*, pp. 48–52.

27. Letter from Kate E. Ainslie to J. Barton, 6 July 1915: Toynbee, *The Treatment of Armenians in the Ottoman Empire*, *op. cit.*, doc. 121, p. 484; letter from the American consul in Aleppo, J. B. Jackson, to H. Morgenthau, 21 April 1915: Ara Sarafian (ed.), *United States Official Records on the Armenian Genocide, 1915–1917*, *op. cit.*, p. 7, summarizes a report on the situation in the *mutesarifat* of Marash made by Reverand John Merril the very same day; it confirms that the Armenians were deported from these areas.

28. Kévorkian & Paboudjian, *Les Arméniens dans l'Empire ottoman*, *op. cit.*, pp. 311–12.

29. Letter from the Dr. Shepard, missionary in Ayntab, 20 June 1915: Toynbee, *The Treatment of Armenians in the Ottoman Empire*, *op. cit.*, doc. 120, p. 482.

30. Kévorkian & Paboudjian, *Les Arméniens dans l'Empire ottoman*, *op. cit.*, p. 318.

31. Letter from Kate E. Ainslie to J. Barton, 6 July 1915: Toynbee, *The Treatment of Armenians in the Ottoman Empire*, *op. cit.*, doc. 121, p. 484. She also witnessed the arrival of the wife of the minister of Göksun.

32. J. Merril met these deportees on the road between Ayntab and Aleppo; he observes that they were being sent toward Iraq: letter from the American consul in Aleppo, J. B. Jackson, to H. Morgenthau, 21 April 1915, in Ara Sarafian (ed.), *United States Official Records on the Armenian Genocide, 1915–1917*, *op. cit.*, p. 11.

33. Letter from Kate E. Ainslie to J. Barton, 6 July 1915: Toynbee, *The Treatment of Armenians in the Ottoman Empire*, *op. cit.*, doc. 121, p. 484. In a letter to Morgenthau, 28 May 1915 (Ara Sarafian [ed.], *United States Official Records on the Armenian Genocide, 1915–1917*, *op. cit.*, p. 49), the consul of Mersina, Edward I. Nathan, confirms that it was *muhacirs* from Macedonia who were settled near Marash and Zeitun.

34. Letter from the American consul in Aleppo, J. B. Jackson, to H. Morgenthau, 21 April 1915: Ara Sarafian (ed.), *United States Official Records on the Armenian Genocide, 1915–1917, op. cit.,* p. 11.

35. Toynbee, *The Treatment of Armenians in the Ottoman Empire, op. cit.,* p. 397.

36. Diary of Pierre Briquet, from the Saint-Paul Institute of Tarsus, from 14 March to May 1915: Toynbee, *The Treatment of Armenians in the Ottoman Empire, op. cit.,* p. 492–4.

37. "Զէյթունցիներու Տարագրութիւնը [The Deportation of the Zeituntsi]," *Zhoghovurti Tsayn,* 15 May 1919.

38. *Verchin Lur,* 26 May/8 June 1915, repeats information given in the *Official Gazette* of the day, which published the decree announcing that the name had been changed; Summary of the story of the Rev. Dikran Andreasian, from Zeytoun, by Father Stephen Trowbridge, Cairo, 6 July 1915: Toynbee, *The Treatment of Armenians in the Ottoman Empire, op. cit.,* doc. 121, p. 489

39. Kévorkian & Paboudjian, *Les Arméniens dans l'Empire ottoman, op. cit.,* pp. 302–3.

40. Puzant Yeghiayan (ed.), Ատանայի Հայոց Պատմութիւն [*History of Armenians of Adana*], Antelias 1970, p. 320.

41. Aguni, *op. cit.,* p. 294.

42. *Ibidem*; letter from the German consul in Alexandretta, P. Hoffmann, to H. von Wangenheim, 7 March 1915: Lepsius (ed.), *Archives du génocide des Arméniens, op. cit.,* doc. 18, pp. 72–3.

43. Hilmar Kaiser, *Bagdad Railways. Politics and the Socio-Economic Transformation of the çukurova,* doctoral thesis, European University of Florence, 2001, p. 308.

44. Yeghiayan (ed.), *History of Armenians of Adana, op. cit.,* pp. 321–2.

45. *Ibidem,* p. 323 (ff. 186–90 of the ms. report).

46. *Ibidem.*

47. Report by a witness, 12 March, annexed to a letter from the Dr. Eugen Büge, German consul in Adana, to Wangenheim, 13 March 1915: Lepsius (ed.), *Archives du génocide des Arméniens, op. cit.,* doc. 19, pp. 74–6.

48. Yeghiayan (ed.), *History of Armenians of Adana, op. cit.,* pp. 321–2; Kaiser, *Bagdad Railways, these cit.,* p. 309; chiffred telegram from the minister of Interior to the vilayet of Adana, 2 March 1915: BOA.DH. şfr, nr. 50/141 (*Osmanli Belgelerinde Ermeniler (1915–1920), Armenians in Ottoman Documents (1915–1920), op. cit.,* doc. no. 2, p. 22).

49. Aguni, *op. cit.,* p. 295, reveals who these notables were: Hovhannes Balian, Krikor Gökpanosian, Hovhannes Aprahamian, Dikran and Sarkis Balian, Baghdasar Balian and Hagop Küchükian.

50. *Ibidem.*

20 *Deportations in the* Mutesarifat *of Marash*

1. Kévorkian & Paboudjian, *Les Arméniens dans l'Empire ottoman, op. cit.,* pp. 305–11.

2. *Ibidem,* p. 311.

3. Telegram from the consul Rössler to Wangenheim, Marash, 31 March 1915: Lepsius (ed.), *Archives du génocide des Arméniens, op. cit.,* doc. 22, pp. 76–7.

4. Report by Drs Caroline F. Hamilton and C. F. Ranney, doctors in Ayntab's American hospital, attached to a 21 April 1915 letter from the American consul in Aleppo, Jackson, to Morgenthau, 21 April 1915: Ara Sarafian (ed.), *United States Official Records on the Armenian Genocide, 1915–1917, op. cit.,* p. 9. In this report, Kherlakian is referred to as "Horlkahian."

5. *Ibidem,* pp. 11–12.

6. Aguni, *op. cit.,* p. 298.

7. *Cf.* n. 4, pp. 12–13.

8. Aguni, *op. cit.,* p. 298. According to an Armenian balance-sheet of the operations, around 900 men were arrested and tortured, 328 were hanged, and 314 worker-soldiers were shot in June-July 1916: BNu/Fonds A. Andonian, P.J.1/3, file 34, Marash, assessment of the deportations and massacres, Aleppo, 23 December 1918, f° 31.

9. *Ibidem,* p. 301. Wolffskeel notes that the Armenians collected money to bribe the judge presiding over the court-martial (Kaiser [ed.], *Eberhard Count Wolffskeel ... Letters, op. cit.,* p. 15, letter to his wife, 24 April 1915), which suggests that, thanks to bribes, certain inhabitants of Marash managed to secure more favorable deportation conditions or avoided a death sentence.

10. BNu/Fonds A. Andonian, P.J.1/3, file 34, Marash, assessment of the deportations and massacres, Aleppo, 23 December 1918, f° 32.
11. BNu/Fonds A. Andonian, P.J.1/3, file 34, list of responsibles for deportations in Marash and his area, ff. 6–9.

21   Deportations in the Vilayet of Adana

1. Kévorkian & Paboudjian, *Les Arméniens dans l'Empire ottoman*, op. cit., pp. 265–78.
2. *Cf. supra*, pp. 87 and sqq.
3. Kaiser, *Bagdad Railways, thesis cit.*, p. 306.
4. Report, 14 December 1914, with a letter from Büge to Wangenheim, 2 February 1915; letter from general Sanders to Wangenheim, 8 February 1915: Kaiser, *Bagdad Railways, thesis cit.*, p. 308.
5. Diary of Miss H. E. Wallis, Adana, from September 1914 to September 1915: Toynbee, *The Treatment of Armenians in the Ottoman Empire*, op. cit., doc. 129, p. 515.
6. Report by William N. Chambers, a British missionary who had been working in Adana for the American Board of Turkey for thirty-seven years, 3 December 1915: Toynbee, *The Treatment of Armenians in the Ottoman Empire*, op. cit., doc. 128, p. 511.
7. Aguni, *op. cit.*, p. 305.
8. In service from 4 April 1914 to 22 February 1916.
9. Aguni, *op. cit.*, p. 305.
10. Diary of Miss Wallis, *doc. cit.*: Toynbee, *The Treatment of Armenians in the Ottoman Empire*, op. cit., doc. 129, p. 515; letters from the consul in Mersina, Edward I. Nathan, to Henry Morgenthau, 18 and 28 May 1915: Ara Sarafian (ed.), *United States Official Records on the Armenian Genocide, 1915–1917*, op. cit., pp. 43 et 46; Yeghiayan (ed.), *History of Armenians of Adana*, op. cit., pp. 340–1, notes, however, that systematic searches for weapons and possibly compromising documents were carried out in Armenian neighborhoods and institutions in the last week of May 1915. The catholicos tendered his resignation when an officer came to search his apartments.
11. *Ibidem*, p. 323.
12. Report by Harriet J. Fischer, missionary in Adana, 13 April 1917, Wheaton (Illinois): Barton, "Turkish Atrocities," op. cit., p. 161.
13. Report from Büge to Wangenheim, 18 May 1915: Kaiser, *Bagdad Railways, thesis cit.*, p. 311.
14. Telegram from Ali Münîf to the vilayet of Adana, 25 May 1915: BOA. DH. şfr, nr. 53/113, in *Osmanli Belgelerinde Ermeniler (1915–1920), Armenians in Ottoman Documents (1915–1920)*, op. cit., doc. no. 21, p. 38.
15. Yeghiayan (ed.), *History of Armenians of Adana*, op. cit., p. 342, cited the unpublished *Memories* of the principal secretary, Kerovpe Papazian, f° 210, as an indication that the catholicos left for Aleppo on 25 May.
16. *Ibidem*, pp. 343–4, the unpublished *Memories* of the principal secretary, Kerovpe Papazian, ff. 210–11.
17. *Ibidem*, pp. 344–5, ff. 211–13.
18. Letter from Nathan to Morgenthau, 28 May 1915: Ara Sarafian (ed.), *United States Official Documents on the Armenian Genocide, 1915–1917*, II, op. cit., doc. no. 44, pp. 78–9.
19. Aguni, *op. cit.*, p. 306.
20. *Ibidem*; in a letter to Morgenthau, 11 September 1915 (Ara Sarafian [ed.], *United States Official Records on the Armenian Genocide, 1915–1917*, op. cit., p. 270), the consul Nathan confirms that Ali Münîf was responsible for the new, harsher policy, for he had decided that there would be "without any exception."
21. Letter from the consul in Mersina, E. Nathan, to H. Morgenthau, 26 July 1915: Ara Sarafian (ed.), *United States Official Records on the Armenian Genocide, 1915–1917*, op. cit., p. 89.
22. Report, 7 July: Kaiser, *Bagdad Railways, thesis cit.*, p. 314.
23. Aguni, *op. cit.*, p. 307; William N. Chambers, missionary in Adana, in a report, 3 December 1915 (Toynbee, *The Treatment of Armenians in the Ottoman Empire*, op. cit., doc. 128, p. 513), confirms that the Protestants were not spared.
24. *Ibidem*, p. 512.

25. Report by Miss H. E. Wallis, from September 1914 to September 1915: Toynbee, *The Treatment of Armenians in the Ottoman Empire, op. cit.*, doc. 129, pp. 516–17; Elizabeth S. Webb, a missionary in Adana, confirms the figure of twenty thousand deportees in a report written on 13 April 1917 in Wheaton, Illinois (Barton, "*Turkish Atrocities*," *op. cit.*, p. 169).

26. *Ibidem*, p. 169.

27. Report of Elizabeth S. Webb, missionary in Adana, 13 April 1917, Wheaton (Illinois): Barton, "*Turkish Atrocities*," *op. cit.*, p. 170.

28. Yeghiayan (ed.), *History of Armenians of Adana, op. cit.*, pp. 337, 347–9.

29. Aguni, *op. cit.*, p. 308.

30. Letter from the consul E. Nathan, to H. Morgenthau, 11 September 1915: Ara Sarafian (ed.), *United States Official Records on the Armenian Genocide, 1915–1917, op. cit.*, p. 270.

31. Report from Stöckel to Pallavicini, in Kaiser, *Bagdad Railways, thesis cit.*, pp. 314–15.

32. Yeghiayan (ed.), *History of Armenians of Adana, op. cit.*, p. 335, cited the unpublished *Memories* of the principal secretary, Kerovpe Papazian, ff. 198–201.

33. *Ibidem*, p. 336.

34. *Cf. supra*, p. 524.

35. Unpublished *Memories* of the principal secretary, Kerovpe Papazian, ff. 201–3: *ibidem*, pp. 336–7.

36. Yervant Odian, *The cursed years, 1914–1919, op. cit.*, no. 39–40.

37. Report by Miss H. E. Wallis, from September 1914 to September 1915: Toynbee, *The Treatment of Armenians in the Ottoman Empire, op. cit.*, doc. 129, pp. 515–16.

38. Yervant Odian, *The cursed years, 1914–1919, op. cit.*, no. 40–1.

39. Report of Elizabeth S. Webb, missionary in Adana, 13 April 1917, Wheaton (Illinois): Barton, "*Turkish Atrocities*," *op. cit.*, p. 170.

40. Aguni, *op. cit.*, p. 308.

41. Yervant Odian, *The cursed years, 1914–1919, op. cit.*, no. 45.

42. *Ibidem*, no. 43. Odian reports that Andonian left Çangırı with a group of other intellectuals, but fell out of the car and broke his leg; this led to a stay in a hospital in Angora, whose chief physician refused to treat him when he learned that he was Armenian. It was while treating himself and then trying to obtain crutches that, late in August, he managed to flee the hospital and slip into the convoys of the deportees from Angora. His companions had long since been put to death in the vicinity of Yozgat.

43. *Ibidem*, no. 44. Odian noted that the two brothers ensure all the support expenses for the four men.

44. Report by Elizabeth S. Webb, missionary in Adana, 13 April 1917, Wheaton (Illinois): Barton, "*Turkish Atrocities*," *op. cit.*, pp. 171–2.

45. *Cf. supra*, p. 520.

46. Report by Elizabeth S. Webb, missionary in Adana, 13 April 1917, Wheaton (Illinois): Barton, "*Turkish Atrocities*," *op. cit.*, p. 173.

47. Kévorkian & Paboudjian, *Les Arméniens dans l'Empire ottoman, op. cit.*, pp. 279–6.

48. Aguni, *op. cit.*, p. 297.

49. *Ibidem*, p. 296. Among the six arrested men were three important entrepreneurs: Abraham Elagözian, Abraham and Garabed Abrahamian.

50. Letter from the consul E. Nathan, to H. Morgenthau, 18 May 1915: Ara Sarafian (ed.), *United States Official Records on the Armenian Genocide, 1915–1917, op. cit.*, p. 43, according to information provided by Dr. Christie, the director of the American mission in Tarsus.

51. Aguni, *op. cit.*, p. 297.

52. *Ibidem.*

53. *Ibidem*, pp. 308–9.

54. Letter from the consul E. Nathan, to H. Morgenthau, 11 September 1915: Ara Sarafian (ed.), *United States Official Records on the Armenian Genocide, 1915–1917, op. cit.*, p. 270.

55. Aguni, *op. cit.*, pp. 270, 310.

56. Kévorkian & Paboudjian, *Les Arméniens dans l'Empire ottoman, op. cit.*, pp. 290–3.

57. *Ibidem*, p. 292.

58. *Ibidem*, pp. 297–300.

59. Hagop Boghosian, Հաճընի Ընդհանուր Պատմությիւնը [*General History of Hadjen*], Los Angeles 1942, pp. 585–6.

60. *Ibidem*, pp. 586–7. Those condemned to death were Garabed Kizirian, Nazareth Shekerdemian, Drtad Melkonian and the young Aram Boyajian, whose "confessions" had not been enough to save him.

61. Cf. *supra*, p. 590.

62. Aguni, *op. cit.*, pp. 305–30?; report by Edith M. Cold, missionary in Hacın, 16 December 1915: Toynbee, *The Treatment of Armenians in the Ottoman Empire, op. cit.*, doc. 126, p. 502; Boghosian, *General History of Hadjen, op. cit.*, pp. 588–90, gives a complete account of the meeting organized at the archbishopric by the primate, which was attended by 70 to 80 notables from the city.

63. *Ibidem*, p. 590; report by Edith M. Cold, missionary in Hacın, 16 December 1915: Toynbee, *The Treatment of Armenians in the Ottoman Empire, op. cit.*, doc. 126, p. 502.

64. *Ibidem*, pp. 502–3; Boghosian, *General History of Hadjen, op. cit.*, p. 590.

65. *Ibidem*, p. 592.

66. Report by Edith M. Cold, missionary in Hacın, 16 December 1915: Toynbee, *The Treatment of Armenians in the Ottoman Empire, op. cit.*, doc. 126, p. 503.

67. *Ibidem*, p. 504; Aguni, *op. cit.*, p. 305.

68. *Ibidem*; Boghosian, *General History of Hadjen, op. cit.*, p. 592.

69. Report by Edith M. Cold, missionary in Hacın, 16 December 1915: Toynbee, *The Treatment of Armenians in the Ottoman Empire, op. cit.*, doc. 126, p. 505.

70. *Ibidem*, p. 507.

71. *Ibidem*, p. 509.

72. *Ibidem*, p. 505.

73. Boghosian, *General History of Hadjen, op. cit.*, p. 593.

74. Aguni, *op. cit.*, p. 305.

75. Report by Edith M. Cold, missionary in Hacın, 16 December 1915: Toynbee, *The Treatment of Armenians in the Ottoman Empire, op. cit.*, doc. 126, p. 505.

76. *Ibidem*, p. 507.

77. APC/APJ, PCI Bureau, file 59, list of responsibles for the deportations in Cilicia, Hacın and Sis: Asum effendi, Hasanağazâde Ali, Şadi effendi, Mafazâde İbrahim, Mafazâde Süleyman, Suzekzâde Hasan, Suzekzâde Haci Ali, Suzekzâde Mustafa, Cemalzâde Mustafa, Dr. Ali effendi, Muhtar Haci effendi and sons, Haci Mahmud effendi and his son, Kürdzâde Hulis, çulhacizâde Haci Halil, Yarimzâde İbrahim, Kısacıkzâde Ali, Kısacıkzâde Ahmed, Haci Hasan effendi, doctor of the municipality, Fodoş Ahmed, Dede effendi Zâde Şeyh Ca, Haci Mehmedzâde Cemil effendi, Haci Mehmedzâde Mahmud, Total Mustafa Bey, lawyer, Aşuk Yusufoğlu Hakkı, Abdurrahman çavuş, Lepeci Zâde, Vezirzâde Mahmud, Yurik Velizâde İbrahim, Mufti Hafız, Kusacıkzâde Mahmud, Şamlızâde Mehmed, Şamlızâde Durmuş, Muallim İbrahim, Gök Mustafa effendi, Gök Cemil, Topaloğlu Molla Halil effendi, Üçtatlı Şükrü, Hamamköyli Haci Bey, Şeyh Alioğlu Tahir, Ankuzoğlu Ahmed, brothers Hökeş, Haci and Yusuf, Ormanci Mehmed, Fekeli Ummet çavuş, Kösezâde Ahmed, Kürd Kuzuoğlu Mehmed, and çamurdanzâde Mehmed.

78. Telegram from Talât to the *sancak* of Kozan, 17 June 1915: BOA.DH. Şfr, nr. 54/51: *Armenians in Ottoman Documents (1915–1920), op. cit.*, doc. no. 37, p. 50; Misak Keleshian, Սիս Սատեան [*Book of Sis*], Beirut 1949, pp. 553–61

79. Kévorkian & Paboudjian, *Les Arméniens dans l'Empire ottoman, op. cit.*, p. 300.

80. *Ibidem*, pp. 300–1.

81. Kaiser, "The Bagdad Railway and the Armenian Genocide," *art. cit.*, p. 79; cf. *supra*, pp. 578–9.

82. SHAT, Syrie-Liban, 1-V, b.d., dossier 2351, "Rapport sur les mesures d'anéantissement prises contre les Arméniens des régions des monts de l'Amanus" [Report on the Measures Taken to Annihilate the Armenians in the Mountainous Amanus Region], signed by the Dr P. Hovnanian, Bagdadbahn physician in Intilli, Vartivar Kabayan and Garabed Geukjeian, who furnished the Bagdadbahn with supplies, Aleppo, 5 January 1919, pp. 8, 11 of annexe.

83. *Ibidem*, p. II.

84. *Ibidem*. Demirji Khodja, Harmanda Samuel, Lapashli Hovsep, Simon oghlu Peniamin, Haji Mattheos, Darakji Ohannes oghlu Arakel and Darakji Baghdasar. Three of them were hanged, one killed and four sent to Der Zor.

85. *Ibidem*, pp. IV, VII.
86. *Ibidem*, annexe.
87. APC/APJ, PCI Bureau, file XXIII, doc. n° 158, telegram no. 67, from the presiding judge at the court of appeals of Constantinople, Asım Bey, to the Ministry of Interior, Adana, 14/27 November 1915.
88. Asım Bey had held posts under Abdül Hamid in Damascus, Salonika, and in Uskub as the presiding judge of a penal tribunal. In 1908, as a member of the CUP, he had served as a court inspector in Salonika and as interim vali of Kosovo. Later, he was promoted to the rank of Director of the Criminal Investigations Department at the Ministry of Justice, member of the commission that appointed civil servants, and, finally, presiding judge at the criminal court and the court of appeals: APC/APJ, PCI Bureau, Ə 25-26-27-28-29-30-31-32-33-34, "Second report on Turks responsible for the armenian atrocities."
89. APC/APJ, PCI Bureau, file XXIII, doc. n° 158, telegram no. 67, from the presiding judge at the court of appeals of Constantinople, Asım bey, to the Ministry of Interior, Adana, 14/27 November 1915.
90. *Ibidem.*
91. Keleshian, *Book of Sis, op. cit.*, pp. 562–3.

22   Deportations in the Sancaks of Ayntab and Antakya

1. Kévorkian & Paboudjian, *Les Arméniens dans l'Empire ottoman, op. cit.*, pp. 318–23. There were another two Armenian villages, Arel and Orul, on the road leading to Rumkale and Nisibin, with eight and 50 Armenian households, respectively.
2. *Ibidem*, p. 323.
3. BNu/Fonds A. Andonian, P.J.1/3, file 4, Ayntab, "The deportation of Armenians in Ayntab," f° 1r°-v°, notes that much of the land on which the Armenian cemetery lay was confiscated on the eve of the war; this led to a lawsuit that, obviously, was never terminated.
4. *Ibidem.*
5. *Ibidem*, f° 3.
6. *Ibidem.* Wolffskeel confirms that certain circles in Marash sent a blatantly "make up telegram" to Istanbul in which they affirmed that the Armenians had "occupy a mosque" and "begin to kill the Muslims": Kaiser (ed.), *Eberhard Count Wolffskeel ... Letters, op. cit.*, p. 14, letter to his wife, 24 April 1915.
7. *Ibidem*, f° 3v°. Among the men arrested were Father Movses, Hrant Sülahian, Nazaret Manushagian, Hagop and Nazar Ghazarian, Movses Vartavarian, Hovsep Biulbiulian, Avedis Khanzadian, and Khoren Minasian: Aguni, *op. cit.*, p. 310.
8. Kevork Sarafian (ed.), Պատմութիւն Անթէպի Հայոց [*History of the Armenians in Ayntab*], I, Los Angeles 1953, p. 1019.
9. *Ibidem*, p. 1020.
10. BNu/Fonds A. Andonian, P.J.1/3, file 4, Ayntab, f° 4.
11. Report by Miss Fearson, a resident of Ayntab, written in September 1915 after her departure from Turkey: missionary in Ayntab and then assistant to the American vice-consul in Urfa, written on 11 April 1918: Toynbee, *The Treatment of Armenians in the Ottoman Empire, op. cit.*, doc. 137, pp. 541–50; Report by Elvesta T. Leslie, an assistant to the American vice-consul in Urfa (report by 11 April 1918): Barton, "*Turkish Atrocities,*" *op. cit.*, p. 107.
12. BNu/Fonds A. Andonian, P.J.1/3, file 4, Ayntab, f° 9.
13. *Ibidem*, f° 4.
14. Telegram from the German consul in Alep, Walter Rössler, to the embassy in Constantinople, 30 July 1915: Lepsius (ed.), *Archives du génocide des Arméniens, op. cit.*, doc. 125, pp. 119–20.
15. Letter from the Consul Jackson to Morgenthau, 3 August 1915: Ara Sarafian (ed.), *United States Official Records on the Armenian Genocide, 1915–1917, op. cit.*, p. 169.
16. Aguni, *op. cit.*, p. 310; BNu/Fonds A. Andonian, P.J.1/3, file 4, Ayntab, f° 4v°.
17. Sarafian (ed.), *Ayntab*, I, *op. cit.*, p. 1024.
18. Report by Miss Fearson, written on 11 April 1918: Toynbee, *The Treatment of Armenians in the Ottoman Empire, op. cit.*, doc. 137, pp. 543–4.

19. BNu/Fonds A. Andonian, P.J.1/3, file 4, Ayntab, f° 4v°.

20. *Ibidem*, f° 6; report by Miss Fearson, written on 11 April 1918: Toynbee, *The Treatment of Armenians in the Ottoman Empire, op. cit.*, doc. 137, p. 544.

21. BNu/Fonds A. Andonian, P.J.1/3, file 4, Ayntab, f° 7.

22. Sarafian (ed.), *Ayntab*, I, *op. cit.*, p. 1026. The director of the deportation was someone named Yasin; he organized the pillage of the Armenians waiting for a train.

23. Letter from the Consul Jackson to Morgenthau, 19 August 1915: Ara Sarafian (ed.), United States Official Records on the Armenian Genocide, 1915–1917, *op. cit.*, p. 207.

24. Telegram from the vali of Aleppo, Bekir Sâmi, to the Ministry of Interior, 1 September 1915: BOA.DH. EUM, 2. Şb, nr. 68/76: *Armenians in Ottoman Documents (1915–1920), op. cit.*, doc. n° 105, p. 100.

25. Sarafian (ed.), *Ayntab*, I, *op. cit.*, p. 1026.

26. *Ibidem*, p. 1027.

27. Aguni, *op. cit.*, p. 312.

28. BNu/Fonds A. Andonian, P.J.1/3, file 4, Ayntab, f° 5.

29. Sarafian (ed.), *Ayntab*, I, *op. cit.*, p. 1026.

30. *Ibidem*, pp. 1029–30.

31. *Ibidem*, p. 1032.

32. *Ibidem*, p. 1033.

33. The report by Elvesta T. Leslie, an assistant to the American vice-consul in Urfa (report by 11 April 1918): Barton, "Turkish Atrocities," *op. cit.*, p. 107, gives 1 December as the first convoy's departure date.

34. Report by Miss Fearson, written on 11 April 1918: Toynbee, *The Treatment of Armenians in the Ottoman Empire, op. cit.*, doc. 137, pp. 546–9.

35. BNu/Fonds A. Andonian, P.J.1/3, file 4, Ayntab, f° 9.

36. *Ibidem*, f° 7v°. Oddly, there is never any mention of a committee responsible for "abandoned property" in the sources at our disposal, even if auctions are mentioned.

37. *Ibidem*, f° 5v°.

38. *Ibidem*.

39. Sarafian (ed.), *Ayntab*, I, *op. cit.*, pp. 1036–7.

40. *Ibidem*, pp. 1037–9.

41. *Ibidem*, pp. 1039–40.

42. *Ibidem*, p. 1041.

43. BNu/Fonds A. Andonian, P.J.1/3, file 4, Ayntab, f° 6.

44. Sarafian (ed.), *Ayntab*, I, *op. cit.*, pp. 1043–4.

45. *Ibidem*, p. 1042.

46. *Ibidem*, p. 1045.

47. BNu/Fonds A. Andonian, P.J.1/3, file 4, Ayntab, f° 10v°.

48. *Ibidem*, ff. 11–17.

49. BNu/Fonds A. Andonian, P.J.1/3, file 60, Kilis, report by the Committee of the deportes from Kilis, 18 December 1918, f° 1. Those present at this meeting were: Haci Mustafa, deputy of Kilis, Hüsni, president of the CUP's Club, Mesud, member of the Regional Council, Haci Ahmed, president of the municipality, Muhtar, director of the Evkaf, Razi, civil servant, Nihad, director of the Regie, and all the senior civil servants of the *Kaza*.

50. *Ibidem*.

51. *Ibidem*, f° 2.

52. *Ibidem*, ff. 3–4.

53. *Ibidem*, f° 5.

54. *Ibidem*, ff. 7–8.

55. Kévorkian & Paboudjian, *Les Arméniens dans l'Empire ottoman, op. cit.*, pp. 343–8.

56. *Ibidem*, p. 348.

57. *Ibidem*, pp. 349–51.

58. *Cf. supra*, pp. 606–7.

59. Telegram from Rössler to the embassy in Constantinople, 30 July 1915: Lepsius (ed.), *Archives du génocide des Arméniens, op. cit.*, doc. 125, pp. 119–20.

60. Zora Iskenderian, "Ժողովուրդը Ինչո՞ւ Զէնքին Փարեցաւ [Why the Population Take up Arms]," in M. Kushakjian & B. Madurian (ed.), Յուշամատեան Մուսա Լերան [Memorial Book of Musa Dagh], Beirut 1970, p. 315.

61. Report by the Rev. Dikran Andreasian [c. October 1915]: Toynbee, The Treatment of Armenians in the Ottoman Empire, op. cit., doc. 130, p. 522. The Protestant minister mistakenly dated the deportation order to 13 July. Obviously, he used the Julian calendar, but that is not enough to explain this date.

62. Report by Bishop Torgom Kushagian, primate of the Armenians of Egypt, 28 September 1915: ibidem, doc. 131, pp. 528–9.

63. Iskenderian, art. cit., in Kushakjian & Madurian (ed.), Memorial Book of Musa Dagh, op. cit., p. 316.

64. Ibidem, p. 327; Report by Bishop Torgom Kushagian: The Treatment of Armenians in the Ottoman Empire, op. cit., doc. 131, pp. 528–9.

65. Report by the Rev. Dikran Andreasian [c. October 1915]: Toynbee, The Treatment of Armenians in the Ottoman Empire, op. cit., doc. 130, p. 522.

66. Ibidem, pp. 523–4. The defense committee included, notably, Reverand Dikran Andreasian, Mikayel Gegejian, Hetum Filian, Sahag Andekian, Khacher Mardirian, Hovnan Iskenderian, Iskender Kelemian, Jabra Kazanjian, Boghos Kabayan, Hovhannes Kebburian, Movses Der Kalustian, Melkon and Krikor Kuyumjian, Krikor Tovmasian, Yesayi Ibrahimian, Simon Shemmasian and Thomas Azayan: Kushakjian & Madurian (ed.), Memorial Book of Musa Dagh, op. cit., pp. 329, 336.

67. Report by the Rev. Dikran Andreasian [c. October 1915]: Toynbee, The Treatment of Armenians in the Ottoman Empire, op. cit., doc. 130, pp. 524–5.

68. Ibidem, pp. 525–6.

69. Ibidem, pp. 525–7.

70. Ibidem, p. 527; Report by Bishop Torgom Kushagian: ibidem, p. 530.

71. Iskenderian, art. cit., in Kushakjian & Madurian (ed.), Memorial Book of Musa Dagh, op. cit., p. 318. The principal Armenian figures arrested in Antioch were Sahag Aramian, the lawyer Dikran Aramian, Setrak and Misak Iskenderian, Mukhtar Hagop, Movses Kazanjian, Abraham Renjilian, Kerovpe Aslanian, Khacher Hagopian, Movses Boyajian, Hovhannes Zararsız, and Stepan Movsesian. Only Alexandre Iskenderian managed to elude the police and flee to Musa Dağ.

72. Ibidem, p. 327.

23   Deportations in the Mutesarifat of Urfa

1. Kévorkian & Paboudjian, Les Arméniens dans l'Empire ottoman, op. cit., pp. 323–6.

2. Ephraim K. Jernazian, Judgement unto Truth. Witnessing the Armenian Genocide, transl. Alice Haug, New Brunswick & London 2003, p. 3.

3. Ibidem, pp. 46–8.

4. Aram Sahagian, Դիւցազնական Ուրֆան եւ իր Հայորդիները [Heroic Urfa and His Armenians], Beirut 1955, pp. 763–4.

5. Ibidem, p. 765.

6. Ibidem, p. 766.

7. Telegram from Walter Rössler to the embassy in Constantinople, 13 August 1915: Lepsius (ed.), Archives du génocide, op. cit., doc. 137, pp. 130–2. The engineer also saw how the corpses of deportees were burned on the road between Urfa and Arabpunar (ibidem, p. 133).

8. Jernazian, op. cit., p. 48; Sahagian, Heroic Urfa, op. cit., pp. 774–6.

9. Ibidem, p. 771.

10. Jernazian, op. cit., p. 49.

11. Ibidem, pp. 50–4.

12. Sahagian, Heroic Urfa, op. cit., p. 771.

13. Ibidem, pp. 772–3; Jernazian, op. cit., p. 54.

14. Ibidem, p. 56.

15. *Ibidem.* The date has been determined on the basis of an indication provided by the witness, who points out that the deportation order was issued "one week" after he began working in his new position.

16. *Ibidem,* p. 56.

17. *Ibidem,* p. 59; Sahagian, *Heroic Urfa, op. cit.,* pp. 776–7.

18. Letter from Francis Leslie, American vice-consul in Urfa, to the Consul Jackson, Urfa, 14 June 1915: Toynbee, *The Treatment of Armenians in the Ottoman Empire, op. cit.,* doc. 133, p. 536.

19. Sahagian, *Heroic Urfa, op. cit.,* pp. 776–7. The *mutesarif* summoned their families and told them to reveal where the weapons were hidden if they wished to see their husbands come back home alive (*ibidem,* p. 777); Elvesta T. Leslie, an assistant to the American vice-consul in Urfa, reports (report by 11 April 1918, in Barton, "*Turkish Atrocities," op. cit.,* p. 109) that Jacob Künzler and Franz Eckart, as well as Francis Leslie and Dr. Shepard, made great efforts to ensure that these families would be deported to Rakka, which probably was deemed safer for them.

20. *Ibidem,* pp. 778–9; Jernazian, *op. cit.,* p. 60, points out that the Dashnak leader Antranig Bozajian was brought before the Aleppo court-martial together with a schoolteacher.

21. Sahagian, *Heroic Urfa, op. cit.,* pp. 780–1.

22. *Ibidem,* p. 781; Jernazian, *op. cit.,* pp. 59–60.

23. Letter from Kate E. Ainslie to J. Barton, 6 July 1915: Toynbee, *The Treatment of Armenians in the Ottoman Empire, op. cit.,* doc. 121, p. 484.

24. Jernazian, *op. cit.,* pp. 60–1.

25. *Ibidem,* pp. 62–3, 70; Sahagian, *Heroic Urfa, op. cit.,* p. 782.

26. *Ibidem,* pp. 788–9.

27. *Ibidem,* pp. 790–2.

28. *Ibidem,* pp. 793–5.

29. *Ibidem,* p. 797; Report by Elvesta T. Leslie, an assistant to the American vice-consul in Urfa, 11 April 1918: Barton, "*Turkish Atrocities," op. cit.,* p. 110.

30. Sahagian, *Heroic Urfa, op. cit.,* p. 771; Jernazian, *op. cit.,* p. 71.

31. *Ibidem;* Sahagian, *Heroic Urfa, op. cit.,* p. 782.

32. Cf. *supra,* p. 327, n. 58–60; Dadrian, "Documentation of the Armenian Genocide in Turkish Sources," in *Genocide: A Critical Bibliographic Review, art. cit.,* pp. 118–20, provides an annotated bibliography that reveals Çerkez Ahmed's criminal activities in Van and, subsequently, the vilayet of Dyarbekir.

33. Hans-Lukas Kieser, *Der Verpasste Fiede. Mission, Ethnie und Staat in den Ostrprovinzen der Türkey, 1839–1938,* Zürich 2000, p. 470, n. 149.

34. Sahagian, *Heroic Urfa, op. cit.,* pp. 801–2.

35. Dadrian, "Documentation of the Armenian Genocide in Turkish Sources," in *Genocide: A Critical Bibliographic Review, art. cit.,* pp. 119–20, provides a list of the Turkish sources on these murders, as well as the commentaries in Rafaël de Nogales, *Four Years Beneath the Crescent, op. cit.,* p. 73, on Major Ahmed. The next day, Zohrab's watch and ring were on sale in Urfa: Sahagian, *Heroic Urfa, op. cit.,* p. 802.

36. *Ibidem,* p. 803, mentions the two labor battalions liquidated on 4 August; Kieser, *Der Verpasste Fiede, op. cit.,* p. 471, n. 150, cites reports by Künzler and Eckart; Jernazian, *op. cit.,* p. 73, also says that the "gendarmes" Halil and Ahmed left for Karaköprü on 4 August, and further notes that the Syriacs who were spared reported on these events when they returned.

37. *Ibidem,* pp. 73–4; Sahagian, *Heroic Urfa, op. cit.,* pp. 804–6, 812.

38. Jernazian, *op. cit.,* p. 74. Elvesta T. Leslie, an assistant to the American vice-consul in Urfa (Barton, "*Turkish Atrocities," op. cit.,* p. 110) confirms that Urfa was attached to the vilayet of Dyarbekir in her report by 11 April 1918

39. *Ibidem,* p. 75.

40. *Ibidem,* p. 75.

41. *Ibidem.*

42. Sahagian, *Heroic Urfa, op. cit.,* p. 807; interview by Mrs. J. Vance Young, wife of Dr. Vance, doctor in the American Hospital of Urfa, in *Egyptian Gazette,* 11 October 1915: Toynbee, *The Treatment of Armenians in the Ottoman Empire, op. cit.,* doc. 135, p. 539.

43. Report by Elvesta T. Leslie, an assistant to the American vice-consul in Urfa, 11 April 1918: Barton, "*Turkish Atrocities," op. cit.,* p. 110.

44. Interview by Mrs. J. Vance Young, in *Egyptian Gazette*, 11 October 1915: Toynbee, *The Treatment of Armenians in the Ottoman Empire*, op. cit., doc. 135, p. 539.

45. Letter from Jackson to Morgenthau, 25 August 1915: Ara Sarafian (ed.), *United States Official Records on the Armenian Genocide, 1915–1917*, op. cit., p. 234; Jehan de Rohé [ps. of Jean-Baptiste Rebours], *Chouchanik, la jeune Arménienne*, Paris 1928, p. 115, a Frenchman held in Urfa, together with other nationals of countries at war with Turkey, witnessed these massacres.

46. Jernazian, op. cit., p. 75.

47. Sahagian, *Heroic Urfa*, op. cit., pp. 810–12. According to Jernazian, the decision was taken when a squadron of gendarmes entered the Armenian quarter in order, it was said, to look for deserters there: Jernazian, op. cit., p. 83.

48. Sahagian, *Heroic Urfa*, op. cit., p. 817.

49. *Ibidem*, p. 818.

50. *Ibidem*.

51. *Ibidem*, p. 819.

52. *Ibidem*, p. 821. A "military committee" charged with coordinating the defense effort was then formed; it comprised: Mgrdich Yotneghperian, Harutiun Rastgelenian, Harutiun Simian, Khoren Kupelian, Levon Eghperlerian, Hovhannes Izmirlian and Armenag Attarian (*ibidem*, p. 823).

53. *Ibidem*, pp. 824–5.

54. *Ibidem*, pp. 827–9.

55. Kaiser (ed.), *Eberhard Count Wolffskeel Von Reichenberg…Letters*, op. cit., pp. 20–1, letter to his wife, 1 October 1915.

56. Sahagian, *Heroic Urfa*, op. cit., p. 831; Memorandum by an American missionary in Urfa [c. October 1915]: Toynbee, *The Treatment of Armenians in the Ottoman Empire*, op. cit., doc. 136, p. 540; Jehan de Rohé, *Chouchanik*, op. cit., p. 115, witnessed the arrival of the regular forces.

57. Kaiser (ed.), *Eberhard Count Wolffskeel Von Reichenberg…Letters*, op. cit., p. XV.

58. *Ibidem*, pp. 20–1, letter to his wife, 16 October 1915; Jernazian, op. cit., p. 85.

59. *Ibidem*; Sahagian, *Heroic Urfa*, op. cit., p. 832.

60. *Ibidem*, pp. 833–5; Jernazian, op. cit., p. 85.

61. *Ibidem*; Sahagian, *Heroic Urfa*, op. cit., p. 835–40.

62. Memorandum by an American missionary in Urfa [c. October 1915]: Toynbee, *The Treatment of Armenians in the Ottoman Empire*, op. cit., doc. 136, p. 540.

63. Jehan de Rohé, *Chouchanik*, op. cit., p. 120.

64. Kaiser (ed.), *Eberhard Count Wolffskeel Von Reichenberg…Letters*, op. cit., p. 28, letter to his wife, 16 October 1915.

65. Sahagian, *Heroic Urfa*, op. cit., p. 943.

66. *Ibidem*, p. 843.

67. *Ibidem*, p. 847.

68. *Ibidem*, p. 856.

69. *Ibidem*, p. 858.

70. *Ibidem*, p. 1015.

71. *Ibidem*, p. 947; Sarafian (ed.), *Ayntab*, I, op. cit., p. 1031, notes that it was Ğalib Bey who had Rev. Soghomon Akelian hanged.

72. Report by Elvesta T. Leslie, 11 April 1918, Barton, "*Turkish Atrocities*," op. cit., p. 110.

73. *Ibidem*, p. 111.

74. Kaiser (ed.), *Eberhard Count Wolffskeel…Letters*, op. cit., p. 25, letter to his wife, 16 October 1915.

75. *Ibidem*, p. 28.

76. Hyacinthe Simon, *Mardine, la ville héroïque. Autel et tombeau de l'Arménie durant les massacres de 1915*, Jounieh, s. d., p. 91.

77. Jacob Künzler, *Im Lande des Blutes. Erlebnisse in Mesopotamien während des Weltkireges (1914–1918)*, introduction by Hans-Lukas Kieser, Zurich 2004, p. 92.

78. Jehan de Rohé, *Chouchanik*, op. cit., p. 121.

79. *Ibidem*, pp. 833–5; Jernazian, op. cit., p. 86.

80. SHAT, Service Historique de la Marine, Service de Renseignements de la Marine, Turquie, 1BB7 231, doc. No. 299, Constantinople, 11 February 1919, "Les crimes de Franz Ec[k]art à Ourfa." He

was arrested in Constantinople by the British occupation forces in February 1919 on the basis of these accusations: APC/APJ, PCI Bureau, Ց 327–8, file no. 34, report by Gabriel Daghavarian, Constantinople, 15 January 1919.

81. Letter from F. Leslie to J. Jackson, Urfa, 14 June 1915: Toynbee, *The Treatment of Armenians in the Ottoman Empire, op. cit.*, doc. 133, p. 536.

82. Jehan de Rohé, *Chouchanik, op. cit.*, p. 111.

83. Künzler, *Im Lande des Blutes, op. cit.*, p. 98.

84. *Ibidem.*

85. APC/APJ, PCI Bureau, dossier 59, List of those responsible for the massacres and deportations in Urfa and its environs.

86. Kévorkian & Paboudjian, *Les Arméniens dans l'Empire ottoman, op. cit.*, pp. 337–40.

87. Letter from J. Jackson to H. Morgenthau, 25 August 1915: Ara Sarafian (ed.), *United States Official Records on the Armenian Genocide, 1915–1917, op. cit.*, p. 234, letter from John Merrill, president of the Central Turkey College in Ayntab, 17 August 1915.

88. BNu/Fonds A. Andonian, P.J.1/3, file 4, Ayntab, ff. 26–30, about the deportation of the Armenians of Eneş.

Part V   The Second Phase of the Genocide Fall 1915–December 1916

1   The Aleppo Sub-Directorate for Deportees: An Agency in the Service of the Party-State's Liquidation Policy

1. Fuat Dündar, *İttihat ve Terakki'nin Müslümanları İskân Politikası (1913–1918)*, Istanbul 2001, pp. 92–174 and the map, p. 93.

2. *Ibidem*, pp. 201–25; APC/APJ, PCI Bureau, Ղ 370, "Muslims who Emigrated during the Balkan war and the General War," gives the following breakdown: vilayet of Andrinople 132,500; vilayet of Adana 9,059; vilayet of Angora 10,000; vilayet of Aydın 145,868; vilayet of Alep 10,504; vilayet of Bursa 20,853; vilayet of Sıvas 10,806; vilayet of Konya 8,512, etc., for a total of 413,922 people.

3. FO 371/6500, Turkish War Criminals, file of the prisoner Şükrü Bey, edited by Vartkes Yeghiayan, *British Foreign Office Dossiers on the Turkish War Criminals, op. cit.*, pp. 143–6. Şükrü became minister during the kemalist period.

4. APC/APJ, PCI Bureau, Բ 125–128–129–130.

5. APC/APJ, PCI Bureau, Ս 456, no. 24, chiffred telegram from the minister of interior, Talât, to the vilayet of Erzerum, 10/23 May 1915.

6. T. C. Başbakanlik Arşivi, 22 Sh 1333, IAMM, circular from Ali Münîf, şf 54/ 315, doc. no. 63; APC/APJ, PCI Bureau, Ս 455, no. 51, directive annexed to chiffred telegram from the commandant by interim of the 15th division, the Colonel Şahabeddin, in Kayseri, to the commandant of the 3th Army, 24 June/7 July 1915 [24 Haziran 1331]. According to Fuat Dündar, the IAMM was renamed *Aşâyir ve Muhâcirîn Müdîriyeti Umumiyesi* (AMMU) in 1916.

7. Report by J. Mordtmann, Pera, 130 June 1915: J. No. zu. 4018 AA-PA Konstantinopel 169, in Kaiser, *Bagdad Railways*, thesis cit., pp. 321–2, and n. 790. Fuat Dündar has very recently unearthed ethnographic maps and censuses established just before or during the First World War, which we had previously known about only from accounts by witnesses such as Mordtmann: Fuat Dündar, "La dimension ingénierie de la Turcisation de l'Anatolie: Les cartes ethnographiques et les recensements," conference, Salzburg, 14–17 April 2005.

8. APC/APJ, PCI Bureau, Ց 313, List of those responsible for massacres in the Aleppo-Der Zor-Mosul.

9. Falih Rıfkı Atay, *Zeytindağı*, Istanbul 1981, p. 64. The author, an officer in the Fourth Army, who was traveling by rail to Aleppo with the Young Turk feminist Halide Edib, saw him board a train in the Adana train station, and heard the story of his exploits in the provinces.

10. Ali Fuad Erden, *Birinci Dünya harbinde Suriye hatıraları* [*Memories of the WWI in Syria*], Istanbul 1954, p. 217, cited in Dadrian, "Documentation of the Armenian Genocide in Turkish Sources," *art. cit.*, pp. 118–19.

11. Hilmar Kaiser, *At the Crossroads of Der Zor, Death, Survival and Humanitarian Resistance in Aleppo, 1915–1917*, Princeton 2001, p. 15, n. 5 and 6, provides a list of the many different dispatches about the new arrival that Rössler sent his ambassador in June 1915.

12. We have discussed the role Kemal played in May 1909 as a member of the parliamentary commission of inquiry after the massacres in Cilicia. It was Kemal who, on behalf of the government, defended the law authorizing recruitment of criminals to the Special Organization before the Senate at its 12/25 September 1916 session (two years late!): Vahakn Dadrian, "The Complicity of the Party, the Government, and the Military," *Journal of Political and Military Sociology* 22/1 (summer 1994), pp. 57–9.

13. Declaration of Ihsan Bey, head of the Interior Minister's cabinet and former assistant prefect of Kilis, at the first session of the trial of Ittihadistes, 27 April 1919: *Takvim-ı Vakayi*, no. 3540, 5 May 1919, p. 5.

14. *Cf. supra*, p. 524.

15. APC/APJ, PCI Bureau, Ч 104–5, Memorandum from the Dr. A. Nakashian to the British Intelligence, Colonel Ballard, Galata, July 1920.

16. Österreichisches Staatsarchiv, HHStA PA LX, Internal, file 272, no. 397.

17. *Cf. supra*, p. 602.

18. V. Dadrian, "The Naïm-Andonian Documents on the World War I Destruction of the Ottoman Armenians," *International Journal of Middle Eastern Studies*, vol. 18/3 (1986), pp. 331–2 and n. 35.

19. FO 371/6501, War Criminals, file of the prisoner Mustafa Abdülhalik: Yeghiayan, *British Foreign Office Dossiers on the Turkish War Criminals, op. cit.*, pp. 305–19.

20. J. Kheroyan, who was appointed to the Ras ul-Ayn camp late in October 1915, presented a letter of credentials signed by Nuri, "chief of the Directorate of Deportees": *cf.* Raymond Kévorkian, *L'Extermination des déportés arméniens ottomans dans les camps de concentration de Syrie-Mésopotamie (1915–1916), la Deuxième phase du génocide*, Paris, RHAC II (1998), p. 110.

2   Displaced Populations and the Main Deportation Routes

1. Österreichisches Staatsarchiv, HHStA PA XL, file 275, no. 26.

2. US National Archives, State Department Record Group 59, 867.4016/225, no. 278, letter and report from Jackson, to the State Department, 16 October 1915: Sarafian, *United States Official Documents, op. cit.*, I, pp. 105–8.

3. *Ibidem*, State Department RG 59, 867.4016/219, no. 382, letter and report from Jackson, to Morgenthau, 29 September 1915: Sarafian, *op. cit.*, I, p. 100.

4. BNu, Archives de la délégation nationale arménienne, "Statistique de la population arménienne en Turquie [in 1920]," IV. 46. 2, ff. 1–3.

5. *Ibidem*.

6. T. C. Başbakanlik Arşivi, 9Za1333/18 Eylul [September] 1915, DN, letter from the vali of Dyarbekir, the Dr. Reşid, to Ministry of Interior [12 August 1331/1915], DH.EUM, 2 şube, 68/71, doc. no. 112.

7. Djemal Pasha, *Memories of a Turkish Statesman, 1913–1919*, London 1922, p. 277.

8. A.A., Türkei 183/376, K169, no. 48: Lepsius, *Archives du génocide des Arméniens, op. cit.*, p. 93.

9. A.A., Türkei 183/38, A23991: Lepsius, *Archives du génocide des Arméniens, op. cit.*, pp. 112–13.

10. French translation of the indictment in the Unionists' trial: Marcus Fisch, *Justicier du génocide arménien, le procès de Tehlirian*, Paris 1981, p. 266.

11. A.A., Türkei 183/38, A23991: Lepsius, *Archives du génocide des Arméniens, op. cit.*, p. 114.

12. Telegram to the ambassador: *ibidem*, p. 120.

13. Beylerian, *op. cit.*, p. 51.

14. Kévorkian, *L'Extermination des déportés arméniens, op. cit.*, p. 78, on the camp of Bab.

15. *Ibidem*, p. 79.

16. US National Archives, State Department RG 59, 867.4016/219, no. 382, letter and report from Jackson to Morgenthau, 29 September 1915: Sarafian, *United States Official Documents on the Armenian Genocide*, I, *op. cit.*, pp. 94–8.

17. SHAT, Syrie-Liban, 1-V, b.d., dossier 2351, "Rapport sur les mesures d'anéantissement prises contre les Arméniens des régions des monts de l'Amanus" [Report on the Measures Taken to Annihilate the Armenians in the Mountainous Amanus Region], signed by the Dr. Ph. Hovnanian, Bagdadbahn physician in Intilli, Vartivar Kabayan and Garabed Geukjeian, who furnished the Bagdadbahn with supplies, Aleppo, 5 January 1919, 11 pp. III–VI.

18. Report by Elizabeth S. Webb, missionary in Adana, 13 April 1917, in Wheaton (Illinois): Barton, "*Turkish Atrocities,*" *op. cit.*, pp. 170–1; Balakian, *Le Golgotha arménien*, *op. cit.*, p. 238. This information is corroborated by the account of Aleksan Tarpinian (Kévorkian, *L'Extermination des déportés arméniens, op. cit.*, pp. 63–4), who passed by way of Osmaniye/Mamura in early September; he puts the number of deportees at 37,000.

19. Balakian, *Le Golgotha arménien*, *op. cit.*, p. 238.

20. Yervant Odian, *The Cursed Years, 1914–1919*, *op. cit.*, no. 45.

21. Reports about the camp of Mamura, 16 and 26 November, 1 and 13 December 1915, by Paula Schäfer and Beatrice Rohner: Toynbee, *The Treatment of Armenians*, *op. cit.*, doc. 117, pp. 469–72.

22. Report of Paula Schäfer about the camp of Mamura, 1 December 1915: *ibidem*, doc. 117, pp. 470–1.

23. Balakian, *Le Golgotha arménien*, *op. cit.*, p. 253; Yervant Odian, *The Cursed Years, 1914–1919*, *op. cit.*, no 47, confirms that, in late November 1915, traffic on the road was hindered by corpses, abandoned children, and crying babies lying alongside lifeless mothers. In Hasanbeyli, Odian encountered worker-soldiers in an *amele taburi* that was building a road; among them were two compositors from the Istanbul daily *Zhamanag*. Of the 800 men originally in the labor battalion, only 160 were left; they lived in the open and worked ten hours a day.

24. *Ibidem*, puts the mortality rate in the Islahiye camp at 150 per day; Balakian, *op. cit.*, p. 253.

25. Lepsius, *Archives du génocide des Arméniens*, *op. cit.*, doc. 185, p. 161.

26. Kévorkian, *L'Extermination des déportés arméniens*, *op. cit.*, pp. 68–74.

27. Vahram Dadian, *To the Desert, Pages from my Diary*, trans. H. Hacikyan, Princeton & London 2003, p. 51. His convoy had left Çorum on 30 July (*ibidem*, pp. 20–1).

28. *Ibidem*, pp. 52–3.

29. *Ibidem*, pp. 54–5.

30. Lepsius, *Archives du génocide des Arméniens*, *op. cit.*, doc. 193, p. 164.

31. Kévorkian, *L'Extermination des déportés arméniens*, *op. cit.*, p. 72.

32. *Ibidem*.

33. Aram Andonian, *Documents officiels concernant les massacres arméniens*, Paris 1920, p. 20.

34. Kévorkian, *L'Extermination des déportés arméniens*, *op. cit.*, p. 73.

35. Report from Rössler to Wolf-Metternich, 9 February 1916: Lepsius, *Archives du génocide des Arméniens*, *op. cit.*, doc. 235, p. 198. Zaven Der Yeghiayan, *Memoirs*, *op. cit.*, *op. cit.*, p. 205, traveled through Katma, on his road into exile, around 10 or 11 November 1916; he saw deportees still living in the open there.

36. Kévorkian, *L'Extermination des déportés arméniens*, *op. cit.*, pp. 77–8, report by Aram Andonian.

37. BNu/Fonds A. Andonian, P.J. 1/3, file 14, Konya, collective report by Armenians native to Akşehir, Aleppo, 23 February 1919, f° 3.

38. Kévorkian, *L'Extermination des déportés arméniens*, *op. cit.*, p. 75, report by Hovhannes Khacherian.

39. *Ibidem*, p. 79, report by Aram Andonian.

40. *Ibidem*, pp. 77–85.

41. *Ibidem*.

42. *Ibidem*. "It was also in the course of this operation," Andonian notes, "that we, too, were sent to Meskene."

43. *Ibidem*, pp. 87–8, report; Kaiser, *At the Crossroads of Der Zor ... 1915–1917*, *op. cit.*, p. 58, n. 52, cites the many telegrams from Rössler to Ambassador Metternich, sent in January and February 1916, which mention the evacuation of the camp in Bab.

44. *Ibidem*; Lepsius, *Archives du génocide des Arméniens*, *op. cit.*, p. 199.

45. Kévorkian, *L'Extermination des déportés arméniens*, *op. cit.*, pp. 76–7.

46. *Ibidem*, pp. 93–7, reports about Munbuc.

47. Yervant Odian, *The Cursed Years, 1914–1919*, *op. cit.*, no. 48.

48. *Ibidem*.

3　Aleppo, the Center of the Genocidal System and of Relief Operations for the Deportees

1. Letter from the consul J. Jackson to H. Morgenthau, 5 June 1915: Ara Sarafian (ed.), *United States Official Records on the Armenian Genocide, 1915–1917, op. cit.*, p. 57.
2. Puzant Yeghiayan (ed.), *History of Armenians in Adana, op. cit.*, p. 345, cites the unpublished *Memories* of the principal secretary, Kerovpe Papazian, f° 214.
3. Kaiser, *At the Crossroads of Der Zor ... 1915–1917, op. cit.*, p. 15, n. 5.
4. Letter from Kate E. Ainslie to J. Barton, 6 July 1915: Toynbee, *The Treatment of Armenians in the Ottoman Empire, op. cit.*, doc. 121, p. 485. Ainslie points out (*ibidem*, p. 486) that horses, mules, and donkeys were "requisitioned" by the authorities "for the army," with the result that the deportees had very few animals at their disposal.
5. Zohrab, *Complete Works, op. cit.*, IV, letters to Clara Zohrab, Aleppo, 16 June, 12 and 15 July 1915, pp. 304–15. Zohrab wrote his last will and testament, dated 15 July, and entrusted it to the German consul, Dr. Rössler (*ibidem*, pp. 319–21, the testament).
6. Telegram from Rössler to the embassy, Aleppo, 15 August 1915: Kaiser, *At the Crossroads of Der Zor ... 1915–1917, op. cit.*, p. 18, n. 13.
7. *Ibidem*, p. 24, cites some telegrams from Rössler and Jackson on this subject
8. An initial report by Martin Niepage, sent to the German embassy in Constantinople by way of the consul, Rössler, on 15 October 1915, was published by J. Lepsius (*Deutschland und Armenien, op. cit.*, pp. 165–7, doc. 182). This second report, which points out German complicity, was published only in the French translation of *Livre bleu du gouvernement britannique*, Paris 1916 (réédition 1987), pp. 507–16, by A. Toynbee.
9. Kaiser, *At the Crossroads of Der Zor ... 1915–1917, op. cit.*, p. 28
10. *Ibidem*, p. 29.
11. Cf. *supra*, p. 174, n. 55.
12. On the committee were Father Harutiun Yesayan, T. Jidejian, Vahan Kavafian, Sarkis Jierjian, H. Barsumian and the Reverend Rupen Gejghajian: Zaven Der Yeghiayan, *Memoirs, op. cit.*, pp. 178–9.
13. Puzant Yeghiayan, Ժամանակակից Պատմութիւն Կաթողիկոսութեան Հայոց Կիլիկիոյ [*Contemporary History of the Armenian Catholicosate of Cilicia*], Beirut 1975, pp. 46–56.
14. Telegram from Rössler to the embassy, Aleppo, 27 October 1915: Kaiser, *At the Crossroads of Der Zor ... 1915–1917, op. cit.*, p. 27. The religious dignitaries who accompanied Sahag II in his exile in Jerusalem were Bishop Yeghishe Garoyan, Yeprem Dohmuni and Kud Mkhitarian, and Fathers Khat and Giragos Markarian. In the following months, other Apostolic and Catholic Armenian clergymen who had been deported from different provinces of Asia Minor also came together in Jerusalem. The Patriarch Zaven says that Sahag was initially isolated in a village near Aleppo. On 21 October, he left for Idlib, although the vali wanted to send him to Munbuc (where all the clergymen had been concentrated), and on 9 November for Jerusalem. Cemal is supposed to have forced through the decision to exile him to Jerusalem at a meeting held in Istanbul in fall 1915: Zaven Der Yeghiayan, *Memoirs, op. cit.*, p. 175.
15. Cf. *supra*, pp. 524, 539, his stay with the political prisoners in Ayaş and, p. 905, his provisional actions in the camp for deportees in Tarsus.
16. Cf. *supra*, p. 539.
17. Cf. *supra*, p. 539, n. 51.
18. Charek, *Marzbed (Haji Hüseyin), op. cit.*, I, pp. 26–7.
19. Kaiser, *At the Crossroads of Der Zor ... 1915–1917, op. cit.*, pp. 31–57.
20. *Ibidem*, provides a good summary of what the Armenian emissaries did in Aleppo and the vicinity, noting that all the work involved in distributing the financial aid was carried out by an Armenian network.
21. T. C. Başbakanlik Arşivi, telegram from the Ministry of Interior to the vilayet of Aleppo, 22 July 1915, EUM BOA.DH.şfr 54A/71, and, telegram from Talât to *mutesarifat* of Zor, 24 July 1915, EUM Special 28 BOA.DH. şfr 54A/91: Kaiser, *At the Crossroads of Der Zor ... 1915–1917, op. cit.*, p. 17 et n. 11.
22. Charek, *Marzbed (Haji Hüseyin), op. cit.*, I, pp. 26–8.
23. Yervant Odian, *The Cursed Years, 1914–1919, op. cit.*, no. 49 and 50.

24. Central Archives of AGBU/Cairo, Aleppo, no. 23, April 1910–December 1919, C8, letter from Stephen Markarian (nephew of the Dr. Shmavonian) to Central Board in Cairo, 2 May 1916.

25. Bishop Yeghishe Chilingirian, who lived in Aleppo from November 1916 to February 1917, puts the number of Armenian deportees in the city at between 25,000 and 30,000: Yeghishe Chilingirian, Նկարագրութիւնք Երուսաղէմի-Հալէպի-Դամասկոսի Գաղթականական եւ Վանական Ջանազան Դիպաց եւ Անցքերու, 1914–1918 [*Descriptions of Various Events and Developments Bearing on the Refugees and Monks in Jerusalem, Aleppo, and Damascus, 1914–1918*], Alexandria 1922, p. 31.

26. Stanley E. Kerr, The Lions of Marash: *Personal Experiences with American Near East Relief, 1919–1922*, New York 1973, p. 28. According to Zaven Der Yeghiayan, *Memoirs, op. cit.*, pp. 171, 173–4, the Patriarchate sent large sums to Aleppo and other regions, tapping endowments that were in principle inalienable and making use of the network established by Dr. Peet, the head of the Bible House of Istanbul, which was run by American missionaries.

27. Report from J. Jackson to the State Secretary, Washington, 4 March 1918: Sarafian (ed.), *United States Official Documents on the Armenian Genocide*, I, *op. cit.*, pp. 149–52, "The Armenian atrocities."

28. "Dr. Altunian," *Veradznunt*, no. 12, 12 June 1919, p. 203.

29. These employees held a certificate issued by Cemal Pasha that exempted them from the deportation: Sarafian (ed.), *United States Official Documents on the Armenian Genocide*, I, *op. cit.*, p. 152.

30. Central Archives of AGBU/Cairo, Aleppo, no. 12, 21 July 1910–26 March 1931, CII-1, letter from the Comity of Damascus to Central Board in Cairo, 13 November 1918; Chilingirian, *op. cit.*, pp. 32–3.

31. Kaiser, *At the Crossroads of Der Zor ... 1915–1917, op. cit.*, p. 27.

32. *Ibidem*.

33. Antranig Dzarugian, Մանկութիւն Չունեցող Մարդիկ [*Men without Childhood*], Erevan 1985, pp. 64–6

34. Report from J. Jackson to the State Secretary, Washington, 4 March 1918: Sarafian (ed.), *United States Official Documents on the Armenian Genocide*, I, *op. cit.*, p. 154, "The Armenian atrocities."

35. Elmas Boyajian, "Հայկական Որբանոցի Կեանքէն [Fragments of the Life in an Armenian Orphanage]," *Chanaser*, no. 19, 1 October 1964, p. 415; Karl Meyer, *L'Arménie et la Suisse*, s.l. 1986, p. 287.

36. *Ibidem*, p. 416.

37. "Հայկական Որբանոցը, Հալէպ [*The Armenian Orphanage in Aleppo*]," *Chanaser*, no. 19, 1 October 1964, p. 414.

38. "Dr. Altunian," *Veradznunt*, no. 12, 12 June 1919, p. 202.

39. Meyer, *op. cit.*, p. 117.

40. Central Archives of AGBU/Cairo, C6, "Rapport sur l'orphelinat arménien (from 31 July 1915 to 30 September 1919), by the Reverend Aharon Shirajian, Aleppo, 30 November 1919.

41. Kaiser, *At the Crossroads of Der Zor ... 1915–1917, op. cit.*, p. 54.

42. *Ibidem*, p. 59. Harriet J. Fischer, a missionary in Adana who was traveling through Aleppo on 1 January 1916 met a Protestant minister from Adana, Rev. Sisag, who was working in the orphanage headed by Rohner; Sisag estimated the number of children residing in the orphanage at 700: report by Harriet J. Fischer, 13 April 1917, Wheaton (Illinois), in Barton, "*Turkish Atrocities*," *op. cit.*, p. 162.

43. T. C. Başbakanlik Arşivi, telegrams from the Ministry of Interior to the vilayets, 23 March 1916 (EUM général 44298 BOA.DH.şfr 62/ 90) and 3 April 1916 (EUM Special 71 BOA.DH.şfr 62/ 210): *ibidem*, p. 61, n. 4, 5. The orphanage directed by Rohner was finally shut down in February 1917. Around 70 children were sent to the Turkish orphanage in Ayntura, Lebanon; 370 others slipped off to the city to avoid being sent there (Kaiser, *At the Crossroads of Der Zor ... 1915–1917, op. cit.*, pp. 69–70).

44. Chilingirian, *op. cit.*, p. 34. Zaven Der Yeghiayan, *Memoirs, op. cit.*, p. 179, indicates that this institution cared for 800 children, 300 of whom were put in Rohner's hands in December 1915.

45. BNu/Fonds A. Andonian, P.J.1/3, file 14, Konya, collective report by peoples native from Akşehir, Aleppo, 23 February 1919, f° 2v°.

46. Kévorkian, *L'Extermination des déportés arméniens, op. cit.*, p. 27.
47. Report, 8 November 1915: Lepsius, *Archives du génocide des Arméniens, op. cit.*, p. 164.
48. US National Archives, State Department RG 59, 867.4016/373, report, 4 March 1918: Sarafian (ed.), *United States Official Documents on the Armenian Genocide*, I, *op. cit.*, p. 146.
49. Yervant Odian, *The cursed years, 1914–1919, op. cit.*, no. 51.
50. *Ibidem.*
51. *Ibidem*, no. 54.
52. Kévorkian, *L'Extermination des déportés arméniens, op. cit.*, pp. 98–104, report on Aleppo.
53. *Ibidem*, pp. 104–5; Report, 27 April 1916: Lepsius, *Archives du génocide des Arméniens, op. cit.*, p. 203.
54. Zaven Der Yeghiayan, *Memoirs, op. cit.*, p. 175.
55. Chiffred telegram from Talât, minister of Interior, to the vali of Aleppo, Mustafa Abdülhalik, 18 November/1 December 1915: APC/APJ, PCI Bureau, ¶ 54, p. 7. The stamp indicating that Nuri received the telegram bears the date 21 November/4 December 1915 and is accompanied by a handwritten note: "I was sure that there were people like this and, on a few occasions, asked the police chief to pursue them, but his investigations failed to produce results."

4   The Camps in Suruc, Arabpunar, and Ras ul-Ayn and the Zones of Relegation in the Vilayet of Mosul

1. Kapigian, *op. cit.*, pp. 346–7.
2. *Ibidem*, pp. 351–2.
3. *Ibidem*, pp. 353–4.
4. *Ibidem*, pp. 356–7.
5. *Ibidem*, p. 358.
6. *Ibidem*, pp. 358–9. According to the confidences of the municipal physician in Suruc, 27,000 Armenian "patients" died in the town's "hospital" between July and December 1915 (*ibidem*, p. 380).
7. *Ibidem*, pp. 358–9.
8. *Cf. supra*, p. 296.
9. Kapigian, *op. cit.*, pp. 368–9.
10. *Ibidem*, p. 376.
11. *Ibidem*, pp. 376–7.
12. *Ibidem*, pp. 381–2.
13. *Ibidem*, p. 383. Kapigian notes that the pharmacists Drtad Tarpinian, from Amasia, and Harutiun Bakalian, from Samsun, "the only surviving male representatives of their cities," were able to treat the 15,000 inmates of the camp and prevent epidemics from wreaking havoc there. Several convoys of unaccompanied women were also sent to Birecik, Nisib, and Ayntab.
14. *Ibidem*, pp. 394–5.
15. *Ibidem*, pp. 397–8.
16. *Ibidem*, pp. 401–2.
17. *Ibidem*, pp. 403–4.
18. *Ibidem*, pp. 409–10. Kapigian notes that around 15 Armenians from a village near the Euphrates who had been Kurdified and Islamicized during the 1895 massacres were incorporated into their convoy en route and then deported to Rakka.
19. *Ibidem*, p. 364.
20. *Ibidem*, pp. 365–7.
21. A.A., Türkei 183/38, A23991, report from Walter Rössler to the chancellor Bethmann Hollweg, 27 July 1915: Lepsius, *Archives du génocide des Arméniens, op. cit.*, doc. 120, p. 114.
22. US National Archives, State Department RG 59, 867.4016/191, no. 372, report to H. Morgenthau, 29 August 1915: Sarafian (ed.), *United States Official Documents on the Armenian Genocide*, I, *op. cit.*, pp. 262–3. The vali in question, a former mutesarif of Marash, was Hayret Bey, who held his post from May 1915 to August 1917: APC/APJ, PCI Bureau, ẞ 314, list of those guilty of perpetrating massacres in Mosul.

23. Lepsius, *Archives du génocide des Arméniens*, *op. cit.*, doc. 137, pp. 130–1.
24. *Ibidem*.
25. *Ibidem*, pp. 131–3, report by Lismayer (not signed).
26. Balakian, *op. cit.*, p. 294.
27. *Ibidem*.
28. *Cf. supra*, p. 967, n. 28, the notes bearing on Martin Niepage's report.
29. Lepsius, *Archives du génocide des Arméniens*, *op. cit.*, doc. 195, pp. 166–7.
30. *Cf. supra*, p. 635.
31. Kévorkian, *L'Extermination des déportés arméniens*, *op. cit.*, pp. 65–6, report by Kalust Hazarabedian.
32. *Ibidem*, pp. 107–8, report by Aram Andonian.
33. *Ibidem*, pp. 110–14, report by J. Kheroyan.
34. Lepsius, *Archives du génocide des Arméniens*, *op. cit.*, doc. 137, pp. 130–1.
35. This is the figure advanced by Naim Bey in his memoirs:: Andonian, *op. cit.*, p. 39.
36. Kévorkian, *L'Extermination des déportés arméniens*, op. cit., pp. 107–9, report by Aram Andonian on Ras ul-Ayn.
37. *Ibidem*.
38. The information provided by Andonian is corroborated by this telegram of Rössler's: Lepsius, *Archives du génocide des Arméniens*, *op. cit.*, doc. 257, p. 200.
39. A.A., Türkei 183/38, A27200: *ibidem*, pp. 203–5. This information is corroborated by the summary report written by the American Consul Jackson: US National Archives, State Department RG 59, 867.4016/ 373, report, 4 March 1918, in Sarafian (ed.), *United States Official Documents on the Armenian Genocide*, I, *op. cit.*, pp. 148–9. This information is supplemented by Garabed K. Muradian's account: Kévorkian, *L'Extermination des déportés arméniens*, *op. cit.*, pp. 119–20; in her report, written on 11 April 1918, Elvesta T. Leslie, a missionary in Ayntab (Barton, "*Turkish Atrocities*," *op. cit.*, p. 109), relates the testimony of a coachman who told her that, in fall 1915, on the road between Urfa and Rakka, on the banks of the Euphrates, 400 to 500 babies were burned alive together and that in March 1916, "thirty thousand" deportees from the camp in Ras ul-Ayn were massacred.
40. Kévorkian, *L'Extermination des déportés arméniens*, *op. cit.*, pp. 113–14.
41. Andonian, *op. cit.*, p. 48.
42. Telegram from Holstein, consul in Mosul, to the ambassador in Constantinople, 21 July 1915: Lepsius, *Archives du génocide des Arméniens*, *op. cit.*, doc. 118, p. 111. Armenian sources put the number of survivors from the second convoy from Siirt to reach Mosul at 50 (*supra*, p. 340), and the number of survivors from Bitlis at 130 (*supra*, p. 353).
43. Zaven Der Yeghiayan, *Memoirs*, *op. cit.*, p. 237.
44. *Ibidem*; *cf. supra*, p. 300.
45. *Cf. supra*, p. 317.
46. Report, 5 September 1916: Lepsius, *Archives du génocide des Arméniens*, *op. cit.*, doc. 298, p. 227. Zaven Der Yeghiayan, *Memoirs*, *op. cit.*, p. 237, confirms these facts, adding that these deportees were subsequently transferred to Kirkuk.
47. National Archives, State Department RG 867. 48/271, report from Jackson to Morgenthau, 8 February 1916, no. 534.
48. Lepsius, *Archives du génocide des Arméniens*, *op. cit.*, doc. 263, pp. 211–12.
49. *Cf. supra*, p. 592.
50. APC/APJ, PCI Bureau, Ց 314, list of those guilty of perpetrating massacres in Mosul.
51. APC/APJ, PCI Bureau, Ց 82, file on the colonel Abdülkadri Hilmi, a native of Kastamonu and member of the Ottoman General Staff who was also involved in the massacres that took place in Alexandropol in summer 1918. According to an Armenian source, of a battalion of 400 worker-soldiers put under his command, only 60 to 80 men were still alive, "in an appalling state," when the English arrived in Mosul (APC/APJ, PCI Bureau, Ց 321–2).
52. APC/APJ, PCI Bureau, Ց 781, Cevdet Bey and the massacres of Armenians in Mosul. Mehmed Halid also held a post in Van, where he rendered his compatriots great services and participated in the underground network based in Aleppo and Bozanti (*cf. supra*, pp. 632–3).
53. Zaven Der Yeghiayan, *Memoirs*, *op. cit.*, pp. 230–3.

54. *Ibidem*, p. 235.

55. *Ibidem*. *La Renaissance*, no. 113, 13 April 1919, provides an account of the third session in the trial of Nevzâde Bey, a close associate of Halil's; at this trial session, it was revealed that most of these men had founded businesses in Mosul and that it was Halil who had them deported and then killed.

56. APC/APJ, PCI Bureau, Ә 781, Cevdet Bey and the massacres of Armenians in Mosul.

57. *La Renaissance*, no. 115, 15 April 1919, and no. 120, 22 April 1919.

58. *La Renaissance*, no. 111, 10 April 1919.

59. *La Renaissance*, no. 113, 13 April 1919.

60. APC/APJ, PCI Bureau, Ә 239–40, file on lieutenant-colonel Basri Bey, member of the General Staff of Halil pasha.

61. APC/APJ, PCI Bureau, Ә 781, Cevdet Bey and the massacres of Armenians in Mosul.

62. S. Zurlinden, *Der Weltkrieg*, II, Zurich 1918, p. 707, in V. N. Dadrian, "Documentation of the Armenian Genocide in Turkish Sources," *art. cit.*, pp. 116–17. Be it noted that while another of Halil's henchmen, Ferid Bey, formerly second in command in Mosul, was brought before the court-martial in Istanbul in December 1919 (*La Renaissance*, no. 332, 27 December 1919), but Halil himself was never brought to justice. The chief of Halil Pasha's General Staff, Ernest Paraquin, further notes that, in spring 1918, the Armenians of Mosul were put to work "on the construction of roads in the desert": SHAT, Service Historique de la Marine, Service de Renseignements de la Marine, Turquie, 1BB7 235, doc. no. 1992, Constantinople, 16 April 1920, "La politique pantouranienne," by Ernest Paraquin, p. 5.

63. Zaven Der Yeghiayan, *Memoirs*, *op. cit.*, pp. 220–1. In fall 1916, Halil also held a post in Baghdad (*ibidem*, p. 222).

5   The Concentration Camps along "The Euphrates Line"

1. Report from J. Jackson to State Department, 3 August 1915: Toynbee, *The Treatment of Armenians in the Ottoman Empire*, *op. cit.*, doc. 139, p. 55, the mutesarif of Zor, then in Aleppo, announced that there were, at this time, around 15,000 Armenians in Zor. In a wire that Rössler sent to the embassy from Aleppo in July 1915 (Kaiser, *At the Crossroads of Der Zor ... 1915–1917*, *op. cit.*, p. 16), he is more precise, putting the number of Armenians in Zor in late July at 15,328.

2. US National Archives, State Department RG 59, 867.4016/219, letter and annexe from the consul Jackson to Morgenthau, 29 September 1915: Sarafian (ed.), *United States Official Documents on the Armenian Genocide*, I, *op. cit.*, pp. 100–1.

3. US National Archives, State Department RG 59, 867.48/271, letter and annexe, 8 and 3 February 1916: *ibidem*, I, pp. 112–13.

4. Kévorkian, *L'Extermination des déportés arméniens*, *op. cit.*, pp. 128–9, report by Aram Andonian. The director of the camp was "a man of sixty, 'married' to some young Armenian girls from Zeitun": BNu/Fonds A. Andonian, P.J.1/3, file 14, Konya, collective report, Aleppo, 14 December 1918.

5. Kévorkian, *L'Extermination des déportés arméniens*, *op. cit.*, p. 129, report by Aram Andonian.

6. Sticks on which one cut marks in order to record deaths.

7. Kévorkian, *L'Extermination des déportés arméniens*, *op. cit.*, pp. 124–5, report by Aram Andonian.

8. Lepsius, *Archives du génocide des Arméniens*, *op. cit.*, doc. 290, p. 219.

9. US National Archives, State Department RG 59, 867.4016/302: Sarafian (ed.), *United States Official Documents on the Armenian Genocide*, I, *op. cit.*, p. 131.

10. Zaven Der Yeghiayan, *Memoirs*, *op. cit.*, p. 208.

11. BNu/Fonds A. Andonian, P.J.1/3, file 14, Konya, collective report, Aleppo, 14 December 1918, f° 8; *ibidem*, report by T. Tajirian, native of Karaman, [Aleppo, 1919], f° 12.

12. Kévorkian, *L'Extermination des déportés arméniens*, *op. cit.*, pp. 125–7.

13. *Ibidem*, pp. 121–43, reports by survivors of Meskene.

14. *Ibidem*, pp. 144–6, report by Krikor Ankout.

15. *Ibidem*, p. 144.

16. *Ibidem*.

17. *Ibidem*, pp. 146–9, report by Krikor Ankout.
18. *Ibidem*.
19. *Ibidem*, pp. 155–6, report by Krikor Ankout.
20. *Ibidem*.
21. Zaven Der Yeghiayan, *Memoirs*, *op. cit.*, p. 210.
22. Kévorkian, *L'Extermination des déportés arméniens*, *op. cit.*, pp. 158–73, report by Krikor Ankout.
23. *Ibidem*.
24. *Ibidem*.
25. *Ibidem*. This information is confirmed in Auguste Bernau's 10 September 1916 report: US National Archives, State Department RG 59, 867.4016/302: Sarafian (ed.), *United States Official Documents on the Armenian Genocide*, I, *op. cit.*, pp. 132–3. There were then 5,000 to 6,000 Armenians left in Rakka at this time: "Although the Armenians of Rakka are treated better than at other places, their misery is terrible."
26. Zaven Der Yeghiayan, *Memoirs*, *op. cit.*, p. 211.
27. Kapigian, *op. cit.*, pp. 415–503.
28. *Ibidem*, p. 415.
29. *Ibidem*, p. 416.
30. *Ibidem*, pp. 416–17. Kapigian escaped their fate, along with a few other deportees who did not come from Erzerum, by joining the families of two of his fellow teachers, Sarkis Manukian and Levon Karakashian. The *kaymakam*'s name is given in *ibidem*, p. 430.
31. *Ibidem*, pp. 418–19.
32. *Ibidem*, p. 430–1.
33. *Ibidem*, pp. 432–3.
34. *Ibidem*, pp. 440–2.
35. *Ibidem*, pp. 442–3. In spring 1919, Dr. Selian organized the transfer of the remaining deportees to Aleppo as well as the campaign to liberate the women and children being held by the Bedouin tribes of the region.
36. *Ibidem*, pp. 444–5.
37. *Ibidem*, pp. 450–2.
38. *Ibidem*, pp. 454–6.
39. *Ibidem*, p. 457.
40. *Ibidem*, pp. 458–9.
41. *Ibidem*, pp. 460–1.
42. *Ibidem*, pp. 462–5.
43. *Ibidem*, pp. 462–5.
44. *Ibidem*, pp. 468–9; APC/APJ, PCI Bureau, Ч 611, "Accusations against İsmail Hakkı bey, the tormenter of Der Zor" (French version: Ց 323).
45. Kapigian, *op. cit.*, pp. 470–1.
46. *Ibidem*, pp. 471–2.
47. *Ibidem*, pp. 472–3. Kapigian gives the names of the families that converted: the Chakmajian brothers from Nevşehir, two households in Ereyli, a Protestant couple from Yozgat, Eftian from Erzerum, two people from Birecik, two from Kastamonu, one from Bardizag, Dr. Levon Ohnigian from Istanbul, and Hovhannes Zeki from the Dardanelles.
48. *Ibidem*, pp. 475–9.
49. Report by Elvesta T. Leslie, 11 April 1918: Barton, *"Turkish Atrocities,"* *op. cit.*, p. 113.
50. Kapigian, *op. cit.*, pp. 484–6. In spring 1917, some fifty boys in Rakka were also rounded up and sent to Urfa: *ibidem*, p. 496.
51. *Ibidem*, pp. 496–8.
52. *Ibidem*, p. 504.
53. Report annexed to a letter from Rössler to Bethmann Hollweg, 16 November 1915: Lepsius, *Archives du génocide des Arméniens*, *op. cit.*, doc. 203, p. 182.
54. Kévorkian, *L'Extermination des déportés arméniens*, *op. cit.*, p. 174.
55. *Ibidem*, p. 175, report by Aram Andonian.
56. *Ibidem*, pp. 137–41, report by Aram Andonian.

57. Zeki began by personally murdering Levon Shashian and his closest collaborators: "Shashian's group was made up of fifteen people guarded by five Chechens and seven gendarmes. They had all been tied up, and were then stripped ... They tortured Levon Effendi brutally: they pulled out his teeth with pliers, gouged out his eyes and placed them in his hand, cut off his ears, nose, and testicles, pulled flesh from his buttocks with pliers four times, and cut his hands off at the wrists, until he finally breathed his last (this happened near Marât)": *ibidem*, p. 178, report by Aram Andonian; APC/APJ, PCI Bureau, Ց 304–305–309, Memorandum about the legal prosecution of Mustafa Sidki, one of those responsible for the massacres in Zor, before Court-Martial No. 1, chief of the police in Zor from 1914 to 20 October 1918.

58. *Cf. supra*, p. 655.

59. Documents published in *Takvim-ı Vakayi*, no. 3540 (read out at the 12 April 1919 trial session), 5 May 1919, p. 5, as an appendix to the indictment of the Young Turk leaders

60. T. C. Başbakanlik Arşivi, 2R1334, 3R1334, 6R1334, 7R1334, 7, 8, 11 and 12 Şubat 1916, DN, telegram from Ali Suad, [DH. EUM, 2.Ş.69/6, 7, 8, 9], doc. no. 158, 159, 161, 160.

61. *Cf. supra*, p. 652. That these massacres took place so early may find its explanation in the fact that the deportees here were concentrated in a single site; this was far from being the case on the line of the Euphrates.

62. Lepsius, *Archives du génocide des Arméniens, op. cit.*, doc. 260, p. 203.

63. *Ibidem*, report of 5 September 1916, p. 227.

64. Kévorkian, *L'Extermination des déportés arméniens, op. cit.*, p. 177, report by Aram Andonian.

65. T. C. Başbakanlik Arşivi, 16Ş1334, 16 Haziran [June] 1916, IAMM, Talât au vilayet d'Aleppo, [Şfr 65/32–1], documents no. 187.

66. Figures cited in the indictment read out at the 27 April 1919 Ittihadiste trial session: *Takvim-ı Vakayi*, no. 3540, 5 May 1919.

67. *Cf. supra*, p. 654, n. 63; APC/APJ, PCI Bureau, Ց 332, "The famous Zeki."

68. APC/APJ, PCI Bureau, Ч 611, "Accusations against İsmail Hakkı bey, the tormenter of Der Zor" (French version: Ց 323).

69. Kévorkian, *L'Extermination des déportés arméniens, op. cit.*, pp. 183–4, report by Aram Andonian.

70. *Ibidem*.

71. *Ibidem*, p. 175 and sqq, report by Aram Andonian.

72. *Ibidem*, p. 178.

73. *Ibidem*, p. 176.

74. *Ibidem*, p. 177.

75. *Ibidem*, p. 185.

76. *Ibidem*, pp. 179–80.

77. Lepsius, *Archives du génocide des Arméniens, op. cit.*, p. 219.

78. *Ibidem*, letter of 29 August 1916, pp. 223–4. The report by Auguste Bernau submitted to the American consul, Jackson, on 10 September 1916, says nothing different.

79. Kévorkian, *L'Extermination des déportés arméniens, op. cit.*

80. *Ibidem*, p. 186, report by A. Andonian, and the report by the director of the Orphanage, M. Aghazarian, pp. 219–27.

81. *Ibidem*, pp. 188–9.

82. APC/APJ, PCI Bureau, Ց 301–9, Memorandum about the legal prosecution of Mustafa Sidki, one of those responsible for the massacres in Zor, before Court-Martial No. 1. This document mentions the names of witnesses who survived, from Rodosto, Geyve, Erzincan and Adabazar, as well as those of Ottoman officers who served in the region.

83. Kévorkian, *L'Extermination des déportés arméniens, op. cit.*, p. 190, report by A. Andonian, and the report by the director of the Orphanage, M. Aghazarian, p. 224. It seems reasonable to suppose that this information was taken from the source mentioned below, but with a typographical error in the number.

84. *Takvim-ı Vakayi*, no. 3540, 5 May 1919.

85. APC/APJ, PCI Bureau, Ց 304–9, Memorandum about the legal prosecution of Mustafa Sidki. The figures on those massacred between Marât and Shedaddiye were furnished by the head of Zor's Department of Statistic, Urfali Mahmud bey.

86. APC/APJ, PCI Bureau, Ӡ 314, List of those responsible for massacres in Der Zor; . Zaven Der Yeghiayan, *Memories*, *op. cit.*, pp. 214–15.
87. *Ibidem*, pp. 217–18.
88. *Ibidem*, p. 218.
89. Yervant Odian, *The cursed years, 1914–1919*, *op. cit.*, no. 75–6.
90. *Ibidem*, no. 77.
91. *Ibidem*, no. 80.
92. *Ibidem*, no. 82.
93. *Ibidem*, no. 83.
94. *Ibidem*, no. 85–6.
95. *Ibidem*, no. 86–90.
96. *Ibidem*, no. 96–100.
97. *Ibidem*, no. 102.
98. *Ibidem*, no. 103.
99. *Ibidem*, no. 104–5.
100. *Ibidem*, no. 112–13.
101. *Ibidem*, no. 114.
102. *Ibidem*, no. 116.
103. *Ibidem*, no. 117.
104. *Ibidem*, no. 121.
105. Kévorkian, *L'Extermination des déportés arméniens*, *op. cit.*

6 The Deportees on the Hama-Homs-Damascus-Dera'a-Jerusalem-Amman-Maan Line

1. *Cf. supra*, p. 609.
2. T. C. Başbakanlik Arşivi, 22Sh1333, 5 July 1915, IAMM, circular send by Ali Münîf, [Şf 54/315], doc. no. 63.
3. T. C. Başbakanlik Arşivi, 10Za1333, 19 September 1915, DN, [DH. EUM, 2 Şube, 68/ 78], document no. 116.
4. US National Archives, State Department RG 59, 867.4016/212, letter from Damas to Morgenthau: Sarafian (ed.), *United States Official Documents on the Armenian Genocide*, I, *op. cit.*, pp. 82–6; this document was published anonymously in 1916 in the French version of the *British government's Blue Book*: Toynbee, *op. cit.*, pp. 497–500.
5. *Ibidem*, p. 500.
6. *Ibidem*, pp. 166–7, Memorandum.
7. US National Archives, State Department RG 59, 867.4016/219, letter to H. Morgenthau: Sarafian (ed.), *United States Official Documents on the Armenian Genocide*, I, *op. cit.*, pp. 94–5.
8. *Ibidem*, p. 100.
9. *Ibidem*, pp. 112–13.
10. *Cf. supra*, p. 645. Yervant Odian, *The cursed years, 1914–1919*, *op. cit.*, no. 51.
11. *Ibidem*, no. 52.
12. Archives de la Bibl. Nubar, A. Genjian, "Հայերը Տամասկոսի մէջ Ազատագրումէն Առաջ եւ Վերջ [The Armenians in Damascus before and after liberation]," p. 1. Vahé Tachjian kindly put the materials mentioned here at my disposal.
13. Malakia Ormanian, Խոհք եւ Խօսք [*Reflections and Things*], Jerusalem 1929, p. 352.
14. Chilingirian, *op. cit.*, pp. 29, 42.
15. Genjian, *doc. cit.*, p. 5.
16. *Ibidem*, p. 2.
17. Chilingirian, *op. cit.*, p. 30.
18. *Ibidem*, p. 32.
19. Zaven Der Yeghiayan, *Memories*, *op. cit.*, pp. 173, 180.
20. Ormanian, *Reflections and Things*, *op. cit.*, p. 353.

21. *Ibidem*, p. 348. The two men continued to receive a monthly salary from the state (*ibidem*, pp. 304, 350). These religious dignitaries were assigned residences in the presbytery of the church of Saint Sarkis in Damascus.

22. *Ibidem*, pp. 353–4.

23. *Ibidem*.

24. *Ibidem*, p. 318.

25. Bibl. Nubar, AGBU Archives, correspondence of the administrative Headquarters, vol. 25, letter from the Central committee to the Prof. Muradian, 29 March 1918, ff. 339–41; Zaven Der Yeghiayan, *Memories, op. cit.*, p. 177.

26. *Cf. supra*, p. 641, n. 14. According to the patriarch, Sahag sent him, as soon as he had arrived in Jerusalem, a report indicating that tens of thousands of Armenians were on the road; they were living out in the open and suffering from famine: Zaven Der Yeghiayan, *Memories, op. cit.*, p. 177.

27. Ormanian, *op. cit.*, p. 346.

28. Bibl. Nubar, AGBU Archives, correspondence of the administrative Headquarters, vol. 25, letter from the Central committee to the Prof. Muradian, 29 March 1918, ff. 339–41.

29. Report by Harriet J. Fischer, missionary in Adana, 13 April 1917, Wheaton (Illinois): Barton, "*Turkish Atrocities,*" *op. cit.*, pp. 164–5.

30. *Cf. supra*, p. 644; Kaiser, *At the Crossroads of Der Zor ... 1915–1917, op. cit.*, pp. 69–70. Late in 1916, the Mazlumian brothers were themselves deported from Aleppo, but their friend Cemal succeeded in having them sent to Beirut, in Zahle, with Aram Andonian: Yervant Odian, *The cursed years, 1914–1919, op. cit.*, no. 63.

31. Yervant Odian, *The cursed years, 1914–1919, op. cit.*, no. 55.

32. Archives of the Catholicosate, Antelias, 26/1, Homs-Hama (1916–40), II/22, letter from bishop Yeghishe Garoyan to Sahag II, Hama, 27 June 1916, kindly put at my disposal by Vahé Tachjian.

33. Yervant Odian, *The cursed years, 1914–1919, op. cit.*, no. 54–5. Odian states that he was able to leave for Hama with a family from Adana because Onnig Mazlumian interceded with Cemal on his behalf.

34. *Ibidem*, no. 55. Odian mentions, notably, the case of Maritsa Mserian, the wife of a tobacco producer, who told him that her 30 companions had survived by swallowing their gold coins day after day in order to escape the body searches that their torturers imposed on them daily. The other members of their convoy died on the road.

35. *Ibidem*, no. 56. Odian says that Mihran Boyajian, Samuel and Avedis Avedisian, Artin Nersesian, native of Tarsus, Sarkis Kantsabedian and the lawyer Hampartsum Sarafian were among those he met.

36. *Ibidem*, no. 56–7.

37. *Ibidem*, no. 58.

38. *Ibidem*, no. 59.

39. Zaven Der Yeghiayan, *Memories, op. cit.*, p. 177. There is every reason to believe that it was the underground network that allowed him to remain abreast of the situation and transmit his recommendations to the deportees.

40. Yervant Odian, *The cursed years, 1914–1919, op. cit.*, no. 60.

41. *Ibidem*, no. 60/1.

42. *Ibidem*, no. 60/2.

43. *Ibidem*, no. 61.

44. *Ibidem*, no. 61 and [62] (cited 61).

45. *Ibidem*, no. [62] (cited 61).

46. *Ibidem*, no. 63.

47. Archives of the Catholicosate, Antelias, 26/1, Homs-Hama (1916–1940), II/13, letter from father Nerses Tavukjian to Sahag II, Hama, 3 November 1918.

48. Bibl. Nubar, arch. of the DNA, 1–15, correspondence February-March 1919, letter no. 32 from the UNA of Beyrouth to Boghos Nubar, 2 December 1918.

49. *Ibidem*.

50. Zaven Der Yeghiayan, *Memories, op. cit.*, p. 177.

51. After the Armistice, in June 1919, Hasan Amca published a series of four articles in the Istanbul daily *Alemdar* in which he related the fate of these deportees; the reactions of "public opinion" forced the paper to suspend publication of the series. The French-language Istanbul daily *La Renaissance* published an unabridged translation of these articles, under the title *Faits et documents*, in no. 186, p. 3, 8 July 1919, no. 189, pp. 2, 11 July 1919, no. 192, p. 2, 15 July 1919, and no. 198, pp. 2–3, 22 July 1919.

52. *Ibidem*, no. 186, 8 July 1919, p. 3.

53. *Ibidem*, no. 189, 11 July 1919, p. 2.

54. *Ibidem*, no. 192, 15 July 1919, p. 2.

55. *Ibidem*.

56. Djemal pasha, *Memories of a Turkish Statesman, 1913–1918, op. cit.*, p. 279.

7 The Peculiar Case of Ahmed Cemal: The Ittihad's Independent Spirit or an Agent of the Genocide?

1. Kouyoumdjian, *Le Liban à la veille et au début de la Grande Guerre. Memories d'un gouverneur, op. cit.*

2. Djemal pacha, *La vérité sur la Question Syrienne*, Istanbul 1916.

3. The law of 26 October 1915: Lepsius (ed.), *Archives du génocide des Arméniens, op. cit.*, p. 282,

4. Letter to the imperial chancellor, 11 May 1916: *ibidem*, pp. 212–13.

5. Letter to Metternich: *ibidem*, p. 214.

6. In a letter from Metternich to the imperial chancellor, 10 July 1916: *ibidem*, pp. 216–17.

7. Letter from Hoffmann to Metternich, 29 August 1916: *ibidem*, pp. 223–5.

8. Zaven Der Yeghiayan, *Memories, op. cit.*, p. 177. An anonymous report by an inhabitant of Athlit (near Mt. Carmel in Syria) that the War Office transmitted to the French military attaché in London in November 1916 mentions a voyage that Cemal is supposed to have made to Istanbul, during which he is said to have called for an end to the massacres that would make it possible to profit from the deportees' labor-power. Constantinople, the report says, nicknamed him the "Armenian Pasha" as a result. The same document confirms that a campaign had been conducted in the Hauran to save several thousand genocide survivors: SHAT (Vincennes), box 7N1253, rapport annexed to a letter from colonel de la Panouse to the minister of the War, London, 1 December 1916, 8.

9. T. C. Başbakanlik Arşivi, 30Ra1334, 5 February 1915, EUM, [Dh. Şfr, 60/239], doc. no. 167.

10. Public Record Office, FO 371/2492, file 200 744, reports of 29, 30 and 31 December 1915.

11. *Cf. supra*, p. 160, n. 66.

12. Bibl. Nubar, Archives of the Délégation nationale arménienne, P.I. 1.2, Correspondence Arménie, I, letter from Y. Zavriev to Boghos Nubar, 1 February 1916; Arménie III, January-March 1916, letters from Zavriev to Nubar; G. Gavelin, "Sazonov, Zavriev and Cemal pacha," Erevan, 5 June 1927.

13. Beylérian, *Les grandes puissances, l'Empire ottoman et les Arméniens, op. cit.*, pp. 156–62; C. Jay Smith, *The Russian Struggle for Power (1914–1917)*, New York 1956; documents edited in *Razdel Aziatskoi Turtsii* (RAT), Moscou, Commissariat du peuple aux Affaires étrangères, pp. 141–51; German edition, *Die europäischen Mächte und die Türkei während des Weltkrieges: Konstantinopel und die Meerengen*, ed. E. A. Adamov, 4 vol., Dresde 1930–1932.

14. Beylérian, *Les grandes puissances, l'Empire ottoman et les Arméniens, op. cit.*, p. 156.

15. AMAE, Guerre 1914–1918, Turquie, vol. 871, 125 r°-v°: *ibidem*.

16. An army doctor, Zavriev had from 1912–14 played crucial roles in the affair surrounding the reforms in the eastern provinces of the empire and then as vice-governor of the Ottoman provinces occupied by the Russian army: Gabriel Lazian, Յեղափոխական Դէմքեր [*Revolutionary Figures*], Cairo 1945, pp. 250–8.

17. Bibl. Nubar, Archives of the Délégation nationale arménienne, P.I. 1.2, Correspondence Arménie, I, letter-report from Zavriev to Nubar, London, 9 August 1915, 15 pp.

18. Lazian, *op. cit.*, p. 259.

19. AMAE, Guerre 1914–1918, Turquie, vol. 871, f° 125r°-v°: Beylerian, *op. cit.*, pp. 156–62.
20. AMAE, Guerre 1914–1918, Turquie, vol. 871, ff. 128–9, letter to the French ambassadors in Rome, London and Petrograd, 28 December 1915: *ibidem*, pp. 157–8.
21. AMAE, Guerre 1914–1918, Turquie, vol. 871, f° 132, letter from Petrograd, 30 December 1915: *ibidem*, p. 159.
22. AMAE, Guerre 1914–1918, Turquie, vol. 871, f° 134r°-v°, note from the Russian ambassador in Paris, 31 December 1915: *ibidem*, p. 159.
23. Bibl. Nubar, Archives of the Délégation nationale arménienne, P.I. 1.2, Correspondence Arménie III, January-March 1916.
24. *Ibidem*, letter from Paris, 18 February 1916.
25. *Ibidem*.
26. Jay Smith, *The Russian Struggle for Power*, *op. cit.*, pp. 354–8.

8   The Armenian Deportees on the Bagdadbahn Construction Sites in the Taurus and Amanus Mountains

1. *Cf. supra*, pp. 577–80.
2. Teotig, "'Ազգը չէ մեռա եւ անհնար է որ մեռնի'. Բանտի եւ Աքսորի Տարիներ [*The Nation Is Not Dead and It Is Impossible That It Should Die: Years of Prison and Exile*]," Antelias 1985, p. 69.
3. Aguni, *op. cit.*, p. 292.
4. *Ibidem*, pp. 292–3. Kévork was brought before the court-martial in Adana two months before the armistice, with 80 other Armenian management-level employees, but avoided being condemned to death by bribing his judges. Teotig met, for example, Father Krikoris Balakian, dressed as a layman (and without a beard), as well as Aguni in Belemedik: Teotig, "*The nation is not dead*," *op. cit.*, pp. 60, 66.
5. *Ibidem*, pp. 62–3.
6. Kévorkian, *L'Extermination des déportés arméniens*, *op. cit.*, p. 66, report by Kaloust Hazarabedian.
7. Aguni, *op. cit.*, p. 289.
8. *Ibidem*, pp. 290–1.
9. Kaiser, "The Bagdad Railway," *art. cit.*, p. 87.
10. SHAT, Syrie-Liban, 1-V, b.d., file 2351, "Report on the annihilation measure taken against the Armenians in the Amanus mountain region," signed by the Dr Ph. Hovnanian, Bagdadbahn physician in Intilli, Vartivar Kabayan and Garabed Geukjian, suppliers of the Bagdadbahn, Aleppo, 5 January 1919, 11 pp.
11. *Cf. supra*, pp. 575–6.
12. Kaiser, "The Bagdad Railway," *art. cit.*, p. 87.
13. APC/APJ, PCI Bureau, Հ 185: Sublime Porte, copy of the chiffred telegram no. 2676, from the minister of interior, to the vali of Konya, 7/20 January 1916. Certified copy, 27 March 1335 [1919] (*Takvim-ı Vakayi*, no. 3540).
14. Balakian, *op. cit.*, p. 303.
15. Kaiser, "The Bagdad Railway," *art. cit.*, p. 87.
16. Aguni, *op. cit.*, pp. 290–1.
17. APC/APJ, PCI Bureau, Յ 169, file of Ağia bey, a Circassian officer.
18. Kévorkian, *L'Extermination des déportés arméniens*, *op. cit.*, pp. 63–5, reports by Aleksan Tarpinian and Sahag Cheghekjian.
19. Kaiser, "The Bagdad Railway," *art. cit.*, p. 87.
20. Aguni, *op. cit.*, pp. 290–1.
21. Kaiser, "The Bagdad Railway," *art. cit.*, pp. 88–9. Even the doctors in Intilli were deported.
22. *Ibidem*.
23. *Ibidem*, p. 90 and n. 25.
24. Kévorkian, *L'Extermination des déportés arméniens*, *op. cit.*, pp. 65–6.
25. *Ibidem*; Kaiser, "The Bagdad Railway," *art. cit.*, p. 91.
26. Kévorkian, *L'Extermination des déportés arméniens*, *op. cit.*, pp. 67–8.

27. Kaiser, "The Bagdad Railway," *art. cit.*, p. 92.

28. Report by Harriet J. Fischer, 13 April 1917, Wheaton (Illinois): Barton, *"Turkish Atrocities,"* op. cit., p. 163.

29. SHAT, Syrie-Liban, 1-V, b.d., file 2351, "Report on the annihilation measure taken against the Armenians in the Amanus mountain region," signed by the Dr Ph. Hovnanian, Bagdadbahn physician in Intilli, Vartivar Kabayan and Garabed Geukjian, suppliers of the Bagdadbahn, Aleppo, 5 January 1919, pp. VI–X.

30. Teotig, *"The nation is not dead,"* op. cit., p. 65; Aguni, *op. cit.*, p. 292.

31. *Ibidem*, p. 294.

32. *Ibidem*, p. 292.

33. Teotig, *"The nation is not dead,"* op. cit., p. 72.

9   The Second Phase of the Genocide: The Dissolution of the Armenian Patriarchate and the Decision to Liquidate the Last Deportees

1. *Takvim-ı Vakayi*, no. 2611, 28 July 1916, pp. 1–5.

2. Ormanian, *Reflections and Things*, op. cit., p. 342.

3. Zaven Der Yeghiayan, *Memories*, op. cit., p. 191.

4. Father Yervant Perdahjian, Անցքեր ու Դէպքեր Պոլսոյ մէջ Փոխանորդարանի Կողմէ [*Events and Facts Observed in Constantinople by the [Patriarchal] Vicariate*], Bibl. Nubar, ms. 288 (P.I. 2/6), French translation and edition by Raymond Kévorkian, *Revue d'Histoire Arménienne Contemporaine* I (1995), pp. 247–87. The manuscript was completed in Jerusalem, the 14 February 1918.

5. *Ibidem*, pp. 270–1.

6. *Ibidem*, p. 273.

7. *Ibidem*.

8. *Ibidem*, pp. 273–4.

9. *Ibidem*, pp. 274–5.

10. *Ibidem*, p. 275. Perdahdjian point out that the *Official Gazette* is distributed only in evening "afin que personne ne soit informé de ce qui allait se passer."

11. *Ibidem*.

12. *Ibidem*, p. 276.

13. *Ibidem*, p. 278.

14. *Ibidem*, p. 279.

15. Zaven Der Yeghiayan, *Memories*, op. cit., pp. 191 et sqq.

16. *Ibidem*, p. 174.

17. National Archives, State Department, R. G. 867.48/ 271, letter from J. Jackson to H. Morgenthau, 8 February 1916, no. 534.

18. The camp in Bozanti (summer–fall 1915): about 10,000 dead; Mamura (summer–fall 1915): around 40,000 dead; Islahiye (August 1915–early 1916): around 60,000 dead; work camps near the Amanus tunnels (May–June 1916): 20,000 dead; Rajo, Katma and Azaz (fall 1915–spring 1916): around 60 000 dead; Bab and Akhterim (October 1915–spring 1916): about 50,000 to 60,000 dead; Lale and Tefrice (December 1915–February 1916): around 5,000 dead; Munbuc (fall 1915–February 1916): ?; Aleppo and the camps in its outskirts (summer 1915–fall 1918): around 10,000 dead; Ras ul-Ayn (summer 1915–April 1916): around 13,000 deaths due to famine or epidemics and 40,000 massacred in the environs; Meskene (November 1915–April 1916): around 30,000 dead; Dipsi (November 1915–April 1916): around 30,000 dead; Abuharar (November 1915–April 1916): ?; Hamam (November 1915–April 1916): ?; Sebka (opposite Rakka, November 1915–June 1916): around 5,000 dead; Zor-Marât (November 1915–December 1916): 195, 750 massacred between Suvar and Sheddadiye; Mosul region (fall 1915–1917): 15,000 thousand people massacred by General Halil; the regions of Hama/Homs/ Damas/Amman/Hauran/ Maan (fall 1915–summer 1916): around 20,000 deaths, notably in the Hauran.

19. BNu/Fonds Andonian, P.J.1/3, file 59, Erzerum, report by Boghos Vartanian, native of Erzerum, 5 August 1916, f° 61 v°. We have noted, on the other hand, the non-public opposition of several Central Committee members to the liquidation of the Armenians (*cf. supra*, p. 249).
20. Letters from Metternich to Bethmann Hollweg, 9 and 21 December 1915, and 24 January 1916: Lepsius (ed.), *op. cit.*, doc. 210, p. 203, doc. 217, p. 208, doc. 230, p. 229.
21. Weber, *Eagles on the Crescent: Germany, Austria and the Diplomacy of the Turkish Alliance, 1914–1918*, *op. cit.*, pp. 159–67.
22. APC/APJ, PCI Bureau, Հ 183: Sublime Porte, copy of chiffred telegram no. 2351, from the minister of interior, to the vilayet of Konya, 3/18 December 1915. [Certified copy, 28 March 1335 (1919)] (in *Takvim-ı Vakayi*, no. 3540, pp. 8–14).
23. Kaiser, *At the Crossroads of Der Zor ... 1915–1917*, *op. cit.*, pp. 36–7.
24. Weber, *Eagles on the Crescent: Germany, Austria and the Diplomacy of the Turkish Alliance, 1914–1918*, *op. cit.*, p. 184.
25. Istanbul 1916.
26. Letter of 25 December 1916: Lepsius (ed.), *Archives du génocide des Arméniens*, *op. cit.*, p. 240.
27. Weber, *Eagles on the Crescent: Germany, Austria and the Diplomacy of the Turkish Alliance, 1914–1918*, *op. cit.*, pp. 184–6.
28. Autheman, *La Banque impériale ottomane*, *op. cit.*, p. 240.
29. Weber, *Eagles on the Crescent: Germany, Austria and the Diplomacy of the Turkish Alliance, 1914–1918*, *op. cit.*, pp. 201–2.
30. Aguni, *op. cit.*, pp. 98–9.
31. Österreichisches Staatsarchiv, HHStA PA XL, file 275, no. 34. Remarks made "spontaneously" in the presence of the parliamentary deputy Natanian Effendi that the Ottoman press was careful not to make public. The Ambassador does, however, add that "this volte-face by Talât is due, first and foremost, to Javid Bey, who is supposed to have agreed to join the Cabinet only on that condition."
32. Österreichisches Staatsarchiv, HHStA PA XL, file 275, no. 39.
33. Ormanian, *Reflections and Things*, *op. cit.*, p. 338.

Part VI   The Last Days of the Ottoman Empire: The Executioners and Their Judges Face-to-Face

1   Grand Vizier Talât Pasha's New Turkey; or, Reanimating Pan-Turkism

1. *Cf. infra*, p. 833, n. 45.
2. *Cf. supra*, p. 123, n. 22.
3. *Cf. supra*, p. 181, n. 119.
4. AMAE, Série Guerre 1914–1918, vol. 862, report attached to the dispatch from the French ambassador in Bern to the foreign minister, 28 November 1917, p. 49.
5. *Cf. supra*, p. 181, n. 118.
6. *Cf. supra*, p. 123, n. 32.
7. *Cf. supra*, p. 181, n. 117.
8. *Cf. supra*, p. 219, n. 21.
9. AMAE, Série Guerre 1914–1918, vol. 862, report attached to the dispatch from the French ambassador in Bern to the foreign minister, 28 November 1917, p. 49.
10. Astourian, "The Armenian Genocide: An Interpretation," *art. cit.*, pp. 138–40, n. 15–16, 122–3, provides an exhaustive list of these sources.
11. Published in full in the 25 September 1917 *Ikdam*. The French translation is attached to a 28 November 1917 dispatch from the French ambassador in Bern to the foreign minister: AMAE, Série Guerre 1914–1918, vol. 862, pp. 50–60.
12. *Ibidem*, p. 51.
13. *Ibidem*, pp. 52–3. Echos of this speech appear in R.L.C., "L'Arménie et l'Allemagne," *La Croix*, 13 October 1917; *La Suisse*, 7 October 1917.

14. AMAE, Série Guerre 1914–1918, vol. 862, p. 54.

15. *Ibidem*, pp. 55–6.

16. *Ibidem*, pp. 56–7.

17. *Ibidem*, p. 57.

18. *Ibidem*.

19. *Ibidem*, p. 60.

20. Arif Cemil, *The Special Organisation*, art. cit., Vakıt/Haratch 89.

21. Hovannisian, *Armenia on the Road to Independence*, op. cit., pp. 109–10; an 8 December 1917 telegram from France's military attaché in London, General de La Panouse, to Georges Clemenceau (8 December 1917) announces negotiations for a truce agreement: AMAE, Guerre 1914–1918, Turquie, vol. 894, f° 57: Beylerian, *Les Grandes Puissances*, op. cit., p. 431.

22. *Ibidem*, pp. 119–20.

23. *Ibidem*.

24. *Ibidem*, pp. 121–2; Dadrian, *Histoire du génocide arménien*, op. cit., p. 550. The newly created Ninth Army was made up of four divisions comprising a total of 30,000 men and a group of auxiliaries comprising 20,000 militiamen and gendarmes: Zürcher, *The Unionist*, op. cit., p. 94.

25. Hovannisian, *Armenia on the Road to Independence*, op. cit., pp. 121–3.

26. *Ibidem*, pp. 113–15; A. Poidebard, *Rôle militaire des Arméniens sur le Front du Caucase après la défection de l'Armée russe*, Paris 1920, p. 13. This corps comprised three divisions commanded by General Areshian, General Silikov, and General Antranig, and a cavalry brigade under the orders of Colonel Korganov.

27. Hovannisian, *Armenia on the Road to Independence*, op. cit., pp. 131–7.

28. *Ibidem*, p. 172.

29. *Ibidem*, pp. 172–4.

30. A.A. Türkei 183/51, A21877, 23 May 1918: Dadrian, *Histoire du génocide arménien*, op. cit., p. 552, n. 2.

31. Deutsches Zentralarchiv (Postdam), Bestand Reicheskanzlei, no. 2458/9, Blatt 292, report of 3 June 1918, p. 2: *ibidem*, p. 552, n. 3.

32. A.A. Türkei 183/53, A32123, 10 July 1918: *ibidem*, p. 552, n. 4.

33. A.A. Türkei 183/53, A32145, 11 July 1918: *ibidem*, p. 552, n. 5.

34. A.A. Türkei 158/20, A31679, 13 July 1918: *ibidem*, pp. 552–3, n. 7.

35. Deutsches Zentralarchiv, Blatt 287, 31 July 1918: *ibidem*, p. 553, n. 8.

36. A.A. Türkei 183/54, A39244, 3 September 1918.

37. SHAT, Service Historique de la Marine, Service de renseignements de la Marine, Turquie, 1BB7 235, doc. no. 1992, Constantinople, 16 April 1920, "La politique pantouranienne," by Ernest Paraquin, p. 1.

38. *Ibidem*, p. 2. In Persia, it was Azerbaijan that the CUP, Halil said, hoped to incorporate "in the near future," despite confessional divisions (*ibidem*, p. 3).

39. *Ibidem*, pp. 3–4. Paraquin notes that Mosul served as a pivot for external propaganda campaigns aiming to create a network of "proselytes of Pan-Turkish national aspirations." "Messengers" were designated there. Among them were Arabs used as "Pan-Turkish propagandists in the Caucasus, where they enjoyed great prestige" as representatives of a holy people, blessed by the Prophet."

40. *Ibidem*, p. 4.

41. *Ibidem*, p. 5.

42. APC/APJ, PCI Bureau, 3 82, file of Colonel Abdülkadri Hilmi, a native of Kastamonu and member of the Ottoman General Staff who was arrested by the British and deported to Malta in May 1919. Hilmi also supervised massacres of worker-soldiers in Mosul: *cf. supra*, p. 653.

43. Hovannisian, *Armenia on the Road to Independence*, op. cit., pp. 175–6.

44. *Ibidem*, p. 176.

45. *Ibidem*, p. 180.

46. *Ibidem*, p. 178.

47. *Ibidem*, p. 182.

48. *Ibidem*, pp. 188–9. On 2 June, Vehib Pasha informed Enver that, in response to an Azerbaijani appeal, the Turkish forces were joining the struggle against the Bolsheviks.

49. *Ibidem*, pp. 191–4.

50. *Ibidem*, pp. 194–6.

51. Ibidem, p. 204, reports that it was after Berlin had threatened to withdraw all its officers from the Turkish contingents that Enver ordered the release of the German prisoners being held in Kars and gave up the idea of taking control of the Georgian rail network; SHAT, Service Historique de la Marine, Service de renseignements de la Marine, Turquie, 1BB7 235, doc. no. 1992, Constantinople, 16 April 1920, "La politique pantouranienne," by Ernest Paraquin, p. 6.

52. A.A. Türkei 183/51, A28553, no. 1178, 3 June 1918: Dadrian, *Histoire du génocide, op. cit.*, p. 555, n. 17.

53. Österreichisches Staatsarchiv, 10 Russland/155, no. 61/P.A., report from the ambassador Hohenlohe to the minister Burian, 29 May 1918: *ibidem*, p. 556, n. 19.

54. *Ibidem*, n. 20: Kriegsarchiv, KM. Präs. 47/-I/26–1917, letter from Pomiankowski to the Austrian Headquarter commandant, 20 August 1918.

55. Hovannisian, *Armenia on the Road to Independence, op. cit.*, pp. 216–18.

56. Golnazarian-Nichanian, *Les Arméniens d'Azerbaïdjan, thesis cit.*, p. 173.

57. APC/APJ, PCI Bureau, ♂ 60–61–62, list of the accused transmitted to the British high commissioner in February 1919 that mentions the massacres of worker-soldiers and civilians in the Mosul region. Lieutenant Lüttichau, who had completed an inspection tour in the East, mentions the atrocities committed by Ali Ihasan, who "on untold occasions deliberately gave the Germans to understand that he would not leave a single Armenian alive in the area under his control": A.A. Türkei 183/54, A44066, pp. 12–13, report of the summer 1918, in Dadrian, *Histoire du génocide arménien, op. cit.*, p. 558, n. 25. In his memoirs, Ihsan states that the operations in Persia were intended to justify the Caucasian campaign in the Germans' eyes: Zürcher, *The Unionist, op. cit.*, p. 95, n. 23.

58. Arsen-Trchnig, Վասպուրականի վերջին անցքերը եւ նահանջը [*The Final Events in Vasburagan and the Exodus*], Bibl. Nubar, file P.I. 1/4, f° 1. According to Arsen-Trchnig, from 3,000 to 4,000 people incapable of walking were taken to the island of Lim; he does not know what became of them (*ibidem*, f° 3).

59. L.C. Dunsterville, "Military Mission to North-West Persia, 1918," in *Journal of the Central Asian Society*, VIII/2 (1921), pp. 79–98.

60. Telegram from Lecomte to the MAE, Tehran, 24 April 1918, AMAE, N. S. Perse, vol. 21, f° 317: Golnazarian-Nichanian, *Les Arméniens d'Azerbaïdjan, thesis cit.*, p. 176.

61. Vazgen, "Ատրպատականի Գոյամարտը [The Battle of Azerbaijan]," *Hayrenik amsagir*, December 1930, p. 157.

62. Golnazarian-Nichanian, *Les Arméniens d'Azerbaïdjan, thesis cit.*, p. 171, points out that the Syriacs vainly offered him 300 rifles.

63. Mohammad Amin Riâhi, *Târikh-e Khoy* [*History of Khoy*], Tehran 1372 (1993), pp. 504–5; Riâhi makes use of a notebook belonging to Mollâ Ja'far-e Khoyi, an eyewitness to these events; it indicates that there were 7,000 refugees. Another source puts their number at 15,000 (*ibidem*, p. 504, n. 7). According to Sister Marie de Lapeyrière, Simko left Mâku for Salmâs on 8 April, accompanied by his men: Archives de la Mission Lazariste, "Compte-rendu des événements qui eurent lieu en Perse, années 1918–1919," pp. 37bis-40.

64. Arsen-Trchnig, *The Final Events in Van and the Exodus, doc. cit.*, f° 3. Arsen-Trchnig states that in their panicked flight to Salmâs, the refugees abandoned their property.

65. Golnazarian-Nichanian, *Les Arméniens d'Azerbaïdjan, thesis cit.*, p. 169.

66. Arsen-Trchnig, *The Final Events in Van and the Exodus, doc. cit.*, f° 3.

67. *Ibidem*.

68. *Ibidem*, p. 168.

69. *Ibidem*, p. 169.

70. Riâhi, *Târikh-e Khoy, op. cit.*, p. 508: Golnazarian-Nichanian, *Les Arméniens d'Azerbaïdjan, thesis cit.*, p. 169.

71. *Ibidem*, pp. 178–80; Arsen-Trchnig, *The Final Events in Van and the Exodus, doc. cit.*, ff. 6–7. Under pressure from the French and American governments, the Persian authorities opened an inquiry in October 1919 in order to establish who was responsible for these massacres; the inquiry brought

out the participation of the local population in these atrocities (Golnazarian-Nichanian, *Les Arméniens d'Azerbaïdjan*, thesis cit., pp. 179–80).

72. *Ibidem*, pp. 180–1.
73. *Ibidem*, p. 182.
74. *Ibidem*, p. 185.
75. Father Franssen gives a translation in its *Mémoires d'un missionnaire*, p. 79: *ibidem*, p. 185.
76. *Ibidem*, p. 186.
77. *Ibidem*.
78. *Ibidem*, pp. 186–7.
79. *Ibidem*, p. 187. Franssen provides the rest of Munir's declaration, which mentions six "enemies of Islam" from Julfa who were hanged by the "Ottoman Army" because they had given assistance to "infidels." (*Mémoires*, p. 82).
80. *Ibidem*, pp. 188–9.
81. *Ibidem*, p. 190.
82. *Mémoires*, p. 92: *ibidem*, p. 190. The speech is mentioned in a corroborating report by the French consul, Saugon, sent to the French Foreign Ministry on 8 March 1919; there are a few minor variations in Saugon's account of it: AMAE, série E. Levant, 1918–1940. Arménie 4, 1919, ff. 41–2.
83. *Ibidem*, f° 43.
84. SHAT, Service Historique de la Marine, Service de Renseignements de la Marine, Turquie, 1BB7 235, doc. no. 1992, Constantinople, 16 April 1920, "La politique pantouranienne," by Ernest Paraquin, p. 12.
85. Golnazarian-Nichanian, *Les Arméniens d'Azerbaïdjan*, thesis cit., p. 191.
86. Report by the French consul, Saugon, sent to the French Foreign Ministry on 8 March 1919: AMAE, Asie 1918–1940, Perse, vol. 16, ff. 21–3, in Golnazarian-Nichanian, *Les Arméniens d'Azerbaïdjan*, thesis cit., p. 200, n. 19, gives a fairly complete account of the Syriac and Armenian losses.
87. *Ibidem*, pp. 200–1, cites a report from The Armenian Prelacy Archives of Tabriz, 27 December 1918.
88. Riâhi, *Târikh-e Khoy*, op. cit., p. 505: Golnazarian-Nichanian, *Les Arméniens d'Azerbaïdjan*, thesis cit., p. 201.
89. Riâhi, *Târikh-e Khoy*, op. cit., p. 515: *ibidem*.
90. National Archives of Armenia, Fonds 57, vol. 5, file 198, ff. 1a-2a: *Ibidem*, pp. 202–3.
91. G. Korganoff, *La participation des Arméniens à la Guerre mondiale sur le front du Caucase (1914–1918)*, Paris 1927, pp. 172–3.
92. Hovannisian, *Armenia on the Road to Independence*, op. cit., pp. 220–1.
93. *Ibidem*, pp. 222–5.
94. *Ibidem*, pp. 225–7.
95. A.A. Türkei 183/54, A34707, 26 September 1918, report to the General Seeckt, chief of the Ottoman General Headquarter: Dadrian, *Histoire du génocide arménien*, op. cit., p. 554, n. 12. Shortly thereafter, Paraquin was relieved of his functions by Halil for having denounced the Baku massacres.
96. Murat Çulcu, *Ermeni Entrikalarının Perde Arkası. "Torlakyan Davası"* [History of Armenian Intrigues As Seen from Inside: "The Torlakyan Trial"], Istanbul 1990, p. 240.
97. *Cf. supra*, p. 44, n. 9.
98. Muhittin Bergen, "Bizimkiler ve Azerbaycan [Us and the Azerbaijan]," *Yakın Tarihiniz* 2 (1962), p. 158: Dadrian, *Histoire du génocide arménien*, op. cit., p. 555, n. 15.
99. Amaduni Virabian (ed.), Հայերի Կոտորածները Բաքվի եւ Ելիզավետպոլի Նահանգներում [*The Armenian Massacres in the Provinces of Bakou and Elisabethpol, 1918–1920*], Erevan 2003, p. 116, doc. 107, 9 October 1918 dispatch from Arshag Jamalian to the Armenian delegation in Constantinople.
100. *Ibidem*, pp. 120–1, 19 October 1918 dispatch.
101. Arshavir Shakhatuni, "Խալիլ Փաշայի Հանդիպումները Արամին Հետ [Halil Pasha's exchanges with Aram]," in *Aram*, Erevan 1991, pp. 495–506.

2 The Refounding of the Young Turk Party Shortly Before and Shortly After the Armistice

1. *Zhoghovurt*, 23, 25 October and 7 November 1918; Zürcher, *The Unionist, op. cit.*, p. 73. The new party was officially registered on 11 November (*ibidem*).
2. *Ibidem*.
3. *Ibidem*, pp. 68–9.
4. *Ibidem*, p. 74. Most of the provincial clubs were converted into offices of *Teceddüt Fırkası*. Mahmut Celâl [Bayar] (1884–1987), the CUP's responsible secretary in Smyrna and, later, a member of the Special Organization, was charged with establishing *Teceddüt* in Smyrna before he joined the Kemalists in Anatolia. He ended his career as president of the republic (1950–1960).
5. *Ibidem*, p. 85.
6. *Ibidem*, p. 95.
7. *Ibidem*, pp. 76–7.
8. *Ibidem*, p. 77.
9. *Ibidem*, p. 78.
10. Zürcher, *Turkey: A Modern History, op. cit.*, p. 141.
11. *Cf. supra*, p. 69, n. 141.
12. Zürcher, *The Unionist, op. cit.*, pp. 81–2, cites, as an example, the first cell created by Baha Said and Kara Vasıf in a tearoom located opposite the Mahmudpaşa Mosque, with Kel Ali [Çetinkaya], Major Yenibahçeli Şükrü ([Oğuz)], Major Çerkez Reşid, Refik İsmail, Major Sevkiyatçı Ali Rıza, and, according to certain sources, Colonel Galatalı Şevket (the commander of the Tenth Division of the Army of the Caucasus) and Edip Servet [Tör], a CUP member since 1906.
13. *Ibidem*, p. 82–3. Halide Edip [Adıvar] played an important role in this network that organized escapes until spring 1920 and her flight after the British occupation.
14. *Ibidem*, pp. 83–4.
15. *Ibidem*, p. 86. Çerkez Ethem (1885–1948), an officer of the Special Organization, collaborated with Rauf [Orbay]'s group in Bandırma, based on a farm in Salihli belonging to the former leader of the Special Organization, Kuşçubaşizâde Eşref, which served as a hiding place for weapons.
16. *Ibidem*, p. 103.
17. *Ibidem*, p. 104.
18. *Ibidem*, p. 105. This plan is described in detail in the memoirs of a Unionist, Şeref [Çavuşoğlu].
19. Harry Stuermer, *Deux ans de guerre à Constantinople*, Paris 1917, pp. 107–9.
20. Archives nationales (Paris), F12/7962, Turquie (secret) m.a. 44905, Financial, C.X.E.014722, report on the "economic conditions" in Turkey, Berne, 11 January 1918, provides indications about the system that was established to ensure these monopolies. Mehmed Cavid and Rahmi Bey, the vali of Smyrna, seem to have granted themselves the monopoly on exporting opium (*ibidem*, f° 2).
21. SHAT, Service Historique de la Marine, Service de renseignements de la Marine, Turquie, 1BB7 236. The record of these hearings was partially published in 1933 by the newspaper *Vakit*, under the title *Harb Kabinelerının ısticvabi* [Hearings of Members of the Ministry of War], and published in full, in Turkish written in Latin letters, in Osman Selim Kocahanoğlu, *Ittihat-Terakki'nin sorgulanması ve Yargılanması (1918–1919)*, Istanbul 1998.
22. Zürcher, *The Unionist, op. cit.*, p. 83.
23. *Cf. supra*, p. 200.
24. Archives nationales (Paris), F12/7962, Turquie (secret) m.a. 57805, Financial, C.X.E.051596, Geneva, 27 September 1918, London, 2 October 1918.
25. Zürcher, *Turkey: A Modern History, op. cit.*, pp. 138–40.
26. Zürcher, *The Unionist, op. cit.*, p. 87.
27. *Cf. supra*, pp. 175, 180, 218, 219, 222, 289, etc.
28. Zürcher, *The Unionist, op. cit.*, p. 98. He was dismissed only on the 18 February 1919 demand of General George Milne, the Commander-in-Chief of the British army of the Black Sea.
29. Zürcher, *Turkey: A Modern History, op. cit.*, p. 147.
30. Zürcher, *The Unionist, op. cit.*, pp. 75, 89.

31. Ibidem, pp. 90–1. The *Vilayâti Şarkiye Müdafaai Hukuku Milliye Cemiyeti* was created on 4 December 1918; it included many former parliamentary deputies and prefects. Its official organ was the newspaper *Hadisat* (*The Event*), published by Süleyman Nazıf.

32. *Ibidem*, p. 91. Hoca Raïf [Dinç] (1874–1949), a Unionist parliamentary deputy from Erzerum, who returned from Constantinople in late December 1918, was particularly active in this regard.

33. *La Renaissance*, no. 80, 5 March 1919; *La Renaissance*, no. 142, 17 May 1919; *La Renaissance*, no. 266, 10 October 1919, announced the fall of Ferid's government and its replacement by Ali Rıza Pasha. In an article entitled "La Dislocation de la Turquie," published in the 22 October 1918 *Matin*, General Şerif Pasha describes the nomination of the İzzet cabinet as "a last disguise, to give the impression of a change." The French secret service noted that "the Committee is supposed to have verbally threatened the Sultan, whom it held responsible for the legal prosecution of the party." It also seems that the military commander of the city, Fayzi, was "dependent on the Committee" and threatened the prefect of police "when arrests of the members of the CUP" continued to be made: SHAT, Service Historique de la Marine, Service de renseignements de la Marine, Turquie, 1BB7 231, doc. no. 43, Constantinople, report of 21 December 1918.

34. Zürcher, *The Unionist, op. cit.*, p. 75.

35. *La Renaissance*, no. 85, 11 March 1919.

36. *La Renaissance*, no. 57, 5 February 1919; SHAT, Service Historique de la Marine, Service de renseignements de la Marine, Turquie, 1BB7 231, doc. no. 200, Constantinople, report of 30 January 1919.

37. *Ibidem*.

38. *La Renaissance*, no. 59, 7 February 1919.

39. *La Renaissance*, no. 61, 8 February 1919.

40. *La Renaissance*, no. 69, 20 February 1919.

41. *La Renaissance*, no. 74, 26 February 1919.

42. *La Renaissance*, no. 79, 4 March 1919.

43. *La Renaissance*, no. 86, 12 March 1919.

44. *La Renaissance*, no. 94, 21 March 1919.

45. *La Renaissance*, no. 100, 28 March 1919.

46. *La Renaissance*, no. 104, 2 April 1919.

47. *La Renaissance*, no. 105, 3 April 1919.

48. *La Renaissance*, no. 118, 18 April 1919. The pace of arrests was slowed in May. Among the other Ittihadists arrested were Mustafa Abdülhalik, 27 October (*La Renaissance*, no. 281, 28 October 1919) and Dr. Ali Saib, 16 December (*La Renaissance*, no. 324, 17 December 1919).

49. Ahmed Bedevi Kuran, *Osmanlı İperatorlugunda İnkilâp Hareketleri ve Milli Mücadele* [*The Revolutionary Movements in the Ottoman Empire and the National Struggle*], Istanbul 1959, p. 772.

50. M. Larcher, *La guerre turque dans la Guerre mondiale*, Paris, E. Chiron, 1926, pp. 540, 635, indicates that, out of a total of 2,850,000 Ottoman soldiers, 1,565,000 deserted in the course of the First World War. *La Renaissance*, no. 68 and 87, 18 February and 13 March 1919, indicates similar evaluation.

51. Zürcher, *The Unionist, op. cit.*, p. 85.

52. *Ibidem*, p. 101.

53. *La Renaissance*, no. 12, 21 December 1918.

54. *Takvim-ı Vakayi*, no. 3425, 22 Kanunuvel.

55. Zürcher, *The Unionist, op. cit.*, p. 80.

3   The Debates in the Ottoman Parliament in the Wake of the Mudros Armistice

1. The president of the *Hürryet İttilaf*, Mustafa Sabri, declared, in the daily *Sabah* (reprinted in *Nor Gyank*, no. 107, 3 February 1919) that they were able to escape thanks to İzzet pacha.

2. Dadrian, *Histoire du génocide arménien, op. cit.*, pp. 505–6.

3. *Meclisi Mebusan Zabıt Ceridesi* [*Minutes of the Sessions of the Ottoman Parliament*], 3th legislature, 5th session, vol. 1, 4 November 1334 [1918], pp. 95, 100, 109, in V. Dadrian, Հայկական

Ցեղասպանութիւնը Խորհրդարանային եւ Պատմագիտական Քննարկումներով [*The Treatment of the Armenian Genocide by the Ottoman Parliament and Its Historical Analysis*], Watertown 1995, pp. 7–8 and n. 1.

4. *Ibidem*, pp. 100, 109.

5. *Ibidem*, pp. 12–13.

6. Haigazn K. Kazarian, an Ottoman academic who took part in the Battle of Gallipoli and later served as an officer in the English forces – notably from March 1920 on, on the General Staff of the British navy in Constantinople – reveals in his book. In his book, Ցեղասպան Թուրքը [*The Genocidaire Turk*], Beirut 1968 – Haigazn K. Kazarian, that the General Staff set up its offices on the premises of the Ministry of the Ottoman navy in Kasım Pasha (*ibidem*, p. 6). He worked under the direction of Intelligence Service officer, Ryan, on the archives of *Evrak odası*, Kazarian had access to, and copied, certain of the documents preserved there, notably the version of the deportation law including the four paragraphs that were never made public, in addition to the four published in the version of the law that was signed by Sultan Reşad and Grand Vizier Said Halim and published in the *Takvim-ı Vakayi* (*ibidem*, pp. 179–80).

7. *Meclisi Mebusan Zabıt Ceridesi* [*Record of the Sessions of the Ottoman Parliament*], 3th legislature, 5th session, vol. 1, 18 November 1334 [1918], pp. 143–61, 109, in V. Dadrian, *The Treatment of the Armenian Genocide, op. cit.*, pp. 56–7.

8. *Ibidem*, note 17. V. Dadrian provides precise information about Sâmi's criminal activities, and also about his abduction of young girls whom he generously offered to his colleagues in Constantinople. Indicted by the Ottoman court-martial, Sâmi was arrested and then released after pretending to be insane; he was later apprehended by the British and exiled to Malta while waiting to be tried. For more details, *cf. supra*, pp. 346–8.

9. *Meclisi Mebusan Zabıt Ceridesi* [*Minutes of the Sessions of the Ottoman Parliament*], 3th legislature, 5th session, vol. 1, 9 December 1334 [1918], pp. 257–8, 109, in V. Dadrian, *The Treatment of the Armenian Genocide, op. cit.*, pp. 56–7.

10. *Ibidem*, 11 December 1334 [1918], pp. 286–301, in Dadrian, *op. cit.*, pp. 61–74.

11. *Ibidem*, pp. 300–1, in Dadrian, *op. cit.*, pp. 70–1.

12. *Ibidem*, 12 December 1334 [1918], pp. 305–17, in Dadrian, *op. cit.*, pp. 74–86.

13. *Ibidem*, p. 322, in Dadrian, *op. cit.*, p. 86.

14. SHAT, Service Historique de la Marine, Service de renseignements de la Marine, Turquie, 1BB7 236. These hearings saw only partial publication in 1933 in the newspaper *Vakıt*, under the title *Harb Kabinelerının Isticvabi* (Interrogations of the members of the War Ministry), and were published in full in Latin letters in Osman Selim Kocahanoğlu, *İttihat-Terakki'nin Sorgulanması ve Yargılanması (1918–1919)*, Istanbul 1998.

15. SHAT, SHM, S.R. Marine, Turquie, 1BB7 236, doc. no. 1651 B-9, Constantinople, 24 January 1920, lieutenant de vaisseau Goybet: p. 3, annexe 14; *İttihat-Terakki'nin Sorgulanması ve Yargılanması (1918–1919), op. cit.*, pp. 293–382, also details the makeup of the commission, headed by Abdüllah Azmi, and the dates of the hearings.

16. *Ibidem*, p. 7.

17. SHM, S.R. Marine, Turquie, 1BB7 236, doc. no. 1654 B-9, Constantinople, 26 January 1920, lieutenant de vaisseau Goybet, annexe 15, p. 10.

18. *Ibidem*, p. 11.

19. *Ibidem*, p. 12.

20. SHAT, SHM, S.R. Marine, Turquie, 1BB7 236, doc. no. 1687 B-9, Constantinople, 31 January 1920, lieutenant de vaisseau Goybet, annexe 17, p. 17.

21. *Ibidem*, doc. no. 1724 B-9, Constantinople, 7 February 1920, L. Feuillet, annexe 19, examination of Halil Bey, pp. 4, 6; *İttihat-Terakki'nin Sorgulanması ve Yargılanması (1918–1919), op. cit.*, pp. 265–91.

22. *Ibidem*, p. 22.

23. SHAT, SHM, S.R. Marine, Turquie, 1BB7 236, doc. no. 1805 B-9, Constantinople, 26 February 1920, L. Feuillet, annexe 20, examination of Said Halim, p. 18; *İttihat-Terakki'nin Sorgulanması ve Yargılanması (1918–1919), op. cit.*, pp. 55–97.

24. *Ibidem*, p. 19.

25. *Ibidem*, p. 20.

26. *Ibidem*, pp. 21–2.
27. *Ibidem*, pp. 23–4.
28. *Ibidem*, pp. 25–6.
29. *Ibidem*, pp. 29–30.
30. Kazarian, *op. cit.*, p. 34. A former *mutesarif* of Serez, where he took part in the massacre of the Macedonians in 1912, Şükrü was implicated in the murder of journalists and liberal politicians.
31. SHAT, SHM, S.R. Marine, Turquie, 1BB7 236, doc. no. 1862 B-9, Constantinople, 19 March 1920, L. Feuillet, annexe 20, examination of Ahmed Şükrü Bey, pp. 21–4; *İttihat-Terakki'nin Sorgulanması ve Yargılanması (1918–1919)*, *op. cit.*, pp. 171–207.
32. *Ibidem*, pp. 25, 36.
33. SHAT, SHM, S.R. Marine, Turquie, 1BB7 236, doc. no. 1968 B-9, Constantinople, 15 April 1920, transl. L. Feuillet, examination of Ahmed Nesimi Bey in front of the Fifth Commission of the Ottoman parliament, pp. 1–2, 10; *İttihat-Terakki'nin Sorgulanması ve Yargılanması (1918–1919)*, *op. cit.*, pp. 209–51.
34. *Ibidem*, pp. 11–12.
35. *Ibidem*, pp. 13–18, 43.
36. SHAT, SHM, S.R. Marine, Turquie, 1BB7 236, doc. no. 2054 B-9, Constantinople, 3 May 1920, L. Feuillet, examination of İbrahim Bey, pp. 12, 27–8; *İttihat-Terakki'nin Sorgulanması ve Yargılanması (1918–1919)*, *op. cit.*, pp. 133–69.
37. *Ibidem*, pp. 27–41.
38. SHAT, SHM, S.R. Marine, Turquie, 1BB7 236, doc. no. 2000 B-9, Constantinople, 21 April 1920, transl. L. Feuillet, examination of the head of State Security and second in command at the Ministry of the Interior, İsmail Canbolat Bey, pp. 7–8; *İttihat-Terakki'nin Sorgulanması ve Yargılanması (1918–1919)*, *op. cit.*, pp. 417–36. It was a department of this Directorate for Emigrés, the Sub-Directorate for Deportees based in Aleppo, which ran the 25 concentration camps in Syria where several hundred thousand Armenians lost their lives.
39. Krieger, *Yozgat*, *op. cit.*, p. 51.
40. Minute of the session: *La Renaissance*, no. 13, 22 December 1918, p. 1.

4   The Mazhar Governmental Commission of Inquiry and the Creation of Courts Martial

1. Taner Akçam, *Insan Haklari ve Ermeni Sorunu*, Ankara 1999, pp. 445–6, indicates in detail how the Commission of Inquiry was formed; also serving on it were a judge on the Final Court of Appeal, Avramakis; Artin Mosdichian, a judge on the Istanbul Court of Appeal; and two civil inspectors, Husni and Emin Bey: Krieger, *Yozgat*, *op. cit.*, p. 305.
2. V. Dadrian, *Histoire du génocide arménien*, *op. cit.*, p. 507.
3. Krieger, *Yozgat*, *op. cit.*, p. 33, cites the Turkish newspapers: *Adalet, Akçam, Alemdar, Sabah, Peyam, Tasviri Efkâr, Vakıt, Yeni Gün, Zaman*; the Armenian newspapers: *Aravod, Ariamard, Artsakank, Azadamard, Darakir, Giligia, Horizon, Hay Lur, Jagadamard, Zhamanag, Nor Giank, Nor Or, Puzantion, Veradznunt, Verchin Lur*; the French newspapers: *Le Bosphore, Le Moniteur Oriental, La Renaissance, Le Spectateur d'Orient, L'Officiel*, which reported on the various sessions of the trials.
4. Cf. *supra*, pp. 286–7.
5. The indictment, drawn up on 12 April 1919, was read out before the court-martial on 27 April 1919, as were a whole series of letters and documents on which the accusation was based: *Takvim-ı Vakayi*, no. 3540, 5 May 1919, p. 6.
6. APC/APJ, PCI Bureau, Ɛ 152 and Ɔ 281 (in English), doc. no. 14/1, file of Midhat Şükrü Bey.
7. Indictment and various documents in support of the accusation: *Takvim-ı Vakayi*, no. 3540, 5 May 1919, p. 6.
8. *Ibidem*, extract from General Vehib's written deposition (p. 17), which also mentions a large number of "directives, circulars, encrypted telegrams sent by the Interior Ministry and the Ministry of War to the valis of the provinces and army commanders with a view to massacring the Armenians rapidly and without exception." Vehib's deposition also reveals that Kâmil Effendi,

a parliamentary deputy from Istanbul and the chairman of the Second Parliamentary Sub-Commission, told *Ikdam* of the disappearance of the files pertaining to the Fifth Commission's inquiry that had been deposed in the parliament's archives after parliament was dissolved. At the request of Mustafa Asim, the parliament's general secretary turned these archives over to the government; according to information gathered by the Minster of War and the court-martial, the stolen documents were those attached to the minutes of the interrogations: *Zhoghovurti Tsayn*, no. 456, 6 April 1920.

9. *Nor Giank*, no. 107, 3 February 1919.

10. *La Renaissance*, no. 7, 15 December 1918, p. 1, and *Ariamard*, 18 December 1918, p. 2.

11. Cf. *supra*, pp. 286–7.

12. Fifth session of the Unionists' trial, 12 May 1919: *Takvim-ı Vakayi*, no. 3554, 21 May 1919, pp. 67–9. The bureau's telegram, signed by Aziz, Atıf, Nâzım, and Halil, is dated 13 November 1914. The judge presiding at the court had another telegram read out and then asked Colonel Cevad whether he had been the one who had written "to be destroyed" in the margins of this telegram, and whether he had received instructions to do so (*ibidem*, p. 68).

13. Cf. *supra*, pp. 184–6.

14. *Takvim-ı Vakayi*, no. 3554, 21 May 1919, pp. 67–8. The marginal note in one of the telegrams reads "*Teşkilât-i Mahsusa*. The rules state that one must send the originals of the telegrams. The 8th of the present month [November 1914]. Cevad."

15. Krieger, *Yozgat*, op. cit., p. 33.

16. Public Record Office, FO 371/4174, no. 102551, from the high commissioner in Constantinople, Arthur Calthorpe, to Lord Curzon, Constantinople, 27 June 1919, concerning official documents in the possession of the *mutesarif* of Ayntab seized by the British military authorities on 4 February 1919. A 12 May 1919 telegram sent by the delegate in Trebizond to the high commissioner in Constantinople, M. Defrance (CADN, Trébizonde, file 77, no. 38), indicates that, according to the Syrian doctor Reshid Kavak Bey, part of the archives of the Committee of Union and Progress were transported to Nakhichevan the previous December by way of Erzerum and Trebizond and were still to be found in that city, in the house of someone named Jaffar Bey.

17. Dadrian, *Histoire du génocide arménien*, op. cit., p. 507.

18. APC/APJ, PCI Bureau, Ż 186, chiffred telegram no. 197, from the secretary of the vilayet of Konya to the acting vali, transmitted to the Ministry of Interior, 27 March 1335 (1919) or 24 Cemazi ul-Akher 1337.

19. APC/APJ, PCI Bureau, Ż 247–8, letter from the Ministry of Interior to the president of the court-martial, 27 July 1919, accompanying the decrypted version of a telegram from Dr. Reşid to İsmail Hakkı, vali of Adana, 17 May 1915.

20. APC/APJ, PCI Bureau, Ż 183–5, letter confirming reception of documents transmitted by the authorities in Konya, certified on 27 March 1919 by the interior minister.

21. APC/APJ, PCI Bureau, Ż 146, Sublime Porte, Ministry of Interior, special bureau of the direction General Security, letter from Cemal Bey to the president of the court-martial, 30 Cemazi ul-Akhr 1337 (2 April 1335 [1919]).

22. APC/APJ, PCI Bureau, Ż 247–8, letter from the Ministry of Interior to the president of the court-martial, 27 July 1919, accompanying the decrypted version of a telegram from Dr Reşid to İsmail Hakkı, vali of Adana, 17 May 1915.

23. *La Renaissance*, no. 5, 13 December 1918. The two civilian magistrates were Şevket Bey and Artin Mosdichian, both from the Appeals Court. Two other members were to be designated by the military authorities (*La Renaissance*, no. 8, 16 December 1918).

24. Dadrian, *Histoire du génocide arménien*, op. cit., pp. 508–9, cites the imperial decrees published in *Takvim-ı Vakayi* officially creating the courts martial.

25. *La Renaissance*, no. 34, 13 January 1919.

26. *La Renaissance*, no. 82, 7 March 1919.

27. V. Dadrian refers to two court sessions in March 1919: 1) that of 8 March, at which the presiding judge was Fevzi Pasha (*Takvim-ı Vakayi*, no. 3493); 2) that of 19 March, at which the presiding judge was Nâzım Pasha (*Journal d'Orient*, 23 April 1919; *Takvim-ı Vakayi*, no. 3503).

28. Krieger, op. cit., pp. 309–10.

29. *La Renaissance*, no. 113, 12 April 1919, p. 1.

30. *La Renaissance*, no. 43, 26 January 1919. This founding member of the CUP committed suicide some ten days later: Kieser, "Dr Mehmed Reshid (1873–1919)," *art. cit.*, p. 265.
31. *La Renaissance*, no. 286, 4 November 1919.
32. *La Renaissance*, no. 140, 141 and 142, 15, 16 and 17 May 1919.
33. *La Renaissance*, no. 208, 2 August 1919, from *Turkçe Stambul*.
34. *La Renaissance*, no. 281, 28 October 1919.
35. *La Renaissance*, no. 307, 27 November 1919.
36. *La Renaissance*, no. 313, 4 December 1919.
37. *La Renaissance*, no. 318, 10 December 1919.
38. Extract from General Vehib's written deposition, 5 December 1918: *Takvim-ı Vakayi*, no. 3540, 5 May 1919, p. 7, col. 2 and 12 pp. full written deposition: APC/APJ, PCI Bureau, Z 171–82.
39. *La Renaissance*, no. 310, 30 November 1919.
40. *La Renaissance*, no. 313, 4 December 1919.
41. *La Renaissance*, no. 366, 7 February 1920.
42. *La Renaissance*, no. 323, 16 December 1919.
43. APC/APJ, PCI Bureau, 3 662–6, file no. 1, June 1919 letter from Setrag Karageuzian about Trebizond and the investigations conducted there after the armistice. CADN, Consulat de Trébizonde, file 77, telegram no. 48 from the high commissioner delegate in Trebizond to the high commissioner in Constantinople, M. Defrance, 1 June 1919, referring to a meeting with Karageuzian, who complained "confidentially of the problems he had encountered on his mission and his intention to resign from his post."
44. *Ibidem*.

5   The Armenian Survivors in their Places of "Relegation" in the Last Days of the War

1. Bibl. Nubar, AGBU Archives, correspondence, vol. 23, letter from the Central Committee to the Colonel Deeds, chief of the Intelligence Department, War Office, 5 November 1917, f° 225.
2. *Ibidem*, vol. 23, letter from the Central Committee to the Colonel Brémond, 16 November 1917, f° 272.
3. *Ibidem*, vol. 23, letter from the Central Committee to chief of the Intelligence Department in Cairo, 16 November 1917, f° 276.
4. *Ibidem*, vol. 24, letter from the Central Committee to chief of the Intelligence Department in Cairo, 31 December 1917, f° 139.
5. *Ibidem*, vol. 26, letter from the Central Committee to Boghos Nubar, 22 April 1918, f° 48.
6. "900 déportés libérés à leur tour à Tafile (Sinai)," *Miutiun*, January-February 1918, no. 61, p. 5.
7. Bibl. Nubar, AGBU Archives, correspondence, vol. 26, f° 91; SHAT, Service Historique de la Marine, Service de renseignements de la Marine, sous-série Q87, report by Guassen, dated Jerusalem, 19 January 1919, confirms, based on information communicated by Ar. Mindikian, that tensions were running high in this region and that the harems contained many girls and young women whom the Armenian delegates were unable to recover.
8. *La Renaissance*, no. 46, 25 January 1919.
9. *Ibidem*.
10. Zaven Der Yeghiayan, *Memories*, *op. cit.*, p. 179.
11. Yervant Odian, *The Cursed Years, 1914–1919*, *op. cit.*, no. 124, 134.
12. *Ibidem*, no. 137–40.
13. *Ibidem*, no. 145–7.
14. *Ibidem*, no. 149.
15. Zaven Der Yeghiayan, *Memories*, *op. cit.*, pp. 242–3.
16. *Ibidem*, p. 247. Bibl. Nubar, Archives of the DNA, 1–15, letter from bishop M. Seropian to Boghos Nubar, Mosul, 6 January 1919, mentions 100 prostitutes.
17. Zaven Der Yeghiayan, *Memories*, *op. cit.*, pp. 249–50, 269, 273. Father Barsegh Torosian, of Arslanbeg, and Father Ghevont, of Geyve, helped gather up these survivors and provide them with food and lodging.

18. *Ibidem*, p. 254. The patriarch put together a makeshift orphanage in a house in Mosul rented on 10 January 1919 (*ibidem*, p. 255).
19. *Ibidem*, p. 256.
20. *Ibidem*, p. 270.
21. Golnazarian-Nichanian, *Les Arméniens d'Azerbaïdjan*, thesis cit., pp. 198–9.
22. A.M.G., 16 N 3186: A. Beylerian, *Les grandes Puissances*, op. cit., p. 670.
23. Report to the Ministry of Foreign Affairs, 26 December 1918: National Archives of Armenia, fonds 276, vol. 1, file 79, no. 1–7: Golnazarian-Nichanian, *Les Arméniens d'Azerbaïdjan*, thesis cit., p. 200.
24. National Archives of Armenia, fonds 57, vol. 5, liasse 198, ff. 1a–2a: *ibidem*, pp. 202–3.
25. AGBU's Central Archives (Cairo), Baghdad, 1910–1937, CIII-7, letter from the Baghdad Committee to the headquarters of Cairo, 18 June 1920.
26. Zaven Der Yeghiayan, *Memories*, op. cit., p. 257.
27. *Ibidem*, p. 262.
28. *Ibidem*, pp. 266–8.
29. *La Renaissance*, no. 291, 8 November 1919.
30. BNu/Fonds A. Andonian, P.J.1/3, file 26, Kayseri, report of Yervant Der Mardirosian, a 23-year-old native of Talas who taught in Talas's American College, f° 46.
31. *Ibidem*, f° 46v°.
32. Yervant Odian, *The Cursed Years, 1914–1919*, op. cit., no. 153, 159 and 164.
33. *Ibidem*, no. 167.
34. *Ibidem*, no. 170–1; *Zhamanag*, 15 October 1918.
35. *La Renaissance*, no. 47, 26 January 1919.
36. APC/APJ, PCI Bureau, Ч 808–9, exactions committed in the province since the armistice. Among the victims were the Dr. Sisak, Aida Boyajian, Aghavni and Hagop Kirkirian, etc. In Zara 140 survivors and 325 in the *sancak* of Şabinkarahisar: APC/APJ, PCI Bureau, Ч 485–7, statistics for the vilayet of Sıvas.
37. *Ibidem*.
38. Zürcher, *The Unionist*, op. cit., p. 69.
39. *Ibidem*, p. 73. The distinction between the Kemalist movement and the CUP made by official Turkish historiography would seem to be artificial as far as the period of the Congress of Sıvas is concerned (*ibidem*, pp. 68–9).
40. *Cf.* n. 36.
41. APC/APJ, PCI Bureau, Ч 810.
42. *Ibidem*. According to the Patriarchate's report, 2,797 people were condemned and executed; 2,040 were Armenians and 757 were Greeks.
43. APC/APJ, PCI Bureau, Ч 811, "La situation des chrétiens dans le vilayet de Trébizonde depuis l'Armistice de Moudros [The Christians' Situation in the Vilayet of Trebizond since the Mudros Armistice]."
44. CADN, Consulat de Trébizonde, file 77, telegram no. 6 from the high commissioner delegate in Trebizond to the high commissioner in Constantinople, M. Defrance, 13 January 1919.
45. APC/APJ, PCI Bureau, Ч 815–29.
46. APC/APJ, PCI Bureau, Ł 101, report, Trebizond, 25 June 1919.
47. APC/APJ, PCI Bureau, Ձ 914, report on the situation in Ismit, 30 September 1920 (in arm.)
48. APC/APJ, PCI Bureau, Յ 282–90, report on the pillaging and exactions in 1919–1921 in the region of Ismit.
49. APC/APJ, PCI Bureau, Ч 851–6, report on the situation in the vilayet of Bursa in 1919; on the exactions in Çengiler, *cf. ibidem*, Ч 856.
50. *Cf. supra*, p. 558, on the massacres of the males held in Orhaneli in the Atranos regions.
51. SHAT, Service Historique de la Marine, Service de Renseignements de la Marine, Turquie, 1BB7 231, doc. no. 1992, report by lieutenant Rollin, Constantinople, 15 April 1919, pp. 2–3.
52. *Ibidem*, p. 4.
53. APC/APJ, PCI Bureau, Ч 873, file no. 144, Bursa.
54. CADN, Consulat de Trébizonde, file 66, telegram no. 6 from the high commissioner delegate in Trebizond to the high commissioner in Constantinople, M. Defrance, June 1919.

55. CADN, Consulat de Trébizonde, file 77, report no. 1 from the agent Kevork Aharonian to the high commissioner delegate in Trebizond, 1 May 1919.

56. *Ibidem*, p. 3.

57. CADN, Consulat de Trébizonde, file 76, report from the agent Kevork Aharonian to the high commissioner delegate in Trebizond, 15 August 1919.The agent states that Hulusi had been sent to Erzerum in order to be tried before the court-martial, adding that he thinks that there are people who are going to help him "flee."

58. *Cf. supra*, p. 291, n. 27.

59. APC/APJ, PCI Bureau, Ʉ 367, list of the regions where the Armenians and the Greeks was repatriate.

60. APC/APJ, PCI Bureau, Ʉ 543–4, Arméniens présents dans l'Empire ottoman lors du traité de Sèvres.

61. Vahé Tachjian, *La France en Cilicie et en Haute-Mésopotamie (1919–1933)*, Paris 2004, pp. 36–44.

62. *Ibidem*, pp. 45–53.

63. Julien Zarifian, *Le sancak de Sis/Kozan*, Master thesis, University Paris VIII 2003.

64. APC/APJ, PCI Bureau, Ч 543, Tableau des exactions commises contre la population arménienne depuis l'armistice.

65. APC/APJ, PCI Bureau, Ը 375, telegram from Gibbons to the *Monitor* of Boston, Trebizond, 24 May 1920. On the deportations of Greeks in the vilayet of Sıvas and the exactions to which they were subjected after the war, cf. APC/APJ, PCI Bureau, Ч 793.

66. APC/APJ, PCI Bureau, Ʉ 368. An Armenian-Greek committee, created by the inter-allied commission, met continuously with representatives of the Patriarchates and the American Near East Relief from 26 February 1919 to spring 1922 in order to oversee the rehabilitation of the survivors, recover people who had been Islamicized, and so on: FO 371–3658, first session, 26 February 1919.

67. *La Renaissance*, no. 50, 29 January 1919.

68. *Ibidem*.

69. *Spectateur d'Orient*, no. 116, 29 April 1919, "Le procès de l'Union et Progrès."

70. *La Renaissance*, no. 43, 22 January 1919.

71. Public Record Office, FO 371/4174, no. 118377, letter from the Admiral Calthorpe to Lord Curzon, 1 August 1919.

72. APC/APJ, PCI Bureau, Ֆ 900–2, report on the activities of the Informations Bureau for the years 1919–1920, by Garabed Nurian, member of the Politic Council, June 1920.

73. Zaven Der Yeghiyan, *Memories, op. cit.*, pp. 301–2, 304.

74. *Ibidem*, p. 277; *La Renaissance*, no. 71, 22 February 1919.

75. The bureau's reports were often published in the French-language daily *La Renaissance*, which was published from December 1918 to spring 1920 under the direction of Dikran Chayan, a former member of the Council of State, and Garabed Nurian, with the assistance of Dr. Topjian. Zaven points out that the Patriarchate financed publication of this journal: Zaven Der Yeghiyan, *Memories, op. cit.*, pp. 302–3.

76. *Ibidem*, p. 304.

77. *Ibidem*, p. 305.

78. *Ibidem*, p. 307.

79. *Ibidem*, p. 308.

80. APC/APJ, PCI Bureau, Ֆ 578, report by the Armenian Patriarchat of Constantinople, 27 December 1918, report on Turks responsibles for the Armenian atrocities.

81. *Ibidem*.

82. APC/APJ, PCI Bureau, Ի 114–25, Primary list of the chief instigators and perpetrators of the Armenian massacres and deportations of the Years of the Great War (1914–1918).

83. *Ibidem*, Ի 117–19.

84. *Ibidem*, Ի 124.

85. APC/APJ, PCI Bureau, Յ 25–34, Second report on Turks responsibles for the Armenian atrocities of the Bureau of Information: the question of Turkish witnesses (Part 1).

86. *Cf. supra*, pp. 737–8.

87. *Cf. supra*, p. 359, n. 24 (report of 20 December 1915 on Dyarbekir), p. 417, n. 353 (report of 9 December on Harput) and p. 417, n. 353.

88. APC/APJ, PCI Bureau, Ց 25–34, Second report on Turks responsibles.

89. *Ibidem.*

90. *Ibidem.* According to the same report, Asim's secretary, someone named Şevfik Bey provided valuable information not only on his own activities, but also on those of the valis Cevdet Bey in Adana and Abdülhalik in Aleppo, as well as on these *mutesarifs* and military commanders in these vilayets.

91. APC/APJ, PCI Bureau, Ч 104–5, Memorandum from Dr. A. Nakashian to the colonel Ballard, member of the British Intelligence Service, Galata, July 1920.

92. *Ibidem.*

93. Zaven Der Yeghiayan, *Memories, op. cit.*, pp. 299–300.

94. *Ibidem*, pp. 313–14.

95. Cf. *supra*, p. 204. The patriarch was aided here by the Armenian-Greek committee created by the inter-allied commission, in which these questions were settled on an ad hoc basis in the course of the 85 coordinating meetings (held from 19 February 1919 to 29 March 1922) attended by representatives of the Greek and Armenian Patriarchates and American Near East Relief: FO 371/ 3658, 371/4195, 371/4196, 371/4197, 371/5087, 371/ 5213, 371/5214, 371/6548, 371/6549, 371–7879.

96. Zaven Der Yeghiayan, *Memories, op. cit.*, p. 321.

97. *Ibidem; La Renaissance*, no. 140–141–142, 15, 16 and 18 May 1919.

98. Kévorkian et Paboudjian, *Les Arméniens dans l'Empire ottoman, op. cit.*, p. 60.

99. Zaven Der Yeghiayan, *Memories, op. cit.*, p. 312. Those present: Stepan Karayan, le Dr. Krikor Tavitian, Tavit Der Movsesian, Hayg Khojasarian, Nerses Ohanian, Khachig Sevajian, etc.

100. *Ibidem*, pp. 321–22.

101. APC/APJ, PCI Bureau, Ч 126.

102. APC/APJ, PCI Bureau, Ը 181–6, no. 193, letter from the Patriarchate to the Ministry of Justice, 3 January 1920, about the law of "abandoned property."

103. *Takvim-ı Vakayi*, no. 3747, 12/25 January 1920, p. 6, col. 1 and 2.

104. APC/APJ, PCI Bureau, Ը 192, "Movable property."

105. *La Renaissance*, no. 382, 26 February 1920, and no. 388, 4 March 1920. *La Renaissance*, no. 355, 25 January 1920, announces the promulgation of the new law about the assets of massacre victims. According to the paper, the law made the despoliation legal: "no one can accept," we read there, "the idea that the Turkish state should inherit all the assets of those massacred."

106. Such was, in any case, the patriarch's interpretation: Zaven Der Yeghiayan, *Memories, op. cit.*, p. 321; *Traité de paix entre les Puissances alliées et associées et la Turquie du 10 août 1920 (Sèvres)*, texte français, article 288, pp. 107–8.

107. SHAT, Service Historique de la Marine, Service de Renseignements de la Marine, Turquie, 1BB7 231, doc. no. 302, Constantinople, 13 February 1919; the Armenian-Greek committee and representatives of the Greek and Armenian Patriarchs and American Near East Relief coordinated operations; the British High Commissariat enforced their decisions: FO 371/ 3658, 371/4195, 371/4196, 371/4197, 371/ 5087, 371/ 5213, 371/5214, 371/6548, 371/6549, 371–7879.

108. The materials cited in the following thirteen notes were kindly put at our disposal by Vahe Tachjian. Bibl. Nubar, Archives of AGBU, correspondance du siège, vol. 26, letter from the Central Committee to the director of the Intelligence Department, 25 April 1918, ff. 61–3.

109. Bibl. Nubar, Archives of the DNA 1–16, correspondance April-May 1919, memoir from the UNA of Marseille to Boghos Nubar, 28 April 1919.

110. Bibl. Nubar, Archives of AGBU, correspondence, vol. 26, letter from the Central Committee to the director of the Intelligence Department, 25 April 1918, ff. 163–4.

111. Levon Yotneghperian, *Diary* (unpublished), pp. 26–30; Sahagian, *The Urfa, op. cit.*, pp. 1166–77.

112. Yotneghperian, *op. cit.*, pp. 40–1.

113. *Ibidem*, pp. 43–8.

114. Archives Bibl. Nubar, Armenian Orphans, "Herian file: extract of newspapers."

115. Dzovinar Kévonian, *Réfugiés et diplomatie humanitaire: les acteurs européens et la scène proche-orientale pendant l'entre-deux-guerres*, Doctoral thesis, University of Paris I, 1998, p. 106.

116. Archives Bibl. Nubar, Armenian Orphans, "Herian file: extract of newspapers." R. Herian is dead in 1921, in Alexandria.

117. Kévonian, *op. cit.*, pp. 105–6.

118. APC/APJ, PCI Bureau, Դ 543–4, "Arméniens présents dans l'Empire ottoman lors du traité de Sèvres."

119. Raymond Kévorkian & Vahé Tachjian, *Un siècle d'histoire de l'Union générale arménienne de bienfaisance*, I, Paris 2006, pp. 64–89.

120. James L. Barton, *Story of Near East Relief (1915–1930)*, New York 1930.

121. Kévorkian & Tachjian, *Un siècle d'histoire, op. cit.*, pp. 60–8.

122. APC/APJ, PCI Bureau, Ը 181–6, no. 193, letter from the Patriarchat to the Ministry of Justice, 3 January 1920.

123. APC/APJ, PCI Bureau, Դ 543–4, "Arméniens présents dans l'Empire ottoman lors du traité de Sèvres."

124. Zaven Der Yeghiayan, *Memories, op. cit.*, pp. 279–80; Azkayin Khnamadarutiun, Ազգային Խնամատարութիւն, Ընդհանուր Տեղեկագիր [*General Report*, 1 May 31-October 1919], Constantinople 1920, p. 3.

125. Zaven Der Yeghiayan, *Memories, op. cit.*, p. 283; Barton, *Story of Near East Relief (1915–1930), op. cit.*, pp. 207–14. The Armenian-Greek committee created by the inter-allied commission dealt with these questions together with representatives of the High Commissioners in the course of the 85 coordinating meetings (which took place from 19 February 1919 to 29 March 1922) that the representatives of the Greek and Armenian Patriarchates and American Near East Relief held with the Allies, who intervened wherever they were in a position to do so: FO 371/ 3658, 371/4195, 371/ 4196, 371/4197, 371/5087, 371/ 5213, 371/5214, 371/ 6548, 371/6549, 371–7879.

126. Zaven Der Yeghiayan, *Memories, op. cit.*, p. 284.

127. SHAT, Service Historique de la Marine, Service de Renseignements de la Marine, Turquie, 1BB7 231, doc. no. 256, Constantinople, letter, 6 February 1919, and "Liste des orphelins qui se trouvent chez les Turcs."

128. Zaven Der Yeghiayan, *Memories, op. cit.*, p. 287.

129. *Ibidem*, p. 289. Chakrian's team also concerned itself with obtaining the prisoners' release, recovering churches' "confiscated" property, and finding the Young Turk cadres' caches. *La Renaissance*, no. 42, 19 January 1919, p. 2, notes that, in Kayseri, five hundred young female converts "had not yet been given back."

130. Zaven Der Yeghiayan, *Memories, op. cit.*, p. 291.

131. *Ibidem*, pp. 292–8. The "maison neutre" was closed in August 1922 by the British high commissioner.

132. APC/APJ, PCI Bureau, Յ 260, transl. of an article from *Ileri*, 3 June 1919, "Les enfants battus au Patriarcat."

133. *Ibidem*.

134. APC/APJ, PCI Bureau, Յ 266, transl. of an article from *Ileri*, 3 June 1919, "Pauvre Djemile Hanoum."

135. *Cf. supra*, pp. 716, 718.

136. APC/APJ, PCI Bureau, Յ 259–260–261, transl. of an article from *Hadisat*, no. 158, 5 June 1919.

137. *Ibidem*.

138. *Ibidem*.

139. APC/APJ, PCI Bureau, Յ 261, "Réponse des journaux arméniens aux allégations des journaux turcs [The Armenian Newspapers' Response to the Allegations of the Turkish Newspapers]."

6   The Great Powers and the Question of "Crimes Against Humanity"

1. AMAE, Guerre 1914–1918, Turquie, 887. I. Arménie (26 May 1915); FO 371/ 2488/51010 (28 May 1915); A.A. Türkey 183/37, A17667; Foreign Relations of the United States , 1915 Supp., p. 981 (1928); U.S. National Archives, RG 59, p. 867. 4016/67 (28 May): Dadrian, *Histoire du génocide arménien, op. cit.*, p. 356, n. 26. Eric Avebury and Ara Sarafian (ed.), *British Parliamentary Debates on the Armenian Genocide, 1915–1918*, Princeton & London 2003, Annexe I, pp. 59–60, notes that the Russian version of the declaration speaks of "crimes against Christianity and civilization."

2. A. Nasibian, *Britain and the Armenian Question from 1915 to 1923*, London 1984, pp. 124–9.

3. PRO, FO 371/4141, file 71, no. 6781, letter from to Calthorpe to Foreign Office, 13 January 1919, recommending extradition procedures for Enver, Talât "and others."

4. PRO, FO 371/4174, file 1270, ff. 251–62, describes the organization of the activities of the Armenian-Greek committee that worked alongside the British High Commission.

5. AMAE, Série Archives du Bureau français de la SDN (1920–1940), vol. 10, Commission de la Société Des Nations; vol. 11, Conférence des préliminaires de Paix. This copious documentation has been studied by Céline Mouradian, *Le traitement juridique et politique des crimes commis contre les minorités ottomanes de l'Armistice de Moudros jusqu'à la préparation du traité de Sèvres*, Master thesis, University Paris VII 2003.

6. AMAE, Série Conférence de la Paix, Sous-Série Recueil des actes (1918–1932), vol. 40, *Commission des Responsabilités des auteurs de la guerre et Sanctions*, Paris, Imprimerie Nationale, 1922.

7. *Ibidem*, pp. 5–6.

8. *Ibidem*. Albert de Lapradelle, professor of international public law, and Lieutenant Colonel O. M. Biggar were put at the disposition of this committee.

9. *Ibidem*, p. 324.

10. *Ibidem*, Procès-Verbal no. 2, session of 7 February 1919, p. 29. N. Politis spells out that these are "acts contrary to what might be called human law or moral law."

11. *Ibidem*, *Rapport présenté par la Troisième sous-commission de la Commission des Responsabilités*, 5 March 1919, pp. 75–6.

12. *Ibidem*, p. 78.

13. *Ibidem*, p. 80.

14. *Ibidem*, pp. 431–55.

15. *Ibidem*, pp. 511–14.

16. *Ibidem*, pp. 162–79.

17. *Ibidem*, p. 173.

18. *Ibidem*, pp. 176–7.

19. *Ibidem*, pp. 178–9.

20. *Ibidem*, pp. 178–9.

21. Paul Mantoux, *Les délibérations du Conseil des Quatre (24 March- 28 June 1919)*, I, Paris 1955.

22. *Ibidem*, p. 124.

23. *Ibidem*, pp. 184–5.

24. *Ibidem*, II, p. 445–6.

25. *Ibidem*, II, p. 519.

26. *Ibidem*, II, p. 517.

27. FO 371/5104, E 1477, propositions unanimously adopted by the Committee for the Protection of Minorities in Turkey, pp. 6–16. The members of the committee designated by the League of Nations were: Great Britain, R. Vansittart; United States, Forbes Adam; France, M. Kammerer, Italie, Colonel Castoldi; Japon, I. Yoshida (*ibidem*, p. 6) [French version: FO 371/5105, pp. 135–41].

28. *Ibidem*, p. 7.

29. *Ibidem*, pp. 10–11.

30. *Ibidem*, pp. 11–15.

31. *Ibidem*, p. 16. FO 371/5107, E 2409, 26 March 1920: the draft treaty on the protection of minorities in Armenia, in English and French versions (13 pp. and 12 articles) was probably meant to show that these principles would apply everywhere.

32. FO 371/5105, E 2109, telegram no. 241, from the Admiral de Robeck to the Foreign Office, 17 March 1920, relatif to the law of "abandoned property," with the note to the Sublime Porte, 2 December 1919.

33. FO 371/ 5105, f° 21.

34. FO 371/5105, E 2109, Cambon to Lloyd George, 11 March 1920.

35. FO 371/5109, pp. 116 and *sqq.*, "Observations présentées par la Délégation ottomane à la Conférence de la Paix," 25 June 1920.

36. FO 371/ 5110, E 8687, response from the president of the Peace Conference, Lloyd George, to the "Observations présentées par la délégation ottomane," Spa, 16 July 1920, pp. 128–30.

37. The Allies consequently introduced most of the recommendations of the Committee on Reparations and of the London Conference in the Peace Treaty of 10 August 1920 between the Allied and Associated Powers and Turkey (the Treaty of Sèvres), French version, articles 226–30, pp. 83–4.

38. *La Renaissance*, no. 197, 20 July 1919, text of the memorandum ready by Grand Vizier Damad Ferid Pasha before the Peace Conference.

39. FO 371/4174, no. 118377, letter from Arthur Calthorpe to Lord Curzon, 1 August 1919, in which the high commissioner reviews the history of his interventions with the Turkish authorities and mentions his 22 January 1919 telegram no. 158 to the Foreign Office in which he describes his intervention with the Sublime Porte.

40. FO 371/4173/53351, ff. 192–3, telegram from the assistant high commissioner, Richard Webb, to the Conférence de la Paix, 3 April 1919: Dadrian, *Histoire du génocide arménien, op. cit.*, p. 486, n. 23.

41. FO 371/4174, no. 118377, letter from Arthur Calthorpe to Lord Curzon, 1 August 1919, which recapitulates these recommendations.

42. *Ibidem*, p. 1.

43. *Ibidem*, p. 2.

44. FO 218/1552, letter from the Admiral Webb to Balfour, 25 February 1919.

45. FO 371/4173, no. 47293, telegram from the Admiral Calthorpe to Balfour, 26 March 1919.

46. FO 371/4174, report by the Admiral Calthorpe, "Deportations," August 1919, p. 5.

47. FO 371/4174, no. 98243, report by the Admiral Calthorpe, on the trials, 10 July 1919, p. 6.

48. *Ibidem*.

49. *Ibidem*.

50. FO 371/4174, no. 88761, telegram from the Admiral Calthorpe to Lord Curzon, 30 May 1919. Initial plans were to put the accused under a guard of French and British soldiers, but this proposed solution was dropped because of the reluctance of the French.

51. *Ibidem*.

52. *La Renaissance*, no. 153, 30 May 1919.

53. FO 371/4174, no. 136069, telegram from the Admiral Calthorpe to Lord Curzon, 21 September 1919.

54. FO 371/6500, Turkish War Criminals: Vartkès Yeghiayan (ed.), *British Foreign Office dossiers on Turkish War Criminals, op. cit.*

55. FO 371/5089, no. 1054, Turks deported in Malta, Parliamentary Question, 4 March 1920.

56. FO 371/5089, no. 2293, John de Robeck, the high commissioner in Constantinople, to Lord Curzon, 11 March 1920, f° 108. Among the prisoners classified "A/T" (prisoners detained "for direct or indirect participation in outrages on subject christians"), Robeck mentions Ali Ihsan Pasha, Hüseyin Cahid, Tevfik Hadi, Yusuf Rıza, Sabit Bey, Veli Neced, Fethi Bey, Tahir Cevdet, Rahmi Bey, İsmail Canbolat, Nevzâde Bey, Mumtaz Bey, Fazıl Berki, and İbrahim Bedreddin.

57. Zürcher, *Turkey: A Modern History, op. cit.*, p. 101.

58. *Ibidem*, p. 145.

59. FO 371/5089, no. 2301, f° 91, telegram from John de Robeck, the high commissioner in Constantinople, to Lord Curzon, 20 March 1920.

60. FO 371/5089, no. 2322, telegram from John de Robeck to Lord Curzon, 27 March 1920. Salih Pasha's government succeeded Ali Rıza's on 20 March 1920 for ten days; it fell in its turn after the declaration by the Entente that made Constantinople a conquered city. Damad Ferid took the reins of government again in April 1920: FO 371/5046, no. 328, f° 140, chiffred telegram from John de Robeck to Foreign Office, 5 April 1920, announcing the appointment, on the same day, of Damad Ferid, the leader of the Liberal Entente, to the post of grand vizier; FO 371/5166, E 4278, 14 April 1920, reports from the British Intelligence services to Lord Curzon, p. 221, on the composition of Damad Ferid's cabinet, with, notably, as interior minister, Reşid Bey, a liberal who had spent the war years in Switzerland.

61. Bibl. Nubar, Archives of the DNA, The House of Lords and the House of Commons, ff. 116–17.

62. *Ibidem*, f° 28.

63. Vahakn Dadrian, "Raphael Lemkin, International Law and the Armenian Genocide," in *The Key Elements in the Turkish Denial of the Armenian Genocide: a Case Study of Distortion and Falsification,*

Watertown, Zorian Institute, 2001, p. 37; Yves Ternon, "Comparer les génocides," in *Ailleurs, hier, autrement: connaissance et reconnaissance du génocide des Arméniens, Revue d'histoire de la Shoah* 177–8 (2003), p. 41.

64. Annette Becker, "L'extermination des Arméniens, entre dénonciation, indifférence et oubli, de 1915 aux années vingt," *Revue d'Histoire de la Shoah* 177–8 (2003), p. 309; Raphaël Lemkin, *Axis Rule in occupied Europe, Laws of Occupation, Analysis of Government, Proposals for Redress,* Washington, 1944, p. 80.

65. Raphaël Lemkin, "Le crime de génocide," *Revue de Droit international, des Sciences diplomatiques et Politiques,* no. 24 (1946), pp. 213–14.

66. *Ibidem.*

67. The text of this talk may be found in the Lemkin archives, which were given to the Jewish-American Archives in 1965 and are available on the internet at www.preventgenocide.org.

68. AMAE, Série Conférence de la Paix, Sous-Série Recueil des actes (1918–1932), vol. 40, *Commission des responsabilités des auteurs de la guerre et sanctions,* Paris, Imprimerie Nationale, 1922, pp. 176–7.

69. Anne-Marie La Rosa & Santiago Villalpando, "Le crime de génocide revisité," in Katia Boustany and Daniel Dormoy (eds.), *Génocide (s),* Bruxelles 1999 (Collection de droit international; 42), pp. 56–7.

7 The First Trial of the Young Turk Criminals Before the Istanbul Court-Martial

1. *La Renaissance,* no. 151, 28 May 1919, a French translation of an article from *Alemdar.*

2. *La Renaissance,* no. 128, 1 May 1919, from *Sabah.*

3. *Cf. supra,* p. 252. Münîf Bey later adopted the family name Yeğena. He also seems to have played a major role in organizing the famine in Lebanon in his capacity as governor of the province.

4. FO 371/5091, no. 11834/1670.

5. *Cf. supra,* pp. 508–13.

6. Krieger, *Yozgat, op. cit.,* pp. 309–10. The 5 February trial session, the first, was opened at 10:30 a.m. by the judge presiding over the extraordinary court-martial, Mahmud Hayret Pasha. The military judges on the court were General Ali Nâzım Pasha and General Kürd Mustafa Pasha; the civilian judges were, to the presiding judge's left, Harutiun Mostichian, a judge on the Constantinople Appeals Court, and, to his right, Şevket Bey, a judge on the Constantinople Appeals Court.

7. *Ibidem,* pp. 311–12, n. 5: the court-martial held lists of massacred people, but not the places and dates of extermination. The plaintiff is presented again by Hayg [Hmayag] Khosrovian, Hagop Bahri and Avedis Surenian, chosen by the Armenian Bar Association.

8. *Ibidem,* pp. 312–15.

9. SHAT, Service Historique de la Marine, Service de renseignements de la Marine, Turquie, 1BB7 231, doc. no. 259, Constantinople, 7 February 1919, "Rapport sur les atrocités de Yozgat, dressé par un fonctionnaire turc [Report on the Atrocities in Yozgat, Drawn up by a Turkish Official]."

10. Krieger, *op. cit.,* p. 224.

11. Fourth trial session, 11 February 1919: Krieger, *op. cit.,* pp. 315–16. At the 15 February fifth trial session, a medical report showed that Eugenie Varvarian had sustained a head injury several years earlier; a certificate attested that she was 18 years old.

12. Fifth trial session, 15 February 1919: *ibidem.*

13. *Cf. supra,* pp. 516–8.

14. *Cf. supra,* p. 739.

15. Krieger, *op. cit.,* p. 312. Remzi, speaking on his own behalf, demanded that the court award him one and a half million Turkish pounds in compensation for damages in his capacity as the only survivor and representative of a family from the region 117 of whose members had been murdered. The court observed, however, that of the 8,000 Armenians living in Yozgat before the massacres, 80 were still alive (*ibidem,* p. 311, n. 5)..

16. Hüsameddin Ertürk, *İki Devrin Perde Arkası [Behind the Curtain during Two Times],* ed. by Samih Hafız Tansu, Istanbul 1964, p. 299.

17. *Ibidem*; *Zhamanag*, 25 March 1919, p. 3, col. 5 and p. 4, col. 1–3. The court was made up of the following members: General Mustafa Nâzım pasha, president; General Zeki pasha, General Mustafa Pasha (known as Nemrud or Kurd Mustafa), General Ali Nâzım Pasha, and colonel Receb Ferdi Bey; Sâmi Bey, prosecutor, with three assistant prosecutors.

18. APC/APJ, PCI Bureau, U' 350, telegram from the civil inspector Nedim Bey, charged with conducting an investigation in the *sancak* of Yozgat, to Emin Bey, 28 December 1918.

19. Verdict of the trial of Yozgat, 8 April 1919: *Takvim-ı Vakayi*, no. 3617, 7 August 1919, p. 2. The verdict was submitted to the Sultan, who promptly ratified it: *Zhamanag*, 9 April 1919, p. 1.

20. *Ibidem*.

21. Public Record Office, FO 371/4173, no. 61185, 17 April 1919, telegram from the high commissioner, Calthorpe, to the Foreign Office, describing the execution of Kemal Bey; FO 371/4173, no. 72536, 21 April 1919, letter from Calthorpe to the Foreign Office, about Kemal Bey's burial, and a 24 April 1919 report by Captain H. A. D. Hoyland, to General Staff Intelligence, 24 April 1919. According to a report of French Intelligence Services, the "peine de mort n'aurait été prononcée qu'à une voix de majorité."

22. Hüsameddin Ertürk, *op. cit.*, p. 297.

23. *Ibidem*, pp. 297–8.

24. *Ibidem*, p. 300.

25. Krieger, *op. cit.*, p. 300. A French source indicates that he added: "Long live Muslims and Turkey! Death to the Armenians, the eternal enemies of the Empire": SHAT, Service Historique de la Marine, Service de renseignements de la Marine, Turquie, 1BB7 231, doc. no. 563, Constantinople, report of 12 April 1919, "L'exécution de Kemal bey."

26. Hüsameddin Ertürk, *op. cit.*, pp. 220–1. SHAT, Service Historique de la Marine, Service de renseignements de la Marine, Turquie, 1BB7 231, doc. no. 563, Constantinople, report of 12 April 1919, "L'exécution de Kemal bey."

27. *Ibidem*.

28. *La Renaissance*, no. 232, 31 August 1919, p. 1.

29. *Ibidem*.

8 The Truncated Trial of the Main Young Turk Leaders

1. First session of the trial of the Unionists, 27 April 1919: *Takvim-ı Vakayi*, no. 3540, 5 May 1919, p. 1, List of the accused, present or fugitives from justice. The court-martial comprised: General Mustafa Nâzım Pasha, president; General Zeki Pasha, General Nemrud Mustafa Pasha, General Ali Nâzım Pasha, Colonel Receb Ferdi Bey, judges; Reşat Bey, prosecutor.

2. First session of the trial of the War Cabinets, 3 June 1919: *Takvim-ı Vakayi*, no. 3571, 11 June 1919, p. 127. Our count indicates that only three of the 23 members of the Ittihad's Central Committee were not indicted: Haci Adıl, Mehmed Cavid, and Hüseyin Cahid.

3. This probably explains why a few people among the leadership of the Special Organization, such as Aziz Bey or Ahmed Cevad, were indicted along with the members of the Central Committee.

4. Indictment of 12 April 1919, read out at the 27 April first session of the trial of the Unionists: *Takvim-ı Vakayi*, no. 3540, 5 May 1919.

5. *Ibidem*.

6. *Ibidem*, p. 17.

7. *Ibidem*.

8. SHAT, Service Historique de la Marine, S. R. Marine, Turquie, 1BB7 231, doc. no. 614, Constantinople, 29 April 1919, "Le procès des Unionistes [The Trial of the Unionists]."

9. Dadrian, *Histoire du génocide*, *op. cit.*, pp. 519–22, explains the procedure followed by the defense.

10. SHAT (cf. n. 8), 1BB7 232, doc. no. 658, translation of the decree of competency, attached to an 8 May 1919 report entitled "The Trial of the Unionists."

11. *Ibidem*, pp. 1–2 (annexe).

12. *Ibidem*, pp. 1–3 (report).

13. Second session of the trial of the Unionists, 4 May 1919: *Takvim-ı Vakayi*, no. 3543, 12 May 1919, pp. 15–31.

14. *Ibidem*, p. 21, col. 2.
15. *Ibidem*, p. 23, col. 2.
16. *Ibidem*, pp. 24–6.
17. *Ibidem*, pp. 29–31.
18. Third session of the trial of the Unionists, 6 May 1335/1919: *Takvim-ı Vakayi*, no. 3547, 15 May 1919: pp. 33–6, examination of Midhat Şükrü; pp. 37–41, examination of Ziya Gökalp; pp. 42–6, examination of Küçük Talât; pp. 47–8, examination of Atıf Bey; p. 49, examination of Yusuf Rıza.
19. SHAT, Service Historique de la Marine, S. R. Marine, Turquie,1BB7 232, doc. no. 663, Constantinople, May 1919, "The Trial of the Unionists."
20. Fourth session of the trial of the Unionists, 8 May 1919: *Takvim-ı Vakayi*, no. 3547, 15 May 1919, pp. 52–66.
21. *Ibidem*, pp. 54–5; SHAT (*cf*. n. 8), 1BB7 232, doc. no. 663, p. 3.
22. Ibidem; Fourth session of the trial of the Unionists, 8 May 1919: *Takvim-ı Vakayi*, no. 3547, 15 May 1919, pp. 55–7.
23. Fifth session of the trial of the Unionists, 12 May 1919: *Takvim-ı Vakayi*, no. 3554, 21 May 1919, pp. 66–90.
24. *Ibidem*, pp. 67–9.
25. *Ibidem*, p. 85.
26. *Ibidem*, pp. 85–6.
27. *Ibidem*, p. 89.
28. Sixth session of the trial of the Unionists, 17 May 1919: *Takvim-ı Vakayi*, no. 3557, 25 May 1919, p. 107.
29. Seventh session of the trial of the Unionists, 19 May 1919: *Takvim-ı Vakayi*, no. 3561, 29 May 1919, p. 119. Five members of the Central Committee's Bureau directed the Special Organization.
30. SHAT (*cf*. n. 8), 1BB7 232, doc. no. 680, report by L. Feuillet, Constantinople, 13 May 1919.
31. FO 371/4174, no. 88761, telegram from Calthorpe to Lord Curzon, 30 May 1919; *La Renaissance*, no. 153, 30 May 1919, from *Alemdar*.
32. First session of the trial of the ministers, 3 June 1919: *Takvim-ı Vakayi*, no. 3571, 11 June 1919, pp. 128–31.
33. The court decided to try Şakir separately, together with those who had organized the massacres of Mamuret ul-Aziz.
34. Dadrian, *Histoire du génocide arménien, op. cit.*, p. 488.
35. First session of the trial of the ministers, 3 June 1919: *Takvim-ı Vakayi*, no. 3571, 11 June 1919, p. 141.
36. *Ibidem.*
37. *Ibidem*, pp. 132–40.
38. Second session of the trial of the ministers, 5 June 1919: *Takvim-ı Vakayi*, no. 3573, 12 June 1919, pp. 144, col. 2 and 145, on Esad effendi, former şeyh ul-Islam.
39. *Ibidem*, pp. 147–8.
40. Third session of the trial of the ministers, 9 June 1919: *Takvim-ı Vakayi*, no. 3575, 15 June 1919, pp. 149–55.
41. Fourth session of the trial of the ministers, 12 June 1919: *Takvim-ı Vakayi*, no. 3577, 17 June 1919, pp. 157–9.
42. Fifth session of the trial of the ministers, 24 June 1919: *Takvim-ı Vakayi*, no. 3593, 9 July 1919 (10 Temmuz 1335), pp. 177–83.
43. Sixth session of the trial of the ministers, 25 June 1919: *Takvim-ı Vakayi*, no. 3594, 10 July 1919, pp. 188–93.
44. *L'Entente*, 26 June 1919.
45. Seventh session of the trial of the ministers, le 26 June 1919: *Takvim-ı Vakayi*, no. 3595, 12 July 1919, p. 198.
46. In addition to Musa Kâzım, Esad effendi, Rifât bey, Hüseyin Haşim, all of whom were present, those affected were Talât, Enver, Cemal, Dr. Nâzım, Cavid Bey, Süleyman el-Bustani, Mustafa Şeref, and – another oddity of this trial – Oskan effendi (Mardikian), a former minister of the post and telegraph office who had resigned his post at the outbreak of the war, p. 1, verdict rendered on

5 July 1919: *Takvim-ı Vakayi*, no. 3604, 5 August 1919, pp. 217–24; English and French translations of the court-martial's verdict, dated 6 Shewal 1335 [5 July 1919], sent to Lord Curzon by the British high commissioner on 7 July 1919: FO 371/4174, no. 1310.

47. *Takvim-ı Vakayi*, no. 3604, 5 August 1919, pp. 217–20.
48. *Ibidem.*

9   The Trial of the Responsible Secretaries and the Vicissitudes of the Subsidiary Trials in the Provinces

1. The first session of the trial of the CUP's responsible secretaries and delegated inspectors, 21 June 1919: *Takvim-ı Vakayi*, no. 3586, 28 June 1919, pp. 161–4, 168. Sitting on the court were many of the same judges who had tried the ministers.
2. The second session of the trial of the CUP's responsible secretaries and delegated inspectors, 23 June 1919: *Takvim-ı Vakayi*, no. 3589, 5 July 1919, pp. 165–75; Third session of the trial, 28 June 1919: *Takvim-ı Vakayi*, no. 3596, 13 July 1919, pp. 205–15 (pagination error for pp. 209–10, which are mentioned twice)
3. Vahakn Dadrian, "The Turkish Military Tribunal's Prosecution of the authors of the Armenian Genocide: Four Major Court-Martial Series," *Holocaust & Genocide Studies*, vol. 11/1 (1997), p. 42. Convicted *in absentia*: Hilmi Bey (deputy of Angora), Ağaoğlu Ahmed (deputy of Karahisar), Colonel Mümtaz Bey (CUP's delegate in Suvar), Hasan Fehmi Bey (delegate in Kastamonu) [*cf. supra*, p. 527, n. 1947]; Sabri Bey (deputy of Sarukhan), Hüseyin Tosun (CUP's delegate and deputy of Erzerum [*cf. supra*, p. 316]), Samih Rifât Bey (former vali of Konya), Haci Ahmed, the father of Enver, etc.
4. *Cf. supra*, pp. 530, 560; on Ahmed Midhat, former chief of the police in Istanbul: APC/APJ, PCI Bureau, ٩ 19 and ٥ 396, "List of responsibles in the vilayet of Angora"; ٥ 457–9, 432, file 70 (in French).
5. *Cf. supra*, pp. 560–2.
6. *Cf. supra*, p. 570.
7. *Cf. supra*, p. 672.
8. The first session of the trial of the CUP's responsible secretaries and delegated inspectors, 21 June 1919: *Takvim-ı Vakayi*, no. 3586, 28 June 1919, pp. 161–4, 168.
9. *La Renaissance*, no. 295, 13 November 1919, reports that the trial of the responsible secretaries was continued on Wednesday, 12 November. The presiding judge was Esad Pasha.
10. Verdict in the trial of the responsible secretaries, 8 January 1920: *Takvim-ı Vakayi*, no. 3772, February 1920, p. 2, col. 2, p. 3, col. 1.
11. *Ibidem.* Sitting on the court at the time were Esad Pasha (presiding judge), and Ihsan Pasha, Mustafa Kerimi Pasha, İsmail Hakkı Pasha, Süleyman Şakir Bey.
12. *Takvim-ı Vakayi*, no. 3771, 9 February 1920, pp. 48–9.
13. *La Renaissance*, no. 330, 24 December 1919, reports that his trial had begun.
14. *La Renaissance*, no. 357, 27 January 1920.
15. *La Renaissance*, no. 363, 4 February 1920, no. 365, 6 February 1920.
16. *La Renaissance*, no. 369, 10 February 1920.
17. *La Renaissance*, no. 374, 17 February 1920.
18. *Cf. supra*, p. 471.
19. Verdict of the trial of Trebizond, 8 July 1919: *Takvim-ı Vakayi*, no. 3616, du 6 August 1919, pp. 50–2. It is noteworthy that the verdict was published two months after the end of the trial and one month after the verdict was announced.
20. *La Renaissance*, no. 324, 17 December 1919; no. 329, 23 December 1919.
21. *La Renaissance*, no. 605, 6 September 1920.
22. *Cf. supra*, with regard to his activities.
23. *Cf. supra*, p. 297.
24. Under the number 2696: FO 371/6504, f° 348. Another document indicates that the American missionaries Dr. H. Atkinson and Henry Diggs were state's witnesses who gave evidence incriminating Sabit: FO 371/6503, no. 264.

25. *Le Spectateur d'Orient*, 13 June 1919.
26. *La Renaissance*, no. 276, 22 October 1919.
27. *La Renaissance*, no. 284, 31 October 1919, no. 302, 21 November, no. 344, 11 January 1920.
28. Chiffred Telegram no. 5, from the head of the Teşkilât-ı Mahsusa, Bahaeddin Şakir, Erzerum, 21 Haziran 1331 (4 July 1915), to the vali of Mamuret ul-Aziz, Sabit Bey, attention: Resneli Nâzım Bey: *Takvim-ı Vakayi*, no. 3540 (read at the trial session of 12 April 1919), 5 May 1919, p. 6, col. 1–2, and no. 3771, 9 February 1920, p. 48, col. 1.
29. *Ibidem*, pp. 48–9.
30. FO 371/5089, no. 949, from Robeck to Lord Curzon, 18 February 1920.
31. *La Renaissance*, no. 423, 23 April 1920.
32. *Cf. supra*, pp. 301–2, with regard to their activities at the practical level.
33. Judgement of the court-martial, 20 July 1920: *Tercüman-ı Hakikat*, no. 14136, 5 August 1920, p. 5.
34. *Ibidem*. Necati was not executed.
35. *Cf. supra*, p. 301; Kazarian, *op. cit.*, pp. 292–300.
36. *Cf. supra*, pp. 308–9, with regard to the activities of Memduh. Many of the exhibits presented during the hearings have been preserved in the archives of PCI Bureau: APC/APJ, PCI Bureau, U' 372–4, 376–401 and 555–70.
37. *Takvim-ı Vakayi*, no. 3917, 31 July 1920, pp. 5–6.
38. *Le Bosphore*, 23 July 1920.
39. *La Renaissance*, no. 111, 10 April 1919.
40. *La Renaissance*, no. 156, 3 June 1919.
41. FO 371/5043, E 1363, ff. 123–5, dispatch of 18 February 1920, with attached a 4 February 1920 report bearing on General Halil Pasha. *La Renaissance*, no. 332, 27 December 1919, specifies that the trial of Ferid Bey began in the court-martial the 27 December 1919. But we have not information to a sentence.
42. *La Renaissance*, no. 290, 7 November 1919, no. 375, 18 February 1920.
43. *La Renaissance*, no. 347, 16 January 1920.
44. *La Renaissance*, no. 382, 26 February 1920, no. 386, 2 March 1920.
45. *La Renaissance*, no. 347, 16 January 1920, no. 369, 11 February 1920, no. 387, 3 March 1920.
46. *La Renaissance*, no. 388, 4 March 1920.
47. *La Renaissance*, no. 402, 20 March 1920.
48. *La Renaissance*, no. 410, 31 March 1920.
49. *Cf. supra*, pp. 543. Verdict of the trial of deportations in Büyükdere/San Stefano, 24 May 1919: *Takvim-ı Vakayi*, no. 3618, 8 August 1919, pp. 6–7.
50. *Cf. supra*, pp. 69, 103.
51. *Cf. supra*, p. 249; Astourian, "The Armenian Genocide: An Interpretation," *The History Teacher*, *art. cit.*, p. 141, n. 23–4.
52. First session of the trial of Sabancali Hakkı, 9 August 1919: *Takvim-ı Vakayi*, no. 3623, 14 August 1919, pp. 1–3.
53. Second session of the trial, 12 August 1919: *Takvim-ı Vakayi*, no. 3632, 25 August 1919, pp. 5–17, 12–17; third session of the trial, 27 August 1919: *Takvim-ı Vakayi*, no. 3636, 27 August 1919, pp. 18–23; Fourth session of the trial, 31 August 1919: *Takvim-ı Vakayi*, no. 3637, pp. 24–31; Fifth session of the trial, 10 September 1919: *Takvim-ı Vakayi*, no. 3656, pp. 32–9.
54. *La Renaissance*, no. 282, 29 October 1919.
55. *Aravod*, no. 46, 7 February 1921.
56. *Cf. supra*, pp. 467–82.
57. *La Renaissance*, no. 340, 7 January 1920.
58. *La Renaissance*, no. 383, 27 February 1920; *Le Spectateur d'Orient*, 12 July 1919: 12 people sent to Yozgat to be tried locally, one sent to Amasia, and two sent to Akşehir. *Le Spectateur d'Orient*, 14 July 1919, reports that warrants had been issued for the arrest of Bedros Halajian, Mansurizâde Said (Sarouhan) and Nori (Kerbela). *Le Spectateur d'Orient*, 18 July 1919, also reports a planned trial of "people implicated in the massacres and deportations in Angora, as well as those implicated in atrocities committed in Kerasund, Sıvas, Adabazar, Bilejik, Bitlis, Ismit, Mamuret ul-Aziz, Amasia, Der Zor, Kırşehir, Dyiarbekir, Kayseri, Konya, Kangri, Andrinople, Karahisar, Adana, Çataldja, Dardanelle, Bafra, Marash, Akhisar and, finally,

Constantinople. Among the people involved in the Constantinople atrocities were Bedri Bey, the former police chief and, at the time, a fugitive from justice, Reşad Bey, the former head of the political section of the police department, and Şehab Bey, the former military commander of Constantinople...One is never forbidden to wait," the newspaper concluded, "and one can always hope."

59. *La Renaissance*, no. 307, 27 November 1919, no. 313, 4 December 1919, no. 318, 10 December 1919. His file was transmitted to Court-martial No. 3 as early as June 1919 (*Le Spectateur d'Orient*, 25 June 1919), which seems to indicate that even Damad Ferid's government did not appreciate the written statement that he submitted to the Mazhar Commission in December 1918.

60. *Cf. supra*, pp. 627, and 646.

61. *Aravod*, no. 31, 25 October 1920.

62. "A la cour martiale, un réquisitoire éloquent," in *La Renaissance*, no. 352, 22 January 1920; *Le Bosphore*, 22 January 1920.

63. *Ibidem*.

64. "Choses de Turquie, Autour d'un procès," in *La Renaissance*, no. 354, 24 January 1920, from *Peyam Eyam*.

65. "Le cas de Mustafa pacha," in *Le Bosphore*, 25 October 1920.

66. *Takvim-ı Vakayi*, no. 3995, 31 October 1920; *Aravod*, no. 32, 1 November 1920, also reports these appointments.

67. *Alemdar*, 31 October 1920.

68. "Le procès de Mustafa pacha," in *Le Bosphore*, 8 November 1920.

69. "Réparations, réintégrations, etc. Mustafa pacha," in *Le Bosphore*, 21 November 1920.

70. "L'affaire du général Mustafa pacha," in *Le Bosphore*, 24 November 1920.

71. "Le procès de Mustafa pacha," in *Le Bosphore*, 21 December 1920.

72. *La Renaissance*, no. 281, 28 October 1919.

73. *La Renaissance*, no. 282, 29 October 1919.

10   Mustafa Kemal: From the Young Turk Connection to the Construction of the Nation-State

1. Zürcher, *The Unionist, op. cit.*, p. 107. After entrusting the command of his army to Nihat Pasha [Anılmış], Kemal left Adana for the capital. According to Zürcher, he presented the British, in vain, with a plan for a British mandate over Anatolia; he would have been the governor of the area under mandate. This episode is omitted in his memoirs.

2. *Ibidem*, p. 114.

3. *Ibidem*, pp. 114–1–15.

4. *Ibidem*, pp. 111–12. But Kemal seems to have considered Esad to be a man who was "obstinate, with limited capability." (*ibidem*, p. 79).

5. *Ibidem*.

6. *Ibidem*, p. 92.

7. *Ibidem*, p. 118.

8. *Ibidem*, p. 119.

9. *Ibidem*, p. 121. *Karakol's* representative with the Bolsheviks, Baha Said, signed a mutual assistance pact with the representative of the Bolshevik government on 11 January 1920.

10. *Ibidem*, pp. 85, 122.

11. *Ibidem*, p. 123. Zürcher mentions a public demonstration for Enver that took place in Trebizond in May 1920.

12. *Ibidem*, p. 130.

13. FO 371/5043, E 1363, ff. 123–5, letter of 18 February 1920, with a 4 February 1920 report on the newly elected deputies to the Ottoman parliament.

14. *Ibidem*, f° 125.

15. *Ibidem*, f° 126.

16. *Cf. supra*, p. 340. The evidence he gave the court directly incriminated Halil [Kut].

17. FO 371/5043, E 1363, f° 126.

18. The Greek-Armenian Committee dealt systematically with questions of security in the 85 coordinating meetings that it held between 19 February and 29 March 1922: FO 371/ 3658, 371/4195, 371/ 4196, 371/4197, 371/5087, 371/ 5213, 371/5214, 371/ 6548, 371/6549, 371/7879.

19. 34th session, 10 March 1920: FO 371/ 5087, ff. 141–5.

20. FO 371/ 5041, E 432, report of Intelligence Services; FO 371/5042, E 875, 16 March 1920, about the withdrawal of French troops from Marash and the massacre of the Armenian population by the Kemalists.

21. FO 371/5046, E 3318, f. 89, report of 15 April 1920.

22. FO 371/5045, E. 2804, ff. 191 and 196, report of 25 March 1920, "Extortion of contributions by Nationalists."

23. FO 371/5043, E 1297, ff. 35 and sq., report of 10 March 1920.

24. FO 371/5043, E 1462, ff. 146–55, letter from Lord Curzon to Robeck, 12 March 1920, on the Allied decision to occupy Istanbul.

25. FO 371/5043, E 1550, about the naval tactics and the deployment of battleships.

26. FO 371/5043, E 1531, report of 15 March 1920, about the reinforcement of the British troops in Turkey; FO 371/5043, E 1642, second report of 15 March 1920.

27. FO 371/5043, E 1693, report of 17 March 1920.

28. FO 371/5046, E 3649, report of 2 April 1920, about Turkish reactions to the pursuit of the military occupation of the capital.

29. FO 371/5173, no. 6709, letter from the British ambassador in Berlin to Lord Curzon, 14 juin 1920, report on the Representatives of the Young Turks, f. 100 (report in French).

30. FO 371/5173, E 4154, from the French embassy in London to the Ministry of Foreign Affairs, 1 May 1920.

31. FO 371/5173, E 3404, telegram from Robeck to G. Buchanan, British ambassador in Rome, 16 April 1920. It is probable that the Italian authorities closed their eyes to these movements and were already considering cooperating with the Ittihadist-Kemalist forces.

32. FO 371/5171, E 12472, report of British Intelligence Services (the Istanbul branch of the S.I.S.), on the week beginning 9 September 1920, passed by Robeck to Lord Curzon, pp. 14–16.

33. FO 371/5178, E 14638, Constantinople, 7 September 1920, report of British Intelligence Services (the Istanbul branch of the S.I.S.), f° 195.

34. Ibidem, f° 196.

35. FO 371/5089, appendix, copy of a Circular of the Ottoman League, Geneve, 6 January 1920.

36. FO 371/5050, f° 198, copy of the Journal d'Orient, 3 June 1920.

37. FO 371/5171, E 12803, report of British Intelligence Services (the Istanbul branch of the S.I.S.), on the week beginning 21 September 1920, passed by Robeck to Lord Curzon, f° 153.

38. Telegram from the foreign minister of the Ankara government, Ahmed Muhtar, to Kâzım Karabekir, 8 November 1920, published in the collection: Kâzım Karabekir, İstiklâl Harbimiz (Our War of Independence), Istanbul 1969, pp. 844–5, coted in Dadrian, Histoire du génocide arménien, op. cit., pp. 564–5, n. 4.

39. FO 371/5178, E 14269, report of British Intelligence Services (the Istanbul branch of the S.I.S.), on the week beginning 28 October 1920, passed by Robeck to Lord Curzon, f° 226.

40. Ibidem, ff. 227–8.

41. Kâzım Karabekir, İstiklâl Harbimiz (Our War of Independence), op. cit., p. 845, coted in Dadrian, Histoire du génocide arménien, op. cit., p. 565.

42. FO 371/6503, no. 6902, letter from the War Office to the State secretary of Foreign Office, London, 15 June 1921.

43. FO 371/6506, f° 335chiffred telegram from Sir H. Rumbold, 27 September 1921.

44. FO 371/6505, f° 93, telegram from the governor of Malta to the War Office, 29 October 1921. An attached 9 November 1921 report recalls that these men had been arrested under Damad Ferid in 1919 and sent to Malta in May–June 1919, and a second group in March 1920; that Chapter VII, Articles 225 to 230 of the Treaty of Sèvres stipulate that Turks guilty of committing acts of violence should be tried, and so on.

45. Zürcher, The Unionist, op. cit., pp. 132–3.

46. Ibidem, p. 134. The first article in the program announces that "Union and Progress is a radical political party that defends all freedoms."

47. *Ibidem.*
48. *Ibidem,* p. 143. The killers, including the man who laid the assassination plan, Ziya Hurşit, were discovered in the hotels of the port.
49. *Ibidem,* p. 143. On 8 February 1925, Kel Ali, a loyal follower of Kemal's, personally killed the deputy from Ardahan, Deli Halit, a member of the opposition, in the midst of a session of the National Assembly (*ibidem,* pp. 146–14–7). Those tried before Ali Fuad [Cebesoy], Kâzım Karabekir, Refet [Bele], Cafer Tayyar [Eğilmez], Colonel Arif (1882–1926), Rüştü (1873–1926), Bekir Sâmi (1867–1932), Sabit [Sağiroğlu] (1881–1960), Ahmed Şükrü, Halis Turgut (1886–1926), Necati [Kurtuluş] (1882–1956), Haret [Sağıroğlu] (1880–1947), Münir Hüsrev [Göle] (1890–1955), Halil [Işık] (1879–1935), Zeki [Kadirbeyoğlu] (1884–1952), İsmail Canbolat, Kâmil [Mitas] (1875–1957), Hulusi [Zarğı] (1883–1968), Abidin (1890–1926), Besim [Özbek] (1882–1965), Faik [Günday] (1884–1964), brother of Ziya Hurşid, Ahmed Muhtar [Cilli] (1871–1958): *ibidem,* pp. 147–14–8. The cases of the other Ittihadists were judged in the second trial, which took place in Ankara.
50. *Ibidem,* pp. 149–53. On his return from Malta, Şükrü was appointed vali of Trebizond and elected deputy from Ismit to the Grand National Assembly. The prosecutor alluded, in his closing speech, to a very dubious connection to the 1925 Kurdish revolt.
51. *Ibidem,* p. 153. Kara Kemal committed suicide on 27 July before he could be transferred to Ankara.
52. *Ibidem,* pp. 154–7. The presiding judge, Ali [Çetinkaya], was on intimate terms with Dr. Nâzım's and a close associate of Enver's.
53. *Ibidem,* p. 159.
54. *Ibidem.* The case of Muftizâde Şükrü Kaya, the head of the Department for the Settlement of Tribes and Emigrants in 1915, is perhaps the most revealing.

Conclusion

1. Currently held in the archives of the Armenian Patriarchate in Jerusalem.
2. APC/APJ, PCI Bureau, Ի 125–128-129–130.

Index